Department for Economic and Social
Information and Policy Analysis
Statistics Division

Département de l'information économique
et sociale et de l'analyse des politiques
Division de statistique

NATIONAL ACCOUNTS STATISTICS: MAIN AGGREGATES AND DETAILED TABLES, 1993
PART I

**UNITED NATIONS
NEW YORK, 1996**

NOTE

Symbols of United Nations documents are composed of capital letters combined with figures.
The first 14 editions of the Yearbook were issued without series symbols.

ST/ESA/STAT/SER.X/22, PART I

UNITED NATIONS PUBLICATION
Sales No. E.96.XVII.5

ISBN 92-1-161381-7

Inquiries should be directed to:
SALES SECTION
UNITED NATIONS
NEW YORK, NY 10017

Copyright © United Nations, 1996
All rights reserved
Printed by the United Nations Reproduction Section, New York

CONTENTS

	Page
Introduction	v
I. System of National Accounts (SNA)	ix
II. System of Material Product Balances (MPS)	xxiii
III. Country Tables	1

Afghanistan	3	Cuba	270
Albania	4	Cyprus	274
Algeria	5	Czech Republic	287
Angola	7	Denmark	289
Anguilla	10	Dominica	322
Antigua and Barbuda	13	Dominican Republic	324
Argentina	15	Ecuador	327
Armenia	17	Egypt	363
Australia	18	El Salvador	366
Austria	44	Equatorial Guinea	374
Bahamas	72	Estonia	377
Bahrain	78	Ethiopia (Former)	437
Bangladesh	81	Fiji	388
Barbados	89	Finland	394
Belarus	91	France	439
Belgium	95	French Guiana	476
Belize	127	French Polynesia	479
Benin	130	Gabon	482
Bermuda	132	Gambia	484
Bhutan	135	Germany	487
Bolivia	139	Ghana	528
Botswana	145	Greece	532
Brazil	152	Grenada	553
British Virgin Islands	155	Guadeloupe	555
Brunei Darussalam	159	Guatemala	558
Bulgaria	160	Guinea-Bissau	562
Burkina Faso	163	Guyana	564
Burundi	166	Haiti	566
Cameroon	169	Honduras	570
Canada	175	Hong Kong	575
Cape Verde	214	Hungary	585
Cayman Islands	219	Iceland	598
Central African Republic	227	India	625
Chad	228	Indonesia	652
Chile	229	Iran (Islamic Rep. of)	655
China	233	Iraq	662
Colombia	234	Ireland	666
Congo	256	Israel	686
Cook Islands	260	Italy	696
Costa Rica	261	Jamaica	726
Côte d'Ivoire	268	Japan	733
Croatia	269	Jordan	771

INTRODUCTION

This is the thirty-seventh issue of *National Accounts Statistics: Main Aggregates and Detailed Tables* 1/, showing detailed national accounts estimates for 182 countries and areas. Like the previous issues, it has been prepared by the Statistics Division of the Department for Economic and Social Information and Policy Analysis of the United Nations Secretariat with the generous co-operation of national statistical services. It is issued in accordance with the request of the Statistical Commission 2/ that the most recent available data on national accounts for as many countries and areas as possible be published regularly.

SCOPE OF PUBLICATION

National accounts estimates for countries or areas whose data are in terms of the United Nations System of National Accounts (SNA) are shown, where available, for each of the following tables:

Part I. Summary information

1.1 Expenditures on the gross domestic product (current prices)

1.2 Expenditures on the gross domestic product (constant prices)

1.3 Cost components of the gross domestic product

1.4 General government current receipts and expenditures, summary

1.5 Current income and outlay of corporate and quasi-corporate enterprises, summary

1.6 Current income and outlay of households and non-profit institutions, summary

1.7 External transactions on current account, summary

1.8 Capital transactions of the nation, summary.

1.9 Gross domestic product by institutional sector of origin

1.10 Gross domestic product by kind of activity (current prices)

1.11 Gross domestic product by kind of activity (constant prices)

1.12 Relations among national accounting aggregates

Part 2. Final expenditures on gross domestic product: detailed breakdowns and supporting tables

2.1 General government final consumption expenditure by function (current prices)

2.2 General government final consumption expenditure by function (constant prices)

2.3 Total government outlays by function and type (current prices)

2.4 Composition of general government social security benefits and social assistance grants to households

2.5 Private final consumption expenditure by type (current prices)

2.6 Private final consumption expenditure by type (constant prices)

2.7 Gross capital formation by type of good and owner (current prices)

2.8 Gross capital formation by type of good and owner (constant prices)

2.9 Gross capital formation by kind of activity of owner, ISIC major divisions (current prices)

2.10 Gross capital formation by kind of activity of owner, ISIC major divisions (constant prices)

2.11 Gross fixed capital formation by kind of activity of owner, ISIC divisions (current prices)

2.12 Gross fixed capital formation by kind of activity of owner, ISIC divisions (constant prices)

2.13 Stocks of reproducible fixed assets, by type of good and owner (current prices)

2.14 Stocks of reproducible fixed assets, by type of good and owner (constant prices)

2.15 Stocks of reproducible fixed assets by kind of activity (current prices)

2.16 Stocks of reproducible fixed assets by kind of activity (constant prices)

2.17 Exports and imports of goods and services, detail

Part 3. Institutional sector accounts: detailed flow accounts 3/

1. General government

    3.11 Production account: total and subsectors

    3.12 Income and outlay account: total and subsectors

    3.13 Capital accumulation account: total and subsectors

    3.14 Capital finance account: total and subsectors

    3.15 Balance sheet: total and subsectors

2. Corporate and quasi-corporate enterprises

    3.21 Production account: total and sectors

    3.22 Income and outlay account: total and sectors

    3.23 Capital accumulation account: total and sectors

    3.24 Capital finance account: total and sectors

    3.25 Balance sheet: total and sectors

    3.26 Financial transactions of financial institutions: detail

3. Households and private unincorporated enterprises

    3.31 Production account: total and subsectors

    3.32 Income and outlay account: total and subsectors

    3.33 Capital accumulation account: total and subsectors

    3.34 Capital finance account: total and subsectors

    3.35 Balance sheet

4. Private non-profit institutions serving households

    3.41 Production account

    3.42 Income and outlay account

    3.43 Capital accumulation account

    3.44 Capital finance account

5. External transactions

    3.51 Current account, detail

    3.52 Capital accumulation account

    3.53 Capital finance account

Part 4. Production by kind of activity: detailed breakdowns and supporting tables

4.1 Derivation of value added by kind of activity (current prices)

4.2 Derivation of value added by kind of activity (constant prices)

4.3 Cost components of value added

For the countries or areas whose data are in terms of the System of Material Product Balances (MPS), the estimates are shown, where available, for each of the following tables:

1. Net material product by use

2. Net material product by kind of activity of the material sphere

3. Primary incomes by kinds of activity of the material sphere

4. Primary incomes from net material product

5. Supply and disposition of goods and material services

6. Capital formation by kind of activity of the material and non-material spheres

7. Final consumption

8. Personal consumption according to source of supply of goods and material services

9. Total consumption of the population by object, commodity and service, and mode of acquisition

Estimates for all tables are shown for the years 1980, 1982 through 1992.

For countries formerly using MPS and are now compiling national accounts estimates in accordance to SNA, only the SNA tables are shown in this publication. However, when only selected aggregates in terms of SNA are available, both SNA and MPS tables are presented.

CONCEPTUAL REFERENCES

The form and concepts of the statistical tables in the present publication generally conform, for the countries or areas with SNA data, to the recommendations in *A System of National Accounts* 4/, Studies in Methods, Series F, No. 2, Rev. 3. For the countries or areas with MPS data, the form and concepts generally conform to the recommendations in *Basic Methodological Principles Governing the Compilation of the System of Statistical Balances of the National Economy: Vol. I and Vol. II* 5/, Series F, No. 17/Rev. I, New York 1989. A summary of the conceptual framework of both systems, their classifications and definitions of transactions is provided in chapters I and II of the present publication.

COMPILATION OF DATA

To compile the large volume of national accounts data, the Statistics Division each year sends to countries or areas pre-filled SNA questionnaire and/or MPS questionnaire. The recipients are requested to update the questionnaire with the latest available national accounts estimates and to indicate where the scope and coverage of the country estimates differ for conceptual or statistical reasons from the definitions and classifications recommended in SNA or in MPS. Data obtained from these replies are supplemented by information gathered from correspondence with the national statistical services and from national and international source publications.

In the present publication, the data for each country or area are presented in separate chapters, as far as possible, under uniform table headings and classifications of SNA or MPS, as the case may be. Important deviations from the two systems, where known, are described in the general note, while differences in definition and coverage of specific items are indicated in footnotes to the relevant tables.

Country data in chapter III are presented in alphabetical order. Unless otherwise stated, the data in the country tables relate to the calendar year against which they are shown.

COMPARABILITY OF THE NATIONAL ESTIMATES

Every effort has been made to present the estimates of the various countries or areas in a form designed to facilitate international comparability. To this end, important differences in concept, scope, coverage and classification have been described in the notes which precede and accompany the country tables. Such differences should be taken into account if misleading comparisons among countries or areas are to be avoided.

REVISIONS

The figures shown are the most recent estimates and revisions available at the time of compilation. In general, figures for the most recent year are to be regarded as provisional. For more up to date information, reference is made to selected issues of the United Nations *Monthly Bulletin of Statistics* 6/.

NOMENCLATURE

The information for the countries and areas shown in this publication reflect what is available to the Statistics Division of the United Nations as of 15 September 1994.

Designations which have changed in recent years are as follows:

Czech Republic, Slovakia - Data for Czech Republic and Slovakia are shown separately under the appropriate country name. For period prior to 1 January 1993, data for the former Czechoslovakia are shown under the country name "Czechoslovakia (Former)"

USSR (Former) - In 1991, the Union of Soviet Socialist Republics formally dissolved into fifteen independent republics (Armenia, Azerbaijan, Belarus, Georgia, Kazakstan, Kyrgyzstan, Latvia, Lithuania, Republic of Moldova, Russian Federation, Tajikistan, Turkmenistan, Ukraine and Uzbekistan). When available, data are shown for the individual republics. All data for the former USSR are shown under the country name "USSR (Former)"

Yugoslavia (Former)- All data for Yugoslavia prior to 1 January 1992 refer to the Socialist Federal Republic of Yugoslavia which was composed of six republics. After that date, when available, data for the republics, Bosnia and Herzegovina, Croatia, Slovenia, The Former Yugoslav Republic of Macedonia and Yugoslavia which is composed of two republics (Serbia and Montenegro) are shown separately.

EXPLANATION OF SYMBOLS

The following symbols have been employed:
Data not available.......................... ...
Category not applicable.................... ..
Magnitude nil or less than half of the unit employed................................... -
Decimal figures are always preceded by a point(.)

When a series is not homogeneous, it is indicated by presenting the data in separate rows.

Decimals and percentages in tables do not necessarily add to totals shown because of rounding.

GENERAL DISCLAIMER

The designations employed and the presentation of material in this publication do not imply the expression of any opinion whatsoever on the part of the Secretariat of the United Nations concerning the legal status of any country, territory, city or area or of its authorities, or concerning the delimitation of its frontiers and boundaries.

Where the designation "country or area" appears in the headings of tables, it covers countries, territories, cities or areas. In prior issues of this publication, where the designation "country" appears in the headings of tables, it covers countries, territories, cities or areas.

In some tables, the designations "developed" and "developing" economies are intended for statistical convenience and do not, necessarily, express a judgment about the stage reached by a particular country or area in the development process.

1/ United Nations publication. The first 25 editions of this publication were issued under the title Yearbook of National Accounts Statistics under the following sales number: 1957, 58.XVII.3; 1958, 59.XVII.3; 1959, 60.XVII.3; 1960, 61.XVII.4; 1961, 62.XVII.2; 1962, 63.XVII.2; 1963, 64.XVII.4; 1964, 65.XVII.2; 1965, 66.XVII.2; 1966, 67.XVII.14; 1967, E.69.XVII.6; 1968, vol.I, E.70.XVII.2, vol.II, E.70.XVII.3; 1969, vol.I, E.71.XVII.2, vol.II, E.71.XVII.3; 1970, (2 volumes), E.72.XVII.3; 1971, (3 volumes), E.73.XVII.3; 1972, (3 volumes), E.74.XVII.3; 1973, (3 volumes), E.75.XVII.2; 1974, (3 volumes), E.75.XVII.5; 1975, (3 volumes), E.76.XVII.2: 1976, (2 volumes), E.77.XVII.2; 1977, (2 volumes), E.78.XVII.2; 1978, (2 volumes), E.79.XVII.8; 1979, (2 volumes), E.8O.XVII.11; 1980, (2 volumes), E.82.XVII.6; 1981, (2 volumes), E.83.XVII.3; Beginning with the twenty-sixth edition, this publication replaced Volume 1. individual country data, of the Yearbook and it was issued under the following sales number: 1982, E.85.XVII.3; 1983, E.86.XVII.3; 1984, E.86.XVII.26; 1985, E.87.XVII.10; 1986, E.89.XVII.7 (Parts I and II); 1987, E.90.XVII.2 (Parts I and II); 1988, E.90.XVII.18 (Parts I and II); 1989, E.91 XVII.16 (Parts I and II); 1990, E.93.XIII.3 (Parts I and II); 1991, E.94.XVII.5 (Parts I and II); 1992, E.95.XVII.4 (Parts I and II);

2/ See Official Records of the Economic and Social Council, First Year, Second Session, (E/39), annex III, chap. IV.

3/ Institutional sector accounts are shown only for those countries which have tables for all the institutional sectors.

4/ United Nations publication, Sales No. E.69.XVII.3. The first addition of the report, published in 1953, was prepared by an expert committee appointed by the Secretary-General of the United Nations.

5/ United Nations publication, Sales No. E.89.XVII.5.

6/ United Nations publication, ST/ESA/STAT/SER.Q.

SYSTEM OF NATIONAL ACCOUNTS (SNA)

The revised System of National Accounts (SNA) was adopted by the Statistical Commission at its fifteenth session [1] for the use of national statistical authorities and in the international reporting of comparable national accounting data. The present System [2] is a revision and extension of the former SNA which was first formulated in 1952.

A. STRUCTURE OF SNA

SNA provides a comprehensive and detailed framework for the systematic and integrated recording of transaction flows in an economy. It brings together into an articulated and coherent system data ranging in degree of aggregation from consolidated accounts of the nation to detailed input-output and flow-of-funds tables. It includes production and goods and services and outlay and capital finance accounts for institutional sectors and subsectors.

The country tables are divided into four parts. These are listed in the above introduction. Part 1 contains summary but comprehensive information, at current and, where appropriate, constant prices. This part includes not only the basic gross domestic product (final expenditures and cost composition) but also summary information on government receipts and disbursements, enterprise and household income and outlay, and external transactions, a summary capital transactions account, information on gross product by institutional sector of origin and kind of activity and, finally, a table showing the relations among the aggregate concepts used in the revised SNA and also commonly in national statistical systems. Tables 1.1, 1.3, 1.4, 1.5, 1.6, 1.7 and 1.8 form a simple, closed and balancing set of flow accounts, drawn from the much more complex and elaborate standard accounts of SNA; these tables can therefore be used not only to provide an overview of the operation of the economic system but also as a guide to the more detailed data that follow and as a framework to enforce conceptual and statistical consistency.

Part 2 shows detailed breakdowns of the final expenditure components on gross domestic product (consumption, capital formation, imports and exports), in current and constant prices, together with supporting tables giving additional information on government outlays and capital stock. This part also shows tables relating to stocks of reproducible tangible assets at current and constant prices.

Part 3 shows detailed institutional sector accounts. For each sector and subsector, five accounts are given: a production account, an income and outlay account, a capital formation account, a capital finance account, and a balance sheet. The latter four are standard SNA accounts, as shown in annex 8.3 to *A System of National Accounts* [2] and in annex 8.2 to *Provisional Guidelines on National and Sector Balance Sheets and Reconciliation Accounts of the System of National Accounts* [3].

The SNA standard accounts do not include institutional sector production accounts, but provision is made for this information in the supporting tables.

The sectors and subsectors distinguished in part 3 are: general government (central, state or provincial, local, social security funds), corporate and quasi-corporate enterprises (non-financial, financial), households and private unincorporated enterprises (farm entrepreneurial, other farm, non-farm entrepreneurial, non-farm wage earner, other) and non-profit institutions serving households.

Part 4 contains kind-of-activity breakdowns. Two levels of detail are employed. All of the information is asked for at the major division (1-digit) level of the *International Standard Industrial Classification of All Economic Activities* [4] (ISIC). In some cases, data are also asked for at the ISIC division (2-digit) level, with a very small amount of further breakdown to the 3-digit level. Where appropriate, both current and constant prices are specified. The tables show the derivation of value added (gross output less intermediate consumption), the cost components of value added, and employment.

B. STANDARD CLASSIFICATIONS OF THE SNA

Detailed discussions of definitions and classifications are to be found in *A System of National Accounts* [2] and in the other publications on SNA cited above. SNA distinguishes between transactive and transaction classifications. Below is a short summary of the main characteristics of each of the classifications used by the system.

I. *Classifications of transactors*

1. *Kind of activity*

The kind-of-activity classification employed is the major division (1-digit) level or, in some tables the division (2-digit) level of ISIC.

In SNA, this classification is intended to be applied to establishment-type units, defined as the smallest units for which separate production accounts can be compiled. SNA also employs a much broader kind of activity classification which divides producers into "industries" and three categories of "other producers". Industries are, broadly, establishments whose activities are intended to be self-sustaining, whether through production for the market or for own use, and it is to this category that the ISIC breakdown is generally applied.

All establishments falling into ISIC major divisions 1-8 should be classed as industries. Producers of government services, private non-profit services to households, and domestic services are classed as "other producers"; all of these should fall into ISIC category 9 "Community, social and personal services". ISIC category 9 also may, of course, include some establishments classed as industries. Where countries consider, however, that some establishments classed as other producers should appear in ISIC categories other than 9, the nature of the exceptions would be specified in footnotes to tables 1.10 and 1.11.

2. *Institutional sectors*

The basic SNA institutional sectoring is given in *A System of National Accounts* [2], table 5.1.

Institutional sectoring, in SNA, is intended to be applied to enterprise-type units, that is, units for which complete accounts can be compiled, as opposed to the establishment-type units employed in the kind-of-activity classification. This distinction is applicable mainly to the corporate and quasi corporate enterprise sector.

The sectoring and subsectoring employed in the institutional sector accounts in part 3 is as follows:

General government

    Central

    State or provincial

    Local

    Social security funds

Corporate and quasi-corporate enterprises

    Non-financial

    Financial

Households and private unincorporated enterprises

    Farm entrepreneurial

    Other farm

    Non-farm entrepreneurial

    Non-farm wage earner

    Other

Non-profit institutions serving households

Rest of the world

(a) *General government.* This sector includes (1) *producers of government services*, all bodies, departments and establishments of any level of government that engage in administration, defense, regulation of the public order and health, cultural, recreational and other social services and social security arrangements that are furnished but not normally sold to the public; and (2) *industries of government*, ancillary departments and establishments mainly engaged in supplying goods and services to other units of government, such as printing plants, central transport pools and arsenals, and agencies mainly selling goods and services to the public but operating on a small scale and financially integrated with general government, such as government restaurant facilities in public buildings. Non-profit institutions which, while not an official part of any organ of government, are wholly or mainly financed and controlled by it should be included in producers of government services. Ancillary agencies may occur in any kind of activity. Producers of government services normally occur only in major division 9 (which of course may also include ancillary agencies).

Provision is made for four subsectors of general government, all of which may include the two components noted above. However, it is not intended that artificial distinctions should be introduced where they do not exist in the institutions of a particular country. It will, for instance, usually be desirable to separate state or provincial government from local government only in countries in which state or provincial governments exercise a considerable degree of autonomy. Similarly, social security funds should in general be distinguished separately only where they are organized separately from the other activities of general government and exercise substantial autonomy in their operations.

(b) *Corporate and quasi-corporate enterprises.* SNA defines this sector to include enterprises which meet any one of the following criteria: (1) they are incorporated; (2) they are owned by a non-resident; (3) they are relatively large partnerships or proprietorships with complete income statements and balance sheets; (4) they are non-profit institutions mainly serving business and financed and controlled by business; or (5) they are engaged in financial activities. Because of the difficulty that may be encountered in compiling separate production account data for incorporated and unincorporated units, a combined production account for these two sectors has also been provided for.

(c) *Households and private unincorporated enterprises.* This sector includes all private unincorporated enterprises not classed as quasi-corporations. SNA also includes in this sector private non-profit institutions serving households that employ less than the equivalent of two full-time persons.

The criterion for classifying the subsectors of the household sector in these tables differs slightly from that tentatively proposed in SNA. There, the subsectoring is based on the occupational status of the person designated "head of household". Here, the classification is based on the most important source of household income, taking all household members into account. It is considered that this criterion more accurately reflects both changing social views and changing labour force participation practices; it also responds to recent directives relating to the elimination of sex-based stereotypes.

(d) *Private non-profit institutions serving households.* This sector includes institutions, not mainly financed and controlled by general governments and employing the equivalent of two or more persons, that furnish educational, health, cultural, recreational and other social and community services to households free of charge or at prices that do not fully cover their costs of production.

As in the case of general government, SNA includes two components in this sector: (1) *producers of private non-profit services to households*, which engage in the activities enumerated above, and (2) *commercial activities* of these institutions, such as owning and letting dwellings, operating eating and lodging facilities, and publishing and selling books, for which it is possible to compile separate production accounts but not complete separate financial accounts. (Where separate financial accounts can be compiled, such activities would be classed as ordinary quasi-corporations.) In SNA, these commercial activities are considered to be "industries" and should be classed in the appropriate ISIC categories, whereas the non-profit services proper will all fall into ISIC category 9.

II. Classifications of transactions

1. Classification of the functions of government

Table 5.3 of *A System of National Accounts* [2] contains a classification of the purposes of government, the 1-digit level of which was used in previous publications for classifying general government outlays. This classification has now been superseded by the *Classification of the Functions of Government* [5].

2. Household consumption expenditure

Table 6.1 of SNA provides a classification of household goods and services. The classification used in the present publication is a slightly condensed version of the second level of this classification, in which some second-level categories have been combined.

3. *Purposes of private non-profit bodies serving households*

This classification appears in table 5.4 of SNA. It is used for classifying the final consumption expenditures of private non-profit institutions serving households.

4. *Gross capital formation*

Table 6.2 of SNA classifies stocks according to type, and table 6.3 classifies gross fixed capital formation according to type. These classifications are used in the present publication in slightly modified form, calling for less detail in some areas and slightly more detail in others (specifically, transport equipment).

5. *Exports and imports of goods and services*

This classification is given in table 6.4 of SNA.

6. *Transfers*

Table 7.1 of SNA contains a classification of unrequired current transfers, including direct taxes. This classification is not employed directly in the present publication but it is the source of the definitions of a number of flows, and will be referred to in that connection.

7. *Financial assets and liabilities*

Table 7.2 of SNA gives a classification of items appearing in the capital finance account.

8. *Balance sheet categories*

Classifications of the various types of assets not included in the previous classification are given in tables 5.1 and 5.2 of *Provisional Guidelines on National and Sector Balance Sheets and Reconciliation Accounts of the System of National Accounts,* 3/ which deal respectively, with stocks and fixed assets, and non-reproducible tangible assets. These classifications are used in the capital stock tables in part 2 and the balance sheet tables in part 3 of the present publication.

C. DEFINITIONS OF FLOWS

The following section briefly defines the content of the flows appearing in the SNA tables of chapter III of the present publication.

I. *Total supply of goods and services*

1. *Gross output of goods and services*

Gross output of goods and services covers both the value of goods and services produced for sale and the value of goods and services produced for own use. It includes (a) the domestic production of goods and services which are either for sale or for transfer to others, (b) net additions to work in progress valued at cost and to stocks of finished goods valued in producers' prices; (c) products made on own account for government or private consumption or for gross fixed capital formation; and (d) rents received on structures, machinery and equipment (but not on land) and imputed rent for owner-occupied dwellings.

Production for own consumption of households includes all own-account production of primary products (agricultural, fishing, forestry, mining and quarrying), own-account production of such items as butter, flour, wine, cloth or furniture made from primary products, and other goods and services that are also commonly sold. Gross output of the distributive trades is defined as the difference between sales and purchase values of goods sold. Gross output of banks and similar financial institutions is defined as the sum of actual service charges and imputed service charges; the latter is equal to the excess of property income received over interest paid out on deposits. For casualty insurance companies, gross output is defined as the excess of premiums received over claims paid, and for life insurance schemes it is the excess of premiums received over the sum of claims paid and net additions to actuarial reserves, excluding the accrued interest of the policy-holders in these reserves. Gross output of general government includes the market value of sales and goods and services produced for own use. The latter should be valued at cost, that is, the sum of net purchases of goods and services for intermediate consumption (at purchasers' prices), consumption of fixed capital, compensation of employees and any indirect taxes paid.

The concept of gross output appears in the tables in both part 3 and part 4. In part 3, each sector production account aggregates to its gross output. In part 4, gross output of various kind-of-activity sectors appears in tables 4.1-4.2 and 4.5-4.10. In the sector production accounts (tables 3.11, 3.21, 3.31 and 3.41) and the supply tables (4.5, 4.6, 4.9 and 4.10), gross output is divided into marketed and non-marketed components. The marketed component includes all output offered for sale (whether or not a buyer is actually found) or valued on the basis of a market transaction, even if it reaches the ultimate recipient through a transfer.

2. Imports of goods and services

Imports of goods and services include broadly the equivalent of general imports of merchandise as defined in external trade statistics, plus imports of services and direct purchases abroad made by resident households and by the government on current account. Transfer of migrants' household and personal effects and gifts between households are also included. The following additions and deductions are required, however, to move from the general trade concept to the national accounting concept. Additions required include (1) the value of purchases of bankers, stores and ballast for ships, aircraft, etc., (2) fish and salvage purchased from foreign vessels, and (3) purchases from abroad of gold ore and gold for industrial uses Deductions required include (4) goods imported solely for improvement or repair and subsequently re-exported; and (5) leased or rented machinery, equipment and other goods; the value of the repairs or leasing and rental services is included, however. The valuation of imports is c.i.f. In principle, transactions should be recorded at the moment the transfer of ownership takes place and not when goods physically enter the domestic territory, but in practice the time of recording used in the national accounts usually must follow that used in the external trade statistics.

Total imports of goods and services appear in tables 1.1, 1.2, 1.7 and 3.51. A detailed breakdown is given in table 2.17.

II. *Disposition of total supply: intermediate and final uses*

1. *Intermediate consumption*

Intermediate consumption covers non-durable goods and services used up in production, including repair and maintenance, research and development and exploration costs. It also includes indirect outlays on financing capital formation, such as flotation costs for loans and transfer costs involved in the purchase and sale of intangible assets and financial claims. Intermediate consumption is, as far as possible, valued in purchasers' prices at the moment of use. For producers of government services and private non-profit services to households, intermediate consumption includes (1) purchases of goods and services on current account *less* sales of similar second-hand goods and scraps and wastes, (2) value of goods in kind received as transfers or gifts from foreign governments, except those received for distribution to households without renovation or alteration, (3) durable goods acquired primarily for military purposes, and (4) goods and services paid for by government but furnished by private suppliers to individuals (e.g., medical services), provided that the individuals have no choice of supplier. However, intermediate consumption of these producers does not include (1) goods and services acquired for use in constructing capital assets, such as roads or buildings, (2) goods and services paid for by government but furnished by private suppliers to individuals, when the individuals can choose the supplier and (3) purchases of strategic materials for government stockpiles.

Intermediate consumption appears in each institutional sector production account in part 3, and in tables 4.1-4.2 by kind of activity. In addition to the flow numbers assigned in SNA, flow numbers have been introduced for two categories of intermediate consumption not separately numbered in *A System of National Accounts* [2]. The first is imputed bank service charges. The imputed bank service charge is defined as the excess of property income accruing to banks and similar financial institutions from the investment of deposits over the interest accruing to their depositors. This imputation is made because of the view that banks perform services for depositors for which no explicit payment is made, in return for the use of the deposits as earning assets. It is not possible to allocate the imputation to specific recipients of the services, however, so that it cannot be included, as would be desirable, as part of the intermediate consumption of each reception. It is therefore deducted as a lump-sum adjustment. The adjustment appears in the tables showing kind-of-activity breakdowns of value added or intermediate consumption, including tables 1.10, 1.11 and 4.1-4.2. The second addition is intermediate consumption of industries of government, required for constructing a production account for general government (table 3.11).

2. *Government final consumption expenditure*

Government final consumption expenditure is equal to the service produced by general government for its own use. Since these services are not sold, they are valued in the gross domestic product at their cost to the government. This cost is defined as the sum of (1) intermediate consumption, (2) compensation of employees, (3) consumption of fixed capital and (4) payments of indirect taxes, *less* (5) the value of own account production of fixed assets, and *less* (6) sales of goods and services.

The latter item, government sales, includes all payments made by individuals for services received (whether nominal or full cost) and it also includes the provision of second-hand goods from government stores as transfers in kind to foreign governments. Sales of such items as timber from forest preserves, seeds from agricultural experiment stations and government publications would also appear here. Compensation of employees, consumption of fixed capital and indirect taxes paid (if any) should preferably relate to all general government activity, with inter-governmental purchases and sales of goods and services eliminated in order to avoid double counting. With this treatment, there will be no operating surplus for any general government unit. Where countries consider that ancillary agencies and/or unincorporated government enterprises selling to the general public are operated on commercial principles and that the prices charged reflect market values, treatment of these entities on a net basis is an acceptable alternative. In this treatment, their sales to other government agencies will appear as intermediate consumption of the latter, and their operating surplus will appear as an item of general government income. This treatment has a number of disadvantages: the boundary between ancillary agencies and other government agencies is very difficult to specify precisely, and variations in treatment are likely to lead to incomparability among countries. Also, the net treatment makes it impossible to obtain figures for such flows as total compensation of general government employees. Finally, the level of gross domestic product will vary when the government's internal transfer prices are altered, a result that is somewhat incongruous.

Total government consumption expenditures appear in tables 1.1, 1.2, 4.7 and 4.8. A breakdown by government subsectors appears in table 3.12. Tables 2.1-2.2 show detailed breakdowns by function.

3. *Private final consumption expenditure*

Private consumption expenditure measures the final consumption expenditure of all resident nongovernmental units. Thus, it is the sum of final consumption expenditure of households and that of private non-profit institutions serving households.

(a) *Private non-profit institutions serving households.* Final consumption expenditure of these units, as in the case of government, is equal to services they produce for their own use and is valued at cost. Cost includes purchases and the value (in purchasers' prices) of transfers of goods and services received in kind, compensation of employees, consumption of fixed capital, and indirect taxes paid by these institutions, *less* their sales of goods and services. The definitions of purchases and sales on current account are much the same as those for general government. Private non-profit institutions serving households are defined to include units employing the equivalent of two or more full-time persons and providing educational, health, cultural, recreational, and other social and community services to households free of charge or at prices that are not intended to cover the full costs of their production. Units mainly financed and controlled by general government, however, are included in general government rather than here. Units primarily serving business, such as trade associations, are included with corporate and quasi-corporate enterprises. In applying these definitions, some judgment is required, and it will often be necessary to examine intent, as well as outcome. A normally profit-making unit that sustains a loss does not thereby become a non-profit institution.

Final expenditures of private non-profit institutions serving households appear in tables 1.1, 1.2 and 3.42, and a breakdown by purpose appears in tables 2.5 and 2.6. Definitions of the purpose categories are given in SNA classification 5.4

(b) *Resident households.* What is wanted as a component of the final uses of gross domestic product is the final consumption expenditure of resident households. What is most commonly available in the statistics, however, is not expenditure of resident units but expenditure in the domestic market. To adjust expenditure in the domestic market to expenditure of resident units, purchases abroad and net gifts in kind received from abroad have been added, and subtracted are purchases in the domestic market of non-resident units. Corresponding adjustments are made to exports (to ensure that they include purchases of non-residents in the domestic market) and to imports (to ensure that they include purchases of residents abroad). These adjustments include expenditures by tourists, ships' crews, border and seasonal workers and diplomatic and military personnel on goods and services, including local transportation, but they exclude expenditures reimbursable as travel expenses (which are counted as intermediate consumption). These adjustments are shown in tables 2.5 and 2.6.

Household final consumption expenditure includes outlays on non-durable and durable goods and services, *less* sales of second-hand goods and of scraps and wastes. In addition to market purchases, household final consumption expenditure includes the imputed gross rent of owner-occupied dwellings, food and other items produced on own account and consumed, and items provided as wages and salaries in kind by an employer, such as food, shelter or clothing, and other fringe benefits included in compensation of employees, except those considered to add to household saving. The imputed gross rent of owner-occupied dwellings should, in principle, be valued at the rent of similar facilities on the market but has been approximated by costs, including operating maintenance and repair charges, depreciation, mortgage interest, and interest on the owner's equity. Other non-marketed output included in final consumption is valued at producers' prices.

Total resident final consumption expenditure appears in tables 1.1, 1.2, 1.6 and 1.12. It is broken down by institutional subsectors in tables 3.32, and in tables 4.7 and 4.8 it is broken down by industrial origin. A detailed breakdown by type of good is shown in tables 2.5 and 2.6. The type of good categories are defined in SNA classification 6.1.

4. *Gross capital formation*

Gross capital formation is the sum of the increase in stocks and gross fixed capital formation, defined below. It appears in tables 1.1, 1.2 and 1.8. Breakdowns of gross capital formation appear in tables 2.7-2.12, 4.7 and 4.8. Gross capital formation of individual institutional sectors appears in tables 3.13, 3.23, 3.33. and 3.43.

(a) *Increase in stocks.* This flow includes the value of the physical change in (a) stocks of raw materials, work in progress and finished goods held by private producers, and (b) stocks of strategic materials held by the government. Work put in place on buildings and other structures, roads and other construction projects is treated as gross fixed capital formation rather than increase in stocks but is distinguished separately there to facilitate analysis. Increases in livestock raised for slaughter should be included in the increase in stocks, but breeding and draft animals, dairy cattle, and animals raised for wool clips are treated as fixed capital. The physical change in stocks during a period of account should be valued at average purchasers' prices during the period. In some cases, the available data relate to the change in the value of stocks held rather than the value of the physical change.

A classification of the increase in stocks by type is given in tables 2.7 and 2.8, and defined in SNA classification 6.2. The increase in stocks by kind of activity of owner is shown in tables 2.9 and 2.10.

(b) *Gross capital formation.* This flow is defined to include purchases and own-account production of new producers' durable goods, reduced by net sales to the rest of the world of similar second-hand or scrapped goods. Outlays of producers of government services for military purposes (except on land and certain civilian-type items, such as schools, hospitals, family-type housing and, in some cases, roads when for civilian use) are, however, considered to be current expenditures. "Military purposes" are here construed in terms of final expenditures: they include the military airport, but not the bulldozer used in constructing the airport. Gross fixed capital formation includes outlays on reclamation and improvement of land and development and extension of timber tracts, mines, plantations, orchards, vineyards etc., and on breeding and dairy cattle, draft animals, and animals raised for wool. Outlays on alteration or extension of fixed assets, which significantly extend their life or increase their productivity, are included, but outlays on repair and maintenance to keep fixed assets in good working order are not. All costs are included that are directly connected with the acquisition and installation of the fixed assets, such as customs duties and other indirect taxes, transport, delivery and installation charges, site clearing, planning and designing costs, legal fees and other transfer costs with respect to transactions in land, mineral deposits, timber tracts etc. However, the costs of financing, such as flotation costs, underwriters' commissions and the cost of advertising bond issues, are excluded; these items are included in intermediate consumption. The acquisition of fixed assets is to be recorded at the moment that the ownership of the goods passes to the buyer. In the case of construction projects, this is taken to be the time that the work is put in place but, as noted above, uncompleted construction projects are shown separately from completed ones.

A classification of fixed assets by type is given in tables 1.7 and 2.8, and the categories are defined in SNA classification 6.3. A classification by kind of activity of purchaser is given in tables 2.9, 2.10, 2.11 and 3.12, and a classification by producing industry is given in tables 4.7 and 4.8. Breakdowns by institutional sector are given in tables 3.13, 3.23, 3.33 and 3.43.

5. *Exports of goods and services*

Exports of goods and services are defined to be parallel to the definition of imports given above, and they are shown in the same tables and classifications. Exports are, however, valued f.o.b., whereas imports are valued c.i.f.

III. *Cost components and income shares*

1. *Value added and gross domestic product*

The value added of industries at producers' prices is equal to the gross output of the industries at producers' prices *less* the value of their intermediate consumption at purchasers' prices. Value added for the total of all domestic producers *plus* import duties and value added tax which are not included in the value added of any domestic producer, and *less* imputed bank service charges which are deducted in a single line) is equal to the gross domestic product is shown in tables 1.9-1.11, and 4.1-4.2. Gross domestic product may be defined alternatively as the sum of final expenditures in the domestic economy (tables 1.1 and 1.2) or as the sum of incomes received in the domestic economy (tables 1.3, 1.9 and 4.3). In principle, all three methods should yield the same result but in statistical practice there are likely to be small discrepancies. Such statistical discrepancies are shown where they exist.

2. *Compensation of employees*

Compensation of employees appears in SNA as a domestic concept and as a national concept. Table 1.3 employs the domestic concept, that is, compensation of employees paid by resident producers. This includes payments to non-resident employees working in the country but excludes payments to resident employees temporarily working abroad. In order to show the relation of this concept to compensation received by resident households (shown in tables 1.6 and 3.32) and compensation paid to the rest of the world (shown in tables 1.7 and 3.51), the two components are shown separately in table 1.3. Each component includes (a) wages and salaries, (b) employers' contributions to social security schemes and (c) employers' contributions to private pension, insurance and similar schemes. The national concept of compensation of employees is shown in the household sector income and outlay account (tables 1.6 and 3.31), where compensation received by resident households from domestic producers and that received from the rest of the world are gathered together. The portion paid by resident producers appears in table 1.3;

that paid by the rest of the world appears in table 1.7.

Wages and salaries include all payments to employees for their labour, whether in cash or in kind, before deduction of employee contributions to social security schemes, withholding taxes and the like. They include commissions, bonuses and tips, and cost of living, vacation and sick leave allowances paid directly by the employers to the employee but exclude reimbursement for travel and other expenses incurred by employees for business purposes, which is included in intermediate consumption. The pay and allowances of members of the armed forces, the fees, salaries and bonuses of members of boards of directors, managing directors, executives and other employees of incorporated enterprises and the fees of ministers of religion are included. Wages and salaries in kind are valued at their cost to the employer, and include goods and services furnished to employees free of charge or at markedly reduced cost that are clearly and primarily of benefit to the employees as consumers.

Employers' contributions to social security schemes include all social security contributions that employers make on behalf of their employees, but not the employees' own share of such contributions. Social security contributions may be broader than payments to social security funds, since not all social security arrangements are funded.

Employers' contributions to pension, insurance and similar schemes include paid and imputed contributions by employers on behalf of their employees to private funds, reserves or other schemes for providing pensions, family allowances, lay-off and severance pay, maternity leave, workmen's compensation, health and other casualty insurance, life insurance and the like. Where employers make payments to employees for such benefits without the establishment of a formal fund for this purpose, the contributions that would be required to support such a fund are imputed both here and subsequently as an imputed transfer from households to their employers, since of course the employees do not control the use of the fund.

3. *Operating surplus*

Operating surplus is the balancing item in the SNA production account. For an individual establishment, it is defined as the excess of value added over the sum of compensation of employees, consumption of fixed capital, and net indirect taxes. The operating surplus of all types of establishments – corporate, quasi-corporate, and unincorporated, public and private – is included in the figure shown in table 1.3. Operating surplus for each of the institutional sectors individually is shown in tables 3.11, 3.21 and 3.31; its breakdown by kind of activity is shown in table 4.3. It is also included in the totals for property and entrepreneurial income shown in tables 1.4, 1.5 and 1.6.

4. *Consumption of fixed capital*

Consumption of fixed capital includes allowances for normal wear and tear, foreseen obsolescence and probable (normally expected) accidental damage to fixed capital not made good by repair, all valued at current replacement cost. Unforeseen obsolescence, damages due to calamities, and depletion of natural resources are not included, since these are capital losses and should appear as changes in the balance sheet. Also not included is the revaluation of past allowances for consumption of fixed capital due to changes in the current replacement cost of fixed assets; this also will appear as part of the change in accumulated allowances shown in the balance sheet. Total consumption of fixed capital appears in tables 1.3, 1.8 and 1.12, consumption of fixed capital of individual institutional sectors in tables 3.11, 3.21, 3.31 and 3.41, and consumption of fixed capital by kind of activity in table 4.3. The accumulated consumption of fixed capital for specific types of assets and kind-of-activity sectors appears as the difference between the gross and net capital stock in tables 2.13-2.16, and for individual institutional sectors it appears in tables 3.15, 3.25, 3.35 and 3.45.

5. *Indirect taxes*

Indirect taxes are defined as taxes chargeable to the cost of production or sale of goods and services. They include (a) import and export duties, (b) excise, sales, entertainment and turnover taxes, (c) real estate and land taxes, unless they are merely an administrative device for collecting income tax, (d) levies on value added and the employment of labour (but not social security contributions), (e) motor-vehicle. driving-test, license, airport and passport fees, when paid by producers, and (f) the operating surplus of government fiscal monopolies on such items as alcoholic beverages and tobacco (in principle reduced by the normal profit margin of similar business units). In the present publication, indirect taxes paid and subsidies received from supranational organizations (e.g., the European Economic Community) are shown separately. Also, the net treatment of value added taxes recommended by the European Economic Community has been employed.

Unlike all other indirect taxes, SNA does not allocate import duties among producers in tables by kind of activity. Indirect taxes are only allocated to a particular kind of activity where they are levied directly on the output of that activity (e.g., excise duties) or on the process of producing that output (e.g., employment taxes). Import duties, however, are levied on the output of foreign rather than domestic producers, and are therefore shown separately in tables by kind of activity, including tables 1.10, 1.11, 4.1, 4.2, 4.3, 4.5 and 4.6.

Total indirect taxes appear in table 1.3. Indirect taxes paid by individual institutional sectors appear in tables 3.11, 3.21, 3.31, and 3.41. Indirect taxes paid to supranational organizations appear in tables 1.7 and 1.12. Indirect taxes retained by government are shown in table 3.12.

6. *Subsidies*

Subsidies are grants on current account by the government to (a) private enterprises and public corporations, or (b) unincorporated public enterprises when clearly intended to compensate for losses resulting from the price policies of government. Total subsidies, including those paid by supranational organizations, as well as by government, appear in table 1.3; subsidies paid by supranational organizations in tables 1.7 and 1.12; and those paid by government in tables 1.4 and 3.12. Subsidies received by individual institutional sectors appear in tables 3.21, 3.31 and 3.41.

7. *Withdrawals from quasi-corporations*

Withdrawals from the entrepreneurial income of quasi-corporations consist of the actual payments made to the proprietors of quasi-corporations from the entrepreneurial income of these units. Entrepreneurial income of quasi-corporations is equal to their income from production (net operating surplus) *plus* their net income (receipts *less* payments) from property. In some cases, the whole of the entrepreneurial income will be treated as if paid out to the proprietors; in other cases, some of it is retained as net saving within the quasi-corporation. Withdrawals from quasi-corporations also include withdrawals from foreign branches of domestic companies or from domestic branches of foreign companies, since both of these categories are treated as quasi-corporations. The withdrawals may be negative, since proprietors may provide funds to the enterprises to compensate for losses.

SNA assigns separate flow numbers to withdrawals as they appear in the paying sectors (flow 4.4) and in the receiving sectors (flow 4.5). As disbursements, they appear in table 3.22 and as part of a larger total in table 1.5. As receipts, they appear in tables 3.12, 3.22, 3.32 and 3.42, and as parts of the larger total in tables 1.4, 1.5 and 1.6.

8. *Property income*

Property income consists of payments of interest, dividends and land rents and royalties, all of which are assigned separate SNA flow numbers, both as payments and as receipts. Interest is defined as income payable and receivable on financial claims, such as bank and other deposits, bills and bonds, including public debt, and the equity of households in life insurance actuarial reserves and pension funds. Dividends consist of income payable and receivable on corporate equity securities and other forms of participation in the equity of private incorporated enterprises, public corporations and cooperatives. Rent payments include, in addition to net land rent, royalty payments for concessions to exploit mineral deposits or for the use of patents, copyrights, trademarks and the like. They exclude rent payments on machinery and equipment or buildings, which are treated as the purchase of a service rather than property income and appear in gross output of the seller and intermediate consumption of the purchaser. Payments of land rent are always treated as a domestic flow since the foreign owners are, for national accounting purposes, dealt with as residents of the country in which the land is located. When it is not possible to separate rent of buildings and rent of the land on which the buildings stand, the whole flow is attributed to the buildings, that is, excluded from property income and included in intermediate consumption.

Property income paid and received by individual institutional sectors is shown in tables 3.12, 3.22, 3.32 and 3.42. As part of a larger total it appears in the summary tables 1.4, 1.5 and 1.6.

IV. *Taxes and unrequited transfers*

The categories of taxes and unrequited transfers are classified and defined in SNA classification 7.1. SNA does not provide the full articulation of the to-whom from-whom relationships of these flows, but assigns flow numbers to the various combinations of them used in specific standard tables and accounts. In order to define less ambiguously the flows used in the present publication, a somewhat fuller listing of individual flow components is used.

1. *Casualty insurance transactions*

Casualty insurance transactions refer to health, accident fire, theft, unemployment and similar insurance schemes. The total of net premiums for the economy as a whole is equal to the total premiums payable *less* an imputed service charge which in turn is defined to be equal to the difference between premiums and claims. As a consequence, for the economy as a whole, net premiums and claims are equal. However, the total service charge is distributed to sectors of receipt and disbursement in proportion to the total (not net) premiums paid, so that net premiums and claims are not necessarily equal for each sector. In the former SNA, these insurance transactions were considered to be in part capital items, and this practice continues in the accounts of a number of countries. In the revised SNA, however, all casualty insurance transactions, including compensation for capital losses, are considered to be current flows. They are shown in detail in tables 3.12, 3.22, 3.32 and 3.42.

2. *Taxes and other government receipts*

Taxes and other government receipts include direct taxes, compulsory fees, fines and penalties, social security contributions, and other current transfers received by general government.

Direct taxes include two components. Direct taxes on income cover levies by public authorities at regular intervals (except social security contributions) on income from employment, property, capital gains or any other source. Real estate and land taxes are included only if they are merely administrative procedures for the assessment and collection of income tax. Other direct taxes cover levies by public authorities at regular intervals on the financial assets and the net of total worth of enterprises, private non-profit institutions and households, and on the possession or use of goods by households. Direct taxes received are shown in tables 1.4 and 3.2; payments of other sectors are shown in tables 3.22, 3.32 and 3.42.

Compulsory fees are payments to public authorities by households for services that are obligatory and unavoidable in the only circumstances in which they are useful. Examples of such fees are payments by households for driving tests and licenses, airport and court fees and the like. Similar payments by business units are treated as indirect taxes. Fines and penalties, however, include not only those paid by households but also those paid by corporate and quasi-corporate enterprises and private non-profit institutions serving households. They appear in the same tables as direct taxes.

Social security contributions consist of contributions for the account of employees, whether made by employees or by employers on their behalf, to the social security arrangements that are imposed, controlled or financed by the government for the purpose of providing social security benefits for the community or large sections of the community. They appear as receipts in tables 1.4 and 3.12, and as payments in tables 1.6 and 3.32.

Current transfers n.e.c. received by general government consist primarily of transfers received from the rest of the world and imputed employee welfare contributions. Transfers from the rest of the world include grants between governments to finance military outlays, outlays for health and educational purposes, and similar transfers in kind of military equipment, food, clothing etc. Payments and assessments and other periodic contributions to international organizations are also included. In addition to actual transfers, this item also includes imputed transfers arising from the obligation of the government as an employer to pay directly to its employees pensions, family allowances, severance and lay-off pay and other welfare benefits when there is no special fund, reserve or insurance for these purposes. In these circumstances, SNA provides for the establishment of an imputed fund to which imputed contributions are made, of a magnitude sufficient to support the unfunded benefit payments. The imputed contributions are included in compensation of employees, as an addition to actual payments, and are then shown as an imputed payment by the employees back to the government as an employer. These transfers appear in table 1.4 as an aggregate, and in table 3.12 in more detail.

3. *Household transfer receipts*

Household transfer receipts include social security benefits, social assistance grants, and unfunded employee welfare benefits. These flows, in varying detail, are shown in tables 1.6, 2.4 and 3.32.

Social security benefits are payments to individuals under the social security arrangements described above. The payments are often made out of a special fund and may be related to the income of individuals from employment or to contributions to social security arrangements made on their behalf. Examples are unemployment insurance benefits, old age, disability and survivors pensions, family allowances and reimbursements for medical and hospital expenses. It may be difficult to distinguish social security benefits from social assistance grants, on the one hand, and insurance benefits, on the other. The main criterion is method of finance; the actual content will vary from country to country. Medical services, for instance, may be supplied as social assistance, as a part of social security, as a casualty insurance benefit, or as a free government service.

Social assistance grants are cash grants to individuals and households, except social security benefits and unfunded employee welfare benefits. They may be made by public authorities, private non-profit institutions, or corporate and quasi-corporate enterprises. Examples are relief payments; widows', guardians' and family allowances and payments of medical and dental expenses which are not part of social insurance schemes; war bonuses, pensions and service grants; and scholarships, fellowships and maintenance allowances for educational, training and similar purposes. They include payments made by public authorities for services provided by business enterprises and private non-profit institutions directly and individually to persons, whether these payments are made to the individuals or directly to the providers of the services that the persons are considered to have purchased. They exclude, however, transfers to persons or households as indemnities for property losses during floods, wars and similar calamities; these are considered to be capital items.

Unfunded employee welfare benefits are pensions, family allowances, severance and lay-off pay, maternity leave pay, workmen's and disability compensation and reimbursements for medical expenses and other casualties which employers pay directly to their former or present employees when there is no special fund, reserve or insurance for these purposes.

4. *Transfers received by private non-profit institutions*

Transfers received by private non-profit institutions serving households include grants and gifts, in cash and in kind, to non-profit institutions serving households which are intended to cover partially the cost of the provision of services by these institutions. They also include membership dues paid to political organizations, fraternal bodies and the like. They appear as a receipt in table 3.42, and as payments sometimes as part of a larger total, in tables 3.12, 3.22 and 3.32.

5. *Other current transfers n.e.c.*

Other current transfers n.e.c. include transfers to and from resident sectors that are not specifically included in any other flows. They may include migrants' remittances, transfers of immigrants' personal and household goods, and transfers between resident and non-resident households, in cash and in kind. They include allowances for bad debts.

V. *Finance of gross accumulation*

1. Net saving

Net saving is the balancing item in the SNA income and outlay account. It is defined as the difference between current receipts and current disbursements. Net saving for the nation as a whole appears in tables 1.8 and 1.12. Net saving for individual institutional sectors appears in tables 3.12, 3.13, 3.22, 3.23, 3.32, 3.33, 3.42 and 3.43.

2. Surplus of the nation on current transactions

The surplus of the nation on current transactions is the balancing item in the external transactions current accounts (tables 1.7 and 3.51). It also appears in table 1.8, the capital transactions account, in table 1.12, the table showing relationships among the national accounting aggregates, and table 3.52, the external transactions capital accumulation account.

3. Purchases of land, net

Purchases of land, net, include purchases *less* sales of land, subsoil deposits, forests and inland waters, including any improvements that are an integral part of these assets except buildings and other structures. The purchases and sales are valued at the transaction (sales) price of the land, forests etc., not including the transfer costs involved; such transfer costs are included in gross capital formation. Purchases and sales are assumed to take place when the legal title to the land is passed. They are considered to take place between resident institutions only. Where the land is purchased by a non-resident, a nominal resident institution is considered to be the owner of the land. The foreign owner is assigned equity in the resident institution equivalent to the purchase price of the land. The value recorded in the flow is the same for both the buyer and the seller. For the country as a whole, therefore, purchases and sales will cancel out. If the sales value of the structures situated on the land cannot be separated from the sales value of the land itself, the entire transaction should be recorded as a purchase and sale of structures (i.e., of second-hand assets), unless the structures are intended for immediate demolition. Purchases of land appear in the capital accumulation accounts of the individual institutional sectors, (tables 3.13, 3.23, 3.33 and 3.43).

4. Purchases of intangible assets, net

Purchases of intangible assets, net, are defined as purchases, *less* sales, of exclusive rights to mineral, fishing and other concessions and of patents, copyrights etc. These transactions involve the once-and-for-all relinquishment and acquisition of the exclusive rights, although they may be paid for over a period of years; they do not include concessions, leases, licenses to use patents and permission to publish copyrighted materials which involve the periodic payment of royalties or rents, with eventual reversion of the rights to the seller. The purchases and sales are valued at the transaction (sales) value of the mineral concession, lease, patent, etc., not including any transfer costs involved. (The transfer costs are included in gross capital formation.) Purchases of intangible assets appear in the individual institutional sector capital accumulation accounts (tables 3.13, 3.23, 3.33 and 3.43) as a part of gross accumulation. Purchases from the rest of the world appear in table 3.52.

5. Capital transfers

Capital transfers are defined as unrequited transfers, in cash or in kind, which are used for purposes of capital formation or other forms of capital accumulation, are made out of wealth, or are non-recurrent. Examples of capital transfers are grants from one government to another to finance deficits in external trade, investment grants, unilateral transfers of capital goods, legacies, death duties and inheritance taxes, migrants' transfers of financial assets and indemnities in respect of calamities. Mixed transfers, considered by one party to the transaction as capital and the other as current, are treated as capital. Capital transfers appear in tables 3.13, 3.23, 3.33, 3.43 and 3.52.

6. Net lending

Net lending is defined as the excess of the sources of finance of accumulation (i.e., net saving, consumption of fixed capital and capital transfers received) over the uses of these funds for gross capital formation, net purchases of land and intangibles, and capital transfers paid. It appears in the capital accumulation accounts of the individual institutional sectors (tables 3.13, 3.23, 3.33 and 3.43), and in the external transactions capital accumulation account (table 3.52). Net lending is also equal to the difference between a sector's net acquisition of financial assets and its net incurrence of financial liabilities. it thus also appears in the institutional sector capital finance accounts (tables 3.14, 3.24, 3.34, 3.44 and 3.53). Although not for all countries, net lending derived in these two different ways are statistically identical.

VI. *Financial assets and liabilities*

Net acquisition of financial assets is defined as the difference between, on the one hand, acquisitions or purchases and, on the other, relinquishment or sales by given transactors of financial claims on second parties. Net incurrence of liabilities is equal to the issue or sale *less* redemption or payment of financial claims of second parties. A classification and definitions of financial assets and liabilities is given in SNA classification 7.2. Changes in financial assets and liabilities for individual institutional sectors appear in the capital finance accounts (tables 3.14, 3.24, 3.34, 3.44 and 3.53). Their total amount is shown in the sector balance sheets (tables 3.15, 3.25, 3.35 and 3.45).

VII. *Other assets*

1. *Reproducible tangible assets*

Reproducible tangible assets are classified and defined in table 5.1 of the *Provisional Guidelines on National and Sector Balance Sheets and Reconciliation Accounts of the System of National Accounts* [3]. They appear, classified by type of asset and broad sector, in tables 2.13 and 2.14, by kind of activity in tables 2.15 and 2.16 and for individual institutional sectors, in the sector balance sheets in tables 3.15, 3.25, 3.35 and 3.45.

2. *Non-reproducible tangible assets*

Non-reproducible tangible assets are classified and defined in table 5.2 of the *Provisional Guidelines* (see above). Only the total appears in the tables, in the sector balance sheets (tables 3.15, 3.25, and 3.45).

3. *Non-financial intangible assets*

Non-financial intangible assets include the mineral, fishing and other concessions, leases, patents, copyrights etc., the purchase and sale of which is recorded in the capital accumulation account. These intangible assets are created at the time of the purchase or sale, that is, when a once-and-for-all lumpsum payment has been made for the lease, concession, patent or copyright. They appear in the sector balance sheets (tables 3.15, 3.25, 3.35 and 3.45).

---

[1] *Official records of the Economic and Social Council. Forty Fourth Session. Supplement No. 10*, (E/4471), paras. 8-24.

[2] The present system is published in *A System of National Accounts*, Studies in Methods, Series F, No. 2, Rev. 3 (United Nations publication, Sales No. E.69.XVII.3).

[3] Statistical Papers, Series M, No. 60 United Nations publication, Sales No. 77.XVII.10.

[4] Statistical Papers, Series M, No. 4, Rev. 2, Add. I (United Nations publication, Sales No. E.71.XVII.8).

[5] Statistical Papers, Series M, No. 70 (United Nations publication, Sales No. 80.XVII.17).

II. SYSTEM OF MATERIAL PRODUCT BALANCES (MPS)

The System of Material Product Balances (MPS) furnishes the means for standardizing the national accounting data which the Statistics Division of the Department for Economic and Social Information and Policy Analysis of the United Nations Secretariat receives from countries with centrally planned economies. Data collection follows the principles found in the *Basic Methodological Rules for the Compilation of the Statistical Balance of the National Economy* 1/. This system is also described in the *Basic Principles of the System of Balances of the National Economy* 2/.

A. STRUCTURE OF MPS

MPS is based on a system of balances. It includes material and financial balances, the balance of manpower resources and the balance of fixed capital and indicators of national wealth. The material balance is a presentation of the volume of the supply of goods and material services originating in domestically produced global product and imports and their disposition to consumption, capital formation and exports, classified by different production activity categories. The financial balance is a presentation of income flows generated in production in the material sphere, their redistribution through transactions in the non-material sphere and through other transfers flows and, finally, their disbursement to consumption and capital formation. The income flows of the financial balance are classified by institutional (social) sectors. The presentation is therefore comparable to that of production, income and outlay and capital finance accounts by institutional sectors in the System of National Accounts (SNA). The third type of balance, that is, the manpower balance, presents the allocation of available manpower to production activities and institutional or social sectors. This balance is expressed in the number of persons employed. The last balance is the one of national wealth and capital assets. It is a presentation of the volume of the stocks of tangible fixed and other assets available at the beginning and the end of the year and the increase that has taken place during the year. The tangible assets are classified by type of asset and by form of ownership and production activities of the national economy.

The MPS tables that are presented in chapter III and are listed in the introduction provide further detail on the material balances. Table 1 on net material product by use is similar to the SNA table on gross domestic product by kind of economic activity. Data regarding the production and goods and services transactions are included in tables 2, 3, 4 and 5 which present, respectively, activity breakdowns of net material product and of primary incomes, of the population and of enterprises, a breakdown by socio-economic sectors of these two types of primary incomes, and a breakdown of supply and disposition of goods and material services by kind of activity of the producers. Tables 6, 7, 8 and 9 present further details on the expenditure categories, such as a breakdown of fixed capital formation by kind of economic activity and by socio-economic sector and of increases in material circulating assets and of stocks by kind of activity, and a classification of final consumption, personal consumption and of total consumption of the population by type of expenditure.

B. DIFFERENCES BETWEEN MPS AND SNA

Apart from the differences in structure of the two systems, there are considerable differences between the coverage of the concepts used in MPS and in SNA. Since these differences limit the use of MPS and SNA data in cross-country types of analyses, a summary of those that are relevant to the MPS data published in chapter III of the present publication is reproduced below 3/.

1. *The treatment of material and non-material services*

In MPS there is a distinction different to that made in SNA, between the production of material and non-material services. Only the production of material services, together with that of goods, is covered by the gross output (global product) concept of MPS. The production of non-material services is excluded. Material goods and services used as input in the production of non-material services are considered to be a part of final consumption expenditure, while income flows resulting from this type of production are treated as income transfers. The material services are those that are directly linked to the production of goods and cover the services related to the repair, transportation and distribution of goods. All other services are treated as non-material services. This important difference between MPS and the present SNA results in the following concrete differences between the two systems;

(a) Expenditures by enterprises on cultural, sports and similar facilities for their employees are excluded in MPS from intermediate consumption. Instead, a transfer between enterprises and households is included, while the material goods and services involved in the above expenditures are allocated to final consumption of the population. SNA treats these expenditures as intermediate consumption;

(b) Depreciation of dwellings and other material goods and services involved in the provision of housing are allocated in MPS to final consumption expenditure. Since these are non-material services, no value-added contribution is included in net material product. In SNA, this contribution is included in gross domestic product;

(c) Travel expenses in connection with business are not included in intermediate consumption in MPS as they are in the present SNA. Instead, they are treated as a part of compensation of employees and the material goods and services involved are allocated to private final consumption expenditure;

(d) In SNA and MPS a different distinction is drawn between uniforms to be treated as intermediate consumption and those to be included in compensation of employees and final consumption expenditure of households. In SNA, the distinction is drawn between civilian (intermediate consumption) and military uniforms and in MPS, between dress and working uniforms;

(e) Tips are treated in SNA as a part of compensation of employees, while in MPS they are treated as income transfers, when they exceed the normal service charge.

2. *Capital formation*

The MPS and SNA guidelines differ, on the one hand, with regard to the treatment of capital gains and losses and the coverage of depreciation and, on the other, in the coverage of fixed capital formation and increases in stocks. The main differences are the following:

(a) In MPS, depreciation, as well as the replacement for losses due to certain foreseeable and non-foreseeable damages to fixed assets and stocks, including those caused by accidents and calamities, are deducted in order to arrive at net fixed capital formation. In SNA, the concept of gross fixed capital formation is generally used. However, if net capital formation were to be estimated, only depreciation on fixed assets would have to be deducted in that system. Losses in stocks or fixed assets would never be considered for deduction. Losses on fixed assets would be treated as capital losses and dealt with outside the national accounts flows, while losses in stocks would be treated as a part of intermediate consumption or as capital losses, depending on whether they are due to normal events in production or to calamities. The dividing line between losses and depreciation of fixed assets also differs in the two systems. In SNA, depreciation is assumed to cover, among other things, the average amount of accidental damage to fixed assets that is not made good by repair or replacement of parts–for example, damage arising from fire and accidents. In MPS, such damages are not reflected in depreciation but covered under losses;

(b) Depreciation in MPS is based on the original cost of the assets. However, every eight to ten years, adjustments to replacement cost are made to this asset value and these adjustments are also reflected in a corrected value of depreciation. Furthermore, differences that arise between the actual value and the written-off book value at the moment the assets are scrapped or sold are included in the value of depreciation for the year in which the sale or scrapping occurs. In SNA, instead, the replacement value of the assets is used as a basis for depreciation. Any change in this value, whether it happens at the moment the asset is sold or during the time it is used, is considered to be a capital gain or loss and is not accounted for in the national accounting flows;

(c) In addition, in MPS, depreciation includes capital consumption allowances with respect to afforestation, land improvements, roads. bridges and similar structures. In SNA, no imputations for depreciation of this type of asset are included;

(d) Expenditures on fixed assets for military purposes are treated in MPS as a part of net fixed capital formation. In SNA, these outlays are allocated to government final consumption expenditure, except for outlays by government on the construction and alteration of family dwellings for personnel of the armed forces, which are included in gross fixed capital formation;

(e) Transfer cost with regard to purchases and sales of existing fixed assets are treated in MPS as transfers since these are non-material services. In SNA, these costs are included in gross fixed capital formation;

(f) Work put in place on structures, roads, dams, ports and other forms of construction is allocated in MPS to increases in material circulating assets and stocks. Only when the construction is finished is its total value transferred to net fixed capital formation. In SNA, these outlays are immediately allocated to gross fixed capital formation.

3. *External transactions*

The third area in which MPS and SNA differ is in the coverage of exports and imports of goods and services, in the distinction between residents and non-residents and in the treatment of monetary, as opposed to non-monetary gold. The differences are the following:

(a) In MPS, embassies, consulates and international bodies are treated as residents of the country in which they are located, while in SNA they are treated as residents of the country they represent. This difference in the residence concept has consequences for the allocation between countries of capital formation and government final consumption expenditure and also for the allocation of the income flows. Wages and salaries paid to local employees of these extraterritorial bodies are not included in SNA concept of gross domestic product. They are dealt with, however, as factor income from abroad and therefore accounted for in the national income concept in SNA. In MPS, such wages and salaries, if earned in the sphere of material production, are included in primary incomes of the population, as well as in net material product;

(b) In MPS, the territorial concept of final consumption expenditure, which includes purchases by non-residents in the domestic market and excludes purchases abroad by residents, is used. As a result, such flows are not accounted for in exports or imports. On the other hand, it does include, in exports and imports, transactions that, though they take place in the domestic market, are conducted in foreign currency. These transactions are treated as if they were transactions with non-residents. In SNA, the national concept of final consumption expenditure is used; taken into account in exports and imports, respectively, are the direct purchases in the domestic market by non-residents and the direct purchases abroad by non-residents. Furthermore, no distinction is made in SNA between transactions that are conducted in local or in foreign currency;

(c) Purchases and sales by external trade organizations of goods that do not cross the border of the country in question and also imported goods that are re-exported without being processed are treated in MPS as part of respectively, imports and exports. In SNA, they are not accounted for in the export and import flows, except for the margins received by resident units as payments for services rendered;

(d) Gifts in kind by households to and from abroad are included in exports and imports in SNA. In MPS, they are excluded from these flows;

(e) Transactions in intangible assets (patents, copyrights, trade-marks, exclusive rights to exploit mineral deposits, etc.) with the rest of the world are included in MPS in exports and imports. In SNA, they are treated as property income or as sales or purchases of intangible assets to or from abroad, depending on whether the payment is for the use of the rights or for the outright transfer of those rights;

(f) Transactions with the rest of the world in monetary and non-monetary gold are included in MPS in exports and imports. In SNA, included in exports and imports are actual transactions in non-monetary gold only. Exports in addition include newly mined gold (whether actually exported or not) in order to transform gold as a commodity into a financial asset.

C. STANDARD CLASSIFICATIONS OF MPS

Two classifications are used in the MPS standard tables presented, that is, the kind-of-activity classification and the classification by socio-economic group. Contrary to SNA usage with respect to the activity and institutional classifications for different groups of transactions, the two MPS classifications are parallel ones that are applied to the same transaction categories: net material product and its component primary incomes and capital formation. Each of these classifications is described briefly below.

I. Kind of activity

All forms of activity in production are classified according to groups or branches, depending on the nature and results of the application of labour. The two major categories constitute branches of the material sphere and branches of the non-material sphere. The first category covers the production of goods, and services that are related to the production of goods, such as repair services, transportation services and goods distribution services. The second category includes the remaining services-producing activities. Each of the two categories is further broken down by branches which are similar in character to the ISIC categories used in SNA. The unit of classification is not the organizational unit (i.e., enterprise) but a smaller unit that performs one type of activity (i.e., establishment). If the enterprise or institution or other organizational unit carries on more than one type of economic activity, it is considered to consist of two or more establishments that perform different activities.

For the subclassification of net material product by kind of activity, only the activity breakdown of the material sphere is used since net material product originates in this sphere only. For capital formation, however, the activity categories of the non-material sphere are also used, since capital formation relates not only to the material sphere but also to non-material branches.

A rough correspondence based on the names of the activity categories can be established between the activity categories presented in SNA and in the MPS branches. The user should be aware, however, of the limitations that such a linkage may entail, as indicated in the following points:

(a) Mining and quarrying, manufacturing, and electricity, gas and water are shown as three separate categories in the SNA presentation and as one category (industrial production), in the MPS presentation;

(b) Hunting and the collection of forestry products is treated as a part of agriculture in the SNA presentation and as a part of forestry and logging in MPS;

(c) The distribution of gas, electricity and water to households is treated in MPS as a non-material service (including in housing). This activity is therefore not reflected in net material product, while its capital formation is dealt with as capital formation of the non-material sphere. In SNA, these distribution activities are an integral part of the activity category for electricity, gas and water;

(d) Printing and publishing, which is treated as a material activity in MPS, is allocated to the MPS category known as "other activities of the material sphere". In SNA, this activity is included with manufacturing;

(e) Cleaning, dyeing and repair services are included with industrial activity (manufacturing) in the MPS presentation and with community, social and personal services in SNA;

(f) In comparing the activity breakdown of net material product and gross domestic product, the user should be aware that the coverage of the MPS category known as "other activities of the material sphere" falls far short of the combined coverage of the two SNA categories for finance, insurance, real estate and business services and for community, social and personal services. The SNA categories include all non-material activities that are excluded from the MPS coverage of net material product. In addition, the shifts between activity categories that were outlined in the previous points affect this group. Other activities in the presentation of net material product include telegraph, news-gathering and editorial agencies, industrial services other than architectural design services, printing and publishing services, the production of motion pictures, phonograph records and prerecorded tapes, data-processing and tabulating services, waterway-maintenance services and the operation of flood-control systems, and services related to the conservation of natural resources and the protection of the environment.

2. *Socio-economic sectors*

The rates of development of the national economy and the basic features of production that support this development are largely determined by the social structure of the community. In order to study the process, the various activities involved in the production of material goods and services are classified in MPS by socio-economic sector. This classification is based on the form of ownership of the fixed and circulating capital. The form of ownership of the means of production determines the forms of ownership of the product and of the incomes generated by its disposal.

The basic socio-economic sectors are the socialist sector and the private sector.

The socialist sector embraces the enterprises and institutions in public, socialist ownership. The fixed and circulating assets of these enterprises are public property. The socialist sector also includes the personal plots of employees and members of cooperatives.

Within the socialist sector, the following socio-economic subsectors are distinguished: the state subsector, the cooperative subsector, which includes agricultural producers' cooperatives; associations; personal plots of employees; personal plots of members of co-operatives.

The state subsector includes the enterprises and institutions in state ownership. The state furnishes them with the fixed and circulating assets required for their operation. These economic units are administratively subordinated to central or local organs of state authority. The production of the state subsector and the income generated in it belong to the people as a country.

The co-operative subsector embraces the enterprises and institutions in collective or group ownership. The fixed and circulating assets of these economic bodies are originally built up from the entrance fees (initiation fees) of their members and the proceeds of sales of shares to them; and are later supplemented from part of their operating surplus. The output and income of the enterprises and institutions of the co-operative subsector are the property of their members.

The association subsector includes the enterprises and institutions owned by voluntary or semi-voluntary associations. The fixed and circulating assets of the economic bodies of this subsector are built up from the voluntary contributions of their members and from part of the operating surplus of such bodies. The output and income of this subsector belong to the associations.

The personal plots of employees and members of co-operatives embrace agricultural output, construction and other forms of activity (gathering of wild fruits and berries, scrap collection etc.).

The private sector includes the enterprises and institutions, the fixed and circulating assets of which are privately owned. The classification of enterprises and institutions of the private sector is based on the specific economic conditions in the country concerned. Within this sector, the subsector of craftsmen, artisans and peasants who are not members of co-operatives may be distinguished.

Peasants, craftsmen and artisans who do not belong to co-operatives operate small private ventures in which the productive process is carried out by their owners in person, as a rule without recourse to hired labour. This group also includes the subsidiary activities of the population occupied in the private sector of the national economy.

D. DEFINITIONS OF FLOWS

Given below are the definitions of the flows that appear in the MPS standard tables of chapter III. To make possible a comparison between SNA and MPS data, a description of the differences between the MPS and the SNA coverage is added to each of the sections. The items needed in order to convert the MPS coverage into a coverage that conforms to the SNA definition are only summarily indicated. For more information on these items, the user is therefore referred to the description of the differences between the two systems in section B above. The items described below have been grouped together into categories similar to those used for the SNA flows (see chap. I above, sect. C).

I. *Total supply and disposition of goods and material services*

1. *Gross output*

Global product covers the value of goods and material services produced. Deliveries of goods and material services within the same enterprise are generally excluded. Included are, among other things, the value of own-account constructed capital goods and capital repairs to fixed assets, the value of work-in-progress and the value of finished goods added to stocks. Covered is, furthermore, the value of goods and material services provided free to employees (the material services are valued at the material cost involved). Included in the contribution to global product by agriculture are seeds and feed produced and consumed at the same farm and agricultural and other goods produced on personal plots for own consumption or for sale, including the cost of their processing. This concept of gross output appears in MPS table 5.

To derive gross output in producers' prices as defined in SNA, global product as described above needs to be increased by:

plus: the gross output value of non-material services (including those of government), including the transfer cost on purchases and sales of existing second-hand fixed assets and land.

2. *Trade margins and transport charges*

The gross output of material goods and services is valued at both producers' and purchasers' values. The difference between the two sets of values gives the distributive trade margins (including restaurants, cafes and other catering) and the transportation margins. The gross output of the distributive-trade units is equal to the value of their gross margins on internal and external trade.

The gross margins on external trade are equivalent to the sum in domestic currency of (a) the value of imports of goods and material services in the domestic market *less* the actual value at which these imports are purchased from abroad and (b) the actual value at which exports of goods and material services are sold to abroad *less* the value of these exports in the domestic market. Trade margins and transport charges appear in MPS table 5.

3. *Intermediate material consumption, including depreciation*

Intermediate material consumption consists of the value of the goods and material services used up in the process of production during a period of account by units of the material sphere, including the consumption of fixed assets during the period. Consistent with the scope of the gross output of goods and material services included in intermediate consumption are certain items, for example, seeds and animal feed, which are produced and used by the same unit. The intermediate output of raw materials etc., is valued net of the value of scraps and wastes originating in the process of production. Purchased items are valued at purchasers' values; items produced on own account are valued at cost in the case of state and co-operative enterprises and at average purchasers' prices in the case of personal plots of households. This concept of intermediate material consumption appears in MPS table 5.

Depreciation or consumption of fixed assets includes an allowance for normal wear and tear and foreseen obsolescence of fixed assets based on standard rates of depreciation and, furthermore, the difference between the book value of scrapped fixed assets and their scrap value. The allowances for depreciation are often based on the original cost of the assets which may be periodically adjusted to replacement cost.

To arrive from intermediate material consumption, including depreciation as defined above, at the SNA concept of intermediate consumption, the MPS coverage needs to be increased and decreased by the following items:

plus: (i) material cost of non-material services;

plus: (ii) material expenditures by enterprises on cultural, sports and similar facilities for their employees;

plus: (iii) reimbursable expenditures for material goods and services purchased during business trips;

minus: (iv) consumption of fixed capital in the material sphere.

4. *Personal consumption*

This consists of all consumer goods, irrespective of durability, and material services (repair, transport, communication and similar services) which are purchased by households, received in kind as payment for work in state and collective enterprises and in private plots, or produced on own account on personal plots. Excluded is the purchase by households of dwellings (which is dealt with as capital formation) but included is the maintenance and depreciation of dwellings. Also included are reimbursable expenditures for material goods and services purchased during business trips. This concept of personal consumption appears in MPS tables 1 and 7. It appears according to source of supply of goods and material services in MPS table 8. In MPS, the domestic concept of consumption is used, so that direct purchases by foreign tourists, diplomatic personnel and other non-residents in the domestic market are included, while similar purchases abroad by residents are excluded.

5. *Material consumption in the units of the non-material sphere serving individuals*

This flow covers expenditures on non-durable goods and material services by units of the non-material sphere serving individuals, reduced by the increases in their stocks of goods. Also included is consumption of fixed assets used by these units. It appears in MPS tables 1 and 7.

6. *Material consumption in the units of the non-material sphere serving the community as a whole*

This flow consists of non-durable goods and material services purchased during a period of account by units of the non-material sphere serving the community as a whole, reduced by the increases in their stocks of goods during the period of account. Also included is consumption of fixed assets of these units. It appears in MPS tables 1 and 7.

To arrive from this concept at government final consumption expenditure as defined in SNA, the following additions to and subtraction from the MPS concept have to be made:

plus: (i) the difference between the value of non-material services produced by government and their material cost and depreciation;

plus: (ii) government expenditures on fixed assets that have military uses;

plus: (iii) the difference between consumption expenditures (i.e., material and non-material cost, depreciation and compensation of employees) of extraterritorial bodies that represent the country abroad *minus* consumption expenditures incurred by extraterritorial bodies of other countries and international organizations located in the country in question;

plus: (iv) material expenditures by government (units in the non-material sphere serving individuals) on education, health, culture and other services provided free to individuals.

7. *Final consumption*

This flow is equal to the sum of personal consumption and material consumption in the units of the non-material sphere serving individuals and of those serving the community as a whole. Each of these concepts has been defined above. They appear in MPS tables 5 and 7.

8. *Consumption of the population*

Consumption of the population is the sum of personal consumption and material consumption in the units of the non-material sphere serving individuals. This concept is comparable to private final consumption expenditure in SNA, which can be derived from this MPS concept by adding and subtracting the following items:

plus: (i) the difference between the value of non-material services purchased by households, including housing services and the material cost and depreciation included in the value of these services;

minus: (ii) material expenditures by government (units in the non-material sphere serving individuals) on education, health, culture and other services provided free to individuals;

plus: (iii) the difference between direct purchases abroad by resident households and direct purchases in the domestic market by non-resident households as well as the difference between gifts sent abroad by household *minus* gifts received from abroad;

minus: (iv) reimbursable expenditures for material goods and services purchased during business trips;

minus: (v) material expenditures by enterprises on cultural sports and similar facilities for their employees.

9. *Total consumption of the population*

Total consumption of the population covers the consumption by the population of goods and material services and of non-material services, whether purchased by households or furnished free of charge. It therefore exceeds the consumption of the population (i.e., the sum of personal consumption and material consumption in the units of the non-material sphere serving individuals) by the value of the services of the units of the non-material sphere serving individuals, reduced by the consumption of goods and material services by these units. The value of the services of the units is equivalent to their costs of production, including operating surplus in some instances. In the case of dwellings provided by these units, their depreciation is not included when evaluating costs of production, since charges in respect of depreciation of these dwellings are included in personal consumption. Total consumption of the population appears classified by object in MPS table 9.

10. *Net fixed capital formation*

Net fixed capital formation consists of the value of new fixed assets purchased or constructed on own account and of completed capital repairs to these assets reduced by consumption of fixed assets for renewal of assets and capital repairs, and capital losses due to fire, floods and other calamities and furthermore reduced by the remaining value of scrapped fixed assets. Thus, it measures the net increase in the value of fixed assets during a period of account. This flow appears in MPS tables 5 and 6.

Fixed assets include completed dwellings, buildings and other structures; machinery, equipment and other durable goods acquired by units of the material and non-material sphere; cattle, excluding young cattle and cattle raised for meat; perennial plants; and expenditures on the improvement of land, forests and other natural resources. New fixed assets put into use are generally valued inclusive of acquisition and installation cost.

Capital repairs cover outlays on repairs that make up at least in part for the physical depreciation of the fixed assets and/or significantly raise the capacity and productivity of the fixed assets.

In order to convert the MPS concept of net fixed capital formation into gross fixed capital formation as defined in SNA, the following additions to and subtractions from the MPS concept have to be made:

plus: (i) consumption of fixed capital in the material and non-material sphere, including that on afforestation, roads, bridges and similar structures;

plus: (ii) losses due to foreseeable as well as non-foreseeable damages to fixed assets;

plus: (iii) transfer cost with regard to purchases and sales of existing second-hand fixed assets, including land;

plus: (iv) work in progress on the construction of structures, roads, dams and ports or others forms of construction;

plus: (v) the difference between outlays on fixed capital formation by extraterritorial bodies representing the country in question abroad, *less* similar outlays by extraterritorial bodies of other countries and international organizations located in the country in question;

minus: (vi) government expenditures on fixed assets that have military uses.

11. *Gross fixed capital formation*

Gross fixed capital formation is equal to net fixed capital formation as defined above *plus* depreciation. Depreciation is defined in section 3 above, together with intermediate material consumption. Gross fixed capital formation classified by kind of activity appears in MPS table 6.

12. *Increases in material circulating assets and stocks*

This item consists of increases during the period of account in the stocks of enterprises in the material sphere, including wholesale and retail trade units, reduced by losses. Also covered are increases in government stockpiles, including stocks of defense items and state reserves of precious metals and precious stones. The stocks in the material sphere consist of raw materials, fuels, supplies and other nondurable goods; young cattle and cattle raised for meat; work in progress, including uncompleted construction projects; and finished goods not yet sold. Increases in material circulating assets and stocks appear in MPS tables 1 and 6.

In order to convert the MPS concept of increases in material circulating assets and stocks into increases in stocks as defined in SNA, the following addition to and subtractions from the MPS concept are needed:

plus: (i) losses due to foreseeable and non-foreseeable damages to stocks;

minus: (ii) work in progress on the construction of structures, roads, dams and ports and on other forms of construction;

minus: (iii) net increases in the holdings of gold ingots and other monetary gold.

13. *Losses*

This item is the sum of the value of the losses in fixed assets and losses in material circulating assets and stocks. Included are losses (a) due to fires, floods and other calamities, (b) in adult productive and working cattle, (c) due to abandoned or interrupted construction works and (d) in agricultural products in storage at state and co-operative agricultural enterprises and at farms. This flow appears in MPS tables 1 and 5.

In SNA, this final demand category is not identified separately from gross capital formation.

14. *Exports and imports of goods and material services*

Exports are defined to include: (a) outward-bound goods that cross the border of the country, including imported goods which are exported without being processed; (b) goods which are purchased outside the country by an external trade organization of the country in question and shipped directly to a third country; (c) outward-bound monetary and non-monetary gold and other precious metals; (d) unilateral transfers of goods by the government and public organizations of the country (uncompensated foreign aid); (e) material services, such as transport, forwarding and communication services, rental, including rental payments for time-charter of ships and other transport equipment and, furthermore, export contract services rendered to other countries. The imports cover the same categories of goods and material services which are inward bound exports are valued f.o.b. while imports are valued c.i.f. They appear in MPS tables 1 and 5.

To arrive at the SNA coverage of exports of goods and services, the following additions to and subtractions from the MPS concept are needed:

plus: (i) the difference between the export value of non-material services and the material cost and depreciation included in these services;

plus: (ii) consumption expenditure (material and non-material cost, depreciation and compensation of employees) and outlays on fixed capital formation by extraterritorial bodies of foreign governments and international organizations located in the country in question;

plus: (iii) direct purchases in the domestic market by non-resident households and gifts sent abroad by households;

minus: (iv) sales abroad by an external trade organization of the country of goods that have not crossed the border of the country in question; as well as of goods that have crossed the border but that are re-exported without being processed;

minus: (v) the difference between exported monetary gold and the value of sales of newly produced gold ingots and bars.

MPS imports have to be adjusted in a similar manner. To be added are the import value of non-material services *minus* material cost and depreciation, consumption expenditure and fixed capital formation of extraterritorial bodies that represent the country abroad and direct purchases abroad by residents. To be deducted are re-exports and purchases abroad by external trade organizations of goods that do not cross the border of the country, and also the value of imported monetary gold and gifts received by households from abroad.

III. *Cost components and income shares*

1. *Net material product*

Net material product is defined in MPS and is used in countries with centrally planned economies. It can be estimated from the production income and expenditure side in the same manner, as is indicated in chapter I above, section C.III, in which the SNA coverage of gross domestic product is described. Following the production approach, net material product is the difference between global product (i.e., gross output) of goods and material services and intermediate material consumption, including consumption of fixed assets. Net material product defined from the income side is the sum of primary incomes of the population (comparable to compensation of employees in SNA) and primary incomes of enterprises (comparable to operating surplus in SNA). The expenditure approach finally defines net material product as the sum of the final uses of goods and material services, that is, personal consumption, and material consumption of units in the non-material sphere serving individuals and that of similar units serving the community as a whole, net capital formation (i.e., net of depreciation), replacement for losses and the balance between exports and imports of goods and material services. These three different methods for deriving net material product are shown in MPS tables 1, 2 and 4.

To arrive at the SNA concept of gross domestic product, net material product needs to be increased and reduced as follows:

plus: (i) the excess value of non-material services (i.e., the gross output value *minus* material cost and depreciation) consumed by households and by government *plus* the difference between these excess values of exported and imported non-material services;

minus: (ii) material expenditures by enterprises on cultural, sports and similar facilities for their employees;

minus: (iii) reimbursable expenditures for material goods and services purchased during business trips;

plus: (iv) consumption of fixed capital in the material and non-material sphere, including that on afforestation, roads, bridges and similar structures;

plus: (v) losses of fixed assets and stocks due to accidental damage, such as fire, accidents etc.;

plus: (vi) transfer cost with regard to purchases and sales of existing second-hand fixed assets, including land.

2. *Primary income of the population*

The primary income of the population consists of (a) wages and salaries, including receipts in kind, and related income, such as bonuses and reimbursements of expenses on business trips received from state, cooperative and private units of the material sphere; (b) the net material product (net value added) originating from the personal plots of households; and (c) the net material product of self-employed craftsmen, artisans and peasants. This flow appears in MPS tables 3 and 4.

Primary income of the population is roughly comparable to the SNA concept of compensation of employees. However, several differences remain and in order to arrive from the MPS concept at compensation of employees as defined in SNA, the following additions and subtractions are needed:

plus: (i) compensation of employees, including employers' contributions to social security funds, paid out in connection with non-material activities, inclusive of those that are paid out in connection with the provision of cultural, sports and similar facilities by industries in the material sphere;

plus: (ii) employers' contributions to social security funds paid out in connection with material activities;

minus: (iii) income from private enterprises;

minus: (iv) reimbursable expenditures for material goods and services purchased during business trips.

3. *Primary income of enterprises*

Primary income of enterprises consists of the sum of the net material product of the units of the material sphere which have employees *less* the wages and salaries and related incomes which they pay out. The primary incomes of these units are the source of such items as their net income, turnover taxes, contributions to social insurance, payments of taxes, fines and other compulsory items, finance of purchases of non-material services, insurance premiums, interest on bank loans and other business costs. This flow appears in MPS tables 3 and 4.

Although the coverage of primary income of enterprises is similar to that of operating surplus in SNA, the following additions to and subtractions from the MPS concept are needed in order to arrive at operating surplus as defined in SNA:

plus: (i) the remaining value of non-material services (i.e., the gross output value *minus* material cost, depreciation and compensation of employees) consumed by households and government, *plus* the difference between the remaining values of exported and imported non-material services;

minus: (ii) material expenditures by enterprises on cultural, sports and similar facilities for their employees;

plus: (iii) consumption of fixed capital in the material and non-material sphere, including that on afforestation, roads, bridges and similar structures;

plus: (iv) losses of fixed assets and stocks due to accidental damage, such as fire, accidents etc.;

plus: (v) transfer cost with regard to purchases and sales of existing fixed assets, including land;

minus: (vi) employers' contributions to social security funds, paid out in connection with material activities;

plus: (vii) income from private plots and private enterprises.

1/ Standing Statistical Commission, Council of Mutual Economic Assistance (Moscow, 1969).

2/ Studies in Methods, Series F, No. 17 (United Nations publication, Sales No.E.71.XVII.10).

3/ For a more exhaustive list of differences between MPS and SNA, the user should refer to *Comparisons of the System of National Accounts and the System of Balances of the National Economy*, part One, *Conceptual Relationships* (United Nations publication, Sales No. 77.XVII.6).

III. COUNTRY TABLES

Afghanistan

Source. Reply to the United Nations national accounts questionnaire from the Central Statistical Office, Kabul.

General note. The estimates shown in the following tables have been prepared in accordance with the United Nations System of National Accounts so far as the existing data would permit.

1.11 Gross Domestic Product by Kind of Activity, in Constant Prices

Thousand Million Afghanis — Fiscal year beginning 21 March

	1980	1983	1984	1985	1986	1987	1988	1989	1990	1991	1992	1993
					At constant prices of: 1978							
1 Agriculture, hunting, forestry and fishing	83.6	88.5	88.1	87.6	89.0	72.1	67.3	64.6	59.6	...	...	...
2 Mining and quarrying										...	...	...
3 Manufacturing	28.8	32.5	33.2	36.2	37.9	37.3	32.8	30.1	30.4	...	...	...
4 Electricity, gas and water										...	...	...
5 Construction	5.9	7.4	8.0	8.0	9.1	10.6	10.2	7.1	7.5	...	...	...
6 Wholesale and retail trade, restaurants and hotels	9.8	11.2	12.4	12.1	12.6	12.0	10.6	10.1	10.5	...	...	...
7 Transport, storage and communication	4.8	5.5	5.9	4.3	4.0	4.9	4.6	4.6	4.7	...	...	...
8 Finance, insurance, real estate and business services	...	...	...	...	...	...	...	...	...	...	...	...
9 Community, social and personal services	...	...	...	...	...	...	...	...	...	...	...	...
Total, Industries	132.9	145.1	147.6	148.2	152.6	136.9	125.5	116.5	112.7	...	...	...
Producers of Government Services	...	...	...	...	...	...	...	...	...	...	...	...
Other Producers	1.8	2.2	2.4	2.2	2.3	2.1	2.0	2.0	2.1	...	...	...
Subtotal	134.7	147.3	150.0	150.4	154.9	139.0	127.5	118.5	114.8	...	...	...
Less: Imputed bank service charge	...	...	...	...	...	...	...	...	...	...	...	...
Plus: Import duties	...	...	...	...	...	...	...	...	...	...	...	...
Plus: Value added tax	...	...	...	...	...	...	...	...	...	...	...	...
Equals: Gross Domestic Product	134.7	147.3	150.0	150.4	154.9	139.0	127.5	118.5	114.8	...	...	...

Albania

Source. Reply to the United Nations National Accounts Questionnaire from the Statistical Directory of the Ministry of Economy, Tirana.
General note. The estimates shown in the following tables have been prepared in accordance with the United Nations System of National Accounts so far as the existing data would permit.

1.1 Expenditure on the Gross Domestic Product, in Current Prices

Million Albanian leks

		1980	1983	1984	1985	1986	1987	1988	1989	1990	1991	1992	1993
1	Government final consumption expenditure	1395	1467	1553	1568	1612	1663	1608	1645	1715	...	...	...
2	Private final consumption expenditure	8755	9519	9833	9881	10345	10785	10764	11392	12227	...	...	...
3	Gross capital formation	5233	5963	5235	5672	5456	4817	4971	5926	4108	...	...	...
	A Increase in stocks	99	110	-864	78	-	-685	-447	72	-1702	...	...	...
	B Gross fixed capital formation	5134	5853	6099	5594	5456	5502	5418	5854	5810	...	...	...
4	Exports of goods and services	149	-231	-118	-265	-30	-19	-342	-289	-1239	...	...	...
5	Less: Imports of goods and services										...	...	...
	Equals: Gross Domestic Product [a]	15532	16718	16503	16856	17383	17246	17001	18674	16812	...	...	...

a) For the years 1986-1990, prices have been unchanged, therefore the estimates in the current prices table are equal to those shown in the constant price table.

1.2 Expenditure on the Gross Domestic Product, in Constant Prices

Million Albanian leks

		1980	1983	1984	1985	1986	1987	1988	1989	1990	1991	1992	1993
						At constant prices of: 1986							
1	Government final consumption expenditure	1385	1455	1536	1551	1612	1663	1608	1645	1715	...	...	...
2	Private final consumption expenditure	8677	9530	9845	9893	10345	10785	10764	11392	12227	...	...	...
3	Gross capital formation	4670	5625	4911	5283	5456	4817	4971	5926	4108	...	...	...
	A Increase in stocks	93	105	-823	74	-	-685	-447	72	-1702	...	...	...
	B Gross fixed capital formation	4577	5520	5734	5209	5456	5502	5418	5854	5810	...	...	...
4	Exports of goods and services	149	-231	-118	-265	-30	-19	-342	-289	-1239	...	...	...
5	Less: Imports of goods and services										...	...	...
	Equals: Gross Domestic Product [a]	14881	16379	16174	16462	17383	17246	17001	18674	16812	...	...	...

a) For the years 1986-1990, prices have been unchanged, therefore the estimates in the current prices table are equal to those shown in the constant price table.

1.3 Cost Components of the Gross Domestic Product

Million Albanian leks

		1980	1983	1984	1985	1986	1987	1988	1989	1990	1991	1992	1993
1	Indirect taxes, net	...	...	...	...	...	...	...	...	...	...	...	...
2	Consumption of fixed capital	1682	1903	1982	2052	2100	2146	2089	2198	2238	...	...	...
3	Compensation of employees paid by resident producers to:	7380	8190	8279	8432	8894	9091	9058	9684	10399	...	...	...
4	Operating surplus	5820	6286	5913	5978	6389	6009	5854	6792	4175	...	...	...
	Equals: Gross Domestic Product	15532	16718	16503	16856	17383	17246	17001	18674	16812	...	...	...

Algeria

Source. Direction des Statistiques et de la Comptabilite Nationale, Secretariat d'Etat au Plan, Alger. Official estimates are published in 'Comptes Economiques'.
General note. The estimates shown in the following tables have been prepared in accordance with the United Nations System of National Accounts so far as the existing data would permit.

1.1 Expenditure on the Gross Domestic Product, in Current Prices

Million Algerian dinars

	1980	1983	1984	1985	1986	1987	1988	1989	1990	1991	1992	1993
1 Government final consumption expenditure	22351	34693	39366	45945	52924	58072	65139	70615	...	...	...	...
2 Private final consumption expenditure	70179	106183	125829	139719	156414	154882	175453	210331	...	...	...	...
3 Gross capital formation	63512	87819	92531	96765	99333	93880	94705	121100	...	...	...	...
A Increase in stocks	8631	7500	5049	4000	-2000	1000	6061	12580	...	...	...	...
B Gross fixed capital formation	54881	80319	87482	92765	101333	92880	88644	108520	...	...	...	...
Residential buildings	...	...	...	...	...	...	...	...	...	...	...	...
Non-residential buildings	...	...	...	...	...	...	...	...	...	...	...	...
Other construction and land improvement etc.	30224	47325	...	...	...	...	...	...	...	...	...	...
Other	24657	32994	...	...	...	...	...	...	...	...	...	...
4 Exports of goods and services	55802	65344	67688	68630	38714	45834	49898	77792	...	...	...	...
5 Less: Imports of goods and services	49338	60286	61558	59462	50833	39962	50588	76378	...	...	...	...
Equals: Gross Domestic Product	162507	233752	263856	291597	296552	312706	334607	403460	...	...	...	...

1.3 Cost Components of the Gross Domestic Product

Million Algerian dinars

	1980	1983	1984	1985	1986	1987	1988	1989	1990	1991	1992	1993
1 Indirect taxes, net	31134	44469	53785	55291	55561	62009	64438	71554	...	...	...	...
2 Consumption of fixed capital	13692	21504	23104	28195	31660	32525	32622	33050	...	...	...	...
3 Compensation of employees paid by resident producers to:	57133	88642	94177	102983	120091	125754	137648	156145	...	...	...	...
A Resident households	...	...	94177	102983	120091	125754	137648	156145	...	...	...	...
B Rest of the world	...	...	...	...	...	...	...	...	...	...	...	...
4 Operating surplus	60549	79138	92791	105128	89240	92418	99900	142711	...	...	...	...
Equals: Gross Domestic Product	162507	233752	263856	291597	296552	312706	334607	403460	...	...	...	...

1.7 External Transactions on Current Account, Summary

Million Algerian dinars

	1980	1983	1984	1985	1986	1987	1988	1989	1990	1991	1992	1993
Payments to the Rest of the World												
1 Imports of goods and services	49338	60286	61558	59462	50833	39962	50588	76378	...	...	...	...
A Imports of merchandise c.i.f.	40519	49772	51257	49491	43393	34153	43427	70072	...	...	...	...
B Other	8819	10514	10301	9971	7440	5809	7161	6306	...	...	...	...
2 Factor income to the rest of the world	6232	6969	7789	7793	7583	7953	12360	14274	...	...	...	...
A Compensation of employees	...	...	...	...	...	...	...	...	...	...	...	...
B Property and entrepreneurial income	6232	6969	7789	7793	7583	7953	12360	14274	...	...	...	...
3 Current transfers to the rest of the world	876	853	868	760	719	539	513	500	...	...	...	...
4 Surplus of the nation on current transactions	2627	28	154	4282	-15271	963	-10367	-7913	...	...	...	...
Payments to the Rest of the World and Surplus of the Nation on Current Transactions	59073	68136	70369	72297	43862	49416	53094	83239	...	...	...	...
Receipts From The Rest of the World												
1 Exports of goods and services	55802	65344	67688	68630	38714	45834	49898	77792	...	...	...	...
A Exports of merchandise f.o.b.	52400	60722	63758	65146	35391	41986	45421	71937	...	...	...	...
B Other	3402	4622	3930	3484	3323	3848	4477	5855	...	...	...	...
2 Factor income from rest of the world	1560	1064	1079	1225	1012	685	615	1096	...	...	...	...
A Compensation of employees	...	...	...	...	...	...	...	...	...	...	...	...
B Property and entrepreneurial income	1560	1064	1079	1225	1012	685	615	1096	...	...	...	...
3 Current transfers from rest of the world	1711	1728	1602	2443	4137	2897	2581	4350	...	...	...	...
Receipts from the Rest of the World on Current Transactions	59073	68136	70369	72297	43862	49416	53094	83238	...	...	...	...

Algeria

1.12 Relations Among National Accounting Aggregates

Million Algerian dinars

	1980	1983	1984	1985	1986	1987	1988	1989	1990	1991	1992	1993
Gross Domestic Product	162507	233752	263856	291597	296552	312706	334607	403460	...	...	...	...
Plus: Net factor income from the rest of the world	-4672	-5904	-6710	-6568	-6571	-7268	-11745	-13178	...	...	...	...
Factor income from the rest of the world	1560	1064	1079	1225	1012	685	615	1096	...	...	...	...
Less: Factor income to the rest of the world	6232	6969	7789	7793	7583	7953	12360	14274	...	...	...	...
Equals: Gross National Product	157835	227848	257146	285029	289981	305438	322862	390282	...	...	...	...
Less: Consumption of fixed capital	13692	21504	23104	28195	31660	32525	32622	33050	...	...	...	...
Equals: National Income	144143	206344	234042	256834	258321	272913	290240	357232	...	...	...	...
Plus: Net current transfers from the rest of the world	836	874	734	1683	3418	2358	2068	3850	...	...	...	...
Current transfers from the rest of the world	1711	1728	1602	2443	4137	2897	2581	4350	...	...	...	...
Less: Current transfers to the rest of the world	876	853	868	760	719	539	513	500	...	...	...	...
Equals: National Disposable Income	144979	207218	234776	258517	261739	275271	292308	361082	...	...	...	...
Less: Final consumption	92530	140876	165195	185664	209338	212954	240592	280946	...	...	...	...
Equals: Net Saving	52449	66342	69581	72853	52401	62317	51716	80136	...	...	...	...
Less: Surplus of the nation on current transactions	2627	28	154	4282	-15271	963	-10367	-7913	...	...	...	...
Equals: Net Capital Formation	49822	66314	69427	68571	67672	61354	62083	88049	...	...	...	...

Angola

Source. Reply to the United Nations national accounts questionnaire from the Instituto Nacional de Estadistica. The official estimates were published in 'Contas Nacionais de Angola, 1985-1990' by the Secretaria de Estado do Planeamento, Departamento de Contas Nacionais. Detailed description of the sources and methods used for the national accounts estimates is found in 'Metodologia de Contas Nacionais de Republica Popular de Angola' published in 1989 by the Ministerio do Plano.

General note. The estimates shown in the following tables have been prepared in accordance with the United Nations System of National Accounts so far as the existing data would permit.

1.1 Expenditure on the Gross Domestic Product, in Current Prices

Million Angolan kwanza

		1980	1983	1984	1985	1986	1987	1988	1989	1990	1991	1992	1993
1	Government final consumption expenditure	...	...	...	63665	68980	73169	78949	80605	87814	...	...	...
2	Private final consumption expenditure	...	...	...	96480	94195	93203	108946	134383	137768	...	...	...
3	Gross capital formation	...	...	...	36572	34972	40815	34810	33898	35958	...	...	...
	A Increase in stocks	...	...	...	1419	1252	2509	-58	2547	1792	...	...	...
	B Gross fixed capital formation	...	...	...	35153	33720	38306	34868	31351	34166	...	...	...
	Residential buildings	...	...	...							...	...	...
	Non-residential buildings	...	...	...	14219	14573	17376	16086	15667	15886	...	...	...
	Other construction and land improvement etc.	...	...	...							...	...	...
	Other	...	...	...	20934	19147	20930	18782	15684	18280	...	...	...
4	Exports of goods and services	...	...	...	67584	44324	72783	78674	94308	119851	...	...	...
5	Less: Imports of goods and services	...	...	...	58901	49710	58002	61739	64328	73329	...	...	...
	Equals: Gross Domestic Product	...	...	...	205400	192761	221968	239640	278866	308062	...	...	...

1.2 Expenditure on the Gross Domestic Product, in Constant Prices

Million Angolan kwanza

		1980	1983	1984	1985	1986	1987	1988	1989	1990	1991	1992	1993
					At constant prices of:1987								
1	Government final consumption expenditure	...	...	...	65702	70173	73169	77325	72879	73362	...	...	...
2	Private final consumption expenditure	...	...	...	106028	96086	93202	92971	101449	98615	...	...	...
3	Gross capital formation	...	...	...	41878	35565	40815	30775	28589	30798	...	...	...
	A Increase in stocks	...	...	...	1678	1003	2509	-510	2708	2888	...	...	...
	B Gross fixed capital formation	...	...	...	40200	34562	38306	31285	25881	27910	...	...	...
	Residential buildings	...	...	...							...	...	...
	Non-residential buildings	...	...	...	18203	14774	17376	13908	12750	12807	...	...	...
	Other construction and land improvement etc.	...	...	...							...	...	...
	Other	...	...	...	21997	19788	20930	17377	13131	15103	...	...	...
4	Exports of goods and services	...	...	...	49723	57125	72783	92116	90505	94064	...	...	...
5	Less: Imports of goods and services	...	...	...	62271	51502	58002	58849	58176	62639	...	...	...
	Equals: Gross Domestic Product	...	...	...	201060	207446	221968	234338	235246	234200	...	...	...

1.3 Cost Components of the Gross Domestic Product

Million Angolan kwanza

		1980	1983	1984	1985	1986	1987	1988	1989	1990	1991	1992	1993
1	Indirect taxes, net	...	...	...	9457	11010	12324	14244	18182	22741	...	...	...
	A Indirect taxes	...	...	...	19622	15873	17018	17561	19861	23486	...	...	...
	B Less: Subsidies	...	...	...	10165	4863	4694	3317	1679	745	...	...	...
2	Consumption of fixed capital	...	...	...							...	...	...
3	Compensation of employees paid by resident producers to:	...	...	...	83443	91542	96521	103428	108592	119913	...	...	...
4	Operating surplus	...	...	...	112500	90209	113123	121968	152092	165408	...	...	...
	Equals: Gross Domestic Product	...	...	...	205400	192761	221968	239640	278866	308062	...	...	...

1.7 External Transactions on Current Account, Summary

Million Angolan kwanza

		1980	1983	1984	1985	1986	1987	1988	1989	1990	1991	1992	1993
					Payments to the Rest of the World								
1	Imports of goods and services	...	...	...	58901	49710	58002	61739	64328	73329	...	...	...
	A Imports of merchandise c.i.f.	...	...	...	49416	40010	47594	48182	47417	54615	...	...	...
	B Other	...	...	...	9485	9700	10408	13557	16911	18714	...	...	...
2	Factor income to the rest of the world	...	...	...	9702	9670	9005	27088	29874	38707	...	...	...

Angola

1.7 External Transactions on Current Account, Summary
(Continued)

Million Angolan kwanza

	1980	1983	1984	1985	1986	1987	1988	1989	1990	1991	1992	1993
A Compensation of employees	...	...	...	1885	2124	2064	1885	1047	300	...	...	...
B Property and entrepreneurial income	...	...	...	7817	7546	6941	25203	28827	38407	...	...	...
3 Current transfers to the rest of the world	...	...	...	1978	1539	240	5799	5564	14768	...	...	...
4 Surplus of the nation on current transactions	...	...	...	-1232	-11479	7541	-14247	-3783	-4561	...	...	...
Payments to the Rest of the World and Surplus of the Nation on Current Transactions	...	...	...	69349	49440	74788	80379	95983	122243	...	...	...

Receipts From The Rest of the World

	1980	1983	1984	1985	1986	1987	1988	1989	1990	1991	1992	1993
1 Exports of goods and services	...	...	...	67584	44324	72783	78674	94308	119851	...	...	...
A Exports of merchandise f.o.b.	...	...	...	62499	39312	67365	73256	89039	114432	...	...	...
B Other	...	...	...	5085	5012	5418	5418	5269	5419	...	...	...
2 Factor income from rest of the world	...	...	...	658	359	209	419	568	430	...	...	...
A Compensation of employees	...	...	...	-	-	-	-	-	-	...	...	...
B Property and entrepreneurial income	...	...	...	658	359	209	419	568	430	...	...	...
3 Current transfers from rest of the world	...	...	...	1107	4757	1795	1286	1107	1962	...	...	...
Receipts from the Rest of the World on Current Transactions	...	...	...	69349	49440	74788	80379	95983	122243	...	...	...

1.10 Gross Domestic Product by Kind of Activity, in Current Prices

Million Angolan kwanza

	1980	1983	1984	1985	1986	1987	1988	1989	1990	1991	1992	1993
1 Agriculture, hunting, forestry and fishing	...	...	...	27583	27362	28402	37981	53187	55067	...	...	...
2 Mining and quarrying	...	...	...	58083	34394	63067	64137	81866	100657	...	...	...
3 Manufacturing	...	...	...	19739	20768	16152	19673	17065	15354	...	...	...
4 Electricity, gas and water	...	...	...	494	457	530	463	443	380	...	...	...
5 Construction	...	...	...	9768	9239	11449	9695	8988	9003	...	...	...
6 Wholesale and retail trade, restaurants and hotels [a]	...	...	...	26536	25405	25926	27648	31354	32827	...	...	...
7 Transport, storage and communication	...	...	...	9914	9629	8768	8195	8389	9822	...	...	...
8 Finance, insurance, real estate and business services [b]	...	...	...	3391	2533	619	1074	1543	214	...	...	...
9 Community, social and personal services [ab]	...	...	...	5979	8049	9087	9880	10051	12526	...	...	...
Total, Industries	...	...	...	161487	137836	164000	178746	212887	235849	...	...	...
Producers of Government Services	...	...	...	41329	51023	53881	57936	63189	69982	...	...	...
Other Producers	...	...	...							...	...	...
Subtotal	...	...	...	202816	188860	217881	236682	276076	305831	...	...	...
Less: Imputed bank service charge	...	...	...	1332	793	-722	364	326	-478	...	...	...
Plus: Import duties	...	...	...	3916	4694	3365	3322	3116	1753	...	...	...
Plus: Value added tax	...	...	...	...	...	...	...	...	...	...	...	...
Equals: Gross Domestic Product	...	...	...	205400	192761	221968	239640	278866	308062	...	...	...

a) Restaurants and hotels are included in item 'Community, social and personal services'.
b) Item 'Finance, insurance, real estate and business services' includes finance and insurance only.
Real estate and business services are included in item 'Community, social and personal services'.

1.11 Gross Domestic Product by Kind of Activity, in Constant Prices

Million Angolan kwanza

	1980	1983	1984	1985	1986	1987	1988	1989	1990	1991	1992	1993
				At constant prices of:1987								
1 Agriculture, hunting, forestry and fishing	...	...	...	27985	27579	28402	27606	28648	28554	...	...	...
2 Mining and quarrying	...	...	...	44298	44624	63067	75371	79186	81018	...	...	...
3 Manufacturing	...	...	...	22662	21643	16152	17953	14740	12301	...	...	...
4 Electricity, gas and water	...	...	...	474	474	530	483	437	370	...	...	...
5 Construction	...	...	...	12204	9549	11449	8567	7271	7169	...	...	...

Angola

1.11 Gross Domestic Product by Kind of Activity, in Constant Prices
(Continued)

Million Angolan kwanza

	1980	1983	1984	1985	1986	1987	1988	1989	1990	1991	1992	1993
				\multicolumn{6}{c}{At constant prices of:1987}				
6 Wholesale and retail trade, restaurants and hotels [a]	...	...	...	29313	25975	25926	25298	27674	27335	...	...	...
7 Transport, storage and communication	...	...	...	9969	10002	8768	8217	7537	8098	...	...	...
8 Finance, insurance, real estate and business services [b]	...	...	...	3461	2614	619	1113	1396	165	...	...	...
9 Community, social and personal services [ab]	...	...	...	6485	8421	9087	9506	8173	8896	...	...	...
Total, Industries	...	...	...	156851	150881	164000	174114	175063	173906	...	...	...
Producers of Government Services	...	...	...	41413	52534	53881	57436	56998	58214	...	...	...
Other Producers	...	...	...							...	...	...
Subtotal	...	...	...	198264	203415	217881	231550	232061	232120	...	...	...
Less: Imputed bank service charge	...	...	...	1291	780	-722	372	-361	-572	...	...	...
Plus: Import duties	...	...	...	4087	4810	3365	3160	2823	1508	...	...	...
Plus: Value added tax	...	...	...	...	...	...	...	...	...	...	...	...
Equals: Gross Domestic Product	...	...	...	201060	207445	221968	234338	235245	234200	...	...	...

a) Restaurants and hotels are included in item 'Community, social and personal services'.
b) Item 'Finance, insurance, real estate and business services' includes finance and insurance only.
   Real estate and business services are included in item 'Community, social and personal services'.

1.12 Relations Among National Accounting Aggregates

Million Angolan kwanza

	1980	1983	1984	1985	1986	1987	1988	1989	1990	1991	1992	1993
Gross Domestic Product	...	...	...	205400	192761	221968	239640	278866	308062	...	...	...
Plus: Net factor income from the rest of the world	...	...	...	-9043	-9311	-8796	-26669	-29306	-38277	...	...	...
Factor income from the rest of the world	...	...	...	658	359	209	419	568	430	...	...	...
Less: Factor income to the rest of the world	...	...	...	9702	9670	9005	27088	29874	38707	...	...	...
Equals: Gross National Product	...	...	...	196357	183450	213172	212971	249560	269785	...	...	...
Less: Consumption of fixed capital	...	...	...	...	...	...	...	...	...	...	...	...
Equals: National Income	...	...	...	196357	183450	213172	212971	249560	269785	...	...	...
Plus: Net current transfers from the rest of the world	...	...	...	-871	3218	1555	-4513	-4457	-12806	...	...	...
Current transfers from the rest of the world	...	...	...	1107	4757	1795	1286	1107	1962	...	...	...
Less: Current transfers to the rest of the world	...	...	...	1978	1539	240	5799	5564	14768	...	...	...
Equals: National Disposable Income	...	...	...	195485	186668	214728	208458	245103	256979	...	...	...
Less: Final consumption	...	...	...	160145	163175	166372	187895	214988	225582	...	...	...
Equals: Net Saving	...	...	...	35340	23493	48356	20563	30115	31397	...	...	...
Less: Surplus of the nation on current transactions	...	...	...	-1232	-11479	7541	-14247	-3783	-4561	...	...	...
Equals: Net Capital Formation	...	...	...	36572	34972	40815	34810	33898	35958	...	...	...

Anguilla

Source. The official estimates of the National Accounts of Anguilla was published for the first time in 'Anguilla - National Accounts Statistics, 1984-1987' by the Ministry of Finance and Economic Development on May 1988.

General note. The estimates shown in the following tables have been prepared in accordance with the United Nations System of National Accounts so far as the existing data would permit.

1.1 Expenditure on the Gross Domestic Product, in Current Prices

Thousand East Caribbean dollars

	1980	1983	1984	1985	1986	1987	1988	1989	1990	1991	1992	1993
1 Government final consumption expenditure	...	...	7116	7843	9219	11984	14970	17875	20069	23497	...	...
2 Private final consumption expenditure	...	...	19765	21277	24732	33613	39242	42730	45307		...	...
3 Gross capital formation	...	...	19430	22779	37277	50934	59959	80271	99564		...	...
A Increase in stocks	...	...	-	-	-	-	-	-	-		...	...
B Gross fixed capital formation	...	...	19430	22779	37277	50934	59959	80271	99564			
4 Exports of goods and services	...	...	22570	35870	46600	51750	82530	101610	110300		...	...
5 Less: Imports of goods and services	...	...	26820	35010	49630	63220	87220	105750	118900		...	...
Equals: Gross Domestic Product	...	...	42061	52759	68198	85061	109481	136736	156340	158590	...	...

1.4 General Government Current Receipts and Disbursements

Thousand East Caribbean dollars

	1980	1983	1984	1985	1986	1987	1988	1989	1990	1991	1992	1993
Receipts												
1 Operating surplus	...	...	...	...	...	...	...	...	...	...	...	...
2 Property and entrepreneurial income	...	...	883	350	1136	780	1778	1791	1171	1443	...	...
3 Taxes, fees and contributions	...	...	5887	7914	11276	14811	18346	24315	24710	27675	...	...
A Indirect taxes	...	...	4973	6941	9993	12846	15776	21169	21055	23513	...	...
B Direct taxes	...	...	93	56	64	109	132	44	84	148	...	...
C Social security contributions	...	...	821	917	1219	1856	2438	3102	3571	4014	...	...
D Compulsory fees, fines and penalties	...	...	...	...	...	...	...	...	...	...	...	...
4 Other current transfers	...	...	2309	1317	1872	1749	1754	1627	2198	2425	...	...
Total Current Receipts of General Government	...	...	9079	9581	14284	17340	21878	27733	28079	31543	...	...
Disbursements												
1 Government final consumption expenditure	...	...	7116	7843	9219	11984	14970	17875	20069	23497	...	...
A Compensation of employees	...	...	6004	6922	8386	9886	13102	14895	16896	18429	...	...
B Consumption of fixed capital	...	...	...	...	...	...	...	...	...	...	...	...
C Purchases of goods and services, net	...	...	2549	2579	3398	4323	4432	5886	7172	9128	...	...
D Less: Own account fixed capital formation	...	...	...	...	...	...	...	...	...	...	...	...
E Indirect taxes paid, net	...	...	...	...	...	...	...	...	...	...	...	...
2 Property income	...	...	-	-	-	61	135	397	290	322	...	...
3 Subsidies	...	...	292	182	15	15	15	23	15	332	...	...
4 Other current transfers	...	...	1075	1152	1334	1547	1829	2101	2444	2630	...	...
A Social security benefits	...	...	48	67	109	182	259	292	405	442	...	...
B Social assistance grants	...	...	...	...	...	...	...	...	...	...	...	...
C Other	...	...	1027	1085	1225	1365	1570	1809	2039	2188	...	...
5 Net saving	...	...	596	404	3716	3733	4929	7337	5261	4762	...	...
Total Current Disbursements and Net Saving of General Government	...	...	9079	9581	14284	17340	21878	27733	28079	31543	...	...

1.10 Gross Domestic Product by Kind of Activity, in Current Prices

Thousand East Caribbean dollars

	1980	1983	1984	1985	1986	1987	1988	1989	1990	1991	1992	1993
1 Agriculture, hunting, forestry and fishing	...	...	2480	2810	2990	3130	3290	4520	6040	3940	...	...
2 Mining and quarrying	...	...	680	540	770	890	800	750	660	1160	...	...
3 Manufacturing	...	...	380	500	540	770	780	810	910	1050	...	...
4 Electricity, gas and water	...	...	640	700	1530	1250	2290	2030	1570	2520	...	...
5 Construction	...	...	6070	7080	11690	15840	18780	25020	30880	27160	...	...

Anguilla

1.10 Gross Domestic Product by Kind of Activity, in Current Prices
(Continued)

Thousand East Caribbean dollars

	1980	1983	1984	1985	1986	1987	1988	1989	1990	1991	1992	1993
6 Wholesale and retail trade, restaurants and hotels	...	...	11920	16920	19950	24450	35350	45680	52590	54250	...	...
7 Transport, storage and communication	...	...	5400	6810	8180	10760	13660	14410	16340	18070	...	...
8 Finance, insurance, real estate and business services	...	...	5080	5350	6430	8230	10800	15110	17400	18930	...	...
9 Community, social and personal services [a]	...	...	690	780	940	1290	1380	1930	2090	2290	...	...
Total, Industries	...	...	33340	41490	53020	66610	87130	110260	128480	129370	...	...
Producers of Government Services	...	...	6010	6930	8400	9900	13120	14910	17110	18480	...	...
Other Producers [a]	...	...	...	...	...	...	...	...	...	...	...	...
Subtotal [b]	...	...	39350	48420	61420	76510	100250	125170	145590	147850	...	...
Less: Imputed bank service charge	...	...	1970	2420	3200	4280	6530	9580	10290	12440	...	...
Plus: Import duties	...	...	...	...	...	...	...	...	...	...	...	...
Plus: Value added tax	...	...	...	...	...	...	...	...	...	...	...	...
Plus: Other adjustments [c]	...	...	4681	6759	9978	12831	15761	21146	21040	23180	...	...
Equals: Gross Domestic Product	...	...	42061	52759	68198	85061	109481	136736	156340	158590	...	...

a) Item 'Other producers' is included in item 'Community, social and personal services'.
b) Gross domestic product in factor values.
c) Item 'Other adjustments' refers to indirect taxes net of subsidies.

1.11 Gross Domestic Product by Kind of Activity, in Constant Prices

Thousand East Caribbean dollars

	1980	1983	1984	1985	1986	1987	1988	1989	1990	1991	1992	1993
			\multicolumn{10}{c}{At constant prices of: 1984}		
1 Agriculture, hunting, forestry and fishing	...	...	2480	2710	2850	2910	3040	3650	4110	2970	...	...
2 Mining and quarrying	...	...	680	580	740	840	760	660	450	740	...	...
3 Manufacturing	...	...	380	440	470	610	630	640	720	820	...	...
4 Electricity, gas and water	...	...	640	760	820	690	1350	1560	1690	1750	...	...
5 Construction	...	...	6070	5900	8190	9500	10430	13900	16540	12200	...	...
6 Wholesale and retail trade, restaurants and hotels	...	...	11920	14740	16620	18080	22970	23720	25640	26010	...	...
7 Transport, storage and communication	...	...	5400	6580	7470	9400	10420	10720	11870	12590	...	...
8 Finance, insurance, real estate and business services	...	...	5080	5250	5580	6100	6990	7840	8800	8940	...	...
9 Community, social and personal services [a]	...	...	690	770	900	1210	1250	1620	1720	1800	...	...
Total, Industries	...	...	33340	37730	43640	49340	57840	64310	71540	67820	...	...
Producers of Government Services	...	...	6010	6230	6650	7290	7570	7710	8120	8640	...	...
Other Producers [a]	...	...	...	...	...	...	...	...	...	...	...	...
Subtotal	...	...	39350	43960	50290	56630	65410	72020	79660	76460	...	...
Less: Imputed bank service charge	...	...	1970	2410	2830	3680	5240	6010	6460	7560	...	...
Plus: Import duties	...	...	...	...	...	...	...	...	...	...	...	...
Plus: Value added tax	...	...	...	...	...	...	...	...	...	...	...	...
Equals: Gross Domestic Product [b]	...	...	37380	41550	47460	52950	60170	66010	73200	68900	...	...

a) Item 'Other producers' is included in item 'Community, social and personal services'.
b) Gross domestic product in factor values.

2.1 Government Final Consumption Expenditure by Function, in Current Prices

Thousand East Caribbean dollars

	1980	1983	1984	1985	1986	1987	1988	1989	1990	1991	1992	1993
1 General public services	...	...	1665	1790	1691	3166	3772	4030	3880	6085	...	...
2 Defence	...	...	...	...	...	...	...	...	...	...	...	...
3 Public order and safety	...	...	771	969	1213	1394	1798	2162	2469	2727	...	...
4 Education	...	...	1658	1872	2149	2817	3314	4201	4742	5210	...	...
5 Health	...	...	1022	1158	1456	1531	2116	2945	3150	3587	...	...
6 Social security and welfare	...	...	122	140	343	359	362	370	480	584	...	...
7 Housing and community amenities	...	...	563	502	735	880	978	1288	1471	1576	...	...
8 Recreational, cultural and religious affairs	...	...	...	...	...	...	...	...	...	...	...	...
9 Economic services	...	...	559	695	506	1056	946	1918	2786	2512	...	...

Anguilla

2.1 Government Final Consumption Expenditure by Function, in Current Prices
(Continued)

Thousand East Caribbean dollars

	1980	1983	1984	1985	1986	1987	1988	1989	1990	1991	1992	1993
A Fuel and energy	...	...	...	...	...	...	...	...	...	...	...	...
B Agriculture, forestry, fishing and hunting	...	...	192	223	232	263	417	489	609	486	...	...
C Mining, manufacturing and construction, except fuel and energy	...	...	...	...	...	...	...	...	...	...	...	...
D Transportation and communication	...	...	307	323	227	700	434	767	1807	1221	...	...
E Other economic affairs	...	...	60	149	47	93	95	662	370	805	...	...
10 Other functions	...	...	756	717	1126	781	1684	961	1091	1216	...	...
Total Government Final Consumption Expenditure	...	...	7116	7843	9219	11984	14970	17875	20069	23497	...	...

Antigua and Barbuda

Source. 'Economic Survey and Projections', British Development Division in the Caribbean.
General note. The estimates shown in the following tables have been prepared in accordance with the United Nations System of National Accounts so far as the existing data would permit.

1.1 Expenditure on the Gross Domestic Product, in Current Prices

Million East Caribbean dollars

	1980	1983	1984	1985	1986	1987	1988	1989	1990	1991	1992	1993
1 Government final consumption expenditure	57.4	83.2	86.5	98.7	121.2	...	...	...	...	...	...	...
2 Private final consumption expenditure	204.0	225.0	327.0	386.5	447.6	...	...	...	...	...	...	...
3 Gross capital formation	93.5	84.6	110.6	151.6	231.9	...	...	...	...	...	...	...
A Increase in stocks	-	-	-	-	-	...	...	...	...	...	...	...
B Gross fixed capital formation	93.5	84.6	110.6	151.6	231.9	...	...	...	...	...	...	...
4 Exports of goods and services	200.0	270.3	345.3	409.5	482.7	...	...	...	...	...	...	...
5 Less: Imports of goods and services	257.6	249.2	401.0	505.6	641.5	...	...	...	...	...	...	...
Equals: Gross Domestic Product	297.3	413.9	468.4	540.7	641.9	647.5	771.1	874.2	901.8	973.0	1009.8	...

1.10 Gross Domestic Product by Kind of Activity, in Current Prices

Million East Caribbean dollars

	1980	1983	1984	1985	1986	1987	1988	1989	1990	1991	1992	1993
1 Agriculture, hunting, forestry and fishing	18.3	21.8	19.3	23.2	24.6	29.3	32.1	...	...	...	...	...
2 Mining and quarrying	1.5	2.3	3.0	4.6	9.9	14.4	16.8	...	...	...	...	...
3 Manufacturing	13.7	17.6	19.3	20.3	21.5	23.0	24.1	...	...	...	...	...
4 Electricity, gas and water	8.2	10.3	12.5	17.2	19.9	22.4	31.3	...	...	...	...	...
5 Construction	23.2	20.5	27.3	35.7	50.6	73.1	98.9	...	...	...	...	...
6 Wholesale and retail trade, restaurants and hotels	66.4	84.2	101.8	121.7	133.6	156.3	183.9	...	...	...	...	...
7 Transport, storage and communication	41.6	63.5	70.9	81.4	88.4	101.0	110.8	...	...	...	...	...
8 Finance, insurance, real estate and business services	42.2	65.3	74.5	79.9	85.0	94.2	103.7	...	...	...	...	...
9 Community, social and personal services	16.7	28.1	33.2	39.2	43.9	46.6	49.5	...	...	...	...	...
Total, Industries	231.8	313.6	361.8	423.2	477.4	560.3	651.1	...	...	...	...	...
Producers of Government Services	35.6	59.5	63.4	67.9	89.7	88.5	125.3	...	...	...	...	...
Other Producers	...	...	...	...	...	...	...	...	...	...	...	...
Subtotal [a]	267.4	373.1	425.2	491.1	567.1	648.8	776.4	...	...	...	...	...
Less: Imputed bank service charge	10.3	17.0	21.9	26.1	30.0	32.7	35.8	...	...	...	...	...
Plus: Import duties	...	...	...	...	...	...	...	...	...	...	...	...
Plus: Value added tax	...	...	...	...	...	...	...	...	...	...	...	...
Plus: Other adjustments [b]	40.0	57.7	65.0	75.9	104.7	...	...	...	...	...	...	...
Equals: Gross Domestic Product	297.1	413.8	468.3	540.9	641.8	...	...	...	...	...	...	...

a) Beginning 1977, gross domestic product in factor values.
b) Item 'Other adjustments' refers to indirect taxes net of subsidies.

1.11 Gross Domestic Product by Kind of Activity, in Constant Prices

Million East Caribbean dollars

	1980	1983	1984	1985	1986	1987	1988	1989	1990	1991	1992	1993
					At constant prices of:1977							
1 Agriculture, hunting, forestry and fishing	13.9	11.6	9.3	9.5	10.1	11.3	11.9	...	...	...	...	...
2 Mining and quarrying	1.2	1.1	1.6	2.5	5.6	7.6	8.3	...	...	...	...	...
3 Manufacturing	11.4	14.2	14.8	15.2	15.8	16.5	16.8	...	...	...	...	...
4 Electricity, gas and water	6.1	8.1	8.0	9.0	9.9	10.6	12.6	...	...	...	...	...
5 Construction	17.2	10.8	13.0	16.8	22.7	31.0	35.4	...	...	...	...	...
6 Wholesale and retail trade, restaurants and hotels	46.5	52.7	62.1	67.2	71.7	76.7	83.7	...	...	...	...	...
7 Transport, storage and communication	35.5	48.8	52.4	55.6	58.6	61.9	66.8	...	...	...	...	...
8 Finance, insurance, real estate and business services	34.6	37.8	38.9	40.6	42.3	44.1	46.3	...	...	...	...	...
9 Community, social and personal services	13.0	16.3	17.3	18.7	18.9	19.3	19.7	...	...	...	...	...

Antigua and Barbuda

1.11 Gross Domestic Product by Kind of Activity, in Constant Prices
(Continued)

Million East Caribbean dollars

	1980	1983	1984	1985	1986	1987	1988	1989	1990	1991	1992	1993
				At constant prices of:1977								
Total, Industries	179.4	201.4	217.4	235.1	255.6	279.0	301.5	...	...	...	...	...
Producers of Government Services	23.7	26.1	26.9	27.8	29.2	30.4	31.1	...	...	...	...	...
Other Producers	...	...	...	...	...	...	...	...	...	...	...	...
Subtotal	203.1	227.5	244.3	262.9	284.8	309.4	332.6	...	...	...	...	...
Less: Imputed bank service charge	8.9	8.9	9.4	9.8	10.4	11.0	11.7	...	...	...	...	...
Plus: Import duties	...	...	...	...	...	...	...	...	...	...	...	...
Plus: Value added tax	...	...	...	...	...	...	...	...	...	...	...	...
Equals: Gross Domestic Product [a]	194.2	218.6	234.9	253.1	274.4	298.3	320.9	...	...	...	...	...

a) Gross domestic product in factor values.

2.1 Government Final Consumption Expenditure by Function, in Current Prices

Thousand East Caribbean dollars

		1980	1983	1984	1985	1986	1987	1988	1989	1990	1991	1992	1993
1	General public services	12625	13821	15232	20238	28170	...	...	...	...	...	...	...
2	Defence	505	1445	1475	1757	2453	...	...	...	...	...	...	...
3	Public order and safety	4581	6732	7643	9203	12527	...	...	...	...	...	...	...
4	Education	7286	10871	10595	11267	15885	...	...	...	...	...	...	...
5	Health	3823	5831	6496	9252	10754	...	...	...	...	...	...	...
6	Social security and welfare	4234	5770	5634	5329	7815	...	...	...	...	...	...	...
7	Housing and community amenities	2846	4831	4468	6171	6858	...	...	...	...	...	...	...
8	Recreational, cultural and religious affairs	201	229	317	458	556	...	...	...	...	...	...	...
9	Economic services	13743	18541	15085	16855	22846	...	...	...	...	...	...	...
	A Fuel and energy	-	24	24	91	175	...	...	...	...	...	...	...
	B Agriculture, forestry, fishing and hunting	2164	2637	2570	3414	4906	...	...	...	...	...	...	...
	C Mining, manufacturing and construction, except fuel and energy	7823	11590	8901	8889	11095	...	...	...	...	...	...	...
	D Transportation and communication						...	...	...	...	...	...	...
	E Other economic affairs	3756	4290	3590	4461	6670	...	...	...	...	...	...	...
10	Other functions	7	38	-	-	40	...	...	...	...	...	...	...
	Total Government Final Consumption Expenditure [a]	49851	68109	66945	80530	107904	...	...	...	...	...	...	...

a) Only central government data are included in the general government estimates.

Argentina

General note. The preparation of national accounts statistics in Argentina is undertaken by Banco Central de la Republica Argentina, Buenos Aires. The official estimates are published on a quarterly basis in the 'Economic Reports'. In 1975 the publication 'Sistema de Cuentas del Producto e Ingreso de la Argentina' was presented. Volume I 'Metodologia y Fuentes' contains a detailed description of the sources and methods used for the national accounts estimation. Volume II 'Cuadros Estadisticos' presents estimates for the period 1950-1973, in accordance with the United Nations System of National Accounts (SNA). On 1 June 1983, the peso argentino equal to 10,000 pesos, was introduced. On 4 June 1985, a new currency called the Austral was introduced. One Austral is equivalent to 1,000 peso argentinos. On 1 January 1992, the peso argentino equal to 10,000 Australes was introduced. The following tables have been prepared from successive replies to the United Nations national accounts questionnaire. When the scope and coverage of the estimates differ for conceptual or statistical reasons from the definitions and classifications recommended in SNA, a footnote is indicated to the relevant tables.

Sources and methods:

(a) **Gross domestic product.** The main approach used to estimate GDP is the production approach.

(b) **Expenditure on the gross domestic product.** The expenditure approach is used to estimate government final consumption expenditure, increase in stocks, investment in construction, and exports and imports of goods and services. The commodity-flow approach is used to estimate the current value of gross investment other than for construction. Private final consumption expenditure is taken as a residual. Government final consumption expenditure, consisting of compensation of employees and net purchases of goods and services, is obtained from government accounts. Investment in construction is estimated through the use of accounting data for the public sector, agricultural census data for the agricultural sector, and construction licenses and miscellaneous sources for the urban private construction. The estimation of domestically produced capital goods is done on the basis of the industrial censuses. For the years between censuses, the data are up-dated through a combination of indexes of physical output and price indexes. Data on exports and imports of goods and services are obtained from the balance of payments accounts. Constant values of government consumption expenditures are obtained through extrapolating wages and salaries by the number of persons employed and through deflating purchases of goods and services by the wholesale price index for non-agricultural goods. Private consumption expenditure at constant prices is obtained as a residual. The current values of construction are deflated by indexes of construction costs or extrapolated by input volumes. Domestic machinery and equipment products are deflated by index of producer prices or extrapolated by volume of production. Imported machinery and equipment are deflated by price indexes. Price deflation is used for exports and imports of goods and services.

(c) **Cost-structure of the gross domestic product.** The estimates of compensation of employees are based on employment data, remuneration data and collective wage agreement data. Intercensal estimates are rough, except for those activities for which accounting data are available. Operating surplus is, in general, obtained as a residual. Consumption of fixed capital is calculated on the basis of accounting data from public enterprises, capital stock data in the case of private construction, gross investment data and estimated depreciation rates in the case of durable production equipment. Information on indirect taxes is obtained by type of government authority.

(d) **Gross domestic product by kind of economic activity.** The table of gross domestic product by kind of economic activity is prepared in factor values. The production approach is used to estimate value added of most industries. The basic statistics on agricultural production are obtained from the Secretaria de Agricultura y Ganaderia de la Nacion. The production is valued at farmers' prices, which are obtained by subtracting transportation costs and commercial mark-ups from wholesale prices. Production estimates for beef, mutton and pork, are defined as the value of sales for slaughter, adjusted for changes in stocks and exports of live animal. Own account consumption of agricultural products and meat is included in the estimates. Since no annual information is available, indirect indicators are used to estimate the value of intermediate consumption. For mining, information on quantities and prices is obtained from the government authorities concerned. Input data are supplied by state companies and balance sheets of a representative sample of mining enterprises. The general method used in estimating industrial production is by interpolating prices and quantities between census years. After the latest industrial census of 1963, extrapolation is used, based on changes in the production volume. Information on prices is obtained from the wholesale price index and miscellaneous sources for products not included in that index. Data on the number of construction permits issued are used to estimate the value of construction in the private sector. The data are converted into value figures by using the cost of construction index. Intermediate consumption is estimated from analysis of budgets, surveys, etc. For the public sector, data are obtained from the accounts of official organizations and state enterprises. Intermediate consumption is estimated on the basis of coefficients obtained from a study of records in the field of public works. Gross output of the trade sector is estimated through applying gross percentage mark-up rates to the value of goods recorded as entering the various marketing channels. Input values are based on information from balance sheets of joint stock companies and other inquiries. Value added in the transport sector is estimated from financial statements and accounts data, direct information or from survey data. For financial intermediaries the data used is based on the financial statements of all credit institutions in the country. The data needed to calculate value added of insurance services is provided by the Super-intendencia de Seguros de la Nacion. The value of rents paid is calculated on the basis of the population censuses and the rent component of the consumer price index. In the case of owner-occupied dwellings, the average gross rent for rented dwellings is applied. The value added of the producers of government, provincial government and local government services is based on the accounts and budget data of the concerned authorities. Business services and other professional services are estimated through population census data and income data. The value of domestic services is obtained by multiplying the number of employees by their average compensation. For the estimates in constant prices, extrapolation of the base year value by indexes of production volume or output quantity and occasionally of employment data are used for all sectors except public construction, in which case the current values are deflated by an index of construction costs.

1.1 Expenditure on the Gross Domestic Product, in Current Prices

Pesos

		1980	1983	1984	1985	1986	1987	1988	1989	1990	1991	1992	1993
1	Government final consumption expenditure	2925	82990	610610	4082100	8057200	19	87	2531	55326	151531	192261	...
2	Private final consumption expenditure												...
3	Gross capital formation	970	22870	157900	933100	1743400	5	21	503	9647	26478	37854	...
4	Exports of goods and services	194	10020	60030	622600	814900	2	11	424	7140	13884	14954	
5	Less: Imports of goods and services	249	6390	37620	332800	631400	2	7	213	3192	10995	18432	
	Equals: Gross Domestic Product [a]	3840	109500	790920	5305000	9984100	23	111	3244	68922	180898	226638	...

a) Beginning 1987, the estimates are in million pesos.

1.2 Expenditure on the Gross Domestic Product, in Constant Prices

Thousand Pesos

		1980	1983	1984	1985	1986	1987	1988	1989	1990	1991	1992	1993
						At constant prices of: 1986							
1	Government final consumption expenditure	8091	7669	7963	7427	8057	8167	7788	7469	7439	8379	9288	
2	Private final consumption expenditure												...
3	Gross capital formation	2749	1907	1842	1513	1743	2002	1962	...	...	...	...	...
	A Increase in stocks	...	...	...	...	...	...	...	...	...	...	...	
	B Gross fixed capital formation	...	...	...	...	...	...	...	1484	1336	1672	2189	...
4	Exports of goods and services	723	811	790	912	815	787	932	990	1177	1080	1086	
5	Less: Imports of goods and services	1231	604	632	550	631	715	633	518	522	860	1404	...
	Equals: Gross Domestic Product	10331	9783	9962	9303	9984	10242	10049	9424	9430	10270	11159	...

Argentina

1.10 Gross Domestic Product by Kind of Activity, in Current Prices

Pesos

	1980	1983	1984	1985	1986	1987	1988	1989	1990	1991	1992	1993
1 Agriculture, hunting, forestry and fishing	244	9480	66010	405000	778800	2	10	312	5599	12420	13577	...
2 Mining and quarrying	48	2340	15050	104000	202200	-	3	103	1972	3733	4067	...
3 Manufacturing	1132	33580	234970	1572500	2737600	6	31	1004	18464	44115	49541	...
4 Electricity, gas and water	71	1700	13230	104000	195400	-	2	66	1328	2924	3826	...
5 Construction	332	7880	50810	303100	596900	2	7	201	3064	8422	12107	...
6 Wholesale and retail trade, restaurants and hotels	635	18170	132520	874000	1626100	4	17	550	10750	28725	34929	...
7 Transport, storage and communication	172	4290	34140	26230	468000	1	6	138	3614	9429	11719	...
8 Finance, insurance, real estate and business services	534	15930	106040	781100	1522100	4	17	418	10239	27675	38133	...
9 Community, social and personal services	684	16850	135580	933900	1856900	4	19	479	14679	44876	59022	...
Total, Industries	...	...	...	...	...	...	...	...	...	...	...	...
Producers of Government Services	...	...	...	...	...	...	...	...	...	...	...	...
Other Producers	...	...	...	...	...	...	...	...	...	...	...	...
Subtotal	3851	110240	788340	5339900	9983900	23	111	3270	69709	182050	226921	...
Less: Imputed bank service charge	11	740	-2580	34900	-200	-	-	26	786	1152	283	...
Plus: Import duties	...	...	...	...	...	...	...	...	...	...	...	...
Plus: Value added tax	...	...	...	...	...	...	...	...	...	...	...	...
Equals: Gross Domestic Product [a]	3840	109500	790920	5305000	9984100	23	111	3244	68922	180898	226638	...

a) Beginning 1987, the estimates are in million pesos.

1.11 Gross Domestic Product by Kind of Activity, in Constant Prices

Thousand Pesos

	1980	1983	1984	1985	1986	1987	1988	1989	1990	1991	1992	1993
					At constant prices of: 1986							
1 Agriculture, hunting, forestry and fishing	714	790	792	778	779	756	830	753	839	872	872	...
2 Mining and quarrying	231	227	225	217	202	216	231	239	252	238	257	...
3 Manufacturing	2890	2658	2729	2458	2738	2786	2650	2461	2512	2811	3017	...
4 Electricity, gas and water	151	171	185	188	195	205	191	182	198	203	214	...
5 Construction	841	657	584	498	597	683	663	502	423	513	624	...
6 Wholesale and retail trade, restaurants and hotels	1843	1612	1688	1536	1626	1637	1599	1438	1464	1705	1863	...
7 Transport, storage and communication	415	406	443	437	468	485	483	497	476	497	553	...
8 Finance, insurance, real estate and business services	1470	1501	1485	1425	1522	1535	1494	1444	1410	1552	1756	...
9 Community, social and personal services	1727	1796	1830	1772	1857	1904	1881	1903	1904	1877	1895	...
Total, Industries	...	...	...	...	...	...	...	...	...	...	...	...
Producers of Government Services	...	...	...	...	...	...	...	...	...	...	...	...
Other Producers	...	...	...	...	...	...	...	...	...	...	...	...
Subtotal	10283	9829	9960	9313	9984	10207	10022	9418	9478	10266	11050	...
Less: Imputed bank service charge	-48	46	-2	10	-	-35	-28	-6	48	-4	-108	...
Plus: Import duties	...	...	...	...	...	...	...	...	...	...	...	...
Plus: Value added tax	...	...	...	...	...	...	...	...	...	...	...	...
Equals: Gross Domestic Product	10331	9783	9962	9303	9984	10242	10049	9424	9430	10270	11159	...

Armenia

Source. Reply to the United Nations national accounts questionnaire from the State Department of Statistics.

General note. The estimates shown in the following tables have been prepared in accordance with the United Nations System of National Accounts so far as the existing data would permit.

1.12 Relations Among National Accounting Aggregates

Million Roubles

	1980	1983	1984	1985	1986	1987	1988	1989	1990	1991	1992	1993
Gross Domestic Product	6501	7500	7983	8101	8199	8292	8054	9490	9693	11567	...	...
Plus: Net factor income from the rest of the world	...	...	...	...	...	...	...	...	...	...	...	...
Equals: Gross National Product	...	...	...	...	...	...	...	...	...	...	...	...
Less: Consumption of fixed capital	...	...	...	...	...	...	...	...	...	...	...	...
Equals: National Income	4922	5666	5975	6144	6081	6065	5779	6915	6976	11232	...	...
Plus: Net current transfers from the rest of the world	...	...	...	...	...	...	...	...	...	...	...	...
Equals: National Disposable Income	...	...	...	...	...	...	...	...	...	...	...	...
Less: Final consumption	...	...	...	...	...	...	...	...	...	...	...	...
Equals: Net Saving	...	...	...	...	...	...	...	...	...	...	...	...
Less: Surplus of the nation on current transactions	...	...	...	...	...	...	...	...	...	...	...	...
Equals: Net Capital Formation	...	...	...	...	...	...	...	...	...	...	...	...

Australia

General note. The preparation of national accounts statistics in Australia is undertaken by the Australian Bureau of Statistics (ABS), Canberra. The Australian National Accounts System corresponds closely to the United Nations System of National Accounts (SNA). Detailed descriptions of the concepts, definitions, sources and methods used are published in 'Australian National Accounts, Concepts, Sources and Methods'. Preliminary annual estimates for the latest financial year are published about 6 to 7 weeks after the end of the financial year in the Commonwealth Budget Paper 'National Income and Expenditure' while quarterly estimates are released usually about 8 weeks after the end of the quarter in the quarterly publication 'Australian National Accounts, National Income and Expenditure ' (5206.0). The most comprehensive national accounts publication is 'Australian National Accounts, National Income and Expenditure' (5204.0) which is released annually. In addition to these National Income and Expenditure publications, input-output tables have been published for the years 1958-59, 1962-63, 1968-69, 1974-75, 1986-87 and annually from 1977-78 to 1983-84 in 'Australian National Accounts, Input-Output Tables' (5209.0). Annual estimates of gross product at constant prices and indexes of gross product at constant prices per person employed and per hour worked, by industry, are published in 'Australian National Accounts, Gross Product, Employment and Hours Worked' (5211.0) until 1989-90. From 1990-91 these estimates are included in 5204.0. Quarterly estimates of gross product at constant prices, by industry, are published in 'Australian National Accounts: Gross Product, Employment and Hours Worked' (5222.0). The following tables have been prepared from successive replies to the United Nations national accounts questionnaire. When the scope and coverage of the estimates differ for conceptual or statistical reasons from the definitions and classifications recommended in SNA, a footnote is placed on the relevant tables. Estimates relate to the fiscal year beginning 1 July. All data at constant prices are at average 1984-85 prices. Data in all tables (except table 4.4) are expressed in million of dollars. In table 4.4, data on number of persons are in units of thousand persons, while hours worked data are shown in units of millions of hours. More detailed employment data have become available from 1983-84 (see Table 4.4). This has resulted in some industry reclassifications which are explained in the footnotes to this table.

Sources and methods Sources and Methods

(a) **Gross domestic product.** Gross domestic product is estimated using both the income and expenditure approaches. The difference between the two approaches is shown as a statistical discrepancy and, by convention, recorded on the expenditure side of the account.

(b) **Expenditure on the gross domestic product.** Government final consumption expenditure and public gross fixed capital formation are estimated from the accounting records of the government sector. Private final consumption expenditure on goods is mainly derived from information collected in retail censuses (held every five years) as well as data on production, imports and exports, and motor vehicle registrations. The results of a monthly survey of retail sales are used to interpolate between census benchmarks and to extrapolate for the period since the last retail census. Benchmarks for dwellings rent are derived from population census data collected every five years. The consumer price index is used in conjunction with a perpetual inventory model of the stock of dwellings to interpolate between census year estimates and extrapolate from the most recent census. Estimates of expenditure on other services are based mainly on revenue or earnings data. Increase in stocks is based on book value levels of stocks reported in ABS economic censuses, taxation statistics and quarterly ABS surveys of stocks (less the stock valuation adjustment). Estimates of private gross fixed capital expenditure are obtained from a quarterly collections of building and engineering construction statistics and from a quarterly survey of new capital expenditure by private businesses on plant and equipment. Exports and imports of goods are estimated from customs data while exports and imports of services are derived from transportation survey data and from data obtained as a by-product of the administration of foreign exchange transactions. Constant price estimates are derived quarterly with annual estimates obtained by summing the quarterly series. Government consumption expenditures are deflated by composite wage rate and material price indexes. Substantial use is made of data from consumer price index in the revaluation of private final consumption expenditure. Estimates of gross fixed capital expenditure are revalued using (output) building price indexes for building; composite wage material price indexes for engineering construction; domestic and overseas producer price indexes (including the computer equipment price index produced by the United States Bureau of Economic Analysis) and import price indexes for equipment; and quantity revaluation for real estate transfer expenses. For exports and imports, considerable use is made of the quantity revaluation technique with the remainder deflated using price indexes (including the BEA index). Increase in stocks estimates are derived using detailed price indexes to revalue book value levels.

(c) **Cost-structure of the gross domestic product.** The components of indirect taxes (net) are estimated from government accounting records. Estimates of gross operating surplus are mainly based on taxation statistics. Estimates of the consumption of fixed capital are derived at current replacement cost using the Perpetual Inventory Method. Since December quarter 1981 the compensation of employees data have been based on a quarterly survey of employers - prior to that quarter, estimates were mainly based on payroll tax data.

(d) **Gross domestic product by kind of economic activity.** The table of gross domestic product by kind of economic activity is prepared at market prices. Constant price estimates of gross product for Agriculture, Mining and Gas industries are derived using double deflation. Estimates for Finance, property and business services, and Public administration and defence are derived by extrapolating the base year value of gross product using hours worked estimates. Estimates for the Community services are derived by extrapolating the base year value of gross product using the sum of the relevant components of government and private final consumption expenditure. Estimates for the remaining industries are derived using the gross output method.

1.1 Expenditure on the Gross Domestic Product, in Current Prices

Million Australian dollars — Fiscal year beginning 1 July

		1980	1983	1984	1985	1986	1987	1988	1989	1990	1991	1992	1993
1	Government final consumption expenditure	25075	35860	40188	44755	49053	52571	56820	61639	66694	71500	74775	77165
2	Private final consumption expenditure	82871	116722	128163	143653	157097	175147	195548	217817	231075	242559	252890	264235
3	Gross capital formation [a]	35657	45701	52029	60630	62423	71539	88926	93945	79869	74771	79130	83776
	A Increase in stocks [a]	465	1376	1013	1386	-1526	-466	3799	4469	-1782	-1905	-436	881
	B Gross fixed capital formation [a]	35192	44325	51016	59244	63949	72005	85127	89476	81651	76676	79566	82895
	Residential buildings	8516	9473	11326	12319	11858	13414	18515	19924	18330	18056	20472	22277
	Non-residential buildings	10639	13750	15695	18878	20769	23421	25525	28956	26639	23457	21735	22003
	Other construction and land improvement etc.												
	Other [b]	16037	21102	23995	28047	31322	35170	41087	40596	36682	35163	37359	38615
4	Exports of goods and services	22539	28773	35566	38936	44119	51727	55489	61029	66300	70075	76507	82208
5	Less: Imports of goods and services	25075	31304	39697	46400	48376	53249	61549	67917	66363	68499	78326	84105
	Statistical discrepancy	-787	-872	7	-1604	187	1259	4571	3773	1678	-3081	-1124	2287
	Equals: Gross Domestic Product [c]	140280	194880	216256	239970	264503	298994	339805	370286	379253	387325	403852	425566

a) Livestock is excluded from items 'Increase in Stocks' and 'Gross Fixed Capital Formation'.
b) Item 'Statistical discrepancy' in tables 2.7 and 2.8 refers to real estate transfer expenses and the expenses are included in item 'other' in tables 1.1 and 1.2.
c) Data in this table have not been revised, therefore they are not comparable with the data in other tables.

1.2 Expenditure on the Gross Domestic Product, in Constant Prices

Million Australian dollars — Fiscal year beginning 1 July

		1980	1983	1984	1985	1986	1987	1988	1989	1990	1991	1992	1993
		\multicolumn{12}{c}{At constant prices of:1989}											
1	Government final consumption expenditure	45668	49290	52069	54462	56476	58190	59543	61639	63374	65322	66760	68134
2	Private final consumption expenditure	163604	176853	183115	189994	191259	199074	208070	217817	219976	225540	231243	237716
3	Gross capital formation [a]	70523	70464	76080	79221	74163	80681	93921	93945	79207	73571	76890	80089
	A Increase in stocks [a]	933	2408	1771	1764	-1869	-383	4043	4469	-1278	-2109	-139	740
	B Gross fixed capital formation [a]	69590	68056	74309	77457	76032	81064	89878	89476	80485	75680	77029	79349

Australia

1.2 Expenditure on the Gross Domestic Product, in Constant Prices
(Continued)

Million Australian dollars — Fiscal year beginning 1 July

	1980	1983	1984	1985	1986	1987	1988	1989	1990	1991	1992	1993
					At constant prices of:1989							
Residential buildings	18891	16222	18088	18089	16333	17383	20671	19924	17715	17405	19760	...
Non-residential buildings	21961	20987	22493	24745	25328	26790	27276	28956	25848	22980	21437	
Other construction and land improvement etc.												...
Other [b]	29275	30983	33728	34623	34371	36891	41931	40596	36922	35295	35832	...
4 Exports of goods and services	35788	39620	45683	47615	52456	56969	57793	61029	67902	74042	78237	85181
5 Less: Imports of goods and services	40066	43074	49806	50380	47177	52047	64485	67917	64470	66779	71378	76384
Statistical discrepancy	-1319	-773	108	-2084	261	1489	4873	3773	1630	-2947	-1069	2122
Equals: Gross Domestic Product [c]	274198	292380	307249	318828	327438	344356	359715	370286	367619	368749	380683	396858

a) Livestock is excluded from items 'Increase in Stocks' and 'Gross Fixed Capital Formation'.
b) Item 'Statistical discrepancy' in tables 2.7 and 2.8 refers to real estate transfer expenses and the expenses are included in item 'other' in tables 1.1 and 1.2.
c) Data in this table have not been revised, therefore they are not comparable with the data in other tables.

1.3 Cost Components of the Gross Domestic Product

Million Australian dollars — Fiscal year beginning 1 July

	1980	1983	1984	1985	1986	1987	1988	1989	1990	1991	1992	1993
1 Indirect taxes, net	15062	22478	25840	28527	31744	37121	41276	44466	44743	44436	45612	50592
A Indirect taxes	17297	26001	29758	32841	36342	41521	45808	49056	50476	50357	52142	56904
B Less: Subsidies [a]	2235	3523	3918	4314	4598	4400	4532	4590	5733	5921	6530	6312
2 Consumption of fixed capital	21207	29940	32539	37424	42650	46703	51279	55858	58307	59926	62570	64658
3 Compensation of employees paid by resident producers to: [b]	74054	100618	110982	122517	134026	147367	164991	183623	191379	195475	202355	211298
A Resident households [b]	73944	100460	110804	122353	133847	147157	164712	183217	190950	195149	202044	211012
B Rest of the world	110	158	178	164	179	210	279	406	429	326	311	286
4 Operating surplus	29957	41844	46895	51502	56083	67803	82259	86339	84824	87488	93315	99018
A Corporate and quasi-corporate enterprises	9344	15253	18735	20173	21426	27437	33964	34718	33367	34792	37674	41449
B Private unincorporated enterprises	20613	26591	28160	31329	34657	40366	48295	51621	51457	52696	55641	57569
C General government	...	...	...	...	...	...	...	...	...	...	...	...
Equals: Gross Domestic Product [c]	140280	194880	216256	239970	264503	298994	339805	370286	379253	387325	403852	425566

a) Subsidies on wheat and wool are recorded on an accrual basis.
b) Some government contributions to superannuation are only recorded in compensation when benefits are paid.
c) Data in this table have not been revised, therefore they are not comparable with the data in other tables.

1.4 General Government Current Receipts and Disbursements

Million Australian dollars — Fiscal year beginning 1 July

	1980	1983	1984	1985	1986	1987	1988	1989	1990	1991	1992	1993
					Receipts							
1 Operating surplus	-	-	-	-	-	-	-	-	-	-	-	...
2 Property and entrepreneurial income [a]	2605	4647	5707	8214	9637	9923	11175	12921	13891	14474	14386	...
3 Taxes, fees and contributions	40375	56740	66368	73676	83359	94753	106451	115691	119611	116006	119273	...
A Indirect taxes	17297	26001	29758	32841	36342	41521	45808	49028	50481	50354	52264	...
B Direct taxes	22399	29621	35331	39437	45434	51367	58544	64266	66568	62899	64048	...
C Social security contributions	...	...	...	...	...	...	...	...	...	...	...	...
D Compulsory fees, fines and penalties	679	1118	1279	1398	1583	1865	2099	2397	2562	2753	2961	...
4 Other current transfers	-	-	-	-	-	-	-	-	-	-	-	...
Total Current Receipts of General Government	42980	61387	72075	81890	92996	104676	117626	128612	133502	130480	133659	...
					Disbursements							
1 Government final consumption expenditure	25075	35860	40188	44755	49053	52571	56820	61767	66655	71324	74344	...
A Compensation of employees	18751	26110	28487	31142	33786	36373	39675	42168	45056	47611	...	...
B Consumption of fixed capital	3256	4320	4582	5046	5407	5688	6031	6492	6825	6974	...	...
C Purchases of goods and services, net	...	...	...	...	...	...	...	...	...	...	...	...
D Less: Own account fixed capital formation	...	...	...	...	...	...	...	...	...	...	...	...
E Indirect taxes paid, net	...	...	...	...	...	...	...	...	...	...	...	...
2 Property income	2996	5159	7101	9329	11276	12235	14075	16804	16379	15658	15337	...
A Interest	2996	5159	7101	9329	11276	12235	14075	16804	16379	15658	15337	...
B Net land rent and royalties	-	-	-	-	-	-	-	-	-	-	-	...

Australia

1.4 General Government Current Receipts and Disbursements
(Continued)

Million Australian dollars — Fiscal year beginning 1 July

	1980	1983	1984	1985	1986	1987	1988	1989	1990	1991	1992	1993
3 Subsidies b	2235	3523	3918	4314	4598	4400	4532	4543	5720	5899	6500	...
4 Other current transfers c	13341	22072	24839	26850	29102	32106	34169	37802	42898	48807	52984	...
A Social security benefits	...	...	...	...	...	...	...	...	...	...	...	...
B Social assistance grants	11431	18902	21224	22932	24897	27770	29358	32449	37200	42236	45752	...
C Other	1910	3170	3615	3918	4205	4336	4811	5353	5698	6571	7232	...
5 Net saving	-667	-5227	-3971	-3358	-1033	3364	8030	7696	1850	-11208	-15506	...
Total Current Disbursements and Net Saving of General Government	42980	61387	72075	81890	92996	104676	117626	128612	133502	130480	133659	...

a) All public enterprises are treated as if they were quasi-corporate.
b) Subsidies on wheat and wool are recorded on an accrual basis.
c) The Australian accounts do not distinguish between current and capital transfers to the rest of the world. They have all been treated as current transfers.

1.5 Current Income and Outlay of Corporate and Quasi-Corporate Enterprises, Summary

Million Australian dollars — Fiscal year beginning 1 July

	1980	1983	1984	1985	1986	1987	1988	1989	1990	1991	1992	1993
Receipts												
1 Operating surplus	9344	15253	18735	20173	21426	27437	33964	34428	33518	35183	38661	...
2 Property and entrepreneurial income received	9542	15198	17180	22625	27555	28021	34959	42837	42101	35005	31719	...
3 Current transfers	-	75	-	-	-	-	-	333	150	-	-	...
Total Current Receipts	18886	30526	35915	42798	48981	55458	68923	77598	75769	70188	70380	...
Disbursements												
1 Property and entrepreneurial income	13626	24688	28537	36709	43091	45013	55421	67176	67428	56795	49088	...
2 Direct taxes and other current payments to general government	4590	4512	5541	6068	6648	8739	10229	13292	15401	15296	15864	...
3 Other current transfers	375	720	951	941	1068	1047	1194	1942	1286	1311	1366	...
4 Net saving	295	606	886	-920	-1826	659	2079	-4812	-8346	-3214	4062	...
Total Current Disbursements and Net Saving	18886	30526	35915	42798	48981	55458	68923	77598	75769	70188	70380	...

1.6 Current Income and Outlay of Households and Non-Profit Institutions

Million Australian dollars — Fiscal year beginning 1 July

	1980	1983	1984	1985	1986	1987	1988	1989	1990	1991	1992	1993
Receipts												
1 Compensation of employees	74063	100638	111005	122530	134006	147328	165690	184588	192814	197449	204779	...
A From resident producers a	73944	100463	110805	122353	133847	147157	165451	184201	192362	196977	204265	...
B From rest of the world	119	175	200	177	159	171	239	387	452	472	514	...
2 Operating surplus of private unincorporated enterprises	20613	26591	28160	31329	34657	40366	48393	51551	51743	52380	54289	...
3 Property and entrepreneurial income	9360	16224	18157	23339	27673	29551	36480	44052	43632	34101	28099	...
4 Current transfers	13989	23672	26848	29168	32015	35409	38203	41919	47199	53181	55955	...
A Social security benefits	...	...	...	...	...	...	...	...	...	...	...	...
B Social assistance grants	11431	18902	21224	22932	24897	27770	29358	32449	37200	42236	45752	...
C Other	2558	4770	5624	6236	7118	7639	8845	9470	9999	10945	10203	...
Total Current Receipts	118025	167125	184170	206366	228351	252654	288766	322110	335388	337111	343122	...
Disbursements												
1 Private final consumption expenditure	82871	116748	128216	143738	157236	175367	195804	218071	231320	242750	253952	...
2 Property income	7028	10953	11941	15826	19150	20460	26733	33441	33646	26963	24081	...
3 Direct taxes and other current transfers n.e.c. to general government	18211	25789	30535	34070	39583	43674	49517	52263	52607	49452	50295	...
A Social security contributions	...	...	...	...	...	...	...	...	...	...	...	...
B Direct taxes	17532	24671	29256	32672	38000	41809	47418	49866	50045	46699	47334	...
C Fees, fines and penalties	679	1118	1279	1398	1583	1865	2099	2397	2562	2753	2961	...
4 Other current transfers	690	1203	1394	1365	1418	1410	1529	1608	1709	1726	1728	...
5 Net saving	9225	12432	12084	11367	10964	11743	15183	16727	16106	16220	13066	...
Total Current Disbursements and Net Saving	118025	167125	184170	206366	228351	252654	288766	322110	335388	337111	343122	...

a) Some government contributions to superannuation are only recorded in compensation when benefits are paid.

Australia

1.7 External Transactions on Current Account, Summary

Million Australian dollars — Fiscal year beginning 1 July

	1980	1983	1984	1985	1986	1987	1988	1989	1990	1991	1992	1993
Payments to the Rest of the World												
1 Imports of goods and services	25071	31192	39505	46111	48069	52819	61109	67363	65764	67807	77074	...
A Imports of merchandise c.i.f. [a]	20483	25678	32420	38683	39910	43360	50282	54696	52158	54285	63479	...
B Other	4588	5514	7085	7428	8159	9459	10827	12667	13606	13522	13595	...
2 Factor income to the rest of the world	2816	6147	8068	9293	10571	12131	15847	20795	21424	19389	17607	...
A Compensation of employees	110	158	178	164	179	210	279	406	429	326	311	...
B Property and entrepreneurial income	2706	5989	7890	9129	10392	11921	15568	20389	20995	19063	17296	...
By general government	374	671	931	1428	2265	2941	3140	4044	3804	3905	3537	...
By corporate and quasi-corporate enterprises	2332	5318	6959	7701	8127	8980	12428	16345	17191	15158	13759	...
By other	...	...	...	...	...	...	...	...	...	...	...	...
3 Current transfers to the rest of the world [b]	1126	1643	1754	1808	1804	1880	2002	2189	2283	2343	2392	...
A Indirect taxes to supranational organizations	...	...	...	...	...	...	...	...	...	...	...	...
B Other current transfers	1126	1643	1754	1808	1804	1880	2002	2189	2283	2343	2392	...
4 Surplus of the nation on current transactions	-4840	-7142	-10547	-14536	-11925	-10326	-17828	-22381	-15838	-12428	-15568	...
Payments to the Rest of the World and Surplus of the Nation on Current Transactions	24173	31840	38780	42676	48519	56504	61130	67966	73633	77111	81505	...
Receipts From The Rest of the World												
1 Exports of goods and services	22505	28574	35273	38539	43603	51080	54728	60133	65154	68828	74878	...
A Exports of merchandise f.o.b.	18689	23695	29717	32196	36032	41369	43880	49119	52349	54800	60004	...
B Other	3816	4879	5556	6343	7571	9711	10848	11014	12805	14028	14874	...
2 Factor income from rest of the world	682	1433	1555	1620	1899	1879	2192	3165	3618	3699	3508	...
A Compensation of employees	119	175	200	177	159	171	239	387	452	472	514	...
B Property and entrepreneurial income	563	1258	1355	1443	1740	1708	1953	2778	3166	3227	2994	...
By general government	3	20	24	37	43	46	59	104	105	16	3	...
By corporate and quasi-corporate enterprises	560	1238	1331	1406	1697	1662	1894	2674	3061	3211	2991	...
By other	-	-	-	-	-	-	-	-	...	...	...	...
3 Current transfers from rest of the world [b]	986	1833	1952	2517	3017	3545	4210	4668	4861	4584	3119	...
A Subsidies from supranational organisations	...	...	...	...	...	...	...	...	...	...	...	...
B Other current transfers	986	1833	1952	2517	3017	3545	4210	4668	4861	4584	3119	...
Receipts from the Rest of the World on Current Transactions	24173	31840	38780	42676	48519	56504	61130	67966	73633	77111	81505	...

a) Item 'Imports of merchandise C.I.F.' excludes freight on imports paid to resident carriers.
b) The Australian accounts do not distinguish between current and capital transfers to the rest of the world. They have all been treated as current transfers.

1.8 Capital Transactions of The Nation, Summary

Million Australian dollars — Fiscal year beginning 1 July

	1980	1983	1984	1985	1986	1987	1988	1989	1990	1991	1992	1993
Finance of Gross Capital Formation												
Gross saving	30060	37751	41538	44513	50755	62469	76571	75940	67917	61724	64192	...
1 Consumption of fixed capital	21207	29940	32539	37424	42650	46703	51279	55858	58307	59926	62570	...
A General government	3256	4320	4582	5051	5415	5685	6011	6478	6868	7132	7354	...
B Corporate and quasi-corporate enterprises	10493	15305	16546	19237	22217	24318	26155	28498	30303	31388	33150	...
Public	3297	5010	5517	6124	6847	7295	7784	8418	8838	9069	9288	...
Private	7196	10295	11029	13113	15370	17023	18371	20082	21465	22319	23862	...
C Other	7458	10315	11411	13136	15018	16700	19113	20882	21136	21406	22066	...
2 Net saving	8853	7811	8999	7089	8105	15766	25292	20080	9610	1798	1622	...
A General government	-667	-5227	-3971	-3358	-1033	3364	8030	7696	1850	-11208	-15506	...
B Corporate and quasi-corporate enterprises	295	606	886	-920	-1826	659	2079	-4812	-8346	-3214	4062	...
C Other [a]	9225	12432	12084	11367	10964	11743	15183	17198	16106	16220	13066	...
Less: Surplus of the nation on current transactions	-4840	-7142	-10547	-14536	-11925	-10326	-17828	-22381	-15838	-12428	-15568	...

Australia

1.8 Capital Transactions of The Nation, Summary
(Continued)

Million Australian dollars — Fiscal year beginning 1 July

	1980	1983	1984	1985	1986	1987	1988	1989	1990	1991	1992	1993
Statistical discrepancy	757	806	-54	1581	222	-918	-5278	-4413	-3992	361	-948	...
Finance of Gross Capital Formation	35657	45699	52031	60630	62902	71877	89121	93908	79763	74513	78812	...
Gross Capital Formation												
Increase in stocks b	465	1376	1013	1386	-1526	-466	3799	4460	-1726	-1832	-477	...
Gross fixed capital formation b	35192	44323	51018	59244	64428	72343	85322	89448	81489	76345	79289	...
1 General government	3750	5311	6171	7167	7821	7510	7572	8635	8775	8975	8912	...
2 Corporate and quasi-corporate enterprises	16870	22822	25298	31463	35904	39755	45123	49886	44957	39862	40346	...
A Public	5588	8839	8934	10822	11284	9895	10348	13011	12026	11747	10925	...
B Private	11282	13983	16364	20641	24620	29860	34775	36875	32931	28115	29421	...
3 Other	14572	16190	19549	20614	20703	25078	32627	30927	27757	27508	30031	...
Gross Capital Formation	35657	45699	52031	60630	62902	71877	89121	93908	79763	74513	78812	...

a) Item 'Other' of net saving includes extraordinary insurance claim paid.
b) Livestock is excluded from items 'Increase in Stocks' and 'Gross Fixed Capital Formation'.

1.10 Gross Domestic Product by Kind of Activity, in Current Prices

Million Australian dollars — Fiscal year beginning 1 July

	1980	1983	1984	1985	1986	1987	1988	1989	1990	1991	1992	1993
1 Agriculture, hunting, forestry and fishing	7425	9604	9673	9619	10462	12486	14873	15068	12698	11911	12869	...
2 Mining and quarrying	8831	12985	14392	15480	13580	14181	13106	16266	18594	16527	17315	...
3 Manufacturing	26981	34862	38183	41369	43764	48415	53446	57179	56722	55915	59771	...
4 Electricity, gas and water a	4072	6949	7613	8352	9424	10130	11204	11919	12648	13517	14076	...
5 Construction	11306	14487	16372	18337	20405	22325	26253	29251	28724	27518	28177	...
6 Wholesale and retail trade, restaurants and hotels b	21792	30395	35176	40738	46439	52363	61674	65551	66403	68281	70707	...
7 Transport, storage and communication	9762	13489	15279	16777	18441	21785	24461	25771	27113	29363	30384	...
8 Finance, insurance, real estate and business services	24332	36144	39894	43968	51923	62928	74836	81988	87171	90883	95432	...
9 Community, social and personal services b	20839	30544	33791	37422	41853	46358	52308	57978	62863	67459	70735	...
Total, Industries	135340	189459	210373	232062	256291	290971	332161	360986	372936	381374	399466	...
Producers of Government Services	6457	8256	8899	9838	10767	11867	12947	13461	14403	15718	16355	...
Other Producers	...	...	...	...	...	...	...	...	...	...	...	...
Subtotal	141797	197715	219272	241900	267058	302838	345108	374447	387339	397092	415821	...
Less: Imputed bank service charge	3317	5161	5942	5212	5792	7476	8219	7472	9539	11144	13292	...
Plus: Import duties	1800	2329	2927	3282	3237	3632	3753	3954	3320	3299	3331	...
Plus: Value added tax	...	...	...	...	...	...	...	...	...	...	...	...
Equals: Gross Domestic Product	140280	194883	216257	239970	264503	298994	340642	370929	381120	389247	405860	...

a) Item 'Electricity, gas and water' includes sewage services.
b) Restaurants and hotels are included in item 'Community, social and personal services'.

1.11 Gross Domestic Product by Kind of Activity, in Constant Prices

Million Australian dollars — Fiscal year beginning 1 July

	1980	1983	1984	1985	1986	1987	1988	1989	1990	1991	1992	1993
At constant prices of: 1989												
1 Agriculture, hunting, forestry and fishing	10931	14243	14271	13917	14447	13842	13914	15068	16095	15333	16065	...
2 Mining and quarrying	9948	10961	12488	13764	12934	14665	15056	16266	16995	17323	17507	...
3 Manufacturing	50411	48131	50589	51498	52068	55186	58077	57194	56112	55133	56864	...
4 Electricity, gas and water a	8125	9167	9736	10093	10303	10834	11350	11919	12161	12347	12509	...
5 Construction	24368	22599	24549	25716	25060	26284	28545	29251	27439	24544	25444	...
6 Wholesale and retail trade, restaurants and hotels b	50922	52335	55339	55977	55138	58341	63680	65551	62620	63627	64593	...
7 Transport, storage and communication	16936	18104	19556	20853	21604	23194	24738	25771	26487	27086	28595	...
8 Finance, insurance, real estate and business services	54850	59161	62212	66176	69956	74183	78016	81988	81630	80735	82960	...
9 Community, social and personal services b	39641	44632	46130	47930	50417	52731	55505	57978	58665	60539	62469	...
Total, Industries	266132	279333	294870	305924	311927	329260	348881	360986	358204	356667	367006	...
Producers of Government Services	9892	10847	11231	11752	12239	12960	13468	13461	13813	14697	15055	...

Australia

1.11 Gross Domestic Product by Kind of Activity, in Constant Prices
(Continued)

Million Australian dollars — Fiscal year beginning 1 July

	1980	1983	1984	1985	1986	1987	1988	1989	1990	1991	1992	1993
					At constant prices of:1989							
Other Producers	...	...	...	...	...	...	...	...	...	...	...	...
Subtotal	276024	290180	306101	317676	324166	342220	362349	374447	372017	371364	382061	...
Less: Imputed bank service charge	6507	7052	7355	6813	7081	7589	8011	7472	7970	7898	8215	...
Plus: Import duties	2392	2479	2977	3065	2782	2968	3794	3954	3708	3749	3997	...
Plus: Value added tax	...	...	...	...	...	...	...	...	...	...	...	...
Plus: Other adjustments	-1028	-729	-	-	-	-	-	-	-	-	-	...
Equals: Gross Domestic Product	270881	284878	301723	313928	319867	337599	358132	370929	367755	367215	377843	...

a) Item 'Electricity, gas and water' includes sewage services.
b) Restaurants and hotels are included in item 'Community, social and personal services'.

1.12 Relations Among National Accounting Aggregates

Million Australian dollars — Fiscal year beginning 1 July

	1980	1983	1984	1985	1986	1987	1988	1989	1990	1991	1992	1993
Gross Domestic Product	140280	194880	216256	239970	264503	298994	339805	370286	379253	387325	403852	425566
Plus: Net factor income from the rest of the world	-2134	-4639	-6513	-7673	-8672	-10252	-13655	-17512	-17694	-15591	-13858	-14414
Factor income from the rest of the world	682	1508	1555	1620	1899	1879	2192	3315	3768	3702	3642	3143
Less: Factor income to the rest of the world	2816	6147	8068	9293	10571	12131	15847	20827	21462	19293	17500	17557
Equals: Gross National Product	138146	190241	209743	232297	255831	288742	326150	352774	361559	371734	389994	411152
Less: Consumption of fixed capital	21207	29940	32539	37424	42650	46703	51279	55858	58307	59926	62570	64658
Equals: National Income	116939	160301	177204	194873	213181	242039	274871	296916	303252	311808	327424	346494
Plus: Net current transfers from the rest of the world a	-140	115	198	709	1213	1665	2208	2329	2428	2241	727	275
Current transfers from the rest of the world	986	1758	1952	2517	3017	3545	4210	4518	4711	4584	3119	2810
Less: Current transfers to the rest of the world	1126	1643	1754	1808	1804	1880	2002	2189	2283	2343	2392	2535
Equals: National Disposable Income	116799	160416	177402	195582	214394	243704	277079	299245	305680	314049	328151	346769
Less: Final consumption b	107946	152582	168351	188408	206150	227718	252368	279456	297769	314059	327665	341400
Equals: Net Saving	8853	7834	9051	7174	8244	15986	24711	19789	7911	-10	486	5369
Less: Surplus of the nation on current transactions	-4810	-7055	-10446	-14428	-11716	-10109	-17507	-22071	-15329	-11774	-14950	-16036
Statistical discrepancy	787	872	-7	1604	-187	-1259	-4571	-3773	-1678	3081	1124	-2287
Equals: Net Capital Formation c	14450	15761	19490	23206	19773	24836	37647	38087	21562	14845	16560	19118

a) The Australian accounts do not distinguish between current and capital transfers to the rest of the world. They have all been treated as current transfers.
b) Item 'Final consumption expenditure' includes some expenditure of non-profit organisations.
c) Data in this table have not been revised, therefore they are not comparable with the data in other tables.

2.1 Government Final Consumption Expenditure by Function, in Current Prices

Million Australian dollars — Fiscal year beginning 1 July

		1980	1983	1984	1985	1986	1987	1988	1989	1990	1991	1992	1993
1	General public services	3139	4640	5112	5812	6829	7937	7974	8242	9249	10345	10925	...
2	Defence	3389	4530	5401	6224	6683	6617	7381	7985	7923	8608	9059	...
3	Public order and safety	1652	2398	2625	2953	3247	3531	3941	4528	4808	5140	5313	...
4	Education	6309	8802	9477	10373	11031	11637	12468	13200	14179	15158	15820	...
5	Health	4334	6039	7073	7762	8732	9538	10669	11363	11965	12494	12600	...
6	Social security and welfare	650	1174	1337	1584	1860	2062	2121	2681	3535	3900	4240	...
7	Housing and community amenities	358	580	641	723	774	860	879	1032	1142	1197	1154	...
8	Recreational, cultural and religious affairs	912	1416	1717	1936	2074	2205	2453	2532	2718	2808	2931	...
9	Economic services	4288	6260	6848	7426	7876	8290	8955	10012	11063	11582	11852	...
	A Fuel and energy	96	142	155	214	164	177	170	209	166	192	207	...
	B Agriculture, forestry, fishing and hunting	951	1338	1440	1569	1702	1801	1938	2096	2279	2210	2187	...
	C Mining, manufacturing and construction, except fuel and energy	252	342	362	444	382	422	505	533	567	589	547	...
	D Transportation and communication	2239	3316	3508	3747	3970	4243	4574	5265	5825	6080	5991	...
	E Other economic affairs	750	1122	1383	1452	1658	1647	1768	1909	2226	2511	2920	...
10	Other functions	44	21	-43	-38	-53	-106	-21	192	73	92	450	...
	Total Government Final Consumption Expenditure	25075	35860	40188	44755	49053	52571	56820	61767	66655	71324	74344	...

Australia

2.3 Total Government Outlays by Function and Type

Million Australian dollars — Fiscal year beginning 1 July

	Final Consumption Expenditures Total	Compensation of Employees	Other	Subsidies	Other Current Transfers & Property Income	Total Current Disbursements	Gross Capital Formation	Other Capital Outlays	Total Outlays
1980									
1 General public services	3139	...	...	26	616	3781	385	-2	4164
2 Defence	3389	...	...	-	41	3430	-	-	3430
3 Public order and safety	1652	...	...	-	18	1670	155	1	1826
4 Education	6309	...	...	5	1096	7410	625	41	8076
5 Health	4334	...	...	80	1668	6077	281	7	6365
6 Social security and welfare	650	...	...	12	9726	10388	32	69	10489
7 Housing and community amenities	358	...	...	61	19	438	216	127	781
8 Recreation, culture and religion	912	...	...	12	77	1001	340	30	1371
9 Economic services	4288	...	...	2027	60	6375	1754	15	8144
A Fuel and energy	96	...	...	82	4	182	27	-122	87
B Agriculture, forestry, fishing and hunting	951	...	...	325	1	1277	203	-3	1477
C Mining (except fuels), manufacturing and construction	252	...	...	430	3	685	9	14	708
D Transportation and communication	2239	...	...	908	3	3150	1458	125	4733
E Other economic affairs	750	...	...	282	49	1081	57	1	1139
10 Other functions [a]	44	...	...	17	3016	3077	28	-11	3094
Total	25075	...	...	2240	16337	43647	3816	277	47745
1985									
1 General public services	5812	...	...	29	935	6776	737	-1	7512
2 Defence	6224	...	...	-	54	6278	-	-	6278
3 Public order and safety	2953	...	...	-	44	2997	346	1	3344
4 Education	10373	...	...	8	2173	12554	1038	90	13682
5 Health	7762	...	...	142	4523	12427	518	7	12952
6 Social security and welfare	1584	...	...	72	18592	20248	146	112	20506
7 Housing and community amenities	723	...	...	287	63	1073	446	675	2194
8 Recreation, culture and religion	1936	...	...	23	168	2127	696	105	2928
9 Economic services	7426	...	...	3736	263	11425	3241	156	14822
A Fuel and energy	214	...	...	519	2	735	23	50	808
B Agriculture, forestry, fishing and hunting	1569	...	...	482	6	2057	355	-1	2411
C Mining (except fuels), manufacturing and construction	444	...	...	453	2	899	30	38	967
D Transportation and communication	3747	...	...	1714	8	5469	2774	58	8301
E Other economic affairs	1452	...	...	568	245	2265	59	11	2335
10 Other functions [a]	-38	...	...	17	9364	9343	29	-32	9340
Total	44755	...	...	4314	36179	85248	7197	1113	93558
1990									
1 General public services	9249	...	...	74	1050	10373	1001	44	11418
2 Defence	7923	...	...	-	93	8016	-	-72	7944
3 Public order and safety	4808	...	...	-	90	4898	701	1	5600
4 Education	14179	...	...	23	3766	17968	1358	89	19415
5 Health	11965	...	...	25	7669	19659	906	46	20611
6 Social security and welfare	3535	...	...	6	29404	32945	124	136	33205
7 Housing and community amenities	1142	...	...	513	196	1851	489	897	3237
8 Recreation, culture and religion	2718	...	...	31	266	3015	623	119	3757
9 Economic services	11063	...	...	4919	363	16345	3411	893	20649
A Fuel and energy	166	...	...	527	16	709	28	89	826
B Agriculture, forestry, fishing and hunting	2279	...	...	1655	10	3944	289	-47	4186
C Mining (except fuels), manufacturing and construction	567	...	...	338	3	908	37	4	949
D Transportation and communication	5825	...	...	1873	7	7705	2846	602	11153
E Other economic affairs	2226	...	...	526	327	3079	211	245	3535
10 Other functions [a]	73	...	...	129	16380	16582	185	76	16843
Total	66655	...	...	5720	59277	131652	8798	2229	142679

Australia

2.3 Total Government Outlays by Function and Type
(Continued)

Million Australian dollars — Fiscal year beginning 1 July

		Final Consumption Expenditures Total	Compensation of Employees	Other	Subsidies	Other Current Transfers & Property Income	Total Current Disbursements	Gross Capital Formation	Other Capital Outlays	Total Outlays
					1991					
1	General public services	10345	...	...	75	1216	11636	1223	18	12877
2	Defence	8608	...	...	-	76	8684	1	-8	8677
3	Public order and safety	5140	...	...	2	89	5231	666	7	5904
4	Education	15158	...	...	37	4310	19505	1239	127	20871
5	Health	12494	...	...	49	8158	20701	827	74	21602
6	Social security and welfare	3900	...	...	5	34063	37968	239	205	38412
7	Housing and community amenities	1197	...	...	602	115	1914	566	849	3329
8	Recreation, culture and religion	2808	...	...	42	257	3107	659	107	3873
9	Economic services	11582	...	...	4670	523	16775	3239	1032	21046
	A Fuel and energy	192	...	...	584	11	787	18	64	869
	B Agriculture, forestry, fishing and hunting	2210	...	...	1168	24	3402	274	6	3682
	C Mining (except fuels), manufacturing and construction	589	...	...	350	11	950	24	12	986
	D Transportation and communication	6080	...	...	1838	10	7928	2762	634	11324
	E Other economic affairs	2511	...	...	730	467	3708	161	316	4185
10	Other functions [a]	92	...	...	417	15658	16167	307	181	16655
	Total	71324	...	...	5899	64465	141688	8966	2592	153246
					1992					
1	General public services	10925	...	...	82	1302	12309	891	39	13239
2	Defence	9059	...	...	-	77	9136	-	-1	9135
3	Public order and safety	5313	...	...	-	142	5455	444	4	5903
4	Education	15820	...	...	63	4567	20450	1403	146	21999
5	Health	12600	...	...	61	8984	21645	905	70	22620
6	Social security and welfare	4240	...	...	-1	36779	41018	190	204	41412
7	Housing and community amenities	1154	...	...	682	83	1919	479	853	3251
8	Recreation, culture and religion	2931	...	...	39	282	3252	718	155	4125
9	Economic services	11852	...	...	4666	759	17277	3673	795	21745
	A Fuel and energy	207	...	...	610	13	830	32	82	944
	B Agriculture, forestry, fishing and hunting	2187	...	...	950	28	3165	265	8	3438
	C Mining (except fuels), manufacturing and construction	547	...	...	338	11	896	27	-27	896
	D Transportation and communication	5991	...	...	1765	16	7772	3217	630	11619
	E Other economic affairs	2920	...	...	1003	691	4614	132	102	4848
10	Other functions [a]	450	...	...	908	15346	16704	229	63	16996
	Total	74344	...	...	6500	68321	149165	8932	2328	160425

a) Property income disbursements are classified to 'Other functions'.

2.4 Composition of General Government Social Security Benefits and Social Assistance Grants to Households

Million Australian dollars — Fiscal year beginning 1 July

		1980 SSB	1980 SAG	1985 SSB	1985 SAG	1990 SSB	1990 SAG	1991 SSB	1991 SAG	1992 SSB	1992 SAG
1	Education benefits	...	455	...	825	...	1750	...	2030	...	2188
	A Pre-primary and primary	...	-	...	4	...	10	...	7	...	-
	B Secondary	...	36	...	141	...	68	...	346	...	657
	C Tertiary	...	215	...	359	...	724	...	898	...	711
	D Other	...	204	...	321	...	948	...	779	...	820
2	Health benefits	...	1454	...	4045	...	7121	...	7570	...	8320
	A Hospital	...	393	...	708	...	1573	...	1617	...	1693
	B Clinics and practitioners	...	747	...	2704	...	4290	...	4623	...	5024
	C Public health	...	5	...	17	...	1	...	11	...	3
	D Medicaments, etc.	...	309	...	616	...	1257	...	1319	...	1600
3	Social security and welfare benefits	...	9481	...	17932	...	27910	...	32235	...	34763
	A Social security	...	9424	...	17807	...	27709	...	32020	...	34623

Australia

2.4 Composition of General Government Social Security Benefits and Social Assistance Grants to Households
(Continued)

Million Australian dollars — Fiscal year beginning 1 July

		1980 SSB	1980 SAG	1985 SSB	1985 SAG	1990 SSB	1990 SAG	1991 SSB	1991 SAG	1992 SSB	1992 SAG
	Temporary sickness	...	174	...	392	...	651	...	445	...	371
	Old age and permanent disability	...	4864	...	7644	...	12243	...	13363	...	14299
	Unemployment	...	996	...	3122	...	4562	...	6736	...	7491
	Family assistance	...	1365	...	2825	...	5231	...	6216	...	7204
	Other	...	2025	...	3824	...	5022	...	5260	...	5258
B	Welfare	...	57	...	125	...	201	...	215	...	140
4	Housing and community amenities	...	5	...	45	...	158	...	94	...	58
5	Recreation and cultural benefits	...	3	...	2	...	4	...	6	...	4
6	Other	...	33	...	83	...	257	...	301	...	419
Total		...	11431	...	22932	...	37200	...	42236	...	45752

2.5 Private Final Consumption Expenditure by Type and Purpose, in Current Prices

Million Australian dollars — Fiscal year beginning 1 July

		1980	1983	1984	1985	1986	1987	1988	1989	1990	1991	1992	1993
	Final Consumption Expenditure of Resident Households												
1	Food, beverages and tobacco [a]	19939	26788	28758	32255	35047	37908	41056	44936	47639	49921	52623	...
A	Food	13841	18728	20101	22740	24705	26513	28947	31623	33223	34966	36682	...
B	Non-alcoholic beverages												...
C	Alcoholic beverages	4517	5860	6268	6858	7342	8148	8554	9329	10039	10329	10571	...
D	Tobacco	1581	2200	2389	2657	3000	3247	3555	3984	4377	4626	5370	...
2	Clothing and footwear [b]	5794	7839	8539	9635	10470	11606	12450	12914	13104	13846	13992	...
3	Gross rent, fuel and power	15460	22690	24928	27970	31351	35293	39913	44296	47827	49962	51809	...
A	Fuel and power	1756	2867	3074	3377	3681	3926	4216	4659	5047	5268	5677	...
B	Other	13704	19823	21854	24593	27670	31367	35697	39637	42780	44694	46132	...
4	Furniture, furnishings and household equipment and operation [b]	6418	8816	9609	10718	11573	12923	14109	15373	15292	16023	16781	...
5	Medical care and health expenses	5084	7898	8328	9248	10575	12006	13485	14948	16463	17483	18650	...
6	Transport and communication	12745	17072	19031	21204	21925	24400	27908	32424	35034	36386	37782	...
A	Personal transport equipment	3545	4298	5112	5729	5233	5734	7651	9470	8938	8847	9752	...
B	Other	9200	12774	13919	15475	16692	18666	20257	22954	26096	27539	28030	...
7	Recreational, entertainment, education and cultural services	6647	10050	11416	12885	14375	16082	18280	20543	22004	23518	24956	...
A	Education	967	1653	1879	2103	2422	2704	3253	3941	4304	4614	4914	...
B	Other	5680	8397	9537	10782	11953	13378	15027	16602	17700	18904	20042	...
8	Miscellaneous goods and services	10423	15135	16852	19370	21852	25652	29451	32832	34631	36764	38342	...
	Total Final Consumption Expenditure in the Domestic Market by Households, of which	82510	116288	127461	143285	157168	175870	196652	218266	231994	243903	254935	...
	Plus: Direct purchases abroad by resident households	1449	2016	2454	2542	2783	3268	3767	4582	4741	4618	5045	...
	Less: Direct purchases in the domestic market by non-resident households	1088	1556	1699	2089	2715	3771	4615	4777	5415	5771	6028	...
	Equals: Final Consumption Expenditure of Resident Households [c]	82871	116748	128216	143738	157236	175367	195804	218071	231320	242750	253952	...
	Final Consumption Expenditure of Private Non-profit Institutions Serving Households												
	Equals: Final Consumption Expenditure of Private Non-profit Organisations Serving Households	...	...	...	...	...	...	...	...	...	...	...	...
	Private Final Consumption Expenditure	82871	116748	128216	143738	157236	175367	195804	218071	231320	242750	253952	...

a) Item 'Food, beverages and tobacco' includes food, beverages and tobacco consumed in institutions except hospitals and nursing homes.
b) Drapery is included in item 'Clothing and footwear'.
c) Item 'Final consumption expenditure of resident households' includes consumption expenditure of private non-profit institutions serving households.

Australia

2.6 Private Final Consumption Expenditure by Type and Purpose, in Constant Prices

Million Australian dollars — Fiscal year beginning 1 July

At constant prices of: 1989

Final Consumption Expenditure of Resident Households

	1980	1983	1984	1985	1986	1987	1988	1989	1990	1991	1992	1993
1 Food, beverages and tobacco [a]	40735	41706	42163	43636	43486	44297	44109	44936	45622	46342	47330	...
A Food	27032	28623	29159	30509	30552	31170	30961	31623	32348	33287	34425	...
B Non-alcoholic beverages												...
C Alcoholic beverages	9226	8972	8952	9091	8858	9050	9112	9329	9378	9291	9302	...
D Tobacco	4477	4111	4052	4036	4076	4077	4036	3984	3896	3764	3603	...
2 Clothing and footwear [b]	10668	11950	12309	12778	12653	13034	13091	12914	12548	13045	13080	...
3 Gross rent, fuel and power	33238	36648	37432	38818	40067	41172	42609	44296	45598	46652	48120	...
A Fuel and power	3737	3936	3964	4101	4253	4274	4381	4659	4783	4793	4991	...
B Other	29501	32712	33468	34717	35814	36898	38228	39637	40815	41859	43129	...
4 Furniture, furnishings and household equipment and operation [b]	10415	11838	12717	13307	13124	13828	14538	15373	15026	15677	16441	...
5 Medical care and health expenses	9837	11828	11648	12210	12958	13624	14394	14948	15381	15812	16673	...
6 Transport and communication	24691	24983	26380	27294	26015	27164	29827	32424	33138	34355	35381	...
A Personal transport equipment	8052	7620	8526	8548	6611	6470	7994	9470	8915	8440	9019	...
B Other	16639	17363	17854	18746	19404	20694	21833	22954	24223	25915	26362	...
7 Recreational, entertainment, education and cultural services	13782	15408	16592	17247	17627	18285	19104	20003	20160	20606	21254	...
A Education	1742	2267	2433	2575	2705	2902	3135	3401	3468	3491	3672	...
B Other	12040	13141	14159	14672	14922	15383	15969	16602	16692	17115	17582	...
8 Miscellaneous goods and services	19533	21738	22964	24702	26043	28945	31486	33372	33519	34566	35433	...
Total Final Consumption Expenditure in the Domestic Market by Households, of which	162541	176099	182205	189992	191973	200349	209158	218266	220992	227055	233712	...
Plus: Direct purchases abroad by resident households	2686	3109	3410	115	-543	-1022	-813	-195	-791	-1354	-1572	...
Less: Direct purchases in the domestic market by non-resident households	2239	2385	2462									...
Equals: Final Consumption Expenditure of Resident Households [c]	162988	176854	183153	190107	191430	199327	208345	218071	220201	225701	232140	...

Final Consumption Expenditure of Private Non-profit Institutions Serving Households

	1980	1983	1984	1985	1986	1987	1988	1989	1990	1991	1992	1993
Equals: Final Consumption Expenditure of Private Non-profit Organisations Serving Households	...	...	...	...	...	...	...	...	...	...	...	...
Private Final Consumption Expenditure	162988	176854	183153	190107	191430	199327	208345	218071	220201	225701	232140	...

a) Item 'Food, beverages and tobacco' includes food, beverages and tobacco consumed in institutions except hospitals and nursing homes.
b) Drapery is included in item 'Clothing and footwear'.
c) Item 'Final consumption expenditure of resident households' includes consumption expenditure of private non-profit institutions serving households.

2.7 Gross Capital Formation by Type of Good and Owner, in Current Prices

Million Australian dollars — Fiscal year beginning 1 July

	1980 TOTAL	1980 Total Private	1980 Public Enterprises	1980 General Government	1985 TOTAL	1985 Total Private	1985 Public Enterprises	1985 General Government	1990 TOTAL	1990 Total Private	1990 Public Enterprises	1990 General Government
Increase in stocks, total [a]	465	737	-338	66	1386	1723	-367	30	-1726	-2986	1237	23
1 Goods producing industries [a]	1220	1220	...	...	1443	1443	...	...	-1087	-1087	...	...
2 Wholesale and retail trade	956	1519	-563	...	1464	2277	-813	...	-526	-1034	508	...
3 Other, except government stocks	585	404	181	...	229	110	119	...	338	556	-218	...
4 Government stocks	66	...	...	66	30	...	...	30	23	...	...	23
Statistical discrepancy [b]	-2362	-2406	44	...	-1780	-2107	327	...	-474	-1421	947	...
Gross Fixed Capital Formation, Total [a]	35192	25854	5588	3750	59244	41255	10822	7167	81489	60688	12026	8775

Australia

2.7 Gross Capital Formation by Type of Good and Owner, in Current Prices
(Continued)

Million Australian dollars — Fiscal year beginning 1 July

	1980 TOTAL	1980 Total Private	1980 Public Enterprises	1980 General Government	1985 TOTAL	1985 Total Private	1985 Public Enterprises	1985 General Government	1990 TOTAL	1990 Total Private	1990 Public Enterprises	1990 General Government
1 Residential buildings	8516	8199	290	27	12319	11239	955	125	18327	17106	1046	175
2 Non-residential buildings												
3 Other construction	10639	4556	2931	3152	18878	8400	4745	5733	26638	14020	6394	6224
4 Land improvement and plantation and orchard development												
5 Producers' durable goods	14356	11418	2367	571	25230	18799	5122	1309	31756	24794	4586	2376
6 Breeding stock, dairy cattle, etc.	...	...	...	...	...	...	...	...	...	...	...	...
Statistical discrepancy c	1681	1681	...	...	2817	2817	...	...	4768	4768	...	...
Total Gross Capital Formation a	35657	26591	5250	3816	60630	42978	10455	7197	79763	57702	13263	8798

	1991 TOTAL	1991 Total Private	1991 Public Enterprises	1991 General Government	1992 TOTAL	1992 Total Private	1992 Public Enterprises	1992 General Government
Increase in stocks, total a	-1832	-1489	-334	-9	-477	-707	210	20
1 Goods producing industries a	-553	-553	...	...	579	579	...	...
2 Wholesale and retail trade	-504	-242	-262	...	692	447	245	...
3 Other, except government stocks	-164	-240	76	...	-376	-111	-265	...
4 Government stocks	-9	...	...	-9	20	...	...	20
Statistical discrepancy b	-602	-454	-148	...	-1392	-1622	230	...
Gross Fixed Capital Formation, Total a	76345	55623	11747	8975	79289	59452	10925	8912
1 Residential buildings	18042	16906	860	276	20454	19146	1137	171
2 Non-residential buildings								
3 Other construction	23556	11164	6069	6323	22256	10253	5567	6436
4 Land improvement and plantation and orchard development								
5 Producers' durable goods	29563	22369	4818	2376	31308	24782	4221	2305
6 Breeding stock, dairy cattle, etc.	...	...	...	...	...	...	...	...
Statistical discrepancy c	5184	5184	...	...	5271	5271	...	...
Total Gross Capital Formation a	74513	54134	11413	8966	78812	58745	11135	8932

a) Livestock is excluded from items 'Increase in Stocks' and 'Gross Fixed Capital Formation'.
b) Item 'Statistical discrepancy' refers to stock valuation adjustment. The detailed data on changes in stock are based on book values.
c) Item 'Statistical discrepancy' in tables 2.7 and 2.8 refers to real estate transfer expenses and the expenses are included in item 'other' in tables 1.1 and 1.2.

Australia

2.8 Gross Capital Formation by Type of Good and Owner, in Constant Prices

Million Australian dollars
Fiscal year beginning 1 July

	1980				1985				1990			
	TOTAL	Total Private	Public Enterprises	General Government	TOTAL	Total Private	Public Enterprises	General Government	TOTAL	Total Private	Public Enterprises	General Government
					At constant prices of:1989							
Increase in stocks, total [a,b]	933	1155	-453	123	1764	2247	-523	40	-1279	-2823	1525	22
1 Goods producing industries [b]	134	134	...	...	909	909	...	...	-1418	-1418	...	...
2 Wholesale and retail trade	-192	598	-790	...	627	1308	-681	...	-55	-1786	1731	...
3 Other, except government stocks	760	423	337	...	188	30	158	...	175	381	-206	...
4 Government stocks	123	...	...	123	40	...	...	40	22	...	...	22
Gross Fixed Capital Formation, Total	69730	51935	10834	7099	77457	55438	13370	8649	80331	59990	11737	8604
1 Residential buildings	18891	18202	632	57	18089	16560	1349	180	17709	16514	1018	177
2 Non-residential buildings												
3 Other construction	21961	9493	6090	6244	24745	11060	6336	7349	25848	13717	6153	5978
4 Land improvement and plantation and orchard development												
5 Producers' durable goods	24201	19426	4112	663	29466	22661	5685	1120	31310	24295	4566	2449
6 Breeding stock, dairy cattle, etc.	...	...	...	...	...	...	...	...	...	...	...	...
Statistical discrepancy [c]	5074	5074	...	...	5157	5157	...	...	5464	5464	...	...
Total Gross Capital Formation [a,b]	70663	53090	10381	7222	79221	57685	12847	8689	79052	57167	13262	8626

	1991				1992			
	TOTAL	Total Private	Public Enterprises	General Government	TOTAL	Total Private	Public Enterprises	General Government
				At constant prices of:1989				
Increase in stocks, total [a,b]	-2020	-1435	-577	-9	-61	-481	400	19
1 Goods producing industries [b]	-600	-600	...	...	339	339	...	...
2 Wholesale and retail trade	-1334	-684	-650	...	65	-582	647	...
3 Other, except government stocks	-78	-151	73	...	-485	-238	-247	...
4 Government stocks	-9	...	...	-9	19	...	...	19
Gross Fixed Capital Formation, Total [a,b]	75362	55079	11436	8847	76858	57559	10600	8699
1 Residential buildings	17396	16255	863	278	19747	18422	1152	173
2 Non-residential buildings								
3 Other construction	23077	11199	5859	6019	21995	10471	5388	6136
4 Land improvement and plantation and orchard development								
5 Producers' durable goods	28878	21614	4714	2550	29066	22616	4060	2390
6 Breeding stock, dairy cattle, etc.	...	...	...	...	...	...	...	...
Statistical discrepancy [c]	6011	6011	...	...	6050	6050	...	...
Total Gross Capital Formation [a,b]	73342	53644	10859	8838	76797	57078	11000	8718

a) For years prior to 1984-1985, the sum of the component items does not equal its total.
b) Livestock is excluded from items 'Increase in Stocks' and 'Gross Fixed Capital Formation'.
c) Item 'Statistical discrepancy' in tables 2.7 and 2.8 refers to real estate transfer expenses and the expenses are included in item 'other' in tables 1.1 and 1.2.

Australia

2.17 Exports and Imports of Goods and Services, Detail

Million Australian dollars — Fiscal year beginning 1 July

	1980	1983	1984	1985	1986	1987	1988	1989	1990	1991	1992	1993
Exports of Goods and Services												
1 Exports of merchandise, f.o.b. [a,b]	18689	23695	29717	32196	36032	41369	43880	49119	52349	54800	60004	...
2 Transport and communication	1895	2102	2480	2759	3028	3471	3588	3795	4252	4494	5077	...
3 Insurance service charges	10	10	13	7	24	38	33	36	36	41	40	...
4 Other commodities [b]	755	1178	1275	1451	1679	2146	2450	2798	3121	3455	3526	...
5 Adjustments of merchandise exports to change-of-ownership basis	29	-34	13	-48	6	146	14	-555	-194	74	11	...
6 Direct purchases in the domestic market by non-residential households	1088	1556	1699	2089	2715	3771	4615	4777	5415	5771	6028	...
7 Direct purchases in the domestic market by extraterritorial bodies	39	67	76	85	119	139	148	163	175	193	192	...
Total Exports of Goods and Services	22505	28574	35273	38539	43603	51080	54728	60133	65154	68828	74878	...
Imports of Goods and Services												
1 Imports of merchandise, c.i.f. [c]	20483	25678	32420	38683	39910	43360	50282	54696	52158	54285	63479	...
A Imports of merchandise, f.o.b. [d]	18755	23648	29881	35832	37102	40437	47032	51253	48970	51028	59707	...
B Transport of services on merchandise imports	1717	2018	2523	2827	2784	2899	3226	3419	3164	3233	3748	...
By residents	...	...	...	...	...	...	...	...	...	...	...	...
By non-residents	1717	2018	2523	2827	2784	2899	3226	3419	3164	3233	3748	...
C Insurance service charges on merchandise imports	11	12	16	24	24	24	24	24	24	24	24	...
By residents	...	...	...	...	...	...	...	...	...	...	...	...
By non-residents	11	12	16	24	24	24	24	24	24	24	24	...
2 Adjustments of merchandise imports to change-of-ownership basis	422	-151	212	-156	57	-51	72	-262	286	28	-281	...
3 Other transport and communication [e]	1494	1699	2092	2197	2114	2510	2912	3424	3443	3642	3756	...
4 Other insurance service charges	48	197	184	312	283	288	357	360	378	379	382	...
5 Other commodities	1020	1530	1875	2217	2581	3133	3484	4178	4311	4468	4264	...
6 Direct purchases abroad by government	1449	2016	2454	2542	2783	3268	3767	4582	4741	4618	5045	...
7 Direct purchases abroad by resident households	155	223	268	316	341	311	307	385	447	387	429	...
Total Imports of Goods and Services	25071	31192	39505	46111	48069	52819	61109	67363	65764	67807	77074	...
Balance of Goods and Services	-2566	-2618	-4232	-7572	-4466	-1739	-6381	-7230	-610	1021	-2196	...
Total Imports and Balance of Goods and Services	22505	28574	35273	38539	43603	51080	54728	60133	65154	68828	74878	...

a) Item 'Exports of merchandise, f.o.b.' refers to exports recorded at the time the goods cross the customs frontier. Sales of ships and aircraft stores, bunkers and ballasts are excluded.
b) Prior to January 1976, exports of gold are included in item 'Other commodities'. Since January 1976, they are included in item 'Export of merchandise, f.o.b.'.
c) Merchandise valued at Free Along Side (F.A.S.).
d) Item 'Imports of merchandise f.o.b.' is adjusted in respect to coverage and valuation. It is recorded at the time the goods cross the customs frontiers. It excludes purchase of ships and aircraft stores etc. which are included in net acquisition of foreign financial assets.
e) Item 'Other transport and communication' includes purchases of ships' stores etc. and crews' expenditure in foreign ports.

Australia

3.12 General Government Income and Outlay Account: Total and Subsectors

Million Australian dollars — Fiscal year beginning 1 July

	1980 Total General Government	1980 Central Government	1980 State or Provincial Government	1980 Local Government	1980 Social Security Funds	1985 Total General Government	1985 Central Government	1985 State or Provincial Government	1985 Local Government	1985 Social Security Funds
Receipts										
1 Operating surplus	-	-	...	-	...	-	-	...	-	...
2 Property and entrepreneurial income [a]	2605	2501	...	1673	...	8214	5990	...	4576	...
A Withdrawals from public quasi-corporations [a]	365	272	...	93	...	2555	2108	...	447	...
B Interest	1613	2127	...	1064	...	4461	3452	...	3361	...
C Dividends	4	4	...	-	...	10	3	...	7	...
D Net land rent and royalties	623	98	...	516	...	1188	427	...	761	...
3 Taxes, fees and contributions	40375	32770	...	7605	...	73676	59196	...	14480	...
A Indirect taxes	17297	10336	...	6961	...	32841	19664	...	13177	...
B Direct taxes	22399	22399	...	...	...	39437	39437	...	...	...
Income	22399	22399	...	...	...	39437	39437	...	...	...
Other [b]	...	...	...	...	...	...	...	...	...	...
C Social security contributions	...	...	...	...	...	...	...	...	...	...
D Fees, fines and penalties [b]	679	35	...	644	...	1398	95	...	1303	...
4 Other current transfers	-	-	...	10309	...	-	-	...	17961	...
A Casualty insurance claims	...	...	...	...	...	...	...	...	...	...
B Transfers from other government subsectors	...	-	...	10309	...	...	-	...	17961	...
C Transfers from the rest of the world	...	...	...	...	...	...	...	...	...	...
D Other transfers, except imputed	-	...	...	...	...	...	...	...	-	...
E Imputed unfunded employee pension and welfare contributions	...	...	...	...	...	...	...	...	...	...
Total Current Receipts [c]	42980	35271	...	19587	...	81890	65186	...	37017	...
Disbursements										
1 Government final consumption expenditure	25075	7740	...	17335	...	44755	14960	...	29795	...
2 Property income	2996	2569	...	1996	...	9329	7068	...	4613	...
A Interest	2996	2569	...	1996	...	9329	7068	...	4613	...
B Net land rent and royalties	-	...	...	...	...	...	...	...	...	...
3 Subsidies [d]	2235	1133	...	1102	...	4314	1923	...	2391	...
4 Other current transfers [e]	13341	22409	...	1241	...	26850	42239	...	2572	...
A Casualty insurance premiums, net	...	...	...	...	...	...	...	...	...	...
B Transfers to other government subsectors	...	10309	...	-	...	...	17961	...	-	...
C Social security benefits	...	...	...	...	...	...	...	...	...	...
D Social assistance grants	11431	11031	...	400	...	22932	22219	...	713	...
E Unfunded employee pension and welfare benefits	-	-	...	...	...	...	...	...	...	...
F Transfers to private non-profit institutions serving households	1223	382	...	841	...	2830	971	...	1859	...
G Other transfers n.e.c.	...	...	...	...	...	...	...	...	...	...
H Transfers to the rest of the world [e]	687	687	...	-	...	1088	1088	...	-	...
Net saving	-667	1420	...	-2087	...	-3358	-1004	...	-2354	...
Total Current Disbursements and Net Saving [c]	42980	35271	...	19587	...	81890	65186	...	37017	...

	1990 Total General Government	1990 Central Government	1990 State or Provincial Government	1990 Local Government	1990 Social Security Funds	1991 Total General Government	1991 Central Government	1991 State or Provincial Government	1991 Local Government	1991 Social Security Funds
Receipts										
1 Operating surplus	-	-	...	-	...	-	-	...	-	...
2 Property and entrepreneurial income [a]	13891	4890	...	11475	...	14474	5577	...	11123	...
A Withdrawals from public quasi-corporations [a]	2479	1145	...	1334	...	4254	2422	...	1832	...
B Interest	9890	3341	...	9023	...	8912	3004	...	8134	...

Australia

3.12 General Government Income and Outlay Account: Total and Subsectors
(Continued)

Million Australian dollars — Fiscal year beginning 1 July

	1990 Total General Government	1990 Central Government	1990 State or Provincial Government	1990 Local Government	1990 Social Security Funds	1991 Total General Government	1991 Central Government	1991 State or Provincial Government	1991 Local Government	1991 Social Security Funds
C Dividends	15	15	...	-	...	14	13	...	1	...
D Net land rent and royalties	1507	389	...	1118	...	1294	138	...	1156	...
3 Taxes, fees and contributions	119611	93766	...	25845	...	116006	88461	...	27545	...
A Indirect taxes	50481	26799	...	23682	...	50354	25163	...	25191	...
B Direct taxes	66568	66568	...	...	...	62899	62899	...	...	...
Income	66568	66568	...	...	...	62899	62899	...	...	...
Other [b]	...	...	...	...	...	...	...	...	...	...
C Social security contributions	...	...	...	...	...	...	...	...	...	...
D Fees, fines and penalties [b]	2562	399	...	2163	...	2753	399	...	2354	...
4 Other current transfers	-	32	...	24195	...	-	32	...	25856	...
A Casualty insurance claims	...	...	...	...	...	...	...	...	...	...
B Transfers from other government subsectors	...	32	...	24195	...	...	32	...	25856	...
C Transfers from the rest of the world	...	...	...	...	...	...	...	...	...	...
D Other transfers, except imputed	...	...	...	-	...	...	...	...	-	...
E Imputed unfunded employee pension and welfare contributions	...	...	...	...	...	...	...	...	...	...
Total Current Receipts [c]	133502	98688	...	61515	...	130480	94070	...	64524	...

Disbursements

1 Government final consumption expenditure	66655	20976	...	45679	...	71324	22695	...	48629	...
2 Property income	16379	6188	...	12665	...	15658	5741	...	12143	...
A Interest	16379	6188	...	12665	...	15658	5741	...	12143	...
B Net land rent and royalties	-	...	...	...	...	-	...	...	...	...
3 Subsidies [d]	5720	2836	...	2884	...	5899	2487	...	3412	...
4 Other current transfers [e]	42898	62502	...	4623	...	48807	69516	...	5179	...
A Casualty insurance premiums, net	...	...	...	...	...	...	...	...	...	...
B Transfers to other government subsectors	...	24195	...	32	...	...	25856	...	32	...
C Social security benefits	...	...	...	...	...	...	...	...	...	...
D Social assistance grants	37200	35820	...	1380	...	42236	40763	...	1473	...
E Unfunded employee pension and welfare benefits	-	-	...	-	...	...	...	...	-	...
F Transfers to private non-profit institutions serving households	4414	1203	...	3211	...	5244	1570	...	3674	...
G Other transfers n.e.c.	...	...	...	...	...	...	...	...	...	...
H Transfers to the rest of the world [e]	1284	1284	...	-	...	1327	1327	...	-	...
Net saving	1850	6186	...	-4336	...	-11208	-6369	...	-4839	...
Total Current Disbursements and Net Saving [c]	133502	98688	...	61515	...	130480	94070	...	64524	...

	1992 Total General Government	1992 Central Government	1992 State or Provincial Government	1992 Local Government	1992 Social Security Funds

Receipts

1 Operating surplus	-	-	...	-	...
2 Property and entrepreneurial income [a]	14386	5650	...	10659	...
A Withdrawals from public quasi-corporations [a]	4882	3009	...	1873	...
B Interest	8172	2513	...	7582	...
C Dividends	24	19	...	5	...
D Net land rent and royalties	1308	109	...	1199	...
3 Taxes, fees and contributions	119273	89864	...	29409	...
A Indirect taxes	52264	25429	...	26835	...
B Direct taxes	64048	64048	...	...	...
Income	64048	64048	...	...	...

Australia

3.12 General Government Income and Outlay Account: Total and Subsectors
(Continued)

Million Australian dollars — Fiscal year beginning 1 July

	Total General Government	Central Government	State or Provincial Government	Local Government	Social Security Funds
	1992				
Other [b]	...	...	...	...	...
C Social security contributions	...	...	...	...	...
D Fees, fines and penalties [b]	2961	387	...	2574	...
4 Other current transfers	-	36	...	27049	...
A Casualty insurance claims	...	...	...	...	...
B Transfers from other government subsectors	...	36	...	27049	...
C Transfers from the rest of the world	...	...	...	...	...
D Other transfers, except imputed	-	...	...	-	...
E Imputed unfunded employee pension and welfare contributions	...	...	...	...	...
Total Current Receipts [c]	133659	95550	...	67117	...
Disbursements					
1 Government final consumption expenditure	74344	23989	...	50355	...
2 Property income	15337	5418	...	11842	...
A Interest	15337	5418	...	11842	...
B Net land rent and royalties	-	...	...	...	...
3 Subsidies [d]	6500	2558	...	3942	...
4 Other current transfers [e]	52984	74631	...	5438	...
A Casualty insurance premiums, net	...	...	...	...	...
B Transfers to other government subsectors	...	27049	...	36	...
C Social security benefits	...	...	...	...	...
D Social assistance grants	45752	44291	...	1461	...
E Unfunded employee pension and welfare benefits	-	-	...	-	...
F Transfers to private non-profit institutions serving households	5842	1901	...	3941	...
G Other transfers n.e.c.	...	...	...	...	...
H Transfers to the rest of the world [e]	1390	1390	...	-	...
Net saving	-15506	-11046	...	-4460	...
Total Current Disbursements and Net Saving [c]	133659	95550	...	67117	...

a) All public enterprises are treated as if they were quasi-corporate.
b) Other direct taxes are included in item 'Taxes, fees and penalties'.
c) State or Provincial government is included in Local government.
d) Subsidies on wheat and wool are recorded on an accrual basis.
e) The Australian accounts do not distinguish between current and capital transfers to the rest of the world. They have all been treated as current transfers.

3.13 General Government Capital Accumulation Account: Total and Subsectors

Million Australian dollars — Fiscal year beginning 1 July

	1980					1985				
	Total General Government	Central Government	State or Provincial Government	Local Government	Social Security Funds	Total General Government	Central Government	State or Provincial Government	Local Government	Social Security Funds
Finance of Gross Accumulation										
1 Gross saving	2589	1729	...	860	...	1693	-458	...	2151	...
A Consumption of fixed capital	3256	309	...	2947	...	5051	546	...	4505	...
B Net saving	-667	1420	...	-2087	...	-3358	-1004	...	-2354	...
2 Capital transfers	292	18	...	1930	...	245	1	...	3490	...
A From other government subsectors	23	...	...	1679	...	71	...	...	3317	...
B From other resident sectors	269	18	...	251	...	174	1	...	173	...
C From rest of the world	...	...	...	...	...	...	...	...	...	...
Finance of Gross Accumulation [a]	2881	1747	...	2790	...	1938	-457	...	5641	...
Gross Accumulation										
1 Gross capital formation [b]	3816	390	...	3426	...	7197	1059	...	6138	...
A Increase in stocks [b]	66	64	...	2	...	30	12	...	18	...
B Gross fixed capital formation [b]	3750	326	...	3424	...	7167	1047	...	6120	...

Australia

3.13 General Government Capital Accumulation Account: Total and Subsectors
(Continued)

Million Australian dollars — Fiscal year beginning 1 July

	1980 Total General Government	1980 Central Government	1980 State or Provincial Government	1980 Local Government	1980 Social Security Funds	1985 Total General Government	1985 Central Government	1985 State or Provincial Government	1985 Local Government	1985 Social Security Funds
2 Purchases of land, net [c]	-129	-154	...	25	...	-118	-89	...	-29	...
3 Purchases of intangible assets, net	...	...	...	...	...	...	...	...	...	...
4 Capital transfers [d]	406	1798	...	264	...	1231	3617	...	860	...
A To other government subsectors	201	1660	...	197	...	720	3251	...	715	...
B To other resident sectors	205	138	...	67	...	511	366	...	145	...
C To rest of the world [d]	...	...	...	...	...	...	...	...	...	...
Net lending	-1212	-287	...	-925	...	-6372	-5044	...	-1328	...
Gross Accumulation [a]	2881	1747	...	2790	...	1938	-457	...	5641	...

	1990 Total General Government	1990 Central Government	1990 State or Provincial Government	1990 Local Government	1990 Social Security Funds	1991 Total General Government	1991 Central Government	1991 State or Provincial Government	1991 Local Government	1991 Social Security Funds
Finance of Gross Accumulation										
1 Gross saving	8718	6891	...	1827	...	-4076	-5640	...	1564	...
A Consumption of fixed capital	6868	705	...	6163	...	7132	729	...	6403	...
B Net saving	1850	6186	...	-4336	...	-11208	-6369	...	-4839	...
2 Capital transfers	195	3	...	4549	...	178	5	...	3894	...
A From other government subsectors	15	...	...	4372	...	-	...	...	3721	...
B From other resident sectors	180	3	...	177	...	178	5	...	173	...
C From rest of the world	...	...	...	...	...	...	...	...	...	...
Finance of Gross Accumulation [a]	8913	6894	...	6376	...	-3898	-5635	...	5458	...
Gross Accumulation										
1 Gross capital formation [b]	8798	1345	...	7453	...	8966	1590	...	7376	...
A Increase in stocks [b]	23	4	...	19	...	-9	-15	...	6	...
B Gross fixed capital formation [b]	8775	1341	...	7434	...	8975	1605	...	7370	...
2 Purchases of land, net [c]	-105	-44	...	-61	...	-101	16	...	-117	...
3 Purchases of intangible assets, net	...	...	...	...	...	...	...	...	...	...
4 Capital transfers [d]	2334	4854	...	1837	...	2693	4346	...	2068	...
A To other government subsectors	1860	4601	...	1616	...	2031	4047	...	1705	...
B To other resident sectors	474	253	...	221	...	662	299	...	363	...
C To rest of the world [d]	...	...	...	...	...	...	...	...	...	...
Net lending	-2114	739	...	-2853	...	-15456	-11587	...	-3869	...
Gross Accumulation [a]	8913	6894	...	6376	...	-3898	-5635	...	5458	...

	1992 Total General Government	1992 Central Government	1992 State or Provincial Government	1992 Local Government	1992 Social Security Funds
Finance of Gross Accumulation					
1 Gross saving	-8152	-10268	...	2116	...
A Consumption of fixed capital	7354	778	...	6576	...
B Net saving	-15506	-11046	...	-4460	...
2 Capital transfers	275	7	...	5478	...
A From other government subsectors	45	...	...	5255	...
B From other resident sectors	230	7	...	223	...
C From rest of the world	...	...	...	...	...
Finance of Gross Accumulation [a]	-7877	-10261	...	7594	...
Gross Accumulation					
1 Gross capital formation [b]	8932	1068	...	7864	...
A Increase in stocks [b]	20	7	...	13	...
B Gross fixed capital formation [b]	8912	1061	...	7851	...

Australia

3.13 General Government Capital Accumulation Account: Total and Subsectors
(Continued)

Million Australian dollars — Fiscal year beginning 1 July

		1992			
		Total General Government	Central Government	State or Provincial Government	Local Government	Social Security Funds
2	Purchases of land, net c	-194	-42	...	-152	...
3	Purchases of intangible assets, net	...	...	...	...	...
4	Capital transfers d	2522	5550	...	2182	...
	A To other government subsectors	1933	5299	...	1844	...
	B To other resident sectors	589	251	...	338	...
	C To rest of the world d	...	...	...	...	...
	Net lending	-19137	-16837	...	-2300	...
	Gross Accumulation a	-7877	-10261	...	7594	...

a) State or Provincial government is included in Local government.
b) Livestock is excluded from items 'Increase in Stocks' and 'Gross Fixed Capital Formation'.
c) Item 'Purchases of land, net' refers mainly to purchases less sales of land and existing building, other than dwellings, from and to other sectors.
d) The Australian accounts do not distinguish between current and capital transfers to the rest of the world. They have all been treated as current transfers.

3.22 Corporate and Quasi-Corporate Enterprise Income and Outlay Account: Total and Sectors

Million Australian dollars — Fiscal year beginning 1 July

		1980			1985			1990			1991		
		TOTAL	Non-Financial	Financial	TOTAL	Non-Financial	Financial	TOTAL	Non-Financial	Financial	TOTAL	Non-Financial	Financial
	Receipts												
1	Operating surplus a	9344	12253	-2909	20173	27075	-6902	33518	42942	-9424	35183	44301	-9118
2	Property and entrepreneurial income	9542	2529	13793	22625	7005	35234	42101	10928	68823	35005	8254	55183
	A Withdrawals from quasi-corporate enterprises	...	...	...	...	...	...	...	...	...	...	...	...
	B Interest	9255	2154	13204	22002	6247	33914	41331	9954	64955	34219	7279	51816
	C Dividends	218	277	589	453	588	1320	552	756	3868	534	723	3367
	D Net land rent and royalties	69	98	-	170	170	-	218	218	-	252	252	-
3	Current transfers	-	-	-	-	-	-	150	-	150	-	-	-
	A Casualty insurance claims	-	-	-	-	-	-	...	...	...	...	...	...
	B Casualty insurance premiums, net, due to be received by insurance companies	...	...	...	...	...	...	...	...	...	...	...	...
	C Current transfers from the rest of the world	-	-	-	-	-	-	150	-	150	-	-	-
	D Other transfers except imputed	...	...	...	...	...	...	...	...	...	...	...	...
	E Imputed unfunded employee pension and welfare contributions	...	...	...	...	...	...	...	...	...	...	...	...
	Total Current Receipts	18886	14782	10884	42798	34080	28332	75769	53870	59549	70188	52555	46065
	Disbursements												
1	Property and entrepreneurial income	13626	10343	10063	36709	26986	29337	67428	52136	52942	56795	44472	40755
	A Withdrawals from quasi-corporations	365	43	322	2555	309	2246	2479	1396	1083	4254	1751	2503
	Public	365	43	322	2555	309	2246	2479	1396	1083	4254	1751	2503
	Private	...	...	...	...	...	...	...	...	...	...	...	...
	B Interest	10236	6895	9410	29224	21079	26304	54917	38224	50271	42989	31154	36711
	C Dividends	2136	2487	297	2850	3544	761	7257	9764	1565	6773	8819	1510
	D Net land rent and royalties	889	918	34	2080	2054	26	2775	2752	23	2779	2748	31
2	Direct taxes and other current transfers n.o.c. to general government	4590	4017	573	6068	5035	1033	15401	11951	3450	15296	11567	3729
	A Direct taxes	4590	4017	573	6068	5035	1033	15401	11951	3450	15296	11567	3729
	On income	4590	4017	573	6068	5035	1033	15401	11951	3450	15296	11567	3729
	Other	...	...	...	...	...	...	...	...	...	...	...	...
	B Fines, fees, penalties and other current transfers n.e.c.	-	-	...	-	-	...	-	-	...	-	-	...

Australia

3.22 Corporate and Quasi-Corporate Enterprise Income and Outlay Account: Total and Sectors
(Continued)

Million Australian dollars — Fiscal year beginning 1 July

	1980 TOTAL	1980 Non-Financial	1980 Financial	1985 TOTAL	1985 Non-Financial	1985 Financial	1990 TOTAL	1990 Non-Financial	1990 Financial	1991 TOTAL	1991 Non-Financial	1991 Financial
3 Other current transfers	375	375	-	941	941	-	1286	1286	-	1311	1311	-
A Casualty insurance premiums, net	304	304	...	798	798	...	935	935	...	911	911	...
B Casualty insurance claims liability of insurance companies	-	...	...	-	...	...	-	...	-	-	...	-
C Transfers to private non-profit institutions	71	71	...	143	143	...	351	351	...	400	400	...
D Unfunded employee pension and welfare benefits	...	...	...	...	...	...	...	...	...	...	...	...
E Social assistance grants	...	...	...	...	...	...	...	...	...	...	...	...
F Other transfers n.e.c.	...	...	...	...	...	...	...	...	...	...	...	...
G Transfers to the rest of the world	...	...	...	...	...	...	...	...	...	...	...	...
Net saving	295	47	248	-920	1118	-2038	-8346	-11503	3157	-3214	-4795	1581
Total Current Disbursements and Net Saving	18886	14782	10884	42798	34080	28332	75769	53870	59549	70188	52555	46065

	1992 TOTAL	1992 Non-Financial	1992 Financial

Receipts

	TOTAL	Non-Financial	Financial
1 Operating surplus [a]	38661	47055	-8394
2 Property and entrepreneurial income	31719	6532	48415
A Withdrawals from quasi-corporate enterprises	...	...	...
B Interest	30879	5546	44983
C Dividends	652	798	3432
D Net land rent and royalties	188	188	-
3 Current transfers	-	-	-
A Casualty insurance claims	...	...	...
B Casualty insurance premiums, net, due to be received by insurance companies	...	...	...
C Current transfers from the rest of the world	-	-	-
D Other transfers except imputed	...	...	...
E Imputed unfunded employee pension and welfare contributions	...	...	...
Total Current Receipts	70380	53587	40021

Disbursements

	TOTAL	Non-Financial	Financial
1 Property and entrepreneurial income	49088	39505	32811
A Withdrawals from quasi-corporations	4882	1851	3031
Public	4882	1851	3031
Private	...	...	...
B Interest	34891	26156	28385
C Dividends	6474	8686	1366
D Net land rent and royalties	2841	2812	29
2 Direct taxes and other current transfers n.e.c. to general government	15864	11951	3913
A Direct taxes	15864	11951	3913
On income	15864	11951	3913
Other	...	...	...
B Fines, fees, penalties and other current transfers n.e.c.	-	-	...

Australia

3.22 Corporate and Quasi-Corporate Enterprise Income and Outlay Account: Total and Sectors
(Continued)

Million Australian dollars — Fiscal year beginning 1 July

	1992 TOTAL	Non-Financial	Financial
3 Other current transfers	1366	1366	-
A Casualty insurance premiums, net	941	941	...
B Casualty insurance claims liability of insurance companies	-	...	-
C Transfers to private non-profit institutions	425	425	...
D Unfunded employee pension and welfare benefits	...	...	...
E Social assistance grants	...	...	...
F Other transfers n.e.c.	...	...	...
G Transfers to the rest of the world	...	...	...
Net saving	4062	765	3297
Total Current Disbursements and Net Saving	70380	53587	40021

a) Item 'Net operating surplus' of financial enterprises includes a deduction for the imputed bank service charge.

3.23 Corporate and Quasi-Corporate Enterprise Capital Accumulation Account: Total and Sectors

Million Australian dollars — Fiscal year beginning 1 July

	1980 TOTAL	Non-Financial	Financial	1985 TOTAL	Non-Financial	Financial	1990 TOTAL	Non-Financial	Financial	1991 TOTAL	Non-Financial	Financial
Finance of Gross Accumulation												
1 Gross saving	10788	9826	962	18317	18930	-613	21957	16284	5673	28174	24002	4172
A Consumption of fixed capital	10493	9779	714	19237	17812	1425	30303	27787	2516	31388	28797	2591
B Net saving	295	47	248	-920	1118	-2038	-8346	-11503	3157	-3214	-4795	1581
2 Capital transfers	231	231	-	807	802	5	2107	1867	240	2439	2183	256
A From resident sectors	231	231	-	807	802	5	2107	1867	240	2439	2183	256
B From the rest of the world	...	...	...	...	...	...	...	...	...	...	...	...
Finance of Gross Accumulation	11019	10057	962	19124	19732	-608	24064	18151	5913	30613	26185	4428
Gross Accumulation												
1 Gross capital formation a	17038	15601	1437	32584	29639	2945	43652	39110	4542	38042	34562	3480
A Increase in stocks a	168	168	-	1121	1121	-	-1305	-1305	-	-1820	-1820	-
B Gross fixed capital formation a	16870	15433	1437	31463	28518	2945	44957	40415	4542	39862	36382	3480
2 Purchases of land, net b	129	118	11	118	86	32	105	228	-123	101	147	-46
3 Purchases of intangible assets, net	...	...	...	...	...	...	...	...	...	...	...	...
4 Capital transfers	23	23	-	71	71	-	15	15	-	-	-	-
A To resident sectors	23	23	-	71	71	-	15	15	-	-	-	-
B To the rest of the world	...	...	...	...	...	...	...	...	...	...	...	...
Net lending	-6171	-5685	-486	-13649	-10064	-3585	-19708	-21202	1494	-7530	-8524	994
Gross Accumulation	11019	10057	962	19124	19732	-608	24064	18151	5913	30613	26185	4428

	1992 TOTAL	Non-Financial	Financial
Finance of Gross Accumulation			
1 Gross saving	37212	31219	5993
A Consumption of fixed capital	33150	30454	2696
B Net saving	4062	765	3297
2 Capital transfers	2261	2202	59
A From resident sectors	2261	2202	59
B From the rest of the world	...	...	...
Finance of Gross Accumulation	39473	33421	6052
Gross Accumulation			
1 Gross capital formation a	40446	37418	3028
A Increase in stocks a	100	100	-
B Gross fixed capital formation a	40346	37318	3028

Australia

3.23 Corporate and Quasi-Corporate Enterprise Capital Accumulation Account: Total and Sectors
(Continued)

Million Australian dollars — Fiscal year beginning 1 July

		1992 TOTAL	Non-Financial	Financial
2	Purchases of land, net [b]	194	203	-9
3	Purchases of intangible assets, net	-	...	...
4	Capital transfers	45	45	-
	A To resident sectors	45	45	-
	B To the rest of the world	...	...	...
	Net lending	-1212	-4245	3033
	Gross Accumulation	39473	33421	6052

a) Livestock is excluded from items 'Increase in Stocks' and 'Gross Fixed Capital Formation'.
b) Item 'Purchases of land, net' refers mainly to purchases less sales of land and existing building, other than dwellings, from and to other sectors.

3.32 Household and Private Unincorporated Enterprise Income and Outlay Account

Million Australian dollars — Fiscal year beginning 1 July

		1980	1983	1984	1985	1986	1987	1988	1989	1990	1991	1992	1993
	Receipts												
1	Compensation of employees [a]	74063	100638	111005	122530	134006	147328	165690	184588	192814	197449	204779	...
2	Operating surplus of private unincorporated enterprises	20613	26591	28160	31329	34657	40366	48393	51551	51743	52380	54289	...
3	Property and entrepreneurial income	9360	16224	18157	23339	27673	29551	36480	44052	43632	34101	28099	...
	A Withdrawals from private quasi-corporations	...	...	...	...	...	...	...	...	...	...	...	...
	B Interest	8294	15074	16912	21876	26045	27691	34081	41483	40836	31246	25724	...
	C Dividends	1015	1140	1235	1450	1614	1846	2384	2554	2781	2840	2360	...
	D Net land rent and royalties	51	10	10	13	14	14	15	15	15	15	15	...
3	Current transfers	13989	23672	26848	29168	32015	35409	38203	42390	47199	53181	55955	...
	A Casualty insurance claims	555	1128	1517	1443	1554	1474	1620	1686	1645	1621	1667	...
	B Social security benefits	...	...	...	...	...	...	...	...	...	...	...	...
	C Social assistance grants	11431	18902	21224	22932	24897	27770	29358	32449	37200	42236	45752	...
	D Unfunded employee pension and welfare benefits	...	...	...	...	...	...	...	...	...	...	...	...
	E Transfers from general government	1294	2322	2689	2973	3333	3439	3912	4374	4765	5644	6267	...
	F Transfers from the rest of the world	709	1320	1418	1820	2231	2726	3313	3410	3589	3680	2269	...
	G Other transfers n.e.c.	...	...	...	...	...	...	...	471	...	...	...	...
	Total Current Receipts	118025	167125	184170	206366	228351	252654	288766	322581	335388	337111	343122	...
	Disbursements												
1	Final consumption expenditures	82871	116748	128216	143738	157236	175367	195804	218071	231320	242750	253952	...
	A Market purchases	...	...	...	...	...	...	...	...	...	...	...	...
	B Gross rents of owner-occupied housing	10165	14864	16431	18537	20853	23548	26706	...	...	...	...	...
	C Consumption from own-account production	...	...	...	...	...	...	...	...	...	...	...	...
2	Property income	7028	10953	11941	15826	19150	20460	26733	33441	33646	26963	24081	...
	A Interest	6902	10864	11841	15686	19015	20310	26588	33278	33459	26798	23911	...
	Consumer debt	1239	2374	2681	3636	4523	4507	5861	8064	7212	5068	3885	...
	Mortgage	3606	5140	5307	6671	8065	8441	10371	12644	13092	11682	11185	...
	Other	2057	3350	3853	5379	6427	7362	10356	12570	13155	10048	8841	...
	B Net land rent and royalties	126	89	100	140	135	150	145	163	187	165	170	...
3	Direct taxes and other current transfers n.e.c. to government	18211	25789	30535	34070	39583	43674	49517	52263	52607	49452	50295	...
	A Social security contributions	...	...	...	...	...	...	...	...	...	...	...	...
	B Direct taxes	17532	24671	29256	32672	38000	41809	47418	49866	50045	46699	47334	...
	Income taxes	17532	24671	29256	32672	38000	41809	47418	49866	50045	46699	47334	...
	Other [b]	...	...	...	...	...	...	...	...	...	...	...	...
	C Fees, fines and penalties [b]	679	1118	1279	1398	1583	1865	2099	2397	2562	2753	2961	...

Australia

3.32 Household and Private Unincorporated Enterprise Income and Outlay Account
(Continued)

Million Australian dollars — Fiscal year beginning 1 July

	1980	1983	1984	1985	1986	1987	1988	1989	1990	1991	1992	1993
4 Other current transfers	690	1203	1394	1365	1418	1410	1529	1608	1709	1726	1728	...
A Net casualty insurance premiums	251	511	690	645	672	628	684	716	710	710	726	...
B Transfers to private non-profit institutions serving households	...	...	...	...	...	...	...	...	...	...	...	...
C Transfers to the rest of the world	439	692	704	720	746	782	845	892	999	1016	1002	...
D Other current transfers, except imputed	...	...	...	...	...	...	...	...	...	...	...	...
E Imputed employee pension and welfare contributions	...	...	...	...	...	...	...	...	...	...	...	...
Net saving	9225	12432	12084	11367	10964	11743	15183	17198	16106	16220	13066	...
Total Current Disbursements and Net Saving	118025	167125	184170	206366	228351	252654	288766	322581	335388	337111	343122	...

a) Some government contributions to superannuation are only recorded in compensation when benefits are paid.
b) Other direct taxes are included in item 'Taxes, fees and penalties'.

3.33 Household and Private Unincorporated Enterprise Capital Accumulation Account

Million Australian dollars — Fiscal year beginning 1 July

	1980	1983	1984	1985	1986	1987	1988	1989	1990	1991	1992	1993
Finance of Gross Accumulation												
1 Gross saving	16683	22747	23495	24503	25982	28443	34296	38080	37242	37626	35132	...
A Consumption of fixed capital	7458	10315	11411	13136	15018	16700	19113	20882	21136	21406	22066	...
Owner-occupied housing	3690	5161	5887	6668	7468	8519	10474	11767	11933	12211	12566	...
Other unincorporated enterprises	3768	5154	5524	6468	7550	8181	8639	9115	9203	9195	9500	...
B Net saving	9225	12432	12084	11367	10964	11743	15183	17198	16106	16220	13066	...
2 Capital transfers	192	333	395	256	214	223	152	99	47	76	31	...
A From resident sectors	192	333	395	256	214	223	152	99	47	76	31	...
B From the rest of the world	...	...	...	...	...	...	...	...	...	...	...	...
Total Finance of Gross Accumulation	16875	23080	23890	24759	26196	28666	34448	38179	37289	37702	35163	...
Gross Accumulation												
1 Gross Capital Formation [a]	14803	16776	19538	20849	20446	25219	33336	30759	27313	27505	29434	...
A Increase in stocks [a]	231	586	-11	235	-257	141	709	-168	-444	-3	-597	...
B Gross fixed capital formation [a]	14572	16190	19549	20614	20703	25078	32627	30927	27757	27508	30031	...
2 Purchases of land, net	...	...	...	...	...	...	...	...	...	...	...	...
3 Purchases of intangibles, net	...	...	...	...	...	...	...	...	...	...	...	...
4 Capital transfers	286	44	13	6	4	3	2	1	-	-	-	...
A To resident sectors	286	44	13	6	4	3	2	1	-	-	-	...
B To the rest of the world	...	...	...	...	...	...	...	...	...	...	...	...
Net lending	1786	6260	4339	3904	5746	3444	1110	7419	9976	10197	5729	...
Total Gross Accumulation	16875	23080	23890	24759	26196	28666	34448	38179	37289	37702	35163	...

a) Livestock is excluded from items 'Increase in Stocks' and 'Gross Fixed Capital Formation'.

3.51 External Transactions: Current Account: Detail

Million Australian dollars — Fiscal year beginning 1 July

	1980	1983	1984	1985	1986	1987	1988	1989	1990	1991	1992	1993
Payments to the Rest of the World												
1 Imports of goods and services	25071	31192	39505	46111	48069	52819	61109	67363	65764	67807	77074	...
A Imports of merchandise c.i.f. [a]	20483	25678	32420	38683	39910	43360	50282	54696	52158	54285	63479	...
B Other	4588	5514	7085	7428	8159	9459	10827	12667	13606	13522	13595	...
2 Factor income to the rest of the world	2816	6147	8068	9293	10571	12131	15847	20795	21424	19389	17607	...
A Compensation of employees	110	158	178	164	179	210	279	406	429	326	311	...
B Property and entrepreneurial income	2706	5989	7890	9129	10392	11921	15568	20389	20995	19063	17296	...
By general government	374	671	931	1428	2265	2941	3140	4044	3804	3905	3537	...
By corporate and quasi-corporate enterprises	2332	5318	6959	7701	8127	8980	12428	16345	17191	15158	13759	...

Australia

3.51 External Transactions: Current Account: Detail
(Continued)

Million Australian dollars

Fiscal year beginning 1 July

	1980	1983	1984	1985	1986	1987	1988	1989	1990	1991	1992	1993
By other	...	...	...	...	...	...	...	...	...	...	...	...
3 Current transfers to the rest of the world [b]	1126	1643	1754	1808	1804	1880	2002	2189	2283	2343	2392	...
A Indirect taxes by general government to supranational organizations	...	...	...	...	...	...	...	...	...	...	...	...
B Other current transfers	1126	1643	1754	1808	1804	1880	2002	2189	2283	2343	2392	...
By general government	687	951	1050	1088	1058	1098	1157	1297	1284	1327	1390	...
By other resident sectors	439	692	704	720	746	782	845	892	999	1016	1002	...
4 Surplus of the nation on current transactions	-4840	-7142	-10547	-14536	-11925	-10326	-17828	-22381	-15838	-12428	-15568	...
Payments to the Rest of the World, and Surplus of the Nation on Current Transfers	24173	31840	38780	42676	48519	56504	61130	67966	73633	77111	81505	...

Receipts From The Rest of the World

	1980	1983	1984	1985	1986	1987	1988	1989	1990	1991	1992	1993
1 Exports of goods and services	22505	28574	35273	38539	43603	51080	54728	60133	65154	68828	74878	...
A Exports of merchandise f.o.b.	18689	23695	29717	32196	36032	41369	43880	49119	52349	54800	60004	...
B Other	3816	4879	5556	6343	7571	9711	10848	11014	12805	14028	14874	...
2 Factor income from the rest of the world	682	1433	1555	1620	1899	1879	2192	3165	3618	3699	3508	...
A Compensation of employees	119	175	200	177	159	171	239	387	452	472	514	...
B Property and entrepreneurial income	563	1258	1355	1443	1740	1708	1953	2778	3166	3227	2994	...
By general government	3	20	24	37	43	46	59	104	105	16	3	...
By corporate and quasi-corporate enterprises	560	1238	1331	1406	1697	1662	1894	2674	3061	3211	2991	...
By other	...	...	...	...	...	...	...	...	...	...	...	...
3 Current transfers from the rest of the world [b]	986	1833	1952	2517	3017	3545	4210	4668	4861	4584	3119	...
A Subsidies to general government from supranational organizations	...	...	...	...	...	...	...	...	...	...	...	...
B Other current transfers	986	1833	1952	2517	3017	3545	4210	4668	4861	4584	3119	...
To general government	277	438	534	697	786	819	897	1108	1122	904	850	...
To other resident sectors	709	1395	1418	1820	2231	2726	3313	3560	3739	3680	2269	...
Receipts from the Rest of the World on Current Transfers	24173	31840	38780	42676	48519	56504	61130	67966	73633	77111	81505	...

a) Item 'Imports of merchandise C.I.F.' excludes freight on imports paid to resident carriers.
b) The Australian accounts do not distinguish between current and capital transfers to the rest of the world. They have all been treated as current transfers.

3.53 External Transactions: Capital Finance Account

Million Australian dollars

Fiscal year beginning 1 July

	1980	1983	1984	1985	1986	1987	1988	1989	1990	1991	1992	1993

Acquisitions of Foreign Financial Assets

	1980	1983	1984	1985	1986	1987	1988	1989	1990	1991	1992	1993
1 Gold and SDR's	1016	1853	-1520	-2140	3394	3924	873	2156	1446	-3929	-3950	...
2 Currency and transferable deposits	...	...	...	...	...	...	...	...	...	...	...	...
3 Other deposits	...	...	...	...	...	...	...	...	...	...	...	...
4 Bills and bonds, short term	...	...	...	...	...	...	...	...	...	...	...	...
5 Bonds, long term	...	...	...	...	...	...	...	...	...	...	...	...
6 Corporate equity securities	189	1174	2537	4777	7821	7497	6289	1123	-1982	3163	610	...
A Subsidiaries abroad	168	1073	1840	2153	4229	7587	2771	3157	-3887	854	2234	...
B Other	21	101	697	2624	3592	-90	3518	-2034	1905	2309	-1624	...
7 Short-term loans, n.e.c.	...	...	...	...	...	...	...	...	...	...	...	...
8 Long-term loans	-9	169	358	1007	-516	2387	2505	829	3401	851	2434	...
A Subsidiaries abroad	145	-179	-532	-330	-1341	198	1389	-1936	2648	-205	-1779	...
B Other	-154	348	890	1337	825	2189	1116	2765	753	1056	4213	...
9 Prproprietors' net additions to accumulation of quasi-corporate, non-resident enterprises	18	57	113	282	429	143	261	-177	224	-162	627	...
10 Trade credit and advances	41	872	1292	145	349	679	592	164	123	-1000	-177	...
11 Other	110	10	61	110	215	-519	43	-44	399	-466	343	...
Total Acquisitions of Foreign Financial Assets	1365	4135	2841	4181	11692	14111	10563	4051	3611	-1543	-113	...

Incurrence of Foreign Liabilities

	1980	1983	1984	1985	1986	1987	1988	1989	1990	1991	1992	1993
1 Currency and transferable deposits	...	...	...	...	...	...	...	...	...	...	...	...

Australia

3.53 External Transactions: Capital Finance Account
(Continued)

Million Australian dollars — Fiscal year beginning 1 July

		1980	1983	1984	1985	1986	1987	1988	1989	1990	1991	1992	1993
2	Other deposits	-132	-15	-10	-16	18	-8	-	24	-22	21	39	...
3	Bills and bonds, short term	...	...	...	...	...	...	...	...	...	...	...	...
4	Bonds, long term	...	...	...	...	...	...	...	...	...	...	...	...
5	Corporate equity securities	1887	1184	1104	2751	6170	4164	6025	4009	8348	3948	7784	...
	A Subsidiaries of non-resident incorporated units	579	583	340	2523	1948	1827	3894	2437	5131	2871	3704	...
	B Other	1308	601	764	228	4222	2337	2131	1572	3217	1077	4080	...
6	Short-term loans, n.e.c.	...	...	...	...	...	...	...	...	...	...	...	...
7	Long-term loans	2830	8146	12685	16595	15064	20069	21644	18863	12155	9407	7847	...
	A Subsidiaries of non-residents	577	1032	1152	497	1429	2344	3483	2531	1501	2349	-1511	...
	B Other	2253	7114	11533	16098	13635	17725	18161	16332	10654	7058	9358	...
8	Non-resident proprietors' net additions to accumulation of resident quasi-corporate enterprises	188	-769	99	-575	411	1470	2222	1562	1549	712	422	...
9	Trade credit and advances	111	556	233	-31	235	80	609	-477	-171	444	213	...
10	Other	354	511	383	334	-302	-29	172	-369	-314	140	88	...
	Total Incurrence of Liabilities	5238	9613	14494	19058	21596	25746	30672	23612	21545	14672	16393	...
	Statistical discrepancy	967	1664	-1106	-341	2021	-1309	-2281	2820	-2096	-3787	-938	...
	Net Lending	-4840	-7142	-10547	-14536	-11925	-10326	-17828	-22381	-15838	-12428	-15568	...
	Total Incurrence of Liabilities and Net Lending	1365	4135	2841	4181	11692	14111	10563	4051	3611	-1543	-113	...

4.3 Cost Components of Value Added

Million Australian dollars — Fiscal year beginning 1 July

	1980						1985					
	Compensation of Employees	Capital Consumption	Net Operating Surplus	Indirect Taxes	Less: Subsidies Received	Value Added	Compensation of Employees	Capital Consumption	Net Operating Surplus	Indirect Taxes	Less: Subsidies Received	Value Added

All Producers

1	Agriculture, hunting, forestry and fishing	1325	1876	3819	499	94	7425	2223	2838	4048	704	194	9619
2	Mining and quarrying	1975	1171	2392	3347	54	8831	3714	2480	5023	4435	172	15480
3	Manufacturing	17324	3040	4269	2758	410	26981	24497	4978	8175	4634	915	41369
4	Electricity, gas and water [a]	1972	1581	439	199	119	4072	3531	2922	1639	467	207	8352
5	Construction	6168	1775	3103	276	16	11306	9999	2940	4997	427	26	18337
6	Wholesale and retail trade, restaurants and hotels [b]	10643	1587	5476	4442	356	21792	17975	2868	9062	11075	242	40738
7	Transport, storage and communication	6210	2286	1758	482	974	9762	9507	4140	4253	831	1954	16777
	A Transport and storage	4571	1602	1499	462	974	7160	6796	2889	3180	794	1954	11705
	B Communication	1639	684	259	20	...	2602	2711	1251	1073	37	...	5072
8	Finance, insurance, real estate and business services	6799	5321	9784	2462	34	24332	12897	9998	16220	5026	173	43968
9	Community, social and personal services [b]	15855	1886	2234	1014	150	20839	29295	3263	3297	1942	375	37422
	Total, Industries	68271	20523	33275	15479	2207	135340	113638	36427	56714	29541	4258	232062
	Producers of Government Services	5783	684	-	18	28	6457	8879	997	-	18	56	9838
	Other Producers	...	...	...	...	...	...	...	...	...	...	...	...
	Total	74054	21207	33275	15497	2235	141797	122517	37424	56714	29559	4314	241900
	Less: Imputed bank service charge	...	...	3317	...	...	3317	...	...	5212	...	...	5212
	Import duties	...	...	...	1800	...	1800	...	...	...	3282	...	3282
	Value added tax	...	...	...	...	...	...	...	...	...	...	...	...
	Total	74054	21207	29958	17297	2235	140280	122517	37424	51502	32841	4314	239970

of which General Government:

1	Agriculture, hunting, forestry and fishing	134	65	...	...	...	199	217	93	...	...	...	310
2	Mining and quarrying	10	9	...	...	...	19	15	13	...	...	...	28
3	Manufacturing	348	29	...	...	...	377	462	43	...	...	...	505
4	Electricity, gas and water	176	13	...	...	...	189	444	19	...	...	...	463

Australia

4.3 Cost Components of Value Added
(Continued)

Million Australian dollars — Fiscal year beginning 1 July

	\multicolumn{6}{c	}{1980}	\multicolumn{6}{c	}{1985}
	Compensation of Employees	Capital Consumption	Net Operating Surplus	Indirect Taxes	Less: Subsidies Received	Value Added	Compensation of Employees	Capital Consumption	Net Operating Surplus	Indirect Taxes	Less: Subsidies Received	Value Added
5 Construction	1651	1219	...	...	...	2870	2255	1930	...	...	...	4185
6 Wholesale and retail trade, restaurants and hotels	11	3	...	...	...	14	17	4	...	...	...	21
7 Transport and communication	375	108	...	...	...	483	636	154	...	...	...	790
8 Finance, insurance, real estate & business services	187	34	...	...	...	221	347	58	...	...	...	405
9 Community, social and personal services	10076	1092	...	...	...	11168	17915	1740	...	...	...	19655
Total, Industries of General Government	12968	2572	...	...	...	15540	22308	4054	...	...	...	26362
Producers of Government Services	5783	684	...	18	28	6457	8879	997	...	18	56	9838
Total, General Government	18751	3256	...	18	28	21997	31187	5051	...	18	56	36200

	\multicolumn{6}{c	}{1990}	\multicolumn{6}{c	}{1991}
	Compensation of Employees	Capital Consumption	Net Operating Surplus	Indirect Taxes	Less: Subsidies Received	Value Added	Compensation of Employees	Capital Consumption	Net Operating Surplus	Indirect Taxes	Less: Subsidies Received	Value Added

All Producers

1 Agriculture, hunting, forestry and fishing	3127	3621	4617	1823	490	12698	2987	3546	4769	1312	703	11911
2 Mining and quarrying	5154	3871	8141	1926	498	18594	4955	4021	7492	680	621	16527
3 Manufacturing	34250	6968	9477	6617	590	56722	33487	7178	9568	6398	716	55915
4 Electricity, gas and water [a]	4151	3894	4161	728	286	12648	4222	3874	4892	807	278	13517
5 Construction	15670	4189	8095	787	17	28724	14222	4340	8212	780	36	27518
6 Wholesale and retail trade, restaurants and hotels [b]	30091	4632	12643	20160	1123	66403	30451	4829	12738	20748	485	68281
7 Transport, storage and communication	13397	6554	7255	1941	2034	27113	14047	6912	8338	2090	2024	29363
A Transport and storage	9326	4654	3998	1868	2034	17812	9821	4895	4545	2010	2024	19247
B Communication	4071	1900	3257	73	...	9301	4226	2017	3793	80	...	10116
8 Finance, insurance, real estate and business services	25159	18250	34313	9518	69	87171	25648	18683	36505	10278	231	90883
9 Community, social and personal services [b]	48768	4992	6098	3561	556	62863	52997	5170	6193	3851	752	67459
Total, Industries	179767	56971	94800	47061	5663	372936	183016	58553	98707	46944	5846	381374
Producers of Government Services	13024	1336	-	100	57	14403	14287	1373	-	111	53	15718
Other Producers	...	...	...	...	...	...	...	...	...	...	...	...
Total	192791	58307	94800	47161	5720	387339	197303	59926	98707	47055	5899	397092
Less: Imputed bank service charge	...	...	9539	...	...	9539	...	...	11144	...	...	11144
Import duties	...	...	...	3320	...	3320	...	...	...	3299	...	3299
Value added tax	...	...	...	...	...	...	...	...	...	...	...	...
Total	192791	58307	85261	50481	5720	381120	197303	59926	87563	50354	5899	389247

of which General Government:

1 Agriculture, hunting, forestry and fishing	260	121	...	...	...	381	253	121	...	...	...	374
2 Mining and quarrying	12	17	...	...	...	29	3	18	...	...	...	21
3 Manufacturing	430	57	...	...	...	487	275	60	...	...	...	335
4 Electricity, gas and water	829	24	...	...	...	853	856	24	...	...	...	880
5 Construction	2615	2629	...	...	...	5244	2685	2755	...	...	...	5440
6 Wholesale and retail trade, restaurants and hotels	21	5	...	...	...	26	30	6	...	...	...	36
7 Transport and communication	760	203	...	...	...	963	824	204	...	...	...	1028
8 Finance, insurance, real estate & business services	881	94	...	...	...	975	686	100	...	...	...	786
9 Community, social and personal services	26860	2382	...	...	...	29242	28902	2471	...	...	...	31373
Total, Industries of General Government	32668	5532	...	...	...	38200	34514	5759	...	...	...	40273
Producers of Government Services	13024	1336	...	100	57	14403	14287	1373	...	111	53	15718
Total, General Government	45692	6868	...	100	57	52603	48801	7132	...	111	53	55991

Australia

4.3 Cost Components of Value Added

Million Australian dollars

Fiscal year beginning 1 July

1992

	Compensation of Employees	Capital Consumption	Net Operating Surplus	Indirect Taxes	Less: Subsidies Received	Value Added
All Producers						
1 Agriculture, hunting, forestry and fishing	2916	3620	5735	1262	664	12869
2 Mining and quarrying	4973	4296	7931	700	585	17315
3 Manufacturing	35374	7634	11009	6547	793	59771
4 Electricity, gas and water [a]	4126	3871	5685	875	481	14076
5 Construction	14675	4448	8299	800	45	28177
6 Wholesale and retail trade, restaurants and hotels [b]	31603	5101	12806	21490	293	70707
7 Transport, storage and communication	14274	7461	8531	2042	1924	30384
A Transport and storage	9724	5334	4873	1960	1924	19967
B Communication	4550	2127	3658	82	...	10417
8 Finance, insurance, real estate and business services	26429	19266	39736	10891	890	95432
9 Community, social and personal services [b]	55395	5433	6510	4151	754	70735
Total, Industries	189765	61130	106242	48758	6429	399466
Producers of Government Services	14811	1440	-	175	71	16355
Other Producers	...	...	...	...	...	...
Total	204576	62570	106242	48933	6500	415821
Less: Imputed bank service charge	...	...	13292	...	...	13292
Import duties	...	...	...	3331	...	3331
Value added tax	...	...	...	...	...	...
Total	204576	62570	92950	52264	6500	405860
of which General Government:						
1 Agriculture, hunting, forestry and fishing	209	124	...	...	...	333
2 Mining and quarrying	-	19	...	...	...	19
3 Manufacturing	288	63	...	...	...	351
4 Electricity, gas and water	795	25	...	...	...	820
5 Construction	2614	2790	...	...	...	5404
6 Wholesale and retail trade, restaurants and hotels	23	6	...	...	...	29
7 Transport and communication	710	209	...	...	...	919
8 Finance, insurance, real estate & business services	667	106	...	...	...	773
9 Community, social and personal services	30281	2572	...	...	...	32853
Total, Industries of General Government	35587	5914	...	...	...	41501
Producers of Government Services	14811	1440	...	175	71	16355
Total, General Government	50398	7354	...	175	71	57856

a) Item 'Electricity, gas and water' includes sewage services.
b) Restaurants and hotels are included in item 'Community, social and personal services'.

Austria

General note. The preparation of annual national accounts statistics in Austria is undertaken by the Austrian Central Statistical Office, Vienna. The official estimates are published annually in 'Oesterreichs Volkseinkommen', (Austrian Central Statistcal Office, Beitrage zur Osterreichischen Statistik). The concepts, definitions, sources of basic statistics and methods of estima tion are described in the 1964-1977 and 1970-1980 issue of the above mentioned publication. The estimates are generally in accordance with the classifications and definitions recommended in the United Nations System of National Accounts (SNA). Input-output tables have been published for the years 1961, 1964 and 1976. The following tables have been prepared from successive replies to the United Nations national accounts questionnaire. When the scope and coverage of The estimates differ for conceptual or statistical reasons fromthe definitions and classifications recommended in SNA, a footnote is indic ated to the relevant tables.

Sources and methods :

(a) Gross domestic product. Gross domestic product is estimated mainly through the production approach.

(b) Expenditure on the gross domestic product. The estimates of government final consumption expenditure are derived from production accounts compiled on the basis of the accounting records of the various authorities. The values of private expenditure on goods are mostly obtained by means of the commodity flow method, either by multiplying the quantity data by average consumer prices or by adding distributive margins and turnover tax and indirect taxes to the value of goods produced domestically or imported. The sources of data include statistics on agricultural produce, industrial output data by commodities,data on energy and foreign trade by commodities, motor vehicle registration statistics, closed accounts for public transportation enterprises, communication, insurance and others. For price data the consumer price index is largely referred to. In addition, decennial household surveys provide bench-mark information on average prices. Own account consumption is valued at producers' prices, for use of owner occupied dwellings the corresponding market rents are imputed. For private expenditure on services, the estimates are mostly based on value added tax statistics. The data on increase in stocks are based on regular stock surveys covering almost all branches, those that are not covered are included in statistical discrepancy. For gross fixed capital formation in machinery and electrical equipment, the value of domestic production plus imports minus exports is adjusted to include transport costs, trade margins, customs duties, etc. The estimates of transport equipment are based on registration statistics and are obtained by multiplying the quantity by the current prices. For construction, the gross value is derived from data on characteristic gross output, with additions for material supplied, non-characteristic construction (including own account-construction, e.g. residential buildings). The estimates of exports and imports of goods and services are based on foreign trade statistics and the balance of payments. Constant price estimates of government final consumption expenditure are based on deflation for intermediate consumption and non-commodity sales. Compensation of employees is in certain activities also deflated, for others quantum indicators are used. For private consumption expenditure, direct revaluation at base-year prices is used where information is available on quantities of commodities consumed. Otherwise, the current estimates are deflated by appropriate price indexes. This same method is used for increase in stocks, exports and imports of goods and services and for gross fixed capital formation.

(c) Cost-structure of the gross domestic product. Estimates of compensation of employees are based on contributions paid by employers to government funds and wage statistics. Direct information is available on compensation of government employees. Operating surplus is basically derived as a residual item. Further breakdown is based on income tax statistics for unincorporated enterprises, independent professions and property. Corporate balance sheets and tax statistics are used for undistributed profits of corporations: for agriculture and forestry income is derived from the production account. In the case of the public sector, data are obtained from the accounting records of public bodies. Depreciation estimates of stocks are obtained either by using the perpetual inventory concept or, in some instances, are extrapolated by net output at constant prices and inflated by national accounts' price index for fixed capital formation. Indirect taxes and subsidies are obtained directly from the records of the various governments.

(d) Gross domestic product by kind of economic activity. The table of GDP by kind of economic activity is prepared at market prices, i.e. producers' values. The production approach is used to estimate value added of nearly all industries. The income approach is used to est imate value added of public administration and defense. The value added of agriculture is obtained by deducting the cost of all non-factor inputs from the gross value of production, which include an imputation for produce consumed on the farms. The calculations are based on production statistics for quantities, and on agricultural price surveys. Mining and quarrying, electricity, gas and water as well as large-scale manufacturing are surveyed by annual over-all censuses while small-scale manufacturing is surveyed annually by samples. Bench-mark estimates have been prepared for 1964, 1971, 1976 and 1983. When necessary extrapolation is based on output statistics, sample survey and turnover statistics. For construction, census type data on gross output and input have been available annually since 1968, own account construction is imputed for housing and agriculture. The estimates of turnover in retail and wholesale trade are based on the 1964, 1976 and 1983 census of non-agricultural establishments, the 1971 census of turnover and, since 1973, an annual sample survey. Estimates of restaurants and hotels are based on the 1964 industrial census and on a special survey in 1972, and 1976 and 1983 Censuses. For the intermediate years, value added tax and turnover tax statistics as well as other suitable indicators (private accommodation) are used. For railways and air transportation and communication, value added is derived from the accounts of concerned enterprises. For the other activities of the transport sector, bench-mark data have been provided by the 1964, 1976 and 1983 industrial censuses, extrapolated by various indicators. From 1973 onward, value added tax statistics provide the output indicators for most transportation other than large enterprises mentioned before. For the financial institutions, value added is derived from accounting records for banking, and other financial institutions from statistics of the supervisory board for insurance. Data on real estate are obtained from decennial housing censuses and micro-census data on housing and rents. In the case of owner-occupied dwellings, rents paid for comparable dwellings are applied. The value added of government services is estimated by adding the cost items obtained from accounting records. The estimates of other services are based on annual turnover statistics, value added tax statistics and various net to gross ratios obtained from the 1964 and 1976 census of non-agricultural establishments. The value of domestic and health services is calculated by means of VAT, social security and wage statistics. For the constant price estimates, double deflation is used, but not invariably, for agriculture, electricity, gas and water, construction, transportation and ownership of dwellings. In manufacturing, a combination of double deflation and fixed net ratios is applied. The turnover of wholesale and retail trade is deflated by appropriate price indexes. For the producers of government services, partly quantum indicators, partly suitable price (wage) indexes are used. For most of the remaining activities, value added is mostly calculated by deflation.

1.1 Expenditure on the Gross Domestic Product, in Current Prices

Million Austrian schillings

		1980	1983	1984	1985	1986	1987	1988	1989	1990	1991	1992	1993
1	Government final consumption expenditure	178697	226891	237759	254999	270655	280436	288356	302881	319888	349632	377059	405598
2	Private final consumption expenditure	552532	694839	733182	775529	804407	837778	880527	935287	999181	1064037	1127091	1168262
3	Gross capital formation	282890	263729	303904	315578	334261	355949	388656	419883	459889	497227	515354	519991
	A Increase in stocks [a]	27433	-5821	20984	11165	10255	13837	17488	14133	17497	8844	4249	8714
	B Gross fixed capital formation [b]	255457	269550	282920	304413	324006	342112	371168	405750	442392	488383	511105	511277
	Residential buildings	52564	61577	62336	62490	65011	68839	76978	79242	83737	98907	115709	133315
	Non-residential buildings	82412	83412	86261	90849	98216	107746	115893	130541	145707	157109	163687	161154
	Other construction and land improvement etc.												
	Other	105999	107977	116065	131811	140059	144418	155358	171889	186596	202512	201571	185287
4	Exports of goods and services [c]	366244	449686	497645	549126	522970	527054	587545	664267	724313	770412	803356	803368
5	Less: Imports of goods and services [c]	385659	433928	495715	546807	509796	519829	578645	649418	701962	752994	776780	779378
	Statistical discrepancy	-	-	-	-	-	-	-	-	-	-	-	-
	Equals: Gross Domestic Product	994704	1201217	1276775	1348425	1422497	1481388	1566439	1672900	1801309	1928314	2046080	2117841

a) Item 'Increase in stocks' includes breeding stock, draught animals and a statistical discrepancy.
b) Item 'Gross fixed capital formation' includes value added tax on investments of investors not entitled to deduct invoiced value added tax. This component is not included in the sub-items. For years 1973-1975, 1977 and 1978 of the current prices table, special investment tax is included. These estimates are shown separately as 'Statistical discrepancy' in tables 2.7, 2.8, 2.9, 2.10 and 2.11.
c) The estimates on transit trade are on a net basis.

Austria

1.2 Expenditure on the Gross Domestic Product, in Constant Prices

Million Austrian schillings

	1980	1983	1984	1985	1986	1987	1988	1989	1990	1991	1992	1993
					At constant prices of:1983							
1 Government final consumption expenditure	212270	226891	227378	231800	235652	236594	237369	239241	242087	249481	255494	263212
2 Private final consumption expenditure	651890	694839	694309	710861	723426	746147	773044	799812	828622	852981	869581	871153
3 Gross capital formation	328498	263729	295709	301289	307534	316390	344021	358497	385111	398876	402887	395642
A Increase in stocks [a]	29170	-5821	20467	12277	7885	7394	16354	10615	17279	7805	6773	7693
B Gross fixed capital formation [b]	299328	269550	275242	289012	299649	308996	327667	347882	367832	391071	396114	387949
Residential buildings	62993	61577	61114	60086	61447	62866	68182	67902	68806	76613	86029	95910
Non-residential buildings	98185	83412	85031	87936	91503	98376	103356	111952	121398	125010	125786	120472
Other construction and land improvement etc.												
Other	121238	107977	112828	124208	128995	130220	137557	148983	157419	167593	161570	148330
4 Exports of goods and services [c]	404606	449686	477069	509958	496138	507911	553725	610644	659913	699154	718744	711700
5 Less: Imports of goods and services [c]	428601	433928	476898	506366	500451	523817	572885	621770	670405	712611	731305	727212
Statistical discrepancy	-	-	-	-	-	-	-	-	-	-	-	-
Equals: Gross Domestic Product	1168663	1201217	1217567	1247542	1262299	1283225	1335274	1386424	1445328	1487881	1515401	1514495

a) Item 'Increase in stocks' includes breeding stock, draught animals and a statistical discrepancy. These estimates are shown separately as 'Statistical discrepancy' in tables 2.7, 2.8, 2.9, 2.10 and 2.11.
b) Item 'Gross fixed capital formation' includes value added tax on investments of investors not entitled to deduct invoiced value added tax. This component is not included in the sub-items. For years 1973-1975, 1977 and 1978 of the current prices table, special investment tax is included. c) The estimates on transit trade are on a net basis.

1.3 Cost Components of the Gross Domestic Product

Million Austrian schillings

	1980	1983	1984	1985	1986	1987	1988	1989	1990	1991	1992	1993
1 Indirect taxes, net	132774	161686	180154	186728	187997	197773	209808	226304	240026	249343	264667	275048
A Indirect taxes	162828	197080	216087	225931	234044	245154	254887	271413	287880	305779	325823	338559
B Less: Subsidies	30054	35394	35933	39203	46047	47381	45079	45109	47854	56436	61156	63511
2 Consumption of fixed capital	116098	149238	158193	167526	176195	183870	194114	205630	218486	235173	252575	270063
3 Compensation of employees paid by resident producers to:	545631	642438	676330	717091	761254	792734	821941	874476	940062	1020817	1088971	1135998
4 Operating surplus	200201	247855	262098	277080	297051	307011	340576	366490	402735	422981	439867	436732
Statistical discrepancy	-	-	-	-	-	-	-	-	-	-	-	-
Equals: Gross Domestic Product	994704	1201217	1276775	1348425	1422497	1481388	1566439	1672900	1801309	1928314	2046080	2117841

1.4 General Government Current Receipts and Disbursements

Million Austrian schillings

	1980	1983	1984	1985	1986	1987	1988	1989	1990	1991	1992	1993
					Receipts							
1 Operating surplus	...	...	...	...	...	...	...	...	...	...	...	...
2 Property and entrepreneurial income	18493	22400	23058	26153	25909	29436	30724	33339	38069	40787	45733	42772
3 Taxes, fees and contributions	418681	502925	549418	591184	617660	635784	665260	694568	752338	816876	890971	928701
A Indirect taxes	162828	197080	216087	225931	234044	245154	254887	271413	287880	305779	325823	338559
B Direct taxes	128390	156637	173768	193628	203767	203357	214461	214465	238931	267125	297765	304938
C Social security contributions	124578	145462	155463	167804	175993	183339	191817	204269	220619	238882	262307	279759
D Compulsory fees, fines and penalties	2885	3746	4100	3821	3856	3934	4095	4421	4908	5090	5076	5445
4 Other current transfers	24444	31737	33668	36190	38508	40491	42019	44422	47055	51104	54314	57482
Total Current Receipts of General Government	461618	557062	606144	653527	682077	705711	738003	772329	837462	908767	991018	1028955
					Disbursements							
1 Government final consumption expenditure	178697	226891	237759	254999	270655	280436	288356	302881	319888	349632	377059	405598
A Compensation of employees	119658	152695	160925	171732	182910	191440	195816	205391	218514	238794	257802	277476
B Consumption of fixed capital	7481	9596	10095	10690	11310	11561	11803	12218	12770	13502	13809	14468
C Purchases of goods and services, net	49617	62265	64269	69932	73568	74525	77823	81919	85032	93485	101327	108964
D Less: Own account fixed capital formation	...	...	...	...	...	...	...	...	...	...	...	...
E Indirect taxes paid, net	1941	2335	2470	2645	2867	2910	2914	3353	3572	3851	4121	4690
2 Property income	24739	36618	43089	47847	51880	58355	61792	66410	73118	82130	87928	93023
A Interest	24739	36618	43089	47847	51880	58355	61792	66410	73118	82130	87928	93023
B Net land rent and royalties	...	...	...	...	...	...	...	...	...	...	...	...

Austria

1.4 General Government Current Receipts and Disbursements
(Continued)

Million Austrian schillings

	1980	1983	1984	1985	1986	1987	1988	1989	1990	1991	1992	1993
3 Subsidies	30054	35394	35933	39203	46047	47381	45079	45109	47854	56436	61156	63511
4 Other current transfers	191983	243978	259035	278618	295518	316037	323595	338030	363129	391272	423989	462413
A Social security benefits	94500	121479	130792	142344	151079	161466	167759	176423	188672	199860	212291	227906
B Social assistance grants	56161	69913	72285	76271	80443	87039	85223	86354	94142	103715	117278	133239
C Other	41322	52586	55958	60003	63996	67532	70613	75253	80315	87697	94420	101268
5 Net saving	36145	14181	30328	32860	17977	3502	19181	19899	33473	29297	40886	4410
Total Current Disbursements and Net Saving of General Government	461618	557062	606144	653527	682077	705711	738003	772329	837462	908767	991018	1028955

1.5 Current Income and Outlay of Corporate and Quasi-Corporate Enterprises, Summary

Million Austrian schillings

	1980	1983	1984	1985	1986	1987	1988	1989	1990	1991	1992	1993
Receipts												
1 Operating surplus	...	...	...	...	...	...	...	...	...	...	...	...
2 Property and entrepreneurial income received	...	...	...	...	...	...	...	...	...	...	...	...
3 Current transfers	...	...	...	...	...	...	...	...	...	...	...	...
Total Current Receipts	...	...	...	...	...	...	...	...	...	...	...	...
Disbursements												
1 Property and entrepreneurial income	...	...	...	...	...	...	...	...	...	...	...	...
2 Direct taxes and other current payments to general government	17650	19790	22624	25795	26176	26191	28067	35715	37887	42781	50834	50020
3 Other current transfers	...	...	...	...	...	...	...	...	...	...	...	...
4 Net saving	39860	45802	45540	42895	45752	47280	56429	59594	60810	61218	58830	79657
Total Current Disbursements and Net Saving	...	...	...	...	...	...	...	...	...	...	...	...

1.6 Current Income and Outlay of Households and Non-Profit Institutions

Million Austrian schillings

	1980	1983	1984	1985	1986	1987	1988	1989	1990	1991	1992	1993
Receipts												
1 Compensation of employees	545631	642438	676330	717091	761254	792734	821941	874476	940062	1020817	1095653	1142371
2 Operating surplus of private unincorporated enterprises	...	...	...	...	...	...	...	...	...	...	...	...
3 Property and entrepreneurial income	152198	201679	219348	237244	254857	266828	292623	312605	356136	379635	398872	385137
4 Current transfers	215287	274138	292498	314506	333585	360669	371692	388205	414124	447252	478422	519547
A Social security benefits	94500	121479	130792	142344	151079	161466	167759	176423	188672	199860	212291	227906
B Social assistance grants	56161	69913	72285	76271	80443	87039	85223	86354	94142	103715	117278	133239
C Other	64626	82746	89421	95891	102063	112164	118710	125428	131310	143677	148853	158402
Total Current Receipts	913116	1118255	1188176	1268841	1349696	1420231	1486256	1575286	1710322	1847704	1972947	2047055
Disbursements												
1 Private final consumption expenditure	552532	694839	733182	775529	804407	837778	880527	935287	999181	1064037	1127091	1168262
2 Property income	11620	14007	13934	14229	15729	17274	19174	22735	30213	38826	42816	43333
3 Direct taxes and other current transfers n.e.c. to general government	238201	285715	310707	339458	357440	364439	382306	387440	426571	468316	514314	540122
A Social security contributions	124578	145462	155463	167804	175993	183339	191817	204269	220619	238882	262307	279759
B Direct taxes	110738	136507	151144	167833	177591	177166	186394	178750	201044	224344	246931	254918
C Fees, fines and penalties	2885	3746	4100	3821	3856	3934	4095	4421	4908	5090	5076	5445
4 Other current transfers	46408	60537	64446	69821	74033	82176	89223	92880	94073	104166	127291	140087
5 Net saving	64355	63157	65907	69804	98087	118564	115026	136944	160284	172359	161435	155251
Total Current Disbursements and Net Saving	913116	1118255	1188176	1268841	1349696	1420231	1486256	1575286	1710322	1847704	1972947	2047055

Austria

1.7 External Transactions on Current Account, Summary

Million Austrian schillings

	1980	1983	1984	1985	1986	1987	1988	1989	1990	1991	1992	1993
Payments to the Rest of the World												
1 Imports of goods and services [a]	385659	433928	495715	546807	509796	519829	578645	649418	701962	752994	776780	779378
A Imports of merchandise c.i.f. [a]	313265	345306	389180	427125	404383	408411	444802	508894	550863	585907	588666	562239
B Other	72394	88622	106535	119682	105413	111418	133843	140524	151099	167087	188114	217139
2 Factor income to the rest of the world	41200	56013	66918	73556	70414	70266	80328	105109	117760	131349	112732	116868
A Compensation of employees [b]	-	-	-	-	-	-	-	-	-	-	2256	2359
B Property and entrepreneurial income	41200	56013	66918	73556	70414	70266	80328	105109	117760	131349	110476	114509
By general government [c]	4385	6907	7761	7437	7348	7423	6898	8489	8779	10189	10315	12096
By corporate and quasi-corporate enterprises	...	...	...	...	...	...	...	...	...	...	...	...
By other	...	...	...	...	...	...	...	...	...	...	...	...
3 Current transfers to the rest of the world [b]	11607	13100	13813	13895	14131	14794	18601	18857	19341	22633	39654	47205
A Indirect taxes to supranational organizations	...	...	...	...	...	...	...	...	...	...	...	...
B Other current transfers	11607	13100	13813	13895	14131	14794	18601	18857	19341	22633	39654	47205
4 Surplus of the nation on current transactions	-26428	8309	-3936	-2493	3750	-2733	-3906	2184	13164	820	-1628	-10610
Payments to the Rest of the World and Surplus of the Nation on Current Transactions	412038	511350	572510	631765	598091	602156	673668	775568	852227	907796	927538	932841
Receipts From The Rest of the World												
1 Exports of goods and services [a]	366244	449686	497645	549126	522970	527054	587545	664267	724313	770412	803356	803368
A Exports of merchandise f.o.b. [a]	225782	274553	312396	359455	342152	342714	374434	427167	466919	479309	486038	467406
B Other	140462	175133	185249	189671	180818	184340	213111	237100	257394	291103	317318	335962
2 Factor income from rest of the world	32847	47204	58367	66487	58448	57361	66629	90727	104596	111833	103072	107739
A Compensation of employees [b]	-	-	-	-	-	-	-	-	-	-	8938	8732
B Property and entrepreneurial income	32847	47204	58367	66487	58448	57361	66629	90727	104596	111833	94134	99007
3 Current transfers from rest of the world [b]	12947	14460	16498	16152	16673	17741	19494	20574	23318	25551	21110	21734
A Subsidies from supranational organisations	...	...	...	...	...	...	...	...	...	...	...	...
B Other current transfers	12947	14460	16498	16152	16673	17741	19494	20574	23318	25551	21110	21734
Receipts from the Rest of the World on Current Transactions	412038	511350	572510	631765	598091	602156	673668	775568	852227	907796	927538	932841

a) The estimates on transit trade are on a net basis.
b) Item 'Compensation of employees' is included in current transfers to/from the rest of the world.
c) Only central government data are included in the general government estimates.

1.8 Capital Transactions of The Nation, Summary

Million Austrian schillings

	1980	1983	1984	1985	1986	1987	1988	1989	1990	1991	1992	1993
Finance of Gross Capital Formation												
Gross saving	256462	272038	299968	313085	338011	353216	384750	422067	473053	498047	513726	509381
1 Consumption of fixed capital	116098	149238	158193	167526	176195	183870	194114	205630	218486	235173	252575	270063
A General government	7481	9596	10095	10690	11310	11561	11803	12218	12770	13502	13809	14468
B Corporate and quasi-corporate enterprises	108617	139642	148098	156836	164885	172309	182311	193412	205716	221671	238766	255595
C Other	-	-	-	-	-	-	-	-	-	-	-	-
2 Net saving	140364	122800	141775	145559	161816	169346	190636	216437	254567	262874	261151	239318
A General government	36145	14181	30328	32860	17977	3502	19181	19899	33473	29297	40886	4410
B Corporate and quasi-corporate enterprises	39864	45462	45540	42895	45752	47280	56429	59594	60810	61218	58830	79657
C Other	64355	63157	65907	69804	98087	118564	115026	136944	160284	172359	161435	155251
Less: Surplus of the nation on current transactions	-26428	8309	-3936	-2493	3750	-2733	-3906	2184	13164	820	-1628	-10610
Finance of Gross Capital Formation	282890	263729	303904	315578	334261	355949	388656	419883	459889	497227	515354	519991

Austria

1.8 Capital Transactions of The Nation, Summary
(Continued)

Million Austrian schillings

	1980	1983	1984	1985	1986	1987	1988	1989	1990	1991	1992	1993
					Gross Capital Formation							
Increase in stocks [a]	27433	-5821	20984	11165	10255	13837	17488	14133	17497	8844	4249	8714
Gross fixed capital formation [b]	255457	269550	282920	304413	324006	342112	371168	405750	442392	488383	511105	511277
1 General government	41568	45189	46288	48004	52092	50728	50676	55192	57293	63043	67334	65946
2 Corporate and quasi-corporate enterprises	...	...	...	...	...	...	...	...	...	...	...	...
3 Other	...	...	...	...	...	...	...	...	...	...	...	...
Gross Capital Formation	282890	263729	303904	315578	334261	355949	388656	419883	459889	497227	515354	519991

a) Item 'Increase in stocks' includes breeding stock, draught animals and a statistical discrepancy.
b) Item 'Gross fixed capital formation' includes value added tax on investments of investors not entitled to deduct invoiced value added tax. This component is not included in the sub-items. For years 1973-1975, 1977 and 1978 of the current prices table, special investment tax is included. These estimates are shown separately as 'Statistical discrepancy' in tables 2.7, 2.8, 2.9, 2.10 and 2.11.

1.9 Gross Domestic Product by Institutional Sectors of Origin

Million Austrian schillings

	1980	1983	1984	1985	1986	1987	1988	1989	1990	1991	1992	1993
					Domestic Factor Incomes Originating							
1 General government	119658	152695	160925	171732	182910	191440	195816	205391	218514	238794	257802	277476
2 Corporate and quasi-corporate enterprises	...	...	...	...	...	...	...	...	...	...	...	...
3 Households and private unincorporated enterprises	...	...	...	...	...	...	...	...	...	...	...	...
4 Non-profit institutions serving households	5810	7856	8263	8769	9250	9724	9766	10104	10860	11644	12682	13413
Subtotal: Domestic Factor Incomes	745832	890293	938428	994171	1058305	1099745	1162517	1240966	1342797	1443798	1528838	1572730
Indirect taxes, net	132774	161686	180154	186728	187997	197773	209808	226304	240026	249343	264667	275048
A Indirect taxes	162828	197080	216087	225931	234044	245154	254887	271413	287880	305779	325823	338559
B Less: Subsidies	30054	35394	35933	39203	46047	47381	45079	45109	47854	56436	61156	63511
Consumption of fixed capital	116098	149238	158193	167526	176195	183870	194114	205630	218486	235173	252575	270063
Statistical discrepancy	-	-	-	-	-	-	-	-	-	-	-	-
Gross Domestic Product	994704	1201217	1276775	1348425	1422497	1481388	1566439	1672900	1801309	1928314	2046080	2117841

1.10 Gross Domestic Product by Kind of Activity, in Current Prices

Million Austrian schillings

	1980	1983	1984	1985	1986	1987	1988	1989	1990	1991	1992	1993
1 Agriculture, hunting, forestry and fishing	44292	44139	48695	44993	47114	48473	49066	52286	56679	52992	50080	48395
2 Mining and quarrying	4866	5322	5538	5874	5649	6293	5592	5459	5627	7259	5399	4731
3 Manufacturing	276671	322806	340063	362803	375646	383843	410001	432101	463722	488803	501577	495443
4 Electricity, gas and water	30673	39087	38605	39852	45127	48146	46018	48427	49035	52820	57044	60098
5 Construction	81207	87447	87056	89060	93504	99664	105344	113528	124270	140043	153328	161794
6 Wholesale and retail trade, restaurants and hotels	166750	201833	206861	215063	228973	236020	256264	273428	300145	319869	342205	345794
7 Transport, storage and communication	57830	68105	74757	78422	81703	87699	97991	105900	112413	121776	130621	134410
8 Finance, insurance, real estate and business services	119062	166217	183139	204393	223012	235048	250863	276736	304347	330612	366264	401216
9 Community, social and personal services	32225	40544	43541	46781	51243	57260	62648	68111	73549	79554	89600	96024
Total, Industries	813576	975500	1028255	1087241	1151971	1202446	1283787	1375976	1489787	1593728	1696118	1747905
Producers of Government Services	129080	164626	173490	185067	197087	205911	210533	220962	234856	256147	275732	296634
Other Producers	7169	9230	9701	10231	10817	11256	11350	11713	12529	13431	14469	15458
Subtotal	949825	1149356	1211446	1282539	1359875	1419613	1505670	1608651	1737172	1863306	1986319	2059997
Less: Imputed bank service charge	45118	61064	63296	68556	75029	82048	87492	94396	104714	114567	124514	136849
Plus: Import duties	5745	7707	8621	9077	8996	9861	10631	11507	12026	12642	13269	13122
Plus: Value added tax	84252	105218	120004	125365	128655	133962	137630	147138	156825	166933	171006	181571
Plus: Other adjustments	-	-	-	-	-	-	-	-	-	-	-	-
Equals: Gross Domestic Product	994704	1201217	1276775	1348425	1422497	1481388	1566439	1672900	1801309	1928314	2046080	2117841

1.11 Gross Domestic Product by Kind of Activity, in Constant Prices

Million Austrian schillings

	1980	1983	1984	1985	1986	1987	1988	1989	1990	1991	1992	1993
					At constant prices of:1983							
1 Agriculture, hunting, forestry and fishing	41959	44139	46405	44199	44638	44657	46527	46135	48091	44895	43566	44221
2 Mining and quarrying	5649	5322	5248	5015	4446	5497	5204	4631	4571	6541	5134	4530
3 Manufacturing	320585	322806	332096	344817	346598	343527	370820	386208	405639	415801	416572	402091
4 Electricity, gas and water	38662	39087	39689	41432	40148	45976	42703	46623	47338	49078	49819	50954
5 Construction	98143	87447	86334	86795	87921	89343	91973	95991	99113	104981	110611	112928

Austria

1.11 Gross Domestic Product by Kind of Activity, in Constant Prices
(Continued)

Million Austrian schillings

	1980	1983	1984	1985	1986	1987	1988	1989	1990	1991	1992	1993
					At constant prices of:1983							
6 Wholesale and retail trade, restaurants and hotels	189408	201833	200866	206947	212522	215439	225940	235233	251039	258182	261898	259267
7 Transport, storage and communication	65079	68105	71894	74778	75454	79053	82191	87514	92389	98542	102842	104904
8 Finance, insurance, real estate and business services	151650	166217	172019	175947	180993	184027	188878	197910	205898	213792	222376	226893
9 Community, social and personal services	38588	40544	41105	42689	44225	46840	50479	52624	55595	58070	58802	60512
Total, Industries	949723	975500	995656	1022619	1036945	1054359	1104715	1152869	1209673	1249882	1271620	1266300
Producers of Government Services	154666	164626	166611	169124	171380	173219	174505	175629	179012	183359	188086	194061
Other Producers	9056	9230	9281	9306	9413	9433	9426	9459	9559	9721	9835	9955
Subtotal	1113445	1149356	1171548	1201049	1217738	1237011	1288646	1337957	1398244	1442962	1469541	1470316
Less: Imputed bank service charge	51801	61064	63067	63984	67504	70283	71985	75603	80477	85919	87590	89371
Plus: Import duties	7877	7707	8188	8411	8992	9573	10214	11021	11239	11257	11094	10972
Plus: Value added tax	99142	105218	100898	102066	103073	106924	108399	113049	116321	119581	122356	122578
Plus: Other adjustments	-	-	-	-	-	-	-	-	-	-	-	-
Equals: Gross Domestic Product	1168663	1201217	1217567	1247542	1262299	1283225	1335274	1386424	1445327	1487881	1515401	1514495

1.12 Relations Among National Accounting Aggregates

Million Austrian schillings

	1980	1983	1984	1985	1986	1987	1988	1989	1990	1991	1992	1993
Gross Domestic Product	994704	1201217	1276775	1348425	1422497	1481388	1566439	1672900	1801309	1928314	2046080	2117841
Plus: Net factor income from the rest of the world	-8353	-8809	-8551	-7069	-11966	-12905	-13699	-14382	-13164	-19516	-9660	-9129
Factor income from the rest of the world	32847	47204	58367	66487	58448	57361	66629	90727	104596	111833	103072	107739
Less: Factor income to the rest of the world	41200	56013	66918	73556	70414	70266	80328	105109	117760	131349	112732	116868
Equals: Gross National Product	986351	1192408	1268224	1341356	1410531	1468483	1552740	1658518	1788145	1908798	2036420	2108712
Less: Consumption of fixed capital	116098	149238	158193	167526	176195	183870	194114	205630	218486	235173	252575	270063
Equals: National Income	870253	1043170	1110031	1173830	1234336	1284613	1358626	1452888	1569659	1673625	1783845	1838649
Plus: Net current transfers from the rest of the world	1340	1360	2685	2257	2542	2947	893	1717	3977	2918	-18544	-25471
Current transfers from the rest of the world	12947	14460	16498	16152	16673	17741	19494	20574	23318	25551	21110	21734
Less: Current transfers to the rest of the world	11607	13100	13813	13895	14131	14794	18601	18857	19341	22633	39654	47205
Equals: National Disposable Income	871593	1044530	1112716	1176087	1236878	1287560	1359519	1454605	1573636	1676543	1765301	1813178
Less: Final consumption	731229	921730	970941	1030528	1075062	1118214	1168883	1238168	1319069	1413669	1504150	1573860
Equals: Net Saving	140364	122800	141775	145559	161816	169346	190636	216437	254567	262874	261151	239318
Less: Surplus of the nation on current transactions	-26428	8309	-3936	-2493	3750	-2733	-3906	2184	13164	820	-1628	-10610
Equals: Net Capital Formation	166792	114491	145711	148052	158066	172079	194542	214253	241403	262054	262779	249928

2.1 Government Final Consumption Expenditure by Function, in Current Prices

Million Austrian schillings

	1980	1983	1984	1985	1986	1987	1988	1989	1990	1991	1992	1993
1 General public services	30445	36148	37870	42057	44066	45237	45995	47924	50863	59518	63398	...
2 Defence	11391	15495	15674	16774	18094	16954	16516	18333	17877	18192	18521	19320
3 Public order and safety	8883	11264	11896	12328	13086	13359	13245	13783	14592	15887	16951	...
4 Education	38553	49473	52362	56053	59870	62678	64061	67228	71385	77479	83875	...
5 Health	43666	52991	55375	59895	64081	69754	72715	76852	82695	90229	100027	...
6 Social security and welfare	32380	42336	43941	46885	49387	50001	53047	55269	58455	64322	69804	...
7 Housing and community amenities	400	258	167	414	558	577	445	641	-302	9	-377	...
8 Recreational, cultural and religious affairs	3100	4060	4439	4828	5116	5352	5512	5963	6400	7265	7912	...
9 Economic services	9879	14866	16035	15765	16397	16524	16820	16888	17923	16731	16948	...

Austria

2.1 Government Final Consumption Expenditure by Function, in Current Prices
(Continued)

Million Austrian schillings

	1980	1983	1984	1985	1986	1987	1988	1989	1990	1991	1992	1993
A Fuel and energy	-	-	1	-	-	1	-	1	2	3	-	...
B Agriculture, forestry, fishing and hunting	1858	2835	2936	1724	1769	1849	1943	1983	1932	702	747	...
C Mining, manufacturing and construction, except fuel and energy	4973	6000	6286	6945	7498	7922	8373	8488	8991	9732	10084	...
D Transportation and communication	2932	5716	6453	6701	6706	6340	6081	6062	6651	5940	5738	...
E Other economic affairs	116	315	359	395	424	412	423	354	347	354	379	...
10 Other functions	-	-	-	-	-	-	-	-	-	-	-	...
Total Government Final Consumption Expenditure	178697	226891	237759	254999	270655	280436	288356	302881	319888	349632	377059	405598

2.2 Government Final Consumption Expenditure by Function, in Constant Prices

Million Austrian schillings

	1980	1983	1984	1985	1986	1987	1988	1989	1990	1991	1992	1993
					At constant prices of:1983							
1 General public services	35212	36148	36120	38197	38431	38616	38515	38674	39457	43181	45086	...
2 Defence	13826	15495	14764	14950	15540	14116	13373	14647	13897	13349	13056	...
3 Public order and safety	10488	11264	11530	11368	11537	11518	11263	11197	11233	11359	11896	...
4 Education	45248	49473	50473	51760	52568	53146	53716	54120	55135	55921	57514	...
5 Health	52405	52991	52822	53789	55395	57689	58012	58313	59247	62137	62153	...
6 Social security and welfare	39361	42336	42134	42743	42980	42262	43447	43341	44333	46112	48211	...
7 Housing and community amenities	475	258	160	376	486	487	366	506	-222	6	-255	...
8 Recreational, cultural and religious affairs	3808	4060	4233	4401	4488	4597	4627	4829	5003	5330	5669	...
9 Economic services	11447	14866	15142	14216	14227	14163	14050	13614	14004	12086	12164	...
A Fuel and energy	-	-	1	-	-	1	-	1	2	-	-	...
B Agriculture, forestry, fishing and hunting	2150	2835	2771	1554	1533	1579	1624	1590	1488	408	476	...
C Mining, manufacturing and construction, except fuel and energy	5709	6000	5942	6269	6513	6796	6992	6854	7048	7160	7299	...
D Transportation and communication	3452	5716	6092	6038	5812	5431	5082	4881	5189	4245	4108	...
E Other economic affairs	136	315	336	355	369	356	352	288	277	271	281	...
10 Other functions	-	-	-	-	-	-	-	-	-	-	-	...
Total Government Final Consumption Expenditure	212270	226891	227378	231800	235652	236594	237369	239241	242087	249481	255494	263212

2.3 Total Government Outlays by Function and Type

Million Austrian schillings

	Final Consumption Expenditures Total	Compensation of Employees	Other	Subsidies	Other Current Transfers & Property Income	Total Current Disbursements	Gross Capital Formation	Other Capital Outlays	Total Outlays
					1980				
1 General public services	30445	21068	9377	...	...	...	...	...	...
2 Defence	11391	6149	5242	...	...	...	...	...	...
3 Public order and safety	8883	8851	32	...	...	...	...	...	...
4 Education	38553	30774	7779	...	...	...	...	...	...
5 Health	43666	15423	28243	...	...	...	...	...	...
6 Social security and welfare	32380	28241	4139	...	...	...	...	...	...
7 Housing and community amenities	400	1510	-1110	...	...	...	...	...	...
8 Recreation, culture and religion	3100	1685	1415	...	...	...	...	...	...
9 Economic services	9879	5957	3922	...	...	...	...	...	...
A Fuel and energy	-	-	-	...	...	...	...	...	...
B Agriculture, forestry, fishing and hunting	1858	1452	406	...	...	...	...	...	...
C Mining (except fuels), manufacturing and construction	4973	2459	2514	...	...	...	...	...	...
D Transportation and communication	2932	2035	897	...	...	...	...	...	...
E Other economic affairs	116	11	105	...	...	...	...	...	...
10 Other functions	-	-	-	...	...	...	...	...	...
Total	178697	119658	59039	30054	216722	425473	41568	19030	486071

Austria

2.3 Total Government Outlays by Function and Type
(Continued)

Million Austrian schillings

		Final Consumption Expenditures Total	Compensation of Employees	Other	Subsidies	Other Current Transfers & Property Income	Total Current Disbursements	Gross Capital Formation	Other Capital Outlays	Total Outlays
					1985					
1	General public services	42057	29408	12649	-	2566	44623	...	...	...
2	Defence	16774	8567	8207	-	110	16884	...	...	...
3	Public order and safety	12328	12156	172	3	96	12427	...	...	...
4	Education	56053	44550	11503	458	3214	59725	...	...	...
5	Health	59895	22923	36972	5414	2112	67421	...	...	...
6	Social security and welfare	46885	40972	5913	2053	263677	312615	...	...	...
7	Housing and community amenities	414	2079	-1665	761	2340	3515	...	...	...
8	Recreation, culture and religion	4828	2603	2225	1964	1518	8310	...	...	...
9	Economic services	15765	8474	7291	28550	2985	47300	...	...	...
	A Fuel and energy	-	-	-	-	12	12	...	...	...
	B Agriculture, forestry, fishing and hunting	1724	1457	267	11498	473	13695	...	...	...
	C Mining (except fuels), manufacturing and construction	6945	3458	3487	3205	1499	11649	...	...	...
	D Transportation and communication	6701	3542	3159	13086	526	20313	...	...	...
	E Other economic affairs	395	17	378	761	475	1631	...	...	...
10	Other functions	-	-	-	-	47847	47847	...	...	...
	Total	254999	171732	83267	39203	326465	620667	48004	28888	697568
					1990					
1	General public services	50863	36161	14702	144	3585	54592	...	...	...
2	Defence	17877	9543	8334	2	43	17922	...	...	...
3	Public order and safety	14592	14672	-80	-3	159	14748	...	...	...
4	Education	71385	57320	14065	617	4407	76409	...	...	...
5	Health	82695	32128	50567	6941	3469	93105	...	...	...
6	Social security and welfare	58455	52255	6200	1202	343047	402704	...	...	...
7	Housing and community amenities	-302	2534	-2836	921	2780	3399	...	...	...
8	Recreation, culture and religion	6400	3649	2751	2685	2147	11232	...	...	...
9	Economic services	17923	10252	7671	35345	3492	56760	...	...	...
	A Fuel and energy	2	-	2	87	16	105	...	...	...
	B Agriculture, forestry, fishing and hunting	1932	1766	166	14135	751	16818	...	...	...
	C Mining (except fuels), manufacturing and construction	8991	4369	4622	2975	1408	13374	...	...	...
	D Transportation and communication	6651	4102	2549	16761	444	23856	...	...	...
	E Other economic affairs	347	15	332	1387	873	2607	...	...	...
10	Other functions	-	-	-	-	73118	73118	...	...	...
	Total	319888	218514	101374	47854	436247	803989	57293	27679	888961
					1991					
1	General public services	59518	39403	20115	-4	4256	63770	...	...	...
2	Defence	18192	10476	7716	-	52	18244	...	...	...
3	Public order and safety	15887	15948	-61	1	146	16034	...	...	...
4	Education	77479	62591	14888	618	5077	83174	...	...	...
5	Health	90229	35497	54732	7454	3902	101585	...	...	...
6	Social security and welfare	64322	56941	7381	1622	368947	434891	...	...	...
7	Housing and community amenities	9	2825	-2816	1191	2994	4194	...	...	...
8	Recreation, culture and religion	7265	4141	3124	2690	2449	12404	...	...	...
9	Economic services	16731	10972	5759	42864	3449	63044	...	...	...
	A Fuel and energy	3	-	3	87	43	133	...	...	...
	B Agriculture, forestry, fishing and hunting	702	1853	-1151	16801	802	18305	...	...	...
	C Mining (except fuels), manufacturing and construction	9732	4726	5006	5671	1306	16709	...	...	...
	D Transportation and communication	5940	4376	1564	18703	395	25038	...	...	...
	E Other economic affairs	354	17	337	1602	903	2859	...	...	...
10	Other functions	-	-	-	-	82130	82130	...	...	...
	Total	349632	238794	110838	56436	473402	879470	63043	26938	969451

Austria

2.3 Total Government Outlays by Function and Type
(Continued)

Million Austrian schillings

	Final Consumption Expenditures Total	Compensation of Employees	Other	Subsidies	Other Current Transfers & Property Income	Total Current Disbursements	Gross Capital Formation	Other Capital Outlays	Total Outlays
1992									
1 General public services	63398	42113	21285	2344	4846	70588	...	...	...
2 Defence	18521	10633	7888	-	37	18558	...	...	...
3 Public order and safety	16951	17016	-65	1	141	17093	...	...	...
4 Education	83875	67863	16012	860	5300	90035	...	...	...
5 Health	100027	39371	60656	7963	4830	112820	...	...	...
6 Social security and welfare	69804	61582	8222	1866	398019	469689	...	...	...
7 Housing and community amenities	-377	3037	-3414	1195	3523	4341	...	...	...
8 Recreation, culture and religion	7912	4522	3390	3219	2785	13916	...	...	...
9 Economic services	16948	11665	5283	43708	4508	65164	...	...	...
A Fuel and energy	-	-	-	83	48	131	...	...	...
B Agriculture, forestry, fishing and hunting	747	1938	-1191	17944	1042	19733	...	...	...
C Mining (except fuels), manufacturing and construction	10084	5153	4931	5006	1993	17083	...	...	...
D Transportation and communication	5738	4555	1183	19486	429	25653	...	...	...
E Other economic affairs	379	19	360	1189	996	2564	...	...	...
10 Other functions	-	-	-	-	87928	87928	...	...	...
Total	377059	257802	119257	61156	511917	950132	67334	28948	1046414
1993									
1 General public services	...	...	...	...	...	...	...	...	...
2 Defence	19320	11000	8320	...	...	19320	...	...	...
3 Public order and safety	...	...	...	...	...	...	...	...	...
4 Education	...	...	...	...	...	...	...	...	...
5 Health	...	...	...	...	...	...	...	...	...
6 Social security and welfare	...	...	...	...	...	...	...	...	...
7 Housing and community amenities	...	...	...	...	...	...	...	...	...
8 Recreation, culture and religion	...	...	...	...	...	...	...	...	...
9 Economic services	...	...	...	...	...	...	...	...	...
A Fuel and energy	...	...	...	...	...	...	...	...	...
B Agriculture, forestry, fishing and hunting	...	...	...	...	...	...	...	...	...
C Mining (except fuels), manufacturing and construction	...	...	...	...	...	...	...	...	...
D Transportation and communication	...	...	...	...	...	...	...	...	...
E Other economic affairs	...	...	...	...	...	...	...	...	...
10 Other functions	...	...	...	...	93023	93023	...	...	...
Total	405598	277476	128122	63511	555436	1024545	65946	40306	1130797

2.4 Composition of General Government Social Security Benefits and Social Assistance Grants to Households

Million Austrian schillings

	1980 Social Security Benefits	Social Assistance Grants	1985 Social Security Benefits	Social Assistance Grants	1990 Social Security Benefits	Social Assistance Grants	1991 Social Security Benefits	Social Assistance Grants	1992 Social Security Benefits	Social Assistance Grants	1993 Social Security Benefits	Social Assistance Grants
1 Education benefits	1	...	1	3092	3	4203	3	4669	4	5069	...	...
2 Health benefits	5	...	264	1669	407	2813	341	3253	379	4002	...	...
3 Social security and welfare benefits	94248	...	140985	64049	187605	77279	198735	85060	210308	96118	...	...
4 Housing and community amenities	...	...	...	2340	...	2779	...	2993	...	3522	...	...
5 Recreation and cultural benefits	...	...	...	1508	...	2131	...	2431	...	2765	...	...
6 Other	246	...	1094	3613	657	4937	781	5109	1600	5802	...	...
Total	94500	56161	142344	76271	188672	94142	199860	103715	212291	117278	227906	133239

Austria

2.5 Private Final Consumption Expenditure by Type and Purpose, in Current Prices

Million Austrian schillings

	1980	1983	1984	1985	1986	1987	1988	1989	1990	1991	1992	1993
Final Consumption Expenditure of Resident Households												
1 Food, beverages and tobacco	141869	167087	176586	181983	187191	189993	195062	201952	212274	223427	233602	238030
A Food	110144	128644	136569	139896	141449	143460	147211	153919	163176	172402	179807	183823
B Non-alcoholic beverages	3858	4388	4620	4959	5485	6017	6233	6387	7111	7706	8721	8706
C Alcoholic beverages	14675	17004	17084	17791	20211	20488	21660	21720	21442	21801	23385	24142
D Tobacco	13192	17051	18312	19337	20045	20028	19958	19926	20545	21518	21689	21359
2 Clothing and footwear	63533	79946	83175	85187	86678	89228	89737	94638	100056	104178	105680	105562
3 Gross rent, fuel and power	93078	124214	138910	152189	159527	163301	164052	174291	185645	202422	215225	230086
A Fuel and power	29557	36422	40567	44845	43195	42558	39786	40228	42893	48052	47003	49445
B Other	63521	87792	98343	107344	116332	120743	124266	134063	142752	154370	168222	180641
4 Furniture, furnishings and household equipment and operation	43446	53928	53064	55357	57301	60809	71721	75675	82657	85810	91773	96799
A Household operation	7575	9453	10115	10626	10755	11237	12073	12890	14035	15679	17179	18505
B Other	35871	44475	42949	44731	46546	49572	59648	62785	68622	70131	74594	78294
5 Medical care and health expenses	25518	33513	35804	38636	40674	43708	46623	52332	55042	60961	67134	71787
6 Transport and communication	98073	122959	125232	133009	130110	132529	141375	160584	174638	190718	201911	203257
A Personal transport equipment	23373	30777	26383	30865	33162	32259	37489	42981	48595	52877	58002	53463
B Other	74700	92182	98849	102144	96948	100270	103886	117603	126043	137841	143909	149794
7 Recreational, entertainment, education and cultural services	34732	42703	44678	47062	50187	55051	67263	72919	79316	85372	90080	92984
A Education	1910	1742	2054	2103	2333	2684	3332	3720	4332	4784	4757	4643
B Other	32822	40961	42624	44959	47854	52367	63931	69199	74984	80588	85323	88341
8 Miscellaneous goods and services	93582	115143	121253	127615	135323	141627	151151	159362	171180	183159	197050	204650
A Personal care	16058	19402	19874	20759	21655	22714	24487	25386	27516	29574	31156	32466
B Expenditures in restaurants, cafes and hotels	63723	77613	81865	85808	91494	93900	98895	105562	112857	121929	130383	133386
C Other	13801	18128	19514	21048	22174	25013	27769	28414	30807	31656	35511	38798
Total Final Consumption Expenditure in the Domestic Market by Households, of which	593830	739493	778702	821037	846991	876245	926985	991752	1060809	1136047	1202455	1243155
A Durable goods	67761	85081	79334	86625	91498	94933	117067	122294	133660	140418	150275	148580
B Semi-durable goods	77392	96385	99478	101955	104337	107375	109067	115341	122951	127180	129785	130618
C Non-durable goods	212869	255100	271585	282824	279898	282640	287308	302514	320922	343115	355292	363748
D Services	235808	302928	328305	349633	371259	391297	413542	451603	483276	525335	567103	600209
Plus: Direct purchases abroad by resident households	39984	47041	53026	56783	59027	69287	73206	80407	88919	92771	96014	99092
Less: Direct purchases in the domestic market by non-resident households	81282	91695	98546	102291	101611	107754	119664	136872	150547	164781	171378	173985
Equals: Final Consumption Expenditure of Resident Households a	552532	694839	733182	775529	804407	837778	880527	935287	999181	1064037	1127091	1168262
Final Consumption Expenditure of Private Non-profit Institutions Serving Households												
Equals: Final Consumption Expenditure of Private Non-profit Organisations Serving Households	...	...	...	...	...	...	...	...	...	...	...	...
Private Final Consumption Expenditure	552532	694839	733182	775529	804407	837778	880527	935287	999181	1064037	1127091	1168262

a) Item 'Final consumption expenditure of resident households' includes consumption expenditure of private non-profit institutions serving households.

2.6 Private Final Consumption Expenditure by Type and Purpose, in Constant Prices

Million Austrian schillings

	1980	1983	1984	1985	1986	1987	1988	1989	1990	1991	1992	1993
At constant prices of: 1983												
Final Consumption Expenditure of Resident Households												
1 Food, beverages and tobacco	162042	167087	166295	168701	170221	171735	175473	180194	184918	187689	190189	190347
A Food	124425	128644	128294	130319	130360	131702	135431	139965	143962	145853	148144	149035
B Non-alcoholic beverages	4450	4388	4441	4724	5129	5622	5828	5959	6635	6871	7406	7273
C Alcoholic beverages	16551	17004	16737	16593	17607	17550	18006	18436	18033	18130	18160	18069
D Tobacco	16617	17051	16823	17066	17125	16861	16208	15834	16287	16836	16480	15971
2 Clothing and footwear	70287	79946	80067	79004	77879	78642	76755	78211	79793	79929	78061	75169
3 Gross rent, fuel and power	119943	124214	129243	134207	137380	140209	140124	144112	147574	155350	155887	160481
A Fuel and power	38179	36422	38128	41055	41904	44209	42441	43003	44480	49036	47063	49570

Austria

2.6 Private Final Consumption Expenditure by Type and Purpose, in Constant Prices
(Continued)

Million Austrian schillings

	1980	1983	1984	1985	1986	1987	1988	1989	1990	1991	1992	1993
				At constant prices of:1983								
B Other	81764	87792	91115	93152	95476	96000	97683	101109	103094	106314	108824	110911
4 Furniture, furnishings and household equipment and operation	48934	53928	51019	51759	51982	54690	63676	65507	69429	70187	72895	74067
A Household operation	8807	9453	9673	9920	9790	10082	10675	11101	11655	12471	13040	13477
B Other	40127	44475	41346	41839	42192	44608	53001	54406	57774	57716	59855	60590
5 Medical care and health expenses	31280	33513	33735	34695	34704	35362	36375	38874	38495	40872	41717	42459
6 Transport and communication	116344	122959	118148	121917	122224	123621	129419	144447	153415	165070	170392	167637
A Personal transport equipment	26306	30777	25046	28392	29372	27776	31457	35202	38941	41121	44170	39358
B Other	90038	92182	93102	93525	92852	95845	97962	109245	114474	123949	126222	128279
7 Recreational, entertainment, education and cultural services	41282	42703	42821	43906	45506	48853	59170	61511	65984	68314	69323	68879
A Education	2228	1742	1984	1968	2056	2222	2636	2630	3111	3035	2844	2555
B Other	39054	40961	40837	41938	43450	46631	56534	58881	62873	65279	66479	66324
8 Miscellaneous goods and services	109496	115143	114747	116309	118469	121732	125945	129566	135051	138993	143141	141132
A Personal care	17891	19402	18809	19305	19792	21016	22499	23173	25128	26533	27420	27479
B Expenditures in restaurants, cafes and hotels	74697	77613	77171	77451	78560	78684	79699	82773	85503	88314	89829	86773
C Other	16908	18128	18767	19553	20117	22032	23747	23620	24420	24146	25892	26880
Total Final Consumption Expenditure in the Domestic Market by Households, of which	699608	739493	736074	750499	758365	774843	806936	842423	874659	906404	921605	920172
A Durable goods	74636	85081	75908	80621	83051	86222	105138	107432	115331	118688	124402	119194
B Semi-durable goods	86043	96385	95778	94736	94018	94988	94077	96432	99611	99310	97571	94811
C Non-durable goods	249706	255100	256364	261932	263698	268998	273873	284968	293648	306738	307120	310717
D Services	289223	302928	308023	313210	317599	324635	333849	353590	366069	381668	392511	395448
Plus: Direct purchases abroad by resident households	47255	47041	51481	53705	55292	65633	68250	72138	76814	76787	77318	77205
Less: Direct purchases in the domestic market by non-resident households	94973	91695	93246	93343	90231	94329	102142	114749	122851	130210	129342	126224
Equals: Final Consumption Expenditure of Resident Households a	651890	694839	694309	710861	723426	746147	773044	799812	828622	852981	869581	871153
	Final Consumption Expenditure of Private Non-profit Institutions Serving Households												
Equals: Final Consumption Expenditure of Private Non-profit Organisations Serving Households	...	...	...	...	...	...	...	...	...	...	...	...
Private Final Consumption Expenditure	651890	694839	694309	710861	723426	746147	773044	799812	828622	852981	869581	871153

a) Item 'Final consumption expenditure of resident households' includes consumption expenditure of private non-profit institutions serving households.

2.11 Gross Fixed Capital Formation by Kind of Activity of Owner, ISIC Divisions, in Current Prices

Million Austrian schillings

	1980	1983	1984	1985	1986	1987	1988	1989	1990	1991	1992	1993
	All Producers											
1 Agriculture, hunting, forestry and fishing	13033	14453	14692	15622	14252	14248	14643	15100	17722	17795	16684	16471
2 Mining and quarrying	760	660	632	691	670	616	855	853	825	568	...	...
3 Manufacturing	41639	37643	41489	47113	56986	58062	58996	60845	71701	76212	...	...
A Manufacturing of food, beverages and tobacco	4858	5723	5767	6418	6390	6989	7632	8047	8897	8745	...	...

Austria

2.11 Gross Fixed Capital Formation by Kind of Activity of Owner, ISIC Divisions, in Current Prices
(Continued)

Million Austrian schillings

	1980	1983	1984	1985	1986	1987	1988	1989	1990	1991	1992	1993
B Textile, wearing apparel and leather industries	2616	2362	2381	2948	3204	2899	3015	3248	3945	4117	...	...
C Manufacture of wood, and wood products, including furniture	3428	3176	3486	3566	3502	3900	5443	5490	6097	6159	...	...
D Manufacture of paper and paper products, printing and publishing	2799	4386	7900	4778	7557	8083	5676	6932	10972	10873	...	...
E Manufacture of chemicals and chemical petroleum, coal, rubber and plastic products	7311	5327	5605	7635	11611	12588	9386	9446	10431	11311	...	...
F Manufacture of non-metalic mineral products except products of petroleum and coal	3385	2803	3144	3799	3862	4050	4875	4838	6273	6203	...	...
G Basic metal industries	5321	3005	2369	4030	4158	2527	4675	4623	4793	4954	...	...
H Manufacture of fabricated metal products, machinery and equipment	11921	10861	10837	13939	16702	17026	18294	18221	20293	23850	...	...
I Other manufacturing industries	...	...	...	...	...	...	...	...	...	...	...	...
4 Electricity, gas and water	13992	18401	20615	21511	19827	15810	15683	17215	18065	17436	...	...
A Electricity, gas and steam	13214	17454	19719	20689	18874	14657	14526	16095	16794	16212	...	...
B Water works and supply	778	947	896	822	953	1153	1157	1120	1271	1224	...	...
5 Construction	5634	4826	5010	5267	5359	6040	7275	7698	8316	8644	...	...
6 Wholesale and retail trade, restaurants and hotels	...	...	...	...	...	...	...	...	...	...	...	...
7 Transport, storage and communication	...	...	...	...	...	...	...	...	...	...	...	...
8 Finance, insurance, real estate and business services	...	...	...	...	...	...	...	...	...	...	...	...
9 Community, social and personal services	...	...	...	...	...	...	...	...	...	...	...	...
Total Industries [a]	203355	215853	227482	246897	261420	279667	307826	336394	370155	406668	424538	...
Producers of Government Services	37620	37113	37180	38253	41866	41336	40403	44648	45885	51860	56429	...
Private Non-Profit Institutions Serving Households [a]	...	...	...	...	...	...	...	...	...	...	...	...
Statistical discrepancy [b]	14482	16584	18258	19263	20720	21109	22939	24708	26352	29855	30138	...
Total	255457	269550	282920	304413	324006	342112	371168	405750	442392	488383	511105	...

a) Item 'Private non-profit institutions serving households' is included with various industries above.
b) Item 'Gross fixed capital formation' includes value added tax on investments of investors not entitled to deduct invoiced value added tax. This component is not included in the sub-items. For years 1973-1975, 1977 and 1978 of the current prices table, special investment tax is included. These estimates are shown separately as 'Statistical discrepancy' in tables 2.7, 2.8, 2.9, 2.10 and 2.11.

2.17 Exports and Imports of Goods and Services, Detail

Million Austrian schillings

	1980	1983	1984	1985	1986	1987	1988	1989	1990	1991	1992	1993
Exports of Goods and Services
1 Exports of merchandise, f.o.b. [a]	225782	274553	312396	359455	342152	342714	374434	427167	466919	479309	486038	467406
2 Transport and communication												
3 Insurance service charges	34439	40809	44615	46744	47121	49364	53469	59608	65871	67685	92487	99194
4 Other commodities												
5 Adjustments of merchandise exports to change-of-ownership basis	...	...	...	...	...	...	...	...	...	...	...	...
6 Direct purchases in the domestic market by non-residential households	81282	91695	98546	102291	101611	107754	119664	136872	150547	164781	171378	173985
7 Direct purchases in the domestic market by extraterritorial bodies	...	...	...	...	...	...	...	...	...	...	...	...
Statistical discrepancy [b]	24741	42629	42088	40636	32086	27222	39978	40620	40976	58637	53453	62783
Total Exports of Goods and Services [a]	366244	449686	497645	549126	522970	527054	587545	664267	724313	770412	803356	803368
Imports of Goods and Services
1 Imports of merchandise, c.i.f. [a]	313265	345306	389180	427125	404383	408411	444802	508894	550863	585907	588666	562239

Austria

2.17 Exports and Imports of Goods and Services, Detail
(Continued)

Million Austrian schillings

	1980	1983	1984	1985	1986	1987	1988	1989	1990	1991	1992	1993
2 Adjustments of merchandise imports to change-of-ownership basis	...	...	...	...	...	...	...	...	...	...	...	...
3 Other transport and communication												
4 Other insurance service charges	26867	33900	36164	39443	38032	37454	41434	46356	50908	51028	68064	67498
5 Other commodities												
6 Direct purchases abroad by government	40827	47870	53908	57648	59926	70375	74264	81389	89906	93771	97053	100158
7 Direct purchases abroad by resident households												
Statistical discrepancy [b]	4700	6852	16463	22591	7455	3589	18145	12779	10285	22288	22997	49483
Total Imports of Goods and Services [a]	385659	433928	495715	546807	509796	519829	578645	649418	701962	752994	776780	779378
Balance of Goods and Services	-19415	15758	1930	2319	13174	7225	8900	14849	22351	17418	26576	23990
Total Imports and Balance of Goods and Services [a]	366244	449686	497645	549126	522970	527054	587545	664267	724313	770412	803356	803368

a) The estimates on transit trade are on a net basis.
b) Item 'Statistical discrepancy' refers to exports/imports of commodities not yet identified as merchandise or services. Before 1979, also including item 'Adjustments of merchandise export/import to change of ownership basis'.

3.11 General Government Production Account: Total and Subsectors

Million Austrian schillings

	1980					1985				
	Total General Government	Central Government	State or Provincial Government	Local Government	Social Security Funds	Total General Government	Central Government	State or Provincial Government	Local Government	Social Security Funds
Gross Output										
1 Sales	34869	6459	8866	17495	2049	50813	9881	13134	24785	3013
2 Services produced for own use	178697	63610	39998	34373	40716	254999	95568	56106	49373	53952
3 Own account fixed capital formation	...	...	...	...	...	...	...	...	...	...
Gross Output [a]	213566	70069	48864	51868	42765	305812	105449	69240	74158	56965
Gross Input										
Intermediate Consumption	84486	19730	11464	18744	34548	120745	32412	15597	26999	45737
Subtotal: Value Added	129080	50339	37400	33124	8217	185067	73037	53643	47159	11228
1 Indirect taxes, net	1941	885	660	396	-	2645	1307	809	529	-
A Indirect taxes	1941	885	660	396	...	2645	1307	809	529	...
B Less: Subsidies	...	...	...	...	...	...	...	...	...	...
2 Consumption of fixed capital	7481	1698	1152	4362	269	10690	2423	1646	6229	392
3 Compensation of employees	119658	47756	35588	28366	7948	171732	69307	51188	40401	10836
4 Net Operating surplus	...	...	...	...	...	...	...	...	...	...
Gross Input [a]	213566	70069	48864	51868	42765	305812	105449	69240	74158	56965

	1990					1991				
	Total General Government	Central Government	State or Provincial Government	Local Government	Social Security Funds	Total General Government	Central Government	State or Provincial Government	Local Government	Social Security Funds
Gross Output										
1 Sales	68337	13548	17709	33519	3561	72755	14000	19362	36087	3306
2 Services produced for own use	319888	113723	71467	62445	72253	349632	122846	78242	70504	78040
3 Own account fixed capital formation	...	...	...	...	...	...	...	...	...	...
Gross Output [a]	388225	127271	89176	95964	75814	422387	136846	97604	106591	81346
Gross Input										
Intermediate Consumption	153369	36073	20280	35254	61762	166240	37529	22077	40515	66119
Subtotal: Value Added	234856	91198	68896	60710	14052	256147	99317	75527	66076	15227
1 Indirect taxes, net	3572	1883	1027	662	-	3851	1990	1121	740	-
A Indirect taxes	3572	1883	1027	662	...	3851	1990	1121	740	...
B Less: Subsidies	...	...	...	...	...	...	...	...	...	...
2 Consumption of fixed capital	12770	2895	1966	7441	468	13502	3061	2078	7868	495
3 Compensation of employees	218514	86420	65903	52607	13584	238794	94266	72328	57468	14732
4 Net Operating surplus	...	...	...	...	...	...	...	...	...	...
Gross Input [a]	388225	127271	89176	95964	75814	422387	136846	97604	106591	81346

Austria

3.11 General Government Production Account: Total and Subsectors

Million Austrian schillings

	1992					1993				
	Total General Government	Central Government	State or Provincial Government	Local Government	Social Security Funds	Total General Government	Central Government	State or Provincial Government	Local Government	Social Security Funds
Gross Output											
1 Sales	79610	15018	20728	40285	3579	86777	17223	22261	43392	3901
2 Services produced for own use	377059	130063	85883	75398	85715	405598	138850	93461	83441	89846
3 Own account fixed capital formation	...	...	...	...	...	...	...	...	...	...
Gross Output a	456669	145081	106611	115683	89294	492375	156073	115722	126833	93747
Gross Input											
Intermediate Consumption	180937	39293	24265	44189	73190	195741	42847	26601	49609	76684
Subtotal: Value Added	275732	105788	82346	71494	16104	296634	113226	89121	77224	17063
1 Indirect taxes, net	4121	2068	1216	837	-	4690	2311	1325	1054	-
A Indirect taxes	4121	2068	1216	837	...	4690	2311	1325	1054	...
B Less: Subsidies	...	...	...	...	...	...	...	...	...	...
2 Consumption of fixed capital	13809	3130	2126	8047	506	14468	3280	2227	8431	530
3 Compensation of employees	257802	100590	79004	62610	15598	277476	107635	85569	67739	16533
4 Net Operating surplus	...	...	...	...	...	...	...	...	...	...
Gross Input a	456669	145081	106611	115683	89294	492375	156073	115722	126833	93747

a) Column 'State or Provincial Government' includes chambers.

3.12 General Government Income and Outlay Account: Total and Subsectors

Million Austrian schillings

	1980					1985				
	Total General Government	Central Government	State or Provincial Government	Local Government	Social Security Funds	Total General Government	Central Government	State or Provincial Government	Local Government	Social Security Funds
Receipts											
1 Operating surplus	...	...	...	...	...	...	...	...	...	...
2 Property and entrepreneurial income a	18493	12527	2210	2173	1583	26153	18941	2935	2319	1958
A Withdrawals from public quasi-corporations	5122	5370	-107	-148	7	6642	6933	-87	-208	4
B Interest	7720	1980	1946	2239	1555	9321	2899	2148	2359	1915
C Dividends	2878	2570	308	-	-	6646	5869	746	31	-
D Net land rent and royalties	2303	2303	2173	...	-	2464	2464	2319	...	-
3 Taxes, fees and contributions	418681	194495	44900	59213	120073	591184	287422	64898	78829	160035
A Indirect taxes	162828	112682	18252	31894	...	225931	157915	25912	42104	...
B Direct taxes	128390	77251	25145	25994	...	193628	122244	36642	34742	...
Income	110191	63982	22283	23926	...	154838	88176	32717	33945	...
Other	18199	13269	2862	2068	...	38790	34068	3925	797	...
C Social security contributions	124578	2625	1159	907	119887	167804	4483	1886	1410	160025
D Fees, fines and penalties	2885	1937	344	418	186	3821	2780	458	573	10
4 Other current transfers	24444	16339	31721	11737	25241	36190	23840	43151	18392	46496
A Casualty insurance claims	180	120	30	30	-	240	170	35	35	-
B Transfers from other government subsectors	...	3157	26301	6748	24388	...	4980	34675	11182	44852
C Transfers from the rest of the world	597	433	1	...	163	699	362	2	...	335
D Other transfers, except imputed	...	...	...	...	...	...	...	...	...	...
E Imputed unfunded employee pension and welfare contributions	23667	12629	5389	4959	690	35251	18328	8439	7175	1309
Total Current Receipts b	461618	223361	78831	73123	146897	653527	330203	110984	99540	208489
Disbursements											
1 Government final consumption expenditure	178697	63610	39998	34373	40716	254999	95568	56106	49373	53952
2 Property income	24739	17595	2048	5037	59	47847	38396	3458	5961	32
A Interest	24739	17595	2048	5037	59	47847	38396	3458	5961	32
B Net land rent and royalties	...	...	...	...	...	...	...	...	...	...
3 Subsidies	30054	21127	1505	1492	5930	39203	29950	2324	1549	5380

Austria

3.12 General Government Income and Outlay Account: Total and Subsectors
(Continued)

Million Austrian schillings

	1980					1985				
	Total General Government	Central Government	State or Provincial Government	Local Government	Social Security Funds	Total General Government	Central Government	State or Provincial Government	Local Government	Social Security Funds
4 Other current transfers	191983	120062	17485	15781	98639	278618	176476	26708	22912	149706
A Casualty insurance premiums, net	180	120	30	30	-	240	170	35	35	-
B Transfers to other government subsectors	...	50096	3058	5316	1514	...	81953	4866	6996	3369
C Social security benefits cd	94500	...	...	...	94500	142344	...	...	...	142344
D Social assistance grants e	56161	44987	7843	3331	...	76271	59137	11466	5668	...
E Unfunded employee pension and welfare benefits	38604	24202	6548	7104	750	56169	34244	10325	10211	1389
F Transfers to private non-profit institutions serving households d	...	...	...	...	...	...	...	...	...	...
G Other transfers n.e.c.	...	...	...	...	...	...	...	...	...	...
H Transfers to the rest of the world	2538	657	6	-	1875	3594	972	16	2	2604
Net saving	36145	967	17795	16440	1553	32860	-10187	22388	19745	-581
Total Current Disbursements and Net Saving b	461618	223361	78831	73123	146897	653527	330203	110984	99540	208489

	1990					1991				
	Total General Government	Central Government	State or Provincial Government	Local Government	Social Security Funds	Total General Government	Central Government	State or Provincial Government	Local Government	Social Security Funds

Receipts

1 Operating surplus	...	...	...	...	...	...	...	...	...	...
2 Property and entrepreneurial income a	38069	27568	4484	2863	3154	40787	29125	4428	3700	3534
A Withdrawals from public quasi-corporations	12416	12726	-48	-273	11	12155	12434	-18	-268	7
B Interest	15734	6645	3340	2944	2805	17796	7656	3744	3208	3188
C Dividends	7523	6618	866	39	-	8069	7625	403	41	-
D Net land rent and royalties	266	266	...	...	-	335	335	...	...	-
3 Taxes, fees and contributions	752338	377930	67642	98083	208683	816876	408251	75938	106780	225907
A Indirect taxes	287880	201184	31880	54816	...	305779	213197	34014	58568	...
B Direct taxes	238931	166429	32247	40255	...	267125	184156	38148	44821	...
Income	190237	119087	31474	39676	...	215256	133709	37146	44401	...
Other	48694	47342	773	579	...	51869	50447	1002	420	...
C Social security contributions	220619	6958	2842	2138	208681	238882	7521	3046	2411	225904
D Fees, fines and penalties	4908	3359	673	874	2	5090	3377	730	980	3
4 Other current transfers	47055	31751	57414	23438	64326	51104	35767	63365	25580	67829
A Casualty insurance claims	387	257	65	65	...	400	260	70	70	...
B Transfers from other government subsectors	...	7793	45816	14118	62147	...	9650	50773	15597	65417
C Transfers from the rest of the world	679	251	2	...	426	887	405	1	...	481
D Other transfers, except imputed	...	...	...	...	...	...	...	...	...	...
E Imputed unfunded employee pension and welfare contributions	45989	23450	11531	9255	1753	49817	25452	12521	9913	1931
Total Current Receipts b	837462	437249	129540	124384	276163	908767	473143	143731	136060	297270

Disbursements

1 Government final consumption expenditure	319888	113723	71467	62445	72253	349632	122846	78242	70504	78040
2 Property income	73118	64337	3219	5291	271	82130	73052	3365	5375	338
A Interest	73118	64337	3219	5291	271	82130	73052	3365	5375	338
B Net land rent and royalties	...	...	...	...	...	...	...	...	...	...
3 Subsidies	47854	35199	3421	2313	6921	56436	42918	3645	2446	7427

Austria

3.12 General Government Income and Outlay Account: Total and Subsectors
(Continued)

Million Austrian schillings

	1990					1991				
	Total General Government	Central Government	State or Provincial Government	Local Government	Social Security Funds	Total General Government	Central Government	State or Provincial Government	Local Government	Social Security Funds
4 Other current transfers	363129	228161	36854	29346	199782	391272	250087	40765	32841	213414
A Casualty insurance premiums, net	387	257	65	65	...	400	260	70	70	...
B Transfers to other government subsectors	...	110959	5813	8833	5409	...	121444	7114	10259	7018
C Social security benefits cd	188672	...	...	...	188672	199860	...	...	...	199860
D Social assistance grants e	94142	70295	16566	7281	...	103715	77486	17967	8262	...
E Unfunded employee pension and welfare benefits	74454	45024	14373	13164	1893	80827	48924	15567	14249	2087
F Transfers to private non-profit institutions serving households d	...	...	...	...	...	...	...	...	...	...
G Other transfers n.e.c.	...	...	...	...	...	...	...	...	...	...
H Transfers to the rest of the world	5474	1626	37	3	3808	6470	1973	47	1	4449
Net saving	33473	-4171	14579	24989	-3064	29297	-15760	17714	24894	-1949
Total Current Disbursements and Net Saving b	837462	437249	129540	124384	276163	908767	473143	143731	136060	297270

	1992					1993				
	Total General Government	Central Government	State or Provincial Government	Local Government	Social Security Funds	Total General Government	Central Government	State or Provincial Government	Local Government	Social Security Funds

Receipts

1 Operating surplus	...	...	...	...	...	...	...	...	...	...
2 Property and entrepreneurial income a	45733	33599	4690	3889	3555	42772	30584	4934	3644	3610
A Withdrawals from public quasi-corporations	12937	13254	-30	-296	9	13605	13945	-20	-330	10
B Interest	17918	6924	4206	3720	3068	18496	7546	4350	3500	3100
C Dividends	11332	10870	413	49	-	7764	7284	430	50	-
D Net land rent and royalties	263	263	...	...	-	219	219	...	...	-
3 Taxes, fees and contributions	890971	445337	80865	116138	248631	928701	454559	87110	121764	265268
A Indirect taxes	325823	229040	34666	62117	...	338559	236118	37781	64660	...
B Direct taxes	297765	205087	42162	50516	...	304938	206606	44989	53343	...
Income	239653	148958	40951	49744	...	242883	152081	43174	47628	...
Other	58112	56129	1211	772	...	62055	54525	1815	5715	...
C Social security contributions	262307	7888	3304	2486	248629	279759	8297	3535	2661	265266
D Fees, fines and penalties	5076	3322	733	1019	2	5445	3538	805	1100	2
4 Other current transfers	54314	40072	70070	29982	67835	57482	41084	73557	31092	79605
A Casualty insurance claims	420	270	75	75	...	424	272	76	76	...
B Transfers from other government subsectors	...	12357	56732	19278	65278	...	11701	59455	19800	76900
C Transfers from the rest of the world	728	229	4	...	495	737	213	4	...	520
D Other transfers, except imputed	...	...	...	...	...	...	...	...	...	...
E Imputed unfunded employee pension and welfare contributions	53166	27216	13259	10629	2062	56321	28898	14022	11216	2185
Total Current Receipts b	991018	519008	155625	150009	320021	1028955	526227	165601	156500	348483

Disbursements

1 Government final consumption expenditure	377059	130063	85883	75398	85715	405598	138850	93461	83441	89846
2 Property income	87928	78727	3438	5346	417	93023	83973	3380	5270	400
A Interest	87928	78727	3438	5346	417	93023	83973	3380	5270	400
B Net land rent and royalties	...	...	...	...	...	...	...	...	...	...
3 Subsidies	61156	44645	6027	2644	7840	63511	49361	4250	2800	7100

Austria

3.12 General Government Income and Outlay Account: Total and Subsectors
(Continued)

Million Austrian schillings

	1992					1993				
	Total General Government	Central Government	State or Provincial Government	Local Government	Social Security Funds	Total General Government	Central Government	State or Provincial Government	Local Government	Social Security Funds
4 Other current transfers	423989	266708	44824	35328	231526	462413	298322	48095	37821	247467
A Casualty insurance premiums, net	420	270	75	75	...	424	272	76	76	...
B Transfers to other government subsectors	...	125422	7055	10739	11181	...	139996	7110	11384	10802
C Social security benefits cd	212291	...	...	...	212291	227906	...	...	...	227906
D Social assistance grants e	117278	86885	21085	9308	...	133239	99639	23300	10300	...
E Unfunded employee pension and welfare benefits	86000	52006	16563	15206	2225	91717	55740	17557	16061	2359
F Transfers to private non-profit institutions serving households d	...	...	...	...	...	...	...	...	...	...
G Other transfers n.e.c.	...	...	...	...	...	...	...	...	...	...
H Transfers to the rest of the world	8000	2125	46	1	5829	9127	2675	52	-	6400
Net saving	40886	-1135	15453	31293	-5477	4410	-44279	16415	27168	3670
Total Current Disbursements and Net Saving b	991018	519008	155625	150009	320021	1028955	526227	165601	156500	348483

a) The item 'Property and entrepreneurial income' is greater than the sum of its sub-items. The difference being the unspecified items.
b) Column 'State or Provincial Government' includes chambers.
c) Item 'Social security benefits' includes social security funds only.
d) Item 'Transfers to private non-profit institutions serving households' is included in item 'Social assistance grants'.
e) Item 'Social assistance grants' includes unemployment benefits.

3.13 General Government Capital Accumulation Account: Total and Subsectors

Million Austrian schillings

	1980					1985				
	Total General Government	Central Government	State or Provincial Government	Local Government	Social Security Funds	Total General Government	Central Government	State or Provincial Government	Local Government	Social Security Funds
Finance of Gross Accumulation										
1 Gross saving	43626	2665	18947	20802	1822	43550	-7764	24034	25974	-189
A Consumption of fixed capital	7481	1698	1152	4362	269	10690	2423	1646	6229	392
B Net saving	36145	967	17795	16440	1553	32860	-10187	22388	19745	-581
2 Capital transfers a	-16465	-13971	-4191	1945	11	-27106	-23984	-5400	2009	-3
A From other government subsectors	...	-2329	-747	3327	8	...	-5004	146	4587	-1
B From other resident sectors	-16411	-11592	-3442	-1380	3	-27091	-18965	-5546	-2578	-2
C From rest of the world	-54	-50	-2	-2	-	-15	-15	-	-	-
Finance of Gross Accumulation b	27161	-11306	14756	22747	1833	16444	-31748	18634	27983	-192
Gross Accumulation										
1 Gross capital formation	41568	13397	5220	21323	1628	48004	16920	6321	23802	961
A Increase in stocks	...	...	...	...	...	...	...	...	...	...
B Gross fixed capital formation	41568	13397	5220	21323	1628	48004	16920	6321	23802	961
2 Purchases of land, net	2565	1275	313	977	-	1782	913	273	374	222
3 Purchases of intangible assets, net	...	...	...	...	...	...	...	...	...	...
4 Capital transfers a	...	...	...	...	...	...	...	...	...	...
Net lending	-16972	-25978	9223	447	205	-33342	-49581	12040	3807	-1375
Gross Accumulation b	27161	-11306	14756	22747	1833	16444	-31748	18634	27983	-192

	1990					1991				
	Total General Government	Central Government	State or Provincial Government	Local Government	Social Security Funds	Total General Government	Central Government	State or Provincial Government	Local Government	Social Security Funds
Finance of Gross Accumulation										
1 Gross saving	46243	-1276	16545	32430	-2596	42799	-12699	19792	32762	-1454
A Consumption of fixed capital	12770	2895	1966	7441	468	13502	3061	2078	7868	495
B Net saving	33473	-4171	14579	24989	-3064	29297	-15760	17714	24894	-1949
2 Capital transfers a	-26993	-38123	5659	6371	21	-26423	-38382	6026	6477	21
A From other government subsectors	...	-23271	12721	11450	21	...	-26345	14081	12807	22
B From other resident sectors	-26872	-14738	-7059	-5075	-1	-26172	-11837	-8008	-6326	-1
C From rest of the world	-121	-114	-3	-4	-	-251	-200	-47	-4	-
Finance of Gross Accumulation b	19250	-39399	22204	38801	-2575	16376	-51081	25818	39239	-1433
Gross Accumulation										
1 Gross capital formation	57293	16390	7594	32517	792	63043	16686	8307	36931	1119

Austria

3.13 General Government Capital Accumulation Account: Total and Subsectors
(Continued)

Million Austrian schillings

	1990					1991				
	Total General Government	Central Government	State or Provincial Government	Local Government	Social Security Funds	Total General Government	Central Government	State or Provincial Government	Local Government	Social Security Funds
A Increase in stocks	...	...	...	...	...	...	...	...	...	...
B Gross fixed capital formation	57293	16390	7594	32517	792	63043	16686	8307	36931	1119
2 Purchases of land, net	686	-358	288	701	55	515	108	343	112	-48
3 Purchases of intangible assets, net	...	...	...	...	...	...	...	...	...	...
4 Capital transfers a	...	...	...	...	...	...	...	...	...	...
Net lending	-38729	-55431	14322	5583	-3422	-47182	-67875	17168	2196	-2504
Gross Accumulation b	19250	-39399	22204	38801	-2575	16376	-51081	25818	39239	-1433

	1992					1993				
	Total General Government	Central Government	State or Provincial Government	Local Government	Social Security Funds	Total General Government	Central Government	State or Provincial Government	Local Government	Social Security Funds

Finance of Gross Accumulation

1 Gross saving	54695	1995	17579	39340	-4971	18878	-40999	18642	35599	4200
A Consumption of fixed capital	13809	3130	2126	8047	506	14468	3280	2227	8431	530
B Net saving	40886	-1135	15453	31293	-5477	4410	-44279	16415	27168	3670
2 Capital transfers a	-28975	-41537	7138	7234	40	-37208	-46068	6961	2921	40
A From other government subsectors	...	-28292	15745	14357	40	...	-29763	16585	14200	40
B From other resident sectors	-28729	-13027	-8601	-7101	-	-36804	-15931	-9614	-11259	-
C From rest of the world	-246	-218	-6	-22	-	-404	-374	-10	-20	-
Finance of Gross Accumulation b	25720	-39542	24717	46574	-4931	-18330	-87067	25603	38520	4240

Gross Accumulation

1 Gross capital formation	67334	15843	9524	40790	1177	65946	15727	10335	38884	1000
A Increase in stocks	...	...	...	...	...	...	...	...	...	...
B Gross fixed capital formation	67334	15843	9524	40790	1177	65946	15727	10335	38884	1000
2 Purchases of land, net	-27	-669	-686	1303	25	3098	108	650	2320	20
3 Purchases of intangible assets, net	...	...	...	...	...	...	...	...	...	...
4 Capital transfers a	...	...	...	...	...	...	...	...	...	...
Net lending	-41587	-54716	15879	4481	-6133	-87374	-102902	14618	-2684	3220
Gross Accumulation b	25720	-39542	24717	46574	-4931	-18330	-87067	25603	38520	4240

a) Capital transfers received are recorded net of capital transfers paid.
b) Column 'State or Provincial Government' includes chambers.

3.32 Household and Private Unincorporated Enterprise Income and Outlay Account

Million Austrian schillings

	1980	1983	1984	1985	1986	1987	1988	1989	1990	1991	1992	1993

Receipts

1 Compensation of employees	545631	642438	676330	717091	761254	792734	821941	874476	940062	1020817	1095653	1142371
A Wages and salaries	453666	528322	552393	584807	622320	647949	669524	712486	766839	833714	893723	928540
B Employers' contributions for social security	91965	114116	123937	132284	138934	144785	152417	161990	173223	187103	201930	213831
C Employers' contributions for private pension & welfare plans	...	...	...	...	...	...	...	...	...	...	...	...
2 Operating surplus of private unincorporated enterprises	...	...	...	...	...	...	...	...	...	...	...	...
3 Property and entrepreneurial income	152198	201679	219348	237244	254857	266828	292623	312605	356136	379635	398872	385137
3 Current transfers	215287	274138	292498	314506	333585	360669	371692	388205	414124	447252	478422	519547
A Casualty insurance claims	13672	19750	21263	24269	26142	31682	33808	35353	34217	38186	42471	45688
B Social security benefits a	94500	121479	130792	142344	151079	161466	167759	176423	188672	199860	212291	227906
C Social assistance grants b	56161	69913	72285	76271	80443	87039	85223	86354	94142	103715	117278	133239
D Unfunded employee pension and welfare benefits	38604	49166	52273	56169	59909	63406	66026	70137	74454	80827	86000	91717
E Transfers from general government	...	...	...	...	...	...	...	...	...	...	...	...
F Transfers from the rest of the world	12350	13830	15885	15453	16012	17076	18876	19938	22639	24664	20382	20997
G Other transfers n.e.c.	...	...	...	...	...	...	...	...	...	...	...	...
Total Current Receipts	913116	1118255	1188176	1268841	1349696	1420231	1486256	1575286	1710322	1847704	1972947	2047055

Disbursements

1 Final consumption expenditures	552532	694839	733182	775529	804407	837778	880527	935287	999181	1064037	1127091	1168262

Austria

3.32 Household and Private Unincorporated Enterprise Income and Outlay Account
(Continued)

Million Austrian schillings

	1980	1983	1984	1985	1986	1987	1988	1989	1990	1991	1992	1993
A Market purchases	512693	640234	672184	707360	729260	759061	801419	848911	907528	966776	1022528	1055642
B Gross rents of owner-occupied housing	32997	47423	53528	60784	67795	71227	72140	79266	84387	90193	97887	106231
C Consumption from own-account production	6842	7182	7470	7385	7352	7490	6968	7110	7266	7068	6676	6389
2 Property income	11620	14007	13934	14229	15729	17274	19174	22735	30213	38826	42816	43333
A Interest	11620	14007	13934	14229	15729	17274	19174	22735	30213	38826	42816	43333
Consumer debt	11620	14007	13934	14229	15729	17274	19174	22735	30213	38826	42816	43333
Mortgage	...	...	...	...	...	...	...	...	...	...	...	...
Other	...	...	...	...	...	...	...	...	...	...	...	...
B Net land rent and royalties	...	...	...	...	...	...	...	...	...	...	...	...
3 Direct taxes and other current transfers n.e.c. to government	238201	285715	310707	339458	357440	364439	382306	387440	426571	468316	514314	540122
A Social security contributions	124578	145462	155463	167804	175993	183339	191817	204269	220619	238882	262307	279759
B Direct taxes	110738	136507	151144	167833	177591	177166	186394	178750	201044	224344	246931	254918
Income taxes	110738	136507	151144	167833	177591	177166	186394	178750	201044	224344	246931	254918
Other	...	...	...	...	...	...	...	...	...	...	...	...
C Fees, fines and penalties	2885	3746	4100	3821	3856	3934	4095	4421	4908	5090	5076	5445
4 Other current transfers	46408	60537	64446	69821	74033	82176	89223	92880	94073	104166	127291	140087
A Net casualty insurance premiums	13672	19750	21263	24269	26142	31682	33808	35353	34217	38186	42471	45688
B Transfers to private non-profit institutions serving households	...	...	...	...	...	...	...	...	...	...	...	...
C Transfers to the rest of the world	9069	9893	10348	10301	10304	10938	14304	14108	13867	16163	31654	38078
D Other current transfers, except imputed	...	...	...	...	...	...	...	...	...	...	...	...
E Imputed employee pension and welfare contributions	23667	30894	32835	35251	37587	39556	41111	43419	45989	49817	53166	56321
Net saving	64355	63157	65907	69804	98087	118564	115026	136944	160284	172359	161435	155251
Total Current Disbursements and Net Saving	913116	1118255	1188176	1268841	1349696	1420231	1486256	1575286	1710322	1847704	1972947	2047055

a) Item 'Social security benefits' includes social security funds only.
b) Item 'Social assistance grants' includes unemployment benefits.

3.51 External Transactions: Current Account: Detail

Million Austrian schillings

	1980	1983	1984	1985	1986	1987	1988	1989	1990	1991	1992	1993
Payments to the Rest of the World												
1 Imports of goods and services [a]	385659	433928	495715	546807	509796	519829	578645	649418	701962	752994	776780	779378
A Imports of merchandise c.i.f. [a]	313265	345306	389180	427125	404383	408411	444802	508894	550863	585907	588666	562239
B Other	72394	88622	106535	119682	105413	111418	133843	140524	151099	167087	188114	217139
2 Factor income to the rest of the world	41200	56013	66918	73556	70414	70266	80328	105109	117760	131349	112732	116868
A Compensation of employees [b]	-	-	-	-	-	-	-	-	-	-	2256	2359
B Property and entrepreneurial income	41200	56013	66918	73556	70414	70266	80328	105109	117760	131349	110476	114509
By general government [c]	4385	6907	7761	7437	7348	7423	6898	8489	8779	10189	10315	12096
By corporate and quasi-cororate enterprises	...	...	...	...	...	...	...	...	...	...	...	...
By other	...	...	...	...	...	...	...	...	...	...	...	...
3 Current transfers to the rest of the world [b]	11607	13100	13813	13895	14131	14794	18601	18857	19341	22633	39654	47205
A Indirect taxes by general government to supranational organizations	...	...	...	...	...	...	...	...	...	...	...	...
B Other current transfers	11607	13100	13813	13895	14131	14794	18601	18857	19341	22633	39654	47205
By general government	2538	3207	3465	3594	3827	3856	4297	4749	5474	6470	8000	9127
By other resident sectors	9069	9893	10348	10301	10304	10938	14304	14108	13867	16163	31654	38078
4 Surplus of the nation on current transactions	-26428	8309	-3936	-2493	3750	-2733	-3906	2184	13164	820	-1628	-10610
Payments to the Rest of the World, and Surplus of the Nation on Current Transfers	412038	511350	572510	631765	598091	602156	673668	775568	852227	907796	927538	932841
Receipts From The Rest of the World												
1 Exports of goods and services [a]	366244	449686	497645	549126	522970	527054	587545	664267	724313	770412	803356	803368

Austria

3.51 External Transactions: Current Account: Detail
(Continued)

Million Austrian schillings

	1980	1983	1984	1985	1986	1987	1988	1989	1990	1991	1992	1993
A Exports of merchandise f.o.b. [a]	225782	274553	312396	359455	342152	342714	374434	427167	466919	479309	486038	467406
B Other	140462	175133	185249	189671	180818	184340	213111	237100	257394	291103	317318	335962
2 Factor income from the rest of the world	32847	47204	58367	66487	58448	57361	66629	90727	104596	111833	103072	107739
A Compensation of employees [b]	-	-	-	-	-	-	-	-	-	-	8938	8732
B Property and entrepreneurial income	32847	47204	58367	66487	58448	57361	66629	90727	104596	111833	94134	99007
3 Current transfers from the rest of the world [b]	12947	14460	16498	16152	16673	17741	19494	20574	23318	25551	21110	21734
A Subsidies to general government from supranational organizations	...	...	...	...	...	...	...	...	...	...	...	...
B Other current transfers	12947	14460	16498	16152	16673	17741	19494	20574	23318	25551	21110	21734
To general government	597	630	613	699	661	665	618	636	679	887	728	737
To other resident sectors	12350	13830	15885	15453	16012	17076	18876	19938	22639	24664	20382	20997
Receipts from the Rest of the World on Current Transfers	412038	511350	572510	631765	598091	602156	673668	775568	852227	907796	927538	932841

a) The estimates on transit trade are on a net basis.
b) Item 'Compensation of employees' is included in current transfers to/from the rest of the world.
c) Only central government data are included in the general government estimates.

4.1 Derivation of Value Added by Kind of Activity, in Current Prices

Million Austrian schillings

	1980 Gross Output	1980 Intermediate Consumption	1980 Value Added	1985 Gross Output	1985 Intermediate Consumption	1985 Value Added	1990 Gross Output	1990 Intermediate Consumption	1990 Value Added	1991 Gross Output	1991 Intermediate Consumption	1991 Value Added
					All Producers							
1 Agriculture, hunting, forestry and fishing	66230	21938	44292	70817	25824	44993	82170	25491	56679	78475	25483	52992
2 Mining and quarrying	10749	5883	4866	13158	7284	5874	11203	5576	5627	12758	5499	7259
3 Manufacturing	783808	507137	276671	1012450	649647	362803	1217412	753690	463722	1273460	784657	488803
A Manufacture of food, beverages and tobacco	135834	94154	41680	173993	120819	53174	190135	128434	61701	199681	133629	66052
B Textile, wearing apparel and leather industries	60787	37191	23596	71191	44701	26490	73881	46213	27668	72878	45544	27334
C Manufacture of wood and wood products, including furniture	57283	36515	20768	61936	37995	23941	86983	52959	34024	87968	52700	35268
D Manufacture of paper and paper products, printing and publishing	45770	27218	18552	68729	43540	25189	92312	57786	34526	96029	59696	36333
E Manufacture of chemicals and chemical petroleum, coal, rubber and plastic products [a]	139091	100524	38567	180974	129756	51218	188957	120177	68780	198158	122055	76103
F Manufacture of non-metallic mineral products, except products of petroleum and coal	36556	20686	15870	47418	26359	21059	59241	32264	26977	61653	33625	28028
G Basic metal industries	64367	42592	21775	81437	53572	27865	84339	55278	29061	78913	52285	26628
H Manufacture of fabricated metal products, machinery and equipment	244120	148260	95860	326772	192909	133863	441564	260578	180986	478180	285120	193060
I Other manufacturing industries	...	...	...	...	...	...	...	...	...	...	...	...
4 Electricity, gas and water	68624	37951	30673	99041	59189	39852	108873	59838	49035	117728	64908	52820
A Electricity, gas and steam	66415	37209	29206	96119	58256	37863	104840	58440	46400	113403	63416	49987
B Water works and supply	2209	742	1467	2922	933	1989	4033	1398	2635	4325	1492	2833
5 Construction	149217	68010	81207	169626	80566	89060	238307	114037	124270	263259	123216	140043
6 Wholesale and retail trade, restaurants and hotels	247261	80511	166750	334116	119053	215063	453666	153521	300145	478944	159075	319869
A Wholesale and retail trade	184082	50152	133930	251213	81218	169995	344305	107164	237141	360948	109702	251246
B Restaurants and hotels	63179	30359	32820	82903	37835	45068	109361	46357	63004	117996	49373	68623
7 Transport, storage and communication	115991	58161	57830	156760	78338	78422	246212	133799	112413	264950	143174	121776
A Transport and storage	91843	55103	36740	121193	73456	47737	198361	128598	69763	214347	137948	76399
B Communication	24148	3058	21090	35567	4882	30685	47851	5201	42650	50603	5226	45377
8 Finance, insurance, real estate and business services	164748	45686	119062	271724	67331	204393	411608	107261	304347	449458	118846	330612
A Financial institutions	52008	9021	42987	76795	13582	63213	120884	27314	93570	130495	29970	100525

Austria

4.1 Derivation of Value Added by Kind of Activity, in Current Prices
(Continued)

Million Austrian schillings

	1980 Gross Output	1980 Intermediate Consumption	1980 Value Added	1985 Gross Output	1985 Intermediate Consumption	1985 Value Added	1990 Gross Output	1990 Intermediate Consumption	1990 Value Added	1991 Gross Output	1991 Intermediate Consumption	1991 Value Added
B Insurance	17520	4533	12987	28145	7708	20437	38659	10727	27932	40421	11548	28873
C Real estate and business services	95220	32132	63088	166784	46041	120743	252065	69220	182845	278542	77328	201214
Real estate, except dwellings	64675	23322	41353	117208	30812	86396	161212	43576	117636	174060	48921	125139
Dwellings												
9 Community, social and personal services	48397	16172	32225	69619	22838	46781	106521	32972	73549	116273	36719	79554
A Sanitary and similar services bc	...	...	...	...	...	...	...	...	...	...	...	...
B Social and related community services c	23376	6201	17175	33036	8750	24286	45303	12106	33197	49665	13363	36302
Educational services d	...	...	...	...	...	...	...	...	...	...	...	...
Medical, dental, other health and veterinary services c	23376	6201	17175	33036	8750	24286	45303	12106	33197	49665	13363	36302
C Recreational and cultural services dc	13773	6063	7710	20327	8636	11691	39340	14366	24974	43020	16548	26472
D Personal and household services bc	11248	3908	7340	16256	5452	10804	21878	6500	15378	23588	6808	16780
Total, Industries	1655025	841449	813576	2197311	1110070	1087241	2875972	1386185	1489787	3055305	1461577	1593728
Producers of Government Services	213566	84486	129080	305812	120745	185067	388225	153369	234856	422387	166240	256147
Other Producers b	8282	1113	7169	12422	2191	10231	15244	2715	12529	16459	3028	13431
Total	1876873	927048	949825	2515545	1233006	1282539	3279441	1542269	1737172	3494151	1630845	1863306
Less: Imputed bank service charge	...	-45118	45118	...	-68556	68556	...	-104714	104714	...	-114567	114567
Import duties	5745	...	5745	9077	...	9077	12026	...	12026	12642	...	12642
Value added tax	84252	...	84252	125365	...	125365	156825	...	156825	166933	...	166933
Other adjustments	...	...	-10	...	...	-20	...	...	...	...	...	...
Total	1966870	972166	994704	2649987	1301562	1348425	3448292	1646983	1801309	3673726	1745412	1928314

	1992 Gross Output	1992 Intermediate Consumption	1992 Value Added	1993 Gross Output	1993 Intermediate Consumption	1993 Value Added
	All Producers					
1 Agriculture, hunting, forestry and fishing	76049	25969	50080	73685	25290	48395
2 Mining and quarrying	10604	5205	5399	9580	4849	4731
3 Manufacturing	1279141	777564	501577	1238407	742964	495443
A Manufacture of food, beverages and tobacco	204638	133539	71099	205257	133205	72052
B Textile, wearing apparel and leather industries	71835	43904	27931	63670	39550	24120
C Manufacture of wood and wood products, including furniture	94162	55286	38876	92098	51306	40792
D Manufacture of paper and paper products, printing and publishing	94699	58941	35758	88532	53500	35032
E Manufacture of chemicals and chemical petroleum, coal, rubber and plastic products a	193487	115277	78210	187047	108953	78094
F Manufacture of non-metallic mineral products, except products of petroleum and coal	65368	34954	30414	65035	35025	30010
G Basic metal industries	75406	51100	24306	69636	45514	24122
H Manufacture of fabricated metal products, machinery and equipment	479546	284562	194984	467132	275911	191221
I Other manufacturing industries	...	...	...	...	...	...
4 Electricity, gas and water	121509	64465	57044	126315	66217	60098
A Electricity, gas and steam	116823	62909	53914	121064	64616	56448
B Water works and supply	4686	1556	3130	5251	1601	3650
5 Construction	286036	132708	153328	301114	139320	161794
6 Wholesale and retail trade, restaurants and hotels	503940	161735	342205	507629	161835	345794
A Wholesale and retail trade	377865	108498	269367	378319	107916	270403
B Restaurants and hotels	126075	53237	72838	129310	53919	75391
7 Transport, storage and communication	285405	154784	130621	297374	162964	134410
A Transport and storage	231699	149149	82550	239930	156194	83736

Austria

4.1 Derivation of Value Added by Kind of Activity, in Current Prices
(Continued)

Million Austrian schillings

	1992 Gross Output	1992 Intermediate Consumption	1992 Value Added	1993 Gross Output	1993 Intermediate Consumption	1993 Value Added
B Communication	53706	5635	48071	57444	6770	50674
8 Finance, insurance, real estate and business services	489519	123255	366264	534066	132850	401216
A Financial institutions	138313	29665	108648	153107	32658	120449
B Insurance	45191	12185	33006	50387	13243	37144
C Real estate and business services	306015	81405	224611	330572	86949	243623
Real estate, except dwellings	189245	51198	138047	201859	53462	148397
Dwellings						
9 Community, social and personal services	128951	39351	89600	139135	43111	96024
A Sanitary and similar services [bc]	...	...	...	...	...	...
B Social and related community services [c]	55781	15298	40483	61631	16957	44674
Educational services [d]	...	...	...	...	...	...
Medical, dental, other health and veterinary services [c]	55781	15298	40483	61631	16957	44674
C Recreational and cultural services [dc]	46916	16658	30258	49072	18372	30700
D Personal and household services [bc]	26254	7395	18859	28432	7782	20650
Total, Industries	3181154	1485036	1696118	3227305	1479400	1747905
Producers of Government Services	456669	180937	275732	492375	195741	296634
Other Producers [b]	17548	3079	14469	18684	3226	15458
Total	3655371	1669052	1986319	3738364	1678367	2059997
Less: Imputed bank service charge	...	-124514	124514	...	-136849	136849
Import duties	13269	...	13269	13122	...	13122
Value added tax	171006	...	171006	181571	...	181571
Other adjustments	...	...	...	...	...	...
Total	3839646	1793566	2046080	3933057	1815216	2117841

a) Item 'Crude petroleum and natural gas production' is included in item 'Manufacture of chemicals and chemical petroleum, coal, rubber and plastic products.'
b) Item 'Sanitary and similar services' is included in item 'Personal and household services' which excludes domestic services and caretakers that are included in item 'Other producers'.
c) Non-governmental only.
d) Item 'Educational services' is included in item 'Recreational and cultural services'.

4.2 Derivation of Value Added by Kind of Activity, in Constant Prices

Million Austrian schillings

	1980 Gross Output	1980 Intermediate Consumption	1980 Value Added	1985 Gross Output	1985 Intermediate Consumption	1985 Value Added	1990 Gross Output	1990 Intermediate Consumption	1990 Value Added	1991 Gross Output	1991 Intermediate Consumption	1991 Value Added
At constant prices of: 1983												
All Producers												
1 Agriculture, hunting, forestry and fishing	67995	26036	41959	69350	25151	44199	73655	25564	48091	70019	25124	44895
2 Mining and quarrying	12491	6842	5649	11719	6704	5015	9501	4930	4571	11211	4670	6541
3 Manufacturing	899390	578805	320585	956268	611451	344817	1106059	700420	405639	1139399	723598	415801
A Manufacture of food, beverages and tobacco	154700	107901	46799	165311	111519	53792	177255	115769	61486	182130	118390	63740

Austria

4.2 Derivation of Value Added by Kind of Activity, in Constant Prices
(Continued)

Million Austrian schillings

At constant prices of: 1983

	1980 Gross Output	1980 Intermediate Consumption	1980 Value Added	1985 Gross Output	1985 Intermediate Consumption	1985 Value Added	1990 Gross Output	1990 Intermediate Consumption	1990 Value Added	1991 Gross Output	1991 Intermediate Consumption	1991 Value Added
B Textile, wearing apparel and leather industries	70579	43121	27458	67199	40934	26265	65020	41296	23724	63783	40931	22852
C Manufacture of wood and wood products, including furniture	59822	36820	23002	59654	35931	23723	75401	45477	29924	76243	44530	31713
D Manufacture of paper and paper products, printing and publishing	51915	31543	20372	64939	40966	23973	85689	52875	32814	87741	53765	33976
E Manufacture of chemicals and chemical petroleum, coal, rubber and plastic products [a]	171831	119864	51967	173057	123291	49766	204366	141535	62831	211556	145577	65979
F Manufacture of non-metallic mineral products, except products of petroleum and coal	42225	24259	17966	44156	24749	19407	51554	29027	22527	51514	29044	22470
G Basic metal industries	71142	48186	22956	74272	50384	23888	80989	49105	31884	79799	48591	31208
H Manufacture of fabricated metal products, machinery and equipment	277176	167109	110067	307680	183678	124002	365785	225339	140446	386633	242772	143861
I Other manufacturing industries	...	...	...	...	...	...	...	...	...	...	...	...
4 Electricity, gas and water	86865	48203	38662	97245	55813	41432	112027	64689	47338	119117	70039	49078
A Electricity, gas and steam	84147	47396	36751	94402	54967	39435	108828	63507	45321	115880	68841	47039
B Water works and supply	2718	807	1911	2843	846	1997	3199	1182	2017	3237	1198	2039
5 Construction	177376	79233	98143	163321	76526	86795	196326	97213	99113	206774	101793	104981
6 Wholesale and retail trade, restaurants and hotels	281560	92152	189408	307515	100568	206947	399338	148299	251039	410741	152559	258182
A Wholesale and retail trade	208291	58171	150120	231289	64801	166488	315094	108210	206884	323759	111274	212485
B Restaurants and hotels	73269	33981	39288	76226	35767	40459	84244	40089	44155	86982	41285	45697
7 Transport, storage and communication	130501	65422	65079	147879	73101	74778	208536	116147	92389	220756	122214	98542
A Transport and storage	103817	61995	41822	114544	68505	46039	168360	111083	57277	178265	117169	61096
B Communication	26684	3427	23257	33335	4596	28739	40176	5064	35112	42491	5045	37446
8 Finance, insurance, real estate and business services	206866	55216	151650	240586	64639	175947	284009	78111	205898	296243	82451	213792
A Financial institutions	59762	10887	48875	71971	13101	58870	88503	16607	71896	94035	17588	76447
B Insurance	19864	5054	14810	24589	6253	18336	26156	6785	19371	25828	7096	18732
C Real estate and business services	127240	39275	87965	144026	45285	98741	169350	54719	114631	176380	57767	118613
Real estate, except dwellings	88269	27405	60864	101135	32167	68968	115351	37786	77565	118919	39778	79141
Dwellings												
9 Community, social and personal services	58629	20041	38588	63370	20681	42689	81522	25927	55595	84650	26580	58070
A Sanitary and similar services [bc]	...	...	...	...	...	...	...	...	...	...	...	...
B Social and related community services [c]	27838	7603	20235	30656	8027	22629	35158	8954	26204	36341	9191	27150
Educational services [d]	...	...	...	...	...	...	...	...	...	...	...	...
Medical, dental, other health and veterinary services [c]	27838	7603	20235	30656	8027	22629	35158	8954	26204	36341	9191	27150
C Recreational and cultural services [dc]	16830	7696	9134	18213	7790	10423	29925	11773	18152	31220	12065	19155
D Personal and household services [bc]	13961	4742	9219	14501	4864	9637	16439	5200	11239	17089	5324	11765
Total, Industries	1921673	971950	949723	2057253	1034634	1022619	2470973	1261299	1209673	2558910	1309028	1249882
Producers of Government Services	254781	100115	154666	277599	108475	169124	294611	115599	179012	302675	119316	183359
Other Producers [b]	10927	1871	9056	11269	1963	9306	11604	2045	9559	11800	2079	9721
Total	2187381	1073936	1113445	2346121	1145072	1201049	2777188	1378943	1398244	2873385	1430423	1442962
Less: Imputed bank service charge	...	-51801	51801	...	-63984	63984	...	-80477	80477	...	-85919	85919
Import duties	7877	...	7877	8411	...	8411	11239	...	11239	11257	...	11257
Value added tax	99142	...	99142	102066	...	102066	116321	...	116321	119581	...	119581
Other adjustments	...	...	-10	...	...	-10	...	...	...	...	...	...
Total	2294400	1125737	1168663	2456598	1209056	1247542	2904748	1459420	1445327	3004223	1516342	1487881

Austria

4.2 Derivation of Value Added by Kind of Activity, in Constant Prices

Million Austrian schillings

		1992			1993		
		Gross Output	Intermediate Consumption	Value Added	Gross Output	Intermediate Consumption	Value Added

At constant prices of: 1983

All Producers

		Gross Output 1992	Intermediate Consumption 1992	Value Added 1992	Gross Output 1993	Intermediate Consumption 1993	Value Added 1993
1	Agriculture, hunting, forestry and fishing	68844	25278	43566	69007	24786	44221
2	Mining and quarrying	9470	4336	5134	8496	3966	4530
3	Manufacturing	1135543	718971	416572	1100984	698893	402091
	A Manufacture of food, beverages and tobacco	182800	117133	65667	180781	116462	64319
	B Textile, wearing apparel and leather industries	61967	39195	22772	56018	35738	20280
	C Manufacture of wood and wood products, including furniture	79824	46497	33327	79002	46120	32882
	D Manufacture of paper and paper products, printing and publishing	87323	55014	32309	83801	52513	31288
	E Manufacture of chemicals and chemical petroleum, coal, rubber and plastic products [a]	208146	143007	65139	204320	140479	63841
	F Manufacture of non-metallic mineral products, except products of petroleum and coal	53376	29759	23617	52533	29557	22976
	G Basic metal industries	79816	49872	29944	74894	46049	28845
	H Manufacture of fabricated metal products, machinery and equipment	382291	238494	143797	369635	231974	137661
	I Other manufacturing industries	...	...	...	...	...	...
4	Electricity, gas and water	116621	66802	49819	118982	68028	50954
	A Electricity, gas and steam	113302	65592	47710	115703	66830	48873
	B Water works and supply	3319	1210	2109	3279	1198	2081
5	Construction	216611	106000	110611	221585	108657	112928
6	Wholesale and retail trade, restaurants and hotels	415813	153915	261898	411940	152673	259267
	A Wholesale and retail trade	327421	111977	215444	326299	111910	214389
	B Restaurants and hotels	88392	41938	46454	85641	40763	44878
7	Transport, storage and communication	232780	129938	102842	237027	132123	104904
	A Transport and storage	188614	124500	64114	189446	125581	63865
	B Communication	44166	5438	38728	47581	6542	41039
8	Finance, insurance, real estate and business services	304270	81894	222376	310208	83315	226893
	A Financial institutions	95086	16506	78580	95612	17613	77999
	B Insurance	27109	7143	19966	28596	7485	21111
	C Real estate and business services	182075	58245	123831	186000	58217	127783
	Real estate, except dwellings	121441	39277	82164	123012	38403	84609
	Dwellings						
9	Community, social and personal services	85645	26843	58802	87910	27398	60512
	A Sanitary and similar services [bc]	...	...	...	...	...	...
	B Social and related community services [c]	36666	9345	27321	38494	9741	28753
	Educational services [d]	...	...	...	...	...	...
	Medical, dental, other health and veterinary services [c]	36666	9345	27321	38494	9741	28753
	C Recreational and cultural services [dc]	31616	12157	19459	31479	12161	19318
	D Personal and household services [bc]	17363	5341	12022	17937	5496	12441
	Total, Industries	2585597	1313977	1271620	2566139	1299839	1266300
	Producers of Government Services	309428	121342	188086	319196	125135	194061

Austria

4.2 Derivation of Value Added by Kind of Activity, in Constant Prices
(Continued)

Million Austrian schillings

	1992 Gross Output	1992 Intermediate Consumption	1992 Value Added	1993 Gross Output	1993 Intermediate Consumption	1993 Value Added
	At constant prices of: 1983					
Other Producers b	11941	2106	9835	12111	2156	9955
Total	2906966	1437425	1469541	2897446	1427130	1470316
Less: Imputed bank service charge	...	-87590	87590	...	-89371	89371
Import duties	11094	...	11094	10972	...	10972
Value added tax	122356	...	122356	122578	...	122578
Other adjustments	...	...	...	...	...	...
Total	3040416	1525015	1515401	3030996	1516501	1514495

a) Item 'Crude petroleum and natural gas production' is included in item 'Manufacture of chemicals and chemical petroleum, coal, rubber and plastic products.'
b) Item 'Sanitary and similar services' is included in item 'Personal and household services' which excludes domestic services and caretakers that are included in item 'Other producers'.
c) Non-governmental only.
d) Item 'Educational services' is included in item 'Recreational and cultural services'.

4.3 Cost Components of Value Added

Million Austrian schillings

	1980 Compensation of Employees	1980 Capital Consumption	1980 Net Operating Surplus	1980 Indirect Taxes	1980 Less: Subsidies Received	1980 Value Added	1985 Compensation of Employees	1985 Capital Consumption	1985 Net Operating Surplus	1985 Indirect Taxes	1985 Less: Subsidies Received	1985 Value Added
	All Producers											
1 Agriculture, hunting, forestry and fishing	...	12172	...	611	1381	44292	...	15046	...	561	1949	44993
2 Mining and quarrying	...	499	...	401	364	4866	...	646	...	420	275	5874
3 Manufacturing	...	28928	...	29996	12448	276671	...	41837	...	37260	15231	362803
A Manufacture of food, beverages and tobacco	...	...	...	...	...	41680	...	...	...	...	...	53174
B Textile, wearing apparel and leather industries	...	...	...	...	...	23596	...	...	...	...	...	26490
C Manufacture of wood and wood products, including furniture	...	...	...	...	...	20768	...	...	...	...	...	23941
D Manufacture of paper and paper products, printing and publishing	...	...	...	...	...	18552	...	...	...	...	...	25189
E Manufacture of chemicals and chemical petroleum, coal, rubber and plastic products a	...	...	...	...	...	38567	...	...	...	...	...	51218
F Manufacture of non-metallic mineral products, except products of petroleum and coal	...	...	...	...	...	15870	...	...	...	...	...	21059
G Basic metal industries	...	...	...	...	...	21775	...	...	...	...	...	27865
H Manufacture of fabricated metal products, machinery and equipment	...	...	...	...	...	95860	...	...	...	...	...	133863
I Other manufacturing industries	...	...	...	...	...	...	...	...	...	...	...	...
4 Electricity, gas and water	...	8162	...	924	667	30673	...	12049	...	1057	835	39852
A Electricity, gas and steam	...	...	...	...	...	29206	...	...	...	...	...	37863
B Water works and supply	...	...	...	...	...	1467	...	...	...	...	...	1989
5 Construction	...	3982	...	3404	1369	81207	...	4936	...	3353	1204	89060
6 Wholesale and retail trade, restaurants and hotels	...	10720	...	20779	2135	166750	...	17671	...	25249	3221	215063
A Wholesale and retail trade	...	8866	...	16465	1508	133930	...	14398	...	18832	2457	169995
B Restaurants and hotels	...	1854	...	4314	627	32820	...	3273	...	6417	764	45068
7 Transport, storage and communication	...	11755	...	3308	9814	57830	...	17551	...	3272	12593	78422
A Transport and storage	...	...	...	...	...	36740	...	...	...	...	...	47737
B Communication	...	...	...	...	...	21090	...	...	...	...	...	30685
8 Finance, insurance, real estate and business services	...	30577	...	8531	585	119062	...	44418	...	12434	1790	204393
A Financial institutions	...	...	...	...	...	42987	...	...	...	...	...	63213
B Insurance	...	...	...	...	...	12987	...	...	...	...	...	20437
C Real estate and business services	...	...	...	...	...	63088	...	...	...	...	...	120743
Real estate, except dwellings	...	...	...	...	...	41353	...	...	...	...	...	86396
Dwellings	...	...	...	...	...		...	...	...	...	...	
9 Community, social and personal services	...	1140	...	2897	1310	32225	...	1679	...	5196	1883	46781
A Sanitary and similar services bc	...	...	...	...	...	...	...	...	...	...	...	...
B Social and related community services c	...	...	...	...	...	17175	...	...	...	...	...	24286

Austria

4.3 Cost Components of Value Added
(Continued)

Million Austrian schillings

	1980						1985					
	Compensation of Employees	Capital Consumption	Net Operating Surplus	Indirect Taxes	Less: Subsidies Received	Value Added	Compensation of Employees	Capital Consumption	Net Operating Surplus	Indirect Taxes	Less: Subsidies Received	Value Added
Educational services d	...	...	...	...	...	...	...	...	...	...	...	...
Medical, dental, other health and veterinary services c	...	...	...	...	...	17175	...	...	...	...	...	24286
C Recreational and cultural services dc	...	...	...	...	...	7710	...	...	...	...	...	11691
D Personal and household services bc	...	...	...	...	...	7340	...	...	...	...	...	10804
Total, Industries	...	107935	...	70851	30073	813576	...	155833	...	88802	38981	1087241
Producers of Government Services	...	7481	...	1941	-	129080	...	10690	...	2645	-	185067
Other Producers b	...	682	...	36	7	7169	...	1003	...	45	222	10231
Total	545631	116098	245319	72828	30054	949825	717091	167526	345636	91492	39203	1282539
Less: Imputed bank service charge	...	...	45118	...	...	45118	...	...	68556	...	...	68556
Import duties	...	...	...	5745	...	5745	...	...	...	9077	...	9077
Value added tax	...	...	...	84252	...	84252	...	...	...	125365	...	125365
Other adjustments	...	...	...	...	...	-	...	...	...	...	...	-
Total	545631	116098	200201	162825	30054	994704	717091	167526	277080	225934	39203	1348425

	1990						1991					
	Compensation of Employees	Capital Consumption	Net Operating Surplus	Indirect Taxes	Less: Subsidies Received	Value Added	Compensation of Employees	Capital Consumption	Net Operating Surplus	Indirect Taxes	Less: Subsidies Received	Value Added

All Producers

1 Agriculture, hunting, forestry and fishing	...	16916	...	1298	4630	56679	...	17669	...	1754	5282	52992
2 Mining and quarrying	...	759	...	499	337	5627	...	789	...	480	315	7259
3 Manufacturing	...	54747	...	46256	14407	463722	...	58691	...	48166	18214	488803
A Manufacture of food, beverages and tobacco	...	...	...	...	...	61701	...	...	...	...	...	66052
B Textile, wearing apparel and leather industries	...	...	...	...	...	27668	...	...	...	...	...	27334
C Manufacture of wood and wood products, including furniture	...	...	...	...	...	34024	...	...	...	...	...	35268
D Manufacture of paper and paper products, printing and publishing	...	...	...	...	...	34526	...	...	...	...	...	36333
E Manufacture of chemicals and chemical petroleum, coal, rubber and plastic products a	...	...	...	...	...	68780	...	...	...	...	...	76103
F Manufacture of non-metallic mineral products, except products of petroleum and coal	...	...	...	...	...	26977	...	...	...	...	...	28028
G Basic metal industries	...	...	...	...	...	29061	...	...	...	...	...	26628
H Manufacture of fabricated metal products, machinery and equipment	...	...	...	...	...	180986	...	...	...	...	...	193060
I Other manufacturing industries	...	...	...	...	...	...	...	...	...	...	...	...
4 Electricity, gas and water	...	16170	...	1385	854	49035	...	17462	...	1367	1039	52820
A Electricity, gas and steam	...	...	...	...	...	46400	...	...	...	...	...	49987
B Water works and supply	...	...	...	...	...	2635	...	...	...	...	...	2833
5 Construction	...	6055	...	4955	1538	124270	...	6177	...	4926	1648	140043
6 Wholesale and retail trade, restaurants and hotels	...	23530	...	30830	5604	300145	...	25526	...	31220	6718	319869
A Wholesale and retail trade	...	19299	...	22869	4782	237141	...	20911	...	22642	5904	251246
B Restaurants and hotels	...	4231	...	7961	822	63004	...	4615	...	8578	814	68623
7 Transport, storage and communication	...	23632	...	3873	16122	112413	...	25634	...	4564	17886	121776
A Transport and storage	...	...	...	...	...	69763	...	...	...	...	...	76399
B Communication	...	...	...	...	...	42650	...	...	...	...	...	45377
8 Finance, insurance, real estate and business services	...	60547	...	20306	2046	304347	...	66103	...	21376	2413	330612
A Financial institutions	...	...	...	...	...	93570	...	...	...	...	...	100525

Austria

4.3 Cost Components of Value Added
(Continued)

Million Austrian schillings

	Compensation of Employees	Capital Consumption	Net Operating Surplus	Indirect Taxes	Less: Subsidies Received	Value Added	Compensation of Employees	Capital Consumption	Net Operating Surplus	Indirect Taxes	Less: Subsidies Received	Value Added
	\multicolumn{6}{c}{1990}	\multicolumn{6}{c}{1991}
B Insurance	...	...	...	...	...	27932	...	...	...	...	...	28873
C Real estate and business services	...	...	...	...	...	182845	...	...	...	...	...	201214
Real estate, except dwellings	...	...	...	...	...	117636]	...	...	...	...	...	125139]
Dwellings	...	...	...	...	...		...	...	...	...	...	
9 Community, social and personal services	...	2117	...	5999	2089	73549	...	2282	...	8442	2674	79554
A Sanitary and similar services [bc]	...	...	...	...	...	...	...	...	...	...	...	...
B Social and related community services [c]	...	...	...	...	...	33197	...	...	...	...	...	36302
Educational services [d]	...	...	...	...	...	...	...	...	...	...	...	...
Medical, dental, other health and veterinary services [c]	...	...	...	...	...	33197	...	...	...	...	...	36302
C Recreational and cultural services [dc]	...	...	...	...	...	24974	...	...	...	...	...	26472
D Personal and household services [bc]	...	...	...	...	...	15378	...	...	...	...	...	16780
Total, Industries	...	204473	...	115401	47627	1489787	...	220333	...	122295	56189	1593728
Producers of Government Services	...	12770	...	3572	-	234856	...	13502	...	3851	-	256147
Other Producers [b]	...	1243	...	53	226	12529	...	1338	...	58	248	13431
Total	940062	218486	507449	119026	47854	1737172	1020817	235173	537548	126204	56436	1863306
Less: Imputed bank service charge	...	...	104714	...	...	104714	...	...	114567	...	...	114567
Import duties	...	...	...	12026	...	12026	...	...	...	12642	...	12642
Value added tax	...	...	...	156825	...	156825	...	...	...	166933	...	166933
Other adjustments	...	...	...	...	...	-	...	...	...	...	...	...
Total	940062	218486	402735	287877	47854	1801309	1020817	235173	422981	305779	56436	1928314

	Compensation of Employees	Capital Consumption	Net Operating Surplus	Indirect Taxes	Less: Subsidies Received	Value Added	Compensation of Employees	Capital Consumption	Net Operating Surplus	Indirect Taxes	Less: Subsidies Received	Value Added
	\multicolumn{6}{c}{1992}	\multicolumn{6}{c}{1993}
	\multicolumn{12}{c}{**All Producers**}
1 Agriculture, hunting, forestry and fishing	...	18353	...	1371	8549	50080	...	18793	...	1670	7510	48395
2 Mining and quarrying	...	850	...	491	276	5399	...	893	...	489	304	4731
3 Manufacturing	...	64005	...	53801	17311	501577	...	68706	...	53265	18301	495443
A Manufacture of food, beverages and tobacco	...	...	...	...	...	71099	...	...	...	...	...	72052
B Textile, wearing apparel and leather industries	...	...	...	...	...	27931	...	...	...	...	...	24120
C Manufacture of wood and wood products, including furniture	...	...	...	...	...	38876	...	...	...	...	...	40792
D Manufacture of paper and paper products, printing and publishing	...	...	...	...	...	35758	...	...	...	...	...	35032
E Manufacture of chemicals and chemical petroleum, coal, rubber and plastic products [a]	...	...	...	...	...	78210	...	...	...	...	...	78094
F Manufacture of non-metallic mineral products, except products of petroleum and coal	...	...	...	...	...	30414	...	...	...	...	...	30010
G Basic metal industries	...	...	...	...	...	24306	...	...	...	...	...	24122
H Manufacture of fabricated metal products, machinery and equipment	...	...	...	...	...	194984	...	...	...	...	...	191221
I Other manufacturing industries	...	...	...	...	...	...	...	...	...	...	...	...
4 Electricity, gas and water	...	19145	...	1499	969	57044	...	20626	...	1561	922	60098
A Electricity, gas and steam	...	...	...	...	...	53914	...	...	...	...	...	56448
B Water works and supply	...	...	...	...	...	3130	...	...	...	...	...	3650
5 Construction	...	6823	...	5500	1970	153328	...	7205	...	5813	1919	161794
6 Wholesale and retail trade, restaurants and hotels	...	27992	...	38136	8170	342205	...	30217	...	38116	7724	345794
A Wholesale and retail trade	...	22959	...	30890	7139	269367	...	24787	...	31290	6833	270403
B Restaurants and hotels	...	5033	...	7246	1031	72838	...	5430	...	6826	891	75391
7 Transport, storage and communication	...	28057	...	4493	19028	130621	...	30257	...	4691	21121	134410

Austria

4.3 Cost Components of Value Added
(Continued)

Million Austrian schillings

	1992						1993					
	Compensation of Employees	Capital Consumption	Net Operating Surplus	Indirect Taxes	Less: Subsidies Received	Value Added	Compensation of Employees	Capital Consumption	Net Operating Surplus	Indirect Taxes	Less: Subsidies Received	Value Added
A Transport and storage	...	...	...	...	...	82550	...	...	...	...	...	83736
B Communication	...	...	...	...	...	48071	...	...	...	...	...	50674
8 Finance, insurance, real estate and business services	...	69614	...	23429	1569	366264	...	74695	...	24588	2630	401216
A Financial institutions	...	...	...	...	...	108648	...	...	...	...	...	120449
B Insurance	...	...	...	...	...	33006	...	...	...	...	...	37144
C Real estate and business services	...	...	...	...	...	224611	...	...	...	...	...	243623
Real estate, except dwellings	...	...	...	...	...	[138047	...	...	...	...	...	[148397
Dwellings	...	...	...	...	...		...	...	...	...	...	
9 Community, social and personal services	...	2478	...	8638	2933	89600	...	2654	...	8917	2824	96024
A Sanitary and similar services [bc]	...	...	...	...	...	...	...	...	...	...	...	...
B Social and related community services [c]	...	...	...	...	...	40483	...	...	...	...	...	44674
Educational services [d]	...	...	...	...	...	...	...	...	...	...	...	...
Medical, dental, other health and veterinary services [c]	...	...	...	...	...	40483	...	...	...	...	...	44674
C Recreational and cultural services [dc]	...	...	...	...	...	30258	...	...	...	...	...	30700
D Personal and household services [bc]	...	...	...	...	...	18859	...	...	...	...	...	20650
Total, Industries	...	237317	...	137358	60775	1696118	...	254046	...	139110	63255	1747905
Producers of Government Services	...	13809	...	4121	-	275732	...	14468	...	4690	-	296634
Other Producers [b]	...	1449	...	65	384	14469	...	1549	...	69	257	15458
Total	1088971	252575	564381	141544	61156	1986319	1135998	270063	573581	143869	63511	2059997
Less: Imputed bank service charge	...	...	124514	...	...	124514	...	...	136849	...	...	136849
Import duties	...	...	...	13269	...	13269	...	...	...	13122	...	13122
Value added tax	...	...	...	171006	...	171006	...	...	...	181571	...	181571
Other adjustments	...	-	...	...	...	...	...	...	...	...	...	...
Total	1088971	252575	439867	325819	61156	2046080	1135998	270063	436732	338562	63511	2117841

a) Item 'Crude petroleum and natural gas production' is included in item 'Manufacture of chemicals and chemical petroleum, coal, rubber and plastic products.'
b) Item 'Sanitary and similar services' is included in item 'Personal and household services' which excludes domestic services and caretakers that are included in item 'Other producers'.
c) Non-governmental only.
d) Item 'Educational services' is included in item 'Recreational and cultural services'.

Bahamas

Source. Reply to the United Nations national accounts questionnaire from the Department of Statistics, Nassau. Official estimates are published in a series of reports entitled 'Expenditure on Gross Domestic Product'.

General note. The estimates shown in the following tables have been prepared in accordance with the United Nations System of National Accounts so far as the existing data would permit.

1.1 Expenditure on the Gross Domestic Product, in Current Prices

Million Bahamian dollars

	1980	1983	1984	1985	1986	1987	1988	1989	1990	1991	1992	1993
1 Government final consumption expenditure	...	...	...	...	...	...	...	409	428	443	448	...
2 Private final consumption expenditure	...	...	...	...	...	...	...	2302	2323	2381	2269	...
A Households	...	...	...	...	...	...	...	2302	2323	2381	2269	...
B Private non-profit institutions serving households	...	...	...	...	...	...	...					...
3 Gross capital formation	...	...	...	...	...	...	...	725	696	633	639	...
A Increase in stocks	...	...	...	...	...	...	...	13	24	-11	5	...
B Gross fixed capital formation	...	...	...	...	...	...	...	712	671	644	635	...
Residential buildings	...	...	...	...	...	...	...	90	86	82	77	...
Non-residential buildings	...	...	...	...	...	...	...	160	143	133	142	...
Other construction and land improvement etc.	...	...	...	...	...	...	...					...
Other	...	...	...	...	...	...	...	462	443	429	416	...
4 Exports of goods and services	...	...	...	...	...	...	...	1424	1516	1416	1405	...
5 Less: Imports of goods and services	...	...	...	...	...	...	...	1789	1840	1761	1689	...
Statistical discrepancy	...	...	...	...	...	...	...	-64	11	-21	-13	...
Equals: Gross Domestic Product	...	...	...	...	...	...	...	3006	3134	3090	3059	...

1.3 Cost Components of the Gross Domestic Product

Million Bahamian dollars

	1980	1983	1984	1985	1986	1987	1988	1989	1990	1991	1992	1993
1 Indirect taxes, net	...	...	...	...	...	...	...	381	411	388	430	...
A Indirect taxes	...	...	...	...	...	...	...	381	411	388	430	...
B Less: Subsidies	...	...	...	...	...	...	...	...	...	...	...	...
2 Consumption of fixed capital	...	...	...	...	...	...	...	...	...	...	...	...
3 Compensation of employees paid by resident producers to:	...	...	...	...	...	...	...	1534	1624	1572	1587	...
4 Operating surplus [a]	...	...	...	...	...	...	...	1027	1110	1109	1029	...
Statistical discrepancy	...	...	...	...	...	...	...	64	-11	21	13	...
Equals: Gross Domestic Product	...	...	...	...	...	...	...	3006	3134	3090	3059	...

a) Gross operating surplus.

1.4 General Government Current Receipts and Disbursements

Million Bahamian dollars

	1980	1983	1984	1985	1986	1987	1988	1989	1990	1991	1992	1993
Receipts												
1 Operating surplus	-	-	-	-	-	-	-	...	...	...	...	...
2 Property and entrepreneurial income	17	43	55	48	48	41	39	55	50	59	56	...
3 Taxes, fees and contributions	239	299	315	377	401	412	473	480	523	503	568	...
A Indirect taxes	201	249	260	308	328	341	393	381	411	388	430	...
B Direct taxes	4	6	7	7	8	8	7	21	26	33	50	...
C Social security contributions	23	30	34	48	50	50	55	59	66	63	61	...
D Compulsory fees, fines and penalties	11	14	14	15	16	14	18	19	19	18	28	...
4 Other current transfers	5	10	10	9	9	10	12	12	17	15	16	...
Total Current Receipts of General Government	261	352	380	435	458	463	524	547	590	577	641	...
Disbursements												
1 Government final consumption expenditure	173	251	268	295	306	334	370	409	428	443	448	...

Bahamas

1.4 General Government Current Receipts and Disbursements
(Continued)

Million Bahamian dollars

	1980	1983	1984	1985	1986	1987	1988	1989	1990	1991	1992	1993
A Compensation of employees	124	182	203	220	227	251	276	... 303	325	327	336	...
B Consumption of fixed capital	3	4	4	6	7	7	6	... 5	5	4	5	...
C Purchases of goods and services, net	46	65	60	69	73	76	88	... 100	98	111	107	...
D Less: Own account fixed capital formation	...	...	...	...	...	...	...	... ...	...	...	...	...
E Indirect taxes paid, net	-	-	-	-	-	-	-	... ...	...	...	...	...
2 Property income	22	40	43	50	47	40	46	... 54	62	70	68	...
A Interest	22	40	43	50	47	40	46	... 54	62	70	68	...
B Net land rent and royalties	...	...	...	...	...	...	...	... ...	...	...	...	...
3 Subsidies	3	8	6	4	5	6	6	... ...	...	...	...	...
4 Other current transfers	20	38	42	44	49	51	59	... 45	46	48	56	...
A Social security benefits	5	15	18	21	24	26	28	... 31	34	37	40	...
B Social assistance grants	3	8	9	8	7	8	8	... 8	9	8	9	...
C Other	12	15	15	14	17	17	23	... 6	4	4	7	...
5 Net saving	44	15	21	43	51	33	42	... 40	53	16	69	...
Total Current Disbursements and Net Saving of General Government	261	352	380	435	458	463	524	... 547	590	577	641	...

1.7 External Transactions on Current Account, Summary

Million Bahamian dollars

	1980	1983	1984	1985	1986	1987	1988	1989	1990	1991	1992	1993
				Payments to the Rest of the World								
1 Imports of goods and services	...	...	...	...	...	...	...	1789	1840	1761	1689	...
A Imports of merchandise c.i.f.	...	...	...	...	...	...	...	1329	1304	1243	1234	...
B Other	...	...	...	...	...	...	...	460	536	518	454	...
2 Factor income to the rest of the world	...	...	...	...	...	...	...	169	150	182	161	...
A Compensation of employees	...	...	...	...	...	...	...	...	...	...	...	...
B Property and entrepreneurial income	...	...	...	...	...	...	...	169	150	182	161	...
By general government	...	...	...	...	...	...	...	9	10	11	10	...
By corporate and quasi-corporate enterprises	...	...	...	...	...	...	...	44	38	42	36	...
By other	...	...	...	...	...	...	...	115	102	129	115	...
3 Current transfers to the rest of the world	...	...	...	...	...	...	...	21	14	11	18	...
4 Surplus of the nation on current transactions	...	...	...	...	...	...	...	-517	-448	-492	-419	...
Payments to the Rest of the World and Surplus of the Nation on Current Transactions	...	...	...	...	...	...	...	1461	1556	1462	1448	...
				Receipts From The Rest of the World								
1 Exports of goods and services	...	...	...	...	...	...	...	1424	1516	1416	1405	...
A Exports of merchandise f.o.b.	...	...	...	...	...	...	...	155	190	217	194	...

Bahamas

1.7 External Transactions on Current Account, Summary
(Continued)

Million Bahamian dollars

	1980	1983	1984	1985	1986	1987	1988	1989	1990	1991	1992	1993
B Other	...	...	...	...	...	...	...	1269	1326	1199	1210	...
2 Factor income from rest of the world	...	...	...	...	...	...	...	16	15	15	12	...
A Compensation of employees	...	...	...	...	...	...	...	...	...	...	...	...
B Property and entrepreneurial income	...	...	...	...	...	...	...	16	15	15	12	...
By general government	...	...	...	...	...	...	...	-	-	-	-	...
By corporate and quasi-corporate enterprises	...	...	...	...	...	...	...	-	-	1	-	...
By other	...	...	...	...	...	...	...	16	15	14	11	...
3 Current transfers from rest of the world	...	...	...	...	...	...	...	22	25	31	31	...
Receipts from the Rest of the World on Current Transactions	...	...	...	...	...	...	...	1461	1556	1462	1447	...

1.10 Gross Domestic Product by Kind of Activity, in Current Prices

Million Bahamian dollars

	1980	1983	1984	1985	1986	1987	1988	1989	1990	1991	1992	1993
1 Agriculture, hunting, forestry and fishing	...	...	...	...	...	...	...	69	82	104	89	...
2 Mining and quarrying	...	...	...	...	...	...	...	98	86	103	105	...
3 Manufacturing	...	...	...	...	...	...	...					...
4 Electricity, gas and water	...	...	...	...	...	...	...	63	67	77	88	...
5 Construction	...	...	...	...	...	...	...	115	109	104	91	...
6 Wholesale and retail trade, restaurants and hotels	...	...	...	...	...	...	...	844	929	800	705	...
7 Transport, storage and communication	...	...	...	...	...	...	...	199	229	205	227	...
8 Finance, insurance, real estate and business services	...	...	...	...	...	...	...	547	573	601	610	...
9 Community, social and personal services	...	...	...	...	...	...	...	286	290	305	310	...
Statistical discrepancy	...	...	...	...	...	...	...	64	-11	21	13	...
Total, Industries	...	...	...	...	...	...	...	2385	2354	2320	2238	...
Producers of Government Services	...	...	...	...	...	...	...	297	324	327	336	...
Other Producers	...	...	...	...	...	...	...	43	45	54	55	...
Subtotal	...	...	...	...	...	...	...	2625	2723	2701	2629	...
Less: Imputed bank service charge	...	...	...	...	...	...	...	...	...	...	...	...
Plus: Import duties	...	...	...	...	...	...	...	290	289	266	268	...
Plus: Value added tax	...	...	...	...	...	...	...	...	...	...	...	...
Plus: Other adjustments a	...	...	...	...	...	...	...	92	122	122	162	...
Equals: Gross Domestic Product	...	...	...	...	...	...	...	3006	3134	3090	3059	...

a) Item 'other adjustments' refers to other indirect taxes.

1.12 Relations Among National Accounting Aggregates

Million Bahamian dollars

	1980	1983	1984	1985	1986	1987	1988	1989	1990	1991	1992	1993
Gross Domestic Product	...	...	...	...	...	...	...	3006	3134	3090	3059	...
Plus: Net factor income from the rest of the world	...	...	...	...	...	...	...	-153	-135	-167	-149	...
Factor income from the rest of the world	...	...	...	...	...	...	...	16	15	15	12	...
Less: Factor income to the rest of the world	...	...	...	...	...	...	...	169	150	182	161	...
Equals: Gross National Product	...	...	...	...	...	...	...	2853	2999	2923	2910	...
Less: Consumption of fixed capital	...	...	...	...	...	...	...	...	...	...	...	...
Equals: National Income	...	...	...	...	...	...	...	...	...	...	...	...
Plus: Net current transfers from the rest of the world	...	...	...	...	...	...	...	1	11	20	13	...
Current transfers from the rest of the world	...	...	...	...	...	...	...	22	25	31	31	...
Less: Current transfers to the rest of the world	...	...	...	...	...	...	...	21	14	11	18	...
Equals: National Disposable Income	...	...	...	...	...	...	...	...	...	...	...	...
Less: Final consumption	...	...	...	...	...	...	...	2711	2751	2824	2717	...
Equals: Net Saving	...	...	...	...	...	...	...	...	...	...	...	...
Less: Surplus of the nation on current transactions	...	...	...	...	...	...	...	-517	-448	-492	-419	...
Equals: Net Capital Formation	...	...	...	...	...	...	...	...	...	...	...	...

Bahamas

2.1 Government Final Consumption Expenditure by Function, in Current Prices

Million Bahamian dollars

		1980	1983	1984	1985	1986	1987	1988	1989	1990	1991	1992	1993
1	General public services	21	29	33	36	37	41	37	66	73	73	80	...
2	Defence	5	9	9	10	11	12	17	17	19	18	18	...
3	Public order and safety	22	32	34	37	39	42	51	52	56	60	60	...
4	Education	48	70	73	81	84	92	92	97	99	99	105	...
5	Health	35	50	54	59	62	67	83	87	83	83	80	...
6	Social security and welfare	4	7	7	7	8	8	15	17	18	21	23	...
7	Housing and community amenities	-	-	-	-	-	-	1	6	7	6	7	...
8	Recreational, cultural and religious affairs	2	3	3	3	4	4	6					...
9	Economic services	37	51	54	61	63	68	71	67	73	84	76	...
	A Fuel and energy	...	...	...	...	...	...	...	...	...	...	...	...
	B Agriculture, forestry, fishing and hunting	4	6	6	7	7	7	8	7	8	11	10	...
	C Mining, manufacturing and construction, except fuel and energy [a]	20	29	29	32	34	38	39	35	39	51	42	...
	D Transportation and communication	11	13	16	18	18	20	22	21	23	19	21	...
	E Other economic affairs	2	3	3	4	4	4	3	3	3	3	3	...
10	Other functions	...	...	...	...	...	...	...	...	...	...	...	...
	Total Government Final Consumption Expenditure	173	251	268	295	306	334	370	409	428	443	448	...

a) Item 'Mining, manufacturing and construction, except fuel and energy' refers to tourism.

2.3 Total Government Outlays by Function and Type

Million Bahamian dollars

		Final Consumption Expenditures Total	Compensation of Employees	Other	Subsidies	Other Current Transfers & Property Income	Total Current Disbursements	Gross Capital Formation	Other Capital Outlays	Total Outlays
					1980					
1	General public services	21	18	3	3	7	31	-12	3	22
2	Defence	5	2	3	...	-	5	-	...	5
3	Public order and safety	22	18	4	...	-	22	1	...	23
4	Education	48	42	5	...	6	53	4	-	57
5	Health	35	26	10	...	-	35	2	...	38
6	Social security and welfare	4	3	1	...	7	11	1	-	11
7	Housing and community amenities	-	-	-	...	-	-	-	...	-
8	Recreation, culture and religion	2	1	1	...	-	2	1	...	3
9	Economic services	37	15	23	-	-	37	8	4	49
	A Fuel and energy	...	...	...	...	...	...	...	...	...
	B Agriculture, forestry, fishing and hunting	4	3	1	...	-	4	2	...	6
	C Mining (except fuels), manufacturing and construction [a]	20	4	16	...	-	20	-	...	20
	D Transportation and communication	11	5	6	...	-	11	5	4	20
	E Other economic affairs	2	2	-	...	-	2	-	-	2
10	Other functions	-	-	-	...	22	22	-	...	22
	Total	173	124	49	3	41	217	5	6	228
					1985					
1	General public services	36	30	6	4	14	54	1	5	60
2	Defence	10	5	5	...	-	10	-	...	10
3	Public order and safety	37	32	6	...	-	38	1	...	38
4	Education	81	73	8	...	10	91	3	-	94
5	Health	59	46	14	...	-	60	1	...	60

Bahamas

2.3 Total Government Outlays by Function and Type
(Continued)

Million Bahamian dollars

	Final Consumption Expenditures Total	Compensation of Employees	Other	Subsidies	Other Current Transfers & Property Income	Total Current Disbursements	Gross Capital Formation	Other Capital Outlays	Total Outlays
6 Social security and welfare	7	5	2	...	19	26	1	-	26
7 Housing and community amenities	-	-	-	...	-	-	-	...	-
8 Recreation, culture and religion	3	2	1	...	-	4	-	...	4
9 Economic services	60	26	34	-	-	60	5	1	66
A Fuel and energy	...	...	...	...	...	...	...	...	...
B Agriculture, forestry, fishing and hunting	7	5	1	...	-	7	1	...	8
C Mining (except fuels), manufacturing and construction a	32	7	25	...	-	32	-	...	32
D Transportation and communication	18	10	8	...	-	18	4	1	22
E Other economic affairs	4	4	-	...	-	4	-	-	4
10 Other functions	-	-	-	...	50	50	-	...	50
Total	294	220	75	4	93	392	11	6	408

a) Item 'Mining, manufacturing and construction, except fuel and energy' refers to tourism.

2.3 Total Government Outlays by Function and Type

Million Bahamian dollars

	Final Consumption Expenditures Total	Compensation of Employees	Other	Subsidies	Other Current Transfers & Property Income	Total Current Disbursements	Gross Capital Formation	Other Capital Outlays	Total Outlays
1990									
1 General public services	73	57	16	...	3	76	1	...	78
2 Defence	19	15	4	...	-	19	-	...	19
3 Public order and safety	56	48	9	...	-	56	1	...	57
4 Education	99	88	11	...	6	105	2	...	107
5 Health	83	63	19	...	-	83	5	...	88
6 Social security and welfare	18	11	7	...	37	55	1	...	55
7 Housing and community amenities	7	5	1	...	-	7	-	...	7
8 Recreation, culture and religion				...			...		
9 Economic services	73	36	37	...	-	73	9	...	82
A Fuel and energy	...	...	...	...	...	...	...	...	...
B Agriculture, forestry, fishing and hunting	8	7	1	...	-	8	-	...	8
C Mining (except fuels), manufacturing and construction a	39	13	26	...	-	39	-	...	39
D Transportation and communication	23	14	10	...	-	23	9	...	32
E Other economic affairs	3	3	-	...	-	3	-	...	3
10 Other functions	...	...	...	...	62	62	-	...	62
Total	428	325	103	...	108	536	19	...	555
1991									
1 General public services	73	57	16	...	3	77	2	...	79
2 Defence	18	15	3	...	-	18	-	...	18
3 Public order and safety	60	50	10	...	-	60	1	...	60
4 Education	99	89	9	...	5	103	6	...	109
5 Health	83	64	18	...	-	83	2	...	85
6 Social security and welfare	21	13	8	...	39	60	-	...	60
7 Housing and community amenities	6	5	1	...	-	6	-	...	6
8 Recreation, culture and religion				...			...		
9 Economic services	84	34	50	...	-	84	6	...	90
A Fuel and energy	...	...	...	...	...	...	...	...	...
B Agriculture, forestry, fishing and hunting	11	6	4	...	-	11	1	...	11
C Mining (except fuels), manufacturing and construction a	51	13	38	...	-	51	-	...	51
D Transportation and communication	19	12	8	...	-	19	5	...	24
E Other economic affairs	3	3	-	...	-	3	-	...	3
10 Other functions	...	...	...	...	70	70	-	...	70
Total	443	327	115	...	118	561	16	...	578

Bahamas

2.3 Total Government Outlays by Function and Type
(Continued)

Million Bahamian dollars

		Final Consumption Expenditures			Subsidies	Other Current Transfers & Property Income	Total Current Disbursements	Gross Capital Formation	Other Capital Outlays	Total Outlays
		Total	Compensation of Employees	Other						

1992

		Total	Comp.	Other	Subs.	Other Curr.	Total Curr. Disb.	GCF	Other Cap.	Total Outlays
1	General public services	80	59	21	...	6	86	3	...	89
2	Defence	18	15	3	...	-	18	-	...	18
3	Public order and safety	60	51	10	...	-	60	-	...	60
4	Education	105	93	11	...	4	109	5	...	114
5	Health	80	64	16	...	-	80	1	...	80
6	Social security and welfare	23	15	8	...	45	68	1	...	69
7	Housing and community amenities	7	5	1	...	1	8	-	...	8
8	Recreation, culture and religion				...				...	
9	Economic services	76	34	42	...	-	76	6	...	82
	A Fuel and energy	...	...	...	...	...	...	...	...	...
	B Agriculture, forestry, fishing and hunting	10	6	4	...	-	10	...	...	11
	C Mining (except fuels), manufacturing and construction [a]	42	13	29	...	-	42	-	...	42
	D Transportation and communication	21	12	9	...	...	21	6	...	27
	E Other economic affairs	3	3	-	...	...	3	-	...	3
10	Other functions	...	...	...	...	68	68	...	...	68
	Total	448	336	112	...	124	571	17	...	588

a) Item 'Mining, manufacturing and construction, except fuel and energy' refers to tourism.

2.17 Exports and Imports of Goods and Services, Detail

Million Bahamian dollars

	1980	1983	1984	1985	1986	1987	1988	1989	1990	1991	1992	1993
Exports of Goods and Services												
1 Exports of merchandise, f.o.b.	...	...	...	...	...	...	...	155	190	217	194	...
2 Transport and communication	...	...	...	...	...	...	...	90	116	81	67	...
3 Insurance service charges	...	...	...	...	...	...	...	...	...	...	...	...
4 Other commodities	...	...	...	...	...	...	...	...	...	...	...	...
5 Adjustments of merchandise exports to change-of-ownership basis	...	...	...	...	...	...	...	...	...	...	...	...
6 Direct purchases in the domestic market by non-residential households	...	...	...	...	...	...	...	1056	1095	1011	1039	...
7 Direct purchases in the domestic market by extraterritorial bodies	...	...	...	...	...	...	...	123	115	108	104	...
Total Exports of Goods and Services	...	...	...	...	...	...	...	1424	1516	1416	1405	...
Imports of Goods and Services												
1 Imports of merchandise, c.i.f.	...	...	...	...	...	...	...	1329	1304	1243	1234	...
2 Adjustments of merchandise imports to change-of-ownership basis	...	...	...	...	...	...	...	...	...	...	...	...
3 Other transport and communication	...	...	...	...	...	...	...	61	63	47	38	...
4 Other insurance service charges	...	...	...	...	...	...	...	18	20	21	23	...
5 Other commodities	...	...	...	...	...	...	...	167	204	203	166	...
6 Direct purchases abroad by government	...	...	...	...	...	...	...	31	53	48	40	...
7 Direct purchases abroad by resident households	...	...	...	...	...	...	...	184	196	200	187	...
Total Imports of Goods and Services	...	...	...	...	...	...	...	1789	1840	1761	1689	...
Balance of Goods and Services	...	...	...	...	...	...	...	-366	-324	-345	-284	...
Total Imports and Balance of Goods and Services	...	...	...	...	...	...	...	1424	1516	1416	1405	...

Bahrain

Source. The estimates are published by the Ministry of Finance and National Economy in the National Accounts of Bahrain.
General note. The estimates shown in the following tables have been prepared by the Statistics Department in accordance with the United Nations System of National Accounts so far as the existing data would permit.

1.1 Expenditure on the Gross Domestic Product, in Current Prices

Million Bahraini dinars

	1980	1983	1984	1985	1986	1987	1988	1989	1990	1991	1992	1993
1 Government final consumption expenditure	150.9	254.5	302.2	312.8	312.4	310.9	339.9	356.7	378.7	...	...	...
2 Private final consumption expenditure	370.3	481.6	499.2	438.3	399.8	389.5	440.7	505.0	526.2	...	...	...
3 Gross capital formation	520.6	618.5	593.3	477.9	325.6	368.0	330.3	415.0	460.2	...	...	...
A Increase in stocks	163.7	42.4	-42.7	-9.9	-65.2	8.8	-14.5	29.0	59.4	...	...	...
B Gross fixed capital formation	356.9	576.1	636.0	487.8	390.8	359.2	344.8	386.0	400.8	...	...	...
4 Exports of goods and services	1421.1	1344.2	1455.0	1397.4	1133.8	1216.5	1228.6	1341.7	1742.4	...	...	...
5 Less: Imports of goods and services	1304.8	1294.4	1381.3	1233.6	973.4	1093.1	1076.7	1270.9	1500.9	...	...	...
Equals: Gross Domestic Product	1158.1	1404.4	1468.5	1392.9	1198.2	1191.8	1262.9	1347.5	1467.5	...	...	...

1.2 Expenditure on the Gross Domestic Product, in Constant Prices

Million Bahraini dinars

	1980	1983	1984	1985	1986	1987	1988	1989	1990	1991	1992	1993
				At constant prices of:1985								
1 Government final consumption expenditure	201.3	269.0	294.6	312.8	343.0	354.2	382.7	397.2	416.7	...	...	...
2 Private final consumption expenditure	451.0	476.4	483.7	438.3	405.9	401.5	504.8	513.0	527.8	...	...	...
3 Gross capital formation	750.4	597.7	725.5	477.9	399.6	430.1	373.1	549.7	383.0	...	...	...
A Increase in stocks	423.0	8.4	81.5	-9.9	-8.5	59.6	-3.3	166.7	-9.8	...	...	...
B Gross fixed capital formation	327.4	589.3	644.0	487.8	408.1	370.5	376.4	383.0	392.8	...	...	...
4 Exports of goods and services	1329.9	1266.4	1422.3	1397.4	1639.9	1599.4	1676.6	1668.1	1815.1	...	...	...
5 Less: Imports of goods and services	1285.5	1254.0	1443.0	1233.6	1373.1	1387.4	1436.7	1590.0	1585.7	...	...	...
Equals: Gross Domestic Product	1447.1	1355.4	1421.8	1392.8	1415.2	1397.8	1500.5	1538.0	1556.9	...	...	...

1.3 Cost Components of the Gross Domestic Product

Million Bahraini dinars

	1980	1983	1984	1985	1986	1987	1988	1989	1990	1991	1992	1993
1 Indirect taxes, net	39.9	62.1	57.6	44.1	26.3	27.7	32.6	34.2	37.5	...	...	...
2 Consumption of fixed capital	120.6	166.9	199.1	203.9	210.0	208.8	225.9	224.6	229.3	...	...	...
3 Compensation of employees paid by resident producers to:	355.6	527.6	591.2	594.5	597.4	593.5	612.5	641.0	688.8	...	...	...
4 Operating surplus	642.0	647.8	620.6	550.4	364.6	361.8	391.9	447.7	511.8	...	...	...
Equals: Gross Domestic Product	1158.1	1404.4	1468.5	1392.9	1198.2	1191.8	1262.9	1347.5	1467.5	...	...	...

1.7 External Transactions on Current Account, Summary

Million Bahraini dinars

	1980	1983	1984	1985	1986	1987	1988	1989	1990	1991	1992	1993
				Payments to the Rest of the World								
1 Imports of goods and services	1304.8	1294.4	1381.3	1233.6	973.4	1093.1	1076.7	1270.9	1500.9	...	...	...
A Imports of merchandise c.i.f.	1251.3	1226.4	1308.3	1166.1	904.3	1020.3	975.2	1178.2	1395.5	...	...	...
B Other	53.5	68.0	73.0	67.5	69.1	72.8	101.5	92.7	105.4	...	...	...
2 Factor income to the rest of the world	251.1	330.4	406.4	408.9	353.3	312.3	381.6	347.9	389.3	...	...	...
A Compensation of employees	88.3	92.2	102.5	206.9	191.1	179.9	178.4	186.2	232.6	...	...	...
B Property and entrepreneurial income	163.8	238.2	303.9	202.0	162.2	132.4	203.2	161.7	156.7	...	...	...
By general government	11.6	11.9	21.5	5.8	3.0	3.5	6.2	4.7	6.5	...	...	...
By corporate and quasi-corporate enterprises	105.2	203.9	229.3	157.4	106.3	80.0	147.6	100.8	93.6	...	...	...
By other	46.0	22.4	53.1	38.8	52.9	48.9	49.4	56.2	56.6	...	...	...
3 Current transfers to the rest of the world	...	...	...	...	...	...	...	...	...	...	...	...
4 Surplus of the nation on current transactions	68.7	-49.4	-31.0	-34.2	-15.7	-75.9	-63.1	-91.4	-128.7	...	...	...
Payments to the Rest of the World and Surplus of the Nation on Current Transactions [a]	...	...	...	...	...	...	...	...	...	...	...	...

Bahrain

1.7 External Transactions on Current Account, Summary
(Continued)

Million Bahraini dinars

	1980	1983	1984	1985	1986	1987	1988	1989	1990	1991	1992	1993
	\multicolumn{12}{c}{Receipts From The Rest of the World}
1 Exports of goods and services	1421.1	1344.2	1455.0	1397.4	1133.8	1216.5	1228.6	1341.7	1742.4	...	...	...
A Exports of merchandise f.o.b.	1294.3	1172.9	1204.7	1089.2	828.0	913.5	906.3	1064.5	1414.1	...	...	...
B Other	126.8	171.3	250.3	308.2	305.8	303.0	322.3	277.2	328.3	...	...	...
2 Factor income from rest of the world	204.5	269.6	348.9	299.2	240.2	204.6	213.6	249.2	260.6	...	...	...
A Compensation of employees	-	-	-	-	-	-	-	-	...	...	...	...
B Property and entrepreneurial income	204.5	269.6	348.9	299.2	240.2	204.6	213.6	249.2	260.6	...	...	...
By general government	16.3	30.0	33.6	31.3	27.3	24.0	13.4	35.7	55.1	...	...	...
By corporate and quasi-corporate enterprises	38.2	5.7	34.8	23.3	14.2	26.7	35.4	73.8	59.9	...	...	...
By other	150.0	233.9	280.5	244.6	198.7	153.9	164.8	139.7	145.6	...	...	...
3 Current transfers from rest of the world [b]	...	-38.4	-47.2	-88.3	-99.5	-91.6	-72.6	-74.8	-102.4	...	...	...
A Subsidies from supranational organisations	...	...	...	...	...	...	...	...	...	...	...	...
B Other current transfers	...	-38.4	-47.2	-88.3	-99.5	-91.6	-72.6	-74.8	-102.4	...	...	...
Receipts from the Rest of the World on Current Transactions [a]	...	...	...	...	...	...	...	...	...	...	...	...

a) Estimates are derived from Balance of Payment Accounts, therefore are not strictly comparable to those in other tables.
b) Current transfers from the rest of the world is net of current transfers to the rest of the world.

1.10 Gross Domestic Product by Kind of Activity, in Current Prices

Million Bahraini dinars

	1980	1983	1984	1985	1986	1987	1988	1989	1990	1991	1992	1993
1 Agriculture, hunting, forestry and fishing	11.4	16.2	16.4	16.4	16.4	16.0	15.4	15.8	14.3	...	...	...
2 Mining and quarrying	403.4	350.4	355.7	398.6	231.7	225.0	196.0	236.4	323.9	...	...	...
3 Manufacturing	187.9	167.2	182.8	138.8	166.1	191.0	235.3	239.8	252.7	...	...	...
4 Electricity, gas and water	12.0	22.0	24.5	25.5	20.9	21.9	23.2	27.8	28.7	...	...	...
5 Construction	81.0	137.2	156.7	133.7	102.8	86.8	90.1	87.6	94.1	...	...	...
6 Wholesale and retail trade, restaurants and hotels	135.3	177.3	141.9	119.5	108.9	117.8	135.5	137.0	147.9	...	...	...
7 Transport, storage and communication	101.1	183.3	182.3	165.9	147.9	139.9	147.3	152.5	140.2	...	...	...
8 Finance, insurance, real estate and business services	164.8	356.2	378.9	318.2	275.3	214.0	238.6	213.5	192.4	...	...	...
9 Community, social and personal services	39.1	52.3	55.8	62.0	61.1	63.8	69.5	70.4	78.9	...	...	...
Total, Industries	1136.0	1462.1	1495.0	1378.6	1131.1	1076.2	1150.9	1180.8	1273.1	...	...	...
Producers of Government Services	135.4	205.9	241.1	253.7	261.3	271.3	288.0	299.6	314.3	...	...	...
Other Producers	...	...	...	...	...	...	...	...	...	...	...	...
Subtotal	1271.4	1668.0	1736.1	1632.3	1392.4	1347.5	1438.9	1480.4	1587.4	...	...	...
Less: Imputed bank service charge	113.8	263.6	267.6	239.4	194.2	155.7	176.0	132.9	120.0	...	...	...
Plus: Import duties	...	...	...	...	...	...	...	...	...	...	...	...
Plus: Value added tax	...	...	...	...	...	...	...	...	...	...	...	...
Equals: Gross Domestic Product	1158.1	1404.4	1468.5	1392.9	1198.2	1191.8	1262.9	1347.5	1467.5	...	...	...

1.11 Gross Domestic Product by Kind of Activity, in Constant Prices

Million Bahraini dinars

	1980	1983	1984	1985	1986	1987	1988	1989	1990	1991	1992	1993
	\multicolumn{12}{c}{At constant prices of:1985}
1 Agriculture, hunting, forestry and fishing	14.5	16.4	16.0	16.4	17.4	17.4	15.7	16.4	15.9	...	...	...
2 Mining and quarrying	641.4	356.5	402.2	398.6	422.1	377.2	384.7	397.3	411.9	...	...	...
3 Manufacturing	126.5	139.9	155.1	138.8	139.9	141.5	157.9	158.6	166.9	...	...	...
4 Electricity, gas and water	15.3	21.3	23.6	25.5	21.4	21.9	24.1	30.5	30.9	...	...	...
5 Construction	79.7	119.4	118.0	133.7	108.0	105.1	119.4	112.1	114.3	...	...	...
6 Wholesale and retail trade, restaurants and hotels	139.0	186.5	152.1	119.5	112.9	128.3	147.1	146.9	152.1	...	...	...
7 Transport, storage and communication	148.8	171.4	179.9	165.9	145.3	143.3	159.9	158.6	135.4	...	...	...
8 Finance, insurance, real estate and business services	121.4	301.2	294.9	318.2	315.4	256.2	271.0	216.9	203.9	...	...	...
9 Community, social and personal services	42.1	55.5	58.9	62.0	67.4	73.0	78.8	81.7	86.4	...	...	...

Bahrain

1.11 Gross Domestic Product by Kind of Activity, in Constant Prices
(Continued)

Million Bahraini dinars

	1980	1983	1984	1985	1986	1987	1988	1989	1990	1991	1992	1993
					At constant prices of:1985							
Total, Industries	1328.7	1368.1	1400.7	1378.6	1349.8	1263.9	1358.6	1319.0	1317.7	...	...	...
Producers of Government Services	188.1	220.0	238.3	253.7	291.0	313.1	328.3	337.7	349.7	...	...	...
Other Producers	...	...	...	...	...	...	...	...	...	...	...	...
Subtotal	1516.8	1588.1	1639.0	1632.3	1640.8	1577.0	1686.9	1656.7	1667.4	...	...	...
Less: Imputed bank service charge	72.7	233.3	217.2	239.4	225.6	178.8	186.2	118.8	110.6	...	...	...
Plus: Import duties	...	...	...	...	...	...	...	...	...	...	...	...
Plus: Value added tax	...	...	...	...	...	...	...	...	...	...	...	...
Equals: Gross Domestic Product	1443.7	1354.8	1421.8	1392.9	1415.2	1397.6	1500.5	1537.9	1556.9	...	...	...

1.12 Relations Among National Accounting Aggregates

Million Bahraini dinars

	1980	1983	1984	1985	1986	1987	1988	1989	1990	1991	1992	1993
Gross Domestic Product	1158.1	1404.4	1468.5	1392.9	1198.2	1191.8	1262.9	1347.5	1467.5	...	...	...
Plus: Net factor income from the rest of the world	-46.6	-60.8	-57.5	-109.7	-113.1	-107.7	-168.0	-98.7	-128.7	...	...	...
Factor income from the rest of the world	204.5	269.6	348.9	299.2	240.2	204.6	213.6	249.2	260.6	...	...	...
Less: Factor income to the rest of the world	251.1	330.4	406.4	408.9	353.3	312.3	381.6	347.9	389.3	...	...	...
Equals: Gross National Product	1111.5	1343.6	1411.0	1283.2	1085.1	1084.1	1094.9	1248.8	1338.8	...	...	...
Less: Consumption of fixed capital	120.6	166.8	199.0	203.9	210.0	208.8	225.9	224.6	229.3	...	...	...
Equals: National Income	990.9	1176.8	1212.0	1079.3	875.1	875.3	869.0	1024.2	1109.5	...	...	...
Plus: Net current transfers from the rest of the world	...	-38.4	-47.2	-88.3	-99.5	-91.6	-72.6	-74.8	-102.4	...	...	...
Equals: National Disposable Income	...	1138.4	1164.8	991.0	775.6	783.7	796.4	949.4	1007.1	...	...	...
Less: Final consumption	...	736.1	801.4	751.1	712.2	700.4	780.6	861.7	904.9	...	...	...
Equals: Net Saving	...	402.3	363.4	239.9	63.4	83.3	15.8	87.7	102.2	...	...	...
Less: Surplus of the nation on current transactions	...	-49.4	-31.0	-34.2	-15.7	-75.9	-63.1	-91.4	-128.7	...	...	...
Equals: Net Capital Formation	...	451.7	394.4	274.1	79.1	159.2	78.9	179.1	230.9	...	...	...

Bangladesh

Source. Reply to the United Nations National Accounts Questionnaire from the Bureau of Statistics, Dhake.
General note. The estimates shown in the following tables have been prepared by the Bureau of Statistics in accordance with the United Nations System of National Acounts so far as the existing data would permit.

1.1 Expenditure on the Gross Domestic Product, in Current Prices

Million Bangladesh taka — Fiscal year beginning 1 July

	1980	1983	1984	1985	1986	1987	1988	1989	1990	1991	1992	1993
1 Government final consumption expenditure	30825	44033	49690	58438	61245	69969	90455	103218	114732	124937	131575	146826
2 Private final consumption expenditure	192810	306491	347748	392801	458991	509429	551725	614255	685204	728632	753034	806495
3 Gross capital formation	37529	43548	52667	58446	69490	74306	85191	94427	95955	109851	132612	150711
A Increase in stocks	...	...	...	...	...	...	...	...	...	...	...	...
B Gross fixed capital formation	37529	43548	52667	58446	69490	74306	85191	94427	95955	109851	132612	150711
Residential buildings	12259	13570	17723	16685	19167	22322	24937	26960	27422	33714	...	...
Non-residential buildings	2670	2461	2217	2001	2953	3215	3553	3946	5206	4249	...	...
Other construction and land improvement etc.	8063	9175	10325	13804	13860	15605	20509	21907	24540	29731	...	...
Other	14537	18342	22402	25956	33510	33164	36192	41614	38787	42157	...	...
4 Exports of goods and services [a]	16977	26065	31189	33856	37587	45015	51185	61422	73634	90696	104169	126734
5 Less: Imports of goods and services [b]	46708	64952	74361	77314	88112	101583	118958	135751	135133	147614	173494	200405
Equals: Gross Domestic Product	231433	355185	406933	466227	539201	597136	659598	737571	834392	906502	947896	1030361

a) Item 'Exports of goods and services' refers to exports of goods and non-factor services.
b) Item 'Imports of goods and services' refers to imports of goods and non-factor services.

1.2 Expenditure on the Gross Domestic Product, in Constant Prices

Million Bangladesh taka — Fiscal year beginning 1 July

	1980	1983	1984	1985	1986	1987	1988	1989	1990	1991	1992	1993
					At constant prices of:1984							
1 Government final consumption expenditure	45701	49210	49690	53652	50457	52482	61450	64150	67095	69611	...	...
2 Private final consumption expenditure	296838	331644	347748	323331	356070	372376	400740	413296	403790	417303	...	...
3 Gross capital formation	52129	49786	52667	76785	61563	57988	60189	61460	57982	61181	...	...
A Increase in stocks	...	...	...	...	...	...	...	...	...	...	...	...
B Gross fixed capital formation	52129	49786	52667	76785	61563	57988	60189	61460	57982	61181	...	...
4 Exports of goods and services	32343	37721	31189	39653	48764	52313	53681	68728	73392	90398	...	...
5 Less: Imports of goods and services	74128	73326	74361	68828	74507	80024	109457	110107	87817	102304	...	...
Equals: Gross Domestic Product	352883	395035	406933	424593	442347	455135	466603	497527	514442	536189	...	...

1.3 Cost Components of the Gross Domestic Product

Million Bangladesh taka — Fiscal year beginning 1 July

	1980	1983	1984	1985	1986	1987	1988	1989	1990	1991	1992	1993
1 Indirect taxes, net	13464	18854	21794	25516	30082	32695	37601	41807	50070	57492	65589	72739
2 Consumption of fixed capital	16468	24872	27983	32045	36665	41247	46399	51640	58860	63882	68239	74942
3 Compensation of employees paid by resident producers to:	...	...	...	...	...	...	...	...	...	...	...	...
4 Operating surplus	...	...	...	...	...	...	...	...	...	...	...	...
Equals: Gross Domestic Product	231433	355185	406933	466227	539201	597136	659598	737571	834392	906502	947896	1030361

1.10 Gross Domestic Product by Kind of Activity, in Current Prices

Million Bangladesh taka — Fiscal year beginning 1 July

	1980	1983	1984	1985	1986	1987	1988	1989	1990	1991	1992	1993
1 Agriculture, hunting, forestry and fishing	94800	148264	169970	188382	219761	231623	245392	271790	300596	312438	288842	314945
2 Mining and quarrying	3	4	4	3	4	3	4	89	112	134	160	190
3 Manufacturing	25188	37733	40112	43563	47631	50437	55608	64506	72801	82571	92009	102822
4 Electricity, gas and water	744	1939	2348	2713	3545	4597	6719	8824	11201	14011	17002	20607
5 Construction	13008	18095	22518	26058	28839	34602	39262	43110	47261	53590	56717	60134
6 Wholesale and retail trade, restaurants and hotels	20778	33898	40039	43139	48028	53073	58103	65251	72309	78282	78306	82213
7 Transport, storage and communication	28677	41797	45655	54605	61901	65945	71774	75061	97697	108672	122466	129221
8 Finance, insurance, real estate and business services	24967	36521	41583	48968	54960	66188	78442	87897	97229	104754	106816	118232
9 Community, social and personal services	16655	28000	31469	41430	53665	65933	75091	88279	96995	108644	136368	151952
Statistical discrepancy	...	...	...	...	...	...	...	...	...	...	...	-5103

Bangladesh

1.10 Gross Domestic Product by Kind of Activity, in Current Prices
(Continued)

Million Bangladesh taka

Fiscal year beginning 1 July

	1980	1983	1984	1985	1986	1987	1988	1989	1990	1991	1992	1993
Total, Industries	224820	346251	393698	448861	518334	572401	630395	704807	796201	863096	898686	975213
Producers of Government Services	6613	8934	13235	17366	20867	24735	29203	32764	38191	43406	49210	55148
Other Producers	...	...	...	...	...	...	...	...	...	...	...	...
Subtotal	231433	355185	406933	466227	539201	597136	659598	737571	834392	906502	947896	1030361
Less: Imputed bank service charge	...	...	...	...	...	...	...	...	...	...	...	...
Plus: Import duties	...	...	...	...	...	...	...	...	...	...	...	...
Plus: Value added tax	...	...	...	...	...	...	...	...	...	...	...	...
Equals: Gross Domestic Product	231433	355185	406933	466227	539201	597136	659598	737571	834392	906502	947896	1030361

1.11 Gross Domestic Product by Kind of Activity, in Constant Prices

Million Bangladesh taka

Fiscal year beginning 1 July

	1980	1983	1984	1985	1986	1987	1988	1989	1990	1991	1992	1993
					At constant prices of:1984							
1 Agriculture, hunting, forestry and fishing	156068	168813	169970	175549	176250	174901	173037	190354	193421	197662	201230	204769
2 Mining and quarrying	4	4	4	3	4	2	3	66	80	94	107	121
3 Manufacturing	37118	40765	40112	41156	44403	44682	45927	49256	50423	54117	59033	64518
4 Electricity, gas and water	1114	2165	2348	2642	3217	3743	4822	5561	6704	7876	8933	10220
5 Construction	16705	20072	22518	22908	24469	27475	28816	29749	31087	32471	34032	35918
6 Wholesale and retail trade, restaurants and hotels	33552	39516	40039	40729	41845	43311	45423	46853	48712	50615	50631	52909
7 Transport, storage and communication	37518	43508	45655	47115	52341	54293	56611	59024	60840	63349	66416	69604
8 Finance, insurance, real estate and business services	36231	40234	41583	44568	46323	47873	49334	50862	52585	54354	52489	54188
9 Community, social and personal services	24769	29974	31469	33979	36304	40302	42791	45439	48256	51467	61108	65263
Total, Industries	343079	385051	393698	408649	425156	436582	446764	477164	492108	512005	533979	557510
Producers of Government Services	9804	9984	13235	15944	17191	18553	19839	20363	22334	24184	26240	28540
Other Producers	...	...	...	...	...	...	...	...	...	...	...	...
Subtotal	352883	395035	406933	424593	442347	455135	466603	497527	514442	536189	560219	586050
Less: Imputed bank service charge	...	...	...	...	...	...	...	...	...	...	...	...
Plus: Import duties	...	...	...	...	...	...	...	...	...	...	...	...
Plus: Value added tax	...	...	...	...	...	...	...	...	...	...	...	...
Equals: Gross Domestic Product	352883	395035	406933	424593	442347	455135	466603	497527	514442	536189	560219	586050

1.12 Relations Among National Accounting Aggregates

Million Bangladesh taka

Fiscal year beginning 1 July

	1980	1983	1984	1985	1986	1987	1988	1989	1990	1991	1992	1993
Gross Domestic Product	231433	355185	406933	466227	539201	597136	659598	737571	834392	906502	947896	1030361
Plus: Net factor income from the rest of the world	5820	12154	8618	11926	15548	20457	22529	22266	26513	33851	38798	45394
Equals: Gross National Product	237253	367339	415551	478153	554749	617593	682127	759837	860905	940353	986694	1075755
Less: Consumption of fixed capital	16468	24872	27983	32045	36665	41247	46399	51640	58860	63882	68239	74942
Equals: National Income	220785	342467	387568	446108	518084	576346	635728	708197	802045	876471	918455	1000813
Plus: Net current transfers from the rest of the world	11005	18409	19609	18214	23560	25786	21854	25265	29663	31176	32026	32987
Equals: National Disposable Income	231790	360876	407177	464322	541644	602132	657582	733462	831708	907647	950481	1033800
Less: Final consumption	223635	350524	397438	451239	520236	579398	642180	717473	799936	853569	884609	953321
Equals: Net Saving	8155	10352	9739	13083	21408	22734	15402	15989	31772	54078	65872	80479
Less: Surplus of the nation on current transactions	-12906	-8324	-14945	-13318	-11417	-10325	-23390	-26798	-5323	8109	1499	6079
Statistical discrepancy	...	...	...	...	...	...	...	...	...	...	...	1369
Equals: Net Capital Formation	21061	18676	24684	26401	32825	33059	38792	42787	37095	45969	64373	75769

Bangladesh

2.3 Total Government Outlays by Function and Type

Million Bangladesh taka — Fiscal year beginning 1 July

	Final Consumption Expenditures Total	Compensation of Employees	Other	Subsidies	Other Current Transfers & Property Income	Total Current Disbursements	Gross Capital Formation	Other Capital Outlays	Total Outlays
1980									
1 General public services	4675	1296	3379	1143	2026	7844	4049	129	12022
2 Defence	1949	1015	934	-	-	1949	169	-	2118
3 Public order and safety	1693	872	821	8	-	1701	19	-	1720
4 Education	1486	1224	262	-	846	2332	629	24	2985
5 Health	909	640	269	10	-	919	569	19	1507
6 Social security and welfare	226	87	139	-	21	247	121	4	372
7 Housing and community amenities	308	160	148	-	1067	1375	1226	15	2616
8 Recreation, culture and religion	38	3	35	-	37	75	-	-	75
9 Economic services	3905	999	2906	1467	693	6065	9019	141	15225
A Fuel and energy	441	10	431	15	200	656	685	41	1382
B Agriculture, forestry, fishing and hunting	2074	347	1727	1437	90	3601	1174	47	4822
C Mining (except fuels), manufacturing and construction	665	218	447	15	324	1004	2132	37	3173
D Transportation and communication	654	381	273	-	77	731	5028	16	5775
E Other economic affairs	71	43	28	-	2	73	-	-	73
10 Other functions	...	...	...	...	...	...	...	...	...
Total	15189	6296	8893	2628	4690	22507	15801	332	38640
1985									
1 General public services	11160	2094	9066	1590	2856	15606	171	-	15777
2 Defence	5350	5349	1	-	-	5350	465	-	5815
3 Public order and safety	3093	1828	1265	-	1	3094	348	-	3442
4 Education	4163	3491	672	15	2437	6615	579	1	7195
5 Health	2503	1574	929	9	22	2534	1142	9	3685
6 Social security and welfare	245	105	140	-	29	274	98	-	372
7 Housing and community amenities	1275	383	892	-	11	1286	1295	15	2596
8 Recreation, culture and religion	160	91	69	-	132	292	1	-	293
9 Economic services	7017	2625	4392	46	1401	8464	22759	335	31558
A Fuel and energy	1308	187	1121	32	474	1814	10228	44	12086
B Agriculture, forestry, fishing and hunting	3444	1599	1845	6	148	3598	3723	276	7597
C Mining (except fuels), manufacturing and construction	1438	437	1001	8	209	1655	4682	10	6347
D Transportation and communication	622	250	372	-	200	822	4126	5	4953
E Other economic affairs	205	152	53	-	370	575	-	-	575
10 Other functions	50	25	25	-	7	57	98	-	155
Total	35016	17565	17451	1660	6896	43572	26956	360	70888
1990									
1 General public services	18211	6065	12146	7618	5238	31067	270	2	31339
2 Defence	10307	5363	4944	-	3	10310	895	-	11205
3 Public order and safety	5557	3481	2076	-	-	5557	373	-	5930
4 Education	7172	6512	660	9	4569	11750	775	3	12528
5 Health	5150	4116	1034	-	46	5196	1951	-	7147
6 Social security and welfare	526	296	230	-	70	596	268	42	906
7 Housing and community amenities	2049	727	1322	6	1	2056	2082	14	4152
8 Recreation, culture and religion	265	157	108	-	237	502	2	-	504
9 Economic services	14355	4618	9737	1518	3143	19016	32436	256	51708
A Fuel and energy	1514	235	1279	20	909	2443	9648	33	12124
B Agriculture, forestry, fishing and hunting	6301	2862	3439	1494	749	8544	5793	208	14545
C Mining (except fuels), manufacturing and construction	3340	506	2834	4	803	4147	7529	15	11691
D Transportation and communication	2850	752	2098	-	135	2985	9466	-	12451
E Other economic affairs	350	263	87	-	547	897	-	-	897
10 Other functions	27	9	18	-	-	27	103	-	130
Total	63619	31344	32275	9151	13307	86077	39155	317	125549

Bangladesh

2.3 Total Government Outlays by Function and Type
(Continued)

Million Bangladesh taka

Fiscal year beginning 1 July

		Final Consumption Expenditures			Other Current Transfers & Property Income	Total Current Disbursements	Gross Capital Formation	Other Capital Outlays	Total Outlays
		Total	Compensation of Employees	Other	Subsidies				

1991

		Total	Comp.	Other	Subsidies	Other Current	Total Current	Gross Capital	Other Capital	Total Outlays
1	General public services	23430	7046	16384	5716	1675	30821	563	-	31384
2	Defence	11900	6192	5708	-	3	11903	1034	-	12937
3	Public order and safety	6500	4205	2295	-	-	6500	417	-	6917
4	Education	8424	7984	440	17	5380	13821	1105	46	14972
5	Health	6557	4800	1757	3	80	6640	1661	-	8301
6	Social security and welfare	587	323	264	-	79	666	281	18	965
7	Housing and community amenities	2450	858	1592	-	-	2450	2782	222	5454
8	Recreation, culture and religion	250	174	76	-	281	531	2	-	533
9	Economic services	14337	5731	8606	1624	3886	19847	36712	510	57069
	A Fuel and energy	1789	275	1514	35	2238	4062	11347	79	15488
	B Agriculture, forestry, fishing and hunting	5866	3380	2486	1579	367	7812	6673	388	14873
	C Mining (except fuels), manufacturing and construction	2507	643	1864	10	430	2947	5237	41	8225
	D Transportation and communication	3766	1103	2663	-	234	4000	13454	2	17456
	E Other economic affairs	409	330	79	-	617	1026	1	-	1027
10	Other functions	29	9	20	-	-	29	65	-	94
	Total	74464	37322	37142	7360	11384	93208	44622	796	138626

1992

		Total	Comp.	Other	Subsidies	Other Current	Total Current	Gross Capital	Other Capital	Total Outlays
1	General public services	24201	8510	15691	2872	1803	28876	953	-	29829
2	Defence	13761	7160	6601	-	3	13764	1196	-	14960
3	Public order and safety	7703	5431	2272	-	5	7708	428	-	8136
4	Education	9831	9228	603	-	7166	16997	381	6	17384
5	Health	8414	6008	2406	-	84	8498	2527	29	11054
6	Social security and welfare	747	411	336	-	115	862	146	-	1008
7	Housing and community amenities	2398	1028	1370	-	51	2449	898	268	3615
8	Recreation, culture and religion	336	232	104	-	418	754	5	-	759
9	Economic services	17828	8200	9628	1431	4752	24011	38298	1870	64179
	A Fuel and energy	4597	1402	3195	115	1948	6660	17541	175	24376
	B Agriculture, forestry, fishing and hunting	5797	4014	1783	414	763	6974	8559	1394	16927
	C Mining (except fuels), manufacturing and construction	2399	735	1664	6	655	3060	5474	153	8687
	D Transportation and communication	4522	1677	2845	896	417	5835	6722	148	12705
	E Other economic affairs	513	372	141	-	969	1482	2	-	1484
10	Other functions	276	29	247	-	-	276	120	-	396
	Total	85495	46237	39258	4303	14397	104195	44952	2173	151320

1993

		Total	Comp.	Other	Subsidies	Other Current	Total Current	Gross Capital	Other Capital	Total Outlays
1	General public services	26401	8992	17409	2030	1731	30162	901	64	31127
2	Defence	14953	7780	7173	-	4	14957	1299	-	16256
3	Public order and safety	7893	5628	2265	-	19	7912	388	-	8300
4	Education	10548	9890	658	-	8070	18618	450	6	19074
5	Health	8588	6011	2577	-	726	9314	4828	99	14241
6	Social security and welfare	558	341	217	-	86	644	36	-	680
7	Housing and community amenities	2270	1009	1261	-	83	2353	1598	169	4120
8	Recreation, culture and religion	350	240	110	-	337	687	4	-	691
9	Economic services	18997	8618	10379	1409	6308	26714	39795	2941	69450
	A Fuel and energy	4736	2038	2698	83	2402	7221	13523	255	20999
	B Agriculture, forestry, fishing and hunting	5542	3786	1756	1313	761	7616	9722	1565	18903
	C Mining (except fuels), manufacturing and construction	2844	810	2034	13	1458	4315	8155	694	13164
	D Transportation and communication	5358	1585	3773	-	597	5955	8394	427	14776
	E Other economic affairs	517	399	118	-	1090	1607	1	-	1608
10	Other functions	2852	50	2802	-	10	2862	333	6	3201
	Total	93410	48559	44851	3439	17374	114223	49632	3285	167140

Bangladesh

4.1 Derivation of Value Added by Kind of Activity, in Current Prices

Million Bangladesh taka
Fiscal year beginning 1 July

	1980 Gross Output	1980 Intermediate Consumption	1980 Value Added	1985 Gross Output	1985 Intermediate Consumption	1985 Value Added	1990 Gross Output	1990 Intermediate Consumption	1990 Value Added	1991 Gross Output	1991 Intermediate Consumption	1991 Value Added
All Producers												
1 Agriculture, hunting, forestry and fishing	...	...	94800	...	...	188382	...	...	300596	...	...	312438
A Agriculture and hunting	...	...	83440	...	...	154890	...	...	244387	...	...	250566
B Forestry and logging	...	...	5366	...	...	18981	...	...	28639	...	...	31005
C Fishing	...	...	5994	...	...	14511	...	...	27570	...	...	30867
2 Mining and quarrying	...	...	3	...	...	3	...	...	112	...	...	134
3 Manufacturing	...	...	25188	...	...	43563	...	...	72801	...	...	82571
4 Electricity, gas and water	...	...	744	...	...	2713	...	...	11201	...	...	14011
A Electricity, gas and steam	...	...	699	...	...	2584	...	...	10767	...	...	13623
B Water works and supply	...	...	45	...	...	129	...	...	434	...	...	388
5 Construction	...	...	13008	...	...	26058	...	...	47261	...	...	53590
6 Wholesale and retail trade, restaurants and hotels	...	...	20778	...	...	43139	...	...	72309	...	...	78282
A Wholesale and retail trade	...	...	20153	...	...	41505	...	...	68279	...	...	73766
B Restaurants and hotels	...	...	625	...	...	1634	...	...	4030	...	...	4516
7 Transport, storage and communication	...	...	28677	...	...	54605	...	...	97697	...	...	108672
A Transport and storage	...	...	28326	...	...	53199	...	...	93039	...	...	103513
B Communication	...	...	351	...	...	1406	...	...	4658	...	...	5159
8 Finance, insurance, real estate and business services	...	...	24967	...	...	48968	...	...	97229	...	...	104754
A Financial institutions	...	...	3436	...	...	8100	...	...	15188	...	...	16050
B Insurance	...	...	417	...	...	835	...	...	1111	...	...	1743
C Real estate and business services	...	...	21114	...	...	40033	...	...	80930	...	...	86961
Real estate, except dwellings	...	...	19913	...	...	37066	...	...	73867	...	...	79055
Dwellings	...	...	...	...	...	...	...	...	...	...	...	...
9 Community, social and personal services	...	...	16655	...	...	41430	...	...	96995	...	...	108644
A Sanitary and similar services	...	...	...	...	...	...	...	...	...	...	...	...
B Social and related community services	...	...	6915	...	...	15338	...	...	32749	...	...	36683
Educational services	...	...	5427	...	...	11545	...	...	24196	...	...	27107
Medical, dental, other health and veterinary services	...	...	1488	...	...	3793	...	...	8553	...	...	9576
C Recreational and cultural services	...	...	315	...	...	650	...	...	1327	...	...	1489
D Personal and household services	...	...	9425	...	...	25442	...	...	62919	...	...	70472
Statistical discrepancy	...	...	...	...	...	...	...	...	...	...	...	...
Total, Industries	...	...	224820	...	...	448861	...	...	796201	...	...	863096
Producers of Government Services	...	...	6613	...	...	17366	...	...	38191	...	...	43406
Other Producers	...	...	...	...	...	...	...	...	...	...	...	...
Total	...	...	231433	...	...	466227	...	...	834392	...	...	906502
Less: Imputed bank service charge	...	...	...	...	...	...	...	...	...	...	...	...
Import duties	...	...	...	...	...	...	...	...	...	...	...	...
Value added tax	...	...	...	...	...	...	...	...	...	...	...	...
Total	...	...	231433	...	...	466227	...	...	834392	...	...	906502

	1992 Gross Output	1992 Intermediate Consumption	1992 Value Added	1993 Gross Output	1993 Intermediate Consumption	1993 Value Added
All Producers						
1 Agriculture, hunting, forestry and fishing	...	...	288842	...	...	314945
A Agriculture and hunting	...	...	216273	...	...	232565
B Forestry and logging	...	...	32442	...	...	33975
C Fishing	...	...	40127	...	...	48405
2 Mining and quarrying	...	...	160	...	...	190
3 Manufacturing	...	...	92009	...	...	102822
4 Electricity, gas and water	...	...	17002	...	...	20607
A Electricity, gas and steam	...	...	...	...	...	...
B Water works and supply	...	...	...	...	...	...

Bangladesh

4.1 Derivation of Value Added by Kind of Activity, in Current Prices
(Continued)

Million Bangladesh taka — Fiscal year beginning 1 July

	1992 Gross Output	1992 Intermediate Consumption	1992 Value Added	1993 Gross Output	1993 Intermediate Consumption	1993 Value Added
5 Construction	...	...	56717	...	...	60134
6 Wholesale and retail trade, restaurants and hotels	...	...	78306	...	...	82213
A Wholesale and retail trade	...	...	...	...	...	...
B Restaurants and hotels	...	...	...	...	...	...
7 Transport, storage and communication	...	...	122466	...	...	129221
A Transport and storage	...	...	...	...	...	...
B Communication	...	...	...	...	...	...
8 Finance, insurance, real estate and business services	...	...	106816	...	...	118232
A Financial institutions	...	...	...	...	...	...
B Insurance	...	...	...	...	...	...
C Real estate and business services	...	...	...	...	...	...
Real estate, except dwellings	...	...	...	...	...	...
Dwellings	...	...	...	...	...	...
9 Community, social and personal services	...	...	136368	...	...	151952
A Sanitary and similar services	...	...	...	...	...	...
B Social and related community services	...	...	...	...	...	...
Educational services	...	...	...	...	...	...
Medical, dental, other health and veterinary services	...	...	...	...	...	...
C Recreational and cultural services	...	...	...	...	...	...
D Personal and household services	...	...	...	...	...	...
Statistical discrepancy	...	...	...	...	...	-5103
Total, Industries	...	...	898686	...	...	975213
Producers of Government Services	...	...	49210	...	...	55148
Other Producers	...	...	...	...	...	...
Total	...	...	947896	...	...	1030361
Less: Imputed bank service charge	...	...	...	...	...	...
Import duties	...	...	...	...	...	...
Value added tax	...	...	...	...	...	...
Total	...	...	947896	...	...	1030361

4.2 Derivation of Value Added by Kind of Activity, in Constant Prices

Million Bangladesh taka — Fiscal year beginning 1 July

At constant prices of: 1984 — All Producers

	1980 Gross Output	1980 Intermediate Consumption	1980 Value Added	1985 Gross Output	1985 Intermediate Consumption	1985 Value Added	1990 Gross Output	1990 Intermediate Consumption	1990 Value Added	1991 Gross Output	1991 Intermediate Consumption	1991 Value Added
1 Agriculture, hunting, forestry and fishing	...	...	156068	...	...	175549	...	...	193421	...	...	197662
A Agriculture and hunting	...	...	135982	...	...	151730	...	...	166677	...	...	169716
B Forestry and logging	...	...	9572	...	...	11413	...	...	12845	...	...	13147
C Fishing	...	...	10514	...	...	12406	...	...	13899	...	...	14799
2 Mining and quarrying	...	...	4	...	...	3	...	...	80	...	...	94
3 Manufacturing	...	...	37118	...	...	41156	...	...	50423	...	...	54117
4 Electricity, gas and water	...	...	1114	...	...	2642	...	...	6704	...	...	7876
A Electricity, gas and steam	...	...	1047	...	...	2516	...	...	6444	...	...	7658
B Water works and supply	...	...	67	...	...	126	...	...	260	...	...	218
5 Construction	...	...	16705	...	...	22908	...	...	31087	...	...	32471
6 Wholesale and retail trade, restaurants and hotels	...	...	33552	...	...	40729	...	...	48712	...	...	50615
A Wholesale and retail trade	...	...	32546	...	...	39389	...	...	46707	...	...	48561
B Restaurants and hotels	...	...	1006	...	...	1340	...	...	2005	...	...	2054
7 Transport, storage and communication	...	...	37518	...	...	47115	...	...	60840	...	...	63349
A Transport and storage	...	...	37064	...	...	45928	...	...	57513	...	...	59664

Bangladesh

4.2 Derivation of Value Added by Kind of Activity, in Constant Prices
(Continued)

Million Bangladesh taka — Fiscal year beginning 1 July

	1980 G.O.	1980 I.C.	1980 V.A.	1985 G.O.	1985 I.C.	1985 V.A.	1990 G.O.	1990 I.C.	1990 V.A.	1991 G.O.	1991 I.C.	1991 V.A.
				At constant prices of:1984								
B Communication	...	...	454	...	...	1187	...	...	3327	...	...	3685
8 Finance, insurance, real estate and business services	...	...	36231	...	...	44568	...	...	52585	...	...	54354
A Financial institutions	...	...	5147	...	...	7887	...	...	9090	...	...	9023
B Insurance	...	...	624	...	...	813	...	...	665	...	...	979
C Real estate and business services	...	...	30460	...	...	35868	...	...	42830	...	...	44352
Real estate, except dwellings	...	...	28668	...	...	33435	...	...	39316	...	...	40656
Dwellings	...	...	...	...	...	...	...	...	...	...	...	...
9 Community, social and personal services	...	...	24769	...	...	33979	...	...	48256	...	...	51467
A Sanitary and similar services	...	...	...	...	...	...	...	...	...	...	...	...
B Social and related community services	...	...	8739	...	...	12580	...	...	16293	...	...	18681
Educational services	...	...	6556	...	...	9469	...	...	12038	...	...	13949
Medical, dental, other health and veterinary services	...	...	2183	...	...	3111	...	...	4225	...	...	4732
C Recreational and cultural services	...	...	364	...	...	533	...	...	660	...	...	784
D Personal and household services	...	...	15666	...	...	20866	...	...	31303	...	...	32002
Total, Industries	...	...	343079	...	...	408649	...	...	492108	...	...	512005
Producers of Government Services	...	...	9804	...	...	15944	...	...	22334	...	...	24184
Other Producers	...	...	...	...	...	...	...	...	...	...	...	...
Total	...	...	352883	...	...	424593	...	...	514442	...	...	536189
Less: Imputed bank service charge	...	...	...	...	...	...	...	...	...	...	...	...
Import duties	...	...	...	...	...	...	...	...	...	...	...	...
Value added tax	...	...	...	...	...	...	...	...	...	...	...	...
Total	...	...	352883	...	...	424593	...	...	514442	...	...	536189

	1992 Gross Output	1992 Intermediate Consumption	1992 Value Added	1993 Gross Output	1993 Intermediate Consumption	1993 Value Added
	At constant prices of:1984					
	All Producers					
1 Agriculture, hunting, forestry and fishing	...	...	201230	...	...	204769
A Agriculture and hunting	...	...	171914	...	...	173687
B Forestry and logging	...	...	13536	...	...	13937
C Fishing	...	...	15780	...	...	17145
2 Mining and quarrying	...	...	107	...	...	121
3 Manufacturing	...	...	59033	...	...	64518
4 Electricity, gas and water	...	...	8933	...	...	10220
A Electricity, gas and steam	...	...	...	...	...	...
B Water works and supply	...	...	...	...	...	...
5 Construction	...	...	34032	...	...	35918
6 Wholesale and retail trade, restaurants and hotels	...	...	50631	...	...	52909
A Wholesale and retail trade	...	...	...	...	...	...
B Restaurants and hotels	...	...	...	...	...	...
7 Transport, storage and communication	...	...	66416	...	...	69604
A Transport and storage	...	...	...	...	...	...
B Communication	...	...	...	...	...	...
8 Finance, insurance, real estate and business services	...	...	52489	...	...	54188
A Financial institutions	...	...	...	...	...	...
B Insurance	...	...	...	...	...	...
C Real estate and business services	...	...	...	...	...	...
Real estate, except dwellings	...	...	...	...	...	...

Bangladesh

4.2 Derivation of Value Added by Kind of Activity, in Constant Prices
(Continued)

Million Bangladesh taka
Fiscal year beginning 1 July

	1992 Gross Output	1992 Intermediate Consumption	1992 Value Added	1993 Gross Output	1993 Intermediate Consumption	1993 Value Added
	\multicolumn{6}{c}{At constant prices of:1984}
Dwellings	...	...	...	...	...	...
9 Community, social and personal services	...	...	61108	...	...	65263
A Sanitary and similar services	...	...	...	...	...	...
B Social and related community services	...	...	...	...	...	...
Educational services	...	...	...	...	...	...
Medical, dental, other health and veterinary services	...	...	...	...	...	...
C Recreational and cultural services	...	...	...	...	...	...
D Personal and household services	...	...	...	...	...	...
Total, Industries	...	...	533979	...	...	557510
Producers of Government Services	...	...	26240	...	...	28540
Other Producers	...	...	...	...	...	...
Total	...	...	560219	...	...	586050
Less: Imputed bank service charge	...	...	...	...	...	...
Import duties	...	...	...	...	...	...
Value added tax	...	...	...	...	...	...
Total	...	...	560219	...	...	586050

Barbados

Source. Reply to the United Nations National Accounts Questionnaire from the Barbados Statistical Service, Garrison, St. Michael. Information on concepts, sources and methods of estimation utilized, are published by the same Service in 'National Income and Product, 1960-1962'.

General note. The estimates have been prepared in accordance with the United Nations System of National Accounts so far as the existing data would permit.

1.1 Expenditure on the Gross Domestic Product, in Current Prices

Million Barbados dollars

		1980	1983	1984	1985	1986	1987	1988	1989	1990	1991	1992	1993
1	Government final consumption expenditure	258.2	346.1	387.6	456.3	468.8	497.5	537.3	614.1	693.7	642.0	639.6	732.2
2	Private final consumption expenditure	1081.1	1321.2	1431.9	1396.7	1692.3	1934.0	2004.0	2144.8	2188.5	2262.2	1987.7	2019.3
3	Gross capital formation	424.3	421.2	373.9	371.8	423.8	466.7	543.3	656.3	648.3	580.4	300.8	451.8
	A Increase in stocks	29.0	6.2	-5.7	7.5	-3.5	6.8	8.4	11.1	-3.1	29.5	-48.8	12.1
	B Gross fixed capital formation	395.3	415.0	379.6	364.3	427.3	459.9	534.9	645.2	651.4	551.0	349.6	439.7
4	Exports of goods and services	1213.7	1489.8	1656.4	1632.7	1495.9	1340.1	1509.7	1724.0	1689.3	1610.1	1587.2	1577.1
5	Less: Imports of goods and services	1246.8	1465.6	1547.1	1447.6	1434.7	1324.6	1495.1	1725.2	1779.5	1701.3	1343.9	1499.7
	Equals: Gross Domestic Product	1730.5	2112.7	2302.8	2409.9	2646.0	2913.7	3099.2	3414.0	3440.2	3393.4	3171.3	3280.6

1.10 Gross Domestic Product by Kind of Activity, in Current Prices

Million Barbados dollars

		1980	1983	1984	1985	1986	1987	1988	1989	1990	1991	1992	1993
1	Agriculture, hunting, forestry and fishing	152.3	135.5	139.2	138.0	146.3	171.6	172.9	153.0	159.5	161.8	147.0	146.7
2	Mining and quarrying	11.5	16.3	31.1	27.9	16.9	18.4	17.1	17.5	19.5	18.6	17.0	15.2
3	Manufacturing	183.5	238.7	264.1	231.7	229.3	223.6	240.2	233.3	237.6	230.8	203.2	210.0
4	Electricity, gas and water	33.1	52.9	68.0	72.7	72.2	80.7	84.8	91.6	91.7	99.8	105.2	101.6
5	Construction	118.2	132.5	130.0	117.9	131.4	144.3	170.3	196.7	193.9	161.9	112.6	116.3
6	Wholesale and retail trade, restaurants and hotels	501.9	565.0	619.0	676.0	719.6	799.9	862.9	942.3	927.6	890.9	816.2	868.7
7	Transport, storage and communication	86.9	154.1	171.0	185.0	197.5	225.4	226.6	227.8	244.5	254.2	248.6	255.1
8	Finance, insurance, real estate and business services	172.6	258.9	270.9	297.8	311.0	313.0	358.5	424.8	432.9	435.5	453.1	437.1
9	Community, social and personal services	57.6	80.9	85.7	89.6	94.1	97.3	99.2	106.1	109.3	109.7	107.7	110.6
	Total, Industries	1317.6	1634.8	1779.0	1836.6	1918.3	2074.2	2232.5	2393.1	2416.6	2363.2	2210.6	2261.3
	Producers of Government Services	218.2	264.3	295.5	344.0	379.0	424.8	435.1	503.4	548.7	530.1	486.7	509.2
	Other Producers	...	...	...	...	...	...	...	...	...	...	...	...
	Subtotal [a]	1535.8	1898.9	2074.6	2180.7	2297.3	2498.9	2667.6	2896.5	2965.3	2893.4	2697.2	2770.6
	Less: Imputed bank service charge	...	...	...	...	...	...	...	...	...	...	...	...
	Plus: Import duties	...	...	...	...	...	...	...	...	...	...	...	...
	Plus: Value added tax	...	...	...	...	...	...	...	...	...	...	...	...
	Plus: Other adjustments [b]	194.7	213.7	228.2	229.3	348.7	414.8	431.6	517.5	474.9	500.0	474.1	509.9
	Equals: Gross Domestic Product	1730.5	2112.7	2302.8	2409.9	2646.0	2913.7	3099.2	3414.0	3440.2	3393.4	3171.3	3280.6

a) Gross domestic product in factor values.
b) Item 'Other adjustments' refers to indirect taxes net of subsidies.

1.11 Gross Domestic Product by Kind of Activity, in Constant Prices

Million Barbados dollars

		1980	1983	1984	1985	1986	1987	1988	1989	1990	1991	1992	1993
		\multicolumn{12}{c	}{At constant prices of:1974}
1	Agriculture, hunting, forestry and fishing	82.6	69.3	75.8	75.4	78.8	70.0	65.9	60.0	65.1	62.1	56.4	52.4
2	Mining and quarrying	4.3	4.9	6.8	7.3	7.7	7.2	6.7	6.2	6.5	6.3	5.7	5.9
3	Manufacturing	94.8	88.7	90.4	81.8	86.0	80.3	85.7	90.3	87.9	83.0	76.0	75.7
4	Electricity, gas and water	16.8	19.5	20.4	21.4	22.8	23.7	25.3	26.1	26.4	27.2	27.6	27.6
5	Construction	56.4	51.2	50.7	49.9	53.5	56.8	61.9	66.9	60.1	55.6	51.1	52.2
6	Wholesale and retail trade, restaurants and hotels	267.6	228.5	240.2	244.7	260.0	283.7	299.7	316.5	299.2	277.0	261.9	269.1
7	Transport, storage and communication	49.7	54.3	57.0	58.7	61.4	64.5	64.8	68.9	62.9	67.6	65.2	66.0
8	Finance, insurance, real estate and business services	128.1	134.1	135.4	140.8	145.0	145.7	150.1	155.5	151.4	147.7	139.9	141.1
9	Community, social and personal services												

Barbados

1.11 Gross Domestic Product by Kind of Activity, in Constant Prices
(Continued)

Million Barbados dollars

	1980	1983	1984	1985	1986	1987	1988	1989	1990	1991	1992	1993
					At constant prices of:1974							
Total, Industries	700.3	650.5	676.7	680.0	715.2	731.9	760.1	790.4	759.5	726.5	683.8	690.0
Producers of Government Services	102.0	101.3	101.8	106.9	111.8	116.2	117.4	118.6	120.4	117.8	108.1	112.0
Other Producers	...	...	...	...	...	...	...	...	...	...	...	...
Subtotal a	802.3	751.8	778.5	786.9	827.0	848.1	877.5	909.1	880.9	844.3	791.9	802.1
Less: Imputed bank service charge	...	...	...	...	...	...	...	...	...	...	...	...
Plus: Import duties	...	...	...	...	...	...	...	...	...	...	...	...
Plus: Value added tax	...	...	...	...	...	...	...	...	...	...	...	...
Equals: Gross Domestic Product	...	...	...	...	...	...	...	...	...	...	...	...

a) Gross domestic product in factor values.

Belarus

Source. Reply to the United Nations national accounts questionnaire from the State Committee of Republic of Belarus on Statistics and Analysis.

General note. The estimates shown in the following tables have been prepared in accordance with the System of National Accounts so far as existing data would permit.

1.1 Expenditure on the Gross Domestic Product, in Current Prices

Thousand Million Roubles

	1980	1983	1984	1985	1986	1987	1988	1989	1990	1991	1992	1993
1 Government final consumption expenditure	...	...	...	...	...	...	...	...	10.2	18.2	146.2	1920.7
2 Private final consumption expenditure	...	...	...	...	...	...	...	...	20.1	39.5	459.2	5760.1
A Households	...	...	...	...	...	...	...	...	18.7	35.9	420.0	5299.2
B Private non-profit institutions serving households	...	...	...	...	...	...	...	...	1.4	3.6	39.3	460.9
3 Gross capital formation	...	...	...	...	...	...	...	...	11.5	25.3	295.1	3752.6
A Increase in stocks	...	...	...	...	...	...	...	...	2.0	6.0	60.5	703.0
B Gross fixed capital formation	...	...	...	...	...	...	...	...	9.5	19.3	234.6	3049.6
4 Exports of goods and services	...	...	...	...	...	...	...	...	19.9	32.1	548.0	5777.3
5 Less: Imports of goods and services	...	...	...	...	...	...	...	...	18.9	29.1	534.7	6834.4
Equals: Gross Domestic Product	...	...	...	...	...	...	...	...	42.7	85.9	914.0	10376.4

1.2 Expenditure on the Gross Domestic Product, in Constant Prices

Thousand Million Roubles

	1980	1983	1984	1985	1986	1987	1988	1989	1990	1991	1992	1993
					At constant prices of:1990							
1 Government final consumption expenditure	...	...	...	...	...	...	...	...	10.2	9.4	15.4	130.9
2 Private final consumption expenditure	...	...	...	...	...	...	...	...	20.1	18.9	36.3	452.2
A Households	...	...	...	...	...	...	...	...	18.7	17.4	33.1	413.9
B Private non-profit institutions serving households	...	...	...	...	...	...	...	...	1.4	1.5	3.3	38.3
3 Gross capital formation	...	...	...	...	...	...	...	...	11.5	13.3	21.3	258.2
A Increase in stocks	...	...	...	...	...	...	...	...	2.0	3.3	5.5	59.8
B Gross fixed capital formation	...	...	...	...	...	...	...	...	9.5	10.0	15.8	198.4
4 Exports of goods and services	...	...	...	...	...	...	...	...	19.9	19.7	21.2	330.8
5 Less: Imports of goods and services	...	...	...	...	...	...	...	...	18.9	19.0	16.6	354.7
Equals: Gross Domestic Product [a]	...	...	...	...	...	...	...	...	42.7	42.2	77.6	817.3

a) Beginning 1991, the base year for this table is the preceding year (T-1).

1.3 Cost Components of the Gross Domestic Product

Thousand Million Roubles

	1980	1983	1984	1985	1986	1987	1988	1989	1990	1991	1992	1993
1 Indirect taxes, net	...	...	...	...	...	...	...	...	2.6	4.2	74.1	962.9
A Indirect taxes	...	...	...	...	...	...	...	...	9.7	11.5	177.0	1985.5
B Less: Subsidies	...	...	...	...	...	...	...	...	7.2	7.2	102.8	1022.6
2 Consumption of fixed capital	...	...	...	...	...	...	...	...	6.3	11.9	157.6	2054.3
3 Compensation of employees paid by resident producers to:	...	...	...	...	...	...	...	...	20.1	36.3	383.4	5118.9
A Resident households	...	...	...	...	...	...	...	...	20.1	36.3	383.4	5118.9
B Rest of the world	...	...	...	...	...	...	...	...	...	...	...	...
4 Operating surplus	...	...	...	...	...	...	...	...	13.7	33.4	298.8	2240.2
A Corporate and quasi-corporate enterprises	...	...	...	...	...	...	...	...	11.5	28.6	205.7	1355.5
B Private unincorporated enterprises	...	...	...	...	...	...	...	...	2.2	4.8	93.1	884.7
C General government	...	...	...	...	...	...	...	...	...	...	...	...
Equals: Gross Domestic Product	...	...	...	...	...	...	...	...	42.7	85.9	914.0	10376.4

Belarus

1.4 General Government Current Receipts and Disbursements

Thousand Million Roubles

	1980	1983	1984	1985	1986	1987	1988	1989	1990	1991	1992	1993
Receipts												
1 Operating surplus	...	...	...	...	...	...	...	...	...	...	...	...
2 Property and entrepreneurial income	...	...	...	...	...	...	...	...	0.4	0.5	14.2	0.1
3 Taxes, fees and contributions	...	...	...	...	...	...	...	...	9.7	11.5	177.0	1985.5
A Indirect taxes	...	...	...	...	...	...	...	...	9.7	11.5	177.0	1985.5
B Direct taxes	...	...	...	...	...	...	...	...	...	...	...	...
C Social security contributions	...	...	...	...	...	...	...	...	...	...	...	...
D Compulsory fees, fines and penalties	...	...	...	...	...	...	...	...	...	...	...	...
4 Other current transfers	...	...	...	...	...	...	...	...	5.0	10.6	195.4	2675.9
Total Current Receipts of General Government	...	...	...	...	...	...	...	...	15.1	22.6	386.6	4661.6
Disbursements												
1 Government final consumption expenditure	...	...	...	...	...	...	...	...	10.2	18.2	146.2	1920.7
A Compensation of employees	...	...	...	...	...	...	...	...	3.8	7.7	70.6	861.6
B Consumption of fixed capital	...	...	...	...	...	...	...	...	0.6	0.9	13.7	202.3
C Purchases of goods and services, net	...	...	...	...	...	...	...	...	5.7	9.6	61.4	854.3
D Less: Own account fixed capital formation	...	...	...	...	...	...	...	...	...	...	...	...
E Indirect taxes paid, net	...	...	...	...	...	...	...	...	-	-	0.5	2.4
2 Property income	...	...	...	...	...	...	...	...	0.5	1.6	6.3	48.5
A Interest	...	...	...	...	...	...	...	...	0.5	1.6	6.3	48.5
B Net land rent and royalties	...	...	...	...	...	...	...	...	-	-	-	-
3 Subsidies	...	...	...	...	...	...	...	...	7.2	7.2	102.8	1022.6
4 Other current transfers	...	...	...	...	...	...	...	...	3.7	8.8	80.2	1020.9
5 Net saving	...	...	...	...	...	...	...	...	-6.4	-13.2	51.1	648.9
Total Current Disbursements and Net Saving of General Government	...	...	...	...	...	...	...	...	15.1	22.6	386.6	4661.6

1.5 Current Income and Outlay of Corporate and Quasi-Corporate Enterprises, Summary

Thousand Million Roubles

	1980	1983	1984	1985	1986	1987	1988	1989	1990	1991	1992	1993
Receipts												
1 Operating surplus	...	...	...	...	...	...	...	...	11.5	28.6	205.7	1355.5
2 Property and entrepreneurial income received	...	...	...	...	...	...	...	...	-	2.8	35.8	1209.3
3 Current transfers	...	...	...	...	...	...	...	...	0.9	0.8	8.3	135.5
Total Current Receipts	...	...	...	...	...	...	...	...	12.4	32.2	249.9	2700.3
Disbursements												
1 Property and entrepreneurial income	...	...	...	...	...	...	...	...	0.3	2.5	47.3	1225.2
2 Direct taxes and other current payments to general government	...	...	...	...	...	...	...	...	...	...	...	...
3 Other current transfers	...	...	...	...	...	...	...	...	4.3	11.1	140.0	1954.9
4 Net saving	...	...	...	...	...	...	...	...	7.9	18.6	62.6	-479.8
Total Current Disbursements and Net Saving	...	...	...	...	...	...	...	...	12.4	32.2	249.9	2700.3

1.6 Current Income and Outlay of Households and Non-Profit Institutions

Thousand Million Roubles

	1980	1983	1984	1985	1986	1987	1988	1989	1990	1991	1992	1993
Receipts												
1 Compensation of employees	...	...	...	...	...	...	...	...	20.1	36.3	383.4	5118.9
A From resident producers	...	...	...	...	...	...	...	...	20.1	36.3	383.4	5118.9
B From rest of the world	...	...	...	...	...	...	...	...	...	...	...	...
2 Operating surplus of private unincorporated enterprises	...	...	...	...	...	...	...	...	2.2	4.8	93.1	884.7
3 Property and entrepreneurial income	...	...	...	...	...	...	...	...	0.4	0.7	3.6	70.1
4 Current transfers	...	...	...	...	...	...	...	...	5.5	13.7	161.1	1927.0
Total Current Receipts	...	...	...	...	...	...	...	...	28.2	55.5	641.1	8000.7

Belarus

1.6 Current Income and Outlay of Households and Non-Profit Institutions
(Continued)

Thousand Million Roubles

	1980	1983	1984	1985	1986	1987	1988	1989	1990	1991	1992	1993
					Disbursements							
1 Private final consumption expenditure	...	...	...	...	...	...	...	...	20.1	39.5	459.2	5760.1
2 Property income	...	...	...	...	...	...	...	...	-	-	-	1.2
3 Direct taxes and other current transfers n.e.c. to general government	...	...	...	...	...	...	...	...	3.4	5.2	118.0	1661.6
4 Other current transfers	...	...	...	...	...	...	...	...	...	...	...	...
5 Net saving	...	...	...	...	...	...	...	...	4.7	10.8	63.9	577.8
Total Current Disbursements and Net Saving	...	...	...	...	...	...	...	...	28.2	55.5	641.1	8000.7

1.8 Capital Transactions of The Nation, Summary

Thousand Million Roubles

	1980	1983	1984	1985	1986	1987	1988	1989	1990	1991	1992	1993
					Finance of Gross Capital Formation							
Gross saving	...	...	...	...	...	...	...	...	12.5	28.2	335.3	2801.2
1 Consumption of fixed capital	...	...	...	...	...	...	...	...	6.3	11.9	157.6	2054.3
A General government	...	...	...	...	...	...	...	...	0.6	0.9	13.7	202.3
B Corporate and quasi-corporate enterprises	...	...	...	...	...	...	...	...	5.3	10.3	137.0	1676.3
C Other	...	...	...	...	...	...	...	...	0.5	0.7	6.9	175.7
2 Net saving	...	...	...	...	...	...	...	...	6.1	16.3	177.6	746.9
A General government	...	...	...	...	...	...	...	...	-6.4	-13.2	51.1	648.9
B Corporate and quasi-corporate enterprises	...	...	...	...	...	...	...	...	7.9	18.6	62.6	-479.8
C Other	...	...	...	...	...	...	...	...	4.7	10.8	63.9	577.8
Less: Surplus of the nation on current transactions	...	...	...	...	...	...	...	...	1.0	3.0	40.1	-951.4
Finance of Gross Capital Formation	...	...	...	...	...	...	...	...	11.5	25.3	295.1	3752.6
					Gross Capital Formation							
Increase in stocks	...	...	...	...	...	...	...	...	2.0	6.0	60.5	703.0
Gross fixed capital formation	...	...	...	...	...	...	...	...	9.5	19.3	234.6	3049.6
1 General government	...	...	...	...	...	...	...	...	0.9	1.6	20.8	553.4
2 Corporate and quasi-corporate enterprises	...	...	...	...	...	...	...	...	6.8	13.9	171.3	1771.6
3 Other	...	...	...	...	...	...	...	...	1.8	3.9	42.5	724.6
Gross Capital Formation	...	...	...	...	...	...	...	...	11.5	25.3	295.1	3752.6

1.10 Gross Domestic Product by Kind of Activity, in Current Prices

Thousand Million Roubles

	1980	1983	1984	1985	1986	1987	1988	1989	1990	1991	1992	1993
1 Agriculture, hunting, forestry and fishing	...	...	...	...	...	...	...	...	9.9	17.4	207.5	1833.1
2 Mining and quarrying	...	...	...	...	...	...	...	...	0.1	0.1	0.7	11.3
3 Manufacturing	...	...	...	...	...	...	...	...	16.3	34.5	334.7	3338.1
4 Electricity, gas and water	...	...	...	...	...	...	...	...				
5 Construction	...	...	...	...	...	...	...	...	3.3	6.5	63.7	817.3
6 Wholesale and retail trade, restaurants and hotels	...	...	...	...	...	...	...	...	1.5	4.0	44.8	864.6
7 Transport, storage and communication	...	...	...	...	...	...	...	...	2.9	4.9	78.5	1121.8
8 Finance, insurance, real estate and business services	...	...	...	...	...	...	...	...	1.8	4.1	53.0	1330.3
9 Community, social and personal services	...	...	...	...	...	...	...	...	3.3	7.1	69.8	868.3
Statistical discrepancy [a]	...	...	...	...	...	...	...	...	0.6	1.3	12.8	195.5
Total, Industries	...	...	...	...	...	...	...	...	39.7	80.0	865.4	10380.4
Producers of Government Services	...	...	...	...	...	...	...	...	1.8	3.5	18.9	229.7

Belarus

1.10 Gross Domestic Product by Kind of Activity, in Current Prices
(Continued)

Thousand Million Roubles

	1980	1983	1984	1985	1986	1987	1988	1989	1990	1991	1992	1993
Other Producers	...	...	...	...	...	...	...	...	0.1	0.2	1.1	10.6
Subtotal	...	...	...	...	...	...	...	...	41.6	83.7	885.4	10620.7
Less: Imputed bank service charge	...	...	...	...	...	...	...	...	-	1.3	15.8	855.0
Plus: Import duties	...	...	...	...	...	...	...	...	0.8	1.3	0.9	63.9
Plus: Value added tax	...	...	...	...	...	...	...	...	...	...	...	...
Plus: Other adjustments [b]	...	...	...	...	...	...	...	...	0.3	2.2	43.4	546.9
Equals: Gross Domestic Product	...	...	...	...	...	...	...	...	42.7	85.9	914.0	10376.4

a) Item 'Statistical discrepancy' refers to other activities of the material sphere.
b) Item 'Other adjustments' refers to indirect taxes net of subsidies.

1.11 Gross Domestic Product by Kind of Activity, in Constant Prices

Thousand Million Roubles

	1980	1983	1984	1985	1986	1987	1988	1989	1990	1991	1992	1993
				At constant prices of: 1990								
1 Agriculture, hunting, forestry and fishing	...	...	...	...	...	...	...	...	9.9	9.6	14.9	185.9
2 Mining and quarrying	...	...	...	...	...	...	...	...	0.1	0.1	0.1	0.6
3 Manufacturing	...	...	...	...	...	...	...	...	16.3	16.4	32.7	300.1
4 Electricity, gas and water	...	...	...	...	...	...	...	...				
5 Construction	...	...	...	...	...	...	...	...	3.3	3.3	6.0	52.5
6 Wholesale and retail trade, restaurants and hotels	...	...	...	...	...	...	...	...	1.5	1.4	3.3	39.0
7 Transport, storage and communication	...	...	...	...	...	...	...	...	2.9	2.8	3.9	64.0
8 Finance, insurance, real estate and business services	...	...	...	...	...	...	...	...	1.8	1.8	4.1	54.8
9 Community, social and personal services	...	...	...	...	...	...	...	...	3.3	3.3	6.6	67.5
Statistical discrepancy [a]	...	...	...	...	...	...	...	...	0.6	0.6	1.2	11.7
Total, Industries	...	...	...	...	...	...	...	...	39.7	39.3	72.8	775.9
Producers of Government Services	...	...	...	...	...	...	...	...	1.8	1.6	2.5	17.7
Other Producers	...	...	...	...	...	...	...	...	0.1	0.1	1.1	0.9
Subtotal	...	...	...	...	...	...	...	...	41.6	41.0	75.5	794.5
Less: Imputed bank service charge	...	...	...	...	...	...	...	...	-	1.3	1.4	18.2
Plus: Import duties	...	...	...	...	...	...	...	...	0.8	0.9	1.5	3.1
Plus: Value added tax	...	...	...	...	...	...	...	...	...	...	...	...
Plus: Other adjustments [b]	...	...	...	...	...	...	...	...	0.3	0.3	2.0	37.9
Equals: Gross Domestic Product [c]	...	...	...	...	...	...	...	...	42.7	42.2	77.6	817.3

a) Item 'Statistical discrepancy' refers to other activities of the material sphere.
b) Item 'Other adjustments' refers to indirect taxes net of subsidies.
c) Beginning 1991, the base year for this table is the preceding year (T-1).

2.1 Government Final Consumption Expenditure by Function, in Current Prices

Thousand Million Roubles

	1980	1983	1984	1985	1986	1987	1988	1989	1990	1991	1992	1993
1 General public services	...	...	...	...	...	...	...	...	...	...	...	...
2 Defence	...	...	...	...	...	...	...	...	5.7	8.3	22.3	...
3 Public order and safety	...	...	...	...	...	...	...	...	0.2	1.7	26.1	...
4 Education	...	...	...	...	...	...	...	...	1.3	2.8	36.4	...
5 Health	...	...	...	...	...	...	...	...	0.7	2.4	28.8	...
6 Social security and welfare	...	...	...	...	...	...	...	...				...
7 Housing and community amenities	...	...	...	...	...	...	...	...	0.2	0.3	6.6	...
8 Recreational, cultural and religious affairs	...	...	...	...	...	...	...	...	0.1	0.2	3.8	...
9 Economic services	...	...	...	...	...	...	...	...	0.4	0.6	6.2	...
A Fuel and energy	...	...	...	...	...	...	...	...	...	...	...	...
B Agriculture, forestry, fishing and hunting	...	...	...	...	...	...	...	...	0.2	0.3	3.2	...
C Mining, manufacturing and construction, except fuel and energy	...	...	...	...	...	...	...	...	...	...	0.1	...
D Transportation and communication	...	...	...	...	...	...	...	...	0.2	0.3	2.9	...
E Other economic affairs	...	...	...	...	...	...	...	...	...	...	...	...
10 Other functions	...	...	...	...	...	...	...	...	1.3	1.4	7.9	...
Total Government Final Consumption Expenditure [a]	...	...	...	...	...	...	...	...	10.2	18.2	146.2	1920.7

a) Data in this series has been revised. The breakdown, if any, may not add up to the total.

Belgium

Source. Reply to the United Nations National Accounts Questionnaire from the Institut National de Statistique, Brussels. The official estimates are published annually by the Institut National in the July-August issue of the 'Bulletin de Statistique'.

General note. The estimates shown in the following tables have been prepared in accordance with the United Nations System of National Accounts so far as the existing data would permit.

1.1 Expenditure on the Gross Domestic Product, in Current Prices

Million Belgian francs

		1980	1983	1984	1985	1986	1987	1988	1989	1990	1991	1992	1993
1	Government final consumption expenditure	613889	725508	760210	815164	846686	851782	852950	891381	933255	1005569	1045387	1111531
2	Private final consumption expenditure	2171908	2687506	2875382	3105122	3198743	3358594	3506403	3769923	4012088	4242981	4445416	4514296
3	Gross capital formation	752953	639442	724849	706552	752704	844983	1001865	1177611	1302832	1305677	1357169	1286277
A	Increase in stocks [a]	24668	-29566	15821	-34733	-30211	10837	18831	24261	-2729	-8836	-31	-12790
B	Gross fixed capital formation	728285	669008	709028	741285	782915	834146	983034	1153350	1305561	1314513	1357200	1299067
	Residential buildings	203517	115639	118092	130896	138521	152661	195510	243862	277994	280537	331464	331365
	Non-residential buildings	285919	275007	265172	268102	274084	278843	313629	328571	360516	388266	399021	401923
	Other construction and land improvement etc.												
	Other	238849	278362	325764	342287	370310	402642	473895	580917	667051	645710	626715	565779
4	Exports of goods and services	2170200	3078900	3505200	3644900	3522900	3608800	4028800	4629800	4738900	4846500	4978100	5010600
5	Less: Imports of goods and services	2257800	3004300	3429000	3525900	3327200	3452300	3826000	4436400	4565000	4657300	4724400	4637500
	Equals: Gross Domestic Product	3451150	4127056	4436641	4745838	4993833	5211859	5564018	6032315	6422075	6743427	7101672	7285204

a) Item 'Increase in stocks' includes the statistical adjustment concerning gross capital formation.

1.2 Expenditure on the Gross Domestic Product, in Constant Prices

Million Belgian francs

		1980	1983	1984	1985	1986	1987	1988	1989	1990	1991	1992	1993
					At constant prices of: 1985								
1	Government final consumption expenditure	796654	792666	795302	815164	830017	832524	825294	827631	830067	850073	853883	870330
2	Private final consumption expenditure	3053065	3009926	3046327	3105122	3176852	3273146	3364709	3491576	3584900	3698761	3796499	3758110
3	Gross capital formation	955965	694832	760493	706552	751719	831915	966824	1083469	1165862	1149956	1169097	1093782
A	Increase in stocks [a]	38309	-28571	24479	-34733	-22328	14458	23682	24072	-1874	-1816	16535	9687
B	Gross fixed capital formation	917656	723403	736014	741285	774047	817457	943142	1059397	1167736	1151772	1152562	1084095
	Residential buildings	241185	127286	124268	130896	133719	140179	175110	207759	230101	228647	258787	252388
	Non-residential buildings	379721	300226	277288	268102	277334	283225	311316	310309	331386	351297	350551	346943
	Other construction and land improvement etc.												
	Other	296750	295891	334458	342287	362994	394053	456716	541329	606249	571828	543224	484764
4	Exports of goods and services	3202600	3417500	3604500	3644900	3845200	4096400	4445900	4772200	4968600	5097400	5294600	5380300
5	Less: Imports of goods and services	3449100	3309300	3500100	3525900	3793200	4127600	4456100	4849100	5050700	5173400	5386700	5472800
	Equals: Gross Domestic Product	4559184	4605624	4706522	4745838	4810588	4906385	5146627	5325776	5498729	5622790	5727379	5629722

a) Item 'Increase in stocks' includes the statistical adjustment concerning gross capital formation.

1.3 Cost Components of the Gross Domestic Product

Million Belgian francs

		1980	1983	1984	1985	1986	1987	1988	1989	1990	1991	1992	1993
1	Indirect taxes, net	289515	351659	368648	391249	403805	466148	491927	571162	597734	611431	672288	707866
A	Indirect taxes	428031	530053	554687	582009	594658	645134	675499	737455	785722	821753	870549	905299
B	Less: Subsidies	138516	178394	186039	190760	190853	178986	183572	166293	187988	210322	198261	197433
2	Consumption of fixed capital	312145	398532	423312	455805	471497	497013	550515	583981	637596	651663	689460	698963
3	Compensation of employees paid by resident producers to:	2071027	2387242	2534834	2664691	2802495	2867036	2984075	3125143	3394237	3663293	3856338	3953319
A	Resident households	2057027	2368642	2515834	2644191	2781195	2843336	2957775	3093843	3355837	3619793	3807838	3900419
B	Rest of the world	14000	18600	19000	20500	21300	23700	26300	31300	38400	43500	48500	52900
4	Operating surplus	778463	989623	1109847	1234093	1316036	1381662	1537501	1752029	1792508	1817040	1883586	1925056
A	Corporate and quasi-corporate enterprises	211760	311526	378084	466797	499338	523675	608041	722073	702476	670535	677527	705060
B	Private unincorporated enterprises	563288	675829	729351	765728	815175	856716	928035	1028929	1088470	1144340	1203001	1216935
C	General government	3415	2268	2412	1568	1523	1271	1425	1027	1562	2165	3058	3061
	Equals: Gross Domestic Product	3451150	4127056	4436641	4745838	4993833	5211859	5564018	6032315	6422075	6743427	7101672	7285204

Belgium

1.4 General Government Current Receipts and Disbursements

Million Belgian francs

	1980	1983	1984	1985	1986	1987	1988	1989	1990	1991	1992	1993
Receipts												
1 Operating surplus	3415	2268	2412	1568	1523	1271	1425	1027	1562	2165	3058	3061
2 Property and entrepreneurial income	58185	72962	77115	81347	70333	60812	63032	74820	82696	90719	87695	85971
3 Taxes, fees and contributions	1533972	1922975	2114821	2268532	2352995	2477014	2563994	2683660	2875512	3017302	3178087	3300504
A Indirect taxes	428031	530053	554687	582009	594658	645134	675499	737455	785722	821753	870549	905299
B Direct taxes	639589	795568	879258	939341	963966	989877	1012352	1021589	1098666	1123270	1169732	1210837
C Social security contributions	466352	597354	680876	747182	794371	842003	876143	924616	991124	1072279	1137806	1184368
D Compulsory fees, fines and penalties [a]	...	...	...	...	...	...	...	...	...	...	...	...
4 Other current transfers [a]	105537	161700	169606	183577	188814	191690	187736	182230	213565	247618	247819	260038
Total Current Receipts of General Government	1701109	2159905	2363954	2535024	2613665	2730787	2816187	2941737	3173335	3357804	3516659	3649574
Disbursements												
1 Government final consumption expenditure	613889	725508	760210	815164	846686	851782	852950	891381	933255	1005569	1045387	1111531
2 Property income	215622	389304	439217	507625	562709	557504	568196	631088	687468	694869	758813	767027
A Interest	215622	389304	439217	507625	562709	557504	568196	631088	687468	694869	758813	767027
B Net land rent and royalties	-	-	-	-	-	-	-	-	-	-	-	-
3 Subsidies	138516	178394	186039	190760	190853	178986	183572	166293	187988	210322	198261	197433
4 Other current transfers	893843	1184807	1243461	1297718	1344873	1420597	1457552	1534185	1611401	1764385	1853705	1947993
A Social security benefits	685886	909355	956533	992491	1030131	1072403	1096464	1149167	1216029	1322037	1408411	1470392
B Social assistance grants	69967	96840	103555	111475	114454	122832	127253	144566	147022	157288	162114	169675
C Other	137990	178612	183373	193752	200288	225362	233835	240452	248350	285060	283180	307926
5 Net saving	-160761	-318108	-264973	-276243	-331456	-278082	-246083	-281210	-246777	-317341	-339507	-374410
Total Current Disbursements and Net Saving of General Government	1701109	2159905	2363954	2535024	2613665	2730787	2816187	2941737	3173335	3357804	3516659	3649574

a) Item 'Other current transfers' includes item 'Fees, fines and penalties'.

1.5 Current Income and Outlay of Corporate and Quasi-Corporate Enterprises, Summary

Million Belgian francs

	1980	1983	1984	1985	1986	1987	1988	1989	1990	1991	1992	1993
Receipts												
1 Operating surplus	211760	311526	378084	466797	499338	523675	608041	722073	702476	670535	677527	...
2 Property and entrepreneurial income received	747074	1090519	1287773	1319276	1248802	1261101	1405190	1748840	1923141	1999349	2113511	...
3 Current transfers	166668	210621	227482	244772	241640	260363	280395	313838	385891	376294	367861	394723
Total Current Receipts	1125502	1612666	1893339	2030845	1989780	2045139	2293626	2784751	3011508	3046178	3158899	...
Disbursements												
1 Property and entrepreneurial income	845246	1241726	1452300	1504735	1382361	1397778	1576957	1950876	2177839	2300451	2450546	...
2 Direct taxes and other current payments to general government	89749	99610	111634	126378	140149	143709	159347	175013	165175	173481	147341	...
3 Other current transfers	163963	206374	223638	238578	236584	253442	275282	301800	365043	360300	359522	386683
4 Net saving	26544	64956	105767	161154	230686	250210	282040	357062	303451	211946	201490	206073
Total Current Disbursements and Net Saving	1125502	1612666	1893339	2030845	1989780	2045139	2293626	2784751	3011508	3046178	3158899	...

1.6 Current Income and Outlay of Households and Non-Profit Institutions

Million Belgian francs

	1980	1983	1984	1985	1986	1987	1988	1989	1990	1991	1992	1993
Receipts												
1 Compensation of employees	2087927	2410742	2561434	2691591	2838095	2904036	3026075	3169343	3440937	3714893	3911238	4040419
A From resident producers	2057027	2368642	2515834	2644191	2781195	2843336	2957775	3093843	3355837	3619793	3807838	3900419
B From rest of the world	30900	42100	45600	47400	56900	60700	68300	75500	85100	95100	103400	140000
2 Operating surplus of private unincorporated enterprises	563288	675829	729351	765728	815175	856716	928035	1028929	1088470	1144340	1203001	1216935
3 Property and entrepreneurial income	314112	495536	564247	635398	656662	677468	727523	852310	940745	1039965	1139249	1204338
4 Current transfers	954278	1244217	1311701	1376581	1424266	1500858	1555022	1648594	1751838	1895488	1998228	2102432
A Social security benefits	685886	909355	956533	992491	1030131	1072403	1096464	1149167	1216029	1322037	1408411	1470392
B Social assistance grants	69967	96840	103555	111475	114454	122832	127253	144566	147022	157288	162114	169675
C Other	198425	238022	251613	272615	279681	305623	331305	354861	388787	416163	427703	462365
Total Current Receipts	3919605	4826324	5166733	5469298	5734198	5939078	6236655	6699176	7221990	7794686	8251716	8564124

Belgium

1.6 Current Income and Outlay of Households and Non-Profit Institutions
(Continued)

Million Belgian francs

	1980	1983	1984	1985	1986	1987	1988	1989	1990	1991	1992	1993
					Disbursements							
1 Private final consumption expenditure	2171908	2687506	2875382	3105122	3198743	3358594	3506403	3769923	4012088	4242981	4445416	4514296
2 Property income	101603	114287	123918	126961	126027	130499	142292	172606	193975	212713	226696	235541
3 Direct taxes and other current transfers n.e.c. to general government	1016192	1293312	1448500	1560145	1618188	1688171	1729148	1771192	1924615	2022068	2160197	2229919
A Social security contributions	466352	597354	680876	747182	794371	842003	876143	924616	991124	1072279	1137806	1184368
B Direct taxes	549840	695958	767624	812963	823817	846168	853005	846576	933491	949789	1022391	1045551
C Fees, fines and penalties a	...	...	...	...	...	...	...	...	...	...	...	...
4 Other current transfers a	203430	271491	282771	297787	306344	319865	345673	362978	422255	436049	460423	492233
5 Net saving	426472	459728	436162	379283	484896	441949	513139	622477	669057	880875	958984	1092135
Total Current Disbursements and Net Saving	3919605	4826324	5166733	5469298	5734198	5939078	6236655	6699176	7221990	7794686	8251716	8564124

a) Item 'Other current transfers' includes item 'Fees, fines and penalties'.

1.7 External Transactions on Current Account, Summary

Million Belgian francs

	1980	1983	1984	1985	1986	1987	1988	1989	1990	1991	1992	1993
					Payments to the Rest of the World							
1 Imports of goods and services	2257800	3004300	3429000	3525900	3327200	3452300	3826000	4436400	4565000	4657300	4724400	4637500
A Imports of merchandise c.i.f.	2029900	2714800	3106400	3165600	2941300	3027100	3340200	3833500	3944700	3954800	3990800	3872000
B Other	227900	289500	322600	360300	385900	425200	485800	602900	620300	702500	733600	765500
2 Factor income to the rest of the world	243500	571000	668500	798500	712700	681700	808200	1165800	1314400	1495700	1709800	1643200
A Compensation of employees	14000	18600	19000	20500	21300	23700	26300	31300	38400	43500	48500	52900
B Property and entrepreneurial income	229500	552400	649500	778000	691400	658000	781900	1134500	1276000	1452200	1661300	1590300
3 Current transfers to the rest of the world	95786	138695	147336	156210	152585	167069	181940	192445	235547	249094	246733	264767
A Indirect taxes to supranational organizations	41606	56573	57261	59412	64613	77013	75711	80718	83257	91933	88738	84572
B Other current transfers	54180	82122	90075	96798	87972	90056	106229	111727	152290	157161	157995	180195
4 Surplus of the nation on current transactions	-148553	-34334	-24581	13447	102919	66107	97746	104699	60495	121466	153258	336484
Payments to the Rest of the World and Surplus of the Nation on Current Transactions	2448533	3679661	4220255	4494057	4295404	4367176	4913886	5899344	6175442	6523560	6834191	6881951
					Receipts From The Rest of the World							
1 Exports of goods and services	2170200	3078900	3505200	3644900	3522900	3608800	4028800	4629800	4738900	4846500	4978100	5010600
A Exports of merchandise f.o.b.	1802200	2531000	2903700	3012800	2874100	2904300	3252200	3722200	3763100	3765100	3854000	3847600
B Other	368000	547900	601500	632100	648800	704500	776600	907600	975800	1081400	1124100	1163000
2 Factor income from rest of the world	217300	508200	608800	722100	653000	632300	758500	1131400	1248400	1469300	1669100	1676300
A Compensation of employees	30900	42100	45600	47400	56900	60700	68300	75500	85100	95100	103400	140000
B Property and entrepreneurial income	186400	466100	563200	674700	596100	571600	690200	1055900	1163300	1374200	1565700	1536300
3 Current transfers from rest of the world	61033	92561	106255	127057	119504	126076	126586	138144	188142	207760	186991	195051
A Subsidies from supranational organisations	23902	29726	33100	42281	44627	42801	32129	27049	46950	66287	58274	51641
B Other current transfers	37131	62835	73155	84776	74877	83275	94457	111095	141192	141473	128717	143410
Receipts from the Rest of the World on Current Transactions	2448533	3679661	4220255	4494057	4295404	4367176	4913886	5899344	6175442	6523560	6834191	6881951

1.8 Capital Transactions of The Nation, Summary

Million Belgian francs

	1980	1983	1984	1985	1986	1987	1988	1989	1990	1991	1992	1993
					Finance of Gross Capital Formation							
Gross saving	604400	605108	700268	719999	855623	911090	1099611	1282310	1363327	1427143	1510427	1622761
1 Consumption of fixed capital	312145	398532	423312	455805	471497	497013	550515	583981	637596	651663	689460	698963
A General government	12234	13809	14611	15454	16606	18175	19581	21724	22334	23751	24749	25311
B Corporate and quasi-corporate enterprises	212109	274340	291412	314610	326412	346161	389187	415765	458519	466309	494532	503370
C Other	87802	110383	117289	125741	128479	132677	141747	146492	156743	161603	170179	170282

Belgium

1.8 Capital Transactions of The Nation, Summary
(Continued)

Million Belgian francs

	1980	1983	1984	1985	1986	1987	1988	1989	1990	1991	1992	1993
2 Net saving	292255	206576	276956	264194	384126	414077	549096	698329	725731	775480	820967	923798
A General government	-160761	-318108	-264973	-276243	-331456	-278082	-246083	-281210	-246777	-317341	-339507	-374410
B Corporate and quasi-corporate enterprises	26544	64956	105767	161154	230686	250210	282040	357062	303451	211946	201490	206073
C Other	426472	459728	436162	379283	484896	441949	513139	622477	669057	880875	958984	1092135
Less: Surplus of the nation on current transactions	-148553	-34334	-24581	13447	102919	66107	97746	104699	60495	121466	153258	336484
Finance of Gross Capital Formation	752953	639442	724849	706552	752704	844983	1001865	1177611	1302832	1305677	1357169	1286277
					Gross Capital Formation							
Increase in stocks a	24668	-29566	15821	-34733	-30211	10837	18831	24261	-2729	-8836	-31	-12790
Gross fixed capital formation	728285	669008	709028	741285	782915	834146	983034	1153350	1305561	1314513	1357200	1299067
1 General government	125662	124069	114146	106001	100175	93370	100184	81781	88693	98895	105586	109500
2 Corporate and quasi-corporate enterprises	344763	359831	401057	422296	450548	485373	572774	700387	806056	810063	786833	724179
3 Other	257860	185108	193825	212988	232192	255403	310076	371182	410812	405555	464781	465388
Gross Capital Formation	752953	639442	724849	706552	752704	844983	1001865	1177611	1302832	1305677	1357169	1286277

a) Item 'Increase in stocks' includes the statistical adjustment concerning gross capital formation.

1.10 Gross Domestic Product by Kind of Activity, in Current Prices

Million Belgian francs

	1980	1983	1984	1985	1986	1987	1988	1989	1990	1991	1992	1993
1 Agriculture, hunting, forestry and fishing	73108	102399	105037	106104	107902	103403	107067	132978	119656	124227	120002	114586
2 Mining and quarrying	7399	14172	11432	10975	6542	4071	1185	1405	1151	...	...	...
3 Manufacturing	833834	966028	1027023	1115004	1156661	1157057	1231094	1363783	1446335	...	...	...
4 Electricity, gas and water a	75002	101410	106295	118997	123245	126731	131782	133796	139157	...	...	...
5 Construction	259389	232464	233695	245768	250228	248749	285029	315876	347022	363750	385712	372944
6 Wholesale and retail trade, restaurants and hotels b	546968	658005	685077	759256	863508	924310	969338	1028937	1151577	1231439	1309165	1348093
7 Transport, storage and communication	268450	304125	344850	372747	369732	396756	442198	479507	514311	548343	569912	575248
8 Finance, insurance, real estate and business services	149581	205685	247868	263389	297516	316447	323094	328819	303237	333762	363349	372435
9 Community, social and personal services c	532987	712968	793818	843267	913808	984743	1062666	1165929	1248502	1334498	1431778	1505494
Statistical discrepancy	96	-825	24364	-6947	-23507	-13956	-23947	-13112	-12135	6237	32031	40090
Total, Industries	2746814	3302198	3590712	3845286	4087078	4270344	4588779	4975512	5280860	5532262	5844772	5967602
Producers of Government Services	482609	572029	601526	641226	666400	665178	671318	713851	757169	815107	859909	917096
Other Producers d	40830	45501	47304	49496	50667	50564	50584	50661	52419	54588	57284	59303
Subtotal	3270253	3919728	4239542	4536008	4804145	4986086	5310681	5740024	6090448	6401957	6761965	6944001
Less: Imputed bank service charge	109122	150629	178145	186425	207845	204228	200496	196065	184037	198480	213273	218262
Plus: Import duties	34508	44930	45289	47013	42012	51354	48578	53723	55698	60421	58172	55243
Plus: Value added tax	255511	313027	329955	349242	355521	378647	405255	434633	459966	479529	494808	504222
Equals: Gross Domestic Product e	3451150	4127056	4436641	4745838	4993833	5211859	5564018	6032315	6422075	6743427	7101672	7285204
Memorandum Item: Mineral fuels and power	162592	199000	205711	223544	221876	221893	228399	243902	264003	...	...	...

a) Item 'Electricity, gas and water' includes also other energy products.
b) Including repairs and recovery.
c) Item 'Community, social and personal services' refers to health services only. All other market services are included in item 'Finance, insurance, real estate and business services'.
d) Item 'Other producers' refers to domestic services only. All other non-marketed services are included in item 'Finance, insurance, real estate and business services'.
e) The breakdown by kind of economic activity used in this table is according to the classification NACE/CLIO.

1.11 Gross Domestic Product by Kind of Activity, in Constant Prices

Million Belgian francs

	1980	1983	1984	1985	1986	1987	1988	1989	1990	1991	1992	1993
					At constant prices of:1985							
1 Agriculture, hunting, forestry and fishing	89589	97356	106390	106104	111107	102909	108841	110635	106548	113900	125610	132127
2 Mining and quarrying	15751	14534	12508	10975	9221	9013	5228	3953	2261	...	...	...
3 Manufacturing	982602	1077005	1105899	1115004	1113706	1141057	1209901	1276018	1328212	...	...	...
4 Electricity, gas and water a	113789	114253	114800	118997	116867	123825	131813	136353	141247	...	...	...
5 Construction	347614	254355	244099	245768	255022	257909	288496	304051	325707	336004	345267	326891
6 Wholesale and retail trade, restaurants and hotels b	800195	778042	763506	759256	778364	780370	805267	806392	828180	870074	902797	891000
7 Transport, storage and communication	349055	336395	363094	372747	353474	371627	400976	429268	453097	463880	471914	367579
8 Finance, insurance, real estate and business services	214880	242041	261547	263389	286489	314432	334972	349207	329718	358892	388117	404427
9 Community, social and personal services c	738645	795727	834520	843267	874760	914393	967241	1032438	1066091	1085279	1107484	1103859
Statistical discrepancy	-1717	17083	5972	-6947	-21371	-24671	-12836	-43268	1672	-10823	-33809	-49811

Belgium

1.11 Gross Domestic Product by Kind of Activity, in Constant Prices
(Continued)

Million Belgian francs

	1980	1983	1984	1985	1986	1987	1988	1989	1990	1991	1992	1993
				At constant prices of:1985								
Total, Industries	3650408	3734075	3826134	3845286	3899343	3995021	4237100	4398517	4542991	4663069	4763687	4683469
Producers of Government Services	618394	623307	629895	641226	650932	648867	647860	660827	669483	680965	694299	707576
Other Producers d	52373	49991	49570	49496	48737	47663	46946	45907	45885	46223	46792	46816
Subtotal	4321175	4407373	4505599	4536008	4599012	4691551	4931906	5105251	5258359	5390257	5504778	5437861
Less: Imputed bank service charge	161892	186037	189883	186425	196660	208159	223909	237197	238066	258753	279931	302283
Plus: Import duties	47028	42674	46859	47013	50956	56000	60416	64851	68113	69158	72340	72345
Plus: Value added tax	352873	341614	343947	349242	357280	366993	378214	392871	410323	422128	430192	421799
Equals: Gross Domestic Product e	4559184	4605624	4706522	4745838	4810588	4906385	5146627	5325776	5498729	5622790	5727379	5629722
Memorandum Item: Mineral fuels and power	216118	226577	225910	223544	219308	233385	245374	251743	255296	...	...	...

a) Item 'Electricity, gas and water' includes also other energy products.
b) Including repairs and recovery.
c) Item 'Community, social and personal services' refers to health services only. All other market services are included in item 'Finance, insurance, real estate and business services'.
d) Item 'Other producers' refers to domestic services only. All other non-marketed services are included in item 'Finance, insurance, real estate and business services'.
e) The breakdown by kind of economic activity used in this table is according to the classification NACE/CLIO.

1.12 Relations Among National Accounting Aggregates

Million Belgian francs

	1980	1983	1984	1985	1986	1987	1988	1989	1990	1991	1992	1993
Gross Domestic Product	3451150	4127056	4436641	4745838	4993833	5211859	5564018	6032315	6422075	6743427	7101672	7285204
Plus: Net factor income from the rest of the world	-26200	-62800	-59700	-76400	-59700	-49400	-49700	-34400	-66000	-26400	-40700	33100
Factor income from the rest of the world	217300	508200	608800	722100	653000	632300	758500	1131400	1248400	1469300	1669100	1676300
Less: Factor income to the rest of the world	243500	571000	668500	798500	712700	681700	808200	1165800	1314400	1495700	1709800	1643200
Equals: Gross National Product	3424950	4064256	4376941	4669438	4934133	5162459	5514318	5997915	6356075	6717027	7060972	7318304
Less: Consumption of fixed capital	312145	398532	423312	455805	471497	497013	550515	583981	637596	651663	689460	698963
Equals: National Income	3112805	3665724	3953629	4213633	4462636	4665446	4963803	5413934	5718479	6065364	6371512	6619341
Plus: Net current transfers from the rest of the world	-34753	-46134	-41081	-29153	-33081	-40993	-55354	-54301	-47405	-41334	-59742	-69716
Current transfers from the rest of the world	61033	92561	106255	127057	119504	126076	126586	138144	188142	207760	186991	195051
Less: Current transfers to the rest of the world	95786	138695	147336	156210	152585	167069	181940	192445	235547	249094	246733	264767
Equals: National Disposable Income	3078052	3619590	3912548	4184480	4429555	4624453	4908449	5359633	5671074	6024030	6311770	6549625
Less: Final consumption	2785797	3413014	3635592	3920286	4045429	4210376	4359353	4661304	4945343	5248550	5490803	5625827
Equals: Net Saving	292255	206576	276956	264194	384126	414077	549096	698329	725731	775480	820967	923798
Less: Surplus of the nation on current transactions	-148553	-34334	-24581	13447	102919	66107	97746	104699	60495	121466	153258	336484
Equals: Net Capital Formation	440808	240910	301537	250747	281207	347970	451350	593630	665236	654014	667709	587314

2.5 Private Final Consumption Expenditure by Type and Purpose, in Current Prices

Million Belgian francs

	1980	1983	1984	1985	1986	1987	1988	1989	1990	1991	1992	1993
				Final Consumption Expenditure of Resident Households								
1 Food, beverages and tobacco	462494	593666	634290	668606	682022	689389	696937	717870	753507	780786	787931	774230
A Food	379518	486802	524868	555296	565021	569174	576343	593276	617568	641806	639148	627010
B Non-alcoholic beverages	9542	11952	11940	12874	15035	16351	17544	20340	22568	22588	24466	23898
C Alcoholic beverages	38034	45753	44041	46014	46331	49235	47341	47028	55193	55629	58876	57034
D Tobacco	35400	49159	53441	54422	55635	54629	55709	57226	58178	60763	65441	66288
2 Clothing and footwear	175913	210197	218803	232751	243629	255261	268958	285603	317426	335654	343443	340219
3 Gross rent, fuel and power	364289	498035	543835	585435	569512	578308	589844	622711	658601	707340	748314	801525
A Fuel and power	136239	184595	202886	220543	183016	167473	154983	161616	171898	189394	186742	195396
B Other	228050	313440	340949	364892	386496	410835	434861	461095	486703	517946	561572	606129
4 Furniture, furnishings and household equipment and operation	252577	280791	289362	304842	333427	353666	377820	401439	430504	459681	472553	467138
A Household operation	30013	37158	40075	40818	44754	46928	47419	50769	52536	54701	56679	56942
B Other	222564	243633	249287	264024	288673	306738	330401	350670	377968	404980	415874	410196
5 Medical care and health expenses	209535	280988	300117	323514	342923	362706	386074	414348	442011	484617	525197	548621
6 Transport and communication	268644	341510	366053	388467	385399	406859	438703	479816	524813	552025	584982	577347
A Personal transport equipment	84498	101254	116086	123455	133657	143572	161655	176936	203520	209694	225247	200143

Belgium

2.5 Private Final Consumption Expenditure by Type and Purpose, in Current Prices
(Continued)

Million Belgian francs

	1980	1983	1984	1985	1986	1987	1988	1989	1990	1991	1992	1993
B Other	184146	240256	249967	265012	251742	263287	277048	302880	321293	342331	359735	377204
7 Recreational, entertainment, education and cultural services	128239	160215	176872	187666	204660	218955	234575	246976	263711	274296	277843	283940
A Education	...	...	...	...	...	...	...	...	...	...	...	...
B Other	128239	160215	176872	187666	204660	218955	234575	246976	263711	274296	277843	283940
8 Miscellaneous goods and services	290270	360520	392902	417556	449675	488134	519612	565788	610073	649153	708806	727824
A Personal care	38299	47835	49864	50792	54345	55273	57044	58802	61601	65062	69634	81513
B Expenditures in restaurants, cafes and hotels	160419	204238	220315	234923	247707	261175	280315	306628	339735	365913	409995	411511
C Other	91552	108447	122723	131841	147623	171686	182253	200358	208737	218178	229177	234800
Statistical discrepancy	-13353	-32116	-38352	685	-14804	-884	-17620	21172	-8658	-26571	-41653	-43648
Total Final Consumption Expenditure in the Domestic Market by Households, of which	2138608	2693806	2883882	3109522	3196443	3352394	3494903	3755723	3991988	4216981	4407416	4477196
Plus: Direct purchases abroad by resident households	78500	88500	93300	100700	107100	121000	138800	139700	148500	155900	173400	179500
Less: Direct purchases in the domestic market by non-resident households	45200	94800	101800	105100	104800	114800	127300	125500	128400	129900	135400	142400
Equals: Final Consumption Expenditure of Resident Households [a]	2171908	2687506	2875382	3105122	3198743	3358594	3506403	3769923	4012088	4242981	4445416	4514296

Final Consumption Expenditure of Private Non-profit Institutions Serving Households

	1980	1983	1984	1985	1986	1987	1988	1989	1990	1991	1992	1993
Equals: Final Consumption Expenditure of Private Non-profit Organisations Serving Households	...	...	...	...	...	...	...	...	...	...	...	...
Private Final Consumption Expenditure	2171908	2687506	2875382	3105122	3198743	3358594	3506403	3769923	4012088	4242981	4445416	4514296

a) Item 'Final consumption expenditure of resident households' includes consumption expenditure of private non-profit institutions serving households.

2.6 Private Final Consumption Expenditure by Type and Purpose, in Constant Prices

Million Belgian francs

	1980	1983	1984	1985	1986	1987	1988	1989	1990	1991	1992	1993

At constant prices of: 1985

Final Consumption Expenditure of Resident Households

	1980	1983	1984	1985	1986	1987	1988	1989	1990	1991	1992	1993
1 Food, beverages and tobacco	666372	666070	659963	668606	672905	680937	686262	686699	697925	712573	722522	712103
A Food	542362	546429	543567	555296	561092	569096	574988	577816	584785	602147	610266	605216
B Non-alcoholic beverages	13120	12804	12384	12874	14499	15243	16240	18663	20408	19944	21007	20069
C Alcoholic beverages	54806	49353	45840	46014	45104	47666	45454	43282	47740	44988	46921	46077
D Tobacco	56084	57484	58172	54422	52210	48932	49580	46938	44992	45494	44328	40741
2 Clothing and footwear	230446	237323	234238	232751	227865	227750	231784	239147	259154	264689	263611	255434
3 Gross rent, fuel and power	547221	555455	568225	585435	588786	600730	599201	607476	622153	651954	662492	675842
A Fuel and power	222938	205743	211262	220543	215926	219803	209136	208075	213309	232935	232952	235655
B Other	324283	349712	356963	364892	372860	380927	390065	399401	408844	419019	429540	440187
4 Furniture, furnishings and household equipment and operation	328314	311524	304107	304842	319942	331445	349033	364354	382278	396561	398318	386588
A Household operation	43756	43856	43216	40818	42359	43433	44157	46038	46887	47740	46449	45438
B Other	284558	267668	260891	264024	277583	288012	304876	318316	335391	348821	351869	341150
5 Medical care and health expenses	286005	313911	315118	323514	326557	336799	352880	368709	375125	385748	398434	391233
6 Transport and communication	384459	377341	383579	388467	396287	411434	436079	455188	479733	489639	504021	484948
A Personal transport equipment	126145	115577	121577	123455	127993	133264	144196	151299	166522	168981	176695	151703
B Other	258314	261764	262002	265012	268294	278170	291883	303889	313211	320658	327326	333245
7 Recreational, entertainment, education and cultural services	166661	178780	185167	187666	198947	208556	221333	231445	243586	249794	256170	260425
A Education	...	...	...	...	...	...	...	...	...	...	...	...
B Other	166661	178780	185167	187666	198947	208556	221333	231445	243586	249794	256170	260425
8 Miscellaneous goods and services	399450	395392	414801	417556	431033	455095	473090	498414	514935	524968	543041	532523
A Personal care	55096	52721	52117	50792	50842	49676	49933	50350	51674	52666	52630	52776
B Expenditures in restaurants, cafes and hotels	214184	221078	233260	234923	235964	242575	254288	267410	280257	285695	298376	288257
C Other	130170	121593	129424	131841	144227	162844	168869	180654	183004	186607	192035	191490

Belgium

2.6 Private Final Consumption Expenditure by Type and Purpose, in Constant Prices
(Continued)

Million Belgian francs

	1980	1983	1984	1985	1986	1987	1988	1989	1990	1991	1992	1993
					At constant prices of:1985							
Statistical discrepancy	-1463	-18869	-9871	685	12330	14700	4547	27744	-6589	2535	20190	33114
Total Final Consumption Expenditure in the Domestic Market by Households, of which	3007465	3016927	3055327	3109522	3174652	3267446	3354209	3479176	3568300	3678461	3768799	3732210
Plus: Direct purchases abroad by resident households	107300	98600	99400	100700	102000	112300	126000	121800	122400	121700	126000	124700
Less: Direct purchases in the domestic market by non-resident households	61700	105600	108400	105100	99800	106600	115500	109400	105800	101400	98300	98800
Equals: Final Consumption Expenditure of Resident Households [a]	3053065	3009927	3046327	3105122	3176852	3273146	3364709	3491576	3584900	3698761	3796499	3758110

Final Consumption Expenditure of Private Non-profit Institutions Serving Households

	1980	1983	1984	1985	1986	1987	1988	1989	1990	1991	1992	1993
Equals: Final Consumption Expenditure of Private Non-profit Organisations Serving Households	...	...	...	...	...	...	...	...	...	...	...	...
Private Final Consumption Expenditure	3053065	3009927	3046327	3105122	3176852	3273146	3364709	3491576	3584900	3698761	3796499	3758110

a) Item 'Final consumption expenditure of resident households' includes consumption expenditure of private non-profit institutions serving households.

2.7 Gross Capital Formation by Type of Good and Owner, in Current Prices

Million Belgian francs

	1980				1985				1990			
	TOTAL	Total Private	Public Enterprises	General Government	TOTAL	Total Private	Public Enterprises	General Government	TOTAL	Total Private	Public Enterprises	General Government
Increase in stocks, total [a]	24668	...	...	...	-34733	...	...	...	-2729	...	...	...
1 Goods producing industries	24668	...	...	...	-34733	...	...	...	-2729	...	...	...
A Materials and supplies	...	...	...	...	...	...	...	...	...	...	...	...
B Work in progress	12616	...	...	...	-3784	...	...	...	-357	...	...	...
C Livestock, except breeding stocks, dairy cattle, etc.	-603	...	...	...	-1189	...	...	...	2547	...	...	...
D Finished goods [b]	12655	...	...	...	-31295	...	...	...	14080	...	...	...
2 Wholesale and retail trade	...	...	...	...	...	...	...	...	...	...	...	...
3 Other, except government stocks	...	...	...	...	...	...	...	...	...	...	...	...
4 Government stocks	...	...	...	...	...	...	...	...	...	...	...	...
Gross Fixed Capital Formation, Total	728285	...	...	...	741285	...	...	...	1305561	...	...	...
1 Residential buildings	203517	...	...	...	130896	...	...	...	277994	...	...	...
2 Non-residential buildings		...	...	...		...	...	...		...	...	...
3 Other construction	285919	...	...	...	268102	...	...	...	360516	...	...	...
4 Land improvement and plantation and orchard development		...	...	...		...	...	...		...	...	...
5 Producers' durable goods	218144	...	...	...	322033	...	...	...	619697	...	...	...
A Transport equipment	51617	...	...	...	69792	...	...	...	135439	...	...	...
B Machinery and equipment	166527	...	...	...	252241	...	...	...	484258	...	...	...
6 Breeding stock, dairy cattle, etc.	50	...	...	...	465	...	...	...	2397	...	...	...
Statistical discrepancy [c]	20655	...	...	...	19789	...	...	...	44957	...	...	...
Total Gross Capital Formation	752953	...	...	...	706552	...	...	...	1302832	...	...	...

	1991				1992				1993			
	TOTAL	Total Private	Public Enterprises	General Government	TOTAL	Total Private	Public Enterprises	General Government	TOTAL	Total Private	Public Enterprises	General Government
Increase in stocks, total [a]	-8836	...	...	...	-31	...	...	...	-12790	...	...	...
1 Goods producing industries	-8836	...	...	...	-31	...	...	...	-12790	...	...	...
A Materials and supplies	...	...	...	...	...	...	...	...	...	...	...	...
B Work in progress	282	...	...	...	...	...	...	...	...	...	...	...
C Livestock, except breeding stocks, dairy cattle, etc.	1613	...	...	...	...	...	...	...	...	...	...	...
D Finished goods [b]	-11586	...	...	...	...	...	...	...	...	...	...	...
2 Wholesale and retail trade	...	...	...	...	...	...	...	...	...	...	...	...
3 Other, except government stocks	...	...	...	...	...	...	...	...	...	...	...	...
4 Government stocks	...	...	...	...	...	...	...	...	...	...	...	...
Gross Fixed Capital Formation, Total	1314513	...	...	...	1357200	...	...	...	1299067	...	...	...

Belgium

2.7 Gross Capital Formation by Type of Good and Owner, in Current Prices
(Continued)

Million Belgian francs

	1991 TOTAL	Total Private	Public Enterprises	General Government	1992 TOTAL	Total Private	Public Enterprises	General Government	1993 TOTAL	Total Private	Public Enterprises	General Government
1 Residential buildings	280537	...	...	...	331464	...	...	...	331365	...	...	...
2 Non-residential buildings		...	...	...		...	...	...		...	...	...
3 Other construction	388266	...	...	...	399021	...	...	...	401923	...	...	...
4 Land improvement and plantation and orchard development		...	...	...		...	...	...		...	...	...
5 Producers' durable goods	604180	...	...	...	579159	...	...	...	513474	...	...	...
A Transport equipment	121664	...	...	...	114331	...	...	...	113370	...	...	...
B Machinery and equipment	482516	...	...	...	464828	...	...	...	400104	...	...	...
6 Breeding stock, dairy cattle, etc.	-384	...	...	...	171	...	...	...	-72	...	...	...
Statistical discrepancy c	41914	...	...	...	47385	...	...	...	52377	...	...	...
Total Gross Capital Formation	1305677	...	...	...	1357169	...	...	...	1286277	...	...	...

a) Item 'Increase in stocks' includes the statistical adjustment concerning gross capital formation. 'Finished goods'.
b) Items 'Wholesale and retail trade' and 'Other, except government stocks' are included in item   c) Item 'Statistical discrepancy' refers to other products.

2.8 Gross Capital Formation by Type of Good and Owner, in Constant Prices

Million Belgian francs

	1980 TOTAL	Total Private	Public Enterprises	General Government	1985 TOTAL	Total Private	Public Enterprises	General Government	1990 TOTAL	Total Private	Public Enterprises	General Government
				At constant prices of:1985								
Increase in stocks, total a	38309	...	...	...	-34733	...	...	...	-1874	...	...	...
1 Goods producing industries	38309	...	...	...	-34733	...	...	...	-1874	...	...	...
A Materials and supplies	...	...	...	...	...	...	...	...	...	...	...	...
B Work in progress	16779	...	...	...	-3784	...	...	...	-309	...	...	...
C Livestock, except breeding stocks, dairy cattle, etc.	-733	...	...	...	-1189	...	...	...	2556	...	...	...
D Finished goods b	22740	...	...	...	-31295	...	...	...	19718	...	...	...
2 Wholesale and retail trade	...	...	...	...	...	...	...	...	...	...	...	...
3 Other, except government stocks	...	...	...	...	...	...	...	...	...	...	...	...
4 Government stocks	...	...	...	...	...	...	...	...	...	...	...	...
Gross Fixed Capital Formation, Total	917656	...	...	...	741285	...	...	...	1167736	...	...	...
1 Residential buildings	241185	...	...	...	130896	...	...	...	230101	...	...	...
2 Non-residential buildings		...	...	...		...	...	...		...	...	...
3 Other construction	379721	...	...	...	268102	...	...	...	331386	...	...	...
4 Land improvement and plantation and orchard development		...	...	...		...	...	...		...	...	...
5 Producers' durable goods	268581	...	...	...	322033	...	...	...	562455	...	...	...
A Transport equipment	71366	...	...	...	69792	...	...	...	114273	...	...	...
B Machinery and equipment	197215	...	...	...	252241	...	...	...	448182	...	...	...
6 Breeding stock, dairy cattle, etc.	86	...	...	...	465	...	...	...	2430	...	...	...
Statistical discrepancy b	28083	...	...	...	19789	...	...	...	41364	...	...	...
Total Gross Capital Formation	955965	...	...	...	706552	...	...	...	1165862	...	...	...

	1991 TOTAL	Total Private	Public Enterprises	General Government	1992 TOTAL	Total Private	Public Enterprises	General Government	1993 TOTAL	Total Private	Public Enterprises	General Government
				At constant prices of:1985								
Increase in stocks, total a	-1816	...	...	...	16535	...	...	...	9687	...	...	...
1 Goods producing industries	-1816	...	...	...	16535	...	...	...	9687	...	...	...
A Materials and supplies	...	...	...	...	...	...	...	...	...	...	...	...
B Work in progress	238	...	...	...	...	...	...	...	...	...	...	...
C Livestock, except breeding stocks, dairy cattle, etc.	1965	...	...	...	...	...	...	...	...	...	...	...
D Finished goods b	2550	...	...	...	...	...	...	...	...	...	...	...
2 Wholesale and retail trade	...	...	...	...	...	...	...	...	...	...	...	...
3 Other, except government stocks	...	...	...	...	...	...	...	...	...	...	...	...
4 Government stocks	...	...	...	...	...	...	...	...	...	...	...	...
Gross Fixed Capital Formation, Total	1151772	...	...	...	1152562	...	...	...	1084095	...	...	...

Belgium

2.8 Gross Capital Formation by Type of Good and Owner, in Constant Prices
(Continued)

Million Belgian francs

	1991 TOTAL	1991 Total Private	1991 Public Enterprises	1991 General Government	1992 TOTAL	1992 Total Private	1992 Public Enterprises	1992 General Government	1993 TOTAL	1993 Total Private	1993 Public Enterprises	1993 General Government
				At constant prices of:1985								
1 Residential buildings	228647	...	...	...	258787	...	...	...	252388	...	...	...
2 Non-residential buildings		...	...	...		...	...	...		...	...	...
3 Other construction	351297	...	...	...	350551	...	...	...	346943	...	...	...
4 Land improvement and plantation and orchard development		...	...	...		...	...	...		...	...	...
5 Producers' durable goods	534215	...	...	...	501155	...	...	...	439468	...	...	...
A Transport equipment	97846	...	...	...	87744	...	...	...	87051	...	...	...
B Machinery and equipment	436369	...	...	...	413411	...	...	...	352417	...	...	...
6 Breeding stock, dairy cattle, etc.	-446	...	...	...	356	...	...	...	268	...	...	...
Statistical discrepancy b	38059	...	...	...	41713	...	...	...	45028	...	...	...
Total Gross Capital Formation	1149956	...	...	...	1169097	...	...	...	1093782	...	...	...

a) Item 'Increase in stocks' includes the statistical adjustment concerning gross capital formation.
b) Items 'Wholesale and retail trade' and 'Other, except government stocks' are included in item 'Finished goods'.

2.11 Gross Fixed Capital Formation by Kind of Activity of Owner, ISIC Divisions, in Current Prices

Million Belgian francs

	1980	1983	1984	1985	1986	1987	1988	1989	1990	1991	1992	1993
					All Producers							
1 Agriculture, hunting, forestry and fishing	15213	16956	17662	18223	18871	20246	19803	20788	24731	18715	19925	19233
2 Mining and quarrying	...	...	...	...	...	...	...	...	...	...	...	...
3 Manufacturing	106540	125658	138873	155000	178004	190137	235532	297274	358185	360186	329914	242811
A Manufacturing of food, beverages and tobacco	17078	20109	18710	19865	24164	25841	33410	37048	45452	46854	50586	39117
B Textile, wearing apparel and leather industries	5913	11716	15529	12478	14521	18164	19218	18452	20427	19836	20912	16159
C Manufacture of wood, and wood products, including furniture a	...	...	...	...	...	...	...	...	...	...	...	...
D Manufacture of paper and paper products, printing and publishing	7985	8787	12302	11309	17825	18801	21194	26445	27213	29328	24522	17090
E Manufacture of chemicals and chemical petroleum, coal, rubber and plastic products	20070	23809	25396	30430	37895	39662	64420	83459	111617	92722	76116	62498
F Manufacture of non-metalic mineral products except products of petroleum and coal	7366	6433	8086	9020	11736	16473	17451	19743	28525	29043	22112	21068
G Basic metal industries	14083	18635	13359	19452	14696	15524	19998	30983	26533	31931	25805	17578
H Manufacture of fabricated metal products, machinery and equipment	28207	28936	37621	45220	47793	43566	46443	64442	75475	92305	95023	57188
I Other manufacturing industries a	5838	7233	7870	7226	9374	12106	13398	16702	22943	18167	14838	12113
4 Electricity, gas and water b	43982	45502	50496	52811	43207	38577	39735	51413	58683	58395	66475	71100
5 Construction	12226	8806	11347	12614	15107	15200	22945	25282	29716	27414	27194	23752
6 Wholesale and retail trade, restaurants and hotels	55411	65203	73456	82020	94179	110023	135309	151230	167914	173004	172207	164187
A Wholesale and retail trade c	48021	57496	64762	72581	82062	94018	116058	131478	147890	150144	147899	140160
B Restaurants and hotels	7390	7707	8694	9439	12117	16005	19251	19752	20024	22860	24308	24027
7 Transport, storage and communication	87544	89871	96311	88272	82367	88263	83540	97171	105654	102369	103387	133588
A Transport and storage	69110	67465	71923	65101	60458	66648	63610	69778	75683	71107	73477	87569
B Communication	18434	22406	24388	23171	21909	21615	19930	27393	29971	31262	29910	46019
8 Finance, insurance, real estate and business services d	18796	19614	23659	26634	30628	30471	33074	36575	35287	29845	27175	22894
A Financial institutions	18796	19614	23659	26634	30628	30471	33074	36575	35287	29845	27175	22894

Belgium

2.11 Gross Fixed Capital Formation by Kind of Activity of Owner, ISIC Divisions, in Current Prices
(Continued)

Million Belgian francs

	1980	1983	1984	1985	1986	1987	1988	1989	1990	1991	1992	1993
B Insurance	...	...	...	...	...	...	...	...	...	...	...	...
C Real estate and business services [d]	...	...	...	...	...	...	...	...	...	...	...	...
Real estate except dwellings	...	...	...	...	...	...	...	...	...	...	...	...
Dwellings	224725	132666	138250	152207	163835	183567	230438	288362	322701	...	...	...
9 Community, social and personal services [d]	262911	173329	183078	199710	220377	247859	312912	391836	436698	445690	505337	512002
Total Industries	602623	544939	594882	635284	682740	740776	882850	1071569	1216868	1215618	1251614	1189567
Producers of Government Services	125662	124069	114146	106001	100175	93370	100184	81781	88693	98895	105586	109500
Private Non-Profit Institutions Serving Households	...	...	...	...	...	...	...	...	...	...	...	...
Total [e]	728285	669008	709028	741285	782915	834146	983034	1153350	1305561	1314513	1357200	1299067

a) Item 'Manufacture of wood and wood products, including furniture' is included in item 'Other manufacturing industries'.
b) Item 'Electricity, gas and water' includes also other energy products.
c) Including repairs and recovery.
d) Business services and real estate except dwellings are included in item 'Community, social and personal services'.
e) The breakdown by kind of economic activity used in this table is according to the classification NACE/CLIO.

2.12 Gross Fixed Capital Formation by Kind of Activity of Owner, ISIC Divisions, in Constant Prices

Million Belgian francs

	1980	1983	1984	1985	1986	1987	1988	1989	1990	1991	1992	1993
				At constant prices of:1985								
				All Producers								
1 Agriculture, hunting, forestry and fishing	19488	18238	18325	18223	18553	19883	19109	19523	22581	16444	17374	16697
2 Mining and quarrying	...	...	...	...	...	...	...	...	...	...	...	...
3 Manufacturing	129766	133163	142407	155000	175392	187613	229166	279795	329585	323988	291064	211733
A Manufacturing of food, beverages and tobacco	21031	21359	19237	19865	23820	25484	32424	34832	41766	42090	44534	34037
B Textile, wearing apparel and leather industries	7193	12421	15943	12478	14300	17924	18701	17382	18795	17834	18443	14093
C Manufacture of wood, and wood products, including furniture [a]	...	...	...	...	...	...	...	...	...	...	...	...
D Manufacture of paper and paper products, printing and publishing	9696	9285	12596	11309	17576	18561	20626	24904	25072	26429	21669	14927
E Manufacture of chemicals and chemical petroleum, coal, rubber and plastic products	24277	25313	26039	30430	37341	39173	62734	78585	102872	83534	67289	54659
F Manufacture of non-metalic mineral products except products of petroleum and coal	9099	6799	8302	9020	11545	16219	16945	18489	25981	25821	19224	18129
G Basic metal industries	16933	19679	13673	19452	14444	15319	19488	29215	24495	28822	22875	15412
H Manufacture of fabricated metal products, machinery and equipment	34313	30613	38535	45220	47119	42989	45200	60652	69483	83097	83931	49914
I Other manufacturing industries [a]	7224	7694	8082	7226	9247	11944	13048	15736	21121	16361	13099	10562
4 Electricity, gas and water [b]	56150	49123	52459	52811	43210	38698	39028	48384	53941	52553	58459	61583
5 Construction	15291	9445	11692	12614	14812	14828	22052	23339	26794	24077	23310	20177
6 Wholesale and retail trade, restaurants and hotels	72146	71196	76579	82020	93297	108718	130797	139694	150284	151006	146061	137614
A Wholesale and retail trade [c]	62630	62784	67475	72581	81136	92619	111828	121112	131954	130464	124789	116960
B Restaurants and hotels	9516	8412	9104	9439	12161	16099	18969	18582	18330	20542	21272	20654
7 Transport, storage and communication	112127	96184	99018	88272	81755	87376	81267	90779	96217	91330	90621	115837
A Transport and storage	89992	72596	74116	65101	60215	66060	61842	64917	68514	63066	64093	75470
B Communication	22135	23588	24902	23171	21540	21316	19425	25862	27703	28264	26528	40367
8 Finance, insurance, real estate and business services [d]	24156	21129	24558	26634	30445	30393	32420	34453	32453	26888	23933	19887
A Financial institutions	24156	21129	24558	26634	30445	30393	32420	34453	32453	26888	23933	19887

Belgium

2.12 Gross Fixed Capital Formation by Kind of Activity of Owner, ISIC Divisions, in Constant Prices
(Continued)

Million Belgian francs

	1980	1983	1984	1985	1986	1987	1988	1989	1990	1991	1992	1993
					At constant prices of:1985							
B Insurance	...	...	...	...	...	...	...	...	...	...	...	...
C Real estate and business services [d]	...	...	...	...	...	...	...	...	...	...	...	...
Real estate except dwellings	...	...	...	...	...	...	...	...	...	...	...	...
Dwellings	269641	146044	145509	152207	159276	171457	209672	249630	270688	...	...	...
9 Community, social and personal services [e]	319785	190268	192231	199710	215424	235290	289904	345957	374088	375335	408876	405768
Total Industries	748909	588746	617269	635284	672888	722799	843743	981924	1085943	1061621	1059698	989296
Producers of Government Services	168747	134657	118745	106001	101159	94658	99399	77473	81793	90151	92864	94799
Private Non-Profit Institutions Serving Households	...	...	...	...	...	...	...	...	...	...	...	...
Total [f]	917656	723403	736014	741285	774047	817457	943142	1059397	1167736	1151772	1152562	1084095

a) Item 'Manufacture of wood and wood products, including furniture' is included in item 'Other manufacturing industries'.
b) Item 'Electricity, gas and water' includes also other energy products.
c) Including repairs and recovery.
d) Business services and real estate except dwellings are included in item 'Community, social and personal services'.
e) Item 'Finance, insurance, real estate and business services' includes only rented and owner-occupied dwellings.
f) The breakdown by kind of economic activity used in this table is according to the classification NACE/CLIO.

2.17 Exports and Imports of Goods and Services, Detail

Million Belgian francs

	1980	1983	1984	1985	1986	1987	1988	1989	1990	1991	1992	1993
					Exports of Goods and Services							
1 Exports of merchandise, f.o.b.	1802200	2531000	2903700	3012800	2874100	2904300	3252200	3722200	3763100	3765100	3854000	3847600
2 Transport and communication												
3 Insurance service charges	322800	453100	499700	527000	544000	589700	649300	782100	847400	951500	988700	1020600
4 Other commodities												
5 Adjustments of merchandise exports to change-of-ownership basis	...	...	...	...	...	...	...	...	...	...	...	...
6 Direct purchases in the domestic market by non-residential households	45200	94800	101800	105100	104800	114800	127300	125500	128400	129900	135400	142400
7 Direct purchases in the domestic market by extraterritorial bodies	...	...	...	...	...	...	...	...	...	...	...	...
Total Exports of Goods and Services	2170200	3078900	3505200	3644900	3522900	3608800	4028800	4629800	4738900	4846500	4978100	5010600
					Imports of Goods and Services							
1 Imports of merchandise, c.i.f.	2029900	2714800	3106400	3165600	2941300	3027100	3340200	3833500	3944700	3954800	3990800	3872000
2 Adjustments of merchandise imports to change-of-ownership basis	...	...	...	...	...	...	...	...	...	...	...	...
3 Other transport and communication												
4 Other insurance service charges	149400	201000	229300	259600	278800	304200	347000	463200	471800	546600	560200	586000
5 Other commodities												
6 Direct purchases abroad by government	...	...	...	...	...	...	...	...	...	...	...	...
7 Direct purchases abroad by resident households	78500	88500	93300	100700	107100	121000	138800	139700	148500	155900	173400	179500
Total Imports of Goods and Services	2257800	3004300	3429000	3525900	3327200	3452300	3826000	4436400	4565000	4657300	4724400	4637500
Balance of Goods and Services	-87600	74600	76200	119000	195700	156500	202800	193400	173900	189200	253700	373100
Total Imports and Balance of Goods and Services	2170200	3078900	3505200	3644900	3522900	3608800	4028800	4629800	4738900	4846500	4978100	5010600

3.11 General Government Production Account: Total and Subsectors

Million Belgian francs

	1980					1985				
	Total General Government	Central Government	State or Provincial Government	Local Government	Social Security Funds	Total General Government	Central Government	State or Provincial Government	Local Government	Social Security Funds
					Gross Output					
1 Sales	...	...	...	...	...	...	...	...	...	...
2 Services produced for own use	613889	412547	...	165843	35499	815164	539227	...	224724	51213
3 Own account fixed capital formation	...	...	...	...	...	...	...	...	...	...
Gross Output [a]	626968	421129	...	168642	37197	829923	551706	...	225999	52218

Belgium

3.11 General Government Production Account: Total and Subsectors
(Continued)

Million Belgian francs

	\multicolumn{5}{c	}{1980}	\multicolumn{5}{c}{1985}
	Total General Government	Central Government	State or Provincial Government	Local Government	Social Security Funds	Total General Government	Central Government	State or Provincial Government	Local Government	Social Security Funds

Gross Input

Intermediate Consumption	139748	110250	...	19702	9796	186170	144119	...	26264	15787
Subtotal: Value Added	487220	310879	...	148940	27401	643753	407587	...	199735	36431
1 Indirect taxes, net	-	-	...	-	-	-	-	...	-	-
2 Consumption of fixed capital	12234	7799	...	3948	487	15454	10681	...	4413	360
3 Compensation of employees	471571	303080	...	142753	25738	626731	396906	...	194302	35523
4 Net Operating surplus	3415	-	...	2239	1176	1568	-	...	1020	548
Gross Input a	626968	421129	...	168642	37197	829923	551706	...	225999	52218

	\multicolumn{5}{c	}{1990}	\multicolumn{5}{c}{1991}
	Total General Government	Central Government	State or Provincial Government	Local Government	Social Security Funds	Total General Government	Central Government	State or Provincial Government	Local Government	Social Security Funds

Gross Output

1 Sales	...	...	...	...	...	...	...	...	...	...
2 Services produced for own use	933255	614318	...	267188	51749	1005569	664498	...	285782	55289
3 Own account fixed capital formation	...	...	...	...	...	...	...	...	...	...
Gross Output a	951524	629788	...	268982	52754	1026187	681580	...	287647	56960

Gross Input

Intermediate Consumption	191630	146821	...	28090	16719	207594	160184	...	29801	17609
Subtotal: Value Added	759894	482967	...	240892	36035	818593	521396	...	257846	39351
1 Indirect taxes, net	-	-	...	-	-	-	-	...	-	-
2 Consumption of fixed capital	22334	14778	...	7107	449	23751	15437	...	7712	602
3 Compensation of employees	735998	468189	...	232350	35459	792677	505959	...	248642	38076
4 Net Operating surplus	1562	-	...	1435	127	2165	-	...	1492	673
Gross Input a	951524	629788	...	268982	52754	1026187	681580	...	287647	56960

	\multicolumn{5}{c	}{1992}	\multicolumn{5}{c}{1993}
	Total General Government	Central Government	State or Provincial Government	Local Government	Social Security Funds	Total General Government	Central Government	State or Provincial Government	Local Government	Social Security Funds

Gross Output

1 Sales	...	...	...	...	...	...	...	...	...	...
2 Services produced for own use	1045387	688849	...	297842	58696	1111531	726680	...	318261	66590
3 Own account fixed capital formation	...	...	...	...	...	...	...	...	...	...
Gross Output a	1067078	706714	...	300006	60358	1135939	747259	...	320425	68255

Gross Input

Intermediate Consumption	203268	154175	...	30590	18503	214939	161349	...	32688	20902
Subtotal: Value Added	863810	552539	...	269416	41855	921000	585910	...	287737	47353
1 Indirect taxes, net	-	-	...	-	-	-	-	...	-	-
2 Consumption of fixed capital	24749	15951	...	8181	617	25311	16147	...	8535	629
3 Compensation of employees	836003	536588	...	259504	39911	892628	569763	...	277471	45394
4 Net Operating surplus	3058	-	...	1731	1327	3061	-	...	1731	1330
Gross Input a	1067078	706714	...	300006	60358	1135939	747259	...	320425	68255

a) State or Provincial government is included in Local government.

3.12 General Government Income and Outlay Account: Total and Subsectors

Million Belgian francs

	\multicolumn{5}{c	}{1980}	\multicolumn{5}{c}{1985}
	Total General Government	Central Government	State or Provincial Government	Local Government	Social Security Funds	Total General Government	Central Government	State or Provincial Government	Local Government	Social Security Funds

Receipts

1 Operating surplus	3415	-	...	2239	1176	1568	-	...	1020	548
2 Property and entrepreneurial income	58185	27856	...	11423	19746	81347	48977	...	17180	24841
A Withdrawals from public quasi-corporations	4455	4190	...	265	-	3077	19	...	3058	-
B Interest	26744	3629	...	4218	19737	36085	19246	...	1701	24789
C Dividends	24522	19495	...	5018	9	38458	28409	...	9997	52
D Net land rent and royalties	2464	542	...	1922	-	3727	1303	...	2424	-
3 Taxes, fees and contributions	1533972	1025004	...	63648	445320	2268532	1437152	...	118562	712818
A Indirect taxes	428031	418016	...	10015	-	582009	563510	...	18499	-

Belgium

3.12 General Government Income and Outlay Account: Total and Subsectors
(Continued)

Million Belgian francs

	1980					1985				
	Total General Government	Central Government	State or Provincial Government	Local Government	Social Security Funds	Total General Government	Central Government	State or Provincial Government	Local Government	Social Security Funds
B Direct taxes	639589	591346	...	48243	-	939341	847490	...	91851	-
C Social security contributions	466352	15642	...	5390	445320	747182	26152	...	8212	712818
D Fees, fines and penalties a	...	...	...	...	...	...	...	...	...	...
4 Other current transfers	105537	80458	...	152289	233319	183577	140386	...	225185	315670
A Casualty insurance claims	2978	1298	...	1665	15	5435	2370	...	3038	27
B Transfers from other government subsectors	...	1009	...	132295	227225	...	1825	...	190496	305343
C Transfers from the rest of the world	24188	24188	...	-	-	43277	43277	...	-	-
D Other transfers, except imputed a	16541	10680	...	817	5044	46329	34591	...	2960	8778
E Imputed unfunded employee pension and welfare contributions	61830	43283	...	17512	1035	88536	58323	...	28691	1522
Total Current Receipts b	1701109	1133318	...	229599	699561	2535024	1626515	...	361947	1053877

Disbursements

1 Government final consumption expenditure	613889	412547	...	165843	35499	815164	539227	...	224724	51213
2 Property income	215622	171553	...	39969	4940	507625	452875	...	57665	6736
A Interest	215622	171553	...	39969	4940	507625	452875	...	57665	6736
B Net land rent and royalties	-	-	...	-	-	-	-	...	-	-
3 Subsidies	138516	131505	...	7011	-	190760	184535	...	6225	-
4 Other current transfers	893843	543920	...	39513	670939	1297718	764838	...	61637	968907
A Casualty insurance premiums, net	3104	1354	...	1735	15	5855	2553	...	3273	29
B Transfers to other government subsectors	...	359520	...	1009	-	...	495839	...	1825	-
C Social security benefits	685886	15642	...	5390	664854	992491	26152	...	8212	958127
D Social assistance grants c	69967	59567	...	10400	-	111475	95885	...	15590	-
E Unfunded employee pension and welfare benefits	61830	43283	...	17512	1035	88536	58323	...	28691	1522
F Transfers to private non-profit institutions serving households c	-	-	...	-	-	-	-	...	-	-
G Other transfers n.e.c.	20250	11748	...	3467	5035	24361	11086	...	4046	9229
H Transfers to the rest of the world	52806	52806	...	-	-	75000	75000	...	-	-
Net saving	-160761	-126207	...	-22737	-11817	-276243	-314960	...	11696	27021
Total Current Disbursements and Net Saving b	1701109	1133318	...	229599	699561	2535024	1626515	...	361947	1053877

	1990					1991				
	Total General Government	Central Government	State or Provincial Government	Local Government	Social Security Funds	Total General Government	Central Government	State or Provincial Government	Local Government	Social Security Funds

Receipts

1 Operating surplus	1562	-	...	1435	127	2165	-	...	1492	673
2 Property and entrepreneurial income	82696	36569	...	27670	31448	90719	45908	...	28506	31600
A Withdrawals from public quasi-corporations	2602	3	...	2599	-	2310	10	...	2300	-
B Interest	30040	7103	...	4584	31344	27227	6993	...	4127	31402
C Dividends	45958	28362	...	17492	104	57775	38491	...	19086	198
D Net land rent and royalties	4096	1101	...	2995	-	3407	414	...	2993	-
3 Taxes, fees and contributions	2875512	1789335	...	132954	953223	3017302	1833650	...	151122	1032530
A Indirect taxes	785722	759242	...	26480	-	821753	794189	...	27564	-
B Direct taxes	1098666	1000917	...	97749	-	1123270	1008703	...	114567	-
C Social security contributions	991124	29176	...	8725	953223	1072279	30758	...	8991	1032530
D Fees, fines and penalties a	...	...	...	...	...	...	...	...	...	...

Belgium

3.12 General Government Income and Outlay Account: Total and Subsectors
(Continued)

Million Belgian francs

	1990					1991				
	Total General Government	Central Government	State or Provincial Government	Local Government	Social Security Funds	Total General Government	Central Government	State or Provincial Government	Local Government	Social Security Funds
4 Other current transfers	213565	152970	...	249513	286835	247618	183604	...	264371	263926
A Casualty insurance claims	8803	3838	...	4921	44	8416	3669	...	4705	42
B Transfers from other government subsectors	...	1321	...	203586	270846	...	1458	...	215910	246915
C Transfers from the rest of the world	47571	47571	...	-	-	67129	67129	...	-	-
D Other transfers, except imputed [a]	42369	22191	...	6099	14079	44765	23450	...	6268	15047
E Imputed unfunded employee pension and welfare contributions	114822	78049	...	34907	1866	127308	87898	...	37488	1922
Total Current Receipts [b]	3173335	1978874	...	411572	1271633	3357804	2063162	...	445491	1328729

Disbursements

1 Government final consumption expenditure	933255	614318	...	267188	51749	1005569	664498	...	285782	55289
2 Property income	687468	654884	...	39766	5809	694869	664858	...	40564	4742
A Interest	687468	654884	...	39766	5809	694869	664858	...	40564	4742
B Net land rent and royalties	-	-	...	-	-	-	-	...	-	-
3 Subsidies	187988	185630	...	2358	-	210322	207910	...	2412	-
4 Other current transfers	1611401	827100	...	76164	1183890	1764385	857128	...	80112	1291428
A Casualty insurance premiums, net	9299	4054	...	5198	47	9119	3976	...	5097	46
B Transfers to other government subsectors	...	474432	...	1321	-	...	462825	...	1458	-
C Social security benefits	1216029	29176	...	8725	1178128	1322037	30758	...	8991	1282288
D Social assistance grants [c]	147022	126078	...	20944	-	157288	135519	...	21769	-
E Unfunded employee pension and welfare benefits	114822	78049	...	34907	1866	127308	87898	...	37488	1922
F Transfers to private non-profit institutions serving households [c]	-	-	...	-	-	-	-	...	-	-
G Other transfers n.e.c.	25292	16374	...	5069	3849	31909	19428	...	5309	7172
H Transfers to the rest of the world	98937	98937	...	-	-	116724	116724	...	-	-
Net saving	-246777	-303058	...	26096	30185	-317341	-331232	...	36621	-22730
Total Current Disbursements and Net Saving [b]	3173335	1978874	...	411572	1271633	3357804	2063162	...	445491	1328729

	1992					1993				
	Total General Government	Central Government	State or Provincial Government	Local Government	Social Security Funds	Total General Government	Central Government	State or Provincial Government	Local Government	Social Security Funds

Receipts

1 Operating surplus	3058	-	...	1731	1327	3061	-	...	1731	1330
2 Property and entrepreneurial income	87695	43528	...	30589	30085	85971	41003	...	32009	30474
A Withdrawals from public quasi-corporations	2322	22	...	2300	-	2302	2	...	2300	-
B Interest	23831	6244	...	4009	30085	25079	8110	...	4010	30474
C Dividends	58437	37160	...	21277	-	55324	32628	...	22696	-
D Net land rent and royalties	3105	102	...	3003	-	3266	263	...	3003	-
3 Taxes, fees and contributions	3178087	1919525	...	162916	1095646	3300504	2001370	...	155999	1143135
A Indirect taxes	870549	841059	...	29490	-	905299	873151	...	32148	-
B Direct taxes	1169732	1045018	...	124714	-	1210837	1095675	...	115162	-
C Social security contributions	1137806	33448	...	8712	1095646	1184368	32544	...	8689	1143135
D Fees, fines and penalties [a]	...	...	...	...	...	...	...	...	...	...
4 Other current transfers	247819	183830	...	274260	292452	260038	191170	...	292813	293309
A Casualty insurance claims	8713	3799	...	4871	43	9447	4119	...	5281	47
B Transfers from other government subsectors	...	4447	...	224794	273482	...	1676	...	237978	277600
C Transfers from the rest of the world	59230	59230	...	-	-	54260	54260	...	-	-
D Other transfers, except imputed [a]	47372	23919	...	6667	16786	50229	29769	...	6952	13508
E Imputed unfunded employee pension and welfare contributions	132504	92435	...	37928	2141	146102	101346	...	42602	2154
Total Current Receipts [b]	3516659	2146883	...	469496	1419510	3649574	2233543	...	482552	1468248

Belgium

3.12 General Government Income and Outlay Account: Total and Subsectors
(Continued)

Million Belgian francs

	1992 Total General Government	1992 Central Government	1992 State or Provincial Government	1992 Local Government	1992 Social Security Funds	1993 Total General Government	1993 Central Government	1993 State or Provincial Government	1993 Local Government	1993 Social Security Funds
					Disbursements					
1 Government final consumption expenditure	1045387	688849	...	297842	58696	1111531	726680	...	318261	66590
2 Property income	758813	728961	...	41577	4782	767027	738099	...	42704	3739
A Interest	758813	728961	...	41577	4782	767027	738099	...	42704	3739
B Net land rent and royalties	-	-	...	-	-	-	-	...	-	-
3 Subsidies	198261	195958	...	2303	-	197433	195545	...	1888	-
4 Other current transfers	1853705	900337	...	85671	1370420	1947993	939138	...	89291	1436818
A Casualty insurance premiums, net	9094	3965	...	5084	45	9825	4284	...	5492	49
B Transfers to other government subsectors	...	498276	...	4447	-	...	515578	...	1676	-
C Social security benefits	1408411	33448	...	8712	1366251	1470392	32544	...	8689	1429159
D Social assistance grants [c]	162114	138354	...	23760	-	169675	145064	...	24611	-
E Unfunded employee pension and welfare benefits	132504	92435	...	37928	2141	146102	101346	...	42602	2154
F Transfers to private non-profit institutions serving households [c]	-	-	...	-	-	-	-	...	-	-
G Other transfers n.e.c.	27449	19726	...	5740	1983	32582	20905	...	6221	5456
H Transfers to the rest of the world	114133	114133	...	-	-	119417	119417	...	-	-
Net saving	-339507	-367222	...	42103	-14388	-374410	-365919	...	30408	-38899
Total Current Disbursements and Net Saving [b]	3516659	2146883	...	469496	1419510	3649574	2233543	...	482552	1468248

a) Item 'Other current transfers' includes item 'Fees, fines and penalties'.
b) State or Provincial government is included in Local government.
c) Item 'Transfers to private non-profit institutions serving households' is included in item 'Social assistance grants'.

3.13 General Government Capital Accumulation Account: Total and Subsectors

Million Belgian francs

	1980 Total General Government	1980 Central Government	1980 State or Provincial Government	1980 Local Government	1980 Social Security Funds	1985 Total General Government	1985 Central Government	1985 State or Provincial Government	1985 Local Government	1985 Social Security Funds
					Finance of Gross Accumulation					
1 Gross saving	-148527	-118408	...	-18789	-11330	-260789	-304279	...	16109	27381
A Consumption of fixed capital	12234	7799	...	3948	487	15454	10681	...	4413	360
B Net saving	-160761	-126207	...	-22737	-11817	-276243	-314960	...	11696	27021
2 Capital transfers	13274	13472	...	15639	490	16931	17053	...	18002	4839
A From other government subsectors	...	198	...	15639	490	...	122	...	18002	4839
B From other resident sectors	12765	12765	...	-	-	16907	16907	...	-	-
C From rest of the world	509	509	...	-	-	24	24	...	-	-
Finance of Gross Accumulation [a]	-135253	-104936	...	-3150	-10840	-243858	-287226	...	34111	32220
					Gross Accumulation					
1 Gross capital formation	125662	74614	...	50761	287	106001	73921	...	31531	549
A Increase in stocks	-	-	...	-	-	-	-	...	-	-
B Gross fixed capital formation	125662	74614	...	50761	287	106001	73921	...	31531	549
2 Purchases of land, net	12985	6836	...	6149	-	6514	4834	...	1680	-
3 Purchases of intangible assets, net	-	-	...	-	-	-	-	...	-	-
4 Capital transfers	47656	63235	...	748	-	60304	82050	...	1217	-
A To other government subsectors	...	16129	...	198	-	...	22841	...	122	-
B To other resident sectors	43356	42806	...	550	-	51392	50297	...	1095	-
C To rest of the world	4300	4300	...	-	-	8912	8912	...	-	-
Net lending	-321556	-249621	...	-60808	-11127	-416677	-448031	...	-317	31671
Gross Accumulation [a]	-135253	-104936	...	-3150	-10840	-243858	-287226	...	34111	32220

Belgium

3.13 General Government Capital Accumulation Account: Total and Subsectors

Million Belgian francs

	1990					1991				
	Total General Government	Central Government	State or Provincial Government	Local Government	Social Security Funds	Total General Government	Central Government	State or Provincial Government	Local Government	Social Security Funds
Finance of Gross Accumulation											
1 Gross saving	-224443	-288280	...	33203	30634	-293590	-315795	...	44333	-22128
A Consumption of fixed capital	22334	14778	...	7107	449	23751	15437	...	7712	602
B Net saving	-246777	-303058	...	26096	30185	-317341	-331232	...	36621	-22730
2 Capital transfers	22210	22220	...	15528	3468	23013	23052	...	14027	3540
A From other government subsectors	...	10	...	15528	3468	...	39	...	14027	3540
B From other resident sectors	21070	21070	...	-	-	22018	22018	...	-	-
C From rest of the world	1140	1140	...	-	-	995	995	...	-	-
Finance of Gross Accumulation a	-202233	-266060	...	48731	34102	-270577	-292743	...	58360	-18588
Gross Accumulation											
1 Gross capital formation	88693	39596	...	48405	692	98895	46311	...	51822	762
A Increase in stocks	-	-	...	-	-	-	-	...	-	-
B Gross fixed capital formation	88693	39596	...	48405	692	98895	46311	...	51822	762
2 Purchases of land, net	409	-1854	...	2263	-	516	-777	...	1293	-
3 Purchases of intangible assets, net	-	-	...	-	-	-	-	...	-	-
4 Capital transfers	57223	74722	...	1507	-	65365	81428	...	1543	-
A To other government subsectors	...	18996	...	10	-	...	17567	...	39	-
B To other resident sectors	41228	39731	...	1497	-	50438	48934	...	1504	-
C To rest of the world	15995	15995	...	-	-	14927	14927	...	-	-
Net lending	-348558	-378524	...	-3444	33410	-435353	-419705	...	3702	-19350
Gross Accumulation a	-202233	-266060	...	48731	34102	-270577	-292743	...	58360	-18588

	1992					1993				
	Total General Government	Central Government	State or Provincial Government	Local Government	Social Security Funds	Total General Government	Central Government	State or Provincial Government	Local Government	Social Security Funds
Finance of Gross Accumulation											
1 Gross saving	-314758	-351271	...	50284	-13771	-349099	-349772	...	38943	-38270
A Consumption of fixed capital	24749	15951	...	8181	617	25311	16147	...	8535	629
B Net saving	-339507	-367222	...	42103	-14388	-374410	-365919	...	30408	-38899
2 Capital transfers	24762	24809	...	19200	3883	57572	57613	...	21646	3129
A From other government subsectors	...	47	...	19200	3883	...	41	...	21646	3129
B From other resident sectors	23237	23237	...	-	-	56354	56354	...	-	-
C From rest of the world	1525	1525	...	-	-	1218	1218	...	-	-
Finance of Gross Accumulation a	-289996	-326462	...	69484	-9888	-291527	-292159	...	60589	-35141
Gross Accumulation											
1 Gross capital formation	105586	49308	...	55483	795	109500	37877	...	70741	882
A Increase in stocks	-	-	...	-	-	-	-	...	-	-
B Gross fixed capital formation	105586	49308	...	55483	795	109500	37877	...	70741	882
2 Purchases of land, net	4446	1130	...	3316	-	2848	1027	...	1821	-
3 Purchases of intangible assets, net	-	-	...	-	-	-	-	...	-	-
4 Capital transfers	73126	94873	...	1383	-	76778	100213	...	1381	-
A To other government subsectors	...	23083	...	47	-	...	24775	...	41	-
B To other resident sectors	55580	54244	...	1336	-	59863	58523	...	1340	-
C To rest of the world	17546	17546	...	-	-	16915	16915	...	-	-
Net lending	-473154	-471773	...	9302	-10683	-480653	-431276	...	-13354	-36023
Gross Accumulation a	-289996	-326462	...	69484	-9888	-291527	-292159	...	60589	-35141

a) State or Provincial government is included in Local government.

Belgium

3.21 Corporate and Quasi-Corporate Enterprise Production Account: Total and Sectors

Million Belgian francs

	1980 TOTAL	1980 Non-Financial	1980 Financial	1980 ADDENDUM: Total, including Unincorporated	1985 TOTAL	1985 Non-Financial	1985 Financial	1985 ADDENDUM: Total, including Unincorporated	1990 TOTAL	1990 Non-Financial	1990 Financial	1990 ADDENDUM: Total, including Unincorporated
Gross Output												
1 Output for sale	...	...	...	...	...	...	...	...	...	...	...	...
2 Imputed bank service charge	...	...	109121	109121	...	...	186425	186425	...	...	184036	184036
3 Own-account fixed capital formation	...	...	...	...	...	...	...	...	...	...	...	...
Gross Output	...	...	216075	...	...	...	378060	...	...	...	493655	...
Gross Input												
Intermediate consumption	...	...	173772	...	...	...	295299	...	...	...	357544	...
1 Imputed banking service charge	...	...	109121	109121	...	...	186425	186425	...	...	184036	184036
2 Other intermediate consumption	...	...	64651	...	...	...	108874	...	...	...	173508	...
Subtotal: Value Added	...	...	42303	2673911	...	...	82761	3705830	...	...	136111	5146517
1 Indirect taxes, net	...	...	7617	-504	...	...	16800	-5006	...	...	28832	82070
A Indirect taxes	...	...	16855	138012	...	...	26698	185692	...	...	37484	270058
B Less: Subsidies	...	...	9238	138516	...	...	9898	190698	...	...	8652	187988
2 Consumption of fixed capital	...	...	14520	299911	...	...	23670	440351	...	...	31900	615262
3 Compensation of employees	...	...	115190	1599456	...	...	174336	2037960	...	...	224831	2658239
4 Net operating surplus	...	...	-95024	775048	...	...	-132045	1232525	...	...	-149452	1790946
Gross Input	...	...	216075	2673911	...	...	378060	3705830	...	...	493655	5146517

	1991 TOTAL	1991 Non-Financial	1991 Financial	1991 ADDENDUM: Total, including Unincorporated	1992 TOTAL	1992 Non-Financial	1992 Financial	1992 ADDENDUM: Total, including Unincorporated	1993 TOTAL	1993 Non-Financial	1993 Financial	1993 ADDENDUM: Total, including Unincorporated
Gross Output												
1 Output for sale	...	...	...	...	...	...	...	...	...	...	...	...
2 Imputed bank service charge	...	...	198479	198479	...	...	213273	213273	...	...	218261	218261
3 Own-account fixed capital formation	...	...	...	...	...	...	...	...	...	...	...	...
Gross Output	...	...	529166	...	...	...	566122	...	...	...	581236	...
Gross Input												
Intermediate consumption	...	...	377699	...	...	...	399506	...	...	...	409913	...
1 Imputed banking service charge	...	...	198479	198479	...	...	213273	213273	...	...	218261	218261
2 Other intermediate consumption	...	...	179220	...	...	...	186233	...	...	...	191652	...
Subtotal: Value Added	...	...	151467	5384884	...	...	166616	5684882	...	...	171323	5804739
1 Indirect taxes, net	...	...	31243	71481	...	...	34463	119308	...	...	37091	148401
A Indirect taxes	...	...	40259	281803	...	...	45665	317569	...	...	48421	345834
B Less: Subsidies	...	...	9016	210322	...	...	11202	198261	...	...	11330	197433
2 Consumption of fixed capital	...	...	31840	624912	...	...	31790	664711	...	...	31880	673652
3 Compensation of employees	...	...	235201	2870616	...	...	243847	3020335	...	...	249976	3060691
4 Net operating surplus	...	...	-146817	1817875	...	...	-143484	1880528	...	...	-147624	1921995
Gross Input	...	...	529166	5384884	...	...	566122	5684882	...	...	581236	5804739

3.22 Corporate and Quasi-Corporate Enterprise Income and Outlay Account: Total and Sectors

Million Belgian francs

	1980 TOTAL	1980 Non-Financial	1980 Financial	1985 TOTAL	1985 Non-Financial	1985 Financial	1990 TOTAL	1990 Non-Financial	1990 Financial	1991 TOTAL	1991 Non-Financial	1991 Financial
Receipts												
1 Operating surplus	211760	306784	-95024	466797	598842	-132045	702476	851928	-149452	670535	817352	-146817
2 Property and entrepreneurial income	747074	...	747074	1319276	...	1319276	1923141	...	1923141	1999349	...	1999349
A Withdrawals from quasi-corporate enterprises	...	...	...	...	...	...	...	...	...	...	...	...
B Interest	740561	...	740561	1300268	...	1300268	1885342	...	1885342	1961470	...	1961470
C Dividends	6498	...	6498	18983	...	18983	37764	...	37764	37839	...	37839
D Net land rent and royalties	15	...	15	25	...	25	35	...	35	40	...	40

Belgium

3.22 Corporate and Quasi-Corporate Enterprise Income and Outlay Account: Total and Sectors
(Continued)

Million Belgian francs

	1980			1985			1990			1991		
	TOTAL	Non-Financial	Financial	TOTAL	Non-Financial	Financial	TOTAL	Non-Financial	Financial	TOTAL	Non-Financial	Financial
3 Current transfers	166668	79275	87393	244772	99641	145131	385891	154088	231803	376294	152099	224195
A Casualty insurance claims	36140	26020	10120	58793	33973	24820	105081	59176	45905	95101	52636	42465
B Casualty insurance premiums, net, due to be received by insurance companies	73973	...	73973	115276	...	115276	179458	...	179458	175205	...	175205
C Current transfers from the rest of the world	...	...	...	...	...	...	...	...	...	...	...	...
D Other transfers except imputed	...	...	...	...	...	...	...	...	...	...	...	...
E Imputed unfunded employee pension and welfare contributions	56555	53255	3300	70703	65668	5035	101352	94912	6440	105988	99463	6525
Total Current Receipts	1125502	386059	739443	2030845	698483	1332362	3011508	1006016	2005492	3046178	969451	2076727
					Disbursements							
1 Property and entrepreneurial income [a]	845246	219116	626130	1504735	383862	1120873	2177839	468776	1709063	2300451	537157	1763294
A Withdrawals from quasi-corporations	160	...	160	176	...	176	333	...	333	364	...	364
B Interest	813297	208835	604462	1443081	366798	1076283	2101394	443617	1657777	2221587	513026	1708561
C Dividends	21508	...	21508	44414	...	44414	50953	...	50953	54369	...	54369
D Net land rent and royalties	10281	10281	...	17064	17064	...	25159	25159	...	24131	24131	...
2 Direct taxes and other current transfers n.e.c. to general government	89749	76689	13060	126378	98978	27400	165175	131441	33734	173481	139410	34071
A Direct taxes	89749	76689	13060	126378	98978	27400	165175	131441	33734	173481	139410	34071
B Fines, fees, penalties and other current transfers n.e.c. [b]	...	...	...	...	...	...	...	...	...	...	...	...
3 Other current transfers	163963	80790	83173	238578	103205	135373	365043	157013	208030	360300	156975	203325
A Casualty insurance premiums, net	33140	27535	5605	52112	37537	14575	83616	62101	21515	78467	57512	20955
B Casualty insurance claims liability of insurance companies	73973	...	73973	115276	...	115276	179458	...	179458	175205	...	175205
C Transfers to private non-profit institutions	...	...	...	...	...	...	...	...	...	...	...	...
D Unfunded employee pension and welfare benefits	56555	53255	3300	70703	65668	5035	101352	94912	6440	105988	99463	6525
E Social assistance grants	...	...	...	...	...	...	...	...	...	...	...	...
F Other transfers n.e.c. [b]	295	...	295	487	...	487	617	...	617	640	...	640
G Transfers to the rest of the world	...	...	...	...	...	...	...	...	...	...	...	...
Net saving	26544	9464	17080	161154	112438	48716	303451	248786	54665	211946	135909	76037
Total Current Disbursements and Net Saving	1125502	386059	739443	2030845	698483	1332362	3011508	1006016	2005492	3046178	969451	2076727

	1992			1993		
	TOTAL	Non-Financial	Financial	TOTAL	Non-Financial	Financial
			Receipts			
1 Operating surplus	677527	821011	-143484	...	...	-147624
2 Property and entrepreneurial income	2113511	...	2113511	...	...	...
A Withdrawals from quasi-corporate enterprises	...	...	...	...	...	...
B Interest	2077433	...	2077433	2052439	...	2052439
C Dividends	36038	...	36038	...	...	...
D Net land rent and royalties	40	...	40	-	...	...
3 Current transfers	367861	157253	210608	394723	169439	225284
A Casualty insurance claims	85070	53065	32005	93470	60320	33150
B Casualty insurance premiums, net, due to be received by insurance companies	171858	...	171858	185104	...	185104
C Current transfers from the rest of the world	...	...	...	...	...	...
D Other transfers except imputed	...	...	...	...	...	...
E Imputed unfunded employee pension and welfare contributions	110933	104188	6745	116149	109119	7030
Total Current Receipts	3158899	978264	2180635	...	...	...

Belgium

3.22 Corporate and Quasi-Corporate Enterprise Income and Outlay Account: Total and Sectors
(Continued)

Million Belgian francs

	1992 TOTAL	1992 Non-Financial	1992 Financial	1993 TOTAL	1993 Non-Financial	1993 Financial
Disbursements						
1 Property and entrepreneurial income a	2450546	580921	1869625	...	...	...
A Withdrawals from quasi-corporations	396	...	396	401	...	401
B Interest	2377138	564417	1812721	...	...	...
C Dividends	56508	...	56508	...	...	...
D Net land rent and royalties	16504	16504	...	...	...	...
2 Direct taxes and other current transfers n.e.c. to general government	147341	109431	37910	...	...	...
A Direct taxes	147341	109431	37910	...	...	...
B Fines, fees, penalties and other current transfers n.e.c. b	...	...	...	...	...	...
3 Other current transfers	359522	158497	201025	386683	171009	215674
A Casualty insurance premiums, net	76069	54309	21760	84745	61890	22855
B Casualty insurance claims liability of insurance companies	171858	...	171858	185104	...	185104
C Transfers to private non-profit institutions	...	...	...	...	...	...
D Unfunded employee pension and welfare benefits	110933	104188	6745	116149	109119	7030
E Social assistance grants	...	...	...	...	...	...
F Other transfers n.e.c. b	662	...	662	685	...	685
G Transfers to the rest of the world	...	...	...	...	...	...
Net saving	201490	129415	72075	206073	...	...
Total Current Disbursements and Net Saving	3158899	978264	2180635	...	...	...

a) Property and entrepreneurial income paid by non-financial corporate and quasi-corporate enterprises is net of property income received.
b) Item 'Other current transfers' includes item 'Fees, fines and penalties'.

3.23 Corporate and Quasi-Corporate Enterprise Capital Accumulation Account: Total and Sectors

Million Belgian francs

	1980 TOTAL	1980 Non-Fin	1980 Fin	1985 TOTAL	1985 Non-Fin	1985 Fin	1990 TOTAL	1990 Non-Fin	1990 Fin	1991 TOTAL	1991 Non-Fin	1991 Fin
Finance of Gross Accumulation												
1 Gross saving	238653	207053	31600	475764	403378	72386	761970	675405	86565	678255	570378	107877
A Consumption of fixed capital	212109	197589	14520	314610	290940	23670	458519	426619	31900	466309	434469	31840
B Net saving	26544	9464	17080	161154	112438	48716	303451	248786	54665	211946	135909	76037
2 Capital transfers	41005	41005	...	46596	45900	696	34616	32147	2469	43199	40766	2433
Finance of Gross Accumulation	279658	248058	31600	522360	449278	73082	796586	707552	89034	721454	611144	110310
Gross Accumulation												
1 Gross capital formation	370034	351238	18796	388752	362118	26634	801645	766358	35287	801486	771641	29845
A Increase in stocks	25271	25271	...	-33544	-33544	...	-4411	-4411	...	-8577	-8577	...
B Gross fixed capital formation	344763	325967	18796	422296	395662	26634	806056	770769	35287	810063	780218	29845
2 Purchases of land, net	2532	2265	267	3557	3443	114	4536	4400	136	4838	4691	147
3 Purchases of intangible assets, net	...	...	...	...	...	...	...	...	...	...	...	...
4 Capital transfers	182	182	...	3652	703	2949	878	34	844	-846	-	-846
Net lending	-93090	-105627	12537	126399	83014	43385	-10473	-63240	52767	-84024	-165188	81164
Gross Accumulation	279658	248058	31600	522360	449278	73082	796586	707552	89034	721454	611144	110310

	1992 TOTAL	1992 Non-Financial	1992 Financial	1993 TOTAL	1993 Non-Financial	1993 Financial
Finance of Gross Accumulation						
1 Gross saving	696022	592157	103865	709443	471490	31880
A Consumption of fixed capital	494532	462742	31790	503370	471490	31880
B Net saving	201490	129415	72075	206073	...	...
2 Capital transfers	47119	44403	2716	51683	49571	2112
Finance of Gross Accumulation	743141	636560	106581	...	...	...

Belgium

3.23 Corporate and Quasi-Corporate Enterprise Capital Accumulation Account: Total and Sectors
(Continued)

Million Belgian francs

		1992			1993		
		TOTAL	Non-Financial	Financial	TOTAL	Non-Financial	Financial
		Gross Accumulation					
1	Gross capital formation	786716	759541	27175	711642	688748	22894
	A Increase in stocks	-117	-117	...	-12537	-12537	...
	B Gross fixed capital formation	786833	759658	27175	724179	701285	22894
2	Purchases of land, net	4835	4745	90	6395	6295	100
3	Purchases of intangible assets, net	...	...	...	...	...	...
4	Capital transfers	-509	-	-509	...	-	31767
	Net lending	-47901	-127726	79825	...	...	45398
	Gross Accumulation	743141	636560	106581	...	...	...

3.32 Household and Private Unincorporated Enterprise Income and Outlay Account

Million Belgian francs

		1980	1983	1984	1985	1986	1987	1988	1989	1990	1991	1992	1993
						Receipts							
1	Compensation of employees	2087927	2410742	2561434	2691591	2838095	2904036	3026075	3169343	3440937	3714893	3911238	4040419
	A Wages and salaries	1649714	1907239	2002421	2066117	2160253	2177255	2252844	2343965	2552649	2749462	2898569	2959019
	B Employers' contributions for social security	297028	335958	387074	437635	472734	504707	527986	568926	613834	668195	697942	716769
	C Employers' contributions for private pension & welfare plans	141185	167545	171939	187839	205108	222074	245245	256452	274454	297236	314727	364631
2	Operating surplus of private unincorporated enterprises	563288	675829	729351	765728	815175	856716	928035	1028929	1088470	1144340	1203001	1216935
3	Property and entrepreneurial income	314112	495536	564247	635398	656662	677468	727523	852310	940745	1039965	1139249	1204338
	A Withdrawals from private quasi-corporations	160	151	160	176	200	238	268	300	333	364	396	401
	B Interest	230614	330415	381366	413318	416784	414827	425887	450553	507388	561399	609104	643877
	C Dividends	79298	160715	178347	217110	234840	257521	296545	396633	428439	473278	524674	554960
	D Net land rent and royalties	4040	4255	4374	4794	4838	4882	4823	4824	4585	4924	5075	5100
3	Current transfers	954278	1244217	1311701	1376581	1424266	1500858	1555022	1648594	1751838	1895488	1998228	2102432
	A Casualty insurance claims	38595	48499	50200	52028	54170	58445	61521	67907	80104	80518	85155	89147
	B Social security benefits	685886	909355	956533	992491	1030131	1072403	1096464	1149167	1216029	1322037	1408411	1470392
	C Social assistance grants	69967	96840	103555	111475	114454	122832	127253	144566	147022	157288	162114	169675
	D Unfunded employee pension and welfare benefits	118385	143175	148859	159239	168828	179874	192625	202702	216174	233296	243437	262251
	E Transfers from general government	20250	16652	20705	24361	22992	27380	25876	24677	25292	31909	27449	32582
	F Transfers from the rest of the world	20900	29300	31400	36500	33200	39400	50700	59000	66600	69800	71000	77700
	G Other transfers n.e.c.	295	396	449	487	491	524	583	575	617	640	662	685
	Total Current Receipts	3919605	4826324	5166733	5469298	5734198	5939078	6236655	6699176	7221990	7794686	8251716	8564124
						Disbursements							
1	Final consumption expenditures	2171908	2687506	2875382	3105122	3198743	3358594	3506403	3769923	4012088	4242981	4445416	4514296
2	Property income	101603	114287	123918	126961	126027	130499	142292	172606	193975	212713	226696	235541
	A Interest	97465	109929	119452	122079	121074	125500	137338	167627	188918	207673	221580	230100
	B Net land rent and royalties	4138	4358	4466	4882	4953	4999	4954	4979	5057	5040	5116	5441
3	Direct taxes and other current transfers n.e.c. to government	1016192	1293312	1448500	1560145	1618188	1688171	1729148	1771192	1924615	2022068	2160197	2229919
	A Social security contributions	466352	597354	680876	747182	794371	842003	876143	924616	991124	1072279	1137806	1184368
	B Direct taxes	549840	695958	767624	812963	823817	846168	853005	846576	933491	949789	1022391	1045551
	Income taxes	...	...	...	...	...	...	...	...	...	...	...	...
	Other	...	...	...	...	...	...	...	...	...	...	...	...
	C Fees, fines and penalties [a]	...	...	...	...	...	...	...	...	...	...	...	...

Belgium

3.32 Household and Private Unincorporated Enterprise Income and Outlay Account
(Continued)

Million Belgian francs

	1980	1983	1984	1985	1986	1987	1988	1989	1990	1991	1992	1993
4 Other current transfers	203430	271491	282771	297787	306344	319865	345673	362978	422255	436049	460423	492233
A Net casualty insurance premiums	39809	50224	52714	55099	56530	60197	64567	71733	85023	86779	89585	93564
B Transfers to private non-profit institutions serving households	...	...	...	...	...	...	...	...	...	...	...	...
C Transfers to the rest of the world	31800	38500	41400	43900	42800	43700	49200	57000	86500	79500	87300	98200
D Other current transfers, except imputed [a]	13436	39592	39798	39549	38186	36094	39281	31543	34558	36474	40101	38218
E Imputed employee pension and welfare contributions	118385	143175	148859	159239	168828	179874	192625	202702	216174	233296	243437	262251
Net saving	426472	459728	436162	379283	484896	441949	513139	622477	669057	880875	958984	1092135
Total Current Disbursements and Net Saving	3919605	4826324	5166733	5469298	5734198	5939078	6236655	6699176	7221990	7794686	8251716	8564124

a) Item 'Other current transfers' includes item 'Fees, fines and penalties'.

3.33 Household and Private Unincorporated Enterprise Capital Accumulation Account

Million Belgian francs

	1980	1983	1984	1985	1986	1987	1988	1989	1990	1991	1992	1993
Finance of Gross Accumulation												
1 Gross saving	514274	570111	553451	505024	613375	574626	654886	768969	825800	1042478	1129163	1262417
A Consumption of fixed capital	87802	110383	117289	125741	128479	132677	141747	146492	156743	161603	170179	170282
B Net saving	426472	459728	436162	379283	484896	441949	513139	622477	669057	880875	958984	1092135
2 Capital transfers	2727	3781	5426	5696	5644	6395	7665	8613	7312	8239	9661	9680
Total Finance of Gross Accumulation	517001	573892	558877	510720	619019	581021	662551	777582	833112	1050717	1138824	1272097
Gross Accumulation												
1 Gross Capital Formation	257257	186283	194714	211799	233564	254963	311542	373930	412494	405296	464867	465135
A Increase in stocks	-603	1175	889	-1189	1372	-440	1466	2748	1682	-259	86	-253
B Gross fixed capital formation	257860	185108	193825	212988	232192	255403	310076	371182	410812	405555	464781	465388
2 Purchases of land, net	-15517	-8265	-6743	-10071	-7172	-8191	-10965	-8201	-4945	-5354	-9281	-9243
3 Purchases of intangibles, net	...	...	...	...	...	...	...	...	...	...	...	...
4 Capital transfers	12583	12727	13329	13255	14303	15754	16686	16901	20192	22864	23746	24587
Net lending	262678	383147	357577	295737	378324	318495	345288	394952	405371	627911	659492	791618
Total Gross Accumulation	517001	573892	558877	510720	619019	581021	662551	777582	833112	1050717	1138824	1272097

3.51 External Transactions: Current Account: Detail

Million Belgian francs

	1980	1983	1984	1985	1986	1987	1988	1989	1990	1991	1992	1993
Payments to the Rest of the World												
1 Imports of goods and services	2257800	3004300	3429000	3525900	3327200	3452300	3826000	4436400	4565000	4657300	4724400	4637500
A Imports of merchandise c.i.f.	2029900	2714800	3106400	3165600	2941300	3027100	3340200	3833500	3944700	3954800	3990800	3872000
B Other	227900	289500	322600	360300	385900	425200	485800	602900	620300	702500	733600	765500
2 Factor income to the rest of the world	243500	571000	668500	798500	712700	681700	808200	1165800	1314400	1495700	1709800	1643200
A Compensation of employees	14000	18600	19000	20500	21300	23700	26300	31300	38400	43500	48500	52900
B Property and entrepreneurial income	229500	552400	649500	778000	691400	658000	781900	1134500	1276000	1452200	1661300	1590300
3 Current transfers to the rest of the world	95786	138695	147336	156210	152585	167069	181940	192445	235547	249094	246733	264767
A Indirect taxes by general government to supranational organizations	41606	56573	57261	59412	64613	77013	75711	80718	83257	91933	88738	84572
B Other current transfers	54180	82122	90075	96798	87972	90056	106229	111727	152290	157161	157995	180195
By general government	11200	18302	16125	15588	14602	17296	23019	19097	15680	24791	25395	34845
By other resident sectors	42980	63820	73950	81210	73370	72760	83210	92630	136610	132370	132600	145350
4 Surplus of the nation on current transactions	-148553	-34334	-24581	13447	102919	66107	97746	104699	60495	121466	153258	336484
Payments to the Rest of the World, and Surplus of the Nation on Current Transfers	2448533	3679661	4220255	4494057	4295404	4367176	4913886	5899344	6175442	6523560	6834191	6881951
Receipts From The Rest of the World												
1 Exports of goods and services	2170200	3078900	3505200	3644900	3522900	3608800	4028800	4629800	4738900	4846500	4978100	5010600
A Exports of merchandise f.o.b.	1802200	2531000	2903700	3012800	2874100	2904300	3252200	3722200	3763100	3765100	3854000	3847600

Belgium

3.51 External Transactions: Current Account: Detail
(Continued)

Million Belgian francs

	1980	1983	1984	1985	1986	1987	1988	1989	1990	1991	1992	1993
B Other	368000	547900	601500	632100	648800	704500	776600	907600	975800	1081400	1124100	1163000
2 Factor income from the rest of the world	217300	508200	608800	722100	653000	632300	758500	1131400	1248400	1469300	1669100	1676300
A Compensation of employees	30900	42100	45600	47400	56900	60700	68300	75500	85100	95100	103400	140000
B Property and entrepreneurial income	186400	466100	563200	674700	596100	571600	690200	1055900	1163300	1374200	1565700	1536300
3 Current transfers from the rest of the world	61033	92561	106255	127057	119504	126076	126586	138144	188142	207760	186991	195051
A Subsidies to general government from supranational organizations	23902	29726	33100	42281	44627	42801	32129	27049	46950	66287	58274	51641
B Other current transfers	37131	62835	73155	84776	74877	83275	94457	111095	141192	141473	128717	143410
To general government	286	1072	543	996	690	1030	989	693	621	842	956	2619
To other resident sectors	36845	61763	72612	83780	74187	82245	93468	110402	140571	140631	127761	140791
Receipts from the Rest of the World on Current Transfers	2448533	3679661	4220255	4494057	4295404	4367176	4913886	5899344	6175442	6523560	6834191	6881951

3.52 External Transactions: Capital Accumulation Account

Million Belgian francs

	1980	1983	1984	1985	1986	1987	1988	1989	1990	1991	1992	1993
Finance of Gross Accumulation												
1 Surplus of the nation on current transactions	-148553	-34334	-24581	13447	102919	66107	97746	104699	60495	121466	153258	336484
2 Capital transfers from the rest of the world	885	565	1005	924	813	1045	1043	1264	1840	1995	2725	2718
A By general government	509	65	305	24	213	45	143	64	1140	995	1525	1218
B By other resident sectors	376	500	700	900	600	1000	900	1200	700	1000	1200	1500
Total Finance of Gross Accumulation	-147668	-33769	-23576	14371	103732	67152	98789	105963	62335	123461	155983	339202
Gross Accumulation												
1 Capital transfers to the rest of the world	4300	6825	7898	8912	8698	10304	10984	11177	15995	14927	17546	16915
A By general government	4300	6825	7898	8912	8698	10304	10984	11177	15995	14927	17546	16915
B By other resident sectors	...	...	...	...	...	...	...	...	...	...	...	...
2 Purchases of intangible assets, n.e.c., net, from the rest of the world	...	...	...	...	...	...	...	...	...	...	...	...
Net lending to the rest of the world	-151968	-40594	-31474	5459	95034	56848	87805	94786	46340	108534	138437	322287
Total Gross Accumulation	-147668	-33769	-23576	14371	103732	67152	98789	105963	62335	123461	155983	339202

4.1 Derivation of Value Added by Kind of Activity, in Current Prices

Million Belgian francs

	1980			1985			1990			1991		
	Gross Output	Intermediate Consumption	Value Added	Gross Output	Intermediate Consumption	Value Added	Gross Output	Intermediate Consumption	Value Added	Gross Output	Intermediate Consumption	Value Added
	All Producers												
1 Agriculture, hunting, forestry and fishing	...	...	73108	...	...	106104	...	...	119656	...	...	124227
2 Mining and quarrying	...	...	7399	...	...	10975	...	...	1151	...	...	...
A Coal mining [a]	...	...	7399	...	...	10975	...	...	1151	...	...	...
B Crude petroleum and natural gas production	...	...	...	...	...	...	...	...	...	...	...	...
C Metal ore mining	...	...	...	...	...	...	...	...	...	...	...	...
D Other mining [b]	...	...	...	...	...	...	...	...	...	...	...	...

Belgium

4.1 Derivation of Value Added by Kind of Activity, in Current Prices
(Continued)

Million Belgian francs

	1980 Gross Output	1980 Intermediate Consumption	1980 Value Added	1985 Gross Output	1985 Intermediate Consumption	1985 Value Added	1990 Gross Output	1990 Intermediate Consumption	1990 Value Added	1991 Gross Output	1991 Intermediate Consumption	1991 Value Added
3 Manufacturing	...	...	833834	...	...	1115004	...	...	1446335	...	...	...
A Manufacture of food, beverages and tobacco	...	...	119190	...	...	171501	...	...	195266	...	...	205326
B Textile, wearing apparel and leather industries	...	...	63655	...	...	81546	...	...	101009	...	...	97729
C Manufacture of wood and wood products, including furniture	...	...	37070	...	...	42413	...	...	61626	...	...	...
D Manufacture of paper and paper products, printing and publishing	...	...	44448	...	...	60554	...	...	89282	...	...	88539
E Manufacture of chemicals and chemical petroleum, coal, rubber and plastic products [c]	...	...	189136	...	...	268619	...	...	344743	...	...	...
F Manufacture of non-metallic mineral products, except products of petroleum and coal [b]	...	...	49986	...	...	51489	...	...	77620	...	...	74970
G Basic metal industries	...	...	70258	...	...	100677	...	...	135398	...	...	106447
H Manufacture of fabricated metal products, machinery and equipment	...	...	247649	...	...	320042	...	...	440447	...	...	423645
I Other manufacturing industries	...	...	12442	...	...	12705	...	...	15647	...	...	...
4 Electricity, gas and water [c]	...	...	75002	...	...	118997	...	...	139157	...	...	...
5 Construction	...	...	259389	...	...	245768	...	...	347022	...	...	363750
6 Wholesale and retail trade, restaurants and hotels [d]	...	...	546968	...	...	759256	...	...	1151577	...	...	1231439
A Wholesale and retail trade [d]	...	...	464159	...	...	636279	...	...	969343	...	...	1034285
B Restaurants and hotels	...	...	82809	...	...	122977	...	...	182234	...	...	197154
7 Transport, storage and communication	...	...	268450	...	...	372747	...	...	514311	...	...	548343
A Transport and storage	...	...	216281	...	...	292908	...	...	401496	...	...	429811
B Communication	...	...	52169	...	...	79839	...	...	112815	...	...	118532
8 Finance, insurance, real estate and business services [e]	...	...	149581	...	...	263389	...	...	303237	...	...	333762
A Financial institutions	...	...	149581	...	...	263389	...	...	303237	...	...	333762
B Insurance	...	...	...	...	...	...	...	...	...	...	...	...
C Real estate and business services [e]	...	...	...	...	...	...	...	...	...	...	...	...
Real estate, except dwellings	...	...	...	...	...	...	...	...	...	...	...	...
Dwellings	...	...	168448	...	...	277822	...	...	377197	...	...	...
9 Community, social and personal services [e]	...	...	532987	...	...	843267	...	...	1248502	...	...	1334498
Educational services	...	...	...	...	...	...	...	...	...	...	...	...
Medical, dental, other health and veterinary services	...	...	122740	...	...	194740	...	...	265719	...	...	...
Statistical discrepancy	...	...	96	...	...	-6947	...	...	-12135	...	...	6237
Total, Industries	...	...	2746814	...	...	3845286	...	...	5280860	...	...	5532262
Producers of Government Services	...	...	482609	...	...	641226	...	...	757169	...	...	815107
Other Producers [f]	...	...	40830	...	...	49496	...	...	52419	...	...	54588
Total	...	...	3270253	...	...	4536008	...	...	6090448	...	...	6401957
Less: Imputed bank service charge	...	...	109122	...	...	186425	...	...	184037	...	...	198480
Import duties	...	...	34508	...	...	47013	...	...	55698	...	...	60421
Value added tax	...	...	255511	...	...	349242	...	...	459966	...	...	479529
Total [g]	...	...	3451150	...	...	4745838	...	...	6422075	...	...	6743427
Memorandum Item: Mineral fuels and power	...	...	162592	...	...	223544	...	...	264003	...	...	...

of which General Government:

1 Agriculture, hunting, forestry and fishing	...	...	...	...	...	...	...	...	...	...	...	...
2 Mining and quarrying	...	...	...	...	...	...	...	...	...	...	...	...
3 Manufacturing	...	...	...	...	...	...	...	...	...	...	...	...
4 Electricity, gas and water	...	...	...	...	...	...	...	...	...	...	...	...

Belgium

4.1 Derivation of Value Added by Kind of Activity, in Current Prices
(Continued)

Million Belgian francs

	1980			1985			1990			1991		
	Gross Output	Intermediate Consumption	Value Added	Gross Output	Intermediate Consumption	Value Added	Gross Output	Intermediate Consumption	Value Added	Gross Output	Intermediate Consumption	Value Added
5 Construction	...	...	...	...	...	...	...	...	...	...	...	...
6 Wholesale and retail trade, restaurants and hotels	...	...	...	...	...	...	...	...	...	...	...	...
7 Transport and communication	...	...	...	...	...	...	...	...	...	...	...	...
8 Finance, insurance, real estate and business services	...	...	...	...	...	...	...	...	...	...	...	...
9 Community, social and personal services	...	...	...	...	...	...	...	...	...	...	...	...
Total, Industries of General Government	...	...	4611	...	...	2527	...	...	3433	...	...	...
Producers of Government Services	...	...	...	...	...	...	...	...	...	...	...	...
Total, General Government	...	...	...	...	...	...	...	...	...	...	...	...

	1992			1993		
	Gross Output	Intermediate Consumption	Value Added	Gross Output	Intermediate Consumption	Value Added

All Producers

1 Agriculture, hunting, forestry and fishing	...	...	120002	...	...	114586
2 Mining and quarrying	...	...	...	...	...	...
A Coal mining [a]	...	...	...	...	...	...
B Crude petroleum and natural gas production	...	...	...	...	...	...
C Metal ore mining	...	...	...	...	...	...
D Other mining [b]	...	...	...	...	...	...
3 Manufacturing	...	...	...	...	...	...
A Manufacture of food, beverages and tobacco	...	...	210718	...	...	210342
B Textile, wearing apparel and leather industries	...	...	100679	...	...	100295
C Manufacture of wood and wood products, including furniture	...	...	...	...	...	...
D Manufacture of paper and paper products, printing and publishing	...	...	89494	...	...	88607
E Manufacture of chemicals and chemical petroleum, coal, rubber and plastic products [c]	...	...	...	...	...	...
F Manufacture of non-metallic mineral products, except products of petroleum and coal [b]	...	...	85195	...	...	84380
G Basic metal industries	...	...	110027	...	...	97964
H Manufacture of fabricated metal products, machinery and equipment	...	...	417289	...	...	440698
I Other manufacturing industries	...	...	...	...	...	...
4 Electricity, gas and water [c]	...	...	...	...	...	...
5 Construction	...	...	385712	...	...	372944
6 Wholesale and retail trade, restaurants and hotels [d]	...	...	1309165	...	...	1348093
A Wholesale and retail trade [d]	...	...	1083648	...	...	1120310
B Restaurants and hotels	...	...	225517	...	...	227783
7 Transport, storage and communication	...	...	569912	...	...	575248
A Transport and storage	...	...	447227	...	...	448434
B Communication	...	...	122685	...	...	126814
8 Finance, insurance, real estate and business services [e]	...	...	363349	...	...	372435
A Financial institutions	...	...	363349	...	...	372435
B Insurance	...	...	...	...	...	...
C Real estate and business services [e]	...	...	...	...	...	...
Real estate, except dwellings	...	...	...	...	...	...
Dwellings	...	...	...	...	...	...
9 Community, social and personal services [e]	...	...	1431778	...	...	1505494
Educational services	...	...	...	...	...	...
Medical, dental, other health and veterinary services	...	...	...	...	...	...

Belgium

4.1 Derivation of Value Added by Kind of Activity, in Current Prices
(Continued)

Million Belgian francs

	1992 Gross Output	1992 Intermediate Consumption	1992 Value Added	1993 Gross Output	1993 Intermediate Consumption	1993 Value Added
Statistical discrepancy	...	...	32031	...	...	40090
Total, Industries	...	...	5844772	...	...	5967602
Producers of Government Services	...	...	859909	...	...	917096
Other Producers [f]	...	...	57284	...	...	59303
Total	...	...	6761965	...	...	6944001
Less: Imputed bank service charge	...	...	213273	...	...	218262
Import duties	...	...	58172	...	...	55243
Value added tax	...	...	494808	...	...	504222
Total [g]	...	...	7101672	...	...	7285204
Memorandum Item: Mineral fuels and power	...	...	...	...	...	...
of which General Government:						
1 Agriculture, hunting, forestry and fishing	...	...	...	...	...	...
2 Mining and quarrying	...	...	...	...	...	...
3 Manufacturing	...	...	...	...	...	...
4 Electricity, gas and water	...	...	...	...	...	...
5 Construction	...	...	...	...	...	...
6 Wholesale and retail trade, restaurants and hotels	...	...	...	...	...	...
7 Transport and communication	...	...	...	...	...	...
8 Finance, insurance, real estate and business services	...	...	...	...	...	...
9 Community, social and personal services	...	...	...	...	...	...
Total, Industries of General Government	...	...	...	...	...	...
Producers of Government Services	...	...	...	...	...	...
Total, General Government	...	...	...	...	...	...

a) Agglomeration and briquettes of coal are included in item 'Coal mining'.
b) Item 'Manufacture of non-metallic mineral products, etc.' includes 'Other mining'.
c) Item 'Manufacture of chemicals and chemical petroleum, etc.' excludes energy products which are included in item 'Electricity, gas and water'.
d) Including repairs and recovery.
e) Business services and real estate except dwellings are included in item 'Community, social and personal services'.
f) Item 'Other producers' refers to domestic services only. All other non-marketed services are included in item 'Finance, insurance, real estate and business services'.
g) The breakdown by kind of economic activity used in this table is according to the classification NACE/CLIO.

4.2 Derivation of Value Added by Kind of Activity, in Constant Prices

Million Belgian francs

	1980 Gross Output	1980 Intermediate Consumption	1980 Value Added	1985 Gross Output	1985 Intermediate Consumption	1985 Value Added	1990 Gross Output	1990 Intermediate Consumption	1990 Value Added	1991 Gross Output	1991 Intermediate Consumption	1991 Value Added
At constant prices of: 1985												
All Producers												
1 Agriculture, hunting, forestry and fishing	...	...	89589	...	...	106104	...	...	106548	...	...	113900
2 Mining and quarrying	...	...	15751	...	...	10975	...	...	2261	...	...	...
A Coal mining [a]	...	...	15751	...	...	10975	...	...	2261	...	...	...
B Crude petroleum and natural gas production	...	...	...	...	...	...	...	...	...	...	...	...
C Metal ore mining	...	...	...	...	...	...	...	...	...	...	...	...
D Other mining [b]	...	...	...	...	...	...	...	...	...	...	...	...

Belgium

4.2 Derivation of Value Added by Kind of Activity, in Constant Prices
(Continued)

Million Belgian francs

		1980			1985			1990			1991	
	Gross Output	Intermediate Consumption	Value Added	Gross Output	Intermediate Consumption	Value Added	Gross Output	Intermediate Consumption	Value Added	Gross Output	Intermediate Consumption	Value Added
					At constant prices of:1985							
3 Manufacturing	...	...	982602	...	...	1115004	...	...	1328212	...	...	...
A Manufacture of food, beverages and tobacco	...	...	163653	...	...	171501	...	...	183420	...	...	189761
B Textile, wearing apparel and leather industries	...	...	85206	...	...	81546	...	...	104212	...	...	101260
C Manufacture of wood and wood products, including furniture	...	...	41759	...	...	42413	...	...	48572	...	...	...
D Manufacture of paper and paper products, printing and publishing	...	...	56894	...	...	60554	...	...	86489	...	...	84033
E Manufacture of chemicals and chemical petroleum, coal, rubber and plastic products [c]	...	...	196392	...	...	268619	...	...	337878	...	...	...
F Manufacture of non-metallic mineral products, except products of petroleum and coal [b]	...	...	63094	...	...	51489	...	...	75591	...	...	71538
G Basic metal industries	...	...	83120	...	...	100677	...	...	108823	...	...	104910
H Manufacture of fabricated metal products, machinery and equipment	...	...	270271	...	...	320042	...	...	305068	...	...	299909
I Other manufacturing industries	...	...	22213	...	...	12705	...	...	14961	...	...	...
4 Electricity, gas and water [c]	...	...	113789	...	...	118997	...	...	141247	...	...	...
5 Construction	...	...	347614	...	...	245768	...	...	325707	...	...	336004
6 Wholesale and retail trade, restaurants and hotels [d]	...	...	800195	...	...	759256	...	...	828180	...	...	870074
A Wholesale and retail trade [d]	...	...	685127	...	...	636279	...	...	681453	...	...	720815
B Restaurants and hotels	...	...	115068	...	...	122977	...	...	146727	...	...	149259
7 Transport, storage and communication	...	...	349055	...	...	372747	...	...	453097	...	...	463880
A Transport and storage	...	...	275367	...	...	292908	...	...	352029	...	...	357174
B Communication	...	...	73688	...	...	79839	...	...	101068	...	...	106706
8 Finance, insurance, real estate and business services [e]	...	...	214880	...	...	263389	...	...	329718	...	...	358892
A Financial institutions	...	...	214880	...	...	263389	...	...	329718	...	...	358892
B Insurance	...	...	...	...	...	...	...	...	...	...	...	...
C Real estate and business services [d]	...	...	...	...	...	...	...	...	...	...	...	...
Real estate, except dwellings	...	...	...	...	...	...	...	...	...	...	...	...
Dwellings	...	...	246561	...	...	277822	...	...	311499	...	...	...
9 Community, social and personal services [e]	...	...	738645	...	...	843267	...	...	1066091	...	...	1085279
Educational services	...	...	...	...	...	...	...	...	...	...	...	...
Medical, dental, other health and veterinary services	...	...	168642	...	...	194740	...	...	227783	...	...	...
Statistical discrepancy	...	...	-1717	...	...	-6947	...	...	1672	...	...	-10823
Total, Industries	...	...	3650408	...	...	3845286	...	...	4542991	...	...	4663069
Producers of Government Services	...	...	618394	...	...	641226	...	...	669483	...	...	680965
Other Producers [f]	...	...	52373	...	...	49496	...	...	45885	...	...	46223
Total	...	...	4321175	...	...	4536008	...	...	5258359	...	...	5390257
Less: Imputed bank service charge	...	...	161892	...	...	186425	...	...	238066	...	...	258753
Import duties	...	...	47028	...	...	47013	...	...	68113	...	...	69158
Value added tax	...	...	352873	...	...	349242	...	...	410323	...	...	422128
Total [g]	...	...	4559184	...	...	4745838	...	...	5498729	...	...	5622790
Memorandum Item: Mineral fuels and power	...	...	216118	...	...	223544	...	...	255296	...	...	...
					of which General Government:							
1 Agriculture, hunting, forestry and fishing	...	...	...	...	...	...	...	...	...	...	...	...
2 Mining and quarrying	...	...	...	...	...	...	...	...	...	...	...	...
3 Manufacturing	...	...	...	...	...	...	...	...	...	...	...	...
4 Electricity, gas and water	...	...	...	...	...	...	...	...	...	...	...	...

Belgium

4.2 Derivation of Value Added by Kind of Activity, in Constant Prices
(Continued)

Million Belgian francs

	1980			1985			1990			1991		
	Gross Output	Intermediate Consumption	Value Added	Gross Output	Intermediate Consumption	Value Added	Gross Output	Intermediate Consumption	Value Added	Gross Output	Intermediate Consumption	Value Added
		At constant prices of:1985
5 Construction	...	...	...	...	...	...	...	...	...	...	...	...
6 Wholesale and retail trade, restaurants and hotels	...	...	...	...	...	...	...	...	...	...	...	...
7 Transport and communication	...	...	...	...	...	...	...	...	...	...	...	...
8 Finance, insurance, real estate and business services	...	...	...	...	...	...	...	...	...	...	...	...
9 Community, social and personal services	...	...	...	...	...	...	...	...	...	...	...	...
Total, Industries of General Government	...	...	6606	...	...	2527	...	...	2891	...	...	...
Producers of Government Services	...	...	...	...	...	...	...	...	...	...	...	...
Total, General Government	...	...	...	...	...	...	...	...	...	...	...	...

	1992			1993		
	Gross Output	Intermediate Consumption	Value Added	Gross Output	Intermediate Consumption	Value Added
		At constant prices of:1985
		**All Producers**
1 Agriculture, hunting, forestry and fishing	...	...	125610	...	...	132127
2 Mining and quarrying	...	...	...	...	...	...
A Coal mining [a]	...	...	...	...	...	...
B Crude petroleum and natural gas production	...	...	...	...	...	...
C Metal ore mining	...	...	...	...	...	...
D Other mining [b]	...	...	...	...	...	...
3 Manufacturing	...	...	...	...	...	...
A Manufacture of food, beverages and tobacco	...	...	187369	...	...	183453
B Textile, wearing apparel and leather industries	...	...	103760	...	...	104609
C Manufacture of wood and wood products, including furniture	...	...	...	...	...	...
D Manufacture of paper and paper products, printing and publishing	...	...	84783	...	...	85018
E Manufacture of chemicals and chemical petroleum, coal, rubber and plastic products [c]	...	...	...	...	...	...
F Manufacture of non-metallic mineral products, except products of petroleum and coal [b]	...	...	78495	...	...	76470
G Basic metal industries	...	...	97040	...	...	91200
H Manufacture of fabricated metal products, machinery and equipment	...	...	290239	...	...	277612
I Other manufacturing industries	...	...	...	...	...	...
4 Electricity, gas and water [c]	...	...	...	...	...	...
5 Construction	...	...	345267	...	...	326891
6 Wholesale and retail trade, restaurants and hotels [d]	...	...	902797	...	...	891000
A Wholesale and retail trade [d]	...	...	746388	...	...	739828
B Restaurants and hotels	...	...	156409	...	...	151172
7 Transport, storage and communication	...	...	471914	...	...	367579
A Transport and storage	...	...	363487	...	...	255544
B Communication	...	...	108427	...	...	112035
8 Finance, insurance, real estate and business services [e]	...	...	388117	...	...	404427
A Financial institutions	...	...	388117	...	...	404427
B Insurance	...	...	...	...	...	...
C Real estate and business services [d]	...	...	...	...	...	...
Real estate, except dwellings	...	...	...	...	...	...
Dwellings	...	...	...	...	...	...
9 Community, social and personal services [e]	...	...	1107484	...	...	1103859

Belgium

4.2 Derivation of Value Added by Kind of Activity, in Constant Prices
(Continued)

Million Belgian francs

	1992 Gross Output	1992 Intermediate Consumption	1992 Value Added	1993 Gross Output	1993 Intermediate Consumption	1993 Value Added
			At constant prices of:1985			
Educational services	...	...	...	...	...	...
Medical, dental, other health and veterinary services	...	...	...	...	...	...
Statistical discrepancy	...	...	-33809	...	...	-49811
Total, Industries	...	...	4763687	...	...	4683469
Producers of Government Services	...	...	694299	...	...	707576
Other Producers f	...	...	46792	...	...	46816
Total	...	...	5504778	...	...	5437861
Less: Imputed bank service charge	...	...	279931	...	...	302283
Import duties	...	...	72340	...	...	72345
Value added tax	...	...	430192	...	...	421799
Total g	...	...	5727379	...	...	5629722
Memorandum Item: Mineral fuels and power	...	...	...	...	...	...
			of which General Government:			
1 Agriculture, hunting, forestry and fishing	...	...	...	...	...	...
2 Mining and quarrying	...	...	...	...	...	...
3 Manufacturing	...	...	...	...	...	...
4 Electricity, gas and water	...	...	...	...	...	...
5 Construction	...	...	...	...	...	...
6 Wholesale and retail trade, restaurants and hotels	...	...	...	...	...	...
7 Transport and communication	...	...	...	...	...	...
8 Finance, insurance, real estate and business services	...	...	...	...	...	...
9 Community, social and personal services	...	...	...	...	...	...
Total, Industries of General Government	...	...	...	...	...	...
Producers of Government Services	...	...	...	...	...	...
Total, General Government	...	...	...	...	...	...

a) Agglomeration and briquettes of coal are included in item 'Coal mining'.
b) Item 'Manufacture of non-metallic mineral products, etc.' includes 'Other mining'.
c) Item 'Manufacture of chemicals and chemical petroleum, etc.' excludes energy products which are included in item 'Electricity, gas and water'.
d) Including repairs and recovery.
e) Business services and real estate except dwellings are included in item 'Community, social and personal services'.
f) Item 'Other producers' refers to domestic services only. All other non-marketed services are included in item 'Finance, insurance, real estate and business services'.
g) The breakdown by kind of economic activity used in this table is according to the classification NACE/CLIO.

4.3 Cost Components of Value Added

Million Belgian francs

	1980 Compensation of Employees	1980 Capital Consumption	1980 Net Operating Surplus	1980 Indirect Taxes	1980 Less: Subsidies Received	1980 Value Added	1985 Compensation of Employees	1985 Capital Consumption	1985 Net Operating Surplus	1985 Indirect Taxes	1985 Less: Subsidies Received	1985 Value Added
				All Producers								
1 Agriculture, hunting, forestry and fishing	4205	...	...	-4863	...	73108	5836	...	...	-5131	...	106104
2 Mining and quarrying	...	...	...	...	...	7399	...	...	...	...	...	10975
A Coal mining a	...	...	...	...	...	7399	...	...	...	...	...	10975
B Crude petroleum and natural gas production	...	...	...	...	...	...	...	...	...	...	...	...
C Metal ore mining	...	...	...	...	...	...	...	...	...	...	...	...
D Other mining b	...	...	...	...	...	...	...	...	...	...	...	...

Belgium

4.3 Cost Components of Value Added
(Continued)

Million Belgian francs

	1980						1985					
	Compensation of Employees	Capital Consumption	Net Operating Surplus	Indirect Taxes	Less: Subsidies Received	Value Added	Compensation of Employees	Capital Consumption	Net Operating Surplus	Indirect Taxes	Less: Subsidies Received	Value Added
3 Manufacturing	573395	...	...	16548	...	833834	704874	...	...	21319	...	1115004
A Manufacture of food, beverages and tobacco	66684	...	...	18927	...	119190	85062	...	...	28036	...	171501
B Textile, wearing apparel and leather industries	50780	...	...	-277	...	63655	62555	...	...	-898	...	81546
C Manufacture of wood and wood products, including furniture c	...	...	...	...	...	37070	...	...	...	...	...	42413
D Manufacture of paper and paper products, printing and publishing	35955	...	...	-150	...	44448	46782	...	...	-357	...	60554
E Manufacture of chemicals and chemical petroleum, coal, rubber and plastic products d	77381	...	...	-1083	...	189136	107369	...	...	-993	...	268619
F Manufacture of non-metallic mineral products, except products of petroleum and coal b	37872	...	...	137	...	49986	37369	...	...	-58	...	51489
G Basic metal industries	66481	...	...	545	...	70258	75533	...	...	-627	...	100677
H Manufacture of fabricated metal products, machinery and equipment	210627	...	...	-1523	...	247649	259454	...	...	-3683	...	320042
I Other manufacturing industries c	27615	...	...	-28	...	12442	30750	...	...	-101	...	12705
4 Electricity, gas and water d	61661	...	36729	...	...	75002	81053	...	...	47663	...	118997
5 Construction	156797	...	...	716	...	259389	129956	...	...	569	...	245768
6 Wholesale and retail trade, restaurants and hotels	291438	...	...	-3086	...	546968	385272	...	...	-10632	...	759256
A Wholesale and retail trade	270587	...	...	-3147	...	464159	353726	...	...	-10628	...	636279
B Restaurants and hotels	20851	...	...	61	...	82809	31546	...	...	-4	...	122977
7 Transport, storage and communication	171794	...	...	-64914	...	268450	225602	...	...	-87501	...	372747
A Transport and storage	129711	...	...	-55625	...	216281	165900	...	...	-73913	...	292908
B Communication	42083	...	...	-9289	...	52169	59702	...	...	-13588	...	79839
8 Finance, insurance, real estate and business services e	114699	...	...	7618	...	149581	173452	...	...	16754	...	263389
A Financial institutions	114699	...	...	7618	...	149581	173754	...	...	16754	...	263389
B Insurance	...	...	...	...	...	...	...	...	...	...	...	...
C Real estate and business services e	...	...	...	...	...	...	...	...	...	...	...	...
Real estate, except dwellings	...	...	...	...	...	...	...	...	...	...	...	...
Dwellings	...	...	...	...	...	168448	...	...	...	...	...	277822
9 Community, social and personal services e	184936	...	...	10748	...	532987	277815	...	...	11953	...	843267
Educational services	...	...	...	...	...	...	...	...	...	...	...	...
Medical, dental, other health and veterinary services	...	...	...	...	...	122740	...	...	...	...	...	194740
Statistical discrepancy	-	...	...	...	...	96	5109	...	...	...	...	-6947
Total, Industries	1558925	...	...	-504	...	2746814	1988969	...	...	-5006	...	3845286
Producers of Government Services	471272	...	...	...	...	482609	626226	...	...	...	...	641226
Other Producers	40830	...	...	...	...	40830	49496	...	...	...	...	49496
Total	2071027	...	...	-504	...	3270253	2664691	...	...	-5006	...	4536008
Less: Imputed bank service charge	...	...	...	...	...	109122	...	...	...	...	...	186425
Import duties	...	...	...	34508	...	34508	...	...	...	47013	...	47013
Value added tax	...	...	...	255511	...	255511	...	...	...	349242	...	349242
Total fg	2071027	312145	778463	289515	...	3451150	2664691	455805	1234093	391249	...	4745838

of which General Government:

1 Agriculture, hunting, forestry and fishing	...	...	...	...	...	...	...	...	...	...	...	...
2 Mining and quarrying	...	...	...	...	...	...	...	...	...	...	...	...
3 Manufacturing	...	...	...	...	...	...	...	...	...	...	...	...
4 Electricity, gas and water	...	...	...	...	...	...	...	...	...	...	...	...

Belgium

4.3 Cost Components of Value Added
(Continued)

Million Belgian francs

	1980						1985					
	Compensation of Employees	Capital Consumption	Net Operating Surplus	Indirect Taxes	Less: Subsidies Received	Value Added	Compensation of Employees	Capital Consumption	Net Operating Surplus	Indirect Taxes	Less: Subsidies Received	Value Added
5 Construction	...	...	...	...	...	...	...	...	...	...	...	...
6 Wholesale and retail trade, restaurants and hotels	...	...	...	...	...	...	...	...	...	...	...	...
7 Transport and communication	...	...	...	...	...	...	...	...	...	...	...	...
8 Finance, insurance, real estate & business services	...	...	...	...	...	...	...	...	...	...	...	...
9 Community, social and personal services	...	...	...	...	...	...	...	...	...	...	...	...
Total, Industries of General Government	299	...	...	...	...	4611	505	...	...	...	...	2527
Producers of Government Services	...	...	...	...	...	...	...	...	...	...	...	...
Total, General Government	...	...	...	...	...	...	...	...	...	...	...	...

	1990						1991					
	Compensation of Employees	Capital Consumption	Net Operating Surplus	Indirect Taxes	Less: Subsidies Received	Value Added	Compensation of Employees	Capital Consumption	Net Operating Surplus	Indirect Taxes	Less: Subsidies Received	Value Added

All Producers

1 Agriculture, hunting, forestry and fishing	8954	...	...	-10148	...	119656	9531	...	...	-6183	...	124227
2 Mining and quarrying	...	...	...	...	...	1151	...	...	...	...	...	...
A Coal mining [a]	...	...	...	...	...	1151	...	...	...	...	...	...
B Crude petroleum and natural gas production	...	...	...	...	...	...	...	...	...	...	...	...
C Metal ore mining	...	...	...	...	...	...	...	...	...	...	...	...
D Other mining [b]	...	...	...	...	...	...	...	...	...	...	...	...
3 Manufacturing	854814	...	...	18397	...	1446335	905133	...	...	24912	...	...
A Manufacture of food, beverages and tobacco	103885	...	...	25444	...	195266	113308	...	...	30713	...	205326
B Textile, wearing apparel and leather industries	67905	...	...	-713	...	101009	69154	...	...	-711	...	97729
C Manufacture of wood and wood products, including furniture [c]	...	...	...	...	...	61626	...	...	...	...	...	...
D Manufacture of paper and paper products, printing and publishing	61600	...	...	-525	...	89282	65364	...	...	-532	...	88539
E Manufacture of chemicals and chemical petroleum, coal, rubber and plastic products [d]	147837	...	...	-1172	...	344743	160146	...	...	-2653	...	...
F Manufacture of non-metallic mineral products, except products of petroleum and coal [b]	47019	...	...	156	...	77620	49526	...	...	324	...	74970
G Basic metal industries	74322	...	...	-419	...	135398	79801	...	...	-8	...	106447
H Manufacture of fabricated metal products, machinery and equipment	314817	...	...	-4062	...	440447	327738	...	...	-1285	...	423645
I Other manufacturing industries [c]	37429	...	...	-312	...	15647	40096	...	...	-936	...	...
4 Electricity, gas and water [d]	76428	...	...	75926	...	139157	80345	...	...	83156	...	...
5 Construction	194417	...	...	1029	...	347022	208932	...	...	1150	...	363750
6 Wholesale and retail trade, restaurants and hotels	535110	...	...	14917	...	1151577	585696	...	...	-12584	...	1231439
A Wholesale and retail trade	485587	...	...	14737	...	969343	533492	...	...	-12764	...	1034285
B Restaurants and hotels	49523	...	...	180	...	182234	52204	...	...	180	...	197154
7 Transport, storage and communication	269452	...	...	-92864	...	514311	289309	...	...	-93463	...	548343
A Transport and storage	202148	...	...	-79120	...	401496	213778	...	...	-78641	...	429811
B Communication	67304	...	...	-13744	...	112815	75531	...	...	-14822	...	118532
8 Finance, insurance, real estate and business services [e]	222299	...	...	28765	...	303237	232261	...	...	31178	...	333762
A Financial institutions	222077	...	...	28765	...	303237	230562	...	...	31178	...	333762
B Insurance	...	...	...	...	...	...	...	...	...	...	...	...
C Real estate and business services [e]	...	...	...	...	...	...	...	...	...	...	...	...
Real estate, except dwellings	...	...	...	...	...	...	...	...	...	...	...	...
Dwellings	...	...	...	...	...	377197	...	...	...	...	...	...
9 Community, social and personal services [e]	425572	...	...	46048	...	1248502	481836	...	...	43315	...	1334498

Belgium

4.3 Cost Components of Value Added
(Continued)

Million Belgian francs

	1990 Compensation of Employees	Capital Consumption	Net Operating Surplus	Indirect Taxes	Less: Subsidies Received	Value Added	1991 Compensation of Employees	Capital Consumption	Net Operating Surplus	Indirect Taxes	Less: Subsidies Received	Value Added
Educational services	...	...	...	...	...	...	...	...	...	...	...	...
Medical, dental, other health and veterinary services	...	...	...	...	...	265719	...	...	...	...	...	...
Statistical discrepancy	19377	...	...	...	...	-12135	23599	...	...	...	...	6237
Total, Industries	2606423	...	...	82070	...	5280860	2816642	...	...	71481	...	5532262
Producers of Government Services	735395	...	...	...	...	757169	792063	...	...	...	...	815107
Other Producers	52419	...	...	...	...	52419	54588	...	...	...	...	54588
Total	3394237	...	...	82070	...	6090448	3663293	...	...	71481	...	6401957
Less: Imputed bank service charge	...	...	...	...	...	184037	...	...	...	...	...	198480
Import duties	...	...	...	55698	...	55698	...	...	...	60421	...	60421
Value added tax	...	...	...	459966	...	459966	...	...	...	479529	...	479529
Total fg	3394237	637596	1792508	597734	...	6422075	3663293	651663	1817040	611431	...	6743427

of which General Government:

1 Agriculture, hunting, forestry and fishing	...	...	...	...	...	...	...	...	...	...	...	...
2 Mining and quarrying	...	...	...	...	...	...	...	...	...	...	...	...
3 Manufacturing	...	...	...	...	...	...	...	...	...	...	...	...
4 Electricity, gas and water	...	...	...	...	...	...	...	...	...	...	...	...
5 Construction	...	...	...	...	...	...	...	...	...	...	...	...
6 Wholesale and retail trade, restaurants and hotels	...	...	...	...	...	...	...	...	...	...	...	...
7 Transport and communication	...	...	...	...	...	...	...	...	...	...	...	...
8 Finance, insurance, real estate & business services	...	...	...	...	...	...	...	...	...	...	...	...
9 Community, social and personal services	...	...	...	...	...	...	...	...	...	...	...	...
Total, Industries of General Government	652	...	...	...	...	3433	...	...	...	...	...	...
Producers of Government Services	...	...	...	...	...	...	...	...	...	...	...	...
Total, General Government	...	...	...	...	...	...	...	...	...	...	...	...

	1992 Compensation of Employees	Capital Consumption	Net Operating Surplus	Indirect Taxes	Less: Subsidies Received	Value Added	1993 Compensation of Employees	Capital Consumption	Net Operating Surplus	Indirect Taxes	Less: Subsidies Received	Value Added
				All Producers								
1 Agriculture, hunting, forestry and fishing	10461	...	...	-5466	...	120002	...	...	...	-9260	...	114586
2 Mining and quarrying	...	...	...	...	...	...	...	...	...	...	...	...
A Coal mining a	...	...	...	...	...	...	...	...	...	...	...	...
B Crude petroleum and natural gas production	...	...	...	...	...	...	...	...	...	...	...	...
C Metal ore mining	...	...	...	...	...	...	...	...	...	...	...	...
D Other mining b	...	...	...	...	...	...	...	...	...	...	...	...
3 Manufacturing	932612	...	...	29906	...	...	...	...	...	31734	...	...
A Manufacture of food, beverages and tobacco	118126	...	...	31811	...	210718	...	...	...	30647	...	210342
B Textile, wearing apparel and leather industries	70044	...	...	-647	...	100679	...	...	...	-750	...	100295
C Manufacture of wood and wood products, including furniture c	...	...	...	...	...	...	...	...	...	...	...	...
D Manufacture of paper and paper products, printing and publishing	67264	...	...	-535	...	89494	...	...	...	-550	...	88607
E Manufacture of chemicals and chemical petroleum, coal, rubber and plastic products d	170697	...	...	-1504	...	...	...	...	...	-1002	...	...
F Manufacture of non-metallic mineral products, except products of petroleum and coal b	51812	...	...	489	...	85195	...	...	...	432	...	84380
G Basic metal industries	78218	...	...	389	...	110027	...	...	...	673	...	97964
H Manufacture of fabricated metal products, machinery and equipment	335147	...	...	801	...	417289	...	...	...	3182	...	440698
I Other manufacturing industries c	41304	...	...	-898	...	...	...	...	...	-898	...	...
4 Electricity, gas and water d	83157	...	...	99945	...	...	...	...	...	108025	...	...

125

Belgium

4.3 Cost Components of Value Added
(Continued)

Million Belgian francs

	1992						1993					
	Compensation of Employees	Capital Consumption	Net Operating Surplus	Indirect Taxes	Less: Subsidies Received	Value Added	Compensation of Employees	Capital Consumption	Net Operating Surplus	Indirect Taxes	Less: Subsidies Received	Value Added
5 Construction	228062	...	...	1303	...	385712	...	...	...	1553	...	372944
6 Wholesale and retail trade, restaurants and hotels	623379	...	...	167	...	1309165	...	...	...	22486	...	1348093
A Wholesale and retail trade	565923	...	...	-138	...	1083648	...	...	...	22193	...	1120310
B Restaurants and hotels	57456	...	...	305	...	225517	...	...	...	293	...	227783
7 Transport, storage and communication	310061	...	...	-89778	...	569912	...	...	...	-95634	...	575248
A Transport and storage	228469	...	...	-75314	...	447227	...	...	...	-77954	...	448434
B Communication	81592	...	...	-14464	...	122685	...	...	...	-17680	...	126814
8 Finance, insurance, real estate and business services [e]	241245	...	...	34398	...	363349	...	...	...	37026	...	372435
A Financial institutions	239318	...	...	34398	...	363349	...	...	...	37026	...	372435
B Insurance	...	...	...	...	...	...	...	...	...	...	...	...
C Real estate and business services [e]	...	...	...	...	...	...	...	...	...	...	...	...
Real estate, except dwellings	...	...	...	...	...	...	...	...	...	...	...	...
Dwellings	...	...	...	...	...	...	...	...	...	...	...	...
9 Community, social and personal services [e]	515589	...	...	48833	...	1431778	...	...	...	52471	...	1505494
Educational services	...	...	...	...	...	...	...	...	...	...	...	...
Medical, dental, other health and veterinary services	...	...	...	...	...	...	...	...	...	...	...	...
Statistical discrepancy	18560	...	...	...	...	32031	...	...	...	...	...	40090
Total, Industries	2963126	...	...	119308	...	5844772	...	...	...	148401	...	5967602
Producers of Government Services	835928	...	...	...	...	859909	...	...	...	...	...	917096
Other Producers	57284	...	...	...	...	57284	...	...	...	...	...	59303
Total	3856338	...	...	119308	...	6761965	...	...	...	148401	...	6944001
Less: Imputed bank service charge	...	...	...	...	...	213273	...	...	...	...	...	218262
Import duties	...	...	...	58172	...	58172	...	...	...	55243	...	55243
Value added tax	...	...	...	494808	...	494808	...	...	...	504222	...	504222
Total [fg]	3856338	689460	1883586	672288	...	7101672	3953319	698963	1925056	707866	...	7285204

of which General Government:

	1992						1993					
1 Agriculture, hunting, forestry and fishing	...	...	...	...	...	...	...	...	...	...	...	...
2 Mining and quarrying	...	...	...	...	...	...	...	...	...	...	...	...
3 Manufacturing	...	...	...	...	...	...	...	...	...	...	...	...
4 Electricity, gas and water	...	...	...	...	...	...	...	...	...	...	...	...
5 Construction	...	...	...	...	...	...	...	...	...	...	...	...
6 Wholesale and retail trade, restaurants and hotels	...	...	...	...	...	...	...	...	...	...	...	...
7 Transport and communication	...	...	...	...	...	...	...	...	...	...	...	...
8 Finance, insurance, real estate & business services	...	...	...	...	...	...	...	...	...	...	...	...
9 Community, social and personal services	...	...	...	...	...	...	...	...	...	...	...	...
Total, Industries of General Government	...	...	...	...	...	...	...	...	...	...	...	...
Producers of Government Services	...	...	...	...	...	...	...	...	...	...	...	...
Total, General Government	...	...	...	...	...	...	...	...	...	...	...	...

a) Agglomeration and briquettes of coal are included in item 'Coal mining'.
b) Item 'Manufacture of non-metallic mineral products, etc.' includes 'Other mining'.
c) Item 'Other manufacturing industries' includes item 'Manufacture of wood and paper products'.
d) Item 'Manufacture of chemicals and chemical petroleum, etc.' excludes energy products which are included in item 'Electricity, gas and water'.
e) Business services and real estate except dwellings are included in item 'Community, social and personal services'.
f) The breakdown by kind of economic activity used in this table is according to the classification NACE/CLIO.
g) Column 4 refers to indirect taxes less subsidies received.

Belize

Source. Central Planning Unit, Ministry of Finance and Economic Planning, Belize. Official estimates are published in 'National Accounts Statistics'. Information on sources and methods of estimation can be found in 'National Accounts Statistics - Sources and Methods' and in 'Economic Accounts of the Public Sector'.

General note. The estimates shown in the following tables have been prepared in accordance with the United Nations System of National Accounts so far as the existing data would permit.

1.1 Expenditure on the Gross Domestic Product, in Current Prices

Million Belize dollars

	1980	1983	1984	1985	1986	1987	1988	1989	1990	1991	1992	1993
1 Government final consumption expenditure	66.8	89.7	93.0	95.4	102.8	127.1	132.0	146.5	155.1	166.6	175.5	...
2 Private final consumption expenditure	280.2	272.1	265.0	215.0	260.1	286.9	328.5	389.8	344.1	570.6	602.9	...
3 Gross capital formation	93.9	76.4	99.3	90.4	92.8	121.3	159.8	220.0	226.3	260.0	289.5	...
A Increase in stocks	5.7	4.9	13.6	17.7	13.3	2.5	-1.8	21.2	18.3	14.6	11.6	...
B Gross fixed capital formation	88.2	71.5	85.7	72.7	79.5	118.8	161.6	198.8	208.0	245.4	277.9	...
4 Exports of goods and services	215.7	185.5	345.2	391.9	398.2	467.5	571.5	619.3	709.5	609.0	643.5	...
5 Less: Imports of goods and services	267.1	245.7	380.7	374.4	398.2	449.7	562.0	649.5	642.1	745.2	775.3	...
Equals: Gross Domestic Product	389.4	378.0	421.8	418.4	455.8	553.0	629.8	726.0	792.9	860.9	936.1	...

1.2 Expenditure on the Gross Domestic Product, in Constant Prices

Million Belize dollars

	1980	1983	1984	1985	1986	1987	1988	1989	1990	1991	1992	1993
					At constant prices of:1984							
1 Government final consumption expenditure	86.3	92.8	93.0	91.9	98.3	119.1	119.9	130.3	133.9	135.8	138.5	...
2 Private final consumption expenditure	389.5	311.9	268.7	156.6	198.7	223.3	255.5	272.6	225.9	362.2	370.4	...
3 Gross capital formation	105.6	74.1	95.6	87.1	89.9	115.5	148.5	195.0	195.4	211.9	228.6	...
A Increase in stocks	7.4	5.1	13.6	17.1	12.7	2.3	-1.6	18.9	15.8	11.9	9.2	...
B Gross fixed capital formation	98.2	69.0	82.0	70.1	77.2	113.2	150.1	176.1	179.6	200.0	219.4	...
4 Exports of goods and services	182.1	189.0	345.2	451.2	439.5	461.0	528.8	588.4	663.9	590.1	616.9	...
5 Less: Imports of goods and services	345.1	254.1	380.7	360.7	380.7	421.5	510.4	577.8	554.5	607.5	611.9	...
Equals: Gross Domestic Product	418.4	413.6	421.8	426.1	445.7	497.5	542.2	608.4	664.7	692.5	742.4	...

1.3 Cost Components of the Gross Domestic Product

Million Belize dollars

	1980	1983	1984	1985	1986	1987	1988	1989	1990	1991	1992	1993
1 Indirect taxes, net	49.1	44.3	50.3	52.2	62.9	73.8	98.5	112.8	117.5	134.4	143.0	...
2 Consumption of fixed capital	21.6	27.2	29.3	29.3	30.4	36.7	41.1	44.8	49.6	55.0	59.4	...
3 Compensation of employees paid by resident producers to:	318.7	306.5	342.2	336.9	362.5	442.6	490.2	568.4	625.8	671.5	733.7	...
4 Operating surplus												...
Equals: Gross Domestic Product	389.4	378.0	421.8	418.4	455.8	553.0	629.8	726.0	792.9	860.9	936.1	...

1.10 Gross Domestic Product by Kind of Activity, in Current Prices

Million Belize dollars

	1980	1983	1984	1985	1986	1987	1988	1989	1990	1991	1992	1993
1 Agriculture, hunting, forestry and fishing	93.4	72.0	77.4	74.6	82.3	109.0	118.4	131.0	148.5	145.4	159.7	152.2
2 Mining and quarrying	0.8	1.0	1.1	1.3	1.6	1.9	2.2	3.0	4.1	5.9	5.8	6.9
3 Manufacturing	81.4	60.9	73.0	61.2	61.2	88.9	98.3	105.8	106.1	112.1	109.3	111.0
4 Electricity, gas and water	3.3	2.5	6.2	9.2	13.3	14.9	16.9	15.5	15.4	19.2	23.7	29.3
5 Construction	19.6	16.4	20.0	19.7	20.3	26.6	33.8	46.1	53.8	59.4	63.4	70.2
6 Wholesale and retail trade, restaurants and hotels	57.7	52.2	57.4	56.3	62.3	73.1	86.7	108.8	127.0	131.7	140.5	147.2
7 Transport, storage and communication	17.2	29.3	32.3	35.1	40.9	48.0	48.7	61.3	73.0	84.3	94.4	106.8
8 Finance, insurance, real estate and business services	32.2	36.6	38.7	41.0	40.0	40.5	48.7	64.9	63.5	76.4	87.7	93.6
9 Community, social and personal services	21.8	35.1	36.4	36.3	37.6	39.4	41.7	43.8	46.3	48.1	50.6	53.0
Total, Industries	327.4	306.0	342.5	334.7	359.5	442.3	495.4	580.2	637.7	682.5	735.1	770.2
Producers of Government Services	24.4	39.3	41.3	41.7	45.4	51.5	57.0	63.3	70.3	76.2	94.3	95.1

Belize

1.10 Gross Domestic Product by Kind of Activity, in Current Prices
(Continued)

Million Belize dollars

	1980	1983	1984	1985	1986	1987	1988	1989	1990	1991	1992	1993
Other Producers	...	...	...	...	...	...	...	...	...	...	...	...
Subtotal [a]	351.7	345.3	383.8	376.4	404.9	493.8	552.4	643.6	708.0	758.7	829.4	865.3
Less: Imputed bank service charge	11.5	11.8	12.4	10.2	12.1	14.5	21.2	30.5	32.5	32.1	36.3	38.0
Plus: Import duties	...	...	...	...	...	...	...	...	...	...	...	...
Plus: Value added tax	...	...	...	...	...	...	...	...	...	...	...	...
Plus: Other adjustments [b]	49.1	44.3	50.3	52.2	62.9	73.8	98.5	112.8	117.5	134.4	143.0	167.8
Equals: Gross Domestic Product	389.4	378.0	421.8	418.4	455.8	553.0	629.8	726.0	792.9	860.9	936.1	995.0

a) Gross domestic product in factor values.
b) Item 'Other adjustments' refers to indirect taxes net of subsidies.

1.11 Gross Domestic Product by Kind of Activity, in Constant Prices

Million Belize dollars

	1980	1983	1984	1985	1986	1987	1988	1989	1990	1991	1992	1993
					At constant prices of: 1984							
1 Agriculture, hunting, forestry and fishing	74.8	75.9	77.4	77.5	74.1	89.4	89.6	94.6	106.6	110.5	123.2	122.2
2 Mining and quarrying	0.8	1.0	1.1	1.3	1.5	1.8	2.1	2.8	3.8	5.3	5.1	6.0
3 Manufacturing	78.5	79.8	73.0	73.7	75.5	81.7	80.3	89.2	96.8	94.4	104.6	104.3
4 Electricity, gas and water	4.9	6.1	6.2	6.6	7.2	7.7	8.5	9.0	10.1	12.0	13.8	15.7
5 Construction	20.3	16.2	20.0	19.2	20.0	26.4	28.7	36.9	40.7	43.6	45.6	49.4
6 Wholesale and retail trade, restaurants and hotels	74.5	54.0	57.4	54.2	59.6	68.5	78.7	96.8	109.6	107.8	110.0	113.2
7 Transport, storage and communication	22.1	30.4	32.3	33.3	37.0	40.9	51.0	64.0	71.7	79.9	90.6	99.9
8 Finance, insurance, real estate and business services	40.9	38.8	38.7	40.2	41.5	45.9	50.2	50.1	53.6	54.1	57.2	58.7
9 Community, social and personal services	32.6	35.4	36.4	37.3	38.3	39.4	40.5	41.6	42.7	43.9	45.1	46.4
Total, Industries	349.4	337.6	342.5	343.3	354.7	401.6	429.6	485.0	535.6	551.5	595.2	615.8
Producers of Government Services	30.1	40.1	41.3	42.7	43.2	45.4	45.8	47.8	50.9	53.1	55.1	56.2
Other Producers	...	...	...	...	...	...	...	...	...	...	...	...
Subtotal [a]	379.5	377.7	383.8	386.0	397.9	447.0	475.4	532.8	586.5	604.6	650.3	672.0
Less: Imputed bank service charge	13.9	12.5	12.4	13.1	13.8	15.9	18.0	18.9	20.3	20.1	21.4	22.3
Plus: Import duties	...	...	...	...	...	...	...	...	...	...	...	...
Plus: Value added tax	...	...	...	...	...	...	...	...	...	...	...	...
Plus: Other adjustments [b]	52.9	48.5	50.4	53.2	61.6	66.4	84.8	94.5	98.5	108.0	113.5	...
Equals: Gross Domestic Product	418.4	413.6	421.8	426.1	445.7	497.5	542.2	608.4	664.7	692.5	742.4	...

a) Gross domestic product in factor values.
b) Item 'Other adjustments' refers to indirect taxes net of subsidies.

1.12 Relations Among National Accounting Aggregates

Million Belize dollars

	1980	1983	1984	1985	1986	1987	1988	1989	1990	1991	1992	1993
Gross Domestic Product	389.4	378.0	421.8	418.4	455.8	553.0	629.8	726.0	792.9	860.9	936.1	995.0
Plus: Net factor income from the rest of the world	-3.8	-11.0	-18.6	-19.8	-8.8	-14.2	-17.8	-24.9	-13.5	-21.5	-22.0	-22.5
Equals: Gross National Product	385.6	367.0	403.2	398.6	447.0	538.9	612.0	701.1	779.4	839.4	914.1	972.4
Less: Consumption of fixed capital	21.6	27.2	29.3	29.3	30.4	36.7	41.1	44.8	49.6	55.0	59.4	64.2
Equals: National Income	364.0	339.8	373.9	369.3	416.6	502.2	570.9	656.3	729.8	784.5	854.7	908.2
Plus: Net current transfers from the rest of the world	29.6	25.0	...	...	...	...	...	...	...	...	...	...
Equals: National Disposable Income	393.6	364.8	...	...	...	...	...	...	...	...	...	...
Less: Final consumption	347.0	361.8	...	...	...	...	...	...	...	...	...	...
Equals: Net Saving	46.6	3.0	...	...	...	...	...	...	...	...	...	...
Less: Surplus of the nation on current transactions	...	...										
Equals: Net Capital Formation	...	...										

2.1 Government Final Consumption Expenditure by Function, in Current Prices

Million Belize dollars

Fiscal year beginning 1 April

	1980	1983	1984	1985	1986	1987	1988	1989	1990	1991	1992	1993
1 General public services	...	...	...	...	...	23.5	25.7	29.0	35.3	53.1	...	...
2 Defence	...	...	...	...	...	8.3	8.8	9.8	9.4	11.0	...	...
3 Public order and safety	...	...	...	...	...	8.3	8.1	12.2	21.9	22.3	...	...
4 Education	...	...	...	...	...	27.7	33.3	37.8	42.8	53.8	...	...
5 Health	...	...	...	...	...	13.8	15.3	18.0	19.1	21.1	...	...

Belize

2.1 Government Final Consumption Expenditure by Function, in Current Prices
(Continued)

Million Belize dollars

Fiscal year beginning 1 April

	1980	1983	1984	1985	1986	1987	1988	1989	1990	1991	1992	1993
6 Social security and welfare	...	...	...	...	...	2.0	2.3	1.5	9.1	12.7	...	...
7 Housing and community amenities	...	...	...	...	...	3.5	5.8	14.3	18.7	19.4	...	...
8 Recreational, cultural and religious affairs	...	...	...	...	...	1.8	2.7	3.1	7.3	7.8	...	...
9 Economic services	...	...	...	...	...	50.3	87.1	92.1	104.5	104.5	...	...
A Fuel and energy	...	...	...	...	...	1.0	-	-	9.4	15.3	...	...
B Agriculture, forestry, fishing and hunting	...	...	...	...	...	17.8	16.0	29.4	30.1	24.0	...	...
C Mining, manufacturing and construction, except fuel and energy	...	...	...	...	...	1.0	6.5	-	1.0	-	...	...
D Transportation and communication	...	...	...	...	...	27.2	61.8	48.8	44.6	54.6	...	...
E Other economic affairs	...	...	...	...	...	3.8	2.4	13.5	19.7	10.3	...	...
10 Other functions	...	...	...	...	...	13.4	13.4	11.0	10.8	14.9	...	...
Total Government Final Consumption Expenditure	...	...	...	...	...	152.6	202.5	228.8	278.9	320.6	...	...

Benin

Source. Reply to the United Nations National Accounts Questionnaire from the Institut National de la Statistique et de l'Analyse Economique, Direction Generale, Cotonou. Official estimates are published in 'Comptes de la Nation 1974-1975 et les estimations des aggregats de comptes nationaux a prix courants et a prix constants de 1970 a 1977'.

General note. The estimates shown in the following tables have been prepared in accordance with the United Nations System of National Accounts so far as the existing data would permit.

1.1 Expenditure on the Gross Domestic Product, in Current Prices

Million CFA francs

	1980	1983	1984	1985	1986	1987	1988	1989	1990	1991	1992	1993
1 Government final consumption expenditure	...	60213	62561	58842	63782	68699	57244	62300	66200	64300	...	...
2 Private final consumption expenditure	...	354119	371999	374128	381144	384549	402584	390100	404100	442200	...	...
3 Gross capital formation	...	72332	58801	74217	68072	66562	72988	56600	71400	77600	...	...
A Increase in stocks	...	2923	1453	11246	-486	-348	1852	-3100	4000	5000	...	...
B Gross fixed capital formation	...	69409	57348	62971	68558	66910	71135	59700	67400	72600	...	...
4 Exports of goods and services	...	83546	130718	156544	129461	128730	142482	87600	102400	118000	...	...
5 Less: Imports of goods and services	...	152772	164741	193953	179924	178986	192864	117400	141600	166600	...	...
Equals: Gross Domestic Product	...	417438	459340	469778	462535	469554	482434	479200	502300	535500	...	...

1.3 Cost Components of the Gross Domestic Product

Million CFA francs

	1980	1983	1984	1985	1986	1987	1988	1989	1990	1991	1992	1993
1 Indirect taxes, net	...	35456	37232	38309	39930	38754	31354	21790	...	...	...	...
A Indirect taxes	...	38425	40011	43706	43767	42150	38638	...	...	...	...	...
B Less: Subsidies	...	2970	2779	5397	3837	3396	7285	...	...	...	...	...
2 Consumption of fixed capital	...	...	...	...	...	...	...	...	...	...	...	...
3 Compensation of employees paid by resident producers to:	...	86607	90984	93240	98455	102136	93302	96333	...	...	...	...
4 Operating surplus	...	295376	331123	338229	324149	328663	357778	369402	...	...	...	...
Equals: Gross Domestic Product	...	417438	459340	469778	462535	469554	482434	487525	...	...	...	...

1.7 External Transactions on Current Account, Summary

Million CFA francs

	1980	1983	1984	1985	1986	1987	1988	1989	1990	1991	1992	1993
Payments to the Rest of the World												
1 Imports of goods and services	...	152772	164741	193953	179924	178986	192864	137507	...	...	...	...
2 Factor income to the rest of the world	...	11854	13033	11600	10000	9600	10000	12300	...	...	...	...
3 Current transfers to the rest of the world	...	1824	1342	2000	2000	2000	2000	2000	...	...	...	...
4 Surplus of the nation on current transactions	...	-37879	-5858	-6009	-19863	-17856	-15482	2941	...	...	...	...
Payments to the Rest of the World and Surplus of the Nation on Current Transactions	...	128571	173258	201544	172061	172730	189382	154748	...	...	...	...
Receipts From The Rest of the World												
1 Exports of goods and services	...	83546	130718	156544	129461	128730	142482	99738	...	...	...	...
2 Factor income from rest of the world	...	1885	1331	2000	1000	1000	-	-	...	...	...	...
3 Current transfers from rest of the world	...	43140	41209	43000	41600	43000	46900	55010	...	...	...	...
Receipts from the Rest of the World on Current Transactions	...	128571	173258	201544	172061	172730	189382	154748	...	...	...	...

1.10 Gross Domestic Product by Kind of Activity, in Current Prices

Million CFA francs

	1980	1983	1984	1985	1986	1987	1988	1989	1990	1991	1992	1993
1 Agriculture, hunting, forestry and fishing	...	138578	153224	150147	155796	156270	167932	177129	...	...	...	...
2 Mining and quarrying	...	9292	22926	21237	3828	5252	4184	4406	...	...	...	...
3 Manufacturing	...	34725	35113	35456	33226	33676	40226	42882	...	...	...	...
4 Electricity, gas and water	...	1471	3211	3447	3854	4047	4316	4107	...	...	...	...
5 Construction	...	16103	14363	15218	15115	15141	14759	15225	...	...	...	...
6 Wholesale and retail trade, restaurants and hotels [a]	...	63655	67221	74521	72940	73416	84358	82110	...	...	...	...
7 Transport, storage and communication	...	27637	31346	37443	37205	36664	36497	36475	...	...	...	...
8 Finance, insurance, real estate and business services	...	41515	43168	44903	47490	49863	51747	54808	...	...	...	...
9 Community, social and personal services [a]	...								...	...	...	...

Benin

1.10 Gross Domestic Product by Kind of Activity, in Current Prices
(Continued)

Million CFA francs

	1980	1983	1984	1985	1986	1987	1988	1989	1990	1991	1992	1993
Total, Industries	...	332976	370572	382373	369455	374329	404019	417141	...	...	...	...
Producers of Government Services	...	49007	51536	49096	53150	56471	47061	48594	...	...	...	...
Other Producers	...	...	...	...	...	...	...	...	...	...	...	...
Subtotal b	...	381982	422100	431469	422603	430800	451080	465735	...	...	...	...
Less: Imputed bank service charge	...	...	...	...	...	...	...	...	...	...	...	...
Plus: Import duties c	...	35456	37232	38309	39930	38754	31354	21790	...	...	...	...
Plus: Value added tax	...	...	...	...	...	...	...	...	...	...	...	...
Equals: Gross Domestic Product	...	417438	459340	469778	462533	469554	482434	487525	...	...	...	...

a) Restaurants and hotels are included in item 'Community, social and personal services'.
b) Gross domestic product in factor values.
c) Item 'Import duties' refers to indirect taxes net of subsidies.

1.11 Gross Domestic Product by Kind of Activity, in Constant Prices

Million CFA francs

	1980	1983	1984	1985	1986	1987	1988	1989	1990	1991	1992	1993
				At constant prices of: 1985								
1 Agriculture, hunting, forestry and fishing	...	115322	137262	150147	157699	148592	167661	177167	...	...	...	...
2 Mining and quarrying	...	10680	21878	21237	13427	15082	13703	12725	...	...	...	...
3 Manufacturing	...	33848	31701	35456	33981	35877	42620	44283	...	...	...	...
4 Electricity, gas and water	...	3858	3130	3447	2881	2996	3617	3617	...	...	...	...
5 Construction	...	18036	15337	15218	14785	14387	13051	13134	...	...	...	...
6 Wholesale and retail trade, restaurants and hotels a	...	65176	66919	74521	80402	81542	84176	79546	...	...	...	...
7 Transport, storage and communication	...	32163	34781	37443	35215	33146	30937	30164	...	...	...	...
8 Finance, insurance, real estate and business services	...	44219	44352	44903	46475	47754	48588	50395	...	...	...	...
9 Community, social and personal services a	...								...	...	...	...
Total, Industries	...	323303	355360	382373	384866	379376	404353	411033	...	...	...	...
Producers of Government Services	...	50306	52377	49096	50815	50612	50308	49903	...	...	...	...
Other Producers	...	...	...	...	...	...	...	...	...	...	...	...
Subtotal	...	373609	407737	431469	435681	429988	454661	460936	...	...	...	...
Less: Imputed bank service charge	...	...	...	...	...	...	...	...	...	...	...	...
Plus: Import duties	...	31177	29149	38309	44190	42685	32355	22634	...	...	...	...
Plus: Value added tax	...	...	...	...	...	...	...	...	...	...	...	...
Equals: Gross Domestic Product	...	404786	436886	469778	479871	472673	487016	483570	...	...	...	...

a) Restaurants and hotels are included in item 'Community, social and personal services'.

1.12 Relations Among National Accounting Aggregates

Million CFA francs

	1980	1983	1984	1985	1986	1987	1988	1989	1990	1991	1992	1993
Gross Domestic Product	...	417438	459340	469778	462535	469554	482434	487525	...	...	...	...
Plus: Net factor income from the rest of the world	...	-9969	-11702	-9600	-9000	-8600	-10000	-12300	...	...	...	...
Factor income from the rest of the world	...	1885	1331	2000	1000	1000	-	-	...	...	...	...
Less: Factor income to the rest of the world	...	11854	13033	11600	10000	9600	10000	12300	...	...	...	...
Equals: Gross National Product	...	407469	447638	460178	453535	460954	472434	475225	...	...	...	...
Less: Consumption of fixed capital	...	...	...	...	...	...	...	...	...	...	...	...
Equals: National Income a	...	407469	447638	460178	453535	460954	472434	475225	...	...	...	...
Plus: Net current transfers from the rest of the world	...	41316	39862	41000	39600	41000	44900	53010	...	...	...	...
Current transfers from the rest of the world	...	43140	41209	43000	41600	43000	46900	55010	...	...	...	...
Less: Current transfers to the rest of the world	...	1824	1342	2000	2000	2000	2000	2000	...	...	...	...
Equals: National Disposable Income b	...	448785	487505	501178	493135	501954	517334	528235	...	...	...	...
Less: Final consumption	...	414332	434560	432970	444926	453248	459828	467672	...	...	...	...
Equals: Net Saving c	...	34453	52945	68208	48209	48706	57506	60563	...	...	...	...
Less: Surplus of the nation on current transactions	...	-37879	-5858	-6009	-19863	-17856	-15482	2941	...	...	...	...
Equals: Net Capital Formation d	...	72332	58801	74217	68072	66562	72988	57622	...	...	...	...

a) Item 'National income' includes consumption of fixed capital.
b) Item 'National disposable income' includes consumption of fixed capital.
c) Item 'Net saving' includes consumption of fixed capital.
d) Item 'Net capital formation' includes consumption of fixed capital.

Bermuda

Source. Reply to the United Nations national accounts questionnaire from the Statistical Department of Bermuda, Hamilton.

General note. The estimates shown in the following tables have been prepared in accordance with the United Nations System of National Accounts so far as the existing data would permit.

1.1 Expenditure on the Gross Domestic Product, in Current Prices

Million Bermuda dollars — Fiscal year beginning 1 April

	1980	1983	1984	1985	1986	1987	1988	1989	1990	1991	1992	1993
1 Government final consumption expenditure	73.2	114.2	126.7	137.8	141.2	157.3	173.4	192.1	207.8	216.6	218.0	...
2 Private final consumption expenditure	518.3	663.4	725.8	781.0	837.1	927.3	1018.5	1094.4	1157.2	1165.7	1197.0	...
A Households	...	652.7	714.2	768.1	823.2	912.8	1003.3	1078.3	1140.4	1148.2	1178.7	...
B Private non-profit institutions serving households	...	10.7	11.6	12.9	13.9	14.5	15.2	16.1	16.8	17.5	18.3	...
3 Gross capital formation	119.7	169.9	211.5	207.6	187.1	228.2	295.2	257.2	237.0	225.7	236.4	...
A Increase in stocks	...	...	...	...	...	...	...	...	...	...	...	...
B Gross fixed capital formation	119.7	169.9	211.5	207.6	187.1	228.2	295.2	257.2	237.0	225.7	236.4	...
Residential buildings	17.7	41.3	65.4	73.2	51.1	57.3	62.9	68.2	75.8	62.4	49.3	...
Non-residential buildings	34.1	44.7	45.5	63.4	44.8	61.2	82.2	38.3	42.9	58.1	60.3	...
Other construction and land improvement etc.	8.6	5.8	0.8	1.0	2.5	12.3	21.2	2.9	2.8	3.6	2.8	...
Other	59.3	78.1	99.8	70.0	88.7	97.4	128.9	147.8	115.5	101.6	124.0	...
4 Exports of goods and services	495.2	616.1	644.9	701.9	821.6	874.1	904.6	963.3	992.5	955.8	999.3	...
5 Less: Imports of goods and services	454.1	560.2	669.4	654.8	690.5	771.8	890.2	914.6	959.6	883.9	953.1	...
Equals: Gross Domestic Product	752.3	1003.4	1039.5	1173.5	1296.5	1415.1	1501.5	1592.4	1634.9	1679.9	1697.6	...

1.2 Expenditure on the Gross Domestic Product, in Constant Prices

Million Bermuda dollars — Fiscal year beginning 1 April

At constant prices of:1975

	1980	1983	1984	1985	1986	1987	1988	1989	1990	1991	1992	1993
1 Government final consumption expenditure	48.3	53.6	55.0	56.6	54.5	57.0	58.9	61.6	62.5	61.2	60.1	...
2 Private final consumption expenditure	330.6	339.8	353.4	369.1	380.0	402.8	419.8	426.8	421.7	406.9	406.8	...
3 Gross capital formation	79.0	89.7	105.4	95.5	85.4	97.3	117.1	95.8	83.7	76.2	78.3	...
A Increase in stocks	...	...	...	...	...	...	...	...	...	...	...	...
B Gross fixed capital formation	79.0	89.7	105.4	95.5	85.4	97.3	117.1	95.8	83.7	76.2	78.3	...
4 Exports of goods and services	322.6	299.8	298.0	308.1	340.2	344.7	338.2	342.9	336.6	311.6	316.3	...
5 Less: Imports of goods and services	302.5	319.6	361.8	349.2	362.1	383.6	413.5	406.5	402.3	354.7	371.4	...
Equals: Gross Domestic Product	478.0	463.3	450.0	480.1	498.0	518.2	520.5	520.6	502.2	501.2	490.1	...

1.4 General Government Current Receipts and Disbursements

Thousand Bermuda dollars — Fiscal year beginning 1 April

	1980	1983	1984	1985	1986	1987	1988	1989	1990	1991	1992	1993
Receipts												
1 Operating surplus	...	...	...	...	...	...	...	...	...	...	...	...
2 Property and entrepreneurial income	8001	13428	11904	16338	26338	20223	21654	14805	...	...	...	...
3 Taxes, fees and contributions	111720	154754	171514	191432	223201	251676	277758	278199	...	...	...	...
A Indirect taxes	51142	77975	84962	97077	110853	127957	141132	143101	...	...	...	...
B Direct taxes	60578	76779	86552	94335	112348	123719	136626	135098	...	...	...	...
C Social security contributions	...	...	...	...	...	...	...	...	...	...	...	...
D Compulsory fees, fines and penalties	...	...	...	...	...	...	...	...	...	...	...	...
4 Other current transfers	12204	27697	25777	31276	35444	35152	58680	65604	...	...	...	...
Total Current Receipts of General Government	131925	195879	209195	239046	284983	307051	358092	358068	...	...	...	...
Disbursements												
1 Government final consumption expenditure	73216	114228	126726	137827	141228	156969	177407	192286	...	...	...	...
A Compensation of employees	...	...	...	...	...	...	...	...	...	...	...	...
B Consumption of fixed capital	...	...	...	...	...	...	...	...	...	...	...	...
C Purchases of goods and services, net	73216	114228	126726	137827	141228	156969	177407	192286	...	...	...	...
D Less: Own account fixed capital formation	...	...	...	...	...	...	...	...	...	...	...	...
E Indirect taxes paid, net	...	...	...	...	...	...	...	...	...	...	...	...

Bermuda

1.4 General Government Current Receipts and Disbursements
(Continued)

Thousand Bermuda dollars — Fiscal year beginning 1 April

	1980	1983	1984	1985	1986	1987	1988	1989	1990	1991	1992	1993
2 Property income	1981	1946	4234	5169	5346	6732	7198	6890	...	...	...	...
A Interest	1981	1946	4234	5169	5346	6732	7198	6890	...	...	...	...
B Net land rent and royalties	...	...	...	...	...	...	...	...	...	...	...	...
3 Subsidies	...	...	...	...	...	...	...	...	...	...	...	...
4 Other current transfers	29283	49883	54551	59006	64348	75397	94664	109775	...	...	...	...
5 Net saving	27445	29822	23684	37044	74061	67953	78823	49657	...	...	...	...
Total Current Disbursements and Net Saving of General Government	131925	195879	209195	239046	284983	307051	358092	358068	...	...	...	...

1.7 External Transactions on Current Account, Summary

Million Bermuda dollars — Fiscal year beginning 1 April

	1980	1983	1984	1985	1986	1987	1988	1989	1990	1991	1992	1993
Payments to the Rest of the World												
1 Imports of goods and services	...	...	669.4	654.8	690.5	771.8	890.2	914.6	959.6	883.9	953.1	...
A Imports of merchandise c.i.f.	...	...	440.9	426.3	426.3	475.1	499.6	511.6	...	...	...	...
B Other	...	...	228.5	228.5	264.2	296.7	390.6	403.0	...	...	...	...
2 Factor income to the rest of the world	...	...	26.0	21.0	25.0	22.0	26.0	46.0	53.0	59.0	59.0	...
3 Current transfers to the rest of the world	...	...	41.0	61.0	61.0	67.0	73.0	81.0	81.0	73.0	91.0	...
4 Surplus of the nation on current transactions	...	...	...	...	...	...	...	...	...	...	...	...
Payments to the Rest of the World and Surplus of the Nation on Current Transactions	...	...	...	...	...	...	...	...	...	...	...	...
Receipts From The Rest of the World												
1 Exports of goods and services	...	...	644.9	701.9	821.6	874.1	904.6	963.3	992.5	955.8	999.3	...
2 Factor income from rest of the world	...	...	53.0	57.0	57.0	57.0	35.0	63.0	59.0	61.0	74.0	...
3 Current transfers from rest of the world	...	...	...	...	...	7.0	7.0	8.0	8.0	10.0	11.0	...
Receipts from the Rest of the World on Current Transactions	...	...	...	...	...	...	...	...	...	...	...	...

1.12 Relations Among National Accounting Aggregates

Million Bermuda dollars — Fiscal year beginning 1 April

	1980	1983	1984	1985	1986	1987	1988	1989	1990	1991	1992	1993
Gross Domestic Product	752.3	1003.4	1039.5	1173.5	1296.5	1415.1	1501.5	1592.4	1634.9	1679.9	1697.6	...
Plus: Net factor income from the rest of the world	24.1	24.0	27.0	37.0	32.0	35.0	9.0	17.0	6.0	2.0	15.0	...
Factor income from the rest of the world	...	46.0	53.0	57.0	57.0	57.0	35.0	63.0	59.0	61.0	74.0	...
Less: Factor income to the rest of the world	...	22.0	26.0	21.0	25.0	22.0	26.0	46.0	53.0	59.0	59.0	...
Equals: Gross National Product	776.4	1027.4	1066.5	1210.5	1328.5	1450.1	1510.5	1609.4	1640.9	1681.9	1712.6	...
Less: Consumption of fixed capital	...	...	...	...	...	...	...	...	...	...	...	...
Equals: National Income	...	...	...	...	...	...	...	...	...	...	...	...
Plus: Net current transfers from the rest of the world	...	...	...	...	...	...	...	...	...	...	...	...
Equals: National Disposable Income	...	...	...	...	...	...	...	...	...	...	...	...
Less: Final consumption	...	...	...	...	...	...	...	...	...	...	...	...
Equals: Net Saving	...	...	...	...	...	...	...	...	...	...	...	...
Less: Surplus of the nation on current transactions	...	...	...	...	...	...	...	...	...	...	...	...
Equals: Net Capital Formation	...	...	...	...	...	...	...	...	...	...	...	...

Bermuda

2.1 Government Final Consumption Expenditure by Function, in Current Prices

Thousand Bermuda dollars
Fiscal year beginning 1 April

	1980	1983	1984	1985	1986	1987	1988	1989	1990	1991	1992	1993
1 General public services	27029	43898	48387	50924	48515	53434	59400	66525	73285	74984	76116	...
2 Defence	1547	2435	2566	2805	2997	3556	3177	3596	3520	3906	3356	...
3 Public order and safety	...	...	...	...	...	...	...	...	...	...	...	...
4 Education	16531	25131	27350	29293	31343	33806	39629	40211	45067	49226	49231	...
5 Health	2588	4030	4657	5165	5452	6041	7015	7605	8630	8852	9122	...
6 Social security and welfare	2304	3905	3716	4911	5370	5901	6128	6534	7570	8286	8371	...
7 Housing and community amenities	5653	7626	7670	8214	9087	9750	10251	11951	13004	13017	13738	...
8 Recreational, cultural and religious affairs	2097	3165	3483	3947	4152	4569	5311	6785	8068	8243	8007	...
9 Economic services	18340	28340	33527	37369	40020	47355	51095	57003	58057	58905	59791	...
10 Other functions [a]	-2873	-4302	-4630	-4801	-5718	-7143	-8599	-8124	-9365	-8802	-9645	...
Total Government Final Consumption Expenditure	73216	114228	126726	137827	141228	157269	173407	192086	207836	216617	218087	...

a) Item 'Other functions' refers to fees, sales and recoveries.

Bhutan

Source. Reply to the United Nations National Accounts Questionnaire from the Central Statistical Office. The official estimates are published in 'Revised Series on Gross Domestic Product of Bhutan: 1980-1987' and 'National Accounts Statistics, 1980-1988'.

General note. The estimates shown in the following tables have been prepared in accordance with the United Nations System of National Accounts so far as the existing data would permit.

1.1 Expenditure on the Gross Domestic Product, in Current Prices

Million Ngultrum

	1980	1983	1984	1985	1986	1987	1988	1989	1990	1991	1992	1993
1 Government final consumption expenditure	275.9	442.9	513.2	560.9	576.3	633.6	641.1	879.0	972.3	1042.6	...	...
2 Private final consumption expenditure	748.6	1195.1	1435.8	1506.7	1837.9	2321.0	2558.2	2581.8	2968.5	3335.0	...	...
3 Gross capital formation	345.1	712.0	765.3	1084.5	1135.1	1088.2	1518.4	1452.4	1635.9	1879.2	...	...
A Increase in stocks	14.7	21.3	10.4	81.6	32.0	-161.5	10.4	-121.1	-33.9	-71.3	...	...
B Gross fixed capital formation	330.4	690.7	754.9	1002.9	1103.1	1249.7	1508.0	1573.5	1669.8	1950.5	...	...
Residential buildings											...	...
Non-residential buildings	229.6	541.3	594.6	631.8	644.8	743.8	723.5	830.4	889.2	871.4	...	...
Other construction and land improvement etc.											...	...
Other	100.8	149.4	160.3	371.1	458.3	505.9	784.5	743.1	780.6	1079.1	...	...
4 Exports of goods and services	145.4	227.8	290.2	367.5	550.5	767.5	1200.8	1348.7	1484.4	1743.4	...	...
5 Less: Imports of goods and services	402.1	789.0	898.9	1127.8	1297.8	1202.6	1984.5	1879.7	2100.0	2431.3	...	...
Equals: Gross Domestic Product	1112.9	1788.8	2105.6	2391.8	2802.0	3607.5	3933.7	4381.6	4961.0	5568.9	6337.3	...

1.2 Expenditure on the Gross Domestic Product, in Constant Prices

Million Ngultrum

	1980	1983	1984	1985	1986	1987	1988	1989	1990	1991	1992	1993
					At constant prices of:1980							
1 Government final consumption expenditure	...	...	...	...	...	...	...	...	...	...	...	...
2 Private final consumption expenditure	...	...	...	...	...	...	...	...	...	...	...	...
3 Gross capital formation	345.1	549.2	503.6	677.8	573.5	562.6	788.9	670.6	717.1	805.0	...	...
A Increase in stocks	14.7	14.9	8.8	53.4	22.1	-90.0	4.8	-53.8	-9.2	-14.3	...	...
B Gross fixed capital formation	330.4	534.3	494.8	624.4	551.4	652.6	784.1	724.4	726.3	819.3	...	...
Residential buildings											...	...
Non-residential buildings	229.6	409.2	371.2	366.6	244.0	319.9	296.8	298.0	306.6	283.8	...	...
Other construction and land improvement etc.											...	...
Other	100.8	125.1	123.6	257.8	307.4	332.7	487.3	426.4	419.7	535.5	...	...
4 Exports of goods and services	...	...	...	...	...	...	...	...	...	...	...	...
5 Less: Imports of goods and services	...	...	...	...	...	...	...	...	...	...	...	...
Equals: Gross Domestic Product	...	...	...	...	...	...	...	...	...	...	...	...

1.3 Cost Components of the Gross Domestic Product

Million Ngultrum

	1980	1983	1984	1985	1986	1987	1988	1989	1990	1991	1992	1993
1 Indirect taxes, net [a]	17.9	34.8	45.6	41.8	43.0	76.7	82.8	73.7	134.2	159.4	159.4	...
2 Consumption of fixed capital [b]	61.2	103.0	118.9	137.6	191.6	330.6	362.3	399.0	451.0	518.5	594.3	...
3 Compensation of employees paid by resident producers to:	1033.8	1651.0	1941.1	2212.4	2567.4	3200.2	3488.6	3908.9	4375.8	4891.0	5583.6	...
4 Operating surplus												...
Equals: Gross Domestic Product	1112.9	1788.8	2105.6	2391.8	2802.0	3607.5	3933.7	4381.6	4961.0	5568.9	6337.3	...

a) Item 'Net indirect taxes' excludes excise refunds from the government of India.
b) The sharp increase in 1987 for 'Consumption of fixed capital' is due to the operation of the Chukha Hydel Project.

1.7 External Transactions on Current Account, Summary

Million Ngultrum

	1980	1983	1984	1985	1986	1987	1988	1989	1990	1991	1992	1993
					Payments to the Rest of the World							
1 Imports of goods and services	402.1	789.0	898.9	1127.7	1297.8	1202.6	1984.5	1879.7	2100.0	2431.3	...	...
A Imports of merchandise c.i.f.	394.6	730.0	825.2	1041.6	1205.4	1124.2	1817.0	1770.2	1994.6	2319.9	...	...
B Other	7.5	59.0	73.7	86.1	92.4	78.4	167.5	109.5	105.3	111.4	...	...
2 Factor income to the rest of the world	217.0	496.6	437.7	515.4	523.6	432.9	467.3	362.4	460.1	552.6	...	...

Bhutan

1.7 External Transactions on Current Account, Summary
(Continued)

Million Ngultrum

	1980	1983	1984	1985	1986	1987	1988	1989	1990	1991	1992	1993
A Compensation of employees	217.0	495.8	436.3	511.6	517.9	425.2	443.9	321.8	425.2	514.6	...	...
B Property and entrepreneurial income	-	0.8	1.4	3.8	5.7	7.7	23.4	40.6	34.9	38.0	...	...
3 Current transfers to the rest of the world	-	-	-	-	-	-	-	-	-	-	...	...
4 Surplus of the nation on current transactions	-450.2	-928.6	-887.2	-1089.4	-1079.6	-635.3	-967.2	-538.8	-751.7	-905.6	...	...
Payments to the Rest of the World and Surplus of the Nation on Current Transactions	168.9	357.0	449.4	553.7	741.8	1000.2	1484.6	1703.3	1808.4	2078.3	...	...
Receipts From The Rest of the World
1 Exports of goods and services	145.4	227.8	290.2	367.5	550.5	767.5	1200.8	1348.7	1484.4	1743.4	...	...
A Exports of merchandise f.o.b.	131.5	160.7	206.4	272.0	427.1	711.9	1072.6	1224.9	1387.6	1632.0	...	...
B Other	13.9	67.1	83.8	95.5	123.4	55.6	128.2	123.8	96.8	111.4	...	...
2 Factor income from rest of the world	17.0	40.6	49.9	65.6	56.6	83.4	123.0	190.8	163.7	112.8	...	...
A Compensation of employees	-	-	-	-	-	-	-	-	-	-	...	...
B Property and entrepreneurial income	17.0	40.6	49.9	65.6	56.6	83.4	123.0	190.8	163.7	112.8	...	...
3 Current transfers from rest of the world	6.5	88.6	109.3	120.6	134.7	149.3	160.8	163.8	160.3	222.1	...	...
Receipts from the Rest of the World on Current Transactions	168.9	357.0	449.4	553.7	741.8	1000.2	1484.6	1703.3	1808.4	2078.3	...	...

1.10 Gross Domestic Product by Kind of Activity, in Current Prices

Million Ngultrum

	1980	1983	1984	1985	1986	1987	1988	1989	1990	1991	1992	1993
1 Agriculture, hunting, forestry and fishing	621.4	934.2	1117.6	1236.2	1399.2	1623.5	1746.3	1924.3	2087.8	2331.0	2622.1	...
2 Mining and quarrying	6.8	10.2	23.3	20.2	37.4	37.0	33.4	41.8	44.8	94.1	199.0	...
3 Manufacturing	35.8	96.5	109.5	128.3	137.1	204.7	226.5	302.5	396.7	499.5	579.4	...
4 Electricity, gas and water [a]	2.5	6.7	5.9	6.8	96.6	377.0	388.0	391.0	384.7	419.8	461.8	...
5 Construction	88.5	238.6	276.5	290.5	267.5	349.9	309.0	365.4	397.1	369.7	428.9	...
6 Wholesale and retail trade, restaurants and hotels	121.5	170.0	182.4	203.0	234.1	248.2	258.5	282.3	321.6	382.9	444.2	...
7 Transport, storage and communication	47.9	76.8	80.6	104.1	114.2	126.0	180.6	235.6	341.5	385.9	447.6	...
8 Finance, insurance, real estate and business services	70.2	100.5	129.6	149.3	170.7	210.5	263.9	306.9	370.5	414.0	462.6	...
9 Community, social and personal services [b]	120.4	155.0	178.5	262.2	350.8	416.0	507.8	525.1	540.5	564.4	590.2	...
Total, Industries	1115.0	1789.0	2104.0	2401.0	2808.0	3592.8	3914.0	4374.9	4885.2	5461.3	6235.8	...
Producers of Government Services [b]												
Other Producers	...	...	...	...	...	...	...	...	...	...	...	
Subtotal [c]	1115.0	1789.0	2104.0	2401.0	2808.0	3592.8	3914.0	4374.9	4885.2	5461.3	6235.8	...
Less: Imputed bank service charge	20.0	35.0	44.0	51.0	49.0	62.0	63.1	67.0	58.4	51.8	57.9	...
Plus: Import duties	...	...	...	...	...	...	...	...	...	...	...	
Plus: Value added tax	...	...	...	...	...	...	...	...	...	...	...	
Plus: Other adjustments [d]	17.9	34.8	45.6	41.8	43.0	76.7	82.8	73.7	134.2	159.4	159.4	...
Equals: Gross Domestic Product	1112.9	1788.8	2105.6	2391.8	2802.0	3607.5	3933.7	4381.6	4961.0	5568.9	6337.3	...

a) The sharp increase beginning 1986 for item 'Electricity, gas and water' is the result of the completion of Chukha Hydel Project.
b) Item 'Producers of government services' is included in item 'Community, social and personal services'.
c) Gross domestic product in factor values.
d) Item 'Other adjustments' refers to indirect taxes net of subsidies.

1.11 Gross Domestic Product by Kind of Activity, in Constant Prices

Million Ngultrum

	1980	1983	1984	1985	1986	1987	1988	1989	1990	1991	1992	1993
At constant prices of: 1980
1 Agriculture, hunting, forestry and fishing	621.4	742.2	806.5	833.9	881.0	925.8	939.7	962.9	992.8	1024.6	1060.0	...
2 Mining and quarrying	6.8	8.9	15.8	12.6	22.2	21.6	19.0	21.7	19.3	27.7	30.0	...
3 Manufacturing	35.8	62.9	67.2	75.4	71.0	105.0	110.3	129.2	149.3	176.9	200.4	...
4 Electricity, gas and water [a]	2.5	6.0	5.2	6.0	60.4	229.0	225.1	222.3	203.8	213.1	215.8	...
5 Construction	88.5	185.2	173.5	169.0	141.8	152.3	129.0	136.2	136.8	119.3	124.0	...

Bhutan

1.11 Gross Domestic Product by Kind of Activity, in Constant Prices
(Continued)

Million Ngultrum

	1980	1983	1984	1985	1986	1987	1988	1989	1990	1991	1992	1993
At constant prices of: 1980												
6 Wholesale and retail trade, restaurants and hotels	121.5	122.0	123.4	132.4	143.4	142.4	129.2	133.6	138.6	147.8	157.6	...
7 Transport, storage and communication	47.9	64.8	66.4	79.4	83.9	91.3	122.1	142.4	169.5	185.9	192.4	...
8 Finance, insurance, real estate and business services	70.2	91.1	109.4	110.1	126.2	135.7	141.0	162.9	199.2	214.2	225.4	...
9 Community, social and personal services [b]	120.4	113.1	130.3	126.0	168.6	200.0	210.0	217.0	217.1	226.7	237.0	...
Total, Industries	1115.0	1396.2	1497.7	1544.8	1698.5	2003.1	2025.4	2128.2	2226.4	2336.2	2442.6	...
Producers of Government Services [b]	...	...	...	...	...	...	...	...	...	...	...	...
Other Producers	...	...	...	...	...	...	...	...	...	...	...	...
Subtotal	1115.0	1396.2	1497.7	1544.8	1698.5	2003.1	2025.4	2128.2	2226.4	2336.2	2442.6	...
Less: Imputed bank service charge	20.0	26.0	32.0	25.0	24.0	30.0	31.8	41.1	28.8	21.0	22.1	...
Plus: Import duties	...	...	...	...	...	...	...	...	...	...	...	...
Plus: Value added tax	...	...	...	...	...	...	...	...	...	...	...	...
Equals: Gross Domestic Product [c]	1095.0	1370.2	1465.7	1519.8	1674.5	1973.1	1993.6	2087.1	2197.6	2315.2	2420.5	...

a) The sharp increase beginning 1986 for item 'Electricity, gas and water' is the result of the completion of Chukha Hydel Project.
b) Item 'Producers of government services' is included in item 'Community, social and personal services'.
c) Gross domestic product in factor values.

1.12 Relations Among National Accounting Aggregates

Million Ngultrum

	1980	1983	1984	1985	1986	1987	1988	1989	1990	1991	1992	1993
Gross Domestic Product	1112.9	1788.8	2105.6	2391.8	2802.0	3607.7	3933.7	4381.6	4961.0	5568.9	6337.3	...
Plus: Net factor income from the rest of the world	-200.0	-456.1	-387.8	-449.7	-467.0	-349.5	-344.3	-171.6	-296.3	-439.8	-439.8	...
Factor income from the rest of the world	17.0	40.6	49.9	65.7	56.6	83.4	123.0	190.8	163.7	112.8	...	...
Less: Factor income to the rest of the world	217.0	496.7	437.7	515.4	523.6	432.9	467.3	362.4	460.1	552.6	...	...
Equals: Gross National Product	912.9	1332.7	1717.8	1942.1	2335.0	3258.2	3589.4	4210.0	4664.7	5129.1	5897.5	...
Less: Consumption of fixed capital	61.2	103.0	118.9	137.6	191.6	330.6	362.3	399.0	451.0	518.5	594.3	...
Equals: National Income	851.7	1229.7	1598.9	1804.5	2143.4	2927.6	3227.1	3811.0	4213.7	4610.6	5303.2	...
Plus: Net current transfers from the rest of the world	6.5	88.6	109.3	120.6	134.7	149.3	160.8	163.8	160.3	222.1	...	...
Current transfers from the rest of the world	6.5	88.6	109.3	120.6	134.7	149.3	160.8	163.8	160.3	222.1	...	...
Less: Current transfers to the rest of the world	-	-	-	-	-	-	-	-	-	-	...	...
Equals: National Disposable Income	858.2	1318.3	1708.2	1925.1	2278.1	3076.9	3387.9	3974.8	4374.0	4832.7	...	...
Less: Final consumption	1024.5	1638.0	1949.0	2067.6	2414.2	2954.6	3199.3	3460.8	3940.8	4377.6	...	...
Equals: Net Saving	-166.3	-319.7	-240.8	-142.5	-136.1	122.3	188.6	514.0	433.2	455.1	...	...
Less: Surplus of the nation on current transactions	-450.2	-928.6	-887.2	-1089.4	-1079.6	-635.3	-967.2	-538.8	-751.7	-905.6	...	...
Equals: Net Capital Formation	283.9	608.9	646.4	946.9	943.5	757.6	1155.8	1052.8	1184.9	1360.7	...	...

2.17 Exports and Imports of Goods and Services, Detail

Million Ngultrum

	1980	1983	1984	1985	1986	1987	1988	1989	1990	1991	1992	1993
Exports of Goods and Services												
1 Exports of merchandise, f.o.b.	131.5	160.7	206.4	272.0	427.1	711.9	1072.6	1224.9	1387.6	1632.0	...	...
2 Transport and communication	-	1.6	2.1	3.5	4.1	4.2	3.5	45.0	12.3	16.4	...	...
3 Insurance service charges	...	...	...	...	...	...	...	...	...	...	...	...
4 Other commodities	...	...	...	...	...	...	...	...	...	...	...	...
5 Adjustments of merchandise exports to change-of-ownership basis	...	...	...	...	...	...	...	...	...	...	...	...
6 Direct purchases in the domestic market by non-residential households	9.5	58.6	73.6	83.0	109.0	46.1	118.3	73.1	78.1	86.5	...	...
7 Direct purchases in the domestic market by extraterritorial bodies	4.4	6.9	8.1	9.0	10.3	5.3	6.4	5.7	6.4	8.5	...	...
Total Exports of Goods and Services	145.4	227.8	290.2	367.5	550.5	767.5	1200.8	1348.7	1484.4	1743.4	...	...
Imports of Goods and Services												
1 Imports of merchandise, c.i.f.	394.6	730.0	825.2	1041.6	1205.4	1124.2	1816.9	1770.2	1994.6	2319.9	...	...

Bhutan

2.17 Exports and Imports of Goods and Services, Detail
(Continued)

Million Ngultrum

	1980	1983	1984	1985	1986	1987	1988	1989	1990	1991	1992	1993
2 Adjustments of merchandise imports to change-of-ownership basis	...	...	...	...	...	...	...	...	...	...	...	...
3 Other transport and communication	-	1.5	2.1	2.2	1.5	1.4	37.7	19.2	19.3	5.2	...	...
4 Other insurance service charges	...	...	...	...	...	...	...	...	...	...	...	...
5 Other commodities	...	...	...	...	...	...	...	...	...	...	...	...
6 Direct purchases abroad by government	4.5	17.5	21.6	24.0	20.9	27.0	39.8	56.1	48.7	64.3	...	...
7 Direct purchases abroad by resident households	3.0	40.0	50.0	60.0	70.0	50.0	90.0	34.2	37.4	41.9	...	...
Total Imports of Goods and Services	402.1	789.0	898.9	1127.8	1297.8	1202.6	1984.5	1879.7	2100.0	2431.3	...	...
Balance of Goods and Services	-256.7	-561.2	-608.7	-760.3	-747.3	-435.1	-783.7	-531.0	-615.6	-687.9	...	...
Total Imports and Balance of Goods and Services	145.4	227.8	290.2	367.5	550.5	767.5	1200.8	1348.7	1484.4	1743.4	...	...

Bolivia

General note. The preparation of national accounts statistics in Bolivia is undertaken by the Instituto Nacional de Estadistica, La Paz. The official estimates together with methodological notes are published in a series of publications entitled 'Boletin de Cuentas Nacionales'. The most detailed description of the sources and methods used for the national accounts estimation is found in 'Cuentas Nacionales, 1958-1966, Planeamiento'. On 1 January 1987, the Bolivian pesos has been re-denominated from pesos to Bolivianos. One Boliviano is equivalent to one million pesos. The estimates are generally in accordance with the classifications and recommendations recommended in the United Nations System of National Accounts (SNA). Input-output table for 1958 has been published in 'La Matriz de Transacciones Intersectoriales de Bienes Nacionales e Importados'. The following tables have been prepared from successive replies to the United Nations national accounts questionnaire. When the scope and coverage of the estimates differ for conceptual or statistical reasons from the definitions and classifications recommended in SNA, a footnote is indicated to the relevant tables.

Sources and methods :

(a) **Gross domestic product.** Gross domestic product is estimated mainly through the production approach.

(b) **Expenditure on the gross domestic product.** All components of GDP by expenditure type are estimated through the expenditure approach except private final consumption expenditure which is obtained as a residual. The estimates of the government final consumption expenditure are based on the annual government accounts furnished by the respective government agencies. Increase in stocks estimates are based on information obtained from the enterprises. For public capital information, estimates are obtained from financial statements of the public institutions. The estimates are classified by type of goods and sub-divisions of the public sector. For the estimates of private capital formation, the Instituto Nacional de Estadistica requests detailed information from the enterprises. The estimates of imported machinery and equipment are based on c.i.f. import values classified by use or economic destination. Trade margins and transport expenses are then added. The estimation of domestically produced capital goods is done on the basis of annual industrial statistics. Data on exports of goods and services are obtained from the balance of payments accounts. The value of non-monetary gold export is added to the f.o.b. figures while imports are estimated by the Banco Central. For the constant price estimates, government expenditure on wages and salaries are revalued at base-year prices while purchases of goods and services are deflated by implicit price or cost-of-living indexes. The estimates of private consumption expenditure is obtained as a residual. For the remaining items, price deflation is used.

(c) **Cost-structure of the gross domestic product.** The cost structure of the gross domestic product has not been estimated since 1969.

(d) **Gross domestic product by kind of economic activity.** The table of gross domestic product by kind of economic activity is prepared at market prices, i.e. producers' values. The production approach is used to estimate value added of most industries, but due to lack of information on intermediate consumption, value added coefficients established from the input-output table of 1958 have been utilized. The income approach is used to estimate value added of public administration and defence and some private industries. For agriculture, information relating to production volume is used, estimated on the basis of information on areas sown and production yields prepared by the Ministerio de Asuntos Campensinos y Agropecuarios and by special institutions. The gross value of production is estimated by using data on physical volumes and producer prices. Estimates of livestock production is based on existing livestock, information on meat cutting for domestic consumption and export data. The mining sector consists of the Corporacion Minera de Bolivia (COMIBOL), and of medium and small mines. The basic statistics are obtained from the accounts of COMIBOL, from Ministerio de Minera, from financial statements of medium-sized mines and from export statistics for small mines. The estimates for the manufacturing sector are based on information obtained from the annual industrial statistics published by the Instituto Nacional de Estadistica supplemented by statistics from private and public institutions and other studies. Information on electricity is obtained from the Direccion Nacional de Electricidad which controls all the public and private enterprises. The sources used for the construction estimates are the accounts of public institutions permits issued by municipalities and financial statements submitted by the construction enterprises. The value of production of private construction, which is based on permits issued and classified by surface area, is adjusted by a percentage for planned unfulfilled work. Information on trade margins and trade volumes is furnished by various concerned institutions. The gross trade margins are estimated from the price differences between the wholesale and producers prices as well as the consumer and wholesale prices for all the agricultural products and a sample of manufactured and imported goods entering the distribution channels. Restaurants and hotels estimates are based on a sample survey of the principal establishments in La Paz, blown up to cover the whole country by using the number of establishments as indicators. The estimates of railway transport are based on the accounts of the public railway enterprise. The gross value of production for urban passenger transport is estimated on the basis of the number of buses in operation, mileage, passenger volumes and average tariffs. Air transport estimates are based on the accounting statements of the national airline as well as taxes charged on foreign airlines. The accounting statements of the financial institutions are used for the financial sector. For ownership of dwellings, census information on population and housing is used supplemented by statistics on real estate. For public administration and defense, the main source is the annual financial statement requested by the Banco Central de Bolivia. Estimates for private services are obtained from concerned entities and institutions. For constant price estimates, value added for agriculture, mining and quarrying, manufacturing and transport sectors is extrapolatd by quantity index for output. Value added of construction is estimated by multiplying the annual authorized construction volume by the base-year prices. For the remaining industries, value added is deflated by appropriate price indexes.

1.1 Expenditure on the Gross Domestic Product, in Current Prices

Thousand Bolivianos

	1980	1983	1984	1985	1986	1987	1988	1989	1990	1991	1992	1993
1 Government final consumption expenditure	16	113	2555	238275	705309	942	1354	1620	1829	2234	2779	3322
2 Private final consumption expenditure	82	969	14157	1793045	6213741	7440	8591	10392	13472	16874	19542	21888
3 Gross capital formation	18	165	3374	484282	1193574	1514	1998	1451	2262	3146	4292	5175
A Increase in stocks	1	2	542	148441	234110	368	186	-243	-16	414	772	911
B Gross fixed capital formation	18	163	2832	335841	959464	1146	1812	1694	2278	2732	3520	4264
Residential buildings	4	...	...	...	...	...	...	...	...	...	...	...
Non-residential buildings	1	...	...	...	...	...	...	...	...	...	...	...
Other construction and land improvement etc.	5	...	...	...	...	...	...	...	...	...	...	...
Other	7	...	...	...	...	...	...	...	...	...	...	...
4 Exports of goods and services	32	513	7896	830101	2586796	2494	2036	3951	3567	4083	3960	4488
5 Less: Imports of goods and services	25	298	4759	478994	1775326	2211	2618	2665	4192	5421	7054	8816
Equals: Gross Domestic Product [a,b]	123	1463	23224	2866709	8924094	10178	11361	14749	16937	20916	23520	26057

a) The estimates for the years 1970-1982 were prepared by the Central Bank. Beginning 1983, they were prepared by the Instituto Nacional de Estadistica.
b) Beginning 1987, the estimates are in million Bolivianos.

Bolivia

1.2 Expenditure on the Gross Domestic Product, in Constant Prices

Thousand Bolivianos

	1980	1983	1984	1985	1986	1987	1988	1989	1990	1991	1992	1993
	\multicolumn{8}{c}{At constant prices of: 1980}		1990			
1 Government final consumption expenditure	16	15	15	14	12	14	13	14	14 / 1829	1885	1951	2000
2 Private final consumption expenditure	82	73	74	77	82	85	87	89	90 / 13472	13927	14393	14854
3 Gross capital formation	18	12	16	21	18	20	15	14	13 / 2261	2692	3217	3241
A Increase in stocks	1	1	4	7	4	5	-	-2	-3 / -16	349	599	485
B Gross fixed capital formation	18	10	11	14	15	15	16	16	15 / 2277	2343	2618	2756
4 Exports of goods and services	32	32	30	27	30	28	30	33	38 / 3567	3752	3769	4408
5 Less: Imports of goods and services	25	18	23	27	33	35	30	32	35 / 4192	4535	5117	5540
Equals: Gross Domestic Product	123[a]	113[a]	113[a]	112[a]	109[a]	112[a]	115[a]	118[a]	121[a] / 16937[b]	17721[b]	18214[b]	18962[b]

a) The estimates for the years 1970-1982 were prepared by the Central Bank. Beginning 1983, they were prepared by the Instituto Nacional de Estadistica.
b) The estimates for the series beginning 1990 are in million Bolivianos.

1.3 Cost Components of the Gross Domestic Product

Thousand Bolivianos

	1980	1983	1984	1985	1986	1987	1988	1989	1990	1991	1992	1993
1 Indirect taxes, net	12	76	1150	262666	920655	...	928	...	...	...	...	...
A Indirect taxes	14	84	1183	285995	923486	...	937	...	...	...	...	...
B Less: Subsidies	2	8	33	23329	2831	...	9	...	...	...	...	...
2 Consumption of fixed capital	...	...	...	...	...	...	...	...	...	...	...	...
3 Compensation of employees paid by resident producers to:	42	464	10013	926100	2153247	...	2908	...	...	...	...	...
A Resident households	42	464	10007	923746	2147885	...	2896	...	...	...	...	...
B Rest of the world	-	-	6	2354	5362	...	12	...	...	...	...	...
4 Operating surplus	70	923	12061	1677943	5850192	...	7525	...	...	...	...	...
A Corporate and quasi-corporate enterprises	19	211	1026	185325	1591285	...	1727	...	...	...	...	...
B Private unincorporated enterprises	51	712	11035	1492618	4258907	...	5799	...	...	...	...	...
C General government	...	...	...	...	...	...	...	...	...	...	...	...
Equals: Gross Domestic Product [a]	123	1463	23224	2866709	8924094	...	11361	...	...	...	...	...

a) Beginning 1987, the estimates are in million Bolivianos.

1.4 General Government Current Receipts and Disbursements

Thousand Bolivianos

	1980	1983	1984	1985	1986	1987	1988	1989	1990	1991	1992	1993
	\multicolumn{12}{c}{Receipts}
1 Operating surplus	...	...	...	...	...	...	...	...	...	...	...	...
2 Property and entrepreneurial income	-	4	62	4126	6931	...	508848	...	...	...	...	...
3 Taxes, fees and contributions	19	126	1879	349224	1160370	...	1353621	...	...	...	...	...
A Indirect taxes	14	84	1183	285995	923486	...	936790	...	...	...	...	...
B Direct taxes	2	10	27	8685	41065	...	133275	...	...	...	...	...
C Social security contributions	4	31	651	52509	184972	...	260270	...	...	...	...	...
D Compulsory fees, fines and penalties	-	2	18	2035	10847	...	23286	...	...	...	...	...
4 Other current transfers	2	21	542	47639	185806	...	441721	...	...	...	...	...
Total Current Receipts of General Government	22	151	2483	400989	1353107	...	2304190	...	...	...	...	...
	\multicolumn{12}{c}{Disbursements}
1 Government final consumption expenditure	16	113	2555	238275	705309	...	1353840	...	...	...	...	...

Bolivia

1.4 General Government Current Receipts and Disbursements
(Continued)

Thousand Bolivianos

	1980	1983	1984	1985	1986	1987	1988	1989	1990	1991	1992	1993
A Compensation of employees	13	95	2072	177659	484056	...	1026878	...	...	...	...	...
B Consumption of fixed capital	-	-	-	-	-	...	-	...	...	...	...	...
C Purchases of goods and services, net	3	19	483	60609	221253	...	326962	...	...	...	...	...
D Less: Own account fixed capital formation	-	-	-	-	-	...	-	...	...	...	...	...
E Indirect taxes paid, net	-	-	-	7	-	...	-	...	...	...	...	...
2 Property income	2	10	329	312443	52737	...	199863	...	...	...	...	...
A Interest	2	10	329	312443	52737	...	199863	...	...	...	...	...
B Net land rent and royalties	...	...	...	...	...	...	...	...	...	...	...	...
3 Subsidies	2	8	33	23329	2831	...	8592	...	...	...	...	...
4 Other current transfers	6	50	1677	317657	461088	...	486060	...	...	...	...	...
A Social security benefits	3	26	672	40780	118032	...	187064	...	...	...	...	...
B Social assistance grants	-	-	-	-	-	...	-	...	...	...	...	...
C Other	3	25	1005	276877	343056	...	298996	...	...	...	...	...
5 Net saving	-4	-31	-2111	-490715	131142	...	255835	...	...	...	...	...
Total Current Disbursements and Net Saving of General Government	22	151	2483	400989	1353107	...	2304190	...	...	...	...	...

1.7 External Transactions on Current Account, Summary

Thousand Bolivianos

	1980	1983	1984	1985	1986	1987	1988	1989	1990	1991	1992	1993
Payments to the Rest of the World												
1 Imports of goods and services	25	298	4759	478994	1775326	...	2617794	...	...	...	...	...
A Imports of merchandise c.i.f.	22	250	3976	409579	1510030	...	2323809	...	...	...	...	...
B Other	2	47	783	69415	265296	...	293985	...	...	...	...	...
2 Factor income to the rest of the world	7	104	1903	176118	329963	...	386810	...	...	...	...	...
A Compensation of employees	-	-	6	2354	5362	...	11750	...	...	...	...	...
B Property and entrepreneurial income	7	103	1897	173764	324601	...	375060	...	...	...	...	...
3 Current transfers to the rest of the world	-	7	91	11559	40407	...	61335	...	...	...	...	...
4 Surplus of the nation on current transactions	2	139	1622	222559	665927	...	-18295	...	...	...	...	...
Payments to the Rest of the World and Surplus of the Nation on Current Transactions	34	547	8375	889230	2811623	...	3047644	...	...	...	...	...
Receipts From The Rest of the World												
1 Exports of goods and services	32	513	7896	830101	2586796	...	2036184	...	...	...	...	...
A Exports of merchandise f.o.b.	30	487	7480	780914	2418488	...	1770399	...	...	...	...	...
B Other	2	26	416	49187	168308	...	265785	...	...	...	...	...
2 Factor income from rest of the world	-	7	89	10677	29876	...	676115	...	...	...	...	...
A Compensation of employees	-	-	7	1501	4788	...	172819	...	...	...	...	...
B Property and entrepreneurial income	-	7	82	9176	25088	...	503296	...	...	...	...	...
3 Current transfers from rest of the world	2	26	390	48452	194951	...	335345	...	...	...	...	...
Receipts from the Rest of the World on Current Transactions	34	547	8375	889230	2811623	...	3047644	...	...	...	...	...

1.8 Capital Transactions of The Nation, Summary

Thousand Bolivianos

	1980	1983	1984	1985	1986	1987	1988	1989	1990	1991	1992	1993
Finance of Gross Capital Formation												
Gross saving	20	304	4996	706841	1859501	...	1979918	...	...	...	...	...
1 Consumption of fixed capital	-	-	-	-	-	...	-	...	...	...	...	...
2 Net saving	20	304	4996	706841	1859501	...	1979918	...	...	...	...	...
Less: Surplus of the nation on current transactions	2	139	1622	222559	665927	...	-18295	...	...	...	...	...
Finance of Gross Capital Formation	18	165	3374	484282	1193574	...	1998213	...	...	...	...	...

Bolivia

1.8 Capital Transactions of The Nation, Summary
(Continued)

Thousand Bolivianos

	1980	1983	1984	1985	1986	1987	1988	1989	1990	1991	1992	1993
				Gross Capital Formation								
Increase in stocks	1	2	542	148441	234110	...	185806	...	...	...	...	...
Gross fixed capital formation	18	163	2832	335841	959464	...	1812407	...	...	...	...	...
1 General government	4	33	1220	163249	238171	...	333004	...	...	...	...	...
2 Corporate and quasi-corporate enterprises	9	110	1010	106128	393440	...	1006781	...	...	...	...	...
A Public	4	79	785	75574	242136	...	514812	...	...	...	...	...
B Private	5	32	225	30554	151304	...	491969	...	...	...	...	...
3 Other	4	20	602	66464	327853	...	472622	...	...	...	...	...
Gross Capital Formation	18	165	3374	484282	1193574	...	1998213	...	...	...	...	...

1.9 Gross Domestic Product by Institutional Sectors of Origin

Thousand Bolivianos

	1980	1983	1984	1985	1986	1987	1988	1989	1990	1991	1992	1993
				Domestic Factor Incomes Originating								
1 General government	13	95	2072	177659	484056	...	1027	...	...	...	...	...
2 Corporate and quasi-corporate enterprises	35	416	5681	703389	2274513	...	2541	...	...	...	...	...
A Non-financial	34	409	5366	714389	2227142	...	2518	...	...	...	...	...
Public	13	174	2247	216257	747209	...	1277	...	...	...	...	...
Private	21	235	3119	498132	1479933	...	1241	...	...	...	...	...
B Financial	1	7	315	-11000	47371	...	23	...	...	...	...	...
3 Households and private unincorporated enterprises	64	877	14321	1722995	5244870	...	6865	...	...	...	...	...
4 Non-profit institutions serving households	...	...	...	...	...	...	...	...	...	...	...	...
Subtotal: Domestic Factor Incomes	112	1387	22074	2604043	8003439	...	10433	...	...	...	...	...
Indirect taxes, net	12	76	1150	262666	920655	...	928	...	...	...	...	...
A Indirect taxes	14	84	1183	285995	923486	...	937	...	...	...	...	...
B Less: Subsidies	2	8	33	23329	2831	...	9	...	...	...	...	...
Consumption of fixed capital	...	...	...	...	...	...	...	...	...	...	...	...
Gross Domestic Product [a]	123	1463	23224	2866709	8924094	...	11361	...	...	...	...	...

a) Beginning 1987, the estimates are in million Bolivianos.

1.10 Gross Domestic Product by Kind of Activity, in Current Prices

Thousand Bolivianos

	1980	1983	1984	1985	1986	1987	1988	1989	1990	1991	1992	1993
1 Agriculture, hunting, forestry and fishing	23	370	7027	832528	2450257	...	2095	...	2805	3540	3742	4231
2 Mining and quarrying	19	215	2753	337557	890331	...	850	...	1654	1514	1458	1521
3 Manufacturing	18	142	2052	343156	1184356	...	1776	...	2379	3169	3546	3778
4 Electricity, gas and water	1	5	124	25665	96333	...	132	...	249	396	557	657
5 Construction	5	54	1181	121481	254744	...	364	...	620	701	998	1146
6 Wholesale and retail trade, restaurants and hotels	13	255	3203	310571	970203	...	1581	...	2236	2655	2756	3102
7 Transport, storage and communication	7	81	1289	304425	1056002	...	1226	...	1805	2511	3052	3518
8 Finance, insurance, real estate and business services	17	142	2309	303562	777652	...	947	...	1808	2146	2589	3112
9 Community, social and personal services	5	105	1228	133835	635561	...	568	...	716	843	968	1133
Total, Industries	108	1369	21167	2712780	8315439	...	9539	...	14272	17475	19666	22198
Producers of Government Services	13	95	2072	177666	484056	...	1027	...	1547	1943	2285	2213
Other Producers	1	8	110	13153	49743	...	67	...	93	113	128	135
Subtotal	122	1472	23349	2903599	8849238	...	10632	...	15912	19531	22079	24546
Less: Imputed bank service charge	2	17	272	61883	66211	...	172	...	253	354	494	620
Plus: Import duties	3	8	147	24993	141067	...	189	...	1279	1739	1933	2131
Plus: Value added tax	...	...	...	...	...	...	352	...				
Plus: Other adjustments	...	...	...	...	...	...	361	...	...	...	...	...
Equals: Gross Domestic Product [a,b]	123	1463	23224	2866709	8924094	...	11361	...	16937	20916	23520	26057

a) The estimates for the years 1970-1982 were prepared by the Central Bank. Beginning 1983, they were prepared by the Instituto Nacional de Estadistica.
b) Beginning 1987, the estimates are in million Bolivianos.

Bolivia

1.11 Gross Domestic Product by Kind of Activity, in Constant Prices

Thousand Bolivianos

	1980	1983	1984	1985	1986	1987	1988	1989	1990	1991	1992	1993
	\multicolumn{8}{c}{At constant prices of: 1980}	\multicolumn{4}{c}{1990}
1 Agriculture, hunting, forestry and fishing	23	20	24	25	24	25	26	26	25 / 2805	3089	2952	3057
2 Mining and quarrying	19	18	16	14	12	12	15	17	18 / 1654	1684	1712	1828
3 Manufacturing	18	15	15	13	14	14	15	15	16 / 2379	2473	2575	2688
4 Electricity, gas and water	1	1	1	1	1	1	1	1	1 / 249	273	297	321
5 Construction	5	4	4	3	3	3	3	3	3 / 620	637	716	745
6 Wholesale and retail trade, restaurants and hotels	13	16	13	13	15	16	15	15	16 / 2236	2344	2467	2575
7 Transport, storage and communication	7	8	8	9	9	10	10	10	10 / 1805	1876	2011	2133
8 Finance, insurance, real estate and business services	17	15	15	15	15	14	14	15	15 / 1808	1849	1972	2075
9 Community, social and personal services	5	4	4	4	4	4	4	4	4 / 716	736	761	781
Total, Industries	108	100	100	99	97	99	103	106	109 / 14272	14961	15463	16203
Producers of Government Services	13	13	13	12	10	10	10	10	11 / 1547	1617	1675	1709
Other Producers	1	1	1	1	1	1	1	1	1 / 93	94	96	98
Subtotal	122	114	113	112	108	110	114	117	121 / 15912	16672	17234	18010
Less: Imputed bank service charge	2	1	1	1	1	1	1	1	1 / 253	283	342	390
Plus: Import duties	3	1	1	1	2	2	2	2	2 / 1279[a]	1333	1322	1343
Plus: Value added tax	...	...	...	...	...	...	...	...	...			
Equals: Gross Domestic Product	123[b]	113[b]	113[b]	112[b]	109[b]	112[b]	115[b]	118[b]	121[b] / 16937[c]	17721[c]	18214[c]	18962[c]

a) Including item 'Plus: Value added tax'.
b) The estimates for the years 1970-1982 were prepared by the Central Bank. Beginning 1983, they were prepared by the Instituto Nacional de Estadistica.
c) The estimates for the series beginning 1990 are in million Bolivianos.

1.12 Relations Among National Accounting Aggregates

Thousand Bolivianos

	1980	1983	1984	1985	1986	1987	1988	1989	1990	1991	1992	1993
Gross Domestic Product	123	1463	23224	2866709	8924094	...	...	...	...	...	...	...
Plus: Net factor income from the rest of the world	-7	-96	-1815	-165441	-300087	...	...	...	...	...	...	...
Factor income from the rest of the world	-	7	89	10677	29876	...	...	...	...	...	...	...
Less: Factor income to the rest of the world	7	104	1903	176118	329963	...	...	...	...	...	...	...
Equals: Gross National Product	116	1366	21410	2701268	8624007	...	...	...	...	...	...	...
Less: Consumption of fixed capital	-	-	-	-	-	...	...	...	...	...	...	...
Equals: National Income	116	1366	21410	2701268	8624007	...	...	...	...	...	...	...
Plus: Net current transfers from the rest of the world	1	20	298	36893	154544	...	...	...	...	...	...	...
Current transfers from the rest of the world	2	26	390	48452	194951	...	...	...	...	...	...	...
Less: Current transfers to the rest of the world	-	7	91	11559	40407	...	...	...	...	...	...	...
Equals: National Disposable Income	118	1386	21708	2738161	8778551	...	...	...	...	...	...	...
Less: Final consumption	98	1082	16712	2031320	6919050	...	...	...	...	...	...	...
Equals: Net Saving	20	304	4996	706841	1859501	...	...	...	...	...	...	...
Less: Surplus of the nation on current transactions	2	139	1622	222559	665927	...	...	...	...	...	...	...
Equals: Net Capital Formation	18	165	3374	484282	1193574	...	...	...	...	...	...	...

Bolivia

2.5 Private Final Consumption Expenditure by Type and Purpose, in Current Prices

Thousand Bolivianos

	1980	1983	1984	1985	1986	1987	1988	1989	1990	1991	1992	1993
Final Consumption Expenditure of Resident Households												
1 Food, beverages and tobacco	34	474	7437	933297	2965270	...	3443707	...	...	...	...	...
A Food	31	442	6986	882566	2764485	...	3056568	...	...	...	...	...
B Non-alcoholic beverages	1	12	117	14334	62105	...	105005	...	...	...	...	...
C Alcoholic beverages	1	8	149	16738	69860	...	229266	...	...	...	...	...
D Tobacco	1	12	185	19659	68820	...	52868	...	...	...	...	...
2 Clothing and footwear	7	49	631	63868	203174	...	438689	...	...	...	...	...
3 Gross rent, fuel and power	11	77	1016	140187	497615	...	1071639	...	...	...	...	...
A Fuel and power	1	4	49	12593	54073	...	400551	...	...	...	...	...
B Other	11	73	967	127594	443542	...	671088	...	...	...	...	...
4 Furniture, furnishings and household equipment and operation	6	70	918	93896	416219	...	830542	...	...	...	...	...
A Household operation	1	11	150	14586	54880	...	202937	...	...	...	...	...
B Other	6	60	768	79310	361339	...	627605	...	...	...	...	...
5 Medical care and health expenses	4	25	326	37978	155983	...	177825	...	...	...	...	...
6 Transport and communication	9	100	1517	265928	1026172	...	1522520	...	...	...	...	...
A Personal transport equipment	2	19	250	37338	172620	...	20648	...	...	...	...	...
B Other	7	81	1268	228590	853552	...	1501872	...	...	...	...	...
7 Recreational, entertainment, education and cultural services	4	38	461	61519	260365	...	259330	...	...	...	...	...
A Education	2	12	131	17600	73802	...	26500	...	...	...	...	...
B Other	2	26	330	43919	186563	...	232830	...	...	...	...	...
8 Miscellaneous goods and services	6	129	1763	189941	662526	...	857710	...	...	...	...	...
A Personal care	-	4	51	5284	19433	...	20194	...	...	...	...	...
B Expenditures in restaurants, cafes and hotels	4	112	1440	151455	570069	...	617779	...	...	...	...	...
C Other	1	13	272	33202	73024	...	219737	...	...	...	...	...
Total Final Consumption Expenditure in the Domestic Market by Households, of which	82	962	14070	1786614	6187324	...	8601962	...	...	...	...	...
Plus: Direct purchases abroad by resident households	-	7	87	6431	26417	...	-11072	...	...	...	...	...
Less: Direct purchases in the domestic market by non-resident households												
Equals: Final Consumption Expenditure of Resident Households [a]	82	969	14157	1793045	6213741	...	8590890	...	...	...	...	...
Final Consumption Expenditure of Private Non-profit Institutions Serving Households												
Equals: Final Consumption Expenditure of Private Non-profit Organisations Serving Households	...	...	...	...	...	...	...	...	...	...	...	...
Private Final Consumption Expenditure	82	969	14157	1793045	6213741	...	8590890	...	...	...	...	...

a) Item 'Final consumption expenditure of resident households' includes consumption expenditure of private non-profit institutions serving households.

2.6 Private Final Consumption Expenditure by Type and Purpose, in Constant Prices

Bolivianos

	1980	1983	1984	1985	1986	1987	1988	1989	1990	1991	1992	1993
At constant prices of: 1980												
Final Consumption Expenditure of Resident Households												
1 Food, beverages and tobacco	34152	32023	34201	36536	36919	...	...	...	...	...	...	...
A Food	31046	29589	32335	34763	34373	...	...	...	...	...	...	...
B Non-alcoholic beverages	1209	951	570	484	754	...	...	...	...	...	...	...
C Alcoholic beverages	948	943	876	832	1239	...	...	...	...	...	...	...
D Tobacco	949	540	420	457	553	...	...	...	...	...	...	...
2 Clothing and footwear	7366	3926	3742	3674	4154	...	...	...	...	...	...	...
3 Gross rent, fuel and power	11394	11770	11901	11987	12136	...	...	...	...	...	...	...
A Fuel and power	732	939	988	1032	1143	...	...	...	...	...	...	...
B Other	10662	10831	10913	10955	10993	...	...	...	...	...	...	...
4 Furniture, furnishings and household equipment and operation	6390	4483	4234	4218	5534	...	...	...	...	...	...	...
A Household operation	781	696	648	667	945	...	...	...	...	...	...	...

Bolivia

2.6 Private Final Consumption Expenditure by Type and Purpose, in Constant Prices
(Continued)

Bolivianos

	1980	1983	1984	1985	1986	1987	1988	1989	1990	1991	1992	1993
				At constant prices of:1980								
B Other	5609	3787	3586	3551	4589	...	...	...	...	...	...	...
5 Medical care and health expenses	3580	3742	3553	3409	3654	...	...	...	...	...	...	...
6 Transport and communication	9048	8759	9171	9727	10788	...	...	...	...	...	...	...
A Personal transport equipment	1742	818	1066	1109	1327	...	...	...	...	...	...	...
B Other	7306	7941	8105	8618	9461	...	...	...	...	...	...	...
7 Recreational, entertainment, education and cultural services	4275	3072	2697	3101	3742	...	...	...	...	...	...	...
A Education	1792	1383	1224	1400	1688	...	...	...	...	...	...	...
B Other	2483	1689	1473	1701	2054	...	...	...	...	...	...	...
8 Miscellaneous goods and services	5599	4918	4656	4399	4417	...	...	...	...	...	...	...
A Personal care	272	248	228	230	268	...	...	...	...	...	...	...
B Expenditures in restaurants, cafes and hotels	3934	3707	3354	3101	3098	...	...	...	...	...	...	...
C Other	1393	963	1074	1068	1051	...	...	...	...	...	...	...
Total Final Consumption Expenditure in the Domestic Market by Households, of which	81804	72693	74155	77053	81344	...	...	...	...	...	...	...
Plus: Direct purchases abroad by resident households	454	231	168	160	159	...	...	...	...	...	...	...
Less: Direct purchases in the domestic market by non-resident households						...	...	...	...	...	...	...
Equals: Final Consumption Expenditure of Resident Households	82258	72924	74323	77213	81503	...	...	...	...	...	...	...

Final Consumption Expenditure of Private Non-profit Institutions Serving Households

	1980	1983	1984	1985	1986	1987	1988	1989	1990	1991	1992	1993
Equals: Final Consumption Expenditure of Private Non-profit Organisations Serving Households	...	...	...	...	...	...	...	...	...	...	...	...
Private Final Consumption Expenditure	82258	72924	74323	77213	81503	...	...	...	...	...	...	...

Botswana

General note. The preparation of national accounts statistics in Botswana is undertaken by the Central Statistics Office of the Ministry of Finance and Development Planning, Gaborone. Official estimates together with methodological notes are published in a series of reports entitled 'National Accounts of Botswana'. The most detailed description of the sources and methods used for the national accounts estimation is found in the fifth edition of this report published in July 1976 for the fiscal year 1973/74. The estimates are generally in accordance with the classifications and definitions recommended in the United Nations System of National Acconts (SNA). The following tables have been prepared from successive replies to the United Nations national accounts questionnaire. The estimates relate to fiscal year beginning 1 July. When the scope and coverage of the estimates differ for conceptual or statistical reasons from the definitions and classifications recommended in SNA, a footnote is indicated to the relevant tables.

Sources and methods:

(a) **Gross domestic product.** Gross domestic product is estimated mainly through the production approach.

(b) **Expenditure on the gross domestic product.** All components of GDP by expenditure type are estimated through the expenditure approach except private final consumption expenditure which is obtained as a residual. The estimates of government final consumption expenditure are based on annual statements of the accounts of central and local governments. Change in stocks is estimated on the basis of the production census for all sectors. Gross fixed capital formation of the government sector is estimated from the government accounts and of the private sector from the production census figures for sectors covered by the census questionnaire. Included in the capital formation estimates are the cost of land clearings and imputed values of new huts. The estimates of exports and imports of goods and services are based on balance-of-payments data. Exports and imports of goods have to be adjusted for duty content, in accordance with the Southern African customs union agreement. GDP by expenditure type at constant price is not estimated.

(c) **Cost-structure of the gross domestic product.** Estimates of compensation of employees are obtained from the Census of Production and Distribution (CPD). Data on payment of wages and salaries are distinguished whether paid to residents or to non-residents and are also classified by type. The main source for estimating consumption of fixed capital formation in the private sector is the CPD. For government assets, straight line depreciation is applied, the constant percentage varying for different types of assets. Indirect taxes are extracted from the Accountant-General's annual statement of accounts, the CPD and the Customs Statistics Unit.

(d) **Gross domestic product by kind of economic activity.** The table of gross domestic product by kind of economic activity is prepared at market prices, i.e. producers' values. The production approach is used to estimate value added of almost all industries. The income approach is used for some sub-groups of private services and for producers of government services. For the traditional farming of the agricultural sector, the main source used for crops is the annual agricultural sample survey and for cattle, the sources used include Rural Income Distribution Survey 1974/75 and annual reports of Botswana Meat Commission and the Ministry of Agriculture. The method has been to obtain quantities of production from the above-mentioned sources and apply unit values. Data from the 1974/75 Rural Income Distribution Survey also provided information on milk production for own use and the value of meat consumed. From this survey, detailed input-output activity analysis of the traditional farming sector is being carried out. For the freehold agriculture, the main source has been an attempted census of the accounts of all freehold farmers. For the non-respondents, a scaling up is made by reference to other farms of the same type. The small firms of the mining sector fill in a questionnaire about their accounts, whereas the two large groups of mining companies are interviewed at length. Manufacturing is dominated by Botswana Meat Commission which contributes more than 40 per cent of the sector's product. The main source is the questionnaire for Census of Production and Distribution (CPD). The CPD is based on the income and outlay accounts and balance sheets of a stratified sample of establishments within Botswana, covering all ISIC sectors. The census gives information for estimating the cost of intermediate consumption. The Government Printer's services are included in manufacturing and valued at cost. For construction, the private contractors and the brigades are covered by the CPD. Estimates of construction outlays for sites and services of low-cost housing are supplied by city and town councils while rural hut construction estimates are derived from the Rural Income Distribution Survey 1974/75. Estimates of construction carried out by government departments are derived from the analysis of government accounts. The main source of information for the trade sector is the CPD. The data obtained from this census are inflated to allow for under-coverage. Gross margins are estimated as the difference between sales and purchases of goods for resale. Taxes levied on imported goods are treated as indirect taxes collected by the trade sector. For transport, the main contributor is the transport service rendered by the Rhodesia Railways. The source of information is a series of returns received from General Manager of the Accounting Branch of Rhodesia Railways. Adjustments are made to convert the data to national accounts framework and significant imputations have to be made on the expenditure side. For other private firms of the transport sector, the financial sector and other services, the main source of information is the CPD. Gross output of financial institutions is made up of the actual sale of services and an imputed service charge. Estimates for producers of government services are based on the Annual Statement of Accounts of the Central Government. For the constant price estimates, the CPD data are deflated by a cost-of-living index.

1.1 Expenditure on the Gross Domestic Product, in Current Prices

Million Botswana pula — Fiscal year beginning 1 July

	1980	1983	1984	1985	1986	1987	1988	1989	1990	1991	1992	1993
1 Government final consumption expenditure	203.2	362.8	443.1	531.8	722.6	1052.3	1208.2	...	...	...	...	...
2 Private final consumption expenditure	460.3	615.1	784.8	901.8	987.4	1116.0	1236.5	...	...	...	...	...
A Households	452.9	607.6	771.9	891.6	972.2	1095.5	1211.0	...	...	...	...	...
B Private non-profit institutions serving households	7.4	7.5	12.9	10.2	15.2	20.5	25.5	...	...	...	...	...
3 Gross capital formation	355.8	366.3	555.6	393.3	688.5	277.5	2288.1	...	...	...	...	...
A Increase in stocks	49.2	28.7	71.6	-64.6	18.6	-804.3	56.1	...	...	...	...	...
B Gross fixed capital formation	306.6	337.6	484.0	457.9	669.9	1081.8	2232.0	...	...	...	...	...
Residential buildings	37.4	31.7	37.8	41.0	36.3	119.8	...	...	...	...	...	...
Non-residential buildings	50.8	50.6	46.9	68.5	92.5	178.0	...	...	...	...	...	...
Other construction and land improvement etc.	90.7	114.8	137.3	114.5	177.1	213.6	...	...	...	...	...	...
Other	127.7	140.5	262.0	233.9	364.0	570.4	...	...	...	...	...	...
4 Exports of goods and services [a]	464.5	884.9	1074.5	1737.5	1838.8	3119.0	3706.0	...	...	...	...	...
5 Less: Imports of goods and services [b]	608.3	838.2	1029.4	1143.8	1427.5	1769.2	2966.8	...	...	...	...	...
Statistical discrepancy	-	-	-	-	-	-	...	...	...	...	...	...
Equals: Gross Domestic Product	875.5	1390.9	1828.6	2420.6	2809.8	3795.6	5472.0	6130.1	6995.0	7810.1	...	...

a) Item 'Exports of goods and services' includes exports of goods only.
b) Item 'Imports of goods and services' includes imports of goods plus net imports of services.

1.2 Expenditure on the Gross Domestic Product, in Constant Prices

Million Botswana pula — Fiscal year beginning 1 July

	1980	1983	1984	1985	1986	1987	1988	1989	1990	1991	1992	1993
	\multicolumn{12}{c}{At constant prices of: 1985}											
1 Government final consumption expenditure	302.1	418.7	489.6	531.4	648.8	869.1	...	...	...	...	...	...
2 Private final consumption expenditure	740.0	651.3	772.2	901.8	901.6	941.0	...	...	...	...	...	...
A Households	730.1	643.0	758.7	891.6	887.5	922.0	...	...	...	...	...	...
B Private non-profit institutions serving households	9.9	8.3	13.5	10.2	14.1	18.5	...	...	...	...	...	...
3 Gross capital formation	562.2	454.6	646.4	393.2	577.7	162.0	...	...	...	...	...	...

Botswana

1.2 Expenditure on the Gross Domestic Product, in Constant Prices
(Continued)

Million Botswana pula — Fiscal year beginning 1 July

	1980	1983	1984	1985	1986	1987	1988	1989	1990	1991	1992	1993
					At constant prices of:1985							
A Increase in stocks	80.7	72.5	101.4	-64.7	16.0	-629.1	...	...	...	...	...	...
B Gross fixed capital formation	481.5	382.1	545.0	457.9	561.7	791.1	...	...	...	...	...	...
Residential buildings	60.6	35.2	41.9	41.0	30.2	89.0	...	...	...	...	...	...
Non-residential buildings	78.4	56.2	51.9	68.5	77.0	132.2	...	...	...	...	...	...
Other construction and land improvement etc.	141.1	127.2	151.7	111.5	149.6	158.7	...	...	...	...	...	...
Other	201.4	163.5	299.5	236.9	304.9	411.2	...	...	...	...	...	...
4 Exports of goods and services	844.2	1481.1	1429.8	1737.5	1728.9	2352.3	...	...	...	...	...	...
5 Less: Imports of goods and services	971.1	980.3	1164.0	1143.8	1209.9	1461.0	...	...	...	...	...	...
Statistical discrepancy	33.7	75.8	77.9	0.5	-10.9	175.3	...	...	...	...	...	...
Equals: Gross Domestic Product	1511.1	2101.2	2251.9	2420.6	2636.2	3038.7	3437.4	3633.6	3954.5	4209.5	...	...

1.3 Cost Components of the Gross Domestic Product

Million Botswana pula — Fiscal year beginning 1 July

	1980	1983	1984	1985	1986	1987	1988	1989	1990	1991	1992	1993
1 Indirect taxes, net	120.6	165.4	155.0	153.4	215.5	232.1	292.7	...	...	...	...	...
A Indirect taxes	121.7	166.1	160.4	160.4	226.2	251.2	313.9	...	...	...	...	...
B Less: Subsidies	1.1	0.7	5.4	7.0	10.7	19.1	21.2	...	...	...	...	...
2 Consumption of fixed capital	135.5	243.7	278.4	349.8	432.4	575.6	811.2	...	...	...	...	...
3 Compensation of employees paid by resident producers to:	315.3	507.3	602.2	700.7	849.6	1051.6	1492.7	...	...	...	...	...
A Resident households	312.5	506.7	601.9	700.5	849.5	1051.6	1492.7	...	...	...	...	...
B Rest of the world	2.6	0.6	0.3	0.2	0.1	-	-	...	...	...	...	...
4 Operating surplus	304.1	474.5	793.0	1216.7	1312.3	1936.3	2875.4	...	...	...	...	...
A Corporate and quasi-corporate enterprises	226.4	403.1	709.6	993.5	1205.8	...	...	...	...	...	...	...
B Private unincorporated enterprises	77.7	71.4	80.8	89.7	106.1	...	...	...	...	...	...	...
C General government	-	-	2.6	1.6	0.4	...	...	...	...	...	...	...
Equals: Gross Domestic Product	875.5	1390.9	1828.6	2420.6	2809.8	3795.6	5472.0	...	...	...	...	...

1.4 General Government Current Receipts and Disbursements

Million Botswana pula — Fiscal year beginning 1 July

	1980	1983	1984	1985	1986	1987	1988	1989	1990	1991	1992	1993
					Receipts							
1 Operating surplus	-	-	2.6	1.6	0.4	-	...	...	...	...	...	...
2 Property and entrepreneurial income	61.5	111.3	192.1	524.4	701.2	742.9	...	...	...	...	...	...
3 Taxes, fees and contributions	221.6	320.7	440.8	433.4	932.1	1233.3	...	...	...	...	...	...
A Indirect taxes	120.9	165.4	160.4	166.5	222.8	274.0	...	...	...	...	...	...
B Direct taxes	98.4	155.3	280.4	266.9	709.3	959.3	...	...	...	...	...	...
C Social security contributions	-	-	-	-	-	-	...	...	...	...	...	...
D Compulsory fees, fines and penalties	2.3	-	-	-	-	-	...	...	...	...	...	...
4 Other current transfers	13.0	37.2	40.6	321.8	112.0	138.4	...	...	...	...	...	...
Total Current Receipts of General Government	296.1	469.2	676.1	1281.2	1745.7	2114.6	...	...	...	...	...	...
					Disbursements							
1 Government final consumption expenditure	203.2	362.8	443.1	531.8	722.6	1052.3	...	...	...	...	...	...
A Compensation of employees	103.9	161.6	200.9	232.5	289.6	362.1	...	...	...	...	...	...
B Consumption of fixed capital	31.0	63.0	73.8	93.2	138.7	200.8	...	...	...	...	...	...
C Purchases of goods and services, net	68.2	138.2	168.4	206.1	294.3	489.4	...	...	...	...	...	...
D Less: Own account fixed capital formation	...	...	...	...	...	...	...	...	...	...	...	...
E Indirect taxes paid, net	0.1	-	-	-	-	-	...	...	...	...	...	...
2 Property income	4.9	13.9	21.7	23.6	40.5	44.9	...	...	...	...	...	...
A Interest	4.9	13.9	21.7	23.6	40.5	44.9	...	...	...	...	...	...
B Net land rent and royalties	...	...	...	...	...	...	...	...	...	...	...	...

Botswana

1.4 General Government Current Receipts and Disbursements
(Continued)

Million Botswana pula — Fiscal year beginning 1 July

	1980	1983	1984	1985	1986	1987	1988	1989	1990	1991	1992	1993
3 Subsidies	...	...	...	...	...	...	...	...	...	...	...	...
4 Other current transfers	31.0	58.7	72.8	101.5	140.5	158.5	...	...	...	...	...	...
A Social security benefits	...	...	...	...	...	...	...	...	...	...	...	...
B Social assistance grants	20.4	40.6	40.1	24.4	35.5	...	...	...	...	...	...	...
C Other	10.6	18.1	32.7	77.1	105.0	...	...	...	...	...	...	...
5 Net saving	57.0	33.8	138.5	624.3	842.1	858.9	...	...	...	...	...	...
Total Current Disbursements and Net Saving of General Government	296.1	469.2	676.1	1281.2	1745.7	2114.6	...	...	...	...	...	...

1.5 Current Income and Outlay of Corporate and Quasi-Corporate Enterprises, Summary

Million Botswana pula — Fiscal year beginning 1 July

	1980	1983	1984	1985	1986	1987	1988	1989	1990	1991	1992	1993
Receipts												
1 Operating surplus	226.4	403.1	709.6	993.5	1205.8	1701.8	...	...	...	...	...	...
2 Property and entrepreneurial income received	81.7	118.9	283.4	213.8	286.6	355.3	...	...	...	...	...	...
3 Current transfers [a]	77.3	48.4	80.4	155.2	137.4	178.9	...	...	...	...	...	...
Total Current Receipts	385.4	570.4	1073.4	1362.5	1629.8	2236.0	...	...	...	...	...	...
Disbursements												
1 Property and entrepreneurial income	277.7	389.8	673.6	1074.6	1301.3	1518.5	...	...	...	...	...	...
2 Direct taxes and other current payments to general government	77.0	121.0	240.4	208.5	609.5	956.1	...	...	...	...	...	...
3 Other current transfers	88.4	90.6	142.3	328.8	107.0	390.9	...	...	...	...	...	...
4 Net saving	-57.7	-31.0	17.1	-249.4	-388.0	-629.5	...	...	...	...	...	...
Total Current Disbursements and Net Saving	385.4	570.4	1073.4	1362.5	1629.8	2236.0	...	...	...	...	...	...

a) Item 'Current transfers' includes imputed intercompany transfers.

1.6 Current Income and Outlay of Households and Non-Profit Institutions

Million Botswana pula — Fiscal year beginning 1 July

	1980	1983	1984	1985	1986	1987	1988	1989	1990	1991	1992	1993
Receipts												
1 Compensation of employees	333.2	536.4	630.8	731.7	893.3	1112.1	...	...	...	...	...	...
A From resident producers	312.7	506.7	601.9	700.5	849.5	1051.6	...	...	...	...	...	...
B From rest of the world	20.5	29.7	28.9	31.2	43.8	60.5	...	...	...	...	...	...
2 Operating surplus of private unincorporated enterprises	77.7	71.4	80.8	89.7	106.1	234.5	...	...	...	...	...	...
3 Property and entrepreneurial income	17.9	44.2	5.0	18.2	65.5	6.8	...	...	...	...	...	...
4 Current transfers	23.0	91.9	120.5	70.9	59.2	164.6	...	...	...	...	...	...
Total Current Receipts	451.8	743.9	837.1	910.5	1124.1	1518.0	...	...	...	...	...	...
Disbursements												
1 Private final consumption expenditure	460.2	615.1	784.8	851.4	958.5	1116.0	...	...	...	...	...	...
2 Property income	3.4	6.2	7.0	-	-	43.5	...	...	...	...	...	...
3 Direct taxes and other current transfers n.e.c. to general government	21.4	34.3	40.0	69.4	99.8	30.0	...	...	...	...	...	...
A Social security contributions	-	-	-	-	-	-	...	...	...	...	...	...
B Direct taxes	21.4	34.3	40.0	69.4	99.8	30.0	...	...	...	...	...	...
C Fees, fines and penalties	...	...	...	...	...	...	...	...	...	...	...	...
4 Other current transfers	16.1	5.0	7.0	46.5	23.8	44.3	...	...	...	...	...	...
5 Net saving	-49.3	83.3	-1.7	-56.8	42.0	284.2	...	...	...	...	...	...
Total Current Disbursements and Net Saving	451.8	743.9	837.1	910.5	1124.1	1518.0	...	...	...	...	...	...

Botswana

1.7 External Transactions on Current Account, Summary

Million Botswana pula — Fiscal year beginning 1 July

	1980	1983	1984	1985	1986	1987	1988	1989	1990	1991	1992	1993
Payments to the Rest of the World												
1 Imports of goods and services [a]	608.3	838.2	1029.4	1143.8	1427.5	1769.2	...	...	...	...	...	...
A Imports of merchandise c.i.f.	495.1	682.1	870.9	991.0	1248.0	1556.6	...	...	...	...	...	...
B Other	113.2	156.1	158.5	152.8	179.5	212.6	...	...	...	...	...	...
2 Factor income to the rest of the world	157.4	196.5	313.2	495.8	477.9	773.8	...	...	...	...	...	...
A Compensation of employees	2.6	0.6	0.3	0.2	0.1	-	...	...	...	...	...	...
B Property and entrepreneurial income	154.8	195.9	312.9	495.6	477.8	773.8	...	...	...	...	...	...
3 Current transfers to the rest of the world	24.2	5.9	5.0	68.5	78.6	233.3	...	...	...	...	...	...
A Indirect taxes to supranational organizations	...	...	...	...	...	...	...	...	...	...	...	...
B Other current transfers	24.2	5.9	5.0	68.5	78.6	233.3	...	...	...	...	...	...
4 Surplus of the nation on current transactions	-270.9	-34.7	-128.7	343.9	203.8	766.5	...	...	...	...	...	...
Payments to the Rest of the World and Surplus of the Nation on Current Transactions	519.0	1005.9	1218.9	2052.0	2187.8	3542.8	...	...	...	...	...	...
Receipts From The Rest of the World												
1 Exports of goods and services [b]	464.5	884.9	1074.5	1737.5	1838.8	3119.0	...	...	...	...	...	...
A Exports of merchandise f.o.b.	398.0	772.3	970.3	1591.6	1696.4	2989.3	...	...	...	...	...	...
B Other	66.5	112.6	104.2	145.9	142.4	129.7	...	...	...	...	...	...
2 Factor income from rest of the world	46.4	91.6	118.0	173.0	225.9	308.7	...	...	...	...	...	...
A Compensation of employees	20.5	29.7	28.9	31.2	43.8	60.5	...	...	...	...	...	...
B Property and entrepreneurial income	25.9	61.9	89.1	141.8	182.1	248.2	...	...	...	...	...	...
3 Current transfers from rest of the world [c]	8.1	29.4	26.4	141.5	123.1	115.1	...	...	...	...	...	...
A Subsidies from supranational organisations	...	...	...	...	...	...	...	...	...	...	...	...
B Other current transfers	8.1	29.4	26.4	141.5	123.1	115.1	...	...	...	...	...	...
Receipts from the Rest of the World on Current Transactions	519.0	1005.9	1218.9	2052.0	2187.8	3542.8	...	...	...	...	...	...

a) Item 'Imports of goods and services' includes imports of goods plus net imports of services.
b) Item 'Exports of goods and services' includes exports of goods only.
c) For 1973-75, item 'Current transfers from the rest of the world' refers to current and capital transfers which are net. Beginning 1976, current and capital transfers are gross, excluding loan waivers and direct grants which are assumed to be capital transfers.

1.8 Capital Transactions of The Nation, Summary

Million Botswana pula — Fiscal year beginning 1 July

	1980	1983	1984	1985	1986	1987	1988	1989	1990	1991	1992	1993
Finance of Gross Capital Formation												
Gross saving	84.9	331.6	426.9	737.2	892.3	1044.0	...	...	...	...	...	...
1 Consumption of fixed capital	135.5	243.7	278.4	349.8	432.4	575.6	...	...	...	...	...	...
A General government	31.0	63.0	73.8	93.2	138.7	200.8	...	...	...	...	...	...
B Corporate and quasi-corporate enterprises	96.2	168.1	191.5	241.5	275.8	351.8	...	...	...	...	...	...
Public	8.2	29.1	23.0	31.1	33.1	51.4	...	...	...	...	...	...
Private	88.0	139.0	168.5	210.4	242.7	300.4	...	...	...	...	...	...
C Other	8.3	12.6	13.1	15.1	17.9	23.0	...	...	...	...	...	...
2 Net saving	-50.6	87.9	148.5	387.4	459.9	468.4	...	...	...	...	...	...
A General government	57.0	33.8	138.5	624.3	842.1	...	...	...	...	...	...	...
B Corporate and quasi-corporate enterprises	-57.7	-31.0	17.1	-249.4	-388.0	...	...	...	...	...	...	...
Public	-1.0	2.6	13.1	3.1	35.1	...	...	...	...	...	...	...
Private	-56.7	-33.6	4.0	-252.5	-423.1	...	...	...	...	...	...	...
C Other	-49.9	85.1	-7.1	12.5	5.8	...	...	...	...	...	...	...
Less: Surplus of the nation on current transactions	-270.9	-34.7	-128.7	343.9	203.8	766.5	...	...	...	...	...	...
Finance of Gross Capital Formation	355.8	366.3	555.6	393.3	688.5	277.5	...	...	...	...	...	...
Gross Capital Formation												
Increase in stocks	49.2	28.7	71.6	-64.6	18.6	-804.3	...	...	...	...	...	...

Botswana

1.8 Capital Transactions of The Nation, Summary
(Continued)

Million Botswana pula — Fiscal year beginning 1 July

	1980	1983	1984	1985	1986	1987	1988	1989	1990	1991	1992	1993
Gross fixed capital formation	306.6	337.6	484.0	457.9	669.9	1081.8	...	...	...	...	...	...
1 General government	90.1	126.3	184.1	197.1	312.5	588.9	...	...	...	...	...	...
2 Corporate and quasi-corporate enterprises	205.5	197.4	284.1	184.9	229.1	...	...	...	...	...	...	...
A Public [a]	35.7	90.7	210.8	39.0	101.4	...	...	...	...	...	...	...
B Private	169.8	106.7	73.3	145.9	127.7	...	...	...	...	...	...	...
3 Other	11.0	13.9	15.8	75.9	128.3	...	...	...	...	...	...	...
Gross Capital Formation	355.8	366.3	555.6	393.3	688.5	277.5	...	...	...	...	...	...

a) Item 'Public' of Corporate and quasi-corporate enterprises refers to non-financial sector only.

1.10 Gross Domestic Product by Kind of Activity, in Current Prices

Million Botswana pula — Fiscal year beginning 1 July

	1980	1983	1984	1985	1986	1987	1988	1989	1990	1991	1992	1993
1 Agriculture, hunting, forestry and fishing	109.1	103.5	118.8	132.4	143.9	268.0	300.8	334.5	361.3	397.4	...	...
2 Mining and quarrying	241.3	466.4	753.1	1133.9	1229.8	1702.5	2918.4	2846.4	2960.3	3072.3	...	...
3 Manufacturing	48.3	80.6	86.6	124.2	167.9	192.4	239.5	268.3	299.6	340.7	...	...
4 Electricity, gas and water	19.3	32.3	42.9	57.7	72.2	107.0	122.4	136.7	161.1	179.0	...	...
5 Construction	69.0	94.8	97.4	96.0	132.3	185.2	259.3	337.1	393.4	460.3	...	...
6 Wholesale and retail trade, restaurants and hotels	64.6	88.0	113.5	164.7	180.9	213.0	563.6	767.8	974.7	1183.3	...	...
7 Transport, storage and communication	21.8	41.4	49.7	66.5	59.1	97.9	117.1	137.0	175.6	215.6	...	...
8 Finance, insurance, real estate and business services	53.8	87.4	112.0	145.2	167.4	190.6	241.7	273.5	336.3	389.7	...	...
9 Community, social and personal services	7.7	10.3	16.8	21.5	28.7	35.0	118.4	137.2	166.0	199.2	...	...
Total, Industries	634.9	1004.7	1390.8	1942.1	2182.2	2991.6	4881.2	5238.5	5828.3	6437.5	...	...
Producers of Government Services	135.0	224.6	274.7	325.7	428.3	562.9	685.1	998.4	1284.2	1507.7	...	...
Other Producers	19.5	33.2	38.5	45.2	52.8	67.8	...	...	...	...	...	...
Subtotal	789.4	1262.5	1704.0	2313.0	2663.3	3622.3	5566.3	6236.9	7112.5	7945.2	...	...
Less: Imputed bank service charge	17.6	28.9	30.6	47.6	56.7	74.2	94.3	106.8	117.5	135.1	...	...
Plus: Import duties	103.7	157.3	155.2	155.2	203.2	247.5	...	...	...	...	...	...
Plus: Value added tax	...	...	...	...	...	...	...	...	...	...	...	...
Equals: Gross Domestic Product [a]	875.5	1390.9	1828.6	2420.6	2809.8	3795.6	5472.0	6130.1	6995.0	7810.1	...	...

a) Data in this table have not been revised, therefore they are not comparable with the data in other tables.

1.11 Gross Domestic Product by Kind of Activity, in Constant Prices

Million Botswana pula — Fiscal year beginning 1 July

	1980	1983	1984	1985	1986	1987	1988	1989	1990	1991	1992	1993
	\multicolumn{12}{c}{At constant prices of:1985}
1 Agriculture, hunting, forestry and fishing	158.3	122.4	119.5	132.4	122.8	203.2	202.6	209.9	215.6	219.9	...	...
2 Mining and quarrying	530.3	1065.6	1099.7	1133.9	1225.6	1260.0	1474.2	1425.6	1521.1	1550.0	...	...
3 Manufacturing	100.6	119.9	95.5	124.2	146.4	190.1	200.4	210.0	223.8	238.2	...	...
4 Electricity, gas and water	28.1	35.8	43.2	57.7	63.9	73.1	82.4	84.2	91.3	96.5	...	...
5 Construction	116.4	105.1	108.1	96.0	111.4	131.6	171.4	188.2	202.0	211.2	...	...
6 Wholesale and retail trade, restaurants and hotels	265.8	239.9	287.7	319.9	340.8	394.7	453.9	513.8	558.0	642.5	...	...
7 Transport, storage and communication	28.3	39.9	50.9	66.5	65.7	103.4	110.3	117.9	136.3	150.1	...	...
8 Finance, insurance, real estate and business services	72.6	93.9	119.2	145.2	145.7	155.7	172.4	193.4	209.6	217.8	...	...
9 Community, social and personal services	35.0	47.7	58.6	66.7	74.2	96.9	101.2	103.2	110.4	116.4	...	...
Total, Industries	1335.4	1870.2	1982.4	2142.5	2296.5	2608.7	2968.8	3046.2	3268.1	3442.6	...	...
Producers of Government Services	199.8	263.3	301.7	325.7	392.2	491.0	538.6	659.3	756.2	839.1	...	...
Other Producers	...	...	...	...	...	...	...	...	...	...	...	...
Subtotal	1535.2	2133.5	2284.1	2468.2	2688.7	3099.7	3507.4	3705.5	4024.3	4281.7	...	...
Less: Imputed bank service charge	24.1	32.3	32.2	47.6	52.5	61.0	70.0	71.9	69.9	72.1	...	...
Plus: Import duties	...	...	...	...	...	...	...	...	...	...	...	...
Plus: Value added tax	...	...	...	...	...	...	...	...	...	...	...	...
Equals: Gross Domestic Product [a]	1511.1	2101.2	2251.9	2420.6	2636.2	3038.7	3437.4	3633.6	3954.5	4209.5	...	...

a) Data in this table have not been revised, therefore they are not comparable with the data in other tables.

Botswana

1.12 Relations Among National Accounting Aggregates

Million Botswana pula — Fiscal year beginning 1 July

	1980	1983	1984	1985	1986	1987	1988	1989	1990	1991	1992	1993
Gross Domestic Product	875.5	1390.9	1828.6	2420.6	2809.8	3795.6	...	...	...	...	...	...
Plus: Net factor income from the rest of the world	-111.0	-104.9	-195.2	-322.8	-252.0	-465.1	...	...	...	...	...	...
Factor income from the rest of the world	46.4	91.6	118.0	173.0	225.9	308.7	...	...	...	...	...	...
Less: Factor income to the rest of the world	157.4	196.5	313.2	495.8	477.9	773.8	...	...	...	...	...	...
Equals: Gross National Product	764.5	1286.0	1633.4	2097.8	2557.8	3330.5	...	...	...	...	...	...
Less: Consumption of fixed capital	135.5	243.7	278.4	349.8	432.4	575.6	...	...	...	...	...	...
Equals: National Income	629.0	1042.3	1355.0	1748.0	2125.4	2754.9	...	...	...	...	...	...
Plus: Net current transfers from the rest of the world	-16.1	23.5	21.4	73.0	44.5	-118.2	...	...	...	...	...	...
Current transfers from the rest of the world	8.1	29.4	26.4	141.5	123.2	115.1	...	...	...	...	...	...
Less: Current transfers to the rest of the world	24.2	5.9	5.0	68.5	78.6	233.3	...	...	...	...	...	...
Equals: National Disposable Income	612.9	1065.8	1376.4	1821.0	2169.9	2636.7	...	...	...	...	...	...
Less: Final consumption	663.5	977.9	1227.9	1433.6	1710.0	2168.3	...	...	...	...	...	...
Statistical discrepancy [a]	-	-	-	-	-	-	...	...	...	...	...	...
Equals: Net Saving	-50.6	87.9	148.5	387.4	459.9	468.4	...	...	...	...	...	...
Less: Surplus of the nation on current transactions	-270.9	-34.7	-128.7	343.9	203.8	766.5	...	...	...	...	...	...
Statistical discrepancy [b]	-	-	-	-	-	-	...	...	...	...	...	...
Equals: Net Capital Formation	220.3	122.6	277.2	43.5	256.1	-298.1	...	...	...	...	...	...

a) Item 'Statistical discrepancy' refers to discrepancy in income and outlay account.
b) Item 'Statistical discrepancy' refers to discrepancy in capital finance account.

Brazil

Source. Reply to the United Nations National Accounts Questionnaire from the Instituto Brasileiro de Geografia e Estatística, in the DECNA, Departamento de Contas Nacionais, Rio de Janeiro. The official estimates are shown in a series of publications entitled 'Conjuntura Economica'. On 28 February 1986, the cruzado, equal to 1,000 cruzeiros, was introduced. On 15 January 1989, the new cruzado, equal to 1,000 old cruzado, was introduced. On 16 March 1990, the cruzeiro, equal to 1 new cruzado, was introduced. On 1 August 1993, the cruzeiro real, equal to 1,000 cruzeiros, was introduced. On July 1, 1994 the Real, equal to 2,750 cruzeiros reais was introduced. However, the estimates are in cruzeiros reais.

General note. The estimates shown in the following tables have been prepared in accordance with the United Nations System of National Accounts so far as the existing data would permit.

1.1 Expenditure on the Gross Domestic Product, in Current Prices

Thousand Cruzeiros reais

	1980	1983	1984	1985	1986	1987	1988	1989	1990	1991	1992	1993
1 Government final consumption expenditure	1	11	32	137	391	1403	10865	181356	... 5058	23812	280325	...
2 Private final consumption expenditure	9	84	272	909	2482	7183	51169	729530	... 20019	106206	1152717	...
3 Gross capital formation	3	19	61	265	699	2573	19666	314869	... 7037	31272	352288	...
A Increase in stocks	-	-2	-4	31	-	-	-	-	... ...	...	...	...
B Gross fixed capital formation	3	21	65	234	699	2573	19666	314869	... 7037	31272	352288	...
Residential buildings									...	...	...	...
Non-residential buildings	2	14	44	159	493	1848	13200	224153	...	...	...	...
Other construction and land improvement etc.									...	...	...	...
Other	1	7	21	75	206	725	6466	90716	...	...	...	...
4 Exports of goods and services	1	13	52	169	323	1091	9425	104511	... 2345	14044	178249	...
5 Less: Imports of goods and services	1	11	31	98	233	714	4928	63918	... 1814	10848	116766	...
Equals: Gross Domestic Product [a]	12	117	386	1383	3662	11537	86197	1266348	32646	164486	1846813	...

a) Beginning 1990, the estimates are in million Cruzeiros Reais.

1.2 Expenditure on the Gross Domestic Product, in Constant Prices

Cruzeiros reais

	1980	1983	1984	1985	1986	1987	1988	1989	1990	1991	1992	1993
					At constant prices of:1980							
1 Government final consumption expenditure	10000	9000	9000	10000	11000	11000	11000	11000	...	...	...	...
2 Private final consumption expenditure									...	...	...	...
3 Gross capital formation	3000	2000	2000	2000	3000	3000	3000	3000	...	...	...	...
A Increase in stocks	-	-	-	-	-	-	-	-	...	...	...	...
B Gross fixed capital formation	3000	2000	2000	2000	3000	3000	3000	3000	...	...	...	...
4 Exports of goods and services	1000	1000	2000	2000	2000	2000	2000	2000	...	...	...	...
5 Less: Imports of goods and services	1000	1000	1000	1000	1000	1000	1000	1000	...	...	...	...
Equals: Gross Domestic Product	12000	12000	12000	13000	14000	15000	15000	15000	...	...	...	...

1.3 Cost Components of the Gross Domestic Product

Thousand Cruzeiros reais

	1980	1983	1984	1985	1986	1987	1988	1989	1990	1991	1992	1993
1 Indirect taxes, net	2	12	34	124	403	1154	8328	111992	...	...	...	...
A Indirect taxes	2	15	40	146	457	1337	9384	136407	...	...	...	...
B Less: Subsidies	-	3	6	22	54	183	1056	24415	...	...	...	...
2 Consumption of fixed capital [a]	...	...	...	...	...	...	...	...	...	...	...	...
3 Compensation of employees paid by resident producers to:	11	105	352	1258	3259	10383	77869	1154356	...	...	...	...
4 Operating surplus [a]									...	...	...	...
Equals: Gross Domestic Product	12	117	386	1383	3662	11537	86197	1266348	...	...	...	...

a) Item 'Operating surplus' includes consumption of fixed capital.

Brazil

1.4 General Government Current Receipts and Disbursements

Thousand Cruzeiros reais

	1980	1983	1984	1985	1986	1987	1988	1989	1990	1991	1992	1993
Receipts												
1 Operating surplus	...	...	...	...	...	...	...	...	...	...	...	...
2 Property and entrepreneurial income	...	...	...	...	...	...	...	...	...	...	...	...
3 Taxes, fees and contributions	3	29	84	311	929	2693	18868	277873	...	...	...	...
A Indirect taxes	2	15	40	146	457	1337	9384	136407	...	...	...	...
B Direct taxes	1	14	44	165	472	1356	9484	141466	...	...	...	...
C Social security contributions	...	...	...	...	...	...	...	...	...	...	...	...
D Compulsory fees, fines and penalties	...	...	...	...	...	...	...	...	...	...	...	...
4 Other current transfers	-	-2	-3	-12	-61	204	2351	52638	...	...	...	...
Total Current Receipts of General Government	3	28	81	299	868	2897	21220	330512	...	...	...	...
Disbursements												
1 Government final consumption expenditure	1	11	32	137	391	1403	10865	181356	...	...	...	...
2 Property income	...	...	...	...	...	...	...	...	...	...	...	...
3 Subsidies	-	3	6	22	54	183	1056	24415	...	...	...	...
4 Other current transfers	1	15	54	254	683	2018	20108	378778	...	...	...	...
5 Net saving	-	-2	-11	-113	-261	-707	-10810	-254037	...	...	...	...
Total Current Disbursements and Net Saving of General Government	3	28	81	299	868	2897	21220	330512	...	...	...	...

1.7 External Transactions on Current Account, Summary

Thousand Cruzeiros reais

	1980	1983	1984	1985	1986	1987	1988	1989	1990	1991	1992	1993
Payments to the Rest of the World												
1 Imports of goods and services	1	11	31	98	233	714	4928	63918	...	...	...	...
2 Factor income to the rest of the world	1	7	25	86	182	475	3729	43116	...	...	...	...
A Compensation of employees	-	-	-	-	-	4	33	351	...	...	...	...
B Property and entrepreneurial income	1	7	25	86	182	471	3696	42765	...	...	...	...
3 Current transfers to the rest of the world	-	-	-	-	1	4	10	59	...	...	...	...
4 Surplus of the nation on current transactions	-1	-4	-	-1	-72	-56	1103	2906	...	...	...	...
Payments to the Rest of the World and Surplus of the Nation on Current Transactions	1	14	56	183	343	1137	9769	109999	...	...	...	...
Receipts From The Rest of the World												
1 Exports of goods and services	1	13	52	169	323	1091	9425	104511	...	...	...	...
2 Factor income from rest of the world	-	1	3	13	19	39	309	4744	...	...	...	...
A Compensation of employees	-	-	-	-	-	-	2	14	...	...	...	...
B Property and entrepreneurial income	-	1	3	13	18	39	307	4730	...	...	...	...
3 Current transfers from rest of the world	-	-	-	1	2	6	35	745	...	...	...	...
Receipts from the Rest of the World on Current Transactions	1	14	56	183	343	1137	9769	109999	...	...	...	...

1.10 Gross Domestic Product by Kind of Activity, in Current Prices

Thousand Cruzeiros reais

	1980	1983	1984	1985	1986	1987	1988	1989	1990	1991	1992	1993
1 Agriculture, hunting, forestry and fishing	1	12	40	145	364	1039	7914	98799	...	...	...	...
2 Mining and quarrying	-	2	13	41	87	231	1500	18086	...	...	...	...
3 Manufacturing	4	35	119	425	1074	3318	24218	342465	...	...	...	...
4 Electricity, gas and water	-	2	8	29	77	339	2173	28083	...	...	...	...
5 Construction	1	7	21	76	234	876	6257	106250	...	...	...	...

Brazil

1.10 Gross Domestic Product by Kind of Activity, in Current Prices
(Continued)

Thousand Cruzeiros reais

	1980	1983	1984	1985	1986	1987	1988	1989	1990	1991	1992	1993
6 Wholesale and retail trade, restaurants and hotels	1	11	34	114	283	838	6314	90176	...	...	...	...
7 Transport, storage and communication	1	6	19	67	165	543	4247	63983	...	...	...	...
8 Finance, insurance, real estate and business services	2	24	76	277	573	2693	21093	416165	...	...	...	...
9 Community, social and personal services	1	13	42	147	382	1194	9490	147752	...	...	...	...
Total, Industries	11	112	372	1321	3239	11071	83206	1311759	...	...	...	...
Producers of Government Services	1	8	22	96	267	896	6830	123056	...	...	...	...
Other Producers	...	...	...	...	...	...	...	...	...	...	...	...
Subtotal a	12	120	394	1417	3506	11967	90036	1434815	...	...	...	...
Less: Imputed bank service charge	1	14	42	159	247	1584	12165	280458	...	...	...	...
Plus: Import duties	...	...	...	...	...	...	...	...	...	...	...	...
Plus: Value added tax	...	...	...	...	...	...	...	...	...	...	...	...
Plus: Other adjustments b	1	11	34	125	403	1154	8326	111991	...	...	...	...
Equals: Gross Domestic Product	12	117	386	1383	3662	11537	86197	1266348	...	...	...	...

a) Gross domestic product in factor values.
b) Item 'Other adjustments' refers to indirect taxes net of subsidies.

1.12 Relations Among National Accounting Aggregates

Thousand Cruzeiros reais

	1980	1983	1984	1985	1986	1987	1988	1989	1990	1991	1992	1993
Gross Domestic Product a	12	117	386	1383	3662	11537	86197	1266348	32646	164486	1846813	...
Plus: Net factor income from the rest of the world a	-	-7	-22	-74	-163	-436	-3420	-38373	-646	-4407	-42280	...
Factor income from the rest of the world	-	1	3	13	19	39	309	4744	...	...	...	...
Less: Factor income to the rest of the world	1	7	25	86	182	475	3729	43116	...	...	...	...
Equals: Gross National Product a	12	110	364	1309	3499	11101	82777	1227975	31802	160079	1804533	...
Less: Consumption of fixed capital	...	...	...	...	...	...	...	...	...	...	...	...
Equals: National Income b	12	110	364	1309	3499	11101	82777	1227975	...	...	...	...
Plus: Net current transfers from the rest of the world	-	-	-	1	1	3	25	686	...	...	...	...
Current transfers from the rest of the world	-	-	-	1	2	6	35	745	...	...	...	...
Less: Current transfers to the rest of the world	-	-	-	-	1	4	10	59	...	...	...	...
Equals: National Disposable Income c	12	110	364	1310	3500	11103	82803	1228661	...	...	...	...
Less: Final consumption	10	95	304	1046	2873	8586	62034	910887	...	...	...	...
Equals: Net Saving d	2	16	61	264	627	2517	20768	317775	...	...	...	...
Less: Surplus of the nation on current transactions	-1	-4	-	-1	-72	-56	1103	2906	...	...	...	...
Equals: Net Capital Formation e	3	20	61	265	699	2573	19665	314869	...	...	...	...

a) Beginning 1990, the estimates are in million Cruzeiros Reais.
b) Item 'National income' includes consumption of fixed capital.
c) Item 'National disposable income' includes consumption of fixed capital.
d) Item 'Net saving' includes consumption of fixed capital.
e) Item 'Net capital formation' includes consumption of fixed capital.

British Virgin Islands

Source. Statistics Office, Finance Department, Road Town, Tortola. The official estimates are published by the Development Planning Unit in 'National Accounts Statistics'.

General note. The estimates shown in the following tables have been prepared in accordance with the United Nations System of National Accounts so far as the existing data would permit.

1.1 Expenditure on the Gross Domestic Product, in Current Prices

Thousand United States dollars

		1980	1983	1984	1985	1986	1987	1988	1989	1990	1991	1992	1993
1	Government final consumption expenditure	7120	14290	16840	16910	18730	20230	26350	32400	...	...	...	...
2	Private final consumption expenditure	40010	57210	63110	66990	71310	85930	90460	101330	...	...	...	...
3	Gross capital formation	22320	33170	34960	35970	39810	45700	48580	53350	...	...	...	...
	A Increase in stocks [a]	2350	2000	2120	2260	2420	2680	3520	4050	...	...	...	...
	B Gross fixed capital formation	19970	31170	32840	33710	37390	43020	45060	49300	...	...	...	...
4	Exports of goods and services	36850	68580	75910	87280	98370	111410	141300	163760	...	...	...	...
5	Less: Imports of goods and services	52120	94670	104520	117270	130400	146610	175350	194640	...	...	...	...
	Equals: Gross Domestic Product	54170	78570	86300	89880	97820	116660	131340	156200	...	...	...	...

a) Item 'Increase in stocks' includes also unrecorded increase in stocks.

1.3 Cost Components of the Gross Domestic Product

Thousand United States dollars

		1980	1983	1984	1985	1986	1987	1988	1989	1990	1991	1992	1993
1	Indirect taxes, net	...	...	8400	9480	11240	15140	17620	23750	...	...	...	...
	A Indirect taxes	...	...	9710	10580	12030	15970	18320	24850	...	...	...	...
	B Less: Subsidies	...	...	1310	1100	790	830	700	1100	...	...	...	...
2	Consumption of fixed capital	...	...	11590	9580	9550	13530	14250	23220	...	...	...	...
3	Compensation of employees paid by resident producers to:	...	...	41380	41550	42960	47810	54820	59830	...	...	...	...
4	Operating surplus	...	...	24930	29270	34070	40180	44650	49400	...	...	...	...
	Equals: Gross Domestic Product	...	...	86300	89880	97820	116660	131340	156200	...	...	...	...

1.4 General Government Current Receipts and Disbursements

Thousand United States dollars

		1980	1983	1984	1985	1986	1987	1988	1989	1990	1991	1992	1993
						Receipts							
1	Operating surplus	...	...	...	...	...	...	...	...	...	...	...	...
2	Property and entrepreneurial income	678	1005	2500	2500	2690	3040	3370	3780	...	...	...	...
3	Taxes, fees and contributions	10645	17873	19010	18660	20900	25700	29660	40610	...	...	...	...
	A Indirect taxes	6389	9373	9700	10570	12010	15970	18320	24850	...	...	...	...
	B Direct taxes	3447	5899	6550	5290	5850	6350	7500	11570	...	...	...	...
	C Social security contributions	809	2601	2760	2800	3040	3380	3840	4190	...	...	...	...
	D Compulsory fees, fines and penalties	...	...	...	...	...	...	...	...	...	...	...	...
4	Other current transfers	1369	1695	1920	1860	2060	2240	3410	3510	...	...	...	...
	Total Current Receipts of General Government	12692	20573	23430	23020	25650	30980	36440	47900	...	...	...	...
						Disbursements							
1	Government final consumption expenditure	7120	14286	16840	16910	18730	20460	25850	32400	...	...	...	...
2	Property income	99	48	50	40	30	50	50	70	...	...	...	...
3	Subsidies	490	880	1310	1100	790	830	700	1100	...	...	...	...
4	Other current transfers	810	1394	1970	1940	2740	2900	3440	4130	...	...	...	...
	A Social security benefits	-	214	210	280	300	370	470	560	...	...	...	...
	B Social assistance grants	...	...	790	910	1170	1260	1560	1920	...	...	...	...
	C Other	810	1180	970	750	1270	1270	1410	1650	...	...	...	...
5	Net saving	4173	3965	3260	3030	3360	6740	6400	10200	...	...	...	...
	Total Current Disbursements and Net Saving of General Government	12692	20573	23430	23020	25650	30980	36440	47900	...	...	...	...

British Virgin Islands

1.5 Current Income and Outlay of Corporate and Quasi-Corporate Enterprises, Summary

Thousand United States dollars

	1980	1983	1984	1985	1986	1987	1988	1989	1990	1991	1992	1993
Receipts												
1 Operating surplus	...	...	7620	11190	15400	20380	25940	30340	...	...	...	...
2 Property and entrepreneurial income received	...	...	16530	19430	20660	23310	27370	30830	...	...	...	...
3 Current transfers	...	...	160	210	240	260	290	360	...	...	...	...
Total Current Receipts	...	...	24310	30830	36300	43950	53600	61530	...	...	...	...
Disbursements												
1 Property and entrepreneurial income	...	...	16730	19820	20810	24540	28080	31100	...	...	...	...
2 Direct taxes and other current payments to general government	...	...	3020	1970	2250	2570	2880	6530	...	...	...	...
3 Other current transfers	...	...	410	1390	1620	1970	2210	2310	...	...	...	...
4 Net saving	...	...	4150	7650	11620	14870	20430	21590	...	...	...	...
Total Current Disbursements and Net Saving	...	...	24310	30830	36300	43950	53600	61530	...	...	...	...

1.6 Current Income and Outlay of Households and Non-Profit Institutions

Thousand United States dollars

	1980	1983	1984	1985	1986	1987	1988	1989	1990	1991	1992	1993
Receipts												
1 Compensation of employees	...	...	42620	42800	44250	49210	56260	61320	...	...	...	...
A From resident producers	...	...	41380	41550	42960	47810	54820	59830	...	...	...	...
B From rest of the world	...	...	1240	1250	1290	1400	1440	1490	...	...	...	...
2 Operating surplus of private unincorporated enterprises	...	...	17310	18070	18650	21370	24600	27010	...	...	...	...
3 Property and entrepreneurial income	...	...	7960	9570	10220	11020	12100	12610	...	...	...	...
4 Current transfers	...	...	4220	5080	6110	6770	7460	8200	...	...	...	...
Total Current Receipts	...	...	72110	75520	79230	88370	100420	109140	...	...	...	...
Disbursements												
1 Private final consumption expenditure	...	...	63110	66990	71310	85930	90460	101330	...	...	...	...
2 Property income	...	...	3450	3830	4060	4430	5020	5320	...	...	...	...
3 Direct taxes and other current transfers n.e.c. to general government	...	...	7940	8060	8890	10000	12650	13040	...	...	...	...
A Social security contributions	...	...	2760	2800	3040	3380	3840	4190	...	...	...	...
B Direct taxes	...	...	4540	4590	5060	5790	7900	7820	...	...	...	...
C Fees, fines and penalties	...	...	640	670	790	830	910	1030	...	...	...	...
4 Other current transfers	...	...	850	910	980	1110	1170	1290	...	...	...	...
5 Net saving	...	...	-3240	-4270	-6010	-13100	-8880	-11840	...	...	...	...
Total Current Disbursements and Net Saving	...	...	72110	75520	79230	88370	100420	109140	...	...	...	...

1.7 External Transactions on Current Account, Summary

Thousand United States dollars

	1980	1983	1984	1985	1986	1987	1988	1989	1990	1991	1992	1993
Payments to the Rest of the World												
1 Imports of goods and services	52120	94670	104520	117270	130400	146610	175350	194640	...	...	...	...
A Imports of merchandise c.i.f.	40490	70570	77360	...	...	...	...	...	...	...	...	...
B Other	11630	24100	27160	...	...	...	...	...	...	...	...	...
2 Factor income to the rest of the world	...	...	1910	2240	2050	2220	2410	2560	...	...	...	...
A Compensation of employees	...	...	30	50	60	60	130	140	...	...	...	...
B Property and entrepreneurial income	...	...	1880	2190	1990	2160	2280	2420	...	...	...	...
3 Current transfers to the rest of the world	...	...	1060	1140	1260	1700	1930	2150	...	...	...	...
4 Surplus of the nation on current transactions	...	...	-19230	-19520	-20460	-22450	-20370	-15410	...	...	...	...
Payments to the Rest of the World and Surplus of the Nation on Current Transactions	...	...	88260	101130	113250	128080	159320	183940	...	...	...	...
Receipts From The Rest of the World												
1 Exports of goods and services	36850	68580	75910	87280	98370	111410	141300	163760	...	...	...	...

British Virgin Islands

1.7 External Transactions on Current Account, Summary
(Continued)

Thousand United States dollars

	1980	1983	1984	1985	1986	1987	1988	1989	1990	1991	1992	1993
A Exports of merchandise f.o.b.	510	2250	2290	2340	2490	...	...	...	...	...	...	...
B Other	36340	66330	73620	84940	95880	...	...	...	...	...	...	...
2 Factor income from rest of the world	...	...	10250	11350	11730	13040	14030	15760	...	...	...	...
A Compensation of employees	...	...	1270	1300	1350	1460	1570	1630	...	...	...	...
B Property and entrepreneurial income	...	...	8980	10050	10380	11580	12460	14130	...	...	...	...
3 Current transfers from rest of the world	...	...	2100	2500	3150	3630	3990	4420	...	...	...	...
Receipts from the Rest of the World on Current Transactions	...	...	88260	101130	113250	128080	159320	183940	...	...	...	...

1.10 Gross Domestic Product by Kind of Activity, in Current Prices

Thousand United States dollars

	1980	1983	1984	1985	1986	1987	1988	1989	1990	1991	1992	1993
1 Agriculture, hunting, forestry and fishing	2660	3390	3560	3660	3730	4350	4400	4760	...	...	...	...
2 Mining and quarrying	40	60	110	160	160	210	240	300	...	...	...	...
3 Manufacturing	1380	2110	2270	2310	2870	3450	3730	4300	...	...	...	...
4 Electricity, gas and water	790	2260	2680	2870	3600	4100	4780	5210	...	...	...	...
5 Construction	2680	6330	6830	5910	5430	6530	7340	9450	...	...	...	...
6 Wholesale and retail trade, restaurants and hotels	17220	22300	23240	24610	26140	32190	34200	39450	...	...	...	...
7 Transport, storage and communication	5580	6970	7730	8700	9740	12280	14410	21280	...	...	...	...
8 Finance, insurance, real estate and business services	12560	19070	20750	22440	23540	26020	27520	31210	...	...	...	...
9 Community, social and personal services	2490	4010	4610	4700	4820	6000	6290	6500	...	...	...	...
Total, Industries	45400	66500	71780	75360	80030	95130	102910	122460	...	...	...	...
Producers of Government Services	5010	8280	11280	10250	11820	12910	17790	19000	...	...	...	...
Other Producers	...	...	...	...	...	...	...	...	...	...	...	...
Subtotal [a]	50410	74780	83060	85610	91850	108040	120700	141460	...	...	...	...
Less: Imputed bank service charge	2140	4690	5160	5210	5270	6520	7180	9010	...	...	...	...
Plus: Import duties	...	...	...	...	...	...	...	...	...	...	...	...
Plus: Value added tax	...	...	...	...	...	...	...	...	...	...	...	...
Plus: Other adjustments [b]	5900	8480	8400	9480	11240	15140	17620	23750	...	...	...	...
Equals: Gross Domestic Product	54170	78570	86300	89880	97820	116660	131140	156200	...	...	...	...

a) Gross domestic product in factor values.
b) Item 'Other adjustments' refers to indirect taxes net of subsidies.

1.11 Gross Domestic Product by Kind of Activity, in Constant Prices

Thousand United States dollars

	1980	1983	1984	1985	1986	1987	1988	1989	1990	1991	1992	1993
	At constant prices of:
		1977					1984					
1 Agriculture, hunting, forestry and fishing	2150	2170	2190 / 3560	3550	3550	4050	4280	4540	...	...	...	...
2 Mining and quarrying	40	50	80 / 110	160	110	160	240	290	...	...	...	...
3 Manufacturing	1040	1270	1360 / 1790	1760	2240	3070	3120	3290	...	...	...	...
4 Electricity, gas and water	570	1450	1260 / 2680	2900	3500	4060	4390	4570	...	...	...	...
5 Construction	2210	3730	4030 / 6830	5980	5500	6190	7450	8680	...	...	...	...
6 Wholesale and retail trade, restaurants and hotels	15070	13280	13280 / 23240	24100	25400	29250	30970	32000	...	...	...	...
7 Transport, storage and communication	4580	5000	5040 / 7380	8020	8130	9470	14110	16330	...	...	...	...
8 Finance, insurance, real estate and business services	8040	9260	9890 / 20750	23030	24740	28430	30940	33270	...	...	...	...
9 Community, social and personal services	1880	2170	2300 / 4610	4600	4380	6710	7160	8130	...	...	...	...

British Virgin Islands

1.11 Gross Domestic Product by Kind of Activity, in Constant Prices
(Continued)

Thousand United States dollars

	1980	1983	1984	1985	1986	1987	1988	1989	1990	1991	1992	1993
		1977		At constant prices of:				1984				
Total, Industries	35580	38380	39430									
			70950	74100	77550	91390	102660	111100	...	...	...	...
Producers of Government Services	3600	4660	5890									
			11280	10130	11150	11170	12590	13550	...	...	...	...
Other Producers	...	...	...	...	...	...	...	...	...	...	...	...
Subtotal	39240	43040	45320									
			82230	84230	88700	102560	115250	124650	...	...	...	...
Less: Imputed bank service charge	1280	1680	1660									
			5160	6100	7590	9540	11750	12210	...	...	...	...
Plus: Import duties	...	...	...	...	...	...	...	...	...	...	...	...
Plus: Value added tax	...	...	...	...	...	...	...	...	...	...	...	...
Equals: Gross Domestic Product	37960	41360	43660									
			77070	78130	81110	93020	103500	112440	...	...	...	...

1.12 Relations Among National Accounting Aggregates

Thousand United States dollars

	1980	1983	1984	1985	1986	1987	1988	1989	1990	1991	1992	1993
Gross Domestic Product	...	...	86300	89880	97820	116660	131340	156200	...	...	...	...
Plus: Net factor income from the rest of the world	...	...	8340	9110	9680	10820	11620	13200	...	...	...	...
Factor income from the rest of the world	...	...	10250	11350	11730	13040	14030	15760	...	...	...	...
Less: Factor income to the rest of the world	...	...	1910	2240	2050	2220	2410	2560	...	...	...	...
Equals: Gross National Product	...	...	94640	98990	107500	127480	142960	169400	...	...	...	...
Less: Consumption of fixed capital	...	...	11590	9580	9550	13530	14250	23220	...	...	...	...
Equals: National Income	...	...	83050	89410	97950	113950	128710	146180	...	...	...	...
Plus: Net current transfers from the rest of the world	...	...	1040	1360	1890	1930	2060	2270	...	...	...	...
Current transfers from the rest of the world	...	...	2100	2500	3150	3630	3990	4420	...	...	...	...
Less: Current transfers to the rest of the world	...	...	1060	1140	1260	1700	1930	2150	...	...	...	...
Equals: National Disposable Income	...	...	84090	90770	99840	115880	130770	148450	...	...	...	...
Less: Final consumption	...	...	79950	83900	90040	106160	116810	133730	...	...	...	...
Equals: Net Saving	...	...	4140	6870	9800	9720	13960	14720	...	...	...	...
Less: Surplus of the nation on current transactions	...	...	-19230	-19520	-20460	-22450	-20370	-15410	...	...	...	...
Equals: Net Capital Formation	...	...	23370	26390	30260	32170	34330	30130	...	...	...	...

2.1 Government Final Consumption Expenditure by Function, in Current Prices

Thousand United States dollars

		1980	1983	1984	1985	1986	1987	1988	1989	1990	1991	1992	1993
1	General public services	1229	3115	3488	3891	4043	4869	...	...	...	...	...	...
2	Defence	...	...	...	...	...	...	...	...	...	...	...	...
3	Public order and safety	762	1392	1810	1813	2103	2301	...	...	...	...	...	...
4	Education	1837	3111	3879	3943	4208	4417	...	...	...	...	...	...
5	Health	977	1862	2518	2498	2686	3302	...	...	...	...	...	...
6	Social security and welfare	145	305	345	300	438	535	...	...	...	...	...	...
7	Housing and community amenities	342	670	740	680	817	1146	...	...	...	...	...	...
8	Recreational, cultural and religious affairs	34	112	129	133	132	102	...	...	...	...	...	...
9	Economic services	1743	3572	3653	3467	4087	4221	...	...	...	...	...	...
	A Fuel and energy	...	...	...	...	...	...	...	...	...	...	...	...
	B Agriculture, forestry, fishing and hunting	238	555	537	499	612	706	...	...	...	...	...	...
	C Mining, manufacturing and construction, except fuel and energy	1193	1912	1889	1656	2006	1838	...	...	...	...	...	...
	D Transportation and communication	...	...	...	...	...	...	...	...	...	...	...	...
	E Other economic affairs	312	1105	1227	1312	1469	1677	...	...	...	...	...	...
10	Other functions	...	...	...	...	...	...	...	...	...	...	...	...
	Total Government Final Consumption Expenditure [a]	7069	14139	16562	16725	18514	20893	...	...	...	...	...	...

a) Only central government data are included in the general government estimates.

Brunei Darussalam

Source. Reply to the United Nations National Accounts Questionnaire from the Statistics Division, Economic Planning Unit, Ministry of Finance.
General note. The estimates shown in the following tables have been prepared by the Government of Brunei in accordance with the United Nations System of National Accounts so far as the existing data would permit.

1.10 Gross Domestic Product by Kind of Activity, in Current Prices

Million Brunei dollars

	1980	1983	1984	1985	1986	1987	1988	1989	1990	1991	1992	1993
1 Agriculture, hunting, forestry and fishing	67.3	79.6	85.7	94.3	98.9	112.3	120.5	144.4	153.7	171.5	191.5	207.2
2 Mining and quarrying	7546.1	5183.2	4889.4	4592.7	2286.2	2652.9	2044.9	2209.3	2644.6	2550.0	2654.4	2416.6
3 Manufacturing	1246.8	816.0	816.7	783.7	532.6	583.1	547.1	557.6	584.7	546.0		
4 Electricity, gas and water	-9.1	15.8	15.3	31.2	30.9	33.3	42.8	53.9	59.3	61.6	64.1	67.3
5 Construction	168.1	265.5	207.0	159.2	170.1	183.1	195.3	254.6	277.4	291.3	311.7	341.1
6 Wholesale and retail trade, restaurants and hotels	955.1	880.1	909.8	821.5	630.4	686.5	707.7	769.0	818.2	846.1	782.4	787.9
7 Transport, storage and communication	58.0	143.8	116.6	136.1	123.2	233.0	244.8	266.3	281.2	297.1	309.8	331.5
8 Finance, insurance, real estate and business services	159.2	267.7	285.3	292.2	260.2	288.1	321.2	361.3	410.7	433.0	459.8	487.2
9 Community, social and personal services	421.4	573.3	855.7	918.7	1090.2	1126.8	1292.9	1349.2	1420.6	1556.7	1754.8	2000.2
Total, Industries	10612.9	8225.0	8181.5	7829.6	5222.7	5899.1	5517.2	5965.6	6650.4	6753.3	6528.5	6639.0
Producers of Government Services	...	...	...	...	...	...	...	...	...	...	...	...
Other Producers	...	...	...	...	...	...	...	...	...	...	...	...
Subtotal	10612.9	8225.0	8181.5	7829.6	5222.7	5899.1	5517.2	5965.6	6650.4	6753.3	6528.5	6639.0
Less: Imputed bank service charge	59.3	101.1	113.1	77.2	87.1	98.3	102.7	120.7	141.9	149.0	156.5	164.3
Plus: Import duties	...	...	...	...	...	...	...	...	...	...	...	...
Plus: Value added tax	...	...	...	...	...	...	...	...	...	...	...	...
Equals: Gross Domestic Product	10553.6	8123.9	8068.5	7752.3	5135.6	5800.9	5414.5	5845.0	6508.6	6604.3	6372.0	6474.7

1.11 Gross Domestic Product by Kind of Activity, in Constant Prices

Million Brunei dollars

	1980	1983	1984	1985	1986	1987	1988	1989	1990	1991	1992	1993
					At constant prices of:1974							
1 Agriculture, hunting, forestry and fishing	42.0	40.6	41.7	43.1	46.2	49.0	49.5	56.1	56.5	59.2	63.0	65.3
2 Mining and quarrying	2957.4	2333.7	2223.5	2193.3	2076.6	1958.9	1889.1	1760.5	1785.9	1964.5	2071.9	1903.0
3 Manufacturing	404.1	245.6	252.7	239.0	216.6	286.2	285.1	288.2	303.5	234.8		
4 Electricity, gas and water	-6.3	9.3	8.8	17.4	16.9	18.0	22.9	28.5	30.7	31.1	32.2	32.3
5 Construction	98.3	123.0	94.5	72.9	79.5	80.0	80.5	98.7	102.0	100.6	103.3	108.3
6 Wholesale and retail trade, restaurants and hotels	358.6	320.0	339.0	285.4	304.9	350.0	364.5	388.6	405.9	374.4	364.8	315.5
7 Transport, storage and communication	37.2	80.7	65.2	73.7	56.6	106.3	109.9	115.6	121.0	115.5	124.2	127.7
8 Finance, insurance, real estate and business services	146.0	175.6	184.0	172.2	120.9	129.2	139.1	151.2	166.2	168.0	172.7	179.1
9 Community, social and personal services	277.5	333.9	485.7	510.7	595.4	606.1	683.1	703.7	720.5	781.4	860.5	914.7
Total, Industries	4314.8	3662.4	3695.1	3607.7	3513.6	3583.7	3623.7	3591.1	3692.2	3829.5	3792.6	3645.9
Producers of Government Services	...	...	...	...	...	...	...	...	...	...	...	...
Other Producers	...	...	...	...	...	...	...	...	...	...	...	...
Subtotal	4314.8	3662.4	3695.1	3607.7	3513.6	3583.7	3623.7	3591.1	3692.2	3829.5	3792.6	3645.9
Less: Imputed bank service charge	55.8	95.1	106.3	72.6	73.9	75.3	76.7	82.3	87.1	93.1	94.5	97.7
Plus: Import duties	...	...	...	...	...	...	...	...	...	...	...	...
Plus: Value added tax	...	...	...	...	...	...	...	...	...	...	...	...
Equals: Gross Domestic Product	4259.0	3567.3	3588.8	3535.3	3439.6	3508.4	3546.9	3508.8	3605.1	3736.4	3698.1	3548.2

Bulgaria

Source. Reply to the United Nations National Accounts Questionnaire from the National Statistical Institute, Sofia. Official estimates and descriptions are published annually by the same Institute in 'Statisticheski Godishnik' (Statistical Yearbook).
General note. As estimates for years till 1990 are based on the principal methodological differences between MPS ans SNA, they are not comparable to the data for 1991 and thereafter. Volume indices, on the basis of constant price estimates, are not consistent because of methodological and structural differences over the years. Since 1991, the estimates are compiled according to the current national accounts and the capital account, taking into account, as far as possible, the main guidelines of SNA, 1993 revision. Branches included in the sectors are classified according to the present national classification of branches. Since 1991, branches are aggregated on the basis of the establishment-type-of-unit. Data for 1991 and the following years are revised and differ from the ones published so far. Estimates at constant prices are calculated year to year whereas for 1991 there are no constant price estimates.

1.1 Expenditure on the Gross Domestic Product, in Current Prices
Million Bulgarian leva

	1980	1983	1984	1985	1986	1987	1988	1989	1990	1991	1992	1993
1 Government final consumption expenditure [a]	1457	2356	2384	2757	2954	2713	2745	2819	3286	10441	17713	25644
2 Private final consumption expenditure	16049	18310	19198	20031	21247	22660	23418	25180	30298	88813	154929	252849
A Households [b]	13973	16045	16789	17385	18367	19209	19903	21454	25330	75586	131370	220897
B Private non-profit institutions serving households [c]	2076	2264	2408	2646	2880	3451	3515	3725	4969	13227	23559	31952
3 Gross capital formation	8768	9807	10516	10495	12350	12020	13197	13105	13800	30662	39937	42427
A Increase in stocks	1479	1832	2404	1882	3059	2203	2937	2776	4148	6027	7360	6999
B Gross fixed capital formation	7289	7975	8112	8613	9291	9817	10260	10328	9652	24635	32577	35428
4 Exports of goods and services [d]	-483	-658	-426	-687	-2128	-861	-1015	-1524	-1995	58976	94549	111680
5 Less: Imports of goods and services										53184	106305	133676
Statistical discrepancy	...	...	...	...	...	...	...	...	...	3	9	10
Equals: Gross Domestic Product	25791	29815	31671	32595	34424	36531	38345	39579	45390	135711	200832	298934

a) Government consumption expenditure on collective goods.
b) Household consumption includes the consumption of goods and services of resident and non-resident units in the country, without adjustments with purchases abroad and net gifts in kind, received from abroad. The imputed rent of owner-occupied dwellings is estimated with the volume of the current costs up to the year 1990; since 1991, by market prices.
c) Including government consumption expenditure on individual goods.
d) Upto 1993, the external balance includes exports of goods less imports of goods, and the statistical discrepancy.

1.2 Expenditure on the Gross Domestic Product, in Constant Prices
Million Bulgarian leva

	1980	1983	1984	1985	1986	1987	1988	1989	1990	1991	1992	1993
	\multicolumn{9}{c}{At constant prices of: 1989}		1991	1992
1 Government final consumption expenditure [a]	...	...	...	...	...	...	...	...	2909	...	9470	16343
2 Private final consumption expenditure	...	...	...	...	...	...	...	...	25258	...	87946	151658
A Households	...	...	...	...	...	...	...	...	21128	...	75140	131489
B Private non-profit institutions serving households [b]	...	...	...	...	...	...	...	...	4130	...	12806	20169
3 Gross capital formation	...	...	...	...	...	...	...	...	9812	...	27294	29603
A Increase in stocks	...	...	...	...	...	...	...	...	1397	...	4464	4998
B Gross fixed capital formation	...	...	...	...	...	...	...	...	8415	...	22830	24605
4 Exports of goods and services	...	...	...	...	...	...	...	...	-2009[c]	...	...	...
5 Less: Imports of goods and services	...	...	...	...	...	...	...	...		...	...	...
Equals: Gross Domestic Product	...	...	...	...	...	...	...	...	35970	...	127139	197859

a) Government consumption expenditure on collective goods.
b) Including government consumption expenditure on individual goods.
c) Upto 1993, the external balance includes exports of goods less imports of goods, and the statistical discrepancy.

Bulgaria

1.3 Cost Components of the Gross Domestic Product

Million Bulgarian leva

	1980	1983	1984	1985	1986	1987	1988	1989	1990	1991	1992	1993
1 Indirect taxes, net	...	...	...	...	...	...	...	...	...	9238	13559	18902
A Indirect taxes	...	...	...	...	...	...	...	...	...	11940	17126	27574
B Less: Subsidies	...	...	...	...	...	...	...	...	...	2702	3567	8672
2 Consumption of fixed capital	3559	4011	4361	4465	4761	5255	5892	5589	6366	18999	26001	39704
3 Compensation of employees paid by resident producers to:	13094	15145	15776	16475	17525	18315	19248	20308	24361	56137	106378	155929
4 Operating surplus [a]	9138	10659	11535	11656	12138	12962	13205	13682	14663	63946	58578	80033
A Corporate and quasi-corporate enterprises	...	...	...	...	...	...	...	...	...	43917	22046	7215
B Private unincorporated enterprises	...	...	...	...	...	...	...	...	...	20029	36532	72814
C General government	...	...	...	...	...	...	...	...	...	-	-	4
Statistical discrepancy [b]	...	...	...	...	...	...	...	...	...	-12609	-3684	4366
Equals: Gross Domestic Product	25791	29815	31671	32595	34424	36531	38345	39579	45390	135711	200832	298934

a) Upto 1990, it includes net indirect taxes and operating surplus. Since 1991, includes operating surplus and mixed income.
b) Adjustments - including import duties on goods, financial intermediation services indirectly measured.

1.9 Gross Domestic Product by Institutional Sectors of Origin

Million Bulgarian leva

	1980	1983	1984	1985	1986	1987	1988	1989	1990	1991	1992	1993
					Domestic Factor Incomes Originating							
1 General government	...	...	...	...	...	...	...	...	...	10506	21976	34899
2 Corporate and quasi-corporate enterprises	...	...	...	...	...	...	...	...	...	89436	101949	115680
A Non-financial	...	...	...	...	...	...	...	...	...	75330	94381	111986
Public	...	...	...	...	...	...	...	...	...	72793	89667	101891
Private	...	...	...	...	...	...	...	...	...	2537	4714	10095
B Financial	...	...	...	...	...	...	...	...	...	14106	7568	3694
Public	...	...	...	...	...	...	...	...	...	13475	6904	2907
Private	...	...	...	...	...	...	...	...	...	631	664	787
3 Households and private unincorporated enterprises	...	...	...	...	...	...	...	...	...	20017	40654	84800
A Owner-occupied housing	...	...	...	...	...	...	...	...	...	8303	14201	31459
B Subsistence production	...	...	...	...	...	...	...	...	...	8719	17098	27481
C Other	...	...	...	...	...	...	...	...	...	2995	9353	25860
4 Non-profit institutions serving households	...	...	...	...	...	...	...	...	...	124	377	583
Subtotal: Domestic Factor Incomes	...	...	...	...	...	...	...	...	...	120083	164956	235962
Indirect taxes, net	...	...	...	...	...	...	...	...	...	9238	13559	18902
A Indirect taxes	...	...	...	...	...	...	...	...	...	11940	17126	27574
B Less: Subsidies	...	...	...	...	...	...	...	...	...	2702	3567	8672
Consumption of fixed capital	...	...	...	...	...	...	...	...	...	18999	26001	39704
Statistical discrepancy [a]	...	...	...	...	...	...	...	...	...	-12609	-3684	4366
Gross Domestic Product	...	...	...	...	...	...	...	...	...	135711	200832	298934

a) Adjustments - including import duties on goods, financial intermediation services indirectly measured.

1.10 Gross Domestic Product by Kind of Activity, in Current Prices

Million Bulgarian leva

	1980	1983	1984	1985	1986	1987	1988	1989	1990	1991	1992	1993
1 Agriculture, hunting, forestry and fishing	3719	4317	5008	3869	4447	4309	4394	4331	8316	20988	23533	29910
2 Mining and quarrying												
3 Manufacturing	11866	15567	16460	17744	19292	19549	20349	20444	19990	56832	78723	100809
4 Electricity, gas and water												
5 Construction	2003	2417	2528	2639	2743	2905	3029	3063	3159	6627	11785	16324
6 Wholesale and retail trade, restaurants and hotels	2907	1580	1377	1856	1319	2592	2571	3009	3548	12852	20792	31455
7 Transport, storage and communication	1745	2059	2094	2002	1954	2322	2907	3412	3267	9313	13112	19831
8 Finance, insurance, real estate and business services [a]	3551	3874	4204	4486	4668	4854	5094	5320	7208	15396	9530	8235
9 Community, social and personal services [b]										26312	47041	88004
Total, Industries	25791	29815	31671	32595	34424	36531	38345	39579	45488	148320	204516	294568
Producers of Government Services	...	...	...	...	...	...	...	...	...	...	...	...

161

Bulgaria

1.10 Gross Domestic Product by Kind of Activity, in Current Prices
(Continued)

Million Bulgarian leva

	1980	1983	1984	1985	1986	1987	1988	1989	1990	1991	1992	1993
Other Producers	...	...	...	...	...	...	...	...	...	...	...	...
Subtotal	25791	29815	31671	32595	34424	36531	38345	39579	45488	148320	204516	294568
Less: Imputed bank service charge	...	...	...	...	...	...	...	...	...	13645	7649	4742
Plus: Import duties	...	...	...	...	...	...	...	...	...	1036	3965	9108
Plus: Value added tax	...	...	...	...	...	...	...	...	...	...	...	...
Plus: Other adjustments c	...	...	...	...	...	...	...	...	-98	...	...	...
Equals: Gross Domestic Product	25791	29815	31671	32595	34424	36531	38345	39579	45390	135711	200832	298934

a) Upto 1990, includes 'Community, Social and Personal Services'.
b) Including item 'Producers of government services'.
c) Item 'Other adjustments' refers to statistical discrepancy.

1.11 Gross Domestic Product by Kind of Activity, in Constant Prices

Million Bulgarian leva

	1980	1983	1984	1985	1986	1987	1988	1989	1990	1991	1992	1993
					At constant prices of: 1989						1991	1992
1 Agriculture, hunting, forestry and fishing	...	...	...	...	...	...	...	...	4170	...	19332	16407
2 Mining and quarrying	...	...	...	...	...	...	...	...	⎡	...	⎡	⎡
3 Manufacturing	...	...	...	...	...	...	...	...	17934	...	50874	77583
4 Electricity, gas and water	...	...	...	...	...	...	...	...	⎣	...	⎣	⎣
5 Construction	...	...	...	...	...	...	...	...	2625	...	7281	10929
6 Wholesale and retail trade, restaurants and hotels	...	...	...	...	...	...	...	...	2344	...	11077	21290
7 Transport, storage and communication	...	...	...	...	...	...	...	...	2857	...	9701	14237
8 Finance, insurance, real estate and business services a	...	...	...	...	...	...	...	...	6040	...	4116	5240
9 Community, social and personal services b	...	...	...	...	...	...	...	...		...	25729	49164
Total, Industries	...	...	...	...	...	...	...	...	35970	...	128110	194850
Producers of Government Services	...	...	...	...	...	...	...	...	...	...	...	...
Other Producers	...	...	...	...	...	...	...	...	...	...	...	...
Subtotal	...	...	...	...	...	...	...	...	35970	...	128110	194850
Less: Imputed bank service charge	...	...	...	...	...	...	...	...	...	...	3512	3028
Plus: Import duties	...	...	...	...	...	...	...	...	...	...	2541	6037
Plus: Value added tax	...	...	...	...	...	...	...	...	...	...	...	...
Equals: Gross Domestic Product	...	...	...	...	...	...	...	...	35970	...	127139	197859

a) Upto 1990, includes 'Community, Social and Personal Services'.
b) Including item 'Producers of government services'.

Burkina Faso

Source. Reply to the United Nations National Accounts Questionnaire from the Institut National de la Statistique et de la Demographie, Ouagadougou. Official estimates are published by the Institut in 'Comptes Nationaux du Burkina Faso'.

General note. The estimates shown in the following tables have been prepared in accordance with the United Nations System of National Accounts so far as the existing data would permit.

1.1 Expenditure on the Gross Domestic Product, in Current Prices

Million CFA francs

	1980	1983	1984	1985	1986	1987	1988	1989	1990	1991	1992	1993
1 Government final consumption expenditure	47439	78795	76922	72602	...	...	...	...	...	...	...	...
2 Private final consumption expenditure	231272	327566	308282	411900	...	...	...	...	...	...	...	...
A Households	228324	322316	300014	...	...	...	...	...	...	...	...	...
B Private non-profit institutions serving households	2948	5250	8268	...	...	...	...	...	...	...	...	...
3 Gross capital formation	72444	92987	94105	128992	...	...	...	...	...	...	...	...
A Increase in stocks	6445	2633	3277	15501	...	...	...	...	...	...	...	...
B Gross fixed capital formation	65999	90354	90828	113491	...	...	...	...	...	...	...	...
4 Exports of goods and services	43571	55853	88094	79155	...	...	...	...	...	...	...	...
5 Less: Imports of goods and services	122708	174188	176837	223336	...	...	...	...	...	...	...	...
Equals: Gross Domestic Product	272018	381013	390565	469313	503500	...	...	...	...	...	...	...

1.2 Expenditure on the Gross Domestic Product, in Constant Prices

Million CFA francs

	1980	1983	1984	1985	1986	1987	1988	1989	1990	1991	1992	1993
				At constant prices of: 1975								
1 Government final consumption expenditure	24477	25676	24717	...	...	...	...	...	...	...	...	...
2 Private final consumption expenditure	144195	148672	140072	...	...	...	...	...	...	...	...	...
3 Gross capital formation	39178	35267	33684	...	...	...	...	...	...	...	...	...
A Increase in stocks	4027	715	402	...	...	...	...	...	...	...	...	...
B Gross fixed capital formation	35151	34552	33282	...	...	...	...	...	...	...	...	...
4 Exports of goods and services	30279	25653	27056	...	...	...	...	...	...	...	...	...
5 Less: Imports of goods and services	89048	81346	74880	...	...	...	...	...	...	...	...	...
Equals: Gross Domestic Product	149080	153922	150650	...	...	...	...	...	...	...	...	...

1.3 Cost Components of the Gross Domestic Product

Million CFA francs

	1980	1983	1984	1985	1986	1987	1988	1989	1990	1991	1992	1993
1 Indirect taxes, net	19443	24084	22530	28498	...	...	...	...	...	...	...	...
2 Consumption of fixed capital	...	...	...	...	...	...	...	...	...	...	...	...
3 Compensation of employees paid by resident producers to:	71443	110072	114251	115346	...	...	...	...	...	...	...	...
4 Operating surplus	181132	246858	253784	312038	...	...	...	...	...	...	...	...
Equals: Gross Domestic Product	272018	381013	390565	455882	...	...	...	...	...	...	...	...

1.7 External Transactions on Current Account, Summary

Million CFA francs

	1980	1983	1984	1985	1986	1987	1988	1989	1990	1991	1992	1993
				Payments to the Rest of the World								
1 Imports of goods and services	122708	174188	176837	223336	...	...	...	...	...	...	...	...
A Imports of merchandise c.i.f.	77821	...	...	...	...	...	...	...	...	...	...	...
B Other	44887	...	...	...	...	...	...	...	...	...	...	...
2 Factor income to the rest of the world	3483	5636	5884	5996	...	...	...	...	...	...	...	...
A Compensation of employees	67	134	140	143	...	...	...	...	...	...	...	...
B Property and entrepreneurial income	3415	5502	5744	5853	...	...	...	...	...	...	...	...
3 Current transfers to the rest of the world	13680	17569	18195	18589	...	...	...	...	...	...	...	...
4 Surplus of the nation on current transactions	-54135	-72122	-45358	-100760	...	...	...	...	...	...	...	...
Payments to the Rest of the World and Surplus of the Nation on Current Transactions	85735	125271	155559	147161	...	...	...	...	...	...	...	...

Burkina Faso

1.7 External Transactions on Current Account, Summary
(Continued)

Million CFA francs

	1980	1983	1984	1985	1986	1987	1988	1989	1990	1991	1992	1993
				Receipts From The Rest of the World								
1 Exports of goods and services	43571	55853	88094	79155	...	...	...	...	...	...	...	...
A Exports of merchandise f.o.b.	33929	...	...	...	...	...	...	...	...	...	...	...
B Other	9642	...	...	...	...	...	...	...	...	...	...	...
2 Factor income from rest of the world	4537	3986	4162	4241	...	...	...	...	...	...	...	...
A Compensation of employees	1285	1762	1840	1875	...	...	...	...	...	...	...	...
B Property and entrepreneurial income	3252	2224	2322	2366	...	...	...	...	...	...	...	...
3 Current transfers from rest of the world	37627	65432	63304	63766	...	...	...	...	...	...	...	...
Receipts from the Rest of the World on Current Transactions	85735	125271	155559	147161	...	...	...	...	...	...	...	...

1.10 Gross Domestic Product by Kind of Activity, in Current Prices

Million CFA francs

	1980	1983	1984	1985	1986	1987	1988	1989	1990	1991	1992	1993
1 Agriculture, hunting, forestry and fishing	107982	152052	164205	213968	...	...	...	...	...	...	...	...
2 Mining and quarrying	386	77	304	294	...	...	...	...	...	...	...	...
3 Manufacturing	29856	48053	47457	50901	...	...	...	...	...	...	...	...
4 Electricity, gas and water	2841	4055	4246	3192	...	...	...	...	...	...	...	...
5 Construction	7801	7749	4934	5333	...	...	...	...	...	...	...	...
6 Wholesale and retail trade, restaurants and hotels	36698	46344	42187	45418	...	...	...	...	...	...	...	...
7 Transport, storage and communication	22654	24211	29011	30913	...	...	...	...	...	...	...	...
8 Finance, insurance, real estate and business services	11519	14009	14510	15488	...	...	...	...	...	...	...	...
9 Community, social and personal services	1324	1877	1771	2026	...	...	...	...	...	...	...	...
Total, Industries	221061	298427	308625	367533	...	...	...	...	...	...	...	...
Producers of Government Services	38452	67556	67455	67405	...	...	...	...	...	...	...	...
Other Producers	2068	3675	5788	6552	...	...	...	...	...	...	...	...
Subtotal	261581	369658	381868	441490	...	...	...	...	...	...	...	...
Less: Imputed bank service charge	5591	6778	7523	6758	...	...	...	...	...	...	...	...
Plus: Import duties	16028	18131	16219	21151	...	...	...	...	...	...	...	...
Plus: Value added tax	...	...	...	...	...	...	...	...	...	...	...	...
Equals: Gross Domestic Product	272018	381013	390565	455882	...	...	...	...	...	...	...	...

1.11 Gross Domestic Product by Kind of Activity, in Constant Prices

Million CFA francs

	1980	1983	1984	1985	1986	1987	1988	1989	1990	1991	1992	1993
				At constant prices of: 1979								
1 Agriculture, hunting, forestry and fishing	96058	102766	102588	126027	...	...	...	...	...	...	...	...
2 Mining and quarrying	330	193	207	225	...	...	...	...	...	...	...	...
3 Manufacturing	31499	32345	32047	32140	...	...	...	...	...	...	...	...
4 Electricity, gas and water	1816	2181	2166	2201	...	...	...	...	...	...	...	...
5 Construction	7466	4992	5292	5681	...	...	...	...	...	...	...	...
6 Wholesale and retail trade, restaurants and hotels	33990	34156	33763	34775	...	...	...	...	...	...	...	...
7 Transport, storage and communication	19699	19480	15733	16497	...	...	...	...	...	...	...	...
8 Finance, insurance, real estate and business services	10125	10584	10540	10633	...	...	...	...	...	...	...	...
9 Community, social and personal services	1162	1182	1008	999	...	...	...	...	...	...	...	...
Total, Industries	202145	207879	203344	229178	...	...	...	...	...	...	...	...
Producers of Government Services	43186	55155	64573	72593	...	...	...	...	...	...	...	...
Other Producers	1877	2154	3170	3421	...	...	...	...	...	...	...	...
Subtotal	247208	265188	271087	305192	...	...	...	...	...	...	...	...
Less: Imputed bank service charge	5070	5061	4831	4744	...	...	...	...	...	...	...	...
Plus: Import duties	14571	10622	8878	10629	...	...	...	...	...	...	...	...
Plus: Value added tax	...	...	...	...	...	...	...	...	...	...	...	...
Equals: Gross Domestic Product	256709	270747	275134	311077	...	...	...	...	...	...	...	...

Burkina Faso

1.12 Relations Among National Accounting Aggregates

Million CFA francs

	1980	1983	1984	1985	1986	1987	1988	1989	1990	1991	1992	1993
Gross Domestic Product	272018	381013	390565	455882	...	...	...	...	...	...	...	...
Plus: Net factor income from the rest of the world	1055	-1651	-1723	-1756	...	...	...	...	...	...	...	...
Factor income from the rest of the world	4537	3986	4162	4241	...	...	...	...	...	...	...	...
Less: Factor income to the rest of the world	3482	5636	5884	5996	...	...	...	...	...	...	...	...
Equals: Gross National Product	273073	379362	388845	454126	...	...	...	...	...	...	...	...
Less: Consumption of fixed capital	...	...	...	...	...	...	...	...	...	...	...	...
Equals: National Income	...	...	...	...	...	...	...	...	...	...	...	...
Plus: Net current transfers from the rest of the world	23947	47863	45108	45177	...	...	...	...	...	...	...	...
Current transfers from the rest of the world	37627	65432	63304	63766	...	...	...	...	...	...	...	...
Less: Current transfers to the rest of the world	13680	17569	18195	18589	...	...	...	...	...	...	...	...
Equals: National Disposable Income	...	...	...	...	...	...	...	...	...	...	...	...
Less: Final consumption	278711	406361	385204	471071	...	...	...	...	...	...	...	...
Equals: Net Saving [a]	18309	20865	48746	28232	...	...	...	...	...	...	...	...
Less: Surplus of the nation on current transactions	-54135	-72122	-45358	-100760	...	...	...	...	...	...	...	...
Equals: Net Capital Formation	...	...	...	...	...	...	...	...	...	...	...	...

a) Item 'Net saving' includes consumption of fixed capital.

Burundi

Source. Reply to the United Nations National Accounts Questionnaire from the Departement des Etudes et Statistiques, Bujumbura.
General note. The estimates shown in the following tables have been prepared in accordance with the United Nations System of National Accounts so far as the existing data would permit.

1.1 Expenditure on the Gross Domestic Product, in Current Prices

Million Burundi francs

	1980	1983	1984	1985	1986	1987	1988	1989	1990	1991	1992	1993
1 Government final consumption expenditure	13746	20414	21132	22793	24252	28570	31491	36547	38343	36113	35212	...
2 Private final consumption expenditure	70133	77516	92484	109478	104340	107015	114298	135449	163216	177692	187784	...
3 Gross capital formation	11876	18458	21774	20187	22107	24876	21672	29362	31058	37264	48784	...
A Increase in stocks	921	-1083	1410	73	3247	3763	-4029	3247	-1177	-1043	1005	...
B Gross fixed capital formation	10955	19542	20364	20113	18860	21114	25701	26115	32235	38307	47779	...
4 Exports of goods and services	7328	9683	11782	13937	15625	13015	17298	15697	15641	21231	20309	...
5 Less: Imports of goods and services	17476	23179	26721	25047	25482	29886	31852	37507	51602	60402	65705	...
Equals: Gross Domestic Product [a]	85607	102892	120451	141347	140842	143590	152907	179548	196656	211898	226384	...

a) Data in this table have not been revised, therefore they are not comparable with the data in other tables.

1.2 Expenditure on the Gross Domestic Product, in Constant Prices

Million Burundi francs

	1980	1983	1984	1985	1986	1987	1988	1989	1990	1991	1992	1993
	\multicolumn{12}{c}{At constant prices of: 1980}
1 Government final consumption expenditure	13746	18751	18338	19204	19895	20313	...	...	...	...	...	...
2 Private final consumption expenditure	70133	72000	72512	80168	83474	86066	...	...	...	...	...	...
3 Gross capital formation	11876	17204	18807	17051	17604	17528	...	...	...	...	...	...
A Increase in stocks	921	-1149	1016	-21	2475	626	...	...	...	...	...	...
B Gross fixed capital formation	10955	18353	17790	17072	15129	16902	...	...	...	...	...	...
4 Exports of goods and services	7328	12360	10622	12819	11349	12192	...	...	...	...	...	...
5 Less: Imports of goods and services	17476	22836	22897	20480	19406	18559	...	...	...	...	...	...
Equals: Gross Domestic Product	85607	97479	97382	108762	112916	117539	...	...	...	...	...	...

1.3 Cost Components of the Gross Domestic Product

Million Burundi francs

	1980	1983	1984	1985	1986	1987	1988	1989	1990	1991	1992	1993
1 Indirect taxes, net	8646	8849	13009	15124	17724	15638	17834	24393	21557	...	...	...
A Indirect taxes	9331	9157	13370	15548	18096	16117	18515	25368	24533	...	...	...
B Less: Subsidies	685	309	361	424	372	479	681	976	2976	...	...	...
2 Consumption of fixed capital	1541	2572	3132	3534	4110	5038	5898	9075	8206	...	...	...
3 Compensation of employees paid by resident producers to:	15837	21093	24211	26856	28319	30107	33255	38139	47979	...	...	...
4 Operating surplus	59582	70378	80100	95833	90689	92807	95921	107942	118914	...	...	...
A Corporate and quasi-corporate enterprises	...	5666	4407	5135	6328	...	...	...	...	...	...	...
B Private unincorporated enterprises	...	64708	75659	90544	84201	...	...	...	...	...	...	...
C General government	...	5	35	154	160	...	...	...	...	...	...	...
Equals: Gross Domestic Product [a]	85607	102891	120451	141347	140842	143590	152907	179548	196656	...	...	...

a) Data in this table have not been revised, therefore they are not comparable with the data in other tables.

1.7 External Transactions on Current Account, Summary

Million Burundi francs

	1980	1983	1984	1985	1986	1987	1988	1989	1990	1991	1992	1993
	\multicolumn{12}{c}{Payments to the Rest of the World}
1 Imports of goods and services	17476	23179	26721	25047	25482	29886	31852	...	...	...	...	...
2 Factor income to the rest of the world	163	558	1161	1614	1925	2512	2862	...	...	...	...	...
A Compensation of employees	...	...	...	...	...	...	...	...	...	...	...	...
B Property and entrepreneurial income	163	558	1161	1614	1925	2512	2862	...	...	...	...	...

Burundi

1.7 External Transactions on Current Account, Summary
(Continued)

Million Burundi francs

	1980	1983	1984	1985	1986	1987	1988	1989	1990	1991	1992	1993
3 Current transfers to the rest of the world	1981	4541	5431	6007	6331	7120	10213	...	...	...	...	...
4 Surplus of the nation on current transactions	-4952	-11266	-13069	-10498	-9376	-16627	-15482	...	...	...	...	...
Payments to the Rest of the World and Surplus of the Nation on Current Transactions	14668	17012	20244	22169	24362	22891	29445	...	...	...	...	...

Receipts From The Rest of the World

	1980	1983	1984	1985	1986	1987	1988	1989	1990	1991	1992	1993
1 Exports of goods and services	7328	9683	11782	13937	15625	13015	17298	...	...	...	...	...
2 Factor income from rest of the world	986	176	182	178	228	361	405	...	...	...	...	...
A Compensation of employees	...	...	...	...	...	...	...	...	...	...	...	...
B Property and entrepreneurial income	986	176	182	178	228	361	405	...	...	...	...	...
3 Current transfers from rest of the world	6355	7153	8280	8054	8509	9515	11742	...	...	...	...	...
Receipts from the Rest of the World on Current Transactions	14668	17012	20244	22169	24362	22891	29445	...	...	...	...	...

1.10 Gross Domestic Product by Kind of Activity, in Current Prices

Million Burundi francs

	1980	1983	1984	1985	1986	1987	1988	1989	1990	1991	1992	1993
1 Agriculture, hunting, forestry and fishing	47875	53726	64398	77474	71872	70447	72852	82609	100602	...	...	...
2 Mining and quarrying a	234	620	447	649	923	1425	1470	2020	1583	...	...	...
3 Manufacturing	6971	11652	15185	17152	17405	23451	24630	32505	32306	...	...	...
4 Electricity, gas and water a	...	...	...	...	...	...	...	...	...	...	...	...
5 Construction	3762	3991	5276	5709	5047	3899	4287	5773	6588	...	...	...
6 Wholesale and retail trade, restaurants and hotels	6714	7837	13680	16060	18182	15261	19209	18973	9474	...	...	...
7 Transport, storage and communication	1677	2288	2748	3142	3732	3918	3918	5718	5989	...	...	...
8 Finance, insurance, real estate and business services	1427	1612	65	102	134	138	139	224	470	...	...	...
9 Community, social and personal services			1837	1898	1943	2341	2734	3451	3858	...	...	...
Total, Industries	68659	81736	103636	122186	119238	120880	129239	151273	160870	...	...	...
Producers of Government Services	8771	12173	13970	16035	17363	18074	19828	24354	31180	...	...	...
Other Producers			564	568	594	583				...	...	...
Subtotal	77430	93909	118170	138789	137195	139537	149067	175627	192050	...	...	...
Less: Imputed bank service charge	...	...	...	...	...	...	...	...	...	...	...	...
Plus: Import duties	2831	2334	2282	2557	3647	4054	3841	3921	4606	...	...	...
Plus: Value added tax	...	...	...	...	...	...	...	...	...	...	...	...
Plus: Other adjustments	5346	6649	...	...	...	...	...	...	...	...	...	...
Equals: Gross Domestic Product b	85607	102892	120451	141347	140842	143590	152908	179549	196656	...	...	...

a) Item 'Electricity, gas and water' is included in item 'Mining and Quarrying'.
b) Data in this table have not been revised, therefore they are not comparable with the data in other tables.

1.12 Relations Among National Accounting Aggregates

Million Burundi francs

	1980	1983	1984	1985	1986	1987	1988	1989	1990	1991	1992	1993
Gross Domestic Product	85607	102892	120451	141347	140842	143590	152907	179548	196656	211898	226384	...
Plus: Net factor income from the rest of the world	822	-382	-980	-1436	-1697	-2151	-2457	-2008	-3886	-2041	-8845	...
Factor income from the rest of the world	986	176	182	178	228	361	405	...	...	...	...	...
Less: Factor income to the rest of the world	163	558	1161	1614	1925	2512	2862	...	...	...	...	...
Equals: Gross National Product	86429	102510	119471	139912	139145	141439	150450	177540	192770	209857	223539	...
Less: Consumption of fixed capital	1541	2572	3132	3534	4110	5038	5898	9075	8206	...	...	...

Burundi

1.12 Relations Among National Accounting Aggregates
(Continued)

Million Burundi francs

	1980	1983	1984	1985	1986	1987	1988	1989	1990	1991	1992	1993
Equals: National Income	84888	99938	116339	136377	135035	136401	144552	168465	184564	...	...	...
Plus: Net current transfers from the rest of the world	4374	2612	2850	2047	2178	2395	1529	...	...	...	...	...
Current transfers from the rest of the world	6355	7153	8280	8055	8509	9515	11742	...	...	...	...	...
Less: Current transfers to the rest of the world	1981	4540	5431	6007	6331	7120	10213	...	...	...	...	...
Equals: National Disposable Income	89262	102550	119189	138424	137213	138796	146081	...	...	...	...	...
Less: Final consumption	83879	97930	113616	132270	128592	135585	145789	...	...	...	...	...
Equals: Net Saving	5383	4620	5573	6154	8621	3211	292	...	...	...	...	...
Less: Surplus of the nation on current transactions	-4952	-11266	-13069	-10498	-9376	-16627	-15482	...	...	...	...	...
Equals: Net Capital Formation	10335	15886	18642	16652	17997	19838	15774	...	...	...	...	...

Cameroon

Source. Reply to the United Nations National Accounts Questionnaire from the Direction de la Statistique et de la Comptabilite Nationale, Ministere de L'economie et du Plan, Yaounde. The official estimates are published annually in 'Comptes de la Nation'.

General note. The estimates shown in the following tables have been prepared in accordance with the United Nations System of National Accounts so far as the existing data would permit.

1.1 Expenditure on the Gross Domestic Product, in Current Prices

Thousand Million CFA francs — Fiscal year beginning 1 July

	1980	1983	1984	1985	1986	1987	1988	1989	1990	1991	1992	1993
1 Government final consumption expenditure	159.1	306.4	345.3	465.5	476.7	391.0	378.4	370.0	350.1	...	...	...
2 Private final consumption expenditure	1222.5	2008.0	2466.3	2570.2	2630.7	2489.3	2430.9	2366.3	2353.8	...	...	...
3 Gross capital formation	488.4	828.9	955.3	1047.6	968.7	761.7	600.6	581.2	561.6	...	...	...
A Increase in stocks	47.0	19.4	16.3	29.4	6.4	4.1	-37.6	-	-	...	...	...
B Gross fixed capital formation	441.4	809.5	939.0	1018.2	962.3	757.6	638.2	581.2	561.6	...	...	...
Residential buildings	116.7	234.4	278.3	287.9	305.1	254.5	228.1			...	...	...
Non-residential buildings								...	...	...	...	...
Other construction and land improvement etc.	100.9	209.8	251.9	312.7	317.9	264.6	163.1	...	...	...	...	...
Other	223.8	365.3	408.8	417.5	339.2	238.5	247.0	...	...	...	...	...
4 Exports of goods and services	388.5	646.5	799.9	881.9	635.6	573.8	667.2	732.8	721.5	...	...	...
5 Less: Imports of goods and services	462.1	594.7	727.9	859.0	789.8	571.4	564.1	629.4	563.4	...	...	...
Equals: Gross Domestic Product [a]	1796.4	3195.0	3838.9	4106.2	3921.9	3644.5	3513.0	3420.9	3423.6	...	...	...

a) Data in this table have not been revised, therefore they are not comparable with the data in other tables.

1.2 Expenditure on the Gross Domestic Product, in Constant Prices

Thousand Million CFA francs — Fiscal year beginning 1 July

	1980	1983	1984	1985	1986	1987	1988	1989	1990	1991	1992	1993
				At constant prices of: 1980								
1 Government final consumption expenditure	151.8	201.1	217.2	226.9	213.4	205.5	192.3	196.2	...	...	...	...
2 Private final consumption expenditure	1141.3	1307.8	1392.4	1457.3	1407.5	1390.0	1283.4	1311.6	...	...	...	...
3 Gross capital formation	431.3	489.5	553.4	592.5	560.2	490.0	470.9	477.5	...	...	...	...
A Increase in stocks	41.5	11.5	9.4	18.9	15.3	9.5	15.6	10.9	...	...	...	...
B Gross fixed capital formation	389.8	478.0	544.0	573.6	544.9	480.5	455.3	466.6	...	...	...	...
4 Exports of goods and services	298.5	347.3	366.6	416.9	389.1	299.9	285.2	290.4	...	...	...	...
5 Less: Imports of goods and services	372.1	296.3	297.2	299.7	295.3	275.0	248.0	250.2	...	...	...	...
Equals: Gross Domestic Product	1650.7	2049.3	2232.4	2393.7	2274.7	2110.4	1983.8	2025.5	...	...	...	...

1.3 Cost Components of the Gross Domestic Product

Thousand Million CFA francs — Fiscal year beginning 1 July

	1980	1983	1984	1985	1986	1987	1988	1989	1990	1991	1992	1993
1 Indirect taxes, net	236.8	416.8	473.0	483.9	391.0	317.7	293.0	...	...	...	...	...
A Indirect taxes	241.3	434.1	485.4	529.8	430.2	337.9	299.3	...	...	...	...	...
B Less: Subsidies	4.5	17.4	12.4	45.9	39.2	20.2	6.3	...	...	...	...	...
2 Consumption of fixed capital	125.5	165.2	194.7	172.3	190.8	232.6	230.4	...	...	...	...	...
3 Compensation of employees paid by resident producers to:	504.6	875.5	989.5	1110.2	1142.4	1091.2	1055.1	...	...	...	...	...
A Resident households	493.9	855.7	986.3	...	...	...	...	...	...	...	...	...
B Rest of the world	10.7	19.8	3.2	...	...	...	...	...	...	...	...	...
4 Operating surplus	929.6	1737.5	2181.7	2339.7	2197.7	2003.0	1934.5	...	...	...	...	...
Equals: Gross Domestic Product	1796.5	3195.0	3838.9	4106.2	3921.9	3644.5	3513.0	...	...	...	...	...

1.4 General Government Current Receipts and Disbursements

Thousand Million CFA francs — Fiscal year beginning 1 July

	1980	1983	1984	1985	1986	1987	1988	1989	1990	1991	1992	1993
					Receipts							
1 Operating surplus	-	-	-	-	-	-	...	...	...	...	...	...
2 Property and entrepreneurial income	12.5	21.7	22.8	32.0	160.7	186.8	...	...	...	...	...	...
3 Taxes, fees and contributions	350.5	632.9	719.0	830.8	789.1	582.0	...	...	...	...	...	...
A Indirect taxes	241.3	434.1	485.4	529.8	430.2	337.9	...	...	...	...	...	...

Cameroon

1.4 General Government Current Receipts and Disbursements
(Continued)

Thousand Million CFA francs — Fiscal year beginning 1 July

	1980	1983	1984	1985	1986	1987	1988	1989	1990	1991	1992	1993
B Direct taxes	88.3	160.7	193.1	252.4	312.6	202.0	...	...	...	...	...	...
C Social security contributions	20.3	37.1	38.6	47.6	42.2	35.0	...	...	...	...	...	...
D Compulsory fees, fines and penalties	0.6	1.0	1.9	1.0	4.1	7.1	...	...	...	...	...	...
4 Other current transfers	18.3	17.9	18.1	21.9	21.5	21.4	...	...	...	...	...	...
Total Current Receipts of General Government	381.3	672.6	759.9	884.7	971.3	790.2	...	...	...	...	...	...

Disbursements

	1980	1983	1984	1985	1986	1987	1988	1989	1990	1991	1992	1993
1 Government final consumption expenditure	159.0	306.4	345.3	465.5	476.7	391.0	...	...	...	...	...	...
A Compensation of employees	107.9	209.2	239.2	286.9	313.4	305.1	...	...	...	...	...	...
B Consumption of fixed capital	2.4	3.6	9.6	7.9	8.6	12.6	...	...	...	...	...	...
C Purchases of goods and services, net	...	...	...	...	...	...	...	...	...	...	...	...
D Less: Own account fixed capital formation	...	...	...	...	...	...	...	...	...	...	...	...
E Indirect taxes paid, net	...	...	...	...	...	...	...	...	...	...	...	...
2 Property income	31.6	38.9	53.6	80.7	151.7	157.4	...	...	...	...	...	...
3 Subsidies	4.5	17.4	12.4	45.9	39.2	20.2	...	...	...	...	...	...
4 Other current transfers	50.2	90.9	117.7	127.9	182.3	153.2	...	...	...	...	...	...
A Social security benefits	8.2	12.6	13.9	16.6	18.3	17.8	...	...	...	...	...	...
B Social assistance grants	2.1	4.9	6.5	16.4	7.1	8.7	...	...	...	...	...	...
C Other	39.9	73.4	97.3	94.9	156.9	126.7	...	...	...	...	...	...
5 Net saving	136.0	218.9	231.0	164.8	121.5	68.3	...	...	...	...	...	...
Total Current Disbursements and Net Saving of General Government	381.3	672.6	759.9	884.7	971.3	790.2	...	...	...	...	...	...

1.5 Current Income and Outlay of Corporate and Quasi-Corporate Enterprises, Summary

Thousand Million CFA francs — Fiscal year beginning 1 July

	1980	1983	1984	1985	1986	1987	1988	1989	1990	1991	1992	1993

Receipts

	1980	1983	1984	1985	1986	1987	1988	1989	1990	1991	1992	1993
1 Operating surplus	...	526.6	694.1	723.0	676.8	618.2	...	...	...	...	...	...
2 Property and entrepreneurial income received	...	45.7	50.0	71.7	73.9	68.9	...	...	...	...	...	...
3 Current transfers	...	28.0	40.4	42.6	46.2	48.4	...	...	...	...	...	...
Total Current Receipts	...	600.3	784.4	837.3	796.9	735.4	...	...	...	...	...	...

Disbursements

	1980	1983	1984	1985	1986	1987	1988	1989	1990	1991	1992	1993
1 Property and entrepreneurial income	...	185.8	195.1	203.2	230.7	247.7	...	...	...	...	...	...
2 Direct taxes and other current payments to general government	...	123.6	145.5	194.3	238.9	159.8	...	...	...	...	...	...
3 Other current transfers	...	53.1	172.0	164.3	147.9	167.2	...	...	...	...	...	...
4 Net saving	...	237.8	271.8	275.4	179.5	160.8	...	...	...	...	...	...
Total Current Disbursements and Net Saving	...	600.3	784.4	837.3	796.9	735.4	...	...	...	...	...	...

1.6 Current Income and Outlay of Households and Non-Profit Institutions

Thousand Million CFA francs — Fiscal year beginning 1 July

	1980	1983	1984	1985	1986	1987	1988	1989	1990	1991	1992	1993

Receipts

	1980	1983	1984	1985	1986	1987	1988	1989	1990	1991	1992	1993
1 Compensation of employees	...	864.4	990.3	1107.1	1139.9	1089.8	...	...	...	...	...	...
2 Operating surplus of private unincorporated enterprises	...	1210.9	1487.7	1616.8	1520.9	1384.8	...	...	...	...	...	...
3 Property and entrepreneurial income	...	99.5	79.6	80.0	91.4	78.2	...	...	...	...	...	...
4 Current transfers	...	243.5	324.7	85.7	79.3	77.5	...	...	...	...	...	...
A Social security benefits	...	12.6	13.9	16.6	18.3	17.8	...	...	...	...	...	...
B Social assistance grants	...	4.9	6.5	16.4	7.1	8.7	...	...	...	...	...	...
C Other	...	226.0	304.3	52.7	53.9	51.0	...	...	...	...	...	...
Total Current Receipts	...	2418.2	2882.1	2889.6	2831.5	2630.3	...	...	...	...	...	...

Disbursements

	1980	1983	1984	1985	1986	1987	1988	1989	1990	1991	1992	1993
1 Private final consumption expenditure	...	2008.0	2466.3	2570.2	2630.7	2489.3	...	...	...	...	...	...

Cameroon

1.6 Current Income and Outlay of Households and Non-Profit Institutions
(Continued)

Thousand Million CFA francs — Fiscal year beginning 1 July

	1980	1983	1984	1985	1986	1987	1988	1989	1990	1991	1992	1993
2 Property income	...	9.8	11.0	32.8	23.8	27.4	...	...	...	...	...	...
3 Direct taxes and other current transfers n.e.c. to general government	...	75.2	88.0	106.7	120.0	84.3	...	...	...	...	...	...
A Social security contributions	...	37.1	38.6	47.6	42.2	35.0	...	...	...	...	...	...
B Direct taxes	...	37.3	48.1	58.5	75.7	45.0	...	...	...	...	...	...
C Fees, fines and penalties	...	0.8	1.3	0.6	2.1	4.3	...	...	...	...	...	...
4 Other current transfers	...	134.1	84.3	-128.6	-139.1	-99.2	...	...	...	...	...	...
5 Net saving	...	191.1	232.5	308.6	196.1	128.5	...	...	...	...	...	...
Total Current Disbursements and Net Saving	...	2418.2	2882.1	2889.6	2831.5	2630.3	...	...	...	...	...	...

1.7 External Transactions on Current Account, Summary

Thousand Million CFA francs — Fiscal year beginning 1 July

	1980	1983	1984	1985	1986	1987	1988	1989	1990	1991	1992	1993
Payments to the Rest of the World												
1 Imports of goods and services	462.1	594.7	727.9	859.0	789.8	571.4	...	...	...	...	...	...
A Imports of merchandise c.i.f.	364.1	462.9	482.3	588.8	558.3	432.6	...	...	...	...	...	...
B Other	98.0	131.8	245.6	270.2	231.5	138.8	...	...	...	...	...	...
2 Factor income to the rest of the world	61.9	76.2	121.8	151.7	88.0	103.5	...	...	...	...	...	...
A Compensation of employees	10.7	19.8	3.2	3.9	3.4	2.2	...	...	...	...	...	...
B Property and entrepreneurial income	51.2	56.4	118.6	147.8	84.6	101.3	...	...	...	...	...	...
3 Current transfers to the rest of the world	22.7	23.8	13.5	30.1	57.0	82.8	...	...	...	...	...	...
4 Surplus of the nation on current transactions	-132.8	-15.8	-25.3	-124.6	-280.9	-171.5	...	...	...	...	...	...
Payments to the Rest of the World and Surplus of the Nation on Current Transactions	413.9	678.9	837.9	916.2	654.0	586.2	...	...	...	...	...	...
Receipts From The Rest of the World												
1 Exports of goods and services	388.5	646.5	799.9	881.9	635.6	573.8	...	...	...	...	...	...
A Exports of merchandise f.o.b.	290.8	483.2	577.7	693.0	508.2	444.6	...	...	...	...	...	...
B Other	97.7	163.3	222.2	188.9	127.4	129.2	...	...	...	...	...	...
2 Factor income from rest of the world	10.7	14.1	23.6	15.6	5.3	3.4	...	...	...	...	...	...
A Compensation of employees	4.9	8.7	4.0	0.8	0.9	0.7	...	...	...	...	...	...
B Property and entrepreneurial income	5.8	5.4	19.6	14.8	4.4	2.7	...	...	...	...	...	...
3 Current transfers from rest of the world	14.7	18.4	14.5	18.7	13.1	8.9	...	...	...	...	...	...
Receipts from the Rest of the World on Current Transactions	413.9	678.9	838.0	916.2	654.0	586.2	...	...	...	...	...	...

1.8 Capital Transactions of The Nation, Summary

Thousand Million CFA francs — Fiscal year beginning 1 July

	1980	1983	1984	1985	1986	1987	1988	1989	1990	1991	1992	1993
Finance of Gross Capital Formation												
Gross saving	355.7	813.2	930.1	921.1	687.8	590.3	522.7	...	...	...	...	...
1 Consumption of fixed capital	125.5	165.2	194.7	172.3	190.8	232.6	230.4	...	...	...	...	...
A General government	...	3.6	9.6	7.9	8.6	12.6	8.7	...	...	...	...	...
B Corporate and quasi-corporate enterprises	...	120.6	141.9	124.5	137.9	167.5	166.2	...	...	...	...	...
C Other	...	41.0	43.2	39.8	44.3	52.4	55.8	...	...	...	...	...
2 Net saving	230.2	647.9	735.4	748.8	497.0	357.7	292.3	...	...	...	...	...
A General government	...	218.9	231.1	164.8	121.5	68.3	...	...	...	...	...	...
B Corporate and quasi-corporate enterprises	...	237.8	271.8	275.4	179.5	160.8	...	...	...	...	...	...
C Other	...	191.1	232.5	308.6	196.1	128.5	...	...	...	...	...	...
Less: Surplus of the nation on current transactions	-132.7	-15.8	-25.3	-124.6	-280.9	-171.5	-77.9	...	...	...	...	...
Finance of Gross Capital Formation	488.4	828.9	955.3	1047.6	968.7	761.7	600.6	...	...	...	...	...

Cameroon

1.8 Capital Transactions of The Nation, Summary
(Continued)

Thousand Million CFA francs
Fiscal year beginning 1 July

	1980	1983	1984	1985	1986	1987	1988	1989	1990	1991	1992	1993
				Gross Capital Formation								
Increase in stocks	47.0	19.4	16.3	29.4	6.4	4.1	-37.6	...	...	...	...	...
Gross fixed capital formation	441.4	809.5	939.0	1018.2	962.3	757.6	638.2	...	...	...	...	...
1 General government	...	209.7	295.4	427.8	447.3	334.3	...	...	...	...	...	...
2 Corporate and quasi-corporate enterprises	...	9.2	6.7	4.2	16.0	12.6	...	...	...	...	...	...
3 Other	...	590.6	636.9	586.2	499.0	410.8	...	...	...	...	...	...
Gross Capital Formation	488.4	828.9	955.3	1047.6	968.7	761.7	600.6	...	...	...	...	...

1.9 Gross Domestic Product by Institutional Sectors of Origin

Thousand Million CFA francs
Fiscal year beginning 1 July

	1980	1983	1984	1985	1986	1987	1988	1989	1990	1991	1992	1993
				Domestic Factor Incomes Originating								
1 General government	107.9	209.2	239.2	286.9	313.4	305.1	299.5	...	...	...	...	...
2 Corporate and quasi-corporate enterprises	...	...	1346.8	1415.4	1396.5	1300.6	1291.7	...	...	...	...	...
A Non-financial	...	...	1210.9	1264.2	1230.2	1167.4	1162.6	...	...	...	...	...
B Financial	...	...	136.0	151.3	166.3	133.2	129.1	...	...	...	...	...
3 Households and private unincorporated enterprises	...	...	1570.6	1730.8	1613.4	1471.5	1384.4	...	...	...	...	...
4 Non-profit institutions serving households	7.2	12.8	14.5	16.7	16.8	17.1	14.1	...	...	...	...	...
Subtotal: Domestic Factor Incomes	1434.3	2613.0	3171.2	3449.8	3340.1	3094.3	2989.7	...	...	...	...	...
Indirect taxes, net	236.7	416.8	473.0	483.9	391.0	317.7	293.0	...	...	...	...	...
A Indirect taxes	...	...	485.4	529.8	430.2	337.9	299.3	...	...	...	...	...
B Less: Subsidies	...	...	12.4	45.9	39.2	20.2	6.3	...	...	...	...	...
Consumption of fixed capital	125.5	165.2	194.7	172.3	190.8	232.6	230.4	...	...	...	...	...
Gross Domestic Product	1796.5	3195.0	3838.9	4106.2	3921.9	3644.5	3513.0	...	...	...	...	...

1.10 Gross Domestic Product by Kind of Activity, in Current Prices

Thousand Million CFA francs
Fiscal year beginning 1 July

	1980	1983	1984	1985	1986	1987	1988	1989	1990	1991	1992	1993
1 Agriculture, hunting, forestry and fishing	488.2	702.0	790.4	888.1	940.7	872.6	896.1	827.9	857.4	...	...	...
2 Mining and quarrying	201.5	520.5	629.7	518.2	326.8	319.7	310.8	320.0	310.7	...	...	...
3 Manufacturing	173.7	358.5	422.4	492.0	500.5	480.2	493.6	485.0	465.5	...	...	...
4 Electricity, gas and water	17.5	35.2	37.7	45.1	46.8	47.5	49.2	59.5	59.3	...	...	...
5 Construction	103.3	192.6	227.6	278.6	265.4	184.8	163.9	144.4	130.7	...	...	...
6 Wholesale and retail trade, restaurants and hotels	232.3	414.9	564.6	658.4	585.0	563.0	529.9	519.6	526.6	...	...	...
7 Transport, storage and communication	103.6	147.3	230.7	248.8	231.5	257.6	213.3	238.1	248.5	...	...	...
8 Finance, insurance, real estate and business services	248.0	396.8	455.3	470.4	490.7	435.7	406.3	389.0	377.0	...	...	...
9 Community, social and personal services	22.9	39.2	46.3	54.0	56.3	50.2	49.7	48.5	47.5	...	...	...
Total, Industries	1591.0	2806.9	3404.7	3653.6	3443.7	3211.3	3112.8	3032.0	3023.2	...	...	...
Producers of Government Services	110.3	212.8	248.8	295.1	325.0	299.7	296.9	282.4	301.0	...	...	...
Other Producers	23.0	40.2	43.3	48.7	50.0	49.6	41.7	45.4	45.2	...	...	...
Subtotal	1724.3	3059.9	3696.8	3997.4	3818.7	3560.6	3451.4	3359.8	3369.4	...	...	...
Less: Imputed bank service charge	30.5	38.1	32.2	26.0	27.8	22.6	19.8	18.1	18.0	...	...	...
Plus: Import duties	102.6	173.0	174.4	134.8	131.0	106.5	81.4	79.2	72.2	...	...	...
Plus: Value added tax	...	...	...	...	...	...	...	...	...	...	...	...
Equals: Gross Domestic Product	1796.4	3194.8	3839.0	4106.2	3921.9	3644.5	3513.0	3420.9	3423.6	...	...	...

1.11 Gross Domestic Product by Kind of Activity, in Constant Prices

Thousand Million CFA francs
Fiscal year beginning 1 July

	1980	1983	1984	1985	1986	1987	1988	1989	1990	1991	1992	1993
				At constant prices of: 1980								
1 Agriculture, hunting, forestry and fishing	460.6	480.9	458.7	497.8	537.2	488.9	541.7	534.7	563.5	...	...	...
2 Mining and quarrying	159.3	284.6	306.7	300.3	273.0	252.3	244.2	247.3	196.9	...	...	...
3 Manufacturing	157.8	243.6	269.2	324.5	324.4	339.6	337.8	320.2	307.3	...	...	...
4 Electricity, gas and water	17.0	22.3	19.6	28.5	27.9	26.4	26.9	32.7	32.6	...	...	...
5 Construction	92.9	111.6	126.1	133.4	120.5	74.8	65.4	59.5	53.9	...	...	...

Cameroon

1.11 Gross Domestic Product by Kind of Activity, in Constant Prices
(Continued)

Thousand Million CFA francs — Fiscal year beginning 1 July

At constant prices of: 1980

	1980	1983	1984	1985	1986	1987	1988	1989	1990	1991	1992	1993
6 Wholesale and retail trade, restaurants and hotels										...	...	...
7 Transport, storage and communication	541.1	638.4	778.6	850.4	769.4	707.0	635.5	570.0	572.2	...	...	...
8 Finance, insurance, real estate and business services										...	...	...
9 Community, social and personal services	122.3	159.0	171.1	173.5	179.3	165.6	162.7	155.8	166.1	...	...	...
Total, Industries	...	...	...	...	...	...	...	...	...	...	...	...
Producers of Government Services	...	...	...	...	...	...	...	...	...	...	...	...
Other Producers	...	...	...	...	...	...	...	...	...	...	...	...
Subtotal	1551.0	1940.4	2129.9	2308.4	2231.7	2054.6	2014.2	1920.2	1892.4	...	...	...
Less: Imputed bank service charge	...	...	...	...	...	...	...	...	...	...	...	...
Plus: Import duties	99.7	108.9	102.5	85.4	109.4	90.3	75.6	64.9	69.3	...	...	...
Plus: Value added tax	...	...	...	...	...	...	...	...	...	...	...	...
Equals: Gross Domestic Product	1650.7	2049.3	2232.4	2393.8	2341.2	2144.9	2089.8	1985.1	1961.6	...	...	...

1.12 Relations Among National Accounting Aggregates

Thousand Million CFA francs — Fiscal year beginning 1 July

	1980	1983	1984	1985	1986	1987	1988	1989	1990	1991	1992	1993
Gross Domestic Product	1796.5	3195.0	3838.9	4106.2	3921.9	3644.5	3513.0	...	...	...	...	...
Plus: Net factor income from the rest of the world	-51.2	-62.1	-98.2	-136.1	-82.8	-100.1	-121.0	...	...	...	...	...
Factor income from the rest of the world	10.7	14.1	23.6	15.6	5.3	3.4	...	...	...	...	...	...
Less: Factor income to the rest of the world	61.9	76.2	121.8	151.7	88.1	103.5	...	...	...	...	...	...
Equals: Gross National Product	1745.3	3132.9	3740.7	3970.1	3839.1	3544.5	3392.0	...	...	...	...	...
Less: Consumption of fixed capital	125.5	165.2	194.7	172.3	190.8	232.6	230.4	...	...	...	...	...
Equals: National Income	1619.8	2967.7	3546.1	3797.8	3648.4	3311.9	3161.6	...	...	...	...	...
Plus: Net current transfers from the rest of the world	-8.0	-5.5	1.0	-11.4	-43.9	-73.9	-60.0	...	...	...	...	...
Current transfers from the rest of the world	14.7	18.4	14.5	18.7	13.1	8.9	...	...	...	...	...	...
Less: Current transfers to the rest of the world	22.7	23.8	13.5	30.1	57.0	82.8	...	...	...	...	...	...
Equals: National Disposable Income	1611.8	2962.2	3547.0	3784.4	3604.5	3238.0	3101.6	...	...	...	...	...
Less: Final consumption	1381.6	2314.3	2811.6	3035.6	3107.4	2880.3	2809.3	...	...	...	...	...
Equals: Net Saving	230.2	647.9	735.4	748.8	497.0	357.7	292.3	...	...	...	...	...
Less: Surplus of the nation on current transactions	-132.8	-15.8	-25.3	-124.6	-280.9	-171.5	-77.9	...	...	...	...	...
Equals: Net Capital Formation	363.0	663.7	760.7	873.4	777.9	529.2	370.2	...	...	...	...	...

2.1 Government Final Consumption Expenditure by Function, in Current Prices

Thousand Million CFA francs — Fiscal year beginning 1 July

	1980	1983	1984	1985	1986	1987	1988	1989	1990	1991	1992	1993
1 General public services	54.5	102.1	110.3	139.4	145.7	110.8	134.3	...	...	...	...	...
2 Defence	23.0	48.7	42.6	53.8	57.3	57.5	46.9	...	...	...	...	...
3 Public order and safety								...	...	...	...	...
4 Education	31.5	62.1	69.0	82.0	91.0	84.6	81.3	...	...	...	...	...
5 Health	10.6	24.3	23.4	26.2	27.0	23.9	22.6	...	...	...	...	...
6 Social security and welfare	0.7	2.2	2.9	2.9	3.5	3.2	3.4	...	...	...	...	...
7 Housing and community amenities	6.3	11.8	17.1	25.4	28.6	19.4	18.7	...	...	...	...	...
8 Recreational, cultural and religious affairs	2.7	5.6	7.2	8.4	9.8	8.9	8.2	...	...	...	...	...
9 Economic services	12.9	22.1	35.0	52.8	50.3	28.7	23.3	...	...	...	...	...
10 Other functions	16.9	27.4	37.8	74.6	63.5	54.0	39.7	...	...	...	...	...
Total Government Final Consumption Expenditure	159.1	306.4	345.3	465.5	476.7	391.0	378.4	...	...	...	...	...

Cameroon

2.17 Exports and Imports of Goods and Services, Detail

Thousand Million CFA francs

Fiscal year beginning 1 July

	1980	1983	1984	1985	1986	1987	1988	1989	1990	1991	1992	1993
Exports of Goods and Services												
1 Exports of merchandise, f.o.b.	290.8	483.2	577.7	693.0	508.2	444.6	...	...	...	...	...	...
2 Transport and communication	47.7	87.1	84.3	97.9	64.9	59.9	...	...	...	...	...	...
3 Insurance service charges				6.2	3.9	3.2	...	...	...	...	...	...
4 Other commodities	26.1	37.1	107.4	55.2	35.9	9.2	...	...	...	...	...	...
5 Adjustments of merchandise exports to change-of-ownership basis	...	...	...	...	...	...	...	...	...	...	...	...
6 Direct purchases in the domestic market by non-residential households	14.2	25.3	26.6	14.9	14.1	39.6	...	...	...	...	...	...
7 Direct purchases in the domestic market by extraterritorial bodies	9.7	13.8	3.9	14.8	8.5	8.2	...	...	...	...	...	...
Total Exports of Goods and Services	388.5	646.5	799.9	881.9	635.5	564.7	...	...	...	...	...	...
Imports of Goods and Services												
1 Imports of merchandise, c.i.f.	364.2	462.9	482.3	588.8	558.3	432.6	...	...	...	...	...	...
2 Adjustments of merchandise imports to change-of-ownership basis	...	...	...	...	...	...	...	...	...	...	...	...
3 Other transport and communication	15.3	21.6	18.5	32.0	21.0	19.6	...	...	...	...	...	...
4 Other insurance service charges	3.5	7.1	7.4	13.6	11.7	9.4	...	...	...	...	...	...
5 Other commodities	70.3	89.6	155.9	140.1	108.9	81.7	...	...	...	...	...	...
6 Direct purchases abroad by government	3.3	3.8	13.1	20.3	10.6	9.0	...	...	...	...	...	...
7 Direct purchases abroad by resident households	5.5	9.7	50.6	64.2	79.4	18.9	...	...	...	...	...	...
Total Imports of Goods and Services	462.1	594.7	727.9	859.0	789.8	571.4	...	...	...	...	...	...
Balance of Goods and Services	-73.6	51.8	72.0	22.9	-154.3	-6.5	...	...	...	...	...	...
Total Imports and Balance of Goods and Services	388.5	646.5	799.9	881.9	635.5	564.7	...	...	...	...	...	...

Canada

General note. The preparation of national accounts statistics in Canada is undertaken by Statistics Canada, in Ottawa, Ontario, Canada. Official estimates are published quarterly and annually in 'National Income and Expenditure Accounts', Statistics Canada 13-001 and 13-201. A detailed description of the sources and methods used for the national accounts estimation is found in 'Guide to the Income and Expenditure Accounts', Statistics Canada Catalogue 13-603E (English) and 13-603F (French), published in November, 1990. The estimates are generally in accordance with the classifications and definitions recommended in the United Nations System of National Accounts (SNA). Annual input-output tables at current and constant prices are published in 'The Input-Output Structure of the Canadian Economy', Statistics Canada Catalogue 15-201. Quarterly statistics on flows of funds are published in 'Financial Flow Accounts' catalogue 13-014 and annual estimates of balance sheets are published in 'National Balance Sheet Accounts' catalogue 13-214. Detailed sources and methods are published in 'A Guide to the Financial Flow and National Balance Sheet Accounts' catalogue 13-585e (English) and 13-585f (French). The following tables have been from successive replies to the United Nations national accounts questionnaire. When the scope and coverage of the estimates differ for conceptual or statistical reasons from the definitions and classifications recommended in SNA, a footnote is indicated to the relevant tables.

Sources and methods:

(a) Gross domestic product. All components of GDP by expenditure type are estimated through the expenditure approach.

(b) Expenditure on the gross domestic product. Government final consumption expenditure is based on public accounts and financial records and statements of the government bodies. At the federal and provincial levels, the figures are derived by eliminating from total government budgetary expenditure on all outlays that are not made directly to purchase new goods and services. At the local level, the estimates are built up directly on a gross basis from the data sources, subtracting revenues from sales of goods and services. Bench-mark estimates of consumption expenditure are based on the censuses of merchandising and services conducted in 1951, 1961, 1966, and 1971 and on the retail commodity survey of 1974 and 1989 as well as the Family Expenditure Surveys (most recently in 1986, 1990 and 1992). These estimates are first adjusted to include commodities purchased through non-retail trade outlets and then broken down into trade groupings. For the non-census years, the bench-mark estimates of each trade group are interpolated or projected by using the movement of sales of equivalent kind-of-business groupings. For non-retail trade groups, surveys of wholesale trade and service industries are used. Estimates of consumer expenditure on services such as transport, health care and education are based on annual surveys or published reports. Comprehensive figures on the quantities of physical stocks held on farms and grains in commercial channels are available from the Agriculture Division of Statistics Canada. Inventories held by government agencies are obtained from government records. Estimates of inventory book values of non-farm business are based on annual censuses or sample surveys. The estimates of gross fixed capital investment are based on the results of annual surveys which are published in 'Private and Public Investment in Canada: Outlook' reports. Data are available separately for non-residential construction and machinery and equipment. Residential construction are derived from housing starts as counted by Canada Mortgage and Housing Corporation, building permit values and quarterly work-put-in-place coefficients. The estimates of exports and imports of goods and services are based on information available in the balance of payments. For merchandise, the import and export figures are obtained from Customs entries while for services, the estimates draw upon a number of sources such as surveys of business firms and Statistics Canada's international travel surveys. Constant dollar values of government consumption expenditure are obtained through extrapolating base-year wages and salaries by employment data and through deflating other current expenditure by base-weighted price indexes. Price deflation is also used for private final consumption expenditure, non-farm stocks, non-residential construction and machinery and equipment, and exports and imports of goods and services. The constant price series for farm inventories is derived by valuing the physical quantities of stocks in prices from the base period chosen. For residential construction, the estimates are derived by deflating current dollar component estimates with price indexes. Exports and imports of merchandise are each revalued by specially constructed current-weighted indexes.

(c) Cost-structure of the gross domestic product. The general method used in the preparation of the labour income estimates consists of calculating the payments made on labour account by the various industrial groups and summing the results. The estimates are based on monthly and annual samples of full-coverage surveys conducted by Statistics Canada, decennial or quinquennial censuses and published statements of governments. A principal benchmark source of information is the tabulation of total wages and salaries submitted by employers with respect to employees' earnings. Undertaken by the Revenue Canada -- Taxation in connection with the administration of the Income Tax Act. The estimates of corporation profits are obtained from the publication 'Financial Statistics for Enterprises'. Estimates of interest and miscellaneous investment income are based on information obtained from various sources such as Revenue Canada -- Taxation, the Bank of Canada, accounts and financial statements of governments and others. For unincorporated business, estimates are obtained either through direct inquiry, projections from bench-mark data, subtracting expenses from gross income or through applying the ratio of net to gross income based on survey or income-tax data. The estimates of depreciation are calculated on an original cost valuation basis with a close link to the figures of book depreciation reported in the accounting records of business firms. For the government sector, capital consumption allowances are imputed while for the agricultural and housing sectors, replacement cost estimates of capital consumption are prepared from estimates of fixed reproducible capital at market values. The estimates of indirect taxes are based on accounting records of the various levels of government. Subsidies consist of federal and provincial production subsidies.

(d) Gross domestic product by kind of economic activity. The table of GDP of economic activity is prepared in factor values. The income approach is used to estimate the value added of the various industries, except in the case of agriculture, for which the income approach is combined with the activity. The components of GDP at factor cost are classified by industry on the basis of establishment data. Wages, salaries and supplementary labour income as well as net incomes of farms and non-farm unincorporated businesses, corporation profits and capital consumption allowances are built up by assembling data on an industry-by-industry basis. Certain imputations are made to include non-market activities. They are allocated to their appropriate industry of origin. For the estimates at constant prices, double deflation is used for agriculture, manufacturing, electricity and railway and air transport. Price deflation is used for non-residential and other engineering construction, road transport and advertising services. For producers of government services and producers of private non-profit services to households, various indicators are used to extrapolate or deflate value added. For the remaining industries, value added is expralopated by various quantity indicators or indexes.

1.1 Expenditure on the Gross Domestic Product, in Current Prices

Million Canadian dollars

	1980	1983	1984	1985	1986	1987	1988	1989	1990	1991	1992	1993
1 Government final consumption expenditure [a]	59097	84314	88882	95274	99878	105570	114164	123770	134763	144047	149386	152775
2 Private final consumption expenditure	170408	228221	248428	271099	293489	318216	345179	373670	393055	405283	416353	430806
3 Gross capital formation [b]	72624	78329	89460	96479	104117	119788	136585	149682	138541	129013	124875	128205
A Increase in stocks [b]	336	-2898	4761	2281	2557	3071	3795	3607	-2835	-3675	-3280	1263
B Gross fixed capital formation [a]	72288	81227	84699	94198	101560	116717	132790	146075	141376	132688	128155	126942
Residential buildings	17455	21423	22348	25238	30823	39539	43899	49152	44018	39809	43727	42907
Non-residential buildings	10921	11362	12009	14519	15507	18305	20953	23948	23646	21023	18064	16368
Other construction and land improvement etc.	18556	21470	21549	22709	20159	19537	22261	23704	26493	27207	24098	23630
Other [c]	25356	26972	28793	31733	35071	39336	45677	49271	47219	44649	42266	44037
4 Exports of goods and services	87579	103444	126035	134919	138119	145416	159309	163903	168917	163943	180406	208223
5 Less: Imports of goods and services	81933	89832	110632	123388	133369	140502	156384	166079	171223	172453	186738	212508
Statistical discrepancy	-45	-2247	-862	-44	-808	-1710	1987	201	-1244	-2419	-2938	-2672
Equals: Gross Domestic Product	307730	402229	441311	474339	501426	546778	600840	645147	662809	667414	681344	704829

a) Acquisitions on embassies, consulates and military establishments abroad are included under government current expenditure and imports.
b) Increase in stocks of gross capital formation includes stocks of breeding stocks, draught animals, dairy cattle, etc. Stocks of commodities internally processed are valued at cost.
c) Producers durable goods of gross fixed capital formation includes work put in place on uncompleted heavy machinery and equipment.

Canada

1.2 Expenditure on the Gross Domestic Product, in Constant Prices

Million Canadian dollars

	1980	1983	1984	1985	1986	1987	1988	1989	1990	1991	1992	1993
					At constant prices of: 1986							
1 Government final consumption expenditure [a]	88415	94160	95360	98328	99878	101602	105766	110032	113560	116752	118176	118815
2 Private final consumption expenditure	247918	255567	267524	281316	293489	306164	319745	330182	333339	328290	332908	338535
3 Gross capital formation [bc]	86901	83319	90772	97786	104117	115764	126620	135408	125225	121281	117211	121426
A Increase in stocks [b]	313	-2215	3412	2162	2557	3222	2515	3778	-1737	-2906	-3469	985
B Gross fixed capital formation [ac]	86588	85534	87360	95624	101560	112542	124105	131630	126962	124187	120680	120441
Residential buildings	23666	24747	24774	27201	30823	35857	36879	38625	34874	30508	32927	31460
Non-residential buildings	14278	12263	12966	15203	15507	17251	18471	19801	19095	17579	15040	13521
Other construction and land improvement etc.	24041	23058	21955	22504	20159	19252	21057	21865	23447	24282	21421	20714
Other [d]	26110	25890	27879	30912	35071	40182	47698	51339	49546	51818	51292	54746
4 Exports of goods and services	97564	106017	124785	132218	138119	142942	156528	157799	164312	165984	178797	197436
5 Less: Imports of goods and services	97035	97395	114058	123935	133369	142678	162385	172584	175960	181359	192127	208958
Statistical discrepancy	-2913	-5821	-757	-140	-808	-1608	1834	248	-1029	-1987	-2371	-2136
Equals: Gross Domestic Product [e]	420850	435847	463626	485573	501426	522186	548108	561085	559447	548961	552594	565118

a) Acquisitions on embassies, consulates and military establishments abroad are included under government current expenditure and imports.
b) Increase in stocks of gross capital formation includes stocks of breeding stocks, draught animals, dairy cattle, etc. Stocks of commodities internally processed are valued at cost.
c) Prior to 1986, the estimates of the total is not equal to the sum of its sub-items. The difference refers to an adjusting entry which is not shown.
d) Producers durable goods of gross fixed capital formation includes work put in place on uncompleted heavy machinery and equipment.
e) The period beginning 1970 was deflated in four time segments, 1970, 1971-1981, 1981-1986 and 1986 to date, with price indexes based on prices of 1961, 1971, 1981 and 1986 respectively. The four series are then linked arithmetically at the major group, component and total gross domestic product levels to a 1986 base. An adjusting entry which refers to the differences between rebased aggregates and the sum of their rebased components is not shown explicitly.

1.3 Cost Components of the Gross Domestic Product

Million Canadian dollars

	1980	1983	1984	1985	1986	1987	1988	1989	1990	1991	1992	1993
1 Indirect taxes, net	27272	40135	42714	47212	53827	59719	67790	76214	76662	79985	84849	88862
A Indirect taxes	35505	50150	54957	58789	64338	71365	79030	86868	87694	93518	98161	100482
B Less: Subsidies	8233	10015	12243	11577	10511	11646	11240	10654	11032	13533	13312	11620
2 Consumption of fixed capital	35527	47060	50884	55926	60595	64116	68128	72352	78594	81622	84388	86882
3 Compensation of employees paid by resident producers to:	171424	221800	238849	257518	274801	298834	327823	353632	372087	381645	390741	400533
A Resident households	171424	221800	238849	257518	274801	298834	327823	353632	372087	381645	390741	400533
B Rest of the world	-	-	-	-	-	-	-	-	-	...	...	...
4 Operating surplus	73462	90987	108001	113638	111394	122399	139086	143150	134222	121743	118428	125879
Statistical discrepancy	45	2247	863	45	809	1710	-1987	-201	1244	2419	2938	2673
Equals: Gross Domestic Product	307730	402229	441311	474339	501426	546778	600840	645147	662809	667414	681344	704829

1.4 General Government Current Receipts and Disbursements

Million Canadian dollars

	1980	1983	1984	1985	1986	1987	1988	1989	1990	1991	1992	1993
					Receipts							
1 Operating surplus	...	...	...	...	...	...	...	...	...	...	...	...
2 Property and entrepreneurial income	17787	25010	27975	29411	28236	29307	32219	36589	38350	38031	39101	40272
3 Taxes, fees and contributions	93743	130487	142887	154218	169742	189317	210086	225014	241797	249727	256944	262774
A Indirect taxes	35505	50150	54957	58789	64338	71365	79030	86868	87694	93518	98161	100482
B Direct taxes	48658	64555	70867	76372	84824	95414	105772	113002	127097	126011	124904	126572
C Social security contributions	7856	13285	14402	16305	17692	19464	21894	21428	24966	27926	31417	32763
D Compulsory fees, fines and penalties	1724	2497	2661	2752	2888	3074	3390	3716	2040	2272	2462	2957
4 Other current transfers	...	...	...	...	...	...	...	...	...	...	...	...
Total Current Receipts of General Government	111530	155497	170862	183629	197978	218624	242305	261603	280147	287758	296045	303046
					Disbursements							
1 Government final consumption expenditure	59097	84314	88882	95274	99878	105570	114164	123770	134763	144047	149386	152775
A Compensation of employees	39345	55885	58871	61226	64637	68647	73047	78698	86297	93261	97709	99955
B Consumption of fixed capital	4553	6297	6773	7092	7371	7699	8269	8896	9489	9465	9715	10093
C Purchases of goods and services, net	15199	22132	23238	26956	27870	29224	32848	36176	38977	41321	41962	42727
D Less: Own account fixed capital formation	...	...	...	...	...	...	...	...	...	...	...	...
E Indirect taxes paid, net	...	...	...	...	...	...	...	...	...	...	...	...
2 Property income	16790	29419	34752	40183	42754	45903	50410	57933	63725	64591	63596	65061

Canada

1.4 General Government Current Receipts and Disbursements
(Continued)

Million Canadian dollars

	1980	1983	1984	1985	1986	1987	1988	1989	1990	1991	1992	1993
A Interest	16790	29419	34752	40183	42754	45903	50410	57933	63725	64591	63596	65061
B Net land rent and royalties	...	...	...	...	...	...	...	...	...	...	...	...
3 Subsidies	8233	10015	12243	11577	10511	11646	11240	10654	11032	13533	13312	11620
4 Other current transfers	31283	51141	55107	59638	63391	68391	73699	79245	88239	101077	110073	116228
A Social security benefits	16655	29135	31151	33963	36904	40292	43469	46952	51197	58736	63351	64865
B Social assistance grants	13811	20812	22385	24032	24692	25930	27736	29895	34002	39651	44024	48676
C Other	817	1194	1571	1643	1795	2169	2494	2398	3040	2690	2698	2687
5 Net saving	-3873	-19392	-20122	-23043	-18556	-12886	-7208	-9999	-17612	-35490	-40322	-42638
Total Current Disbursements and Net Saving of General Government	111530	155497	170862	183629	197978	218624	242305	261603	280147	287758	296045	303046

1.5 Current Income and Outlay of Corporate and Quasi-Corporate Enterprises, Summary

Million Canadian dollars

	1980	1983	1984	1985	1986	1987	1988	1989	1990	1991	1992	1993
					Receipts							
1 Operating surplus	59025	70846	84118	88032	82832	93351	107009	111248	103956	91868	86924	92338
2 Property and entrepreneurial income received	16162	27191	32393	37849	38067	39629	45731	48787	51998	51267	48322	48966
3 Current transfers	3713	3785	3791	4233	4496	5268	6205	8218	9056	7820	5893	4822
Total Current Receipts	78900	101822	120302	130114	125395	138248	158945	168253	165010	150955	141139	146126
					Disbursements							
1 Property and entrepreneurial income	54686	79769	90228	95787	96877	99487	114419	128855	142321	132712	128246	124108
2 Direct taxes and other current payments to general government	12078	12320	14984	15563	14573	16990	17586	18566	16834	14710	13582	15077
3 Other current transfers	647	735	744	697	734	786	835	966	1013	1060	1040	1091
4 Net saving	11489	8998	14346	18067	13211	20985	26105	19866	4842	2473	-1729	5850
Total Current Disbursements and Net Saving	78900	101822	120302	130114	125395	138248	158945	168253	165010	150955	141139	146126

1.6 Current Income and Outlay of Households and Non-Profit Institutions

Million Canadian dollars

	1980	1983	1984	1985	1986	1987	1988	1989	1990	1991	1992	1993
					Receipts							
1 Compensation of employees	171424	221800	238849	257518	274801	298834	327823	353632	372087	381645	390741	400533
A From resident producers	171424	221800	238849	257518	274801	298834	327823	353632	372087	381645	390741	400533
B From rest of the world	...	...	...	...	...	...	...	...	...	...	...	...
2 Operating surplus of private unincorporated enterprises	16598	23629	27307	29255	32802	33867	37143	37503	36924	37227	38551	40370
3 Property and entrepreneurial income	27539	41896	47702	50729	52686	55191	63101	74316	85181	78751	73073	68971
4 Current transfers	31503	51159	54741	59215	62966	67701	72736	78492	82697	95361	104086	110124
A Social security benefits	16655	29135	31151	33963	36904	40292	43469	46952	46898	53801	58054	59297
B Social assistance grants	13811	20812	22385	24032	24692	25930	27736	29895	34002	39651	44024	48676
C Other	1037	1212	1205	1220	1370	1479	1531	1645	1797	1909	2008	2151
Total Current Receipts	247064	338484	368599	396717	423255	455593	500803	543943	576889	592984	606451	619998
					Disbursements							
1 Private final consumption expenditure	170408	228221	248428	271099	293489	318216	345179	373670	393055	405283	416353	430806
2 Property income	3713	3785	3791	4233	4496	5268	6205	8218	9056	7820	5893	4822
3 Direct taxes and other current transfers n.e.c. to general government	45165	66974	71846	78797	89156	99748	111800	118043	135550	139991	143633	145574
A Social security contributions	10591	17156	18582	20847	22785	25162	28283	28345	31833	34659	38264	39454
B Direct taxes	32850	47321	50603	55198	63483	71512	80127	85982	101677	103060	102907	103163
C Fees, fines and penalties	1724	2497	2661	2752	2888	3074	3390	3716	2040	2272	2462	2957
4 Other current transfers	364	473	500	554	602	629	709	784	736	775	933	980
5 Net saving	27414	39031	44034	42034	35512	31732	36910	43228	38492	39115	39639	37816
Total Current Disbursements and Net Saving	247064	338484	368599	396717	423255	455593	500803	543943	576889	592984	606451	619998

Canada

1.7 External Transactions on Current Account, Summary

Million Canadian dollars

	1980	1983	1984	1985	1986	1987	1988	1989	1990	1991	1992	1993
Payments to the Rest of the World
1 Imports of goods and services	81933	89832	110632	123388	133369	140502	156384	166079	171223	172453	186738	212508
A Imports of merchandise c.i.f.	70912	75961	95404	106680	114426	119546	133404	140112	141789	141602	154399	177903
B Other	11021	13871	15228	16708	18943	20956	22980	25967	29434	30851	32339	34605
2 Factor income to the rest of the world	11466	17197	19849	21906	24118	24471	30705	31829	34438	32790	33739	34076
A Compensation of employees	-	-	-	-	-	-	-	-	...	...	...	...
B Property and entrepreneurial income	11466	17197	19849	21906	24118	24471	30705	31829	34438	32790	33739	34076
By general government	1592	3245	3755	4743	6502	7453	8527	10140	11130	12212	13451	15316
By corporate and quasi-corporate enterprises	9874	13952	16094	17163	17616	17018	22178	21689	23308	20578	20288	18760
By other	...	...	...	...	...	...	...	...	...	...	...	...
3 Current transfers to the rest of the world	1310	1800	2239	2355	2538	2926	3356	3359	3925	3625	3756	3800
A Indirect taxes to supranational organizations	...	...	...	...	...	...	...	...	...	...	...	...
B Other current transfers	1310	1800	2239	2355	2538	2926	3356	3359	3925	3625	3756	3800
4 Surplus of the nation on current transactions	-1977	1862	1407	-3406	-11738	-12421	-16624	-24637	-27438	-31520	-31726	-29382
Payments to the Rest of the World and Surplus of the Nation on Current Transactions	92732	110691	134127	144243	148287	155478	173821	176630	182148	177348	192507	221002
Receipts From The Rest of the World
1 Exports of goods and services	87579	103444	126035	134919	138119	145416	159309	163903	168917	163943	180406	208223
A Exports of merchandise f.o.b.	78946	93311	114849	122468	123691	129976	141983	145594	149858	144342	160063	185840
B Other	8633	10133	11186	12451	14428	15440	17326	18309	19059	19601	20343	22383
2 Factor income from rest of the world	3639	5594	6363	7574	7716	8027	11993	10334	10579	10888	9440	9945
A Compensation of employees	-	-	-	-	-	-	-	-	...	...	...	...
B Property and entrepreneurial income	3639	5594	6363	7574	7716	8027	11993	10334	10579	10888	9440	9945
By general government	80	35	60	48	243	472	1072	1374	1403	1477	1192	665
By corporate and quasi-corporate enterprises	3125	4505	4820	6058	6055	5998	8914	6595	6061	6240	5224	6050
By other	434	1054	1483	1468	1418	1557	2007	2365	3115	3171	3024	3230
3 Current transfers from rest of the world	1514	1653	1729	1750	2452	2035	2519	2393	2652	2517	2661	2834
A Subsidies from supranational organisations	...	...	...	...	...	...	...	...	...	...	...	...
B Other current transfers	1514	1653	1729	1750	2452	2035	2519	2393	2652	2517	2661	2834
Receipts from the Rest of the World on Current Transactions	92732	110691	134127	144243	148287	155478	173821	176630	182148	177348	192507	221002

1.8 Capital Transactions of The Nation, Summary

Million Canadian dollars

	1980	1983	1984	1985	1986	1987	1988	1989	1990	1991	1992	1993
Finance of Gross Capital Formation
Gross saving	70557	75697	89142	92984	90762	103947	123935	125447	108615	92655	87273	93478
1 Consumption of fixed capital	35527	47060	50884	55926	60595	64116	68128	72352	78594	81622	84388	86882
A General government	4553	6297	6773	7092	7371	7699	8269	8896	9489	9465	9715	10093
B Corporate and quasi-corporate enterprises	20753	27659	29887	33521	36779	38512	41297	43543	47629	49483	51401	52653
Public	2268	3329	3863	4268	4433	4654	4757	4852	4981	5206	5482	5782
Private	18485	24330	26024	29253	32346	33858	36540	38691	42648	44277	45919	46871
C Other	10221	13104	14224	15313	16445	17905	18562	19913	21476	22674	23272	24136
2 Net saving	35030	28637	38258	37058	30167	39831	55807	53095	30021	11033	2885	6596
A General government	-3873	-19392	-20122	-23043	-18556	-12886	-7208	-9999	-17612	-35490	-40322	-42638
B Corporate and quasi-corporate enterprises [a]	11489	8998	14346	18067	13211	20985	26105	19866	4842	2473	-1729	5850
Public [a]	1929	1219	1486	1529	1377	2508	2687	1967	1068	1434	1896	1968
Private [a]	9560	7779	12860	16538	11834	18477	23418	17899	3774	1039	-3625	3882

Canada

1.8 Capital Transactions of The Nation, Summary
(Continued)

Million Canadian dollars

	1980	1983	1984	1985	1986	1987	1988	1989	1990	1991	1992	1993
C Other [a]	27414	39031	44034	42034	35512	31732	36910	43228	42791	44050	44936	43384
Less: Surplus of the nation on current transactions	-1977	1862	1407	-3406	-11738	-12421	-16624	-24637	-27438	-31520	-31726	-29382
Statistical discrepancy	90	4494	1725	89	1617	3420	-3974	-402	2488	4838	5876	5345
Finance of Gross Capital Formation	72624	78329	89460	96479	104117	119788	136585	149682	138541	129013	124875	128205
					Gross Capital Formation							
Increase in stocks	336	-2898	4761	2281	2557	3071	3795	3607	-2835	-3675	-3280	1263
Gross fixed capital formation	72288	81227	84699	94198	101560	116717	132790	146075	141376	132688	128155	126942
1 General government	8223	10395	11390	12886	12567	12886	13690	15263	16610	16434	16079	16448
2 Corporate and quasi-corporate enterprises	43689	47076	48287	54385	57210	64705	74711	83120	81848	77825	70090	68680
3 Other	20376	23756	25022	26927	31783	39126	44389	47692	42918	38429	41986	41814
Gross Capital Formation	72624	78329	89460	96479	104117	119788	136585	149682	138541	129013	124875	128205

a) All inventory valuation adjustments have been allocated to private corporate enterprises.

1.9 Gross Domestic Product by Institutional Sectors of Origin

Million Canadian dollars

	1980	1983	1984	1985	1986	1987	1988	1989	1990	1991	1992	1993
					Domestic Factor Incomes Originating							
1 General government	39651	56219	59235	61902	65282	69278	73709	79451	87160	94068	98482	100729
2 Corporate and quasi-corporate enterprises [a]	182470	224120	250677	269578	276968	306197	343148	365983	366965	355746	355157	367716
3 Households and private unincorporated enterprises	22765	32448	36938	39676	43945	45758	50052	51348	52184	53574	55530	57967
A Owner-occupied housing	2750	7182	8386	9421	10205	10472	10611	10710	10675	10794	11223	11677
B Subsistence production	266	261	266	203	198	201	198	196	195	187	186	168
C Other	19749	25005	28286	30052	33542	35085	39243	40442	41314	42593	44121	46121
4 Non-profit institutions serving households	...	...	...	...	...	...	...	...	...	...	...	...
Subtotal: Domestic Factor Incomes	244886	312787	346850	371156	386195	421233	466909	496782	506309	503388	509169	526412
Indirect taxes, net	27272	40135	42714	47212	53827	59719	67790	76214	76662	79985	84849	88862
A Indirect taxes	35505	50150	54957	58789	64338	71365	79030	86868	87694	93518	98161	100482
B Less: Subsidies	8233	10015	12243	11577	10511	11646	11240	10654	11032	13533	13312	11620
Consumption of fixed capital	35527	47060	50884	55926	60595	64116	68128	72352	78594	81622	84388	86882
Statistical discrepancy	45	2247	863	45	809	1710	-1987	-201	1244	2419	2938	2673
Gross Domestic Product	307730	402229	441311	474339	501426	546778	600840	645147	662809	667414	681344	704829

a) A small amount of wages, salaries and supplementary labour income paid by unincorporated business is included in the corporate and quasi-corporate sector. Owner-occupied housing is net imputed rent. Subsistence production is income-in-kind.

1.10 Gross Domestic Product by Kind of Activity, in Current Prices

Million Canadian dollars

	1980	1983	1984	1985	1986	1987	1988	1989	1990	1991	1992	1993
1 Agriculture, hunting, forestry and fishing	11698	12080	13604	13337	14728	14612	16390	15685	14903	13993	...	...
2 Mining and quarrying	18067	21610	25565	27115	17503	20298	20510	20437	21397	17731	...	...
3 Manufacturing	55043	65262	75504	81673	86789	94499	105838	109154	105478	98771	...	...
4 Electricity, gas and water	8172	11890	13371	14668	15533	16305	17506	17777	18121	20387	...	...
5 Construction [a]	20266	25061	24481	26141	28082	32393	36324	40930	41438	38387	...	...
6 Wholesale and retail trade, restaurants and hotels	38520	47682	52663	57872	63190	69209	76063	81676	83921	81929	...	...
7 Transport, storage and communication	19554	25460	28366	29845	31466	33458	34355	36174	37678	38797	...	...
8 Finance, insurance, real estate and business services	48005	67452	72871	78506	85820	95370	105774	117000	122938	127283	...	...
9 Community, social and personal services	13680	18874	21033	23348	26139	28231	31911	35065	36846	39555	...	...
Total, Industries	233003	295371	327458	352503	369249	404375	444672	473897	482722	476834	...	...
Producers of Government Services	43016	60801	64322	67184	70724	74838	79673	85842	93787	100576	...	...
Other Producers	6602	9409	10241	11090	11866	12666	13770	14794	16296	17370	...	...
Subtotal [b]	282621	365581	402021	430776	451839	491879	538116	574533	592805	594780	603542	622796
Less: Imputed bank service charge	2161	3488	3424	3649	4240	4819	5066	5601	6658	7352	7047	6829
Plus: Import duties	3124	3208	3802	3910	4169	4220	4644	4494	4237	3742	4125	3368
Plus: Value added tax	-	-	-	-	-	-	-	-	-	-	18466	18887
Plus: Other adjustments [c,d]	24146	36928	38912	43302	49658	55499	63146	71720	72425	76243	62258	66607
Equals: Gross Domestic Product	307730	402229	441311	474340	501426	546779	600839	645146	662809	667413	681344	704829

a) The construction industry is defined on an activity basis. It includes all contract and own-account construction put in place.
b) Gross domestic product in factor values.
c) Item 'Other adjustments' refers to net indirect taxes other than import duties.
d) Beginning 1991, item 'Other adjustments' includes goods and services tax (V.A.T.).

Canada

1.11 Gross Domestic Product by Kind of Activity, in Constant Prices

Million Canadian dollars

	1980	1983	1984	1985	1986	1987	1988	1989	1990	1991	1992	1993
					At constant prices of:1986							
1 Agriculture, hunting, forestry and fishing	12076	13435	13312	12915	14728	13859	13442	14383	14832	14317	13596	14518
2 Mining and quarrying	17244	15838	18029	18827	17503	18631	20422	19622	19570	19936	20294	21691
3 Manufacturing	75134	72234	81553	86150	86789	90967	95599	96453	92857	86483	87092	91434
4 Electricity, gas and water	12843	13504	14147	15184	15533	16053	16277	15957	15174	15885	16073	16353
5 Construction [a]	24379	26697	25013	26953	28082	29687	30815	32502	32396	29864	27337	26034
6 Wholesale and retail trade, restaurants and hotels	52149	53086	56212	60356	63190	66940	69939	72359	71563	67855	70574	73569
7 Transport, storage and communication	25490	26792	29343	30364	31466	33762	35983	37239	37967	37418	37972	39145
8 Finance, insurance, real estate and business services	67572	71405	76401	80793	85820	90731	95639	99026	99837	101244	102474	105109
9 Community, social and personal services	21640	22482	23687	24960	26139	26884	28669	29707	29493	30580	30613	31247
Statistical discrepancy	-687	1070	813	496	...	...	...	...	...	...	...	...
Total, Industries	307831	316543	338511	356998	369249	387517	406786	417250	413692	403583	406026	419098
Producers of Government Services	65706	68507	69355	69992	70724	71891	73197	74735	76513	77364	78001	77918
Other Producers	9128	10566	11204	11586	11866	12111	12604	13064	13457	13586	13764	13931
Subtotal [bc]	381992	394995	418716	438450	451839	471520	492587	505050	503661	494532	497791	510947
Less: Imputed bank service charge	3687	3601	3541	3864	4240	4544	4850	5401	5708	5774	5571	5423
Plus: Import duties	...	...	...	...	...	...	...	...	...	...	...	...
Plus: Value added tax	...	...	...	...	...	...	...	...	...	...	...	...
Plus: Other adjustments [de]	42545	44454	48451	50987	53827	55211	60370	61436	61493	60202	60375	59593
Equals: Gross Domestic Product	420850	435848	463626	485573	501426	522186	548107	561084	559447	548961	552595	565117

a) The construction industry is defined on an activity basis. It includes all contract and own-account construction put in place.
b) Gross domestic product in factor values.
c) The period beginning 1970 was deflated in four time segments, 1970, 1971-1981, 1981-1986 and 1986 to date, with price indexes based on prices of 1961, 1971, 1981 and 1986 respectively. The four series are then linked arithmetically at the major group, component and total gross domestic product levels to a 1986 base. An adjusting entry which refers to the differences between rebased aggregates and the sum of their rebased components is not shown explicitly.
d) Item 'Other adjustments' relates to indirect taxes less subsidies and import duties.
e) Beginning 1991, item 'Other adjustments' includes goods and services tax (V.A.T.).

1.12 Relations Among National Accounting Aggregates

Million Canadian dollars

	1980	1983	1984	1985	1986	1987	1988	1989	1990	1991	1992	1993
Gross Domestic Product	307730	402229	441311	474339	501426	546778	600840	645147	662809	667414	681344	704829
Plus: Net factor income from the rest of the world	-7827	-11603	-13486	-14332	-16402	-16444	-18712	-21495	-23859	-21902	-24299	-24131
Factor income from the rest of the world	3639	5594	6363	7574	7716	8027	11993	10334	10579	10888	9440	9945
Less: Factor income to the rest of the world	11466	17197	19849	21906	24118	24471	30705	31829	34438	32790	33739	34076
Equals: Gross National Product	299903	390626	427825	460007	485024	530334	582128	623652	638950	645512	657045	680698
Less: Consumption of fixed capital	35527	47060	50884	55926	60595	64116	68128	72352	78594	81622	84388	86882
Equals: National Income [a]	264331	341319	376078	404036	423620	464508	515987	551501	559112	561471	569719	591143
Plus: Net current transfers from the rest of the world	204	-147	-510	-605	-86	-891	-837	-966	-1273	-1108	-1095	-966
Current transfers from the rest of the world	1514	1653	1729	1750	2452	2035	2519	2393	2652	2517	2661	2834
Less: Current transfers to the rest of the world	1310	1800	2239	2355	2538	2926	3356	3359	3925	3625	3756	3800
Equals: National Disposable Income	264535	341172	375568	403431	423534	463617	515150	550535	557839	560363	568624	590177
Less: Final consumption	229505	312535	337310	366373	393367	423786	459343	497440	527818	549330	565739	583581
Equals: Net Saving	35030	28637	38258	37058	30167	39831	55807	53095	30021	11033	2885	6596
Less: Surplus of the nation on current transactions	-1977	1862	1407	-3406	-11738	-12421	-16624	-24637	-27438	-31520	-31726	-29382
Statistical discrepancy	90	4494	1725	89	1617	3420	-3974	-402	2488	4838	5876	5345
Equals: Net Capital Formation [bc]	37097	31269	38576	40553	43522	55672	68457	77330	59947	47391	40487	41323

a) Item 'National income' includes a statistical discrepancy.
b) Increase in stocks of gross capital formation includes stocks of breeding stocks, draught animals, dairy cattle, etc. Stocks of commodities internally processed are valued at cost.
c) Acquisitions on embassies, consulates and military establishments abroad are included under government current expenditure and imports.

2.5 Private Final Consumption Expenditure by Type and Purpose, in Current Prices

Million Canadian dollars

	1980	1983	1984	1985	1986	1987	1988	1989	1990	1991	1992	1993
				Final Consumption Expenditure of Resident Households								
1 Food, beverages and tobacco	32058	41695	44478	47199	50469	53255	55933	59265	61251	65085	65772	66746
A Food	23316	29183	31324	32806	34942	37148	38543	40371	41850	43284	43854	45406
B Non-alcoholic beverages												
C Alcoholic beverages	5530	7627	7962	8471	9094	9432	10140	10569	10632	11347	11442	11375
D Tobacco	3212	4885	5192	5922	6433	6675	7250	8325	8769	10454	10476	9965

Canada

2.5 Private Final Consumption Expenditure by Type and Purpose, in Current Prices
(Continued)

Million Canadian dollars

	1980	1983	1984	1985	1986	1987	1988	1989	1990	1991	1992	1993
2 Clothing and footwear	11673	13984	15225	16592	18011	19210	20155	21116	21589	21465	21315	22182
3 Gross rent, fuel and power	34905	52247	56057	60299	64314	68561	75362	83087	89648	95647	100661	105030
4 Furniture, furnishings and household equipment and operation	16750	20878	22877	24796	27529	30255	32860	34508	35214	34948	35964	37161
5 Medical care and health expenses	6319	9132	10314	11314	12501	13727	14611	15905	16913	17566	18548	19543
6 Transport and communication	25446	33713	37757	43070	45690	49652	54362	57707	59523	58391	58898	60816
A Personal transport equipment	8364	9824	12050	15225	16597	17946	19858	20476	19508	18600	19191	19648
B Other	17082	23889	25707	27845	29093	31706	34504	37231	40015	39791	39707	41168
7 Recreational, entertainment, education and cultural services	17727	23439	26235	28589	32013	35009	39062	41973	43675	44742	45945	47614
A Education	5031	7011	7570	7982	8624	9219	10038	10777	11772	12602	13053	13269
B Other	12696	16428	18665	20607	23389	25790	29024	31196	31903	32140	32892	34345
8 Miscellaneous goods and services	24907	31686	34222	38121	42842	47224	51269	57097	60236	62011	63356	66371
A Personal care	4326	5396	5815	6648	7404	7985	8522	9169	9550	10063	10220	10795
B Expenditures in restaurants, cafes and hotels	12026	14616	15634	17068	18865	20268	22992	25954	26445	25879	26098	26657
C Other	8555	11674	12773	14405	16573	18971	19755	21974	24241	26069	27038	28919
Total Final Consumption Expenditure in the Domestic Market by Households, of which	169785	226774	247165	269980	293369	316893	343614	370658	388049	399855	410459	425463
A Durable goods	25466	30032	34699	40278	44628	49430	54570	57533	56267	53656	53759	56203
B Semi-durable goods	19706	24131	26082	28147	30604	33148	35220	37068	37997	37742	38045	39252
C Non-durable goods	51180	69688	74632	79959	83597	88019	93646	99736	104561	109981	112670	115920
D Services	73433	102923	111752	121596	134540	146296	160178	176321	189224	198476	205985	214088
Plus: Direct purchases abroad by resident households	3972	5288	5679	6125	6453	7622	8459	10244	12754	13230	13953	14147
Less: Direct purchases in the domestic market by non-resident households	3349	3841	4416	5006	6333	6299	6894	7232	7748	7802	8059	8804
Equals: Final Consumption Expenditure of Resident Households [a]	170408	228221	248428	271099	293489	318216	345179	373670	393055	405283	416353	430806

Final Consumption Expenditure of Private Non-profit Institutions Serving Households

Equals: Final Consumption Expenditure of Private Non-profit Organisations Serving Households	...	...	...	...	...	...	...	...	...	...	...	...
Private Final Consumption Expenditure	170408	228221	248428	271099	293489	318216	345179	373670	393055	405283	416353	430806

a) Item 'Final consumption expenditure of resident households' includes consumption expenditure of private non-profit institutions serving households.

2.6 Private Final Consumption Expenditure by Type and Purpose, in Constant Prices

Million Canadian dollars

	1980	1983	1984	1985	1986	1987	1988	1989	1990	1991	1992	1993

At constant prices of: 1986

Final Consumption Expenditure of Resident Households

	1980	1983	1984	1985	1986	1987	1988	1989	1990	1991	1992	1993
1 Food, beverages and tobacco [a]	49333	49471	49616	50420	50469	50652	51276	51725	50902	51135	51445	51607
A Food	32625	33232	33699	34488	34942	35543	36092	36705	36619	37049	38061	38682
B Non-alcoholic beverages												
C Alcoholic beverages	9846	9298	9146	9236	9094	8964	9005	8994	8589	8717	8387	8189
D Tobacco	7667	7506	7147	6930	6433	6145	6179	6026	5694	5369	4997	4736
2 Clothing and footwear	15068	15178	16100	17006	18011	18374	18294	18429	18284	16605	16356	16851
3 Gross rent, fuel and power	52104	57852	59992	62013	64314	66449	70089	73388	76074	78037	80262	82407
4 Furniture, furnishings and household equipment and operation	23170	22837	24310	25708	27529	29148	30383	30521	30363	28764	29447	30206
5 Medical care and health expenses	9987	10613	11365	11866	12501	12892	12962	13411	13547	13263	13504	13724
6 Transport and communication [a]	38149	36421	39565	43690	45690	48343	51709	52452	51565	49864	49869	50381
A Personal transport equipment	11923	11555	13630	16461	16597	17660	18698	18214	17235	16741	16563	16235
B Other	26482	24938	25970	27215	29093	30683	33011	34238	34330	33123	33306	34146
7 Recreational, entertainment, education and cultural services [a]	23512	25823	28124	29775	32013	33565	35793	36908	37085	36449	37554	38499
A Education	6774	7951	8376	8411	8624	8852	9228	9409	9774	9883	10066	10031

Canada

2.6 Private Final Consumption Expenditure by Type and Purpose, in Constant Prices
(Continued)

Million Canadian dollars

	1980	1983	1984	1985	1986	1987	1988	1989	1990	1991	1992	1993
				At constant prices of:1986								
B Other	17175	18078	19866	21406	23389	24713	26565	27499	27311	26566	27488	28468
8 Miscellaneous goods and services [a]	36550	35860	37262	39982	42842	45166	47031	49305	49494	47547	48142	50129
A Personal care	5353	5778	6110	6883	7404	7596	7830	8140	8140	8057	8100	8403
B Expenditures in restaurants, cafes and hotels	18222	16871	17275	18043	18865	19422	20993	22535	21936	19574	19427	19590
C Other	13199	13274	13924	15049	16573	18148	18208	18630	19418	19916	20615	22136
Statistical discrepancy	-751	-506	-323	-191	...	...	...	...	...	...	...	...
Total Final Consumption Expenditure in the Domestic Market by Households, of which [a]	247122	253549	266011	280269	293369	304589	317537	326139	327314	321664	326579	333804
A Durable goods	32322	32493	36814	41961	44628	48226	51442	51983	50252	47735	47860	49341
B Semi-durable goods	26488	26436	27793	29036	30604	31698	32091	32379	32274	29671	29770	30476
C Non-durable goods	79904	79238	80216	82329	83597	84128	86661	88208	87152	86884	88631	90029
D Services	109371	116280	121726	127075	134540	140537	147343	153569	157636	157374	160318	163958
Plus: Direct purchases abroad by resident households	6541	6747	6616	6463	6453	7534	8719	10503	12477	12684	12538	11327
Less: Direct purchases in the domestic market by non-resident households	5560	4511	4942	5311	6333	5959	6511	6460	6452	6058	6209	6596
Equals: Final Consumption Expenditure of Resident Households [bc]	247918	255567	267524	281316	293489	306164	319745	330182	333339	328290	332908	338535
	Final Consumption Expenditure of Private Non-profit Institutions Serving Households
Equals: Final Consumption Expenditure of Private Non-profit Organisations Serving Households	...	...	...	...	...	...	...	...	...	...	...	...
Private Final Consumption Expenditure [c]	247918	255567	267524	281316	293489	306164	319745	330182	333339	328290	332908	338535

a) Prior to 1986, the estimates of the total is not equal to the sum of its sub-items. The difference refers to an adjusting entry which is not shown.
b) Item 'Final consumption expenditure of resident households' includes consumption expenditure of private non-profit institutions serving households.
c) The period beginning 1970 was deflated in four time segments, 1970, 1971-1981, 1981-1986 and 1986 to date, with price indexes based on prices of 1961, 1971, 1981 and 1986 respectively. The four series are then linked arithmetically at the major group, component and total gross domestic product levels to a 1986 base. An adjusting entry which refers to the differences between rebased aggregates and the sum of their rebased components is not shown explicitly.

2.7 Gross Capital Formation by Type of Good and Owner, in Current Prices

Million Canadian dollars

	1980					1985					1990				
	TOTAL	Total Private	Public Enterprises	General Government	TOTAL	Total Private	Public Enterprises	General Government	TOTAL	Total Private	Public Enterprises	General Government
Increase in stocks, total [ab]	336	267	...	69	2281	2345	...	-64	-2835	-2902	...	67
1 Goods producing industries	344	344	...	...	695	695	...	...	-734	-734	...	...
2 Wholesale and retail trade	-633	-633	...	...	1583	1583	...	...	-2203	-2203	...	...
3 Other, except government stocks	556	556	...	...	67	67	...	...	35	35	...	...
4 Government stocks	69	...	...	69	-64	...	...	-64	67	...	...	67
Gross Fixed Capital Formation, Total [cbd]	72288	64065	...	8223	94198	81312	...	12886	141376	124766	...	16610
1 Residential buildings	17455	17402	...	53	25238	25222	...	16	44018	44006	...	12
2 Non-residential buildings	10921	8790	...	2131	14518	11133	...	3385	23646	19006	...	4640
3 Other construction	18556	13723	...	4833	22709	15614	...	7095	26493	17955	...	8538
4 Land improvement and plantation and orchard development [d]	...	...	...	...	...	...	...	...	...	...	...	...
5 Producers' durable goods [e]	25356	24150	...	1206	31733	29343	...	2390	47219	43799	...	3420
A Transport equipment [f]	7483	...	...	...	7985	7283	...	702	10680	10020	...	660
Passenger cars	...	...	...	...	3000	2855	...	145	4531	4330	...	201
Other	...	...	...	...	4985	4428	...	557	6149	5690	...	459
B Machinery and equipment [e]	17873	...	...	...	23748	22060	...	1688	36539	33779	...	2760
6 Breeding stock, dairy cattle, etc. [a]	...	...	...	...	...	...	...	...	...	...	...	...
Total Gross Capital Formation [cb]	72624	64332	...	8292	96479	83657	...	12822	138541	121864	...	16677

Canada

2.7 Gross Capital Formation by Type of Good and Owner, in Current Prices

Million Canadian dollars

	1991 TOTAL	1991 Total Private	1991 Public Enterprises	1991 General Government	1992 TOTAL	1992 Total Private	1992 Public Enterprises	1992 General Government	1993 TOTAL	1993 Total Private	1993 Public Enterprises	1993 General Government
Increase in stocks, total [a,b]	-3675	-3638	...	-37	-3280	-3240	...	-40	1263	1267	...	-4
1 Goods producing industries	-2810	-2810	...	...	-2657	-2657	...	...	83	83	...	...
2 Wholesale and retail trade	-713	-713	...	...	-1128	-1128	...	...	1143	1143	...	...
3 Other, except government stocks	-115	-115	...	...	545	545	...	...	41	41	...	...
4 Government stocks	-37	...	...	-37	-40	...	...	-40	-4	...	...	-4
Gross Fixed Capital Formation, Total [c,b,d]	132688	116254	...	16434	128155	112076	...	16079	126942	110494	...	16448
1 Residential buildings	39809	39791	...	18	43727	43705	...	22	42907	42884	...	23
2 Non-residential buildings	21023	15603	...	5420	18064	12377	...	5687	16368	10855	...	5513
3 Other construction	27207	19565	...	7642	24098	17142	...	6956	23630	16330	...	7300
4 Land improvement and plantation and orchard development [d]	...		...	...	...	...	...	...	...	...	...	...
5 Producers' durable goods [e]	44649	41295	...	3354	42266	38852	...	3414	44037	40425	...	3612
A Transport equipment [f]	10124	9586	...	538	9223	8692	...	531	9424	8847	...	577
Passenger cars	4424	4298	...	126	3870	3746	...	124	3765	3641	...	124
Other	5700	5288	...	412	5353	4946	...	407	5659	5206	...	453
B Machinery and equipment [e]	34525	31709	...	2816	33043	30160	...	2883	34613	31578	...	3035
6 Breeding stock, dairy cattle, etc. [a]	...	...	...	...	...	...	...	...	...	...	...	...
Total Gross Capital Formation [c,b]	129013	112616	...	16397	124875	108836	...	16039	128205	111761	...	16444

a) Increase in stocks of gross capital formation includes stocks of breeding stocks, draught animals, dairy cattle, etc. Stocks of commodities internally processed are valued at cost.
b) Column 'Public enterprises' is included in column 'Total private'.
c) Acquisitions on embassies, consulates and military establishments abroad are included under government current expenditure and imports.
d) Item 'Land improvement and plantation and orchard development' comprises construction outlays on dams and reservoirs along with irrigation and land reclamation projects for primary industries.
e) Producers durable goods of gross fixed capital formation includes work put in place on uncompleted heavy machinery and equipment.
f) From 1981, the methodology has been changed in order to derive the estimates in greater detail. There is, therefore, a statistical break in the detail of producers' durable goods between 1980 and 1981.

2.8 Gross Capital Formation by Type of Good and Owner, in Constant Prices

Million Canadian dollars

	1980 TOTAL	1980 Total Private	1980 Public Enterprises	1980 General Government	1985 TOTAL	1985 Total Private	1985 Public Enterprises	1985 General Government	1990 TOTAL	1990 Total Private	1990 Public Enterprises	1990 General Government
				At constant prices of: 1986								
Increase in stocks, total [a,b]	313	236	...	77	2162	2229	...	-67	-1737	-1800	...	63
1 Goods producing industries	799	799	...	...	723	723	...	...	57	57	...	...
2 Wholesale and retail trade	-1105	-1105	...	...	1866	1866	...	...	-1899	-1899	...	...
3 Other, except government stocks	469	469	...	...	53	53	...	...	42	42	...	...
4 Government stocks	77	...	...	77	-67	...	...	-67	63	...	...	63
Statistical discrepancy	73	73	...	...	-413	-413	...	...	...	...	...	...
Gross Fixed Capital Formation, Total [c,b,d]	86588	76394	...	10286	95624	82863	...	12776	126962	111492	...	15470
1 Residential buildings	23666	23593	...	72	27201	27184	...	17	34874	34864	...	10
2 Non-residential buildings	14278	11570	...	2700	15203	11689	...	3502	19095	15316	...	3779
3 Other construction	24041	17306	...	6633	22504	15418	...	7085	23447	15689	...	7758
4 Land improvement and plantation and orchard development [d]	...	...	...	...	...	...	...	...	...	...	...	...
5 Producers' durable goods [e]	26110	24875	...	1235	30912	28694	...	2218	49546	45623	...	3923
A Transport equipment [f]	...	...	...	...	8373	7670	...	703	10327	9725	...	602
Passenger cars	...	...	...	...	3187	3039	...	148	4081	3895	...	186
Other	...	...	...	...	5186	4631	...	555	6246	5830	...	416
B Machinery and equipment [e]	...	...	...	...	23586	21984	...	1602	39219	35898	...	3321
6 Breeding stock, dairy cattle, etc. [a]	...	...	...	...	...	...	...	...	...	...	...	...
Statistical discrepancy	-1507	-950	...	-354	-196	-122	...	-46	...	...	...	...
Statistical discrepancy	...	-557	...	-17	...	-51	...	4	...	...	...	...
Total Gross Capital Formation [c,b,g]	86901	76073	...	10346	97786	85041	...	12713	125225	109692	...	15533

Canada

2.8 Gross Capital Formation by Type of Good and Owner, in Constant Prices

Million Canadian dollars

	1991 TOTAL	1991 Total Private	1991 Public Enterprises	1991 General Government	1992 TOTAL	1992 Total Private	1992 Public Enterprises	1992 General Government	1993 TOTAL	1993 Total Private	1993 Public Enterprises	1993 General Government
At constant prices of:1986												
Increase in stocks, total [a,b]	-2906	-2874	...	-32	-3469	-3434	...	-35	985	988	...	-3
1 Goods producing industries	-2327	-2327	...	...	-2970	-2970	...	...	18	18	...	...
2 Wholesale and retail trade	-482	-482	...	...	-1155	-1155	...	...	962	962	...	...
3 Other, except government stocks	-65	-65	...	...	691	691	...	...	8	8	...	...
4 Government stocks	-32	...	...	-32	-35	...	...	-35	-3	...	...	-3
Statistical discrepancy	...	...	...	...	...	...	...	...	...	...	...	...
Gross Fixed Capital Formation, Total [c,b,d]	124187	107985	...	16202	120680	104580	...	16100	120441	103635	...	16806
1 Residential buildings	30508	30493	...	15	32927	32907	...	20	31460	31443	...	17
2 Non-residential buildings	17579	13035	...	4544	15040	10283	...	4757	13521	8937	...	4584
3 Other construction	24282	17110	...	7172	21421	14971	...	6450	20714	13981	...	6733
4 Land improvement and plantation and orchard development [d]	...	...	...	...	...	...	...	...	...	...	...	...
5 Producers' durable goods [e]	51818	47347	...	4471	51292	46419	...	4873	54746	49274	...	5472
A Transport equipment [f]	10440	9929	...	511	9090	8605	...	485	8878	8371	...	507
Passenger cars	4436	4306	...	130	3839	3712	...	127	3657	3531	...	126
Other	6004	5623	...	381	5251	4893	...	358	5221	4840	...	381
B Machinery and equipment [e]	41378	37418	...	3960	42202	37814	...	4388	45868	40903	...	4965
6 Breeding stock, dairy cattle, etc. [a]	...	...	...	...	...	...	...	...	...	...	...	...
Statistical discrepancy	...	...	...	...	...	...	...	...	...	...	...	...
Statistical discrepancy	...	...	...	...	...	...	...	...	...	...	...	...
Total Gross Capital Formation [c,b,g]	121281	105111	...	16170	117211	101146	...	16065	121426	104623	...	16803

a) Increase in stocks of gross capital formation includes stocks of breeding stocks, draught animals, dairy cattle, etc. Stocks of commodities internally processed are valued at cost.
b) Column 'Public enterprises' is included in column 'Total private'.
c) Acquisitions on embassies, consulates and military establishments abroad are included under government current expenditure and imports.
d) Item 'Land improvement and plantation and orchard development' comprises construction outlays on dams and reservoirs along with irrigation and land reclamation projects for primary industries.
e) Producers durable goods of gross fixed capital formation includes work put in place on uncompleted heavy machinery and equipment.
f) From 1981, the methodology has been changed in order to derive the estimates in greater detail. There is, therefore, a statistical break in the detail of producers' durable goods between 1980 and 1981.
g) The period beginning 1970 was deflated in four time segments, 1970, 1971-1981, 1981-1986 and 1986 to date, with price indexes based on prices of 1961, 1971, 1981 and 1986 respectively. The four series are then linked arithmetically at the major group, component and total gross domestic product levels to a 1986 base. An adjusting entry which refers to the differences between rebased aggregates and the sum of their rebased components is not shown explicitly.

2.9 Gross Capital Formation by Kind of Activity of Owner, ISIC Major Divisions, in Current Prices

Million Canadian dollars

	1980 Total Gross Capital Formation	1980 Increase in Stocks	1980 Gross Fixed Capital Formation	1985 Total Gross Capital Formation	1985 Increase in Stocks	1985 Gross Fixed Capital Formation	1990 Total Gross Capital Formation	1990 Increase in Stocks	1990 Gross Fixed Capital Formation	1991 Total Gross Capital Formation	1991 Increase in Stocks	1991 Gross Fixed Capital Formation
All Producers												
1 Agriculture, hunting, fishing and forestry	4541	-204	4745	4079	561	3518	3713	653	3060	2572	-66	2638
2 Mining and quarrying	8576	196	8380	10854	147	10707	8009	436	7573	7802	-53	7855
3 Manufacturing	9673	245	9428	11254	86	11168	17060	-2108	19168	14299	-2539	16838
4 Electricity, gas and water	6663	117	6546	6268	-144	6412	11486	390	11096	12632	-21	12653
5 Construction	1098	-10	1108	1396	45	1351	1959	-105	2064	1563	-131	1694
6 Wholesale and retail trade, restaurants and hotels [a]	1067	-633	1700	4017	1583	2434	1053	-2203	3256	2391	-713	3104
7 Transport, storage and communication	6030	18	6012	6995	64	6931	10755	61	10694	10755	-114	10869
8 Finance, insurance, real estate and business services [b,c]	21983	538	21445	31332	3	31329	55838	-26	55864	49583	-1	49584
9 Community, social and personal services [b,c,a]	4701	...	4701	7462	...	7462	11991	...	11991	11019	...	11019
Total Industries	64332	267	64065	83657	2345	81312	121864	-2902	124766	112616	-3638	116254
Producers of Government Services	8292	69	8223	12822	-64	12886	16677	67	16610	16397	-37	16434
Private Non-Profit Institutions Serving Households	...	...	...	...	...	...	...	...	...	...	...	...
Total [d,e]	72624	336	72288	96479	2281	94198	138541	-2835	141376	129013	-3675	132688

Canada

2.9 Gross Capital Formation by Kind of Activity of Owner, ISIC Major Divisions, in Current Prices

Million Canadian dollars

		1992			1993		
		Total Gross Capital Formation	Increase in Stocks	Gross Fixed Capital Formation	Total Gross Capital Formation	Increase in Stocks	Gross Fixed Capital Formation

All Producers

1	Agriculture, hunting, fishing and forestry	2355	-559	2914	4172	886	3286
2	Mining and quarrying	6067	99	5968	7634	41	7593
3	Manufacturing	11112	-1970	13082	12354	-322	12676
4	Electricity, gas and water	11634	-221	11855	10300	-424	10724
5	Construction	1758	-6	1764	1810	-98	1908
6	Wholesale and retail trade, restaurants and hotels [a]	1709	-1128	2837	4015	1143	2872
7	Transport, storage and communication	10437	-77	10514	9359	-9	9368
8	Finance, insurance, real estate and business services [bc]	52460	622	51838	50763	50	50713
9	Community, social and personal services [bca]	11304	...	11304	11354	...	11354
	Total Industries	108836	-3240	112076	111761	1267	110494
	Producers of Government Services	16039	-40	16079	16444	-4	16448
	Private Non-Profit Institutions Serving Households	...	...	...	...	...	...
	Total [de]	124875	-3280	128155	128205	1263	126942

a) Restaurants and hotels are included in item 'Community, social and personal services'.
b) For column 'Increase in stocks', item 'Community, social and personal services' is included in item 'Finance, insurance, real estate and business services'.
c) Business services are included in item 'Community, social and personal services'.
d) Acquisitions on embassies, consulates and military establishments abroad are included under government current expenditure and imports.
e) Increase in stocks of gross capital formation includes stocks of breeding stocks, draught animals, dairy cattle, etc. Stocks of commodities internally processed are valued at cost.

2.17 Exports and Imports of Goods and Services, Detail

Million Canadian dollars

		1980	1983	1984	1985	1986	1987	1988	1989	1990	1991	1992	1993

Exports of Goods and Services

1	Exports of merchandise, f.o.b.	78946	93311	114849	122468	123691	129976	141983	145594	149858	144342	160063	185840
2	Transport and communication [a]	1696	1347	1225	1197	1098	1104	1105	1337	1239	1321	1213	1393
3	Insurance service charges	...	...	...	...	...	...	...	...	...	...	...	...
4	Other commodities [a]	3588	4945	5545	6248	6997	8037	9327	9740	10072	10478	11071	12186
5	Adjustments of merchandise exports to change-of-ownership basis	...	...	...	...	...	...	...	...	...	...	...	...
6	Direct purchases in the domestic market by non-residential households [a]	3349	3841	4416	5006	6333	6299	6894	7232	7748	7802	8059	8804
7	Direct purchases in the domestic market by extraterritorial bodies	...	...	...	...	...	...	...	...	...	...	...	...
	Total Exports of Goods and Services	87579	103444	126035	134919	138119	145416	159309	163903	168917	163943	180406	208223

Imports of Goods and Services

1	Imports of merchandise, c.i.f.	70912	75961	95404	106680	114426	119546	133404	140112	141789	141602	154399	177903
	A Imports of merchandise, f.o.b.	69576	74836	94088	105274	113021	118094	132022	138521	140174	140108	152740	176014
	B Transport of services on merchandise imports	1336	1125	1316	1406	1405	1452	1382	1591	1615	1494	1659	1889
	C Insurance service charges on merchandise imports	...	...	...	...	...	...	...	...	...	...	...	...
2	Adjustments of merchandise imports to change-of-ownership basis	...	...	...	...	...	...	...	...	...	...	...	...
3	Other transport and communication	439	395	382	385	435	390	393	467	423	403	502	487
4	Other insurance service charges	5726	7212	8122	9137	11100	11973	13236	14276	15092	15905	16775	18855
5	Other commodities												
6	Direct purchases abroad by government	887	978	1046	1063	956	973	893	986	1171	1319	1205	1213
7	Direct purchases abroad by resident households	3969	5286	5678	6123	6452	7620	8458	10238	12748	13224	13857	14050
	Total Imports of Goods and Services	81933	89832	110632	123388	133369	140502	156384	166079	171223	172453	186738	212508
	Balance of Goods and Services	5646	13612	15403	11531	4750	4914	2925	-2176	-2306	-8510	-6332	-4285
	Total Imports and Balance of Goods and Services	87579	103444	126035	134919	138119	145416	159309	163903	168917	163943	180406	208223

a) Item 'Direct purchases in the domestic market by non-residential households' excludes crew expenditures which are included in item 'Transport and communication'. Diplomatic and military personnel expenditure are included in item 'Other commodities'.

Canada

3.12 General Government Income and Outlay Account: Total and Subsectors

Million Canadian dollars

	1980					1985				
	Total General Government	Central Government	State or Provincial Government	Local Government	Social Security Funds	Total General Government	Central Government	State or Provincial Government	Local Government	Social Security Funds
Receipts										
1 Operating surplus	...	...	...	...	...	...	...	...	...	...
2 Property and entrepreneurial income	17787	4618	10236	804	2129	29411	7594	16246	1375	4196
A Withdrawals from public quasi-corporations	...	...	...	...	...	...	...	...	...	...
B Interest	10923	3749	4301	744	2129	20879	6158	9220	1305	4196
C Dividends [a]	1564	851	653	60	...	2445	1428	947	70	...
D Net land rent and royalties [b]	5300	18	5282	...	...	6087	8	6079	...	...
3 Taxes, fees and contributions	93743	45127	34669	10406	3541	154218	74271	58537	15714	5696
A Indirect taxes	35505	12254	13015	10236	...	58789	18897	24459	15433	...
B Direct taxes	48658	29731	18927	...	...	76372	46599	29773	...	...
Income	45213	28532	16681	...	...	70835	44796	26039	...	...
Other	3445	1199	2246	...	...	5537	1803	3734	...	...
C Social security contributions	7856	3125	1190	...	3541	16305	8753	1856	...	5696
D Fees, fines and penalties	1724	17	1537	170	...	2752	22	2449	281	...
4 Other current transfers	...	...	12641	19811	...	...	...	21329	31891	...
A Casualty insurance claims	...	...	...	...	...	...	...	...	...	...
B Transfers from other government subsectors	...	...	12641	19811	...	...	...	21329	31891	...
C Transfers from the rest of the world	...	...	...	...	...	...	...	...	...	...
D Other transfers, except imputed	...	...	...	...	...	...	...	...	...	...
E Imputed unfunded employee pension and welfare contributions	...	...	...	...	...	...	...	...	...	...
Total Current Receipts [cd]	111530	49745	57546	31021	5670	183629	81865	96112	48980	9892
Disbursements										
1 Government final consumption expenditure	59097	13804	18847	26359	87	95274	23262	30056	41790	166
2 Property income	16790	9897	4828	2065	...	40183	24620	12128	3435	...
A Interest	16790	9897	4828	2065	...	40183	24620	12128	3435	...
B Net land rent and royalties	...	...	...	...	...	...	...	...	...	...
3 Subsidies	8233	5646	2175	412	...	11577	6369	4610	598	...
4 Other current transfers	31283	30105	30462	588	2580	59638	55093	50259	955	6551
A Casualty insurance premiums, net	...	...	...	...	...	...	...	...	...	...
B Transfers to other government subsectors	...	12831	19512	109	...	...	21746	31385	89	...
C Social security benefits	16655	12448	1640	...	2567	33963	24229	3217	...	6517
D Social assistance grants	13811	4022	9310	479	...	24032	7509	15657	866	...
E Unfunded employee pension and welfare benefits	...	...	...	...	...	...	...	...	...	...
F Transfers to private non-profit institutions serving households	...	...	...	...	...	...	...	...	...	...
G Other transfers n.e.c.	...	...	...	...	...	...	...	...	...	...
H Transfers to the rest of the world	817	804	...	...	13	1643	1609	...	...	34
Net saving	-3873	-9707	1234	1597	3003	-23043	-27479	-941	2202	3175
Total Current Disbursements and Net Saving [cd]	111530	49745	57546	31021	5670	183629	81865	96112	48980	9892

	1990					1991				
	Total General Government	Central Government	State or Provincial Government	Local Government	Social Security Funds	Total General Government	Central Government	State or Provincial Government	Local Government	Social Security Funds
Receipts										
1 Operating surplus	...	...	...	...	...	...	...	...	...	...
2 Property and entrepreneurial income	38350	12129	18372	2247	5602	38031	12468	17682	2253	5628
A Withdrawals from public quasi-corporations	...	...	...	...	...	...	...	...	...	...
B Interest	28022	8799	11497	2124	5602	29193	9495	11954	2116	5628

Canada

3.12 General Government Income and Outlay Account: Total and Subsectors
(Continued)

Million Canadian dollars

		1990				1991				
		Total General Government	Central Government	State or Provincial Government	Local Government	Social Security Funds	Total General Government	Central Government	State or Provincial Government	Local Government	Social Security Funds
	C Dividends a	5912	3322	2467	123	...	4665	2965	1563	137	...
	D Net land rent and royalties b	4416	8	4408	...	...	4173	8	4165	...	...
3	Taxes, fees and contributions	241797	113248	93674	24757	10118	249727	118212	94125	26543	10847
	A Indirect taxes	87694	26567	36853	24274	...	93518	30189	37305	26024	...
	B Direct taxes	127097	73619	53478	...	...	126011	72917	53094	...	...
	Income	118741	71420	47321	...	...	117696	70085	47611	...	...
	Other	8356	2199	6157	...	...	8315	2832	5483	...	...
	C Social security contributions	24966	13027	1821	...	10118	27926	15064	2015	...	10847
	D Fees, fines and penalties	2040	35	1522	483	...	2272	42	1711	519	...
4	Other current transfers	...	...	26017	45630	...	...	...	26789	49280	...
	A Casualty insurance claims	...	...	...	...	...	...	...	...	...	...
	B Transfers from other government subsectors	...	...	26017	45630	...	...	...	26789	49280	...
	C Transfers from the rest of the world	...	...	...	...	...	...	...	...	...	...
	D Other transfers, except imputed	...	...	...	...	...	...	...	...	...	...
	E Imputed unfunded employee pension and welfare contributions	...	...	...	...	...	...	...	...	...	...
	Total Current Receipts cd	280147	125377	138063	72634	15720	287758	130680	138596	78076	16475

Disbursements

1	Government final consumption expenditure	134763	30332	44052	60174	205	144047	31037	48007	64801	202
2	Property income	63725	41808	18077	3840	...	64591	41496	19111	3984	...
	A Interest	63725	41808	18077	3840	...	64591	41496	19111	3984	...
	B Net land rent and royalties	...	...	...	...	...	...	...	...	...	...
3	Subsidies	11032	4841	5316	875	...	13533	7001	5598	934	...
4	Other current transfers	88239	72148	72423	1865	13450	101077	80012	79223	3013	14898
	A Casualty insurance premiums, net	...	...	...	...	...	...	...	...	...	...
	B Transfers to other government subsectors	...	26856	44673	118	...	...	27597	48362	110	...
	C Social security benefits	51197	32824	5005	...	13368	58736	38731	5198	...	14807
	D Social assistance grants	34002	9510	22745	1747	...	39651	11085	25663	2903	...
	E Unfunded employee pension and welfare benefits	...	...	...	...	...	...	...	...	...	...
	F Transfers to private non-profit institutions serving households	...	...	...	...	...	...	...	...	...	...
	G Other transfers n.e.c.	...	...	...	...	...	...	...	...	...	...
	H Transfers to the rest of the world	3040	2958	...	...	82	2690	2599	...	...	91
	Net saving	-17612	-23752	-1805	5880	2065	-35490	-28866	-13343	5344	1375
	Total Current Disbursements and Net Saving cd	280147	125377	138063	72634	15720	287758	130680	138596	78076	16475

		1992					1993				
		Total General Government	Central Government	State or Provincial Government	Local Government	Social Security Funds	Total General Government	Central Government	State or Provincial Government	Local Government	Social Security Funds

Receipts

1	Operating surplus	...	...	...	...	...	...	...	...	...	...
2	Property and entrepreneurial income	39101	12549	18535	2525	5492	40272	12318	19854	2657	5443
	A Withdrawals from public quasi-corporations	...	...	...	...	...	...	...	...	...	...
	B Interest	30381	10061	12421	2407	5492	31635	10609	13053	2530	5443
	C Dividends a	4530	2480	1932	118	...	3901	1701	2073	127	...
	D Net land rent and royalties b	4190	8	4182	...	...	4736	8	4728	...	...
3	Taxes, fees and contributions	256944	122621	94407	28290	11626	262774	123343	97693	29528	12210
	A Indirect taxes	98161	31636	38783	27742	...	100482	31313	40211	28958	...
	B Direct taxes	124904	73001	51903	...	...	126572	73343	53229	...	...
	Income	116376	70323	46053	...	...	118130	70768	47362	...	...

Canada

3.12 General Government Income and Outlay Account: Total and Subsectors
(Continued)

Million Canadian dollars

	1992 Total General Government	1992 Central Government	1992 State or Provincial Government	1992 Local Government	1992 Social Security Funds	1993 Total General Government	1993 Central Government	1993 State or Provincial Government	1993 Local Government	1993 Social Security Funds
Other	8528	2678	5850	...	...	8442	2575	5867	...	...
C Social security contributions	31417	17922	1869	...	11626	32763	18619	1934	...	12210
D Fees, fines and penalties	2462	62	1852	548	...	2957	68	2319	570	...
4 Other current transfers	...	...	28803	51073	...	...	...	30342	51892	...
A Casualty insurance claims	...	...	...	...	...	...	...	...	...	...
B Transfers from other government subsectors	...	...	28803	51073	...	...	...	30342	51892	...
C Transfers from the rest of the world	...	...	...	...	...	...	...	...	...	...
D Other transfers, except imputed	...	...	...	...	...	...	...	...	...	...
E Imputed unfunded employee pension and welfare contributions	...	...	...	...	...	...	...	...	...	...
Total Current Receipts [cd]	296045	135170	141745	81888	17118	303046	135661	147889	84077	17653
Disbursements										
1 Government final consumption expenditure	149386	31923	49302	67957	204	152775	33095	49639	69808	233
2 Property income	63596	38807	20598	4191	...	65061	38338	22440	4283	...
A Interest	63596	38807	20598	4191	...	65061	38338	22440	4283	...
B Net land rent and royalties	...	...	...	...	...	...	...	...	...	...
3 Subsidies	13312	5548	6554	1210	...	11620	4736	5658	1226	...
4 Other current transfers	110073	85607	83858	3602	16882	116228	90385	85550	4055	18472
A Casualty insurance premiums, net	...	...	...	...	...	...	...	...	...	...
B Transfers to other government subsectors	...	29637	50143	96	...	...	31191	50948	95	...
C Social security benefits	63351	41148	5425	...	16778	64865	40994	5510	...	18361
D Social assistance grants	44024	12228	28290	3506	...	48676	15624	29092	3960	...
E Unfunded employee pension and welfare benefits	...	...	...	...	...	...	...	...	...	...
F Transfers to private non-profit institutions serving households	...	...	...	...	...	...	...	...	...	...
G Other transfers n.e.c.	...	...	...	...	...	...	...	...	...	...
H Transfers to the rest of the world	2698	2594	...	...	104	2687	2576	...	...	111
Net saving	-40322	-26715	-18567	4928	32	-42638	-30893	-15398	4705	-1052
Total Current Disbursements and Net Saving [cd]	296045	135170	141745	81888	17118	303046	135661	147889	84077	17653

a) Item 'Dividends' refers to remitted profits of government business enterprises.
b) Item 'Net land rent and royalties' refers to royalties only.
c) Local government includes hospitals.
d) Social security funds refers to Canada and Quebec pension plans only.

3.13 General Government Capital Accumulation Account: Total and Subsectors

Million Canadian dollars

	1980 Total General Government	1980 Central Government	1980 State or Provincial Government	1980 Local Government	1980 Social Security Funds	1985 Total General Government	1985 Central Government	1985 State or Provincial Government	1985 Local Government	1985 Social Security Funds
Finance of Gross Accumulation										
1 Gross saving	680	-8897	2841	3733	3003	-15951	-26243	1490	5627	3175
A Consumption of fixed capital	4553	810	1607	2136	-	7092	1236	2431	3425	-
B Net saving	-3873	-9707	1234	1597	3003	-23043	-27479	-941	2202	3175
2 Capital transfers	72	1	71	...	...	65	-	65	...	...
A From other government subsectors	...	...	...	...	...	...	...	...	...	...
B From other resident sectors	72	1	71	...	...	65	-	65	...	...
C From rest of the world	...	...	...	...	...	...	...	...	...	...
Finance of Gross Accumulation [ab]	752	-8896	2912	3733	3003	-15886	-26243	1555	5627	3175
Gross Accumulation										
1 Gross capital formation	8292	992	3162	4138	...	12822	2197	4720	5905	...
A Increase in stocks	69	69	...	...	...	-64	-64	...	...	...
B Gross fixed capital formation	8223	923	3162	4138	...	12886	2261	4720	5905	...

Canada

3.13 General Government Capital Accumulation Account: Total and Subsectors
(Continued)

Million Canadian dollars

	1980					1985				
	Total General Government	Central Government	State or Provincial Government	Local Government	Social Security Funds	Total General Government	Central Government	State or Provincial Government	Local Government	Social Security Funds
2 Purchases of land, net	...	...	...	...	...	...	...	...	...	...
3 Purchases of intangible assets, net	...	...	...	...	...	...	...	...	...	...
4 Capital transfers	1077	775	302	...	...	3828	2984	844	...	...
A To other government subsectors	...	...	...	...	...	...	...	...	...	...
B To other resident sectors	1077	775	302	...	...	3828	2984	844	...	...
C To rest of the world	...	...	...	...	...	...	...	...	...	...
Net lending [c]	-8617	-10663	-552	-405	3003	-32536	-31424	-4009	-278	3175
Gross Accumulation [ab]	752	-8896	2912	3733	3003	-15886	-26243	1555	5627	3175

	1990					1991				
	Total General Government	Central Government	State or Provincial Government	Local Government	Social Security Funds	Total General Government	Central Government	State or Provincial Government	Local Government	Social Security Funds

Finance of Gross Accumulation

1 Gross saving	-8123	-22163	1262	10713	2065	-26025	-27329	-10301	10230	1375
A Consumption of fixed capital	9489	1589	3067	4833	...	9465	1537	3042	4886	...
B Net saving	-17612	-23752	-1805	5880	2065	-35490	-28866	-13343	5344	1375
2 Capital transfers	3	-	3	...	...	2	-	2	...	...
A From other government subsectors	...	...	...	...	...	...	...	...	...	...
B From other resident sectors	3	-	3	...	...	2	-	2	...	...
C From rest of the world	...	...	...	...	...	...	...	...	...	...
Finance of Gross Accumulation [ab]	-8120	-22163	1265	10713	2065	-26023	-27329	-10299	10230	1375

Gross Accumulation

1 Gross capital formation	16677	2291	4896	9490	...	16397	2246	4920	9231	...
A Increase in stocks	67	67	...	...	...	-37	-37	...	...	...
B Gross fixed capital formation	16610	2224	4896	9490	...	16434	2283	4920	9231	...
2 Purchases of land, net	...	...	...	...	...	...	...	...	...	...
3 Purchases of intangible assets, net	...	...	...	...	...	...	...	...	...	...
4 Capital transfers	2332	1493	839	...	...	2353	1430	923	...	...
A To other government subsectors	...	...	...	...	...	...	...	...	...	...
B To other resident sectors	2332	1493	839	...	...	2353	1430	923	...	...
C To rest of the world	...	...	...	...	...	...	...	...	...	...
Net lending [c]	-27129	-25947	-4470	1223	2065	-44773	-31005	-16142	999	1375
Gross Accumulation [ab]	-8120	-22163	1265	10713	2065	-26023	-27329	-10299	10230	1375

	1992					1993				
	Total General Government	Central Government	State or Provincial Government	Local Government	Social Security Funds	Total General Government	Central Government	State or Provincial Government	Local Government	Social Security Funds

Finance of Gross Accumulation

1 Gross saving	-30607	-25162	-15455	9978	32	-32545	-29296	-12198	10001	-1052
A Consumption of fixed capital	9715	1553	3112	5050	...	10093	1597	3200	5296	...
B Net saving	-40322	-26715	-18567	4928	32	-42638	-30893	-15398	4705	-1052
2 Capital transfers	5	-	5	...	...	3	-	3	...	...
A From other government subsectors	...	...	...	...	...	...	...	...	...	...
B From other resident sectors	5	-	5	...	...	3	-	3	...	...
C From rest of the world	...	...	...	...	...	...	...	...	...	...
Finance of Gross Accumulation [ab]	-30602	-25162	-15450	9978	32	-32542	-29296	-12195	10001	-1052

Gross Accumulation

1 Gross capital formation	16039	2498	4308	9233	...	16444	2679	4320	9445	...
A Increase in stocks	-40	-40	...	...	...	-4	-4	...	...	...
B Gross fixed capital formation	16079	2538	4308	9233	...	16448	2683	4320	9445	...

Canada

3.13 General Government Capital Accumulation Account: Total and Subsectors
(Continued)

Million Canadian dollars

		1992					1993				
		Total General Government	Central Government	State or Provincial Government	Local Government	Social Security Funds	Total General Government	Central Government	State or Provincial Government	Local Government	Social Security Funds
2	Purchases of land, net	...	...	...	...	...	...	...	...	...	...
3	Purchases of intangible assets, net	...	...	...	...	...	...	...	...	...	...
4	Capital transfers	2079	1297	782	...	...	1529	775	754	...	...
	A To other government subsectors	...	...	...	...	...	...	...	...	...	...
	B To other resident sectors	2079	1297	782	...	...	1529	775	754	...	...
	C To rest of the world	...	...	...	...	...	...	...	...	...	...
	Net lending [c]	-48720	-28957	-20540	745	32	-50515	-32750	-17269	556	-1052
	Gross Accumulation [ab]	-30602	-25162	-15450	9978	32	-32542	-29296	-12195	10001	-1052

a) Local government includes hospitals.
b) Social security funds refers to Canada and Quebec pension plans only.
c) Net lending of the capital accumulation account and the capital finance account have not been reconciled and are different due to different statistical sources.

3.14 General Government Capital Finance Account, Total and Subsectors

Million Canadian dollars

		1980					1985				
		Total General Government	Central Government	State or Provincial Government	Local Government	Social Security Funds	Total General Government	Central Government	State or Provincial Government	Local Government	Social Security Funds
					Acquisition of Financial Assets						
1	Gold and SDRs	...	...	...	...	...	...	...	...	...	...
2	Currency and transferable deposits	1983	1744	-74	313	...	2039	2093	-428	374	...
3	Other deposits					...					...
4	Bills and bonds, short term	309	5	300	4	...	4145	4	3769	372	...
5	Bonds, long term	5512	-148	3630	106	1924	3437	-80	1219	187	2111
	A Corporations	140	4	96	40	...	-72	-	107	-179	...
	B Other government subsectors	5372	-152	3534	66	1924	3509	-80	1112	366	2111
	C Rest of the world	-	-	-	-	...	-	-	-	-	...
6	Corporate equity securities [a]	14	6	8	-	...	389	119	270	-	...
7	Short-term loans, n.e.c. [b]	771	458	315	-2	...	824	778	46	-	...
8	Long-term loans, n.e.c. [b]	69	-39	108	-	...	-113	-33	-80	-	...
	A Mortgages	69	-39	108	-	...	-113	-33	-80	-	...
	B Other	...	...	...	...	...	...	...	...	...	...
9	Other receivables	173	38	16	119	...	204	22	37	145	...
10	Other assets	5709	1655	2878	97	1079	1644	1003	-183	-240	1064
	Total Acquisition of Financial Assets [c]	14540	3719	7181	637	3003	12569	3906	4650	838	3175
					Incurrence of Liabilities						
1	Currency and transferable deposits	61	61	-	-	...	75	75	-	-	...
2	Other deposits	...	...	...	...	...	...	...	...	...	...
3	Bills and bonds, short term	5662	5298	366	-2	...	10026	9892	109	25	...
4	Bonds, long term	12366	6460	4912	994	...	29276	21654	7120	502	...
5	Short-term loans, n.e.c. [b]	1234	566	813	-145	...	3526	2131	1067	328	...
6	Long-term loans, n.e.c. [b]	2	-	-	2	...	9	-	-	9	...
7	Other payables	135	14	31	90	...	217	6	15	196	...
8	Other liabilities	2152	1941	-17	228	...	4091	3271	700	120	...
	Total Incurrence of Liabilities	21612	14340	6105	1167	...	47220	37029	9011	1180	...
	Statistical discrepancy [d]	1339	55	1229	55	...	-882	-691	-127	-64	...
	Net Lending [e]	-8411	-10676	-153	-585	3003	-33769	-32432	-4234	-278	3175
	Incurrence of Liabilities and Net Worth [c]	14540	3719	7181	637	3003	12569	3906	4650	838	3175

		1990					1991				
		Total General Government	Central Government	State or Provincial Government	Local Government	Social Security Funds	Total General Government	Central Government	State or Provincial Government	Local Government	Social Security Funds
					Acquisition of Financial Assets						
1	Gold and SDRs	...	...	...	...	...	...	...	...	...	...
2	Currency and transferable deposits	1338	771	706	-139	...	-1204	-1070	46	-180	...
3	Other deposits					...					...
4	Bills and bonds, short term	-5310	4	-5499	185	...	76	-3	-211	290	...
5	Bonds, long term	3478	-77	2698	143	714	3650	-50	2135	345	1220
	A Corporations	201	4	248	-51	...	664	5	617	42	...
	B Other government subsectors	3277	-81	2450	194	714	2986	-55	1518	303	1220

Canada

3.14 General Government Capital Finance Account, Total and Subsectors
(Continued)

Million Canadian dollars

	1990					1991				
	Total General Government	Central Government	State or Provincial Government	Local Government	Social Security Funds	Total General Government	Central Government	State or Provincial Government	Local Government	Social Security Funds
C Rest of the world	...	...	...	...	...	...	...	...	...	...
6 Corporate equity securities a	2885	101	2784	...	...	2615	240	2375	...	...
7 Short-term loans, n.e.c. b	622	-238	899	-39	...	844	132	601	111	...
8 Long-term loans, n.e.c. b	-12	-14	2	...	...	-	-13	13	...	...
A Mortgages	-12	-14	2	...	...	-	-13	13	...	...
B Other	...	...	...	...	...	...	...	...	...	...
9 Other receivables	437	27	13	397	...	346	15	23	308	...
10 Other assets	4913	-2977	4147	2392	1351	7100	803	3578	2564	155
Total Acquisition of Financial Assets c	8351	-2403	5750	2939	2065	13427	54	8560	3438	1375

Incurrence of Liabilities

1 Currency and transferable deposits	130	130	...	...	...	44	44	...	...	...
2 Other deposits	...	...	...	...	...	...	...	...	...	...
3 Bills and bonds, short term	16467	14485	1841	141	...	11803	12226	-302	-121	...
4 Bonds, long term	15134	6769	7279	1086	...	45388	20145	22589	2654	...
5 Short-term loans, n.e.c. b	1419	-1	16	1404	...	1803	-1	1300	504	...
6 Long-term loans, n.e.c. b	12	...	...	12	...	...	...	...	...	...
7 Other payables	914	12	531	371	...	844	19	681	144	...
8 Other liabilities	1420	231	1217	-28	...	-485	-2437	2178	-226	...
Total Incurrence of Liabilities	35496	21626	10884	2986	...	59397	29996	26446	2955	...
Statistical discrepancy d	-22	1902	-654	-1270	...	-1131	1069	-1684	-516	...
Net Lending e	-27123	-25931	-4480	1223	2065	-44839	-31011	-16202	999	1375
Incurrence of Liabilities and Net Worth c	8351	-2403	5750	2939	2065	13427	54	8560	3438	1375

	1992					1993				
	Total General Government	Central Government	State or Provincial Government	Local Government	Social Security Funds	Total General Government	Central Government	State or Provincial Government	Local Government	Social Security Funds

Acquisition of Financial Assets

1 Gold and SDRs	...	...	...	...	...	...	...	...	...	...
2 Currency and transferable deposits	-655	-1016	49	312	...	2073	1232	850	-9	...
3 Other deposits					...					...
4 Bills and bonds, short term	-2819	-12	-3040	233	...	-2711	6	-3249	532	...
5 Bonds, long term	1275	48	110	552	565	1420	-11	2320	84	-973
A Corporations	133	-	108	25	...	-117	1	6	-124	...
B Other government subsectors	1142	48	2	527	565	1537	-12	2314	208	-973
C Rest of the world	...	...	...	...	...	...	...	...	...	...
6 Corporate equity securities a	1382	170	1212	...	...	190	11	179	...	...
7 Short-term loans, n.e.c. b	485	43	438	4	...	38	-480	517	1	...
8 Long-term loans, n.e.c. b	184	-13	197	...	...	67	-10	77	...	...
A Mortgages	184	-13	197	...	...	67	-10	77	...	...
B Other	...	...	...	...	...	...	...	...	...	...
9 Other receivables	187	15	-25	197	...	370	28	239	103	...
10 Other assets	7661	636	6571	987	-533	12303	1755	9095	1532	-79
Total Acquisition of Financial Assets c	7700	-129	5512	2285	32	13750	2531	10028	2243	-1052

Incurrence of Liabilities

1 Currency and transferable deposits	84	84	...	...	...	209	209	...	...	...
2 Other deposits	...	...	...	...	...	...	...	...	...	...
3 Bills and bonds, short term	16851	12977	4102	-228	...	13399	12908	485	6	...
4 Bonds, long term	35090	12527	21376	1187	...	47222	21964	23387	1871	...
5 Short-term loans, n.e.c. b	1222	-2	1264	-40	...	3329	-3	3250	82	...

Canada

3.14 General Government Capital Finance Account, Total and Subsectors
(Continued)

Million Canadian dollars

	1992 Total General Government	1992 Central Government	1992 State or Provincial Government	1992 Local Government	1992 Social Security Funds	1993 Total General Government	1993 Central Government	1993 State or Provincial Government	1993 Local Government	1993 Social Security Funds
6 Long-term loans, n.e.c. b	2	...	...	2	...	...	...	...	...	...
7 Other payables	1147	60	949	138	...	990	100	342	548	...
8 Other liabilities	3664	3311	-21	374	...	1582	1987	-711	306	...
Total Incurrence of Liabilities	58060	28957	27670	1433	...	66731	37165	26753	2813	...
Statistical discrepancy d	-1535	-109	-1533	107	...	-2453	-1863	536	-1126	...
Net Lending e	-48825	-28977	-20625	745	32	-50528	-32771	-17261	556	-1052
Incurrence of Liabilities and Net Worth c	7700	-129	5512	2285	32	13750	2531	10028	2243	-1052

a) Investment in short-term papers, bonds and corporate equity securities of the rest of the world cannot be split between long-term and short-term by purchasers, the total investment has been allocated to the item 'Corporate equity securities'.
b) Loans other than mortgages are included in item 'Short-term loans, n.e.c.'.
c) Social security funds refers to Canada and Quebec pension plans only.
d) The statistical discrepancy equals the diffrence between net lending in the Income and Expenditure Accounts and net acquisition of financial assets in the Financial Flow Accounts (change in financial assets less change in liabilities).
e) The net lending in the Capital Finance Accounts differs from that in the Capital Accumulation Accounts because net transactions in land (and other existing assets) are included in the former but not the latter.

3.15 General Government Balance Sheet, Total and Subsectors

Million Canadian dollars

	1980 Total General Government	1980 Central Government	1980 State or Provincial Government	1980 Local Government	1980 Social Security Funds	1985 Total General Government	1985 Central Government	1985 State or Provincial Government	1985 Local Government	1985 Social Security Funds
Assets										
Non-financial assets	151415	18555	53345	79515	...	217059	24492	76788	115779	...
1 Tangible assets	151415	18555	53345	79515	...	217059	24492	76788	115779	...
A Stocks	455	455	...	...	...	230	230	...	...	...
B Reproducible fixed assets	122890	15084	42861	64945	...	175519	20279	61173	94067	...
Gross	444	...	444	...	...	839	...	839	...	...
Less: Accumulated consumption of fixed capital	...	...	...	...	...	...	...	...	...	...
C Land and other non-reproducible tangible assets	27626	3016	10040	14570	...	40471	3983	14776	21712	...
2 Intangible assets	...	...	...	...	...	...	...	...	...	...
Financial assets	136708	43254	59380	8700	25374	209259	50158	99125	17944	42032
1 Gold and SDRs	...	...	...	...	...	...	...	...	...	...
2 Currency and transferable deposits	9739	3453	3586	2700	...	12008	5164	2204	4640	...
3 Other deposits	...	...	...	...	...	...	...	...	...	...
4 Bills and bonds, short term	2116	11	2012	93	...	9917	27	8392	1498	...
5 Bonds, long term	40126	133	20992	1228	17773	63685	289	31433	2390	29573
A Corporate	1203	34	1015	154	...	2058	29	1576	453	...
B Other government subsectors	38923	99	19977	1074	17773	61627	260	29857	1937	29573
C Rest of the world	...	...	...	...	...	...	...	...	...	...
6 Corporate equity securities	301	64	237	-	...	3255	935	2320	-	...
7 Short term loans, n.e.c.	7822	4746	3068	8	...	7185	4461	2686	38	...
8 Long term loans, n.e.c.	3279	337	2942	...	...	3955	186	3769	...	...
A Mortgages	3279	337	2942	...	...	3955	186	3769	...	...
B Other	...	...	...	...	...	...	...	...	...	...
9 Other receivables	733	192	67	474	...	2278	180	149	1949	...
10 Other assets	72592	34318	26476	4197	7601	106976	38916	48172	7429	12459
Total Assets	288123	61809	112725	88215	25374	426318	74650	175913	133723	42032
Liabilities and Net Worth										
Liabilities	178429	93521	57582	27326	...	375941	220492	117670	37779	...
1 Currency and transferable deposits	1111	1111	...	...	...	1423	1423	...	...	...
2 Other deposits	21444	20735	619	90	...	65964	59401	6287	276	...
3 Other deposits	...	...	...	...	...	...	...	...	...	...
4 Bonds, long term	127888	59417	46775	21696	...	254549	136124	91446	26979	...
5 Short term loans, n.e.c.	9645	1952	4681	3012	...	16903	3638	8845	4420	...
6 Long term loans, n.e.c.	47	...	-	47	...	80	...	-	80	...
7 Other payables	2638	404	1279	955	...	7666	457	4041	3168	...
8 Other liabilities	15656	9902	4228	1526	...	29356	19449	7051	2856	...
Net worth	109694	-31712	55143	60889	25374	50377	-145842	58243	95944	42032
Total Liabilities and Net Worth	288123	61809	112725	88215	25374	426318	74650	175913	133723	42032

Canada

3.15 General Government Balance Sheet, Total and Subsectors

Million Canadian dollars

	1990					1991				
	Total General Government	Central Government	State or Provincial Government	Local Government	Social Security Funds	Total General Government	Central Government	State or Provincial Government	Local Government	Social Security Funds

Assets

	1990					1991				
Non-financial assets	273200	29775	87169	156256	...	279460	30018	89640	159802	...
1 Tangible assets	273200	29775	87169	156256	...	279460	30018	89640	159802	...
A Stocks	285	285	...	...	...	248	248	...	...	...
B Reproducible fixed assets	219504	24504	68663	126337	...	223992	24653	70349	128990	...
Gross	1345	...	1345	...	...	1490	...	1490	...	...
Less: Accumulated consumption of fixed capital	...	...	...	...	...	...	...	...	...	...
C Land and other non-reproducible tangible assets	52066	4986	17161	29919	...	53730	5117	17801	30812	...
2 Intangible assets	...	...	...	...	...	...	...	...	...	...
Financial assets	279921	60681	141129	22761	55350	293999	61669	151853	23007	57470
1 Gold and SDRs	...	...	...	...	...	...	...	...	...	...
2 Currency and transferable deposits	12544	4669	3710	4165	...	11057	3600	3769	3688	...
3 Other deposits	...	...	...	...	...	...	...	...	...	...
4 Bills and bonds, short term	19032	56	14623	4353	...	20615	61	15849	4705	...
5 Bonds, long term	78753	150	37881	3481	37241	82336	93	39761	4021	38461
A Corporate	3298	29	2903	366	...	3917	26	3483	408	...
B Other government subsectors	75455	121	34978	3115	37241	78419	67	36278	3613	38461
C Rest of the world	...	...	...	...	...	...	...	...	...	...
6 Corporate equity securities	8477	333	8144	-	...	10411	198	10213	-	...
7 Short term loans, n.e.c.	14677	8858	5764	55	...	15266	9630	5529	107	...
8 Long term loans, n.e.c.	3979	80	3899	...	...	3954	65	3889	...	...
A Mortgages	3979	80	3899	...	...	3954	65	3889	...	...
B Other	...	...	...	...	...	...	...	...	...	...
9 Other receivables	2917	167	232	2518	...	3018	188	252	2578	...
10 Other assets	139542	46368	66876	8189	18109	147342	47834	72591	7908	19009
Total Assets	553121	90456	228298	179017	55350	573459	91687	241493	182809	57470

Liabilities and Net Worth

	1990					1991				
Liabilities	570939	345724	180772	44443	...	629143	375717	205987	47439	...
1 Currency and transferable deposits	2241	2241	...	...	...	2285	2285	...	...	...
2 Other deposits	153003	136522	15891	590	...	163706	147644	15593	469	...
3 Other deposits	...	...	...	...	...	...	...	...	...	...
4 Bonds, long term	344303	181573	130432	32298	...	389819	201609	153537	34673	...
5 Short term loans, n.e.c.	17627	18	12308	5301	...	19135	15	13630	5490	...
6 Long term loans, n.e.c.	80	...	-	80	...	80	...	-	80	...
7 Other payables	9024	563	4742	3719	...	8348	607	3902	3839	...
8 Other liabilities	44661	24807	17399	2455	...	45770	23557	19325	2888	...
Net worth	-17818	-255268	47526	134574	55350	-55684	-284030	35506	135370	57470
Total Liabilities and Net Worth	553121	90456	228298	179017	55350	573459	91687	241493	182809	57470

	1992				
	Total General Government	Central Government	State or Provincial Government	Local Government	Social Security Funds

Assets

	1992				
Non-financial assets	283884	29057	91990	162837	...
1 Tangible assets	283884	29057	91990	162837	...
A Stocks	208	208	...	...	...
B Reproducible fixed assets	227276	23910	72070	131296	...
Gross	1524	...	1524	...	...
Less: Accumulated consumption of fixed capital	...	...	...	...	...
C Land and other non-reproducible tangible assets	54874	4939	18394	31541	...
2 Intangible assets	...	...	...	...	...
Financial assets	297221	64686	151895	23546	57094
1 Gold and SDRs	...	...	...	...	...
2 Currency and transferable deposits	9944	2333	3886	3725	...

Canada

3.15 General Government Balance Sheet, Total and Subsectors
(Continued)

Million Canadian dollars

	1992 Total General Government	Central Government	State or Provincial Government	Local Government	Social Security Funds
3 Other deposits	...	...	...	...	...
4 Bills and bonds, short term	16084	49	12196	3839	...
5 Bonds, long term	84627	136	40882	4583	39026
A Corporate	4217	26	3679	512	...
B Other government subsectors	80410	110	37203	4071	39026
C Rest of the world	...	...	...	...	...
6 Corporate equity securities	11347	368	10979	-	...
7 Short term loans, n.e.c.	15155	9644	5424	87	...
8 Long term loans, n.e.c.	3924	53	3871	...	...
A Mortgages	3924	53	3871	...	...
B Other	...	...	...	...	...
9 Other receivables	2882	215	255	2412	...
10 Other assets	153258	51888	74402	8900	18068
Total Assets	581105	93743	243885	186383	57094
Liabilities and Net Worth					
Liabilities	690204	408570	231932	49702	...
1 Currency and transferable deposits	2369	2369	...	...	...
2 Other deposits	180245	160396	19579	270	...
3 Other deposits	...	...	...	...	...
4 Bonds, long term	427890	215085	176037	36768	...
5 Short term loans, n.e.c.	19605	15	14172	5418	...
6 Long term loans, n.e.c.	80	...	-	80	...
7 Other payables	7189	669	2561	3959	...
8 Other liabilities	52826	30036	19583	3207	...
Net worth	-109099	-314827	11953	136681	57094
Total Liabilities and Net Worth	581105	93743	243885	186383	57094

3.22 Corporate and Quasi-Corporate Enterprise Income and Outlay Account: Total and Sectors

Million Canadian dollars

	1980 TOTAL	1980 Non-Financial	1980 Financial	1985 TOTAL	1985 Non-Financial	1985 Financial	1990 TOTAL	1990 Non-Financial	1990 Financial	1991 TOTAL	1991 Non-Financial	1991 Financial
Receipts												
1 Operating surplus	59025	...	...	88032	...	...	103956	...	...	91868	...	...
2 Property and entrepreneurial income	16162	...	...	37849	...	...	51998	...	...	51267	...	...
3 Current transfers	3713	...	...	4233	...	...	9056	...	...	7820	...	...
A Casualty insurance claims	...	...	...	...	...	...	...	...	...	...	...	...
B Casualty insurance premiums, net, due to be received by insurance companies	...	...	...	...	...	...	...	...	...	...	...	...
C Current transfers from the rest of the world	...	...	...	...	...	...	...	...	...	...	...	...
D Other transfers except imputed	3713	...	...	4233	...	...	9056	...	...	7820	...	...
E Imputed unfunded employee pension and welfare contributions	...	...	...	...	...	...	...	...	...	...	...	...
Total Current Receipts [a]	78900	...	...	130114	...	...	165010	...	...	150955	...	...
Disbursements												
1 Property and entrepreneurial income	54686	...	...	95787	...	...	142321	...	...	132712	...	...
2 Direct taxes and other current transfers n.e.c. to general government	12078	...	...	15563	...	...	16834	...	...	14710	...	...
A Direct taxes	12078	...	...	15563	...	...	16834	...	...	14710	...	...
On income	12078	...	...	15563	...	...	16834	...	...	14710	...	...
Other	...	...	...	...	...	...	...	...	...	...	...	...
B Fines, fees, penalties and other current transfers n.e.c.	...	...	...	...	...	...	...	...	...	...	...	...

Canada

3.22 Corporate and Quasi-Corporate Enterprise Income and Outlay Account: Total and Sectors
(Continued)

Million Canadian dollars

	1980			1985			1990			1991		
	TOTAL	Non-Financial	Financial	TOTAL	Non-Financial	Financial	TOTAL	Non-Financial	Financial	TOTAL	Non-Financial	Financial
3 Other current transfers	647	...	...	697	...	...	1013	...	...	1060	...	...
A Casualty insurance premiums, net	...	...	...	...	...	...	...	...	...	...	...	...
B Casualty insurance claims liability of insurance companies	...	...	...	...	...	...	...	...	...	...	...	...
C Transfers to private non-profit institutions	518	...	...	539	...	...	864	...	...	900	...	...
D Unfunded employee pension and welfare benefits	...	...	...	...	...	...	...	...	...	...	...	...
E Social assistance grants	...	...	...	...	...	...	...	...	...	...	...	...
F Other transfers n.e.c.	...	...	...	...	...	...	...	...	...	...	...	...
G Transfers to the rest of the world	129	...	...	158	...	...	149	...	...	160	...	...
Net saving	11489	...	...	18067	...	...	4842	...	...	2473	...	...
Total Current Disbursements and Net Saving [a]	78900	...	...	130114	...	...	165010	...	...	150955	...	...

	1992			1993		
	TOTAL	Non-Financial	Financial	TOTAL	Non-Financial	Financial

Receipts

1 Operating surplus	86924	...	...	92338	...	...
2 Property and entrepreneurial income	48322	...	...	48966	...	...
3 Current transfers	5893	...	...	4822	...	...
A Casualty insurance claims	...	...	...	...	...	...
B Casualty insurance premiums, net, due to be received by insurance companies	...	...	...	...	...	...
C Current transfers from the rest of the world	...	...	...	...	...	...
D Other transfers except imputed	5893	...	...	4822	...	...
E Imputed unfunded employee pension and welfare contributions	...	...	...	...	...	...
Total Current Receipts [a]	141139	...	...	146126	...	...

Disbursements

1 Property and entrepreneurial income	128246	...	...	124108	...	...
2 Direct taxes and other current transfers n.e.c. to general government	13582	...	...	15077	...	...
A Direct taxes	13582	...	...	15077	...	...
On income	13582	...	...	15077	...	...
Other	...	...	...	...	...	...
B Fines, fees, penalties and other current transfers n.e.c.	...	...	...	...	...	...
3 Other current transfers	1040	...	...	1091	...	...
A Casualty insurance premiums, net	...	...	...	...	...	...
B Casualty insurance claims liability of insurance companies	...	...	...	...	...	...
C Transfers to private non-profit institutions	915	...	...	958	...	...
D Unfunded employee pension and welfare benefits	...	...	...	...	...	...
E Social assistance grants	...	...	...	...	...	...
F Other transfers n.e.c.	...	...	...	...	...	...
G Transfers to the rest of the world	125	...	...	133	...	...
Net saving	-1729	...	...	5850	...	...
Total Current Disbursements and Net Saving [a]	141139	...	...	146126	...	...

a) Tables 3.22 and 3.23 cover corporate and government business enterprises only.

Canada

3.23 Corporate and Quasi-Corporate Enterprise Capital Accumulation Account: Total and Sectors

Million Canadian dollars

	1980 TOTAL	1980 Non-Financial	1980 Financial	1985 TOTAL	1985 Non-Financial	1985 Financial	1990 TOTAL	1990 Non-Financial	1990 Financial	1991 TOTAL	1991 Non-Financial	1991 Financial
Finance of Gross Accumulation												
1 Gross saving	32242	...	...	51588	...	...	52471	...	...	51956	...	...
A Consumption of fixed capital	20753	...	...	33521	...	...	47629	...	...	49483	...	...
B Net saving	11489	...	...	18067	...	...	4842	...	...	2473	...	...
2 Capital transfers	679	...	...	3308	...	...	2002	...	...	1820	...	...
A From resident sectors	679	...	...	3308	...	...	2002	...	...	1820	...	...
B From the rest of the world	...	...	...	...	...	...	...	...	...	...	...	...
Finance of Gross Accumulation [a]	32921	...	...	54896	...	...	54473	...	...	53776	...	...
Gross Accumulation												
1 Gross capital formation	44429	...	...	56382	...	...	78322	...	...	74142	...	...
A Increase in stocks	740	...	...	1997	...	...	-3526	...	...	-3683	...	...
B Gross fixed capital formation	43689	...	...	54385	...	...	81848	...	...	77825	...	...
2 Purchases of land, net	...	...	...	...	...	...	...	...	...	...	...	...
3 Purchases of intangible assets, net	...	...	...	...	...	...	...	...	...	...	...	...
4 Capital transfers	...	...	...	...	...	...	...	...	...	...	...	...
Net lending [b]	-11508	...	...	-1486	...	...	-23849	...	...	-20366	...	...
Gross Accumulation [a]	32921	...	...	54896	...	...	54473	...	...	53776	...	...

	1992 TOTAL	1992 Non-Financial	1992 Financial	1993 TOTAL	1993 Non-Financial	1993 Financial
Finance of Gross Accumulation						
1 Gross saving	49672	...	...	58503	...	...
A Consumption of fixed capital	51401	...	...	52653	...	...
B Net saving	-1729	...	...	5850	...	...
2 Capital transfers	1809	...	...	1275	...	...
A From resident sectors	1809	...	...	1275	...	...
B From the rest of the world	...	...	...	...	...	...
Finance of Gross Accumulation [a]	51481	...	...	59778	...	...
Gross Accumulation						
1 Gross capital formation	67424	...	...	68947	...	...
A Increase in stocks	-2666	...	...	267	...	...
B Gross fixed capital formation	70090	...	...	68680	...	...
2 Purchases of land, net	...	...	...	...	...	...
3 Purchases of intangible assets, net	...	...	...	...	...	...
4 Capital transfers	...	...	...	...	...	...
Net lending [b]	-15943	...	...	-9169	...	...
Gross Accumulation [a]	51481	...	...	59778	...	...

a) Tables 3.22 and 3.23 cover corporate and government business enterprises only.
b) The net lending in the Capital Finance Accounts differs from that in the Capital Accumulation Accounts because net transactions in land (and other existing assets) are included in the former but not the latter.

3.24 Corporate and Quasi-Corporate Enterprise Capital Finance Account: Total and Sectors

Million Canadian dollars

	1980 TOTAL	1980 Non-Financial	1980 Financial	1985 TOTAL	1985 Non-Financial	1985 Financial	1990 TOTAL	1990 Non-Financial	1990 Financial	1991 TOTAL	1991 Non-Financial	1991 Financial
Acquisition of Financial Assets												
1 Gold and SDRs	-541	...	-541	-111	...	-111	649	...	649	-2831	...	-2831
2 Currency and transferable deposits	6977	2041	4936	-3064	-1860	-1204	1373	2500	-1127	5391	1259	4132
3 Other deposits	...	...	...	...	...	...	...	...	...	...	...	...
4 Bills and bonds, short term	4441	961	3480	6588	1132	5456	10774	1328	9446	3818	-6119	9937
5 Bonds, long term	9035	-105	9140	12924	513	12411	13997	1105	12892	27001	811	26190
A Corporate, resident	1448	-159	1607	1822	209	1613	4604	864	3740	5116	349	4767
B Government	7587	54	7533	11102	304	10798	9393	241	9152	21885	462	21423
C Rest of the world	...	...	...	...	...	...	...	...	...	...	...	...
6 Corporate equity securities [a]	3415	1012	2403	10357	489	9868	11362	936	10426	14112	-954	15066
7 Short term loans, n.e.c. [b]	21713	707	21006	15272	1085	14187	11670	1753	9917	3619	695	2924
8 Long term loans, n.e.c. [b]	10730	79	10651	15545	226	15319	27915	627	27288	23236	779	22457

Canada

3.24 Corporate and Quasi-Corporate Enterprise Capital Finance Account: Total and Sectors
(Continued)

Million Canadian dollars

	1980 TOTAL	1980 Non-Financial	1980 Financial	1985 TOTAL	1985 Non-Financial	1985 Financial	1990 TOTAL	1990 Non-Financial	1990 Financial	1991 TOTAL	1991 Non-Financial	1991 Financial
A Mortgages	10730	79	10651	15545	226	15319	27915	627	27288	23236	779	22457
B Other	...	...	...	...	...	...	...	...	...	...	...	...
9 Trade credits and advances	13675	8757	4918	11745	4486	7259	6134	474	5660	5013	2729	2284
A Consumer credit	4690	-92	4782	7013	120	6893	5215	...	5215	1580	...	1580
B Other	8985	8849	136	4732	4366	366	919	474	445	3433	2729	704
10 Other receivables	...	...	...	...	...	...	...	...	...	...	...	...
11 Other assets	25547	13005	12542	20518	10818	9700	28220	13218	15002	29888	22227	7661
Total Acquisition of Financial Assets	94992	26457	68535	89774	16889	72885	112094	21941	90153	109247	21427	87820

Incurrence of Liabilities

	TOTAL	Non-Fin	Fin	TOTAL	Non-Fin	Fin	TOTAL	Non-Fin	Fin	TOTAL	Non-Fin	Fin
1 Currency and transferable deposits	38762	-	38762	24567	-	24567	37358	...	37358	21295	...	21295
2 Other deposits	...	...	...	...	...	...	...	...	...	...	...	...
3 Bills and bonds, short term	5410	2532	2878	3584	2277	1307	2476	1889	587	-8302	-6465	-1837
4 Bonds, long term	7864	5711	2153	5657	3503	2154	12117	9728	2389	20755	16797	3958
5 Corporate equity securities	7703	5528	2175	19197	10306	8891	13956	6498	7458	31487	8515	22972
6 Short-term loans, n.e.c. [b]	12412	11794	618	11690	5674	6016	14575	13423	1152	6096	1586	4510
7 Long-term loans, n.e.c. [b]	1887	1813	74	2538	2580	-42	9334	9277	57	7300	7019	281
8 Net equity of households in life insurance and pension fund reserves	12155	-	12155	17882	-	17882	28330	...	28330	29220	...	29220
9 Proprietors' net additions to the accumulation of quasi-corporations [c]	9157	3789	5368	3007	-290	3297	7286	5644	1642	8153	6160	1993
10 Trade credit and advances	4913	4955	-42	2261	2295	-34	1464	1362	102	2445	2333	112
11 Other accounts payable	...	...	...	...	...	...	...	...	...	...	...	...
12 Other liabilities	8031	4346	3685	6394	260	6134	12073	1771	10302	13386	5611	7775
Total Incurrence of Liabilities	108294	40468	67826	96777	26605	70172	138969	49592	89377	131835	41556	90279
Statistical discrepancy	-1445	-2144	699	-6727	-7699	972	-2988	-2127	-861	-2256	360	-2616
Net Lending [d]	-11857	-11867	10	-276	-2017	1741	-23887	-25524	1637	-20332	-20489	157
Incurrence of Liabilities and Net Lending	94992	26457	68535	89774	16889	72885	112094	21941	90153	109247	21427	87820

	1992 TOTAL	1992 Non-Financial	1992 Financial	1993 TOTAL	1993 Non-Financial	1993 Financial

Acquisition of Financial Assets

	TOTAL	Non-Fin	Fin	TOTAL	Non-Fin	Fin
1 Gold and SDRs	-6986	...	-6986	-599	...	-599
2 Currency and transferable deposits	8075	8560	-485	1728	5593	-3865
3 Other deposits	...	...	...	...	...	...
4 Bills and bonds, short term	1112	-3128	4240	18102	1655	16447
5 Bonds, long term	24198	509	23689	34232	-1300	35532
A Corporate, resident	3169	-169	3338	4650	-154	4804
B Government	21029	678	20351	29582	-1146	30728
C Rest of the world	...	...	...	...	...	...
6 Corporate equity securities [a]	18933	-61	18994	22779	-341	23120
7 Short term loans, n.e.c. [b]	8729	-117	8846	-1374	-331	-1043
8 Long term loans, n.e.c. [b]	23312	283	23029	15290	281	15009
A Mortgages	23312	283	23029	15290	281	15009
B Other	...	...	...	...	...	...
9 Trade credits and advances	5953	5832	121	9538	3324	6214
A Consumer credit	-545	...	-545	5643	...	5643
B Other	6498	5832	666	3895	3324	571
10 Other receivables	...	...	...	...	...	...
11 Other assets	27517	9541	17976	50602	21912	28690
Total Acquisition of Financial Assets	110843	21419	89424	150298	30793	119505

Incurrence of Liabilities

	TOTAL	Non-Fin	Fin	TOTAL	Non-Fin	Fin
1 Currency and transferable deposits	29089	...	29089	10109	...	10109
2 Other deposits	...	...	...	...	...	...
3 Bills and bonds, short term	-12634	-14612	1978	5278	6426	-1148
4 Bonds, long term	7818	6941	877	11854	6909	4945
5 Corporate equity securities	31822	8967	22855	58899	15083	43816
6 Short-term loans, n.e.c. [b]	8123	6224	1899	-5904	-5020	-884

Canada

3.24 Corporate and Quasi-Corporate Enterprise Capital Finance Account: Total and Sectors
(Continued)

Million Canadian dollars

	1992 TOTAL	1992 Non-Financial	1992 Financial	1993 TOTAL	1993 Non-Financial	1993 Financial
7 Long-term loans, n.e.c. [b]	7184	6865	319	4857	5217	-360
8 Net equity of households in life insurance and pension fund reserves	27916	...	27916	23007	...	23007
9 Proprietors' net additions to the accumulation of quasi-corporations [c]	3385	6529	-3144	4784	2406	2378
10 Trade credit and advances	4397	4244	153	5784	5390	394
11 Other accounts payable	...	...	...	...	...	...
12 Other liabilities	18127	8108	10019	43896	10324	33572
Total Incurrence of Liabilities	125227	33266	91961	162564	46735	115829
Statistical discrepancy	1486	2045	-559	-3078	-2971	-107
Net Lending [d]	-15870	-13892	-1978	-9188	-12971	3783
Incurrence of Liabilities and Net Lending	110843	21419	89424	150298	30793	119505

a) Investment in short-term papers, bonds and corporate equity securities of the rest of the world cannot be split between long-term and short-term by purchasers, the total investment has been allocated to the item 'Corporate equity securities'.
b) Loans other than mortgages are included in item 'Short-term loans, n.e.c.'.
c) Item 'Proprietors' net additions to the accumulation of quasi-corporations' consists of corporate and government claims on their associated enterprises.
d) The net lending in the Capital Finance Accounts differs from that in the Capital Accumulation Accounts because net transactions in land (and other existing assets) are included in the former but not the latter.

3.25 Corporate and Quasi-Corporate Enterprise Balance Sheet: Total and Sectors

Million Canadian dollars

	1980 TOTAL	1980 Non-Financial	1980 Financial	1985 TOTAL	1985 Non-Financial	1985 Financial	1990 TOTAL	1990 Non-Financial	1990 Financial	1991 TOTAL	1991 Non-Financial	1991 Financial
Assets												
Non-financial assets	513558	496130	17428	716688	684220	32468	990579	940112	50467	990740	937913	52827
1 Tangible assets	513558	496130	17428	716688	684220	32468	990579	940112	50467	990740	937913	52827
A Stocks	72672	72672	...	87997	87997	...	106046	106046	...	103294	103294	...
B Reproducible fixed assets	322492	310518	11974	463650	440226	23424	637411	601125	36286	630188	592491	37697
Gross	43257	41047	2210	58812	55579	3233	91959	86968	4991	97225	91925	5300
Less: Accumulated consumption	...	...	...	...	...	...	...	...	...	...	...	...
C Land and other non-reproducible tangible assets	75137	71893	3244	106229	100418	5811	155163	145973	9190	160033	150203	9830
2 Intangible assets	...	...	...	...	...	...	...	...	...	...	...	...
Financial assets	690619	165944	524675	1084307	282011	802296	1721105	420758	1300347	1835953	433676	1402277
1 Gold and SDRs	4810	...	4810	4581	...	4581	21552	...	21552	19529	...	19529
2 Currency and transferable deposits	67631	24942	42689	93507	43412	50095	108607	59056	49551	112236	59987	52249
3 Other deposits	...	...	...	...	...	...	...	...	...	...	...	...
4 Bills and bonds, short term	30271	3303	26968	64656	11211	53445	134191	25815	108376	138304	22081	116223
5 Bonds, long term	83312	1553	81759	137811	2824	134987	210859	6964	203895	240974	7762	233212
A Corporate, resident	24719	559	24160	33339	462	32877	57177	2283	54894	60347	2692	57655
B Government	58593	994	57599	104472	2362	102110	153682	4681	149001	180627	5070	175557
C Rest of the world	...	...	...	...	...	...	...	...	...	...	...	...
6 Corporate equity securities [a]	38532	4006	34526	84938	5711	79227	141074	7541	133533	157953	6392	151561
7 Short-term loans, n.e.c. [b]	121671	4304	117367	180177	6879	173298	213728	9896	203832	216470	9067	207403
8 Long-term loans, n.e.c. [b]	120890	4185	116705	167766	6021	161745	315718	7433	308285	340657	7895	332762
A Mortgages	120890	4185	116705	167766	6021	161745	315718	7433	308285	340657	7895	332762
B Other	...	...	...	...	...	...	...	...	...	...	...	...
9 Trade credits and allowances	108990	64385	44605	149286	89933	59353	206406	106571	99835	210796	109021	101775
A Consumer credit	44344	1084	43260	58809	1700	57109	97236	1700	95536	98557	1700	96857
B Other	64646	63301	1345	90477	88233	2244	109170	104871	4299	112239	107321	4918
10 Other receivables	...	...	...	...	...	...	...	...	...	...	...	...
11 Other assets	114512	59266	55246	201585	116020	85565	368970	197482	171488	399034	211471	187563
Total Assets	1204177	662074	542103	1800995	966231	834764	2711684	1360870	1350814	2826693	1371589	1455104
Liabilities and Net Worth												
Liabilities	1003031	522432	480599	1539591	784458	755133	2292714	1089781	1202933	2442305	1134800	1307505
1 Currency and transferable deposits	283689	...	283689	394848	...	394848	581324	...	581324	601572	...	601572
2 Other deposits	...	...	...	...	...	...	...	...	...	...	...	...
3 Bills and bonds, short term	21427	7662	13765	28031	18720	9311	70342	53147	17195	61673	47344	14329

Canada

3.25 Corporate and Quasi-Corporate Enterprise Balance Sheet: Total and Sectors
(Continued)

Million Canadian dollars

	1980 TOTAL	1980 Non-Financial	1980 Financial	1985 TOTAL	1985 Non-Financial	1985 Financial	1990 TOTAL	1990 Non-Financial	1990 Financial	1991 TOTAL	1991 Non-Financial	1991 Financial
4 Bonds, long term	88080	71726	16354	135143	109328	25815	186822	140549	46273	206533	155768	50765
5 Corporate equity securities	223655	180067	43588	364783	274050	90733	559751	385880	173871	597010	397581	199429
6 Short-term loans, n.e.c. b	89911	76373	13538	145303	120754	24549	180110	149743	30367	184178	148763	35415
7 Long-term loans, n.e.c. b	27964	27428	536	35625	34906	719	72446	71097	1349	79597	78089	1508
8 Net equity of households in life insurance and pension fund reserves	96986	...	96986	185864	...	185864	327869	...	327869	358731	...	358731
9 Proprietors' net equity in quasi-corporations	111755	64596	47159	155133	101943	53190	238256	152607	85649	255074	160312	94762
1 Trade credit and advances	60312	59762	550	80968	80204	764	95421	94305	1116	99158	98003	1155
1 Other accounts payable	...	...	...	...	...	...	...	...	...	...	...	...
12 Other liabilities	56633	34818	21815	85076	44553	40523	112986	42453	70533	131468	48940	82528
Net worth	201146	139642	61504	261404	181773	79631	418970	271089	147881	384388	236789	147599
Total Liabilities and Net Worth	1204177	662074	542103	1800995	966231	834764	2711684	1360870	1350814	2826693	1371589	1455104

	1992 TOTAL	1992 Non-Financial	1992 Financial

Assets

	TOTAL	Non-Financial	Financial
Non-financial assets	1010956	955421	55535
1 Tangible assets	1010956	955421	55535
A Stocks	105806	105806	...
B Reproducible fixed assets	637415	597926	39489
Gross	101888	96332	5556
Less: Accumulated consumption	...	...	...
C Land and other non-reproducible tangible assets	165847	155357	10490
2 Intangible assets	...	...	...
Financial assets	1959770	455833	1503937
1 Gold and SDRs	15132	...	15132
2 Currency and transferable deposits	120190	68955	51235
3 Other deposits	...	...	...
4 Bills and bonds, short term	139711	20081	119630
5 Bonds, long term	267699	8040	259659
A Corporate, resident	64696	2562	62134
B Government	203003	5478	197525
C Rest of the world	...	...	...
6 Corporate equity securities a	179873	7417	172456
7 Short-term loans, n.e.c. b	222635	9233	213402
8 Long-term loans, n.e.c. b	365847	8498	357349
A Mortgages	365847	8498	357349
B Other	...	...	...
9 Trade credits and allowances	215438	113744	101694
A Consumer credit	97591	1700	95891
B Other	117847	112044	5803
10 Other receivables	...	...	...
11 Other assets	433245	219865	213380
Total Assets	2970726	1411254	1559472

Liabilities and Net Worth

	TOTAL	Non-Financial	Financial
Liabilities	2593828	1173340	1420488
1 Currency and transferable deposits	636002	...	636002
2 Other deposits	...	...	...
3 Bills and bonds, short term	46667	32937	13730

Canada

3.25 Corporate and Quasi-Corporate Enterprise Balance Sheet: Total and Sectors
(Continued)

Million Canadian dollars

	1992 TOTAL	Non-Financial	Financial
4 Bonds, long term	220044	168011	52033
5 Corporate equity securities	638184	406715	231469
6 Short-term loans, n.e.c. [b]	190013	154894	35119
7 Long-term loans, n.e.c. [b]	86853	85062	1791
8 Net equity of households in life insurance and pension fund reserves	386890	...	386890
9 Proprietors' net equity in quasi-corporations	259845	167898	91947
1 Trade credit and advances	103163	101876	1287
1 Other accounts payable	...	...	...
12 Other liabilities	152257	55947	96310
Net worth	376898	237914	138984
Total Liabilities and Net Worth	2970726	1411254	1559472

a) Investment in short-term papers, bonds and corporate equity securities of the rest of the world cannot be split between long-term and short-term by purchasers, the total investment has been allocated to the item 'Corporate equity securities'. b) Loans other than mortgages are included in item 'Short-term loans, n.e.c.'.

3.26 Financial Transactions of Financial Institutions: Detail

Million Canadian dollars

	1980 ALL FINANCIAL INSTITUTIONS	Central Bank	Other Monetary Institutions	Insurance	Other Financial Institutions	1985 ALL FINANCIAL INSTITUTIONS	Central Bank	Other Monetary Institutions	Insurance	Other Financial Institutions
Acquisition of Financial Assets										
1 Gold and SDRs	-541	-541	...	...	...	-112	-112	...	...	...
A Gold	-647	-647	...	...	...	-233	-233	...	...	...
B Net acquisitions of SDRs	-131	-131	...	...	...	184	184	...	...	...
2 Currency and transferable deposits	4936	...	4493	725	-282	-1204	...	-1023	-410	229
A Liability of resident institutions	1467	...	1073	723	-329	433	...	732	-403	104
B Liability of rest of the world	3469	...	3420	2	47	-1637	...	-1755	-7	125
3 Other deposits	...	...	...	...	...	...	...	...	...	...
4 Bills and bonds, short term	3480	1012	1863	4	601	5456	466	824	1192	2974
5 Bonds, long term	9140	1230	-15	6639	1286	12411	-1986	-133	12749	1781
6 Corporate equity securities [a]	2403	...	111	1988	304	9868	-	4664	2551	2653
7 Short-term loans, n.e.c. [b]	21280	...	16321	158	4801	10733	...	7971	23	2739
8 Long-term loans, n.e.c. [b]	10651	...	7690	2083	878	15319	...	12476	1973	870
A Mortgages	10651	...	7690	2083	878	15319	...	12476	1973	870
B Other	...	...	...	...	...	...	...	...	...	...
9 Trade credit and advances	4918	...	4427	446	45	7259	...	6122	308	829
A Consumer credit	4782	...	4427	300	55	6893	...	6122	-25	796
B Other	136	...	...	146	-10	366	...	...	333	33
10 Other assets	12542	13	9593	469	2467	9700	-13	3158	1440	5115
Total Acquisition of Financial Assets	68535	1440	44483	12512	10100	72884	1809	34059	19826	17190
Incurrence of Liabilities										
1 Currency and transferable deposits	38762	1470	36760	...	532	24567	1266	22575	...	726
2 Other deposits	...	...	...	...	...	...	...	...	...	...
3 Bills and bonds, short term	2878	...	87	...	2791	1307	...	-46	...	1353
4 Bonds, long term	2153	...	392	...	1761	2154	...	1383	...	771
5 Corporate equity securities	2175	...	777	74	1324	8891	...	1328	448	7115
6 Short-term loans, n.e.c. [b]	618	...	583	48	-13	6016	...	3699	184	2133
7 Long-term loans, n.e.c. [b]	74	...	20	30	24	-42	...	-60	28	-10
8 Net equity of households in life insurance and pension fund reserves	12252	...	...	12252	...	17665	...	...	17665	...
9 Other liabilities	9011	-30	5087	618	3336	9396	569	1276	2307	5244
Total Incurrence of liabilities	67923	1440	43706	13022	9755	69954	1835	30155	20632	17332
Statistical discrepancy [c]	-602	-	-5	97	-694	-1189	1	719	-217	-1692
Net Lending [d]	10	-	772	-413	-349	1741	-25	4623	-1023	-1834
Incurrence of Liabilities and Net Lending	68535	1440	44483	12512	10100	72884	1809	34059	19826	17190

Canada

3.26 Financial Transactions of Financial Institutions: Detail

Million Canadian dollars

		1990				1991			
	ALL FINANCIAL INSTITUTIONS	Central Bank	Other Monetary Institutions	Insurance	Other Financial Institutions	ALL FINANCIAL INSTITUTIONS	Central Bank	Other Monetary Institutions	Insurance	Other Financial Institutions

Acquisition of Financial Assets

1 Gold and SDRs	649	649	...	...	...	-2831	-2831	...	...	...
A Gold	674	674	...	...	...	-2966	-2966	...	...	...
B Net acquisitions of SDRs	35	35	...	...	...	51	51	...	...	...
2 Currency and transferable deposits	-1127	...	-354	173	-946	3377	...	3206	218	-47
A Liability of resident institutions	-1413	...	-333	165	-1245	1622	...	1321	149	152
B Liability of rest of the world	286	...	-21	8	299	1755	...	1885	69	-199
3 Other deposits	...	...	...	...	...	...	...	...	...	...
4 Bills and bonds, short term	9446	-568	5967	2760	1287	8941	2571	5788	-4600	5182
5 Bonds, long term	12942	-258	1702	9855	1643	27088	-474	9348	14327	3887
6 Corporate equity securities [a]	10425	-	2717	6639	1069	16579	-	-608	13691	3496
7 Short-term loans, n.e.c. [b]	9858	...	8972	-71	957	4330	...	4055	192	83
8 Long-term loans, n.e.c. [b]	27388	...	21789	6458	-859	23096	...	17763	4243	1090
A Mortgages	27388	...	21789	6458	-859	23096	...	17763	4243	1090
B Other	...	...	...	...	...	...	...	...	...	...
9 Trade credit and advances	5660	...	4681	567	412	1760	...	1759	712	-711
A Consumer credit	5215	...	4681	157	377	1186	...	1759	52	-625
B Other	445	...	...	410	35	574	...	...	660	-86
10 Other assets	17485	-3	3845	3177	10466	14436	22	-6117	1362	19169
Total Acquisition of Financial Assets	92885	-21	49319	29558	14029	97479	-9	35194	30145	32149

Incurrence of Liabilities

1 Currency and transferable deposits	39961	489	38969	...	503	19119	1863	16817	...	439
2 Other deposits	...	...	...	...	...	...	...	...	...	...
3 Bills and bonds, short term	587	...	-	...	587	-3107	...	-	...	-3107
4 Bonds, long term	2389	...	1591	...	798	3196	...	3053	...	143
5 Corporate equity securities	7508	...	1379	479	5650	22825	...	2658	754	19413
6 Short-term loans, n.e.c. [b]	547	...	-156	-141	844	9408	...	1449	-188	8147
7 Long-term loans, n.e.c. [b]	60	...	5	-11	66	-14	...	13	-9	-18
8 Net equity of households in life insurance and pension fund reserves	28330	...	...	28330	...	30354	...	...	30354	...
9 Other liabilities	13574	-488	4605	1690	7767	16394	-1842	8023	1628	8585
Total Incurrence of liabilities	92956	1	46393	30347	16215	98175	21	32013	32539	33602
Statistical discrepancy [c]	805	-5	383	-	427	369	1	842	-	-474
Net Lending [d]	734	-27	3309	-789	-1759	-327	-29	4023	-2394	-1927
Incurrence of Liabilities and Net Lending	92885	-21	49319	29558	14029	97479	-9	35194	30145	32149

	1992				
	ALL FINANCIAL INSTITUTIONS	Central Bank	Other Monetary Institutions	Insurance	Other Financial Institutions

Acquisition of Financial Assets

1 Gold and SDRs	-6986	-6986	...	...	...
A Gold	-6929	-6929	...	...	...
B Net acquisitions of SDRs	-623	-623	...	...	...
2 Currency and transferable deposits	-420	...	-4943	857	3666
A Liability of resident institutions	3046	...	-1081	862	3265
B Liability of rest of the world	-3466	...	-3862	-5	401
3 Other deposits	...	...	...	...	...
4 Bills and bonds, short term	5058	1575	472	2605	406
5 Bonds, long term	25296	-1304	7771	13195	5634
6 Corporate equity securities [a]	17644	-	49	10752	6843
7 Short-term loans, n.e.c. [b]	9345	...	9467	137	-259
8 Long-term loans, n.e.c. [b]	22885	...	18659	2226	2000
A Mortgages	22885	...	18659	2226	2000
B Other	...	...	...	...	...
9 Trade credit and advances	332	...	365	1010	-1043
A Consumer credit	-647	...	365	70	-1082
B Other	979	...	...	940	39

201

Canada

3.26 Financial Transactions of Financial Institutions: Detail
(Continued)

Million Canadian dollars

	1992 ALL FINANCIAL INSTITUTIONS	Central Bank	Other Monetary Institutions	Insurance	Other Financial Institutions
10 Other assets	30105	-96	6888	559	22754
Total Acquisition of Financial Assets	102309	-7761	38728	31341	40001
Incurrence of Liabilities					
1 Currency and transferable deposits	28824	457	28039	...	328
2 Other deposits	...	...	...	...	...
3 Bills and bonds, short term	-142	...	-	...	-142
4 Bonds, long term	1379	...	-1237	...	2616
5 Corporate equity securities	32516	...	1505	714	30297
6 Short-term loans, n.e.c. b	1224	...	645	134	445
7 Long-term loans, n.e.c. b	352	...	-5	-50	407
8 Net equity of households in life insurance and pension fund reserves	28549	...	...	28549	...
9 Other liabilities	13674	-8181	5740	3946	12169
Total Incurrence of liabilities	106376	-7724	34687	33293	46120
Statistical discrepancy c	389	4	336	-	49
Net Lending d	-3678	-33	4377	-1952	-6070
Incurrence of Liabilities and Net Lending	102309	-7761	38728	31341	40001

a) Investment in short-term papers, bonds and corporate equity securities of the rest of the world cannot be split between long-term and short-term by purchasers, the total investment has been allocated to the item 'Corporate equity securities'.
b) Loans other than mortgages are included in item 'Short-term loans, n.e.c.'.
c) The statistical discrepancy equals the diffrence between net lending in the Income and Expenditure Accounts and net acquisition of financial assets in the Financial Flow Accounts (change in financial assets less change in liabilities).
d) The net lending in the Capital Finance Accounts differs from that in the Capital Accumulation Accounts because net transactions in land (and other existing assets) are included in the former but not the latter.

3.32 Household and Private Unincorporated Enterprise Income and Outlay Account

Million Canadian dollars

	1980	1983	1984	1985	1986	1987	1988	1989	1990	1991	1992	1993
Receipts												
1 Compensation of employees	171424	221800	238849	257518	274801	298834	327823	353632	372087	381645	390741	400533
A Wages and salaries	156819	200449	215699	232257	247943	269468	295619	316369	330741	335795	341204	348291
B Employers' contributions for social security	6357	10212	11269	12573	13857	14962	16876	23275	25043	26550	31514	33946
C Employers' contributions for private pension & welfare plans	8248	11139	11881	12688	13001	14404	15328	13987	16303	19300	18023	18296
2 Operating surplus of private unincorporated enterprises a	16598	23629	27307	29255	32802	33867	37143	37503	36927	37227	38555	40368
3 Property and entrepreneurial income	27539	41896	47702	50729	52686	55191	63101	74316	85178	78751	73069	68973
A Withdrawals from private quasi-corporations	...	...	...	...	...	...	...	...	...	...	...	...
B Interest	22432	34564	40374	43084	44100	45506	53294	65347	76551	71143	65679	61290
C Dividends	5107	7332	7328	7645	8586	9685	9807	8969	8627	7608	7390	7683
D Net land rent and royalties	...	...	...	...	...	...	...	...	...	...	...	...
3 Current transfers	31503	51159	54741	59215	62966	67701	72736	78492	82697	95361	104086	110124
A Casualty insurance claims	...	...	...	...	...	...	...	...	...	...	...	...
B Social security benefits	16655	29135	31151	33963	36904	40292	43469	46952	46898	53801	58054	59297
C Social assistance grants	13811	20612	22385	24032	24692	25930	27736	29895	34002	39651	44024	48676
D Unfunded employee pension and welfare benefits	...	...	...	...	...	...	...	...	...	...	...	...
E Transfers from general government	...	...	...	...	...	...	...	...	...	...	...	...
F Transfers from the rest of the world	519	610	629	681	777	821	849	856	933	1009	1093	1193
G Other transfers n.e.c.	518	602	576	539	593	658	682	789	864	900	915	958
Total Current Receipts	247064	338484	368599	396717	423255	455593	500803	543943	576889	592984	606451	619998
Disbursements												
1 Final consumption expenditures	170408	228221	248428	271099	293489	318216	345179	373670	393055	405283	416353	430806
2 Property income	3713	3785	3791	4233	4496	5268	6205	8218	9056	7820	5893	4822
A Interest	3713	3785	3791	4233	4496	5268	6205	8218	9056	7820	5893	4822
Consumer debt	3713	3785	3791	4233	4496	5268	6205	8218	9056	7820	5893	4822
Mortgage	...	...	...	...	...	...	...	...	...	...	...	...

Canada

3.32 Household and Private Unincorporated Enterprise Income and Outlay Account
(Continued)

Million Canadian dollars

	1980	1983	1984	1985	1986	1987	1988	1989	1990	1991	1992	1993
Other	...	...	...	...	...	...	...	...	...	...	...	...
B Net land rent and royalties	...	...	...	...	...	...	...	...	...	...	...	...
3 Direct taxes and other current transfers n.e.c. to government	45165	66974	71846	78797	89156	99748	111800	118043	135550	139991	143633	145574
A Social security contributions	10591	17156	18582	20847	22785	25162	28283	28345	31833	34659	38264	39454
B Direct taxes	32850	47321	50603	55198	63483	71512	80127	85982	101677	103060	102907	103163
Income taxes	32140	46384	49594	54203	62378	70333	78888	84643	100188	101478	101226	101412
Other	710	937	1009	995	1105	1179	1239	1339	1489	1582	1681	1751
C Fees, fines and penalties	1724	2497	2661	2752	2888	3074	3390	3716	2040	2272	2462	2957
4 Other current transfers	364	473	500	554	602	629	709	784	736	775	933	980
A Net casualty insurance premiums	...	...	...	...	...	...	...	...	...	...	...	...
B Transfers to private non-profit institutions serving households	...	...	...	...	...	...	...	...	...	...	...	...
C Transfers to the rest of the world	364	473	500	554	602	629	709	784	736	775	933	980
D Other current transfers, except imputed	...	...	...	...	...	...	...	...	...	...	...	...
E Imputed employee pension and welfare contributions	...	...	...	...	...	...	...	...	...	...	...	...
Net saving	27414	39031	44034	42034	35512	31732	36910	43228	38492	39115	39639	37816
Total Current Disbursements and Net Saving	247064	338484	368599	396717	423255	455593	500803	543943	576889	592984	606451	619998

a) Item 'Operating surplus' refers to net income of unincorporated business including net rent.

3.33 Household and Private Unincorporated Enterprise Capital Accumulation Account

Million Canadian dollars

	1980	1983	1984	1985	1986	1987	1988	1989	1990	1991	1992	1993
Finance of Gross Accumulation												
1 Gross saving	37635	52135	58258	57347	51957	49637	55472	63141	59968	61789	62911	61952
A Consumption of fixed capital	10221	13104	14224	15313	16445	17905	18562	19913	21476	22674	23272	24136
B Net saving	27414	39031	44034	42034	35512	31732	36910	43228	38492	39115	39639	37816
2 Capital transfers	1559	2857	2280	2297	2204	1263	1558	1820	1787	1971	1821	1811
A From resident sectors	398	1306	644	520	247	216	210	334	330	533	270	254
B From the rest of the world	1161	1551	1636	1777	1957	1047	1348	1486	1457	1438	1551	1557
Total Finance of Gross Accumulation	39194	54992	60538	59644	54161	50900	57030	64961	61755	63760	64732	63763
Gross Accumulation												
1 Gross Capital Formation	19903	23009	23995	27275	32630	38683	43801	48273	43542	38474	41412	42814
A Increase in stocks	-473	-747	-1027	348	847	-443	-588	581	624	45	-574	1000
B Gross fixed capital formation	20376	23756	25022	26927	31783	39126	44389	47692	42918	38429	41986	41814
2 Purchases of land, net	...	...	...	...	...	...	...	...	...	...	...	...
3 Purchases of intangibles, net	...	...	...	...	...	...	...	...	...	...	...	...
4 Capital transfers	389	414	393	426	388	236	226	241	257	317	342	348
A To resident sectors	72	65	47	65	13	8	7	2	3	2	5	3
B To the rest of the world	317	349	346	361	375	228	219	239	254	315	337	345
Net lending [a]	18902	31569	36150	31943	21143	11981	13003	16447	17956	24969	22978	20601
Total Gross Accumulation	39194	54992	60538	59644	54161	50900	57030	64961	61755	63760	64732	63763

a) The net lending in the Capital Finance Accounts differs from that in the Capital Accumulation Accounts because net transactions in land (and other existing assets) are included in the former but not the latter.

3.34 Household and Private Unincorporated Enterprise Capital Finance Account

Million Canadian dollars

	1980	1983	1984	1985	1986	1987	1988	1989	1990	1991	1992	1993
Acquisition of Financial Assets												
1 Gold	...	...	...	...	...	...	...	...	...	...	...	...
2 Currency and transferable deposits	22265	7488	22061	15619	27289	17938	44713	48081	28804	21356	21124	10026
3 Other deposits	...	...	...	...	...	...	...	...	...	...	...	...
4 Bills and bonds, short term	5229	7863	1932	3439	5451	2618	1888	13771	7836	-4819	1025	-5923
5 Bonds, long term	2186	7164	7496	7625	-6804	12271	7080	-19769	-4678	9198	-136	-3974
A Corporate	216	289	126	-215	-2270	-1003	3214	-3683	706	5371	-2421	2055
B Government	1970	6875	7370	7840	-4534	13274	3866	-16086	-5384	3827	2285	-6029

Canada

3.34 Household and Private Unincorporated Enterprise Capital Finance Account
(Continued)

Million Canadian dollars

	1980	1983	1984	1985	1986	1987	1988	1989	1990	1991	1992	1993
C Rest of the world	-	-	-	-	-	-	-	-	...	...	...	...
6 Corporate equity securities [a]	-207	2195	486	6202	7233	8808	-2525	2080	3424	16694	16208	36576
7 Short term loans, n.e.c.	...	...	...	...	...	...	...	...	...	...	...	...
8 Long term loans, n.e.c.	436	-276	328	-77	554	2283	2182	3349	2912	4198	6845	6267
A Mortgages	436	-276	328	-77	554	2283	2182	3349	2912	4198	6845	6267
B Other	-	-	-	-	-	-	-	-	...	...	...	...
9 Trade credit and advances	...	...	...	...	...	...	...	...	...	...	...	...
10 Net equity of households in life insurance and pension fund reserves	12142	15884	18015	17849	18699	18349	21934	24963	28290	29180	27869	22972
11 Proprietors' net additions to the accumulation of quasi-corporations	...	...	...	...	...	...	...	...	...	...	...	...
12 Other	-2140	598	-3530	5852	-1012	-4758	-19526	-14529	-11899	-20085	-12399	-13123
Total Acquisition of Financial Assets	39911	40916	46788	56509	51410	57509	55746	57946	54689	55722	60536	52821
Incurrence of Liabilities												
1 Short term loans, n.e.c. [b]	10040	2555	4745	8392	10170	15055	15203	11926	6790	487	783	5956
2 Long term loans, n.e.c. [b]	9342	10443	7910	12664	19981	25630	25457	28078	21454	20265	23207	16764
A Mortgages	9342	10443	7910	12664	19981	25630	25457	28078	21454	20265	23207	16764
B Other	-	-	-	-	-	-	-	-	...	...	...	...
3 Trade credit and advances	2313	-3640	-673	3000	1060	3008	2197	854	408	-578	868	-384
4 Other accounts payable	...	...	...	...	...	...	...	...	...	...	...	...
5 Other liabilities	37	80	-34	136	80	-194	-10	-98	-108	1	-49	97
Total Incurrence of Liabilities	21732	9438	11948	24192	31291	43499	42847	40760	28544	20175	24809	22433
Statistical discrepancy [c]	-866	711	-352	1456	190	2005	-136	707	3858	5611	7420	4187
Net Lending [d]	19045	30767	35192	30861	19929	12005	13035	16479	22287	29936	28307	26201
Incurrence of Liabilities and Net Lending	39911	40916	46788	56509	51410	57509	55746	57946	54689	55722	60536	52821

a) Investment in short-term papers, bonds and corporate equity securities of the rest of the world cannot be split between long-term and short-term by purchasers, the total investment has been allocated to the item 'Corporate equity securities'.
b) Loans other than mortgages are included in item 'Short-term loans, n.e.c.'.
c) The statistical discrepancy equals the diffrence between net lending in the Income and Expenditure Accounts and net acquisition of financial assets in the Financial Flow Accounts (change in financial assets less change in liabilities).
d) The net lending in the Capital Finance Accounts differs from that in the Capital Accumulation Accounts because net transactions in land (and other existing assets) are included in the former but not the latter.

3.35 Household and Private Unincorporated Enterprise Balance Sheet

Million Canadian dollars

	1980	1983	1984	1985	1986	1987	1988	1989	1990	1991	1992	1993
Assets												
Non-financial assets	399109	528720	556523	580055	594063	665200	764151	817219	845372	902858	949550	...
1 Tangible assets	399109	528720	556523	580055	594063	665200	764151	817219	845372	902858	949550	...
A Stocks of household enterprises	14560	14658	13917	13934	14063	13640	13698	14283	14636	13348	13611	...
B Dwellings	217710	279381	298298	322570	360425	406340	468676	488169	518417	546540	571304	...
C Other reproducible fixed assets of unincorporated enterprises	35796	42706	42724	42810	44879	45152	45925	47032	47286	45749	44227	...
D Land and other non-reproducible tangible assets	166839	191975	201584	200741	219575	245220	281777	314767	312319	342970	364635	...
2 Intangible assets	...	...	...	...	...	...	...	...	...	...	...	...
Financial assets	477185	632876	693082	757942	835081	913595	998134	1096992	1167748	1243779	1321051	...
1 Gold	...	...	...	...	...	...	...	...	...	...	...	...
2 Currency and transferable deposits	183716	223703	240787	252369	282205	299610	343939	394811	421647	444450	468713	...
3 Other deposits	...	...	...	...	...	...	...	...	...	...	...	...
4 Bills and bonds, short term	6177	10968	10397	13879	20026	21699	24248	35847	43721	35926	34970	...
5 Bonds, long term	38481	62200	71188	77452	68686	78604	85139	65086	63506	70065	65118	...
A Corporate	3115	5376	8159	9075	6913	5527	9472	3458	6994	14371	10585	...
B Government	35366	56824	63029	68377	61773	73077	75667	61628	56512	55694	54533	...
C Rest of the world	...	...	...	...	...	...	...	...	...	...	...	...
6 Corporate equitry securities	119368	149468	161947	182343	203746	227619	238280	245513	253290	270049	285353	...
7 Short-term loans, n.e.c.	...	...	...	...	...	...	...	...	...	...	...	...
8 Long-term loans, n.e.c.	9007	9936	10264	10187	10741	13024	15206	18555	21467	25245	31521	...
A Mortgages	9007	9936	10264	10187	10741	13024	15206	18555	21467	25245	31521	...

Canada

3.35 Household and Private Unincorporated Enterprise Balance Sheet
(Continued)

Million Canadian dollars

	1980	1983	1984	1985	1986	1987	1988	1989	1990	1991	1992	1993
B Other	...	...	...	...	...	...	...	...	...	...	...	...
9 Trade credit and advances of unincorporated enterprises	...	...	...	...	...	...	...	...	...	...	...	...
1 Net equity in life insurance and pension fund reserves	98122	146246	164373	186877	213041	237934	262593	301788	328698	359521	387689	...
1 Proprietors' equity in quasi-corporations	...	...	...	...	...	...	...	...	...	...	...	...
12 Other	22314	30355	34126	34835	36636	35105	28729	35392	35419	38523	47687	...
Total Assets	876294	1161596	1249605	1337997	1429144	1578795	1762285	1914211	2013120	2146637	2270601	...
Memorandum Item: Consumer Durable Goods	116806	140888	148437	159780	178335	193848	214565	231199	239188	243749	249205	...
Liabilities and Net Worth												
Liabilities	175704	205197	215505	239767	270626	312162	354679	395534	424648	445951	469209	...
1 Short-term loans, n.e.c.	67893	75039	78259	87954	96984	112005	126256	137989	145913	147118	145179	...
2 Long-term loans, n.e.c.	106575	127118	134342	147018	167985	194286	221039	248634	269025	290539	314719	...
A Mortgages	106575	127118	134342	147018	167985	194286	221039	248634	269025	290539	314719	...
B Other	...	...	...	...	...	...	...	...	...	...	...	...
3 Trade credit and advances	499	1965	1863	3618	4400	4808	6331	7956	8863	7446	8511	...
4 Other accounts payable	...	...	...	...	...	...	...	...	...	...	...	...
5 Other liabilities	737	1075	1041	1177	1257	1063	1053	955	847	848	800	...
Net worth	700590	956399	1034100	1098230	1158518	1266633	1407606	1518677	1588472	1700686	1801392	...
Total Liabilities and Net Worth	876294	1161596	1249605	1337997	1429144	1578795	1762285	1914211	2013120	2146637	2270601	...

3.51 External Transactions: Current Account: Detail

Million Canadian dollars

	1980	1983	1984	1985	1986	1987	1988	1989	1990	1991	1992	1993
Payments to the Rest of the World												
1 Imports of goods and services	81933	89832	110632	123388	133369	140502	156384	166079	171223	172453	186738	212508
A Imports of merchandise c.i.f.	70912	75961	95404	106680	114426	119546	133404	140112	141789	141602	154399	177903
B Other	11021	13871	15228	16708	18943	20956	22980	25967	29434	30851	32339	34605
2 Factor income to the rest of the world	11466	17197	19849	21906	24118	24471	30705	31829	34438	32790	33739	34076
A Compensation of employees	-	-	-	-	-	-	-	-	...	...	...	...
B Property and entrepreneurial income	11466	17197	19849	21906	24118	24471	30705	31829	34438	32790	33739	34076
By general government	1592	3245	3755	4743	6502	7453	8527	10140	11130	12212	13451	15316
By corporate and quasi-cororate enterprises	9874	13952	16094	17163	17616	17018	22178	21689	23308	20578	20288	18760
By other	...	...	...	...	...	...	...	...	...	...	...	...
3 Current transfers to the rest of the world	1310	1800	2239	2355	2538	2926	3356	3359	3925	3625	3756	3800
A Indirect taxes by general government to supranational organizations	...	...	...	...	...	...	...	...	...	...	...	...
B Other current transfers	1310	1800	2239	2355	2538	2926	3356	3359	3925	3625	3756	3800
By general government	817	1194	1571	1643	1795	2169	2494	2398	3040	2690	2698	2687
By other resident sectors	493	606	668	712	743	757	862	961	885	935	1058	1113
4 Surplus of the nation on current transactions	-1977	1862	1407	-3406	-11738	-12421	-16624	-24637	-27438	-31520	-31726	-29382
Payments to the Rest of the World, and Surplus of the Nation on Current Transfers	92732	110691	134127	144243	148287	155478	173821	176630	182148	177348	192507	221002
Receipts From The Rest of the World												
1 Exports of goods and services	87579	103444	126035	134919	138119	145416	159309	163903	168917	163943	180406	208223
A Exports of merchandise f.o.b.	78946	93311	114849	122468	123691	129976	141983	145594	149858	144342	160063	185840
B Other	8633	10133	11186	12451	14428	15440	17326	18309	19059	19601	20343	22383
2 Factor income from the rest of the world	3639	5594	6363	7574	7716	8027	11993	10334	10579	10888	9440	9945
A Compensation of employees	-	-	-	-	-	-	-	-	...	...	...	...
B Property and entrepreneurial income	3639	5594	6363	7574	7716	8027	11993	10334	10579	10888	9440	9945
By general government	80	35	60	48	243	472	1072	1374	1403	1477	1192	665
By corporate and quasi-corporate enterprises	3125	4505	4820	6058	6055	5998	8914	6595	6061	6240	5224	6050

Canada

3.51 External Transactions: Current Account: Detail
(Continued)

Million Canadian dollars

	1980	1983	1984	1985	1986	1987	1988	1989	1990	1991	1992	1993
By other	434	1054	1483	1468	1418	1557	2007	2365	3115	3171	3024	3230
3 Current transfers from the rest of the world	1514	1653	1729	1750	2452	2035	2519	2393	2652	2517	2661	2834
A Subsidies to general government from supranational organizations	...	...	...	...	...	...	...	...	...	...	...	...
B Other current transfers	1514	1653	1729	1750	2452	2035	2519	2393	2652	2517	2661	2834
To general government	995	1043	1100	1069	1675	1214	1670	1537	1719	1508	1568	1641
To other resident sectors	519	610	629	681	777	821	849	856	933	1009	1093	1193
Receipts from the Rest of the World on Current Transfers	92732	110691	134127	144243	148287	155478	173821	176630	182148	177348	192507	221002

3.52 External Transactions: Capital Accumulation Account

Million Canadian dollars

	1980	1983	1984	1985	1986	1987	1988	1989	1990	1991	1992	1993
Finance of Gross Accumulation												
1 Surplus of the nation on current transactions	-1977	1862	1407	-3406	-11738	-12421	-16624	-24637	-27438	-31520	-31726	-29382
2 Capital transfers from the rest of the world	1161	1551	1636	1777	1957	1047	1348	1486	1457	1438	1551	1557
A By general government	-	-	-	-	-	-	-	-	...	...	...	...
B By other resident sectors	1161	1551	1636	1777	1957	1047	1348	1486	1457	1438	1551	1557
Total Finance of Gross Accumulation	-816	3413	3043	-1629	-9781	-11374	-15276	-23151	-25981	-30082	-30175	-27825
Gross Accumulation												
1 Capital transfers to the rest of the world	317	349	346	361	375	228	219	239	254	315	337	345
A By general government	-	-	-	-	-	-	-	-	...	...	...	...
B By other resident sectors	317	349	346	361	375	228	219	239	254	315	337	345
2 Purchases of intangible assets, n.e.c., net, from the rest of the world	-	-	-	-	-	-	-	-	...	...	...	...
Net lending to the rest of the world	-1133	3064	2697	-1990	-10156	-11602	-15495	-23390	-26235	-30397	-30512	-28170
Total Gross Accumulation	-816	3413	3043	-1629	-9781	-11374	-15276	-23151	-25981	-30082	-30175	-27825

3.53 External Transactions: Capital Finance Account

Million Canadian dollars

	1980	1983	1984	1985	1986	1987	1988	1989	1990	1991	1992	1993
Acquisitions of Foreign Financial Assets												
1 Gold and SDR's [a]	-541	550	-1093	-111	663	4464	9450	344	649	-2831	-6986	-599
2 Currency and transferable deposits	3416	1187	3412	-6287	6160	-4907	-1954	833	111	2022	-4832	-3610
3 Other deposits	...	...	...	...	...	...	...	...	...	...	...	...
4 Bills and bonds, short term	...	...	...	...	...	...	...	...	...	...	...	...
5 Bonds, long term	...	...	...	...	...	...	...	...	...	...	...	...
6 Corporate equity securities	...	...	...	...	...	...	...	...	...	...	...	...
7 Short-term loans, n.e.c.	4386	72	2375	-27	-2456	3697	4678	2039	-258	590	1246	1269
8 Long-term loans	4	-	-	-	-	-	-	-	-	-	-	...
9 Proprietors' net additions to accumulation of quasi-corporate, non-resident enterprises [b]	9683	4488	4200	7272	12702	8656	781	8334	9581	-736	8926	3011
10 Trade credit and advances	1869	3780	1423	87	-427	1210	310	6	-259	1222	2368	-1734
11 Other	262	1874	778	5442	2463	100	744	2623	4897	6259	6394	12881
Total Acquisitions of Foreign Financial Assets	19079	11951	11095	6376	19105	13220	14009	14179	14721	6526	7116	11218
Incurrence of Foreign Liabilities												
1 Currency and transferable deposits	11014	2620	2053	3819	325	358	-449	1324	6084	-2182	-4203	-7119
2 Other deposits	...	...	...	...	...	...	...	...	...	...	...	...
3 Bills and bonds, short term	1093	1680	1587	-562	2388	2528	9197	1249	5643	4426	4899	9209
4 Bonds, long term	3534	4797	7725	11083	22556	7551	15587	17474	14346	26295	17522	27495
5 Corporate equity securities	1489	913	154	1552	1877	6640	-2379	3884	-1735	-990	1037	11911
6 Short-term loans, n.e.c.	906	933	1261	472	-931	3909	2853	8013	5019	2933	2705	343

Canada

3.53 External Transactions: Capital Finance Account
(Continued)

Million Canadian dollars

		1980	1983	1984	1985	1986	1987	1988	1989	1990	1991	1992	1993
7	Long-term loans	-	-72	-108	-144	-100	-62	-14	-89	-15	131	52	-3
8	Non-resident proprietors' net additions to accumulation of resident quasi-corporate enterprises c	3091	1890	1163	-2248	5881	6290	3995	3485	10188	7378	11438	2750
9	Trade credit and advances	72	1580	1450	629	-215	1096	-421	888	1171	154	2095	391
10	Other	75	430	297	1170	1414	-338	1720	710	1895	1392	588	1100
	Total Incurrence of Liabilities	21274	14771	15582	15771	33195	27972	30089	36938	42596	39537	36133	46077
	Statistical discrepancy	-1062	-4917	-6176	-6300	-2696	-3150	-585	631	-1640	-2614	1495	-6689
	Net Lending	-1133	2097	1689	-3095	-11394	-11602	-15495	-23390	-26235	-30397	-30512	-28170
	Total Incurrence of Liabilities and Net Lending	19079	11951	11095	6376	19105	13220	14009	14179	14721	6526	7116	11218

a) Item 'Gold and SDRs' refers to official international reserves.
b) Item 'Proprietors net additions to accumulation of quasi-corporate, non-resident enterprises' relates to claims on associated enterprises aboard.
c) Item 'Non-resident proprietors net additions to accumulation of resident quasi-corporate enterprises' relates to liabilities to associated enterprises abroad.

4.1 Derivation of Value Added by Kind of Activity, in Current Prices

Million Canadian dollars

		1980			1985			1990			1991		
		Gross Output	Intermediate Consumption	Value Added	Gross Output	Intermediate Consumption	Value Added	Gross Output	Intermediate Consumption	Value Added	Gross Output	Intermediate Consumption	Value Added

All Producers

		Gross Output	Int. Cons.	Value Added	Gross Output	Int. Cons.	Value Added	Gross Output	Int. Cons.	Value Added	Gross Output	Int. Cons.	Value Added
1	Agriculture, hunting, forestry and fishing	22023	10324	11698	30768	17432	13337	35580	20677	14903	33771	19779	13993
	A Agriculture and hunting	16490	7373	9116	23443	13413	10030	25102	14701	10401	23830	14024	9805
	B Forestry and logging	4689	2661	2028	6136	3594	2542	8749	5346	3403	8154	5048	3107
	C Fishing	844	290	554	1189	425	765	1729	630	1099	1787	707	1081
2	Mining and quarrying	31940	13873	18067	45467	18352	27115	40690	19291	21397	36007	18276	17731
	A Coal mining	792	362	430	1594	661	932	1620	791	828	1546	793	752
	B Crude petroleum and natural gas production	17199	8022	9177	29889	11203	18686	21783	10943	10840	18704	10246	8458
	C Metal ore mining	8182	2986	5195	6724	3130	3595	10204	4116	6087	8706	3840	4866
	D Other mining	5767	2503	3264	7260	3358	3902	7083	3441	3642	7051	3397	3655
3	Manufacturing	178067	123026	55043	257848	176177	81673	315109	209631	105478	292793	194018	98771
	A Manufacture of food, beverages and tobacco	30069	22798	7271	40461	28673	11788	47943	32592	15351	47795	31533	16262
	B Textile, wearing apparel and leather industries	10059	6181	3878	12409	7444	4965	14485	8762	5723	13061	7727	5334
	C Manufacture of wood and wood products, including furniture	10801	6824	3976	14644	9145	5499	19725	12897	6828	17239	11525	5713
	D Manufacture of paper and paper products, printing and publishing	20262	11448	8815	28141	16739	11403	38628	21955	16673	34899	20842	14056
	E Manufacture of chemicals and chemical petroleum, coal, rubber and plastic products	31745	25482	6264	49869	39973	9896	52389	38738	13651	48416	33928	14487
	F Manufacture of non-metallic mineral products, except products of petroleum and coal	4349	2531	1818	6023	3448	2575	7682	4313	3369	6494	3714	2780
	G Basic metal industries	17677	12815	4862	19980	13901	6080	23436	17060	6376	21553	15843	5710
	H Manufacture of fabricated metal products, machinery and equipment	49136	32414	16723	80797	53598	27199	104275	69610	34666	96843	65369	31473
	I Other manufacturing industries	3969	2533	1435	5524	3256	2268	6546	3704	2841	6493	3537	2956
4	Electricity, gas and water	9641	1916	8172	17345	3345	14668	23106	5930	18121	24920	5526	20387
	A Electricity, gas and steam	9641	1916	7724	17345	3345	14001	23106	5930	17176	24920	5526	19393
	B Water works and supply	...	...	447	...	...	667	...	...	945	...	...	994
5	Construction a	51043	30777	20266	68032	41891	26141	100453	59015	41438	90855	52468	38387
6	Wholesale and retail trade, restaurants and hotels	58534	20014	38520	88567	30695	57872	132537	48616	83921	129082	47153	81929
	A Wholesale and retail trade	45654	14579	31075	70477	23088	47389	103927	35695	68231	102492	35162	67330
	B Restaurants and hotels	12880	5435	7445	18090	7607	10483	28610	12921	15690	26590	11991	14599
7	Transport, storage and communication	33090	13535	19554	50605	20759	29845	65781	28103	37678	65630	26833	38797
	A Transport and storage	24967	11837	13129	36907	17929	18977	47011	23515	23496	46323	22503	23821
	B Communication	8123	1698	6425	13698	2830	10868	18770	4588	14182	19307	4330	14976
8	Finance, insurance, real estate and business services	69607	21601	48005	116549	38043	78506	189878	66941	122938	197386	70103	127283
	A Financial institutions	5405	1777	3628	9739	2882	6858	18287	4909	13378	19271	5619	13652

Canada

4.1 Derivation of Value Added by Kind of Activity, in Current Prices
(Continued)

Million Canadian dollars

	1980 Gross Output	1980 Intermediate Consumption	1980 Value Added	1985 Gross Output	1985 Intermediate Consumption	1985 Value Added	1990 Gross Output	1990 Intermediate Consumption	1990 Value Added	1991 Gross Output	1991 Intermediate Consumption	1991 Value Added
B Insurance	4041	2676	1364	6591	4798	1793	10985	7797	3188	11025	8054	2971
C Real estate and business services	60161	17148	43013	100219	30363	69855	160606	54235	106372	167090	56430	110660
Real estate, except dwellings	40361	12085	28276	65432	22547	42885	106760	42422	64339	109967	44084	65884
Dwellings	19800	5063	14737	34787	7816	26970	53846	11813	42033	57123	12346	44776
9 Community, social and personal services	52682	39002	13680	82805	59456	23348	123021	86175	36846	126913	87357	39555
A Sanitary and similar services	312	145	167	674	323	350	1687	1025	662	1840	1194	646
B Social and related community services	7102	1863	5239	12554	3106	9448	18905	4690	14215	20587	4853	15734
Educational services	783	238	545	1330	492	838	2000	788	1212	2173	854	1319
Medical, dental, other health and veterinary services	6319	1625	4694	11224	2614	8610	16905	3902	13003	18414	3999	14415
C Recreational and cultural services	4497	1671	2826	7904	2879	5025	13793	5859	7934	14360	6036	8323
D Personal and household services [b]	40771	35323	5448	61673	53148	8525	88636	74601	14035	90126	75274	14852
Total, Industries	506626	274070	233003	757984	406149	352503	1026157	544380	482722	997356	521515	476834
Producers of Government Services	...	...	43016	...	...	67184	...	...	93787	...	...	100576
Other Producers	...	...	6602	...	...	11090	...	...	16296	...	...	17370
Total [c]	...	...	282621	...	...	430776	...	...	592805	...	...	594780
Less: Imputed bank service charge	...	...	2161	...	...	3649	...	...	6658	...	...	7352
Import duties	...	...	3124	...	...	3910	...	...	4237	...	...	3742
Value added tax	...	...	...	...	...	...	...	...	...	...	...	...
Other adjustments [de]	...	...	24146	...	...	43302	...	...	72425	...	...	76243
Total	...	...	307730	...	...	474340	...	...	662809	...	...	667413

a) The construction industry is defined on an activity basis. It includes all contract and own-account construction put in place.
b) Columns 'Gross output' and 'Intermediate consumption' of item 'Personal and household services' include dummy industries.
c) Gross domestic product in factor values.
d) Item 'Other adjustments' refers to net indirect taxes other than import duties.
e) Beginning 1991, item 'Other adjustments' includes goods and services tax (V.A.T.).

4.2 Derivation of Value Added by Kind of Activity, in Constant Prices

Million Canadian dollars

	1980 Gross Output	1980 Intermediate Consumption	1980 Value Added	1985 Gross Output	1985 Intermediate Consumption	1985 Value Added	1990 Gross Output	1990 Intermediate Consumption	1990 Value Added	1991 Gross Output	1991 Intermediate Consumption	1991 Value Added
	At constant prices of: 1986											
	All Producers											
1 Agriculture, hunting, forestry and fishing	23606	11811	12076	29155	16260	12915	33346	18514	14832	32898	18580	14317
A Agriculture and hunting	16991	8317	9019	21651	12269	9404	24190	13352	10838	24427	13710	10717
B Forestry and logging	5445	3194	2246	6217	3577	2635	7445	4580	2865	6781	4246	2534
C Fishing	1136	393	730	1338	398	946	1711	582	1129	1690	624	1066
2 Mining and quarrying	31830	15001	17244	35180	16307	18827	37731	18160	19570	37966	18030	19936
A Coal mining	856	512	377	1474	636	825	1774	745	1029	1732	731	1001
B Crude petroleum and natural gas production	16923	7463	10192	19779	9192	10595	21837	10516	11320	22339	10732	11607
C Metal ore mining	7375	4274	3500	6852	3113	3695	8018	3764	4254	7919	3486	4433
D Other mining	6960	3188	3761	7157	3345	3808	6102	3135	2967	5976	3081	2895

Canada

4.2 Derivation of Value Added by Kind of Activity, in Constant Prices
(Continued)

Million Canadian dollars

	1980 Gross Output	1980 Intermediate Consumption	1980 Value Added	1985 Gross Output	1985 Intermediate Consumption	1985 Value Added	1990 Gross Output	1990 Intermediate Consumption	1990 Value Added	1991 Gross Output	1991 Intermediate Consumption	1991 Value Added
				At constant prices of: 1986								
3 Manufacturing	231561	156596	75134	256849	170819	86150	285706	192850	92857	269726	183240	86483
A Manufacture of food, beverages and tobacco	39802	27746	12130	42003	29382	12682	42852	30460	12393	42281	30213	12068
B Textile, wearing apparel and leather industries	12590	7664	4958	12608	7550	5063	12999	8130	4868	11679	7242	4436
C Manufacture of wood and wood products, including furniture	13545	8328	5214	15597	9349	6263	17992	11530	6463	15901	10229	5672
D Manufacture of paper and paper products, printing and publishing	27413	15078	12423	29267	16802	12480	32203	18955	13248	30683	18323	12359
E Manufacture of chemicals and chemical petroleum, coal, rubber and plastic products	41514	32460	8833	41504	30652	10928	45782	33198	12584	43083	31242	11841
F Manufacture of non-metallic mineral products, except products of petroleum and coal	6468	3550	2919	6293	3458	2846	6880	3984	2896	5884	3432	2452
G Basic metal industries	19433	14055	5346	20347	14000	6352	20805	14367	6438	20890	14440	6451
H Manufacture of fabricated metal products, machinery and equipment	64951	43246	21803	83303	56071	27229	100389	68721	31668	93591	64717	28873
I Other manufacturing industries	5025	3057	1976	5736	3415	2323	5804	3505	2299	5734	3402	2331
4 Electricity, gas and water	14816	2565	12843	17677	3137	15184	19547	5158	15174	20436	5333	15885
A Electricity, gas and steam	14816	2565	12191	17677	3137	14506	19547	5158	14388	20436	5333	15103
B Water works and supply	...	...	647	...	...	679	...	...	786	...	...	782
5 Construction a	67965	44059	24379	70198	43363	26953	84757	52360	32396	78894	49030	29864
6 Wholesale and retail trade, restaurants and hotels	80746	28610	52149	91830	31451	60356	113294	41731	71563	108415	40559	67855
A Wholesale and retail trade	61718	21073	40694	72724	23570	49116	89575	30245	59330	87105	29999	57106
B Restaurants and hotels	19303	7522	11877	19127	7878	11274	23719	11486	12233	21310	10560	10749
7 Transport, storage and communication	44284	18886	25490	50428	20067	30364	63310	25343	37967	61631	24214	37418
A Transport and storage	33828	16554	17281	36709	16947	19764	43282	21359	21923	41286	20381	20905
B Communication	10769	2325	8439	13708	3117	10590	20028	3984	16044	20345	3833	16513
8 Finance, insurance, real estate and business services	98122	30645	67572	120572	39800	80793	156465	56627	99837	158641	57395	101244
A Financial institutions	9676	2260	7726	10721	2926	7881	13442	4223	9218	13634	4567	9066
B Insurance	5679	4110	1646	7654	5412	2329	9427	6490	2937	9555	6468	3087
C Real estate and business services	82932	24321	58626	102186	31505	70691	133596	45914	87682	135452	46360	89091
Real estate, except dwellings	53775	17564	36044	66158	23207	42880	87770	35575	52195	87968	36021	51947
Dwellings	29181	6668	22530	36073	8235	27853	45826	10339	35487	47484	10339	37144
9 Community, social and personal services	75237	53579	21640	85062	60105	24960	106109	76616	29493	107937	77357	30580
A Sanitary and similar services	468	231	238	684	307	378	1384	825	559	1524	946	578
B Social and related community services	11164	2659	8513	13161	3195	9973	15916	4358	11558	16651	4490	12162
Educational services	1098	358	735	1416	514	900	1662	687	975	1707	723	984
Medical, dental, other health and veterinary services	10073	2298	7777	11742	2681	9069	14254	3671	10583	14944	3767	11178
C Recreational and cultural services	7200	2275	4981	8392	2885	5512	10825	4636	6189	11048	4745	6303
D Personal and household services b	56276	48398	7861	62750	53709	9050	77984	66797	11187	78714	67176	11537
Statistical discrepancy	...	...	-687	...	...	496	...	...	...	...	...	...
Total, Industries	668677	361426	307831	758194	401887	356998	900269	487364	413692	876541	473740	403583
Producers of Government Services	...	...	65706	...	...	69992	...	...	76513	...	...	77364
Other Producers	...	...	9128	...	...	11586	...	...	13457	...	...	13586
Total cd	...	...	381992	...	...	438450	...	...	503661	...	...	494532
Less: Imputed bank service charge	...	...	3687	...	...	3864	...	...	5708	...	...	5774
Import duties	...	...	...	...	...	...	...	...	...	...	...	...
Value added tax	...	...	...	...	...	...	...	...	...	...	...	...
Other adjustments ef	...	...	42545	...	...	50987	...	...	61493	...	...	60202
Total	...	...	420850	...	...	485573	...	...	559447	...	...	548961

Canada

4.2 Derivation of Value Added by Kind of Activity, in Constant Prices

Million Canadian dollars

	1992 Gross Output	1992 Intermediate Consumption	1992 Value Added	1993 Gross Output	1993 Intermediate Consumption	1993 Value Added
			At constant prices of: 1986			
			All Producers			
1 Agriculture, hunting, forestry and fishing	...	...	13596	...	...	14518
A Agriculture and hunting	...	...	9934	...	...	10617
B Forestry and logging	...	...	2607	...	...	2815
C Fishing	...	...	1055	...	...	1086
2 Mining and quarrying	...	...	20294	...	...	21691
A Coal mining	...	...	822	...	...	941
B Crude petroleum and natural gas production	...	...	12383	...	...	13340
C Metal ore mining	...	...	4340	...	...	3967
D Other mining	...	...	2749	...	...	3443
3 Manufacturing	...	...	87092	...	...	91434
A Manufacture of food, beverages and tobacco	...	...	12267	...	...	12483
B Textile, wearing apparel and leather industries	...	...	4257	...	...	4343
C Manufacture of wood and wood products, including furniture	...	...	5901	...	...	6141
D Manufacture of paper and paper products, printing and publishing	...	...	12030	...	...	12124
E Manufacture of chemicals and chemical petroleum, coal, rubber and plastic products	...	...	12154	...	...	12652
F Manufacture of non-metallic mineral products, except products of petroleum and coal	...	...	2356	...	...	2389
G Basic metal industries	...	...	6587	...	...	7292
H Manufacture of fabricated metal products, machinery and equipment	...	...	29257	...	...	31645
I Other manufacturing industries	...	...	2284	...	...	2366
4 Electricity, gas and water	...	...	16073	...	...	16353
A Electricity, gas and steam	...	...	15310	...	...	15584
B Water works and supply	...	...	763	...	...	769
5 Construction [a]	...	...	27337	...	...	26034
6 Wholesale and retail trade, restaurants and hotels	...	...	70574	...	...	73569
A Wholesale and retail trade	...	...	59678	...	...	62390
B Restaurants and hotels	...	...	10896	...	...	11180
7 Transport, storage and communication	...	...	37972	...	...	39145
A Transport and storage	...	...	21083	...	...	21703
B Communication	...	...	16890	...	...	17441
8 Finance, insurance, real estate and business services	...	...	102474	...	...	105109
A Financial institutions	...	...	9267	...	...	9565
B Insurance	...	...	3205	...	...	3344
C Real estate and business services	...	...	90003	...	...	92200
Real estate, except dwellings	...	...	51642	...	...	52597
Dwellings	...	...	38360	...	...	39603
9 Community, social and personal services	...	...	30613	...	...	31247
A Sanitary and similar services	...	...	572	...	...	592
B Social and related community services	...	...	12223	...	...	12420
Educational services	...	...	1003	...	...	1014
Medical, dental, other health and veterinary services	...	...	11221	...	...	11406
C Recreational and cultural services	...	...	6422	...	...	6509
D Personal and household services [b]	...	...	11395	...	...	11726
Statistical discrepancy	...	...	...	...	...	...

Canada

4.2 Derivation of Value Added by Kind of Activity, in Constant Prices
(Continued)

Million Canadian dollars

	1992			1993		
	Gross Output	Intermediate Consumption	Value Added	Gross Output	Intermediate Consumption	Value Added
			At constant prices of: 1986			
Total, Industries	...	...	406026	...	...	419098
Producers of Government Services	...	...	78001	...	...	77918
Other Producers	...	...	13764	...	...	13931
Total cd	...	...	497791	...	...	510947
Less: Imputed bank service charge	...	...	5571	...	...	5423
Import duties	...	...	...	...	...	...
Value added tax	...	...	...	...	...	...
Other adjustments ef	...	...	60375	...	...	59593
Total	...	...	552595	...	...	565117

a) The construction industry is defined on an activity basis. It includes all contract and own-account construction put in place.
b) Columns 'Gross output' and 'Intermediate consumption' of item 'Personal and household services' include dummy industries.
c) Gross domestic product in factor values.
d) The period beginning 1970 was deflated in four time segments, 1970, 1971-1981, 1981-1986 and 1986 to date, with price indexes based on prices of 1961, 1971, 1981 and 1986 respectively. The four series are then linked arithmetically at the major group, component and total gross domestic product levels to a 1986 base. An adjusting entry which refers to the differences between rebased aggregates and the sum of their rebased components is not shown explicitly.
e) Item 'Other adjustments' relates to indirect taxes less subsidies and import duties.
f) Beginning 1991, item 'Other adjustments' includes goods and services tax (V.A.T.).

4.3 Cost Components of Value Added

Million Canadian dollars

		1980						1985					
		Compensation of Employees	Capital Consumption	Net Operating Surplus	Indirect Taxes	Less: Subsidies Received	Value Added	Compensation of Employees	Capital Consumption	Net Operating Surplus	Indirect Taxes	Less: Subsidies Received	Value Added
						All Producers							
1	Agriculture, hunting, forestry and fishing	2745	...	8953	851	916	11698	3850	...	9487	1389	2470	13337
	A Agriculture and hunting	1092	...	8024	723	898	9116	1913	...	8117	1203	2421	10030
	B Forestry and logging	1477	...	551	112	12	2028	1732	...	810	161	20	2542
	C Fishing	176	...	378	16	6	554	205	...	560	25	29	765
2	Mining and quarrying	4395	...	13673	952	74	18067	6675	...	20439	1258	1184	27115
	A Coal mining	186	...	245	24	2	430	398	...	534	79	2	932
	B Crude petroleum and natural gas production	1151	...	8027	596	60	9177	2115	...	16570	811	1093	18686
	C Metal ore mining	1495	...	3700	208	4	5195	1811	...	1784	186	78	3595
	D Other mining	1563	...	1701	124	8	3264	2351	...	1551	182	11	3902
3	Manufacturing	37545	...	17497	2855	4273	55043	53435	...	28237	5051	1643	81673
	A Manufacture of food, beverages and tobacco	4558	...	2713	283	169	7271	6465	...	5323	463	321	11788
	B Textile, wearing apparel and leather industries	2897	...	981	79	12	3878	3621	...	1344	115	15	4965
	C Manufacture of wood and wood products, including furniture	3222	...	754	151	24	3976	4238	...	1261	222	16	5499
	D Manufacture of paper and paper products, printing and publishing	5199	...	3615	286	63	8815	7724	...	3679	486	44	11403
	E Manufacture of chemicals and chemical petroleum, coal, rubber and plastic products	3725	...	2539	1190	3885	6264	5654	...	4242	2376	885	9896
	F Manufacture of non-metallic mineral products, except products of petroleum and coal	1214	...	605	112	3	1818	1596	...	978	166	5	2575
	G Basic metal industries	3284	...	1579	216	18	4862	4499	...	1580	315	18	6080
	H Manufacture of fabricated metal products, machinery and equipment	12353	...	4369	489	89	16723	18035	...	9164	830	331	27199
	I Other manufacturing industries	1093	...	342	49	10	1435	1603	...	666	78	8	2268
4	Electricity, gas and water	2082	...	5642	297	332	8172	3219	...	10781	718	555	14668
	A Electricity, gas and steam	2082	...	5642	297	332	7724	3219	...	10781	718	555	14001
	B Water works and supply a	...	...	...	...	...	447	...	...	...	...	...	667
5	Construction b	14649	...	5617	2604	9	20266	18526	...	7615	4049	14	26141
6	Wholesale and retail trade, restaurants and hotels	27987	...	10531	1648	66	38520	41901	...	15972	2718	261	57872
	A Wholesale and retail trade	22775	...	8299	1275	59	31075	34150	...	13240	2078	199	47389
	B Restaurants and hotels	5212	...	2232	373	7	7445	7751	...	2732	640	62	10483
7	Transport, storage and communication	12745	...	6809	1474	1009	19554	18280	...	11565	2733	2075	29845
	A Transport and storage	8819	...	4310	1121	1008	13129	12474	...	6503	2050	1798	18977

Canada

4.3 Cost Components of Value Added
(Continued)

Million Canadian dollars

	1980						1985					
	Compensation of Employees	Capital Consumption	Net Operating Surplus	Indirect Taxes	Less: Subsidies Received	Value Added	Compensation of Employees	Capital Consumption	Net Operating Surplus	Indirect Taxes	Less: Subsidies Received	Value Added
B Communication	3926	...	2499	353	1	6425	5806	...	5062	683	277	10868
8 Finance, insurance, real estate and business services	17166	...	30837	7324	916	48005	28448	...	50058	12125	2253	78506
A Financial institutions	3396	...	231	212	2	3628	5321	...	1537	409	13	6858
B Insurance	2035	...	-671	402	16	1364	3176	...	-1383	829	30	1793
C Real estate and business services	11735	...	31277	6710	898	43013	19951	...	49904	10887	2210	69855
Real estate, except dwellings	11735	...	16540	2862	654	28276	19951	...	22934	5159	1836	42885
Dwellings	...	...	14737	3848	244	14737	...	...	26970	5728	374	26970
9 Community, social and personal services	7056	...	6622	468	638	13680	12036	...	11313	911	1123	23348
A Sanitary and similar services	102	...	65	17	-	167	223	...	128	51	1	350
B Social and related community services	2051	...	3187	116	2	5239	3964	...	5484	218	81	9448
Educational services	445	...	99	19	-	545	705	...	133	34	7	838
Medical, dental, other health and veterinary services	1606	...	3088	97	2	4694	3259	...	5351	184	74	8610
C Recreational and cultural services	1500	...	1326	155	620	2826	2565	...	2460	298	1035	5025
D Personal and household services	3403	...	2044	180	16	5448	5284	...	3241	344	6	8525
Total, Industries	126372	...	106184	18472	8232	233003	186369	...	165467	30955	11577	352503
Producers of Government Services [a]	38909	...	4554	1480	...	43016	60761	...	7091	1624	...	67184
Other Producers	6141	...	461	15553	...	6602	10389	...	700	26210	...	11090
Total [cd]	171423	...	111198	35504	8232	282621	257518	...	173258	58789	11577	430776
Less: Imputed bank service charge	...	...	2161	...	...	2161	...	...	3649	...	...	3649
Import duties	...	...	...	...	...	3124	...	...	...	...	...	3910
Value added tax	...	...	...	...	...	...	...	...	...	...	...	...
Other adjustments [ef]	...	...	...	...	...	24146	...	...	...	...	...	43302
Total	171423	...	109037	35504	8232	307730	257518	...	169609	58789	11577	474340

	1990						1991					
	Compensation of Employees	Capital Consumption	Net Operating Surplus	Indirect Taxes	Less: Subsidies Received	Value Added	Compensation of Employees	Capital Consumption	Net Operating Surplus	Indirect Taxes	Less: Subsidies Received	Value Added
	All Producers											
1 Agriculture, hunting, forestry and fishing	5069	...	9835	2095	2773	14903	5157	...	8836	2253	3813	13993
A Agriculture and hunting	2330	...	8071	1716	2699	10401	2389	...	7416	1945	3736	9805
B Forestry and logging	2415	...	988	317	33	3403	2464	...	643	244	40	3107
C Fishing	324	...	776	62	41	1099	304	...	777	64	37	1081
2 Mining and quarrying	7282	...	14115	1563	72	21397	7524	...	10208	1422	59	17731
A Coal mining	450	...	378	94	3	828	451	...	302	81	2	752
B Crude petroleum and natural gas production	2399	...	8441	983	6	10840	2520	...	5938	931	3	8458
C Metal ore mining	2229	...	3858	252	34	6087	2308	...	2558	216	31	4866
D Other mining	2204	...	1438	234	29	3642	2245	...	1410	194	23	3655

Canada

4.3 Cost Components of Value Added
(Continued)

Million Canadian dollars

		1990					1991				
	Compensation of Employees	Capital Consumption	Net Operating Surplus	Indirect Taxes	Less: Subsidies Received	Value Added	Compensation of Employees	Capital Consumption	Net Operating Surplus	Indirect Taxes	Less: Subsidies Received	Value Added
3 Manufacturing	69224	...	36256	4476	714	105478	67903	...	30870	3883	694	98771
A Manufacture of food, beverages and tobacco	7812	...	7540	550	285	15351	7979	...	8283	492	294	16262
B Textile, wearing apparel and leather industries	4174	...	1549	156	18	5723	3917	...	1417	134	18	5334
C Manufacture of wood and wood products, including furniture	5654	...	1174	287	15	6828	5120	...	593	229	19	5713
D Manufacture of paper and paper products, printing and publishing	10649	...	6024	624	51	16673	10643	...	3414	541	52	14056
E Manufacture of chemicals and chemical petroleum, coal, rubber and plastic products	7585	...	6066	963	86	13651	7564	...	6923	893	58	14487
F Manufacture of non-metallic mineral products, except products of petroleum and coal	2065	...	1304	199	5	3369	1911	...	869	169	4	2780
G Basic metal industries	5062	...	1314	415	71	6376	5164	...	547	357	61	5710
H Manufacture of fabricated metal products, machinery and equipment	24059	...	10607	1159	168	34666	23408	...	8065	960	172	31473
I Other manufacturing industries	2164	...	678	123	15	2841	2197	...	759	108	16	2956
4 Electricity, gas and water	4531	...	12645	1178	340	18121	5032	...	14362	1207	281	20387
A Electricity, gas and steam	4531	...	12645	1178	340	17176	5032	...	14362	1207	281	19393
B Water works and supply [a]	...	...	...	...	...	945	...	...	...	...	...	994
5 Construction [b]	31281	...	10157	7109	4	41438	29532	...	8855	3936	166	38387
6 Wholesale and retail trade, restaurants and hotels	63015	...	20906	4777	113	83921	62876	...	19054	4276	487	81929
A Wholesale and retail trade	51599	...	16632	3731	91	68231	51921	...	15409	3359	388	67330
B Restaurants and hotels	11416	...	4274	1046	22	15690	10955	...	3645	917	99	14599
7 Transport, storage and communication	22984	...	14694	4335	2591	37678	23828	...	14968	3802	2842	38797
A Transport and storage	15775	...	7721	3304	2375	23496	16141	...	7679	2880	2652	23821
B Communication	7209	...	6973	1031	216	14182	7687	...	7289	922	190	14976
8 Finance, insurance, real estate and business services	48878	...	74060	20135	2782	122938	50675	...	76608	22068	3271	127283
A Financial institutions	7423	...	5955	743	47	13378	7955	...	5697	981	38	13652
B Insurance	4547	...	-1359	1493	3	3188	4796	...	-1825	1599	5	2971
C Real estate and business services	36908	...	69464	17899	2732	106372	37924	...	72736	19488	3228	110660
Real estate, except dwellings	36908	...	27431	9433	2529	64339	37924	...	27960	10204	3039	65884
Dwellings	...	...	42033	8466	203	42033	...	...	44776	9284	189	44776
9 Community, social and personal services	19390	...	17457	1869	1644	36846	20752	...	18802	1873	1920	39555
A Sanitary and similar services	435	...	227	190	4	662	484	...	162	261	5	646
B Social and related community services	6491	...	7724	418	385	14215	7283	...	8450	473	479	15734
Educational services	1030	...	182	61	2	1212	1110	...	209	63	4	1319
Medical, dental, other health and veterinary services	5461	...	7542	357	383	13003	6173	...	8241	410	475	14415
C Recreational and cultural services	4014	...	3921	573	1127	7934	4119	...	4205	518	1177	8323
D Personal and household services	8450	...	5585	688	128	14035	8866	...	5985	621	259	14852
Total, Industries	271654	...	210124	47536	11032	482722	273278	...	202562	44719	13532	476834
Producers of Government Services [a]	85249	...	9483	2224	...	93787	92111	...	9459	2118	...	100576
Other Producers	15185	...	1112	37933	...	16296	16256	...	1114	46681	...	17370
Total [cd]	372088	...	220719	87693	11032	592805	381645	...	213135	93518	13532	594780
Less: Imputed bank service charge	...	...	6658	...	...	6658	...	...	7352	...	...	7352
Import duties	...	...	...	...	...	4237	...	...	...	...	...	3742
Value added tax	...	...	...	...	...	...	...	...	...	...	...	...
Other adjustments [ef]	...	...	...	...	...	72425	...	...	...	...	...	76243
Total	372088	...	228621	87693	11032	662809	381645	...	222906	93518	13532	667413

a) Columns 'Compensation of employees' and 'Operating surplus' of item 'Producers of government services' include item 'Water works and supply'.
b) The construction industry is defined on an activity basis. It includes all contract and own-account construction put in place.
c) Gross domestic product in factor values.
d) Column 'Consumption of fixed capital' is included in column 'Net operating surplus'.
e) Item 'Other adjustments' refers to net indirect taxes other than import duties.
f) Beginning 1991, item 'Other adjustments' includes goods and services tax (V.A.T.).

Cape Verde

Source. Reply to the United Nations National Accounts Questionnaire from the Ministerio do Plano e da Cooperacao, Direccao Geral de Estatistica. The official estimates are published in 'Boletim Anual de Estatistica' and 'Boletim de Contas Nacionais'.

General note. The official estimates have been adjusted by the Direccao Geral de Estatistica to conform to the United Nations System of National Accounts so far as the existing data would permit.

1.1 Expenditure on the Gross Domestic Product, in Current Prices

Million Cape Verde escudos

	1980	1983	1984	1985	1986	1987	1988	1989	1990	1991	1992	1993
1 Government final consumption expenditure	807	1954	2438	2748	3380	3673	3968	...	...	...	...	...
2 Private final consumption expenditure	5386	8498	10193	11471	13407	15134	17848	...	...	...	...	...
3 Gross capital formation	2429	4860	4930	5712	6880	7381	7287	...	...	...	...	...
A Increase in stocks	214	21	-37	-246	439	328	-434	...	...	...	...	...
B Gross fixed capital formation	2214	4840	4966	5957	6440	7053	7721	...	...	...	...	...
Residential buildings	491	782	806	1029	1139	1785	2249	...	...	...	...	...
Non-residential buildings	362	744	744	1038	1243	1095	1295	...	...	...	...	...
Other construction and land improvement etc.	533	1618	1521	1971	1977	1303	1404	...	...	...	...	...
Other	829	1696	1895	1919	2082	2870	2773	...	...	...	...	...
4 Exports of goods and services	1089	2451	2562	2887	2733	2984	3190	...	...	...	...	...
5 Less: Imports of goods and services	3793	7622	8575	9736	10841	11189	11653	...	...	...	...	...
Equals: Gross Domestic Product	5919	10140	11548	13081	15558	17984	20640	...	...	...	...	...

1.2 Expenditure on the Gross Domestic Product, in Constant Prices

Million Cape Verde escudos

	1980	1983	1984	1985	1986	1987	1988	1989	1990	1991	1992	1993
				At constant prices of:1980								
1 Government final consumption expenditure	807	1386	1543	1684	1797	1947	2060	...	...	...	...	...
2 Private final consumption expenditure	5386	5855	6352	6760	7098	7491	8370	...	...	...	...	...
3 Gross capital formation	2429	3120	2987	3172	3715	3737	3318	...	...	...	...	...
A Increase in stocks	214	17	-91	-123	321	217	-358	...	...	...	...	...
B Gross fixed capital formation	2214	3103	3078	3296	3394	3520	3675	...	...	...	...	...
Residential buildings	491	531	512	586	606	954	1138	...	...	...	...	...
Non-residential buildings	362	506	458	603	676	591	667	...	...	...	...	...
Other construction and land improvement etc.	533	1143	1029	1198	1142	750	805	...	...	...	...	...
Other	829	923	1080	909	970	1226	1066	...	...	...	...	...
4 Exports of goods and services	1089	1570	1473	1571	1412	1666	1632	...	...	...	...	...
5 Less: Imports of goods and services	3793	4810	4974	5176	5792	5990	5851	...	...	...	...	...
Equals: Gross Domestic Product	5919	7121	7381	8011	8229	8852	9528	...	...	...	...	...

1.7 External Transactions on Current Account, Summary

Million Cape Verde escudos

	1980	1983	1984	1985	1986	1987	1988	1989	1990	1991	1992	1993
				Payments to the Rest of the World								
1 Imports of goods and services	...	...	...	9736	10841	11189	11653	...	...	...	...	...
A Imports of merchandise c.i.f.	...	...	...	7663	8601	8596	8626	...	...	...	...	...
B Other	...	...	...	2073	2240	2593	3027	...	...	...	...	...
2 Factor income to the rest of the world	...	...	...	485	365	400	215	...	...	...	...	...
3 Current transfers to the rest of the world	...	...	...	82	107	492	541	...	...	...	...	...
4 Surplus of the nation on current transactions	...	...	...	-299	105	-1062	-399	...	...	...	...	...
Payments to the Rest of the World and Surplus of the Nation on Current Transactions	...	...	...	10004	11418	11019	12010	...	...	...	...	...

Cape Verde

1.7 External Transactions on Current Account, Summary
(Continued)

Million Cape Verde escudos

	1980	1983	1984	1985	1986	1987	1988	1989	1990	1991	1992	1993
				Receipts From The Rest of the World								
1 Exports of goods and services	...	...	...	2887	2733	2984	3190	...	...	...	...	...
A Exports of merchandise f.o.b.	...	...	...	524	355	561	241	...	...	...	...	...
B Other	...	...	...	2364	2378	2424	2950	...	...	...	...	...
2 Factor income from rest of the world	...	...	...	198	161	256	541	...	...	...	...	...
3 Current transfers from rest of the world	...	...	...	6919	8525	7778	8278	...	...	...	...	...
Receipts from the Rest of the World on Current Transactions	...	...	...	10004	11418	11019	12010	...	...	...	...	...

1.10 Gross Domestic Product by Kind of Activity, in Current Prices

Million Cape Verde escudos

	1980	1983	1984	1985	1986	1987	1988	1989	1990	1991	1992	1993
1 Agriculture, hunting, forestry and fishing	1099	1379	1599	2043	2493	3615	4177	...	...	...	...	...
2 Mining and quarrying	37	88	85	119	124	103	127	...	...	...	...	...
3 Manufacturing	267	487	509	723	816	1033	1113	...	...	...	...	...
4 Electricity, gas and water	-20	-18	8	16	86	172	208	...	...	...	...	...
5 Construction	692	1150	1330	1398	1705	1881	2238	...	...	...	...	...
6 Wholesale and retail trade, restaurants and hotels	1850	3181	3375	3607	4029	4377	5123	...	...	...	...	...
7 Transport, storage and communication	513	1357	1626	1834	2143	2303	2595	...	...	...	...	...
8 Finance, insurance, real estate and business services	516	932	1108	1247	1482	1608	1846	...	...	...	...	...
9 Community, social and personal services	59	113	134	159	205	236	277	...	...	...	...	...
Total, Industries	5013	8669	9773	11145	13081	15328	17703	...	...	...	...	...
Producers of Government Services	547	933	1153	1288	1653	1877	2026	...	...	...	...	...
Other Producers	...	...	...	...	...	...	...	...	...	...	...	...
Subtotal	5560	9602	10926	12433	14733	17204	19729	...	...	...	...	...
Less: Imputed bank service charge	109	177	212	236	285	348	367	...	...	...	...	...
Plus: Import duties	468	715	834	884	1111	1128	1279	...	...	...	...	...
Plus: Value added tax	...	...	...	...	...	...	...	...	...	...	...	...
Equals: Gross Domestic Product	5919	10140	11548	13081	15559	17984	20640	...	...	...	...	...

1.11 Gross Domestic Product by Kind of Activity, in Constant Prices

Million Cape Verde escudos

	1980	1983	1984	1985	1986	1987	1988	1989	1990	1991	1992	1993
				At constant prices of:1980								
1 Agriculture, hunting, forestry and fishing	1099	867	923	1177	1263	1672	1830	...	...	...	...	...
2 Mining and quarrying	37	59	54	68	68	68	77	...	...	...	...	...
3 Manufacturing	267	326	310	422	422	533	430	...	...	...	...	...
4 Electricity, gas and water	-20	16	22	53	57	26	10	...	...	...	...	...
5 Construction	692	880	881	927	967	1051	1224	...	...	...	...	...
6 Wholesale and retail trade, restaurants and hotels	1850	2170	2192	2224	2196	2160	2395	...	...	...	...	...
7 Transport, storage and communication	513	878	959	938	935	950	1002	...	...	...	...	...
8 Finance, insurance, real estate and business services	516	595	628	668	704	736	796	...	...	...	...	...
9 Community, social and personal services	59	78	82	86	101	110	120	...	...	...	...	...
Total, Industries	5013	5867	6051	6562	6713	7305	7882	...	...	...	...	...
Producers of Government Services	547	735	812	897	973	1104	1193	...	...	...	...	...
Other Producers	...	...	...	...	...	...	...	...	...	...	...	...
Subtotal	5560	6602	6863	7459	7686	8409	9075	...	...	...	...	...
Less: Imputed bank service charge	109	113	121	127	136	160	161	...	...	...	...	...
Plus: Import duties	468	632	639	679	679	603	615	...	...	...	...	...
Plus: Value added tax	...	...	...	...	...	...	...	...	...	...	...	...
Equals: Gross Domestic Product	5919	7121	7381	8011	8229	8852	9529	...	...	...	...	...

Cape Verde

1.12 Relations Among National Accounting Aggregates

Million Cape Verde escudos

	1980	1983	1984	1985	1986	1987	1988	1989	1990	1991	1992	1993
Gross Domestic Product	5919	10140	11548	13081	15558	17984	20640	...	...	...	...	...
Plus: Net factor income from the rest of the world	33	-309	-334	-287	-204	-144	326	...	...	...	...	...
Factor income from the rest of the world	...	...	...	198	161	256	541	...	...	...	...	...
Less: Factor income to the rest of the world	...	...	...	485	365	400	215	...	...	...	...	...
Equals: Gross National Product	5952	9831	11214	12794	15354	17840	20966	...	...	...	...	...
Less: Consumption of fixed capital	...	...	...	...	...	...	...	...	...	...	...	...
Equals: National Income	...	...	...	...	...	...	...	...	...	...	...	...
Plus: Net current transfers from the rest of the world	2955	5100	6091	6837	8418	7286	7737	...	...	...	...	...
Current transfers from the rest of the world	...	...	...	6919	8525	7778	8278	...	...	...	...	...
Less: Current transfers to the rest of the world	...	...	...	82	107	492	541	...	...	...	...	...
Equals: National Disposable Income	...	...	...	...	...	...	...	...	...	...	...	...
Less: Final consumption	...	...	...	...	...	...	...	...	...	...	...	...
Equals: Net Saving	...	...	...	...	...	...	...	...	...	...	...	...
Less: Surplus of the nation on current transactions	...	...	...	...	...	...	...	...	...	...	...	...
Equals: Net Capital Formation	...	...	...	...	...	...	...	...	...	...	...	...

2.5 Private Final Consumption Expenditure by Type and Purpose, in Current Prices

Million Cape Verde escudos

	1980	1983	1984	1985	1986	1987	1988	1989	1990	1991	1992	1993
Final Consumption Expenditure of Resident Households												
1 Food, beverages and tobacco	3426	5382	6301	6968	8202	9136	11177	...	...	...	...	...
A Food	2815	4368	5165	5542	6575	7177	9115	...	...	...	...	...
B Non-alcoholic beverages	62	106	112	138	200	212	170	...	...	...	...	...
C Alcoholic beverages	433	723	833	1050	1128	1366	1471	...	...	...	...	...
D Tobacco	115	184	190	237	299	381	421	...	...	...	...	...
2 Clothing and footwear	285	379	417	363	367	439	447	...	...	...	...	...
3 Gross rent, fuel and power	645	1167	1396	1579	1887	2052	2409	...	...	...	...	...
A Fuel and power	253	462	557	638	742	794	885	...	...	...	...	...
B Other	392	706	839	942	1146	1259	1525	...	...	...	...	...
4 Furniture, furnishings and household equipment and operation	420	574	670	883	965	1097	1230	...	...	...	...	...
A Household operation	122	187	252	313	332	357	433	...	...	...	...	...
B Other	298	387	418	570	634	740	798	...	...	...	...	...
5 Medical care and health expenses	43	43	102	93	65	90	87	...	...	...	...	...
6 Transport and communication	362	590	725	954	1186	1524	1579	...	...	...	...	...
A Personal transport equipment	285	429	494	708	871	941	933	...	...	...	...	...
B Other	77	161	231	246	315	583	646	...	...	...	...	...
7 Recreational, entertainment, education and cultural services	212	428	625	680	795	871	1003	...	...	...	...	...
8 Miscellaneous goods and services								...	...	...	...	...
Total Final Consumption Expenditure in the Domestic Market by Households, of which	5395	8564	10237	11520	13469	15210	17935	...	...	...	...	...
Plus: Direct purchases abroad by resident households	83	137	163	178	210	229	265	...	...	...	...	...
Less: Direct purchases in the domestic market by non-resident households	91	203	207	228	273	305	352	...	...	...	...	...
Equals: Final Consumption Expenditure of Resident Households [a]	5386	8497	10193	11470	13406	15134	17848	...	...	...	...	...
Final Consumption Expenditure of Private Non-profit Institutions Serving Households												
Equals: Final Consumption Expenditure of Private Non-profit Organisations Serving Households	...	...	...	...	...	...	...	...	...	...	...	...
Private Final Consumption Expenditure	5386	8497	10193	11470	13406	15134	17848	...	...	...	...	...

a) Item 'Final consumption expenditure of resident households' includes consumption expenditure of private non-profit institutions serving households.

Cape Verde

2.6 Private Final Consumption Expenditure by Type and Purpose, in Constant Prices

Million Cape Verde escudos

		1980	1983	1984	1985	1986	1987	1988	1989	1990	1991	1992	1993
		\multicolumn{12}{c}{At constant prices of:1980}												
		\multicolumn{12}{c}{Final Consumption Expenditure of Resident Households}												
1	Food, beverages and tobacco	3426	3678	3994	4186	4424	4579	5282	...	...	...	...	...
	A Food	2815	2976	3253	3325	3545	3578	4316	...	...	...	...	...
	B Non-alcoholic beverages	62	58	80	108	100	133	92	...	...	...	...	...
	C Alcoholic beverages	434	549	594	682	705	795	806	...	...	...	...	...
	D Tobacco	115	95	68	70	74	73	68	...	...	...	...	...
2	Clothing and footwear	286	266	258	228	201	231	225	...	...	...	...	...
3	Gross rent, fuel and power	645	764	807	854	917	975	1093	...	...	...	...	...
	A Fuel and power	253	304	319	342	358	379	413	...	...	...	...	...
	B Other	392	460	488	513	559	597	680	...	...	...	...	...
4	Furniture, furnishings and household equipment and operation	420	395	416	512	519	569	617	...	...	...	...	...
	A Household operation	122	136	156	165	174	201	236	...	...	...	...	...
	B Other	298	259	259	346	345	368	380	...	...	...	...	...
5	Medical care and health expenses	43	25	39	53	35	49	39	...	...	...	...	...
6	Transport and communication	362	442	466	574	605	720	703	...	...	...	...	...
	A Personal transport equipment	285	329	325	427	444	445	418	...	...	...	...	...
	B Other	77	113	141	147	161	275	285	...	...	...	...	...
7	Recreational, entertainment, education and cultural services	213	327	396	381	428	404	448	...	...	...	...	...
8	Miscellaneous goods and services								...	...	...	...	...
	Total Final Consumption Expenditure in the Domestic Market by Households, of which	5395	5896	6376	6787	7128	7526	8408	...	...	...	...	...
	Plus: Direct purchases abroad by resident households	83	87	92	96	100	105	116	...	...	...	...	...
	Less: Direct purchases in the domestic market by non-resident households	91	129	118	123	130	140	154	...	...	...	...	...
	Equals: Final Consumption Expenditure of Resident Households [a]	5386	5855	6352	6760	7098	7491	8370	...	...	...	...	...
	\multicolumn{12}{c}{Final Consumption Expenditure of Private Non-profit Institutions Serving Households}												
	Equals: Final Consumption Expenditure of Private Non-profit Organisations Serving Households	...	...	...	...	...	...	...	...	...	...	...	...
	Private Final Consumption Expenditure	5386	5855	6352	6760	7098	7491	8370	...	...	...	...	...

a) Item 'Final consumption expenditure of resident households' includes consumption expenditure of private non-profit institutions serving households.

2.17 Exports and Imports of Goods and Services, Detail

Million Cape Verde escudos

		1980	1983	1984	1985	1986	1987	1988	1989	1990	1991	1992	1993
		\multicolumn{12}{c}{Exports of Goods and Services}												
1	Exports of merchandise, f.o.b.	216	246	212	523	355	560	241	...	...	...	...	...
2	Transport and communication	352	1116	1366	1516	1458	1508	2018	...	...	...	...	...
3	Insurance service charges	37	42	36	39	22	60	49	...	...	...	...	...
4	Other commodities	3	72	64	80	136	217	166	...	...	...	...	...
5	Adjustments of merchandise exports to change-of-ownership basis	390	772	678	501	491	334	365	...	...	...	...	...
6	Direct purchases in the domestic market by non-residential households	91	203	207	228	273	305	352	...	...	...	...	...
7	Direct purchases in the domestic market by extraterritorial bodies	...	...	...	...	...	...	...	...	...	...	...	...
	Total Exports of Goods and Services	1089	2451	2562	2887	2733	2984	3190	...	...	...	...	...
		\multicolumn{12}{c}{Imports of Goods and Services}												
1	Imports of merchandise, c.i.f.	3349	6237	7036	7663	8601	8596	8626	...	...	...	...	...

Cape Verde

2.17 Exports and Imports of Goods and Services, Detail
(Continued)

Million Cape Verde escudos

	1980	1983	1984	1985	1986	1987	1988	1989	1990	1991	1992	1993
2 Adjustments of merchandise imports to change-of-ownership basis	...	...	...	...	...	...	...	...	...	...	...	...
3 Other transport and communication	139	265	308	486	524	758	964	...	...	...	...	...
4 Other insurance service charges	15	50	58	72	73	92	123	...	...	...	...	...
5 Other commodities	207	933	1010	1338	1433	1514	1675	...	...	...	...	...
6 Direct purchases abroad by government	...	...	...	...	...	...	...	...	...	...	...	...
7 Direct purchases abroad by resident households	83	137	163	178	210	229	265	...	...	...	...	...
Total Imports of Goods and Services	3793	7622	8575	9736	10841	11189	11653	...	...	...	...	...
Balance of Goods and Services	-2704	-5171	-6013	-6849	-8108	-8205	-8463	...	...	...	...	...
Total Imports and Balance of Goods and Services	1089	2451	2562	2887	2733	2984	3190	...	...	...	...	...

Cayman Islands

Source. Reply to the United Nations National Accounts Questionnaire from the Government Statistics Office, Grand Cayman. The official estimates are published in 'National Income Estimates of the Cayman Islands'.

General note. The estimates shown in the following tables have been prepared by the Statistical Office in accordance with the United Nations System of National Accounts so far as the existing data would permit.

1.1 Expenditure on the Gross Domestic Product, in Current Prices

Million Cayman Islands Dollars

	1980	1983	1984	1985	1986	1987	1988	1989	1990	1991	1992	1993
1 Government final consumption expenditure	...	34	41	43	44	53	60	67	84	93	...	...
2 Private final consumption expenditure	...	137	152	166	181	215	268	308	369	385	...	...
A Households	...	137	152	166	181	215	268	308	369	385	...	...
B Private non-profit institutions serving households	...	...	...	...	...	...	...	...	...	...	...	...
3 Gross capital formation	...	49	62	53	67	74	105	110	126	134	...	...
A Increase in stocks	...	...	...	...	...	...	...	...	...	...	...	...
B Gross fixed capital formation	...	49	62	53	67	74	105	110	126	134	...	...
4 Exports of goods and services	...	159	171	184	200	243	261	285	378	363	...	...
5 Less: Imports of goods and services	...	161	176	185	204	246	295	326	345	325	...	...
Statistical discrepancy [a]	...	-	-6	3	2	-	15	30	-22	-34	...	...
Equals: Gross Domestic Product	...	218	244	264	290	339	414	474	590	616	...	...

a) Item 'Statistical discrepancy' relates to the difference between the estimate of GDP through industrial origin approach and that of expenditure approach.

1.2 Expenditure on the Gross Domestic Product, in Constant Prices

Million Cayman Islands Dollars

	1980	1983	1984	1985	1986	1987	1988	1989	1990	1991	1992	1993
					At constant prices of:1986							
1 Government final consumption expenditure	...	38	44	44	44	50	53	56	63	68	...	...
2 Private final consumption expenditure	...	152	162	169	181	201	235	256	279	283	...	...
A Households	...	152	162	169	181	201	235	256	279	283	...	...
B Private non-profit institutions serving households	...	...	...	...	...	...	...	...	...	...	...	...
3 Gross capital formation	...	55	66	54	67	70	92	92	95	98	...	...
A Increase in stocks	...	...	...	...	...	...	...	...	...	...	...	...
B Gross fixed capital formation	...	55	66	54	67	70	92	92	95	98	...	...
4 Exports of goods and services	...	176	182	187	200	227	229	237	286	267	...	...
5 Less: Imports of goods and services	...	179	188	189	204	230	259	271	261	239	...	...
Statistical discrepancy	...	-	-6	4	2	-1	12	24	-16	-25	...	...
Equals: Gross Domestic Product	...	242	260	269	290	317	362	394	446	452	...	...

1.3 Cost Components of the Gross Domestic Product

Million Cayman Islands Dollars

	1980	1983	1984	1985	1986	1987	1988	1989	1990	1991	1992	1993
1 Indirect taxes, net	...	38	40	42	48	57	69	75	82	90	...	...
A Indirect taxes	...	39	41	43	49	58	70	76	83	91	...	...
B Less: Subsidies	...	1	1	1	1	1	1	1	1	1	...	...
2 Consumption of fixed capital	...	13	17	20	23	28	34	38	42	47	...	...
3 Compensation of employees paid by resident producers to:	...	128	143	156	175	200	238	274	327	342	...	...
A Resident households	...	124	138	150	168	192	226	261	310	323	...	...
B Rest of the world	...	4	5	6	7	8	12	13	17	19	...	...
4 Operating surplus	...	39	44	46	44	54	73	87	139	137	...	...
Equals: Gross Domestic Product	...	218	244	264	290	339	414	474	590	616	...	...

1.4 General Government Current Receipts and Disbursements

Million Cayman Islands Dollars

	1980	1983	1984	1985	1986	1987	1988	1989	1990	1991	1992	1993
					Receipts							
1 Operating surplus	...	...	...	...	...	...	...	...	...	...	...	...
2 Property and entrepreneurial income	...	4	3	4	5	5	4	6	6	4	...	...
3 Taxes, fees and contributions	...	42	45	47	54	64	78	83	92	101	...	...
A Indirect taxes	...	39	41	43	49	59	70	75	83	90	...	...

Cayman Islands

1.4 General Government Current Receipts and Disbursements
(Continued)

Million Cayman Islands Dollars

	1980	1983	1984	1985	1986	1987	1988	1989	1990	1991	1992	1993
B Direct taxes	...	-	4	4	4	-	1	1	1	1	...	...
C Social security contributions	...	...	...	...	...	...	...	...	...	...	...	...
D Compulsory fees, fines and penalties	...	3	-	-	1	5	7	8	8	10	...	...
4 Other current transfers	...	...	...	...	...	...	...	...	...	...	...	...
Statistical discrepancy	...	-	1	1	2	-	-	-	-	-	...	...
Total Current Receipts of General Government	...	46	49	52	61	69	82	90	98	105	...	...

Disbursements

	1980	1983	1984	1985	1986	1987	1988	1989	1990	1991	1992	1993
1 Government final consumption expenditure	...	31	41	43	44	51	61	69	87	98	...	...
A Compensation of employees	...	20	25	28	29	33	39	44	57	63	...	...
B Consumption of fixed capital	...	1	2	2	2	2	3	4	4	5	...	...
C Purchases of goods and services, net	...	10	14	13	13	16	19	21	26	30	...	...
D Less: Own account fixed capital formation	...	...	...	...	...	...	...	...	...	...	...	...
E Indirect taxes paid, net	...	...	...	...	...	...	...	...	...	...	...	...
2 Property income	...	1	1	1	1	1	2	2	2	2	...	...
A Interest	...	1	1	1	1	1	2	2	1	2	...	...
B Net land rent and royalties	...	...	...	...	...	...	...	...	...	...	...	...
3 Subsidies	...	2	1	1	1	1	1	1	1	1	...	...
4 Other current transfers	...	1	1	1	4	3	5	4	7	6	...	...
5 Net saving	...	11	5	6	11	13	13	13	4	-2	...	...
Total Current Disbursements and Net Saving of General Government	...	46	49	52	61	69	82	90	98	105	...	...

1.7 External Transactions on Current Account, Summary

Million Cayman Islands Dollars

	1980	1983	1984	1985	1986	1987	1988	1989	1990	1991	1992	1993

Payments to the Rest of the World

	1980	1983	1984	1985	1986	1987	1988	1989	1990	1991	1992	1993
1 Imports of goods and services	...	161	176	185	204	246	295	326	345	326	...	...
A Imports of merchandise c.i.f.	...	110	118	122	133	162	192	215	237	221	...	...
B Other	...	51	58	63	71	84	103	111	108	105	...	...
2 Factor income to the rest of the world	...	30	25	27	27	37	48	60	70	65	...	...
A Compensation of employees	...	2	2	2	3	4	5	6	8	8	...	...
B Property and entrepreneurial income	...	28	23	25	24	33	43	54	62	57	...	...
By general government	...	-	-	1	1	1	1	1	1	2	...	...
By corporate and quasi-corporate enterprises	...	28	23	24	23	32	42	53	61	55	...	...
By other	...	...	...	...	...	...	...	...	...	...	...	...
3 Current transfers to the rest of the world	...	4	6	6	7	9	11	13	15	15	...	...
4 Surplus of the nation on current transactions	...	-31	-30	-27	-30	-42	-85	-106	-43	-36	...	...
Payments to the Rest of the World and Surplus of the Nation on Current Transactions	...	164	177	191	208	250	269	293	387	370	...	...

Receipts From The Rest of the World

	1980	1983	1984	1985	1986	1987	1988	1989	1990	1991	1992	1993
1 Exports of goods and services	...	159	171	184	200	243	261	284	378	363	...	...
A Exports of merchandise f.o.b.	...	1	1	1	2	2	2	2	2	1	...	...

Cayman Islands

1.7 External Transactions on Current Account, Summary
(Continued)

Million Cayman Islands Dollars

	1980	1983	1984	1985	1986	1987	1988	1989	1990	1991	1992	1993
B Other	...	158	170	183	198	241	259	282	376	362	...	...
2 Factor income from rest of the world	...	5	6	7	8	7	8	9	9	7	...	...
A Compensation of employees	...	-	-	-	-	-	-	-	-	-	...	...
B Property and entrepreneurial income	...	5	6	7	8	7	8	9	9	7	...	...
By general government	...	2	3	3	4	3	3	4	3	2	...	...
By corporate and quasi-corporate enterprises	...	1	1	1	1	2	2	2	2	1	...	...
By other	...	2	2	3	3	3	3	3	4	4	...	...
3 Current transfers from rest of the world	...	...	...	...	...	...	...	...	...	...	...	...
Receipts from the Rest of the World on Current Transactions	...	164	177	191	208	250	269	293	387	370	...	...

1.9 Gross Domestic Product by Institutional Sectors of Origin

Million Cayman Islands Dollars

	1980	1983	1984	1985	1986	1987	1988	1989	1990	1991	1992	1993
Domestic Factor Incomes Originating												
1 General government	...	19	25	28	29	34	40	45	58	63	...	...
2 Corporate and quasi-corporate enterprises [a]	...	132	141	150	165	199	250	300	347	365	...	...
3 Households and private unincorporated enterprises [b]	...	19	21	23	25	29	37	41	46	52	...	...
4 Non-profit institutions serving households	...	...	...	...	...	...	...	...	...	...	...	...
Subtotal: Domestic Factor Incomes	...	170	187	201	219	262	327	386	451	480	...	...
Indirect taxes, net	...	38	40	43	48	57	67	72	82	90	...	...
A Indirect taxes	...	39	41	43	49	59	70	75	83	91	...	...
B Less: Subsidies	...	1	1	-	1	2	3	3	1	1	...	...
Consumption of fixed capital	...	13	17	20	23	28	34	38	42	47	...	...
Statistical discrepancy	...	-3	-	-	-	-8	-14	-22	15	-1	...	...
Gross Domestic Product	...	218	244	264	290	339	414	474	590	616	...	...

a) Item 'Corporate and quasi-corporate enterprises' includes private unincorporated enterprises.
b) Only domestic servants and rental of dwellings are included in item 'Households and private unincorporated enterprises'.

1.10 Gross Domestic Product by Kind of Activity, in Current Prices

Million Cayman Islands Dollars

	1980	1983	1984	1985	1986	1987	1988	1989	1990	1991	1992	1993
1 Agriculture, hunting, forestry and fishing	...	1	1	1	2	2	2	2	2	2	...	...
2 Mining and quarrying	...	1	1	1	1	2	3	3	2	2	...	...
3 Manufacturing	...	5	6	6	6	7	8	9	9	9	...	...
4 Electricity, gas and water	...	5	5	6	7	9	12	15	18	19	...	...
5 Construction	...	27	27	25	27	29	40	52	56	55	...	...
6 Wholesale and retail trade, restaurants and hotels	...	45	50	54	60	72	92	116	142	138	...	...
7 Transport, storage and communication	...	24	29	33	38	36	48	52	63	65	...	...
8 Finance, insurance, real estate and business services [a]	...	65	70	79	86	110	134	153	197	210	...	...
9 Community, social and personal services	...	15	17	19	20	22	25	27	34	42	...	...
Total, Industries	...	189	206	224	247	290	364	429	522	542	...	...
Producers of Government Services	...	20	26	29	30	34	40	45	58	63	...	...
Other Producers	...	...	...	...	...	...	...	...	...	...	...	...
Subtotal	...	209	232	253	277	323	404	473	580	605	...	...
Less: Imputed bank service charge	...	5	7	9	7	8	12	15	26	30	...	...
Plus: Import duties	...	18	19	20	22	28	34	37	42	41	...	...
Plus: Value added tax	...	...	...	...	...	...	...	...	...	...	...	...
Plus: Other adjustments	...	-5	-	-	-2	-4	-12	-21	-6	-	...	...
Equals: Gross Domestic Product	...	217	244	264	290	339	414	474	590	616	...	...

a) Item 'Finance, insurance, real estate and business services' excludes banks and insurance companies registered in Cayman Islands but with no physical presence in the Islands.

Cayman Islands

1.11 Gross Domestic Product by Kind of Activity, in Constant Prices

Million Cayman Islands Dollars

	1980	1983	1984	1985	1986	1987	1988	1989	1990	1991	1992	1993
					At constant prices of:1986							
1 Agriculture, hunting, forestry and fishing	...	2	1	1	2	1	1	1	1	2	...	...
2 Mining and quarrying	...	1	1	1	1	2	3	3	2	2	...	...
3 Manufacturing	...	6	6	6	6	7	7	8	7	6	...	...
4 Electricity, gas and water	...	5	6	6	7	8	10	11	13	14	...	...
5 Construction	...	32	30	26	27	27	36	42	44	41	...	...
6 Wholesale and retail trade, restaurants and hotels	...	48	53	56	60	68	79	95	114	107	...	...
7 Transport, storage and communication	...	26	31	34	38	36	43	49	52	54	...	...
8 Finance, insurance, real estate and business services [a]	...	71	76	79	86	100	118	122	132	135	...	...
9 Community, social and personal services	...	17	18	19	20	21	22	25	31	38	...	...
Total, Industries	...	208	222	228	247	270	319	356	396	399	...	...
Producers of Government Services	...	25	26	29	30	32	34	37	43	46	...	...
Other Producers	...	...	...	...	...	...	...	...	...	...	...	...
Subtotal	...	232	248	257	277	302	353	393	439	445	...	...
Less: Imputed bank service charge	...	7	8	9	7	7	10	14	28	33	...	...
Plus: Import duties	...	20	20	20	22	26	30	33	42	44	...	...
Plus: Value added tax	...	...	...	...	...	...	...	...	...	...	...	...
Plus: Other adjustments	...	-3	-	-	-2	-4	-11	-18	-7	-4	...	...
Equals: Gross Domestic Product	...	242	260	269	290	317	362	394	446	452	...	...

a) Item 'Finance, insurance, real estate and business services' excludes banks and insurance companies registered in Cayman Islands but with no physical presence in the Islands.

1.12 Relations Among National Accounting Aggregates

Million Cayman Islands Dollars

	1980	1983	1984	1985	1986	1987	1988	1989	1990	1991	1992	1993
Gross Domestic Product	...	217	244	264	290	339	414	474	590	616	...	...
Plus: Net factor income from the rest of the world	...	-25	-19	-20	-19	-30	-40	-51	-61	-58	...	...
Factor income from the rest of the world	...	5	6	7	8	7	8	9	9	7	...	...
Less: Factor income to the rest of the world	...	30	25	27	27	37	48	60	70	65	...	...
Equals: Gross National Product	...	193	225	244	271	309	374	423	529	558	...	...
Less: Consumption of fixed capital	...	13	17	20	23	28	34	38	42	47	...	...
Equals: National Income	...	180	208	224	248	281	340	385	487	511	...	...
Plus: Net current transfers from the rest of the world	...	5	6	6	7	9	11	13	15	15	...	...
Equals: National Disposable Income	...	185	214	230	255	290	351	398	502	526	...	...
Less: Final consumption	...	171	193	209	225	268	329	376	453	478	...	...
Equals: Net Saving	...	14	21	21	30	22	22	22	49	48	...	...
Less: Surplus of the nation on current transactions	...	-31	-30	-27	-30	-42	-86	-106	-43	-35	...	...
Statistical discrepancy	...	-9	-6	-15	-16	-18	-37	-56	-8	4	...	...
Equals: Net Capital Formation	...	36	45	33	44	46	71	72	84	87	...	...

2.1 Government Final Consumption Expenditure by Function, in Current Prices

Million Cayman Islands Dollars

	1980	1983	1984	1985	1986	1987	1988	1989	1990	1991	1992	1993
1 General public services	...	11	13	14	16	14	21	23	25	28	...	...
2 Defence	...	...	...	...	...	...	...	...	...	...	...	...
3 Public order and safety	...	4	6	7	7	9	10	11	14	15	...	...
4 Education	...	5	6	7	7	8	9	10	14	15	...	...
5 Health	...	6	7	7	7	8	9	10	15	15	...	...
6 Social security and welfare	...	1	1	1	1	2	3	3	4	6	...	...
7 Housing and community amenities	...	-	-	-	1	1	1	1	1	2	...	...
8 Recreational, cultural and religious affairs	...	...	...	...	...	...	...	...	...	...	...	...
9 Economic services	...	6	7	8	9	11	14	15	18	21	...	...

Cayman Islands

2.1 Government Final Consumption Expenditure by Function, in Current Prices
(Continued)

Million Cayman Islands Dollars

	1980	1983	1984	1985	1986	1987	1988	1989	1990	1991	1992	1993
A Fuel and energy	...	...	...	...	...	...	...	...	...	...	...	...
B Agriculture, forestry, fishing and hunting	...	-	1	1	1	1	2	2	2	2	...	...
C Mining, manufacturing and construction, except fuel and energy	...	-	-	-	-	-	-	-	-	1	...	...
D Transportation and communication	...	3	3	3	4	4	5	5	5	6	...	...
E Other economic affairs	...	3	4	4	4	6	7	8	10	12	...	...
10 Other functions	...	-	1	1	2	3	2	2	3	1	...	...
Total Government Final Consumption Expenditure [a]	...	33	41	45	50	55	67	74	94	103	...	...

a) The estimates include only the total government current expenditure.

2.2 Government Final Consumption Expenditure by Function, in Constant Prices

Million Cayman Islands Dollars

	1980	1983	1984	1985	1986	1987	1988	1989	1990	1991	1992	1993
					At constant prices of:1986							
1 General public services	...	12	14	14	16	13	18	19	18	20	...	...
2 Defence	...	...	...	...	...	...	...	...	...	...	...	...
3 Public order and safety	...	4	6	7	7	8	9	10	10	11	...	...
4 Education	...	6	6	7	7	8	8	8	10	11	...	...
5 Health	...	7	7	7	7	7	8	8	11	11	...	...
6 Social security and welfare	...	1	1	1	1	2	2	2	3	4	...	...
7 Housing and community amenities	...	-	-	-	1	1	1	1	1	1	...	...
8 Recreational, cultural and religious affairs	...	...	...	...	...	...	...	...	...	...	...	...
9 Economic services	...	7	8	9	9	10	12	12	13	15	...	...
A Fuel and energy	...	...	...	...	...	...	...	...	...	...	...	...
B Agriculture, forestry, fishing and hunting	...	-	1	1	1	1	2	2	2	2	...	...
C Mining, manufacturing and construction, except fuel and energy	...	-	-	-	-	-	-	-	-	-	...	...
D Transportation and communication	...	3	3	3	4	4	1	1	4	4	...	...
E Other economic affairs	...	4	4	5	4	6	6	7	7	9	...	...
10 Other functions	...	-	1	2	2	3	2	2	2	1	...	...
Total Government Final Consumption Expenditure [a]	...	37	44	46	50	53	58	61	68	74	...	...

a) The estimates include only the total government current expenditure.

2.17 Exports and Imports of Goods and Services, Detail

Million Cayman Islands Dollars

	1980	1983	1984	1985	1986	1987	1988	1989	1990	1991	1992	1993
					Exports of Goods and Services							
1 Exports of merchandise, f.o.b.	...	1	1	2	2	2	2	2	2	1	...	...
2 Transport and communication	...	27	31	34	38	49	56	57	66	63	...	...
3 Insurance service charges	...	...	...	...	...	...	...	...	...	...	...	...
4 Other commodities [a]	...	49	54	61	67	82	88	112	173	171	...	...
5 Adjustments of merchandise exports to change-of-ownership basis	...	...	...	...	...	...	...	...	...	...	...	...
6 Direct purchases in the domestic market by non-residential households	...	81	84	87	92	110	116	113	137	128	...	...
7 Direct purchases in the domestic market by extraterritorial bodies	...	...	...	...	...	...	...	...	...	...	...	...
Total Exports of Goods and Services	...	159	171	184	200	243	261	285	378	363	...	...
					Imports of Goods and Services							
1 Imports of merchandise, c.i.f.	...	110	118	122	133	162	192	215	237	221	...	...

Cayman Islands

2.17 Exports and Imports of Goods and Services, Detail
(Continued)

Million Cayman Islands Dollars

	1980	1983	1984	1985	1986	1987	1988	1989	1990	1991	1992	1993
A Imports of merchandise, f.o.b.	...	98	105	109	119	145	172	192	212	197	...	...
B Transport of services on merchandise imports	...	11	11	12	13	16	19	21	23	22	...	...
C Insurance service charges on merchandise imports	...	1	1	1	1	2	2	2	2	2	...	...
2 Adjustments of merchandise imports to change-of-ownership basis	...	...	...	...	...	...	...	...	...	...	...	...
3 Other transport and communication	...	23	26	29	31	37	42	48	36	39	...	...
4 Other insurance service charges	...	...	...	...	...	...	...	...	...	...	...	...
5 Other commodities [a]	...	14	15	17	19	23	21	23	32	27	...	...
6 Direct purchases abroad by government	...	5	4	5	6	7	8	9	10	11	...	...
7 Direct purchases abroad by resident households	...	9	13	13	14	17	31	30	30	28	...	...
Total Imports of Goods and Services	...	161	176	185	204	246	295	326	345	325	...	...
Balance of Goods and Services	...	-3	-5	-2	-5	-3	-34	-41	33	38	...	...
Total Imports and Balance of Goods and Services	...	159	171	184	200	243	261	285	378	363	...	...

a) Item 'Other commodities' refers to services only.

4.1 Derivation of Value Added by Kind of Activity, in Current Prices

Million Cayman Islands Dollars

	1985 Gross Output	1985 Intermediate Consumption	1985 Value Added	1990 Gross Output	1990 Intermediate Consumption	1990 Value Added	1991 Gross Output	1991 Intermediate Consumption	1991 Value Added
				All Producers					
1 Agriculture, hunting, forestry and fishing	2	1	1	6	2	4	7	3	4
2 Mining and quarrying	2	1	1						
3 Manufacturing	11	5	6	15	6	9	16	7	9
4 Electricity, gas and water	17	11	6	36	18	18	44	25	19
5 Construction	50	24	25	110	54	56	106	51	55
6 Wholesale and retail trade, restaurants and hotels	103	48	54	268	126	142	260	121	138
A Wholesale and retail trade	52	19	33	147	57	90	149	58	91
B Restaurants and hotels	50	29	19	121	69	52	111	63	48
7 Transport, storage and communication	75	42	33	141	78	63	140	75	65
8 Finance, insurance, real estate and business services [a]	123	44	79	266	69	197	277	67	210
A Financial institutions	56	22	34	132	33	99	136	30	106
B Insurance									
C Real estate and business services	...	...	...	134	36	98	141	37	104
9 Community, social and personal services	31	12	19	58	24	34	64	22	42
A Sanitary and similar services	...	...	...	...	...	...	...	...	...
B Social and related community services	...	...	...	...	...	...	...	...	...
Educational services	...	...	...	4	1	2	...	...	...
Medical, dental, other health and veterinary services	...	...	...	8	2	5	...	...	...
C Recreational and cultural services	...	...	...	11	6	5	...	...	...
D Personal and household services	...	...	...	9	-	9	...	...	...
Total, Industries	414	190	224	900	378	522	914	372	542
Producers of Government Services	41	12	29	82	24	58	91	28	63

Cayman Islands

4.1 Derivation of Value Added by Kind of Activity, in Current Prices
(Continued)

Million Cayman Islands Dollars

	1985 Gross Output	1985 Intermediate Consumption	1985 Value Added	1990 Gross Output	1990 Intermediate Consumption	1990 Value Added	1991 Gross Output	1991 Intermediate Consumption	1991 Value Added
Other Producers	...	...	...	...	...	...	...	...	...
Total	455	202	253	982	402	580	1005	400	605
Less: Imputed bank service charge	...	-9	9	...	-26	26	...	-30	30
Import duties	20	-	20	42	-	42	41	-	41
Value added tax	...	...	...	...	...	...	...	...	...
Other adjustments	...	-	-	...	6	-6	...	-	-
Total	475	211	264	1024	434	590	1046	430	616

a) Item 'Finance, insurance, real estate and business services' excludes banks and insurance companies registered in Cayman Islands but with no physical presence in the Islands.

4.3 Cost Components of Value Added

Million Cayman Islands Dollars

	1985 Compensation of Employees	1985 Capital Consumption	1985 Net Operating Surplus	1985 Indirect Taxes	1985 Less: Subsidies Received	1985 Value Added	1990 Compensation of Employees	1990 Capital Consumption	1990 Net Operating Surplus	1990 Indirect Taxes	1990 Less: Subsidies Received	1990 Value Added
					All Producers							
1 Agriculture, hunting, forestry and fishing	1	...	...	...	...	1	1	...	...	...	...	1
2 Mining and quarrying	1	...	...	...	...	1	1	...	...	...	...	3
3 Manufacturing	2	...	...	...	...	6	4	...	...	...	...	9
4 Electricity, gas and water	2	...	...	...	...	6	8	...	...	...	...	18
5 Construction	16	...	...	...	...	25	30	...	...	...	...	56
6 Wholesale and retail trade, restaurants and hotels	35	...	...	...	...	54	93	...	...	...	...	142
A Wholesale and retail trade	21	...	...	...	...	33	59	...	...	...	...	90
B Restaurants and hotels	14	...	...	...	...	21	35	...	...	...	...	52
7 Transport, storage and communication	16	...	...	...	...	33	25	...	...	...	...	63
8 Finance, insurance, real estate and business services [a]	42	...	...	...	...	79	84	...	...	...	...	197
A Financial institutions	25	...	...	...	...	34	52	...	...	...	...	99
B Insurance		...	...	...	...			...	...	...	...	
C Real estate and business services	16	...	...	...	...	45	32	...	...	...	...	98
9 Community, social and personal services	14	...	...	...	...	19	28	...	...	...	...	34
Total, Industries	129	...	...	...	...	224	274	...	...	...	...	522
Producers of Government Services	27	...	...	...	...	29	54	...	...	...	...	58
Other Producers	...	...	...	...	...	...	...	...	...	...	...	...
Total	156	...	...	...	...	253	328	...	...	...	...	580
Less: Imputed bank service charge	...	...	...	...	...	9	...	...	...	...	...	26
Import duties	...	...	...	...	...	20	...	...	...	...	...	42
Value added tax	...	...	...	...	...	...	...	...	...	...	...	...
Other adjustments	...	...	...	...	...	-	...	...	...	...	...	-6
Total	156	...	...	...	...	264	328	...	...	...	...	590

	1991 Compensation of Employees	1991 Capital Consumption	1991 Net Operating Surplus	1991 Indirect Taxes	1991 Less: Subsidies Received	1991 Value Added
			All Producers			
1 Agriculture, hunting, forestry and fishing	1	...	...	...	...	1
2 Mining and quarrying	1	...	...	...	...	3
3 Manufacturing	5	...	...	...	...	9
4 Electricity, gas and water	9	...	...	...	...	19

Cayman Islands

4.3 Cost Components of Value Added
(Continued)

Million Cayman Islands Dollars

	\multicolumn{6}{c	}{1991}
	Compensation of Employees	Capital Consumption	Net Operating Surplus	Indirect Taxes	Less: Subsidies Received	Value Added
5 Construction	28	...	...	...	...	55
6 Wholesale and retail trade, restaurants and hotels	91	...	...	...	...	138
A Wholesale and retail trade	59	...	...	...	...	91
B Restaurants and hotels	32	...	...	...	...	48
7 Transport, storage and communication	28	...	...	...	...	65
8 Finance, insurance, real estate and business services [a]	89	...	...	...	...	210
A Financial institutions	56	...	...	...	...	106
B Insurance		...	...	...	...	
C Real estate and business services	33	...	...	...	...	104
9 Community, social and personal services	32	...	...	...	...	42
Total, Industries	284	...	...	...	...	542
Producers of Government Services	58	...	...	...	...	63
Other Producers	...	...	...	...	...	...
Total	342	...	...	...	...	605
Less: Imputed bank service charge	...	...	...	...	...	30
Import duties	...	...	...	...	...	41
Value added tax	...	...	...	...	...	...
Other adjustments	...	...	...	...	...	-
Total	342	...	...	...	...	616

a) Item 'Finance, insurance, real estate and business services' excludes banks and insurance companies registered in Cayman Islands but with no physical presence in the Islands.

Central African Rep.

Source. Reply to the United Nations National Accounts Questionnaire from the Ministere du Plan, de la Cooperation International et des Statistiques, Bangui.
General note. The estimates shown in the following tables have been prepared and adjusted by the Ministere Francais de la Cooperation to conform to the United Nations System of National Accounts so far as the existing data would permit.

1.1 Expenditure on the Gross Domestic Product, in Current Prices

Million CFA francs

	1980	1983	1984	1985	1986	1987	1988	1989	1990	1991	1992	1993
1 Government final consumption expenditure	...	...	...	58781	60580	63032	60777	...	...	...	...	...
2 Private final consumption expenditure	...	...	...	307397	318960	290962	303914	...	...	...	...	...
3 Gross capital formation	...	...	...	59774	49667	45591	39594	...	...	...	...	...
A Increase in stocks	...	...	...	11595	-331	-810	2490	...	...	...	...	...
B Gross fixed capital formation	...	...	...	48179	49998	46401	37104	...	...	...	...	...
4 Exports of goods and services	...	...	...	85513	70681	64407	66853	...	...	...	...	...
5 Less: Imports of goods and services	...	...	...	122920	111241	103050	94390	...	...	...	...	...
Equals: Gross Domestic Product [a]	...	...	...	388545	388647	360942	376748 327500	340600	353000	362100	354500	...

a) Data in this table have not been revised, therefore they are not comparable with the data in other tables.

1.11 Gross Domestic Product by Kind of Activity, in Constant Prices

Million CFA francs

	1980	1983	1984	1985	1986	1987	1988	1989	1990	1991	1992	1993
			At constant prices of:									
		1982					1984					
1 Agriculture, hunting, forestry and fishing	94497	93925	104696 104900	107330	116250	114250	119470	...	...	...	...	...
2 Mining and quarrying	5722	5766	5877 7620	7640	7910	9220	8930	...	...	...	...	...
3 Manufacturing	18000	19678	20268 21650	22380	22250	20380	22530	...	...	...	...	...
4 Electricity, gas and water	1549	923	1452 1300	1180	1290	1840	1240	...	...	...	...	...
5 Construction	4014	4447	5856 6200	5630	5600	7260	6960	...	...	...	...	...
6 Wholesale and retail trade, restaurants and hotels	51723	43774	47317 51930	56623	58508	57168	57880	...	...	...	...	...
7 Transport, storage and communication	9997	8703	9447 10070	10987	11352	11092	11230	...	...	...	...	...
8 Finance, insurance, real estate and business services	7846	8387	8446 10120[a]	10030	7960	5080	4580	...	...	...	...	...
9 Community, social and personal services	36421[b]	38284[b]	35619[b]					...	...	...	...	...
Total, Industries	229768	223887	238977 213790	221800	231120	226290	232820	...	...	...	...	...
Producers of Government Services	...	...	... 39360	39630	40760	40340	41570	...	...	...	...	...
Other Producers	...	...	...	...	...	...	...	...	...	...	...	...
Subtotal	229768	223887	238977 253150	261430	271880	266630	274390	...	...	...	...	...
Less: Imputed bank service charge	4627	5069	5069	...	...	...	...	...	...	...	...	...
Plus: Import duties	12802	12151	13749 13930	13900	14900	12600	12360	...	...	...	...	...
Plus: Value added tax	...	...	8650	9600	10030	8800	9010	...	...	...	...	...
Equals: Gross Domestic Product	237943	230969	247657 275730	284930	296810	288030	295760	...	...	...	...	...

a) Including item 'Community, social and personal services'.
b) Item 'Producers of government services' is included in item 'Community, social and personal services'.

Chad

Source. Reply to the United Nations National Accounts Questionnaire from the Sous-Direction de la Statistique, Direction du Plan et du Developpement, Ministere des Finances, de L'Economie et du Plan, Ndjamena.

General note. The official estimates have been adjusted by the Sous-Direction de la Statistique to conform to the United Nations System of National Accounts so far as the existing data would permit.

1.1 Expenditure on the Gross Domestic Product, in Current Prices

Thousand Million CFA francs

	1980	1983	1984	1985	1986	1987	1988	1989	1990	1991	1992	1993
1 Government final consumption expenditure	...	...	...	...	...	...	...	...	...	...	...	...
2 Private final consumption expenditure	...	...	...	...	...	...	...	...	...	...	...	...
3 Gross capital formation	...	...	...	...	...	...	...	...	...	...	...	...
4 Exports of goods and services	...	...	...	...	...	...	...	...	...	...	...	...
5 Less: Imports of goods and services	...	...	...	...	...	...	...	...	...	...	...	...
Equals: Gross Domestic Product	...	...	...	...	283.00	246.00	311.00	325.00	332.00	364.00	366.00	...

1.11 Gross Domestic Product by Kind of Activity, in Constant Prices

Thousand Million CFA francs

	1980	1983	1984	1985	1986	1987	1988	1989	1990	1991	1992	1993
					At constant prices of:1977							
1 Agriculture, hunting, forestry and fishing	63.38	61.06	51.37	74.35	70.31	67.42	83.07	79.24	...	...	...	...
2 Mining and quarrying	0.06	0.10	0.21	0.36	0.39	0.41	0.42	0.48	...	...	...	...
3 Manufacturing	13.30	22.16	27.22	25.41	24.14	21.56	24.81	30.25	...	...	...	...
4 Electricity, gas and water	0.41	0.68	0.87	0.87	1.02	1.07	1.15	1.24	...	...	...	...
5 Construction	0.28	0.50	1.00	1.72	1.89	1.97	2.02	2.31	...	...	...	...
6 Wholesale and retail trade, restaurants and hotels									...	...	...	...
7 Transport, storage and communication	32.74	41.64	44.28	53.08	53.60	50.42	56.53	59.28	...	...	...	...
8 Finance, insurance, real estate and business services									...	...	...	...
9 Community, social and personal services [a]									...	...	...	...
Total, Industries	110.17	126.14	124.96	155.79	151.37	142.84	167.99	172.80	...	...	...	...
Producers of Government Services	8.28	16.91	18.10	19.33	16.44	19.18	19.85	21.62	...	...	...	...
Other Producers [a]	...	...	...	...	...	...	...	...	...	...	...	...
Subtotal [b]	118.45	143.05	143.06	175.12	167.81	162.02	187.84	194.42	...	...	...	...
Less: Imputed bank service charge	...	...	...	...	...	...	...	...	...	...	...	...
Plus: Import duties	...	...	...	...	...	...	...	...	...	...	...	...
Plus: Value added tax	...	...	...	...	...	...	...	...	...	...	...	...
Plus: Other adjustments [c]	0.38	3.24	6.29	6.94	6.79	8.37	8.59	10.60	...	...	...	...
Equals: Gross Domestic Product	118.83	146.29	149.35	182.06	174.60	170.39	196.43	205.02	...	...	...	...

a) Item 'Producers of government services' is included in item 'Community, social and personal services'.
b) Gross domestic product in factor values.
c) Item 'Other adjustments' refers to indirect taxes net of subsidies.

Chile

General note. The preparation of national accounts statistics in Chile is undertaken by Banco Central de Chile, Santiago. The official estimates are published in 'Cuentas Nacionales de Chile'. The following presentation of sources and methods is mainly based on a detailed description received by the United Nations from ODEPLAN. However, descriptions can also be found in 'Cuentas Nacionales de Chile, 1960-1975', published in 1976. The estimates are generally in accordance with the classifications and definitions recommended in the United Nations System of National Accounts (SNA). The following tables have been prepared from successive replies to the United Nations national accounts questionnaire. When the scope and coverage of the estimates differ for conceptual or statistical reasons from the definitions and classifications recommended in SNA, a footnote is indicated to the relevant tables.

Sources and methods:

(a) Gross domestic product. The main approach used to estimate GDP is the production approach.

(b) Expenditure on the gross domestic product. The expenditure approach is used to estimate government final consumption expenditure, increase in stocks, exports and imports of goods and services and capital formation in new construction. The commodity-flow approach is used to estimate other construction. Private final consumption expenditure is estimated as a residual. Data on government consumption expenditure is obtained i.a. through special inquiries and direct information from the concerned authorities. Values of locally produced and imported capital goods are adjusted by coefficients by type of capital goods to arrive at purchasers' values. Estimates of exports and imports of goods and services are obtained from the balance of payments statements prepared by the Central Bank. To arrive at constant prices, value added of government services is deflated by index of wages and salaries. Purchases of goods and services are deflated by the wholesale price index and the price index of intermediate imported goods. For private consumption expenditure most domestically produced items are deflated by appropriate components of the consumer price index. Imported goods are deflated by the price index of imported consumer goods. For gross fixed capital formation, buildings and other construction are devalued using double deflation. Base year estimates of transport equipment, machinery and equipment are extrapolated by a quantity index for each industrial group, except for imports which are deflated by price indexes of imported capital goods. Price deflation is used for exports and imports of goods and services.

(c) Cost-structure of the gross domestic product. Wages and salaries are in most cases estimated from company accounts and/or direct information from the enterprises. Employers' contributions to social security schemes as well as wages and salaries in kind are included in the estimates. Operating surplus is obtained as a residual. Depreciation data are obtained from accounting statements of enterprises or computed from data of fixed assets by type of capital and useful life time. For indirect taxes, published fiscal statements by type of tax, are used.

(d) Gross domestic product by kind of economic activity. This table is prepared at market prices, i.e. producers' values. The production approach is used to estimate value added of most industries. The income approach is however used for government services, business services and domestic services. The general method of estimating gross value of agricultural production involves the use of physical quantities of production together with the respective wholesale or producers' prices. Quantities of livestock production are obtained from published data and directly from Instituto Nacional de Estadistica (INE). The estimates include both marketed and non-marketed production. The inputs into agriculture and forestry are based on information from the suppliers of input products. The estimates for the mining and quarrying sector are mainly based on data on sales and change in stocks, but in some cases on physical production valued at average sales price or on expenditure data in the construction and industrial sectors. For manufacturing, the required statistics for companies with 1 to 49 employees are found in their annual industrial declarations. For units with 50 or more employees, the industrial yearbook of INE is used. The gross value of construction in the public sector is obtained from accounts of the respective institutions. For the private sector the construction expenditure on all buildings is calculated on the basis of the municipal building permits. In order to estimate intermediate consumption and the components of value added, cost-structure by type of construction are applied to the gross value of production. Estimates of private sector trade is made on the basis of a continuous survey. For public enterprises, information provided in their accounting statements and in their budget statements is used. For transport, information is based on accounts, sales data and on the stock of motor vehicles. The production and input estimates for financial institutions and corporations, real estate and insurance are made possible through data from the Superintendencia de Bancos. Bench-mark estimates for actual rents paid and imputed rent for owner-occupied dwellings have been made on the basis of the housing censuses in 1960 and 1970. These estimates are projected annually by a value index which combines the increase in physical stock with a price index for rent. For public administration and defense, budgets and accounts provide the required basic data. For the constant price estimates, double deflation is used in the agricultural sector, the output value is extrapolated by quantity indexes by product, whereas intermediate inputs are deflated by an index of input prices. Value added of fishing, mining and quarrying, manufacturing and electricity is extrapolated by quantity indexes of production. Double deflation is used for construction, current gross values are deflated by price indexes for each type of construction. For intermediate consumption, input-structures are used. For trade, value added of the base year is extrapolated by a quantity index. Double deflation is used for the transport and financing, insurance, real estate and business services sector. For transport, current output is deflated separately for different uses and types of transport. For financial institutions, output is deflated by an implicit price index for expenditure. Output of ownership of dwellings is extrapolated by an index based on the change in the housing stock, whereas inputs are deflated by the value index for repairs. For community, social and personal services, double deflation is used.

1.1 Expenditure on the Gross Domestic Product, in Current Prices

Thousand Million Chilean pesos

	1980	1983	1984	1985	1986	1987	1988	1989	1990	1991	1992	1993
1 Government final consumption expenditure	134	220	256	335 / 356	430	494	613	742	906	1147	1457	1788
2 Private final consumption expenditure	760	1100	1327	1853 / 1776	2239	2906	3545	4527	5609	7450	9664	11778
3 Gross capital formation	226	171	337	473 / 456	646	1010	1347	1920	2435	2945	4153	5306
A Increase in stocks	47	-20	70	54 / 9	60	128	146	187	276	435	636	591
B Gross fixed capital formation	179	192	267	420 / 447	586	882	1202	1733	2159	2510	3517	4715
Residential buildings	45	46	51	85 / 77	108	153	216	...	...	...	...	...
Non-residential buildings	16	16	19	28 / 29	40	47	78	...	...	...	...	...
Other construction and land improvement etc.	44	69	94	138 / 165	197	259	308	...	...	...	...	...
Other	74	60	102	168 / 175	241	422	599	...	...	...	...	...
4 Exports of goods and services	245	376	441	748 / 746	995	1374	2046	2639	3194	3943	4615	4916
5 Less: Imports of goods and services	290	332	458	668 / 682	890	1244	1634	2298	2875	3468	4390	5335
Equals: Gross Domestic Product	1076	1536	1903	2741 / 2652	3419	4541	5918	7529	9270	12017	15500	18454

Chile

1.2 Expenditure on the Gross Domestic Product, in Constant Prices

Million Chilean pesos

	1980	1983	1984	1985	1986	1987	1988	1989	1990	1991	1992	1993
			1977		At constant prices of:			1986				
1 Government final consumption expenditure	44916	42183	41844	42940 / 425550	430168	419089	434140	449847	454628	474215	499300	515771
2 Private final consumption expenditure	256505	233733	235201	232893 / 2129737	2238746	2400565	2569303	2836164	2847234	3100432	3460139	3741696
3 Gross capital formation	86961	34512	59558	49287 / 604126	645698	819023	914078	1118976	1163565	1182675	1490011	1675924
A Increase in stocks	22848	-4729	12920	-2002 / 31938	59675	105760	99869	110717	137041	178241	224558	186246
B Gross fixed capital formation	64113	39241	46638	51289 / 572188	586023	713263	814209	1008259	1026524	1004434	1265453	1489678
Residential buildings	15669	10363	10173	13633 / 91257	108391	123163	146686					
Non-residential buildings	5560	3780	3806	4219 / 35085	39623	38958	53377	485575	503207	515573	582386	660592
Other construction and land improvement etc.	13426	13086	15096	16296 / 196193	196851	221343	216127					
Other	29458	12012	17563	17140 / 249653	241158	329799	398019	522684	523317	488861	683067	829086
4 Exports of goods and services	86077	82151	84022	94342 / 903429	994634	1061675	1184359	1375171	1508335	1669676	1895505	1974801
5 Less: Imports of goods and services	110461	67863	76795	68866 / 824839	890037	1055671	1190726	1482821	1536408	1667579	2060073	2291778
Equals: Gross Domestic Product	363998	324717	343828	350596 / 3238003	3419209	3644681	3911154	4297337	4437355	4759419	5284882	5616414

1.7 External Transactions on Current Account, Summary

Million Chilean pesos

	1980	1983	1984	1985	1986	1987	1988	1989	1990	1991	1992	1993
				Payments to the Rest of the World								
1 Imports of goods and services [a]	290099	332069	458024	667866 / 681892	890037	1243994	1633819	2298171	2874658	...	...	...
2 Factor income to the rest of the world	48274	153625	229517	337967 / ...	408105	412776	515648	578027	649010	...	...	...
3 Current transfers to the rest of the world	3151	5090	5636	9056 / ...	9608	9479	6885	6807	8629	...	...	...
Statistical discrepancy	...	...	...	... / ...	8175	29306	-9350	-55263	-66661	...	...	...
4 Surplus of the nation on current transactions	-76552	-86283	-204779	-214595 / -248912	-251048	-226493	-29464	-133532	-188488	...	...	...
Payments to the Rest of the World and Surplus of the Nation on Current Transactions	264973	404500	488399	800294 / ...	1064877	1469062	2117538	2694210	3277148	...	...	...
				Receipts From The Rest of the World								
1 Exports of goods and services [a]	245387	375860	440922	747886 / 746455	994634	1374296	2045598	2638730	3193645	...	...	...
2 Factor income from rest of the world	12008	15939	31390	32172 / ...	43988	39911	45327	63854	108575	...	...	...
3 Current transfers from rest of the world	7578	12701	16087	20236 / ...	26721	34886	50178	64362	69334	...	...	...
Statistical discrepancy	...	...	...	... / ...	-466	19969	-23565	-72736	-94406	...	...	...
Receipts from the Rest of the World on Current Transactions	264973	404500	488399	800294 / ...	1064877	1469062	2117538	2694210	3277148	...	...	...

a) Data for this table have not been revised, therefore, data for some years are not comparable with those of other tables.

Chile

1.10 Gross Domestic Product by Kind of Activity, in Current Prices

Thousand Million Chilean pesos

	1980	1983	1984	1985	1986	1987	1988	1989	1990	1991	1992	1993
1 Agriculture, hunting, forestry and fishing	78	90	136	205 / 196	293	399	502	...	...	...	...	...
2 Mining and quarrying	92	158	160	281 / 349	343	517	915	...	...	...	...	...
3 Manufacturing	231	320	437	602 / 416	611	795	1069	...	...	...	...	...
4 Electricity, gas and water	23	45	54	81 / 69	92	113	151	...	...	...	...	...
5 Construction	56	69	80	113 / 131	164	219	304	...	...	...	...	...
6 Wholesale and retail trade, restaurants and hotels	198	234	281	441 / 356	483	701	796	...	...	...	...	...
7 Transport, storage and communication	55	85	107	149 / 160	217	276	356	...	...	...	...	...
8 Finance, insurance, real estate and business services	182	245	261	418 / 343	418	520	602	...	...	...	...	...
9 Community, social and personal services	66	100	117	154 / 418	499	613	751	...	...	...	...	...
Total, Industries	980	1346	1632	2444 / 2438	3119	4153	5444	...	...	...	...	...
Producers of Government Services	92	149	171	213 / 128	150	176	215	...	...	...	...	...
Other Producers	...	...	...	...	...	...	...	...	...	...	...	...
Subtotal	1072	1495	1804	2657 / 2567	3268	4328	5658	...	...	...	...	...
Less: Imputed bank service charge	56	48	42	119 / 226	234	298	290	...	...	...	...	...
Plus: Import duties	60	88	141	204 / 215	272	350	363	...	...	...	...	...
Plus: Value added tax	...	...	...	97	113	161	186	...	...	...	...	...
Equals: Gross Domestic Product	1076	1536	1903	2741 / 2652	3419	4541	5918	...	...	...	...	...

1.11 Gross Domestic Product by Kind of Activity, in Constant Prices

Million Chilean pesos

	1980	1983	1984	1985	1986	1987	1988	1989	1990	1991	1992	1993
	\multicolumn{4}{c}{1977}	\multicolumn{8}{c}{At constant prices of: 1986}
1 Agriculture, hunting, forestry and fishing	30031	30312	33027	35354 / 272263	293013	320921	357873	377942	400532	411500	442055	448649
2 Mining and quarrying	26077	29291	30894	31899 / 339740	342852	341729	368478	403515	425712	445469	454460	458665
3 Manufacturing	78332	65466	71289	73204 / 567684	610935	643172	699852	776409	784984	836466	928593	975604
4 Electricity, gas and water	7754	8246	8834	9171 / 86467	91757	96767	102226	99378	95138	122084	147343	153614
5 Construction	19420	15398	15742	18510 / 149024	163546	178494	193826	227087	237306	246324	277927	316800
6 Wholesale and retail trade, restaurants and hotels	71896	62103	64520	61371 / 459163	482799	535403	563842	643206	667943	744991	880689	956597
7 Transport, storage and communication	20313	17762	18590	19561 / 203461	216927	237678	258553	291171	310430	340873	387800	418308
8 Finance, insurance, real estate and business services	55855	44666	42845	51365 / 385398	418315	451792	493020	742318	766734	818421	881821	932766
9 Community, social and personal services	20145	18668	20035	21479 / 482976	498538	508310	523097	334542	344726	356837	369946	384779

Chile

1.11 Gross Domestic Product by Kind of Activity, in Constant Prices
(Continued)

Million Chilean pesos

	1980	1983	1984	1985	1986	1987	1988	1989	1990	1991	1992	1993
		1977			At constant prices of:			1986				
Total, Industries	329823	291912	305776	321914 / 2946176	3118682	3314266	3560767	3895568	4033505	4322965	4770633	5045782
Producers of Government Services	29215	28749	28526	29065 / 146588	149736	147255	147928	147455	149159	151646	156052	158790
Other Producers	...	...	...	... / ...	...	...	...	...	...	...	...	...
Subtotal	359038	320661	334302	350979 / 3092764	3268418	3461521	3708695	4043023	4182664	4474611	4926685	5204572
Less: Imputed bank service charge	18889	10116	7652	15489 / 215743	234428	249736	273286	299774	306297	329004	363113	383732
Plus: Import duties	23850	14170	17179	15106 / 255194	271748	293445	318286	208041	212579	237156	301020	340412
Plus: Value added tax	...	...	...	... / 105788	113471	139451	157459	346046	348409	376656	420289	455162
Equals: Gross Domestic Product	363998	324717	343828	350596 / 3238003	3419209	3644681	3911154	4297337	4437355	4759419	5284882	5616414

1.12 Relations Among National Accounting Aggregates

Thousand Million Chilean pesos

	1980	1983	1984	1985	1986	1987	1988	1989	1990	1991	1992	1993
Gross Domestic Product	1076	1536	1903	2741 / 2652	3419	4541	5918	7529	9270	12017	15500	18454
Plus: Net factor income from the rest of the world	-36	-138	-198	-306 / -335	-374	-384	-485	-532	-568	-647	-692	-629
Factor income from the rest of the world	12	16	31	32 / ...	...	...	...	...	...	...	...	...
Less: Factor income to the rest of the world	48	154	230	338 / ...	...	...	...	...	...	...	...	...
Equals: Gross National Product	1039	1398	1705	2436 / 2317	3045	4156	5433	6998	8701	11370	14808	17824
Less: Consumption of fixed capital	103	181	226	328 / ...	...	...	...	...	...	...	...	...
Equals: National Income	936	1217	1478	2108 / ...	...	...	...	...	...	...	...	...
Plus: Net current transfers from the rest of the world	4	8	10	11 / 22	18	28	43	58	61	119	156	155
Current transfers from the rest of the world	8	13	16	20 / ...	...	...	...	...	...	...	...	...
Less: Current transfers to the rest of the world	3	5	6	9 / ...	...	...	...	...	...	...	...	...
Equals: National Disposable Income	940	1225	1489	2119 / ...	...	...	...	...	...	...	...	...
Less: Final consumption	894	1321	1583	2188 / 2131	2669	3400	4159	5269	6515	8597	11122	13566
Equals: Net Saving	46	-96	-94	-69 / ...	...	...	...	...	...	...	...	...
Less: Surplus of the nation on current transactions	-77	-86	-205	-215 / -249	-251	-226	-29	-134	-188	-53	-311	-892
Equals: Net Capital Formation	123	-10	111	145 / ...	...	...	...	...	...	...	...	...

China

Source. Communication from the State Statistical Bureau of the People's Republic of China, Beijing.

General note. The estimates shown in the following table has been prepared in accordance with the System of National Accounts so far as the existing data would permit.

1.1 Expenditure on the Gross Domestic Product, in Current Prices

Thousand Million Yuan Renminbi

	1980	1983	1984	1985	1986	1987	1988	1989	1990	1991	1992	1993
1 Government final consumption expenditure	...	...	102.00	118.40	136.70	149.00	172.70	203.30	225.20	283.00	349.23	449.97
2 Private final consumption expenditure	...	...	367.45	458.90	517.50	596.12	763.31	852.35	911.32	1031.59	1245.98	1568.25
3 Gross capital formation	...	...	246.86	338.60	384.60	432.20	549.50	609.50	644.40	751.70	963.60	1499.80
A Increase in stocks	...	...	34.30	74.50	74.80	58.00	87.10	175.60	171.20	157.70	131.90	201.80
B Gross fixed capital formation	...	...	212.56	264.10	309.80	374.20	462.40	433.90	473.20	594.00	831.70	1298.00
4 Exports of goods and services	...	...	-0.85	-41.68	-36.39	-7.42	-21.58	-21.99	48.88	56.19	32.29	-58.48
5 Less: Imports of goods and services	...	...										
Statistical discrepancy	...	...	1.64	22.22	17.81	26.35	28.90	47.76	23.27	39.30	72.44	-8.03
Equals: Gross Domestic Product	...	...	717.10	896.44	1020.22	1196.25	1492.83	1690.92	1853.07	2161.78	2663.54	3451.51

1.12 Relations Among National Accounting Aggregates

Thousand Million Yuan Renminbi

	1980	1983	1984	1985	1986	1987	1988	1989	1990	1991	1992	1993
Gross Domestic Product	447.00	578.70	692.80 / 717.10	896.44	1020.22	1196.25	1492.83	1690.92	1853.07	2161.78	2663.54	3451.51
Plus: Net factor income from the rest of the world	...	2.20	3.40 / 3.38	3.02	0.87	-0.61	-0.60	-0.43	1.40	4.80	1.60	-3.84
Equals: Gross National Product	447.00	580.90	696.20 / 720.48	899.46	1021.09	1195.64	1492.23	1690.49	1854.47	2166.58	2665.14	3447.67
Less: Consumption of fixed capital	47.70	62.40	71.10 / 71.10	83.80	102.00	118.90	134.30	159.20	182.00	215.80	250.60	363.10
Equals: National Income	399.30	518.50	625.10 / 649.38	815.66	919.09	1076.74	1357.93	1531.29	1672.47	1950.78	2414.54	3084.57
Plus: Net current transfers from the rest of the world	...	1.00	1.00 / 1.00	0.70	1.30	0.80	1.60	1.40	1.40	4.50	6.40	6.80
Equals: National Disposable Income	...	519.50	626.10 / 650.38	816.36	920.39	1077.54	1359.53	1532.69	1673.87	1955.28	2420.94	3091.37
Less: Final consumption	...	...	... / 469.45	577.30	654.20	745.12	936.01	1055.65	1136.52	1314.59	1595.21	2018.22
Equals: Net Saving	...	...	... / 180.93	239.06	266.19	332.42	423.52	477.04	537.35	640.69	825.73	1073.15
Less: Surplus of the nation on current transactions	...	...	... / 5.17	-15.74	-16.41	19.12	8.32	26.74	74.95	104.79	112.73	-63.55
Equals: Net Capital Formation	...	...	... / 175.76	254.80	282.60	313.30	415.20	450.30	462.40	535.90	713.00	1136.70

Colombia

General note. The preparation of national accounts statistics in Colombia is undertaken by the Departamento Administrativo Nacional de Estadistica (DANE), Bogota. Official estimates together with some methodological notes are published in 'Cuentas Nacionales de Colombia' (Revision 3). The estimates are generally in accordance with the classifications and definitions recommended in the United Nations System of Nationsl Accounts (SNA). The following tables have been prepared from successive replies to the United Nations National Accounts Questionnaire. When the scope and coverage of the estimates differ for conceptual or statistical reasons from the definitions and classifications recommended in SNA, a footnote is indicated to the relevant tables.

Sources and methods:

(a) Gross domestic product. Gross domestic product is estimated mainly through the production approach.

(b) Expenditure on the gross domestic product. The expenditure approach is used to estimate government final consumption expenditure, exports and imports of goods and services, part of increase in stocks and gross fixed capital formation in construction. For other gross fixed capital formation, the commodity-flow approach is used. Private final consumption expenditure and part of increase in stocks are obtained as a residual. The estimates of government final consumption expenditures are based on official sources such as Informe Financiero de la Contraloria General de la Republica. The estimates of private consumption expenditure are obtained as a residual except for the bench-mark year 1970 which were based on results from the family budget survey conducted that year. The estimates for changes in stocks are based on information obtained from various sources such as manufacturing surveys, commercial census, and the Federacion Nacional de Cafeteros. For gross fixed capital formation, the c.i.f. values of imported capital goods in the foreign trade statistics are adjusted to include customs duties, other taxes and transport and insurance costs. Adjustments are also made for trade margins and installation costs on goods passing through trade channels. For domestic production, estimates are based on manufacturing surveys. Estimates of capital formation in construction are obtained as by-product in the calculation of the construction sector's contribution to GDP whereas investments in the government sector is obtained from the government accounts. The estimates of exports and imports of goods are derived from foreign trade statistics while that of services are derived from the balance of payments. For the constant price estimates, current values of government expenditure and gross fixed capital formation estimates are deflated by appropriate price indexes. Estimates of private consumption expenditure at constant prices are obtained as a residual. No specific information is available for the remaining expenditure items.

(c) Cost-structure of the gross domestic product. The estimates of compensation of employees are obtained in the process of estimating value added by industrial origin. The estimates are obtained from the statistical surveys held in 1970 and from accounting data. In the case of agriculture, hunting, forestry and fishing, the estimates are based on projections from census data on employment and statistics of average wages and salaries. Depreciation of assets owned by general government are not included in the estimates. Operating surplus is obtained as a residual and no information is available for the estimates of consumption of fixed capital and of net indirect taxes.

(d) Gross domestic product by kind of economic activity. The table of gross domestic product by kind of economic activity is prepared at market prices, i.e. producers' values. The production approach is used to estimate value added of almost all industries. The income approach is used to estimate the value added of producers of government services and some private services, while the expenditure approach is used for ownership of dwellings. Gross output of the trade sector is estimated by the commodity-flow approach. For agriculture, the gross value of production is obtained by multiplying the output of each commodity by the price paid to producers. The production and price data are derived from agricultural sample surveys and from various concerned institutions. The Federacion Nacional de Cafeteros supplies information on data for coffee. For livestock, the estimates are based on statistics of government controlled slaughterings and net exports with rough estimates made for uncontrolled slaughterings. Data for the petroleum industry are obtained directly from the oil companies. Information on the output and value of minerals is available from censuses of mines and concerned institutions. For manufacturing, results of surveys carried out by the Departamento Administrativo Nacional de Estadistica are used. The estimates are projected by applying volume and price indexes to both output and input. The basic data for electricity, gas and water are obtained from concerned enterprises and surveys. Coefficients calculated from these surveys are used to estimate value added of plants not covered. For urban construction, estimates are derived from building permits issued while rural construction estimates are based on an estimation of economic life of existing constructions and on demographic data. Estimates of public construction are obtained from the government records. For the trade sector, value added is based on estimates of the flow of goods through trade channels. The gross margins are based on data provided by the Banco de la Republica or recalculated from the Commercial Census 1967. The mark-ups are kept constant over the period of analysis. For transport, estimates are based on indormation provided by the Banco de la Republica. Data to measure the contribution of the communication sector are obtained by direct inquiries. Estimates for the financial institutions are obtained directly from the enterprises concerned through the Superintendencia Bancaria. The contribution of the government sector is measured by the wages and salaries paid to employees. Value added of other private services is estimated by the Banco de la Republica using the results of the Census of services in 1970. Constant input-output ratios have been assumed. For the constant price estimates, value added of the majority of industries is extrapolated by quantity index for output. For ownership of dwellings and producers of government services, value added is deflated by an index of rents and an index of wages and salaries, respectively.

1.1 Expenditure on the Gross Domestic Product, in Current Prices

Thousand Million Colombian pesos

	1980	1983	1984	1985	1986	1987	1988	1989	1990	1991	1992	1993
1 Government final consumption expenditure	159	335	426	531	666	868	1182	1597	2076	2685	3656	...
2 Private final consumption expenditure	1105	2208	2734	3446	4479	5919	7714	9943	13270	17348	23183	...
3 Gross capital formation	301	608	731	946	1222	1765	2580	3021	3752	4164	5707	...
A Increase in stocks	36	83	77	75	18	227	292	288	387	354	493	...
B Gross fixed capital formation	265	525	654	870	1204	1537	2288	2733	3365	3810	5214	...
Residential buildings	36	80	98	122	167	245	310	396	459	657	1004	...
Non-residential buildings	9	15	13	21	33	64	98	111	128	173	237	...
Other construction and land improvement etc.	98	211	280	427	547	508	858	956	1078	1268	1646	...
Other	122	219	264	301	457	721	1023	1270	1700	1712	2327	...
4 Exports of goods and services	275	340	486	717	1365	1588	2059	2866	4390	5902	6255	...
5 Less: Imports of goods and services	261	436	520	674	944	1317	1803	2300	3260	3992	5658	...
Equals: Gross Domestic Product	1579	3054	3857	4966	6788	8824	11731	15127	20228	26107	33143	...

1.2 Expenditure on the Gross Domestic Product, in Constant Prices

Million Colombian pesos

	1980	1983	1984	1985	1986	1987	1988	1989	1990	1991	1992	1993
	\multicolumn{12}{c}{At constant prices of: 1975}											
1 Government final consumption expenditure	54364	58652	61070	63818	64711	68330	75061	79281	81729	84385	90155	...
2 Private final consumption expenditure [a]	384698	403572	415128	422917	436600	453079	470019	485203	499839	507693	528842	...
3 Gross capital formation	103358	120628	113521	102574	107038	116901	126264	117013	115641	105537	146659	...
A Increase in stocks	15337	23184	14865	9069	6388	15430	13762	10402	12595	8852	33818	...
B Gross fixed capital formation	88021	97444	98656	93505	100650	101471	112502	106611	103046	96685	112841	...

Colombia

1.2 Expenditure on the Gross Domestic Product, in Constant Prices
(Continued)

Million Colombian pesos

	1980	1983	1984	1985	1986	1987	1988	1989	1990	1991	1992	1993
	\multicolumn{12}{c}{At constant prices of:1975}
Residential buildings	10788	14224	14327	14848	15931	17247	16705	16705	15504	18230	21513	...
Non-residential buildings	2414	2312	1632	2203	2723	3927	4579	4061	3761	4171	4386	...
Other construction and land improvement etc.	29496	33478	36300	38214	39682	30753	37407	32693	29145	26030	26867	...
Other	45323	47430	46397	38240	42314	49544	53811	53152	54636	48254	60075	...
4 Exports of goods and services	84450	72643	80129	91629	110601	119215	119514	129559	152353	170573	179598	...
5 Less: Imports of goods and services	101105	104115	99993	93377	97169	102361	109067	105988	114303	118212	166545	...
Equals: Gross Domestic Product	525765	551380	569855	587561	621781	655164	681791	705068	735259	749976	778709	...

a) Item 'Private final consumption expenditure' excludes direct purchases abroad by resident households and direct purchases in the domestic market by non-resident households.

1.3 Cost Components of the Gross Domestic Product

Thousand Million Colombian pesos

	1980	1983	1984	1985	1986	1987	1988	1989	1990	1991	1992	1993
1 Indirect taxes, net	158	254	361	517	799	1033	1254	1595	1990	2461	3247	...
A Indirect taxes	172	279	395	552	838	1076	1314	1666	2099	2610	3366	...
B Less: Subsidies	14	26	34	35	39	43	59	71	109	149	119	...
2 Consumption of fixed capital [a]	...	...	...	...	...	...	...	...	...	...	...	...
3 Compensation of employees paid by resident producers to:	657	1340	1673	2017	2575	3351	4466	5788	7555	9846	13079	...
A Resident households	656	1336	1666	2005	2560	3329	4455	5771	7519	9761	13021	...
B Rest of the world	1	4	6	13	16	22	11	17	36	85	58	...
4 Operating surplus [a]	764	1461	1823	2432	3414	4440	6011	7742	10682	13799	16817	...
Equals: Gross Domestic Product	1579	3054	3857	4966	6788	8824	11731	15127	20228	26107	33143	...

a) Item 'Operating surplus' includes consumption of fixed capital.

1.4 General Government Current Receipts and Disbursements

Thousand Million Colombian pesos

	1980	1983	1984	1985	1986	1987	1988	1989	1990	1991	1992	1993
	\multicolumn{12}{c}{Receipts}
1 Operating surplus	-14	-26	-18	-17	3	-209	-54	-72	-120	20	-24	...
2 Property and entrepreneurial income	15	31	40	57	80	129	178	259	419	549	752	...
3 Taxes, fees and contributions	266	457	624	853	1250	1656	2164	2795	3671	5315	6768	...
A Indirect taxes	172	279	395	552	838	1076	1314	1666	2099	2610	3366	...
B Direct taxes	51	84	106	143	204	303	496	633	885	1770	2135	...
C Social security contributions	39	89	114	146	193	257	336	467	650	867	1133	...
D Compulsory fees, fines and penalties	3	5	8	12	16	20	19	29	37	68	134	...
4 Other current transfers	58	132	170	200	281	370	498	650	812	1182	1844	...
Total Current Receipts of General Government	324	594	815	1092	1614	1946	2787	3632	4782	7066	9340	...
	\multicolumn{12}{c}{Disbursements}
1 Government final consumption expenditure	159	335	426	531	666	868	1182	1597	2076	2685	3656	...
2 Property income	14	39	54	63	97	129	193	251	399	472	681	...
3 Subsidies	14	26	34	35	39	43	59	71	109	149	119	...
4 Other current transfers	88	215	277	331	460	607	810	1103	1439	2008	3052	...
A Social security benefits	17	44	60	80	105	141	191	265	359	502	730	...
B Social assistance grants [a]	12	35	44	48	68	87	111	161	223	299	445	...
C Other	59	135	173	203	287	380	509	677	857	1207	1877	...
5 Net saving	49	-21	25	131	352	298	542	610	759	1752	1832	...
Total Current Disbursements and Net Saving of General Government	324	594	815	1092	1614	1946	2787	3632	4782	7066	9340	...

a) Item 'Social assistance grants' refers to health only.

Colombia

1.5 Current Income and Outlay of Corporate and Quasi-Corporate Enterprises, Summary

Thousand Million Colombian pesos

	1980	1983	1984	1985	1986	1987	1988	1989	1990	1991	1992	1993
					Receipts							
1 Operating surplus	241	457	579	837	1278	1860	2436	3295	4694	5472	6598	...
2 Property and entrepreneurial income received	158	339	426	552	692	902	1336	1895	2522	3393	4201	...
3 Current transfers	21	48	64	79	101	143	238	347	457	710	941	...
Total Current Receipts	420	844	1069	1468	2072	2905	4010	5537	7673	9575	11740	...
					Disbursements							
1 Property and entrepreneurial income	248	530	676	924	1221	1600	2148	3104	4220	5534	6854	...
2 Direct taxes and other current payments to general government	32	56	70	91	134	203	370	481	695	1451	1798	...
3 Other current transfers	23	52	70	90	120	170	293	390	522	805	1082	...
4 Net saving	118	207	253	363	596	932	1200	1562	2236	1785	2006	...
Total Current Disbursements and Net Saving	420	844	1069	1468	2072	2905	4010	5537	7673	9575	11738	...

1.6 Current Income and Outlay of Households and Non-Profit Institutions

Thousand Million Colombian pesos

	1980	1983	1984	1985	1986	1987	1988	1989	1990	1991	1992	1993
					Receipts							
1 Compensation of employees	658	1337	1669	2007	2563	3333	4460	5777	7528	9780	13039	...
2 Operating surplus of private unincorporated enterprises	537	1029	1262	1612	2133	2789	3629	4520	6108	8308	10243	...
3 Property and entrepreneurial income	105	204	241	310	413	516	690	958	1302	1798	1547	...
4 Current transfers	67	159	221	304	477	683	886	1160	1626	2543	4114	...
A Social security benefits	32	86	110	139	186	248	331	474	653	924	1329	...
B Social assistance grants												...
C Other	35	74	111	165	291	435	555	686	974	1619	2785	...
Total Current Receipts	1367	2730	3393	4233	5586	7322	9666	12415	16565	22429	28943	...
					Disbursements							
1 Private final consumption expenditure	1105	2208	2734	3446	4479	5919	7714	9943	13270	17348	23183	...
2 Property income	29	78	102	128	157	229	343	513	673	898	1041	...
3 Direct taxes and other current transfers n.e.c. to general government	62	122	160	210	278	377	481	648	877	1254	1604	...
A Social security contributions	39	89	114	146	193	257	336	467	650	867	1133	...
B Direct taxes	20	30	40	56	76	109	134	164	207	359	402	...
C Fees, fines and penalties	2	3	5	8	9	11	11	17	20	28	69	...
4 Other current transfers	29	59	79	97	127	176	231	318	419	546	752	...
5 Net saving	142	262	320	353	545	620	898	993	1326	2383	2363	...
Total Current Disbursements and Net Saving	1367	2730	3393	4233	5586	7322	9666	12415	16565	22429	28943	...

1.7 External Transactions on Current Account, Summary

Thousand Million Colombian pesos

	1980	1983	1984	1985	1986	1987	1988	1989	1990	1991	1992	1993
					Payments to the Rest of the World							
1 Imports of goods and services	261	436	520	674	944	1317	1803	2300	3260	3992	5658	...
2 Factor income to the rest of the world	36	99	145	226	336	481	565	883	1259	1495	1605	...
A Compensation of employees	1	4	6	13	16	22	11	18	37	85	58	...
B Property and entrepreneurial income	35	96	138	213	320	459	554	865	1222	1410	1547	...
3 Current transfers to the rest of the world	2	2	3	4	4	5	9	11	8	29	94	...
4 Surplus of the nation on current transactions	8	-159	-134	-98	271	85	60	143	570	1755	494	...
Payments to the Rest of the World and Surplus of the Nation on Current Transactions	307	378	534	805	1555	1888	2437	3337	5097	7271	7851	...

Colombia

1.7 External Transactions on Current Account, Summary
(Continued)

Thousand Million Colombian pesos

	1980	1983	1984	1985	1986	1987	1988	1989	1990	1991	1992	1993
					Receipts From The Rest of the World							
1 Exports of goods and services	275	340	486	717	1365	1588	2059	2866	4390	5902	6255	...
2 Factor income from rest of the world	24	23	16	20	34	52	81	116	183	265	323	...
A Compensation of employees	2	1	2	3	3	4	5	6	9	18	18	...
B Property and entrepreneurial income	23	22	14	17	31	48	76	110	174	247	305	...
3 Current transfers from rest of the world	8	15	32	68	156	248	297	355	524	1103	1273	...
Receipts from the Rest of the World on Current Transactions	307	378	534	805	1555	1888	2437	3337	5097	7271	7851	...

1.8 Capital Transactions of The Nation, Summary

Thousand Million Colombian pesos

	1980	1983	1984	1985	1986	1987	1988	1989	1990	1991	1992	1993
					Finance of Gross Capital Formation							
Gross saving	309	448	598	847	1493	1850	2640	3165	4322	5920	6201	...
1 Consumption of fixed capital	...	...	...	...	...	...	...	...	...	...	...	...
2 Net saving a	309	448	598	847	1493	1850	2640	3165	4322	5920	6201	...
A General government	49	-21	25	131	352	298	542	610	759	1752	1832	...
B Corporate and quasi-corporate enterprises	118	207	253	363	596	932	1200	1562	2236	1785	2006	...
C Other	142	262	320	353	545	620	898	993	1327	2383	2363	...
Less: Surplus of the nation on current transactions	8	-159	-134	-98	271	85	60	143	570	1755	494	...
Finance of Gross Capital Formation	...	...	...	...	...	...	...	...	...	...	...	...
					Gross Capital Formation							
Increase in stocks	36	83	77	75	18	227	292	288	387	354	493	...
Gross fixed capital formation	265	525	654	870	1204	1537	2288	2733	3364	3810	5214	...
1 General government	59	113	133	137	203	280	421	564	671	808	995	...
2 Corporate and quasi-corporate enterprises	139	281	370	563	747	875	1360	1536	1946	2042	2825	...
3 Other	66	131	152	170	255	382	507	633	747	960	1394	...
Gross Capital Formation	301	608	731	946	1222	1765	2580	3022	3752	4164	5707	...

a) Item 'Net saving' includes consumption of fixed capital.

1.10 Gross Domestic Product by Kind of Activity, in Current Prices

Thousand Million Colombian pesos

	1980	1983	1984	1985	1986	1987	1988	1989	1990	1991	1992	1993
1 Agriculture, hunting, forestry and fishing	306	572	671	844	1186	1594	1965	2429	3284	4445	5196	...
2 Mining and quarrying	36	89	127	207	332	578	722	1158	1884	2141	2348	...
3 Manufacturing	367	641	853	1062	1526	1793	2482	3159	4035	5332	6440	...
4 Electricity, gas and water	21	63	83	107	151	201	271	377	509	691	884	...
5 Construction	75	170	220	342	447	495	776	894	1001	1312	1883	...
6 Wholesale and retail trade, restaurants and hotels	210	414	535	698	921	1240	1684	2154	2861	3763	5148	...
7 Transport, storage and communication	141	254	318	405	527	713	969	1270	1843	2515	3457	...
8 Finance, insurance, real estate and business services	217	439	504	608	766	985	1323	1668	2255	2978	3796	...
9 Community, social and personal services	83	178	216	256	332	431	555	743	987	1348	1822	...
Total, Industries	1454	2819	3527	4529	6188	8030	10746	13852	18659	24525	30974	...
Producers of Government Services	121	267	349	424	547	714	932	1239	1607	1972	2715	...
Other Producers	...	...	...	...	...	...	...	...	...	...	...	...
Subtotal	1576	3085	3876	4953	6736	8743	11679	15091	20266	26497	33689	...
Less: Imputed bank service charge	40	105	104	119	156	227	369	474	657	986	1199	...
Plus: Import duties	44	74	85	131	208	308	421	510	619	596	653	...
Plus: Value added tax	...	...	...	...	...	...	...	...	...	...	...	...
Equals: Gross Domestic Product	1579	3054	3857	4966	6788	8824	11731	15127	20228	26107	33143	...

Colombia

1.11 Gross Domestic Product by Kind of Activity, in Constant Prices

Million Colombian pesos

	1980	1983	1984	1985	1986	1987	1988	1989	1990	1991	1992	1993
					At constant prices of:1975							
1 Agriculture, hunting, forestry and fishing	119314	124196	126375	128456	132792	141270	145182	151423	160245	166918	163825	...
2 Mining and quarrying	6661	8156	9948	13730	22262	27624	28876	32237	34146	33928	32991	...
3 Manufacturing	117672	114197	121035	124610	132021	140229	142887	150913	157290	158583	167924	...
4 Electricity, gas and water	5210	5640	5930	6111	6478	7056	7429	7819	8114	8362	7854	...
5 Construction	17632	22193	23606	25641	26890	24191	27382	25154	21866	21920	23752	...
6 Wholesale and retail trade, restaurants and hotels	66681	68598	69984	71239	73800	77059	80928	82420	84741	85104	88878	...
7 Transport, storage and communication	48944	53131	54486	55044	55569	57426	59396	61307	63597	65782	69228	...
8 Finance, insurance, real estate and business services	73463	84284	81764	83299	86953	91560	98816	101026	107289	112588	117164	...
9 Community, social and personal services	25811	27945	28214	28324	29410	30950	31518	32153	32978	34186	34869	...
Total, Industries	481388	508340	521342	536454	566175	597365	622414	644452	670266	687371	706485	...
Producers of Government Services	40840	43371	47242	49272	52290	55989	59905	62274	64049	63842	66840	...
Other Producers	...	...	...	...	...	...	...	...	...	...	...	...
Subtotal	522228	551711	568584	585726	618461	653354	682319	706726	734315	751213	773325	...
Less: Imputed bank service charge	14095	19071	15503	14409	14380	16708	20584	21057	20349	22241	23220	...
Plus: Import duties	17632	18740	16774	16244	17696	18518	20056	19399	21293	21004	28604	...
Plus: Value added tax	...	...	...	...	...	...	...	...	...	...	...	...
Equals: Gross Domestic Product	525765	551380	569855	587561	621781	655164	681791	705068	735259	749976	778709	...

1.12 Relations Among National Accounting Aggregates

Thousand Million Colombian pesos

	1980	1983	1984	1985	1986	1987	1988	1989	1990	1991	1992	1993
Gross Domestic Product	1579	3054	3857	4966	6788	8824	11731	15127	20228	26107	33143	...
Plus: Net factor income from the rest of the world	-11	-76	-128	-206	-302	-429	-484	-766	-1075	-1229	-1282	...
Factor income from the rest of the world	24	23	16	20	34	52	81	116	183	265	323	...
Less: Factor income to the rest of the world	36	99	145	226	336	481	565	882	1258	1494	1605	...
Equals: Gross National Product	1568	2978	3728	4760	6486	8395	11248	14361	19153	24878	31861	...
Less: Consumption of fixed capital	...	...	...	...	...	...	...	...	...	...	...	...
Equals: National Income [a]	1568	2978	3728	4760	6486	8395	11248	14361	19153	24878	31861	...
Plus: Net current transfers from the rest of the world	6	13	29	64	152	243	288	344	516	1074	1180	...
Current transfers from the rest of the world	8	15	32	68	156	248	297	355	524	1103	1273	...
Less: Current transfers to the rest of the world	2	2	3	4	4	5	9	11	8	29	93	...
Equals: National Disposable Income [b]	1573	2991	3757	4824	6638	8638	11536	14705	19669	25952	33041	...
Less: Final consumption	1264	2543	3160	3977	5145	6788	8896	11539	15347	20032	26840	...
Equals: Net Saving [c]	309	448	598	847	1493	1850	2640	3165	4322	5920	6201	...
Less: Surplus of the nation on current transactions	8	-159	-134	-98	271	85	60	143	570	1756	494	...
Equals: Net Capital Formation [d]	301	608	731	946	1222	1765	2580	3023	3752	4164	5707	...

a) Item 'National income' includes consumption of fixed capital.
b) Item 'National disposable income' includes consumption of fixed capital.
c) Item 'Net saving' includes consumption of fixed capital.
d) Item 'Net capital formation' includes consumption of fixed capital.

2.1 Government Final Consumption Expenditure by Function, in Current Prices

Million Colombian pesos

	1980	1983	1984	1985	1986	1987	1988	1989	1990	1991	1992	1993
1 General public services	44344	104278	132433	166107	207161	267555	354711	469582	640031	798463	...	...
2 Defence	16614	36105	43597	61574	73822	99066	150136	209996	251995	309467	...	...
3 Public order and safety	...	...	...	...	...	...	...	...	...	...	...	...
4 Education	42555	91368	127906	151915	197219	256184	332570	425965	546058	721003	...	...
5 Health	14103	31101	31086	51851	62259	83983	113203	158312	204522	252560	...	...
6 Social security and welfare	11694	21046	29359	33334	37157	48191	69336	101750	149628	199354	...	...
7 Housing and community amenities	1212	1137	1534	2139	3798	5865	7415	9105	11885	16945	...	...
8 Recreational, cultural and religious affairs	1216	2993	3770	5252	6707	6629	10418	13358	18843	23242	...	...
9 Economic services	27471	44323	52205	57715	76928	98954	141675	204614	250618	343402	...	...
10 Other functions	162	2214	3741	1377	763	1956	2906	3872	2879	20105	...	...
Total Government Final Consumption Expenditure	159371	334565	425631	531264	665814	868383	1182370	1596555	2076459	2684541	...	...

Colombia

2.3 Total Government Outlays by Function and Type

Million Colombian pesos

		Final Consumption Expenditures				Other Current Transfers & Property Income	Total Current Disbursements	Gross Capital Formation	Other Capital Outlays	Total Outlays
		Total	Compensation of Employees	Other	Subsidies					

1980

1	General public services	44344	35678	8666	22	1209	45575	6134	243	51952
2	Defence	16614	9974	6640	...	12	16626	301	3	16930
3	Public order and safety	...	...	...	...	...	...	...	...	...
4	Education	42555	39789	2766	735	607	43897	5344	33	49274
5	Health	14103	9120	4983	192	448	14743	2162	20	16925
6	Social security and welfare	11694	16721	-5027	5	30597	42296	6943	110	49349
7	Housing and community amenities	1212	805	407	1545	183	2940	2575	61	5576
8	Recreation, culture and religion	1216	866	350	65	247	1528	1335	27	2890
9	Economic services	27471	21942	5529	11096	3843	42410	30451	3787	76648
10	Other functions	162	...	162	...	9673	9835	...	...	9835
	Total	159371	134895	24476	13660	46819	219850	55245	4284	279379

1985

1	General public services	166107	138820	27287	204	9976	176287	12225	417	188929
2	Defence	61574	34111	27463	-	15	61589	292	1100	62981
3	Public order and safety	...	...	...	...	...	...	...	...	...
4	Education	151915	141394	10521	3700	2253	157868	14384	43	172295
5	Health	51851	34663	17188	416	684	52951	8766	104	61821
6	Social security and welfare	33334	58839	-25505	8	80751	114093	8366	84	122543
7	Housing and community amenities	2139	1732	407	1242	1118	4499	4539	925	9963
8	Recreation, culture and religion	5252	3818	1434	49	996	6297	3253	64	9614
9	Economic services	57715	63018	-5303	29551	23766	111032	78523	73844	263399
10	Other functions	1377	-	1377	-	34440	35817	126	-	35943
	Total	531264	476395	54869	35170	153999	720433	130474	76581	927488

1990

1	General public services	640031	507920	...	573	...	...	73313	...	790220
2	Defence	251995	143395	...	...	...	...	1583	...	253600
3	Public order and safety	...	...	...	...	...	...	...	...	...
4	Education	546058	508942	...	2058	...	...	43777	...	604302
5	Health	204522	131532	...	135	...	...	27016	...	237914
6	Social security and welfare	149628	239496	...	65	...	...	48990	...	586737
7	Housing and community amenities	11885	10150	...	178	...	...	41273	...	63934
8	Recreation, culture and religion	18843	14499	...	361	...	...	24349	...	54695
9	Economic services	250618	246427	...	105461	...	...	410333	...	952395
10	Other functions	2879	...	...	...	...	...	428	...	245599
	Total	2076459	1802361	...	108831	...	...	671062	...	3789396

1991

1	General public services	798463	616273	...	1269	...	...	94669	...	997558
2	Defence	309467	172074	...	...	...	...	13939	...	324686
3	Public order and safety	...	...	...	...	...	...	...	...	...
4	Education	721003	640419	...	1831	...	...	66893	...	803819
5	Health	252560	160469	...	438	...	...	23849	...	295922
6	Social security and welfare	199354	319162	...	3876	...	...	67776	...	805606
7	Housing and community amenities	16945	12121	...	35582	...	...	50784	...	115130
8	Recreation, culture and religion	23242	16006	...	646	...	...	35591	...	69067
9	Economic services	343402	293299	...	105831	...	...	454178	...	1285874
10	Other functions	20105	...	...	...	...	...	-	...	321078
	Total	2684541	2229823	...	149473	...	...	807679	...	5018740

Colombia

2.5 Private Final Consumption Expenditure by Type and Purpose, in Current Prices

Thousand Million Colombian pesos

	1980	1983	1984	1985	1986	1987	1988	1989	1990	1991	1992	1993
Final Consumption Expenditure of Resident Households											
1 Food, beverages and tobacco	420	814	990	1277	1650	2102	2702	3454	4602	6003	7931	...
A Food	353	685	832	1065	1371	1739	2251	2870	3812	5030	6615	...
B Non-alcoholic beverages	13	24	27	35	47	68	84	109	154	196	266	...
C Alcoholic beverages	41	79	100	135	183	239	296	388	525	636	862	...
D Tobacco	13	26	32	42	49	56	71	82	111	141	188	...
2 Clothing and footwear	76	132	178	219	272	364	489	582	668	782	1035	...
3 Gross rent, fuel and power	139	290	353	425	528	654	817	1053	1376	1819	2316	...
A Fuel and power	15	40	54	71	98	126	167	233	315	423	519	...
B Other	124	249	298	355	429	528	651	820	1061	1396	1797	...
4 Furniture, furnishings and household equipment and operation	62	116	149	191	254	349	490	631	841	1003	1328	...
A Household operation	28	57	74	100	135	183	253	339	466	544	754	...
B Other	34	60	75	91	118	166	236	292	375	459	574	...
5 Medical care and health expenses	61	132	164	204	280	377	486	656	885	1084	1487	...
6 Transport and communication	160	312	394	483	637	883	1210	1551	2252	3119	4285	...
A Personal transport equipment	59	104	127	154	200	281	384	465	601	784	1067	...
B Other	101	208	267	330	437	602	826	1086	1651	2335	3218	...
7 Recreational, entertainment, education and cultural services	58	123	150	191	258	351	454	604	788	995	1261	...
A Education	16	37	43	56	72	94	122	167	223	299	402	...
B Other	42	86	108	135	187	257	332	437	565	696	859	...
8 Miscellaneous goods and services	133	279	343	435	557	755	1036	1344	1826	2512	3528	...
A Personal care	10	20	26	37	47	61	87	120	168	206	271	...
B Expenditures in restaurants, cafes and hotels	101	213	259	317	405	549	736	955	1300	1876	2682	...
C Other	21	46	59	81	105	144	214	269	358	430	575	...
Total Final Consumption Expenditure in the Domestic Market by Households, of which	1109	2197	2722	3425	4436	5835	7684	9876	13238	17317	23171	...
Plus: Direct purchases abroad by resident households	15	32	39	52	130	177	177	210	262	361	385	...
Less: Direct purchases in the domestic market by non-resident households	19	21	27	32	87	93	148	143	230	330	373	...
Equals: Final Consumption Expenditure of Resident Households [a]	1105	2208	2734	3446	4479	5919	7714	9943	13270	17348	23183	...
Final Consumption Expenditure of Private Non-profit Institutions Serving Households											
Equals: Final Consumption Expenditure of Private Non-profit Organisations Serving Households	...	...	...	...	...	...	...	...	...	...	...	...
Private Final Consumption Expenditure	1105	2208	2734	3446	4479	5919	7714	9943	13270	17348	23183	...

a) Item 'Final consumption expenditure of resident households' includes consumption expenditure of private non-profit institutions serving households.

2.6 Private Final Consumption Expenditure by Type and Purpose, in Constant Prices

Million Colombian pesos

	1980	1983	1984	1985	1986	1987	1988	1989	1990	1991	1992	1993
At constant prices of: 1975											
Final Consumption Expenditure of Resident Households											
1 Food, beverages and tobacco	156402	161241	164559	169747	174805	178345	186048	194143	200823	201105	209847	...
A Food	134192	138878	142072	146134	150794	153633	162177	169799	176125	175720	183650	...
B Non-alcoholic beverages	3820	3871	3534	3655	3908	4365	4382	4431	4592	4468	4620	...
C Alcoholic beverages	13452	13575	13860	14585	15207	15808	15473	15941	16320	16942	17511	...
D Tobacco	4938	4917	5093	5373	4896	4539	4016	3972	3786	3975	4066	...
2 Clothing and footwear	27635	26512	27143	26376	26993	27727	28344	29879	29697	29236	31707	...
3 Gross rent, fuel and power	43790	48835	50642	52452	54351	56858	58833	60848	62828	64963	65920	...
A Fuel and power	4060	4755	5043	5298	5510	5843	6080	6427	6765	6970	6640	...
B Other	39730	44080	45599	47154	48841	51015	52753	54421	56063	57993	59280	...
4 Furniture, furnishings and household equipment and operation	22589	22827	23250	22871	23819	25219	26774	26992	28022	28760	30192	...
A Household operation	10285	10972	11094	11225	11952	12349	13193	13436	14261	14653	15523	...

Colombia

2.6 Private Final Consumption Expenditure by Type and Purpose, in Constant Prices
(Continued)

Million Colombian pesos

	1980	1983	1984	1985	1986	1987	1988	1989	1990	1991	1992	1993
					At constant prices of:1975							
B Other	12304	11855	12156	11646	11867	12870	13581	13556	13761	14107	14669	...
5 Medical care and health expenses	19670	21164	21854	22729	23309	25421	25312	26188	26965	27931	29686	...
6 Transport and communication	50594	54536	55613	55245	56257	58491	61012	62921	64109	66154	69268	...
A Personal transport equipment	16046	15167	15424	14784	15074	16774	17821	17337	17375	17334	19037	...
B Other	34548	39369	40189	40461	41183	41717	43191	45584	46734	48820	50231	...
7 Recreational, entertainment, education and cultural services	20835	22233	25318	24851	26787	28947	29338	30307	30829	31686	32261	...
A Education	6006	6456	6026	6268	6692	7119	7486	7592	7815	8142	8478	...
B Other	14829	15777	19292	18583	20095	21828	21852	22715	23014	23544	23783	...
8 Miscellaneous goods and services	43183	46224	46749	48646	50279	52071	54358	53925	56566	57858	59961	...
A Personal care	4155	4326	4081	4705	5032	5137	5470	5607	6195	6375	6691	...
B Expenditures in restaurants, cafes and hotels	31522	33442	33944	34623	35662	36732	37828	37828	38963	40162	41272	...
C Other	7506	8456	8724	9318	9585	10202	11060	10490	11408	11321	11998	...
Total Final Consumption Expenditure in the Domestic Market by Households, of which	384698	403572	415128	422917	436600	453079	470019	485203	499839	507693	528842	
Plus: Direct purchases abroad by resident households	5958	8193	8201	7798	15528	15882	11905	10660	11905	11770	12154	...
Less: Direct purchases in the domestic market by non-resident households	6117	4670	4773	4241	7490	7393	9269	6813	9269	10104	11377	...
Equals: Final Consumption Expenditure of Resident Households [a]	384539	407095	418556	426474	444638	461568	472655	489050	502475	509359	529619	

Final Consumption Expenditure of Private Non-profit Institutions Serving Households

| Equals: Final Consumption Expenditure of Private Non-profit Organisations Serving Households | ... | ... | ... | ... | ... | ... | ... | ... | ... | ... | ... | |
| Private Final Consumption Expenditure | 384539 | 407095 | 418556 | 426474 | 444638 | 461568 | 472655 | 489050 | 502475 | 509359 | 529619 | ... |

a) Item 'Final consumption expenditure of resident households' includes consumption expenditure of private non-profit institutions serving households.

3.12 General Government Income and Outlay Account: Total and Subsectors

Million Colombian pesos

	1980					1985				
	Total General Government	Central Government	State or Provincial Government	Local Government	Social Security Funds	Total General Government	Central Government	State or Provincial Government	Local Government	Social Security Funds
					Receipts					
1 Operating surplus	-14163	-14740	...	492	85	-17318	-18521	...	734	469
2 Property and entrepreneurial income	14943	7085	...	5050	2808	56914	26200	...	18633	12081
A Withdrawals from public quasi-corporations	2146	...	...	2146	...	4363	...	...	4363	...
B Interest	10139	6420	...	1037	2682	36988	22556	...	2544	11888
C Dividends	1678	370	...	1182	126	6444	2624	...	3636	184
D Net land rent and royalties	980	295	...	685	...	9119	1020	...	8090	9
3 Taxes, fees and contributions	265749	187887	...	38281	39581	852669	578220	...	126957	147492
A Indirect taxes	172044	134648	...	37396	...	551948	430711	...	121237	...
B Direct taxes	50946	50407	...	406	133	142593	137082	...	4319	1192
Income	49855	49855	...	...	...	129035	129035	...	...	...
Other	1091	552	...	406	133	13558	8047	...	4319	1192
C Social security contributions	39361	...	...	...	39361	145887	...	...	...	145887
D Fees, fines and penalties	3398	2832	...	479	87	12241	10427	...	1401	413
4 Other current transfers	57549	10398	...	44330	2821	199539	30177	...	164465	4897
A Casualty insurance claims	...	...	...	...	...	...	...	...	...	...
B Transfers from other government subsectors	43553	371	...	41290	1892	157446	1592	...	151794	4060
C Transfers from the rest of the world	1607	1607	...	...	...	3415	3281	...	134	...
D Other transfers, except imputed	1143	513	...	625	5	4649	2528	...	2106	15
E Imputed unfunded employee pension and welfare contributions	11246	7907	...	2415	924	34029	22776	...	10431	822
Total Current Receipts	324078	190630	...	88153	45295	1091804	616076	...	310789	164939

Colombia

3.12 General Government Income and Outlay Account: Total and Subsectors
(Continued)

Million Colombian pesos

		1980					1985			
		Total General Government	Central Government	State or Provincial Government	Local Government	Social Security Funds	Total General Government	Central Government	State or Provincial Government	Local Government	Social Security Funds

Disbursements

1	Government final consumption expenditure	159371	85866	...	70035	3470	531264	269005	...	250511	11748
2	Property income	13612	13034	...	576	2	62636	54351	...	8161	124
	A Interest	13612	13034	...	576	2	62636	54351	...	8161	124
	B Net land rent and royalties	...	...	...	...	...	...	...	...	...	...
3	Subsidies	13660	12416	...	1232	12	35170	32991	...	2173	6
4	Other current transfers	88006	54291	...	3784	29931	331262	185331	...	15786	130145
	A Casualty insurance premiums, net	...	...	...	...	...	...	...	...	...	...
	B Transfers to other government subsectors	43553	42962	...	534	57	157446	155057	...	1891	498
	C Social security benefits	16696	...	...	...	16696	79734	...	...	...	79734
	D Social assistance grants	12244	...	...	...	12244	48424	...	...	...	48424
	E Unfunded employee pension and welfare benefits	11246	7907	...	2415	924	34029	22776	...	10431	822
	F Transfers to private non-profit institutions serving households	3889	3060	...	821	8	9921	5811	...	3464	646
	G Other transfers n.e.c.	...	...	...	...	...	...	...	...	...	...
	H Transfers to the rest of the world	378	362	...	14	2	1708	1687	...	-	21
	Net saving	49429	25023	...	12526	11880	131472	74398	...	34158	22916
	Total Current Disbursements and Net Saving	324078	190630	...	88153	45295	1091804	616076	...	310789	164939

		1990					1991				
		Total General Government	Central Government	State or Provincial Government	Local Government	Social Security Funds	Total General Government	Central Government	State or Provincial Government	Local Government	Social Security Funds

Receipts

1	Operating surplus	-120787	-124409	...	1540	2082	19801	13972	...	2357	3472
2	Property and entrepreneurial income	419226	198350	...	181262	39614	549379	271372	...	208150	69857
	A Withdrawals from public quasi-corporations	13711	...	...	13711	...	19015	...	...	19015	...
	B Interest	189776	128471	...	23307	37998	267981	164179	...	36125	67677
	C Dividends	76254	58406	...	16232	1616	111494	91584	...	17730	2180
	D Net land rent and royalties	139485	11473	...	128012	...	150889	15609	...	135280	...
3	Taxes, fees and contributions	3671872	2495299	...	517679	658894	5315432	3786380	...	650529	878523
	A Indirect taxes	2099540	1611495	...	488045	...	2610355	1993328	...	617027	...
	B Direct taxes	885216	857878	...	18890	8448	1769741	1737137	...	22612	9992
	Income	771977	771977	...	...	...	1659388	1659388	...	...	...
	Other	113239	85901	...	18890	8448	110353	77749	...	22612	9992
	C Social security contributions	649751	...	...	...	649751	867343	...	...	...	867343
	D Fees, fines and penalties	37365	25926	...	10744	695	67993	55915	...	10890	1188
4	Other current transfers	811876	93295	...	705721	12860	1181804	129265	...	1011428	41111
	A Casualty insurance claims	...	...	...	...	...	...	...	...	...	...
	B Transfers from other government subsectors	650692	6170	...	634388	10134	986170	11358	...	938412	36400
	C Transfers from the rest of the world	2069	1655	...	414	...	26415	26380	...	35	...
	D Other transfers, except imputed	22405	6461	...	15925	19	31496	9737	...	21520	239
	E Imputed unfunded employee pension and welfare contributions	136710	79009	...	54994	2707	137723	81790	...	51461	4472
	Total Current Receipts	4782187	2662535	...	1406202	713450	7066416	4200989	...	1872464	992963

Disbursements

1	Government final consumption expenditure	2076459	1088533	...	941700	46226	2684541	1431518	...	1189355	63668
2	Property income	398677	339414	...	58007	1256	471459	389132	...	81249	1078
	A Interest	398677	339414	...	58007	1256	471459	389132	...	81249	1078
	B Net land rent and royalties	...	...	...	...	...	...	...	...	...	...
3	Subsidies	108831	92215	...	16616	...	149473	133631	...	15842	...

Colombia

3.12 General Government Income and Outlay Account: Total and Subsectors
(Continued)

Million Colombian pesos

		1990				1991			
	Total General Government	Central Government	State or Provincial Government	Local Government	Social Security Funds	Total General Government	Central Government	State or Provincial Government	Local Government	Social Security Funds
4 Other current transfers	1439293	745197	...	98494	595602	2008474	1091274	...	103662	813538
A Casualty insurance premiums, net	...	...	...	...	...	...	...	...	...	...
B Transfers to other government subsectors	650692	642905	...	5984	1803	986170	973106	...	10479	2585
C Social security benefits	359840	...	...	...	359840	501971	...	...	...	501971
D Social assistance grants	222925	...	...	...	222925	299476	...	...	...	299476
E Unfunded employee pension and welfare benefits	136710	79009	...	54994	2707	137723	81790	...	51461	4472
F Transfers to private non-profit institutions serving households	62257	16620	...	37329	8308	75337	28711	...	41621	5005
G Other transfers n.e.c.	...	...	...	...	...	...	...	...	...	...
H Transfers to the rest of the world	6869	6663	...	187	19	7797	7667	...	101	29
Net saving	758927	397176	...	291385	70366	1752469	1155434	...	482356	114679
Total Current Disbursements and Net Saving	4782187	2662535	...	1406202	713450	7066416	4200989	...	1872464	992963

		1992			
	Total General Government	Central Government	State or Provincial Government	Local Government	Social Security Funds
					Receipts
1 Operating surplus	-23694	-28387	...	4219	474
2 Property and entrepreneurial income	752098	403536	...	259037	89525
A Withdrawals from public quasi-corporations	25485	...	...	25485	...
B Interest	330156	197472	...	46102	86582
C Dividends	160019	134841	...	22235	2943
D Net land rent and royalties	236438	71223	...	165215	...
3 Taxes, fees and contributions	6768414	4710129	...	909832	1148453
A Indirect taxes	3365912	2499943	...	865969	...
B Direct taxes	2135386	2091049	...	30807	13530
Income	2039235	2039235	...	...	...
Other	96151	51814	...	30807	13530
C Social security contributions	1133406	...	...	...	1133406
D Fees, fines and penalties	133710	119137	...	13056	1517
4 Other current transfers	1843606	181178	...	1598397	64031
A Casualty insurance claims	...	...	...	...	...
B Transfers from other government subsectors	1565871	7244	...	1501470	57157
C Transfers from the rest of the world	30801	30758	...	43	...
D Other transfers, except imputed	47504	21371	...	25809	324
E Imputed unfunded employee pension and welfare contributions	199430	121805	...	71075	6550
Total Current Receipts	9340424	5266456	...	2771485	1302483
					Disbursements
1 Government final consumption expenditure	3656324	2020061	...	1543221	93042
2 Property income	681510	575595	...	104344	1571
A Interest	681510	575595	...	104344	1571
B Net land rent and royalties	...	...	...	...	...
3 Subsidies	118753	97958	...	20795	...

Colombia

3.12 General Government Income and Outlay Account: Total and Subsectors
(Continued)

Million Colombian pesos

		1992			
	Total General Government	Central Government	State or Provincial Government	Local Government	Social Security Funds
4 Other current transfers	3051676	1730337	...	130090	1191249
A Casualty insurance premiums, net	...	...	...	...	...
B Transfers to other government subsectors	1565871	1556268	...	7384	2219
C Social security benefits	729598	...	...	...	729598
D Social assistance grants	445136	...	...	...	445136
E Unfunded employee pension and welfare benefits	199430	121805	...	71075	6550
F Transfers to private non-profit institutions serving households	102357	43022	...	51631	7704
G Other transfers n.e.c.	...	...	...	...	...
H Transfers to the rest of the world	9284	9242	...	-	42
Net saving	1832161	842505	...	973035	16621
Total Current Disbursements and Net Saving	9340424	5266456	...	2771485	1302483

3.13 General Government Capital Accumulation Account: Total and Subsectors

Million Colombian pesos

	1980					1985				
	Total General Government	Central Government	State or Provincial Government	Local Government	Social Security Funds	Total General Government	Central Government	State or Provincial Government	Local Government	Social Security Funds
					Finance of Gross Accumulation					
1 Gross saving	49429	25023	...	12526	11880	131472	74398	...	34158	22916
2 Capital transfers	29255	22735	...	2315	4205	-67387	-86840	...	5804	13649
A From other government subsectors	...	-4247	...	-	4247	...	-13649	...	...	13649
B From other resident sectors	...	...	...	...	...	...	...	...	...	...
C From rest of the world	29255	26982	...	2315	-42	-67387	-73191	...	5804	...
Finance of Gross Accumulation	78684	47758	...	14841	16085	64085	-12442	...	39962	36565
					Gross Accumulation					
1 Gross capital formation	55245	31830	...	18033	5382	130474	74598	...	51716	4160
A Increase in stocks	-3974	-3974	...	...	...	-6339	-6339	...	...	...
B Gross fixed capital formation	59219	35804	...	18033	5382	136813	80937	...	51716	4160
2 Purchases of land, net	482	160	...	276	46	2537	1652	...	885	-
3 Purchases of intangible assets, net	...	...	...	...	...	...	...	...	...	...
4 Capital transfers	...	...	...	...	...	...	...	...	...	...
Net lending	22957	15768	...	-3468	10657	-68926	-88692	...	-12639	32405
Gross Accumulation	78684	47758	...	14841	16085	64085	-12442	...	39962	36565

	1990					1991				
	Total General Government	Central Government	State or Provincial Government	Local Government	Social Security Funds	Total General Government	Central Government	State or Provincial Government	Local Government	Social Security Funds
					Finance of Gross Accumulation					
1 Gross saving	758927	397176	...	291385	70366	1752469	1155434	...	482356	114679
2 Capital transfers	11411	-46567	...	-21454	79432	-138973	-184851	...	-25229	71107
A From other government subsectors	...	...	...	...	...	...	...	...	...	...
B From other resident sectors	...	...	...	...	...	...	...	...	...	...
C From rest of the world	...	...	...	...	...	...	...	...	...	...
Finance of Gross Accumulation	770338	350609	...	269931	149798	1613496	970583	...	457127	185786
					Gross Accumulation					
1 Gross capital formation	642349	264964	...	327157	50228	956843	391896	...	488232	76715
A Increase in stocks	-28713	-39709	...	...	10996	149164	134709	...	...	14455
B Gross fixed capital formation	671062	304673	...	327157	39232	807679	257187	...	488232	62260
2 Purchases of land, net	14797	8345	...	2995	3457	16976	8691	...	3576	4709
3 Purchases of intangible assets, net	...	...	...	...	...	...	...	...	...	...
4 Capital transfers	...	...	...	...	...	...	...	...	...	...
Net lending	113192	77300	...	-60221	96113	639677	569996	...	-34681	104362
Gross Accumulation	770338	350609	...	269931	149798	1613496	970583	...	457127	185786

Colombia

3.13 General Government Capital Accumulation Account: Total and Subsectors

Million Colombian pesos

	1992			
	Total General Government	Central Government	State or Provincial Government	Local Government	Social Security Funds
Finance of Gross Accumulation					
1 Gross saving	1832161	842505	...	973035	16621
2 Capital transfers	-160080	-186539	...	-14065	40524
A From other government subsectors	...	...	...	...	...
B From other resident sectors	...	...	...	...	...
C From rest of the world	...	...	...	...	...
Finance of Gross Accumulation	1672081	655966	...	958970	57145
Gross Accumulation					
1 Gross capital formation	1006566	232367	...	662546	111653
A Increase in stocks	11416	-9399	...	...	20815
B Gross fixed capital formation	995150	241766	...	662546	90838
2 Purchases of land, net	20875	9652	...	4443	6780
3 Purchases of intangible assets, net	...	...	...	...	...
4 Capital transfers	...	...	...	...	...
Net lending	644640	413947	...	291981	-61288
Gross Accumulation	1672081	655966	...	958970	57145

3.22 Corporate and Quasi-Corporate Enterprise Income and Outlay Account: Total and Sectors

Million Colombian pesos

	1980			1985			1990			1991		
	TOTAL	Non-Financial	Financial	TOTAL	Non-Financial	Financial	TOTAL	Non-Financial	Financial	TOTAL	Non-Financial	Financial
Receipts												
1 Operating surplus	240597	259190	-18593	837314	920164	-82850	4694460	4896600	-202140	5471527	5987984	-516457
2 Property and entrepreneurial income	158459	29253	129206	551801	92626	459175	2521803	472142	2049661	3393106	640869	2752237
A Withdrawals from quasi-corporate enterprises	718	325	393	1825	995	830	33727	...	33727	44849	...	44849
B Interest	147094	22958	124136	521485	76074	445411	2304575	353459	1951116	3148557	517300	2631257
C Dividends	10251	5574	4677	27254	14320	12934	166372	101767	64605	183493	107413	76080
D Net land rent and royalties	396	396	...	1237	1237	...	17129	16916	213	16207	16156	51
3 Current transfers	21208	14001	7207	78718	54353	24365	457059	279449	177610	710173	412242	297931
A Casualty insurance claims	2657	2461	196	10769	10117	652	98360	90904	7456	166324	155524	10800
B Casualty insurance premiums, net, due to be received by insurance companies	3693	...	3693	15255	...	15255	141726	...	141726	247664	...	247664
C Current transfers from the rest of the world	...	...	...	...	...	...	...	...	...	...	...	...
D Other transfers except imputed	...	...	...	...	...	...	...	...	...	...	...	...
E Imputed unfunded employee pension and welfare contributions	14858	11540	3318	52694	44236	8458	216973	188545	28428	296185	256718	39467
Total Current Receipts	420264	302444	117820	1467833	1067143	400690	7673322	5648191	2025131	9574806	7041095	2533711
Disbursements												
1 Property and entrepreneurial income	247684	172804	74880	924108	585593	338515	4203952	2882714	1321238	5533524	3738857	1794667
A Withdrawals from quasi-corporations	5707	5691	16	38207	38171	36	382684	382684	...	474777	456014	18763
Public	...	2146	...	...	4363	...	...	...	...	...	...	...
Private	...	3545	...	...	33808	...	...	...	...	...	...	...
B Interest	154200	84849	69351	713067	382408	330659	2860559	1588066	1272493	3773144	2130643	1642501
C Dividends	85928	80415	5513	162196	154376	7820	802940	754260	48680	1115405	982002	133403
D Net land rent and royalties	1849	1849	...	10638	10638	...	157769	157704	65	170198	170198	-
2 Direct taxes and other current transfers n.e.c. to general government	31712	28775	2937	90859	83360	7499	695149	644457	50692	1442444	1345771	96673
A Direct taxes	30496	27626	2870	86214	79524	6690	678130	633380	44750	1410532	1325666	84866
B Fines, fees, penalties and other current transfers n.e.c.	1216	1149	67	4645	3836	809	17019	11077	5942	31912	20105	11807

Colombia

3.22 Corporate and Quasi-Corporate Enterprise Income and Outlay Account: Total and Sectors
(Continued)

Million Colombian pesos

	1980 TOTAL	1980 Non-Financial	1980 Financial	1985 TOTAL	1985 Non-Financial	1985 Financial	1990 TOTAL	1990 Non-Financial	1990 Financial	1991 TOTAL	1991 Non-Financial	1991 Financial
3 Other current transfers	23057	15453	7604	89779	60421	29358	521489	322098	199391	805955	458845	347110
A Casualty insurance premiums, net	2657	2461	196	10666	10025	641	103367	97502	5865	177714	160551	17163
B Casualty insurance claims liability of insurance companies	3693	...	3693	15255	...	15255	141726	...	141726	247664	...	247664
C Transfers to private non-profit institutions	...	...	...	...	...	...	...	...	...	...	...	...
D Unfunded employee pension and welfare benefits	14858	11540	3318	52694	44236	8458	216973	188545	28428	296185	256718	39467
E Social assistance grants	...	...	...	...	...	...	...	...	...	...	...	...
F Other transfers n.e.c.	...	...	...	...	...	...	...	...	...	...	...	...
G Transfers to the rest of the world [a]	1849	1452	397	11164	6160	5004	59423	36051	23372	84392	41576	42816
Net saving	117811	85412	32399	363087	337769	25318	2252732	1798922	453810	1784897	1497622	287275
Total Current Disbursements and Net Saving	420264	302444	117820	1467833	1067143	400690	7673322	5648191	2025131	9574806	7041095	2533711

	1992 TOTAL	1992 Non-Financial	1992 Financial
Receipts			
1 Operating surplus	6597561	7208371	-610810
2 Property and entrepreneurial income	4201265	879237	3322028
A Withdrawals from quasi-corporate enterprises	52922	...	52922
B Interest	3802555	685436	3117119
C Dividends	313021	161100	151921
D Net land rent and royalties	32767	32701	66
3 Current transfers	940806	552194	388612
A Casualty insurance claims	210553	197270	13283
B Casualty insurance premiums, net, due to be received by insurance companies	312777	...	312777
C Current transfers from the rest of the world	...	...	...
D Other transfers except imputed	...	...	...
E Imputed unfunded employee pension and welfare contributions	417476	354924	62552
Total Current Receipts	1739632	8639802	3099830
Disbursements			
1 Property and entrepreneurial income	6854767	4724303	2130464
A Withdrawals from quasi-corporations	648106	625028	23078
Public	...	...	...
Private	...	...	...
B Interest	4462827	2497656	1965171
C Dividends	1466532	1324317	142215
D Net land rent and royalties	277302	277302	-
2 Direct taxes and other current transfers n.e.c. to general government	1790668	1684345	106323
A Direct taxes	1733420	1644808	88612
B Fines, fees, penalties and other current transfers n.e.c.	57248	39537	17711

Colombia

3.22 Corporate and Quasi-Corporate Enterprise Income and Outlay Account: Total and Sectors
(Continued)

Million Colombian pesos

		1992		
		TOTAL	Non-Financial	Financial
3	Other current transfers	1080831	626912	453919
	A Casualty insurance premiums, net	231228	208711	22517
	B Casualty insurance claims liability of insurance companies	312777	...	312777
	C Transfers to private non-profit institutions	...	...	...
	D Unfunded employee pension and welfare benefits	417476	354924	62552
	E Social assistance grants	...	...	...
	F Other transfers n.e.c.	...	...	...
	G Transfers to the rest of the world [a]	119350	63277	56073
Net saving		2006114	1604242	401872
Total Current Disbursements and Net Saving		1739632	8639802	3099830

a) Item 'Transfers to the rest of the world' refers to net current transfers n. e. c.

3.23 Corporate and Quasi-Corporate Enterprise Capital Accumulation Account: Total and Sectors

Million Colombian pesos

	1980			1985			1990			1991		
	TOTAL	Non-Financial	Financial	TOTAL	Non-Financial	Financial	TOTAL	Non-Financial	Financial	TOTAL	Non-Financial	Financial
Finance of Gross Accumulation												
1 Gross saving	117811	85412	32399	363087	337769	25318	2236396	1798922	437474	1784897	1497622	287275
2 Capital transfers [a]	-27152	3888	-31040	76293	45891	30402	-69764	78730	-148494	192232	118795	73437
Finance of Gross Accumulation	90659	89300	1359	439380	383660	55720	2166632	1877652	288980	1977129	1616417	360712
Gross Accumulation												
1 Gross capital formation	167450	157111	10339	608807	596102	12705	2185282	2087160	98122	2153415	2018296	135119
A Increase in stocks	28061	27224	837	45624	46883	-1259	239306	225413	13893	111239	75796	35443
B Gross fixed capital formation	139389	129887	9502	563183	549219	13964	1945976	1861747	84229	2042176	1942500	99676
2 Purchases of land, net	3211	1916	1295	10865	11092	-227	100524	96976	3548	168982	151167	17815
3 Purchases of intangible assets, net	...	...	...	-3	-3	...	...	...	...	...	...	...
4 Capital transfers [a]	...	...	...	...	...	...	...	...	...	...	...	...
Net lending	-80002	-69727	-10275	-180289	-223531	43242	-119174	-306484	187310	-345268	-553046	207778
Gross Accumulation	90659	89300	1359	439380	383660	55720	2166632	1877652	288980	1977129	1616417	360712

	1992		
	TOTAL	Non-Financial	Financial
Finance of Gross Accumulation			
1 Gross saving	2006114	1604242	401872
2 Capital transfers [a]	207365	156603	50762
Finance of Gross Accumulation	2213479	1760845	452634
Gross Accumulation			
1 Gross capital formation	2882591	2693978	188613
A Increase in stocks	57042	28681	28361
B Gross fixed capital formation	2825549	2665297	160252
2 Purchases of land, net	191651	163226	28425
3 Purchases of intangible assets, net	...	...	...
4 Capital transfers [a]	...	...	...
Net lending	-860763	1096359	235596
Gross Accumulation	2213479	1760845	452634

a) Capital transfers received are recorded net of capital transfers paid.

Colombia

3.33 Household and Private Unincorporated Enterprise Capital Accumulation Account
Million Colombian pesos

	1980	1983	1984	1985	1986	1987	1988	1989	1990	1991	1992	1993
Finance of Gross Accumulation												
1 Gross saving	141982	262213	319645	352722	544784	620275	897687	992631	1326413	2382510	2363075	...
2 Capital transfers [a]	-2103	-4458	-5263	-8906	-13561	-8088	61082	2345	58353	-53259	-47285	...
Total Finance of Gross Accumulation	139879	257755	314382	343816	531223	612187	958769	994976	1384766	2329251	2315790	...
Gross Accumulation												
1 Gross Capital Formation	78422	161712	182201	206268	300895	463620	705162	792752	924024	1054135	1818019	...
A Increase in stocks	12136	30947	30231	35798	46210	81418	198328	159468	176562	93836	424353	...
B Gross fixed capital formation	66286	130765	151970	170470	254685	382202	506834	633284	747462	960299	1393666	...
2 Purchases of land, net	-3693	-7951	-6149	-13402	-14117	-23468	-20896	-36991	-115321	-185958	-212526	...
3 Purchases of intangibles, net	...	-14	-15	3	-2	-8	...	...	...	...	...	...
4 Capital transfers [a]	...	...	...	...	...	...	...	...	...	...	...	...
Net lending	65150	104008	138345	150947	244447	172043	274503	239215	576063	1461074	710297	...
Total Gross Accumulation	139879	257755	314382	343816	531223	612187	958769	994976	1384766	2329251	2315790	...

a) Capital transfers received are recorded net of capital transfers paid.

4.1 Derivation of Value Added by Kind of Activity, in Current Prices
Thousand Million Colombian pesos

	1980 Gross Output	1980 Intermediate Consumption	1980 Value Added	1985 Gross Output	1985 Intermediate Consumption	1985 Value Added	1990 Gross Output	1990 Intermediate Consumption	1990 Value Added	1991 Gross Output	1991 Intermediate Consumption	1991 Value Added
All Producers												
1 Agriculture, hunting, forestry and fishing	376	70	306	1063	220	844	4209	925	3284	5588	1144	4444
A Agriculture and hunting [a]	361	69	293	1014	217	797	4033	914	3119	5342	1128	4214
B Forestry and logging	7	-	7	24	1	23	83	3	80	112	4	108
C Fishing [a]	7	1	6	26	2	24	93	8	85	133	11	123
2 Mining and quarrying	49	13	36	270	63	207	2258	374	1884	2602	461	2141
3 Manufacturing	959	592	367	2835	1773	1062	11700	7665	4035	14697	9365	5332
A Manufacture of food, beverages and tobacco	459	291	169	1319	838	481	4782	3348	1434	6128	4103	2025
B Textile, wearing apparel and leather industries	105	60	45	270	149	121	1278	707	571	1661	913	747
C Manufacture of wood and wood products, including furniture	13	7	6	42	21	21	192	94	98	236	116	120
D Manufacture of paper and paper products, printing and publishing	46	29	17	152	95	57	642	414	228	822	514	307
E Manufacture of chemicals and chemical petroleum, coal, rubber and plastic products	176	112	64	603	417	186	2595	1850	745	3286	2292	994
F Manufacture of non-metallic mineral products, except products of petroleum and coal	34	16	18	105	51	54	498	245	253	625	300	325
G Basic metal industries	...	...	...	...	...	...	...	...	...	...	...	...
H Manufacture of fabricated metal products, machinery and equipment	117	73	44	305	185	119	1544	934	610	1748	1043	704
I Other manufacturing industries	9	4	5	39	17	22	169	73	96	191	82	109
4 Electricity, gas and water	33	13	21	149	43	107	709	200	509	953	262	691
5 Construction	134	60	75	567	225	342	1650	649	1001	2083	770	1312
6 Wholesale and retail trade, restaurants and hotels [b]	231	78	153	722	207	515	2924	805	2119	3645	1020	2625
A Wholesale and retail trade	231	78	153	722	207	515	2924	805	2119	3645	1020	2625
B Restaurants and hotels	...	...	...	...	...	...	...	...	...	...	...	...
7 Transport, storage and communication	223	82	141	646	242	405	2858	1015	1843	3876	1361	2515
A Transport and storage	202	75	126	558	215	343	2425	887	1538	3282	1189	2093
B Communication	21	7	14	88	27	62	433	128	305	594	172	422
8 Finance, insurance, real estate and business services	252	36	217	718	110	608	2740	486	2254	3616	637	2978
A Financial institutions [c]	135	29	106	389	87	302	1789	405	1384	2366	534	1832
B Insurance												
C Real estate and business services [c]	117	7	110	329	23	306	951	81	870	1249	103	1146
Real estate, except dwellings	...	...	...	...	...	...	...	...	...	...	...	...

Colombia

4.1 Derivation of Value Added by Kind of Activity, in Current Prices
(Continued)

Thousand Million Colombian pesos

	1980 Gross Output	1980 Intermediate Consumption	1980 Value Added	1985 Gross Output	1985 Intermediate Consumption	1985 Value Added	1990 Gross Output	1990 Intermediate Consumption	1990 Value Added	1991 Gross Output	1991 Intermediate Consumption	1991 Value Added
Dwellings	117	7	110	329	23	306	951	81	870	1249	103	1146
9 Community, social and personal services [b]	198	58	140	615	177	439	2448	719	1729	3411	924	2487
A Sanitary and similar services	...	...	...	...	...	...	...	...	...	...	...	...
B Social and related community services	...	...	...	...	...	...	...	...	...	...	...	...
C Recreational and cultural services	...	...	...	...	...	...	...	...	...	...	...	...
D Personal and household services	198	58	140	615	177	439	2448	719	1729	3411	924	2487
Total, Industries	2456	1001	1454	7587	3058	4529	31496	12838	18658	40471	15944	24525
Producers of Government Services	166	45	121	557	133	424	2199	592	1607	2880	907	1972
Other Producers	...	...	...	...	...	...	...	...	...	...	...	...
Total	2622	1046	1576	8144	3190	4953	33695	13430	20265	43351	16851	26497
Less: Imputed bank service charge	...	-40	40	...	-119	119	...	-657	657	...	-986	986
Import duties	44	...	44	131	...	131	619	...	619	596	...	596
Value added tax	...	...	...	...	...	...	...	...	...	...	...	...
Total	2666	1086	1579	8275	3309	4966	34314	14087	20227	43947	17837	26107

1992 — All Producers

	Gross Output	Intermediate Consumption	Value Added
1 Agriculture, hunting, forestry and fishing	6557	1361	5196
A Agriculture and hunting [a]	6237	1343	4895
B Forestry and logging	134	5	128
C Fishing [a]	186	13	173
2 Mining and quarrying	3084	736	2348
3 Manufacturing	17894	11454	6440
A Manufacture of food, beverages and tobacco	6514	4245	2269
B Textile, wearing apparel and leather industries	2013	1132	881
C Manufacture of wood and wood products, including furniture	...	...	...
D Manufacture of paper and paper products, printing and publishing	...	...	...
E Manufacture of chemicals and chemical petroleum, coal, rubber and plastic products	...	...	...
F Manufacture of non-metallic mineral products, except products of petroleum and coal	...	...	...
G Basic metal industries	...	...	...
H Manufacture of fabricated metal products, machinery and equipment	...	...	...
I Other manufacturing industries	...	...	...
4 Electricity, gas and water	1185	301	884
5 Construction	2877	994	1883
6 Wholesale and retail trade, restaurants and hotels [b]	4654	1330	3324
A Wholesale and retail trade	4654	1330	3324
B Restaurants and hotels	...	...	...
7 Transport, storage and communication	5267	1810	3457
A Transport and storage	4486	1585	2901
B Communication	781	225	556
8 Finance, insurance, real estate and business services	4627	831	3796
A Financial institutions [c]	3031	701	2330
B Insurance			
C Real estate and business services [c]	1597	130	1467
Real estate, except dwellings	...	...	...

Colombia

4.1 Derivation of Value Added by Kind of Activity, in Current Prices
(Continued)

Thousand Million Colombian pesos

	1992 Gross Output	1992 Intermediate Consumption	1992 Value Added
Dwellings	1597	130	1467
9 Community, social and personal services [b]	4860	1215	3645
A Sanitary and similar services	...	...	...
B Social and related community services	...	...	...
C Recreational and cultural services	...	...	...
D Personal and household services	4860	1215	3645
Total, Industries	51005	20032	30973
Producers of Government Services	3924	1208	2715
Other Producers	...	...	...
Total	54929	21240	33688
Less: Imputed bank service charge	...	-1199	1199
Import duties	653	...	653
Value added tax	...	...	...
Total	55582	22439	33142

a) Hunting is included in item 'Fishing'.
b) Restaurants and hotels are included in item 'Community, social and personal services'.
c) Business services are included in the financial institutions.

4.2 Derivation of Value Added by Kind of Activity, in Constant Prices

Million Colombian pesos

At constant prices of: 1975
All Producers

	1980 Gross Output	1980 Intermediate Consumption	1980 Value Added	1985 Gross Output	1985 Intermediate Consumption	1985 Value Added	1990 Gross Output	1990 Intermediate Consumption	1990 Value Added	1991 Gross Output	1991 Intermediate Consumption	1991 Value Added
1 Agriculture, hunting, forestry and fishing	145051	25737	119314	156113	27657	128456	195186	34941	160245	203613	36695	166918
A Agriculture and hunting [a]	140256	25407	114849	150616	27270	123346	188600	34478	154122	196660	36202	160458
B Forestry and logging	2366	109	2257	2662	128	2534	3194	152	3042	3267	156	3111
C Fishing [a]	2429	221	2208	2835	259	2576	3392	311	3081	3686	337	3349
2 Mining and quarrying	10803	4142	6661	22566	8836	13730	50133	15987	34146	49882	15954	33928
3 Manufacturing	329176	211504	117672	343770	219160	124610	434458	277168	157290	435639	277056	158583
A Manufacture of food, beverages and tobacco	153624	104423	49201	164180	110975	53205	195550	133389	62161	192953	131273	61680
B Textile, wearing apparel and leather industries	39800	23488	16312	35877	20708	15169	49275	28439	20836	51013	29384	21629
C Manufacture of wood and wood products, including furniture	4371	2038	2333	4420	2036	2384	6191	2880	3311	6227	2893	3334
D Manufacture of paper and paper products, printing and publishing	18890	11221	7669	21208	12470	8738	27058	15950	11108	28038	16549	11489
E Manufacture of chemicals and chemical petroleum, coal, rubber and plastic products	55717	37135	18582	65099	42866	22233	84793	55670	29123	86787	56949	29838
F Manufacture of non-metallic mineral products, except products of petroleum and coal	10621	4597	6024	11459	4912	6547	15668	6785	8883	16631	7202	9428
G Basic metal industries	...	...	...	...	...	...	...	...	...	...	...	...
H Manufacture of fabricated metal products, machinery and equipment	42880	26934	15946	37569	23201	14368	51276	31687	19589	49569	30553	19016
I Other manufacturing industries	3273	1668	1605	3958	1992	1966	4647	2368	2279	4421	2253	2168
4 Electricity, gas and water	8672	3462	5210	10056	3945	6111	13318	5204	8114	13724	5362	8362
5 Construction	39964	22332	17632	54813	29172	25641	47713	25847	21866	47831	25911	21920
6 Wholesale and retail trade, restaurants and hotels [b]	76857	23866	52991	80331	24521	55810	97707	29934	67773	97341	29814	67527
A Wholesale and retail trade	76857	23866	52991	80331	24521	55810	97707	29934	67773	97341	29814	67527
B Restaurants and hotels	...	...	...	...	...	...	...	...	...	...	...	...
7 Transport, storage and communication	72307	23363	48944	80449	25405	55044	92699	29102	63597	95749	29967	65782
A Transport and storage	62957	20883	42074	66805	21828	44977	74633	24369	50264	76372	24890	51482

Colombia

4.2 Derivation of Value Added by Kind of Activity, in Constant Prices
(Continued)

Million Colombian pesos

	1980 Gross Output	1980 Intermediate Consumption	1980 Value Added	1985 Gross Output	1985 Intermediate Consumption	1985 Value Added	1990 Gross Output	1990 Intermediate Consumption	1990 Value Added	1991 Gross Output	1991 Intermediate Consumption	1991 Value Added
				At constant prices of:1975								
B Communication	9350	2480	6870	13644	3577	10067	18066	4733	13333	19377	5077	14300
8 Finance, insurance, real estate and business services	87075	13612	73463	98163	14864	83299	126888	19599	107289	133277	20684	112588
A Financial institutions c	48813	10902	37911	52589	11635	40954	72750	15716	57034	77244	16685	60559
B Insurance												
C Real estate and business services c	38262	2710	35552	45574	3229	42345	54138	3883	50255	56033	4004	52029
Real estate, except dwellings	...	...	...	...	...	...	...	...	...	...	...	...
Dwellings	38262	2710	35552	45574	3229	42345	54138	3883	50255	56033	4004	52029
9 Community, social and personal services b	62497	22996	39501	68398	24645	43753	78587	28641	49946	81309	29546	51763
A Sanitary and similar services	...	...	...	...	...	...	...	...	...	...	...	...
B Social and related community services	...	...	...	...	...	...	...	...	...	...	...	...
C Recreational and cultural services	...	...	...	...	...	...	...	...	...	...	...	...
D Personal and household services	62497	22996	39501	68398	24645	43753	78587	28641	49946	81309	29546	51763
Total, Industries	832402	351014	481388	914659	378205	536454	1136689	466423	670266	1158365	470994	687371
Producers of Government Services	56706	15866	40840	66687	17415	49272	86530	22481	64049	90522	26680	63842
Other Producers	...	...	...	...	...	...	...	...	...	...	...	...
Total	889108	366880	522228	981346	395620	585726	1223219	488904	734315	1248887	497674	751213
Less: Imputed bank service charge	...	-14095	14095	...	-14409	14409	...	-20349	20349	...	-22241	22241
Import duties	17632	...	17632	16244	...	16244	21293	...	21293	21004	...	21004
Value added tax												
Total	906740	380975	525765	997590	410029	587561	1244512	509253	735259	1269891	519915	749976

	1992 Gross Output	1992 Intermediate Consumption	1992 Value Added
	At constant prices of:1975		
	All Producers		
1 Agriculture, hunting, forestry and fishing	200783	36958	163825
A Agriculture and hunting a	193742	36461	157281
B Forestry and logging	3381	162	3219
C Fishing a	3660	335	3325
2 Mining and quarrying	53239	20248	32991
3 Manufacturing	456567	288643	167924
A Manufacture of food, beverages and tobacco	198548	132687	65861
B Textile, wearing apparel and leather industries	53204	30884	22320
C Manufacture of wood and wood products, including furniture	6461	3026	3435
D Manufacture of paper and paper products, printing and publishing	29741	17625	12116
E Manufacture of chemicals and chemical petroleum, coal, rubber and plastic products	90595	59750	30845
F Manufacture of non-metallic mineral products, except products of petroleum and coal	17436	7584	9852
G Basic metal industries	...	...	...
H Manufacture of fabricated metal products, machinery and equipment	56306	34897	21409
I Other manufacturing industries	4276	2190	2086
4 Electricity, gas and water	12968	5114	7854
5 Construction	52180	28428	23752
6 Wholesale and retail trade, restaurants and hotels b	102494	31680	70814
A Wholesale and retail trade	102494	31680	70814
B Restaurants and hotels	...	...	...
7 Transport, storage and communication	101541	32313	69228

Colombia

4.2 Derivation of Value Added by Kind of Activity, in Constant Prices
(Continued)

Million Colombian pesos

	1992 Gross Output	1992 Intermediate Consumption	1992 Value Added
			At constant prices of: 1975
A Transport and storage	81337	26971	54366
B Communication	20204	5342	14862
8 Finance, insurance, real estate and business services	139058	21894	117164
A Financial institutions c	81624	17790	63834
B Insurance			
C Real estate and business services c	57434	4104	53330
Real estate, except dwellings	...	...	...
Dwellings	57434	4104	53330
9 Community, social and personal services b	83502	30569	52933
A Sanitary and similar services	...	...	...
B Social and related community services	...	...	...
C Recreational and cultural services	...	...	...
D Personal and household services	83502	30569	52933
Total, Industries	1202332	495847	706485
Producers of Government Services	96988	30148	66840
Other Producers	...	...	...
Total	1299320	525995	773325
Less: Imputed bank service charge	...	-23220	23220
Import duties	28604	...	28604
Value added tax	...	...	...
Total	1327924	549215	778709

a) Hunting is included in item 'Fishing'.
b) Restaurants and hotels are included in item 'Community, social and personal services'.
c) Business services are included in the financial institutions.

4.3 Cost Components of Value Added

Thousand Million Colombian pesos

	1980 Compensation of Employees	1980 Capital Consumption	1980 Net Operating Surplus	1980 Indirect Taxes	1980 Less: Subsidies Received	1980 Value Added	1985 Compensation of Employees	1985 Capital Consumption	1985 Net Operating Surplus	1985 Indirect Taxes	1985 Less: Subsidies Received	1985 Value Added
					All Producers							
1 Agriculture, hunting, forestry and fishing	133	...	172	-	...	306	326	...	520	-3	...	844
A Agriculture and hunting a	131	...	161	-	...	293	320	...	480	-3	...	797
B Forestry and logging	1	...	6	-	...	7	5	...	18	-	...	23
C Fishing a	-	...	6	-	...	6	1	...	23	-	...	24
2 Mining and quarrying	9	...	27	-	...	36	38	...	167	2	...	207
3 Manufacturing	122	...	146	100	...	367	340	...	451	271	...	1062
A Manufacture of food, beverages and tobacco	29	...	65	74	...	169	92	...	207	183	...	481
B Textile, wearing apparel and leather industries	29	...	15	2	...	45	66	...	48	7	...	121
C Manufacture of wood and wood products, including furniture	4	...	2	-	...	6	11	...	9	1	...	21
D Manufacture of paper and paper products, printing and publishing	7	...	9	1	...	17	21	...	33	4	...	57
E Manufacture of chemicals and chemical petroleum, coal, rubber and plastic products	19	...	30	15	...	64	58	...	79	49	...	186
F Manufacture of non-metallic mineral products, except products of petroleum and coal	8	...	8	1	...	18	24	...	25	4	...	54
G Basic metal industries	...	...	...	...	...	...	...	...	...	...	...	...
H Manufacture of fabricated metal products, machinery and equipment	24	...	14	6	...	44	60	...	39	20	...	119
I Other manufacturing industries	3	...	2	-	...	5	10	...	11	2	...	22
4 Electricity, gas and water	9	...	11	-	...	21	38	...	69	-	...	107

Colombia

4.3 Cost Components of Value Added
(Continued)

Thousand Million Colombian pesos

	1980						1985					
	Compensation of Employees	Capital Consumption	Net Operating Surplus	Indirect Taxes	Less: Subsidies Received	Value Added	Compensation of Employees	Capital Consumption	Net Operating Surplus	Indirect Taxes	Less: Subsidies Received	Value Added
5 Construction	43	...	28	3	...	75	160	...	166	17	...	342
6 Wholesale and retail trade, restaurants and hotels [b]	32	...	116	5	...	153	108	...	355	53	...	515
A Wholesale and retail trade	32	...	116	5	...	153	108	...	355	53	...	515
B Restaurants and hotels	...	...	...	...	...	...	...	...	...	...	...	...
7 Transport, storage and communication	58	...	86	-3	...	141	180	...	219	6	...	405
A Transport and storage	50	...	81	-4	...	126	140	...	202	1	...	343
B Communication	8	...	5	1	...	14	39	...	17	5	...	62
8 Finance, insurance, real estate and business services	63	...	148	6	...	217	194	...	387	28	...	608
A Financial institutions [c]	63	...	43	-	...	106	194	...	97	11	...	302
B Insurance	...	...	...	...	...	...	...	...	...	...	...	...
C Real estate and business services [c]	...	...	105	5	...	110	...	...	290	17	...	306
Real estate, except dwellings	...	...	...	...	...	...	...	...	...	...	...	...
Dwellings	...	...	105	5	...	110	...	...	290	17	...	306
9 Community, social and personal services [b]	67	...	70	3	...	140	213	...	217	9	...	439
A Sanitary and similar services	...	...	...	...	...	...	...	...	...	...	...	...
B Social and related community services	...	...	...	...	...	...	...	...	...	...	...	...
C Recreational and cultural services	...	...	...	...	...	...	...	...	...	...	...	...
D Personal and household services	67	...	70	3	...	140	213	...	217	9	...	439
Total, Industries [de]	536	...	804	114	...	1454	1596	...	2551	382	...	4529
Producers of Government Services	120	...	...	1	...	121	421	...	...	3	...	424
Other Producers	...	...	...	...	...	...	...	...	...	...	...	...
Total [de]	657	...	804	115	...	1576	2017	...	2551	386	...	4953
Less: Imputed bank service charge	...	...	40	...	...	40	...	...	119	...	...	119
Import duties	...	...	...	44	...	44	...	...	...	131	...	131
Value added tax	...	...	...	...	...	...	...	...	...	...	...	...
Total [de]	657	...	764	158	...	1579	2017	...	2432	517	...	4966

	1990						1991					
	Compensation of Employees	Capital Consumption	Net Operating Surplus	Indirect Taxes	Less: Subsidies Received	Value Added	Compensation of Employees	Capital Consumption	Net Operating Surplus	Indirect Taxes	Less: Subsidies Received	Value Added

All Producers

1 Agriculture, hunting, forestry and fishing	1337	...	1942	5	...	3284	1762	...	2670	13	...	4445
A Agriculture and hunting [a]	1316	...	1798	5	...	3119	1733	...	2468	13	...	4214
B Forestry and logging	16	...	64	...	...	80	22	...	86	...	...	108
C Fishing [a]	5	...	80	...	...	85	7	...	116	...	...	123
2 Mining and quarrying	171	...	1629	84	...	1884	211	...	1865	65	...	2141

Colombia

4.3 Cost Components of Value Added
(Continued)

Thousand Million Colombian pesos

	1990						1991					
	Compensation of Employees	Capital Consumption	Net Operating Surplus	Indirect Taxes	Less: Subsidies Received	Value Added	Compensation of Employees	Capital Consumption	Net Operating Surplus	Indirect Taxes	Less: Subsidies Received	Value Added
3 Manufacturing	1306	...	1981	748	...	4035	1691	...	2664	977	...	5332
A Manufacture of food, beverages and tobacco	337	...	705	392	...	1434	444	...	1085	495	...	2024
B Textile, wearing apparel and leather industries	259	...	303	9	...	571	352	...	379	19	...	750
C Manufacture of wood and wood products, including furniture	46	...	46	6	...	98	55	...	58	7	...	120
D Manufacture of paper and paper products, printing and publishing	73	...	139	16	...	228	89	...	197	21	...	307
E Manufacture of chemicals and chemical petroleum, coal, rubber and plastic products	222	...	325	198	...	745	293	...	411	289	...	993
F Manufacture of non-metallic mineral products, except products of petroleum and coal	93	...	140	20	...	253	119	...	181	25	...	325
G Basic metal industries	...	...	...	...	...	...	...	...	...	...	...	...
H Manufacture of fabricated metal products, machinery and equipment	238	...	272	100	...	610	296	...	294	114	...	704
I Other manufacturing industries	38	...	51	7	...	96	43	...	59	7	...	109
4 Electricity, gas and water	158	...	349	2	...	509	212	...	470	8	...	690
5 Construction	365	...	581	55	...	1001	461	...	778	73	...	1312
6 Wholesale and retail trade, restaurants and hotels [b]	390	...	1496	233	...	2119	491	...	1714	419	...	2624
A Wholesale and retail trade	390	...	1496	233	...	2119	491	...	1714	419	...	2624
B Restaurants and hotels	...	...	...	...	...	...	...	...	...	...	...	...
7 Transport, storage and communication	737	...	1043	63	...	1843	968	...	1480	67	...	2515
A Transport and storage	589	...	913	36	...	1538	772	...	1292	29	...	2093
B Communication	148	...	130	27	...	305	196	...	188	38	...	422
8 Finance, insurance, real estate and business services	690	...	1428	136	...	2254	986	...	1811	181	...	2978
A Financial institutions [c]	690	...	635	59	...	1384	986	...	773	73	...	1832
B Insurance	...	...	...	...	...	...	...	...	...	...	...	...
C Real estate and business services [c]	...	...	793	77	...	870	...	...	1038	108	...	1146
Real estate, except dwellings	...	...	...	...	...	...	...	...	...	...	...	...
Dwellings	...	...	793	77	...	870	...	...	1038	108	...	1146
9 Community, social and personal services [b]	816	...	890	23	...	1729	1116	...	1333	39	...	2488
A Sanitary and similar services	...	...	...	...	...	...	...	...	...	...	...	...
B Social and related community services	...	...	...	...	...	...	...	...	...	...	...	...
C Recreational and cultural services	...	...	...	...	...	...	...	...	...	...	...	...
D Personal and household services	816	...	890	23	...	1729	1116	...	1333	39	...	2488
Total, Industries [de]	5970	...	11339	1349	...	18658	7898	...	14785	1842	...	24525
Producers of Government Services	1585	...	...	22	...	1607	1949	...	...	23	...	1972
Other Producers	...	...	...	...	...	...	...	...	...	...	...	...
Total [de]	7555	...	11339	1371	...	20265	9847	...	14785	1865	...	26497
Less: Imputed bank service charge	...	...	657	...	...	657	...	...	986	...	...	986
Import duties	...	...	...	620	...	620	...	...	...	596	...	596
Value added tax	...	...	...	...	...	...	...	...	...	...	...	...
Total [de]	7555	...	10682	1991	...	20228	9847	...	13799	2461	...	26107

	1992						
	Compensation of Employees	Capital Consumption	Net Operating Surplus	Indirect Taxes	Less: Subsidies Received	Value Added

All Producers

1 Agriculture, hunting, forestry and fishing	2131	...	3048	17	...	5196
A Agriculture and hunting [a]	2095	...	2783	17	...	4895
B Forestry and logging	26	...	102	...	...	128
C Fishing [a]	10	...	163	...	...	173

Colombia

4.3 Cost Components of Value Added
(Continued)

Thousand Million Colombian pesos

		1992				
		Compensation of Employees	Capital Consumption	Net Operating Surplus	Indirect Taxes	Less: Subsidies Received	Value Added
2	Mining and quarrying	306	...	2009	33	...	2348
3	Manufacturing	2318	...	2876	1247	...	6441
	A Manufacture of food, beverages and tobacco	582	...	1104	583	...	2269
	B Textile, wearing apparel and leather industries	469	...	368	44	...	881
	C Manufacture of wood and wood products, including furniture	73	...	70	10	...	153
	D Manufacture of paper and paper products, printing and publishing	126	...	246	29	...	401
	E Manufacture of chemicals and chemical petroleum, coal, rubber and plastic products	398	...	508	389	...	1295
	F Manufacture of non-metallic mineral products, except products of petroleum and coal	165	...	240	34	...	439
	G Basic metal industries	...	...	...	...	...	...
	H Manufacture of fabricated metal products, machinery and equipment	450	...	278	148	...	876
	I Other manufacturing industries	55	...	62	10	...	127
4	Electricity, gas and water	264	...	611	9	...	884
5	Construction	617	...	1164	102	...	1883
6	Wholesale and retail trade, restaurants and hotels [b]	653	...	2119	552	...	3324
	A Wholesale and retail trade	653	...	2119	552	...	3324
	B Restaurants and hotels	...	...	...	...	...	...
7	Transport, storage and communication	1313	...	2036	108	...	3457
	A Transport and storage	1065	...	1807	29	...	2901
	B Communication	248	...	229	79	...	556
8	Finance, insurance, real estate and business services	1267	...	2249	280	...	3796
	A Financial institutions [c]	1267	...	932	131	...	2330
	B Insurance	...	...	...	...	...	...
	C Real estate and business services [c]	...	...	1317	149	...	1466
	Real estate, except dwellings	...	...	...	...	...	...
	Dwellings	...	...	1317	149	...	1466
9	Community, social and personal services [b]	1571	...	1905	170	...	3646
	A Sanitary and similar services	...	...	...	...	...	...
	B Social and related community services	...	...	...	...	...	...
	C Recreational and cultural services	...	...	...	...	...	...
	D Personal and household services	1571	...	1905	170	...	3646
Total, Industries [de]		10440	...	18017	2518	...	30975
Producers of Government Services		2639	...	...	76	...	2715
Other Producers		...	...	...	...	...	...
Total [de]		13079	...	18017	2594	...	33690
Less: Imputed bank service charge		...	...	1199	...	...	1199
Import duties		...	...	...	653	...	653
Value added tax		...	...	...	...	...	...
Total [de]		13079	...	16818	3247	...	33144

a) Hunting is included in item 'Fishing'.
b) Restaurants and hotels are included in item 'Community, social and personal services'.
c) Business services are included in the financial institutions.
d) Column 4 refers to indirect taxes less subsidies received.
e) Column 'Consumption of fixed capital' is included in column 'Net operating surplus'.

Congo

Source. Reply to the United Nations National Accounts Questionnaire from the Centre National de la Statistique et des Etudes Economique, Brazzaville.
General note. The estimates shown in the following tables have been prepared by the Centre National in accordance with the United Nations System of National Accounts so far as the existing data would permit.

1.1 Expenditure on the Gross Domestic Product, in Current Prices

Million CFA francs

		1980	1983	1984	1985	1986	1987	1988	1989	1990	1991	1992	1993
1	Government final consumption expenditure	63385	124245	141696	159693	159804	142115	138722	144600	...	...	...	...
2	Private final consumption expenditure	147924	318459	372192	403583	380534	390669	396328	408500	...	...	...	...
	A Households	147324	317199	370712	401955	378934	389229	394828	...	...	...	...	...
	B Private non-profit institutions serving households	600	1260	1480	1628	1600	1440	1500	...	...	...	...	...
3	Gross capital formation	128901	307122	291239	293982	188598	136205	122640	122924	...	...	...	...
	A Increase in stocks	10157	4268	13974	17080	5742	-7811	-6518	-3776	...	...	...	...
	B Gross fixed capital formation	118744	302854	277265	276902	182856	144016	129158	126700	...	...	...	...
4	Exports of goods and services	203029	463133	590696	551863	255152	288254	267723	368100	...	...	...	...
5	Less: Imports of goods and services	182842	413714	437314	438271	343681	266720	266448	270600	...	...	...	...
	Equals: Gross Domestic Product	360397	799245	958509	970850	640407	690523	658964	773524	773100	820600	748400	...

1.2 Expenditure on the Gross Domestic Product, in Constant Prices

Million CFA francs

		1980	1983	1984	1985	1986	1987	1988	1989	1990	1991	1992	1993
						At constant prices of:1978							
1	Government final consumption expenditure	56869	83667	94077	100530	98384	84894	82080	83886	...	...	...	...
2	Private final consumption expenditure	128582	205073	220678	229054	213466	216324	217361	215622	...	...	...	...
	A Households	128043	204104	219678	227969	212526	...	...	...	...	...	...	...
	B Private non-profit institutions serving households	539	969	1000	1085	940	...	...	...	...	...	...	...
3	Gross capital formation	103238	181474	161402	153359	98947	68068	58080	49771	...	...	...	...
	A Increase in stocks	9192	2392	10306	8412	3035	-3103	-2649	-5796	...	...	...	...
	B Gross fixed capital formation	94046	179082	151096	144947	95912	71171	60729	55567	...	...	...	...
4	Exports of goods and services	104687	154170	169264	158300	152812	153452	173179	186514	...	...	...	...
5	Less: Imports of goods and services	144774	231121	223770	224452	175501	133895	134989	133099	...	...	...	...
	Equals: Gross Domestic Product	248602	393263	421651	416791	388108	388843	395711	402694	...	...	...	...

1.3 Cost Components of the Gross Domestic Product

Million CFA francs

		1980	1983	1984	1985	1986	1987	1988	1989	1990	1991	1992	1993
1	Indirect taxes, net	57077	125075	153724	148591	86690	89122	80672	106175	...	...	...	...
	A Indirect taxes	60164	134529	162290	154437	91444	90790	82358	...	...	...	...	...
	B Less: Subsidies	3087	9454	8566	5846	4754	1668	1686	...	...	...	...	...
2	Consumption of fixed capital	41191	120807	176986	167228	156074	164360	144647	148975	...	...	...	...
3	Compensation of employees paid by resident producers to:	119568	226115	257713	264454	264296	253198	245033	247514	...	...	...	...
4	Operating surplus	142561	327248	370086	390577	133347	183843	188612	270860	...	...	...	...
	A Corporate and quasi-corporate enterprises	94831	212395	237834	248081	-4228	41403	34329	...	...	...	...	...
	B Private unincorporated enterprises	47730	114853	132252	142496	137575	142440	154283	...	...	...	...	...
	C General government	...	...	...	...	...	...	...	...	...	...	...	...
	Equals: Gross Domestic Product	360397	799245	958509	970850	640407	690523	658964	773524	...	...	...	...

1.4 General Government Current Receipts and Disbursements

Million CFA francs

		1980	1983	1984	1985	1986	1987	1988	1989	1990	1991	1992	1993
						Receipts							
1	Operating surplus	...	...	...	...	...	...	...	...	...	...	...	...
2	Property and entrepreneurial income	10	1453	5954	4427	-	10883	7798	...	...	...	...	...
3	Taxes, fees and contributions	126351	287767	342227	307933	179767	133749	130495	...	...	...	...	...
	A Indirect taxes	60164	134529	162290	154437	91444	90331	81898	...	...	...	...	...

Congo

1.4 General Government Current Receipts and Disbursements
(Continued)

Million CFA francs

	1980	1983	1984	1985	1986	1987	1988	1989	1990	1991	1992	1993
B Direct taxes	59522	137629	165601	138070	72375	23697	25597	...	...	...	...	...
C Social security contributions	5656	15236	13365	15000	15600	19621	22890	...	...	...	...	...
D Compulsory fees, fines and penalties	1009	373	971	426	348	100	110	...	...	...	...	...
4 Other current transfers	3306	23222	5635	13169	13915	14712	23377	...	...	...	...	...
Total Current Receipts of General Government	129667	312442	353816	325529	193682	159344	161670	...	...	...	...	...

Disbursements

	1980	1983	1984	1985	1986	1987	1988	1989	1990	1991	1992	1993
1 Government final consumption expenditure	63385	124245	141696	159693	159804	142115	138722	...	...	...	...	...
2 Property income	9100	20053	30225	42268	21683	40125	43394	...	...	...	...	...
A Interest	9100	20053	30225	42268	21683	40125	43394	...	...	...	...	...
B Net land rent and royalties	...	...	...	...	...	...	...	...	...	...	...	...
3 Subsidies	3087	9454	8566	5846	4754	...	...	...	...	...	...	...
4 Other current transfers	11180	33805	23265	28821	25355	43327	44154	...	...	...	...	...
A Social security benefits	2911	4494	4981	5731	5800	12571	13850	...	...	...	...	...
B Social assistance grants		1120		100	900	8287	8517	...	...	...	...	...
C Other	8269	28191	18284	22990	18655	22469	21787	...	...	...	...	...
5 Net saving	42915	124885	150064	88901	-17914	-66223	-66402	...	...	...	...	...
Total Current Disbursements and Net Saving of General Government	129667	312442	353816	325529	193682	159344	161670	...	...	...	...	...

1.7 External Transactions on Current Account, Summary

Million CFA francs

	1980	1983	1984	1985	1986	1987	1988	1989	1990	1991	1992	1993

Payments to the Rest of the World

	1980	1983	1984	1985	1986	1987	1988	1989	1990	1991	1992	1993
1 Imports of goods and services	182842	413714	437314	438271	343681	266720	266448	...	...	...	...	...
2 Factor income to the rest of the world	34877	68147	72723	106547	44717	86030	93328	...	...	...	...	...
A Compensation of employees	-	-	-	-	-	140	200	...	...	...	...	...
B Property and entrepreneurial income	34877	68147	72723	106547	44717	85890	93128	...	...	...	...	...
3 Current transfers to the rest of the world	19070	41346	43645	32167	25512	36255	36264	...	...	...	...	...
4 Surplus of the nation on current transactions	-27366	-41823	57152	-1934	-138507	-66015	-101106	...	...	...	...	...
Payments to the Rest of the World and Surplus of the Nation on Current Transactions	209423	481384	610834	575051	275403	322990	294934	...	...	...	...	...

Receipts From The Rest of the World

	1980	1983	1984	1985	1986	1987	1988	1989	1990	1991	1992	1993
1 Exports of goods and services	203029	463133	590696	551863	255152	288254	267722	...	...	...	...	...
2 Factor income from rest of the world	2201	5258	5077	4103	2781	9333	3112	...	...	...	...	...
A Compensation of employees	506	-	-	-	-	150	1320	...	...	...	...	...
B Property and entrepreneurial income	1695	5258	5077	4103	2781	9183	1792	...	...	...	...	...
3 Current transfers from rest of the world	4193	12993	15061	19085	17470	25403	24100	...	...	...	...	...
Receipts from the Rest of the World on Current Transactions	209423	481384	610834	575051	275403	322990	294934	...	...	...	...	...

1.8 Capital Transactions of The Nation, Summary

Million CFA francs

	1980	1983	1984	1985	1986	1987	1988	1989	1990	1991	1992	1993

Finance of Gross Capital Formation

	1980	1983	1984	1985	1986	1987	1988	1989	1990	1991	1992	1993
Gross saving	101535	265299	348391	292048	50091	70190	21534	...	...	...	...	...
1 Consumption of fixed capital	41191	120807	176986	167228	156074	164360	144647	...	...	...	...	...
A General government	...	...	...	...	...	...	...	...	...	...	...	...
B Corporate and quasi-corporate enterprises	31939	105083	161038	149632	138039	144657	124116	...	...	...	...	...
Public	8178	24146	29513	30798	35141	34277	35158	...	...	...	...	...
Private	23761	80937	131525	118834	102898	110380	88958	...	...	...	...	...
C Other	9252	15724	15948	17596	18035	19703	20531	...	...	...	...	...

Congo

1.8 Capital Transactions of The Nation, Summary
(Continued)

Million CFA francs

	1980	1983	1984	1985	1986	1987	1988	1989	1990	1991	1992	1993
2 Net saving	60344	144492	171405	124820	-105983	-94170	-123113	...	...	...	...	...
A General government	42915	124885	150064	88901	-17914	-66223	-64602	...	...	...	...	...
B Corporate and quasi-corporate enterprises	14460	12567	16965	33991	-90636	-17604	-47834	...	...	...	...	...
Public	-1229	-9526	-1845	13040	4946	-3194	-10331	...	...	...	...	...
Private	15689	22093	18810	20951	-95582	-14410	-37503	...	...	...	...	...
C Other	2969	7040	4376	1928	2567	-10343	-10677	...	...	...	...	...
Less: Surplus of the nation on current transactions	-27366	-41823	57152	-1934	-138507	-66015	-101106	...	...	...	...	...
Finance of Gross Capital Formation	128901	307122	291239	293982	188598	136205	122640	...	...	...	...	...
Gross Capital Formation												
Increase in stocks	10157	4268	13974	17080	5742	-7811	-6518	...	...	...	...	...
Gross fixed capital formation	118744	302854	277265	276902	182856	144016	129158	...	...	...	...	...
1 General government	15256	76426	92300	70166	36502	18632	14178	...	...	...	...	...
2 Corporate and quasi-corporate enterprises	91838	205224	167605	188578	132824	111584	101980	...	...	...	...	...
A Public	22991	90145	78487	97539	49317	32424	25569	...	...	...	...	...
B Private	68847	115079	89118	91039	83507	79160	76411	...	...	...	...	...
3 Other	11650	21204	17360	18158	13530	13800	13000	...	...	...	...	...
Gross Capital Formation	128901	307122	291239	293982	188598	136205	122640	...	...	...	...	...

1.9 Gross Domestic Product by Institutional Sectors of Origin

Million CFA francs

	1980	1983	1984	1985	1986	1987	1988	1989	1990	1991	1992	1993
Domestic Factor Incomes Originating												
1 General government	45352	74616	88605	97680	101495	102716	102603	...	...	...	...	...
2 Corporate and quasi-corporate enterprises	154879	348387	390706	397555	142154	174067	157855	...	...	...	...	...
A Non-financial	154288	345602	386443	386274	140676	172984	155721	...	...	...	...	...
Public	21879	42939	57254	62835	70569	66485	65668	...	...	...	...	...
Private	132409	302663	329189	323439	70107	106499	90053	...	...	...	...	...
B Financial	591	2785	4263	11281	1478	1083	2134	...	...	...	...	...
Public	591	2785	4263	11281	1478	1083	2134	...	...	...	...	...
Private	...	...	...	...	...	...	...	...	...	...	...	...
3 Households and private unincorporated enterprises	61498	129600	147988	159246	153258	159763	172687	...	...	...	...	...
4 Non-profit institutions serving households	400	760	500	550	550	495	500	...	...	...	...	...
Subtotal: Domestic Factor Incomes	262129	553363	627799	655031	397643	437041	433645	...	...	...	...	...
Indirect taxes, net	57077	125075	153724	148591	86690	89122	80672	...	...	...	...	...
A Indirect taxes	60164	134529	162290	154437	91444	90331	81898	...	...	...	...	...
B Less: Subsidies	3087	9454	8566	5846	4754	1209	1226	...	...	...	...	...
Consumption of fixed capital	41191	120807	176986	167228	156074	164360	144647	...	...	...	...	...
Gross Domestic Product	360397	799245	958509	970850	640407	690523	658964	...	...	...	...	...

1.10 Gross Domestic Product by Kind of Activity, in Current Prices

Million CFA francs

	1980	1983	1984	1985	1986	1987	1988	1989	1990	1991	1992	1993
1 Agriculture, hunting, forestry and fishing	42128	60651	66348	72331	77424	82434	91384	100839	...	...	...	...
2 Mining and quarrying	120980	324772	413699	398041	99444	155188	110399	216192	...	...	...	...
3 Manufacturing	27079	44114	46449	54587	61277	59757	56917	54483	...	...	...	...
4 Electricity, gas and water	2906	9351	10119	11906	9054	10614	12714	14014	...	...	...	...
5 Construction	17060	55866	72112	58895	38806	21580	17117	13955	...	...	...	...
6 Wholesale and retail trade, restaurants and hotels	35053	95787	104487	110463	104377	102153	107588	111321	...	...	...	...
7 Transport, storage and communication	32781	57701	68529	70799	71067	71294	72600	70075	...	...	...	...
8 Finance, insurance, real estate and business services	26042	60666	63122	76240	64402	70975	71108	70503	...	...	...	...
9 Community, social and personal services									...	...	...	...

Congo

1.10 Gross Domestic Product by Kind of Activity, in Current Prices
(Continued)

Million CFA francs

	1980	1983	1984	1985	1986	1987	1988	1989	1990	1991	1992	1993
Total, Industries	304029	708908	844865	853262	525851	573995	539827	651382	...	...	...	...
Producers of Government Services	45352	74616	88605	97680	101495	102716	102603	104306	...	...	...	...
Other Producers	700	1380	1700	1750	1550	1395	1400	1400	...	...	...	...
Subtotal	350081	784904	935170	952692	628896	678106	643830	757088	...	...	...	...
Less: Imputed bank service charge	7178	14711	13730	16054	16466	13116	13054	12500	...	...	...	...
Plus: Import duties	17494	29052	37069	34212	27977	25533	28188	28936	...	...	...	...
Plus: Value added tax	...	...	...	...	...	...	...	...	...	...	...	...
Equals: Gross Domestic Product	360397	799245	958509	970850	640407	690523	658964	773524	...	...	...	...

1.11 Gross Domestic Product by Kind of Activity, in Constant Prices

Million CFA francs

	1980	1983	1984	1985	1986	1987	1988	1989	1990	1991	1992	1993
				At constant prices of:1978								
1 Agriculture, hunting, forestry and fishing	39609	41766	40942	41325	43635	45722	48758	51711	...	...	...	...
2 Mining and quarrying	38362	61469	63228	61838	66930	77255	82145	95206	...	...	...	...
3 Manufacturing	21166	36309	38463	42213	39601	39883	42467	37562	...	...	...	...
4 Electricity, gas and water	3435	9743	9670	10719	8084	10108	10634	11336	...	...	...	...
5 Construction	13597	36970	45521	34617	21807	11344	7466	5237	...	...	...	...
6 Wholesale and retail trade, restaurants and hotels	28655	54100	54345	54088	52610	50597	49544	49818	...	...	...	...
7 Transport, storage and communication	26907	41043	42423	42921	39875	37254	37689	36017	...	...	...	...
8 Finance, insurance, real estate and business services	23604	42369	41259	45156	37637	41705	40044	37398	...	...	...	...
9 Community, social and personal services									...	...	...	...
Total, Industries	195335	323769	335851	332877	310179	313868	318747	324285	...	...	...	...
Producers of Government Services	42455	53632	62735	65766	67304	66379	65980	66000	...	...	...	...
Other Producers	655	992	1204	1178	1046	1032	1026	1004	...	...	...	...
Subtotal	238445	378393	399790	399821	378529	381279	385753	391289	...	...	...	...
Less: Imputed bank service charge	6508	10817	10095	11804	11812	11254	10230	9796	...	...	...	...
Plus: Import duties	16665	25687	31956	28774	21391	18818	20188	21201	...	...	...	...
Plus: Value added tax	...	...	...	...	...	...	...	...	...	...	...	...
Equals: Gross Domestic Product	248602	393263	421651	416791	388108	388843	395711	402694	...	...	...	...

1.12 Relations Among National Accounting Aggregates

Million CFA francs

	1980	1983	1984	1985	1986	1987	1988	1989	1990	1991	1992	1993
Gross Domestic Product	360397	799245	958509	970850	640407	690523	658964	...	...	...	...	...
Plus: Net factor income from the rest of the world	-32676	-62889	-67646	-102444	-41936	-76697	-90216	...	...	...	...	...
Factor income from the rest of the world	2201	5258	5077	4103	2781	9333	3112	...	...	...	...	...
Less: Factor income to the rest of the world	34877	68147	72723	106547	44717	86030	93328	...	...	...	...	...
Equals: Gross National Product	327721	736356	890863	868406	598471	613826	568748	...	...	...	...	...
Less: Consumption of fixed capital	41191	120807	176986	167228	156074	164360	144647	...	...	...	...	...
Equals: National Income	286530	615549	713877	701178	442397	449466	424101	...	...	...	...	...
Plus: Net current transfers from the rest of the world	-14877	-28353	-28584	-13082	-8042	-10852	-12164	...	...	...	...	...
Current transfers from the rest of the world	4193	12993	15061	19085	17470	25403	24100	...	...	...	...	...
Less: Current transfers to the rest of the world	19070	41346	43645	32167	25512	36255	36264	...	...	...	...	...
Equals: National Disposable Income	271653	587196	685293	688096	434355	438614	411937	...	...	...	...	...
Less: Final consumption	211309	442704	513888	563276	540338	532784	535050	...	...	...	...	...
Equals: Net Saving	60344	144492	171405	124820	-105983	-94170	-123113	...	...	...	...	...
Less: Surplus of the nation on current transactions	-27366	-41823	57152	-1934	-138507	-66015	-101106	...	...	...	...	...
Equals: Net Capital Formation	87710	186315	114253	126754	32524	-28155	-22007	...	...	...	...	...

Cook Islands

Source. Reply to the United Nations national accounts questionnaire from the Statistical Office of the Cook Islands, Rarotonga. The first comprehensive estimates of gross domestic product for the period 1982-1986 was published in 'National Accounts of the Cook Islands, 1982-1986' in September 1990. This was the result of the joint efforts of the Statistics Office of Cook Islands with the Asian Development Bank.

General note. The estimates shown in the following tables have been prepared by the Statistical Office in accordance with the United Nations System of National Accounts so far as the existing data would permit.

1.1 Expenditure on the Gross Domestic Product, in Current Prices

Thousand New Zealand dollars

	1980	1983	1984	1985	1986	1987	1988	1989	1990	1991	1992	1993
1 Government final consumption expenditure	...	...	...	...	...	...	...	...	...	...	...	...
2 Private final consumption expenditure	...	...	...	...	...	...	...	...	...	...	...	...
3 Gross capital formation	...	...	...	...	...	...	...	...	...	...	...	...
4 Exports of goods and services [a]	4190	4890	6509	6072	9060	11956	6627	4667	...	...	...	...
5 Less: Imports of goods and services [b]	23610	35086	36167	49663	50309	56982	64526	73078	...	...	...	...
Equals: Gross Domestic Product	...	...	...	...	...	...	...	...	...	...	...	...

a) Item 'Exports of goods and services' refers to exports of goods, f.o.b. only.
b) Item 'Imports of goods and services' refers to imports of goods, c.i.f. only.

1.10 Gross Domestic Product by Kind of Activity, in Current Prices

Thousand New Zealand dollars

	1980	1983	1984	1985	1986	1987	1988	1989	1990	1991	1992	1993
1 Agriculture, hunting, forestry and fishing	...	6135	6592	7449	8034	...	...	...	...	...	...	...
2 Mining and quarrying	...	47	93	74	47	...	...	...	...	...	...	...
3 Manufacturing	...	1521	2125	2407	3203	...	...	...	...	...	...	...
4 Electricity, gas and water	...	137	420	56	715	...	...	...	...	...	...	...
5 Construction	...	857	920	1375	2357	...	...	...	...	...	...	...
6 Wholesale and retail trade, restaurants and hotels	...	8908	11228	13571	14526	...	...	...	...	...	...	...
7 Transport, storage and communication	...	3486	4567	5634	7743	...	...	...	...	...	...	...
8 Finance, insurance, real estate and business services	...	3544	4326	5636	7714	...	...	...	...	...	...	...
9 Community, social and personal services	...	652	816	984	1487	...	...	...	...	...	...	...
Total, Industries	...	25287	31087	37186	45826	...	...	...	...	...	...	...
Producers of Government Services	...	10892	13077	15761	18540	...	...	...	...	...	...	...
Other Producers	...	...	...	...	...	...	...	...	...	...	...	...
Subtotal	...	36179	44164	52947	64366	...	...	...	...	...	...	...
Less: Imputed bank service charge	...	820	865	1035	1095	...	...	...	...	...	...	...
Plus: Import duties	...	...	...	...	...	...	...	...	...	...	...	...
Plus: Value added tax	...	...	...	...	...	...	...	...	...	...	...	...
Equals: Gross Domestic Product	...	35359	43299	51912	63271	...	...	...	...	...	...	...

1.11 Gross Domestic Product by Kind of Activity, in Constant Prices

Thousand New Zealand dollars

	1980	1983	1984	1985	1986	1987	1988	1989	1990	1991	1992	1993
				At constant prices of:1985								
1 Agriculture, hunting, forestry and fishing	...	4901	6359	7449	7756	...	...	...	...	...	...	...
2 Mining and quarrying	...	57	104	74	42	...	...	...	...	...	...	...
3 Manufacturing	...	1860	2376	2407	2896	...	...	...	...	...	...	...
4 Electricity, gas and water	...	168	470	56	646	...	...	...	...	...	...	...
5 Construction	...	1067	1053	1375	2085	...	...	...	...	...	...	...
6 Wholesale and retail trade, restaurants and hotels	...	10896	12552	13571	13134	...	...	...	...	...	...	...
7 Transport, storage and communication	...	4264	5105	5634	7001	...	...	...	...	...	...	...
8 Finance, insurance, real estate and business services	...	4517	5084	5636	6858	...	...	...	...	...	...	...
9 Community, social and personal services	...	798	912	984	1345	...	...	...	...	...	...	...
Total, Industries	...	28528	34015	37186	41763	...	...	...	...	...	...	...
Producers of Government Services	...	13205	14249	15761	16272	...	...	...	...	...	...	...
Other Producers	...	...	...	...	...	...	...	...	...	...	...	...
Subtotal	...	41733	48264	52947	58035	...	...	...	...	...	...	...
Less: Imputed bank service charge	...	328	541	1035	1875	...	...	...	...	...	...	...
Plus: Import duties	...	...	...	...	...	...	...	...	...	...	...	...
Plus: Value added tax	...	...	...	...	...	...	...	...	...	...	...	...
Equals: Gross Domestic Product	...	41405	47722	51912	56161	...	...	...	...	...	...	...

Costa Rica

Source. Reply to the United Nations National Accounts Questionnaire from the Banco Central de Costa Rica, Departamento de Estudios Economicos, Seccion Cuentas Nacionales, San Jose. Official estimates are published in 'Cifras de Cuentas Nacionales de Costa Rica'.

General note. The estimates shown in the tables below have been prepared in accordance with the United Nations System of National Accounts so far as the existing data would permit.

1.1 Expenditure on the Gross Domestic Product, in Current Prices

Million Costa Rican colones

	1980	1983	1984	1985	1986	1987	1988	1989	1990	1991	1992	1993
1 Government final consumption expenditure	7544	19527	25503	31175	37951	42652	54630	72283	94948	111876	144448	175028
2 Private final consumption expenditure	27140	79481	99837	118974	144381	176475	215794	256923	321143	411105	544609	648335
3 Gross capital formation	11003	31270	37003	51240	62162	77169	85569	112743	142676	173646	261902	314206
A Increase in stocks	1109	8001	4324	13000	16139	20856	19358	25519	25606	37547	73584	65671
B Gross fixed capital formation	9895	23270	32679	38240	46023	56313	66211	87224	117071	136098	188318	248535
4 Exports of goods and services	10963	46601	56046	60807	77280	90005	118998	148435	179509	264408	342014	422107
5 Less: Imports of goods and services	15245	47565	55377	64277	75195	101767	125246	164473	215352	270928	388871	485265
Equals: Gross Domestic Product	41406	129314	163011	197920	246579	284533	349743	425911	522925	690107	904102	1074411

1.2 Expenditure on the Gross Domestic Product, in Constant Prices

Million Costa Rican colones

	1980	1983	1984	1985	1986	1987	1988	1989	1990	1991	1992	1993
	At constant prices of: 1966											
1 Government final consumption expenditure	1276	1140	1184	1196	1225	1252	1290	1335	1362	1349	1388	1458
2 Private final consumption expenditure	6238	5447	5842	6093	6413	6652	6795	7144	7440	7367	7974	8494
3 Gross capital formation	2753	1701	1887	2033	2665	2756	2562	2822	2921	2563	3364	3744
A Increase in stocks	329	278	92	141	546	420	311	225	-53	-30	208	-131
B Gross fixed capital formation	2425	1423	1795	1892	2119	2336	2251	2598	2974	2593	3156	3875
4 Exports of goods and services	3367	3491	3885	3729	3865	4674	5019	5811	6314	6842	7827	8765
5 Less: Imports of goods and services	3987	2785	3082	3267	3841	4517	4476	5288	5793	5601	7064	8106
Equals: Gross Domestic Product	9648	8993	9715	9785	10326	10818	11190	11824	12245	12521	13489	14355

1.3 Cost Components of the Gross Domestic Product

Million Costa Rican colones

	1980	1983	1984	1985	1986	1987	1988	1989	1990	1991	1992	1993
1 Indirect taxes, net	4862	18624	23914	26671	33642	39128	44584	54846	64587	89339	132612	140871
A Indirect taxes	5245	19561	25180	28663	36271	41994	49156	61042	71816	99591	141545	154226
B Less: Subsidies	383	937	1266	1992	2629	2867	4572	6196	7229	10252	8933	13355
2 Consumption of fixed capital	2181	4210	4862	5488	6130	7114	8919	10621	13245	18400	22229	26029
3 Compensation of employees paid by resident producers to:	20495	56432	73430	92373	112667	134065	166356	209001	264381	327436	429729	534121
4 Operating surplus	13867	50048	60806	73388	94140	104227	129884	151441	180712	254932	319532	373390
Equals: Gross Domestic Product	41406	129314	163011	197920	246579	284533	349743	425911	522925	690107	904102	1074411

1.4 General Government Current Receipts and Disbursements

Million Costa Rican colones

	1980	1983	1984	1985	1986	1987	1988	1989	1990	1991	1992	1993
	Receipts											
1 Operating surplus	...	...	...	...	...	...	...	...	...	...	...	...
2 Property and entrepreneurial income	229	957	1757	2315	3273	4767	7426	9581	10495	14691	15025	18628
3 Taxes, fees and contributions	8607	32836	41557	49404	60573	71562	85309	105543	131544	175814	241082	283754
A Indirect taxes	5245	19561	25180	28663	36271	41994	49156	61042	71816	99591	141545	154225
B Direct taxes	1014	4719	4756	5025	5696	6317	8236	9507	11820	14545	19016	26942
C Social security contributions	2274	8309	11172	15133	17896	21801	26432	32878	44027	54447	71260	90544
D Compulsory fees, fines and penalties	73	247	449	583	710	1450	1485	2116	3880	7230	9261	12043
4 Other current transfers	105	271	417	1056	8720	11848	7493	7145	6487	7645	9420	16927
Total Current Receipts of General Government	8941	34064	43730	52775	72565	88178	100227	122270	148526	198151	265527	319310
	Disbursements											
1 Government final consumption expenditure	7544	19527	25503	31175	37951	42652	54630	72283	94948	111876	144448	175028

Costa Rica

1.4 General Government Current Receipts and Disbursements
(Continued)

Million Costa Rican colones

	1980	1983	1984	1985	1986	1987	1988	1989	1990	1991	1992	1993
A Compensation of employees	6289	15799	20543	25778	31580	36260	...	...	...	...	...	...
B Consumption of fixed capital	...	...	...	...	...	...	...	...	...	...	...	...
C Purchases of goods and services, net	...	...	...	...	...	...	...	...	...	...	...	...
D Less: Own account fixed capital formation	...	...	...	...	...	...	...	...	...	...	...	...
E Indirect taxes paid, net	...	...	...	...	...	...	...	...	...	...	...	...
2 Property income	935	3738	3571	3866	5253	6716	11344	14971	25895	33449	46573	47616
A Interest	935	3738	3571	3866	5253	6716	11344	14971	25895	33449	46573	47616
B Net land rent and royalties	...	...	...	...	...	...	...	...	...	...	...	...
3 Subsidies	383	937	1266	1992	2629	2867	4572	6196	7229	10252	8933	13355
4 Other current transfers	749	2531	3608	5941	12529	19983	16078	17350	24202	29198	28468	40311
A Social security benefits	358	1303	1611	2304	3590	3892	5113	6491	8532	11363	14371	17357
B Social assistance grants	56	47	64	104	165	182	206	283	313	386	394	569
C Other	335	1180	1933	3533	8774	15909	10759	10576	15358	17449	13703	22385
5 Net saving	-672	7331	9783	9800	14204	15960	13604	11470	-3748	13375	37106	39575
Total Current Disbursements and Net Saving of General Government	8941	34064	43730	52774	72565	88178	100227	122270	148526	198151	265527	319310

1.7 External Transactions on Current Account, Summary

Million Costa Rican colones

	1980	1983	1984	1985	1986	1987	1988	1989	1990	1991	1992	1993
Payments to the Rest of the World												
1 Imports of goods and services	15245	47565	55377	64277	75195	101768	125246	164473	215352	270928	388871	485265
A Imports of merchandise c.i.f.	13989	41120	48741	55834	64882	86626	104564	138939	183173	229463	328695	411894
B Other	1256	6446	6636	8443	10313	15142	20683	25534	32178	41463	60175	73371
2 Factor income to the rest of the world	2283	15810	16085	17408	18587	22265	30073	41491	34729	37289	41406	44413
A Compensation of employees	72	154	229	297	294	540	491	774	515	1184	1128	1424
B Property and entrepreneurial income	2211	15656	15856	17110	18293	21725	29582	40717	34213	36105	40278	42989
3 Current transfers to the rest of the world	176	407	462	537	603	703	856	334	368	427	752	1026
4 Surplus of the nation on current transactions	-6134	-13765	-11623	-14847	-9453	-24130	-22766	-37494	-47296	-15714	-52804	-70280
Payments to the Rest of the World and Surplus of the Nation on Current Transactions	11570	50017	60301	67375	84932	100606	133409	168805	203152	292930	378224	460423
Receipts From The Rest of the World												
1 Exports of goods and services	10963	46601	56046	60807	77280	90005	118998	148435	179509	264408	342014	422107
A Exports of merchandise f.o.b.	9248	35430	44288	47388	60838	69505	87845	108779	124681	181990	230149	277074
B Other	1715	11171	11758	13419	16442	20500	31152	39656	54828	82418	111865	145033
2 Factor income from rest of the world	296	2136	2281	3293	3488	3649	4412	10752	13249	15470	16165	16936
A Compensation of employees	104	490	627	802	966	1099	1533	1777	2247	3187	3894	4416
B Property and entrepreneurial income	191	1646	1654	2491	2522	2550	2879	8974	11002	12283	12271	12521
3 Current transfers from rest of the world	311	1280	1974	3275	4164	6952	10000	9618	10395	13053	20045	21380
Receipts from the Rest of the World on Current Transactions	11570	50017	60301	67375	84932	100606	133409	168805	203152	292930	378224	460423

1.8 Capital Transactions of The Nation, Summary

Million Costa Rican colones

	1980	1983	1984	1985	1986	1987	1988	1989	1990	1991	1992	1993
Finance of Gross Capital Formation												
Gross saving	4869	17506	25380	36393	52709	53039	62802	75249	95381	157932	209098	243924
1 Consumption of fixed capital	2181	4210	4862	5488	6130	7114	8919	10621	13245	18400	22228	26026
2 Net saving	2688	13296	20518	30905	46579	45925	53883	64628	82136	139532	186870	217898
A General government	-672	7331	9783	9800	14204	15733	13604	11470	...	...	...	...
B Corporate and quasi-corporate enterprises [a]	254	5537	3961	2607	3940	10987	7627	5131	...	...	...	...

Costa Rica

1.8 Capital Transactions of The Nation, Summary
(Continued)

Million Costa Rican colones

	1980	1983	1984	1985	1986	1987	1988	1989	1990	1991	1992	1993
Public	254	5537	3961	2607	3940	10987	7627	5131	...	...	...	...
Private [a]	...	...	...	...	...	...	...	...	...	...	...	...
C Other [a]	3106	428	6775	18498	28436	19205	32653	48027	...	...	...	...
Less: Surplus of the nation on current transactions	-6134	-13765	-11623	-14847	-9453	-24130	-22766	-37494	-47295	-15714	-52804	-70282
Finance of Gross Capital Formation	11003	31270	37003	51240	62162	77169	85569	112743	142676	173645	261902	314206
Gross Capital Formation												
Increase in stocks	1109	8001	4324	13000	16139	20856	19358	25519	25606	37547	73584	65671
Gross fixed capital formation	9895	23270	32679	38240	46023	56313	66211	87224	117071	136098	188318	248535
1 General government	1987	3398	4920	6444	5997	4871	5351	...	...	...	...	...
2 Corporate and quasi-corporate enterprises	1838	4817	5444	7496	8375	7698	9073	...	...	...	...	...
A Public	1838	4817	5444	7496	8375	7698	9073	...	...	...	...	...
B Private	...	...	...	...	...	...	...	...	...	...	...	...
3 Other	6069	15054	22315	24300	31651	43744	51787	...	...	...	...	...
Gross Capital Formation	11003	31270	37003	51240	62162	77169	85569	112743	142676	173645	261902	314206

a) Private corporate and quasi-corporate enterprises are included in item 'Other'.

1.10 Gross Domestic Product by Kind of Activity, in Current Prices

Million Costa Rican colones

	1980	1983	1984	1985	1986	1987	1988	1989	1990	1991	1992	1993
1 Agriculture, hunting, forestry and fishing	7372	28446	34571	37341	51530	51417	62774	73344	82622	119569	147830	169265
2 Mining and quarrying	7701	28263	36667	43715	52573	60698	74397	86688	101328	137469	185616	211602
3 Manufacturing												
4 Electricity, gas and water	882	4950	5536	6348	7413	8598	10292	13437	16227	24210	31960	39631
5 Construction	2584	3789	5807	7072	8127	9160	10544	14455	16796	19549	23294	29886
6 Wholesale and retail trade, restaurants and hotels	8315	25498	31701	40507	47367	58505	70592	83087	105048	139460	193287	222667
7 Transport, storage and communication	1744	6283	7842	9774	11639	14069	17367	20949	26484	35884	47582	60192
8 Finance, insurance, real estate and business services	4686	10884	13194	17796	24522	31071	39424	49690	64398	76525	96771	120131
9 Community, social and personal services [a]	1835	5401	7150	9589	11829	14756	18380	24260	32103	44623	58763	76215
Total, Industries	35119	113514	142468	172142	215000	248273	303769	365910	445006	597289	785103	929589
Producers of Government Services	6289	15800	20543	25778	31580	36260	45974	60001	77920	92818	118999	144822
Other Producers [a]	...	...	...	...	...	...	...	...	...	...	...	...
Subtotal	41406	129314	163011	197920	246580	284533	349743	425911	522925	690107	904102	1074411
Less: Imputed bank service charge	...	...	...	...	...	...	...	...	...	...	...	...
Plus: Import duties	...	...	...	...	...	...	...	...	...	...	...	...
Plus: Value added tax	...	...	...	...	...	...	...	...	...	...	...	...
Equals: Gross Domestic Product	41406	129314	163011	197920	246580	284533	349743	425911	522925	690107	904102	1074411

a) Item 'Other producers' is included in item 'Community, social and personal services'.

1.11 Gross Domestic Product by Kind of Activity, in Constant Prices

Million Costa Rican colones

	1980	1983	1984	1985	1986	1987	1988	1989	1990	1991	1992	1993
	At constant prices of: 1966											
1 Agriculture, hunting, forestry and fishing	1736	1808	1990	1880	1971	2053	2148	2308	2366	2513	2614	2681
2 Mining and quarrying	2120	1902	2100	2142	2299	2425	2478	2563	2629	2685	2961	3151
3 Manufacturing												
4 Electricity, gas and water	225	304	313	290	308	332	340	357	380	397	421	445
5 Construction	603	337	416	439	453	458	458	515	502	466	478	556
6 Wholesale and retail trade, restaurants and hotels	1741	1418	1580	1653	1768	1839	1863	1962	2057	2061	2319	2493
7 Transport, storage and communication	676	676	701	717	770	838	909	994	1060	1091	1245	1384
8 Finance, insurance, real estate and business services	1165	1211	1252	1284	1344	1413	1494	1580	1663	1689	1799	1936
9 Community, social and personal services [a]	416	396	408	420	435	456	477	502	527	550	573	607

Costa Rica

1.11 Gross Domestic Product by Kind of Activity, in Constant Prices
(Continued)

Million Costa Rican colones

	1980	1983	1984	1985	1986	1987	1988	1989	1990	1991	1992	1993
				At constant prices of:1966								
Total, Industries	8681	8052	8760	8826	9347	9815	10167	10780	11184	11452	12410	13253
Producers of Government Services	967	941	955	959	979	1003	1023	1044	1059	1070	1081	1102
Other Producers [a]	...	...	...	...	...	...	...	...	...	...	...	...
Subtotal	9648	8993	9715	9785	10326	10818	11190	11824	12246	12522	13491	14355
Less: Imputed bank service charge	...	...	...	...	...	...	...	...	...	...	...	...
Plus: Import duties	...	...	...	...	...	...	...	...	...	...	...	...
Plus: Value added tax	...	...	...	...	...	...	...	...	...	...	...	...
Equals: Gross Domestic Product	9648	8993	9715	9785	10326	10818	11190	11824	12246	12522	13491	14355

a) Item 'Other producers' is included in item 'Community, social and personal services'.

1.12 Relations Among National Accounting Aggregates

Million Costa Rican colones

	1980	1983	1984	1985	1986	1987	1988	1989	1990	1991	1992	1993
Gross Domestic Product	41406	129314	163011	197920	246579	284533	349743	425911	522925	690107	904102	1074411
Plus: Net factor income from the rest of the world	-1988	-13673	-13804	-14115	-15098	-18616	-25661	-30740	-21480	-21819	-25241	-27477
Factor income from the rest of the world	296	2136	2281	3293	3489	3649	4412	10752	...	...	...	...
Less: Factor income to the rest of the world	2283	15809	16085	17408	18587	22265	30073	41491	...	...	...	...
Equals: Gross National Product	39418	115641	149207	183805	231481	265917	324082	395171	501445	668287	878861	1046934
Less: Consumption of fixed capital	2181	4210	4862	5488	6130	7114	8919	10621	13245	18400	22228	26029
Equals: National Income	37237	111431	144345	178317	225351	258803	315163	384550	488201	649888	856633	1020905
Plus: Net current transfers from the rest of the world	135	873	1512	2738	3560	6249	9144	9284	10027	12625	19293	20355
Current transfers from the rest of the world	...	...	...	...	...	...	10000	9618	10395	...	...	...
Less: Current transfers to the rest of the world	...	...	...	...	...	...	856	334	368	...	...	...
Equals: National Disposable Income	37372	112304	145857	181055	228911	265052	324306	393834	498227	662513	875926	1041260
Less: Final consumption	34684	99008	125339	150149	182332	219127	270423	329206	416092	522981	689057	823362
Equals: Net Saving	2688	13296	20518	30905	46579	45925	53883	64628	82136	139532	186870	217898
Less: Surplus of the nation on current transactions	-6134	-13765	-11623	-14847	-9453	-24130	-22766	-37494	-47296	-15714	-52805	-70280
Equals: Net Capital Formation	8822	27061	32141	45752	56032	70056	76650	102122	129432	155246	239674	288177

2.9 Gross Capital Formation by Kind of Activity of Owner, ISIC Major Divisions, in Current Prices

Million Costa Rican colones

	1980 Total Gross Capital Formation	1980 Increase in Stocks	1980 Gross Fixed Capital Formation	1985 Total Gross Capital Formation	1985 Increase in Stocks	1985 Gross Fixed Capital Formation	1990 Total Gross Capital Formation	1990 Increase in Stocks	1990 Gross Fixed Capital Formation	1991 Total Gross Capital Formation	1991 Increase in Stocks	1991 Gross Fixed Capital Formation
					All Producers							
1 Agriculture, hunting, fishing and forestry	727	6	721	2703	-	2703	15381	1061	14320	17518	319	17198
2 Mining and quarrying	2527	978	1548	14776	6693	8083	42172	12269	29903	53641	22479	31162
3 Manufacturing												
4 Electricity, gas and water	952	44	907	3495	-120	3615	10321	337	9984	13035	1833	11202
5 Construction	477	-	477	1374	-	1374	4471	...	4471	6455	...	6455
6 Wholesale and retail trade, restaurants and hotels	429	-	429	7379	6175	1204	16191	11554	4637	18796	11681	7115
7 Transport, storage and communication	1641	62	1579	7083	-251	7334	22420	441	21979	26198	753	25445
8 Finance, insurance, real estate and business services	2054	13	2041	6748	67	6681	19581	112	19469	20809	48	20762
9 Community, social and personal services	205	-	205	803	-	803	4407	...	4407	5044	...	5044
Total Industries	9012	1104	7908	44359	12564	31795	134944	25774	109172	161496	37113	124384
Producers of Government Services	1992	5	1987	6880	436	6444	7733	-168	7901	12150	435	11714
Private Non-Profit Institutions Serving Households	...	...	...	...	...	...	...	...	...	...	...	...
Total	11003	1109	9895	51240	13000	38240	142677	25606	117071	173645	37547	136098

Costa Rica

2.9 Gross Capital Formation by Kind of Activity of Owner, ISIC Major Divisions, in Current Prices

Million Costa Rican colones

	1992 Total Gross Capital Formation	1992 Increase in Stocks	1992 Gross Fixed Capital Formation	1993 Total Gross Capital Formation	1993 Increase in Stocks	1993 Gross Fixed Capital Formation
			All Producers			
1 Agriculture, hunting, fishing and forestry	29482	4258	25222	33753	4588	29165
2 Mining and quarrying	87367	42852	44515	85722	26259	59463
3 Manufacturing						
4 Electricity, gas and water	17045	1335	15710	25404	578	24826
5 Construction	8749	...	8749	12253	...	12253
6 Wholesale and retail trade, restaurants and hotels	34932	24298	10634	45984	33380	12603
7 Transport, storage and communication	38578	299	38280	52183	495	51689
8 Finance, insurance, real estate and business services	24630	52	24578	30696	39	30657
9 Community, social and personal services	7053	...	7053	9334	...	9334
Total Industries	247836	73094	174742	295329	65339	229990
Producers of Government Services	14064	488	13576	18877	332	18545
Private Non-Profit Institutions Serving Households	...	...	...	...	...	...
Total	261900	73582	188318	314206	65671	248535

2.17 Exports and Imports of Goods and Services, Detail

Million Costa Rican colones

	1980	1983	1984	1985	1986	1987	1988	1989	1990	1991	1992	1993
					Exports of Goods and Services							
1 Exports of merchandise, f.o.b.	9248	35430	44288	47388	60838	69505	87845	108779	124681	181990	230149	277074
2 Transport and communication	191	744	1006	1003	1232	1570	2039	2496	3591	5959	7693	8945
3 Insurance service charges	106	183	262	290	357	371	603	702	994	1258	1544	1781
4 Other commodities	484	3213	3708	4730	5658	7888	12232	15720	19832	28132	34988	41350
5 Adjustments of merchandise exports to change-of-ownership basis	...	...	...	...	...	...	...	...	...	...	...	...
6 Direct purchases in the domestic market by non-residential households	933	7032	6783	7396	9196	10670	16279	20738	30411	47070	67640	92956
7 Direct purchases in the domestic market by extraterritorial bodies	...	...	...	...	...	...	...	...	...	...	...	...
Total Exports of Goods and Services	10963	46601	56046	60807	77280	90005	118998	148435	179509	264408	342014	422107
					Imports of Goods and Services							
1 Imports of merchandise, c.i.f.	13989	41120	48741	55834	64882	86626	104564	138939	183173	229463	328696	411893
A Imports of merchandise, f.o.b.	12707	37313	44253	50707	58843	78204	94750	125560	165422	207290	296715	371825
B Transport of services on merchandise imports	1283	3807	4488	5127	6038	8422	9814	13379	17751	22173	31981	40068
C Insurance service charges on merchandise imports	...	...	...	...	...	...	...	...	...	...	...	...
2 Adjustments of merchandise imports to change-of-ownership basis	...	...	...	...	...	...	...	...	...	...	...	...
3 Other transport and communication	213	1293	962	1038	1092	1357	2195	2423	3582	6056	7183	8433
4 Other insurance service charges	...	...	...	...	...	...	...	...	...	...	...	...
5 Other commodities [a]	348	2568	2740	3349	4176	7536	12090	12555	13295	15226	20045	23446
6 Direct purchases abroad by government	695	2585	2935	4056	5046	6249	6399	10556	15302	20183	32947	41493
7 Direct purchases abroad by resident households												
Total Imports of Goods and Services	15245	47565	55377	64277	75195	101768	125246	164473	215352	270928	388871	485265
Balance of Goods and Services	-4282	-964	669	-3470	2085	-11763	-6248	-16038	-35843	-6520	-46857	-63158
Total Imports and Balance of Goods and Services	10963	46601	56046	60807	77280	90005	118998	148435	179509	264408	342014	422107

a) Item 'Other commodities' relates to non-factor services.

Costa Rica

4.3 Cost Components of Value Added

Million Costa Rican colones

	1980						1985					
	Compensation of Employees	Capital Consumption	Net Operating Surplus	Indirect Taxes	Less: Subsidies Received	Value Added	Compensation of Employees	Capital Consumption	Net Operating Surplus	Indirect Taxes	Less: Subsidies Received	Value Added
	All Producers											
1 Agriculture, hunting, forestry and fishing	2694	271	3860	...	...	7372	12490	581	...	...	...	37341
2 Mining and quarrying	2740	503	2552	...	...	7701	13521	1261	...	...	...	43715
3 Manufacturing				...	...				...	...	...	
4 Electricity, gas and water	268	148	463	...	...	882	1376	835	...	...	...	6348
5 Construction	1868	184	482	...	...	2584	5926	295	...	...	...	7072
6 Wholesale and retail trade, restaurants and hotels	3299	172	2530	...	...	8315	15853	420	...	...	...	40507
7 Transport, storage and communication	922	278	693	...	...	1744	4828	727	...	...	...	9774
8 Finance, insurance, real estate and business services	1146	548	2919	...	...	4686	5721	1196	...	...	...	17795
9 Community, social and personal services [a]	1268	79	367	...	...	1835	6880	175	...	...	...	9589
Total, Industries	14205	2181	13867	...	...	35119	66595	5488	...	...	...	172142
Producers of Government Services	6289	...	...	...	...	6289	25778	...	...	...	...	25778
Other Producers [a]	...	...	...	...	...	...	...	...	...	...	...	...
Total	20495	2181	13867	...	...	41406	92373	5488	...	...	...	197920
Less: Imputed bank service charge	...	...	...	...	...	...	...	...	...	...	...	...
Import duties	...	...	...	...	...	...	...	...	...	...	...	...
Value added tax	...	...	...	...	...	...	...	...	...	...	...	...
Total	20495	2181	13867	5245	383	41406	92373	5488	...	...	...	197920

	1990						1991					
	Compensation of Employees	Capital Consumption	Net Operating Surplus	Indirect Taxes	Less: Subsidies Received	Value Added	Compensation of Employees	Capital Consumption	Net Operating Surplus	Indirect Taxes	Less: Subsidies Received	Value Added
	All Producers											
1 Agriculture, hunting, forestry and fishing	38736	1315	...	...	...	82622	50266	1832	...	...	...	119569
2 Mining and quarrying	33142	2973	...	...	...	101328	43889	4195	...	...	...	137469
3 Manufacturing			...	...	...				...	...	...	
4 Electricity, gas and water	4269	2184	...	...	...	16227	6314	2924	...	...	...	24210
5 Construction	14118	401	...	...	...	16796	16397	587	...	...	...	19549
6 Wholesale and retail trade, restaurants and hotels	44535	925	...	...	...	105048	53875	1418	...	...	...	139459
7 Transport, storage and communication	14215	1638	...	...	...	26484	18781	2279	...	...	...	35884
8 Finance, insurance, real estate and business services	18641	3279	...	...	...	64398	22925	4389	...	...	...	76525
9 Community, social and personal services [a]	18804	530	...	...	...	32103	22170	774	...	...	...	44623
Total, Industries	186460	13245	...	...	...	445006	234618	18399	...	...	...	597289
Producers of Government Services	77920	...	...	...	...	77920	92818	...	...	...	...	92818
Other Producers [a]	...	...	...	...	...	...	...	...	...	...	...	...
Total	264380	13245	...	...	...	522925	327436	18399	...	...	...	690107
Less: Imputed bank service charge	...	...	...	...	...	...	...	...	...	...	...	...
Import duties	...	...	...	...	...	...	...	...	...	...	...	...
Value added tax	...	...	...	...	...	...	...	...	...	...	...	...
Total	264380	13245	...	...	...	522925	327436	18399	...	...	...	690107

	1992						1993					
	Compensation of Employees	Capital Consumption	Net Operating Surplus	Indirect Taxes	Less: Subsidies Received	Value Added	Compensation of Employees	Capital Consumption	Net Operating Surplus	Indirect Taxes	Less: Subsidies Received	Value Added
	All Producers											
1 Agriculture, hunting, forestry and fishing	...	...	...	...	...	147830	...	...	...	...	...	169265
2 Mining and quarrying	...	...	...	...	...	185616	...	...	...	...	...	211602
3 Manufacturing	...	...	...	...	...		...	...	...	...	...	
4 Electricity, gas and water	...	...	...	...	...	31960	...	...	...	...	...	39631

Costa Rica

4.3 Cost Components of Value Added
(Continued)

Million Costa Rican colones

	Compensation of Employees	Capital Consumption	Net Operating Surplus	Indirect Taxes	Less: Subsidies Received	Value Added	Compensation of Employees	Capital Consumption	Net Operating Surplus	Indirect Taxes	Less: Subsidies Received	Value Added
	\multicolumn{6}{c}{1992}	\multicolumn{6}{c}{1993}
5 Construction	...	...	...	...	...	23294	...	...	...	...	...	29886
6 Wholesale and retail trade, restaurants and hotels	...	...	...	...	...	193287	...	...	...	...	...	222667
7 Transport, storage and communication	...	...	...	...	...	47582	...	...	...	...	...	60192
8 Finance, insurance, real estate and business services	...	...	...	...	...	96771	...	...	...	...	...	120131
9 Community, social and personal services [a]	...	...	...	...	...	58763	...	...	...	...	...	76215
Total, Industries	...	...	...	...	...	785103	...	...	...	...	...	929589
Producers of Government Services	...	...	...	...	...	118999	...	...	...	...	...	144822
Other Producers [a]	...	...	...	...	...	...	...	...	...	...	...	...
Total	...	...	...	...	...	904102	...	...	...	...	...	1074411
Less: Imputed bank service charge	...	...	...	...	...	...	...	...	...	...	...	...
Import duties	...	...	...	...	...	...	...	...	...	...	...	...
Value added tax	...	...	...	...	...	...	...	...	...	...	...	...
Total	...	...	...	...	...	904102	...	...	...	...	...	1074411

a) Item 'Other producers' is included in item 'Community, social and personal services'.

Cote d'Ivoire

Source. Communication from the Direction des Etudes de Developpement, Ministere du Plan, Abidjan. The official estimates are published annually in 'Comptes de la Nation'.

General note. The official estimates of Cote d'Ivoire have been adjusted by the Direction des Etudes de Developpement to conform to the present United Nations System of National Accounts so far as the existing data would permit.

1.1 Expenditure on the Gross Domestic Product, in Current Prices

Million CFA francs

	1980	1983	1984	1985	1986	1987	1988	1989	1990	1991	1992	1993
1 Government final consumption expenditure	357603	439300	453300	441600	485900	501800	530000	576000	499000	488000	...	...
2 Private final consumption expenditure	1388110	1663500	1783700	1836400	2007700	2041000	2058000	2168000	2109000	2162000	...	...
3 Gross capital formation	570461	470700	348200	406100	382500	373400	387000	277000	197000	221000	...	...
A Increase in stocks	46856	8900	-39300	37000	7700	16600	36000	-44000	-53000	-33000	...	...
B Gross fixed capital formation	523605	461800	387500	369100	374800	356800	351000	321000	250000	254000	...	...
Residential buildings		...	...	...	...	...	...	...	...	...	...	...
Non-residential buildings	346117	...	...	...	...	...	...	...	...	...	...	...
Other construction and land improvement etc.		...	...	...	...	...	...	...	...	...	...	...
Other	177488	...	...	...	...	...	...	...	...	...	...	...
4 Exports of goods and services	773515	963100	1354600	1466300	1252800	1013500	931000	997000	931000	888000	...	...
5 Less: Imports of goods and services	939803	930700	950400	1015600	957200	898000	852000	905000	797000	799000	...	...
Equals: Gross Domestic Product [a]	2149886	2605913	2989400	3134800	3171700	3031700	3054000	3113000	2939000	2960000	...	...

a) Data for this table have not been revised, therefore, data for some years are not comparable with those of other tables.

1.10 Gross Domestic Product by Kind of Activity, in Current Prices

Million CFA francs

	1980	1983	1984	1985	1986	1987	1988	1989	1990	1991	1992	1993
1 Agriculture, hunting, forestry and fishing	616278	...	791517	...	...	...	...	...	...	...	...	...
2 Mining and quarrying	5718	...	84075	...	...	...	...	...	...	...	...	...
3 Manufacturing	241025	...	341556	...	...	...	...	...	...	...	...	...
4 Electricity, gas and water	34439	...	35884	...	...	...	...	...	...	...	...	...
5 Construction	148943	...	62014	...	...	...	...	...	...	...	...	...
6 Wholesale and retail trade, restaurants and hotels [a]	392139	...	...	...	...	...	...	...	...	...	...	...
7 Transport, storage and communication	159691	...	212759	...	...	...	...	...	...	...	...	...
8 Finance, insurance, real estate and business services	210517	...	...	...	...	...	...	...	...	...	...	...
9 Community, social and personal services	21967	...	...	...	...	...	...	...	...	...	...	...
Total, Industries	1830717	...	2358321	...	...	...	...	...	...	...	...	...
Producers of Government Services	213688	...	...	...	...	...	...	...	...	...	...	...
Other Producers	15553	...	...	...	...	...	...	...	...	...	...	...
Subtotal	2059958	...	...	...	...	...	...	...	...	...	...	...
Less: Imputed bank service charge	67651	...	...	...	...	...	...	...	...	...	...	...
Plus: Import duties	157579	...	170199	...	...	...	...	...	...	...	...	...
Plus: Value added tax	...	...	...	...	...	...	...	...	...	...	...	...
Equals: Gross Domestic Product	2149886	...	2855779	...	...	...	...	...	...	...	...	...

a) Item 'Wholesale and retail trade, restaurants and hotels' includes the profit or loss of the Marketing Board.

Croatia

Source. Reply to the United Nations national accounts questionnaire from the Central Bureau of Statistics. The official estimates and detailed description on the concepts, sources and methods of estimation used in the compilation of national accounts estimates are published in 'National Accounts of the Republic of Croatia for 1986-1988 and for 1989-1990' and the 'Statistical Yearbook of the Republic of Croatia'.

General note. The estimates shown in the following tables have been prepared in accordance with the System of Material Product Balances (MPS). Gross social product and the elements of its initial distribution are calculated according to the so-called real or production method, except for the non-agricultural private sector where the personal or earnings method is used.

1a Net Material Product by Use at Current Market Prices

Million Croatian dinars

		1980	1983	1984	1985	1986	1987	1988	1989	1990	1991	1992	1993
1	Personal consumption	22	56	75	145	252	553	1682	25505	138298	...	...	...
2	Material consumption in the units of the non-material sphere serving individuals [a]	2	6	10	18	46	103	281	2628	24923	...	...	...
	Consumption of the Population	24	62	85	163	298	656	1963	28133	163221	...	...	...
3	Material consumption in the units of the non-material sphere serving the community as a whole [a]	...	...	...	...	...	...	...	...	...	...	...	...
4	Net fixed capital formation [b]	13	21	29	55	114	210	622	7162	37682	...	...	...
5	Increase in material circulating assets and in stocks	5	17	33	54	84	244	662	13928	32997	...	...	...
6	Losses	...	...	...	...	...	...	...	...	...	...	...	...
7	Exports of goods and material services	9	21	46	71	493	995	3297	42539	183090	...	...	...
8	Less: Imports of goods and material services	12	18	40	59	450	934	3105	42358	181117	...	...	...
	Statistical discrepancy	2	-	8	7	7	92	396	6800	6482	...	...	...
	Net Material Product [c]	41	103	161	291	546	1263	3835	56204	242355	383524	2685537	...

a) Item 'Material consumption in the units of the non-material sphere serving the community as a whole' is included in item 'Material consumption in the units of the non-material sphere serving individuals'.
b) Gross fixed capital formation rather than net.
c) The data refer to Social Product and not to Net Material Product.

2a Net Material Product by Kind of Activity of the Material Sphere in Current Market Prices

Million Croatian dinars

		1980	1983	1984	1985	1986	1987	1988	1989	1990	1991	1992	1993
1	Agriculture and forestry	5	15	22	33	65	133	383	5664	27469	49093	425541	...
	A Agriculture and livestock	...	...	...	...	...	...	...	...	...	...	...	...
	B Forestry	-	1	2	4	7	14	42	671	3115	5189	32684	...
	C Other	5	14	20	29	58	119	341	4993	24354	43904	392857	...
2	Industrial activity	14	35	58	114	201	500	1562	24832	80431	125765	1125852	...
3	Construction	4	9	14	24	39	89	255	3789	20532	26073	149884	...
4	Wholesale and retail trade and restaurants and other eating and drinking places [a]	10	26	38	66	137	306	923	11621	64614	99817	545759	...
5	Transport and communication	4	9	15	27	52	112	367	5614	24831	43649	209722	...
6	Other activities of the material sphere	4	9	14	27	52	123	345	4684	24478	39127	228779	...
	Net material product [b]	41	103	161	291	546	1263	3835	56204	242355	383524	2685537	...

a) Item 'Wholesale and retail trade and restaurants and other eating and drinking places' refers to trade, catering trade and tourism.
b) The data refer to Social Product and not to Net Material Product.

2b Net Material Product by Kind of Activity of the Material Sphere in Constant Market Prices

Thousand Croatian dinars

		1980	1983	1984	1985	1986	1987	1988	1989	1990	1991	1992	1993
						At constant prices of:1972							
1	Agriculture and forestry	1233	1373	1430	1316	1433	1416	1332	1401	1360	...	...	...
	A Agriculture and livestock	...	...	...	...	...	...	...	...	...	...	...	...
	B Forestry	95	110	115	114	115	120	123	120	105	...	...	...
	C Other	1138	1263	1315	1202	1318	1296	1209	1281	1255	...	...	...
2	Industrial activity	3471	3438	3613	3684	3854	3920	3864	3848	3401	...	...	...
3	Construction	1066	877	832	803	745	684	694	659	612	...	...	...
4	Wholesale and retail trade and restaurants and other eating and drinking places [a]	2148	2091	2077	2098	2116	2011	1981	1848	1688	...	...	...
5	Transport and communication	1158	1109	1150	1187	1257	1362	1410	1349	1281	...	...	...
6	Other activities of the material sphere	777	826	819	847	805	807	824	845	758	...	...	...
	Net material product [b]	9853	9714	9921	9935	10210	10200	10105	9950	9100	...	...	...

a) Item 'Wholesale and retail trade and restaurants and other eating and drinking places' refers to trade, catering trade and tourism.
b) The data refer to Social Product and not to Net Material Product.

Cuba

Source. Correspondence from the Oficina Nacional de Estadisticas, Habana.
General note. The estimates shown in the following tables have been prepared in accordance with the United Nations System of National Accounts.

1a Net Material Product by Use at Current Market Prices
Million Cuban pesos

		1980	1983	1984	1985	1986	1987	1988	1989	1990	1991	1992	1993
1	Personal consumption	6692.4	8666.6	9277.1	9683.3	10047.8	10133.4	10390.6	10658.8	...	...	...	...
2	Material consumption in the units of the non-material sphere serving individuals	980.1	1357.0	1460.2	1497.1	1553.5	1432.2	1472.8	1454.2	...	...	...	...
	Consumption of the Population	7672.5	10023.6	10737.3	11180.4	11601.3	11565.6	11863.4	12113.0	...	...	...	...
3	Material consumption in the units of the non-material sphere serving the community as a whole	663.8	1016.3	1133.2	1186.2	1208.5	1122.8	1119.2	1113.6	...	...	...	...
4	Net fixed capital formation	1529.3	2242.6	2894.9	3098.3	2728.9	1994.3	2054.1	2233.0	...	...	...	...
5	Increase in material circulating assets and in stocks	576.9	552.7	590.3	663.0	-246.9	-260.0	-78.3	137.1	...	...	...	...
6	Losses	20.0	38.4	41.4	81.8	86.1	73.9	82.4	82.2	...	...	...	...
7	Exports of goods and material services	4129.4	5674.4	5743.7	-2220.6	-2304.4	-2072.5	-2211.4	-2681.2	...	...	...	...
8	Less: Imports of goods and material services	4766.1	6445.7	7416.9						...	...	...	...
	Statistical discrepancy	27.3	-176.4	-28.9	-37.4	-216.1	-139.8	-65.5	-206.8	...	...	...	...
	Net Material Product	9853.1	12925.9	13695.0	13951.7	12857.4	12284.3	12763.9	12790.9	...	...	...	...

1b Net Material Product by Use at Constant Market Prices
Million Cuban pesos

		1980	1983	1984	1985	1986	1987	1988	1989	1990	1991	1992	1993
					At constant prices of:1981								
1	Personal consumption	7131.5	7683.4	7961.1	8144.3	8333.6	8290.1	8470.8	8597.3	...	...	...	...
2	Material consumption in the units of the non-material sphere serving individuals	1015.3	1265.1	1360.2	1374.7	1413.2	1314.3	1347.0	1330.0	...	...	...	...
	Consumption of the Population	8146.8	8948.5	9321.3	9519.0	9746.8	9604.4	9817.8	9927.3	...	...	...	...
3	Material consumption in the units of the non-material sphere serving the community as a whole	669.7	1000.0	1115.8	1171.5	1205.5	1110.9	1106.4	1100.4	...	...	...	...
4	Net fixed capital formation	1615.1	2242.6	2894.9	3098.3	2771.2	2119.2	2225.3	2417.1	...	...	...	...
5	Increase in material circulating assets and in stocks	621.9	536.2	560.0	615.7	-179.3	-187.2	-56.4	98.8	...	...	...	...
6	Losses	22.7	38.4	41.4	81.6	82.0	73.9	83.1	83.0	...	...	...	...
7	Exports of goods and material services	3993.3	5612.5	5484.5	-267.2	383.4	383.5	209.8	-163.0	...	...	...	...
8	Less: Imports of goods and material services	5518.1	5625.1	5869.1						...	...	...	...
	Statistical discrepancy	-28.3	-7.9	147.4	41.7	-65.8	168.5	179.0	31.9	...	...	...	...
	Net Material Product	9523.1	12745.2	13696.0	14260.6	13943.8	13273.2	13565.0	13495.5	...	...	...	...

2a Net Material Product by Kind of Activity of the Material Sphere in Current Market Prices
Million Cuban pesos

		1980	1983	1984	1985	1986	1987	1988	1989	1990	1991	1992	1993
1	Agriculture and forestry	616.9	1342.1	1369.6	1362.2	1428.7	1440.8	1532.9	1554.6	...	...	...	...
	A Agriculture and livestock	578.9	1251.5	1260.3	1252.3	1318.1	1333.1	1442.9	1456.5	...	...	...	...
	B Forestry	44.6	78.3	88.4	93.7	94.9	92.7	76.7	82.2	...	...	...	...
	C Other	-6.6	12.3	20.9	16.2	15.7	15.0	13.3	15.9	...	...	...	...
2	Industrial activity	3816.7	4134.9	4734.4	5071.8	4806.3	4498.5	4782.2	4656.2	...	...	...	...
3	Construction	784.8	1078.5	1321.0	1312.6	1198.5	997.6	1082.5	1171.8	...	...	...	...
4	Wholesale and retail trade and restaurants and other eating and drinking places	3803.3	5336.4	5124.5	5080.9	4333.7	4205.1	4209.5	4294.5	...	...	...	...
5	Transport and communication	782.1	957.9	1051.2	1039.6	986.3	1053.9	1073.4	1037.8	...	...	...	...
	A Transport	669.4	807.7	890.0	871.8	823.1	867.6	879.8	851.0	...	...	...	...
	B Communication	112.7	150.2	161.2	167.8	163.2	186.3	193.6	186.8	...	...	...	...
6	Other activities of the material sphere	49.3	76.1	94.3	84.6	103.9	88.4	83.4	76.0	...	...	...	...
	Net material product	9853.1	12925.9	13695.0	13951.7	12857.4	12284.3	12763.9	12790.9	...	...	...	...

Cuba

2b Net Material Product by Kind of Activity of the Material Sphere in Constant Market Prices

Million Cuban pesos

		1980	1983	1984	1985	1986	1987	1988	1989	1990	1991	1992	1993
						At constant prices of:1981							
1	Agriculture and forestry	1241.4	1305.9	1335.0	1268.7	1236.2	1290.5	1318.3	1332.6	...	...	...	...
	A Agriculture and livestock	1178.8	1210.7	1225.7	1162.9	1129.6	1186.4	1215.6	1217.3	...	...	...	...
	B Forestry	50.3	78.3	88.4	87.3	88.5	86.7	87.1	96.9	...	...	...	...
	C Other	12.3	16.9	20.9	18.5	18.1	17.4	15.6	18.4	...	...	...	...
2	Industrial activity	2748.2	4059.6	4586.9	5098.5	4803.5	4586.3	4797.5	4720.9	...	...	...	...
3	Construction	746.5	1078.0	1320.5	1279.5	1225.5	1079.9	1181.8	1296.6	...	...	...	...
4	Wholesale and retail trade and restaurants and other eating and drinking places	4032.8	5275.4	5304.8	5472.7	5566.3	5177.1	5116.0	5031.9	...	...	...	...
5	Transport and communication	709.0	942.8	1044.6	1011.7	991.8	1010.8	1035.2	984.0	...	...	...	...
	A Transport	597.4	794.3	885.2	845.7	815.1	830.2	847.3	795.5	...	...	...	...
	B Communication	111.6	148.5	159.4	166.0	176.7	180.6	187.9	188.5	...	...	...	...
6	Other activities of the material sphere	45.2	83.5	104.4	129.5	120.5	128.6	116.2	129.5	...	...	...	...
	Net material product	9523.1	12745.2	13696.2	14260.6	13943.8	13273.2	13565.0	13495.5	...	...	...	...

6a Capital Formation by Kind of Activity of the Material and Non-Material Spheres in Current Market Prices

Million Cuban pesos

		1980	1983	1984	1985	1986	1987	1988	1989	1990	1991	1992	1993
						Gross Fixed Capital Formation							
1	Agriculture and forestry	638.8	890.6	1011.1	1089.6	1152.6	1025.7	1013.1	1145.2	...	...	...	...
2	Industrial activity	1088.1	1386.7	1571.3	1850.4	1691.9	1449.6	1609.6	1655.2	...	...	...	...
3	Construction	139.0	255.5	312.4	278.4	273.6	237.0	268.1	304.2	...	...	...	...
4	Wholesale and retail trade and restaurants and other eating and drinking places	78.7	139.1	189.2	190.3	178.2	146.3	122.7	150.6	...	...	...	...
5	Transport and communication	438.8	577.4	592.1	585.5	698.4	616.9	672.6	698.6	...	...	...	...
6	Other activities of the material sphere	8.9	13.3	16.7	16.6	34.0	27.8	24.5	33.6	...	...	...	...
	Total Material Sphere	2392.3	3262.6	3692.8	4010.8	4028.7	3503.3	3710.4	3987.4	...	...	...	...
7	Housing except owner-occupied, communal and miscellaneous personal services	252.4	223.3	328.0	281.6	314.0	291.6	353.0	395.4	...	...	...	...
8	Education, culture and art	150.4	95.1	143.3	139.7	142.4	174.6	159.2	166.3	...	...	...	...
9	Health and social welfare services and sports	59.7	73.4	90.1	115.8	167.6	186.1	195.7	184.6	...	...	...	...
	Total Non-Material Sphere Serving Individuals	462.5	391.8	561.4	537.1	624.0	652.3	707.9	746.5	...	...	...	...
10	Government	51.8	323.9	487.3	537.2	273.3	170.9	139.8	134.3	...	...	...	...
11	Finance, credit and insurance	1.6	4.0	3.2	1.9	2.4	4.6	1.8	2.5	...	...	...	...
12	Research, scientific and technological institutes	19.2	25.8	34.7	42.5	50.0	44.7	45.2	55.8	...	...	...	...
13	Other activities of the non-material sphere	1.4	12.8	8.4	2.3	4.3	1.8	0.7	2.6	...	...	...	...
	Total Non-Material Sphere Serving the Community as a Whole	74.0	366.5	533.6	583.9	330.0	222.0	187.5	195.2	...	...	...	...
14	Owner-occupied dwellings	-	-	-	-	-	-	-	-	...	...	...	...
	Total Gross Fixed Capital Formation	2928.8	4020.9	4787.8	5131.8	4982.7	4377.6	4606.0	4929.1	...	...	...	...
						Increases in Material Circulating Assets and Stocks							
1	Agriculture and forestry	...	...	...	...	...	-14.9	129.9	-42.9	...	...	...	...
2	Industrial activity	...	...	...	...	...	-187.3	-18.8	195.0	...	...	...	...
3	Construction	...	...	...	...	...	-87.1	82.3	-5.7	...	...	...	...
4	Wholesale and retail trade and restaurants and other eating and drinking places	...	...	...	...	...	0.1	-331.8	-50.0	...	...	...	...
5	Transport and communication	...	...	...	...	...	-43.9	9.4	-6.7	...	...	...	...
6	Other activities of the non-material sphere	...	...	...	...	...	6.4	11.5	26.5	...	...	...	...
	Total increase in material circulating assets	...	...	...	...	...	-326.7	-117.5	116.2	...	...	...	...
	Statistical discrepancy	...	...	...	...	...	...	...	...	...	...	...	...
	Increase in stocks of the non-material sphere [a]	576.9	552.7	590.3	663.0	-246.9	66.7	39.2	20.9	...	...	...	...

a) Prior to 1987, estimates include the increase in stocks of both material and non-material sphere.

Cuba

6b Capital Formation by Kind of Activity of the Material and Non-Material Spheres in Constant Market Prices
Million Cuban pesos

	1980	1983	1984	1985	1986	1987	1988	1989	1990	1991	1992	1993
	\multicolumn{12}{c}{At constant prices of: 1981}
	\multicolumn{12}{c}{Gross Fixed Capital Formation}
1 Agriculture and forestry	678.7	890.6	1011.1	1089.6	1136.9	1065.8	1072.8	1213.1	...	...	...	...
2 Industrial activity	1138.0	1386.7	1571.3	1850.4	1718.4	1510.1	1656.7	1686.3	...	...	...	...
3 Construction	140.0	255.5	312.4	278.4	274.4	238.7	273.6	283.9	...	...	...	...
4 Wholesale and retail trade and restaurants and other eating and drinking places	78.2	139.1	189.2	190.3	180.8	147.3	125.6	151.9	...	...	...	...
5 Transport and communication	435.3	577.4	592.1	585.5	704.5	622.0	691.0	684.0	...	...	...	...
6 Other activities of the material sphere	9.1	13.3	16.7	16.6	34.2	28.4	25.1	35.4	...	...	...	...
Total Material Sphere	2479.3	3262.6	3692.8	4010.8	4049.2	3612.3	3844.8	4054.6	...	...	...	...
7 Housing except owner-occupied, communal and miscellaneous personal services	251.3	223.3	328.0	281.6	318.1	295.1	367.2	450.1	...	...	...	...
8 Education, culture and art	149.2	95.1	143.3	139.7	144.7	177.7	164.8	112.7	...	...	...	...
9 Health and social welfare services and sports	59.2	73.4	90.1	115.8	171.4	187.4	205.3	272.6	...	...	...	...
Total Non-Material Sphere Serving Individuals	459.7	391.8	561.4	537.1	634.2	660.2	737.3	845.4	...	...	...	...
10 Government	52.7	323.9	487.3	537.2	282.6	173.8	143.2	146.1	...	...	...	...
11 Finance, credit and insurance	2.0	4.0	3.2	1.9	2.4	5.5	1.8	5.1	...	...	...	...
12 Research, scientific and technological institutes	19.1	25.8	34.7	42.5	52.2	45.1	47.9	61.2	...	...	...	...
13 Other activities of the non-material sphere	1.8	12.8	8.4	2.3	4.4	3.1	0.8	5.1	...	...	...	...
Total Non-Material Sphere Serving the Community as a Whole	75.6	366.5	533.6	583.9	341.6	227.5	193.7	217.5	...	...	...	...
14 Owner-occupied dwellings	-	-	-	-	-	-	-	-	...	...	...	...
Total Gross Fixed Capital Formation	3014.6	4020.9	4787.8	5131.8	5025.0	4500.0	4775.8	5117.5	...	...	...	...
	\multicolumn{12}{c}{Increases in Material Circulating Assets and Stocks}
1 Agriculture and forestry	...	...	...	...	...	...	...	...	...	...	...	...
2 Industrial activity	...	...	...	...	...	...	...	...	...	...	...	...
3 Construction	...	...	...	...	...	...	...	...	...	...	...	...
4 Wholesale and retail trade and restaurants and other eating and drinking places	...	...	...	...	...	...	...	...	...	...	...	...
5 Transport and communication	...	...	...	...	...	...	...	...	...	...	...	...
6 Other activities of the non-material sphere	...	...	...	...	...	...	...	...	...	...	...	...
Total increase in material circulating assets	...	...	...	...	...	...	...	...	...	...	...	...
Statistical discrepancy	...	...	...	...	...	...	...	...	...	...	...	...
Increase in stocks of the non-material sphere [a]	621.9	536.2	560.0	615.7	-179.3	-187.2	-56.4	98.8	...	...	...	...

a) Estimates include the increase in stocks of both material and non-material sphere.

7a Final Consumption at Current Market Prices
Million Cuban pesos

	1980	1983	1984	1985	1986	1987	1988	1989	1990	1991	1992	1993
1 Personal consumption	6692.4	8666.6	9277.1	9683.3	10047.8	10133.4	10390.6	10658.8	...	...	...	...
	\multicolumn{12}{c}{a) Material Consumption in the Units of the Non-Material Sphere Serving Individuals}
Housing except owner-occupied, communal and miscellaneous personal services	203.6	371.0	423.5	437.5	435.6	397.0	386.5	381.7	...	...	...	...
Education, culture and art	552.1	704.7	732.0	734.6	742.2	662.8	683.9	650.0	...	...	...	...
Health and social welfare services and sports	224.4	281.3	304.7	325.0	375.7	372.4	402.4	422.5	...	...	...	...
Other	-	-	-	-	-	-	-	-	...	...	...	...
2 Total non-material sphere serving individuals	980.1	1357.0	1460.2	1497.1	1553.5	1432.2	1472.8	1454.2	...	...	...	...

Cuba

7a Final Consumption at Current Market Prices
(Continued)

Million Cuban pesos

	1980	1983	1984	1985	1986	1987	1988	1989	1990	1991	1992	1993
b) Material Consumption in the Units of the Non-Material Sphere Serving the Community as a Whole												
Government	588.1	886.5	994.2	1042.9	1049.4	958.8	961.6	945.8	...	...	...	...
Finance, credit and insurance	8.3	15.2	16.1	15.3	17.5	19.9	19.4	19.6	...	...	...	...
Research, scientific and technological institutes	19.4	43.2	50.9	54.4	66.4	72.5	68.6	78.5	...	...	...	...
Other activities of the non-material sphere	48.0	71.4	72.0	73.6	75.2	71.6	69.6	69.7	...	...	...	...
3 Total non-material sphere serving the community as a whole	663.8	1016.3	1133.2	1186.2	1208.5	1122.8	1119.2	1113.6	...	...	...	...
Final consumption	8336.3	11039.9	11870.5	12366.6	12809.8	12688.4	12982.6	13226.6	...	...	...	...

7b Final Consumption at Constant Market Prices

Million Cuban pesos

	1980	1983	1984	1985	1986	1987	1988	1989	1990	1991	1992	1993
					At constant prices of:1981							
1 Personal consumption	7131.5	7683.4	7961.1	8144.3	8333.6	8290.1	8470.8	8597.3	...	...	...	...
a) Material Consumption in the Units of the Non-Material Sphere Serving Individuals												
Housing except owner-occupied, communal and miscellaneous personal services	218.9	367.8	420.1	433.8	423.5	393.9	383.4	378.6	...	...	...	...
Education, culture and art	567.1	633.3	654.7	639.1	641.4	571.6	587.3	556.5	...	...	...	...
Health and social welfare services and sports	229.3	264.0	285.4	301.8	348.3	348.8	376.3	394.9	...	...	...	...
Other	-	-	-	-	-	-	-	-	...	...	...	...
2 Total non-material sphere serving individuals	1015.3	1265.1	1360.2	1374.7	1413.2	1314.3	1347.0	1330.0	...	...	...	...
b) Material Consumption in the Units of the Non-Material Sphere Serving the Community as a Whole												
Government	592.0	878.8	985.9	1034.9	1056.4	954.0	956.5	940.7	...	...	...	...
Finance, credit and insurance	8.3	15.2	16.0	15.3	17.4	19.8	19.3	19.5	...	...	...	...
Research, scientific and technological institutes	20.5	41.1	48.8	52.3	62.8	71.4	67.4	77.0	...	...	...	...
Other activities of the non-material sphere	48.9	64.9	65.1	69.0	68.9	65.7	63.2	63.2	...	...	...	...
3 Total non-material sphere serving the community as a whole	669.7	1000.0	1115.8	1171.5	1205.5	1110.9	1106.4	1100.4	...	...	...	...
Final consumption	8816.5	9948.5	10437.1	10690.5	10952.3	10715.3	10924.2	11027.7	...	...	...	...

8 Personal Consumption According to Source of Supply of Goods and Material Services in Current Market Prices

Million Cuban pesos

	1980	1983	1984	1985	1986	1987	1988	1989	1990	1991	1992	1993
1 Purchases of goods in state and co-operative retail trade	5906.5	7719.6	8274.8	8612.2	8907.4	8850.3	9083.1	9295.5	...	...	...	...
2 Purchases of goods in the free market and from private retail trade	...	...	...	...	...	...	...	...	...	...	...	...
3 Goods produced on own account and received in kind	116.3	134.8	132.2	151.3	150.0	148.3	159.1	158.7	...	...	...	...
4 Payments for transport and communication services	385.5	448.1	489.4	518.0	562.0	638.6	622.5	640.4	...	...	...	...
5 Purchases of electricity, gas and water	95.1	154.5	164.8	176.5	186.8	247.4	262.9	285.0	...	...	...	...
6 Purchases directly from handicrafts, repair shops and the like	96.5	109.6	113.8	119.9	128.4	128.1	131.9	144.5	...	...	...	...
7 Consumption of fixed assets in respect of all dwellings	92.5	100.0	102.1	105.4	113.2	120.7	131.1	134.7	...	...	...	...
8 Other	-	-	-	-	-	-	-	-	...	...	...	...
Personal consumption	6692.4	8666.6	9277.1	9683.3	10047.8	10133.4	10390.6	10658.8	...	...	...	...

Cyprus

General note. The preparation of national accounts statistics in Cyprus is undertaken by the Department of Statistics and Research, Ministry of Finance, Nicosia. The official estimates are published annually in the 'Economic Report' and the 'Statistical Abstract', issued by the same Department. Information on concepts, sources and methods of estimation used can be found in the 'History and Analysis of the Methodology of National Accounts in Cyprus', published in 1977 and covers the period 1960-1975 and the 'New National Accounts of Cyprus 1976-1983', published in 1985 and covers the years 1976 and after. The estimates are generally in accordance with the classifications and definitions of the United Nations System of National Accounts (SNA). For the years 1950-1975 the 1958 SNA was used and since 1976 the 1968 SNA. To compare national accounts estimates based on the 1968 SNA and those based on the 1958 SNA the following differences should be taken into consideration: (1) Under the 1968 SNA, rents are treated as intermediate inputs instead of value added, (2) operating surplus is not equal to profits as it includes property income paid to owners, and (3) GDP is at market prices (instead of the factor cost pricing), under the 1958 SNA. The following tables have been prepared from successive replies to the United Nations National Accounts Questionnaire. Where the scope and coverage of the estimates differ for conceptual or statistical reasons from the definitions and classifications recommended in the SNA, a footnote is indicated to the relevant tables.

Sources and methods:

(a) Gross domestic product. Prior to 1976 gross domestic product was estimated through a combination of the income and the production methods. Since 1976 GDP is solely estimated through the production method.

(b) Expenditure on the gross domestic product. The expenditure method is used to estimate all the components of the expenditure account (i.e. government and private final consumption expenditure, capital formation, stocks and imports and exports of goods and services). Sources of data are the Treasury Report for Government financial accounts, the publications of the Department of Statistics and Research on industtrial, agriculture, services, imports and exports which provide annual data. The Central Bank of Cyprus provide detailed data on balance of payments and its components. For constant price estimates the total cost of living allowance index is used to deflate wages and salaries in government final consumtion expenditure and partial price indices from the retail price index are used to deflate the private final consumption expenditure. For the other expenditure items, various price deflators are used.

(c) Cost-structure of the gross domestic product. Separate estimates for compensation of employees and operating surplus were not available prior to 1976. Since 1976 separate estimates for compensation of employees and operating surplus are compiled from annual production surveys and other secondary sources. These estimates are published in the Economic Report. The estimate of consumption of fixed capital is based on a fixed percentage (10.5%) of the gross national product. An effort is being made to calculate consumption of fixed capital based on the existing capital stock. Net indirect taxes are available in the Financial Report, issued by the Treasury Department.

(d) Gross domestic product by kind of economic activity. Agricultural estimates were based mainly on ad-hoc inquiries of the Ministry of Agriculture and Natural Resources for years prior to 1969. From 1969 to 1974, estimates were derived from area sample surveys conducted twice a year. From 1975, the area sample was replaced by an annual survey of crop and livestock holders. Data on fishing and forestry are supplied by the Fisheries and Forestry Departments respectively. Estimates for Mining and Quarrying, Manufacturing and Electricity, Gas and Water are derived from the annual industrial production surveys and the censuses of industrial production held every five years since 1956. Construction sector consists of public and private construction. Public construction estimates are compiled from the annual Financial Report of the Treasury Department and the Annual Reports of semi-government organizations and Local Government Authorities. For private construction data are derived from the annual construction surveys conducted since 1978 and based on the building permits. While since 1987 an additional survey is conducted through building contractors. In addition ad hoc inquiries are undertaken for collecting data on inputs, labour, materials, investments etc. supplementing the surveys data. Prior to 1978 the same surveys were conducted every three years. Prior to 1981 Wholesale and Retail Trade estimates were based on gross trade margins, calculated through the commodity flow method. Since the 1981 Census of Wholesale and Retail, estiamtes are derived from an annual survey. For transport, prior to 1980, estimates were based on extrapolation of value added by using indices of the number of buses in use and bus fares, rented cars and fares as well as the number of taxis and their revenues. For lorry transport, estimates were based on the transport margins derived from the commodity flow method. Estimates for Port Services and Civil Aviation were compiled from the annual Financial Report of the Treasury Department and for Cyprus Airways data were obtained regularly from their annual report. For Storage, data were compiled from ad hoc inquiries collected through the Agricultural Surveys and later by conducting Special Surveys. For Communication, estimates were obtained for Postal Services from the Financial Report and for the Cyprus Telecommunication Authority data were compiled from its annual report. Since 1980 estimates are based on annual surveys on all activities of the Transport Sector. Data on financial institutions are collected by the Central Bank of Cyprus. Data on insurance activities are extracted from the records of the Office of the Supervisor of Insurance Companies and ad hoc surveys conducted by the Department of Statistics and Research. Data on Real Estate are based on land and buildings transfer fees and ad hoc surveys. Data on Business Services are derived from annual surveys. The main source of information for public administration and defence and public services is the annual Financial Report of the Treasury Department and annual returns submitted by the local authorities. Estimates for the private services are derived from the annual Services Survey. For the constant price estimates, the double deflation method is used for all items of agricultural outputs and inputs to arrive at value added estimates. Special price deflators for each category and or product items are constructed for both the output and inputs. Prior to 1976, value added was deflated by using a combination of indices for the remaining industries. Quantity indices for mining and quarrying, manufacturing and construction, price indices for wholesale and retail trade, base-year average prices for electricity, gas and water, employment and wage rate indices for all the other services sectors. Since 1976, double deflation method of output and inputs is used. For producers of Government services, the cost of living allowance index is used to deflate their value added which comprises mainly of compensation of employees.

1.1 Expenditure on the Gross Domestic Product, in Current Prices

Million Cyprus pounds

		1980	1983	1984	1985	1986	1987	1988	1989	1990	1991	1992	1993
1	Government final consumption expenditure	103.4	171.9	188.7	208.5	229.9	295.7	332.5	360.7	443.1	493.7	591.2	...
2	Private final consumption expenditure	508.4	765.8	851.5	945.8	979.2	1059.8	1210.2	1343.3	1532.2	1754.1	1961.2	...
	A Households	504.4	758.0	841.6	933.5	966.6	1045.0	1193.8	1324.5	1510.9	1729.7	1933.4	...
	B Private non-profit institutions serving households	4.0	7.8	9.9	12.3	12.6	14.8	16.4	18.8	21.3	24.4	27.8	...
3	Gross capital formation	287.5	342.3	449.3	449.7	415.0	454.5	548.0	697.2	691.2	691.4	878.9	...
	A Increase in stocks	27.5	26.3	36.8	46.7	31.0	36.6	57.2	75.8	62.3	41.0	86.4	...
	B Gross fixed capital formation	260.0	316.0	412.5	403.0	384.0	417.9	490.8	621.4	628.9	650.4	792.5	...
	Residential buildings	105.3	115.4	125.0	145.3	150.2	151.3	170.7	190.4	218.7	244.2	259.4	...
	Non-residential buildings	47.2	56.9	66.3	66.4	68.5	79.4	97.1	112.0	121.5	133.8	161.3	...
	Other construction and land improvement etc.	34.2	51.3	59.4	56.4	65.7	79.3	71.0	80.5	84.1	90.1	94.9	...
	Other	73.3	92.4	161.8	134.9	99.6	107.9	152.0	238.5	204.6	182.3	276.9	...
4	Exports of goods and services	344.1	573.0	731.0	722.4	721.0	841.8	959.6	1161.4	1315.9	1259.4	1536.1	...
5	Less: Imports of goods and services	479.5	727.2	897.4	872.0	775.2	894.9	1067.9	1351.3	1459.8	1527.1	1880.6	...
	Statistical discrepancy	-3.5	10.9	14.3	27.8	30.7	23.5	14.0	46.2	24.5	-5.5	-5.5	
	Equals: Gross Domestic Product	760.4	1136.7	1337.4	1482.2	1600.6	1780.4	1996.4	2257.5	2547.1	2666.0	3081.3	...

Cyprus

1.2 Expenditure on the Gross Domestic Product, in Constant Prices

Million Cyprus pounds

	1980	1983	1984	1985	1986	1987	1988	1989	1990	1991	1992	1993
		At constant prices of:										
		1980						1985				
1 Government final consumption expenditure	103.4	122.7	127.4	132.1 / 208.5	216.0	276.4	299.9	309.2	362.4	373.0	435.2	...
2 Private final consumption expenditure	508.4	618.4	646.3	684.5 / 945.8	962.2	1014.6	1121.2	1198.6	1305.9	1435.4	1500.7	...
A Households	504.4	612.8	640.1	676.8 / 933.5	949.9	999.7	1105.5	1182.0	1287.8	1415.0	1480.1	...
B Private non-profit institutions serving households	4.0	5.6	6.2	7.7 / 12.3	12.3	14.9	15.7	16.5	18.2	20.4	20.6	...
3 Gross capital formation	287.5	268.3	328.3	310.8 / 449.7	404.5	430.5	489.6	592.5	564.7	537.0	646.9	...
A Increase in stocks	27.5	21.4	28.2	33.9 / 46.7	30.0	37.4	54.8	70.6	57.3	36.1	70.3	...
B Gross fixed capital formation	260.0	246.9	300.1	276.9 / 403.0	374.5	393.1	434.8	521.9	507.4	500.9	576.6	...
Residential buildings	105.3	88.4	88.8	96.0 / 145.3	147.7	145.8	154.0	160.8	174.5	186.1	185.6	...
Non-residential buildings	47.2	43.5	47.1	43.7 / 66.4	67.3	76.3	87.4	94.5	97.2	101.4	115.5	...
Other construction and land improvement etc.	34.2	38.5	41.2	36.3 / 56.4	64.6	75.4	64.4	67.8	67.1	66.9	67.8	...
Other	73.3	76.5	123.0	100.9 / 134.9	94.9	95.6	129.0	198.8	168.6	146.9	207.7	...
4 Exports of goods and services	344.1	458.2	527.4	521.7 / 722.4	710.2	807.5	916.8	1069.9	1141.2	1044.8	1239.6	...
5 Less: Imports of goods and services	479.5	585.0	680.7	649.8 / 872.0	780.6	886.9	1004.3	1206.0	1281.3	1309.1	1539.6	...
Statistical discrepancy	-3.5	-5.4	5.9	0.1 / 27.8	21.0	3.6	-35.1	-33.3	-21.5	8.3	26.0	...
Equals: Gross Domestic Product	760.4	877.2	954.6	999.4 / 1482.2	1533.2	1645.7	1788.1	1930.7	2071.4	2089.4	2308.8	...

1.3 Cost Components of the Gross Domestic Product

Million Cyprus pounds

	1980	1983	1984	1985	1986	1987	1988	1989	1990	1991	1992	1993
1 Indirect taxes, net	50.4	82.6	97.6	124.7	137.9	150.5	165.0	192.8	222.7	226.3	258.5	...
A Indirect taxes	71.9	114.8	136.9	153.0	155.2	171.9	199.3	232.5	249.4	252.2	292.2	...
B Less: Subsidies	21.5	32.2	39.3	28.3	17.3	21.4	34.3	39.7	26.7	25.9	33.7	...
2 Consumption of fixed capital	70.4	119.0	140.5	160.3	170.3	189.5	212.4	240.8	272.8	284.6	328.3	...
3 Compensation of employees paid by resident producers to:	639.6	935.1	1099.3	1195.8	1292.4	1440.4	1619.0	1823.9	2051.6	2155.1	2494.5	...
4 Operating surplus												...
Equals: Gross Domestic Product	760.4	1136.7	1337.4	1480.8	1600.6	1780.4	1996.4	2257.5	2547.1	2666.0	3081.3	...

1.7 External Transactions on Current Account, Summary

Million Cyprus pounds

	1980	1983	1984	1985	1986	1987	1988	1989	1990	1991	1992	1993
				Payments to the Rest of the World								
1 Imports of goods and services	479.5	727.2	897.4	872.0	779.2	894.9	1067.9	1351.3	1459.8	1527.1	1880.6	...
A Imports of merchandise c.i.f.	424.3	642.0	796.5	762.3	659.1	758.2	921.8	1189.9	1274.6	1317.7	1648.8	...
B Other	55.2	85.2	100.9	109.7	120.1	136.7	146.1	161.4	185.2	209.4	231.8	...
2 Factor income to the rest of the world	20.4	50.7	59.6	62.9	66.5	68.5	75.0	85.4	89.8	107.2	106.2	...
A Compensation of employees	2.3	2.5	2.2	2.9	3.6	3.5	5.1	4.8	5.5	8.5	11.3	...
B Property and entrepreneurial income	18.1	48.2	57.4	60.0	62.9	65.0	69.9	80.6	84.3	98.7	94.9	...
3 Current transfers to the rest of the world	1.4	1.6	1.8	1.5	1.5	1.3	1.5	1.7	2.0	2.5	2.5	...
4 Surplus of the nation on current transactions	-82.9	-93.4	-116.7	-98.8	-13.6	-7.9	-54.3	-131.7	-71.8	-204.1	-282.4	...
Payments to the Rest of the World and Surplus of the Nation on Current Transactions	418.4	686.1	842.1	837.6	833.6	956.8	1090.1	1306.7	1479.8	1432.7	1707.7	...
				Receipts From The Rest of the World								
1 Exports of goods and services	344.1	573.0	731.0	722.4	721.0	841.8	959.6	1161.4	1315.9	1259.4	1536.1	...

Cyprus

1.7 External Transactions on Current Account, Summary
(Continued)

Million Cyprus pounds

	1980	1983	1984	1985	1986	1987	1988	1989	1990	1991	1992	1993
A Exports of merchandise f.o.b.	185.0	257.9	334.2	287.3	257.8	295.6	328.1	389.4	431.1	438.3	448.9	...
B Other	159.1	315.1	396.8	435.1	463.2	546.2	631.5	772.0	884.8	821.1	1087.2	...
2 Factor income from rest of the world	47.0	72.5	83.8	88.7	87.6	92.6	101.3	120.8	140.9	152.0	152.0	...
A Compensation of employees	34.0	46.8	49.5	51.3	51.0	54.2	58.7	60.3	65.6	68.2	79.4	...
B Property and entrepreneurial income	13.0	25.7	34.3	37.4	36.6	38.4	42.6	60.5	75.2	83.8	72.6	...
3 Current transfers from rest of the world	27.3	40.6	27.3	26.5	25.0	22.4	29.2	24.5	23.1	21.3	18.9	...
Receipts from the Rest of the World on Current Transactions	418.4	686.1	842.1	837.6	833.6	956.8	1090.1	1306.7	1479.8	1432.7	1707.7	...

1.10 Gross Domestic Product by Kind of Activity, in Current Prices

Million Cyprus pounds

	1980	1983	1984	1985	1986	1987	1988	1989	1990	1991	1992	1993
1 Agriculture, hunting, forestry and fishing	72.9	89.8	119.6	111.0	117.3	132.3	143.2	156.4	175.3	165.6	177.6	...
2 Mining and quarrying	9.9	8.0	8.0	7.1	7.5	6.7	7.1	6.2	6.7	7.6	7.7	...
3 Manufacturing	133.4	187.9	215.2	231.9	240.5	273.9	309.1	332.3	363.8	382.4	411.9	...
4 Electricity, gas and water	10.0	22.2	28.0	33.3	37.2	39.1	44.0	46.4	51.8	55.6	60.9	...
5 Construction	102.5	123.9	137.0	148.6	156.5	170.0	189.2	215.5	242.3	272.2	307.1	...
6 Wholesale and retail trade, restaurants and hotels	115.6	187.0	231.7	277.0	303.9	346.4	386.3	468.7	546.5	532.8	652.0	...
7 Transport, storage and communication	60.5	100.6	120.6	138.3	155.9	168.0	182.2	205.8	230.9	233.0	263.9	...
8 Finance, insurance, real estate and business services	108.9	161.4	189.2	208.3	230.6	254.1	289.0	324.0	381.2	414.2	479.5	...
9 Community, social and personal services	25.8	46.9	56.8	68.4	78.9	90.1	104.6	121.8	139.8	161.4	193.9	...
Total, Industries	639.5	927.7	1106.1	1223.9	1328.3	1480.6	1654.7	1877.1	2138.3	2224.8	2554.5	...
Producers of Government Services [a]	89.5	150.9	166.6	183.7	200.9	218.2	240.9	261.7	295.8	332.6	369.3	...
Other Producers	3.1	5.9	7.7	8.1	9.1	9.8	11.4	13.3	16.1	18.7	21.3	...
Subtotal [b]	732.1	1084.5	1280.4	1415.7	1538.3	1708.6	1907.0	2152.1	2450.2	2576.1	2945.1	...
Less: Imputed bank service charge	23.0	31.1	37.8	39.9	40.8	42.7	47.9	57.6	74.9	81.3	92.8	...
Plus: Import duties	51.3	83.3	94.8	105.0	103.1	114.5	137.3	163.0	171.8	171.2	192.5	...
Plus: Value added tax	...	...	...	...	...	...	...	...	...	...	36.5	...
Equals: Gross Domestic Product	760.4	1136.7	1337.4	1480.8	1600.6	1780.4	1996.4	2257.5	2547.1	2666.0	3081.3	...

a) For the first series, item 'Producers of Government Services' includes public administration and defence only. All other activities of government are included in the corresponding industries.
b) For the first series, gross domestic product in factor values.

1.11 Gross Domestic Product by Kind of Activity, in Constant Prices

Million Cyprus pounds

	1980	1983	1984	1985	1986	1987	1988	1989	1990	1991	1992	1993
			1980		At constant prices of:			1985				
1 Agriculture, hunting, forestry and fishing	72.9	71.9	78.6	78.4 / 111.0	110.4	114.2	126.7	130.9	131.9	112.0	135.9	...
2 Mining and quarrying	9.9	7.5	7.1	7.2 / 7.1	7.1	6.7	6.6	5.2	5.7	5.9	6.0	...
3 Manufacturing	133.4	153.3	163.1	166.8 / 231.9	232.6	251.3	268.5	276.1	286.9	289.5	299.1	...
4 Electricity, gas and water	10.0	12.8	14.3	15.5 / 33.3	39.8	46.0	51.9	56.9	62.2	63.2	74.2	...
5 Construction	102.5	86.2	87.8	86.6 / 148.6	149.1	153.7	159.8	170.2	178.7	187.1	196.4	...
6 Wholesale and retail trade, restaurants and hotels	115.6	151.2	169.3	186.2 / 277.0	287.9	316.9	350.2	399.6	442.4	437.1	498.6	...
7 Transport, storage and communication	60.5	76.9	88.8	93.8 / 138.3	143.6	151.3	165.8	190.1	204.0	197.4	215.0	...
8 Finance, insurance, real estate and business services	108.9	141.2	157.1	165.9 / 208.3	225.0	240.0	263.8	284.1	320.1	334.7	368.8	...
9 Community, social and personal services	25.8	30.3	35.0	37.4 / 68.4	73.2	79.0	87.3	98.2	104.4	115.2	127.1	...

Cyprus

1.11 Gross Domestic Product by Kind of Activity, in Constant Prices
(Continued)

Million Cyprus pounds

	1980	1983	1984	1985	1986	1987	1988	1989	1990	1991	1992	1993
		1980		At constant prices of:				1985				
Total, Industries	639.5	731.3	801.1	837.9 / 1223.9	1268.7	1359.1	1480.6	1611.3	1736.3	1742.1	1921.1	...
Producers of Government Services	89.5	106.6	111.7	116.4 / 183.7	189.8	198.9	212.8	220.0	235.5	248.3	269.1	...
Other Producers	3.1	4.2	4.5	4.7 / 8.1	8.7	10.3	10.8	12.1	13.5	14.2	15.0	...
Subtotal	732.1	842.1	917.3	959.0 / 1415.7	1467.4	1568.3	1704.2	1843.4	1985.3	2004.6	2205.2	...
Less: Imputed bank service charge	23.0	24.1	27.1	27.0 / 39.9	38.9	39.2	42.8	49.3	60.7	63.3	69.5	...
Plus: Import duties	51.3	59.2	64.4	67.4 / 105.0	108.9	116.6	126.7	136.8	146.8	148.1	144.1	...
Plus: Value added tax	...	...	...	...	...	...	...	...	...	...	29.0	...
Equals: Gross Domestic Product	760.4	877.2	954.6	999.4 / 1480.8	1537.2	1645.7	1788.1	1930.9	2071.4	2089.4	2308.8	...

1.12 Relations Among National Accounting Aggregates

Million Cyprus pounds

	1980	1983	1984	1985	1986	1987	1988	1989	1990	1991	1992	1993
Gross Domestic Product	760.4	1136.7	1337.4	1480.8	1600.6	1780.4	1996.4	2257.5	2547.1	2666.0	3081.3	...
Plus: Net factor income from the rest of the world	26.6	21.8	24.2	25.8	21.1	24.1	26.3	35.4	51.0	44.8	45.7	...
Factor income from the rest of the world	47.0	72.5	83.8	88.7	87.6	92.6	101.3	120.8	140.8	152.0	152.0	...
Less: Factor income to the rest of the world	20.4	50.7	59.6	62.9	66.5	68.5	75.0	85.4	89.8	107.2	106.2	...
Equals: Gross National Product	787.0	1158.5	1361.6	1506.6	1621.7	1804.5	2022.7	2292.9	2598.1	2710.8	3127.0	...
Less: Consumption of fixed capital	70.4	119.0	140.5	160.3	170.3	189.5	212.4	240.8	272.8	284.6	328.3	...
Equals: National Income	716.6	1039.5	1221.1	1346.3	1451.4	1615.0	1810.3	2052.1	2325.3	2426.2	2798.7	...
Plus: Net current transfers from the rest of the world	25.9	39.0	25.5	25.0	23.5	21.1	27.7	22.8	21.1	18.8	16.4	...
Current transfers from the rest of the world	27.3	40.6	27.3	26.5	25.0	22.4	29.2	24.5	23.1	21.3	18.9	...
Less: Current transfers to the rest of the world	1.4	1.6	1.8	1.5	1.5	1.3	1.5	1.7	2.0	2.5	2.5	...
Equals: National Disposable Income	742.5	1078.5	1246.6	1371.3	1474.9	1636.1	1838.0	2074.9	2346.4	2445.0	2815.1	...
Less: Final consumption	611.8	937.7	1040.2	1154.3	1209.1	1355.5	1542.7	1704.0	1975.3	2247.8	2552.4	...
Statistical discrepancy	3.5	-10.9	-14.3	-26.4	-34.7	-23.5	-14.0	-46.2	-24.5	5.5	5.5	...
Equals: Net Saving	134.2	129.9	192.1	190.6	231.1	257.1	281.3	324.7	346.6	202.7	268.2	...
Less: Surplus of the nation on current transactions	-82.9	-93.4	-116.7	-98.8	-13.6	-7.9	-54.3	-131.7	-71.8	-204.1	-282.4	...
Equals: Net Capital Formation	217.1	223.3	308.8	289.4	244.7	265.0	335.6	456.4	418.4	406.8	550.6	...

2.1 Government Final Consumption Expenditure by Function, in Current Prices

Million Cyprus pounds

	1980	1983	1984	1985	1986	1987	1988	1989	1990	1991	1992	1993
1 General public services [a]	15.5	24.3	26.3	29.1	31.5	35.2	38.6	42.4	48.9	56.4	61.4	...
2 Defence [b]	9.8	11.4	11.1	12.6	17.0	64.7	76.7	81.7	126.9	130.8	190.9	...
3 Public order and safety [a]	15.3	24.9	27.7	29.9	32.1	34.6	36.9	39.9	42.2	48.8	51.8	...
4 Education	23.7	40.0	43.6	48.5	52.4	57.5	64.4	69.9	77.3	87.3	96.4	...
5 Health	11.2	19.6	21.7	24.6	26.9	29.8	32.2	36.1	40.1	45.4	55.9	...
6 Social security and welfare	10.9	23.4	26.5	29.4	32.5	35.7	41.4	44.2	55.7	63.0	68.8	...
7 Housing and community amenities	4.2	6.3	7.9	8.5	10.0	10.1	12.5	12.7	15.4	17.0	21.6	...
8 Recreational, cultural and religious affairs	0.7	1.2	1.3	1.6	1.7	1.9	2.1	2.4	2.8	3.4	3.2	...
9 Economic services	11.7	20.0	22.4	24.2	25.7	26.2	27.7	31.4	33.6	41.4	41.1	...

Cyprus

2.1 Government Final Consumption Expenditure by Function, in Current Prices
(Continued)

Million Cyprus pounds

	1980	1983	1984	1985	1986	1987	1988	1989	1990	1991	1992	1993
A Fuel and energy	-	-	-	-	-	-	-	-	-	...	...	...
B Agriculture, forestry, fishing and hunting	4.8	7.6	8.2	8.5	8.9	9.5	10.3	11.2	11.8	13.0	13.7	...
C Mining, manufacturing and construction, except fuel and energy	1.4	2.6	2.9	3.1	3.3	3.3	3.4	3.8	4.0	4.2	5.4	...
D Transportation and communication	0.3	0.6	0.6	0.7	1.1	1.1	1.0	1.0	0.7	1.2	1.2	...
E Other economic affairs	5.2	9.2	10.7	11.9	12.4	12.3	13.0	15.3	17.1	23.0	20.8	...
10 Other functions	0.4	0.8	0.2	0.1	0.1	-	-	0.1	0.2	0.2	0.1	...
Total Government Final Consumption Expenditure	103.4	171.9	188.7	208.5	229.9	295.7	332.5	360.7	443.1	493.7	591.2	...

a) For the first series, item 'Public order and safety' is included in 'General public services'.
b) Beginning 1986, item 'Defence' includes military expenditure of government.

2.5 Private Final Consumption Expenditure by Type and Purpose, in Current Prices

Million Cyprus pounds

	1980	1983	1984	1985	1986	1987	1988	1989	1990	1991	1992	1993
Final Consumption Expenditure of Resident Households												
1 Food, beverages and tobacco	174.5	252.8	317.7	346.4	357.2	401.7	452.7	494.8	538.2	584.5	667.1	...
A Food	141.5	205.8	258.7	281.3	291.4	323.4	359.7	376.6	398.1	438.4	496.7	...
B Non-alcoholic beverages	7.5	11.7	16.2	18.5	14.0	15.8	17.5	27.3	42.0	44.5	51.2	...
C Alcoholic beverages	13.1	17.1	21.9	24.9	27.3	31.3	38.2	52.4	54.2	53.0	59.8	...
D Tobacco	12.4	18.2	20.9	21.7	24.5	31.2	37.3	38.5	43.9	48.6	59.6	...
2 Clothing and footwear	55.9	107.2	116.3	125.2	130.8	135.8	144.9	173.3	209.4	239.1	267.6	...
3 Gross rent, fuel and power	49.5	88.4	96.7	107.0	109.7	116.2	124.1	136.7	150.1	167.1	182.5	...
A Fuel and power	11.9	17.6	21.3	23.7	18.0	18.3	19.1	22.3	26.6	31.7	34.4	...
B Other	37.6	70.8	75.4	83.3	91.7	97.9	105.0	114.4	123.5	135.4	148.1	...
4 Furniture, furnishings and household equipment and operation	66.3	116.2	126.8	136.1	136.0	155.6	171.9	196.0	214.3	231.8	280.1	...
A Household operation	19.5	29.8	34.0	37.6	40.5	45.0	48.2	51.5	58.0	68.8	76.7	...
B Other	46.8	86.4	92.8	98.5	95.5	110.6	123.7	144.5	156.3	163.0	203.4	...
5 Medical care and health expenses	10.2	23.8	28.6	34.4	36.2	44.1	51.4	56.7	64.2	70.7	83.1	...
6 Transport and communication	132.4	171.3	179.5	187.0	197.6	208.9	261.0	307.1	335.1	377.6	418.2	...
A Personal transport equipment	34.6	51.1	52.6	55.9	63.0	64.1	95.2	111.6	117.5	147.4	158.8	...
B Other	97.8	120.3	126.9	131.1	134.6	144.8	165.8	195.5	217.6	230.2	259.4	...
7 Recreational, entertainment, education and cultural services	40.3	73.6	79.0	91.6	88.9	98.9	118.1	140.2	168.2	176.9	207.4	...
A Education	5.7	7.5	9.8	12.1	14.1	16.5	19.4	23.0	28.4	33.0	38.8	...
B Other	34.6	66.1	69.2	79.5	74.8	82.4	98.7	117.2	139.8	143.9	168.6	...
8 Miscellaneous goods and services	83.8	135.3	151.6	180.3	206.7	247.8	296.2	369.4	444.8	416.3	570.8	...
A Personal care	22.6	13.0	14.8	18.5	18.8	23.1	26.8	33.3	38.5	42.6	52.4	...
B Expenditures in restaurants, cafes and hotels	43.9	92.8	105.4	126.9	145.2	176.8	215.6	264.7	313.3	271.5	364.8	...
C Other	17.3	29.5	31.4	34.9	42.7	47.9	53.8	71.4	93.0	102.2	153.6	...
Statistical discrepancy a	-7.3	-	-	-	-	-	-	-	-	-	-	...
Total Final Consumption Expenditure in the Domestic Market by Households, of which	605.6	968.6	1096.2	1208.0	1263.1	1409.0	1620.2	1874.2	2124.3	2264.0	2676.8	...
A Durable goods	...	142.8	146.5	160.2	163.6	178.6	224.8	264.1	291.2	325.1	365.3	...
B Semi-durable goods	...	184.5	201.2	217.6	225.0	245.2	270.2	324.2	377.4	424.3	490.4	...
C Non-durable goods	...	374.4	445.2	478.0	477.1	532.9	599.3	663.8	734.9	800.0	904.9	...
D Services	...	266.9	303.2	352.2	397.4	452.3	525.9	622.1	720.8	714.6	916.2	...
Plus: Direct purchases abroad by resident households	16.4	28.8	34.4	39.1	41.8	46.0	52.0	54.3	66.6	72.4	82.3	...
Less: Direct purchases in the domestic market by non-resident households	110.7	231.5	277.5	299.2	326.5	392.4	464.5	580.7	666.0	587.7	808.2	...
Equals: Final Consumption Expenditure of Resident Households bc	504.3	758.0	841.6	933.5	966.6	1044.9	1193.8	1324.5	1510.9	1729.7	1933.4	...
Final Consumption Expenditure of Private Non-profit Institutions Serving Households												
1 Research and science	...	-	-	-	-	-	-	-	-	-	-	...
2 Education	...	-	-	-	-	-	-	-	-	-	-	...
3 Medical and other health services	...	-	-	-	-	-	-	-	-	-	-	...

Cyprus

2.5 Private Final Consumption Expenditure by Type and Purpose, in Current Prices
(Continued)

Million Cyprus pounds

		1980	1983	1984	1985	1986	1987	1988	1989	1990	1991	1992	1993
4	Welfare services	...	0.4	0.4	0.6	0.7	0.7	0.7	0.9	1.0	1.2	1.4	...
5	Recreational and related cultural services	...	2.3	3.4	4.3	3.8	5.7	6.4	7.0	7.6	8.7	10.5	...
6	Religious organisations	...	2.8	3.4	4.1	4.3	4.5	4.8	5.5	6.6	7.5	7.9	...
7	Professional and labour organisations serving households	...	2.2	2.6	3.2	3.6	3.7	4.1	4.9	5.5	6.3	7.2	...
8	Miscellaneous	...	0.1	0.1	0.1	0.2	0.3	0.4	0.5	0.6	0.7	0.8	...
	Equals: Final Consumption Expenditure of Private Non-profit Organisations Serving Households	4.1	7.8	9.9	12.3	12.6	14.8	16.4	18.8	21.3	24.4	27.8	...
	Private Final Consumption Expenditure	508.4	765.8	851.5	945.8	979.2	1059.8	1210.2	1343.3	1532.2	1754.1	1961.2	...

a) Item 'Statistical discrepancy' represents unclassified estimates.
b) First series, item 'Final consumption expenditure of resident households' includes consumption expenditure of private non-profit institutions serving households.
c) Beginning 1976, the components do not add up to the total. The difference refers to changes in stocks.

2.6 Private Final Consumption Expenditure by Type and Purpose, in Constant Prices

Million Cyprus pounds

		1980	1983	1984	1985	1986	1987	1988	1989	1990	1991	1992	1993
		At constant prices of: 1980							1985				

Final Consumption Expenditure of Resident Households

		1980	1983	1984	1985	1986	1987	1988	1989	1990	1991	1992	1993
1	Food, beverages and tobacco	174.5	203.1	236.4	246.0 / 346.4	348.3	382.6	415.5	433.2	452.9	458.3	485.2	...
	A Food	141.5	163.1	190.2	197.3 / 281.3	283.7	306.8	327.7	323.9	326.8	336.4	359.9	...
	B Non-alcoholic beverages	7.5	10.1	12.1	13.7 / 18.5	13.6	15.0	16.0	24.8	36.7	37.5	39.8	...
	C Alcoholic beverages	13.1	15.1	17.6	19.1 / 24.9	26.8	30.1	35.0	46.5	48.1	43.8	41.2	...
	D Tobacco	12.4	14.8	16.5	15.9 / 21.7	24.2	30.7	36.8	38.0	41.3	40.6	44.3	...
2	Clothing and footwear	55.9	86.3	87.6	87.2 / 125.2	126.4	127.5	128.1	144.5	163.4	184.7	195.8	...
3	Gross rent, fuel and power	49.5	74.0	76.1	79.8 / 106.9	113.4	119.7	127.9	135.4	140.4	147.6	159.7	...
	A Fuel and power	11.9	11.8	12.2	12.9 / 23.6	26.2	29.8	35.1	38.0	39.8	42.5	51.6	...
	B Other	37.6	62.2	63.9	66.9 / 83.3	87.2	89.9	92.8	97.4	100.6	105.1	108.1	...
4	Furniture, furnishings and household equipment and operation	66.3	96.0	101.3	105.4 / 136.2	133.0	150.1	161.8	178.9	189.8	199.1	222.8	...
	A Household operation	19.5	24.3	26.5	28.2 / 37.7	39.4	43.0	44.9	47.0	51.3	57.6	60.4	...
	B Other	46.8	71.7	74.8	77.2 / 98.5	93.6	107.1	116.9	131.9	138.5	141.5	162.4	...
5	Medical care and health expenses	10.2	17.5	19.5	22.4 / 34.4	35.1	41.0	46.7	49.6	52.8	54.6	59.7	...
6	Transport and communication	132.4	140.1	141.1	143.0 / 187.0	198.6	204.9	248.9	291.8	310.2	329.3	348.5	...
	A Personal transport equipment	34.6	44.4	43.1	45.7 / 55.9	60.6	56.6	80.2	91.3	100.1	128.5	133.7	...
	B Other	97.8	95.7	98.0	97.3 / 131.1	138.0	148.3	168.7	200.5	210.1	200.8	214.8	...
7	Recreational, entertainment, education and cultural services	40.3	65.7	67.4	73.1 / 91.6	87.7	95.2	109.8	125.5	142.3	142.7	151.7	...
	A Education	5.7	6.6	9.1	10.7 / 12.1	15.0	16.7	18.3	20.5	23.7	25.8	28.7	...
	B Other	34.6	59.1	58.3	62.4 / 79.5	72.7	78.5	91.5	105.0	118.6	116.9	123.0	...
8	Miscellaneous goods and services	83.8	100.5	103.9	115.8 / 180.3	198.3	227.2	262.2	314.6	358.7	336.7	427.4	...
	A Personal care	22.6	9.8	10.4	12.2 / 18.5	17.9	21.0	23.7	27.9	30.8	33.1	38.0	...
	B Expenditures in restaurants, cafes and hotels	43.9	65.2	67.1	76.0 / 126.9	138.2	160.7	188.5	220.5	244.1	214.3	264.7	...
	C Other	17.3	25.5	26.4	27.6 / 34.9	42.2	45.5	50.0	66.2	83.8	89.3	124.7	...

Cyprus

2.6 Private Final Consumption Expenditure by Type and Purpose, in Constant Prices
(Continued)

Million Cyprus pounds

	1980	1983	1984	1985	1986	1987	1988	1989	1990	1991	1992	1993
		1980		At constant prices of:				1985				
Statistical discrepancy	-7.3a	-a	-a	-a						...	...	...
Total Final Consumption Expenditure in the Domestic Market by Households, of which	605.6	783.2	832.3	872.7 / 1208.0	1240.9	1348.3	1500.9	1673.5	1810.5	1853.0	2050.8	...
A Durable goods	...	128.9	126.9	136.0 / 160.2	160.7	169.4	206.2	237.2	263.2	293.5	312.9	...
B Semi-durable goods	...	149.6	152.7	155.1 / 217.6	217.5	230.1	242.4	277.3	306.8	337.4	369.6	...
C Non-durable goods	...	295.5	328.7	336.6 / 478.0	481.2	530.4	583.1	623.0	654.9	664.9	710.2	...
D Services	...	209.2	225.0	245.0 / 352.2	381.5	418.3	469.2	535.9	585.6	557.2	658.1	...
Plus: Direct purchases abroad by resident households	16.4	23.3	26.3	28.4 / 39.1	41.4	44.3	48.4	48.7	44.9	59.1	63.1	...
Less: Direct purchases in the domestic market by non-resident households	110.7	187.2	211.0	216.5 / 299.2	320.8	375.4	430.3	518.5	567.6	481.0	619.2	...
Equals: Final Consumption Expenditure of Resident Households [b]	504.3	612.8	640.0	674.0 / 933.5	949.9	999.7	1105.5	1182.0	1287.8	1415.0	1480.1	...

Final Consumption Expenditure of Private Non-profit Institutions Serving Households

	1980	1983	1984	1985	1986	1987	1988	1989	1990	1991	1992	1993
1 Research and science	...	-	-	-								...
2 Education	...	-	-	-								...
3 Medical and other health services	...	-	-	-								...
4 Welfare services	...	0.2	0.2	0.3 / 0.6	0.6	0.5	0.6	0.6	0.7	0.9	0.9	...
5 Recreational and related cultural services	...	1.3	1.6	2.4 / 4.3	3.9	6.4	6.8	6.7	6.6	7.8	7.4	...
6 Religious organisations	...	2.4	2.6	2.9 / 4.1	4.2	4.2	4.4	4.7	6.0	6.2	6.7	...
7 Professional and labour organisations serving households	...	1.6	1.8	2.0 / 3.2	3.4	3.5	3.6	4.0	4.4	4.9	5.1	...
8 Miscellaneous	...	0.1	0.1	0.1 / 0.1	0.2	0.3	0.3	0.5	0.5	0.6	0.5	...
Equals: Final Consumption Expenditure of Private Non-profit Organisations Serving Households	4.1	5.6	6.3	7.7 / 12.3	12.3	14.9	15.7	16.5	18.2	20.4	20.6	...
Private Final Consumption Expenditure	508.4	618.4	646.3	681.7 / 945.8	962.2	1014.6	1121.2	1198.5	1306.0	1435.4	1500.7	...

a) Item 'Statistical discrepancy' represents unclassified estimates.
b) Beginning 1976, the components do not add up to the total. The difference refers to changes in stocks.

2.11 Gross Fixed Capital Formation by Kind of Activity of Owner, ISIC Divisions, in Current Prices

Million Cyprus pounds

	1980	1983	1984	1985	1986	1987	1988	1989	1990	1991	1992	1993
					All Producers							
1 Agriculture, hunting, forestry and fishing	16.7	27.4	35.8	35.1	43.1	49.8	34.7	31.3	28.9	26.5	25.6	...
A Agriculture and hunting	...	...	...	34.2	42.0	48.6	33.2	29.7	28.2	25.2	24.6	...
B Forestry and logging	...	...	...	0.4	0.4	0.6	0.6	0.6	0.6	0.6	0.6	...
C Fishing	...	...	...	0.5	0.7	0.6	0.9	1.0	1.0	0.7	0.4	...
2 Mining and quarrying	1.3	0.4	0.8	0.5	0.7	0.4	0.5	0.9	1.6	1.4	1.3	...
A Coal mining	...	...	...	...	...	...	...	...	...	...	...	...
B Crude petroleum and natural gas production	...	...	...	...	...	...	...	...	...	...	...	...
C Metal ore mining	...	...	...	-	0.2	0.2	-	-	0.2	-	-	...
D Other mining	...	...	...	0.5	0.5	0.2	0.5	0.9	1.4	1.4	1.3	...

Cyprus

2.11 Gross Fixed Capital Formation by Kind of Activity of Owner, ISIC Divisions, in Current Prices
(Continued)

Million Cyprus pounds

	1980	1983	1984	1985	1986	1987	1988	1989	1990	1991	1992	1993
3 Manufacturing	27.6	24.5	31.4	34.7	31.4	37.1	43.6	51.0	50.7	51.8	54.4	...
A Manufacturing of food, beverages and tobacco	...	...	...	9.8	10.5	10.4	15.5	16.9	12.3	13.9	18.1	...
B Textile, wearing apparel and leather industries	...	...	...	6.1	4.9	8.2	7.6	9.1	9.4	8.1	7.3	...
C Manufacture of wood, and wood products, including furniture	...	...	...	2.6	2.1	2.8	4.4	4.1	3.0	3.7	3.8	...
D Manufacture of paper and paper products, printing and publishing	...	...	...	1.3	1.9	3.1	3.2	3.9	5.8	6.3	5.0	...
E Manufacture of chemicals and chemical petroleum, coal, rubber and plastic products	...	...	...	4.8	2.7	3.9	5.2	5.7	7.3	6.9	6.6	...
F Manufacture of non-metallic mineral products except products of petroleum and coal	...	...	...	2.7	3.0	3.3	3.1	3.7	5.7	5.3	7.4	...
G Basic metal industries	...	...	...	...	...	...	...	...	...	...	...	...
H Manufacture of fabricated metal products, machinery and equipment	...	...	...	6.4	5.8	4.9	3.9	6.2	6.0	6.3	4.8	...
I Other manufacturing industries	...	...	...	1.0	0.5	0.5	0.7	1.4	1.2	1.3	1.4	...
4 Electricity, gas and water	10.9	11.5	7.5	8.6	9.0	14.0	28.5	16.0	19.2	28.0	65.5	...
A Electricity, gas and steam	...	...	...	6.3	6.8	10.5	25.4	12.0	16.4	20.5	61.1	...
B Water works and supply	...	...	...	2.3	2.2	3.5	3.1	4.0	2.8	7.5	4.4	...
5 Construction	7.5	13.3	15.2	10.2	9.9	7.6	15.6	14.2	17.4	13.5	13.6	...
6 Wholesale and retail trade, restaurants and hotels a	37.3	53.7	61.3	59.4	61.3	73.8	86.4	107.7	116.3	123.6	148.3	...
A Wholesale and retail trade	...	...	...	29.9	30.2	36.8	45.6	49.0	53.1	54.4	71.0	...
B Restaurants and hotels	...	...	...	29.5	31.1	37.0	40.8	58.7	63.2	69.2	77.3	...
7 Transport, storage and communication	28.6	44.9	107.1	75.2	46.8	50.5	60.2	158.8	101.8	84.3	134.3	...
A Transport and storage	...	...	...	55.4	28.8	37.0	46.5	144.9	89.3	71.0	119.5	...
B Communication	...	...	...	19.8	18.0	13.5	13.7	13.9	12.5	13.3	14.8	...
8 Finance, insurance, real estate and business services b	107.7	119.9	129.5	151.8	155.8	157.7	180.6	202.7	237.1	263.6	281.4	...
A Financial institutions	...	...	...	3.0	2.2	2.5	5.8	7.1	9.6	11.8	13.8	...
B Insurance	...	...	...	1.1	0.9	1.4	1.6	1.4	2.5	2.8	3.8	...
C Real estate and business services	...	...	...	147.7	152.7	153.7	173.0	193.2	224.2	248.4	263.6	...
Real estate except dwellings	...	...	...	0.2	0.2	-	-	1.0	0.8	0.6	0.8	...
Dwellings	...	...	...	145.3	150.2	151.3	170.7	190.4	218.7	244.2	259.4	...
9 Community, social and personal services ab	2.5	4.0	5.7	6.5	7.7	10.2	13.1	16.9	22.1	24.8	26.7	...
Total Industries	240.1	299.6	394.3	382.0	365.7	403.1	463.2	599.5	596.0	617.5	751.1	...
Producers of Government Services	4.0	6.2	4.6	6.0	7.8	11.2	22.9	17.4	28.3	27.7	34.7	...
Private Non-Profit Institutions Serving Households	0.9	1.7	2.1	4.4	4.5	3.6	4.7	4.5	4.6	5.2	6.7	...
Statistical discrepancy	15.0	8.5	11.5	10.6	6.0	-	-	-	-	-	-	...
Total	260.0	316.0	412.5	403.0	384.0	417.9	490.8	621.4	628.9	650.4	792.5	...

a) For the first series, restaurants and hotels are included in item 'Community, social and personal services'. b) For the first series, business services are included in item 'Community, social and personal services'.

2.12 Gross Fixed Capital Formation by Kind of Activity of Owner, ISIC Divisions, in Constant Prices

Million Cyprus pounds

	1980	1983	1984	1985	1986	1987	1988	1989	1990	1991	1992	1993
		1980			At constant prices of:			1985				
					All Producers							
1 Agriculture, hunting, forestry and fishing	16.7	21.3	25.9	23.5 / 35.1	41.9	46.9	31.2	26.8	24.6	20.5	18.6	...
2 Mining and quarrying	1.3	0.4	0.5	0.4 / 0.5	0.6	0.4	0.4	0.8	1.3	1.1	0.9	...
3 Manufacturing	27.6	20.3	24.4	25.8 / 34.7	30.3	34.3	36.6	41.5	39.3	37.9	38.9	...
4 Electricity, gas and water	10.9	9.2	5.4	5.8 / 8.6	8.6	12.9	25.2	13.6	13.7	18.1	40.4	...

Cyprus

2.12 Gross Fixed Capital Formation by Kind of Activity of Owner, ISIC Divisions, in Constant Prices
(Continued)

Million Cyprus pounds

	1980	1983	1984	1985	1986	1987	1988	1989	1990	1991	1992	1993
		At constant prices of:										
		1980						1985				
5 Construction	7.5	11.0	12.3	7.5 / 10.2	9.3	6.7	13.4	11.7	14.0	11.1	9.8	...
6 Wholesale and retail trade, restaurants and hotels	37.3	42.0	44.8	40.9 / 59.4	59.8	69.7	76.1	90.5	93.1	95.2	106.9	...
7 Transport, storage and communication	28.6	34.8	76.2	53.0 / 75.2	45.2	45.8	51.8	131.1	81.6	64.9	101.3	...
8 Finance, insurance, real estate and business services	107.7	92.1	92.3	100.9 / 151.8	154.1	153.7	164.2	173.2	194.0	206.2	208.4	...
9 Community, social and personal services	2.5	3.2	4.2	4.8 / 6.5	7.4	9.2	11.1	14.0	18.3	19.9	20.2	...
Total Industries	240.1	234.3	286.0	262.6 / 382.0	357.2	379.6	410.1	503.2	479.9	474.9	545.4	...
Producers of Government Services	4.0	4.9	3.3	4.0 / 6.0	7.5	10.1	20.5	15.0	23.8	21.9	26.2	...
Private Non-Profit Institutions Serving Households	0.9	1.4	1.6	3.0 / 4.4	4.4	3.4	4.2	3.7	3.7	4.1	5.0	...
Statistical discrepancy	15.0	6.3	9.2	7.3 / 10.6	5.4	-	-	-	-	-	-	...
Total	260.0	246.9	300.1	276.9 / 403.0	374.5	393.1	434.8	521.9	507.4	500.9	576.6	...

2.17 Exports and Imports of Goods and Services, Detail

Million Cyprus pounds

	1980	1983	1984	1985	1986	1987	1988	1989	1990	1991	1992	1993
	Exports of Goods and Services
1 Exports of merchandise, f.o.b.	185.0	257.9	334.2	287.3	257.8	295.6	328.1	389.4	431.1	438.3	448.9	...
2 Transport and communication	31.5	50.0	66.6	80.8	81.0	92.0	94.9	105.8	118.5	124.2	141.6	...
3 Insurance service charges	0.6	0.8	1.0	1.0	0.7	0.7	0.7	0.7	0.7	0.7	0.7	...
4 Other commodities	55.3	89.5	117.2	121.3	124.9	132.8	149.9	175.5	192.6	220.2	250.9	...
5 Adjustments of merchandise exports to change-of-ownership basis	71.7	174.8	212.0	232.0	256.6	320.7	386.0	490.0	573.0	476.0	694.0	...
6 Direct purchases in the domestic market by non-residential households	...	...	...	...	...	...	...	...	...	...	...	...
7 Direct purchases in the domestic market by extraterritorial bodies	...	...	...	...	...	...	...	...	...	...	...	...
Total Exports of Goods and Services	344.1	573.0	731.0	722.4	721.0	841.8	959.6	1163.4	1315.9	1259.4	1536.1	...
	Imports of Goods and Services
1 Imports of merchandise, c.i.f.	424.3	642.0	796.5	762.3	661.2	758.2	921.8	1189.9	1274.6	1317.7	1648.8	...
A Imports of merchandise, f.o.b.	381.0	575.9	720.7	687.2	595.1	682.6	829.6	1078.9	1148.8	1185.9	1488.8	...
B Transport of services on merchandise imports	39.1	59.7	68.5	67.8	59.5	68.0	83.0	99.9	113.2	118.6	144.0	...
C Insurance service charges on merchandise imports	4.2	6.4	7.3	7.3	6.6	7.6	9.2	11.1	12.6	13.2	16.0	...
2 Adjustments of merchandise imports to change-of-ownership basis	...	...	...	...	...	...	...	...	...	...	...	...
3 Other transport and communication	22.1	29.3	34.4	37.1	40.5	47.3	48.2	53.7	62.3	72.6	79.1	...
4 Other insurance service charges	...	...	...	...	...	...	...	...	...	...	...	...
5 Other commodities	13.3	21.0	24.7	25.1	26.5	33.0	35.2	41.4	41.7	48.0	52.0	...
6 Direct purchases abroad by government	...	...	...	...	...	...	...	...	...	...	...	...
7 Direct purchases abroad by resident households	19.8	34.9	41.8	47.5	51.0	56.2	62.7	66.3	81.2	88.8	100.7	...
Total Imports of Goods and Services	479.5	727.2	897.4	872.0	779.2	894.9	1067.9	1351.3	1459.8	1527.1	1880.6	...
Balance of Goods and Services	-135.4	-154.2	-166.4	-149.6	-58.2	-53.1	-108.3	-187.9	-143.9	-267.7	-344.5	...
Total Imports and Balance of Goods and Services	344.1	573.0	731.0	722.4	721.0	841.8	959.6	1163.4	1315.9	1259.4	1536.1	...

Cyprus

4.1 Derivation of Value Added by Kind of Activity, in Current Prices

Million Cyprus pounds

	1980 Gross Output	1980 Intermediate Consumption	1980 Value Added	1985 Gross Output	1985 Intermediate Consumption	1985 Value Added	1990 Gross Output	1990 Intermediate Consumption	1990 Value Added	1991 Gross Output	1991 Intermediate Consumption	1991 Value Added
						All Producers						
1 Agriculture, hunting, forestry and fishing	126.7	53.8	72.9	198.0	87.0	111.0	278.7	103.4	175.3	271.3	105.7	165.6
A Agriculture and hunting	123.3	53.1	70.2	191.5	86.2	105.3	266.1	101.3	164.8	259.4	103.7	155.7
B Forestry and logging	1.4	0.5	0.9	1.7	0.5	1.2	3.2	1.0	2.2	2.8	0.8	2.0
C Fishing	2.0	0.2	1.8	4.8	0.3	4.5	9.4	1.1	8.3	9.1	1.2	7.9
2 Mining and quarrying	18.9	9.0	9.9	15.2	8.1	7.1	13.5	6.5	6.7	14.3	6.7	7.6
A Coal mining	-	-	-	-	-	-		-		-		-
B Crude petroleum and natural gas production	-	-	-	-	-	-	...	-		-	...	-
C Metal ore mining	2.9	1.1	1.8	1.7	0.9	0.8	0.6	0.3	0.3	0.4	0.3	0.1
D Other mining	16.0	7.9	8.1	13.5	7.2	6.3	12.9	6.5	6.4	13.9	6.4	7.5
3 Manufacturing	404.7	271.3	133.4	685.9	454.0	231.9	1006.3	642.5	363.8	1061.1	678.7	382.4
A Manufacture of food, beverages and tobacco	102.0	65.0	37.0	181.7	118.2	63.5	259.7	161.3	98.4	271.8	169.6	102.2
B Textile, wearing apparel and leather industries	83.7	52.5	31.2	145.9	89.1	56.8	227.8	140.7	87.1	238.8	149.8	89.0
C Manufacture of wood and wood products, including furniture	27.5	15.5	12.0	61.8	34.5	27.3	78.1	44.6	34.3	83.7	46.5	37.2
D Manufacture of paper and paper products, printing and publishing	23.1	14.5	8.6	40.8	25.3	15.5	69.1	44.4	24.7	64.7	39.3	25.4
E Manufacture of chemicals and chemical petroleum, coal, rubber and plastic products	81.1	70.4	10.7	115.8	97.0	18.8	137.4	107.4	30.0	154.1	119.6	34.5
F Manufacture of non-metallic mineral products, except products of petroleum and coal	39.7	24.2	15.5	42.4	27.1	15.3	78.8	45.7	33.1	81.5	47.5	34.0
G Basic metal industries	-	-	-	-	-	-	-	-	-	-	-	-
H Manufacture of fabricated metal products, machinery and equipment	40.1	24.9	15.2	81.3	52.1	29.2	122.9	77.7	45.5	131.1	81.9	49.2
I Other manufacturing industries	7.5	4.3	3.2	16.2	10.7	5.5	32.5	21.8	10.7	35.4	24.5	10.9
4 Electricity, gas and water	30.6	20.6	10.0	77.0	43.7	33.3	87.1	35.3	51.8	94.1	38.5	55.6
A Electricity, gas and steam	29.0	19.9	9.1	70.4	40.3	30.1	70.2	28.8	41.4	79.6	32.9	46.7
B Water works and supply	1.6	0.7	0.9	6.6	3.4	3.2	16.9	6.5	10.4	14.5	5.4	8.9
5 Construction	197.1	94.6	102.5	286.6	138.0	148.6	466.1	223.8	242.3	515.5	243.3	272.2
6 Wholesale and retail trade, restaurants and hotels	169.1	53.5	115.6	427.5	150.5	277.0	826.0	279.5	546.5	797.5	264.7	532.8
A Wholesale and retail trade	121.7	32.6	89.1	257.9	80.3	177.6	409.6	123.9	285.7	436.9	126.2	310.7
B Restaurants and hotels	47.4	20.9	26.5	169.6	70.2	99.4	416.5	155.6	260.9	360.6	138.5	222.1
Restaurants	22.8	10.1	12.7	80.9	35.8	45.1	192.0	83.0	108.9	173.7	76.1	97.6
Hotels and other lodging places	24.6	10.8	13.8	88.7	34.4	54.3	224.5	72.5	152.0	186.9	62.4	124.5
7 Transport, storage and communication	106.5	46.0	60.5	216.9	78.6	138.3	336.6	105.7	230.9	340.0	107.0	233.0
A Transport and storage	88.4	44.1	44.3	171.8	74.0	97.8	258.9	99.9	159.0	258.0	99.2	159.1
B Communication	18.1	1.9	16.2	45.1	4.6	40.5	77.7	5.8	71.9	81.7	7.8	73.9
8 Finance, insurance, real estate and business services	128.1	19.2	108.9	254.9	46.6	208.3	463.3	82.1	381.2	506.8	92.6	414.2
A Financial institutions	29.4	3.8	25.6	56.3	11.8	44.5	112.6	22.6	90.0	126.6	28.1	98.5
B Insurance	6.8	1.5	5.3	13.0	3.3	9.7	24.8	7.0	17.8	26.5	7.1	19.4
C Real estate and business services	91.9	13.9	78.0	185.6	32.1	153.5	325.9	52.4	273.5	353.7	57.4	206.3
Real estate, except dwellings	28.3	2.9	25.4	68.1	7.1	61.0	125.3	12.8	112.5	129.2	12.3	116.9
Dwellings	50.8	5.6	45.2	77.7	9.6	68.1	117.1	14.8	102.3	128.4	16.5	111.9
9 Community, social and personal services	36.4	10.6	25.8	94.5	26.1	68.4	190.9	51.1	139.8	219.3	57.9	161.4
A Sanitary and similar services	0.7	0.2	0.5	1.2	0.3	0.9	2.5	0.4	2.1	4.0	0.5	3.5
B Social and related community services [a]	9.0	2.1	6.9	29.9	7.3	22.6	68.4	18.0	50.4	80.0	20.6	59.4
Educational services	3.4	0.6	2.8	13.4	2.8	10.6	30.3	6.1	24.2	35.4	7.2	28.2
Medical, dental, other health and veterinary services	5.2	1.4	3.8	14.9	4.0	10.9	34.2	10.6	23.6	39.9	11.7	28.2
C Recreational and cultural services	8.6	3.7	4.9	23.6	8.8	14.8	43.6	14.8	28.8	47.9	16.0	31.9
D Personal and household services	18.1	4.6	13.5	39.8	9.7	30.1	76.4	17.9	58.5	87.4	20.8	66.6

Cyprus

4.1 Derivation of Value Added by Kind of Activity, in Current Prices
(Continued)

Million Cyprus pounds

	1980 Gross Output	1980 Intermediate Consumption	1980 Value Added	1985 Gross Output	1985 Intermediate Consumption	1985 Value Added	1990 Gross Output	1990 Intermediate Consumption	1990 Value Added	1991 Gross Output	1991 Intermediate Consumption	1991 Value Added
Total, Industries	1218.1	578.6	639.5	2256.5	1033.5	1223.9	3668.5	1530.2	2138.3	3819.9	1595.1	2224.8
Producers of Government Services	109.0	19.5	89.5	218.1	34.4	183.7	355.5	59.7	295.8	405.1	72.5	332.6
Other Producers	4.7	1.6	3.1	13.3	5.2	8.1	23.5	7.4	16.1	27.5	8.8	18.7
Total	1331.8	599.7	732.1	2487.9	1072.2	1415.7	4047.5	1597.3	2450.2	4252.5	1676.4	2576.1
Less: Imputed bank service charge	...	-23.0	23.0	...	-39.9	39.9	...	-74.9	74.9	...	-81.3	81.3
Import duties	51.3	...	51.3	105.0	...	105.0	171.8	...	171.8	171.2	...	171.2
Value added tax	...	...	...	...	...	...	...	...	...	...	...	...
Total	1383.1	622.7	760.4	2592.9	1112.1	1480.8	4219.3	1672.2	2547.1	4423.7	1757.7	2666.0

	1992 Gross Output	1992 Intermediate Consumption	1992 Value Added

All Producers

	Gross Output	Intermediate Consumption	Value Added
1 Agriculture, hunting, forestry and fishing	297.1	119.5	177.6
A Agriculture and hunting	284.4	117.3	167.1
B Forestry and logging	2.7	0.8	1.9
C Fishing	10.0	1.4	8.6
2 Mining and quarrying	14.7	7.0	7.7
A Coal mining	-	...	-
B Crude petroleum and natural gas production	-	...	-
C Metal ore mining	0.4	0.3	0.1
D Other mining	14.3	6.7	7.6
3 Manufacturing	1129.1	717.2	411.9
A Manufacture of food, beverages and tobacco	302.1	188.1	114.0
B Textile, wearing apparel and leather industries	245.0	153.3	91.7
C Manufacture of wood and wood products, including furniture	91.7	50.9	40.8
D Manufacture of paper and paper products, printing and publishing	69.1	42.0	27.1
E Manufacture of chemicals and chemical petroleum, coal, rubber and plastic products	155.6	118.2	37.4
F Manufacture of non-metallic mineral products, except products of petroleum and coal	88.5	51.6	36.9
G Basic metal industries	-	-	-
H Manufacture of fabricated metal products, machinery and equipment	140.9	87.9	53.0
I Other manufacturing industries	36.2	25.2	11.0
4 Electricity, gas and water	102.5	41.6	60.9
A Electricity, gas and steam	85.0	35.2	49.8
B Water works and supply	17.5	6.4	11.1
5 Construction	570.8	263.7	307.1
6 Wholesale and retail trade, restaurants and hotels	980.0	328.0	652.0
A Wholesale and retail trade	493.3	141.7	351.6
B Restaurants and hotels	486.7	186.3	300.4
Restaurants	233.7	101.4	132.3
Hotels and other lodging places	253.0	84.9	168.1
7 Transport, storage and communication	402.1	138.2	263.9
A Transport and storage	316.6	129.2	187.4
B Communication	85.5	9.0	76.5
8 Finance, insurance, real estate and business services	590.5	111.0	479.5
A Financial institutions	147.5	36.4	111.1
B Insurance	36.7	8.9	27.8
C Real estate and business services	406.3	65.8	340.5
Real estate, except dwellings	155.7	14.9	140.8

Cyprus

4.1 Derivation of Value Added by Kind of Activity, in Current Prices
(Continued)

Million Cyprus pounds

	1992 Gross Output	1992 Intermediate Consumption	1992 Value Added
Dwellings	140.7	17.7	123.0
9 Community, social and personal services	260.4	66.5	193.9
A Sanitary and similar services	5.9	0.5	5.4
B Social and related community services [a]	93.9	22.6	71.3
Educational services	41.5	8.3	33.2
Medical, dental, other health and veterinary services	46.8	12.6	34.2
C Recreational and cultural services	55.6	17.8	37.8
D Personal and household services	105.0	25.6	79.4
Total, Industries	4347.2	1792.7	2554.5
Producers of Government Services	445.2	75.9	369.3
Other Producers	31.1	9.8	21.3
Total	4823.5	1878.4	2945.1
Less: Imputed bank service charge	...	-92.8	92.8
Import duties	192.5	...	192.5
Value added tax	36.5	...	36.5
Total	5052.5	1971.2	3081.3

a) Social and related community services include in addition to educational and health services also the services of commercial and professional associations, welfare institutions and other social and related community services.

4.2 Derivation of Value Added by Kind of Activity, in Constant Prices

Million Cyprus pounds

At constant prices of: 1985

All Producers

	1990 Gross Output	1990 Interm. Cons.	1990 Value Added	1991 Gross Output	1991 Interm. Cons.	1991 Value Added	1992 Gross Output	1992 Interm. Cons.	1992 Value Added
1 Agriculture, hunting, forestry and fishing	232.2	100.3	131.9	210.4	98.4	112.0	243.2	107.3	135.9
A Agriculture and hunting	222.8	98.4	124.4	202.2	96.7	105.5	234.4	105.5	128.9
B Forestry and logging	2.2	0.6	1.6	1.9	0.6	1.3	1.8	0.5	1.3
C Fishing	7.2	1.3	5.9	6.3	1.1	5.2	7.0	1.3	5.7
2 Mining and quarrying	12.4	6.9	5.5	12.4	6.5	5.9	12.6	6.6	6.0
A Coal mining	-	-	-	-	-	-	-	-	-
B Crude petroleum and natural gas production	-	-	-	-	-	-	-	-	-
C Metal ore mining	0.5	0.3	0.2	0.4	0.3	0.1	0.3	0.2	0.1
D Other mining	12.1	6.6	5.5	12.0	6.2	5.8	12.3	6.4	5.9
3 Manufacturing	918.4	631.5	286.9	948.5	659.0	289.5	975.5	676.4	299.1
A Manufacture of food, beverages and tobacco	228.2	149.1	79.1	230.3	151.1	79.2	252.7	165.8	86.9
B Textile, wearing apparel and leather industries	204.1	135.0	69.1	204.2	136.1	68.1	193.0	128.3	64.7
C Manufacture of wood and wood products, including furniture	63.3	34.4	28.7	64.7	36.0	28.7	65.3	36.3	29.0
D Manufacture of paper and paper products, printing and publishing	57.5	39.0	18.5	52.7	34.0	18.7	55.8	36.0	19.8
E Manufacture of chemicals and chemical petroleum, coal, rubber and plastic products	163.7	137.4	26.3	186.9	160.0	26.9	188.8	160.5	28.3
F Manufacture of non-metallic mineral products, except products of petroleum and coal	76.1	50.9	25.2	77.0	50.7	26.3	78.2	51.6	26.7
G Basic metal industries	-	...	-	-	...	-	-	...	-
H Manufacture of fabricated metal products, machinery and equipment	97.2	66.1	31.1	102.0	69.7	32.3	109.6	75.6	34.0
I Other manufacturing industries	28.3	19.4	8.9	30.7	21.4	9.3	32.0	22.3	9.7
4 Electricity, gas and water	126.4	64.2	62.2	128.5	65.3	63.2	149.3	75.1	74.2
A Electricity, gas and steam	112.7	57.4	55.3	117.0	59.2	57.8	136.7	68.6	68.1
B Water works and supply	13.7	6.8	6.9	11.5	6.1	5.4	12.6	6.5	6.1

Cyprus

4.2 Derivation of Value Added by Kind of Activity, in Constant Prices
(Continued)

Million Cyprus pounds

	1990 Gross Output	1990 Intermediate Consumption	1990 Value Added	1991 Gross Output	1991 Intermediate Consumption	1991 Value Added	1992 Gross Output	1992 Intermediate Consumption	1992 Value Added
				At constant prices of: 1985					
5 Construction	370.9	192.2	178.7	389.0	201.9	187.1	406.4	210.0	196.4
6 Wholesale and retail trade, restaurants and hotels	686.7	244.3	442.4	653.7	216.6	437.1	755.1	256.5	498.6
A Wholesale and retail trade	358.9	108.8	250.1	370.1	104.0	266.1	405.7	113.3	292.4
B Restaurants and hotels	327.8	135.5	192.3	283.6	112.6	171.0	349.4	143.2	206.2
Restaurants	159.1	70.9	88.2	134.0	60.4	73.6	159.0	75.9	83.1
Hotels and other lodging places	168.7	64.6	104.1	149.6	52.2	97.4	190.4	67.3	123.1
7 Transport, storage and communication	304.0	100.0	204.0	293.7	96.3	197.4	336.8	121.8	215.0
A Transport and storage	228.1	94.4	133.7	214.5	89.5	125.0	253.5	114.4	139.1
B Communication	75.9	5.6	70.3	79.2	6.8	72.4	83.3	7.4	75.9
8 Finance, insurance, real estate and business services	387.1	67.0	320.1	404.7	70.0	334.7	447.5	78.7	368.8
A Financial institutions	96.6	18.1	78.5	103.4	21.5	81.9	114.4	26.6	87.8
B Insurance	21.3	5.7	15.6	21.7	5.5	16.2	28.5	6.5	22.0
C Real estate and business services	269.2	43.2	226.0	279.6	43.0	236.6	304.6	45.6	259.0
Real estate, except dwellings	102.9	10.2	92.7	162.1	74.7	87.4	110.4	4.8	105.6
Dwellings	94.3	10.5	83.8	99.1	6.6	92.5	102.9	12.0	90.9
9 Community, social and personal services	150.5	46.1	104.4	165.2	50.0	115.2	183.2	56.1	127.1
A Sanitary and similar services	1.5	0.3	1.2	2.4	0.4	2.0	3.3	0.4	2.9
B Social and related community services	51.2	15.8	35.4	56.3	17.1	39.2	60.5	18.1	42.4
Educational services	22.5	5.3	17.2	24.6	5.9	18.7	26.8	6.5	20.3
Medical, dental, other health and veterinary services	25.8	9.4	16.4	28.4	9.9	18.5	29.9	10.3	19.6
C Recreational and cultural services	39.3	13.7	25.6	43.0	14.5	28.5	47.8	16.1	31.7
D Personal and household services	58.5	16.3	42.2	63.5	18.0	45.5	71.6	21.5	50.1
Total, Industries	3188.8	1452.5	1736.3	3206.1	1464.0	1742.1	3509.5	1588.4	1921.1
Producers of Government Services	287.2	51.7	235.5	306.1	57.8	248.3	326.9	57.8	269.1
Other Producers	20.0	6.5	13.5	21.4	7.2	14.2	22.7	7.7	15.0
Total	3496.0	1510.7	1985.3	3533.6	1529.0	2004.6	3859.1	1653.9	2205.2
Less: Imputed bank service charge	...	-60.7	60.7	...	-63.3	63.3	...	-69.5	69.5
Import duties	146.8	...	146.8	148.1	...	148.1	144.1	...	144.1
Value added tax	...	...	...	...	...	...	29.0	...	29.0
Total	3642.8	1571.4	2071.4	3681.7	1592.3	2089.4	4032.2	1723.4	2308.8

Czech Republic

Source. Reply to the United Nations national accounts questionnaire from the Czech Statistical Office.

General note. The estimates shown in the following tables have been prepared in accordance with the System of National Accounts so far as the existing data would permit.

1.1 Expenditure on the Gross Domestic Product, in Current Prices

Million Koruna

	1980	1983	1984	1985	1986	1987	1988	1989	1990	1991	1992	1993
1 Government final consumption expenditure [a]	...	...	...	...	...	106800	108364	112897	112610	134740	163700	211600
2 Private final consumption expenditure	...	...	...	...	...	233339	242886	251264	284824	318900	406300	496600
A Households	...	...	...	...	...	233339	242886	251264	284824	318900	406300	496600
B Private non-profit institutions serving households [a]	...	...	...	...	...	...	...	...	...	...	...	...
3 Gross capital formation	...	...	...	130775	143068	145026	140905	140510	162528	214177	210400	162200
A Increase in stocks	...	...	...	9614	12739	19908	4694	4079	13235	48921	-15300	-79700
B Gross fixed capital formation	...	...	...	121161	130329	125118	136211	136431	149293	165256	225700	241900
Residential buildings	...	...	...	...	...	11924	15704	14233	15401	16978	...	...
Non-residential buildings	...	...	...	...	...						...	...
Other construction and land improvement etc.	...	...	...	...	...	57652	59224	65819	78173	84921	...	...
Other	...	...	...	...	...	55542	61283	56379	55719	63357	...	...
4 Exports of goods and services	...	...	...	...	...	9908	21293	19894	7360	412276	447900	522500
5 Less: Imports of goods and services	...	...	...	...	...					363500	437300	483200
Equals: Gross Domestic Product	415300	436900	462800	473700	483000	495073	513448	524565	567322	716593	791000	909700

a) The consumption expenditure of the private non-profit institutions serving households is included in item 'Government final consumption expenditure'.

1.2 Expenditure on the Gross Domestic Product, in Constant Prices

Million Koruna

	1980	1983	1984	1985	1986	1987	1988	1989	1990	1991	1992	1993
					At constant prices of:1984							
1 Government final consumption expenditure [a]	...	...	...	...	...	100900	98000	102500	103400	94100	91200	89900
2 Private final consumption expenditure	...	...	...	...	...	225100	234000	237400	253200	181100	206600	210900
A Households	...	...	...	...	...	225100	234000	237400	253200	181100	206600	210900
B Private non-profit institutions serving households [a]	...	...	...	...	...	...	...	...	...	...	...	...
3 Gross capital formation	...	...	...	...	...	147900	140600	143600	148900	126700	103100	92200
A Increase in stocks	...	...	...	...	...	20100	4600	3800	12100	14100	-19500	-21000
B Gross fixed capital formation	...	...	...	...	...	127800	136000	139800	136800	112600	122600	113200
4 Exports of goods and services	...	...	...	...	...	4100	15200	26400	-1800	239000	255200	277200
5 Less: Imports of goods and services	...	...	...	...	...					208800	251600	267900
Equals: Gross Domestic Product	...	...	462800	465600	475300	478000	487800	509900	503700	432100	404500	402300

a) The consumption expenditure of the private non-profit institutions serving households is included in item 'Government final consumption expenditure'.

1.10 Gross Domestic Product by Kind of Activity, in Current Prices

Million Koruna

	1980	1983	1984	1985	1986	1987	1988	1989	1990	1991	1992	1993
1 Agriculture, hunting, forestry and fishing	...	...	...	...	...	33304	32866	46476	41436	39902	...	...
2 Mining and quarrying	...	...	...	...	...						...	...
3 Manufacturing	...	...	...	...	...	207386	214765	219462	222679	314916	...	...
4 Electricity, gas and water	...	...	...	...	...						...	...
5 Construction	...	...	...	...	...	39074	41442	41166	46224	44981	...	...
6 Wholesale and retail trade, restaurants and hotels	...	...	...	...	...	60269	63589	60008	74878	75180	...	...
7 Transport, storage and communication	...	...	...	...	...	26789	26839	25325	24508	29144	...	...
8 Finance, insurance, real estate and business services	...	...	...	...	...	25599	24251	30080	30242	68709	...	...
9 Community, social and personal services	...	...	...	...	...	18069	18327	20089	25406	35343	...	...
Total, industries	...	...	...	...	...	410490	422079	442606	465373	608175	...	...
Producers of Government Services	...	...	...	...	...	42835	44581	46565	47318	53573	...	...

Czech Republic

1.10 Gross Domestic Product by Kind of Activity, in Current Prices
(Continued)

Million Koruna

	1980	1983	1984	1985	1986	1987	1988	1989	1990	1991	1992	1993
Other Producers	...	...	...	...	...	2557	2672	2885	2354	1987	...	...
Subtotal	...	...	...	...	...	455882	469332	492056	515045	663735	...	...
Less: Imputed bank service charge	...	...	...	...	...	13794	12498	14985	15721	45279	...	...
Plus: Import duties [a]	...	...	...	...	...	3218	3785	5585	4886	17109	...	...
Plus: Value added tax [b]	...	...	...	...	...	51719	55528	44427	64613	81028	...	...
Plus: Other adjustments	...	...	...	...	...	-1952	-2699	-2518	-1501	-	...	...
Equals: Gross Domestic Product	415300	436900	462800	473700	483000	495073	513448	524565	567322	716593	791000	909700

a) Item 'Import duties' refers to the differences between retail and import prices. Beginning 1991, it includes customs and import tax.
b) Item 'value added tax' refers to turnover tax.

1.11 Gross Domestic Product by Kind of Activity, in Constant Prices

Million Koruna

	1980	1983	1984	1985	1986	1987	1988	1989	1990	1991	1992	1993
					At constant prices of:1984							
1 Agriculture, hunting, forestry and fishing	...	...	...	...	...	...	...	33923	31838	31758	...	...
2 Mining and quarrying	...	...	...	...	...	...	...				...	...
3 Manufacturing	...	...	...	...	...	...	...	225930	222327	193173	...	...
4 Electricity, gas and water	...	...	...	...	...	...	...				...	...
5 Construction	...	...	...	...	...	...	...	40186	42321	30018	...	...
6 Wholesale and retail trade, restaurants and hotels	...	...	...	...	...	...	...	51715	52360	38256	...	...
7 Transport, storage and communication	...	...	...	...	...	...	...	25497	21287	18287	...	...
8 Finance, insurance, real estate and business services	...	...	...	...	...	...	...	30121	29691	60382	...	...
9 Community, social and personal services	...	...	...	...	...	...	...	21423	25496	28752	...	...
Total, Industries	...	...	...	...	...	...	...	428795	425320	400626	...	...
Producers of Government Services	...	...	...	...	...	...	...	45747	43387	41690	...	...
Other Producers	...	...	...	...	...	...	...	2890	2224	1745	...	...
Subtotal	...	...	...	...	...	...	...	477432	470931	444061	...	...
Less: Imputed bank service charge	...	...	...	...	...	...	...	14985	15721	45279	...	...
Plus: Import duties	...	...	...	...	...	...	...	47494	48502	33308	...	...
Plus: Value added tax	...	...	...	...	...	...	...				...	...
Equals: Gross Domestic Product	...	...	...	...	...	478000	487800	509941	503712	432090	404500	402300

Denmark

General note. The preparation of national accounts statistics in Denmark is undertaken by the Danmarks Statistik, Copenhagen. The official estimates are published three times annually in 'Statistiske Efterretninger (Nationalregnskab. Offentlige Finanser, Betalingsbalance)' and in more detail in the annual publication 'Nationalregnskabsstatistik'. The following presentation of sources and methods is mainly based on a report prepared by the Statistical Office of the European Communities in 1976 entitled 'Base statistics needed for the ESA accounts and tables: present situation and prospects for improvements' and on 'Input-output tabeller for Danmark 1966' published by Danmarks Statistik in 1973. The estimates are generally in accordance with the classifications and definitions recommended in the United Nations System of National Accounts (SNA). The following tables have been prepared from successive replies to the United Nations national accounts questionnaire. When the scope and coverage of the estimates differ for conceptual or statistical reasons from the definitions and classifications recommended in SNA, a footnote is indicated to the relevant tables.

Sources and methods:

(a) Gross domestic product. Gross domestic product is estimated mainly through the production approach.

(b) Expenditure on the gross domestic product. The expenditure approach is used to estimate government final consumption expenditure, increase in stocks and exports and imports of goods and services. The commodity-flow approach is used for private final consumption expenditure and gross fixed capital formation. The estimates of government consumption expenditure are mainly based on the accounts of the central and local government and on social secutiry funds. The estimates of private consumption expenditure, using the commodity-flow method, have a time-lag of two years. Therefore, short-term estimates are made, using turnover statistics for the retail trade. This is supplemented by family budget surveys which are conducted every five years. Changes in stocks are estimated on the basis of inventory statistics. For gross fixed capital formation, information is classified by product and by ownership branch. The valuation is made net of deductible value added tax. Estimates of investments in buildings are based partly on data available on construction starts, work under construction and work completed and partly on information from accounting data. Estimates of investments in machinery and equipment are based on production and foreign trade statistics adjusted to include gross margins, duties etc. Exports and imports of goods and services are estimated mainly form the balance-of-payments and foreign trade statistics. Special surveys are available for shipping and for payments to and receipts from the rest of the world by Danish enterprises. For the constant price estimates, price indexes arrived at for the supply of goods and services, broken down into 4,000 groups, are used for all components of GDP by expenditure type except that of exports for which the indexes for domestic output are used.

(c) Cost-structure of the gross domestic product. Data on the compensation of employees are taken directly from the annual surveys on current transactions. For consumption of fixed capital, only rough estimates are made. Total indirect taxes and subsidies are obtained from government accounts. Operating surplus is estimated as a residual.

(d) Gross domestic product by kind of economic activity. The table of GDP by kind of economic activity is prepared in factor values. The production approach is used to estimate the value added of almost all industries. The income approach is used to estimate the value added of producers of government services, parts of business services and other private services. The gross output of the trade sector is primarily estimated by means of the commodity-flow approach. The estimates of agricultural production are based on product-by-product data in terms of volume and prices which are obtained from the annual agricultural statistics. The estimates of gross output are supplemented by survey data on total costs and cost structure. For forestry and fishing, the main sources used are the annual agricultural reports and the annual reports of the Ministry of Fisheries. For manufacturing, estimates are based on an annual survey covering all enterprises employing 20 or more persons and on a quarterly survey on the turnover of 4,000 products. Censuses taken in 1966 and 1975 provide a product-by-product breakdown of intermediate inputs. The value-added tax returns of enterprises are used to make estimates for small enterprises and services not covered by direct surveys. For electricity, gas and water, the estimates are based on annual electricity statistics, accunting statistics of the municipalities and on local government reports, respectively. For private construction, various sources are used such as an annual accounting survey and investment statistics. Construction in the public sector is estimated from government accounts. The estimates of gross trade and trasnport margins are based on data obtained from a sample survey of trade enterprises adjusted for under-coverage, mark-ups and other non-available margins. Another method used is to estimate the size of the gross margins of each commodity and its share in the distributive channel. These estimates are partly based on information from the Price Directorate. For restaurants and hotels, value-added tax statistics are used. For the transport sector, the information is taken from the accounts of the exterprises concerned except road transport which makes use of the vaue-added tax returns. For the finanacial sector, the balance-sheets and complete accounts of the companies' current transactions are used. A bench-mark survey of housing rents is carried out every five years. For intervening years, changes in the average rent and total stock of residential buildings are used. Rents of rented dwellings are used for the imputation of rents of owner-occupied dwellings. Value-added tax statistics, population census and accouting data of advertising services are used for the business services sector. The main sources for the producers of government services are the account of the central and local government and social secutiry funds. For other services, value-added tax statistics are used except for professions like doctors and dentists, for which social security data are used. For the constant price estimates, double deflation is used. The data are deflated by means of a price index related to each of the 4,000 groups of goods and services. The price indexes are applied to domestic output as well as imports.

1.1 Expenditure on the Gross Domestic Product, in Current Prices

Million Danish kroner

	1980	1983	1984	1985	1986	1987	1988	1989	1990	1991	1992	1993
1 Government final consumption expenditure	99734	140544	146176	155481	159359	176214	188487	196546	202504	211201	219128	229808
2 Private final consumption expenditure	208814	279963	307889	337215	366747	377878	388806	403894	415032	430202	442968	457904
A Households	207048	277680	305198	334191	363338	374135	384819	399688	409998	424927	437547	451359
B Private non-profit institutions serving households	1766	2283	2691	3024	3409	3743	3987	4207	5034	5275	5421	6545
3 Gross capital formation	69187	81862	104104	120290	143386	132958	130738	140838	138441	136026	129621	124398
A Increase in stocks	-1125	-187	6852	5098	5016	-5075	-1488	1885	-916	-667	-892	-7270
B Gross fixed capital formation	70312	82049	97252	115192	138370	138033	132226	138953	139357	136693	130513	131668
Residential buildings	19833	20264	25788	26532	33429	33846	32288	30960	28026	25308	25862	25495
Non-residential buildings	15194	12186	14831	19529	23078	27211	26973	24630	24657	23268	31373	31161
Other construction and land improvement etc.	9149	14350	13066	15260	17247	17235	18421	21139	22582	20277	14831	12097
Other	26136	35249	43567	53870	64617	59742	54543	62224	64092	67841	58446	62916
4 Exports of goods and services	122256	186311	207523	225566	213559	220084	238916	264908	283575	306005	310677	299863
5 Less: Imports of goods and services	126205	176140	200408	223480	216555	207226	214891	238936	240442	255567	251141	238735
Equals: Gross Domestic Product	373786	512540	565284	615072	666496	699908	732056	767250	799110	827867	851253	873238

1.2 Expenditure on the Gross Domestic Product, in Constant Prices

Million Danish kroner

	1980	1983	1984	1985	1986	1987	1988	1989	1990	1991	1992	1993
					At constant prices of:1980							
1 Government final consumption expenditure	99734	105465	105030	107682	108205	110873	111920	111234	110752	110588	112100	115212
2 Private final consumption expenditure	208814	212292	219469	230365	243583	239929	237481	236539	236644	239429	242060	247775
A Households	207048	210541	217539	228287	241352	237660	235163	234187	233967	236691	239240	244508
B Private non-profit institutions serving households	1766	1751	1930	2077	2231	2269	2318	2352	2677	2738	2820	3267
3 Gross capital formation	69187	62364	75009	82870	94682	85932	82205	86198	82318	77803	71399	66702

Denmark

1.2 Expenditure on the Gross Domestic Product, in Constant Prices
(Continued)

Million Danish kroner

	1980	1983	1984	1985	1986	1987	1988	1989	1990	1991	1992	1993
	\multicolumn{12}{c}{At constant prices of:1980}
A Increase in stocks	-1125	417	5079	4156	2506	-2771	-603	2559	139	292	-498	-3558
B Gross fixed capital formation	70312	61947	69930	78714	92176	88703	82808	83639	82179	77511	71897	70260
Residential buildings	19833	15023	18072	17697	21475	20780	18817	17149	14804	13079	12429	12060
Non-residential buildings	15194	9116	10567	13167	15226	17284	16369	14225	13743	12559	16260	15665
Other construction and land improvement etc.	9149	10656	9218	10376	11982	11178	11337	12333	12715	11007	7827	6322
Other	26136	27152	32073	37473	43493	39461	36285	39931	40918	40867	35381	36213
4 Exports of goods and services	122256	142176	147108	154406	154454	162295	174922	182193	194833	209792	215532	211276
5 Less: Imports of goods and services	126205	131040	138184	149373	159457	156265	158606	165718	167669	174594	174257	167157
Equals: Gross Domestic Product	373786	391257	408432	425950	441467	442764	447922	450446	456878	463018	466834	473808

1.3 Cost Components of the Gross Domestic Product

Million Danish kroner

	1980	1983	1984	1985	1986	1987	1988	1989	1990	1991	1992	1993
1 Indirect taxes, net	57797	74671	83607	94555	110820	113963	114211	113246	113167	115735	114366	118476
A Indirect taxes	69591	91426	102228	112913	130880	135974	139551	140201	141521	144461	148593	153351
B Less: Subsidies	11794	16755	18621	18358	20060	22011	25340	26955	28354	28726	34227	34875
2 Consumption of fixed capital	33670	46900	50200	54800	57600	61600	64800	69100	72100	76400	79600	83800
3 Compensation of employees paid by resident producers to:	212722	283353	306095	330841	356230	388891	407106	422094	439262	452933	468410	473890
A Resident households	212426	282782	305445	330180	355526	388244	406362	421263	438342	452000	467446	472854
B Rest of the world	296	571	650	661	704	647	744	831	921	932	964	1036
4 Operating surplus	69597	107617	125382	134876	141847	135454	145937	162809	174580	182800	188877	197070
Equals: Gross Domestic Product	373786	512541	565284	615072	666497	699908	732054	767249	799109	827868	851253	873236

1.4 General Government Current Receipts and Disbursements

Million Danish kroner

	1980	1983	1984	1985	1986	1987	1988	1989	1990	1991	1992	1993
	\multicolumn{12}{c}{Receipts}
1 Operating surplus	-	-	-	-	-	-	-	-	-	-	-	-
2 Property and entrepreneurial income	15119	23041	28479	30240	32654	31369	34127	37849	38390	37902	45754	45754
3 Taxes, fees and contributions	169531	237914	268802	301149	337759	359647	377223	387762	388490	403559	419463	435275
A Indirect taxes	69591	91426	102228	112913	130879	135974	139552	140201	141523	144461	148593	153351
B Direct taxes	96343	136551	155156	175661	195466	208943	226248	235426	233268	245202	255988	265866
C Social security contributions	3168	9377	10688	11749	10619	13798	10228	10843	12325	12571	13599	14545
D Compulsory fees, fines and penalties	429	560	730	826	795	932	1195	1292	1374	1325	1283	1513
4 Other current transfers	10327	13900	16351	16110	18189	20721	21640	20885	22083	23440	23884	27755
Total Current Receipts of General Government	194977	274855	313632	347499	388602	411737	432990	446496	448963	464901	489101	508784
	\multicolumn{12}{c}{Disbursements}
1 Government final consumption expenditure	99734	140544	146176	155481	159359	176214	188487	196546	202504	211201	219128	229808
A Compensation of employees	69515	101183	104850	110282	114398	125773	136347	142219	146755	152411	157954	163867
B Consumption of fixed capital	2925	4027	4328	4948	5412	5997	6420	7025	7542	7912	8558	9053
C Purchases of goods and services, net	26841	34798	36243	39391	38578	43243	44891	46464	47391	50064	51699	54975
D Less: Own account fixed capital formation	...	...	...	...	...	...	...	...	...	...	...	...
E Indirect taxes paid, net	453	536	755	860	971	1201	829	838	816	814	917	1913
2 Property income	14747	41306	54149	60639	58692	57746	58305	57464	58505	61078	58489	67827
A Interest	14747	41306	54149	60639	58692	57746	58305	57464	58505	61078	58489	67827
B Net land rent and royalties	...	...	...	...	...	...	...	...	...	...	...	...

Denmark

1.4 General Government Current Receipts and Disbursements
(Continued)

Million Danish kroner

	1980	1983	1984	1985	1986	1987	1988	1989	1990	1991	1992	1993
3 Subsidies	11794	16756	18621	18358	20060	22011	25340	26955	28354	28726	34227	34875
4 Other current transfers	68819	100824	106973	112584	117881	128971	144268	158595	164644	178361	188533	201434
A Social security benefits	62155	91183	96155	100396	103307	113716	126956	140360	147423	157661	167767	179023
B Social assistance grants												
C Other	6664	9641	10818	12188	14574	15255	17312	18235	17221	20701	20765	22411
5 Net saving	-117	-24575	-12287	437	32610	26795	16590	6936	-5044	-14464	-11277	-25159
Total Current Disbursements and Net Saving of General Government	194977	274855	313632	347499	388602	411737	432990	446496	448963	464902	489100	508785

1.5 Current Income and Outlay of Corporate and Quasi-Corporate Enterprises, Summary

Million Danish kroner

	1980	1983	1984	1985	1986	1987	1988	1989	1990	1991	1992	1993
Receipts												
1 Operating surplus	...	40020	47533	53881	55840	50329	52842	63845	66930	70940	74433	82387
2 Property and entrepreneurial income received	...	17829	21464	26133	27621	33071	29736	23568	23669	18767	11683	13189
3 Current transfers	...	20309	23294	25588	26556	29188	32239	31953	35957	37222	38931	42331
Statistical discrepancy	...	194	213	394	422	533	528	-	-	-	-	-
Total Current Receipts	...	78352	92504	105996	110439	113121	115345	119366	126556	126929	125047	137907
Disbursements												
1 Property and entrepreneurial income	...	...	...	...	...	...	...	...	...	...	...	...
2 Direct taxes and other current payments to general government	...	9025	17240	19128	27220	24982	26404	26849	20895	21548	23081	31200
3 Other current transfers	...	18818	20177	23520	25327	27611	30066	29480	29232	31169	31471	36032
Statistical discrepancy	...	3797	3752	3912	3651	3914	4351	4197	5247	4785	5068	5426
4 Net saving	...	46712	51335	59436	54241	56614	54524	58840	71182	69428	65426	65249
Total Current Disbursements and Net Saving	...	78352	92504	105996	110439	113121	115345	119366	126556	126930	125046	137907

1.6 Current Income and Outlay of Households and Non-Profit Institutions

Million Danish kroner

	1980	1983	1984	1985	1986	1987	1988	1989	1990	1991	1992	1993
Receipts												
1 Compensation of employees	...	283615	306309	331116	356440	389186	407367	422355	439556	454786	470346	475851
2 Operating surplus of private unincorporated enterprises	...	67597	77849	80994	86006	85125	93094	98964	107650	111859	114445	114682
3 Property and entrepreneurial income	...	-18432	-19946	-21905	-29200	-34886	-34170	-36101	-38140	-31537	-32773	-21750
4 Current transfers	...	99930	106530	112552	117316	128882	143831	157358	166441	178234	190101	203941
A Social security benefits	...	90458	96418	101315	105215	115522	128887	141245	148847	159142	169699	181917
B Social assistance grants	...	...	...	...	...	...	...	...	...	...	...	...
C Other	...	9472	10111	11237	12101	13360	14944	16113	17594	19092	20402	22024
Statistical discrepancy	...	3797	3752	3912	3651	3914	4351	4197	5247	4785	5068	5426
Total Current Receipts	...	436507	474494	506669	534213	572221	614473	646773	680754	718127	747187	778150
Disbursements												
1 Private final consumption expenditure	...	279963	307889	337215	366747	377878	388806	403894	415032	430201	442968	457904
2 Property income	...	...	...	...	...	...	...	...	...	...	...	...
3 Direct taxes and other current transfers n.e.c. to general government	...	143713	156056	176703	188384	208001	221920	231592	239255	250791	262598	267260
A Social security contributions	...	16187	18140	20170	20137	24039	22076	23015	26882	27137	29691	32594
B Direct taxes	...	127526	137916	156533	168247	183962	199844	208577	212373	223654	232907	234666
C Fees, fines and penalties [a]	...	...	...	...	...	...	...	...	...	...	...	...
4 Other current transfers [a]	...	13365	14593	16249	17310	19108	21019	20833	22187	23385	24199	26823
5 Net saving	...	-534	-4044	-23498	-38228	-32765	-17272	-9546	4280	13750	17422	26163
Total Current Disbursements and Net Saving	...	436507	474494	506669	534213	572222	614473	646773	680754	718127	747187	778150

a) Item 'Other current transfers' includes item 'Fees, fines and penalties'.

Denmark

1.7 External Transactions on Current Account, Summary

Million Danish kroner

	1980	1983	1984	1985	1986	1987	1988	1989	1990	1991	1992	1993
	Payments to the Rest of the World											
1 Imports of goods and services	126205	176140	200408	223480	216555	207226	214891	238936	240442	255567	251141	238735
A Imports of merchandise c.i.f.	109673	148896	171826	191282	184388	173651	175786	195705	196348	208642	204675	191078
B Other	16532	27244	28582	32198	32167	33575	39106	43231	44094	46925	46466	47657
2 Factor income to the rest of the world	16845	28842	38960	43905	46612	48430	55479	68885	75124	96349	131040	182041
A Compensation of employees	296	571	650	661	704	647	744	831	921	932	964	1036
B Property and entrepreneurial income	16549	28271	38310	43244	45908	47783	54735	68054	74203	95417	130076	181005
3 Current transfers to the rest of the world	6035	8894	9553	11612	15029	14807	16225	15579	15309	17151	15607	18953
A Indirect taxes to supranational organizations	1236	1810	2033	2150	2260	2201	2383	2639	2475	7609	7199	6810
B Other current transfers	4799	7084	7520	9462	12769	12606	13842	12940	12834	9542	8408	12143
4 Surplus of the nation on current transactions	-13658	-13232	-18540	-28381	-36215	-20602	-9429	-11342	4077	9088	21549	25656
Payments to the Rest of the World and Surplus of the Nation on Current Transactions	135427	200644	230381	250616	241981	249861	277166	312058	334952	378155	419337	465385
	Receipts From The Rest of the World											
1 Exports of goods and services	122256	186311	207523	225566	213559	220084	238916	264908	283574	306005	310677	299863
A Exports of merchandise f.o.b.	96161	147474	166117	180090	171723	175132	186333	208544	221412	235164	245463	236483
B Other	26095	38837	41406	45476	41836	44952	52582	56365	62162	70841	65214	63380
2 Factor income from rest of the world	7563	10412	15101	17735	19119	20863	27746	38015	40831	62257	99151	153368
A Compensation of employees	434	833	864	937	914	942	1005	1092	1214	2786	2901	2997
B Property and entrepreneurial income	7129	9579	14237	16798	18205	19921	26741	36923	39617	59471	96250	150371
3 Current transfers from rest of the world	5608	3921	7758	7315	9303	8913	10505	9135	10546	9892	9509	12154
A Subsidies from supranational organisations	4915	5641	7089	6531	8424	9837	9362	8828	9415	9714	9491	11609
B Other current transfers	693	-1720	669	784	879	-924	1143	307	1131	178	18	545
Receipts from the Rest of the World on Current Transactions	135427	200644	230382	250616	241981	249860	277167	312058	334951	378154	419337	465385

1.8 Capital Transactions of The Nation, Summary

Million Danish kroner

	1980	1983	1984	1985	1986	1987	1988	1989	1990	1991	1992	1993
	Finance of Gross Capital Formation											
Gross saving	55528	68631	85564	91909	107171	112355	121308	129494	142517	145114	151169	150053
1 Consumption of fixed capital	33670	46900	50200	54800	57600	61600	64800	69100	72100	76400	79600	83800
A General government	2925	4027	4328	4948	5412	5997	6420	7025	7542	7912	8558	9053
B Corporate and quasi-corporate enterprises	...	24377	26615	29782	31195	33298	40378	37786	43680	46607	48316	50832
C Other	...	18496	19257	20070	20993	22305	18002	24289	20879	21881	22726	23915
2 Net saving	21858	21731	35364	37109	49571	50755	56508	60394	70417	68714	71569	66253
A General government	-117	-24575	-12287	437	32610	26795	16590	6936	-5044	-14464	-11277	-25159
B Corporate and quasi-corporate enterprises	...	46712	51335	59436	54241	56614	54524	58840	71182	69428	65426	65249
C Other	...	-534	-4044	-23498	-38228	-32765	-17272	-9546	4280	13750	17422	26163
Less: Surplus of the nation on current transactions	-13658	-13232	-18540	-28381	-36215	-20603	-9429	-11342	4077	9088	21549	25656
Finance of Gross Capital Formation	69186	81863	104104	120290	143386	132958	130737	140836	138440	136026	129620	124397
	Gross Capital Formation											
Increase in stocks	-1125	-187	6852	5098	5016	-5075	-1488	1885	-916	-667	-892	-7270
Gross fixed capital formation	70312	82049	97252	115192	138370	138033	132226	138953	139357	136693	130513	131668
1 General government	12883	10905	11845	14064	13869	15581	16836	16618	15570	12966	19619	19182
2 Corporate and quasi-corporate enterprises	...	46857	53075	65885	80178	80990	81509	85325	89219	90033	78357	80938
3 Other	...	24287	32332	35243	44323	41462	33881	37010	34568	33694	32535	31546
Gross Capital Formation	69187	81862	104104	120290	143386	132958	130738	140838	138441	136026	129621	124398

Denmark

1.9 Gross Domestic Product by Institutional Sectors of Origin

Million Danish kroner

	1980	1983	1984	1985	1986	1987	1988	1989	1990	1991	1992	1993
					Domestic Factor Incomes Originating							
1 General government	69515	101182	104850	110283	114399	125773	136348	142219	146756	152413	157954	163868
2 Corporate and quasi-corporate enterprises	...	187744	210910	234077	255831	268690	276126	298289	313525	324812	334514	341689
A Non-financial	...	188862	211776	236012	257875	271276	278757	300930	316827	329347	338939	342913
B Financial	-397	-1118	-866	-1935	-2044	-2586	-2631	-2641	-3302	-4535	-4425	-1224
3 Households and private unincorporated enterprises	...	102044	115717	121357	127847	129882	140569	144395	153561	158508	164819	165403
4 Non-profit institutions serving households	...	...	...	...	...	...	...	...	...	...	...	...
Subtotal: Domestic Factor Incomes	282319	390970	431477	465717	498077	524345	553043	584903	613842	635733	657287	670960
Indirect taxes, net	57797	74671	83607	94555	110820	113963	114211	113246	113167	115735	114366	118476
A Indirect taxes	69591	91426	102228	112913	130880	135974	139551	140201	141521	144461	148593	153351
B Less: Subsidies	11794	16755	18621	18358	20060	22011	25340	26955	28354	28726	34227	34875
Consumption of fixed capital	33670	46900	50200	54800	57600	61600	64800	69100	72100	76400	79600	83800
Gross Domestic Product	373786	512541	565284	615072	666497	699908	732054	767249	799109	827868	851253	873236

1.10 Gross Domestic Product by Kind of Activity, in Current Prices

Million Danish kroner

	1980	1983	1984	1985	1986	1987	1988	1989	1990	1991	1992	1993
1 Agriculture, hunting, forestry and fishing	17818	24940	31002	30100	30005	27338	27593	31669	30301	29614	27140	26492
2 Mining and quarrying	373	3339	4156	6039	5327	5389	4459	6259	7299	6889	7437	7683
3 Manufacturing	64311	86043	97505	105073	111703	113869	119875	123572	129919	134238	141815	142591
4 Electricity, gas and water	4520	7289	5872	6796	8508	9228	9935	11726	12511	14752	12783	15225
5 Construction	24383	24921	28640	30958	37686	43331	42939	40728	40601	38331	39838	39589
6 Wholesale and retail trade, restaurants and hotels	45257	65893	70659	80892	88350	87952	86348	91443	95467	99765	104475	103574
7 Transport, storage and communication	25899	35216	40391	43220	44770	48016	53232	58283	62373	65423	67278	70592
8 Finance, insurance, real estate and business services	52303	71595	82796	89995	100890	107231	114889	127777	135951	139211	139549	149429
9 Community, social and personal services	16229	21682	23577	25317	27774	30342	32897	33692	35352	37082	39874	39083
Total, Industries	251094	340918	384597	418391	455014	472697	492166	525149	549775	565306	580190	594258
Producers of Government Services	72440	105210	109178	115230	119810	131770	142766	149244	154296	160323	166512	172920
Other Producers	2285	2779	3122	3400	3702	4009	4125	4350	4994	5300	5648	6260
Subtotal [a]	325818	448907	496897	537021	578526	608476	639058	678744	709065	730930	752350	773439
Less: Imputed bank service charge	9830	11037	15220	16504	22850	22530	21215	24741	23123	18797	15463	18678
Plus: Import duties	...	...	...	...	...	...	...	...	...	...	...	...
Plus: Value added tax	...	...	...	...	...	...	...	...	...	...	...	...
Plus: Other adjustments [b]	57797	74671	83607	94555	110820	113963	114211	113246	113169	115736	114366	118476
Equals: Gross Domestic Product	373786	512541	565284	615072	666496	699909	732053	767248	799111	827868	851253	873236
Memorandum Item: Mineral fuels and power	5532	10726	9673	12297	13011	13569	13366	17238	18993	20256	19325	20937

a) Gross domestic product in factor values.
b) Item 'Other adjustments' relates to indirect taxes less subsidies and import duties.

1.11 Gross Domestic Product by Kind of Activity, in Constant Prices

Million Danish kroner

	1980	1983	1984	1985	1986	1987	1988	1989	1990	1991	1992	1993
					At constant prices of: 1980							
1 Agriculture, hunting, forestry and fishing	17818	19404	23289	23191	22368	21311	23447	25274	25486	25082	23604	27151
2 Mining and quarrying	373	2508	3125	4991	7841	10074	10242	12402	12671	15293	16232	17992
3 Manufacturing	64311	67510	70673	72920	72920	69933	71036	71869	71130	71058	71744	69512
4 Electricity, gas and water	4520	5153	5244	6064	6528	6356	6544	6397	6903	8638	7638	8808
5 Construction	24383	18499	20124	21431	25486	26573	24749	23045	22054	20447	18634	18376
6 Wholesale and retail trade, restaurants and hotels	45257	49110	49828	53516	56545	57106	57273	55377	57446	59115	59876	58458
7 Transport, storage and communication	25899	25532	26726	26477	26816	30349	32489	34130	37578	38177	40841	46035
8 Finance, insurance, real estate and business services	52303	53771	58369	60030	64293	65132	65967	68775	69702	67664	65221	65036
9 Community, social and personal services	16229	16166	16357	16695	17695	17248	17535	17108	17072	17060	18381	17544
Total, Industries	251094	257652	273735	285316	300493	304083	309282	314377	320041	322535	322169	328911
Producers of Government Services	72440	80074	79874	81615	82950	83398	84769	84689	84599	83907	84851	86144
Other Producers	2285	2106	2218	2309	2401	2403	2429	2451	2734	2826	2979	3274

Denmark

1.11 Gross Domestic Product by Kind of Activity, in Constant Prices
(Continued)

Million Danish kroner

	1980	1983	1984	1985	1986	1987	1988	1989	1990	1991	1992	1993
					At constant prices of:1980							
Subtotal [a]	325818	339832	355827	369240	385844	389884	396480	401518	407375	409267	409999	418329
Less: Imputed bank service charge	9830	8410	11043	11312	15291	14359	12854	14233	12874	10014	7868	10922
Plus: Import duties	...	...	...	...	...	...	...	...	...	...	...	...
Plus: Value added tax	...	...	...	...	...	...	...	...	...	...	...	...
Plus: Other adjustments [b]	57797	59836	63649	68021	70916	67240	64295	63160	62379	63764	64701	66402
Equals: Gross Domestic Product	373786	391258	408433	425949	441469	442765	447921	450444	456879	463018	466832	473809
Memorandum Item: Mineral fuels and power	5532	8195	8654	11311	14319	16445	16878	19055	19928	24085	23520	26357

a) Gross domestic product in factor values.
b) Item 'Other adjustments' relates to indirect taxes less subsidies and import duties.

1.12 Relations Among National Accounting Aggregates

Million Danish kroner

	1980	1983	1984	1985	1986	1987	1988	1989	1990	1991	1992	1993
Gross Domestic Product	373785	512541	565284	615072	666496	699908	732055	767249	799109	827868	851253	873237
Plus: Net factor income from the rest of the world	-9282	-18430	-23860	-26171	-27492	-27566	-27733	-30870	-34293	-34092	-31889	-28673
Factor income from the rest of the world	7563	10412	15101	17735	19119	20863	27746	38015	40831	62257	99151	153368
Less: Factor income to the rest of the world	16845	28842	38960	43905	46612	48430	55479	68885	75124	96349	131040	182041
Equals: Gross National Product	364503	494111	541424	588901	639004	672342	704322	736379	764816	793776	819364	844564
Less: Consumption of fixed capital	33670	46900	50200	54800	57600	61600	64800	69100	72100	76400	79600	83800
Equals: National Income	330833	447211	491224	534101	581404	610742	639521	667279	692716	717376	739764	760764
Plus: Net current transfers from the rest of the world	-427	-4973	-1795	-4296	-5727	-5895	-5720	-6444	-4763	-7259	-6098	-6799
Current transfers from the rest of the world	5608	3921	7758	7315	9303	8913	10505	9135	10546	9892	9509	12154
Less: Current transfers to the rest of the world	6035	8894	9553	11612	15029	14807	16225	15579	15309	17151	15607	18953
Equals: National Disposable Income	330406	442238	489429	529805	575677	604847	633802	660835	687953	710117	733666	753965
Less: Final consumption	308548	420507	454065	492696	526106	554092	577293	600440	617536	641403	662096	687712
Equals: Net Saving	21858	21731	35364	37109	49571	50755	56508	60395	70417	68714	71569	66253
Less: Surplus of the nation on current transactions	-13658	-13232	-18540	-28381	-36215	-20603	-9429	-11342	4077	9088	21549	25656
Equals: Net Capital Formation	35517	34963	53904	65490	85786	71358	65937	71737	66340	59626	50020	40597

2.1 Government Final Consumption Expenditure by Function, in Current Prices

Million Danish kroner

	1980	1983	1984	1985	1986	1987	1988	1989	1990	1991	1992	1993
1 General public services [a]	...	...	16935	18156	19035	20664	22096	23119	22919	...	...	...
2 Defence	...	...	13270	13135	12945	14192	15561	15611	16193	...	...	...
3 Public order and safety [a]	...	...	...	...	...	...	...	...	...	...	...	...
4 Education	...	...	34898	36742	37763	41810	44873	46736	48019	...	...	...
5 Health	...	...	28748	30688	32147	35121	37537	38920	40099	...	...	...
6 Social security and welfare	...	...	31421	34774	37169	42001	44909	47350	49263	...	...	...
7 Housing and community amenities	...	...	2001	2057	1006	1135	1244	1375	1529	...	...	...
8 Recreational, cultural and religious affairs	...	...	5683	6189	6297	6804	7762	8023	8371	...	...	...
9 Economic services	...	...	13220	13740	12997	14487	14505	15412	16111	...	...	...
10 Other functions [a]	...	...	...	...	...	...	...	...	...	...	...	...
Total Government Final Consumption Expenditure	...	...	146176	155481	159359	176214	188487	196546	202504	...	...	...

a) Item 'Public order and safety' and 'Other functions' are included in item 'General public services'.

Denmark

2.2 Government Final Consumption Expenditure by Function, in Constant Prices

Million Danish kroner

	1980	1983	1984	1985	1986	1987	1988	1989	1990	1991	1992	1993
					At constant prices of:1980							
1 General public services [a]	...	...	12253	12636	12873	12993	13087	12990	12431	...	...	...
2 Defence	...	...	9118	8575	8469	8752	9215	8629	8876	...	...	...
3 Public order and safety [a]	...	...	...	...	...	...	...	...	...	...	...	...
4 Education	...	...	25421	25894	26034	26688	26984	26817	26584	...	...	...
5 Health	...	...	20720	21330	21999	22252	22269	22033	21944	...	...	...
6 Social security and welfare	...	...	22570	24080	25119	26195	26507	26835	26801	...	...	...
7 Housing and community amenities	...	...	1437	1414	676	688	737	752	790	...	...	...
8 Recreational, cultural and religious affairs	...	...	4083	4261	4247	4268	4581	4538	4562	...	...	...
9 Economic services	...	...	9430	9492	8788	9036	8538	8640	8764	...	...	...
10 Other functions [a]	...	...	...	...	...	...	...	...	...	...	...	...
Total Government Final Consumption Expenditure	...	...	105030	107682	108205	110873	111920	111234	110752	...	...	...

a) Item 'Public order and safety' and 'Other functions' are included in item 'General public services'.

2.5 Private Final Consumption Expenditure by Type and Purpose, in Current Prices

Million Danish kroner

	1980	1983	1984	1985	1986	1987	1988	1989	1990	1991	1992	1993
					Final Consumption Expenditure of Resident Households							
1 Food, beverages and tobacco	52239	69215	75428	78377	81641	81422	84341	86726	87274	89961	93807	93600
A Food	35894	47182	52049	53872	55594	55859	58263	60905	60679	63062	65183	66197
B Non-alcoholic beverages	1262	1628	1751	1872	2016	2067	2182	2397	2417	2383	2905	3198
C Alcoholic beverages	7953	11113	11458	12033	12851	12764	13121	12794	12838	12863	12951	11724
D Tobacco	7130	9292	10170	10600	11180	10731	10774	10630	11339	11652	12768	12481
2 Clothing and footwear	12236	16225	17832	19881	22117	22089	21803	21799	22333	23341	23031	23473
3 Gross rent, fuel and power	55832	73477	78716	84790	90374	98045	102108	107837	114187	120736	124281	131392
A Fuel and power	16473	19243	19655	21508	22875	25034	23210	22757	23527	25190	24640	27507
B Other	39359	54234	59061	63281	67498	73011	78898	85080	90660	95546	99641	103885
4 Furniture, furnishings and household equipment and operation	15333	19112	20808	23097	25010	24790	26129	26048	26346	27338	27308	27621
A Household operation	3739	4940	5344	5683	6178	6092	6526	6723	6870	7212	7953	7714
B Other	11594	14171	15464	17413	18831	18698	19603	19325	19476	20126	19356	19907
5 Medical care and health expenses	3760	5100	5572	6001	5788	6933	7848	8409	9155	9031	9752	10114
6 Transport and communication	30229	45246	51869	59137	64437	63875	61714	62359	62981	65824	67996	70066
A Personal transport equipment	6234	12935	16573	20776	23417	19539	14830	13889	14776	16327	16583	16593
B Other	23995	32311	35296	38361	41020	44336	46883	48470	48205	49497	51413	53474
7 Recreational, entertainment, education and cultural services	18992	26383	29608	32440	35629	36048	37003	40062	41825	43879	44115	46193
A Education	2734	4397	4737	5108	5488	5919	6598	7090	7490	7899	8480	8749
B Other	16258	21986	24871	27332	30141	30129	30405	32972	34335	35980	35635	37443
8 Miscellaneous goods and services	18392	25967	28845	32308	36945	39103	41848	44567	45460	47139	49287	50203
A Personal care	2843	4003	4330	4792	5300	5731	6149	6512	6744	6978	7321	7250
B Expenditures in restaurants, cafes and hotels	9738	13721	15290	16978	19622	20638	22064	23668	24130	24716	26652	26859
C Other	5811	8242	9225	10538	12023	12734	13635	14387	14585	15445	15314	16093
Total Final Consumption Expenditure in the Domestic Market by Households, of which	207013	280725	308678	336030	361942	372306	382794	397806	409559	427249	439577	452662
A Durable goods	19153	29842	35657	42042	46492	41351	37251	36785	37737	40046	39414	40054
B Semi-durable goods	29986	40146	44295	49439	54865	57214	57976	58618	60105	63090	63760	65213
C Non-durable goods	83874	107003	114655	120894	126601	129103	130804	133492	134928	139107	143672	147721

Denmark

2.5 Private Final Consumption Expenditure by Type and Purpose, in Current Prices
(Continued)

Million Danish kroner

	1980	1983	1984	1985	1986	1987	1988	1989	1990	1991	1992	1993
D Services	74000	103734	114071	123654	133985	144638	156764	168912	176790	185005	192730	199674
Plus: Direct purchases abroad by resident households	8402	10589	12116	14444	17089	18810	20558	20736	23114	21886	23228	20997
Less: Direct purchases in the domestic market by non-resident households	8367	13634	15596	16282	15693	16981	18533	18855	22676	24208	25258	22300
Equals: Final Consumption Expenditure of Resident Households	207048	277680	305198	334191	363338	374135	384819	399688	409997	424926	437547	451359

Final Consumption Expenditure of Private Non-profit Institutions Serving Households

	1980	1983	1984	1985	1986	1987	1988	1989	1990	1991	1992	1993
Equals: Final Consumption Expenditure of Private Non-profit Organisations Serving Households	1766	2283	2691	3024	3409	3743	3987	4207	5034	5275	5421	6545
Private Final Consumption Expenditure	208814	279963	307889	337215	366747	377878	388806	403895	415031	430201	442968	457904

2.6 Private Final Consumption Expenditure by Type and Purpose, in Constant Prices

Million Danish kroner

	1980	1983	1984	1985	1986	1987	1988	1989	1990	1991	1992	1993

At constant prices of: 1980

Final Consumption Expenditure of Resident Households

	1980	1983	1984	1985	1986	1987	1988	1989	1990	1991	1992	1993
1 Food, beverages and tobacco	52239	54009	54276	54312	55561	54897	55310	54977	54564	55983	57242	58105
A Food	35894	36480	36836	36912	37916	37881	38368	38492	37890	39260	39818	41237
B Non-alcoholic beverages	1262	1124	999	1030	1093	1074	1071	1156	1127	1130	1404	1545
C Alcoholic beverages	7953	8824	8641	8751	8951	8756	8797	8429	8370	8591	8741	8322
D Tobacco	7130	7582	7800	7619	7601	7186	7074	6900	7176	7002	7280	7000
2 Clothing and footwear	12236	12486	12997	13852	14841	14350	13646	13444	13810	13940	13296	13809
3 Gross rent, fuel and power	55832	54454	55168	56869	57748	58311	58171	57669	57831	58693	58941	60593
A Fuel and power	16473	13790	14025	15284	15724	15764	15148	14258	14083	14661	14788	16080
B Other	39359	40663	41143	41585	42024	42548	43023	43411	43748	44031	44153	44513
4 Furniture, furnishings and household equipment and operation	15333	14206	14480	15191	15945	15214	15470	14801	14519	14724	14385	14852
A Household operation	3739	3761	3754	3777	3985	3714	3778	3715	3718	3853	4126	3998
B Other	11594	10444	10726	11414	11961	11500	11692	11086	10801	10871	10259	10854
5 Medical care and health expenses	3760	3839	3909	3998	3756	4234	4524	4687	4811	4622	5080	5153
6 Transport and communication	30229	34324	37735	41479	43827	40717	37112	36393	36220	36840	38172	39072
A Personal transport equipment	6234	11076	13523	16128	17263	13237	9556	8724	8875	9528	9709	10025
B Other	23995	23249	24212	25351	26564	27480	27556	27669	27345	27312	28463	29047
7 Recreational, entertainment, education and cultural services	18992	20450	21879	22998	24796	23978	24184	25426	26139	27303	26617	28281
A Education	2734	3329	3422	3525	3620	3545	3737	3830	3913	3925	4119	4182
B Other	16258	17120	18457	19472	21175	20434	20447	21596	22225	23378	22497	24099
8 Miscellaneous goods and services	18392	19715	20425	21654	23753	24096	24802	25542	25299	25890	26467	26662
A Personal care	2843	2863	2901	2990	3201	3283	3381	3541	3525	3866	4080	3845
B Expenditures in restaurants, cafes and hotels	9738	10428	10734	11311	12541	12758	13185	13648	13466	13584	14207	14443
C Other	5811	6424	6790	7353	8011	8056	8236	8353	8308	8440	8181	8374
Total Final Consumption Expenditure in the Domestic Market by Households, of which	207013	213483	220869	230353	240227	235797	233218	232939	233192	237994	240200	246527
A Durable goods	19153	24521	28093	31611	33775	28332	24736	24241	24543	25873	25168	26540
B Semi-durable goods	29986	29763	30889	32888	35492	35322	34314	34067	34122	34994	34111	35222
C Non-durable goods	83874	81501	82053	83935	85895	85199	84946	83934	83651	85738	88277	90785

Denmark

2.6 Private Final Consumption Expenditure by Type and Purpose, in Constant Prices
(Continued)

Million Danish kroner

	1980	1983	1984	1985	1986	1987	1988	1989	1990	1991	1992	1993
					At constant prices of:1980							
D Services	74000	77697	79835	81918	85065	86944	89222	90697	90877	91390	92644	93979
Plus: Direct purchases abroad by resident households	8402	7501	7878	9084	11480	12711	13250	12284	13818	12297	12991	11526
Less: Direct purchases in the domestic market by non-resident households	8367	10442	11208	11149	10354	10848	11305	11037	13044	13600	13951	13544
Equals: Final Consumption Expenditure of Resident Households	207048	210541	217539	228287	241352	237660	235163	234187	233967	236691	239240	244509
			Final Consumption Expenditure of Private Non-profit Institutions Serving Households									
Equals: Final Consumption Expenditure of Private Non-profit Organisations Serving Households	1766	1751	1930	2077	2231	2269	2318	2352	2677	2738	2820	3267
Private Final Consumption Expenditure	208814	212292	219469	230364	243583	239929	237481	236539	236644	239429	242060	247776

2.7 Gross Capital Formation by Type of Good and Owner, in Current Prices

Million Danish kroner

	1980				1985				1990			
	TOTAL	Total Private	Public Enterprises	General Government	TOTAL	Total Private	Public Enterprises	General Government	TOTAL	Total Private	Public Enterprises	General Government
Increase in stocks, total	-1125	...	...	...	5098	...	...	...	-916	...	...	...
1 Goods producing industries	1173	...	...	...	2950	...	...	...	1051	...	...	...
A Materials and supplies	-78	...	...	...	1660	...	...	...	598	...	...	...
B Work in progress a	...	...	...	...	...	...	...	...	...	...	...	...
C Livestock, except breeding stocks, dairy cattle, etc.	33	...	...	...	-90	...	...	...	-9	...	...	...
D Finished goods a	1218	...	...	...	1380	...	...	...	462	...	...	...
2 Wholesale and retail trade	-2105	...	...	...	3154	...	...	...	-1562	...	...	...
3 Other, except government stocks	-268	...	...	...	-1520	...	...	...	-819	...	...	...
4 Government stocks	75	...	...	...	514	...	...	...	413	...	...	...
Gross Fixed Capital Formation, Total	70312	...	...	...	115192	...	...	...	139357	...	...	...
1 Residential buildings	19833	...	...	...	26532	...	...	...	28026	...	...	...
2 Non-residential buildings	15194	...	...	...	19529	...	...	...	24657	...	...	...
3 Other construction	9149	...	...	...	15260	...	...	...	22582	...	...	...
4 Land improvement and plantation and orchard development	...	...	...	...	...	...	...	...	...	...	...	...
5 Producers' durable goods	26396	...	...	...	53961	...	...	...	63858	...	...	...
A Transport equipment	5500	...	...	...	12228	...	...	...	13916	...	...	...
B Machinery and equipment	20896	...	...	...	41733	...	...	...	49942	...	...	...
6 Breeding stock, dairy cattle, etc.	-260	...	...	...	-91	...	...	...	234	...	...	...
Total Gross Capital Formation	69187	...	...	...	120290	...	...	...	138441	...	...	...

	1991				1992				1993			
	TOTAL	Total Private	Public Enterprises	General Government	TOTAL	Total Private	Public Enterprises	General Government	TOTAL	Total Private	Public Enterprises	General Government
Increase in stocks, total	-667	...	...	...	-892	...	...	...	-7270	...	...	...
1 Goods producing industries	-396	...	...	...	1370	...	...	...	-312	...	...	...
A Materials and supplies	-111	...	...	...	283	...	...	...	-287	...	...	...
B Work in progress a	...	...	...	...	...	...	...	...	...	...	...	...
C Livestock, except breeding stocks, dairy cattle, etc.	87	...	...	...	225	...	...	...	-80	...	...	...
D Finished goods a	-372	...	...	...	862	...	...	...	55	...	...	...
2 Wholesale and retail trade	363	...	...	...	1756	...	...	...	-2965	...	...	...
3 Other, except government stocks	-826	...	...	...	-4152	...	...	...	-4094	...	...	...
4 Government stocks	192	...	...	...	133	...	...	...	100	...	...	...
Gross Fixed Capital Formation, Total	136693	...	...	...	130513	...	...	...	131668	...	...	...
1 Residential buildings	25308	...	...	...	25862	...	...	...	25495	...	...	...
2 Non-residential buildings	23268	...	...	...	31373	...	...	...	31161	...	...	...

Denmark

2.7 Gross Capital Formation by Type of Good and Owner, in Current Prices
(Continued)

Million Danish kroner

	1991 TOTAL	Total Private	Public Enterprises	General Government	1992 TOTAL	Total Private	Public Enterprises	General Government	1993 TOTAL	Total Private	Public Enterprises	General Government
3 Other construction	20277	...	...	...	14831	...	...	...	12097	...	...	...
4 Land improvement and plantation and orchard development	...	...	...	...	...	...	...	...	...	...	...	...
5 Producers' durable goods	67912	...	...	...	58502	...	...	...	62872	...	...	...
A Transport equipment	18574	...	...	...	12650	...	...	...	15920	...	...	...
B Machinery and equipment	49338	...	...	...	45852	...	...	...	46952	...	...	...
6 Breeding stock, dairy cattle, etc.	-71	...	...	...	-56	...	...	...	44	...	...	...
Total Gross Capital Formation	136026	...	...	...	129621	...	...	...	124398	...	...	...

a) Item 'Work in progress' is included in item 'Finished goods'.

2.8 Gross Capital Formation by Type of Good and Owner, in Constant Prices

Million Danish kroner

	1980 TOTAL	Total Private	Public Enterprises	General Government	1985 TOTAL	Total Private	Public Enterprises	General Government	1990 TOTAL	Total Private	Public Enterprises	General Government
				At constant prices of:1980								
Increase in stocks, total	-1125	...	...	...	4156	...	...	...	139	...	...	...
1 Goods producing industries	1173	...	...	...	2062	...	...	...	889	...	...	...
A Materials and supplies	-78	...	...	...	1100	...	...	...	458	...	...	...
B Work in progress a	...	...	...	...	...	...	...	...	...	...	...	...
C Livestock, except breeding stocks, dairy cattle, etc.	33	...	...	...	-68	...	...	...	-7	...	...	...
D Finished goods a	1218	...	...	...	1030	...	...	...	438	...	...	...
2 Wholesale and retail trade	-2105	...	...	...	2743	...	...	...	-932	...	...	...
3 Other, except government stocks	-193	...	...	...	-649	...	...	...	182	...	...	...
4 Government stocks		...	...	...		...	...	...		...	...	...
Gross Fixed Capital Formation, Total	70312	...	...	...	78714	...	...	...	82179	...	...	...
1 Residential buildings	19833	...	...	...	17697	...	...	...	14804	...	...	...
2 Non-residential buildings	15194	...	...	...	13167	...	...	...	13743	...	...	...
3 Other construction	9149	...	...	...	10376	...	...	...	12715	...	...	...
4 Land improvement and plantation and orchard development	...	...	...	...	...	...	...	...	...	...	...	...
5 Producers' durable goods	26396	...	...	...	37540	...	...	...	40720	...	...	...
A Transport equipment	5500	...	...	...	8111	...	...	...	8008	...	...	...
B Machinery and equipment	20896	...	...	...	29429	...	...	...	32712	...	...	...
6 Breeding stock, dairy cattle, etc.	-260	...	...	...	-67	...	...	...	198	...	...	...
Total Gross Capital Formation	69187	...	...	...	82870	...	...	...	82318	...	...	...

	1991 TOTAL	Total Private	Public Enterprises	General Government	1992 TOTAL	Total Private	Public Enterprises	General Government	1993 TOTAL	Total Private	Public Enterprises	General Government
				At constant prices of:1980								
Increase in stocks, total	292	...	...	...	-498	...	...	...	-3558	...	...	...
1 Goods producing industries	-290	...	...	...	982	...	...	...	-121	...	...	...
A Materials and supplies	32	...	...	...	230	...	...	...	-180	...	...	...
B Work in progress a	...	...	...	...	...	...	...	...	...	...	...	...
C Livestock, except breeding stocks, dairy cattle, etc.	72	...	...	...	183	...	...	...	-60	...	...	...
D Finished goods a	-394	...	...	...	569	...	...	...	119	...	...	...
2 Wholesale and retail trade	211	...	...	...	870	...	...	...	-1936	...	...	...
3 Other, except government stocks	371	...	...	...	-2350	...	...	...	-1501	...	...	...
4 Government stocks		...	...	...		...	...	...		...	...	...
Gross Fixed Capital Formation, Total	77511	...	...	...	71897	...	...	...	70260	...	...	...
1 Residential buildings	13079	...	...	...	12429	...	...	...	12060	...	...	...
2 Non-residential buildings	12559	...	...	...	16260	...	...	...	15665	...	...	...

Denmark

2.8 Gross Capital Formation by Type of Good and Owner, in Constant Prices
(Continued)

Million Danish kroner

	1991				1992				1993			
	TOTAL	Total Private	Public Enterprises	General Government	TOTAL	Total Private	Public Enterprises	General Government	TOTAL	Total Private	Public Enterprises	General Government
					At constant prices of:1980							
3 Other construction	11007	...	...	...	7827	...	...	...	6322	...	...	...
4 Land improvement and plantation and orchard development	...	...	...	...	...	...	...	...	...	...	...	...
5 Producers' durable goods	40937	...	...	...	35441	...	...	...	36163	...	...	...
A Transport equipment	9509	...	...	...	6854	...	...	...	7579	...	...	...
B Machinery and equipment	31428	...	...	...	28587	...	...	...	28584	...	...	...
6 Breeding stock, dairy cattle, etc.	-70	...	...	...	-60	...	...	...	50	...	...	...
Total Gross Capital Formation	77803	...	...	...	71399	...	...	...	66702	...	...	...

a) Item 'Work in progress' is included in item 'Finished goods'.

2.11 Gross Fixed Capital Formation by Kind of Activity of Owner, ISIC Divisions, in Current Prices

Million Danish kroner

	1980	1983	1984	1985	1986	1987	1988	1989	1990	1991	1992	1993
					All Producers							
1 Agriculture, hunting, forestry and fishing	5289	4698	6247	8108	7552	6504	5799	7252	8433	6549	6611	5633
A Agriculture and hunting	4895	4147	5457	6895	6657	5695	5079	6577	7593	5704	...	...
B Forestry and logging	99	109	102	164	156	143	142	144	114	124	...	...
C Fishing	295	442	688	1048	740	666	577	532	726	721	...	...
2 Mining and quarrying	838	4586	1724	2205	2002	1315	1089	1323	1905	2609	2586	3348
A Coal mining	...	...	...	...	...	...	...	...	...	...	...	...
B Crude petroleum and natural gas production	753	4526	1631	2094	1788	1166	902	1170	1763	2301	...	...
C Metal ore mining	...	...	...	...	...	...	...	...	...	...	...	...
D Other mining	85	59	93	111	214	149	187	153	142	308	...	...
3 Manufacturing	9262	10094	13509	18032	20942	19738	19491	20036	20209	22428	20856	22316
A Manufacturing of food, beverages and tobacco	2204	2180	3016	3253	3723	3859	4306	4010	3897	4907	...	...
B Textile, wearing apparel and leather industries	282	405	607	719	902	771	779	904	706	600	...	...
C Manufacture of wood, and wood products, including furniture	464	450	791	1265	1204	976	900	1131	1305	1129	...	...
D Manufacture of paper and paper products, printing and publishing	604	1143	1239	1960	2673	2590	2394	2313	1844	2352	...	...
E Manufacture of chemicals and chemical petroleum, coal, rubber and plastic products	1669	1788	2341	2879	3276	3159	3340	3732	3526	4341	...	...
F Manufacture of non-metalic mineral products except products of petroleum and coal	901	481	762	1407	1513	1686	1598	1059	1341	1092	...	...
G Basic metal industries	244	175	178	216	234	202	187	235	303	354	...	...
H Manufacture of fabricated metal products, machinery and equipment	2774	3367	4423	6118	6951	5980	5542	6216	6635	6940	...	...
I Other manufacturing industries	120	106	152	216	465	515	444	435	652	713	...	...
4 Electricity, gas and water	2932	6421	5733	6859	7980	7650	8006	9043	9623	7828	7540	6377
5 Construction	1878	2110	2924	4659	4751	4091	3572	3651	3915	3432	3497	3475
6 Wholesale and retail trade, restaurants and hotels	3066	3770	5090	6062	8524	8327	8721	8782	8794	7515	...	...
A Wholesale and retail trade	3066	3770	5090	6062	8524	8327	8721	8782	8794	7515	...	...
B Restaurants and hotels	...	...	...	...	...	...	...	...	...	...	...	...
7 Transport, storage and communication	8256	9190	11279	13975	19605	17896	19296	24481	24797	28186	...	...
A Transport and storage	5918	6792	8572	10767	15642	13421	14152	19278	20548	24783	...	...
B Communication	2339	2398	2707	3208	3963	4474	5145	5203	4249	3403	...	...
8 Finance, insurance, real estate and business services	21891	22130	28102	28981	36219	37509	36520	33281	31270	29722	...	...
A Financial institutions	2006	1768	2185	2318	2632	3488	4061	2149	3021	4155	...	...
B Insurance											...	...
C Real estate and business services	19885	20362	25917	26663	33587	34021	32459	31132	28249	25567		
Real estate except dwellings	...	...	...	...	...	...	...	...	...	...	...	...

Denmark

2.11 Gross Fixed Capital Formation by Kind of Activity of Owner, ISIC Divisions, in Current Prices
(Continued)

Million Danish kroner

	1980	1983	1984	1985	1986	1987	1988	1989	1990	1991	1992	1993
Dwellings	19885	20362	25917	26663	33587	34021	32459	31132	28249	25567	...	...
9 Community, social and personal services	456	522	697	770	1076	1114	1200	1158	1738	1197	...	...
A Sanitary and similar services	...	...	...	...	...	...	...	...	...	...	...	...
B Social and related community services	...	...	...	...	...	...	...	...	...	...	...	...
C Recreational and cultural services	456	522	697	770	1076	1114	1200	1158	1738	1197	...	...
D Personal and household services	...	...	...	...	...	...	...	...	...	...	...	...
Statistical discrepancy	3658	7541	10079	11453	15652	18175	11388	13253	12975	11406	...	...
Total Industries	57526	71062	85385	101106	124304	122318	115083	122261	123660	120872	112275	112752
Producers of Government Services	12785	10987	11867	14086	14066	15715	17143	16692	15698	15821	18238	18916
Private Non-Profit Institutions Serving Households	...	...	...	...	...	...	...	...	...	...	...	...
Total	70311	82049	97252	115192	138370	138033	132226	138953	139358	136693	130513	131668

2.12 Gross Fixed Capital Formation by Kind of Activity of Owner, ISIC Divisions, in Constant Prices

Million Danish kroner

	1980	1983	1984	1985	1986	1987	1988	1989	1990	1991	1992	1993
	\multicolumn{12}{c}{At constant prices of:1980}
	\multicolumn{12}{c}{All Producers}
1 Agriculture, hunting, forestry and fishing	5289	3433	4327	5461	4841	3995	3427	4224	4785	3500	3560	2905
A Agriculture and hunting	4895	3019	3762	4649	4251	3469	2954	3820	4305	3035	...	...
B Forestry and logging	99	80	69	105	96	86	84	81	66	67	...	...
C Fishing	295	334	496	707	494	440	389	324	413	399	...	...
2 Mining and quarrying	838	3393	1115	1400	1320	823	674	785	1079	1411	1418	1778
A Coal mining	...	...	...	...	...	...	...	...	...	...	...	...
B Crude petroleum and natural gas production	753	3347	1044	1319	1171	722	548	686	991	1235	...	...
C Metal ore mining	...	...	...	...	...	...	...	...	...	...	...	...
D Other mining	85	46	70	82	149	100	126	99	88	175	...	...
3 Manufacturing	9262	7559	9607	12250	13664	12324	11993	11899	11567	12487	11204	11329
A Manufacturing of food, beverages and tobacco	2204	1609	2097	2167	2416	2367	2578	2300	2181	2616	...	...
B Textile, wearing apparel and leather industries	282	305	437	494	602	498	500	555	422	338	...	...
C Manufacture of wood, and wood products, including furniture	464	329	570	879	817	650	585	698	769	622	...	...
D Manufacture of paper and paper products, printing and publishing	604	857	822	1229	1559	1443	1350	1290	983	1301	...	...
E Manufacture of chemicals and chemical petroleum, coal, rubber and plastic products	1669	1346	1673	1958	2150	1946	1988	2095	1896	2303	...	...
F Manufacture of non-metalic mineral products except products of petroleum and coal	901	357	567	1001	1016	1069	1003	613	757	586	...	...
G Basic metal industries	244	126	117	139	139	118	111	131	173	200	...	...
H Manufacture of fabricated metal products, machinery and equipment	2774	2551	3214	4239	4662	3913	3608	3986	4052	4156	...	...
I Other manufacturing industries	120	80	109	146	301	320	271	231	334	363	...	...
4 Electricity, gas and water	2932	4787	4038	4635	5446	4900	4944	5292	5488	4314	4122	3460
5 Construction	1878	1668	2182	3306	3202	2650	2292	2198	2247	1832	1881	1776
6 Wholesale and retail trade, restaurants and hotels	3066	2939	3760	4258	5720	5426	5625	5576	5521	4439	...	...
A Wholesale and retail trade	3066	2939	3760	4258	5720	5426	5625	5576	5521	4439	...	...
B Restaurants and hotels	...	...	...	...	...	...	...	...	...	...	...	...
7 Transport, storage and communication	8256	7022	8318	9343	13233	11767	12376	14700	14753	15617	...	...
A Transport and storage	5918	5207	6364	7098	10262	8579	9017	11437	12124	13631	...	...

Denmark

2.12 Gross Fixed Capital Formation by Kind of Activity of Owner, ISIC Divisions, in Constant Prices
(Continued)

Million Danish kroner

	1980	1983	1984	1985	1986	1987	1988	1989	1990	1991	1992	1993
	\multicolumn{12}{c}{At constant prices of:1980}
B Communication	2339	1815	1954	2245	2971	3189	3359	3264	2629	1985	...	...
8 Finance, insurance, real estate and business services	21891	16556	19865	19597	23442	23290	21746	18958	17340	16150	...	...
A Financial institutions	2006	1454	1694	1801	1870	2405	2810	1686	2389	2913	...	...
B Insurance											...	...
C Real estate and business services	19885	15102	18171	17796	21572	20885	18936	17272	14951	13237	...	...
Real estate except dwellings	...	...	...	...	...	...	...	...	...	...	...	...
Dwellings	19885	15102	18171	17796	21572	20885	18936	17272	14951	13237	...	...
9 Community, social and personal services	456	418	548	584	799	834	917	836	1177	807	...	...
A Sanitary and similar services	...	...	...	...	...	...	...	...	...	...	...	...
B Social and related community services	...	...	...	...	...	...	...	...	...	...	...	...
C Recreational and cultural services	456	418	548	584	799	834	917	836	1177	807	...	...
D Personal and household services	...	...	...	...	...	...	...	...	...	...	...	...
Statistical discrepancy	3658	5979	7787	8557	11257	12840	8528	9510	9300	8369	...	...
Total Industries	57526	53754	61545	69390	82924	78849	72521	73977	73257	68925	61998	60221
Producers of Government Services	12785	8193	8385	9324	9252	9854	10287	9661	8922	8585	9898	10039
Private Non-Profit Institutions Serving Households	...	...	...	...	...	...	...	...	...	...	...	...
Total	70311	61947	69930	78714	92176	88703	82808	83638	82179	77510	71896	70260

2.17 Exports and Imports of Goods and Services, Detail

Million Danish kroner

	1980	1983	1984	1985	1986	1987	1988	1989	1990	1991	1992	1993
	\multicolumn{12}{c}{**Exports of Goods and Services**}
1 Exports of merchandise, f.o.b.	96161	147474	166117	180090	171723	175132	186333	208544	221412	235164	245463	236483
2 Transport and communication	16350	22868	25071	26339	22213	22076	27534	33716	33585	39596	36821	40866
A In respect of merchandise imports	160	200	230	270	255	260	322	285	720	748	720	520
B Other	16190	22668	24841	26069	21958	21816	27212	33431	32865	38848	36101	40346
3 Insurance service charges	-122	-490	-1001	-1032	-1008	-877	-900	-814	72	-428	-561	-1220
4 Other commodities	1500	2825	1740	3887	4938	6772	7415	4608	5829	7465	3696	1434
5 Adjustments of merchandise exports to change-of-ownership basis	...	...	...	...	...	...	...	...	...	...	...	...
6 Direct purchases in the domestic market by non-residential households	8367	13634	15596	16282	15693	16981	18533	18855	22676	24208	25258	22300
7 Direct purchases in the domestic market by extraterritorial bodies	...	...	...	...	...	...	...	...	...	...	...	...
Total Exports of Goods and Services	122256	186311	207523	225566	213559	220084	238916	264908	283574	306005	310677	299863
	\multicolumn{12}{c}{**Imports of Goods and Services**}
1 Imports of merchandise, c.i.f.	109673	148896	171826	191282	184388	173651	175786	195705	196348	208642	204675	191078
A Imports of merchandise, f.o.b. [a]	105313	143396	165426	184232	177578	167205	169200	188406	189023	200861	197004	183854
B Transport of services on merchandise imports	4360	5500	6400	7050	6810	6446	6586	7299	7325	7781	7671	7224
By residents	160	200	230	270	255	260	322	285	720	748	720	520

Denmark

2.17 Exports and Imports of Goods and Services, Detail
(Continued)

Million Danish kroner

	1980	1983	1984	1985	1986	1987	1988	1989	1990	1991	1992	1993
By non-residents	4200	5300	6170	6780	6555	6186	6264	7014	6605	7033	6951	6704
C Insurance service charges on merchandise imports [a]	...	...	...	...	...	...	...	...	...	...	...	...
2 Adjustments of merchandise imports to change-of-ownership basis	...	...	...	...	...	...	...	...	...	...	...	...
3 Other transport and communication	7679	13864	14978	16064	13935	14012	17955	21698	20299	23827	22080	25270
4 Other insurance service charges	...	...	...	...	...	...	...	...	...	...	...	...
5 Other commodities	451	2791	1488	1690	1143	753	593	797	681	1212	1158	1390
6 Direct purchases abroad by government	...	...	...	...	...	...	...	...	...	...	...	...
7 Direct purchases abroad by resident households	8402	10589	12116	14444	17089	18810	20558	20736	23114	21886	23228	20997
Total Imports of Goods and Services	126205	176140	200408	223480	216555	207226	214891	238936	240442	255567	251141	238735
Balance of Goods and Services	-3949	10171	7115	2086	-2996	12858	24025	25972	43132	50438	59536	61128
Total Imports and Balance of Goods and Services	122256	186311	207523	225566	213559	220084	238916	264908	283574	306005	310677	299863

a) Item 'Insurance service charges in respect of merchandise imports' is included in item 'Import of merchandise, f.o.b.'.

3.12 General Government Income and Outlay Account: Total and Subsectors

Million Danish kroner

	1980					1985				
	Total General Government	Central Government	State or Provincial Government	Local Government	Social Security Funds	Total General Government	Central Government	State or Provincial Government	Local Government	Social Security Funds

Receipts

1 Operating surplus	-	-	...	-	-	-	-	...	-	-
2 Property and entrepreneurial income	15119	8094	...	3396	3629	30240	18011	...	4621	7608
A Withdrawals from public quasi-corporations	2116	1670	...	444	2	6820	5438	...	1376	6
B Interest	12858	6360		2871	3627	22871	12138		3131	7602
C Dividends			...					...		
D Net land rent and royalties	145	64	...	81	-	549	435	...	114	-
3 Taxes, fees and contributions	169531	115721	...	51451	2359	301149	208381	...	85360	7408
A Indirect taxes	69591	64092	...	5499	-	112913	107350	...	5563	-
B Direct taxes	96343	50418	...	45925	-	175661	95882	...	79779	-
C Social security contributions	3168	809	...	-	2359	11749	4341	...	-	7408
D Fees, fines and penalties	429	402	...	27	-	826	808	...	18	-
4 Other current transfers	10327	10697	...	68147	15247	16110	20250	...	93652	27613
A Casualty insurance claims	...	...	...	...	...	...	...	...	...	...
B Transfers from other government subsectors	...	3312	...	65229	15223	...	8784	...	89086	27535
C Transfers from the rest of the world	5147	5147	...	-	-	7638	7633	...	5	-
D Other transfers, except imputed	1386	198	...	1164	24	2483	408	...	1997	78
E Imputed unfunded employee pension and welfare contributions	3794	2040	...	1754	-	5989	3425	...	2564	-
Total Current Receipts	194977	134512	...	122994	21235	347499	246642	...	183633	42629

Disbursements

1 Government final consumption expenditure	99734	31174	...	68155	405	155481	48422	...	105960	1099
2 Property income	14747	12323	...	2424	-	60639	57885	...	2752	2
A Interest	14747	12323	...	2424	-	60639	57885	...	2752	2
B Net land rent and royalties	...	...	...	...	...	...	...	...	...	...
3 Subsidies	11794	9923	...	1870	-	18358	15017	...	3336	5

Denmark

3.12 General Government Income and Outlay Account: Total and Subsectors
(Continued)

Million Danish kroner

	1980					1985				
	Total General Government	Central Government	State or Provincial Government	Local Government	Social Security Funds	Total General Government	Central Government	State or Provincial Government	Local Government	Social Security Funds
4 Other current transfers	68819	91298	...	44586	16699	112584	137301	...	67044	33644
A Casualty insurance premiums, net	...	...	...	...	...	...	...	...	...	...
B Transfers to other government subsectors	...	80452	...	2249	1063	...	116621	...	3372	5412
C Social security benefits	62155	4704	...	41815	15636	100396	8947	...	63217	28232
D Social assistance grants			...					...		
E Unfunded employee pension and welfare benefits	-	...	...	...	...	-	...	...	...	...
F Transfers to private non-profit institutions serving households	618	96	...	522	-	640	185	...	455	-
G Other transfers n.e.c.	...	...	...	...	...	...	...	...	...	...
H Transfers to the rest of the world	6046	6046	...	-	-	11548	11548	...	-	-
Net saving	-117	-10206	...	5959	4131	437	-11983	...	4541	7879
Total Current Disbursements and Net Saving	194977	134512	...	122994	21235	347499	246642	...	183633	42629

	1990					1991				
	Total General Government	Central Government	State or Provincial Government	Local Government	Social Security Funds	Total General Government	Central Government	State or Provincial Government	Local Government	Social Security Funds

Receipts

1 Operating surplus	-	-	...	-	-	-	-	...	-	-
2 Property and entrepreneurial income	38390	23625	...	4293	10472	37902	21786	...	5017	11098
A Withdrawals from public quasi-corporations	6054	4457	...	1522	75	5376	2813	...	2531	33
B Interest	31671	18531	...	2743	10397	31808	18281	...	2462	11065
C Dividends			...					...		
D Net land rent and royalties	665	637	...	28	-	718	693	...	25	-
3 Taxes, fees and contributions	388490	256556	...	119991	11943	403559	266507	...	124851	12201
A Indirect taxes	141523	132632	...	8891	-	144461	135771	...	8690	-
B Direct taxes	233268	122184	...	111084	-	245202	129054	...	116148	-
C Social security contributions	12325	382	...	-	11943	12571	370	...	-	12201
D Fees, fines and penalties	1374	1358	...	16	-	1325	1312	...	13	-
4 Other current transfers	22083	27879	...	115663	37325	23440	29634	...	120752	41844
A Casualty insurance claims	...	...	...	...	...	...	...	...	...	...
B Transfers from other government subsectors	...	12215	...	109313	37256	...	12814	...	114204	41772
C Transfers from the rest of the world	9980	9975	...	5	-	10669	10662	...	7	-
D Other transfers, except imputed	3685	639	...	2977	69	3750	735	...	2942	72
E Imputed unfunded employee pension and welfare contributions	8418	5050	...	3368	-	9021	5422	...	3599	-
Total Current Receipts	448963	308060	...	239947	59740	464901	317927	...	250620	65143

Disbursements

1 Government final consumption expenditure	202504	61936	...	138705	1863	211201	64406	...	144933	1861
2 Property income	58505	55486	...	3002	17	61078	58016	...	3044	18
A Interest	58505	55486	...	3002	17	61078	58016	...	3044	18
B Net land rent and royalties	...	...	...	...	...	...	...	...	...	...
3 Subsidies	28354	24279	...	3550	525	28726	23878	...	4080	768

Denmark

3.12 General Government Income and Outlay Account: Total and Subsectors
(Continued)

Million Danish kroner

	1990					1991				
	Total General Government	Central Government	State or Provincial Government	Local Government	Social Security Funds	Total General Government	Central Government	State or Provincial Government	Local Government	Social Security Funds
4 Other current transfers	164644	182783	...	93742	46903	178361	196690	...	98750	51713
A Casualty insurance premiums, net	...	...	...	...	...	...	...	...	...	...
B Transfers to other government subsectors	...	146569	...	3154	9061	...	155976	...	3425	9390
C Social security benefits	147423	19550	...	90031	37842	157661	20567	...	94772	42323
D Social assistance grants			...					...		
E Unfunded employee pension and welfare benefits	-	...	...	...	...	-	...	...	...	...
F Transfers to private non-profit institutions serving households	922	365	...	557	-	1151	597	...	553	-
G Other transfers n.e.c.	...	...	...	...	...	...	...	...	...	...
H Transfers to the rest of the world	16299	16299	...	-	-	19550	19550	...	-	-
Net saving	-5044	-16424	...	948	10432	-14464	-25061	...	-186	10783
Total Current Disbursements and Net Saving	448963	308060	...	239947	59740	464902	317929	...	250621	65143

	1992					1993				
	Total General Government	Central Government	State or Provincial Government	Local Government	Social Security Funds	Total General Government	Central Government	State or Provincial Government	Local Government	Social Security Funds

Receipts

1 Operating surplus	-	-	...	-	-	-	-	...	-	-
2 Property and entrepreneurial income	45754	28741	...	4944	12069	45754	28924	...	4838	11992
A Withdrawals from public quasi-corporations	10868	8611	...	2225	32	8712	6726	...	2033	-46
B Interest	34136	19410	...	2690	12036	36257	21444	...	2776	12039
C Dividends			...					...		
D Net land rent and royalties	750	720	...	30	-	785	755	...	30	-
3 Taxes, fees and contributions	419463	275424	...	130824	13216	435275	285939	...	135181	14154
A Indirect taxes	148593	139606	...	8987	-	153351	142650	...	10701	-
B Direct taxes	255988	134173	...	121816	-	265866	141408	...	124457	-
C Social security contributions	13599	383	...	-	13216	14545	391	...	-	14154
D Fees, fines and penalties	1283	1262	...	21	-	1513	1490	...	23	-
4 Other current transfers	23884	30895	...	127206	46036	27755	36679	...	134449	51694
A Casualty insurance claims	...	...	...	...	...	...	...	...	...	...
B Transfers from other government subsectors	...	13917	...	120376	45959	...	16338	...	127134	51595
C Transfers from the rest of the world	10352	10345	...	7	-	12880	12873	...	8	-
D Other transfers, except imputed	3953	925	...	2952	77	4660	1373	...	3187	99
E Imputed unfunded employee pension and welfare contributions	9579	5708	...	3871	-	10215	6095	...	4120	-
Total Current Receipts	489101	335060	...	262974	71321	508784	351542	...	274468	77840

Disbursements

1 Government final consumption expenditure	219128	66676	...	150108	2344	229808	70073	...	157256	2479
2 Property income	58489	55274	...	3197	18	67827	64470	...	3345	11
A Interest	58489	55274	...	3197	18	67827	64470	...	3345	11
B Net land rent and royalties	...	...	...	...	...	...	...	...	...	...
3 Subsidies	34227	28839	...	4453	935	34875	28960	...	4919	996

Denmark

3.12 General Government Income and Outlay Account: Total and Subsectors
(Continued)

Million Danish kroner

		1992					1993			
		Total General Government	Central Government	State or Provincial Government	Local Government	Social Security Funds	Total General Government	Central Government	State or Provincial Government	Local Government	Social Security Funds
4	Other current transfers	188533	208455	...	103257	57073	201434	223448	...	108457	64594
	A Casualty insurance premiums, net	...	...	...	...	...	...	...	...	...	...
	B Transfers to other government subsectors	...	166334	...	3374	10544	...	178728	...	3999	12338
	C Social security benefits	167767	21975	...	99264	46529	179023	23068	...	103699	52256
	D Social assistance grants			...					...		
	E Unfunded employee pension and welfare benefits	-	...	...	...	...	-	...	...	...	...
	F Transfers to private non-profit institutions serving households	1339	719	...	619	-	1645	887	...	758	-
	G Other transfers n.e.c.	...	...	...	...	...	...	...	...	...	...
	H Transfers to the rest of the world	19426	19426	...	-	-	20766	20766	...	-	-
	Net saving	-11277	-24186	...	1958	10950	-25159	-35410	...	491	9759
	Total Current Disbursements and Net Saving	489100	335058	...	262973	71320	508785	351541	...	274468	77839

3.13 General Government Capital Accumulation Account: Total and Subsectors

Million Danish kroner

		1980					1985			
		Total General Government	Central Government	State or Provincial Government	Local Government	Social Security Funds	Total General Government	Central Government	State or Provincial Government	Local Government	Social Security Funds
				Finance of Gross Accumulation							
1	Gross saving	2808	-9505	...	8183	4131	5385	-10842	...	8339	7888
	A Consumption of fixed capital	2925	701	...	2224	-	4948	1141	...	3798	9
	B Net saving	-117	-10206	...	5959	4131	437	-11983	...	4541	7879
2	Capital transfers	2607	1347	...	4770	-	3460	1811	...	1730	-
	A From other government subsectors	...	31	...	3479	-	...	3	...	78	-
	B From other resident sectors	2483	1192	...	1291	-	3220	1568	...	1652	-
	C From rest of the world	124	124	...	-	-	240	240	...	-	-
	Finance of Gross Accumulation	5415	-8158	...	12953	4131	8845	-9031	...	10069	7888
				Gross Accumulation							
1	Gross capital formation	12958	43	...	12913	2	14578	4896	...	9673	9
	A Increase in stocks	75	75	...	-	-	514	514	...	-	-
	B Gross fixed capital formation	12883	-32	...	12913	2	14064	4382	...	9673	9
	Own account	...	...	...	...	...	...	...	...	...	...
	Other	12883	-32	...	12913	2	14064	4382	...	9673	9
2	Purchases of land, net	-288	-391	...	103	-	-1212	-33	...	-1231	52
3	Purchases of intangible assets, net			...					...		
4	Capital transfers	4976	7081	...	1405	-	7923	5280	...	1692	1032
	A To other government subsectors	...	3479	...	31	-	...	78	...	3	-
	B To other resident sectors	4233	2859	...	1374	-	7119	4398	...	1689	1032
	C To rest of the world	743	743	...	-	-	804	804	...	-	-
	Net lending	-12231	-14891	...	-1468	4129	-12444	-19174	...	-65	6795
	Gross Accumulation	5415	-8158	...	12953	4131	8845	-9031	...	10069	7888

		1990					1991			
		Total General Government	Central Government	State or Provincial Government	Local Government	Social Security Funds	Total General Government	Central Government	State or Provincial Government	Local Government	Social Security Funds
				Finance of Gross Accumulation							
1	Gross saving	2498	-14594	...	6655	10437	-6554	-23191	...	5851	10786
	A Consumption of fixed capital	7542	1830	...	5707	5	7912	1871	...	6038	3
	B Net saving	-5044	-16424	...	948	10432	-14466	-25062	...	-187	10783
2	Capital transfers	5332	4824	...	544	60	6344	5865	...	498	95
	A From other government subsectors	...	-	...	96	-	...	3	...	110	-
	B From other resident sectors	5021	4513	...	448	60	5962	5480	...	388	95
	C From rest of the world	311	311	...	-	-	382	382	...	-	-
	Finance of Gross Accumulation	7830	-9770	...	7199	10497	-210	-17326	...	6349	10881

Denmark

3.13 General Government Capital Accumulation Account: Total and Subsectors
(Continued)

Million Danish kroner

	1990					1991				
	Total General Government	Central Government	State or Provincial Government	Local Government	Social Security Funds	Total General Government	Central Government	State or Provincial Government	Local Government	Social Security Funds

Gross Accumulation

1 Gross capital formation	15983	5209	...	10770	4	13159	2600	...	10559	-
A Increase in stocks	413	413	...	-	-	192	192	...	-	-
B Gross fixed capital formation	15570	4796	...	10770	4	12967	2408	...	10559	-
Own account	...	...	...	...	...	...	...	...	...	...
Other	15570	4796	...	10770	4	12967	2408	...	10559	-
2 Purchases of land, net	-3203	27		-3230		-2832	31		-2863	
3 Purchases of intangible assets, net			...					...		
4 Capital transfers	7131	4484	...	1818	925	6993	4068	...	2009	1028
A To other government subsectors	...	96	...	-	-	...	110	...	3	-
B To other resident sectors	7052	4309	...	1818	925	6882	3847	...	2007	1028
C To rest of the world	79	79	...	-	-	111	111	...	-	-
Net lending	-12081	-19490	...	-2159	9568	-17530	-24025	...	-3356	9852
Gross Accumulation	7830	-9770	...	7199	10497	-210	-17326	...	6349	10880

	1992					1993				
	Total General Government	Central Government	State or Provincial Government	Local Government	Social Security Funds	Total General Government	Central Government	State or Provincial Government	Local Government	Social Security Funds

Finance of Gross Accumulation

1 Gross saving	-2718	-22067	...	8396	10953	-16105	-33123	...	7255	9763
A Consumption of fixed capital	8558	2118	...	6437	3	9053	2285	...	6764	4
B Net saving	-11276	-24185	...	1959	10950	-25158	-35408	...	491	9759
2 Capital transfers	3783	3165	...	655	30	4160	3733	...	520	31
A From other government subsectors	...	-	...	68	-	...	-	...	124	-
B From other resident sectors	3353	2736	...	587	30	3649	3222	...	396	31
C From rest of the world	429	429	...	-	-	511	511	...	-	-
Finance of Gross Accumulation	1065	-18902	...	9051	10983	-11945	-29390	...	7775	9794

Gross Accumulation

1 Gross capital formation	19753	7777	...	11957	19	19282	6526	...	12752	4
A Increase in stocks	133	133	...	-	-	100	100	...	-	-
B Gross fixed capital formation	19620	7644	...	11957	19	19182	6426	...	12752	4
Own account	...	...	...	...	...	...	...	...	...	...
Other	19620	7644	...	11957	19	19182	6426	...	12752	4
2 Purchases of land, net	-2440	30		-2471	-	-1866	56		-1922	-
3 Purchases of intangible assets, net			...					...		
4 Capital transfers	8333	4928	...	2160	1313	9925	5629	...	2559	1862
A To other government subsectors	...	68	...	-	-	...	126	...	-	-
B To other resident sectors	8121	4648	...	2160	1313	9847	5425	...	2559	1862
C To rest of the world	212	212	...	-	-	79	78	...	-	-
Net lending	-24581	-31637	...	-2595	9651	-39287	-41600	...	-5615	7928
Gross Accumulation	1065	-18902	...	9051	10983	-11946	-29389	...	7774	9794

3.21 Corporate and Quasi-Corporate Enterprise Production Account: Total and Sectors

Million Danish kroner

	1980				1985				1990			
	\multicolumn{3}{c}{Corporate and Quasi-Corporate Enterprises}	ADDENDUM: Total, including Unincorporated	\multicolumn{3}{c}{Corporate and Quasi-Corporate Enterprises}	ADDENDUM: Total, including Unincorporated	\multicolumn{3}{c}{Corporate and Quasi-Corporate Enterprises}	ADDENDUM: Total, including Unincorporated
	TOTAL	Non-Financial	Financial		TOTAL	Non-Financial	Financial		TOTAL	Non-Financial	Financial	

Gross Output

1 Output for sale	...	...	...	...	...	...	...	...	...	...	...	...
2 Imputed bank service charge	...	...	...	...	...	...	...	...	...	...	...	...
3 Own-account fixed capital formation	...	...	...	...	...	...	...	...	...	...	...	...
Gross Output	14449	-	14449	...	616290	591306	24984	...	768949	730659	38290	...

Gross Input

Intermediate consumption	...	...	14242	...	355600	330169	25431	...	417575	379133	38442	...

Denmark

3.21 Corporate and Quasi-Corporate Enterprise Production Account: Total and Sectors
(Continued)

Million Danish kroner

	1980				1985				1990			
	\multicolumn{3}{c}{Corporate and Quasi-Corporate Enterprises}	ADDENDUM: Total, including Unincorporated	\multicolumn{3}{c}{Corporate and Quasi-Corporate Enterprises}	ADDENDUM: Total, including Unincorporated	\multicolumn{3}{c}{Corporate and Quasi-Corporate Enterprises}	ADDENDUM: Total, including Unincorporated
	TOTAL	Non-Financial	Financial		TOTAL	Non-Financial	Financial		TOTAL	Non-Financial	Financial	
1 Imputed banking service charge	...	...	9630	...	16504	-	16504	...	23123	-	23123	...
2 Other intermediate consumption	...	...	4412	...	339095	330168	8927	...	394452	379133	15319	...
Subtotal: Value Added	...	...	207	...	260690	261137	-447	...	351374	351526	-152	...
1 Indirect taxes, net	...	...	87	...	-3169	-3280	111	...	-5831	-7205	1374	...
A Indirect taxes	...	...	112	...	4197	3975	222	...	6677	5002	1675	...
B Less: Subsidies	...	...	25	...	7366	7255	111	...	12508	12207	301	...
2 Consumption of fixed capital	...	...	518	...	29782	28405	1377	...	43680	41904	1776	...
3 Compensation of employees	...	...	8991	...	180196	164957	15239	...	246595	223485	23110	...
4 Net operating surplus	...	...	-9388	...	53881	71055	-17174	...	66930	93342	-26412	...
Gross Input	...	...	14450	...	616290	591306	24984	...	768949	730659	38290	...

	1991				1992				1993			
	\multicolumn{3}{c}{Corporate and Quasi-Corporate Enterprises}	ADDENDUM: Total, including Unincorporated	\multicolumn{3}{c}{Corporate and Quasi-Corporate Enterprises}	ADDENDUM: Total, including Unincorporated	\multicolumn{3}{c}{Corporate and Quasi-Corporate Enterprises}	ADDENDUM: Total, including Unincorporated
	TOTAL	Non-Financial	Financial		TOTAL	Non-Financial	Financial		TOTAL	Non-Financial	Financial	
\multicolumn{13}{c}{**Gross Output**}
1 Output for sale	...	...	...	...	...	...	...	...	...	...	...	...
2 Imputed bank service charge	...	...	...	...	...	...	...	...	...	...	...	...
3 Own-account fixed capital formation	...	...	...	...	...	...	...	...	...	...	...	...
Gross Output	793983	760722	33261	...	807485	777538	29947	...	819035	783233	35802	...
\multicolumn{13}{c}{**Gross Input**}
Intermediate consumption	427282	393386	33896	...	433933	403408	30525	...	432652	399962	32690	...
1 Imputed banking service charge	18797	-	18797	...	15462	-	15462	...	18679	-	18679	...
2 Other intermediate consumption	408485	393386	15099	...	418471	403408	15063	...	413974	399962	14012	...
Subtotal: Value Added	366701	367336	-635	...	373552	374130	-578	...	386383	383271	3112	...
1 Indirect taxes, net	-4719	-6663	1944	...	-9279	-11158	1879	...	-6138	-8416	2278	...
A Indirect taxes	7497	5442	2055	...	7590	5262	2328	...	8973	6418	2555	...
B Less: Subsidies	12216	12105	111	...	16869	16420	449	...	15111	14834	277	...
2 Consumption of fixed capital	46607	44652	1955	...	48316	46349	1967	...	50832	48774	2058	...
3 Compensation of employees	253872	229677	24195	...	260081	235233	24848	...	259302	235320	23982	...
4 Net operating surplus	70940	99670	-28730	...	74433	103706	-29273	...	82387	107593	-25206	...
Gross Input	793982	760722	33260	...	807484	777538	29946	...	819035	783233	35802	...

3.22 Corporate and Quasi-Corporate Enterprise Income and Outlay Account: Total and Sectors

Million Danish kroner

	1980			1985			1990			1991		
	TOTAL	Non-Financial	Financial	TOTAL	Non-Financial	Financial	TOTAL	Non-Financial	Financial	TOTAL	Non-Financial	Financial
\multicolumn{13}{c}{**Receipts**}
1 Operating surplus [a]	...	...	-9388	53881	71055	-17174	66930	93342	-26412	70940	99670	-28730
2 Property and entrepreneurial income	...	...	18741	26133	-6830	32963	23669	-18280	41949	18767	-19143	37910
3 Current transfers	...	...	13024	25588	4239	21349	35957	5769	30188	37222	5924	31298
A Casualty insurance claims	...	...	33	4865	4789	76	5282	5204	78	6792	6701	91
B Casualty insurance premiums, net, due to be received by insurance companies	...	...	7034	12040	-	12040	14245	-	14245	16641	-	16641
C Current transfers from the rest of the world	...	...	...	...	...	...	...	...	...	...	...	...
D Other transfers except imputed	...	...	5957	8683	-550	9233	16430	565	15865	13789	-777	14566
E Imputed unfunded employee pension and welfare contributions												
Statistical discrepancy	...	...	270	394	-	394	-	-	-	-	-	-
Total Current Receipts	...	...	22647	105996	68464	37532	126556	80831	45725	126929	86451	40478
\multicolumn{13}{c}{**Disbursements**}
1 Property and entrepreneurial income [a]	...	...	...	...	...	...	...	...	...	...	...	...
2 Direct taxes and other current transfers n.e.c. to general government	...	...	1279	19128	13208	5920	20895	10168	10727	21548	11790	9758

Denmark

3.22 Corporate and Quasi-Corporate Enterprise Income and Outlay Account: Total and Sectors
(Continued)

Million Danish kroner

	1980			1985			1990			1991		
	TOTAL	Non-Financial	Financial	TOTAL	Non-Financial	Financial	TOTAL	Non-Financial	Financial	TOTAL	Non-Financial	Financial
3 Other current transfers	...	...	8869	23520	6888	16632	29232	5597	23635	31169	4656	26513
A Casualty insurance premiums, net	...	...	33	4865	4789	76	5282	5204	78	6792	6701	91
B Casualty insurance claims liability of insurance companies	...	...	7034	12040	-	12040	14245	-	14245	16641	-	16641
C Transfers to private non-profit institutions	...	...	...	...	...	...	...	...	...	...	...	...
D Unfunded employee pension and welfare benefits	...	...	...	...	...	...	...	...	...	...	...	...
E Social assistance grants	...	...	...	...	...	...	...	...	...	...	...	...
F Other transfers n.e.c.	...	...	1802	6615	2099	4516	9705	393	9312	7736	-2045	9781
G Transfers to the rest of the world	...	...	...	...	...	...	...	...	...	...	...	...
Statistical discrepancy [b]	...	...	3678	3912	-	3912	5247	-	5247	4785	-	4785
Net saving	...	...	8821	59436	48368	11068	71182	65066	6116	69428	70005	-577
Total Current Disbursements and Net Saving	...	...	22647	105996	68464	37532	126556	80831	45725	126930	86451	40479

	1992			1993		
	TOTAL	Non-Financial	Financial	TOTAL	Non-Financial	Financial

Receipts

1 Operating surplus [a]	74433	103706	-29273	82387	107593	-25206
2 Property and entrepreneurial income	11683	-20671	32354	13189	-16648	29837
3 Current transfers	38931	5816	33115	42331	6244	36087
A Casualty insurance claims	6909	6817	92	7322	7224	98
B Casualty insurance premiums, net, due to be received by insurance companies	16930	-	16930	17940	-	17940
C Current transfers from the rest of the world	...	...	...	...	...	...
D Other transfers except imputed	15091	-1001	16092	17069	-980	18049
E Imputed unfunded employee pension and welfare contributions						
Statistical discrepancy	-	-	-	-	-	-
Total Current Receipts	125047	88851	36196	137907	97189	40718

Disbursements

1 Property and entrepreneurial income [a]	...	...	...	...	...	...
2 Direct taxes and other current transfers n.e.c. to general government	23081	11536	11545	31200	17070	14130
3 Other current transfers	31471	3425	28046	36032	5371	30661
A Casualty insurance premiums, net	6909	6817	92	7322	7224	98
B Casualty insurance claims liability of insurance companies	16930	-	16930	17940	-	17940
C Transfers to private non-profit institutions	...	...	...	...	...	...
D Unfunded employee pension and welfare benefits	...	...	...	...	...	...
E Social assistance grants	...	...	...	...	...	...
F Other transfers n.e.c.	7632	-3392	11024	10770	-1853	12623
G Transfers to the rest of the world	...	...	...	...	...	...
Statistical discrepancy [b]	5068	-	5068	5426	-	5426
Net saving	65426	73890	-8464	65249	74748	-9499
Total Current Disbursements and Net Saving	125046	88851	36195	137907	97189	40718

a) Item 'Property and entrepreneurial income' received is net of item 'Property income' paid.
b) Item 'Statistical discrepancy' refers to change in the actuarial reserves for pensions.

Denmark

3.23 Corporate and Quasi-Corporate Enterprise Capital Accumulation Account: Total and Sectors

Million Danish kroner

	1980			1985			1990			1991		
	TOTAL	Non-Financial	Financial	TOTAL	Non-Financial	Financial	TOTAL	Non-Financial	Financial	TOTAL	Non-Financial	Financial
				Finance of Gross Accumulation								
1 Gross saving	...	...	9339	89218	76773	12445	114862	106970	7892	116035	114657	1378
A Consumption of fixed capital	...	...	518	29782	28405	1377	43680	41904	1776	46607	44652	1955
B Net saving	...	...	8821	59436	48368	11068	71182	65066	6116	69428	70005	-577
2 Capital transfers	...	...	-	6023	6023	-	5146	5146	-	5089	5089	-
Finance of Gross Accumulation	...	...	9339	95241	82796	12445	120008	112116	7892	121124	119746	1378
				Gross Accumulation								
1 Gross capital formation	...	...	1834	69442	65041	4401	87848	84633	3215	88999	84593	4406
A Increase in stocks	...	...	-	3557	3557	-	-1371	-1371	-	-1034	-1034	-
B Gross fixed capital formation	...	...	1834	65885	61484	4401	89219	86004	3215	90033	85627	4406
2 Purchases of land, net	...	...	-	909	909	-	1709	1709	-	1445	1445	-
3 Purchases of intangible assets, net	...	...										
4 Capital transfers	...	...	9	66	42	24	333	247	86	384	383	1
Net lending	...	...	7496	24824	16804	8020	30118	25527	4591	30296	33325	-3029
Gross Accumulation	...	...	9339	95241	82796	12445	120008	112116	7892	121124	119746	1378

	1992			1993		
	TOTAL	Non-Financial	Financial	TOTAL	Non-Financial	Financial
			Finance of Gross Accumulation			
1 Gross saving	113742	120239	-6497	116081	123522	-7441
A Consumption of fixed capital	48316	46349	1967	50832	48774	2058
B Net saving	65426	73890	-8464	65249	74748	-9499
2 Capital transfers	5653	5653	-	7184	7184	-
Finance of Gross Accumulation	119395	125892	-6497	123265	130706	-7441
			Gross Accumulation			
1 Gross capital formation	77180	76704	476	73598	73047	551
A Increase in stocks	-1177	-1177	-	-7340	-7340	-
B Gross fixed capital formation	78357	77881	476	80938	80387	551
2 Purchases of land, net	1191	1191	-	944	944	-
3 Purchases of intangible assets, net						
4 Capital transfers	122	122	-	139	114	25
Net lending	40903	47875	-6973	48583	56601	-8018
Gross Accumulation	119396	125892	-6497	123264	130706	-7442

3.31 Household and Private Unincorporated Enterprise Production Account

Million Danish kroner

	1980	1983	1984	1985	1986	1987	1988	1989	1990	1991	1992	1993
						Gross Output						
1 Output for sale	...	...	...	...	...	...	...	...	...	...	...	...
2 Non-marketed output	...	...	...	...	...	...	...	...	...	...	...	...
Gross Output [a]	...	212444	234135	244946	258098	264961	270470	283353	288791	293476	307041	309676
						Gross Input						
Intermediate consumption	...	91899	99335	103382	108716	110918	111631	114583	114726	113901	120078	121353
Subtotal: Value Added	...	120545	134800	141564	149382	154043	158839	168770	174065	179575	186963	188323
1 Indirect taxes net liability of unincorporated enterprises	...	5	-174	137	542	1856	268	86	-375	-814	-582	-995
A Indirect taxes	...	3756	3840	4274	4658	5951	5755	5986	5886	5734	6216	7588
B Less: Subsidies	...	3751	4014	4137	4116	4095	5487	5900	6261	6548	6798	8583
2 Consumption of fixed capital	...	18496	19257	20070	20993	22305	18002	24289	20879	21881	22726	23915
3 Compensation of employees	...	34447	37868	40363	41841	44757	47475	45431	45911	46649	50374	50721
4 Net operating surplus	...	67597	77849	80994	86006	85125	93094	98964	107650	111859	114445	114682
Gross Input [a]	...	212444	234135	244946	258098	264961	270470	283353	288791	293476	307041	309676

a) Private non-profit institutions serving households are included in household and private unincorporated enterprises.

Denmark

3.32 Household and Private Unincorporated Enterprise Income and Outlay Account

Million Danish kroner

	1980	1983	1984	1985	1986	1987	1988	1989	1990	1991	1992	1993
Receipts												
1 Compensation of employees	...	283615	306309	331116	356440	389186	407367	422355	439556	454786	470346	475851
2 Operating surplus of private unincorporated enterprises	...	67597	77849	80994	86006	85125	93094	98964	107650	111859	114445	114682
3 Property and entrepreneurial income	...	-18432	-19946	-21905	-29200	-34886	-34170	-36101	-38140	-31537	-32773	-21750
3 Current transfers	...	99930	106530	112552	117316	128882	143831	157358	166441	178234	190101	203941
A Casualty insurance claims	...	5131	5926	7002	7523	8252	8640	8172	8786	9643	9811	10396
B Social security benefits	...											
C Social assistance grants	...	90458	96418	101315	105215	115522	128887	141245	148847	159142	169699	181917
D Unfunded employee pension and welfare benefits	...											
E Transfers from general government	...											
F Transfers from the rest of the world	...	4341	4185	4235	4578	5108	6304	7941	8808	9449	10591	11628
G Other transfers n.e.c.	...											
Statistical discrepancy a	...	3797	3752	3912	3651	3914	4351	4197	5247	4785	5068	5426
Total Current Receipts b	...	436507	474494	506669	534213	572221	614473	646773	680754	718127	747187	778150
Disbursements												
1 Final consumption expenditures	...	279963	307889	337215	366747	377878	388806	403894	415032	430201	442968	457904
2 Property income c	...	...	...	...	...	...	...	...	...	...	...	...
3 Direct taxes and other current transfers n.e.c. to government	...	143713	156056	176703	188384	208001	221920	231592	239255	250791	262598	267260
A Social security contributions	...	16187	18140	20170	20137	24039	22076	23015	26882	27137	29691	32594
B Direct taxes	...	127526	137916	156533	168247	183962	199844	208577	212373	223654	232907	234666
Income taxes	...	...	...	...	...	...	...	...	...	...	...	...
Other	...	...	...	...	...	...	...	...	...	...	...	...
C Fees, fines and penalties	...	...	...	...	...	...	...	...	...	...	...	...
4 Other current transfers	...	13365	14593	16249	17310	19108	21019	20833	22187	23385	24199	26823
A Net casualty insurance premiums	...	5131	5926	7002	7523	8252	8640	8172	8786	9643	9811	10396
B Transfers to private non-profit institutions serving households	...											
C Transfers to the rest of the world	...	2788	2942	3258	3506	3796	4710	4425	4983	4721	4809	6212
D Other current transfers, except imputed	...											
E Imputed employee pension and welfare contributions	...	5446	5725	5989	6281	7060	7669	8236	8418	9021	9579	10215
Net saving	...	-534	-4044	-23498	-38228	-32765	-17272	-9546	4280	13750	17422	26163
Total Current Disbursements and Net Saving b	...	436507	474494	506669	534213	572222	614473	646773	680754	718127	747187	778150

a) Item 'Statistical discrepancy' refers to change in the actuarial reserves for pensions.
b) Private non-profit institutions serving households are included in household and private unincorporated enterprises.
c) Item 'Property and entrepreneurial income' received is net of item 'Property income' paid.

3.33 Household and Private Unincorporated Enterprise Capital Accumulation Account

Million Danish kroner

	1980	1983	1984	1985	1986	1987	1988	1989	1990	1991	1992	1993
Finance of Gross Accumulation												
1 Gross saving	...	17962	15213	-3428	-17235	-10460	730	14743	25159	35631	40148	50078
A Consumption of fixed capital	...	18496	19257	20070	20993	22305	18002	24289	20879	21881	22726	23915
B Net saving	...	-534	-4044	-23498	-38228	-32765	-17272	-9546	4280	13750	17422	26163
2 Capital transfers	...	1790	1803	1616	1426	1926	1955	3253	2540	2193	2762	2997
Total Finance of Gross Accumulation a	...	19752	17016	-1812	-15809	-8534	2685	17996	27699	37824	42910	53075
Gross Accumulation												
1 Gross Capital Formation	...	23668	34099	36270	44011	40990	34632	37540	34611	33869	32686	31515

Denmark

3.33 Household and Private Unincorporated Enterprise Capital Accumulation Account
(Continued)

Million Danish kroner

	1980	1983	1984	1985	1986	1987	1988	1989	1990	1991	1992	1993
A Increase in stocks	...	-619	1767	1027	-312	-472	751	530	43	175	151	-31
B Gross fixed capital formation	...	24287	32332	35243	44323	41462	33881	37010	34568	33694	32535	31546
2 Purchases of land, net	...	84	192	303	847	827	965	1458	1494	1387	1249	922
3 Purchases of intangibles, net	...											
4 Capital transfers	...	3392	3301	3785	2651	2901	3120	2960	5049	6432	3703	4048
Net lending	...	-7392	-20576	-42170	-63318	-53252	-36032	-23962	-13455	-3864	5272	16590
Total Gross Accumulation [a]	...	19752	17016	-1812	-15809	-8534	2685	17996	27699	37824	42910	53075

a) Private non-profit institutions serving households are included in household and private unincorporated enterprises.

3.51 External Transactions: Current Account: Detail

Million Danish kroner

	1980	1983	1984	1985	1986	1987	1988	1989	1990	1991	1992	1993
Payments to the Rest of the World												
1 Imports of goods and services	126205	176140	200408	223480	216555	207226	214891	238936	240442	255567	251141	238735
A Imports of merchandise c.i.f.	109673	148896	171826	191282	184388	173651	175786	195705	196348	208642	204675	191078
B Other	16532	27244	28582	32198	32167	33575	39106	43231	44094	46925	46466	47657
2 Factor income to the rest of the world	16845	28842	38960	43905	46612	48430	55479	68885	75124	96349	131040	182041
A Compensation of employees	296	571	650	661	704	647	744	831	921	932	964	1036
B Property and entrepreneurial income	16549	28271	38310	43244	45908	47783	54735	68054	74203	95417	130076	181005
3 Current transfers to the rest of the world	6035	8894	9553	11612	15029	14807	16225	15579	15309	17151	15607	18953
A Indirect taxes by general government to supranational organizations	1236	1810	2033	2150	2260	2201	2383	2639	2475	7609	7199	6810
B Other current transfers	4799	7084	7520	9462	12769	12606	13842	12940	12834	9542	8408	12143
4 Surplus of the nation on current transactions	-13658	-13232	-18540	-28381	-36215	-20602	-9429	-11342	4077	9088	21549	25656
Payments to the Rest of the World, and Surplus of the Nation on Current Transfers	135427	200644	230381	250616	241981	249861	277166	312058	334952	378155	419337	465385
Receipts From The Rest of the World												
1 Exports of goods and services	122256	186311	207523	225566	213559	220084	238916	264908	283574	306005	310677	299863
A Exports of merchandise f.o.b.	96161	147474	166117	180090	171723	175132	186333	208544	221412	235164	245463	236483
B Other	26095	38837	41406	45476	41836	44952	52582	56365	62162	70841	65214	63380
2 Factor income from the rest of the world	7563	10412	15101	17735	19119	20863	27746	38015	40831	62257	99151	153368
A Compensation of employees	434	833	864	937	914	942	1005	1092	1214	2786	2901	2997
B Property and entrepreneurial income	7129	9579	14237	16798	18205	19921	26741	36923	39617	59471	96250	150371
3 Current transfers from the rest of the world	5608	3921	7758	7315	9303	8913	10505	9135	10546	9892	9509	12154
A Subsidies to general government from supranational organizations	4915	5641	7089	6531	8424	9837	9362	8828	9415	9714	9491	11609
B Other current transfers	693	-1720	669	784	879	-924	1143	307	1131	178	18	545
Receipts from the Rest of the World on Current Transfers	135427	200644	230382	250616	241981	249860	277167	312058	334951	378154	419337	465385

Denmark

3.52 External Transactions: Capital Accumulation Account

Million Danish kroner

	1980	1983	1984	1985	1986	1987	1988	1989	1990	1991	1992	1993
Finance of Gross Accumulation												
1 Surplus of the nation on current transactions	-13658	-13232	-18540	-28381	-36215	-20602	-9429	-11342	4077	9088	21549	25656
2 Capital transfers from the rest of the world	457	906	1157	736	782	994	784	1736	859	781	723	845
Total Finance of Gross Accumulation	-13201	-12326	-17383	-27645	-35433	-19608	-8645	-9606	4936	9869	22272	26501
Gross Accumulation												
1 Capital transfers to the rest of the world	1124	1777	1386	1411	1526	618	790	635	354	963	683	617
2 Purchases of intangible assets, n.e.c., net, from the rest of the world	...	...	...	...	...	...	...	...	...	...	...	...
Net lending to the rest of the world	-14325	-14103	-18769	-29056	-36959	-20226	-9435	-10241	4582	8906	21589	25884
Total Gross Accumulation	-13201	-12326	-17383	-27645	-35433	-19608	-8645	-9606	4936	9869	22272	26501

4.1 Derivation of Value Added by Kind of Activity, in Current Prices

Million Danish kroner

	1980 Gross Output	1980 Intermediate Consumption	1980 Value Added	1985 Gross Output	1985 Intermediate Consumption	1985 Value Added	1990 Gross Output	1990 Intermediate Consumption	1990 Value Added	1991 Gross Output	1991 Intermediate Consumption	1991 Value Added
All Producers												
1 Agriculture, hunting, forestry and fishing	39786	21967	17818	60811	30710	30100	60077	29776	30301	58505	28891	29614
A Agriculture and hunting	36252	20975	15276	55780	28854	26925	55144	27949	27194	53256	27092	26164
B Forestry and logging	699	5	694	993	47	945	1156	36	1121	1208	-30	1238
C Fishing	2835	987	1848	4038	1809	2230	3777	1791	1986	4041	1829	2212
2 Mining and quarrying	1119	746	373	9192	3153	6039	9373	2076	7299	9591	2701	6889
A Coal mining	...	...	...	...	...	...	...	...	...	...	...	...
B Crude petroleum and natural gas production	419	388	31	7961	2548	5413	7946	1633	6314	8205	2214	5990
C Metal ore mining	...	...	...	...	...	...	...	...	...	...	...	...
D Other mining	700	358	342	1231	605	626	1427	443	985	1386	487	899
3 Manufacturing	198037	133727	64311	318521	213448	105073	356613	226694	129919	365509	231271	134238
A Manufacture of food, beverages and tobacco	70605	56238	14367	98517	75483	23033	101213	74532	26681	105285	76563	28721
B Textile, wearing apparel and leather industries	10279	6315	3964	16869	10733	6136	16860	10828	6032	17043	10761	6282
C Manufacture of wood and wood products, including furniture	8585	5536	3049	15409	9673	5737	19315	12036	7279	19999	12372	7628
D Manufacture of paper and paper products, printing and publishing	16383	9410	6974	28130	17311	10819	35480	21350	14130	36016	21498	14518
E Manufacture of chemicals and chemical petroleum, coal, rubber and plastic products	28907	21140	7768	48694	36100	12594	49345	31789	17556	50371	33045	17327
F Manufacture of non-metallic mineral products, except products of petroleum and coal	7679	4223	3456	10839	5963	4877	12457	6700	5757	12582	6926	5656
G Basic metal industries	3223	2283	940	4458	3119	1338	4507	2843	1664	4248	2632	1616
H Manufacture of fabricated metal products, machinery and equipment	50003	27402	22601	91044	52629	38415	110935	63431	47504	113127	64151	48975
I Other manufacturing industries	2373	1180	1193	4561	2437	2124	6501	3185	3316	6838	3323	3515
4 Electricity, gas and water	11932	7413	4520	19398	12602	6796	23166	10655	12511	26395	11643	14752
A Electricity, gas and steam	11258	7208	4050	18310	12292	6018	21971	10220	11751	25118	11191	13927
B Water works and supply	674	205	470	1088	310	778	1195	435	760	1277	452	825
5 Construction	52148	27766	24383	76506	45548	30958	96359	55757	40601	90624	52293	38331
6 Wholesale and retail trade, restaurants and hotels	67559	22301	45257	116760	35868	80892	140124	44656	95467	147490	47725	99765
A Wholesale and retail trade	58003	16775	41228	100473	26679	73794	119439	33153	86286	125830	35520	90310
B Restaurants and hotels	9556	5526	4030	16287	9189	7098	20685	11503	9181	21660	12205	9455
7 Transport, storage and communication	48170	22271	25899	86753	43533	43220	112707	50334	62373	123728	58306	65423
A Transport and storage	41700	20258	21442	73159	39286	33873	92575	44513	48062	102575	51214	51362
B Communication	6470	2013	4457	13594	4247	9347	20132	5821	14311	21153	7092	14061
8 Finance, insurance, real estate and business services	73324	21020	52303	130331	40336	89995	199696	63746	135951	203222	64011	139211
A Financial institutions	12259	3508	8750	21383	6793	14590	30963	13059	17905	27095	13199	13896

Denmark

4.1 Derivation of Value Added by Kind of Activity, in Current Prices
(Continued)

Million Danish kroner

	1980 Gross Output	1980 Intermediate Consumption	1980 Value Added	1985 Gross Output	1985 Intermediate Consumption	1985 Value Added	1990 Gross Output	1990 Intermediate Consumption	1990 Value Added	1991 Gross Output	1991 Intermediate Consumption	1991 Value Added
B Insurance	2190	991	1200	3601	2245	1356	7326	3634	3692	6166	3925	2241
C Real estate and business services	58875	16521	42353	105347	31298	74049	161407	47053	114354	169961	46887	123074
Real estate, except dwellings	...	...	...	...	...	...	...	...	...	...	...	...
Dwellings	38956	10018	28938	62636	15670	46966	89922	21655	68267	94757	21211	73546
9 Community, social and personal services	23684	7454	16229	39084	13767	25317	53612	18261	35352	56121	19038	37082
A Sanitary and similar services	...	...	...	...	...	...	...	...	...	...	...	...
B Social and related community services	5356	852	4504	7584	1349	6234	10503	1732	8772	11109	1865	9244
Educational services	434	119	315	640	190	450	964	283	681	1007	306	701
Medical, dental, other health and veterinary services	4922	733	4189	6944	1159	5784	9539	1449	8091	10102	1559	8543
C Recreational and cultural services	3551	554	2996	6188	1423	4765	9077	2404	6673	10031	2623	7408
D Personal and household services	14777	6048	8729	25312	10995	14317	34032	14125	19907	34981	14550	20430
Total, Industries	515757	264663	251094	857355	438964	418391	1051728	501953	549775	1081184	515878	565306
Producers of Government Services	105241	32801	72440	168887	53657	115230	223879	69583	154296	234844	74521	160323
Other Producers	2577	292	2285	3881	481	3400	6012	1018	4994	6276	975	5300
Total [a]	623574	297756	325818	1030123	493103	537021	1281619	572554	709065	1322304	591374	730930
Less: Imputed bank service charge	...	-9830	9830	...	-16504	16504	...	-23123	23123	...	-18797	18797
Import duties	...	...	...	...	...	...	...	...	...	...	...	...
Value added tax	...	...	...	...	...	...	...	...	...	...	...	...
Other adjustments [b]	57797	...	57797	94555	...	94555	113169	-	113169	115736	-	115736
Total	681371	307586	373786	1124678	509607	615072	1394788	595677	799111	1438040	610171	827868
Memorandum Item: Mineral fuels and power	23218	17685	5532	43323	31026	12297	39408	20415	18993	42598	22342	20256

	1992 Gross Output	1992 Intermediate Consumption	1992 Value Added	1993 Gross Output	1993 Intermediate Consumption	1993 Value Added
			All Producers			
1 Agriculture, hunting, forestry and fishing	56806	29667	27140	53758	27265	26492
A Agriculture and hunting	51808	27833	23976	49824	25603	24221
B Forestry and logging	1136	-74	1210	882	-29	910
C Fishing	3862	1908	1954	3052	1691	1361
2 Mining and quarrying	10122	2685	7437	11140	3458	7683
A Coal mining	...	...	...	...	...	...
B Crude petroleum and natural gas production	8506	2145	6361	9165	2897	6268
C Metal ore mining	...	...	...	...	...	...
D Other mining	1616	540	1076	1975	561	1415

Denmark

4.1 Derivation of Value Added by Kind of Activity, in Current Prices
(Continued)

Million Danish kroner

		1992			1993		
		Gross Output	Intermediate Consumption	Value Added	Gross Output	Intermediate Consumption	Value Added
3	Manufacturing	380975	239158	141815	373091	230501	142591
	A Manufacture of food, beverages and tobacco	111120	82287	28833	108929	78756	30173
	B Textile, wearing apparel and leather industries	17927	11501	6426	16616	10835	5781
	C Manufacture of wood and wood products, including furniture	21730	13026	8703	22008	13241	8767
	D Manufacture of paper and paper products, printing and publishing	36810	21651	15159	35067	19796	15271
	E Manufacture of chemicals and chemical petroleum, coal, rubber and plastic products	52953	31902	21051	52316	32303	20013
	F Manufacture of non-metallic mineral products, except products of petroleum and coal	12610	6519	6091	11964	6013	5951
	G Basic metal industries	3907	2391	1516	3555	2247	1309
	H Manufacture of fabricated metal products, machinery and equipment	116753	66907	49846	116362	64961	51401
	I Other manufacturing industries	7165	2974	4190	6274	2349	3925
4	Electricity, gas and water	25272	12489	12783	26609	11384	15225
	A Electricity, gas and steam	23897	11925	11972	25232	10919	14313
	B Water works and supply	1375	564	811	1377	465	912
5	Construction	94982	55145	39838	94052	54463	39589
6	Wholesale and retail trade, restaurants and hotels	149738	45264	104475	152061	48487	103574
	A Wholesale and retail trade	127176	32716	94460	129553	36581	92972
	B Restaurants and hotels	22562	12548	10015	22508	11906	10602
7	Transport, storage and communication	125848	58569	67278	134139	63548	70592
	A Transport and storage	103619	51199	52419	110107	54243	55864
	B Communication	22229	7370	14859	24032	9305	14728
8	Finance, insurance, real estate and business services	204521	64972	139549	215580	66151	149429
	A Financial institutions	24010	12892	11118	31171	12745	18426
	B Insurance	5937	4049	1888	4631	3545	1086
	C Real estate and business services	174574	48031	126543	179778	49861	129917
	Real estate, except dwellings	...	...	...	...	...	...
	Dwellings	98852	22826	76026	103253	25196	78056
9	Community, social and personal services	59511	19637	39874	60692	21608	39083
	A Sanitary and similar services	...	...	...	...	...	...
	B Social and related community services	12105	2077	10028	12012	2047	9964
	Educational services	1036	326	710	1063	337	726
	Medical, dental, other health and veterinary services	11069	1751	9318	10949	1710	9238
	C Recreational and cultural services	11225	2772	8453	12465	3719	8746
	D Personal and household services	36181	14788	21393	36215	15842	20373
Total, Industries		1107775	527584	580190	1121123	526865	594258
Producers of Government Services		244554	78042	166512	257441	84521	172920
Other Producers		6751	1104	5648	7589	1329	6260
Total [a]		1359080	606730	752350	1386153	612714	773439
Less: Imputed bank service charge		...	-15463	15463	...	-18678	18678
Import duties		...	...	...	...	...	...
Value added tax		...	...	...	...	...	...
Other adjustments [b]		114366	-	114366	118476	-	118476
Total		1473446	622193	851253	1504629	631392	873236
Memorandum Item: Mineral fuels and power		41374	22050	19325	43205	22268	20937

a) Gross domestic product in factor values.
b) Item 'Other adjustments' refers to indirect taxes net of subsidies.

Denmark

4.2 Derivation of Value Added by Kind of Activity, in Constant Prices

Million Danish kroner

		1980 Gross Output	1980 Intermediate Consumption	1980 Value Added	1985 Gross Output	1985 Intermediate Consumption	1985 Value Added	1990 Gross Output	1990 Intermediate Consumption	1990 Value Added	1991 Gross Output	1991 Intermediate Consumption	1991 Value Added
					At constant prices of: 1980 All Producers								
1	Agriculture, hunting, forestry and fishing	39786	21967	17818	46105	22914	23191	49156	23671	25486	47803	22722	25082
	A Agriculture and hunting	36252	20975	15276	42334	21741	20593	46131	22419	23712	44744	21431	23313
	B Forestry and logging	699	5	694	722	1	722	719	-1	721	827	-	828
	C Fishing	2835	987	1848	3049	1172	1876	2306	1253	1053	2232	1291	941
2	Mining and quarrying	1119	746	373	6745	1754	4991	13886	1215	12671	16802	1508	15293
	A Coal mining	...	...	...	...	...	...	...	...	...	...	...	...
	B Crude petroleum and natural gas production	419	388	31	5925	1347	4578	13117	935	12182	16078	1210	14867
	C Metal ore mining	...	...	...	...	...	...	...	...	...	...	...	...
	D Other mining	700	358	342	820	407	413	769	280	489	724	298	426
3	Manufacturing	198037	133727	64311	219271	146352	72920	227278	156147	71130	230887	159828	71058
	A Manufacture of food, beverages and tobacco	70605	56238	14367	71017	54254	16763	73725	55362	18364	77902	57892	20010
	B Textile, wearing apparel and leather industries	10279	6315	3964	12003	7336	4668	10359	7152	3207	10235	7018	3217
	C Manufacture of wood and wood products, including furniture	8585	5536	3049	10537	6399	4138	10733	7130	3603	10793	7330	3463
	D Manufacture of paper and paper products, printing and publishing	16383	9410	6974	18338	11367	6971	18386	12026	6360	18180	11966	6214
	E Manufacture of chemicals and chemical petroleum, coal, rubber and plastic products	28907	21140	7768	32191	23708	8483	36405	27211	9195	37038	28230	8808
	F Manufacture of non-metallic mineral products, except products of petroleum and coal	7679	4223	3456	6988	3903	3085	6854	4149	2705	6732	4133	2599
	G Basic metal industries	3223	2283	940	3146	2155	991	3100	1935	1164	2907	1862	1044
	H Manufacture of fabricated metal products, machinery and equipment	50003	27402	22601	61961	35517	26444	63996	39102	24893	63240	39350	23890
	I Other manufacturing industries	2373	1180	1193	3090	1713	1377	3720	2080	1639	3860	2047	1813
4	Electricity, gas and water	11932	7413	4520	13977	7913	6064	15605	8701	6903	18804	10166	8638
	A Electricity, gas and steam	11258	7208	4050	13278	7707	5571	14974	8435	6538	18181	9897	8284
	B Water works and supply	674	205	470	699	206	493	631	266	365	623	269	354
5	Construction	52148	27766	24383	51313	29881	21431	52910	30856	22054	48457	28010	20447
6	Wholesale and retail trade, restaurants and hotels	67559	22301	45257	78536	25019	53516	84942	27496	57446	87221	28106	59115
	A Wholesale and retail trade	58003	16775	41228	67608	18476	49131	73183	19840	53343	75220	20345	54875
	B Restaurants and hotels	9556	5526	4030	10928	6543	4385	11759	7656	4103	12001	7761	4240
7	Transport, storage and communication	48170	22271	25899	54250	27774	26477	70199	32622	37578	73905	35727	38177
	A Transport and storage	41700	20258	21442	45850	24919	20932	59509	29188	30322	62907	31690	31216
	B Communication	6470	2013	4457	8400	2855	5546	10690	3434	7256	10998	4037	6961
8	Finance, insurance, real estate and business services	73324	21020	52303	87131	27101	60030	102493	32791	69702	100030	32367	67664
	A Financial institutions	12259	3508	8750	14656	4480	10176	17239	6359	10880	14435	5958	8478
	B Insurance	2190	991	1200	2430	1417	1013	3714	1664	2050	2851	1723	1128
	C Real estate and business services	58875	16521	42353	70045	21204	48841	81540	24768	56772	82744	24686	58058
	Real estate, except dwellings	...	...	...	...	...	...	...	...	...	...	...	...
	Dwellings	38956	10018	28938	41175	10861	30314	43371	11049	32322	43657	11141	32516
9	Community, social and personal services	23684	7454	16229	26041	9346	16695	27873	10803	17072	28081	11021	17060
	A Sanitary and similar services	...	...	...	...	...	...	...	...	...	...	...	...
	B Social and related community services	5356	852	4504	5223	934	4289	5810	1103	4708	5985	1134	4851
	Educational services	434	119	315	445	136	309	502	178	325	510	182	329
	Medical, dental, other health and veterinary services	4922	733	4189	4778	798	3980	5308	925	4383	5475	952	4522
	C Recreational and cultural services	3551	554	2996	4279	986	3293	5231	1463	3769	5592	1635	3957
	D Personal and household services	14777	6048	8729	16539	7426	9113	16832	8237	8595	16504	8252	8252

Denmark

4.2 Derivation of Value Added by Kind of Activity, in Constant Prices
(Continued)

Million Danish kroner

	1980 Gross Output	1980 Intermediate Consumption	1980 Value Added	1985 Gross Output	1985 Intermediate Consumption	1985 Value Added	1990 Gross Output	1990 Intermediate Consumption	1990 Value Added	1991 Gross Output	1991 Intermediate Consumption	1991 Value Added
				At constant prices of: 1980								
Total, Industries	515757	264663	251094	583370	298054	285316	644344	324303	320041	651989	329454	322535
Producers of Government Services	105241	32801	72440	116911	35297	81615	122386	37787	84599	122854	38947	83907
Other Producers	2577	292	2285	2637	328	2309	3163	429	2734	3216	390	2826
Total a	623574	297756	325818	702918	333678	369240	769893	362518	407375	778059	368791	409267
Less: Imputed bank service charge	...	-9830	9830	...	-11312	11312	-	-12874	12874	-	-10014	10014
Import duties	...	...	...	...	...	...	...	...	...	...	...	...
Value added tax	...	...	...	...	...	...	...	...	...	...	...	...
Other adjustments b	57797	...	57797	68021	...	68021	62379	-	62379	63764	-	63764
Total	681371	307586	373786	770939	344990	425949	832272	375392	456879	841823	378805	463018
Memorandum Item: Mineral fuels and power	23218	17685	5532	30443	19133	11311	40698	20770	19928	47291	23206	24085

		1992 Gross Output	1992 Intermediate Consumption	1992 Value Added	1993 Gross Output	1993 Intermediate Consumption	1993 Value Added
		At constant prices of: 1980					
		All Producers					
1	Agriculture, hunting, forestry and fishing	47145	23540	23604	49443	22293	27151
	A Agriculture and hunting	44008	22300	21707	46822	21194	25628
	B Forestry and logging	797	-1	798	722	-	722
	C Fishing	2340	1241	1099	1899	1099	801
2	Mining and quarrying	17786	1555	16232	19939	1946	17992
	A Coal mining	...	...	...	...	...	...
	B Crude petroleum and natural gas production	16967	1210	15757	18895	1537	17358
	C Metal ore mining	...	...	...	...	...	...
	D Other mining	819	345	475	1044	409	634
3	Manufacturing	237606	165862	71744	237150	167637	69512
	A Manufacture of food, beverages and tobacco	79117	59954	19163	83264	64765	18499
	B Textile, wearing apparel and leather industries	10645	7577	3068	9963	7150	2813
	C Manufacture of wood and wood products, including furniture	11763	7823	3940	12182	8106	4076
	D Manufacture of paper and paper products, printing and publishing	18191	12130	6061	17174	11307	5867
	E Manufacture of chemicals and chemical petroleum, coal, rubber and plastic products	38992	29521	9471	38755	29244	9511
	F Manufacture of non-metallic mineral products, except products of petroleum and coal	7427	3953	3474	6134	3658	2475
	G Basic metal industries	2955	1718	1237	2573	1618	955
	H Manufacture of fabricated metal products, machinery and equipment	64553	41381	23172	63764	40326	23438
	I Other manufacturing industries	3963	1805	2158	3341	1463	1878
4	Electricity, gas and water	17982	10344	7638	20069	11261	8808
	A Electricity, gas and steam	17183	10007	7176	19427	10984	8443
	B Water works and supply	799	337	462	642	277	365
5	Construction	48177	29543	18634	46594	28217	18376
6	Wholesale and retail trade, restaurants and hotels	86789	26912	59876	86783	28325	58458
	A Wholesale and retail trade	74365	19310	55054	74695	20308	54387
	B Restaurants and hotels	12424	7602	4822	12088	8017	4071
7	Transport, storage and communication	75717	34876	40841	84063	38028	46035
	A Transport and storage	64271	30786	33485	71814	32835	38979
	B Communication	11446	4090	7356	12249	5193	7056
8	Finance, insurance, real estate and business services	95863	30643	65221	99581	34546	65036
	A Financial institutions	12204	5895	6309	15744	6821	8923

Denmark

4.2 Derivation of Value Added by Kind of Activity, in Constant Prices
(Continued)

Million Danish kroner

	1992 Gross Output	1992 Intermediate Consumption	1992 Value Added	1993 Gross Output	1993 Intermediate Consumption	1993 Value Added
			At constant prices of:1980			
B Insurance	2814	932	1883	2056	1856	200
C Real estate and business services	80845	23816	57029	81781	25869	55913
Real estate, except dwellings	...	...	...	...	...	...
Dwellings	43800	10968	32832	44220	12353	31866
9 Community, social and personal services	29657	11277	18381	28960	11417	17544
A Sanitary and similar services	...	...	...	...	...	...
B Social and related community services	6368	1202	5167	6218	1176	5043
Educational services	513	181	332	516	184	333
Medical, dental, other health and veterinary services	5855	1021	4835	5702	992	4710
C Recreational and cultural services	6646	1779	4867	6617	2002	4615
D Personal and household services	16643	8296	8347	16125	8239	7886
Total, Industries	656721	334551	322169	672583	343672	328911
Producers of Government Services	125000	40149	84851	128800	42656	86144
Other Producers	3456	477	2979	3740	465	3274
Total [a]	785176	375177	409999	805122	386793	418329
Less: Imputed bank service charge	-	-7868	7868	-	-10922	10922
Import duties	...	...	...	...	...	...
Value added tax	...	...	...	...	...	...
Other adjustments [b]	64701	-	64701	66402	-	66402
Total	849877	383045	466832	871524	397715	473809
Memorandum Item: Mineral fuels and power	47828	24309	23520	51670	25314	26357

a) Gross domestic product in factor values.
b) Item 'Other adjustments' refers to indirect taxes net of subsidies.

4.3 Cost Components of Value Added

Million Danish kroner

	1980 Compensation of Employees	1980 Capital Consumption	1980 Net Operating Surplus	1980 Indirect Taxes	1980 Less: Subsidies Received	1980 Value Added	1985 Compensation of Employees	1985 Capital Consumption	1985 Net Operating Surplus	1985 Indirect Taxes	1985 Less: Subsidies Received	1985 Value Added
					All Producers							
1 Agriculture, hunting, forestry and fishing	3433	...	14386	...	...	17818	5220	...	24880	...	...	30100
A Agriculture and hunting	2272	...	13005	...	...	15276	3682	...	23244	...	...	26925
B Forestry and logging	433	...	262	...	...	694	555	...	390	...	...	945
C Fishing	728	...	1119	...	...	1848	983	...	1246	...	...	2230
2 Mining and quarrying	261	...	112	...	...	373	487	...	5552	...	...	6039
A Coal mining	...	...	...	...	...	...	...	...	...	...	...	...
B Crude petroleum and natural gas production	101	...	-70	...	...	31	263	...	5150	...	...	5413
C Metal ore mining	...	...	...	...	...	...	...	...	...	...	...	...
D Other mining	160	...	182	...	...	342	224	...	402	...	...	626

Denmark

4.3 Cost Components of Value Added
(Continued)

Million Danish kroner

	1980 Compensation of Employees	1980 Capital Consumption	1980 Net Operating Surplus	1980 Indirect Taxes	1980 Less: Subsidies Received	1980 Value Added	1985 Compensation of Employees	1985 Capital Consumption	1985 Net Operating Surplus	1985 Indirect Taxes	1985 Less: Subsidies Received	1985 Value Added
3 Manufacturing	47647	...	16664	...	...	64311	72922	...	32149	...	...	105073
A Manufacture of food, beverages and tobacco	9201	...	5166	...	...	14367	13337	...	9696	...	...	23033
B Textile, wearing apparel and leather industries	2824	...	1140	...	...	3964	4438	...	1698	...	...	6136
C Manufacture of wood and wood products, including furniture	2474	...	575	...	...	3049	4237	...	1499	...	...	5737
D Manufacture of paper and paper products, printing and publishing	5870	...	1103	...	...	6974	8421	...	2398	...	...	10819
E Manufacture of chemicals and chemical petroleum, coal, rubber and plastic products	4474	...	3294	...	...	7768	7072	...	5522	...	...	12594
F Manufacture of non-metallic mineral products, except products of petroleum and coal	2642	...	813	...	...	3456	3216	...	1660	...	...	4877
G Basic metal industries	855	...	85	...	...	940	939	...	399	...	...	1338
H Manufacture of fabricated metal products, machinery and equipment	18497	...	4105	...	...	22601	30035	...	8380	...	...	38415
I Other manufacturing industries	810	...	383	...	...	1193	1227	...	897	...	...	2124
4 Electricity, gas and water	1847	...	2674	...	...	4520	2863	...	3934	...	...	6796
A Electricity, gas and steam	1588	...	2463	...	...	4050	2481	...	3537	...	...	6018
B Water works and supply	259	...	211	...	...	470	382	...	397	...	...	778
5 Construction	16902	...	7480	...	...	24383	23694	...	7264	...	...	30958
6 Wholesale and retail trade, restaurants and hotels	28985	...	16273	...	...	45257	43807	...	37086	...	...	80892
A Wholesale and retail trade	26197	...	15031	...	...	41228	38840	...	34954	...	...	73794
B Restaurants and hotels	2788	...	1242	...	...	4030	4967	...	2132	...	...	7098
7 Transport, storage and communication	15493	...	10406	...	...	25899	24470	...	18750	...	...	43220
A Transport and storage	11831	...	9611	...	...	21442	18889	...	14984	...	...	33873
B Communication	3662	...	795	...	...	4457	5581	...	3766	...	...	9347
8 Finance, insurance, real estate and business services	18008	...	34296	...	...	52303	31024	...	58970	...	...	89995
A Financial institutions	6710	...	2041	...	...	8750	11266	...	3324	...	...	14590
B Insurance	2281	...	-1082	...	...	1200	3973	...	-2618	...	...	1356
C Real estate and business services	9017	...	33337	...	...	42353	15785	...	58264	...	...	74049
Real estate, except dwellings	...	...	...	...	...	...	...	...	...	...	...	...
Dwellings	1280	...	27658	...	...	28938	2005	...	44961	...	...	46966
9 Community, social and personal services	8417	...	7811	...	...	16229	12807	...	12508	...	...	25317
A Sanitary and similar services	...	...	...	...	...	...	...	...	...	...	...	...
B Social and related community services	1162	...	3341	...	...	4504	1841	...	4393	...	...	6234
Educational services	28	...	287	...	...	315	44	...	406	...	...	450
Medical, dental, other health and veterinary services	1134	...	3054	...	...	4189	1797	...	3987	...	...	5784
C Recreational and cultural services	1859	...	1137	...	...	2996	3014	...	1751	...	...	4765
D Personal and household services	5396	...	3333	...	...	8729	7952	...	6364	...	...	14317
Total, Industries [a]	140993	...	110101	...	...	251094	217297	...	201094	...	...	418391
Producers of Government Services	69515	...	2925	...	...	72440	110282	...	4948	...	...	115230
Other Producers	2214	...	70	...	...	2285	3262	...	138	...	...	3400
Total [ba]	212722	...	113096	...	...	325818	330841	...	206180	...	...	537021
Less: Imputed bank service charge	...	...	9830	...	...	9830	...	...	16504	...	...	16504
Import duties	...	...	...	...	...	...	...	...	...	...	...	...
Value added tax	...	...	...	...	...	...	...	...	...	...	...	...
Other adjustments	...	...	...	69591	11794	57797	...	...	...	112913	18358	94555
Total [a]	212722	...	103266	69591	11794	373786	330841	...	189676	112913	18358	615072

Denmark

4.3 Cost Components of Value Added

Million Danish kroner

		1990					1991				
	Compensation of Employees	Capital Consumption	Net Operating Surplus	Indirect Taxes	Less: Subsidies Received	Value Added	Compensation of Employees	Capital Consumption	Net Operating Surplus	Indirect Taxes	Less: Subsidies Received	Value Added

All Producers

	Comp. Emp. 1990	Cap. Cons. 1990	Net Op. Surp. 1990	Ind. Tax 1990	Subs. 1990	VA 1990	Comp. Emp. 1991	Cap. Cons. 1991	Net Op. Surp. 1991	Ind. Tax 1991	Subs. 1991	VA 1991
1 Agriculture, hunting, forestry and fishing	6056	...	24246	...	...	30301	6250	...	23364	...	...	29614
A Agriculture and hunting	4535	...	22660	...	...	27194	4595	...	21569	...	...	26164
B Forestry and logging	559	...	562	...	...	1121	601	...	637	...	...	1238
C Fishing	962	...	1024	...	...	1986	1054	...	1158	...	...	2212
2 Mining and quarrying	583	...	6716	...	...	7299	627	...	6262	...	...	6889
A Coal mining	...	...	...	...	...	...	...	...	...	...	...	...
B Crude petroleum and natural gas production	293	...	6021	...	...	6314	339	...	5652	...	...	5990
C Metal ore mining	...	...	...	...	...	...	...	...	...	...	...	...
D Other mining	290	...	695	...	...	985	288	...	610	...	...	899
3 Manufacturing	91862	...	38057	...	...	129919	93562	...	40674	...	...	134238
A Manufacture of food, beverages and tobacco	15952	...	10729	...	...	26681	16355	...	12366	...	...	28721
B Textile, wearing apparel and leather industries	4432	...	1600	...	...	6032	4361	...	1920	...	...	6282
C Manufacture of wood and wood products, including furniture	5489	...	1790	...	...	7279	5638	...	1990	...	...	7628
D Manufacture of paper and paper products, printing and publishing	11322	...	2809	...	...	14130	11550	...	2968	...	...	14518
E Manufacture of chemicals and chemical petroleum, coal, rubber and plastic products	9852	...	7704	...	...	17556	10295	...	7032	...	...	17327
F Manufacture of non-metallic mineral products, except products of petroleum and coal	3838	...	1919	...	...	5757	3856	...	1799	...	...	5656
G Basic metal industries	1139	...	525	...	...	1664	1147	...	469	...	...	1616
H Manufacture of fabricated metal products, machinery and equipment	38038	...	9466	...	...	47504	38452	...	10523	...	...	48975
I Other manufacturing industries	1800	...	1515	...	...	3316	1908	...	1607	...	...	3515
4 Electricity, gas and water	3854	...	8657	...	...	12511	3999	...	10754	...	...	14752
A Electricity, gas and steam	3404	...	8347	...	...	11751	3540	...	10387	...	...	13927
B Water works and supply	450	...	310	...	...	760	459	...	367	...	...	825
5 Construction	30252	...	10349	...	...	40601	29433	...	8898	...	...	38331
6 Wholesale and retail trade, restaurants and hotels	58043	...	37424	...	...	95467	59735	...	40030	...	...	99765
A Wholesale and retail trade	51381	...	34905	...	...	86286	52807	...	37503	...	...	90310
B Restaurants and hotels	6662	...	2519	...	...	9181	6928	...	2527	...	...	9455
7 Transport, storage and communication	31324	...	31049	...	...	62373	32650	...	32773	...	...	65423
A Transport and storage	24286	...	23776	...	...	48062	25651	...	25711	...	...	51362
B Communication	7038	...	7273	...	...	14311	6999	...	7062	...	...	14061
8 Finance, insurance, real estate and business services	48358	...	87593	...	...	135951	50441	...	88770	...	...	139211
A Financial institutions	16593	...	1312	...	...	17905	17489	...	-3593	...	...	13896
B Insurance	6518	...	-2826	...	...	3692	6706	...	-4465	...	...	2241
C Real estate and business services	25247	...	89107	...	...	114354	26246	...	96828	...	...	123074
Real estate, except dwellings	...	...	...	...	...	...	...	...	...	...	...	...
Dwellings	2302	...	65964	...	...	68267	2385	...	71161	...	...	73546
9 Community, social and personal services	17474	...	17878	...	...	35352	18789	...	18294	...	...	37082
A Sanitary and similar services	...	...	...	...	...	...	...	...	...	...	...	...
B Social and related community services	2677	...	6095	...	...	8772	2744	...	6501	...	...	9244
Educational services	66	...	615	...	...	681	69	...	633	...	...	701
Medical, dental, other health and veterinary services	2611	...	5480	...	...	8091	2675	...	5868	...	...	8543
C Recreational and cultural services	4210	...	2463	...	...	6673	4388	...	3020	...	...	7408
D Personal and household services	10587	...	9320	...	...	19907	11657	...	8773	...	...	20430

Denmark

4.3 Cost Components of Value Added
(Continued)

Million Danish kroner

	1990						1991					
	Compensation of Employees	Capital Consumption	Net Operating Surplus	Indirect Taxes	Less: Subsidies Received	Value Added	Compensation of Employees	Capital Consumption	Net Operating Surplus	Indirect Taxes	Less: Subsidies Received	Value Added
Total, Industries [a]	287804	...	261971	...	...	549775	295487	...	269819	...	...	565306
Producers of Government Services	146755	...	7541	...	...	154296	152411	...	7912	...	...	160323
Other Producers	4703	...	291	...	...	4994	5035	...	266	...	...	5300
Total [ba]	439262	...	269803	...	...	709065	452933	...	277997	...	...	730930
Less: Imputed bank service charge	...	...	23123	...	...	23123	...	...	18797	...	...	18797
Import duties	...	...	...	...	...	...	...	...	...	...	...	...
Value added tax	...	...	...	...	...	...	...	...	...	...	...	...
Other adjustments	...	...	...	141523	28354	113169	...	...	...	144462	28726	115736
Total [a]	439262	...	246680	141523	28354	799111	452933	...	259200	144462	28726	827868

	1992						1993					
	Compensation of Employees	Capital Consumption	Net Operating Surplus	Indirect Taxes	Less: Subsidies Received	Value Added	Compensation of Employees	Capital Consumption	Net Operating Surplus	Indirect Taxes	Less: Subsidies Received	Value Added

All Producers

1 Agriculture, hunting, forestry and fishing	6320	...	20819	...	...	27140	6260	...	20232	...	...	26492
A Agriculture and hunting	4736	...	19239	...	...	23976	4874	...	19347	...	...	24221
B Forestry and logging	589	...	621	...	...	1210	470	...	440	...	...	910
C Fishing	995	...	959	...	...	1954	916	...	445	...	...	1361
2 Mining and quarrying	662	...	6775	...	...	7437	680	...	7002	...	...	7683
A Coal mining	...	...	...	...	...	...	...	...	...	...	...	...
B Crude petroleum and natural gas production	...	...	...	...	...	6361	...	...	...	...	...	6268
C Metal ore mining	...	...	...	...	...	...	...	...	...	...	...	...
D Other mining	...	...	...	...	...	1076	...	...	...	...	...	1415
3 Manufacturing	96397	...	45419	...	...	141815	95633	...	46960	...	...	142591
A Manufacture of food, beverages and tobacco	16690	...	12143	...	...	28833	17026	...	13147	...	...	30173
B Textile, wearing apparel and leather industries	4408	...	2018	...	...	6426	4252	...	1530	...	...	5781
C Manufacture of wood and wood products, including furniture	5966	...	2738	...	...	8703	6015	...	2752	...	...	8767
D Manufacture of paper and paper products, printing and publishing	11802	...	3357	...	...	15159	12079	...	3193	...	...	15271
E Manufacture of chemicals and chemical petroleum, coal, rubber and plastic products	11609	...	9442	...	...	21051	11919	...	8094	...	...	20013
F Manufacture of non-metallic mineral products, except products of petroleum and coal	3767	...	2324	...	...	6091	3696	...	2255	...	...	5951
G Basic metal industries	1131	...	385	...	...	1516	1021	...	288	...	...	1309
H Manufacture of fabricated metal products, machinery and equipment	39144	...	10702	...	...	49846	37657	...	13744	...	...	51401
I Other manufacturing industries	1880	...	2310	...	...	4190	1968	...	1957	...	...	3925
4 Electricity, gas and water	4203	...	8580	...	...	12783	4253	...	10971	...	...	15225
A Electricity, gas and steam	4203	...	8580	...	...	12783	4253	...	10971	...	...	15224
B Water works and supply	...	...	...	...	...	...	...	...	...	...	...	...
5 Construction	31114	...	8723	...	...	39838	30987	...	8602	...	...	39589
6 Wholesale and retail trade, restaurants and hotels	61637	...	42837	...	...	104475	61951	...	41624	...	...	103574
A Wholesale and retail trade	54455	...	40005	...	...	94460	54706	...	38266	...	...	92972
B Restaurants and hotels	7182	...	2832	...	...	10015	7245	...	3358	...	...	10602
7 Transport, storage and communication	33912	...	33366	...	...	67278	34024	...	36568	...	...	70592
A Transport and storage	26709	...	25710	...	...	52419	26917	...	28947	...	...	55864
B Communication	7203	...	7656	...	...	14859	7107	...	7621	...	...	14728
8 Finance, insurance, real estate and business services	51420	...	88129	...	...	139549	51050	...	98380	...	...	149429
A Financial institutions	24848	...	-11842	...	...	13006	23983	...	-4470	...	...	19512
B Insurance	...	...	...	...	...	...	...	...	...	...	...	...
C Real estate and business services	26572	...	99971	...	...	126543	27067	...	102850	...	...	129917
Real estate, except dwellings	...	...	...	...	...	...	...	...	...	...	...	...

Denmark

4.3 Cost Components of Value Added
(Continued)

Million Danish kroner

	1992 Compensation of Employees	1992 Capital Consumption	1992 Net Operating Surplus	1992 Indirect Taxes	1992 Less: Subsidies Received	1992 Value Added	1993 Compensation of Employees	1993 Capital Consumption	1993 Net Operating Surplus	1993 Indirect Taxes	1993 Less: Subsidies Received	1993 Value Added
Dwellings	2515	...	73511	...	...	76026	2627	...	75430	...	...	78056
9 Community, social and personal services	19498	...	20376	...	...	39874	19990	...	19092	...	...	39083
A Sanitary and similar services	...	...	...	...	...	...	...	...	...	...	...	...
B Social and related community services	2927	...	7101	...	...	10028	3037	...	6927	...	...	9964
Educational services	2927	...	7101	...	...	10028	3037	...	6927	...	...	9964
Medical, dental, other health and veterinary services		...		...	...			...		...	...	
C Recreational and cultural services	4598	...	3855	...	...	8453	4570	...	4176	...	...	8746
D Personal and household services	11973	...	9420	...	...	21393	12383	...	7989	...	...	20373
Total, Industries [a]	305165	...	275026	...	...	580190	304826	...	289432	...	...	594258
Producers of Government Services	157954	...	8558	...	...	166512	163867	...	9053	...	...	172920
Other Producers	5291	...	357	...	...	5648	5197	...	1063	...	...	6260
Total [ba]	468410	...	283940	...	...	752350	473890	...	299548	...	...	773439
Less: Imputed bank service charge	...	...	15463	...	...	15463	...	...	18678	...	...	18678
Import duties	...	...	...	...	...	...	...	...	...	...	...	...
Value added tax	...	...	...	...	...	...	...	...	...	...	...	...
Other adjustments	...	...	...	148593	34227	114366	...	...	...	153351	34875	118476
Total [a]	468410	...	268477	148593	34227	851253	473890	...	280870	153351	34875	873236

a) Column 'Consumption of fixed capital' is included in column 'Net operating surplus'.
b) Gross domestic product in factor values.

Dominica

Source. Reply to the United Nations National Accounts Questionnaire from the Ministry of Finance, Trade and Industry, Roseau.
General note. The estimates shown in the following tables have been prepared in accordance with the United Nations System of National Accounts so far as the existing data would permit.

1.1 Expenditure on the Gross Domestic Product, in Current Prices

Thousand East Caribbean dollars

	1980	1983	1984	1985	1986	1987	1988	1989	1990	1991	1992	1993
1 Government final consumption expenditure	43540	52270	60230	59890	62070	68150	75030	86710	91860	95670	...	...
2 Private final consumption expenditure	147470	144860	172490	192780	188900	224470	259000	302160	289370	341860	...	...
3 Gross capital formation	81160	60570	89370	75820	67510	79330	120570	170670	184200	197650		
A Increase in stocks	7000	-	-	-	-	-	-	6500	4950	5150		
B Gross fixed capital formation	74160	60570	89370	75820	67510	79330	120570	164170	179250	192500		
Residential buildings											...	...
Non-residential buildings	47520	32350	44150	38580	30380	37070	54120	64210	72420	74830		
Other construction and land improvement etc.											...	...
Other	26640	28220	45220	37240	37130	42260	66450	99960	106830	117670	...	...
4 Exports of goods and services	35100	88800	86400	97270	148320	162620	190640	173430	226010	222280	...	...
5 Less: Imports of goods and services	147700	130700	165900	159580	164200	195300	252000	310250	339900	378630	...	...
Equals: Gross Domestic Product	159570	215800	242590	266180	302600	339270	393240	422720	451540	478830	511500	...

1.3 Cost Components of the Gross Domestic Product

Thousand East Caribbean dollars

	1980	1983	1984	1985	1986	1987	1988	1989	1990	1991	1992	1993
1 Indirect taxes, net	15830	35380	39900	42900	49330	57510	68950	76550	77270	80940	...	...
A Indirect taxes	23930	37180	42100	44560	51180	59280	70800	78490	78700	82890	...	...
B Less: Subsidies	8100	1800	2200	1660	1850	1770	1850	1940	1430	1950	...	...
2 Consumption of fixed capital	...	...	...	...	...	...	...	...	...	...	...	...
3 Compensation of employees paid by resident producers to:	...	...	...	...	...	...	...	...	...	...	...	...
4 Operating surplus	...	...	...	...	...	...	...	...	...	...	...	...
Equals: Gross Domestic Product	159570	215800	242590	266180	302600	339270	393240	422720	451540	478830	...	...

1.10 Gross Domestic Product by Kind of Activity, in Current Prices

Thousand East Caribbean dollars

	1980	1983	1984	1985	1986	1987	1988	1989	1990	1991	1992	1993
1 Agriculture, hunting, forestry and fishing	44050	52500	56800	62390	76640	82590	95900	89550	96920	101610	...	...
2 Mining and quarrying	1170	1330	1500	1460	1380	1760	2570	2910	3080	3810	...	...
3 Manufacturing	6930	14120	12360	14370	16880	18250	20990	24530	26430	27430	...	...
4 Electricity, gas and water	3470	5230	5920	6240	6680	7390	8970	10040	11180	12930	...	...
5 Construction	18480	12580	17170	15000	11820	14420	21050	24970	28160	29100	...	...
6 Wholesale and retail trade, restaurants and hotels	14380	15980	16890	23700	28850	34050	37980	43590	48700	52550	...	...
7 Transport, storage and communication	10490	22260	26520	29340	34350	41760	49520	53810	59840	64800	...	...
8 Finance, insurance, real estate and business services	16170	20860	26110	28040	30010	33050	40100	47270	55160	58470	...	...
9 Community, social and personal services	1620	2310	2400	2490	2660	2910	3080	3630	3900	4210	...	...
Total, Industries	116760	147170	165670	183030	209270	236180	280160	300300	333370	354910	...	...
Producers of Government Services	33740	40630	47050	50120	54360	57630	59520	66980	69010	72500	...	...
Other Producers	...	...	...	...	...	...	...	...	...	...	...	...
Subtotal [a]	150500	187800	212720	233150	263630	293810	339680	367280	402380	427410	...	...
Less: Imputed bank service charge	6760	7380	10030	9870	10360	12050	15390	21110	28110	29520	...	...
Plus: Import duties	...	...	...	...	...	...	...	...	...	...	...	...
Plus: Value added tax	...	...	...	...	...	...	...	...	...	...	...	...
Plus: Other adjustments [b]	15830	35380	39900	42900	49330	57510	68950	76550	77270	80940	...	...
Equals: Gross Domestic Product	159570	215800	242590	266180	302600	339270	393240	422720	451540	478830	...	...

a) Gross domestic product in factor values.
b) Item 'Other adjustments' refers to indirect taxes net of subsidies.

Dominica

1.11 Gross Domestic Product by Kind of Activity, in Constant Prices

Thousand East Caribbean dollars

	1980	1983	1984	1985	1986	1987	1988	1989	1990	1991	1992	1993
					At constant prices of:1977							
1 Agriculture, hunting, forestry and fishing	23660	29840	31470	30680	36500	38340	40650	34810	38050	38670	...	...
2 Mining and quarrying	720	790	1000	970	920	1120	1380	1460	1490	1530	...	...
3 Manufacturing	6200	8740	7870	8900	9280	9830	10830	11480	11820	11580	...	...
4 Electricity, gas and water	1670	1980	2120	2270	2400	2570	2740	2920	3240	4040	...	...
5 Construction	11900	8260	11640	10370	8750	9860	12880	13590	15820	15660	...	...
6 Wholesale and retail trade, restaurants and hotels	12360	12920	13110	14150	15600	17350	18840	20540	21920	22190	...	...
7 Transport, storage and communication	5860	7900	8290	9220	10210	11690	12800	13490	14280	14840	...	...
8 Finance, insurance, real estate and business services	11160	11650	11830	12190	12450	12890	13650	14320	14870	15530	...	...
9 Community, social and personal services	1090	1190	1210	1230	1270	1310	1360	1440	1490	1520	...	...
Total, Industries	74620	83270	88540	89980	97380	104960	115130	114050	122980	125560	...	...
Producers of Government Services	21090	22930	23390	23970	24210	24820	25560	25870	26700	27500	...	...
Other Producers	...	...	...	...	...	...	...	...	...	...	...	...
Subtotal a	95710	106200	111930	113950	121590	129780	140690	139920	149680	153060	...	...
Less: Imputed bank service charge	3500	3630	3780	3970	4090	4290	5260	6010	6960	7410	...	...
Plus: Import duties	...	...	...	...	...	...	...	...	...	...	...	...
Plus: Value added tax	...	...	...	...	...	...	...	...	...	...	...	...
Plus: Other adjustments b	10150	20120	21290	21130	22880	25610	28800	29610	29470	29630	...	...
Equals: Gross Domestic Product	102360	122690	129440	131110	140380	151100	164230	163520	172190	175280	...	...

a) Gross domestic product in factor values.
b) Item 'Other adjustments' refers to indirect taxes net of subsidies.

1.12 Relations Among National Accounting Aggregates

Thousand East Caribbean dollars

	1980	1983	1984	1985	1986	1987	1988	1989	1990	1991	1992	1993
Gross Domestic Product	159570	215800	242590	266180	302600	339270	393240	422720	451540	478830	...	...
Plus: Net factor income from the rest of the world	810	1080	-2700	-3400	-6100	-6000	-1600	4410	4870	4960	...	...
Equals: Gross National Product	160380	216880	239890	262780	296500	333270	391640	427130	456410	483790	...	...
Less: Consumption of fixed capital	...	...	...	...	...	...	...	...	...	...	...	...
Equals: National Income	...	...	...	...	...	...	...	...	...	...	...	...
Plus: Net current transfers from the rest of the world	...	...	...	...	...	...	...	...	...	...	...	...
Equals: National Disposable Income	...	...	...	...	...	...	...	...	...	...	...	...
Less: Final consumption	...	...	...	...	...	...	...	...	...	...	...	...
Equals: Net Saving	...	...	...	...	...	...	...	...	...	...	...	...
Less: Surplus of the nation on current transactions	...	...	...	...	...	...	...	...	...	...	...	...
Equals: Net Capital Formation	...	...	...	...	...	...	...	...	...	...	...	...

Dominican Republic

General note. The preparation of national accounts statistics in Dominican Republic is undertaken by Banco Central de la Republica Dominicana, Santo Domingo. The official estimates are published in the series 'Cuentas Nacionales, Producto Nacional Bruto', which also includes a detailed description of the sources and methods used for the national accounts estimation. The estimates are generally in accordance with the classifications and definitions recommended in the United Nations System of National Accounts (SNA). The following tables have been prepared from successive replies to the United Nations national accounts questionnaire. When the scope and coverage of the estimates differ for conceptual or statistical reasons from the definitions and classifications recommended in SNA a footnote is indicated to the relevant tables.

Sources and methods:

(a) Gross domestic product. The main approach used to estimate GDP is the production approach.

(b) Expenditure on the gross domestic product. The expenditure approach is used to estimate government final consumption expenditure, increase in stocks and exports and imports of goods and services. Gross fixed capital formation is mainly estimated by the commodity-flow method, whereas private final consumption expenditure is taken as a residual, which also includes changes in stocks which could not be computed directly. Government consumption expenditure data for the central government is obtained from the Ministry of Finance and the National Budget Office. For gross fixed capital formation, import statistics are utilized for capital goods such as machinery, equipment and transport and communication equipment, since no such products are produced locally. To the import values are added customs duties, surcharges, mark-ups, etc. The data on exports and imports of goods and services are taken from the publication on balance of payments, prepared by the Central Bank. For the calculation of constant prices, price deflation is used for government consumption expenditure. Compensation of employees is deflated by means of the cost of living index, whereas for government purchases and sales general price indexes are used. Constant value of private consumption expenditure is obtained as a residual. The value of construction is deflated by a construction costs index. In the case of rural dwellings base-year prices are multiplied by number of dwellings built. The import price index is used as a deflator for exports and imports of goods and services.

(c) Cost-structure of the gross domestic product. The data on indirect taxes and subsidies are based on the annual reports of the Ministry of Finance and on information from the Treasury and the National Budget Office.

(d) Gross domestic product by kind of economic activity. The production approach is the basic method of estimation used for most sectors. The income approach is used for trade, transport and communication, finance, general government and other services. In agriculture gross output is estimated by multiplying the quantities harvested by the average price paid to the producers. Quantity data are available from the agricultural censuses of 1950, 1960 and 1970 and from estimates by the Banco Agricola, the Ministry of Agriculture and others. Own account consumption is included in the production series. Data on the volume of livestock production is provided by the Ministry of Agriculture, which also estimates the quantity of unreported slaughter and herd changes in livestock. The basic information for calculating gross output of the mining and quarrying sector is obtained directly from the reports on production and sales of enterprises. For manufacturing the main source of information is the series of annual bulletins of industrial statistics. The value of construction for 1960, which is taken as a bench-mark, is extrapolated by means of a value index. This index is a combination of a price index of construction costs and an index of main materials used. Value added is obtained by applying to gross output a coefficient representing the ratio of gross factor income. Data for the trade sector are available from the first national trade census carried out in 1955, and from total wholesale and retail sales figures published periodically by the National Statistical Office. Wages and salaries are calculated by combining average remunerations series with sectoral employment series. The Dominican merchant marine and the Dominican airline provide the data needed to estimate incomes, inputs and value added for shipping and air transport. For land transport the information obtained include data from transport enterprises and surveys among owners of trucks and taxis. For financial institutions the estimates are based on complete accounting information which is available for all banks and finance companies and most insurance companies. Value added of ownership of dwellings is taken as the difference between gross rents paid or imputed based on census data and the inputs for maintenance, upkeep and management and property taxes. For public administration and defence, data are obtained from Government Authorities, publications and from independent institutions. For other private services, data on the number of persons employed and mean income are used. The bench-mark data are extrapolated according to a specially constructed income index. For the computation of constant prices, the value added for agriculture is estimated by a revaluation at base-year prices of the harvested quantities. In the case of livestock products, estimates of annual changes in average meat yield per animal are utilized. For mining and quarrying value added is estimated by revaluating the different minerals at their respective 1962 prices. Value added of manufacturing is extrapolated by a quantity index of output. Current values of public and private construction are deflated by means of an index of construction costs. Wholesale and retail sales of locally produced and imported goods are deflated using the respective price indexes. For transport, storage and communication, value added is extrapolated by quantity index of output. For financial institutions value added is extrapolated by quantity indicators of personnel employed. For ownership of dwellings the indicator used is the number of urban and rural dwellings. Value added for public administration, defence and other services is extrapolated by an indicator of the number of personnel employed.

1.1 Expenditure on the Gross Domestic Product, in Current Prices

Million Dominican pesos

	1980	1983	1984	1985	1986	1987	1988	1989	1990	1991	1992	1993
1 Government final consumption expenditure	504	786	871	1112	1297	1205	1783	1824	2308	4074	5681	6865
2 Private final consumption expenditure	5109	6356	7845	10832	11606	14542	19096	31237	51577	82539	91274	92742
3 Gross capital formation [a]	1665	1817	2203	2799	3577	5437	8123	11605	13398	17019	23721	26955
A Increase in stocks [a]	82	62	33	52	85	118	89	100	120	127	150	195
B Gross fixed capital formation	1584	1754	2169	2747	3492	5319	8034	11505	13278	16892	23571	26760
4 Exports of goods and services [b]	1271	1242	3780	4088	4041	5847	11000	13149	16903	24569	26558	28269
5 Less: Imports of goods and services [b]	1919	1578	4343	4859	4741	7495	11649	15422	19318	28131	34865	34259
Equals: Gross Domestic Product [c]	6631	8623	10355	13972	15780	19536	28353	42393	64867	100070	112369	120572

a) Item 'Gross capital formation' includes only increase of stocks of mining, manufacturing, peanuts, raw tobacco and beans.
b) Beginning 1984, estimates were converted from dollars to pesos by using the annual average exchange rates fixed by the Central Bank.
c) Data in this table have not been revised, therefore they are not comparable with the data in other tables.

1.2 Expenditure on the Gross Domestic Product, in Constant Prices

Million Dominican pesos

	1980	1983	1984	1985	1986	1987	1988	1989	1990	1991	1992	1993
					At constant prices of: 1970							
1 Government final consumption expenditure	260.7	347.4	345.9	361.0	385.8	318.3	348.6	349.3	351.2	384.9	407.1	410.4
2 Private final consumption expenditure	2254.3	2457.0	2387.6	2388.7	2488.7	2736.9	2689.2	2696.6	2470.6	2552.0	2632.6	2648.9
3 Gross capital formation [a]	748.0	594.7	622.8	593.5	617.2	783.3	857.7	946.3	782.8	702.3	942.5	1003.5
A Increase in stocks [a]	52.3	35.2	14.5	22.1	26.0	39.9	24.8	19.5	17.0	32.7	35.6	45.0
B Gross fixed capital formation	695.7	559.5	608.3	571.4	591.2	743.4	832.9	926.8	765.8	669.6	906.9	958.5
4 Exports of goods and services [b]	560.0	544.4	572.0	564.3	581.1	696.3	721.7	763.4	874.1	885.1	1011.5	1027.9
5 Less: Imports of goods and services [b]	866.6	663.1	606.8	656.5	708.3	828.8	831.3	803.1	723.9	740.7	916.7	891.3
Equals: Gross Domestic Product	2956.4	3280.4	3321.5	3251.0	3365.5	3706.0	3785.9	3952.5	3754.8	3783.6	4077.0	4199.4

a) Item 'Gross capital formation' includes only increase of stocks of mining, manufacturing, peanuts, raw tobacco and beans.
b) The estimates of imports and exports of goods and services are deflated by imports and exports price indexes.

Dominican Republic

1.3 Cost Components of the Gross Domestic Product

Million Dominican pesos

	1980	1983	1984	1985	1986	1987	1988	1989	1990	1991	1992	1993
1 Indirect taxes, net	507.2	574.2	789.3	1169.7	1569.2	1985.8	2948.4	3856.8	4287.8	6565.0	12619.0	14639.0
A Indirect taxes	507.2	574.3	789.4	1173.1	1570.9	1985.8	2948.4	3856.8	4374.5	6773.0	12815.0	14810.0
B Less: Subsidies	-	0.1	0.1	3.4	1.7	-	-	-	86.7	208.0	196.0	171.6
2 Consumption of fixed capital	394.5	513.1	616.1	831.4	938.9	1162.4	1687.0	2522.4	3860.0	5954.0	6686.0	7174.0
3 Compensation of employees paid by resident producers to:	5729.0	7535.9	8949.9	11971.3	13272.3	16387.9	23717.3	36013.8	56719.1	87551.2	93063.8	98758.7
4 Operating surplus												
Equals: Gross Domestic Product	6630.7	8623.2	10355.3	13972.4	15780.4	19536.1	28352.7	42393.0	64866.9	00070.2	12368.8	20571.7

1.7 External Transactions on Current Account, Summary

Million Dominican pesos

	1980	1983	1984	1985	1986	1987	1988	1989	1990	1991	1992	1993
Payments to the Rest of the World												
1 Imports of goods and services	1919.0	1578.0	4343.0	4859.0	4741.0	7495.0	11649.0	15422.0	19318.0	28131.0	34865.0	34259.0
2 Factor income to the rest of the world	252.4	303.8	682.6	773.1	1121.8	1615.2	1950.5	1375.5	2225.5	3815.1	3161.3	4811.4
3 Current transfers to the rest of the world	...	...	...	...	...	...	...	...	...	...	...	...
4 Surplus of the nation on current transactions	-670.8	-417.9	-498.2	-376.6	-952.5	-1983.5	-310.0	-1140.0	-517.1	-1404.6	-5381.1	-4612.9
Payments to the Rest of the World and Surplus of the Nation on Current Transactions	1500.6	1463.9	4527.4	5255.5	4910.7	7126.7	13289.5	15657.5	21026.4	30541.5	32645.2	34457.5
Receipts From The Rest of the World												
1 Exports of goods and services	1271.0	1242.0	3780.0	4088.0	4041.0	5847.0	11000.0	13149.0	16903.0	24569.0	26558.0	28269.0
2 Factor income from rest of the world	41.8	6.9	16.0	66.5	48.5	43.3	51.2	67.5	917.7	1110.3	689.7	668.5
3 Current transfers from rest of the world	187.8	215.0	731.4	1101.0	821.1	1236.4	2238.3	2441.0	3205.7	4862.2	5397.5	5520.0
Receipts from the Rest of the World on Current Transactions	1500.6	1463.9	4527.4	5255.5	4910.7	7126.7	13289.5	15657.5	21026.4	30541.5	32645.2	34457.5

1.10 Gross Domestic Product by Kind of Activity, in Current Prices

Million Dominican pesos

	1980	1983	1984	1985	1986	1987	1988	1989	1990	1991	1992	1993
1 Agriculture, hunting, forestry and fishing	1336.3	1484.9	1915.7	2426.5	2588.8	3654.7	5173.0	7557.8	11157.0	17813.5	19627.5	21060.3
2 Mining and quarrying	351.7	229.2	243.6	624.8	607.2	1043.1	1397.0	1997.0	2659.5	3973.8	3374.4	3620.7
3 Manufacturing [a][b]	1015.4	1527.5	1707.6	2436.6	2738.8	2866.0	3979.0	5866.2	8756.9	13504.5	15823.8	16978.9
4 Electricity, gas and water	30.0	77.5	94.1	108.4	122.5	126.8	137.8	143.0	259.5	441.3	597.8	641.4
5 Construction	479.4	669.0	881.6	888.6	1100.4	1771.0	2786.0	4043.8	5189.3	7102.0	9208.6	9880.8
6 Wholesale and retail trade, restaurants and hotels [c]	1047.8	1450.6	1781.9	2268.6	2485.0	3069.0	3946.0	6048.9	8886.6	13747.6	15794.6	16947.6
7 Transport, storage and communication	362.3	462.9	522.7	1157.5	1296.2	1050.0	1520.0	2307.2	4216.2	6692.7	7761.3	8327.9
8 Finance, insurance, real estate and business services [d]	793.9	1090.4	1242.1	1462.9	1692.6	2074.5	2995.0	7066.2	11351.6	17754.5	18600.4	19958.2
9 Community, social and personal services [c][d]	662.0	927.1	1153.7	1052.3	1473.9	1924.0	3670.1	3298.7	6682.1	10275.2	12085.2	12967.6
Total, Industries	6078.8	7919.1	9543.0	12426.2	14105.4	17579.1	25603.9	38328.8	59158.7	91305.1	02873.6	10383.4
Producers of Government Services	551.9	704.2	812.3	1546.2	1675.0	1957.0	2748.8	4064.2	5708.2	8765.1	9495.2	10188.3
Other Producers	...	...	...	...	...	...	...	...	...	...	...	...
Subtotal	6630.7	8623.3	10355.3	13972.4	15780.4	19536.1	28352.7	42393.0	64866.9	00070.2	12368.8	20571.7
Less: Imputed bank service charge	...	...	...	...	...	...	...	...	...	...	...	...
Plus: Import duties	...	...	...	...	...	...	...	...	...	...	...	...
Plus: Value added tax	...	...	...	...	...	...	...	...	...	...	...	...
Equals: Gross Domestic Product	6630.7	8623.3	10355.3	13972.4	15780.4	19536.1	28352.7	42393.0	64866.9	00070.2	12368.8	20571.7

a) Item 'Manufacturing' includes handicrafts.
b) Repair services are included in item 'Manufacturing'.
c) Restaurants and hotels are included in item 'Community, social and personal services'.
d) Business services are included in item 'Community, social and personal services'.

Dominican Republic

1.11 Gross Domestic Product by Kind of Activity, in Constant Prices

Million Dominican pesos

	1980	1983	1984	1985	1986	1987	1988	1989	1990	1991	1992	1993
	\multicolumn{12}{c}{At constant prices of:1970}											
1 Agriculture, hunting, forestry and fishing	484.2	550.8	550.9	531.3	528.5	543.8	536.6	548.7	501.6	522.9	554.5	558.4
2 Mining and quarrying	124.6	124.8	135.1	134.7	119.7	150.7	140.2	139.3	116.6	111.5	90.9	57.2
3 Manufacturing [ab]	545.4	585.9	578.2	548.1	598.2	674.4	670.0	701.1	671.9	684.4	761.7	779.2
4 Electricity, gas and water	49.1	50.6	57.0	59.9	63.3	70.1	68.0	62.1	56.3	58.8	75.9	87.7
5 Construction	197.5	226.7	226.8	192.0	221.8	297.4	306.9	347.5	280.8	245.9	305.9	336.7
6 Wholesale and retail trade, restaurants and hotels [c]	511.1	575.8	593.5	571.6	587.8	655.0	682.9	694.6	645.0	665.0	724.4	767.2
7 Transport, storage and communication	230.5	259.5	257.0	241.7	249.2	308.6	311.4	332.0	331.5	351.4	401.8	428.8
8 Finance, insurance, real estate and business services [d]	268.5	285.5	292.0	332.2	351.2	370.1	398.1	433.5	449.0	451.9	454.6	454.5
9 Community, social and personal services [cd]	265.4	300.3	300.4	305.9	313.9	321.3	332.4	344.7	344.0	337.8	346.2	356.3
Total, Industries	2676.3	2959.9	2990.9	2917.4	3033.6	3391.4	3446.4	3603.5	3395.8	3429.6	3715.9	3826.0
Producers of Government Services	280.1	320.5	330.6	333.6	331.9	314.6	339.5	349.0	358.8	354.0	361.1	373.4
Other Producers	...	...	...	...	...	...	...	...	...	...	...	...
Subtotal	2956.4	3280.4	3321.5	3251.0	3365.5	3706.0	3785.9	3952.5	3754.7	3783.6	4077.0	4199.4
Less: Imputed bank service charge	...	...	...	...	...	...	...	...	...	...	...	...
Plus: Import duties	...	...	...	...	...	...	...	...	...	...	...	...
Plus: Value added tax	...	...	...	...	...	...	...	...	...	...	...	...
Equals: Gross Domestic Product	2956.4	3280.4	3321.5	3251.0	3365.5	3706.0	3785.9	3952.5	3754.7	3783.6	4077.0	4199.4

a) Item 'Manufacturing' includes handicrafts.
b) Repair services are included in item 'Manufacturing'.
c) Restaurants and hotels are included in item 'Community, social and personal services'.
d) Business services are included in item 'Community, social and personal services'.

1.12 Relations Among National Accounting Aggregates

Million Dominican pesos

	1980	1983	1984	1985	1986	1987	1988	1989	1990	1991	1992	1993
Gross Domestic Product	6630.7	8623.3	10355.3	13972.4	15780.4	19536.1	28352.7	42393.0	64866.9	00070.2	12368.8	20571.7
Plus: Net factor income from the rest of the world [a]	-211.5	-297.1	-666.3	-706.0	-1074.0	-1572.0	-1899.0	-1308.0	-1308.0	-2705.0	-3035.0	-4952.5
Equals: Gross National Product	6419.2	8326.2	9689.0	13266.4	14706.4	17964.1	26453.7	41085.0	63558.9	97365.2	09333.8	15619.2
Less: Consumption of fixed capital	394.5	513.1	616.1	831.4	938.9	1162.4	1687.0	2522.4	3860.0	5954.0	6686.0	7174.0
Equals: National Income	6024.7	7813.1	9072.9	12435.0	13767.5	16801.7	24766.7	38562.6	59698.9	91411.2	02647.8	08445.2
Plus: Net current transfers from the rest of the world [ba]	187.8	215.0	731.4	1101.0	821.1	1236.4	2238.3	2441.0	3205.7	4862.2	5397.5	5520.0
Equals: National Disposable Income	6212.5	8028.1	9804.3	13536.0	14588.6	18038.1	27005.0	41003.6	62904.6	96273.4	08045.3	13965.2
Less: Final consumption	5612.8	7142.2	8715.6	11945.0	12903.0	15747.0	20879.0	33061.0	53883.6	86613.4	96955.0	99607.0
Statistical discrepancy	...	...	...	...	...	...	...	...	...	...	563.8	809.7
Equals: Net Saving	599.7	885.9	1088.7	1591.0	1685.6	2291.1	6126.0	7942.6	9021.0	9660.0	11654.1	15167.9
Less: Surplus of the nation on current transactions [a]	-670.8	-417.9	-498.2	-376.6	-952.5	-1983.5	-310.0	-1140.0	-517.1	-1404.6	-5381.1	-4612.9
Statistical discrepancy	-0.3	-	-0.5	...	...	...	...	...	...	...	...	...
Equals: Net Capital Formation [c]	1270.8	1303.8	1586.4	1967.6	2638.1	4274.6	6436.0	9082.6	9538.1	11064.6	17035.2	19780.8

a) Beginning 1984, estimates were converted from dollars to pesos by using the annual average exchange rates fixed by the Central Bank.
b) Item 'Net current transfers from the rest of the world' includes mainly net interest receipts.
c) Item 'Gross capital formation' includes only increase of stocks of mining, manufacturing, peanuts, raw tobacco and beans.

Ecuador

Source. Reply to the United Nations National Accounts Questionnaire from the Subgerencia de Cuentas Nacionales, Banco Central del Ecuador, Quito. The official estimates are published annually in 'Memoria del Gerente General del Banco Central del Ecuador'.

General note. The estimates shown in the following tables have been prepared in accordance with the United Nations System of National Accounts so far as the existing data would permit.

1.1 Expenditure on the Gross Domestic Product, in Current Prices

Thousand Million Ecuadoran sucres

	1980	1983	1984	1985	1986	1987	1988	1989	1990	1991	1992	1993
1 Government final consumption expenditure	43	70	100	127	167	230	347	485	706	936	1407	2117
2 Private final consumption expenditure	175	369	521	716	926	1269	2087	3706	5622	8432	13148	19374
A Households	175	369	521	716	926	1269	2087	3706	5622	8432	13148	19374
B Private non-profit institutions serving households	...	...	...	...	...	...	...	...	...	...	...	...
3 Gross capital formation	77	98	140	202	288	407	649	1070	1435	2726	4117	5787
A Increase in stocks	7	5	15	23	28	-	6	-1	-77	309	333	330
B Gross fixed capital formation	69	93	125	178	260	407	643	1071	1512	2416	3785	5457
Residential buildings	8	15	21	25	31	41	75	98	144	241	347	502
Non-residential buildings	11	18	22	28	35	43	62	112	189	291	464	619
Other construction and land improvement etc.	18	29	36	51	73	126	163	304	354	554	784	1275
Other	32	31	46	75	121	197	343	556	826	1330	2189	3060
4 Exports of goods and services	74	133	210	297	315	432	859	1520	2686	3858	6119	7184
5 Less: Imports of goods and services	75	111	157	232	313	544	922	1611	2246	3655	5378	7011
Equals: Gross Domestic Product	293	560	813	1110	1383	1795	3020	5170	8204	12296	19414	27451

1.2 Expenditure on the Gross Domestic Product, in Constant Prices

Million Ecuadoran sucres

	1980	1983	1984	1985	1986	1987	1988	1989	1990	1991	1992	1993
	\multicolumn{12}{c}{At constant prices of:1975}												
1 Government final consumption expenditure	23611	22828	21997	21076	20904	21245	21562	20980	21431	20950	20289	20036
2 Private final consumption expenditure	99686	103785	106597	110441	111397	114115	116312	119225	122259	125264	128107	131332
A Households	99686	103785	106597	110441	111397	114115	116312	119225	122259	125264	128107	131332
B Private non-profit institutions serving households	...	...	...	...	...	...	...	...	...	...	...	...
3 Gross capital formation	39216	26294	25914	27975	28816	27915	26876	27656	23449	30452	30084	28836
A Increase in stocks	4241	2167	2879	3357	3139	1115	1411	2405	-512	3850	1650	94
B Gross fixed capital formation	34975	24127	23035	24618	25677	26800	25465	25251	23961	26602	28434	28742
Residential buildings										3077	2783	2536
Non-residential buildings	16016	14696	14160	14399	14367	14982	13017	13175	11559	3208	3357	2986
Other construction and land improvement etc.										5788	5440	5905
Other	18959	9431	8875	10219	11310	11818	12448	12076	12402	14529	16854	17315
4 Exports of goods and services	30792	31396	35331	39562	42944	36027	47235	46440	51159	56523	61940	64552
5 Less: Imports of goods and services	45683	33418	32613	35000	34925	40286	36243	38106	36692	42551	42984	43309
Equals: Gross Domestic Product	147622	150885	157226	164054	169136	159016	175742	176195	181531	190638	197436	201447

1.3 Cost Components of the Gross Domestic Product

Thousand Million Ecuadoran sucres

	1980	1983	1984	1985	1986	1987	1988	1989	1990	1991	1992	1993
1 Indirect taxes, net	24	47	68	128	156	205	357	694	1133	1443	2308	3271
A Indirect taxes	27	49	72	152	191	229	397	761	1279	1706	2626	3649
B Less: Subsidies	3	2	5	24	34	24	40	67	146	263	318	378
2 Consumption of fixed capital [a]	...	...	...	...	...	...	...	...	...	...	...	...
3 Compensation of employees paid by resident producers to:	94	136	180	232	302	401	550	787	1115	1566	2461	3968

Ecuador

1.3 Cost Components of the Gross Domestic Product
(Continued)

Thousand Million Ecuadoran sucres

	1980	1983	1984	1985	1986	1987	1988	1989	1990	1991	1992	1993
A Resident households	93	134	176	230	298	394	540	765	1075	1510	2354	3836
B Rest of the world	1	2	3	2	4	7	10	22	40	56	106	132
4 Operating surplus [a]	175	378	565	749	925	1189	2113	3690	5955	9287	14645	20212
A Corporate and quasi-corporate enterprises [b]	52	102	168	214	218	214	432	574	1068	1416	2264	2078
B Private unincorporated enterprises [c]	123	275	396	534	705	971	1677	3117	4889	7873	12383	18138
C General government	-	-	2	2	2	4	4	-1	-2	-2	-2	-4
Equals: Gross Domestic Product	293	560	813	1110	1383	1795	3020	5170	8204	12296	19414	27451

a) Item 'Operating surplus' includes consumption of fixed capital.
b) Beginning 1976, item 'Corporate and quasi-corporate enterprises' includes quasi-corporate enterprises that up to 1975 were included with households.
c) Item 'Private unincorporated enterprises' relates to households.

1.4 General Government Current Receipts and Disbursements

Million Ecuadoran sucres

	1980	1983	1984	1985	1986	1987	1988	1989	1990	1991	1992	1993
Receipts												
1 Operating surplus	300	473	1677	1716	2381	3844	4007	-1106	-2000	-2000	-2000	-3000
2 Property and entrepreneurial income	10954	25204	33566	31298	29120	30644	60584	105028	235000	232000	301000	383000
3 Taxes, fees and contributions	58631	106049	161792	273900	299440	339389	592746	1090743	1870000	2588000	3843000	5383000
A Indirect taxes	26931	48693	72358	152141	190845	228830	397276	761063	1279000	1706000	2626000	3649000
B Direct taxes	22390	41137	69653	93216	70004	63400	112254	178608	373000	555000	721000	1051000
C Social security contributions	8092	14786	17597	25042	33454	41297	72469	131431	197000	297000	457000	625000
D Compulsory fees, fines and penalties	1218	1433	2184	3501	5137	5862	10747	19641	21000	30000	39000	58000
4 Other current transfers	10540	18031	22770	44256	62386	70527	94530	155903	260000	345000	457000	676000
Total Current Receipts of General Government	80425	149757	219805	351170	393327	444404	751867	1350568	2363000	3161000	4599000	6439000
Disbursements												
1 Government final consumption expenditure	42562	70055	99628	127330	166731	230417	346895	484989	706000	936000	1407000	2117000
2 Property income	7590	24536	31184	48591	57085	56821	77753	174638	332000	337000	499000	543000
A Interest	7588	24534	31184	48591	57085	56821	77753	174638	332000	337000	499000	543000
B Net land rent and royalties	2	2	-	-	-	-	-	-	-	-	-	...
3 Subsidies	2543	2030	4668	23762	34392	24295	40482	67110	146000	263000	318000	378000
4 Other current transfers	16916	28506	37051	49195	60872	88223	121295	203606	351000	475000	759000	1029000
A Social security benefits	6746	12639	15629	20673	22385	39535	55348	87672	141000	204000	375000	469000
B Social assistance grants	1353	1520	2090	2625	2875	4214	5911	10785	...	...	...	...
C Other	8817	14347	19332	25897	35612	44474	60036	105149	...	...	...	...
5 Net saving [a]	10814	24630	47274	102292	74247	44648	165442	420225	829000	1148000	1616000	2371000
Total Current Disbursements and Net Saving of General Government	80425	149757	219805	351170	393327	444404	751867	1350568	2363000	3159000	4599000	6438000

a) Item 'Net saving' includes consumption of fixed capital.

1.5 Current Income and Outlay of Corporate and Quasi-Corporate Enterprises, Summary

Million Ecuadoran sucres

	1980	1983	1984	1985	1986	1987	1988	1989	1990	1991	1992	1993
Receipts												
1 Operating surplus [a]	52003	102234	168068	214248	217661	214309	432382	574034	1068000	1416000	2264000	2077000
2 Property and entrepreneurial income received	15780	43860	77216	103952	144072	205295	296009	432077	703000	1177000	1984000	2756000
3 Current transfers	1786	3669	4690	7839	11436	19446	29446	42036	74000	130000	226000	384000
Total Current Receipts	69569	149763	249974	326039	373169	439050	757837	1048147	1845000	2723000	4474000	5217000
Disbursements												
1 Property and entrepreneurial income	32576	87750	154293	186170	246288	321598	474643	749802	1238000	1838000	2913000	3561000
2 Direct taxes and other current payments to general government	20187	37764	64648	86072	59537	49863	95754	141967	325000	479000	592000	833000
3 Other current transfers	2866	5836	7222	25539	38898	46987	65861	106339	148000	230000	352000	600000
4 Net saving [b]	13940	18413	23811	28258	28446	20602	121579	50039	135000	176000	617000	223000
Total Current Disbursements and Net Saving	69569	149763	249974	326039	373169	439050	757837	1048147	1845000	2723000	4474000	5217000

a) Item 'Operating surplus' includes consumption of fixed capital.
b) Item 'Net saving' includes consumption of fixed capital.

Ecuador

1.6 Current Income and Outlay of Households and Non-Profit Institutions

Thousand Million Ecuadoran sucres

	1980	1983	1984	1985	1986	1987	1988	1989	1990	1991	1992	1993
					Receipts							
1 Compensation of employees	93	134	176	230	298	394	541	767	1078	1515	2361	3844
A From resident producers	93	134	176	230	298	394	540	765	1075	1510	2354	3836
B From rest of the world	-	-	-	-	-	1	1	2	3	5	7	8
2 Operating surplus of private unincorporated enterprises	123	275	396	534	705	971	1677	3117	4889	7873	12383	18138
3 Property and entrepreneurial income	6	17	24	45	62	84	87	126	213	351	908	995
4 Current transfers	10	19	24	34	41	90	119	203	325	480	845	1159
A Social security benefits	7	13	16	21	22	40	55	88	141	204	375	469
B Social assistance grants												
C Other	3	6	8	13	19	51	64	115	184	276	470	690
Total Current Receipts	232	445	620	843	1107	1540	2424	4213	6505	10219	16498	24135
					Disbursements							
1 Private final consumption expenditure	175	369	521	716	926	1269	2087	3706	5622	8432	13147	19375
2 Property income	7	14	19	26	40	58	90	103	173	270	612	1003
3 Direct taxes and other current transfers n.e.c. to general government	12	20	25	36	49	61	100	188	266	404	625	899
A Social security contributions	8	15	18	25	33	41	72	131	197	297	457	625
B Direct taxes	3	4	6	9	13	16	22	45	56	86	143	234
C Fees, fines and penalties	1	1	1	2	3	3	5	12	13	21	25	40
4 Other current transfers	2	4	5	9	13	20	29	41	78	129	231	357
5 Net saving a	37	38	51	57	79	132	119	175	366	985	1884	2501
Total Current Disbursements and Net Saving	232	445	620	843	1107	1540	2424	4213	6505	10220	16498	24135

a) Item 'Net saving' includes consumption of fixed capital.

1.7 External Transactions on Current Account, Summary

Million Ecuadoran sucres

	1980	1983	1984	1985	1986	1987	1988	1989	1990	1991	1992	1993
					Payments to the Rest of the World							
1 Imports of goods and services	74527	110617	157412	231668	312507	543702	922375	1610751	2246000	3655000	5378000	7011000
A Imports of merchandise c.i.f.	63512	85154	127264	177399	242639	448150	725271	1317900	1811000	3053000	4465000	5816000
B Other	11015	25463	30148	54269	69868	95552	197104	292851	435000	602000	913000	1195000
2 Factor income to the rest of the world	16932	43696	76962	84409	115517	126115	212451	399908	656000	777000	992000	1165000
A Compensation of employees	783	2187	3375	2337	3761	7391	9746	22034	40000	56000	106000	132000
B Property and entrepreneurial income	16149	41509	73587	82072	111756	118724	202705	377874	616000	721000	886000	1033000
3 Current transfers to the rest of the world	1011	2026	2497	3366	3833	6368	9963	18227	34000	44000	84000	100000
4 Surplus of the nation on current transactions	-14423	-17401	-18313	-14378	-107219	-209221	-243299	-424558	-106000	-414000	-2000	-692000
Payments to the Rest of the World and Surplus of the Nation on Current Transactions	78047	138938	218558	305065	324638	466964	901490	1604328	2830000	4062000	6452000	7584000
					Receipts From The Rest of the World							
1 Exports of goods and services	73797	133061	209858	296922	314740	431538	859062	1520090	2686000	3858000	6119000	7184000
A Exports of merchandise f.o.b.	64389	110999	183425	255387	250181	348095	673104	1221020	2251000	3214000	5075000	5813000
B Other	9408	22062	26433	41535	64559	83443	185958	299070	435000	644000	1044000	1371000
2 Factor income from rest of the world	2395	1904	4391	2654	3868	3821	5648	15636	27000	41000	61000	66000
A Compensation of employees	45	157	175	267	480	733	1118	2135	3000	5000	7000	8000
B Property and entrepreneurial income	2350	1747	4216	2387	3388	3088	4530	13501	24000	37000	54000	58000
3 Current transfers from rest of the world	1855	3973	4309	5489	6030	31605	36780	68602	117000	163000	272000	334000
Receipts from the Rest of the World on Current Transactions	78047	138938	218558	305065	324638	466964	901490	1604328	2830000	4062000	6452000	7584000

Ecuador

1.8 Capital Transactions of The Nation, Summary

Million Ecuadoran sucres

	1980	1983	1984	1985	1986	1987	1988	1989	1990	1991	1992	1993
Finance of Gross Capital Formation												
Gross saving	62000	81000	122000	187000	181000	198000	406000	645000	1330000	2311000	4115000	5096000
1 Consumption of fixed capital	26000	63000	97000	136000	200000	315000	542000	935000	1416000	2026000	3007000	4368000
2 Net saving	36000	18000	25000	51000	-19000	-117000	-136000	-290000	-86000	285000	1108000	728000
Less: Surplus of the nation on current transactions	-14000	-17000	-18000	-14000	-107000	-209000	-243000	-425000	-105000	-415000	-2000	-691000
Finance of Gross Capital Formation	77000	98000	140000	202000	288000	407000	649000	1070000	1435000	2726000	4117000	5787000
Gross Capital Formation												
Increase in stocks	7000	5000	15000	23000	28000	234	6000	-1000	-77000	309000	333000	330000
Gross fixed capital formation	69000	93000	125000	178000	260000	407000	643000	1071000	1512000	2417000	3784000	5457000
1 General government	19000	27000	36000	54000	82000	116000	165000	237000	328000	470000	754000	996000
2 Corporate and quasi-corporate enterprises	36000	47000	63000	88000	133000	226000	366000	639000	790000	1367000	2127000	3169000
A Public	9000	18000	17000	19000	45000	51000	96000	236000	219000	435000	691000	1137000
B Private	27000	29000	46000	69000	88000	175000	270000	403000	571000	932000	1436000	2032000
3 Other	14000	19000	27000	36000	45000	65000	112000	194000	395000	580000	903000	1292000
Gross Capital Formation	77000	98000	140000	202000	288000	407000	649000	1070000	1435000	2726000	4117000	5787000

1.9 Gross Domestic Product by Institutional Sectors of Origin

Thousand Million Ecuadoran sucres

	1980	1983	1984	1985	1986	1987	1988	1989	1990	1991	1992	1993
Domestic Factor Incomes Originating												
1 General government	29	47	71	97	128	169	237	311	444	586	950	1518
2 Corporate and quasi-corporate enterprises	104	202	288	401	441	538	957	1459	2358	3191	5191	6526
A Non-financial	93	184	272	381	415	485	860	1375	2227	2950	4803	5796
Public	32	68	106	173	152	160	300	627	1190	1471	2632	3669
Private	61	116	166	208	263	325	560	748	1037	1480	2171	2127
B Financial	11	18	16	20	26	52	97	84	131	241	388	730
Public	6	10	4	2	6	27	58	27	34	87	138	186
Private	5	8	12	18	20	25	39	57	97	154	250	544
3 Households and private unincorporated enterprises	156	315	443	592	779	1064	1802	3302	5101	8161	12812	18799
4 Non-profit institutions serving households	...	...	...	...	...	...	...	...	...	...	...	...
Subtotal: Domestic Factor Incomes [a,b]	290	564	803	1090	1347	1771	2997	5072	7903	11938	18953	26843
Indirect taxes, net [c]	12	16	27	42	64	77	121	196	450	646	951	1486
A Indirect taxes	13	16	27	42	64	77	121	196	450	646	951	1486
B Less: Subsidies	1	-	-	-	-	-	-	-	-	-	-	...
Consumption of fixed capital	...	...	...	...	...	...	...	...	...	...	...	...
Statistical discrepancy [d]	-9	-19	-17	-22	-29	-54	-98	-97	-149	-288	-490	-878
Gross Domestic Product	293	560	813	1110	1383	1795	3020	5170	8204	12296	19413	27451

a) Item 'Domestic factor incomes' includes consumption of fixed capital.
b) Item 'Domestic factor incomes' includes net indirect taxes other than import duties.
c) Item 'Indirect taxes, net' refers to import duties only.
d) Item 'Statistical discrepancy' relates to imputed bank service charges.

1.10 Gross Domestic Product by Kind of Activity, in Current Prices

Thousand Million Ecuadoran sucres

	1980	1983	1984	1985	1986	1987	1988	1989	1990	1991	1992	1993
1 Agriculture, hunting, forestry and fishing	36	73	110	148	209	275	433	722	1100	1762	2466	3323
2 Mining and quarrying [a]	36	86	127	190	138	123	297	605	1218	1368	2440	2942
3 Manufacturing [a]	52	104	168	210	274	350	645	1090	1588	2554	4280	5969
4 Electricity, gas and water	2	3	4	3	6	7	2	4	-15	-13	23	76
5 Construction	22	34	37	49	67	99	140	236	329	556	882	1340
6 Wholesale and retail trade, restaurants and hotels	43	76	130	173	247	363	611	1119	1737	2723	4168	5551
7 Transport, storage and communication	23	54	58	95	126	170	296	461	708	1064	1505	2450
8 Finance, insurance, real estate and business services	34	59	68	84	105	151	244	334	502	857	1393	2255
9 Community, social and personal services	15	30	35	47	57	77	115	215	331	537	943	1564

Ecuador

1.10 Gross Domestic Product by Kind of Activity, in Current Prices
(Continued)

Thousand Million Ecuadoran sucres

	1980	1983	1984	1985	1986	1987	1988	1989	1990	1991	1992	1993
Total, Industries	262	520	736	999	1229	1615	2782	4785	7498	11408	18100	25470
Producers of Government Services	27	42	63	86	113	148	205	272	387	504	813	1309
Other Producers	2	2	3	4	6	8	10	14	19	26	40	65
Subtotal	290	564	803	1090	1347	1771	2997	5072	7903	11938	18953	26844
Less: Imputed bank service charge	9	19	17	22	29	54	98	97	149	288	490	879
Plus: Import duties	12	16	27	42	64	77	121	196	215	280	339	537
Plus: Value added tax	...	...	...	...	...	...	...	...	234	366	612	949
Equals: Gross Domestic Product	293	560	813	1110	1383	1795	3020	5170	8204	12296	19414	27451

a) Petroleum refining is included in item 'Crude petroleum and natural gas production'.

1.11 Gross Domestic Product by Kind of Activity, in Constant Prices

Million Ecuadoran sucres

	1980	1983	1984	1985	1986	1987	1988	1989	1990	1991	1992	1993
					At constant prices of:1975							
1 Agriculture, hunting, forestry and fishing	21198	19891	22007	24178	26656	27323	29416	30230	32080	33988	35154	34555
2 Mining and quarrying [a]	15070	19893	21879	23875	24513	11107	23964	21642	21442	23251	24599	27298
3 Manufacturing [a]	26807	29183	28643	28710	28241	28729	29312	27858	28055	28951	29989	30731
4 Electricity, gas and water	1115	1426	1836	1833	2232	2616	2721	2899	2781	2841	2919	2980
5 Construction	6906	6728	6583	6742	6841	7011	6024	6264	5333	5274	5256	5032
6 Wholesale and retail trade, restaurants and hotels	24789	22537	23467	24268	24793	25397	25925	26470	27469	28557	29420	29919
7 Transport, storage and communication	10038	10511	10914	11506	12571	12829	13620	14700	15362	16289	17223	17992
8 Finance, insurance, real estate and business services	17694	18972	17679	18162	18579	21095	22679	19188	19589	20806	21479	23455
9 Community, social and personal services	7612	9098	9366	9529	9773	10067	10082	10388	10434	10757	11112	11264
Total, Industries	131229	138239	142374	148803	154199	146174	163743	159639	162545	170714	177151	183226
Producers of Government Services	13709	14493	14775	14842	14898	15002	15617	15636	16015	16169	16114	15754
Other Producers	675	705	714	723	735	756	778	800	819	844	864	881
Subtotal	145613	153437	157863	164368	169832	161932	180138	176075	179379	187727	194129	199861
Less: Imputed bank service charge	5006	6158	4485	4519	4934	7122	8510	4692	4881	5661	5984	7811
Plus: Import duties	7015	3606	3848	4205	4238	4206	4114	4812	3624	4815	5324	5369
Plus: Value added tax	...	...	...	...	...	...	...	...	3409	3757	3967	4028
Equals: Gross Domestic Product	147622	150885	157226	164054	169136	159016	175742	176195	181531	190638	197436	201447

a) Petroleum refining is included in item 'Crude petroleum and natural gas production'.

1.12 Relations Among National Accounting Aggregates

Thousand Million Ecuadoran sucres

	1980	1983	1984	1985	1986	1987	1988	1989	1990	1991	1992	1993
Gross Domestic Product	293	560	813	1110	1383	1795	3020	5170	8204	12296	19414	27451
Plus: Net factor income from the rest of the world	-15	-42	-73	-82	-112	-122	-207	-384	-629	-737	-931	-1098
Factor income from the rest of the world	2	2	4	3	4	4	6	16	27	41	61	66
Less: Factor income to the rest of the world	17	44	77	84	116	126	212	400	656	778	992	1164
Equals: Gross National Product	279	518	740	1028	1272	1272	2813	4786	7575	11559	18483	26353
Less: Consumption of fixed capital	26	63	97	136	200	315	542	935	1416	2026	3007	4368
Equals: National Income	253	455	643	892	1072	1357	2271	3851	6159	9533	15476	21985
Plus: Net current transfers from the rest of the world	1	2	2	2	2	25	27	50	83	119	187	234
Current transfers from the rest of the world	2	4	4	5	6	32	37	69	117	163	273	334
Less: Current transfers to the rest of the world	1	2	2	3	4	6	10	18	34	44	84	100
Equals: National Disposable Income	254	457	645	894	1074	1382	2298	3901	6242	9652	15663	22219
Less: Final consumption	217	439	620	843	1093	1500	2434	4191	6328	9367	14555	21491
Equals: Net Saving	37	18	25	51	-19	-118	-136	-290	-86	285	1108	728
Less: Surplus of the nation on current transactions	-14	-17	-18	-14	-107	-209	-243	-425	-106	-415	-2	-691
Equals: Net Capital Formation	51	35	43	65	88	91	107	135	20	700	1110	1419

Ecuador

2.1 Government Final Consumption Expenditure by Function, in Current Prices

Million Ecuadoran sucres

	1980	1983	1984	1985	1986	1987	1988	1989	1990	1991	1992	1993
1 General public services	6181	7546	10270	14758	27376	38301	47670	67861	101104	131000	192000	...
2 Defence	5136	9611	17391	25063	21386	29770	68903	82646	113059	151000	238000	...
3 Public order and safety	2348	3697	5431	7601	10608	13939	29084	36165	54579	72000	109000	...
4 Education	13136	20691	29911	42950	56854	85060	101046	134474	213726	281000	402000	...
5 Health	2309	6009	7817	8685	10757	13653	20700	31150	37118	46000	59000	...
6 Social security and welfare	1910	4175	5489	6946	9264	12376	19193	27302	47502	63000	117000	...
7 Housing and community amenities	1338	1861	3059	3885	5233	6678	11912	19699	34103	50000	64000	...
8 Recreational, cultural and religious affairs	131	188	329	379	472	647	897	1277	1547	3000	3000	...
9 Economic services	5062	8997	11059	16083	27178	41061	56411	69714	107965	150000	241000	...
A Fuel and energy	1094	2463	2440	4335	4864	6348	10005	313	542	1000	36000	...
B Agriculture, forestry, fishing and hunting	1530	2388	3641	4920	6547	9647	12318	19162	29985	40000	53000	...
C Mining, manufacturing and construction, except fuel and energy	386	634	1034	1486	2877	5574	6900	9483	13625	18000	28000	...
D Transportation and communication	1700	2292	2813	3901	11190	17051	23464	34948	56761	79000	111000	...
E Other economic affairs	352	1220	1131	1441	1700	2441	3724	5808	7052	12000	13000	...
10 Other functions	7791	12802	15774	10650	9133	3867	16656	54059	66428	63000	73000	...
Total Government Final Consumption Expenditure [a]	45342	75577	106530	137000	178261	245352	372472	524347	777131	1009000	1498000	...

a) Government final consumption expenditure in this table includes compensation of employees and intermediate consumption of the following departmental enterprises: electricity, gas and steam, water works and supply and medical and other health services.

2.3 Total Government Outlays by Function and Type

Million Ecuadoran sucres

	Final Consumption Expenditures Total	Compensation of Employees	Other	Subsidies	Other Current Transfers & Property Income	Total Current Disbursements	Gross Capital Formation	Other Capital Outlays	Total Outlays
					1980				
1 General public services	6181	2932	3249	...	94	6275	469	91	6835
2 Defence	5136	2668	2468	...	...	5136	36	...	5172
3 Public order and safety	2348	2020	328	...	60	2408	125	...	2533
4 Education	13136	11978	1158	...	797	13933	1660	48	15641
5 Health	2309	1885	424	...	2207	4516	802	...	5318
6 Social security and welfare	1910	1587	323	...	5761	7671	720	70	8461
7 Housing and community amenities	1338	947	391	...	2	1340	2071	493	3904
8 Recreation, culture and religion	131	74	57	...	16	147	31	...	178
9 Economic services	5062	2632	2430	2543	131	7736	13644	1394	22774
A Fuel and energy	1094	526	568	242	33	1369	5221	1008	7598
B Agriculture, forestry, fishing and hunting	1530	942	588	146	41	1717	979	318	3014
C Mining (except fuels), manufacturing and construction	386	265	121	1722	42	2150	98	3	2251
D Transportation and communication	1700	725	975	420	1	2121	6296	59	8476
E Other economic affairs	352	174	178	13	14	379	1050	6	1435
10 Other functions	7791	26	7765	...	6772	14563	...	127	14690
Total [abc]	45342	26749	18593	2543	15840	63725	19558	2223	85506
					1985				
1 General public services	14758	...	...	...	950	15708	1593	3	17304
2 Defence	25063	...	...	...	1	25064	66	...	25130
3 Public order and safety	7601	...	...	...	159	7760	748	...	8508
4 Education	42950	...	...	...	1205	44155	6169	49	50373
5 Health	8685	...	...	...	6916	15601	3245	454	19300
6 Social security and welfare	6946	...	...	...	18041	24987	1379	626	26992
7 Housing and community amenities	3885	...	...	36	18	3939	6102	1196	11237
8 Recreation, culture and religion	379	...	...	...	50	429	203	...	632
9 Economic services	16083	...	...	23726	461	40270	34228	559	75057

Ecuador

2.3 Total Government Outlays by Function and Type
(Continued)

Million Ecuadoran sucres

		Final Consumption Expenditures			Subsidies	Other Current Transfers & Property Income	Total Current Disbursements	Gross Capital Formation	Other Capital Outlays	Total Outlays
		Total	Compensation of Employees	Other						
A	Fuel and energy	4335	...	...	21485	46	25866	7756	12	33634
B	Agriculture, forestry, fishing and hunting	4920	...	...	177	36	5133	3265	3	8401
C	Mining (except fuels), manufacturing and construction	1486	...	...	823	146	2455	117	411	2983
D	Transportation and communication	3901	...	...	840	189	4930	17673	6	22609
E	Other economic affairs	1441	...	...	401	44	1886	5417	127	7430
10	Other functions	10650	...	...	...	44763	55413	380	-	55793
Total abc		137000	...	...	23762	72564	233326	54113	2887	290326

1990

1	General public services	101104	...	...	108	1911	103123	14054	39	117216
2	Defence	113059	...	...	...	22	113081	146	-	113227
3	Public order and safety	54579	...	...	...	666	55245	7503	-	62748
4	Education	213726	...	...	...	8671	222397	37589	275	260261
5	Health	37118	...	...	...	5724	42842	36517	14	79373
6	Social security and welfare	47502	...	...	...	6709	54211	9972	435	64618
7	Housing and community amenities	34103	...	...	-	2415	36518	47928	19034	103480
8	Recreation, culture and religion	1547	...	...	...	3	1550	562	-	2112
9	Economic services	107965	...	...	130438	2861	241264	173391	64482	479137
A	Fuel and energy	542	...	...	124140	32	124714	253	60842	185809
B	Agriculture, forestry, fishing and hunting	29985	...	...	170	290	30445	15126	785	46356
C	Mining (except fuels), manufacturing and construction	13625	...	...	98	1033	14756	1631	-	16387
D	Transportation and communication	56761	...	...	4425	1332	62518	120139	1455	184112
E	Other economic affairs	7052	...	...	1605	174	8831	36242	1400	46473
10	Other functions	66428	...	...	...	326795	393223	1525	-	394748
Total abc		777131	...	...	130546	355777	1263454	329187	84279	1676920

1991

1	General public services	131000	...	...	...	2000	133000	18000	...	151000
2	Defence	151000	...	...	...	-	151000	...	...	151000
3	Public order and safety	72000	...	...	...	1000	73000	8000	...	81000
4	Education	281000	...	...	...	12000	293000	49000	...	342000
5	Health	46000	...	...	...	75000	121000	56000	...	177000
6	Social security and welfare	63000	...	...	...	143000	206000	14000	...	220000
7	Housing and community amenities	50000	...	...	...	50000	100000	71000	...	171000
8	Recreation, culture and religion	3000	...	...	...	-	3000	1000	...	4000
9	Economic services	150000	...	...	...	396000	546000	257000	...	803000
A	Fuel and energy	1000	...	...	...	364000	365000	1000	...	366000
B	Agriculture, forestry, fishing and hunting	40000	...	...	...	3000	43000	23000	...	66000
C	Mining (except fuels), manufacturing and construction	18000	...	...	...	1000	19000	2000	...	21000
D	Transportation and communication	79000	...	...	...	24000	103000	160000	...	263000
E	Other economic affairs	12000	...	...	...	5000	17000	71000	...	88000
10	Other functions	63000	...	...	...	334000	397000	2000	...	399000
Total abc		1009000	...	...	...	1013000	2022000	476000	...	2498000

1992

1	General public services	192000	...	...	...	4000	196000	46000	...	242000
2	Defence	238000	...	...	...	1000	239000	...	...	239000
3	Public order and safety	109000	...	...	...	1000	110000	7000	...	117000
4	Education	402000	...	...	...	19000	421000	78000	...	499000
5	Health	59000	...	...	...	157000	216000	123000	...	339000
6	Social security and welfare	117000	...	...	...	240000	357000	23000	...	380000
7	Housing and community amenities	64000	...	...	...	104000	168000	94000	...	262000
8	Recreation, culture and religion	3000	...	...	...	...	3000	1000	...	4000
9	Economic services	241000	...	...	...	495000	736000	387000	...	1123000

Ecuador

2.3 Total Government Outlays by Function and Type
(Continued)

Million Ecuadoran sucres

	Final Consumption Expenditures Total	Compensation of Employees	Other	Subsidies	Other Current Transfers & Property Income	Total Current Disbursements	Gross Capital Formation	Other Capital Outlays	Total Outlays
A Fuel and energy	36000	...	...	...	434000	470000	81000	...	551000
B Agriculture, forestry, fishing and hunting	53000	...	...	...	1000	54000	27000	...	81000
C Mining (except fuels), manufacturing and construction	28000	...	...	...	2000	30000	2000	...	32000
D Transportation and communication	111000	...	...	...	47000	158000	235000	...	393000
E Other economic affairs	13000	...	...	...	11000	24000	42000	...	66000
10 Other functions	73000	...	...	...	494000	567000	1000	...	568000
Total abc	1498000	...	...	...	1515000	3013000	760000	...	3773000

a) Government final consumption expenditure in this table includes compensation of employees and intermediate consumption of the following departmental enterprises: electricity, gas and steam, water works and supply and medical and other health services.
b) Column 5 (Other current transfers and property income) includes current transfers n.e.c. and social security benefits. Column 8 (Other capital outlays) includes purchases of land, net, capital transfers and increase in stocks.
c) Beginning 1984, the estimates of total gross fixed capital formation (column 9) shown in this table is different from the estimates shown in table 3.13. This is because some functions of the general government which are included in the detailed account of table 3.13 could not be allocated to the items included in this table.

2.5 Private Final Consumption Expenditure by Type and Purpose, in Current Prices

Thousand Million Ecuadoran sucres

	1980	1983	1984	1985	1986	1987	1988	1989	1990	1991	1992	1993
Final Consumption Expenditure of Resident Households												
1 Food, beverages and tobacco	61	146	211	275	348	453	759	1435	2181	3277	5088	7326
A Food	49	124	178	233	290	374	632	1203	1831	2730	4251	6052
B Non-alcoholic beverages	2	5	8	11	17	22	34	59	85	131	209	311
C Alcoholic beverages	6	11	16	21	26	34	56	103	164	251	391	622
D Tobacco	3	6	9	10	15	23	36	71	101	165	237	341
2 Clothing and footwear	18	35	57	78	105	142	248	394	567	838	1243	1790
3 Gross rent, fuel and power a	20	33	42	51	63	82	117	193	288	443	664	1011
A Fuel and power a	3	6	7	9	13	18	25	43	65	107	172	269
B Other	17	27	34	42	50	64	92	151	224	336	492	742
4 Furniture, furnishings and household equipment and operation	13	20	31	43	67	106	178	300	438	626	942	1285
5 Medical care and health expenses	7	14	20	27	38	54	87	154	230	354	594	893
6 Transport and communication a	18	45	54	89	114	163	257	451	720	1078	1666	2690
7 Recreational, entertainment, education and cultural services	...	...	...	...	...	...	...	...	...	...	...	...
8 Miscellaneous goods and services	37	76	105	144	192	272	444	791	1215	1835	2982	4460
A Personal care	...	...	...	...	...	...	...	...	...	...	...	...
B Expenditures in restaurants, cafes and hotels	8	16	21	26	34	45	68	131	232	357	575	851
C Other	29	60	84	117	158	226	376	660	983	1478	2407	3609
Total Final Consumption Expenditure in the Domestic Market by Households, of which	173	369	520	708	927	1271	2089	3719	5639	8451	13179	19455
Plus: Direct purchases abroad by resident households	2	1	-	8	-2	-2	-2	-12	-17	-19	-32	-81
Less: Direct purchases in the domestic market by non-resident households	-	-	-	-	-	-	-	-	-	-	-	...
Equals: Final Consumption Expenditure of Resident Households b	175	369	521	716	926	1269	2087	3706	5622	8432	13147	19374
Final Consumption Expenditure of Private Non-profit Institutions Serving Households												
Equals: Final Consumption Expenditure of Private Non-profit Organisations Serving Households	...	...	...	...	...	...	...	...	...	...	...	...
Private Final Consumption Expenditure	175	369	521	716	926	1269	2087	3706	5622	8432	13147	19374

a) Fuel is included in item 'Transport and communication'.
b) Item 'Final consumption expenditure of resident households' includes consumption expenditure of private non-profit institutions serving households.

Ecuador

2.6 Private Final Consumption Expenditure by Type and Purpose, in Constant Prices

Million Ecuadoran sucres

At constant prices of: 1975

Final Consumption Expenditure of Resident Households

	1980	1983	1984	1985	1986	1987	1988	1989	1990	1991	1992	1993
1 Food, beverages and tobacco	35303	35320	36170	36647	37052	37693	38645	39332	39512	40067	40841	42048
A Food	29339	29741	30531	30876	31276	31869	32870	33405	33594	34089	34709	35712
B Non-alcoholic beverages	1328	1488	1522	1522	1518	1496	1497	1525	1567	1574	1623	1662
C Alcoholic beverages	3554	3216	3190	3291	3267	3337	3400	3525	3470	3546	3629	3781
D Tobacco	1082	875	927	958	991	991	878	877	881	858	880	893
2 Clothing and footwear	11167	11510	11711	11803	11653	11783	12073	12298	12623	12782	13130	13441
3 Gross rent, fuel and power [a]	9845	11005	11456	12285	12822	13395	13744	14221	14806	15865	15826	16150
A Fuel and power [a]	1593	2255	2457	2719	3004	3263	3347	3566	3828	4162	4321	4392
B Other	8252	8750	8999	9566	9818	10132	10397	10655	10978	11703	11505	10758
4 Furniture, furnishings and household equipment and operation	7365	5808	5482	5767	6330	6510	6585	6655	6747	6553	7096	7240
5 Medical care and health expenses	3655	4469	4436	4881	4866	5412	5142	4965	5081	5212	5368	5470
6 Transport and communication [a]	9998	11323	11521	12126	12585	12842	13701	14456	15468	16028	16486	17098
7 Recreational, entertainment, education and cultural services	...	...	...	...	...	...	...	...	...	...	...	...
8 Miscellaneous goods and services	20516	23021	24537	25076	26127	26581	26680	27741	28421	29029	29738	30435
A Personal care	...	...	...	...	...	...	...	...	...	...	...	...
B Expenditures in restaurants, cafes and hotels	4451	4905	4980	4995	5074	5263	5464	5668	5825	5956	6094	6215
C Other	16065	18116	19557	20081	21053	21318	21216	22073	22596	23073	23644	24220
Total Final Consumption Expenditure in the Domestic Market by Households, of which	97849	102456	105313	108585	111435	114216	116570	119668	122658	125536	128485	131882
Plus: Direct purchases abroad by resident households	1837	1329	1284	1856	-38	-101	-258	-443	-399	-272	-378	-550
Less: Direct purchases in the domestic market by non-resident households	-	-	-	-	-	-	-	-	-	-	-	...
Equals: Final Consumption Expenditure of Resident Households [b]	99686	103785	106597	110441	111397	114115	116312	119225	122259	125264	128107	131332

Final Consumption Expenditure of Private Non-profit Institutions Serving Households

	1980	1983	1984	1985	1986	1987	1988	1989	1990	1991	1992	1993
Equals: Final Consumption Expenditure of Private Non-profit Organisations Serving Households	...	...	...	...	...	...	...	...	...	...	...	...
Private Final Consumption Expenditure	99686	103785	106597	110441	111397	114115	116312	119225	122259	125264	128107	131332

a) Fuel is included in item 'Transport and communication'.
b) Item 'Final consumption expenditure of resident households' includes consumption expenditure of private non-profit institutions serving households.

2.7 Gross Capital Formation by Type of Good and Owner, in Current Prices

Million Ecuadoran sucres

	1980				1985				1990			
	TOTAL	Total Private	Public Enterprises	General Government	TOTAL	Total Private	Public Enterprises	General Government	TOTAL	Total Private	Public Enterprises	General Government
Increase in stocks, total	7304	5647	945	712	23442	20440	1972	1030	-77000	-185000	103000	4000
Gross Fixed Capital Formation, Total	69326	42001	8479	18846	178255	106054	18088	54113	1512000	966000	219000	328000
1 Residential buildings	8456	8447	...	9	25126	25111	...	15	144000	144000	...	-
2 Non-residential buildings	10864	6824	1087	2953	27903	18019	1286	8598	189000	116000	11000	61000
3 Other construction	17613	419	4256	12938	50622	2016	10406	38200	354000	8000	114000	232000
4 Land improvement and plantation and orchard development	...	...	...	...	...	...	...	...	...	...	...	...
5 Producers' durable goods	31739	25657	3136	2946	70146	56458	6395	7293	799000	671000	94000	34000
6 Breeding stock, dairy cattle, etc.	654	654	-	-	4458	4450	1	7	27000	27000	...	-
Total Gross Capital Formation	76630	47648	9424	19558	201697	126494	20060	55143	1435000	781000	323000	332000

Ecuador

2.7 Gross Capital Formation by Type of Good and Owner, in Current Prices

Million Ecuadoran sucres

	1991 TOTAL	Total Private	Public Enterprises	General Government	1992 TOTAL	Total Private	Public Enterprises	General Government	1993 TOTAL	Total Private	Public Enterprises	General Government
Increase in stocks, total	309000	192000	112000	5000	333000	198000	126000	9000	330000	157000	161000	12000
Gross Fixed Capital Formation, Total	2416000	1511000	435000	470000	3784000	2339000	691000	754000	5457000	3324000	1137000	996000
1 Residential buildings	241000	241000	...	-	347000	347000	...	-	502000	502000	...	...
2 Non-residential buildings	291000	182000	14000	95000	464000	264000	36000	164000	619000	411000	24000	184000
3 Other construction	554000	5000	219000	330000	784000	6000	281000	497000	1275000	10000	540000	725000
4 Land improvement and plantation and orchard development	...	...	...	...	...	...	...	...	...	...	...	...
5 Producers' durable goods	1286000	1039000	202000	45000	2132000	1665000	374000	93000	2971000	2311000	573000	87000
6 Breeding stock, dairy cattle, etc.	44000	44000	...	-	57000	57000	...	-	90000	90000	...	...
Total Gross Capital Formation	2725000	1703000	547000	475000	4117000	2537000	817000	763000	5787000	3481000	1298000	1008000

2.8 Gross Capital Formation by Type of Good and Owner, in Constant Prices

Million Ecuadoran sucres

	1980 TOTAL	Total Private	Public Enterprises	General Government	1985 TOTAL	Total Private	Public Enterprises	General Government	1990 TOTAL	Total Private	Public Enterprises	General Government
					At constant prices of:1975							
Increase in stocks, total	4241	...	...	...	3357	...	...	...	-512	...	...	...
Gross Fixed Capital Formation, Total	34975	22447	4096	8432	24618	14818	2623	7177	23961	14436	4344	5181
1 Residential buildings									...	...	...	
2 Non-residential buildings	16016	7041	2258	6717	14399	6694	1547	6158	11559			4646
3 Other construction									...	...		
4 Land improvement and plantation and orchard development									...	...		
5 Producers' durable goods	18576	15023	1838	1715	9594	7501	1075	1018	11660	...	...	535
6 Breeding stock, dairy cattle, etc.	383	383	-	-	625	623	1	1	742	...	...	-
Total Gross Capital Formation	39216	...	...	...	27975	...	...	...	23449	...	...	...

	1991 TOTAL	Total Private	Public Enterprises	General Government	1992 TOTAL	Total Private	Public Enterprises	General Government	1993 TOTAL	Total Private	Public Enterprises	General Government
					At constant prices of:1975							
Increase in stocks, total	3850	...	...	...	1650	...	...	...	94	...	...	...
Gross Fixed Capital Formation, Total	26602	17034	4572	4996	28434	18071	5011	5352	28742	18216	5780	4746
1 Residential buildings			...	...			...	...			...	...
2 Non-residential buildings	3077	3077	149	1046	2783	2783	262	1188	2536	2536	117	885
3 Other construction			2289	3447			1953	3443			2499	3358
4 Land improvement and plantation and orchard development			...	...			...	...			...	...
5 Producers' durable goods	13754	11117	2134	503	16117	12600	2796	721	16499	12832	3164	503
6 Breeding stock, dairy cattle, etc.	775	775	...	-	737	737	...	...	816	816	...	...
Total Gross Capital Formation	30452	...	...	...	30084	...	...	...	28836	...	...	...

2.17 Exports and Imports of Goods and Services, Detail

Million Ecuadoran sucres

	1980	1983	1984	1985	1986	1987	1988	1989	1990	1991	1992	1993
				Exports of Goods and Services								
1 Exports of merchandise, f.o.b.	64389	110999	183425	255387	250181	348095	673104	1221020	2251000	3214000	5075000	5813000
2 Transport and communication	5116	9849	12580	23143	33623	44672	99865	173105	250000	389000	658000	828000
A In respect of merchandise imports	1939	...	...	...	...	...	...	...	...	...	...	...
B Other	3177	...	...	...	...	...	...	...	...	...	...	...
3 Insurance service charges	98	129	189	485	448	525	437	563	1000	1000	...	3000
A In respect of merchandise imports	96	...	...	...	...	...	...	...	...	...	...	...
B Other	2	...	...	...	...	...	...	...	...	...	...	...

Ecuador

2.17 Exports and Imports of Goods and Services, Detail
(Continued)

Million Ecuadoran sucres

	1980	1983	1984	1985	1986	1987	1988	1989	1990	1991	1992	1993
4 Other commodities	499	1440	1521	483	1141	656	1131	3221	5000	11000	28000	41000
5 Adjustments of merchandise exports to change-of-ownership basis	-	-	-	-	-	-	-	-	-	-	...	...
6 Direct purchases in the domestic market by non-residential households	3270	9960	11072	15790	26410	33114	77696	108989	159000	214000	314000	409000
7 Direct purchases in the domestic market by extraterritorial bodies	425	684	1071	1634	2937	4476	6829	13192	20000	29000	43000	90000
Total Exports of Goods and Services [a]	73797	133061	209858	296922	314740	431538	859062	1520090	2686000	3858000	6119000	7184000
				Imports of Goods and Services								
1 Imports of merchandise, c.i.f.	63512	85154	127264	177399	242639	448150	725271	1317900	1811000	3053000	4465000	5816000
A Imports of merchandise, f.o.b.	56881	...	...	...	...	...	...	...	...	...	...	...
B Transport of services on merchandise imports	6591	...	...	...	...	...	...	...	...	...	...	...
By residents	1378	...	...	...	...	...	...	...	...	...	...	...
By non-residents	5213	...	...	...	...	...	...	...	...	...	...	...
C Insurance service charges on merchandise imports	40	...	...	...	...	...	...	...	...	...	...	...
By residents	40	...	...	...	...	...	...	...	...	...	...	...
By non-residents	...	...	...	...	...	...	...	...	...	...	...	...
2 Adjustments of merchandise imports to change-of-ownership basis	...	...	...	...	...	...	...	...	...	...	...	...
3 Other transport and communication	3128	6614	7690	18469	25080	31941	69728	97585	142000	222000	339000	414000
4 Other insurance service charges	392	2316	975	1677	4882	6432	8034	25915	40000	34000	21000	89000
5 Other commodities	1290	4846	8185	7855	11110	18811	32049	48780	74000	108000	198000	250000
6 Direct purchases abroad by government	500	458	911	830	1161	2656	5158	10788	16000	14000	29000	42000
7 Direct purchases abroad by resident households	5705	11229	12387	25438	27635	35712	82135	109783	162000	224000	326000	400000
Total Imports of Goods and Services	74527	110617	157412	231668	312507	543702	922375	1610751	2246000	3655000	5378000	7011000
Balance of Goods and Services	-730	22444	52446	65254	2233	-112164	-63313	-90661	440000	203000	741000	173000
Total Imports and Balance of Goods and Services [a]	73797	133061	209858	296922	314740	431538	859062	1520090	2686000	3858000	6119000	7184000

a) Data for this table have not been revised, therefore, data for some years are not comparable with those of other tables.

3.11 General Government Production Account: Total and Subsectors

Million Ecuadoran sucres

	1980					1985				
	Total General Government	Central Government	State or Provincial Government	Local Government	Social Security Funds	Total General Government	Central Government	State or Provincial Government	Local Government	Social Security Funds
					Gross Output					
1 Sales	5612	2853	...	847	1912	20111	11764	...	1762	6585
2 Services produced for own use	1897	869	...	971	57	6244	3770	...	2429	45
3 Own account fixed capital formation	43080	36792	...	5098	1190	128135	107261	...	16794	4080
Gross Output [a]	50589	40514	...	6916	3159	154490	122795	...	20985	10710
					Gross Input					
Intermediate Consumption	21153	18156	...	2184	813	57591	48346	...	5856	3389
Subtotal: Value Added	29436	22358	...	4732	2346	96899	74449	...	15129	7321
1 Indirect taxes, net	...	...	...	...	...	...	...	...	...	...
2 Consumption of fixed capital [b]	...	...	...	...	...	...	...	...	...	...
3 Compensation of employees	29136	21954	...	4836	2346	95183	72600	...	15262	7321
4 Net Operating surplus [b]	300	404	...	-104	...	1716	1849	...	-133	...
Gross Input [a]	50589	40514	...	6916	3159	154490	122795	...	20985	10710

Ecuador

3.11 General Government Production Account: Total and Subsectors

Million Ecuadoran sucres

	1990					1991				
	Total General Government	Central Government	State or Provincial Government	Local Government	Social Security Funds	Total General Government	Central Government	State or Provincial Government	Local Government	Social Security Funds
Gross Output										
1 Sales	126000	73000	...	6000	47000	174207	97881	...	8074	68252
2 Services produced for own use	65000	48000	...	17000	-	69969	52726	...	17243	-
3 Own account fixed capital formation	709000	596000	...	88000	25000	939365	773428	...	130666	35271
Gross Output a	901000	717000	...	111000	72000	1183541	924035	...	155983	103523
Gross Input										
Intermediate Consumption	457000	392000	...	34000	31000	594144	501808	...	49640	42696
Subtotal: Value Added	444000	325000	...	78000	41000	589397	422227	...	106343	60827
1 Indirect taxes, net	...	...	...	...	...	...	...	...	...	...
2 Consumption of fixed capital b	...	...	...	...	...	...	...	...	...	...
3 Compensation of employees	446000	327000	...	78000	41000	591189	424019	...	106343	60827
4 Net Operating surplus b	-2000	1000	...	-	...	-1792	-1792	...	-	...
Gross Input a	901000	717000	...	111000	72000	1183541	924035	...	155983	103523

	1992			
	Total General Government	Central Government	State or Provincial Government	Local Government	Social Security Funds
Gross Output				
1 Sales	304860	150571	...	13059	141230
2 Services produced for own use	85849	63089	...	22760	-
3 Own account fixed capital formation	1396324	1165545	...	166602	64177
Gross Output a	1787033	1379205	...	202421	205407
Gross Input				
Intermediate Consumption	798775	631505	...	68294	98976
Subtotal: Value Added	988258	747700	...	134127	106431
1 Indirect taxes, net	...	...	...	...	...
2 Consumption of fixed capital b	...	...	...	...	...
3 Compensation of employees	990498	749940	...	134127	106431
4 Net Operating surplus b	-2240	-2240	...	-	...
Gross Input a	1787033	1379205	...	202421	205407

a) Data for this table have not been revised, therefore, data for some years are not comparable with those of other tables.
b) Item 'Operating surplus' includes consumption of fixed capital.

3.12 General Government Income and Outlay Account: Total and Subsectors

Million Ecuadoran sucres

	1980					1985				
	Total General Government	Central Government	State or Provincial Government	Local Government	Social Security Funds	Total General Government	Central Government	State or Provincial Government	Local Government	Social Security Funds
Receipts										
1 Operating surplus	300	404	...	-104	-	1716	1849	...	-133	-
2 Property and entrepreneurial income	10954	7656	...	342	2956	31298	21581	...	854	8863
A Withdrawals from public quasi-corporations	...	...	...	...	...	...	...	...	...	...
B Interest	2974	70	...	34	2870	9345	582	...	168	8595
C Dividends	104	-	...	18	86	1768	1479	...	21	268
D Net land rent and royalties	7876	7586	...	290	-	20185	19520	...	665	-
3 Taxes, fees and contributions	58631	46156	...	4349	8126	273900	237713	...	11072	25115
A Indirect taxes	26931	25393	...	1538	-	152141	146672	...	5469	-
B Direct taxes	22390	19906	...	2484	-	93216	88541	...	4675	-
Income	22025	19770	...	2255	-	92169	88284	...	3885	-
Other	365	136	...	229	-	1047	257	...	790	-
C Social security contributions	8092	-	...	-	8092	25042	-	...	-	25042
D Fees, fines and penalties	1218	857	...	327	34	3501	2500	...	928	73

Ecuador

3.12 General Government Income and Outlay Account: Total and Subsectors
(Continued)

Million Ecuadoran sucres

	1980					1985				
	Total General Government	Central Government	State or Provincial Government	Local Government	Social Security Funds	Total General Government	Central Government	State or Provincial Government	Local Government	Social Security Funds
4 Other current transfers	10540	2561	...	7896	83	44256	21138	...	22755	363
A Casualty insurance claims	...	...	...	...	...	...	...	...	...	...
B Transfers from other government subsectors	8072	270	...	7763	39	21748	306	...	21433	9
C Transfers from the rest of the world	931	931	...	-	-	2853	2853	...	-	-
D Other transfers, except imputed	943	922	...	21	-	16181	15245	...	936	-
E Imputed unfunded employee pension and welfare contributions	594	438	...	112	44	3474	2734	...	386	354
Total Current Receipts	80425	56777	...	12483	11165	351170	282281	...	34548	34341
	Disbursements										
1 Government final consumption expenditure	42562	36645	...	4727	1190	127330	107046	...	16204	4080
2 Property income	7590	6515	...	219	856	48591	43042	...	1707	3842
A Interest	7588	6513	...	219	856	48591	43042	...	1707	3842
B Net land rent and royalties	2	2	...	-	-	-	-	...	-	-
3 Subsidies	2543	2543	...	-	-	23762	23741	...	21	-
4 Other current transfers	16916	9365	...	724	6827	49195	27044	...	1077	21074
A Casualty insurance premiums, net	...	...	...	...	...	...	...	...	...	...
B Transfers to other government subsectors	8072	7802	...	257	13	21748	21442	...	272	34
C Social security benefits	6746	-	...	-	6746	20673	-	...	-	20673
D Social assistance grants	1353	974	...	355	24	2625	2193	...	419	13
E Unfunded employee pension and welfare benefits	594	438	...	112	44	3474	2734	...	386	354
F Transfers to private non-profit institutions serving households	...	...	...	...	...	...	...	...	...	...
G Other transfers n.e.c.	46	46	...	-	-	71	71	...	-	-
H Transfers to the rest of the world	105	105	...	-	-	604	604	...	-	-
Net saving a	10814	1709	...	6813	2292	102292	81408	...	15539	5345
Total Current Disbursements and Net Saving	80425	56777	...	12483	11165	351170	282281	...	34548	34341

	1990					1991				
	Total General Government	Central Government	State or Provincial Government	Local Government	Social Security Funds	Total General Government	Central Government	State or Provincial Government	Local Government	Social Security Funds
	Receipts										
1 Operating surplus	-2000	-1000	...	...	-	-2000	-2000	...	-	-
2 Property and entrepreneurial income	235000	194000	...	8000	33000	232000	171000	...	7000	54000
A Withdrawals from public quasi-corporations	...	...	...	...	...	...	...	...	...	...
B Interest	39000	2000	...	5000	31000	57000	2000	...	5000	50000
C Dividends	5000	3000	...	1000	1000	8000	4000	...	...	4000
D Net land rent and royalties	191000	189000	...	2000	-	167000	166000	...	2000	-
3 Taxes, fees and contributions	1870000	1619000	...	53000	198000	2588000	2202000	...	88000	298000
A Indirect taxes	1279000	1243000	...	36000	-	1706000	1645000	...	61000	-
B Direct taxes	373000	361000	...	12000	-	555000	535000	...	20000	-
Income	367000	361000	...	6000	-	542000	534000	...	8000	-
Other	6000	...	...	6000	-	13000	1000	...	12000	-
C Social security contributions	197000	-	...	-	197000	297000	...	...	-	297000
D Fees, fines and penalties	21000	15000	...	5000	1000	30000	22000	...	7000	1000
4 Other current transfers	260000	89000	...	167000	3000	345000	118000	...	221000	6000
A Casualty insurance claims	...	...	...	...	...	...	...	...	...	...
B Transfers from other government subsectors	...	...	...	...	...	...	...	...	...	...
C Transfers from the rest of the world	7000	7000	...	...	-	3000	1000	...	2000	-
D Other transfers, except imputed	232000	71000	...	161000	...	313000	103000	...	210000	...
E Imputed unfunded employee pension and welfare contributions	21000	11000	...	7000	3000	29000	14000	...	9000	6000

Ecuador

3.12 General Government Income and Outlay Account: Total and Subsectors
(Continued)

Million Ecuadoran sucres

	1990					1991				
	Total General Government	Central Government	State or Provincial Government	Local Government	Social Security Funds	Total General Government	Central Government	State or Provincial Government	Local Government	Social Security Funds
Total Current Receipts	2363000	1902000	...	228000	233000	3161000	2489000	...	314000	357000

Disbursements

	Total	Central	State	Local	SSF	Total	Central	State	Local	SSF
1 Government final consumption expenditure	706000	596000	...	85000	25000	935000	773000	...	127000	35000
2 Property income	332000	325000	...	1000	5000	338000	330000	...	4000	4000
A Interest	332000	325000	...	1000	5000	338000	330000	...	4000	4000
B Net land rent and royalties	...	...	...	...	...	...	...	...	...	...
3 Subsidies	146000	146000	...	-	-	263000	263000	...	-	-
4 Other current transfers	351000	191000	...	15000	144000	475000	246000	...	19000	210000
A Casualty insurance premiums, net	...	...	...	...	...	...	...	...	...	...
B Transfers to other government subsectors	...	...	...	...	...	...	...	...	...	...
C Social security benefits	141000	-	...	-	141000	204000	-	...	-	204000
D Social assistance grants	...	...	...	...	...	...	...	...	...	...
E Unfunded employee pension and welfare benefits	21000	11000	...	7000	3000	29000	14000	...	9000	6000
F Transfers to private non-profit institutions serving households	185000	176000	...	9000	...	...	...	...	...	...
G Other transfers n.e.c.	...	...	...	...	...	237000	227000	...	10000	...
H Transfers to the rest of the world	4000	4000	...	-	...	5000	5000	...	-	...
Net saving a	829000	644000	...	126000	59000	1149000	876000	...	163000	108000
Total Current Disbursements and Net Saving	2363000	1902000	...	228000	233000	3160000	2489000	...	314000	357000

	1992					1993				
	Total General Government	Central Government	State or Provincial Government	Local Government	Social Security Funds	Total General Government	Central Government	State or Provincial Government	Local Government	Social Security Funds

Receipts

	Total	Central	State	Local	SSF	Total	Central	State	Local	SSF
1 Operating surplus	-2000	-2000	...	-	-	-3000	-3000	...	...	...
2 Property and entrepreneurial income	301000	206000	...	8000	87000	383000	279000	...	9000	95000
A Withdrawals from public quasi-corporations	...	...	...	...	...	...	...	...	...	...
B Interest	84000	2000	...	5000	77000	91000	3000	...	6000	82000
C Dividends	16000	5000	...	...	11000	20000	7000	...	-	13000
D Net land rent and royalties	201000	199000	...	2000	-	271000	269000	...	2000	...
3 Taxes, fees and contributions	3843000	3254000	...	131000	458000	5383000	4592000	...	163000	628000
A Indirect taxes	2626000	2534000	...	92000	-	3649000	3528000	...	121000	...
B Direct taxes	721000	692000	...	29000	-	1051000	1021000	...	30000	...
Income	701000	691000	...	10000	-	1034000	1020000	...	14000	...
Other	20000	1000	...	19000	-	17000	1000	...	16000	...
C Social security contributions	457000	-	...	-	457000	625000	...	...	...	625000
D Fees, fines and penalties	39000	28000	...	10000	1000	58000	43000	...	12000	3000
4 Other current transfers	457000	149000	...	301000	7000	676000	218000	...	450000	8000
A Casualty insurance claims	...	...	...	...	...	...	...	...	...	...
B Transfers from other government subsectors	289000	...	...	289000	...	597000	161000	...	436000	...
C Transfers from the rest of the world	14000	13000	...	1000	-	17000	16000	...	1000	...
D Other transfers, except imputed	112000	112000	...	...	...	...	...	...	...	...
E Imputed unfunded employee pension and welfare contributions	41000	24000	...	11000	6000	62000	41000	...	13000	8000
Total Current Receipts	4599000	3607000	...	439000	553000	6439000	5085000	...	622000	732000

Disbursements

	Total	Central	State	Local	SSF	Total	Central	State	Local	SSF
1 Government final consumption expenditure	1407000	1174000	...	163000	70000	2117000	1800000	...	212000	105000
2 Property income	499000	488000	...	6000	5000	543000	518000	...	8000	17000
A Interest	499000	488000	...	6000	5000	543000	518000	...	8000	17000
B Net land rent and royalties	...	...	...	...	...	...	...	...	...	...
3 Subsidies	318000	318000	...	-	-	378000	378000	...	...	...

Ecuador

3.12 General Government Income and Outlay Account: Total and Subsectors
(Continued)

Million Ecuadoran sucres

		1992				1993				
		Total General Government	Central Government	State or Provincial Government	Local Government	Social Security Funds	Total General Government	Central Government	State or Provincial Government	Local Government	Social Security Funds
4	Other current transfers	757000	352000	...	24000	382000	1030000	...	...	...	477000
	A Casualty insurance premiums, net	...	...	...	...	...	...	...	...	...	...
	B Transfers to other government subsectors	...	...	...	...	...	...	...	...	...	...
	C Social security benefits	375000	-	...	-	375000	469000	...	...	...	469000
	D Social assistance grants	...	...	...	...	...	...	...	...	...	...
	E Unfunded employee pension and welfare benefits	41000	23000	...	11000	7000	61000	41000	...	13000	8000
	F Transfers to private non-profit institutions serving households	334000	334000	...	...	...	...	...	...	...	...
	G Other transfers n.e.c.	...	...	...	...	...	...	...	...	...	...
	H Transfers to the rest of the world	8000	8000	...	-	...	...	...	...	...	...
	Net saving [a]	1616000	1275000	...	248000	93000	2371000	1869000	...	374000	128000
	Total Current Disbursements and Net Saving	4599000	3607000	...	439000	553000	6439000	5085000	...	622000	732000

a) Item 'Net saving' includes consumption of fixed capital.

3.13 General Government Capital Accumulation Account: Total and Subsectors

Million Ecuadoran sucres

		1980					1985				
		Total General Government	Central Government	State or Provincial Government	Local Government	Social Security Funds	Total General Government	Central Government	State or Provincial Government	Local Government	Social Security Funds
					Finance of Gross Accumulation						
1	Gross saving	10814	1709	...	6813	2292	102292	81408	...	15539	5345
2	Capital transfers	...	...	...	...	...	...	...	...	...	...
	Finance of Gross Accumulation	10814	1709	...	6813	2292	102292	81408	...	15539	5345
					Gross Accumulation						
1	Gross capital formation	19558	12810	...	5833	915	55143	36644	...	15684	2815
	A Increase in stocks	712	...	...	...	712	1030	...	...	...	1030
	B Gross fixed capital formation	18846	12810	...	5833	203	54113	36644	...	15684	1785
2	Purchases of land, net	200	170	...	-40	70	-280	-60	...	-220	-
3	Purchases of intangible assets, net	...	...	...	...	...	...	...	...	...	...
4	Capital transfers	1820	1385	...	435	-	1603	913	...	690	-
	A To other government subsectors	...	...	...	...	...	...	...	...	...	...
	B To other resident sectors	1820	1385	...	435	...	1603	913	...	690	...
	C To rest of the world	...	...	...	...	...	...	...	...	...	...
	Net lending [a]	-10764	-12656	...	585	1307	45826	43911	...	-615	2530
	Gross Accumulation	10814	1709	...	6813	2292	102292	81408	...	15539	5345
		1990					1991				
		Total General Government	Central Government	State or Provincial Government	Local Government	Social Security Funds	Total General Government	Central Government	State or Provincial Government	Local Government	Social Security Funds
					Finance of Gross Accumulation						
1	Gross saving	829000	644000	...	126000	59000	1149000	876000	...	165000	108000
2	Capital transfers	...	...	...	...	...	...	...	...	...	...
	Finance of Gross Accumulation	829000	644000	...	126000	59000	1149000	876000	...	165000	108000
					Gross Accumulation						
1	Gross capital formation	332000	235000	...	84000	12000	475000	331000	...	123000	21000
	A Increase in stocks	4000	4000	...	...	...	5000	5000	...	...	...
	B Gross fixed capital formation	328000	232000	...	84000	12000	470000	326000	...	123000	21000
2	Purchases of land, net	-1000	...	...	-1000	...	-1000	...	...	-2000	-
3	Purchases of intangible assets, net	...	...	...	...	...	...	...	...	...	...
4	Capital transfers	89000	83000	...	6000	-	177000	168000	...	9000	-
	A To other government subsectors	...	...	...	...	...	...	...	...	...	...
	B To other resident sectors	89000	83000	...	6000	-	173000	165000	...	8000	-
	C To rest of the world	...	...	...	...	...	...	...	...	...	...
	Net lending [a]	409000	325000	...	37000	47000	497000	377000	...	34000	87000
	Gross Accumulation	829000	644000	...	126000	59000	1149000	876000	...	165000	108000

Ecuador

3.13 General Government Capital Accumulation Account: Total and Subsectors
Million Ecuadoran sucres

	1992 Total General Government	1992 Central Government	1992 State or Provincial Government	1992 Local Government	1992 Social Security Funds	1993 Total General Government	1993 Central Government	1993 State or Provincial Government	1993 Local Government	1993 Social Security Funds
Finance of Gross Accumulation										
1 Gross saving	1616000	1275000	...	248000	93000	2371000	1869000	...	374000	128000
2 Capital transfers	...	...	...	...	...	...	...	...	...	...
Finance of Gross Accumulation	1616000	1275000	...	248000	93000	2371000	1869000	...	374000	128000
Gross Accumulation										
1 Gross capital formation	762000	508000	...	179000	75000	1009000	758000	...	230000	20000
A Increase in stocks	9000	8000	...	-	...	13000	11000	...	1000	...
B Gross fixed capital formation	753000	500000	...	178000	75000	996000	747000	...	229000	20000
2 Purchases of land, net	1000	1000	...	...	-	1000	1000	...	...	...
3 Purchases of intangible assets, net	...	...	...	...	...	...	...	...	...	...
4 Capital transfers	276000	261000	...	15000	...	417000	413000	...	4000	...
A To other government subsectors	...	...	...	...	...	...	...	...	...	...
B To other resident sectors	...	...	...	...	...	...	...	...	...	...
C To rest of the world	...	...	...	...	...	...	...	...	...	...
Net lending [a]	577000	505000	...	54000	18000	944000	697000	...	140000	108000
Gross Accumulation	1616000	1275000	...	248000	93000	2371000	1869000	...	374000	128000

a) Net lending of the capital accumulation account and the capital finance account have not been reconciled and are different due to different statistical sources.

3.21 Corporate and Quasi-Corporate Enterprise Production Account: Total and Sectors
Thousand Million Ecuadoran sucres

	1980 TOTAL	1980 Non-Financial	1980 Financial	ADDENDUM: Total, including Unincorporated	1985 TOTAL	1985 Non-Financial	1985 Financial	ADDENDUM: Total, including Unincorporated	1990 TOTAL	1990 Non-Financial	1990 Financial	ADDENDUM: Total, including Unincorporated
Gross Output												
1 Output for sale	206	201	5	...	830	817	13	...	6320	6210	110	...
2 Imputed bank service charge	9	-	9	...	22	-	22	...	149	-	149	...
3 Own-account fixed capital formation	...	...	...	...	...	...	...	...	...	...	...	...
Gross Output [a]	215	201	14	...	852	817	35	...	6469	6210	259	...
Gross Input												
Intermediate consumption	120	108	12	...	473	436	37	...	4259	3983	276	...
1 Imputed banking service charge	9	-	9	...	22	-	22	...	149	-	149	...
2 Other intermediate consumption	111	108	3	...	451	436	15	...	4111	3983	128	...
Subtotal: Value Added [a]	96	93	2	...	379	381	-2	...	2209	2227	-17	...
1 Indirect taxes, net	10	9	-	...	77	74	3	...	646	638	8	...
A Indirect taxes	11	11	-	...	100	97	3	...	792	784	8	...
B Less: Subsidies	2	2	-	...	24	24	-	...	146	146	-	...
2 Consumption of fixed capital [b]	...	...	...	...	...	...	...	...	...	...	...	...
3 Compensation of employees	34	29	5	...	89	71	18	...	495	363	131	...
4 Net operating surplus [b]	52	55	-3	...	214	237	-22	...	1068	1225	-157	...
Gross Input [a]	215	201	14	...	852	817	35	...	6469	6210	259	...

	1991 TOTAL	1991 Non-Financial	1991 Financial	ADDENDUM: Total, including Unincorporated	1992 TOTAL	1992 Non-Financial	1992 Financial	ADDENDUM: Total, including Unincorporated
Gross Output								
1 Output for sale	7928	7783	145	...	14650	14451	199	...
2 Imputed bank service charge	288	-	288	...	446	-	446	...
3 Own-account fixed capital formation	...	...	...	...	...	...	...	...
Gross Output [a]	8216	7783	433	...	15096	14451	644	...
Gross Input								
Intermediate consumption	5311	4846	465	...	9999	9250	749	...
1 Imputed banking service charge	288	-	288	...	446	...	446	...
2 Other intermediate consumption	5023	4846	177	...	9553	9250	303	...
Subtotal: Value Added [a]	2905	2937	-32	...	5097	5201	-104	...

Ecuador

3.21 Corporate and Quasi-Corporate Enterprise Production Account: Total and Sectors
(Continued)

Thousand Million Ecuadoran sucres

		1991				1992		
		Corporate and Quasi-Corporate Enterprises		ADDENDUM: Total, including Unincorporated		Corporate and Quasi-Corporate Enterprises		ADDENDUM: Total, including Unincorporated
	TOTAL	Non-Financial	Financial		TOTAL	Non-Financial	Financial	
1 Indirect taxes, net	768	757	11	...	1206	1188	18	...
A Indirect taxes	1029	1019	11	...	1509	1491	18	...
B Less: Subsidies	261	261	-	...	303	303	-	...
2 Consumption of fixed capital [b]	...	...	...	...	...	...	...	...
3 Compensation of employees	687	478	209	...	1130	762	369	...
4 Net operating surplus [b]	1450	1702	-252	...	2761	3252	-491	...
Gross Input [a]	8216	7783	433	...	15096	14451	644	...

a) Data for this table have not been revised, therefore, data for some years are not comparable with those of other tables.
b) Item 'Operating surplus' includes consumption of fixed capital.

3.22 Corporate and Quasi-Corporate Enterprise Income and Outlay Account: Total and Sectors

Million Ecuadoran sucres

	1980			1985			1990			1991		
	TOTAL	Non-Financial	Financial	TOTAL	Non-Financial	Financial	TOTAL	Non-Financial	Financial	TOTAL	Non-Financial	Financial
						Receipts						
1 Operating surplus [a]	52003	55087	-3084	214248	236520	-22272	1068000	1225000	-157000	1416000	1679000	-263000
2 Property and entrepreneurial income	15780	2948	12832	103952	19890	84062	703000	105000	597000	1177000	180000	997000
A Withdrawals from quasi-corporate enterprises	...	...	...	...	...	...	...	...	...	...	...	...
B Interest	15283	2617	12666	101161	17913	83248	681000	95000	586000	1141000	160000	981000
C Dividends	493	327	166	2791	1977	814	22000	11000	11000	36000	20000	16000
D Net land rent and royalties	4	4	-	-	-	-	...	...	...	...	-	-
3 Current transfers	1786	1473	313	7839	5669	2170	74000	48000	26000	130000	87000	43000
A Casualty insurance claims	619	594	25	2451	2351	100	25000	23000	1000	37000	35000	2000
B Casualty insurance premiums, net, due to be received by insurance companies	197	-	197	1011	-	1011	12000	-	12000	21000	-	21000
C Current transfers from the rest of the world	...	...	...	...	...	...	...	...	...	...	...	...
D Other transfers except imputed	...	...	...	...	...	...	...	...	...	...	...	...
E Imputed unfunded employee pension and welfare contributions	970	879	91	4377	3318	1059	37000	25000	12000	72000	52000	20000
Total Current Receipts	69569	59508	10061	326039	262079	63960	1845000	1379000	467000	2723000	1946000	777000
						Disbursements						
1 Property and entrepreneurial income	32576	27949	4627	186170	120801	65369	1238000	781000	457000	1838000	1109000	729000
A Withdrawals from quasi-corporations	92	16	76	246	168	78	3000	1000	1000	5000	2000	3000
Public	...	...	...	...	...	...	...	...	...	...	...	...
Private	92	16	76	246	168	78	3000	1000	1000	5000	2000	3000
B Interest	17440	13626	3814	129731	67727	62004	817000	374000	444000	1346000	645000	701000
C Dividends [b]	6156	5419	737	29972	26685	3287	191000	179000	12000	270000	245000	25000
D Net land rent and royalties	8888	8888	-	26221	26221	-	227000	227000	-	217000	217000	-
2 Direct taxes and other current transfers n.e.c. to general government	20187	19893	294	86072	85159	913	325000	319000	5000	479000	469000	10000
A Direct taxes	19679	19385	294	84538	83760	778	317000	313000	4000	470000	461000	9000
On income	19585	19291	294	84133	83355	778	315000	311000	4000	466000	457000	9000
Other	94	94	-	405	405	-	2000	2000	-	4000	4000	...
B Fines, fees, penalties and other current transfers n.e.c.	508	508	-	1534	1399	135	8000	7000	1000	9000	8000	1000

Ecuador

3.22 Corporate and Quasi-Corporate Enterprise Income and Outlay Account: Total and Sectors
(Continued)

Million Ecuadoran sucres

	1980 TOTAL	1980 Non-Financial	1980 Financial	1985 TOTAL	1985 Non-Financial	1985 Financial	1990 TOTAL	1990 Non-Financial	1990 Financial	1991 TOTAL	1991 Non-Financial	1991 Financial
3 Other current transfers	2866	1734	1132	25539	20704	4835	148000	115000	32000	230000	177000	53000
A Casualty insurance premiums, net	655	629	26	2484	2363	121	18000	16000	1000	27000	25000	2000
B Casualty insurance claims liability of insurance companies	197	...	197	1011	-	1011	12000	-	12000	21000	-	21000
C Transfers to private non-profit institutions	...	...	...	...	...	...	...	...	...	...	...	...
D Unfunded employee pension and welfare benefits	970	879	91	4377	3318	1059	37000	25000	12000	72000	52000	20000
E Social assistance grants	1035	223	812	17667	15023	2644	...	...	...	...	...	...
F Other transfers n.e.c.	...	...	...	...	...	...	80000	74000	6000	110000	100000	10000
G Transfers to the rest of the world	9	3	6	...	...	...	...	...	...	...	...	...
Net saving c	13940	9932	4008	28258	35415	-7157	135000	163000	-28000	176000	191000	-15000
Total Current Disbursements and Net Saving	69569	59508	10061	326039	262079	63960	1845000	1379000	467000	2723000	1946000	777000

	1992 TOTAL	1992 Non-Financial	1992 Financial	1993 TOTAL	1993 Non-Financial	1993 Financial
Receipts						
1 Operating surplus a	2264000	2749000	-485000	2077000	2865000	-788000
2 Property and entrepreneurial income	1984000	243000	1741000	2756000	356000	2400000
A Withdrawals from quasi-corporate enterprises	...	...	...	...	...	...
B Interest	1949000	222000	1727000	2715000	330000	2385000
C Dividends	35000	21000	14000	41000	26000	15000
D Net land rent and royalties	...	-	-	...	...	...
3 Current transfers	226000	132000	94000	384000	203000	181000
A Casualty insurance claims	56000	52000	4000	77000	66000	11000
B Casualty insurance premiums, net, due to be received by insurance companies	42000	-	42000	51000	...	51000
C Current transfers from the rest of the world	...	...	...	...	...	...
D Other transfers except imputed	1000	...	...	1000	1000	...
E Imputed unfunded employee pension and welfare contributions	128000	80000	48000	256000	137000	119000
Total Current Receipts	4474000	3124000	1350000	5217000	3425000	1793000
Disbursements						
1 Property and entrepreneurial income	2913000	1629000	1284000	3562000	1997000	1565000
A Withdrawals from quasi-corporations	8000	2000	6000	11000	2000	9000
Public	...	...	...	...	...	...
Private	8000	2000	6000	9000	...	9000
B Interest	2269000	1031000	1238000	2705000	1198000	1507000
C Dividends b	365000	325000	40000	475000	426000	49000
D Net land rent and royalties	271000	271000	-	371000	371000	...
2 Direct taxes and other current transfers n.e.c. to general government	592000	576000	16000	833000	811000	22000
A Direct taxes	578000	567000	11000	816000	797000	19000
On income	572000	561000	11000	810000	791000	19000
Other	6000	6000	...	6000	6000	...
B Fines, fees, penalties and other current transfers n.e.c.	14000	9000	5000	17000	14000	3000

Ecuador

3.22 Corporate and Quasi-Corporate Enterprise Income and Outlay Account: Total and Sectors
(Continued)

Million Ecuadoran sucres

		1992			1993	
	TOTAL	Non-Financial	Financial	TOTAL	Non-Financial	Financial
3 Other current transfers	352000	246000	106000	600000	336000	264000
A Casualty insurance premiums, net	52000	47000	5000	90000	67000	23000
B Casualty insurance claims liability of insurance companies	42000	-	42000	51000	-	51000
C Transfers to private non-profit institutions	...	...	...	...	...	...
D Unfunded employee pension and welfare benefits	128000	80000	48000	256000	137000	119000
E Social assistance grants	...	...	...	...	...	...
F Other transfers n.e.c.	130000	119000	11000	203000	132000	71000
G Transfers to the rest of the world	...	...	...	...	...	...
Net saving c	617000	673000	-56000	223000	281000	-58000
Total Current Disbursements and Net Saving	4474000	3124000	1350000	5218000	3425000	1793000

a) Item 'Operating surplus' includes consumption of fixed capital.
b) Item 'Dividends' includes profit-sharing by employees.
c) Item 'Net saving' includes consumption of fixed capital.

3.23 Corporate and Quasi-Corporate Enterprise Capital Accumulation Account: Total and Sectors

Million Ecuadoran sucres

	1980			1985			1990			1991		
	TOTAL	Non-Financial	Financial	TOTAL	Non-Financial	Financial	TOTAL	Non-Financial	Financial	TOTAL	Non-Financial	Financial
Finance of Gross Accumulation											
1 Gross saving	13940	9932	4008	28258	35415	-7157	135000	163000	-28000	177000	192000	-15000
2 Capital transfers a	1405	1755	-350	445	514	-69	85000	94000	-9000	176000	180000	-4000
Finance of Gross Accumulation	15345	11687	3658	28703	35929	-7226	220000	257000	-37000	353000	372000	-19000
Gross Accumulation											
1 Gross capital formation	41606	38647	2959	105736	95741	9995	769000	696000	73000	1622000	1551000	71000
A Increase in stocks	5400	4085	1315	17357	11794	5563	-21000	-73000	52000	256000	221000	35000
B Gross fixed capital formation	36206	34562	1644	88379	83947	4432	790000	769000	21000	1366000	1330000	36000
2 Purchases of land, net	1703	1742	-39	6489	5350	1139	38000	31000	7000	46000	43000	3000
3 Purchases of intangible assets, net	79	79	-	1124	1124	-	16000	16000	-	20000	20000	-
4 Capital transfers	...	...	...	...	...	...	...	...	...	...	...	...
Net lending b	-28043	-28781	738	-84646	-66286	-18360	-602000	-486000	-116000	1335000	1242000	-93000
Gross Accumulation	15345	11687	3658	28703	35929	-7226	220000	257000	-37000	353000	372000	-19000

	1992			1993		
	TOTAL	Non-Financial	Financial	TOTAL	Non-Financial	Financial
Finance of Gross Accumulation						
1 Gross saving	617000	673000	-56000	223000	281000	-58000
2 Capital transfers a	272000	273000	-1000	423000	377000	46000
Finance of Gross Accumulation	889000	946000	-57000	645000	657000	-12000
Gross Accumulation						
1 Gross capital formation	2431000	2352000	79000	3519000	3455000	64000
A Increase in stocks	304000	267000	37000	350000	323000	27000
B Gross fixed capital formation	2127000	2085000	42000	3169000	3132000	37000
2 Purchases of land, net	79000	54000	25000	82000	68000	14000
3 Purchases of intangible assets, net	24000	24000	-	33000	33000	-
4 Capital transfers	...	...	...	...	...	...
Net lending b	1644000	1484000	-160000	2989000	2899000	-90000
Gross Accumulation	889000	946000	-57000	645000	657000	-12000

a) Capital transfers received are recorded net of capital transfers paid.
b) Net lending of the capital accumulation account and the capital finance account have not been reconciled and are different due to different statistical sources.

Ecuador

3.24 Corporate and Quasi-Corporate Enterprise Capital Finance Account: Total and Sectors

Million Ecuadoran sucres

	1980			1985			1990			1991		
	TOTAL	Non-Financial	Financial	TOTAL	Non-Financial	Financial	TOTAL	Non-Financial	Financial	TOTAL	Non-Financial	Financial
Acquisition of Financial Assets											
1 Gold and SDRs	460	-	460	4759	-	4759	63000	...	63000	8000	...	8000
2 Currency and transferable deposits	2955	2245	710	12777	9576	3201	178000	135000	43000	245000	190000	55000
3 Other deposits	9704	1620	8084	14157	-7912	22069	356000	109000	246000	344000	166000	178000
4 Bills and bonds, short term	...	...	...	...	...	...	...	...	...	...	...	...
5 Bonds, long term [a]	3236	904	2332	11245	2755	8490	-11000	...	-11000	43000	33000	10000
6 Corporate equity securities	3535	2463	1072	9247	5294	3953	38000	21000	17000	82000	55000	27000
7 Short term loans, n.e.c.	19602	562	19040	55668	5931	49737	452000	151000	301000	543000	21000	522000
8 Long term loans, n.e.c.	6059	610	5449	64383	355	64028	192000	76000	116000	1244000	87000	1157000
9 Trade credits and advances	19260	15196	4064	82729	65547	17182	847000	642000	205000	1384000	1220000	164000
10 Other receivables	2598	2056	542	41881	18342	23539	48000	32000	16000	134000	118000	16000
11 Other assets	...	...	...	...	...	...	...	...	...	...	...	...
Total Acquisition of Financial Assets	67409	25656	41753	296846	99888	196958	2163000	1166000	997000	4026000	1889000	2137000
Incurrence of Liabilities											
1 Currency and transferable deposits	13429	-	13429	47433	-	47433	476000	-	476000	540000	-	540000
2 Other deposits	14721	1408	13313	91414	7649	83765	647000	86000	561000	769000	84000	685000
3 Bills and bonds, short term	...	...	...	...	...	...	...	...	...	...	...	...
4 Bonds, long term [a]	2715	9	2706	11974	2434	9540	69000	1000	68000	1000	13000	-12000
5 Corporate equity securities	11312	5856	5456	47359	22868	24491	205000	148000	57000	432000	356000	76000
6 Short-term loans, n.e.c.	25215	21547	3668	32247	32784	-537	371000	363000	8000	484000	465000	19000
7 Long-term loans, n.e.c.	5551	4789	762	52217	11612	40605	68000	200000	-132000	1185000	365000	820000
8 Net equity of households in life insurance and pension fund reserves	149	-	149	582	-	582	43000	-	4000	45000	38000	7000
9 Proprietors' net additions to the accumulation of quasi-corporations	...	...	...	...	...	...	...	39000	...	...	...	...
10 Trade credit and advances	14283	12726	1557	81787	71855	9932	795000	672000	122000	1867000	1715000	152000
11 Other accounts payable	1773	1294	479	12914	21033	-8119	133000	123000	9000	186000	170000	16000
12 Other liabilities [b]	-398	...	-398	7804	...	7804	-62000	...	-62000	-78000	...	-78000
Total Incurrence of Liabilities	88750	47629	41121	385731	170235	215496	2744000	1632000	1112000	5432000	3207000	2225000
Net Lending [c]	-21341	-21973	632	-88885	-70347	-18538	-581000	-466000	-115000	1405000	1317000	-88000
Incurrence of Liabilities and Net Lending	67409	25656	41753	296846	99888	196958	2163000	1166000	997000	4035000	1889000	2145000

	1992			1993		
	TOTAL	Non-Financial	Financial	TOTAL	Non-Financial	Financial
Acquisition of Financial Assets					
1 Gold and SDRs	-110000	...	-110000	-47000	...	-47000
2 Currency and transferable deposits	263000	207000	56000	26000	...	26000
3 Other deposits	317000	68000	249000	1198000	...	1198000
4 Bills and bonds, short term	...	...	...	...	...	...
5 Bonds, long term [a]	175000	65000	110000	52000	...	52000
6 Corporate equity securities	142000	86000	56000	47000	...	47000
7 Short term loans, n.e.c.	904000	29000	875000	1720000	...	1720000
8 Long term loans, n.e.c.	2662000	188000	2474000	4051000	...	4051000
9 Trade credits and advances	1962000	1652000	310000	369000	...	369000
10 Other receivables	146000	85000	61000	51000	...	51000
11 Other assets	...	...	...	...	...	...
Total Acquisition of Financial Assets	6462000	2380000	4082000	7466000	...	7466000
Incurrence of Liabilities					
1 Currency and transferable deposits	754000	...	754000	1335000	...	1335000
2 Other deposits	1312000	117000	1195000	1423000	...	1423000
3 Bills and bonds, short term	...	...	...	...	...	...
4 Bonds, long term [a]	262000	6000	256000	76000	...	76000
5 Corporate equity securities	316000	182000	134000	326000	...	326000
6 Short-term loans, n.e.c.	814000	730000	84000	197000	...	197000

Ecuador

3.24 Corporate and Quasi-Corporate Enterprise Capital Finance Account: Total and Sectors
(Continued)

Million Ecuadoran sucres

		1992			1993	
		TOTAL	Non-Financial	Financial	TOTAL	Non-Financial	Financial
7	Long-term loans, n.e.c.	2261000	609000	1652000	3481000	...	3481000
8	Net equity of households in life insurance and pension fund reserves	57000	47000	10000	37000	...	37000
9	Proprietors' net additions to the accumulation of quasi-corporations	...	...	...	...	...	...
10	Trade credit and advances	2046000	1742000	304000	317000	...	317000
11	Other accounts payable	214000	186000	28000	422000	...	422000
12	Other liabilities [b]	-149000	...	-149000	-52000	...	-52000
	Total Incurrence of Liabilities	7887000	3619000	4268000	7563000	...	7563000
	Net Lending [c]	1424000	1239000	-185000	-97000	...	-97000
	Incurrence of Liabilities and Net Lending	6462000	2380000	4082000	7466000	...	7466000

a) Item 'Bonds, long-term' includes short-term bonds.
b) Item 'Other liabilities' refers to gold and SDRS.
c) Net lending of the capital accumulation account and the capital finance account have not been reconciled and are different due to different statistical sources.

3.31 Household and Private Unincorporated Enterprise Production Account

Thousand Million Ecuadoran sucres

	1980	1983	1984	1985	1986	1987	1988	1989	1990	1991	1992	1993
					Gross Output							
1 Output for sale	238	439	668	922	1209	1690	2818	5112	7915	13156	18728	...
2 Non-marketed output	2	2	3	4	6	8	10	14	19	26	40	...
Gross Output [a]	240	441	671	927	1215	1698	2828	5126	7934	13182	18768	...
					Gross Input							
Intermediate consumption	83	126	228	335	436	634	1026	1824	2832	5124	6413	...
Subtotal: Value Added	156	315	443	592	779	1064	1802	3302	5101	8058	12356	...
1 Indirect taxes net liability of unincorporated enterprises	3	4	7	10	15	18	33	52	37	58	76	...
A Indirect taxes	3	4	7	10	15	18	33	52	37	61	92	...
B Less: Subsidies	...	...	...	...	...	...	...	...	...	2	16	...
2 Consumption of fixed capital [b]	...	...	...	...	...	...	...	...	...	...	...	...
3 Compensation of employees	31	36	41	48	59	75	92	133	174	285	383	...
4 Net operating surplus [b]	123	275	396	534	705	971	1677	3117	4889	7714	11896	...
Gross Input [a]	240	441	671	927	1215	1698	2828	5126	7934	13182	18768	...

a) Data for this table have not been revised, therefore, data for some years are not comparable with those of other tables.
b) Item 'Operating surplus' includes consumption of fixed capital.

3.32 Household and Private Unincorporated Enterprise Income and Outlay Account

Thousand Million Ecuadoran sucres

	1980	1983	1984	1985	1986	1987	1988	1989	1990	1991	1992	1993
					Receipts							
1 Compensation of employees	93	134	176	230	298	394	541	767	1078	1515	2361	3844
A Wages and salaries	88	124	164	211	272	...	...	...	946	1295	2016	3247
B Employers' contributions for social security	4	7	8	11	15	...	...	...	74	119	177	279
C Employers' contributions for private pension & welfare plans	2	3	5	8	12	...	...	...	58	101	168	318
2 Operating surplus of private unincorporated enterprises [a]	123	275	396	534	705	971	1677	3117	4889	7873	12383	18138
3 Property and entrepreneurial income	6	17	24	45	62	84	87	126	213	351	908	995
A Withdrawals from private quasi-corporations	...	...	...	...	...	...	...	...	...	...	...	...
B Interest	3	10	15	33	47	64	61	86	144	254	781	840
C Dividends [b]	3	6	8	11	13	18	24	37	64	90	117	141
D Net land rent and royalties	-	1	1	1	1	2	3	3	5	7	10	14

Ecuador

3.32 Household and Private Unincorporated Enterprise Income and Outlay Account
(Continued)

Thousand Million Ecuadoran sucres

	1980	1983	1984	1985	1986	1987	1988	1989	1990	1991	1992	1993
3 Current transfers	10	19	24	34	41	90	119	203	325	480	845	1159
A Casualty insurance claims	-	1	1	1	1	2	4	6	12	18	57	51
B Social security benefits	7	13	16	21	22	40	55	88	141	204	375	469
C Social assistance grants	...	...	...	...	...	...	...	...	...	...	...	...
D Unfunded employee pension and welfare benefits	2	3	5	8	12	18	26	36	58	101	169	318
E Transfers from general government	...	...	...	...	...	...	...	...	24	28	44	54
F Transfers from the rest of the world	...	...	...	...	...	...	...	...	...	...	...	...
G Other transfers n.e.c.	2	2	3	4	6	31	34	73	89	129	200	267
Total Current Receipts	232	445	620	843	1107	1540	2424	4213	6505	10218	16498	24135
					Disbursements							
1 Final consumption expenditures	175	369	521	716	926	1269	2087	3706	5622	8432	13147	19375
2 Property income	7	14	19	26	40	58	90	103	173	270	612	1003
A Interest	7	14	19	26	40	58	90	103	173	270	612	1003
B Net land rent and royalties	...	...	...	...	...	...	...	...	...	...	...	...
3 Direct taxes and other current transfers n.e.c. to government	12	20	25	36	49	61	100	188	266	404	625	899
A Social security contributions	8	15	18	25	33	41	72	131	197	297	457	625
B Direct taxes	3	4	6	9	13	16	22	45	56	86	143	234
Income taxes	2	4	5	8	12	16	21	42	52	78	130	224
Other	-	-	-	1	1	1	1	2	4	8	13	10
C Fees, fines and penalties	1	1	1	2	3	3	5	12	13	21	25	40
4 Other current transfers	2	4	5	9	13	20	29	41	78	129	231	357
A Net casualty insurance premiums	-	1	1	1	1	2	3	5	19	28	61	38
B Transfers to private non-profit institutions serving households	...	...	...	...	...	...	...	...	...	...	...	...
C Transfers to the rest of the world	...	...	...	...	...	...	...	...	...	...	...	...
D Other current transfers, except imputed	...	...	...	...	...	...	...	...	...	...	1	1
E Imputed employee pension and welfare contributions	2	3	5	8	12	18	26	36	58	101	169	318
Net saving [c]	37	38	51	57	79	132	119	175	366	985	1884	2501
Total Current Disbursements and Net Saving	232	445	620	843	1107	1540	2424	4213	6505	10220	16498	24135

a) Item 'Operating surplus' includes consumption of fixed capital.
b) Item 'Dividends' includes profit-sharing by employees.
c) Item 'Net saving' includes consumption of fixed capital.

3.33 Household and Private Unincorporated Enterprise Capital Accumulation Account

Million Ecuadoran sucres

	1980	1983	1984	1985	1986	1987	1988	1989	1990	1991	1992	1993
					Finance of Gross Accumulation							
1 Gross saving	37453	37998	50564	56769	78581	132361	118890	175093	366052	985000	1884000	2501000
2 Capital transfers [a]	422	-781	576	1158	1769	1834	3255	4958	3989	2000	4000	-3000
A From resident sectors	...	...	...	...	...	...	...	...	...	...	...	-3000
B From the rest of the world	...	...	...	...	...	...	...	...	...	...	...	...
Total Finance of Gross Accumulation	37875	37218	51140	57927	80350	134195	122145	180051	370041	987000	1888000	2498000
					Gross Accumulation							
1 Gross Capital Formation	15466	20578	30746	40818	49781	63478	112478	165610	335153	627000	924000	1260000

Ecuador

3.33 Household and Private Unincorporated Enterprise Capital Accumulation Account
(Continued)

Million Ecuadoran sucres

	1980	1983	1984	1985	1986	1987	1988	1989	1990	1991	1992	1993
A Increase in stocks	1192	1615	3652	5055	5167	-1760	298	-28525	-60005	47000	21000	-33000
B Gross fixed capital formation	14274	18963	27094	35763	44614	65238	112180	194135	395158	580000	903000	1293000
Owner-occupied housing	8447	15192	21021	25111	30965	41037	...	...	...	...	...	...
Other gross fixed capital formation	5827	3771	6073	10652	13649	24201	...	...	...	...	...	...
2 Purchases of land, net	-1903	-3755	-4752	-6209	-9142	-9753	-11462	-13281	-36470	-45000	-80000	-83000
3 Purchases of intangibles, net	...	...	...	...	...	...	...	...	...	...	...	...
4 Capital transfers	...	...	...	...	...	...	...	...	...	...	...	...
Net lending [b]	24312	20394	25146	23318	39711	80470	21129	27722	71358	405000	1044000	1321000
Total Gross Accumulation	37875	37217	51140	57927	80350	134195	122145	180051	370041	987000	1888000	2498000

a) Capital transfers received are recorded net of capital transfers paid.
b) Net lending of the capital accumulation account and the capital finance account have not been reconciled and are different due to different statistical sources.

3.34 Household and Private Unincorporated Enterprise Capital Finance Account

Million Ecuadoran sucres

	1980	1983	1984	1985	1986	1987	1988	1989	1990	1991	1992	1993
Acquisition of Financial Assets											
1 Gold	...	...	...	...	...	...	...	...	...	143000	...	...
2 Currency and transferable deposits	7756	6415	17648	16919	22616	16529	102976	100669	150168	485000	395000	...
3 Other deposits	5346	12633	27494	72448	50405	107404	102405	193150	314990	...	872000	...
4 Bills and bonds, short term	...	...	...	...	...	...	...	...	...	...	...	...
5 Bonds, long term [a]	-2726	-2396	-6780	-793	1884	3834	-14285	-19698	66932	-54000	158000	...
6 Corporate equity securities	2221	1529	2798	9980	6275	14296	15289	3656	20937	49000	22000	...
7 Short term loans, n.e.c.	...	...	...	...	...	...	...	...	...	...	...	...
8 Long term loans, n.e.c.	...	...	...	...	...	...	...	...	...	...	...	...
9 Trade credit and advances	-7222	14434	-10251	-	-	-	-	-	...	...	...	...
10 Net equity of households in life insurance and pension fund reserves	3626	6442	9179	10452	13311	18705	22688	43813	96430	110000	114000	...
11 Proprietors' net additions to the accumulation of quasi-corporations	...	...	...	...	...	...	...	...	...	...	...	...
12 Other	...	...	...	...	...	...	...	...	...	...	...	...
Total Acquisition of Financial Assets [b]	9001	39057	40088	109006	94491	160768	229073	321590	649457	733000	1561000	...
Incurrence of Liabilities											
1 Short term loans, n.e.c.	2440	7853	12483	21135	24636	32933	63201	75572	132401	128000	240000	...
2 Long term loans, n.e.c.	4704	13428	22340	20453	36415	31519	40662	100677	116542	168000	286000	...
3 Trade credit and advances	...	...	...	...	...	...	...	...	...	...	...	...
4 Other accounts payable	-9764	3291	-18412	42554	-33951	10852	86804	32375	230988	-40000	475000	...
5 Other liabilities	...	...	...	...	...	...	...	...	...	...	...	...
Total Incurrence of Liabilities	-2620	24572	16411	84142	27100	75304	190667	208624	479931	257000	1001000	...
Net Lending [c]	11621	14485	23677	24864	67391	85464	38406	112966	169526	476000	560000	...
Incurrence of Liabilities and Net Lending [b]	9001	39057	40088	109006	94491	160768	229073	321590	649457	733000	1561000	...

a) Item 'Bonds, long-term' includes short-term bonds.
b) Data for this table have not been revised, therefore, data for some years are not comparable with those of other tables.
c) Net lending of the capital accumulation account and the capital finance account have not been reconciled and are different due to different statistical sources.

3.51 External Transactions: Current Account: Detail

Million Ecuadoran sucres

	1980	1983	1984	1985	1986	1987	1988	1989	1990	1991	1992	1993
Payments to the Rest of the World											
1 Imports of goods and services	74527	110617	157412	231668	312507	543702	922375	1610751	2246000	3655000	5378000	7012000
A Imports of merchandise c.i.f.	63512	85154	127264	177399	242639	448150	725271	1317900	1811000	3053000	4465000	5816000
B Other	11015	25463	30148	54269	69868	95552	197104	292851	435000	602000	913000	1196000
2 Factor income to the rest of the world	16932	43696	76962	84409	115517	126115	212451	399908	656000	778000	991000	1164000

Ecuador

3.51 External Transactions: Current Account: Detail
(Continued)

Million Ecuadoran sucres

	1980	1983	1984	1985	1986	1987	1988	1989	1990	1991	1992	1993
A Compensation of employees	783	2187	3375	2337	3761	7391	9746	22034	40000	56000	106000	132000
B Property and entrepreneurial income	16149	41509	73587	82072	111756	118724	202705	377874	616000	722000	885000	1032000
3 Current transfers to the rest of the world	1011	2026	2497	3366	3833	6368	9963	18227	34000	44000	84000	100000
A Indirect taxes by general government to supranational organizations	...	...	...	...	...	...	...	...	...	...	...	...
B Other current transfers	1011	2026	2497	3366	3833	6368	9963	18227	34000	44000	84000	100000
By general government	105	287	387	604	643	...	...	...	...	...	...	...
By other resident sectors	906	1739	2110	2762	3190	...	...	...	...	...	...	...
4 Surplus of the nation on current transactions	-14423	-17401	-18313	-14378	-107219	-209221	-243299	-424558	-106000	-415000	-2000	-692000
Payments to the Rest of the World, and Surplus of the Nation on Current Transfers	78047	138938	218558	305065	324638	466964	901490	1604328	2830000	4062000	6451000	7584000
Receipts From The Rest of the World												
1 Exports of goods and services	73797	133061	209858	296922	314740	431538	859062	1520090	2686000	3858000	6119000	7184000
A Exports of merchandise f.o.b.	64389	110999	183425	255387	250181	348095	673104	1221020	2251000	3214000	5075000	5813000
B Other	9408	22062	26433	41535	64559	83443	185958	299070	435000	644000	1044000	1371000
2 Factor income from the rest of the world	2395	1904	4391	2654	3868	3821	5648	15636	27000	42000	61000	66000
A Compensation of employees	45	157	175	267	480	733	1118	2135	3000	5000	7000	8000
B Property and entrepreneurial income	2350	1747	4216	2387	3388	3088	4530	13501	24000	37000	54000	58000
3 Current transfers from the rest of the world	1855	3973	4309	5489	6030	31605	36780	68602	117000	163000	272000	334000
A Subsidies to general government from supranational organizations	...	...	...	...	...	...	...	...	...	...	...	...
B Other current transfers	1855	3973	4309	5489	6030	31605	36780	68602	117000	163000	272000	334000
To general government	931	2273	2292	2853	2963	3271	...	...	...	...	...	...
To other resident sectors	924	1700	2017	2636	3067	28334	...	...	...	...	...	...
Receipts from the Rest of the World on Current Transfers	78047	138938	218558	305065	324638	466964	901490	1604328	2830000	4063000	6452000	7584000

3.52 External Transactions: Capital Accumulation Account

Million Ecuadoran sucres

	1980	1983	1984	1985	1986	1987	1988	1989	1990	1991	1992	1993
Finance of Gross Accumulation												
1 Surplus of the nation on current transactions	-14423	-17401	-18313	-14378	-107219	-209221	-243299	-424558	-106000	-415000	-2000	-692000
2 Capital transfers from the rest of the world	7	7	-	-	-	-	-	-	-	1000	1000	1000
A By general government	...	...	...	...	...	...	...	...	...	...	...	...
B By other resident sectors	7	7	-	-	-	-	-	-	-	-	-	...
Total Finance of Gross Accumulation	-14416	-17394	-18313	-14378	-107219	-209221	-243299	-424558	-106000	-414000	-1000	-691000
Gross Accumulation												
1 Capital transfers to the rest of the world	...	...	...	...	...	...	...	...	...	...	...	...
2 Purchases of intangible assets, n.e.c., net, from the rest of the world	79	735	948	1124	1388	2321	5457	8652	16000	19000	23000	33000
Net lending to the rest of the world a	-14495	-18129	-19261	-15502	-108607	-211542	-248756	-433210	-122000	-433000	-24000	-724000
Total Gross Accumulation	-14416	-17394	-18313	-14378	-107219	-209221	-243299	-424558	-106000	-414000	-1000	-691000

a) Net lending of the capital accumulation account and the capital finance account have not been reconciled and are different due to different statistical sources.

3.53 External Transactions: Capital Finance Account

Million Ecuadoran sucres

	1980	1983	1984	1985	1986	1987	1988	1989	1990	1991	1992	1993
Acquisitions of Foreign Financial Assets												
1 Gold and SDR's	-158	7949	3202	5239	5484	-262	-17801	-25281	-80000	-103000	-89000	-64000
2 Currency and transferable deposits	23	149	126	218	779	106	612	1615	4000	3000	3000	93000
3 Other deposits	2285	-644	5564	-386	9913	-7124	36134	18445	-10000	15000	43000	-92000
4 Bills and bonds, short term	-	-	-	-	-	-	-	-	-	-	-	...

Ecuador

3.53 External Transactions: Capital Finance Account
(Continued)

Million Ecuadoran sucres

		1980	1983	1984	1985	1986	1987	1988	1989	1990	1991	1992	1993
5	Bonds, long term [a]	-350	-489	-779	-117	-7	-	-	-	-	...	...	...
6	Corporate equity securities	1750	2210	3115	4224	8362	13969	26972	27385	45000	62000	98000	128000
7	Short-term loans, n.e.c.	9707	-31672	-4763	-2022	-19981	1562	65862	-7527	92000	78000	157000	250000
8	Long-term loans	15958	60539	17080	14860	58509	113361	56427	261696	-3000	103000	-190000	641000
9	Proprietors' net additions to accumulation of quasi-corporate, non-resident enterprises	...	...	...	...	...	...	...	...	...	...	...	...
10	Trade credit and advances	5711	-1250	10498	23540	26446	94743	203251	185521	243000	719000	639000	563000
11	Other [b]	-529	...	...	...	...	...	-	60507	157000	-	-	...
	Total Acquisitions of Foreign Financial Assets	34397	36792	34043	45556	89505	216355	371457	522361	448000	877000	661000	1519000

Incurrence of Foreign Liabilities

		1980	1983	1984	1985	1986	1987	1988	1989	1990	1991	1992	1993
1	Currency and transferable deposits	700	1453	-3230	2194	15274	-10009	9430	-29664	45000	-18000	-49000	-59000
2	Other deposits	6061	15154	2331	15641	-32243	20229	47416	87297	156000	12000	26000	912000
3	Bills and bonds, short term	-	-	-	-	-	-	-	-	-	-	-	...
4	Bonds, long term [a]	-9	-484	898	-831	-95	-475	25	1138	2000	3000	16000	-6000
5	Corporate equity securities	298	497	627	823	2299	1592	4854	8416	8000	18000	29000	78000
6	Short-term loans, n.e.c.	122	12	-	-1052	-1197	-6366	-93	3357	2000	...	-	1000
7	Long-term loans	...	...	...	...	...	...	...	...	...	...	...	...
8	Non-resident proprietors' net additions to accumulation of resident quasi-corporate enterprises	...	...	...	...	...	...	...	...	...	...	...	...
9	Trade credit and advances	2395	8225	5579	6459	11108	34225	53706	122253	110000	268000	247000	27000
10	Other [b]	6007	-9892	1197	4042	-5436	-18113	-	-	-	-	-	...
	Total Incurrence of Liabilities	15574	14965	7402	27276	-10290	21083	115338	192797	323000	283000	269000	953000
	Statistical discrepancy	...	...	...	...	...	...	...	...	3000	161000	369000	-158000
	Net Lending [c]	18823	21827	26641	18280	99795	195272	256119	329564	122000	433000	24000	724000
	Total Incurrence of Liabilities and Net Lending	34397	36792	34043	45556	89505	216355	371457	522361	448000	877000	662000	1519000

a) Item 'Bonds, long-term' includes short-term bonds.
b) Item 'Other' refers to other receivables/payables and accounting discrepancies.
c) Net lending of the capital accumulation account and the capital finance account have not been reconciled and are different due to different statistical sources.

4.1 Derivation of Value Added by Kind of Activity, in Current Prices

Thousand Million Ecuadoran sucres

		1980			1985			1990			1991		
		Gross Output	Intermediate Consumption	Value Added	Gross Output	Intermediate Consumption	Value Added	Gross Output	Intermediate Consumption	Value Added	Gross Output	Intermediate Consumption	Value Added
						All Producers							
1	Agriculture, hunting, forestry and fishing	42	7	36	182	34	148	1417	317	1100	2253	491	1762
	A Agriculture and hunting	36	6	30	154	28	125	1077	244	834	1725	378	1347
	B Forestry and logging	3	-	3	10	2	8	94	17	77	144	25	119
	C Fishing	3	-	3	18	4	15	245	57	189	385	89	296
2	Mining and quarrying	76	41	36	299	109	190	2338	1120	1218	2682	1314	1368
	A Coal mining [a]	...	...	...	...	...	...	...	...	...	...	...	...
	B Crude petroleum and natural gas production [b]	75	40	35	290	106	184	2232	1079	1153	2547	1253	1294
	C Metal ore mining [a]	...	...	...	...	...	...	...	...	...	...	...	...
	D Other mining [a]	1	-	1	9	4	6	107	41	65	134	60	74

Ecuador

4.1 Derivation of Value Added by Kind of Activity, in Current Prices
(Continued)

Thousand Million Ecuadoran sucres

	1980 Gross Output	1980 Intermediate Consumption	1980 Value Added	1985 Gross Output	1985 Intermediate Consumption	1985 Value Added	1990 Gross Output	1990 Intermediate Consumption	1990 Value Added	1991 Gross Output	1991 Intermediate Consumption	1991 Value Added
3 Manufacturing	130	78	52	562	351	210	4584	2996	1588	7100	4546	2554
A Manufacture of food, beverages and tobacco	61	37	24	282	171	111	2246	1233	1013	3502	1880	1622
B Textile, wearing apparel and leather industries	22	12	10	85	46	38	634	441	193	933	659	274
C Manufacture of wood and wood products, including furniture	8	6	3	31	24	8	248	218	30	382	336	46
D Manufacture of paper and paper products, printing and publishing	8	4	3	29	18	11	313	177	137	520	248	272
E Manufacture of chemicals and chemical petroleum, coal, rubber and plastic products	10	7	4	40	32	8	322	295	28	498	460	38
F Manufacture of non-metallic mineral products, except products of petroleum and coal	13	7	6	58	35	23	446	330	116	664	475	189
G Basic metal industries												
H Manufacture of fabricated metal products, machinery and equipment	6	5	1	28	22	7	271	254	17	463	434	29
I Other manufacturing industries	2	1	1	9	5	4	103	49	54	140	56	84
4 Electricity, gas and water	5	3	2	18	14	3	138	153	-15	224	237	-13
5 Construction	42	20	22	121	73	49	830	501	329	1260	704	556
6 Wholesale and retail trade, restaurants and hotels	69	26	43	282	108	173	2660	924	1737	4161	1438	2723
A Wholesale and retail trade	58	21	37	245	83	162	2341	717	1625	3667	1112	2555
B Restaurants and hotels	11	5	6	36	25	11	319	207	112	494	326	168
7 Transport, storage and communication	35	11	23	152	57	95	1271	563	708	1885	821	1064
A Transport and storage	32	11	21	145	54	91	1174	500	675	1720	705	1015
B Communication	2	-	2	7	3	4	96	63	33	165	116	49
8 Finance, insurance, real estate and business services	41	7	34	114	30	84	760	258	502	1232	375	857
A Financial institutions	14	3	11	35	15	20	251	128	124	419	178	241
B Insurance												
C Real estate and business services	27	4	23	79	15	64	509	131	378	814	197	617
9 Community, social and personal services	18	4	15	65	18	47	511	180	331	797	260	537
A Sanitary and similar services	...	...	...	...	...	...	...	...	...	...	...	...
B Social and related community services	...	...	...	...	...	...	...	...	...	...	...	...
C Recreational and cultural services	...	...	...	...	...	...	...	...	...	...	...	...
D Personal and household services	18	4	15	65	18	47	511	180	331	797	260	537
Total, Industries	459	197	262	1794	796	999	14510	7012	7498	21594	10186	11408
Producers of Government Services	45	18	27	134	48	86	775	388	387	1010	506	504
Other Producers	2	...	2	4	...	4	19	...	19	26	...	26
Total	505	215	290	1933	844	1090	15303	7400	7903	22630	10692	11938
Less: Imputed bank service charge	...	-9	9	...	-22	22	...	-149	149	...	-288	288
Import duties	12	...	12	42	...	42	215	...	215	280	...	280
Value added tax	...	...	...	...	...	...	234	...	234	366	...	366
Total	517	224	293	1975	865	1110	15753	7548	8204	23276	10980	12296

of which General Government:

	1980 GO	1980 IC	1980 VA	1985 GO	1985 IC	1985 VA	1990 GO	1990 IC	1990 VA	1991 GO	1991 IC	1991 VA
1 Agriculture, hunting, forestry and fishing	...	...	...	...	...	...	...	...	...	...	...	...
2 Mining and quarrying	...	...	...	...	...	...	...	...	...	...	...	...
3 Manufacturing	...	...	...	...	...	...	...	...	...	...	...	...
4 Electricity, gas and water	1	-	-	4	2	3	1	1	-	1	1	-

Ecuador

4.1 Derivation of Value Added by Kind of Activity, in Current Prices
(Continued)

Thousand Million Ecuadoran sucres

	1980 Gross Output	1980 Intermediate Consumption	1980 Value Added	1985 Gross Output	1985 Intermediate Consumption	1985 Value Added	1990 Gross Output	1990 Intermediate Consumption	1990 Value Added	1991 Gross Output	1991 Intermediate Consumption	1991 Value Added
5 Construction	3	2	1	9	5	4	79	44	35	107	60	47
6 Wholesale and retail trade, restaurants and hotels	...	...	...	...	...	...	...	...	...	...	...	...
7 Transport and communication	...	...	...	...	...	...	...	...	...	...	...	...
8 Finance, insurance, real estate and business services	...	...	...	...	...	...	...	...	...	...	...	...
9 Community, social and personal services	2	1	1	7	3	4	46	23	23	67	31	36
Total, Industries of General Government	6	3	3	20	10	10	126	68	58	175	92	83
Producers of Government Services	45	18	27	134	48	86	775	388	387	1010	506	504
Total, General Government	51	21	29	154	58	97	901	456	445	1185	598	587

	1992 Gross Output	1992 Intermediate Consumption	1992 Value Added	1993 Gross Output	1993 Intermediate Consumption	1993 Value Added
All Producers						
1 Agriculture, hunting, forestry and fishing	3237	771	2466	4368	1045	3323
A Agriculture and hunting	2406	589	1817	3274	803	2471
B Forestry and logging	233	40	193	347	61	286
C Fishing	597	142	455	747	181	566
2 Mining and quarrying	4539	2099	2440	5245	2303	2942
A Coal mining [a]	...	...	...	...	...	...
B Crude petroleum and natural gas production [b]	4335	2003	2332	4939	2157	2782
C Metal ore mining [a]	...	...	...	...	...	...
D Other mining [a]	204	96	108	306	146	160
3 Manufacturing	11279	6999	4280	15917	9948	5969
A Manufacture of food, beverages and tobacco	5552	2838	2714	7628	3920	3708
B Textile, wearing apparel and leather industries	1376	957	419	1916	1320	596
C Manufacture of wood and wood products, including furniture	612	533	79	846	737	109
D Manufacture of paper and paper products, printing and publishing	963	440	523	1381	639	742
E Manufacture of chemicals and chemical petroleum, coal, rubber and plastic products	829	757	72	1215	1122	93
F Manufacture of non-metallic mineral products, except products of petroleum and coal	1049	733	316	1623	1132	491
G Basic metal industries						
H Manufacture of fabricated metal products, machinery and equipment	695	661	34	1031	969	62
I Other manufacturing industries	202	80	122	276	109	167
4 Electricity, gas and water	402	379	23	636	560	76
5 Construction	1912	1030	882	2837	1497	1340
6 Wholesale and retail trade, restaurants and hotels	6433	2264	4169	8981	3430	5551
A Wholesale and retail trade	5635	1765	3870	7796	2699	5097
B Restaurants and hotels	798	499	299	1185	731	454
7 Transport, storage and communication	2855	1350	1505	4534	2084	2450
A Transport and storage	2594	1162	1432	4101	1792	2309

Ecuador

4.1 Derivation of Value Added by Kind of Activity, in Current Prices
(Continued)

Thousand Million Ecuadoran sucres

		1992 Gross Output	1992 Intermediate Consumption	1992 Value Added	1993 Gross Output	1993 Intermediate Consumption	1993 Value Added
	B Communication	261	188	73	433	292	141
8	Finance, insurance, real estate and business services	2002	609	1393	3208	953	2255
	A Financial institutions	692	303	389	1228	498	730
	B Insurance						
	C Real estate and business services	1310	306	1004	1980	455	1525
9	Community, social and personal services	1334	391	943	2111	547	1564
	A Sanitary and similar services	...	...	...	...	...	...
	B Social and related community services	...	...	...	...	...	...
	C Recreational and cultural services	...	...	...	...	...	...
	D Personal and household services	1334	391	943	2111	547	1564
Total, Industries		33993	15892	18101	47837	22367	25470
Producers of Government Services		1498	685	813	2281	972	1309
Other Producers		40	...	40	65	...	65
Total		35531	16577	18954	50183	23339	26844
Less: Imputed bank service charge		...	-491	491	...	-878	878
Import duties		339	...	339	537	...	537
Value added tax		612	...	612	949	...	949
Total		36482	17068	19414	51669	24217	27452

of which General Government:

		1992 GO	1992 IC	1992 VA	1993 GO	1993 IC	1993 VA
1	Agriculture, hunting, forestry and fishing	...	...	...	...	...	...
2	Mining and quarrying	...	...	...	...	...	...
3	Manufacturing	...	...	...	...	...	...
4	Electricity, gas and water	1	1	-	1	2	-1
5	Construction	168	95	73	258	147	111
6	Wholesale and retail trade, restaurants and hotels	...	...	...	...	...	...
7	Transport and communication	...	...	...	...	...	...
8	Finance, insurance, real estate and business services	...	...	...	...	...	...
9	Community, social and personal services	145	81	64	163	64	99
Total, Industries of General Government		314	177	137	422	213	209
Producers of Government Services		1498	685	813	2281	972	1309
Total, General Government		1812	862	950	2703	1185	1518

a) Items 'Coal mining' and 'Metal ore mining' are included in item 'Other mining'.
b) Petroleum refining is included in item 'Crude petroleum and natural gas production'.

4.2 Derivation of Value Added by Kind of Activity, in Constant Prices

Million Ecuadoran sucres

		1980 GO	1980 IC	1980 VA	1985 GO	1985 IC	1985 VA	1990 GO	1990 IC	1990 VA	1991 GO	1991 IC	1991 VA
					At constant prices of: 1975								
					All Producers								
1	Agriculture, hunting, forestry and fishing	25678	4480	21198	29578	5400	24178	39431	7351	32080	41991	8003	33988
	A Agriculture and hunting	21995	3948	18047	24333	4630	19703	30757	6000	24757	32469	6495	25974
	B Forestry and logging	1782	242	1540	1980	268	1712	2174	303	1871	2317	324	1993
	C Fishing	1901	290	1611	3265	502	2763	6500	1048	5452	7205	1184	6021
2	Mining and quarrying	30114	15044	15070	38378	14503	23875	41297	19855	21442	43467	20216	23251
	A Coal mining [a]	...	...	...	...	...	...	...	...	...	...	...	...
	B Crude petroleum and natural gas production [b]	29493	14876	14617	37011	14150	22861	39335	19329	20006	41441	19669	21772
	C Metal ore mining [a]	...	...	...	...	...	...	...	...	...	...	...	...
	D Other mining [a]	621	168	453	1367	353	1014	1962	526	1436	2026	547	1479

Ecuador

4.2 Derivation of Value Added by Kind of Activity, in Constant Prices
(Continued)

Million Ecuadoran sucres

	1980 Gross Output	1980 Intermediate Consumption	1980 Value Added	1985 Gross Output	1985 Intermediate Consumption	1985 Value Added	1990 Gross Output	1990 Intermediate Consumption	1990 Value Added	1991 Gross Output	1991 Intermediate Consumption	1991 Value Added
				At constant prices of:1975								
3 Manufacturing	76120	49313	26807	85216	56506	28710	97164	69109	28055	103109	74158	28951
A Manufacture of food, beverages and tobacco	35477	23885	11592	37991	27143	10848	43741	34073	9668	46136	36356	9780
B Textile, wearing apparel and leather industries	13608	7927	5681	14113	7533	6580	15865	9425	6440	16077	9648	6429
C Manufacture of wood and wood products, including furniture	4876	3398	1478	5829	4255	1574	6104	4700	1404	6594	5102	1492
D Manufacture of paper and paper products, printing and publishing	4306	2649	1657	5004	3122	1882	6223	3704	2519	6464	3898	2566
E Manufacture of chemicals and chemical petroleum, coal, rubber and plastic products	6131	4392	1739	7184	5365	1819	7654	5780	1874	8163	6190	1973
F Manufacture of non-metallic mineral products, except products of petroleum and coal	6685	3712	2973	8849	5076	3773	8898	5974	2924	9689	6510	3179
G Basic metal industries												
H Manufacture of fabricated metal products, machinery and equipment	3878	2919	959	4154	3183	971	6059	4555	1504	7365	5543	1822
I Other manufacturing industries	1159	431	728	2092	829	1263	2620	898	1722	2621	911	1710
4 Electricity, gas and water	3163	2048	1115	4463	2630	1833	6025	3244	2781	6583	3742	2841
5 Construction	18325	11419	6906	17223	10481	6742	14375	9042	5333	14445	9171	5274
6 Wholesale and retail trade, restaurants and hotels	39439	14650	24789	40141	15873	24268	46715	19246	27469	49073	20516	28557
A Wholesale and retail trade	33169	11521	21648	33237	11964	21273	38672	14440	24232	40777	15440	25337
B Restaurants and hotels	6270	3129	3141	6904	3909	2995	8043	4806	3237	8296	5076	3220
7 Transport, storage and communication	17223	7185	10038	19856	8350	11506	26049	10687	15362	27704	11415	16289
A Transport and storage	15888	6871	9017	17542	7784	9758	20341	9141	11200	20970	9558	11412
B Communication	1335	314	1021	2314	566	1748	5708	1546	4162	6734	1857	4877
8 Finance, insurance, real estate and business services	21412	3718	17694	23039	4877	18162	25334	5745	19589	26774	5968	20806
A Financial institutions	7280	1555	5725	6886	2432	4454	7264	2976	4288	8198	3088	5110
B Insurance												
C Real estate and business services	14132	2163	11969	16153	2445	13708	18070	2769	15301	18576	2880	15696
9 Community, social and personal services	9819	2207	7612	12318	2789	9529	13559	3125	10434	14028	3271	10757
A Sanitary and similar services	...	...	...	...	...	...	...	...	...	...	...	...
B Social and related community services	...	...	...	...	...	...	...	...	...	...	...	...
C Recreational and cultural services	...	...	...	...	...	...	...	...	...	...	...	...
D Personal and household services	9819	2207	7612	12318	2789	9529	13559	3125	10434	14028	3271	10757
Total, Industries	241293	110064	131229	270212	121409	148803	309949	147404	162545	327174	156460	170714
Producers of Government Services	24882	11173	13709	21946	7104	14842	23032	7017	16015	22591	6422	16169
Other Producers	675	...	675	723	...	723	819	...	819	844	...	844
Total	266850	121237	145613	292881	128513	164368	333800	154421	179379	350609	162882	187727
Less: Imputed bank service charge	...	-5006	5006	...	-4519	4519	...	-4881	4881	...	-5661	5661
Import duties	7015	...	7015	4205	...	4205	3624	...	3624	4815	...	4815
Value added tax	...	...	...	...	...	...	3409	...	3409	3757	...	3757
Total	273865	126243	147622	297086	133032	164054	340833	159302	181531	359181	168543	190638
				of which General Government:								
1 Agriculture, hunting, forestry and fishing	...	...	...	...	...	...	...	...	...	...	...	...
2 Mining and quarrying	...	...	...	...	...	...	...	...	...	...	...	...
3 Manufacturing	...	...	...	...	...	...	...	...	...	...	...	...
4 Electricity, gas and water	...	...	...	...	...	...	...	...	...	...	...	...

Ecuador

4.2 Derivation of Value Added by Kind of Activity, in Constant Prices
(Continued)

Million Ecuadoran sucres

	1980 Gross Output	1980 Intermediate Consumption	1980 Value Added	1985 Gross Output	1985 Intermediate Consumption	1985 Value Added	1990 Gross Output	1990 Intermediate Consumption	1990 Value Added	1991 Gross Output	1991 Intermediate Consumption	1991 Value Added
					At constant prices of: 1975							
5 Construction	...	...	...	...	...	...	...	...	...	...	...	...
6 Wholesale and retail trade, restaurants and hotels	...	...	...	...	...	...	...	...	...	...	...	...
7 Transport and communication	...	...	...	...	...	...	...	...	...	...	...	...
8 Finance, insurance, real estate and business services	...	...	...	...	...	...	...	...	...	...	...	...
9 Community, social and personal services	...	...	...	...	...	...	...	...	...	...	...	...
Total, Industries of General Government	...	...	...	...	...	...	...	...	...	...	...	...
Producers of Government Services	24882	11173	13709	21946	7104	14842	23032	7017	16015	22591	6422	16169
Total, General Government	...	...	...	...	...	...	...	...	...	...	...	...

	1992 Gross Output	1992 Intermediate Consumption	1992 Value Added	1993 Gross Output	1993 Intermediate Consumption	1993 Value Added
		At constant prices of: 1975				
		All Producers				
1 Agriculture, hunting, forestry and fishing	43387	8233	35154	42882	8327	34555
A Agriculture and hunting	33519	6697	26822	33562	6901	26661
B Forestry and logging	2403	335	2068	2500	347	2153
C Fishing	7465	1201	6264	6820	1079	5741
2 Mining and quarrying	45868	21269	24599	48144	20846	27298
A Coal mining [a]	...	...	...	...	...	...
B Crude petroleum and natural gas production [b]	43794	20709	23085	46018	20272	25746
C Metal ore mining [a]	...	...	...	...	...	...
D Other mining [a]	2074	560	1514	2126	574	1552
3 Manufacturing	107368	77379	29989	109657	78926	30731
A Manufacture of food, beverages and tobacco	47901	37827	10074	48146	37952	10194
B Textile, wearing apparel and leather industries	16176	9843	6333	16400	9985	6415
C Manufacture of wood and wood products, including furniture	6862	5322	1540	7151	5544	1607
D Manufacture of paper and paper products, printing and publishing	6809	4102	2707	6939	4212	2727
E Manufacture of chemicals and chemical petroleum, coal, rubber and plastic products	8508	6470	2038	8911	6773	2138
F Manufacture of non-metallic mineral products, except products of petroleum and coal	10563	7002	3561	11173	7390	3783
G Basic metal industries						
H Manufacture of fabricated metal products, machinery and equipment	7815	5868	1947	8119	6101	2018
I Other manufacturing industries	2734	945	1789	2818	969	1849
4 Electricity, gas and water	6778	3859	2919	6971	3991	2980
5 Construction	14403	9147	5256	14077	9045	5032
6 Wholesale and retail trade, restaurants and hotels	50971	21551	29420	52215	22296	29919
A Wholesale and retail trade	42448	16323	26125	43478	16814	26664
B Restaurants and hotels	8523	5228	3295	8737	5482	3255
7 Transport, storage and communication	29243	12020	17223	30606	12614	17992
A Transport and storage	21861	9981	11880	22582	10377	12205

Ecuador

4.2 Derivation of Value Added by Kind of Activity, in Constant Prices
(Continued)

Million Ecuadoran sucres

	1992 Gross Output	1992 Intermediate Consumption	1992 Value Added	1993 Gross Output	1993 Intermediate Consumption	1993 Value Added
			At constant prices of:1975			
B Communication	7382	2039	5343	8024	2237	5787
8 Finance, insurance, real estate and business services	27865	6386	21479	30338	6883	23455
A Financial institutions	8728	3404	5324	10559	3753	6806
B Insurance						
C Real estate and business services	19137	2982	16155	19779	3130	16649
9 Community, social and personal services	14508	3396	11112	14723	3459	11264
A Sanitary and similar services	...	...	...	...	...	...
B Social and related community services	...	...	...	...	...	...
C Recreational and cultural services	...	...	...	...	...	...
D Personal and household services	14508	3396	11112	14723	3459	11264
Total, Industries	340391	163240	177151	349613	166387	183226
Producers of Government Services	21961	5847	16114	21747	5993	15754
Other Producers	864	...	864	881	...	881
Total	363216	169087	194129	372241	172380	199861
Less: Imputed bank service charge	...	-5984	5984	...	-7811	7811
Import duties	5324	...	5324	5369	...	5369
Value added tax	3967	...	3967	4028	...	4028
Total	372507	175071	197436	381638	180191	201447
			of which General Government:			
1 Agriculture, hunting, forestry and fishing	...	...	...	...	...	...
2 Mining and quarrying	...	...	...	...	...	...
3 Manufacturing	...	...	...	...	...	...
4 Electricity, gas and water	...	...	...	...	...	...
5 Construction	...	...	...	...	...	...
6 Wholesale and retail trade, restaurants and hotels	...	...	...	...	...	...
7 Transport and communication	...	...	...	...	...	...
8 Finance, insurance, real estate and business services	...	...	...	...	...	...
9 Community, social and personal services	...	...	...	...	...	...
Total, Industries of General Government	...	...	...	...	...	...
Producers of Government Services	21961	5847	16114	21747	5993	15754
Total, General Government	...	...	...	...	...	...

a) Items 'Coal mining' and 'Metal ore mining' are included in item 'Other mining'.
b) Petroleum refining is included in item 'Crude petroleum and natural gas production'.

4.3 Cost Components of Value Added

Thousand Million Ecuadoran sucres

	1980 Compensation of Employees	1980 Capital Consumption	1980 Net Operating Surplus	1980 Indirect Taxes	1980 Less: Subsidies Received	1980 Value Added	1985 Compensation of Employees	1985 Capital Consumption	1985 Net Operating Surplus	1985 Indirect Taxes	1985 Less: Subsidies Received	1985 Value Added
				All Producers								
1 Agriculture, hunting, forestry and fishing	7	...	28	-	...	36	13	...	135	1	...	148
A Agriculture and hunting	7	...	23	-	...	30	12	...	112	1	...	125
B Forestry and logging	-	...	3	-	...	3	-	...	8	-	...	8
C Fishing	-	...	2	-	...	3	1	...	14	-	...	15
2 Mining and quarrying	2	...	29	5	...	36	7	...	132	51	...	190
A Coal mining [a]	...	...	...	...	...	...	...	...	...	...	...	...
B Crude petroleum and natural gas production [b]	1	...	29	5	...	35	4	...	129	51	...	184
C Metal ore mining [a]	...	...	...	...	...	...	...	...	...	...	...	...
D Other mining [a]	-	...	1	-	...	1	3	...	3	-	...	6

Ecuador

4.3 Cost Components of Value Added
(Continued)

Thousand Million Ecuadoran sucres

	1980 Compensation of Employees	Capital Consumption	Net Operating Surplus	Indirect Taxes	Less: Subsidies Received	Value Added	1985 Compensation of Employees	Capital Consumption	Net Operating Surplus	Indirect Taxes	Less: Subsidies Received	Value Added
3 Manufacturing	15	...	32	5	...	52	28	...	163	19	...	210
A Manufacture of food, beverages and tobacco	4	...	17	3	...	24	7	...	94	11	...	111
B Textile, wearing apparel and leather industries	3	...	6	-	...	10	7	...	29	2	...	38
C Manufacture of wood and wood products, including furniture	2	...	1	-	...	3	2	...	5	-	...	8
D Manufacture of paper and paper products, printing and publishing	1	...	2	-	...	3	2	...	9	-	...	11
E Manufacture of chemicals and chemical petroleum, coal, rubber and plastic products	2	...	1	1	...	4	3	...	3	2	...	8
F Manufacture of non-metallic mineral products, except products of petroleum and coal	2	...	4	-	...	6	4	...	18	2	...	23
G Basic metal industries		...			...			...			...	
H Manufacture of fabricated metal products, machinery and equipment	1	...	-	-	...	1	2	...	3	2	...	7
I Other manufacturing industries	-	...	1	-	...	1	-	...	4	-	...	4
4 Electricity, gas and water	2	...	1	-	...	2	6	...	-3	1	...	3
A Electricity, gas and steam	...	...	...	...	...	...	...	...	...	...	...	...
B Water works and supply	...	...	...	...	...	...	...	...	...	...	...	...
5 Construction	12	...	9	-	...	22	22	...	25	1	...	49
6 Wholesale and retail trade, restaurants and hotels	12	...	31	-	...	43	21	...	147	5	...	173
A Wholesale and retail trade	11	...	26	-	...	37	18	...	139	5	...	162
B Restaurants and hotels	1	...	5	-	...	6	3	...	8	1	...	11
7 Transport, storage and communication	6	...	17	1	...	23	14	...	79	2	...	95
A Transport and storage	5	...	16	-	...	21	11	...	77	2	...	91
B Communication	1	...	1	-	...	2	3	...	1	1	...	4
8 Finance, insurance, real estate and business services	7	...	26	1	...	34	22	...	56	6	...	84
A Financial institutions	5	...	6	-	...	11	18	...	-1	3	...	20
B Insurance		...			...			...			...	
C Real estate and business services	2	...	21	1	...	23	4	...	57	3	...	64
9 Community, social and personal services	4	...	10	-	...	15	9	...	37	-	...	47
A Sanitary and similar services	...	...	...	...	...	...	...	...	...	...	...	...
B Social and related community services	...	...	...	...	...	...	...	...	...	...	...	...
C Recreational and cultural services	...	...	...	...	...	...	...	...	...	...	...	...
D Personal and household services	4	...	10	-	...	15	9	...	37	-	...	47
Statistical discrepancy	...	...	...	...	...	...	...	...	...	...	...	...
Total, Industries [cd]	65	...	184	12	...	262	141	...	771	86	...	999
Producers of Government Services	27	...	...	...	...	27	86	...	...	...	...	86
Other Producers	2	...	...	...	...	2	4	...	...	...	...	4
Total [cd]	94	...	184	12	...	290	232	...	771	86	...	1090
Less: Imputed bank service charge	...	...	9	...	...	9	...	...	22	...	...	22
Import duties	...	...	...	12	...	12	...	...	...	42	...	42
Value added tax	...	...	...	...	...	...	...	...	...	...	...	...
Total [cd]	94	...	175	24	...	293	232	...	749	128	...	1110

of which General Government:

1 Agriculture, hunting, forestry and fishing	...	...	...	...	...	...	...	...	...	...	...	...
2 Mining and quarrying	...	...	...	...	...	...	...	...	...	...	...	...
3 Manufacturing	...	...	...	...	...	...	...	...	...	...	...	...
4 Electricity, gas and water	-	...	-	...	...	-	1	...	2	...	...	3

Ecuador

4.3 Cost Components of Value Added
(Continued)

Thousand Million Ecuadoran sucres

	1980						1985					
	Compensation of Employees	Capital Consumption	Net Operating Surplus	Indirect Taxes	Less: Subsidies Received	Value Added	Compensation of Employees	Capital Consumption	Net Operating Surplus	Indirect Taxes	Less: Subsidies Received	Value Added
5 Construction	1	...	...	...	...	1	4	...	...	...	...	4
6 Wholesale and retail trade, restaurants and hotels	...	...	...	...	...	...	...	...	...	...	...	...
7 Transport and communication	...	...	...	...	...	...	...	...	...	...	...	...
8 Finance, insurance, real estate & business services	...	...	...	...	...	...	...	...	...	...	...	...
9 Community, social and personal services	1	...	...	...	...	1	4	...	...	...	...	4
Total, Industries of General Government	3	...	-	...	...	3	9	...	2	...	...	10
Producers of Government Services	27	...	...	...	...	27	86	...	...	...	...	86
Total, General Government	29	...	-	...	...	29	95	...	2	...	...	97

	1990						1991					
	Compensation of Employees	Capital Consumption	Net Operating Surplus	Indirect Taxes	Less: Subsidies Received	Value Added	Compensation of Employees	Capital Consumption	Net Operating Surplus	Indirect Taxes	Less: Subsidies Received	Value Added

All Producers

1 Agriculture, hunting, forestry and fishing	80	...	1015	5	...	1100	116	...	1635	10	...	1762
A Agriculture and hunting	76	...	753	5	...	834	111	...	1227	9	...	1347
B Forestry and logging	1	...	76	-	...	77	1	...	116	1	...	118
C Fishing	3	...	186	-	...	189	4	...	292	-	...	296
2 Mining and quarrying	61	...	610	547	...	1218	93	...	715	559	...	1368
A Coal mining [a]	...	...	...	...	...	...	...	...	...	...	...	...
B Crude petroleum and natural gas production [b]	47	...	559	547	...	1153	73	...	662	559	...	1294
C Metal ore mining [a]	...	...	...	...	...	...	...	...	...	...	...	...
D Other mining [a]	14	...	51	-	...	65	20	...	53	-	...	73
3 Manufacturing	126	...	1400	62	...	1588	176	...	2257	122	...	2554
A Manufacture of food, beverages and tobacco	31	...	928	54	...	1013	42	...	1470	110	...	1622
B Textile, wearing apparel and leather industries	34	...	157	2	...	193	49	...	221	4	...	274
C Manufacture of wood and wood products, including furniture	10	...	19	1	...	30	14	...	31	1	...	46
D Manufacture of paper and paper products, printing and publishing	8	...	128	1	...	137	11	...	260	1	...	272
E Manufacture of chemicals and chemical petroleum, coal, rubber and plastic products	13	...	14	1	...	28	18	...	18	2	...	38
F Manufacture of non-metallic mineral products, except products of petroleum and coal	17	...	97	2	...	116	23	...	163	3	...	189
G Basic metal industries		...			...			...			...	
H Manufacture of fabricated metal products, machinery and equipment	11	...	5	1	...	17	15	...	13	1	...	29
I Other manufacturing industries	2	...	52	-	...	54	3	...	81	-	...	84
4 Electricity, gas and water	23	...	-40	2	...	-15	33	...	-49	3	...	-13
A Electricity, gas and steam	...	...	...	...	...	...	...	...	...	...	...	...
B Water works and supply	...	...	...	...	...	...	...	...	...	...	...	...
5 Construction	80	...	245	4	...	329	111	...	439	6	...	556
6 Wholesale and retail trade, restaurants and hotels	83	...	1632	21	...	1736	117	...	2569	37	...	2723
A Wholesale and retail trade	71	...	1533	20	...	1624	100	...	2419	36	...	2555
B Restaurants and hotels	12	...	99	1	...	112	17	...	150	1	...	168
7 Transport, storage and communication	63	...	628	17	...	708	93	...	951	20	...	1064
A Transport and storage	45	...	623	7	...	675	64	...	944	7	...	1015

Ecuador

4.3 Cost Components of Value Added
(Continued)

Thousand Million Ecuadoran sucres

	1990						1991					
	Compensation of Employees	Capital Consumption	Net Operating Surplus	Indirect Taxes	Less: Subsidies Received	Value Added	Compensation of Employees	Capital Consumption	Net Operating Surplus	Indirect Taxes	Less: Subsidies Received	Value Added
B Communication	18	...	5	10	...	33	29	...	7	13	...	49
8 Finance, insurance, real estate and business services	148	...	330	23	...	501	234	...	588	34	...	857
A Financial institutions	131	...	-16	8	...	124	209	...	25	6	...	240
B Insurance		...			...			...			...	
C Real estate and business services	17	...	346	15	...	378	25	...	563	28	...	616
9 Community, social and personal services	45	...	284	2	...	331	62	...	470	4	...	537
A Sanitary and similar services	...	...	...	...	...	...	...	...	...	...	...	...
B Social and related community services	...	...	...	...	...	...	...	...	...	...	...	...
C Recreational and cultural services	...	...	...	...	...	...	...	...	...	...	...	...
D Personal and household services	45	...	284	3	...	331	62	...	470	4	...	536
Statistical discrepancy	...	...	...	...	...	...	...	...	...	...	...	...
Total, Industries cd	709	...	6104	683	...	7496	1035	...	9578	795	...	11408
Producers of Government Services	387	...	...	...	...	387	504	...	...	...	...	504
Other Producers	19	...	...	...	...	19	26	...	...	...	...	26
Total cd	1115	...	6104	683	...	7902	1565	...	9578	795	...	11938
Less: Imputed bank service charge	...	...	149	...	...	149	...	...	288	...	...	288
Import duties	...	...	...	215	...	215	...	...	...	280	...	280
Value added tax	...	...	...	234	...	234	...	...	...	366	...	366
Total cd	1115	...	5955	1132	...	8202	1565	...	9290	1441	...	12296

of which General Government:

1 Agriculture, hunting, forestry and fishing	...	...	...	...	...	...	...	...	...	...	...	...
2 Mining and quarrying	...	...	...	...	...	...	...	...	...	...	...	...
3 Manufacturing	...	...	...	...	...	...	...	...	...	...	...	...
4 Electricity, gas and water	2	...	-2	...	...	-	2	...	-2	...	...	2
5 Construction	35	...	...	...	...	35	47	...	...	...	...	47
6 Wholesale and retail trade, restaurants and hotels	...	...	...	...	...	...	...	...	...	...	...	...
7 Transport and communication	...	...	...	...	...	...	...	...	...	...	...	...
8 Finance, insurance, real estate & business services	...	...	...	...	...	...	...	...	...	...	...	...
9 Community, social and personal services	23	...	...	...	...	23	36	...	...	...	...	36
Total, Industries of General Government	60	...	-2	...	...	58	85	...	-2	...	...	83
Producers of Government Services	387	...	...	...	...	387	504	...	...	...	...	504
Total, General Government	446	...	-2	...	...	445	589	...	-2	...	...	587

	1992						1993					
	Compensation of Employees	Capital Consumption	Net Operating Surplus	Indirect Taxes	Less: Subsidies Received	Value Added	Compensation of Employees	Capital Consumption	Net Operating Surplus	Indirect Taxes	Less: Subsidies Received	Value Added

All Producers

1 Agriculture, hunting, forestry and fishing	204	...	2244	17	...	2465	380	...	2924	18	...	3322
A Agriculture and hunting	196	...	1605	16	...	1817	365	...	2089	17	...	2471
B Forestry and logging	1	...	191	1	...	193	2	...	283	1	...	286
C Fishing	7	...	448	-	...	455	12	...	553	...	...	565
2 Mining and quarrying	120	...	1311	1009	...	2440	142	...	1414	1386	...	2942
A Coal mining [a]	...	...	...	...	...	...	...	...	...	...	...	...
B Crude petroleum and natural gas production [b]	90	...	1233	1009	...	2332	90	...	1306	1386	...	2782
C Metal ore mining [a]	...	...	...	...	...	...	...	...	...	...	...	...
D Other mining [a]	30	...	78	-	...	108	52	...	108	...	...	160

Ecuador

4.3 Cost Components of Value Added
(Continued)

Thousand Million Ecuadoran sucres

		1992						1993				
	Compensation of Employees	Capital Consumption	Net Operating Surplus	Indirect Taxes	Less: Subsidies Received	Value Added	Compensation of Employees	Capital Consumption	Net Operating Surplus	Indirect Taxes	Less: Subsidies Received	Value Added
3 Manufacturing	261	...	3830	190	...	4281	438	...	5270	257	...	5965
A Manufacture of food, beverages and tobacco	64	...	2479	171	...	2714	107	...	3365	236	...	3708
B Textile, wearing apparel and leather industries	73	...	339	6	...	418	124	...	465	7	...	596
C Manufacture of wood and wood products, including furniture	22	...	56	2	...	80	37	...	70	2	...	109
D Manufacture of paper and paper products, printing and publishing	16	...	505	3	...	523	26	...	714	2	...	742
E Manufacture of chemicals and chemical petroleum, coal, rubber and plastic products	24	...	45	4	...	72	46	...	43	3	...	92
F Manufacture of non-metallic mineral products, except products of petroleum and coal	35	...	278	1	...	317	56	...	429	5	...	490
G Basic metal industries		...			...			...			...	
H Manufacture of fabricated metal products, machinery and equipment	23	...	10	1	...	34	36	...	24	1	...	61
I Other manufacturing industries	4	...	118	1	...	123	6	...	160	1	...	167
4 Electricity, gas and water	45	...	-27	4	...	22	61	...	10	5	...	76
A Electricity, gas and steam	...	...	...	...	...	...	61	...	10	5	...	76
B Water works and supply	...	...	...	...	...	...	...	...	...	...	...	...
5 Construction	161	...	712	8	...	881	266	...	1065	9	...	1340
6 Wholesale and retail trade, restaurants and hotels	175	...	3938	55	...	4168	274	...	5272	4	...	5550
A Wholesale and retail trade	148	...	3667	54	...	3869	228	...	4865	3	...	5096
B Restaurants and hotels	27	...	271	1	...	299	46	...	407	1	...	454
7 Transport, storage and communication	133	...	1358	14	...	1505	200	...	2251	-2	...	2449
A Transport and storage	91	...	1344	-3	...	1432	128	...	2208	-28	...	2308
B Communication	42	...	14	17	...	73	72	...	43	26	...	141
8 Finance, insurance, real estate and business services	405	...	933	53	...	1393	1227	...	509	146	...	2255
A Financial institutions	370	...	6	12	...	388	614	...	69	47	...	730
B Insurance		...			...			...			...	
C Real estate and business services	36	...	927	41	...	1004	613	...	813	99	...	1525
9 Community, social and personal services	102	...	836	5	...	943	169	...	1394	1	...	1564
A Sanitary and similar services	...	...	...	...	...	...	...	...	...	...	...	...
B Social and related community services	...	...	...	...	...	...	...	...	...	...	...	...
C Recreational and cultural services	...	...	...	...	...	...	...	...	...	...	...	...
D Personal and household services	102	...	836	5	...	943	169	...	1394	1	...	1564
Statistical discrepancy	...	...	...	...	...	...	...	...	...	...	...	7
Total, Industries cd	1606	...	15135	1355	...	18098	3157	...	20090	1824	...	25470
Producers of Government Services	813	...	...	...	...	813	1309	...	...	...	...	1309
Other Producers	40	...	...	...	...	40	65	...	...	...	...	65
Total cd	2459	...	15135	1355	...	18951	3968	...	21090	1784	...	26844
Less: Imputed bank service charge	...	...	490	...	...	490	...	...	878	...	...	878
Import duties	...	...	...	339	...	339	...	...	...	537	...	537
Value added tax	...	...	...	612	...	612	...	...	...	949	...	949
Total cd	2459	...	14645	2306	...	19412	3968	...	20212	3272	...	27452

of which General Government:

1 Agriculture, hunting, forestry and fishing	...	...	...	...	...	...	...	...	...	...	...	...
2 Mining and quarrying	...	...	...	...	...	...	...	...	...	...	...	...
3 Manufacturing	...	...	...	...	...	...	...	...	...	...	...	...
4 Electricity, gas and water	2	...	-2	...	...	...	2	...	-3	...	...	...

Ecuador

4.3 Cost Components of Value Added
(Continued)

Thousand Million Ecuadoran sucres

	1992						1993					
	Compensation of Employees	Capital Consumption	Net Operating Surplus	Indirect Taxes	Less: Subsidies Received	Value Added	Compensation of Employees	Capital Consumption	Net Operating Surplus	Indirect Taxes	Less: Subsidies Received	Value Added
5 Construction	74	...	...	...	...	74	112	...	...	...	...	112
6 Wholesale and retail trade, restaurants and hotels	...	...	...	...	...	...	...	...	...	...	...	...
7 Transport and communication	...	...	...	...	...	...	...	...	...	...	...	...
8 Finance, insurance, real estate & business services	...	...	...	...	...	...	...	...	...	...	...	...
9 Community, social and personal services	64	...	...	...	...	64	99	...	...	...	...	99
Total, Industries of General Government	140	...	-2	...	...	138	214	...	-3	...	...	211
Producers of Government Services	813	...	...	...	...	813	1309	...	...	...	...	1309
Total, General Government	953	...	-2	...	...	951	1523	...	-3	...	...	1520

a) Items 'Coal mining' and 'Metal ore mining' are included in item 'Other mining'.
b) Petroleum refining is included in item 'Crude petroleum and natural gas production'.
c) Column 'Consumption of fixed capital' is included in column 'Net operating surplus'.
d) Column 4 refers to indirect taxes less subsidies received.

Egypt

General note. The preparation of national accounts statistics in Egypt is undertaken by the Ministry of Planning, Cairo. Official estimates are published in the annual 'Statistical Yearbook' published by the same agency. The estimates are generally in accordance with the classifications and definitions recommended in the United Nations System of National Accounts (SNA). An input-output table for the year 1966-67 has been completed by CAPMAS. The following tables have been prepared from successive replies to the United Nations national accounts questionnaire. When the scope and coverage of the estimates differ for conceptual or statistical reasons from the definitions and classifications recommended in SNA, a footnote is indicated to the relevant tables.

Sources and methods:

(a) Gross domestic product. Gross domestic product is estimated mainly through the production approach.

(b) Expenditure on the gross domestic product. All components of GDP by expenditure type are estimated through the expenditure approach. The estimates of government final consumption expenditure are based on government budgets and accounts. For private consumption expenditures, the estimates are based on family budgets and household expenditure surveys. The Department of Statistics prepares data on inventories of cotton, covering both commercial stocks and stocks of spinning industry. Other sources of information for changes in stocks include data collected regularly by the Ministry of Supply. For gross fixed capital formation, the government sector is estimated directly together with government consumption expenditure. The private sector estimate is obtained by deducting the government estimate from total capital formation. Capital formation in machinery and equipment is estimated through the commodity-flow approach using information on domestic production, imports and exports of capital goods. The estimates of exports and imports of merchandise are generally based on foreign trade statistics. The estimates of GDP by expenditure type in constant prices are prepared by the CAPMAS on the basis of official index numbers of prices and quantities.

(c) Cost-structure of the gross domestic product. The estimates of wages and salaries are based on government accounts and on various sectoral surveys. No specific information is available for operating surplus, which is computed as a gross estimate, i.e., including consumption of fixed capital. Indirect taxes and subsidies are seperately available for all economic units in the compulsory standard accounts for public enterprises and in the economic surveys for the private sector.

(d) Gross domestic product by kind of economic activity. The table of gross domestic product by kind of economic activity is prepared in factor values. The production approach is used to estimate value added of most industries. The income approach is used to estimate value added of community, social and personal services. The Ministry of Agriculture collects, through annual sample surveys, data on crop area, yield and crop-cutting. Livestock data are obtained through special censuses every two years and prices received by farmers are collected annually. The estimated acreage of each of the main crops is multiplied by average productivity of the basic area of measurement. The gross output is evaluated at farm-gate prices and estimates of intermediate consumption are based on data collected from the co-operative societies and from censuses. For the industrial activity sector, annual statistics on industrial production, capital formation, employment, wages and salaries are available for industrial establishments with ten workers or more which form the organized sector of the economy. For the non-organized sector, estimates are made by using data from industrial censuses and by studying the cost-structure of each industry, productivity and degree of mechanization. The output of construction is estimated indirectly from the input side by means of employment data and data on intermediate consumption. The value of gross output and components of value added are obtained by using the relationship between available data on intermediate consumption and primary inputs in organized enterprises and applying this relationship on the estimated intermediate consumption of this industry. For trade, annual basic statistics are available for establishments with five or more workers, while those with less than five workers are covered by sample surveys conducted every three years. Estimates for restaurants are made by using data on establishments, wages and salaries, working hours and data from sample surveys. Estimates for hotels are obtained through annual questionnaires. Data on input, output and other elements of large-scale transport are available through annual accounts. For unorganized transport, estimates are based on information on the number of establishments and workers, on wages and salaries and on other sources. Indicators such as input-ratios are used to estimate value added. Gross output and input of public financial institutions and insurance companies are based on data collected annually. The estimates of real estate, business services, and imputed rents of owner-occupied dwellings are based on family budget surveys. The government accounts provide information to estimate government services. Annual data are available for non-profit institutions serving households. For the service activities of unincorporated enterprises, gross output and inputs are estimated by using available censuses of establishments, wages and salaries statistics. The constant prices of GDP by kind of economic activity are estimated by CAPMAS on the basis of official index numbers of prices and quantities such as wholesale prices, consumer prices and quantities of imported and exported merchandise.

1.1 Expenditure on the Gross Domestic Product, in Current Prices

Million Egyptian pounds — Fiscal year beginning 1 July

	1980	1983	1984	1985	1986	1987	1988	1989	1990	1991	1992	1993
1 Government final consumption expenditure	2840	...	...	...	6632	7728	8621	9671	11010	12130	...	...
2 Private final consumption expenditure	11155	...	...	...	34800	42317	50653	62911	84048	110026	...	...
3 Gross capital formation	5208	...	...	...	15778	22076	23614	27335	23964	24617	...	...
A Increase in stocks	100	...	...	...	1526	1919	3405	4845	-655	200	...	...
B Gross fixed capital formation	5108	...	...	...	14252	20157	20209	22490	24619	24417	...	...
4 Exports of goods and services	5307	...	...	...	6476	10688	13741	19274	30943	40122	...	...
5 Less: Imports of goods and services	7361	...	...	...	11740	21699	24843	31450	39822	50705	...	...
Equals: Gross Domestic Product [a]	17149	31247	36618	40820	51946	61109	71786	87741	110143	136190	...	...

a) Data in this table have not been revised, therefore they are not comparable with the data in other tables.

1.2 Expenditure on the Gross Domestic Product, in Constant Prices

Million Egyptian pounds — Fiscal year beginning 1 July

	1980	1983	1984	1985	1986	1987	1988	1989	1990	1991	1992	1993
					At constant prices of:1981							
1 Government final consumption expenditure	...	4330	4406	4663	4572	...	...	...	...	...	...	...
2 Private final consumption expenditure	...	19196	21018	20851	22283	...	...	...	...	...	...	...
3 Gross capital formation	...	5729	5712	5552	5409	...	...	...	...	...	...	...
A Increase in stocks	...	121	133	146	161	...	...	...	...	...	...	...
B Gross fixed capital formation	...	5608	5579	5406	5248	...	...	...	...	...	...	...
4 Exports of goods and services	...	6561	6709	6749	7421	...	...	...	...	...	...	...
5 Less: Imports of goods and services	...	10041	10330	9751	9355	...	...	...	...	...	...	...
Equals: Gross Domestic Product	...	25775	27515	28063	30269	...	...	...	...	...	...	...

Egypt

1.3 Cost Components of the Gross Domestic Product

Million Egyptian pounds — Fiscal year beginning 1 July

	1980	1983	1984	1985	1986	1987	1988	1989	1990	1991	1992	1993
1 Indirect taxes, net	431	2291	2486	1760	3181	2723	4532	6400	6799	10705	...	...
A Indirect taxes	2598	...	...	...	...	...	...	...	...	...	...	...
B Less: Subsidies	2167	...	...	...	...	...	...	...	...	...	...	...
2 Consumption of fixed capital [a]	...	...	...	...	...	...	...	...	...	...	...	...
3 Compensation of employees paid by resident producers to:	16718	28956	34132	39060	40832	58386	67254	81341	103344	125485	...	...
4 Operating surplus [a]											...	...
Equals: Gross Domestic Product	17149	31247	36618	40820	51946	61109	71786	87741	110143	136190	...	...

a) Item 'Operating surplus' includes consumption of fixed capital.

1.10 Gross Domestic Product by Kind of Activity, in Current Prices

Million Egyptian pounds — Fiscal year beginning 1 July

	1980	1983	1984	1985	1986	1987	1988	1989	1990	1991	1992	1993
1 Agriculture, hunting, forestry and fishing	3392	5722	6380	7669	10111	11216	13046	15834	17823	20675	...	...
2 Mining and quarrying [a]	2768	3229	3581	3184	1873	2589	2408	3921	10986	13342	...	...
3 Manufacturing	2254	4050	5266	6351	8137	10633	12675	14669	17417	21409	...	...
4 Electricity, gas and water [b]	108	229	316	465	528	675	775	1033	1435	2009	...	...
5 Construction	740	1582	1876	2298	2822	3242	3804	4490	5226	6076	...	...
6 Wholesale and retail trade, restaurants and hotels	2255	5610	7013	8886	11306	12849	14787	17832	21744	26658	...	...
7 Transport, storage and communication	1458	2881	3079	3532	4043	5004	5873	7484	10822	14172	...	...
8 Finance, insurance, real estate and business services	1284	540	631	718	851	971	1101	1285	1475	1677	...	...
9 Community, social and personal services [cb]	644	5414	6612	7700	9094	11207	12785	14793	16416	19467	...	...
Total, Industries	...	29257	34754	40803	48765	58386	67254	81341	103344	125485	...	...
Producers of Government Services	1815	...	...	...	4549	...	...	...	...	...	...	...
Other Producers [c]	...	...	...	...	...	...	...	...	...	...	...	...
Subtotal [d]	16718	29257	34754	40403	48765	58386	67254	81341	103344	125485	...	...
Less: Imputed bank service charge	...	...	...	...	...	...	...	...	...	...	...	...
Plus: Import duties	...	...	...	...	...	...	...	...	...	...	...	...
Plus: Value added tax	...	...	...	...	...	...	...	...	...	...	...	...
Plus: Other adjustments [e]	431	...	...	...	3181	2723	4532	6400	6799	10705	...	...
Equals: Gross Domestic Product	17149	...	...	...	51946	61109	71786	87741	110143	136190	...	...

a) Item 'Mining and quarrying' refers to oil and its products.
b) Item 'Electricity, gas and water' refers to electricity only. Gas and water are included in item 'Community, social and personal services'.
c) Item 'Other producers' is included in item 'Community, social and personal services'.
d) Gross domestic product in factor values.
e) Item 'Other adjustments' refers to indirect taxes net of subsidies.

1.11 Gross Domestic Product by Kind of Activity, in Constant Prices

Million Egyptian pounds — Fiscal year beginning 1 July

	1980	1983	1984	1985	1986	1987	1988	1989	1990	1991	1992	1993
		At constant prices of: 1981							At constant prices of: 1986			
1 Agriculture, hunting, forestry and fishing	...	4258	4394	4540	4670	...	8930	9180	9440	...	...	...
2 Mining and quarrying	...	3536[a]	3911[a]	3949[a]	3867[a]	...	9234	9727	10292	...	...	...
3 Manufacturing	...	3260	3584	3849	4129					...	...	...
4 Electricity, gas and water	...	163[b]	179[b]	219[b]	241[b]	...	746	796	905	...	...	...
5 Construction	...	1179	1224	1273	1242	...	2145	2259	2381	...	...	...
6 Wholesale and retail trade, restaurants and hotels	...	3239	3477	3545	3728	...	10151	10618	11110	...	...	...
7 Transport, storage and communication	...	2484	2541	2705	2840	...	3996	4368	4678	...	...	...
8 Finance, insurance, real estate and business services	...	2007	2236	2348	2500	...	...	...	...	...	...	...
9 Community, social and personal services	...	1008[cb]	1097[cb]	1201[cb]	1303[cb]	...	8048	8655	9104	...	...	...
Statistical discrepancy	...	257	277	258	299	...	...	...	...	...	...	...

Egypt

1.11 Gross Domestic Product by Kind of Activity, in Constant Prices
(Continued)

Million Egyptian pounds — Fiscal year beginning 1 July

	1980	1983	1984	1985	1986	1987	1988	1989	1990	1991	1992	1993
			1981		At constant prices of:				1986			
Total, Industries	...	21390	22920	23887	24817	...	...	...	...	...	...	...
Producers of Government Services	...	...	...	...	...	...	...	...	...	...	...	...
Other Producers	...	...	...	...	...	...	...	...	...	...	...	...
Subtotal	...	23848[d]	25610[d]	26829[d]	27957[d]	43249	45603	47911	...	...	...	...
Less: Imputed bank service charge	...	...	...	...	...	...	...	...	...	...	...	...
Plus: Import duties	...	...	...	...	...	...	...	...	...	...	...	...
Plus: Value added tax	...	...	...	...	...	...	...	...	...	...	...	...
Equals: Gross Domestic Product	...	...	...	...	...	...	...	...	...	...	...	...

a) Item 'Mining and quarrying' refers to oil and its products.
b) Item 'Electricity, gas and water' refers to electricity only. Gas and water are included in item 'Community, social and personal services'.
c) Item 'Other producers' is included in item 'Community, social and personal services'.
d) Gross domestic product in factor values.

2.11 Gross Fixed Capital Formation by Kind of Activity of Owner, ISIC Divisions, in Current Prices

Million Egyptian pounds — Fiscal year beginning 1 July

		1980	1983	1984	1985	1986	1987	1988	1989	1990	1991	1992	1993
						All Producers							
1	Agriculture, hunting, forestry and fishing	370	520	665	772	889	1435	1599	1791	...	...	...	...
2	Mining and quarrying	606	292	375	281	179	1770	2153	2335	...	...	...	...
3	Manufacturing	1288	1541	1616	1524	1611	5068	4730	5230	...	...	...	...
4	Electricity, gas and water	482	503	487	588	546	3252	1973	2447	...	...	...	...
5	Construction	184	210	195	170	245	267	331	437	...	...	...	...
6	Wholesale and retail trade, restaurants and hotels	181	133	141	97	87	...	...	...	...	...	...	...
7	Transport, storage and communication	986	1612	1745	1637	1397	3668	3435	3719	...	...	...	...
8	Finance, insurance, real estate and business services	678	831	943	1353	1551	...	...	...	...	...	...	...
9	Community, social and personal services	559	1066	1105	1329	1195	1487	1829	2054	...	...	...	...
	Total Industries	5334	6710	7272	7752	7700	20157	20209	22490	...	...	...	...
	Producers of Government Services	...	...	...	...	...	...	...	...	...	...	...	...
	Private Non-Profit Institutions Serving Households	...	...	...	...	...	...	...	...	...	...	...	...
	Total [a]	5334	6710	7272	7752	7700	20157	20209	22490	...	...	...	...

a) Gross fixed capital formation includes the value of land for estimates prior to 1981/82.

El Salvador

General note. The preparation of national accounts statistics in El Salvador is undertaken by the Departamento de Investigaciones Economicas del Banco Central, San Salvador. The official estimates are published monthly in 'Revista Mensual'. A detailed description of the sources and methods used for the national accounts estimation is contained in 'Metodologia de Cuentas Nacionales de los Paises Centroamericanos' published by the Consejo Monetario Centroamericano Secretaria Ejecutiva in October 1976. The estimates are generally in accordance with the classifications and definitions recommended in the United Nations System of National Accounts (SNA). The following tables have been prepared from successive replies to the United Nations national accounts questionnaire. When the scope and coverage of the estimates differ for conceptual or statistical reasons from the definitions and classifications recommended in SNA, a footnote is indicated to the relevant tables.

Sources and methods:

(a) Gross domestic product. Gross domestic product is estimated mainly through the production approach.

(b) Expenditure on the gross domestic product. The expenditure approach is used to estimate government final consumption expenditure, increase in stocks, and exports and imports of goods and services. The commodity-flow approach supplemented by the expenditure approach is used for private final consumption expenditure and gross fixed capital formation. The estimates of government consumption expenditure are obtained directly from government sources. For private consumption expenditure, the commodity-flow approach is used with adjustments made for distribution and other costs which are included in the retail value. The estimates of increase in stocks are based on information on stored agricultural products, the stocks of the manufacturing and trade industries and the stocks of public construction. Private capital formation is estimated on the basis of data on domestically produced and imported capital goods and on statistics of construction and repair work. The imports data are adjusted to include import duties, trade margins and installation costs. For public expenditure on capital formation, data are obtained from official sources. Data on exports and imports of goods and services are obtained from the balance of payments. Export data on coffee are obtained from the Compania Salvadorena de Cafe, while other merchandise data are furnished by the Direccion General de Estadistica y Censos. GDP by expenditure at constant prices is not estimated.

(c) Cost-structure of the gross domestic product. Compensation of employees, combined with operating surplus, is obtained as a residual. The estimates of net indirect taxes are derived from the government accounts. No specific information is available on how consumption of fixed capital is estimated.

(d) Gross domestic product by kind of economic activity. The table of gross domestic product by kind of economic activity is prepared at market prices, i.e. producers' values. The production approach is used to estimate value added of most industries. The income approach is used for domestic services and public administration and defence while an indirect method is used for the trade sector. The agricultural data, which are provided by Ministerio de Agricultura y Ganaderia, are obtained through various periodic surveys. Data on the coffee harvest are supplied by the Compania Salvadorena de Cafe while coffee prices are taken from the Compania de Cafe's export prices. Information on the production of cotton is provided by the Cooperative Algodonera Salvadorena Ltda. The gross value of production is calculated by applying producers' prices to the quantity of each commodity produced. For the livestock sector, information is obtained from the Direccion General de Estadistica y Censos, external trade data and through direct studies on prices. Value added of forestry and logging is estimated by means of indirect methods. For the mining and quarrying sector, the estimates are based on 1961 census figures combined with a volume index constructed from square-metre construction data and on price index. The gross value of production in manufacturing is based on the results of annual surveys and industrial censuses held every five years. Estimates for small-scale manufacturing is extrapolated from census data. The estimates for electricity are based on industrial census results and on information furnished by the concerned agencies. For private construction, the information is obtained from the Direccion General de Estadistica y Censos. The basic sources include permits issued for urban construction. Rural population figures are used to determine the number of new dwellings in rural areas. The estimates for public construction are obtained from concerned institutions. For both public and private constructions, intermediate consumption is determined by using a fixed percentage of gross value of production. Gross output of the trade sector is determined on the basis of the values of domestic and imported goods marketed. The gross value of production of domestic goods and the c.i.f. values of imported goods are adjusted for changes in stocks and trade margin are added. An estimate of inputs, which is made from survey based on percentages for electricity, transport, etc., is deducted from the total gross value of production to arrive at value added. Estimates of restaurants and hotels are inter-and extrapolated on the basis of census figures. The enterprises concerned with road transport are classified into international, interdepartamental, urban and interurban transport. A sample from each category is taken in order to obtain average figures for estimating receipts per ton, which are multiplied by quantity figures to arrive at gross value of production and value added. For railways, air transport and communication, information is obtained directly from concerned companies. The estimates of the financial sector are based on financial statements furnished by the banks and insurance companies. Imputation is made for service charges by deducting interest from investment income. The estimate of ownership of dwellings are based on the number of urban and rural dwellings obtained from the population censuses and rents data from surveys, and using the cost of living index as an inflator. Ten percent of the gross value of production are deducted for inputs. The estimates of government services are based on information published by the Ministerio de Hacienda. For other services such as education, hospitals, religion, the estimates are obtained from concerned institutions or from publications such as Indicadores Economicas and Boletin Estadistico. For domestic services, the annual average wages for four regional areas of the country are applied to an estimate of the number of persons engaged. The latter is based on the 1961 census figures and average growth rates while the wage is estimated annually, applying the cost of living index. For the constant price estimates, value added for the agricultural, electricity, trade, transport and financial sectors is estimated by using volume or quantity indexes. Double deflation is used for the manufacturing sector. Price deflation is used for mining and quarrying, construction, restaurants and hotels and government services. For domestic services, wages paid in the base-year are applied to the number employed in the current year.

1.1 Expenditure on the Gross Domestic Product, in Current Prices

Million Salvadoran colones

		1980	1983	1984	1985	1986	1987	1988	1989	1990	1991	1992	1993
1	Government final consumption expenditure	1247	1607	1869	2220	2803	3181	3484	3930	4649	5272	5789	...
2	Private final consumption expenditure	6405	7871	9184	11640	15206	18744	22153	26729	36132	41821	48798	...
3	Gross capital formation	1183	1224	1394	1554	2619	2861	3501	4940	4851	6606	8874	...
	A Increase in stocks	-27	44	58	-169	26	-297	45	646	17	171	280	...
	B Gross fixed capital formation	1210	1180	1336	1723	2594	3158	3456	4293	4834	6435	8594	...
	Residential buildings	182	315	326	488	537	637	644	841	1120	1303	1329	...
	Non-residential buildings	21	6	8	7	110	146	231	181	212	245	435	...
	Other construction and land improvement etc.	436	386	387	404	425	633	781	938	840	1096	1380	...
	Other	571	473	614	824	1522	1742	1800	2333	2662	3791	5450	...
4	Exports of goods and services	3046	2486	2536	3199	4875	4395	4327	4267	6538	7055	7459	...
5	Less: Imports of goods and services	2964	3036	3327	4283	5740	6040	6099	7636	11113	12963	16068	...
	Equals: Gross Domestic Product	8917	10152	11657	14331	19763	23141	27366	32230	41057	47792	54853	...

El Salvador

1.2 Expenditure on the Gross Domestic Product, in Constant Prices

Million Salvadoran colones

	1980	1983	1984	1985	1986	1987	1988	1989	1990	1991	1992	1993
					At constant prices of:1962							
1 Government final consumption expenditure	422	440	461	492	511	526	539	533	538	561	562	...
2 Private final consumption expenditure	2496	2096	2175	2251	2245	2259	2275	2330	2377	2424	2497	...
3 Gross capital formation	412	326	335	317	385	368	446	551	390	478	600	...
A Increase in stocks	-10	12	14	-37	5	-46	16	81	2	16	27	...
B Gross fixed capital formation	422	314	321	354	380	415	430	469	388	461	572	...
4 Exports of goods and services	838	705	674	648	566	637	577	499	719	707	787	...
5 Less: Imports of goods and services	879	696	710	714	694	697	693	735	738	769	870	...
Equals: Gross Domestic Product	3289	2870	2936	2994	3013	3094	3144	3177	3285	3401	3576	...

1.3 Cost Components of the Gross Domestic Product

Million Salvadoran colones

	1980	1983	1984	1985	1986	1987	1988	1989	1990	1991	1992	1993
1 Indirect taxes, net	642	751	982	1245	2014	1764	1680	1649	2195	2771	3400	...
A Indirect taxes	677	774	1009	1275	2056	1806	1724	1699	2270	2834	3426	...
B Less: Subsidies	35	23	27	30	42	42	44	50	76	63	26	...
2 Consumption of fixed capital	369	420	482	591	815	955	1129	1329	1694	1972	2265	...
3 Compensation of employees paid by resident producers to: [a]	7904	8981	10193	12495	16934	20422	24557	29252	37168	43049	49188	...
4 Operating surplus												...
Equals: Gross Domestic Product	8916	10152	11657	14331	19763	23141	27366	32230	41057	47792	54853	...

a) Items 'Compensation of employees paid by resident producers' and 'Operating surplus' have been obtained as a residual.

1.7 External Transactions on Current Account, Summary

Million Salvadoran colones

	1980	1983	1984	1985	1986	1987	1988	1989	1990	1991	1992	1993
					Payments to the Rest of the World							
1 Imports of goods and services	2964	3036	3327	4283	5740	6040	6099	7636	11113	12963	16068	...
A Imports of merchandise c.i.f.	2405	2463	2742	3413	4674	4972	5035	6503	9594	11276	14216	...
B Other	559	573	585	870	1066	1068	1064	1133	1519	1687	1852	...
2 Factor income to the rest of the world	258	495	511	521	675	721	710	757	1113	1225	1107	...
A Compensation of employees	3	17	20	18	...	...	...	...	...	...	...	...
B Property and entrepreneurial income	255	478	491	503	...	...	...	...	...	...	...	...
3 Current transfers to the rest of the world	10	7	9	8	12	12	12	12	18	20	21	...
4 Surplus of the nation on current transactions	77	-241	-365	-579	583	696	262	-988	-1029	-945	-1268	...
Payments to the Rest of the World and Surplus of the Nation on Current Transactions	3309	3298	3482	4234	7011	7469	7082	7417	11215	13263	15928	...
					Receipts From The Rest of the World							
1 Exports of goods and services	3046	2486	2536	3199	4876	4395	4327	4267	6538	7055	7459	...
A Exports of merchandise f.o.b.	2688	2025	1920	2339	3775	2955	3044	2786	4419	4716	5001	...
B Other	358	461	616	860	1101	1440	1283	1481	2119	2339	2458	...
2 Factor income from rest of the world	131	126	168	168	203	196	200	230	337	403	627	...
A Compensation of employees	85	83	111	...	...	...	...	...	...	...	...	...
B Property and entrepreneurial income	46	43	57	...	...	...	...	...	...	...	...	...
3 Current transfers from rest of the world	132	686	778	867	1932	2878	2555	2921	4340	5805	7842	...
Receipts from the Rest of the World on Current Transactions	3309	3298	3482	4234	7011	7469	7082	7418	11215	13263	15928	...

El Salvador

1.8 Capital Transactions of The Nation, Summary

Million Salvadoran colones

	1980	1983	1984	1985	1986	1987	1988	1989	1990	1991	1992	1993
Finance of Gross Capital Formation												
Gross saving	1260	983	1029	975	3202	3557	3765	3952	3822	5661	7606	...
1 Consumption of fixed capital	369	420	482	591	815	955	1128	1328	1694	1972	2265	...
2 Net saving	891	563	547	384	2387	2602	2637	2624	2128	3689	5341	...
Less: Surplus of the nation on current transactions	77	-241	-365	-579	583	696	262	-988	-1029	-945	-1268	...
Finance of Gross Capital Formation	1183	1224	1394	1554	2619	2861	3501	4940	4851	6606	8874	...
Gross Capital Formation												
Increase in stocks	-27	44	59	-169	26	-297	45	646	17	171	280	...
Gross fixed capital formation	1210	1180	1336	1723	2594	3158	3456	4293	4834	6435	8594	...
1 General government	214	89	79	83	90	103	129	256	144	214	601	...
2 Corporate and quasi-corporate enterprises	...	...	...	...	...	...	...	...	...	...	...	...
3 Other	...	...	...	...	...	...	...	...	...	...	...	...
Gross Capital Formation	1183	1224	1394	1554	2619	2861	3501	4940	4851	6606	8874	...

1.10 Gross Domestic Product by Kind of Activity, in Current Prices

Million Salvadoran colones

	1980	1983	1984	1985	1986	1987	1988	1989	1990	1991	1992	1993
1 Agriculture, hunting, forestry and fishing	2480	2161	2320	2611	3969	3199	3801	3767	4599	4881	5167	...
2 Mining and quarrying	11	15	18	21	27	38	47	58	65	82	99	...
3 Manufacturing	1339	1572	1837	2346	3086	4045	4808	5836	7647	8957	10348	...
4 Electricity, gas and water	189	244	281	335	418	497	535	606	793	1082	1284	...
5 Construction	306	343	355	437	547	711	815	984	1072	1310	1557	...
6 Wholesale and retail trade, restaurants and hotels [a]	2038	2510	2995	3898	5627	7275	8721	10831	14187	16751	19647	...
7 Transport, storage and communication	314	412	481	613	816	1061	1206	1416	1897	2274	2660	...
8 Finance, insurance, real estate and business services	686	896	1032	1189	1503	1822	2299	2688	3290	3892	4522	...
9 Community, social and personal services [a]	637	823	982	1278	1794	2286	2749	3330	4275	4986	5709	...
Total, Industries	8001	8976	10291	12728	17786	20934	24981	29516	37825	44214	50993	...
Producers of Government Services	916	1177	1366	1603	1977	2207	2385	2714	3232	3578	3860	...
Other Producers	...	...	...	...	...	...	...	...	...	...	...	...
Subtotal	8917	10153	11657	14331	19763	23141	27366	32230	41057	47792	54853	...
Less: Imputed bank service charge	...	...	...	...	...	...	...	...	...	...	...	...
Plus: Import duties	...	...	...	...	...	...	...	...	...	...	...	...
Plus: Value added tax	...	...	...	...	...	...	...	...	...	...	...	...
Equals: Gross Domestic Product	8917	10152	11657	14331	19763	23141	27366	32230	41057	47792	54853	...

a) Restaurants and hotels are included in item 'Community, social and personal services'.

1.11 Gross Domestic Product by Kind of Activity, in Constant Prices

Million Salvadoran colones

	1980	1983	1984	1985	1986	1987	1988	1989	1990	1991	1992	1993
At constant prices of: 1962												
1 Agriculture, hunting, forestry and fishing	841	727	751	743	720	735	728	731	785	785	856	...
2 Mining and quarrying	4	4	4	4	4	5	5	5	5	5	6	...
3 Manufacturing	586	491	497	515	528	544	560	574	592	620	658	...
4 Electricity, gas and water	106	105	108	113	116	118	120	121	128	137	146	...
5 Construction	111	92	87	91	93	104	112	116	101	112	122	...
6 Wholesale and retail trade, restaurants and hotels [a]	625	478	487	490	491	498	500	517	533	556	579	...
7 Transport, storage and communication	194	171	176	179	180	183	187	189	201	215	227	...
8 Finance, insurance, real estate and business services	233	239	242	247	249	255	262	255	261	269	280	...
9 Community, social and personal services [a]	248	198	200	201	202	205	208	211	214	223	231	...

El Salvador

1.11 Gross Domestic Product by Kind of Activity, in Constant Prices
(Continued)

Million Salvadoran colones

	1980	1983	1984	1985	1986	1987	1988	1989	1990	1991	1992	1993
				At constant prices of:1962								
Total, Industries	2947	2505	2552	2583	2583	2647	2681	2719	2820	2921	3105	...
Producers of Government Services	342	366	384	412	430	447	463	458	465	479	471	...
Other Producers	...	...	...	...	...	...	...	...	...	...	...	...
Subtotal	3289	2870	2936	2994	3013	3094	3144	3177	3285	3401	3576	...
Less: Imputed bank service charge	...	...	...	...	...	...	...	...	...	...	...	...
Plus: Import duties	...	...	...	...	...	...	...	...	...	...	...	...
Plus: Value added tax	...	...	...	...	...	...	...	...	...	...	...	...
Equals: Gross Domestic Product	3289	2870	2936	2994	3013	3094	3144	3177	3285	3401	3576	...

a) Restaurants and hotels are included in item 'Community, social and personal services'.

1.12 Relations Among National Accounting Aggregates

Million Salvadoran colones

	1980	1983	1984	1985	1986	1987	1988	1989	1990	1991	1992	1993
Gross Domestic Product	8917	10152	11657	14331	19763	23141	27366	32230	41057	47792	54853	...
Plus: Net factor income from the rest of the world	-128	-370	-343	-353	-472	-525	-509	-527	-775	-822	-481	...
Factor income from the rest of the world	131	126	168	168	203	196	201	230	337	403	627	...
Less: Factor income to the rest of the world	258	495	511	521	675	721	710	757	1113	1225	1107	...
Equals: Gross National Product	8789	9782	11314	13978	19291	22616	26857	31703	40282	46970	54372	...
Less: Consumption of fixed capital	369	420	482	591	815	955	1129	1329	1694	1972	2265	...
Equals: National Income	8420	9362	10832	13387	18476	21661	25728	30374	38588	44998	52107	...
Plus: Net current transfers from the rest of the world	122	679	769	859	1920	2866	2543	2909	4322	5785	7821	...
Current transfers from the rest of the world	132	686	778	867	1932	2878	2555	2921	4340	5805	7842	...
Less: Current transfers to the rest of the world	10	7	9	8	12	12	12	12	18	20	21	...
Equals: National Disposable Income	8542	10041	11601	14246	20396	24527	28271	33283	42910	50783	59928	...
Less: Final consumption	7652	9478	11054	13860	18009	21926	25637	30660	40781	47093	54588	...
Equals: Net Saving	890	563	547	386	2387	2601	2634	2623	2129	3690	5340	...
Less: Surplus of the nation on current transactions	77	-241	-365	-579	583	696	262	-988	-1029	-945	-1268	...
Equals: Net Capital Formation	813	804	912	965	1804	1905	2372	3611	3158	4635	6608	...

2.11 Gross Fixed Capital Formation by Kind of Activity of Owner, ISIC Divisions, in Current Prices

Million Salvadoran colones

	1980	1983	1984	1985	1986	1987	1988	1989	1990	1991	1992	1993
					All Producers							
1 Agriculture, hunting, forestry and fishing	20	40	48	61	81	85	53	67	102	148	196	...
2 Mining and quarrying	...	...	...	...	...	...	...	...	...	...	...	...
3 Manufacturing	158	149	187	220	484	469	522	567	811	1179	1562	...
4 Electricity, gas and water	12	14	11	16	94	100	86	109	133	146	255	...
5 Construction	655	721	741	928	1126	1485	1729	2085	2267	2759	3327	...
6 Wholesale and retail trade, restaurants and hotels [a]	11	20	35	39	77	72	82	102	124	136	239	...
7 Transport, storage and communication	120	123	208	333	600	803	804	1037	1170	1761	2254	...
8 Finance, insurance, real estate and business services [b]	1	-	1	4	4	1	2	5	6	7	11	...
9 Community, social and personal services [a,b]	20	23	26	40	38	41	50	64	77	85	149	...
Total Industries	996	1091	1257	1640	2504	3055	3327	4037	4690	6221	7993	...
Producers of Government Services	214	89	79	83	90	103	129	256	144	214	601	...
Private Non-Profit Institutions Serving Households	...	...	...	...	...	...	...	...	...	...	...	...
Total	1210	1180	1336	1723	2594	3158	3456	4293	4834	6435	8594	...

a) Restaurants and hotels are included in item 'Community, social and personal services'.
b) Business services are included in item 'Community, social and personal services'.

El Salvador

4.1 Derivation of Value Added by Kind of Activity, in Current Prices

Million Salvadoran colones

	1980 Gross Output	1980 Intermediate Consumption	1980 Value Added	1985 Gross Output	1985 Intermediate Consumption	1985 Value Added	1990 Gross Output	1990 Intermediate Consumption	1990 Value Added	1991 Gross Output	1991 Intermediate Consumption	1991 Value Added
					All Producers							
1 Agriculture, hunting, forestry and fishing	3075	595	2480	3179	568	2611	6264	1665	4599	6923	2042	4881
A Agriculture and hunting	2988	583	2405	3048	550	2498	5959	1642	4317	6607	2018	4589
B Forestry and logging	34	-	34	43	-	43	77	-	77	82	-	82
C Fishing	53	12	41	88	18	70	228	23	205	234	24	210
2 Mining and quarrying	17	6	11	31	10	21	96	31	65	120	38	82
A Coal mining	...	...	...	...	...	...	...	...	...	...	...	...
B Crude petroleum and natural gas production	...	...	...	...	...	...	...	...	...	...	...	...
C Metal ore mining	17	6	11	31	10	21	96	31	65	120	38	82
D Other mining	...	...	...	...	...	...	...	...	...	...	...	...
3 Manufacturing	3397	2058	1339	5950	3604	2346	18111	10464	7647	21218	12261	8957
A Manufacture of food, beverages and tobacco	1531	870	661	3116	1826	1290	9893	5562	4331	11472	6447	5025
B Textile, wearing apparel and leather industries	577	354	223	706	441	265	2237	1364	873	2674	1630	1044
C Manufacture of wood and wood products, including furniture	58	25	33	150	66	84	462	176	286	542	206	336
D Manufacture of paper and paper products, printing and publishing	119	75	44	191	124	67	613	379	234	744	460	284
E Manufacture of chemicals and chemical petroleum, coal, rubber and plastic products	705	501	204	1052	713	339	2600	1665	935	3064	1962	1102
F Manufacture of non-metallic mineral products, except products of petroleum and coal	116	48	68	206	88	118	718	323	395	855	385	470
G Basic metal industries	74	53	21	183	132	51	521	324	197	611	380	231
H Manufacture of fabricated metal products, machinery and equipment	143	83	60	205	118	87	663	412	251	784	488	296
I Other manufacturing industries	76	51	25	141	96	45	403	259	144	471	303	168
4 Electricity, gas and water	246	57	189	436	101	335	1016	223	793	1387	305	1082
A Electricity, gas and steam	...	...	164	...	...	295	894	196	698	1220	268	952
B Water works and supply	...	...	25	...	...	40	122	27	95	167	37	130
5 Construction	649	343	306	918	481	437	2172	1100	1072	2634	1324	1310
6 Wholesale and retail trade, restaurants and hotels	2166	128	2038	4147	249	3898	15150	963	14187	17889	1138	16751
A Wholesale and retail trade	...	...	2038	4147	249	3898	15150	963	14187	17889	1138	16751
B Restaurants and hotels [a]	...	...	...	...	...	...	...	...	...	...	...	...
Restaurants	...	...	...	...	...	...	...	...	...	...	...	...
Hotels and other lodging places	...	...	16	...	...	...	...	...	...	...	...	...
7 Transport, storage and communication	490	177	313	905	292	613	2790	893	1897	3344	1070	2274
8 Finance, insurance, real estate and business services	780	94	686	1348	159	1189	3754	464	3290	4451	559	3892
A Financial institutions	...	...	...	521	79	442	1139	215	924	1445	274	1171
B Insurance	...	...	...									
C Real estate and business services	...	...	...	827	80	747	2615	249	2366	3006	285	2721
9 Community, social and personal services [a]	1298	661	637	1908	630	1278	6290	2015	4275	7336	2350	4986
Total, Industries	12118	4119	8001	18820	6092	12728	55427	17602	37825	65302	21088	44214
Producers of Government Services	1247	331	916	2220	617	1603	4649	1417	3232	5272	1694	3578
Other Producers	...	...	...	...	...	...	...	...	...	...	...	...
Total	13365	4450	8917	21040	6709	14331	60076	19019	41057	70574	22782	47792
Less: Imputed bank service charge	...	...	...	...	...	...	...	...	...	...	...	...
Import duties	...	...	...	...	...	...	...	...	...	...	...	...
Value added tax	...	...	...	...	...	...	...	...	...	...	...	...
Total	...	...	...	...	...	...	...	...	...	...	...	...

El Salvador

4.1 Derivation of Value Added by Kind of Activity, in Current Prices

Million Salvadoran colones

	1992 Gross Output	1992 Intermediate Consumption	1992 Value Added
			All Producers
1 Agriculture, hunting, forestry and fishing	7081	1914	5167
A Agriculture and hunting	6736	1884	4852
B Forestry and logging	87	-	87
C Fishing	258	30	228
2 Mining and quarrying	144	46	99
A Coal mining	...	...	...
B Crude petroleum and natural gas production	...	...	...
C Metal ore mining	144	46	99
D Other mining	...	...	...
3 Manufacturing	24514	14166	10348
A Manufacture of food, beverages and tobacco	13115	7367	5748
B Textile, wearing apparel and leather industries	3304	2013	1291
C Manufacture of wood and wood products, including furniture	624	238	386
D Manufacture of paper and paper products, printing and publishing	862	533	329
E Manufacture of chemicals and chemical petroleum, coal, rubber and plastic products	3485	2230	1255
F Manufacture of non-metallic mineral products, except products of petroleum and coal	972	437	535
G Basic metal industries	725	450	275
H Manufacture of fabricated metal products, machinery and equipment	913	568	345
I Other manufacturing industries	514	330	184
4 Electricity, gas and water	1646	362	1284
A Electricity, gas and steam	1483	326	1157
B Water works and supply	163	36	127
5 Construction	3144	1587	1557
6 Wholesale and retail trade, restaurants and hotels	20981	1335	19647
A Wholesale and retail trade	20981	1335	19647
B Restaurants and hotels [a]	...	...	...
Restaurants	...	...	...
Hotels and other lodging places	...	...	...
7 Transport, storage and communication	3912	1252	2660
8 Finance, insurance, real estate and business services	5182	660	4522
A Financial institutions	1782	337	1445
B Insurance			
C Real estate and business services	3400	323	3077
9 Community, social and personal services [a]	8401	2691	5710
Total, Industries	75005	24013	50993
Producers of Government Services	5789	1929	3860
Other Producers	...	...	...
Total	80794	25942	54853
Less: Imputed bank service charge	...	...	...
Import duties	...	...	...
Value added tax	...	...	...
Total	...	...	...

a) Restaurants and hotels are included in item 'Community, social and personal services'.

El Salvador

4.2 Derivation of Value Added by Kind of Activity, in Constant Prices

Million Salvadoran colones

At constant prices of: 1962

All Producers

	1980 Gross Output	1980 Intermediate Consumption	1980 Value Added	1985 Gross Output	1985 Intermediate Consumption	1985 Value Added	1990 Gross Output	1990 Intermediate Consumption	1990 Value Added	1991 Gross Output	1991 Intermediate Consumption	1991 Value Added
1 Agriculture, hunting, forestry and fishing	...	...	841	...	...	743	...	...	785	...	...	785
A Agriculture and hunting	...	...	801	...	...	699	...	...	745	...	...	743
B Forestry and logging	...	...	27	...	...	29	...	...	29	...	...	30
C Fishing	...	...	13	...	...	15	...	...	12	...	...	12
2 Mining and quarrying	...	...	4	...	...	4	...	...	5	...	...	5
A Coal mining	...	...	...	...	...	...	...	...	...	...	...	...
B Crude petroleum and natural gas production	...	...	...	...	...	...	...	...	...	...	...	...
C Metal ore mining	...	...	4	...	...	4	...	...	5	...	...	5
D Other mining	...	...	...	...	...	...	...	...	...	...	...	...
3 Manufacturing	...	...	586	...	...	515	...	...	592	...	...	620
A Manufacture of food, beverages and tobacco	...	...	360	...	...	347	...	...	392	...	...	412
B Textile, wearing apparel and leather industries	...	...	52	...	...	30	...	...	36	...	...	38
C Manufacture of wood and wood products, including furniture	...	...	18	...	...	21	...	...	25	...	...	27
D Manufacture of paper and paper products, printing and publishing	...	...	24	...	...	13	...	...	13	...	...	13
E Manufacture of chemicals and chemical petroleum, coal, rubber and plastic products	...	...	53	...	...	44	...	...	50	...	...	53
F Manufacture of non-metallic mineral products, except products of petroleum and coal	...	...	27	...	...	23	...	...	29	...	...	30
G Basic metal industries	...	...	9	...	...	9	...	...	12	...	...	12
H Manufacture of fabricated metal products, machinery and equipment	...	...	32	...	...	20	...	...	24	...	...	25
I Other manufacturing industries	...	...	12	...	...	8	...	...	11	...	...	11
4 Electricity, gas and water	...	...	106	...	...	113	...	...	128	...	...	137
A Electricity, gas and steam	...	...	98	...	...	102	...	...	128	...	...	137
B Water works and supply	...	...	8	...	...	11	...	...	...	...	...	...
5 Construction	...	...	111	...	...	91	...	...	101	...	...	111
6 Wholesale and retail trade, restaurants and hotels	...	...	625	...	...	490	...	...	533	...	...	556
A Wholesale and retail trade	...	...	625	...	...	490	...	...	533	...	...	556
B Restaurants and hotels [a]	...	...	...	...	...	...	...	...	...	...	...	...
Restaurants	...	...	...	...	...	...	...	...	...	...	...	...
Hotels and other lodging places	...	...	6	...	...	...	...	...	...	...	...	...
7 Transport, storage and communication	...	...	194	...	...	179	...	...	201	...	...	215
8 Finance, insurance, real estate and business services	...	...	233	...	...	247	...	...	261	...	...	270
A Financial institutions	...	...	...	...	...	103	...	...	101	...	...	105
B Insurance	...	...	...	...	...	...	...	...	...	...	...	...
C Real estate and business services	...	...	...	...	...	144	...	...	160	...	...	165
9 Community, social and personal services [a]	...	...	248	...	...	201	...	...	214	...	...	223
Total, Industries	...	...	2948	...	...	2583	...	...	2820	...	...	2922
Producers of Government Services	...	...	342	...	...	412	...	...	465	...	...	479
Other Producers	...	...	...	...	...	...	...	...	...	...	...	...
Total	...	...	3289	...	...	2994	...	...	3285	...	...	3401
Less: Imputed bank service charge	...	...	...	...	...	...	...	...	...	...	...	...
Import duties	...	...	...	...	...	...	...	...	...	...	...	...
Value added tax	...	...	...	...	...	...	...	...	...	...	...	...
Total	...	...	...	...	...	...	...	...	...	...	...	...

El Salvador

4.2 Derivation of Value Added by Kind of Activity, in Constant Prices

Million Salvadoran colones

At constant prices of: 1962
All Producers

		1992 Gross Output	1992 Intermediate Consumption	1992 Value Added
1	Agriculture, hunting, forestry and fishing	...	...	856
	A Agriculture and hunting	...	...	817
	B Forestry and logging	...	...	29
	C Fishing	...	...	10
2	Mining and quarrying	...	...	6
	A Coal mining	...	...	...
	B Crude petroleum and natural gas production	...	...	...
	C Metal ore mining	...	...	6
	D Other mining	...	...	...
3	Manufacturing	...	...	658
	A Manufacture of food, beverages and tobacco	...	...	436
	B Textile, wearing apparel and leather industries	...	...	41
	C Manufacture of wood and wood products, including furniture	...	...	28
	D Manufacture of paper and paper products, printing and publishing	...	...	14
	E Manufacture of chemicals and chemical petroleum, coal, rubber and plastic products	...	...	55
	F Manufacture of non-metallic mineral products, except products of petroleum and coal	...	...	32
	G Basic metal industries	...	...	13
	H Manufacture of fabricated metal products, machinery and equipment	...	...	27
	I Other manufacturing industries	...	...	12
4	Electricity, gas and water	...	...	146
	A Electricity, gas and steam	...	...	146
	B Water works and supply	...	...	...
5	Construction	...	...	122
6	Wholesale and retail trade, restaurants and hotels	...	...	579
	A Wholesale and retail trade	...	...	579
	B Restaurants and hotels [a]	...	...	...
	Restaurants	...	...	...
	Hotels and other lodging places	...	...	...
7	Transport, storage and communication	...	...	227
8	Finance, insurance, real estate and business services	...	...	280
	A Financial institutions	...	...	110
	B Insurance	...	...	...
	C Real estate and business services	...	...	170
9	Community, social and personal services [a]	...	...	231
Total, Industries		...	...	3105
Producers of Government Services		...	...	471
Other Producers		...	...	...
Total		...	...	3576
Less: Imputed bank service charge		...	...	...
Import duties		...	...	...
Value added tax		...	...	...
Total		...	...	...

a) Restaurants and hotels are included in item 'Community, social and personal services'.

Equatorial Guinea

Source. Reply to the United Nations National Accounts Questionnaire from the Ministerio de Planificación y Desarrollo Economico, Direccion General de Estadistica, Malabo. The official estimates and information on concepts, sources and methods of estimation can be found in 'Las Cuentas Nacionales de Guinea Ecuatorial' published in July 1987.

General note. The estimates shown in the following tables have been prepared in accordance with the United Nations System of National Accounts (SNA) so far as the existing data would permit. The monetary unit was ekwele. On 2 January 1985, the ekwele was replaced by CFA francs. 4 bipkwele is equivalent to 1 CFA franc.

1.1 Expenditure on the Gross Domestic Product, in Current Prices

Million CFA francs

	1980	1983	1984	1985	1986	1987	1988	1989	1990	1991	1992	1993
1 Government final consumption expenditure	...	7080	8505	... 5909	7240	5210	7804	9397	6765	6696	...	...
2 Private final consumption expenditure	...	16083	17511	... 30566	28754	26630	29096	22956	23593	35225	...	...
A Households	...	16083	17511	...	...	...	...	...	...	...	...	...
B Private non-profit institutions serving households	...	-	-	...	...	...	...	...	...	...	...	...
3 Gross capital formation	...	2860	3642	... 2830	6966	10844	10448	8278	13963	7434	...	...
A Increase in stocks	...	-158	418	-1721	-624	654	-685	-7	-1365	-1091	...	...
B Gross fixed capital formation	...	3018	3224	... 4551	7590	10190	11133	8285	15328	8525	...	...
Residential buildings	...	...	...								...	...
Non-residential buildings	...	...	...	... 2933	3079	3004	4293	3492	4993	4502	...	...
Other construction and land improvement etc.	...	...	...								...	...
Other	...	...	...	1618	4511	7186	6840	4793	10335	4023	...	...
4 Exports of goods and services	...	1477	1886	... 10388	12092	18568	19187	17083	26483	13174	...	...
5 Less: Imports of goods and services	...	1851	2012	... 11626	17847	21930	23786	15458	26455	16100	...	...
Equals: Gross Domestic Product	...	25649	29532	... 38067	37205	39322	42749	42256	44349	46429	...	...

1.2 Expenditure on the Gross Domestic Product, in Constant Prices

Million CFA francs

	1980	1983	1984	1985	1986	1987	1988	1989	1990	1991	1992	1993
				At constant prices of:1985								
1 Government final consumption expenditure	...	...	...	5909	5583	3202	4588	5612	...	...	...	...
2 Private final consumption expenditure	...	...	...	30547	29390	26158	29432	25845	...	...	...	...
3 Gross capital formation	...	...	...	3493	6224	7677	7236	6593	...	...	...	...
A Increase in stocks	...	...	...	-1721	-595	666	-1066	-143	...	...	...	...
B Gross fixed capital formation	...	...	...	5214	6819	7011	8302	6736	...	...	...	...
4 Exports of goods and services	...	...	...	10432	9194	16408	14637	13081	...	...	...	...
5 Less: Imports of goods and services	...	...	...	11625	13104	13371	13704	10106	...	...	...	...
Equals: Gross Domestic Product [a]	...	...	...	38756	37286	40074	42189	41025	...	...	...	...

a) Data for this table have not been revised, therefore, data for some years are not comparable with those of other tables.

1.10 Gross Domestic Product by Kind of Activity, in Current Prices

Million CFA francs

	1980	1983	1984	1985	1986	1987	1988	1989	1990	1991	1992	1993
1 Agriculture, hunting, forestry and fishing	...	16404	18149	22777 21695	22108	23146	22361	22991	22924	23328	...	...
2 Mining and quarrying	...	...	...	...	...	...	...	...	...	...	...	...
3 Manufacturing	...	212	240	563 695	471	857	532	545	556	597	...	...
4 Electricity, gas and water	...	181	176	456 977	762	685	1119	1277	1469	1358	...	...
5 Construction	...	2703	2690	2071 1231	1248	1465	1907	1496	1638	1299	...	...

Equatorial Guinea

1.10 Gross Domestic Product by Kind of Activity, in Current Prices
(Continued)

Million CFA francs

	1980	1983	1984	1985	1986	1987	1988	1989	1990	1991	1992	1993
6 Wholesale and retail trade, restaurants and hotels	...	1291	1376	2648 / 3211	2926	3370	4735	3597	3266	3319	...	...
7 Transport, storage and communication	...	269	240	656 / 1098	878	632	760	823	923	855	...	...
8 Finance, insurance, real estate and business services	...	359	360	686 / 862	886	918	947	966	989	1005	...	...
9 Community, social and personal services	...	...	...	3257	2970	3086	3658	3997	5572	5817	...	...
Total, Industries	...	21420	23231	29857 / 33026	32249	34161	36019	35692	37337	37578	...	...
Producers of Government Services	...	3931	5700	5362 / 2712	2892	3283	5201	5256	5428	6354	...	...
Other Producers	...	42	38	476	...	...	...	...	...	...	...	...
Subtotal	...	25394	28970	35695 / 35738	35141	37444	41220	40948	42765	43932	...	...
Less: Imputed bank service charge	...	...	...	...	...	...	...	...	...	...	...	...
Plus: Import duties	...	255	562	2328 / 2328	2064	1878	1529	1309	1585	2497	...	...
Plus: Value added tax	...	...	...	...	...	...	...	...	...	...	...	...
Equals: Gross Domestic Product	...	25649	29532	38023 / 38067	37205	39322	42749	42257	44350	46429	...	...

1.11 Gross Domestic Product by Kind of Activity, in Constant Prices

Million CFA francs

	1980	1983	1984	1985	1986	1987	1988	1989	1990	1991	1992	1993
				At constant prices of: 1985								
1 Agriculture, hunting, forestry and fishing	...	...	...	21695	22841	25193	24553	24963	...	...	...	...
2 Mining and quarrying	...	...	...	...	...	...	...	...	...	...	...	...
3 Manufacturing	...	...	...	695	413	680	403	410	...	...	...	...
4 Electricity, gas and water	...	...	...	977	762	685	1076	1228	...	...	...	...
5 Construction	...	...	...	1921	1564	1924	2326	1806	...	...	...	...
6 Wholesale and retail trade, restaurants and hotels	...	...	...	3211	2681	2925	3819	2830	...	...	...	...
7 Transport, storage and communication	...	...	...	1098	770	502	576	619	...	...	...	...
8 Finance, insurance, real estate and business services	...	...	...	862	812	799	764	761	...	...	...	...
9 Community, social and personal services	...	...	...	5969	5378	5487	7144	7100	...	...	...	...
Total, Industries	...	...	...	...	...	...	...	...	...	...	...	...
Producers of Government Services	...	...	...	...	...	...	...	...	...	...	...	...
Other Producers	...	...	...	...	...	...	...	...	...	...	...	...
Subtotal	...	...	...	36428	35222	38196	40660	39716	...	...	...	...
Less: Imputed bank service charge	...	...	...	...	...	...	...	...	...	...	...	...
Plus: Import duties	...	...	...	2328	2064	1878	1529	1309	...	...	...	...
Plus: Value added tax	...	...	...	...	...	...	...	...	...	...	...	...
Equals: Gross Domestic Product [a]	...	...	...	38756	37286	40074	42189	41025	...	...	...	...

a) Data for this table have not been revised, therefore, data for some years are not comparable with those of other tables.

4.1 Derivation of Value Added by Kind of Activity, in Current Prices

Million CFA francs

	1985			1990			1991		
	Gross Output	Intermediate Consumption	Value Added	Gross Output	Intermediate Consumption	Value Added	Gross Output	Intermediate Consumption	Value Added
				All Producers					
1 Agriculture, hunting, forestry and fishing	...	...	21695	...	...	22924	...	...	23328
A Agriculture and hunting	...	...	18082	...	...	18106	...	...	18348
B Forestry and logging	...	...	2676	...	...	3812	...	...	3949
C Fishing	...	...	937	...	...	1006	...	...	1031
2 Mining and quarrying	...	...	...	...	...	...	...	...	...

Equatorial Guinea

4.1 Derivation of Value Added by Kind of Activity, in Current Prices
(Continued)

Million CFA francs

		1985 Gross Output	1985 Intermediate Consumption	1985 Value Added	1990 Gross Output	1990 Intermediate Consumption	1990 Value Added	1991 Gross Output	1991 Intermediate Consumption	1991 Value Added
3	Manufacturing	...	...	695	...	...	556	...	...	597
	A Manufacture of food, beverages and tobacco	...	...	361	...	...	130	...	...	140
	B Textile, wearing apparel and leather industries	...	...	3	...	...	4	...	...	5
	C Manufacture of wood and wood products, including furniture	...	...	219	...	...	291	...	...	313
	D Manufacture of paper and paper products, printing and publishing	...	...	56	...	...	64	...	...	68
	E Manufacture of chemicals and chemical petroleum, coal, rubber and plastic products	...	...	17	...	...	23	...	...	25
	F Manufacture of non-metallic mineral products, except products of petroleum and coal	...	...	...	...	...	...	...	...	...
	G Basic metal industries	...	...	7	...	...	8	...	...	9
	H Manufacture of fabricated metal products, machinery and equipment	...	...	...	...	...	...	...	...	...
	I Other manufacturing industries	...	...	32	...	...	35	...	...	38
4	Electricity, gas and water	...	...	977	...	...	1469	...	...	1358
5	Construction	...	...	1231	...	...	1638	...	...	1299
6	Wholesale and retail trade, restaurants and hotels	...	...	3211	...	...	3266	...	...	3319
	A Wholesale and retail trade	...	...	3001	...	...	3032	...	...	3079
	B Restaurants and hotels	...	...	210	...	...	234	...	...	240
	Restaurants	...	...	107	...	...	121	...	...	123
	Hotels and other lodging places	...	...	103	...	...	113	...	...	117
7	Transport, storage and communication	...	...	1098	...	...	923	...	...	855
	A Transport and storage	...	...	858	...	...	540	...	...	458
	B Communication	...	...	240	...	...	383	...	...	397
8	Finance, insurance, real estate and business services	...	...	862	...	...	989	...	...	1005
	A Financial institutions	...	...	236	...	...	258	...	...	262
	B Insurance	...	...	578	...	...	645	...	...	654
	C Real estate and business services	...	...	48	...	...	86	...	...	88
9	Community, social and personal services	...	...	3257	...	...	5572	...	...	5817
	A Sanitary and similar services	...	...	...	...	...	...	...	...	...
	B Social and related community services	...	...	2617	...	...	4873	...	...	5019
	Educational services	...	...	1681	...	...	3084	...	...	3145
	Medical, dental, other health and veterinary services	...	...	936	...	...	1789	...	...	1874
	C Recreational and cultural services	...	...	18	...	...	21	...	...	21
	D Personal and household services	...	...	624	...	...	678	...	...	777
Total, Industries		...	...	33026	...	...	37337	...	...	37578
Producers of Government Services		...	...	2712	...	...	5428	...	...	6354
Other Producers		...	...	...	...	...	...	...	...	...
Total		...	...	35738	...	...	42765	...	...	43932
Less: Imputed bank service charge		...	...	...	...	...	...	...	...	...
Import duties		...	...	2328	...	...	1585	...	...	2497
Value added tax		...	...	...	...	...	...	...	...	...
Total		...	...	38067	...	...	44349	...	...	46429

Estonia

Source. Reply to the United Nations National Accounts Questionnaire from the State Statistical Office of Estonia, Tallinn. The official estimates for the years 1980-1990 are published in 'National Accounts in Estonia'.

General note. The estimates shown in the following tables have been prepared in accordance with the United Nations document F.20 entitled 'Comparison of the System of National Accounts and the System of Balances of the National Economy, Part 1: Conceptual Relationships' for the years 1980-1990. For the year beginning 1991, the estimates are in accordance with the provisional 'Revised System of National Accounts (1993)'. The shift from the Soviet rouble to the Estonian national currency (Kroon) was made on June 20, 1992 at the rate of 10 roubles = 1 Kroon. From this date, the Kroon has been the only legal currency in Estonia.

1.1 Expenditure on the Gross Domestic Product, in Current Prices

Million Estonian kroons

	1980	1983	1984	1985	1986	1987	1988	1989	1990	1991	1992	1993
1 Government final consumption expenditure	56	70	75	80	86	91	89	89	105	... / 241	1775 / 2084	4053
2 Private final consumption expenditure	281	306	311	318	329	351	352	387	514	... / 1055	8480 / 7260	12711
A Households	281	306	311	318	329	351	352	387	514	... / 1002	7698 / 7163	12591
B Private non-profit institutions serving households	...	...	...	...	...	...	...	...	...	... / 53	782 / 97	120
3 Gross capital formation	128	153	162	163	168	166	189	210	241	... / 448	3738 / 3518	5866
A Increase in stocks	8	23	23	13	7	3	20	25	52	... / 90	983 / 763	541
B Gross fixed capital formation	120	129	139	150	161	163	169	185	190	... / 357	2755 / 2755	5325
4 Exports of goods and services	253	294	298	272	284	300	328	340	335	... / 584	7893 / 7893	15196
5 Less: Imports of goods and services	264	309	324	336	350	363	383	384	398	... / 495	7631 / 7121	15908
Statistical discrepancy	-5	-4	1	-2	-1	-	-	-	-	... / -	- / -580	-
Equals: Gross Domestic Product	448	510	522	495	516	544	576	642	798	... / 1832	14255 / 13054	21918

Estonia

1.2 Expenditure on the Gross Domestic Product, in Constant Prices

Million Estonian kroons

	1980	1983	1984	1985	1986	1987	1988	1989	1990	1991	1992	1993
	\multicolumn{9}{c}{At constant prices of: 1980}	1991	1993	
1 Government final consumption expenditure	56	70	74	79	84	89	88	86	93	... 241	224 3548	4053
2 Private final consumption expenditure	281	291	296	301	305	320	322	343	390	... 1055	844 14157	12711
A Households	281	291	296	301	305	320	322	343	390	... 1002	757 ...	...
B Private non-profit institutions serving households	...	...	...	...	...	...	...	...	...	... 53	87 ...	...
3 Gross capital formation	128	145	133	129	128	123	132	134	132	... 448	304 5917	5866
A Increase in stocks	8	19	21	12	5	2	12	15	24	... 91	89 1075	541
B Gross fixed capital formation	120	126	113	118	123	121	120	119	108	... 357	215 4842	5325
4 Exports of goods and services	253	288	284	250	252	265	288	289	214	... 584	607 11840	15196
5 Less: Imports of goods and services	264	294	290	304	311	316	325	307	319	... 495	408 11482	15908
Statistical discrepancy	-5	...	...	...	...	...	...	...	...	... ...	... ...	...
Equals: Gross Domestic Product	448	499	498	455	458	481	505	546	510	441 1832	1571 23980	21918

1.3 Cost Components of the Gross Domestic Product

Million Estonian kroons

	1980	1983	1984	1985	1986	1987	1988	1989	1990	1991	1992	1993
1 Indirect taxes, net	27	4	-5	-5	4	-1	-5	2	50	... 211	1283 1280	2668
A Indirect taxes	62	75	74	72	73	71	72	78	100	... 252	1607 1604	2996
B Less: Subsidies	35	71	79	76	69	72	77	77	50	... 41	324 324	328
2 Consumption of fixed capital	76	89	94	100	102	112	116	122	127	... 102	637 640	2674
3 Compensation of employees paid by resident producers to:	208	229	239	248	255	265	286	328	421	... 860	6021 6257	10993
A Resident households	...	...	...	...	...	...	...	...	...	... 860	6021 6257	10993
B Rest of the world										... ...	... ...	...
4 Operating surplus	137	188	193	151	155	169	179	191	200	... 659	6314 4877	5583
A Corporate and quasi-corporate enterprises	...	...	...	...	...	...	...	...	...	... 537	... ...	...
B Private unincorporated enterprises	...	...	...	...	...	...	...	...	...	... 122	... ...	...
C General government	...	...	...	...	...	...	...	...	...	... ...	... ...	...
Equals: Gross Domestic Product	448	510	522	495	516	544	576	642	798	... 1832	14255 13054	21918

Estonia

1.4 General Government Current Receipts and Disbursements

Million Estonian kroons

	1980	1983	1984	1985	1986	1987	1988	1989	1990	1991	1992	1993
Receipts												
1 Operating surplus	...	...	...	...	...	...	...	...	...	-	156	258
2 Property and entrepreneurial income	...	...	...	...	...	...	...	...	...	2	58	95
3 Taxes, fees and contributions	...	...	...	...	...	...	...	...	...	635	4364	8524
A Indirect taxes	...	...	...	...	...	...	...	...	...	252	1607	2996
B Direct taxes	...	...	...	...	...	...	...	...	...	257	1576	2869
C Social security contributions	...	...	...	...	...	...	...	...	...	126	1170	2600
D Compulsory fees, fines and penalties	...	...	...	...	...	...	...	...	...	-	11	59
4 Other current transfers	...	...	...	...	...	...	...	...	...	3	2347	1747
Statistical discrepancy	...	...	...	...	...	...	...	...	...	...	-156	-555
Total Current Receipts of General Government	...	...	...	...	...	...	...	...	...	640	6769	10069
Disbursements												
1 Government final consumption expenditure	...	...	...	...	...	...	...	...	...	241	1775	4053
A Compensation of employees	...	...	...	...	...	...	...	...	...	97	815	1981
B Consumption of fixed capital	...	...	...	...	...	...	...	...	...	6	75	558
C Purchases of goods and services, net	...	...	...	...	...	...	...	...	...	138	881	1506
D Less: Own account fixed capital formation	...	...	...	...	...	...	...	...	...	-	-	-
E Indirect taxes paid, net	...	...	...	...	...	...	...	...	...	-	4	8
2 Property income	...	...	...	...	...	...	...	...	...	1	9	44
A Interest	...	...	...	...	...	...	...	...	...	1	9	43
B Net land rent and royalties	...	...	...	...	...	...	...	...	...	-	-	-
3 Subsidies	...	...	...	...	...	...	...	...	...	41	324	328
4 Other current transfers	...	...	...	...	...	...	...	...	...	165	2828	3099
A Social security benefits	...	...	...	...	...	...	...	...	...	165	375	1063
B Social assistance grants	...	...	...	...	...	...	...	...	...	-	-	62
C Other	...	...	...	...	...	...	...	...	...	-	2453	1974
5 Net saving	...	...	...	...	...	...	...	...	...	193	1833	2545
Total Current Disbursements and Net Saving of General Government	...	...	...	...	...	...	...	...	...	640	6769	10069

1.5 Current Income and Outlay of Corporate and Quasi-Corporate Enterprises, Summary

Million Estonian kroons

	1980	1983	1984	1985	1986	1987	1988	1989	1990	1991	1992	1993
Receipts												
1 Operating surplus	...	...	...	...	...	...	...	...	...	537	4689	2457
2 Property and entrepreneurial income received	...	...	...	...	...	...	...	...	...	6	130	155
3 Current transfers	...	...	...	...	...	...	...	...	...	1	23	37
Statistical discrepancy	...	...	...	...	...	...	...	...	...	-10	...	...

Estonia

1.5 Current Income and Outlay of Corporate and Quasi-Corporate Enterprises, Summary
(Continued)

Million Estonian kroons

	1980	1983	1984	1985	1986	1987	1988	1989	1990	1991	1992	1993
Total Current Receipts	...	...	...	...	...	...	...	...	...	534	4842	2649

Disbursements

	1980	1983	1984	1985	1986	1987	1988	1989	1990	1991	1992	1993
1 Property and entrepreneurial income	...	...	...	...	...	...	...	...	...	21	471	845
2 Direct taxes and other current payments to general government	...	...	...	...	...	...	...	...	...	132	717	810
3 Other current transfers	...	...	...	...	...	...	...	...	...	2	1114	246
4 Net saving	...	...	...	...	...	...	...	...	...	379	2540	748
Total Current Disbursements and Net Saving	...	...	...	...	...	...	...	...	...	534	4842	2649

1.6 Current Income and Outlay of Households and Non-Profit Institutions

Million Estonian kroons

	1980	1983	1984	1985	1986	1987	1988	1989	1990	1991	1992	1993

Receipts

	1980	1983	1984	1985	1986	1987	1988	1989	1990	1991	1992	1993
1 Compensation of employees	...	...	...	...	...	...	...	...	...	720	6464	11272
A From resident producers	...	...	...	...	...	...	...	...	...	...	6021	10992
B From rest of the world	...	...	...	...	...	...	...	...	...	...	443	280
2 Operating surplus of private unincorporated enterprises	...	...	...	...	...	...	...	...	...	122	1469	2868
3 Property and entrepreneurial income	...	...	...	...	...	...	...	...	...	14	117	203
4 Current transfers	...	...	...	...	...	...	...	...	...	171	2482	2604
A Social security benefits	...	...	...	...	...	...	...	...	...	165	283	497
B Social assistance grants	...	...	...	...	...	...	...	...	...	-	92	409
C Other	...	...	...	...	...	...	...	...	...	6	2107	1698
Total Current Receipts	...	...	...	...	...	...	...	...	...	1027	10532	16947

Disbursements

	1980	1983	1984	1985	1986	1987	1988	1989	1990	1991	1992	1993
1 Private final consumption expenditure	...	...	...	...	...	...	...	...	...	919	8480	12711
2 Property income	...	...	...	...	...	...	...	...	...	...	...	...
3 Direct taxes and other current transfers n.e.c. to general government	...	...	...	...	...	...	...	...	...	246	2027	4487
A Social security contributions	...	...	...	...	...	...	...	...	...	127	1170	2507
B Direct taxes	...	...	...	...	...	...	...	...	...	119	857	1980
C Fees, fines and penalties	...	...	...	...	...	...	...	...	...	...	...	...
4 Other current transfers	...	...	...	...	...	...	...	...	...	11	242	84
5 Net saving	...	...	...	...	...	...	...	...	...	-149	-216	-335
Total Current Disbursements and Net Saving	...	...	...	...	...	...	...	...	...	1027	10532	16947

Estonia

1.7 External Transactions on Current Account, Summary

Million Estonian kroons

	1980	1983	1984	1985	1986	1987	1988	1989	1990	1991	1992	1993
Payments to the Rest of the World
1 Imports of goods and services	...	...	...	...	...	...	...	...	...	...	7631	16940
A Imports of merchandise c.i.f.	...	...	...	...	...	...	...	...	...	...	5922	13528
B Other	...	...	...	...	...	...	...	...	...	...	1709	3412
2 Factor income to the rest of the world	...	...	...	...	...	...	...	...	...	...	83	544
A Compensation of employees	...	...	...	...	...	...	...	...	...	...	-	-
B Property and entrepreneurial income	...	...	...	...	...	...	...	...	...	...	83	544
By general government	...	...	...	...	...	...	...	...	...	...	-	...
By corporate and quasi-corporate enterprises	...	...	...	...	...	...	...	...	...	...	38	...
By other	...	...	...	...	...	...	...	...	...	...	45	...
3 Current transfers to the rest of the world	...	...	...	...	...	...	...	...	...	...	680	6
4 Surplus of the nation on current transactions	...	...	...	...	...	...	...	...	...	...	1326	-259
Payments to the Rest of the World and Surplus of the Nation on Current Transactions	...	...	...	...	...	...	...	...	...	...	9720	17231
Receipts From The Rest of the World
1 Exports of goods and services	...	...	...	...	...	...	...	...	...	...	7893	15196
A Exports of merchandise f.o.b.	...	...	...	...	...	...	...	...	...	...	5549	10763
B Other	...	...	...	...	...	...	...	...	...	...	2345	4433
2 Factor income from rest of the world	...	...	...	...	...	...	...	...	...	...	448	637
A Compensation of employees	...	...	...	...	...	...	...	...	...	...	443	280
B Property and entrepreneurial income	...	...	...	...	...	...	...	...	...	...	5	357
By general government	...	...	...	...	...	...	...	...	...	...	-	...
By corporate and quasi-corporate enterprises	...	...	...	...	...	...	...	...	...	...	2	...
By other	...	...	...	...	...	...	...	...	...	...	3	...
3 Current transfers from rest of the world	...	...	...	...	...	...	...	...	...	...	1379	1398
Receipts from the Rest of the World on Current Transactions [a]	...	...	...	...	...	...	...	...	...	...	9720	17231

a) Data for this table have not been revised, therefore, data for some years are not comparable with those of other tables.

1.8 Capital Transactions of The Nation, Summary

Million Estonian kroons

	1980	1983	1984	1985	1986	1987	1988	1989	1990	1991	1992	1993
Finance of Gross Capital Formation
Gross saving	112	134	137	97	102	102	135	166	178	... / 532	5062 / 5062	6505
1 Consumption of fixed capital	76	89	94	100	102	112	116	122	127	... / 102	637 / 637	2674
A General government	...	...	...	...	...	...	...	...	...	... / 6	75 / 75	558
B Corporate and quasi-corporate enterprises	...	...	...	...	...	...	...	...	...	... / 87	543 / 543	2036
C Other	...	...	...	...	...	...	...	...	...	... / 9	19 / 19	80
2 Net saving	35	45	43	-3	-	-9	19	44	52	... / 430	4425 / 4425	3831
A General government	...	...	...	...	...	...	...	...	...	... / 193	1833 / 1833	2843
B Corporate and quasi-corporate enterprises	...	...	...	...	...	...	...	...	...	... / 386	2503 / 2503	748

Estonia

1.8 Capital Transactions of The Nation, Summary
(Continued)

Million Estonian kroons

	1980	1983	1984	1985	1986	1987	1988	1989	1990	1991	1992	1993
C Other	...	...	...	...	...	...	...	...	...	-149	89 / 89	240
Less: Surplus of the nation on current transactions	-11	-14	-26	-64	-66	-64	-54	-44	-63	... / 84	1324 / 1544	639
Statistical discrepancy	5	4	-1	2	1	-	-	-	-	... / -	- / -	-
Finance of Gross Capital Formation	128	153	162	163	168	166	189	210	241	... / 448	3738 / 3518	5866
Gross Capital Formation												
Increase in stocks	8	23	23	13	7	3	20	25	52	... / 90	983 / 763	541
Gross fixed capital formation	120	129	139	150	161	163	169	185	190	... / 358	2755 / 2755	5325
1 General government	...	...	...	...	...	...	...	...	...	... / 63	504 / 504	1054
2 Corporate and quasi-corporate enterprises	...	...	...	...	...	...	...	...	...	279	2131 / 2131	3638
3 Other	...	...	...	...	...	...	...	...	...	16	120 / 120	633
Gross Capital Formation	128	153	162	163	168	166	189	210	241	... / 448	3738 / 3518	5866

1.9 Gross Domestic Product by Institutional Sectors of Origin

Million Estonian kroons

	1980	1983	1984	1985	1986	1987	1988	1989	1990	1991	1992	1993
Domestic Factor Incomes Originating												
1 General government	...	...	...	...	...	...	...	...	...	97	815 / 993	1981
2 Corporate and quasi-corporate enterprises	...	...	...	...	...	...	...	...	...	1158	10027 / 8491	11581
A Non-financial	...	...	...	...	...	...	...	...	...	1144	9797 / 8208	11072
B Financial	...	...	...	...	...	...	...	...	...	14	230 / 283	509
3 Households and private unincorporated enterprises	...	...	...	...	...	...	...	...	...	122	1474 / 1631	2976
4 Non-profit institutions serving households	...	...	...	...	...	...	...	...	...	2	19 / 19	37
Subtotal: Domestic Factor Incomes	...	...	...	...	...	...	...	...	...	1379	12335 / 11134	16575
Indirect taxes, net	...	...	...	...	...	...	...	...	...	211	1283 / 1280	2669
A Indirect taxes	...	...	...	...	...	...	...	...	...	252	1607 / 1604	2997
B Less: Subsidies	...	...	...	...	...	...	...	...	...	41	324 / 324	328
Consumption of fixed capital	...	...	...	...	...	...	...	...	...	102	637 / 640	2674
Statistical discrepancy	...	...	...	...	...	...	...	...	...	140	- / -	-
Gross Domestic Product	...	...	...	...	...	...	...	...	...	1832	14255 / 13054	21918

Estonia

1.10 Gross Domestic Product by Kind of Activity, in Current Prices

Million Estonian kroons

	1980	1983	1984	1985	1986	1987	1988	1989	1990	1991	1992	1993
1 Agriculture, hunting, forestry and fishing	64	99	106	102	110	107	112	127	125	... / 310	1779 / 1647	2203
2 Mining and quarrying	...	...	...	...	...	...	...	...	...	... / 30	349 / 310	367
3 Manufacturing	187	188	186	193	205	213	218	230	316	... / 599	4084 / 2773	3751
4 Electricity, gas and water	...	...	...	...	...	...	...	...	...	... / 31	614 / 537	692
5 Construction	31	33	38	40	40	42	46	52	57	... / 111	654 / 603	1298
6 Wholesale and retail trade, restaurants and hotels	62	71	72	37	38	42	43	52	64	... / 147	2064 / 1980	3725
7 Transport, storage and communication	22	26	26	28	29	34	39	41	51	... / 114	1698 / 1715	2453
8 Finance, insurance, real estate and business services	...	...	...	...	...	...	...	...	...	... / 44	999 / 1076	1905
9 Community, social and personal services	82	93	94	96	94	106	119	141	184	... / 162	312 / 620	1062
Total, Industries	448	510	522	495	516	544	576	642	798	... / 1548	12553 / 11261	17456
Producers of Government Services	...	...	...	...	...	...	...	...	...	... / 103	869 / 960	2313
Other Producers	...	...	...	...	...	...	...	...	...	... / ...	... / ...	...
Subtotal	448	510	522	495	516	544	576	642	798	... / 1651	13422 / 12221	19769
Less: Imputed bank service charge	...	...	...	...	...	...	...	...	...	... / ...	... / ...	...
Plus: Import duties	...	...	...	...	...	...	...	...	...	... / ...	... / ...	...
Plus: Value added tax	...	...	...	...	...	...	...	...	...	... / ...	... / ...	...
Plus: Other adjustments	...	...	...	...	...	...	...	...	...	... / 181	833 / 833	2149
Equals: Gross Domestic Product	448	510	522	495	516	544	576	642	798	... / 1832	14255 / 13054	21918

1.11 Gross Domestic Product by Kind of Activity, in Constant Prices

Million Estonian kroons

	1980	1983	1984	1985	1986	1987	1988	1989	1990	1991	1992	1993
	At constant prices of: 1980										1991	
1 Agriculture, hunting, forestry and fishing	64	62	60	50	55	54	53	58	48	35 / 310	238	...
2 Mining and quarrying	...	...	...	...	...	...	...	...	...	... / 30	33	...
3 Manufacturing	187	210	208	209	208	218	228	224	213	188 / 599	426	...
4 Electricity, gas and water	...	...	...	...	...	...	...	...	...	... / 31	27	...
5 Construction	31	35	36	38	38	39	41	46	36	34 / 111	51	...

Estonia

1.11 Gross Domestic Product by Kind of Activity, in Constant Prices
(Continued)

Million Estonian kroons

	1980	1983	1984	1985	1986	1987	1988	1989	1990	1991	1992	1993
	\multicolumn{9}{c}{At constant prices of: 1980}		1991	
6 Wholesale and retail trade, restaurants and hotels	62	75	78	39	39	42	42	52	48	39 / 147	205	...
7 Transport, storage and communication	22	24	23	24	25	28	32	32	30	22 / 114	170	...
8 Finance, insurance, real estate and business services	...	...	...	...	...	...	...	...	...	... / 44	65	...
9 Community, social and personal services	82	93	92	95	93	100	109	135	135	124 / 162	72	...
Total, Industries	448	499	498	455	458	481	505	546	510	441 / 1548	1286	...
Producers of Government Services	...	...	...	...	...	...	...	...	...	... / 103	118	...
Other Producers	...	...	...	...	...	...	...	...	...	... / ...	...	...
Subtotal	448	499	498	455	458	481	505	546	510	441 / 1651	1404	...
Less: Imputed bank service charge	...	...	...	...	...	...	...	...	...	... / ...	...	...
Plus: Import duties	...	...	...	...	...	...	...	...	...	... / ...	...	...
Plus: Value added tax	...	...	...	...	...	...	...	...	...	... / ...	...	...
Plus: Other adjustments	...	...	...	...	...	...	...	...	...	... / 181	168	...
Equals: Gross Domestic Product	448	499	498	455	458	481	505	546	510	441 / 1832	1571	...

1.12 Relations Among National Accounting Aggregates

Million Estonian kroons

	1980	1983	1984	1985	1986	1987	1988	1989	1990	1991	1992	1993
Gross Domestic Product	448	510	522	495	516	544	576	642	798	... / 1832	14255	... / 21918
Plus: Net factor income from the rest of the world	...	...	...	...	...	...	...	...	...	... / ...	365	... / 93
Factor income from the rest of the world	...	...	...	...	...	...	...	...	...	... / ...	448	... / 637
Less: Factor income to the rest of the world	...	...	...	...	...	...	...	...	...	... / ...	83	... / 544
Equals: Gross National Product	448	510	522	495	516	544	576	642	798	... / 1832	14620	... / 22011
Less: Consumption of fixed capital	76	89	94	100	102	112	116	122	127	... / 102	637	... / 2674

Estonia

1.12 Relations Among National Accounting Aggregates
(Continued)

Million Estonian kroons

	1980	1983	1984	1985	1986	1987	1988	1989	1990	1991	1992	1993
Equals: National Income	372	421	428	395	414	432	460	520	671	... 1730	13983	... 19337
Plus: Net current transfers from the rest of the world	...	...	...	...	...	...	...	...	...	... ...	701	... 1392
Current transfers from the rest of the world	...	...	...	...	...	...	...	...	...	... ...	1381	... 1398
Less: Current transfers to the rest of the world	...	...	...	...	...	...	...	...	...	... ...	680	... 6
Equals: National Disposable Income	372	421	428	395	414	432	460	520	671	... 1730	14684	... 20730
Less: Final consumption	336	376	385	398	414	441	441	476	620	... 1296	10255	... 16765
Statistical discrepancy	...	...	...	...	...	...	...	...	...	... ...	...	-134
Equals: Net Saving	35	45	43	-3	-	-9	19	44	52	... 434	4429	... 3831
Less: Surplus of the nation on current transactions	-11	-14	-26	-64	-66	-64	-54	-44	-63	... 84	1328	... 639
Statistical discrepancy	5	4	-1	2	1	-	-	-	-	... ...	...	...
Equals: Net Capital Formation	51	64	68	63	67	54	74	88	114	... 350	3101	... 3192

2.1 Government Final Consumption Expenditure by Function, in Current Prices

Million Estonian kroons

	1980	1983	1984	1985	1986	1987	1988	1989	1990	1991	1992	1993
1 General public services	...	...	...	...	...	...	...	...	...	...	217 217	475
2 Defence	...	...	...	...	...	...	...	...	...	...	44 44	135
3 Public order and safety	...	...	...	...	...	...	...	...	...	...	176 176	462
4 Education	...	...	...	...	...	...	...	...	...	...	711 711	1521
5 Health	...	...	...	...	...	...	...	...	...	...	43 352	437
6 Social security and welfare	...	...	...	...	...	...	...	...	...	...	64 64	196
7 Housing and community amenities	...	...	...	...	...	...	...	...	...	...	- -	311
8 Recreational, cultural and religious affairs	...	...	...	...	...	...	...	...	...	...	115 115	197
9 Economic services	...	...	...	...	...	...	...	...	...	...	404 405	320
A Fuel and energy	...	...	...	...	...	...	...	...	...	...	... ...	16
B Agriculture, forestry, fishing and hunting	...	...	...	...	...	...	...	...	...	...	... ...	93
C Mining, manufacturing and construction, except fuel and energy	...	...	...	...	...	...	...	...	...	...	... ...	40
D Transportation and communication	...	...	...	...	...	...	...	...	...	...	... ...	77
E Other economic affairs	...	...	...	...	...	...	...	...	...	...	... ...	94
10 Other functions	...	...	...	...	...	...	...	...	...	...	... ...	...
Total Government Final Consumption Expenditure	...	...	...	...	...	...	...	...	...	...	1775 2084	4054

Estonia

4.1 Derivation of Value Added by Kind of Activity, in Current Prices

Million Estonian kroons

	1992 Gross Output	1992 Intermediate Consumption	1992 Value Added	1993 Gross Output	1993 Intermediate Consumption	1993 Value Added
			All Producers			
1 Agriculture, hunting, forestry and fishing	3901	2254	1647	5830	3627	2203
A Agriculture and hunting	3584	2024	1560	5459	3395	2064
B Forestry and logging						
C Fishing	317	230	87	371	232	139
2 Mining and quarrying	580	270	310	731	365	366
3 Manufacturing	10208	7435	2773	12762	9011	3751
4 Electricity, gas and water	1955	1418	537	2499	1807	692
5 Construction	1690	1087	603	3443	2146	1297
6 Wholesale and retail trade, restaurants and hotels	3190	1210	1980	7501	3776	3725
A Wholesale and retail trade	2824	1051	1773	6689	3321	3368
B Restaurants and hotels	366	159	207	811	454	357
7 Transport, storage and communication	3884	2169	1715	6132	3679	2453
8 Finance, insurance, real estate and business services	1731	655	1076	3867	1962	1905
A Financial institutions	416	119	297	1008	448	560
B Insurance						
C Real estate and business services	1315	536	779	2859	1514	1345
9 Community, social and personal services	1178	558	620	1882	820	1062
Total, Industries	28317	17056	11261	44647	27193	17454
Producers of Government Services	1752	792	960	3686	1372	2314
Other Producers	...	...	...	...	...	...
Total	30069	17848	12221	48333	28565	19768
Less: Imputed bank service charge	...	...	...	...	...	...
Import duties	...	...	...	...	...	...
Value added tax	...	...	...	...	...	...
Other adjustments	833	...	833	2150	...	2150
Total	30902	17848	13054	50483	28565	21918

4.2 Derivation of Value Added by Kind of Activity, in Constant Prices

Million Estonian kroons

	1992 Gross Output	1992 Intermediate Consumption	1992 Value Added	1993 Gross Output	1993 Intermediate Consumption	1993 Value Added
			At constant prices of: 1991			
			All Producers			
1 Agriculture, hunting, forestry and fishing	6298	3771	2527	5830	3627	2203
2 Mining and quarrying	1038	518	520	731	364	367
3 Manufacturing	18286	12902	5384	12762	9011	3751
4 Electricity, gas and water	3247	2348	899	2499	1807	692
5 Construction	2864	1787	1077	3443	2146	1297
6 Wholesale and retail trade, restaurants and hotels	5965	2790	3175	7501	3776	3725
A Wholesale and retail trade	5297	2416	2881	6689	3322	3367
B Restaurants and hotels	668	374	294	812	454	358
7 Transport, storage and communication	5929	3590	2339	6132	3679	2453
8 Finance, insurance, real estate and business services	3779	1650	2129	3867	1962	1905
9 Community, social and personal services	2498	1116	1382	1882	820	1062
Total, Industries	49904	30472	19432	44647	27192	17455
Producers of Government Services	3509	1300	2209	3686	1373	2313

Estonia

4.2 Derivation of Value Added by Kind of Activity, in Constant Prices
(Continued)

Million Estonian kroons

	1992			1993		
	Gross Output	Intermediate Consumption	Value Added	Gross Output	Intermediate Consumption	Value Added
				At constant prices of:1991		
Other Producers	...	...	...	...	...	...
Total	53413	31772	21641	48333	28565	19768
Less: Imputed bank service charge	...	...	...	...	...	...
Import duties	...	...	...	...	...	...
Value added tax	...	...	...	...	...	...
Other adjustments	2339	...	2339	2150	...	2150
Total	55752	31772	23980	50483	28565	21918

Fiji

General note. The preparation of national accounts statistics in Fiji is undertaken by the Bureau of Statistics, Suva. The official estimates together with methodological notes are published in a series of reports entitled 'National Accounts Studies'. The third volume of this series, 'The National Accounts of Fiji 1968-1972', contains a detailed description of the sources and methods used for the national accounts estimation. The estimates are generally in accordance with the classifications and definitions recommended in the United Nations System of National Accounts (SNA). Input-output tables have been compiled for the years 1966 and 1967. The 1967 tables were published in 1970 in 'An Input-Output Table for Fiji 1967'. The following tables have been prepared from successive replies to the United Nations national accounts questionnaire. When the scope and coverage of the estimates differ for conceptual or statistical reasons from the definitions and classifications recommended in SNA, a footnote is indicated to the relevant tables.

Sources and methods:

(a) **Gross domestic product.** Gross domestic product is estimated mainly through the production approach.

(b) **Expenditure on the gross domestic product.** All components of GDP by expenditure type are estimated through the expenditure approach except private final consumption expenditure which is mostly based on the commodity-flow approach. The estimates of government final consumption expenditure are based on the annual report 'An Economic and Functional Classification of Government Accounts'. For private consumption expenditure estimates, all imported items valued at landed cost from foreign trade statistics and producers' values from industrial censuses are grossed up by margins established in the 1970 Census of Distribution and Services. Special estimates are made for those items after consumer expenditure, such as food, electricity, gas and water, medical services and recreations, which are not covered by the commodity-flow approach. For these estimates data from the household budget survey in 1972, income tax statistics and the 1970 census of distribution are used. Estimates of gross capital formation for the private industry are based on surveys of capital investment, for government industry and producers of government services the estimates are derived from government account and for the producers of private non-profit services to households from the 1970/1971 survey of non-profit making institutions. Value of imports and exports of goods and services are obtained from the balance of payments and annual shipping and aircraft statistics. For the constant price estimates, the current values of expenditure items are deflated by various price indexes such as consumer price index, index of rural produce prices, implicit price index of value added of building and construction, trade index of exports, etc.

(c) **Cost-structure of the gross domestic product.** Estimates of the cost-structure of GDP are made from the various sectoral surveys and taxation data. Estimates of indirect taxes and subsidies are based on government accounts.

(d) **Gross domestic product by kind of economic activity.** The table of GDP by kind of economic activity is prepared at market price, i.e. producers' values. The production approach is used to estimate value added of most industries, such as agriculture, mining, manufacturing, electricity, gas and water, construction, and for the trade sector in combination with the commodity-flow approach. The income approach is used to estimate value added of restaurants and hotels and most of the sub-sectors of the service industries. For agricultural sector, the total output of sugar-cane and copra are estimated from material inputs revealed by annual industrial censuses. The bench-mark estimates of substance output is based on the 1968 Agricultural Census, the 1965 Rural-Urban Household Expenditure Survey and Bureau of Statistics Data. The annual increases are based on estimates of population growth and an index of rural produce prices. For other agricultural produce gross output is based on 1968 and 1972 household budget surveys and intermediate consumption is based on case studies. The gross output and intermediate consumption of the industrial activity sectors are based on annual industrial censuses carried out since 1970. Estimates of gross output, intermediate consumption and compensation of employees of private construction are obtained from annual censuses of building and construction conducted annually since 1970. Government bodies engaged in construction are covered through their annual reports and operating budgets. For the trade sector, the estimates are based on statistics from the Inland Revenue Departments and on the Census of Distribution 1970. The producers' values and c.i.f. import values are grossed up by the margin established in the 1970 Census of Distribution. Banking estimates are obtained from income tax statistics while insurance estimates are derived from annual surveys. Imputed rent per urban household is derived from the household budget survey in 1968, grossed up by the consumer price index for rent and the growth in urban population. For rural areas, an estimated rent has been assumed in 1968 and grossed up annually by a rural price factor and growth in rural population. Estimates for producers of government services are based on the operating budgets and government accounts and finance. Other services estimates are derived from income tax statistics, the 1970/71 survey of non-profit institutions and 1970 Census of Distribution and Services. For the constant price estimates, the general approach used for the major crops of agriculture, industrial activity, transport, insurance and private services is extrapolated. Value added is extrapolated by production indexes. Price deflation is used for construction, trade, restaurants and hotels, real estate, banking and producers of government services, the current value being deflated by various price indexes such as consumer price index, index of wage rates, etc.

1.1 Expenditure on the Gross Domestic Product, in Current Prices

Million Fiji dollars

	1980	1983	1984	1985	1986	1987	1988	1989	1990	1991	1992	1993
1 Government final consumption expenditure	157	232	245	252	267	269	263	305	340	397	449	514
2 Private final consumption expenditure	575	748	794	838	873	960	1094	1210	1366	1484	1580	1689
3 Gross capital formation	313	241	241	251	266	234	204	257	357	293	311	384
A Increase in stocks	63	2	23	12	51	4	13	25	35	26	30	40
B Gross fixed capital formation	250	239	218	239	215	230	191	232	322	267	281	344
4 Exports of goods and services	477	498	546	584	609	664	894	1163	1310	1279	1316	1425
5 Less: Imports of goods and services	511	560	560	589	577	616	815	1059	1330	1236	1259	1487
Statistical discrepancy	-27	-17	9	-20	24	-46	-53	-15	2	-41	-20	15
Equals: Gross Domestic Product [a]	984	1142	1275	1316	1462	1465	1587	1861	2045	2176	2377	2540

a) Data in this table have not been revised, therefore they are not comparable with the data in other tables.

1.2 Expenditure on the Gross Domestic Product, in Constant Prices

Million Fiji dollars

	1980	1983	1984	1985	1986	1987	1988	1989	1990	1991	1992	1993
	\multicolumn{8}{c}{At constant prices of:1977}				
1 Government final consumption expenditure	123	136	149	150	150	166	163	156	...	...	...	...
2 Private final consumption expenditure	423	442	444	462	448	466	483	553	...	...	...	...
3 Gross capital formation	239	153	146	145	149	105	99	132	...	...	...	...
A Increase in stocks	48	1	15	7	27	2	6	13	...	...	...	...
B Gross fixed capital formation	191	152	131	138	122	103	93	119	...	...	...	...
4 Exports of goods and services	341	331	367	399	374	349	414	481	...	...	...	...
5 Less: Imports of goods and services	349	355	337	343	369	336	437	547	...	...	...	...
Statistical discrepancy	-35	43	43	-33	81	29	71	123	...	...	...	...
Equals: Gross Domestic Product [a]	742	750	812	780	833	779	793	898	...	...	...	...

a) Data in this table have not been revised, therefore they are not comparable with the data in other tables.

Fiji

1.3 Cost Components of the Gross Domestic Product

Million Fiji dollars

	1980	1983	1984	1985	1986	1987	1988	1989	1990	1991	1992	1993
1 Indirect taxes, net	83	110	124	139	136	136	155	200	234	234	283	334
A Indirect taxes	85	111	125	140	137	136	155	200	234	234	283	334
B Less: Subsidies	2	1	1	1	1	-	-	-	...	...	...	...
2 Consumption of fixed capital	64	80	88	95	103	111	119	138	154	168	183	183
3 Compensation of employees paid by resident producers to:	426	559	603	596	641	612	661	766	783	810	843	861
4 Operating surplus	411	393	460	487	582	606	653	757	874	964	1068	1162
Equals: Gross Domestic Product	984	1142	1275	1317	1462	1465	1588	1861	2045	2176	2377	2540

1.4 General Government Current Receipts and Disbursements

Million Fiji dollars

	1980	1983	1984	1985	1986	1987	1988	1989	1990	1991	1992	1993
Receipts												
1 Operating surplus	...	...	...	...	...	...	...	...				
2 Property and entrepreneurial income	19	20	18	23	25	32	41	36	...	...	...	...
3 Taxes, fees and contributions	200	257	298	304	300	288	321	409	...	...	...	...
A Indirect taxes	84	111	125	140	137	137	155	199	...	...	...	...
B Direct taxes	105	131	154	147	144	135	147	185	...	...	...	...
C Social security contributions	-	-	-	1	-	-	-	-	...	...	...	...
D Compulsory fees, fines and penalties	11	14	19	19	19	16	19	25	...	...	...	...
4 Other current transfers	30	38	31	40	56	39	53	32	...	...	...	...
Total Current Receipts of General Government	250	314	346	367	381	359	415	477	...	...	...	...
Disbursements												
1 Government final consumption expenditure	157	232	246	252	267	269	264	305	...	...	...	...
2 Property income	17	35	41	45	51	59	71	69	...	...	...	...
A Interest	17	35	41	45	51	59	71	69	...	...	...	...
B Net land rent and royalties	-	-	-	-	-	-	-	-	...	...	...	...
3 Subsidies	1	1	1	1	1	-	-	-	...	...	...	...
4 Other current transfers	20	33	50	43	43	48	50	56	...	...	...	...
A Social security benefits	2	3	3	2	4	6	6	23	...	...	...	...
B Social assistance grants									...	...	...	...
C Other	18	30	46	40	39	42	44	33	...	...	...	...
5 Net saving	55	13	9	26	19	-17	30	47	...	...	...	...
Total Current Disbursements and Net Saving of General Government	250	314	346	367	381	359	415	477	...	...	...	...

1.7 External Transactions on Current Account, Summary

Million Fiji dollars

	1980	1983	1984	1985	1986	1987	1988	1989	1990	1991	1992	1993
Payments to the Rest of the World												
1 Imports of goods and services	511	560	560	589	577	616	815	1059	1330	1236	1259	1487
2 Factor income to the rest of the world	33	49	53	53	56	82	88	112	108	105	119	96
A Compensation of employees	-	-	-	-	-	-	-	-	-	-	-	-
B Property and entrepreneurial income	33	49	53	53	56	82	88	112	108	105	119	96
3 Current transfers to the rest of the world	26	23	25	34	33	46	36	65	71	87	80	85
4 Surplus of the nation on current transactions	-41	-87	-45	-47	-8	-23	46	52	-86	-16	-4	-87
Payments to the Rest of the World and Surplus of the Nation on Current Transactions	529	545	593	629	659	722	985	1288	1423	1412	1454	1581

Fiji

1.7 External Transactions on Current Account, Summary
(Continued)

Million Fiji dollars

	1980	1983	1984	1985	1986	1987	1988	1989	1990	1991	1992	1993
	\multicolumn{12}{c}{Receipts From The Rest of the World}											
1 Exports of goods and services	477	498	546	584	609	664	894	1163	1310	1279	1316	1425
2 Factor income from rest of the world	18	21	23	16	22	34	53	76	73	76	79	82
A Compensation of employees	3	7	10	7	8	9	19	34	32	28	34	40
B Property and entrepreneurial income	15	14	13	9	14	25	34	42	41	48	45	42
3 Current transfers from rest of the world	34	26	24	29	28	24	37	50	40	55	60	73
Receipts from the Rest of the World on Current Transactions	529	545	593	629	659	722	984	1289	1423	1410	1455	1580

1.8 Capital Transactions of The Nation, Summary

Million Fiji dollars

	1980	1983	1984	1985	1986	1987	1988	1989	1990	1991	1992	1993
	\multicolumn{12}{c}{Finance of Gross Capital Formation}											
Gross saving	244	137	205	184	282	166	196	295	274	236	287	312
1 Consumption of fixed capital	65	80	88	95	103	111	119	138	154	168	183	183
2 Net saving	179	57	117	89	179	55	77	157	120	68	104	129
Less: Surplus of the nation on current transactions	-41	-87	-45	-47	-7	-23	46	52	-86	-16	-4	-87
Statistical discrepancy	28	17	-9	20	-23	45	54	12	-3	41	20	-15
Finance of Gross Capital Formation	313	241	241	251	266	234	204	257	357	293	311	384
	\multicolumn{12}{c}{Gross Capital Formation}											
Increase in stocks	63	2	23	12	51	4	13	25	35	26	30	40
Gross fixed capital formation	250	239	218	239	215	230	191	232	322	267	281	344
Gross Capital Formation	313	241	241	251	266	234	204	257	357	293	311	384

1.10 Gross Domestic Product by Kind of Activity, in Current Prices

Million Fiji dollars

	1980	1983	1984	1985	1986	1987	1988	1989	1990	1991	1992	1993
1 Agriculture, hunting, forestry and fishing	200	190	220	216	277	306	280	326	...	...	...	...
2 Mining and quarrying	-3	6	1	14	18	31	62	56	...	...	...	...
3 Manufacturing	108	94	112	111	137	157	137	175	...	...	...	...
4 Electricity, gas and water	15	27	42	40	48	44	52	55	...	...	...	...
5 Construction	73	75	61	64	64	50	60	66	...	...	...	...
6 Wholesale and retail trade, restaurants and hotels	162	183	204	210	223	209	282	379	...	...	...	...
7 Transport, storage and communication	80	98	108	122	132	133	163	169	...	...	...	...
8 Finance, insurance, real estate and business services	112	141	154	166	182	182	197	216	...	...	...	...
9 Community, social and personal services	107	153	165	160	169	153	165	179	...	...	...	...
Total, Industries	854	967	1069	1104	1250	1265	1397	1621	...	...	...	...
Producers of Government Services	61	90	101	94	113	105	90	105	...	...	...	...
Other Producers	16	22	23	27	27	29	30	33	...	...	...	...
Subtotal [a]	932	1079	1192	1224	1391	1399	1518	1759	...	...	...	...
Less: Imputed bank service charge	31	47	41	47	65	70	85	98	...	...	...	...
Plus: Import duties	...	...	...	...	...	...	...	...	...	...	...	...
Plus: Value added tax	...	...	...	...	...	...	...	...	...	...	...	...
Plus: Other adjustments [b]	83	110	124	139	136	136	155	200	...	...	...	...
Equals: Gross Domestic Product [c]	984	1142	1275	1316	1462	1465	1588	1861	...	...	...	...

a) Gross domestic product in factor values.
b) Item 'Other adjustments' refers to indirect taxes net of subsidies.
c) Data in this table have not been revised, therefore they are not comparable with the data in other tables.

Fiji

1.11 Gross Domestic Product by Kind of Activity, in Constant Prices

Million Fiji dollars

	1980	1983	1984	1985	1986	1987	1988	1989	1990	1991	1992	1993
					At constant prices of:1977							
1 Agriculture, hunting, forestry and fishing	153	144	181	156	186	174	170	190	182	179	185	186
2 Mining and quarrying	-	1	1	1	1	1	2	2	2	1	2	2
3 Manufacturing	81	78	91	79	95	84	83	93	99	104	103	108
4 Electricity, gas and water	7	7	8	8	9	9	10	10	11	11	12	12
5 Construction	60	51	40	38	39	29	31	34	37	46	57	43
6 Wholesale and retail trade, restaurants and hotels	117	122	122	125	136	117	130	161	183	173	169	183
7 Transport, storage and communication	67	78	88	90	90	88	95	111	120	120	127	133
8 Finance, insurance, real estate and business services	84	94	96	98	98	95	96	99	106	111	116	120
9 Community, social and personal services	128	131	136	132	130	135	133	139	141	143	147	150
Statistical discrepancy	...	...	...	...	...	...	...	...	30	...	...	...
Total, Industries	697	706	763	727	784	732	750	839	911	888	918	937
Producers of Government Services	...	...	...	...	...	...	...	...	...	...	...	...
Other Producers	...	...	...	...	...	...	...	...	...	...	...	...
Subtotal a	697	706	763	727	784	732	750	839	911	888	918	937
Less: Imputed bank service charge	18	22	22	23	24	22	23	24	29	32	34	36
Plus: Import duties	...	...	...	...	...	...	...	...	...	...	...	...
Plus: Value added tax	...	...	...	...	...	...	...	...	...	...	...	...
Plus: Other adjustments b	63	66	71	76	73	69	66	83	91	91	100	100
Equals: Gross Domestic Product	742	750	812	780	833	779	793	898	973	947	984	1001

a) Gross domestic product in factor values.
b) Item 'Other adjustments' refers to indirect taxes net of subsidies.

1.12 Relations Among National Accounting Aggregates

Million Fiji dollars

	1980	1983	1984	1985	1986	1987	1988	1989	1990	1991	1992	1993
Gross Domestic Product	984	1142	1275	1316	1462	1465	1587	1861	2045	2176	2377	2540
Plus: Net factor income from the rest of the world	-15	-28	-30	-36	-34	-48	-35	-36	-35	-29	-40	-14
Factor income from the rest of the world	18	21	23	17	22	34	53	76	73	76	79	82
Less: Factor income to the rest of the world	33	49	53	53	56	82	88	112	108	105	119	96
Equals: Gross National Product	969	1114	1245	1280	1427	1417	1552	1825	2010	2147	2337	2526
Less: Consumption of fixed capital	65	80	88	95	103	111	119	138	154	168	183	183
Equals: National Income	904	1034	1157	1185	1324	1306	1433	1687	1856	1979	2154	2343
Plus: Net current transfers from the rest of the world	8	3	-1	-6	-5	-22	1	-15	-31	-32	-20	-12
Current transfers from the rest of the world	34	26	24	28	28	24	37	50	40	55	60	73
Less: Current transfers to the rest of the world	26	23	25	34	33	46	36	65	71	87	80	85
Equals: National Disposable Income	912	1037	1156	1179	1319	1284	1434	1672	1825	1947	2134	2331
Less: Final consumption	732	980	1039	1091	1140	1229	1358	1515	1706	1881	2029	2203
Equals: Net Saving	180	57	117	88	179	55	77	157	119	66	105	128
Less: Surplus of the nation on current transactions	-41	-88	-45	-47	-8	-23	46	52	-86	-16	-4	-87
Statistical discrepancy	27	17	-9	20	-23	46	54	15	-2	41	20	-15
Equals: Net Capital Formation	248	162	153	155	164	124	85	120	203	123	129	200

2.1 Government Final Consumption Expenditure by Function, in Current Prices

Million Fiji dollars

	1980	1983	1984	1985	1986	1987	1988	1989	1990	1991	1992	1993
1 General public services	36	60	59	72	74	75	87	88	...	...	...	...
2 Defence	8	14	15	15	15	26	28	37	...	...	...	...
3 Public order and safety	...	...	...	...	...	...	...	...	...	...	...	...
4 Education	47	67	74	70	70	69	63	78	...	...	...	...
5 Health	19	30	33	31	32	31	28	33	...	...	...	...
6 Social security and welfare	1	1	1	1	1	1	1	1	...	...	...	...
7 Housing and community amenities	3	3	3	4	5	3	4	6	...	...	...	...
8 Recreational, cultural and religious affairs	1	2	1	2	2	3	3	4	...	...	...	...
9 Economic services	42	55	59	57	67	60	50	57	...	...	...	...

Fiji

2.1 Government Final Consumption Expenditure by Function, in Current Prices
(Continued)

Million Fiji dollars

	1980	1983	1984	1985	1986	1987	1988	1989	1990	1991	1992	1993
A Fuel and energy	-	-	-	-	-	-	-	-	...	...	...	...
B Agriculture, forestry, fishing and hunting	5	7	7	7	16	9	8	7	...	...	...	...
C Mining, manufacturing and construction, except fuel and energy	8	10	11	13	20	18	12	12	...	...	...	...
D Transportation and communication	14	17	18	17	16	15	12	16	...	...	...	...
E Other economic affairs	15	21	23	20	15	17	18	22	...	...	...	...
10 Other functions	...	...	...	...	...	...	...	...	...	...	...	...
Total Government Final Consumption Expenditure	157	232	245	252	266	268	264	304	...	...	...	...

2.5 Private Final Consumption Expenditure by Type and Purpose, in Current Prices

Million Fiji dollars

	1980	1983	1984	1985	1986	1987	1988	1989	1990	1991	1992	1993
Final Consumption Expenditure of Resident Households												
1 Food, beverages and tobacco	177	246	262	273	281	289	342	370	403	439	...	...
A Food	135	191	200	210	216	225	263	281	299	329	...	...
B Non-alcoholic beverages	9	12	16	17	16	13	17	28	30	32	...	...
C Alcoholic beverages	20	26	28	28	29	31	38	42	45	53	...	...
D Tobacco	13	17	18	18	20	20	24	19	29	25	...	...
2 Clothing and footwear	34	37	38	40	50	49	111	103	105	111	...	...
3 Gross rent, fuel and power	77	103	112	114	125	127	130	148	167	186	...	...
4 Furniture, furnishings and household equipment and operation	51	63	65	70	74	83	85	103	99	111	...	...
5 Medical care and health expenses	12	14	15	15	16	16	23	24	26	28	...	...
6 Transport and communication	72	97	107	110	111	120	123	146	155	165	...	...
7 Recreational, entertainment, education and cultural services	24	31	35	36	37	36	44	52	51	51	...	...
8 Miscellaneous goods and services	35	46	50	48	49	60	69	87	97	104	...	...
Statistical discrepancy	64	85	81	102	92	102	104	103	115	150	...	...
Total Final Consumption Expenditure in the Domestic Market by Households, of which	546	722	765	808	835	882	1031	1137	1217	1345	...	...
A Durable goods	30	39	43	41	35	47	43	64	64	73	...	...
B Semi-durable goods	57	65	68	70	78	75	145	151	159	166	...	...
C Non-durable goods	293	397	413	445	453	483	551	604	655	734	...	...
D Services	166	221	241	252	269	277	292	318	339	372	...	...
Plus: Direct purchases abroad by resident households	14	17	19	20	27	66	50	60	60	60	...	...
Less: Direct purchases in the domestic market by non-resident households	-	-	-	-	-	-	-	-	...	...	...	...
Equals: Final Consumption Expenditure of Resident Households	560	739	784	828	862	948	1081	1197	1277	1405	...	...
Final Consumption Expenditure of Private Non-profit Institutions Serving Households												
Equals: Final Consumption Expenditure of Private Non-profit Organisations Serving Households	15	9	10	10	11	12	12	13	15	16	...	...
Statistical discrepancy	...	...	...	...	...	...	...	...	74	63	...	...
Private Final Consumption Expenditure	575	748	794	838	873	960	1093	1210	1366	1484	...	...

2.6 Private Final Consumption Expenditure by Type and Purpose, in Constant Prices

Million Fiji dollars

	1980	1983	1984	1985	1986	1987	1988	1989	1990	1991	1992	1993
At constant prices of: 1977												
Final Consumption Expenditure of Resident Households												
1 Food, beverages and tobacco	146	151	150	148	147	140	150	158	152	156	...	...
A Food	114	120	120	120	116	113	119	125	114	121	...	...
B Non-alcoholic beverages	8	9	9	9	9	7	8	10	10	10	...	...
C Alcoholic beverages	15	13	12	11	14	13	15	17	16	18	...	...
D Tobacco	9	9	9	8	8	7	8	6	12	7	...	...

Fiji

2.6 Private Final Consumption Expenditure by Type and Purpose, in Constant Prices
(Continued)

Million Fiji dollars

	1980	1983	1984	1985	1986	1987	1988	1989	1990	1991	1992	1993
					At constant prices of:1977							
2 Clothing and footwear	20	23	23	24	20	18	28	29	30	32	...	...
3 Gross rent, fuel and power	48	50	51	52	51	54	55	57	62	61	...	...
4 Furniture, furnishings and household equipment and operation	34	38	38	46	46	47	45	49	44	46	...	...
5 Medical care and health expenses	10	7	8	7	7	6	8	8	8	7	...	...
6 Transport and communication	51	58	61	62	63	68	68	77	79	77	...	...
7 Recreational, entertainment, education and cultural services	19	20	22	22	18	17	20	22	20	18	...	...
8 Miscellaneous goods and services	24	29	29	28	25	29	27	30	31	31	...	...
Statistical discrepancy	49	51	46	45	52	47	48	48	49	67	...	...
Total Final Consumption Expenditure in the Domestic Market by Households, of which	401	427	428	434	429	426	449	478	475	495	...	...
A Durable goods	24	23	26	25	23	28	24	31	29	36	...	...
B Semi-durable goods	32	39	39	39	36	30	42	47	49	42	...	...
C Non-durable goods	229	240	233	239	240	231	241	254	248	271	...	...
D Services	116	125	130	131	130	137	142	146	149	146	...	...
Plus: Direct purchases abroad by resident households	11	10	11	11	15	34	22	26	24	22	...	...
Less: Direct purchases in the domestic market by non-resident households	...	...	...	...	...	...	...	...	...	...	...	...
Equals: Final Consumption Expenditure of Resident Households	412	437	439	445	444	460	471	504	499	517	...	...
			Final Consumption Expenditure of Private Non-profit Institutions Serving Households									
Equals: Final Consumption Expenditure of Private Non-profit Organisations Serving Households	11	5	5	6	6	6	6	6	...	...	...	...
Statistical discrepancy	...	...	...	11	...	...	6	43	6	6	...	...
Private Final Consumption Expenditure	423	442	444	462	450	466	483	553	505	523	...	...

Finland

Source. Reply to the United Nations National Accounts Questionnaire from the Central Statistical Office, Helsinki. Official estimates are published annually in 'Tilastotiedotus Kansantalouden Tilinpito' (Statistical Report, National Accounting) issued by the same office. Information on concepts, sources and methods of estimation utilized can be found in 'Heikki Sourama-Olli Saariaho, Kansantalouden tilinipito, Rakenne, Maaritelmat ja luokitukset, Central Statistical Office of Finland, Studies No. 63, Helsinki, 1980'.

General note. The estimates shown in the following tables have been prepared by the Central Statistical Office in accordance with the United Nations System of National Accounts so far as the existing data would permit.

1.1 Expenditure on the Gross Domestic Product, in Current Prices

Million Finnish markkaa

	1980	1983	1984	1985	1986	1987	1988	1989	1990	1991	1992	1993
1 Government final consumption expenditure	34392	52451	58842	66967	72849	80046	87199	96019	108535	118719	118453	112542
2 Private final consumption expenditure	103551	149624	165149	180887	194007	211534	232580	254588	269754	274709	272114	271753
A Households	99873	144066	159140	174165	186830	203783	223918	245058	259157	263886	261136	260814
B Private non-profit institutions serving households	3678	5558	6009	6722	7177	7751	8662	9530	10597	10823	10978	10939
3 Gross capital formation	55403	69430	74497	78983	80697	91652	112264	142572	142068	100563	82120	68616
A Increase in stocks	6700	-116	1487	-440	-2211	-889	3006	6424	2924	-9498	-5833	-2735
B Gross fixed capital formation	48703	69546	73010	79423	82908	92541	109258	136148	139144	110061	87953	71351
Residential buildings	13970	18959	19954	20730	20074	21882	28395	38241	38410	29791	22127	17636
Non-residential buildings	10895	17678	17776	19091	20226	22670	26848	32792	35822	30179	21112	14304
Other construction and land improvement etc.	6163	8097	8695	9338	10261	10529	10669	12632	13781	13510	12176	11014
Other	17675	24812	26585	30264	32347	37460	43346	52483	51131	36581	32538	28397
4 Exports of goods and services	63489	82735	94190	98034	95634	100048	108750	116702	118828	109289	128272	159438
5 Less: Imports of goods and services	65016	81361	86137	94639	89898	97775	109866	125996	126600	112422	121878	133341
Statistical discrepancy	-443	-1272	-1944	1396	1705	1350	3414	3113	2845	10	-2303	1462
Equals: Gross Domestic Product	191376	271607	304597	331628	354994	386855	434341	486998	515430	490868	476778	480470

1.2 Expenditure on the Gross Domestic Product, in Constant Prices

Million Finnish markkaa

	1980	1983	1984	1985	1986	1987	1988	1989	1990	1991	1992	1993
	\multicolumn{12}{c}{At constant prices of: 1990}
1 Government final consumption expenditure	77552	86507	88878	92900	95792	99878	102132	104526	108535	111256	108799	103004
2 Private final consumption expenditure	191933	210290	216906	225002	234000	246163	258821	269879	269754	260031	247363	237793
A Households	183794	201100	207739	215488	224238	236228	248631	259445	259157	249612	236968	227620
B Private non-profit institutions serving households	8139	9190	9167	9514	9762	9935	10190	10434	10597	10419	10395	10173
3 Gross capital formation	112179	109857	109696	109561	107087	113746	129337	153032	142068	101398	86166	72862
A Increase in stocks	12522	-138	1967	-577	-2620	-1321	2967	7978	2924	-9567	-6071	-2202
B Gross fixed capital formation	99657	109995	107729	110138	109707	115067	126370	145054	139144	110965	92237	75064
Residential buildings	32930	33626	32849	31887	29342	29676	34256	40739	38410	30442	25545	21914
Non-residential buildings	24464	29913	27951	28027	28262	29032	31496	35065	35822	31774	24724	18042
Other construction and land improvement etc.	11937	12008	12164	12348	12958	12732	12136	13396	13781	13064	11986	11061
Other	30326	34448	34765	37876	39145	43627	48482	55854	51131	35685	29982	24047
4 Exports of goods and services	95192	101143	106215	107365	108673	111632	115761	117241	118828	110965	122059	142459
5 Less: Imports of goods and services	85908	86811	88216	93868	96281	105175	116898	127311	126600	111755	112989	113752
Statistical discrepancy	-11654	-11296	-11431	-4702	-2665	-1327	-1434	-2003	2845	7116	10605	12266
Equals: Gross Domestic Product	379294	409690	422048	436258	446606	464917	487719	515364	515430	479011	462003	454632

1.3 Cost Components of the Gross Domestic Product

Million Finnish markkaa

	1980	1983	1984	1985	1986	1987	1988	1989	1990	1991	1992	1993
1 Indirect taxes, net	19368	27980	33586	37292	41008	45704	55396	61878	63269	57556	54615	55237
A Indirect taxes	25593	36848	43380	47639	52316	57388	66667	75595	78025	74730	71643	71556
B Less: Subsidies	6225	8868	9794	10347	11308	11684	11271	13717	14756	17174	17028	16319
2 Consumption of fixed capital	28343	40487	44489	48516	52202	57102	63366	71813	79512	82170	81892	83568
3 Compensation of employees paid by resident producers to:	104064	147913	164641	183327	196548	213873	236454	264582	288768	289775	273616	258088

Finland

1.3 Cost Components of the Gross Domestic Product
(Continued)

Million Finnish markkaa

	1980	1983	1984	1985	1986	1987	1988	1989	1990	1991	1992	1993
A Resident households	104016	147842	164565	183248	196480	213805	236379	264519	288660	289619	273514	257956
B Rest of the world	48	71	76	79	68	68	75	63	108	156	102	132
4 Operating surplus	39601	55227	61881	62493	65236	70176	79125	88725	83881	61367	66655	83577
A Corporate and quasi-corporate enterprises	11720	16523	20072	20811	21236	28014	33981	38300	30919	12257	17970	31584
B Private unincorporated enterprises	27940	38476	41704	41604	43947	42130	45072	50355	52918	49261	48810	52150
C General government	-59	228	105	78	53	32	72	70	44	-151	-125	-157
Equals: Gross Domestic Product	191376	271607	304597	331628	354994	386855	434341	486998	515430	490868	476778	480470

1.4 General Government Current Receipts and Disbursements

Million Finnish markkaa

	1980	1983	1984	1985	1986	1987	1988	1989	1990	1991	1992	1993
Receipts												
1 Operating surplus	-59	228	105	78	53	32	72	70	44	-151	-125	-157
2 Property and entrepreneurial income	4578	8272	9856	11220	11790	12387	13666	16211	19786	23010	25422	28497
3 Taxes, fees and contributions	72133	104444	121349	137581	152101	158341	191102	214797	237177	232536	226366	222877
A Indirect taxes	25593	36848	43380	47639	52316	57388	66667	75595	78025	74730	71643	71556
B Direct taxes	27718	42866	49381	55741	63127	61308	74454	82179	92741	88138	82270	74900
C Social security contributions	18196	23712	27303	32714	34931	37809	46999	53108	63356	66806	69566	73920
D Compulsory fees, fines and penalties	626	1018	1285	1487	1727	1836	2982	3915	3055	2862	2887	2501
4 Other current transfers	3090	4903	5500	6134	6729	7342	3745	4021	4472	1977	2180	2233
Total Current Receipts of General Government	79742	117847	136810	155013	170673	178102	208585	235099	261479	257372	253843	253450
Disbursements												
1 Government final consumption expenditure	34392	52451	58842	66967	72849	80046	87199	96019	108535	118719	118453	112542
A Compensation of employees	23526	36634	41341	46868	50885	55765	61032	67522	75449	84015	84141	79397
B Consumption of fixed capital	1905	2840	3190	3566	3918	4448	5037	5671	6673	6743	6631	6748
C Purchases of goods and services, net	8952	12964	14297	16519	18027	19813	21108	22804	26387	27936	27658	26378
D Less: Own account fixed capital formation	...	...	...	...	...	...	...	...	...	...	...	...
E Indirect taxes paid, net	9	13	14	14	19	20	22	22	26	25	23	19
2 Property income	1996	4212	5167	6147	6195	6571	7201	7260	7511	9598	12608	22155
A Interest	1993	4206	5160	6138	6185	6559	7186	7240	7487	9570	12583	22105
B Net land rent and royalties	3	6	7	9	10	12	15	18	20	21	19	49
3 Subsidies	6225	8868	9794	10347	11308	11684	11271	13717	14756	17174	17028	16319
4 Other current transfers	24971	41412	46577	53513	59347	65476	70864	77735	90227	106482	123238	133058
A Social security benefits	15877	26820	30452	35083	38936	42486	49136	53787	62387	77566	89081	90090
B Social assistance grants	3406	5767	6326	7376	7913	8871	9273	9929	11779	15745	20546	28482
C Other	5688	8825	9799	11054	12498	14119	12455	14019	16061	13171	13611	14486
5 Net saving	12158	10904	16430	18039	20974	14325	32050	40368	40450	5399	-17484	-30624
Total Current Disbursements and Net Saving of General Government	79742	117847	136810	155013	170673	178102	208585	235099	261479	257372	253843	253450

Finland

1.5 Current Income and Outlay of Corporate and Quasi-Corporate Enterprises, Summary

Million Finnish markkaa

	1980	1983	1984	1985	1986	1987	1988	1989	1990	1991	1992	1993
Receipts												
1 Operating surplus	11720	16523	20072	20811	21236	28014	33981	38300	30919	12257	17970	31584
2 Property and entrepreneurial income received	17553	28870	38238	45284	45046	51974	67272	93778	116619	118373	111058	88341
3 Current transfers [a]	6480	10398	13131	12676	14662	15581	17534	19086	18147	17380	21134	20163
Total Current Receipts	35753	55791	71441	78771	80944	95569	118787	151164	165685	148010	150162	140088
Disbursements												
1 Property and entrepreneurial income	24729	40526	51692	58450	59587	67489	82857	112685	139390	146498	144474	118740
2 Direct taxes and other current payments to general government	2293	4427	4577	4637	5469	4482	5995	7197	10458	10045	8196	4451
3 Other current transfers [a]	6924	11891	13833	13630	15266	15911	18181	21037	18604	19771	24835	23839
4 Net saving	1807	-1053	1339	2054	622	7687	11754	10245	-2767	-28304	-27343	-6942
Total Current Disbursements and Net Saving	35753	55791	71441	78771	80944	95569	118787	151164	165685	148010	150162	140088

a) All transfers include reinvested earnings.

1.6 Current Income and Outlay of Households and Non-Profit Institutions

Million Finnish markkaa

	1980	1983	1984	1985	1986	1987	1988	1989	1990	1991	1992	1993
Receipts												
1 Compensation of employees	104429	148401	164879	183582	196900	214194	236874	264901	288978	289915	273736	258124
A From resident producers	104016	147842	164565	183248	196480	213805	236379	264519	288660	289619	273514	257956
B From rest of the world	413	559	314	334	420	389	495	382	318	296	222	168
2 Operating surplus of private unincorporated enterprises	27940	38476	41704	41604	43947	42130	45072	50355	52918	49261	48810	52150
3 Property and entrepreneurial income	6267	9596	11617	12669	13016	14823	17932	22028	25258	28610	31580	26236
4 Current transfers	29787	48483	54624	62005	68397	74991	82559	90492	101575	117647	135349	144946
A Social security benefits	16359	27652	31366	36038	40044	43577	50542	55271	64096	79391	91147	92332
B Social assistance grants	3515	6027	6625	7675	8275	9171	9594	10279	12279	16325	21176	29072
C Other	9913	14804	16633	18292	20078	22243	22423	24942	25200	21931	23026	23542
Total Current Receipts	168423	244956	272824	299860	322260	346138	382437	427776	468729	485433	489475	481456
Disbursements												
1 Private final consumption expenditure	103551	149624	165149	180887	194007	211534	232580	254588	269754	274709	272114	271753
2 Property income	5280	8282	10194	11539	12006	13458	17599	23487	28908	30606	30915	25432
3 Direct taxes and other current transfers n.e.c. to general government	44996	64495	74808	86907	96056	98498	121008	135450	152796	151659	150269	150652
A Social security contributions	18931	24940	28626	34206	36527	39706	49437	56383	67248	70474	72993	77066
B Direct taxes	25439	38537	44897	51214	57802	56956	68589	75152	82493	78323	74389	71085
C Fees, fines and penalties	626	1018	1285	1487	1727	1836	2982	3915	3055	2862	2887	2501
4 Other current transfers	7107	11037	12513	13440	15212	16309	14073	15866	16066	13848	15460	14287
5 Net saving	7489	11518	10160	7087	4979	6339	-2823	-1615	1205	14611	20717	19332
Total Current Disbursements and Net Saving	168423	244956	272824	299860	322260	346138	382437	427776	468729	485433	489475	481456

1.7 External Transactions on Current Account, Summary

Million Finnish markkaa

	1980	1983	1984	1985	1986	1987	1988	1989	1990	1991	1992	1993
Payments to the Rest of the World												
1 Imports of goods and services	65016	81361	86137	94639	89898	97775	109866	125996	126600	112422	121878	133341
A Imports of merchandise c.i.f.	58046	70731	73496	80764	76736	81867	91232	104400	101967	86348	93188	101559
B Other	6970	10630	12641	13875	13162	15908	18634	21596	24633	26074	28690	31782
2 Factor income to the rest of the world	5249	9459	11987	12929	12560	13599	16864	22318	28960	31006	32491	36446

Finland

1.7 External Transactions on Current Account, Summary
(Continued)

Million Finnish markkaa

	1980	1983	1984	1985	1986	1987	1988	1989	1990	1991	1992	1993
A Compensation of employees	48	71	76	79	68	68	75	63	108	156	102	132
B Property and entrepreneurial income	5201	9388	11911	12850	12492	13531	16789	22255	28852	30850	32389	36314
3 Current transfers to the rest of the world	1631	3892	4779	4796	5217	5616	7301	7126	6981	7897	8280	8524
A Indirect taxes to supranational organizations	...	...	...	...	...	...	...	...	...	...	...	...
B Other current transfers [a]	1631	3892	4779	4796	5217	5616	7301	7126	6981	7897	8280	8524
4 Surplus of the nation on current transactions	-5163	-6302	-135	-4683	-3625	-7549	-11331	-24874	-26513	-26697	-22035	-4744
Payments to the Rest of the World and Surplus of the Nation on Current Transactions	66733	88410	102768	107681	104050	109441	122700	130566	136028	124628	140614	173567

Receipts From The Rest of the World

	1980	1983	1984	1985	1986	1987	1988	1989	1990	1991	1992	1993
1 Exports of goods and services	63489	82735	94190	98034	95634	100048	108750	116702	118828	109289	128272	159438
A Exports of merchandise f.o.b.	52594	67960	78961	82475	81066	83826	91313	98265	99750	91100	105809	132550
B Other	10895	14775	15229	15559	14568	16222	17437	18437	19078	18189	22463	26888
2 Factor income from rest of the world	2007	3665	4883	6221	4976	5586	8497	11222	15024	14437	12674	13229
A Compensation of employees	413	559	314	334	420	389	495	382	318	296	222	168
B Property and entrepreneurial income	1594	3106	4569	5887	4556	5197	8002	10840	14706	14141	12452	13061
3 Current transfers from rest of the world	1237	2010	3695	3426	3440	3807	5453	2642	2176	902	-332	900
A Subsidies from supranational organisations	...	...	...	...	...	...	...	...	...	...	...	...
B Other current transfers [a]	1237	2010	3695	3426	3440	3807	5453	2642	2176	902	-332	900
Receipts from the Rest of the World on Current Transactions	66733	88410	102768	107681	104050	109441	122700	130566	136028	124628	140614	173567

a) All transfers include reinvested earnings.

1.8 Capital Transactions of The Nation, Summary

Million Finnish markkaa

	1980	1983	1984	1985	1986	1987	1988	1989	1990	1991	1992	1993

Finance of Gross Capital Formation

	1980	1983	1984	1985	1986	1987	1988	1989	1990	1991	1992	1993
Gross saving	49797	61856	72418	75696	78777	85453	104347	120811	118400	73876	57782	65334
1 Consumption of fixed capital	28343	40487	44489	48516	52202	57102	63366	71813	79512	82170	81892	83568
A General government	2196	3295	3618	4014	4470	5067	5696	6294	7383	7481	7401	7481
B Corporate and quasi-corporate enterprises	16435	23019	25140	27678	29543	32164	35236	39918	43637	45657	47525	50262
C Other	9712	14173	15731	16824	18189	19871	22434	25601	28492	29032	26966	25825
2 Net saving	21454	21369	27929	27180	26575	28351	40981	48998	38888	-8294	-24110	-18234
A General government	12158	10904	16430	18039	20974	14325	32050	40368	40450	5399	-17484	-30624
B Corporate and quasi-corporate enterprises	1807	-1053	1339	2054	622	7687	11754	10245	-2767	-28304	-27343	-6942
C Other	7489	11518	10160	7087	4979	6339	-2823	-1615	1205	14611	20717	19332
Less: Surplus of the nation on current transactions	-5163	-6302	-135	-4683	-3625	-7549	-11331	-24874	-26513	-26697	-22035	-4744
Statistical discrepancy	443	1272	1944	-1396	-1705	-1350	-3414	-3113	-2845	-10	2303	-1462
Finance of Gross Capital Formation	55403	69430	74497	78983	80697	91652	112264	142572	142068	100563	82120	68616

Gross Capital Formation

	1980	1983	1984	1985	1986	1987	1988	1989	1990	1991	1992	1993
Increase in stocks	6700	-116	1487	-440	-2211	-889	3006	6424	2924	-9498	-5833	-2735
Gross fixed capital formation	48703	69546	73010	79423	82908	92541	109258	136148	139144	110061	87953	71351
1 General government	6794	10275	10567	11594	11948	14171	15846	15119	18464	18285	16601	13403
2 Corporate and quasi-corporate enterprises	22073	32493	34447	38486	42268	47106	55234	70457	69697	53198	42192	33312
3 Other	19836	26778	27996	29343	28692	31264	38178	50572	50983	38578	29160	24636
Gross Capital Formation	55403	69430	74497	78983	80697	91652	112264	142572	142068	100563	82120	68616

Finland

1.10 Gross Domestic Product by Kind of Activity, in Current Prices

Million Finnish markkaa

	1980	1983	1984	1985	1986	1987	1988	1989	1990	1991	1992	1993
1 Agriculture, hunting, forestry and fishing	16871	21369	23580	24310	24239	22612	24739	28077	29043	24073	21468	21948
2 Mining and quarrying	928	1085	1185	1258	1227	1246	1603	2037	1733	1729	1800	1743
3 Manufacturing	48563	63496	70911	75644	78197	87145	95972	105225	105383	89667	92426	101962
4 Electricity, gas and water	4976	7826	8050	8429	9522	10018	10065	9245	9504	11059	11003	11016
5 Construction	13692	20887	22750	23222	25199	27461	32940	42035	43467	36962	26041	19766
6 Wholesale and retail trade, restaurants and hotels	22280	31863	35242	39179	40958	45712	50944	56344	57971	52144	48409	47518
7 Transport, storage and communication	13628	18967	21408	23483	25424	27251	30136	33591	36406	36126	36484	37556
8 Finance, insurance, real estate and business services	23136	34463	39112	43317	49118	53993	60135	68820	78211	78829	75503	83366
9 Community, social and personal services	3502	5166	5872	6523	7404	8412	9245	10650	12082	12355	12738	12950
Total, Industries	147576	205122	228110	245365	261288	283850	315779	356024	373800	342944	325872	337825
Producers of Government Services	25440	39487	44545	50448	54822	60233	66091	73215	82148	90783	90795	86164
Other Producers	2986	4464	5012	5628	6140	6609	7507	8240	9164	9378	9558	9538
Subtotal	176002	249073	277667	301441	322250	350692	389377	437479	465112	443105	426225	433527
Less: Imputed bank service charge	4682	6411	7440	8023	8989	10576	12180	14873	17000	15329	10513	14205
Plus: Import duties [a]	20056	28945	34370	38210	41733	46739	57144	64392	67318	63092	61066	61148
Plus: Value added tax	...	...	...	...	...	...	...	...	...	...	...	...
Equals: Gross Domestic Product	191376	271607	304597	331628	354994	386855	434341	486998	515430	490868	476778	480470

a) Item 'Import duties' includes also commodity indirect taxes net of subsidies.

1.11 Gross Domestic Product by Kind of Activity, in Constant Prices

Million Finnish markkaa

	1980	1983	1984	1985	1986	1987	1988	1989	1990	1991	1992	1993
	\multicolumn{12}{c}{At constant prices of: 1990}											
1 Agriculture, hunting, forestry and fishing	28967	28287	28927	28712	27158	24981	26363	28333	29043	25808	25532	26689
2 Mining and quarrying	993	1160	1178	1262	1376	1416	1538	1705	1733	1597	1562	1524
3 Manufacturing	77875	83772	87420	90734	92536	98019	102024	106104	105383	93911	95751	100999
4 Electricity, gas and water	6792	7295	7758	8418	8470	9076	9322	9324	9504	9798	9752	10166
5 Construction	32646	35195	34254	34578	35274	35725	38998	44490	43467	38446	32702	28111
6 Wholesale and retail trade, restaurants and hotels	40237	42907	44745	46679	48474	51863	54734	59062	57971	50785	44803	42571
7 Transport, storage and communication	24397	25693	26268	27267	27509	29472	31336	34325	36406	35048	34872	35558
8 Finance, insurance, real estate and business services	48071	55067	58605	61674	66140	69585	72796	76971	78211	75542	72046	73229
9 Community, social and personal services	8935	9711	9899	10210	10522	10812	11002	11596	12082	11374	11163	11129
Total, Industries	268913	289087	299054	309534	317459	330949	348113	371910	373800	342309	328183	329976
Producers of Government Services	62766	70032	71555	73569	74732	77311	79314	80915	82148	83140	81329	77556
Other Producers	7171	7943	8168	8430	8600	8605	8860	9064	9164	8917	8949	8877
Subtotal	338850	367062	378777	391533	400791	416865	436287	461889	465112	434366	418461	416409
Less: Imputed bank service charge	8723	9614	10268	10727	12270	13679	15169	16943	17000	17343	14339	15585
Plus: Import duties [a]	49167	52242	53539	55452	58085	61731	66601	70418	67318	61988	57881	53808
Plus: Value added tax	...	...	...	...	...	...	...	...	...	...	...	...
Equals: Gross Domestic Product	379294	409690	422048	436258	446606	464917	487719	515364	515430	479011	462003	454632

a) Item 'Import duties' includes also commodity indirect taxes net of subsidies.

1.12 Relations Among National Accounting Aggregates

Million Finnish markkaa

	1980	1983	1984	1985	1986	1987	1988	1989	1990	1991	1992	1993
Gross Domestic Product	191376	271607	304597	331628	354994	386855	434341	486998	515430	490868	476778	480470
Plus: Net factor income from the rest of the world	-3242	-5794	-7104	-6708	-7584	-8013	-8367	-11096	-13936	-16569	-19817	-23217
Factor income from the rest of the world	2007	3665	4883	6221	4976	5586	8497	11222	15024	14437	12674	13229
Less: Factor income to the rest of the world	5249	9459	11987	12929	12560	13599	16864	22318	28960	31006	32491	36446
Equals: Gross National Product	188134	265813	297493	324920	347410	378842	425974	475902	501494	474299	456961	457253
Less: Consumption of fixed capital	28343	40487	44489	48516	52202	57102	63366	71813	79512	82170	81892	83568

Finland

1.12 Relations Among National Accounting Aggregates
(Continued)

Million Finnish markkaa

	1980	1983	1984	1985	1986	1987	1988	1989	1990	1991	1992	1993
Equals: National Income	159791	225326	253004	276404	295208	321740	362608	404089	421982	392129	375069	373685
Plus: Net current transfers from the rest of the world	-394	-1882	-1084	-1370	-1777	-1809	-1848	-4484	-4805	-6995	-8612	-7624
Current transfers from the rest of the world [a]	1237	2010	3695	3426	3440	3807	5453	2642	2176	902	-332	900
Less: Current transfers to the rest of the world [a]	1631	3892	4779	4796	5217	5616	7301	7126	6981	7897	8280	8524
Equals: National Disposable Income	159397	223444	251920	275034	293431	319931	360760	399605	417177	385134	366457	366061
Less: Final consumption	137943	202075	223991	247854	266856	291580	319779	350607	378289	393428	390567	384295
Equals: Net Saving	21454	21369	27929	27180	26575	28351	40981	48998	38888	-8294	-24110	-18234
Less: Surplus of the nation on current transactions	-5163	-6302	-135	-4683	-3625	-7549	-11331	-24874	-26513	-26697	-22035	-4744
Statistical discrepancy	443	1272	1944	-1396	-1705	-1350	-3414	-3113	-2845	-10	2303	-1462
Equals: Net Capital Formation	27060	28943	30008	30467	28495	34550	48898	70759	62556	18393	228	-14952

a) All transfers include reinvested earnings.

2.1 Government Final Consumption Expenditure by Function, in Current Prices

Million Finnish markkaa

	1980	1983	1984	1985	1986	1987	1988	1989	1990	1991	1992	1993
1 General public services	3585	5182	5694	6388	6655	7503	8237	9070	10033	11123	10842	9906
2 Defence	2712	4367	4297	5183	5824	6203	6573	6820	7498	8200	9489	8648
3 Public order and safety	2120	3178	3490	3857	4094	4414	4838	5230	5813	6526	6492	6093
4 Education	9361	13739	14960	16867	18528	20405	22432	24862	27276	29708	29585	27943
5 Health	7441	11341	13269	15284	16616	18077	19354	21494	24546	26522	26129	24681
6 Social security and welfare	4250	6736	8277	9775	10963	12172	13562	15269	17718	19494	18829	17984
7 Housing and community amenities	1113	1942	2188	2218	2271	2474	2639	2857	3250	3544	3299	2927
8 Recreational, cultural and religious affairs	1075	1737	2009	2362	2625	2916	3151	3464	3883	4149	3976	3929
9 Economic services	2567	3931	4315	4690	4861	5388	6010	6583	8203	9134	9259	9567
A Fuel and energy	...	...	...	...	...	...	...	...	...	...	...	...
B Agriculture, forestry, fishing and hunting	...	...	...	...	...	...	...	...	...	...	...	...
C Mining, manufacturing and construction, except fuel and energy	...	...	...	...	...	...	...	...	...	...	...	...
D Transportation and communication	1793	2642	2902	3114	3145	3389	3673	3949	5080	5594	5657	5784
E Other economic affairs	...	...	...	...	...	...	...	...	...	...	...	...
10 Other functions	168	298	343	343	412	494	403	370	315	319	553	864
Total Government Final Consumption Expenditure	34392	52451	58842	66967	72849	80046	87199	96019	108535	118719	118453	112542

2.2 Government Final Consumption Expenditure by Function, in Constant Prices

Million Finnish markkaa

	1980	1983	1984	1985	1986	1987	1988	1989	1990	1991	1992	1993
					At constant prices of: 1990							
1 General public services	7889	8352	8501	8776	8793	9377	9592	9861	10033	10495	10098	9238
2 Defence	5376	6556	6058	6768	7225	7297	7290	7233	7498	7578	8612	7670
3 Public order and safety	4857	5356	5452	5522	5561	5584	5630	5688	5813	5891	5765	5481
4 Education	21508	22585	22625	23688	24318	25358	26024	26709	27276	28217	27530	25862
5 Health	17112	19141	20107	20997	21887	22799	23248	23713	24546	24460	23535	22174
6 Social security and welfare	10059	11595	12738	13763	14603	15408	16107	16950	17718	18451	17250	16457
7 Housing and community amenities	2487	3316	3402	3097	3009	3111	3131	3140	3250	3308	3012	2636
8 Recreational, cultural and religious affairs	2478	2961	3145	3328	3501	3673	3758	3801	3883	3941	3709	3614
9 Economic services	5475	6234	6404	6538	6392	6694	6900	7039	8203	8606	8762	9077
A Fuel and energy	...	...	...	...	...	...	...	...	...	...	...	...
B Agriculture, forestry, fishing and hunting	...	...	...	...	...	...	...	...	...	...	...	...
C Mining, manufacturing and construction, except fuel and energy	...	...	...	...	...	...	...	...	...	...	...	...
D Transportation and communication	3775	4174	4296	4357	4118	4211	4216	4200	5080	5350	5494	5642
E Other economic affairs	...	...	...	...	...	...	...	...	...	...	...	...
10 Other functions	311	411	446	423	503	577	452	392	315	309	526	795
Total Government Final Consumption Expenditure	77552	86507	88878	92900	95792	99878	102132	104526	108535	111256	108799	103004

Finland

2.3 Total Government Outlays by Function and Type

Million Finnish markkaa

	Final Consumption Expenditures Total	Compensation of Employees	Other	Subsidies	Other Current Transfers & Property Income	Total Current Disbursements	Gross Capital Formation	Other Capital Outlays	Total Outlays
1980									
1 General public services	3585	2216	1369	...	...	...	...	...	...
2 Defence	2712	1238	1474	...	...	...	...	...	...
3 Public order and safety	2120	1748	372	...	...	...	...	...	...
4 Education	9361	6447	2914	...	...	...	...	...	...
5 Health	7441	5574	1867	...	...	...	...	...	...
6 Social security and welfare	4250	3455	795	...	...	...	...	...	...
7 Housing and community amenities	1113	981	132	...	...	...	...	...	...
8 Recreation, culture and religion	1075	664	411	...	...	...	...	...	...
9 Economic services	2567	1168	1399	...	...	...	...	...	...
A Fuel and energy	...	...	...	...	...	...	...	...	...
B Agriculture, forestry, fishing and hunting	...	...	...	...	...	...	...	...	...
C Mining (except fuels), manufacturing and construction	...	...	...	...	...	...	...	...	...
D Transportation and communication	1793	510	1283	...	...	...	...	...	...
E Other economic affairs	...	...	...	...	...	...	...	...	...
10 Other functions	168	35	133	...	...	...	...	...	...
Total	34392	23526	10866	6225	26967	67584	...	...	...
1985									
1 General public services	6388	3960	2428	...	...	...	...	...	...
2 Defence	5183	2492	2691	...	...	...	...	...	...
3 Public order and safety	3857	3188	669	...	...	...	...	...	...
4 Education	16867	12095	4772	...	...	...	...	...	...
5 Health	15284	11599	3685	...	...	...	...	...	...
6 Social security and welfare	9775	7653	2122	...	...	...	...	...	...
7 Housing and community amenities	2218	2124	94	...	...	...	...	...	...
8 Recreation, culture and religion	2362	1495	867	...	...	...	...	...	...
9 Economic services	4690	2197	2493	...	...	...	...	...	...
A Fuel and energy	...	...	...	...	...	...	...	...	...
B Agriculture, forestry, fishing and hunting	...	...	...	...	...	...	...	...	...
C Mining (except fuels), manufacturing and construction	...	...	...	...	...	...	...	...	...
D Transportation and communication	3114	876	2238	...	...	...	...	...	...
E Other economic affairs	...	...	...	...	...	...	...	...	...
10 Other functions	343	65	278	...	...	...	...	...	...
Total	66967	46868	20099	10347	59660	136974	...	...	...
1990									
1 General public services	10033	6248	3785	...	...	...	...	...	...
2 Defence	7498	3414	4084	...	...	...	...	...	...
3 Public order and safety	5813	4983	830	...	...	...	...	...	...
4 Education	27276	19563	7713	...	...	...	...	...	...
5 Health	24546	18442	6104	...	...	...	...	...	...
6 Social security and welfare	17718	13507	4211	...	...	...	...	...	...
7 Housing and community amenities	3250	3030	220	...	...	...	...	...	...
8 Recreation, culture and religion	3883	2454	1429	...	...	...	...	...	...
9 Economic services	8203	3695	4508	...	...	...	...	...	...
A Fuel and energy	...	...	...	...	...	...	...	...	...
B Agriculture, forestry, fishing and hunting	...	...	...	...	...	...	...	...	...
C Mining (except fuels), manufacturing and construction	...	...	...	...	...	...	...	...	...
D Transportation and communication	5080	1221	3859	...	...	...	...	...	...
E Other economic affairs	...	...	...	...	...	...	...	...	...
10 Other functions	315	113	202	...	...	...	...	...	...
Total	108535	75449	33086	14756	97738	221029	...	...	...

Finland

2.3 Total Government Outlays by Function and Type
(Continued)

Million Finnish markkaa

		Final Consumption Expenditures Total	Compensation of Employees	Other	Subsidies	Other Current Transfers & Property Income	Total Current Disbursements	Gross Capital Formation	Other Capital Outlays	Total Outlays
	1991									
1	General public services	11123	7135	3988	...	...	...	...	...	...
2	Defence	8200	3969	4231	...	...	...	...	...	...
3	Public order and safety	6526	5660	866	...	...	...	...	...	...
4	Education	29708	21355	8353	...	...	...	...	...	...
5	Health	26522	20466	6056	...	...	...	...	...	...
6	Social security and welfare	19494	15126	4368	...	...	...	...	...	...
7	Housing and community amenities	3544	3338	206	...	...	...	...	...	...
8	Recreation, culture and religion	4149	2683	1466	...	...	...	...	...	...
9	Economic services	9134	4214	4920	...	...	...	...	...	...
	A Fuel and energy	...	...	...	...	...	...	...	...	...
	B Agriculture, forestry, fishing and hunting	...	...	...	...	...	...	...	...	...
	C Mining (except fuels), manufacturing and construction	...	...	...	...	...	...	...	...	...
	D Transportation and communication	5594	1316	4278	...	...	...	...	...	...
	E Other economic affairs	...	...	...	...	...	...	...	...	...
10	Other functions	319	69	250	...	...	...	...	...	...
	Total	118719	84015	34704	17174	116080	251973	...	...	...
	1992									
1	General public services	10842	7054	3788	...	...	...	...	...	...
2	Defence	9489	4004	5485	...	...	...	...	...	...
3	Public order and safety	6492	5734	758	...	...	...	...	...	...
4	Education	29585	21382	8203	...	...	...	...	...	...
5	Health	26129	20613	5516	...	...	...	...	...	...
6	Social security and welfare	18829	15107	3722	...	...	...	...	...	...
7	Housing and community amenities	3299	3238	61	...	...	...	...	...	...
8	Recreation, culture and religion	3976	2637	1339	...	...	...	...	...	...
9	Economic services	9259	4301	4958	...	...	...	...	...	...
	A Fuel and energy	...	...	...	...	...	...	...	...	...
	B Agriculture, forestry, fishing and hunting	...	...	...	...	...	...	...	...	...
	C Mining (except fuels), manufacturing and construction	...	...	...	...	...	...	...	...	...
	D Transportation and communication	5657	1327	4330	...	...	...	...	...	...
	E Other economic affairs	...	...	...	...	...	...	...	...	...
10	Other functions	553	71	482	...	...	...	...	...	...
	Total	118453	84141	34312	17028	135846	271327	...	...	...
	1993									
1	General public services	9906	6533	3373	...	...	...	...	...	...
2	Defence	8648	3778	4870	...	...	...	...	...	...
3	Public order and safety	6093	5370	723	...	...	...	...	...	...
4	Education	27943	20574	7369	...	...	...	...	...	...
5	Health	24681	19455	5226	...	...	...	...	...	...
6	Social security and welfare	17984	14262	3722	...	...	...	...	...	...
7	Housing and community amenities	2927	2925	2	...	...	...	...	...	...
8	Recreation, culture and religion	3929	2646	1283	...	...	...	...	...	...
9	Economic services	9567	3850	5717	...	...	...	...	...	...
	A Fuel and energy	...	...	...	...	...	...	...	...	...
	B Agriculture, forestry, fishing and hunting	...	...	...	...	...	...	...	...	...
	C Mining (except fuels), manufacturing and construction	...	...	...	...	...	...	...	...	...
	D Transportation and communication	5784	1021	4763	...	...	...	...	...	...
	E Other economic affairs	...	...	...	...	...	...	...	...	...
10	Other functions	864	4	860	...	...	...	...	...	...
	Total	112542	79397	33145	16319	155213	284074	...	...	...

Finland

2.5 Private Final Consumption Expenditure by Type and Purpose, in Current Prices

Million Finnish markkaa

	1980	1983	1984	1985	1986	1987	1988	1989	1990	1991	1992	1993
Final Consumption Expenditure of Resident Households												
1 Food, beverages and tobacco	27816	39237	42868	45107	48266	50720	53846	57080	59013	61262	61305	60029
A Food	21038	29248	31909	33845	35651	36826	38428	40020	40903	42011	41885	41595
B Non-alcoholic beverages	487	698	782	831	919	993	1112	1204	1285	1311	1358	1235
C Alcoholic beverages	4108	6061	6569	6912	7778	8495	9590	10618	11405	12026	11885	11403
D Tobacco	2183	3230	3608	3519	3918	4406	4716	5238	5420	5914	6177	5796
2 Clothing and footwear	6143	7689	8691	9561	10527	11938	12939	13850	14397	14058	12515	12148
3 Gross rent, fuel and power	18547	27327	29766	32623	34381	36041	38764	42479	47253	53589	58053	64089
A Fuel and power	5105	6803	7082	7995	7491	8319	8223	8554	9972	10881	11235	12432
B Other	13442	20524	22684	24628	26890	27722	30541	33925	37281	42708	46818	51657
4 Furniture, furnishings and household equipment and operation	7453	10283	11411	12078	13027	14407	15821	17063	17264	16608	15583	14978
A Household operation	1136	1490	1718	1883	2084	2231	2356	2538	2695	2983	3026	3203
B Other	6317	8793	9693	10195	10943	12176	13465	14525	14569	13625	12557	11775
5 Medical care and health expenses	3532	5353	5991	6729	7459	8361	9479	10399	11580	12666	13385	13674
6 Transport and communication	16340	23425	25729	29230	30154	33734	39144	43401	43553	39278	37226	37539
A Personal transport equipment	4965	7427	8384	10338	11433	13279	16651	18313	15894	11173	8537	7495
B Other	11375	15998	17345	18892	18721	20455	22493	25088	27659	28105	28689	30044
7 Recreational, entertainment, education and cultural services	9404	13411	14633	15816	17334	19162	20929	23100	24563	24932	24229	23854
8 Miscellaneous goods and services	10958	16593	18840	21248	23290	26345	29369	33214	35417	35448	33967	32345
A Personal care	1792	2627	2936	3123	3415	3731	4057	4469	4947	5247	5334	5220
B Expenditures in restaurants, cafes and hotels	6430	9639	10881	12319	13371	14895	16825	18830	20201	19890	19129	18369
C Other	2736	4327	5023	5806	6504	7719	8487	9915	10269	10311	9504	8756
Total Final Consumption Expenditure in the Domestic Market by Households, of which	100193	143318	157929	172392	184438	200708	220291	240586	253040	257841	256263	258656
A Durable goods	11332	16749	18621	21234	23232	26258	31115	33922	31366	25135	20527	18723
B Semi-durable goods	11338	14339	15820	17250	18822	21105	23020	24884	25872	25835	23777	23108
C Non-durable goods	43450	60600	65713	69921	72528	77314	81886	87115	93138	97808	98446	99319
D Services	34073	51630	57775	63987	69856	76031	84270	94665	102664	109063	113513	117506
Plus: Direct purchases abroad by resident households	2294	3599	4250	5031	5587	6811	7907	8969	10767	11089	10962	9237
Less: Direct purchases in the domestic market by non-resident households	2614	2851	3039	3258	3195	3736	4280	4497	4650	5044	6089	7079
Equals: Final Consumption Expenditure of Resident Households	99873	144066	159140	174165	186830	203783	223918	245058	259157	263886	261136	260814
Final Consumption Expenditure of Private Non-profit Institutions Serving Households												
1 Research and science	57	74	84	89	96	103	114	140	164	177	196	208
2 Education	764	1053	1133	1275	1381	1428	1556	1691	1869	1899	2029	2045
3 Medical and other health services	261	491	557	682	754	899	1021	1125	1225	1243	1126	1198
4 Welfare services	257	352	300	346	362	384	477	506	585	604	554	598
5 Recreational and related cultural services	425	697	774	856	897	947	1089	1256	1405	1444	1475	1442
6 Religious organisations	1033	1576	1716	1878	2010	2209	2392	2631	2899	2919	2933	2837
7 Professional and labour organisations serving households	446	681	756	841	886	938	1061	1171	1305	1359	1332	1288
8 Miscellaneous	435	634	689	755	791	843	952	1010	1145	1178	1333	1323
Equals: Final Consumption Expenditure of Private Non-profit Organisations Serving Households	3678	5558	6009	6722	7177	7751	8662	9530	10597	10823	10978	10939
Private Final Consumption Expenditure	103551	149624	165149	180887	194007	211534	232580	254588	269754	274709	272114	271753

Finland

2.6 Private Final Consumption Expenditure by Type and Purpose, in Constant Prices

Million Finnish markkaa

		1980	1983	1984	1985	1986	1987	1988	1989	1990	1991	1992	1993
		\multicolumn{12}{c}{At constant prices of: 1990}
		\multicolumn{12}{c}{**Final Consumption Expenditure of Resident Households**}
1	Food, beverages and tobacco	51823	54190	55159	54214	55921	57151	58417	59895	59013	58578	57777	56222
	A Food	37171	38753	39179	38751	39321	39863	40914	41407	40903	40932	40770	40586
	B Non-alcoholic beverages	1063	1112	1140	1097	1164	1177	1279	1307	1285	1243	1292	1189
	C Alcoholic beverages	8426	8983	9230	9222	9997	10331	10643	11313	11405	11102	10501	9940
	D Tobacco	5163	5342	5610	5144	5439	5780	5581	5868	5420	5301	5214	4507
2	Clothing and footwear	10237	10305	11003	11468	12032	13216	14108	14572	14397	13507	11623	10866
3	Gross rent, fuel and power	33364	36627	38012	39723	41084	42942	44210	45456	47253	49090	50184	52166
	A Fuel and power	7432	7467	7745	8554	8628	9411	9327	9263	9972	10625	10541	10819
	B Other	25932	29160	30267	31169	32456	33531	34883	36193	37281	38465	39643	41347
4	Furniture, furnishings and household equipment and operation	13295	14719	14990	14997	15494	16438	17350	17873	17264	15948	14505	13526
	A Household operation	2714	2809	2707	2720	2816	2780	2778	2782	2695	2796	2749	2741
	B Other	10581	11910	12283	12277	12678	13658	14572	15091	14569	13152	11756	10785
5	Medical care and health expenses	8258	9256	9206	9733	10251	10873	11165	11268	11580	11700	11622	11272
6	Transport and communication	28143	31802	32914	36225	37521	39670	43570	46067	43553	38247	35132	33240
	A Personal transport equipment	8040	10133	10911	13308	13811	14737	17597	18667	15894	11236	8131	6547
	B Other	20103	21669	22003	22917	23710	24933	25973	27400	27659	27011	27001	26693
7	Recreational, entertainment, education and cultural services	18045	19441	19565	20032	20718	21622	22771	24010	24563	23949	22199	21274
8	Miscellaneous goods and services	22511	24425	25943	27449	28825	31140	33243	35500	35417	33321	31168	29268
	A Personal care	3299	3641	3771	3846	3998	4224	4496	4725	4947	4866	4772	4589
	B Expenditures in restaurants, cafes and hotels	14519	15094	15792	16384	16961	18054	19110	20147	20201	18568	17569	16749
	C Other	4693	5690	6380	7219	7866	8862	9637	10628	10269	9887	8827	7930
	Total Final Consumption Expenditure in the Domestic Market by Households, of which	185676	200765	206792	213841	221846	233052	244834	254641	253040	244340	234210	227834
	A Durable goods	17835	22240	23415	26152	27269	28958	32869	34627	31366	24896	19479	16857
	B Semi-durable goods	19593	19444	20136	20824	21595	23335	24914	25974	25872	24829	21974	20537
	C Non-durable goods	78032	81127	82541	82734	85607	88826	90903	92918	93138	93620	92522	90134
	D Services	70216	77954	80700	84131	87375	91933	96148	101122	102664	100995	100235	100306
	Plus: Direct purchases abroad by resident households	3723	4669	5260	5928	6406	7664	8675	9611	10767	10101	8577	6481
	Less: Direct purchases in the domestic market by non-resident households	5605	4334	4313	4281	4014	4488	4878	4807	4650	4829	5819	6695
	Equals: Final Consumption Expenditure of Resident Households	183794	201100	207739	215488	224238	236228	248631	259445	259157	249612	236968	227620
		\multicolumn{12}{c}{**Final Consumption Expenditure of Private Non-profit Institutions Serving Households**}
1	Research and science	131	124	130	132	136	137	140	160	164	170	188	193
2	Education	1652	1686	1693	1770	1841	1792	1798	1822	1869	1830	1913	1890
3	Medical and other health services	626	820	902	1012	1075	1194	1277	1271	1225	1186	1064	1108
4	Welfare services	594	605	477	514	509	514	561	560	585	577	515	526
5	Recreational and related cultural services	901	1107	1142	1180	1192	1200	1278	1385	1405	1399	1400	1364
6	Religious organisations	2333	2656	2647	2640	2724	2817	2767	2851	2899	2804	2780	2660
7	Professional and labour organisations serving households	1004	1203	1167	1216	1234	1217	1265	1286	1305	1317	1265	1192
8	Miscellaneous	898	989	1009	1050	1051	1064	1104	1099	1145	1136	1270	1240
	Equals: Final Consumption Expenditure of Private Non-profit Organisations Serving Households	8139	9190	9167	9514	9762	9935	10190	10434	10597	10419	10395	10173
	Private Final Consumption Expenditure	191933	210290	216906	225002	234000	246163	258821	269879	269754	260031	247363	237793

Finland

2.11 Gross Fixed Capital Formation by Kind of Activity of Owner, ISIC Divisions, in Current Prices

Million Finnish markkaa

		1980	1983	1984	1985	1986	1987	1988	1989	1990	1991	1992	1993
						All Producers							
1	Agriculture, hunting, forestry and fishing	4555	5998	6072	6352	6165	5856	6332	7149	7106	5549	3977	3646
	A Agriculture and hunting	3380	4567	4508	4689	4480	4133	4418	5063	5080	3751	2279	2084
	B Forestry and logging	1075	1332	1461	1552	1571	1604	1786	1954	1892	1670	1590	1478
	C Fishing	100	99	103	111	114	119	128	132	134	128	108	84
2	Mining and quarrying	199	244	162	344	312	241	227	375	278	173	136	135
	A Coal mining	...	...	...	...	...	...	...	...	...	...	...	...
	B Crude petroleum and natural gas production	...	...	...	...	...	...	...	...	...	...	...	...
	C Metal ore mining	36	18	38	151	100	17	21	73	31	26	13	32
	D Other mining	163	226	124	193	212	224	206	302	247	147	123	103
3	Manufacturing	8738	10951	11739	13271	14037	17647	15341	21822	21770	15888	14102	12843
	A Manufacturing of food, beverages and tobacco	1141	1488	1256	1342	1452	1994	1547	2120	2311	1967	2689	1522
	B Textile, wearing apparel and leather industries	401	397	364	277	391	495	-48	412	399	180	153	228
	C Manufacture of wood, and wood products, including furniture [a]	767	622	546	638	666	681	771	1376	1334	1026	788	844
	D Manufacture of paper and paper products, printing and publishing	2513	3218	3814	4585	4596	5675	5977	8310	8223	6314	5031	4524
	E Manufacture of chemicals and chemical petroleum, coal, rubber and plastic products	1037	1415	1608	1598	1856	2963	2412	2791	2791	1964	2004	2090
	F Manufacture of non-metalic mineral products except products of petroleum and coal	387	535	608	531	704	719	644	866	1154	463	314	284
	G Basic metal industries	524	447	473	757	1140	1530	1116	1368	967	962	675	665
	H Manufacture of fabricated metal products, machinery and equipment	1782	2520	2714	3191	2928	3269	2831	4061	4219	2758	2155	2558
	I Other manufacturing industries [a]	186	309	356	352	304	321	91	518	372	254	293	128
4	Electricity, gas and water	2250	3599	3549	4172	4339	4432	4143	5777	5434	5957	4901	4097
	A Electricity, gas and steam	1847	3176	3091	3666	3792	3866	3602	5188	4812	5151	4305	3517
	B Water works and supply	403	423	458	506	547	566	541	589	622	806	596	580
5	Construction	995	1822	1667	1004	1160	1600	2334	2916	2856	1865	374	329
6	Wholesale and retail trade, restaurants and hotels	3057	5403	5714	6303	6697	8011	7473	12767	12401	9482	7255	5451
	A Wholesale and retail trade	2683	4976	5233	5808	6147	7410	6889	10949	10821	8164	6604	4989
	B Restaurants and hotels	374	427	481	495	550	601	584	1818	1580	1318	651	462
	Restaurants	188	182	197	208	219	270	297	570	563	559	287	252
	Hotels and other lodging places	186	245	284	287	331	331	287	1248	1017	759	364	210
7	Transport, storage and communication	4760	6121	5984	5948	6835	7127	8186	10920	10223	6900	8007	7273
	A Transport and storage	3715	4539	4529	4025	4678	4665	5384	7877	6969	4005	5482	4793
	B Communication	1045	1582	1455	1923	2157	2462	2802	3043	3254	2895	2525	2480
8	Finance, insurance, real estate and business services	16078	23831	25988	28613	29392	31188	46794	56083	56845	42204	29341	21077
	A Financial institutions [b]	509	883	1046	991	1921	1531	-802	1783	753	927	351	-968
	B Insurance	310	230	502	9	387	-39	678	259	825	529	1042	-197
	C Real estate and business services	15259	22718	24440	27613	27084	29696	46918	54041	55267	40748	27948	22242
	Real estate except dwellings	646	2463	2878	4806	4580	5122	14716	11687	12919	8020	3440	2776
	Dwellings	14208	19504	20548	21386	20762	22661	29375	39468	39701	30937	23138	18435
9	Community, social and personal services	941	1281	1440	1622	1711	1768	1956	2516	3277	3169	2503	2264
	A Sanitary and similar services	645	763	780	849	953	921	946	1144	1433	1389	1208	1093
	B Social and related community services	90	135	164	193	216	267	330	398	493	418	312	224

Finland

2.11 Gross Fixed Capital Formation by Kind of Activity of Owner, ISIC Divisions, in Current Prices
(Continued)

Million Finnish markkaa

	1980	1983	1984	1985	1986	1987	1988	1989	1990	1991	1992	1993
Educational services	50	67	77	80	91	106	120	131	165	104	82	75
Medical, dental, other health and veterinary services	29	48	64	82	88	115	131	170	216	210	136	81
C Recreational and cultural services	170	327	428	501	457	482	562	811	1177	1163	860	840
D Personal and household services	36	56	68	79	85	98	118	163	174	199	123	107
Total Industries	41573	59250	62315	67629	70648	77870	92786	120325	120190	91187	70596	57115
Producers of Government Services	6465	9521	9862	10877	11281	13371	15046	14295	17286	17067	15897	12918
Private Non-Profit Institutions Serving Households	665	775	833	917	979	1300	1426	1528	1668	1807	1460	1318
Total	48703	69546	73010	79423	82908	92541	109258	136148	139144	110061	87953	71351

a) Furniture is included in item 'Other manufacturing industries'.
b) Item 'Financial institutions' include activities auxiliary to financial intermediation and insurance.

2.12 Gross Fixed Capital Formation by Kind of Activity of Owner, ISIC Divisions, in Constant Prices

Million Finnish markkaa

	1980	1983	1984	1985	1986	1987	1988	1989	1990	1991	1992	1993
					At constant prices of:1990							
					All Producers							
1 Agriculture, hunting, forestry and fishing	8336	8641	8043	8140	7596	6951	7160	7617	7106	5506	3907	3515
A Agriculture and hunting	6096	6493	5989	5989	5473	4844	4966	5387	5080	3760	2273	2018
B Forestry and logging	2067	2010	1917	2012	1987	1971	2054	2090	1892	1619	1534	1425
C Fishing	173	138	137	139	136	136	140	140	134	127	100	72
2 Mining and quarrying	360	353	214	445	386	286	251	393	278	168	130	127
A Coal mining	...	...	...	...	...	...	...	...	...	...	...	...
B Crude petroleum and natural gas production	...	...	...	...	...	...	...	...	...	...	...	...
C Metal ore mining	61	30	50	199	127	20	23	76	31	25	13	30
D Other mining	299	323	164	246	259	266	228	317	247	143	117	97
3 Manufacturing	15721	16265	16295	17416	17761	21473	17847	23903	21770	15579	13373	11566
A Manufacturing of food, beverages and tobacco	2189	2325	1836	1844	1880	2459	1854	2337	2311	1947	2626	1397
B Textile, wearing apparel and leather industries	746	614	531	380	504	612	-15	459	399	176	144	189
C Manufacture of wood, and wood products, including furniture a	1233	835	687	755	777	773	844	1466	1334	1030	757	796
D Manufacture of paper and paper products, printing and publishing	5035	5245	5816	6591	6392	7630	7393	9314	8223	6054	4573	3928
E Manufacture of chemicals and chemical petroleum, coal, rubber and plastic products	1653	1934	1982	1887	2177	3336	2601	2989	2791	1960	1974	1951
F Manufacture of non-metalic mineral products except products of petroleum and coal	683	800	854	699	898	866	725	944	1154	458	300	255
G Basic metal industries	867	589	597	894	1316	1712	1216	1475	967	944	621	556
H Manufacture of fabricated metal products, machinery and equipment	3010	3502	3525	3923	3459	3718	3119	4362	4219	2754	2075	2381
I Other manufacturing industries a	305	421	467	443	358	367	110	557	372	256	303	113
4 Electricity, gas and water	4400	5425	5012	5628	5557	5397	4725	6155	5434	5797	4720	3908
A Electricity, gas and steam	3585	4775	4352	4933	4847	4696	4100	5526	4812	5019	4129	3334
B Water works and supply	815	650	660	695	710	701	625	629	622	778	591	574
5 Construction	1764	2580	2193	1126	1314	1831	2589	3067	2856	1777	336	277
6 Wholesale and retail trade, restaurants and hotels	6144	8308	8250	8565	8671	9634	8388	13530	12401	9594	7359	5291
A Wholesale and retail trade	5410	7642	7545	7884	7946	8903	7722	11591	10821	8250	6669	4815
B Restaurants and hotels	734	666	705	681	725	731	666	1939	1580	1344	690	476
Restaurants	348	269	274	274	276	320	335	606	563	558	284	235
Hotels and other lodging places	386	397	431	407	449	411	331	1333	1017	786	406	241
7 Transport, storage and communication	8491	8461	7921	7469	8246	8253	9267	11477	10223	6815	7582	6254
A Transport and storage	6804	6345	6099	5202	5777	5516	6246	8333	6969	3939	5130	3956

Finland

2.12 Gross Fixed Capital Formation by Kind of Activity of Owner, ISIC Divisions, in Constant Prices
(Continued)

Million Finnish markkaa

	1980	1983	1984	1985	1986	1987	1988	1989	1990	1991	1992	1993
					At constant prices of:1990							
B Communication	1687	2116	1822	2267	2469	2737	3021	3144	3254	2876	2452	2298
8 Finance, insurance, real estate and business services	37849	41792	42039	42899	41867	41095	55029	59487	56845	43451	33736	26336
A Financial institutions [b]	981	1294	1444	1208	2405	1748	-1066	1861	753	918	329	-1351
B Insurance	671	364	767	-160	515	-64	775	271	825	551	1194	-271
C Real estate and business services	36197	40134	39828	41851	38947	39411	55320	57355	55267	41982	32213	27958
Real estate except dwellings	2001	4534	4711	7218	6539	6562	16784	12288	12919	8548	4163	4123
Dwellings	33464	34548	33783	32849	30303	30672	35406	42051	39701	31648	26728	22914
9 Community, social and personal services	1827	1952	2035	2162	2170	2105	2192	2649	3277	3160	2585	2313
A Sanitary and similar services	1245	1180	1125	1155	1235	1127	1077	1210	1433	1371	1219	1096
B Social and related community services	175	202	229	254	272	309	364	415	493	417	305	209
Educational services	100	103	110	109	119	124	131	137	165	102	76	66
Medical, dental, other health and veterinary services	55	69	87	105	108	133	144	177	216	211	135	77
C Recreational and cultural services	345	493	594	657	561	557	620	852	1177	1171	940	905
D Personal and household services	62	77	87	96	102	112	131	172	174	201	121	103
Total Industries	84892	93777	92002	93850	93568	97025	107448	128278	120190	91847	73728	59587
Producers of Government Services	13343	14961	14468	14990	14821	16421	17275	15149	17286	17243	16899	13959
Private Non-Profit Institutions Serving Households	1422	1257	1259	1298	1318	1621	1647	1627	1668	1875	1610	1518
Total	99657	109995	107729	110138	109707	115067	126370	145054	139144	110965	92237	75064

a) Furniture is included in item 'Other manufacturing industries'.
b) Item 'Financial institutions' include activities auxiliary to financial intermediation and insurance.

2.13 Stocks of Reproducible Fixed Assets, by Type of Good and Owner, in Current Prices

Million Finnish markkaa

	TOTAL Gross	TOTAL Net	Total Private Gross	Total Private Net	Public Enterprises Gross	Public Enterprises Net	General Government Gross	General Government Net
				1980				
1 Residential buildings	294985	207127	294985	207127	...	...	-	-
2 Non-residential buildings	239836	157597	165906	104930	...	...	73930	52667
3 Other construction [a]	182815	121481	111166	66762	...	...	71649	54719
4 Land improvement and plantation and orchard development [a]	...	...	...	...	...	...	...	...
5 Producers' durable goods	240626	134233	233643	130357	...	...	6983	3876
6 Breeding stock, dairy cattle, etc.	...	...	...	...	...	...	...	...
Total	958262	620438	805700	509176	...	...	152562	111262
				1985				
1 Residential buildings	546027	374235	546027	374235	...	...	-	-
2 Non-residential buildings	438968	285636	298576	188610	...	...	140392	97026
3 Other construction [a]	303376	193101	182294	104044	...	...	121082	89057
4 Land improvement and plantation and orchard development [a]	...	...	...	...	...	...	...	...
5 Producers' durable goods	395792	217024	383239	209669	...	...	12553	7355
6 Breeding stock, dairy cattle, etc.	...	...	...	...	...	...	...	...
Total	1684163	1069996	1410136	876558	...	...	274027	193438
				1990				
1 Residential buildings	988585	655831	988585	655831	...	...	-	-
2 Non-residential buildings	771330	494624	528540	334169	...	...	242790	160455
3 Other construction [a]	454128	278519	242449	128029	...	...	211679	150490
4 Land improvement and plantation and orchard development [a]	...	...	...	...	...	...	...	...
5 Producers' durable goods	610976	345493	587811	330959	...	...	23165	14534
6 Breeding stock, dairy cattle, etc.	...	...	...	...	...	...	...	...
Total	2825019	1774467	2347385	1448988	...	...	477634	325479

Finland

2.13 Stocks of Reproducible Fixed Assets, by Type of Good and Owner, in Current Prices
(Continued)

Million Finnish markkaa

		TOTAL Gross	TOTAL Net	Total Private Gross	Total Private Net	Public Enterprises Gross	Public Enterprises Net	General Government Gross	General Government Net
					1991				
1	Residential buildings	993384	652504	993384	652504	...	...	-	-
2	Non-residential buildings	759965	484225	522413	328774	...	...	237552	155451
3	Other construction a	477656	290961	253521	132632	...	...	224135	158329
4	Land improvement and plantation and orchard development a	...	...	...	...	...	...	...	...
5	Producers' durable goods	642192	356453	616814	340638	...	...	25378	15815
6	Breeding stock, dairy cattle, etc.	...	...	...	...	...	...	...	...
	Total	2873197	1784143	2386132	1454548	...	...	487065	329595
					1992				
1	Residential buildings	900978	581615	900978	581615	...	...	-	-
2	Non-residential buildings	699925	439485	480280	298103	...	...	219645	141382
3	Other construction a	477732	286886	250419	128497	...	...	227313	158389
4	Land improvement and plantation and orchard development a	...	...	...	...	...	...	...	...
5	Producers' durable goods	636800	339087	608886	321985	...	...	27914	17102
6	Breeding stock, dairy cattle, etc.	...	...	...	...	...	...	...	...
	Total	2715435	1647073	2240563	1330200	...	...	474872	316873
					1993				
1	Residential buildings	845717	537883	845717	537883	...	...	-	-
2	Non-residential buildings	666005	411284	456026	277838	...	...	209979	133446
3	Other construction a	474307	283010	244847	124504	...	...	229460	158506
4	Land improvement and plantation and orchard development a	...	...	...	...	...	...	...	...
5	Producers' durable goods	682843	349735	652004	331457	...	...	30839	18278
6	Breeding stock, dairy cattle, etc.	...	...	...	...	...	...	...	...
	Total	2668872	1581912	2198594	1271682	...	...	470278	310230

a) Item 'Land improvement and plantation and orchard development' is included in item 'Other construction'.

2.14 Stocks of Reproducible Fixed Assets, by Type of Good and Owner, in Constant Prices

Million Finnish markkaa

		TOTAL Gross	TOTAL Net	Total Private Gross	Total Private Net	Public Enterprises Gross	Public Enterprises Net	General Government Gross	General Government Net
				At constant prices of:1990					
					1980				
1	Residential buildings	692453	486214	692453	486214	...	...	-	-
2	Non-residential buildings	528233	348918	362468	230826	...	...	165765	118092
3	Other construction a	364410	241322	222431	132943	...	...	141979	108379
4	Land improvement and plantation and orchard development a	...	...	...	...	...	...	...	...
5	Producers' durable goods	422565	234673	411998	228841	...	...	10567	5832
6	Breeding stock, dairy cattle, etc.	...	...	...	...	...	...	...	...
	Total	2007661	1311127	1689350	1078824	...	...	318311	232303
					1985				
1	Residential buildings	837464	573980	837464	573980	...	...	-	-
2	Non-residential buildings	639600	416920	433745	274654	...	...	205855	142266
3	Other construction a	409605	260350	245892	140020	...	...	163713	120330
4	Land improvement and plantation and orchard development a	...	...	...	...	...	...	...	...
5	Producers' durable goods	493724	270577	479256	262105	...	...	14468	8472
6	Breeding stock, dairy cattle, etc.	...	...	...	...	...	...	...	...
	Total	2380393	1521827	1996357	1250759	...	...	384036	271068

Finland

2.14 Stocks of Reproducible Fixed Assets, by Type of Good and Owner, in Constant Prices
(Continued)

Million Finnish markkaa

	TOTAL Gross	TOTAL Net	Total Private Gross	Total Private Net	Public Enterprises Gross	Public Enterprises Net	General Government Gross	General Government Net
	\multicolumn{8}{c}{At constant prices of:1990}							
	\multicolumn{8}{c}{1990}							
1 Residential buildings	988585	655831	988585	655831	...	...	-	-
2 Non-residential buildings	771330	494624	528540	334169	...	...	242790	160455
3 Other construction a	454128	278519	242449	128029	...	...	211679	150490
4 Land improvement and plantation and orchard development a	...	...	...	...	...	...	...	...
5 Producers' durable goods	610976	345493	587811	330959	...	...	23165	14534
6 Breeding stock, dairy cattle, etc.	...	...	...	...	...	...	...	...
Total	2825019	1774467	2347385	1448988	...	...	477634	325479
	\multicolumn{8}{c}{1991}							
1 Residential buildings	1014278	666228	1014278	666228	...	...	-	-
2 Non-residential buildings	796925	508047	546874	344416	...	...	250051	163631
3 Other construction a	462434	281660	244747	127891	...	...	217687	153769
4 Land improvement and plantation and orchard development a	...	...	...	...	...	...	...	...
5 Producers' durable goods	620659	344083	595498	328402	...	...	25161	15681
6 Breeding stock, dairy cattle, etc.	...	...	...	...	...	...	...	...
Total	2894296	1800018	2401397	1466937	...	...	492899	333081
	\multicolumn{8}{c}{1992}							
1 Residential buildings	1032048	666226	1032048	666226	...	...	-	-
2 Non-residential buildings	811360	509786	554501	344451	...	...	256859	165335
3 Other construction a	466734	280623	243421	124942	...	...	223313	155681
4 Land improvement and plantation and orchard development a	...	...	...	...	...	...	...	...
5 Producers' durable goods	579620	308446	553039	292148	...	...	26581	16298
6 Breeding stock, dairy cattle, etc.	...	...	...	...	...	...	...	...
Total	2889762	1765081	2383009	1427767	...	...	506753	337314
	\multicolumn{8}{c}{1993}							
1 Residential buildings	1048626	666935	1048626	666935	...	...	-	-
2 Non-residential buildings	822610	508415	559824	341416	...	...	262786	166999
3 Other construction a	472238	281217	243952	123474	...	...	228286	157743
4 Land improvement and plantation and orchard development a	...	...	...	...	...	...	...	...
5 Producers' durable goods	572326	293346	544589	276884	...	...	27737	16462
6 Breeding stock, dairy cattle, etc.	...	...	...	...	...	...	...	...
Total	2915800	1749913	2396991	1408709	...	...	518809	341204

a) Item 'Land improvement and plantation and orchard development' is included in item 'Other construction'.

2.15 Stocks of Reproducible Fixed Assets by Kind of Activity, in Current Prices

Million Finnish markkaa

	1980 Gross	1980 Net	1985 Gross	1985 Net	1990 Gross	1990 Net	1991 Gross	1991 Net	1992 Gross	1992 Net	1993 Gross	1993 Net
1 Residential buildings	294985	207127	546027	374235	988585	655831	993384	652504	900978	581615	845717	537883
2 Non-residential buildings	239836	157597	438968	285636	771330	494624	759965	484225	699925	439485	666005	411284
A Industries	158088	99562	283641	178350	501635	315833	495647	310523	455359	281225	431948	261618
1 Agriculture	20147	9742	30650	16350	42260	23903	43208	24582	41113	23570	40897	23292
2 Mining and quarrying	1050	596	1575	803	2261	1038	2111	935	1811	768	1653	670
3 Manufacturing	46851	29757	82416	50574	131542	75971	127070	72601	115148	64714	108343	59835
4 Electricity, gas and water	9716	6417	16426	10288	25908	15238	25226	14775	22822	13116	21534	12203
5 Construction	3274	2348	6385	4424	10449	6659	10283	6489	9148	5551	8498	4975
6 Wholesale and retail trade	31463	19410	55043	33494	93664	55615	91730	54221	83415	48617	78581	44918
7 Transport and communication	6178	4585	11770	8279	21212	13981	21255	13721	19519	12328	18947	11771

Finland

2.15 Stocks of Reproducible Fixed Assets by Kind of Activity, in Current Prices
(Continued)

Million Finnish markkaa

	1980 Gross	1980 Net	1985 Gross	1985 Net	1990 Gross	1990 Net	1991 Gross	1991 Net	1992 Gross	1992 Net	1993 Gross	1993 Net
8 Finance, etc.	33973	22887	69413	47324	157480	112332	157971	112121	146736	102317	138290	94026
9 Community, social and personal services	5436	3820	9963	6814	16859	11096	16793	11078	15647	10244	15205	9928
B Producers of government services	73930	52667	140392	97026	242790	160455	237552	155451	219645	141382	209979	133446
C Other producers	7818	5368	14935	10260	26905	18336	26766	18251	24921	16878	24078	16220
3 Other construction [a]	182815	121481	303376	193101	454128	278519	477656	290961	477732	286886	474307	283010
A Industries	110323	66206	180857	103098	240147	126497	251091	131020	247964	126883	242343	122863
1 Agriculture	35425	19452	56889	28989	80814	38200	83035	38683	81807	36977	74635	33214
2 Mining and quarrying	732	477	1296	787	1820	986	1878	987	1790	913	1777	889
3 Manufacturing	8882	5322	13510	7326	18764	9351	19632	9618	19009	9080	18867	8829
4 Electricity, gas and water	31597	18376	53013	30044	78936	43393	83671	45762	81781	44246	81879	43897
5 Construction	4	4	22	20	28	21	30	22	31	22	32	21
6 Wholesale and retail trade	552	326	980	599	1587	954	1703	1016	1712	1008	1724	992
7 Transport and communication	24976	16808	40732	26307	35806	20468	37539	21275	38137	21238	39535	21724
8 Finance, etc.	-	-	-	-	58	54	60	55	59	52	59	51
9 Community, social and personal services	8155	5441	14415	9026	22334	13070	23543	13602	23638	13347	23835	13246
B Producers of government services	71649	54719	121082	89057	211679	150490	224135	158329	227313	158389	229460	158506
C Other producers	843	556	1437	946	2302	1532	2430	1612	2455	1614	2504	1641
4 Land improvement and development and plantation and orchard development [a]	...	...	...	...	...	...	...	...	...	...	...	...
5 Producers' durable goods	240626	134233	395792	217024	610976	345493	642192	356453	636800	339087	682843	349735
A Industries	232397	129633	381015	208384	583990	328694	612687	338205	604551	319489	647300	328824
1 Agriculture	25904	13341	40353	20250	49033	23390	46969	21518	43265	18637	43801	17727
2 Mining and quarrying	2662	1570	4215	2406	5567	2892	5722	2873	4802	2152	4875	2110
3 Manufacturing	94493	54015	160640	90035	252052	144924	271469	153726	258996	140419	275449	145006
4 Electricity, gas and water	23742	16714	39429	25391	60279	35904	64338	37776	67247	37657	72935	39572
5 Construction	8015	3732	11594	6001	18016	10081	18704	10029	18080	8826	18187	8008
6 Wholesale and retail trade	23858	11979	40283	21393	70261	41241	74672	43044	76035	42514	82048	43537
7 Transport and communication	46322	24323	68135	33070	85804	43419	84029	41729	87667	43261	98660	47723
8 Finance, etc.	4829	2573	11764	7348	33513	21172	36015	21127	36844	19461	38834	18522
9 Community, social and personal services	2572	1386	4602	2490	9465	5671	10769	6383	11615	6562	12511	6619
B Producers of government services	6983	3876	12553	7355	23165	14534	25378	15815	27914	17102	30839	18278
C Other producers	1246	724	2224	1285	3821	2265	4127	2433	4335	2496	4704	2633
6 Breeding stock, dairy cattle, etc.	...	...	...	...	...	...	...	...	...	...	...	...
Total	958262	620438	1684163	1069996	2825019	1774467	2873197	1784143	2715435	1647073	2668872	1581912

a) Item 'Land improvement and plantation and orchard development' is included in item 'Other construction'.

2.16 Stocks of Reproducible Fixed Assets by Kind of Activity, in Constant Prices

Million Finnish markkaa

	1980 Gross	1980 Net	1985 Gross	1985 Net	1990 Gross	1990 Net	1991 Gross	1991 Net	1992 Gross	1992 Net	1993 Gross	1993 Net
	\multicolumn{12}{c}{At constant prices of: 1990}											
1 Residential buildings	692453	486214	837464	573980	988585	655831	1014278	666228	1032048	666226	1048626	666935
2 Non-residential buildings	528233	348918	639600	416920	771330	494624	796925	508047	811360	509786	822610	508415
A Industries	344941	218793	411846	259609	501635	315833	518700	325204	525354	324712	529688	321115
1 Agriculture	35160	17003	39718	21187	42260	23903	42608	24238	41690	23895	41586	23677
2 Mining and quarrying	2355	1336	2309	1179	2261	1038	2222	984	2118	898	2068	838
3 Manufacturing	105052	66721	120845	74157	131542	75971	133758	76419	134675	75690	135596	74889
4 Electricity, gas and water	21785	14389	24086	15085	25908	15238	26554	15552	26692	15341	26951	15273
5 Construction	7342	5264	9362	6487	10449	6659	10824	6830	10700	6492	10635	6226
6 Wholesale and retail trade	70546	43519	80709	49112	93664	55615	96559	57074	97562	56864	98350	56218
7 Transport and communication	13429	10028	17205	12141	21212	13981	21599	13955	21995	13885	22392	13889

Finland

2.16 Stocks of Reproducible Fixed Assets by Kind of Activity, in Constant Prices
(Continued)

Million Finnish markkaa

	1980 Gross	1980 Net	1985 Gross	1985 Net	1990 Gross	1990 Net	1991 Gross	1991 Net	1992 Gross	1992 Net	1993 Gross	1993 Net
					At constant prices of:1990							
8 Finance, etc.	77059	51949	102996	70263	157480	112332	166886	118481	171620	119667	173078	117679
9 Community, social and personal services	12213	8584	14616	9998	16859	11096	17690	11671	18302	11980	19032	12426
B Producers of government services	165765	118092	205855	142266	242790	160455	250051	163631	256859	165335	262786	166999
C Other producers	17527	12033	21899	15045	26905	18336	28174	19212	29147	19739	30136	20301
3 Other construction [a]	364410	241322	409605	260350	454128	278519	462434	281660	466734	280623	472238	281217
A Industries	220731	131822	243935	138730	240147	126497	242392	126329	241023	123366	241497	121866
1 Agriculture	76821	42204	80351	41035	80814	38200	80570	37414	79189	35787	78608	34774
2 Mining and quarrying	1476	961	1763	1072	1820	986	1807	952	1773	906	1768	888
3 Manufacturing	17939	10747	18404	9979	18764	9351	18778	9197	18562	8867	18496	8656
4 Electricity, gas and water	63807	37109	72205	40921	78936	43393	80029	43771	79865	43209	80273	43037
5 Construction	9	9	30	27	28	21	29	21	30	21	31	21
6 Wholesale and retail trade	1115	659	1335	816	1587	954	1649	984	1671	985	1691	973
7 Transport and communication	43094	29145	50213	32586	35806	20468	36665	20761	36791	20506	37204	20481
8 Finance, etc.	-	-	-	-	58	54	58	53	58	51	58	50
9 Community, social and personal services	16470	10988	19634	12294	22334	13070	22807	13176	23084	13034	23368	12986
B Producers of government services	141979	108379	163713	120330	211679	150490	217687	153769	223313	155681	228286	157743
C Other producers	1700	1121	1957	1290	2302	1532	2355	1562	2398	1576	2455	1608
4 Land improvement and development and plantation and orchard development [a]	...	...	...	...	...	...	...	...	...	...	...	...
5 Producers' durable goods	422565	234673	493724	270577	610976	345493	620659	344083	579620	308446	572326	293346
A Industries	410074	227723	476599	260572	583990	328694	591432	326005	548890	289760	540313	274491
1 Agriculture	45498	23456	49968	25088	49033	23390	47331	21679	42219	18183	38947	15764
2 Mining and quarrying	4380	2578	5153	2943	5567	2892	5514	2769	4409	1977	4180	1804
3 Manufacturing	166741	94510	202447	112988	252052	144924	255880	144935	225805	122464	223550	117809
4 Electricity, gas and water	42285	29742	51288	33019	60279	35904	61968	36383	61311	34332	61509	33378
5 Construction	13412	6248	13682	7080	18016	10081	18047	9677	16396	8004	15196	6690
6 Wholesale and retail trade	43885	22004	52140	27713	70261	41241	72484	41785	71435	39978	71270	38002
7 Transport and communication	81396	42471	81804	39672	85804	43419	84757	42052	81669	40300	80247	38746
8 Finance, etc.	7979	4265	14283	8925	33513	21172	34982	20522	34772	18374	34306	16394
9 Community, social and personal services	4498	2449	5834	3144	9465	5671	10469	6203	10874	6148	11108	5904
B Producers of government services	10567	5832	14468	8472	23165	14534	25161	15681	26581	16298	27737	16462
C Other producers	1924	1118	2657	1533	3821	2265	4066	2397	4149	2388	4276	2393
6 Breeding stock, dairy cattle, etc.	...	...	...	...	...	...	...	...	...	...	...	...
Total	2007661	1311127	2380393	1521827	2825019	1774467	2894296	1800018	2889762	1765081	2915800	1749913

a) Item 'Land improvement and plantation and orchard development' is included in item 'Other construction'.

2.17 Exports and Imports of Goods and Services, Detail

Million Finnish markkaa

	1980	1983	1984	1985	1986	1987	1988	1989	1990	1991	1992	1993
					Exports of Goods and Services							
1 Exports of merchandise, f.o.b. [a]	52594	67960	78961	82475	81066	83826	91313	98265	99750	91100	105809	132550
2 Transport and communication	4515	5765	6580	6216	5757	6387	7026	7662	8347	7508	8643	10430
A In respect of merchandise imports [b]	834	842	952	967	861	870	963	1060	1091	974	1085	1300
B Other	3681	4923	5628	5249	4896	5517	6063	6602	7256	6534	7558	9130
3 Insurance service charges	295	244	12	-335	-121	-313	-575	-603	-816	-1190	-1650	-1468
A In respect of merchandise imports [b]	-	-	-	-	-	-	-	-	-	-	-	-
B Other	295	244	12	-335	-121	-313	-575	-603	-816	-1190	-1650	-1468

Finland

2.17 Exports and Imports of Goods and Services, Detail
(Continued)

Million Finnish markkaa

		1980	1983	1984	1985	1986	1987	1988	1989	1990	1991	1992	1993
4	Other commodities	3349	5781	5426	6370	5628	6292	6535	6625	6779	6745	9196	10646
5	Adjustments of merchandise exports to change-of-ownership basis	...	...	...	...	...	...	...	...	...	...	...	...
6	Direct purchases in the domestic market by non-residential households	2614	2851	3039	3258	3195	3736	4260	4497	4650	5045	6089	7079
7	Direct purchases in the domestic market by extraterritorial bodies	122	134	172	51	109	120	171	256	118	81	184	201
	Total Exports of Goods and Services	63489	82735	94190	98034	95634	100048	108750	116702	118828	109289	128272	159438

Imports of Goods and Services

		1980	1983	1984	1985	1986	1987	1988	1989	1990	1991	1992	1993
1	Imports of merchandise, c.i.f. [a]	58046	70731	73496	80764	76736	81867	91232	104400	101967	86348	93188	101559
2	Adjustments of merchandise imports to change-of-ownership basis	...	...	...	...	...	...	...	...	...	...	...	...
3	Other transport and communication	1692	2565	2572	2545	2160	2610	3338	3869	4363	3974	4360	5537
4	Other insurance service charges	201	180	182	179	294	274	94	172	-288	-37	23	184
5	Other commodities	2648	3970	5349	6022	4857	5921	7120	8393	9571	10647	12964	16200
6	Direct purchases abroad by government	135	318	289	99	264	294	176	194	221	401	382	624
7	Direct purchases abroad by resident households	2294	3599	4250	5031	5587	6811	7907	8969	10767	11089	10962	9237
	Total Imports of Goods and Services	65016	81361	86137	94639	89898	97775	109866	125996	126600	112422	121878	133341
	Balance of Goods and Services	-1527	1374	8053	3395	5736	2273	-1116	-9294	-7772	-3133	6394	26097
	Total Imports and Balance of Goods and Services	63489	82735	94190	98034	95634	100048	108750	116702	118828	109289	128272	159438

a) Exports and imports of merchandise are recorded on the basis of the crossing of frontiers. No data are available on the basis of changes in the ownership of the goods. b) Insurance service charges in respect of merchandise imports are included in transport and communication in respect of merchandise imports.

3.12 General Government Income and Outlay Account: Total and Subsectors

Million Finnish markkaa

		1980					1985				
		Total General Government	Central Government	State or Provincial Government	Local Government	Social Security Funds	Total General Government	Central Government	State or Provincial Government	Local Government	Social Security Funds

Receipts

1	Operating surplus	-59	-66	...	7	-	78	107	...	-29	-
2	Property and entrepreneurial income	4578	991	...	960	2627	11220	2986	...	1893	6341
	A Withdrawals from public quasi-corporations	369	-24	...	393	-	1206	650	...	556	-
	B Interest	3911	948	...	379	2584	9178	2013	...	966	6199
	C Dividends	114	66	...	5	43	468	321	...	5	142
	D Net land rent and royalties	184	1	...	183	-	368	2	...	366	-
3	Taxes, fees and contributions	72133	38711	...	15354	18068	137581	75141	...	30397	32043
	A Indirect taxes	25593	25593	...	-	-	47639	47639	...	-	-
	B Direct taxes	27718	12387	...	15331	-	55741	25384	...	30357	-
	Income	27718	12387	...	15331	-	55448	25384	...	30064	-
	Other	-	-	...	-	-	293	-	...	293	-
	C Social security contributions	18196	128	...	-	18068	32714	671	...	-	32043
	D Fees, fines and penalties	626	603	...	23	-	1487	1447	...	40	-
4	Other current transfers	3090	1381	...	12655	2481	6134	2244	...	25277	8013
	A Casualty insurance claims	21	-	...	6	15	36	-	...	17	19
	B Transfers from other government subsectors	-	419	...	10608	2400	-	471	...	21202	7727
	C Transfers from the rest of the world	-	-	...	-	-	-	-	...	-	-
	D Other transfers, except imputed	70	38	...	-	32	269	66	...	-	203
	E Imputed unfunded employee pension and welfare contributions	2999	924	...	2041	34	5829	1707	...	4058	64
	Total Current Receipts	79742	41017	...	28976	23176	155013	80478	...	57538	46397

Disbursements

1	Government final consumption expenditure	34392	11134	...	22450	808	66967	20245	...	45154	1568
2	Property income	1996	1222	...	739	35	6147	4625	...	1362	160

411

Finland

3.12 General Government Income and Outlay Account: Total and Subsectors
(Continued)

Million Finnish markkaa

	1980 Total General Government	1980 Central Government	1980 State or Provincial Government	1980 Local Government	1980 Social Security Funds	1985 Total General Government	1985 Central Government	1985 State or Provincial Government	1985 Local Government	1985 Social Security Funds
A Interest	1993	1221	...	737	35	6138	4623	...	1355	160
B Net land rent and royalties	3	1	...	2	-	9	2	...	7	-
3 Subsidies	6225	5954	...	271	-	10347	9878	...	469	-
4 Other current transfers	24971	19773	...	3117	15508	53513	40471	...	6695	35747
A Casualty insurance premiums, net	36	-	...	21	15	60	-	...	41	19
B Transfers to other government subsectors	-	12097	...	914	416	-	27357	...	1603	440
C Social security benefits	15877	1453	...	-	14424	35083	2480	...	-	32603
D Social assistance grants	3406	2386	...	488	532	7376	3545	...	1604	2227
E Unfunded employee pension and welfare benefits	3453	2147	...	1289	17	6496	3796	...	2664	36
F Transfers to private non-profit institutions serving households	1683	1265	...	405	13	2822	2013	...	783	26
G Other transfers n.e.c.	187	96	...	-	91	616	220	...	-	396
H Transfers to the rest of the world	329	329	...	-	-	1060	1060	...	-	-
Net saving	12158	2934	...	2399	6825	18039	5259	...	3858	8922
Total Current Disbursements and Net Saving	79742	41017	...	28976	23176	155013	80478	...	57538	46397

	1990 Total General Government	1990 Central Government	1990 State or Provincial Government	1990 Local Government	1990 Social Security Funds	1991 Total General Government	1991 Central Government	1991 State or Provincial Government	1991 Local Government	1991 Social Security Funds
Receipts										
1 Operating surplus	44	118	...	-74	-	-151	-18	...	-133	-
2 Property and entrepreneurial income	19786	5772	...	2720	11294	23010	6472	...	3124	13414
A Withdrawals from public quasi-corporations	1443	617	...	826	-	1931	745	...	1186	-
B Interest	16531	4431	...	1258	10842	19227	5101	...	1231	12895
C Dividends	1125	723	...	11	391	1064	625	...	13	426
D Net land rent and royalties	687	1	...	625	61	788	1	...	694	93
3 Taxes, fees and contributions	237177	124298	...	51078	61801	232536	124203	...	48188	60145
A Indirect taxes	78025	78025	...	-	-	74730	74730	...	-	-
B Direct taxes	92741	41741	...	51000	-	88138	40064	...	48074	-
Income	92287	41741	...	50546	-	87643	40064	...	47579	-
Other	454	-	...	454	-	495	-	...	495	-
C Social security contributions	63356	1555	...	-	61801	66806	6661	...	-	60145
D Fees, fines and penalties	3055	2977	...	78	-	2862	2748	...	114	-
4 Other current transfers	4472	3605	...	37209	11379	1977	1394	...	40824	21832
A Casualty insurance claims	49	-	...	19	30	43	-	...	14	29
B Transfers from other government subsectors	-	699	...	36092	10930	-	940	...	39656	21477
C Transfers from the rest of the world	1	1	...	-	-	1	1	...	-	-
D Other transfers, except imputed	535	215	...	-	320	602	276	...	-	326
E Imputed unfunded employee pension and welfare contributions	3887	2690	...	1098	99	1331	177	...	1154	-
Total Current Receipts	261479	133793	...	90933	84474	257372	132051	...	92003	95391
Disbursements										
1 Government final consumption expenditure	108535	31824	...	74014	2697	118719	36592	...	79158	2969
2 Property income	7511	4912	...	2316	283	9598	6378	...	2965	255
A Interest	7487	4910	...	2299	278	9570	6375	...	2950	245
B Net land rent and royalties	20	2	...	17	1	21	3	...	15	3
3 Subsidies	14756	13999	...	757	-	17174	16402	...	772	-

Finland

3.12 General Government Income and Outlay Account: Total and Subsectors
(Continued)

Million Finnish markkaa

	1990					1991				
	Total General Government	Central Government	State or Provincial Government	Local Government	Social Security Funds	Total General Government	Central Government	State or Provincial Government	Local Government	Social Security Funds
4 Other current transfers	90227	68766	...	8994	60188	106482	85313	...	10228	73014
A Casualty insurance premiums, net	75	-	...	45	30	72	-	...	43	29
B Transfers to other government subsectors	-	44207	...	2707	807	-	57395	...	3030	1648
C Social security benefits	62387	6458	...	-	55929	77566	12379	...	-	65187
D Social assistance grants	11779	5054	...	4317	2408	15745	5549	...	5149	5047
E Unfunded employee pension and welfare benefits	7029	6257	...	694	78	3085	2266	...	727	92
F Transfers to private non-profit institutions serving households	4995	3693	...	1231	71	5404	4051	...	1279	74
G Other transfers n.e.c.	1528	663	...	-	865	1664	727	...	-	937
H Transfers to the rest of the world	2434	2434	...	-	-	2946	2946	...	-	-
Net saving	40450	14292	...	4852	21306	5399	-12634	...	-1120	19153
Total Current Disbursements and Net Saving	261479	133793	...	90933	84474	257372	132051	...	92003	95391

	1992					1993				
	Total General Government	Central Government	State or Provincial Government	Local Government	Social Security Funds	Total General Government	Central Government	State or Provincial Government	Local Government	Social Security Funds

Receipts

1 Operating surplus	-125	-19	...	-106	-	-157	141	...	-298	-
2 Property and entrepreneurial income	25422	6802	...	3906	14714	28497	9016	...	4743	14738
A Withdrawals from public quasi-corporations	1983	459	...	1524	-	2853	760	...	2093	-
B Interest	22074	6042	...	1638	14394	24273	8002	...	1784	14487
C Dividends	555	300	...	15	240	447	250	...	16	181
D Net land rent and royalties	810	1	...	729	80	924	4	...	850	70
3 Taxes, fees and contributions	226366	117261	...	46196	62909	222877	108464	...	47208	67205
A Indirect taxes	71643	71643	...	-	-	71556	71556	...	-	-
B Direct taxes	82270	36201	...	46069	-	74900	27822	...	47078	-
Income	81728	36201	...	45527	-	72668	27822	...	44846	-
Other	542	-	...	542	-	2232	-	...	2232	-
C Social security contributions	69566	6657	...	-	62909	73920	6715	...	-	67205
D Fees, fines and penalties	2887	2760	...	127	-	2501	2371	...	130	-
4 Other current transfers	2180	1727	...	41349	24493	2233	1266	...	42402	41179
A Casualty insurance claims	43	-	...	7	36	39	-	...	10	29
B Transfers from other government subsectors	-	1029	...	40206	24154	-	797	...	41295	40522
C Transfers from the rest of the world	136	136	...	-	-	1	1	...	-	-
D Other transfers, except imputed	685	382	...	-	303	1096	468	...	-	628
E Imputed unfunded employee pension and welfare contributions	1316	180	...	1136	-	1097	-	...	1097	-
Total Current Receipts	253843	125771	...	91345	102116	253450	118887	...	94055	123122

Disbursements

1 Government final consumption expenditure	118453	38399	...	77223	2831	112542	36038	...	73506	2998
2 Property income	12608	8687	...	3563	358	22155	17907	...	3721	527
A Interest	12583	8687	...	3546	350	22105	17879	...	3700	526
B Net land rent and royalties	19	-	...	17	2	49	28	...	21	-
3 Subsidies	17028	16218	...	810	-	16319	15388	...	931	-

Finland

3.12 General Government Income and Outlay Account: Total and Subsectors
(Continued)

Million Finnish markkaa

	1992 Total General Government	1992 Central Government	1992 State or Provincial Government	1992 Local Government	1992 Social Security Funds	1993 Total General Government	1993 Central Government	1993 State or Provincial Government	1993 Local Government	1993 Social Security Funds
4 Other current transfers	123238	90036	...	12247	86344	133058	97351	...	13792	104529
A Casualty insurance premiums, net	76	-	...	40	36	74	-	...	45	29
B Transfers to other government subsectors	-	58794	...	4234	2361	-	70052	...	8590	3972
C Social security benefits	89081	13766	...	-	75315	90090	8616	...	-	81474
D Social assistance grants	20546	7039	...	6054	7453	28482	7339	...	3176	17967
E Unfunded employee pension and welfare benefits	3297	2575	...	722	-	3435	2716	...	719	-
F Transfers to private non-profit institutions serving households	5270	4000	...	1197	73	6001	4666	...	1262	73
G Other transfers n.e.c.	2462	1356	...	-	1106	2731	1717	...	-	1014
H Transfers to the rest of the world	2506	2506	...	-	-	2245	2245	...	-	-
Net saving	-17484	-27569	...	-2498	12583	-30624	-47797	...	2105	15068
Total Current Disbursements and Net Saving	253843	125771	...	91345	102116	253450	118887	...	94055	123122

3.13 General Government Capital Accumulation Account: Total and Subsectors

Million Finnish markkaa

	1980 Total General Government	1980 Central Government	1980 State or Provincial Government	1980 Local Government	1980 Social Security Funds	1985 Total General Government	1985 Central Government	1985 State or Provincial Government	1985 Local Government	1985 Social Security Funds
	\multicolumn{10}{c}{Finance of Gross Accumulation}
1 Gross saving	14354	3695	...	3779	6880	22053	6554	...	6451	9048
A Consumption of fixed capital	2196	761	...	1380	55	4014	1295	...	2593	126
B Net saving	12158	2934	...	2399	6825	18039	5259	...	3858	8922
2 Capital transfers a	-485	-1213	...	728	-	-94	-1805	...	1220	491
A From other government subsectors	-	-729	...	729	-	-	-1224	...	1224	-
B From other resident sectors	-435	-434	...	-1	-	-94	-581	...	-4	491
C From rest of the world	-50	-50	...	-	-	-	-	...	-	-
Finance of Gross Accumulation	13869	2482	...	4507	6880	21959	4749	...	7671	9539
	\multicolumn{10}{c}{Gross Accumulation}
1 Gross capital formation	7001	2797	...	4079	125	11787	4217	...	7093	477
A Increase in stocks	207	207	...	-	-	193	193	...	-	-
B Gross fixed capital formation	6794	2590	...	4079	125	11594	4024	...	7093	477
2 Purchases of land, net	382	144	...	238	-	540	156	...	384	-
3 Purchases of intangible assets, net	...	...	...	...	...	...	...	...	...	...
4 Capital transfers a	...	...	...	...	...	...	...	...	...	...
Net lending	6486	-459	...	190	6755	9632	376	...	194	9062
Gross Accumulation	13869	2482	...	4507	6880	21959	4749	...	7671	9539

	1990 Total General Government	1990 Central Government	1990 State or Provincial Government	1990 Local Government	1990 Social Security Funds	1991 Total General Government	1991 Central Government	1991 State or Provincial Government	1991 Local Government	1991 Social Security Funds
	\multicolumn{10}{c}{Finance of Gross Accumulation}
1 Gross saving	47833	16691	...	9596	21546	12880	-10173	...	3664	19389
A Consumption of fixed capital	7383	2399	...	4744	240	7481	2461	...	4784	236
B Net saving	40450	14292	...	4852	21306	5399	-12634	...	-1120	19153
2 Capital transfers a	-757	-3098	...	2341	-	-1202	-3478	...	2276	-
A From other government subsectors	-	-2347	...	2347	-	-	-2283	...	2283	-
B From other resident sectors	-757	-751	...	-6	-	-903	-896	...	-7	-
C From rest of the world	-	-	...	-	-	-299	-299	...	-	-
Finance of Gross Accumulation	47076	13593	...	11937	21546	11678	-13651	...	5940	19389
	\multicolumn{10}{c}{Gross Accumulation}
1 Gross capital formation	18641	7218	...	11243	180	18661	8232	...	10215	214

Finland

3.13 General Government Capital Accumulation Account: Total and Subsectors
(Continued)

Million Finnish markkaa

	1990					1991				
	Total General Government	Central Government	State or Provincial Government	Local Government	Social Security Funds	Total General Government	Central Government	State or Provincial Government	Local Government	Social Security Funds
A Increase in stocks	177	177	...	-	-	376	376	...	-	-
B Gross fixed capital formation	18464	7041	...	11243	180	18285	7856	...	10215	214
2 Purchases of land, net	362	156	...	206	-	213	157	...	54	2
3 Purchases of intangible assets, net	381	...	...	...	381	171	...	...	...	171
4 Capital transfers [a]	...	...	...	...	...	...	...	...	...	...
Net lending	27692	6219	...	488	20985	-7367	-22040	...	-4329	19002
Gross Accumulation	47076	13593	...	11937	21546	11678	-13651	...	5940	19389

	1992					1993				
	Total General Government	Central Government	State or Provincial Government	Local Government	Social Security Funds	Total General Government	Central Government	State or Provincial Government	Local Government	Social Security Funds

Finance of Gross Accumulation

1 Gross saving	-10083	-25037	...	2143	12811	-23143	-45109	...	6671	15295
A Consumption of fixed capital	7401	2532	...	4641	228	7481	2688	...	4566	227
B Net saving	-17484	-27569	...	-2498	12583	-30624	-47797	...	2105	15068
2 Capital transfers [a]	-896	-3021	...	2125	-	-684	-1870	...	1186	-
A From other government subsectors	-	-2130	...	2130	-	-	-1191	...	1191	-
B From other resident sectors	-896	-891	...	-5	-	-684	-679	...	-5	-
C From rest of the world	-	-	...	-	-	-	-	...	-	-
Finance of Gross Accumulation	-10979	-28058	...	4268	12811	-23827	-46979	...	7857	15295

Gross Accumulation

1 Gross capital formation	16734	8089	...	8153	492	13750	7226	...	6100	424
A Increase in stocks	133	133	...	-	-	347	347	...	-	-
B Gross fixed capital formation	16601	7956	...	8153	492	13403	6879	...	6100	424
2 Purchases of land, net	179	219	...	-40	-	58	48	...	10	-
3 Purchases of intangible assets, net	-	...	...	...	-	-	...	...	...	-
4 Capital transfers [a]	...	...	...	...	...	...	...	...	...	...
Net lending	-27892	-36366	...	-3845	12319	-37635	-54253	...	1747	14871
Gross Accumulation	-10979	-28058	...	4268	12811	-23827	-46979	...	7857	15295

a) Capital transfers received are recorded net of capital transfers paid.

3.14 General Government Capital Finance Account, Total and Subsectors

Million Finnish markkaa

	1980					1985				
	Total General Government	Central Government	State or Provincial Government	Local Government	Social Security Funds	Total General Government	Central Government	State or Provincial Government	Local Government	Social Security Funds

Acquisition of Financial Assets

1 Gold and SDRs	...	...	...	...	...	...	...	...	...	...
2 Currency and transferable deposits	-778	-206	...	-285	-287	667	167	...	22	478
3 Other deposits	665	399	...	215	51	285	-17	...	478	-176
4 Bills and bonds, short term	...	...	...	...	...	...	...	...	...	...
5 Bonds, long term	796	237	...	110	449	224	82	...	160	-18
A Corporations	...	237	...	8	...	...	82	...	-	...
B Other government subsectors	...	-	...	102	...	...	-	...	160	...
C Rest of the world	...	...	...	-	...	...	...	...	...	...
6 Corporate equity securities	1987	312	...	1089	586	4590	922	...	1841	1827
7 Short-term loans, n.e.c.	570	-32	...	198	404	1838	455	...	542	841
8 Long-term loans, n.e.c.	8580	2413	...	1205	4962	8922	2145	...	428	6349
A Mortgages	...	1579	...	-	-	...	742	...	457	-2
B Other	...	834	...	1205	4962	...	1403	...	-29	6351
9 Other receivables	308	117	...	-388	579	695	-580	...	559	716
10 Other assets	1413	707	...	706	-	1143	840	...	303	-
Total Acquisition of Financial Assets	13541	3947	...	2850	6744	18364	4014	...	4333	10017

Incurrence of Liabilities

1 Currency and transferable deposits	...	...	...	...	...	...	...	...	...	...

Finland

3.14 General Government Capital Finance Account, Total and Subsectors
(Continued)

Million Finnish markkaa

	1980					1985				
	Total General Government	Central Government	State or Provincial Government	Local Government	Social Security Funds	Total General Government	Central Government	State or Provincial Government	Local Government	Social Security Funds
2 Other deposits	...	...	...	...	...	...	...	...	...	...
3 Bills and bonds, short term	56	40	...	14	2	-78	-	...	-15	-63
4 Bonds, long term	2837	2878	...	-41	6	5034	4644	...	390	-31
5 Short-term loans, n.e.c.	109	18	...	85	3	556	-15	...	602	282
6 Long-term loans, n.e.c.	2073	402	...	1668	-232	593	-1009	...	1320	333
7 Other payables	500	972	...	-240	5	817	132	...	352	2
8 Other liabilities	820	-	...	815	-	1318	-	...	1316	-
Total Incurrence of Liabilities	6395	4310	...	2301	-216	8240	3752	...	3965	523
Statistical discrepancy a	660	96	...	359	205	492	-114	...	174	432
Net Lending	6486	-459	...	190	6755	9632	376	...	194	9062
Incurrence of Liabilities and Net Worth	13541	3947	...	2850	6744	18364	4014	...	4333	10017

	1990					1991				
	Total General Government	Central Government	State or Provincial Government	Local Government	Social Security Funds	Total General Government	Central Government	State or Provincial Government	Local Government	Social Security Funds

Acquisition of Financial Assets

1 Gold and SDRs	...	...	...	...	...	...	...	...	...	...
2 Currency and transferable deposits	4073	3792	...	412	-131	-8266	-9385	...	216	903
3 Other deposits	-3199	-4004	...	-232	1037	-2947	-1317	...	-769	-861
4 Bills and bonds, short term	...	...	...	...	...	...	...	...	...	...
5 Bonds, long term	187	-105	...	-	292	878	-121	...	-	999
A Corporations	...	-105	...	...	...	...	-121	...	-	...
B Other government subsectors	...	-	...	-	...	...	-	...	-	...
C Rest of the world	...	-	...	-	...	...	-	...	...	...
6 Corporate equity securities	10059	5276	...	3632	1151	3703	373	...	1568	1762
7 Short-term loans, n.e.c.	5091	2039	...	1730	1322	7444	4221	...	682	2541
8 Long-term loans, n.e.c.	20863	4772	...	730	15361	23717	7178	...	2407	14132
A Mortgages	...	...	...	...	...	...	...	...	...	...
B Other	...	...	...	...	...	...	...	...	...	...
9 Other receivables	365	-714	...	-30	1109	4043	39	...	402	3602
10 Other assets	-1313	-2042	...	729	-	-300	-638	...	338	-
Total Acquisition of Financial Assets	36126	9014	...	6971	20141	28272	350	...	4844	23078

Incurrence of Liabilities

1 Currency and transferable deposits	...	...	...	...	...	...	...	...	...	...
2 Other deposits	185	185	...	...	...	59	59	...	...	...
3 Bills and bonds, short term	85	-	...	109	-24	11	-	...	11	-
4 Bonds, long term	1188	1256	...	-68	386	22629	21341	...	1288	1849
5 Short-term loans, n.e.c.	1122	145	...	591	-1134	8023	4774	...	1400	68
6 Long-term loans, n.e.c.	4006	2743	...	2397	230	4229	-1036	...	5197	3005
7 Other payables	2131	-735	...	2636	30	2647	-417	...	59	-
8 Other liabilities	2037	-	...	2007	-	567	-	...	567	-
Total Incurrence of Liabilities	10754	3594	...	7672	-512	38165	24721	...	8522	4922
Statistical discrepancy a	-2320	-799	...	-1189	-332	-2526	-2331	...	651	-846
Net Lending	27692	6219	...	488	20985	-7367	-22040	...	-4329	19002
Incurrence of Liabilities and Net Worth	36126	9014	...	6971	20141	28272	350	...	4844	23078

	1992				
	Total General Government	Central Government	State or Provincial Government	Local Government	Social Security Funds

Acquisition of Financial Assets

1 Gold and SDRs	...	...	...	...	...
2 Currency and transferable deposits	-374	-1278	...	149	755
3 Other deposits	311	-3	...	854	-540
4 Bills and bonds, short term	...	...	...	...	...
5 Bonds, long term	21870	16502	...	-	5368
A Corporations	...	16502	...	-	...
B Other government subsectors	...	-	...	-	...

Finland

3.14 General Government Capital Finance Account, Total and Subsectors
(Continued)

Million Finnish markkaa

	1992 Total General Government	Central Government	State or Provincial Government	Local Government	Social Security Funds
C Rest of the world	...	-	...	-	...
6 Corporate equity securities	6735	5030	...	416	1289
7 Short-term loans, n.e.c.	3479	4111	...	217	-849
8 Long-term loans, n.e.c.	14302	7153	...	3299	3850
A Mortgages	...	...	...	...	...
B Other	...	...	...	...	...
9 Other receivables	8425	3188	...	2236	3001
10 Other assets	-1595	-1114	...	-481	-
Total Acquisition of Financial Assets	53153	33589	...	6690	12874

Incurrence of Liabilities

1 Currency and transferable deposits	74	74	...	...	...
2 Other deposits	-	-	...	...	...
3 Bills and bonds, short term	-66	-	...	-66	...
4 Bonds, long term	59749	56385	...	3364	-
5 Short-term loans, n.e.c.	9980	11151	...	-260	-911
6 Long-term loans, n.e.c.	9395	2269	...	6654	472
7 Other payables	1157	483	...	-491	1165
8 Other liabilities	379	-	...	369	10
Total Incurrence of Liabilities	80668	70362	...	9570	736
Statistical discrepancy [a]	377	-407	...	965	-181
Net Lending	-27892	-36366	...	-3845	12319
Incurrence of Liabilities and Net Worth	53153	33589	...	6690	12874

a) Statistical discrepancy refers to adjustment made in order to reconcile the net lending of the Capital Accumulation Account and the Capital Finance Account.

3.22 Corporate and Quasi-Corporate Enterprise Income and Outlay Account: Total and Sectors

Million Finnish markkaa

	1980 TOTAL	Non-Financial	Financial	1985 TOTAL	Non-Financial	Financial	1990 TOTAL	Non-Financial	Financial	1991 TOTAL	Non-Financial	Financial
Receipts												
1 Operating surplus	11720	14520	-2800	20811	26584	-5773	30919	40872	-9953	12257	23840	-11583
2 Property and entrepreneurial income	17553	3091	14462	45284	9625	35659	116619	22262	94357	118373	24138	94235
A Withdrawals from quasi-corporate enterprises	-	-	-	-	-	-	-	-	-	-	-	-
B Interest	17121	2805	14316	43714	8585	35129	111469	18718	92751	112777	20047	92730
C Dividends	374	230	144	1431	906	525	4889	3314	1575	5264	3851	1413
D Net land rent and royalties	58	56	2	139	134	5	261	230	31	332	240	92
3 Current transfers	6480	2115	4365	12676	3491	9185	18147	3987	14160	17380	2051	15329
A Casualty insurance claims	1830	1413	417	3018	2188	830	5614	3974	1640	6110	4161	1949
B Casualty insurance premiums, net, due to be received by insurance companies	3159	-	3159	6847	-	6847	9670	-	9670	10738	-	10738
C Current transfers from the rest of the world	...	...	...	10	10	...	-1777	-711	-1066	-3918	-2867	-1051
D Other transfers except imputed	800	65	735	1750	258	1492	4460	568	3892	4234	566	3668
E Imputed unfunded employee pension and welfare contributions	691	637	54	1051	1035	16	180	156	24	216	191	25
Total Current Receipts	35753	19726	16027	78771	39700	39071	165685	67121	98564	148010	50029	97981
Disbursements												
1 Property and entrepreneurial income	24729	14584	10145	58450	30237	28213	139390	60813	78577	146498	67216	79282
A Withdrawals from quasi-corporations	1382	1382	-	2791	2791	-	4116	4116	-	4190	4190	-
Public	369	369	-	1206	1206	-	1443	1443	-	1931	1931	-
Private	1013	1013	-	1585	1585	-	2673	2673	-	2259	2259	-
B Interest	21683	11794	9889	50786	23381	27405	123589	46627	76962	130634	52317	78317

Finland

3.22 Corporate and Quasi-Corporate Enterprise Income and Outlay Account: Total and Sectors
(Continued)

Million Finnish markkaa

	1980 TOTAL	1980 Non-Financial	1980 Financial	1985 TOTAL	1985 Non-Financial	1985 Financial	1990 TOTAL	1990 Non-Financial	1990 Financial	1991 TOTAL	1991 Non-Financial	1991 Financial
C Dividends	1113	857	256	3636	2835	801	9805	8192	1613	9501	8536	965
D Net land rent and royalties	551	551	...	1237	1230	7	1880	1878	2	2173	2173	-
2 Direct taxes and other current transfers n.e.c. to general government	2293	2033	260	4637	3983	654	10458	8515	1943	10045	8876	1169
A Direct taxes	2263	2033	230	4444	3983	461	10127	8505	1622	9709	8856	853
On income	2263	2033	230	4371	3916	455	10013	8401	1612	9584	8742	842
Other	...	...	...	73	67	6	114	104	10	125	114	11
B Fines, fees, penalties and other current transfers n.e.c.	30	...	30	193	...	193	331	10	321	336	20	316
3 Other current transfers	6924	2821	4103	13630	4915	8715	18604	4514	14090	19771	4402	15369
A Casualty insurance premiums, net	1805	1388	417	2985	2155	830	5562	3922	1640	6072	4123	1949
B Casualty insurance claims liability of insurance companies	3159	-	3159	6847	-	6847	9670	-	9670	10738	-	10738
C Transfers to private non-profit institutions	232	220	12	447	420	27	766	700	66	683	627	56
D Unfunded employee pension and welfare benefits	1246	1213	33	2079	2048	31	613	566	47	522	471	51
E Social assistance grants	482	-	482	955	-	955	1709	-	1709	1825	-	1825
F Other transfers n.e.c. [a]	...	-	...	25	-	25	957	-	957	849	-	849
G Transfers to the rest of the world [b]	-	-	-	292	292	-	-673	-674	1	-918	-819	-99
Net saving	1807	288	1519	2054	565	1489	-2767	-6721	3954	-28304	-30465	2161
Total Current Disbursements and Net Saving	35753	19726	16027	78771	39700	39071	165685	67121	98564	148010	50029	97981

	1992 TOTAL	1992 Non-Financial	1992 Financial	1993 TOTAL	1993 Non-Financial	1993 Financial
Receipts						
1 Operating surplus	17970	28184	-10214	31584	40366	-8782
2 Property and entrepreneurial income	111058	24303	86755	88341	19120	69221
A Withdrawals from quasi-corporate enterprises	-	-	-	-	-	-
B Interest	106213	20667	85546	83800	15517	68283
C Dividends	4587	3394	1193	4283	3354	929
D Net land rent and royalties	258	242	16	258	249	9
3 Current transfers	21134	2949	18185	20163	3341	16822
A Casualty insurance claims	8394	6108	2286	7844	6319	1525
B Casualty insurance premiums, net, due to be received by insurance companies	13296	-	13296	12425	-	12425
C Current transfers from the rest of the world	-5750	-4901	-849	-4928	-4608	-320
D Other transfers except imputed	4406	979	3427	4475	1329	3146
E Imputed unfunded employee pension and welfare contributions	788	763	25	347	301	46
Total Current Receipts	150162	55436	94726	140088	62827	77261
Disbursements						
1 Property and entrepreneurial income	144474	67663	76811	118740	61906	56834
A Withdrawals from quasi-corporations	4101	4101	-	4865	4865	-
Public	1983	1983	-	2853	2853	-
Private	2118	2118	-	2012	2012	-
B Interest	131885	55455	76430	106026	49414	56612
C Dividends	6446	6065	381	5308	5086	222
D Net land rent and royalties	2042	2042	-	2541	2541	-
2 Direct taxes and other current transfers n.e.c. to general government	8196	7453	743	4451	3255	1196
A Direct taxes	7814	7373	441	3657	3158	499
On income	7669	7240	429	2752	2296	456

Finland

3.22 Corporate and Quasi-Corporate Enterprise Income and Outlay Account: Total and Sectors
(Continued)

Million Finnish markkaa

	1992 TOTAL	1992 Non-Financial	1992 Financial	1993 TOTAL	1993 Non-Financial	1993 Financial
Other	145	133	12	905	862	43
B Fines, fees, penalties and other current transfers n.e.c.	382	80	302	794	97	697
3 Other current transfers	24835	6383	18452	23839	6842	16997
A Casualty insurance premiums, net	8358	6072	2286	7805	6280	1525
B Casualty insurance claims liability of insurance companies	13296	-	13296	12425	-	12425
C Transfers to private non-profit institutions	500	460	40	257	230	27
D Unfunded employee pension and welfare benefits	771	715	56	329	253	76
E Social assistance grants	2066	-	2066	2242	-	2242
F Other transfers n.e.c. [a]	600	-	600	650	-	650
G Transfers to the rest of the world [b]	-756	-864	108	131	79	52
Net saving	-27343	-26063	-1280	-6942	-9176	2234
Total Current Disbursements and Net Saving	150162	55436	94726	140088	62827	77261

a) Item 'Other transfers n.e.c.' refers to transfers to households.
b) Item 'Transfers to the rest of the world' includes re-invested earnings.

3.23 Corporate and Quasi-Corporate Enterprise Capital Accumulation Account: Total and Sectors

Million Finnish markkaa

	1980 TOTAL	1980 Non-Financial	1980 Financial	1985 TOTAL	1985 Non-Financial	1985 Financial	1990 TOTAL	1990 Non-Financial	1990 Financial	1991 TOTAL	1991 Non-Financial	1991 Financial
Finance of Gross Accumulation												
1 Gross saving	18242	16249	1993	29732	27312	2420	40870	35196	5674	17353	13411	3942
A Consumption of fixed capital	16435	15961	474	27678	26747	931	43637	41917	1720	45657	43876	1781
B Net saving	1807	288	1519	2054	565	1489	-2767	-6721	3954	-28304	-30465	2161
2 Capital transfers [a]	90	90	...	-305	186	-491	528	515	13	594	2092	-1498
A From resident sectors	90	90	...	-305	186	-491	528	515	13	594	2092	-1498
B From the rest of the world	...	...	...	...	...	...	...	...	...	...	...	...
Finance of Gross Accumulation	18332	16339	1993	29427	27498	1929	41398	35711	5687	17947	15503	2444
Gross Accumulation												
1 Gross capital formation	28412	27264	1148	38020	36837	1183	72118	70589	1529	43403	41889	1514
A Increase in stocks	6339	6339	-	-466	-466	-	2421	2421	-	-9795	-9795	-
B Gross fixed capital formation	22073	20925	1148	38486	37303	1183	69697	68168	1529	53198	51684	1514
2 Purchases of land, net	103	55	48	630	415	215	972	905	67	98	-17	115
3 Purchases of intangible assets, net	-	-	-	-	-	-	-381	-381	-	-171	-171	-
4 Capital transfers [a]	...	...	...	...	...	...	...	...	...	...	...	...
Net lending	-10183	-10980	797	-9223	-9754	531	-31311	-35402	4091	-25383	-26198	815
Gross Accumulation	18332	16339	1993	29427	27498	1929	41398	35711	5687	17947	15503	2444

	1992 TOTAL	1992 Non-Financial	1992 Financial	1993 TOTAL	1993 Non-Financial	1993 Financial
Finance of Gross Accumulation						
1 Gross saving	20182	19693	489	43320	39276	4044
A Consumption of fixed capital	47525	45756	1769	50262	48452	1810
B Net saving	-27343	-26063	-1280	-6942	-9176	2234
2 Capital transfers [a]	493	488	5	405	517	-112
A From resident sectors	493	488	5	405	517	-112
B From the rest of the world	...	...	...	...	...	...
Finance of Gross Accumulation	20675	20181	494	43725	39793	3932
Gross Accumulation						
1 Gross capital formation	37494	36061	1433	29869	30816	-947

Finland

3.23 Corporate and Quasi-Corporate Enterprise Capital Accumulation Account: Total and Sectors
(Continued)

Million Finnish markkaa

	1992 TOTAL	1992 Non-Financial	1992 Financial	1993 TOTAL	1993 Non-Financial	1993 Financial
A Increase in stocks	-4698	-4698	-	-3443	-3443	-
B Gross fixed capital formation	42192	40759	1433	33312	34259	-947
2 Purchases of land, net	-8	304	-312	-340	60	-400
3 Purchases of intangible assets, net	-	-	-	-	-	-
4 Capital transfers [a]	...	...	...	...	...	...
Net lending	-16811	-16184	-627	14196	8917	5279
Gross Accumulation	20675	20181	494	43725	39793	3932

[a] Capital transfers received are recorded net of capital transfers paid.

3.24 Corporate and Quasi-Corporate Enterprise Capital Finance Account: Total and Sectors

Million Finnish markkaa

	1980 TOTAL	1980 Non-Financial	1980 Financial	1985 TOTAL	1985 Non-Financial	1985 Financial	1990 TOTAL	1990 Non-Financial	1990 Financial	1991 TOTAL	1991 Non-Financial	1991 Financial
Acquisition of Financial Assets												
1 Gold and SDRs	127	-	127	397	-	397	-300	-	-300	239	-	239
2 Currency and transferable deposits	3960	1156	2804	1241	2998	-1757	20644	-800	21444	-8264	824	-9088
3 Other deposits	2719	460	2259	5034	1624	3410	-12116	-2951	-9165	-2468	2668	-5136
4 Bills and bonds, short term	3662	-	3662	4717	-	4717	-4136	-	-4136	-8628	-	-8628
A Corporate and quasi-corporate, resident	3600	-	3600	4027	-	4027	-4620	-	-4620	...	-	...
B Government	54	-	54	-19	-	-19	109	-	109	...	-	...
C Rest of the world	8	-	8	709	-	709	375	-	375	...	-	...
5 Bonds, long term	2301	147	2154	6372	32	6340	5554	6369	-815	10448	-2233	12681
A Corporate, resident	...	147	...	...	32	...	...	6369	...	...	-2233	...
B Government	...	-	...	...	-	...	...	-	...	...	-	...
C Rest of the world	...	-	...	...	-	...	...	-	...	...	-	...
6 Corporate equity securities	2130	1444	686	14005	10244	3761	32315	26700	5615	26180	11178	15002
7 Short term loans, n.e.c.	1733	13	1720	13916	5090	8826	-18308	-1451	-16857	36515	12716	23799
8 Long term loans, n.e.c.	13509	131	13378	24935	-186	25121	77211	13046	64165	36426	13736	22690
A Mortgages	...	-	...	...	-	...	...	-	...	...	-	...
B Other	...	131	...	...	-186	...	...	13046	...	...	13736	...
9 Trade credits and advances	8799	8732	67	3025	2626	399	-6345	-5601	-744	-11348	-10807	-541
10 Other receivables	2354	1277	1077	3950	1193	2757	9167	1463	7704	4652	3884	768
11 Other assets	-	-	-	-	-	-	-	-	-	-	-	-
Total Acquisition of Financial Assets	41294	13360	27934	77592	23621	53971	103686	36775	66911	83752	31966	51786
Incurrence of Liabilities												
1 Currency and transferable deposits	5573	-	5573	6973	-	6973	23980	-	23980	-8110	-	-8110
2 Other deposits	11820	-27	11847	15417	15	15402	-5906	165	-6071	3123	435	2688
3 Bills and bonds, short term	3616	2941	675	3950	3363	587	-5327	4031	-9358	-6949	-2793	-4156
4 Bonds, long term	791	-578	1369	13150	5271	7879	33141	2322	30819	29921	5400	24521
5 Corporate equity securities	1646	1133	513	14790	13420	1370	23838	22027	1811	23707	12750	10957
6 Short-term loans, n.e.c.	2493	-434	2927	10385	-3849	14234	-10539	-8659	-1880	11179	6187	4992
7 Long-term loans, n.e.c.	11741	10128	1613	18062	14659	3403	86059	73143	12916	55921	43393	12528
8 Net equity of households in life insurance and pension fund reserves	1060	-	1060	2075	-	2075	2804	-	2804	3269	-	3269
9 Proprietors' net additions to the accumulation of quasi-corporations	1413	1413	-	1143	1143	-	-1313	-1313	-	-300	-300	-
10 Trade credit and advances	9940	9852	88	1700	1893	-193	-7524	-6737	-787	-11010	-9947	-1063
11 Other accounts payable	2243	821	1422	3485	2265	1220	7845	2983	4862	4802	2594	2208
12 Other liabilities	...	...	...	...	...	...	...	...	...	...	...	...
Total Incurrence of Liabilities	52336	25249	27087	91130	38180	52950	147058	87962	59096	105553	57719	47834
Statistical discrepancy [a]	-859	-909	50	-4315	-4805	490	-12061	-15785	3724	3582	445	3137
Net Lending	-10183	-10980	797	-9223	-9754	531	-31311	-35402	4091	-25383	-26198	815
Incurrence of Liabilities and Net Lending	41294	13360	27934	77592	23621	971	103686	36775	66911	83752	31966	51786

Finland

3.24 Corporate and Quasi-Corporate Enterprise Capital Finance Account: Total and Sectors

Million Finnish markkaa

	1992 TOTAL	Non-Financial	Financial
Acquisition of Financial Assets			
1 Gold and SDRs	-217	-	-217
2 Currency and transferable deposits	-3433	150	-3583
3 Other deposits	163	-7336	7499
4 Bills and bonds, short term	-2188	-	-2188
A Corporate and quasi-corporate, resident	...	-	...
B Government	...	-	...
C Rest of the world	...	-	...
5 Bonds, long term	3404	-686	4090
A Corporate, resident	...	-686	...
B Government	...	-	...
C Rest of the world	...	-	...
6 Corporate equity securities	2288	13395	-11107
7 Short term loans, n.e.c.	-4755	16200	-20955
8 Long term loans, n.e.c.	12117	9643	2474
A Mortgages	...	-	...
B Other	...	9643	...
9 Trade credits and advances	-8819	-8568	-251
10 Other receivables	2833	1054	1779
11 Other assets	-	-	-
Total Acquisition of Financial Assets	1393	23852	-22459
Incurrence of Liabilities			
1 Currency and transferable deposits	4574	-	4574
2 Other deposits	5427	-167	5594
3 Bills and bonds, short term	-1865	-3944	2079
4 Bonds, long term	9878	2064	7814
5 Corporate equity securities	6044	7825	-1781
6 Short-term loans, n.e.c.	-32808	-5241	-27567
7 Long-term loans, n.e.c.	16389	32872	-16483
8 Net equity of households in life insurance and pension fund reserves	4101	-	4101
9 Proprietors' net additions to the accumulation of quasi-corporations	-1595	-1595	-
10 Trade credit and advances	-1697	-2652	955
11 Other accounts payable	9881	6464	3417
12 Other liabilities	...	...	...
Total Incurrence of Liabilities	18329	35626	-17297
Statistical discrepancy [a]	-125	4410	-4535
Net Lending	-16811	-16184	-627
Incurrence of Liabilities and Net Lending	1393	23852	-22459

a) Statistical discrepancy refers to adjustment made in order to reconcile the net lending of the Capital Accumulation Account and the Capital Finance Account.

3.32 Household and Private Unincorporated Enterprise Income and Outlay Account

Million Finnish markkaa

	1980	1983	1984	1985	1986	1987	1988	1989	1990	1991	1992	1993
Receipts												
1 Compensation of employees	104429	148401	164879	183582	196900	214194	236874	264901	288978	289915	273736	258124
A Wages and salaries	85058	122228	135861	149722	160309	174395	192161	213839	229910	229721	216736	201564
B Employers' contributions for social security	19371	26173	29018	33860	36591	39799	44713	51062	59068	60194	57000	56560
C Employers' contributions for private pension & welfare plans	...	...	...	...	...	...	...	...	...	...	...	...
2 Operating surplus of private unincorporated enterprises	28823	39896	43538	43791	46207	45090	48870	56236	58535	54701	53031	55469
3 Property and entrepreneurial income	6055	9229	11152	12130	12405	14179	17196	21172	24270	27543	30652	25394
A Withdrawals from private quasi-corporations	1013	1352	1484	1585	1696	1772	1985	2372	2673	2259	2118	2012
B Interest	4529	7087	8729	9371	9388	10961	13605	16838	19024	22084	26210	21287

Finland

3.32 Household and Private Unincorporated Enterprise Income and Outlay Account
(Continued)

Million Finnish markkaa

	1980	1983	1984	1985	1986	1987	1988	1989	1990	1991	1992	1993
C Dividends	344	550	671	865	975	1073	1194	1513	2124	2705	1825	1590
D Net land rent and royalties	169	240	268	309	346	373	412	449	449	495	499	505
3 Current transfers	25846	42597	48215	55021	60753	66668	73325	80298	90182	106114	124099	133408
A Casualty insurance claims	791	1331	1631	1651	1802	2056	2394	3268	3044	3143	3475	3210
B Social security benefits	16359	27652	31366	36038	40044	43577	50542	55271	64096	79391	91147	92332
C Social assistance grants	3515	6027	6625	7675	8275	9171	9594	10279	12279	16325	21176	29072
D Unfunded employee pension and welfare benefits	4813	7000	7862	8782	9795	10807	8395	9227	7989	4002	4478	4178
E Transfers from general government	106	141	192	275	353	447	550	677	839	992	1416	1244
F Transfers from the rest of the world	250	432	500	554	412	474	1529	820	953	1385	1787	2702
G Other transfers n.e.c.	12	14	39	46	72	136	321	756	982	876	620	670
Total Current Receipts	165153	240123	267784	294524	316265	340131	376265	422607	461965	478273	481518	472395

Disbursements

	1980	1983	1984	1985	1986	1987	1988	1989	1990	1991	1992	1993
1 Final consumption expenditures	99873	144066	159140	174165	186830	203783	223918	245058	259157	263886	261136	260814
2 Property income	4235	6846	8515	9742	10269	11646	15402	20797	25528	26689	26550	21548
A Interest	4121	6675	8321	9529	10033	11387	15129	20505	25242	26367	26230	21238
B Net land rent and royalties	114	171	194	213	236	259	273	292	286	322	320	310
3 Direct taxes and other current transfers n.e.c. to government	44928	64313	74608	86684	95806	98260	120749	135143	152414	151251	149857	150087
A Social security contributions	18931	24940	28626	34206	36527	39706	49437	56383	67248	70474	72993	77066
B Direct taxes	25371	38355	44697	50991	57552	56718	68330	74845	82111	77915	73977	70520
Income taxes	25371	38304	44639	50924	57472	56638	68251	74751	82007	77801	73844	69769
Other	-	51	58	67	80	80	79	94	104	114	133	751
C Fees, fines and penalties	626	1018	1285	1487	1727	1836	2982	3915	3055	2862	2887	2501
4 Other current transfers	6725	10344	11733	12623	14302	15403	13003	14660	14581	12151	13679	12542
A Net casualty insurance premiums	791	1331	1631	1651	1802	2056	2394	3268	3044	3143	3475	3210
B Transfers to private non-profit institutions serving households	1768	2602	2946	3233	3494	3697	4061	4450	4890	4660	4664	4500
C Transfers to the rest of the world	281	474	539	489	1109	1054	1727	1727	2015	2210	2804	2793
D Other current transfers, except imputed	...	...	...	...	...	...	...	...	...	...	...	...
E Imputed employee pension and welfare contributions	3885	5937	6617	7250	7897	8596	4821	5215	4632	2138	2736	2039
Net saving	9392	14554	13788	11310	9058	11039	3193	6949	10285	24296	30296	27404
Total Current Disbursements and Net Saving	165153	240123	267784	294524	316265	340131	376265	422607	461965	478273	481518	472395

3.33 Household and Private Unincorporated Enterprise Capital Accumulation Account

Million Finnish markkaa

	1980	1983	1984	1985	1986	1987	1988	1989	1990	1991	1992	1993

Finance of Gross Accumulation

	1980	1983	1984	1985	1986	1987	1988	1989	1990	1991	1992	1993
1 Gross saving	16753	25017	25358	23487	22121	25153	18766	24041	29103	43471	48236	44766
A Consumption of fixed capital	7361	10463	11570	12177	13063	14114	15573	17092	18818	19175	17940	17362
B Net saving	9392	14554	13788	11310	9058	11039	3193	6949	10285	24296	30296	27404
2 Capital transfers [a]	163	152	121	131	47	-15	1367	-105	-394	-467	-514	-234
A From resident sectors	163	152	121	131	47	-15	1367	-105	-394	-467	-514	-234
B From the rest of the world	...	...	...	...	...	...	...	...	...	...	...	...
Total Finance of Gross Accumulation	16916	25169	25479	23618	22168	25138	20133	23936	28709	43004	47722	44532

Gross Accumulation

	1980	1983	1984	1985	1986	1987	1988	1989	1990	1991	1992	1993
1 Gross Capital Formation	14142	18855	19127	19504	19476	19487	23377	31138	30907	24354	17587	16300

Finland

3.33 Household and Private Unincorporated Enterprise Capital Accumulation Account
(Continued)

Million Finnish markkaa

		1980	1983	1984	1985	1986	1987	1988	1989	1990	1991	1992	1993
	A Increase in stocks	154	63	47	-167	-251	-959	-404	670	326	-79	-1268	361
	B Gross fixed capital formation	13988	18792	19080	19671	19727	20446	23781	30468	30581	24433	18855	15939
2	Purchases of land, net	-658	-1140	-1051	-1438	-1179	-1030	-2639	-1433	-1530	-394	-244	243
3	Purchases of intangibles, net	-	-	-	-	-	-	-	-	-	-	-	-
4	Capital transfers [a]	...	...	...	...	...	...	...	...	...	...	...	...
	Net lending	3432	7454	7403	5552	3871	6681	-605	-5769	-668	19044	30379	27989
	Total Gross Accumulation	16916	25169	25479	23618	22168	25138	20133	23936	28709	43004	47722	44532

a) Capital transfers received are recorded net of capital transfers paid.

3.34 Household and Private Unincorporated Enterprise Capital Finance Account

Million Finnish markkaa

		1980	1983	1984	1985	1986	1987	1988	1989	1990	1991	1992	1993
					Acquisition of Financial Assets								
1	Gold	...	...	...	...	...	...	...	...	...	...	...	...
2	Currency and transferable deposits	486	207	1496	-419	-227	372	499	1144	78	1010	1883	...
3	Other deposits	8324	10002	10497	10653	10391	14603	28773	11080	6801	9295	1994	...
4	Bills and bonds, short term	...	...	...	...	...	...	...	...	...	...	...	...
5	Bonds, long term	616	3462	2913	5775	3077	8386	4351	1229	1200	3600	5453	...
6	Corporate equity securities	2729	4105	4055	4798	4500	5096	7008	9591	3450	3300	4720	...
7	Short term loans, n.e.c.	-6	20	21	-24	-17	60	117	-123	44	-13	29	...
8	Long term loans, n.e.c.	-	-	-	-	-	-	-	-	-	-	-	-
	A Mortgages	...	...	...	...	...	...	...	...	...	...	...	...
	B Other	-	-	-	-	-	-	-	-	-	-	-	-
9	Trade credit and advances	2	15	136	-39	20	256	-280	488	-203	-168	4101	...
10	Net equity of households in life insurance and pension fund reserves	1060	1797	2073	2075	2322	2828	2519	2839	2804	3269	-40	...
11	Proprietors' net additions to the accumulation of quasi-corporations	-	-	-	-	-	-	-	-	-	-	-	...
12	Other	29	72	316	256	212	94	94	-273	1486	-312	288	...
	Total Acquisition of Financial Assets	13240	19680	21507	23075	20278	31695	43081	25975	15660	19981	18428	...
					Incurrence of Liabilities								
1	Short term loans, n.e.c.	1063	994	1277	1675	509	1741	2389	3908	2641	1224	-2030	...
2	Long term loans, n.e.c.	7555	10454	11116	12198	13800	21532	38547	22111	8158	3383	-4570	...
	A Mortgages	4670	7251	6833	8864	8764	...	...	...	...	...	...	...
	B Other	2885	3203	4283	3334	5036	...	...	...	...	...	...	...
3	Trade credit and advances	265	480	605	144	502	-98	891	9	-296	-1083	-715	...
4	Other accounts payable	385	416	325	405	-113	1529	378	867	300	642	814	...
5	Other liabilities	...	...	...	...	...	...	...	...	...	...	...	...
	Total Incurrence of Liabilities	9268	12344	13323	14422	14698	24704	42205	26895	10803	4166	-6501	...
	Statistical discrepancy [a]	540	-118	781	3101	1709	310	1481	4849	5525	-3229	-5450	...
	Net Lending	3432	7454	7403	5552	3871	6681	-605	-5769	-668	19044	30379	...
	Incurrence of Liabilities and Net Lending	13240	19680	21507	23075	20278	31695	43081	25975	15660	19981	18428	...

a) Statistical discrepancy refers to adjustment made in order to reconcile the net lending of the Capital Accumulation Account and the Capital Finance Account.

3.42 Private Non-Profit Institutions Serving Households: Income and Outlay Account

Million Finnish markkaa

		1980	1983	1984	1985	1986	1987	1988	1989	1990	1991	1992	1993
						Receipts							
1	Operating surplus	-883	-1420	-1834	-2187	-2260	-2960	-3798	-5881	-5617	-5440	-4221	-3319
2	Property and entrepreneurial income	212	367	465	539	611	644	736	856	988	1067	928	842
	A Withdrawals from quasi-corporations	-	-	-	-	-	-	-	-	-	-	-	-
	B Interest	136	227	255	299	269	298	323	376	508	619	619	563
	C Dividends	59	117	183	211	311	312	372	436	432	400	259	229
	D Net land rent and royalties	17	23	27	29	31	34	41	44	48	48	50	50

Finland

3.42 Private Non-Profit Institutions Serving Households: Income and Outlay Account
(Continued)

Million Finnish markkaa

	1980	1983	1984	1985	1986	1987	1988	1989	1990	1991	1992	1993
3 Current transfers	3941	5886	6409	6984	7644	8323	9234	10194	11393	11533	11250	11538
A Casualty insurance claims	58	88	98	103	110	107	127	146	166	184	173	178
B Current transfers from general government	1683	2535	2619	2822	3147	3550	3924	4370	4995	5404	5270	6001
C Other transfers from resident sectors	2	3	4	4	4	5	5	6	6	6	6	6
D Current transfers received from the rest of the world	2003	2972	3359	3685	3981	4232	4690	5147	5661	5348	5169	4758
E Imputed unfunded employee pension and welfare contributions	195	288	329	370	402	429	488	525	565	591	632	595
Total Current Receipts	3270	4833	5040	5336	5995	6007	6172	5169	6764	7160	7957	9061

Disbursements

	1980	1983	1984	1985	1986	1987	1988	1989	1990	1991	1992	1993
1 Final consumption expenditures	3678	5558	6009	6722	7177	7751	8662	9530	10597	10823	10978	10939
A Compensation of employees	...	...	...	...	...	...	...	...	...	...	...	...
B Consumption of fixed capital	...	...	...	...	...	...	...	...	...	...	...	...
C Purchases of goods and services, net	3678	5558	6009	6722	7177	7751	8662	9530	10597	10823	10978	10939
Purchases	3678	5558	6009	6722	7177	7751	8662	9530	10597	10823	10978	10939
Less: Sales	-	-	-	-	-	-	-	-	-	-	-	-
2 Property income	1045	1436	1679	1797	1737	1812	2197	2690	3380	3917	4365	3884
A Interest	967	1336	1567	1665	1597	1672	2035	2524	3163	3707	4182	3691
B Net land rent and royalties	73	92	102	119	127	129	146	149	198	186	165	193
3 Direct taxes and other transfers to general government	68	182	200	223	250	238	259	307	382	408	412	565
A Direct taxes	68	182	200	223	250	238	259	307	382	408	412	565
B Fees, fines and penalties	-	-	-	-	-	-	-	-	-	-	-	-
4 Other current transfers	382	693	780	817	910	906	1070	1206	1485	1697	1781	1745
A Net casualty insurance premiums	58	88	98	103	110	114	130	153	171	189	173	178
B Social assistance grants	109	260	299	299	362	300	321	350	500	580	630	590
C Unfunded employee pension and welfare benefits	114	176	183	207	238	262	293	319	347	395	410	414
D Current transfers to the rest of the world	46	89	100	106	102	132	171	202	233	235	240	240
E Other current transfers n.e.c.	55	80	100	102	98	98	155	182	234	298	328	323
Net saving	-1903	-3036	-3628	-4223	-4079	-4700	-6016	-8564	-9080	-9685	-9579	-8072
Total Current Disbursements	3270	4833	5040	5336	5995	6007	6172	5169	6764	7160	7957	9061

3.43 Private Non-Profit Institutions Serving Households: Capital Accumulation Account

Million Finnish markkaa

	1980	1983	1984	1985	1986	1987	1988	1989	1990	1991	1992	1993

Finance of Gross Accumulation

	1980	1983	1984	1985	1986	1987	1988	1989	1990	1991	1992	1993
1 Gross saving	448	674	533	424	1047	1057	845	-55	594	172	-553	391
A Consumption of fixed capital	2351	3710	4161	4647	5126	5757	6861	8509	9674	9857	9026	8463
B Net saving	-1903	-3036	-3628	-4223	-4079	-4700	-6016	-8564	-9080	-9685	-9579	-8072
2 Capital transfers [a]	182	245	260	268	287	388	527	555	623	776	917	513
A From resident sectors	182	245	260	268	287	388	527	555	623	776	917	513
Private	-	-	-	-	-	-	-	-	-	-	-	-
Public	182	245	260	268	287	388	527	555	623	776	917	513
B From the rest of the world	-	-	-	-	-	-	-	-	-	-	-	-
Finance of Gross Accumulation	630	919	793	692	1334	1445	1372	500	1217	948	364	904

Gross Accumulation

	1980	1983	1984	1985	1986	1987	1988	1989	1990	1991	1992	1993
1 Gross capital formation	5848	7986	8916	9672	8965	10818	14397	20104	20402	14145	10305	8697

Finland

3.43 Private Non-Profit Institutions Serving Households: Capital Accumulation Account
(Continued)

Million Finnish markkaa

	1980	1983	1984	1985	1986	1987	1988	1989	1990	1991	1992	1993
A Increase in stocks	-	-	-	-	-	-	-	-	-	-	-	-
B Gross fixed capital formation	5848	7986	8916	9672	8965	10818	14397	20104	20402	14145	10305	8697
2 Purchases of land, net	173	219	256	268	237	235	315	162	196	83	73	39
3 Purchases of intangible assets, net	...	...	...	...	...	...	...	...	...	...	...	...
4 Capital transfers [a]	...	...	...	...	...	...	...	...	...	...	...	...
Net lending	-5391	-7286	-8379	-9248	-7868	-9608	-13340	-19766	-19381	-13280	-10014	-7832
Gross Accumulation	630	919	793	692	1334	1445	1372	500	1217	948	364	904

a) Capital transfers received are recorded net of capital transfers paid.

3.44 Private Non-Profit Institutions Serving Households: Capital Finance Account

Million Finnish markkaa

	1980	1983	1984	1985	1986	1987	1988	1989	1990	1991	1992	1993
Acquisition of Financial Assets												
1 Gold	...	...	...	...	...	...	...	...	...	...	...	...
2 Currency and transferable deposits	69	100	76	-41	176	126	92	6	175	644	240	...
3 Other deposits	90	54	143	11	281	365	370	101	1957	331	67	...
4 Bills and bonds, short term	...	...	...	...	...	...	...	...	...	...	...	...
5 Bonds, long term	23	36	64	-40	31	40	49	-5	7	316	588	...
A Corporate, resident	23	36	64	-40	31	40	49	-5	7	316	588	...
B Government	...	...	...	...	...	...	...	...	...	...	...	...
C Rest of the world	-	-	-	-	-	-	-	-	-	-	-	...
6 Corporate equity securities	290	225	251	309	330	251	401	392	143	135	609	...
7 Short-term loans, n.e.c.	48	18	38	-204	-32	205	173	473	-1331	111	274	...
8 Long-term loans, n.e.c.	149	107	84	134	64	127	178	-19	40	1	77	...
9 Other receivables	-187	123	337	-71	88	204	45	170	82	113	171	...
10 Proprietors' net additions to the accumulation of quasi-corporations	-	-	-	-	-	-	-	-	-	-	-	...
11 Other assets	-	-	-	-	-	-	-	-	-	-	-	...
Total Acquisition of Financial Assets	482	663	993	98	938	1318	1308	1118	1073	1651	2026	...
Incurrence of Liabilities												
1 Short-term loans	167	120	423	116	88	297	229	284	302	-6	-191	...
2 Long-term loans	1062	1679	1578	2405	2223	3643	5045	6075	5872	7800	4502	...
3 Other liabilities	4473	5802	6849	6601	6161	6502	8596	13270	12448	6976	7780	...
Total Incurrence of Liabilities	5702	7601	8850	9122	8472	10442	13870	19629	18622	14770	12091	...
Statistical discrepancy [a]	171	348	522	224	334	484	778	1255	1832	161	-51	...
Net Lending	-5391	-7286	-8379	-9248	-7868	-9608	-13340	-19766	-19381	-13280	-10014	...
Incurrence of Liabilities and Net Lending	482	663	993	98	938	1318	1308	1118	1073	1651	2026	...

a) Statistical discrepancy refers to adjustment made in order to reconcile the net lending of the Capital Accumulation Account and the Capital Finance Account.

3.51 External Transactions: Current Account: Detail

Million Finnish markkaa

	1980	1983	1984	1985	1986	1987	1988	1989	1990	1991	1992	1993
Payments to the Rest of the World												
1 Imports of goods and services	65016	81361	86137	94639	89898	97775	109866	125996	126600	112422	121878	133341
A Imports of merchandise c.i.f.	58046	70731	73496	80764	76736	81867	91232	104400	101967	86348	93188	101559
B Other	6970	10630	12641	13875	13162	15908	18634	21596	24633	26074	28690	31782
2 Factor income to the rest of the world	5249	9459	11987	12929	12560	13599	16864	22318	28960	31006	32491	36446

Finland

3.51 External Transactions: Current Account: Detail
(Continued)

Million Finnish markkaa

	1980	1983	1984	1985	1986	1987	1988	1989	1990	1991	1992	1993
A Compensation of employees	48	71	76	79	68	68	75	63	108	156	102	132
B Property and entrepreneurial income	5201	9388	11911	12850	12492	13531	16789	22255	28852	30850	32389	36314
3 Current transfers to the rest of the world	1631	3892	4779	4796	5217	5616	7301	7126	6981	7897	8280	8524
A Indirect taxes by general government to supranational organizations	...	...	...	...	...	...	...	...	...	...	...	...
B Other current transfers	1631	3892	4779	4796	5217	5616	7301	7126	6981	7897	8280	8524
By general government	329	669	871	1060	1189	1447	1764	2170	2434	2946	2506	2245
By other resident sectors [a]	1302	3223	3908	3736	4028	4169	5537	4956	4547	4951	5774	6279
4 Surplus of the nation on current transactions	-5163	-6302	-135	-4683	-3625	-7549	-11331	-24874	-26513	-26697	-22035	-4744
Payments to the Rest of the World, and Surplus of the Nation on Current Transfers	66733	88410	102768	107681	104050	109441	122700	130566	136028	124628	140614	173567

Receipts From The Rest of the World

	1980	1983	1984	1985	1986	1987	1988	1989	1990	1991	1992	1993
1 Exports of goods and services	63489	82735	94190	98034	95634	100048	108750	116702	118828	109289	128272	159438
A Exports of merchandise f.o.b.	52594	67960	78961	82475	81066	83826	91313	98265	99750	91100	105809	132550
B Other	10895	14775	15229	15559	14568	16222	17437	18437	19078	18189	22463	25888
2 Factor income from the rest of the world	2007	3665	4883	6221	4976	5586	8497	11222	15024	14437	12674	13229
A Compensation of employees	413	559	314	334	420	389	495	382	318	296	222	168
B Property and entrepreneurial income	1594	3106	4569	5887	4556	5197	8002	10840	14706	14141	12452	13061
3 Current transfers from the rest of the world	1237	2010	3695	3426	3440	3807	5453	2642	2176	902	-332	900
A Subsidies to general government from supranational organizations	...	...	...	...	...	...	...	...	...	...	...	...
B Other current transfers	1237	2010	3695	3426	3440	3807	5453	2642	2176	902	-332	900
To general government	-	-	-	-	-	-	-	-	-	1	136	1
To other resident sectors [a]	1237	2010	3695	3426	3440	3807	5453	2642	2175	901	-468	899
Receipts from the Rest of the World on Current Transfers	66733	88410	102768	107681	104050	109441	122700	130566	136028	124628	140614	173567

a) All transfers include reinvested earnings.

3.53 External Transactions: Capital Finance Account

Million Finnish markkaa

	1980	1983	1984	1985	1986	1987	1988	1989	1990	1991	1992	1993

Acquisitions of Foreign Financial Assets

	1980	1983	1984	1985	1986	1987	1988	1989	1990	1991	1992	1993
1 Gold and SDR's	127	-132	1072	397	92	46	364	-4	-300	239	-217	...
2 Currency and transferable deposits	3595	1703	18261	-3089	4597	18420	3700	-13017	18544	-8152	-6670	...
3 Other deposits	-22	-104	-2163	566	-203	1806	175	-1009	-651	1550	1468	...
4 Bills and bonds, short term	8	719	1078	709	1278	-1364	1297	-945	375	-1107	827	...
5 Bonds, long term	781	116	-416	3048	4124	2097	1878	-1003	-281	-2	321	...
6 Corporate equity securities	528	917	2745	2069	3585	4352	7511	8979	8299	2653	1593	...
A Subsidiaries abroad	423	...	...	...	...	...	...	...	...	...	...	...
B Other	105	...	...	...	...	...	...	...	...	...	...	...
7 Short-term loans, n.e.c.	122	876	2587	3612	8085	3350	4264	11230	-1045	8710	3654	...
A Subsidiaries abroad	-	-	-	-	-	-	-	-	-	-	-	...
B Other	122	876	2587	3612	8085	3350	4264	11230	-1045	8710	3654	...
8 Long-term loans	167	-34	3314	293	1232	1397	3552	8995	13910	1538	2438	...
A Subsidiaries abroad	64	-3	355	162	620	...	...	...	...	...	...	...
B Other	103	-31	2959	131	612	...	...	...	...	...	...	...
9 Proprietors' net additions to accumulation of quasi-corporate, non-resident enterprises	-	-	-	-	-	-	-	-	-	-	-	...
10 Trade credit and advances	2613	1934	-1801	58	-441	-1339	1235	-507	1663	2696	1385	...
11 Other	303	559	617	-111	1042	126	2754	2618	1880	-	100	...
Total Acquisitions of Foreign Financial Assets	8222	6554	25294	7552	23391	28891	26730	15337	42394	8125	4899	...

Incurrence of Foreign Liabilities

	1980	1983	1984	1985	1986	1987	1988	1989	1990	1991	1992	1993
1 Currency and transferable deposits	5431	7132	10137	2436	9098	32493	12678	-709	17739	-1327	-338	...
2 Other deposits	-	-	-	-	-	-	-	-	-	462	-	...
3 Bills and bonds, short term	358	105	1016	1024	-89	301	1128	164	125	-	4360	...

Finland

3.53 External Transactions: Capital Finance Account
(Continued)

Million Finnish markkaa

		1980	1983	1984	1985	1986	1987	1988	1989	1990	1991	1992	1993
4	Bonds, long term	673	2241	6070	8909	8791	8126	14010	14578	27109	37238	38261	...
5	Corporate equity securities	145	468	1485	870	2755	1117	2879	4044	437	177	1639	...
	A Subsidiaries of non-resident incorporated units	145	88	332	365	1623	...	...	...	...	...	...	...
	B Other	-	380	1153	505	1132	...	...	...	...	...	...	...
6	Short-term loans, n.e.c.	1539	447	6360	1353	13529	-4780	5171	2086	8739	-13462	-22357	...
	A Subsidiaries of non-residents	-	-	-	-	-	-	-	-	-	-	-	...
	B Other	1539	447	6360	1353	13529	-4780	5171	2086	8739	-13462	-22357	...
7	Long-term loans	360	296	-487	-448	-1922	2854	118	8874	19882	12795	2030	...
	A Subsidiaries of non-residents	-41	-	-8	25	...	...	...	...	...	...	...	...
	B Other	401	296	-479	-473	...	...	...	...	...	...	...	...
8	Non-resident proprietors' net additions to accumulation of resident quasi-corporate enterprises	-	-	-	-	-	-	-	-	-	-	-	...
9	Trade credit and advances	4038	1725	-43	-1383	-1633	-558	-238	1379	626	1247	8329	...
10	Other	238	152	567	-28	530	2702	1000	4329	1274	3	40	...
	Total Incurrence of Liabilities	12782	12566	25105	12733	31059	42255	36746	34745	75931	37133	31964	...
	Statistical discrepancy [a]	653	290	368	-498	-4043	-5815	1315	5466	-7024	-2012	-5030	...
	Net Lending	-5213	-6302	-179	-4683	-3625	-7549	-11331	-24874	-26513	-26996	-22035	...
	Total Incurrence of Liabilities and Net Lending [b]	8222	6554	25294	7552	23391	28891	26730	15337	42394	8125	4899	...

a) Statistical discrepancy refers to adjustment made in order to reconcile the net lending of the Capital Accumulation Account and the Capital Finance Account.
b) Total incurrence of liabilities includes allocated Special Drawing Rights.

4.1 Derivation of Value Added by Kind of Activity, in Current Prices

Million Finnish markkaa

		1980 Gross Output	1980 Intermediate Consumption	1980 Value Added	1985 Gross Output	1985 Intermediate Consumption	1985 Value Added	1990 Gross Output	1990 Intermediate Consumption	1990 Value Added	1991 Gross Output	1991 Intermediate Consumption	1991 Value Added
		All Producers											
1	Agriculture, hunting, forestry and fishing	24797	7926	16871	36874	12564	24310	42589	13546	29043	36886	12813	24073
	A Agriculture and hunting	15651	7206	8445	24532	11404	13128	27545	12143	15402	24865	11531	13334
	B Forestry and logging	8681	585	8096	11658	958	10700	14216	1158	13058	11210	1043	10167
	C Fishing	465	135	330	684	202	482	828	245	583	811	239	572
2	Mining and quarrying	1755	827	928	2724	1466	1258	3454	1721	1733	3287	1558	1729
	A Coal mining	...	...	...	...	...	...	...	...	...	...	...	...
	B Crude petroleum and natural gas production	...	...	...	...	...	...	...	...	...	...	...	...
	C Metal ore mining	682	324	358	832	474	358	765	329	436	681	290	391
	D Other mining	1073	503	570	1892	992	900	2689	1392	1297	2606	1268	1338
3	Manufacturing	155064	106501	48563	234387	158743	75644	297738	192355	105383	265223	175556	89667
	A Manufacture of food, beverages and tobacco	26703	21575	5128	42404	33638	8766	51329	38938	12391	50991	37848	13143
	B Textile, wearing apparel and leather industries	9427	5323	4104	11990	6721	5269	9415	5334	4081	7636	4242	3394
	C Manufacture of wood and wood products, including furniture [a]	12195	7942	4253	13272	9495	3777	19280	12719	6561	14869	10402	4467
	D Manufacture of paper and paper products, printing and publishing	31538	20952	10586	49735	33126	16609	64367	42350	22017	59495	41113	18382
	E Manufacture of chemicals and chemical petroleum, coal, rubber and plastic products	25148	19382	5766	35476	27075	8401	36444	24598	11846	33913	22889	11024
	F Manufacture of non-metallic mineral products, except products of petroleum and coal	4446	2472	1974	6897	3829	3068	10770	5653	5117	8932	4824	4108
	G Basic metal industries	11238	8864	2374	16444	13278	3166	19377	14755	4622	17791	13526	4265
	H Manufacture of fabricated metal products, machinery and equipment	30620	18017	12603	53104	29076	24028	79548	44393	35155	65324	37374	27950
	I Other manufacturing industries [a]	3749	1974	1775	5065	2505	2560	7208	3615	3593	6272	3338	2934
4	Electricity, gas and water	18593	13617	4976	29767	21338	8429	32719	23215	9504	33918	22859	11059
	A Electricity, gas and steam	17934	13417	4517	28769	21042	7727	31253	22863	8390	32339	22453	9886
	B Water works and supply	659	200	459	998	296	702	1466	352	1114	1579	406	1173

Finland

4.1 Derivation of Value Added by Kind of Activity, in Current Prices
(Continued)

Million Finnish markkaa

	1980 Gross Output	1980 Intermediate Consumption	1980 Value Added	1985 Gross Output	1985 Intermediate Consumption	1985 Value Added	1990 Gross Output	1990 Intermediate Consumption	1990 Value Added	1991 Gross Output	1991 Intermediate Consumption	1991 Value Added
5 Construction	35640	21948	13692	57201	33979	23222	102189	58722	43467	88306	51344	36962
6 Wholesale and retail trade, restaurants and hotels	40237	17957	22280	67614	28435	39179	103550	45579	57971	97476	45332	52144
A Wholesale and retail trade	33108	13863	19245	54341	20813	33528	81761	32964	48797	76335	32786	43549
B Restaurants and hotels	7129	4094	3035	13273	7622	5651	21789	12615	9174	21141	12546	8595
Restaurants	4946	2878	2068	9206	5362	3844	15106	8905	6201	14819	8891	5928
Hotels and other lodging places	2183	1216	967	4067	2260	1807	6683	3710	2973	6322	3655	2667
7 Transport, storage and communication	23997	10369	13628	40914	17431	23483	62011	25605	36406	60994	24868	36126
A Transport and storage	19589	9442	10147	32606	15716	16890	48814	22407	26407	47167	21390	25777
B Communication	4408	927	3481	8308	1715	6593	13197	3198	9999	13827	3478	10349
8 Finance, insurance, real estate and business services	37304	14168	23136	73708	30391	43317	129306	51095	78211	130960	52131	78829
A Financial institutions [b]	6510	1707	4803	13212	4357	8855	26320	8201	18119	24078	8476	15602
B Insurance	1711	765	946	2395	1414	981	3204	1225	1979	3486	1104	2382
C Real estate and business services	29083	11696	17387	58101	24620	33481	99782	41669	58113	103396	42551	60845
Real estate, except dwellings	5516	3031	2485	11441	6893	4548	19762	11103	8659	20910	12380	8530
Dwellings	15048	4878	10170	27244	8522	18722	39962	11737	28225	45621	12494	33127
9 Community, social and personal services	5828	2326	3502	11154	4631	6523	20208	8126	12082	20515	8160	12355
A Sanitary and similar services	628	235	393	1362	494	868	2629	830	1799	2698	802	1896
B Social and related community services	2167	678	1489	4246	1398	2848	7098	2531	4567	7384	2640	4744
Educational services	281	88	193	480	157	323	785	307	478	763	281	482
Medical, dental, other health and veterinary services	1187	352	835	2585	802	1783	4546	1523	3023	4929	1653	3276
C Recreational and cultural services	2155	1054	1101	3873	2063	1810	7556	3761	3795	7259	3617	3642
D Personal and household services	878	359	519	1673	676	997	2925	1004	1921	3174	1101	2073
Total, Industries	343215	195639	147576	554343	308978	245365	793764	419964	373800	737565	394621	342944
Producers of Government Services	38461	13021	25440	75832	25384	50448	123834	41686	82148	136377	45594	90783
Other Producers	5005	2019	2986	9729	4101	5628	15304	6140	9164	15604	6226	9378
Total	386681	210679	176002	639904	338463	301441	932902	467790	465112	889546	446441	443105
Less: Imputed bank service charge	...	-4682	4682	...	-8023	8023	...	-17000	17000	...	-15329	15329
Import duties [c]	20056	...	20056	38210	...	38210	67318	...	67318	63092	...	63092
Value added tax	...	...	...	...	...	...	...	...	...	...	...	...
Total	406737	215361	191376	678114	346486	331628	1000220	484790	515430	952638	461770	490868

	1992 Gross Output	1992 Intermediate Consumption	1992 Value Added	1993 Gross Output	1993 Intermediate Consumption	1993 Value Added
			All Producers			
1 Agriculture, hunting, forestry and fishing	34435	12967	21468	35156	13208	21948
A Agriculture and hunting	22781	11635	11146	23739	11822	11917
B Forestry and logging	10683	1046	9637	10345	1070	9275
C Fishing	971	286	685	1072	316	756
2 Mining and quarrying	3334	1534	1800	3295	1552	1743
A Coal mining	...	...	...	...	...	...
B Crude petroleum and natural gas production	...	...	...	...	...	...
C Metal ore mining	625	272	353	582	285	297
D Other mining	2709	1262	1447	2713	1267	1446

Finland

4.1 Derivation of Value Added by Kind of Activity, in Current Prices
(Continued)

Million Finnish markkaa

	1992 Gross Output	1992 Intermediate Consumption	1992 Value Added	1993 Gross Output	1993 Intermediate Consumption	1993 Value Added
3 Manufacturing	269231	176805	92426	291994	190032	101962
A Manufacture of food, beverages and tobacco	50034	36879	13155	50830	37100	13730
B Textile, wearing apparel and leather industries	7030	3796	3234	6972	3726	3246
C Manufacture of wood and wood products, including furniture [a]	14754	9709	5045	16612	10527	6085
D Manufacture of paper and paper products, printing and publishing	60356	40579	19777	64837	42291	22546
E Manufacture of chemicals and chemical petroleum, coal, rubber and plastic products	34431	23759	10672	37609	26056	11553
F Manufacture of non-metallic mineral products, except products of petroleum and coal	7443	4135	3308	7187	3956	3231
G Basic metal industries	20928	15567	5361	24128	17964	6164
H Manufacture of fabricated metal products, machinery and equipment	68468	39246	29222	78162	45314	32848
I Other manufacturing industries [a]	5787	3135	2652	5657	3098	2559
4 Electricity, gas and water	35111	24108	11003	37414	26398	11016
A Electricity, gas and steam	33429	23681	9748	35663	25938	9725
B Water works and supply	1682	427	1255	1751	460	1291
5 Construction	69004	42963	26041	57188	37422	19766
6 Wholesale and retail trade, restaurants and hotels	92035	43626	48409	90602	43084	47518
A Wholesale and retail trade	71845	31229	40616	71305	30907	40398
B Restaurants and hotels	20190	12397	7793	19297	12177	7120
Restaurants	14137	8794	5343	13614	8590	5024
Hotels and other lodging places	6053	3603	2450	5683	3587	2096
7 Transport, storage and communication	61240	24756	36484	63133	25577	37556
A Transport and storage	46992	21126	25866	48808	21680	27128
B Communication	14248	3630	10618	14325	3897	10428
8 Finance, insurance, real estate and business services	125262	49759	75503	134836	51470	83366
A Financial institutions [b]	19186	7736	11450	23123	8072	15051
B Insurance	2894	1361	1533	4127	1230	2897
C Real estate and business services	103182	40662	62520	107586	42168	65418
Real estate, except dwellings	20523	12793	7730	21684	13909	7775
Dwellings	49745	12361	37384	54835	13656	41179
9 Community, social and personal services	20950	8212	12738	21187	8237	12950
A Sanitary and similar services	2955	878	2077	3121	902	2219
B Social and related community services	7194	2556	4638	7100	2478	4622
Educational services	772	282	490	791	289	502
Medical, dental, other health and veterinary services	4792	1608	3184	4750	1588	3162
C Recreational and cultural services	7599	3712	3887	7751	3777	3974
D Personal and household services	3202	1066	2136	3215	1080	2135
Total, Industries	710602	384730	325872	734805	396980	337825
Producers of Government Services	137645	46850	90795	145218	59054	86164
Other Producers	15657	6099	9558	15662	6124	9538
Total	863904	437679	426225	895685	462158	433527
Less: Imputed bank service charge	...	-10513	10513	...	-14205	14205
Import duties [c]	61066	...	61066	61148	...	61148
Value added tax	...	...	...	...	...	...
Total	924970	448192	476778	956833	476363	480470

a) Furniture is included in item 'Other manufacturing industries'.
b) Item 'Financial institutions' include activities auxiliary to financial intermediation and insurance.
c) Item 'Import duties' includes also commodity indirect taxes net of subsidies.

Finland

4.2 Derivation of Value Added by Kind of Activity, in Constant Prices

Million Finnish markkaa

	1980 Gross Output	1980 Intermediate Consumption	1980 Value Added	1985 Gross Output	1985 Intermediate Consumption	1985 Value Added	1990 Gross Output	1990 Intermediate Consumption	1990 Value Added	1991 Gross Output	1991 Intermediate Consumption	1991 Value Added
						At constant prices of: 1990 — All Producers						
1 Agriculture, hunting, forestry and fishing	42329	13362	28967	42100	13388	28712	42589	13546	29043	38005	12197	25808
A Agriculture and hunting	26337	12131	14206	26943	12063	14880	27545	12143	15402	25462	10955	14507
B Forestry and logging	15339	1093	14246	14398	1155	13243	14216	1158	13058	11714	998	10716
C Fishing	653	138	515	759	170	589	828	245	583	829	244	585
2 Mining and quarrying	2061	1068	993	2556	1294	1262	3454	1721	1733	3158	1561	1597
A Coal mining	...	...	...	...	...	...	...	...	...	...	...	...
B Crude petroleum and natural gas production	...	...	...	...	...	...	...	...	...	...	...	...
C Metal ore mining	669	345	324	685	341	344	765	329	436	745	320	425
D Other mining	1392	723	669	1871	953	918	2689	1392	1297	2413	1241	1172
3 Manufacturing	228586	150711	77875	260883	170149	90734	297738	192355	105383	270553	176642	93911
A Manufacture of food, beverages and tobacco	44426	34334	10092	48281	37141	11140	51329	38938	12391	50567	38429	12138
B Textile, wearing apparel and leather industries	14295	8188	6107	13910	7925	5985	9415	5334	4081	7617	4305	3312
C Manufacture of wood and wood products, including furniture [a]	18323	12279	6044	16908	11196	5712	19280	12719	6561	15298	10120	5178
D Manufacture of paper and paper products, printing and publishing	46123	30608	15515	54761	36079	18682	64367	42350	22017	61555	40759	20796
E Manufacture of chemicals and chemical petroleum, coal, rubber and plastic products	27033	18726	8307	29799	20169	9630	36444	24598	11846	34993	23836	11157
F Manufacture of non-metallic mineral products, except products of petroleum and coal	7632	4003	3629	8701	4577	4124	10770	5653	5117	9070	4745	4325
G Basic metal industries	13307	10080	3227	16370	12468	3902	19377	14755	4622	19133	14635	4498
H Manufacture of fabricated metal products, machinery and equipment	51390	29455	21935	65913	37463	28450	79548	44393	35155	66000	36647	29353
I Other manufacturing industries [a]	6057	3038	3019	6240	3131	3109	7208	3615	3593	6320	3166	3154
4 Electricity, gas and water	23122	16330	6792	29023	20605	8418	32719	23215	9504	33868	24070	9798
A Electricity, gas and steam	21908	16038	5870	27718	20291	7427	31253	22863	8390	32421	23722	8699
B Water works and supply	1214	292	922	1305	314	991	1466	352	1114	1447	348	1099
5 Construction	78828	46182	32646	83370	48792	34578	102189	58722	43467	90173	51727	38446
6 Wholesale and retail trade, restaurants and hotels	76783	36546	40237	86293	39614	46679	103550	45579	57971	91540	40755	50785
A Wholesale and retail trade	60508	26882	33626	68310	28968	39342	81761	32964	48797	71512	29176	42336
B Restaurants and hotels	16275	9664	6611	17983	10646	7337	21789	12615	9174	20028	11579	8449
Restaurants	11244	6799	4445	12426	7491	4935	15106	8905	6201	13896	8187	5709
Hotels and other lodging places	5031	2865	2166	5557	3155	2402	6683	3710	2973	6132	3392	2740
7 Transport, storage and communication	41572	17175	24397	46859	19592	27267	62011	25605	36406	58693	23645	35048
A Transport and storage	35261	15749	19512	37980	17535	20445	48814	22407	26407	45203	20343	24860
B Communication	6311	1426	4885	8879	2057	6822	13197	3198	9999	13490	3302	10188
8 Finance, insurance, real estate and business services	73996	25925	48071	97904	36230	61674	129306	51095	78211	125749	50207	75542
A Financial institutions [b]	13290	3163	10127	19449	5267	14182	26320	8201	18119	25123	8112	17011
B Insurance	2154	1035	1119	2643	1356	1287	3204	1225	1979	3564	1071	2493
C Real estate and business services	58552	21727	36825	75812	29607	46205	99782	41669	58113	97062	41024	56038
Real estate, except dwellings	10565	4796	5769	14030	7187	6843	19762	11103	8659	20669	12009	8660
Dwellings	27999	8845	19154	33646	10507	23139	39962	11737	28225	41361	12136	29225
9 Community, social and personal services	14189	5254	8935	16484	6274	10210	20208	8126	12082	19213	7839	11374
A Sanitary and similar services	1424	489	935	1932	623	1309	2629	830	1799	2468	740	1728
B Social and related community services	6188	1740	4448	6603	2002	4601	7098	2531	4567	6647	2439	4208

Finland

4.2 Derivation of Value Added by Kind of Activity, in Constant Prices
(Continued)

Million Finnish markkaa

	1980 Gross Output	1980 Intermediate Consumption	1980 Value Added	1985 Gross Output	1985 Intermediate Consumption	1985 Value Added	1990 Gross Output	1990 Intermediate Consumption	1990 Value Added	1991 Gross Output	1991 Intermediate Consumption	1991 Value Added
				At constant prices of: 1990								
Educational services	695	177	518	735	203	532	785	307	478	691	265	426
Medical, dental, other health and veterinary services	3820	1086	2734	4105	1217	2888	4546	1523	3023	4360	1509	2851
C Recreational and cultural services	4540	2312	2228	5554	2811	2743	7556	3761	3795	7094	3613	3481
D Personal and household services	2037	713	1324	2395	838	1557	2925	1004	1921	3004	1047	1957
Total, Industries	581466	312553	268913	665472	355938	309534	793764	419964	373800	730952	388643	342309
Producers of Government Services	86749	23983	62766	105183	31614	73569	123834	41686	82148	127716	44576	83140
Other Producers	10926	3755	7171	13584	5154	8430	15304	6140	9164	15003	6086	8917
Total	679141	340291	338850	784239	392706	391533	932902	467790	465112	873671	439305	434366
Less: Imputed bank service charge	...	-8723	8723	...	-10727	10727	...	-17000	17000	...	-17343	17343
Import duties c	49167	...	49167	55452	...	55452	67318	...	67318	61988	...	61988
Value added tax	...	...	...	...	...	...	...	...	...	...	...	...
Total	728308	349014	379294	839691	403433	436258	1000220	484790	515430	935659	456648	479011

	1992 Gross Output	1992 Intermediate Consumption	1992 Value Added	1993 Gross Output	1993 Intermediate Consumption	1993 Value Added
	At constant prices of: 1990					
	All Producers					
1 Agriculture, hunting, forestry and fishing	37547	12015	25532	38505	11816	26689
A Agriculture and hunting	23435	10713	12722	23841	10500	13341
B Forestry and logging	13138	1015	12123	13650	1017	12633
C Fishing	974	287	687	1014	299	715
2 Mining and quarrying	3163	1601	1562	3084	1560	1524
A Coal mining	...	...	...	...	...	...
B Crude petroleum and natural gas production	...	...	...	...	...	...
C Metal ore mining	662	284	378	621	267	354
D Other mining	2501	1317	1184	2463	1293	1170
3 Manufacturing	276489	180738	95751	290049	189050	100999
A Manufacture of food, beverages and tobacco	50675	38348	12327	51693	38947	12746
B Textile, wearing apparel and leather industries	7016	3959	3057	6858	3883	2975
C Manufacture of wood and wood products, including furniture [a]	15943	10609	5334	18166	12109	6057
D Manufacture of paper and paper products, printing and publishing	62091	41278	20813	65730	43917	21813
E Manufacture of chemicals and chemical petroleum, coal, rubber and plastic products	35759	24426	11333	36390	24787	11603
F Manufacture of non-metallic mineral products, except products of petroleum and coal	7882	4099	3783	7350	3803	3547
G Basic metal industries	21307	16324	4983	22748	17410	5338
H Manufacture of fabricated metal products, machinery and equipment	69878	38720	31158	75229	41249	33980
I Other manufacturing industries [a]	5938	2975	2963	5885	2945	2940
4 Electricity, gas and water	33711	23959	9752	35355	25189	10166
A Electricity, gas and steam	32275	23614	8661	33974	24857	9117
B Water works and supply	1436	345	1091	1381	332	1049
5 Construction	76788	44086	32702	65787	37676	28111
6 Wholesale and retail trade, restaurants and hotels	83049	38246	44803	79059	36488	42571
A Wholesale and retail trade	64163	27172	36991	60856	25793	35063
B Restaurants and hotels	18886	11074	7812	18203	10695	7508
Restaurants	13116	7829	5287	12539	7507	5032
Hotels and other lodging places	5770	3245	2525	5664	3188	2476
7 Transport, storage and communication	57593	22721	34872	58366	22808	35558
A Transport and storage	43673	19285	24388	44278	19301	24977

Finland

4.2 Derivation of Value Added by Kind of Activity, in Constant Prices
(Continued)

Million Finnish markkaa

	1992 Gross Output	1992 Intermediate Consumption	1992 Value Added	1993 Gross Output	1993 Intermediate Consumption	1993 Value Added
				At constant prices of:1990		
B Communication	13920	3436	10484	14088	3507	10581
8 Finance, insurance, real estate and business services	119469	47423	72046	121326	48097	73229
A Financial institutions b	20743	7285	13458	21734	7257	14477
B Insurance	3944	1275	2669	4236	1072	3164
C Real estate and business services	94782	38863	55919	95356	39768	55588
Real estate, except dwellings	21491	12142	9349	22180	12818	9362
Dwellings	42387	12037	30350	44204	13157	31047
9 Community, social and personal services	18805	7642	11163	18673	7544	11129
A Sanitary and similar services	2495	786	1709	2472	781	1691
B Social and related community services	6140	2264	3876	5928	2140	3788
Educational services	689	260	429	720	264	456
Medical, dental, other health and veterinary services	3970	1395	2575	3821	1336	2485
C Recreational and cultural services	7182	3597	3585	7299	3624	3675
D Personal and household services	2988	995	1993	2974	999	1975
Total, Industries	706614	378431	328183	710204	380228	329976
Producers of Government Services	126381	45052	81329	121715	44159	77556
Other Producers	14812	5863	8949	14535	5658	8877
Total	847807	429346	418461	846454	430045	416409
Less: Imputed bank service charge	...	-14339	14339	...	-15585	15585
Import duties c	57881	...	57881	53808	...	53808
Value added tax	...	...	...	...	...	...
Total	905688	443685	462003	900262	445630	454632

a) Furniture is included in item 'Other manufacturing industries'.
b) Item 'Financial institutions' include activities auxiliary to financial intermediation and insurance.
c) Item 'Import duties' includes also commodity indirect taxes net of subsidies.

4.3 Cost Components of Value Added

Million Finnish markkaa

	1980 Compensation of Employees	1980 Capital Consumption	1980 Net Operating Surplus	1980 Indirect Taxes	1980 Less: Subsidies Received	1980 Value Added	1985 Compensation of Employees	1985 Capital Consumption	1985 Net Operating Surplus	1985 Indirect Taxes	1985 Less: Subsidies Received	1985 Value Added
				All Producers								
1 Agriculture, hunting, forestry and fishing	3020	3523	11084	90	846	16871	4351	5539	16266	174	2020	24310
A Agriculture and hunting	1026	2462	5703	76	822	8445	1625	3902	9424	145	1968	13128
B Forestry and logging	1978	962	5164	4	12	8096	2691	1506	6518	8	23	10700
C Fishing	16	99	217	10	12	330	35	131	324	21	29	482
2 Mining and quarrying	506	168	289	3	38	928	742	273	260	8	25	1258
A Coal mining	...	...	...	...	...	...	...	...	...	...	...	...
B Crude petroleum and natural gas production	...	...	...	...	...	...	...	...	...	...	...	...
C Metal ore mining	289	124	-21	1	35	358	340	160	-122	2	22	358
D Other mining	217	44	310	2	3	570	402	113	382	6	3	900

Finland

4.3 Cost Components of Value Added
(Continued)

Million Finnish markkaa

	1980						1985					
	Compensation of Employees	Capital Consumption	Net Operating Surplus	Indirect Taxes	Less: Subsidies Received	Value Added	Compensation of Employees	Capital Consumption	Net Operating Surplus	Indirect Taxes	Less: Subsidies Received	Value Added
3 Manufacturing	30073	5629	13020	348	507	48563	46792	9628	19121	811	708	75644
A Manufacture of food, beverages and tobacco	3350	674	1105	40	41	5128	5209	1159	2355	84	41	8766
B Textile, wearing apparel and leather industries	2804	268	1050	24	42	4104	3750	440	1115	50	86	5269
C Manufacture of wood and wood products, including furniture [a]	2485	412	1371	29	44	4253	3013	647	92	64	39	3777
D Manufacture of paper and paper products, printing and publishing	5931	1745	2950	79	119	10586	9682	3029	3854	186	142	16609
E Manufacture of chemicals and chemical petroleum, coal, rubber and plastic products	2336	707	2709	33	19	5766	3815	1197	3367	75	53	8401
F Manufacture of non-metallic mineral products, except products of petroleum and coal	1151	209	617	10	13	1974	1884	376	807	22	21	3068
G Basic metal industries	1304	406	673	26	35	2374	2014	654	467	55	24	3166
H Manufacture of fabricated metal products, machinery and equipment	9578	1070	2028	98	171	12603	15857	1896	6294	251	270	24028
I Other manufacturing industries [a]	1134	138	517	9	23	1775	1568	230	770	24	32	2560
4 Electricity, gas and water	1783	1784	1448	27	66	4976	3067	3000	2392	34	64	8429
A Electricity, gas and steam	1608	1514	1435	25	65	4517	2791	2570	2396	32	62	7727
B Water works and supply	175	270	13	2	1	459	276	430	-4	2	2	702
5 Construction	10206	850	2612	30	6	13692	17349	1242	4459	182	10	23222
6 Wholesale and retail trade, restaurants and hotels	16009	2463	3676	157	25	22280	26192	4202	8390	487	92	39179
A Wholesale and retail trade	13602	2219	3282	148	6	19245	22009	3769	7324	454	28	33528
B Restaurants and hotels	2407	244	394	9	19	3035	4183	433	1066	33	64	5651
Restaurants	1681	140	246	6	5	2068	2916	240	684	23	19	3844
Hotels and other lodging places	726	104	148	3	14	967	1267	193	382	10	45	1807
7 Transport, storage and communication	7648	4265	1580	142	7	13628	13042	6231	3969	264	23	23483
A Transport and storage	5429	3401	1184	140	7	10147	8985	4839	2831	258	23	16890
B Communication	2219	864	396	2	-	3481	4057	1392	1138	6	-	6593
8 Finance, insurance, real estate and business services	7932	6986	8198	65	45	23136	15517	13389	14271	216	76	43317
A Financial institutions [b]	2811	397	1614	8	27	4803	5403	762	2722	15	47	8855
B Insurance	721	77	151	-	3	946	1240	174	-439	10	4	981
C Real estate and business services	4400	6512	6433	57	15	17387	8874	12453	11988	191	25	33481
Real estate, except dwellings	1126	432	917	10	-	2485	2008	953	1540	47	-	4548
Dwellings	-	5814	4315	41	-	10170	-	10913	7711	101	3	18722
9 Community, social and personal services	1911	536	1076	22	43	3502	3648	1005	1972	64	166	6523
A Sanitary and similar services	153	319	-82	4	1	393	359	623	-106	12	20	868
B Social and related community services	685	68	748	6	18	1489	1357	119	1389	19	36	2848
Educational services	143	41	15	-	6	193	233	66	36	-	12	323
Medical, dental, other health and veterinary services	310	19	500	6	-	835	698	38	1028	19	-	1783
C Recreational and cultural services	829	101	187	5	21	1101	1459	201	243	14	107	1810
D Personal and household services	244	48	223	7	3	519	473	62	446	19	3	997
Total, Industries	79088	26204	42983	884	1583	147576	130700	44509	71100	2240	3184	245365
Producers of Government Services	23526	1905	-	9	-	25440	46868	3566	-	14	-	50448
Other Producers	2750	234	-	2	-	2986	5175	441	-	12	-	5628
Total	105364	28343	42983	895	1583	176002	182743	48516	71100	2266	3184	301441
Less: Imputed bank service charge	...	...	4682	...	...	4682	...	...	8023	...	...	8023
Import duties	...	...	...	...	...	20056	...	...	...	...	...	38210
Value added tax	...	...	...	...	...	...	...	...	...	...	...	...
Other adjustments	-1300	...	1300	24698	4642	...	584	...	-584	45373	7163	...
Total	104064	28343	39601	25593	6225	191376	183327	48516	62493	47639	10347	331628

Finland

4.3 Cost Components of Value Added

Million Finnish markkaa

		1990					1991				
	Compensation of Employees	Capital Consumption	Net Operating Surplus	Indirect Taxes	Less: Subsidies Received	Value Added	Compensation of Employees	Capital Consumption	Net Operating Surplus	Indirect Taxes	Less: Subsidies Received	Value Added

All Producers

	Comp. Emp. 1990	Cap. Cons. 1990	Net Op. Surp. 1990	Ind. Tax 1990	Subs. 1990	VA 1990	Comp. Emp. 1991	Cap. Cons. 1991	Net Op. Surp. 1991	Ind. Tax 1991	Subs. 1991	VA 1991
1 Agriculture, hunting, forestry and fishing	5109	7215	20832	151	4264	29043	5180	7260	16752	145	5264	24073
A Agriculture and hunting	2173	4909	12392	110	4182	15402	2435	4826	11119	105	5151	13334
B Forestry and logging	2898	2164	8016	11	31	13058	2704	2290	5215	10	52	10167
C Fishing	38	142	424	30	51	583	41	144	418	30	61	572
2 Mining and quarrying	659	381	714	15	36	1733	671	386	696	13	37	1729
A Coal mining	...	...	...	...	...	...	...	...	...	...	...	...
B Crude petroleum and natural gas production	...	...	...	...	...	...	...	...	...	...	...	...
C Metal ore mining	168	190	89	3	14	436	177	185	42	3	16	391
D Other mining	491	191	625	12	22	1297	494	201	654	10	21	1338
3 Manufacturing	64538	14935	26493	589	1172	105383	60912	15779	13699	540	1263	89667
A Manufacture of food, beverages and tobacco	7458	1784	3147	62	60	12391	7380	1846	3925	56	64	13143
B Textile, wearing apparel and leather industries	3189	587	372	23	90	4081	2721	586	153	19	85	3394
C Manufacture of wood and wood products, including furniture [a]	4084	865	1653	55	96	6561	3474	898	125	52	82	4467
D Manufacture of paper and paper products, printing and publishing	13936	5118	3039	138	214	22017	13665	5641	-829	132	227	18382
E Manufacture of chemicals and chemical petroleum, coal, rubber and plastic products	5785	1824	4252	65	80	11846	5828	1896	3322	61	83	11024
F Manufacture of non-metallic mineral products, except products of petroleum and coal	2927	611	1591	22	34	5117	2623	643	860	22	40	4108
G Basic metal industries	2670	959	988	32	27	4622	2565	992	699	31	22	4265
H Manufacture of fabricated metal products, machinery and equipment	22325	2874	10324	171	539	35155	20634	2962	4823	145	614	27950
I Other manufacturing industries [a]	2164	313	1127	21	32	3593	2022	315	621	22	46	2934
4 Electricity, gas and water	4449	4535	530	54	64	9504	4590	4766	1743	51	91	11059
A Electricity, gas and steam	4091	3913	373	50	37	8390	4202	4111	1593	48	68	9886
B Water works and supply	358	622	157	4	27	1114	388	655	150	3	23	1173
5 Construction	30780	1946	10622	194	75	43467	27903	2061	6876	174	52	36962
6 Wholesale and retail trade, restaurants and hotels	42044	7203	8457	563	296	57971	40207	7568	4143	511	285	52144
A Wholesale and retail trade	34923	6563	6921	520	130	48797	33469	6892	2785	473	70	43549
B Restaurants and hotels	7121	640	1536	43	166	9174	6738	676	1358	38	215	8595
Restaurants	4944	318	957	30	48	6201	4674	338	951	27	62	5928
Hotels and other lodging places	2177	322	579	13	118	2973	2064	338	407	11	153	2667
7 Transport, storage and communication	20915	7835	7413	371	128	36406	20381	8011	7580	396	242	36126
A Transport and storage	14578	5756	5841	353	121	26407	13931	5828	5846	380	208	25777
B Communication	6337	2079	1572	18	7	9999	6450	2183	1734	16	34	10349
8 Finance, insurance, real estate and business services	29907	26202	21982	458	338	78211	30164	26837	21824	415	411	78829
A Financial institutions [b]	9236	1421	7517	17	72	18119	9293	1466	4909	16	82	15602
B Insurance	2069	317	-405	3	5	1979	2037	332	16	3	6	2382
C Real estate and business services	18602	24464	14870	438	261	58113	18834	25039	16899	396	323	60845
Real estate, except dwellings	3347	2926	2241	147	2	8659	3372	3115	1918	129	4	8530
Dwellings	-	19845	8372	114	106	28225	-	20067	13082	99	121	33127
9 Community, social and personal services	6546	1808	3850	136	258	12082	6658	1972	3910	137	322	12355
A Sanitary and similar services	690	1014	83	28	16	1799	697	1069	114	30	14	1896
B Social and related community services	2524	245	1871	40	113	4567	2576	274	2021	40	167	4744

Finland

4.3 Cost Components of Value Added
(Continued)

Million Finnish markkaa

	1990						1991					
	Compensation of Employees	Capital Consumption	Net Operating Surplus	Indirect Taxes	Less: Subsidies Received	Value Added	Compensation of Employees	Capital Consumption	Net Operating Surplus	Indirect Taxes	Less: Subsidies Received	Value Added
Educational services	380	107	24	5	38	478	344	110	88	5	65	482
Medical, dental, other health and veterinary services	1394	95	1504	35	5	3023	1487	111	1648	35	5	3276
C Recreational and cultural services	2524	474	850	31	84	3795	2527	542	645	30	102	3642
D Personal and household services	808	75	1046	37	45	1921	858	87	1130	37	39	2073
Total, Industries	204947	72060	100893	2531	6631	373800	196666	74640	77223	2382	7967	342944
Producers of Government Services	75449	6673	-	26	-	82148	84015	6743	-	25	-	90783
Other Producers	8360	779	-	25	-	9164	8567	787	-	24	-	9378
Total	288756	79512	100893	2582	6631	465112	289248	82170	77223	2431	7967	443105
Less: Imputed bank service charge	...	...	17000	...	...	17000	...	...	15329	...	...	15329
Import duties	...	...	...	...	...	67318	...	...	...	...	...	63092
Value added tax	...	...	...	...	...	...	...	...	...	...	...	...
Other adjustments	12	...	-12	75443	8125	...	527	...	-527	72299	9207	...
Total	288768	79512	83881	78025	14756	515430	289775	82170	61367	74730	17174	490868

	1992						1993					
	Compensation of Employees	Capital Consumption	Net Operating Surplus	Indirect Taxes	Less: Subsidies Received	Value Added	Compensation of Employees	Capital Consumption	Net Operating Surplus	Indirect Taxes	Less: Subsidies Received	Value Added

All Producers

1 Agriculture, hunting, forestry and fishing	4701	7133	15084	135	5585	21468	4487	7098	15009	130	4776	21948
A Agriculture and hunting	2287	4735	9504	99	5479	11146	2183	4717	9616	93	4692	11917
B Forestry and logging	2367	2251	5060	9	50	9637	2255	2227	4818	8	33	9275
C Fishing	47	147	520	27	56	685	49	154	575	29	51	756
2 Mining and quarrying	642	371	809	12	34	1800	625	369	772	10	33	1743
A Coal mining	...	...	...	...	...	...	...	...	...	...	...	...
B Crude petroleum and natural gas production	...	...	...	...	...	...	...	...	...	...	...	...
C Metal ore mining	172	162	27	2	10	353	160	146	-1	2	10	297
D Other mining	470	209	782	10	24	1447	465	223	773	8	23	1446
3 Manufacturing	57142	16611	19651	488	1466	92426	56280	17571	29495	491	1875	101962
A Manufacture of food, beverages and tobacco	7167	1978	4037	51	78	13155	6844	2098	4818	48	78	13730
B Textile, wearing apparel and leather industries	2267	595	449	17	94	3234	2099	601	592	15	61	3246
C Manufacture of wood and wood products, including furniture [a]	3156	929	987	48	75	5045	3262	961	1973	54	165	6085
D Manufacture of paper and paper products, printing and publishing	12996	6022	846	119	206	19777	12836	6468	3456	122	336	22546
E Manufacture of chemicals and chemical petroleum, coal, rubber and plastic products	5606	1961	3154	55	104	10672	5758	2060	3795	63	123	11553
F Manufacture of non-metallic mineral products, except products of petroleum and coal	2170	661	496	20	39	3308	1961	682	642	18	72	3231
G Basic metal industries	2620	1062	1684	28	33	5361	2685	1119	2426	32	98	6164
H Manufacture of fabricated metal products, machinery and equipment	19394	3081	7387	131	771	29222	19178	3245	10966	121	662	32848
I Other manufacturing industries [a]	1766	322	611	19	66	2652	1657	337	827	18	280	2559
4 Electricity, gas and water	4572	4907	1561	46	83	11003	4332	5124	1659	51	150	11016
A Electricity, gas and steam	4195	4255	1318	43	63	9748	3963	4470	1358	48	114	9725
B Water works and supply	377	652	243	3	20	1255	369	654	301	3	36	1291
5 Construction	23122	2110	711	158	60	26041	19076	2114	-1487	140	77	19766
6 Wholesale and retail trade, restaurants and hotels	36904	7728	3780	462	465	48409	35924	8214	3287	431	338	47518
A Wholesale and retail trade	30749	7046	2615	428	222	40616	30071	7522	2588	402	185	40398
B Restaurants and hotels	6155	682	1165	34	243	7793	5853	692	699	29	153	7120
Restaurants	4335	349	705	24	70	5343	4078	365	604	21	44	5024
Hotels and other lodging places	1820	333	460	10	173	2450	1775	327	95	8	109	2096
7 Transport, storage and communication	20007	8345	8051	359	278	36484	19348	9017	9025	402	236	37556

Finland

4.3 Cost Components of Value Added
(Continued)

Million Finnish markkaa

	1992						1993					
	Compensation of Employees	Capital Consumption	Net Operating Surplus	Indirect Taxes	Less: Subsidies Received	Value Added	Compensation of Employees	Capital Consumption	Net Operating Surplus	Indirect Taxes	Less: Subsidies Received	Value Added
A Transport and storage	13529	6013	6223	345	244	25866	13384	6517	7065	389	227	27128
B Communication	6478	2332	1828	14	34	10618	5964	2500	1960	13	9	10428
8 Finance, insurance, real estate and business services	28333	25175	21970	371	346	75503	27496	24301	31587	331	349	83366
A Financial institutions b	8673	1460	1425	14	122	11450	8122	1461	5653	12	197	15051
B Insurance	1994	337	-793	3	8	1533	1961	349	591	3	7	2897
C Real estate and business services	17666	23378	21338	354	216	62520	17413	22491	25343	316	145	65418
Real estate, except dwellings	3674	3041	907	117	9	7730	3890	3016	769	102	2	7775
Dwellings	-	18361	18933	90	-	37384	-	17332	23770	77	...	41179
9 Community, social and personal services	6648	2091	4209	123	333	12738	6650	2212	4188	123	223	12950
A Sanitary and similar services	716	1095	254	27	15	2077	712	1152	381	28	54	2219
B Social and related community services	2576	301	1923	36	198	4638	2538	324	1843	35	118	4622
Educational services	333	117	114	3	77	490	341	124	80	3	46	502
Medical, dental, other health and veterinary services	1496	124	1549	33	18	3184	1496	132	1513	32	11	3162
C Recreational and cultural services	2539	598	819	27	96	3887	2558	632	799	26	41	3974
D Personal and household services	817	97	1213	33	24	2136	842	104	1165	34	10	2135
Total, Industries	182071	74471	75826	2154	8650	325872	174218	76020	93535	2109	8057	337825
Producers of Government Services	84141	6631	-	23	-	90795	79397	6748	-	19	-	86164
Other Producers	8746	790	-	22	-	9558	8720	800	-	18	-	9538
Total	274958	81892	75826	2199	8650	426225	262335	83568	93535	2146	8057	433527
Less: Imputed bank service charge	...	...	10513	...	...	10513	...	...	14205	...	...	14205
Import duties	...	...	...	...	...	61066	...	...	...	...	...	61148
Value added tax	...	...	...	...	...	...	...	...	...	...	...	...
Other adjustments	-1342	...	1342	69444	8378	...	-4247	...	4247	69410	8262	...
Total	273616	81892	66655	71643	17028	476778	258088	83568	83577	71556	16319	480470

a) Furniture is included in item 'Other manufacturing industries'.
b) Item 'Financial institutions' include activities auxiliary to financial intermediation and insurance.

Former Ethiopia

General note. The preparation of national accounts statistics in Ethiopia is undertaken by the Central Statistical Office, Addis Ababa. The official estimates with methodological notes are published annually in the 'Statistical Abstract'. The estimates are generally in accordance with the classifications and definitions recommended in the United Nations Systems of National Accounts (SNA). The following tables have been prepared from successive replies to the United Nations national accounts questionnaire. The Ethiopian Fiscal year which is from June to July has been used for all estimates except the 'External Transactions' table. When the scope and coverage of the estimates differ for conceptual or statistical reasons from the definitions and classifications recommended in SNA, a footnote is indicated to the relevant tables.

Sources and methods :

(a) Gross domestic product. Gross domestic product is estimated mainly through the production approach.

(b) Expenditure on the gross domestic product. The expenditure approach is used to estimate government final consumption expenditure and exports and imports of goods and services. This approach, in combination with the commodity-flow approach, is also used for estimating gross fixed capital formation. Private consumption expenditure is obtained as a residual which also includes increase in stocks. Government final consumption expenditure, consisting of compensation of employees and net purchases of goods and services, is obtained from the annual Budgetary Revenue and Expenditure report, from the Ministry of Finance and from municipalities. These sources are also used for estimating the public sector's capital formation in building and construction. The estimates of private construction in urban areas are based on building permits which are adjusted for timing by taking the average of the last two years and adding 5 percent for underreporting. Other urban private construction is estimated by applying the ratio of per capita consumption expenditure in Addis Ababa to the per capita consumption expenditure in other urban areas. Construction in the rural areas is estimated by multiplying the assumed number of tukuls built in a given year by an assumed average cost per tukul. For capital formation in machinery and equipment, import statistics are used. To the import values are added import duties, transport costs, trade margins and installation costs. The data on exports and imports of goods and services are obtained from the external trade statistics. GDP by expenditure type at constant prices is not estimated.

(c) Cost-structure of the gross domestic product. The cost-structure of the gross domestic product is not estimated.

(d) Gross domestic product by kind of economic activity. The table of GDP by kind of economic activity is prepared in factor values. The production approach is used to estimate value added of most industries. The income approach is also used in measuring the output of the modern sectors of the economy such as the industrial activity and the services sectors. The estimates of the value added of agriculture for the bench-mark years 1961-1963 are based on various sources such as population figures, assumed per capita consumption of food grains and wholesale prices. Recent years' estimates are also based on qualitative crop surveys and surveys on cultivated area. The net output by type of plant product is multiplied by wholesale prices adjusted for trade and transport margins. The 1961-1963 bench-mark estimates of livestock production were based on the number of livestock by type, on gross output and on value added. For subsequent years, gross output and value added are derived by applying growth factors linked to the population growth rate. For forestry, the sources include the Forestry Dept., the survey of wood working industries, family budget studies in 1967/68 and the annual surveys of manufacturing industries. Value added is derived by deducting 10 percent from gross value of production of industrial wood and firewood. The Ministry of Mines and the annual budgetary reports provide data for the mining sector. The value of production is estimated by multiplying the quantity produced of each mineral product by its average price. The source of data for large-scale manufacturing is the annual surveys of manufacturing industries. Values added is obtained by deducting the cost of inputs of raw materials, fuel and energy from the gross value of production. For small scale manufacturing and handicraft, value added is derived by assuming that the growth rate is half of the one observed for output of large-scale manufacturing. Data for electricity are obtained from annual returns to questionnaires submitted to concerned enterprises. Data on the number of building permits issued, the 1968 household expenditure survey and population estimates are used to estimate the value of construction in the private sector. The total value of Addis Ababa building permits is adjusted for timing and underreporting. Work done in other towns is estimated by applying the ratio of per capita consumption expenditure in Addis Ababa to the per capita consumption expenditure in other towns. For the public sector, data are obtained from the Budgetary Revenue and Expenditure reports as well as from questionnaires sent to municipalities and public agencies. The gross trade margin of imported goods is estimated at 15 percent of the value of imports based on the 1963 trade inquiry. Similar assumptions are made for locally produced goods. Value added in the transport sector is based on the annual reports of concerned enterprises for the railway, water and air transports. For road transport, data on passenger or ton kilometres, registration statistics, and passenger fares and freight rates are used. For the financial institutions the profit and loss statement and the annual reports of concerned institutions are used. Bench-mark estimates for 1961-1963 are available for ownership of dwellings. The gross rental income of the urban areas is obtained by multiplying the total number of housing units by assumed actual and imputed average annual rental rates, while for the rural areas the total number of tukuls is multiplied by the assumed average value per tukul. Value added of public administration and defence is equal to total wages and salaries paid to government employees, including payment in kind. The sources of data include annual reports and questionnaires sent to different agencies. For other government services such as education and health, value added is based on government reports. Value added per student enrolled in non-governmental schools is estimated as two-thirds of the value added per student in government schools. The value of domestic services is obtained by multiplying the number of employees by assumed average pay rates. For the constant price estimates, the current net output of plant products in the agricultural sector is revalued at base-year producer prices. For livestock, water supply and construction, value added at current factor costs is assumed to be equal to the value added at constant factor costs. Price indexes are used to deflate the the current value added of mining and quarrying, small-scale manufacturing, trade, finance and most of the services sectors. For large-scale manufacturing, electricity, transport and domestic services, value added is extrapolated by volume indexes.

1.1 Expenditure on the Gross Domestic Product, in Current Prices

Million Birr — Fiscal year ending 7 July

	1980	1983	1984	1985	1986	1987	1988	1989	1990	1991	1992	1993
1 Government final consumption expenditure	1293.2	1997.0	1879.0	1957.0	2103.0	2230.0	2846.0	3040.0	3386.0	3753.0	2165.0	...
2 Private final consumption expenditure	6794.6	7371.0	7431.0	7529.0	8376.0	8623.0	8421.0	8768.0	8856.0	9321.0	11706.0	...
3 Gross capital formation	854.0	1240.0	1570.0	1541.0	1563.0	1797.0	1873.0	1661.0	1535.0	1421.0	1215.0	...
A Increase in stocks	...	...	...	...	...	...	...	...	...	...	...	...
B Gross fixed capital formation	854.0	1240.0	1570.0	1541.0	1563.0	1797.0	1873.0	1661.0	1535.0	1421.0	1215.0	...
4 Exports of goods and services	1209.5	1142.0	1267.0	1137.0	1371.0	1290.0	1353.0	1436.0	1369.0	1450.0	1039.0	...
5 Less: Imports of goods and services	1652.4	1991.0	2311.0	2240.0	2508.0	2541.0	2592.0	2534.0	2613.0	2613.0	2617.0	...
Equals: Gross Domestic Product	8498.9	9759.0	9836.0	9924.0	10905.0	11399.0	11901.0	12371.0	12533.0	13332.0	13508.0	...

1.10 Gross Domestic Product by Kind of Activity, in Current Prices

Million Birr — Fiscal year ending 7 July

	1980	1983	1984	1985	1986	1987	1988	1989	1990	1991	1992	1993
1 Agriculture, hunting, forestry and fishing	3906.9	4383.5	3955.4	3863.8	4370.4	4361.6	4307.6	4594.7	4699.6	5039.8	6311.3	...
2 Mining and quarrying	8.1	9.7	12.0	15.1	15.3	12.0	14.3	14.5	21.7	36.6	39.5	...
3 Manufacturing	830.0	923.0	929.0	1003.1	1058.9	1267.7	1254.9	1286.8	1265.4	1263.7	1138.0	...
4 Electricity, gas and water	55.4	62.0	67.6	73.6	109.9	134.8	143.8	159.0	171.2	181.6	163.4	...
5 Construction	295.9	362.0	406.0	401.2	416.3	444.1	442.1	439.7	415.5	394.4	346.2	...
6 Wholesale and retail trade, restaurants and hotels [a]	812.2	980.4	997.5	962.1	1036.3	1056.9	1080.2	1119.8	1098.3	1152.5	1279.5	...
7 Transport, storage and communication	355.1	523.0	564.8	614.0	723.9	701.4	718.8	783.0	826.1	875.7	678.5	...
8 Finance, insurance, real estate and business services [b]	444.7	604.6	572.2	618.0	614.1	678.2	758.5	745.9	753.4	957.9	987.6	...
9 Community, social and personal services [a,b]	445.2	484.7	525.8	563.0	602.6	654.2	676.5	708.5	748.3	787.9	690.1	...
Total, Industries	7153.5	8332.9	8030.3	8113.9	8947.7	9311.1	9396.7	9851.9	9999.5	10690.1	11634.5	...
Producers of Government Services	535.3	721.0	739.7	815.3	869.0	915.9	1175.3	1277.3	1436.7	1604.8	909.4	...

Former Ethiopia

1.10 Gross Domestic Product by Kind of Activity, in Current Prices
(Continued)

Million Birr — Fiscal year ending 7 July

	1980	1983	1984	1985	1986	1987	1988	1989	1990	1991	1992	1993
Other Producers	...	...	...	...	...	...	...	...	...	...	...	...
Subtotal c	7688.8	9053.9	8770.0	8929.2	9816.7	10227.0	10572.0	11129.2	11436.2	12294.9	12543.5	...
Less: Imputed bank service charge	...	...	...	...	...	...	...	...	...	...	...	...
Plus: Import duties	...	...	...	...	...	...	...	...	...	...	...	...
Plus: Value added tax	...	...	...	...	...	...	...	...	...	...	...	...
Plus: Other adjustments d	810.1	705.1	1066.0	994.8	1088.3	1172.0	1329.0	1241.8	1096.8	1037.1	964.5	...
Equals: Gross Domestic Product	8498.9	9759.0	9836.0	9924.0	10905.0	11399.0	11901.0	12371.0	12533.0	13332.0	13508.0	...

a) Restaurants and hotels are included in item 'Community, social and personal services'.
b) Business services are included in item 'Community, social and personal services'.
c) Gross domestic product in factor values.
d) Item 'Other adjustments' refers to indirect taxes net of subsidies.

1.11 Gross Domestic Product by Kind of Activity, in Constant Prices

Million Birr — Fiscal year ending 7 July

	1980	1983	1984	1985	1986	1987	1988	1989	1990	1991	1992	1993
At constant prices of: 1981												
1 Agriculture, hunting, forestry and fishing	3969.8	4204.2	3685.7	3125.3	3480.6	4008.7	3923.7	4011.4	4020.5	4042.7	6701.9	...
2 Mining and quarrying	8.1	9.1	11.3	14.1	14.2	11.1	13.2	13.4	19.6	39.9	48.4	...
3 Manufacturing	834.3	952.5	994.8	1009.3	1041.4	1096.1	1114.9	1136.6	1089.1	902.3	1370.4	...
4 Electricity, gas and water	55.6	69.4	74.5	81.2	85.6	91.9	98.9	102.0	107.0	101.7	169.0	...
5 Construction	319.2	345.1	379.5	368.9	374.8	389.5	377.9	359.6	322.2	257.8	355.2	...
6 Wholesale and retail trade, restaurants and hotels a	828.5	934.3	938.4	887.4	938.6	1013.2	1025.8	1049.6	1005.1	912.6	1753.3	...
7 Transport, storage and communication	350.9	411.9	429.2	469.2	525.6	526.9	570.3	577.8	592.3	526.7	751.2	...
8 Finance, insurance, real estate and business services b	466.2	593.3	559.6	589.9	579.5	645.5	717.3	693.9	692.1	689.7	844.1	...
9 Community, social and personal services ab	457.3	436.0	448.3	459.9	474.9	500.8	521.6	539.2	554.7	570.8	1025.4	...
Total, Industries	7289.9	7955.8	7521.3	7005.2	7515.2	8283.7	8363.6	8483.5	8402.6	8044.2	13018.9	...
Producers of Government Services	564.7	654.6	663.8	698.7	721.6	740.5	829.2	858.3	898.4	935.2	1012.7	...
Other Producers	...	...	...	...	...	...	...	...	...	...	...	...
Subtotal c	7854.6	8610.4	8185.1	7703.9	8236.8	9024.2	9192.8	9341.8	9301.0	8979.4	14031.6	...
Less: Imputed bank service charge	...	...	...	...	...	...	...	...	...	...	...	...
Plus: Import duties	...	...	...	...	...	...	...	...	...	...	...	...
Plus: Value added tax	...	...	...	...	...	...	...	...	...	...	...	...
Equals: Gross Domestic Product c	7854.6	8610.4	8185.1	7703.9	8236.8	9024.2	9192.8	9341.8	9301.0	8979.4	14031.6	...

a) Restaurants and hotels are included in item 'Community, social and personal services'.
b) Business services are included in item 'Community, social and personal services'.
c) Gross domestic product in factor values.

1.12 Relations Among National Accounting Aggregates

Million Birr — Fiscal year ending 7 July

	1980	1983	1984	1985	1986	1987	1988	1989	1990	1991	1992	1993
Gross Domestic Product	...	9759.0	9836.0	9924.0	10905.0	11399.0	11901.0	12371.0	12533.0	13332.0	13508.0	...
Plus: Net factor income from the rest of the world	...	-28.0	-40.0	-68.0	-60.0	-77.0	-139.0	-156.0	-94.0	-97.0	-84.0	...
Equals: Gross National Product	...	9731.0	9796.0	9856.0	10845.0	11322.0	11762.0	12215.0	12439.0	13235.0	13424.0	...
Less: Consumption of fixed capital	...	...	...	...	...	...	...	...	...	...	...	...
Equals: National Income	...	...	...	...	...	...	...	...	...	...	...	...
Plus: Net current transfers from the rest of the world	...	...	...	...	...	...	...	...	...	...	...	...
Equals: National Disposable Income	...	...	...	...	...	...	...	...	...	...	...	...
Less: Final consumption	...	...	...	...	...	...	...	...	...	...	...	...
Equals: Net Saving	...	...	...	...	...	...	...	...	...	...	...	...
Less: Surplus of the nation on current transactions	...	...	...	...	...	...	...	...	...	...	...	...
Equals: Net Capital Formation	...	...	...	...	...	...	...	...	...	...	...	...

France

General note. The preparation of national accounts statistics in France is undertaken by the Institut National de la Statistique et des Etudes Economiques (INSEE) Paris, with the co-operation of some other administrative bodies. The official estimates are published in 'Comptes et indicateurs economiques - Rapport sur les Comptes de la Nation', which is issued annually on June in the 'INSEE-Resultats' series. The estimates are generally in accordance with the classifications and definitions recommended in the United Nations System of National Accounts (SNA). However, it is worth noting that they are elaborated according to French classifications and guidelines of the 'Systeme Elargi de Comptabilite Nationale', which is the French version of the 'European System of Integrated Economic Accounts' (ESA). Input-output tables valued at market prices are an integral part of the French national accounts and are published every year at the same time. When the scope and coverage of the estimates differ for conceptual or statistical reasons from the definitions and classifications recommended in SNA, a footnote is indicated to the relevant tables.

Sources and methods:

(a) Gross domestic product. Gross domestic product (GDP) is estimated through three different approaches the production, the expenditure and the income approach, which are used to derived GDP by kind of economic activity, by expenditure and by cost structure, respectively. The input-output table allows a partial synthesis between the production and the expenditure approaches. The final synthesis is based on the production accounts by industry. It actually concerns a part of the national economy only: some accounts (government and private non-profit administrations, financial institutions, insurance companies, large public corporations) which are integratedly built for the industries and for the corresponding sectors are taken to be final and are not questioned at this stage. Reconciling estimates relating to industries and to sectors is performed by distributing value added discrepancies among them or adjusting the global value added estimate: in this case, the distribution of total supply between intermediate consumption and final uses is revised and/or production accounts are corrected for institutional sectors which are considered to be questionable.

(b) Expenditure on the gross domestic product. For each commodity of the input-output table classification, a commodity-flow balance is built, generally by aggregating and completing balances elaborated at a more detailed level of the classification. Sources allowing the household private consumption to be estimated are infra-annual inquiries on production combined with foreign trade data at a very detailed level of the classification, households surveys and specific informations relating to such expenses as health or dwelling. Estimates relating to goods are compared with informations about the retail trade turnover. Gross fixed capital formation estimates proceed from the commodity flow balances compared with informations originating in the investors business accounts at a rather aggregated level. Changes in producers stocks come from the breakdown, by product, of stocks held at the beginning and at the end of the year by enterprises and from an estimate of the holding gains accruing on goods held in stock. Users and trade stocks are estimated by composing intermediate and households consumptions estimates in the commodity flows. Foreign trade comes from the customs statistics and the balance of payments services exchanges, completed by some ad hoc sources.

(c) Cost-structure of the gross domestic product. Three basic sources are used to estimate the cost-components of the different institutional sectors. First, individual accounting data which are not adjusted: government administrations, large public corporations, financial institutions and insurance companies. Second, data on firms (non-financial corporations excluding large public corporations and private unincorporated non-agricultural enterprises) originating from fiscal informations which are adjusted to take into account absences, tax cheating and evading and made consistent with corresponding data obtain from the first source. Third, statistics not originating in the centralization of individual accounting data: unincorporated agricultural enterprises, some productions of households (rental services of dwellings, self consumption of agricultural products, domestic services), private non-profit institutions.

(d) Gross domestic product by kind of economic activity. The estimates of the production of non-financial and non-agricultural firms by industry, except large public national firm start from the sales as reported in the firms' fiscal returns. The part of the production which is not properly reported in the sales - inter-establishment deliveries, production for own capital formation, subcontracting and processing of customers owned materials - is added up in order to obtain non-stocked production estimates. Accounting data of financial institutions, insurance companies and large public corporations which are processed separately make it possible to estimate the output of the corresponding industries. Agriculture production indirectly estimated from products sources while trade output is estimated from trade margins by product and type of use. The estimates of the production of government industries come from data supplied by concerned units. Non-market services output is obtained as the sum of the costs. With the exception of some rows or columns, or more generally of some cells, of the intermediate consumptions table, the intermediate consumptions are calculated, for current year in an indirect way, that is, the principle consists in projecting the preceding year table assuming that the technical coefficients remain unchanged at constant prices. The adding up of the estimates in row, i.e., the projected total intermediate consumption for each product, is compared with the intermediate demand as estimated from the commodity-flow balances (see GDP by expenditure).

1.1 Expenditure on the Gross Domestic Product, in Current Prices

Million French francs

	1980	1983	1984	1985	1986	1987	1988	1989	1990	1991	1992	1993
1 Government final consumption expenditure	509274	782134	854300	910315	959509	1004657	1058400	1106075	1170435	1238998	1320526	1405383
2 Private final consumption expenditure	1653311	2435547	2651305	2871097	3062808	3249514	3444407	3671748	3878580	4055649	4208390	4310136
A Households	1645072	2424143	2639171	2858393	3049520	3235582	3429508	3655793	3861322	4037525	4189834	4291627
B Private non-profit institutions serving households	8239	11404	12134	12704	13288	13932	14899	15955	17258	18124	18556	18509
3 Gross capital formation	680079	795547	827948	887420	994673	1075447	1228608	1373822	1462303	1457983	1387052	1212681
A Increase in stocks	34326	-14054	-12416	-17871	17156	20679	40295	59270	70945	21061	-14875	-106541
B Gross fixed capital formation	645753	809601	840364	905291	977517	1054768	1188313	1314552	1391358	1436922	1401927	1319222
Residential buildings	208861	250437	254374	257751	268128	283307	308052	331217	...	...	...	...
Non-residential buildings	185267	232603	244092	258826	283324	304266	345184	379770				
Other construction and land improvement etc.									...	...	...	...
Other	251625	326561	341898	388714	426065	467195	535077	603565				
4 Exports of goods and services	604422	900658	1053328	1123930	1074095	1101383	1221304	1411087	1467972	1538062	1587935	1558742
5 Less: Imports of goods and services	638791	907388	1024968	1092619	1021789	1094349	1217627	1403052	1469802	1514461	1493363	1404152
Equals: Gross Domestic Product	2808295	4006498	4361913	4700143	5069296	5336652	5735092	6159680	6509488	6776231	7010540	7082790

1.2 Expenditure on the Gross Domestic Product, in Constant Prices

Million French francs

	1980	1983	1984	1985	1986	1987	1988	1989	1990	1991	1992	1993
	At constant prices of:1980											
1 Government final consumption expenditure	509274	556461	563017	575863	585855	602353	622838	625494	638447	656280	679112	702169
2 Private final consumption expenditure	1653311	1761576	1780452	1823159	1894291	1948459	2012059	2073624	2129872	2158815	2188128	2192153
A Households	1645072	1753269	1772234	1814929	1886019	1939871	2003042	2064262	2119975	2148656	2177988	2182268
B Private non-profit institutions serving households	8239	8307	8218	8230	8272	8588	9017	9362	9897	10159	10140	9885
3 Gross capital formation	680079	601618	586790	603289	656419	690068	757943	824667	852684	826608	788024	677480

France

1.2 Expenditure on the Gross Domestic Product, in Constant Prices
(Continued)

Million French francs

	1980	1983	1984	1985	1986	1987	1988	1989	1990	1991	1992	1993
					At constant prices of: 1980							
A Increase in stocks	34326	-972	-139	-2648	23251	26306	30494	39969	45652	19174	5470	-59719
B Gross fixed capital formation	645753	602590	586929	605937	633168	663762	727449	784698	807032	807434	782554	737199
Residential buildings	208861	188817	180466	176519	177377	181141	191270	201810	...	...	...	...
Non-residential buildings	185267	176264	174061	176804	188960	196935	217083	233647				
Other construction and land improvement etc.									...	...	...	...
Other	251625	237509	232402	252614	266831	285686	319096	349241	...	...	...	...
4 Exports of goods and services	604422	638799	683480	696510	686413	707373	764552	842590	887719	924058	968980	965931
5 Less: Imports of goods and services	638791	624550	641275	670442	718342	773744	840080	908005	963623	992992	1003270	969851
Equals: Gross Domestic Product	2808295	2933904	2972464	3028379	3104636	3174509	3317312	3458370	3545099	3572769	3620974	3567882

1.3 Cost Components of the Gross Domestic Product

Million French francs

	1980	1983	1984	1985	1986	1987	1988	1989	1990	1991	1992	1993
1 Indirect taxes, net	356953	506002	554910	599896	627563	667420	747551	796725	846942	851103	861395	861918
A Indirect taxes	428590	619647	688426	742648	785542	836125	891710	934229	983429	995345	1015855	1036157
B Less: Subsidies	71637	113645	133516	142752	157979	168705	144159	137504	136487	144242	154460	174239
2 Consumption of fixed capital	346185	508546	551642	589380	631975	673500	725034	776143	828961	880117	907100	925227
3 Compensation of employees paid by resident producers to:	1575784	2259282	2425773	2582446	2708114	2821197	2976425	3161614	3371797	3531792	3669277	3723188
A Resident households	1570224	2248486	2411189	2562757	2688804	2804228	2956067	3146024	3354073	3511656	3646390	3701705
B Rest of the world	5560	10796	14584	19689	19310	16969	20358	15590	17724	20136	22887	21483
4 Operating surplus	529373	732668	829588	928421	1101644	1174535	1286082	1425198	1461788	1513219	1572768	1572457
A Corporate and quasi-corporate enterprises	124476	154920	207225	253615	368361	414130	493672	545243	506886	535948	537415	535387
B Private unincorporated enterprises [a]	406094	578741	624687	678238	732714	756472	794645	885146	944150	979219	1032115	1034711
C General government	-1197	-993	-2324	-3432	569	3933	-2235	-5191	10752	-1948	3238	2359
Equals: Gross Domestic Product	2808295	4006498	4361913	4700143	5069296	5336652	5735092	6159680	6509488	6776231	7010540	7082790

a) Private unincorporated enterprises includes households.

1.4 General Government Current Receipts and Disbursements

Million French francs

	1980	1983	1984	1985	1986	1987	1988	1989	1990	1991	1992	1993
					Receipts							
1 Operating surplus	-1197	-993	-2324	-3432	569	3933	-2235	-5191	10752	-1948	3238	2359
2 Property and entrepreneurial income	25696	54382	53411	66917	73895	66531	62550	70708	80021	78550	77495	76026
3 Taxes, fees and contributions	1150935	1706934	1905876	2046957	2170224	2310033	2439819	2616467	2769595	2875589	2953964	3027421
A Indirect taxes	410607	586917	653822	705103	736494	781946	829419	873123	922814	926557	950946	978316
B Direct taxes	236244	358740	407431	429321	469768	499110	514221	553220	581504	632890	630102	651003
C Social security contributions	500068	755445	837392	905143	955257	1019205	1086937	1179692	1253800	1304210	1360258	1385198
D Compulsory fees, fines and penalties	4016	5832	7231	7390	8705	9772	9242	10432	11477	11932	12658	12904
4 Other current transfers	74852	105819	115214	125977	134054	142355	171395	159181	164123	195912	205478	209034
Total Current Receipts of General Government	1250286	1866142	2072177	2236419	2378742	2522852	2671529	2841165	3024491	3148103	3240175	3314840
					Disbursements							
1 Government final consumption expenditure	509274	782134	854300	910315	959509	1004657	1058400	1106075	1170435	1238998	1320526	1405383
A Compensation of employees	376678	572947	626251	669198	712439	733702	763439	799813	841269	886661	941529	996294
B Consumption of fixed capital	37945	59123	65923	72304	77663	83510	90288	97715	105885	115546	123868	131361
C Purchases of goods and services, net	84712	131718	140435	153290	153324	170706	187572	190105	203423	215910	232504	253228
D Less: Own account fixed capital formation	...	...	...	...	...	...	...	...	...	...	...	...
E Indirect taxes paid, net	9939	18346	21691	15523	16083	16739	17101	18442	19858	20881	22625	24500
2 Property income	41312	102230	116539	135075	145927	147570	152362	168485	191321	208554	237141	260884
A Interest	41251	102176	116484	135010	145859	147497	152287	168366	191222	208442	237011	260746
B Net land rent and royalties	61	54	55	65	68	73	75	119	99	112	130	138

France

1.4 General Government Current Receipts and Disbursements
(Continued)

Million French francs

	1980	1983	1984	1985	1986	1987	1988	1989	1990	1991	1992	1993
3 Subsidies	54407	87423	107248	109854	118625	117683	102041	102657	101086	102748	113088	114359
4 Other current transfers	584378	948589	1044978	1140101	1212164	1269650	1350189	1425546	1520469	1635045	1744819	1867456
A Social security benefits	439730	705473	762685	823173	880391	913086	978761	1039064	1107756	1183483	1262220	1335942
B Social assistance grants	45387	76992	97336	117926	129284	130718	138284	143098	152362	163752	170441	192188
C Other	99261	166124	184957	199002	202489	225846	233144	243384	260351	287810	312158	339326
5 Net saving	60915	-54234	-50888	-58926	-57483	-16708	8537	38402	41180	-37242	-175399	-333242
Total Current Disbursements and Net Saving of General Government	1250286	1866142	2072177	2236419	2378742	2522852	2671529	2841165	3024491	3148103	3240175	3314840

1.5 Current Income and Outlay of Corporate and Quasi-Corporate Enterprises, Summary

Million French francs

	1980	1983	1984	1985	1986	1987	1988	1989	1990	1991	1992	1993
Receipts												
1 Operating surplus	124476	154920	207225	253615	368361	414130	493672	545243	506886	535948	537415	535387
2 Property and entrepreneurial income received	510717	881268	994270	1111299	1155200	1161873	1286828	1489734	1663361	1842918	1915474	2074621
3 Current transfers	144908	234090	256632	270947	280272	305376	313287	318409	370217	381647	411231	426291
Total Current Receipts	780101	1270278	1458127	1635861	1803833	1881379	2093787	2353386	2540464	2760513	2864120	3036299
Disbursements												
1 Property and entrepreneurial income	558388	967417	1077183	1199622	1216143	1230903	1340292	1574577	1768150	2003767	2071921	2215767
2 Direct taxes and other current payments to general government	65902	88612	105134	115852	136134	150124	162539	180722	186607	168871	146550	147382
3 Other current transfers	151771	228551	252238	275294	294334	308091	343499	340248	386143	403073	433363	450491
4 Net saving	4040	-14302	23572	45093	157222	192261	247457	257839	199564	184802	212286	222659
Total Current Disbursements and Net Saving	780101	1270278	1458127	1635861	1803833	1881379	2093787	2353386	2540464	2760513	2864120	3036299

1.6 Current Income and Outlay of Households and Non-Profit Institutions

Million French francs

	1980	1983	1984	1985	1986	1987	1988	1989	1990	1991	1992	1993
Receipts												
1 Compensation of employees	1573880	2255615	2419226	2573107	2700561	2816655	2972468	3161822	3370516	3531133	3665726	3721760
A From resident producers	1570224	2248486	2411189	2562757	2688804	2804228	2956067	3146024	3354073	3511656	3646390	3701705
B From rest of the world	3656	7129	8037	10350	11757	12427	16401	15798	16443	19477	19336	20055
2 Operating surplus of private unincorporated enterprises	406094	578741	624687	678238	732714	756472	794645	885146	944150	979219	1032115	1034711
3 Property and entrepreneurial income	167378	257749	274798	304443	306159	329982	349034	422604	460835	532224	556342	550209
4 Current transfers	683149	1073605	1184248	1295273	1386675	1440181	1543753	1627775	1749096	1860171	1981001	2098737
A Social security benefits	443334	711500	770207	834620	896206	930719	999470	1061412	1131617	1209285	1289790	1366380
B Social assistance grants	46879	79021	99437	120179	131665	133238	140997	146029	155572	167145	173921	195677
C Other	192936	283084	314604	340474	358804	376224	403286	420334	461907	483741	517290	536680
Total Current Receipts	2830501	4165710	4502959	4851061	5126109	5343290	5659900	6097347	6524597	6902747	7235184	7405417
Disbursements												
1 Private final consumption expenditure	1653311	2435547	2651305	2871097	3062808	3249514	3444407	3671748	3878580	4055649	4208390	4310136
2 Property income	89600	131812	145715	164302	182239	187838	213448	250163	275549	278999	293828	278092
3 Direct taxes and other current transfers n.e.c. to general government	683552	1045082	1161790	1241441	1317128	1402602	1475078	1595046	1695219	1816203	1893947	1942999
A Social security contributions	511363	772521	856208	924924	979420	1048753	1119307	1217772	1294247	1346155	1403867	1432712
B Direct taxes	169455	268116	300447	311356	331724	347117	348497	368774	391866	460760	480155	499956
C Fees, fines and penalties	2734	4445	5135	5161	5984	6732	7274	8500	9106	9288	9925	10331
4 Other current transfers	151799	229710	241012	259964	277099	286446	297139	311250	344988	358805	387222	405085
5 Net saving	252239	323559	303137	314257	286835	216890	229828	269140	330261	393091	451797	469105
Total Current Disbursements and Net Saving	2830501	4165710	4502959	4851061	5126109	5343290	5659900	6097347	6524597	6902747	7235184	7405417

France

1.7 External Transactions on Current Account, Summary

Million French francs

	1980	1983	1984	1985	1986	1987	1988	1989	1990	1991	1992	1993
Payments to the Rest of the World												
1 Imports of goods and services	638791	907388	1024968	1092619	1021789	1094349	1217627	1403052	1469802	1514461	1493363	1404152
A Imports of merchandise c.i.f.	576505	808900	914542	970814	893847	952251	1063873	1229621	1273885	1302876	1268897	1172006
B Other	62286	98488	110426	121805	127942	142098	153754	173431	195917	211585	224466	232146
2 Factor income to the rest of the world	79595	170399	206772	226699	190134	184380	202977	247784	295867	367291	402655	449683
A Compensation of employees	5560	10796	14584	19689	19310	16969	20358	15590	17724	20136	22887	21483
B Property and entrepreneurial income	74035	159603	192188	207010	170824	167411	182619	232194	278143	347155	379768	428200
3 Current transfers to the rest of the world	66436	112491	110528	122924	128709	137175	158742	161310	163981	193977	195086	208844
A Indirect taxes to supranational organizations	17983	32730	34604	37545	49048	54179	62291	61106	60615	68788	64909	57841
B Other current transfers	48453	79761	75924	85379	79661	82996	96451	100204	103366	125189	130177	151003
4 Surplus of the nation on current transactions	-16700	-31978	-485	2384	23876	-9504	-17752	-32298	-62337	-37215	8732	71068
Payments to the Rest of the World and Surplus of the Nation on Current Transactions	768122	1158300	1341783	1444626	1364508	1406400	1561594	1779848	1867313	2038514	2099836	2133747
Receipts From The Rest of the World												
1 Exports of goods and services	604422	900658	1053328	1123930	1074095	1101383	1221304	1411087	1467972	1538062	1587935	1558742
A Exports of merchandise f.o.b.	488877	720442	845218	901379	860303	886740	992606	1135583	1173049	1218530	1247213	1204225
B Other	115545	180216	208110	222551	213792	214643	228698	275504	294923	319532	340722	354517
2 Factor income from rest of the world	92182	158672	183267	201020	173526	171913	191330	237813	263783	329004	345525	394368
A Compensation of employees	3656	7129	8037	10350	11757	12427	16401	15798	16443	19477	19336	20055
B Property and entrepreneurial income	88526	151543	175230	190670	161769	159486	174929	222015	247340	309527	326189	374313
3 Current transfers from rest of the world	71518	98970	105188	119676	116887	133104	148960	130948	135558	171448	166376	180637
A Subsidies from supranational organisations	17230	26222	26268	32898	39354	51022	42118	34847	35401	41494	41372	59880
B Other current transfers	54288	72748	78920	86778	77533	82082	106842	96101	100157	129954	125004	120757
Receipts from the Rest of the World on Current Transactions	768122	1158300	1341783	1444626	1364508	1406400	1561594	1779848	1867313	2038514	2099836	2133747

1.8 Capital Transactions of The Nation, Summary

Million French francs

	1980	1983	1984	1985	1986	1987	1988	1989	1990	1991	1992	1993
Finance of Gross Capital Formation												
Gross saving	663379	763569	827463	889804	1018549	1065943	1210856	1341524	1399966	1420768	1395784	1283749
1 Consumption of fixed capital	346185	508546	551642	589380	631975	673500	725034	776143	828961	880117	907100	925227
A General government	44431	68303	75808	82842	88614	95049	102336	110785	119557	129829	138978	146927
B Corporate and quasi-corporate enterprises	198981	297608	323047	346588	370246	392148	417385	439559	475522	518085	541517	543960
C Other	102773	142635	152787	159950	173115	186303	205313	225799	233882	232203	226605	234340
2 Net saving	317194	255023	275821	300424	386574	392443	485822	565381	571005	540651	488684	358522
A General government	60915	-54234	-50888	-58926	-57483	-16708	8537	38402	41180	-37242	-175399	-333242
B Corporate and quasi-corporate enterprises	4040	-14302	23572	45093	157222	192261	247457	257839	199564	184802	212286	222659
C Other	252239	323559	303137	314257	286835	216890	229828	269140	330261	393091	451797	469105
Less: Surplus of the nation on current transactions	-16700	-31978	-485	2384	23876	-9504	-17752	-32298	-62337	-37215	8732	71068
Finance of Gross Capital Formation	680079	795547	827948	887420	994673	1075447	1228608	1373822	1462303	1457983	1387052	1212681
Gross Capital Formation												
Increase in stocks	34326	-14054	-12416	-17871	17156	20679	40295	59270	70945	21061	-14875	-106541
Gross fixed capital formation	645753	809601	840364	905291	977517	1054768	1188313	1314552	1391358	1436922	1401927	1319222
1 General government	86602	119346	126127	144277	152435	161760	188556	205077	212033	230440	242317	241684
2 Corporate and quasi-corporate enterprises	292619	373546	393575	433249	475315	525833	595681	655612	706495	738335	716435	650269
3 Other	266532	316709	320662	327765	349767	367175	404076	453863	472830	468147	443175	427269
Gross Capital Formation	680079	795547	827948	887420	994673	1075447	1228608	1373822	1462303	1457983	1387052	1212681

France

1.9 Gross Domestic Product by Institutional Sectors of Origin

Million French francs

	1980	1983	1984	1985	1986	1987	1988	1989	1990	1991	1992	1993
					Domestic Factor Incomes Originating							
1 General government	385982	587471	640678	684315	731510	755915	779105	813899	871844	905459	967196	1022451
2 Corporate and quasi-corporate enterprises	1182119	1654790	1810362	1958147	2152300	2286812	2482333	2667976	2784296	2923055	2996712	2990066
A Non-financial	1173068	1650098	1799486	1944671	2125522	2263031	2474535	2669008	2814249	2939374	3003487	2971135
B Financial [a]	9051	4692	10876	13476	26778	23781	7798	-1032	-29953	-16319	-6775	18931
3 Households and private unincorporated enterprises	529672	739543	793562	857058	914116	940604	987840	1090799	1162204	1200564	1261895	1266884
4 Non-profit institutions serving households	7384	10146	10759	11347	11832	12401	13229	14138	15241	15933	16242	16244
Subtotal: Domestic Factor Incomes	2105157	2991950	3255361	3510867	3809758	3995732	4262507	4586812	4833585	5045011	5242045	5295645
Indirect taxes, net	356953	506002	554910	599896	627563	667420	747551	796725	846942	851103	861395	861918
A Indirect taxes	428590	619647	688426	742648	785542	836125	891710	934229	983429	995345	1015855	1036157
B Less: Subsidies	71637	113645	133516	142752	157979	168705	144159	137504	136487	144242	154460	174239
Consumption of fixed capital	346185	508546	551642	589380	631975	673500	725034	776143	828961	880117	907100	925227
Gross Domestic Product	2808295	4006498	4361913	4700143	5069296	5336652	5735092	6159680	6509488	6776231	7010540	7082790

a) Financial of Corporate and quasi-corporate enterprises refers to net of imputed bank service charges.

1.10 Gross Domestic Product by Kind of Activity, in Current Prices

Million French francs

	1980	1983	1984	1985	1986	1987	1988	1989	1990	1991	1992	1993
1 Agriculture, hunting, forestry and fishing	119024	169591	175216	182310	189495	189002	191278	215282	221865	204959	198222	165587
2 Mining and quarrying	23821	33492	35563	40112	35657	34723	30772	31738	29754	30476	32237	31994
3 Manufacturing	679520	900970	956273	1033139	1120100	1143222	1242136	1324621	1394503	1407648	1430849	1400791
4 Electricity, gas and water	50308	87500	104907	116869	118093	122784	126454	128259	138739	153193	165272	176357
5 Construction	193609	234603	242001	243898	262953	278086	309643	320643	335812	358171	364538	363974
6 Wholesale and retail trade, restaurants and hotels	395042	579607	635917	685011	747077	797082	854082	928578	990699	1026489	1049443	1064768
7 Transport, storage and communication	164194	235988	259504	289050	310759	322383	334976	357487	378473	396727	416003	414880
8 Finance, insurance, real estate and business services	472578	696287	782100	861137	977594	1086928	1198252	1322401	1390152	1466932	1520684	1584400
9 Community, social and personal services	121265	189704	211658	231374	256333	276677	306334	335181	363473	387469	414298	435101
Total, Industries	2219361	3127742	3403139	3682900	4018061	4250887	4593927	4964190	5243470	5432064	5591546	5637852
Producers of Government Services	448211	684995	750506	795561	845325	873976	913641	961363	1015534	1076279	1145098	1206414
Other Producers												
Subtotal	2667572	3812737	4153645	4478461	4863386	5124863	5507568	5925553	6259004	6508343	6736644	6844266
Less: Imputed bank service charge	107503	162385	175627	192340	223272	246505	262490	279423	278020	271159	269255	281275
Plus: Import duties [a]	6339	7938	8696	8904	8976	9667	10747	11030	10946	11954	10644	10492
Plus: Value added tax	242015	348956	375609	405281	420379	449074	479572	502698	517561	514827	520879	515121
Plus: Other adjustments	-128	-748	-410	-163	-173	-447	-305	-178	-3	-16	-1	-
Equals: Gross Domestic Product [b]	2808295	4006498	4361913	4700143	5069296	5336652	5735092	6159680	6509488	6776231	7010540	7082790

a) Item 'Import duties' includes also value added tax (VAT) on products.
b) Data in this series has been revised. The breakdown, if any, may not add up to the total.

1.11 Gross Domestic Product by Kind of Activity, in Constant Prices

Million French francs

	1980	1983	1984	1985	1986	1987	1988	1989	1990	1991	1992	1993
					At constant prices of:1980							
1 Agriculture, hunting, forestry and fishing	119024	131217	137323	138441	139457	141354	140801	145962	148989	145288	158528	146649
2 Mining and quarrying	23821	21209	20407	21700	20745	21054	20275	19729	18338	19629	21868	22423
3 Manufacturing	679520	683532	671038	668425	667256	661095	700521	736640	750400	738680	735100	713042
4 Electricity, gas and water	50308	63797	70040	74085	77261	81682	83221	82712	84444	88534	90933	94355
5 Construction	193609	187519	183153	180406	185861	187684	202688	212123	217515	219090	213623	206012
6 Wholesale and retail trade, restaurants and hotels	395042	418314	425030	431301	443225	448663	457080	476416	492158	493822	493119	482929
7 Transport, storage and communication	164194	179319	184483	191249	198339	209271	228695	246655	259184	265932	275765	276115
8 Finance, insurance, real estate and business services	472578	490559	507082	528799	566336	601553	623157	649334	650680	656620	650002	657483
9 Community, social and personal services	121265	138083	146489	152209	160419	165288	174073	185046	196265	203855	209637	214384

France

1.11 Gross Domestic Product by Kind of Activity, in Constant Prices
(Continued)

Million French francs

	1980	1983	1984	1985	1986	1987	1988	1989	1990	1991	1992	1993
					At constant prices of:1980							
Total, Industries	2219361	2313549	2345045	2386615	2458899	2517644	2630511	2754617	2817973	2831450	2848575	2813392
Producers of Government Services	448211	481600	489752	498414	505807	512351	526532	531650	539211	552151	562138	570796
Other Producers												
Subtotal	2667572	2795149	2834797	2885029	2964706	3029995	3157043	3286267	3357184	3383601	3410713	3384188
Less: Imputed bank service charge	107503	114024	114264	118696	131917	140115	143561	145827	138811	130858	120451	118940
Plus: Import duties a	6339	7049	7271	7626	8482	9437	10318	11127	11878	12426	12581	12468
Plus: Value added tax	242015	245888	244808	254556	263514	275354	293687	306977	315001	308337	312896	301673
Plus: Other adjustments	-128	-158	-148	-136	-149	-162	-175	-174	-153	-153	-16	-16
Equals: Gross Domestic Product	2808295	2933904	2972464	3028379	3104636	3174509	3317312	3458370	3545099	3572769	3620974	3567882

a) Item 'Import duties' includes also value added tax (VAT) on products.

1.12 Relations Among National Accounting Aggregates

Million French francs

	1980	1983	1984	1985	1986	1987	1988	1989	1990	1991	1992	1993
Gross Domestic Product	2808295	4006498	4361913	4700143	5069296	5336652	5735092	6159680	6509488	6776231	7010540	7082790
Plus: Net factor income from the rest of the world	12587	-11727	-23505	-25679	-16608	-12467	-11647	-9971	-32084	-38287	-57130	-55315
Factor income from the rest of the world	92182	158672	183267	201020	173526	171913	191330	237813	263783	329004	345525	394368
Less: Factor income to the rest of the world	79595	170399	206772	226699	190134	184380	202977	247784	295867	367291	402655	449683
Equals: Gross National Product	2820882	3994771	4338408	4674464	5052688	5324185	5723445	6149709	6477404	6737944	6953410	7027475
Less: Consumption of fixed capital	346185	508546	551642	589380	631975	673500	725034	776143	828961	880117	907100	925227
Equals: National Income	2474697	3486225	3786766	4085084	4420713	4650685	4998411	5373566	5648443	5857827	6046310	6102248
Plus: Net current transfers from the rest of the world	5082	-13521	-5340	-3248	-11822	-4071	-9782	-30362	-28423	-22529	-28710	-28207
Current transfers from the rest of the world	71518	98970	105188	119676	116887	133104	148960	130948	135558	171448	166376	180637
Less: Current transfers to the rest of the world	66436	112491	110528	122924	128709	137175	158742	161310	163981	193977	195086	208844
Equals: National Disposable Income	2479779	3472704	3781426	4081836	4408891	4646614	4988629	5343204	5620020	5835298	6017600	6074041
Less: Final consumption	2162585	3217681	3505605	3781412	4022317	4254171	4502807	4777823	5049015	5294647	5528916	5715519
Equals: Net Saving	317194	255023	275821	300424	386574	392443	485822	565381	571005	540651	488684	358522
Less: Surplus of the nation on current transactions	-16700	-31978	-485	2384	23876	-9504	-17752	-32298	-62337	-37215	8732	71068
Equals: Net Capital Formation	333894	287001	276306	298040	362698	401947	503574	597679	633342	577866	479952	287454

2.1 Government Final Consumption Expenditure by Function, in Current Prices

Million French francs

	1980	1983	1984	1985	1986	1987	1988	1989	1990	1991	1992	1993
1 General public services	...	92422	102254	118110	129631	132760	138014	144190	138791	...	...	...
2 Defence	...	130039	139304	150324	153648	162885	182210	180818	194532	...	...	...
3 Public order and safety	...	35186	38957	41122	43522	45947	47865	50682	53999	...	...	...
4 Education	...	203236	222305	233901	249379	255929	266166	280022	300718	...	...	...
5 Health	...	128282	141328	149970	156086	168687	172667	188635	198781	...	...	...
6 Social security and welfare	...	65093	69620	73729	75293	75112	83781	83802	90850	...	...	...
7 Housing and community amenities	...	44286	49497	54033	58538	62372	65245	70796	74258	...	...	...
8 Recreational, cultural and religious affairs	...	22193	24232	26878	28944	30757	31935	34728	36871	...	...	...
9 Economic services	...	56273	58912	60420	62597	67828	66803	68961	73266	...	...	...
A Fuel and energy	...	...	...	...	...	...	...	...	...	...	...	...
B Agriculture, forestry, fishing and hunting	...	...	...	...	...	...	...	...	...	...	...	...
C Mining, manufacturing and construction, except fuel and energy	...	...	...	...	...	...	...	...	...	...	...	...
D Transportation and communication	...	26541	27950	29158	28170	32549	30026	29911	32712	...	...	...
E Other economic affairs	...	29732	30962	31262	34427	35279	36777	39050	40554	...	...	...
10 Other functions	...	5124	7891	1828	1871	2380	3714	3441	3930	...	...	...
Total Government Final Consumption Expenditure a	...	782134	854300	910315	959509	1004657	1058400	1106075	1170435	...	...	...

a) Data in this series has been revised. The breakdown, if any, may not add up to the total.

France

2.5 Private Final Consumption Expenditure by Type and Purpose, in Current Prices

Million French francs

	1980	1983	1984	1985	1986	1987	1988	1989	1990	1991	1992	1993
Final Consumption Expenditure of Resident Households												
1 Food, beverages and tobacco	351554	510629	558718	592432	623560	646863	672382	709369	743698	773552	782880	799189
A Food	288155	416615	458512	486534	509730	528628	547656	577486	603019	625546	626619	630802
B Non-alcoholic beverages	7225	11760	12874	14047	15430	16296	17131	18606	21278	23128	23995	24873
C Alcoholic beverages	38625	54129	56389	59598	64017	65477	67905	71188	76001	79883	82754	87330
D Tobacco	17549	28125	30943	32253	34383	36462	39690	42089	43400	44995	49512	56184
2 Clothing and footwear [a]	120714	171928	185120	200547	218764	226660	232664	241271	252991	257797	260810	257567
3 Gross rent, fuel and power	287562	436138	491281	546046	571375	604634	644247	688292	733360	803480	852808	908260
A Fuel and power	85641	128364	144445	161183	148789	141755	133463	135902	144635	163847	164128	167883
B Other	201921	307774	346836	384863	422586	462879	510784	552390	588725	639633	688680	740377
4 Furniture, furnishings and household equipment and operation	156976	216449	226027	239196	254969	268124	284086	297066	307973	315509	319544	324534
A Household operation	45594	66318	71441	76968	80124	83850	88686	93782	97916	104785	109918	114029
B Other	111382	150131	154586	162228	174845	184274	195400	203284	210057	210724	209626	210505
5 Medical care and health expenses	127284	195354	222606	246474	270716	284184	311542	340028	367837	394348	419864	443021
6 Transport and communication	273642	416585	444418	482204	501845	545823	577636	624266	655844	660809	688010	683239
A Personal transport equipment	66340	102777	99827	105787	124556	140101	149484	165108	168806	155624	162646	143413
B Other	207302	313808	344591	376417	377289	405722	428152	459158	487038	505185	525364	539826
7 Recreational, entertainment, education and cultural services	119956	173581	188423	201960	220494	238155	255153	277347	294010	304264	316817	323484
A Education	6115	9956	11402	12968	14467	16967	18789	21323	21167	21564	23500	24998
B Other	113841	163625	177021	188992	206027	221188	236364	256024	272843	282700	293317	298486
8 Miscellaneous goods and services	216562	325283	351141	379609	409379	440803	475216	516915	548704	577871	605408	619664
A Personal care [a]	24838	39006	43216	47960	53063	57983	63129	68789	73650	78711	83278	86762
B Expenditures in restaurants, cafes and hotels	105639	161007	172931	187816	200733	215735	235227	257656	277819	292201	303924	305579
C Other	86085	125270	134994	143833	155583	167085	176860	190470	197235	206959	218206	227323
Total Final Consumption Expenditure in the Domestic Market by Households, of which	1654250	2445947	2667734	2888468	3071102	3255246	3452926	3694554	3904417	4087630	4246141	4358958
A Durable goods	147062	211432	209656	219514	250825	274648	295255	315919	325584	309818	315094	293458
B Semi-durable goods	275165	385612	411866	438835	472428	494899	516467	544382	571453	588266	600036	601121
C Non-durable goods	620991	916032	1008634	1092037	1113117	1147280	1187160	1260091	1327938	1396465	1422082	1462705
D Services	611032	932871	1037578	1138082	1234732	1338419	1454044	1574162	1679442	1793081	1908929	2001674
Plus: Direct purchases abroad by resident households	25360	32865	37482	41421	45113	51328	58000	64162	66576	69835	74060	72569
Less: Direct purchases in the domestic market by non-resident households	34538	54669	66045	71496	66695	70992	81418	102923	109671	119735	131809	131344
Equals: Final Consumption Expenditure of Resident Households [b]	1645072	2424143	2639171	2858393	3049520	3235582	3429508	3655793	3861322	4037525	4189834	4291627
Final Consumption Expenditure of Private Non-profit Institutions Serving Households												
Equals: Final Consumption Expenditure of Private Non-profit Organisations Serving Households	8239	11404	12134	12704	13288	13932	14899	15955	17258	18124	18556	18509
Private Final Consumption Expenditure	1653311	2435547	2651305	2871097	3062808	3249514	3444407	3671748	3878580	4055649	4208390	4310136

a) Personal effects are included in item 'Clothing and footwear'.
b) Data in this series has been revised. The breakdown, if any, may not add up to the total.

2.6 Private Final Consumption Expenditure by Type and Purpose, in Constant Prices

Million French francs

	1980	1983	1984	1985	1986	1987	1988	1989	1990	1991	1992	1993
At constant prices of: 1980												
Final Consumption Expenditure of Resident Households												
1 Food, beverages and tobacco	351554	363311	369402	374428	380978	387976	395200	400249	404756	409126	410167	414063
A Food	288155	297428	303066	306667	311833	318254	323954	326946	329386	332444	333380	335791
B Non-alcoholic beverages	7225	8442	8635	8893	9346	9567	10266	11580	12977	13576	13586	13905
C Alcoholic beverages	38625	38729	38316	38417	39328	39500	40429	40801	41011	41194	41420	43653
D Tobacco	17549	18712	19385	20451	20471	20655	20551	20922	21382	21912	21781	20714
2 Clothing and footwear [a]	120714	130524	127675	127757	130997	129361	128457	129565	131910	130130	128386	125511
3 Gross rent, fuel and power	287562	306636	319267	333269	345566	355874	361046	367889	377790	395658	404828	414534
A Fuel and power	85641	82720	86469	90893	93341	94114	89488	89281	90399	98977	99509	101145

France

2.6 Private Final Consumption Expenditure by Type and Purpose, in Constant Prices
(Continued)

Million French francs

	1980	1983	1984	1985	1986	1987	1988	1989	1990	1991	1992	1993
					At constant prices of:1980							
B Other	201921	223916	232798	242376	252225	261760	271558	278608	287391	296681	305319	313389
4 Furniture, furnishings and household equipment and operation	156976	157593	153303	153569	157412	160728	167190	169824	170560	168579	166273	166029
A Household operation	45594	45427	45455	45954	46061	46945	48884	50052	50726	52028	53163	54004
B Other	111382	112166	107848	107615	111351	113783	118306	119772	119834	116551	113110	112025
5 Medical care and health expenses	127284	148943	160606	171655	183496	188712	202304	218954	237289	251415	262513	273973
6 Transport and communication	273642	302188	296481	298476	310825	325426	338833	352783	361031	354528	363617	353261
A Personal transport equipment	66340	77375	69330	68924	75784	82485	86637	92735	94196	84460	86961	74913
B Other	207302	224813	227151	229552	235041	242941	252196	260048	266835	270068	276656	278348
7 Recreational, entertainment, education and cultural services	119956	131038	132696	135004	142217	149589	160763	171795	181072	183318	185090	185822
A Education	6115	6830	7247	7836	8310	9173	9602	10337	9691	9372	9790	9990
B Other	113841	124208	125449	127168	133907	140416	151161	161458	171381	173946	175300	175832
8 Miscellaneous goods and services	216562	228810	231990	239846	247843	253949	262841	274920	278986	282628	286079	286031
A Personal care [a]	24838	26548	27468	28897	30604	31659	33112	34680	35457	36110	36690	36963
B Expenditures in restaurants, cafes and hotels	105639	110082	110278	112651	114887	115598	119505	124686	127293	127488	126965	123323
C Other	86085	921..	94244	98298	102352	106692	110224	115554	116236	119030	122424	125745
Total Final Consumption Expenditure in the Domestic Market by Households, of which	1654250	1769043	1791420	1834004	1899334	1951615	2016634	2085979	2143394	2175382	2206953	2219224
A Durable goods	147062	164185	153475	154169	168722	180341	193699	203711	210729	199389	200994	187683
B Semi-durable goods	275165	288084	283595	282131	287767	289595	293926	301550	307522	306370	304279	301002
C Non-durable goods	620991	647975	663927	680764	698900	713715	729414	747787	764029	784429	792640	803958
D Services	611032	668799	690423	716940	743945	767964	799595	832931	861114	885194	909040	926581
Plus: Direct purchases abroad by resident households	25360	23779	25181	26277	27839	30662	33671	35954	36185	36744	38017	36414
Less: Direct purchases in the domestic market by non-resident households	34538	39553	44367	45352	41154	42406	47263	57671	59604	62995	67656	65902
Equals: Final Consumption Expenditure of Resident Households	1645072	1753269	1772234	1814929	1886019	1939871	2003042	2064262	2119975	2148656	2177988	2182268
	Final Consumption Expenditure of Private Non-profit Institutions Serving Households											
Equals: Final Consumption Expenditure of Private Non-profit Organisations Serving Households	8239	8307	8218	8230	8272	8588	9017	9362	9897	10159	10140	9885
Private Final Consumption Expenditure	1653311	1761576	1780452	1823159	1894291	1948459	2012059	2073624	2129872	2158815	2188128	2192153

a) Personal effects are included in item 'Clothing and footwear'.

2.11 Gross Fixed Capital Formation by Kind of Activity of Owner, ISIC Divisions, in Current Prices

Million French francs

	1980	1983	1984	1985	1986	1987	1988	1989	1990	1991	1992	1993
					All Producers							
1 Agriculture, hunting, forestry and fishing	23450	31518	30137	30775	29726	29536	34784	39778	41729	38743	35235	32243
2 Mining and quarrying	1176	1678	1785	1405	1141	941	1146	1058	788	627	546	403
A Coal mining	1176	1678	1785	1405	1141	941	1146	1058	788	627	546	403
B Crude petroleum and natural gas production	...	...	...	...	...	...	...	...	...	...	...	...
C Metal ore mining	...	...	...	...	...	...	...	...	...	...	...	...
D Other mining	...	...	...	...	...	...	...	...	...	...	...	...

France

2.11 Gross Fixed Capital Formation by Kind of Activity of Owner, ISIC Divisions, in Current Prices
(Continued)

Million French francs

	1980	1983	1984	1985	1986	1987	1988	1989	1990	1991	1992	1993
3 Manufacturing	99135	115651	125295	145344	158686	171436	195157	216622	238401	233868	231251	189723
A Manufacturing of food, beverages and tobacco	12986	18108	22021	22389	21919	23450	28988	34100	32600	35078	40463	27896
B Textile, wearing apparel and leather industries	4237	5869	6363	7207	6893	7630	9307	9379	9869	8558	7401	5823
C Manufacture of wood, and wood products, including furniture	3977	4283	5145	5363	5812	6672	7781	9365	9523	9590	7122	6543
D Manufacture of paper and paper products, printing and publishing	5323	6131	6459	8455	12697	14431	15948	18534	21013	20359	18758	15116
E Manufacture of chemicals and chemical petroleum, coal, rubber and plastic products	21905	23048	23353	28965	30708	33887	36780	41001	47671	45603	49352	43624
F Manufacture of non-metallic mineral products except products of petroleum and coal	6669	6702	6718	6650	8145	8863	11534	13177	11063	9706	12038	10157
G Basic metal industries	8784	8990	11927	13307	14295	14062	13637	14112	14554	13762	12181	9702
H Manufacture of fabricated metal products, machinery and equipment	35254	42520	43309	53008	58217	62441	71182	76954	92108	91212	83936	70862
I Other manufacturing industries	...	...	...	...	...	...	...	...	...	...	...	...
4 Electricity, gas and water	38826	50465	49265	51022	48959	46834	45594	45492	43797	44872	44544	46516
5 Construction	21196	23227	22485	23342	23545	25505	29777	36033	32432	35509	29843	35844
6 Wholesale and retail trade, restaurants and hotels	43177	58935	64558	69052	81893	98454	98649	112737	113116	117378	117259	108096
A Wholesale and retail trade	34094	45943	48912	52339	60728	71875	70426	81513	80358	82203	84859	77550
B Restaurants and hotels	9083	12992	15646	16713	21165	26579	28223	31224	32758	35175	32400	30546
7 Transport, storage and communication	60577	69189	70891	78626	78770	85427	101234	109214	119002	134833	119485	120924
A Transport and storage	37289	44388	43973	49579	53211	59086	75286	79456	87581	96126	85935	81640
B Communication	23288	24801	26918	29047	25559	26341	25948	29758	31421	38707	33550	39284
8 Finance, insurance, real estate and business services	266226	326307	334973	349569	382730	410010	464927	516225	548483	561116	544117	506543
A Financial institutions	7660	12029	15512	16714	18546	20987	24340	22575	23844	29645	17119	8589
B Insurance	1390	1334	2343	3120	4484	4636	4391	6168	8194	7045	4949	4571
C Real estate and business services	257176	312944	317118	329735	359700	384387	436196	487482	516445	524426	522049	493383
Real estate except dwellings	18552	27831	27806	36130	45569	45978	63817	70953	85104	93157	106940	95902
Dwellings	238624	285113	289312	293605	314131	338409	372379	416529	431341	431269	415209	397481
9 Community, social and personal services	12865	22566	24202	25184	31172	35986	41858	46339	53735	52297	51800	52116
Total Industries	566628	699536	723591	774319	836622	904129	1013126	1123498	1191483	1219243	1174080	1092408
Producers of Government Services	77674	108052	114631	128731	138551	148182	172559	188241	196839	214488	224580	223538
Private Non-Profit Institutions Serving Households	1451	2013	2142	2241	2344	2457	2628	2813	3036	3191	3267	3276
Total	645753	809601	840364	905291	977517	1054768	1188313	1314552	1391358	1436922	1401927	1319222

2.12 Gross Fixed Capital Formation by Kind of Activity of Owner, ISIC Divisions, in Constant Prices

Million French francs

	1980	1983	1984	1985	1986	1987	1988	1989	1990	1991	1992	1993
					At constant prices of:1980							
					All Producers							
1 Agriculture, hunting, forestry and fishing	23450	22814	20323	20195	18452	17311	19781	22202	22636	20116	18270	17156
2 Mining and quarrying	1176	1257	1244	938	737	592	696	620	455	357	307	227
A Coal mining	1176	1257	1244	938	737	592	696	620	455	357	307	227
B Crude petroleum and natural gas production	...	...	...	...	...	...	...	...	...	...	...	...
C Metal ore mining	...	...	...	...	...	...	...	...	...	...	...	...
D Other mining	...	...	...	...	...	...	...	...	...	...	...	...

France

2.12 Gross Fixed Capital Formation by Kind of Activity of Owner, ISIC Divisions, in Constant Prices
(Continued)

Million French francs

	1980	1983	1984	1985	1986	1987	1988	1989	1990	1991	1992	1993
					At constant prices of:1980							
3 Manufacturing	99135	84371	85433	94312	99177	104487	116128	124282	133506	126827	123877	101538
A Manufacturing of food, beverages and tobacco	12986	13256	15148	14693	13796	14368	17274	19549	18243	19255	21546	14788
B Textile, wearing apparel and leather industries	4237	4262	4306	4647	4282	4642	5517	5336	5489	4587	3920	3097
C Manufacture of wood, and wood products, including furniture	3977	3118	3520	3505	3624	4024	4598	5366	5320	5225	3813	3489
D Manufacture of paper and paper products, printing and publishing	5323	4455	4381	5472	7914	8786	9487	10600	11723	10983	10058	8100
E Manufacture of chemicals and chemical petroleum, coal, rubber and plastic products	21905	16932	16032	18900	19331	20780	21996	23660	26798	24701	26490	23383
F Manufacture of non-metalic mineral products except products of petroleum and coal	6669	4941	4664	4393	5141	5456	6939	7635	6260	5297	6501	5465
G Basic metal industries	8784	6607	8163	8663	8962	8546	8092	8084	8165	7468	6516	5180
H Manufacture of fabricated metal products, machinery and equipment	35254	30800	29219	34039	36127	37885	42225	44052	51508	49311	45033	38036
I Other manufacturing industries	...	...	...	...	...	...	...	...	...	...	...	...
4 Electricity, gas and water	38826	37657	34610	34194	31924	29556	28072	27299	25570	25290	24780	25590
5 Construction	21196	17269	15752	15641	15104	15903	18163	21122	18562	19612	16288	19467
6 Wholesale and retail trade, restaurants and hotels	43177	43728	45171	46019	52587	61442	60269	66709	65066	65557	64004	58857
A Wholesale and retail trade	34094	34041	34151	34784	38969	44818	42947	48108	46145	46019	46226	42145
B Restaurants and hotels	9083	9687	11020	11235	13618	16624	17322	18601	18921	19538	17778	16712
7 Transport, storage and communication	60577	51232	49945	52715	49964	52598	59707	64565	67986	74639	65856	66162
A Transport and storage	37289	32666	30870	33231	33466	36047	43817	46609	49474	52325	46712	43395
B Communication	23288	18566	19075	19484	16498	16551	15890	17956	18512	22314	19144	22767
8 Finance, insurance, real estate and business services	266226	244179	234476	235590	250756	260977	286904	310323	319527	316238	306133	285232
A Financial institutions	7660	8726	9949	10428	11437	12868	14657	13402	14013	16925	10587	5545
B Insurance	1390	971	1610	2117	2977	2990	2747	3786	4907	4031	2576	2655
C Real estate and business services	257176	234482	222917	223045	236342	245119	269500	293135	300607	295282	292970	277032
Real estate except dwellings	18552	19866	17977	22356	28875	29305	40252	43230	52182	56664	65748	61401
Dwellings	238624	214616	204940	200689	207467	215814	229248	249905	248425	238618	227222	215631
9 Community, social and personal services	12865	16726	16748	16705	20344	22867	26387	28630	32503	30738	30465	30928
Total Industries	566628	519233	503702	516309	539045	565733	616107	665752	685811	679374	649980	605157
Producers of Government Services	77674	81820	81702	88080	92557	96428	109663	117174	119337	126141	130621	130077
Private Non-Profit Institutions Serving Households	1451	1537	1525	1548	1566	1601	1679	1772	1884	1919	1953	1965
Total	645753	602590	586929	605937	633168	663762	727449	784698	807032	807434	782554	737199

2.17 Exports and Imports of Goods and Services, Detail

Million French francs

	1980	1983	1984	1985	1986	1987	1988	1989	1990	1991	1992	1993
					Exports of Goods and Services							
1 Exports of merchandise, f.o.b.	488877	720442	845218	901379	860303	886740	992606	1135583	1173049	1218530	1247213	1204225
2 Transport and communication	36946	48150	51029	55823	49486	50045	53717	59151	59532	61673	60610	61255
3 Insurance service charges	1001	1467	1524	1502	1946	2622	2505	1999	1634	1993	2090	2604
4 Other commodities	43060	75930	89512	93730	95665	90984	91058	111431	124086	136131	145473	158898
5 Adjustments of merchandise exports to change-of-ownership basis	...	...	...	...	...	...	...	...	...	...	...	...
6 Direct purchases in the domestic market by non-residential households	34538	54669	66045	71496	66695	70992	81418	102923	109671	119735	132549	131760
7 Direct purchases in the domestic market by extraterritorial bodies	...	...	...	...	...	...	...	...	...	...	...	...
Total Exports of Goods and Services	604422	900658	1053328	1123930	1074095	1101383	1221304	1411087	1467972	1538062	1587935	1558742
					Imports of Goods and Services							
1 Imports of merchandise, c.i.f.	576505	808900	914542	970814	893847	952251	1063873	1229621	1273885	1302876	1268897	1172006

France

2.17 Exports and Imports of Goods and Services, Detail
(Continued)

Million French francs

		1980	1983	1984	1985	1986	1987	1988	1989	1990	1991	1992	1993
2	Adjustments of merchandise imports to change-of-ownership basis	...	...	...	...	...	...	...	...	...	...	...	...
3	Other transport and communication	13693	23034	24048	27398	26416	27358	29920	32048	35285	36546	36782	37785
4	Other insurance service charges	873	2307	2625	1744	2614	4570	6091	4448	3880	4812	4362	7171
5	Other commodities	22360	40282	46271	51242	53799	58842	59743	72773	90176	100392	109262	114220
6	Direct purchases abroad by government	...	...	...	...	...	...	...	...	...	...	...	...
7	Direct purchases abroad by resident households	25360	32865	37482	41421	45113	51328	58000	64162	66576	69835	74060	72970
	Total Imports of Goods and Services	638791	907388	1024968	1092619	1021789	1094349	1217627	1403052	1469802	1514461	1493363	1404152
	Balance of Goods and Services	-34369	-6730	28360	31311	52306	7034	3677	8035	-1830	23601	94572	154590
	Total Imports and Balance of Goods and Services	604422	900658	1053328	1123930	1074095	1101383	1221304	1411087	1467972	1538062	1587935	1558742

3.11 General Government Production Account: Total and Subsectors

Million French francs

	1980					1985				
	Total General Government	Central Government	State or Provincial Government	Local Government	Social Security Funds	Total General Government	Central Government	State or Provincial Government	Local Government	Social Security Funds
Gross Output											
1 Sales	...	...	...	...	...	...	...	...	...	...
2 Services produced for own use	509274	309358	...	99598	100318	910315	527508	...	199878	182929
3 Own account fixed capital formation	97928	39066	...	39250	19612	178881	68932	...	73906	36043
Gross Output	607202	348424	...	138848	119930	1089196	596440	...	273784	218972
Gross Input											
Intermediate Consumption	169058	97068	...	41888	30102	313564	173702	...	82114	57748
Subtotal: Value Added	438144	251356	...	96960	89828	775632	422738	...	191670	161224
1 Indirect taxes, net	7731	4293	...	-689	4127	8475	834	...	-1095	8736
A Indirect taxes	10474	5744	...	603	4127	16438	6424	...	1278	8736
B Less: Subsidies	2743	1451	...	1292	-	7963	5590	...	2373	-
2 Consumption of fixed capital	44431	12968	...	27418	4045	82842	21035	...	53730	8077
3 Compensation of employees	387179	234387	...	71136	81656	687747	403261	...	140075	144411
4 Net Operating surplus	-1197	-292	...	-905	-	-3432	-2392	...	-1040	-
Gross Input	607202	348424	...	138848	119930	1089196	596440	...	273784	218972

	1990					1991				
	Total General Government	Central Government	State or Provincial Government	Local Government	Social Security Funds	Total General Government	Central Government	State or Provincial Government	Local Government	Social Security Funds
Gross Output											
1 Sales	...	...	...	...	...	...	...	...	...	...
2 Services produced for own use	1170435	645966	...	285474	238995	1238998	677839	...	309007	252152
3 Own account fixed capital formation	245453	87768	...	112772	44913	243915	77248	...	119365	47302
Gross Output	1415888	733734	...	398246	283908	1482913	755087	...	428372	299454
Gross Input											
Intermediate Consumption	408146	206447	...	128149	73550	431431	216091	...	136992	78348
Subtotal: Value Added	1007742	527287	...	270097	210358	1051482	538996	...	291380	221106
1 Indirect taxes, net	16341	4857	...	-837	12321	16194	3674	...	-527	13047
A Indirect taxes	21220	6562	...	2337	12321	22673	6758	...	2868	13047
B Less: Subsidies	4879	1705	...	3174	-	6479	3084	...	3395	-
2 Consumption of fixed capital	119557	26784	...	81869	10904	129829	28572	...	89450	11807
3 Compensation of employees	861092	483624	...	190335	187133	907407	507480	...	203675	196252
4 Net Operating surplus	10752	12022	...	-1270	-	-1948	-730	...	-1218	-
Gross Input	1415888	733734	...	398246	283908	1482913	755087	...	428372	299454

France

3.11 General Government Production Account: Total and Subsectors

Million French francs

	1992 Total General Government	1992 Central Government	1992 State or Provincial Government	1992 Local Government	1992 Social Security Funds	1993 Total General Government	1993 Central Government	1993 State or Provincial Government	1993 Local Government	1993 Social Security Funds
					Gross Output					
1 Sales	...	...	...	...	...	...	...	...	...	...
2 Services produced for own use	1320526	720719	...	333217	266590	1405383	765904	...	355449	284030
3 Own account fixed capital formation	260313	83618	...	126503	50192	278591	91114	...	133874	53603
Gross Output	1580839	804337	...	459720	316782	1683974	857018	...	489323	337633
					Gross Input					
Intermediate Consumption	456897	226500	...	148457	81940	495981	249411	...	158699	87871
Subtotal: Value Added	1123942	577837	...	311263	234842	1187993	607607	...	330624	249762
1 Indirect taxes, net	17768	4177	...	-392	13983	18615	4065	...	-410	14960
A Indirect taxes	24524	7376	...	3165	13983	26550	8209	...	3381	14960
B Less: Subsidies	6756	3199	...	3557	-	7935	4144	...	3791	-
2 Consumption of fixed capital	138978	30312	...	96023	12643	146927	31430	...	102123	13374
3 Compensation of employees	963958	537884	...	217858	208216	1020092	567543	...	231121	221428
4 Net Operating surplus	3238	5464	...	-2226	-	2359	4569	...	-2210	-
Gross Input	1580839	804337	...	459720	316782	1683974	857018	...	489323	337633

3.12 General Government Income and Outlay Account: Total and Subsectors

Million French francs

	1980 Total General Government	1980 Central Government	1980 State or Provincial Government	1980 Local Government	1980 Social Security Funds	1985 Total General Government	1985 Central Government	1985 State or Provincial Government	1985 Local Government	1985 Social Security Funds
					Receipts					
1 Operating surplus	-1197	-292	...	-905	-	-3432	-2392	...	-1040	-
2 Property and entrepreneurial income	25696	10804	...	4127	10765	66917	35302	...	7959	23656
A Withdrawals from public quasi-corporations	817	817	...	-	-	16808	16808	...	-	-
B Interest	18164	6368	...	1792	10004	38272	13080	...	3948	21244
C Dividends	5372	3111	...	1500	761	8147	3123	...	2612	2412
D Net land rent and royalties	1343	508	...	835	-	3690	2291	...	1399	-
3 Taxes, fees and contributions	1150935	567368	...	83499	500068	2046957	954903	...	183597	908457
A Indirect taxes	410607	357006	...	47731	5870	705103	588099	...	100893	16111
B Direct taxes	236244	200951	...	35293	-	429321	348345	...	80758	218
Income	177031	177031	...	-	-	292902	292902	...	-	-
Other	59213	23920	...	35293	-	136419	55443	...	80758	218
C Social security contributions	500068	5870	...	-	494198	905143	13015	...	-	892128
D Fees, fines and penalties	4016	3541	...	475	-	7390	5444	...	1946	-
4 Other current transfers	74852	7857	...	77588	68034	125977	2034	...	125544	126309
A Casualty insurance claims	266	-	...	204	62	503	17	...	365	121
B Transfers from other government subsectors	...	-52932	...	71103	60456	...	-95822	...	113033	110699
C Transfers from the rest of the world	4353	4038	...	-	315	9807	9438	...	-	369
D Other transfers, except imputed	19869	9957	...	4044	5868	27877	7547	...	8497	11833
E Imputed unfunded employee pension and welfare contributions	50364	46794	...	2237	1333	87790	80854	...	3649	3287
Total Current Receipts	1250286	585737	...	164309	578867	2236419	989847	...	316060	1058422
					Disbursements					
1 Government final consumption expenditure	509274	309358	...	99598	100318	910315	527508	...	199878	182929
2 Property income	41312	22144	...	17715	1453	135075	88302	...	41569	5204
A Interest	41251	22083	...	17715	1453	135010	88237	...	41569	5204
B Net land rent and royalties	61	61	...	-	-	65	65	...	-	-
3 Subsidies	54407	48741	...	4512	1154	109854	98488	...	7317	4049

France

3.12 General Government Income and Outlay Account: Total and Subsectors
(Continued)

Million French francs

		1980					1985			
		Total General Government	Central Government	State or Provincial Government	Local Government	Social Security Funds	Total General Government	Central Government	State or Provincial Government	Local Government	Social Security Funds
4	Other current transfers	584378	164236	...	30916	447853	1140101	374141	...	48146	845724
	A Casualty insurance premiums, net	583	8	...	441	134	1046	29	...	761	256
	B Transfers to other government subsectors	...	71850	...	4553	2224	...	113912	...	4507	9491
	C Social security benefits	439730	-	...	-	439730	823173	-	...	-	823173
	D Social assistance grants	45387	31336	...	14051	-	117926	98549	...	19377	-
	E Unfunded employee pension and welfare benefits	52794	49224	...	2237	1333	96280	89344	...	3649	3287
	F Transfers to private non-profit institutions serving households	2829	927	...	1527	375	8059	4511	...	2850	698
	G Other transfers n.e.c.	23160	12533	...	8107	2520	55280	33647	...	17002	4631
	H Transfers to the rest of the world	19895	18358	...	-	1537	38337	34149	...	-	4188
	Net saving	60915	21258	...	11568	28089	-58926	-98592	...	19150	20516
	Total Current Disbursements and Net Saving	1250286	585737	...	164309	578867	2236419	989847	...	316060	1058422

		1990					1991			
		Total General Government	Central Government	State or Provincial Government	Local Government	Social Security Funds	Total General Government	Central Government	State or Provincial Government	Local Government	Social Security Funds

Receipts

1	Operating surplus	10752	12022	...	-1270	-	-1948	-730	...	-1218	-
2	Property and entrepreneurial income	80021	49590	...	12500	17931	78550	46681	...	13133	18736
	A Withdrawals from public quasi-corporations	20918	20918	...	-	-	18935	18935	...	-	-
	B Interest	35508	13795	...	5774	15939	37068	14046	...	6251	16771
	C Dividends	20115	13580	...	4543	1992	18344	11870	...	4509	1965
	D Net land rent and royalties	3480	1297	...	2183	-	4203	1830	...	2373	-
3	Taxes, fees and contributions	2769595	1249868	...	267575	1252152	2875589	1288655	...	281509	1305425
	A Indirect taxes	922814	746757	...	156912	19145	926557	742532	...	163951	20074
	B Direct taxes	581504	474502	...	106793	209	632890	518820	...	113837	233
	Income	415280	415280	...	-	-	463221	463221	...	-	-
	Other	166224	59222	...	106793	209	169669	55599	...	113837	233
	C Social security contributions	1253800	21002	...	-	1232798	1304210	19092	...	-	1285118
	D Fees, fines and penalties	11477	7607	...	3870	-	11932	8211	...	3721	-
4	Other current transfers	164123	-23185	...	188047	136448	195912	-31542	...	207558	160648
	A Casualty insurance claims	722	-	...	562	160	698	-	...	562	136
	B Transfers from other government subsectors	...	-149065	...	171331	114921	...	-183161	...	188247	135666
	C Transfers from the rest of the world	12523	12422	...	1	100	27644	27643	...	1	-
	D Other transfers, except imputed	40041	12349	...	11448	16244	49595	16220	...	13718	19657
	E Imputed unfunded employee pension and welfare contributions	110837	101109	...	4705	5023	117975	107756	...	5030	5189
	Total Current Receipts	3024491	1288295	...	466852	1406531	3148103	1303064	...	500982	1484809

Disbursements

1	Government final consumption expenditure	1170435	645966	...	285474	238995	1238998	677839	...	309007	252152
2	Property income	191321	134227	...	51633	5461	208554	146732	...	55645	6177
	A Interest	191222	134128	...	51633	5461	208442	146620	...	55645	6177
	B Net land rent and royalties	99	99	...	-	-	112	112	...	-	-
3	Subsidies	101086	85671	...	9415	6000	102748	85267	...	10031	7450

France

3.12 General Government Income and Outlay Account: Total and Subsectors
(Continued)

Million French francs

	1990					1991				
	Total General Government	Central Government	State or Provincial Government	Local Government	Social Security Funds	Total General Government	Central Government	State or Provincial Government	Local Government	Social Security Funds
4 Other current transfers	1520469	444437	...	69874	1143345	1635045	473056	...	74668	1228073
A Casualty insurance premiums, net	1552	25	...	1189	338	1686	23	...	1339	324
B Transfers to other government subsectors	...	114214	...	4982	17991	...	115910	...	4789	20053
C Social security benefits	1107756	-	...	-	1107756	1183483	-	...	-	1183483
D Social assistance grants	152362	129480	...	22882	-	163752	139385	...	24367	-
E Unfunded employee pension and welfare benefits	122330	112602	...	4705	5023	127242	117023	...	5030	5189
F Transfers to private non-profit institutions serving households	11329	5732	...	4933	664	12221	6099	...	5406	716
G Other transfers n.e.c.	76999	39578	...	31179	6242	80590	36137	...	33733	10720
H Transfers to the rest of the world	48141	42806	...	4	5331	66071	58479	...	4	7588
Net saving	41180	-22006	...	50456	12730	-37242	-79830	...	51631	-9043
Total Current Disbursements and Net Saving	3024491	1288295	...	466852	1406531	3148103	1303064	...	500982	1484809

	1992					1993				
	Total General Government	Central Government	State or Provincial Government	Local Government	Social Security Funds	Total General Government	Central Government	State or Provincial Government	Local Government	Social Security Funds

Receipts

1 Operating surplus	3238	5464	...	-2226	-	2359	4569	...	-2210	-
2 Property and entrepreneurial income	77495	46209	...	13372	17914	76026	45280	...	13409	17337
A Withdrawals from public quasi-corporations	18426	18426	...	-	-	19325	19325	...	-	-
B Interest	38531	15372	...	6575	16584	41086	18210	...	6338	16538
C Dividends	16742	11147	...	4265	1330	12216	6925	...	4492	799
D Net land rent and royalties	3796	1264	...	2532	-	3399	820	...	2579	-
3 Taxes, fees and contributions	2953964	1298176	...	293405	1362383	3027421	1320692	...	314094	1392635
A Indirect taxes	950946	762556	...	167548	20842	978316	774125	...	177027	27164
B Direct taxes	630102	508012	...	121779	311	651003	517782	...	132886	335
Income	454976	454976	...	-	-	469010	469010	...	-	-
Other	175126	53036	...	121779	311	181993	48772	...	132886	335
C Social security contributions	1360258	19028	...	-	1341230	1385198	20062	...	-	1365136
D Fees, fines and penalties	12658	8580	...	4078	-	12904	8723	...	4181	-
4 Other current transfers	205478	-12649	...	220826	184508	209034	-66972	...	229363	202967
A Casualty insurance claims	833	-	...	660	173	880	-	...	702	178
B Transfers from other government subsectors	...	-199289	...	198981	157515	...	-227154	...	206460	177018
C Transfers from the rest of the world	20554	19977	...	577	-	21248	20745	...	503	-
D Other transfers, except imputed	57173	20519	...	15255	21399	52394	16287	...	16049	20058
E Imputed unfunded employee pension and welfare contributions	126918	116144	...	5353	5421	134512	123150	...	5649	5713
Total Current Receipts	3240175	1307200	...	525377	1564805	3314840	1303569	...	554656	1612939

Disbursements

1 Government final consumption expenditure	1320526	720719	...	333217	266590	1405383	765904	...	355449	284030
2 Property income	237141	168242	...	59452	9447	260884	183836	...	62681	14367
A Interest	237011	168112	...	59452	9447	260746	183698	...	62681	14367
B Net land rent and royalties	130	130	...	-	-	138	138	...	-	-
3 Subsidies	113088	94277	...	10100	8711	114359	94054	...	10489	9816

France

3.12 General Government Income and Outlay Account: Total and Subsectors
(Continued)

Million French francs

	1992 Total General Government	Central Government	State or Provincial Government	Local Government	Social Security Funds	1993 Total General Government	Central Government	State or Provincial Government	Local Government	Social Security Funds
4 Other current transfers	1744819	509405	...	81967	1310654	1867456	548749	...	86458	1388573
A Casualty insurance premiums, net	1872	27	...	1461	384	1954	49	...	1520	385
B Transfers to other government subsectors	...	131139	...	5631	20437	...	129878	...	5448	20998
C Social security benefits	1262220	-	...	-	1262220	1335942	-	...	-	1335942
D Social assistance grants	170441	144400	...	26041	-	192188	164268	...	27920	-
E Unfunded employee pension and welfare benefits	134361	123587	...	5353	5421	140541	129179	...	5649	5713
F Transfers to private non-profit institutions serving households	14810	7710	...	6180	920	15705	8577	...	6428	700
G Other transfers n.e.c.	92012	41530	...	37297	13185	99737	45044	...	39489	15204
H Transfers to the rest of the world	69103	61012	...	4	8087	81389	71754	...	4	9631
Net saving	-175399	-185443	...	40641	-30597	-333242	-288974	...	39579	-83847
Total Current Disbursements and Net Saving	3240175	1307200	...	525377	1564805	3314840	1303569	...	554656	1612939

3.13 General Government Capital Accumulation Account: Total and Subsectors

Million French francs

	1980 Total General Government	Central Government	State or Provincial Government	Local Government	Social Security Funds	1985 Total General Government	Central Government	State or Provincial Government	Local Government	Social Security Funds
Finance of Gross Accumulation										
1 Gross saving	105346	34226	...	38986	32134	23916	-77557	...	72880	28593
A Consumption of fixed capital	44431	12968	...	27418	4045	82842	21035	...	53730	8077
B Net saving	60915	21258	...	11568	28089	-58926	-98592	...	19150	20516
2 Capital transfers	24421	8453	...	13867	2101	45763	17354	...	25821	2588
A From other government subsectors	-	-	...	-	-	-	-	...	-	-
B From other resident sectors	8529	6755	...	1274	500	19158	13202	...	4884	1072
C From rest of the world	15892	1698	...	12593	1601	26605	4152	...	20937	1516
Finance of Gross Accumulation	129767	42679	...	52853	34235	69679	-60203	...	98701	31181
Gross Accumulation										
1 Gross capital formation	91104	19328	...	61422	10354	149388	33127	...	103765	12496
A Increase in stocks	4502	4482	...	20	-	5111	5089	...	22	-
B Gross fixed capital formation	86602	14846	...	61402	10354	144277	28038	...	103743	12496
2 Purchases of land, net	2933	988	...	1798	147	2155	838	...	1094	223
3 Purchases of intangible assets, net	86	50	...	36	-	71	1	...	70	-
4 Capital transfers	36144	30495	...	5234	415	52736	40711	...	10418	1607
Net lending	-500	-8182	...	-15637	23319	-134671	-134880	...	-16646	16855
Gross Accumulation	129767	42679	...	52853	34235	69679	-60203	...	98701	31181

	1990 Total General Government	Central Government	State or Provincial Government	Local Government	Social Security Funds	1991 Total General Government	Central Government	State or Provincial Government	Local Government	Social Security Funds
Finance of Gross Accumulation										
1 Gross saving	160737	4778	...	132325	23634	92587	-51258	...	141081	2764
A Consumption of fixed capital	119557	26784	...	81869	10904	129829	28572	...	89450	11807
B Net saving	41180	-22006	...	50456	12730	-37242	-79830	...	51631	-9043
2 Capital transfers	79287	39627	...	37256	2404	103797	62666	...	38311	2820
A From other government subsectors	-	-	...	-	-	-	-	...	-	-
B From other resident sectors	37081	33044	...	3269	768	59857	54977	...	3528	1352
C From rest of the world	42206	6583	...	33987	1636	43940	7689	...	34783	1468
Finance of Gross Accumulation	240024	44405	...	169581	26038	196384	11408	...	179392	5584
Gross Accumulation										
1 Gross capital formation	229662	57454	...	153096	19112	238936	48251	...	167907	22778

France

3.13 General Government Capital Accumulation Account: Total and Subsectors
(Continued)

Million French francs

	1990					1991				
	Total General Government	Central Government	State or Provincial Government	Local Government	Social Security Funds	Total General Government	Central Government	State or Provincial Government	Local Government	Social Security Funds
A Increase in stocks	17629	17587	...	42	-	8496	8459	...	37	-
B Gross fixed capital formation	212033	39867	...	153054	19112	230440	39792	...	167870	22778
2 Purchases of land, net	3467	1209	...	1814	444	4289	1165	...	2673	451
3 Purchases of intangible assets, net	429	130	...	299	-	341	-59	...	400	-
4 Capital transfers	107555	87163	...	18892	1500	99896	75751	...	22603	1542
Net lending	-101089	-101551	...	-4520	4982	-147078	-113700	...	-14191	-19187
Gross Accumulation	240024	44405	...	169581	26038	196384	11408	...	179392	5584

	1992					1993				
	Total General Government	Central Government	State or Provincial Government	Local Government	Social Security Funds	Total General Government	Central Government	State or Provincial Government	Local Government	Social Security Funds
Finance of Gross Accumulation										
1 Gross saving	-36421	-155131	...	136664	-17954	-186315	-257544	...	141702	-70473
A Consumption of fixed capital	138978	30312	...	96023	12643	146927	31430	...	102123	13374
B Net saving	-175399	-185443	...	40641	-30597	-333242	-288974	...	39579	-83847
2 Capital transfers	118888	74103	...	41753	3032	106606	58529	...	44866	3211
A From other government subsectors	-	-	...	-	-	-	-	...	-	-
B From other resident sectors	72041	66756	...	4206	1079	55764	50520	...	3989	1255
C From rest of the world	46847	7347	...	37547	1953	50842	8009	...	40877	1956
Finance of Gross Accumulation	82467	-81028	...	178417	-14922	-79709	-199015	...	186568	-67262
Gross Accumulation										
1 Gross capital formation	246397	45854	...	175163	25380	227763	27711	...	173834	26218
A Increase in stocks	4080	4042	...	38	-	-13921	-13961	...	40	-
B Gross fixed capital formation	242317	41812	...	175125	25380	241684	41672	...	173794	26218
2 Purchases of land, net	5320	1246	...	3409	665	5970	1712	...	3695	563
3 Purchases of intangible assets, net	501	64	...	437	-	572	6	...	566	-
4 Capital transfers	113801	81832	...	24153	7816	121118	88762	...	25496	6860
Net lending	-283552	-210024	...	-24745	-48783	-435132	-317206	...	-17023	-100903
Gross Accumulation	82467	-81028	...	178417	-14922	-79709	-199015	...	186568	-67262

3.14 General Government Capital Finance Account, Total and Subsectors

Million French francs

	1980					1985				
	Total General Government	Central Government	State or Provincial Government	Local Government	Social Security Funds	Total General Government	Central Government	State or Provincial Government	Local Government	Social Security Funds
Acquisition of Financial Assets										
1 Gold and SDRs	242	242	...	...	...	41	41	...	...	...
2 Currency and transferable deposits	23639	11116	...	1951	10572	47214	18950	...	13199	15065
3 Other deposits	1911	312	...	256	1343	723	1073	...	1361	-1711
4 Bills and bonds, short term	-	...	...	-	-	-	...	...	...	-
5 Bonds, long term	1465	110	...	371	984	8022	531	...	571	6920
6 Corporate equity securities	21794	17659	...	-	4135	20691	18889	...	-	1802
7 Short-term loans, n.e.c.	2261	-513	...	-896	3670	-8242	-15023	...	-795	7576
8 Long-term loans, n.e.c.	-4669	-4669	...	-	...	452	452	...	-	...
9 Other receivables	86	...	...	86	...	131	...	...	131	...
10 Other assets	7418	6383	...	518	517	14724	10767	...	6365	-2408
Total Acquisition of Financial Assets	54147	30640	...	2286	21221	83756	35680	...	20832	27244
Incurrence of Liabilities										
1 Currency and transferable deposits	10886	10886	...	...	745	44309	44309	...	...	489
2 Other deposits	2547	1437	...	365	...	-1884	-2043	...	-330	...
3 Bills and bonds, short term	-5949	-5949	...	...	...	20162	20162	...	...	...
4 Bonds, long term	28862	27645	...	1217	-	93083	89807	...	3276	-
5 Short-term loans, n.e.c.	-8074	-694	...	-689	-6691	24685	21890	...	258	2537

France

3.14 General Government Capital Finance Account, Total and Subsectors
(Continued)

Million French francs

1980 / 1985

	Total General Government	Central Government	State or Provincial Government	Local Government	Social Security Funds	Total General Government	Central Government	State or Provincial Government	Local Government	Social Security Funds
6 Long-term loans, n.e.c.	21199	364	...	18598	2237	25711	-7561	...	31746	1526
7 Other payables	-	-	...	...	...	5	-	...	5	...
8 Other liabilities	5176	5133	...	-1568	1611	12356	3996	...	2523	5837
Total Incurrence of Liabilities	54647	38822	...	17923	-2098	218427	170560	...	37478	10389
Statistical discrepancy	...	...	...	...	...	...	...	...	...	...
Net Lending	-500	-8182	...	-15637	23319	-134671	-134880	...	-16646	16855
Incurrence of Liabilities and Net Worth	54147	30640	...	2286	21221	83756	35680	...	20832	27244

1990 / 1991

	Total General Government	Central Government	State or Provincial Government	Local Government	Social Security Funds	Total General Government	Central Government	State or Provincial Government	Local Government	Social Security Funds
Acquisition of Financial Assets										
1 Gold and SDRs	12244	-619	...	2218	10645	4243	-23	...	43	4223
2 Currency and transferable deposits	2534	-4980	...	1864	5650	-20225	-27490	...	-8755	16020
3 Other deposits	-503	-183	...	-442	122	1801	-491	...	103	2189
4 Bills and bonds, short term	-602	-	...	...	-602	383	383	...	-	-
5 Bonds, long term	7402	1762	...	141	5499	3036	-404	...	1941	1499
6 Corporate equity securities	5788	3931	...	-	1857	6855	3374	...	-	3481
7 Short-term loans, n.e.c.	-19292	-16026	...	8300	-11566	-3710	-4235	...	16638	-16113
8 Long-term loans, n.e.c.	-3135	-3135	...	...	...	1553	1553	...	-	-
9 Other receivables	929	...	...	929	...	-75	-	...	-75	-
10 Other assets	31311	13409	...	13217	4685	33393	19153	...	15530	-1290
Total Acquisition of Financial Assets	36676	-5841	...	26227	16290	27254	-8180	...	25425	10009
Incurrence of Liabilities										
1 Currency and transferable deposits	2586	2586	...	...	-	-10284	-10284	...	-	-
2 Other deposits	351	215	...	-	136	-10866	-11004	...	-	138
3 Bills and bonds, short term	29700	29700	...	...	...	7400	7400	...	-	-
4 Bonds, long term	85978	89310	...	-1400	-1932	90789	91747	...	-451	-507
5 Short-term loans, n.e.c.	-13343	-29332	...	9723	6266	46930	20687	...	8860	17383
6 Long-term loans, n.e.c.	41588	19541	...	22851	-804	25600	581	...	26797	-1778
7 Other payables	-	-	...	-	...	-	-	...	-	-
8 Other liabilities	-9095	-16310	...	-427	7642	24265	24265	...	4410	13960
Total Incurrence of Liabilities	137765	95710	...	30747	11308	173834	105022	...	39616	29196
Statistical discrepancy	...	...	...	...	...	498	498	...	-	-
Net Lending	-101089	-101551	...	-4520	4982	-147078	-113700	...	-14191	-19187
Incurrence of Liabilities and Net Worth	36676	-5841	...	26227	16290	27254	-8180	...	25425	10009

1992 / 1993

	Total General Government	Central Government	State or Provincial Government	Local Government	Social Security Funds	Total General Government	Central Government	State or Provincial Government	Local Government	Social Security Funds
Acquisition of Financial Assets										
1 Gold and SDRs	19089	4233	...	1922	12934	-856	-450	...	-1864	1458
2 Currency and transferable deposits	25310	51806	...	-5751	-20745	52132	53097	...	19	-984
3 Other deposits	3054	515	...	-1	2540	3105	3687	...	-661	79
4 Bills and bonds, short term	5500	749	...	-	4751	-4191	418	...	-	-4609
5 Bonds, long term	4282	4124	...	4	154	7593	12907	...	-3	-5311
6 Corporate equity securities	-8630	-11121	...	-	2491	-48252	-43339	...	-	-4913
7 Short-term loans, n.e.c.	21874	11100	...	5824	4950	-9587	-14885	...	8839	-3541
8 Long-term loans, n.e.c.	9381	9381	...	-	-	23100	23100	...	-	-
9 Other receivables	269	-	...	269	-	69	-	...	69	-
10 Other assets	74353	32753	...	14965	26635	69370	41883	...	17511	9976
Total Acquisition of Financial Assets	154482	103540	...	17232	33710	92483	76418	...	23910	-7845
Incurrence of Liabilities										
1 Currency and transferable deposits	-6824	-6824	...	-	-	880	880	...	-	-
2 Other deposits	-8450	-8841	...	-	391	1268	868	...	-	400
3 Bills and bonds, short term	157700	157700	...	-	-	54900	54900	...	-	-
4 Bonds, long term	132377	131286	...	-975	2066	315734	311479	...	2217	2038
5 Short-term loans, n.e.c.	47347	20392	...	-3801	30756	68922	1437	...	3430	64055

455

France

3.14 General Government Capital Finance Account, Total and Subsectors
(Continued)

Million French francs

	1992					1993				
	Total General Government	Central Government	State or Provincial Government	Local Government	Social Security Funds	Total General Government	Central Government	State or Provincial Government	Local Government	Social Security Funds
6 Long-term loans, n.e.c.	41961	-5833	...	34203	13591	22511	-1763	...	22709	1565
7 Other payables	-	-	...	-	-	-	-	...	-	-
8 Other liabilities	73923	25684	...	12550	35689	63400	25823	...	12577	25000
Total Incurrence of Liabilities	438034	313564	...	41977	82493	527615	393624	...	40933	93058
Statistical discrepancy	-	-	-	-	-	-	-	-	-	-
Net Lending	-283552	-210024	...	-24745	-48783	-435132	-317206	...	-17023	-100903
Incurrence of Liabilities and Net Worth	154482	103540	...	17232	33710	92483	76418	...	23910	-7845

3.21 Corporate and Quasi-Corporate Enterprise Production Account: Total and Sectors

Million French francs

	1980				1985				1990			
	\multicolumn{3}{c	}{Corporate and Quasi-Corporate Enterprises}	ADDENDUM: Total, including Unincorporated	\multicolumn{3}{c	}{Corporate and Quasi-Corporate Enterprises}	ADDENDUM: Total, including Unincorporated	\multicolumn{3}{c	}{Corporate and Quasi-Corporate Enterprises}	ADDENDUM: Total, including Unincorporated
	TOTAL	Non-Financial	Financial		TOTAL	Non-Financial	Financial		TOTAL	Non-Financial	Financial	
Gross Output												
1 Output for sale	3276870	3207040	69830	4189155	5416894	5252336	164558	6799907	7768321	7261957	506364	9583038
2 Imputed bank service charge	107503	-	107503	107503	192340	-	192340	192340	271421	-	271421	305643
3 Own-account fixed capital formation	...	...	...	...	...	...	...	...	...	...	...	...
Gross Output	3384373	3207040	177333	4313587	5609234	5252336	356898	7020106	8039742	7261957	777785	9888681
Gross Input												
Intermediate consumption	1913242	1754633	158609	2199771	3134719	2818783	315936	3522172	4493121	3738878	754243	4932305
1 Imputed banking service charge	107503	-	107503	107503	192340	-	192340	192340	278020	-	278020	278020
2 Other intermediate consumption	1805739	1754633	51106	2092268	2942379	2818783	123596	3329832	4215101	3738878	476223	4654285
Subtotal: Value Added	1471131	1452407	18724	2113816	2474515	2433553	40962	3497934	3546621	3523079	23542	4956376
1 Indirect taxes, net	90031	86241	3790	100948	169780	154588	15192	177323	286803	252273	34530	301995
A Indirect taxes	149178	132354	16824	169714	281369	241512	39857	311949	390170	338187	51983	433600
B Less: Subsidies	59147	46113	13034	68766	111589	86924	24665	134626	103367	85914	17453	131605
2 Consumption of fixed capital	198981	193098	5883	301077	346588	334294	12294	505406	475522	456557	18965	707881
3 Compensation of employees	1057643	991844	65799	1180848	1704532	1586647	117885	1882690	2277410	2127376	150034	2494580
4 Net operating surplus	124476	181224	-56748	530943	253615	358024	-104409	932515	506886	686873	-179987	1451920
Gross Input	3384373	3207040	177333	4313587	5609234	5252336	356898	7020106	8039742	7261957	777785	9888681

	1991				1992				1993			
	\multicolumn{3}{c	}{Corporate and Quasi-Corporate Enterprises}	ADDENDUM: Total, including Unincorporated	\multicolumn{3}{c	}{Corporate and Quasi-Corporate Enterprises}	ADDENDUM: Total, including Unincorporated	\multicolumn{3}{c	}{Corporate and Quasi-Corporate Enterprises}	ADDENDUM: Total, including Unincorporated
	TOTAL	Non-Financial	Financial		TOTAL	Non-Financial	Financial		TOTAL	Non-Financial	Financial	
Gross Output												
1 Output for sale	8180781	7583438	597343	14435	8532432	7735584	796848	396735	8842091	7617240	1224851	670660
2 Imputed bank service charge	262753	-	262753	301535	257808	-	257808	300494	272766	-	272766	319410
3 Own-account fixed capital formation	...	...	...	...	...	...	...	...	...	...	...	...
Gross Output	8443534	7583438	860096	315970	8790240	7735584	1054656	697229	9114857	7617240	1497617	990070
Gross Input												
Intermediate consumption	4709756	3891367	818389	5135644	4947453	3944164	1003289	5360184	5254236	3837558	1416678	5638785
1 Imputed banking service charge	269336	-	269336	269336	263193	-	263193	263193	278625	-	278625	278625
2 Other intermediate consumption	4440420	3891367	549053	4866308	4684260	3944164	740096	5096991	4975611	3837558	1138053	5360160
Subtotal: Value Added	3733778	3692071	41707	5180326	3842787	3791420	51367	5337045	3860621	3779682	80939	5351285
1 Indirect taxes, net	292638	255382	37256	308037	304558	268194	36364	311996	326595	285985	40610	317748
A Indirect taxes	401985	350457	51528	445784	417033	365607	51426	459699	439855	386104	53751	484052
B Less: Subsidies	109347	95075	14272	137747	112475	97413	15062	147703	113260	100119	13141	166304
2 Consumption of fixed capital	518085	497315	20770	748670	541517	519739	21778	766442	543960	522562	21398	776587
3 Compensation of employees	2387107	2229700	157407	2607505	2459297	2296281	163016	2688084	2454679	2284582	170097	2685824
4 Net operating surplus	535948	709674	-173726	1516114	537415	707206	-169791	1570523	535387	686553	-151166	1571126
Gross Input	8443534	7583438	860096	315970	8790240	7735584	1054656	697229	9114857	7617240	1497617	990070

France

3.22 Corporate and Quasi-Corporate Enterprise Income and Outlay Account: Total and Sectors

Million French francs

	1980 TOTAL	1980 Non-Financial	1980 Financial	1985 TOTAL	1985 Non-Financial	1985 Financial	1990 TOTAL	1990 Non-Financial	1990 Financial	1991 TOTAL	1991 Non-Financial	1991 Financial
Receipts												
1 Operating surplus	124476	181224	-56748	253615	358024	-104409	506886	686873	-179987	535948	709674	-173726
2 Property and entrepreneurial income	510717	48885	461832	1111299	100203	1011096	1663361	215112	1448249	1842918	268293	1574625
A Withdrawals from quasi-corporate enterprises	-	-	-	-	-	-	-	-	-	-	-	-
B Interest	473110	19956	453154	1025511	41905	983606	1446307	59241	1387066	1583492	77004	1506488
C Dividends	33417	24749	8668	78862	51397	27465	206690	145507	61183	246688	178551	68137
D Net land rent and royalties	4190	4180	10	6926	6901	25	10364	10364	-	12738	12738	-
3 Current transfers	144908	81857	63051	270947	144583	126364	370217	179748	190469	381647	190460	191187
A Casualty insurance claims	11640	11362	278	24473	23928	545	32284	31491	793	37306	36538	768
B Casualty insurance premiums, net, due to be received by insurance companies	48264	-	48264	85940	-	85940	125562	-	125562	129052	-	129052
C Current transfers from the rest of the world	...	...	...	...	...	...	...	...	...	...	...	...
D Other transfers except imputed	55658	42329	13329	110777	73192	37585	151661	90512	61149	151660	93437	58223
E Imputed unfunded employee pension and welfare contributions	29346	28166	1180	49757	47463	2294	60710	57745	2965	63629	60485	3144
Total Current Receipts	780101	311966	468135	1635861	602810	1033051	2540464	1081733	1458731	2760513	1168427	1592086
Disbursements												
1 Property and entrepreneurial income	558388	206134	352254	1199622	413131	786491	1768150	634580	1133570	2003767	701770	1301997
A Withdrawals from quasi-corporations	817	817	-	16808	16808	-	20918	20918	-	18935	18935	-
B Interest	474486	134499	339987	1002776	267840	734936	1293040	340914	952126	1466514	377302	1089212
C Dividends [a]	74964	62697	12267	164151	112596	51555	432168	250724	181444	494518	281733	212785
D Net land rent and royalties	8121	8121	-	15887	15887	-	22024	22024	-	23800	23800	-
2 Direct taxes and other current transfers n.e.c. to general government	65902	51891	14011	115852	81941	33911	186607	136215	50392	168871	122965	45906
A Direct taxes	64650	50639	14011	113703	79792	33911	184376	133984	50392	166342	120436	45906
On income	7825	4968	2857	32463	15690	16773	42039	20736	21303	43013	22139	20874
Other	56825	45671	11154	81240	64102	17138	142337	113248	29089	123329	98297	25032
B Fines, fees, penalties and other current transfers n.e.c.	1252	1252	-	2149	2149	-	2231	2231	-	2529	2529	-
3 Other current transfers	151771	73328	78443	275294	131546	143748	386143	171476	214667	403073	186726	216347
A Casualty insurance premiums, net	15321	15009	312	27568	27057	511	34587	33776	811	41030	40236	794
B Casualty insurance claims liability of insurance companies	56970	-	56970	103779	-	103779	145984	-	145984	149534	-	149534
C Transfers to private non-profit institutions	531	531	-	1240	1240	-	1558	1558	-	1218	1218	-
D Unfunded employee pension and welfare benefits	48687	39060	9627	87286	65443	21843	118589	81024	37565	123773	83899	39874
E Social assistance grants	...	...	...	...	...	...	...	...	...	...	...	...
F Other transfers n.e.c.	30262	18728	11534	55421	37806	17615	85425	55118	30307	87518	61373	26145
G Transfers to the rest of the world	...	...	...	...	...	...	...	...	...	...	...	...
Net saving	4040	-19387	23427	45093	-23808	68901	199564	139462	60102	184802	156966	27836
Total Current Disbursements and Net Saving	780101	311966	468135	1635861	602810	1033051	2540464	1081733	1458731	2760513	1168427	1592086

	1992 TOTAL	1992 Non-Financial	1992 Financial	1993 TOTAL	1993 Non-Financial	1993 Financial
Receipts						
1 Operating surplus	537415	707206	-169791	535387	686553	-151166
2 Property and entrepreneurial income	1915474	306228	1609246	2074621	326161	1748460
A Withdrawals from quasi-corporate enterprises	-	-	-	-	-	-
B Interest	1619429	80632	1538797	1764322	89014	1675308
C Dividends	281843	211394	70449	297014	223862	73152
D Net land rent and royalties	14202	14202	-	13285	13285	-

France

3.22 Corporate and Quasi-Corporate Enterprise Income and Outlay Account: Total and Sectors
(Continued)

Million French francs

	1992 TOTAL	1992 Non-Financial	1992 Financial	1993 TOTAL	1993 Non-Financial	1993 Financial
3 Current transfers	411231	204290	206941	426291	206218	220073
A Casualty insurance claims	42111	41249	862	45034	44168	866
B Casualty insurance premiums, net, due to be received by insurance companies	147095	-	147095	154538	-	154538
C Current transfers from the rest of the world	...	...	...	...	...	...
D Other transfers except imputed	153612	97876	55736	158469	97215	61254
E Imputed unfunded employee pension and welfare contributions	68413	65165	3248	68250	64835	3415
Total Current Receipts	2864120	1217724	1646396	3036299	1218932	1817367
Disbursements						
1 Property and entrepreneurial income	2071921	762390	1309531	2215767	781490	1434277
A Withdrawals from quasi-corporations	18426	18426	-	19325	19325	-
B Interest	1481917	417450	1064467	1652766	420235	1232531
C Dividends a	545602	300538	245064	518470	316724	201746
D Net land rent and royalties	25976	25976	-	25206	25206	-
2 Direct taxes and other current transfers n.e.c. to general government	146550	99019	47531	147382	96452	50930
A Direct taxes	144065	96534	47531	145047	94117	50930
On income	45071	24097	20974	45568	26471	19097
Other	98994	72437	26557	99479	67646	31833
B Fines, fees, penalties and other current transfers n.e.c.	2485	2485	-	2335	2335	-
3 Other current transfers	433363	199768	233595	450491	210545	239946
A Casualty insurance premiums, net	46651	45755	896	48690	47770	920
B Casualty insurance claims liability of insurance companies	169966	-	169966	176929	-	176929
C Transfers to private non-profit institutions	1234	1234	-	1235	1235	-
D Unfunded employee pension and welfare benefits	130674	88026	42648	134712	88351	46361
E Social assistance grants	...	...	...	...	...	...
F Other transfers n.e.c.	84838	64753	20085	88925	73189	15736
G Transfers to the rest of the world	...	...	...	...	...	...
Net saving	212286	156547	55739	222659	130445	92214
Total Current Disbursements and Net Saving	2864120	1217724	1646396	3036299	1218932	1817367

a) Item 'Dividends' includes profit-sharing by employees.

3.23 Corporate and Quasi-Corporate Enterprise Capital Accumulation Account: Total and Sectors

Million French francs

	1980 TOTAL	1980 Non-Financial	1980 Financial	1985 TOTAL	1985 Non-Financial	1985 Financial	1990 TOTAL	1990 Non-Financial	1990 Financial	1991 TOTAL	1991 Non-Financial	1991 Financial
Finance of Gross Accumulation												
1 Gross saving	203021	173711	29310	391681	310486	81195	675086	596019	79067	702887	654281	48606
A Consumption of fixed capital	198981	193098	5883	346588	334294	12294	475522	456557	18965	518085	497315	20770
B Net saving	4040	-19387	23427	45093	-23808	68901	199564	139462	60102	184802	156966	27836
2 Capital transfers	13799	10998	2801	32538	26852	5686	50463	43990	6473	57967	51299	6668
Finance of Gross Accumulation	216820	184709	32111	424219	337338	86881	725549	640009	85540	760854	705580	55274
Gross Accumulation												
1 Gross capital formation	321298	310236	11062	413884	390083	23801	761191	721635	39556	764889	720792	44097

France

3.23 Corporate and Quasi-Corporate Enterprise Capital Accumulation Account: Total and Sectors
(Continued)

Million French francs

	1980 TOTAL	1980 Non-Financial	1980 Financial	1985 TOTAL	1985 Non-Financial	1985 Financial	1990 TOTAL	1990 Non-Financial	1990 Financial	1991 TOTAL	1991 Non-Financial	1991 Financial
A Increase in stocks	28679	28720	-41	-19365	-20004	639	54696	54664	32	26554	26476	78
B Gross fixed capital formation	292619	281516	11103	433249	410087	23162	706495	666971	39524	738335	694316	44019
2 Purchases of land, net	4899	4324	575	5540	4785	755	35893	34162	1731	39371	37938	1433
3 Purchases of intangible assets, net	5460	5464	-4	12046	12042	4	19810	19810	-	27353	27353	-
4 Capital transfers	7479	5947	1532	26077	17634	8443	37015	13698	23317	60682	15513	45169
Net lending	-122316	-141262	18946	-33328	-87206	53878	-128360	-149296	20936	-131441	-96016	-35425
Gross Accumulation	216820	184709	32111	424219	337338	86881	725549	640009	85540	760854	705580	55274

	1992 TOTAL	1992 Non-Financial	1992 Financial	1993 TOTAL	1993 Non-Financial	1993 Financial
Finance of Gross Accumulation						
1 Gross saving	753803	676286	77517	766619	653007	113612
A Consumption of fixed capital	541517	519739	21778	543960	522562	21398
B Net saving	212286	156547	55739	222659	130445	92214
2 Capital transfers	69938	60533	9405	91699	82186	9513
Finance of Gross Accumulation	823741	736819	86922	858318	735193	123125
Gross Accumulation						
1 Gross capital formation	702039	673440	28599	563518	544160	19358
A Increase in stocks	-14396	-14255	-141	-86751	-86728	-23
B Gross fixed capital formation	716435	687695	28740	650269	630888	19381
2 Purchases of land, net	40331	38876	1455	12210	11150	1060
3 Purchases of intangible assets, net	29187	29187	-	16968	16968	-
4 Capital transfers	75061	19505	55556	82987	22064	60923
Net lending	-22877	-24189	1312	182635	140851	41784
Gross Accumulation	823741	736819	86922	858318	735193	123125

3.24 Corporate and Quasi-Corporate Enterprise Capital Finance Account: Total and Sectors

Million French francs

	1980 TOTAL	1980 Non-Financial	1980 Financial	1985 TOTAL	1985 Non-Financial	1985 Financial	1990 TOTAL	1990 Non-Financial	1990 Financial	1991 TOTAL	1991 Non-Financial	1991 Financial
Acquisition of Financial Assets												
1 Gold and SDRs	13445	1220	12225	26390	-2021	28411	118474	13283	105191	-1644	22780	-24424
2 Currency and transferable deposits	67558	4997	62561	64990	-8784	73774	-57258	42113	-99371	-77066	-63346	-13720
3 Other deposits	295263	19785	275478	290650	36729	253921	403448	46798	356650	110981	-14576	125557
4 Bills and bonds, short term	-5619	-	-5619	51645	10358	41287	355293	35544	319749	202805	19714	183091
5 Bonds, long term	45156	5232	39924	237120	6722	230398	185584	14937	170647	223283	-14130	237413
6 Corporate equity securities	35824	10574	25250	120311	63274	57037	446625	363194	83431	279078	194208	84870
7 Short term loans, n.e.c.	137524	11243	126281	167655	32805	134850	153726	12392	141334	551548	334438	217110
8 Long term loans, n.e.c.	239151	-	239151	220907	-	220907	392756	-	392756	224192	-	224192
9 Trade credits and advances	122570	117942	4628	52279	47182	5097	156874	162461	-5587	154351	139453	14898
10 Other receivables	2819	2740	79	4339	4237	102	11781	11502	279	8457	8391	66
11 Other assets	...	...	...	...	...	...	...	...	...	...	...	...
Total Acquisition of Financial Assets	953691	173733	779958	1236286	190502	1045784	2167303	702224	1465079	1675985	626932	1049053
Incurrence of Liabilities												
1 Currency and transferable deposits	96278	-	96278	101128	-	101128	-8194	-	-8194	-104718	-	-104718
2 Other deposits	464912	11002	453910	422980	19227	403753	595019	25593	569426	201371	78922	122449
3 Bills and bonds, short term	330	-	330	31837	3300	28537	421953	27977	393976	208821	6805	202016
4 Bonds, long term	69706	16844	52862	183562	18585	164977	195458	70932	124526	204998	60682	144316
5 Corporate equity securities	71401	51540	19861	302750	99361	203389	546052	221602	324450	500112	242032	258080
6 Short-term loans, n.e.c.	141040	57084	83956	50889	45476	5413	506	141413	-140907	357410	106524	250886

France

3.24 Corporate and Quasi-Corporate Enterprise Capital Finance Account: Total and Sectors
(Continued)

Million French francs

	1980 TOTAL	1980 Non-Financial	1980 Financial	1985 TOTAL	1985 Non-Financial	1985 Financial	1990 TOTAL	1990 Non-Financial	1990 Financial	1991 TOTAL	1991 Non-Financial	1991 Financial
7 Long-term loans, n.e.c.	86836	67356	19480	35208	40062	-4854	199734	199880	-146	148977	141478	7499
8 Net equity of households in life insurance and pension fund reserves	13138	-	13138	47350	-	47350	165866	-	165866	184748	-	184748
9 Proprietors' net additions to the accumulation of quasi-corporations	...	...	...	...	...	...	...	...	...	...	...	...
10 Trade credit and advances	124531	121263	3268	58085	41271	16814	148466	149222	-756	92910	84465	8445
11 Other accounts payable	15944	-	15944	24242	-	24242	17780	-	17780	11082	-	11082
12 Other liabilities	...	...	...	...	...	...	...	...	...	...	...	...
Total Incurrence of Liabilities	1084116	325089	759027	1258031	267282	990749	2282640	836619	1446021	1805711	720908	1084803
Statistical discrepancy [a]	-8109	-10094	1985	11583	10426	1157	13023	14901	-1878	1715	2040	-325
Net Lending	-122316	-141262	18946	-33328	-87206	53878	-128360	-149296	20936	-131441	-96016	-35425
Incurrence of Liabilities and Net Lending	953691	173733	779958	1236286	190502	1045784	2167303	702224	1465079	1675985	626932	1049053

	1992 TOTAL	1992 Non-Financial	1992 Financial	1993 TOTAL	1993 Non-Financial	1993 Financial
Acquisition of Financial Assets						
1 Gold and SDRs	-14524	5701	-20225	13338	1768	11570
2 Currency and transferable deposits	-8561	-2837	-5724	-27392	1894	-29286
3 Other deposits	373224	79834	293390	330636	-27747	358383
4 Bills and bonds, short term	446713	80451	366262	134584	-61580	196164
5 Bonds, long term	164632	-18471	183103	460213	-7934	468147
6 Corporate equity securities	366665	248883	117782	416794	130876	285918
7 Short term loans, n.e.c.	539943	2625	537318	-114393	121167	-235560
8 Long term loans, n.e.c.	116096	-	116096	511389	-	511389
9 Trade credits and advances	170250	161413	8837	118207	77233	40974
10 Other receivables	8201	8035	166	3666	3607	59
11 Other assets	...	...	...	...	...	...
Total Acquisition of Financial Assets	2162639	565634	1597005	1847042	239284	1607758
Incurrence of Liabilities						
1 Currency and transferable deposits	132400	-	132400	68174	-	68174
2 Other deposits	316826	112099	204727	312071	29368	282703
3 Bills and bonds, short term	304253	16880	287373	-13572	-24892	11320
4 Bonds, long term	206801	51623	155178	187752	51301	136451
5 Corporate equity securities	479378	233764	245614	448235	216089	232146
6 Short-term loans, n.e.c.	313338	-1774	315112	22540	-412127	434667
7 Long-term loans, n.e.c.	68770	60409	8361	291576	154650	136926
8 Net equity of households in life insurance and pension fund reserves	210150	-	210150	264462	-	264462
9 Proprietors' net additions to the accumulation of quasi-corporations	...	...	...	...	...	...
10 Trade credit and advances	138937	127053	11884	96576	120333	-23757
11 Other accounts payable	20619	-	20619	13958	-	13958
12 Other liabilities	...	...	...	...	...	...
Total Incurrence of Liabilities	2191472	600054	1591418	1691772	134722	1557050
Statistical discrepancy [a]	-5956	-10231	4275	-27365	-36289	8924
Net Lending	-22877	-24189	1312	182635	140851	41784
Incurrence of Liabilities and Net Lending	2162639	565634	1597005	1847042	239284	1607758

a) Statistical discrepancy refers to adjustment made in order to reconcile the net lending of the Capital Accumulation Account and the Capital Finance Account.

3.31 Household and Private Unincorporated Enterprise Production Account

Million French francs

	1980	1983	1984	1985	1986	1987	1988	1989	1990	1991	1992	1993
Gross Output												
1 Output for sale	912285	1229851	1325834	1383013	1461829	1500035	1590637	1735739	1814717	1833654	1864303	1828569
2 Non-marketed output	16929	24975	26438	27859	27858	28310	30317	32182	34222	38782	42686	46644
Gross Output	929214	1254826	1352272	1410872	1489687	1528345	1620954	1767921	1848939	1872436	1906989	1875213
Gross Input												
Intermediate consumption	286529	364424	399061	387453	396588	395143	414470	441284	439184	425888	412731	384549

France

3.31 Household and Private Unincorporated Enterprise Production Account
(Continued)

Million French francs

	1980	1983	1984	1985	1986	1987	1988	1989	1990	1991	1992	1993
Subtotal: Value Added	642685	890402	953211	1023419	1093099	1133202	1206484	1326637	1409755	1446548	1494258	1490664
1 Indirect taxes net liability of unincorporated enterprises	10917	9208	7931	7543	7073	7566	14682	11467	15192	15399	7438	-8847
A Indirect taxes	20536	25738	28475	30580	33101	34864	40183	38675	43430	43799	42666	44197
B Less: Subsidies	9619	16530	20544	23037	26028	27298	25501	27208	28238	28400	35228	53044
2 Consumption of fixed capital	102096	141651	151718	158818	171910	185032	203962	224371	232359	230585	224925	232627
3 Compensation of employees	123205	160240	168255	178158	180689	183377	192396	204816	217170	220398	228787	231145
4 Net operating surplus	406467	579303	625307	678900	733427	757227	795444	885983	945034	980166	1033108	1035739
Gross Input	929214	1254826	1352272	1410872	1489687	1528345	1620954	1767921	1848939	1872436	1906989	1875213

3.32 Household and Private Unincorporated Enterprise Income and Outlay Account

Million French francs

	1980	1983	1984	1985	1986	1987	1988	1989	1990	1991	1992	1993
					Receipts							
1 Compensation of employees	1573880	2255615	2419226	2573107	2700561	2816655	2972468	3161822	3370516	3531133	3665726	3721760
A Wages and salaries	1162641	1644066	1755254	1855004	1945807	2024989	2138217	2273162	2429113	2548018	2637645	2674969
B Employers' contributions for social security	331529	493327	536059	580556	606927	639739	677157	725118	769856	801511	832750	844029
C Employers' contributions for private pension & welfare plans	79710	118222	127913	137547	147827	151927	157094	163542	171547	181604	195331	202762
2 Operating surplus of private unincorporated enterprises	406467	579303	625307	678900	733427	757227	795444	885983	945034	980166	1033108	1035739
3 Property and entrepreneurial income	166725	256819	273808	303406	305074	328844	347817	421301	459426	530744	554827	548698
A Withdrawals from private quasi-corporations	...	...	...	...	...	...	...	...	...	...	...	...
B Interest	111745	177554	185902	200298	186774	182014	194686	217873	243522	275413	274132	304253
C Dividends	44162	66428	72719	86311	101706	133614	135977	185134	197632	237421	262257	226537
D Net land rent and royalties	10818	12837	15187	16797	16594	13216	17154	18294	18272	17910	18438	17908
3 Current transfers	670050	1053406	1161368	1271035	1361872	1414309	1514816	1597992	1716527	1826103	1943833	2060533
A Casualty insurance claims	47377	72702	79524	84577	87659	92703	98518	99963	117240	121831	137112	142757
B Social security benefits	443334	711500	770207	834620	896206	930719	999470	1061412	1131617	1209285	1289790	1366380
C Social assistance grants	46879	79021	99437	120179	131665	133238	140997	146029	155572	167145	173921	195677
D Unfunded employee pension and welfare benefits	92369	138013	152966	162704	169348	177833	185234	194374	204525	212428	223670	230302
E Transfers from general government	...	...	...	...	...	...	...	...	...	...	...	...
F Transfers from the rest of the world	5801	5947	6421	5807	6207	6628	6523	7276	8094	9085	10354	10298
G Other transfers n.e.c.	34290	46223	52813	63148	70787	73188	84074	88938	99479	106329	108986	115119
Total Current Receipts	2817122	4145143	4479709	4826448	5100934	5317035	5630545	6067098	6491503	6868146	7197494	7366730
					Disbursements							
1 Final consumption expenditures	1645072	2424143	2639171	2858393	3049520	3235582	3429508	3655793	3861322	4037525	4189834	4291627
2 Property income	89538	131726	145623	164206	182139	187733	213336	250043	275419	278862	293688	277952
A Interest	79257	118798	130985	148239	166994	176375	198130	233927	259818	264232	279567	264979
B Net land rent and royalties	10281	12928	14638	15967	15145	11358	15206	16116	15601	14630	14121	12973
3 Direct taxes and other current transfers n.e.c. to government	683517	1045028	1161711	1241350	1317028	1402493	1474957	1594920	1695081	1816055	1893787	1942818
A Social security contributions	511363	772521	856208	924924	979420	1048753	1119307	1217772	1294247	1346155	1403867	1432712
B Direct taxes	169420	268062	300368	311265	331624	347008	348376	368648	391728	460612	479995	499775
Income taxes	119822	189865	210857	210404	223547	238662	237206	251000	271238	338187	354266	367872
Other	49598	78197	89511	100861	108077	108346	111170	117648	120490	122425	125729	131903
C Fees, fines and penalties	2734	4445	5135	5161	5984	6732	7274	8500	9106	9288	9925	10331

France

3.32 Household and Private Unincorporated Enterprise Income and Outlay Account
(Continued)

Million French francs

	1980	1983	1984	1985	1986	1987	1988	1989	1990	1991	1992	1993
4 Other current transfers	149610	226704	237829	256625	273631	282771	293252	307107	340476	354089	382318	400124
A Net casualty insurance premiums	33549	52255	56785	60635	62662	67487	71124	72020	89190	92673	105313	110163
B Transfers to private non-profit institutions serving households	9673	13504	14416	14826	15825	16534	17572	18108	19511	20461	20936	21075
C Transfers to the rest of the world	12783	16674	15890	16728	15525	14736	14249	14205	15142	15565	16305	15640
D Other current transfers, except imputed	13895	26049	22825	26889	31792	32087	33213	39232	45086	43786	44433	50484
E Imputed employee pension and welfare contributions	79710	118222	127913	137547	147827	151927	157094	163542	171547	181604	195331	202762
Net saving	249385	317542	295375	305874	278616	208456	219492	259235	319205	381615	437867	454209
Total Current Disbursements and Net Saving	2817122	4145143	4479709	4826448	5100934	5317035	5630545	6067098	6491503	6868146	7197494	7366730

3.33 Household and Private Unincorporated Enterprise Capital Accumulation Account

Million French francs

	1980	1983	1984	1985	1986	1987	1988	1989	1990	1991	1992	1993
					Finance of Gross Accumulation							
1 Gross saving	351481	459193	447093	464692	450526	393488	423454	483606	551564	612200	662792	686836
A Consumption of fixed capital	102096	141651	151718	158818	171910	185032	203962	224371	232359	230585	224925	232627
B Net saving	249385	317542	295375	305874	278616	208456	219492	259235	319205	381615	437867	454209
2 Capital transfers	11742	10763	10739	10777	10920	13778	30673	23180	20098	24055	28232	29963
Total Finance of Gross Accumulation	363223	469956	457832	475469	461446	407266	454127	506786	571662	636255	691024	716799
					Gross Accumulation							
1 Gross Capital Formation	265604	316513	313197	320945	349295	362483	396472	455335	467110	449595	433944	416713
A Increase in stocks	1145	2679	-4406	-3617	2878	-1180	-3848	5494	-1380	-13989	-4559	-5869
B Gross fixed capital formation	264459	313834	317603	324562	346417	363663	400320	449841	468490	463584	438503	422582
2 Purchases of land, net	-7865	-9142	-10106	-7746	-11265	-15853	-22559	-34319	-39428	-43731	-45724	-18253
3 Purchases of intangibles, net	-5546	-8069	-9754	-12117	-16473	-17067	-22305	-17556	-20239	-27694	-29688	-17540
4 Capital transfers	8737	13237	13841	14722	18979	20974	24613	26546	29466	32363	31020	30381
Net lending	102293	157417	150654	159665	120910	56729	77906	76780	134753	225722	301472	305498
Total Gross Accumulation	363223	469956	457832	475469	461446	407266	454127	506786	571662	636255	691024	716799

3.34 Household and Private Unincorporated Enterprise Capital Finance Account

Million French francs

	1980	1983	1984	1985	1986	1987	1988	1989	1990	1991	1992	1993
					Acquisition of Financial Assets							
1 Gold	1000	-201	-161	51	-8241	-1008	6741	-3658	-1009	-1328	...	-719
2 Currency and transferable deposits	30660	41313	40948	31609	65500	46128	58965	66187	37993	-30320	26299	14847
3 Other deposits	123348	161703	135080	134259	67021	153174	143344	73123	53525	99074	104375	179346
4 Bills and bonds, short term	-	-	-	-	-	7168	7163	-8624	3530	8468	9596	17511
5 Bonds, long term	46561	35531	12448	6278	18111	-29971	-14960	-18767	-9150	19363	8442	75777
6 Corporate equity securities	16324	29046	86487	132274	188604	131481	173869	191263	149771	237437	94483	6220
7 Short term loans, n.e.c.	24894	-21484	15888	-62283	6255	20266	-53904	9719	-28848	-74991	4045	-112154
8 Long term loans, n.e.c.	...	...	...	...	...	...	...	...	...	...	...	...
9 Trade credit and advances	-52	20310	11409	-2060	-7930	-1282	24146	28614	3688	-2921	15307	7499
10 Net equity of households in life insurance and pension fund reserves	13138	25371	34346	47350	67527	81541	124415	163763	165866	184748	210150	264462
11 Proprietors' net additions to the accumulation of quasi-corporations	...	...	...	...	...	...	...	...	...	...	...	...
12 Other	13149	19166	24976	20327	17677	20003	10545	33849	5198	3153	12457	11204
Total Acquisition of Financial Assets	269022	310755	361421	307805	414524	427500	480324	535469	380564	442683	485154	463993
					Incurrence of Liabilities							
1 Short term loans, n.e.c.	25934	-5782	30774	11371	134150	145650	85032	237066	55076	92120	147614	-93725

France

3.34 Household and Private Unincorporated Enterprise Capital Finance Account
(Continued)

Million French francs

	1980	1983	1984	1985	1986	1987	1988	1989	1990	1991	1992	1993
2 Long term loans, n.e.c.	112152	105293	114382	121441	136041	213701	207169	177500	153213	55373	22457	177351
3 Trade credit and advances	9202	32444	59999	12758	21006	15510	97481	31543	44456	67448	783	36477
4 Other accounts payable	...	...	...	...	...	...	...	...	...	...	...	...
5 Other liabilities	-84	135	-138	73	82	-5	797	-898	1519	-439	1049	94
Total Incurrence of Liabilities	147204	132090	205017	145643	291279	374856	390479	445211	254264	214502	171903	120009
Statistical discrepancy [a]	19525	21248	5750	2497	2335	-4085	11939	13478	-8453	2459	11779	38486
Net Lending	102293	157417	150654	159665	120910	56729	77906	76780	134753	225722	301472	305498
Incurrence of Liabilities and Net Lending	269022	310755	361421	307805	414524	427500	480324	535469	380564	442683	485154	463993

a) Statistical discrepancy refers to adjustment made in order to reconcile the net lending of the Capital Accumulation Account and the Capital Finance Account.

3.41 Private Non-Profit Institutions Serving Households: Production Account

Million French francs

	1980	1983	1984	1985	1986	1987	1988	1989	1990	1991	1992	1993
Gross Output												
1 Sales	9774	13477	14300	15262	15918	16699	17738	18858	20187	21044	21410	21591
2 Non-marketed output	8239	11404	12134	12704	13288	13932	14899	15955	17258	18124	18556	18509
Gross Output	18013	24881	26434	27966	29206	30631	32637	34813	37445	39168	39966	40100
Gross Input												
Intermediate consumption	9904	13684	14534	15411	16090	16876	17969	19153	20579	21510	21935	22034
Subtotal: Value Added	8109	11197	11900	12555	13116	13755	14668	15660	16866	17658	18031	18066
1 Indirect taxes, net	48	67	72	76	79	83	88	94	102	107	109	109
2 Consumption of fixed capital	677	984	1069	1132	1205	1271	1351	1428	1523	1618	1680	1713
3 Compensation of employees	7757	10708	11379	12009	12545	13156	14028	14975	16125	16880	17235	17272
4 Net operating surplus	-373	-562	-620	-662	-713	-755	-799	-837	-884	-947	-993	-1028
Gross Input	18013	24881	26434	27966	29206	30631	32637	34813	37445	39168	39966	40100

3.42 Private Non-Profit Institutions Serving Households: Income and Outlay Account

Million French francs

	1980	1983	1984	1985	1986	1987	1988	1989	1990	1991	1992	1993
Receipts												
1 Operating surplus	-373	-562	-620	-662	-713	-755	-799	-837	-884	-947	-993	-1028
2 Property and entrepreneurial income	653	930	990	1037	1085	1138	1217	1303	1409	1480	1515	1511
A Withdrawals from quasi-corporations	-	-	-	-	-	-	-	-	-	-	-	-
B Interest	653	930	990	1037	1085	1138	1217	1303	1409	1480	1515	1511
C Dividends	-	-	-	-	-	-	-	-	-	-	-	-
D Net land rent and royalties	-	-	-	-	-	-	-	-	-	-	-	-
3 Current transfers	13099	20199	22880	24238	24803	25872	28937	29783	32569	34068	37168	38204
A Casualty insurance claims	66	101	105	113	119	129	132	119	171	168	188	189
B Current transfers from general government	2829	5835	7288	8059	7493	7927	9918	10180	11329	12221	14810	15705
C Other transfers from resident sectors	...	...	...	...	...	...	...	...	...	...	...	...
D Current transfers received from the rest of the world	10204	14263	15487	16066	17191	17816	18887	19484	21069	21679	22170	22310
E Imputed unfunded employee pension and welfare contributions	...	...	...	...	...	...	...	...	...	...	...	...
Total Current Receipts	13379	20567	23250	24613	25175	26255	29355	30249	33094	34601	37690	38687
Disbursements												
1 Final consumption expenditures	8239	11404	12134	12704	13288	13932	14899	15955	17258	18124	18556	18509
2 Property income	62	86	92	96	100	105	112	120	130	137	140	140
A Interest	62	86	92	96	100	105	112	120	130	137	140	140
B Net land rent and royalties	...	...	...	...	...	...	...	...	...	...	...	...
3 Direct taxes and other transfers to general government	35	54	79	91	100	109	121	126	138	148	160	181

France

3.42 Private Non-Profit Institutions Serving Households: Income and Outlay Account
(Continued)

Million French francs

	1980	1983	1984	1985	1986	1987	1988	1989	1990	1991	1992	1993
4 Other current transfers	2189	3006	3183	3339	3468	3675	3887	4143	4512	4716	4904	4961
A Net casualty insurance premiums	46	85	83	87	89	106	108	102	147	135	162	172
B Social assistance grants	...	...	...	...	...	...	...	...	...	...	...	...
C Unfunded employee pension and welfare benefits	1682	2470	2628	2752	2879	3019	3229	3458	3740	3928	4021	4011
D Current transfers to the rest of the world	...	...	...	...	...	...	...	...	...	...	...	...
E Other current transfers n.e.c.	461	451	472	500	500	550	550	583	625	653	721	778
Net saving	2854	6017	7762	8383	8219	8434	10336	9905	11056	11476	13930	14896
Total Current Disbursements	13379	20567	23250	24613	25175	26255	29355	30249	33094	34601	37690	38687

3.43 Private Non-Profit Institutions Serving Households: Capital Accumulation Account

Million French francs

	1980	1983	1984	1985	1986	1987	1988	1989	1990	1991	1992	1993
					Finance of Gross Accumulation							
1 Gross saving	3531	7001	8831	9515	9424	9705	11687	11333	12579	13094	15610	16609
A Consumption of fixed capital	677	984	1069	1132	1205	1271	1351	1428	1523	1618	1680	1713
B Net saving	2854	6017	7762	8383	8219	8434	10336	9905	11056	11476	13930	14896
2 Capital transfers	584	1139	1386	1415	1739	1855	2354	2618	3357	4221	4405	4320
Finance of Gross Accumulation	4115	8140	10217	10930	11163	11560	14041	13951	15936	17315	20015	20929
					Gross Accumulation							
1 Gross capital formation	2073	2875	3059	3203	3350	3512	3756	4022	4340	4563	4672	4687
A Increase in stocks	-	-	-	-	-	-	-	-	-	-	-	-
B Gross fixed capital formation	2073	2875	3059	3203	3350	3512	3756	4022	4340	4563	4672	4687
2 Purchases of land, net	33	46	49	51	53	56	60	63	68	71	73	73
3 Purchases of intangible assets, net	-	-	-	-	-	-	-	-	-	-	-	-
4 Capital transfers	180	250	266	279	291	304	325	348	376	395	404	403
Net lending	1829	4969	6843	7397	7469	7688	9900	9518	11152	12286	14866	15766
Gross Accumulation	4115	8140	10217	10930	11163	11560	14041	13951	15936	17315	20015	20929

3.44 Private Non-Profit Institutions Serving Households: Capital Finance Account

Million French francs

	1980	1983	1984	1985	1986	1987	1988	1989	1990	1991	1992	1993
					Acquisition of Financial Assets							
1 Gold	...	...	...	...	...	...	...	...	...	...	...	...
2 Currency and transferable deposits	194	1857	1297	462	223	7680	903	1000	409	-2073	4500	14130
3 Other deposits	611	844	871	640	1110	1083	-99	152	233	-	-11	5824
4 Bills and bonds, short term	...	...	...	...	...	...	...	...	...	...	...	...
5 Bonds, long term	55	89	157	-	-	-	9579	3902	13395	13684	27058	10333
6 Corporate equity securities	...	...	...	...	...	...	...	...	...	...	...	...
7 Short-term loans, n.e.c.	210	155	551	563	-220	1081	-310	1581	-1764	-1360	1955	3146
8 Long-term loans, n.e.c.	...	...	...	...	...	...	...	...	...	...	...	...
9 Other receivables	15	20	23	20	19	18	29	-187	15	13	34	11
10 Proprietors' net additions to the accumulation of quasi-corporations	...	...	...	...	...	...	...	...	...	...	...	...
11 Other assets	259	2494	4890	7161	6463	1420	2184	4320	1230	6921	-26760	-7446
Total Acquisition of Financial Assets	1344	5459	7789	8846	7595	11282	12286	10768	13518	15218	17484	30021
					Incurrence of Liabilities							
1 Short-term loans	69	278	599	272	-97	3514	1401	768	1044	2325	2499	-2512
2 Long-term loans	-547	202	326	1144	155	-32	978	400	244	500	-	16743
3 Other liabilities	-7	10	21	33	68	112	7	82	175	107	119	24
Total Incurrence of Liabilities	-485	490	946	1449	126	3594	2386	1250	1463	2932	2618	14255
Net Lending	1829	4969	6843	7397	7469	7688	9900	9518	11152	12286	14866	15766
Incurrence of Liabilities and Net Lending	1344	5459	7789	8846	7595	11282	12286	10768	13518	15218	17484	30021

France

3.51 External Transactions: Current Account: Detail

Million French francs

	1980	1983	1984	1985	1986	1987	1988	1989	1990	1991	1992	1993
Payments to the Rest of the World												
1 Imports of goods and services	638791	907388	1024968	1092619	1021789	1094349	1217627	1403052	1469802	1514461	1493363	1404152
A Imports of merchandise c.i.f.	576505	808900	914542	970814	893847	952251	1063873	1229621	1273885	1302876	1268897	1172006
B Other	62286	98488	110426	121805	127942	142098	153754	173431	195917	211585	224466	232146
2 Factor income to the rest of the world	79595	170399	206772	226699	190134	184380	202977	247784	295867	367291	402655	449683
A Compensation of employees	5560	10796	14584	19689	19310	16969	20358	15590	17724	20136	22887	21483
B Property and entrepreneurial income	74035	159603	192188	207010	170824	167411	182619	232194	278143	347155	379768	428200
3 Current transfers to the rest of the world	66436	112491	110528	122924	128709	137175	158742	161310	163981	193977	195086	208844
A Indirect taxes by general government to supranational organizations	17983	32730	34604	37545	49048	54179	62291	61106	60615	68788	64909	57844
B Other current transfers	48453	79761	75924	85379	79661	82996	96451	100204	103366	125189	130177	151003
4 Surplus of the nation on current transactions	-16700	-31978	-485	2384	23876	-9504	-17752	-32298	-62337	-37215	8732	71068
Payments to the Rest of the World, and Surplus of the Nation on Current Transfers	768122	1158300	1341783	1444626	1364508	1406400	1561594	1779848	1867313	2038514	2099836	2133747
Receipts From The Rest of the World												
1 Exports of goods and services	604422	900658	1053328	1123930	1074095	1101383	1221304	1411087	1467972	1538062	1587935	1558742
A Exports of merchandise f.o.b.	488877	720442	845218	901379	860303	886740	992606	1135583	1173049	1218530	1247213	1204225
B Other	115545	180216	208110	222551	213792	214643	228698	275504	294923	319532	340722	354517
2 Factor income from the rest of the world	92182	158672	183267	201020	173526	171913	191330	237813	263783	329004	345525	394368
A Compensation of employees	3656	7129	8037	10350	11757	12427	16401	15798	16443	19477	19336	20055
B Property and entrepreneurial income	88526	151543	175230	190670	161769	159486	174929	222015	247340	309527	326189	374313
3 Current transfers from the rest of the world	71518	98970	105188	119676	116887	133104	148960	130948	135558	171448	166376	180637
A Subsidies to general government from supranational organizations	17230	26222	26268	32898	39354	51022	42118	34847	35401	41494	41372	59880
B Other current transfers	54288	72748	78920	86778	77533	82082	106842	96101	100157	129954	125004	120757
Receipts from the Rest of the World on Current Transfers	768122	1158300	1341783	1444626	1364508	1406400	1561594	1779848	1867313	2038514	2099836	2133747

3.52 External Transactions: Capital Accumulation Account

Million French francs

	1980	1983	1984	1985	1986	1987	1988	1989	1990	1991	1992	1993
Finance of Gross Accumulation												
1 Surplus of the nation on current transactions	-16700	-31978	-485	2384	23876	-9504	-17752	-32298	-62337	-37215	8732	71068
2 Capital transfers from the rest of the world	669	1141	906	785	907	1268	6338	1879	6046	6949	11617	9411
Total Finance of Gross Accumulation	-16031	-30837	421	3169	24783	-8236	-11414	-30419	-56291	-30266	20349	80479
Gross Accumulation												
1 Capital transfers to the rest of the world	2663	4162	4369	4106	4128	12773	5268	5859	27253	10245	10440	11712
2 Purchases of intangible assets, n.e.c., net, from the rest of the world	...	...	...	...	...	...	...	...	...	...	...	...
Net lending to the rest of the world	-18694	-34999	-3948	-937	20655	-21009	-16682	-36278	-83544	-40511	9909	68767
Total Gross Accumulation	-16031	-30837	421	3169	24783	-8236	-11414	-30419	-56291	-30266	20349	80479

3.53 External Transactions: Capital Finance Account

Million French francs

	1980	1983	1984	1985	1986	1987	1988	1989	1990	1991	1992	1993
Acquisitions of Foreign Financial Assets												
1 Gold and SDR's	14953	18010	46187	26617	-8176	-1407	-17563	8826	128448	2632	-6267	9100
2 Currency and transferable deposits	19665	11573	-7092	10021	19336	-22507	-6068	25298	14270	-24181	10037	-42730
3 Other deposits	79666	5425	65132	16932	46224	225527	147195	296564	248100	-4943	248326	241703
4 Bills and bonds, short term	-	-	-	2473	-897	740	2092	2874	3166	30982	50173	35008

France

3.53 External Transactions: Capital Finance Account
(Continued)

Million French francs

	1980	1983	1984	1985	1986	1987	1988	1989	1990	1991	1992	1993
5 Bonds, long term	5535	10828	4874	27347	33441	7360	19934	28598	43470	38607	59056	136487
6 Corporate equity securities	17065	18234	21499	16743	46895	67137	82783	131624	151624	141595	108484	87931
7 Short-term loans, n.e.c.	5678	-585	16014	9036	3900	16114	-5716	59379	83675	10160	129699	-26817
8 Long-term loans	27503	38370	26108	23272	-1477	9093	15259	17578	-5982	-1435	12146	42613
9 Prproietors' net additions to accumulation of quasi-corporate, non-resident enterprises	...	...	...	...	...	...	...	...	...	...	...	...
10 Trade credit and advances	9243	14369	11579	-1743	5209	27410	33645	37174	43093	22827	49885	41534
11 Other	432	598	620	914	915	687	1334	238	242	1011	1169	1183
Total Acquisitions of Foreign Financial Assets	179740	116822	184921	131612	145370	330154	272895	608153	710106	217255	662708	526012

Incurrence of Foreign Liabilities

	1980	1983	1984	1985	1986	1987	1988	1989	1990	1991	1992	1993
1 Currency and transferable deposits	5044	-247	12560	11318	6731	26614	-28852	25728	23723	-8138	77233	-30056
2 Other deposits	125908	25190	50959	11829	61443	220166	148062	344379	388286	-26733	77109	36037
3 Bills and bonds, short term	-	-	-	2827	12418	9570	38965	48811	96598	35547	50317	-71568
4 Bonds, long term	10866	52632	64440	52572	24754	26049	41848	132811	141070	90679	210170	92367
5 Corporate equity securities	14524	14313	20017	46222	48317	47480	51512	107109	82097	104653	108286	151071
6 Short-term loans, n.e.c.	-242	247	1687	-1440	4040	2256	-1060	6943	24039	37458	72680	201396
7 Long-term loans	12661	47517	10450	-14583	-37113	-9622	5928	-2607	-824	3270	19857	16305
8 Non-resident proprietors' net additions to accumulation of resident quasi-corporate enterprises	...	...	...	...	...	...	...	...	...	...	...	...
9 Trade credit and advances	17950	5002	20380	9385	-1567	21969	26134	8730	33992	15813	30497	50381
10 Other	307	395	458	339	269	250	226	624	99	545	827	191
Total Incurrence of Liabilities	187018	145049	180951	118469	119292	344732	282763	672528	789080	253094	646976	446124
Statistical discrepancy [a]	11416	6772	7918	14080	5423	6431	6814	-28097	4570	4672	5823	11121
Net Lending	-18694	-34999	-3948	-937	20655	-21009	-16682	-36278	-83544	-40511	9909	68767
Total Incurrence of Liabilities and Net Lending	179740	116822	184921	131612	145370	330154	272895	608153	710106	217255	662708	526012

a) Statistical discrepancy refers to adjustment made in order to reconcile the net lending of the Capital Accumulation Account and the Capital Finance Account.

4.1 Derivation of Value Added by Kind of Activity, in Current Prices

Thousand Million French francs

	1980			1985			1990			1991		
	Gross Output	Intermediate Consumption	Value Added	Gross Output	Intermediate Consumption	Value Added	Gross Output	Intermediate Consumption	Value Added	Gross Output	Intermediate Consumption	Value Added

All Producers

1 Agriculture, hunting, forestry and fishing	251	132	119	394	212	182	439	217	222	429	224	205
A Agriculture and hunting	237	129	108	373	206	167	410	211	199	401	218	182
B Forestry and logging	10	1	9	13	1	12	19	2	17	19	2	17
C Fishing	4	2	2	7	4	4	9	4	5	9	4	5
2 Mining and quarrying	56	32	24	99	59	40	71	41	30	77	47	30
A Coal mining	14	10	4	19	14	5	12	9	3	11	9	2
B Crude petroleum and natural gas production	30	16	14	65	37	28	43	24	19	50	29	21
C Metal ore mining	3	1	2	4	2	2	3	2	1	2	1	1
D Other mining	8	4	4	12	6	5	14	7	6	14	7	7

France

4.1 Derivation of Value Added by Kind of Activity, in Current Prices
(Continued)

Thousand Million French francs

		1980			1985			1990			1991		
		Gross Output	Intermediate Consumption	Value Added	Gross Output	Intermediate Consumption	Value Added	Gross Output	Intermediate Consumption	Value Added	Gross Output	Intermediate Consumption	Value Added
3	Manufacturing	1910	1231	680	2924	1891	1033	3700	2305	1395	3742	2334	1408
	A Manufacture of food, beverages and tobacco	326	237	88	514	370	144	606	427	179	625	439	186
	B Textile, wearing apparel and leather industries	132	77	55	202	123	79	219	132	87	215	128	86
	C Manufacture of wood and wood products, including furniture	59	35	24	74	44	30	107	63	44	108	63	46
	D Manufacture of paper and paper products, printing and publishing	108	64	43	190	119	71	273	168	105	283	171	112
	E Manufacture of chemicals and chemical petroleum, coal, rubber and plastic products	410	290	120	631	436	195	685	421	264	695	421	274
	F Manufacture of non-metallic mineral products, except products of petroleum and coal	68	35	33	89	48	41	124	66	58	126	67	59
	G Basic metal industries	160	121	39	212	157	55	230	159	71	214	150	64
	H Manufacture of fabricated metal products, machinery and equipment	623	358	265	973	574	398	1406	843	563	1427	868	559
	I Other manufacturing industries	26	14	12	39	20	20	50	26	24	49	27	22
4	Electricity, gas and water	90	40	50	179	62	117	220	81	139	241	88	153
5	Construction	404	211	194	530	286	244	781	445	336	817	459	358
6	Wholesale and retail trade, restaurants and hotels	551	156	395	955	270	685	1374	383	991	1423	397	1026
	A Wholesale and retail trade	448	111	338	773	198	576	1098	286	811	1132	296	836
	B Restaurants and hotels	102	45	57	182	72	110	276	97	179	291	101	190
7	Transport, storage and communication	250	86	164	435	146	289	571	193	378	606	209	397
	A Transport and storage	187	76	111	309	127	182	413	170	243	431	178	253
	B Communication	63	10	53	126	19	107	158	22	136	175	31	144
8	Finance, insurance, real estate and business services	652	179	473	1216	355	861	2294	904	1390	2468	1002	1467
	A Financial institutions	...	...	100	...	...	178	...	...	...	...	...	...
	B Insurance	...	...	22	...	...	47	...	...	...	...	...	...
	C Real estate and business services	...	...	350	...	...	636	...	...	...	...	...	...
	Real estate, except dwellings	...	...	156	...	...	38	...	...	...	...	...	...
	Dwellings	...	...	26	...	...	301	...	...	...	...	...	...
9	Community, social and personal services	168	47	121	323	92	231	497	134	363	533	146	387
	A Sanitary and similar services	...	...	...	...	...	...	...	...	...	...	...	...
	B Social and related community services	...	...	68	...	...	135	...	...	210	...	...	224
	Educational services	...	...	6	...	...	16	...	...	25	...	...	27
	Medical, dental, other health and veterinary services	...	...	61	...	...	120	...	...	185	...	...	199
	C Recreational and cultural services	...	...	50	...	...	90	...	...	144	...	...	150
	D Personal and household services	...	...	4	...	...	7	...	...	12	...	...	13
Total, Industries		4333	2114	2219	7054	3371	3683	9947	4703	5243	10337	4905	5432
Producers of Government Services		606	157	448	1083	287	796	1395	380	1016	1474	398	1076
Other Producers		...	...	...	...	...	...	...	...	...	...	...	...
Total		4939	2271	2668	8137	3659	4478	11342	5083	6259	11812	5303	6508
Less: Imputed bank service charge		...	-108	108	...	-192	192	...	-278	278	...	-271	271
Import duties [a]		6	...	6	9	...	9	11	...	11	12	...	12
Value added tax		242	...	242	405	...	405	518	...	518	515	...	515
Other adjustments		-	...	-	-	...	-	-	...	-	-	...	-
Total [b]		5187	2379	2808	8551	3851	4700	11871	5361	6509	12338	5574	6764

France

4.1 Derivation of Value Added by Kind of Activity, in Current Prices

Thousand Million French francs

	1992 Gross Output	1992 Intermediate Consumption	1992 Value Added	1993 Gross Output	1993 Intermediate Consumption	1993 Value Added
All Producers						
1 Agriculture, hunting, forestry and fishing	418	220	198	379	213	166
A Agriculture and hunting	392	214	178	355	208	148
B Forestry and logging	17	2	16	16	2	14
C Fishing	9	4	5	8	4	4
2 Mining and quarrying	78	46	32	75	43	32
A Coal mining	10	8	2	10	7	3
B Crude petroleum and natural gas production	52	29	23	51	29	22
C Metal ore mining	2	1	-	2	1	-
D Other mining	14	7	6	13	7	6
3 Manufacturing	3748	2317	1431	3572	2172	1401
A Manufacture of food, beverages and tobacco	634	437	197	626	413	213
B Textile, wearing apparel and leather industries	211	124	87	189	110	79
C Manufacture of wood and wood products, including furniture	105	57	48	102	54	48
D Manufacture of paper and paper products, printing and publishing	287	171	116	279	161	119
E Manufacture of chemicals and chemical petroleum, coal, rubber and plastic products	694	416	278	689	409	280
F Manufacture of non-metallic mineral products, except products of petroleum and coal	122	65	57	115	61	54
G Basic metal industries	207	145	62	183	129	54
H Manufacture of fabricated metal products, machinery and equipment	1439	876	563	1340	812	528
I Other manufacturing industries	49	25	24	48	23	26
4 Electricity, gas and water	253	88	165	262	86	176
5 Construction	813	449	365	795	431	364
6 Wholesale and retail trade, restaurants and hotels	1458	408	1049	1477	412	1065
A Wholesale and retail trade	1156	307	850	1174	309	866
B Restaurants and hotels	302	102	200	302	103	199
7 Transport, storage and communication	634	218	416	636	222	415
A Transport and storage	446	184	262	442	187	255
B Communication	187	33	154	195	35	160
8 Finance, insurance, real estate and business services	2729	1209	1521	3376	1792	1584
A Financial institutions	...	...	...	...	...	...
B Insurance	...	...	...	...	...	...
C Real estate and business services	...	...	...	...	...	...
Real estate, except dwellings	...	...	...	...	...	...
Dwellings	...	...	...	...	...	...
9 Community, social and personal services	569	155	414	593	158	435
A Sanitary and similar services	...	...	...	...	...	...
B Social and related community services	...	...	...	...	...	...
Educational services	...	...	...	...	...	...
Medical, dental, other health and veterinary services	...	...	...	...	...	...
C Recreational and cultural services	...	...	...	...	...	...
D Personal and household services	...	...	...	...	...	...
Total, Industries	10700	5109	5592	11166	5528	5638
Producers of Government Services	1569	424	1145	1636	430	1206

France

4.1 Derivation of Value Added by Kind of Activity, in Current Prices
(Continued)

Thousand Million French francs

	1992 Gross Output	1992 Intermediate Consumption	1992 Value Added	1993 Gross Output	1993 Intermediate Consumption	1993 Value Added
Other Producers	...	...	...	...	...	...
Total	12269	5533	6737	12802	5958	6844
Less: Imputed bank service charge	...	-269	269	...	-281	281
Import duties [a]	11	...	11	10	...	10
Value added tax	521	...	521	515	...	515
Other adjustments	-	...	-	-	...	-
Total [b]	12801	5802	6999	13328	6239	7089

a) Item 'Import duties' includes also value added tax (VAT) on products.
b) Data for this table have not been revised, therefore, data for some years are not comparable with those of other tables.

4.2 Derivation of Value Added by Kind of Activity, in Constant Prices

Million French francs

At constant prices of: 1980

All Producers

	1980 Gross Output	1980 Interm. Cons.	1980 Value Added	1985 Gross Output	1985 Interm. Cons.	1985 Value Added	1990 Gross Output	1990 Interm. Cons.	1990 Value Added	1991 Gross Output	1991 Interm. Cons.	1991 Value Added
1 Agriculture, hunting, forestry and fishing	251146	132122	119024	272902	134461	138441	289198	140209	148989	282622	137334	145288
A Agriculture and hunting	237356	129096	108260	258679	131449	127230	272668	135863	136805	266312	133012	133300
B Forestry and logging	9565	690	8875	10059	678	9381	12237	1789	10448	12156	1753	10403
C Fishing	4225	2336	1889	4164	2334	1830	4293	2557	1736	4154	2569	1585
2 Mining and quarrying	56056	32235	23821	52800	31100	21700	50755	32417	18338	53497	33868	19629
A Coal mining	14415	10169	4246	11324	8357	2967	8281	6260	2021	7461	6151	1310
B Crude petroleum and natural gas production	30228	16446	13782	32175	18027	14148	32555	21013	11542	36456	22630	13826
C Metal ore mining	3051	1460	1591	2021	984	1037	2163	914	1249	1886	838	1048
D Other mining	8362	4160	4202	7280	3732	3548	7756	4230	3526	7694	4249	3445
3 Manufacturing	1910470	1230950	679520	1865692	1197267	668425	2173287	1422887	750400	2182176	1443496	738680
A Manufacture of food, beverages and tobacco	325694	237223	88471	340489	248174	92315	379387	282194	97193	388607	288960	99647
B Textile, wearing apparel and leather industries	131954	76844	55110	127337	75584	51753	126192	78232	47960	122384	76898	45486
C Manufacture of wood and wood products, including furniture	58950	34715	24235	51131	30296	20835	63965	38420	25545	62489	37835	24654
D Manufacture of paper and paper products, printing and publishing	107696	64371	43325	119017	75894	43123	146310	97580	48730	148726	101272	47454
E Manufacture of chemicals and chemical petroleum, coal, rubber and plastic products	409759	290151	119608	388139	261395	126744	442805	296619	146186	446921	303591	143330
F Manufacture of non-metallic mineral products, except products of petroleum and coal	67673	34611	33062	58189	29506	28683	69547	37729	31818	68938	37630	31308
G Basic metal industries	160232	121267	38965	133664	99728	33936	146894	106352	40542	143553	104657	38896
H Manufacture of fabricated metal products, machinery and equipment	622908	357877	265031	621725	363618	258107	769844	469440	300404	772185	476114	296071
I Other manufacturing industries	25604	13891	11713	26001	13072	12929	28343	16321	12022	28373	16539	11834
4 Electricity, gas and water	90370	40062	50308	112609	38524	74085	134219	49775	84444	142954	54420	88534
5 Construction	404451	210842	193609	366145	185739	180406	466761	249246	217515	469628	250538	219090
6 Wholesale and retail trade, restaurants and hotels	550630	155588	395042	601054	169753	431301	711663	219505	492158	715824	222002	493822
A Wholesale and retail trade	448462	110702	337760	491138	124650	366488	585689	165287	420402	588978	167939	421039
B Restaurants and hotels	102168	44886	57282	109916	45103	64813	125974	54218	71756	126846	54063	72783
7 Transport, storage and communication	250067	85873	164194	275999	84750	191249	371247	112063	259184	385875	119943	265932
A Transport and storage	186577	75548	111029	187724	72605	115119	242662	97817	144845	245390	99819	145571
B Communication	63490	10325	53165	88275	12145	76130	128585	14246	114339	140485	20124	120361
8 Finance, insurance, real estate and business services	651538	178960	472578	751165	222366	528799	1134965	484285	650680	1175535	518915	656620
A Financial institutions	...	...	100497	...	...	107965	...	...	...	...	...	...
B Insurance	...	...	22101	...	...	21881	...	...	...	...	...	...
C Real estate and business services	...	...	349980	...	...	398953	...	...	...	...	...	...
Real estate, except dwellings	...	...	156231	...	...	27468	...	...	...	...	...	...

France

4.2 Derivation of Value Added by Kind of Activity, in Constant Prices
(Continued)

Million French francs

	1980 Gross Output	1980 Intermediate Consumption	1980 Value Added	1985 Gross Output	1985 Intermediate Consumption	1985 Value Added	1990 Gross Output	1990 Intermediate Consumption	1990 Value Added	1991 Gross Output	1991 Intermediate Consumption	1991 Value Added
				At constant prices of:1980								
Dwellings	...	...	26000	...	...	192982	...	...	...	...	...	...
9 Community, social and personal services	168441	47176	121265	210255	58046	152209	270529	74264	196265	283491	79636	203855
A Sanitary and similar services	...	...	...	...	...	...	...	...	...	...	...	...
B Social and related community services	...	...	67748	...	...	93299	...	...	127611	...	...	133703
Educational services	...	...	6417	...	...	9743	...	...	10997	...	...	11242
Medical, dental, other health and veterinary services	...	...	61331	...	...	83556	...	...	116939	...	...	123151
C Recreational and cultural services	...	...	49906	...	...	55311	...	...	64867	...	...	66593
D Personal and household services	...	...	3611	...	...	3599	...	...	3787	...	...	3558
Total, Industries	4333169	2113808	2219361	4508621	2122006	2386615	5602624	2784651	2817973	5691602	2860152	2831450
Producers of Government Services	605633	157422	448211	682634	184220	498414	756097	216886	539211	773604	221453	552151
Other Producers	...	...	...	...	...	...	...	...	...	...	...	...
Total	4938802	2271230	2667572	5191255	2306226	2885029	6358721	3001537	3357184	6465206	3081605	3383601
Less: Imputed bank service charge	...	-107503	107503	...	-118696	118696	...	-138811	138811	...	-130858	130858
Import duties [a]	6339	...	6339	7626	...	7626	11878	...	11878	12426	...	12426
Value added tax	242015	...	242015	254556	...	254556	315001	...	315001	308337	...	308337
Other adjustments	-128	...	-128	-136	...	-136	-153	...	-153	-153	...	-153
Total	5187028	2378733	2808295	5453301	2424922	3028379	6685447	3140348	3545099	6785816	3212463	3573353

	1992 Gross Output	1992 Intermediate Consumption	1992 Value Added	1993 Gross Output	1993 Intermediate Consumption	1993 Value Added
	At constant prices of:1980					
	All Producers					
1 Agriculture, hunting, forestry and fishing	295495	136967	158528	283515	136866	146649
A Agriculture and hunting	280062	132664	147398	268731	132611	136120
B Forestry and logging	11400	1727	9673	10835	1730	9105
C Fishing	4033	2576	1457	3949	2525	1424
2 Mining and quarrying	54710	32842	21868	53794	31371	22423
A Coal mining	7525	5954	1571	6768	4731	2037
B Crude petroleum and natural gas production	38005	21904	16101	38499	22029	16470
C Metal ore mining	1765	794	971	1634	734	900
D Other mining	7415	4190	3225	6893	3877	3016
3 Manufacturing	2190810	1455710	735100	2109958	1396916	713042
A Manufacture of food, beverages and tobacco	390123	291070	99053	391293	286691	104602
B Textile, wearing apparel and leather industries	118071	75363	42708	108378	68682	39696
C Manufacture of wood and wood products, including furniture	59843	35509	24334	57296	33904	23392
D Manufacture of paper and paper products, printing and publishing	150094	102870	47224	148215	101202	47013
E Manufacture of chemicals and chemical petroleum, coal, rubber and plastic products	456765	310221	146544	459870	312953	146917
F Manufacture of non-metallic mineral products, except products of petroleum and coal	66214	36850	29364	61874	34290	27584
G Basic metal industries	143296	105984	37312	131473	96707	34766
H Manufacture of fabricated metal products, machinery and equipment	778438	482096	296342	724916	447519	277397
I Other manufacturing industries	27966	15747	12219	26643	14968	11675
4 Electricity, gas and water	144417	53484	90933	145426	51071	94355

France

4.2 Derivation of Value Added by Kind of Activity, in Constant Prices
(Continued)

Million French francs

		1992			1993	
	Gross Output	Intermediate Consumption	Value Added	Gross Output	Intermediate Consumption	Value Added

At constant prices of: 1980

5	Construction	457620	243997	213623	439831	233819	206012
6	Wholesale and retail trade, restaurants and hotels	719009	225890	493119	708578	225649	482929
	A Wholesale and retail trade	592426	171499	420927	585971	171232	414739
	B Restaurants and hotels	126583	54391	72192	122607	54417	68190
7	Transport, storage and communication	400983	125218	275765	402181	126066	276115
	A Transport and storage	251922	103722	148200	248528	103658	144870
	B Communication	149061	21496	127565	153653	22408	131245
8	Finance, insurance, real estate and business services	1248148	598146	650002	1475412	817929	657483
	a) Financial institutions	...	...	...	...	...	...
	B Insurance	...	...	...	...	...	...
	C Real estate and business services	...	...	...	...	...	...
	Real estate, except dwellings	...	...	...	...	...	...
	Dwellings	...	...	...	...	...	...
9	Community, social and personal services	293683	84046	209637	298704	84320	214384
	A Sanitary and similar services	...	...	...	...	...	...
	B Social and related community services	...	...	...	...	...	...
	Educational services	...	...	...	...	...	...
	Medical, dental, other health and veterinary services	...	...	...	...	...	...
	C Recreational and cultural services	...	...	...	...	...	...
	D Personal and household services	...	...	...	...	...	...
	Total, Industries	5804875	2956300	2848575	5917399	3104007	2813392
	Producers of Government Services	796506	234368	562138	805591	234795	570796
	Other Producers	...	...	...	...	...	...
	Total	6601381	3190668	3410713	6722990	3338802	3384188
	Less: Imputed bank service charge	...	-120451	120451	...	-118940	118940
	Import duties [a]	12581	...	12581	12468	...	12468
	Value added tax	312896	...	312896	301673	...	301673
	Other adjustments	-16	...	-16	-16	...	-16
	Total	6926842	3311119	3615723	7037115	3457742	3579373

a) Item 'Import duties' includes also value added tax (VAT) on products.

4.3 Cost Components of Value Added

Million French francs

		1980						1985					
		Compensation of Employees	Capital Consumption	Net Operating Surplus	Indirect Taxes	Less: Subsidies Received	Value Added	Compensation of Employees	Capital Consumption	Net Operating Surplus	Indirect Taxes	Less: Subsidies Received	Value Added

All Producers

1	Agriculture, hunting, forestry and fishing	18856	...	102124	2670	4626	119024	29241	...	156238	5271	8440	182310
	A Agriculture and hunting	14948	...	94880	2495	4063	108260	22734	...	146488	4990	7247	166965
	B Forestry and logging	2565	...	6695	116	501	8875	3682	...	8960	145	1005	11782
	C Fishing	1343	...	549	59	62	1889	2825	...	790	136	188	3563
2	Mining and quarrying	16622	...	10357	905	4062	23821	23689	...	22004	1568	7149	40112
	A Coal mining	7570	...	491	209	4024	4246	10011	...	1687	376	7123	4951
	B Crude petroleum and natural gas production	4902	...	8410	501	31	13782	8812	...	17901	915	12	27616
	C Metal ore mining	1588	...	-64	68	1	1591	1259	...	732	66	-1	2058
	D Other mining	2562	...	1520	127	6	4202	3607	...	1684	211	15	5487

France

4.3 Cost Components of Value Added
(Continued)

Million French francs

	1980						1985					
	Compensation of Employees	Capital Consumption	Net Operating Surplus	Indirect Taxes	Less: Subsidies Received	Value Added	Compensation of Employees	Capital Consumption	Net Operating Surplus	Indirect Taxes	Less: Subsidies Received	Value Added
3 Manufacturing	464648	...	154219	75554	14902	679520	685646	...	261592	118211	32310	1033139
A Manufacture of food, beverages and tobacco	47297	...	37049	12903	8778	88471	76781	...	64389	19831	16872	144129
B Textile, wearing apparel and leather industries	41536	...	11927	1879	232	55110	57227	...	18591	3584	352	79050
C Manufacture of wood and wood products, including furniture	15740	...	7555	1005	65	24235	20302	...	8226	1444	-2	29974
D Manufacture of paper and paper products, printing and publishing	32074	...	10245	1448	442	43325	50636	...	19612	2851	2245	70854
E Manufacture of chemicals and chemical petroleum, coal, rubber and plastic products	60684	...	13544	45667	287	119608	92567	...	35393	67980	509	195431
F Manufacture of non-metallic mineral products, except products of petroleum and coal	20571	...	11379	1170	59	33062	26673	...	12043	1977	95	40598
G Basic metal industries	28980	...	8554	1885	454	38965	39520	...	13408	2704	576	55056
H Manufacture of fabricated metal products, machinery and equipment	209494	...	50804	9224	4491	265031	309373	...	83222	17257	11375	398477
I Other manufacturing industries	8272	...	3162	373	94	11713	12567	...	6708	583	288	19570
4 Electricity, gas and water	19057	...	25902	6459	1110	50308	36483	...	69761	12429	1804	116869
5 Construction	126304	...	63476	5809	1980	193609	165140	...	72667	9101	3010	243898
6 Wholesale and retail trade, restaurants and hotels	213167	...	165132	26659	9916	395042	366315	...	271828	66528	19660	685011
A Wholesale and retail trade	184594	...	136746	25401	8981	337760	309257	...	220199	63034	16983	575507
B Restaurants and hotels	28573	...	28386	1258	935	57282	57058	...	51629	3494	2677	109504
7 Transport, storage and communication	105842	...	66593	4193	12434	164194	176966	...	126682	8598	23196	289050
A Transport and storage	75531	...	44660	3221	12383	111029	123327	...	75358	6789	23178	182296
B Communication	30311	...	21933	972	51	53165	53639	...	51324	1809	18	106754
8 Finance, insurance, real estate and business services	167488	...	285953	39767	20630	472578	301497	...	525999	74755	41114	861137
A Financial institutions	...	...	...	...	...	100497	...	...	...	...	...	178162
B Insurance	...	...	...	...	...	22101	...	...	...	...	...	46547
C Real estate and business services	...	...	...	...	...	349980	...	...	...	...	...	636428
Real estate, except dwellings	...	...	...	...	...	156231	...	...	...	...	...	38103
Dwellings	...	...	...	...	...	26000	...	...	...	...	...	301201
9 Community, social and personal services	43905	...	71056	8153	1849	121265	90490	...	130596	16194	5906	231374
A Sanitary and similar services	...	...	...	...	...	...	...	...	...	...	...	...
B Social and related community services	...	...	...	...	...	67748	...	...	...	...	...	135081
Educational services	...	...	...	...	...	6417	...	...	...	...	...	15533
Medical, dental, other health and veterinary services	...	...	...	...	...	61331	...	...	...	...	...	119548
C Recreational and cultural services	...	...	...	...	...	49906	...	...	...	...	...	89549
D Personal and household services	...	...	...	...	...	3611	...	...	...	...	...	6744
Total, Industries	1175889	...	944812	170169	71509	2219361	1875467	...	1637367	312655	142589	3682900
Producers of Government Services	399895	...	38249	10067	...	448211	706979	...	72774	15808	...	795561
Other Producers	...	...	...	...	...	...	...	...	...	...	...	...
Total	1575784	...	983061	180236	71509	2667572	2582446	...	1710141	328463	142589	4478461
Less: Imputed bank service charge	...	...	107503	...	...	107503	...	...	192340	...	...	192340
Import duties	...	...	...	6339	...	6339	...	...	...	8904	...	8904
Value added tax	...	...	...	242015	...	242015	...	...	...	405281	...	405281
Other adjustments	...	...	...	...	128	-128	...	...	...	...	163	-163
Total [b]	1575784	...	875558	428590	71637	2808295	2582446	...	1517801	742648	142752	4700143

France

4.3 Cost Components of Value Added

Million French francs

		1990						1991					
		Compensation of Employees	Capital Consumption	Net Operating Surplus	Indirect Taxes	Less: Subsidies Received	Value Added	Compensation of Employees	Capital Consumption	Net Operating Surplus	Indirect Taxes	Less: Subsidies Received	Value Added
						All Producers							
1	Agriculture, hunting, forestry and fishing	35060	...	192736	8628	14559	221865	...	...	...	...	...	204959
	A Agriculture and hunting	26819	...	177681	8229	13375	199354	...	...	...	...	...	182445
	B Forestry and logging	3864	...	14436	152	1111	17341	...	...	...	...	...	17380
	C Fishing	4377	...	619	247	73	5170	...	...	...	...	...	5134
2	Mining and quarrying	19378	...	11922	1686	3231	29754	...	...	...	...	...	30476
	A Coal mining	5606	...	189	311	3188	2918	...	...	...	...	...	2180
	B Crude petroleum and natural gas production	8758	...	9656	1075	19	19470	...	...	...	...	...	21088
	C Metal ore mining	946	...	-45	45	1	945	...	...	...	...	...	704
	D Other mining	4068	...	2122	255	23	6421	...	...	...	...	...	6504
3	Manufacturing	818074	...	468378	140752	32702	1394503	...	...	...	...	...	1407648
	A Manufacture of food, beverages and tobacco	91566	...	82409	25532	20600	178907	...	...	...	...	...	186166
	B Textile, wearing apparel and leather industries	59321	...	25199	3146	420	87246	...	...	...	...	...	86159
	C Manufacture of wood and wood products, including furniture	25942	...	16563	2100	198	44407	...	...	...	...	...	45741
	D Manufacture of paper and paper products, printing and publishing	67425	...	34745	3683	637	105216	...	...	...	...	...	111635
	E Manufacture of chemicals and chemical petroleum, coal, rubber and plastic products	112803	...	73740	77885	708	263720	...	...	...	...	...	273558
	F Manufacture of non-metallic mineral products, except products of petroleum and coal	32018	...	23647	2303	181	57788	...	...	...	...	...	58721
	G Basic metal industries	39587	...	28091	3123	193	70608	...	...	...	...	...	64094
	H Manufacture of fabricated metal products, machinery and equipment	374679	...	175809	22281	9674	563095	...	...	...	...	...	559159
	I Other manufacturing industries	14733	...	8175	699	91	23516	...	...	...	...	...	22415
4	Electricity, gas and water	44763	...	76162	19706	1892	138739	...	...	...	...	...	153193
5	Construction	219136	...	107336	13019	3679	335812	...	...	...	...	...	358171
6	Wholesale and retail trade, restaurants and hotels	504537	...	401008	104443	19289	990699	...	...	...	...	...	1026489
	A Wholesale and retail trade	411374	...	315290	99237	14556	811345	...	...	...	...	...	836082
	B Restaurants and hotels	93163	...	85718	5206	4733	179354	...	...	...	...	...	190407
7	Transport, storage and communication	219612	...	172348	11108	24595	378473	...	...	...	...	...	396727
	A Transport and storage	153437	...	104265	9753	24586	242869	...	...	...	...	...	253159
	B Communication	66175	...	68083	1355	9	135604	...	...	...	...	...	143568
8	Finance, insurance, real estate and business services	489845	...	816849	112888	29430	1390152	...	...	...	...	...	1466932
	A Financial institutions	...											
	B Insurance												
	C Real estate and business services	...	...	...	...	...	...						
	Real estate, except dwellings			...			...						
	Dwellings			...			...						
9	Community, social and personal services	132702	...	215398	22480	7107	363473	...	...	...	...	...	387469
	A Sanitary and similar services												
	B Social and related community services	...	...	209614	...	...	209614	...	...	224346	...	...	224346
	Educational services						24588						26869
	Medical, dental, other health and veterinary services						185307						198608
	C Recreational and cultural services	...	...	141456	...	...	141456	...	...	150317	...	...	150317
	D Personal and household services	...	...	12405	...	...	12405	...	...	12807	...	...	12807
	Total, Industries	2483107	...	2462137	434710	136484	5243470	...	...	...	...	144297	5432064
	Producers of Government Services	888690	...	106632	20212	...	1015534	...	...	...	...	...	1076279

France

4.3 Cost Components of Value Added
(Continued)

Million French francs

	1990						1991					
	Compensation of Employees	Capital Consumption	Net Operating Surplus	Indirect Taxes	Less: Subsidies Received	Value Added	Compensation of Employees	Capital Consumption	Net Operating Surplus	Indirect Taxes	Less: Subsidies Received	Value Added
Other Producers	...	...	...	...	...	...	...	...	...	...	...	...
Total	3371797	...	2568769	454922	136484	6259004	3538181	...	2645462	468997	144297	6508343
Less: Imputed bank service charge	...	...	278020	...	...	278020	...	...	271159	...	...	271159
Import duties	...	...	...	10946	...	10946	...	...	...	11954	...	11954
Value added tax	...	...	...	517561	...	517561	...	...	...	514827	...	514827
Other adjustments	...	...	...	...	3	-3	...	...	...	...	16	-16
Total b	3371797	...	2290749	983429	136487	6509488	3531792	...	2393336	995345	144242	6776231

	1992						1993					
	Compensation of Employees	Capital Consumption	Net Operating Surplus	Indirect Taxes	Less: Subsidies Received	Value Added	Compensation of Employees	Capital Consumption	Net Operating Surplus	Indirect Taxes	Less: Subsidies Received	Value Added
					**All Producers**							
1 Agriculture, hunting, forestry and fishing	...	...	...	...	...	198222	...	...	...	...	...	165587
A Agriculture and hunting	...	...	...	...	...	177891	...	...	...	...	...	147799
B Forestry and logging	...	...	...	...	...	15698	...	...	...	...	...	14050
C Fishing	...	...	...	...	...	4633	...	...	...	...	...	3738
2 Mining and quarrying	...	...	...	...	...	32237	...	...	...	...	...	31994
A Coal mining	...	...	...	...	...	2320	...	...	...	...	...	3026
B Crude petroleum and natural gas production	...	...	...	...	...	23022	...	...	...	...	...	22442
C Metal ore mining	...	...	...	...	...	439	...	...	...	...	...	304
D Other mining	...	...	...	...	...	6456	...	...	...	...	...	6222
3 Manufacturing	...	...	...	...	...	1430849	...	...	...	...	...	1400791
A Manufacture of food, beverages and tobacco	...	...	...	...	...	196660	...	...	...	...	...	213281
B Textile, wearing apparel and leather industries	...	...	...	...	...	86511	...	...	...	...	...	78960
C Manufacture of wood and wood products, including furniture	...	...	...	...	...	47890	...	...	...	...	...	48013
D Manufacture of paper and paper products, printing and publishing	...	...	...	...	...	115893	...	...	...	...	...	118696
E Manufacture of chemicals and chemical petroleum, coal, rubber and plastic products	...	...	...	...	...	278189	...	...	...	...	...	280279
F Manufacture of non-metallic mineral products, except products of petroleum and coal	...	...	...	...	...	56743	...	...	...	...	...	54004
G Basic metal industries	...	...	...	...	...	61895	...	...	...	...	...	54303
H Manufacture of fabricated metal products, machinery and equipment	...	...	...	...	...	562667	...	...	...	...	...	527652
I Other manufacturing industries	...	...	...	...	...	24401	...	...	...	...	...	25603
4 Electricity gas and water	...	...	...	...	...	165272	...	...	...	...	...	176357
5 Construction	...	...	...	...	...	364538	...	...	...	...	...	363974
6 Wholesale and retail trade, restaurants and hotels	...	...	...	...	...	1049443	...	...	...	...	...	1064768
A Wholesale and retail trade	...	...	...	...	...	849535	...	...	...	...	...	865638
B Restaurants and hotels	...	...	...	...	...	199908	...	...	...	...	...	199130
7 Transport, storage and communication	...	...	...	...	...	416003	...	...	...	...	...	414880
A Transport and storage	...	...	...	...	...	261852	...	...	...	...	...	255134
B Communication	...	...	...	...	...	154151	...	...	...	...	...	159746
8 Finance, insurance, real estate and business services	...	...	...	...	...	1520684	...	...	...	...	...	1584400
A Financial institutions	...	...	...	...	...	...	...	...	...	...	...	...
B Insurance	...	...	...	...	...	...	...	...	...	...	...	...
C Real estate and business services	...	...	...	...	...	...	...	...	...	...	...	...
Real estate, except dwellings	...	...	...	...	...	...	...	...	...	...	...	...
Dwellings	...	...	...	...	...	...	...	...	...	...	...	...
9 Community, social and personal services	...	...	...	...	...	414298	...	...	...	...	...	435101
A Sanitary and similar services	...	...	...	...	...	...	...	...	...	...	...	...
B Social and related community services	...	...	...	...	...	...	...	...	...	...	...	...

France

4.3 Cost Components of Value Added
(Continued)

Million French francs

	1992						1993					
	Compensation of Employees	Capital Consumption	Net Operating Surplus	Indirect Taxes	Less: Subsidies Received	Value Added	Compensation of Employees	Capital Consumption	Net Operating Surplus	Indirect Taxes	Less: Subsidies Received	Value Added
Educational services	...	...	...	...	...	...	...	...	...	...	...	...
Medical, dental, other health and veterinary services	...	...	...	...	...	...	...	...	...	...	...	...
C Recreational and cultural services	...	...	...	...	...	...	...	...	...	...	...	...
D Personal and household services	...	...	...	...	...	...	...	...	...	...	...	...
Total, Industries	...	...	...	...	154262	5591546	...	...	...	...	174805	5637852
Producers of Government Services	...	...	...	...	...	1145098	...	...	...	...	...	1206414
Other Producers	...	...	...	...	...	...	...	...	...	...	...	...
Total	3673084	...	2733110	484712	154262	6736644	3736136	...	2769796	513139	174805	6844266
Less: Imputed bank service charge	...	...	269255	...	...	269255	...	...	281275	...	...	281275
Import duties	...	...	...	10644	...	10644	...	...	...	10492	...	10492
Value added tax	...	...	...	520879	...	520879	...	...	...	515121	...	515121
Other adjustments	...	...	...	...	1	-1	...	...	...	...	-	-
Total [b]	3669277	...	2479868	1015855	154460	7010540	3723188	...	2497684	1036157	174239	7082790

a) Data in this series has been revised. The breakdown, if any, may not add up to the total.
b) Column 'Consumption of fixed capital' is included in column 'Net operating surplus'.

French Guiana

Source. Reply to the United Nations national accounts questionnaire from the Institut National de la Statistique et des Etudes Economiques (INSEE), Paris. Official estimates and descriptions are published annually by the Direction Statistique Economiques of the Institut in 'Les Comptes Economiques de la Guyane'.

General note. The estimates shown in the following tables have been adjusted by the INSEE to conform to the United Nations System of National Accounts so far as the existing data would permit.

1.1 Expenditure on the Gross Domestic Product, in Current Prices

Million French francs

	1980	1983	1984	1985	1986	1987	1988	1989	1990	1991	1992	1993
1 Government final consumption expenditure	648	1091	1184	1324	1405	1573	1779	2027	2285	2548	...	...
2 Private final consumption expenditure	1064	1822	1954	2172	2404	2835	3329	3837	4201	4447	...	...
3 Gross capital formation	498	1152	1126	1206	1243	1304	1777	2620	3109	3111	...	...
A Increase in stocks	15	13	16	3	24	11	52	90	-12	114	...	...
B Gross fixed capital formation	483	1139	1110	1203	1219	1292	1725	2530	3122	2997	...	...
4 Exports of goods and services	102	294	998	1701	1239	1194	3721	4034	4391	6005	...	...
5 Less: Imports of goods and services	1092	2161	2683	3230	3373	3225	5677	6834	7461	8707	...	...
Equals: Gross Domestic Product	1219	2197	2579	3173	2918	3681	4929	5684	6526	7404	...	...

1.3 Cost Components of the Gross Domestic Product

Million French francs

	1980	1983	1984	1985	1986	1987	1988	1989	1990	1991	1992	1993
1 Indirect taxes, net	66	137	143	205	266	368	488	550	667	626	...	...
A Indirect taxes	143	283	302	402	441	489	602	650	803	824	...	...
B Less: Subsidies	77	146	159	197	175	121	114	100	137	198	...	...
2 Consumption of fixed capital	...	...	...	...	...	...	...	...	...	...	...	...
3 Compensation of employees paid by resident producers to:	978	1730	1936	2113	2248	2672	3116	3715	4200	4489	...	...
4 Operating surplus	175	329	500	856	404	641	1326	1419	1659	2289	...	...
Equals: Gross Domestic Product	1219	2197	2579	3173	2918	3681	4929	5684	6526	7404	...	...

1.4 General Government Current Receipts and Disbursements

Million French francs

	1980	1983	1984	1985	1986	1987	1988	1989	1990	1991	1992	1993
Receipts												
1 Operating surplus	...	...	...	...	...	...	...	...	...	...	...	...
2 Property and entrepreneurial income	10	17	18	18	14	11	10	22	16	16	...	...
3 Taxes, fees and contributions	475	915	1032	1250	1325	1456	1730	1924	2175	2424	...	...
4 Other current transfers	747	1259	1384	1266	1412	1647	1689	1951	2370	2543	...	...
Total Current Receipts of General Government	1233	2191	2433	2534	2750	3114	3429	3897	4561	4983	...	...
Disbursements												
1 Government final consumption expenditure	648	1091	1184	1324	1405	1573	1779	2027	2285	2548	...	...
2 Property income	14	27	37	29	50	61	79	107	134	154	...	...
3 Subsidies	8	9	11	10	24	16	22	27	25	40	...	...
4 Other current transfers	308	579	789	725	848	1011	1034	1140	1289	1461	...	...
5 Net saving	256	485	412	446	423	454	514	596	828	779	...	...
Total Current Disbursements and Net Saving of General Government	1233	2191	2433	2534	2750	3114	3429	3897	4561	4983	...	...

1.7 External Transactions on Current Account, Summary

Million French francs

	1980	1983	1984	1985	1986	1987	1988	1989	1990	1991	1992	1993
Payments to the Rest of the World												
1 Imports of goods and services	1092	2161	2683	3230	3373	3225	5677	6834	7461	8707	...	...
2 Factor income to the rest of the world	37	77	104	286	-251	83	560	180	315	634	...	...
A Compensation of employees	...	...	...	...	...	...	...	...	...	...	...	...
B Property and entrepreneurial income	37	77	104	286	-251	83	560	180	315	634	...	...
3 Current transfers to the rest of the world	41	89	224	22	20	22	24	28	52	32	...	...
4 Surplus of the nation on current transactions	-197	-509	-327	-246	-180	-199	-555	-898	-825	-474	...	...
Payments to the Rest of the World and Surplus of the Nation on Current Transactions	973	1819	2684	3292	2962	3130	5706	6145	7003	8899		

French Guiana

1.7 External Transactions on Current Account, Summary
(Continued)

Million French francs

		1980	1983	1984	1985	1986	1987	1988	1989	1990	1991	1992	1993
		\multicolumn{12}{c}{Receipts From The Rest of the World}											
1	Exports of goods and services	102	294	998	1701	1239	1194	3721	4034	4391	6005	...	...
2	Factor income from rest of the world	52	125	149	133	154	184	200	160	194	203	...	...
	A Compensation of employees	...	...	...	...	...	...	...	...	...	...	...	...
	B Property and entrepreneurial income	52	125	149	133	154	184	200	160	194	203	...	...
3	Current transfers from rest of the world	819	1400	1537	1458	1569	1752	1786	1951	2418	2692	...	...
	Receipts from the Rest of the World on Current Transactions	973	1819	2684	3292	2962	3130	5706	6145	7003	8899	...	...

1.8 Capital Transactions of The Nation, Summary

Million French francs

	1980	1983	1984	1985	1986	1987	1988	1989	1990	1991	1992	1993
\multicolumn{12}{c}{Finance of Gross Capital Formation}												
Gross saving	300	643	799	960	1064	1105	1223	1722	2284	2637	...	...
Less: Surplus of the nation on current transactions	-197	-509	-327	-246	-180	-199	-555	-898	-825	-474	...	...
Finance of Gross Capital Formation	498	1152	1126	1206	1243	1304	1777	2620	3109	3111	...	...
\multicolumn{12}{c}{Gross Capital Formation}												
Increase in stocks	15	13	16	3	24	11	52	90	-12	114	...	...
Gross fixed capital formation	483	1139	1110	1203	1219	1292	1725	2530	3122	2997	...	...
1 General government	227	463	570	510	475	597	737	812	911	1091	...	...
2 Corporate and quasi-corporate enterprises	166	546	405	540	549	486	749	1353	1704	1468	...	...
3 Other	90	130	135	153	196	209	240	365	506	438	...	...
Gross Capital Formation	498	1152	1126	1206	1243	1304	1777	2620	3109	3111	...	...

1.10 Gross Domestic Product by Kind of Activity, in Current Prices

Million French francs

	1980	1983	1984	1985	1986	1987	1988	1989	1990	1991	1992	1993
1 Agriculture, hunting, forestry and fishing	68	128	156	202	245	285	439	605	651	546	...	...
2 Mining and quarrying	56	99	121	156	171	208	257	399	492	565	...	...
3 Manufacturing	...	...	...	...	...	...	...	...	...	...	...	...
4 Electricity, gas and water	-23	-37	-27	-15	30	30	36	73	46	35	...	...
5 Construction	99	227	267	337	340	336	479	761	828	891	...	...
6 Wholesale and retail trade, restaurants and hotels	164	268	327	406	413	481	577	672	874	971	...	...
7 Transport, storage and communication	67	145	186	386	-130	214	707	388	498	908	...	...
8 Finance, insurance, real estate and business services	126	256	326	371	439	534	619	704	806	937	...	...
9 Community, social and personal services	165	281	289	331	348	417	466	632	681	782	...	...
Total, Industries	722	1367	1646	2173	1856	2505	3581	4234	4876	5634	...	...
Producers of Government Services	489	801	911	995	1070	1168	1315	1401	1522	1685	...	...
Other Producers	16	24	27	30	32	36	42	50	55	66	...	...
Subtotal	1228	2192	2584	3197	2957	3708	4938	5684	6454	7385	...	...
Less: Imputed bank service charge	95	171	205	228	274	295	347	372	378	417	...	...
Plus: Import duties	86	175	200	205	234	268	338	371	451	436	...	...
Plus: Value added tax	-	-	-	-	-	-	-	-	...	...	...	...
Equals: Gross Domestic Product	1219	2197	2579	3173	2918	3681	4929	5684	6526	7404	...	...

1.12 Relations Among National Accounting Aggregates

Million French francs

	1980	1983	1984	1985	1986	1987	1988	1989	1990	1991	1992	1993
Gross Domestic Product	1219	2197	2579	3173	2918	3681	4929	5684	6526	7404	...	...
Plus: Net factor income from the rest of the world	15	48	45	-153	405	102	-361	-20	-122	-431	...	...
Factor income from the rest of the world	52	125	149	133	154	184	200	160	193	203	...	...
Less: Factor income to the rest of the world	37	77	104	286	-251	83	560	180	315	634	...	...
Equals: Gross National Product	1234	2245	2624	3021	3324	3783	4569	5664	6405	6973	...	...

French Guiana

1.12 Relations Among National Accounting Aggregates
(Continued)

Million French francs

	1980	1983	1984	1985	1986	1987	1988	1989	1990	1991	1992	1993
Less: Consumption of fixed capital	...	...	...	...	...	...	...	...	...	...	...	...
Equals: National Income	1234	2245	2624	3021	3324	3783	4569	5664	6405	6973	...	...
Plus: Net current transfers from the rest of the world	778	1311	1313	1436	1548	1730	1762	1923	2366	2660	...	...
Current transfers from the rest of the world	819	1400	1537	1458	1569	1752	1786	1951	2418	2692	...	...
Less: Current transfers to the rest of the world	41	89	224	22	20	22	24	28	52	32	...	...
Equals: National Disposable Income	2012	3556	3937	4457	4872	5513	6330	7586	8771	9633	...	...
Less: Final consumption	1711	2912	3139	3497	3809	4408	5108	5864	6487	6995	...	...
Equals: Net Saving	301	643	798	960	1063	1105	1222	1722	2284	2637	...	...
Less: Surplus of the nation on current transactions	-197	-509	-327	-246	-180	-199	-555	-898	-825	-474	...	...
Equals: Net Capital Formation	498	1152	1125	1206	1243	1304	1777	2620	3109	3111	...	...

French Polynesia

Source. Reply to the United Nations National Accounts Questionnaire from the Institute National de la Statistique et des Etudes Economiques (INSEE), Paris. Official estimates and descriptions are published by the same Institute in 'Comptes Economiques de la Polynesie Francaise'.

General note. The estimates shown in the following tables have been adjusted by the INSEE to conform to the United Nations System of National Accounts so far as the existing data would permit.

1.1 Expenditure on the Gross Domestic Product, in Current Prices
Million CFP francs

	1980	1983	1984	1985	1986	1987	1988	1989	1990	1991	1992	1993
1 Government final consumption expenditure	48375	82176	92147	94951	104685	99216	110051	115339	120207	...	...	...
2 Private final consumption expenditure	59491	105464	121425	119842	143944	174387	169289	167249	178697	...	...	...
3 Gross capital formation	23597	42972	59108	80994	89389	48792	53005	65882	63515	...	...	...
A Increase in stocks	-700	-800	4000	945	1078	42	-836	520	482	...	...	...
B Gross fixed capital formation	24297	43772	55108	80049	88311	48750	53841	65362	63033	...	...	...
4 Exports of goods and services	6811	14102	14597	19847	21575	24125	23218	24860	27262	...	...	...
5 Less: Imports of goods and services	41442	74225	85470	88862	92658	90554	87487	91663	91926	...	...	...
Equals: Gross Domestic Product	96832	170489	201807	226772	266935	255966	268076	281667	297754	...	...	...

1.3 Cost Components of the Gross Domestic Product
Million CFP francs

	1980	1983	1984	1985	1986	1987	1988	1989	1990	1991	1992	1993
1 Indirect taxes, net	...	...	...	...	...	...	...	...	...	...	...	...
A Indirect taxes	...	...	...	...	...	...	...	...	...	...	...	...
B Less: Subsidies	917	1115	1084	2374	2829	...	...	...	...	...	...	...
2 Consumption of fixed capital	...	...	...	...	...	...	...	...	...	...	...	...
3 Compensation of employees paid by resident producers to:	41992	70018	80327	89347	96924	...	...	...	...	...	...	...
4 Operating surplus	41960	75082	89342	...	...	...	...	...	...	...	...	...
Equals: Gross Domestic Product	96832	170489	201807	226772	266935	...	...	...	...	...	...	...

1.4 General Government Current Receipts and Disbursements
Million CFP francs

	1980	1983	1984	1985	1986	1987	1988	1989	1990	1991	1992	1993
Receipts												
1 Operating surplus	...	...	...	...	...	...	...	...	...	...	...	...
2 Property and entrepreneurial income	355	867	1093	1344	1258	518	45	-215	-226	...	...	...
3 Taxes, fees and contributions	17503	32895	41640	50182	54423	59772	56386	60540	64499	...	...	...
A Indirect taxes	13481	25006	31258	37667	40921	44672	41908	42493	45499	...	...	...
B Direct taxes										...	...	...
C Social security contributions	4022	7889	10382	12515	13502	15100	14478	18047	19000	...	...	...
D Compulsory fees, fines and penalties	...	...	...	...	...	...	...	...	...	...	...	...
4 Other current transfers	57725	99719	110038	120524	144736	135938	153520	158474	163797	...	...	...
Total Current Receipts of General Government	75583	133481	152771	172050	200417	196228	209951	218799	228070	...	...	...
Disbursements												
1 Government final consumption expenditure	48375	82176	92147	94951	104685	99216	110051	115339	120207	...	...	...
A Compensation of employees	27672	45014	50698	56636	60554	62394	70141	73796	79392	...	...	...
B Consumption of fixed capital	...	...	...	...	...	...	...	...	...	...	...	...
C Purchases of goods and services, net	...	...	...	...	...	...	...	...	...	...	...	...
D Less: Own account fixed capital formation	...	...	...	...	...	...	...	...	...	...	...	...
E Indirect taxes paid, net	...	...	...	...	...	...	...	...	...	...	...	...
2 Property income	869	1613	2124	2626	2852	1792	2043	2406	3139	...	...	...
A Interest	869	1613	2124	2626	2852	1792	2043	2406	3139	...	...	...
B Net land rent and royalties	...	...	...	...	...	...	...	...	...	...	...	...
3 Subsidies	917	1115	1084	2374	2829	2760	3154	3327	3857	...	...	...
4 Other current transfers	19299	37560	46010	54937	63726	66268	71238	74822	77561	...	...	...
5 Net saving [a]	6123	11017	11406	17162	26325	26192	23465	22905	23306	...	...	...
Total Current Disbursements and Net Saving of General Government	75583	133481	152771	172050	200417	196228	209951	218799	228070	...	...	...

a) Item 'Net saving' includes consumption of fixed capital.

French Polynesia

1.5 Current Income and Outlay of Corporate and Quasi-Corporate Enterprises, Summary

Million CFP francs

	1980	1983	1984	1985	1986	1987	1988	1989	1990	1991	1992	1993
Receipts												
1 Operating surplus	41765	74770	88995	99891	128832	96095	96939	98485	100928	...	...	...
2 Property and entrepreneurial income received	869	1613	2124	2626	2852	1274	1998	2621	3365	...	...	...
3 Current transfers	...	...	...	...	...	...	...	...	...	...	...	...
Total Current Receipts [a]	42634	76383	91119	102517	131684	97369	98937	101106	104293	...	...	...
Disbursements												
1 Property and entrepreneurial income	18547	32613	37993	43086	50718	40774	41415	45620	45914	...	...	...
2 Direct taxes and other current payments to general government	3735	7207	9064	10683	10801	9166	8064	7567	9453	...	...	...
3 Other current transfers	1260	2232	2697	3108	3708	5660	6079	6220	6530	...	...	...
4 Net saving [b]	19092	34331	41365	45640	66457	41769	43379	41699	42395	...	...	...
Total Current Disbursements and Net Saving [a]	42634	76383	91119	102517	131684	97369	98937	101106	104293	...	...	...

a) Private unincorporated enterprises are included in corporate and quasi-corporate enterprises.
b) Item 'Net saving' includes consumption of fixed capital.

1.6 Current Income and Outlay of Households and Non-Profit Institutions

Million CFP francs

	1980	1983	1984	1985	1986	1987	1988	1989	1990	1991	1992	1993
Receipts												
1 Compensation of employees	41992	70018	80327	89347	96924	114155	127846	135545	147871	...	...	...
2 Operating surplus of private unincorporated enterprises	...	...	...	...	...	...	...	...	...	...	...	...
3 Property and entrepreneurial income	18547	32613	37993	43086	50718	44394	45225	49390	49820	...	...	...
4 Current transfers	8918	17986	20531	26958	31116	29420	30913	32658	34444	...	...	...
Total Current Receipts	69457	120617	138851	159391	178758	187969	203984	217593	232135	...	...	...
Disbursements												
1 Private final consumption expenditure	59491	105464	121425	119842	143944	174387	169289	167249	178697	...	...	...
2 Property income	...	...	...	...	...	...	...	...	...	...	...	...
3 Direct taxes and other current transfers n.e.c. to general government	688	1055	1358	2397	2350	2130	1877	2009	2233	...	...	...
4 Other current transfers	896	2151	3373	4017	5214	6646	7173	7885	8497	...	...	...
5 Net saving [a]	8382	11947	12695	33135	27250	4806	25645	40450	42709	...	...	...
Total Current Disbursements and Net Saving	69457	120617	138851	159391	178758	187969	203984	217593	232135	...	...	...

a) Item 'Net saving' includes consumption of fixed capital.

1.7 External Transactions on Current Account, Summary

Million CFP francs

	1980	1983	1984	1985	1986	1987	1988	1989	1990	1991	1992	1993
Payments to the Rest of the World												
1 Imports of goods and services	41442	74225	85470	88862	92658	90554	87487	91663	91926	...	...	...
2 Factor income to the rest of the world	...	...	...	...	...	...	...	...	...	...	...	...
3 Current transfers to the rest of the world	317	493	555	-	-	...	...	...	...	...	...	...
4 Surplus of the nation on current transactions	10000	14323	6358	14943	30643	24214	40307	40620	46129	...	...	...
Payments to the Rest of the World and Surplus of the Nation on Current Transactions	51759	89041	92383	103805	123301	114768	127794	132283	138055	...	...	...
Receipts From The Rest of the World												
1 Exports of goods and services	6811	14102	14597	19847	21575	24125	23218	24860	27262	...	...	...
2 Factor income from rest of the world	...	...	...	...	...	...	...	...	...	...	...	...
3 Current transfers from rest of the world	44948	74939	77786	83958	101726	90643	104576	107423	110794	...	...	...
Receipts from the Rest of the World on Current Transactions	51759	89041	92383	103805	123301	114768	127794	132283	138055	...	...	...

French Polynesia

1.8 Capital Transactions of The Nation, Summary

Million CFP francs

	1980	1983	1984	1985	1986	1987	1988	1989	1990	1991	1992	1993
Finance of Gross Capital Formation												
Gross saving	...	...	...	...	...	...	...	...	...	...	...	...
1 Consumption of fixed capital	...	...	...	...	...	...	...	...	...	...	...	...
2 Net saving [a]	33597	57295	65466	95937	120032	72767	92489	105054	108410	...	...	...
A General government	6123	11017	11406	17162	26325	26192	23465	22905	23306	...	...	...
B Corporate and quasi-corporate enterprises	19092	34331	41365	45640	66457	41769	43379	41699	42395	...	...	...
C Other	8382	11947	12695	33135	27250	4806	25645	40450	42709	...	...	...
Less: Surplus of the nation on current transactions	10000	14323	6358	14943	30643	24214	40307	40620	46129	...	...	...
Finance of Gross Capital Formation	23597	42972	59108	80994	89389	48792	53005	65882	63515	...	...	...
Gross Capital Formation												
Increase in stocks	-700	-800	4000	945	1078	42	-836	520	482	...	...	...
Gross fixed capital formation	24297	43772	55108	80049	88311	48750	53841	65362	63033	...	...	...
1 General government	6484	12454	11109	18548	20588	25703	30550	31653	31454	...	...	...
2 Corporate and quasi-corporate enterprises	9707	20112	28931	42795	48373	14159	15442	22750	21082	...	...	...
3 Other	8106	11206	15068	18706	19350	8888	7849	10959	10497	...	...	...
Gross Capital Formation	23597	42972	59108	80994	89389	48792	53005	65882	63515	...	...	...

a) Item 'Net saving' includes consumption of fixed capital.

1.10 Gross Domestic Product by Kind of Activity, in Current Prices

Million CFP francs

	1980	1983	1984	1985	1986	1987	1988	1989	1990	1991	1992	1993
1 Agriculture, hunting, forestry and fishing	4533	6650	8142	8557	9249	10401	11170	12439	13849	...	...	...
2 Mining and quarrying	...	...	...	...	...	...	...	...	...	...	...	...
3 Manufacturing [a]	6393	12873	16779	19376	23490	17886	19701	20235	21648	...	...	...
4 Electricity, gas and water [a]	1164	1443	1544	1791	2525	3704	4080	4328	4957	...	...	...
5 Construction	9869	16793	20222	27251	30396	15556	15169	18646	18294	...	...	...
6 Wholesale and retail trade, restaurants and hotels	22502	41893	51117	...	...	65255	61897	64184	67632	...	...	...
7 Transport, storage and communication	5448	10602	11857	13086	17391					...	...	...
8 Finance, insurance, real estate and business services	17562	31972	36404			75433	79894	81392	84436	...	...	...
9 Community, social and personal services				...	...					...	...	...
Total, Industries	67471	122226	146065	164023	200222	188235	191911	201224	210816	...	...	...
Producers of Government Services	28994	47622	55033	61967	65901	66912	75307	79536	85949	...	...	...
Other Producers	367	641	709	782	812	819	858	907	989	...	...	...
Subtotal	96832	170489	201807	226772	266935	255966	268076	281667	297754	...	...	...
Less: Imputed bank service charge	...	...	...	...	...	...	...	...	...	...	...	...
Plus: Import duties	...	...	...	...	...	...	...	...	...	...	...	...
Plus: Value added tax	...	...	...	...	...	...	...	...	...	...	...	...
Equals: Gross Domestic Product	96832	170489	201807	226772	266935	255966	268076	281667	297754	...	...	...

a) Manufacturing of energy-generating products is included in item 'Electricity, gas and water'.

Gabon

Source. Reply to the United Nations National Accounts Questionnaire from the Direction de la Statistique et des Etudes Economiques, Libreville. The official estimates which conform to the present United Nations System of National Accounts are published annually by the same office in 'Comptes Economiques'.

General note. The estimates shown in the following tables have been prepared by the Direction de la Statistique et des Etudes Economiques to conform to the United Nations System of National Accounts so far as the existing data would permit.

1.1 Expenditure on the Gross Domestic Product, in Current Prices

Million CFA francs

		1980	1983	1984	1985	1986	1987	1988	1989	1990	1991	1992	1993
1	Government final consumption expenditure	119659	222300	284400	306300	303900	242200	220600	215387	...	...	...	...
2	Private final consumption expenditure	236670	385700	464700	501200	562100	496300	487900	565201	...	...	...	...
3	Gross capital formation	248967	454800	512900	613600	543482	272500	367300	271672	...	...	...	...
4	Exports of goods and services	585171	792500	919600	935700	475822	421200	377700	587000	...	...	...	...
5	Less: Imports of goods and services	285982	562700	625600	711000	684200	411600	439900	471200	...	...	...	...
	Equals: Gross Domestic Product	904500	1292600	1556000	1645800	1201100	1020600	1013600	1168066 1344400	1494500	1533100	1565200	...

1.3 Cost Components of the Gross Domestic Product

Million CFA francs

		1980	1983	1984	1985	1986	1987	1988	1989	1990	1991	1992	1993
1	Indirect taxes, net	114046	163200	218200	232200	165400	124700	141100	128000	...	...	...	...
2	Consumption of fixed capital	84002	116200	176500	162700	230200	195600	121833	169337	...	...	...	...
3	Compensation of employees paid by resident producers to:	231514	374900	425600	478300	482100	408200	403500	409752	...	...	...	...
4	Operating surplus	419317	560000	649000	667700	231900	228900	271267	396421	...	...	...	...
	Statistical discrepancy	55606	78300	86700	104900	91500	63200	75900	64536	...	...	...	...
	Equals: Gross Domestic Product	904500	1292600	1556000	1645800	1201100	1020600	1013600	1168066				

1.7 External Transactions on Current Account, Summary

Million CFA francs

		1980	1983	1984	1985	1986	1987	1988	1989	1990	1991	1992	1993
	Payments to the Rest of the World												
1	Imports of goods and services	285982	562700	625600	711000	684200	411600	439900	471200	...	...	...	...
	A Imports of merchandise c.i.f.	192312	325700	390400	445000	437778	261600	284000	289200	...	...	...	...
	B Other	93670	237000	235200	266000	246422	150000	155900	182000	...	...	...	...
2	Factor income to the rest of the world	55569	99000	104000	105000	70008	67666	79482	104900	...	...	...	...
	A Compensation of employees	...	...	...	...	...	...	482	...	...	...	...	...
	B Property and entrepreneurial income	55569	99000	104000	105000	70008	67666	79000	104900	...	...	...	...
3	Current transfers to the rest of the world	61655	75200	85000	99600	137326	87656	104376	98545	...	...	...	...
4	Surplus of the nation on current transactions [a]	210869	133400	169000	80300	-358552	-95733	-214172	-55945	...	...	...	...
	Payments to the Rest of the World and Surplus of the Nation on Current Transactions [a]	614075	870300	983600	995900	532982	471189	409586	618700	...	...	...	...
	Receipts From The Rest of the World												
1	Exports of goods and services [a]	585171	792500	919600	935700	475822	421200	377700	587000	...	...	...	...
	A Exports of merchandise f.o.b.	537101	738700	889400	887200	434129	389089	344273	517400	...	...	...	...
	B Other	48070	53800	30200	48500	41693	32111	33427	69600	...	...	...	...
2	Factor income from rest of the world	5262	16500	20900	13100	6270	4800	4362	4200	...	...	...	...
	A Compensation of employees	...	...	...	...	...	...	...	...	...	...	...	...
	B Property and entrepreneurial income	5262	16500	20900	13100	6270	4800	4362	4200	...	...	...	...
3	Current transfers from rest of the world	23642	61300	43100	47100	50890	45189	27524	27500	...	...	...	...
	A Subsidies from supranational organisations	6481	7200	6800	8800	8167	9225	6087	7000	...	...	...	...
	B Other current transfers	17160	54100	36300	38300	42723	35964	21437	20500	...	...	...	...
	Receipts from the Rest of the World on Current Transactions	614075	870300	983600	995900	532982	471189	409586	618700	...	...	...	...

a) Beginning 1976, estimates are not strictly comparable with those of other tables.

Gabon

1.10 Gross Domestic Product by Kind of Activity, in Current Prices

Million CFA francs

	1980	1983	1984	1985	1986	1987	1988	1989	1990	1991	1992	1993
1 Agriculture, hunting, forestry and fishing	66340	82200	96600	102200	109300	107400	108000	117200	...	...	...	...
2 Mining and quarrying	404078	592000	766400	760100	267300	280400	217900	364100	...	...	...	...
3 Manufacturing a	43813	68200	74100	87500	83800	70200	70100	64300	...	...	...	...
4 Electricity, gas and water	13449	20100	23200	30000	26400	26400	28500	27700	...	...	...	...
5 Construction	58971	78300	85500	103500	132600	70600	50300	62300	...	...	...	...
6 Wholesale and retail trade, restaurants and hotels	67256	84800	93300	108600	117200	90400	139400	140000	...	...	...	...
7 Transport, storage and communication	36476	63400	66700	78300	83600	79500	87600	92600	...	...	...	...
8 Finance, insurance, real estate and business services	58119	42100	48500	57500	69200	54500	44400	49000	...	...	...	...
9 Community, social and personal services	42095	79300	98500	87500	97100	65700	82500	77200	...	...	...	...
Total, Industries	790592	1110400	1352800	1415200	986600	845000	828600	994400	...	...	...	...
Producers of Government Services	67511	118800	132100	148700	155800	141000	137100	134000	...	...	...	...
Other Producers	...	...	...	...	...	...	...	...	...	...	...	...
Subtotal	858108	1229200	1484900	1563900	1142300	986000	965700	1128400	...	...	...	...
Less: Imputed bank service charge	9574	14900	15600	23000	32800	28600	28030	24836	...	...	...	...
Plus: Import duties	55606	78200	86700	104900	91500	63200	75900	64536	...	...	...	...
Plus: Value added tax	...	...	...	...	...	...	...	...	...	...	...	...
Equals: Gross Domestic Product	904500	1292600	1556000	1645800	1201100	1020600	1013600	1168066	...	...	...	...

a) Repair services are included in item 'Manufacturing'.

1.12 Relations Among National Accounting Aggregates

Million CFA francs

	1980	1983	1984	1985	1986	1987	1988	1989	1990	1991	1992	1993
Gross Domestic Product	904500	1292600	1556000	1645800	1201100	1020600	1013600	1168066	...	...	...	...
Plus: Net factor income from the rest of the world	-50307	-82500	-83100	-91900	-63730	-62866	-75120	-100700	...	...	...	...
Factor income from the rest of the world	5262	16500	20900	13100	6270	4800	4362	4200	...	...	...	...
Less: Factor income to the rest of the world	55569	99000	104000	105000	70008	67666	79482	104900	...	...	...	...
Equals: Gross National Product	854193	1210100	1472900	1553900	1137370	957734	938480	1067360	...	...	...	...
Less: Consumption of fixed capital	84002	116200	176500	162700	230200	195600	121833	169337	...	...	...	...
Equals: National Income	770191	1093900	1296400	1391200	907170	762134	816642	898023	...	...	...	...
Plus: Net current transfers from the rest of the world	-38013	-13900	-41900	-52500	-86436	-42467	-76852	-71045	...	...	...	...
Current transfers from the rest of the world	23642	61300	43100	47100	50890	45189	27524	27500	...	...	...	...
Less: Current transfers to the rest of the world	61655	75200	85000	99600	137326	87656	104376	98545	...	...	...	...
Equals: National Disposable Income	732178	1080000	1254500	1338700	820730	719667	739795	826978	...	...	...	...
Less: Final consumption	356328	608000	749100	807500	866000	738500	708500	780588	...	...	...	...
Equals: Net Saving	375850	472000	505400	531200	-45270	-18833	31295	46390	...	...	...	...
Less: Surplus of the nation on current transactions	210869	133400	169000	80300	-358552	-95733	-214172	-55945	...	...	...	...
Equals: Net Capital Formation	164981	338600	336400	450900	313282	76900	245467	102335	...	...	...	...

Gambia

Source. Reply to the United Nations National Accounts Questionnaire from the Central Statistics Department, Ministry of Economic Planning and Industrial Development, Banjul. The official estimates are published in 'Sources and Methods of Estimates of National Income at Current Prices in The Gambia', February 1985, 'Estimates of National Income at Constant Prices in The Gambia', July 1985 and 'National Accounts of The Gambia, 1982/83 to 1989/90' January 1991.

General note. The estimates shown in the following tables have been prepared in accordance with the United Nations System of National Accounts so far as the existing data would permit.

1.1 Expenditure on the Gross Domestic Product, in Current Prices

Thousand Gambian dalasis — Fiscal year beginning 1 July

	1980	1983	1984	1985	1986	1987	1988	1989	1990	1991	1992	1993
1 Government final consumption expenditure	88461	118701	133462	161469	186983	243563	264206	316726	380474	369137	...	...
2 Private final consumption expenditure	...	...	...	...	...	...	...	...	...	...	...	...
3 Gross capital formation	...	...	...	...	...	...	...	...	...	...	...	...
A Increase in stocks	...	...	...	...	...	...	...	...	...	...	...	...
B Gross fixed capital formation [a]	59518	58925	72816	77504	103542	126128	134663	111971	132397	156622	...	...
Residential buildings	29550	8426	11241	24287	19771	48041	32344	13559	43389	35594	...	...
Non-residential buildings											...	...
Other construction and land improvement etc.	21828	35556	43204	38064	57146	30811	64187	64286	32145	73935		
Other	8141	14943	18371	15153	26625	47276	38132	34126	56863	47093		
4 Exports of goods and services [b]	93280	313680	325250	470820	763944	790065	1010752	1122120			...	...
5 Less: Imports of goods and services [c]	290900	395050	388570	507400	839972	843460	1066492	1256040	...	...	...	...
Equals: Gross Domestic Product	411681	617837	781863	1085241	1485985	1635517	1942310	2366950	2629565	2947632	...	...

a) The estimates refer to central government capital formation only.
b) Item 'Exports of goods and services' includes net travel and tourism income.
c) Item 'Imports of goods and services' includes net freight and insurance.

1.3 Cost Components of the Gross Domestic Product

Thousand Gambian dalasis — Fiscal year beginning 1 July

	1980	1983	1984	1985	1986	1987	1988	1989	1990	1991	1992	1993
1 Indirect taxes, net	44140	98646	110802	158100	172246	225109	367536	401338	463203	536736	...	...
2 Consumption of fixed capital	50561	80000	100000	124701	169756	211358	227129	248704	273555	302110	...	...
3 Compensation of employees paid by resident producers to:	...	...	...	...	...	...	...	...	...	...	...	...
4 Operating surplus	...	...	...	...	...	...	...	...	...	...	...	...
Equals: Gross Domestic Product	411681	617837	781863	1085241	1485985	1635517	1942310	2366950	2629565	2947632	...	...

1.10 Gross Domestic Product by Kind of Activity, in Current Prices

Thousand Gambian dalasis — Fiscal year beginning 1 July

	1980	1983	1984	1985	1986	1987	1988	1989	1990	1991	1992	1993
1 Agriculture, hunting, forestry and fishing	115825	135776	192641	276989	467130	499213	493711	637611	608123	674920	...	...
2 Mining and quarrying	126	176	202	245	311	342	373	405	486	600	...	...
3 Manufacturing	28104	59663	61318	69150	32531	67000	90127	132321	159205	175273	...	...
4 Electricity, gas and water	1850	2353	1505	6199	12494	14320	14994	17000	21440	25638	...	...
5 Construction	31215	32444	39510	40608	70294	53928	84204	116804	118623	148300	...	...
6 Wholesale and retail trade, restaurants and hotels	100703	223499	270336	370176	515250	565057	747507	861207	1024592	1127954	...	...
7 Transport, storage and communication	34706	50367	66392	102435	133011	161281	190574	221403	262630	311472	...	...
8 Finance, insurance, real estate and business services	49162	44413	57331	120618	168752	176887	190453	205550	210885	247249	...	...
9 Community, social and personal services	8600	14840	18639	26075	39375	45833	56000	65707	71861	81313	...	...
Total, Industries	370291	563531	707874	1012495	1439148	1583861	1867943	2258008	2477845	2792719	...	...
Producers of Government Services	55092	76417	86553	93064	95150	111656	146229	174151	191529	196913	...	...
Other Producers	...	...	...	...	...	...	...	...	...	...	...	...
Subtotal	425383	639948	794427	1105559	1534298	1695517	2014172	2432159	2669374	2989632		
Less: Imputed bank service charge	13702	22111	12564	20318	48313	60000	71862	65209	39809	42000		
Plus: Import duties	...	...	...	...	...	...	...	...	...	...	...	...
Plus: Value added tax	...	...	...	...	...	...	...	...	...	...	...	...
Equals: Gross Domestic Product	411681	617837	781863	1085241	1485985	1635517	1942310	2366950	2629565	2947632	...	...

Gambia

1.11 Gross Domestic Product by Kind of Activity, in Constant Prices

Thousand Gambian dalasis

Fiscal year beginning 1 July

	1980	1983	1984	1985	1986	1987	1988	1989	1990	1991	1992	1993
					At constant prices of: 1976							
1 Agriculture, hunting, forestry and fishing	104457	97169	107158	113602	121407	120205	117035	127345	111434	124479	...	...
2 Mining and quarrying	185	155	160	166	172	178	184	190	209	230	...	...
3 Manufacturing	19103	28859	24929	27457	30911	34554	31811	33261	33223	32859	...	...
4 Electricity, gas and water	1500	1736	1892	2088	2260	2486	2404	2517	3100	3162	...	...
5 Construction	18509	22431	25463	23291	27611	19756	24901	27873	30101	31606	...	...
6 Wholesale and retail trade, restaurants and hotels	95407	146383	135165	140789	143446	143273	155264	161653	170044	176368	...	...
7 Transport, storage and communication	30323	40180	44514	45443	53127	63160	67287	72835	81984	85154	...	...
8 Finance, insurance, real estate and business services	34872	29098	31274	41872	43952	45232	46638	48291	47087	49654	...	...
9 Community, social and personal services	6738	8524	8814	9114	9423	9744	10075	10759	11056	11320	...	...
Total, Industries	311094	374535	379369	403822	432309	438588	455599	484724	488238	514832		
Producers of Government Services	40857	69646	65426	60043	48500	50682	54900	54900	56500	57630		
Other Producers	...	...	...	...	...	...	...	...	...	...		
Subtotal	351951	444181	444795	463865	480809	489270	510499	539624	544738	572462		
Less: Imputed bank service charge	10187	12036	5629	6728	10950	11399	11926	12602	6027	10230		
Plus: Import duties	...	...	...	...	...	...	...	...	...	...		
Plus: Value added tax	...	...	...	...	...	...	...	...	...	...		
Equals: Gross Domestic Product	341764	432145	439166	457137	469859	477871	498573	527022	538711	562232	...	...

1.12 Relations Among National Accounting Aggregates

Thousand Gambian dalasis

Fiscal year beginning 1 July

	1980	1983	1984	1985	1986	1987	1988	1989	1990	1991	1992	1993
Gross Domestic Product	411681	617837	781863	1085241	1485985	1635517	1942310	2366950	2629565	2947632	...	...
Plus: Net factor income from the rest of the world	-6195	-23690	-10640	-66200	-134800	-93900	-80210	-94700	-64300	-76324	...	...
Equals: Gross National Product	405486	594147	771223	1019041	1351185	1541617	1862100	2272250	2565265	2871308	...	...
Less: Consumption of fixed capital	50561	80000	100000	124701	169756	211358	227129	248704	273555	302110	...	...
Equals: National Income	354925	514147	671223	894340	1181429	1330259	1634971	2023546	2291710	2569198	...	...
Plus: Net current transfers from the rest of the world [a]	102090	47980	69190	188100	347400	386400	369700	429200	447000	542621	...	...
Equals: National Disposable Income [b]	457015	562127	740413	1082440	1528829	1716659	2004671	2452746	2738710	3111819	...	...
Less: Final consumption	...	...	...	...	...	...	...	...	...	...	...	...
Equals: Net Saving	...	...	...	...	...	...	...	...	...	...	...	...
Less: Surplus of the nation on current transactions	...	...	...	...	...	...	...	...	...	...	...	...
Equals: Net Capital Formation	...	...	...	...	...	...	...	...	...	...	...	...

a) Item 'Net current transfers from the rest of the world' includes mainly net interest receipts.
b) Item 'National disposable income' includes unrequited private transfers and official transfers.

2.1 Government Final Consumption Expenditure by Function, in Current Prices

Thousand Gambian dalasis

Fiscal year beginning 1 July

	1980	1983	1984	1985	1986	1987	1988	1989	1990	1991	1992	1993
1 General public services	...	...	52515	59813	177283	256275	152961	153778	179915	178219	...	...
2 Defence	...	...	...	...	...	...	...	...	...	...	...	...
3 Public order and safety	...	...	...	...	...	...	...	...	...	...	...	...
4 Education [a]	...	...	25664	27175	29916	33131	49956	67841	105635	101530	...	...
5 Health	...	...	14136	14830	14198	56251	24379	41191	52191	45733	...	...
6 Social security and welfare	...	...	166	151	197	240	422	347	438	560	...	...
7 Housing and community amenities	...	...	11435	10240	18118	32654	23366	24015	24446	30962	...	...
8 Recreational, cultural and religious affairs [a]	...	...	...	...	...	...	...	...	...	...	...	...
9 Economic services	...	...	104717	121272	152988	139468	144284	165929	152451	194056	...	...

Gambia

2.1 Government Final Consumption Expenditure by Function, in Current Prices
(Continued)

Thousand Gambian dalasis — Fiscal year beginning 1 July

	1980	1983	1984	1985	1986	1987	1988	1989	1990	1991	1992	1993
A Fuel and energy	...	...	...	...	...	...	...	...	...	...	...	...
B Agriculture, forestry, fishing and hunting	...	...	24840	53429	71411	60291	36608	32090	48147	59927	...	...
C Mining, manufacturing and construction, except fuel and energy	...	...	16994	7595	14923	7231	7398	29237	15092	16398	...	...
D Transportation and communication	...	...	57737	46762	47030	64159	75807	67323	30402	84663	...	...
E Other economic affairs	...	...	5146	13486	19624	7787	24471	37279	58810	33068	...	...
10 Other functions	...	...	14970	31314	73334	118879	165385	205923	303797	253260	...	...
Total Government Final Consumption Expenditure [b]	...	...	223603	264795	466034	636898	560753	659024	818873	804320	...	...

a) Item 'Education' includes item 'Recreational, cultural and religiious affairs.
b) Only central government data are included in the general government estimates.

Germany

On October 1990, the Federal Republic of Germany and the German Democratic Republic united to form one sovereign State under the designation "Germany".

National Accounts estimates for united Germany (subsequent to 3 October 1990) are not available. The tables shown in the following country chapter are for the territory of the Federal Republic of Germany before the unification. Data for the former German Democratic Republic, prepared in accordance with the System of Material Product Balances, can be found in the 1992 edition of this publication.

Germany, Fed. Rep. of

General note. The preparation of national accounts statistics in the Federal Republic of Germany is undertaken by the Federal Statistical Office, Wiesbaden. The official estimates are published in the monthly bulletin 'Wirtschaft und Statistik'. Detailed data as well as description of the sources and methods used for the national accounts estimation are published annually in Fachserie 18 'Volkswirtschaftliche Gesamtrechnungen', Reihe 1 'Konten und Standardtabellen'. The estimates are in close accordance with the classifications and definitions recommended in the United Nations System of National Accounts (SNA). Input-output tables for 1978 and 1980 have been published in 1982 in Reihe 2 of Fachserie 18. The 1977 tables will be issued together with revised tables for 1978 and 1980 in 1987. The following tables have been prepared from successive replies to the United Nations national accounts questionnaire. Estimates shown include the relevant data relating to Berlin, for which separate data have not been supplied. This is without prejudice to any question of status which may be involved. When the scope and coverage of the estimates differ for conceptual or statistical reasons from the definitions and classifications recommended in SNA, a footnote is indicated to the relevant tables. As a general principle, the statistical units in the case of the data provided in the ISIC classification are institutional units (e.g. enterprises). Only the ownership of dwellings (including owner-occupied housing) is shown in a functional delimitation and fully allocated to the enterprise sector. The enterprise sector comprises all enterprises, i.e. also those which according to SNA should be shown in the sector of private households or general government, respectively.

Sources and methods:

(a) **Gross domestic product.** The main approach used to estimate GDP is the production approach.

(b) **Expenditure on the gross domestic product.** The expenditure approach is used to estimate all components of GDP by expenditure type except gross fixed capital formation which is calculated mainly by the commodity-flow approach. Government final consumption expenditure is based on records from all sectors of general government. Private final consumption expenditure is estimated mainly from data on retail sales. Data for certain base-years are derived mainly from censuses (trade census 1979, crafts census 1977, industrial production census 1977). Annual data are linked with these base-year data by means of current turnover and other supply statistics. The estimates of gross fixed capital formation are based on quarterly production reports, monthly construction reports, statistics on building activity and the previously mentioned censuses. Exports and imports of goods are based on foreign trade statistics, while exports and imports of services are obtained mainly from the Central Bank. For the calculation of constant prices, price deflation is used for all expenditure groups.

(c) **Cost-structure of the gross domestic product.** Compensation of employees is calculated from three sources - social security statistics, census data extrapolated by current data and taxation statistics. Capital consumption is calculated at constant prices and at current replacement costs according to the perpetual inventory method. Indirect taxes and subsidies are taken directly from the general government accounts. Operating surplus is then obtained as a residual.

(d) **Gross domestic product by kind of economic activity.** The table of GDP by kind of economic activity is prepared at market prices, i.e. producers' values. The production approach is used to estimate value added of most industries. The income approach is used to estimate value added of domestic services, private non-profit institutions and producers of government services. The value of agricultural production is defined as the difference between primary gross production and internally used quantities, times average prices, or, as the sum of sales, change in livestock and other stocks, own account consumption, investment and exports. The basic statistics used are mainly data on utilization of agricultural production. Inputs are derived from book-keeping records, foreign trade statistics and production and sales statistics from suppliers of agricultural input goods. The main sources for estimating mining and quarrying, manufacturing, electricity, gas and water and construction are the censuses of production industries, which provide bench-mark data, and annual data taken from several sources. Data on intermediate consumption for these sectors are taken from the censuses and cost-structure statistics. For trade, the bench-mark estimates are mainly based on the trade censuses 1979. Output is extrapolated by turnover data, while input is estimated from the trade censuses, cost-structure statistics and annual trade reports. For the transport sector, cost-structure statistics are used to estimate parts of output and intermediate consumption for most sub-sectors. Turnover tax statistics are utilized for preparing the current output estimates. Banking statistics, collected by Central Bank, and insurance statistics, collected by Federal Supervisory Board, provide the basis for estimating output of financial institutions including insurance. Input is estimated on the basis of bank company reports and insurance company reports. Rents are estimated separately for three different categories - old, medium and new buildings. The rents are based on data from censuses of buildings and dwellings, which include owner-occupied dwellings. The data are extrapolated by quantity and price indexes. The data used to estimate value added of government services, are mainly based on receipts and expenditure statistics of general government. For private non-profit institutions output is estimated as the sum of costs for wages and salaries, estimated capital consumption and indirect taxes. Double deflation is used in the calculations of constant prices, for all sectors except transport and real estate and business services. Output of most sectors is deflated by producer price indexes. However, for most agricultural products, current quantities are multiplied by base year prices, for some transport and communication services output is extrapolated by quantity indexes, and for insurance and business services extrapolation is used. Deflation by purchase price indexes or specially constructed input indexes is done for almost all sectors. For trade, and partly for transportation and communication, however, constant input-ouput ratios are assumed.

1.1 Expenditure on the Gross Domestic Product, in Current Prices

Million Deutsche marks

		1980	1983	1984	1985	1986	1987	1988	1989	1990	1991	1992	1993
1	Government final consumption expenditure	298020	336440	350440	365720	382550	397280	412380	418820	444070	466520	502860	508480
2	Private final consumption expenditure	837020	959280	1001200	1036530	1066430	1108020	1153690	1220950	1320710	1448770	1536320	1588900
	A Households	821690	940130	981230	1014740	1042340	1082150	1126620	1192120	1289980	1414560	1498410	1548090
	B Private non-profit institutions serving households	15330	19150	19970	21790	24090	25870	27070	28830	30730	34210	37910	40810
3	Gross capital formation	343850	339310	355990	357060	376400	385220	420200	464530	519270	583650	584280	540280
	A Increase in stocks	11770	-1500	5320	1250	2920	-560	10300	16010	11490	20430	-2590	-11520
	B Gross fixed capital formation	332080	340810	350670	355810	373480	385780	409900	448520	507780	563220	586870	551800
	Residential buildings	99530	105770	111040	100850	101830	102580	108610	117930	135860	151430	170960	184070
	Non-residential buildings	105710	100090	102500	101930	110780	113770	118830	127120	137350	147890	158360	154400
	Other construction and land improvement etc.												
	Other	126840	134950	137130	153030	160870	169430	182460	203470	234570	263900	257550	213330
4	Exports of goods and services	389140	479630	536320	592740	580540	576610	619830	701430	778900	875220	932650	911260
5	Less: Imports of goods and services	395990	446120	493060	528870	480630	476650	510120	581290	636950	726560	743110	695220
	Equals: Gross Domestic Product	1472040	1668540	1750890	1823180	1925290	1990480	2095980	2224440	2426000	2647600	2813000	2853700

1.2 Expenditure on the Gross Domestic Product, in Constant Prices

Million Deutsche marks

		1980	1983	1984	1985	1986	1987	1988	1989	1990	1991	1992	1993
		At constant prices of: 1991											
1	Government final consumption expenditure	411070	415640	426010	434800	445840	452710	462330	454880	465030	466520	485320	479720
2	Private final consumption expenditure	1115900	1110590	1130550	1150050	1189950	1230610	1264340	1300150	1370010	1448770	1480420	1483010
	A Households	1094100	1087280	1106740	1124430	1162020	1201180	1234370	1269200	1337920	1414560	1444630	1446410
	B Private non-profit institutions serving households	21800	23310	23810	25620	27930	29430	29970	30950	32090	34210	35790	36600
3	Gross capital formation	467980	424170	430770	422740	438590	441630	473900	508740	547370	583650	564490	511050

Germany, Fed. Rep. of

1.2 Expenditure on the Gross Domestic Product, in Constant Prices
(Continued)

Million Deutsche marks

	1980	1983	1984	1985	1986	1987	1988	1989	1990	1991	1992	1993
	\multicolumn{12}{c}{At constant prices of:1991}											
A Increase in stocks	12790	2320	8330	2390	4300	-610	12130	18080	15020	20430	-470	-6980
B Gross fixed capital formation	455190	421850	422440	420350	434290	442240	461770	490660	532350	563220	564960	518030
Residential buildings	142900	136410	139140	125310	124580	123050	127620	133870	145240	151430	161630	166850
Non-residential buildings	141180	126840	126980	125220	133600	135160	138500	143980	146190	147890	150570	142890
Other construction and land improvement etc.												
Other	171110	158600	156320	169820	176110	184030	195650	212810	240920	263900	252760	208290
4 Exports of goods and services	476840	526850	570010	613090	609300	611700	645250	710920	789050	875220	922460	893030
5 Less: Imports of goods and services	453790	441050	463840	484680	497580	518250	544820	590290	651060	726560	758390	718210
Equals: Gross Domestic Product	2018000	2036200	2093500	2136000	2186100	2218400	2301000	2384400	2520400	2647600	2694300	2648600

1.3 Cost Components of the Gross Domestic Product

Million Deutsche marks

	1980	1983	1984	1985	1986	1987	1988	1989	1990	1991	1992	1993
1 Indirect taxes, net	162820	182670	189800	192370	194860	200700	209370	231550	253390	291680	319400	334410
A Indirect taxes	193470	214390	226130	230310	236170	245500	257110	278330	302220	337330	364400	379300
B Less: Subsidies	30650	31720	36330	37940	41310	44800	47740	46780	48830	45650	45000	44890
2 Consumption of fixed capital	175000	214930	226370	235360	243690	252300	263090	279450	303010	332840	359690	379160
3 Compensation of employees paid by resident producers to:	860880	949030	983690	1021420	1074440	1119350	1163780	1216250	1315520	1430300	1527130	1550390
A Resident households	858840	946900	981630	1019340	1072240	1117010	1161220	1213390	1308100	1410270	1499760	1521380
B Rest of the world	2040	2130	2060	2080	2200	2340	2560	2860	7420	20030	27370	29010
4 Operating surplus	273340	321910	351030	374030	412300	418130	459740	497190	554080	592780	606780	589740
A Corporate and quasi-corporate enterprises	273340	321910	351030	374030	412300	418130	459740	497190	554080	592780	606780	589740
B Private unincorporated enterprises	...	...	...	...	...	...	...	...	...	...	...	...
C General government	...	...	...	...	...	...	...	...	...	...	...	...
Equals: Gross Domestic Product	1472040	1668540	1750890	1823180	1925290	1990480	2095980	2224440	2426000	2647600	2813000	2853700

1.4 General Government Current Receipts and Disbursements

Million Deutsche marks

	1980	1983	1984	1985	1986	1987	1988	1989	1990	1991	1992	1993
	\multicolumn{12}{c}{Receipts}											
1 Operating surplus	...	...	...	...	...	...	...	...	...	...	...	...
2 Property and entrepreneurial income	15680	29710	30860	33650	32830	26040	19020	30580	33310	34840	45490	43790
3 Taxes, fees and contributions	617930	692350	730980	766640	796710	828050	865110	929240	969130	1089730	1173290	1206180
A Indirect taxes	193470	214390	226130	230310	236170	245500	257110	278330	302220	337330	364400	379300
B Direct taxes	187750	200360	213020	229640	237040	245940	255410	281760	271000	316000	342660	336040
C Social security contributions	230080	269160	282750	297250	313390	325900	341090	356940	382770	421990	451450	475730
D Compulsory fees, fines and penalties	6630	8440	9080	9440	10110	10710	11500	12210	13140	14410	14780	15110
4 Other current transfers	27590	32260	33360	34010	36750	36210	39460	38890	40600	46260	49590	49440
Total Current Receipts of General Government	661200	754320	795200	834300	866290	890300	923590	998710	1043040	1170830	1268370	1299410
	\multicolumn{12}{c}{Disbursements}											
1 Government final consumption expenditure	298020	336440	350440	365720	382550	397280	412380	418820	444070	466520	502860	508480
A Compensation of employees	162450	183370	187010	193880	203300	211500	216920	222840	236290	252960	269770	278940
B Consumption of fixed capital	9700	12120	12680	13120	13570	14070	14690	15550	16660	18010	19340	20520
C Purchases of goods and services, net	125910	141020	150840	158820	165810	171860	180920	180590	191300	195720	213930	209200
D Less: Own account fixed capital formation	280	320	350	360	380	400	400	410	430	420	430	430
E Indirect taxes paid, net	240	250	260	260	250	250	250	250	250	250	250	250
2 Property income	27480	49070	51570	54180	56130	56780	58940	59590	62390	73500	83220	89930
A Interest	27480	49070	51570	54180	56130	56780	58940	59590	62390	73500	83220	89930
B Net land rent and royalties	...	...	...	...	...	...	...	...	...	...	...	...

Germany, Fed. Rep. of

1.4 General Government Current Receipts and Disbursements
(Continued)

Million Deutsche marks

		1980	1983	1984	1985	1986	1987	1988	1989	1990	1991	1992	1993
3	Subsidies	30650	31720	36330	37940	41310	44800	47740	46780	48830	45650	45000	44890
4	Other current transfers	279000	325910	334670	342040	353850	371390	392530	409620	472900	574610	614820	654690
	A Social security benefits	174390	206830	210200	215260	220980	232050	245000	254320	269050	284350	303000	329530
	B Social assistance grants	43210	48400	48340	49070	52980	55500	55950	58350	60280	63970	69660	74370
	C Other	61400	70680	76130	77710	79890	83840	91580	96950	143570	226290	242160	250790
5	Net saving	26050	11180	22190	34420	32450	20050	12000	63900	14850	10550	22470	1420
	Total Current Disbursements and Net Saving of General Government	661200	754320	795200	834300	866290	890300	923590	998710	1043040	1170830	1268370	1299410

1.5 Current Income and Outlay of Corporate and Quasi-Corporate Enterprises, Summary

Million Deutsche marks

		1980	1983	1984	1985	1986	1987	1988	1989	1990	1991	1992	1993
	Receipts												
1	Operating surplus	273340	321910	351030	374030	412300	418130	459740	497190	554080	592780	606780	589740
2	Property and entrepreneurial income received	229950	286100	308790	318520	321560	322020	337490	379110	458960	533400	603090	633460
3	Current transfers [a]	68200	78710	83510	86700	90830	97210	101940	107740	120120	128980	140700	149910
	Total Current Receipts [a]	533020	646150	691650	729070	808400	810340	895240	974260	1132610	1196930	1270410	1246330
	Disbursements												
1	Property and entrepreneurial income	453400	535870	580020	612920	652050	650720	697680	774110	908130	998050	1084740	1088530
2	Direct taxes and other current payments to general government [a]	27390	31360	36380	41130	40860	36580	39840	45870	41500	45010	45200	43320
3	Other current transfers [a]	57590	68740	72240	77400	82270	87400	92920	99400	108560	116960	126810	136560
4	Net saving [a]	-5360	10180	3010	-2380	33220	35640	64800	54880	74420	36910	13660	-22080
	Total Current Disbursements and Net Saving [a]	533020	646150	691650	729070	808400	810340	895240	974260	1132610	1196930	1270410	1246330

a) Current income and outlay of corporate and quasi-corporate enterprises refers to corporate enterprises only.

1.6 Current Income and Outlay of Households and Non-Profit Institutions

Million Deutsche marks

		1980	1983	1984	1985	1986	1987	1988	1989	1990	1991	1992	1993
	Receipts												
1	Compensation of employees	863880	953440	988330	1026410	1079490	1124700	1169380	1221890	1317100	1422240	1513550	1535920
	A From resident producers	858840	946900	981630	1019340	1072240	1117010	1161220	1213390	1308100	1410270	1499760	1521380
	B From rest of the world	5040	6540	6700	7070	7250	7690	8160	8500	9000	11970	13790	14540
2	Operating surplus of private unincorporated enterprises	...	...	...	...	...	...	...	...	...	...	...	...
3	Property and entrepreneurial income [a]	250800	289740	317470	338930	377480	384090	424700	462490	521370	557650	571300	541700
4	Current transfers	304150	355990	364030	375560	392360	412890	433310	453310	480370	504870	544250	586000
	A Social security benefits	174390	206830	210200	215260	220980	232050	245000	254320	269050	284350	303000	329530
	B Social assistance grants	43210	48400	48340	49070	52980	55500	55950	58350	60280	63970	69660	74370
	C Other	86550	100760	105490	111230	118400	125340	132360	140640	151040	156550	171590	182100
	Total Current Receipts	1418830	1599170	1669830	1740900	1849330	1921680	2027390	2137690	2318840	2484760	2629100	2663620
	Disbursements												
1	Private final consumption expenditure	837020	959280	1001200	1036530	1066430	1108020	1153690	1220950	1320710	1448770	1536320	1588900
2	Property income	13190	17860	17760	17670	17930	17480	18170	19460	22100	25880	31540	36920
3	Direct taxes and other current transfers n.e.c. to general government	394880	444320	466520	493120	517070	543280	564250	602060	619360	697180	749840	768440
	A Social security contributions	229480	268560	282150	296610	312750	325220	340330	356100	380450	415690	442760	466350
	B Direct taxes	160210	169070	177220	188980	196270	209430	214670	236340	228590	270520	295670	289940
	C Fees, fines and penalties	5190	6690	7150	7530	8050	8630	9250	9620	10320	10970	11410	12150
4	Other current transfers	88820	100890	107390	110180	114920	120360	125750	131680	145190	148850	164440	173740
5	Net saving	84920	76820	76960	83400	132980	132540	165530	163540	211480	164080	146960	95620
	Total Current Disbursements and Net Saving [a]	1418830	1599170	1669830	1740900	1849330	1921680	2027390	2137690	2318840	2484760	2629100	2663620

a) Item 'Property and entrepreneural income' includes undistributed profits of unincorporated enterprises.

Germany, Fed. Rep. of

1.7 External Transactions on Current Account, Summary

Million Deutsche marks

	1980	1983	1984	1985	1986	1987	1988	1989	1990	1991	1992	1993
Payments to the Rest of the World												
1 Imports of goods and services [a]	395990	446120	493060	528870	480630	476650	510120	581290	636950	726560	743110	695220
A Imports of merchandise c.i.f. [b]	324020	362800	405350	436870	390690	383890	411770	475320	521240	596210	599420	545990
B Other	71970	83320	87710	92000	89940	92760	98350	105970	115710	130350	143690	149230
2 Factor income to the rest of the world	26160	35450	37070	40600	45670	48390	56020	62200	82890	102700	122970	142900
A Compensation of employees	2040	2130	2060	2080	2200	2340	2560	2860	7420	20030	27370	29010
B Property and entrepreneurial income	24120	33320	35010	38520	43470	46050	53460	59340	75470	82670	95600	113890
By general government	1520	6450	6900	8190	9790	11590	11670	11340	12640	14030	17610	26210
By corporate and quasi-corporate enterprises	22600	26870	28110	30330	33680	34460	41790	48000	62830	68640	77990	87680
By other	...	...	...	...	...	...	...	...	...	...	...	...
3 Current transfers to the rest of the world [c]	34620	39970	45280	45110	44650	44980	51170	55640	100830	185360	198910	206120
A Indirect taxes to supranational organizations	...	...	...	...	...	...	...	...	...	...	...	...
B Other current transfers	34620	39970	45280	45110	44650	44980	51170	55640	100830	185360	198910	206120
4 Surplus of the nation on current transactions	-24770	14370	24220	43920	82230	82330	89150	107020	85040	18960	38660	40620
Payments to the Rest of the World and Surplus of the Nation on Current Transactions	432000	535910	599630	658500	653180	652350	706460	806150	905710	1033580	1103650	1084860
Receipts From The Rest of the World												
1 Exports of goods and services [a]	389140	479630	536320	592740	580540	576610	619830	701430	778900	875220	932650	911260
A Exports of merchandise f.o.b.	339060	416970	467350	517760	508960	506850	548020	616360	663700	738530	800640	787560
B Other	50080	62660	68970	74980	71580	69760	71810	85070	115200	136690	132010	123700
2 Factor income from rest of the world	31520	42610	49480	51920	56480	60910	68040	86860	105490	123100	129770	132000
A Compensation of employees	5040	6540	6700	7070	7250	7690	8160	8500	9000	11970	13790	14540
B Property and entrepreneurial income	26480	36070	42780	44850	49230	53220	59880	78360	96490	111130	115980	117460
By general government	80	110	120	120	120	90	120	140	230	300	230	240
By corporate and quasi-corporate enterprises	25440	32390	38030	38040	41580	45460	49120	62540	80690	96660	102320	104830
By other	960	3570	4630	6690	7530	7670	10640	15680	15570	14170	13430	12390
3 Current transfers from rest of the world [c]	11340	13670	13830	13840	16160	14830	18590	17860	21320	35260	41230	41600
A Subsidies from supranational organisations	...	...	...	...	...	...	...	...	...	...	...	...
B Other current transfers	11340	13670	13830	13840	16160	14830	18590	17860	21320	35260	41230	41600
Receipts from the Rest of the World on Current Transactions	432000	535910	599630	658500	653180	652350	706460	806150	905710	1033580	1103650	1084860

a) Exports and imports of goods for purposes of repair and improvement are reduced to the value of these services.
b) Imports of merchandise, f.o.b. rather than c.i.f.
c) Indirect taxes paid to and subsidies received from supranational organizations are included in 'Current transfers'.

1.8 Capital Transactions of The Nation, Summary

Million Deutsche marks

	1980	1983	1984	1985	1986	1987	1988	1989	1990	1991	1992	1993
Finance of Gross Capital Formation												
Gross saving	319080	353680	380210	400980	458630	467550	509350	571550	604310	602610	622940	580900
1 Consumption of fixed capital	175000	214930	226370	235360	243690	252300	263090	279450	303010	332840	359690	379160
A General government	9700	12120	12680	13120	13570	14070	14690	15550	16660	18010	19340	20520
B Corporate and quasi-corporate enterprises	162730	199650	210370	218820	226600	234570	244600	259900	282060	310210	335420	353450
C Other	2570	3160	3320	3420	3520	3660	3800	4000	4290	4620	4930	5190
2 Net saving	144080	138750	153840	165620	214940	215250	246260	292100	301300	269770	263250	201740
A General government	26050	11180	22190	34420	32450	20050	12000	63900	14850	10550	22470	1420
B Corporate and quasi-corporate enterprises	-5360	10180	3010	-2380	33220	35640	64800	54880	74420	36910	13660	-22080
C Other	123390	117390	128640	133580	149270	159560	169460	173320	212030	222310	227120	222400
Less: Surplus of the nation on current transactions	-24770	14370	24220	43920	82230	82330	89150	107020	85040	18960	38660	40620
Finance of Gross Capital Formation	343850	339310	355990	357060	376400	385220	420200	464530	519270	583650	584280	540280

Germany, Fed. Rep. of

1.8 Capital Transactions of The Nation, Summary
(Continued)

Million Deutsche marks

	1980	1983	1984	1985	1986	1987	1988	1989	1990	1991	1992	1993
					Gross Capital Formation							
Increase in stocks	11770	-1500	5320	1250	2920	-560	10300	16010	11490	20430	-2590	-11520
Gross fixed capital formation	332080	340810	350670	355810	373480	385780	409900	448520	507780	563220	586870	551800
1 General government	49980	40440	40550	41020	45310	46000	47500	50990	54160	58440	62720	61410
2 Corporate and quasi-corporate enterprises [a]	282100	300370	310120	314790	328170	339780	362400	397530	453620	504780	524150	490390
3 Other	...	...	...	...	...	...	...	...	...	...	...	...
Gross Capital Formation	343850	339310	355990	357060	376400	385220	420200	464530	519270	583650	584280	540280

a) Including gross fixed capital formation of private non-profit organizations.

1.9 Gross Domestic Product by Institutional Sectors of Origin

Million Deutsche marks

	1980	1983	1984	1985	1986	1987	1988	1989	1990	1991	1992	1993
					Domestic Factor Incomes Originating							
1 General government	162450	183370	187010	193880	203300	211500	216920	222840	236290	252960	269770	278940
2 Corporate and quasi-corporate enterprises [a]	943050	1052650	1111060	1162330	1240570	1280390	1358760	1440710	1579330	1710220	1798230	1791550
A Non-financial	938350	1051340	1108780	1159600	1237670	1277470	1354160	1433580	1575410	1706870	1795930	1785800
B Financial [a]	4700	1310	2280	2730	2900	2920	4600	7130	3920	3350	2300	5750
3 Households and private unincorporated enterprises	2090	2320	2410	2490	2530	2530	2520	2520	2630	2860	2960	3010
4 Non-profit institutions serving households	26630	32600	34240	36750	40340	43060	45320	47370	51350	57040	62950	66630
Subtotal: Domestic Factor Incomes	1134220	1270940	1334720	1395450	1486740	1537480	1623520	1713440	1869600	2023080	2133910	2140130
Indirect taxes, net	162820	182670	189800	192370	194860	200700	209370	231550	253390	291680	319400	334410
A Indirect taxes	193470	214390	226130	230310	236170	245500	257110	278330	302220	337330	364400	379300
B Less: Subsidies	30650	31720	36330	37940	41310	44800	47740	46780	48830	45650	45000	44890
Consumption of fixed capital	175000	214930	226370	235360	243690	252300	263090	279450	303010	332840	359690	379160
Gross Domestic Product	1472040	1668540	1750890	1823180	1925290	1990480	2095980	2224440	2426000	2647600	2813000	2853700

a) Financial of Corporate and quasi-corporate enterprises refers to net of imputed bank service charges.

1.10 Gross Domestic Product by Kind of Activity, in Current Prices

Million Deutsche marks

	1980	1983	1984	1985	1986	1987	1988	1989	1990	1991	1992	1993
1 Agriculture, hunting, forestry and fishing	30520	33230	34460	31920	34000	30240	33720	37210	36740	33880	32820	29290
2 Mining and quarrying [a]	12230	15670	15720	16050	13580	12780	11180	11740	11390	12450	12650	...
3 Manufacturing [abc]	476250	519420	542600	578850	620440	624690	652670	686010	741550	790810	799890	749040
4 Electricity, gas and water	36410	45580	48260	50480	52330	55890	56660	57560	58840	61670	63380	...
5 Construction [b]	99890	99050	99720	94810	100130	101680	106250	114660	127620	137280	152660	158590
6 Wholesale and retail trade, restaurants and hotels	152150	167840	177260	178530	186050	193910	204470	214350	244650	277100	288380	...
7 Transport, storage and communication	85430	95540	100970	105050	107310	111110	116870	125710	134200	143820	153580	158110
8 Finance, insurance, real estate and business services [d]	155930	211480	223380	231870	239910	243520	257080	273460	288850	318130	350230	386330
9 Community, social and personal services [cd]	163420	203160	220270	236840	256790	279570	309070	338680	386990	444570	505610	...
Total, Industries	1212230	1390970	1462640	1524400	1610540	1653390	1747970	1859380	2030830	2219710	2359200	2380780
Producers of Government Services	172390	195740	199950	207260	217120	225820	231860	238640	253200	271220	289360	299710
Other Producers	31310	38100	39990	42680	46420	49280	51670	53920	58300	64550	70880	74870
Subtotal	1415930	1624810	1702580	1774340	1874080	1928490	2031500	2151940	2342330	2555480	2719440	2755360
Less: Imputed bank service charge	53940	81710	84070	84260	83690	82270	85150	88410	96280	111240	124070	133110
Plus: Import duties	13480	16210	16480	16440	17020	19150	19530	23380	24980	29280	30570	28820
Plus: Value added tax	96570	109230	115900	116660	117880	125110	130100	137530	154970	174080	187060	202630
Equals: Gross Domestic Product	1472040	1668540	1750890	1823180	1925290	1990480	2095980	2224440	2426000	2647600	2813000	2853700

a) Quarrying is included in item 'Manufacturing'.
b) Structural steel erection is included in item 'Manufacturing'.
c) Publishing is included in item 'Community, social and personal services'.
d) Business services and real estate except dwellings are included in item 'Community, social and personal services'.

Germany, Fed. Rep. of

1.11 Gross Domestic Product by Kind of Activity, in Constant Prices

Million Deutsche marks

	1980	1983	1984	1985	1986	1987	1988	1989	1990	1991	1992	1993
					At constant prices of:1991							
1 Agriculture, hunting, forestry and fishing	29250	32050	34110	31850	35150	32090	34480	34970	36430	33880	37570	36010
2 Mining and quarrying [a]	16600	15070	14650	14590	12630	12690	11770	12680	11210	12450	11960	...
3 Manufacturing [abc]	656030	636070	655050	679170	689570	677000	698640	722600	762270	790810	772270	713090
4 Electricity, gas and water	47770	46670	48330	49820	51360	54300	54910	56830	58170	61670	61950	...
5 Construction [b]	139640	131120	131670	124560	126620	124560	127110	132460	136790	137280	141090	139590
6 Wholesale and retail trade, restaurants and hotels	204930	198920	207610	208530	212370	216440	223520	233180	251400	277100	277890	...
7 Transport, storage and communication	97590	101860	105200	109280	109390	113920	121770	127850	137630	143820	151190	152350
8 Finance, insurance, real estate and business services [d]	222960	242260	246720	255120	266700	276310	287570	297550	310100	318130	330580	345720
9 Community, social and personal services [cd]	237060	262180	276250	290250	306300	324480	349890	370510	405800	444570	476600	...
Total, Industries	1651830	1666200	1719590	1763170	1810090	1831790	1909660	1988630	2109800	2219710	2261100	2219790
Producers of Government Services	237360	245760	248420	252020	255610	258960	261700	262620	266910	271220	275910	278080
Other Producers	45100	48750	50110	51940	54150	55790	57470	59120	61570	64550	67340	69170
Subtotal	1934290	1960710	2018120	2067130	2119850	2146540	2228830	2310370	2438280	2555480	2604350	2567040
Less: Imputed bank service charge	70280	76730	78410	82040	86920	91570	95480	98870	105400	111240	119900	125450
Plus: Import duties	15660	17110	17470	18190	19010	21900	22080	23970	25900	29280	29220	27200
Plus: Value added tax	138330	135110	136320	132720	134160	141530	145570	148930	161620	174080	180630	179810
Equals: Gross Domestic Product	2018000	2036200	2093500	2136000	2186100	2218400	2301000	2384400	2520400	2647600	2694300	2648600

a) Quarrying is included in item 'Manufacturing'.
b) Structural steel erection is included in item 'Manufacturing'.
c) Publishing is included in item 'Community, social and personal services'.
d) Business services and real estate except dwellings are included in item 'Community, social and personal services'.

1.12 Relations Among National Accounting Aggregates

Million Deutsche marks

	1980	1983	1984	1985	1986	1987	1988	1989	1990	1991	1992	1993
Gross Domestic Product	1472040	1668540	1750890	1823180	1925290	1990480	2095980	2224440	2426000	2647600	2813000	2853700
Plus: Net factor income from the rest of the world	5360	7160	12410	11320	10810	12520	12020	24660	22600	20400	6800	-10900
Factor income from the rest of the world	31520	42610	49480	51920	56480	60910	68040	86860	105490	123100	129770	132000
Less: Factor income to the rest of the world	26160	35450	37070	40600	45670	48390	56020	62200	82890	102700	122970	142900
Equals: Gross National Product	1477400	1675700	1763300	1834500	1936100	2003000	2108000	2249100	2448600	2668000	2819800	2842800
Less: Consumption of fixed capital	175000	214930	226370	235360	243690	252300	263090	279450	303010	332840	359690	379160
Equals: National Income	1302400	1460770	1536930	1599140	1692410	1750700	1844910	1969650	2145590	2335160	2460110	2463640
Plus: Net current transfers from the rest of the world [a]	-23280	-26300	-31450	-31270	-28490	-30150	-32580	-37780	-79510	-150100	-157680	-164520
Current transfers from the rest of the world	11340	13670	13830	13840	16160	14830	18590	17860	21320	35260	41230	41600
Less: Current transfers to the rest of the world	34620	39970	45280	45110	44650	44980	51170	55640	100830	185360	198910	206120
Equals: National Disposable Income	1279120	1434470	1505480	1567870	1663920	1720550	1812330	1931870	2066080	2185060	2302430	2299120
Less: Final consumption	1135040	1295720	1351640	1402250	1448980	1505300	1566070	1639770	1764780	1915290	2039180	2097380
Equals: Net Saving	144080	138750	153840	165620	214940	215250	246260	292100	301300	269770	263250	201740
Less: Surplus of the nation on current transactions	-24770	14370	24220	43920	82230	82330	89150	107020	85040	18960	38660	40620
Equals: Net Capital Formation	168850	124380	129620	121700	132710	132920	157110	185080	216260	250810	224590	161120

a) Indirect taxes paid to and subsidies received from supranational organizations are included in 'Current transfers'.

2.1 Government Final Consumption Expenditure by Function, in Current Prices

Million Deutsche marks

	1980	1983	1984	1985	1986	1987	1988	1989	1990	1991	1992	1993
1 General public services	31400	34740	35760	37460	39510	42210	42290	43740	46130	...	...	...
2 Defence	40380	47800	48930	49900	51290	52300	52480	53790	52730	...	...	...
3 Public order and safety	23080	26660	27240	28280	29500	30790	31740	32990	35300	...	...	...
4 Education	60490	68100	69960	72410	74810	76370	77700	80060	84070	...	...	...
5 Health	86850	97290	104150	109950	115190	119940	129650	126010	136500	...	...	...
6 Social security and welfare	28340	34000	35670	37210	39830	41710	44260	47510	53160	...	...	...
7 Housing and community amenities	5750	5060	5070	5620	6160	6630	6490	6310	6380	...	...	...
8 Recreational, cultural and religious affairs	6920	7620	8040	8520	9130	9690	10020	10450	11140	...	...	...
9 Economic services	14810	15170	15620	16370	17130	17640	17750	17960	18660	...	...	...

Germany, Fed. Rep. of

2.1 Government Final Consumption Expenditure by Function, in Current Prices
(Continued)

Million Deutsche marks

	1980	1983	1984	1985	1986	1987	1988	1989	1990	1991	1992	1993
A Fuel and energy	80	80	80	120	120	100	110	90	90	...	...	...
B Agriculture, forestry, fishing and hunting	1950	2050	2050	2100	2240	2270	2260	2330	2420	...	...	...
C Mining, manufacturing and construction, except fuel and energy	160	170	190	180	210	220	250	200	210	...	...	...
D Transportation and communication	9850	9640	9830	10370	10710	10960	11040	11220	11590	...	...	...
E Other economic affairs	2770	3230	3470	3600	3850	4090	4090	4120	4350	...	...	...
10 Other functions	-	-	-	-	-	-	-	-	-	...	...	...
Total Government Final Consumption Expenditure	298020	336440	350440	365720	382550	397280	412380	418820	444070	...	...	...

2.3 Total Government Outlays by Function and Type

Million Deutsche marks

	Final Consumption Expenditures Total	Compensation of Employees	Other	Subsidies	Other Current Transfers & Property Income	Total Current Disbursements	Gross Capital Formation	Other Capital Outlays	Total Outlays
1980									
1 General public services	31400	22020	9380	950	16640	48990	2210	6550	57750
2 Defence	40380	19840	20540	-	960	41340	210	210	41760
3 Public order and safety	23080	19300	3780	-	30	23110	2170	80	25360
4 Education	60490	47300	13190	40	6150	66680	8490	910	76080
5 Health	86850	18240	68610	160	530	87540	3970	1460	92970
6 Social security and welfare	28340	14240	14100	420	249140	277900	1220	8070	287190
7 Housing and community amenities	5750	8790	-3040	2090	20	7860	10400	3190	21450
8 Recreation, culture and religion	6920	4510	2410	400	1180	8500	3420	960	12880
9 Economic services	14810	8210	6600	26590	4350	45750	18390	13750	77890
A Fuel and energy	80	-	80	4290	-	4370	500	1420	6290
B Agriculture, forestry, fishing and hunting	1950	1230	720	9210	50	11210	380	1030	12620
C Mining (except fuels), manufacturing and construction	160	-	160	340	-	500	-	510	1010
D Transportation and communication	9850	5420	4430	7340	-	17190	16250	6740	40180
E Other economic affairs	2770	1560	1210	5410	4300	12480	1260	4050	17790
10 Other functions	-	-	-	-	27480	27480	-	-	27480
Total	298020	162450	135570	30650	306480	635150	50480	35180	720810
1985									
1 General public services	37460	...	...	1490	23810	62760	2220	6230	71210
2 Defence	49900	...	...	-	1310	51210	220	270	51700
3 Public order and safety	28280	...	...	-	40	28320	1940	90	30350
4 Education	72410	...	...	90	4840	77340	5230	610	83180
5 Health	109950	...	...	140	590	110680	4610	1300	116590
6 Social security and welfare	37210	...	...	710	304040	341960	1600	5140	348700
7 Housing and community amenities	5620	...	...	3010	80	8710	8720	2750	20180
8 Recreation, culture and religion	8520	...	...	620	1340	10480	2420	1010	13910
9 Economic services	16370	...	...	31880	5990	54240	14060	15880	84180
A Fuel and energy	120	...	...	3400	-	3520	-	930	4450
B Agriculture, forestry, fishing and hunting	2100	...	...	13010	40	15150	210	890	16250
C Mining (except fuels), manufacturing and construction	180	...	...	1170	-	1350	-	500	1850
D Transportation and communication	10370	...	...	7530	-	17900	12850	6710	37460
E Other economic affairs	3600	...	...	6770	5950	16320	1000	6850	24170
10 Other functions	-	...	...	-	54180	54180	-	-	54180
Total	365720	...	...	37940	396220	799880	41020	33280	874180
1990									
1 General public services	46130	...	...	2000	77400	125530	3330	9000	137860
2 Defence	52730	...	...	-	1360	54090	180	150	54420
3 Public order and safety	35300	...	...	-	60	35360	2750	110	38220
4 Education	84070	...	...	50	6530	90650	7160	710	98520
5 Health	136500	...	...	120	430	137050	4840	2240	144130

Germany, Fed. Rep. of

2.3 Total Government Outlays by Function and Type (Continued)

Million Deutsche marks

	Final Consumption Expenditures Total	Compensation of Employees	Other	Subsidies	Other Current Transfers & Property Income	Total Current Disbursements	Gross Capital Formation	Other Capital Outlays	Total Outlays
6 Social security and welfare	53160	...	...	970	374140	428270	1840	2200	432310
7 Housing and community amenities	6380	...	...	3340	80	9800	14140	3800	27740
8 Recreation, culture and religion	11140	...	...	920	1710	13770	3500	1260	18530
9 Economic services	18660	...	...	41430	11190	71280	16420	15340	103040
A Fuel and energy	90	...	...	9380	-	9470	-	660	10130
B Agriculture, forestry, fishing and hunting	2420	...	...	14490	60	16970	210	1380	18560
C Mining (except fuels), manufacturing and construction	210	...	...	750	-	960	-	940	1900
D Transportation and communication	11590	...	...	7980	10	19580	14930	6070	40580
E Other economic affairs	4350	...	...	8830	11120	24300	1280	6290	31870
10 Other functions	-	...	...	-	62390	62390	-	-	62390
Total	444070	...	...	48830	535290	1028190	54160	34810	1117160

2.5 Private Final Consumption Expenditure by Type and Purpose, in Current Prices

Million Deutsche marks

	1980	1983	1984	1985	1986	1987	1988	1989	1990	1991	1992	1993
Final Consumption Expenditure of Resident Households												
1 Food, beverages and tobacco [a]	200100	225270	230470	233190	236670	241060	247360	262310	285500	300580	307310	307680
A Food												
B Non-alcoholic beverages	182650	203570	209000	211110	214200	218550	224300	238110	258400	274620	281480	281410
C Alcoholic beverages												
D Tobacco	17450	21700	21470	22080	22470	22510	23060	24200	27100	25960	25830	26270
2 Clothing and footwear	75850	80020	82550	85320	88630	91720	92830	95580	107040	117840	120260	122480
3 Gross rent, fuel and power [bc]	157030	197170	211930	225760	225450	228720	234150	246560	264260	288660	309740	337070
A Fuel and power [c]	45150	53850	58970	63960	55180	50440	46600	47790	51220	58850	58360	60470
B Other	111880	143320	152960	161800	170270	178280	187550	198770	213040	229810	251380	276600
4 Furniture, furnishings and household equipment and operation [b]	80840	84840	87400	87450	90570	96120	102040	109300	120950	134240	142580	145170
5 Medical care and health expenses	22830	29360	31490	32950	33990	35680	38100	40300	44010	48990	53490	56280
6 Transport and communication [c]	119290	141330	148410	154350	160460	170610	179590	197370	222160	255640	265040	257380
A Personal transport equipment	31380	39680	40950	43320	57670	63570	64450	66890	75500	88510	87700	78810
B Other [c]	87910	101650	107460	111030	102790	107040	115140	130480	146660	167130	177340	178570
7 Recreational, entertainment, education and cultural services	84560	93500	96850	99990	104000	108200	114770	119780	134260	146220	156180	157920
8 Miscellaneous goods and services [a]	63430	73760	79190	83700	87600	92030	98780	106340	115360	127750	135100	144020
A Personal care	14760	17160	17990	18650	19380	20510	21800	22580	24220	26030	27020	27560
B Expenditures in restaurants, cafes and hotels	...	...	...	...	...	...	...	...	...	...	...	...
C Other	...	...	...	...	...	...	...	...	...	...	...	...
Total Final Consumption Expenditure in the Domestic Market by Households, of which	803930	925250	968290	1002710	1027370	1064140	1107620	1177540	1293540	1419920	1489700	1528000
Plus: Direct purchases abroad by resident households	33660	37010	38720	41200	42380	45240	47790	49130	54270	60880	67070	71970
Less: Direct purchases in the domestic market by non-resident households	15900	22130	25780	29170	27410	27230	28790	34550	57830	66240	58360	51880
Equals: Final Consumption Expenditure of Resident Households	821690	940130	981230	1014740	1042340	1082150	1126620	1192120	1289980	1414560	1498410	1548090
Final Consumption Expenditure of Private Non-profit Institutions Serving Households												
Equals: Final Consumption Expenditure of Private Non-profit Organisations Serving Households	15330	19150	19970	21790	24090	25870	27070	28830	30730	34210	37910	40810
Private Final Consumption Expenditure	837020	959280	1001200	1036530	1066430	1108020	1153690	1220950	1320710	1448770	1536320	1588900

a) Expenditure in restaurants and cafes is included in item 'Food, beverages and tobacco', expenditure in hotels, etc., is included in item 'Miscellaneous goods and services'.
b) Indoor repairs and upkeep paid for by tenants are included in household equipment and operation.
c) Fuel for personal transport equipment is included in item 'Transport and communication'.

Germany, Fed. Rep. of

2.6 Private Final Consumption Expenditure by Type and Purpose, in Constant Prices

Million Deutsche marks

	1980	1983	1984	1985	1986	1987	1988	1989	1990	1991	1992	1993
	At constant prices of: 1991											
Final Consumption Expenditure of Resident Households												
1 Food, beverages and tobacco [a]	254040	248780	250850	252130	254350	260740	266440	276680	293020	300580	297960	292290
A Food												
B Non-alcoholic beverages	227820	223750	225720	226780	229260	235470	241120	251110	265760	274620	273520	268620
C Alcoholic beverages												
D Tobacco	26220	25030	25130	25350	25090	25270	25320	25570	27260	25960	24440	23670
2 Clothing and footwear	97870	91390	92160	93230	95310	97530	97330	98940	109390	117840	116890	115830
3 Gross rent, fuel and power [bc]	214280	231580	239810	247520	254540	259890	262300	265690	275630	288660	296410	306940
A Fuel and power [c]	51910	50970	53880	56410	57150	56660	53530	51060	53200	58850	58210	59480
B Other	162370	180610	185930	191110	197390	203230	208770	214630	222430	229810	238200	247460
4 Furniture, furnishings and household equipment and operation [b]	106370	97540	98320	96870	99160	104100	109050	114850	124400	134240	138110	136620
5 Medical care and health expenses	32880	35720	37690	38780	39270	40290	42120	42680	45830	48990	51750	52400
6 Transport and communication [c]	162420	164520	168550	171890	186900	196850	204180	213940	234540	255640	254480	238470
A Personal transport equipment	48990	51800	50820	51870	66940	71770	70640	71360	78570	88510	84460	72120
B Other [c]	113430	112720	117730	120020	119960	125080	133540	142580	155970	167130	170020	166350
7 Recreational, entertainment, education and cultural services	106090	104800	105890	107710	110820	114650	120350	124570	136440	146220	150350	147780
8 Miscellaneous goods and services [a]	88450	90240	95130	99600	101800	103900	109800	115350	121950	127750	126910	127610
A Personal care	19530	19740	20230	20670	21170	22180	23230	23670	24890	26030	26030	25590
B Expenditures in restaurants, cafes and hotels	...	...	...	...	...	...	...	...	...	...	...	...
C Other	...	...	...	...	...	...	...	...	...	...	...	...
Total Final Consumption Expenditure in the Domestic Market by Households, of which	1062400	1064570	1088400	1107730	1142150	1177950	1211570	1252700	1341200	1419920	1432860	1417940
Plus: Direct purchases abroad by resident households	55180	49810	49100	50420	51110	53830	54550	53310	56400	60880	67880	76280
Less: Direct purchases in the domestic market by non-resident households	23480	27100	30760	33720	31240	30600	31750	36810	59680	66240	56110	47810
Equals: Final Consumption Expenditure of Resident Households	1094100	1087280	1106740	1124430	1162020	1201180	1234370	1269200	1337920	1414560	1444630	1446410
Final Consumption Expenditure of Private Non-profit Institutions Serving Households												
Equals: Final Consumption Expenditure of Private Non-profit Organisations Serving Households	21800	23310	23810	25620	27930	29430	29970	30950	32090	34210	35790	36600
Private Final Consumption Expenditure	1115900	1110590	1130550	1150050	1189950	1230610	1264340	1300150	1370010	1448770	1480420	1483010

a) Expenditure in restaurants and cafes is included in item 'Food, beverages and tobacco'; expenditure in hotels, etc., is included in item 'Miscellaneous goods and services'.
b) Indoor repairs and upkeep paid for by tenants are included in household equipment and operation.
c) Fuel for personal transport equipment is included in item 'Transport and communication'.

2.7 Gross Capital Formation by Type of Good and Owner, in Current Prices

Million Deutsche marks

	1980				1985				1990			
	TOTAL	Total Private	Public Enterprises	General Government	TOTAL	Total Private	Public Enterprises	General Government	TOTAL	Total Private	Public Enterprises	General Government
Increase in stocks, total [a]	11770	...	...	...	1250	...	...	...	11490	...	...	...
1 Goods producing industries	8530	...	...	...	-1910	...	...	...	11250	...	...	...
A Materials and supplies	...	...	...	...	...	...	...	...	...	...	...	...
B Work in progress	...	...	...	...	...	...	...	...	...	...	...	...
C Livestock, except breeding stocks, dairy cattle, etc.	...	...	...	...	-100	...	...	...	-200	...	...	...
D Finished goods	...	...	...	...	...	...	...	...	...	...	...	...
2 Wholesale and retail trade	2550	...	...	...	3070	...	...	...	300	...	...	...
3 Other, except government stocks	190	...	...	...	90	...	...	...	-60	...	...	...
4 Government stocks	500	...	...	...	...	...	...	...	...	...	...	...
Gross Fixed Capital Formation, Total	332080	...	...	...	355810	...	...	...	507780	...	...	...

Germany, Fed. Rep. of

2.7 Gross Capital Formation by Type of Good and Owner, in Current Prices
(Continued)

Million Deutsche marks

	1980 TOTAL	Total Private	Public Enterprises	General Government	1985 TOTAL	Total Private	Public Enterprises	General Government	1990 TOTAL	Total Private	Public Enterprises	General Government
1 Residential buildings	99530	...	...	...	100850	...	...	...	135860	...	...	...
2 Non-residential buildings												
3 Other construction	105710	...	...	...	101930	...	...	...	137350	...	...	...
4 Land improvement and plantation and orchard development		...	...	...		...	...	...		...	...	...
5 Producers' durable goods	130510	...	...	...	159220	...	...	...	245480	...	...	...
A Transport equipment [b]	25790	...	...	...	30960	...	...	...	52940	...	...	...
B Machinery and equipment [b]	104720	...	...	...	128260	...	...	...	192540	...	...	...
6 Breeding stock, dairy cattle, etc. [a]	...	...	...	...	...	...	...	...	...	...	...	...
Statistical discrepancy [c]	-3670	...	...	...	-6190	...	...	...	-10910	...	...	...
Total Gross Capital Formation	343850	...	...	...	357060	...	...	...	519270	...	...	...

	1991 TOTAL	Total Private	Public Enterprises	General Government	1992 TOTAL	Total Private	Public Enterprises	General Government	1993 TOTAL	Total Private	Public Enterprises	General Government
Increase in stocks, total [a]	20430	...	...	...	-2590	...	...	...	-11520	...	...	...
1 Goods producing industries	9480	...	...	...	-330	...	...	...	...	...	...	...
A Materials and supplies	...	...	...	...	...	...	...	...	...	...	...	...
B Work in progress	...	...	...	...	...	...	...	...	...	...	...	...
C Livestock, except breeding stocks, dairy cattle, etc.	-400	...	...	...	-200	...	...	...	...	...	...	...
D Finished goods	...	...	...	...	...	...	...	...	...	...	...	...
2 Wholesale and retail trade	10940	...	...	...	-2310	...	...	...	...	...	...	...
3 Other, except government stocks	10	...	...	...	50	...	...	...	...	...	...	...
4 Government stocks	...	...	...	...	...	...	...	...	...	...	...	...
Gross Fixed Capital Formation, Total	563220	...	...	...	586870	...	...	...	551800	...	...	...
1 Residential buildings	151430	...	...	...	170960	...	...	...	184070	...	...	...
2 Non-residential buildings												
3 Other construction	147890	...	...	...	158360	...	...	...	154400	...	...	...
4 Land improvement and plantation and orchard development		...	...	...		...	...	...		...	...	...
5 Producers' durable goods	275110	...	...	...	269200	...	...	...	224450	...	...	...
A Transport equipment [b]	65780	...	...	...	...	...	...	...	...	...	...	...
B Machinery and equipment [b]	209330	...	...	...	...	...	...	...	...	...	...	...
6 Breeding stock, dairy cattle, etc. [a]	...	...	...	...	...	...	...	...	...	...	...	...
Statistical discrepancy [c]	-11210	...	...	...	-11650	...	...	...	-11120	...	...	...
Total Gross Capital Formation	583650	...	...	...	584280	...	...	...	540280	...	...	...

a) Item 'Breeding stocks, dairy cattle, etc.' is included in item 'Increase in stocks'.
b) Railroad equipment is included in item 'Machinery and equipment'.
c) Item 'Statistical discrepancy' includes net sales of used capital goods.

2.8 Gross Capital Formation by Type of Good and Owner, in Constant Prices

Million Deutsche marks

	1980 TOTAL	Total Private	Public Enterprises	General Government	1985 TOTAL	Total Private	Public Enterprises	General Government	1990 TOTAL	Total Private	Public Enterprises	General Government
					At constant prices of:1991							
Increase in stocks, total [a]	12790	...	...	...	2390	...	...	...	15020	...	...	...
A Materials and supplies	...	...	...	...	...	...	...	...	...	...	...	...
B Work in progress	...	...	...	...	...	...	...	...	...	...	...	...
C Livestock, except breeding stocks, dairy cattle, etc.	...	...	...	...	-100	...	...	...	-200	...	...	...
D Finished goods	...	...	...	...	...	...	...	...	...	...	...	...
Gross Fixed Capital Formation, Total	455190	...	...	...	420350	...	...	...	532350	...	...	...

Germany, Fed. Rep. of

2.8 Gross Capital Formation by Type of Good and Owner, in Constant Prices
(Continued)

Million Deutsche marks

	1980 TOTAL	Total Private	Public Enterprises	General Government	1985 TOTAL	Total Private	Public Enterprises	General Government	1990 TOTAL	Total Private	Public Enterprises	General Government
				At constant prices of:1991								
1 Residential buildings	142900	...	...	...	125310	...	...	...	145240	...	...	...
2 Non-residential buildings		...	...	...		...	...	...		...	...	...
3 Other construction	141180	...	...	...	125220	...	...	...	146190	...	...	...
4 Land improvement and plantation and orchard development		...	...	...		...	...	...		...	...	...
5 Producers' durable goods	176360	...	...	...	177210	...	...	...	252390	...	...	...
A Transport equipment [b]	37260	...	...	...	37200	...	...	...	54940	...	...	...
B Machinery and equipment [b]	139100	...	...	...	140010	...	...	...	197450	...	...	...
6 Breeding stock, dairy cattle, etc. [a]	...	...	...	...	...	...	...	...	...	...	...	...
Statistical discrepancy [c]	-5250	...	...	...	-7390	...	...	...	-11470	...	...	...
Total Gross Capital Formation	467980	...	...	...	422740	...	...	...	547370	...	...	...

	1991 TOTAL	Total Private	Public Enterprises	General Government	1992 TOTAL	Total Private	Public Enterprises	General Government	1993 TOTAL	Total Private	Public Enterprises	General Government
				At constant prices of:1991								
Increase in stocks, total [a]	20430	...	...	...	-470	...	...	...	-6980	...	...	...
A Materials and supplies	...	...	...	...	...	...	...	...	...	...	...	...
B Work in progress	...	...	...	...	...	...	...	...	...	...	...	...
C Livestock, except breeding stocks, dairy cattle, etc.	-400	...	...	...	-200	...	...	...	...	...	...	...
D Finished goods	...	...	...	...	...	...	...	...	...	...	...	...
Gross Fixed Capital Formation, Total	563220	...	...	...	564960	...	...	...	518030	...	...	...
1 Residential buildings	151430	...	...	...	161630	...	...	...	166850	...	...	...
2 Non-residential buildings		...	...	...		...	...	...		...	...	...
3 Other construction	147890	...	...	...	150570	...	...	...	142890	...	...	...
4 Land improvement and plantation and orchard development		...	...	...		...	...	...		...	...	...
5 Producers' durable goods	275110	...	...	...	...	...	...	...	...	...	...	...
A Transport equipment [b]	65780	...	...	...	...	...	...	...	...	...	...	...
B Machinery and equipment [b]	209330	...	...	...	...	...	...	...	...	...	...	...
6 Breeding stock, dairy cattle, etc. [a]	...	...	...	...	...	...	...	...	...	...	...	...
Statistical discrepancy [c]	-11210	...	...	...	...	...	...	...	...	...	...	...
Total Gross Capital Formation	583650	...	...	...	564490	...	...	...	511050	...	...	...

a) Item 'Breeding stocks, dairy cattle, etc.' is included in item 'Increase in stocks'.
b) Railroad equipment is included in item 'Machinery and equipment'.
c) Item 'Statistical discrepancy' includes net sales of used capital goods.

2.11 Gross Fixed Capital Formation by Kind of Activity of Owner, ISIC Divisions, in Current Prices

Million Deutsche marks

	1980	1983	1984	1985	1986	1987	1988	1989	1990	1991	1992	1993
					All Producers							
1 Agriculture, hunting, forestry and fishing	9360	10490	9840	9900	9730	9750	10290	11320	12430	13180	12680	11070
A Agriculture and hunting [a]	8840	9920	9360	9440	9200	9130	9550	10560	11590	12260	11750	10260
B Forestry and logging [a]	520	570	480	460	530	620	740	760	840	920	930	810
C Fishing [a]	...	...	...	...	...	...	...	...	...	...	...	...
2 Mining and quarrying [b]	2400	3460	2710	2870	3060	2740	3140	2690	2180	2020	2630	2240
A Coal mining	1820	2870	2130	2210	2380	2250	2610	2040	1530	1290	1680	...
B Crude petroleum and natural gas production	...	...	...	...	...	...	...	...	...	...	...	...
C Metal ore mining	...	...	...	...	...	...	...	...	...	...	...	...
D Other mining	...	...	...	...	...	...	...	...	...	...	...	...

Germany, Fed. Rep. of

2.11 Gross Fixed Capital Formation by Kind of Activity of Owner, ISIC Divisions, in Current Prices
(Continued)

Million Deutsche marks

	1980	1983	1984	1985	1986	1987	1988	1989	1990	1991	1992	1993
3 Manufacturing	59390	57470	57800	67230	74160	79050	81800	91840	105850	114100	107060	89390
A Manufacturing of food, beverages and tobacco	6180	6580	6280	5930	6260	7010	7610	8480	10000	12510	12470	...
B Textile, wearing apparel and leather industries	1990	2030	2060	2260	2380	2440	2560	2840	3130	2970	2550	...
C Manufacture of wood, and wood products, including furniture	1700	1410	1480	1320	1370	1520	1950	2210	2690	3040	3350	...
D Manufacture of paper and paper products, printing and publishing c	3590	3070	2900	3670	4200	4470	5970	6420	6830	7310	6770	...
E Manufacture of chemicals and chemical petroleum, coal, rubber and plastic products	10700	10670	10550	12020	13660	15490	15710	17600	19820	20350	19520	...
F Manufacture of non-metalic mineral products except products of petroleum and coal b	3390	2920	3060	2870	2910	3120	3740	4600	5190	5790	5980	...
G Basic metal industries	5700	4250	4840	6630	5880	5640	5760	6170	7450	7950	7880	...
H Manufacture of fabricated metal products, machinery and equipment d	25830	26230	26330	32180	37140	38900	38010	42900	50160	53550	47950	...
I Other manufacturing industries	310	310	300	350	360	460	490	620	580	630	590	...
4 Electricity, gas and water	16570	19250	20920	20400	20990	20670	20220	20070	20180	20590	24020	26290
A Electricity, gas and steam	14330	17440	19090	18640	19250	18990	18310	17990	18060	18420	21340	...
B Water works and supply	2240	1810	1830	1760	1740	1680	1910	2080	2120	2170	2680	...
5 Construction d	6210	4790	4480	4300	4730	4980	5280	6420	7790	8890	10140	9130
6 Wholesale and retail trade, restaurants and hotels	16690	16670	16910	17670	19820	22500	26950	29240	32800	40120	45510	36860
A Wholesale and retail trade	14350	14120	14280	14980	17070	19660	24010	26190	29570	36970	42270	36860
B Restaurants and hotels	2340	2550	2630	2690	2750	2840	2940	3050	3230	3150	3240	...
7 Transport, storage and communication	26160	29780	30950	34850	36120	35970	36400	39280	41990	45470	43620	...
A Transport and storage	15700	17180	16450	18390	19210	18460	18410	20060	22340	23730	22840	22350
B Communication	10460	12600	14500	16460	16910	17510	17990	19220	19650	21740	20780	...
8 Finance, insurance, real estate and business services	98220	107250	111480	101510	102320	101900	108380	117870	136090	152110	172110	183560
A Financial institutions	3770	5840	5670	6150	5910	5330	5530	5500	6080	8080	10360	9920
B Insurance	1810	2560	2900	2150	2850	2310	3650	4560	5810	6150	6070	5910
C Real estate and business services e	92640	98850	102910	93210	93560	94260	99200	107810	124200	137880	155680	167730
Real estate except dwellings	...	...	...	...	...	...	...	...	...	...	...	...
Dwellings	92640	98850	102910	93210	93560	94260	99200	107810	124200	137880	155680	167730
9 Community, social and personal services ce	45530	50860	55220	56760	58580	64240	72750	82740	98290	112100	110080	...
Educational services	...	...	...	...	...	...	...	...	...	...	...	...
Medical, dental, other health and veterinary services	8700	8950	9750	9220	9450	10430	11060	12070	14220	15190	14980	...
Total Industries	280530	300020	310310	315490	329510	341800	365210	401470	457600	508580	527850	493480
Producers of Government Services	50100	40600	40710	41220	45480	46200	47720	51250	54430	58670	62910	61630
Private Non-Profit Institutions Serving Households	5120	5290	5310	5290	5530	5720	5990	6280	6660	7180	7760	7810
Statistical discrepancy f	-3670	-5100	-5660	-6190	-7040	-7940	-9020	-10480	-10910	-11210	-11650	-11120
Total	332080	340810	350670	355810	373480	385780	409900	448520	507780	563220	586870	551800

a) Hunting and fishing are included in item 'Forestry and logging'.
b) Quarrying is included in item 'Manufacture of non-metalic mineral products except products of petroleum and coal'.
c) Publishing is included in item 'Community, social and personal services'.
d) Structural steel erection is included in item 'Manufacture of fabricated metal products, machinery and equipment'.
e) Business services and real estate except dwellings are included in item 'Community, social and personal services'.
f) Item 'Statistical discrepancy' relates to adjustment for net purchases of used capital goods.

2.12 Gross Fixed Capital Formation by Kind of Activity of Owner, ISIC Divisions, in Constant Prices

Million Deutsche marks

	1980	1983	1984	1985	1986	1987	1988	1989	1990	1991	1992	1993
	\multicolumn{12}{c}{At constant prices of:1991}											
	\multicolumn{12}{c}{All Producers}											
1 Agriculture, hunting, forestry and fishing	13160	12810	11640	11460	11090	11030	11420	12260	12940	13180	12190	10410
A Agriculture and hunting a	12420	12110	11060	10910	10480	10320	10590	11430	12070	12260	11300	9640
B Forestry and logging a	740	700	580	550	610	710	830	830	870	920	890	770
C Fishing a	...	...	...	...	...	...	...	...	...	...	...	...
2 Mining and quarrying b	3210	4080	3120	3230	3390	3000	3390	2800	2230	2020	2550	2150

Germany, Fed. Rep. of

2.12 Gross Fixed Capital Formation by Kind of Activity of Owner, ISIC Divisions, in Constant Prices
(Continued)

Million Deutsche marks

	1980	1983	1984	1985	1986	1987	1988	1989	1990	1991	1992	1993
				At constant prices of:1991								
A Coal mining	2420	3360	2440	2470	2620	2460	2820	2120	1560	1290	1630	...
B Crude petroleum and natural gas production	...	...	...	...	...	...	...	...	...	...	...	...
C Metal ore mining	...	...	...	...	...	...	...	...	...	...	...	...
D Other mining	...	...	...	...	...	...	...	...	...	...	...	...
3 Manufacturing	82850	70340	68810	77760	84270	88530	89860	97930	109740	114100	103970	86080
A Manufacturing of food, beverages and tobacco	9020	8410	7760	7090	7290	8020	8440	9110	10450	12510	12020	...
B Textile, wearing apparel and leather industries	2850	2530	2500	2650	2710	2720	2790	3040	3240	2970	2440	...
C Manufacture of wood, and wood products, including furniture	2370	1720	1770	1530	1550	1700	2180	2390	2820	3040	3250	...
D Manufacture of paper and paper products, printing and publishing c	4940	3630	3340	4110	4620	4810	6390	6730	7010	7310	6660	...
E Manufacture of chemicals and chemical petroleum, coal, rubber and plastic products	15170	13200	12720	14080	15690	17450	17320	18760	20510	20350	18910	...
F Manufacture of non-metalic mineral products except products of petroleum and coal b	4660	3570	3630	3310	3300	3490	4140	4950	5410	5790	5780	...
G Basic metal industries	7950	5170	5740	7620	6650	6280	6310	6500	7680	7950	7650	...
H Manufacture of fabricated metal products, machinery and equipment d	35470	31730	30990	36970	42050	43560	41760	45790	52030	53550	46690	...
I Other manufacturing industries	420	380	360	400	410	500	530	660	590	630	570	...
4 Electricity, gas and water	21020	22970	24430	23410	23710	23060	22150	21520	20920	20590	23120	25050
A Electricity, gas and steam	18160	20730	22210	21310	21690	21120	19990	19240	18700	18420	20560	...
B Water works and supply	2860	2240	2220	2100	2020	1940	2160	2280	2220	2170	2560	...
5 Construction d	8960	6040	5470	5090	5400	5570	5770	6840	8080	8890	9790	8740
6 Wholesale and retail trade, restaurants and hotels	23200	20510	20270	20760	22810	25450	29870	31480	34140	40120	44060	35300
A Wholesale and retail trade	19950	17350	17110	17590	19630	22210	26580	28140	30760	36970	40930	35300
B Restaurants and hotels	3250	3160	3160	3170	3180	3240	3290	3340	3380	3150	3130	...
7 Transport, storage and communication	33460	35400	35950	39660	40580	40110	39930	42220	43640	45470	43140	...
A Transport and storage	20690	20930	19630	21450	22020	20970	20460	21750	23370	23730	22160	21290
B Communication	12770	14470	16320	18210	18560	19140	19470	20470	20270	21740	20980	...
8 Finance, insurance, real estate and business services	140650	137770	139030	125120	124210	121470	126620	133090	145050	152110	163130	167050
A Financial institutions	5020	7050	6550	6850	6470	5790	5960	5730	6210	8080	10100	9540
B Insurance	2510	3160	3500	2460	3270	2630	4110	4980	6070	6150	5850	5580
C Real estate and business services e	133120	127560	128980	115810	114470	113050	116550	122380	132770	137880	147180	151930
Real estate except dwellings	...	...	...	...	...	...	...	...	...	...	...	...
Dwellings	133120	127560	128980	115810	114470	113050	116550	122380	132770	137880	147180	151930
9 Community, social and personal services ce	60730	60780	64150	64910	66310	72170	80820	89470	102390	112100	106850	...
Educational services	...	...	...	...	...	...	...	...	...	...	...	...
Medical, dental, other health and veterinary services	11190	10220	10870	10130	10300	11300	12120	12980	14780	15190	14540	...
Total Industries	387240	370700	372870	371400	381770	390390	409830	437610	479130	508580	508800	464210
Producers of Government Services	66030	50980	50010	49920	54080	54080	54960	57280	57650	58670	59930	57010
Private Non-Profit Institutions Serving Households	7170	6660	6510	6420	6620	6730	6890	7020	7040	7180	7450	7240
Statistical discrepancy f	-5250	-6490	-6950	-7390	-8180	-8960	-9910	-11250	-11470	-11210	-11220	-10430
Total	455190	421850	422440	420350	434290	442240	461770	490660	532350	563220	564960	518030

a) Hunting and fishing are included in item 'Forestry and logging'.
b) Quarrying is included in item 'Manufacture of non-metalic mineral products except products of petroleum and coal'.
c) Publishing is included in item 'Community, social and personal services'.
d) Structural steel erection is included in item 'Manufacture of fabricated metal products, machinery and equipment'.
e) Business services and real estate except dwellings are included in item 'Community, social and personal services'.
f) Item 'Statistical discrepancy' relates to adjustment for net purchases of used capital goods.

Germany, Fed. Rep. of

2.13 Stocks of Reproducible Fixed Assets, by Type of Good and Owner, in Current Prices

Thousand Million Deutsche marks

		TOTAL Gross	TOTAL Net	Total Private Gross	Total Private Net	Public Enterprises Gross	Public Enterprises Net	General Government Gross	General Government Net
				1980					
1	Residential buildings	2793.9	2040.5	2793.9	2040.5	...	...	...	...
2	Non-residential buildings	...	...	...	...	...	...	...	...
3	Other construction	2160.5	1484.6	1730.3	1171.4	...	...	430.3	313.1
4	Land improvement and plantation and orchard development	...	...	...	...	...	...	...	...
5	Producers' durable goods	1426.7	776.0	1360.8	739.0	...	...	65.9	37.0
6	Breeding stock, dairy cattle, etc. [a]	...	...	...	...	...	...	...	...
	Total [bc]	6381.1	4301.0	5885.0	3950.9	...	...	496.1	350.1
				1985					
1	Residential buildings	3641.2	2593.0	3641.2	2593.0	...	...	...	...
2	Non-residential buildings	...	...	...	...	...	...	...	...
3	Other construction	2744.1	1829.1	2187.2	1434.2	...	...	556.9	394.8
4	Land improvement and plantation and orchard development	...	...	...	...	...	...	...	...
5	Producers' durable goods	1859.4	982.3	1774.0	938.8	...	...	85.5	43.5
6	Breeding stock, dairy cattle, etc. [a]	...	...	...	...	...	...	...	...
	Total [bc]	8244.7	5404.4	7602.3	4966.1	...	...	642.4	438.4
				1990					
1	Residential buildings	4839.4	3339.7	4839.4	3339.7	...	...	...	...
2	Non-residential buildings	...	...	...	...	...	...	...	...
3	Other construction	3710.2	2406.9	2970.5	1899.1	...	...	739.7	507.8
4	Land improvement and plantation and orchard development	...	...	...	...	...	...	...	...
5	Producers' durable goods	2373.5	1278.2	2270.4	1224.1	...	...	103.1	54.1
6	Breeding stock, dairy cattle, etc. [a]	...	...	...	...	...	...	...	...
	Total [bc]	10923.0	7024.8	10080.3	6462.8	...	...	842.7	561.9
				1991					
1	Residential buildings	5293.3	3634.4	5293.3	3634.4	...	...	...	...
2	Non-residential buildings	...	...	...	...	...	...	...	...
3	Other construction	4040.7	2609.6	3236.1	2061.0	...	...	804.6	548.6
4	Land improvement and plantation and orchard development	...	...	...	...	...	...	...	...
5	Producers' durable goods	2557.1	1394.0	2447.6	1335.7	...	...	109.6	58.3
6	Breeding stock, dairy cattle, etc. [a]	...	...	...	...	...	...	...	...
	Total [bc]	11891.2	7638.0	10977.0	7031.0	...	...	914.2	606.9
				1992					
1	Residential buildings	5719.8	3909.8	5719.8	3909.8	...	...	...	...
2	Non-residential buildings	...	...	...	...	...	...	...	...
3	Other construction	4321.1	2778.7	3461.5	2196.7	...	...	859.6	582.0
4	Land improvement and plantation and orchard development	...	...	...	...	...	...	...	...
5	Producers' durable goods	2689.6	1468.3	2574.3	1406.3	...	...	115.3	61.9
6	Breeding stock, dairy cattle, etc. [a]	...	...	...	...	...	...	...	...
	Total [bc]	12730.5	8156.7	11755.6	7512.7	...	...	974.9	644.0
				1993					
1	Residential buildings	6040.6	4111.4	6040.6	4111.4	...	...	...	...
2	Non-residential buildings	...	...	...	...	...	...	...	...
3	Other construction	4503.2	2881.6	3604.5	2277.8	...	...	898.7	603.9
4	Land improvement and plantation and orchard development	...	...	...	...	...	...	...	...
5	Producers' durable goods	2747.2	1476.8	2626.9	1412.3	...	...	120.3	64.5
6	Breeding stock, dairy cattle, etc. [a]	...	...	...	...	...	...	...	...
	Total [bc]	13291.0	8469.9	12271.9	7801.5	...	...	1019.0	668.4

a) Item 'Breeding stocks, dairy cattle, etc.' is included in item 'Increase in stocks'.
b) Column 'Public enterprises' is included in column 'Total private'.
c) Value recorded at the beginning of the year (opening stock).

Germany, Fed. Rep. of

2.14 Stocks of Reproducible Fixed Assets, by Type of Good and Owner, in Constant Prices

Thousand Million Deutsche marks

	TOTAL Gross	TOTAL Net	Total Private Gross	Total Private Net	Public Enterprises Gross	Public Enterprises Net	General Government Gross	General Government Net
At constant prices of: 1991								
1980								
1 Residential buildings	3930.3	2870.4	3930.3	2870.4	...	...	...	...
2 Non-residential buildings	...	...	...	...	...	...	...	...
3 Other construction	2917.5	2005.5	2311.9	1565.0	...	...	605.6	440.4
4 Land improvement and plantation and orchard development	...	...	...	...	...	...	...	...
5 Producers' durable goods	1918.3	1040.0	1831.2	990.7	...	...	87.1	49.3
6 Breeding stock, dairy cattle, etc. [a]	...	...	...	...	...	...	...	...
Total [bc]	8766.1	5915.9	8073.4	5426.2	...	...	692.7	489.7
1985								
1 Residential buildings	4499.9	3204.5	4499.9	3204.5	...	...	...	...
2 Non-residential buildings	...	...	...	...	...	...	...	...
3 Other construction	3365.8	2243.0	2677.6	1755.4	...	...	688.2	487.6
4 Land improvement and plantation and orchard development	...	...	...	...	...	...	...	...
5 Producers' durable goods	2109.2	1107.4	2014.5	1058.9	...	...	94.7	48.6
6 Breeding stock, dairy cattle, etc. [a]	...	...	...	...	...	...	...	...
Total [bc]	9974.8	6554.9	9192.0	6018.8	...	...	782.8	536.1
1990								
1 Residential buildings	5035.8	3475.2	5035.8	3475.2	...	...	...	...
2 Non-residential buildings	...	...	...	...	...	...	...	...
3 Other construction	3846.8	2495.5	3078.7	1968.2	...	...	768.1	527.3
4 Land improvement and plantation and orchard development	...	...	...	...	...	...	...	...
5 Producers' durable goods	2419.4	1302.9	2314.6	1247.9	...	...	104.8	55.0
6 Breeding stock, dairy cattle, etc. [a]	...	...	...	...	...	...	...	...
Total [bc]	11302.0	7273.7	10429.1	6691.3	...	...	872.9	582.4
1991								
1 Residential buildings	5159.2	3542.3	5159.2	3542.3	...	...	...	...
2 Non-residential buildings	...	...	...	...	...	...	...	...
3 Other construction	3947.6	2549.3	3164.2	2015.2	...	...	783.5	534.2
4 Land improvement and plantation and orchard development	...	...	...	...	...	...	...	...
5 Producers' durable goods	2534.3	1381.6	2425.8	1323.8	...	...	108.5	57.8
6 Breeding stock, dairy cattle, etc. [a]	...	...	...	...	...	...	...	...
Total [bc]	11641.2	7473.2	10749.2	6881.3	...	...	892.0	591.9
1992								
1 Residential buildings	5291.3	3616.8	5291.3	3616.8	...	...	...	...
2 Non-residential buildings	...	...	...	...	...	...	...	...
3 Other construction	4049.3	2603.7	3250.4	2062.8	...	...	798.9	540.9
4 Land improvement and plantation and orchard development	...	...	...	...	...	...	...	...
5 Producers' durable goods	2634.2	1438.1	2522.0	1377.7	...	...	112.3	60.3
6 Breeding stock, dairy cattle, etc. [a]	...	...	...	...	...	...	...	...
Total [bc]	11974.8	7658.6	11063.6	7057.4	...	...	911.2	601.2
1993								
1 Residential buildings	5427.3	3694.0	5427.3	3694.0	...	...	...	...
2 Non-residential buildings	...	...	...	...	...	...	...	...
3 Other construction	4142.1	2649.8	3328.8	2103.4	...	...	813.3	546.5
4 Land improvement and plantation and orchard development	...	...	...	...	...	...	...	...
5 Producers' durable goods	2682.8	1442.2	2567.8	1380.5	...	...	115.0	61.7
6 Breeding stock, dairy cattle, etc. [a]	...	...	...	...	...	...	...	...
Total [bc]	12252.2	7786.0	11323.9	7177.9	...	...	928.3	608.1

a) Item 'Breeding stocks, dairy cattle, etc.' is included in item 'Increase in stocks'.
b) Column 'Public enterprises' is included in column 'Total private'.
c) Value recorded at the beginning of the year (opening stock).

Germany, Fed. Rep. of

2.15 Stocks of Reproducible Fixed Assets by Kind of Activity, in Current Prices

Thousand Million Deutsche marks

	1980 Gross	1980 Net	1985 Gross	1985 Net	1990 Gross	1990 Net	1991 Gross	1991 Net	1992 Gross	1992 Net	1993 Gross	1993 Net
1 Residential buildings	2793.9	2040.5	3641.2	2593.0	4839.4	3339.7	5293.3	3634.4	5719.8	3909.8	6040.6	4111.4
2 Non-residential buildings [a]	...	...	...	...	...	...	...	...	...	...	...	...
3 Other construction [ab]	2160.5	1484.6	2744.1	1829.1	3710.2	2406.9	4040.7	2609.6	4321.1	2778.7	4503.2	2881.6
A Industries	1613.8	1083.4	2038.0	1324.7	2769.4	1756.7	3018.2	1907.9	3227.4	2033.4	3359.2	2107.9
1 Agriculture	152.1	83.7	171.4	91.9	207.7	107.7	220.6	113.6	231.9	118.7	234.1	119.0
2 Mining and quarrying [c]	20.0	11.2	22.6	12.2	25.0	12.6	25.6	12.7	25.9	12.7	...	...
3 Manufacturing [c]	382.9	217.5	441.0	229.6	554.1	276.3	594.5	295.0	623.2	307.6	...	...
4 Electricity, gas and water	197.0	148.5	246.3	179.5	334.0	234.0	363.4	252.5	389.9	269.1		
5 Construction	25.3	17.7	31.7	20.4	40.3	23.7	43.5	25.3	46.1	26.6		
6 Wholesale and retail trade	178.8	129.3	226.0	155.3	310.6	207.3	344.0	229.6	373.6	249.7		
7 Transport and communication	263.5	171.0	319.5	195.4	432.8	253.0	467.0	269.8	494.9	282.6		
8 Finance, etc.	93.1	72.0	127.9	96.7	179.8	131.8	197.1	144.0	213.6	155.7		
9 Community, social and personal services	301.1	232.4	451.5	343.7	685.2	510.3	762.7	565.4	828.4	610.8		
B Producers of government services [d]	430.3	313.1	556.9	394.8	739.7	507.8	804.6	548.6	859.6	582.0	898.7	603.9
C Other producers	116.4	88.1	149.2	109.6	201.2	142.4	217.8	153.1	234.0	163.3	245.2	169.9
4 Land improvement and development and plantation and orchard development [b]	...	...	...	...	...	...	...	...	...	...	...	...
5 Producers' durable goods	1426.7	776.0	1859.4	982.3	2373.5	1278.2	2557.1	1394.0	2689.6	1468.3	2747.2	1476.8
A Industries	1342.7	729.3	1751.0	927.5	2244.2	1210.9	2420.7	1322.0	2546.5	1392.1	2598.4	1397.7
1 Agriculture	116.0	58.9	135.7	66.2	147.9	73.2	154.4	77.5	158.3	79.8	158.5	79.3
2 Mining and quarrying [c]	25.1	13.0	33.9	18.1	36.8	18.7	36.9	18.4	37.3	18.6	...	...
3 Manufacturing [c]	569.8	297.6	703.8	364.8	904.0	481.5	971.1	523.0	1014.7	545.3	...	...
4 Electricity, gas and water	115.8	62.9	155.7	83.9	184.7	95.1	188.5	95.7	191.9	96.9		
5 Construction	46.4	23.0	46.0	20.4	46.6	23.1	50.1	26.1	54.4	29.5		
6 Wholesale and retail trade	81.9	43.2	96.6	47.7	125.7	69.5	139.5	79.3	154.7	89.7		
7 Transport and communication	189.6	101.9	237.2	126.2	283.2	149.7	297.6	158.8	298.6	159.0		
8 Finance, etc.	17.9	10.5	29.8	17.4	40.6	23.6	44.8	26.3	49.2	29.0		
9 Community, social and personal services	180.1	118.3	312.4	182.9	474.8	276.4	537.8	316.9	587.5	344.3		
B Producers of government services	65.9	37.0	85.5	43.5	103.1	54.1	109.6	58.3	115.3	61.9	120.3	64.5
C Other producers	18.1	9.7	23.0	11.3	26.1	13.2	26.9	13.7	27.8	14.2	28.4	14.6
6 Breeding stock, dairy cattle, etc.	...	...	...	...	...	...	...	...	...	...	...	...
Total [ef]	6381.1	4301.0	8244.7	5404.4	10923.0	7024.8	11891.2	7638.0	12730.5	8156.7	13291.0	8469.9

a) Item 'Non-residential buildings' is included in item 'Other construction'.
b) Item 'Land improvement and plantation and orchard development' is included in item 'Other construction'.
c) Quarrying is included in item 'Manufacturing'.
d) Item 'Producers of government services' does not include government civil engineering works.
e) Public underground construction is not contained in the data of this table (Stocks of Reproducible Fixed Assets by kind of activity).
f) Value recorded at the beginning of the year (opening stock).

2.16 Stocks of Reproducible Fixed Assets by Kind of Activity, in Constant Prices

Thousand Million Deutsche marks

	1980 Gross	1980 Net	1985 Gross	1985 Net	1990 Gross	1990 Net	1991 Gross	1991 Net	1992 Gross	1992 Net	1993 Gross	1993 Net
					At constant prices of: 1991							
1 Residential buildings	3930.3	2870.4	4499.9	3204.5	5035.8	3475.2	5159.2	3542.3	5291.3	3616.8	5427.3	3694.0
2 Non-residential buildings [a]	...	...	...	...	...	...	...	...	...	...	...	...
3 Other construction [ab]	2917.5	2005.5	3365.8	2243.0	3846.8	2495.5	3947.6	2549.3	4049.3	2603.7	4142.1	2649.8
A Industries	2152.4	1444.5	2493.1	1620.1	2870.0	1820.5	2950.6	1865.1	3031.7	1910.2	3105.1	1948.3
1 Agriculture	208.1	114.4	212.7	113.9	215.5	111.7	215.9	111.2	216.3	110.7	216.7	110.2
2 Mining and quarrying [c]	25.5	14.3	27.1	14.6	25.8	13.0	25.0	12.4	24.4	11.9	...	...
3 Manufacturing [c]	524.2	297.9	544.0	283.0	574.9	286.6	581.1	288.4	585.7	289.1	...	...
4 Electricity, gas and water	241.9	182.2	294.3	214.5	344.8	241.5	355.0	246.7	366.4	252.9		
5 Construction	35.2	24.7	39.3	25.3	41.8	24.7	42.5	24.7	43.3	25.0		
6 Wholesale and retail trade	246.8	178.5	278.1	191.2	322.9	215.4	336.4	224.5	351.2	234.7		
7 Transport and communication	323.5	209.9	382.0	233.4	446.8	261.2	456.3	263.6	465.1	265.6		

503

Germany, Fed. Rep. of

2.16 Stocks of Reproducible Fixed Assets by Kind of Activity, in Constant Prices
(Continued)

Thousand Million Deutsche marks

	1980 Gross	1980 Net	1985 Gross	1985 Net	1990 Gross	1990 Net	1991 Gross	1991 Net	1992 Gross	1992 Net	1993 Gross	1993 Net
					At constant prices of:1991							
8 Finance, etc.	130.0	100.5	158.1	119.5	185.4	135.9	192.6	140.8	200.7	146.3	...	...
9 Community, social and personal services	417.3	322.2	557.4	424.7	712.2	530.4	745.8	552.9	778.6	574.1	...	...
B Producers of government services [d]	605.6	440.4	688.2	487.6	768.1	527.3	783.5	534.2	798.9	540.9	813.3	546.5
C Other producers	159.5	120.6	184.5	135.3	208.7	147.7	213.6	150.1	218.7	152.6	223.7	155.0
4 Land improvement and development and plantation and orchard development [b]	...	...	...	...	...	...	...	...	...	...	...	...
5 Producers' durable goods	1918.3	1040.0	2109.2	1107.4	2419.4	1302.9	2534.3	1381.6	2634.2	1438.1	2682.8	1442.2
A Industries	1805.7	977.1	1988.3	1045.8	2288.1	1234.6	2399.3	1310.3	2495.3	1364.1	2541.1	1366.9
1 Agriculture	160.5	81.3	156.2	75.9	150.1	74.3	150.8	75.7	150.5	75.8	148.7	74.4
2 Mining and quarrying [c]	33.4	17.2	38.0	20.1	37.4	19.0	36.4	18.2	36.0	17.9	...	...
3 Manufacturing [c]	787.5	410.4	817.6	420.9	923.6	492.0	960.7	517.2	987.5	530.5	...	...
4 Electricity, gas and water	149.1	81.1	174.5	93.6	187.2	96.4	186.8	94.8	187.5	94.7	...	...
5 Construction	66.2	32.8	54.2	23.9	47.6	23.6	49.4	25.8	52.1	28.3	...	...
6 Wholesale and retail trade	110.5	58.3	109.6	53.8	127.9	70.7	138.3	78.7	151.3	87.7	...	...
7 Transport and communication	250.0	134.4	267.1	141.2	289.2	152.8	299.0	159.7	305.6	163.1	...	...
8 Finance, etc.	21.5	12.5	30.1	17.5	40.9	23.8	44.7	26.3	49.3	29.1	...	...
9 Community, social and personal services	227.1	149.1	341.0	198.9	484.3	282.0	533.2	314.1	575.5	337.0	...	...
B Producers of government services	87.1	49.3	94.7	48.6	104.8	55.0	108.5	57.8	112.3	60.3	115.0	61.7
C Other producers	25.6	13.7	26.3	13.1	26.5	13.3	26.6	13.5	26.7	13.7	26.7	13.7
6 Breeding stock, dairy cattle, etc.	...	...	...	...	...	...	...	...	...	...	...	...
Total [ef]	8766.1	5915.9	9974.8	6554.9	11302.0	7273.7	11641.2	7473.2	11974.8	7658.6	12252.2	7786.0

a) Item 'Non-residential buildings' is included in item 'Other construction'.
b) Item 'Land improvement and plantation and orchard development' is included in item 'Other construction'.
c) Quarrying is included in item 'Manufacturing'.
d) Item 'Producers of government services' does not include government civil engineering works.
e) Public underground construction is not contained in the data of this table (Stocks of Reproducible Fixed Assets by kind of activity).
f) Value recorded at the beginning of the year (opening stock).

2.17 Exports and Imports of Goods and Services, Detail

Million Deutsche marks

	1980	1983	1984	1985	1986	1987	1988	1989	1990	1991	1992	1993
	Exports of Goods and Services
1 Exports of merchandise, f.o.b.	339060	416970	467350	517760	508960	506850	548020	616360	663700	738530	800640	787560
2 Transport and communication	34180	40530	43190	45810	44170	42530	43020	50520	57370	70450	73650	71820
3 Insurance service charges	...	...	...	...	...	...	...	...	...	...	...	...
4 Other commodities	...	...	...	...	...	...	...	...	...	...	...	...
5 Adjustments of merchandise exports to change-of-ownership basis	...	...	...	...	...	...	...	...	...	...	...	...
6 Direct purchases in the domestic market by non-residential households	15900	22130	25780	29170	27410	27230	28790	34550	57830	66240	58360	51880
7 Direct purchases in the domestic market by extraterritorial bodies	...	...	...	...	...	...	...	...	...	...	...	...
Total Exports of Goods and Services [a]	389140	479630	536320	592740	580540	576610	619830	701430	778900	875220	932650	911260
	Imports of Goods and Services
1 Imports of merchandise, c.i.f.	324020	362800	405350	436870	390690	383890	411770	475320	521240	596210	599420	545990

Germany, Fed. Rep. of

2.17 Exports and Imports of Goods and Services, Detail
(Continued)

Million Deutsche marks

	1980	1983	1984	1985	1986	1987	1988	1989	1990	1991	1992	1993
A Imports of merchandise, f.o.b.	324020	362800	405350	436870	390690	383890	411770	475320	521240	596210	599420	545990
B Transport of services on merchandise imports	...	...	...	...	...	...	...	...	...	...	...	...
C Insurance service charges on merchandise imports	...	...	...	...	...	...	...	...	...	...	...	...
2 Adjustments of merchandise imports to change-of-ownership basis	...	...	...	...	...	...	...	...	...	...	...	...
3 Other transport and communication	38310	46310	48990	50800	47560	47520	50560	56840	61440	69470	76620	77260
4 Other insurance service charges	...	...	...	...	...	...	...	...	...	...	...	...
5 Other commodities	...	...	...	...	...	...	...	...	...	...	...	...
6 Direct purchases abroad by government	...	...	...	...	...	...	...	...	...	...	...	...
7 Direct purchases abroad by resident households	33660	37010	38720	41200	42380	45240	47790	49130	54270	60880	67070	71970
Total Imports of Goods and Services [a]	395990	446120	493060	528870	480630	476650	510120	581290	636950	726560	743110	695220
Balance of Goods and Services	-6850	33510	43260	63870	99910	99960	109710	120140	141950	148660	189540	216040
Total Imports and Balance of Goods and Services	389140	479630	536320	592740	580540	576610	619830	701430	778900	875220	932650	911260

a) Exports and imports of goods for purposes of repair and improvement are reduced to the value of these services.

3.11 General Government Production Account: Total and Subsectors

Million Deutsche marks

	1980 Total General Government	Central Government	State or Provincial Government	Local Government	Social Security Funds	1985 Total General Government	Central Government	State or Provincial Government	Local Government	Social Security Funds
Gross Output
1 Sales	40760	2150	9820	28760	30	55010	2730	13420	38810	50
2 Services produced for own use	298020	56440	95590	54060	91930	365720	69020	113860	65140	117700
3 Own account fixed capital formation	280	-	130	150	-	360	-	170	190	-
Gross Output	339060	58590	105540	82970	91960	421090	71750	127450	104140	117750
Gross Input
Intermediate Consumption	166670	30310	18560	35420	82380	213830	38310	23660	46220	105640
Subtotal: Value Added	172390	28280	86980	47550	9580	207260	33440	103790	57920	12110
1 Indirect taxes, net	240	10	100	120	10	260	10	120	120	10
A Indirect taxes	240	10	100	120	10	260	10	120	120	10
B Less: Subsidies	...	...	...	...	...	...	...	...	...	...
2 Consumption of fixed capital	9700	630	2980	5760	330	13120	860	4020	7730	510
3 Compensation of employees	162450	27640	83900	41670	9240	193880	32570	99650	50070	11590
4 Net Operating surplus	...	...	...	...	...	...	...	...	...	...
Gross Input	339060	58590	105540	82970	91960	421090	71750	127450	104140	117750

	1990 Total General Government	Central Government	State or Provincial Government	Local Government	Social Security Funds	1991 Total General Government	Central Government	State or Provincial Government	Local Government	Social Security Funds
Gross Output
1 Sales	74880	6480	17460	50870	70	90020	14200	19470	56210	140
2 Services produced for own use	444070	74780	138950	82260	148080	466520	64230	146880	90230	165180
3 Own account fixed capital formation	430	-	200	230	-	420	-	200	220	-
Gross Output	519380	81260	156610	133360	148150	556960	78430	166550	146660	165320
Gross Input
Intermediate Consumption	266180	41500	32250	59730	132700	285740	37710	34020	65870	148140
Subtotal: Value Added	253200	39760	124360	73630	15450	271220	40720	132530	80790	17180
1 Indirect taxes, net	250	-	120	120	10	250	-	120	120	10
A Indirect taxes	250	-	120	120	10	250	-	120	120	10
B Less: Subsidies	...	...	...	...	...	...	...	...	...	...
2 Consumption of fixed capital	16660	1110	5210	9680	660	18010	1220	5640	10430	720
3 Compensation of employees	236290	38650	119030	63830	14780	252960	39500	126770	70240	16450
4 Net Operating surplus	...	...	...	...	...	...	...	...	...	...
Gross Input	519380	81260	156610	133360	148150	556960	78430	166550	146660	165320

Germany, Fed. Rep. of

3.11 General Government Production Account: Total and Subsectors

Million Deutsche marks

	1992					1993				
	Total General Government	Central Government	State or Provincial Government	Local Government	Social Security Funds	Total General Government	Central Government	State or Provincial Government	Local Government	Social Security Funds
Gross Output										
1 Sales	96610	12840	21230	62320	220	101920	12730	22530	66300	360
2 Services produced for own use	502860	68190	156480	95400	182790	508480	66270	162200	97280	182730
3 Own account fixed capital formation	430	-	200	230	-	430	-	200	230	-
Gross Output	599900	81030	177910	157950	183010	610830	79000	184930	163810	183090
Gross Input										
Intermediate Consumption	310540	38780	36160	71470	164130	311120	36430	37480	73680	163530
Subtotal: Value Added	289360	42250	141750	86480	18880	299710	42570	147450	90130	19560
1 Indirect taxes, net	250	-	120	120	10	250	-	120	120	10
A Indirect taxes	250	-	120	120	10	250	-	120	120	10
B Less: Subsidies	...	...	...	...	...	...	...	...	...	...
2 Consumption of fixed capital	19340	1330	6050	11170	790	20520	1420	6440	11810	850
3 Compensation of employees	269770	40920	135580	75190	18080	278940	41150	140890	78200	18700
4 Net Operating surplus	...	...	...	...	...	...	...	...	...	...
Gross Input	599900	81030	177910	157950	183010	610830	79000	184930	163810	183090

3.12 General Government Income and Outlay Account: Total and Subsectors

Million Deutsche marks

	1980					1985				
	Total General Government	Central Government	State or Provincial Government	Local Government	Social Security Funds	Total General Government	Central Government	State or Provincial Government	Local Government	Social Security Funds
Receipts										
1 Operating surplus	...	...	...	...	...	...	...	...	...	...
2 Property and entrepreneurial income	15680	5720	1630	4050	5350	33650	20900	2750	5350	5740
3 Taxes, fees and contributions	617930	197200	138590	51730	230410	766640	235580	171400	61920	297740
A Indirect taxes	193470	118880	47080	27510	-	230310	138480	59010	32820	-
B Direct taxes	187750	78320	87970	21460	-	229640	97100	107210	25330	-
Income	179340	...	...	...	...	221220	...	...	...	...
Other	8410	...	...	...	...	8420	...	...	...	...
C Social security contributions	230080	-	-	-	230080	297250	-	-	-	297250
D Fees, fines and penalties	6630	-	3540	2760	330	9440	-	5180	3770	490
4 Other current transfers	27590	11970	34700	31720	39130	34010	14570	39940	36850	44130
A Casualty insurance claims	1300	-	-	220	1080	1420	-	-	260	1160
B Transfers from other government subsectors	...	920	22060	29700	37250	...	950	24200	34340	41990
C Transfers from the rest of the world	7880	7770	110	-	...	9730	9600	130	-	...
D Other transfers, except imputed	...	...	...	...	...	...	...	...	...	...
E Imputed unfunded employee pension and welfare contributions	18410	3280	12530	1800	800	22860	4020	15610	2250	980
Total Current Receipts	661200	214890	174920	87500	274890	834300	271050	214090	104120	347610
Disbursements										
1 Government final consumption expenditure	298020	56440	95590	54060	91930	365720	69020	113860	65140	117700
2 Property income	27480	14000	8560	5970	20	54180	29570	18510	7170	20
A Interest	27480	14000	8560	5970	20	54180	29570	18510	7170	20
B Net land rent and royalties	...	...	...	...	...	...	...	...	...	...
3 Subsidies	30650	21190	7070	1390	1000	37940	25360	10250	1710	620

Germany, Fed. Rep. of

3.12 General Government Income and Outlay Account: Total and Subsectors
(Continued)

Million Deutsche marks

	1980					1985				
	Total General Government	Central Government	State or Provincial Government	Local Government	Social Security Funds	Total General Government	Central Government	State or Provincial Government	Local Government	Social Security Funds
4 Other current transfers	279000	116650	58990	14280	179010	342040	135090	66150	19060	223220
A Casualty insurance premiums, net	3780	3560	-	220	-	3840	3580	-	260	-
B Transfers to other government subsectors	-	58550	28620	2320	440	-	64420	32770	3250	1040
C Social security benefits	174390	-	-	-	174390	215260	-	-	-	215260
D Social assistance grants	43210	28630	8870	5710	-	49070	33400	7240	8430	-
E Unfunded employee pension and welfare benefits	26930	7800	14670	3660	800	31440	7960	17950	4550	980
F Transfers to private non-profit institutions serving households	8790	1070	5090	2240	390	11220	1330	6500	2400	990
G Other transfers n.e.c.	...	...	...	...	...	...	...	...	...	...
H Transfers to the rest of the world	21900	17040	1740	130	2990	31210	24400	1690	170	4950
Net saving	26050	6610	4710	11800	2930	34420	12010	5320	11040	6050
Total Current Disbursements and Net Saving	661200	214890	174920	87500	274890	834300	271050	214090	104120	347610

	1990					1991				
	Total General Government	Central Government	State or Provincial Government	Local Government	Social Security Funds	Total General Government	Central Government	State or Provincial Government	Local Government	Social Security Funds

Receipts

1 Operating surplus	...	...	...	...	...	...	...	...	...	...
2 Property and entrepreneurial income	33310	19690	-410	6450	8540	34840	18180	20	7100	10490
3 Taxes, fees and contributions	969130	297120	211710	77200	383100	1089730	346850	236710	83470	422700
A Indirect taxes	302220	183450	77790	40980	-	337330	207860	86700	42770	-
B Direct taxes	271000	113670	126650	30680	-	316000	138990	142040	34970	-
Income	259850	...	...	...	...	303840	...	...	...	...
Other	11150	...	...	...	...	12160	...	...	...	...
C Social security contributions	382770	-	-	-	382770	421990	-	-	-	421990
D Fees, fines and penalties	13140	-	7270	5540	330	14410	-	7970	5730	710
4 Other current transfers	40600	16600	50360	45800	55800	46260	21000	56420	50350	66590
A Casualty insurance claims	1600	-	-	330	1270	1670	-	-	360	1310
B Transfers from other government subsectors	...	730	31400	42640	53190	...	1810	35300	47080	63910
C Transfers from the rest of the world	11310	11060	250	-	...	16280	14420	1860	-	...
D Other transfers, except imputed	...	...	...	...	...	...	...	...	...	...
E Imputed unfunded employee pension and welfare contributions	27690	4810	18710	2830	1340	28310	4770	19260	2910	1370
Total Current Receipts	1043040	333410	261660	129450	447440	1170830	386030	293150	140920	499780

Disbursements

1 Government final consumption expenditure	444070	74780	138950	82260	148080	466520	64230	146880	90230	165180
2 Property income	62390	34150	21850	7320	30	73500	42380	24000	8040	30
A Interest	62390	34150	21850	7320	30	73500	42380	24000	8040	30
B Net land rent and royalties	...	...	...	...	...	...	...	...	...	...
3 Subsidies	48830	33380	12000	2350	1100	45650	30450	11440	2570	1190
4 Other current transfers	472900	211740	84570	26880	277670	574610	276000	103680	28960	314070
A Casualty insurance premiums, net	4530	4200	-	330	-	4920	4560	-	360	-
B Transfers to other government subsectors	-	81390	41050	4360	1160	-	95680	45850	5300	1270
C Social security benefits	269050	-	-	-	269050	284350	-	-	-	284350
D Social assistance grants	60280	37140	10290	12850	-	63970	38900	11930	13140	-
E Unfunded employee pension and welfare benefits	39100	9030	22960	5770	1340	41600	9490	24590	6150	1370
F Transfers to private non-profit institutions serving households	15720	2790	8300	3550	1080	16830	2620	9090	3990	1130
G Other transfers n.e.c.	...	...	...	...	...	...	...	...	...	...
H Transfers to the rest of the world	84220	77190	1970	20	5040	162940	124750	12220	20	25950
Net saving	14850	-20640	4290	10640	20560	10550	-27030	7150	11120	19310
Total Current Disbursements and Net Saving	1043040	333410	261660	129450	447440	1170830	386030	293150	140920	499780

Germany, Fed. Rep. of

3.12 General Government Income and Outlay Account: Total and Subsectors

Million Deutsche marks

	1992					1993				
	Total General Government	Central Government	State or Provincial Government	Local Government	Social Security Funds	Total General Government	Central Government	State or Provincial Government	Local Government	Social Security Funds

Receipts

1 Operating surplus	...	...	...	...	...	...	...	...	...	...
2 Property and entrepreneurial income	45490	27480	120	7780	11310	43790	25340	290	8400	11140
3 Taxes, fees and contributions	1173290	374340	257380	89750	451820	1206180	369670	268580	91790	476140
A Indirect taxes	364400	224330	94470	45600	-	379300	229200	103600	46500	-
B Direct taxes	342660	150010	154240	38410	-	336040	140470	156480	39090	-
Income	329530	...	...	...	...	322580	...	...	...	...
Other	13130	...	...	...	...	13460	...	...	...	...
C Social security contributions	451450	-	-	-	451450	475730	-	-	-	475730
D Fees, fines and penalties	14780	-	8670	5740	370	15110	-	8500	6200	410
4 Other current transfers	49590	25080	59060	55170	67520	49440	30640	57730	60170	78920
A Casualty insurance claims	1820	-	-	390	1430	1860	-	-	440	1420
B Transfers from other government subsectors	...	4830	36110	51640	64660	...	11500	34040	56470	76010
C Transfers from the rest of the world	17720	15330	2390	-	...	16570	14230	2340	-	...
D Other transfers, except imputed	...	...	...	...	...	...	...	...	...	...
E Imputed unfunded employee pension and welfare contributions	30050	4920	20560	3140	1430	31010	4910	21350	3260	1490
Total Current Receipts	1268370	426900	316560	152700	530650	1299410	425650	326600	160360	566200

Disbursements

1 Government final consumption expenditure	502860	68190	156480	95400	182790	508480	66270	162200	97280	182730
2 Property income	83220	50030	25520	8820	50	89930	54890	26950	9420	50
A Interest	83220	50030	25520	8820	50	89930	54890	26950	9420	50
B Net land rent and royalties	...	...	...	...	...	...	...	...	...	...
3 Subsidies	45000	28080	12440	3290	1190	44890	30230	10140	3630	890
4 Other current transfers	614820	276450	115060	33200	347350	654690	293560	128260	37550	373340
A Casualty insurance premiums, net	5430	5040	-	390	-	5720	5280	-	440	-
B Transfers to other government subsectors	-	97140	52990	5950	1160	-	104620	64580	7660	1160
C Social security benefits	303000	-	-	-	303000	329530	-	-	-	329530
D Social assistance grants	69660	41510	13130	15020	-	74370	44800	12850	16720	-
E Unfunded employee pension and welfare benefits	44200	10210	26060	6500	1430	46650	10890	27360	6910	1490
F Transfers to private non-profit institutions serving households	18970	2490	9940	5320	1220	20160	2380	10630	5810	1340
G Other transfers n.e.c.	...	...	...	...	...	...	...	...	...	...
H Transfers to the rest of the world	173560	120060	12940	20	40540	178260	125590	12840	10	39820
Net saving	22470	4150	7060	11990	-730	1420	-19300	-950	12480	9190
Total Current Disbursements and Net Saving	1268370	426900	316560	152700	530650	1299410	425650	326600	160360	566200

3.13 General Government Capital Accumulation Account: Total and Subsectors

Million Deutsche marks

	1980					1985				
	Total General Government	Central Government	State or Provincial Government	Local Government	Social Security Funds	Total General Government	Central Government	State or Provincial Government	Local Government	Social Security Funds

Finance of Gross Accumulation

1 Gross saving	35750	7240	7690	17560	3260	47540	12870	9340	18770	6560
A Consumption of fixed capital	9700	630	2980	5760	330	13120	860	4020	7730	510
B Net saving	26050	6610	4710	11800	2930	34420	12010	5320	11040	6050
2 Capital transfers	7230	260	10830	19620	1560	5670	270	11240	16630	20
A From other government subsectors	-	170	9570	15290	10	-	130	9430	12910	20
B From other resident sectors	7090	20	1190	4330	1550	5490	30	1740	3720	-
C From rest of the world	140	70	70	-	-	180	110	70	-	-
Finance of Gross Accumulation	42980	7500	18520	37180	4820	53210	13140	20580	35400	6580

Germany, Fed. Rep. of

3.13 General Government Capital Accumulation Account: Total and Subsectors
(Continued)

Million Deutsche marks

1980 / 1985

	Total General Government	Central Government	State or Provincial Government	Local Government	Social Security Funds	Total General Government	Central Government	State or Provincial Government	Local Government	Social Security Funds
					1980					1985

Gross Accumulation

1 Gross capital formation	50480	6890	8810	34040	740	41020	5730	8680	25280	1330
A Increase in stocks	500	500	-	-	-	-	-	-	-	-
B Gross fixed capital formation	49980	6390	8810	34040	740	41020	5730	8680	25280	1330
Own account	280	-	130	150	-	360	-	170	190	-
Other	49700	6390	8680	33890	740	40660	5730	8510	25090	1330
2 Purchases of land, net	2760	420	450	1810	80	1890	430	360	1080	20
3 Purchases of intangible assets, net	...	...	...	...	...	...	...	...	...	...
4 Capital transfers	32420	25020	26830	5360	250	31390	24210	24640	4790	240
A To other government subsectors	-	9180	14860	900	100	-	8640	12680	1090	80
B To other resident sectors	28970	12400	11960	4460	150	28780	12980	11940	3700	160
C To rest of the world	3450	3440	10	-	-	2610	2590	20	-	-
Net lending	-42680	-24830	-17570	-4030	3750	-21090	-17230	-13100	4250	4990
Gross Accumulation	42980	7500	18520	37180	4820	53210	13140	20580	35400	6580

1990 / 1991

	Total General Government	Central Government	State or Provincial Government	Local Government	Social Security Funds	Total General Government	Central Government	State or Provincial Government	Local Government	Social Security Funds
					1990					1991

Finance of Gross Accumulation

1 Gross saving	31510	-19530	9500	20320	21220	28560	-25810	12790	21550	20030
A Consumption of fixed capital	16660	1110	5210	9680	660	18010	1220	5640	10430	720
B Net saving	14850	-20640	4290	10640	20560	10550	-27030	7150	11120	19310
2 Capital transfers	7720	720	15520	19740	20	7930	800	16590	20870	30
A From other government subsectors	-	530	12110	15620	20	-	660	13400	16270	30
B From other resident sectors	7470	10	3340	4120	-	7790	70	3120	4600	-
C From rest of the world	250	180	70	-	-	140	70	70	-	-
Finance of Gross Accumulation	39230	-18810	25020	40060	21240	36490	-25010	29380	42420	20060

Gross Accumulation

1 Gross capital formation	54160	7010	11100	34990	1060	58440	7420	11620	37930	1470
A Increase in stocks	-	-	-	-	-	-	-	-	-	-
B Gross fixed capital formation	54160	7010	11100	34990	1060	58440	7420	11620	37930	1470
Own account	430	-	200	230	-	420	-	200	220	-
Other	53730	7010	10900	34760	1060	58020	7420	11420	37710	1470
2 Purchases of land, net	1370	200	310	820	40	1460	170	390	850	50
3 Purchases of intangible assets, net	...	...	...	...	...	...	...	...	...	...
4 Capital transfers	33440	27470	28670	5480	100	66240	61410	29240	5590	360
A To other government subsectors	-	11820	15330	1060	70	-	13210	16000	1060	90
B To other resident sectors	27410	9630	13330	4420	30	39750	21930	13240	4530	50
C To rest of the world	6030	6020	10	-	-	26490	26270	-	-	220
Net lending	-49740	-53490	-15060	-1230	20040	-89650	-94010	-11870	-1950	18180
Gross Accumulation	39230	-18810	25020	40060	21240	36490	-25010	29380	42420	20060

1992 / 1993

	Total General Government	Central Government	State or Provincial Government	Local Government	Social Security Funds	Total General Government	Central Government	State or Provincial Government	Local Government	Social Security Funds
					1992					1993

Finance of Gross Accumulation

1 Gross saving	41810	5480	13110	23160	60	21940	-17880	5490	24290	10040
A Consumption of fixed capital	19340	1330	6050	11170	790	20520	1420	6440	11810	850
B Net saving	22470	4150	7060	11990	-730	1420	-19300	-950	12480	9190
2 Capital transfers	8910	370	17700	22080	30	9190	300	16340	22570	40
A From other government subsectors	-	160	14030	17050	30	-	160	12720	17140	40
B From other resident sectors	8560	30	3500	5030	-	8950	30	3490	5430	-
C From rest of the world	350	180	170	-	-	240	110	130	-	-
Finance of Gross Accumulation	50720	5850	30810	45240	90	31130	-17580	21830	46860	10080

Gross Accumulation

1 Gross capital formation	62720	8610	11920	40580	1610	61410	8000	11540	40240	1630

Germany, Fed. Rep. of

3.13 General Government Capital Accumulation Account: Total and Subsectors
(Continued)

Million Deutsche marks

	1992					1993				
	Total General Government	Central Government	State or Provincial Government	Local Government	Social Security Funds	Total General Government	Central Government	State or Provincial Government	Local Government	Social Security Funds
A Increase in stocks	-	-	-	-	-	-	-	-	-	-
B Gross fixed capital formation	62720	8610	11920	40580	1610	61410	8000	11540	40240	1630
Own account	430	-	200	230	-	430	-	200	230	-
Other	62290	8610	11720	40350	1610	60980	8000	11340	40010	1630
2 Purchases of land, net	1430	350	340	660	80	1270	340	400	340	190
3 Purchases of intangible assets, net	...	...	...	...	...	...	...	...	...	...
4 Capital transfers	51840	47030	29920	5650	510	50280	44270	29990	5700	380
A To other government subsectors	-	13320	16740	1100	110	-	12060	16830	1060	110
B To other resident sectors	26330	8560	13180	4550	40	25790	7900	13160	4640	90
C To rest of the world	25510	25150	-	-	360	24490	24310	-	-	180
Net lending	-65270	-50140	-11370	-1650	-2110	-81830	-70190	-20100	580	7880
Gross Accumulation	50720	5850	30810	45240	90	31130	-17580	21830	46860	10080

3.14 General Government Capital Finance Account, Total and Subsectors

Million Deutsche marks

	1980					1985				
	Total General Government	Central Government	State or Provincial Government	Local Government	Social Security Funds	Total General Government	Central Government	State or Provincial Government	Local Government	Social Security Funds
			Acquisition of Financial Assets							
1 Gold and SDRs	-	-	...	...	-	-	-	...	...	-
2 Currency and transferable deposits	-3230	-3090	...	...	-140	2260	1700	...	...	560
3 Other deposits	9730	6560	...	...	3170	13320	8930	...	...	4390
4 Bills and bonds, short term	10	10	...	...	-	20	20	...	...	-
5 Bonds, long term	-50	-300	...	...	250	-450	-340	...	...	-110
6 Corporate equity securities	910	910	...	...	-	760	760	...	...	-
7 Short-term loans, n.e.c.	400	-280	...	...	680	740	330	...	...	410
8 Long-term loans, n.e.c.	4300	4420	...	...	-120	4970	5140	...	...	-170
9 Other receivables	...	...	...	...	...	...	...	...	...	...
10 Other assets	40	40	...	...	-	90	90	...	...	-
Total Acquisition of Financial Assets	12110	8270	...	...	3840	21710	16630	...	...	5080
			Incurrence of Liabilities							
1 Currency and transferable deposits	-	-	...	...	-	-	-	...	...	-
2 Other deposits	-	-	...	...	-	-	-	...	...	-
3 Bills and bonds, short term	-2170	-2170	...	...	-	-480	-480	...	...	-
4 Bonds, long term	2140	2140	...	...	-	38120	38120	...	...	-
5 Short-term loans, n.e.c.	5350	5270	...	...	80	-2140	-2150	...	...	10
6 Long-term loans, n.e.c.	49470	49460	...	...	10	7280	7220	...	...	60
7 Other payables	...	...	...	...	...	...	...	...	...	...
8 Other liabilities	-	-	...	...	-	-	-	...	...	-
Total Incurrence of Liabilities	54790	54700	...	...	90	42780	42710	...	...	70
Net Lending	-42680	-46430	...	...	3750	-21070	-26080	...	...	5010
Incurrence of Liabilities and Net Worth	12110	8270	...	...	3840	21710	16630	...	...	5080

	1990				
	Total General Government	Central Government	State or Provincial Government	Local Government	Social Security Funds
		Acquisition of Financial Assets		
1 Gold and SDRs	-	-	...	...	-
2 Currency and transferable deposits	8340	7260	...	...	1080
3 Other deposits	11660	4140	...	...	7520
4 Bills and bonds, short term	200	200	...	...	-
5 Bonds, long term	3300	600	...	...	2700
6 Corporate equity securities	1260	1260	...	...	-
7 Short-term loans, n.e.c.	8180	2510	...	...	5670
8 Long-term loans, n.e.c.	8980	5730	...	...	3250
9 Other receivables	...	...	...	...	...
10 Other assets	50	50	...	...	-
Total Acquisition of Financial Assets	41970	21750	...	...	20220

Germany, Fed. Rep. of

3.14 General Government Capital Finance Account, Total and Subsectors
(Continued)

Million Deutsche marks

	1990					
	Total General Government	Central Government	State or Provincial Government	Local Government	Social Security Funds
	Incurrence of Liabilities				
1 Currency and transferable deposits	-	-	...	...	-
2 Other deposits	-	-	...	...	-
3 Bills and bonds, short term	8380	8380	...	...	-
4 Bonds, long term	76740	76740	...	...	-
5 Short-term loans, n.e.c.	740	900	...	...	-160
6 Long-term loans, n.e.c.	7310	7200	...	...	110
7 Other payables	...	...	...	...	...
8 Other liabilities	-	-	...	...	-
Total Incurrence of Liabilities	93170	93220	...	...	-50
Net Lending	-51200	-71470	...	...	20270
Incurrence of Liabilities and Net Worth	41970	21750	...	...	20220

3.21 Corporate and Quasi-Corporate Enterprise Production Account: Total and Sectors

Million Deutsche marks

	1980				1985				1990			
	Corporate and Quasi-Corporate Enterprises			ADDENDUM: Total, including Unincorporated	Corporate and Quasi-Corporate Enterprises			ADDENDUM: Total, including Unincorporated	Corporate and Quasi-Corporate Enterprises			ADDENDUM: Total, including Unincorporated
	TOTAL	Non-Financial	Financial		TOTAL	Non-Financial	Financial		TOTAL	Non-Financial	Financial	
	Gross Output											
1 Output for sale	...	...	...	...	...	...	...	...	...	...	...	...
2 Imputed bank service charge	...	...	...	...	...	...	...	...	...	...	...	...
3 Own-account fixed capital formation	...	...	...	...	...	...	...	...	...	...	...	...
Gross Output a	3464380	3364650	99730	...	4327810	4178520	149290	...	5405620	5223250	182370	...
	Gross Input											
Intermediate consumption	2306090	2218780	87310	...	2887670	2754530	133140	...	3471070	3308920	162150	...
1 Imputed banking service charge	53940	-	53940	...	84260	-	84260	...	96280	-	96280	...
2 Other intermediate consumption	2252150	2218780	33370	...	2803410	2754530	48880	...	3374790	3308920	65870	...
Subtotal: Value Added	1158290	1145870	12420	...	1440140	1423990	16150	...	1934550	1914330	20220	...
1 Indirect taxes, net	52510	47560	4950	...	58990	50020	8970	...	73160	63020	10140	...
A Indirect taxes	83160	78210	4950	...	96930	87960	8970	...	121990	111850	10140	...
B Less: Subsidies	30650	30650	-	...	37940	37940	-	...	48830	48830	-	...
2 Consumption of fixed capital	162730	159960	2770	...	218820	214370	4450	...	282060	275960	6160	...
3 Compensation of employees	669710	635550	34160	...	788300	744380	43920	...	1025250	964350	60900	...
4 Net operating surplus	273340	302800	-29460	...	374030	415220	-41190	...	554080	611060	-56980	...
Gross Input a	3464380	3364650	99730	...	4327810	4178520	149290	...	5405620	5223250	182370	...

	1991				1992				1993			
	Corporate and Quasi-Corporate Enterprises			ADDENDUM: Total, including Unincorporated	Corporate and Quasi-Corporate Enterprises			ADDENDUM: Total, including Unincorporated	Corporate and Quasi-Corporate Enterprises			ADDENDUM: Total, including Unincorporated
	TOTAL	Non-Financial	Financial		TOTAL	Non-Financial	Financial		TOTAL	Non-Financial	Financial	
	Gross Output											
1 Output for sale	...	...	...	...	...	...	...	...	...	...	...	...
2 Imputed bank service charge	...	...	...	...	...	...	...	...	...	...	...	...
3 Own-account fixed capital formation	...	...	...	...	...	...	...	...	...	...	...	...
Gross Output a	5905090	5694590	210500	...	6137820	5906320	231500	...	6035180	...	...	...
	Gross Input											
Intermediate consumption	3796620	3609080	187540	...	3902690	3696790	205900	...	3787510	...	...	...
1 Imputed banking service charge	111240	-	111240	...	124070	-	124070	...	133110	-	133110	...
2 Other intermediate consumption	3685380	3609080	76300	...	3778620	3696790	81830	...	3654400	...	...	...
Subtotal: Value Added	2108470	2085510	22960	...	2235130	2209530	25600	...	2247670	2216200	31470	...

Germany, Fed. Rep. of

3.21 Corporate and Quasi-Corporate Enterprise Production Account: Total and Sectors
(Continued)

Million Deutsche marks

	1991			1991 ADDENDUM: Total, including Unincorporated	1992			1992 ADDENDUM: Total, including Unincorporated	1993			1993 ADDENDUM: Total, including Unincorporated
	TOTAL	Non-Financial	Financial		TOTAL	Non-Financial	Financial		TOTAL	Non-Financial	Financial	
1 Indirect taxes, net	88040	75350	12690	...	101480	85980	15500	...	102670	...	...	...
A Indirect taxes	133690	121000	12690	...	146480	130980	15500	...	147560	...	...	...
B Less: Subsidies	45650	45650	-	...	45000	45000	-	...	44890	44890	-	...
2 Consumption of fixed capital	310210	303290	6920	...	335420	327620	7800	...	353450	...	...	...
3 Compensation of employees	1117440	1050840	66600	...	1191450	1118330	73120	...	1201810	1125380	76430	...
4 Net operating surplus	592780	656030	-63250	...	606780	677600	-70820	...	589740	660420	-70680	...
Gross Input a	5905090	5694590	210500	...	6137820	5906320	231500	...	6035180	...	...	...

a) The estimates of this table exclude private non-profit organizations.

3.22 Corporate and Quasi-Corporate Enterprise Income and Outlay Account: Total and Sectors

Million Deutsche marks

	1980			1985			1990			1991		
	TOTAL	Non-Financial	Financial	TOTAL	Non-Financial	Financial	TOTAL	Non-Financial	Financial	TOTAL	Non-Financial	Financial
Receipts												
1 Operating surplus	234870	264330	-29460	323850	365040	-41190	553530	610460	-56930	534550	597800	-63250
2 Property and entrepreneurial income	229950	28850	201100	318520	38610	279910	458960	71300	387660	533400	87250	446150
A Withdrawals from quasi-corporate enterprises	4590	4100	490	6330	5770	560	8190	7570	620	8320	7670	650
B Interest a	213770	16700	197070	290620	18320	272300	414610	41700	372910	486170	55400	430770
C Dividends	11590	8050	3540	21570	14520	7050	36160	22030	14130	38910	24180	14730
D Net land rent and royalties a	...	...	...	...	...	...	...	...	...	...	...	...
3 Current transfers	68200	28760	39440	86700	33190	53510	120120	43440	76680	128980	45680	83300
A Casualty insurance claims	4980	4790	190	6520	6230	290	8910	8580	330	9500	9140	360
B Casualty insurance premiums, net, due to be received by insurance companies	32540	-	32540	44690	-	44690	63430	-	63430	69080	-	69080
C Current transfers from the rest of the world	...	...	...	...	...	...	...	...	...	...	...	...
D Other transfers except imputed	7800	3560	4240	9590	3580	6010	13150	4200	8950	14230	4560	9670
E Imputed unfunded employee pension and welfare contributions	22880	20410	2470	25900	23380	2520	34630	30660	3970	36170	31980	4190
Total Current Receipts	533020	321940	211080	729070	436840	292230	1132610	725200	407410	1196930	730730	466200
Disbursements												
1 Property and entrepreneurial income	453400	307370	146030	612920	407460	205460	908130	611940	296190	998050	659620	338430
A Withdrawals from quasi-corporations	182430	182430	...	235850	235850	...	377200	377200	...	396500	396500	...
B Interest a	243590	100850	142740	323690	136470	187220	452800	172790	280010	526960	203530	323430
C Dividends	27380	24090	3290	53380	35140	18240	78130	61950	16180	74590	59590	15000
D Net land rent and royalties a	...	...	...	...	...	...	...	...	...	...	...	...
2 Direct taxes and other current transfers n.e.c. to general government	27390	22540	4850	41130	31240	9890	41500	33500	8000	45010	34470	10540
A Direct taxes	25950	21100	4850	39220	29330	9890	38680	30680	8000	41570	31030	10540
B Fines, fees, penalties and other current transfers n.e.c.	1440	1440	-	1910	1910	-	2820	2820	-	3440	3440	-
3 Other current transfers	57590	21590	36000	77400	27280	50120	108560	36270	72290	116960	38310	78650
A Casualty insurance premiums, net	5630	5440	190	7470	7180	290	10100	9770	330	10760	10400	360
B Casualty insurance claims liability of insurance companies	32540	-	32540	44690	-	44690	63430	-	63430	69080	-	69080
C Transfers to private non-profit institutions	...	...	...	...	...	...	...	...	...	...	...	...
D Unfunded employee pension and welfare benefits	17140	16060	1080	21330	19940	1390	28510	26340	2170	30100	27760	2340
E Social assistance grants	2280	90	2190	3910	160	3750	6520	160	6360	7020	150	6870
F Other transfers n.e.c.	...	...	...	...	...	...	...	...	...	...	...	...
G Transfers to the rest of the world	...	...	...	...	...	...	...	...	...	...	...	...
Net saving	-5360	-29560	24200	-2380	-29140	26760	74420	43490	30930	36910	-1670	38580
Total Current Disbursements and Net Saving	533020	321940	211080	729070	436840	292230	1132610	725200	407410	1196930	730730	466200

Germany, Fed. Rep. of

3.22 Corporate and Quasi-Corporate Enterprise Income and Outlay Account: Total and Sectors

Million Deutsche marks

	1992 TOTAL	1992 Non-Financial	1992 Financial	1993 TOTAL	1993 Non-Financial	1993 Financial
Receipts						
1 Operating surplus	526620	597440	-70820	462960	533640	-70680
2 Property and entrepreneurial income	603090	100010	503080	633460	95960	537500
A Withdrawals from quasi-corporate enterprises	8470	7780	690	8660	7910	750
B Interest [a]	553290	67130	486160	580910	62620	518290
C Dividends	41330	25100	16230	43890	25430	18460
D Net land rent and royalties [a]	...	...	...	...	...	...
3 Current transfers	140700	49120	91580	149910	51030	98880
A Casualty insurance claims	9500	9110	390	10550	10110	440
B Casualty insurance premiums, net, due to be received by insurance companies	76360	-	76360	83940	-	83940
C Current transfers from the rest of the world	...	...	...	...	...	...
D Other transfers except imputed	15060	5040	10020	14880	5280	9600
E Imputed unfunded employee pension and welfare contributions	39780	34970	4810	40540	35640	4900
Total Current Receipts	1270410	746570	523840	1246330	680630	565700
Disbursements						
1 Property and entrepreneurial income	1084740	695120	389620	1088530	676240	412290
A Withdrawals from quasi-corporations	392950	392950	...	360110	360110	...
B Interest [a]	603620	237140	366480	642600	251870	390730
C Dividends	88170	65030	23140	85820	64260	21560
D Net land rent and royalties [a]	...	...	...	...	...	...
2 Direct taxes and other current transfers n.e.c. to general government	45200	33630	11570	43320	31150	12170
A Direct taxes	41830	30260	11570	40360	28190	12170
B Fines, fees, penalties and other current transfers n.e.c.	3370	3370	-	2960	2960	-
3 Other current transfers	126810	40250	86560	136560	42490	94070
A Casualty insurance premiums, net	10870	10480	390	12140	11700	440
B Casualty insurance claims liability of insurance companies	76360	-	76360	83940	-	83940
C Transfers to private non-profit institutions	...	...	...	...	...	...
D Unfunded employee pension and welfare benefits	32110	29620	2490	33230	30650	2580
E Social assistance grants	7470	150	7320	7250	140	7110
F Other transfers n.e.c.	...	...	...	...	...	...
G Transfers to the rest of the world	...	...	...	...	...	...
Net saving	13660	-22430	36090	-22080	-69250	47170
Total Current Disbursements and Net Saving	1270410	746570	523840	1246330	680630	565700

a) Item 'Interest' includes item 'Net land rent and royalties'.

3.23 Corporate and Quasi-Corporate Enterprise Capital Accumulation Account: Total and Sectors

Million Deutsche marks

	1980 TOTAL	1980 Non-Financial	1980 Financial	1985 TOTAL	1985 Non-Financial	1985 Financial	1990 TOTAL	1990 Non-Financial	1990 Financial	1991 TOTAL	1991 Non-Financial	1991 Financial
Finance of Gross Accumulation												
1 Gross saving	159940	132970	26970	219860	188650	31210	360770	323680	37090	351740	306240	45500
A Consumption of fixed capital	165300	162530	2770	222240	217790	4450	286350	280190	6160	314830	307910	6920
B Net saving	-5360	-29560	24200	-2380	-29140	26760	74420	43490	30930	36910	-1670	38580
2 Capital transfers	56360	56360	-	65650	65650	-	70070	70070	-	83440	83440	-

Germany, Fed. Rep. of

3.23 Corporate and Quasi-Corporate Enterprise Capital Accumulation Account: Total and Sectors
(Continued)

Million Deutsche marks

	1980 TOTAL	1980 Non-Financial	1980 Financial	1985 TOTAL	1985 Non-Financial	1985 Financial	1990 TOTAL	1990 Non-Financial	1990 Financial	1991 TOTAL	1991 Non-Financial	1991 Financial
A From resident sectors	56360	56360	-	65650	65650	-	70070	70070	-	83440	83440	-
B From the rest of the world	...	...	...	...	...	...	...	...	...	...	...	...
Finance of Gross Accumulation [a]	216300	189330	26970	285510	254300	31210	430840	393750	37090	435180	389680	45500

Gross Accumulation

	1980 TOTAL	1980 Non-Financial	1980 Financial	1985 TOTAL	1985 Non-Financial	1985 Financial	1990 TOTAL	1990 Non-Financial	1990 Financial	1991 TOTAL	1991 Non-Financial	1991 Financial
1 Gross capital formation	293370	287600	5770	316040	307650	8390	465110	453280	11830	525210	510970	14240
A Increase in stocks	11270	11080	190	1250	1160	90	11490	11550	-60	20430	20420	10
B Gross fixed capital formation	282100	276520	5580	314790	306490	8300	453620	441730	11890	504780	490550	14230
2 Purchases of land, net	-2760	-3100	340	-1890	-2430	540	-1370	-1320	-50	-1460	-1670	210
3 Purchases of intangible assets, net	...	...	...	...	...	...	...	...	...	...	...	...
4 Capital transfers	19240	16180	3060	22170	14600	7570	20330	18250	2080	25330	19520	5810
A To resident sectors	19240	16180	3060	22170	14600	7570	20330	18250	2080	25330	19520	5810
B To the rest of the world	...	...	...	...	...	...	...	...	...	...	...	...
Net lending	-93550	-111350	17800	-50810	-65520	14710	-53230	-76460	23230	-113900	-139140	25240
Gross Accumulation [a]	216300	189330	26970	285510	254300	31210	430840	393750	37090	435180	389680	45500

	1992 TOTAL	1992 Non-Financial	1992 Financial	1993 TOTAL	1993 Non-Financial	1993 Financial

Finance of Gross Accumulation

	1992 TOTAL	1992 Non-Financial	1992 Financial	1993 TOTAL	1993 Non-Financial	1993 Financial
1 Gross saving	354010	310120	43890	336560	-69250	47170
A Consumption of fixed capital	340350	332550	7800	358640	...	...
B Net saving	13660	-22430	36090	-22080	-69250	47170
2 Capital transfers	70780	70780	-	73070	73070	-
A From resident sectors	70780	70780	-	73070	73070	-
B From the rest of the world	...	...	...	...	...	...
Finance of Gross Accumulation [a]	424790	380900	43890	409630	362460	47170

Gross Accumulation

	1992 TOTAL	1992 Non-Financial	1992 Financial	1993 TOTAL	1993 Non-Financial	1993 Financial
1 Gross capital formation	521560	505080	16480	478870	...	...
A Increase in stocks	-2590	-2640	50	-11520	...	...
B Gross fixed capital formation	524150	507720	16430	490390	...	...
2 Purchases of land, net	-1430	-1800	370	-1270	...	...
3 Purchases of intangible assets, net	...	...	...	...	...	...
4 Capital transfers	26250	19510	6740	30250	22480	7770
A To resident sectors	26250	19510	6740	30250	22480	7770
B To the rest of the world	...	...	...	...	...	...
Net lending	-121590	-141890	20300	-98220	...	...
Gross Accumulation [a]	424790	380900	43890	409630	362460	47170

a) Capital accumulation account of corporate and quasi-corporate enterprise includes private non-profit organizations.

3.24 Corporate and Quasi-Corporate Enterprise Capital Finance Account: Total and Sectors

Million Deutsche marks

	1980 TOTAL	1980 Non-Financial	1980 Financial	1985 TOTAL	1985 Non-Financial	1985 Financial	1990 TOTAL	1990 Non-Financial	1990 Financial

Acquisition of Financial Assets

	1980 TOTAL	1980 Non-Financial	1980 Financial	1985 TOTAL	1985 Non-Financial	1985 Financial	1990 TOTAL	1990 Non-Financial	1990 Financial
1 Gold and SDRs	-11530	-	-11530	2300	-	2300	1500	-	1500
2 Currency and transferable deposits	-2430	6120	-8550	13910	11580	2330	31470	22470	9000
3 Other deposits	18270	3950	14320	65600	9720	55880	62090	29860	32230
4 Bills and bonds, short term	-14990	-40	-14950	4920	1060	3860	15650	6380	9270
5 Bonds, long term	26950	410	26540	51530	9220	42310	133350	38560	94790
6 Corporate equity securities	9420	7340	2080	7040	1640	5400	51470	32810	18660
7 Short term loans, n.e.c.	70510	13250	57260	29030	11570	17460	164310	37030	127280
8 Long term loans, n.e.c.	133350	4170	129180	112470	7800	104670	197270	16010	181260
9 Trade credits and advances	9400	9400	-	3910	3910	-	4150	4150	-
10 Other receivables	...	...	...	...	...	...	...	...	...
11 Other assets	-580	-580	-	2570	2570	-	1510	1510	-
Total Acquisition of Financial Assets	238370	44020	194350	293280	59070	234210	662770	188780	473990

Germany, Fed. Rep. of

3.24 Corporate and Quasi-Corporate Enterprise Capital Finance Account: Total and Sectors
(Continued)

Million Deutsche marks

	1980 TOTAL	1980 Non-Financial	1980 Financial	1985 TOTAL	1985 Non-Financial	1985 Financial	1990 TOTAL	1990 Non-Financial	1990 Financial
				Incurrence of Liabilities					
1 Currency and transferable deposits	6640	-	6640	22500	-	22500	117650	-	117650
2 Other deposits	75790	-	75790	104240	-	104240	166280	-	166280
3 Bills and bonds, short term	-1520	880	-2400	1800	-	1800	-1250	-1590	340
4 Bonds, long term	42510	820	41690	38440	5390	33050	87070	7300	79770
5 Corporate equity securities	6960	5260	1700	11010	6760	4250	28020	21990	6030
6 Short-term loans, n.e.c.	71930	45090	26840	38150	27330	10820	90960	60580	30380
7 Long-term loans, n.e.c.	88770	88260	510	74530	74570	-40	108610	108760	-150
8 Net equity of households in life insurance and pension fund reserves	35030	11650	23380	45730	10620	35110	53500	10320	43180
9 Proprietors' net additions to the accumulation of quasi-corporations	...	...	...	...	...	...	...	...	...
10 Trade credit and advances	3730	3730	-	430	430	-	7310	7310	-
11 Other accounts payable	...	...	...	...	...	...	...	...	...
12 Other liabilities	2420	-	2420	7760	-	7760	7260	-	7260
Total Incurrence of Liabilities	332260	155690	176570	344590	125100	219490	665410	214670	450740
Net Lending	-93890	-111670	17780	-51310	-66030	14720	-2640	-25890	23250
Incurrence of Liabilities and Net Lending	238370	44020	194350	293280	59070	234210	662770	188780	473990

3.32 Household and Private Unincorporated Enterprise Income and Outlay Account

Million Deutsche marks

	1980	1983	1984	1985	1986	1987	1988	1989	1990	1991	1992	1993
					Receipts							
1 Compensation of employees	863880	953440	988330	1026410	1079490	1124700	1169380	1221890	1317100	1422240	1513550	1535920
A Wages and salaries	709520	777420	802930	833780	876630	912810	948870	992810	1069650	1154680	1226680	1239480
B Employers' contributions for social security	109670	127000	132980	140100	147720	153610	160940	168020	180180	197860	211230	218880
C Employers' contributions for private pension & welfare plans	44690	49020	52420	52530	55140	58280	59570	61060	67270	69700	75640	77560
2 Operating surplus of private unincorporated enterprises	...	...	...	...	...	...	...	...	...	...	...	...
3 Property and entrepreneurial income	289270	330310	369150	389110	393770	411110	428630	472270	521920	615880	651460	668480
A Withdrawals from private quasi-corporations	216310	237030	266320	279700	282920	301140	311730	338650	369560	446410	464640	478230
B Interest [a]	67010	86190	94500	99860	99770	99020	102730	117380	133520	152430	168610	171560
C Dividends	5950	7090	8330	9550	11080	10950	14170	16240	18840	17040	18210	18690
D Net land rent and royalties [a]	...	...	...	...	...	...	...	...	...	...	...	...
3 Current transfers	304150	355990	364030	375560	392360	412890	433310	453310	480370	504870	544250	586000
A Casualty insurance claims	25850	31720	34150	36230	38250	40470	43510	46380	51390	51220	57890	63800
B Social security benefits	174390	206830	210200	215260	220980	232050	245000	254320	269050	284350	303000	329530
C Social assistance grants	43210	48400	48340	49070	52980	55500	55950	58350	60280	63970	69660	74370
D Unfunded employee pension and welfare benefits	45650	51610	52640	54900	58120	61280	63740	66620	70430	74690	79480	83250
E Transfers from general government	8790	10060	10790	11220	12170	13330	14150	14540	15720	16830	18970	20160
F Transfers from the rest of the world	670	940	1110	1360	1540	1340	1450	2900	2190	1720	2120	1770
G Other transfers n.e.c.	5590	6430	6800	7520	8320	8920	9510	10200	11310	12090	13130	13120
Total Current Receipts [b]	1457300	1639740	1721510	1791080	1865620	1948700	2031320	2147470	2319390	2542990	2709260	2790400
					Disbursements							
1 Final consumption expenditures	837020	959280	1001200	1036530	1066430	1108020	1153690	1220950	1320710	1448770	1536320	1588900
A Market purchases	821690	940130	981230	1014740	1042340	1082150	1126620	1192120	1289980	1414560	1498410	1548090
B Gross rents of owner-occupied housing	...	...	...	...	...	...	...	...	...	...	...	...
C Consumption from own-account production	15330	19150	19970	21790	24090	25870	27070	28830	30730	34210	37910	40810
2 Property income	13190	17860	17760	17670	17930	17480	18170	19460	22100	25880	31540	36920
A Interest	13190	17860	17760	17670	17930	17480	18170	19460	22100	25880	31540	36920
Consumer debt	13190	17860	17760	17670	17930	17480	18170	19460	22100	25880	31540	36920
Mortgage	...	...	...	...	...	...	...	...	...	...	...	...

Germany, Fed. Rep. of

3.32 Household and Private Unincorporated Enterprise Income and Outlay Account
(Continued)

Million Deutsche marks

	1980	1983	1984	1985	1986	1987	1988	1989	1990	1991	1992	1993
Other	...	...	...	...	...	...	...	...	...	...	...	...
B Net land rent and royalties	...	...	...	...	...	...	...	...	...	...	...	...
3 Direct taxes and other current transfers n.e.c. to government	394880	444320	466520	493120	517070	543280	564250	602060	619360	697180	749840	768440
A Social security contributions	229480	268560	282150	296610	312750	325220	340330	356100	380450	415690	442760	466350
B Direct taxes	160210	169070	177220	188980	196270	209430	214670	236340	228590	270520	295670	289940
Income taxes	156550	165140	173120	184840	191070	204760	210090	231200	223770	265070	289310	283270
Other	3660	3930	4100	4140	5200	4670	4580	5140	4820	5450	6360	6670
C Fees, fines and penalties	5190	6690	7150	7530	8050	8630	9250	9620	10320	10970	11410	12150
4 Other current transfers	88820	100890	107390	110180	114920	120360	125750	131680	145190	148850	164440	173740
A Net casualty insurance premiums	26500	32410	34810	36770	38710	40930	43910	46850	51810	51530	58230	63930
B Transfers to private non-profit institutions serving households	...	...	...	...	...	...	...	...	...	...	...	...
C Transfers to the rest of the world	11810	12280	13150	12740	12560	11750	12150	12960	14340	14960	17380	19280
D Other current transfers, except imputed	5820	7180	7010	8140	8510	9400	10120	10810	11770	12660	13190	12970
E Imputed employee pension and welfare contributions	44690	49020	52420	52530	55140	58280	59570	61060	67270	69700	75640	77560
Net saving	123390	117390	128640	133580	149270	159560	169460	173320	212030	222310	227120	222400
Total Current Disbursements and Net Saving b	1457300	1639740	1721510	1791080	1865620	1948700	2031320	2147470	2319390	2542990	2709260	2790400

a) Item 'Interest' includes item 'Net land rent and royalties'.
b) Private non-profit institutions serving households are included in household and private unincorporated enterprises.

3.33 Household and Private Unincorporated Enterprise Capital Accumulation Account

Million Deutsche marks

	1980	1983	1984	1985	1986	1987	1988	1989	1990	1991	1992	1993
Finance of Gross Accumulation											
1 Gross saving	123390	117390	128640	133580	149270	159560	169460	173320	212030	222310	227120	222400
A Consumption of fixed capital	...	...	...	...	...	...	...	...	...	...	...	...
B Net saving a	123390	117390	128640	133580	149270	159560	169460	173320	212030	222310	227120	222400
2 Capital transfers	21360	22360	23230	21480	20980	18850	19930	18410	16580	22410	22360	25840
A From resident sectors	21340	22330	23190	21430	20940	18820	19900	18360	16550	22380	22340	25820
B From the rest of the world	20	30	40	50	40	30	30	50	30	30	20	20
Total Finance of Gross Accumulation	144750	139750	151870	155060	170250	178410	189390	191730	228610	244720	249480	248240
Gross Accumulation											
1 Gross Capital Formation	...	...	...	...	...	...	...	...	...	...	...	...
2 Purchases of land, net	...	...	...	...	...	...	...	...	...	...	...	...
3 Purchases of intangibles, net	...	...	...	...	...	...	...	...	...	...	...	...
4 Capital transfers	36990	39120	41550	42040	43780	47070	47440	45010	46860	49020	49670	52370
A To resident sectors	36580	38590	41140	41620	43310	46560	46950	44590	46350	48530	49100	51800
B To the rest of the world	410	530	410	420	470	510	490	420	510	490	570	570
Net lending	107760	100630	110320	113020	126470	131340	141950	146720	181750	195700	199810	195870
Total Gross Accumulation	144750	139750	151870	155060	170250	178410	189390	191730	228610	244720	249480	248240

a) Item 'Net saving' excludes undistributed profits of unincorporated enterprises.

3.34 Household and Private Unincorporated Enterprise Capital Finance Account

Million Deutsche marks

	1980	1983	1984	1985	1986	1987	1988	1989	1990	1991	1992	1993
Acquisition of Financial Assets											
1 Gold	-	-	-	-	-	-	-	-	-	...	...	...
2 Currency and transferable deposits	3900	9490	6140	5380	13290	13750	23270	7630	16370	...	...	...
3 Other deposits	54520	40780	39630	46310	58710	43390	22530	39010	48350	...	...	...
4 Bills and bonds, short term	400	-1370	-630	-410	-290	-1050	-300	3650	5830	...	...	...
5 Bonds, long term	24790	15950	26600	21510	8020	26380	48020	62620	75630	...	...	...
6 Corporate equity securities	-900	4060	700	3470	3640	5910	2540	-6990	-2820	...	...	...
7 Short term loans, n.e.c.	-	-	-	-	-	-	-	-	-	...	...	...

Germany, Fed. Rep. of

3.34 Household and Private Unincorporated Enterprise Capital Finance Account
(Continued)

Million Deutsche marks

	1980	1983	1984	1985	1986	1987	1988	1989	1990	1991	1992	1993
8 Long term loans, n.e.c.	140	370	190	-540	330	180	20	40	40	...	...	...
9 Trade credit and advances	-	-	-	-	-	-	-	-	-	...	...	...
10 Net equity of households in life insurance and pension fund reserves	35030	40290	44140	45730	48010	49480	53030	54850	53500	...	...	...
11 Proprietors' net additions to the accumulation of quasi-corporations	...	...	...	...	...	...	...	...	...	...	...	...
12 Other	2870	4000	4400	4870	5460	5490	5790	7010	5580	...	...	...
Total Acquisition of Financial Assets	120750	113570	121170	126320	137170	143530	154900	167820	202480	...	...	...

Incurrence of Liabilities

	1980	1983	1984	1985	1986	1987	1988	1989	1990	1991	1992	1993
1 Short term loans, n.e.c.	4770	2830	3510	3580	120	-730	10	4680	5250	...	...	...
2 Long term loans, n.e.c.	7890	9690	6970	9200	9880	12300	12960	16360	18550	...	...	...
3 Trade credit and advances	-	-	-	-	-	-	-	-	-	...	...	...
4 Other accounts payable	...	...	...	...	...	...	...	...	...	...	...	...
5 Other liabilities	-	-	-	-	-	-	-	-	-	...	...	...
Total Incurrence of Liabilities	12660	12520	10480	12780	10000	11570	12970	21040	23800	...	...	...
Net Lending	108090	101050	110690	113540	127170	131960	141930	146780	178680	...	...	...
Incurrence of Liabilities and Net Lending	120750	113570	121170	126320	137170	143530	154900	167820	202480	...	...	...

3.41 Private Non-Profit Institutions Serving Households: Production Account

Million Deutsche marks

	1980	1983	1984	1985	1986	1987	1988	1989	1990	1991	1992	1993

Gross Output

	1980	1983	1984	1985	1986	1987	1988	1989	1990	1991	1992	1993
1 Sales	27300	33020	34960	36800	39050	41160	43180	44640	48920	54050	59270	62010
2 Non-marketed output	15330	19150	19970	21790	24090	25870	27070	28830	30730	34210	37910	40810
A Services produced for own use	15330	19150	19970	21790	24090	25870	27070	28830	30730	34210	37910	40810
B Own account fixed capital formation	...	...	...	...	...	...	...	...	...	...	...	...
Gross Output	42630	52170	54930	58590	63140	67030	70250	73470	79650	88260	97180	102820

Gross Input

	1980	1983	1984	1985	1986	1987	1988	1989	1990	1991	1992	1993
Intermediate consumption	13410	16390	17350	18400	19250	20280	21100	22070	23980	26570	29260	30960
Subtotal: Value Added	29220	35780	37580	40190	43890	46750	49150	51400	55670	61690	67920	71860
1 Indirect taxes, net	20	20	20	20	30	30	30	30	30	30	40	40
2 Consumption of fixed capital	2570	3160	3320	3420	3520	3660	3800	4000	4290	4620	4930	5190
3 Compensation of employees	26630	32600	34240	36750	40340	43060	45320	47370	51350	57040	62950	66630
A To residents	26630	32600	34240	36750	40340	43060	45320	47370	51350	57040	62950	66630
B To the rest of the world	...	...	...	...	...	...	...	...	...	...	...	...
4 Net operating surplus	...	...	...	...	...	...	...	...	...	...	...	...
Gross Input	42630	52170	54930	58590	63140	67030	70250	73470	79650	88260	97180	102820

3.51 External Transactions: Current Account: Detail

Million Deutsche marks

	1980	1983	1984	1985	1986	1987	1988	1989	1990	1991	1992	1993

Payments to the Rest of the World

	1980	1983	1984	1985	1986	1987	1988	1989	1990	1991	1992	1993
1 Imports of goods and services [a]	395990	446120	493060	528870	480630	476650	510120	581290	636950	726560	743110	695220
A Imports of merchandise c.i.f. [b]	324020	362800	405350	436870	390690	383890	411770	475320	521240	596210	599420	545990
B Other	71970	83320	87710	92000	89940	92760	98350	105970	115710	130350	143690	149230
2 Factor income to the rest of the world	26160	35450	37070	40600	45670	48390	56020	62200	82890	102700	122970	142900
A Compensation of employees	2040	2130	2060	2080	2200	2340	2560	2860	7420	20030	27370	29010
B Property and entrepreneurial income	24120	33320	35010	38520	43470	46050	53460	59340	75470	82670	95600	113890
By general government	1520	6450	6900	8190	9790	11590	11670	11340	12640	14030	17610	26210
By corporate and quasi-cororate enterprises	22600	26870	28110	30330	33680	34460	41790	48000	62830	68640	77990	87680

Germany, Fed. Rep. of

3.51 External Transactions: Current Account: Detail
(Continued)

Million Deutsche marks

	1980	1983	1984	1985	1986	1987	1988	1989	1990	1991	1992	1993
By other	...	...	...	...	...	...	...	...	...	...	...	...
3 Current transfers to the rest of the world	34620	39970	45280	45110	44650	44980	51170	55640	100830	185360	198910	206120
A Indirect taxes by general government to supranational organizations	...	...	...	...	...	...	...	...	...	...	...	...
B Other current transfers	34620	39970	45280	45110	44650	44980	51170	55640	100830	185360	198910	206120
By general government	21900	26540	30960	31210	30980	32130	37840	41240	84220	162940	173560	178260
By other resident sectors	12720	13430	14320	13900	13670	12850	13330	14400	16610	22420	25350	27860
4 Surplus of the nation on current transactions	-24770	14370	24220	43920	82230	82330	89150	107020	85040	18960	38660	40620
Payments to the Rest of the World, and Surplus of the Nation on Current Transfers	432000	535910	599630	658500	653180	652350	706460	806150	905710	1033580	1103650	1084860

Receipts From The Rest of the World

	1980	1983	1984	1985	1986	1987	1988	1989	1990	1991	1992	1993
1 Exports of goods and services a	389140	479630	536320	592740	580540	576610	619830	701430	778900	875220	932650	911260
A Exports of merchandise f.o.b.	339060	416970	467350	517760	508960	506850	548020	616360	663700	738530	800640	787560
B Other	50080	62660	68970	74980	71580	69760	71810	85070	115200	136690	132010	123700
2 Factor income from the rest of the world	31520	42610	49480	51920	56480	60910	68040	86860	105490	123100	129770	132000
A Compensation of employees	5040	6540	6700	7070	7250	7690	8160	8500	9000	11970	13790	14540
B Property and entrepreneurial income	26480	36070	42780	44850	49230	53220	59880	78360	96490	111130	115980	117460
By general government	80	110	120	120	120	90	120	140	230	300	230	240
By corporate and quasi-corporate enterprises	25440	32390	38030	38040	41580	45460	49120	62540	80690	96660	102320	104830
By other	960	3570	4630	6690	7530	7670	10640	15680	15570	14170	13430	12390
3 Current transfers from the rest of the world	11340	13670	13830	13840	16160	14830	18590	17860	21320	35260	41230	41600
A Subsidies to general government from supranational organizations	...	...	...	...	...	...	...	...	...	...	...	...
B Other current transfers	11340	13670	13830	13840	16160	14830	18590	17860	21320	35260	41230	41600
To general government	10070	11920	12030	11810	13900	12780	16380	14110	17360	26490	31570	31690
To other resident sectors	1270	1750	1800	2030	2260	2050	2210	3750	3960	8770	9660	9910
Receipts from the Rest of the World on Current Transfers	432000	535910	599630	658500	653180	652350	706460	806150	905710	1033580	1103650	1084860

a) Exports and imports of goods for purposes of repair and improvement are reduced to the value of these services.
b) Imports of merchandise, f.o.b. rather than c.i.f.

3.52 External Transactions: Capital Accumulation Account

Million Deutsche marks

	1980	1983	1984	1985	1986	1987	1988	1989	1990	1991	1992	1993

Finance of Gross Accumulation

	1980	1983	1984	1985	1986	1987	1988	1989	1990	1991	1992	1993
1 Surplus of the nation on current transactions	-24770	14370	24220	43920	82230	82330	89150	107020	85040	18960	38660	40620
2 Capital transfers from the rest of the world	160	180	110	230	200	220	180	310	280	170	370	260
A By general government	140	150	70	180	160	190	150	260	250	140	350	240
B By other resident sectors	20	30	40	50	40	30	30	50	30	30	20	20
Total Finance of Gross Accumulation	-24610	14550	24330	44150	82430	82550	89330	107330	85320	19130	39030	40880

Gross Accumulation

	1980	1983	1984	1985	1986	1987	1988	1989	1990	1991	1992	1993
1 Capital transfers to the rest of the world	3860	2780	2760	3030	2820	2770	2980	3320	6540	26980	26080	25060
A By general government	3450	2250	2350	2610	2350	2260	2490	2900	6030	26490	25510	24490
B By other resident sectors	410	530	410	420	470	510	490	420	510	490	570	570
2 Purchases of intangible assets, n.e.c., net, from the rest of the world	...	...	...	...	...	...	...	...	...	...	...	...
Net lending to the rest of the world	-28470	11770	21570	41120	79610	79780	86350	104010	78780	-7850	12950	15820
Total Gross Accumulation	-24610	14550	24330	44150	82430	82550	89330	107330	85320	19130	39030	40880

Germany, Fed. Rep. of

3.53 External Transactions: Capital Finance Account

Million Deutsche marks

	1980	1983	1984	1985	1986	1987	1988	1989	1990	1991	1992	1993
Acquisitions of Foreign Financial Assets												
1 Gold and SDR's	-11530	-2900	-700	2300	-1000	12500	-7900	-4600	1500	...	...	...
2 Currency and transferable deposits	1350	-1880	4010	2000	7780	890	1960	7910	6000	...	...	...
3 Other deposits	10050	-5420	15120	36530	82520	16280	30250	94450	23230	...	...	...
4 Bills and bonds, short term	-10090	-2110	-970	3350	12390	25980	-19820	9760	15320	...	...	...
5 Bonds, long term	7340	5740	15710	27460	16390	25090	67730	46780	76600	...	...	...
6 Corporate equity securities	3570	8320	5680	7460	15890	4390	13740	14720	20510	...	...	...
7 Short-term loans, n.e.c.	4490	5690	5540	7040	14580	8770	8550	35360	90010	...	...	...
8 Long-term loans	16150	22410	22470	24730	20000	31550	14530	25590	74800	...	...	...
9 Proprietors' net additions to accumulation of quasi-corporate, non-resident enterprises	...	...	...	...	...	...	...	...	...	...	...	...
10 Trade credit and advances	9400	7700	11710	3910	520	-1210	16160	15000	4150	...	...	...
11 Other	-	-	-	-	-	-	-	-	-	...	...	...
Total Acquisitions of Foreign Financial Assets	30730	37550	78570	114780	169070	124240	125200	244970	312120	...	...	...
Incurrence of Foreign Liabilities												
1 Currency and transferable deposits	9750	-280	9480	2950	9300	-4010	11780	34810	67450	...	...	...
2 Other deposits	3360	-6770	10480	15580	18980	24710	15500	31400	67410	...	...	...
3 Bills and bonds, short term	820	970	-620	140	-200	-490	70	-50	770	...	...	...
4 Bonds, long term	290	10800	13820	31460	59070	35000	2090	22490	28110	...	...	...
5 Corporate equity securities	1100	2460	4000	7210	15170	-1340	3320	26210	-1370	...	...	...
6 Short-term loans, n.e.c.	15610	-1580	11230	16880	-6550	-1070	1610	20510	14480	...	...	...
7 Long-term loans	24450	18240	5480	-1200	-1860	-9220	-4220	640	2950	...	...	...
8 Non-resident proprietors' net additions to accumulation of resident quasi-corporate enterprises	...	...	...	...	...	...	...	...	...	...	...	...
9 Trade credit and advances	3730	1820	3000	430	-4630	680	7750	4710	7310	...	...	...
10 Other	100	90	130	220	180	190	150	190	130	...	...	...
Total Incurrence of Liabilities	59210	25750	57000	73670	89460	44450	38050	140910	187240	...	...	...
Net Lending	-28480	11800	21570	41110	79610	79790	87150	104060	124880	...	...	...
Total Incurrence of Liabilities and Net Lending	30730	37550	78570	114780	169070	124240	125200	244970	312120	...	...	...

4.1 Derivation of Value Added by Kind of Activity, in Current Prices

Million Deutsche marks

	1980			1985			1990			1991		
	Gross Output	Intermediate Consumption	Value Added	Gross Output	Intermediate Consumption	Value Added	Gross Output	Intermediate Consumption	Value Added	Gross Output	Intermediate Consumption	Value Added
All Producers												
1 Agriculture, hunting, forestry and fishing	65420	34900	30520	70780	38860	31920	72660	35920	36740	69310	35430	33880
A Agriculture and hunting [a]	56290	31270	25020	61430	34820	26610	58420	29500	28920	58200	29690	28510
B Forestry and logging [a]	9130	3630	5500	9350	4040	5310	14240	6420	7820	11110	5740	5370
C Fishing [a]	...	...	...	...	...	...	...	...	...	...	...	...
2 Mining and quarrying [b]	29980	17750	12230	37000	20950	16050	30760	19370	11390	32170	19720	12450
A Coal mining	25350	15100	10250	30340	16870	13470	23470	14800	8670	23750	14570	9180
B Crude petroleum and natural gas production	...	...	...	...	...	...	...	...	...	...	...	...
C Metal ore mining	...	...	...	...	...	...	...	...	...	...	...	...
D Other mining	4630	2650	1980	6660	4080	2580	7290	4570	2720	8420	5150	3270

Germany, Fed. Rep. of

4.1 Derivation of Value Added by Kind of Activity, in Current Prices
(Continued)

Million Deutsche marks

		1980			1985			1990			1991		
		Gross Output	Intermediate Consumption	Value Added	Gross Output	Intermediate Consumption	Value Added	Gross Output	Intermediate Consumption	Value Added	Gross Output	Intermediate Consumption	Value Added
3	Manufacturing	1331030	854780	476250	1638350	1059500	578850	2005610	1264060	741550	2150060	1359250	790810
	A Manufacture of food, beverages and tobacco	190580	135320	55260	221380	158570	62810	247040	168780	78260	268170	186050	82120
	B Textile, wearing apparel and leather industries	69160	44420	24740	74830	49650	25180	83070	55120	27950	84990	57220	27770
	C Manufacture of wood and wood products, including furniture	47890	30440	17450	45060	28150	16910	60620	37780	22840	66240	40250	25990
	D Manufacture of paper and paper products, printing and publishing [c]	50010	29370	20640	64150	38850	25300	86780	52660	34120	94380	57270	37110
	E Manufacture of chemicals and chemical petroleum, coal, rubber and plastic products	283870	199250	84620	363130	254690	108440	377120	244750	132370	397240	259140	138100
	F Manufacture of non-metallic mineral products, except products of petroleum and coal [b]	52130	30420	21710	52370	31300	21070	65980	37950	28030	71740	41640	30100
	G Basic metal industries	118160	80080	38080	134010	89880	44130	150550	96040	54510	146650	91340	55310
	H Manufacture of fabricated metal products, machinery and equipment [d]	511430	300980	210450	674570	403520	271050	923050	564760	358290	1009120	620030	389090
	I Other manufacturing industries	7800	4500	3300	8850	4890	3960	11400	6220	5180	11530	6310	5220
4	Electricity, gas and water	105450	69040	36410	171460	120980	50480	173420	114580	58840	186740	125070	61670
	A Electricity, gas and steam	100440	67020	33420	164610	117860	46750	165150	110780	54370	178650	121240	57410
	B Water works and supply	5010	2020	2990	6850	3120	3730	8270	3800	4470	8090	3830	4260
5	Construction [d]	195960	96070	99890	190100	95290	94810	262380	134760	127620	286660	149380	137280
6	Wholesale and retail trade, restaurants and hotels	1118690	966540	152150	1347910	1169380	178530	1603810	1359160	244650	1768170	1491070	277100
	A Wholesale and retail trade	1071340	938090	133250	1289770	1133360	156410	1524670	1312120	212550	1683790	1440960	242830
	B Restaurants and hotels	47350	28450	18900	58140	36020	22120	79140	47040	32100	84380	50110	34270
7	Transport, storage and communication	158420	72990	85430	198600	93550	105050	259840	125640	134200	277210	133390	143820
	A Transport and storage	119810	67390	52420	148810	85350	63460	193010	111870	81140	207640	121460	86180
	B Communication	38610	5600	33010	49790	8200	41590	66830	13770	53060	69570	11930	57640
8	Finance, insurance, real estate and business services	211610	55680	155930	311090	79220	231870	395410	106560	288850	440310	122180	318130
	A Financial institutions	71190	19850	51340	106810	27900	78910	125750	34760	90990	142190	37470	104720
	B Insurance	28540	13520	15020	42480	20980	21500	56620	31110	25510	68310	38830	29480
	C Real estate and business services [e]	111880	22310	89570	161800	30340	131460	213040	40690	172350	229810	45880	183930
	Real estate, except dwellings	...	...	...	...	...	...	...	...	...	...	...	...
	Dwellings	111880	22310	89570	161800	30340	131460	213040	40690	172350	229810	45880	183930
9	Community, social and personal services [ce]	247820	84400	163420	362520	125680	236840	601730	214740	386990	694460	249890	444570
	Educational services	...	...	...	...	...	...	...	...	...	...	...	...
	Medical, dental, other health and veterinary services	46320	14020	32300	59650	18000	41650	75270	22590	52680	83650	25230	58420
Total, Industries		3464380	2252150	1212230	4327810	2803410	1524400	5405620	3374790	2030830	5905090	3685380	2219710
Producers of Government Services		339060	166670	172390	421090	213830	207260	519380	266180	253200	556960	285740	271220
Other Producers		44720	13410	31310	61080	18400	42680	82280	23980	58300	91120	26570	64550
Total		3848160	2432230	1415930	4809980	3035640	1774340	6007280	3664950	2342330	6553170	3997690	2555480
Less: Imputed bank service charge		...	-53940	53940	...	-84260	84260	...	-96280	96280	...	-111240	111240
Import duties		13480	...	13480	16440	...	16440	24980	...	24980	29280	...	29280
Value added tax		96570	...	96570	116660	...	116660	154970	...	154970	174080	...	174080
Total		3958210	2486170	1472040	4943080	3119900	1823180	6187230	3761230	2426000	6756530	4108930	2647600

		1992			1993		
		Gross Output	Intermediate Consumption	Value Added	Gross Output	Intermediate Consumption	Value Added
		All Producers					
1	Agriculture, hunting, forestry and fishing	68150	35330	32820	62740	33450	29290
	A Agriculture and hunting [a]	57140	29670	27470	...	...	...
	B Forestry and logging [a]	11010	5660	5350	...	...	...
	C Fishing [a]	...	...	...	...	...	...
2	Mining and quarrying [b]	31690	19040	12650	...	...	...

Germany, Fed. Rep. of

4.1 Derivation of Value Added by Kind of Activity, in Current Prices
(Continued)

Million Deutsche marks

		1992			1993		
		Gross Output	Intermediate Consumption	Value Added	Gross Output	Intermediate Consumption	Value Added
	A Coal mining	23740	14470	9270	...	...	...
	B Crude petroleum and natural gas production	...	...	...	...	...	...
	C Metal ore mining	...	...	...	...	...	...
	D Other mining	7950	4570	3380	...	...	...
3	Manufacturing	2157020	1357130	799890	...	...	749040
	A Manufacture of food, beverages and tobacco	271820	188380	83440	...	...	...
	B Textile, wearing apparel and leather industries	82440	54460	27980	...	...	...
	C Manufacture of wood and wood products, including furniture	69260	41790	27470	...	...	...
	D Manufacture of paper and paper products, printing and publishing c	93240	55550	37690	...	...	...
	E Manufacture of chemicals and chemical petroleum, coal, rubber and plastic products	397570	252940	144630	...	...	...
	F Manufacture of non-metallic mineral products, except products of petroleum and coal b	76530	44550	31980	...	...	...
	G Basic metal industries	142100	88030	54070	...	...	...
	H Manufacture of fabricated metal products, machinery and equipment d	1012630	625550	387080	...	...	...
	I Other manufacturing industries	11430	5880	5550	...	...	...
4	Electricity, gas and water	188100	124720	63380	...	...	...
	A Electricity, gas and steam	...	...	...	...	...	...
	B Water works and supply	...	...	...	...	...	...
5	Construction d	316120	163460	152660	...	...	158590
6	Wholesale and retail trade, restaurants and hotels	1802280	1513900	288380	...	...	...
	A Wholesale and retail trade	1714190	1461880	252310	...	...	247490
	B Restaurants and hotels	88090	52020	36070	...	...	...
7	Transport, storage and communication	300540	146960	153580	...	...	158110
	A Transport and storage	221540	130830	90710	...	...	...
	B Communication	79000	16130	62870	...	...	...
8	Finance, insurance, real estate and business services	482880	132650	350230	...	...	386330
	A Financial institutions	157110	40020	117090	...	...	...
	B Insurance	74390	41810	32580	...	...	...
	C Real estate and business services e	251380	50820	200560	...	...	221750
	Real estate, except dwellings	...	...	...	...	...	...
	Dwellings	251380	50820	200560	...	...	221750
9	Community, social and personal services ce	791040	285430	505610	...	...	...
	Educational services	...	...	...	...	...	...
	Medical, dental, other health and veterinary services	93060	28270	64790	...	...	...
Total, Industries		6137820	3778620	2359200	6035180	3654400	2380780
Producers of Government Services		599900	310540	289360	610830	311120	299710
Other Producers		100140	29260	70880	105830	30960	74870
Total		6837860	4118420	2719440	6751840	3996480	2755360
Less: Imputed bank service charge		...	-124070	124070	...	-133110	133110
Import duties		30570	...	30570	28820	...	28820
Value added tax		187060	...	187060	202630	...	202630
Total		7055490	4242490	2813000	6983290	4129590	2853700

a) Hunting and fishing are included in item 'Forestry and logging'.
b) Quarrying is included in item 'Manufacture of non-metalic mineral products except products of petroleum and coal'.
c) Publishing is included in item 'Community, social and personal services'.
d) Structural steel erection is included in item 'Manufacture of fabricated metal products, machinery and equipment'.
e) Business services and real estate except dwellings are included in item 'Community, social and personal services'.

Germany, Fed. Rep. of

4.2 Derivation of Value Added by Kind of Activity, in Constant Prices

Million Deutsche marks

	1980 Gross Output	1980 Intermediate Consumption	1980 Value Added	1985 Gross Output	1985 Intermediate Consumption	1985 Value Added	1990 Gross Output	1990 Intermediate Consumption	1990 Value Added	1991 Gross Output	1991 Intermediate Consumption	1991 Value Added
At constant prices of: 1991 — All Producers												
1 Agriculture, hunting, forestry and fishing	66220	36970	29250	68580	36730	31850	74020	37590	36430	69310	35430	33880
A Agriculture and hunting [a]	...	...	24120	...	...	26450	...	...	29610	...	...	28510
B Forestry and logging [a]	...	...	5130	...	...	5400	...	...	6820	...	...	5370
C Fishing [a]	...	...	...	...	...	...	...	...	...	...	...	...
2 Mining and quarrying [bc]	174740	110370	16600	189080	124670	14590	207770	138390	11210	218910	144790	12450
A Coal mining	...	...	14780	...	...	13230	...	...	8510	...	...	9180
B Crude petroleum and natural gas production	...	...	...	...	...	...	...	...	...	...	...	...
C Metal ore mining	...	...	...	...	...	...	...	...	...	...	...	...
D Other mining	...	...	1820	...	...	1360	...	...	2700	...	...	3270
3 Manufacturing	1666360	1010330	656030	1727210	1048040	679170	2049080	1286810	762270	2150060	1359250	790810
A Manufacture of food, beverages and tobacco	...	...	78690	...	...	78100	...	...	79130	...	...	82120
B Textile, wearing apparel and leather industries	...	...	31540	...	...	28510	...	...	28320	...	...	27770
C Manufacture of wood and wood products, including furniture	...	...	27470	...	...	22310	...	...	23850	...	...	25990
D Manufacture of paper and paper products, printing and publishing [d]	...	...	28270	...	...	29820	...	...	35260	...	...	37110
E Manufacture of chemicals and chemical petroleum, coal, rubber and plastic products	...	...	125540	...	...	135310	...	...	140690	...	...	138100
F Manufacture of non-metallic mineral products, except products of petroleum and coal [b]	...	...	29090	...	...	25080	...	...	28950	...	...	30100
G Basic metal industries	...	...	46340	...	...	46340	...	...	53350	...	...	55310
H Manufacture of fabricated metal products, machinery and equipment [e]	...	...	284660	...	...	309390	...	...	367370	...	...	389090
I Other manufacturing industries	...	...	4430	...	...	4310	...	...	5350	...	...	5220
4 Electricity, gas and water [c]	...	...	47770	...	...	49820	...	...	58170	...	...	61670
A Electricity, gas and steam	...	...	43410	...	...	45570	...	...	53450	...	...	57410
B Water works and supply	...	...	4360	...	...	4250	...	...	4720	...	...	4260
5 Construction [e]	268560	128920	139640	235600	111040	124560	279980	143190	136790	286660	149380	137280
6 Wholesale and retail trade, restaurants and hotels [f]	1271780	1096340	204930	1306630	1126410	208530	1554390	1336270	251400	1683790	1440960	277100
A Wholesale and retail trade	...	...	175440	...	...	180220	...	...	218120	...	...	242830
B Restaurants and hotels	...	...	29490	...	...	28310	...	...	33280	...	...	34270
7 Transport, storage and communication	184430	86840	97590	204480	95200	109280	268470	130840	137630	277210	133390	143820
A Transport and storage	...	...	61990	...	...	66440	...	...	81720	...	...	86180
B Communication	...	...	35600	...	...	42840	...	...	55910	...	...	57640
8 Finance, insurance, real estate and business services	293580	70620	222960	342230	87110	255120	423160	113060	310100	440310	122180	318130
A Financial institutions [g]	131210	40520	70050	151120	51230	78490	200730	68280	100720	210500	76300	104720
B Insurance [g]	...	...	20640	...	...	21400	...	...	31730	...	...	29480
C Real estate and business services [h]	162370	30100	132270	191110	35880	155230	222430	44780	177650	229810	45880	183930
Real estate, except dwellings	...	...	...	...	...	...	...	...	...	...	...	...
Dwellings	...	...	132270	...	...	155230	...	...	177650	...	...	183930
9 Community, social and personal services [dhf]	418470	151920	237060	503390	184830	290250	715850	276770	405800	778840	300000	444570
Educational services	...	...	...	...	...	...	...	...	...	...	...	...
Medical, dental, other health and veterinary services	...	...	42340	...	...	49160	...	...	54490	...	...	58420

Germany, Fed. Rep. of

4.2 Derivation of Value Added by Kind of Activity, in Constant Prices
(Continued)

Million Deutsche marks

	1980 Gross Output	1980 Intermediate Consumption	1980 Value Added	1985 Gross Output	1985 Intermediate Consumption	1985 Value Added	1990 Gross Output	1990 Intermediate Consumption	1990 Value Added	1991 Gross Output	1991 Intermediate Consumption	1991 Value Added
					At constant prices of:1991							
Total, Industries	4344140	2692310	1651830	4577200	2814030	1763170	5572720	3462920	2109800	5905090	3685380	2219710
Producers of Government Services [i]	540840	258380	237360	578180	274220	252020	632000	303520	266910	648080	312310	271220
Other Producers [i]	...	...	45100	...	...	51940	...	...	61570	...	...	64550
Total	4884980	2950690	1934290	5155380	3088250	2067130	6204720	3766440	2438280	6553170	3997690	2555480
Less: Imputed bank service charge	...	-70280	70280	...	-82040	82040	...	-105400	105400	...	-111240	111240
Import duties	...	...	15660	...	...	18190	...	...	25900	...	...	29280
Value added tax	...	...	138330	...	...	132720	...	...	161620	...	...	174080
Total	4884980	3020970	2018000	5155380	3170290	2136000	6204720	3871840	2520400	6553170	4108930	2647600

	1992 Gross Output	1992 Intermediate Consumption	1992 Value Added	1993 Gross Output	1993 Intermediate Consumption	1993 Value Added
		At constant prices of:1991				
		All Producers				
1 Agriculture, hunting, forestry and fishing	72400	34830	37570	69500	33490	36010
A Agriculture and hunting [a]	...	...	32370	...	...	...
B Forestry and logging [a]	...	...	5200	...	...	...
C Fishing [a]	...	...	...	...	...	...
2 Mining and quarrying [bc]	219850	145940	11960	...	...	...
A Coal mining	...	...	8540	...	...	...
B Crude petroleum and natural gas production	...	...	...	...	...	...
C Metal ore mining	...	...	...	...	...	...
D Other mining	...	...	3420	...	...	...
3 Manufacturing	2125890	1353620	772270	...	...	713090
A Manufacture of food, beverages and tobacco	...	...	77830	...	...	...
B Textile, wearing apparel and leather industries	...	...	26860	...	...	...
C Manufacture of wood and wood products, including furniture	...	...	26340	...	...	...
D Manufacture of paper and paper products, printing and publishing [d]	...	...	36980	...	...	...
E Manufacture of chemicals and chemical petroleum, coal, rubber and plastic products	...	...	139090	...	...	...
F Manufacture of non-metallic mineral products, except products of petroleum and coal [b]	...	...	30450	...	...	...
G Basic metal industries	...	...	55510	...	...	...
H Manufacture of fabricated metal products, machinery and equipment [e]	...	...	373950	...	...	...
I Other manufacturing industries	...	...	5260	...	...	...
4 Electricity, gas and water [c]	...	...	61950	...	...	...
A Electricity, gas and steam	...	...	...	...	...	...
B Water works and supply	...	...	...	...	...	...
5 Construction [e]	299350	158260	141090	...	...	139590
6 Wholesale and retail trade, restaurants and hotels [f]	1693210	1449070	277890	...	...	...
A Wholesale and retail trade	...	...	244140	...	...	239120
B Restaurants and hotels	...	...	33750	...	...	...
7 Transport, storage and communication	293340	142150	151190	...	...	152350
A Transport and storage	...	...	88250	...	...	...
B Communication	...	...	62940	...	...	...
8 Finance, insurance, real estate and business services	459750	129170	330580	...	...	345720
A Financial institutions [g]	221550	79580	111860	...	...	...
B Insurance [g]	...	...	30110	...	...	...
C Real estate and business services [h]	238200	49590	188610	...	...	195710
Real estate, except dwellings	...	...	...	...	...	...

Germany, Fed. Rep. of

4.2 Derivation of Value Added by Kind of Activity, in Constant Prices
(Continued)

Million Deutsche marks

	1992 Gross Output	1992 Intermediate Consumption	1992 Value Added	1993 Gross Output	1993 Intermediate Consumption	1993 Value Added
				At constant prices of:1991		
Dwellings	...	...	188610	...	...	195710
9 Community, social and personal services [d,h,f]	835860	325510	476600	...	...	...
Educational services	...	...	...	...	...	...
Medical, dental, other health and veterinary services	...	...	61550	...	...	...
Total, Industries	5999650	3738550	2261100	5827780	3607990	2219790
Producers of Government Services [i]	671350	328100	275910	668920	321670	278080
Other Producers [i]	...	...	67340	...	...	69170
Total	6671000	4066650	2604350	6496700	3929660	2567040
Less: Imputed bank service charge	...	-119900	119900	...	-125450	125450
Import duties	...	...	29220	...	...	27200
Value added tax	...	...	180630	...	...	179810
Total	6671000	4186550	2694300	6496700	4055110	2648600

a) Hunting and fishing are included in item 'Forestry and logging'.
b) Quarrying is included in item 'Manufacture of non-metalic mineral products except products of petroleum and coal'.
c) Gross output and intermediate consumption of electricity, gas and water are included in item 'Mining and quarrying'.
d) Publishing is included in item 'Community, social and personal services'.
e) Structural steel erection is included in item 'Manufacture of fabricated metal products, machinery and equipment'.
f) Gross output and intermediate consumption of restaurants and hotels are included in item 'Community, social and personal services'.
g) Gross output and intermediate consumption of insurance are included in item 'Financial institutions'.
h) Business services and real estate except dwellings are included in item 'Community, social and personal services'.
i) Gross output and intermediate consumption of 'Other producers' are included in item 'Producers of government services'.

4.3 Cost Components of Value Added

Million Deutsche marks

	1980 Compensation of Employees	1980 Capital Consumption	1980 Net Operating Surplus	1980 Indirect Taxes	1980 Less: Subsidies Received	1980 Value Added	1985 Compensation of Employees	1985 Capital Consumption	1985 Net Operating Surplus	1985 Indirect Taxes	1985 Less: Subsidies Received	1985 Value Added
						All Producers						
1 Agriculture, hunting, forestry and fishing	6220	9160	16140	-1000	...	30520	7100	10960	17220	-3360	...	31920
A Agriculture and hunting [a]	3280	8640	14020	-920	...	25020	3760	10300	15890	-3340	...	26610
B Forestry and logging [a]	2940	520	2120	-80	...	5500	3340	660	1330	-20	...	5310
C Fishing [a]	...	...	...	...	...	...	...	...	...	...	...	...
2 Mining and quarrying [b]	11590	2130	390	-1880	...	12230	13250	2840	1650	-1690	...	16050
A Coal mining	10710	1660	-170	-1950	...	10250	11760	2230	1250	-1770	...	13470
B Crude petroleum and natural gas production	...	...	...	...	...	...	...	...	...	...	...	...
C Metal ore mining	...	...	...	...	...	...	...	...	...	...	...	...
D Other mining	880	470	560	70	...	1980	1490	610	400	80	...	2580
3 Manufacturing	330490	48870	54080	42810	...	476250	387310	61530	83410	46600	...	578850
A Manufacture of food, beverages and tobacco	24480	5720	10410	14650	...	55260	27620	6880	11580	16730	...	62810
B Textile, wearing apparel and leather industries	18790	2530	2920	500	...	24740	18360	2620	3720	480	...	25180
C Manufacture of wood and wood products, including furniture	13190	1650	2210	400	...	17450	13390	1850	1410	260	...	16910
D Manufacture of paper and paper products, printing and publishing [c]	14800	2360	3030	450	...	20640	17250	3080	4430	540	...	25300
E Manufacture of chemicals and chemical petroleum, coal, rubber and plastic products	45350	10160	7640	21470	...	84620	58640	11960	14770	23070	...	108440
F Manufacture of non-metallic mineral products, except products of petroleum and coal [b]	14120	3140	3700	750	...	21710	14140	3520	2860	550	...	21070
G Basic metal industries	30770	5860	680	770	...	38080	32600	7050	4690	-210	...	44130
H Manufacture of fabricated metal products, machinery and equipment [d]	166930	17220	22600	3700	...	210450	203130	24250	38600	5070	...	271050
I Other manufacturing industries	2060	230	890	120	...	3300	2180	320	1350	110	...	3960
4 Electricity, gas and water	14560	9640	11080	1130	...	36410	18040	12990	17420	2030	...	50480
A Electricity, gas and steam	13300	8720	10390	1010	...	33420	16590	11850	16360	1950	...	46750
B Water works and supply	1260	920	690	120	...	2990	1450	1140	1060	80	...	3730

Germany, Fed. Rep. of

4.3 Cost Components of Value Added
(Continued)

Million Deutsche marks

	1980						1985					
	Compensation of Employees	Capital Consumption	Net Operating Surplus	Indirect Taxes	Less: Subsidies Received	Value Added	Compensation of Employees	Capital Consumption	Net Operating Surplus	Indirect Taxes	Less: Subsidies Received	Value Added
5 Construction [d]	65690	5130	27010	2060	...	99890	64800	5430	22930	1650	...	94810
6 Wholesale and retail trade, restaurants and hotels	96160	11620	43020	1350	...	152150	115050	14300	48280	900	...	178530
A Wholesale and retail trade	87570	10110	34830	740	...	133250	102990	12340	40840	240	...	156410
B Restaurants and hotels	8590	1510	8190	610	...	18900	12060	1960	7440	660	...	22120
7 Transport, storage and communication	54460	19590	16670	-5290	...	85430	62860	25400	22740	-5950	...	105050
A Transport and storage	35520	13030	9120	-5250	...	52420	40450	15310	13600	-5900	...	63460
B Communication	18940	6560	7550	-40	...	33010	22410	10090	9140	-50	...	41590
8 Finance, insurance, real estate and business services [e]	34160	39060	24480	6830	...	155930	43920	53510	43070	10860	...	231870
A Financial institutions	24240	2050	22710	2340	...	51340	32150	3250	38780	4730	...	78910
B Insurance	9920	720	1770	2610	...	15020	11770	1200	4290	4240	...	21500
C Real estate and business services [f]	...	36290	...	1880	...	89570	...	49060	...	1890	...	131460
Real estate, except dwellings	...	...	...	...	...	...	...	...	...	...	...	...
Dwellings	...	36290	...	1880	...	89570	...	49060	...	1890	...	131460
9 Community, social and personal services [cfe]	56380	17530	134410	6500	...	163420	75970	31860	201570	7950	...	236840
Educational services	...	...	...	...	...	...	...	...	...	...	...	...
Medical, dental, other health and veterinary services	9000	3440	19940	-80	...	32300	13770	5950	22080	-150	...	41650
Total, Industries [g]	669710	162730	327280	52510	...	1212230	788300	218820	458290	58990	...	1524400
Producers of Government Services	162450	9700	-	240	...	172390	193880	13120	-	260	...	207260
Other Producers	28720	2570	-	20	...	31310	39240	3420	-	20	...	42680
Total [g]	860880	175000	327280	52770	...	1415930	1021420	235360	458290	59270	...	1774340
Less: Imputed bank service charge	...	...	53940	...	...	53940	...	...	84260	...	...	84260
Import duties	...	...	...	13480	...	13480	...	...	...	16440	...	16440
Value added tax	...	...	...	96570	...	96570	...	...	...	116660	...	116660
Total [g]	860880	175000	273340	162820	...	1472040	1021420	235360	374030	192370	...	1823180

	1990						1991					
	Compensation of Employees	Capital Consumption	Net Operating Surplus	Indirect Taxes	Less: Subsidies Received	Value Added	Compensation of Employees	Capital Consumption	Net Operating Surplus	Indirect Taxes	Less: Subsidies Received	Value Added
					All Producers							
1 Agriculture, hunting, forestry and fishing	7430	11870	22020	-4580	...	36740	7960	12410	17420	-3910	...	33880
A Agriculture and hunting [a]	3610	11080	18680	-4450	...	28920	3910	11570	16890	-3860	...	28510
B Forestry and logging [a]	3820	790	3340	-130	...	7820	4050	840	530	-50	...	5370
C Fishing [a]	...	...	...	...	...	...	...	...	...	...	...	...
2 Mining and quarrying [b]	13320	3550	-1040	-4440	...	11390	13280	3440	-80	-4190	...	12450
A Coal mining	12010	2840	-1440	-4740	...	8670	11980	2690	-940	-4550	...	9180
B Crude petroleum and natural gas production	...	...	...	...	...	...	...	...	...	...	...	...
C Metal ore mining	...	...	...	...	...	...	...	...	...	...	...	...
D Other mining	1310	710	400	300	...	2720	1300	750	860	360	...	3270

Germany, Fed. Rep. of

4.3 Cost Components of Value Added
(Continued)

Million Deutsche marks

	1990						1991					
	Compensation of Employees	Capital Consumption	Net Operating Surplus	Indirect Taxes	Less: Subsidies Received	Value Added	Compensation of Employees	Capital Consumption	Net Operating Surplus	Indirect Taxes	Less: Subsidies Received	Value Added
3 Manufacturing	499730	76070	111000	54750	...	741550	534970	83090	111420	61330	...	790810
A Manufacture of food, beverages and tobacco	31980	7950	19810	18520	...	78260	35580	8630	16920	20990	...	82120
B Textile, wearing apparel and leather industries	19460	2890	5010	590	...	27950	19850	3060	4240	620	...	27770
C Manufacture of wood and wood products, including furniture	16560	1980	3830	470	...	22840	18360	2180	4920	530	...	25990
D Manufacture of paper and paper products, printing and publishing [c]	22850	4230	6290	750	...	34120	25210	4660	6430	810	...	37110
E Manufacture of chemicals and chemical petroleum, coal, rubber and plastic products	74960	14230	16060	27120	...	132370	78800	15320	12400	31580	...	138100
F Manufacture of non-metallic mineral products, except products of petroleum and coal [b]	17280	3840	5950	960	...	28030	18560	4190	6420	930	...	30100
G Basic metal industries	38590	6860	7910	1150	...	54510	40280	7220	6910	900	...	55310
H Manufacture of fabricated metal products, machinery and equipment [d]	275220	33650	44380	5040	...	358290	295380	37350	51530	4830	...	389090
I Other manufacturing industries	2830	440	1760	150	...	5180	2950	480	1650	140	...	5220
4 Electricity, gas and water	22040	16140	18780	1880	...	58840	24570	16860	17740	2500	...	61670
A Electricity, gas and steam	20410	14780	17380	1800	...	54370	23060	15420	16430	2500	...	57410
B Water works and supply	1630	1360	1400	80	...	4470	1510	1440	1310	-	...	4260
5 Construction [d]	84050	5470	35720	2380	...	127620	89960	5930	38740	2650	...	137280
6 Wholesale and retail trade, restaurants and hotels	152280	18190	71470	2710	...	244650	170800	20360	81280	4660	...	277100
A Wholesale and retail trade	135340	15760	59660	1790	...	212550	151830	17750	69540	3710	...	242830
B Restaurants and hotels	16940	2430	11810	920	...	32100	18970	2610	11740	950	...	34270
7 Transport, storage and communication	77890	32260	29260	-5210	...	134200	85410	35010	27690	-4290	...	143820
A Transport and storage	52210	17490	16610	-5170	...	81140	57500	18870	14090	-4280	...	86180
B Communication	25680	14770	12650	-40	...	53060	27910	16140	13600	-10	...	57640
8 Finance, insurance, real estate and business services [e]	60900	70670	39300	13050	...	288850	66600	77710	47990	15860	...	318130
A Financial institutions	45090	4380	37690	3830	...	90990	48610	4890	45940	5280	...	104720
B Insurance	15810	1780	1610	6310	...	25510	17990	2030	2050	7410	...	29480
C Real estate and business services [f]	...	64510	...	2910	...	172350	...	70790	...	3170	...	183930
Real estate, except dwellings	...	...	...	...	...	...	...	...	...	...	...	...
Dwellings	...	64510	...	2910	...	172350	...	70790	...	3170	...	183930
9 Community, social and personal services [cfe]	107610	47840	323850	12620	...	386990	123890	55400	361820	13430	...	444570
Educational services	...	...	...	...	...	...	...	...	...	...	...	...
Medical, dental, other health and veterinary services	17860	8090	26900	-170	...	52680	20610	9080	28930	-200	...	58420
Total, Industries [g]	1025250	282060	650360	73160	...	2030830	1117440	310210	704020	88040	...	2219710
Producers of Government Services	236290	16660	-	250	...	253200	252960	18010	-	250	...	271220
Other Producers	53980	4290	-	30	...	58300	59900	4620	-	30	...	64550
Total [g]	1315520	303010	650360	73440	...	2342330	1430300	332840	704020	88320	...	2555480
Less: Imputed bank service charge	...	...	96280	...	...	96280	...	...	111240	...	...	111240
Import duties	...	...	...	24980	...	24980	...	...	...	29280	...	29280
Value added tax	...	...	...	154970	...	154970	...	...	...	174080	...	174080
Total [g]	1315520	303010	554080	253390	...	2426000	1430300	332840	592780	291680	...	2647600

	1992						1993					
	Compensation of Employees	Capital Consumption	Net Operating Surplus	Indirect Taxes	Less: Subsidies Received	Value Added	Compensation of Employees	Capital Consumption	Net Operating Surplus	Indirect Taxes	Less: Subsidies Received	Value Added
	All Producers
1 Agriculture, hunting, forestry and fishing	8310	12960	15340	-3790	...	32820	8410	...	...	...	...	29290
A Agriculture and hunting [a]	3990	12060	15140	-3720	...	27470	...	...	...	...	...	...
B Forestry and logging [a]	4320	900	200	-70	...	5350	...	...	...	...	...	...
C Fishing [a]	...	...	...	...	...	...	...	...	...	...	...	...
2 Mining and quarrying [b]	13740	3380	-690	-3780	...	12650	...	...	...	...	...	...

Germany, Fed. Rep. of

4.3 Cost Components of Value Added
(Continued)

Million Deutsche marks

		1992						1993				
		Compensation of Employees	Capital Consumption	Net Operating Surplus	Indirect Taxes	Less: Subsidies Received	Value Added	Compensation of Employees	Capital Consumption	Net Operating Surplus	Indirect Taxes	Less: Subsidies Received	Value Added
	A Coal mining	12550	2580	-1600	-4260	...	9270	...	...	...	...	...	...
	B Crude petroleum and natural gas production	...	...	...	...	...	...	...	...	...	...	...	...
	C Metal ore mining	...	...	...	...	...	...	...	...	...	...	...	...
	D Other mining	1190	800	910	480	...	3380	...	...	...	...	...	...
3	Manufacturing	556330	88680	87760	67120	...	799890	541210	...	...	...	...	749040
	A Manufacture of food, beverages and tobacco	37120	9240	16000	21080	...	83440	...	...	...	...	...	...
	B Textile, wearing apparel and leather industries	19630	3180	4500	670	...	27980	...	...	...	...	...	...
	C Manufacture of wood and wood products, including furniture	18990	2360	5480	640	...	27470	...	...	...	...	...	...
	D Manufacture of paper and paper products, printing and publishing c	26390	4990	5460	850	...	37690	...	...	...	...	...	...
	E Manufacture of chemicals and chemical petroleum, coal, rubber and plastic products	82440	16210	9300	36680	...	144630	...	...	...	...	...	...
	F Manufacture of non-metallic mineral products, except products of petroleum and coal b	19640	4490	6740	1110	...	31980	...	...	...	...	...	...
	G Basic metal industries	40190	7530	5650	700	...	54070	...	...	...	...	...	...
	H Manufacture of fabricated metal products, machinery and equipment d	308970	40170	32690	5250	...	387080	...	...	...	...	...	...
	I Other manufacturing industries	2960	510	1940	140	...	5550	...	...	...	...	...	...
4	Electricity, gas and water	26320	17570	17450	2040	...	63380	...	...	...	...	...	...
	A Electricity, gas and steam	24770	...	...	...	...	...	...	...	...	...	...	...
	B Water works and supply	1550	...	...	...	...	...	...	...	...	...	...	...
5	Construction d	97240	6470	45480	3470	...	152660	100330	...	...	...	...	158590
6	Wholesale and retail trade, restaurants and hotels	187510	22700	71890	6280	...	288380	...	...	...	...	...	...
	A Wholesale and retail trade	165610	19950	61500	5250	...	252310	172030	...	...	...	...	247490
	B Restaurants and hotels	21900	2750	10390	1030	...	36070	...	...	...	...	...	...
7	Transport, storage and communication	91330	36670	30160	-4580	...	153580	91670	...	...	...	...	158110
	A Transport and storage	61170	19880	14250	-4590	...	90710	...	...	...	...	...	...
	B Communication	30160	16790	15910	10	...	62870	...	...	...	...	...	...
8	Finance, insurance, real estate and business services e	73120	84710	53250	19060	...	350230	76430	...	...	...	...	386330
	A Financial institutions	53010	5510	52720	5850	...	117090	...	...	...	...	...	...
	B Insurance	20110	2290	530	9650	...	32580	...	...	...	...	...	...
	C Real estate and business services f	...	76910	...	3560	...	200560	...	...	...	...	...	221750
	Real estate, except dwellings	...	...	...	...	...	...	...	...	...	...	...	...
	Dwellings	...	76910	...	3560	...	200560	...	...	...	...	...	221750
9	Community, social and personal services cde	137550	62280	410210	15660	...	505610	...	...	...	...	...	...
	Educational services	...	...	...	...	...	...	...	...	...	...	...	...
	Medical, dental, other health and veterinary services	22880	9950	32220	-260	...	64790	...	...	...	...	...	...
Total, Industries g		1191450	335420	730850	101480	...	2359200	1201810	353450	722850	102670	...	2380780
Producers of Government Services		269770	19340	-	250	...	289360	278940	20520	-	250	...	299710
Other Producers		65910	4930	-	40	...	70880	69640	5190	-	40	...	74870
Total g		1527130	359690	730850	101770	...	2719440	1550390	379160	722850	102960	...	2755360
Less: Imputed bank service charge		...	...	124070	...	...	124070	...	...	133110	...	...	133110
Import duties		...	...	...	30570	...	30570	...	...	...	28820	...	28820
Value added tax		...	...	...	187060	...	187060	...	...	...	202630	...	202630
Total g		1527130	359690	606780	319400	...	2813000	1550390	379160	589740	334410	...	2853700

a) Hunting and fishing are included in item 'Forestry and logging'.
b) Quarrying is included in item 'Manufacture of non-metalic mineral products except products of petroleum and coal'.
c) Publishing is included in item 'Community, social and personal services'.
d) Structural steel erection is included in item 'Manufacture of fabricated metal products, machinery and equipment'.
e) Dwelling is excluded from columns 1 and 3 of item 'Finance, insurance, real estate and business services' and is included in columns 1 and 3 of item 'Community, social and personal services'.
f) Business services and real estate except dwellings are included in item 'Community, social and personal services'.
g) Column 4 refers to indirect taxes less subsidies received.

Ghana

General note. The preparation of national accounts statistics in Ghana is undertaken by the Central Bureau of Statistics, Accra. The official estimates are published by the bureau in the 'Economic Survey'. A detailed description of the sources and methods used for the national accounts estimation is contained in the publications 'Sources and Methods of Estimation of National Income at Current Prices in Ghana' and 'National Income of Ghana at Constant Prices'. The estimates are generally in accordance with the classifications and definitions recommended in the United Nations System of National Accounts (SNA). Work relating to input-output analysis is being done at present. The following tables have been prepared from successive replies to the United Nations national accounts questionnaire. When the scope and coverage of the estimates differ for conceptual or statistical reasons from the definitions and classifications recommended in SNA, a footnote is indicated to the relevant tables.

Sources and methods:

(a) Gross domestic product. Gross domestic product is estimated mainly through the production approach.

(b) Expenditure on the gross domestic product. Gross fixed capital formation is estimated by using the commodity-flow approach. A combination of commodity-flow and expenditure approach is used for increase in stock. Private consumption expenditure is treated as a residual. Gross fixed capital formation is classified according to type of capital goods and not according to kind of economic activity. The estimates of increase in stocks are mainly based on special inquiries into the stocks held by selected kinds of producers and distributors. Adjustment is made to arrive at estimates on the equivalent of physical changes in the stocks, valued at average market prices during the period of account. Government consumption expenditure is estimated on a cash basis from government records. These records are reclassified according to government purposes. It is feasible to distinguish between acquisition for military purposes and for civilian purposes which exclude durable goods. Sales of goods and services by government to the public are subtracted from total expenditure. Exports and imports of goods and services are mainly estimated from foreign trade statistics of merchandise trade supplemented by information from the Central Bank. For the constant price estimates, no specific information is available for government consumption expenditure, but wages and salaries paid by government are extrapolated by index numbers of employment. For gross capital formation, current values are deflated by appropriate price indexes. In the case of commodity trade, current values are deflated by Paasche indexes of prices specially prepared for this purpose. Private consumption expenditure is obtained as a residual.

(c) Cost-structure of the gross domestic product. In estimating the cost structure components of GDP, the perpetual inventory method is used for estimating consumption of fixed capital. Indirect taxes net of subsidies are obtained by analysing the taxes on production and expenditure in the revenue account of the government. The domestic factor income is obtained as a residual.

(d) Gross domestic product by kind of economic activity. The table of GDP by kind of economic activity is prepared at market prices i.e., producers values. The value added of the majority of industries is estimated through the production approach. A combination of the commodity-flow approach and the expenditure approach is used for the construction sector. For the agricultural sector, statistics of the Ghana Cocoa Marketing Board is the main source of information for the estimation of cocoa, which is the most important crop in Ghana. For other principal crops, information is collected through annual sample surveys. The production of crop is estimated as the product of area sown and yield per acre. The intermediate consumption is estimated on the basis of a small-scale survey in 1969 and projected on the basis of movements in acreage and prices of the crops. Data on gross output of forestry and logging are obtained from the Forestry Department while for intermediate consumption, a small-scale sample survey has been carried out in a bench-mark year and a constant input ratio applied for subsequent years. Annual establishment surveys are undertaken on a census basis for mining, large-scale manufacturing and electricity and water supply. In the case of manufacturing, the surveys provide detailed information on inputs and outputs for commodity-flow purposes. A sample survey was carried out in 1963 for small-scale and medium-scale manufacturing. The data collected formed the basis for the estimates in the subsequent years by using per worker input and output in the bench-mark year and projected employment data, extrapolated from population census. For the construction sector, data on works undertaken by the government are obtained by analysing the government accounts. Information on domestic production, imports and exports of construction materials, trade and transport margins and cost-composition of the total expenditure are available to prepare estimates of gross output. The gross margins of wholesale and retail trade estimates are based partly on spotchecks in a bench-mark year and partly on sample survey, while gross receipts and intermediate consumption estimates are based on income tax records and annual surveys. For the services sectors, information is generally obtained from the institutions concerned. The rental value of residential dwellings are imputed on the basis of cost components, estimated from the record of the Ministry of Local Government. For the constant price estimates, the general approach used for agriculture, industrial activity, electricity, gas and water and construction sectors is double deflation. The value added of the trade, transport and financial services is extrapolated by quantity indexes. Different kinds of price indexes are used to deflate the value added of restaurants and hotels as well as the education and recreational services.

1.1 Expenditure on the Gross Domestic Product, in Current Prices

Million Ghanaian cedis

	1980	1983	1984	1985	1986	1987	1988	1989	1990	1991	1992	1993
1 Government final consumption expenditure	4784	10787	19641	32241	56600	74700	104800	145500	222000	294200	400100	...
2 Private final consumption expenditure	35953	167147	233023	284621	415400	610400	834300	1186700	1736100	2159400	2544300	...
3 Gross capital formation [a]	2410	6901	18607	32828	47800	77900	114900	192000	249100	328000	388000	...
A Increase in stocks [a]	-203	-21	65	139	300	600	800	1000	1400	1600	1900	...
B Gross fixed capital formation	2613	6922	18542	32689	47500	77300	114100	191000	247700	326400	386100	...
Residential buildings	1627	4750	10494	17205	...	...	...	...	...	...	...	...
Non-residential buildings					...	...	...	...	...	...	...	...
Other construction and land improvement etc. [b]	234	381	1096	3291	...	...	...	...	...	...	...	...
Other	752	1791	6952	12192	...	...	...	...	...	...	...	...
4 Exports of goods and services	3628	10225	20161	33185	81800	157800	217700	292000	312600	404700	482900	...
5 Less: Imports of goods and services	3923	11022	20871	39826	90400	174700	220600	398900	488000	611500	806400	...
Equals: Gross Domestic Product	42854	184038	270561	343048	511400	746000	1051200	1417200	2031700	2574800	3008800	...

a) Cocoa is valued at cost to the Ghana Cocoa Marketing Board. Stocks of other export commodities, including minerals, are valued at export prices.
b) Other construction includes expenditure on mining development but excludes minor engineering construction done by the private sector.

1.2 Expenditure on the Gross Domestic Product, in Constant Prices

Million Ghanaian cedis

	1980	1983	1984	1985	1986	1987	1988	1989	1990	1991	1992	1993
	\multicolumn{12}{c}{At constant prices of:1975}
1 Government final consumption expenditure	982	990	862	835	850	...	...	...	...	...	...	...
2 Private final consumption expenditure	4253	3443	3917	4181	4321	...	...	...	...	...	...	...
3 Gross capital formation [a]	491	344	393	490	475	...	...	...	...	...	...	...
A Increase in stocks [a]	-26	-1	1	1	2	...	...	...	...	...	...	...
B Gross fixed capital formation	516	344	392	489	473	...	...	...	...	...	...	...

Ghana

1.2 Expenditure on the Gross Domestic Product, in Constant Prices
(Continued)

Million Ghanaian cedis

	1980	1983	1984	1985	1986	1987	1988	1989	1990	1991	1992	1993
At constant prices of: 1975												
Residential buildings	288	175	202	189	167	...	...	...	...	...	...	...
Non-residential buildings						...	...	...	...	...	...	...
Other construction and land improvement etc. b	42	14	21	36	40	...	...	...	...	...	...	...
Other	186	155	169	264	266	...	...	...	...	...	...	...
4 Exports of goods and services	655	373	409	435	616	...	...	...	...	...	...	...
5 Less: Imports of goods and services	842	402	423	522	560	...	...	...	...	...	...	...
Equals: Gross Domestic Product	5538	4747	5158	5420	5702	...	...	...	...	...	...	...

a) Cocoa is valued at cost to the Ghana Cocoa Marketing Board. Stocks of other export commodities, including minerals, are valued at export prices.   b) Other construction includes expenditure on mining development but excludes minor engineering construction done by the private sector.

1.3 Cost Components of the Gross Domestic Product

Million Ghanaian cedis

	1980	1983	1984	1985	1986	1987	1988	1989	1990	1991	1992	1993
1 Indirect taxes, net	2116	6704	13819	24137	46955	...	...	...	...	...	...	...
2 Consumption of fixed capital	1512	4197	11206	16339	29267	...	...	...	...	...	...	...
3 Compensation of employees paid by resident producers to:	2274	3743	5282	14964	27896	...	...	...	...	...	...	...
4 Operating surplus	...	...	...	...	...	...	...	...	...	...	...	...
Equals: Gross Domestic Product	42854	184038	270561	343048	550515	...	...	...	...	...	...	...

1.7 External Transactions on Current Account, Summary

Million Ghanaian cedis

	1980	1983	1984	1985	1986	1987	1988	1989	1990	1991	1992	1993
Payments to the Rest of the World												
1 Imports of goods and services	3923	11022	20871	39826	69881	...	...	...	...	...	...	...
A Imports of merchandise c.i.f.	3343	11546	16495	32808	48833	...	...	...	...	...	...	...
B Other	580	5482	4376	7018	21048	...	...	...	...	...	...	...
2 Factor income to the rest of the world	189	1644	3707	5867	12648	...	...	...	...	...	...	...
3 Current transfers to the rest of the world	27	320	385	511	1080	...	...	...	...	...	...	...
4 Surplus of the nation on current transactions	-258	-237	2961	-4989	14507	...	...	...	...	...	...	...
Payments to the Rest of the World and Surplus of the Nation on Current Transactions	3880	12749	27924	41215	98116	...	...	...	...	...	...	...
Receipts From The Rest of the World												
1 Exports of goods and services	3628	10225	20161	33185	76948	...	...	...	...	...	...	...
A Exports of merchandise f.o.b.	3334	8782	18963	32070	73768	...	...	...	...	...	...	...
B Other	294	1443	1198	1115	3180	...	...	...	...	...	...	...
2 Factor income from rest of the world	7	4	65	98	72	...	...	...	...	...	...	...
3 Current transfers from rest of the world	246	2520	7698	7933	21096	...	...	...	...	...	...	...
Receipts from the Rest of the World on Current Transactions	3880	12749	27924	41216	98116	...	...	...	...	...	...	...

1.8 Capital Transactions of The Nation, Summary

Million Ghanaian cedis

	1980	1983	1984	1985	1986	1987	1988	1989	1990	1991	1992	1993
Finance of Gross Capital Formation												
Gross saving	2153	6664	21568	27839	63935	...	...	...	...	...	...	...
1 Consumption of fixed capital	1512	4197	11206	16339	29267	...	...	...	...	...	...	...
2 Net saving	641	2467	10363	11500	34668	...	...	...	...	...	...	...
Less: Surplus of the nation on current transactions	-258	-237	2961	-4988	14507	...	...	...	...	...	...	...
Finance of Gross Capital Formation	2410	6901	18607	32827	49428	...	...	...	...	...	...	...
Gross Capital Formation												
Increase in stocks	-203	-21	65	139	340	...	...	...	...	...	...	...
Gross fixed capital formation	2613	6922	18542	32689	49088	...	...	...	...	...	...	...
Gross Capital Formation	2410	6901	18607	32828	49428	...	...	...	...	...	...	...

Ghana

1.10 Gross Domestic Product by Kind of Activity, in Current Prices

Million Ghanaian cedis

	1980	1983	1984	1985	1986	1987	1988	1989	1990	1991	1992	1993
1 Agriculture, hunting, forestry and fishing	24821	109927	133232	154003	244317	...	...	...	...	...	...	...
2 Mining and quarrying	462	1944	3214	3822	8783	...	...	...	...	...	...	...
3 Manufacturing	3346	7101	17306	39562	61864	...	...	...	...	...	...	...
4 Electricity, gas and water	223	358	2166	4045	8957	...	...	...	...	...	...	...
5 Construction	1055	2796	5945	9780	12962	...	...	...	...	...	...	...
6 Wholesale and retail trade, restaurants and hotels	7327	43120	76544	85031	125520	...	...	...	...	...	...	...
7 Transport, storage and communication	1130	7663	17451	18329	25333	...	...	...	...	...	...	...
8 Finance, insurance, real estate and business services	1314	3311	4676	7746	18381	...	...	...	...	...	...	...
9 Community, social and personal services	206	636	1051	2289	4420	...	...	...	...	...	...	...
Total, Industries	39884	176856	261584	324608	510537	...	...	...	...	...	...	...
Producers of Government Services	3136	7822	9141	18701	36831	...	...	...	...	...	...	...
Other Producers	88	212	206	277	489	...	...	...	...	...	...	...
Subtotal	43108	184890	270931	343586	547857	...	...	...	...	...	...	...
Less: Imputed bank service charge	651	2259	2865	5323	6903	...	...	...	...	...	...	...
Plus: Import duties	397	1407	2494	4786	9561	...	...	...	...	...	...	...
Plus: Value added tax	...	...	...	...	...	...	...	...	...	...	...	...
Equals: Gross Domestic Product	42854	184038	270561	343048	550515	...	...	...	...	...	...	...

1.11 Gross Domestic Product by Kind of Activity, in Constant Prices

Million Ghanaian cedis

	1980	1983	1984	1985	1986	1987	1988	1989	1990	1991	1992	1993
					At constant prices of:1975							
1 Agriculture, hunting, forestry and fishing	2957	2533	2780	2798	2890	...	...	...	...	...	...	...
2 Mining and quarrying	71	52	59	63	61	...	...	...	...	...	...	...
3 Manufacturing	575	328	370	460	511	...	...	...	...	...	...	...
4 Electricity, gas and water	43	41	39	46	55	...	...	...	...	...	...	...
5 Construction	206	129	132	135	132	...	...	...	...	...	...	...
6 Wholesale and retail trade, restaurants and hotels	556	463	510	580	632	...	...	...	...	...	...	...
7 Transport, storage and communication	166	192	217	235	248	...	...	...	...	...	...	...
8 Finance, insurance, real estate and business services	372	414	453	465	500	...	...	...	...	...	...	...
9 Community, social and personal services	35	41	49	63	77	...	...	...	...	...	...	...
Total, Industries	4980	4193	4608	4845	5106	...	...	...	...	...	...	...
Producers of Government Services	609	660	663	693	710	...	...	...	...	...	...	...
Other Producers	28	27	25	25	27	...	...	...	...	...	...	...
Subtotal	5617	4880	5296	5563	5843	...	...	...	...	...	...	...
Less: Imputed bank service charge	160	177	191	206	218	...	...	...	...	...	...	...
Plus: Import duties	81	44	53	63	77	...	...	...	...	...	...	...
Plus: Value added tax	...	...	...	...	...	...	...	...	...	...	...	...
Equals: Gross Domestic Product	5538	4747	5158	5420	5702	...	...	...	...	...	...	...

1.12 Relations Among National Accounting Aggregates

Million Ghanaian cedis

	1980	1983	1984	1985	1986	1987	1988	1989	1990	1991	1992	1993
Gross Domestic Product	42854	184038	270561	343048	511400	746000	1051200	1417200	2031700	2574800	3008800	...
Plus: Net factor income from the rest of the world	-182	-1640	-3642	-5768	-12576	-20500	-26500	-28200	-36700	-43900	-46400	...
Factor income from the rest of the world	7	4	65	98	72	...	...	...	...	...	...	...
Less: Factor income to the rest of the world	189	1644	3707	5867	12648	...	...	...	...	...	...	...
Equals: Gross National Product	42671	182398	266918	337280	498824	725500	1024700	1389000	1995000	2530900	2962400	...
Less: Consumption of fixed capital	1512	4197	11206	16339	29267	47600	68800	86100	110700	131000	156400	...

Ghana

1.12 Relations Among National Accounting Aggregates
(Continued)

Million Ghanaian cedis

	1980	1983	1984	1985	1986	1987	1988	1989	1990	1991	1992	1993
Equals: National Income	41159	178201	255713	320941	469557	677900	955900	1302900	1884300	2399900	2806000	...
Plus: Net current transfers from the rest of the world	219	2200	7313	7421	20016	...	...	...	...	...	...	...
Current transfers from the rest of the world	246	2520	7698	7933	21096	...	...	...	...	...	...	...
Less: Current transfers to the rest of the world	27	320	385	511	1080	...	...	...	...	...	...	...
Equals: National Disposable Income	41379	180401	263026	328362	489573	...	...	...	...	...	...	...
Less: Final consumption	40738	177934	252664	316862	471996	...	...	...	...	...	...	...
Equals: Net Saving	641	2467	10363	11500	17577	...	...	...	...	...	...	...
Less: Surplus of the nation on current transactions	-258	-237	2961	-4989	14507	...	...	...	...	...	...	...
Equals: Net Capital Formation	899	2704	7402	16489	3070	...	...	...	...	...	...	...

2.17 Exports and Imports of Goods and Services, Detail

Million Ghanaian cedis

		1980	1983	1984	1985	1986	1987	1988	1989	1990	1991	1992	1993
	Exports of Goods and Services												
1	Exports of merchandise, f.o.b.	3334	8782	18963	32070	73768	...	...	...	...	...	...	...
2	Transport and communication	35	382	792	707	1716	...	...	...	...	...	...	...
3	Insurance service charges	...	...	...	...	...	...	...	...	...	...	...	...
4	Other commodities	259	1061	407	408	1464	...	...	...	...	...	...	...
5	Adjustments of merchandise exports to change-of-ownership basis	...	...	...	...	...	...	...	...	...	...	...	...
6	Direct purchases in the domestic market by non-residential households	...	...	...	...	...	...	...	...	...	...	...	...
7	Direct purchases in the domestic market by extraterritorial bodies	...	...	...	...	...	...	...	...	...	...	...	...
	Total Exports of Goods and Services	3628	10225	20161	33185	76948	...	...	...	...	...	...	...
	Imports of Goods and Services												
1	Imports of merchandise, c.i.f.	3343	11546	16495	32808	48833	...	...	...	...	...	...	...
	A Imports of merchandise, f.o.b.	3106	10622	14566	29649	40733	...	...	...	...	...	...	...
	B Transport of services on merchandise imports	237	924	1929	3159	8100	...	...	...	...	...	...	...
	C Insurance service charges on merchandise imports	...	...	...	...	...	...	...	...	...	...	...	...
2	Adjustments of merchandise imports to change-of-ownership basis	...	...	...	...	...	...	...	...	...	...	...	...
3	Other transport and communication	228	2442	1717	2719	6300	...	...	...	...	...	...	...
4	Other insurance service charges	...	...	...	...	...	...	...	...	...	...	...	...
5	Other commodities	352	3040	2660	4300	14748	...	...	...	...	...	...	...
6	Direct purchases abroad by government	...	...	...	...	...	...	...	...	...	...	...	...
7	Direct purchases abroad by resident households	...	...	...	...	...	...	...	...	...	...	...	...
	Total Imports of Goods and Services	3923	11022	20871	39826	69881	...	...	...	...	...	...	...
	Balance of Goods and Services	-294	-797	-710	-6641	7067	...	...	...	...	...	...	...
	Total Imports and Balance of Goods and Services	3628	10225	20161	33185	76948	...	...	...	...	...	...	...

Greece

General note. The preparation of national accounts statistics in Greece is undertaken by the National Accounts Service, Ministry of National Economy, Athens. Official estimates are published in a series of reports entitled 'National Accounts of Greece'. The estimates are generally in accordance with the classifications and definitions recommended in the United Nations System of National Accounts (SNA). Input-output tables have been published for the years 1958 and 1970 in 'National Accounts of Greece 1970-1976'. The following tables have been prepared from successive replies to the United Nations national accounts questionnaire. When the scope and coverage of the estimates differ for conceptual or statistical reasons from the definitions and classifications recommended in SNA, a footnote is indicated to the relevant tables.

Sources and methods:

(a) Gross domestic product. Gross domestic product is estimated mainly through the production approach.

(b) Expenditure on the gross domestic product. The expenditure approach is used to estimate government final consumption expenditure and exports and imports of goods and services. This approach, in combination with the commodity-flow approach, is also used to estimate gross capital formation. Private final consumption expenditure is estimated on the basis of the direct expenditure approach. The estimates of government final consumption expenditure are obtained from the accounts of the different government units. For private consumption expenditure, sources include the household budget surveys, tax statistics and other statistical sources. In estimating increase in stocks, delayed information from the manufacturing and mining surveys is used to supplement the commodity-flow method. Estimates of investments in private buildings are based on building permits that have been issued, while for the public sector construction, estimates are derived from government budgetary accounts and replies from public enterprises and public funds. Information from the annual manufacturing and mining surveys as well as investments by large industrial units, public enterprises and public funds are used for machinery and equipment. Own-account construction is covered by information on loans granted for such construction works. For exports and imports of goods and services, foreign trade statistics based on the special trade principle are used. For the constant price estimates, price indices are used to deflate the wages and salaries of government employees. For the private expenditure, the annual quantities of food, fuel, light and water charges are multiplied by average base-year prices. Expenditure on other private goods and services are deflated by appropriate price indexes. Value added of residential and non-residential buildings is extrapolated by specially constructed indicators. For other components of gross capital formation, price deflation is used. The base-year values of exports and imports of merchandise are extrapolated by volume indexes while other goods and services are deflated by mean value index of exports and imports.

(c) Cost-structure of the gross domestic product. Estimates of compensation of employees for various services such as finance, insurance and transport are estimated by using data derived from questionnaires sent to them by the National Accounts Service. For manufacturing and mining, data are derived from the annual industrial surveys. The employers' contributions are estimated by using data derived from statements of the social insurance funds. Capital consumption is estimated as a percentage of the corresponding capital stock figure for each industry and type of assests. The current-price estimates of capital stock and depreciation are calculated on a replacement cost basis. The estimates of indirect taxes and subsidies are obtained from government accounts. Operating surplus is calculated as a residual.

(d) Gross domestic product by kind of economic activity. The table of gross domestic product by kind of economic activity is prepared in factor values. The production approach is used to estimate value added of most industries. The income approach is used for lignite mining, electricity, gas and water and parts of the service sectors such as transportation, communication, health and education, and miscellaneous services. For agricultural and animal breeding, the estimate of production is based on annual surveys conducted by the National Statistical Office of Greece. Intermediate consumption estimates are based on data taken from various sources such as Ministry of Agriculture and the Pubic Power Corporation. Agricultural product prices refer to prices obtained by farmers. The estimates of mining and quarrying and manufacturing are based on the annual survey of industrial establishments. The information from the survey is available within 2-3 years, meanwhile, value added is extrapolated by the index of industrial production and the wholesale price index. Value added of electricity, gas and water is estimated on the basis of annual questionnaires sent to the concerned enterprises. For construction, gross value is obtained from investment data of buildings and other construction to which values of military construction and repairs are added. The estimates of gross trade margins for agricultural products are based on traded quantities valued at the difference between consumers' and producers' prices. For industrial and imported products, percentages of gross trade margins are applied to the traded values at current prices. Intermediate consumption estimates are based on a survey conducted in 1970 for the compilation of the input-output table. Value added of transport and communication and finance and insurance services is based on data compiled through questionnaires sent to the concerned enterprises. For ownership of dwellings, the estimation of real or imputed rent is carried out at constant prices, based on the number of dwelling rooms existing and the average annual rent expenditure in a bench-mark year. These data are obtained from dwelling censuses and household budget surveys. Estimates concerning government services are obtained from general government accounts. For private health and educational services, only wages and salaries data are available. Value added of hotel is based on surveys conducted every three years by the National Accounts Service, while that of restaurants is based on data obtained from household budget surveys. For other services, employment data as well as data on average remuneration per person employed or data derived from taxation returns are used. For the constant price estimates, double deflation is used for agriculture and electricity. For water, construction, transport and hotels, value added is extrapolated by quantity indicators. For the remaining sectors of the industries, price deflation is used.

1.1 Expenditure on the Gross Domestic Product, in Current Prices

Thousand Million Greek drachmas

	1980	1983	1984	1985	1986	1987	1988	1989	1990	1991	1992	1993
1 Government final consumption expenditure	280	579	743	942	1067	1225	1530	1819	2251	2555	2925	3201
2 Private final consumption expenditure	1105	2054	2461	3025	3719	4356	5153	6158	7498	9112	10669	12148
3 Gross capital formation	489	673	739	983	1093	1103	1464	1839	2101	2612	2907	3100
A Increase in stocks	76	49	36	103	75	28	145	148	29	236	211	190
B Gross fixed capital formation	414	624	703	880	1018	1075	1318	1690	2072	2376	2696	2910
Residential buildings	138	163	152	178	248	287	329	403	555	560	551	604
Non-residential buildings	59	73	88	96	125	141	195	221	267	293	321	353
Other construction and land improvement etc.	71	133	174	235	246	215	266	337	376	528	632	646
Other	147	255	289	371	399	432	528	729	874	995	1192	1306
4 Exports of goods and services [a]	358	609	825	978	1233	1537	1801	2019	2279	2906	3438	3709
5 Less: Imports of goods and services	449	925	1139	1514	1703	1993	2291	2810	3445	4253	4898	5419
Statistical discrepancy	-72	89	177	203	106	45	-84	-220	-132	-42	-209	21
Equals: Gross Domestic Product	1711	3079	3806	4618	5515	6272	7572	8805	10551	12889	14832	16760

a) Data on Exports of goods and services as well as transport, storage and communication exclude income from ocean-going cargo ships under Greek flag or ownership. However, remittances actually received by the bank of Greece from persons engaged in these enterprises are included in factor income from the rest of the world.

1.2 Expenditure on the Gross Domestic Product, in Constant Prices

Million Greek drachmas

	1980	1983	1984	1985	1986	1987	1988	1989	1990	1991	1992	1993
	\multicolumn{12}{c}{At constant prices of: 1970}
1 Government final consumption expenditure	68940	77400	79760	82300	81626	82348	87078	89960	91948	93742	94589	95462
2 Private final consumption expenditure	319341	339425	345194	358671	361026	365473	378488	394942	403194	412458	420028	420585
3 Gross capital formation	111985	89148	82063	92509	86039	75569	92542	95777	94654	100079	101266	98099
A Increase in stocks	19280	6148	3763	10149	8805	2254	12711	7904	-1485	8353	8126	6807
B Gross fixed capital formation	92705	83000	78300	82360	77234	73315	79831	87873	96139	91726	93140	91292

Greece

1.2 Expenditure on the Gross Domestic Product, in Constant Prices
(Continued)

Million Greek drachmas

	1980	1983	1984	1985	1986	1987	1988	1989	1990	1991	1992	1993
	At constant prices of:1970											
Residential buildings	27291	21124	17083	17097	19399	20044	20691	21742	24646	20912	18396	17766
Non-residential buildings	11622	9529	9848	9241	9752	9849	12257	11901	11878	10965	10711	10385
Other construction and land improvement etc.	15674	15396	15962	17883	14737	11812	12603	13699	13194	15675	16784	15174
Other	38118	36951	35407	38139	33346	31610	34280	40531	46421	44174	47249	47967
4 Exports of goods and services [a]	88563	83488	97628	98882	112766	130789	142516	144429	145719	169651	183241	197694
5 Less: Imports of goods and services	97373	115110	115350	130120	135066	157447	170066	188441	210982	238802	252547	263976
Statistical discrepancy	-17946	3200	1401	3769	7823	15106	4063	16873	23775	28888	24104	25997
Equals: Gross Domestic Product	473510	477551	490696	506011	514214	511838	534621	553540	548308	566016	570681	573861

a) Data on Exports of goods and services as well as transport, storage and communication exclude income from ocean-going cargo ships under Greek flag or ownership. However, remittances actually received by the bank of Greece from persons engaged in these enterprises are included in factor income from the rest of the world.

1.3 Cost Components of the Gross Domestic Product

Thousand Million Greek drachmas

	1980	1983	1984	1985	1986	1987	1988	1989	1990	1991	1992	1993
1 Indirect taxes, net	187	346	443	481	642	794	952	967	1332	1817	2301	2338
A Indirect taxes	229	...	...	...	...	...	...	...	...	...	...	...
B Less: Subsidies	42	...	...	...	...	...	...	...	...	...	...	...
2 Consumption of fixed capital	142	273	329	403	505	578	662	793	942	1108	1276	1447
3 Compensation of employees paid by resident producers to: [a]	647	1249	1533	1916	2165	2436	2978	3600	4376	4936	5455	6005
A Resident households [a]	645	1243	1526	1910	2157	2425	2965	3581	4356	4915	5422	6005
B Rest of the world	3	7	6	6	8	10	14	19	19	22	33	40
4 Operating surplus [a]	734	1211	1501	1818	2202	2464	2981	3445	3901	5027	5800	6931
Equals: Gross Domestic Product	1711	3079	3806	4618	5515	6272	7572	8805	10551	12889	14832	16760

a) Compensation of employees paid by resident producers to resident households excludes wages paid to agricultural workers which are included in item 'Operating surplus'.

1.4 General Government Current Receipts and Disbursements

Thousand Million Greek drachmas

	1980	1983	1984	1985	1986	1987	1988	1989	1990	1991	1992	1993
	Receipts											
1 Operating surplus	...	...	...	...	...	...	...	...	...	...	...	...
2 Property and entrepreneurial income	40	54	75	94	91	113	96	126	195	225	439	488
3 Taxes, fees and contributions	477	968	1228	1488	1848	2142	2460	2767	3654	4577	5457	6182
A Indirect taxes	229	465	579	705	911	1091	1228	1325	1805	2322	2874	3083
B Direct taxes [a]	95	168	226	259	336	378	449	465	651	811	898	1033
C Social security contributions	154	334	423	524	601	672	784	978	1198	1444	1685	2066
D Compulsory fees, fines and penalties [a]	...	...	...	...	...	...	...	...	...	...	...	...
4 Other current transfers	4	12	21	15	18	18	23	28	35	88	53	66
Total Current Receipts of General Government	521	1034	1325	1597	1956	2273	2580	2922	3885	4890	5949	6735
	Disbursements											
1 Government final consumption expenditure	280	579	743	942	1067	1225	1530	1819	2251	2555	2925	3201
A Compensation of employees	196	398	505	648	730	840	1032	1282	1582	1788	...	...
B Consumption of fixed capital	...	...	...	...	...	...	...	...	...	...	...	...
C Purchases of goods and services, net	...	...	...	...	...	...	...	...	...	...	...	...
D Less: Own account fixed capital formation	...	...	...	...	...	...	...	...	...	...	...	...
E Indirect taxes paid, net	...	...	...	...	...	...	...	...	...	...	...	...
2 Property income	41	113	173	247	316	449	592	729	1193	1564	1927	2535
3 Subsidies	42	66	77	138	154	152	122	144	176	151	138	180
4 Other current transfers	160	417	537	690	826	940	1103	1364	1612	2040	2270	2673
A Social security benefits	158	412	533	686	821	936	1098	1359	1607	2034	2263	2662
B Social assistance grants	...	...	...	...	...	...	...	...	...	...	...	...
C Other	2	5	4	4	5	4	5	5	6	6	7	11
5 Net saving	-1	-142	-205	-420	-407	-493	-767	-1134	-1348	-1420	-1311	-1853
Total Current Disbursements and Net Saving of General Government	521	1034	1325	1597	1956	2273	2580	2922	3885	4890	5949	6735

a) Item 'Fees, fines and penalties' is included in item 'Direct taxes'.

Greece

1.6 Current Income and Outlay of Households and Non-Profit Institutions

Thousand Million Greek drachmas

	1980	1983	1984	1985	1986	1987	1988	1989	1990	1991	1992	1993
Receipts												
1 Compensation of employees [a]	671	1287	1575	1963	2204	2480	3007	3628	4405	4983	5525	6160
A From resident producers [a]	645	1243	1526	1910	2157	2425	2965	3581	4356	4915	5422	6005
B From rest of the world	26	45	48	53	47	55	42	47	48	68	103	155
2 Operating surplus of private unincorporated enterprises	...	...	...	...	...	...	...	...	...	...	...	...
3 Property and entrepreneurial income [b]	748	1233	1516	1839	2238	2592	3290	3814	4638	5978	6784	8517
4 Current transfers	204	494	637	796	958	1122	1343	1585	1879	2427	2710	3219
A Social security benefits	158	412	533	686	821	936	1098	1359	1607	2034	2263	2662
B Social assistance grants	...	...	...	...	...	...	...	...	...	...	...	...
C Other	46	82	104	110	137	186	245	226	272	393	447	556
Total Current Receipts	1623	3015	3728	4598	5400	6194	7640	9028	10921	13388	15019	17896
Disbursements												
1 Private final consumption expenditure	1105	2054	2461	3025	3719	4356	5153	6158	7498	9112	10669	12148
2 Property income	...	...	...	...	...	...	...	...	...	...	...	...
3 Direct taxes and other current transfers n.e.c. to general government	228	472	606	731	854	950	1132	1322	1665	1964	2201	2659
A Social security contributions	154	334	423	524	601	672	784	978	1198	1444	1685	2066
B Direct taxes	74	138	183	208	253	278	348	344	466	520	516	593
C Fees, fines and penalties	...	...	...	...	...	...	...	...	...	...	...	...
4 Other current transfers	5	12	21	15	18	18	23	28	35	88	53	66
Statistical discrepancy	-72	89	177	203	106	45	-84	-220	-132	-42	-209	21
5 Net saving	358	387	462	623	704	825	1416	1738	1857	2267	2305	3002
Total Current Disbursements and Net Saving	1623	3015	3728	4598	5400	6194	7640	9028	10921	13388	15019	17896

a) Compensation of employees paid by resident producers to resident households excludes wages paid to agricultural workers which are included in item 'Operating surplus'.
b) Beginning 1975, item 'Property and entrepreneural income' includes savings of corporations.

1.7 External Transactions on Current Account, Summary

Thousand Million Greek drachmas

	1980	1983	1984	1985	1986	1987	1988	1989	1990	1991	1992	1993
Payments to the Rest of the World												
1 Imports of goods and services	449	925	1139	1514	1703	1993	2291	2810	3445	4253	4898	5419
A Imports of merchandise c.i.f.	405	833	1036	1378	1538	1830	2061	2520	3093	3818	4351	...
B Other	44	93	103	135	165	163	230	290	353	436	547	...
2 Factor income to the rest of the world	24	85	131	180	199	218	254	315	324	392	483	541
A Compensation of employees	3	7	6	6	8	10	14	19	19	22	33	...
B Property and entrepreneurial income	21	78	125	173	191	208	241	295	305	371	449	...
3 Current transfers to the rest of the world	2	30	33	44	95	77	91	111	123	183	200	279
A Indirect taxes to supranational organizations	...	25	29	40	90	73	86	105	118	177	193	268
B Other current transfers	2	5	4	4	5	4	5	5	6	6	7	11
4 Surplus of the nation on current transactions	9	-155	-153	-377	-291	-192	-153	-441	-649	-657	-637	-505
Payments to the Rest of the World and Surplus of the Nation on Current Transactions	484	886	1150	1360	1707	2097	2484	2794	3243	4172	4944	5734
Receipts From The Rest of the World												
1 Exports of goods and services [a]	358	609	825	978	1233	1537	1801	2019	2279	2906	3438	3709
A Exports of merchandise f.o.b.	221	393	543	629	790	955	1083	1231	1268	1580	1816	...

Greece

1.7 External Transactions on Current Account, Summary
(Continued)

Thousand Million Greek drachmas

	1980	1983	1984	1985	1986	1987	1988	1989	1990	1991	1992	1993
B Other	137	217	282	348	443	582	717	788	1011	1326	1622	...
2 Factor income from rest of the world	80	116	133	146	132	155	198	230	278	342	431	636
A Compensation of employees	26	45	48	53	47	48	42	47	48	68	103	155
B Property and entrepreneurial income	54	71	85	93	84	107	156	182	230	274	328	480
3 Current transfers from rest of the world	46	161	192	237	343	405	485	546	686	925	1075	1389
A Subsidies from supranational organisations	...	78	88	126	205	219	240	320	414	531	628	833
B Other current transfers	46	82	104	110	137	186	245	226	272	393	447	556
Receipts from the Rest of the World on Current Transactions	484	886	1150	1360	1707	2097	2484	2794	3243	4172	4944	5734

a) Data on Exports of goods and services as well as transport, storage and communication exclude income from ocean-going cargo ships under Greek flag or ownership. However, remittances actually received by the bank of Greece from persons engaged in these enterprises are included in factor income from the rest of the world.

1.8 Capital Transactions of The Nation, Summary

Thousand Million Greek drachmas

	1980	1983	1984	1985	1986	1987	1988	1989	1990	1991	1992	1993
Finance of Gross Capital Formation												
Gross saving	499	518	586	606	802	911	1311	1398	1452	1955	2269	2595
1 Consumption of fixed capital	142	273	329	403	505	578	662	793	942	1108	1276	1447
2 Net saving	357	245	257	203	297	333	650	604	509	847	994	1149
A General government	-1	-142	-205	-420	-407	-493	-767	-1134	-1348	-1420	-1311	-1853
B Corporate and quasi-corporate enterprises [a]	...	...	...	...	...	...	...	...	...	...	...	...
C Other [a]	358	387	462	623	704	825	1416	1738	1857	2267	2305	3002
Less: Surplus of the nation on current transactions	9	-155	-153	-377	-291	-192	-153	-441	-649	-657	-637	-505
Finance of Gross Capital Formation	489	673	739	983	1093	1103	1464	1839	2101	2612	2907	3100
Gross Capital Formation												
Increase in stocks	76	49	36	103	75	28	145	148	29	236	211	190
Gross fixed capital formation	414	624	703	880	1018	1075	1318	1690	2072	2376	2696	2910
1 General government	43	111	162	207	228	202	243	296	326	485	601	607
2 Corporate and quasi-corporate enterprises [b]	52	104	124	168	157	139	156	218	238	284	348	437
A Public	52	104	124	168	157	139	156	218	238	284	348	437
B Private [b]	...	...	...	...	...	...	...	...	...	...	...	...
3 Other [b]	318	409	417	505	634	734	919	1176	1507	1607	1747	1866
Gross Capital Formation	489	673	739	983	1093	1103	1464	1839	2101	2612	2907	3100

a) Beginning 1975, item 'Corporate and quasi-corporate enterprises' is included in item 'Other'.
b) Private corporate and quasi-corporate enterprises are included in item 'Other'.

1.10 Gross Domestic Product by Kind of Activity, in Current Prices

Thousand Million Greek drachmas

	1980	1983	1984	1985	1986	1987	1988	1989	1990	1991	1992	1993
1 Agriculture, hunting, forestry and fishing	270	463	591	714	788	865	1087	1279	1337	1819	1853	1983
2 Mining and quarrying	23	57	77	90	79	99	108	118	141	157	162	173
3 Manufacturing	297	503	615	753	907	971	1149	1347	1511	1736	1941	2220
4 Electricity, gas and water	24	65	77	106	140	156	174	186	253	292	340	377
5 Construction	130	188	214	263	335	348	445	542	676	784	846	946
6 Wholesale and retail trade, restaurants and hotels [a]	196	360	439	540	657	725	853	997	1156	1381	1650	1975
7 Transport, storage and communication [b]	118	223	264	309	373	443	525	585	702	788	894	1016
8 Finance, insurance, real estate and business services [c]	132	223	265	316	383	458	568	683	851	1121	1369	1625
9 Community, social and personal services [acd]	185	361	442	571	675	795	957	1182	1450	1702	2050	2535
Total, Industries	1376	2442	2983	3661	4337	4860	5865	6919	8078	9780	11106	12848
Producers of Government Services	147	291	379	476	536	618	755	919	1141	1291	1425	1574

Greece

1.10 Gross Domestic Product by Kind of Activity, in Current Prices
(Continued)

Thousand Million Greek drachmas

	1980	1983	1984	1985	1986	1987	1988	1989	1990	1991	1992	1993
Other Producers [d]	...	...	...	...	...	...	...	...	...	...	...	...
Subtotal [e]	1524	2733	3363	4137	4873	5478	6621	7838	9219	11072	12531	14423
Less: Imputed bank service charge	...	...	...	...	...	...	...	...	...	...	...	...
Plus: Import duties	...	...	...	...	...	...	...	...	...	...	...	...
Plus: Value added tax	...	...	...	...	...	...	...	...	...	...	...	...
Plus: Other adjustments [f]	187	346	443	481	642	794	952	967	1332	1817	2301	2338
Equals: Gross Domestic Product	1711	3079	3806	4618	5515	6272	7572	8805	10551	12889	14832	16760

a) Restaurants and hotels are included in item 'Community, social and personal services'.
b) Data on Exports of goods and services as well as transport, storage and communication exclude income from ocean-going cargo ships under Greek flag or ownership. However, remittances actually received by the bank of Greece from persons engaged in these enterprises are included in factor income from the rest of the world.
c) Business services are included in item 'Community, social and personal services'.
d) Item 'Other producers' is included in item 'Community, social and personal services'.
e) Gross domestic product in factor values.
f) Item 'Other adjustments' refers to indirect taxes net of subsidies.

1.11 Gross Domestic Product by Kind of Activity, in Constant Prices

Million Greek drachmas

	1980	1983	1984	1985	1986	1987	1988	1989	1990	1991	1992	1993
	\multicolumn{12}{c}{At constant prices of: 1970}												
1 Agriculture, hunting, forestry and fishing	60499	55518	59394	60523	62036	58761	62581	63180	53523	62883	61082	60223
2 Mining and quarrying	6245	6982	7827	7968	8000	8064	9064	9372	9185	8841	9023	8761
3 Manufacturing	89125	85436	86475	89529	89449	87306	91206	93203	90761	90079	88693	84920
4 Electricity, gas and water	13724	15172	16022	17032	17475	18549	19699	20624	20102	21805	22766	23512
5 Construction	26392	23025	21890	22525	23539	23543	25557	26687	28186	27225	26250	25907
6 Wholesale and retail trade, restaurants and hotels [a]	50633	53238	53238	55595	57096	57153	60125	62410	62785	64983	65000	62000
7 Transport, storage and communication [b]	39898	42971	45936	48733	49414	49048	52794	55594	56262	57181	60275	63100
8 Finance, insurance, real estate and business services [c]	49134	54158	55704	57198	59086	60380	62308	64603	67760	71178	75023	76256
9 Community, social and personal services [acd]	45152	45783	46220	47404	49323	50420	51546	54420	55554	55295	58110	59904
Total, Industries	380802	382283	392706	406507	415418	413224	434880	450093	444117	459470	466222	464583
Producers of Government Services	36708	40068	41990	42912	41796	41774	42290	44857	44179	45274	42459	41678
Other Producers [d]	...	...	...	...	...	...	...	...	...	...	...	...
Subtotal [e]	417510	422351	434696	449419	457214	454998	477170	494950	488296	504744	508681	506261
Less: Imputed bank service charge	...	...	...	...	...	...	...	...	...	...	...	...
Plus: Import duties	...	...	...	...	...	...	...	...	...	...	...	...
Plus: Value added tax	...	...	...	...	...	...	...	...	...	...	...	...
Plus: Other adjustments [f]	56000	55200	56000	56592	57000	56840	57451	58590	60012	61272	62000	67600
Equals: Gross Domestic Product	473510	477551	490696	506011	514214	511838	534621	553540	548308	566016	570681	573861

a) Restaurants and hotels are included in item 'Community, social and personal services'.
b) Data on Exports of goods and services as well as transport, storage and communication exclude income from ocean-going cargo ships under Greek flag or ownership. However, remittances actually received by the bank of Greece from persons engaged in these enterprises are included in factor income from the rest of the world.
c) Business services are included in item 'Community, social and personal services'.
d) Item 'Other producers' is included in item 'Community, social and personal services'.
e) Gross domestic product in factor values.
f) Item 'Other adjustments' refers to indirect taxes net of subsidies.

1.12 Relations Among National Accounting Aggregates

Thousand Million Greek drachmas

	1980	1983	1984	1985	1986	1987	1988	1989	1990	1991	1992	1993
Gross Domestic Product	1711	3079	3806	4618	5515	6272	7572	8805	10551	12889	14832	16760
Plus: Net factor income from the rest of the world	57	30	2	-34	-68	-63	-57	-85	-46	-50	-52	94
Factor income from the rest of the world	80	116	133	146	132	155	198	230	278	342	431	636
Less: Factor income to the rest of the world	24	85	131	180	199	218	254	315	324	392	483	541
Equals: Gross National Product	1768	3110	3808	4584	5447	6209	7516	8720	10505	12838	14780	16855
Less: Consumption of fixed capital	142	273	329	403	505	578	662	793	942	1108	1276	1447

Greece

1.12 Relations Among National Accounting Aggregates
(Continued)

Thousand Million Greek drachmas

	1980	1983	1984	1985	1986	1987	1988	1989	1990	1991	1992	1993
Equals: National Income	1625	2837	3478	4181	4942	5631	6854	7926	9562	11730	13505	15408
Plus: Net current transfers from the rest of the world	44	130	159	192	247	328	394	435	563	741	874	1111
Current transfers from the rest of the world	46	161	192	237	343	405	485	546	686	925	1075	1389
Less: Current transfers to the rest of the world	2	30	33	44	95	77	91	111	123	183	200	279
Equals: National Disposable Income	1669	2967	3637	4373	5189	5958	7248	8362	10125	12471	14379	16519
Less: Final consumption	1385	2633	3204	3968	4786	5581	6682	7977	9748	11667	13594	15349
Statistical discrepancy	72	-89	-177	-203	-106	-45	84	220	132	42	209	-21
Equals: Net Saving	357	245	257	203	297	333	650	604	509	847	994	1149
Less: Surplus of the nation on current transactions	9	-155	-153	-377	-291	-192	-153	-441	-649	-657	-637	-505
Equals: Net Capital Formation	347	401	410	580	588	525	802	1045	1158	1504	1631	1654

2.1 Government Final Consumption Expenditure by Function, in Current Prices

Thousand Million Greek drachmas

		1980	1983	1984	1985	1986	1987	1988	1989	1990	1991	1992	1993
1	General public services	98	208	285	370	406	472	616	752	920	1087	...	...
2	Defence	100	196	246	290	320	368	444	470	561	629	...	...
3	Public order and safety	...	...	...	...	...	...	...	...	...	...	...	...
4	Education	37	87	100	138	156	176	214	280	348	397	...	...
5	Health	28	57	73	93	123	136	171	210	264	297	...	...
6	Social security and welfare	4	9	11	15	17	19	22	28	32	34	...	...
7	Housing and community amenities	...	...	...	...	...	...	...	...	...	...	...	...
8	Recreational, cultural and religious affairs	...	...	...	...	...	...	...	...	...	...	...	...
9	Economic services [a]	13	22	28	37	46	54	62	74	95	104	...	...
10	Other functions [a]	...	...	...	...	...	...	...	...	...	...	...	...
	Total Government Final Consumption Expenditure [b]	280	579	743	942	1067	1225	1530	1819	2251	2555	...	...

a) Item 'Other functions' is included in item 'Economic services'.
b) Data in this series has been revised. The breakdown, if any, may not add up to the total.

2.5 Private Final Consumption Expenditure by Type and Purpose, in Current Prices

Thousand Million Greek drachmas

		1980	1983	1984	1985	1986	1987	1988	1989	1990	1991	1992	1993
	Final Consumption Expenditure of Resident Households												
1	Food, beverages and tobacco	474	873	1050	1244	1515	1772	2061	2436	2947	3514	4019	4605
	A Food	408	746	889	1044	1259	1463	1662	1975	2346	2781	3145	3587
	B Non-alcoholic beverages	11	19	24	28	41	48	60	71	89	107	126	157
	C Alcoholic beverages	27	50	60	80	99	125	151	172	231	278	325	372
	D Tobacco	27	59	77	92	115	136	188	218	281	348	423	489
2	Clothing and footwear	112	171	214	273	350	418	502	589	694	829	881	977
3	Gross rent, fuel and power	138	246	294	346	419	515	624	721	891	1156	1406	1709
	A Fuel and power	29	66	84	99	118	145	156	164	203	245	290	308
	B Other	109	180	210	247	301	370	467	557	688	912	1116	1401
4	Furniture, furnishings and household equipment and operation	96	184	215	268	324	392	453	532	637	738	843	932
	A Household operation	29	62	78	101	113	144	173	205	251	307	364	414
	B Other	66	122	137	167	212	248	280	327	385	431	480	518
5	Medical care and health expenses	42	73	88	116	147	163	183	214	263	339	430	529
6	Transport and communication	142	277	332	441	556	597	700	844	1092	1380	1717	1858
	A Personal transport equipment	17	48	65	115	140	125	144	214	290	394	537	456
	B Other	126	229	267	326	416	472	555	629	802	986	1180	1402
7	Recreational, entertainment, education and cultural services	63	123	147	186	229	273	329	383	439	541	595	671
	A Education	11	14	16	19	23	26	32	38	47	62	80	97
	B Other	53	109	132	167	206	248	298	345	392	479	515	574
8	Miscellaneous goods and services	99	179	233	296	363	455	542	631	770	895	1166	1384
	A Personal care	16	34	41	56	69	86	100	115	141	177	217	257
	B Expenditures in restaurants, cafes and hotels	61	113	152	193	231	289	344	402	484	547	715	857

Greece

2.5 Private Final Consumption Expenditure by Type and Purpose, in Current Prices
(Continued)

Thousand Million Greek drachmas

	1980	1983	1984	1985	1986	1987	1988	1989	1990	1991	1992	1993
C Other	21	32	39	47	62	80	97	114	145	170	233	269
Total Final Consumption Expenditure in the Domestic Market by Households, of which	1165	2125	2573	3169	3902	4587	5394	6350	7733	9393	11057	12664
A Durable goods	70	152	182	254	325	339	378	487	602	719	886	815
B Semi-durable goods	153	250	311	394	507	614	739	869	1033	1231	1389	1548
C Non-durable goods	594	1111	1343	1616	1965	2306	2664	3114	3823	4564	5271	6075
D Services	348	612	738	905	1105	1327	1612	1879	2275	2878	3511	4226
Plus: Direct purchases abroad by resident households	13	32	38	51	69	69	105	133	173	186	227	231
Less: Direct purchases in the domestic market by non-resident households	74	104	150	195	252	299	346	325	409	467	615	747
Equals: Final Consumption Expenditure of Resident Households [a]	1105	2054	2461	3025	3719	4356	5153	6158	7498	9112	10669	12148

Final Consumption Expenditure of Private Non-profit Institutions Serving Households

	1980	1983	1984	1985	1986	1987	1988	1989	1990	1991	1992	1993
Equals: Final Consumption Expenditure of Private Non-profit Organisations Serving Households	...	...	...	...	...	...	...	...	...	...	...	...
Private Final Consumption Expenditure	1105	2054	2461	3025	3719	4356	5153	6158	7498	9112	10669	12148

a) Item 'Final consumption expenditure of resident households' includes consumption expenditure of private non-profit institutions serving households.

2.6 Private Final Consumption Expenditure by Type and Purpose, in Constant Prices

Million Greek drachmas

	1980	1983	1984	1985	1986	1987	1988	1989	1990	1991	1992	1993

At constant prices of: 1970

Final Consumption Expenditure of Resident Households

	1980	1983	1984	1985	1986	1987	1988	1989	1990	1991	1992	1993
1 Food, beverages and tobacco	121530	129949	131303	132492	134618	139698	143785	144321	144429	146220	148142	151403
A Food	95136	98951	98273	96961	97653	101067	104807	105173	104225	105415	107481	110915
B Non-alcoholic beverages	2818	2662	2832	2767	3023	3186	3615	3856	4196	4342	4687	5318
C Alcoholic beverages	9784	10806	11563	13221	13160	14395	15083	15068	15713	15645	15765	15450
D Tobacco	13792	17530	18635	19543	20782	21050	20280	20224	20295	20818	20209	19720
2 Clothing and footwear	34684	27308	27200	28363	28924	28363	28636	29161	29171	29554	27415	27498
3 Gross rent, fuel and power	52239	58394	60674	61928	63113	65486	67467	69348	70945	73626	75993	77984
A Fuel and power	9292	11051	11901	12081	12015	12935	13312	13454	13400	14189	14852	15314
B Other	42947	47343	48773	49847	51098	52551	54155	55894	57545	59437	61141	62670
4 Furniture, furnishings and household equipment and operation	28868	28299	27345	28527	27645	28006	28764	30046	30549	29835	29780	29510
A Household operation	8173	8767	9263	9920	8827	9533	10001	10295	10420	10602	10738	10756
B Other	20695	19532	18082	18607	18818	18473	18763	19751	20129	19233	19042	18754
5 Medical care and health expenses	11032	11274	11299	11857	11963	12140	12077	12326	12286	12272	13233	13498
6 Transport and communication	41074	46672	50704	57838	57111	55140	57614	62991	67368	72268	75793	71067
A Personal transport equipment	3630	6381	7406	11417	10046	7717	8153	10983	14305	18837	21864	16351
B Other	37444	40291	43298	46421	47065	47423	49461	52008	53063	53431	53929	54716
7 Recreational, entertainment, education and cultural services	16546	19399	20160	20804	21567	21065	22286	23760	23818	24846	25313	27171
A Education	2257	1862	1803	1880	1907	1876	1983	2093	2077	2150	2237	2349
B Other	14289	17537	18357	18924	19660	19189	20303	21667	21741	22696	23076	24822
8 Miscellaneous goods and services	27283	26501	28027	29662	29863	30611	31514	32320	33794	33180	36081	36436
A Personal care	4366	4725	4778	5809	5702	5624	5909	6151	6624	7065	7339	7486
B Expenditures in restaurants, cafes and hotels	17564	17146	18509	19060	19011	19316	19533	19903	20531	19517	20955	21163
C Other	5353	4630	4740	4793	5150	5671	6072	6266	6639	6598	7787	7787
Total Final Consumption Expenditure in the Domestic Market by Households, of which	333256	347796	356712	371471	374804	380509	392143	404273	412360	421801	431750	434567
A Durable goods	21398	25118	25576	29790	29130	25732	26752	31478	35266	38317	41613	36636
B Semi-durable goods	46562	40282	40058	42155	43185	43236	44594	45988	46691	47380	47014	47008
C Non-durable goods	157072	170134	173889	178313	180452	188293	194134	196249	197391	200222	204276	209071

Greece

2.6 Private Final Consumption Expenditure by Type and Purpose, in Constant Prices
(Continued)

Million Greek drachmas

	1980	1983	1984	1985	1986	1987	1988	1989	1990	1991	1992	1993
					At constant prices of:1970							
D Services	108224	112262	117189	121213	122037	123248	126663	130558	133012	135888	138847	141852
Plus: Direct purchases abroad by resident households	4076	5572	5456	5712	5696	4811	6533	7347	7937	7201	7326	6679
Less: Direct purchases in the domestic market by non-resident households	17991	13943	16974	18512	19474	19847	20188	16678	17103	16544	19048	20661
Equals: Final Consumption Expenditure of Resident Households [a]	319341	339425	345194	358671	361026	365473	378488	394942	403194	412458	420028	420585

Final Consumption Expenditure of Private Non-profit Institutions Serving Households

Equals: Final Consumption Expenditure of Private Non-profit Organisations Serving Households	...	...	...	...	...	...	...	...	...	...	...	...
Private Final Consumption Expenditure	319341	339425	345194	358671	361026	365473	378488	394942	403194	412458	420028	420585

a) Item 'Final consumption expenditure of resident households' includes consumption expenditure of private non-profit institutions serving households.

2.7 Gross Capital Formation by Type of Good and Owner, in Current Prices

Thousand Million Greek drachmas

	1980 TOTAL	1980 Total Private	1980 Public Enterprises	1980 General Government	1985 TOTAL	1985 Total Private	1985 Public Enterprises	1985 General Government	1990 TOTAL	1990 Total Private	1990 Public Enterprises	1990 General Government
Increase in stocks, total	76	67	7	2	103	108	6	-11	29	3	26	-
1 Goods producing industries	63	59	5	...	97	92	5	...	47	37	10	...
2 Wholesale and retail trade	5	4	-	...	12	12	-	...	-39	-39	-	...
3 Other, except government stocks	5	4	2	...	5	4	1	...	21	5	16	...
4 Government stocks	2	...	...	2	-11	...	...	-11	-	...	...	-
Gross Fixed Capital Formation, Total	414	318	52	43	880	505	168	207	2072	1507	238	326
1 Residential buildings	138	136	2	-	178	171	6	2	555	539	15	1
2 Non-residential buildings	59	49	3	7	96	57	9	30	267	192	9	66
3 Other construction	65	21	17	27	220	31	42	147	349	27	87	235
4 Land improvement and plantation and orchard development [a]	6	1	-	6	15	2	-	13	27	6	-	21
5 Producers' durable goods	147	112	31	4	371	244	111	15	874	743	127	4
A Transport equipment	47	39	8	-	90	74	15	1	216	202	14	-
B Machinery and equipment	100	73	23	4	280	171	96	14	658	541	113	3
6 Breeding stock, dairy cattle, etc.	...	...	...	...	...	...	...	...	...	...	...	...
Total Gross Capital Formation	489	384	59	46	983	613	174	196	2101	1510	264	326

	1991 TOTAL	1991 Total Private	1991 Public Enterprises	1991 General Government	1992 TOTAL	1992 Total Private	1992 Public Enterprises	1992 General Government	1993 TOTAL	1993 Total Private	1993 Public Enterprises	1993 General Government
Increase in stocks, total	236	204	32	-	211	...	...	...	190	...	...	...
1 Goods producing industries	220	209	12	...	...	...	...	...	...	...	...	...
2 Wholesale and retail trade	-5	-5	-	...	...	...	...	...	...	...	...	...
3 Other, except government stocks	21	-	21	...	...	...	...	...	...	...	...	...
4 Government stocks	-	...	...	-	...	...	...	...	...	...	...	...
Gross Fixed Capital Formation, Total	2376	1612	284	485	2696	...	...	...	2910	...	...	...
1 Residential buildings	560	542	16	1	551	...	...	...	604	...	...	...
2 Non-residential buildings	293	196	17	81	321	...	...	...	353	...	...	...
3 Other construction	498	25	124	349	...	...	...	...	...	...	...	...
4 Land improvement and plantation and orchard development [a]	33	4	-	29	...	...	...	...	...	...	...	...
5 Producers' durable goods	995	844	126	26	1192	...	...	...	1306	...	...	...
A Transport equipment	250	235	15	-	304	...	...	...	311	...	...	...
B Machinery and equipment	745	609	111	26	889	...	...	...	995	...	...	...
6 Breeding stock, dairy cattle, etc.	...	...	...	...	...	...	...	...	...	...	...	...
Total Gross Capital Formation	2612	1816	316	485	2907	...	...	601	3100	...	...	...

a) Item 'Land improvement and plantation and orchard development' includes outlays on land improvement and transfer costs on purchases and sales of agricultural land only.

Greece

2.8 Gross Capital Formation by Type of Good and Owner, in Constant Prices

Million Greek drachmas

	1980 TOTAL	1980 Total Private	1980 Public Enterprises	1980 General Government	1985 TOTAL	1985 Total Private	1985 Public Enterprises	1985 General Government	1990 TOTAL	1990 Total Private	1990 Public Enterprises	1990 General Government
					At constant prices of:1970							
Increase in stocks, total	19280	16634	1538	1108	10149	10599	557	-1007	-1485	-2716	1229	2
1 Goods producing industries	14636	13577	1059	...	9125	8659	466	...	2006	1511	495	...
2 Wholesale and retail trade	1997	1978	19	...	894	894	-	...	-4420	-4420	-	...
3 Other, except government stocks	1539	1079	460	...	1137	1046	91	...	927	193	734	...
4 Government stocks	1108	...	...	1108	-1007	...	...	-1007	2	...	...	2
Gross Fixed Capital Formation, Total	92705	70465	13231	9009	82360	49670	16672	16018	96139	73412	11099	11628
1 Residential buildings	27291	26929	332	30	17097	16382	546	169	24646	23943	663	40
2 Non-residential buildings	11622	9691	501	1430	9241	5511	877	2853	11878	8538	398	2942
3 Other construction	14273	4493	4410	5370	16740	2300	3939	10501	12193	936	3501	7756
4 Land improvement and plantation and orchard development [a]	1401	150	-	1251	1143	153	-	990	1001	218	-	783
5 Producers' durable goods	38118	29202	7988	928	38139	25324	11310	1505	46421	39777	6537	107
A Transport equipment	13987	11439	2482	66	10354	8429	1763	162	11261	10525	719	17
B Machinery and equipment	24131	17763	5506	862	27785	16895	9547	1343	35160	29252	5818	90
6 Breeding stock, dairy cattle, etc.	...	...	...	...	...	...	...	...	...	...	...	...
Total Gross Capital Formation	111985	87099	14769	10117	92509	60269	17229	15011	94654	70696	12328	11630

	1991 TOTAL	1991 Total Private	1991 Public Enterprises	1991 General Government	1992 TOTAL	1992 Total Private	1992 Public Enterprises	1992 General Government	1993 TOTAL	1993 Total Private	1993 Public Enterprises	1993 General Government
					At constant prices of:1970							
Increase in stocks, total	8353	7006	1347	-	8126	...	...	...	6807	...	...	...
1 Goods producing industries	7861	7367	494	...								
2 Wholesale and retail trade	-348	-348	-	...								
3 Other, except government stocks	840	-13	853	...								
4 Government stocks	-	...	...	-								
Gross Fixed Capital Formation, Total	91726	65943	11141	14811	93140	...	...	...	91292	...	...	...
1 Residential buildings	20912	20264	616	32	18396	...	...	...	17766	...	...	...
2 Non-residential buildings	10965	7327	639	3014	10711	...	...	...	10385	...	...	...
3 Other construction	14735	763	4287	9685	...	...	...	...	...	...	...	...
4 Land improvement and plantation and orchard development [a]	1050	119	-	931	...	...	...	...	...	...	...	...
5 Producers' durable goods	44174	37470	5599	1149	47249	...	...	...	47967	...	...	...
A Transport equipment	11009	10328	662	19	12057	...	678	...	10792	...	...	...
B Machinery and equipment	33165	27142	4937	1130	35192	...	...	...	37175	...	...	...
6 Breeding stock, dairy cattle, etc.	...	...	...	...	...	...	...	...	...	...	...	...
Total Gross Capital Formation	100079	72949	12488	14811	101266	...	...	...	98099	...	...	...

a) Item 'Land improvement and plantation and orchard development' includes outlays on land improvement and transfer costs on purchases and sales of agricultural land only.

2.9 Gross Capital Formation by Kind of Activity of Owner, ISIC Major Divisions, in Current Prices

Thousand Million Greek drachmas

	1980 Total Gross Capital Formation	1980 Increase in Stocks	1980 Gross Fixed Capital Formation	1985 Total Gross Capital Formation	1985 Increase in Stocks	1985 Gross Fixed Capital Formation	1990 Total Gross Capital Formation	1990 Increase in Stocks	1990 Gross Fixed Capital Formation	1991 Total Gross Capital Formation	1991 Increase in Stocks	1991 Gross Fixed Capital Formation
						All Producers						
1 Agriculture, hunting, fishing and forestry	14	-4	18	66	9	57	22	-50	72	149	83	66
2 Mining and quarrying	23	1	22	40	3	37	35	-	36	36	-	36
3 Manufacturing	127	61	65	191	79	111	427	88	339	482	125	357
4 Electricity, gas and water	29	5	24	86	5	81	113	10	103	107	12	96

Greece

2.9 Gross Capital Formation by Kind of Activity of Owner, ISIC Major Divisions, in Current Prices
(Continued)

Thousand Million Greek drachmas

		1980			1985			1990			1991		
		Total Gross Capital Formation	Increase in Stocks	Gross Fixed Capital Formation	Total Gross Capital Formation	Increase in Stocks	Gross Fixed Capital Formation	Total Gross Capital Formation	Increase in Stocks	Gross Fixed Capital Formation	Total Gross Capital Formation	Increase in Stocks	Gross Fixed Capital Formation
5	Construction	...	...	...	...	...	...	...	...	...	...	...	...
6	Wholesale and retail trade, restaurants and hotels [a]	5	5	...	12	12	...	-39	-39	...	-5	-5	...
7	Transport, storage and communication	65	6	59	125	5	120	311	21	290	393	21	372
8	Finance, insurance, real estate and business services [b]	137	-1	137	176	-	176	554	-	554	559	-	559
9	Community, social and personal services [ab]	45	...	45	92	...	92	351	...	351	410	...	410
	Total Industries [c]	444	73	370	787	114	673	1774	29	1745	2131	236	1895
	Producers of Government Services [c]	46	2	43	196	-11	207	326	-	326	485	-	485
	Private Non-Profit Institutions Serving Households	...	...	...	...	...	...	...	...	...	...	...	...
	Total [d]	489	76	414	983	103	880	2101	29	2072	2612	236	2376

		1992		
		Total Gross Capital Formation	Increase in Stocks	Gross Fixed Capital Formation
		All Producers		
1	Agriculture, hunting, fishing and forestry	188	105	83
2	Mining and quarrying	48	3	45
3	Manufacturing	499	110	389
4	Electricity, gas and water	138	15	123
5	Construction	...	...	...
6	Wholesale and retail trade, restaurants and hotels [a]	7	7	...
7	Transport, storage and communication	449	28	421
8	Finance, insurance, real estate and business services [b]	558	-	558
9	Community, social and personal services [ab]	454	...	454
	Total Industries [c]	2341	268	2074
	Producers of Government Services [c]	601	-	601
	Private Non-Profit Institutions Serving Households	...	...	...
	Total [d]	2907	211	2696

a) Gross fixed capital formation of item 'Wholesale and retail trade, restaurants and hotels' is included in item 'Community, social and personal services'.
b) Only ownership of dwellings is included in Gross fixed capital formation, all other activities are included in item 'Community, social and personal services'.
c) Beginning 1979, gross fixed capital formation and increase in stocks of public enterprises are included in item 'Total industries'.
d) Data in this series has been revised. The breakdown, if any, may not add up to the total.

2.10 Gross Capital Formation by Kind of Activity of Owner, ISIC Major Divisions, in Constant Prices

Million Greek drachmas

		1980			1985			1990			1991		
		Total Gross Capital Formation	Increase in Stocks	Gross Fixed Capital Formation	Total Gross Capital Formation	Increase in Stocks	Gross Fixed Capital Formation	Total Gross Capital Formation	Increase in Stocks	Gross Fixed Capital Formation	Total Gross Capital Formation	Increase in Stocks	Gross Fixed Capital Formation
		At constant prices of: 1970											
		All Producers											
1	Agriculture, hunting, fishing and forestry	3069	-1052	4121	6243	1156	5087	708	-2794	3502	4971	2098	2873
2	Mining and quarrying	5232	290	4942	3700	264	3436	1622	-17	1639	1470	13	1457
3	Manufacturing	29097	14278	14819	18169	7239	10930	22115	4322	17793	20796	5256	15540
4	Electricity, gas and water	7026	1119	5907	8340	466	7874	5255	495	4760	4254	494	3760
5	Construction	...	...	...	...	...	...	...	...	...	...	...	...
6	Wholesale and retail trade, restaurants and hotels [a]	1997	1997	...	894	894	...	-4420	-4420	...	-348	-348	...
7	Transport, storage and communication	18376	1572	16804	14340	1145	13195	16495	921	15574	16414	828	15586
8	Finance, insurance, real estate and business services [b]	27230	-32	27262	16920	-8	16928	24612	6	24606	20892	12	20880
9	Community, social and personal services [ab]	9841	...	9841	8892	...	8892	16480	...	16480	16988	...	16988
	Total Industries [c]	101868	18172	83696	77498	11156	66342	82867	-1487	84354	85437	8353	77084
	Producers of Government Services [c]	10117	1108	9009	15011	-1007	16018	11787	2	11785	14811	-	14811
	Private Non-Profit Institutions Serving Households	...	...	...	...	...	...	...	...	...	...	...	...
	Total [d]	111985	19280	92705	92509	10149	82360	94654	-1485	96139	100079	8353	91726

Greece

2.10 Gross Capital Formation by Kind of Activity of Owner, ISIC Major Divisions, in Constant Prices

Million Greek drachmas

At constant prices of: 1970 — All Producers

	1992 Total Gross Capital Formation	Increase in Stocks	Gross Fixed Capital Formation
1 Agriculture, hunting, fishing and forestry	7019	3881	3138
2 Mining and quarrying	1762	108	1654
3 Manufacturing	19393	4122	15271
4 Electricity, gas and water	4899	560	4339
5 Construction	...	...	...
6 Wholesale and retail trade, restaurants and hotels [a]	460	460	...
7 Transport, storage and communication	17489	1056	16433
8 Finance, insurance, real estate and business services [b]	18641	12	18629
9 Community, social and personal services [a,b]	16995	...	16995
Total Industries [c]	86658	10199	76459
Producers of Government Services [c]	16510	-	16510
Private Non-Profit Institutions Serving Households	...	...	...
Total [d]	101266	8126	93140

a) Gross fixed capital formation of item 'Wholesale and retail trade, restaurants and hotels' is included in item 'Community, social and personal services'.
b) Only ownership of dwellings is included in Gross fixed capital formation, all other activities are included in item 'Community, social and personal services'.
c) Beginning 1979, gross fixed capital formation and increase in stocks of public enterprises are included in item 'Total industries'.
d) Data in this series has been revised. The breakdown, if any, may not add up to the total.

2.11 Gross Fixed Capital Formation by Kind of Activity of Owner, ISIC Divisions, in Current Prices

Thousand Million Greek drachmas

All Producers

	1980	1983	1984	1985	1986	1987	1988	1989	1990	1991	1992	1993
1 Agriculture, hunting, forestry and fishing	18	28	46	57	40	34	48	59	72	66	83	...
2 Mining and quarrying	22	24	28	37	21	29	31	34	36	36	45	...
3 Manufacturing	65	90	102	111	168	188	236	288	339	357	389	...
4 Electricity, gas and water	24	53	59	81	59	49	66	94	103	96	123	...
A Electricity, gas and steam	22	51	54	74	54	46	62	90	97	88	115	...
B Water works and supply	2	2	4	7	5	4	4	3	6	7	8	...
5 Construction	...	...	...	...	...	...	...	...	...	...	...	...
6 Wholesale and retail trade, restaurants and hotels	...	...	...	...	...	...	...	...	...	...	...	...
7 Transport, storage and communication	59	93	91	120	118	124	141	207	290	372	421	...
A Transport and storage	50	68	71	97	97	100	108	162	227	278	314	...
B Communication	9	25	21	23	20	24	33	46	63	94	108	...
8 Finance, insurance, real estate and business services	137	162	151	176	247	286	329	403	554	559	558	...
A Financial institutions	...	...	...	...	...	...	...	...	...	...	...	...
B Insurance	...	...	...	...	...	...	...	...	...	...	...	...
C Real estate and business services	137	162	151	176	247	286	329	403	554	559	558	...
Real estate except dwellings	...	...	...	...	...	...	...	...	...	...	...	...
Dwellings	137	162	151	176	247	286	329	403	554	559	558	...
9 Community, social and personal services	45	63	64	92	138	162	225	309	351	410	454	...
A Sanitary and similar services	...	...	...	...	...	...	...	...	...	...	...	...
B Social and related community services	2	2	4	5	11	12	9	14	22	29	36	...

Greece

2.11 Gross Fixed Capital Formation by Kind of Activity of Owner, ISIC Divisions, in Current Prices
(Continued)

Thousand Million Greek drachmas

	1980	1983	1984	1985	1986	1987	1988	1989	1990	1991	1992	1993
Educational services	-	-	-	-	-	-	1	-	1	-	-	...
Medical, dental, other health and veterinary services	2	2	4	5	11	12	9	14	21	29	36	...
C Recreational and cultural services	-	-	-	-	1	2	2	2	2	5	8	...
D Personal and household services	43	60	60	87	127	148	214	293	328	376	410	...
Total Industries	370	513	541	673	791	873	1075	1394	1745	1895	2074	...
Producers of Government Services	43	111	162	207	228	202	243	296	326	485	601	...
Private Non-Profit Institutions Serving Households	...	...	...	...	...	...	...	...	...	...	...	...
Total [a]	414	624	703	880	1018	1075	1318	1690	2072	2376	2696	...

a) Data in this series has been revised. The breakdown, if any, may not add up to the total.

2.12 Gross Fixed Capital Formation by Kind of Activity of Owner, ISIC Divisions, in Constant Prices

Million Greek drachmas

	1980	1983	1984	1985	1986	1987	1988	1989	1990	1991	1992	1993
					At constant prices of:1970							
					All Producers							
1 Agriculture, hunting, forestry and fishing	4121	3592	5026	5087	2827	2305	2836	2975	3502	2873	3138	...
2 Mining and quarrying	4942	3142	3042	3436	1550	2033	1834	1737	1639	1457	1654	...
3 Manufacturing	14819	12112	11958	10930	12996	13385	14956	15503	17793	15540	15271	...
4 Electricity, gas and water	5907	7317	6686	7874	4866	3279	3943	4822	4760	3760	4339	...
A Electricity, gas and steam	5459	7061	6330	7361	4573	3075	3753	4680	4532	3525	4101	...
B Water works and supply	448	256	356	513	293	204	190	142	228	235	238	...
5 Construction	...	...	...	...	...	...	...	...	...	...	...	...
6 Wholesale and retail trade, restaurants and hotels	...	...	...	...	...	...	...	...	...	...	...	...
7 Transport, storage and communication	16804	14949	12162	13195	10665	9567	9375	12057	15574	15586	16433	...
A Transport and storage	14457	11304	9617	10817	8952	7927	7336	9635	12542	11826	12543	...
B Communication	2347	3645	2545	2378	1713	1640	2039	2422	3032	3760	3890	...
8 Finance, insurance, real estate and business services	27262	20949	16934	16928	19277	19956	20646	21700	24606	20880	18629	...
A Financial institutions	...	...	...	...	...	...	...	...	...	...	...	...
B Insurance	...	...	...	...	...	...	...	...	...	...	...	...
C Real estate and business services	27262	20949	16934	16928	19277	19956	20646	21700	24606	20880	18629	...
Real estate except dwellings	...	...	...	...	...	...	...	...	...	...	...	...
Dwellings	27262	20949	16934	16928	19277	19956	20646	21700	24606	20880	18629	...
9 Community, social and personal services	9841	8339	7247	8892	10844	11340	14117	16548	16480	16988	16995	...
A Sanitary and similar services	...	...	...	...	...	...	...	...	...	...	...	...
B Social and related community services	398	320	427	481	956	791	596	773	1171	1275	1416	...
Educational services	13	19	10	6	6	3	39	18	26	18	16	...
Medical, dental, other health and veterinary services	385	301	417	475	950	788	557	755	1145	1257	1400	...
C Recreational and cultural services	22	34	34	46	72	145	119	108	78	178	300	...
D Personal and household services	9421	7985	6786	8365	9816	10404	13402	15667	15231	15535	15279	...
Total Industries	83696	70400	63055	66342	63025	61865	67707	75342	84354	77084	76459	...
Producers of Government Services	9009	12600	15245	16018	14209	11450	12124	12531	11785	14811	16510	...
Private Non-Profit Institutions Serving Households	...	...	...	...	...	...	...	...	...	...	...	...
Total	92705	83000	78300	82360	77234	73315	79831	87873	96139	91726	93140	...

Greece

2.17 Exports and Imports of Goods and Services, Detail

Thousand Million Greek drachmas

	1980	1983	1984	1985	1986	1987	1988	1989	1990	1991	1992	1993
Exports of Goods and Services												
1 Exports of merchandise, f.o.b. [a]	221	393	543	629	790	955	1083	1231	1268	1580	1816	...
2 Transport and communication												...
3 Insurance service charges	58	110	128	149	187	278	369	454	596	845	998	...
4 Other commodities												...
5 Adjustments of merchandise exports to change-of-ownership basis	...	...	...	...	...	...	...	...	...	...	...	...
6 Direct purchases in the domestic market by non-residential households	74	104	150	195	252	299	346	325	409	467	615	747
7 Direct purchases in the domestic market by extraterritorial bodies	4	3	5	4	4	5	3	9	6	14	10	12
Total Exports of Goods and Services	358	609	825	978	1233	1537	1801	2019	2279	2906	3438	3709
Imports of Goods and Services												
1 Imports of merchandise, c.i.f.	405	833	1036	1378	1538	1830	2061	2520	3093	3818	4351	...
A Imports of merchandise, f.o.b.	368	758	943	1254	1361	1620	1824	2256	...	...	...	...
B Transport of services on merchandise imports	36	75	93	124	177	210	237	293	...	...	...	...
C Insurance service charges on merchandise imports	...	...	...	...	...	...	...	...	...	...	...	...
2 Adjustments of merchandise imports to change-of-ownership basis	...	...	...	...	...	...	...	...	...	...	...	...
3 Other transport and communication												...
4 Other insurance service charges	24	51	52	68	77	75	100	124	141	210	273	...
5 Other commodities												...
6 Direct purchases abroad by government	7	9	13	17	19	19	25	32	38	40	47	73
7 Direct purchases abroad by resident households	13	32	38	51	69	69	105	133	173	186	227	231
Total Imports of Goods and Services	449	925	1139	1514	1703	1993	2291	2810	3445	4253	4898	5419
Balance of Goods and Services	-91	-316	-314	-536	-470	-457	-490	-791	-1166	-1348	-1460	-1710
Total Imports and Balance of Goods and Services	358	609	825	978	1233	1537	1801	2019	2279	2906	3438	3709

a) Data on Exports of goods and services as well as transport, storage and communication exclude income from ocean-going cargo ships under Greek flag or ownership. However, remittances actually received by the bank of Greece from persons engaged in these enterprises are included in factor income from the rest of the world.

3.12 General Government Income and Outlay Account: Total and Subsectors

Thousand Million Greek drachmas

	1980					1985				
	Total General Government	Central Government	State or Provincial Government	Local Government	Social Security Funds	Total General Government	Central Government	State or Provincial Government	Local Government	Social Security Funds
Receipts										
1 Operating surplus	...	...	...	...	...	...	...	...	...	...
2 Property and entrepreneurial income	40	9	...	18	13	94	9	...	36	48
3 Taxes, fees and contributions	477	297	...	14	166	1488	869	...	37	582
A Indirect taxes	229	208	...	8	12	705	632	...	14	58
B Direct taxes [a]	95	88	...	6	-	259	237	...	22	-
Income	74	...	...	...	...	208	...	...	...	...
Other	21	...	...	...	...	51	...	...	...	...
C Social security contributions	154	-	...	-	154	524	-	...	-	524
D Fees, fines and penalties [a]	...	...	...	...	...	...	...	...	...	...
4 Other current transfers	4	4	...	43	3	15	12	...	159	30
A Casualty insurance claims	...	...	...	...	...	...	...	...	...	...
B Transfers from other government subsectors	...	1	...	42	3	...	1	...	155	30
C Transfers from the rest of the world	-	-	...	...	...	-	-	...	-	...
D Other transfers, except imputed	4	3	...	1	...	15	11	...	4	...
E Imputed unfunded employee pension and welfare contributions	...	...	...	...	...	...	...	...	...	...
Total Current Receipts [b]	521	310	...	75	182	1597	890	...	231	660

Greece

3.12 General Government Income and Outlay Account: Total and Subsectors
(Continued)

Thousand Million Greek drachmas

		1980					1985				
		Total General Government	Central Government	State or Provincial Government	Local Government	Social Security Funds	Total General Government	Central Government	State or Provincial Government	Local Government	Social Security Funds
		Disbursements									
1	Government final consumption expenditure	280	208	...	51	21	942	665	...	188	90
2	Property income	41	41	...	-	...	247	239	...	-	8
3	Subsidies	42	42	...	-	...	138	138	...	-	...
4	Other current transfers	160	58	...	4	143	690	233	...	12	631
	A Casualty insurance premiums, net	...	...	...	...	...	...	...	...	...	...
	B Transfers to other government subsectors	...	45	...	-	-	...	184	...	1	-
	C Social security benefits	158	11	...	4	142	686	44	...	11	630
	D Social assistance grants	...	...	...	...	...	...	...	...	...	...
	E Unfunded employee pension and welfare benefits	...	...	...	...	...	...	...	...	...	...
	F Transfers to private non-profit institutions serving households	...	...	...	...	...	...	...	...	...	...
	G Other transfers n.e.c.	...	...	...	...	...	...	...	...	...	...
	H Transfers to the rest of the world	2	2	...	-	...	4	4	...	-	...
	Net saving [b]	-1	-39	...	20	18	-420	-384	...	32	-68
	Total Current Disbursements and Net Saving [b]	521	310	...	75	182	1597	890	...	231	660

		1990					1991				
		Total General Government	Central Government	State or Provincial Government	Local Government	Social Security Funds	Total General Government	Central Government	State or Provincial Government	Local Government	Social Security Funds
		Receipts									
1	Operating surplus	...	...	...	...	...	...	...	...	...	...
2	Property and entrepreneurial income	195	-17	...	65	147	225	12	...	79	134
3	Taxes, fees and contributions	3654	2304	...	68	1283	4577	2897	...	79	1600
	A Indirect taxes	1805	1698	...	22	84	2322	2136	...	29	157
	B Direct taxes [a]	651	606	...	46	-	811	761	...	50	-
	Income	466	420	...	46	...	520	470	...	50	...
	Other	185	185	...	...	...	291	291	...	...	...
	C Social security contributions	1198	-	...	-	1198	1444	-	...	-	1444
	D Fees, fines and penalties [a]	...	...	...	...	...	...	...	...	...	...
4	Other current transfers	35	30	...	500	362	88	84	...	560	338
	A Casualty insurance claims	...	...	...	...	...	...	...	...	...	...
	B Transfers from other government subsectors	...	6	...	489	362	...	7	...	549	338
	C Transfers from the rest of the world	-	-	...	-	...	-	-	...	-	...
	D Other transfers, except imputed	35	24	...	11	...	88	77	...	11	...
	E Imputed unfunded employee pension and welfare contributions	...	...	...	...	...	...	...	...	...	...
	Total Current Receipts [b]	3885	2317	...	634	1792	4890	2993	...	719	2072
		Disbursements									
1	Government final consumption expenditure	2251	1510	...	522	219	2555	1711	...	594	250
2	Property income	1193	1164	...	-	29	1564	1561	...	-	3
3	Subsidies	176	176	...	-	...	151	151	...	-	...

Greece

3.12 General Government Income and Outlay Account: Total and Subsectors
(Continued)

Thousand Million Greek drachmas

	1990					1991				
	Total General Government	Central Government	State or Provincial Government	Local Government	Social Security Funds	Total General Government	Central Government	State or Provincial Government	Local Government	Social Security Funds
4 Other current transfers	1612	978	...	16	1476	2040	1079	...	18	1837
A Casualty insurance premiums, net	...	...	...	...	...	...	...	...	...	...
B Transfers to other government subsectors	...	852	...	6	1	...	887	...	7	1
C Social security benefits	1607	120	...	11	1476	2034	186	...	12	1837
D Social assistance grants	...	...	...	...	...	...	...	...	...	...
E Unfunded employee pension and welfare benefits	...	...	...	...	...	...	...	...	...	...
F Transfers to private non-profit institutions serving households	...	...	...	...	...	...	...	...	...	...
G Other transfers n.e.c.	...	...	...	...	...	...	...	...	...	...
H Transfers to the rest of the world	6	6	...	-	...	6	6	...	-	...
Net saving [b]	-1348	-1511	...	95	68	-1420	-1509	...	107	-18
Total Current Disbursements and Net Saving [b]	3885	2317	...	634	1792	4890	2993	...	719	2072

	1992					1993				
	Total General Government	Central Government	State or Provincial Government	Local Government	Social Security Funds	Total General Government	Central Government	State or Provincial Government	Local Government	Social Security Funds

Receipts

1 Operating surplus	...	...	...	...	...	...	...	...	...	...
2 Property and entrepreneurial income	439	176	...	93	170	488	100	...	194	194
3 Taxes, fees and contributions	5457	3480	...	90	1888	6182	3770	...	110	2302
A Indirect taxes	2874	2637	...	35	203	3083	2800	...	47	236
B Direct taxes [a]	898	843	...	55	-	1033	970	...	63	-
Income	516	461	...	55	...	593	530	...	63	...
Other	383	383	...	...	...	440	440	...	...	...
C Social security contributions	1685	-	...	-	1685	2066	-	...	-	2066
D Fees, fines and penalties [a]	...	...	...	...	...	...	...	...	...	...
4 Other current transfers	53	48	...	613	382	66	114	...	497	451
A Casualty insurance claims	...	...	...	...	...	...	...	...	...	...
B Transfers from other government subsectors	...	9	...	600	382	...	63	...	482	451
C Transfers from the rest of the world	-	-	...	-	...	-	-	...	-	...
D Other transfers, except imputed	53	40	...	13	...	66	51	...	15	...
E Imputed unfunded employee pension and welfare contributions	...	...	...	...	...	...	...	...	...	...
Total Current Receipts [b]	5949	3704	...	796	2439	6735	3984	...	801	2947

Disbursements

1 Government final consumption expenditure	2925	1959	...	657	310	3201	2172	...	694	335
2 Property income	1927	1903	...	-	24	2535	2460	...	-	75
3 Subsidies	138	138	...	-	...	180	180	...	-	...
4 Other current transfers	2270	1148	...	20	2092	2673	1110	...	76	2483
A Casualty insurance premiums, net	...	...	...	...	...	...	...	...	...	...
B Transfers to other government subsectors	...	982	...	8	1	...	933	...	62	1
C Social security benefits	2263	159	...	13	2091	2662	166	...	14	2483
D Social assistance grants	...	...	...	...	...	...	...	...	...	...
E Unfunded employee pension and welfare benefits	...	...	...	...	...	...	...	...	...	...
F Transfers to private non-profit institutions serving households	...	...	...	...	...	...	...	...	...	...
G Other transfers n.e.c.	...	...	...	...	...	...	...	...	...	...
H Transfers to the rest of the world	7	7	...	-	...	11	11	...	-	...
Net saving [b]	-1311	-1444	...	119	14	-1853	-1938	...	31	54
Total Current Disbursements and Net Saving [b]	5949	3704	...	796	2439	6735	3984	...	801	2947

a) Item 'Fees, fines and penalties' is included in item 'Direct taxes'.
b) Column 'Local government' includes all public funds.

Greece

3.32 Household and Private Unincorporated Enterprise Income and Outlay Account

Thousand Million Greek drachmas

	1980	1983	1984	1985	1986	1987	1988	1989	1990	1991	1992	1993
Receipts												
1 Compensation of employees	671	1287	1575	1963	2204	2480	3007	3628	4405	4983	5525	6160
2 Operating surplus of private unincorporated enterprises	...	...	...	...	...	...	...	...	...	...	...	...
3 Property and entrepreneurial income	748	1233	1516	1839	2238	2592	3290	3814	4638	5978	6784	8517
3 Current transfers	204	494	637	796	958	1122	1343	1585	1879	2427	2710	3219
A Casualty insurance claims	...	...	...	...	...	...	...	...	...	...	...	...
B Social security benefits	158	412	533	686	821	936	1098	1359	1607	2034	2263	2662
C Social assistance grants	...	...	...	...	...	...	...	...	...	...	...	...
D Unfunded employee pension and welfare benefits	...	...	...	...	...	...	...	...	...	...	...	...
E Transfers from general government	...	...	...	...	...	...	...	...	...	...	...	...
F Transfers from the rest of the world	46	82	104	110	137	186	245	226	272	393	447	556
G Other transfers n.e.c.	...	...	...	...	...	...	...	...	...	...	...	...
Total Current Receipts	1623	3015	3728	4598	5400	6194	7640	9028	10921	13388	15019	17896
Disbursements												
1 Final consumption expenditures	1105	2054	2461	3025	3719	4356	5153	6158	7498	9112	10669	12148
2 Property income	...	...	...	...	...	...	...	...	...	...	...	...
3 Direct taxes and other current transfers n.e.c. to government	228	472	606	731	854	950	1132	1322	1665	1964	2201	2659
A Social security contributions	154	334	423	524	601	672	784	978	1198	1444	1685	2066
B Direct taxes	74	138	183	208	253	278	348	344	466	520	516	593
Income taxes	...	...	...	...	...	...	...	...	...	...	...	...
Other	...	...	...	...	...	...	...	...	...	...	...	...
C Fees, fines and penalties	...	...	...	...	...	...	...	...	...	...	...	...
4 Other current transfers	5	12	21	15	18	18	23	28	35	88	53	66
A Net casualty insurance premiums	...	...	...	...	...	...	...	...	...	...	...	...
B Transfers to private non-profit institutions serving households	...	...	...	...	...	...	...	...	...	...	...	...
C Transfers to the rest of the world	-	-	-	-	-	-	-	-	-	-	-	-
D Other current transfers, except imputed	5	12	21	15	18	18	23	28	35	88	53	66
E Imputed employee pension and welfare contributions	...	...	...	...	...	...	...	...	...	...	...	...
Statistical discrepancy	-72	89	177	203	106	45	-84	-211	-350	-42	-209	21
Net saving	358	387	462	623	704	825	1416	1729	2075	2267	2305	3002
Total Current Disbursements and Net Saving	1623	3015	3728	4598	5400	6194	7640	9028	10921	13388	15019	17896

3.51 External Transactions: Current Account: Detail

Thousand Million Greek drachmas

	1980	1983	1984	1985	1986	1987	1988	1989	1990	1991	1992	1993
Payments to the Rest of the World												
1 Imports of goods and services	449	925	1139	1514	1703	1993	2291	2810	3445	4253	4898	5419
A Imports of merchandise c.i.f.	405	833	1036	1378	1538	1830	2061	2520	3093	3818	4351	...
B Other	44	93	103	135	165	163	230	290	353	436	547	...
2 Factor income to the rest of the world	24	85	131	180	199	218	254	315	324	392	483	541

Greece

3.51 External Transactions: Current Account: Detail
(Continued)

Thousand Million Greek drachmas

	1980	1983	1984	1985	1986	1987	1988	1989	1990	1991	1992	1993
A Compensation of employees	3	7	6	6	8	10	14	19	19	22	33	...
B Property and entrepreneurial income	21	78	125	173	191	208	241	295	305	371	449	...
3 Current transfers to the rest of the world	2	30	33	44	95	77	91	111	123	183	200	279
A Indirect taxes by general government to supranational organizations	...	25	29	40	90	73	86	105	118	177	193	268
B Other current transfers	2	5	4	4	5	4	5	5	6	6	7	11
By general government	2	5	4	4	5	4	5	5	6	6	7	11
By other resident sectors	-	-	-	-	-	-	-	-	-	-	-	-
4 Surplus of the nation on current transactions	9	-155	-153	-377	-291	-192	-153	-441	-649	-657	-637	-505
Payments to the Rest of the World, and Surplus of the Nation on Current Transfers	484	886	1150	1360	1707	2097	2484	2794	3243	4172	4944	5734

Receipts From The Rest of the World

	1980	1983	1984	1985	1986	1987	1988	1989	1990	1991	1992	1993
1 Exports of goods and services [a]	358	609	825	978	1233	1537	1801	2019	2279	2906	3438	3709
A Exports of merchandise f.o.b.	221	393	543	629	790	955	1083	1231	1268	1580	1816	...
B Other	137	217	282	348	443	582	717	788	1011	1326	1622	...
2 Factor income from the rest of the world	80	116	133	146	132	155	198	230	278	342	431	636
A Compensation of employees	26	45	48	53	47	48	42	47	48	68	103	155
B Property and entrepreneurial income	54	71	85	93	84	107	156	182	230	274	328	480
3 Current transfers from the rest of the world	46	161	192	237	343	405	485	546	686	925	1075	1389
A Subsidies to general government from supranational organizations	...	78	88	126	205	219	240	320	414	531	628	833
B Other current transfers	46	82	104	110	137	186	245	226	272	393	447	556
To general government	-	-	-	-	-	-	-	-	-	-	-	-
To other resident sectors	46	82	104	110	137	186	245	226	272	393	447	556
Receipts from the Rest of the World on Current Transfers	484	886	1150	1360	1707	2097	2484	2794	3243	4172	4944	5734

a) Data on Exports of goods and services as well as transport, storage and communication exclude income from ocean-going cargo ships under Greek flag or ownership. However, remittances actually received by the bank of Greece from persons engaged in these enterprises are included in factor income from the rest of the world.

4.1 Derivation of Value Added by Kind of Activity, in Current Prices

Thousand Million Greek drachmas

	1980 Gross Output	1980 Intermediate Consumption	1980 Value Added	1985 Gross Output	1985 Intermediate Consumption	1985 Value Added	1990 Gross Output	1990 Intermediate Consumption	1990 Value Added	1991 Gross Output	1991 Intermediate Consumption	1991 Value Added
					All Producers							
1 Agriculture, hunting, forestry and fishing	...	...	270	...	...	714	...	...	1337	...	...	1819
A Agriculture and hunting	...	...	261	...	...	685	...	...	1262	...	...	1731
B Forestry and logging	...	...	4	...	...	10	...	...	18	...	...	20
C Fishing	...	...	5	...	...	19	...	...	58	...	...	68
2 Mining and quarrying	...	...	23	...	...	90	...	...	141	...	...	157

Greece

4.1 Derivation of Value Added by Kind of Activity, in Current Prices
(Continued)

Thousand Million Greek drachmas

	1980 Gross Output	1980 Intermediate Consumption	1980 Value Added	1985 Gross Output	1985 Intermediate Consumption	1985 Value Added	1990 Gross Output	1990 Intermediate Consumption	1990 Value Added	1991 Gross Output	1991 Intermediate Consumption	1991 Value Added
3 Manufacturing	...	...	297	...	...	753	...	...	1511	...	...	1736
A Manufacture of food, beverages and tobacco	...	...	55	...	...	160	...	...	317	...	...	400
B Textile, wearing apparel and leather industries	...	...	75	...	...	179	...	...	323	...	...	338
C Manufacture of wood and wood products, including furniture	...	...	16	...	...	26	...	...	56	...	...	67
D Manufacture of paper and paper products, printing and publishing	...	...	15	...	...	49	...	...	105	...	...	125
E Manufacture of chemicals and chemical petroleum, coal, rubber and plastic products	...	...	35	...	...	95	...	...	225	...	...	246
F Manufacture of non-metallic mineral products, except products of petroleum and coal	...	...	26	...	...	55	...	...	124	...	...	134
G Basic metal industries	...	...	17	...	...	45	...	...	75	...	...	80
H Manufacture of fabricated metal products, machinery and equipment	...	...	53	...	...	124	...	...	261	...	...	314
I Other manufacturing industries	...	...	6	...	...	19	...	...	26	...	...	33
4 Electricity, gas and water	...	...	24	...	...	106	...	...	253	...	...	292
A Electricity, gas and steam	...	...	24	...	...	106	...	...	253	...	...	292
B Water works and supply	...	...	...	...	...	...	...	...	...	...	...	...
5 Construction	...	...	130	...	...	263	...	...	676	...	...	784
6 Wholesale and retail trade, restaurants and hotels [a]	...	...	196	...	...	540	...	...	1156	...	...	1381
A Wholesale and retail trade	...	...	196	...	...	540	...	...	1156	...	...	1381
B Restaurants and hotels	...	...	...	...	...	...	...	...	...	...	...	...
7 Transport, storage and communication [b]	...	...	118	...	...	309	...	...	702	...	...	788
8 Finance, insurance, real estate and business services [c]	...	...	132	...	...	316	...	...	851	...	...	1121
9 Community, social and personal services [acd]	...	...	185	...	...	571	...	...	1450	...	...	1702
Total, Industries	...	...	1376	...	...	3661	...	...	8078	...	...	9780
Producers of Government Services	...	...	147	...	...	476	...	...	1141	...	...	1291
Other Producers [d]	...	...	...	...	...	...	...	...	...	...	...	...
Total [e]	...	...	1524	...	...	4137	...	...	9219	...	...	11072
Less: Imputed bank service charge	...	...	...	...	...	...	...	...	...	...	...	...
Import duties	...	...	...	...	...	...	...	...	...	...	...	...
Value added tax	...	...	...	...	...	...	...	...	...	...	...	...
Other adjustments [f]	...	...	187	...	...	481	...	...	1332	...	...	1817
Total	...	...	1711	...	...	4618	...	...	10551	...	...	12889

	1992 Gross Output	1992 Intermediate Consumption	1992 Value Added	1993 Gross Output	1993 Intermediate Consumption	1993 Value Added
			All Producers			
1 Agriculture, hunting, forestry and fishing	...	...	1853	...	...	1983
A Agriculture and hunting	...	...	1760	...	...	1884
B Forestry and logging	...	...	22	...	...	22
C Fishing	...	...	71	...	...	77
2 Mining and quarrying	...	...	162	...	...	173

Greece

4.1 Derivation of Value Added by Kind of Activity, in Current Prices
(Continued)

Thousand Million Greek drachmas

		1992 Gross Output	1992 Intermediate Consumption	1992 Value Added	1993 Gross Output	1993 Intermediate Consumption	1993 Value Added
3	Manufacturing	...	...	1941	...	...	2220
	A Manufacture of food, beverages and tobacco	...	...	492	...	...	694
	B Textile, wearing apparel and leather industries	...	...	357	...	...	387
	C Manufacture of wood and wood products, including furniture	...	...	71	...	...	76
	D Manufacture of paper and paper products, printing and publishing	...	...	147	...	...	165
	E Manufacture of chemicals and chemical petroleum, coal, rubber and plastic products	...	...	274	...	...	315
	F Manufacture of non-metallic mineral products, except products of petroleum and coal	...	...	142	...	...	154
	G Basic metal industries	...	...	81	...	...	85
	H Manufacture of fabricated metal products, machinery and equipment	...	...	354	...	...	316
	I Other manufacturing industries	...	...	23	...	...	27
4	Electricity, gas and water	...	...	340	...	...	377
	A Electricity, gas and steam	...	...	340	...	...	377
	B Water works and supply	...	...	...	...	...	...
5	Construction	...	...	846	...	...	946
6	Wholesale and retail trade, restaurants and hotels [a]	...	...	1650	...	...	1975
	A Wholesale and retail trade	...	...	1650	...	...	1975
	B Restaurants and hotels	...	...	...	...	...	...
7	Transport, storage and communication [b]	...	...	894	...	...	1016
8	Finance, insurance, real estate and business services [c]	...	...	1369	...	...	1625
9	Community, social and personal services [acd]	...	...	2050	...	...	2535
Total, Industries		...	...	11106	...	...	12848
Producers of Government Services		...	...	1425	...	...	1574
Other Producers [d]		...	...	...	...	...	...
Total [e]		...	...	12531	...	...	14423
Less: Imputed bank service charge		...	...	...	...	...	...
Import duties		...	...	...	...	...	...
Value added tax		...	...	...	...	...	...
Other adjustments [f]		...	...	2301	...	...	2338
Total		...	...	14832	...	...	16760

a) Restaurants and hotels are included in item 'Community, social and personal services'.
b) Data on Exports of goods and services as well as transport, storage and communication exclude income from ocean-going cargo ships under Greek flag or ownership. However, remittances actually received by the bank of Greece from persons engaged in these enterprises are included in factor income from the rest of the world.
c) Business services are included in item 'Community, social and personal services'.
d) Item 'Other producers' is included in item 'Community, social and personal services'.
e) Gross domestic product in factor values.
f) Item 'Other adjustments' refers to indirect taxes net of subsidies.

4.2 Derivation of Value Added by Kind of Activity, in Constant Prices

Million Greek drachmas

	1980 GO	1980 IC	1980 VA	1985 GO	1985 IC	1985 VA	1990 GO	1990 IC	1990 VA	1991 GO	1991 IC	1991 VA
At constant prices of: 1970 — All Producers											
1 Agriculture, hunting, forestry and fishing	...	...	60499	...	...	60523	...	...	53523	...	...	62883
A Agriculture and hunting	...	...	58029	...	...	58223	...	...	51156	...	...	60415
B Forestry and logging	...	...	1202	...	...	1150	...	...	975	...	...	1019
C Fishing	...	...	1268	...	...	1150	...	...	1392	...	...	1449
2 Mining and quarrying	...	...	6245	...	...	7968	...	...	9185	...	...	8841

Greece

4.2 Derivation of Value Added by Kind of Activity, in Constant Prices
(Continued)

Million Greek drachmas

	1980 Gross Output	1980 Intermediate Consumption	1980 Value Added	1985 Gross Output	1985 Intermediate Consumption	1985 Value Added	1990 Gross Output	1990 Intermediate Consumption	1990 Value Added	1991 Gross Output	1991 Intermediate Consumption	1991 Value Added
					At constant prices of:1970							
3 Manufacturing	...	...	89125	...	...	89529	...	...	90761	...	...	90079
A Manufacture of food, beverages and tobacco	...	...	16977	...	...	20041	...	...	20002	...	...	21034
B Textile, wearing apparel and leather industries	...	...	23697	...	...	21286	...	...	20605	...	...	19279
C Manufacture of wood and wood products, including furniture	...	...	3583	...	...	2551	...	...	2637	...	...	2556
D Manufacture of paper and paper products, printing and publishing	...	...	3568	...	...	4444	...	...	4419	...	...	4522
E Manufacture of chemicals and chemical petroleum, coal, rubber and plastic products	...	...	11384	...	...	13225	...	...	15359	...	...	14383
F Manufacture of non-metallic mineral products, except products of petroleum and coal	...	...	7823	...	...	6926	...	...	7667	...	...	6762
G Basic metal industries	...	...	5396	...	...	5067	...	...	5170	...	...	5422
H Manufacture of fabricated metal products, machinery and equipment	...	...	14558	...	...	13539	...	...	13036	...	...	13801
I Other manufacturing industries	...	...	2139	...	...	2450	...	...	1866	...	...	2320
4 Electricity, gas and water	...	...	13724	...	...	17032	...	...	20102	...	...	21805
A Electricity, gas and steam	...	...	13724	...	...	17032	...	...	20102	...	...	21805
B Water works and supply	...	...	...	...	...	...	...	...	...	...	...	...
5 Construction	...	...	26392	...	...	22525	...	...	28186	...	...	27225
6 Wholesale and retail trade, restaurants and hotels [a]	...	...	50633	...	...	55595	...	...	62785	...	...	64983
A Wholesale and retail trade	...	...	50633	...	...	55595	...	...	62785	...	...	64983
B Restaurants and hotels	...	...	...	...	...	...	...	...	...	...	...	...
7 Transport, storage and communication [b]	...	...	39898	...	...	48733	...	...	56262	...	...	57181
8 Finance, insurance, real estate and business services [c]	...	...	49134	...	...	57198	...	...	67760	...	...	71178
9 Community, social and personal services [acd]	...	...	45152	...	...	47404	...	...	55554	...	...	55295
Total, Industries	...	...	380802	...	...	406507	...	...	444117	...	...	459470
Producers of Government Services	...	...	36708	...	...	42912	...	...	44179	...	...	45274
Other Producers [d]	...	...	...	...	...	...	...	...	...	...	...	...
Total [e]	...	...	417510	...	...	449419	...	...	488296	...	...	504744
Less: Imputed bank service charge	...	...	...	...	...	...	...	...	...	...	...	...
Import duties	...	...	...	...	...	...	...	...	...	...	...	...
Value added tax	...	...	...	...	...	...	...	...	...	...	...	...
Other adjustments [f]	...	...	56000	...	...	56592	...	...	60012	...	...	61272
Total	...	...	473510	...	...	506011	...	...	548308	...	...	566016

	1992 Gross Output	1992 Intermediate Consumption	1992 Value Added	1993 Gross Output	1993 Intermediate Consumption	1993 Value Added
		At constant prices of:1970				
		All Producers				
1 Agriculture, hunting, forestry and fishing	...	...	61082	...	...	60223
A Agriculture and hunting	...	...	58427	...	...	57493
B Forestry and logging	...	...	923	...	...	930
C Fishing	...	...	1732	...	...	1800
2 Mining and quarrying	...	...	9023	...	...	8761

Greece

4.2 Derivation of Value Added by Kind of Activity, in Constant Prices
(Continued)

Million Greek drachmas

	1992 Gross Output	1992 Intermediate Consumption	1992 Value Added	1993 Gross Output	1993 Intermediate Consumption	1993 Value Added
				At constant prices of: 1970		
3 Manufacturing	...	...	88693	...	...	84920
A Manufacture of food, beverages and tobacco	...	...	22256	...	...	22092
B Textile, wearing apparel and leather industries	...	...	18088	...	...	17352
C Manufacture of wood and wood products, including furniture	...	...	2415	...	...	2256
D Manufacture of paper and paper products, printing and publishing	...	...	4531	...	...	4252
E Manufacture of chemicals and chemical petroleum, coal, rubber and plastic products	...	...	14077	...	...	14266
F Manufacture of non-metallic mineral products, except products of petroleum and coal	...	...	6401	...	...	6358
G Basic metal industries	...	...	5536	...	...	5259
H Manufacture of fabricated metal products, machinery and equipment	...	...	14014	...	...	12074
I Other manufacturing industries	...	...	1375	...	...	1011
4 Electricity, gas and water	...	...	22766	...	...	23512
A Electricity, gas and steam	...	...	22766	...	...	23512
B Water works and supply	...	...	...	...	...	...
5 Construction	...	...	26250	...	...	25907
6 Wholesale and retail trade, restaurants and hotels [a]	...	...	65000	...	...	62000
A Wholesale and retail trade	...	...	65000	...	...	62000
B Restaurants and hotels	...	...	...	...	...	...
7 Transport, storage and communication [b]	...	...	60275	...	...	63100
8 Finance, insurance, real estate and business services [c]	...	...	75023	...	...	76256
9 Community, social and personal services [acd]	...	...	58110	...	...	59904
Total, Industries	...	...	466222	...	...	464583
Producers of Government Services	...	...	42459	...	...	41678
Other Producers [d]	...	...	...	...	...	...
Total [e]	...	...	508681	...	...	506261
Less: Imputed bank service charge	...	.	...	...	...	...
Import duties	...	...	...	...	...	...
Value added tax	...	...	...	...	...	...
Other adjustments [f]	...	...	62000	...	...	67600
Total	...	...	570681	...	...	573861

a) Restaurants and hotels are included in item 'Community, social and personal services'.
b) Data on Exports of goods and services as well as transport, storage and communication exclude income from ocean-going cargo ships under Greek flag or ownership. However, remittances actually received by the bank of Greece from persons engaged in these enterprises are included in factor income from the rest of the world.
c) Business services are included in item 'Community, social and personal services'.
d) Item 'Other producers' is included in item 'Community, social and personal services'.
e) Gross domestic product in factor values.
f) Item 'Other adjustments' refers to indirect taxes net of subsidies.

Grenada

Source. 'National Income Estimates of Grenada', St. George's.
General note. The estimates shown in the following tables have been prepared in accordance with the United Nations System of National Accounts so far as the existing data would permit.

1.1 Expenditure on the Gross Domestic Product, in Current Prices

Million E.C. dollars

		1980	1983	1984	1985	1986	1987	1988	1989	1990	1991	1992	1993
1	Government final consumption expenditure	41.7	55.9	59.3	68.1	80.7	77.3	82.8	88.0	110.8	106.8	114.8	...
2	Private final consumption expenditure	171.5	183.9	213.2	240.1	261.6	295.0	320.0	340.0	351.1	392.6	384.1	...
3	Gross capital formation	61.1	101.6	81.7	91.9	116.5	150.0	167.9	196.4	227.5	247.7	199.5	...
	A Increase in stocks	8.4	-5.2	1.7	-5.2	-0.6	8.4	7.4	15.0	17.0	20.9	12.1	...
	B Gross fixed capital formation	52.7	106.8	80.0	97.1	117.1	141.6	160.5	181.4	210.5	226.8	187.4	...
4	Exports of goods and services	106.9	105.3	112.8	149.0	163.4	173.5	181.0	185.0	240.3	257.3	223.2	...
5	Less: Imports of goods and services	179.2	193.8	192.1	237.9	271.8	289.7	303.0	318.0	388.6	437.2	343.6	...
	Equals: Gross Domestic Product	202.0	252.9	274.9	311.2	350.4	406.1	448.7	491.4	541.1	567.2	578.0	...

1.10 Gross Domestic Product by Kind of Activity, in Current Prices

Million E.C. dollars

		1980	1983	1984	1985	1986	1987	1988	1989	1990	1991	1992	1993
1	Agriculture, hunting, forestry and fishing	41.4	41.3	44.9	44.2	52.9	69.5	72.0	73.7	71.3	68.8	...	...
2	Mining and quarrying	0.5	0.6	0.5	0.8	1.1	1.2	1.2	1.4	1.7	1.9	...	...
3	Manufacturing	6.6	10.5	9.8	12.5	13.3	16.0	18.4	20.8	22.6	24.3	...	...
4	Electricity, gas and water	3.4	4.4	4.0	6.4	7.5	8.7	9.9	11.5	13.0	14.3	...	...
5	Construction	11.3	17.3	18.4	19.4	23.4	28.3	33.9	40.5	44.5	48.1	...	...
6	Wholesale and retail trade, restaurants and hotels	33.5	36.5	41.0	48.8	54.9	60.7	67.2	74.1	82.2	90.4	...	...
7	Transport, storage and communication	21.5	27.4	30.1	31.5	38.5	42.5	49.2	54.8	60.2	66.2	...	...
8	Finance, insurance, real estate and business services	19.8	23.3	27.5	31.4	33.7	36.1	38.7	40.7	42.8	44.3	...	...
9	Community, social and personal services	8.5	10.2	10.6	11.0	11.5	12.0	12.5	12.6	12.8	12.9	...	...
	Total, Industries [a]	146.5	171.5	186.8	206.0	236.8	275.0	303.0	311.2	351.1	371.2	...	...
	Producers of Government Services	27.1	41.9	46.6	51.5	58.6	60.2	63.1	82.0	88.9	91.5	...	...
	Other Producers	...	...	...	...	...	...	...	...	...	...	...	...
	Subtotal	173.6	213.4	233.4	257.5	295.4	335.2	366.1	393.2	440.0	462.7	...	...
	Less: Imputed bank service charge	6.0	8.9	10.0	11.3	13.3	14.7	15.9	16.8	18.0	18.9	...	...
	Plus: Import duties	...	...	...	...	...	...	...	...	...	...	...	...
	Plus: Value added tax	...	...	...	...	...	...	...	...	...	...	...	...
	Plus: Other adjustments [b]	34.4	48.4	51.5	65.0	68.4	85.6	98.5	115.0	119.1	123.4	...	...
	Equals: Gross Domestic Product [c]	202.0	252.9	274.9	311.2	350.4	406.1	448.7	491.4	541.1	567.2	...	...

a) Gross domestic product in factor values.
b) Item 'Other adjustments' refers to indirect taxes net of subsidies.
c) For the first series, gross domestic product in factor values.

1.11 Gross Domestic Product by Kind of Activity, in Constant Prices

Million E.C. dollars

		1980	1983	1984	1985	1986	1987	1988	1989	1990	1991	1992	1993
		\multicolumn{12}{c}{At constant prices of: 1984}
1	Agriculture, hunting, forestry and fishing	40.6	39.3	43.9	42.0	41.8	45.4	46.4	47.5	47.1	46.6	...	...
2	Mining and quarrying	0.5	0.6	0.5	0.7	0.9	1.0	1.1	1.2	1.3	1.4	...	...
3	Manufacturing	8.9	11.6	9.8	11.7	11.8	13.8	15.2	17.0	18.4	19.3	...	...
4	Electricity, gas and water	4.0	3.9	4.0	4.7	5.3	5.8	6.5	7.3	8.0	8.4	...	...
5	Construction	16.1	18.2	18.4	19.3	22.2	25.6	29.4	33.8	37.0	38.8	...	...
6	Wholesale and retail trade, restaurants and hotels	39.6	37.8	41.0	45.3	49.2	51.4	54.1	57.6	62.1	64.5	...	...
7	Transport, storage and communication	27.3	28.0	30.1	30.4	33.4	35.9	39.5	42.7	47.0	49.8	...	...
8	Finance, insurance, real estate and business services	23.7	25.9	27.5	28.9	29.7	30.7	31.4	32.4	33.3	34.0	...	...
9	Community, social and personal services	9.5	10.5	10.6	10.7	11.0	11.3	11.4	11.4	11.4	11.4	...	...
	Total, Industries [a]	170.2	175.8	185.8	193.7	205.3	220.9	235.0	250.9	265.6	274.2	...	...
	Producers of Government Services	31.2	45.0	46.6	51.5	54.0	54.0	54.0	54.0	54.8	55.6	...	...

Grenada

1.11 Gross Domestic Product by Kind of Activity, in Constant Prices
(Continued)

Million E.C. dollars

	1980	1983	1984	1985	1986	1987	1988	1989	1990	1991	1992	1993
				At constant prices of:1984								
Other Producers	...	...	...	...	...	...	...	...	...	...	...	...
Subtotal	201.4	220.8	232.4	245.2	259.3	274.9	289.0	304.9	320.4	329.8	...	...
Less: Imputed bank service charge	6.9	9.2	10.0	10.8	12.0	12.8	13.1	13.4	13.7	14.1	...	...
Plus: Import duties	...	...	...	...	...	...	...	...	...	...	...	...
Plus: Value added tax	...	...	...	...	...	...	...	...	...	...	...	...
Plus: Other adjustments [b]	39.9	50.1	51.5	61.9	60.6	...	...	...	...	...	...	...
Equals: Gross Domestic Product	234.4	261.7	273.9	296.3	307.9	...	...	...	...	...	...	...

a) Gross domestic product in factor values.
b) Item 'Other adjustments' refers to indirect taxes net of subsidies.

1.12 Relations Among National Accounting Aggregates

Million E.C. dollars

	1980	1983	1984	1985	1986	1987	1988	1989	1990	1991	1992	1993
Gross Domestic Product	...	252.9	274.9	311.2	350.4	...	...	...	...	...	...	...
Plus: Net factor income from the rest of the world	...	0.5	-3.0	-3.5	-2.8	...	...	...	...	...	...	...
Factor income from the rest of the world	...	4.6	3.8	3.3	2.8	...	...	...	...	...	...	...
Less: Factor income to the rest of the world	...	4.1	6.8	6.8	5.6	...	...	...	...	...	...	...
Equals: Gross National Product	...	253.4	271.9	307.7	347.6	...	...	...	...	...	...	...
Less: Consumption of fixed capital	...	...	...	...	...	...	...	...	...	...	...	...
Equals: National Income	...	...	...	...	...	...	...	...	...	...	...	...
Plus: Net current transfers from the rest of the world	...	...	...	...	...	...	...	...	...	...	...	...
Equals: National Disposable Income	...	...	...	...	...	...	...	...	...	...	...	...
Less: Final consumption	...	...	...	...	...	...	...	...	...	...	...	...
Equals: Net Saving	...	...	...	...	...	...	...	...	...	...	...	...
Less: Surplus of the nation on current transactions	...	...	...	...	...	...	...	...	...	...	...	...
Equals: Net Capital Formation	...	...	...	...	...	...	...	...	...	...	...	...

Guadeloupe

Source. Reply to the United Nations National Accounts Questionnaire from the Institute national de la statistique et des etudes economiques (INSEE), Paris. Official estimates and descriptions are published by the same Institute in 'Comptes Economiques de la Guadeloupe'.

General note. The estimates shown in the following tables have been adjusted by the INSEE to conform to the United Nations System of National Accounts so far as the existing data would permit.

1.1 Expenditure on the Gross Domestic Product, in Current Prices

Million French francs

	1980	1983	1984	1985	1986	1987	1988	1989	1990	1991	1992	1993
1 Government final consumption expenditure	1856.7	2815.2	3107.7	3388.1	3576.8	3813.7	4073.8	4450.3	4679.7	5085.1	...	...
2 Private final consumption expenditure	5101.7	8128.8	8485.3	9335.4	9867.6	10904.5	11818.3	12683.1	14112.4	14331.9	...	...
3 Gross capital formation	1547.9	1998.4	1999.9	2161.7	2315.6	3307.2	3477.3	4221.9	5315.8	5579.5		
A Increase in stocks	82.8	68.4	21.7	28.0	-74.5	251.0	-98.5	112.4	161.0	166.2		
B Gross fixed capital formation	1465.1	1930.0	1978.2	2133.7	2390.1	3056.2	3575.8	4109.5	5154.8	5413.3		
4 Exports of goods and services	458.0	562.8	750.4	728.1	819.0	698.2	1035.6	783.8	743.9	998.3		
5 Less: Imports of goods and services	3104.1	5092.6	5296.5	5810.9	5621.2	6430.1	7379.6	8077.1	9651.3	9580.0		
Equals: Gross Domestic Product	5860.2	8412.6	9046.8	9802.4	10957.8	12293.6	13025.4	14062.0	15200.5	16414.8	...	...

1.3 Cost Components of the Gross Domestic Product

Million French francs

	1980	1983	1984	1985	1986	1987	1988	1989	1990	1991	1992	1993
1 Indirect taxes, net	619.8	890.3	813.1	919.1	1136.3	1411.2	1720.4	1697.5	1939.2	2002.8		
A Indirect taxes	728.4	1183.2	1207.4	1334.4	1500.8	1723.2	1962.0	2122.7	2184.3	2307.8		
B Less: Subsidies [a]	108.6	292.9	394.3	415.3	364.5	312.0	241.6	425.2	245.1	305.0		
2 Consumption of fixed capital [b]	...	...	...	...	...	...	...	...	...	...		
3 Compensation of employees paid by resident producers to:	4108.2	6167.4	6587.0	7242.6	7590.3	8342.4	9310.7	10116.6	11318.7	12664.1		
4 Operating surplus [b]	1132.2	1354.9	1646.7	1640.7	2231.2	2540.0	1994.3	2247.9	1942.5	1747.9		
Equals: Gross Domestic Product	5860.2	8412.6	9046.8	9802.4	10957.8	12293.6	13025.4	14062.0	15200.5	16414.8		

a) Item 'Subsidies' in table 1.3 includes subsidies from the government and from the rest of the world.
b) Item 'Operating surplus' includes consumption of fixed capital.

1.4 General Government Current Receipts and Disbursements

Million French francs

	1980	1983	1984	1985	1986	1987	1988	1989	1990	1991	1992	1993
					Receipts							
1 Operating surplus	-	-	-	-	-	-	-	-	...	...		
2 Property and entrepreneurial income	39.3	44.6	54.0	57.6	48.9	42.9	42.0	53.4	39.2	108.3		
3 Taxes, fees and contributions	2088.7	3480.4	3858.6	4098.3	4326.9	4985.2	5609.4	5984.9	5979.4	7136.0		
4 Other current transfers	2071.3	3002.7	3059.0	3362.7	4060.0	4184.4	4235.9	5282.7	5619.8	5735.6		
Total Current Receipts of General Government	4199.3	6527.7	6971.6	7518.6	8435.8	9212.5	9887.3	11321.0	11638.4	12980.0		
					Disbursements							
1 Government final consumption expenditure	1856.6	2815.2	3107.7	3388.1	3576.8	3813.7	4073.8	4450.3	4679.7	5085.1		
2 Property income	68.1	129.7	158.1	189.1	250.4	251.7	349.3	337.7	386.5	368.1		
3 Subsidies [a]	21.2	68.6	87.7	103.6	72.6	79.5	155.8	165.6	126.2	156.3		
4 Other current transfers	1793.4	3098.6	3380.0	3504.4	3957.8	4379.6	4547.0	5077.9	5194.0	5942.4		
5 Net saving	460.0	415.6	238.1	333.4	578.2	688.0	761.4	1289.5	1252.1	1427.8		
Total Current Disbursements and Net Saving of General Government	4199.3	6527.7	6971.6	7518.6	8435.8	9212.5	9887.3	11321.0	11638.4	12980.0		

a) Item 'Subsidies' in table 1.3 includes subsidies from the government and from the rest of the world.

1.7 External Transactions on Current Account, Summary

Million French francs

	1980	1983	1984	1985	1986	1987	1988	1989	1990	1991	1992	1993
					Payments to the Rest of the World							
1 Imports of goods and services	3104.1	5092.6	5296.5	5810.9	5621.2	6430.1	7379.6	8077.1	9651.3	9580.0	...	...
2 Factor income to the rest of the world	244.9	389.0	484.0	510.5	607.5	680.4	744.2	704.7	783.1	806.6	...	...
A Compensation of employees	-	-	-	-	-	-	-	-	...	...		
B Property and entrepreneurial income	244.9	389.0	484.0	510.5	607.5	680.4	744.2	704.7				

Guadeloupe

1.7 External Transactions on Current Account, Summary
(Continued)

Million French francs

	1980	1983	1984	1985	1986	1987	1988	1989	1990	1991	1992	1993
3 Current transfers to the rest of the world	80.3	95.4	101.0	71.2	81.9	91.5	100.3	96.4	94.4	103.0	...	...
4 Surplus of the nation on current transactions	-712.9	-1614.0	-1596.4	-1808.1	-914.5	-1862.4	-2537.9	-2158.4	-3615.7	-3326.9	...	...
Payments to the Rest of the World and Surplus of the Nation on Current Transactions	2716.4	3963.0	4285.1	4584.5	5396.1	5339.6	5686.2	6719.8	6913.1	7162.7	...	...

Receipts From The Rest of the World

1 Exports of goods and services	458.1	562.8	750.4	728.1	819.0	698.2	1035.6	783.8	743.9	998.3	...	...
2 Factor income from rest of the world	89.2	145.8	139.8	150.0	191.8	253.2	293.8	368.5	401.7	251.9	...	...
A Compensation of employees	-	-	-	-	-	-	-	-	...	...	...	...
B Property and entrepreneurial income	89.2	145.8	139.8	150.0	191.8	253.2	293.8	368.5	401.7	251.9	...	...
3 Current transfers from rest of the world	2169.1	3254.4	3394.9	3706.4	4385.3	4388.2	4356.8	5567.5	5767.5	5912.5	...	...
Receipts from the Rest of the World on Current Transactions	2716.4	3963.0	4285.1	4584.5	5396.1	5339.5	5686.3	6719.8	6913.1	7162.7	...	...

1.8 Capital Transactions of The Nation, Summary

Million French francs

	1980	1983	1984	1985	1986	1987	1988	1989	1990	1991	1992	1993

Finance of Gross Capital Formation

Gross saving	834.9	384.4	403.5	353.6	1401.1	1444.8	939.4	2063.6	1700.0	2252.7	...	...
Less: Surplus of the nation on current transactions	-712.9	-1614.0	-1596.4	-1808.1	-914.5	-1862.4	-2537.9	-2158.4	-3615.7	-3326.9	...	...
Finance of Gross Capital Formation	1547.8	1998.4	1999.9	2161.7	2315.6	3307.2	3477.3	4222.0	5315.8	5579.5	...	...

Gross Capital Formation

Increase in stocks	82.7	68.4	21.7	28.0	-74.5	251.0	-98.5	112.4	161.0	166.2	...	...
Gross fixed capital formation	1465.1	1930.0	1978.2	2133.7	2390.1	3056.2	3575.8	4109.5	5154.8	5413.3	...	...
1 General government	437.4	604.0	628.8	724.7	860.9	971.9	848.5	1065.9	1409.9	1644.9	...	...
2 Corporate and quasi-corporate enterprises	762.5	957.9	977.8	1048.6	1116.6	1514.2	1933.5	2108.4	2561.1	2596.1	...	...
3 Other	265.2	368.1	371.6	360.4	412.6	570.1	793.8	935.2	1183.8	1172.3	...	...
Gross Capital Formation	1547.8	1998.4	1999.9	2161.7	2315.6	3307.2	3477.3	4221.9	5315.8	5579.5	...	...

1.10 Gross Domestic Product by Kind of Activity, in Current Prices

Million French francs

	1980	1983	1984	1985	1986	1987	1988	1989	1990	1991	1992	1993
1 Agriculture, hunting, forestry and fishing	428.9	846.1	940.4	958.9	1094.8	1166.9	1310.6	1177.4	1011.0	1192.2	...	...
2 Mining and quarrying	357.4	381.5	380.8	463.9	547.9	614.8	688.5	758.4	811.7	1000.5	...	...
3 Manufacturing									...	...	...	...
4 Electricity, gas and water	11.2	-81.2	-160.9	-45.9	-12.2	60.1	90.2	38.7	151.6	224.5	...	...
5 Construction	246.2	404.0	450.7	464.3	537.7	625.7	645.8	949.3	1118.5	1145.4	...	...
6 Wholesale and retail trade, restaurants and hotels	1023.5	1462.4	1630.4	1637.4	1805.5	2061.2	2098.6	2499.5	2757.8	2692.6	...	...
7 Transport, storage and communication	255.1	412.5	430.3	546.1	652.1	739.1	774.5	773.3	881.5	984.3	...	...
8 Finance, insurance, real estate and business services	645.9	701.5	789.8	845.0	990.3	1282.9	1361.4	1373.8	1711.9	1891.2	...	...
9 Community, social and personal services	895.8	1250.9	1330.7	1386.8	1581.0	1695.7	1795.9	2031.4	2040.5	2294.0	...	...
Total, Industries	3864.0	5377.7	5792.2	6256.5	7197.1	8246.4	8765.5	9601.8	10484.5	11424.7	...	...
Producers of Government Services	1695.3	2568.6	2810.3	3052.1	3194.9	3448.5	3728.7	4057.9	4235.3	4534.0	...	...
Other Producers	122.5	199.6	212.8	247.9	278.8	281.6	269.6	281.8	316.2	319.7	...	...
Subtotal	5681.8	8145.9	8815.3	9556.5	10670.8	11976.5	12763.8	13941.5	15036.0	16278.4	...	...
Less: Imputed bank service charge	305.9	484.7	560.5	600.6	628.1	794.8	971.9	1160.3	1222.3	1535.2	...	...
Plus: Import duties	238.9	351.6	383.4	400.3	429.8	536.6	614.0	664.5	722.9	738.0	...	...
Plus: Value added tax	245.4	399.8	408.6	446.2	485.3	575.2	619.5	616.2	663.9	933.6	...	...
Equals: Gross Domestic Product	5860.2	8412.6	9046.8	9802.4	10957.8	12293.6	13025.4	14062.0	15200.5	16414.8	...	...

Guadeloupe

1.12 Relations Among National Accounting Aggregates

Million French francs

	1980	1983	1984	1985	1986	1987	1988	1989	1990	1991	1992	1993
Gross Domestic Product	5860.2	8412.6	9046.8	9802.4	10957.8	12293.6	13025.4	14062.0	15200.5	16414.8	...	...
Plus: Net factor income from the rest of the world	-155.7	-243.2	-344.2	-360.5	-415.7	-427.3	-450.4	-336.2	-381.4	-554.7	...	...
Factor income from the rest of the world	89.2	145.8	139.8	150.0	191.8	253.1	293.8	368.5	401.7	251.9	...	...
Less: Factor income to the rest of the world	244.9	389.0	484.0	510.5	607.5	680.4	744.2	704.7	783.1	806.6	...	...
Equals: Gross National Product	5704.5	8169.4	8702.6	9441.9	10542.1	11866.3	12575.0	13725.8	14819.1	15860.1	...	...
Less: Consumption of fixed capital	...	...	...	...	...	...	...	...	...	...	...	...
Equals: National Income	...	...	...	...	...	...	...	...	...	...	...	...
Plus: Net current transfers from the rest of the world	2088.9	3159.0	3293.9	3635.2	4303.4	4296.7	4256.6	5471.2	5673.1	5809.5	...	...
Current transfers from the rest of the world	2169.2	3254.4	3394.9	3706.4	4385.3	4388.2	4356.9	5567.5	5767.5	5912.5	...	...
Less: Current transfers to the rest of the world	80.3	95.4	101.0	71.2	81.9	91.5	100.3	96.3	94.4	103.0	...	...
Equals: National Disposable Income	...	...	...	...	...	...	...	...	...	...	...	...
Less: Final consumption	6958.4	10944.0	11593.0	12723.5	13444.4	14718.2	15892.1	17133.4	18792.1	19417.0	...	...
Equals: Net Saving	...	...	...	...	...	...	...	...	...	...	...	...
Less: Surplus of the nation on current transactions	-712.9	-1614.0	-1596.4	-1808.1	-914.5	-1862.4	-2537.9	-2158.4	-3615.7	-3326.9	...	...
Equals: Net Capital Formation	...	...	...	...	...	...	...	...	...	...	...	...

Guatemala

Source. Reply to the United Nations National Accounts Questionnaire from the Banco de Guatemala, Guatemala City. The official estimates are published in 'Boletin Estadistico del Banco de Guatemala'.

General note. The estimates shown in the following tables have been prepared in accordance with the United Nations System of National Accounts so far as the existing data would permit.

1.1 Expenditure on the Gross Domestic Product, in Current Prices

Million Guatemalan quetzales

		1980	1983	1984	1985	1986	1987	1988	1989	1990	1991	1992	1993
1	Government final consumption expenditure	626.5	687.9	725.9	777.4	1123.9	1399.6	1639.8	1870.0	2323.9	2714.0	3487.4	4064.7
2	Private final consumption expenditure	6216.8	7500.7	7855.9	9295.9	12846.7	14989.2	17289.0	19837.4	28692.1	39693.4	45899.1	53925.9
3	Gross capital formation	1251.7	1002.5	1095.9	1285.4	1636.5	2463.7	2814.4	3201.0	4668.3	6762.1	9851.1	11861.9
	A Increase in stocks	-43.5	52.3	183.5	60.5	43.3	275.4	67.3	-53.9	213.3	1002.0	1493.2	1413.1
	B Gross fixed capital formation	1295.3	950.2	912.4	1224.9	1593.2	2188.3	2747.2	3254.9	4455.0	5760.2	8357.9	10448.8
	Residential buildings	151.5	120.5	104.9	144.7	189.8	226.8	305.9	375.5	431.3	666.6	942.3	1128.1
	Non-residential buildings												
	Other construction and land improvement etc.	437.3	369.6	290.5	271.1	327.4	417.7	530.7	620.1	866.1	999.3	1502.3	1759.9
	Other	706.5	460.1	516.9	809.1	1076.0	1543.8	1910.6	2259.4	3157.6	4094.3	5913.3	7560.7
4	Exports of goods and services	1747.6	1175.8	1256.2	2068.0	2542.1	2807.0	3308.5	4099.2	6775.8	8349.0	9482.7	10616.0
5	Less: Imports of goods and services	1963.3	1317.1	1463.6	2246.9	2311.1	3948.5	4506.8	5322.9	8143.1	10216.2	14771.3	16905.8
	Equals: Gross Domestic Product	7879.4	9049.9	9470.3	11180.0	15838.1	17711.1	20544.9	23684.7	34316.9	47302.3	53949.0	63562.7

1.2 Expenditure on the Gross Domestic Product, in Constant Prices

Million Guatemalan quetzales

		1980	1983	1984	1985	1986	1987	1988	1989	1990	1991	1992	1993
		At constant prices of:1958											
1	Government final consumption expenditure	222.7	229.9	236.0	230.6	243.0	259.9	273.0	283.4	292.7	297.7	315.0	330.7
2	Private final consumption expenditure	2318.8	2247.7	2272.5	2265.6	2283.8	2372.8	2470.1	2544.2	2606.1	2706.3	2842.9	2982.2
3	Gross capital formation	355.4	275.2	292.1	236.1	236.6	313.5	310.2	311.4	307.3	376.9	490.3	516.7
	A Increase in stocks	-17.2	17.0	57.1	15.9	8.0	47.3	10.4	-7.5	21.1	80.1	109.5	93.8
	B Gross fixed capital formation	372.6	258.2	234.9	220.2	228.6	266.1	299.8	318.9	286.2	296.8	380.8	422.9
	Residential buildings	40.6	29.5	25.4	28.4	31.2	33.8	41.1	44.7	36.4	41.3	53.6	56.4
	Non-residential buildings												
	Other construction and land improvement etc.	147.1	112.5	85.2	70.6	70.4	80.4	90.6	96.0	93.2	92.0	116.0	122.8
	Other	184.9	116.2	124.3	121.2	127.0	152.0	168.1	178.2	156.6	163.5	211.1	243.8
4	Exports of goods and services	651.1	454.7	440.2	454.0	390.5	414.0	437.3	495.4	527.8	502.0	543.9	540.4
5	Less: Imports of goods and services	441.2	267.9	287.2	250.3	213.6	315.8	327.7	346.8	344.3	369.2	510.5	541.2
	Equals: Gross Domestic Product	3106.9	2939.6	2953.5	2936.1	2940.2	3044.4	3162.9	3287.6	3389.6	3513.6	3681.5	3828.8

1.7 External Transactions on Current Account, Summary

Million Guatemalan quetzales

		1980	1983	1984	1985	1986	1987	1988	1989	1990	1991	1992	1993
		Payments to the Rest of the World											
1	Imports of goods and services	1963.3	1317.1	1463.6	2246.9	2311.1	3948.5	4506.8	5322.9	8143.1	10216.2	14771.3	16905.8
	A Imports of merchandise c.i.f.	1598.2	1135.0	1304.1	2091.2	2101.3	3574.5	4048.1	4676.9	7089.8	9311.8	13113.3	14929.2
	B Other	365.1	182.1	159.5	155.7	209.8	373.9	458.7	646.0	1053.3	904.4	1657.9	1976.6
2	Factor income to the rest of the world	147.4	142.5	237.0	383.3	508.7	548.9	545.8	585.1	867.1	981.4	970.3	869.8
	A Compensation of employees	...	...	...	...	...	...	...	...	...	...	...	...
	B Property and entrepreneurial income	147.4	142.5	237.0	383.3	508.7	548.9	545.8	585.1	867.1	981.4	970.3	869.8
	By general government	39.4	83.3	124.8	335.6	414.5	430.3	431.9	398.2	662.2	756.8	780.4	...
	By corporate and quasi-corporate enterprises	63.9	16.2	67.4	23.4	25.6	62.2	73.2	128.1	102.0	127.2	85.0	...
	By other	44.1	42.9	44.8	24.4	68.6	56.3	40.6	58.8	102.9	97.4	104.9	...
3	Current transfers to the rest of the world	15.5	3.6	3.0	2.3	2.4	6.4	9.2	15.0	45.5	85.4	81.5	31.3
4	Surplus of the nation on current transactions	-176.4	-224.0	-384.9	-474.5	-40.1	-1136.4	-1086.8	-1055.2	-1045.5	-1077.7	-3606.0	-4349.6
	Payments to the Rest of the World and Surplus of the Nation on Current Transactions	1949.8	1239.1	1318.6	2157.9	2782.1	3367.3	3975.0	4867.8	8010.3	10205.3	12217.0	13457.4

Guatemala

1.7 External Transactions on Current Account, Summary
(Continued)

Million Guatemalan quetzales

	1980	1983	1984	1985	1986	1987	1988	1989	1990	1991	1992	1993
					Receipts From The Rest of the World							
1 Exports of goods and services	1747.6	1175.8	1256.2	2068.0	2542.1	2807.0	3308.5	4099.2	6775.8	8349.0	9482.7	10616.0
A Exports of merchandise f.o.b.	1519.8	1091.7	1154.8	1886.2	2285.8	2415.5	2790.9	3209.4	5209.3	6186.7	6649.1	7398.9
B Other	227.8	84.2	101.4	181.8	256.3	391.6	517.6	889.7	1566.5	2162.3	2833.6	3217.0
2 Factor income from rest of the world	76.8	29.1	30.2	52.5	73.0	76.5	74.6	41.6	194.8	464.8	629.4	753.0
A Compensation of employees	...	...	...	...	...	...	...	...	...	...	...	...
B Property and entrepreneurial income	76.8	29.1	30.2	52.5	73.0	76.5	74.6	41.6	194.8	464.8	629.4	753.0
By general government	73.5	28.9	30.0	51.6	72.1	76.1	66.6	31.2	28.3	112.2	119.8	...
By corporate and quasi-corporate enterprises [a]	2.0	-	0.1	0.7	0.4	-	4.2	8.3	166.5	350.2	508.3	...
By other	1.3	0.2	0.1	0.2	0.5	0.3	3.9	2.2	-	2.3	1.3	...
3 Current transfers from rest of the world	125.3	34.2	32.2	37.4	167.0	483.8	591.8	727.0	1039.7	1391.6	2104.8	2088.4
Receipts from the Rest of the World on Current Transactions	1949.8	1239.1	1318.6	2157.9	2782.1	3367.3	3975.0	4867.8	8010.3	10205.3	12217.0	13457.4

a) For the years 1990-1992, property and entrepreneurial income received by the corporate and quasi-corporate enterprises from the rest of the world includes bank service charges.

1.11 Gross Domestic Product by Kind of Activity, in Constant Prices

Million Guatemalan quetzales

	1980	1983	1984	1985	1986	1987	1988	1989	1990	1991	1992	1993
					At constant prices of:1958							
1 Agriculture, hunting, forestry and fishing	772.0	744.9	756.5	759.3	753.0	782.4	817.6	842.7	877.2	904.4	931.2	949.8
2 Mining and quarrying	14.8	9.4	7.6	6.5	8.5	8.4	8.7	9.0	8.5	9.2	11.9	13.4
3 Manufacturing	517.3	466.1	468.4	464.8	467.9	477.4	487.9	499.1	510.2	522.3	538.4	551.4
4 Electricity, gas and water	53.2	51.5	54.0	56.3	63.2	68.2	74.1	79.9	84.6	88.0	99.6	108.1
5 Construction	97.9	75.8	54.3	49.7	51.3	58.7	67.9	73.2	67.4	68.4	83.1	91.8
6 Wholesale and retail trade, restaurants and hotels	839.1	764.4	773.1	747.0	730.9	752.8	776.2	803.4	816.1	850.2	888.4	925.9
7 Transport, storage and communication	215.8	199.7	206.3	209.8	210.7	220.8	230.4	254.3	269.9	285.9	308.9	332.4
8 Finance, insurance, real estate and business services	244.8	256.5	257.7	263.1	269.3	276.1	285.6	296.7	310.5	324.5	338.3	355.2
9 Community, social and personal services	188.9	186.3	186.8	187.6	186.1	189.5	195.9	200.7	207.5	212.5	218.8	225.3
Total, Industries	2943.9	2754.5	2764.7	2744.1	2740.7	2834.2	2944.3	3059.0	3152.0	3265.2	3418.6	3553.3
Producers of Government Services	163.0	185.1	188.8	192.0	199.5	210.2	218.5	228.6	237.5	248.4	262.9	275.6
Other Producers	...	...	...	...	...	...	...	...	...	...	...	...
Subtotal	3106.9	2939.6	2953.5	2936.1	2940.2	3044.4	3162.9	3287.6	3389.6	3513.6	3681.5	3828.8
Less: Imputed bank service charge	...	...	...	...	...	...	...	...	...	...	...	...
Plus: Import duties	...	...	...	...	...	...	...	...	...	...	...	...
Plus: Value added tax	...	...	...	...	...	...	...	...	...	...	...	...
Equals: Gross Domestic Product	3106.9	2939.6	2953.5	2936.1	2940.2	3044.4	3162.9	3287.6	3389.6	3513.6	3681.5	3828.8

1.12 Relations Among National Accounting Aggregates

Million Guatemalan quetzales

	1980	1983	1984	1985	1986	1987	1988	1989	1990	1991	1992	1993
Gross Domestic Product	7879.4	9049.9	9470.3	11180.0	15838.1	17711.1	20544.9	23684.7	34316.9	47302.3	53949.0	63562.7
Plus: Net factor income from the rest of the world	-70.5	-113.4	-206.8	-330.8	-435.7	-472.4	-471.1	-543.5	-672.3	-516.6	-340.8	-116.8
Factor income from the rest of the world	76.8	29.1	30.2	52.5	73.0	76.5	74.6	41.6	194.8	464.8	629.4	753.0
Less: Factor income to the rest of the world	147.4	142.5	237.0	383.3	508.7	548.9	545.8	585.1	867.1	981.4	970.3	869.8
Equals: Gross National Product	7808.8	8936.5	9263.5	10849.2	15402.4	17238.6	20073.8	23141.2	33644.7	46785.7	53608.2	63445.9
Less: Consumption of fixed capital	...	...	...	...	...	...	...	...	...	...	...	...

Guatemala

1.12 Relations Among National Accounting Aggregates
(Continued)

Million Guatemalan quetzales

	1980	1983	1984	1985	1986	1987	1988	1989	1990	1991	1992	1993
Equals: National Income [a]	7808.8	8936.5	9263.5	10849.2	15402.4	17238.6	20073.8	23141.2	33644.7	46785.7	53608.2	63445.9
Plus: Net current transfers from the rest of the world	109.8	30.6	29.2	35.1	164.6	477.5	582.6	712.0	994.1	1306.2	2023.3	2057.1
Current transfers from the rest of the world	125.3	34.2	32.2	37.4	167.0	483.8	591.8	727.0	1039.7	1391.6	2104.8	2088.4
Less: Current transfers to the rest of the world	15.5	3.6	3.0	2.3	2.4	6.4	9.2	15.0	45.5	85.4	81.5	31.3
Equals: National Disposable Income [b]	7918.6	8967.1	9292.8	10884.3	15567.0	17716.1	20656.4	23853.2	34638.8	48091.9	55631.5	65503.0
Less: Final consumption	6843.3	8188.6	8581.8	10073.4	13970.6	16388.8	18928.7	21707.4	31016.0	42407.4	49386.5	57990.6
Equals: Net Saving [c]	1075.3	778.5	710.9	810.9	1596.4	1327.3	1727.7	2145.8	3622.8	5684.5	6245.1	7512.3
Less: Surplus of the nation on current transactions	-176.4	-224.0	-384.9	-474.5	-40.1	-1136.4	-1086.8	-1055.2	-1045.5	-1077.7	-3606.0	-4349.6
Equals: Net Capital Formation [d]	1251.7	1002.5	1095.9	1285.4	1636.5	2463.7	2814.4	3201.0	4668.3	6762.1	9851.1	11861.9

a) Item 'National income' includes consumption of fixed capital.
b) Item 'National disposable income' includes consumption of fixed capital.
c) Item 'Net saving' includes consumption of fixed capital.
d) Item 'Net capital formation' includes consumption of fixed capital.

2.11 Gross Fixed Capital Formation by Kind of Activity of Owner, ISIC Divisions, in Current Prices

Million Guatemalan quetzales

	1980	1983	1984	1985	1986	1987	1988	1989	1990	1991	1992	1993
					All Producers							
1 Agriculture, hunting, forestry and fishing	74.0	61.8	70.6	93.5	129.0	164.6	186.3	229.1	401.2	496.9	643.9	793.3
2 Mining and quarrying	...	...	...	...	...	...	...	...	...	...	...	...
3 Manufacturing	554.1	402.2	441.9	662.3	873.9	1191.1	1499.3	1774.4	2464.2	3041.9	4341.9	5474.5
4 Electricity, gas and water	...	...	...	...	...	...	...	...	...	...	...	...
5 Construction	151.5	120.5	104.9	144.7	189.8	226.8	305.9	375.5	431.3	666.6	942.3	1128.1
6 Wholesale and retail trade, restaurants and hotels	...	...	...	...	...	...	...	...	...	...	...	...
7 Transport, storage and communication	121.8	41.6	53.1	113.0	151.5	280.5	327.4	375.7	469.9	797.1	1216.7	1615.3
8 Finance, insurance, real estate and business services	...	...	...	...	...	...	...	...	...	...	...	...
9 Community, social and personal services	...	...	...	...	...	...	...	...	...	...	...	...
Total Industries	901.4	626.2	670.5	1013.6	1344.2	1863.1	2318.9	2754.8	3766.6	5002.5	7144.7	9011.2
Producers of Government Services	393.9	324.1	241.8	211.4	249.0	325.3	428.3	500.2	688.3	757.6	1213.2	1437.6
Private Non-Profit Institutions Serving Households	...	...	...	...	...	...	...	...	...	...	...	...
Total	1295.3	950.2	912.4	1224.9	1593.2	2188.3	2747.2	3254.9	4455.0	5760.2	8357.9	10448.8

2.12 Gross Fixed Capital Formation by Kind of Activity of Owner, ISIC Divisions, in Constant Prices

Million Guatemalan quetzales

	1980	1983	1984	1985	1986	1987	1988	1989	1990	1991	1992	1993
					At constant prices of:1958							
					All Producers							
1 Agriculture, hunting, forestry and fishing	23.1	17.4	19.1	18.4	18.9	20.7	21.0	22.9	24.9	25.4	28.6	31.0
2 Mining and quarrying	...	...	...	...	...	...	...	...	...	...	...	...
3 Manufacturing	151.1	103.1	107.7	105.2	107.5	123.1	137.4	145.4	129.9	129.6	163.2	184.9
4 Electricity, gas and water	...	...	...	...	...	...	...	...	...	...	...	...
5 Construction	40.6	29.5	25.4	28.4	31.2	33.8	41.1	44.7	36.4	41.3	53.6	56.4
6 Wholesale and retail trade, restaurants and hotels	...	...	...	...	...	...	...	...	...	...	...	...
7 Transport, storage and communication	27.0	9.4	11.8	12.3	14.6	23.0	24.5	25.4	18.1	25.7	37.1	45.6
8 Finance, insurance, real estate and business services	...	...	...	...	...	...	...	...	...	...	...	...
9 Community, social and personal services	...	...	...	...	...	...	...	...	...	...	...	...
Total Industries	241.7	159.4	163.9	164.3	172.2	200.5	224.0	238.4	209.3	221.9	282.5	317.9
Producers of Government Services	130.8	98.8	71.0	55.9	56.3	65.6	75.8	80.5	76.9	74.9	98.2	105.0
Private Non-Profit Institutions Serving Households	...	...	...	...	...	...	...	...	...	...	...	...
Total	372.6	258.2	234.9	220.2	228.6	266.1	299.8	318.9	286.2	296.8	380.8	422.9

Guatemala

2.17 Exports and Imports of Goods and Services, Detail

Million Guatemalan quetzales

		1980	1983	1984	1985	1986	1987	1988	1989	1990	1991	1992	1993
		\multicolumn{12}{c}{**Exports of Goods and Services**}
1	Exports of merchandise, f.o.b.	1519.8	1091.7	1154.8	1886.2	2285.8	2415.5	2790.9	3209.4	5209.3	6186.7	6649.1	7398.9
2	Transport and communication	30.3	16.8	9.3	11.6	16.3	22.2	44.1	68.7	81.9	121.2	136.3	...
	A In respect of merchandise imports	4.4	1.9	0.3	0.7	-	-	0.9	5.8	29.4	33.8	11.2	...
	B Other	25.9	14.9	9.0	11.0	16.3	22.2	43.1	62.9	52.5	87.4	125.1	...
3	Insurance service charges	11.4	2.1	5.5	1.3	0.7	1.8	5.7	19.3	26.2	27.6	60.8	...
	A In respect of merchandise imports	3.3	0.7	0.3	0.7	0.2	0.5	0.6	4.0	1.6	0.2	2.3	...
	B Other	8.1	1.4	5.2	0.5	0.4	1.3	5.1	15.3	24.6	27.5	58.5	...
4	Other commodities	82.3	20.6	39.4	56.9	106.7	180.8	146.8	267.7	766.5	1097.4	1494.1	...
5	Adjustments of merchandise exports to change-of-ownership basis	...	...	...	...	...	...	...	...	...	...	...	...
6	Direct purchases in the domestic market by non-residential households	61.6	6.8	11.7	23.6	64.1	126.1	161.3	310.4	507.1	730.6	963.4	1169.4
7	Direct purchases in the domestic market by extraterritorial bodies	42.2	37.9	35.5	88.4	68.4	60.7	159.7	223.6	184.7	185.5	178.9	...
	Total Exports of Goods and Services	1747.6	1175.8	1256.2	2068.0	2542.1	2807.0	3308.5	4099.2	6775.8	8349.0	9482.7	10616.0
		\multicolumn{12}{c}{**Imports of Goods and Services**}
1	Imports of merchandise, c.i.f.	1598.2	1135.0	1304.1	2091.2	2101.3	3574.5	4048.1	4676.9	7089.8	9311.8	13113.3	14929.2
	A Imports of merchandise, f.o.b.	1472.6	1056.0	1205.8	1916.6	1919.5	3292.9	3674.3	4230.6	6140.5	8415.3	12058.4	13660.3
	B Transport of services on merchandise imports	119.0	74.8	93.1	165.3	172.2	266.7	354.0	422.7	899.0	849.0	999.0	...
	By residents	...	...	...	...	...	...	...	...	...	...	...	...
	By non-residents	119.0	74.8	93.1	165.3	172.2	266.7	354.0	422.7	899.0	849.0	999.0	...
	C Insurance service charges on merchandise imports	6.7	4.2	5.2	9.3	9.6	14.9	19.8	23.7	50.3	47.5	55.9	...
	By residents	...	...	...	...	...	...	...	...	...	...	...	...
	By non-residents	6.7	4.2	5.2	9.3	9.6	14.9	19.8	23.7	50.3	47.5	55.9	...
2	Adjustments of merchandise imports to change-of-ownership basis	...	...	...	...	...	...	...	...	...	...	...	...
3	Other transport and communication	53.2	19.8	15.9	16.0	19.2	25.7	42.2	54.9	61.7	70.5	88.8	...
4	Other insurance service charges	9.7	12.8	21.4	10.8	12.2	8.8	17.2	28.4	21.1	25.3	43.1	...
5	Other commodities	114.5	45.8	46.2	63.9	107.7	222.9	102.4	150.8	454.6	162.1	827.1	...
6	Direct purchases abroad by government	23.7	14.3	13.3	23.2	37.2	35.3	49.2	59.8	87.9	142.5	165.4	...
7	Direct purchases abroad by resident households	164.0	89.3	62.7	41.9	33.6	81.2	247.6	352.1	428.0	504.0	533.6	683.1
	Total Imports of Goods and Services	1963.3	1317.1	1463.6	2246.9	2311.1	3948.5	4506.8	5322.9	8143.1	10216.2	14771.3	16905.8
	Balance of Goods and Services	-215.7	-141.2	-207.4	-178.9	231.0	-1141.5	-1198.3	-1223.7	-1367.4	-1867.2	-5288.5	-6289.9
	Total Imports and Balance of Goods and Services	1747.6	1175.8	1256.2	2068.0	2542.1	2807.0	3308.5	4099.2	6775.8	8349.0	9482.7	10616.0

Guinea-Bissau

Source. Reply to the United Nations National Accounts Questionnaire from the Ministerio do Plano, Bissau.
General note. The estimates shown in the following tables have been prepared in accordance with the United Nations System of National Accounts so far as the existing data would permit.

1.1 Expenditure on the Gross Domestic Product, in Current Prices

Million Guinea-Bissau pesos

	1980	1983	1984	1985	1986	1987	1988	1989	1990	1991	1992	1993
1 Government final consumption expenditure	...	...	...	...	6423	10776	20134	46925	58013	108032	163100	...
2 Private final consumption expenditure	...	...	...	...	41844	82375	160420	351049	514670	860458	1700380	...
A Households	...	...	...	...	41844	82375	160420	351049	514670	860458	1700380	...
B Private non-profit institutions serving households	...	...	...	...	...	...	...	...	...	...	...	...
3 Gross capital formation	...	...	...	...	9967	21785	49864	72534	75136	96820	405660	...
A Increase in stocks	...	...	...	...	582	879	192	6337	4591	7695	...	...
B Gross fixed capital formation	...	...	...	...	9385	20906	49672	66197	70546	89125	...	...
4 Exports of goods and services	...	...	...	...	2211	13788	22666	28924	61211	114568	125010	...
5 Less: Imports of goods and services	...	...	...	...	13472	36349	81134	140557	198937	324894	864140	...
Equals: Gross Domestic Product	...	...	...	...	46973	92375	171949	358875	510094	854985	1530010	...

1.2 Expenditure on the Gross Domestic Product, in Constant Prices

Million Guinea-Bissau pesos

	1980	1983	1984	1985	1986	1987	1988	1989	1990	1991	1992	1993
					At constant prices of:1986							
1 Government final consumption expenditure	...	...	...	...	6423	5756	6207	6486	6299	6252	...	...
2 Private final consumption expenditure	...	...	...	...	41844	44264	49493	50556	52281	53791	...	...
A Households	...	...	...	...	41844	44264	49493	50556	52281	53791	...	...
B Private non-profit institutions serving households	...	...	...	...	...	...	...	...	...	...	...	...
3 Gross capital formation	...	...	...	...	9967	11711	15384	14579	14431	14568	...	...
A Increase in stocks	...	...	...	...	582	496	53	277	344	295	...	...
B Gross fixed capital formation	...	...	...	...	9385	11214	15331	14302	14087	14273	...	...
4 Exports of goods and services	...	...	...	...	2211	7394	7002	7816	8590	9142	...	...
5 Less: Imports of goods and services	...	...	...	...	13472	19502	25038	24003	24337	24772	...	...
Equals: Gross Domestic Product	...	...	...	...	46973	49623	53047	55434	57263	58981	...	...

1.10 Gross Domestic Product by Kind of Activity, in Current Prices

Million Guinea-Bissau pesos

	1980	1983	1984	1985	1986	1987	1988	1989	1990	1991	1992	1993
1 Agriculture, hunting, forestry and fishing	...	...	...	...	21997	47096	78470	160016	227508	382400	...	...
2 Mining and quarrying	...	...	...	...	31	15	57				...	...
3 Manufacturing	...	...	...	...	6959	7026	11763	28465	41930	72556	...	...
4 Electricity, gas and water	...	...	...	...	16	640	1809				...	...
5 Construction	...	...	...	...	2621	4266	10947	34645	50937	71874	...	...
6 Wholesale and retail trade, restaurants and hotels	...	...	...	...	9267	22874	48341	92338	131250	220356	...	...
7 Transport, storage and communication	...	...	...	...	1337	3550	6375	12824	18874	33364	...	...
8 Finance, insurance, real estate and business services	...	...	...	...	248	1264	5264	11697	16626	27914	...	...
9 Community, social and personal services	...	...	...	...							...	...
Total, Industries	...	...	...	...	42476	86731	163026	339985	487125	808464	...	...
Producers of Government Services	...	...	...	...	4497	5644	8923	18891	22969	46522	...	...
Other Producers	...	...	...	...	...	...	...	...	...	...	...	...
Subtotal	...	...	...	...	46973	92375	171949	358875	510094	854985	...	...
Less: Imputed bank service charge	...	...	...	...	...	...	...	...	...	...	...	...
Plus: Import duties	...	...	...	...	...	...	...	...	...	...	...	...
Plus: Value added tax	...	...	...	...	...	...	...	...	...	...	...	...
Equals: Gross Domestic Product	...	...	...	...	46973	92375	171949	358875	510094	854985	...	...

Guinea-Bissau

1.11 Gross Domestic Product by Kind of Activity, in Constant Prices

Million Guinea-Bissau pesos

	1980	1983	1984	1985	1986	1987	1988	1989	1990	1991	1992	1993
					At constant prices of:1986							
1 Agriculture, hunting, forestry and fishing	...	...	...	...	21997	24313	26630	27883	28918	29785	...	...
2 Mining and quarrying	...	...	...	...	31	10					...	...
3 Manufacturing	...	...	...	...	6959	6077	5729	5932	5841	5780	...	...
4 Electricity, gas and water	...	...	...	...	16	577					...	...
5 Construction	...	...	...	...	2621	1348	1804	1774	1890	1946	...	...
6 Wholesale and retail trade, restaurants and hotels	...	...	...	...	9267	10091	10928	11752	12598	13271	...	...
7 Transport, storage and communication	...	...	...	...	1337	1413	1538	1663	1718	1828	...	...
8 Finance, insurance, real estate and business services	...	...	...	...	248	1054	1220	1330	1432	1416	...	...
9 Community, social and personal services	...	...	...	...							...	...
Total, Industries	...	...	...	...	42476	44883	47849	50334	52397	54026	...	...
Producers of Government Services	...	...	...	...	4497	4740	5199	5100	4867	4954	...	...
Other Producers	...	...	...	...	...	...	...	...	...	...	...	...
Subtotal	...	...	...	...	46973	49623	53047	55434	57263	58981	...	...
Less: Imputed bank service charge	...	...	...	...	...	...	...	...	...	...	...	...
Plus: Import duties	...	...	...	...	...	...	...	...	...	...	...	...
Plus: Value added tax	...	...	...	...	...	...	...	...	...	...	...	...
Equals: Gross Domestic Product	...	...	...	...	46973	49623	53047	55434	57263	58981	...	...

Guyana

Source. Reply to the United Nations National Accounts Questionnaire from the Statistical Bureau, Georgetown. Official estimates have been published by the Statistical Bureau in 'Annual Statistical Abstract'.

General note. The estimates shown in the following tables have been prepared in accordance with the United Nations System of National Accounts so far as the existing data would permit.

1.1 Expenditure on the Gross Domestic Product, in Current Prices

Million Guyana dollars

		1980	1983	1984	1985	1986	1987	1988	1989	1990	1991	1992	1993
1	Government final consumption expenditure	436.0	488.0	550.0	700.0	876.0	952.0	1162.0	1701.0	2133.0	4610.0	6383.0	7377.0
2	Private final consumption expenditure	796.2	879.0	929.0	1055.0	1000.0	1715.0	2279.0	5987.0	9537.0	2150.4	2352.5	2913.4
3	Gross capital formation	449.0	395.0	390.0	410.0	586.0	1123.0	890.0	3536.0	6624.0	13746.0	25113.0	30118.0
	A Increase in stocks	45.0	-	-	-	-	-	-	-	-	-	-	-
	B Gross fixed capital formation	404.0	395.0	390.0	410.0	586.0	1123.0	890.0	3536.0	6624.0	13746.0	25113.0	30118.0
4	Exports of goods and services	1042.0	675.0	897.0	1042.0	1092.0	...	...	...	...	...	...	...
5	Less: Imports of goods and services	1215.0	973.0	1152.0	1243.0	1335.0	...	...	...	...	...	...	...
	Equals: Gross Domestic Product	1508.2	1455.0	1700.0	1964.0	2219.0	3357.0	4137.0	10330.0	15665.0	38966.0	46734.0	56647.0

1.3 Cost Components of the Gross Domestic Product

Million Guyana dollars

		1980	1983	1984	1985	1986	1987	1988	1989	1990	1991	1992	1993
1	Indirect taxes, net	172.2	255.0	290.0	334.0	399.0	506.0	538.0	1256.0	1850.0	5344.0	6343.0	9529.0
2	Consumption of fixed capital	95.0	120.0	125.0	126.0	134.0	140.0	142.0	199.0	220.0	...	...	...
3	Compensation of employees paid by resident producers to:	1241.0	1080.0	1285.0	1504.0	1686.0	2711.0	...	...	...	...	...	...
4	Operating surplus							...	...	...	...	...	...
	Equals: Gross Domestic Product	1508.2	1455.0	1700.0	1964.0	2219.0	3357.0	4137.0	10330.0	15665.0	38966.0	46734.0	56647.0

1.10 Gross Domestic Product by Kind of Activity, in Current Prices

Million Guyana dollars

		1980	1983	1984	1985	1986	1987	1988	1989	1990	1991	1992	1993
1	Agriculture, hunting, forestry and fishing	312.0	291.0	400.0	506.0	544.0	1090.0	1085.0	4278.0	5973.0	15790.0	20467.0	21686.0
2	Mining and quarrying	221.0	17.0	65.0	50.0	116.0	171.0	360.0	1027.0	1392.0	5252.0	4549.0	8150.0
3	Manufacturing	162.0	158.0	130.0	160.0	188.0	234.0	311.0	555.0	713.0	1454.0	1760.0	1977.0
4	Electricity, gas and water												
5	Construction [a]	95.0	98.0	100.0	120.0	124.0	148.0	246.0	434.0	620.0	1170.0	1405.0	1673.0
6	Wholesale and retail trade, restaurants and hotels [b]	115.0	120.0	125.0	133.0	134.0	162.0	290.0	500.0	915.0	1738.0	2016.0	2323.0
7	Transport, storage and communication	75.0	98.0	100.0	128.0	139.0	198.0	299.0	546.0	1056.0	2112.0	2312.0	2645.0
8	Finance, insurance, real estate and business services [c]	72.0	115.0	125.0	132.0	134.0	191.0	250.0	687.0	1661.0	3115.0	3650.0	3922.0
9	Community, social and personal services [bc]	34.0	48.0	50.0	55.0	55.0	72.0	125.0	225.0	310.0	553.0	664.0	746.0
	Total, Industries	1086.0	945.0	1095.0	1284.0	1434.0	2266.0	2966.0	8252.0	12640.0	31184.0	36823.0	43122.0
	Producers of Government Services	250.0	255.0	315.0	346.0	387.0	585.0	633.0	822.0	1175.0	2438.0	3568.0	3996.0
	Other Producers	...	...	...	...	...	...	...	...	...	...	...	...
	Subtotal [d]	1336.0	1200.0	1410.0	1630.0	1821.0	2851.0	3599.0	9074.0	13815.0	33622.0	40391.0	47118.0
	Less: Imputed bank service charge	...	...	...	...	...	...	...	...	...	...	...	...
	Plus: Import duties	...	...	...	...	...	...	...	...	...	...	...	...
	Plus: Value added tax	...	...	...	...	...	...	...	...	...	...	...	...
	Plus: Other adjustments [e]	172.0	255.0	290.0	334.0	399.0	506.0	538.0	1256.0	1850.0	5344.0	6343.0	9529.0
	Equals: Gross Domestic Product	1508.0	1455.0	1700.0	1964.0	2220.0	3357.0	4137.0	10330.0	15665.0	38966.0	46734.0	56647.0

a) Item 'Construction' includes engineering and sewage services.
b) Restaurants and hotels are included in item 'Community, social and personal services'.
c) Business services are included in item 'Community, social and personal services'.
d) Gross domestic product in factor values.
e) Item 'Other adjustments' refers to indirect taxes net of subsidies.

Guyana

1.11 Gross Domestic Product by Kind of Activity, in Constant Prices

Million Guyana dollars

	1980	1983	1984	1985	1986	1987	1988	1989	1990	1991	1992	1993
			1977		At constant prices of:			1988				
1 Agriculture, hunting, forestry and fishing	214.0	208.0	215.0	215.0	223.0 / 1057.0	1023.0	936.0	909.0	784.0	881.0	1095.0	1160.0
2 Mining and quarrying	140.0	51.0	62.0	74.0	68.0 / 368.0	370.0	360.0	266.0	314.0	381.0	337.0	502.0
3 Manufacturing	132.0	102.0	96.0	93.0	93.0 / 499.0	478.0	460.0	426.0	370.0	409.0	488.0	505.0
4 Electricity, gas and water												
5 Construction	70.0[a]	61.0[a]	61.0[a]	61.0[a]	60.0[a] / 232.0	245.0	246.0	241.0	246.0	251.0	256.0	265.0
6 Wholesale and retail trade, restaurants and hotels	89.0[b]	55.0[b]	58.0[b]	58.0[b]	58.0[b] / 259.0	275.0	290.0	278.0	287.0	301.0	316.0	338.0
7 Transport, storage and communication	64.0	63.0	65.0	62.0	63.0 / 257.0	289.0	299.0	284.0	290.0	290.0	299.0	317.0
8 Finance, insurance, real estate and business services	57.0[c]	56.0[c]	57.0[c]	59.0[c]	59.0[c] / 232.0	249.0	250.0	259.0	266.0	266.0	270.0	280.0
9 Community, social and personal services	21.0[bc]	21.0[bc]	20.0[bc]	20.0[bc]	20.0[bc] / 116.0	122.0	125.0	125.0	128.0	131.0	134.0	139.0
Total, Industries	787.0	617.0	634.0	642.0	644.0 / 3020.0	3051.0	2966.0	2788.0	2685.0	2910.0	3195.0	3507.0
Producers of Government Services	207.0	187.0	187.0	187.0	187.0 / 644.0	644.0	644.0	634.0	634.0	634.0	609.0	597.0	597.0
Other Producers	...	...	...	...	...	...	...	...	...	...	...	...
Subtotal	994.0[d]	804.0[d]	821.0[d]	829.0[d]	831.0[d] / 3664.0	3695.0	3600.0	3422.0	3319.0	3519.0	3792.0	4104.0
Less: Imputed bank service charge	...	...	...	...	...	...	...	...	...	...	...	...
Plus: Import duties	...	...	...	...	...	...	...	...	...	...	...	...
Plus: Value added tax	...	...	...	...	...	...	...	...	...	...	...	...
Equals: Gross Domestic Product	...	...	...	...	...	...	...	...	...	...	...	...

a) Item 'Construction' includes engineering and sewage services.
b) Restaurants and hotels are included in item 'Community, social and personal services'.
c) Business services are included in item 'Community, social and personal services'.
d) Gross domestic product in factor values.

1.12 Relations Among National Accounting Aggregates

Million Guyana dollars

	1980	1983	1984	1985	1986	1987	1988	1989	1990	1991	1992	1993
Gross Domestic Product	1508.2	1455.0	1700.0	1964.0	2219.0	3357.0	4137.0	10330.0	15665.0	38966.0	46734.0	56647.0
Plus: Net factor income from the rest of the world	-83.0	-172.0	-182.0	-245.0	-283.0	-606.0	-869.0	-2790.0	-4239.0	15093.0	-8287.0	-9982.0
Equals: Gross National Product	1425.2	1283.0	1518.0	1719.0	1936.0	2751.0	3268.0	7540.0	11426.0	23873.0	38447.0	46665.0
Less: Consumption of fixed capital	95.0	120.0	125.0	126.0	134.0	140.0	142.0	199.0	220.0	...	...	...
Equals: National Income	1330.2	1163.0	1393.0	1593.0	1802.0	2611.0	3126.0	7341.0	11206.0	...	...	...
Plus: Net current transfers from the rest of the world	-2.0	2.0	18.0	20.0	29.0	45.0	...	...	...	...	...	...
Equals: National Disposable Income	1328.2	1165.0	1411.0	1613.0	1831.0	2656.0	...	...	...	...	...	...
Less: Final consumption	1232.2	1358.0	1565.0	1755.0	1876.0	...	...	...	...	...	...	...
Equals: Net Saving	96.0	-193.0	-154.0	-142.0	-45.0	...	...	...	...	...	...	...
Less: Surplus of the nation on current transactions	-258.0	-468.0	-418.0	-426.0	-497.0	...	...	...	...	...	...	...
Equals: Net Capital Formation	354.0	275.0	264.0	284.0	452.0	...	...	...	...	...	...	...

Haiti

Source. Reply to the United Nations National Accounts Questionnaire from the Institut Haitien de Statistique, Port-au-prince. The official estimates are published by the Institut in 'Le Bulletin de Statistique Supplement Annuel de l'Institut'

General note. The estimates shown in the following tables have been prepared in accordance with the United Nations System of National Accounts so far as the existing data would permit.

1.1 Expenditure on the Gross Domestic Product, in Current Prices

Million Haitian gourdes — Fiscal year ending 30 September

	1980	1983	1984	1985	1986	1987	1988	1989	1990	1991	1992	1993
1 Government final consumption expenditure	6835	7866	8678	9471	10472	9203	9367	8575	11609	14015	14902	17799
2 Private final consumption expenditure												
3 Gross capital formation	1238	1331	1441	1673	1620	1545	1500	1791	1815	1914	1219	1259
A Increase in stocks	...	...	...	...	...	...	...	...	...	...	...	...
B Gross fixed capital formation	1238	1331	1441	1673	1620	1545	1500	1791	1815	1914	1219	1259
4 Exports of goods and services	2148	2302	2598	2716	2340	2860	2542	2145	1955	2000	1095	1184
5 Less: Imports of goods and services	3302	3381	3636	3813	3245	3767	3572	3201	2942	3174	1848	2118
Equals: Gross Domestic Product	6919	8118	9081	10047	11188	9840	9837	9309	12437	14755	15368	18124

1.2 Expenditure on the Gross Domestic Product, in Constant Prices

Million Haitian gourdes — Fiscal year ending 30 September

	1980	1983	1984	1985	1986	1987	1988	1989	1990	1991	1992	1993
	\multicolumn{12}{c}{At constant prices of:1976}												
1 Government final consumption expenditure	5161	4575	4675	4683	4759	4749	4859	4064	4708	4735	4547	4465
2 Private final consumption expenditure												
3 Gross capital formation	934	924	967	1078	987	997	955	901	841	916	495	465
A Increase in stocks	...	...	...	...	...	...	...	...	...	...	...	...
B Gross fixed capital formation	934	924	967	1078	987	997	955	901	841	916	495	467
4 Exports of goods and services	1435	1598	1617	1562	1259	1512	1296	1883	1147	1190	651	833
5 Less: Imports of goods and services	2182	2041	2188	2222	1930	2221	2033	1716	1571	1681	979	1117
Equals: Gross Domestic Product	5349	5056	5071	5101	5075	5037	5076	5132	5125	5160	4714	4648

1.7 External Transactions on Current Account, Summary

Million Haitian gourdes — Fiscal year ending 30 September

	1980	1983	1984	1985	1986	1987	1988	1989	1990	1991	1992	1993
	\multicolumn{12}{c}{Payments to the Rest of the World}												
1 Imports of goods and services	3302	3381	3636	3813	3245	3767	3572	3201	2942	3174	1848	2118
2 Factor income to the rest of the world	...	...	...	...	...	131	166	151	148	158	152	...
3 Current transfers to the rest of the world	350	217	225	236	267	285	304	317	321	297	74	...
4 Surplus of the nation on current transactions	-782	-600	-515	-473	-246	-157	-202	-313	-281	-64	-204	...
Payments to the Rest of the World and Surplus of the Nation on Current Transactions	...	...	...	...	...	4026	3840	3356	3130	3565	1870	...
	\multicolumn{12}{c}{Receipts From The Rest of the World}												
1 Exports of goods and services	2148	2302	2598	2716	2340	2860	2542	2145	1955	2000	1095	1184
2 Factor income from rest of the world	...	...	...	...	...	26	31	23	23	27	24	...
3 Current transfers from rest of the world	794	769	840	961	1026	1140	1268	1188	1153	1538	751	...
Receipts from the Rest of the World on Current Transactions	...	...	...	...	...	4026	3840	3356	3130	3565	1870	...

1.11 Gross Domestic Product by Kind of Activity, in Constant Prices

Million Haitian gourdes — Fiscal year ending 30 September

	1980	1983	1984	1985	1986	1987	1988	1989	1990	1991	1992	1993
	\multicolumn{12}{c}{At constant prices of:1976}												
1 Agriculture, hunting, forestry and fishing	1723	1566	1621	1631	1670	1688	1735	1735	1697	1753	1688	1545
2 Mining and quarrying	67	5	5	6	5	8	8	7	7	7	6	5
3 Manufacturing	977	888	836	829	814	783	776	787	806	666	517	484
4 Electricity, gas and water	36	42	45	46	47	49	54	56	56	50	40	42
5 Construction	288	286	291	328	308	315	320	323	310	321	250	240

Haiti

1.11 Gross Domestic Product by Kind of Activity, in Constant Prices
(Continued)

Million Haitian gourdes — Fiscal year ending 30 September

	1980	1983	1984	1985	1986	1987	1988	1989	1990	1991	1992	1993
	\multicolumn{12}{c}{At constant prices of:1976}
6 Wholesale and retail trade, restaurants and hotels	998	937	905	914	912	902	902	901	902	840	758	797
7 Transport, storage and communication	99	106	92	85	88	99	105	108	113	106	97	92
8 Finance, insurance, real estate and business services	263	280	285	283	290	291	297	301	310	335	323	333
9 Community, social and personal services	149	161	188	195	202	177	176	186	193	180	186	202
Total, Industries	4600	4271	4266	4317	4336	4312	4374	4405	4394	4258	3865	3740
Producers of Government Services	515	540	575	580	596	605	605	609	618	755	774	799
Other Producers	...	...	...	...	...	...	...	...	...	...	...	...
Subtotal	5115	4811	4842	4897	4932	4918	4979	5014	5012	5013	4639	4539
Less: Imputed bank service charge	...	...	...	...	...	...	...	...	...	...	...	...
Plus: Import duties	234	245	230	204	143	119	97	118	113	146	74	109
Plus: Value added tax	...	...	...	...	...	...	...	...	...	...	...	...
Equals: Gross Domestic Product	5349	5056	5071	5101	5075	5037	5076	5132	5125	5159	4713	4648

1.12 Relations Among National Accounting Aggregates

Million Haitian gourdes — Fiscal year ending 30 September

	1980	1983	1984	1985	1986	1987	1988	1989	1990	1991	1992	1993
Gross Domestic Product	6919	8118	9081	10047	11188	9840	9837	9309	12437	14755	15368	18124
Plus: Net factor income from the rest of the world	-72	-73	-92	-101	-100	-105	-135	-128	-125	-131	-100	-68
Factor income from the rest of the world	...	...	...	...	...	26	31	23	23	27	...	...
Less: Factor income to the rest of the world	...	...	...	...	...	131	166	151	148	158	152	...
Equals: Gross National Product	6847	8045	8989	9946	11088	9735	9702	9181	12312	14624	15268	18056
Less: Consumption of fixed capital	197	212	230	267	257	240	239	285	289	349	194	201
Equals: National Income	6650	7833	8759	9679	10831	9495	9463	8896	12023	14275	15074	17855
Plus: Net current transfers from the rest of the world	444	552	615	725	759	855	964	871	832	1241	677	1022
Current transfers from the rest of the world	794	769	840	961	1026	1140	1268	1188	1153	1538	751	...
Less: Current transfers to the rest of the world	350	217	225	236	267	285	304	317	321	297	74	...
Equals: National Disposable Income	7094	8385	9374	10404	11590	10350	10427	9767	12855	15516	15751	18877
Less: Final consumption	6835	7866	8678	9471	10472	9203	9367	8575	11609	14015	14902	17799
Equals: Net Saving	259	519	697	933	1117	1147	1059	1192	1245	1501	849	1078
Less: Surplus of the nation on current transactions	-782	-600	-515	-473	-246	-157	-202	-313	-281	-64	-176	20
Equals: Net Capital Formation	1041	1119	1211	1406	1363	1305	1261	1506	1526	1565	1025	1058

4.2 Derivation of Value Added by Kind of Activity, in Constant Prices

Million Haitian gourdes — Fiscal year ending 30 September

	1980 Gross Output	1980 Intermediate Consumption	1980 Value Added	1985 Gross Output	1985 Intermediate Consumption	1985 Value Added	1990 Gross Output	1990 Intermediate Consumption	1990 Value Added	1991 Gross Output	1991 Intermediate Consumption	1991 Value Added
	\multicolumn{12}{c}{At constant prices of:1976}
	\multicolumn{12}{c}{All Producers}
1 Agriculture, hunting, forestry and fishing	...	...	1723	...	...	1631	...	...	1697	...	...	1753
A Agriculture and hunting	...	...	1444	...	...	1387	...	...	1415	...	...	1453
B Forestry and logging	...	...	279 }	...	...	244 }	...	...	282 }	...	...	300 }
C Fishing	...	...		...	...		...	...		...	...	
2 Mining and quarrying	...	...	67	...	...	6	...	...	7	...	...	7

Haiti

4.2 Derivation of Value Added by Kind of Activity, in Constant Prices
(Continued)

Million Haitian gourdes — Fiscal year ending 30 September

	1980 Gross Output	1980 Intermediate Consumption	1980 Value Added	1985 Gross Output	1985 Intermediate Consumption	1985 Value Added	1990 Gross Output	1990 Intermediate Consumption	1990 Value Added	1991 Gross Output	1991 Intermediate Consumption	1991 Value Added
					At constant prices of: 1976							
3 Manufacturing	...	...	977	...	...	829	...	...	806	...	...	666
A Manufacture of food, beverages and tobacco	...	...	348	...	...	332	...	...	291	...	...	282
B Textile, wearing apparel and leather industries	...	...	134	...	...	118	...	...	85	...	...	86
C Manufacture of wood and wood products, including furniture	...	...	...	...	...	...	...	...	...	...	...	...
D Manufacture of paper and paper products, printing and publishing	...	...	...	...	...	...	...	...	...	...	...	...
E Manufacture of chemicals and chemical petroleum, coal, rubber and plastic products	...	...	98	...	...	27	...	...	37	...	...	40
F Manufacture of non-metallic mineral products, except products of petroleum and coal	...	...	36	...	...	41	...	...	28	...	...	32
G Basic metal industries	...	...	...	...	...	...	...	...	...	...	...	...
H Manufacture of fabricated metal products, machinery and equipment	...	...	230	...	...	199	...	...	289	...	...	160
I Other manufacturing industries	...	...	130	...	...	112	...	...	76	...	...	65
4 Electricity, gas and water	...	...	36	...	...	46	...	...	56	...	...	50
5 Construction	...	...	288	...	...	328	...	...	310	...	...	321
6 Wholesale and retail trade, restaurants and hotels	...	...	998	...	...	914	...	...	903	...	...	840
A Wholesale and retail trade	...	...	963	...	...	885	...	...	884	...	...	826
B Restaurants and hotels	...	...	35	...	...	29	...	...	19	...	...	14
7 Transport, storage and communication	...	...	99	...	...	85	...	...	113	...	...	106
8 Finance, insurance, real estate and business services	...	...	263	...	...	283	...	...	308	...	...	335
A Financial institutions	...	...	13	...	...	9	...	...	8	...	...	7
B Insurance	...	...		...	...		...	...		...	...	
C Real estate and business services	...	...	250	...	...	274	...	...	302	...	...	328
9 Community, social and personal services	...	...	149	...	...	195	...	...	193	...	...	180
Total, Industries	...	...	4599	...	...	4316	...	...	4394	...	...	4258
Producers of Government Services	...	...	515	...	...	580	...	...	618	...	...	756
Other Producers	...	...	...	...	...	...	...	...	...	...	...	...
Total	...	...	5114	...	...	4896	...	...	5012	...	...	5014
Less: Imputed bank service charge	...	...	...	...	...	...	...	...	...	...	...	...
Import duties	...	...	234	...	...	204	...	...	113	...	...	146
Value added tax	...	...	...	...	...	...	...	...	...	...	...	...
Total	...	...	5348	...	...	5101	...	...	5125	...	...	5160

	1992 Gross Output	1992 Intermediate Consumption	1992 Value Added	1993 Gross Output	1993 Intermediate Consumption	1993 Value Added
	At constant prices of: 1976					
	All Producers					
1 Agriculture, hunting, forestry and fishing	...	...	1688	...	...	1545
A Agriculture and hunting	...	...	1382	...	...	1233
B Forestry and logging	...	...	305	...	...	312
C Fishing	...	...		...	...	
2 Mining and quarrying	...	...	6	...	...	5

Haiti

4.2 Derivation of Value Added by Kind of Activity, in Constant Prices
(Continued)

Million Haitian gourdes — Fiscal year ending 30 September

	1992 Gross Output	1992 Intermediate Consumption	1992 Value Added	1993 Gross Output	1993 Intermediate Consumption	1993 Value Added
			At constant prices of: 1976			
3 Manufacturing	...	...	517	...	...	484
A Manufacture of food, beverages and tobacco	...	...	261	...	...	263
B Textile, wearing apparel and leather industries	...	...	89	...	...	88
C Manufacture of wood and wood products, including furniture	...	...	...	...	...	...
D Manufacture of paper and paper products, printing and publishing	...	...	...	...	...	...
E Manufacture of chemicals and chemical petroleum, coal, rubber and plastic products	...	...	30	...	...	30
F Manufacture of non-metallic mineral products, except products of petroleum and coal	...	...	17	...	...	19
G Basic metal industries	...	...	...	...	...	...
H Manufacture of fabricated metal products, machinery and equipment	...	...	82	...	...	57
I Other manufacturing industries	...	...	39	...	...	29
4 Electricity, gas and water	...	...	40	...	...	42
5 Construction	...	...	250	...	...	240
6 Wholesale and retail trade, restaurants and hotels	...	...	758	...	...	797
A Wholesale and retail trade	...	...	744	...	...	786
B Restaurants and hotels	...	...	14	...	...	11
7 Transport, storage and communication	...	...	97	...	...	92
8 Finance, insurance, real estate and business services	...	...	323	...	...	333
A Financial institutions	...	...	9	...	...	13
B Insurance	...	...		...	...	
C Real estate and business services	...	...	314	...	...	321
9 Community, social and personal services	...	...	186	...	...	202
Total, Industries	...	...	3865	...	...	3740
Producers of Government Services	...	...	774	...	...	799
Other Producers	...	...	...	...	...	...
Total	...	...	4640	...	...	4537
Less: Imputed bank service charge	...	...	...	...	...	...
Import duties	...	...	74	...	...	110
Value added tax	...	...	...	...	...	...
Total	...	...	4714	...	...	4648

Honduras

General note. The preparation of national accounts statistics in Honduras is undertaken by the Departmento de Estudios Economicos, Banco Central de Honduras, Tegucigalpa, D.C. The official estimates are published in 'Cuentas Nacionales'. A detailed description of sources and methods used for the national accounts estimation is found in 'Metodologia de cuentas nacionales de los paises centroamericanos' issued by the Consejo Monetario Centroamericano in October 1976. The estimates are generally in accordance with the classifications and definitions recommended in the United Nations System of National Accounts (SNA). The following tables have been prepared from successive replies to the United Nations national accounts questionnaire. When the scope and coverage of the estimates differ for conceptual or statistical reasons from the definitions and classifications recommended in SNA, a footnote is indicated to the relevant tables.

Sources and methods:

(a) **Gross domestic product.** Gross domestic product is estimated mainly through the production approach.

(b) **Expenditure on the gross domestic product.** The expenditure approach is used to estimate government final consumption expenditure and exports and imports of goods and services. The commodity-flow approach is used for private final consumption expenditure and for gross capital formation. Government final consumption expenditure is estimated on the basis of government accounts. Changes in stocks are estimated on the basis of information obtained from various sectors such as the banana industry, the mines, the petroleum sector and the trade enterprises. Private investment consists of gross value of production in the construction sector, plus imports and domestic production of capital goods which are adjusted to purchasers' values. Public investment is estimated from public sector data on settlements by type of construction and classes of machinery and equipment. The estimates of exports and imports of goods and services are based on the balance of payment data. Private consumption expenditure is estimated as a residual. For the constant price estimates, private final consumption expenditure is estimated as a residual while all other items of GDP by expenditure type are deflated by various price indexes.

(c) **Cost-structure of the gross domestic product.** Estimates of labour income are derived from sources such as censuses and surveys, supplemented by information on wages and salaries paid by various government agencies and other public bodies. Estimates of profits of enterprises and professional incomes are obtained from the Direccion General del Impuesto sobre la Renta. Estimates of interest and dividend payments received by household and private non-profit institutions are derived as a residual. Indirect taxes and subsidies are estimated on the basis of government sources. For consumption of fixed capital, no specific information is available.

(d) **Gross domestic product by kind of economic activity.** The table of gross domestic product by kind of economic activity is prepared in factor values. The production approach is used to estimate value added of most industries. The income approach is, however, used to estimate value added of producers of government services, part of the transport sectors and other private services. For the agricultural crop production, information is obtained directly from the most important export enterprises while for other products, estimates are obtained from consumption per capita data adjusted for exports and imports. Surveys are conducted to obtain information on basic production of grains. Agricultural censuses were held in 1953, 1965 and 1974. The Instituto Hondureno del Cafe provides complete information for coffee production. The banana companies in the northern zone are visited annually while for the rest of the country, consumption per capita data are taken into account together with prices collected from native producers. Livestock production information is gathered from the most important producers with adjustments made for clandestine or uncontrolled transaction. Inputs are estimated as 30 percent of the gross value of production. The production in the forestry sector is calculated as a function of household and industrial consumption of firewood, and extrapolated by an index. The estimates of fishing are calculated on the basis of information from the Direccion General de Pesca, the foreign trade statistics and per capita consumption data. For metal mining, the statistical information is obtained directly while estimates for non-metallic mineral are based on inputs used in the construction sector using certain coefficients derived from analysis of construction costs. The estimates of manufacturing are based on censuses, surveys and sample data provided by the Direccion General de Industrias and the Departamento de Estudios Industriales. Information on electricity, gas and water is obtained directly from concerned enterprises. The data available cover gross values of production, aggregated values, physical production, installed capacity and personal occupation. Information on public construction is taken directly from the municipalities. Based on the information obtained from them, a sample is taken from which the growth of private construction can be measured. The population and housing censuses are also taken into account for dwellings. For the trade sector, the estimates are based on the gross value of agricultural and industrial production by item. The value of imports and exports are estimated from foreign trade statistics and information received from the Direccion de Tributacion Directa. In estimating road transport, inforamtion on registered vehicles for rental is used. Data on income and expenditure by type of vehicle, depreciation and profits are obtained. Information for financial institutions is obtained from the Superintendencia de Bancos, which provides financial statements for all banks in the system and insurance companies. The estimates of ownership of dwellings are based on census information for 1949, 1961 and 1974 covering the number of dwellings and the average rents paid and imputed. For producers of government services, information is obtained directly from the Contaduria General de la Nacion and the Asesoria Tecnica Municipal. For private services, use is made of employment data, classified by type of service rendered and data on average wages and salaries from other information sources. For domestic services, data on employment and wages are basis for estimating the value added with 75 percent added to the cash figures for board and lodging as wages and salaries in kind. For the constant price estimates, value added of the agricultural sector is either extrapolated by quantity indexes for output or deflated by price indexes. For the industrial activity sector, trade, transport and storage, financial institutions and insurance and private services, value added is extrapolated by quantity index. For the remaining sectors, current values are deflated by various price indexes.

1.1 Expenditure on the Gross Domestic Product, in Current Prices

Million Honduran lempiras

	1980	1983	1984	1985	1986	1987	1988	1989	1990	1991	1992	1993
1 Government final consumption expenditure	650	807	876	953	1087	1181	1308	1475	1621	1769	2171	2520
2 Private final consumption expenditure	3561	4684	5026	5412	5606	5916	6245	7226	8379	11021	12520	14750
3 Gross capital formation	1271	852	1156	1261	1055	1446	1942	1978	2881	4022	4881	6495
A Increase in stocks	13	-176	-95	27	10	314	513	94	348	926	679	823
B Gross fixed capital formation	1258	1028	1251	1234	1045	1132	1429	1884	2533	3096	4202	5672
4 Exports of goods and services	1911	1610	1706	1827	2025	1907	2432	3204	4664	5632	6048	7332
5 Less: Imports of goods and services	2261	1799	2126	2174	2156	2145	2676	3549	5008	6130	6820	8653
Equals: Gross Domestic Product	5132	6154	6638	7279	7617	8305	9251	10334	12537	16314	18800	22444

1.2 Expenditure on the Gross Domestic Product, in Constant Prices

Million Honduran lempiras

	1980	1983	1984	1985	1986	1987	1988	1989	1990	1991	1992	1993
	At constant prices of:1978											
1 Government final consumption expenditure	491	472	489	515	563	597	651	669	579	520	587	616
2 Private final consumption expenditure	2742	2774	2980	2989	3164	3212	3279	3452	3464	3637	3716	3945
3 Gross capital formation	958	557	697	740	596	777	994	957	988	1165	1310	1538
A Increase in stocks	10	-103	-53	14	5	147	230	37	111	286	194	216
B Gross fixed capital formation	948	660	750	726	591	630	764	920	877	879	1116	1322
4 Exports of goods and services	1506	1401	1395	1500	1527	1564	1550	1629	1637	1604	1732	1713
5 Less: Imports of goods and services	1631	1131	1311	1316	1390	1421	1527	1546	1502	1592	1711	1832
Equals: Gross Domestic Product	4066	4073	4250	4428	4460	4729	4947	5161	5166	5334	5634	5980

Honduras

1.3 Cost Components of the Gross Domestic Product

Million Honduran lempiras

	1980	1983	1984	1985	1986	1987	1988	1989	1990	1991	1992	1993
1 Indirect taxes, net	539	617	702	841	811	944	1033	1078	1381	2339	2669	3127
A Indirect taxes	545	627	754	902	880	983	1059	1098	1674	2381	2717	3247
B Less: Subsidies	6	10	52	61	69	39	26	20	293	42	48	120
2 Consumption of fixed capital	321	427	462	487	534	571	608	654	872	1115	1214	1372
3 Compensation of employees paid by resident producers to:	2469	3213	3428	3643	3956	4204	4627	5178	6621	7734	9515	10846
4 Operating surplus	1803	1897	2046	2308	2316	2586	2983	3424	3663	5126	5402	7099
Equals: Gross Domestic Product	5132	6154	6638	7279	7617	8305	9251	10334	12537	16314	18800	22444

1.7 External Transactions on Current Account, Summary

Million Honduran lempiras

	1980	1983	1984	1985	1986	1987	1988	1989	1990	1991	1992	1993
Payments to the Rest of the World												
1 Imports of goods and services	2261	1799	2126	2174	2156	2145	2676	3549	5008	6130	6820	8653
A Imports of merchandise c.i.f.	2189	1728	2026	2045	2025	2008	2503	3303	4687	5695	6342	8069
B Other	72	71	100	129	131	137	173	246	321	435	478	584
2 Factor income to the rest of the world	350	358	393	406	444	498	601	781	1180	1566	1931	2180
3 Current transfers to the rest of the world	32	22	23	24	25	26	30	36	51	54	57	66
4 Surplus of the nation on current transactions	-633	-438	-633	-440	-234	-328	-260	-509	-230	-932	-1433	-2297
Payments to the Rest of the World and Surplus of the Nation on Current Transactions	2010	1741	1909	2164	2391	2341	3047	3857	6009	6818	7375	8602
Receipts From The Rest of the World												
1 Exports of goods and services	1911	1610	1706	1827	2025	1907	2432	3204	4664	5632	6048	7332
A Exports of merchandise f.o.b.	1720	1414	1493	1611	1808	1661	2090	2725	4002	4539	4677	5559
B Other	191	196	213	216	217	247	342	479	663	1092	1371	1773
2 Factor income from rest of the world	24	20	20	22	24	23	31	41	44	67	72	86
3 Current transfers from rest of the world	75	111	183	315	342	411	584	612	1302	1119	1256	1184
Receipts from the Rest of the World on Current Transactions	2010	1741	1909	2164	2391	2341	3047	3857	6009	6818	7375	8602

1.8 Capital Transactions of The Nation, Summary

Million Honduran lempiras

	1980	1983	1984	1985	1986	1987	1988	1989	1990	1991	1992	1993
Finance of Gross Capital Formation												
Gross saving	638	414	523	821	821	1118	1682	1469	2652	3090	3449	4198
1 Consumption of fixed capital	321	427	462	487	534	571	608	654	872	1115	1214	1372
2 Net saving	317	-13	61	334	287	547	1074	815	1780	1975	2235	2826
Less: Surplus of the nation on current transactions	-633	-438	-633	-440	-234	-328	-260	-509	-230	-932	-1432	-2297
Finance of Gross Capital Formation	1271	852	1156	1261	1055	1446	1942	1978	2881	4022	4881	6495
Gross Capital Formation												
Increase in stocks	13	-176	-95	27	10	314	513	94	348	926	679	823
Gross fixed capital formation	1258	1028	1251	1234	1045	1132	1429	1884	2533	3096	4202	5672
1 General government	477	617	737	647	447	425	467	589	823	1168	1948	2824
2 Corporate and quasi-corporate enterprises	781	411	514	587	598	707	962	1295	1710	1928	2254	2848
3 Other	...	...	...	...	...	...	...	...	...	...	...	...
Gross Capital Formation	1271	852	1156	1261	1055	1446	1942	1978	2881	4022	4881	6495

1.10 Gross Domestic Product by Kind of Activity, in Current Prices

Million Honduran lempiras

	1980	1983	1984	1985	1986	1987	1988	1989	1990	1991	1992	1993
1 Agriculture, hunting, forestry and fishing	1087	1171	1236	14C7	1400	1539	1742	1951	2503	3178	3258	3993
2 Mining and quarrying	96	117	131	139	114	83	126	158	191	206	308	369
3 Manufacturing	687	834	915	935	972	1070	1244	1389	1823	2367	2875	3456
4 Electricity, gas and water	64	89	104	113	229	236	241	276	353	497	530	589
5 Construction	270	364	384	356	286	302	365	464	574	745	1061	1457

Honduras

1.10 Gross Domestic Product by Kind of Activity, in Current Prices
(Continued)

Million Honduran lempiras

	1980	1983	1984	1985	1986	1987	1988	1989	1990	1991	1992	1993
6 Wholesale and retail trade, restaurants and hotels	730	809	812	854	915	961	1027	1089	1289	1567	1762	2056
7 Transport, storage and communication	313	373	388	408	462	509	567	648	703	909	1048	1102
8 Finance, insurance, real estate and business services	547	736	843	947	1033	1129	1259	1433	1616	2015	2370	2816
9 Community, social and personal services	453	591	635	695	787	880	963	1075	1290	1441	1704	2033
Statistical discrepancy	...	...	...	...	...	...	...	...	...	...	28	...
Total, Industries	4247	5084	5448	5854	6198	6709	7534	8484	10342	12925	14944	17871
Producers of Government Services	346	453	488	584	608	652	684	773	814	1050	1187	1446
Other Producers	...	...	...	...	...	...	...	...	...	...	...	...
Subtotal [a]	4593	5537	5936	6438	6806	7361	8218	9256	11156	13975	16131	19317
Less: Imputed bank service charge	...	...	...	...	...	...	...	...	...	...	...	...
Plus: Import duties	...	...	...	...	...	...	...	...	...	...	...	...
Plus: Value added tax	...	...	...	...	...	...	...	...	...	...	...	...
Plus: Other adjustments [b]	539	617	702	841	811	944	1033	1078	1381	2339	2669	3127
Equals: Gross Domestic Product	5132	6154	6638	7279	7617	8305	9251	10334	12537	16314	18800	22444

a) Gross domestic product in factor values.
b) Item 'Other adjustments' refers to indirect taxes net of subsidies.

1.11 Gross Domestic Product by Kind of Activity, in Constant Prices

Million Honduran lempiras

	1980	1983	1984	1985	1986	1987	1988	1989	1990	1991	1992	1993
					At constant prices of:1978							
1 Agriculture, hunting, forestry and fishing	985	983	1056	1080	1072	1161	1155	1271	1285	1364	1413	1432
2 Mining and quarrying	66	78	87	89	83	51	69	78	72	75	83	86
3 Manufacturing	529	534	575	582	606	646	678	704	709	721	765	813
4 Electricity, gas and water	52	64	67	77	82	96	108	113	128	129	130	139
5 Construction	202	228	240	221	177	184	211	242	218	212	284	344
6 Wholesale and retail trade, restaurants and hotels	560	480	462	463	507	517	531	507	503	514	529	572
7 Transport, storage and communication	249	305	317	329	334	348	372	396	411	423	441	456
8 Finance, insurance, real estate and business services	418	455	466	489	505	536	587	625	648	690	736	796
9 Community, social and personal services	336	319	313	326	360	384	406	410	406	380	406	433
Total, Industries	3397	3446	3583	3656	3726	3923	4117	4346	4380	4508	4787	5071
Producers of Government Services	262	266	273	316	314	329	331	341	291	280	291	320
Other Producers	...	...	...	...	...	...	...	...	...	...	...	...
Subtotal [a]	3659	3712	3856	3972	4040	4252	4448	4687	4671	4788	5078	5391
Less: Imputed bank service charge	...	...	...	...	...	...	...	...	...	...	...	...
Plus: Import duties	...	...	...	...	...	...	...	...	...	...	...	...
Plus: Value added tax	...	...	...	...	...	...	...	...	...	...	...	...
Plus: Other adjustments [b]	407	361	394	456	420	477	499	474	495	546	556	589
Equals: Gross Domestic Product	4066	4073	4250	4428	4460	4729	4947	5161	5166	5334	5634	5980

a) Gross domestic product in factor values.
b) Item 'Other adjustments' refers to indirect taxes net of subsidies.

1.12 Relations Among National Accounting Aggregates

Million Honduran lempiras

	1980	1983	1984	1985	1986	1987	1988	1989	1990	1991	1992	1993
Gross Domestic Product	5132	6154	6638	7279	7617	8305	9251	10334	12537	16314	18800	22444
Plus: Net factor income from the rest of the world	-326	-338	-373	-384	-420	-475	-570	-740	-1136	-1499	-1859	-2094
Factor income from the rest of the world	24	20	20	22	24	23	31	41	44	67	72	86
Less: Factor income to the rest of the world	350	358	393	406	444	498	601	781	1180	1566	1931	2180
Equals: Gross National Product	4806	5816	6265	6895	7197	7830	8681	9594	11401	14815	16941	20350
Less: Consumption of fixed capital	321	427	462	487	534	571	608	654	872	1115	1214	1372

Honduras

1.12 Relations Among National Accounting Aggregates
(Continued)

Million Honduran lempiras

	1980	1983	1984	1985	1986	1987	1988	1989	1990	1991	1992	1993
Equals: National Income	4485	5389	5803	6408	6663	7259	8073	8940	10529	13700	15727	18978
Plus: Net current transfers from the rest of the world	43	89	160	291	317	385	554	576	1251	1065	1199	1118
Current transfers from the rest of the world	75	111	183	315	342	411	584	612	1302	1119	1256	1184
Less: Current transfers to the rest of the world	32	22	23	24	25	26	30	36	51	54	57	66
Equals: National Disposable Income	4528	5478	5963	6699	6980	7644	8627	9516	11780	14765	16926	20096
Less: Final consumption	4211	5491	5902	6365	6693	7097	7553	8701	10000	12790	14691	17270
Equals: Net Saving	317	-13	61	334	287	547	1074	815	1780	1975	2235	2826
Less: Surplus of the nation on current transactions	-633	-438	-633	-440	-234	-328	-260	-509	-229	-932	-1432	-2297
Equals: Net Capital Formation	950	425	694	774	521	875	1334	1324	2009	2907	3667	5123

2.1 Government Final Consumption Expenditure by Function, in Current Prices

Million Honduran lempiras

	1980	1983	1984	1985	1986	1987	1988	1989	1990	1991	1992	1993
1 General public services	216	263	296	391	468	413	436	412	...	...	...	...
2 Defence	114	140	162	188	211	245	264	276	...	...	...	...
3 Public order and safety	...	...	...	...	...	...	...	...	...	...	...	...
4 Education	151	225	244	269	315	366	404	449	...	...	...	...
5 Health	63	83	92	95	120	141	175	191	...	...	...	...
6 Social security and welfare	...	...	...	...	...	...	...	...	...	...	...	...
7 Housing and community amenities	...	...	...	...	...	...	...	...	...	...	...	...
8 Recreational, cultural and religious affairs	...	...	...	...	...	...	...	...	...	...	...	...
9 Economic services	...	...	...	...	...	...	...	...	...	...	...	...
10 Other functions	134	166	158	142	183	206	189	279	...	...	...	...
Total Government Final Consumption Expenditure [a]	678	877	952	1046	1297	1371	1468	1607	...	...	...	...

a) Data in this table have not been revised, therefore they are not comparable with the data in other tables.

2.17 Exports and Imports of Goods and Services, Detail

Million Honduran lempiras

	1980	1983	1984	1985	1986	1987	1988	1989	1990	1991	1992	1993
Exports of Goods and Services												
1 Exports of merchandise, f.o.b.	1720	1414	1493	1611	1808	1661	2090	2725	4002	4539	4677	5559
2 Transport and communication	...	...	...	...	...	...	...	...	...	...	...	...
3 Insurance service charges	...	...	...	...	...	...	...	...	...	...	...	...
4 Other commodities	...	...	...	...	...	...	...	...	...	...	...	...
5 Adjustments of merchandise exports to change-of-ownership basis	...	...	...	...	...	...	...	...	...	...	...	...
6 Direct purchases in the domestic market by non-residential households	...	...	...	...	...	...	...	...	...	...	...	...
7 Direct purchases in the domestic market by extraterritorial bodies	...	...	...	...	...	...	...	...	...	...	...	...
Total Exports of Goods and Services	1911	1610	1706	1827	2025	1907	2432	3204	4664	5632	6048	7332
Imports of Goods and Services												
1 Imports of merchandise, c.i.f.	2189	1728	2026	2045	2025	2008	2503	3303	4687	5695	6342	8069

Honduras

2.17 Exports and Imports of Goods and Services, Detail
(Continued)

Million Honduran lempiras

	1980	1983	1984	1985	1986	1987	1988	1989	1990	1991	1992	1993
A Imports of merchandise, f.o.b.	1908	1513	1769	1783	1759	1743	2170	2858	4054	4928	5496	7017
B Transport of services on merchandise imports	281	215	257	262	266	265	333	445	633	767	846	1052
C Insurance service charges on merchandise imports												
2 Adjustments of merchandise imports to change-of-ownership basis	...	...	...	...	...	...	...	...	...	...	...	...
3 Other transport and communication	...	...	...	...	...	...	...	...	...	...	...	...
4 Other insurance service charges	...	...	...	...	...	...	...	...	...	...	...	...
5 Other commodities	72	71	100	129	131	137	173	246	321	435	478	584
6 Direct purchases abroad by government	...	...	...	...	...	...	...	...	...	...	...	...
7 Direct purchases abroad by resident households	...	...	...	...	...	...	...	...	...	...	...	...
Total Imports of Goods and Services	2261	1799	2126	2174	2156	2145	2676	3549	5008	6130	6820	8653
Balance of Goods and Services	-350	-189	-420	-347	-131	-238	-244	-345	-344	-498	-772	-1321
Total Imports and Balance of Goods and Services	1911	1610	1706	1827	2025	1907	2432	3204	4664	5632	6048	7332

Hong Kong

General note. The preparation of national accounts statistics in Hong Kong is undertaken by the Census and Statistics Department, Hong Kong. The official estimates together with methodological notes of the estimates have been published in a series of publications entitled 'Estimates of Gross Domestic Product', issued annually since 1973. The estimates are generally in accordance with the definitions and classifications recommended in the United Nations System of National Accounts (SNA). The following tables have been prepared from successive replies to the United Nations national accounts questionnaire received from the Overseas Development Administration, Foreign and Commonwealth Office, London. When the scope and coverage of the estimates differ for conceptual or statistical reasons from the definitions and classifications recommended in SNA, a footnote is indicated to the relevant tables.

Sources and methods:

(a) Gross domestic product. Gross domestic product is estimated mainly through the expenditure approach.

(b) Expenditure on the gross domestic product. The expenditure approach is used to estimate government final consumption expenditure and exports and imports of goods and services. The commodity-flow approach is used for private final consumption expenditure and gross capital formation supplemented by the expenditure approach. Government consumption expenditure data up to 1972 were obtained from the Annual Reports of the Accountant-General which provided data on the actual expenditure of each department by financial year ending 31 March. Since 1973, quarterly figures have been available from the Treasury and adjustment to a calendar year basis is no longer required. The estimates relate to current expenditure on goods and services by government departments not engaged in trading activities. For the large proportion of the commodities included in private consumption expenditure which is imported, adequate and detailed trade statistics are available. Trade statistics of retained imports are supported and complemented by data from the household expenditure surveys, censuses/surveys of manufacturing establishments, sample surveys on sales of business establishments, administrative statistics and other sources. Foodstuffs produced domestically for local consumption are compiled from the annual output estimates made by the Agriculture and Fisheries Department and other government departments concerned. Imported and domestically produced commodities are reported in importers' and producers' values, respectively, and the retail value is arrived at by adding transport expenses and distributors' profit margins. Estimates of change in stock of distributors and manufacturers have been compiled based on results of the censuses/surveys of manufacturing establishments and distributive trades from 1973 onwards. Prior to 1973, token estimates on change in stock were made based on the ratio of the 1980 GDP estimates with and without adjustment for changes in stocks. Information on quantities of hydrocarbon oils kept in stock by oil companies are obtained from the Industry Department. For gross fixed capital formation, investment in machinery and equipment is based mainly on the value of retained imports of capital goods, with a percentage added to allow for profit, transport, assembly charges and installation expenses. Estimates of domestically manufactured machinery and equipment locally purchased are calculated from results of the censuses/surveys of manufacturing establishments. Private sector investment in building and construction prior to 1979 is based on the monthly statistical returns of the Building Ordinance Office. From 1979 it is based on the results of annual Survey of Building, Construction and Real Estate Sectors while investment in the government sector is obtained from an analysis of the accounts of government departments. The estimates of exports and imports of merchandise are obtained from detailed external trade statistics. For port and airport charges and expenditure of non-residents in Hong Kong and that of Hong Kong residents abroad, the main sources of data are the surveys conducted by the Hong Kong Tourist Association, surveys on expenditure of Hong Kong residents abroad, and government accounts. The estimates of other items of imports and exports of services were not available prior to 1978. From 1978 onwards, an annual survey of imports and exports of services has been conducted to provide estimates in respect of the other items of services. Token estimates were made for years prior to 1978 based on benchmark information obtained from the annual survey. For the constant price estimates, price deflation is used for most of the expenditure items. The current values are deflated by various price indexes such as specially constructed salary rate index, consumer price indexes, tourist price index, cost index of building and construction, overall index of unit values of exports and imports, etc. For increase in stocks, unit value index of imports as well as the consumer price index of appropriate commodity groups are used.

(c) Cost-structure of the gross domestic product. The main components of the table: compensation of employees and operating surplus are complied using the production approach. Data, available since 1980, are based on information collected from economic censuses/surveys conducted for the various major economic sectors.

(d) Gross domestic product by kind of economic activity. The estimates are compiled using the production approach. Data, available since 1980, are based on information collected from economic censuses/surveys conducted for the various major economic sectors.

1.1 Expenditure on the Gross Domestic Product, in Current Prices

Million Hong Kong dollars

	1980	1983	1984	1985	1986	1987	1988	1989	1990	1991	1992	1993
1 Government final consumption expenditure	8720	16359	18056	19787	22887	25722	30008	36253	43283	51470	64070	72335
2 Private final consumption expenditure	84660	136840	156223	167483	189159	219315	254682	287677	330459	391098	451670	515312
A Households	80305	128814	147139	157214	177077	205602	238398	267722	306122	362671	421326	480788
B Private non-profit institutions serving households	4355	8026	9084	10269	12082	13713	16284	19955	24337	28427	30344	34524
3 Gross capital formation	49756	57295	63135	58749	73941	101458	130261	139667	159504	181827	221995	248512
A Increase in stocks	3745	4329	5803	1469	6183	9746	14132	3463	5728	4098	8187	2040
B Gross fixed capital formation	46011	52966	57332	57280	67758	91712	116129	136204	153776	177729	213808	246472
Residential buildings [a]	6433	8210	8797	9816	11667	12868	17390	19911	23475	23826	24517	24628
Non-residential buildings	5062	8649	7934	7519	6832	9931	12042	16433	20311	23339	22088	20796
Other construction and land improvement etc. [b]	6304	9713	9207	7792	8687	11797	14166	20020	21824	27226	34368	45627
Other	28212	26394	31394	32153	40572	57116	72531	79840	88166	103338	132835	155421
4 Exports of goods and services	127406	207006	277811	296202	348345	470306	604051	697656	782195	926973	1114304	1263697
5 Less: Imports of goods and services	128746	204827	258732	270566	321771	432313	563980	637392	732892	882856	1072704	1202261
Equals: Gross Domestic Product	141796	212673	256493	271655	312561	384488	455022	523861	582549	668512	779335	897595

a) Item 'Residential buildings' includes also combined residential and non-residential buildings.
b) Land improvement and plantation and orchard development refers to transfer costs of land and buildings.

1.2 Expenditure on the Gross Domestic Product, in Constant Prices

Million Hong Kong dollars

	1980	1983	1984	1985	1986	1987	1988	1989	1990	1991	1992	1993
	At constant prices of: 1990											
1 Government final consumption expenditure	23330	31813	33068	33977	36185	37598	39005	41035	43283	46617	52789	53843
2 Private final consumption expenditure	174813	213146	225373	234956	253618	279138	302329	312682	330459	359019	386519	416165
A Households	161982	196329	207466	215977	233512	258327	280710	290017	306122	333542	361847	390957
B Private non-profit institutions serving households	12831	16817	17907	18979	20106	20811	21619	22665	24337	25477	24672	25208
3 Gross capital formation	108133	109137	113011	108068	120090	139504	151772	145580	159504	172140	191933	192675

Hong Kong

1.2 Expenditure on the Gross Domestic Product, in Constant Prices
(Continued)

Million Hong Kong dollars

	1980	1983	1984	1985	1986	1987	1988	1989	1990	1991	1992	1993
					At constant prices of:1990							
A Increase in stocks	6026	5184	6444	1655	7095	10464	14317	3376	5728	4081	8453	2587
B Gross fixed capital formation	102107	103953	106567	106413	112995	129040	137455	142204	153776	168059	183480	190088
Residential buildings	15728	16292	16902	18850	21083	19834	21645	21519	23475	22576	23024	22994
Non-residential buildings	12999	17996	15883	14543	12372	15248	15191	18005	20311	22034	20502	19395
Other construction and land improvement etc.	16247	21354	19466	16463	17635	21141	20392	21330	21824	24529	27250	33076
Other	57133	48311	54316	56557	61905	72817	80227	81350	88166	98920	112704	114623
4 Exports of goods and services	228778	287729	342624	361896	415496	536680	662009	721293	782195	899622	1064219	1199988
5 Less: Imports of goods and services	221384	270706	310426	330415	374978	484157	605813	657222	732892	865382	1045113	1174327
Statistical discrepancy	-3171	-2948	1222	-1863	...	...	...	...	...	...	...	...
Equals: Gross Domestic Product	310499	368171	404872	406619	450411	508763	549302	563368	582549	612016	650347	688344

1.3 Cost Components of the Gross Domestic Product

Million Hong Kong dollars

	1980	1983	1984	1985	1986	1987	1988	1989	1990	1991	1992	1993
1 Indirect taxes, net	5965	8273	9493	12463	15212	20445	21450	25390	29614	36323	48777	...
2 Consumption of fixed capital [a]	...	...	...	...	...	...	...	...	...	...	...	...
3 Compensation of employees paid by resident producers to:	65535	105503	124213	137628	155954	184569	216828	252498	290838	326002	369292	...
4 Operating surplus [a]	68916	96012	115576	116245	140054	182226	221427	246437	268608	305512	362826	...
Statistical discrepancy [b]	1379	2885	7211	5318	1341	-2752	-4684	-465	-6511	675	-1562	...
Equals: Gross Domestic Product	141796	212673	256493	271655	312561	384488	455022	523861	582549	668512	779335	...

a) Item 'Operating surplus' includes consumption of fixed capital.
b) The estimates shown refers to the difference between production estimate and expenditure estimate.

1.10 Gross Domestic Product by Kind of Activity, in Current Prices

Million Hong Kong dollars

	1980	1983	1984	1985	1986	1987	1988	1989	1990	1991	1992	1993
1 Agriculture, hunting, forestry and fishing	1102	1225	1245	1211	1308	1334	1417	1386	1432	1441	1468	1612
2 Mining and quarrying	213	316	299	356	346	257	229	224	210	222	205	198
3 Manufacturing	31806	46242	58329	56192	66836	80713	90035	96170	98352	97223	99764	94294
4 Electricity, gas and water	1703	4739	5687	6665	8385	9691	10199	10860	12612	13521	15637	17588
5 Construction	8929	12885	12917	12679	14253	17024	20658	25738	30220	34659	37337	41534
6 Wholesale and retail trade, restaurants and hotels	28762	41204	55503	57943	66020	89249	109793	124749	140722	163284	190760	219115
7 Transport, storage and communication	9922	16529	18680	20629	24192	31693	40005	44654	52927	60604	71227	81805
8 Finance, insurance, real estate and business services	42966	58059	61850	67410	80340	101566	126229	148831	172384	212169	259864	306606
9 Community, social and personal services	7419	15077	17360	20059	21450	23521	27202	29966	32444	35472	41125	46991
Statistical discrepancy [a]	1379	2885	7211	5318	1341	-2752	-4684	-465	-6511	675	-1562	17931
Total, Industries	132822	196276	231870	243144	283130	355048	425767	482578	541303	618595	717387	809743
Producers of Government Services	5665	11246	12954	14765	17028	19108	21964	26072	31241	38273	48579	54721
Other Producers	3164	5840	6689	7687	8928	10382	11836	14085	17643	20548	20999	24937
Subtotal [b]	141651	213362	251513	265596	309086	384538	459567	522735	590187	677416	786965	889401
Less: Imputed bank service charge	7200	11848	11725	11722	13079	17743	21313	23800	30741	45902	54846	63015
Plus: Import duties	...	...	...	...	...	...	...	...	...	...	...	...
Plus: Value added tax	1379	2885	7211	5318	1341	-2752	-4684	-465	-6511	675	-1562	17931
Plus: Other adjustments [c]	5965	8273	9493	12463	15212	20445	21450	25390	29614	36323	48777	53278
Equals: Gross Domestic Product	141796	212673	256493	271655	312561	384488	455022	523861	582549	668512	779335	897595

a) The estimates shown refers to the difference between production estimate and expenditure estimate.
b) Gross domestic product in factor values.
c) Item 'Other adjustments' refers to indirect taxes net of subsidies.

2.5 Private Final Consumption Expenditure by Type and Purpose, in Current Prices

Million Hong Kong dollars

	1980	1983	1984	1985	1986	1987	1988	1989	1990	1991	1992	1993
				Final Consumption Expenditure of Resident Households								
1 Food, beverages and tobacco	21408	32870	35824	36075	38219	42124	46752	51114	57451	63276	68008	73360
A Food	19461	29884	32690	32625	34454	37782	41629	45787	51491	56864	60776	65805
B Non-alcoholic beverages												
C Alcoholic beverages	1040	1580	1564	1688	2083	2527	2944	2603	2927	3157	3341	3795

Hong Kong

2.5 Private Final Consumption Expenditure by Type and Purpose, in Current Prices
(Continued)

Million Hong Kong dollars

	1980	1983	1984	1985	1986	1987	1988	1989	1990	1991	1992	1993
D Tobacco	907	1406	1570	1762	1682	1815	2179	2724	3033	3255	3891	3760
2 Clothing and footwear [a]	14646	22826	26629	28810	36526	45328	55895	61529	69778	78318	95670	113755
3 Gross rent, fuel and power	12053	20786	23490	25594	28386	31951	37018	42784	49182	56749	66154	74932
4 Furniture, furnishings and household equipment and operation	8883	14326	17534	18084	21800	27387	33029	35040	36871	47890	57714	61933
A Household operation	1344	2147	2427	2684	3007	3350	3900	4472	5074	5618	6364	6855
B Other	7539	12179	15107	15400	18793	24037	29129	30568	31797	42272	51350	55078
5 Medical care and health expenses [b]	4569	8136	9198	9983	11180	12901	14253	15439	18251	21890	25058	28565
6 Transport and communication	6354	9623	10966	12067	13367	16032	20173	22390	27127	33722	44312	53335
7 Recreational, entertainment, education and cultural services	6571	11262	13350	15170	16841	20016	23370	26266	28626	33424	35877	44184
A Education	966	1616	1890	2035	2335	2654	3003	3496	4079	4576	5056	5751
B Other	5605	9646	11460	13135	14506	17362	20367	22770	24547	28848	30821	38433
8 Miscellaneous goods and services	6353	10441	12412	13910	15335	19552	21660	26561	29594	33456	41563	46028
Statistical discrepancy	-	-	-	-	-	-	-	-	-	-	-	-
Total Final Consumption Expenditure in the Domestic Market by Households, of which	80837	130270	149403	159693	181655	215291	252150	281123	316880	368725	434356	496092
Plus: Direct purchases abroad by resident households	6483	10646	12558	13336	14712	17523	21997	26383	31823	37803	41522	47628
Less: Direct purchases in the domestic market by non-resident households	7015	12102	14822	15815	19290	27212	35749	39784	42581	43857	54552	62932
Equals: Final Consumption Expenditure of Resident Households	80305	128814	147139	157214	177077	205602	238398	267722	306122	362671	421326	480788

Final Consumption Expenditure of Private Non-profit Institutions Serving Households

	1980	1983	1984	1985	1986	1987	1988	1989	1990	1991	1992	1993
Equals: Final Consumption Expenditure of Private Non-profit Organisations Serving Households	4355	8026	9084	10269	12082	13713	16284	19955	24337	28427	30344	34524
Private Final Consumption Expenditure	84660	136840	156223	167483	189159	219315	254682	287677	330459	391098	451670	515312

a) Personal effects are included in item 'Clothing and footwear'.
b) Personal care is included in 'Medical care and health expenses'.

2.6 Private Final Consumption Expenditure by Type and Purpose, in Constant Prices

Million Hong Kong dollars

	1980	1983	1984	1985	1986	1987	1988	1989	1990	1991	1992	1993

At constant prices of: 1990

Final Consumption Expenditure of Resident Households

	1980	1983	1984	1985	1986	1987	1988	1989	1990	1991	1992	1993
1 Food, beverages and tobacco	43316	47718	47728	48751	50923	53275	54711	54635	57451	56901	57080	58437
A Food	36971	41914	42480	43407	45623	47580	48219	48313	51491	51770	52049	53517
B Non-alcoholic beverages												
C Alcoholic beverages	2754	2962	2549	2605	2883	3242	3691	3040	2927	2959	2762	2955
D Tobacco	3591	2842	2699	2739	2417	2453	2801	3282	3033	2172	2269	1965
2 Clothing and footwear	30981	37889	39983	41797	47880	55318	63229	65337	69778	73141	83157	92635
3 Gross rent, fuel and power	22623	29243	31005	32136	34882	38027	42622	46500	49182	51072	54045	57143
4 Furniture, furnishings and household equipment and operation	15503	20359	22602	23169	26198	31278	35431	36260	36871	46185	53899	56560
A Household operation	3547	3856	3937	4059	4302	4484	4748	4925	5074	5222	5436	5544
B Other	11956	16503	18665	19110	21896	26794	30683	31335	31797	40963	48463	51016
5 Medical care and health expenses	11119	13888	13671	14028	15022	16484	16912	16991	18251	20112	21030	22394
6 Transport and communication	14947	16059	16737	17334	17974	20470	24327	24748	27127	30395	38033	43512
7 Recreational, entertainment, education and cultural services	16450	20749	22435	23945	25036	27541	28707	28884	28626	30299	29597	33197
A Education	4299	4450	4540	4356	4314	4384	4255	4194	4079	3895	3691	3609
B Other	12151	16299	17895	19589	20722	23157	24452	24690	24547	26404	25906	29588
8 Miscellaneous goods and services	15213	17267	19144	20876	22634	27304	28143	30219	29594	30041	34318	35808

Hong Kong

2.6 Private Final Consumption Expenditure by Type and Purpose, in Constant Prices
(Continued)

Million Hong Kong dollars

	1980	1983	1984	1985	1986	1987	1988	1989	1990	1991	1992	1993
				At constant prices of:1990								
Statistical discrepancy	-3243	-1645	-698	-960	-	-	-	-	-	-	-	-
Total Final Consumption Expenditure in the Domestic Market by Households, of which	166909	201527	212607	221076	240549	269697	294082	303574	316880	338146	371159	399686
Plus: Direct purchases abroad by resident households	11424	15752	17725	18235	19697	22840	27422	28858	31823	36831	38705	43077
Less: Direct purchases in the domestic market by non-resident households	16351	20950	22866	23334	26734	34210	40794	42415	42581	41435	48017	51800
Equals: Final Consumption Expenditure of Resident Households	161982	196329	207466	215977	233512	258327	280710	290017	306122	333542	361847	390957
			Final Consumption Expenditure of Private Non-profit Institutions Serving Households									
Equals: Final Consumption Expenditure of Private Non-profit Organisations Serving Households	12831	16817	17907	18979	20106	20811	21619	22665	24337	25477	24672	25208
Private Final Consumption Expenditure	174813	213146	225373	234956	253618	279138	302329	312682	330459	359019	386519	416165

2.7 Gross Capital Formation by Type of Good and Owner, in Current Prices

Million Hong Kong dollars

	1980				1985				1990			
	TOTAL	Total Private	Public Enterprises	General Government	TOTAL	Total Private	Public Enterprises	General Government	TOTAL	Total Private	Public Enterprises	General Government
Increase in stocks, total	3745	3745	...	...	1469	1469	...	...	5728	5728	...	...
Gross Fixed Capital Formation, Total	46011	39163	...	6848	57280	48457	...	8823	153776	134006	...	19770
1 Residential buildings a	6433	4553	...	1880	9816	7680	...	2136	23475	18375	...	5100
2 Non-residential buildings	5062	4533	...	529	7519	6013	...	1506	20311	16158	...	4153
3 Other construction	5194	1440	...	3754	5728	1402	...	4326	13528	4639	...	8889
4 Land improvement and plantation and orchard development b	1110	1110	...	...	2064	2064	...	...	8296	8296	...	...
5 Producers' durable goods	14942	14257	...	685	25406	24551	...	855	59811	58183	...	1628
A Transport equipment	3751	3226	...	525	3706	3428	...	278	8468	8043	...	425
B Machinery and equipment	11191	11031	...	160	21700	21123	...	577	51343	50140	...	1203
6 Breeding stock, dairy cattle, etc.	13270	13270	...	...	6747	6747	...	...	28355	28355	...	...
Statistical discrepancy c	...	...	...	-	...	...	...	-	...	...	...	-
Total Gross Capital Formation d	49756	42908	...	6848	58749	49926	...	8823	159504	139734	...	19770

	1991				1992				1993			
	TOTAL	Total Private	Public Enterprises	General Government	TOTAL	Total Private	Public Enterprises	General Government	TOTAL	Total Private	Public Enterprises	General Government
Increase in stocks, total	4098	4098	...	...	8187	8187	...	...	2040	2040	...	...
Gross Fixed Capital Formation, Total	177729	157189	...	20540	213808	191493	...	22315	246472	213203	...	33269
1 Residential buildings a	23826	18929	...	4897	24517	18935	...	5582	24628	19229	...	5399
2 Non-residential buildings	23339	19133	...	4206	22088	18425	...	3663	20796	16197	...	4599
3 Other construction	14268	4825	...	9443	16451	5282	...	11169	25754	5213	...	20541
4 Land improvement and plantation and orchard development b	12958	12958	...	...	17917	17917	...	...	19873	19873	...	...
5 Producers' durable goods	70957	68963	...	1994	88225	86324	...	1901	98767	96037	...	2730
A Transport equipment	10295	9835	...	460	13153	12445	...	708	13987	13455	...	532
B Machinery and equipment	60662	59128	...	1534	75072	73879	...	1193	84780	82582	...	2198
6 Breeding stock, dairy cattle, etc.	32381	32381	...	...	44610	44610	...	...	56654	56654	...	...
Statistical discrepancy c	...	...	...	-	...	...	...	-	...	...	...	-
Total Gross Capital Formation d	181827	161287	...	20540	221995	199680	...	22315	248512	215243	...	33269

a) Item 'Residential buildings' includes also combined residential and non-residential buildings.
b) Land improvement and plantation and orchard development refers to transfer costs of land and buildings.
c) Item 'Statistical discrepancy' refers to real estate developers' margin.
d) Column 'Public Enterprises' is included in column 'General Government'.

Hong Kong

2.8 Gross Capital Formation by Type of Good and Owner, in Constant Prices

Million Hong Kong dollars

	1980				1985				1990			
	TOTAL	Total Private	Public Enterprises	General Government	TOTAL	Total Private	Public Enterprises	General Government	TOTAL	Total Private	Public Enterprises	General Government
	At constant prices of:1990										
Increase in stocks, total	6026	6026	...	...	1655	1655	...	...	5728	5728	...	...
Gross Fixed Capital Formation, Total	102107	86032	...	16290	106413	90052	...	16389	153776	134006	...	19770
1 Residential buildings	15728	11705	...	3856	18850	14847	...	3927	23475	18375	...	5100
2 Non-residential buildings	12999	11650	...	1346	14543	11634	...	2924	20311	16158	...	4153
3 Other construction	13352	3707	...	9645	11120	2718	...	8391	13528	4639	...	8889
4 Land improvement and plantation and orchard development	2895	2895	...	...	5343	5343	...	...	8296	8296		
5 Producers' durable goods	31700	30255	...	1447	35588	34386	...	1193	59811	58183	...	1628
A Transport equipment	7943	6804	...	1108	5174	4778	...	391	8468	8043	...	425
B Machinery and equipment	23669	23415	...	338	30344	29583	...	802	51343	50140	...	1203
6 Breeding stock, dairy cattle, etc.	25066	25066	...	...	21493	21493	...	...	28355	28355	...	...
Statistical discrepancy	367	754	...	-4	-524	-369	...	-46	-	-	...	-
Total Gross Capital Formation	108133	92058	...	16290	108068	91707	...	16389	159504	139734	...	19770

	1991				1992				1993			
	TOTAL	Total Private	Public Enterprises	General Government	TOTAL	Total Private	Public Enterprises	General Government	TOTAL	Total Private	Public Enterprises	General Government
	At constant prices of:1990										
Increase in stocks, total	4081	4081	...	...	8453	8453	...	...	2587	2587	...	...
Gross Fixed Capital Formation, Total	168059	148914	...	19145	183480	163336	...	20144	190088	161677	...	28411
1 Residential buildings	22576	17963	...	4613	23024	17770	...	5254	22994	18000	...	4994
2 Non-residential buildings	22034	18032	...	4002	20502	17084	...	3418	19395	14933	...	4462
3 Other construction	13048	4473	...	8575	14124	4481	...	9643	20595	4121	...	16474
4 Land improvement and plantation and orchard development	11481	11481	...	...	13126	13126	...	...	12481	12481	...	...
5 Producers' durable goods	69886	67931	...	1955	84839	83010	...	1829	89253	86772	...	2481
A Transport equipment	10129	9676	...	453	12618	11936	...	682	12636	12149	...	487
B Machinery and equipment	59757	58255	...	1502	72221	71074	...	1147	76617	74623	...	1994
6 Breeding stock, dairy cattle, etc.	29034	29034	...	...	27865	27865	...	...	25370	25370	...	...
Statistical discrepancy	-	-	...	-	-	-	...	-	-	-	...	-
Total Gross Capital Formation	172140	152995	...	19145	191933	171789	...	20144	192675	164264	...	28411

4.1 Derivation of Value Added by Kind of Activity, in Current Prices

Million Hong Kong dollars

	1980			1985			1990			1991		
	Gross Output	Intermediate Consumption	Value Added	Gross Output	Intermediate Consumption	Value Added	Gross Output	Intermediate Consumption	Value Added	Gross Output	Intermediate Consumption	Value Added
	All Producers											
1 Agriculture, hunting, forestry and fishing	2633	1531	1102	3239	2028	1211	3872	2440	1432	3796	2355	1441
2 Mining and quarrying	352	139	213	623	267	356	402	192	210	405	183	222
3 Manufacturing	116585	84779	31806	196968	140776	56192	341986	243634	98352	338692	241469	97223
A Manufacture of food, beverages and tobacco	...	...	...	...	...	...	...	...	...	...	...	...

Hong Kong

4.1 Derivation of Value Added by Kind of Activity, in Current Prices
(Continued)

Million Hong Kong dollars

		1980 Gross Output	1980 Intermediate Consumption	1980 Value Added	1985 Gross Output	1985 Intermediate Consumption	1985 Value Added	1990 Gross Output	1990 Intermediate Consumption	1990 Value Added	1991 Gross Output	1991 Intermediate Consumption	1991 Value Added
	B Textile, wearing apparel and leather industries	47054	34005	13049	79241	55605	23636	123468	88361	35107	123947	89776	34171
	C Manufacture of wood and wood products, including furniture	...	...	...	...	...	...	...	...	...	...	...	...
	D Manufacture of paper and paper products, printing and publishing	...	...	...	...	...	...	...	...	...	...	...	...
	E Manufacture of chemicals and chemical petroleum, coal, rubber and plastic products	8021	5522	2499	16796	11691	5105	20981	14517	6464	16645	11294	5351
	F Manufacture of non-metallic mineral products, except products of petroleum and coal	...	...	...	...	...	...	...	...	...	...	...	...
	G Basic metal industries	...	...	...	...	...	...	...	...	...	...	...	...
	H Manufacture of fabricated metal products, machinery and equipment	27148	20118	7030	40400	29865	10536	68705	51352	17353	66686	48957	17729
	I Other manufacturing industries	34361	25133	9228	60531	43616	16915	128831	89403	39428	131415	91443	39972
4	Electricity, gas and water	4807	3104	1703	11190	4526	6665	18105	5493	12612	20350	6830	13521
5	Construction	18423	9494	8929	27299	14620	12679	61270	31050	30220	70368	35709	34659
6	Wholesale and retail trade, restaurants and hotels	46620	17859	28762	104963	47020	57943	291627	150904	140722	333528	170244	163284
	A Wholesale and retail trade	38450	14990	23460	86593	39925	46668	251331	136125	115206	289677	153582	136096
	B Restaurants and hotels	8170	2869	5301	18369	7094	11275	40296	14780	25516	43850	16662	27188
7	Transport, storage and communication	21653	11731	9922	46302	25673	20629	106319	53392	52927	114839	54235	60604
	A Transport and storage	17815	10208	7607	38501	23075	15426	85419	44935	40484	88984	43734	45250
	B Communication	3838	1523	2315	7801	2597	5204	20901	8458	12443	25855	10501	15354
8	Finance, insurance, real estate and business services	49640	6674	42966	85821	18411	67410	222217	49833	172384	269610	57442	212169
	A Financial institutions	11726	2965	8760	22281	8003	14278	55851	21250	34600	78945	24803	54142
	B Insurance	1125	257	869	2851	846	2005	6910	2355	4555	8224	2807	5418
	C Real estate and business services	36789	3452	33337	60690	9563	51127	159456	26228	133228	182440	29833	152609
	Real estate, except dwellings	20150	1881	18269	21129	4379	16750	64521	10452	54068	72335	12154	60181
	Dwellings	12661	633	12028	28075	1404	26671	62375	3119	59257	72497	3625	68873
9	Community, social and personal services	12535	5115	7419	37099	17040	20059	62166	29721	32444	66155	30683	35472
	Statistical discrepancy a	...	...	1379	...	...	5318	...	...	-6511	...	...	675
	Total, Industries	273248	140426	132822	513504	270361	243144	1107964	566659	541303	1217743	599150	618595
	Producers of Government Services	9106	3441	5665	20951	6186	14765	45554	14313	31241	54303	16030	38273
	Other Producers	4969	1805	3164	11858	4171	7687	27977	10334	17643	32879	12331	20548
	Total	287323	145672	141651	546313	280718	265596	1181495	591306	590187	1304925	627511	677416
	Less: Imputed bank service charge	...	-7200	7200	...	-11722	11722	...	-30741	30741	...	-45902	45902
	Import duties	...	...	...	...	...	...	...	...	...	...	...	...
	Value added tax	...	...	1379	...	...	5318	...	...	-6511	...	...	675
	Other adjustments b	5965	...	5965	12463	...	12463	29614	...	29614	36323	...	36323
	Total	294667	152872	141796	564094	292440	271655	1204598	622047	582549	1341923	673413	668512

		1992 Gross Output	1992 Intermediate Consumption	1992 Value Added	1993 Gross Output	1993 Intermediate Consumption	1993 Value Added
	All Producers						
1	Agriculture, hunting, forestry and fishing	3705	2237	1468	...	...	...
2	Mining and quarrying	368	163	205	...	...	...
3	Manufacturing	337928	238164	99764	...	...	...
	A Manufacture of food, beverages and tobacco	...	...	...	...	...	...

Hong Kong

4.1 Derivation of Value Added by Kind of Activity, in Current Prices
(Continued)

Million Hong Kong dollars

		1992			1993	
	Gross Output	Intermediate Consumption	Value Added	Gross Output	Intermediate Consumption	Value Added
B Textile, wearing apparel and leather industries	118567	83791	34776	...	...	...
C Manufacture of wood and wood products, including furniture	...	...	...	...	...	...
D Manufacture of paper and paper products, printing and publishing	...	...	...	...	...	...
E Manufacture of chemicals and chemical petroleum, coal, rubber and plastic products	16035	11135	4900	...	...	...
F Manufacture of non-metallic mineral products, except products of petroleum and coal	...	...	...	...	...	...
G Basic metal industries	...	...	...	...	...	...
H Manufacture of fabricated metal products, machinery and equipment	67698	49126	18572	...	...	...
I Other manufacturing industries	135628	94112	41516	...	...	...
4 Electricity, gas and water	22969	7332	15637	...	...	...
5 Construction	74589	37252	37337	...	...	...
6 Wholesale and retail trade, restaurants and hotels	345387	154626	190760	...	...	...
A Wholesale and retail trade	293180	134759	158421	...	...	...
B Restaurants and hotels	52207	19867	32339	...	...	...
7 Transport, storage and communication	135648	64422	71227	...	...	...
A Transport and storage	104516	51770	52746	...	...	...
B Communication	31132	12651	18481	...	...	...
8 Finance, insurance, real estate and business services	323671	63807	259864	...	...	...
A Financial institutions	95017	25415	69602	...	...	...
B Insurance	9806	3196	6609	...	...	...
C Real estate and business services	218849	35196	183653	...	...	...
Real estate, except dwellings	89666	14108	75558	...	...	...
Dwellings	85201	4260	80941	...	...	...
9 Community, social and personal services	76463	35337	41125	...	...	...
Statistical discrepancy a	...	...	-1562	...	...	...
Total, Industries	1320728	603340	717387	...	...	...
Producers of Government Services	67391	18812	48579	...	...	...
Other Producers	35346	14348	20999	...	...	...
Total	1423464	636500	786965	...	...	889401
Less: Imputed bank service charge	...	-54846	54846	...	...	...
Import duties	...	...	...	...	...	...
Value added tax	...	...	-1562	...	...	...
Other adjustments b	48777	...	48777	...	...	...
Total	1470679	691345	779335	...	...	...

a) The estimates shown refers to the difference between production estimate and expenditure estimate.
b) Item 'Other adjustments' refers to indirect taxes net of subsidies.

4.3 Cost Components of Value Added

Million Hong Kong dollars

	1980						1985					
	Compensation of Employees	Capital Consumption	Net Operating Surplus	Indirect Taxes	Less: Subsidies Received	Value Added	Compensation of Employees	Capital Consumption	Net Operating Surplus	Indirect Taxes	Less: Subsidies Received	Value Added
						All Producers						
1 Agriculture, hunting, forestry and fishing	245	...	857	...	...	1102	427	...	784	...	...	1211
2 Mining and quarrying	52	...	161	...	...	213	70	...	286	...	...	356
3 Manufacturing	22635	...	9172	...	...	31806	38063	...	18129	...	...	56192
A Manufacture of food, beverages and tobacco	...	...	...	...	...	...	...	...	...	...	...	...

Hong Kong

4.3 Cost Components of Value Added
(Continued)

Million Hong Kong dollars

	1980						1985				
	Compensation of Employees	Capital Consumption	Net Operating Surplus	Indirect Taxes	Less: Subsidies Received	Value Added	Compensation of Employees	Capital Consumption	Net Operating Surplus	Indirect Taxes	Less: Subsidies Received	Value Added
B Textile, wearing apparel and leather industries	9882	...	3168	...	...	13049	17425	...	6211	...	...	23636
C Manufacture of wood and wood products, including furniture	...	...	...	...	...	...	...	...	...	...	...	...
D Manufacture of paper and paper products, printing and publishing	...	...	...	...	...	...	...	...	...	...	...	...
E Manufacture of chemicals and chemical petroleum, coal, rubber and plastic products	1779	...	720	...	...	2499	3171	...	1934	...	...	5105
F Manufacture of non-metallic mineral products, except products of petroleum and coal	...	...	...	...	...	...	...	...	...	...	...	...
G Basic metal industries	...	...	...	...	...	...	...	...	...	...	...	...
H Manufacture of fabricated metal products, machinery and equipment	4791	...	2239	...	...	7030	7050	...	3486	...	...	10536
I Other manufacturing industries	6183	...	3045	...	...	9228	10417	...	6498	...	...	16915
4 Electricity, gas and water	618	...	1085	...	...	1703	1534	...	5130	...	...	6665
5 Construction	6855	...	2074	...	...	8929	10664	...	2015	...	...	12679
6 Wholesale and retail trade, restaurants and hotels	12061	...	16700	...	...	28762	28781	...	29162	...	...	57943
A Wholesale and retail trade	8459	...	15002	...	...	23460	20569	...	26099	...	...	46668
B Restaurants and hotels	3603	...	1698	...	...	5301	8212	...	3063	...	...	11275
7 Transport, storage and communication	4790	...	5132	...	...	9922	10185	...	10444	...	...	20629
A Transport and storage	3807	...	3800	...	...	7607	8017	...	7409	...	...	15426
B Communication	983	...	1332	...	...	2315	2169	...	3035	...	...	5204
8 Finance, insurance, real estate and business services	5681	...	37285	...	...	42966	15842	...	51567	...	...	67410
A Financial institutions	2875	...	5885	...	...	8760	7678	...	6600	...	...	14278
B Insurance	340	...	528	...	...	869	934	...	1071	...	...	2005
C Real estate and business services	2465	...	30872	...	...	33337	7230	...	43897	...	...	51127
Real estate, except dwellings	974	...	17295	...	...	18269	2493	...	14256	...	...	16750
Dwellings	...	...	12028	...	...	12028	...	...	26671	...	...	26671
9 Community, social and personal services	3770	...	3650	...	...	7419	9609	...	10450	...	...	20059
Statistical discrepancy [a]	...	...	...	...	...	1379	...	...	...	...	...	5318
Total, Industries	56707	...	76116	...	...	132822	115175	...	127967	...	...	243144
Producers of Government Services	5665	...	-	...	...	5665	14765	...	-	...	...	14765
Other Producers	3164	...	-	...	...	3164	7687	...	-	...	...	7687
Total	65535	...	76116	...	...	141651	137628	...	127967	...	...	265596
Less: Imputed bank service charge	...	...	7200	...	...	7200	...	...	11722	...	...	11722
Import duties	...	...	...	...	...	...	...	...	...	...	...	...
Value added tax	...	...	...	...	...	1379	...	...	...	...	...	5318
Other adjustments [b]	...	...	...	...	...	5965	...	...	...	...	...	12463
Total	65535	...	68916	5965	...	141796	137628	...	116245	12463	...	271655

	1990						1991				
	Compensation of Employees	Capital Consumption	Net Operating Surplus	Indirect Taxes	Less: Subsidies Received	Value Added	Compensation of Employees	Capital Consumption	Net Operating Surplus	Indirect Taxes	Less: Subsidies Received	Value Added
					All Producers						
1 Agriculture, hunting, forestry and fishing	607	...	826	...	...	1432	661	...	780	...	...	1441
2 Mining and quarrying	77	...	133	...	...	210	72	...	150	...	...	222
3 Manufacturing	57592	...	40759	...	...	98352	55652	...	41571	...	...	97223
A Manufacture of food, beverages and tobacco	...	...	...	...	...	...	...	...	...	...	...	...

Hong Kong

4.3 Cost Components of Value Added
(Continued)

Million Hong Kong dollars

	1990						1991					
	Compensation of Employees	Capital Consumption	Net Operating Surplus	Indirect Taxes	Less: Subsidies Received	Value Added	Compensation of Employees	Capital Consumption	Net Operating Surplus	Indirect Taxes	Less: Subsidies Received	Value Added
B Textile, wearing apparel and leather industries	23946	...	11162	...	...	35107	23043	...	11128	...	...	34171
C Manufacture of wood and wood products, including furniture	...	...	...	...	...	...	...	...	...	...	...	...
D Manufacture of paper and paper products, printing and publishing	...	...	...	...	...	...	...	...	...	...	...	...
E Manufacture of chemicals and chemical petroleum, coal, rubber and plastic products	3534	...	2930	...	...	6464	2974	...	2377	...	...	5351
F Manufacture of non-metallic mineral products, except products of petroleum and coal	...	...	...	...	...	...	...	...	...	...	...	...
G Basic metal industries	...	...	...	...	...	...	...	...	...	...	...	...
H Manufacture of fabricated metal products, machinery and equipment	9294	...	8059	...	...	17353	8938	...	8790	...	...	17729
I Other manufacturing industries	20820	...	18608	...	...	39428	20697	...	19275	...	...	39972
4 Electricity, gas and water	3153	...	9459	...	...	12612	3625	...	9896	...	...	13521
5 Construction	24797	...	5423	...	...	30220	27480	...	7179	...	...	34659
6 Wholesale and retail trade, restaurants and hotels	72513	...	68210	...	...	140722	85834	...	77450	...	...	163284
A Wholesale and retail trade	54361	...	60846	...	...	115206	65492	...	70603	...	...	136096
B Restaurants and hotels	18152	...	7364	...	...	25516	20342	...	6847	...	...	27188
7 Transport, storage and communication	24790	...	28137	...	...	52927	26452	...	34152	...	...	60604
A Transport and storage	19513	...	20971	...	...	40484	20938	...	24313	...	...	45250
B Communication	5277	...	7166	...	...	12443	5514	...	9839	...	...	15354
8 Finance, insurance, real estate and business services	41943	...	130441	...	...	172384	49277	...	162892	...	...	212169
A Financial institutions	20064	...	14536	...	...	34600	23609	...	30533	...	...	54142
B Insurance	3198	...	1357	...	...	4555	3752	...	1666	...	...	5418
C Real estate and business services	18681	...	114548	...	...	133228	21916	...	130693	...	...	152609
Real estate, except dwellings	6163	...	47906	...	...	54068	7655	...	52526	...	...	60181
Dwellings	...	...	59257	...	...	59257	-	...	68873	...	...	68873
9 Community, social and personal services	16482	...	15962	...	...	32444	18128	...	17344	...	...	35472
Statistical discrepancy [a]	...	...	...	...	...	-6511	...	...	...	...	...	675
Total, Industries	241954	...	299350	...	...	541303	267181	...	351414	...	...	618595
Producers of Government Services	31241	...	-	...	...	31241	38273	...	-	...	...	38273
Other Producers	17643	...	-	...	...	17643	20548	...	-	...	...	20548
Total	290838	...	299350	...	...	590187	326002	...	351414	...	...	677416
Less: Imputed bank service charge	...	...	30741	...	...	30741	-	...	45902	...	...	45902
Import duties	...	...	...	...	...	...	...	...	...	...	...	...
Value added tax	...	...	...	...	...	-6511	...	...	...	...	...	675
Other adjustments [b]	...	...	...	...	...	29614	...	...	...	...	...	36323
Total	290838	...	268608	29614	...	582549	326002	...	305512	36323	...	668512

	1992						
	Compensation of Employees	Capital Consumption	Net Operating Surplus	Indirect Taxes	Less: Subsidies Received	Value Added

All Producers

1 Agriculture, hunting, forestry and fishing	603	...	865	...	...	1468
2 Mining and quarrying	81	...	124	...	...	205
3 Manufacturing	55155	...	44610	...	...	99764
A Manufacture of food, beverages and tobacco	...	...	...	...	...	...

Hong Kong

4.3 Cost Components of Value Added
(Continued)

Million Hong Kong dollars

	1992					
	Compensation of Employees	Capital Consumption	Net Operating Surplus	Indirect Taxes	Less: Subsidies Received	Value Added
B Textile, wearing apparel and leather industries	21832	...	12944	...	...	34776
C Manufacture of wood and wood products, including furniture	...	...	...	...	...	...
D Manufacture of paper and paper products, printing and publishing	...	...	...	...	...	...
E Manufacture of chemicals and chemical petroleum, coal, rubber and plastic products	2848	...	2052	...	...	4900
F Manufacture of non-metallic mineral products, except products of petroleum and coal	...	...	...	...	...	...
G Basic metal industries	...	...	...	...	...	...
H Manufacture of fabricated metal products, machinery and equipment	8840	...	9733	...	...	18572
I Other manufacturing industries	21635	...	19881	...	...	41516
4 Electricity, gas and water	4115	...	11522	...	...	15637
5 Construction	30023	...	7313	...	...	37337
6 Wholesale and retail trade, restaurants and hotels	98254	...	92507	...	...	190760
A Wholesale and retail trade	74264	...	84157	...	...	158421
B Restaurants and hotels	23990	...	8349	...	...	32339
7 Transport, storage and communication	31978	...	39249	...	...	71227
A Transport and storage	24906	...	27840	...	...	52746
B Communication	7072	...	11409	...	...	18481
8 Finance, insurance, real estate and business services	56820	...	203044	...	...	259864
A Financial institutions	27020	...	42582	...	...	69602
B Insurance	4480	...	2129	...	...	6609
C Real estate and business services	25319	...	158333	...	...	183653
Real estate, except dwellings	7944	...	67613	...	...	75558
Dwellings	...	...	80941	...	...	80941
9 Community, social and personal services	22686	...	18439	...	...	41125
Statistical discrepancy [a]	...	...	...	...	...	-1562
Total, Industries	299715	...	417673	...	...	717387
Producers of Government Services	48579	...	-	...	...	48579
Other Producers	20999	...	-	...	...	20999
Total	369292	...	417673	...	...	786965
Less: Imputed bank service charge	...	...	54846	...	...	54846
Import duties	...	...	...	...	...	...
Value added tax	...	...	...	...	...	-1562
Other adjustments [b]	...	...	...	...	...	48777
Total	369292	...	362826	48777	...	779335

a) The estimates shown refers to the difference between production estimate and expenditure estimate.
b) Item 'Other adjustments' refers to indirect taxes net of subsidies.

Hungary

General note. The compilation of national accounts statistics in Hungary is undertaken by the Hungarian Central Statistical Office. The official estimates are published in the 'Statisztikai Evkonyv' (Statistical Yearbook). Detailed data are published in the series of National Accounts Hungary. The most relevant long-time series were published in the 'Nepgazdasagi merlegek 1947-1988' and National Accounts Hungary 1991-1994. The description of the sources and methods used for the national accounts estimation are published in the joint Oecd/HCSO publication: 'National Accounts for Hungary - Sources, Methods and Estimations'. From 1991 the estimations are in accordance with the 1993 SNA and ISIC Rev.3 (Sources and methods) the earlier periods are described in the previous UN National Accounts publications. As a general rule the statistical units are institutional units. Only the government production is shown by establishments. When the scope and coverage of the estimates differ for conceptual or statistical reasons from the definitions and classifications recommended in 1993 SNA, a footnote is indicated to the relevant tables. Substantial changes were introduced in the compilation of national accounts from 1991. The most important ones are as follows: The output of financial intermediaries was measured on cost level before the revision, presently the service charges are accounted as the output of this sector; owner occupied dwellings are valued on imputed market rents (prior to 1991 they were accounted on costs); consumption of fixed capital in the government sector is based on replacement cost (prior to 1991 they were based on historical costs) of gross fixed capital formation from 1991 on financial leasing and capital contribution in kind are included. The base years for the constant price estimations are 1976, 1988 and 1991. (For every base year two data series are given. Some methodological changes were introduced in the base year as well.)

Sources and methods:

(a) Gross domestic product. Gross domestic product is estimated from three approaches: production, expenditure and cost structure (income side). The main approach used for the estimation of GDP is the production approach.

(b) Expenditure on the gross domestic product. The expenditure approach is used to estimate all expenditure type components of GDP. Government final consumption expenditure is based on records from all sub-sectors of general government. Private final consumption expenditure is estimated mainly from household budget survey and partly from trade statistics. The main sources for estimation of gross fixed capital formation are the investment surveys. Exports and imports of goods are based on customs declaration, while exports and imports of services are obtained from the Balance of Payments. For the calculation of constant prices, price deflation is used for all expenditure groups.

(c) Cost-structure of the gross domestic product. Compensation of employees is estimated from tax declarations of corporations, income tax declarations, labour surveys, financial data for general government and social security statistics. Taxes and subsidies on products are taken directly from the general government accounts.

(d) Gross domestic product by kind of economic activity. The table of value added by kind of activity is prepared at basic prices. The main sources of the estimation at current prices are: financial tax reports of corporations, state budget, income tax statistics, agricultural statistics, reports of financial intermediaries and nonprofit surveys. Double deflation is used for the calculations at constant prices, except agriculture and trade margin. Government production is an exception where the cost elements are deflated.

1.1 Expenditure on the Gross Domestic Product, in Current Prices

Million Hungarian forint

		1980	1983	1984	1985	1986	1987	1988	1989	1990	1991	1992	1993
1	Government final consumption expenditure [a]	134875	171584	183274	201539	219335	239078	289989 / 320663	363075	457973	590932 / 650113	796694	1030317
2	Private final consumption expenditure [b]	380465	470481	512524	552294	592144	665723	721924 / 716366	844251	1046338	1303792 / 1375306	1700597	2110620
	A Households	...	...	...	...	...	...	...	...	...	1359229	1674521	2069334
	B Private non-profit institutions serving households	...	...	...	...	...	...	...	...	...	16079	26076	41286
3	Gross capital formation	221256	237155	251775	258423	292739	327484	358947 / 364678	458103	530433	480748 / 490471	445691	687982
	A Increase in stocks [c]	13569	17137	26415	26294	31561	23947	63375 / 53877	85615	129915	39880 / -25827	-131436	26846
	B Gross fixed capital formation	207687	220018	225360	232129	261178	303537	295572 / 310801	372488	400518	440868 / 516298	577127	661136
4	Exports of goods and services [d]	281871	360713	401961	436180	431585	464391	530395 / 530395	620857	650704	834913 / 818407	925322	937046
5	Less: Imports of goods and services [e]	297436	343566	371078	414778	447003	470306	491738 / 491738	563453	596135	901981 / 842627	933248	1228130
	Equals: Gross Domestic Product [f]	721031	896367	978456	1033658	1088800	1226370	1409517 / 1440364	1722833	2089313	2308404 / 2491672	2935056	3537835

a) Item 'Government final consumption expenditure' includes health, social and cultural expenditure of enterprises and final consumption expenditure of non-profit institutions, and gross output of financial services and insurance is valued at cost level.
b) Item 'Private final consumption expenditure' covers total final consumption expenditure in domestic market of households. From 1988, consumption from own-account production is evaluated at basic prices. The wage-like part of the business travel cost (i.e. per diem) is treated as private consumption expenditure.
c) Item 'Increase in stocks' includes gains or losses arising from fluctuations in prices.
d) Item 'Exports of goods and services' excludes direct purchases in the domestic market by non-resident households.
e) Item 'Imports of goods and services' excludes direct purchases abroad by resident households, except purchase of cars by Hungarian individuals for own use from 1991.
f) Data in this table have not been revised, therefore they are not comparable with the data in other tables.

Hungary

1.2 Expenditure on the Gross Domestic Product, in Constant Prices

Million Hungarian forint

	1980	1983	1984	1985	1986	1987	1988	1989	1990	1991	1992	1993
	\multicolumn{7}{c}{At constant prices of: 1981}	\multicolumn{3}{c}{1988}	\multicolumn{3}{c}{1991}		
1 Government final consumption expenditure	142741[a]	153514[a]	155631[a]	160957[a]	166519[a]	168736[a]	171802[a] / 332448[a]	327428[a]	324958[a]	316217[a] / 650113	648823	709081
2 Private final consumption expenditure	401066[b]	415426[b]	420088[b]	424796[b]	433166[b]	450521[b]	430098[b] / 716366[b]	730158[b]	704454[b]	659129[b] / 1375308	1392351	1431562
A Households	...						...	...	...	1359229	1369491	1401606
B Private non-profit institutions serving households	...			...			...	...	...	16079	22860	29956
3 Gross capital formation	226071	197990	193229	186512	202581	208997	202201 / 360742	365214	349747	276224 / 490471	384058	520300
A Increase in stocks	10317	1591	4040	3090	7246	-5560	7214 / 49941	32685	40947	-376 / -25827	-118456	9182
B Gross fixed capital formation	215754	196399	189189	183422	195335	214557	194987 / 310801	332529	308800	276600 / 516298	502514	511118
4 Exports of goods and services	292570[c]	340415[c]	363001[c]	381906[c]	373406[c]	391140[c]	416375[c] / 530395[c]	536815[c]	508132[c]	492506[c] / 818407	835607	750882
5 Less: Imports of goods and services	311422[d]	307096[d]	310429[d]	334730[d]	343653[d]	353668[d]	355315[d] / 491738[d]	500737[d]	479425[d]	505353[d] / 842627	844708	1015714
Equals: Gross Domestic Product	751026	800249	821520	819441	832019	865726	865161 / 1448213	1458878	1407866	1238723 / 2491672	2416131	2396111

a) Item 'Government final consumption expenditure' includes health, social and cultural expenditure of enterprises and final consumption expenditure of non-profit institutions, and gross output of financial services and insurance is valued at cost level.
b) Item 'Private final consumption expenditure' covers total final consumption expenditure in domestic market of households. From 1988, consumption from own-account production is evaluated at basic prices. The wage-like part of the business travel cost (i.e. per diem) is treated as private consumption expenditure.
c) Item 'Exports of goods and services' excludes direct purchases in the domestic market by non-resident households.
d) Item 'Imports of goods and services' excludes direct purchases abroad by resident households, except purchase of cars by Hungarian individuals for own use from 1991.

1.3 Cost Components of the Gross Domestic Product

Million Hungarian forint

	1980	1983	1984	1985	1986	1987	1988	1989	1990	1991	1992	1993
1 Indirect taxes, net	69555	89584	76395	67829	37765	61247	160767	201854	288502	299179 / 363037	446232	548543
A Indirect taxes	206412	257629	245169	255460	257378	300052	377938	403308	465539	443917 / 459179	507984	611409
B Less: Subsidies	136857	168045	168774	187631	219613	238805	217171	201454	177037	144738 / 96142	61752	62866
2 Consumption of fixed capital [a]	89031	99496	105668	108277	116956	124776	132739	154395	163878	185789	...	...
3 Compensation of employees paid by resident producers to:	311270	381368	432534	467777	503221	548142	695106	891472	1118021	1350900 / 1385912	1606402	1927321
4 Operating surplus	242603	314516	349792	376561	418574	477000	402869	463037	509138	472536 / 850462	983065	1186411
A Corporate and quasi-corporate enterprises	185963	230162	247175	259369	281317	330109	254668	303326	307016	204752 / 368615	336213	459736
B Private unincorporated enterprises	55773	81619	99569	114229	134434	143200	144253	155082	194636	259493 / 361668	498157	564992
C General government	867	2735	3048	2963	2823	3691	3948	4629	7486	8291 / 120179	148695	161683
Statistical discrepancy [b]	8572	11403	14067	13214	12284	15205	18036	...	-	... / -107739	-100643	-124440
Equals: Gross Domestic Product	721031	896367	978456	1033658	1088800	1226370	1409517	1710758	2079539	2308404 / 2491672	2935056	3537835

a) Item 'Consumption of fixed capital' is estimated on the basis of the charges actually made by producers.
b) Item 'Statistical discrepancy' refers to the difference between own-account agricultural production valued at approximated basic values and final consumption of goods from own-account production valued at consumer prices. After 1988, own-account agricultural production is valued at purchasers' prices, as in the case of private final consumption.

Hungary

1.5 Current Income and Outlay of Corporate and Quasi-Corporate Enterprises, Summary

Million Hungarian forint

	1980	1983	1984	1985	1986	1987	1988	1989	1990	1991	1992	1993
Receipts												
1 Operating surplus	...	...	...	...	...	...	...	...	...	368615	336213	459736
2 Property and entrepreneurial income received	...	...	...	...	...	...	...	...	...	731386	737751	671469
3 Current transfers	...	...	...	...	...	...	...	...	...	44169	161549	199390
Total Current Receipts	...	...	...	...	...	...	...	...	...	1144170	1235513	1330595
Disbursements												
1 Property and entrepreneurial income	...	...	...	...	...	...	...	...	...	846874	807840	713792
2 Direct taxes and other current payments to general government	...	...	...	...	...	...	...	...	...	87612	64075	71774
3 Other current transfers	...	...	...	...	...	...	...	...	...	44422	184797	226732
Statistical discrepancy	...	...	...	...	...	...	...	...	...	107739	100643	124440
4 Net saving	...	...	...	...	...	...	...	...	...	57523	78158	193857
Total Current Disbursements and Net Saving	...	...	...	...	...	...	...	...	...	1144170	1235513	1330595

1.9 Gross Domestic Product by Institutional Sectors of Origin

Million Hungarian forint

	1980	1983	1984	1985	1986	1987	1988	1989	1990	1991	1992	1993
Domestic Factor Incomes Originating												
1 General government	59633	75104	81229	90236	98694	109676	140530	199847	261544	332472 / 435778	551199	663043
2 Corporate and quasi-corporate enterprises	436049	535453	597395	635047	683281	765075	801568	965523	1117754	1149284 / 1452814	1509679	1817864
A Non-financial	431781	528282	590053	627300	672356	754822	787296	946562	1092095	1118755 / 1350999	1400535	1672269
Public	...	...	...	...	...	...	...	...	...	...	791240	715669
Private	...	...	...	...	...	...	...	...	...	...	609295	956900
B Financial	4268	7171	7342	7747	10925	10253	14272	18961	25659	30529 / 101815	109144	145595
3 Households and private unincorporated enterprises	58191	85327	103702	119055	139820	150391	155877	189139	247861	341680 / 401469	550238	645396
4 Non-profit institutions serving households	...	...	...	...	...	...	...	...	...	8930	13153	14446
Subtotal: Domestic Factor Incomes	553873	695884	782326	844338	921795	1025142	1097975	1354509	1627159	1823436 / 2298991	2624269	3140749
Indirect taxes, net	69555	89584	76395	67829	37765	61247	160767	201854	288502	299179 / 363037	446232	548543
A Indirect taxes	206412	257629	245169	255460	257378	300052	377938	403308	465539	443917 / 459179	507984	611409
B Less: Subsidies	136857	168045	168774	187631	219613	238805	217171	201454	177037	144738 / 96142	61752	62866
Consumption of fixed capital	89031	99496	105668	108277	116956	124776	132739	154395	163878	185789	...	...
Statistical discrepancy	8572	11403	14067	13214	12284	15205	18036	...	...	-170356	-135445	-151457
Gross Domestic Product	721031	896367	978456	1033658	1088800	1226370	1409517	1710758	2079539	2308404 / 2491672	2935056	3537835

Hungary

1.10 Gross Domestic Product by Kind of Activity, in Current Prices

Million Hungarian forint

	1980	1983	1984	1985	1986	1987	1988	1989	1990	1991	1992	1993
1 Agriculture, hunting, forestry and fishing [a]	120652	152927	166144	166664	182569	189222	209454 / 209781	235893	261236	230593 / 195138	189879	209258
2 Mining and quarrying	40106	58414	58670	59392	56512	56360	55446 / 55446	51754	60772	71923 / 81813	32210	20141
3 Manufacturing [b]	190499	227879	254477	272452	275451	308902	327184 / 327317	416202	436523	496464 / 494217	583044	691668
4 Electricity, gas and water [c]	22277	29511	30116	34443	44750	54293	64501 / 64796	68300	83457	76787 / 90486	102003	123788
5 Construction	53467	65447	71120	73950	78966	92233	96775 / 102316	127469	125436	121929 / 123500	153892	166808
6 Wholesale and retail trade, restaurants and hotels	64812	76763	86821	96741	107977	128107	125857 / 127804	159513	266560	329674 / 355643	341615	418002
7 Transport, storage and communication	58513	71425	74176	77731	86250	94425	101170 / 101399	124406	143539	185374 / 209907	245244	281868
8 Finance, insurance, real estate and business services [de]	30130	39967	46688	53500	59926	70275	86511 / 95175	116420	145007	179521 / 336630	426409	557852
9 Community, social and personal services [e]	4754	5690	6357	7490	8280	9430	15220 / 15075	19331	22915	27561 / 411657	549973	671364
Total, Industries [f]	585210	728023	794569	842363	900681	1003247	1082118 / 1099109	1319288	1545445	1719826 / 2298991	2624269	3140749
Producers of Government Services [g]	60324	74171	80605	89066	96538	107092	131957 / 163849	190423	251058	319369 / ...	...	...
Other Producers	...	...	...	...	...	...	... / ...	...	...	... / ...	...	...
Subtotal	645534	802194	875174	931429	997219	1110339	1214075 / 1262958	1509711	1796503	2039195 / 2298991	2624269	3140749
Less: Imputed bank service charge	...	...	...	...	...	...	... / ...	...	...	... / ...	...	...
Plus: Import duties [hi]	66925	82770	89215	89015	79297	100826	177406 / 177406	213122	292810	269209 / 300420	411430	521526
Plus: Value added tax	...	...	...	...	...	...	... / ...	...	...	... / ...	...	...
Plus: Other adjustments [i]	8572	11403	14067	13214	12284	15205	18036 / ...	...	...	-107739	-100643	-124440
Equals: Gross Domestic Product [k]	721031	896367	978456	1033658	1088800	1226370	1409517 / 1440364	1722833	2089313	2308404 / 2491672	2935056	3537835

a) Item 'Agriculture, hunting, forestry and fishing' includes operation of irrigation systems and veterinary services. After 1988, the operation of irrigation systems is included in item 'Electricity, gas and water'.
b) Item 'Manufacturing' includes gas.
c) For the years before 1988, item 'Electricity, gas and water' excludes gas and operation of irrigation systems.
d) Gross output of finance, insurance and that of owner-occupied housing are estimated at cost level.
e) Services - except trade, transport, restaurants, hotels, storage, communications, sanitary and community services - are included in item 'Finance, insurance, real estate and business services'
f) All types of repair services are included in the relevant industries.
g) Item 'Producers of government services' includes non-profit institutions.
h) Item 'Import duties' refers to all net taxes on commodities and are excluded from the value added of industries.
i) Item 'Import duties' include 'other adjustments'.
j) Data in this table have not been revised, therefore they are not comparable with the data in other tables.
k) The estimates beginning 1991 of the new series are according to the ISIC Rev. 3. All the footnotes refer to the first series.

Hungary

1.11 Gross Domestic Product by Kind of Activity, in Constant Prices

Million Hungarian forint

	1980	1983	1984	1985	1986	1987	1988	1989	1990	1991	1992	1993
	\multicolumn{6}{c	}{At constant prices of: 1981}		1988			1991		
1 Agriculture, hunting, forestry and fishing	131563[a]	151948[a]	158969[a]	152521[a]	157851[a]	153117[a]	165153[a] 210153[a]	207618[a]	197943[a]	181672[a] 195138	162730	151853
2 Mining and quarrying	50919	46551	45235	42383	40166	40020	39085 55446	50220	44898	36593 81813	30110	16826
3 Manufacturing	186775[b]	218885[b]	228014[b]	226480[b]	224478[b]	233086[b]	229450[b] 327771[b]	324148[b]	295482[b]	240906[b] 494217	502101	533494
4 Electricity, gas and water	21373[c]	23759[c]	23192[c]	21679[c]	24996[c]	25914[c]	25968[c] 64812[c]	64945[c]	65643[c]	56159[c] 90486	89861	98983
5 Construction	53436	55202	52307	49885	49914	53815	50846 102846	111370	86996	73956 123500	125793	117740
6 Wholesale and retail trade, restaurants and hotels	64992	67701	67475	69900	71279	75244	65483 128008	126301	141165	129387 355643	298219	282747
7 Transport, storage and communication	61060	64819	66730	66117	68010	71045	71975 101632	108621	100655	89153 209907	200779	190495
8 Finance, insurance, real estate and business services	32765[de]	36986[de]	38718[de]	41983[de]	44663[de]	50113[de]	50674[de] 96221[de]	99236[de]	108511[de]	104596[de] 336630	330976	353158
9 Community, social and personal services	4956[e]	5273[e]	5644[e]	5870[e]	6141[e]	6998[e]	7940[e] 15075[e]	14265[e]	13794[e]	13123[e] 411657	442835	444575
Total, Industries	607839[f]	671124[f]	686284[f]	676818[f]	687498[f]	709352[f]	706574[f] 1101964[f]	1106724[f]	1055087[f]	925545[f] 2298991	2183404	2189871
Producers of Government Services	62173[g]	66433[g]	69994[g]	71753[g]	73081[g]	75367[g]	75911[g] 168843[g]	173676[g]	176806[g]	174660[g]	...	...
Other Producers	...	...	...	...	...	...	...	...	...	...	...	...
Subtotal	670012	737557	756278	748571	760579	784719	782485 1270807	1280400	1231893	1100205 2298991	2183404	2189871
Less: Imputed bank service charge	...	...	...	...	...	...	...	...	...	...	...	...
Plus: Import duties	81014[hi]	62692[hi]	65242[hi]	70870[hi]	71440[hi]	81007[hi]	82676[hi] 177406[hi]	178478[hi]	175973[hi]	140237[hi] 300420	313241	292060
Plus: Value added tax							...	...	...	...		
Plus: Other adjustments							...	...	...	-107739	-80514	-85820
Equals: Gross Domestic Product	751026	800249	821520	819441	832019	865726	865161 1448213	1458878	1407866	1240442 2491672[j]	2416131[j]	2396111[j]

a) Item 'Agriculture, hunting, forestry and fishing' includes operation of irrigation systems and veterinary services. After 1988, the operation of irrigation systems is included in item 'Electricity, gas and water'.
b) Item 'Manufacturing' includes gas.
c) For the years before 1988, item 'Electricity, gas and water' excludes gas and operation of irrigation systems.
d) Gross output of finance, insurance and that of owner-occupied housing are estimated at cost level.
e) Services - except trade, transport, restaurants, hotels, storage, communications, sanitary and community services - are included in item 'Finance, insurance, real estate and business services'
f) All types of repair services are included in the relevant industries.
g) Item 'Producers of government services' includes non-profit institutions.
h) Item 'Import duties' refers to all net taxes on commodities and are excluded from the value added of industries.
i) Item 'Import duties' include 'other adjustments'.
j) The estimates beginning 1991 of the new series are according to the ISIC Rev. 3. All the footnotes refer to the first series.

2.1 Government Final Consumption Expenditure by Function, in Current Prices

Million Hungarian forint

	1980	1983	1984	1985	1986	1987	1988	1989	1990	1991	1992	1993
1 General public services	...	...	...	...	...	...	...	...	...	...	124745	160786
2 Defence	...	...	...	...	...	...	...	...	...	...	51966	132334
3 Public order and safety	...	...	...	...	...	...	...	...	...	...	62454	77317
4 Education	...	...	...	...	...	...	...	...	...	...	173529	207090
5 Health	...	...	...	...	...	...	...	...	...	...	127457	146103
6 Social security and welfare	...	...	...	...	...	...	...	...	...	...	73295	88024
7 Housing and community amenities	...	...	...	...	...	...	...	...	...	...	53592	63544
8 Recreational, cultural and religious affairs	...	...	...	...	...	...	...	...	...	...	32090	39966
9 Economic services	...	...	...	...	...	...	...	...	...	...	75444	81711

Hungary

2.1 Government Final Consumption Expenditure by Function, in Current Prices
(Continued)

Million Hungarian forint

	1980	1983	1984	1985	1986	1987	1988	1989	1990	1991	1992	1993
A Fuel and energy	...	...	...	...	...	...	...	...	...	...	...	...
B Agriculture, forestry, fishing and hunting	...	...	...	...	...	...	...	...	...	...	2318	3769
C Mining, manufacturing and construction, except fuel and energy	...	...	...	...	...	...	...	...	...	...	7880	8300
D Transportation and communication	...	...	...	...	...	...	...	...	...	...	65246	69642
E Other economic affairs	...	...	...	...	...	...	...	...	...	...	...	...
10 Other functions	...	...	...	...	...	...	...	...	...	...	22122	33442
Total Government Final Consumption Expenditure	...	...	...	...	...	...	...	...	...	...	796694	1030317

2.2 Government Final Consumption Expenditure by Function, in Constant Prices

Million Hungarian forint

	1980	1983	1984	1985	1986	1987	1988	1989	1990	1991	1992	1993
					At constant prices of:1991							
1 General public services	...	...	...	...	...	...	...	...	...	...	103335	108890
2 Defence	...	...	...	...	...	...	...	...	...	...	43059	105971
3 Public order and safety	...	...	...	...	...	...	...	...	...	...	51750	52366
4 Education	...	...	...	...	...	...	...	...	...	...	139844	137937
5 Health	...	...	...	...	...	...	...	...	...	...	99931	96325
6 Social security and welfare	...	...	...	...	...	...	...	...	...	...	61331	57122
7 Housing and community amenities	...	...	...	...	...	...	...	...	...	...	45263	47097
8 Recreational, cultural and religious affairs	...	...	...	...	...	...	...	...	...	...	25940	27296
9 Economic services	...	...	...	...	...	...	...	...	...	...	59534	52445
A Fuel and energy	...	...	...	...	...	...	...	...	...	...	...	...
B Agriculture, forestry, fishing and hunting	...	...	...	...	...	...	...	...	...	...	1976	2668
C Mining, manufacturing and construction, except fuel and energy	...	...	...	...	...	...	...	...	...	...	6774	6459
D Transportation and communication	...	...	...	...	...	...	...	...	...	...	50784	43318
E Other economic affairs	...	...	...	...	...	...	...	...	...	...	...	...
10 Other functions	...	...	...	...	...	...	...	...	...	...	18836	23632
Total Government Final Consumption Expenditure	...	...	...	...	...	...	...	...	...	...	648823	709081

2.5 Private Final Consumption Expenditure by Type and Purpose, in Current Prices

Million Hungarian forint

	1980	1983	1984	1985	1986	1987	1988	1989	1990	1991	1992	1993
					Final Consumption Expenditure of Resident Households							
1 Food, beverages and tobacco [a]	190053	228447	248817	262550	277533	307677	341257 / 326037	376878	460627	533651 / 535403	641884	770609
A Food	129997	154551	170298	179982	188589	212418	234455 / 225133	262462	316758	368377 / 369879	448538	547490
B Non-alcoholic beverages	4662	5998	6309	7059	7874	8592	9844 / 9844	10949	12316	16300 / 16300	22064	28056
C Alcoholic beverages	44961	54318	58113	61174	65565	67577	74055 / 68157	76944	97322	112327 / 112577	128360	143013
D Tobacco	10433	13580	14097	14335	15505	19090	22903 / 22903	26523	34231	36647 / 36647	42922	52050
2 Clothing and footwear	39853	47486	49673	54868	57872	64586	63856 / 63856	69585	82490	97087 / 97167	117820	139312
3 Gross rent, fuel and power [b]	30673	39745	44688	52281	54594	61968	70974 / 78836	89064	111897	156382 / 234245	290713	350385
A Fuel and power	15972	19275	21262	27043	27195	31216	34075 / 34075	38655	48006	79560 / 79560	100744	120833
B Other	14701	20470	23426	25238	27399	30752	36899 / 44761	50409	63891	76822 / 154685	189969	229552
4 Furniture, furnishings and household equipment and operation [c]	35468	43630	48230	50150	53771	62171	64301 / 64301	78553	88230	114028 / 114028	137739	165840

Hungary

2.5 Private Final Consumption Expenditure by Type and Purpose, in Current Prices
(Continued)

Million Hungarian forint

	1980	1983	1984	1985	1986	1987	1988	1989	1990	1991	1992	1993
A Household operation	8164	9973	11008	11252	11815	12850	13821 13821	16219	17898	25609 25609	31407	41709
B Other	27304	33657	37222	38898	41956	49321	50480 50480	62334	70332	88419 88419	106332	124131
5 Medical care and health expenses	2791	3391	3539	3856	4190	4528	5172 5172	6828	15203	19521 19903	27956	35370
6 Transport and communication	33566	46116	49874	55065	61229	70012	77755 77755	97407	134627	198141 198841	252279	319386
A Personal transport equipment	11331	10778	12105	13291	15626	19174	19073 19073	24206	35422	47555 47555	71916	88641
B Other d	22235	35338	37769	41774	45603	50838	58682 58682	73201	99205	150586 151286	180363	230745
7 Recreational, entertainment, education and cultural services	24442	30397	32946	36993	42419	48176	45385 45385	59129	68565	85721 92589	114103	148473
A Education	4525	5594	5750	5984	6337	6531	6600 6510	6642	7950	8795 9385	11664	14946
B Other	19917	24803	27196	31009	36082	41645	38785 38875	52487	60615	76926 83204	102439	133527
8 Miscellaneous goods and services	23619	31269	34757	36531	40536	46605	53224 55024	66807	84699	99261 104348	137909	181310
A Personal care	5703	7466	8047	8239	9112	10819	12601 12601	14004	17456	20617 20617	24997	35040
B Expenditures in restaurants, cafes and hotels	2959	4570	5273	5710	6407	7801	10316 12116	13960	15714	14300 14300	21300	23400
C Other	14957	19233	21437	22582	25017	27985	30307 30307	38843	51529	64344 69431	91612	122870
Total Final Consumption Expenditure in the Domestic Market by Households, of which e	380465	470481	512524	552294	592144	665723	721924 716366	844251	1046338	1303792 1396524	1720403	2110685
A Durable goods	34077	38936	43677	48800	57212	69795	67894 67894	91068	105753	132800 132800	174642	210250
B Semi-durable goods	69096	83880	89579	95762	102118	114896	116152 116152	132652	163400	206839 206919	250496	306367
C Non-durable goods	229147	282482	307653	329299	347687	386309	428588 413368	482405	601103	749863 751615	917472	1118437

Hungary

2.5 Private Final Consumption Expenditure by Type and Purpose, in Current Prices
(Continued)

Million Hungarian forint

	1980	1983	1984	1985	1986	1987	1988	1989	1990	1991	1992	1993
D Services	48145	65183	71615	78433	85127	94723	109290 118952	138126	176082	214290 305190	377793	475631
Plus: Direct purchases abroad by resident households	...	...	...	...	...	...	...	...	...	... ...	...	...
Less: Direct purchases in the domestic market by non-resident households	...	...	...	...	...	...	...	...	...	... ...	...	...
Equals: Final Consumption Expenditure of Resident Households f	380465	470481	512524	552294	592144	665723	721924 716366	844251	1046338	1303792 1359229	1674521	2069334

Final Consumption Expenditure of Private Non-profit Institutions Serving Households

	1980	1983	1984	1985	1986	1987	1988	1989	1990	1991	1992	1993
Equals: Final Consumption Expenditure of Private Non-profit Organisations Serving Households	...	...	...	...	...	...	...	...	...	16079	26076	41286
Private Final Consumption Expenditure	380465	470481	512524	552294	592144	665723	721924 716366	844252	1046338	1303792 1375308	1700597	2110620

a) Item 'Food, beverages and tobacco' includes expenditure in restaurants, cafes and hotels.
b) Gross rent of owner-occupied housing is evaluated at market rents since 1991.
c) Service for insurance of household property is not taken into account.
d) Service charges on insurance of personal transport equipment is not taken into account.
e) Item 'Private final consumption expenditure' covers total final consumption expenditure in domestic market of households. From 1988, consumption from own-account production is evaluated at basic prices. The wage-like part of the business travel cost (i.e. per diem) is treated as private consumption expenditure.
f) Before 1988, some benefits (like meal contributions of the employers) were accounted as part of social benefit in kind, and was included in the government consumption. From 1988, they are being accounted as part of labour income and are being included in the (purchased) private final consumption.

2.6 Private Final Consumption Expenditure by Type and Purpose, in Constant Prices

Million Hungarian forint

	1980	1983	1984	1985	1986	1987	1988	1989	1990	1991	1992	1993
	\multicolumn{6}{c}{At constant prices of: 1981}	\multicolumn{3}{c}{1988}	\multicolumn{3}{c}{1991}		

Final Consumption Expenditure of Resident Households

	1980	1983	1984	1985	1986	1987	1988	1989	1990	1991	1992	1993
1 Food, beverages and tobacco	197605a	202741a	202987a	205563a	209016a	209637a	204174a 326037a	328046a	301274a	289799a 535403	537096	522588
A Food	135044	139149	138514	139138	141594	145469	141602 225133	226250	206172	201626 369879	374178	363868
B Non-alcoholic beverages	4790	5479	5323	5690	6189	6435	6180 9844	9573	8447	9503 16300	19022	19440
C Alcoholic beverages	47014	46537	47216	48610	48462	45263	43627 68157	68982	66010	60048 112577	109668	105839
D Tobacco	10757	11573	11934	12125	12771	12470	12765 22903	23241	20645	18622 36647	34228	33441
2 Clothing and footwear	42541	42248	39981	39842	38613	39459	32802 63856	58771	56521	50025 97167	95868	97205
3 Gross rent, fuel and power b	32528	36586	38345	39393	39553	42033	42709 78836	81534	83294	79634 234245	231153	234956
A Fuel and power	15967	16759	17995	18935	18619	20115	19778 34075	34996	36470	34271 79560	70712	70535
B Other	16561	19827	20350	20458	20934	21918	22931 44761	46538	46824	45363 154685	160441	164421
4 Furniture, furnishings and household equipment and operation	36999c	39923c	41185c	39717c	40120c	43765c	39769c 62837c	64376c	58656c	55573c 114028	113460	117265
A Household operation	8700	9067	9105	8770	8812	9125	8189 12357	11357	10560	10704 25609	25701	28858

Hungary

2.6 Private Final Consumption Expenditure by Type and Purpose, in Constant Prices
(Continued)

Million Hungarian forint

	1980	1983	1984	1985	1986	1987	1988	1989	1990	1991	1992	1993
				At constant prices of:								
				1981				1988		1991		
B Other	28299	30856	32080	30947	31308	34640	31580					
							50480	53019	48096	44869		
										88419	87759	88407
5 Medical care and health expenses	2846	3221	3219	3395	3544	3750	3694					
							9099	8147	8942	8203		
										19903	18217	16441
6 Transport and communication	37795	35286	37285	38769	42193	47091	48754					
							77755	82057	86051	77003		
										198841	208998	223985
A Personal transport equipment	11390	9447	9907	10541	12073	14757	14661					
							19073	19146	22173	19756		
										47555	64869	70889
B Other	26405	25839	27378	28228	30120	32334	34093					
							58682d	62911d	63878d	57247d		
										151286	144129	153096
7 Recreational, entertainment, education and cultural services	25478	28782	29967	31529	33334	37357	32593					
							45518	53311	50968	47656		
										92589	92574	92889
A Education	4626	5263	5130	5022	4855	5008	4842					
							5937	5536	5378	4621		
										9385	10167	9356
B Other	20852	23519	24837	26507	28479	32349	27751					
							39581	47775	45590	43035		
										83204	82407	83533
8 Miscellaneous goods and services	25274	26639	27119	26588	26793	27429	25603					
							52428	53916	58791	51236		
										104348	106376	114022
A Personal care	6262	6498	6375	6283	6331	6678	6481					
							12601	12044	12325	10822		
										20617	20073	22019
B Expenditures in restaurants, cafes and hotels	3307	3529	3657	3456	3173	3181	3168					
							11088	10487	11248	10080		
										14300	16200	14600
C Other	15705	16612	17087	16849	17289	17570	15954					
							28739	31385	35218	30334		
										69431	70103	77403
Total Final Consumption Expenditure in the Domestic Market by Households, of which	401066e	415426e	420088e	424796e	433166e	450521e	430098e					
							716366e	730158e	704497e	659129e		
										1396524	1403742	1419351
A Durable goods	34512	35562	38183	40452	44898	53665	47531					
							67894	79341	76537	71692		
										132800	153108	164965
B Semi-durable goods	73151	74610	72429	70953	69866	72325	62842					
							116001	111739	111347	100974		
										206919	200192	205033
C Non-durable goods	240928	248343	250786	254443	259550	263594	258111					
							413368	417214	392837	375567		
										751615	741278	731126

Hungary

2.6 Private Final Consumption Expenditure by Type and Purpose, in Constant Prices
(Continued)

Million Hungarian forint

	1980	1983	1984	1985	1986	1987	1988	1989	1990	1991	1992	1993
				At constant prices of:				1988		1991		
				1981								
D Services	52475	56911	58690	58948	58852	60937	61614	121864	123776	110896	309164	318227
							119103			305190		
Plus: Direct purchases abroad by resident households	...	...	...	...	...	...	... ...	...	...	... ...	...	...
Less: Direct purchases in the domestic market by non-resident households	...	...	...	...	...	...	... ...	...	...	... ...	...	...
Equals: Final Consumption Expenditure of Resident Households	401066f	415426f	420088f	424796f	433166f	450521f	430098f 716366f	730158	704497	659129f 1359229	1369491	1401606

Final Consumption Expenditure of Private Non-profit Institutions Serving Households

Equals: Final Consumption Expenditure of Private Non-profit Organisations Serving Households	...	...	...	...	...	...	... ...	...	...	... 16079	22860	29956
Private Final Consumption Expenditure	401066	415426	420088	424796	433166	450521	430098 716366	730158	704497	659129 1375308	1392351	1431562

a) Item 'Food, beverages and tobacco' includes goods consumed in restaurants, cafes, hotels, hospitals, other medical institutions and schools.
b) Gross rent of owner-occupied housing is evaluated at market rents since 1991.
c) Service for insurance of household property is not taken into account.
d) Service charges on insurance of personal transport equipment is not taken into account.
e) Item 'Private final consumption expenditure' covers total final consumption expenditure in domestic market of households. From 1988, consumption from own-account production is evaluated at basic prices. The wage-like part of the business travel cost (i.e. per diem) is treated as private consumption expenditure.
f) Before 1988, some benefits (like meal contributions of the employers) were accounted as part of social benefit in kind, and was included in the government consumption. From 1988, they are being accounted as part of labour income and are being included in the (purchased) private final consumption.

4.1 Derivation of Value Added by Kind of Activity, in Current Prices

Million Hungarian forint

	1991			1992			1993		
	Gross Output	Intermediate Consumption	Value Added	Gross Output	Intermediate Consumption	Value Added	Gross Output	Intermediate Consumption	Value Added
	All Producers
1 Agriculture, hunting, forestry and fishing a	546443	351305	195138	541140	351261	189879	551658	342400	209258
A Agriculture and hunting	522062	334379	187683	516604	339177	177427	519107	325770	193337
B Forestry and logging	22619	15754	6865	22831	10973	11858	29894	14818	15076
C Fishing	1762	1172	590	1705	1111	594	2657	1812	845
2 Mining and quarrying	145438	63625	81813	66565	34355	32210	48421	28280	20141
A Coal mining	47486	25049	22437	45389	21831	23558	22518	14654	7864
B Crude petroleum and natural gas production	83699	29427	54272	9620	5899	3721	12323	6377	5946
C Metal ore mining	8225	5626	2599	5623	2798	2825	6166	2634	3532
D Other mining	6028	3523	2505	5933	3827	2106	7414	4615	2799
3 Manufacturing	1861385	1367168	494217	1912527	1329483	583044	2124856	1433188	691668
A Manufacture of food, beverages and tobacco	520776	404744	116032	524658	400605	124053	583844	440226	143618
B Textile, wearing apparel and leather industries	130012	85887	44125	136773	79655	57118	151909	85566	66343
C Manufacture of wood and wood products, including furniture	71784	47165	24619	99003	62837	36166	100675	61820	38855
D Manufacture of paper and paper products, printing and publishing	102186	74874	27312	115640	83530	32110	125351	84282	41069
E Manufacture of chemicals and chemical petroleum, coal, rubber and plastic products b	408358	301648	106710	417610	272515	145095	463505	288425	175080
F Manufacture of non-metallic mineral products, except products of petroleum and coal	67225	46106	21119	70874	46270	24604	77684	47879	29805
G Basic metal industries	140722	120938	19784	103186	87237	15949	91102	74909	16193
H Manufacture of fabricated metal products, machinery and equipment	216145	140441	75704	235349	151656	83693	256421	165558	90863
I Other manufacturing industries	204177	145365	58812	209434	145178	64256	274365	184523	89842
4 Electricity, gas and water c	311119	220633	90486	294846	192843	102003	363028	239240	123788
A Electricity, gas and steam	272862	203132	69730	256774	175703	81071	315753	217182	98571
B Water works and supply	38257	17501	20756	38072	17140	20932	47275	22058	25217

Hungary

4.1 Derivation of Value Added by Kind of Activity, in Current Prices
(Continued)

Million Hungarian forint

		1991 Gross Output	1991 Intermediate Consumption	1991 Value Added	1992 Gross Output	1992 Intermediate Consumption	1992 Value Added	1993 Gross Output	1993 Intermediate Consumption	1993 Value Added
5	Construction	275590	152090	123500	334857	180965	153892	364336	197528	166808
6	Wholesale and retail trade, restaurants and hotels	672729	317086	355643	796118	454503	341615	864562	446560	418002
7	Transport, storage and communication	348212	138305	209907	439484	194240	245244	504185	222317	281868
	A Transport and storage	281904	120576	161328	347379	160030	187349	384728	181820	202908
	B Communication	66308	17729	48579	92105	34210	57895	119457	40497	78960
8	Finance, insurance, real estate and business services d e	533679	197049	336630	658852	232443	426409	831613	273761	557852
	A Financial institutions	152155	50340	101815	163984	54840	109144	209264	63669	145595
	B Insurance				...	...	...	...	...	...
	C Real estate and business services	381524	146709	234815	494868	177603	317265	622349	210092	412257
9	Community, social and personal services e	629556	217899	411657	841809	291836	549973	1095977	424613	671364
Total, Industries f		5324151	3025160	2298991	5886198	3261929	2624269	6748636	3607887	3140749
Producers of Government Services g		...	...	...	...	...	...	...	...	...
Other Producers		...	...	...	...	...	...	...	...	...
Total		5324151	3025160	2298991	5886198	3261929	2624269	6748636	3607887	3140749
Less: Imputed bank service charge		...	...	...	...	...	...	...	...	...
Import duties h i		300420	...	300420	411430	...	411430	521526	...	521526
Value added tax		...	...	...	...	...	...	...	...	...
Other adjustments i		...	107739	-107739	...	100643	-100643	...	124440	-124440
Total		5624571	3132899	2491672	6297628	3362572	2935056	7270162	3732327	3537835

a) Item 'Agriculture, hunting, forestry and fishing' includes operation of irrigation systems and veterinary services. After 1988, the operation of irrigation systems is included in item 'Electricity, gas and water'.
b) Item 'Manufacturing' includes gas.
c) For the years before 1988, item 'Electricity, gas and water' excludes gas and operation of irrigation systems.
d) Gross output of finance, insurance and that of owner-occupied housing are estimated at cost level.
e) Services - except trade, transport, restaurants, hotels, storage, communications, sanitary and community services - are included in item 'Finance, insurance, real estate and business services'
f) All types of repair services are included in the relevant industries.
g) Item 'Producers of government services' includes non-profit institutions.
h) Item 'Import duties' refers to all net taxes on commodities and are excluded from the value added of industries.
i) Item 'Import duties' include 'other adjustments'.

4.2 Derivation of Value Added by Kind of Activity, in Constant Prices

Million Hungarian forint

		1991 Gross Output	1991 Intermediate Consumption	1991 Value Added	1992 Gross Output	1992 Intermediate Consumption	1992 Value Added	1993 Gross Output	1993 Intermediate Consumption	1993 Value Added
		\multicolumn{9}{c}{At constant prices of: 1991}

All Producers

		1991 GO	1991 IC	1991 VA	1992 GO	1992 IC	1992 VA	1993 GO	1993 IC	1993 VA
1	Agriculture, hunting, forestry and fishing	546443	351305	195138	486097	323367	162730	438067	286214	151853
	A Agriculture and hunting	522062	334379	187683	463895	312366	151529	411239	272127	139112
	B Forestry and logging	22619	15754	6865	20650	9979	10671	24697	12627	12070
	C Fishing	1762	1172	590	1552	1022	530	2131	1460	671
2	Mining and quarrying	145438	63625	81813	61776	31666	30110	41129	24303	16826
	A Coal mining	47486	25049	22437	42635	20379	22256	20086	12742	7344
	B Crude petroleum and natural gas production	83699	29427	54272	8449	5368	3081	10088	5561	4527
	C Metal ore mining	8225	5626	2599	5945	2645	3300	5829	2333	3496
	D Other mining	6028	3523	2505	4747	3274	1473	5126	3667	1459

Hungary

4.2 Derivation of Value Added by Kind of Activity, in Constant Prices
(Continued)

Million Hungarian forint

	1991			1992			1993		
	Gross Output	Intermediate Consumption	Value Added	Gross Output	Intermediate Consumption	Value Added	Gross Output	Intermediate Consumption	Value Added
	At constant prices of: 1991								
3 Manufacturing	1861385	1367168	494217	1688085	1185985	502101	1713876	1180382	533494
A Manufacture of food, beverages and tobacco	520776	404744	116032	461950	355284	106666	455351	353875	101476
B Textile, wearing apparel and leather industries	130012	85887	44125	119472	72522	46950	123675	74064	49611
C Manufacture of wood and wood products, including furniture	71784	47165	24619	84401	55668	28734	79150	50415	28735
D Manufacture of paper and paper products, printing and publishing	102186	74874	27312	102446	74405	28040	97628	67044	30584
E Manufacture of chemicals and chemical petroleum, coal, rubber and plastic products	408358	301648	106710	378355	245777	132577	394035	246093	147942
F Manufacture of non-metallic mineral products, except products of petroleum and coal	67225	46106	21119	62965	42213	20752	60799	38794	22005
G Basic metal industries	140722	120938	19784	100654	82156	18498	86346	67730	18616
H Manufacture of fabricated metal products, machinery and equipment	216145	140441	75704	205487	134451	71038	212530	139079	73451
I Other manufacturing industries	204177	145365	58812	172355	123509	48846	204362	143288	61074
4 Electricity, gas and water	311119	220633	90486	268891	179030	89861	306791	207808	98983
A Electricity, gas and steam	272862	203132	69730	237400	164516	72884	276502	191589	84913
B Water works and supply	38257	17501	20756	31491	14514	16977	30289	16219	14070
5 Construction	275590	152090	123500	284093	158300	125793	271957	154217	117740
6 Wholesale and retail trade, restaurants and hotels	672729	317086	355643	660933	362713	298219	616253	333506	282747
7 Transport, storage and communication	348212	138305	209907	362006	161227	200779	353626	163131	190495
A Transport and storage	281904	120576	161328	285344	132538	152806	275209	135569	139640
B Communication	66308	17729	48579	76662	28689	47973	78417	27562	50855
8 Finance, insurance, real estate and business services	533679	197049	336630	517101	186125	330976	538637	185479	353158
A Financial institutions	152155	50340	101815	131187	44226	86961	144320	44524	99796
B Insurance	...	...	...	...	...	...	...	...	...
C Real estate and business services	381524	146709	234815	385914	141899	244015	394317	140955	253362
9 Community, social and personal services	629556	217899	411657	676617	233782	442835	748310	303735	444575
Total, Industries	5324151	3025160	2298991	5005599	2822195	2183404	5028646	2838775	2189871
Producers of Government Services	...	...	...	...	...	...	...	...	...
Other Producers	...	...	...	...	...	...	...	...	...
Total	5324151	3025160	2298991	5005599	2822195	2183404	5028646	2838775	2189871
Less: Imputed bank service charge	...	...	...	...	...	...	...	...	...
Import duties	300420	...	300420	313241	...	313241	292060	...	292060
Value added tax	...	...	...	...	...	...	...	...	...
Other adjustments	...	107739	-107739	...	80514	-80514	...	85820	-85820
Total	5624571	3132899	2491672	5318840	2902709	2416131	5320706	2924595	2396111

4.3 Cost Components of Value Added

Million Hungarian forint

	1992						1993					
	Compensation of Employees	Capital Consumption	Net Operating Surplus	Indirect Taxes	Less: Subsidies Received	Value Added	Compensation of Employees	Capital Consumption	Net Operating Surplus	Indirect Taxes	Less: Subsidies Received	Value Added
	All Producers											
1 Agriculture, hunting, forestry and fishing [a]	105316	84463	...	7724	7624	189879	103277	116874	...	5489	16382	209258
A Agriculture and hunting	95169	81926	...	5958	5626	177427	89219	114458	...	5059	15399	193337
B Forestry and logging	9548	2519	...	1759	1968	11858	13088	2390	...	422	824	15076
C Fishing	599	18	...	7	30	594	970	26	...	8	159	845
2 Mining and quarrying	25591	8939	...	228	2548	32210	24659	-2430	...	289	2377	20141
A Coal mining	17524	8160	...	133	2259	23558	14015	-4320	...	118	1949	7864
B Crude petroleum and natural gas production	2451	1229	...	43	2	3721	4475	1374	...	99	2	5946
C Metal ore mining	3417	-352	...	26	266	2825	3613	308	...	29	418	3532
D Other mining	2199	-98	...	26	21	2106	2556	208	...	43	8	2799

Hungary

4.3 Cost Components of Value Added
(Continued)

Million Hungarian forint

	1992 Compensation of Employees	1992 Capital Consumption	1992 Net Operating Surplus	1992 Indirect Taxes	1992 Less: Subsidies Received	1992 Value Added	1993 Compensation of Employees	1993 Capital Consumption	1993 Net Operating Surplus	1993 Indirect Taxes	1993 Less: Subsidies Received	1993 Value Added
3 Manufacturing	398396	160906	...	32206	8464	583044	464321	204773	...	31788	9214	691668
A Manufacture of food, beverages and tobacco	79238	44044	...	2083	1312	124053	96248	47520	...	2895	3045	143618
B Textile, wearing apparel and leather industries	45272	12887	...	565	1606	57118	53426	13812	...	734	1629	66343
C Manufacture of wood and wood products, including furniture	22560	13759	...	537	690	36166	24219	15183	...	458	1005	38855
D Manufacture of paper and paper products, printing and publishing	28504	3775	...	571	740	32110	33759	7542	...	753	985	41069
E Manufacture of chemicals and chemical petroleum, coal, rubber and plastic products [b]	64100	56032	...	25997	1035	145095	71638	80869	...	23378	805	175080
F Manufacture of non-metallic mineral products, except products of petroleum and coal	18304	6119	...	279	98	24604	20224	9375	...	368	162	29805
G Basic metal industries	15487	1042	...	369	949	15949	18541	-2533	...	462	277	16193
H Manufacture of fabricated metal products, machinery and equipment	65500	17811	...	948	566	83693	74686	15247	...	1429	499	90863
I Other manufacturing industries	59431	5436	...	857	1468	64256	71580	17758	...	1311	807	89842
4 Electricity, gas and water [c]	51277	46857	...	4069	200	102003	75200	44826	...	4120	358	123788
A Electricity, gas and steam	36707	42399	...	2083	118	81071	55489	41290	...	1959	167	98571
B Water works and supply	14570	4458	...	1986	82	20932	19711	3536	...	2161	191	25217
5 Construction	94258	58287	...	1463	116	153892	119973	45069	...	1992	226	166808
6 Wholesale and retail trade, restaurants and hotels	226759	107875	...	7936	955	341615	267518	141530	...	10775	1821	418002
A Wholesale and retail trade	187637	89627	...	7625	863	284026	221178	124719	...	10372	1752	354517
B Restaurants and hotels	39122	18248	...	311	92	57589	46340	16811	...	403	69	63485
7 Transport, storage and communication	140644	105657	...	2024	3081	245244	162013	119577	...	2025	1747	281868
A Transport and storage	105452	83570	...	1224	2897	187349	116724	86349	...	1424	1589	202908
B Communication	35192	22087	...	800	184	57895	45289	33228	...	601	158	78960
8 Finance, insurance, real estate and business services [d][e]	145862	279244	...	3154	1851	426409	182296	373322	...	3364	1130	557852
A Financial institutions	36941	69677	...	1394	830	107182	51914	79766	...	843	9	132514
B Insurance	12353	-10359	...	-	32	1962	14740	-1676	...	26	9	13081
C Real estate and business services	96568	219926	...	1760	989	317265	115642	295232	...	2495	1112	412257
9 Community, social and personal services [e]	418299	130837	...	1345	508	549973	528064	142870	...	1087	657	671364
Total, Industries [f]	1606402	983065	...	60149	25347	2624269	1927321	1186411	...	60929	33912	3140749
Producers of Government Services [g]	...	...	...	...	...	...	...	...	...	...	...	...
Other Producers	...	...	...	...	...	...	...	...	...	...	...	...
Total	1606402	983065	...	60149	25347	2624269	1927321	1186411	...	60929	33912	3140749
Less: Imputed bank service charge	...	...	...	...	...	...	...	...	...	...	...	...
Import duties [h]	...	...	...	447835	36405	411430	...	...	...	550480	28954	521526
Value added tax	...	...	...	...	...	...	...	...	...	...	...	...
Other adjustments [i]	...	...	...	...	...	-100643	...	...	...	...	...	-124440
Total	1606402	983065	...	507984	61752	2935056	1927321	1186411	...	611409	62866	3537835

a) Item 'Agriculture, hunting, forestry and fishing' includes operation of irrigation systems and veterinary services. After 1988, the operation of irrigation systems is included in item 'Electricity, gas and water'.
b) Item 'Manufacturing' includes gas.
c) For the years before 1988, item 'Electricity, gas and water' excludes gas and operation of irrigation systems.
d) Gross output of finance, insurance and that of owner-occupied housing are estimated at cost level.
e) Services - except trade, transport, restaurants, hotels, storage, communications, sanitary and community services - are included in item 'Finance, insurance, real estate and business services'.
f) All types of repair services are included in the relevant industries.
g) Item 'Producers of government services' includes non-profit institutions.
h) Item 'Import duties' refers to all net taxes on commodities and are excluded from the value added of industries.
i) Item 'Statistical discrepancy' refers to the difference between own-account agricultural production valued at approximated basic values and final consumption of goods from own-account production valued at consumer prices. After 1988, own-account agricultural production is valued at purchasers' prices, as in the case of private final consumption.

Iceland

General note. The preparation of national accounts statistics in Iceland is undertaken by 'THJODHAGSSTOFNUN' (National Economic Institute), Reykjavik. The official estimates are published once or twice a year in 'THJODARBUSKAPURINN' (The Icelandic Economy) and in more detail but irregularly in a special series 'THJODHAGSREIKNINGASKYRSLUR' (National Accounts Publications). A detailed description of the sources and methods is found in that series on national accounts especially in no. 13. The estimates shown in the following tables have been prepared in accordance with the United Nations System of National Accounts.

(a) Gross domestic product. Gross domestic product is estimated mainly through the expenditure approach. The production approach is used in estimating GDP by kind of economic activity as well as cost-structure of GDP as described below. The difference between the two methods is explicitly presented as a 'statistical discrepancy' on the cost components' side of GDP.

(b) Expenditure on the gross domestic product. All components of GDP by expenditure type are estimated through the expenditure approach. Government final consumption expenditure is mainly based on government accounts. Estimates of private consumption expenditure are based on various sources. A vital source is the import of consumer goods plus import duties and trade and transport margin. The Agricultural Production Board is the source for the estimate of consumption of domestically produced agricultural products. A considerable part of the consumption of services is derived from the Industrial Statistics and the Family Expenditure Survey which is used as a weight in consumer price index. Gross capital formation is based on import of investment goods, direct inquiries to the main constructors and domestical producers of investment goods and government accounts. Exports and imports of goods and services are estimated from foreign trade statistics and balance of payment statistics. Price deflation is used for most of the expenditure items in arriving at constant prices. Various price indices are used.

(c) Cost-structure of the gross domestic product. (See 'Gross domestic product by kind of economic activity' below.)

(d) Gross domestic product by kind of economic activity. The production approach is used to estimate both cost-structure of domestic product and GDP by kind of activity. The main source are the annual accounts of enterprises. From the tax assessments data a sample of establishments is drawn from almost every single branch of industry. The sample is drawn from the tax records presenting the total value of wages and salaries of all employees and calculated income of self-employed. These amounts are classified by enterprises and establishments within each enterprise which enables breakdown by activity within enterprises. A sample of annual reports of enterprises, including operating accounts and balance sheets, are compiled from tax authorities. After processing these sources the samples are blown-up according to the total value of wages and salaries statistics on turnover as well as other vital adminstrative registers in each branch of industry. The operating account as presented in operating accounts of the firms is not suitable for national accounting purposes. One of the reason is the price increases during the year and therefore adjustments are made for the effects of inflation on the valuation of stocks at the beginning and the end of a year. By introducing a new concept 'stock appreciation' an attempt is made to correct the value of the stocks at the beginning and end of each year in such a way that both items are revalued at the annual average prices instead of prices at the beginning and end of year. By doing this the increase in stocks during the year is valued at the annual average prices and that value item replaces the former increase in stocks valued at prices in the beginning and the end of year respectively. For the constant price estimates the general approach for almost all industries is the deflation of the gross output or extrapolation of base-year value of output. Double-deflation is not used except in the case of the fishing industry.

1.1 Expenditure on the Gross Domestic Product, in Current Prices

Million Icelandic kronur

		1980	1983	1984	1985	1986	1987	1988	1989	1990	1991	1992	1993
1	Government final consumption expenditure	2663	12050	14701	21130	28776	38981	50537	60341	69989	78157	80375	84037
2	Private final consumption expenditure	9326	41016	55872	77240	99196	133557	161068	190254	223729	248999	249044	248952
3	Gross capital formation	4196	13769	18676	22417	27030	38810	47418	50587	65461	74834	69193	65508
	A Increase in stocks [a]	80	-1070	-661	-3111	-3748	-3783	-3085	-8143	-4546	-1226	-406	557
	B Gross fixed capital formation	4116	14839	19337	25528	30778	42593	50503	58730	70007	76060	69599	64951
	Residential buildings	1157	4194	5657	6455	6923	9303	12586	15936	18666	19104	18912	18551
	Non-residential buildings	694	3448	4266	5842	7640	11108	12481	14849	15552	16397	16259	16397
	Other construction and land improvement etc.	1182	3561	4292	5243	6140	8203	9979	12243	13514	16237	13325	14512
	Other	1083	3635	5123	7988	10076	13979	15456	15702	22276	24322	21103	15491
4	Exports of goods and services	5645	26683	33765	48774	61961	71681	81721	106282	124246	124943	121248	135018
5	Less: Imports of goods and services	5648	25275	33871	48663	55880	73965	84100	99240	119595	130305	121943	122759
	Equals: Gross Domestic Product	16182	68243	89143	120898	161083	209064	256644	308224	363830	396628	397917	410756

a) Item 'Increase in stocks' includes stocks of export products only.

1.2 Expenditure on the Gross Domestic Product, in Constant Prices

Million Icelandic kronur

		1980	1983	1984	1985	1986	1987	1988	1989	1990	1991	1992	1993
		\multicolumn{8}{c}{At constant prices of: 1980}	\multicolumn{4}{c}{1990}			
1	Government final consumption expenditure	2662	3173	3192	3399	3646	3884	4065	4187	4370 / 69989	72194	71581	73370
2	Private final consumption expenditure	9326	9807	10170	10600	11332	13165	12664	12136	12196 / 223729	232978	222645	212696
3	Gross capital formation	4196	3430	4099	3933	3741	4619	4820	4285	4341 / 65461	72554	63546	57851
	A Increase in stocks [a]	80	-207	122	-85	-201	-75	130	-40	-96 / -4546	1126	34	925
	B Gross fixed capital formation	4116	3637	3977	4018	3942	4694	4690	4325	4437 / 70007	71428	63512	56926

Iceland

1.2 Expenditure on the Gross Domestic Product, in Constant Prices
(Continued)

Million Icelandic kronur

	1980	1983	1984	1985	1986	1987	1988	1989	1990	1991	1992	1993
	\multicolumn{9}{c}{At constant prices of: 1980}	\multicolumn{3}{c}{1990}		
Residential buildings	1157	1038	1146	990	853	974	1118	1149	1143 / 18666	17755	17162	16475
Non-residential buildings	694	856	863	895	940	1162	1108	1070	966 / 15552	15257	14786	14584
Other construction and land improvement etc.	1182	847	865	809	792	874	888	886	818 / 13514	15186	12161	12940
Other	1083	896	1103	1325	1357	1684	1576	1220	1510 / 22276	23231	19404	12927
4 Exports of goods and services	5645	5886	6028	6694	7092	7324	7060	7268	7266 / 124246	117090	115091	122453
5 Less: Imports of goods and services	5648	5432	5929	6487	6549	8073	7702	6912	6981 / 119595	126226	116400	106458
Statistical discrepancy	...	...	...	...	...	...	...	...	-	-	-	-
Equals: Gross Domestic Product	16181	16864	17561	18139	19262	20919	20906	20964	21191 / 363830	368590	356463	359912

a) Item 'Increase in stocks' includes stocks of export products only.

1.3 Cost Components of the Gross Domestic Product

Million Icelandic kronur

	1980	1983	1984	1985	1986	1987	1988	1989	1990	1991	1992	1993
1 Indirect taxes, net	3109	12583	18052	23531	30550	42332	52217	59317	66209	71645	70538	68330
A Indirect taxes	3681	15094	20918	27638	35823	48320	61324	72152	79162	83965	83763	78690
B Less: Subsidies	572	2511	2866	4107	5273	5988	9107	12835	12953	12320	13225	10360
2 Consumption of fixed capital	1964	9330	11409	15483	19696	23473	29001	37267	43814	48347	51423	54582
3 Compensation of employees paid by resident producers to:	7725	29513	38352	56216	74404	109893	136137	153392	173696	200380	203000	204800
A Resident households	7716	29474	38311	56166	74315	109718	135806	152873	173014	199497	202277	204098
B Rest of the world	9	39	41	50	89	175	331	519	682	883	723	702
4 Operating surplus	1972	10493	16238	18283	25318	29602	32736	45326	59741	55849	51176	56117
Statistical discrepancy [a]	1412	6323	5092	7386	11117	3762	6552	12922	20371	20407	21779	26926
Equals: Gross Domestic Product	16182	68242	89143	120899	161085	209062	256643	308224	363831	396628	397916	410755

a) The estimates shown refers to the difference between production estimate and expenditure estimate.

1.4 General Government Current Receipts and Disbursements

Million Icelandic kronur

	1980	1983	1984	1985	1986	1987	1988	1989	1990	1991	1992	1993
\multicolumn{13}{c}{Receipts}
1 Operating surplus	-	-	-	-	-	-	-	-	-	-	-	...
2 Property and entrepreneurial income	329	2360	2692	3895	4134	5123	6134	8597	8786	10466	11000	10563
3 Taxes, fees and contributions	5138	20874	28837	37209	50226	65691	89969	106878	122369	137472	139271	136965
A Indirect taxes	3681	15094	20918	27638	35824	48320	61323	72153	79163	83964	83763	77157
B Direct taxes	1228	5061	6773	8140	12296	14448	25267	30442	38422	42644	43741	48050
C Social security contributions	215	654	1056	1333	1996	2729	3137	4033	4529	10487	11321	11386
D Compulsory fees, fines and penalties	14	65	90	98	110	194	242	250	255	377	446	372
4 Other current transfers	-	-	-	-	-	-	-	-	-	-	-	-
Total Current Receipts of General Government	5467	23234	31529	41104	54360	70814	96103	115475	131155	147938	150271	147528
\multicolumn{13}{c}{Disbursements}
1 Government final consumption expenditure	2662	12050	14701	21130	28777	38980	50536	60341	69989	78157	80375	84818
A Compensation of employees	1715	7119	8575	12303	17054	24789	32627	37823	43289	48929	50399	53076
B Consumption of fixed capital	95	427	541	735	948	1151	1357	1680	2029	2319	2454	2600
C Purchases of goods and services, net	852	4505	5584	8092	10774	13041	16552	20838	24672	26909	27522	29142
D Less: Own account fixed capital formation	...	...	...	...	...	...	...	...	...	...	...	...
E Indirect taxes paid, net	...	...	...	...	...	...	...	...	...	...	...	...
2 Property income	256	2030	2544	3668	4434	5132	8290	11207	12903	14717	14508	15381
A Interest	256	2030	2544	3668	4434	5132	8290	11207	12903	14717	14508	15381
B Net land rent and royalties	-	-	-	-	-	-	-	-	-	-	-	...

Iceland

1.4 General Government Current Receipts and Disbursements
(Continued)

Million Icelandic kronur

	1980	1983	1984	1985	1986	1987	1988	1989	1990	1991	1992	1993
3 Subsidies	572	2511	2867	4107	5273	5988	9106	12835	12953	12320	13225	10504
4 Other current transfers	810	3350	4639	6471	8462	11610	17490	21081	25604	28775	30295	32764
A Social security benefits	518	2189	2922	4227	5431	7625	10162	12406	14445	16182	17824	19204
B Social assistance grants	225	776	1196	1453	1909	2467	5058	5404	7729	8483	8641	9504
C Other	67	385	521	791	1122	1518	2270	3271	3430	4110	3830	4056
5 Net saving	1168	3294	6779	5729	7413	9106	10682	10011	9706	13970	11867	4061
Total Current Disbursements and Net Saving of General Government	5468	23235	31530	41105	54359	70816	96104	115475	131155	147939	150270	147528

1.7 External Transactions on Current Account, Summary

Million Icelandic kronur

	1980	1983	1984	1985	1986	1987	1988	1989	1990	1991	1992	1993
Payments to the Rest of the World												
1 Imports of goods and services	5648	25275	33871	48663	55880	73965	84100	99240	119595	130305	121943	122759
A Imports of merchandise c.i.f.	4802	20596	26744	37600	45910	61237	68723	80250	96621	104129	96895	91307
B Other	846	4679	7127	11063	9970	12728	15377	18990	22974	26176	25048	31452
2 Factor income to the rest of the world	478	3444	5051	6255	7042	7281	9461	15087	16872	17463	16717	17912
A Compensation of employees	10	39	41	50	89	175	331	519	682	883	723	702
B Property and entrepreneurial income [a]	468	3405	5010	6205	6953	7106	9130	14568	16190	16580	15994	17210
3 Current transfers to the rest of the world	5	32	43	47	72	66	80	228	358	465	451	539
A Indirect taxes to supranational organizations	...	...	...	...	...	...	...	...	...	...	...	...
B Other current transfers	5	32	43	47	72	66	80	228	358	465	451	539
4 Surplus of the nation on current transactions	-318	-1295	-4173	-4760	707	-7149	-8965	-4350	-8108	-18513	-12451	-386
Payments to the Rest of the World and Surplus of the Nation on Current Transactions	5813	27456	34792	50205	63701	74163	84676	110205	128717	129720	126660	140824
Receipts From The Rest of the World												
1 Exports of goods and services	5645	26683	33765	48774	61961	71681	81721	106282	124246	124943	121248	135018
A Exports of merchandise f.o.b.	4460	18623	23557	33750	44968	53053	61667	80072	92452	91560	87833	94704
B Other	1186	8060	10208	15024	16993	18628	20054	26210	31794	33383	33415	40314
2 Factor income from rest of the world	167	773	1027	1431	1740	2482	2955	3923	4471	4777	5412	5806
A Compensation of employees	104	418	572	831	1013	1589	1998	2306	2658	2994	3037	3175
B Property and entrepreneurial income [a]	63	355	455	600	727	893	957	1617	1813	1783	2375	2631
3 Current transfers from rest of the world	-	-	-	-	-	-	-	-	-	-	-	-
A Subsidies from supranational organisations	...	...	...	...	...	...	...	...	...	...	...	...
B Other current transfers	-	-	-	-	-	-	-	-	-	-	-	-
Receipts from the Rest of the World on Current Transactions	5812	27456	34792	50205	63701	74163	84676	110205	128717	129720	126660	140824

a) Item 'Property and entrepreneurial income' paid/received refers to interest payments.

1.8 Capital Transactions of The Nation, Summary

Million Icelandic kronur

	1980	1983	1984	1985	1986	1987	1988	1989	1990	1991	1992	1993
Finance of Gross Capital Formation												
Gross saving	3878	12473	14503	17658	27738	31660	38452	46237	57353	56321	56742	65121
1 Consumption of fixed capital	1964	9330	11409	15483	19696	23473	29001	37267	43814	48347	51423	54582
A General government	95	427	541	735	948	1151	1357	1680	2029	2319	2454	2600
B Corporate and quasi-corporate enterprises	...	...	...	...	...	...	...	...	...	...	...	...
C Other	...	...	...	...	...	...	...	...	...	...	...	...
2 Net saving	1914	3143	3094	2175	8042	8187	9451	8970	13539	7974	5319	10539
A General government	1169	3294	6780	5728	7413	9104	10682	10011	9707	13972	11867	4061
B Corporate and quasi-corporate enterprises	...	...	...	...	...	...	...	...	...	...	...	...

Iceland

1.8 Capital Transactions of The Nation, Summary
(Continued)

Million Icelandic kronur

	1980	1983	1984	1985	1986	1987	1988	1989	1990	1991	1992	1993
C Other	...	...	...	...	...	...	...	...	...	...	...	...
Less: Surplus of the nation on current transactions	-318	-1295	-4173	-4760	707	-7149	-8965	-4350	-8108	-18513	-12451	-386
Finance of Gross Capital Formation	4196	13768	18676	22418	27031	38809	47417	50587	65461	74834	69193	65507
					Gross Capital Formation							
Increase in stocks [a]	80	-1070	-661	-3111	-3748	-3783	-3085	-8143	-4546	-1226	-406	557
Gross fixed capital formation	4116	14839	19337	25528	30778	42593	50503	58730	70007	76060	69599	64950
1 General government	579	2442	2975	4402	4800	7294	10348	12630	14378	16228	16016	17746
2 Corporate and quasi-corporate enterprises	...	...	...	...	...	...	...	...	...	...	...	...
3 Other	...	...	...	...	...	...	...	...	...	...	...	...
Gross Capital Formation	4196	13769	18676	22417	27030	38810	47418	50587	65461	74834	69193	65507

a) Item 'Increase in stocks' includes stocks of export products only.

1.10 Gross Domestic Product by Kind of Activity, in Current Prices

Million Icelandic kronur

	1980	1983	1984	1985	1986	1987	1988	1989	1990	1991	1992	1993
1 Agriculture, hunting, forestry and fishing	1571	5134	7218	11447	15848	21105	25184	29251	35549	38086	...	...
2 Mining and quarrying	...	...	...	...	...	...	...	...	...	...	...	...
3 Manufacturing	2410	9061	13097	17224	24077	32736	37689	43739	47707	51712	...	...
4 Electricity, gas and water	515	3326	4694	5594	6106	6447	9142	10929	11767	11946	...	...
5 Construction	1065	4317	5724	7395	10306	14596	16343	19930	22777	24063	...	...
6 Wholesale and retail trade, restaurants and hotels	1233	6064	7925	10162	13795	19402	21090	26609	36658	40689	...	...
7 Transport, storage and communication	914	4644	6134	7295	9397	12415	15257	16933	21388	22469	...	...
8 Finance, insurance, real estate and business services	2164	10304	12465	17903	20111	29194	38462	47486	51966	58419	...	...
9 Community, social and personal services	456	2214	2673	4307	5711	8465	11129	12756	14643	16624	...	...
Total, Industries	10327	45066	59929	81327	105351	144359	174297	207634	242455	264007	...	...
Producers of Government Services [a]	1760	7339	8867	12679	17503	25212	33038	38404	44060	51310	...	...
Other Producers	97	400	533	798	1056	1484	2097	2649	3157	3611	...	...
Subtotal	12184	52804	69329	94804	123911	171054	209431	248687	289672	318928	...	...
Less: Imputed bank service charge	523	3468	3330	4822	4493	8085	11557	12702	12422	14352	...	...
Plus: Import duties	-	-	-	-	-	-	-	-	-	-	...	...
Plus: Value added tax	...	...	...	...	...	...	...	...	...	...	...	...
Plus: Other adjustments [b]	4521	18906	23144	30917	41666	46094	58769	72239	86579	92052	...	...
Equals: Gross Domestic Product	16182	68243	89143	120899	161084	209063	256644	308223	363829	396628	...	...

a) Beginning 1980, all accrued pension liabilities of central government employees are included even if they had not become effective. Thus, the estimates of 'Producers of government services' beginning 1980 are not comparable with those of previous years.   b) Item 'Other adjustments' includes import duties, other indirect taxes less subsidies as well as residual error between production and expenditure approaches.

1.11 Gross Domestic Product by Kind of Activity, in Constant Prices

Million Icelandic kronur

	1980	1983	1984	1985	1986	1987	1988	1989	1990	1991	1992	1993
					At constant prices of:1980							
1 Agriculture, hunting, forestry and fishing	1571	1281	1301	1448	1629	1817	1855	1804	1843	1610	...	...
2 Mining and quarrying	...	...	...	...	...	...	...	...	...	...	...	...
3 Manufacturing	2410	2246	2407	2438	2563	2772	2583	2490	2421	2451	...	...
4 Electricity, gas and water	515	692	745	770	802	813	852	870	875	890	...	...
5 Construction	1065	1090	1132	1092	1123	1276	1263	1274	1258	1260	...	...
6 Wholesale and retail trade, restaurants and hotels	1233	1330	1393	1460	1579	1826	1775	1677	1745	1770	...	...
7 Transport, storage and communication	914	999	1057	1135	1233	1386	1366	1331	1422	1445	...	...
8 Finance, insurance, real estate and business services	2164	2505	2687	2862	3006	3183	3308	3331	3339	3401	...	...
9 Community, social and personal services	456	553	567	614	667	737	747	731	723	750	...	...

Iceland

1.11 Gross Domestic Product by Kind of Activity, in Constant Prices
(Continued)

Million Icelandic kronur

	1980	1983	1984	1985	1986	1987	1988	1989	1990	1991	1992	1993
					At constant prices of:1980							
Total, Industries	10327	10696	11289	11820	12602	13811	13748	13507	13627	13577	...	...
Producers of Government Services [a]	1760	2049	2115	2225	2351	2560	2732	2814	2952	3064	...	...
Other Producers	97	125	136	152	167	177	191	197	204	209	...	...
Subtotal	12184	12871	13541	14197	15121	16548	16672	16518	16784	16850	...	...
Less: Imputed bank service charge	523	587	670	748	838	877	946	925	909	946	...	...
Plus: Import duties	...	...	...	...	...	...	...	...	...	...	...	...
Plus: Value added tax	...	...	...	...	...	...	...	...	...	...	...	...
Equals: Gross Domestic Product [b]	11661	12284	12871	13449	14282	15671	15726	15593	15874	15904	...	...

a) Beginning 1980, all accrued pension liabilities of central government employees are included even if they had not become effective. Thus, the estimates of 'Producers of government services' beginning 1980 are not comparable with those of previous years. b) Gross domestic product in factor values.

1.12 Relations Among National Accounting Aggregates

Million Icelandic kronur

	1980	1983	1984	1985	1986	1987	1988	1989	1990	1991	1992	1993
Gross Domestic Product	16182	68242	89144	120899	161085	209063	256644	308224	363830	396628	397917	410755
Plus: Net factor income from the rest of the world	-310	-2671	-4024	-4824	-5302	-4799	-6506	-11164	-12401	-12686	-11305	-12106
Factor income from the rest of the world	167	773	1027	1431	1740	2482	2955	3923	4471	4777	5412	5806
Less: Factor income to the rest of the world	477	3444	5051	6255	7042	7281	9461	15087	16872	17463	16717	17912
Equals: Gross National Product	15872	65571	85119	116075	155782	204264	250138	297060	351429	383942	386612	398649
Less: Consumption of fixed capital	1964	9330	11409	15483	19696	23473	29001	37267	43814	48347	51423	54582
Equals: National Income	13909	56241	73710	100592	136086	180791	221136	259793	307615	335596	335188	344068
Plus: Net current transfers from the rest of the world	-5	-32	-43	-47	-72	-66	-80	-228	-358	-465	-451	-539
Current transfers from the rest of the world	-	-	-	-	-	-	-	-	-	-	-	-
Less: Current transfers to the rest of the world	5	32	43	47	72	66	80	228	358	465	451	539
Equals: National Disposable Income	13904	56209	73667	100545	136014	180725	221056	259565	307257	335131	334737	343529
Less: Final consumption	11989	53066	70573	98370	127972	172538	211605	250595	293718	327156	329419	332989
Statistical discrepancy	-	-	-	-	-	-	-	-	-	-	-	-
Equals: Net Saving	1914	3143	3094	2175	8042	8187	9451	8970	13539	7974	5318	10540
Less: Surplus of the nation on current transactions	-318	-1295	-4173	-4760	707	-7149	-8965	-4350	-8108	-18513	-12451	-386
Statistical discrepancy	-	-	-	-	-	-	-	-	-	-	-	-
Equals: Net Capital Formation	2232	4438	7267	6935	7335	15336	18416	13320	21647	26487	17769	10926

2.1 Government Final Consumption Expenditure by Function, in Current Prices

Million Icelandic kronur

	1980	1983	1984	1985	1986	1987	1988	1989	1990	1991	1992	1993
1 General public services	187	797	1032	1430	1863	2739	3715	4372	5772	6471	6448	6769
2 Defence	-	-	-	-	-	-	-	-	-	-	-	-
3 Public order and safety	223	911	1072	1481	2031	2856	3641	3891	4442	5028	5112	5384
4 Education	565	2316	2822	4225	5791	8051	10350	12280	13764	15438	15951	16398
5 Health	836	4209	5080	7224	10165	13673	17957	21526	24008	26547	26544	27180
6 Social security and welfare	124	592	676	1183	1640	2370	3285	3777	4625	5668	6149	6556
7 Housing and community amenities	84	359	431	589	747	1054	1295	1712	2104	2552	2905	3314
8 Recreational, cultural and religious affairs	104	454	593	792	1123	1417	1887	2444	2965	3467	3763	4481
9 Economic services	324	1476	1883	2515	3252	4066	4743	5962	6944	7308	7602	8391
A Fuel and energy	21	99	103	145	179	279	274	298	230	255	266	218
B Agriculture, forestry, fishing and hunting	67	251	332	478	576	800	901	980	1262	1620	1619	1775
C Mining, manufacturing and construction, except fuel and energy	9	33	59	80	75	116	161	155	203	232	263	238
D Transportation and communication	204	997	1232	1579	2127	2477	2899	3881	4484	4414	4656	5079
E Other economic affairs	24	96	157	234	296	394	508	648	765	787	799	1081
10 Other functions	216	937	1112	1690	2167	2755	3663	4378	5367	5680	5901	6345
Total Government Final Consumption Expenditure	2663	12050	14700	21129	28778	38981	50536	60340	69989	78157	80375	84818

Iceland

2.2 Government Final Consumption Expenditure by Function, in Constant Prices

Million Icelandic kronur

	1980	1983	1984	1985	1986	1987	1988	1989	1990	1991	1992	1993
					At constant prices of:1990							
1 General public services	2920	3382	3618	3714	3804	4384	4803	4861	5772	5985	5746	5816
2 Defence	-	-	-	-	-	-	-	-	-	-	-	...
3 Public order and safety	3498	3860	3772	3856	4131	4497	4627	4302	4442	4635	4542	4626
4 Education	8878	9790	9947	11013	11754	12588	13062	13541	13763	14221	14160	14089
5 Health	13726	18049	17665	18676	20940	22279	23427	24041	24008	24564	23674	23353
6 Social security and welfare	1881	2481	2404	3096	3308	3644	4091	4134	4625	5209	5444	5633
7 Housing and community amenities	1377	1533	1503	1524	1533	1719	1692	1916	2104	2365	2595	2848
8 Recreational, cultural and religious affairs	1643	1913	2082	2057	2294	2243	2415	2711	2965	3203	3353	3850
9 Economic services	5484	6355	6511	6488	6718	6696	6223	6684	6943	6765	6784	7210
A Fuel and energy	315	416	367	379	361	437	342	328	230	234	235	188
B Agriculture, forestry, fishing and hunting	1085	1068	1162	1242	1173	1269	1149	1085	1261	1495	1440	1525
C Mining, manufacturing and construction, except fuel and energy	131	137	206	208	149	172	196	167	203	212	232	204
D Transportation and communication	3564	4325	4228	4054	4426	4179	3874	4379	4484	4100	4169	4364
E Other economic affairs	389	409	547	605	608	639	663	724	765	725	709	929
10 Other functions	3430	3865	3816	4323	4364	4414	4825	4938	5367	5245	5281	5527
Total Government Final Consumption Expenditure	42837	51228	51318	54747	58845	62464	65167	67128	69989	72192	71579	72952

2.3 Total Government Outlays by Function and Type

Million Icelandic kronur

	Final Consumption Expenditures Total	Compensation of Employees	Other	Subsidies	Other Current Transfers & Property Income	Total Current Disbursements	Gross Capital Formation	Other Capital Outlays	Total Outlays
					1980				
1 General public services	187	150	37	-	12	200	5	-	204
2 Defence	-	-	-	-	-	-	-	-	-
3 Public order and safety	223	172	51	-	2	225	13	5	243
4 Education	565	431	134	-	8	573	84	44	701
5 Health	836	481	355	-	4	840	43	2	884
6 Social security and welfare	124	111	13	-	739	863	29	14	906
7 Housing and community amenities	84	48	36	-	-	84	30	89	203
8 Recreation, culture and religion	104	77	27	24	40	168	48	6	221
9 Economic services	324	146	178	548	4	876	314	314	1505
A Fuel and energy	21	18	3	46	-	66	2	81	149
B Agriculture, forestry, fishing and hunting	67	44	23	439	1	507	24	114	645
C Mining (except fuels), manufacturing and construction	9	8	1	15	-	23	1	32	56
D Transportation and communication	204	59	145	38	-	241	286	43	571
E Other economic affairs	24	17	7	11	2	38	2	45	84
10 Other functions	216	100	116	-	256	472	14	-5	481
Total	2663	1716	947	572	1064	4298	579	470	5348
					1985				
1 General public services	1430	904	526	-	110	1540	35	8	1583
2 Defence	-	-	-	-	-	-	-	-	-
3 Public order and safety	1481	1051	430	-	22	1503	209	44	1756
4 Education	4225	3147	1078	-	85	4310	563	837	5710
5 Health	7224	3539	3685	-	9	7233	334	64	7631
6 Social security and welfare	1183	1035	148	-	5770	6953	415	61	7428
7 Housing and community amenities	589	298	291	-	-	589	99	1337	2025
8 Recreation, culture and religion	792	505	287	171	405	1368	503	55	1926
9 Economic services	2515	1062	1453	3935	68	6518	2076	1696	10290

Iceland

2.3 Total Government Outlays by Function and Type
(Continued)

Million Icelandic kronur

	Final Consumption Expenditures Total	Compensation of Employees	Other	Subsidies	Other Current Transfers & Property Income	Total Current Disbursements	Gross Capital Formation	Other Capital Outlays	Total Outlays
A Fuel and energy	145	123	22	651	2	798	12	186	996
B Agriculture, forestry, fishing and hunting	478	318	160	2842	34	3354	135	896	4384
C Mining (except fuels), manufacturing and construction	80	62	18	153	10	243	9	168	420
D Transportation and communication	1579	449	1130	233	-	1811	1920	233	3964
E Other economic affairs	234	111	123	56	23	313	1	212	526
10 Other functions	1690	762	928	-	3669	5359	170	-39	5489
Total	21129	12303	8826	4107	10137	35373	4402	4062	43837
1990									
1 General public services	5772	3401	2371	-	505	6277	921	-	7198
2 Defence	-	-	-	-	-	-	-	-	-
3 Public order and safety	4442	3269	1173	-	71	4513	216	74	4803
4 Education	13764	10675	3089	-	246	14010	1742	2033	17784
5 Health	24008	12722	11286	-	206	24214	787	83	25084
6 Social security and welfare	4625	4218	407	-	22512	27137	1545	-169	28513
7 Housing and community amenities	2104	850	1254	-	1	2105	169	622	2897
8 Recreation, culture and religion	2965	1975	990	884	1967	5816	1764	275	7855
9 Economic services	6944	3223	3721	12069	91	19104	5577	6516	31196
A Fuel and energy	230	226	4	868	5	1102	10	851	1963
B Agriculture, forestry, fishing and hunting	1262	883	379	9859	27	11148	476	2560	14184
C Mining (except fuels), manufacturing and construction	203	222	-19	324	20	547	14	1013	1574
D Transportation and communication	4484	1393	3091	694	-	5178	5049	1035	11262
E Other economic affairs	765	499	266	325	40	1129	29	1057	2214
10 Other functions	5367	2955	2412	-	12908	18275	1656	34	19965
Total	69989	43288	26701	12953	38507	121449	14378	9468	145295
1991									
1 General public services	6471	3637	2834	-	622	7093	932	60	8084
2 Defence	-	-	-	-	-	-	-	-	-
3 Public order and safety	5028	3735	1293	-	93	5121	232	82	5435
4 Education	15438	12072	3366	-	295	15732	2202	2258	20192
5 Health	26547	14326	12221	-	346	26893	920	134	27946
6 Social security and welfare	5668	5143	525	-	25048	30716	1561	-127	32150
7 Housing and community amenities	2552	1145	1407	-	3	2555	78	951	3585
8 Recreation, culture and religion	3467	2169	1298	1197	2178	6842	1448	718	9007
9 Economic services	7308	3735	3574	11123	187	18617	6771	7574	32962
A Fuel and energy	255	231	24	933	6	1194	21	320	1535
B Agriculture, forestry, fishing and hunting	1620	1110	510	8521	42	10183	438	2872	13492
C Mining (except fuels), manufacturing and construction	232	265	-33	261	29	521	7	404	932
D Transportation and communication	4414	1493	2921	743	-	5157	6261	1265	12683
E Other economic affairs	787	635	152	665	109	1561	45	2714	4320
10 Other functions	5680	2968	2712	-	14719	20399	2085	37	22521
Total	78157	48930	29228	12319	43491	133967	16228	11686	161881
1992									
1 General public services	6448	3771	2677	-	519	6967	784	5	7756
2 Defence	-	-	-	-	-	-	-	-	-
3 Public order and safety	5112	3781	1331	-	115	5227	339	62	5627
4 Education	15951	12446	3505	-	324	16275	2485	1937	20696
5 Health	26544	14357	12187	-	246	26791	663	306	27759
6 Social security and welfare	6149	5641	508	-	26689	32838	1873	-173	34538
7 Housing and community amenities	2905	1292	1613	-	16	2920	282	926	4128
8 Recreation, culture and religion	3763	2213	1550	1147	2279	7189	1773	384	9345
9 Economic services	7602	3875	3727	12078	107	19788	6570	6084	32442

Iceland

2.3 Total Government Outlays by Function and Type
(Continued)

Million Icelandic kronur

		Final Consumption Expenditures		Subsidies	Other Current Transfers & Property Income	Total Current Disbursements	Gross Capital Formation	Other Capital Outlays	Total Outlays
		Total	Compensation of Employees	Other						

		Total	Compensation of Employees	Other	Subsidies	Other Current Transfers & Property Income	Total Current Disbursements	Gross Capital Formation	Other Capital Outlays	Total Outlays
A	Fuel and energy	266	233	33	1095	6	1366	-	170	1537
B	Agriculture, forestry, fishing and hunting	1619	1148	471	9239	20	10877	547	2022	13447
C	Mining (except fuels), manufacturing and construction	263	281	-19	283	26	571	22	501	1094
D	Transportation and communication	4656	1563	3093	759	-	5414	5919	929	12262
E	Other economic affairs	799	650	149	704	56	1559	82	2461	4102
10	Other functions	5901	3023	2878	-	14509	20410	1247	-3	21654
Total		80375	50399	29976	13225	44804	138404	16016	9526	163946

1993

		Total	Compensation of Employees	Other	Subsidies	Other Current Transfers & Property Income	Total Current Disbursements	Gross Capital Formation	Other Capital Outlays	Total Outlays
1	General public services	6769	3896	2873	-	692	7461	203	49	7713
2	Defence	-	-	-	-	-	-	-	-	-
3	Public order and safety	5384	4014	1370	-	101	5485	294	97	5876
4	Education	16398	12555	3843	-	345	16743	2413	1599	20755
5	Health	27180	14985	12195	-	245	27425	680	384	28488
6	Social security and welfare	6556	6112	444	-	28927	35483	1622	-11	37093
7	Housing and community amenities	3314	1313	2001	-	21	3336	68	1032	4436
8	Recreation, culture and religion	4481	2686	1795	1296	2241	8018	2596	528	11142
9	Economic services	8391	4096	4295	9208	191	17790	8237	3674	29701
A	Fuel and energy	218	234	-16	1111	6	1336	10	114	1460
B	Agriculture, forestry, fishing and hunting	1775	1180	595	6580	18	8372	499	1354	10225
C	Mining (except fuels), manufacturing and construction	238	288	-50	286	36	561	15	331	906
D	Transportation and communication	5079	1686	3393	538	26	5643	7678	1023	14344
E	Other economic affairs	1081	708	373	694	104	1879	35	852	2767
10	Other functions	6345	3420	2925	-	15381	21726	1633	2	23361
Total		84818	53076	31742	10504	48145	143466	17747	7353	168567

2.4 Composition of General Government Social Security Benefits and Social Assistance Grants to Households

Million Icelandic kronur

	1980 SSB	1980 SAG	1985 SSB	1985 SAG	1990 SSB	1990 SAG	1991 SSB	1991 SAG	1992 SSB	1992 SAG	1993 SSB	1993 SAG
1 Education benefits	...	8	...	85	...	246	...	295	...	324	...	345
2 Health benefits	...	4	...	9	...	206	...	346	...	246	...	245
3 Social security and welfare benefits	519	213	4227	1360	14445	7276	16182	7839	17824	8055	19204	8898
A Social security	519	146	4227	1073	14445	6657	16182	7365	17824	7304	19204	7652
Temporary sickness	12	...	95	...	186	...	220	...	221	...	224	...
Old age and permanent disability	420	...	3164	...	10168	...	11664	...	12351	...	13300	...
Unemployment	9	...	182	...	1066	...	957	...	1824	...	2596	...
Family assistance	26	...	400	...	1795	...	1918	...	2008	...	1493	...
Other	53	...	387	...	1229	...	1423	...	1420	...	1591	...
B Welfare	...	67	...	287	...	619	...	474	...	751	...	1246
4 Housing and community amenities	...	-	...	-	...	1	...	3	...	16	...	16
5 Recreation and cultural benefits	...	-	...	-	...	-	...	-	...	-	...	-
6 Other	...	-	...	-	...	-	...	-	...	-	...	-
Total	519	225	4227	1453	14445	7729	16182	8483	17824	8641	19204	9504

2.5 Private Final Consumption Expenditure by Type and Purpose, in Current Prices

Million Icelandic kronur

	1980	1983	1984	1985	1986	1987	1988	1989	1990	1991	1992	1993
Final Consumption Expenditure of Resident Households												
1 Food, beverages and tobacco	2298	9957	13349	19190	22997	29915	38097	48835	56808	59910	61046	61667
A Food	1678	7511	9895	14274	16652	21338	27578	34579	40555	42150	43181	43337
B Non-alcoholic beverages	186	793	1051	1533	2180	3140	3899	5258	6291	7024	7036	6891
C Alcoholic beverages	227	883	1227	1795	2257	2988	3629	5440	6035	6527	6507	6976

Iceland

2.5 Private Final Consumption Expenditure by Type and Purpose, in Current Prices
(Continued)

Million Icelandic kronur

	1980	1983	1984	1985	1986	1987	1988	1989	1990	1991	1992	1993
D Tobacco	207	770	1176	1588	1909	2449	2991	3557	3928	4208	4322	4464
2 Clothing and footwear	850	3561	4980	7085	9445	12361	13981	15368	17426	19864	19322	18098
3 Gross rent, fuel and power	1889	8591	11192	14605	17914	21320	26062	32572	39304	43147	43850	45276
A Fuel and power	299	1673	2238	2572	2709	3004	3804	4502	5500	6082	6400	6879
B Other	1590	6917	8954	12034	15205	18315	22258	28071	33804	37066	37450	38397
4 Furniture, furnishings and household equipment and operation	1176	4472	5579	7455	9752	13802	14361	16345	17694	20131	19244	18257
A Household operation	344	1530	1717	2672	3572	4808	4409	5276	6221	6797	6661	7135
B Other	833	2942	3862	4784	6179	8994	9952	11069	11473	13334	12583	11122
5 Medical care and health expenses	118	522	812	1142	1668	2092	2801	3522	3877	4161	4654	5474
6 Transport and communication	1390	6249	8996	11595	15985	23087	25610	26929	30875	37051	35038	34666
A Personal transport equipment	1064	4626	6854	8883	12847	19098	20434	20570	23602	28946	26531	25933
B Other	327	1622	2142	2712	3138	3989	5176	6359	7274	8105	8507	8733
7 Recreational, entertainment, education and cultural services	687	3264	4315	6319	8211	11482	16143	19509	22931	25148	25464	26162
A Education	35	143	225	307	431	573	1682	2103	2512	2512	2841	3115
B Other	651	3121	4090	6013	7780	10909	14461	17406	20419	22636	22623	23047
8 Miscellaneous goods and services	747	3345	4959	7554	10196	14406	18479	21410	26432	29953	30959	30084
A Personal care	126	597	740	1192	1719	2303	3239	4020	4893	5831	5847	5865
B Expenditures in restaurants, cafes and hotels	379	2014	3106	4688	6082	8588	11244	12673	15694	17689	18397	17712
C Other	242	734	1113	1674	2394	3516	3996	4717	5845	6433	6715	6507
Total Final Consumption Expenditure in the Domestic Market by Households, of which	9156	39960	54182	74945	96169	128465	155534	184490	215347	239365	239577	239685
Plus: Direct purchases abroad by resident households	293	1788	2852	4142	5632	8581	10348	12196	16770	17954	17126	18528
Less: Direct purchases in the domestic market by non-resident households	123	732	1162	1848	2604	3489	4814	6432	8388	8320	7659	9261
Equals: Final Consumption Expenditure of Resident Households [a]	9326	41016	55872	77240	99196	133557	161068	190254	223729	248999	249044	248952

Final Consumption Expenditure of Private Non-profit Institutions Serving Households

	1980	1983	1984	1985	1986	1987	1988	1989	1990	1991	1992	1993
Equals: Final Consumption Expenditure of Private Non-profit Organisations Serving Households	...	...	...	...	...	...	...	...	...	...	...	...
Private Final Consumption Expenditure	9326	41016	55872	77240	99196	133557	161068	190254	223729	248999	249044	248952

a) Item 'Final consumption expenditure of resident households' includes consumption expenditure of private non-profit institutions serving households.

2.6 Private Final Consumption Expenditure by Type and Purpose, in Constant Prices

Million Icelandic kronur

	1980	1983	1984	1985	1986	1987	1988	1989	1990	1991	1992	1993
	At constant prices of: 1980								1990			

Final Consumption Expenditure of Resident Households

	1980	1983	1984	1985	1986	1987	1988	1989	1990	1991	1992	1993
1 Food, beverages and tobacco	2298	2358	2355	2452	2447	2752	2669	2893	2884 / 56808	57638	56815	55459
A Food	1678	1715	1697	1793	1725	1928	1864	1975	1953 / 40555	41038	40891	39824
B Non-alcoholic beverages	186	158	167	190	215	268	261	279	319 / 6291	6602	6476	6284
C Alcoholic beverages	227	251	252	252	285	315	318	409	394 / 6035	6063	5629	5705
D Tobacco	207	234	240	217	222	240	226	230	218 / 3928	3935	3819	3646
2 Clothing and footwear	850	861	903	990	977	1047	984	921	875 / 17426	18091	16837	15591
3 Gross rent, fuel and power	1889	2036	2082	2102	2133	2171	2220	2272	2335 / 39304	39699	40111	40310
A Fuel and power	299	307	303	287	294	299	304	311	330 / 5500	5252	5319	5345
B Other	1590	1729	1779	1815	1839	1872	1916	1962	2005 / 33804	34447	34792	34966
4 Furniture, furnishings and household equipment and operation	1176	1180	1184	1226	1284	1542	1306	1209	1076 / 17694	19045	17293	16271

Iceland

2.6 Private Final Consumption Expenditure by Type and Purpose, in Constant Prices
(Continued)

Million Icelandic kronur

At constant prices of: 1980 (columns 1980–1990 top row); 1990 (columns 1990 bottom row–1993)

	1980	1983	1984	1985	1986	1987	1988	1989	1990	1991	1992	1993
A Household operation	344	382	350	420	425	483	369	356	361 / 6221	6522	6007	6199
B Other	833	799	834	806	858	1059	937	853	714 / 11473	12524	11286	10072
5 Medical care and health expenses	118	153	141	149	174	190	190	190	180 / 3877	3851	3788	3855
6 Transport and communication	1390	1459	1645	1641	2216	2889	2466	1932	2003 / 30875	34036	30505	27886
A Personal transport equipment	1064	1133	1299	1270	1830	2476	2069	1522	1592 / 23602	26597	23083	20623
B Other	327	326	345	371	387	413	397	410	411 / 7274	7439	7423	7263
7 Recreational, entertainment, education and cultural services	687	773	745	818	810	960	1195	1199	1205 / 22931	23973	22265	21702
A Education	35	37	37	38	38	38	87	89	89 / 2512	2513	2538	2564
B Other	651	736	707	781	772	922	1108	1110	1116 / 20419	21459	19726	19138
8 Miscellaneous goods and services	747	814	885	1003	1052	1187	1224	1227	1278 / 26432	27351	26576	24627
A Personal care	126	133	122	154	151	175	241	261	263 / 4893	5509	5399	5059
B Expenditures in restaurants, cafes and hotels	379	478	534	592	606	654	669	648	687 / 15694	15936	15504	14098
C Other	242	203	229	257	295	358	314	317	328 / 5845	5906	5673	5470
Total Final Consumption Expenditure in the Domestic Market by Households, of which	9156	9634	9940	10381	11093	12737	12253	11844	11836 / 215347	223684	214190	205702
Plus: Direct purchases abroad by resident households	293	346	441	471	535	761	774	690	811 / 16770	17068	15331	14915
Less: Direct purchases in the domestic market by non-resident households	123	173	211	253	296	333	363	397	451 / 8388	7774	6876	7921
Equals: Final Consumption Expenditure of Resident Households	9326[a]	9807[a]	10170[a]	10600[a]	11332[a]	13165[a]	12664[a]	12136[a]	12196[a] / 223729	232978	222645	212696

Final Consumption Expenditure of Private Non-profit Institutions Serving Households

	1980	1983	1984	1985	1986	1987	1988	1989	1990	1991	1992	1993
Equals: Final Consumption Expenditure of Private Non-profit Organisations Serving Households	...	...	...	...	...	...	...	...	...	...	...	...
Private Final Consumption Expenditure	9326	9807	10170	10600	11332	13165	12664	12136	12196 / 223729	232978	222645	212696

a) Item 'Final consumption expenditure of resident households' includes consumption expenditure of private non-profit institutions serving households.

2.11 Gross Fixed Capital Formation by Kind of Activity of Owner, ISIC Divisions, in Current Prices

Million Icelandic kronur

All Producers

	1980	1983	1984	1985	1986	1987	1988	1989	1990	1991	1992	1993
1 Agriculture, hunting, forestry and fishing	396	1414	1855	2512	4814	6559	8386	5831	4152	4742	7578	3750
A Agriculture and hunting	173	616	969	1152	1126	1607	1597	1616	1441	1830	1628	1600
B Forestry and logging	...	...	...	...	...	...	...	...	...	...	...	...
C Fishing	224	798	886	1360	3688	4952	6788	4216	2711	2911	5950	2150
2 Mining and quarrying	555	1785	2805	4160	4815	5701	6180	7130	7116	8055	6839	7120
3 Manufacturing												
4 Electricity, gas and water	774	1885	2120	1862	1739	2107	3532	5443	6526	7101	3857	3750
A Electricity, gas and steam	743	1785	2007	1654	1529	1867	3212	5073	5921	6381	3308	3100
B Water works and supply	31	100	113	208	210	240	320	370	605	720	549	650
5 Construction [a]	104	376	580	603	764	1165	1305	1377	1744	2473	1562	1528
6 Wholesale and retail trade, restaurants and hotels [bc]	226	1493	1970	3214	4234	6950	6693	6535	7033	6998	7043	7022
7 Transport, storage and communication	414	1453	1696	2949	3124	4925	3311	6185	11945	12814	9241	6090

Iceland

2.11 Gross Fixed Capital Formation by Kind of Activity of Owner, ISIC Divisions, in Current Prices
(Continued)

Million Icelandic kronur

	1980	1983	1984	1985	1986	1987	1988	1989	1990	1991	1992	1993
A Transport and storage	353	1091	1223	2396	2321	3809	2559	5280	10941	11348	7387	4190
B Communication	61	362	472	552	802	1116	752	905	1003	1466	1854	1900
8 Finance, insurance, real estate and business services [bdc]	1157	4195	5657	6455	6923	9303	12586	15936	18666	19104	18912	18551
A Financial institutions	...	...	...	...	...	...	...	...	...	...	...	...
B Insurance	...	...	...	...	...	...	...	...	...	...	...	...
C Real estate and business services	1157	4195	5657	6455	6923	9303	12586	15936	18666	19104	18912	18551
Real estate except dwellings	...	...	...	...	...	...	...	...	...	...	...	...
Dwellings	1157	4195	5657	6455	6923	9303	12586	15936	18666	19104	18912	18551
9 Community, social and personal services	...	...	...	...	...	...	...	...	...	...	...	...
Total Industries	3625	12600	16682	21755	26413	36708	41993	48438	57182	61286	55031	47811
Producers of Government Services	491	2238	2656	3773	4365	5884	8510	10293	12825	14775	14568	17140
Private Non-Profit Institutions Serving Households	...	...	...	...	...	...	...	...	...	...	...	...
Total	4116	14839	19337	25528	30778	42593	50503	58730	70007	76060	69599	64951

a) Item 'Construction' includes machinery only.
b) Finance, insurance and business services are included in item 'Wholesale and retail trade, restaurants and hotels'.
c) Computers in all economic activities are included in item 'Wholesale and retail trade'.
d) Real estate refers to owner-occupied dwellings and rent only.

2.12 Gross Fixed Capital Formation by Kind of Activity of Owner, ISIC Divisions, in Constant Prices

Million Icelandic kronur

	1980	1983	1984	1985	1986	1987	1988	1989	1990	1991	1992	1993
	\multicolumn{8}{c}{At constant prices of: 1980}	\multicolumn{4}{c}{1990}
	\multicolumn{12}{c}{All Producers}
1 Agriculture, hunting, forestry and fishing	396	348	388	412	627	744	796	438	264 / 4152	4502	6998	3222
A Agriculture and hunting	173	148	206	188	153	194	159	125	92 / 1441	1750	1527	1422
B Forestry and logging	...	...	...	...	...	...	...	...	... / ...	...	...	...
C Fishing	224	200	183	224	474	550	637	314	172 / 2711	2752	5471	1800
2 Mining and quarrying	555	439	562	636	586	614	562	513	448 / 7116	7637	6263	6051
3 Manufacturing												
4 Electricity, gas and water	774	459	427	285	215	221	315	395	416 / 6526	6653	3506	3317
A Electricity, gas and steam	743	434	404	253	189	196	286	368	382 / 5921	5984	3008	2740
B Water works and supply	31	25	23	32	26	25	28	27	35 / 605	669	498	577
5 Construction [a]	104	87	109	87	87	122	140	115	143 / 1744	2371	1439	1265
6 Wholesale and retail trade, restaurants and hotels [bc]	226	381	451	579	604	835	681	512	532 / 7033	6582	6428	6062
7 Transport, storage and communication	414	357	360	459	419	570	334	468	766 / 11945	12173	8449	5262
A Transport and storage	353	255	239	348	292	421	247	385	684 / 10941	10810	6766	3634
B Communication	61	102	122	111	127	150	87	83	82 / 1003	1363	1682	1628
8 Finance, insurance, real estate and business services [bdc]	1157	1039	1146	990	853	974	1118	1149	1143 / 18666	17755	17162	16475
A Financial institutions	...	...	...	...	...	...	...	...	... / ...	...	...	...

Iceland

2.12 Gross Fixed Capital Formation by Kind of Activity of Owner, ISIC Divisions, in Constant Prices
(Continued)

Million Icelandic kronur

	1980	1983	1984	1985	1986	1987	1988	1989	1990	1991	1992	1993
	\multicolumn{8}{c}{At constant prices of: 1980}		\multicolumn{3}{c}{1990}
B Insurance	...	...	...	...	...	...	...	...	... ...	...	...	...
C Real estate and business services	1157	1039	1146	990	853	974	1118	1149	1143 18666	17755	17162	16475
Real estate except dwellings	...	...	...	...	...	...	...	...	... ...	...	...	...
Dwellings	1157	1039	1146	990	853	974	1118	1149	1143 18666	17755	17162	16475
9 Community, social and personal services	...	...	...	...	...	...	...	...	... ...	...	...	...
Total Industries	3625	3109	3444	3447	3391	4080	3946	3590	3712 57182	57671	50245	41654
Producers of Government Services	491	528	534	571	551	614	744	735	725 12825	13757	13267	15272
Private Non-Profit Institutions Serving Households	...	...	...	...	...	...	...	...	... ...	...	...	...
Total	4116	3637	3977	4018	3942	4694	4690	4325	4437 70007	71428	63512	56926

a) Item 'Construction' includes machinery only.
b) Finance, insurance and business services are included in item 'Wholesale and retail trade, restaurants and hotels'.
c) Computers in all economic activities are included in item 'Wholesale and retail trade'.
d) Real estate refers to owner-occupied dwellings and rent only.

2.13 Stocks of Reproducible Fixed Assets, by Type of Good and Owner, in Current Prices

Million Icelandic kronur

	TOTAL		Total Private		Public Enterprises		General Government	
	Gross	Net	Gross	Net	Gross	Net	Gross	Net
\multicolumn{9}{c}{1980}
1 Residential buildings	...	19574	...	19574	...	...	...	...
2 Non-residential buildings	...	10986	...	6791	...	297	...	3898
3 Other construction	...	12109	...	45	...	7766	...	4298
4 Land improvement and plantation and orchard development	...	1349	...	1349	...	...	...	...
5 Producers' durable goods	...	7336	...	6847	...	489	...	-
A Transport equipment	...	1641	...	1641	...	...	...	...
Passenger cars	...	670	...	670	...	...	...	...
Other	...	1641	...	1641	...	...	...	...
B Machinery and equipment	...	5695	...	5206	...	489	...	-
6 Breeding stock, dairy cattle, etc.	...	611	...	611	...	...	...	...
Total	...	...	...	...	...	...	...	...
\multicolumn{9}{c}{1985}
1 Residential buildings	...	145668	...	145668	...	...	...	...
2 Non-residential buildings	...	86526	...	53075	...	2453	...	30998
3 Other construction	...	91971	...	1112	...	57330	...	33529
4 Land improvement and plantation and orchard development	...	9613	...	9613	...	...	...	...
5 Producers' durable goods	...	57143	...	54005	...	3138	...	-
A Transport equipment	...	12625	...	12625	...	...	...	...
Passenger cars	...	6367	...	6367	...	...	...	...
Other	...	12625	...	12625	...	...	...	...
B Machinery and equipment	...	44518	...	41380	...	3138	...	-
6 Breeding stock, dairy cattle, etc.	...	3946	...	3946	...	...	...	...
Total	...	...	...	...	...	...	...	...

Iceland

2.13 Stocks of Reproducible Fixed Assets, by Type of Good and Owner, in Current Prices
(Continued)

Million Icelandic kronur

		TOTAL Gross	TOTAL Net	Total Private Gross	Total Private Net	Public Enterprises Gross	Public Enterprises Net	General Government Gross	General Government Net
					1990				
1	Residential buildings	...	403167	...	403167	...	...	...	...
2	Non-residential buildings	...	254548	...	141213	...	6072	...	107262
3	Other construction	...	251447	...	9345	...	142078	...	100024
4	Land improvement and plantation and orchard development	...	22984	...	22984	...	...	...	...
5	Producers' durable goods	...	171717	...	162311	...	9406	...	-
	A Transport equipment	...	35025	...	35025	...	...	...	...
	Passenger cars	...	14609	...	14609	...	...	...	...
	Other	...	35025	...	35025	...	...	...	...
	B Machinery and equipment	...	136692	...	127286	...	9406	...	...
6	Breeding stock, dairy cattle, etc.	...	11317	...	11317	...	...	...	...
	Total	...	...	...	...	...	...	...	...
					1991				
1	Residential buildings	...	442068	...	442068	...	...	...	...
2	Non-residential buildings	...	281123	...	153281	...	6513	...	121329
3	Other construction	...	274579	...	9872	...	154819	...	109887
4	Land improvement and plantation and orchard development	...	24214	...	24214	...	...	...	...
5	Producers' durable goods	...	187402	...	177009	...	10393	...	-
	A Transport equipment	...	41112	...	41112	...	...	...	...
	Passenger cars	...	...	...	...	...	...	...	...
	Other	...	41112	...	41112	...	...	...	...
	B Machinery and equipment	...	146290	...	135897	...	10393	...	...
6	Breeding stock, dairy cattle, etc.	...	11808	...	11808	...	...	...	...
	Total	...	...	...	...	...	...	...	...
					1992				
1	Residential buildings	...	460342	...	460342	...	...	...	...
2	Non-residential buildings	...	294663	...	158104	...	6635	...	129923
3	Other construction	...	282731	...	9677	...	158575	...	114479
4	Land improvement and plantation and orchard development	...	25186	...	25186	...	...	...	...
5	Producers' durable goods	...	195782	...	184406	...	11376	...	-
	A Transport equipment	...	41745	...	41745	...	...	...	...
	Passenger cars	...	...	...	...	...	...	...	...
	Other	...	41745	...	41745	...	...	...	...
	B Machinery and equipment	...	154037	...	142661	...	11376	...	...
6	Breeding stock, dairy cattle, etc.	...	11944	...	11944	...	...	...	...
	Total	...	...	...	...	...	...	...	...
					1993				
1	Residential buildings	...	477158	...	477158	...	...	...	...
2	Non-residential buildings	...	308300	...	162627	...	6938	...	138735
3	Other construction	...	293629	...	9448	...	162654	...	121528
4	Land improvement and plantation and orchard development	...	25991	...	25991	...	...	...	...
5	Producers' durable goods	...	208947	...	196269	...	12677	...	-
	A Transport equipment	...	42227	...	42227	...	...	...	...
	Passenger cars	...	...	...	...	...	...	...	...
	Other	...	42227	...	42227	...	...	...	...
	B Machinery and equipment	...	166719	...	154042	...	12677	...	...
6	Breeding stock, dairy cattle, etc.	...	11945	...	11945	...	...	...	...
	Total	...	...	...	...	...	...	...	...

Iceland

2.14 Stocks of Reproducible Fixed Assets, by Type of Good and Owner, in Constant Prices

Million Icelandic kronur

		TOTAL Gross	TOTAL Net	Total Private Gross	Total Private Net	Public Enterprises Gross	Public Enterprises Net	General Government Gross	General Government Net
				At constant prices of:1990					
				1990					
1	Residential buildings	...	403219	...	403219	...	...	...	...
2	Non-residential buildings	...	254609	...	141192	...	6152	...	107265
3	Other construction	...	251444	...	9342	...	142078	...	100024
4	Land improvement and plantation and orchard development	...	23042	...	23042	...	...	...	...
5	Producers' durable goods	...	171757	...	162346	...	9411	...	-
	A Transport equipment	...	35014	...	35014	...	...	...	...
	Passenger cars	...	1091	...	1091	...	...	...	...
	Other	...	35014	...	35014	...	...	...	...
	B Machinery and equipment	...	136743	...	127332	...	9411	...	...
6	Breeding stock, dairy cattle, etc.	...	11317	...	11317	...	...	...	...
	Total	...	1115389	...	750459	...	157641	...	207289
				1991					
1	Residential buildings	...	410894	...	410894	...	...	...	...
2	Non-residential buildings	...	261771	...	142877	...	6133	...	112762
3	Other construction	...	256249	...	9172	...	144474	...	102602
4	Land improvement and plantation and orchard development	...	23251	...	23251	...	...	...	...
5	Producers' durable goods	...	178221	...	168525	...	9696	...	-
	A Transport equipment	...	39382	...	39382	...	...	...	...
	Passenger cars	...	...	...	...	...	...	...	...
	Other	...	39382	...	39382	...	...	...	...
	B Machinery and equipment	...	138839	...	129143	...	9696	...	...
6	Breeding stock, dairy cattle, etc.	...	11317	...	11317	...	...	...	...
	Total	...	1141702	...	766036	...	160303	...	215364
				1992					
1	Residential buildings	...	417783	...	417783	...	...	...	...
2	Non-residential buildings	...	268297	...	144302	...	6094	...	117901
3	Other construction	...	257797	...	8777	...	144187	...	104833
4	Land improvement and plantation and orchard development	...	23519	...	23519	...	...	...	...
5	Producers' durable goods	...	179782	...	169438	...	10344	...	-
	A Transport equipment	...	38449	...	38449	...	...	...	...
	Passenger cars	...	...	...	...	...	...	...	...
	Other	...	38449	...	38449	...	...	...	...
	B Machinery and equipment	...	141333	...	130989	...	10344	...	...
6	Breeding stock, dairy cattle, etc.	...	11317	...	11317	...	...	...	...
	Total	...	1158495	...	775137	...	160624	...	222734
				1993					
1	Residential buildings	...	423813	...	423813	...	...	...	...
2	Non-residential buildings	...	274477	...	145202	...	6062	...	123213
3	Other construction	...	260162	...	8383	...	143079	...	108700
4	Land improvement and plantation and orchard development	...	23743	...	23743	...	...	...	...
5	Producers' durable goods	...	174770	...	163935	...	10835	...	-
	A Transport equipment	...	35230	...	35230	...	...	...	...
	Passenger cars	...	...	...	...	...	...	...	...
	Other	...	35230	...	35230	...	...	...	...
	B Machinery and equipment	...	139539	...	128705	...	10835	...	...
6	Breeding stock, dairy cattle, etc.	...	11318	...	11318	...	...	...	...
	Total	...	1168282	...	776393	...	159975	...	231913

Iceland

2.15 Stocks of Reproducible Fixed Assets by Kind of Activity, in Current Prices

Million Icelandic kronur

		1980 Gross	1980 Net	1985 Gross	1985 Net	1990 Gross	1990 Net	1991 Gross	1991 Net	1992 Gross	1992 Net	1993 Gross	1993 Net
1	Residential buildings	...	19574	...	145668	...	403167	...	442068	...	460342	...	477158
2	Non-residential buildings	...	10986	...	86526	...	254548	...	281123	...	294663	...	308300
A	Industries	...	7088	...	55529	...	147286	...	159794	...	164739	...	169565
1	Agriculture	...	1139	...	7615	...	16029	...	16565	...	16210	...	16257
2	Mining and quarrying	...	...	...	...	...	...	...	...	...	...	...	...
3	Manufacturing	...	3052	...	22571	...	53097	...	56723	...	57623	...	58266
4	Electricity, gas and water	...	...	...	...	...	...	...	...	...	...	...	...
5	Construction	...	...	...	...	...	...	...	...	...	...	...	...
6	Wholesale and retail trade	...	2718	...	23614	...	73550	...	81490	...	85771	...	89577
7	Transport and communication	...	180	...	1728	...	4610	...	5015	...	5135	...	5465
8	Finance, etc.	...	...	...	...	...	...	...	...	...	...	...	...
9	Community, social and personal services	...	...	...	...	...	...	...	...	...	...	...	...
B	Producers of government services	...	3898	...	30998	...	107262	...	121329	...	129923	...	138735
C	Other producers	...	...	...	...	...	...	...	...	...	...	...	...
3	Other construction	...	12109	...	91971	...	251447	...	274579	...	282731	...	293629
A	Industries	...	7811	...	58442	...	151423	...	164692	...	168252	...	172101
1	Agriculture	...	45	...	1112	...	9345	...	9872	...	9677	...	9448
2	Mining and quarrying	...	...	...	...	...	...	...	...	...	...	...	...
3	Manufacturing	...	...	...	...	...	...	...	...	...	...	...	...
4	Electricity, gas and water	...	6085	...	45512	...	104842	...	113693	...	114780	...	117007
5	Construction	...	...	...	...	...	...	...	...	...	...	...	...
6	Wholesale and retail trade	...	...	...	...	...	...	...	...	...	...	...	...
7	Transport and communication	...	1680	...	11817	...	37236	...	41126	...	43795	...	45646
8	Finance, etc.	...	...	...	...	...	...	...	...	...	...	...	...
9	Community, social and personal services	...	...	...	...	...	...	...	...	...	...	...	...
B	Producers of government services	...	4298	...	33529	...	100024	...	109887	...	114479	...	121528
C	Other producers	...	...	...	...	...	...	...	...	...	...	...	...
4	Land improvement and development and plantation and orchard development	...	1349	...	9613	...	22984	...	24214	...	25186	...	25991
5	Producers' durable goods	...	7336	...	57143	...	171717	...	187402	...	195782	...	208947
A	Industries	...	7336	...	57143	...	171717	...	187402	...	195782	...	208947
1	Agriculture	...	2954	...	20236	...	62965	...	65865	...	69800	...	73602
2	Mining and quarrying	...	...	...	...	...	...	...	...	...	...	...	...
3	Manufacturing	...	1608	...	14316	...	43183	...	46243	...	47731	...	52342
4	Electricity, gas and water	...	...	...	...	...	...	...	...	...	...	...	...
5	Construction	...	486	...	4161	...	8872	...	10338	...	10702	...	11657
6	Wholesale and retail trade	...	...	...	...	...	...	...	...	...	...	...	...
7	Transport and communication	...	2096	...	15298	...	43292	...	50404	...	52036	...	53774
8	Finance, etc.	...	...	...	...	...	...	...	...	...	...	...	...
9	Community, social and personal services	...	...	...	...	...	...	...	...	...	...	...	...
	Statistical discrepancy	...	193	...	3133	...	13405	...	14552	...	15513	...	17572
B	Producers of government services	...	...	...	...	...	...	...	...	...	...	...	...
C	Other producers	...	...	...	...	...	...	...	...	...	...	...	...
6	Breeding stock, dairy cattle, etc.	...	611	...	3946	...	11317	...	11808	...	11944	...	11945
Total		...	51965	...	394867	...	1115180	...	1221194	...	1270648	...	1325970

Iceland

2.16 Stocks of Reproducible Fixed Assets by Kind of Activity, in Constant Prices

Million Icelandic kronur

		1990 Gross	1990 Net	1991 Gross	1991 Net	1992 Gross	1992 Net	1993 Gross	1993 Net
		\multicolumn{8}{c	}{At constant prices of: 1990}
1	Residential buildings	...	403219	...	410894	...	417783	...	423813
2	Non-residential buildings	...	254609	...	261771	...	268297	...	274477
	A Industries	...	147344	...	149009	...	150396	...	151264
	1 Agriculture	...	16029	...	15851	...	15602	...	15307
	2 Mining and quarrying	...	...	...	...	...	...	...	...
	3 Manufacturing	...	53155	...	52762	...	52300	...	51719
	4 Electricity, gas and water	...	...	...	...	...	...	...	...
	5 Construction	...	...	...	...	...	...	...	...
	6 Wholesale and retail trade	...	73550	...	75735	...	77832	...	79554
	7 Transport and communication	...	4610	...	4661	...	4662	...	4684
	8 Finance, etc.	...	...	...	...	...	...	...	...
	9 Community, social and personal services	...	...	...	...	...	...	...	...
	B Producers of government services	...	107265	...	112762	...	117901	...	123213
	C Other producers	...	...	...	...	...	...	...	...
3	Other construction	...	251444	...	256249	...	257797	...	260162
	A Industries	...	151420	...	153647	...	152964	...	151461
	1 Agriculture	...	9342	...	9172	...	8777	...	8383
	2 Mining and quarrying	...	...	...	...	...	...	...	...
	3 Manufacturing	...	...	...	...	...	...	...	...
	4 Electricity, gas and water	...	104842	...	106253	...	104446	...	102541
	5 Construction	...	...	...	...	...	...	...	...
	6 Wholesale and retail trade	...	...	...	...	...	...	...	...
	7 Transport and communication	...	37236	...	38221	...	39740	...	40538
	8 Finance, etc.	...	...	...	...	...	...	...	...
	9 Community, social and personal services	...	...	...	...	...	...	...	...
	B Producers of government services	...	100024	...	102602	...	104833	...	108700
	C Other producers	...	...	...	...	...	...	...	...
4	Land improvement and development and plantation and orchard development	...	23042	...	23251	...	23519	...	23743
5	Producers' durable goods	...	171757	...	178221	...	179782	...	174770
	A Industries	...	171757	...	178221	...	179782	...	174770
	1 Agriculture	...	63005	...	62091	...	63924	...	61914
	2 Mining and quarrying	...	...	...	...	...	...	...	...
	3 Manufacturing	...	43195	...	44247	...	43909	...	43535
	4 Electricity, gas and water	...	...	...	...	...	...	...	...
	5 Construction	...	8872	...	9912	...	9864	...	9649
	6 Wholesale and retail trade	...	...	...	...	...	...	...	...
	7 Transport and communication	...	43281	...	48019	...	47787	...	45124
	8 Finance, etc.	...	...	...	...	...	...	...	...
	9 Community, social and personal services	...	...	...	...	...	...	...	...
	Statistical discrepancy	...	13405	...	13952	...	14297	...	14547
	B Producers of government services	...	...	...	...	...	...	...	...
	C Other producers	...	...	...	...	...	...	...	...
6	Breeding stock, dairy cattle, etc.	...	11317	...	11317	...	11317	...	11318
	Total	...	1115389	...	1141702	...	1158495	...	1168282

Iceland

2.17 Exports and Imports of Goods and Services, Detail

Million Icelandic kronur

	1980	1983	1984	1985	1986	1987	1988	1989	1990	1991	1992	1993
					Exports of Goods and Services							
1 Exports of merchandise, f.o.b.	4460	18623	23557	33750	44968	53053	61667	80072	92452	91560	87833	94704
2 Transport and communication												
3 Insurance service charges	1185	8060	10208	15024	16993	18628	20054	26210	31794	33383	33415	40314
4 Other commodities												
5 Adjustments of merchandise exports to change-of-ownership basis	...	...	...	...	...	...	...	...	...	...	...	...
6 Direct purchases in the domestic market by non-residential households	...	...	...	...	...	...	...	...	...	...	...	...
7 Direct purchases in the domestic market by extraterritorial bodies	...	...	...	...	...	...	...	...	...	...	...	...
Total Exports of Goods and Services	5645	26683	33765	48774	61961	71681	81721	106282	124246	124943	121248	135018
					Imports of Goods and Services							
1 Imports of merchandise, c.i.f.	4802	20596	26744	37600	45910	61237	68723	80250	96621	104129	96895	91307
A Imports of merchandise, f.o.b.	4307	18156	23889	33760	40988	55020	61996	72603	87652	94639	87909	82393
B Transport of services on merchandise imports	495	2440	2855	3840	4922	6217	6727	7647	8969	9490	8986	8914
C Insurance service charges on merchandise imports												
2 Adjustments of merchandise imports to change-of-ownership basis	...	...	...	...	...	...	...	...	...	...	...	...
3 Other transport and communication												
4 Other insurance service charges	846	4679	7127	11063	9970	12728	15377	18990	22974	26176	25048	31452
5 Other commodities												
6 Direct purchases abroad by government												
7 Direct purchases abroad by resident households	...	...	...	...	...	...	...	...	...	...	...	...
Total Imports of Goods and Services	5648	25275	33871	48663	55880	73965	84100	99240	119595	130305	121943	122759
Balance of Goods and Services	-3	1408	-106	111	6081	-2284	-2379	7042	4651	-5362	-695	12259
Total Imports and Balance of Goods and Services	5645	26683	33765	48774	61961	71681	81721	106282	124246	124943	121248	135018

3.12 General Government Income and Outlay Account: Total and Subsectors

Million Icelandic kronur

	1980					1985				
	Total General Government	Central Government	State or Provincial Government	Local Government	Social Security Funds	Total General Government	Central Government	State or Provincial Government	Local Government	Social Security Funds
					Receipts					
1 Operating surplus	...	...	...	...	...	...	...	...	...	...
2 Property and entrepreneurial income	329	260	...	66	3	3895	3078	...	748	69
A Withdrawals from public quasi-corporations	17	10	...	7	...	290	180	...	110	...
B Interest	303	250	...	50	3	3490	2892	...	529	69
C Dividends	-	-	...	-	...	11	3	...	8	...
D Net land rent and royalties	9	-	...	9	...	104	3	...	101	...
3 Taxes, fees and contributions	5138	4166	...	972	...	37209	29938	...	7271	...
A Indirect taxes	3681	3240	...	441	...	27638	24147	...	3491	...
B Direct taxes	1228	697	...	531	...	8140	4360	...	3780	...
Income	1148	617	...	531	...	7457	3677	...	3780	...
Other	80	80	...	-	...	683	683	...	-	...
C Social security contributions	215	215	...	...	...	1333	1333	...	...	...
D Fees, fines and penalties	14	14	...	...	...	98	98	...	...	...

Iceland

3.12 General Government Income and Outlay Account: Total and Subsectors
(Continued)

Million Icelandic kronur

	1980					1985				
	Total General Government	Central Government	State or Provincial Government	Local Government	Social Security Funds	Total General Government	Central Government	State or Provincial Government	Local Government	Social Security Funds
4 Other current transfers	-	-	...	11	1149	-	-	...	56	8687
A Casualty insurance claims	...	...	...	...	...	...	...	...	...	...
B Transfers from other government subsectors	...	...	...	11	1149	...	...	...	56	8687
C Transfers from the rest of the world	...	...	...	...	...	...	...	...	...	...
D Other transfers, except imputed	...	...	...	...	...	...	...	...	...	...
E Imputed unfunded employee pension and welfare contributions	...	...	...	...	...	...	...	...	...	...
Total Current Receipts	5467	4426	...	1049	1152	41104	33016	...	8075	8756
Disbursements											
1 Government final consumption expenditure	2662	1507	...	586	569	21130	12255	...	4455	4420
2 Property income	256	215	...	41	-	3668	3300	...	368	-
A Interest	256	215	...	41	-	3668	3300	...	368	-
B Net land rent and royalties	...	...	...	...	...	...	...	...	...	...
3 Subsidies	572	546	...	26	-	4107	3950	...	157	-
4 Other current transfers	810	1341	...	110	518	6471	9942	...	1044	4228
A Casualty insurance premiums, net	...	...	...	...	...	...	...	...	...	...
B Transfers to other government subsectors	-	1087	...	73	...	-	8100	...	643	...
C Social security benefits	518	-	...	-	518	4227	-	...	-	4227
D Social assistance grants	225	199	...	25	1	1453	1182	...	270	1
E Unfunded employee pension and welfare benefits	...	...	...	...	...	...	...	...	...	...
F Transfers to private non-profit institutions serving households	...	...	...	...	...	...	...	...	...	...
G Other transfers n.e.c.	55	43	...	12	-	730	599	...	131	-
H Transfers to the rest of the world	12	12	...	-	-	61	61	...	-	-
Net saving	1168	817	...	286	65	5729	3569	...	2051	109
Total Current Disbursements and Net Saving	5468	4426	...	1049	1152	41105	33016	...	8075	8757

	1990					1991				
	Total General Government	Central Government	State or Provincial Government	Local Government	Social Security Funds	Total General Government	Central Government	State or Provincial Government	Local Government	Social Security Funds
Receipts											
1 Operating surplus	...	...	...	...	...	...	...	...	...	...
2 Property and entrepreneurial income	8786	6699	...	1953	134	10466	8150	...	2268	47
A Withdrawals from public quasi-corporations	2633	2041	...	592	...	2747	1895	...	852	...
B Interest	5728	4596	...	998	134	7325	6210	...	1067	47
C Dividends	77	58	...	19	...	28	12	...	16	...
D Net land rent and royalties	348	4	...	344	...	366	33	...	333	...
3 Taxes, fees and contributions	122369	99080	...	23289	...	137472	111178	...	26294	...
A Indirect taxes	79163	69573	...	9590	...	83964	72622	...	11342	...
B Direct taxes	38422	24723	...	13699	...	42644	27692	...	14952	...
Income	35737	22038	...	13699	...	39324	24372	...	14952	...
Other	2685	2685	...	-	...	3320	3320	...	-	...
C Social security contributions	4529	4529	...	...	...	10487	10487	...	...	...
D Fees, fines and penalties	255	255	...	...	...	377	377	...	...	...
4 Other current transfers	-	-	...	1380	24178	-	-	...	1582	27255
A Casualty insurance claims	...	...	...	...	...	...	...	...	...	...
B Transfers from other government subsectors	...	...	...	1380	24178	...	...	...	1582	27255
C Transfers from the rest of the world	...	...	...	...	...	...	...	...	...	...
D Other transfers, except imputed	...	...	...	...	...	...	...	...	...	...
E Imputed unfunded employee pension and welfare contributions	...	...	...	...	...	...	...	...	...	...

Iceland

3.12 General Government Income and Outlay Account: Total and Subsectors
(Continued)

Million Icelandic kronur

	1990 Total General Government	1990 Central Government	1990 State or Provincial Government	1990 Local Government	1990 Social Security Funds	1991 Total General Government	1991 Central Government	1991 State or Provincial Government	1991 Local Government	1991 Social Security Funds
Total Current Receipts	131155	105779	...	26622	24312	147938	119328	...	30144	27302

Disbursements

1 Government final consumption expenditure	69989	44741	...	15125	10123	78157	49596	...	17620	10941
2 Property income	12903	11370	...	1533	-	14717	12962	...	1755	-
A Interest	12903	11370	...	1533	-	14717	12962	...	1755	-
B Net land rent and royalties	...	...	...	...	...	...	...	...	...	...
3 Subsidies	12953	12281	...	672	-	12320	11351	...	969	-
4 Other current transfers	25604	34871	...	1845	14446	28775	39767	...	1661	16183
A Casualty insurance premiums, net	...	...	...	...	...	...	...	...	...	...
B Transfers to other government subsectors	-	25332	...	226	...	-	28836	...	-	...
C Social security benefits	14445	-	...	-	14445	16182	-	...	-	16182
D Social assistance grants	7729	6940	...	788	1	8483	7680	...	802	1
E Unfunded employee pension and welfare benefits	...	...	...	...	...	...	...	...	...	...
F Transfers to private non-profit institutions serving households	...	...	...	...	...	...	...	...	...	...
G Other transfers n.e.c.	3113	2282	...	831	-	3711	2852	...	859	-
H Transfers to the rest of the world	317	317	...	-	-	399	399	...	-	-
Net saving	9706	2516	...	7447	-257	13970	5653	...	8139	178
Total Current Disbursements and Net Saving	131155	105779	...	26622	24312	147939	119329	...	30144	27302

	1992 Total General Government	1992 Central Government	1992 State or Provincial Government	1992 Local Government	1992 Social Security Funds	1993 Total General Government	1993 Central Government	1993 State or Provincial Government	1993 Local Government	1993 Social Security Funds

Receipts

1 Operating surplus	...	...	...	...	...	...	...	...	...	...
2 Property and entrepreneurial income	11000	8446	...	2402	152	10563	8217	...	2254	92
A Withdrawals from public quasi-corporations	3665	2430	...	1235	...	3378	2328	...	1050	...
B Interest	6828	5868	...	808	152	6795	5870	...	833	92
C Dividends	43	17	...	26	...	49	17	...	32	...
D Net land rent and royalties	464	131	...	333	...	341	2	...	339	...
3 Taxes, fees and contributions	139271	111934	...	27337	...	136965	110240	...	26725	...
A Indirect taxes	83763	72193	...	11570	...	77157	70252	...	6905	...
B Direct taxes	43741	27974	...	15767	...	48050	28230	...	19820	...
Income	40378	24611	...	15767	...	44397	24577	...	19820	...
Other	3363	3363	...	-	...	3653	3653	...	-	...
C Social security contributions	11321	11321	...	...	...	11386	11386	...	...	...
D Fees, fines and penalties	446	446	...	...	...	372	372	...	...	...
4 Other current transfers	-	601	...	1743	28311	-	-	...	2016	29368
A Casualty insurance claims	...	...	...	...	...	...	...	...	...	...
B Transfers from other government subsectors	...	601	...	1743	28311	...	...	...	2016	29368
C Transfers from the rest of the world	...	...	...	...	...	...	...	...	...	...
D Other transfers, except imputed	...	...	...	...	...	...	...	...	...	...
E Imputed unfunded employee pension and welfare contributions	...	...	...	...	...	...	...	...	...	...
Total Current Receipts	150271	120981	...	31482	28463	147528	118457	...	30995	29460

Disbursements

1 Government final consumption expenditure	80375	50112	...	19679	10584	84818	53389	...	21373	10056
2 Property income	14508	12875	...	1633	-	15381	13678	...	1703	-
A Interest	14508	12875	...	1633	-	15381	13678	...	1703	-
B Net land rent and royalties	...	...	...	...	...	...	...	...	...	...
3 Subsidies	13225	12227	...	998	-	10504	9526	...	978	-

Iceland

3.12 General Government Income and Outlay Account: Total and Subsectors
(Continued)

Million Icelandic kronur

	1992					1993				
	Total General Government	Central Government	State or Provincial Government	Local Government	Social Security Funds	Total General Government	Central Government	State or Provincial Government	Local Government	Social Security Funds
4 Other current transfers	30295	40831	...	2295	17824	32764	42200	...	2629	19320
A Casualty insurance premiums, net	...	...	...	...	...	...	...	...	...	...
B Transfers to other government subsectors	-	30054	...	601	...	-	30769	...	500	116
C Social security benefits	17824	-	...	-	17824	19204	-	...	-	19204
D Social assistance grants	8641	7696	...	945	-	9504	8110	...	1394	-
E Unfunded employee pension and welfare benefits	...	...	...	...	...	...	...	...	...	...
F Transfers to private non-profit institutions serving households	...	...	...	...	...	...	...	...	...	...
G Other transfers n.e.c.	3473	2724	...	749	-	3684	2949	...	735	-
H Transfers to the rest of the world	357	357	...	-	-	372	372	...	-	-
Net saving	11867	4935	...	6877	55	4061	-337	...	4312	84
Total Current Disbursements and Net Saving	150270	120980	...	31482	28463	147528	118456	...	30995	29460

3.13 General Government Capital Accumulation Account: Total and Subsectors

Million Icelandic kronur

	1980					1985				
	Total General Government	Central Government	State or Provincial Government	Local Government	Social Security Funds	Total General Government	Central Government	State or Provincial Government	Local Government	Social Security Funds
	Finance of Gross Accumulation										
1 Gross saving	1264	890	...	310	64	6463	4120	...	2235	108
A Consumption of fixed capital	95	71	...	24	-	735	551	...	184	-
B Net saving	1169	819	...	286	64	5728	3569	...	2051	108
2 Capital transfers a	16	16	...	125	-	154	129	...	682	...
A From other government subsectors	...	-	...	125	...	...	-	...	657	...
B From other resident sectors	16	16	...	-	...	154	129	...	25	...
C From rest of the world	...	...	...	...	...	...	...	...	...	...
Finance of Gross Accumulation	1280	906	...	435	64	6617	4249	...	2917	108
	Gross Accumulation										
1 Gross capital formation	579	250	...	329	-	4402	1889	...	2513	-
A Increase in stocks	...	...	...	...	...	...	...	...	...	...
B Gross fixed capital formation	579	250	...	329	-	4402	1889	...	2513	-
2 Purchases of land, net	...	...	...	...	...	...	...	...	...	...
3 Purchases of intangible assets, net	...	...	...	...	...	...	...	...	...	...
4 Capital transfers	486	519	...	92	-	4216	4481	...	392	-
A To other government subsectors	-	125	...	...	...	-	657	...	...	...
B To other resident sectors	486	394	...	92	-	4216	3824	...	392	-
C To rest of the world	...	...	...	...	...	...	...	...	...	...
Net lending	215	137	...	14	64	-2003	-2122	...	11	108
Gross Accumulation	1280	906	...	435	64	6615	4248	...	2916	108

	1990					1991				
	Total General Government	Central Government	State or Provincial Government	Local Government	Social Security Funds	Total General Government	Central Government	State or Provincial Government	Local Government	Social Security Funds
	Finance of Gross Accumulation										
1 Gross saving	11736	4024	...	7969	-257	16291	7389	...	8724	178
A Consumption of fixed capital	2029	1508	...	521	-	2319	1736	...	583	-
B Net saving	9707	2516	...	7448	-257	13972	5653	...	8141	178
2 Capital transfers a	517	468	...	1725	-	711	610	...	1956	-
A From other government subsectors	...	-	...	1676	...	...	-	...	1855	...
B From other resident sectors	517	468	...	49	...	711	610	...	101	...
C From rest of the world	...	...	...	...	...	...	...	...	...	...
Finance of Gross Accumulation	12253	4492	...	9694	-257	17002	7999	...	10680	178
	Gross Accumulation										
1 Gross capital formation	14378	6338	...	8040	-	16228	7100	...	9128	-

Iceland

3.13 General Government Capital Accumulation Account: Total and Subsectors
(Continued)

Million Icelandic kronur

	1990					1991				
	Total General Government	Central Government	State or Provincial Government	Local Government	Social Security Funds	Total General Government	Central Government	State or Provincial Government	Local Government	Social Security Funds
A Increase in stocks	...	...	...	...	...	...	...	...	...	...
B Gross fixed capital formation	14378	6338	...	8040	-	16228	7100	...	9128	-
2 Purchases of land, net	...	...	...	...	...	...	...	...	...	...
3 Purchases of intangible assets, net	...	...	...	...	...	...	...	...	...	...
4 Capital transfers	9980	10198	...	1458	-	12397	12086	...	2166	-
A To other government subsectors	-	1676	...	...	...	-	1855	...	...	...
B To other resident sectors	9980	8522	...	1458	...	12397	10231	...	2166	...
C To rest of the world	...	...	...	...	...	...	...	...	...	...
Net lending	-12105	-12044	...	196	-257	-11623	-11187	...	-614	178
Gross Accumulation	12253	4492	...	9694	-257	17002	7999	...	10680	178

	1992					1993				
	Total General Government	Central Government	State or Provincial Government	Local Government	Social Security Funds	Total General Government	Central Government	State or Provincial Government	Local Government	Social Security Funds

Finance of Gross Accumulation

1 Gross saving	14321	6748	...	7518	55	6661	1580	...	4997	84
A Consumption of fixed capital	2454	1813	...	641	-	2600	1917	...	683	-
B Net saving	11867	4935	...	6877	55	4061	-337	...	4314	84
2 Capital transfers [a]	619	517	...	1904	-	679	531	...	1864	-
A From other government subsectors	...	-	...	1802	...	...	-	...	1716	...
B From other resident sectors	619	517	...	102	...	679	531	...	148	...
C From rest of the world	...	...	...	...	...	...	...	...	...	...
Finance of Gross Accumulation	14940	7265	...	9422	55	7340	2111	...	6861	84

Gross Accumulation

1 Gross capital formation	16016	6434	...	9582	-	17746	8025	...	9721	-
A Increase in stocks	...	...	...	...	...	...	...	...	...	...
B Gross fixed capital formation	16016	6434	...	9582	-	17746	8025	...	9721	-
2 Purchases of land, net	...	...	...	...	...	...	...	...	...	...
3 Purchases of intangible assets, net	...	...	...	...	...	...	...	...	...	...
4 Capital transfers	10145	10394	...	1553	-	8032	7867	...	1881	-
A To other government subsectors	-	1802	...	...	...	-	1716	...	...	...
B To other resident sectors	10145	8592	...	1553	...	8032	6151	...	1881	...
C To rest of the world	...	...	...	...	...	...	...	...	...	...
Net lending	-11221	-9563	...	-1713	55	-18438	-13781	...	-4741	84
Gross Accumulation	14940	7265	...	9422	55	7340	2111	...	6861	84

a) Capital transfers received are recorded net of capital transfers paid.

3.51 External Transactions: Current Account: Detail

Million Icelandic kronur

	1980	1983	1984	1985	1986	1987	1988	1989	1990	1991	1992	1993

Payments to the Rest of the World

1 Imports of goods and services	5648	25275	33871	48663	55880	73965	84100	99240	119595	130305	121943	122759
A Imports of merchandise c.i.f.	4802	20596	26744	37600	45910	61237	68723	80250	96621	104129	96895	91307
B Other	846	4679	7127	11063	9970	12728	15377	18990	22974	26176	25048	31452
2 Factor income to the rest of the world	478	3444	5051	6255	7042	7281	9461	15087	16872	17463	16717	17912

Iceland

3.51 External Transactions: Current Account: Detail
(Continued)

Million Icelandic kronur

	1980	1983	1984	1985	1986	1987	1988	1989	1990	1991	1992	1993
A Compensation of employees	10	39	41	50	89	175	331	519	682	883	723	702
B Property and entrepreneurial income	468	3405	5010	6205	6953	7106	9130	14568	16190	16580	15994	17210
3 Current transfers to the rest of the world	5	32	43	47	72	66	80	228	358	465	451	539
A Indirect taxes by general government to supranational organizations	...	...	...	...	...	...	...	...	...	...	...	...
B Other current transfers	5	32	43	47	72	66	80	228	358	465	451	539
By general government	5	32	43	47	72	66	80	228	358	465	451	539
By other resident sectors	-	-	-	-	-	-	-	-	-	-	-	-
4 Surplus of the nation on current transactions	-318	-1295	-4173	-4760	707	-7149	-8965	-4350	-8108	-18513	-12451	-386
Payments to the Rest of the World, and Surplus of the Nation on Current Transfers	5813	27456	34792	50205	63701	74163	84676	110205	128717	129720	126660	140824

Receipts From The Rest of the World

	1980	1983	1984	1985	1986	1987	1988	1989	1990	1991	1992	1993
1 Exports of goods and services	5645	26683	33765	48774	61961	71681	81721	106282	124246	124943	121248	135018
A Exports of merchandise f.o.b.	4460	18623	23557	33750	44968	53053	61667	80072	92452	91560	87833	94704
B Other	1186	8060	10208	15024	16993	18628	20054	26210	31794	33383	33415	40314
2 Factor income from the rest of the world	167	773	1027	1431	1740	2482	2955	3923	4471	4777	5412	5806
A Compensation of employees	104	418	572	831	1013	1589	1998	2306	2658	2994	3037	3175
B Property and entrepreneurial income	63	355	455	600	727	893	957	1617	1813	1783	2375	2631
3 Current transfers from the rest of the world	-	-	-	-	-	-	-	-	-	-	-	-
A Subsidies to general government from supranational organizations	...	...	...	...	...	...	...	...	...	...	...	...
B Other current transfers	-	-	-	-	-	-	-	-	-	-	-	-
Receipts from the Rest of the World on Current Transfers	5812	27456	34792	50205	63701	74163	84676	110205	128717	129720	126660	140824

3.52 External Transactions: Capital Accumulation Account

Million Icelandic kronur

	1980	1983	1984	1985	1986	1987	1988	1989	1990	1991	1992	1993

Finance of Gross Accumulation

	1980	1983	1984	1985	1986	1987	1988	1989	1990	1991	1992	1993
1 Surplus of the nation on current transactions	-318	-1295	-4173	-4760	707	-7149	-8965	-4350	-8108	-18513	-12451	-386
2 Capital transfers from the rest of the world	-15	-10	68	55	232	42	38	43	364	164	91	384
A By general government	-	-	-	-	-	-	-	-	-	-	-	-
B By other resident sectors	-15	-10	68	55	232	42	38	43	364	164	91	384
Total Finance of Gross Accumulation	-333	-1305	-4105	-4705	939	-7107	-8927	-4307	-7744	-18349	-12360	-2

Gross Accumulation

	1980	1983	1984	1985	1986	1987	1988	1989	1990	1991	1992	1993
1 Capital transfers to the rest of the world	...	...	...	...	...	...	...	...	...	...	...	...
2 Purchases of intangible assets, n.e.c., net, from the rest of the world	...	...	...	...	...	...	...	...	...	...	...	...
Net lending to the rest of the world	-333	-1305	-4105	-4705	939	-7107	-8927	-4307	-7744	-18349	-12360	-2
Total Gross Accumulation	-333	-1305	-4105	-4705	939	-7107	-8927	4307	-7744	-18349	-12360	-2

4.1 Derivation of Value Added by Kind of Activity, in Current Prices

Million Icelandic kronur

	1980			1985			1990			1991		
	Gross Output	Intermediate Consumption	Value Added	Gross Output	Intermediate Consumption	Value Added	Gross Output	Intermediate Consumption	Value Added	Gross Output	Intermediate Consumption	Value Added

All Producers

	Gross Output	Intermediate Consumption	Value Added	Gross Output	Intermediate Consumption	Value Added	Gross Output	Intermediate Consumption	Value Added	Gross Output	Intermediate Consumption	Value Added
1 Agriculture, hunting, forestry and fishing	2949	1382	1567	21557	10043	11514	63486	27525	35961	66933	28386	38548
A Agriculture and hunting	1083	497	586	7527	3329	4198	17475	9561	7914	16703	8978	7725
B Forestry and logging	-	-	-	-	-	-	-	-	-	-	-	-
C Fishing	1866	885	981	14030	6714	7316	46011	17964	28048	50231	19408	30822
2 Mining and quarrying	-	-	-	-	-	-	-	-	-	-	-	-

Iceland

4.1 Derivation of Value Added by Kind of Activity, in Current Prices
(Continued)

Million Icelandic kronur

	1980 Gross Output	1980 Intermediate Consumption	1980 Value Added	1985 Gross Output	1985 Intermediate Consumption	1985 Value Added	1990 Gross Output	1990 Intermediate Consumption	1990 Value Added	1991 Gross Output	1991 Intermediate Consumption	1991 Value Added
3 Manufacturing	8041	5557	2484	61051	43230	17821	151803	107648	44155	163007	114810	48197
A Manufacture of food, beverages and tobacco	4549	3594	955	35247	27568	7679	84818	66824	17995	93317	72065	21252
B Textile, wearing apparel and leather industries	572	360	212	3982	2556	1426	6415	4287	2128	6331	4022	2309
C Manufacture of wood and wood products, including furniture	393	175	218	2460	1242	1218	5998	3582	2416	6640	3891	2749
D Manufacture of paper and paper products, printing and publishing	365	183	182	3507	1810	1697	10558	5108	5451	12225	5939	6286
E Manufacture of chemicals and chemical petroleum, coal, rubber and plastic products	381	255	126	3284	2230	1054	8958	5523	3434	9706	6066	3640
F Manufacture of non-metallic mineral products, except products of petroleum and coal	330	200	130	2365	1373	992	5528	3105	2423	6174	3640	2534
G Basic metal industries	641	426	215	4700	3736	964	12073	9436	2637	10202	8858	1345
H Manufacture of fabricated metal products, machinery and equipment	719	322	397	4142	1795	2347	12141	6064	6077	13154	6724	6430
I Other manufacturing industries	92	42	50	1365	923	442	5314	3720	1594	5257	3604	1653
4 Electricity, gas and water	872	300	572	9670	3703	5967	19582	7934	11648	20616	8778	11838
A Electricity, gas and steam	832	286	546	9316	3554	5762	18490	7535	10954	19363	8429	10934
B Water works and supply	40	15	25	354	149	205	1093	399	694	1253	349	904
5 Construction	3250	2069	1181	22683	14296	8387	71259	47166	24093	82179	57597	24582
6 Wholesale and retail trade, restaurants and hotels	3172	726	2446	28189	8246	19943	68525	22496	46029	75602	25261	50342
A Wholesale and retail trade	2794	511	2283	23432	5513	17919	55475	15374	40102	60789	17159	43630
B Restaurants and hotels	378	215	163	4757	2732	2025	13049	7123	5927	14814	8102	6712
Restaurants	216	130	86	3317	2001	1316	9689	5604	4085	11234	6496	4737
Hotels and other lodging places	162	85	77	1440	731	709	3361	1519	1842	3580	1605	1975
7 Transport, storage and communication	2122	1122	1000	19698	11526	8172	48480	26293	22187	51352	28892	22460
A Transport and storage	1853	1069	784	17307	10812	6495	41906	24261	17646	44178	26554	17623
B Communication	269	53	216	2391	714	1677	6574	2033	4541	7174	2338	4836
8 Finance, insurance, real estate and business services	2730	735	1995	25561	8186	17375	73951	24739	49212	78392	25555	52838
A Financial institutions	676	104	572	6547	1388	5159	20998	6586	14412	23573	7582	15991
B Insurance	217	82	135	1378	394	984	1650	1340	310	2150	1324	826
C Real estate and business services	1837	549	1288	17636	6404	11232	51302	16813	34490	52669	16649	36020
9 Community, social and personal services	1103	435	668	10648	4751	5897	29988	12910	17078	33168	14244	18923
A Sanitary and similar services	...	...	...	...	...	...	...	...	...	...	...	...
B Social and related community services	141	37	104	1343	372	971	4948	1569	3380	5501	1739	3762
Educational services	...	...	...	...	...	...	...	...	...	...	...	...
Medical, dental, other health and veterinary services	141	37	104	1343	372	971	4948	1569	3380	5501	1739	3762
C Recreational and cultural services	258	124	134	3380	1983	1397	9625	4848	4777	10411	4964	5447
D Personal and household services [a]	705	274	431	5925	2396	3529	15414	6493	8921	17255	7542	9713
Total, Industries	24239	12326	11913	199058	103982	95076	527074	276711	250363	571249	303522	267727
Producers of Government Services	2863	1051	1811	23155	10119	13035	79181	33898	45282	88494	37346	51148
Other Producers	174	74	100	1396	572	824	5551	2288	3263	6270	2593	3677
Total	27276	13451	13825	223608	114673	108936	611806	312897	298910	666013	343460	322553
Less: Imputed bank service charge	...	-523	523	...	-4822	4822	...	-12422	12422	...	-14352	14352
Import duties [b]	1166	...	1166	7277	...	7277	51785	...	51785	60590	...	60590
Value added tax	...	...	...	...	...	...	...	...	...	...	...	...
Other adjustments [c]	1220	...	1220	8605	...	8605	16107	...	16107	15263	...	15263
Total	29662	13974	15688	239490	119494	119996	679698	325319	354379	741866	357812	384054

a) Item 'Personal and household services' includes also ISIC-code 96, residents directly employed at the NATO-base.
b) Item 'Import duties' includes all indirect taxes and subsidies not directly allocated to specified activities.
c) Item 'Other adjustments' includes residual error between production and expenditure approaches.

Iceland

4.2 Derivation of Value Added by Kind of Activity, in Constant Prices

Million Icelandic kronur

	1980			1985			1990			1991		
	Gross Output	Intermediate Consumption	Value Added	Gross Output	Intermediate Consumption	Value Added	Gross Output	Intermediate Consumption	Value Added	Gross Output	Intermediate Consumption	Value Added
	At constant prices of: 1980											
	All Producers											
1 Agriculture, hunting, forestry and fishing	...	...	1571	...	...	1448	...	...	1843	...	...	1610
A Agriculture and hunting	...	...	597	...	...	626	...	...	574	...	...	569
B Forestry and logging	...	...	...	...	...	...	...	...	...	...	...	...
C Fishing	...	...	975	...	...	823	...	...	1270	...	...	1042
2 Mining and quarrying	...	...	...	...	...	...	...	...	...	...	...	...
3 Manufacturing	...	...	2410	...	...	2438	...	...	2421	...	...	2451
A Manufacture of food, beverages and tobacco	...	...	1148	...	...	1055	...	...	1061	...	...	1061
B Textile, wearing apparel and leather industries	...	...	201	...	...	215	...	...	128	...	...	121
C Manufacture of wood and wood products, including furniture	...	...	159	...	...	153	...	...	138	...	...	146
D Manufacture of paper and paper products, printing and publishing	...	...	158	...	...	192	...	...	232	...	...	261
E Manufacture of chemicals and chemical petroleum, coal, rubber and plastic products	...	...	98	...	...	132	...	...	139	...	...	142
F Manufacture of non-metallic mineral products, except products of petroleum and coal	...	...	85	...	...	77	...	...	84	...	...	87
G Basic metal industries	...	...	198	...	...	228	...	...	263	...	...	256
H Manufacture of fabricated metal products, machinery and equipment	...	...	320	...	...	328	...	...	304	...	...	307
I Other manufacturing industries	...	...	44	...	...	59	...	...	74	...	...	71
4 Electricity, gas and water	...	...	515	...	...	770	...	...	875	...	...	890
A Electricity, gas and steam	...	...	488	...	...	740	...	...	839	...	...	853
B Water works and supply	...	...	27	...	...	31	...	...	36	...	...	37
5 Construction	...	...	1065	...	...	1092	...	...	1258	...	...	1260
6 Wholesale and retail trade, restaurants and hotels	...	...	1233	...	...	1460	...	...	1745	...	...	1770
A Wholesale and retail trade	...	...	1118	...	...	1273	...	...	1540	...	...	1564
B Restaurants and hotels	...	...	115	...	...	187	...	...	205	...	...	206
Restaurants	...	...	55	...	...	119	...	...	127	...	...	134
Hotels and other lodging places	...	...	47	...	...	45	...	...	20	...	...	20
7 Transport, storage and communication	...	...	914	...	...	1135	...	...	1422	...	...	1445
A Transport and storage	...	...	735	...	...	818	...	...	872	...	...	865
B Communication	...	...	179	...	...	318	...	...	550	...	...	581
8 Finance, insurance, real estate and business services	...	...	2164	...	...	2862	...	...	3339	...	...	3401
A Financial institutions	...	...	574	...	...	821	...	...	998	...	...	1039
B Insurance	...	...	87	...	...	113	...	...	131	...	...	137
C Real estate and business services	...	...	1503	...	...	1929	...	...	2210	...	...	2225
9 Community, social and personal services	...	...	456	...	...	615	...	...	723	...	...	750
Total, Industries	...	...	10327	...	...	11820	...	...	13627	...	...	13577
Producers of Government Services	...	...	1760	...	...	2225	...	...	2952	...	...	3064
Other Producers	...	...	97	...	...	152	...	...	204	...	...	209
Total	...	...	12184	...	...	14197	...	...	16784	...	...	16850
Less: Imputed bank service charge	...	...	523	...	...	748	...	...	909	...	...	946
Import duties	...	...	...	...	...	...	...	...	...	...	...	...
Value added tax	...	...	...	...	...	...	...	...	...	...	...	...
Total [a]	...	...	11661	...	...	13449	...	...	15874	...	...	15904

a) Gross domestic product in factor values.

Iceland

4.3 Cost Components of Value Added

Million Icelandic kronur

		1980					1985				
	Compensation of Employees	Capital Consumption	Net Operating Surplus	Indirect Taxes	Less: Subsidies Received	Value Added	Compensation of Employees	Capital Consumption	Net Operating Surplus	Indirect Taxes	Less: Subsidies Received	Value Added

All Producers

	C of E	CC	NOS	IT	Subs	VA	C of E	CC	NOS	IT	Subs	VA
1 Agriculture, hunting, forestry and fishing	834	351	385	14	16	1568	5937	2745	2751	229	147	11515
A Agriculture and hunting	55	133	408	7	16	587	437	733	3006	166	143	4199
B Forestry and logging	-	-	-	-	-	-	-	-	-	-	-	-
C Fishing	779	218	-23	7	-	981	5500	2012	-255	63	4	7316
2 Mining and quarrying	-	-	-	-	-	-	-	-	-	-	-	-
3 Manufacturing	1978	351	81	417	342	2485	13563	3321	340	2683	2087	17820
A Manufacture of food, beverages and tobacco	959	138	51	137	329	956	6587	1512	690	768	1877	7680
B Textile, wearing apparel and leather industries	159	26	16	23	13	211	1059	191	97	158	80	1425
C Manufacture of wood and wood products, including furniture	148	21	-10	59	-	218	750	84	-50	434	-	1218
D Manufacture of paper and paper products, printing and publishing	137	17	4	25	-	183	1128	229	139	200	-	1696
E Manufacture of chemicals and chemical petroleum, coal, rubber and plastic products	70	24	4	28	-	126	639	254	62	230	130	1055
F Manufacture of non-metallic mineral products, except products of petroleum and coal	68	17	-1	46	-	130	555	199	-67	305	-	992
G Basic metal industries	103	78	17	17	-	215	704	650	-473	83	-	964
H Manufacture of fabricated metal products, machinery and equipment	297	28	-5	77	-	397	1830	185	-134	465	-	2346
I Other manufacturing industries	38	2	5	5	-	50	311	17	75	39	-	442
4 Electricity, gas and water	92	149	273	104	48	570	877	2517	2200	1022	649	5967
A Electricity, gas and steam	91	145	252	104	46	546	864	2435	2095	1014	648	5760
B Water works and supply	1	4	21	-	2	24	13	81	105	7	1	205
5 Construction	755	80	217	129	-	1181	4585	1156	1581	1065	-	8387
6 Wholesale and retail trade, restaurants and hotels	935	135	163	1219	6	2446	7554	1284	1323	9800	18	19943
A Wholesale and retail trade	816	123	179	1171	6	2283	6454	1132	1116	9235	18	17919
B Restaurants and hotels	119	12	-16	48	-	163	1100	152	207	565	-	2024
Restaurants	63	7	-14	31	-	87	697	85	81	453	-	1316
Hotels and other lodging places	56	5	-2	17	-	76	403	67	126	112	-	708
7 Transport, storage and communication	619	260	33	117	30	999	4527	1893	876	1077	200	8173
A Transport and storage	484	194	55	80	30	783	3596	1533	819	748	200	6496
B Communication	135	66	-22	37	-	216	931	360	57	329	-	1677
8 Finance, insurance, real estate and business services	435	413	1006	159	18	1995	4004	3644	8147	1628	48	17375
A Financial institutions	223	15	336	16	18	572	1946	247	2730	284	48	5159
B Insurance	50	5	32	48	-	135	295	61	138	490	-	984
C Real estate and business services	163	393	637	95	-	1288	1763	3336	5279	854	-	11232
9 Community, social and personal services	426	42	90	137	28	667	3296	438	1350	1000	187	5897
A Sanitary and similar services	...	...	...	...	...	...	...	...	...	...	...	...
B Social and related community services	21	3	77	3	-	104	177	32	732	30	-	971
Educational services	...	...	...	...	...	...	...	...	...	...	...	...
Medical, dental, other health and veterinary services	21	3	77	3	-	104	177	32	732	30	-	971
C Recreational and cultural services	105	21	15	20	28	133	811	199	406	167	187	1396
D Personal and household services [a]	300	18	-1	113	-	430	2308	207	212	803	-	3530
Total, Industries	6074	1781	2250	2296	488	11913	44343	16998	18568	18502	3334	95077
Producers of Government Services	1662	95	1	53	-	1811	11893	736	27	379	-	13035

Iceland

4.3 Cost Components of Value Added
(Continued)

Million Icelandic kronur

	1980						1985					
	Compensation of Employees	Capital Consumption	Net Operating Surplus	Indirect Taxes	Less: Subsidies Received	Value Added	Compensation of Employees	Capital Consumption	Net Operating Surplus	Indirect Taxes	Less: Subsidies Received	Value Added
Other Producers	89	10	-2	3	-	100	732	74	-9	27	-	824
Total	7825	1886	2249	2352	488	13825	56968	17808	18586	18908	3334	108936
Less: Imputed bank service charge	...	...	523	...	...	523	...	...	4822	...	...	4822
Import duties bc	...	...	...	1168	2	1166	...	...	...	7433	156	7277
Value added tax	...	...	...	...	...	...	...	...	...	...	...	...
Other adjustments d	...	...	...	...	...	1220	...	...	...	...	...	8605
Total e	7825	1886	1727	3520	490	15688	56968	17808	13764	26341	3490	119996

	1990						1991					
	Compensation of Employees	Capital Consumption	Net Operating Surplus	Indirect Taxes	Less: Subsidies Received	Value Added	Compensation of Employees	Capital Consumption	Net Operating Surplus	Indirect Taxes	Less: Subsidies Received	Value Added
	All Producers											
1 Agriculture, hunting, forestry and fishing	21116	7832	6656	637	280	35961	22144	8286	7693	680	255	38548
A Agriculture and hunting	1063	2154	4630	347	280	7914	1073	2091	4487	329	255	7725
B Forestry and logging	-	-	-	-	-	-	-	-	-	-	-	-
C Fishing	20053	5678	2026	290	-	28048	21071	6195	3206	350	-	30822
2 Mining and quarrying	-	-	-	-	-	-	-	-	-	-	-	-
3 Manufacturing	33774	7704	6230	2728	6280	44155	37996	7686	6030	2829	6344	48197
A Manufacture of food, beverages and tobacco	15501	3956	3185	1461	6108	17995	17532	3989	4463	1596	6329	21252
B Textile, wearing apparel and leather industries	1697	435	6	132	142	2128	1887	232	75	114	-	2308
C Manufacture of wood and wood products, including furniture	1994	249	53	120	-	2416	2252	249	131	116	-	2749
D Manufacture of paper and paper products, printing and publishing	3725	722	811	193	-	5451	4417	739	956	189	15	6286
E Manufacture of chemicals and chemical petroleum, coal, rubber and plastic products	1890	609	781	185	30	3434	2151	699	617	173	-	3640
F Manufacture of non-metallic mineral products, except products of petroleum and coal	1560	406	236	223	-	2423	1846	395	100	194	-	2535
G Basic metal industries	1917	722	-91	90	-	2637	1903	828	-1513	127	-	1345
H Manufacture of fabricated metal products, machinery and equipment	4451	541	806	279	-	6077	4905	486	772	267	-	6430
I Other manufacturing industries	1039	66	444	46	-	1594	1103	68	429	53	-	1653
4 Electricity, gas and water	2730	6775	2262	153	271	11648	2915	6532	2500	203	310	11838
A Electricity, gas and steam	2555	6591	1932	147	271	10954	2736	6273	2033	203	311	10934
B Water works and supply	175	184	330	5	-	694	178	259	467	-	-	904
5 Construction	14099	948	7517	1546	19	24093	16392	1096	6355	739	-	24582
6 Wholesale and retail trade, restaurants and hotels	23880	3571	9207	9371	-	46029	29507	3876	7306	9653	-	50342
A Wholesale and retail trade	19821	2883	8355	9043	-	40102	24223	3246	6737	9424	-	43629
B Restaurants and hotels	4058	689	852	328	-	5927	5284	630	569	229	-	6712
Restaurants	3033	282	555	215	-	4085	4057	210	352	118	-	4737
Hotels and other lodging places	1025	406	297	113	-	1842	1227	420	217	111	-	1975
7 Transport, storage and communication	11511	4204	5672	1329	530	22187	13365	5275	3829	714	723	22460
A Transport and storage	8721	3030	5138	1287	530	17646	10248	3875	3510	714	723	17623
B Communication	2791	1174	534	43	-	4541	3117	1400	319	-	-	4836
8 Finance, insurance, real estate and business services	14362	10476	21573	3688	887	49212	17666	10696	22309	3241	1074	52838
A Financial institutions	6452	1002	7044	802	887	14412	7596	1131	7678	659	1073	15991
B Insurance	1137	146	-1164	192	-	311	1354	163	-860	170	-	827
C Real estate and business services	6773	9329	15694	2694	-	34490	8715	9402	15491	2412	-	36020
9 Community, social and personal services	9684	1224	5993	915	737	17079	10671	1291	7107	681	827	18923
A Sanitary and similar services	...	...	...	...	...	...	...	...	...	...	...	...
B Social and related community services	524	110	2638	108	-	3380	569	91	3055	47	-	3762

Iceland

4.3 Cost Components of Value Added
(Continued)

Million Icelandic kronur

	1990						1991					
	Compensation of Employees	Capital Consumption	Net Operating Surplus	Indirect Taxes	Less: Subsidies Received	Value Added	Compensation of Employees	Capital Consumption	Net Operating Surplus	Indirect Taxes	Less: Subsidies Received	Value Added
Educational services	...	...	...	...	...	...	...	...	...	...	...	...
Medical, dental, other health and veterinary services	524	110	2638	108	-	3380	569	91	3055	47	-	3762
C Recreational and cultural services	2795	569	1734	416	737	4777	3090	713	2060	411	827	5447
D Personal and household services [a]	6365	545	1622	390	1	8921	7011	487	1992	224	-	9714
Total, Industries	131155	42735	65110	20367	9004	250363	150654	44739	63127	18740	9534	267727
Producers of Government Services	41822	2034	94	1332	-	45282	48719	2325	105	-	-	51148
Other Producers	2889	304	-36	107	-	3264	3306	347	-42	67	-	3677
Total	175866	45073	65168	21806	9004	298909	202679	47411	63190	18807	9534	322553
Less: Imputed bank service charge	...	...	12422	...	...	12422	...	...	14352	...	...	14352
Import duties [bc]	...	...	...	53739	1954	51785	...	...	...	61328	738	60590
Value added tax	...	...	...				...	...	...			
Other adjustments [d]	...	...	...	...	...	16107	...	...	...	...	...	15263
Total [e]	175866	45073	52746	75545	10958	354379	202679	47411	48838	80135	10272	384053

a) Item 'Personal and household services' includes also ISIC-code 96, residents directly employed at the NATO-base.
b) Item 'Import duties' includes all indirect taxes and subsidies not directly allocated to specified activities.
c) Beginning 1990, the VAT (Vale Added Tax) was introduced and replacing the former sales tax. The former sales tax was allocated to the industry collecting the tax as far as possible, but after the introduction of VAT, the VAT is unallocated in the item 'Import Duties'.
d) Item 'Other adjustments' includes residual error between production and expenditure approaches.
e) The figures for column 'Capital consumption' are mainly derived from business accounting records and are not consistent with national accounting practices which use perpetual inventory method and a fixed percentage of the remaining value of the stocks of reproducable fixed assets as presented in table 1.3.

India

General note. The preparation of national accounts statistics in India is undertaken by the National Accounts Division of the Central Statistical Organization (CSO), Department of Statistics, Ministry of Planning, New Delhi. Official estimates are published annually in the 'National Accounts Statistics'. The sources of data and methodology followed are given in 'National Accounts Statistics - Sources and Methods', 1989. The estimates are generally in accordance with the classifications and definitions recommended in the United Nations System of National Accounts (SNA). The estimates relate to fiscal year beginning 1 April. Wherever the scope and coverage of the estimates differ for conceptual and statistical reasons from the definitions and classifications recommended in SNA, a footnote has been added to the relevant tables.

Sources and methods:

(a) Gross domestic product. Gross domestic product is estimated mainly through the production approach for the commodity producing sectors and income approach for the services sectors.

(b) Expenditure on the gross domestic product. The expenditure approach is used to estimate government final consumption expenditure, increase in stocks and exports of goods and services. The commodity-flow approach is used to estimate private final consumption expenditure whereas the estimate of gross fixed capital formation is based on the expenditure approach. Estimates of government consumption expenditure are mainly obtained from budget documents and annual reports of the government bodies. Estimates of private expenditure on goods are obtained from commodity production data adjusted for change in stocks and foreign trade and reduced by intermediate consumption and government final consumption and by the quantities used for capital formation. Private expenditure on services is estimated as the value of the total output for each kind of service reduced by the estimated expenditures on service by government and the business. Estimates of increase in stocks for the public sector and organized (i.e. larger or modern) private industries are based on government budget documents and annual accounts and reports of industries respectively. Estimates of change in stocks of unorganized private industries are based on sample survey data, data on bank advances and margins and on livestock censuses. For gross fixed capital formation, estimates of construction are compiled using data from a number of sources such as annual survey of industries, dispatches of cement for domestic consumption, sample surveys and government budget documents and the All-India debt and investment surveys. These estimates are extrapolated by the relevant indicators. For machinery and equipment, estimates are based on the annual survey of industries, foreign trade statistics, customs and excise revenue statements, data on trade, transport and other charges collected from leading manufacturing firms. The estimates of exports and imports of goods and services are based on balance of payment statistics supplemented by information supplied by government agencies. For the constant 1980-81 price estimates, private expenditure on goods is extrapolated by quantity indexes. Changes in stocks of livestock, mining and foodgrains are valued at 1980-81 prices. For government expenditure, private expenditure on services, increase in stock for other sectors and gross fixed capital formation, the current values are deflated by relevant price indexes. Import and export of goods and services are not estimated at constant prices.

(c) Cost-structure of the gross domestic product. Estimates of compensation of employees are based on budget documents, annual reports of enterprises, income and expenditure accounts of institutions and companies and sample surveys. Estimates of operating surplus are based on most of the sources used for compensation of employees. Consumption of fixed capital is estimated for each industry separately on the basis of estimated value of capital stock and the expected age of various types of assets at the aggregate level by following the Perpetual Inventory Method. The sources include the All-India rural debt and investment surveys, livestock censuses, budget documents and annual accounts. Estimates of indirect taxes and subsidies are based on accounts and annual reports of government bodies.

(d) Gross domestic product by kind of economic activity. The table of GDP by kind of economic activity is prepared at factor cost. The production approach is used to estimate value added for all commodity producing sectors and moving the bench-mark estimates for small-scale manufacturing. Value added of construction is based on a combination of the commodity-flow and expenditure approaches. The income approach is used for all other sectors. The production estimates of principal agricultural crops are based on results of the random sample crop-cutting sueveys conducted by the respective state government agencies. The wholesale prices in the primary markets are used to evaluate the total production of each commodity. The annual estimates of livestock products are based on the livestock population by type and the correponding average yield rates. Intermediate consumption is estimated by using a variety of sources such as the National SampleSurvey (NSS), the All-India rural debt and investment survey, and marketing reports. Estimates of the gross output of minerals are based on data available from the Indian Bureau of Mines. For large-scale manufacturing, estimates are prepared for 19 industry groups based on the Annual Surveys of Industries (ASI). Bench-mark estimates for the household and non-household small-scale manufacturing and other unorganised portions of trade, transport etc. have been prepared using data on value added per worker derived from the follow-up surveys of economic census of CSO and NSSO and estimated working force. Other years' estimates are extrapolated by means of indicators of physical output or input and prices. Estimates of pucca construction are compiled by the commodity flow approach using data on steel and cement production, foreign trade statistics, customs and excise revenue, etc. The estimates of kutcha construction are based on expenditure data from NSS, debt and investment surveys and other sources. For public sector trade, transport, administration, banks etc., estimates are based on the analysis of budget documents and annual accounts. The estimates of gross rents for urban and rural dwellings are based on the number of dwellings and estimated gross rental value per dwelling obtained from the NSSO surveys on consumer expenditure. For the constant price estimates, double deflation is used for the agriculture and mining sectors. Current values of large-scale manufacturing and construction are deflated by price indexes. For small-scale manufacturing, electricity, gas and water, trade, transport, ownership of dwellings and other services, value added is extrapolated by quantity indexes. Current price estimates of public administration are deflated with the consumer price index of industrial workers to obtain the constant price estimates.

1.1 Expenditure on the Gross Domestic Product, in Current Prices

Thousand Million Indian rupees — Fiscal year beginning 1 April

		1980	1983	1984	1985	1986	1987	1988	1989	1990	1991	1992	1993
1	Government final consumption expenditure	130.84	211.41	243.52	291.74	346.25	408.43	473.31	542.03	617.79	694.59	785.86	910.52
2	Private final consumption expenditure	981.28	1459.65	1614.55	1768.52	1985.99	2225.51	2574.19	2882.42	3303.71	3815.37	4194.18	4744.49
3	Gross capital formation	284.53	437.90	490.12	634.42	678.99	748.82	970.54	1107.91	1373.91	1408.64	1637.56	1675.53
	A Increase in stocks	21.77	37.99	34.44	91.87	58.47	26.88	113.85	80.16	133.87	40.88	125.78	31.74
	B Gross fixed capital formation a	262.76	399.91	455.68	542.55	620.52	721.94	856.69	1027.75	1240.04	1367.76	1511.78	1643.79
	Residential buildings	31.32	48.55	59.77	68.77	80.80	90.04	101.51	117.72	147.32	168.20	185.04	208.50
	Non-residential buildings	29.32	42.92	49.37	57.74	62.12	72.81	90.94	113.67	137.58	152.30	171.59	186.38
	Other construction and land improvement etc.	75.85	105.02	118.05	148.02	162.81	185.02	222.00	247.53	298.73	351.55	377.40	398.85
	Other	126.27	203.42	228.49	268.02	314.79	374.07	442.24	548.83	656.41	695.71	777.75	850.06
4	Exports of goods and services	90.29	131.39	158.46	149.51	165.43	202.81	259.13	346.09	406.35	562.54	673.12	...
5	Less: Imports of goods and services	135.96	176.75	194.84	217.54	223.59	252.59	320.10	402.12	486.98	562.49	730.00	...
	Statistical discrepancy	9.15	12.29	1.62	-4.22	-23.58	-0.97	0.75	91.88	140.39	241.96	467.57	...
	Equals: Gross Domestic Product	1360.13	2075.89	2313.43	2622.43	2929.49	3332.01	3957.82	4568.21	5355.17	6160.61	7028.29	7863.55

a) Data for gross fixed capital formation are unadjusted for statistical discrepancy and therefore do not coincide with the data shown in the table 'Gross Capital Formation by Kind of Economic Activity of Owners'.

1.2 Expenditure on the Gross Domestic Product, in Constant Prices

Thousand Million Indian rupees — Fiscal year beginning 1 April

		1980	1983	1984	1985	1986	1987	1988	1989	1990	1991	1992	1993
		\multicolumn{12}{c}{At constant prices of: 1980}												
1	Government final consumption expenditure	130.84	157.50	169.83	189.24	208.49	226.60	238.68	252.15	260.59	259.25	267.69	288.32
2	Private final consumption expenditure a	992.92	1150.57	1194.64	1240.54	1302.62	1351.29	1434.68	1497.38	1554.54	1582.04	1603.92	1668.33
3	Gross capital formation	284.53	328.44	334.11	398.47	401.71	417.86	500.08	510.45	580.71	508.92	549.75	528.22
	A Increase in stocks	21.77	32.12	26.27	68.73	41.74	18.31	72.08	45.35	69.54	18.29	51.50	11.26
	B Gross fixed capital formation b	262.76	296.32	307.84	329.74	359.97	399.55	428.00	465.10	511.17	490.63	498.25	516.96

India

1.2 Expenditure on the Gross Domestic Product, in Constant Prices
(Continued)

Thousand Million Indian rupees — Fiscal year beginning 1 April

	1980	1983	1984	1985	1986	1987	1988	1989	1990	1991	1992	1993
					At constant prices of:1980							
Residential buildings	31.32	30.04	32.93	34.35	35.83	36.53	38.55	42.36	36.47	38.06	39.23	40.61
Non-residential buildings	29.32	23.91	23.68	26.88	29.03	31.09	35.87	41.67	47.39	46.53	48.59	48.78
Other construction and land improvement etc.	75.85	71.69	70.57	78.37	81.04	82.83	89.81	86.66	103.72	107.51	105.09	101.78
Other	126.27	170.68	180.66	190.14	214.07	249.10	263.77	294.41	323.59	298.53	305.34	325.79
4 Exports of goods and services	...	...	...	...	...	...	...	...	...	...	...	...
5 Less: Imports of goods and services	...	...	...	...	...	...	...	...	...	...	...	...
Equals: Gross Domestic Product	1360.13	1615.47	1674.89	1766.48	1852.50	1940.85	2133.45	2273.67	2402.61	2414.28	2525.49	2613.20

a) Item 'Private consumption expenditure' refers to expenditure in the domestic market only.
b) Data for gross fixed capital formation are unadjusted for statistical discrepancy and therefore do not coincide with the data shown in the table 'Gross Capital Formation by Kind of Economic Activity of Owners'.

1.3 Cost Components of the Gross Domestic Product

Thousand Million Indian rupees — Fiscal year beginning 1 April

	1980	1983	1984	1985	1986	1987	1988	1989	1990	1991	1992	1993
1 Indirect taxes, net	135.86	208.66	228.10	284.44	329.19	383.50	430.76	481.59	577.20	640.31	751.95	792.10
A Indirect taxes	167.46	264.71	306.40	369.87	427.14	498.47	574.30	667.49	763.29	866.61	956.16	1004.42
B Less: Subsidies	31.60	56.05	78.30	85.43	97.95	114.97	143.54	185.90	186.09	226.30	204.21	212.32
2 Consumption of fixed capital	120.87	192.29	220.91	262.37	298.23	333.41	389.21	456.46	521.95	629.52	722.65	800.69
3 Compensation of employees paid by resident producers to: a	...	...	...	...	...	...	...	...	...	...	...	...
A Resident households	...	...	...	...	...	...	...	...	...	...	...	...
B Rest of the world	0.35	0.72	1.13	1.12	1.78	3.80	3.90	3.32	3.20	2.86	3.47	...
4 Operating surplus	...	...	...	...	...	...	...	...	...	...	...	...
Equals: Gross Domestic Product	1360.13	2075.89	2313.43	2622.43	2929.49	3332.01	3957.82	4568.21	5355.17	6160.61	7028.29	7863.55

a) Item 'Compensation of employees' includes part of net operating surplus of unincorporated enterprises which cannot be separated from labour income of own-account.

1.4 General Government Current Receipts and Disbursements

Thousand Million Indian rupees — Fiscal year beginning 1 April

	1980	1983	1984	1985	1986	1987	1988	1989	1990	1991	1992	1993
					Receipts							
1 Operating surplus	-8.48	-14.93	-15.45	-12.35	-13.13	-13.84	-17.58	-22.69	-25.50	-28.71	-34.47	...
2 Property and entrepreneurial income	17.70	27.78	38.69	42.12	56.87	58.45	60.08	69.64	65.75	116.42	111.01	...
3 Taxes, fees and contributions	206.24	323.32	373.46	448.28	512.25	590.50	694.68	806.08	913.54	1062.63	1195.20	...
A Indirect taxes	167.46	264.71	306.40	369.87	427.14	498.47	574.30	667.49	763.29	866.61	956.16	...
B Direct taxes	35.75	53.55	58.06	65.74	73.28	80.01	103.96	118.88	129.28	174.71	205.95	...
C Social security contributions	...	...	...	...	...	...	...	...	...	...	...	...
D Compulsory fees, fines and penalties	3.03	5.06	9.00	12.67	11.83	12.02	16.42	19.71	20.97	21.31	33.09	...
4 Other current transfers	...	...	...	...	...	...	...	...	...	...	...	...
Total Current Receipts of General Government	215.46	336.17	396.70	478.05	555.99	635.11	737.18	853.03	953.79	1150.34	1271.74	...
					Disbursements							
1 Government final consumption expenditure	130.84	211.41	243.52	291.74	346.25	408.43	473.31	542.03	617.79	694.59	785.86	...
A Compensation of employees	80.37	129.02	149.26	172.03	200.55	241.21	283.67	331.83	382.58	439.14	505.03	...
B Consumption of fixed capital	7.64	13.23	15.78	19.40	22.64	26.23	30.49	35.37	39.01	46.50	53.06	...
C Purchases of goods and services, net	42.83	69.16	78.48	100.31	123.06	140.99	159.15	174.83	196.20	208.95	227.77	...
D Less: Own account fixed capital formation	...	...	...	...	...	...	...	...	...	...	...	...
E Indirect taxes paid, net	...	...	...	...	...	...	...	...	...	...	...	...
2 Property income	15.24	37.39	50.08	61.15	75.92	96.78	118.16	156.67	202.33	262.58	302.80	...

India

1.4 General Government Current Receipts and Disbursements
(Continued)

Thousand Million Indian rupees — Fiscal year beginning 1 April

	1980	1983	1984	1985	1986	1987	1988	1989	1990	1991	1992	1993
A Interest [a]	15.24	37.39	50.08	61.15	75.92	96.78	118.16	156.67	202.33	262.58	302.80	...
B Net land rent and royalties	-	-	-	-	-	-	-	-	-	-	-	...
3 Subsidies	31.60	56.05	78.30	85.43	97.95	114.97	143.54	185.90	186.09	226.30	204.21	...
4 Other current transfers	28.57	46.62	57.75	70.35	87.20	100.16	121.72	141.42	157.17	173.88	200.35	...
Statistical discrepancy [b]	-0.26	0.85	1.43	5.87	8.44	8.68	6.00	1.66	4.69	-4.27	2.13	...
5 Net saving	9.47	-16.15	-34.38	-36.49	-59.77	-93.91	-125.55	-174.65	-214.28	-202.74	-223.61	...
Total Current Disbursements and Net Saving of General Government	215.46	336.17	396.70	478.05	555.99	635.11	737.18	853.03	953.79	1150.34	1271.74	...

a) Item 'Interest' refers to interest on the public debt.
b) Item 'Statistical discrepancy' relates to inter-governmental accounting adjustments. For years prior to 1974, it is included in item 'Net saving'.

1.7 External Transactions on Current Account, Summary

Thousand Million Indian rupees — Fiscal year beginning 1 April

	1980	1983	1984	1985	1986	1987	1988	1989	1990	1991	1992	1993
Payments to the Rest of the World												
1 Imports of goods and services	135.96	176.75	194.84	217.54	223.59	252.59	320.10	402.12	486.98	562.49	730.00	...
A Imports of merchandise c.i.f.	125.58	161.38	188.64	213.15	227.60	258.31	344.82	409.83	503.50	518.64	694.56	...
B Other	10.38	15.37	6.20	4.39	-4.01	-5.72	-24.72	-7.71	-16.52	43.85	35.44	...
2 Factor income to the rest of the world	5.20	14.22	20.26	21.21	24.68	32.22	51.42	65.44	82.95	107.52	128.59	...
A Compensation of employees	0.35	0.72	1.13	1.12	1.78	3.80	3.90	3.32	3.20	2.86	3.47	...
B Property and entrepreneurial income	4.85	13.50	19.13	20.09	22.90	28.42	47.52	62.12	79.75	104.66	125.12	...
3 Current transfers to the rest of the world	0.12	0.11	0.15	0.14	0.15	0.34	0.24	0.26	0.26	0.37	0.35	...
A Indirect taxes to supranational organizations	...	...	...	...	...	...	...	...	...	...	...	...
B Other current transfers	0.12	0.11	0.15	0.14	0.15	0.34	0.24	0.26	0.26	0.37	0.35	...
Statistical discrepancy [a]	-0.06	2.08	15.46	15.06	25.73	34.49	59.67	53.14	68.94	35.67	54.88	...
4 Surplus of the nation on current transactions	-20.94	-25.17	-32.92	-62.34	-63.55	-68.25	-123.04	-122.79	-181.96	-33.77	-138.16	...
Payments to the Rest of the World and Surplus of the Nation on Current Transactions	120.28	167.99	197.79	191.61	210.60	251.39	308.39	398.17	457.17	672.28	775.66	...
Receipts From The Rest of the World												
1 Exports of goods and services	90.29	131.39	158.46	149.51	165.43	202.81	259.13	346.09	406.35	562.54	673.12	...
A Exports of merchandise f.o.b.	65.76	101.68	119.59	115.78	133.15	163.96	206.47	282.29	331.53	449.22	547.62	...
B Other	24.53	29.71	38.87	33.73	32.28	38.85	52.66	63.80	74.82	113.32	125.50	...
2 Factor income from rest of the world	8.65	4.78	6.02	6.92	6.63	6.03	6.46	8.13	7.50	6.75	10.56	...
A Compensation of employees	0.06	0.09	0.12	0.14	0.09	0.17	0.33	1.13	0.74	1.17	0.35	...
B Property and entrepreneurial income	8.59	4.69	5.90	6.78	6.54	5.86	6.13	7.00	6.76	5.58	10.21	...
3 Current transfers from rest of the world	22.69	27.85	31.16	28.35	29.91	35.33	38.65	38.24	37.37	94.19	81.24	...
A Subsidies from supranational organisations	...	...	...	...	...	...	...	...	...	...	...	...
B Other current transfers	22.69	27.85	31.16	28.35	29.91	35.33	38.65	38.24	37.37	94.19	81.24	...
Statistical discrepancy [a]	-1.35	3.97	2.15	6.83	8.63	7.22	4.15	5.71	5.95	8.80	10.74	...
Receipts from the Rest of the World on Current Transactions	120.28	167.99	197.79	191.61	210.60	251.39	308.39	398.17	457.17	672.28	775.66	...

a) Item 'Statistical discrepancy' refers to difference of payment and ownership basis of imports and exports of merchandise.

1.8 Capital Transactions of The Nation, Summary

Thousand Million Indian rupees — Fiscal year beginning 1 April

	1980	1983	1984	1985	1986	1987	1988	1989	1990	1991	1992	1993
Finance of Gross Capital Formation												
Gross saving	287.86	392.94	421.78	519.33	548.01	696.31	852.75	1019.70	1267.93	1420.29	1406.35	1584.93
1 Consumption of fixed capital	120.87	192.29	220.91	262.37	298.23	333.41	389.21	456.46	521.95	629.52	722.65	800.69
A General government	22.25	36.25	42.42	51.30	57.38	64.74	75.12	87.43	95.56	112.41	128.55	143.23
B Corporate and quasi-corporate enterprises	43.70	72.13	83.62	101.89	119.79	134.46	160.85	194.08	228.80	288.45	343.29	389.09
Public	26.70	44.31	51.66	62.58	73.60	84.54	100.41	121.21	141.94	175.30	202.00	219.86

India

1.8 Capital Transactions of The Nation, Summary
(Continued)

Thousand Million Indian rupees — Fiscal year beginning 1 April

	1980	1983	1984	1985	1986	1987	1988	1989	1990	1991	1992	1993
Private [a]	17.00	27.82	31.96	39.31	46.19	49.92	60.44	72.87	86.86	113.15	141.29	169.23
C Other	54.92	83.91	94.87	109.18	121.06	134.21	153.24	174.95	197.59	228.66	250.81	268.37
2 Net saving	166.99	200.65	200.87	256.96	249.78	362.90	463.54	563.24	745.98	790.77	683.70	784.24
A General government	5.79	-17.46	-38.25	-41.85	-66.44	-97.81	-127.41	-174.03	-208.69	-195.93	-214.84	-354.14
B Corporate and quasi-corporate enterprises	-2.36	8.61	16.94	26.41	21.41	28.74	59.76	84.75	83.12	117.32	59.97	152.79
Public	-8.20	4.71	9.43	12.54	15.48	20.76	32.89	39.62	25.55	35.57	-6.78	10.49
Private [a]	5.84	3.90	7.51	13.87	5.93	7.98	26.87	45.13	57.57	81.75	66.75	142.30
C Other	163.56	209.50	222.18	272.40	294.81	431.97	531.19	652.52	871.55	869.38	838.57	985.59
Less: Surplus of the nation on current transactions	-20.94	-25.17	-32.92	-62.34	-63.55	-68.25	-123.04	-122.79	-181.96	-33.77	-138.16	-21.49
Finance of Gross Capital Formation	308.80	418.11	454.70	581.67	611.56	764.56	975.79	1142.49	1449.89	1454.06	1544.51	1606.42
Gross Capital Formation												
Increase in stocks	21.77	37.99	34.44	91.87	58.47	26.88	113.85	80.16	133.87	40.88	125.78	31.74
Gross fixed capital formation	262.76	399.91	455.68	542.55	620.52	721.94	856.69	1027.75	1240.04	1367.76	1511.78	1643.79
1 General government	64.57	97.57	112.45	131.89	143.02	148.94	183.17	181.10	207.01	228.99	274.92	315.00
2 Corporate and quasi-corporate enterprises	87.77	174.25	203.42	243.55	311.46	299.00	336.00	409.62	497.66	701.66	742.85	909.76
A Public	52.36	106.93	121.51	143.12	189.52	196.77	215.49	257.52	294.75	358.15	321.77	345.04
B Private [a]	35.41	67.32	81.91	100.43	121.94	102.23	120.51	152.10	202.91	343.51	421.08	564.72
3 Other	110.42	128.09	139.81	167.11	166.04	274.00	337.52	437.03	535.37	437.11	494.01	419.03
Statistical discrepancy	24.27	-19.79	-35.42	-52.75	-67.43	15.74	5.25	34.58	75.98	45.42	-93.05	-69.11
Gross Capital Formation	308.80	418.11	454.70	581.67	611.56	764.56	975.79	1142.49	1449.89	1454.06	1544.51	1606.42

a) Estimates relate to private corporate sector enterprises only.

1.10 Gross Domestic Product by Kind of Activity, in Current Prices

Thousand Million Indian rupees — Fiscal year beginning 1 April

	1980	1983	1984	1985	1986	1987	1988	1989	1990	1991	1992	1993
1 Agriculture, hunting, forestry and fishing	466.49	674.98	719.50	772.24	824.13	923.79	1140.73	1270.51	1480.01	1728.99	1933.32	2143.82
2 Mining and quarrying	18.87	49.09	54.58	61.98	67.96	70.85	92.08	103.08	117.85	128.75	145.14	169.68
3 Manufacturing	216.44	330.45	372.43	417.75	461.66	528.65	628.63	770.76	891.60	968.81	1113.09	1222.62
4 Electricity, gas and water	20.70	33.62	40.52	48.94	55.67	62.68	73.25	87.23	104.64	127.04	151.45	200.19
5 Construction	61.14	94.21	110.97	129.47	152.17	176.11	206.77	235.86	286.16	323.97	358.33	398.47
6 Wholesale and retail trade, restaurants and hotels	147.13	229.90	266.90	310.50	345.51	384.33	452.22	529.10	618.66	705.33	814.79	919.78
7 Transport, storage and communication	57.24	102.81	118.73	140.98	165.37	199.38	238.72	277.31	339.13	410.64	491.45	575.44
8 Finance, insurance, real estate and business services	107.91	155.91	175.95	198.82	223.09	247.56	282.56	335.77	389.02	475.34	521.50	598.24
9 Community, social and personal services	70.41	103.88	117.39	132.20	155.41	175.68	203.52	235.67	279.81	337.02	385.20	437.19
Total, Industries	1166.33	1774.85	1976.97	2212.88	2450.97	2769.03	3318.48	3845.29	4506.88	5205.89	5914.27	6665.43
Producers of Government Services	57.94	92.38	108.36	125.11	149.33	179.48	208.58	241.33	271.09	314.41	362.07	406.02
Other Producers	...	...	...	...	...	...	...	...	...	...	...	...
Subtotal [a]	1224.27	1867.23	2085.33	2337.99	2600.30	2948.51	3527.06	4086.62	4777.97	5520.30	6276.34	7071.45
Less: Imputed bank service charge [b]	...	...	...	...	...	...	...	...	...	...	...	...
Plus: Import duties	...	...	...	...	...	...	...	...	...	...	...	...
Plus: Value added tax	...	...	...	...	...	...	...	...	...	...	...	...
Plus: Other adjustments [c]	135.86	208.66	228.10	284.44	329.19	383.50	430.76	481.59	577.20	640.31	751.95	792.10
Equals: Gross Domestic Product	1360.13	2075.89	2313.43	2622.43	2929.49	3332.01	3957.82	4568.21	5355.17	6160.61	7028.29	7863.55

a) Gross domestic product in factor values.
b) Imputed bank service charges are adjusted in the respective activity.
c) Item 'Other adjustments' refers to indirect taxes net of subsidies.

1.11 Gross Domestic Product by Kind of Activity, in Constant Prices

Thousand Million Indian rupees — Fiscal year beginning 1 April

	1980	1983	1984	1985	1986	1987	1988	1989	1990	1991	1992	1993
					At constant prices of:1980							
1 Agriculture, hunting, forestry and fishing	466.49	540.80	540.61	542.18	532.81	534.79	622.14	632.63	656.53	641.74	674.25	694.12
2 Mining and quarrying	18.87	24.51	24.86	26.23	29.78	30.80	35.42	38.01	42.07	43.96	44.64	46.77
3 Manufacturing	216.44	273.77	291.53	303.20	324.45	348.18	378.65	422.85	448.63	434.54	448.05	464.21
4 Electricity, gas and water	20.70	25.88	28.63	30.99	34.22	36.92	40.80	45.05	47.97	52.51	56.47	59.82
5 Construction	61.14	65.76	68.28	71.83	75.37	77.77	83.79	88.07	98.33	100.95	101.43	102.65

India

1.11 Gross Domestic Product by Kind of Activity, in Constant Prices
(Continued)

Thousand Million Indian rupees — Fiscal year beginning 1 April

	1980	1983	1984	1985	1986	1987	1988	1989	1990	1991	1992	1993
					At constant prices of:1980							
6 Wholesale and retail trade, restaurants and hotels	147.13	174.17	181.73	196.49	208.52	218.01	233.85	252.31	265.79	267.61	284.97	297.67
7 Transport, storage and communication	57.24	66.92	73.02	79.51	84.83	92.27	98.04	106.63	111.64	118.04	124.53	132.02
8 Finance, insurance, real estate and business services	107.91	128.59	137.14	147.08	159.16	168.71	184.16	204.03	217.24	238.06	245.23	266.09
9 Community, social and personal services	70.41	80.50	84.07	87.99	95.50	98.73	104.34	112.81	121.28	128.45	133.25	140.19
Total, Industries	1166.33	1380.90	1429.87	1485.50	1544.64	1606.18	1781.19	1902.39	2009.48	2025.86	2112.82	2203.54
Producers of Government Services	57.94	67.75	74.46	80.16	88.07	97.04	103.42	112.14	113.28	115.70	121.56	126.88
Other Producers	...	...	...	...	...	...	...	...	...	...	...	...
Subtotal [a]	1224.27	1448.65	1504.33	1565.66	1632.71	1703.22	1884.61	2014.53	2122.76	2141.56	2234.38	2330.42
Less: Imputed bank service charge [b]	...	...	...	...	...	...	...	...	...	...	...	...
Plus: Import duties	...	...	...	...	...	...	...	...	...	...	...	...
Plus: Value added tax	...	...	...	...	...	...	...	...	...	...	...	...
Plus: Other adjustments [c]	135.86	166.82	170.56	200.82	219.79	237.63	248.84	259.14	279.85	272.72	291.11	282.78
Equals: Gross Domestic Product	1360.13	1615.47	1674.89	1766.48	1852.50	1940.85	2133.45	2273.67	2402.61	2414.28	2525.49	2613.20

a) Gross domestic product in factor values.
b) Imputed bank service charges are adjusted in the respective activity.
c) Item 'Other adjustments' refers to indirect taxes net of subsidies.

1.12 Relations Among National Accounting Aggregates

Thousand Million Indian rupees — Fiscal year beginning 1 April

	1980	1983	1984	1985	1986	1987	1988	1989	1990	1991	1992	1993
Gross Domestic Product	1360.13	2075.89	2313.43	2622.43	2929.49	3332.01	3957.82	4568.21	5355.17	6160.61	7028.29	7863.55
Plus: Net factor income from the rest of the world	3.45	-9.44	-14.24	-14.29	-18.05	-26.19	-44.96	-57.31	-75.45	-100.77	-118.03	-118.03
Factor income from the rest of the world	8.65	4.78	6.02	6.92	6.63	6.03	6.46	8.13	7.50	6.75	10.56	10.56
Less: Factor income to the rest of the world	5.20	14.22	20.26	21.21	24.68	32.22	51.42	65.44	82.95	107.52	128.59	128.59
Equals: Gross National Product	1363.58	2066.45	2299.19	2608.14	2911.44	3305.82	3912.86	4510.90	5279.72	6059.84	6910.26	7745.52
Less: Consumption of fixed capital	120.87	192.29	220.91	262.37	298.23	333.41	389.21	456.46	521.95	629.52	722.65	800.69
Equals: National Income	1242.71	1874.16	2078.28	2345.77	2613.21	2972.41	3523.65	4054.44	4757.77	5430.32	6187.61	6944.83
Plus: Net current transfers from the rest of the world	22.57	27.74	31.01	28.21	29.76	34.99	38.41	37.98	37.11	93.82	80.89	80.89
Current transfers from the rest of the world	22.69	27.85	31.16	28.35	29.91	35.33	38.65	38.24	37.37	94.19	81.24	81.24
Less: Current transfers to the rest of the world	0.12	0.11	0.15	0.14	0.15	0.34	0.24	0.26	0.26	0.37	0.35	0.35
Equals: National Disposable Income	1265.28	1901.90	2109.29	2373.98	2642.97	3007.40	3562.06	4092.42	4794.88	5524.14	6268.50	7025.72
Less: Final consumption	1112.12	1671.06	1858.07	2060.26	2332.24	2633.94	3047.50	3424.45	3921.50	4509.96	4980.04	5655.01
Statistical discrepancy	13.83	-30.19	-50.35	-56.76	-60.95	-10.56	-51.02	-104.73	-127.40	-223.41	-604.76	-586.47
Equals: Net Saving [a]	166.99	200.65	200.87	256.96	249.78	362.90	463.54	563.24	745.98	790.77	683.70	784.24
Less: Surplus of the nation on current transactions	-20.94	-25.17	-32.92	-62.34	-63.55	-68.25	-123.04	-122.79	-181.96	-33.77	-138.16	-21.49
Statistical discrepancy	-24.27	19.79	35.42	52.75	67.43	-15.74	-5.25	-34.58	-75.98	-45.42	93.05	69.11
Equals: Net Capital Formation	163.66	245.61	269.21	372.05	380.76	415.41	581.33	651.45	851.96	779.12	914.91	874.84

a) Item 'Net Savings' includes retained earnings of foreign controlled rupee companies and branches of foreign companies in India.

2.1 Government Final Consumption Expenditure by Function, in Current Prices

Thousand Million Indian rupees — Fiscal year beginning 1 April

	1980	1983	1984	1985	1986	1987	1988	1989	1990	1991	1992	1993
1 General public services [a]	25.28	37.64	46.74	53.67	61.40	75.07	87.34	102.39	118.45	142.12	164.55	...
2 Defence	34.61	57.67	66.05	86.55	112.55	133.23	149.98	164.50	176.52	188.02	210.08	...
3 Public order and safety [a]	...	...	...	...	...	...	...	...	...	...	...	...
4 Education	14.11	24.73	28.47	35.54	39.75	45.29	53.23	65.42	79.37	89.66	100.77	...
5 Health	7.45	13.09	15.68	17.44	19.76	22.60	25.84	28.88	35.06	38.08	43.82	...
6 Social security and welfare	3.30	6.72	6.19	6.58	8.35	8.82	12.04	13.99	17.80	20.00	22.04	...
7 Housing and community amenities	2.15	3.19	4.28	5.32	6.21	6.80	7.49	8.62	12.73	13.67	13.94	...
8 Recreational, cultural and religious affairs	1.07	1.75	1.54	1.99	2.47	3.44	3.89	4.37	5.24	4.45	5.13	...
9 Economic services	16.60	25.90	29.18	32.99	39.10	46.82	52.97	61.49	67.84	78.33	86.06	...

India

2.1 Government Final Consumption Expenditure by Function, in Current Prices
(Continued)

Thousand Million Indian rupees — Fiscal year beginning 1 April

	1980	1983	1984	1985	1986	1987	1988	1989	1990	1991	1992	1993
A Fuel and energy	1.47	2.86	3.75	4.13	4.83	6.33	7.76	9.61	10.14	12.29	13.61	...
B Agriculture, forestry, fishing and hunting	6.62	9.85	11.37	11.66	14.22	17.97	19.84	22.00	22.81	26.46	29.38	...
C Mining, manufacturing and construction, except fuel and energy	1.43	2.62	2.98	3.50	3.73	4.20	5.01	5.82	7.28	6.19	6.66	...
D Transportation and communication	4.53	6.41	6.61	8.05	8.88	9.42	11.24	13.79	15.89	19.13	21.87	...
E Other economic affairs	2.55	4.16	4.47	5.65	7.44	8.90	9.12	10.27	11.72	14.26	14.54	...
10 Other functions	1.61	2.23	1.15	1.79	1.17	1.01	2.26	1.26	1.67	0.97	1.98	...
Total Government Final Consumption Expenditure bcd	106.18	172.92	199.28	241.87	290.76	343.08	395.04	450.92	514.68	575.30	648.37	...

a) Item 'Public order and safety' is included in item 'General public services'.
b) Item 'Total government consumption expenditure' includes central and state government but excludes other local authorities. Consumption of fixed capital has also not been accounted for. Therefore, the figures will not tally with figures in table 3.12 to this extent.
c) For series 1, losses of departmental enterprises are treated as consumption expenditure of the government, whereas for series 2, they are treated as losses of the government.
d) For series 1, compensation of employees of the administrative departments includes pension payable to the employees of the departmental enterprises also, whereas in series 2, it has been allocated to the respective departmental enterprises.

2.3 Total Government Outlays by Function and Type

Thousand Million Indian rupees — Fiscal year beginning 1 April

	Final Consumption Expenditures Total	Compensation of Employees	Other	Subsidies	Other Current Transfers & Property Income	Total Current Disbursements	Gross Capital Formation	Other Capital Outlays	Total Outlays
1980									
1 General public services a	25.28	18.28	7.00	0.08	4.40	29.76	2.03	0.65	32.44
2 Defence	34.61	17.46	17.15	0.04	0.08	34.73	0.16	-	34.89
3 Public order and safety a	...	...	...	...	...	...	...	...	...
4 Education	14.11	13.17	0.94	-	23.33	37.44	0.89	0.16	38.49
5 Health	7.45	5.04	2.41	-	1.00	8.45	0.98	-	9.43
6 Social security and welfare	3.30	1.92	1.38	0.14	2.55	5.99	0.35	0.31	6.65
7 Housing and community amenities	2.15	1.31	0.84	-	1.90	4.05	3.64	1.73	9.42
8 Recreation, culture and religion	1.07	0.75	0.32	0.01	0.52	1.60	0.29	0.03	1.92
9 Economic services	16.60	9.46	7.14	31.21	5.97	53.78	14.98	7.62	76.38
A Fuel and energy	1.47	0.81	0.66	1.15	1.24	3.86	3.12	1.82	8.80
B Agriculture, forestry, fishing and hunting	6.62	4.67	1.95	19.80	2.49	28.91	2.95	2.11	33.97
C Mining (except fuels), manufacturing and construction	1.43	1.20	0.23	3.50	0.85	5.78	0.34	1.87	7.99
D Transportation and communication	4.53	0.68	3.85	0.15	0.89	5.57	8.07	1.73	15.37
E Other economic affairs	2.55	2.10	0.45	6.61	0.50	9.66	0.50	0.09	10.25
10 Other functions	1.61	0.18	1.43	0.01	1.10	2.72	0.45	0.21	3.38
Total bc	106.18	67.57	38.61	31.49	40.85	178.52	23.77	10.71	213.00
1985									
1 General public services a	53.67	40.11	13.56	0.03	11.02	64.72	5.03	1.15	70.90
2 Defence	86.55	36.27	50.28	0.07	0.25	86.87	0.25	-	87.12
3 Public order and safety a	...	...	...	...	...	...	...	...	...
4 Education	35.54	32.22	3.32	0.14	49.57	85.25	2.16	0.41	87.82
5 Health	17.44	12.38	5.06	-	2.63	20.07	2.14	0.04	22.25
6 Social security and welfare	6.58	4.40	2.18	2.65	7.91	17.14	0.89	0.36	18.39
7 Housing and community amenities	5.32	3.48	1.84	0.23	4.23	9.78	15.19	6.52	31.49
8 Recreation, culture and religion	1.99	1.08	0.91	-	1.14	3.13	0.46	0.03	3.62
9 Economic services	32.99	19.02	13.97	81.99	11.09	126.07	27.46	13.13	166.66
A Fuel and energy	4.13	1.87	2.26	1.26	1.60	6.99	6.40	3.99	17.38
B Agriculture, forestry, fishing and hunting	11.66	8.96	2.70	40.98	5.05	57.69	5.44	2.90	66.03
C Mining (except fuels), manufacturing and construction	3.50	2.77	0.73	27.33	1.86	32.69	0.88	2.98	36.55
D Transportation and communication	8.05	1.27	6.78	0.62	1.07	9.74	13.94	3.13	26.81
E Other economic affairs	5.65	4.15	1.50	11.80	1.51	18.96	0.80	0.13	19.89
10 Other functions	1.79	0.27	1.52	0.14	4.28	6.21	1.11	0.29	7.61
Total bc	241.87	149.23	92.64	85.25	92.12	419.24	54.69	21.93	495.86

India

2.3 Total Government Outlays by Function and Type
(Continued)

Thousand Million Indian rupees — Fiscal year beginning 1 April

		Final Consumption Expenditures Total	Compensation of Employees	Other	Subsidies	Other Current Transfers & Property Income	Total Current Disbursements	Gross Capital Formation	Other Capital Outlays	Total Outlays
					1990					
1	General public services [a]	118.45	93.65	24.80	0.13	26.19	144.77	10.24	3.57	158.58
2	Defence	176.52	75.37	101.15	0.19	1.12	177.83	0.71	-	178.54
3	Public order and safety [a]	...	...	...	...	...	...	...	...	...
4	Education	79.37	72.54	6.83	-	111.93	191.30	5.33	1.16	197.79
5	Health	35.06	27.68	7.38	0.03	5.90	40.99	3.65	0.41	45.05
6	Social security and welfare	17.80	11.21	6.59	8.13	19.60	45.53	1.06	1.01	47.60
7	Housing and community amenities	12.73	7.33	5.40	0.02	13.33	26.08	16.42	13.91	56.41
8	Recreation, culture and religion	5.24	2.44	2.80	0.01	2.51	7.76	1.25	0.14	9.15
9	Economic services	67.84	41.41	26.43	176.90	29.98	274.72	45.37	37.08	357.17
	A Fuel and energy	10.14	4.55	5.59	7.25	4.93	22.32	6.83	4.57	33.72
	B Agriculture, forestry, fishing and hunting	22.81	17.92	4.89	75.09	15.99	113.89	8.19	24.24	146.32
	C Mining (except fuels), manufacturing and construction	7.28	6.50	0.78	50.19	4.11	61.58	0.97	3.37	65.92
	D Transportation and communication	15.89	3.55	12.34	1.21	2.50	19.60	28.14	4.54	52.28
	E Other economic affairs	11.72	8.89	2.83	43.16	2.45	57.33	1.24	0.36	58.93
10	Other functions	1.67	0.21	1.46	0.15	1.96	3.78	0.64	0.28	4.70
	Total [bc]	514.68	331.84	182.84	185.56	212.52	912.76	84.67	57.56	1054.99
					1991					
1	General public services [a]	142.12	108.83	33.29	0.06	28.31	170.49	10.42	3.79	184.70
2	Defence	188.02	91.05	96.97	0.22	1.00	189.24	1.67	-	190.91
3	Public order and safety [a]	...	...	...	...	...	...	...	...	...
4	Education	89.66	82.63	7.03	0.01	122.66	212.33	5.69	1.01	219.03
5	Health	38.08	29.88	8.20	-	6.71	44.79	3.59	0.48	48.86
6	Social security and welfare	20.00	12.39	7.61	7.85	22.02	49.87	1.83	0.97	52.67
7	Housing and community amenities	13.67	7.70	5.97	0.08	18.12	31.87	18.63	17.11	67.61
8	Recreation, culture and religion	4.45	2.68	1.77	0.02	2.90	7.37	1.36	0.20	8.93
9	Economic services	78.33	46.19	32.14	217.47	34.34	330.14	52.07	32.38	414.59
	A Fuel and energy	12.29	5.23	7.06	46.14	6.21	64.64	9.70	5.43	79.77
	B Agriculture, forestry, fishing and hunting	26.46	21.06	5.40	98.59	14.86	139.91	9.28	20.28	169.47
	C Mining (except fuels), manufacturing and construction	6.19	5.26	0.93	45.76	4.97	56.92	1.23	3.95	62.10
	D Transportation and communication	19.13	4.19	14.94	1.47	3.78	24.38	30.75	2.21	57.34
	E Other economic affairs	14.26	10.45	3.81	25.51	4.52	44.29	1.11	0.51	45.91
10	Other functions	0.97	0.17	0.80	-	1.99	2.96	0.17	0.22	3.35
	Total [bc]	575.30	381.52	193.78	225.71	238.05	1039.06	95.43	56.17	1190.66
					1992					
1	General public services [a]	164.55	127.95	36.60	2.49	32.46	199.50	11.97	2.64	214.11
2	Defence	210.08	101.46	108.62	-	1.29	211.37	1.57	-	212.94
3	Public order and safety [a]	...	...	...	...	...	...	...	...	...
4	Education	100.77	94.30	6.47	-	139.97	240.74	5.64	1.08	247.46
5	Health	43.82	34.75	9.07	-	8.28	52.10	3.82	0.25	56.17
6	Social security and welfare	22.04	14.58	7.46	7.16	25.05	54.25	1.61	1.36	57.22
7	Housing and community amenities	13.94	8.84	5.10	0.03	18.52	32.49	22.67	19.44	74.60
8	Recreation, culture and religion	5.13	3.03	2.10	0.03	3.04	8.20	1.49	0.19	9.88
9	Economic services	86.06	53.08	32.98	193.74	42.74	322.54	59.02	40.01	421.57

India

2.3 Total Government Outlays by Function and Type
(Continued)

Thousand Million Indian rupees — Fiscal year beginning 1 April

	Final Consumption Expenditures Total	Compensation of Employees	Other	Subsidies	Other Current Transfers & Property Income	Total Current Disbursements	Gross Capital Formation	Other Capital Outlays	Total Outlays
A Fuel and energy	13.61	6.24	7.37	17.27	6.00	36.88	11.00	10.00	57.88
B Agriculture, forestry, fishing and hunting	29.38	23.89	5.49	106.86	15.45	151.69	10.51	23.08	185.28
C Mining (except fuels), manufacturing and construction	6.66	6.12	0.54	56.63	10.05	73.34	1.04	3.30	77.68
D Transportation and communication	21.87	4.83	17.04	2.95	4.32	29.14	35.27	3.08	67.49
E Other economic affairs	14.54	12.00	2.54	10.03	6.92	31.49	1.20	0.55	33.24
10 Other functions	1.98	0.21	1.77	0.09	2.50	4.57	0.24	0.13	4.94
Total bc	648.37	438.20	210.17	203.54	273.85	1125.76	108.03	65.10	1298.89

a) Item 'Public order and safety' is included in item 'General public services'. Therefore, the figures will not tally with figures in table 3.12 to this extent.
b) Item 'Total government consumption expenditure' includes central and state government but excludes other local authorities. Consumption of fixed capital has also not been accounted for.
c) For series 1, losses of departmental enterprises are treated as consumption expenditure of the government, whereas for series 2, they are treated as losses of the government.

2.5 Private Final Consumption Expenditure by Type and Purpose, in Current Prices

Thousand Million Indian rupees — Fiscal year beginning 1 April

	1980	1983	1984	1985	1986	1987	1988	1989	1990	1991	1992	1993
Final Consumption Expenditure of Resident Households												
1 Food, beverages and tobacco	574.73	842.43	921.03	977.11	1084.88	1206.44	1385.92	1524.47	1737.56	2068.13	2275.08	2539.46
A Food	536.58	789.53	864.87	919.00	1021.88	1138.23	1307.11	1432.90	1632.90	1951.25	2144.78	2400.73
B Non-alcoholic beverages	0.63	1.01	1.12	1.46	1.82	1.99	2.31	2.84	3.37	4.21	4.44	5.62
C Alcoholic beverages	12.34	19.75	22.74	24.48	25.73	25.38	25.68	25.45	27.22	29.33	30.43	33.77
D Tobacco	25.18	32.14	32.30	32.17	35.45	40.84	50.82	63.28	74.07	83.34	95.43	99.34
2 Clothing and footwear	111.41	157.67	174.88	205.66	228.41	248.92	289.10	326.29	371.48	386.16	390.52	470.46
3 Gross rent, fuel and power	125.00	176.02	195.36	214.33	239.84	266.84	293.00	324.24	356.41	391.69	427.59	473.75
A Fuel and power	46.12	71.24	78.41	85.23	98.13	112.68	124.75	136.52	150.11	164.27	176.98	200.78
B Other	78.88	104.78	116.95	129.10	141.71	154.16	168.25	187.72	206.30	227.42	250.61	272.97
4 Furniture, furnishings and household equipment and operation	37.60	59.46	65.67	77.85	87.31	97.95	113.76	140.58	157.91	167.01	182.28	200.17
A Household operation	15.06	22.95	24.00	30.11	34.41	41.54	45.12	53.41	60.30	68.05	81.93	90.48
B Other	22.54	36.51	41.67	47.74	52.90	56.41	68.64	87.17	97.61	98.96	100.35	109.69
5 Medical care and health expenses	29.70	46.66	48.29	50.89	53.55	59.23	72.64	76.22	82.61	90.29	98.68	109.89
6 Transport and communication	51.07	96.45	112.61	133.10	166.05	199.42	243.28	279.88	356.75	444.72	531.44	622.25
A Personal transport equipment	2.74	6.76	7.84	9.84	11.31	11.02	13.66	14.20	16.95	18.84	20.40	22.10
B Other	48.33	89.69	104.77	123.26	154.74	188.40	229.62	265.68	339.80	425.88	511.04	600.15
7 Recreational, entertainment, education and cultural services	29.85	42.69	48.20	53.47	63.25	73.00	88.51	100.36	118.14	133.32	151.49	168.38
A Education	17.25	23.54	25.48	25.29	33.41	40.03	46.35	55.57	69.90	79.33	89.87	102.42
B Other	12.60	19.15	22.72	28.18	29.84	32.97	42.16	44.79	48.24	53.99	61.62	65.96
8 Miscellaneous goods and services	33.56	48.10	54.86	65.17	76.69	88.81	103.72	128.68	142.78	166.67	188.47	211.50
A Personal care	10.49	12.62	14.48	17.01	22.78	26.64	28.79	38.30	38.32	36.85	42.33	42.47
B Expenditures in restaurants, cafes and hotels	8.72	13.70	15.27	17.42	19.21	21.61	26.12	31.22	36.13	41.82	48.13	54.73
C Other	14.35	21.78	25.11	30.74	34.70	40.56	48.81	59.16	68.33	88.00	98.01	114.30
Total Final Consumption Expenditure in the Domestic Market by Households, of which	992.92	1469.48	1620.90	1777.58	1999.98	2240.61	2589.93	2900.72	3323.64	3847.99	4245.55	4795.86
A Durable goods	15.07	23.66	28.56	38.26	47.29	50.83	61.30	72.84	79.26	77.71	84.04	86.95
B Semi-durable goods	127.79	187.52	207.92	242.03	269.77	296.32	347.34	404.00	458.37	477.07	484.16	570.89
C Non-durable goods	673.78	997.81	1088.84	1165.04	1301.93	1458.71	1679.45	1846.55	2109.95	2498.89	2766.12	3094.42

India

2.5 Private Final Consumption Expenditure by Type and Purpose, in Current Prices
(Continued)

Thousand Million Indian rupees — Fiscal year beginning 1 April

	1980	1983	1984	1985	1986	1987	1988	1989	1990	1991	1992	1993
D Services	176.28	260.49	295.58	332.25	380.99	434.75	501.84	577.33	676.06	794.32	911.23	1043.60
Plus: Direct purchases abroad by resident households	0.85	2.28	3.68	3.98	3.41	4.67	5.94	6.09	6.49	16.59	11.18	11.18
Less: Direct purchases in the domestic market by non-resident households	12.49	12.11	10.03	13.04	17.40	19.77	21.68	24.39	26.42	49.21	62.55	62.55
Equals: Final Consumption Expenditure of Resident Households [a]	981.28	1459.65	1614.55	1768.52	1985.99	2225.51	2574.19	2882.42	3303.71	3815.37	4194.18	4744.49

Final Consumption Expenditure of Private Non-profit Institutions Serving Households

Equals: Final Consumption Expenditure of Private Non-profit Organisations Serving Households	...	...	...	...	...	...	...	...	...	...	...	...
Private Final Consumption Expenditure	981.28	1459.65	1614.55	1768.52	1985.99	2225.51	2574.19	2882.42	3303.71	3815.37	4194.18	4744.49

a) Item 'Final consumption expenditure of resident households' includes consumption expenditure of private non-profit institutions serving households.

2.6 Private Final Consumption Expenditure by Type and Purpose, in Constant Prices

Thousand Million Indian rupees — Fiscal year beginning 1 April

At constant prices of: 1980

Final Consumption Expenditure of Resident Households

	1980	1983	1984	1985	1986	1987	1988	1989	1990	1991	1992	1993
1 Food, beverages and tobacco	574.73	649.79	675.23	683.77	701.05	720.21	758.16	777.52	800.85	825.16	832.57	851.16
A Food	536.58	605.79	630.50	642.36	659.25	680.38	717.21	735.15	760.73	783.28	790.20	808.56
B Non-alcoholic beverages	0.63	0.81	0.92	1.06	1.27	1.09	1.18	1.40	1.55	1.54	1.55	1.68
C Alcoholic beverages	12.34	17.37	19.20	19.47	19.76	16.26	15.86	15.35	15.26	15.46	15.27	15.24
D Tobacco	25.18	25.82	24.61	20.88	20.77	22.48	23.91	25.62	23.31	24.88	25.55	25.68
2 Clothing and footwear	111.41	136.68	138.77	150.99	159.92	163.84	180.63	183.84	190.62	179.63	169.74	187.79
3 Gross rent, fuel and power	125.00	138.56	143.80	148.86	155.05	161.02	167.33	173.33	179.23	185.81	192.23	199.63
A Fuel and power	46.12	51.44	53.82	55.92	59.04	61.82	64.83	67.40	69.74	72.62	75.20	78.62
B Other	78.88	87.12	89.98	92.94	96.01	99.20	102.50	105.93	109.49	113.19	117.03	121.01
4 Furniture, furnishings and household equipment and operation	37.60	52.08	51.53	58.47	62.97	64.24	65.55	73.96	77.71	74.96	76.36	78.64
A Household operation	15.06	19.73	18.18	21.44	22.68	23.40	24.09	28.15	30.29	30.67	33.22	34.80
B Other	22.54	32.35	33.35	37.03	40.29	40.84	41.46	45.81	47.42	44.29	43.14	43.84
5 Medical care and health expenses	29.70	31.68	32.34	33.03	33.70	34.41	35.18	35.98	36.72	37.53	38.19	38.90
6 Transport and communication	51.07	69.72	76.15	81.78	94.87	103.86	113.97	125.57	137.26	145.99	157.05	168.48
A Personal transport equipment	2.74	5.72	6.27	6.86	7.56	6.99	7.75	7.48	8.32	8.64	8.89	9.47
B Other	48.33	64.00	69.88	74.92	87.31	96.87	106.22	118.09	128.94	137.35	148.16	159.01
7 Recreational, entertainment, education and cultural services	29.85	33.51	35.38	37.72	43.08	46.65	52.14	54.87	58.73	58.28	60.23	62.15
A Education	17.25	17.25	17.53	16.25	19.77	21.72	23.10	26.05	29.41	29.41	30.41	32.25
B Other	12.60	16.26	17.85	21.47	23.31	24.93	29.04	28.82	29.32	28.87	29.82	29.90
8 Miscellaneous goods and services	33.56	38.55	41.44	45.92	51.98	57.06	61.72	72.31	73.42	74.68	77.55	81.58
A Personal care	10.49	10.97	11.81	13.11	17.13	19.68	19.86	24.94	24.40	20.82	21.43	21.04
B Expenditures in restaurants, cafes and hotels	8.72	10.60	10.86	11.53	12.12	12.79	14.01	15.51	16.41	16.73	17.74	18.72
C Other	14.35	16.98	18.77	21.28	22.73	24.59	27.85	31.86	32.61	37.13	38.38	41.82
Total Final Consumption Expenditure in the Domestic Market by Households, of which	992.92	1150.57	1194.64	1240.54	1302.62	1351.29	1434.68	1497.38	1554.54	1582.04	1603.92	1668.33
A Durable goods	15.07	21.10	23.21	29.61	35.49	37.80	41.91	46.18	47.02	42.10	42.70	42.24
B Semi-durable goods	127.79	163.33	166.49	180.35	193.87	198.67	215.67	224.34	232.95	220.90	210.12	228.39
C Non-durable goods	673.78	765.77	794.11	810.34	838.37	865.80	913.33	942.33	974.33	1004.64	1022.40	1051.71

India

2.6 Private Final Consumption Expenditure by Type and Purpose, in Constant Prices
(Continued)

Thousand Million Indian rupees — Fiscal year beginning 1 April

	1980	1983	1984	1985	1986	1987	1988	1989	1990	1991	1992	1993
					At constant prices of: 1980							
D Services	176.28	200.37	210.83	220.24	234.89	249.02	263.77	284.53	300.24	314.40	328.70	345.99
Plus: Direct purchases abroad by resident households	...	...	...	...	...	...	...	...	...	...	...	...
Less: Direct purchases in the domestic market by non-resident households	...	...	...	...	...	...	...	...	...	...	...	...
Equals: Final Consumption Expenditure of Resident Households	...	...	...	...	...	...	...	...	...	...	...	...

Final Consumption Expenditure of Private Non-profit Institutions Serving Households

	1980	1983	1984	1985	1986	1987	1988	1989	1990	1991	1992	1993
Equals: Final Consumption Expenditure of Private Non-profit Organisations Serving Households	...	...	...	...	...	...	...	...	...	...	...	...
Private Final Consumption Expenditure	...	...	...	1240.54	1302.62	1351.29	1434.68	1497.38	1554.54	1582.04	1603.92	1668.33

2.7 Gross Capital Formation by Type of Good and Owner, in Current Prices

Thousand Million Indian rupees — Fiscal year beginning 1 April

	1980 TOTAL	1980 Total Private	1980 Public Enterprises	1980 General Government	1985 TOTAL	1985 Total Private	1985 Public Enterprises	1985 General Government	1990 TOTAL	1990 Total Private	1990 Public Enterprises	1990 General Government
Increase in stocks, total	21.77	21.03	2.57	-1.83	91.87	72.71	17.41	1.75	133.87	114.13	18.73	1.01
1 Goods producing industries	4.40	...	...	...	35.07	...	...	...	50.97	...	...	...
A Materials and supplies	...	...	...	...	...	...	...	...	...	...	...	...
B Work in progress	...	...	...	...	...	...	...	...	...	...	...	...
C Livestock, except breeding stocks, dairy cattle, etc.	1.20	...	...	...	2.59	...	...	...	1.91	...	...	...
D Finished goods	...	...	...	...	...	...	...	...	...	...	...	...
2 Wholesale and retail trade	15.85	...	...	...	57.02	...	...	...	77.50	...	...	...
3 Other, except government stocks	1.90	...	...	...	-1.18	...	...	...	4.55	...	...	...
4 Government stocks	-0.38	...	...	...	0.96	...	...	...	0.85	...	...	...
Gross Fixed Capital Formation, Total [ab]	262.76	145.83	52.36	64.57	542.55	267.54	143.12	131.89	1240.04	738.28	294.75	207.01
1 Residential buildings	31.32	29.62	-	1.70	68.77	63.69	-	5.08	147.32	141.16	-	6.16
2 Non-residential buildings [c]	29.32	16.66	5.40	7.26	57.74	28.39	15.55	13.80	137.58	85.74	26.49	25.35
3 Other construction	75.85	21.21	10.00	44.64	148.02	29.49	31.09	87.44	298.73	101.87	63.90	132.96
4 Land improvement and plantation and orchard development	...	...	...	...	...	...	...	...	...	...	...	...
5 Producers' durable goods	124.94	77.01	36.96	10.97	264.96	142.91	96.48	25.57	651.29	404.39	204.36	42.54
A Transport equipment	30.41	21.46	4.95	4.00	62.86	47.69	7.55	7.62	163.31	124.63	26.83	11.85
B Machinery and equipment	94.53	55.55	32.01	6.97	202.10	95.22	88.93	17.95	487.98	279.76	177.53	30.69
6 Breeding stock, dairy cattle, etc.	1.33	1.33	-	-	3.06	3.06	-	-	5.12	5.12	...	...
Statistical discrepancy	24.27	...	...	...	-52.75	...	...	...	75.98	...	...	...
Total Gross Capital Formation	308.80	166.86	54.93	62.74	581.67	340.25	160.53	133.64	1449.89	852.41	313.48	208.02

	1991 TOTAL	1991 Total Private	1991 Public Enterprises	1991 General Government	1992 TOTAL	1992 Total Private	1992 Public Enterprises	1992 General Government	1993 TOTAL	1993 Total Private	1993 Public Enterprises	1993 General Government
Increase in stocks, total	40.88	62.98	-19.00	-3.10	125.78	98.91	27.01	-0.14	31.74	-6.41	36.25	1.90
1 Goods producing industries	-8.17	...	...	...	13.01	...	...	...	-11.41	...	...	...
A Materials and supplies	...	...	...	...	...	...	...	...	...	...	...	...
B Work in progress	...	...	...	...	...	...	...	...	...	...	...	...
C Livestock, except breeding stocks, dairy cattle, etc.	2.19	...	...	...	2.50	...	...	...	2.89	...	...	...
D Finished goods	...	...	...	...	...	...	...	...	...	...	...	...
2 Wholesale and retail trade	50.91	...	...	...	107.94	...	...	...	38.92	...	...	...
3 Other, except government stocks	-1.66	...	...	...	4.13	...	...	...	3.61	...	...	...
4 Government stocks	-0.20	...	...	...	0.70	...	...	...	0.62	...	...	...
Gross Fixed Capital Formation, Total [ab]	1367.76	780.62	358.15	228.99	1511.78	915.09	321.77	274.92	1643.79	983.75	345.04	315.00
1 Residential buildings	168.20	159.54	-	8.66	185.04	175.39	-	9.65	208.50	197.29	-	11.21
2 Non-residential buildings [c]	152.30	100.79	24.26	27.25	171.59	116.46	24.78	30.35	186.38	123.00	28.36	35.02

India

2.7 Gross Capital Formation by Type of Good and Owner, in Current Prices
(Continued)

Thousand Million Indian rupees — Fiscal year beginning 1 April

	1991 TOTAL	Total Private	Public Enterprises	General Government	1992 TOTAL	Total Private	Public Enterprises	General Government	1993 TOTAL	Total Private	Public Enterprises	General Government
3 Other construction	351.55	110.96	93.08	147.51	377.40	125.68	73.83	177.89	398.85	123.90	80.10	194.85
4 Land improvement and plantation and orchard development	...	...	...	...	...	...	...	...	...	...	...	...
5 Producers' durable goods	690.27	403.89	240.81	45.57	771.61	491.42	223.16	57.03	843.20	532.70	236.58	73.92
A Transport equipment	167.91	119.42	35.40	13.09	191.27	144.94	26.44	19.89	222.79	172.39	27.90	22.50
B Machinery and equipment	522.36	284.47	205.41	32.48	580.34	346.48	196.72	37.14	620.41	360.31	208.68	51.42
6 Breeding stock, dairy cattle, etc.	5.44	5.44	...	...	6.14	6.14	...	...	6.86	6.86	...	...
Statistical discrepancy	45.42	...	...	...	-93.05	...	...	...	-69.11	...	...	...
Total Gross Capital Formation	1454.06	843.60	339.15	225.89	1544.51	1014.00	348.78	274.78	1606.42	977.34	381.29	316.90

a) Gross fixed capital formation by kind of activity and by type of goods are prepared independently and therefore, do not always tally.
b) Data for gross fixed capital formation are unadjusted for statistical discrepancy and therefore do not coincide with the data shown in the table 'Gross Capital Formation by Kind of Economic Activity of Owners'.
c) Item 'Non-residential buildings' includes residential house construction of public enterprises and the private corporate sector.

2.8 Gross Capital Formation by Type of Good and Owner, in Constant Prices

Thousand Million Indian rupees — Fiscal year beginning 1 April

	1980 TOTAL	Total Private	Public Enterprises	General Government	1985 TOTAL	Total Private	Public Enterprises	General Government	1990 TOTAL	Total Private	Public Enterprises	General Government
					At constant prices of: 1980							
Increase in stocks, total	21.77	21.03	2.57	-1.83	68.73	54.49	12.96	1.28	69.54	59.67	9.40	0.47
1 Goods producing industries	4.40	...	...	...	25.84	...	...	...	26.03	...	...	...
A Materials and supplies	...	...	...	...	...	...	...	...	...	...	...	...
B Work in progress	...	...	...	...	...	...	...	...	...	...	...	...
C Livestock, except breeding stocks, dairy cattle, etc.	1.20	...	...	...	1.61	...	...	...	0.73	...	...	...
D Finished goods	...	...	...	...	...	...	...	...	...	...	...	...
2 Wholesale and retail trade	15.85	...	...	...	43.03	...	...	...	40.85	...	...	...
3 Other, except government stocks	1.90	...	...	...	-0.84	...	...	...	2.23	...	...	...
4 Government stocks	-0.38	...	...	...	0.70	...	...	...	0.43	...	...	...
Gross Fixed Capital Formation, Total ab	262.76	145.83	52.36	64.57	329.74	158.94	94.24	76.56	511.17	305.16	126.68	79.33
1 Residential buildings	31.32	29.62	-	1.70	34.35	31.79	-	2.56	36.47	34.35	-	2.12
2 Non-residential buildings c	29.32	16.66	5.40	7.26	26.88	11.70	8.04	7.14	47.39	29.53	9.07	8.79
3 Other construction	75.85	21.21	10.00	44.64	78.37	12.15	17.79	48.43	103.72	35.19	21.54	46.99
4 Land improvement and plantation and orchard development	...	...	...	...	...	...	...	...	...	...	...	...
5 Producers' durable goods	124.94	77.01	36.96	10.97	188.15	101.31	68.41	18.43	322.09	204.59	96.07	21.43
A Transport equipment	30.41	21.46	4.95	4.00	47.71	36.99	5.34	5.38	79.81	62.04	12.31	5.46
B Machinery and equipment	94.53	55.55	32.01	6.97	140.44	64.32	63.07	13.05	242.28	142.55	83.76	15.97
6 Breeding stock, dairy cattle, etc.	1.33	1.33	-	-	1.99	1.99	-	-	1.50	1.50	...	...
Statistical discrepancy	24.27	...	...	...	-32.06	...	...	...	31.32	...	...	...
Total Gross Capital Formation	308.80	166.86	54.93	62.74	366.41	213.43	107.20	77.84	612.03	364.83	136.08	79.80

	1991 TOTAL	Total Private	Public Enterprises	General Government	1992 TOTAL	Total Private	Public Enterprises	General Government	1993 TOTAL	Total Private	Public Enterprises	General Government
					At constant prices of: 1980							
Increase in stocks, total	18.29	27.99	-8.32	-1.38	51.50	40.51	11.14	-0.15	11.26	-2.82	13.34	0.74
1 Goods producing industries	-4.12	...	...	...	5.12	...	...	...	-4.62	...	...	...
A Materials and supplies	...	...	...	...	...	...	...	...	...	...	...	...
B Work in progress	...	...	...	...	...	...	...	...	...	...	...	...
C Livestock, except breeding stocks, dairy cattle, etc.	0.76	...	...	...	0.83	...	...	...	0.91	...	...	...
D Finished goods	...	...	...	...	...	...	...	...	...	...	...	...
2 Wholesale and retail trade	23.23	...	...	...	44.44	...	...	...	14.30	...	...	...
3 Other, except government stocks	-0.73	...	...	...	1.66	...	...	...	1.35	...	...	...
4 Government stocks	-0.09	...	...	...	0.28	...	...	...	0.23	...	...	...
Gross Fixed Capital Formation, Total ab	490.63	280.60	132.98	77.05	498.25	304.75	107.84	85.66	516.96	312.56	111.53	92.87

India

2.8 Gross Capital Formation by Type of Good and Owner, in Constant Prices
(Continued)

Thousand Million Indian rupees — Fiscal year beginning 1 April

	1991 TOTAL	1991 Total Private	1991 Public Enterprises	1991 General Government	1992 TOTAL	1992 Total Private	1992 Public Enterprises	1992 General Government	1993 TOTAL	1993 Total Private	1993 Public Enterprises	1993 General Government
				At constant prices of:1980								
1 Residential buildings	38.06	35.42	-	2.64	39.23	36.52	-	2.71	40.61	37.68	-	2.93
2 Non-residential buildings c	46.53	30.84	7.34	8.35	48.59	33.08	6.88	8.63	48.78	32.25	7.27	9.26
3 Other construction	107.51	34.18	27.72	45.61	105.09	35.80	19.05	50.24	101.78	32.53	18.72	50.53
4 Land improvement and plantation and orchard development	...	...	...	...	...	...	...	...	...	...	...	...
5 Producers' durable goods	296.75	178.38	97.92	20.45	303.28	197.29	81.91	24.08	323.39	207.70	85.54	30.15
A Transport equipment	73.54	53.60	14.55	5.39	78.14	60.47	10.08	7.59	89.35	70.45	10.53	8.37
B Machinery and equipment	223.21	124.78	83.37	15.06	225.14	136.82	71.83	16.49	234.04	137.25	75.01	21.78
6 Breeding stock, dairy cattle, etc.	1.78	1.78	...	...	2.06	2.06	...	...	2.40	2.40	...	...
Statistical discrepancy	16.29	...	...	...	-30.67	...	...	...	-21.73	...	...	...
Total Gross Capital Formation	525.21	308.59	124.66	75.67	519.08	345.26	118.98	85.51	506.49	309.74	124.87	93.61

a) Gross fixed capital formation by kind of activity and by type of goods are prepared independently and therefore, do not always tally.
b) Data for gross fixed capital formation are unadjusted for statistical discrepancy and therefore do not coincide with the data shown in the table 'Gross Capital Formation by Kind of Economic Activity of Owners'.
c) Item 'Non-residential buildings' includes residential house construction of public enterprises and the private corporate sector.

2.9 Gross Capital Formation by Kind of Activity of Owner, ISIC Major Divisions, in Current Prices

Thousand Million Indian rupees — Fiscal year beginning 1 April

	1980 Total Gross Capital Formation	1980 Increase in Stocks	1980 Gross Fixed Capital Formation	1985 Total Gross Capital Formation	1985 Increase in Stocks	1985 Gross Fixed Capital Formation	1990 Total Gross Capital Formation	1990 Increase in Stocks	1990 Gross Fixed Capital Formation	1991 Total Gross Capital Formation	1991 Increase in Stocks	1991 Gross Fixed Capital Formation
					All Producers							
1 Agriculture, hunting, fishing and forestry	48.64	0.99	47.65	75.88	4.11	71.77	128.52	3.43	125.09	142.26	1.95	140.31
2 Mining and quarrying	9.62	0.10	9.52	40.28	2.51	37.77	66.26	1.61	64.65	63.36	2.11	61.25
3 Manufacturing	48.44	-1.33	49.77	142.03	20.64	121.39	305.77	44.00	261.77	277.13	-13.62	290.75
4 Electricity, gas and water	31.70	2.76	28.94	70.64	3.04	67.60	144.06	-0.19	144.25	188.95	0.13	188.82
5 Construction	6.96	1.88	5.08	12.62	4.77	7.85	22.11	2.12	19.99	18.76	1.26	17.50
6 Wholesale and retail trade, restaurants and hotels	23.25	15.85	7.40	73.45	57.07	16.38	115.46	77.54	37.92	90.14	50.89	39.25
7 Transport, storage and communication	29.07	1.82	27.25	60.44	-1.45	61.89	143.33	3.95	139.38	160.45	-1.60	162.05
8 Finance, insurance, real estate and business services	33.11	0.07	33.04	74.25	-0.04	74.29	178.21	0.10	178.11	216.96	0.16	216.80
9 Community, social and personal services	5.53	0.01	5.52	14.06	0.26	13.80	26.52	0.46	26.06	26.05	-0.20	26.25
Total Industries a	236.32	22.15	214.17	563.65	90.91	472.74	1130.24	133.02	997.22	1184.06	41.08	1142.98
Producers of Government Services	21.62	-0.38	22.00	48.03	0.96	47.07	75.13	0.85	74.28	82.27	-0.20	82.47
Private Non-Profit Institutions Serving Households	...	...	...	...	...	...	...	...	...	...	...	...
Statistical discrepancy	50.86	...	...	-30.01	...	...	244.52	...	...	187.73	...	...
Total ab	308.80	21.77	236.17	581.67	91.87	519.81	1449.89	133.87	1071.50	1454.06	40.88	1225.45

	1992 Total Gross Capital Formation	1992 Increase in Stocks	1992 Gross Fixed Capital Formation	1993 Total Gross Capital Formation	1993 Increase in Stocks	1993 Gross Fixed Capital Formation
			All Producers			
1 Agriculture, hunting, fishing and forestry	159.65	2.98	156.67	173.68	1.08	172.60
2 Mining and quarrying	65.81	2.12	63.69	66.97	-2.91	69.88
3 Manufacturing	332.32	9.37	322.95	345.89	-10.01	355.90
4 Electricity, gas and water	186.83	-3.19	190.02	210.85	1.13	209.72

India

2.9 Gross Capital Formation by Kind of Activity of Owner, ISIC Major Divisions, in Current Prices
(Continued)

Thousand Million Indian rupees — Fiscal year beginning 1 April

		1992			1993		
		Total Gross Capital Formation	Increase in Stocks	Gross Fixed Capital Formation	Total Gross Capital Formation	Increase in Stocks	Gross Fixed Capital Formation
5	Construction	21.65	1.73	19.92	22.36	-0.70	23.06
6	Wholesale and retail trade, restaurants and hotels	150.19	108.29	41.90	85.94	38.77	47.17
7	Transport, storage and communication	197.48	3.65	193.83	220.65	3.44	217.21
8	Finance, insurance, real estate and business services	228.54	0.08	228.46	248.19	0.12	248.07
9	Community, social and personal services	29.48	0.05	29.43	34.80	0.20	34.60
	Total Industries [a]	1371.95	125.08	1246.87	1409.33	31.12	1378.21
	Producers of Government Services	95.84	0.70	95.14	108.54	0.62	107.92
	Private Non-Profit Institutions Serving Households	...	...	...	...	...	...
	Statistical discrepancy	76.72	...	...	88.55	...	...
	Total [ab]	1544.51	125.78	1342.01	1606.42	31.74	1486.13

a) Gross fixed capital formation by kind of activity and by type of goods are prepared independently and therefore, do not always tally.
b) The estimates of 'Increase in stocks' and 'Gross fixed capital formation' (columns 2 and 3, respectively) are unadjusted for statistical discrepancy and therefore, do not add up to 'Gross capital formation' (column 1).

2.10 Gross Capital Formation by Kind of Activity of Owner, ISIC Major Divisions, in Constant Prices

Thousand Million Indian rupees — Fiscal year beginning 1 April

		1980			1985			1990			1991		
		Total Gross Capital Formation	Increase in Stocks	Gross Fixed Capital Formation	Total Gross Capital Formation	Increase in Stocks	Gross Fixed Capital Formation	Total Gross Capital Formation	Increase in Stocks	Gross Fixed Capital Formation	Total Gross Capital Formation	Increase in Stocks	Gross Fixed Capital Formation

At constant prices of: 1980 — All Producers

1	Agriculture, hunting, fishing and forestry	48.64	0.99	47.65	46.46	2.72	43.74	50.74	1.49	49.25	49.80	0.65	49.15
2	Mining and quarrying	9.62	0.10	9.52	26.52	1.82	24.70	28.45	0.95	27.50	23.80	1.11	22.69
3	Manufacturing	48.44	-1.33	49.77	94.13	16.25	77.88	139.23	22.89	116.34	107.06	-6.36	113.42
4	Electricity, gas and water	31.70	2.76	28.94	45.65	2.44	43.21	61.50	-0.11	61.61	69.32	0.06	69.26
5	Construction	6.96	1.88	5.08	7.99	2.61	5.38	10.39	0.81	9.58	7.69	0.42	7.27
6	Wholesale and retail trade, restaurants and hotels	23.25	15.85	7.40	53.58	43.07	10.51	57.57	40.87	16.70	38.39	23.22	15.17
7	Transport, storage and communication	29.07	1.82	27.25	38.76	-1.04	39.80	60.42	1.92	58.50	59.53	-0.72	60.25
8	Finance, insurance, real estate and business services	33.11	0.07	33.04	37.77	-0.03	37.80	63.45	0.06	63.39	69.06	0.07	68.99
9	Community, social and personal services	5.53	0.01	5.52	7.47	0.19	7.28	10.32	0.23	10.09	8.77	-0.07	8.84
	Total Industries [a]	236.32	22.15	214.17	358.33	68.03	290.30	482.07	69.11	412.96	433.42	18.38	415.04
	Producers of Government Services	21.62	-0.38	22.00	28.21	0.70	27.51	28.39	0.43	27.96	27.11	-0.09	27.20
	Private Non-Profit Institutions Serving Households	...	...	...	...	...	...	...	...	...	...	...	...
	Statistical discrepancy	50.86	...	...	-20.13	...	...	101.57	...	...	64.68	...	...
	Total [ab]	308.80	21.77	236.17	366.41	68.73	317.81	612.03	69.54	440.92	525.21	18.29	442.24

		1992			1993		
		Total Gross Capital Formation	Increase in Stocks	Gross Fixed Capital Formation	Total Gross Capital Formation	Increase in Stocks	Gross Fixed Capital Formation

At constant prices of: 1980 — All Producers

1	Agriculture, hunting, fishing and forestry	51.20	1.02	50.18	52.28	0.24	52.04
2	Mining and quarrying	22.20	1.00	21.20	21.15	-1.22	22.37
3	Manufacturing	119.10	3.95	115.15	117.56	-3.91	121.47
4	Electricity, gas and water	63.34	-1.39	64.73	69.10	0.47	68.63

India

2.10 Gross Capital Formation by Kind of Activity of Owner, ISIC Major Divisions, in Constant Prices
(Continued)

Thousand Million Indian rupees — *Fiscal year beginning 1 April*

	1992 Total Gross Capital Formation	1992 Increase in Stocks	1992 Gross Fixed Capital Formation	1993 Total Gross Capital Formation	1993 Increase in Stocks	1993 Gross Fixed Capital Formation
			At constant prices of:1980			
5 Construction	8.09	0.54	7.55	8.26	-0.20	8.46
6 Wholesale and retail trade, restaurants and hotels	59.37	44.58	14.79	30.17	14.24	15.93
7 Transport, storage and communication	67.76	1.47	66.29	73.37	1.30	72.07
8 Finance, insurance, real estate and business services	67.13	0.03	67.10	66.85	0.04	66.81
9 Community, social and personal services	9.12	0.02	9.10	10.12	0.07	10.05
Total Industries [a]	467.31	51.22	416.09	448.86	11.03	437.83
Producers of Government Services	29.14	0.28	28.86	30.56	0.23	30.33
Private Non-Profit Institutions Serving Households	...	...	...	...	...	...
Statistical discrepancy	22.63	...	...	27.07	...	...
Total [ab]	519.08	51.50	444.95	506.49	11.26	468.16

a) Gross fixed capital formation by kind of activity and by type of goods are prepared independently and therefore, do not always tally.
b) The estimates of 'Increase in stocks' and 'Gross fixed capital formation' (columns 2 and 3, respectively) are unadjusted for statistical discrepancy and therefore, do not add up to 'Gross capital formation' (column 1).

2.11 Gross Fixed Capital Formation by Kind of Activity of Owner, ISIC Divisions, in Current Prices

Thousand Million Indian rupees — *Fiscal year beginning 1 April*

	1980	1983	1984	1985	1986	1987	1988	1989	1990	1991	1992	1993
					All Producers							
1 Agriculture, hunting, forestry and fishing	47.65	58.65	66.03	71.77	73.86	88.28	98.25	107.41	125.09	140.31	156.67	172.60
A Agriculture and hunting	45.37	54.33	61.07	66.25	66.89	80.45	88.98	96.81	112.79	126.48	141.44	155.21
B Forestry and logging	1.01	1.77	1.87	1.82	2.44	2.47	3.01	3.55	4.25	4.40	4.74	4.88
C Fishing	1.27	2.55	3.09	3.70	4.53	5.36	6.26	7.05	8.05	9.43	10.49	12.51
2 Mining and quarrying	9.52	26.97	27.00	37.77	42.01	39.82	44.79	59.76	64.65	61.25	63.69	69.88
3 Manufacturing	49.77	94.16	103.67	121.39	126.00	152.10	171.86	208.94	261.77	290.75	322.95	355.90
4 Electricity, gas and water	28.94	49.19	53.11	67.60	92.56	100.88	114.50	121.21	144.25	188.82	190.02	209.72
A Electricity, gas and steam	25.57	43.67	47.58	60.89	85.00	91.49	105.42	113.49	136.39	178.83	178.17	196.45
B Water works and supply	3.37	5.52	5.53	6.71	7.56	9.39	9.08	7.72	7.86	9.99	11.85	13.27
5 Construction	5.08	8.20	8.82	7.85	9.45	10.85	12.66	19.53	19.99	17.50	19.92	23.06
6 Wholesale and retail trade, restaurants and hotels	7.40	12.89	15.08	16.38	18.88	20.18	26.05	31.73	37.92	39.25	41.90	47.17
A Wholesale and retail trade	5.12	8.59	10.34	11.46	12.90	13.10	17.05	20.07	26.84	26.84	27.03	29.92
B Restaurants and hotels	2.28	4.30	4.74	4.92	5.98	7.08	9.00	11.66	11.08	12.41	14.87	17.25
7 Transport, storage and communication	27.25	44.43	56.08	61.89	80.54	79.50	104.85	126.18	139.38	162.05	193.83	217.21
A Transport and storage	24.24	37.54	48.40	52...	69.95	65.11	83.45	100.12	111.35	127.19	144.55	157.29
B Communication	3.01	6.89	7.68	9.04	10.59	14.39	21.40	26.06	28.03	34.86	49.28	59.92
8 Finance, insurance, real estate and business services	33.04	52.08	64.68	74.29	88.28	104.83	122.81	141.29	178.11	216.80	228.46	248.07
A Financial institutions	1.65	3.51	4.89	5.52	7.45	14.78	21.26	23.54	30.79	48.58	43.42	39.57
B Insurance	...	...	...	...	...	...	...	...	...	...	...	...
C Real estate and business services	31.39	48.57	59.79	68.77	80.83	90.05	101.55	117.75	147.32	168.22	185.04	208.50
Real estate except dwellings	0.07	0.02	0.02	0.01	0.03	0.01	0.05	0.03	-	0.02	-	-
Dwellings [a]	31.32	48.55	59.77	68.76	80.80	90.04	101.50	117.72	147.32	168.20	185.04	208.50
9 Community, social and personal services	5.52	8.58	10.69	13.80	16.06	16.43	20.39	23.72	26.06	26.25	29.43	34.60
Total Industries	214.17	355.15	405.16	472.74	547.64	612.87	716.16	839.77	997.22	1142.98	1246.87	1378.21
Producers of Government Services	22.00	32.25	38.62	47.07	54.53	55.42	62.04	57.01	74.28	82.47	95.14	107.92
Private Non-Profit Institutions Serving Households	...	...	...	...	...	...	...	...	...	...	...	...
Total	236.17	387.40	443.78	519.81	602.17	668.29	778.20	896.78	1071.50	1225.45	1342.01	1486.13

a) Item 'Dwellings' includes residential house construction of general government.

India

2.12 Gross Fixed Capital Formation by Kind of Activity of Owner, ISIC Divisions, in Constant Prices

Thousand Million Indian rupees — Fiscal year beginning 1 April

At constant prices of: 1980

All Producers

	1980	1983	1984	1985	1986	1987	1988	1989	1990	1991	1992	1993
1 Agriculture, hunting, forestry and fishing	47.65	42.59	45.97	43.74	41.47	45.77	46.51	46.14	49.25	49.15	50.18	52.04
A Agriculture and hunting	45.37	39.57	42.87	40.68	37.98	42.19	42.60	41.91	44.59	44.34	45.07	46.66
B Forestry and logging	1.01	1.35	1.27	1.06	1.29	1.18	1.30	1.37	1.52	1.38	1.35	1.27
C Fishing	1.27	1.67	1.83	2.00	2.20	2.40	2.61	2.86	3.14	3.43	3.76	4.11
2 Mining and quarrying	9.52	21.20	19.82	24.70	25.41	22.68	23.36	27.75	27.50	22.69	21.20	22.37
3 Manufacturing	49.77	71.33	73.67	77.88	75.19	88.71	90.52	100.21	116.34	113.42	115.15	121.47
4 Electricity, gas and water	28.94	38.14	37.96	43.21	55.34	56.43	57.56	56.39	61.61	69.26	64.73	68.63
5 Construction	5.08	6.59	6.73	5.38	6.11	6.96	7.26	10.20	9.58	7.27	7.55	8.46
6 Wholesale and retail trade, restaurants and hotels	7.40	9.64	10.51	10.51	11.04	11.66	13.54	15.08	16.70	15.17	14.79	15.93
A Wholesale and retail trade	5.12	6.48	7.27	7.25	7.65	7.67	8.97	9.67	11.95	10.49	9.64	10.23
B Restaurants and hotels	2.28	3.16	3.24	3.26	3.39	3.99	4.57	5.41	4.75	4.68	5.15	5.70
7 Transport, storage and communication	27.25	35.34	41.79	39.80	49.64	45.01	52.86	57.63	58.50	60.25	66.29	72.07
A Transport and storage	24.24	30.04	36.33	34.14	43.53	37.06	42.38	46.22	47.06	47.86	50.48	53.38
B Communication	3.01	5.30	5.46	5.66	6.11	7.95	10.48	11.41	11.44	12.39	15.81	18.69
8 Finance, insurance, real estate and business services	33.04	32.65	36.31	37.80	40.24	45.32	49.99	53.46	63.39	68.99	67.10	66.81
A Financial institutions	1.65	2.60	3.36	3.45	4.39	8.78	11.43	11.38	13.67	18.99	15.55	13.51
B Insurance	...	...	...	...	...	...	...	...	...	...	...	...
C Real estate and business services	31.39	30.05	32.95	34.35	35.85	36.54	38.56	42.08	49.72	50.00	51.55	53.30
Real estate except dwellings	0.07	0.01	0.01	-	-	-	-	-	-	-	-	-
Dwellings a	31.32	30.04	32.94	34.35	35.85	36.54	38.56	42.08	49.72	50.00	51.55	53.30
9 Community, social and personal services	5.52	6.00	6.82	7.28	8.37	8.28	9.36	9.96	10.09	8.84	9.10	10.05
Total Industries	214.17	263.48	279.58	290.30	312.81	330.82	350.96	376.82	412.96	415.04	416.09	437.83
Producers of Government Services	22.00	23.60	26.02	27.51	29.50	27.66	28.58	23.80	27.96	27.20	28.86	30.33
Private Non-Profit Institutions Serving Households	...	...	...	...	...	...	...	...	...	...	...	...
Total	236.17	287.08	305.60	317.81	342.31	358.48	379.54	400.62	440.92	442.24	444.95	468.16

a) Item 'Dwellings' includes residential house construction of general government.

2.17 Exports and Imports of Goods and Services, Detail

Thousand Million Indian rupees — Fiscal year beginning 1 April

Exports of Goods and Services

	1980	1983	1984	1985	1986	1987	1988	1989	1990	1991	1992	1993
1 Exports of merchandise, f.o.b.	65.76	101.68	119.59	115.78	133.15	163.96	206.47	282.29	331.53	449.22	547.62	...
2 Transport and communication	3.62	4.40	6.44	6.04	6.88	8.82	13.00	15.10	17.65	23.08	28.51	...
A In respect of merchandise imports	...	...	...	...	...	...	...	...	...	...	...	...
B Other	3.62	4.40	6.44	6.04	6.88	8.82	13.00	15.10	17.65	23.08	28.51	...
3 Insurance service charges	0.48	1.14	0.89	0.79	0.83	1.05	1.36	1.98	1.98	2.65	4.59	...
A In respect of merchandise imports	...	...	...	...	...	...	...	...	...	...	...	...
B Other	0.48	1.14	0.89	0.79	0.83	1.05	1.36	1.98	1.98	2.65	4.59	...
4 Other commodities	6.59	16.03	23.66	20.69	15.80	16.43	20.77	28.04	34.72	47.18	40.59	...
5 Adjustments of merchandise exports to change-of-ownership basis	1.35	-3.97	-2.15	-6.83	-8.63	-7.22	-4.15	-5.71	-5.95	-8.80	-10.74	...
6 Direct purchases in the domestic market by non-residential households	12.38	11.93	9.92	13.04	17.13	19.38	21.24	24.19	26.30	49.18	60.50	...
7 Direct purchases in the domestic market by extraterritorial bodies	0.11	0.18	0.11	-	0.27	0.39	0.44	0.20	0.12	0.03	2.05	...
Total Exports of Goods and Services	90.29	131.39	158.46	149.51	165.43	202.81	259.13	346.09	406.35	562.54	673.12	...

Imports of Goods and Services

	1980	1983	1984	1985	1986	1987	1988	1989	1990	1991	1992	1993
1 Imports of merchandise, c.i.f.	125.58	161.38	188.64	213.15	227.60	258.31	344.82	409.83	503.50	518.64	694.56	...

India

2.17 Exports and Imports of Goods and Services, Detail
(Continued)

Thousand Million Indian rupees — Fiscal year beginning 1 April

	1980	1983	1984	1985	1986	1987	1988	1989	1990	1991	1992	1993
2 Adjustments of merchandise imports to change-of-ownership basis	0.06	-2.08	-15.46	-15.06	-25.73	-34.49	-59.67	-53.14	-68.94	-35.67	-54.88	...
3 Other transport and communication	3.40	6.17	7.33	6.65	6.57	9.89	12.92	15.16	16.98	19.82	46.16	...
4 Other insurance service charges	0.34	0.75	0.84	0.83	1.02	1.07	0.95	1.40	1.58	3.07	4.49	...
5 Other commodities	5.23	6.95	8.55	6.54	9.07	11.12	12.84	20.38	23.73	36.64	25.30	...
6 Direct purchases abroad by government	0.50	1.30	1.26	1.45	1.65	2.02	2.30	2.40	3.64	3.40	3.19	...
7 Direct purchases abroad by resident households	0.85	2.28	3.68	3.98	3.41	4.67	5.94	6.09	6.49	16.59	11.18	...
Total Imports of Goods and Services	135.96	176.75	194.84	217.54	223.59	252.59	320.10	402.12	486.98	562.49	730.00	...
Balance of Goods and Services	-45.67	-45.36	-36.38	-68.03	-58.16	-49.78	-60.97	-56.03	-80.63	0.05	-56.88	...
Total Imports and Balance of Goods and Services	90.29	131.39	158.46	149.51	165.43	202.81	259.13	346.09	406.35	562.54	673.12	...

3.26 Financial Transactions of Financial Institutions: Detail

Thousand Million Indian rupees — Fiscal year beginning 1 April

	1980 ALL FINANCIAL INSTITUTIONS	Central Bank	Other Monetary Institutions	Insurance	Other Financial Institutions	1985 ALL FINANCIAL INSTITUTIONS	Central Bank	Other Monetary Institutions	Insurance	Other Financial Institutions
Acquisition of Financial Assets										
1 Gold and SDRs	...	...	...	...	...	...	...	...	...	...
2 Currency and transferable deposits	6.46	0.04	6.31	-	0.11	19.50	-0.24	19.77	-	-0.03
3 Other deposits	4.08	-	3.04	0.93	0.11	16.83	-	14.78	-0.74	2.79
4 Bills and bonds, short term	29.79	23.33	5.58	-	0.88	80.51	74.41	1.93	-	4.17
5 Bonds, long term	...	...	...	...	...	...	...	...	...	...
6 Corporate equity securities	46.34	12.17	25.46	5.88	2.83	58.88	-17.76	53.78	13.32	9.54
7 Short-term loans, n.e.c.	66.05	3.77	42.97	2.67	16.64	89.05	-12.86	62.27	4.61	35.03
8 Long-term loans, n.e.c.										
9 Trade credit and advances	...	...	...	...	...	...	...	...	...	...
10 Other assets	1.12	-20.37	19.05	1.82	0.62	34.45	-2.58	28.33	4.53	4.17
Total Acquisition of Financial Assets	153.84	18.94	102.41	11.30	21.19	299.22	40.97	180.86	21.72	55.67
Incurrence of Liabilities										
1 Currency and transferable deposits	99.06	6.96	91.85	-	0.25	166.05	10.65	153.46	-	1.94
2 Other deposits	...	...	...	...	...	...	...	...	...	...
3 Bills and bonds, short term	...	...	...	...	...	...	...	...	...	...
4 Bonds, long term	...	...	...	...	...	...	...	...	...	...
5 Corporate equity securities	1.48	-	0.14	-0.04	1.38	14.48	-	4.66	-	9.82
6 Short-term loans, n.e.c.	12.35	-	1.89	-	10.46	20.82	-	7.68	0.02	13.12
7 Long-term loans, n.e.c.										
8 Net equity of households in life insurance and pension fund reserves	...	...	...	...	...	...	...	...	...	...
9 Other liabilities	33.17	7.48	8.05	10.06	7.58	73.74	26.60	7.99	18.10	21.05
Total Incurrence of liabilities	146.06	14.44	101.93	10.02	19.67	275.09	37.25	173.79	18.12	45.93
Net Lending	7.78	4.50	0.48	1.28	1.52	24.13	3.72	7.07	3.60	9.74
Incurrence of Liabilities and Net Lending	153.84	18.94	102.41	11.30	21.19	299.22	40.97	180.86	21.72	55.67

	1990 ALL FINANCIAL INSTITUTIONS	Central Bank	Other Monetary Institutions	Insurance	Other Financial Institutions	1991 ALL FINANCIAL INSTITUTIONS	Central Bank	Other Monetary Institutions	Insurance	Other Financial Institutions
Acquisition of Financial Assets										
1 Gold and SDRs	...	...	...	...	...	...	...	...	...	...
2 Currency and transferable deposits	34.43	-0.06	33.58	0.86	0.05	3.13	0.02	2.04	-	1.07
3 Other deposits	-1.78	-	-6.23	-1.92	6.37	67.72	-	42.02	4.03	21.67
4 Bills and bonds, short term	-0.07	-13.98	17.02	-	-3.11	18.84	0.14	14.52	-	4.18
5 Bonds, long term	...	...	...	...	...	...	...	...	...	...
6 Corporate equity securities	299.41	139.87	86.13	44.64	28.77	199.72	-75.98	145.31	45.63	84.76
7 Short-term loans, n.e.c.	319.25	45.80	115.65	18.81	138.99	329.90	51.78	122.62	29.28	126.22
8 Long-term loans, n.e.c.										
9 Trade credit and advances	...	...	...	...	...	...	...	...	...	...

India

3.26 Financial Transactions of Financial Institutions: Detail
(Continued)

Thousand Million Indian rupees
Fiscal year beginning 1 April

	1990 ALL FINANCIAL INSTITUTIONS	Central Bank	Other Monetary Institutions	Insurance	Other Financial Institutions	1991 ALL FINANCIAL INSTITUTIONS	Central Bank	Other Monetary Institutions	Insurance	Other Financial Institutions
10 Other assets	131.32	0.67	84.14	4.85	41.66	292.04	144.28	102.26	8.36	37.14
Total Acquisition of Financial Assets	782.56	172.30	330.29	67.24	212.73	911.35	120.24	428.77	87.30	275.04

Incurrence of Liabilities

1 Currency and transferable deposits	349.10	85.60	257.92	-	5.58	486.29	140.88	341.75	-	3.66
2 Other deposits	...	...	...	...	...	...	...	...	...	...
3 Bills and bonds, short term	...	...	...	...	...	...	...	...	...	...
4 Bonds, long term	...	...	...	...	...	...	...	...	...	...
5 Corporate equity securities	51.46	-	8.17	0.99	42.30	96.37	-	8.23	-	88.14
6 Short-term loans, n.e.c.	98.42	-	21.97	-	76.45	-18.30	-	-59.50	-	41.20
7 Long-term loans, n.e.c.										
8 Net equity of households in life insurance and pension fund reserves	...	...	...	...	...	...	...	...	...	...
9 Other liabilities	252.94	81.05	28.16	61.25	82.48	281.72	-20.62	110.09	75.60	116.65
Total Incurrence of liabilities	751.92	166.65	316.22	62.24	206.81	846.08	120.26	400.57	75.60	249.65
Net Lending	30.64	5.65	14.07	5.00	5.92	65.27	-0.02	28.20	11.70	25.39
Incurrence of Liabilities and Net Lending	782.56	172.30	330.29	67.24	212.73	911.35	120.24	428.77	87.30	275.04

	1992 ALL FINANCIAL INSTITUTIONS	Central Bank	Other Monetary Institutions	Insurance	Other Financial Institutions

Acquisition of Financial Assets

1 Gold and SDRs	...	...	...	...	...
2 Currency and transferable deposits	1.95	-0.08	2.32	0.01	-0.30
3 Other deposits	12.23	-	31.32	0.98	-20.07
4 Bills and bonds, short term	34.02	6.32	26.13	-	1.57
5 Bonds, long term	...	...	...	...	...
6 Corporate equity securities	396.12	117.66	140.44	55.17	82.85
7 Short-term loans, n.e.c.	168.94	-59.57	103.39	22.66	102.46
8 Long-term loans, n.e.c.					
9 Trade credit and advances	...	...	...	...	...
10 Other assets	46.76	22.88	2.61	12.77	8.50
Total Acquisition of Financial Assets	660.02	87.21	306.21	91.59	175.01

Incurrence of Liabilities

1 Currency and transferable deposits	380.81	74.22	301.98	-	4.61
2 Other deposits	...	...	...	...	...
3 Bills and bonds, short term	...	...	...	...	...
4 Bonds, long term	...	...	...	...	...
5 Corporate equity securities	71.59	-	7.13	-	64.46
6 Short-term loans, n.e.c.	84.77	-	50.99	-	33.78
7 Long-term loans, n.e.c.					
8 Net equity of households in life insurance and pension fund reserves	...	...	...	...	...
9 Other liabilities	89.21	12.98	-54.36	83.01	47.58
Total Incurrence of liabilities	626.38	87.20	305.74	83.01	150.43
Net Lending	33.64	0.01	0.47	8.58	24.58
Incurrence of Liabilities and Net Lending	660.02	87.21	306.21	91.59	175.01

3.51 External Transactions: Current Account: Detail

Thousand Million Indian rupees
Fiscal year beginning 1 April

	1980	1983	1984	1985	1986	1987	1988	1989	1990	1991	1992	1993
					Payments to the Rest of the World							
1 Imports of goods and services	135.96	176.75	194.84	217.54	223.59	252.59	320.10	402.12	486.98	562.49	730.00	...
A Imports of merchandise c.i.f.	125.58	161.38	188.64	213.15	227.60	258.31	344.82	409.83	503.50	518.64	694.56	...
B Other	10.38	15.37	6.20	4.39	-4.01	-5.72	-24.72	-7.71	-16.52	43.85	35.44	...
2 Factor income to the rest of the world	5.20	14.22	20.26	21.21	24.68	32.22	51.42	65.44	82.95	107.52	128.59	...

641

India

3.51 External Transactions: Current Account: Detail
(Continued)

Thousand Million Indian rupees — Fiscal year beginning 1 April

	1980	1983	1984	1985	1986	1987	1988	1989	1990	1991	1992	1993
A Compensation of employees	0.35	0.72	1.13	1.12	1.78	3.80	3.90	3.32	3.20	2.86	3.47	...
B Property and entrepreneurial income	4.85	13.50	19.13	20.09	22.90	28.42	47.52	62.12	79.75	104.66	125.12	...
3 Current transfers to the rest of the world [a]	0.12	0.11	0.15	0.14	0.15	0.34	0.24	0.26	0.26	0.37	0.35	...
A Indirect taxes by general government to supranational organizations	...	...	...	...	...	...	...	...	...	...	...	...
B Other current transfers	0.12	0.11	0.15	0.14	0.15	0.34	0.24	0.26	0.26	0.37	0.35	...
By general government	...	...	...	...	...	...	...	...	...	...	...	...
By other resident sectors	0.12	0.11	0.15	0.14	0.15	0.34	0.24	0.26	0.26	0.37	0.35	...
Statistical discrepancy [b]	-0.06	2.08	15.46	15.06	25.73	34.49	59.67	53.14	68.94	35.67	54.88	...
4 Surplus of the nation on current transactions	-20.94	-25.17	-32.92	-62.34	-63.55	-68.25	-123.04	-122.79	-181.96	-33.77	-138.16	...
Payments to the Rest of the World, and Surplus of the Nation on Current Transfers	120.28	167.99	197.79	191.61	210.60	251.39	308.39	398.17	457.17	672.28	775.66	...

Receipts From The Rest of the World

	1980	1983	1984	1985	1986	1987	1988	1989	1990	1991	1992	1993
1 Exports of goods and services	90.29	131.39	158.46	149.51	165.43	202.81	259.13	346.09	406.35	562.54	673.12	...
A Exports of merchandise f.o.b.	65.76	101.68	119.59	115.78	133.15	163.96	206.47	282.29	331.53	449.22	547.62	...
B Other	24.53	29.71	38.87	33.73	32.28	38.85	52.66	63.80	74.82	113.32	125.50	...
2 Factor income from the rest of the world	8.65	4.78	6.02	6.92	6.63	6.03	6.46	8.13	7.50	6.75	10.56	...
A Compensation of employees	0.06	0.09	0.12	0.14	0.09	0.17	0.33	1.13	0.74	1.17	0.35	...
B Property and entrepreneurial income	8.59	4.69	5.90	6.78	6.54	5.86	6.13	7.00	6.76	5.58	10.21	...
3 Current transfers from the rest of the world	22.69	27.85	31.16	28.35	29.91	35.33	38.65	38.24	37.37	94.19	81.24	...
A Subsidies to general government from supranational organizations	...	...	...	...	...	...	...	...	...	...	...	...
B Other current transfers	22.69	27.85	31.16	28.35	29.91	35.33	38.65	38.24	37.37	94.19	81.24	...
To general government	...	...	...	...	...	...	...	...	...	...	...	...
To other resident sectors	22.69	27.85	31.16	28.35	29.91	35.33	38.65	38.24	37.37	94.19	81.24	...
Statistical discrepancy [b]	-1.35	3.97	2.15	6.83	8.63	7.22	4.15	5.71	5.95	8.80	10.74	...
Receipts from the Rest of the World on Current Transfers	120.28	167.99	197.79	191.61	210.60	251.39	308.39	398.17	457.17	672.28	775.66	...

a) The estimates of 'Transfers to the rest of the world' shown in the government tables represent the current disbursements by the government in the form of contributions to international bodies appearing in the government budget documents, whereas the estimates shown in the external transaction tables represent the current transfer payments/receipts by private bodies to/from other countries as shown in India's overall balance of payments data supplied by the Reserve Bank of India.

b) Item 'Statistical discrepancy' refers to difference of payment and ownership basis of imports and exports of merchandise.

3.52 External Transactions: Capital Accumulation Account

Thousand Million Indian rupees — Fiscal year beginning 1 April

	1980	1983	1984	1985	1986	1987	1988	1989	1990	1991	1992	1993

Finance of Gross Accumulation

	1980	1983	1984	1985	1986	1987	1988	1989	1990	1991	1992	1993
1 Surplus of the nation on current transactions	-20.94	-25.17	-32.92	-62.34	-63.55	-68.25	-123.04	-122.79	-181.96	-33.77	-138.16	...
2 Capital transfers from the rest of the world	4.39	2.62	4.44	3.20	5.30	5.35	7.33	9.02	8.29	11.42	10.55	...
A By general government [a]	4.39	2.62	4.44	3.20	5.30	5.35	7.33	9.02	8.29	11.42	10.55	...
B By other resident sectors	...	...	...	...	...	...	...	...	...	...	...	...
Total Finance of Gross Accumulation	-16.55	-22.55	-28.48	-59.14	-58.25	-62.90	-115.71	-113.77	-173.67	-22.35	-127.61	...

Gross Accumulation

	1980	1983	1984	1985	1986	1987	1988	1989	1990	1991	1992	1993
1 Capital transfers to the rest of the world [a]	0.01	0.07	0.04	0.13	0.05	0.03	0.09	0.05	0.01	0.02	0.02	...
A By general government	0.01	0.07	0.04	0.13	0.05	0.03	0.09	0.05	0.01	0.02	0.02	...
B By other resident sectors	...	...	...	...	...	...	...	...	...	...	...	...
2 Purchases of intangible assets, n.e.c., net, from the rest of the world	...	...	...	...	...	...	...	...	...	...	...	...
Net lending to the rest of the world	-16.56	-22.62	-28.52	-59.27	-58.30	-62.93	-115.80	-113.82	-173.68	-22.37	-127.63	...
Total Gross Accumulation	-16.55	-22.55	-28.48	-59.14	-58.25	-62.90	-115.71	-113.77	-173.67	-22.35	-127.61	...

a) The estimates of 'Transfers to/received from the rest of the world' shown in the government tables represent the disbursements/receipts by the government in the form of gifts, donations etc. to/from other countries appearing in the government budget documents, whereas the estimates shown in the external transaction tables represent the transfer payments/receipts by official bodies to/from other countries as shown in India's overall balance of payments data supplied by the Reserve Bank of India.

India

4.1 Derivation of Value Added by Kind of Activity, in Current Prices

Thousand Million Indian rupees — Fiscal year beginning 1 April

	1980 Gross Output	1980 Intermediate Consumption	1980 Value Added	1985 Gross Output	1985 Intermediate Consumption	1985 Value Added	1990 Gross Output	1990 Intermediate Consumption	1990 Value Added	1991 Gross Output	1991 Intermediate Consumption	1991 Value Added
All Producers												
1 Agriculture, hunting, forestry and fishing	625.27	158.78	466.49	1014.65	242.41	772.24	1892.32	412.31	1480.01	2210.47	481.48	1728.99
A Agriculture and hunting	579.06	154.40	424.66	934.01	234.37	699.64	1747.45	395.83	1351.62	2057.71	463.44	1594.27
B Forestry and logging	36.25	3.63	32.62	58.73	5.87	52.86	92.01	9.20	82.81	93.22	9.32	83.90
C Fishing	9.96	0.75	9.21	21.91	2.17	19.74	52.86	7.28	45.58	59.54	8.72	50.82
2 Mining and quarrying	24.82	5.95	18.87	87.77	25.79	61.98	156.48	38.63	117.85	175.52	46.77	128.75
A Coal mining	14.58	4.21	10.37	34.46	19.15	15.31	62.77	25.45	37.32	73.72	29.68	44.04
B Crude petroleum and natural gas production	4.03	0.55	3.48	39.88	4.35	35.53	65.84	8.13	57.71	65.40	10.45	54.95
C Metal ore mining	2.66	0.61	2.05	6.09	1.31	4.78	12.62	3.05	9.57	16.20	3.96	12.24
D Other mining	3.55	0.58	2.97	7.34	0.98	6.36	15.25	2.00	13.25	20.20	2.68	17.52
3 Manufacturing	...	...	216.44	...	...	417.75	...	...	891.60	...	...	968.81
A Manufacture of food, beverages and tobacco	...	...	18.99	...	...	38.34	...	...	82.48	...	...	92.05
B Textile, wearing apparel and leather industries	...	...	55.01	...	...	83.00	...	...	157.99	...	...	167.78
C Manufacture of wood and wood products, including furniture	...	...	9.73	...	...	13.14	...	...	13.73	...	...	12.99
D Manufacture of paper and paper products, printing and publishing	...	...	7.22	...	...	14.21	...	...	31.65	...	...	38.80
E Manufacture of chemicals and chemical petroleum, coal, rubber and plastic products	...	...	26.71	...	...	59.30	...	...	137.98	...	...	155.29
F Manufacture of non-metallic mineral products, except products of petroleum and coal	...	...	7.50	...	...	20.54	...	...	40.13	...	...	48.80
G Basic metal industries	...	...	16.41	...	...	34.21	...	...	77.27	...	...	85.56
H Manufacture of fabricated metal products, machinery and equipment	...	...	50.96	...	...	102.05	...	...	232.61	...	...	247.68
I Other manufacturing industries	...	...	23.91	...	...	52.96	...	...	117.76	...	...	119.86
4 Electricity, gas and water	...	...	20.70	...	...	48.94	...	...	104.64	...	...	127.04
A Electricity, gas and steam	...	...	18.74	...	...	44.08	...	...	93.86	...	...	114.58
B Water works and supply	...	...	1.96	...	...	4.86	...	...	10.78	...	...	12.46
5 Construction	160.38	99.24	61.14	343.04	213.57	129.47	726.64	440.48	286.16	831.05	507.08	323.97
6 Wholesale and retail trade, restaurants and hotels	...	...	147.13	...	...	310.50	...	...	618.66	...	...	705.33
A Wholesale and retail trade	...	...	138.39	...	...	293.11	...	...	582.41	...	...	663.37
B Restaurants and hotels	...	...	8.74	...	...	17.39	...	...	36.25	...	...	41.96
7 Transport, storage and communication	...	...	57.24	...	...	140.98	...	...	339.13	...	...	410.64
A Transport and storage	...	...	49.26	...	...	124.96	...	...	291.89	...	...	354.01
B Communication	...	...	7.98	...	...	16.02	...	...	47.24	...	...	56.63
8 Finance, insurance, real estate and business services	...	...	107.91	...	...	198.82	...	...	389.02	...	...	475.34
A Financial institutions	...	...	25.60	...	...	63.38	...	...	167.42	...	...	221.79
B Insurance	...	...	8.48	...	...	19.27	...	...	43.54	...	...	58.14
C Real estate and business services	...	...	73.83	...	...	116.17	...	...	178.06	...	...	195.41
Real estate, except dwellings [a]	...	...	2.00	...	...	5.67	...	...	11.61	...	...	12.86
Dwellings	...	...	71.83	...	...	110.50	...	...	166.45	...	...	182.55
9 Community, social and personal services	...	...	70.41	...	...	132.20	...	...	279.81	...	...	337.02
A Sanitary and similar services	...	...	2.89	...	...	5.06	...	...	11.97	...	...	13.82
B Social and related community services [b]	...	...	67.52	...	...	127.14	...	...	267.84	...	...	323.20
C Recreational and cultural services	...	...	...	...	...	...	...	...	...	...	...	...
D Personal and household services	...	...	...	...	...	...	...	...	...	...	...	...
Total, Industries	...	...	1166.33	...	...	2212.88	...	...	4506.88	...	...	5205.89
Producers of Government Services	...	...	57.94	...	...	125.11	...	...	271.09	...	...	314.41
Other Producers	...	...	...	...	...	...	...	...	...	...	...	...

India

4.1 Derivation of Value Added by Kind of Activity, in Current Prices
(Continued)

Thousand Million Indian rupees — *Fiscal year beginning 1 April*

	1980 Gross Output	1980 Intermediate Consumption	1980 Value Added	1985 Gross Output	1985 Intermediate Consumption	1985 Value Added	1990 Gross Output	1990 Intermediate Consumption	1990 Value Added	1991 Gross Output	1991 Intermediate Consumption	1991 Value Added
Total c	...	...	1224.27	...	...	2337.99	...	...	4777.97	...	...	5520.30
Less: Imputed bank service charge d	...	...	...	...	...	...	...	...	...	...	...	...
Import duties	...	...	...	...	...	...	...	...	...	...	...	...
Value added tax	...	...	...	...	...	...	...	...	...	...	...	...
Other adjustments e	...	...	135.86	...	...	284.44	...	...	577.20	...	...	640.31
Total	...	...	1360.13	...	...	2622.43	...	...	5355.17	...	...	6160.61

of which General Government:

	1980 VA	1985 VA	1990 VA	1991 VA
1 Agriculture, hunting, forestry and fishing	12.62	24.78	42.82	51.83
2 Mining and quarrying	-	-	...	...
3 Manufacturing	0.09	10.42	24.92	28.47
4 Electricity, gas and water	2.31	5.62	8.65	9.34
5 Construction	8.66	18.49	41.51	46.47
6 Wholesale and retail trade, restaurants and hotels	0.15	0.34	0.45	0.38
7 Transport and communication	0.94	1.29	1.76	1.95
8 Finance, insurance, real estate and business services	0.65	1.57	3.82	4.68
9 Community, social and personal services	26.92	58.17	131.35	149.08
Statistical discrepancy	-	-	-	...
Total, Industries of General Government	52.34	120.68	255.28	292.20
Producers of Government Services	57.94	125.11	271.09	314.41
Total, General Government	110.28	245.79	526.37	606.61

	1992 Gross Output	1992 Intermediate Consumption	1992 Value Added	1993 Gross Output	1993 Intermediate Consumption	1993 Value Added
			All Producers			
1 Agriculture, hunting, forestry and fishing	2457.97	524.65	1933.32	...	...	2143.82
A Agriculture and hunting	2286.47	504.19	1782.28	...	...	1977.29
B Forestry and logging	96.32	9.63	86.69	...	...	89.65
C Fishing	75.18	10.83	64.35	...	...	76.88
2 Mining and quarrying	201.68	56.54	145.14	233.49	63.81	169.68
A Coal mining	91.02	37.01	54.01	105.69	42.80	62.89
B Crude petroleum and natural gas production	71.32	12.00	59.32	85.52	11.88	73.64
C Metal ore mining	17.90	4.57	13.33	19.05	4.93	14.12
D Other mining	21.44	2.96	18.48	23.23	4.20	19.03
3 Manufacturing	...	...	1113.09	...	...	1222.62
A Manufacture of food, beverages and tobacco	...	...	102.35	...	...	107.86
B Textile, wearing apparel and leather industries	...	...	200.44	...	...	231.80
C Manufacture of wood and wood products, including furniture	...	...	29.12	...	...	37.06
D Manufacture of paper and paper products, printing and publishing	...	...	46.87	...	...	52.32
E Manufacture of chemicals and chemical petroleum, coal, rubber and plastic products	...	...	185.44	...	...	207.60
F Manufacture of non-metallic mineral products, except products of petroleum and coal	...	...	53.75	...	...	61.04
G Basic metal industries	...	...	98.49	...	...	107.20
H Manufacture of fabricated metal products, machinery and equipment	...	...	264.85	...	...	280.21
I Other manufacturing industries	...	...	131.78	...	...	137.53
4 Electricity, gas and water	...	...	151.45	...	...	200.19
A Electricity, gas and steam	...	...	137.08	...	...	183.44
B Water works and supply	...	...	14.37	...	...	16.75

India

4.1 Derivation of Value Added by Kind of Activity, in Current Prices
(Continued)

Thousand Million Indian rupees
Fiscal year beginning 1 April

	1992 Gross Output	1992 Intermediate Consumption	1992 Value Added	1993 Gross Output	1993 Intermediate Consumption	1993 Value Added
5 Construction	909.41	551.08	358.33	...	...	398.47
6 Wholesale and retail trade, restaurants and hotels	...	...	814.79	...	...	919.78
A Wholesale and retail trade	...	...	766.50	...	...	864.74
B Restaurants and hotels	...	...	48.29	...	...	55.04
7 Transport, storage and communication	...	...	491.45	...	...	575.44
A Transport and storage	...	...	420.61	...	...	482.75
B Communication	...	...	70.84	...	...	92.69
8 Finance, insurance, real estate and business services	...	...	521.50	...	...	598.24
A Financial institutions	...	...	242.38	...	...	...
B Insurance	...	...	63.28	...	...	...
C Real estate and business services	...	...	215.84	...	...	...
Real estate, except dwellings [a]	...	...	14.25	...	...	...
Dwellings	...	...	201.59	...	...	...
9 Community, social and personal services	...	...	385.20	...	...	437.19
A Sanitary and similar services	...	...	16.35	...	...	...
B Social and related community services [b]	...	...	368.85	...	...	...
C Recreational and cultural services	...	...	...	...	...	...
D Personal and household services	...	...	...	...	...	...
Total, Industries	...	...	5914.27	...	...	6665.43
Producers of Government Services	...	...	362.07	...	...	406.02
Other Producers	...	...	...	...	...	...
Total [c]	...	...	6276.34	...	...	7071.45
Less: Imputed bank service charge [d]	...	...	...	...	...	...
Import duties	...	...	...	...	...	...
Value added tax	...	...	...	...	...	...
Other adjustments [e]	...	...	751.95	...	...	792.10
Total	...	...	7028.29	...	...	7863.55

of which General Government:

	1992 Value Added	1993 Value Added
1 Agriculture, hunting, forestry and fishing	57.29	...
2 Mining and quarrying	...	...
3 Manufacturing	30.05	...
4 Electricity, gas and water	12.01	...
5 Construction	53.20	...
6 Wholesale and retail trade, restaurants and hotels	-0.04	...
7 Transport and communication	3.56	...
8 Finance, insurance, real estate and business services	6.09	...
9 Community, social and personal services	170.34	...
Statistical discrepancy	...	...
Total, Industries of General Government	332.50	...
Producers of Government Services	362.07	...
Total, General Government	694.57	...

a) Item 'Real estate, except dwellings' includes also business services other than legal services.
b) Item 'Social and related community services' includes legal services and the rest of the community, social and personal services other than sanitary services but excluding repair services which are included under manufacturing.
c) Gross domestic product in factor values.
d) Imputed bank service charges are adjusted in the respective activity.
e) Item 'Other adjustments' refers to indirect taxes net of subsidies.

India

4.2 Derivation of Value Added by Kind of Activity, in Constant Prices

Thousand Million Indian rupees
Fiscal year beginning 1 April

At constant prices of: 1980 — All Producers

	1980 Gross Output	1980 Intermediate Consumption	1980 Value Added	1985 Gross Output	1985 Intermediate Consumption	1985 Value Added	1990 Gross Output	1990 Intermediate Consumption	1990 Value Added	1991 Gross Output	1991 Intermediate Consumption	1991 Value Added
1 Agriculture, hunting, forestry and fishing	625.27	158.78	466.49	724.19	182.01	542.18	871.60	215.07	656.53	862.04	220.30	641.74
A Agriculture and hunting	579.06	154.40	424.66	675.72	177.17	498.55	818.85	208.94	609.91	808.68	214.14	594.54
B Forestry and logging	36.25	3.63	32.62	35.34	3.53	31.81	34.50	3.45	31.05	34.26	3.43	30.83
C Fishing	9.96	0.75	9.21	13.13	1.31	11.82	18.25	2.68	15.57	19.10	2.73	16.37
2 Mining and quarrying	24.82	5.95	18.87	39.96	13.73	26.23	57.32	15.25	42.07	60.95	16.99	43.96
A Coal mining	14.58	4.21	10.37	19.55	10.87	8.68	26.80	10.85	15.95	29.11	11.70	17.41
B Crude petroleum and natural gas production	4.03	0.55	3.48	12.82	1.55	11.27	19.33	2.36	16.97	19.43	3.09	16.34
C Metal ore mining	2.66	0.61	2.05	3.21	0.68	2.53	4.38	1.13	3.25	4.83	1.17	3.66
D Other mining	3.55	0.58	2.97	4.38	0.63	3.75	6.81	0.91	5.90	7.58	1.03	6.55
3 Manufacturing	...	...	216.44	...	...	303.20	...	...	448.63	...	...	434.54
A Manufacture of food, beverages and tobacco	...	...	18.99	...	...	29.99	...	...	41.03	...	...	40.63
B Textile, wearing apparel and leather industries	...	...	55.01	...	...	64.57	...	...	81.73	...	...	79.18
C Manufacture of wood and wood products, including furniture	...	...	9.73	...	...	9.09	...	...	7.94	...	...	7.40
D Manufacture of paper and paper products, printing and publishing	...	...	7.22	...	...	9.83	...	...	15.55	...	...	16.20
E Manufacture of chemicals and chemical petroleum, coal, rubber and plastic products	...	...	26.71	...	...	44.27	...	...	79.82	...	...	80.01
F Manufacture of non-metallic mineral products, except products of petroleum and coal	...	...	7.50	...	...	12.70	...	...	19.40	...	...	20.30
G Basic metal industries	...	...	16.41	...	...	19.76	...	...	28.38	...	...	29.63
H Manufacture of fabricated metal products, machinery and equipment	...	...	50.96	...	...	72.23	...	...	108.77	...	...	102.03
I Other manufacturing industries	...	...	23.91	...	...	40.76	...	...	66.01	...	...	59.16
4 Electricity, gas and water	...	...	20.70	...	...	30.99	...	...	47.97	...	...	52.51
A Electricity, gas and steam	...	...	18.74	...	...	28.06	...	...	43.68	...	...	48.11
B Water works and supply	...	...	1.96	...	...	2.93	...	...	4.29	...	...	4.40
5 Construction	160.38	99.24	61.14	174.44	102.61	71.83	233.54	135.21	98.33	237.55	136.60	100.95
6 Wholesale and retail trade, restaurants and hotels	...	...	147.13	...	...	196.49	...	...	265.79	...	...	267.61
A Wholesale and retail trade	...	...	138.39	...	...	184.98	...	...	249.32	...	...	250.82
B Restaurants and hotels	...	...	8.74	...	...	11.51	...	...	16.47	...	...	16.79
7 Transport, storage and communication	...	...	57.24	...	...	79.51	...	...	111.64	...	...	118.04
A Transport and storage	...	...	49.26	...	...	68.76	...	...	97.07	...	...	102.47
B Communication	...	...	7.98	...	...	10.75	...	...	14.57	...	...	15.57
8 Finance, insurance, real estate and business services	...	...	107.91	...	...	147.08	...	...	217.24	...	...	238.06
A Financial institutions	...	...	25.60	...	...	45.97	...	...	93.27	...	...	106.58
B Insurance	...	...	8.48	...	...	12.31	...	...	18.42	...	...	22.64
C Real estate and business services	...	...	73.83	...	...	88.80	...	...	105.55	...	...	108.84
Real estate, except dwellings	...	...	2.00	...	...	4.32	...	...	6.10	...	...	5.93
Dwellings	...	...	71.83	...	...	84.48	...	...	99.45	...	...	102.91
9 Community, social and personal services	...	...	70.41	...	...	87.99	...	...	121.28	...	...	128.45
A Sanitary and similar services	...	...	2.89	...	...	3.19	...	...	4.72	...	...	4.78
B Social and related community services [a]	...	...	67.52	...	...	84.80	...	...	116.56	...	...	123.67
C Recreational and cultural services	...	...	...	...	...	...	...	...	...	...	...	...
D Personal and household services	...	...	...	...	...	...	...	...	...	...	...	...
Total, Industries	...	...	1166.33	...	...	1485.50	...	...	2009.48	...	...	2025.86
Producers of Government Services	...	...	57.94	...	...	80.16	...	...	113.28	...	...	115.70
Other Producers	...	...	...	...	...	...	...	...	...	...	...	...

India

4.2 Derivation of Value Added by Kind of Activity, in Constant Prices
(Continued)

Thousand Million Indian rupees — Fiscal year beginning 1 April

	1980 Gross Output	1980 Intermediate Consumption	1980 Value Added	1985 Gross Output	1985 Intermediate Consumption	1985 Value Added	1990 Gross Output	1990 Intermediate Consumption	1990 Value Added	1991 Gross Output	1991 Intermediate Consumption	1991 Value Added
At constant prices of: 1980												
Total b	...	...	1224.27	...	...	1565.66	...	...	2122.76	...	...	2141.56
Less: Imputed bank service charge c	...	...	...	...	...	...	...	...	...	...	...	...
Import duties	...	...	...	...	...	...	...	...	...	...	...	...
Value added tax	...	...	...	...	...	...	...	...	...	...	...	...
Other adjustments d	...	...	135.86	...	...	200.82	...	...	279.85	...	...	272.72
Total	...	...	1360.13	...	...	1766.48	...	...	2402.61	...	...	2414.28
of which General Government:												
1 Agriculture, hunting, forestry and fishing	...	...	12.62	...	...	13.80	...	...	14.39	...	...	15.00
2 Mining and quarrying	...	...	-	...	...	-	...	...	-	...	...	-
3 Manufacturing	...	...	0.09	...	...	5.80	...	...	9.38	...	...	9.69
4 Electricity, gas and water	...	...	2.31	...	...	3.31	...	...	5.67	...	...	5.93
5 Construction	...	...	8.66	...	...	12.00	...	...	17.57	...	...	17.31
6 Wholesale and retail trade, restaurants and hotels	...	...	0.15	...	...	0.21	...	...	0.16	...	...	0.10
7 Transport and communication	...	...	0.94	...	...	0.77	...	...	0.59	...	...	0.57
8 Finance, insurance, real estate and business services	...	...	0.65	...	...	0.84	...	...	1.15	...	...	1.12
9 Community, social and personal services	...	...	26.92	...	...	37.47	...	...	55.21	...	...	55.20
Statistical discrepancy	...	...	-	...	...	...	...	...	-	...	...	...
Total, Industries of General Government	...	...	52.34	...	...	74.20	...	...	104.12	...	...	104.92
Producers of Government Services	...	...	57.94	...	...	80.16	...	...	113.28	...	...	115.70
Total, General Government	...	...	110.28	...	...	154.36	...	...	217.40	...	...	220.62

	1992 Gross Output	1992 Intermediate Consumption	1992 Value Added	1993 Gross Output	1993 Intermediate Consumption	1993 Value Added
At constant prices of: 1980						
All Producers						
1 Agriculture, hunting, forestry and fishing	897.35	223.10	674.25	...	...	694.12
A Agriculture and hunting	842.48	216.59	625.89	...	...	644.56
B Forestry and logging	34.39	3.44	30.95	...	...	31.09
C Fishing	20.48	3.07	17.41	...	...	18.47
2 Mining and quarrying	62.47	17.83	44.64	64.56	17.79	46.77
A Coal mining	30.27	12.29	17.98	31.17	12.62	18.55
B Crude petroleum and natural gas production	19.39	3.23	16.16	20.16	2.79	17.37
C Metal ore mining	4.74	1.15	3.59	4.74	1.15	3.59
D Other mining	8.07	1.16	6.91	8.49	1.23	7.26
3 Manufacturing	...	...	448.05	...	...	464.21
A Manufacture of food, beverages and tobacco	...	...	41.85	...	...	40.91
B Textile, wearing apparel and leather industries	...	...	86.26	...	...	96.22
C Manufacture of wood and wood products, including furniture	...	...	8.42	...	...	8.97
D Manufacture of paper and paper products, printing and publishing	...	...	16.45	...	...	17.42
E Manufacture of chemicals and chemical petroleum, coal, rubber and plastic products	...	...	84.32	...	...	88.01
F Manufacture of non-metallic mineral products, except products of petroleum and coal	...	...	20.72	...	...	21.47
G Basic metal industries	...	...	30.96	...	...	31.27
H Manufacture of fabricated metal products, machinery and equipment	...	...	100.16	...	...	101.31
I Other manufacturing industries	...	...	58.91	...	...	58.63
4 Electricity, gas and water	...	...	56.47	...	...	59.82
A Electricity, gas and steam	...	...	51.82	...	...	54.79
B Water works and supply	...	...	4.65	...	...	5.03

India

4.2 Derivation of Value Added by Kind of Activity, in Constant Prices
(Continued)

Thousand Million Indian rupees
Fiscal year beginning 1 April

	1992 Gross Output	1992 Intermediate Consumption	1992 Value Added	1993 Gross Output	1993 Intermediate Consumption	1993 Value Added
			At constant prices of: 1980			
5 Construction	239.00	137.57	101.43	...	...	102.65
6 Wholesale and retail trade, restaurants and hotels	...	...	284.97	...	...	297.67
A Wholesale and retail trade	...	...	267.17	...	...	278.84
B Restaurants and hotels	...	...	17.80	...	...	18.83
7 Transport, storage and communication	...	...	124.53	...	...	132.02
A Transport and storage	...	...	107.28	...	...	112.88
B Communication	...	...	17.25	...	...	19.14
8 Finance, insurance, real estate and business services	...	...	245.23	...	...	266.09
A Financial institutions	...	...	111.18	...	...	...
B Insurance	...	...	21.65	...	...	...
C Real estate and business services	...	...	112.40	...	...	...
Real estate, except dwellings	...	...	5.97	...	...	...
Dwellings	...	...	106.43	...	...	...
9 Community, social and personal services	...	...	133.25	...	...	140.19
A Sanitary and similar services	...	...	5.05	...	...	...
B Social and related community services [a]	...	...	128.20	...	...	...
C Recreational and cultural services	...	...	...	...	...	...
D Personal and household services	...	...	...	...	...	...
Total, Industries	...	...	2112.82	...	...	2203.54
Producers of Government Services	...	...	121.56	...	...	126.88
Other Producers	...	...	...	...	...	...
Total [b]	...	...	2234.38	...	...	2330.42
Less: Imputed bank service charge [c]	...	...	...	...	...	...
Import duties	...	...	...	...	...	...
Value added tax	...	...	...	...	...	...
Other adjustments [d]	...	...	291.11	...	...	282.78
Total	...	...	2525.49	...	...	2613.20
			of which General Government:			
1 Agriculture, hunting, forestry and fishing	...	...	14.99	...	...	...
2 Mining and quarrying	...	...	-	...	...	...
3 Manufacturing	...	...	8.91	...	...	...
4 Electricity, gas and water	...	...	6.30	...	...	...
5 Construction	...	...	18.08	...	...	...
6 Wholesale and retail trade, restaurants and hotels	...	...	-0.01	...	...	...
7 Transport and communication	...	...	0.89	...	...	...
8 Finance, insurance, real estate and business services	...	...	1.14	...	...	...
9 Community, social and personal services	...	...	57.54	...	...	...
Statistical discrepancy	...	...	...	...	...	...
Total, Industries of General Government	...	...	107.84	...	...	...
Producers of Government Services	...	...	121.56	...	...	...
Total, General Government	...	...	229.40	...	...	...

a) Item 'Social and related community services' includes legal services and the rest of the community, social and personal services other than sanitary services but excluding repair services which are included under manufacturing.
b) Gross domestic product in factor values.
c) Imputed bank service charges are adjusted in the respective activity.
d) Item 'Other adjustments' refers to indirect taxes net of subsidies.

India

4.3 Cost Components of Value Added

Thousand Million Indian rupees — *Fiscal year beginning 1 April*

All Producers

	\multicolumn{6}{c	}{1980}	\multicolumn{6}{c}{1985}
	Compensation of Employees	Capital Consumption	Net Operating Surplus	Indirect Taxes	Less: Subsidies Received	Value Added	Compensation of Employees	Capital Consumption	Net Operating Surplus	Indirect Taxes	Less: Subsidies Received	Value Added
1 Agriculture, hunting, forestry and fishing	97.27	25.58	343.64	...	...	466.49	156.50	49.36	566.38	...	...	772.24
A Agriculture and hunting	92.12	24.10	308.44	...	...	424.66	145.63	45.77	508.24	...	...	699.64
B Forestry and logging	3.45	0.33	28.84	...	...	32.62	7.28	0.86	44.72	...	...	52.86
C Fishing	1.70	1.15	6.36	...	...	9.21	3.59	2.73	13.42	...	...	19.74
2 Mining and quarrying	10.60	4.13	4.14	...	...	18.87	18.92	13.75	29.31	...	...	61.98
3 Manufacturing	69.82	29.46	117.16	...	...	216.44	137.28	59.71	220.76	...	...	417.75
4 Electricity, gas and water	7.80	11.58	1.32	...	...	20.70	18.89	27.78	2.27	...	...	48.94
5 Construction	44.82	3.43	12.89	...	...	61.14	96.48	7.20	25.79	...	...	129.47
6 Wholesale and retail trade, restaurants and hotels	31.27	3.91	111.95	...	...	147.13	66.16	8.53	235.81	...	...	310.50
A Wholesale and retail trade	28.93	2.84	106.62	...	...	138.39	61.41	5.98	225.72	...	...	293.11
B Restaurants and hotels	2.34	1.07	5.33	...	...	8.74	4.75	2.55	10.09	...	...	17.39
7 Transport, storage and communication	28.98	20.00	8.26	...	...	57.24	61.37	42.34	37.27	...	...	140.98
A Transport and storage	23.97	18.15	7.14	...	...	49.26	50.77	38.10	36.09	...	...	124.96
B Communication	5.01	1.85	1.12	...	...	7.98	10.60	4.24	1.18	...	...	16.02
8 Finance, insurance, real estate and business services	16.62	15.27	76.02	...	...	107.91	38.65	35.49	124.68	...	...	198.82
A Financial institutions	15.76	0.64	17.68	...	...	34.08	36.44	1.61	44.60	...	...	82.65
B Insurance				...	...					...	...	
C Real estate and business services	0.86	14.63	58.34	...	...	73.83	2.21	33.88	80.08	...	...	116.17
9 Community, social and personal services	45.72	2.64	22.05	...	...	70.41	91.65	5.57	34.98	...	...	132.20
Total, Industries [a]	352.90	116.00	697.43	...	...	1166.33	685.90	249.73	1277.25	...	...	2212.88
Producers of Government Services	53.07	4.87		...	...	57.94	112.47	12.64	-	...	...	125.11
Other Producers	...	...	...	...	...	...	...	...	...	...	...	...
Total [b]	405.97	120.87	697.43	...	...	1224.27	798.37	262.37	1277.25	...	...	2337.99
Less: Imputed bank service charge [c]	...	...	...	...	...	...	...	...	...	...	...	...
Import duties	...	...	...	...	...	...	...	...	...	...	...	...
Value added tax	...	...	...	...	...	...	...	...	...	...	...	...
Other adjustments [d]	...	...	...	...	...	135.86	...	...	...	...	...	284.44
Total	...	...	...	...	...	1360.13	...	...	...	...	...	2622.43

of which General Government:

	Compensation of Employees	Capital Consumption	Net Operating Surplus	Indirect Taxes	Less: Subsidies Received	Value Added	Compensation of Employees	Capital Consumption	Net Operating Surplus	Indirect Taxes	Less: Subsidies Received	Value Added
1 Agriculture, hunting, forestry and fishing	2.59	3.52	6.51	...	...	12.62	6.25	7.86	10.67	...	...	24.78
2 Mining and quarrying	-	-	-			-	-	-	-			-
3 Manufacturing	6.49	1.37	-7.77	...	...	0.09	14.13	2.63	-6.34	...	...	10.42
4 Electricity, gas and water	1.52	2.39	-1.60	...	...	2.31	4.01	5.79	-4.18	...	...	5.62
5 Construction	8.26	0.40	-	...	...	8.66	17.81	0.68	-	...	...	18.49
6 Wholesale and retail trade, restaurants and hotels	0.02	-	0.13	...	...	0.15	0.06	-	0.28	...	...	0.34
7 Transport and communication	0.86	0.61	-0.53	...	...	0.94	1.49	1.06	-1.26	...	...	1.29
8 Finance, insurance, real estate & business services	0.27	0.38	-	...	...	0.65	0.58	0.99	-	...	...	1.57
9 Community, social and personal services	25.81	1.21	-0.10	...	...	26.92	55.90	2.95	-0.68	...	...	58.17
Total, Industries of General Government	45.82	9.88	-3.36	...	...	52.34	100.23	21.96	-1.51	...	...	120.68
Producers of Government Services	53.07	4.87	-	...	...	57.94	112.47	12.64	-	...	...	125.11
Total, General Government	98.89	14.75	-3.36	...	...	110.28	212.70	34.60	-1.51	...	...	245.79

All Producers

	\multicolumn{6}{c	}{1990}	\multicolumn{6}{c}{1991}
	Compensation of Employees	Capital Consumption	Net Operating Surplus	Indirect Taxes	Less: Subsidies Received	Value Added	Compensation of Employees	Capital Consumption	Net Operating Surplus	Indirect Taxes	Less: Subsidies Received	Value Added
1 Agriculture, hunting, forestry and fishing	275.11	87.03	1117.87	...	...	1480.01	306.38	103.39	1319.22	...	...	1728.99
A Agriculture and hunting	257.45	79.03	1015.14	...	...	1351.62	286.80	94.01	1213.46	...	...	1594.27
B Forestry and logging	9.38	1.86	71.57	...	...	82.81	10.44	2.23	71.23	...	...	83.90
C Fishing	8.28	6.14	31.16	...	...	45.58	9.14	7.15	34.53	...	...	50.82
2 Mining and quarrying	39.03	33.66	45.16	...	...	117.85	37.55	40.96	50.24	...	...	128.75

India

4.3 Cost Components of Value Added
(Continued)

Thousand Million Indian rupees

Fiscal year beginning 1 April

	1990 Compensation of Employees	Capital Consumption	Net Operating Surplus	Indirect Taxes	Less: Subsidies Received	Value Added	1991 Compensation of Employees	Capital Consumption	Net Operating Surplus	Indirect Taxes	Less: Subsidies Received	Value Added
3 Manufacturing	280.55	119.73	491.32	...	...	891.60	312.08	146.69	510.04	...	...	968.81
4 Electricity, gas and water	40.33	62.86	1.45	...	...	104.64	45.99	78.07	2.98	...	...	127.04
5 Construction	210.58	13.94	61.64	...	...	286.16	236.99	16.10	70.88	...	...	323.97
6 Wholesale and retail trade, restaurants and hotels	130.19	17.28	471.19	...	...	618.66	149.05	21.00	535.28	...	...	705.33
A Wholesale and retail trade	120.16	12.15	450.10	...	...	582.41	137.36	14.67	511.34	...	...	663.37
B Restaurants and hotels	10.03	5.13	21.09	...	...	36.25	11.69	6.33	23.94	...	...	41.96
7 Transport, storage and communication	127.60	88.35	123.18	...	...	339.13	146.10	105.08	159.46	...	...	410.64
A Transport and storage	107.55	77.80	106.54	...	...	291.89	123.91	91.63	138.47	...	...	354.01
B Communication	20.05	10.55	16.64	...	...	47.24	22.19	13.45	20.99	...	...	56.63
8 Finance, insurance, real estate and business services	83.15	62.29	243.58	...	...	389.02	97.37	74.33	303.64	...	...	475.34
A Financial institutions	76.98	6.44	127.54	...	...	210.96	90.27	9.17	180.49	...	...	279.93
B Insurance				...	...					...	...	
C Real estate and business services	6.17	55.85	116.04	...	...	178.06	7.10	65.16	123.15	...	...	195.41
9 Community, social and personal services	202.39	10.92	66.50	...	...	279.81	241.80	12.98	82.24	...	...	337.02
Total, Industries [a]	1388.93	496.06	2621.89	...	...	4506.88	1573.31	598.60	3033.98	...	...	5205.89
Producers of Government Services	245.20	25.89	-	...	...	271.09	283.49	30.92	-	...	...	314.41
Other Producers	...	...	...	...	...	...	...	...	...	...	...	...
Total [b]	1634.13	521.95	2621.89	...	...	4777.97	1856.80	629.52	3033.98	...	...	5520.30
Less: Imputed bank service charge [c]	...	...	...	...	...	...	...	...	...	...	...	...
Import duties	...	...	...	...	...	...	...	...	...	...	...	...
Value added tax	...	...	...	...	...	...	...	...	...	...	...	...
Other adjustments [d]	...	...	...	...	...	577.20	...	...	...	...	...	640.31
Total	...	...	...	...	...	5355.17	...	...	...	...	...	6160.61

of which General Government:

1 Agriculture, hunting, forestry and fishing	14.54	14.91	13.37	...	...	42.82	16.54	17.48	17.81	...	...	51.83
2 Mining and quarrying	-	-	-	...	...	-	-	-	-	...	...	-
3 Manufacturing	26.98	4.98	-7.04	...	...	24.92	29.53	5.90	-6.96	...	...	28.47
4 Electricity, gas and water	8.51	10.05	-9.91	...	...	8.65	9.62	11.74	-12.02	...	...	9.34
5 Construction	40.37	1.14	-	...	...	41.51	45.15	1.32	-	...	...	46.47
6 Wholesale and retail trade, restaurants and hotels	0.11	-	0.34	...	...	0.45	0.13	-	0.25	...	...	0.38
7 Transport and communication	2.94	1.51	-2.69	...	...	1.76	3.15	1.70	-2.90	...	...	1.95
8 Finance, insurance, real estate & business services	1.83	1.95	0.04	...	...	3.82	2.34	2.31	0.03	...	...	4.68
9 Community, social and personal services	127.05	5.95	-1.65	...	...	131.35	144.00	7.11	-2.03	...	...	149.08
Total, Industries of General Government	222.33	40.49	-7.54	...	...	255.28	250.46	47.56	-5.82	...	...	292.20
Producers of Government Services	245.20	25.89	-	...	...	271.09	283.49	30.92	-	...	...	314.41
Total, General Government	467.53	66.38	-7.54	...	...	526.37	533.95	78.48	-5.82	...	...	606.61

	1992 Compensation of Employees	Capital Consumption	Net Operating Surplus	Indirect Taxes	Less: Subsidies Received	Value Added
			All Producers			
1 Agriculture, hunting, forestry and fishing	342.60	116.70	1474.02	...	...	1933.32
A Agriculture and hunting	320.36	106.24	1355.68	...	...	1782.28
B Forestry and logging	10.43	2.57	73.69	...	...	86.69
C Fishing	11.81	7.89	44.65	...	...	64.35
2 Mining and quarrying	42.30	46.96	55.88	...	...	145.14
3 Manufacturing	350.22	171.02	591.85	...	...	1113.09
4 Electricity, gas and water	51.72	91.81	7.92	...	...	151.45

India

4.3 Cost Components of Value Added
(Continued)

Thousand Million Indian rupees — Fiscal year beginning 1 April

1992

	Compensation of Employees	Capital Consumption	Net Operating Surplus	Indirect Taxes	Less: Subsidies Received	Value Added
5 Construction	262.91	17.73	77.69	...	...	358.33
6 Wholesale and retail trade, restaurants and hotels	174.97	24.29	615.53	...	...	814.79
A Wholesale and retail trade	161.41	16.79	588.30	...	...	766.50
B Restaurants and hotels	13.56	7.50	27.23	...	...	48.29
7 Transport, storage and communication	169.32	120.99	201.14	...	...	491.45
A Transport and storage	144.97	104.26	171.38	...	...	420.61
B Communication	24.35	16.73	29.76	...	...	70.84
8 Finance, insurance, real estate and business services	112.10	83.12	326.28	...	...	521.50
A Financial institutions	104.61	11.73	189.32	...	...	305.66
B Insurance				...	...	
C Real estate and business services	7.49	71.39	136.96	...	...	215.84
9 Community, social and personal services	275.50	14.75	94.95	...	...	385.20
Total, Industries a	1781.64	687.37	3445.26	...	...	5914.27
Producers of Government Services	326.79	35.28	-	...	...	362.07
Other Producers	...	...	...	...	...	...
Total b	2108.43	722.65	3445.26	...	...	6276.34
Less: Imputed bank service charge c	...	...	...	...	...	...
Import duties	...	...	...	...	...	...
Value added tax	...	...	...	...	...	...
Other adjustments d	...	...	...	...	...	751.95
Total	...	...	...	...	...	7028.29

of which General Government:

1 Agriculture, hunting, forestry and fishing	19.22	19.67	18.40	...	...	57.29
2 Mining and quarrying	-	-	-	...	...	-
3 Manufacturing	34.18	6.61	-10.74	...	...	30.05
4 Electricity, gas and water	11.03	13.26	-12.28	...	...	12.01
5 Construction	51.73	1.47	-	...	...	53.20
6 Wholesale and retail trade, restaurants and hotels	0.15	0.01	-0.20	...	...	-0.04
7 Transport and communication	3.76	1.97	-2.17	...	...	3.56
8 Finance, insurance, real estate & business services	3.28	2.62	0.19	...	...	6.09
9 Community, social and personal services	164.74	8.13	-2.53	...	...	170.34
Total, Industries of General Government	288.09	53.74	-9.33	...	...	332.50
Producers of Government Services	326.79	35.28	-	...	...	362.07
Total, General Government	614.88	89.02	-9.33	...	...	694.57

a) Mixed income of self-employed workers is included in column 'Compensation of employees'.
b) Gross domestic product in factor values.
c) Imputed bank service charges are adjusted in the respective activity.
d) Item 'Other adjustments' refers to indirect taxes net of subsidies.

Indonesia

General note. The preparation of national accounts statistics in Indonesia is undertaken by the Central Bureau of Statistics, Jakarta. The official estimates are generally in accordance with the United Nations System of National Accounts (SNA). The Indonesian Input-output tables were published in 1976 and 1980 for the year 1971 and 1975 respectively, with the title 'Table Input-output Indonesia 1971' and 'Table Input-output Indonesia 1975'. The following tables are prepared for the United Nation's national accounts questionnaire. Whenever the scope and coverage of the estimates differ from those recommended in the SNA, a footnote is indicated to the relevant tables.

Sources and methods:

(a) **Gross domestic product.** Gross domestic product is estimated mainly through the production approach.

(b) **Expenditure on the gross domestic product.** The expenditure approach is used to estimate government final consumption expenditure, exports and imports of goods and services. Private final consumption expenditure is derived as residual. The commodity-flow approach is used for gross fixed capital formation. The main sources of data for the estimation of central government consumption expenditure are the budgetary accounts of the Department of Finance, while local governments provide data directly to the Central Bureau of Statistics (CBS). Bench-mark data for capital formation are based on statistics of imports and domestic production of construction materials and machinery and equipment. For other years, import of machineries and equipments are obtained from import statistics, while domestic production is compiled by using production and implicit price indexes to extrapolate the bench-mark estimates. The input-output ratios for buildings and structures have been established for 1971 on the basis of special surveys on construction projects in that year. Other years' estimates are extrapolated by quantity and price indexes of domestic production and imports of construction materials. Estimates of exports and imports of goods and services are obtained from foreign trade and balance of payment statistics. For the constant price estimates, current values of government expenditure items are deflated by the consumer price index and by the wholesale price index. For gross fixed capital formation referring to buildings and structures, the bench-mark values are extrapolated by quantity indicators of domestic production and volume indicators of imports of construction materials. Values of exports and imports are deflated by the corresponding unit value price indexes.

(c) **Cost-structure of the gross domestic product.** Consumption of fixed capital for manufacturing, electricity, gas and water, is estimated from information available at the CBS. For other sectors the estimates are based on the results of special surveys. The main source of data for net indirect taxes are the budgetary accounts of the central and local governments. Compensation of employees together with operating surplus is obtained as a residual.

(d) **Gross domestic product by kind of economic activity.** The table on gross domestic product by kind of economic activity is prepared at market prices, i.e. producers' values. The production approach is used to estimate value-added of most of the industries. The income approach is used for government and domestic services while gross output of trade and construction is estimated on the basis of the commodity-flow approach. For agriculture, main food crops production is compiled on the basis of information relating to area harvested and average yield for each crop obtained from the CBS. The prices used are based on farm-gate prices obtained from annual surveys. The consumption of vegetables by households is based on per capita consumption estimates derived from the Household Survey 1969/79 and 1976, extrapolated by population and price changes and adding 1 per cent to cover consumption outside households. For main food crops, commercial and estate crops, the value of intermediate inputs is based on cost-structure surveys. Estimates of livestock, forestry, and fishing are obtained from the departments concerned. For livestock, intermediate inputs are calculated as fixed percentages of gross output. The most important mining commodity is crude petroleum for which production data are available for all enterprises concerned. Estimates of prices and input costs are compiled on the basis of returns furnished by the largest firm. For the base-year 1971, data on output and input structure of manufacturing have been compiled for each industry group from statistics maintained by the CBS and from surveys and other studies undertaken. For other years industrial production indexes are compiled on the basis of output of selected manufactured products. For gross output of construction, the information on imports of construction materials is obtained from commodity imports statistics whereas estimates of domestically produced materials are based on the annual industrial surveys. The average ratios of intermediate inputs to gross output are based on data gathered from surveys. Gross output of the trade sector is calculated by multiplying estimates of the producers' values of the marketed surplus of agricultural products, domestically produced manufactured goods, selected mining and quarrying products and the cost of imported goods by the percentage distribution mark-ups gathered from special surveys undertaken in 1971. Estimates for other years are extrapolated by a quantity index of marketed surplus traded and an implicit price index. For railway transport, the annual reports of the State Railway Company constitute the main source of data for estimating gross output, intermediate input and value added. For road transport, gross output and input values are estimated by multiplying the average earning of each type of vehicle by the corresponding number of vehicles. For other transports, estimates are based on cost-structure surveys and data from concerned authorities and companies. The information of gross output and value added of the banking sector is based on the data compiled annually by the Bank of Indonesia supplemented by special inquiries for other financial intermediaries. Basic data relating to real estate and business services are limited and rough procedures are adopted by using information gathered from the special surveys. For government services, estimates are obtained from current budget expenditure and information furnished by local bodies. Estimates of other services are calculated for the year 1971 as the bench-mark year, and estimates of other years are extrapolated by using employment and price indicators. For the constant price estimates, revaluation is used for the agricultural sector, while value added of public administration and defence, is deflated by a moving average of the consumer price index. In all other sectors value added is extrapolated by various quantity indicators and indexes.

1.1 Expenditure on the Gross Domestic Product, in Current Prices

Thousand Million Indonesian rupiahs

		1980	1983	1984	1985	1986	1987	1988	1989	1990	1991	1992	1993
1	Government final consumption expenditure	5148	8077	9122	10893	11329	11764	12756	15698	17573	20785	24731	29893
2	Private final consumption expenditure	25595	47063	54067	57201	63355	71989	81045	88752	106312	125260	137411	158077
3	Gross capital formation	11894	22261	23543	27204	29025	39146	44810	58831	70704	80570	92894	97105
	A Increase in stocks	1345	2794	3406	4837	4243	8166	8007	13171	15071	14933	18745	10373
	B Gross fixed capital formation	10550	19468	20136	22367	24782	30980	36803	45660	55633	65637	74149	86732
4	Exports of goods and services	16162	19847	22999	21534	20010	29874	34666	42505	51953	62264	75776	88552
5	Less: Imports of goods and services	9886	19626	19845	19835	21036	27956	31171	38601	50946	61376	70025	75601
	Equals: Gross Domestic Product	48914	77623	89885	96997	102683	124817	142105	167185	195597	227502	260786	298026

1.2 Expenditure on the Gross Domestic Product, in Constant Prices

Thousand Million Indonesian rupiahs

		1980	1983	1984	1985	1986	1987	1988	1989	1990	1991	1992	1993
						At constant prices of:1983							
1	Government final consumption expenditure	6801	8077	8353	8991	9241	9226	9924	10965	11317	12113	12819	12834
2	Private final consumption expenditure	36037	47063	48942	49448	50530	52200	54225	56476	62053	66724	69277	73998
3	Gross capital formation	12569	22261	22749	26257	27755	27646	26321	29985	36035	34935	36053	37032
	A Increase in stocks	-3077	2794	4452	6641	6333	5049	1120	1417	3303	-105	-362	-957
	B Gross fixed capital formation	15646	19468	18297	19616	21422	22597	25201	28568	32732	35040	36415	37989
4	Exports of goods and services	26182	19847	21145	19495	22460	25745	26016	28733	28863	35846	42133	45356
5	Less: Imports of goods and services	14866	19626	18151	19109	19906	20299	16504	18723	23050	26436	29181	29650
	Equals: Gross Domestic Product	66723	77623	83037	85082	90081	94518	99981	107437	115217	123181	131102	139571

Indonesia

1.3 Cost Components of the Gross Domestic Product

Thousand Million Indonesian rupiahs

	1980	1983	1984	1985	1986	1987	1988	1989	1990	1991	1992	1993
1 Indirect taxes, net	1635	2281 / 2451	2723	3597	6529	7130	9033	12445	13420	15004	17795	20544
2 Consumption of fixed capital	2962	4629 / 3881	4494	4850	5134	6241	7105	8365	9784	11380	13045	14907
3 Compensation of employees paid by resident producers to:	40849	64305 / 71290	82667	88551	91020	111446	125967	146375	172393	201118	229946	262575
4 Operating surplus												
Equals: Gross Domestic Product	45446	71215 / 77623	89885	96997	102683	124817	142105	167185	195597	227502	260786	298026

1.10 Gross Domestic Product by Kind of Activity, in Current Prices

Thousand Million Indonesian rupiahs

	1980	1983	1984	1985	1986	1987	1988	1989	1990	1991	1992	1993
1 Agriculture, hunting, forestry and fishing	11726	17765	20420	22513	24871	29116	34278	39164	42149	44559	50032	54719
2 Mining and quarrying	11238	16107	16938	13571	11503	17267	17162	21823	26119	31482	30908	26433
3 Manufacturing	6353	9896	13113	15503	17185	21150	26252	30323	38910	47544	56560	66892
4 Electricity, gas and water	231	314	354	396	647	747	869	1008	1258	1750	2148	2718
5 Construction	2582	4597	4757	5302	5314	6087	7169	8884	10749	13329	16077	20437
6 Wholesale and retail trade, restaurants and hotels [a]	7323	11419	13435	15417	17122	21048	24379	28856	33000	36900	42779	49616
7 Transport, storage and communication	2211	4098	5051	6100	6407	7443	8140	9306	11000	13792	16998	20850
8 Finance, insurance, real estate and business services [b]	2152	4714	5631	6271	7013	8144	9058	10818	13178	16082	19029	22541
9 Community, social and personal services [cb]	1872	3001	3718	3999	4315	4903	5351	5830	6434	7443	8947	11232
Total, Industries	45688	71911	83415	89072	94376	115905	132659	156012	182797	212881	243478	275438
Producers of Government Services	3225	5712	6470	7925	8307	8912	9446	11174	12801	14622	17309	22588
Other Producers	...	...	...	...	...	...	...	...	...	...	...	...
Subtotal	48914	77623	89885	96997	102683	124817	142105	167185	195597	227503	260787	298026
Less: Imputed bank service charge	...	...	...	...	...	...	...	...	...	...	...	...
Plus: Import duties	...	...	...	...	...	...	...	...	...	...	...	...
Plus: Value added tax	...	...	...	...	...	...	...	...	...	...	...	...
Equals: Gross Domestic Product	48914	77623	89885	96997	102683	124817	142105	167185	195597	227503	260787	298026

a) Restaurants and hotels are included in item 'Community, social and personal services'.
b) Business services are included in item 'Community, social and personal services'.
c) For the first series, restaurants and hotels are included in item 'Community, social and personal services'.

1.11 Gross Domestic Product by Kind of Activity, in Constant Prices

Thousand Million Indonesian rupiahs

	1980	1983	1984	1985	1986	1987	1988	1989	1990	1991	1992	1993
					At constant prices of: 1983							
1 Agriculture, hunting, forestry and fishing	16303	17765	18513	19300	19799	20224	21214	21918	22357	22663	24139	24512
2 Mining and quarrying	16078	16107	17120	15480	16309	16366	15893	16664	17532	19322	18993	19588
3 Manufacturing	7304	9896	12079	13431	14678	16235	18182	19856	22337	24482	26856	29035
4 Electricity, gas and water	312	314	324	361	430	495	549	616	726	843	928	1022
5 Construction	3850	4597	4394	4508	4609	4803	5259	5878	6673	7475	8171	9089
6 Wholesale and retail trade, restaurants and hotels	10303	11419	11811	12399	13399	14356	15657	17338	18569	19606	21103	23114
7 Transport, storage and communication	2911	4098	4443	4487	4668	4939	5212	5812	6368	6869	7595	8418
8 Finance, insurance, real estate and business services [a]	2946	4714	5241	5481	6028	6313	6514	7168	7893	8655	9499	10404
9 Community, social and personal services [a]	2663	3001	3117	3180	3299	3422	3570	3791	3981	4215	4497	4880
Total, Industries	62670	71911	77040	78627	83219	87153	92049	99041	106436	114130	121781	130062
Producers of Government Services	4053	5712	5997	6455	6862	7366	7932	8397	8783	9052	9320	9509
Other Producers	...	...	...	...	...	...	...	...	...	...	...	...
Subtotal	66723	77623	83037	85082	90081	94518	99981	107437	115219	123182	131101	139571
Less: Imputed bank service charge	...	...	...	...	...	...	...	...	...	...	...	...
Plus: Import duties	...	...	...	...	...	...	...	...	...	...	...	...
Plus: Value added tax	...	...	...	...	...	...	...	...	...	...	...	...
Equals: Gross Domestic Product	66723	77623	83037	85082	90081	94518	99981	107437	115219	123182	131101	139571

a) Business services are included in item 'Community, social and personal services'.

Indonesia

1.12 Relations Among National Accounting Aggregates

Thousand Million Indonesian rupiahs

	1980	1983	1984	1985	1986	1987	1988	1989	1990	1991	1992	1993
Gross Domestic Product	45446	71215 77623	89885	96997	102683	124817	142105	167185	195597	227502	260786	...
Plus: Net factor income from the rest of the world	-2011	-3036 -3283	-4183	-3941	-4193	-6022	-6922	-8074	-9614	-10899	-12213	...
Equals: Gross National Product	43435	68179 74340	85702	93056	98490	118795	135183	159111	185983	216603	248573	...
Less: Consumption of fixed capital	2962	4629 3881	4494	4850	5134	6241	7105	8365	9784	11380	13045	...
Equals: National Income	40473	63550 70459	81208	88206	93356	112554	128078	150746	176199	205223	235528	...
Plus: Net current transfers from the rest of the world	...	... ...	...	...	...	...	...	...	...	...	...	...
Equals: National Disposable Income	...	... ...	...	...	...	...	...	...	...	...	...	...
Less: Final consumption	...	... ...	...	...	...	...	...	...	...	...	...	...
Equals: Net Saving	...	... ...	...	...	...	...	...	...	...	...	...	...
Less: Surplus of the nation on current transactions	...	... ...	...	...	...	...	...	...	...	...	...	...
Equals: Net Capital Formation	...	... ...	...	...	...	...	...	...	...	...	...	...

Iran(Islamic Repub.of)

General note. The preparation of national accounts statistics in Iran is undertaken by the National Accounts Department, Bank Markazi Jomhouri Islami Iran, Tehran. The official estimates are published in the annual bulletin 'Bank Markazi Jomhouri Islami Iran, Economic Report and Balance Sheet'. Detailed data as well as description of sources and methods used for national accounts estimation are published in the latest volume of the National Accounts of Iran, 1974-1987. The estimates are generally in accordance with the classifications and definitions recommended in the United Nations System of National Accounts (SNA). Input-output tables have been compiled for the years 1965, 1969, 1973 and 1984. The following tables have been prepared from successive replies to the United Nations national accounts questionnaire. When the scope and coverage of the estimates differ for conceptual or statistical reasons from the definitions and classifications recommended in SNA, a footnote is indicated to the relevant tables.

Sources and methods:

(a) Gross domestic product. Gross Domestic Product is estimated mainly through production approach.

(b) Expenditure on the gross domestic product. The expenditure approach is used to estimate all components of Gross Domestic Product by expenditure type except gross fixed capital formation in machinery which is calculated mainly by commodity-flow approach. Estimates for government final consumption expenditure are based on records from all sectors of general government. Private final consumption expenditure is estimated using data from family budget surveys. The estimates of gross fixed capital formation in private construction are derived from annual surveys on construction. The data on investment in construction by the public sector is obtained from the accounts of different government units. The capital formation in machinery and equipment is estimated through commodity-flow approach using information on domestic production, imports and exports of capital goods. The estimates of exports and imports of goods and services are obtained from the balance of payments accounts and foreign trade statistics. For the constant price estimates all items of Gross Domestic Product by expenditure type are deflated by appropriate price indices.

(c) Cost-structure of the gross domestic product. The estimates of compensation of employees are obtained in the process of estimating value added by industrial origin. Consumption of fixed capital is estimated according to useful lifetime of different type of capital goods. Operating surplus is obtained as a residual. Estimates of indirect taxes and subsidies are based on government accounts.

(d) Gross domestic product by kind of economic activity. The table of Gross Domestic Product by kind of economic activity is prepared in factor values. The production approach is used to estimate the value added of most industries. The income approach is used for producers of government services, communication and part of other services. The agricultural estimates are based on annual surveys of agriculture, carried out by ministry of agriculture. The estimates are checked using the results of the annual family budget surveys. Data on the production of red meat are based on information supplied by slaughter houses in urban areas and on the results of expenditure surveys in rural areas. The data are then converted to current-price estimates by using wholesale price index. Statistics concerning forestry and fishing are obtained from concerned agencies. Mining estimates are based on annual sample surveys and the 1991 Census of Mining. The value added of oil sector is derived from the reports of the Ministry of Oil. The manufacturing estimates for large establishments which employ 10 workers or more are based on the results of the annual surveys of manufacturing. For small establishments, estimates are derived using the sample surveys of 1986 and information from other sources. The estimates of electricity, gas and water are based on information obtained from the government accounts. Estimates for private construction in the urban areas are obtained from the results of Bank Markazi's annual surveys with adjustments made to cover contractors' profits which are not included in the surveys. As for the rural areas, the results of 1973 survey of rural construction by the Statistical Center of Iran are extrapolated using information concerning construction in small towns. For trade sector the gross margin is calculated using the results or survey of wholesale and retail trade in the urban areas. Estimates for transport sector are generally based on the sample surveys by Bank Markazi Jomhouri Islami Iran and financial statements of the government organizations involved. The value added of financial institutions and insurance is obtained directly from the financial statements of concerned institutions. The estimates for dwellings are based on data obtained from family budget surveys and imputations are made for owner-occupied dwellings. For producers of government services estimates are derived from government accounts. Estimates for social and personal services are based on information from various sources mainly the family budget surveys. For constant price estimates, the current values are deflated by an appropriate price index for each kind of economic activity.

1.1 Expenditure on the Gross Domestic Product, in Current Prices

Thousand Million Iranian rials — Fiscal year beginning 21 March

	1980	1983	1984	1985	1986	1987	1988	1989	1990	1991	1992	1993
1 Government final consumption expenditure	1380	2151	2190	2443	2371	2707	3199	3294	4054	5367	7988	...
2 Private final consumption expenditure	3531	7771	8927	9627	10439	12226	14906	18448	24071	31677	41295	...
A Households	3503	7640	8800	9516	10307	12086	14775	18369	23943	...	...	...
B Private non-profit institutions serving households	28	131	127	111	132	139	131	79	127	...	...	...
3 Gross capital formation	1962	3096	3604	3321	3593	5079	4253	6600	10490	16650	22132	...
A Increase in stocks	520	226	508	562	1099	2417	1296	2891	4827	5806	6441	...
B Gross fixed capital formation	1442	2870	3096	2759	2494	2662	2957	3709	5663	10844	15691	...
Residential buildings	623	1285	1383	1366	1269	1318	1315	1572	2030	...	...	...
Non-residential buildings	526	838	851	731	826	881	998	1096	1871	...	...	...
Other construction and land improvement etc.										...	...	...
Other	293	747	862	662	399	463	644	1042	1761	...	...	...
4 Exports of goods and services	883	1878	1570	1251	553	837	1514	2773	5395	7439	9645	...
5 Less: Imports of goods and services	1089	1851	1605	1266	935	950	1756	3594	6792	9749	11446	...
Statistical discrepancy	-35	330	119	400	207	51	189	266	-573	-1277	-1803	...
Equals: Gross Domestic Product	6632	13376	14804	15775	16227	19949	22304	27787	36645	50107	67811	...

1.2 Expenditure on the Gross Domestic Product, in Constant Prices

Thousand Million Iranian rials — Fiscal year beginning 21 March

	1980	1983	1984	1985	1986	1987	1988	1989	1990	1991	1992	1993
	\multicolumn{12}{c}{At constant prices of:1982}											
1 Government final consumption expenditure	1968	1930	1811	1898	1508	1403	1396	1189	1337	...	...	...
2 Private final consumption expenditure	5360	6804	7170	7291	6544	6141	6172	6327	7564	...	...	...
A Households	5316	6693	7072	7206	6460	6075	6120	6298	7523	...	...	...
B Private non-profit institutions serving households	44	111	98	85	84	67	52	29	40	...	...	...
3 Gross capital formation	2575	2710	2880	2439	2057	2058	1432	1766	2201	...	...	...

Iran(Islamic Repub.of)

1.2 Expenditure on the Gross Domestic Product, in Constant Prices
(Continued)

Thousand Million Iranian rials — Fiscal year beginning 21 March

	1980	1983	1984	1985	1986	1987	1988	1989	1990	1991	1992	1993
					At constant prices of:1982							
A Increase in stocks	727	159	318	286	411	698	288	549	822	...	...	...
B Gross fixed capital formation	1848	2551	2562	2153	1646	1361	1144	1217	1379	...	...	...
Residential buildings	817	1100	1063	991	794	665	508	508	493	...	...	...
Non-residential buildings	673	731	671	545	531	451	386	356	425	...	...	...
Other construction and land improvement etc.										...	...	...
Other	358	720	828	617	320	245	249	353	461	...	...	...
4 Exports of goods and services	869	1899	1546	1400	1221	1557	1730	1866	2253	...	...	...
5 Less: Imports of goods and services	1175	1883	1638	1305	946	1006	791	946	1274	...	...	...
Statistical discrepancy a	-42	475	275	350	-134	214	-470	-421	-1149	...	...	...
Equals: Gross Domestic Product	9556	11935	12044	12072	10249	10368	9468	9782	10930	...	...	...

a) Item 'Statistical discrepancy' includes terms of trade adjustment.

1.3 Cost Components of the Gross Domestic Product

Thousand Million Iranian rials — Fiscal year beginning 21 March

	1980	1983	1984	1985	1986	1987	1988	1989	1990	1991	1992	1993
1 Indirect taxes, net	161	446	561	608	613	665	551	758	890	...	...	...
A Indirect taxes	290	611	731	782	799	816	691	998	1410	...	...	...
B Less: Subsidies	129	165	170	175	186	151	140	239	520	...	...	...
2 Consumption of fixed capital	865	1474	1724	1867	2299	2886	3290	3957	5443	...	...	...
3 Compensation of employees paid by resident producers to:	5641	11126	12399	12902	13109	16347	18275	22807	30884	...	...	...
4 Operating surplus	...	...	...	...	...	...	...	...	...	...	...	...
Statistical discrepancy	-35	330	119	400	207	51	189	266	-573	...	...	...
Equals: Gross Domestic Product	6632	13376	14804	15775	16227	19949	22304	27787	36645	...	...	...

1.4 General Government Current Receipts and Disbursements

Thousand Million Iranian rials — Fiscal year beginning 21 March

	1980	1983	1984	1985	1986	1987	1988	1989	1990	1991	1992	1993
					Receipts							
1 Operating surplus	...	...	...	...	...	...	...	...	...	...	...	...
2 Property and entrepreneurial income	916	1815	1408	1229	450	790	1097	1972	1148	...	...	...
3 Taxes, fees and contributions	516	1167	1371	1568	1595	1686	1696	2036	2903	...	...	...
A Indirect taxes	290	611	731	782	799	816	691	998	1410	...	...	...
B Direct taxes	120	335	380	507	511	563	638	642	955	...	...	...
C Social security contributions	104	217	256	274	281	302	362	389	530	...	...	...
D Compulsory fees, fines and penalties	2	3	4	5	5	5	6	8	9	...	...	...
4 Other current transfers	115	186	456	453	281	415	100	111	3061	...	...	...
Total Current Receipts of General Government	1546	3168	3235	3250	2325	2891	2892	4118	7112	...	...	...
					Disbursements							
1 Government final consumption expenditure	1380	2151	2190	2443	2371	2707	3199	3294	4054	...	...	...
A Compensation of employees	1125	1596	1640	1883	1927	2182	2466	2607	3092	...	...	...
B Consumption of fixed capital	...	...	...	...	...	...	...	...	...	...	...	...
C Purchases of goods and services, net	255	555	550	560	443	526	733	688	963	...	...	...
D Less: Own account fixed capital formation	...	...	...	...	...	...	...	...	...	...	...	...
E Indirect taxes paid, net	...	...	...	...	...	...	...	...	...	...	...	...
2 Property income	35	11	6	10	5	4	5	3	3	...	...	...
A Interest	35	11	6	10	5	4	5	3	3	...	...	...
B Net land rent and royalties	-	-	-	-	-	-	-	-	...	...	...	...

Iran(Islamic Repub.of)

1.4 General Government Current Receipts and Disbursements
(Continued)

Thousand Million Iranian rials — Fiscal year beginning 21 March

	1980	1983	1984	1985	1986	1987	1988	1989	1990	1991	1992	1993
3 Subsidies	129	165	170	175	186	151	140	239	520	...	...	...
4 Other current transfers	366	549	560	343	402	614	772	736	1283	...	...	...
A Social security benefits	94	209	246	264	270	290	349	353	502	...	...	...
B Social assistance grants										...	...	...
C Other	272	340	314	80	132	323	423	383	780	...	...	...
5 Net saving	-364	292	309	280	-637	-584	-1223	-153	1252	...	...	...
Total Current Disbursements and Net Saving of General Government	1546	3168	3235	3250	2325	2891	2892	4118	7112	...	...	...

1.7 External Transactions on Current Account, Summary

Thousand Million Iranian rials — Fiscal year beginning 21 March

	1980	1983	1984	1985	1986	1987	1988	1989	1990	1991	1992	1993
Payments to the Rest of the World												
1 Imports of goods and services	1089	1851	1605	1266	935	950	1756	3594	6792	...	...	...
A Imports of merchandise c.i.f.	963	1801	1548	1211	911	931	1729	3494	6624	...	...	...
B Other [a]	126	49	58	55	24	20	28	100	168	...	...	...
2 Factor income to the rest of the world	94	115	102	95	61	65	177	382	531	...	...	...
A Compensation of employees	65	99	89	86	56	61	164	357	505	...	...	...
B Property and entrepreneurial income	29	16	13	9	5	5	12	25	25	...	...	...
3 Current transfers to the rest of the world	...	...	...	...	...	...	...	...	...	...	...	...
4 Surplus of the nation on current transactions	-180	21	-46	-49	-401	-153	-358	-1032	-1660	...	...	...
Payments to the Rest of the World and Surplus of the Nation on Current Transactions	1002	1987	1661	1312	596	863	1574	2944	5662	...	...	...
Receipts From The Rest of the World												
1 Exports of goods and services	883	1878	1570	1251	553	837	1514	2773	5395	...	...	...
A Exports of merchandise f.o.b.	46	31	33	41	70	81	10	27	24	...	...	...
B Other [b]	837	1847	1537	1210	483	756	1504	2746	5371	...	...	...
2 Factor income from rest of the world	119	109	91	61	43	26	60	170	267	...	...	...
A Compensation of employees	48	39	37	26	15	12	27	87	120	...	...	...
B Property and entrepreneurial income	72	69	54	35	28	14	34	84	147	...	...	...
3 Current transfers from rest of the world	...	...	...	...	...	...	...	...	...	...	...	...
Receipts from the Rest of the World on Current Transactions	1002	1987	1661	1312	596	863	1574	2944	5662	...	...	...

a) Item 'Other' of Imports of goods and services refers to imports of services only.
b) Item 'Other' of exports of goods and services includes export of oil.

1.8 Capital Transactions of The Nation, Summary

Thousand Million Iranian rials — Fiscal year beginning 21 March

	1980	1983	1984	1985	1986	1987	1988	1989	1990	1991	1992	1993
Finance of Gross Capital Formation												
Gross saving	1782	3117	3558	3272	3192	4926	3895	5568	8829	...	...	...
1 Consumption of fixed capital	865	1474	1724	1867	2299	2886	3290	3957	5443	...	...	...
2 Net saving	917	1643	1833	1406	894	2040	604	1611	3387	...	...	...
Less: Surplus of the nation on current transactions	-180	21	-46	-49	-401	-153	-358	-1032	-1660	...	...	...
Finance of Gross Capital Formation	1962	3096	3604	3321	3593	5079	4253	6600	10490	...	...	...
Gross Capital Formation												
Increase in stocks	520	226	508	562	1099	2417	1296	2891	4827	...	...	...
Gross fixed capital formation	1442	2870	3096	2759	2494	2662	2957	3709	5663	...	...	...
1 General government [a]	687	1262	1262	1087	1094	1100	1201	1424	2616	...	...	...
2 Corporate and quasi-corporate enterprises [ab]	...	...	...	...	...	...	...	...	...	...	...	...
3 Other [b]	755	1608	1834	1672	1401	1562	1756	2285	3046	...	...	...
Gross Capital Formation	1962	3096	3604	3321	3593	5079	4253	6600	10490	...	...	...

a) Public corporate and quasi corporate enterprises are included in item 'General government'.
b) Private corporate and quasi-corporate enterprises are included in item 'Other'.

Iran(Islamic Repub.of)

1.10 Gross Domestic Product by Kind of Activity, in Current Prices

Thousand Million Iranian rials — Fiscal year beginning 21 March

	1980	1983	1984	1985	1986	1987	1988	1989	1990	1991	1992	1993
1 Agriculture, hunting, forestry and fishing	1164	2335	2827	3110	3753	4891	5209	6670	8419	...	...	...
2 Mining and quarrying [a]	877	2070	1761	1595	747	1005	1100	1845	3967	...	...	...
3 Manufacturing	613	1142	1304	1296	1354	1837	2288	2906	4414	...	...	...
4 Electricity, gas and water	72	138	124	140	163	201	261	305	395	...	...	...
5 Construction	540	1167	1262	1174	1153	1168	1111	1288	1438	...	...	...
6 Wholesale and retail trade, restaurants and hotels	561	1510	1949	2281	2753	3569	4469	5529	6542	...	...	...
7 Transport, storage and communication	560	1031	1169	1182	1133	1316	1491	1791	2652	...	...	...
8 Finance, insurance, real estate and business services	954	1614	1895	2095	2217	2519	3001	3614	4296	...	...	...
9 Community, social and personal services [b]	148	324	318	402	380	454	560	623	817	...	...	...
Total, Industries	5491	11330	12610	13275	13651	16960	19490	24570	32940	...	...	...
Producers of Government Services	1172	1682	1737	1979	2044	2330	2401	2607	3092	...	...	...
Other Producers [b]	...	...	...	...	...	...	...	...	...	...	...	...
Subtotal [c]	6664	13013	14346	15254	15695	19290	21891	27177	36032	...	...	...
Less: Imputed bank service charge	193	83	104	86	81	6	137	148	277	...	...	...
Plus: Import duties	...	...	...	...	...	...	...	...	...	...	...	...
Plus: Value added tax	...	...	...	...	...	...	...	...	...	...	...	...
Plus: Other adjustments [d]	161	446	561	608	613	665	551	758	890	...	...	...
Equals: Gross Domestic Product	6632	13376	14804	15775	16227	19949	22304	27787	36645	...	...	...

a) Oil production is included in item 'Mining and quarrying'.
b) Item 'Other producers' is included in item 'Community, social and personal services'.
c) Gross domestic product in factor values.
d) Item 'Other adjustments' refers to indirect taxes net of subsidies.

1.11 Gross Domestic Product by Kind of Activity, in Constant Prices

Thousand Million Iranian rials — Fiscal year beginning 21 March

At constant prices of: 1982

	1980	1983	1984	1985	1986	1987	1988	1989	1990	1991	1992	1993
1 Agriculture, hunting, forestry and fishing	1915	2193	2354	2538	2651	2716	2648	2746	2968	...	...	...
2 Mining and quarrying [a]	920	2077	1700	1716	1465	1664	1811	1948	2328	...	...	...
3 Manufacturing	965	1115	1252	1226	1148	1276	1302	1418	1644	...	...	...
4 Electricity, gas and water	93	132	148	162	174	193	186	207	247	...	...	...
5 Construction	763	937	890	773	649	550	433	426	438	...	...	...
6 Wholesale and retail trade, restaurants and hotels	786	1072	1231	1172	1045	1042	1008	1069	1136	...	...	...
7 Transport, storage and communication	903	890	906	907	786	643	600	655	796	...	...	...
8 Finance, insurance, real estate and business services	1259	1423	1507	1541	1362	1300	1269	1305	1392	...	...	...
9 Community, social and personal services [b]	190	284	244	285	236	262	282	267	299	...	...	...
Total, Industries	7794	10123	10231	10319	9515	9646	9540	10040	11247	...	...	...
Producers of Government Services	1717	1467	1373	1468	1226	1093	871	805	876	...	...	...
Other Producers [b]	...	...	...	...	...	...	...	...	...	...	...	...
Subtotal [c]	9510	11590	11604	11787	10741	10739	10410	10846	12124	...	...	...
Less: Imputed bank service charge	282	72	82	64	48	3	50	46	78	...	...	...
Plus: Import duties	...	...	...	...	...	...	...	...	...	...	...	...
Plus: Value added tax	...	...	...	...	...	...	...	...	...	...	...	...
Plus: Other adjustments [d]	232	398	457	465	387	348	234	267	265	...	...	...
Equals: Gross Domestic Product	9461	11916	11979	12189	11080	11085	10594	11067	12311	...	...	...

a) Oil production is included in item 'Mining and quarrying'.
b) Item 'Other producers' is included in item 'Community, social and personal services'.
c) Gross domestic product in factor values.
d) Item 'Other adjustments' refers to indirect taxes net of subsidies.

1.12 Relations Among National Accounting Aggregates

Thousand Million Iranian rials — Fiscal year beginning 21 March

	1980	1983	1984	1985	1986	1987	1988	1989	1990	1991	1992	1993
Gross Domestic Product	6632	13376	14804	15775	16227	19949	22304	27787	36645	50107	67811	...
Plus: Net factor income from the rest of the world	26	-7	-11	-34	-19	-39	-116	-212	-263	463	235	...
Factor income from the rest of the world	119	109	91	61	43	26	60	170	267	...	...	...
Less: Factor income to the rest of the world	94	115	102	95	61	65	177	382	531	...	...	...
Equals: Gross National Product	6658	13370	14793	15742	16208	19910	22188	27575	36381	50570	68046	...
Less: Consumption of fixed capital	865	1474	1724	1867	2299	2886	3290	3957	5443	...	...	...

Iran(Islamic Repub.of)

1.12 Relations Among National Accounting Aggregates
(Continued)

Thousand Million Iranian rials — Fiscal year beginning 21 March

	1980	1983	1984	1985	1986	1987	1988	1989	1990	1991	1992	1993
Equals: National Income	5794	11896	13068	13875	13910	17024	18897	23619	30939	...	...	...
Plus: Net current transfers from the rest of the world	...	...	...	...	...	...	...	...	...	...	...	...
Equals: National Disposable Income	5794	11896	13068	13875	13910	17024	18897	23619	30939	...	...	...
Less: Final consumption	4911	9923	11116	12070	12809	14933	18104	21742	28125	...	...	...
Statistical discrepancy	35	-330	-119	-400	-207	-51	-189	-266	573	...	...	...
Equals: Net Saving	917	1643	1833	1406	894	2040	604	1611	3387	...	...	...
Less: Surplus of the nation on current transactions	-180	21	-46	-49	-401	-153	-358	-1032	-1660	...	...	...
Equals: Net Capital Formation	1097	1622	1879	1454	1294	2193	963	2644	5047	...	...	...

2.1 Government Final Consumption Expenditure by Function, in Current Prices

Thousand Million Iranian rials — Fiscal year beginning 21 March

	1980	1983	1984	1985	1986	1987	1988	1989	1990	1991	1992	1993
1 General public services	42	42	50	57	91	87	111	128	133	...	...	...
2 Defence	335	880	831	928	867	1099	1345	1117	1124	...	...	...
3 Public order and safety										...	...	...
4 Education	341	333	376	492	586	561	673	808	1049	...	...	...
5 Health	101	117	127	162	162	152	209	276	301	...	...	...
6 Social security and welfare	37	135	142	183	198	214	227	274	388	...	...	...
7 Housing and community amenities	2	4	4	6	14	9	10	12	14	...	...	...
8 Recreational, cultural and religious affairs	18	29	30	38	41	37	44	48	68	...	...	...
9 Economic services	194	113	223	204	109	214	236	200	293	...	...	...
A Fuel and energy	21	2	6	...	...	...	...	...	...	...	...	...
B Agriculture, forestry, fishing and hunting	36	32	30	...	...	...	...	...	...	...	...	...
C Mining, manufacturing and construction, except fuel and energy	18	7	6	...	...	...	...	...	...	...	...	...
D Transportation and communication	33	25	30	...	...	...	...	...	...	...	...	...
E Other economic affairs	86	47	151	...	...	...	...	...	...	...	...	...
10 Other functions [a]	160	311	192	206	158	200	197	274	458	...	...	...
Total Government Final Consumption Expenditure	1380	2151	2190	2443	2371	2707	3199	3294	4054	...	...	...

a) Beginning 1985, the estimates of 'Other functions' exclude municipalities and social security fund.

2.2 Government Final Consumption Expenditure by Function, in Constant Prices

Thousand Million Iranian rials — Fiscal year beginning 21 March

At constant prices of: 1982

	1980	1983	1984	1985	1986	1987	1988	1989	1990	1991	1992	1993
1 General public services	61	37	40	43	55	41	42	41	38	...	...	...
2 Defence	449	809	723	764	600	639	702	500	505	...	...	...
3 Public order and safety										...	...	...
4 Education	496	294	302	369	354	267	252	256	298	...	...	...
5 Health	147	103	102	121	98	72	78	87	85	...	...	...
6 Social security and welfare	54	119	114	137	120	102	85	87	110	...	...	...
7 Housing and community amenities	3	3	3	4	8	4	4	4	4	...	...	...
8 Recreational, cultural and religious affairs	26	25	24	28	25	18	17	15	19	...	...	...
9 Economic services	282	100	179	153	66	102	88	63	83	...	...	...
A Fuel and energy	30	2	5	...	...	...	...	...	...	...	...	...
B Agriculture, forestry, fishing and hunting	53	29	24	...	...	...	...	...	...	...	...	...
C Mining, manufacturing and construction, except fuel and energy	26	6	5	...	...	...	...	...	...	...	...	...
D Transportation and communication	49	22	24	...	...	...	...	...	...	...	...	...
E Other economic affairs	125	41	121	...	...	...	...	...	...	...	...	...
10 Other functions [a]	233	273	153	154	96	95	73	87	130	...	...	...
Total Government Final Consumption Expenditure	1968	1930	1811	1898	1508	1403	1396	1189	1337	...	...	...

a) Beginning 1985, the estimates of 'Other functions' exclude municipalities and social security fund.

Iran(Islamic Repub.of)

2.5 Private Final Consumption Expenditure by Type and Purpose, in Current Prices

Thousand Million Iranian rials — Fiscal year beginning 21 March

	1980	1983	1984	1985	1986	1987	1988	1989	1990	1991	1992	1993
Final Consumption Expenditure of Resident Households												
1 Food, beverages and tobacco [a]	1537	3343	3844	4156	4834	5736	7023	8573	10204	...	...	...
2 Clothing and footwear	272	791	852	891	851	1136	1658	2220	2823	...	...	...
3 Gross rent, fuel and power	769	1738	2088	2349	2641	2913	3529	4319	5969	...	...	...
4 Furniture, furnishings and household equipment and operation	231	551	562	586	552	678	695	1020	1530	...	...	...
5 Medical care and health expenses	135	303	390	410	380	488	580	624	924	...	...	...
6 Transport and communication	233	479	540	605	617	721	746	853	1210	...	...	...
7 Recreational, entertainment, education and cultural services	49	111	129	150	155	175	202	261	400	...	...	...
8 Miscellaneous goods and services	277	324	395	369	278	239	342	500	883	...	...	...
Total Final Consumption Expenditure in the Domestic Market by Households, of which	3503	7640	8800	9516	10307	12086	14775	18369	23943	...	...	...
A Durable goods	224	576	403	447	341	380	331	432	613	...	...	...
B Semi-durable goods	415	1087	1187	1226	1179	1510	2100	2929	3394	...	...	...
C Non-durable goods	1778	3802	4376	4788	5526	6591	7986	9672	12833	...	...	...
D Services	1086	2176	2835	3055	3261	3605	4357	5336	7104	...	...	...
Plus: Direct purchases abroad by resident households	...	...	...	...	...	...	...	...	...	...	...	...
Less: Direct purchases in the domestic market by non-resident households	...	...	...	...	...	...	...	...	...	...	...	...
Equals: Final Consumption Expenditure of Resident Households	3503	7640	8800	9516	10307	12086	14775	18369	23943	...	...	...
Final Consumption Expenditure of Private Non-profit Institutions Serving Households												
Equals: Final Consumption Expenditure of Private Non-profit Organisations Serving Households	28	131	127	111	132	139	131	79	127	...	...	...
Private Final Consumption Expenditure	3531	7771	8927	9627	10439	12226	14906	18448	24071	...	...	...

a) Item 'Food, beverages and tobacco' includes expenditure in restaurants, cafes and hotels.

2.6 Private Final Consumption Expenditure by Type and Purpose, in Constant Prices

Thousand Million Iranian rials — Fiscal year beginning 21 March

	1980	1983	1984	1985	1986	1987	1988	1989	1990	1991	1992	1993
At constant prices of: 1982												
Final Consumption Expenditure of Resident Households												
1 Food, beverages and tobacco [a]	2471	2987	3156	3139	2920	2838	2956	3075	3463	...	...	...
2 Clothing and footwear	415	658	663	708	638	632	610	630	666	...	...	...
3 Gross rent, fuel and power	987	1511	1645	1735	1667	1510	1569	1507	1927	...	...	...
4 Furniture, furnishings and household equipment and operation	402	476	460	483	350	276	186	241	334	...	...	...
5 Medical care and health expenses	144	279	332	318	263	330	370	345	460	...	...	...
6 Transport and communication	396	414	414	445	391	332	255	270	319	...	...	...
7 Recreational, entertainment, education and cultural services	68	95	95	100	54	42	37	46	74	...	...	...
8 Miscellaneous goods and services	434	274	306	278	178	116	137	185	279	...	...	...
Total Final Consumption Expenditure in the Domestic Market by Households, of which	5316	6693	7072	7206	6460	6075	6120	6298	7523	...	...	...
A Durable goods	376	494	320	350	207	151	89	109	144	...	...	...
B Semi-durable goods	653	913	933	976	827	779	735	812	937	...	...	...
C Non-durable goods	2809	3388	3579	3619	3365	3265	3344	3454	4065	...	...	...

Iran(Islamic Repub.of)

2.6 Private Final Consumption Expenditure by Type and Purpose, in Constant Prices
(Continued)

Thousand Million Iranian rials — Fiscal year beginning 21 March

	1980	1983	1984	1985	1986	1987	1988	1989	1990	1991	1992	1993
				At constant prices of:1982								
D Services	1479	1898	2241	2261	2061	1880	1952	1923	2377	...	...	...
Plus: Direct purchases abroad by resident households	...	...	...	...	...	...	...	...	...	...	...	...
Less: Direct purchases in the domestic market by non-resident households	...	...	...	...	...	...	...	...	...	...	...	...
Equals: Final Consumption Expenditure of Resident Households	5316	6693	7072	7206	6460	6075	6120	6298	7523	...	...	...
	Final Consumption Expenditure of Private Non-profit Institutions Serving Households											
Equals: Final Consumption Expenditure of Private Non-profit Organisations Serving Households	44	111	98	85	84	67	52	29	40	...	...	...
Private Final Consumption Expenditure	5360	6804	7170	7291	6544	6141	6172	6327	7564	...	...	...

a) Item 'Food, beverages and tobacco' includes expenditure in restaurants, cafes and hotels.

2.11 Gross Fixed Capital Formation by Kind of Activity of Owner, ISIC Divisions, in Current Prices

Thousand Million Iranian rials — Fiscal year beginning 21 March

	1980	1983	1984	1985	1986	1987	1988	1989	1990	1991	1992	1993
					All Producers							
1 Agriculture, hunting, forestry and fishing	92	170	128	136	138	169	214	240	425	...	...	...
2 Mining and quarrying ab	76	209	160	126	137	89	122	176	212	...	...	...
3 Manufacturing b	110	189	216	149	156	197	272	356	624	...	...	...
4 Electricity, gas and water c	77	153	226	172	164	168	149	205	349	...	...	...
5 Construction	10	45	46	40	15	13	17	26	60	...	...	...
6 Wholesale and retail trade, restaurants and hotels	...	...	...	...	...	...	...	...	...	...	...	...
7 Transport, storage and communication	202	410	510	418	286	338	417	583	778	...	...	...
8 Finance, insurance, real estate and business services	623	1285	1383	1366	1269	1318	1315	1572	2030	...	...	...
9 Community, social and personal services										...	...	...
Total Industries	1442	2870	3096	2759	2494	2662	2957	3709	5663	...	...	...
Producers of Government Services	...	...	...	...	...	...	...	...	...	...	...	...
Private Non-Profit Institutions Serving Households	...	...	...	...	...	...	...	...	...	...	...	...
Total	1442	2870	3096	2759	2494	2662	2957	3709	5663	...	...	...

a) Item 'Mining and quarrying' refers only to oil and gas production.
b) Mining is included in item 'Manufacturing'.
c) Item 'Electricity, gas and water' excludes gas.

2.12 Gross Fixed Capital Formation by Kind of Activity of Owner, ISIC Divisions, in Constant Prices

Thousand Million Iranian rials — Fiscal year beginning 21 March

	1980	1983	1984	1985	1986	1987	1988	1989	1990	1991	1992	1993
				At constant prices of:1982								
					All Producers							
1 Agriculture, hunting, forestry and fishing	121	151	107	111	94	87	83	78	109	...	...	...
2 Mining and quarrying ab	96	189	140	99	90	46	47	58	48	...	...	...
3 Manufacturing b	138	174	192	124	111	102	105	118	155	...	...	...
4 Electricity, gas and water c	96	138	188	136	110	87	57	68	84	...	...	...
5 Construction	13	43	45	37	12	7	7	9	16	...	...	...
6 Wholesale and retail trade, restaurants and hotels	...	...	...	...	...	...	...	...	...	...	...	...
7 Transport, storage and communication	251	380	459	365	206	176	161	195	191	...	...	...
8 Finance, insurance, real estate and business services	817	1100	1063	991	794	665	508	508	493	...	...	...
9 Community, social and personal services										...	...	...
Total Industries	1848	2551	2562	2153	1646	1361	1144	1217	1379	...	...	...
Producers of Government Services	...	...	...	...	...	...	...	...	...	...	...	...
Private Non-Profit Institutions Serving Households	...	...	...	...	...	...	...	...	...	...	...	...
Total	1848	2551	2562	2153	1646	1361	1144	1217	1379	...	...	...

a) Item 'Mining and quarrying' refers only to oil and gas production.
b) Mining is included in item 'Manufacturing'.
c) Item 'Electricity, gas and water' excludes gas.

Iraq

General note. The preparaton of national accounts statistics in Iraq is undertaken by the Central Statistical Organization, Baghdad. The following presentation of sources and methods is mainly based on information contained in a handbook entitled 'Technical Note on the Estimation of National Income of the Republic of Iraq, 1962-1965'. The estimates are generally in accordance with the classifications and definitions recommended in the United Nations System of National Accounts (SNA). Input-output tables have been published in 'Input-Output and Social Accounts of Iraq 1960-1963'. The following tables have been prepared from successive replies to the United Nations national accounts questionnaire. When the scope and coverage of the estimates differ for conceptual or statistical reasons from the definitions and classifications recommended in SNA, a footnote is indicated to the relevant tables.

Sources and methods:

(a) Gross domestic product. GDP is estimated mainly through the production approach.

(b) Expenditure on the gross domestic product. The expenditure approach is used to estimate government final consumption expenditure, increase in stocks, and exports and imports of goods and services. This approach, in combination with the commodity-flow approach is used for gross fixed capital formation. The commodity-flow approach is used for private consumption expenditure. The estimates of government final consumption expenditure, consisting of wages, salaries and allowances and intermediate consumption of goods and services are obtained from the final accounts of the concerned bodies. The estimates of private final consumption expenditure is obtained as a residual for some years, while family budget surveys are used for other years. The data used for the estimation of increase in stocks are obtained from the final accounts of the establishments of the trade, transport and communication sectors. The industrial surveys provide data for the manufacturing industries. The gross fixed capital formation is classified according to economic activities and kinds of assets. Data are obtained from various sources such as the ordinary budget, actual expenditure on the development planning budget, reports and surveys. Foreign trade statistics provide data on imports of capital goods in c.i.f. values. Exports and imports of goods and services are estimated from foreign trade statistics and balance-of-payments data. GDP by expenditure type at constant prices is not estimated.

(c) Cost-structure of the gross domestic product. The estimates of compensation of employees in the socialist sector are obtained from the final accounts of the government and companies. For the private sector, the data are obtained from service surveys and internal trade surveys. Operating surplus is obtained as a residual. The depreciation estimates are prepared according to kinds of fixed assets and are based on the estimates of fixed capital formation, taking into consideration the prices of fixed assets and the average age of each kind of asset. The data on indirect taxes and subsidies are obtained from the actual accounts of the government or from the final accounts of the establishments of the socialist sector.

(d) Gross domestic product by kind of economic activity. The table of GDP by kind of economic activity is prepared in factor values. The production approach is used to estimate the value added of most industries. The income approach is used for transport and storage, private services and producers of government services. The commodity-flow approach is used to estimate gross output of the trade sector. Data on areas cultivated, average yield, quantity and value of each crop are obtained from the Central Statistical Organization while prices are based on a production survey. The production of various types of vegetables is estimated from data of the Ministry of Agriculture, and the valuation is made by using farm prices collected by the Central Statistical Organization. The results of the 1971 Agricultural census are used for estimating the value of fruit production. Intermediate consumption of these agricultural crops are estimated individually. The estimation of livestock products is based on sample surveys. The quantity of meat is estimated by multiplying the number of animals slaughtered in the abbatoirs by the average weight of the animals. The number of animals slaughtered outside the abbatoirs is estimated on the basis of data on exports of skins and guts. The estimate of the output of crude oil, natural gas and sulphur is based on the final accounts of the producing companies, from which data on the quantity and value of production and other factors of the value added are obtained. The data on manufacturing are obtained from the annual and quarterly industrial surveys which collect data on the number of establishments and employees, wages and salaries, quantity and value of inputs, increase in stocks and capital formation. The data for electricity, gas and water are obtained from the balance sheets and final accounts of the concerned establishments and from the Industrial Department of the Central Statistical Organization. The value added in the construction sector is based on the reports of the Central Statistical Organization and data on fixed capital formation which are based on the national development planning budget. The data used to estimate value added in the trade sector are taken from government final accounts, the internal trade survey and the hotel survey. For restaurants and hotels, a survey of services and hotels comprising the number of employees and establishments, wages and salaries, revenue, purchases, etc. is used. The final accounts of public establishments and the reports issued by the Central Statistical Organization are the basis for estimating transport and communication. The gross value of output is obtained by adding intermediate consumption to value added. Data on banking, insurance and other financing establishments have been obtained directly from concerned establishments. The services survey is used for the value added of real-estate services. For ownership of dwellings, rents are imputed based on the rent survey conducted by the Ministry of Finance and the family budget surveys. For government services, estimates are based on final government accounts and balance-sheets and final accounts of semi-governmental institutions. The services survey and the family budget surveys are used for estimating private services, GDP by kind of economic activity at constant prices is estimated taking 1964, 1969 and 1974 as base year.

1.1 Expenditure on the Gross Domestic Product, in Current Prices

Million Iraqi dinars

	1980	1983	1984	1985	1986	1987	1988	1989	1990	1991	1992	1993
1 Government final consumption expenditure	2451.2	5475.3	4989.1	4431.8	5252.8	5673.8	6260.0	5990.1	6142.0	7033.3	...	...
2 Private final consumption expenditure	3601.9	6848.9	7815.2	8098.7	8397.7	9204.4	10101.4	11232.4	11760.5	9611.1	...	...
3 Gross capital formation	4860.5	1979.9	2700.2	3664.6	2868.3	3533.7	4278.3	3988.0	5243.1	3809.1	...	...
A Increase in stocks	1053.3	-3533.3	-1733.2	-636.5	-990.9	-124.1	-118.3	-2317.5	-976.9	520.0	...	...
B Gross fixed capital formation	3807.1	5513.2	4433.4	4301.2	3859.2	3657.5	4396.6	6305.5	6220.0	3289.1	...	...
Residential buildings	...	...	...	...	...	671.4	998.9	2355.5	2772.0	902.0	...	...
Non-residential buildings	...	...	...	...	...	1141.1	1231.7	901.6	310.8	836.6	...	...
Other construction and land improvement etc.	...	...	...	...	...	1044.0	998.0	1413.6	...	...	...	...
Other	...	...	...	...	...	801.2	1168.0	1634.8	...	...	...	...
4 Exports of goods and services	10012.4	3107.9	3734.3	3774.7	2417.8	4087.1	3825.7	4482.6	4305.4	547.8	...	...
5 Less: Imports of goods and services	4977.6	4156.3	4316.4	4476.0	3873.6	4598.4	4432.9	4667.3	4154.2	1061.6	...	...
Equals: Gross Domestic Product	15948.4	13255.7	14922.4	15493.8	15063.0	17900.6	20032.5	21025.8	23296.8	19939.7	...	...

1.3 Cost Components of the Gross Domestic Product

Million Iraqi dinars

	1980	1983	1984	1985	1986	1987	1988	1989	1990	1991	1992	1993
1 Indirect taxes, net	177.7	634.7	371.5	482.0	411.0	300.6	600.3	617.9	448.5	-1373.6	...	...
A Indirect taxes	504.7	941.4	678.4	837.5	783.3	708.2	1019.6	1035.0	1024.8	485.6	...	...
B Less: Subsidies	327.0	306.7	306.9	355.5	372.3	407.6	419.3	417.1	576.3	1859.2	...	...
2 Consumption of fixed capital	804.3	1034.9	1236.8	1291.0	1304.0	1584.0	1748.9	1836.7	2056.3	1918.2	...	...
3 Compensation of employees paid by resident producers to:	2849.2	4458.7	4765.4	4889.9	5151.2	5697.0	6300.9	6705.2	7855.4	8989.9	...	...
4 Operating surplus	12117.2	7127.4	8548.7	8830.9	8196.8	10319.0	11382.4	11866.0	12936.6	10405.2	...	...
Equals: Gross Domestic Product	15948.4	13255.7	14922.4	15493.8	15063.0	17900.6	20032.5	21025.8	23296.8	19939.7	...	...

Iraq

1.10 Gross Domestic Product by Kind of Activity, in Current Prices

Million Iraqi dinars

	1980	1983	1984	1985	1986	1987	1988	1989	1990	1991	1992	1993
1 Agriculture, hunting, forestry and fishing [a]	741.9	1413.6	1941.9	2160.3	2173.7	2518.7	2834.3	3346.1	4613.3	6047.0	...	...
2 Mining and quarrying	9647.5	2863.8	3565.5	3484.5	2181.2	3594.8	3639.0	3894.8	3330.6	149.4	...	...
3 Manufacturing [abc]	712.2	1012.1	1300.7	1479.9	1755.8	2071.1	2641.0	2694.2	2058.7	1273.9	...	...
4 Electricity, gas and water [c]	49.5	124.3	163.3	200.3	219.9	298.5	325.7	269.0	247.5	162.4	...	...
5 Construction	1256.0	1975.2	1502.3	1413.6	1374.1	1430.8	1527.9	1417.8	1693.2	812.4	...	...
6 Wholesale and retail trade, restaurants and hotels [bc]	811.4	1565.0	1854.9	1931.1	1916.3	2182.7	2524.2	2376.4	3454.7	3608.2	...	...
7 Transport, storage and communication	667.2	801.7	807.9	772.3	1104.3	1269.7	1295.1	1533.3	2103.9	2645.9	...	...
8 Finance, insurance, real estate and business services [d]	651.0	1042.5	1534.9	1300.2	1647.5	1788.6	1981.0	2384.8	2781.2	3150.4	...	...
9 Community, social and personal services [d]	72.4	142.2	154.7	153.0	198.4	200.4	230.2	305.0	292.2	489.8	...	...
Total, Industries	14609.1	10940.4	12826.1	12895.2	12571.2	15355.3	16998.4	18221.4	20575.3	18339.4		
Producers of Government Services	1309.1	2114.4	2445.7	2687.7	2847.8	3228.0	3557.2	3599.1	3823.5	4845.7		
Other Producers											...	...
Subtotal [e]	15918.2	13054.8	15271.8	15582.9	15419.0	18583.3	20555.6	21820.5	24398.8	23185.1		
Less: Imputed bank service charge	147.5	433.8	720.9	571.1	767.0	983.3	1123.4	1412.6	1550.5	1871.8		
Plus: Import duties	...	...	...	...	...	...	...	...	...	...		
Plus: Value added tax	...	...	...	...	...	...	...	...	...	...		
Plus: Other adjustments [f]	177.7	634.7	371.5	482.0	411.0	300.6	600.3	617.9	448.5	-1373.6		
Equals: Gross Domestic Product	15948.4	13255.7	14922.4	15493.8	15063.0	17900.6	20032.5	21025.8	23296.8	19939.7	...	...

a) Agricultural services and related activities such as cotton ginning and pressing are included in item 'Manufacturing'.
b) Distribution of petroleum products is included in item 'Wholesale and retail trade'.
c) Gas distribution is included in item 'Wholesale and retail trade'.
d) Business services are included in item 'Community, social and personal services'.
e) Gross domestic product in factor values.
f) Item 'Other adjustments' refers to indirect taxes net of subsidies.

1.11 Gross Domestic Product by Kind of Activity, in Constant Prices

Million Iraqi dinars

	1980	1983	1984	1985	1986	1987	1988	1989	1990	1991	1992	1993
	\multicolumn{12}{c}{At constant prices of:1975}		
1 Agriculture, hunting, forestry and fishing [a]	370.8	403.2	446.9	517.7	495.5	453.9	483.5	536.3	575.3	404.7	...	...
2 Mining and quarrying	3026.2	1130.2	1399.6	1406.1	1747.2	2793.1	2898.3	2460.5	2253.0	54.3	...	...
3 Manufacturing [abc]	547.2	528.9	522.1	583.4	576.9	786.7	738.7	616.2	475.2	345.3	...	...
4 Electricity, gas and water [c]	37.2	65.7	73.2	79.1	84.8	87.4	97.3	112.8	93.5	48.7	...	...
5 Construction	839.0	1036.3	725.7	630.8	565.7	543.4	535.4	458.4	514.3	95.2	...	...
6 Wholesale and retail trade, restaurants and hotels [bc]	574.5	602.2	660.1	641.4	630.6	618.5	686.3	607.9	797.5	290.7	...	...
7 Transport, storage and communication	454.2	296.0	276.7	253.5	357.7	359.8	352.1	392.2	485.7	213.2	...	...
8 Finance, insurance, real estate and business services [d]	495.3	510.0	607.9	498.0	593.9	577.0	607.7	670.2	706.2	468.6	...	...
9 Community, social and personal services [d]	49.3	60.4	53.0	50.2	64.3	56.8	62.6	78.0	67.5	39.5	...	...
Total, Industries	6393.7	4632.9	4765.2	4660.2	5116.6	6276.6	6461.9	5932.5	5968.2	1960.2		
Producers of Government Services	891.2	897.5	837.5	882.1	922.5	914.7	967.2	920.7	882.6	390.4		
Other Producers											...	...
Subtotal [e]	7284.9	5530.4	5602.7	5542.3	6039.1	7191.3	7429.1	6853.2	6850.8	2350.6		
Less: Imputed bank service charge	100.4	184.1	246.9	187.4	248.5	278.6	305.4	361.4	357.9	150.8		
Plus: Import duties	...	...	...	...	...	...	...	...	...	...		
Plus: Value added tax	...	...	...	...	...	...	...	...	...	...		
Equals: Gross Domestic Product [e]	7184.5	5346.3	5355.8	5354.9	5790.6	6912.7	7123.7	6491.8	6492.9	2199.8	...	...

a) Agricultural services and related activities such as cotton ginning and pressing are included in item 'Manufacturing'.
b) Distribution of petroleum products is included in item 'Wholesale and retail trade'.
c) Gas distribution is included in item 'Wholesale and retail trade'.
d) Business services are included in item 'Community, social and personal services'.
e) Gross domestic product in factor values.

1.12 Relations Among National Accounting Aggregates

Million Iraqi dinars

	1980	1983	1984	1985	1986	1987	1988	1989	1990	1991	1992	1993
Gross Domestic Product	15948.4	13255.7	14922.4	15493.8	15063.0	17900.6	20032.5	21025.8	23296.8	19939.7	...	...
Plus: Net factor income from the rest of the world	474.2	-589.6	-470.5	-558.8	-692.4	-704.7	-700.4	-704.3	-773.9	-650.5	...	...
Factor income from the rest of the world	942.8	42.7	25.7	27.9	39.7	23.7	40.8	37.4	...	...		
Less: Factor income to the rest of the world	468.6	632.3	496.2	586.7	732.1	728.4	741.2	741.7	...	...		
Equals: Gross National Product	16422.6	12666.1	14451.9	14935.0	14370.6	17195.9	19332.1	20321.5	22522.9	19289.2		
Less: Consumption of fixed capital	804.3	1034.9	1236.8	1291.0	1304.0	1584.0	1748.9	1836.7	2056.3	1918.2	...	...

Iraq

1.12 Relations Among National Accounting Aggregates
(Continued)

Million Iraqi dinars

	1980	1983	1984	1985	1986	1987	1988	1989	1990	1991	1992	1993
Equals: National Income	15618.3	11631.2	13215.1	13644.0	13066.6	15611.9	17583.2	18484.8	20466.6	17371.0	...	...
Plus: Net current transfers from the rest of the world	-176.2	-10.5	32.4	-152.6	-89.1	-84.0	-18.7	-149.3	-49.3	122.8	...	...
Equals: National Disposable Income	15442.1	11620.7	13247.3	13491.4	12977.5	15527.9	17564.5	18335.5	20417.3	17493.8	...	...
Less: Final consumption	6053.1	12324.2	12804.3	12530.5	13650.5	14878.2	16361.4	17222.5	17902.5	16644.4	...	...
Equals: Net Saving	9389.0	-703.5	443.2	960.9	-673.0	649.7	1203.1	1113.0	2514.8	849.4	...	...
Less: Surplus of the nation on current transactions	5332.8	-1648.5	-1020.2	-1412.7	-2237.3	-1300.0	-1326.3	-1038.3	-672.0	-1041.5	...	...
Equals: Net Capital Formation	4056.2	945.0	1463.4	2373.6	1564.3	1949.7	2529.4	2151.3	3186.8	1890.9	...	...

2.8 Gross Capital Formation by Type of Good and Owner, in Constant Prices

Million Iraqi dinars

	1980 TOTAL	Total Private	Public Enterprises	General Government	1985 TOTAL	Total Private	Public Enterprises	General Government	1990 TOTAL	Total Private	Public Enterprises	General Government
	\multicolumn{12}{c}{At constant prices of:1975}
Increase in stocks, total	...	...	...	...	...	...	...	...	...	...	...	...
Gross Fixed Capital Formation, Total	2375.9	515.7	...	...	1684.9	378.8	...	...	1966.4	...	...	...
1 Residential buildings	451.3	325.0	...	...	438.9	300.1	...	...	842.0	...	...	...
2 Non-residential buildings	346.3	9.6	...	...	217.4	22.0	...	...	398.2	...	...	...
3 Other construction	623.6	-	...	...	669.2	0.3	...	...	233.2	...	...	...
4 Land improvement and plantation and orchard development	...	...	...	...	...	...	...	...	24.8	...	...	...
5 Producers' durable goods	954.7	181.1	...	...	359.4	56.4	...	...	468.2	...	...	...
A Transport equipment	345.8	121.5	...	...	60.1	26.1	...	...	165.7	...	...	...
B Machinery and equipment	608.9	59.6	...	...	299.3	30.3	...	...	302.4	...	...	...
6 Breeding stock, dairy cattle, etc.	...	...	...	...	...	...	...	...	...	...	...	...
Total Gross Capital Formation	...	...	...	...	...	...	...	...	...	...	...	...

	1991 TOTAL	Total Private	Public Enterprises	General Government	1992 TOTAL	Total Private	Public Enterprises	General Government
	\multicolumn{8}{c}{At constant prices of:1975}
Increase in stocks, total	...	...	...	...	...	...	...	...
Gross Fixed Capital Formation, Total	618.1	...	...	...	1010.7	...	...	...
1 Residential buildings	105.7	...	...	...	255.8	...	...	...
2 Non-residential buildings	98.1	...	...	...	83.7	...	...	...
3 Other construction	55.9	...	...	...	51.6	...	...	...
4 Land improvement and plantation and orchard development	20.4	...	...	...	33.9	...	...	...
5 Producers' durable goods	338.1	...	...	...	585.6	...	...	...
A Transport equipment	108.6	...	...	...	147.9	...	...	...
B Machinery and equipment	229.5	...	...	...	437.7	...	...	...
6 Breeding stock, dairy cattle, etc.	...	...	...	...	...	...	...	...
Total Gross Capital Formation	...	...	...	...	...	...	...	...

2.11 Gross Fixed Capital Formation by Kind of Activity of Owner, ISIC Divisions, in Current Prices

Million Iraqi dinars

	1980	1983	1984	1985	1986	1987	1988	1989	1990	1991	1992	1993
	\multicolumn{12}{c}{All Producers}
1 Agriculture, hunting, forestry and fishing	452.0	507.6	505.7	483.3	416.3	335.0	437.4	471.7	375.6	177.8	...	...
2 Mining and quarrying	191.3	194.3	141.6	333.9	181.3	215.3	379.3	608.2	385.1	134.5	...	...
3 Manufacturing	468.4	563.8	286.1	270.3	282.6	152.8	148.3	913.3	1014.1	710.0	...	...
4 Electricity, gas and water	271.3	607.3	454.5	366.8	492.7	357.0	402.8	434.3	311.5	241.7	...	...

Iraq

2.11 Gross Fixed Capital Formation by Kind of Activity of Owner, ISIC Divisions, in Current Prices
(Continued)

Million Iraqi dinars

		1980	1983	1984	1985	1986	1987	1988	1989	1990	1991	1992	1993
5	Construction	137.1	24.3	69.6	42.8	22.0	20.8	37.5	51.0	57.9	14.9	...	...
6	Wholesale and retail trade, restaurants and hotels [a]	149.1	91.7	93.4	95.9	103.2	45.7	60.9	223.5	57.7	59.3	...	...
7	Transport, storage and communication	662.0	803.1	801.5	744.8	727.0	263.0	186.8	310.3	288.7	271.3	...	...
8	Finance, insurance, real estate and business services [b]	449.7	712.4	725.4	660.7	546.1	521.5	899.2	2251.5	2710.6	853.9	...	...
9	Community, social and personal services [a,b]	1.3	2.6	3.0	4.0	3.4	4.3	4.8	4.6	4.7	4.9	...	...
	Total Industries	2782.2	3507.1	3080.8	3002.5	2774.6	1915.4	2557.1	5268.5	5205.9	2468.3	...	...
	Producers of Government Services	689.3	1205.5	847.6	696.9	597.1	1742.4	1839.5	1037.0	1014.2	820.7	...	...
	Private Non-Profit Institutions Serving Households	...	...	...	...	...	...	...	...	...	...	...	...
	Total [c]	3471.5	4712.6	3928.4	3699.4	3371.7	3657.8	4396.6	6305.5	6220.1	3289.1	...	...

a) Restaurants and hotels are included in item 'Community, social and personal services'.
b) Business services are included in item 'Community, social and personal services'.
c) Data for this table have not been revised, therefore, data for some years are not comparable with those of other tables.

2.12 Gross Fixed Capital Formation by Kind of Activity of Owner, ISIC Divisions, in Constant Prices

Million Iraqi dinars

		1980	1983	1984	1985	1986	1987	1988	1989	1990	1991	1992	1993
		\multicolumn{12}{c	}{At constant prices of:1988}
		\multicolumn{12}{c	}{All Producers}
1	Agriculture, hunting, forestry and fishing	855.9	758.5	696.4	618.0	490.6	363.7	437.4	435.6	254.0	73.0	...	...
2	Mining and quarrying	318.7	257.1	172.5	384.7	191.1	224.0	379.3	571.9	236.9	58.8	...	...
3	Manufacturing	856.5	824.2	386.4	339.8	326.8	164.6	148.3	848.9	637.7	456.1	...	...
4	Electricity, gas and water	502.9	891.1	617.3	461.6	571.7	385.7	402.8	402.1	184.8	152.6	...	...
5	Construction	281.6	36.1	100.3	60.3	30.5	22.3	37.5	47.8	32.6	12.5	...	...
6	Wholesale and retail trade, restaurants and hotels	276.8	136.8	127.2	123.5	120.7	49.2	60.9	206.4	34.9	27.0	...	...
7	Transport, storage and communication	1240.3	1187.9	1097.0	968.5	486.3	282.5	186.8	286.7	202.1	118.2	...	...
8	Finance, insurance, real estate and business services	855.6	124.6	999.4	840.6	641.0	565.0	899.2	2077.1	1430.3	291.8	...	...
9	Community, social and personal services	2.3	3.7	3.9	5.0	3.9	4.6	4.8	4.3	2.5	3.3	...	...
	Total Industries	5190.6	4220.0	4200.4	3802.0	2862.6	2061.6	2557.0	4880.8	3015.8	1193.3	...	...
	Producers of Government Services	1906.1	2994.2	1860.0	1665.7	1293.4	1877.8	1839.5	959.6	684.3	480.8	...	...
	Private Non-Profit Institutions Serving Households	...	...	...	...	...	...	...	...	...	...	...	...
	Total	7096.7	7214.2	6060.5	5467.4	4156.0	3939.5	4396.5	5840.4	3700.1	1674.1	...	...

Ireland

General note. The preparation of national accounts statistics in Ireland is undertaken by the Central Statistics Office, Dublin. The official estimates are published annually in 'National Income and Expenditure'. The following presentation of sources and methods is mainly based on a report entitled 'Basic statistics needed for the ESA accounts and tables: present situation and prospects for improvements' prepared by the Statistical Office of the European Communities in 1976 and on information received from Ireland's Central Statistics Office. The estimates are generally in accordance with the classifications and definitions recommended in the United Nations System of National Accounts (SNA). Official Input-Output tables have been published in respect of the years 1964, 1969 and 1975. The following tables have been prepared from successive replies to the United Nations national accounts questionnaire. When the scope and coverage of the estimates differ for conceptual or statistical reasons from the definitions and classifications recommended in SNA, a footnote is indicated to the relevant tables.

Sources and methods:

(a) Gross domestic product. Gross domestic product is estimated mainly through the income approach.

(b) Expenditure on the gross domestic product. The expenditure approach is used to estimate government final consumption expenditure, increase in stocks, exports and imports of goods and services. The commodity-flow approach is used to estimate private final consumption expenditure and gross fixed capital formation except in the case of building and construction and government capital formation. Government final consumption expenditure is estimated from the accounts of the various government bodies such as the ministries, the local authorities and Health Boards, extrabudgetary funds and the Industrial Development Authority. Data on private consumption expenditure are also estimated from Household Budget Inquiries. Largescale Household Budget Inquiries were carried out in 1951-52, 1965-66, 1973 and 1980. The 1951-52 and 1965-66 surveys were restricted to urban areas. Smallscale annual Household Budget Surveys were undertaken in 1974-1979 and 1981. These were restricted to urban areas for 1974-1979 but covered urban and rural areas in 1981. Estimates of transactions in goods and services are obtained from the censuses of industrial production and the statistics of imports and exports of merchandise. The goods are valued at national average retail prices where volume data are available. Otherwise, they are aggregated at appropriate producers' or import prices and adjusted for distribution costs. In building up the stock figures, industrial stocks from stocks inquiries and censuses of industrial production, and stockpiles of strategic commodities from the Department of Agriculture. Investment in building and construction is estimated through the use of data from the production surveys. Estimates of locally produced goods are obtained from production census data minus exports plus distribution margins. Estimates of imported goods are obtained from detailed import returns. The estimates of imports and exports of goods and services are obtained from balance-of-payments, special studies and surveys. For the constant price estimates, direct revaluation at base-year prices is used for items of private final consumption expenditure where quantity data are available. For all other components of GDP by expenditure type, price deflation is used.

(c) Cost-structure of the gross domestic product. Estimates of compensation of employees are based on wage rates and number of farm worker for the agricultural sector, censuses of industrial production for the industrial sectors, surveys conducted at intervals and updated by indexes of earnings for the trade sector, annual surveys conducted among the relevant companies for the transport, credit and insurance sectors and salary rates and number of employees for the other market services. Operating surplus is calculated from returns made to the revenue authorities and from government accounts. Depreciation is based on the perpetual inventory method for the agricultural sector. For private enterprises, it is taken as the income tax wear-and-tear and other allowances. Indirect taxes and subsidies are estimated from the government accounts.

(d) Gross domestic product by kind of economic activity. The table of GDP by kind of economic activity is prepared in factor values. The income approach is used to estimate the value added of all industries except agriculture, for which the production approach is used. Annual estimates of agricultural output are calculated on a commodity basis for crops, livestock and livestock products. The data on quantities and values are obtained from various sources such as Department of Agriculture and Central Statistics Office. The total quantities purchased and amounts paid by the purchasers for important agricultural items such as wheat and barley are available from various inquiries and adjusted for marketing margins and transport costs. For live exports, f.o.b. export value less an allowance for marketing margins, is taken as the output value. For the remaining items market prices are used as the basis for evaluation. Input data are obtained through the Department of Agriculture for fertilizers. Data for seeds are compiled indirectly from acreages and seedling rates. Own-account consumption of food and fuel is evaluated at agricultural prices. For mining, quarrying and manufacturing enterprises employing more than three persons, the estimates are based on annual censuses. Quarterly surveys of turnover and employment are conducted for manufacturing. For small-scale manufacturing, the number of persons engaged, which is derived as the difference between population census data and data from the production census, interpolated for intercensal years and projected forward, are multiplied by average income per person. The estimates of electricity, gas and water and of construction are based on annual inquiries. For trade, censuses of distribution provide bench-mark data for turnover, purchase of products, wages and salaries and intermediate inputs. For intervening years, monthly turnover figures from a sample of 2,500 establishments are used together with annual estimates of the number of employees and trends in earnings. For restaurants and hotels, annual surveys and revenue data are used. Transport is mainly provided by public enterprises and data are obtained from published accounts. Data obtained from annual reports, direct surveys on wages and salaries and revenue statistics are used for the estimates of the financial sector. For real estate and business services, data from population census, imputed average income and revenue accounts are used. The imputed rent of owner-occupied dwellings is taken as the average rent paid for similar dwellings in similar locations. Estimates of other private services are based on the results of inquiries into wages and salaries and on trends in operating surplus taken from revenue data. Data on government services are obtained from the government accounts. For the constant price estimates, double deflation is used for agriculture. Value added of all other economic activity sectors of GDP is extrapolated by a quantity index.

1.1 Expenditure on the Gross Domestic Product, in Current Prices

Million Irish pounds

		1980	1983	1984	1985	1986	1987	1988	1989	1990	1991	1992	1993
1	Government final consumption expenditure	1860.2	2857.3	3066.6	3300.9	3541.9 3541.9	3574.7	3539.5	3685.6	4082.3	4480.4	4842.4	5166.7
2	Private final consumption expenditure	6157.6	8813.8	9651.7	10597.6	11305.5 12138.4	12845.4	13811.3	15378.3	15800.4	16607.0	17574.5	18065.1
3	Gross capital formation	2604.2	3520.7	3733.4	3549.7	3535.5 3573.7	3480.8	3593.3	4552.2	5608.5	5281.3	4581.5	4628.6
	A Increase in stocks	-73.0	101.7	217.0	163.2	142.0 142.0	11.3	-76.6	188.6	665.1	620.2	-179.4	-190.8
	B Gross fixed capital formation	2677.2	3419.0	3516.4	3386.5	3393.5 3431.7	3469.5	3669.9	4363.6	4943.4	4661.1	4760.9	4819.4
	Residential buildings	578.0	786.6	856.6	845.4	881.7 919.9	910.5	811.2	964.9	1088.2	1120.6	1294.8	1303.5
	Non-residential buildings	829.6	985.5	984.2	928.0	919.3 919.3	870.9	949.8	1054.3	1481.8	1548.2	1482.8	1484.8
	Other construction and land improvement etc.												
	Other	1269.6	1646.8	1675.6	1613.1	1592.5 1592.5	1688.1	1908.9	2344.5	2373.5	1992.3	1983.3	2031.1
4	Exports of goods and services	4638.6	7751.6	9770.0	10738.4	10351.5 10377.3	11855.1	13633.6	16136.8	16115.8	16892.6	18706.9	21871.4
5	Less: Imports of goods and services	5899.9	8164.2	9815.1	10396.6	9860.4 9928.3	10681.3	11920.9	14359.5	14514.0	15072.1	15718.0	17441.9
	Equals: Gross Domestic Product	9360.7	14779.2	16406.6	17790.0	18874.0 19702.8	21074.7	22656.8	25393.4	27093.0	28189.2	29987.3	32289.9

Ireland

1.2 Expenditure on the Gross Domestic Product, in Constant Prices

Million Irish pounds

	1980	1983	1984	1985	1986	1987	1988	1989	1990	1991	1992	1993
					At constant prices of:1985							
1 Government final consumption expenditure	3163.1	3264.6	3241.9	3300.9	3387.5 / 3387.5	3223.3	3062.8	3034.4	3211.9	3297.6	3378.4	3414.7
2 Private final consumption expenditure	10419.8	9932.8	10132.4	10597.6	10810.9 / 11709.6	12098.9	12636.0	13631.4	13805.6	14161.2	14572.9	14740.6
3 Gross capital formation	3773.0	3864.8	3877.6	3549.7	3448.8 / 3507.9	3314.8	3230.0	3929.9	4876.1	4454.2	3701.9	3544.5
A Increase in stocks	-149.4	100.5	208.0	163.2	156.9 / 156.9	1.9	-97.0	176.6	670.7	625.4	-122.1	-181.2
B Gross fixed capital formation	3922.4	3764.3	3669.6	3386.5	3291.9 / 3351.0	3312.9	3327.0	3753.3	4205.4	3828.8	3824.0	3725.7
Residential buildings	...	841.0	875.9	845.4	822.7 / 882.2	832.5	723.9	825.2	865.5	857.8	945.3	901.7
Non-residential buildings	...	1106.4	1032.6	928.0	878.9 / 878.9	809.4	848.8	900.3	1213.6	1234.6	1159.4	1130.9
Other construction and land improvement etc.	...											
Other	...	1816.9	1761.1	1613.1	1590.3 / 1589.9	1670.9	1754.3	2027.8	2126.3	1736.4	1719.4	1693.2
4 Exports of goods and services	7271.4	8641.8	10075.5	10738.4	11048.3 / 11073.1	12592.3	13707.6	15115.1	16455.0	17312.8	19599.7	21489.9
5 Less: Imports of goods and services	8887.8	9166.6	10069.9	10396.6	10981.7 / 11047.3	11729.7	12304.9	13873.3	14639.1	14834.1	15639.1	16557.4
Statistical discrepancy	-53.3	-	-	-	-	...	...	...	...	...	...	...
Equals: Gross Domestic Product	15686.2	16537.4	17257.5	17790.0	17713.8 / 18630.8	19499.6	20331.5	21837.5	23709.5	24391.7	25613.8	26632.3

1.3 Cost Components of the Gross Domestic Product

Million Irish pounds

	1980	1983	1984	1985	1986	1987	1988	1989	1990	1991	1992	1993
1 Indirect taxes, net	830.4	1773.2	1873.6	1816.9	1987.7 / 2172.2	2297.7	2353.2	3197.3	2836.2	2876.2	3317.3	3192.9
A Indirect taxes	1571.2	2794.4	3113.5	3269.6	3475.2 / 3475.2	3672.4	3965.4	4377.0	4445.9	4514.0	4780.7	4902.8
B Less: Subsidies	740.8	1021.2	1239.9	1452.7	1487.5 / 1303.0	1374.7	1612.2	1179.7	1609.7	1637.8	1463.4	1709.9
2 Consumption of fixed capital	1034.2	1528.3	1596.8	1723.9	1835.1 / 1885.1	2062.5	2162.1	2379.3	2558.1	2722.9	2878.3	3043.8
3 Compensation of employees paid by resident producers to:	5585.0	8253.7	8957.1	9600.9	10254.8 / 10264.5	10796.6	11438.0	12253.5	13257.7	14112.0	15077.9	16092.8
A Resident households	5585.0	8253.7	8957.1	9600.9	10254.8 / 10264.5	10796.6	11438.0	12253.5	13257.7	14112.0	15077.9	16092.8
B Rest of the world	-	-	-	-	-	-	-	-	-	-	-	-
4 Operating surplus	1911.1	3224.0	3979.1	4648.2	4796.3 / 5380.9	5917.9	6703.4	7563.3	8441.0	8478.2	8713.8	9960.5
Equals: Gross Domestic Product	9360.7	14779.2	16406.6	17789.9	18873.9 / 19702.7	21074.7	22656.7	25393.4	27093.0	28189.3	29987.3	32290.0

1.4 General Government Current Receipts and Disbursements

Million Irish pounds

	1980	1983	1984	1985	1986	1987	1988	1989	1990	1991	1992	1993
					Receipts							
1 Operating surplus	39.0	114.0	127.3	174.5	177.1 / 177.1	166.6	213.6	143.3	119.7	140.6	150.0	...
2 Property and entrepreneurial income	184.1	367.3	396.4	434.0	331.8 / 331.8	369.9	313.5	286.8	345.6	407.0	425.3	...
3 Taxes, fees and contributions	3310.4	5783.3	6540.1	6930.9	7469.8 / 7469.8	8005.3	8920.3	9168.7	9796.1	10324.0	11119.0	...
A Indirect taxes [a]	1472.1	2581.1	2874.8	3032.5	3191.4 / 3191.4	3343.7	3671.7	4059.0	4144.4	4178.7	4455.4	...
B Direct taxes	1181.5	2051.2	2414.6	2564.2	2880.4 / 2880.4	3178.6	3641.5	3385.3	3775.5	4120.3	4489.1	...
C Social security contributions	656.8	1151.0	1250.7	1334.2	1398.0 / 1398.0	1483.0	1607.1	1724.4	1876.2	2025.0	2174.5	...
D Compulsory fees, fines and penalties [a]	...	...	...	...	...	...	...	...	...	...	...	...

Ireland

1.4 General Government Current Receipts and Disbursements
(Continued)

Million Irish pounds

	1980	1983	1984	1985	1986	1987	1988	1989	1990	1991	1992	1993
4 Other current transfers	96.9	180.2	122.6	170.1	157.8 / 157.8	237.5	181.3	170.5	215.0	366.2	337.3	...
Total Current Receipts of General Government	3630.4	6444.8	7186.4	7709.5	8136.5 / 8136.5	8779.3	9628.7	9769.3	10476.4	11237.8	12031.6	...

Disbursements

	1980	1983	1984	1985	1986	1987	1988	1989	1990	1991	1992	1993
1 Government final consumption expenditure [a]	1860.2	2857.3	3066.6	3300.9	3541.9 / 3541.9	3574.7	3539.4	3685.5	4082.3	4480.3	4842.4	...
A Compensation of employees	1181.2	1876.8	2047.0	2176.1	2334.8 / 2334.8	2418.7	2439.3	2530.9	2738.4	3014.8	3255.9	...
B Consumption of fixed capital	87.5	107.0	119.1	129.9	140.7 / 140.7	149.5	158.4	167.5	176.6	184.9	192.1	...
C Purchases of goods and services, net	...	...	...	...	...	...	...	...	...	...	...	...
D Less: Own account fixed capital formation	...	...	...	...	...	...	...	...	...	...	...	...
E Indirect taxes paid, net	...	...	...	...	...	...	...	...	...	...	...	...
2 Property income	590.6	1350.8	1503.6	1764.6	1758.1 / 1758.1	1944.1	1957.0	1967.4	2125.3	2146.2	2116.5	...
3 Subsidies	356.4	558.1	563.2	588.5	569.2 / 384.7	575.8	705.9	167.5	303.4	277.0	315.9	...
4 Other current transfers	1404.1	2745.5	3006.2	3325.3	3634.5 / 3819.0	3980.3	4156.3	4116.2	4341.4	4781.0	5225.1	...
A Social security benefits	502.4	1044.6	1128.6	1231.8	1303.0 / 1303.0	1339.4	1322.6	1306.6	1336.2	1448.5	1562.4	...
B Social assistance grants	677.3	1362.2	1514.7	1702.1	1897.5 / 2082.0	2188.5	2359.4	2325.8	2500.3	2752.7	3023.9	...
C Other	224.4	338.7	362.9	391.4	434.1 / 434.1	452.4	474.4	483.9	504.9	579.9	638.8	...
5 Net saving	-580.9	-1066.7	-953.3	-1269.9	-1367.2 / -1367.2	-1295.7	-729.8	-167.3	-376.0	-446.7	-468.1	...
Total Current Disbursements and Net Saving of General Government	3630.4	6445.0	7186.3	7709.4	8136.5 / 8136.5	8779.2	9628.8	9769.3	10476.4	11237.8	12031.8	...

a) Item 'Fees, fines and penalties' is included in item 'Indirect taxes' or is offset against item 'Final consumption expenditure'.

1.7 External Transactions on Current Account, Summary

Million Irish pounds

	1980	1983	1984	1985	1986	1987	1988	1989	1990	1991	1992	1993

Payments to the Rest of the World

	1980	1983	1984	1985	1986	1987	1988	1989	1990	1991	1992	1993
1 Imports of goods and services	5899.9	8164.2	9815.1	10396.6	9860.4 / 9928.5	10681.3	11920.9	14359.5	14514.0	15072.1	15718.0	17441.9
A Imports of merchandise c.i.f.	5346.1	7334.2	8892.6	9390.2	8745.5 / 8745.5	9137.0	10047.6	12114.4	12286.1	12688.3	13019.7	14622.7
B Other	553.8	830.0	922.5	1006.4	1114.9 / 1183.0	1544.3	1873.3	2245.1	2227.9	2383.8	2698.3	2819.2
2 Factor income to the rest of the world	832.1	1745.4	2342.9	2772.9	2705.1 / 2768.8	2899.4	3690.1	4577.6	4770.2	4627.3	4937.4	5352.3
A Compensation of employees	-	-	-	-	-	-	-	-	-	-	-	-
B Property and entrepreneurial income	832.1	1745.4	2342.9	2772.9	2705.1 / 2768.8	2899.4	3690.1	4577.6	4770.2	4627.3	4937.4	5352.3
3 Current transfers to the rest of the world	123.4	251.6	283.1	312.5	373.7 / 373.7	378.5	363.1	372.0	381.5	452.5	467.8	568.6
A Indirect taxes to supranational organizations	99.0	213.3	238.7	237.2	283.8 / 283.8	328.8	293.7	318.0	301.5	335.4	325.2	385.6
B Other current transfers	24.4	38.3	44.4	75.3	89.9 / 89.9	49.7	69.4	54.0	80.0	117.1	142.6	183.0
4 Surplus of the nation on current transactions	-1101.0	-1016.7	-952.5	-700.5	-540.2 / -642.0	-46.8	-	-419.8	-182.4	551.2	974.9	2088.5
Payments to the Rest of the World and Surplus of the Nation on Current Transactions	5754.4	9144.5	11488.6	12781.5	12399.0 / 12429.0	13912.4	15974.1	18889.3	19483.3	20703.1	22098.1	25451.3

Receipts From The Rest of the World

	1980	1983	1984	1985	1986	1987	1988	1989	1990	1991	1992	1993
1 Exports of goods and services	4638.6	7751.7	9770.0	10738.4	10351.5 / 10377.3	11855.1	13633.6	16136.8	16115.8	16892.6	18706.9	21871.4

Ireland

1.7 External Transactions on Current Account, Summary
(Continued)

Million Irish pounds

	1980	1983	1984	1985	1986	1987	1988	1989	1990	1991	1992	1993
A Exports of merchandise f.o.b.	4004.4	6812.7	8696.0	9526.8	9180.7 9180.7	10447.1	12073.0	14358.3	14100.5	14675.2	16386.8	19437.4
B Other	634.2	939.0	1074.0	1211.6	1170.8 1196.6	1408.0	1560.6	1778.4	2015.3	2217.4	2320.1	2433.9
2 Factor income from rest of the world	474.0	561.5	704.1	807.2	748.1 752.2	787.0	1028.3	1344.8	1638.9	1762.2	1642.8	1625.4
A Compensation of employees	9.4	12.4	12.0	13.4	16.0 16.0	16.0	16.0	16.0	16.0	15.3	15.8	15.8
B Property and entrepreneurial income	464.6	549.1	692.1	793.8	732.1 736.2	771.0	1012.3	1328.8	1622.9	1747.0	1627.0	1609.7
3 Current transfers from rest of the world	641.8	831.3	1014.4	1235.9	1299.5 1299.5	1270.3	1312.1	1407.7	1728.7	2048.1	1748.4	1954.4
A Subsidies from supranational organisations	384.4	463.1	676.8	864.2	918.3 918.3	798.9	906.3	1012.2	1306.3	1360.8	1147.5	1319.4
B Other current transfers	257.4	368.2	337.6	371.7	381.2 381.2	471.4	405.8	395.5	422.4	687.3	600.9	635.0
Receipts from the Rest of the World on Current Transactions	5754.4	9144.5	11488.5	12781.5	12399.1 12429.0	13912.4	15974.0	18889.3	19483.4	20702.9	22098.1	25451.2

1.8 Capital Transactions of The Nation, Summary

Million Irish pounds

	1980	1983	1984	1985	1986	1987	1988	1989	1990	1991	1992	1993
Finance of Gross Capital Formation												
Gross saving	1503.2	2503.9	2780.8	2849.2	2995.3 2931.6	3434.0	3593.2	4132.4	5426.2	5832.5	5556.3	6717.1
1 Consumption of fixed capital	1034.2	1528.3	1596.8	1723.9	1835.1 1885.1	2062.5	2162.1	2379.3	2558.1	2722.9	2878.3	3043.8
A General government	87.5	107.0	119.1	129.9	140.7 140.7	149.5	158.4	167.5	176.6	184.9	192.1	...
B Corporate and quasi-corporate enterprises	946.7	1421.3	1477.7	1594.0	1694.4 1744.4	1913.0	2003.7	2211.8	2381.5	2538.0	2686.2	...
C Other	...	...	...	...	... ...	...	...	...	...	...	...	...
2 Net saving	469.0	975.6	1184.0	1125.3	1160.2 1046.5	1371.5	1431.1	1753.1	2868.1	3109.6	2678.0	3673.3
A General government	-580.9	-1066.9	-953.3	-1269.9	-1367.2 -1367.2	-1295.7	-729.8	-167.3	-376.0	-446.7	-468.1	...
B Corporate and quasi-corporate enterprises	1049.9	2042.5	2137.3	2395.2	2527.4 2413.7	2667.2	2160.9	1920.4	3244.0	3556.3	3146.1	...
C Other	...	...	...	...	... ...	...	...	...	...	...	...	...
Less: Surplus of the nation on current transactions	-1101.0	-1016.7	-952.5	-700.5	-540.2 -642.0	-46.8	-	-419.8	-182.4	551.2	974.9	2088.5
Finance of Gross Capital Formation	2604.2	3520.6	3733.3	3549.7	3535.5 3573.6	3480.8	3593.2	4552.2	5608.6	5281.3	4581.4	4628.6
Gross Capital Formation												
Increase in stocks	-73.0	101.6	217.0	163.2	142.0 142.0	11.3	-76.6	188.6	665.1	620.2	-179.4	-190.8
Gross fixed capital formation	2677.2	3419.0	3516.4	3386.5	3393.5 3431.7	3469.5	3669.9	4363.6	4943.4	4661.1	4760.9	4819.4
1 General government	412.3	649.1	661.6	717.5	693.4 693.4	554.6	410.9	459.6	559.2	613.5	623.8	...
2 Corporate and quasi-corporate enterprises	2264.9	2769.9	2854.8	2668.9	2700.1 2738.3	2914.9	3259.0	3904.0	4384.3	4047.6	4137.1	...
3 Other	...	...	...	...	... ...	...	...	...	...	...	...	...
Gross Capital Formation	2604.2	3520.6	3733.4	3549.7	3535.5 3573.7	3480.8	3593.3	4552.2	5608.5	5281.3	4581.5	4628.6

Ireland

1.10 Gross Domestic Product by Kind of Activity, in Current Prices

Million Irish pounds

	1980	1983	1984	1985	1986	1987	1988	1989	1990	1991	1992	1993
1 Agriculture, hunting, forestry and fishing	999.4	1479.4	1688.7	1557.7	1531.8 / 1531.8	1803.9	2015.7	2174.1	1986.5	1928.3	2155.1	...
2 Mining and quarrying												...
3 Manufacturing	2520.6	4096.6	4612.8	5365.7	5605.0 / 5891.3	6214.5	6930.8	7835.7	8264.9	8721.6	9236.4	...
4 Electricity, gas and water												
5 Construction	862.6	1023.7	1002.7	967.2	968.0 / 1025.9	1041.1	1092.2	1123.8	1290.3	1364.7	1406.2	...
6 Wholesale and retail trade, restaurants and hotels	985.0	1595.6	1671.3	1929.9	1916.5 / 2003.1	2194.0	2171.8	2713.0	3149.6	3063.5	3025.8	
7 Transport, storage and communication	463.9	656.6	716.1	860.4	982.4 / 1008.9	1141.8	1230.3	1286.5	1392.8	1466.0	1518.6	
8 Finance, insurance, real estate and business services	461.6	715.3	870.4	991.6	1067.4 / 1146.9	1203.8	1397.5	1450.2	1531.6	1744.1	2200.8	
9 Community, social and personal services	1084.7	1716.7	1942.4	2021.4	2260.7 / 2640.6	2800.1	2968.6	3526.7	3881.9	4143.1	4137.4	...
Total, Industries	7377.8	11283.9	12504.4	13693.9	14331.8 / 15248.5	16399.2	17806.8	20109.9	21497.5	22431.2	23680.3	
Producers of Government Services	1541.2	2433.6	2672.2	2865.3	3116.6 / 3028.7	3200.3	3260.4	3441.4	3730.7	3990.5	4382.8	
Other Producers												...
Subtotal	8919.0	13717.7	15176.8	16559.2	17448.4 / 18277.2	19599.5	21067.2	23551.2	25228.2	26421.7	28063.1	...
Less: Imputed bank service charge	388.0	675.4	735.1	817.2	803.6 / 803.6	828.3	964.9	975.9	1006.0	1114.6	1139.0	
Plus: Import duties	359.3	543.3	597.4	633.3	678.3 / 678.3	690.7	790.9	873.2	902.6	869.9	883.6	
Plus: Value added tax	470.4	1193.6	1367.5	1414.6	1550.8 / 1550.8	1612.3	1763.8	1944.0	1968.9	2012.0	2179.3	...
Equals: Gross Domestic Product	9360.7	14779.2	16406.6	17789.9	18873.9 / 19702.7	21074.2	22657.0	25392.6	27093.7	28189.0	29987.0	...

1.12 Relations Among National Accounting Aggregates

Million Irish pounds

	1980	1983	1984	1985	1986	1987	1988	1989	1990	1991	1992	1993
Gross Domestic Product	9360.7	14779.2	16406.6	17789.9	18873.9 / 19702.7	21074.8	22656.7	25393.4	27092.9	28189.2	29987.3	32290.0
Plus: Net factor income from the rest of the world	-358.1	-1183.9	-1638.8	-1965.7	-1957.0 / -2016.6	-2112.4	-2661.8	-3232.8	-3131.3	-2865.0	-3294.6	-3726.8
Factor income from the rest of the world	474.0	561.5	704.1	807.2	748.1 / 752.2	787.0	1028.3	1344.8	1638.9	1762.2	1642.8	1625.4
Less: Factor income to the rest of the world	832.1	1745.4	2342.9	2772.9	2705.1 / 2768.8	2899.4	3690.1	4577.6	4770.2	4627.3	4937.4	5352.3
Equals: Gross National Product	9002.6	13595.3	14767.8	15824.2	16917.0 / 17686.1	18962.5	19994.9	22160.6	23961.6	25324.2	26692.7	28563.1
Less: Consumption of fixed capital	1034.2	1528.3	1596.8	1723.9	1835.1 / 1885.1	2062.5	2162.1	2379.3	2558.1	2722.9	2878.3	3043.8
Equals: National Income	7968.4	12067.0	13171.0	14100.3	15081.9 / 15801.0	16899.9	17832.8	19781.2	21403.5	22601.4	23814.4	25519.3
Plus: Net current transfers from the rest of the world	518.4	579.7	731.3	923.4	925.8 / 925.8	891.8	949.1	1035.8	1347.2	1595.7	1280.6	1385.8
Current transfers from the rest of the world	641.8	831.3	1014.4	1235.9	1299.5 / 1299.5	1270.3	1312.1	1407.7	1728.6	2048.1	1748.4	1954.3
Less: Current transfers to the rest of the world	123.4	251.6	283.1	312.5	373.7 / 373.7	378.5	363.1	371.9	381.4	452.4	467.9	568.6
Equals: National Disposable Income	8486.8	12646.7	13902.3	15023.7	16007.6 / 16726.8	17791.7	18781.9	20817.0	22750.7	24197.1	25094.9	26905.1
Less: Final consumption	8017.8	11671.1	12718.3	13898.5	14847.4 / 15680.3	16420.2	17350.8	19063.9	19882.7	21087.4	22416.9	23231.8
Equals: Net Saving	469.0	975.6	1184.0	1125.3	1160.2 / 1046.5	1371.5	1431.1	1753.1	2868.1	3109.6	2678.0	3673.3
Less: Surplus of the nation on current transactions	-1101.0	-1016.7	-952.5	-700.5	-540.2 / -642.0	-46.8	-	-419.8	-182.4	551.2	974.9	2088.5
Equals: Net Capital Formation	1570.0	1992.3	2136.5	1825.8	1700.4 / 1688.6	1418.3	1431.1	2172.9	3050.5	2558.4	1703.2	1584.8

Ireland

2.5 Private Final Consumption Expenditure by Type and Purpose, in Current Prices

Million Irish pounds

	1980	1983	1984	1985	1986	1987	1988	1989	1990	1991	1992	1993
Final Consumption Expenditure of Resident Households											
1 Food, beverages and tobacco	2562.3	3807.8	4127.6	4297.4	4510.9 / 4495.8	4753.1	5003.1	5595.5	5676.7	6024.3	6358.1	6431.9
A Food	1548.1	2216.6	2383.0	2408.9	2498.1 / 2492.9	2671.4	2747.5	3056.9	3070.3	3239.9	3356.6	3368.5
B Non-alcoholic beverages	79.1	128.8	134.4	155.5	156.0 / 184.8	180.6	217.0	245.6	226.2	231.5	256.8	243.0
C Alcoholic beverages	695.9	1040.5	1155.1	1233.6	1338.3 / 1259.6	1329.1	1462.2	1696.8	1772.5	1859.6	2015.5	2084.6
D Tobacco	239.1	422.0	455.0	499.4	518.5 / 558.6	572.1	576.5	596.3	607.7	693.4	729.1	735.9
2 Clothing and footwear	453.3	582.8	668.4	775.3	797.8 / 881.5	907.3	1006.2	1122.9	1131.3	1200.0	1177.5	1301.1
3 Gross rent, fuel and power	678.1	1033.0	1117.7	1253.4	1323.3 / 1665.9	1727.5	1797.5	1919.0	1953.5	2076.2	2133.1	2245.6
A Fuel and power	350.3	528.2	561.7	628.3	654.4 / 652.6	671.2	670.1	731.0	710.4	749.6	720.1	761.9
B Other	327.8	504.8	556.0	625.1	668.8 / 1013.4	1056.3	1127.3	1188.0	1243.2	1326.6	1413.0	1483.7
4 Furniture, furnishings and household equipment and operation	449.5	589.0	609.5	727.6	802.2 / 863.7	877.8	1064.1	1220.7	1158.7	1216.3	1261.2	1259.1
A Household operation	123.9	196.6	220.0	244.2	298.4 / 328.2	325.9	416.4	495.2	454.1	487.2	517.9	530.1
B Other	325.6	392.3	389.4	483.4	503.8 / 535.5	552.0	647.6	725.6	704.6	729.1	743.3	729.0
5 Medical care and health expenses	128.3	217.9	267.2	383.2	450.7 / 450.7	490.6	532.7	557.1	590.9	644.6	706.8	750.5
6 Transport and communication	824.4	1142.9	1281.1	1391.7	1385.9 / 1549.5	1607.2	1785.0	2040.1	2166.7	2168.3	2287.3	2389.3
A Personal transport equipment	277.7	267.1	311.3	358.2	373.4 / 375.5	373.7	474.8	628.4	707.6	575.3	584.0	604.2
B Other	546.7	875.8	969.8	1033.5	1012.4 / 1174.1	1233.5	1310.2	1411.7	1459.2	1593.0	1703.3	1785.2
7 Recreational, entertainment, education and cultural services	619.3	830.3	903.6	1014.8	1087.3 / 1257.8	1419.5	1457.2	1631.0	1747.3	1881.4	2066.0	2183.1
A Education	137.3	211.9	245.5	279.8	323.4 / 399.0	439.4	458.3	482.2	506.1	526.6	590.1	649.1
B Other	482.0	618.4	658.0	735.0	763.9 / 858.8	980.1	999.0	1148.8	1241.1	1354.8	1475.9	1534.1
8 Miscellaneous goods and services	435.0	637.2	740.8	870.5	928.7 / 1029.6	1169.3	1293.9	1477.5	1671.8	1767.6	1869.7	1904.8
A Personal care [a]	78.9	130.4	141.3	204.9	224.0 / 247.3	263.8	265.1	259.9	294.8	415.5	480.8	436.5
B Expenditures in restaurants, cafes and hotels	89.2	144.3	154.2	176.0	180.1 / 222.3	247.3	292.9	352.9	384.1	375.6	346.8	378.0
C Other	266.9	362.5	445.3	489.6	524.5 / 560.1	658.2	735.9	864.7	992.9	976.5	1042.1	1090.2
Total Final Consumption Expenditure in the Domestic Market by Households, of which	6150.3	8840.8	9715.9	10713.9	11286.6 / 12194.6	12952.3	13939.8	15563.9	16097.0	16978.7	17859.7	18465.4
Plus: Direct purchases abroad by resident households	283.4	363.0	378.0	401.7	511.1 / 435.9	457.1	526.5	565.4	573.4	566.8	664.3	690.6
Less: Direct purchases in the domestic market by non-resident households	281.9	390.0	442.0	518.0	492.2 / 492.2	564.0	655.0	751.0	870.0	939.0	949.0	1091.0
Equals: Final Consumption Expenditure of Resident Households [b]	6151.8	8813.8	9651.7	10597.6	11305.5 / 12138.4	12845.4	13811.3	15378.3	15800.4	16606.5	17575.0	18065.0
Final Consumption Expenditure of Private Non-profit Institutions Serving Households											
Equals: Final Consumption Expenditure of Private Non-profit Organisations Serving Households	...	...	...	...	... / ...	...	...	...	...	...	...	...
Private Final Consumption Expenditure	6151.8	8813.8	9651.7	10597.6	11305.5 / 12138.4	12845.4	13811.3	15378.3	15800.4	16606.5	17575.0	18065.0

a) Item 'Personal care' excludes services of barbers, beauty shops etc.
b) Item 'Final consumption expenditure of resident households' includes consumption expenditure of private non-profit institutions serving households.

Ireland

2.6 Private Final Consumption Expenditure by Type and Purpose, in Constant Prices

Million Irish pounds

At constant prices of: 1985

Final Consumption Expenditure of Resident Households

	1980	1983	1984	1985	1986	1987	1988	1989	1990	1991	1992	1993
1 Food, beverages and tobacco	...	4289.3	4274.8	4297.4	4195.6 / 4226.0	4402.8	4489.9	4863.7	4901.8	5078.7	5152.2	5144.9
A Food	...	2522.7	2443.0	2408.9	2371.2 / 2377.6	2488.9	2499.2	2671.9	2645.8	2754.8	2818.6	2827.9
B Non-alcoholic beverages	...	144.6	143.6	155.5	127.6 / 153.4	191.7	211.3	266.0	292.8	292.5	278.7	279.6
C Alcoholic beverages	...	1110.3	1174.4	1233.6	1224.8 / 1184.7	1228.7	1296.9	1440.7	1467.6	1496.3	1544.0	1549.2
D Tobacco	...	511.7	513.7	499.4	472.1 / 510.4	493.5	482.6	485.0	495.7	535.0	510.8	488.2
2 Clothing and footwear	...	664.0	711.3	775.3	768.3 / 849.0	865.0	947.4	1036.4	1029.2	1075.6	1032.8	1141.6
3 Gross rent, fuel and power	...	1180.3	1215.0	1253.4	1318.4 / 1665.3	1704.6	1724.0	1772.5	1778.1	1853.2	1868.8	1934.6
A Fuel and power	...	604.9	608.6	628.3	683.7 / 679.9	712.4	731.8	790.6	781.4	837.4	830.3	877.0
B Other	...	575.4	606.4	625.1	634.7 / 985.4	992.2	992.1	981.9	996.7	1015.8	1038.4	1057.6
4 Furniture, furnishings and household equipment and operation	...	642.5	624.4	727.6	786.4 / 848.1	847.4	995.4	1100.1	1021.6	1047.4	1070.2	1076.1
A Household operation	...	212.1	219.6	244.2	289.8 / 320.4	308.6	374.3	423.5	382.5	398.7	419.2	434.8
B Other	...	430.4	404.8	483.4	496.5 / 527.7	538.8	621.1	676.6	639.0	648.7	651.0	641.4
5 Medical care and health expenses	...	262.0	288.7	383.2	431.3 / 431.3	419.7	419.4	425.8	434.3	446.1	460.9	468.5
6 Transport and communication	...	1278.3	1347.5	1391.7	1387.1 / 1578.6	1588.0	1725.8	1909.0	1999.3	1962.9	2067.4	2098.8
A Personal transport equipment	...	317.3	333.6	358.2	351.6 / 353.5	327.3	396.4	500.5	559.3	454.0	460.4	453.0
B Other	...	961.0	1013.9	1033.5	1035.5 / 1225.1	1260.7	1329.4	1408.5	1440.0	1508.8	1607.0	1645.8
7 Recreational, entertainment, education and cultural services	...	919.2	958.3	1014.8	1015.6 / 1179.1	1281.0	1279.2	1394.2	1462.4	1537.0	1633.7	1680.9
A Education	...	215.1	261.0	279.8	281.4 / 347.1	354.1	343.9	340.8	342.0	346.1	355.5	359.8
B Other	...	704.1	697.3	735.0	734.2 / 831.9	926.9	935.3	1053.4	1120.5	1191.0	1278.2	1321.1
8 Miscellaneous goods and services	...	728.3	779.8	870.5	890.0 / 986.4	1090.5	1172.6	1292.7	1430.8	1466.9	1514.2	1510.5
A Personal care [a]	...	143.1	145.2	204.9	216.3 / 238.8	249.3	246.4	231.7	255.6	351.6	395.9	356.8
B Expenditures in restaurants, cafes and hotels	...	170.7	166.2	176.0	170.9 / 210.9	227.6	257.0	297.8	313.3	291.4	256.9	269.8
C Other	...	414.4	468.3	489.6	502.7 / 536.7	613.5	669.2	763.2	861.9	823.9	861.4	883.8
Total Final Consumption Expenditure in the Domestic Market by Households, of which	...	9963.7	10199.8	10713.9	10792.7 / 11763.8	12199.0	12753.8	13794.4	14057.6	14467.9	14800.2	15055.9
Plus: Direct purchases abroad by resident households	...	415.8	398.7	401.7	492.4 / 420.0	426.7	481.1	496.6	487.2	466.9	530.4	543.9
Less: Direct purchases in the domestic market by non-resident households	...	446.7	466.1	518.0	474.2 / 474.2	526.8	598.9	659.6	739.2	773.5	757.7	859.3
Equals: Final Consumption Expenditure of Resident Households [b]	...	9932.8	10132.4	10597.6	10810.9 / 11709.6	12098.9	12636.0	13631.4	13805.6	14161.2	14572.9	14740.6

Final Consumption Expenditure of Private Non-profit Institutions Serving Households

Equals: Final Consumption Expenditure of Private Non-profit Organisations Serving Households	...	...	...	...	...	...	...	...	...	...	...	...
Private Final Consumption Expenditure	...	9932.8	10132.4	10597.6	10810.9 / 11709.6	12098.9	12636.0	13631.4	13805.6	14161.2	14572.9	14740.6

a) Item 'Personal care' excludes services of barbers, beauty shops etc.
b) Item 'Final consumption expenditure of resident households' includes consumption expenditure of private non-profit institutions serving households.

Ireland

2.7 Gross Capital Formation by Type of Good and Owner, in Current Prices

Million Irish pounds

	1990				1991				1992			
	TOTAL	Total Private	Public Enterprises	General Government	TOTAL	Total Private	Public Enterprises	General Government	TOTAL	Total Private	Public Enterprises	General Government
Increase in stocks, total	665.1	...	...	...	620.2	...	...	...	-179.4	...	...	...
1 Goods producing industries	121.2	...	...	...	126.7	...	...	...	199.4	...	...	...
A Materials and supplies	84.6	...	...	...	88.0	...	...	...	179.9	...	...	...
B Work in progress		...	...	...		...	...	...		...	...	...
C Livestock, except breeding stocks, dairy cattle, etc.	23.2	...	...	...	15.6	...	...	...	-17.3	...	...	...
D Finished goods	13.4	...	...	...	23.1	...	...	...	36.7	...	...	...
2 Wholesale and retail trade	543.9	...	...	...	493.5	...	...	...	-378.8	...	...	...
3 Other, except government stocks	...	...	...	...	...	...	...	...	...	...	...	...
4 Government stocks	...	...	...	...	...	...	...	...	...	...	...	...
Gross Fixed Capital Formation, Total	4943.4	...	...	...	4661.1	...	...	...	4760.9	...	...	...
1 Residential buildings	1088.2	...	...	...	1120.6	...	...	...	1294.8	...	...	...
2 Non-residential buildings	1246.6	...	...	...	1343.5	...	...	...	1315.9	...	...	...
3 Other construction		...	...	...		...	...	...		...	...	...
4 Land improvement and plantation and orchard development	235.2	...	...	...	204.7	...	...	...	167.0	...	...	...
5 Producers' durable goods	2316.8	...	...	...	1973.4	...	...	...	1882.9	...	...	...
A Transport equipment	933.1	...	...	...	722.8	...	...	...	637.9	...	...	...
Passenger cars	302.0	...	...	...	246.1	...	...	...	255.9	...	...	...
Other	631.1	...	...	...	476.7	...	...	...	381.9	...	...	...
B Machinery and equipment	1383.7	...	...	...	1250.6	...	...	...	1245.1	...	...	...
6 Breeding stock, dairy cattle, etc.	56.7	...	...	...	18.9	...	...	...	100.4	...	...	...
Total Gross Capital Formation	5608.5	...	...	...	5281.3	...	...	...	4581.5	...	...	...

	1993			
	TOTAL	Total Private	Public Enterprises	General Government
Increase in stocks, total	-190.8	...	...	...
1 Goods producing industries	-65.6	...	...	...
A Materials and supplies	-77.0	...	...	...
B Work in progress		...	...	...
C Livestock, except breeding stocks, dairy cattle, etc.	-21.3	...	...	...
D Finished goods	32.7	...	...	...
2 Wholesale and retail trade	-125.2	...	...	...
3 Other, except government stocks	...	...	...	...
4 Government stocks	...	...	...	...
Gross Fixed Capital Formation, Total	4819.4	...	...	...
1 Residential buildings	1303.5	...	...	...
2 Non-residential buildings	1350.4	...	...	...
3 Other construction		...	...	...
4 Land improvement and plantation and orchard development	134.5	...	...	...
5 Producers' durable goods	2019.6	...	...	...
A Transport equipment	661.1	...	...	...
Passenger cars	263.5	...	...	...
Other	397.6	...	...	...
B Machinery and equipment	1358.5	...	...	...
6 Breeding stock, dairy cattle, etc.	11.5	...	...	...
Total Gross Capital Formation	4628.6	...	...	...

Ireland

2.8 Gross Capital Formation by Type of Good and Owner, in Constant Prices

Million Irish pounds

	1990 TOTAL	Total Private	Public Enterprises	General Government	1991 TOTAL	Total Private	Public Enterprises	General Government	1992 TOTAL	Total Private	Public Enterprises	General Government
	\multicolumn{12}{c}{At constant prices of: 1985}
Increase in stocks, total	670.7	...	...	...	625.4	...	...	...	-122.1	...	...	...
1 Goods producing industries	139.3	...	...	...	134.8	...	...	...	211.3	...	...	...
A Materials and supplies	97.8	...	...	...	91.9	...	...	...	196.4	...	...	...
B Work in progress		...	...	...		...	...	...		...	...	...
C Livestock, except breeding stocks, dairy cattle, etc.	24.2	...	...	...	21.6	...	...	...	-18.8	...	...	...
D Finished goods	17.3	...	...	...	21.3	...	...	...	33.8	...	...	...
2 Wholesale and retail trade	531.4	...	...	...	490.6	...	...	...	-333.4	...	...	...
3 Other, except government stocks	...	...	...	...	...	...	...	...	...	...	...	...
4 Government stocks	...	...	...	...	...	...	...	...	...	...	...	...
Gross Fixed Capital Formation, Total	4205.4	...	...	...	3828.8	...	...	...	3824.0	...	...	...
1 Residential buildings	865.5	...	...	...	857.8	...	...	...	945.3	...	...	...
2 Non-residential buildings	1021.0	...	...	...	1071.4	...	...	...	1028.8	...	...	...
3 Other construction		...	...	...		...	...	...		...	...	...
4 Land improvement and plantation and orchard development	192.6	...	...	...	163.2	...	...	...	130.5	...	...	...
5 Producers' durable goods	2075.5	...	...	...	1720.3	...	...	...	1636.4	...	...	...
A Transport equipment	762.2	...	...	...	582.7	...	...	...	508.4	...	...	...
Passenger cars	302.0	...	...	...	246.1	...	...	...	255.9	...	...	...
Other	460.2	...	...	...	336.5	...	...	...	252.5	...	...	...
B Machinery and equipment	1313.3	...	...	...	1137.6	...	...	...	1128.0	...	...	...
6 Breeding stock, dairy cattle, etc.	50.7	...	...	...	16.2	...	...	...	83.0	...	...	...
Total Gross Capital Formation	4876.1	...	...	...	4454.2	...	...	...	3701.9	...	...	...

	1993 TOTAL	Total Private	Public Enterprises	General Government
	\multicolumn{4}{c}{At constant prices of: 1985}
Increase in stocks, total	-181.2	...	...	...
1 Goods producing industries	-69.0	...	...	...
A Materials and supplies	-81.8	...	...	...
B Work in progress		...	...	...
C Livestock, except breeding stocks, dairy cattle, etc.	-16.6	...	...	...
D Finished goods	29.5	...	...	...
2 Wholesale and retail trade	-112.3	...	...	...
3 Other, except government stocks	...	...	...	...
4 Government stocks	...	...	...	...
Gross Fixed Capital Formation, Total	3725.7	...	...	...
1 Residential buildings	901.7	...	...	...
2 Non-residential buildings	1028.5	...	...	...
3 Other construction		...	...	...
4 Land improvement and plantation and orchard development	102.4	...	...	...
5 Producers' durable goods	1689.5	...	...	...
A Transport equipment	507.6	...	...	...
Passenger cars	263.5	...	...	...
Other	244.0	...	...	...
B Machinery and equipment	1181.9	...	...	...
6 Breeding stock, dairy cattle, etc.	3.7	...	...	...
Total Gross Capital Formation	3544.5	...	...	...

Ireland

2.9 Gross Capital Formation by Kind of Activity of Owner, ISIC Major Divisions, in Current Prices

Million Irish pounds

	1990 Total Gross Capital Formation	1990 Increase in Stocks	1990 Gross Fixed Capital Formation	1991 Total Gross Capital Formation	1991 Increase in Stocks	1991 Gross Fixed Capital Formation	1992 Total Gross Capital Formation	1992 Increase in Stocks	1992 Gross Fixed Capital Formation	1993 Total Gross Capital Formation	1993 Increase in Stocks	1993 Gross Fixed Capital Formation
						All Producers						
1 Agriculture, hunting, fishing and forestry	...	...	570.6	...	...	455.8	...	...	485.2	...	...	367.1
2 Mining and quarrying	...	...	59.5	...	...	33.7	...	...	31.5	...	...	25.8
3 Manufacturing	...	...	948.8	...	...	781.5	...	...	792.8	...	...	781.3
4 Electricity, gas and water	...	...	156.3	...	...	208.4	...	...	234.9	...	...	309.4
5 Construction	...	...	118.4	...	...	99.9	...	...	80.4	...	...	69.0
6 Wholesale and retail trade, restaurants and hotels [a]	...	...	348.4	...	...	278.1	...	...	246.0	...	...	228.5
7 Transport, storage and communication	...	...	724.9	...	...	716.2	...	...	652.6	...	...	794.5
8 Finance, insurance, real estate and business services	...	...	1403.8	...	...	1352.2	...	...	1504.5	...	...	1531.4
9 Community, social and personal services [ab]	...	...	410.1	...	...	579.6	...	...	594.6	...	...	589.0
Total Industries	...	...	4740.9	...	...	4505.3	...	...	4622.4	...	...	4695.9
Producers of Government Services [c]	...	...	202.5	...	...	155.8	...	...	138.5	...	...	123.5
Private Non-Profit Institutions Serving Households [b]	...	...	...	...	...	...	...	...	...	...	...	...
Total	...	...	4943.4	...	...	4661.1	...	...	4760.9	...	...	4819.4

a) Restaurants and hotels are included in item 'Community, social and personal services'.
b) Item 'Private non-profit institutions serving households' is included in item 'Community, social and personal services'.
c) Item 'Producers of Government Services' includes public administration and defence only. All other activities of government are included in the corresponding industries.

2.10 Gross Capital Formation by Kind of Activity of Owner, ISIC Major Divisions, in Constant Prices

Million Irish pounds

	1990 Total Gross Capital Formation	1990 Increase in Stocks	1990 Gross Fixed Capital Formation	1991 Total Gross Capital Formation	1991 Increase in Stocks	1991 Gross Fixed Capital Formation	1992 Total Gross Capital Formation	1992 Increase in Stocks	1992 Gross Fixed Capital Formation	1993 Total Gross Capital Formation	1993 Increase in Stocks	1993 Gross Fixed Capital Formation
						At constant prices of:1985						
						All Producers						
1 Agriculture, hunting, fishing and forestry	...	...	493.3	...	...	382.0	...	...	398.7	...	...	286.7
2 Mining and quarrying	...	...	53.4	...	...	28.8	...	...	26.6	...	...	20.7
3 Manufacturing	...	...	857.2	...	...	679.8	...	...	676.3	...	...	635.1
4 Electricity, gas and water	...	...	133.0	...	...	174.2	...	...	196.9	...	...	258.1
5 Construction	...	...	106.6	...	...	84.9	...	...	71.1	...	...	58.0
6 Wholesale and retail trade, restaurants and hotels	...	...	283.8	...	...	224.3	...	...	198.2	...	...	177.3
7 Transport, storage and communication	...	...	617.2	...	...	593.6	...	...	534.0	...	...	633.5
8 Finance, insurance, real estate and business services	...	...	1147.7	...	...	1057.2	...	...	1125.6	...	...	1092.4
9 Community, social and personal services	...	...	344.3	...	...	477.2	...	...	484.8	...	...	466.9
Total Industries	...	...	4036.4	...	...	3702.0	...	...	3712.3	...	...	3628.8
Producers of Government Services	...	...	169.0	...	...	126.9	...	...	111.7	...	...	97.0
Private Non-Profit Institutions Serving Households	...	...	...	...	...	...	...	...	...	...	...	...
Total	...	...	4205.4	...	...	3828.9	...	...	3824.0	...	...	3725.8

2.11 Gross Fixed Capital Formation by Kind of Activity of Owner, ISIC Divisions, in Current Prices

Million Irish pounds

	1980	1983	1984	1985	1986	1987	1988	1989	1990	1991	1992	1993
					All Producers							
1 Agriculture, hunting, forestry and fishing	266.0	296.1	308.1	300.9	246.8 / 246.8	309.7	410.5	520.8	570.6	455.8	485.2	367.1
A Agriculture and hunting	236.2	271.6	280.6	274.1	221.8 / 221.8	274.6	392.9	474.6	539.0	425.6	457.9	342.9
B Forestry and logging	2.0	3.0	2.8	2.8	2.7 / 2.7	2.6	2.4	26.3	24.5	24.8	22.3	20.9
C Fishing	27.8	21.5	24.7	24.0	22.3 / 22.3	32.5	15.2	19.8	7.0	5.3	5.0	3.3
2 Mining and quarrying	33.5	39.2	20.6	18.1	27.2 / 25.3	34.4	40.8	48.6	59.5	33.7	31.5	25.8

Ireland

2.11 Gross Fixed Capital Formation by Kind of Activity of Owner, ISIC Divisions, in Current Prices
(Continued)

Million Irish pounds

	1980	1983	1984	1985	1986	1987	1988	1989	1990	1991	1992	1993
3 Manufacturing	582.4	599.2	650.7	648.6	653.2 / 655.1	629.7	726.7	900.2	948.8	781.5	792.8	781.3
A Manufacturing of food, beverages and tobacco	183.9	198.9	190.6	198.6	223.2 / 223.9	207.0	206.8	247.4	256.5	...	...	...
B Textile, wearing apparel and leather industries	30.3	24.5	20.8	37.6	30.9 / 31.0	29.2	40.4	41.0	44.5	...	...	...
C Manufacture of wood, and wood products, including furniture	18.3	14.4	20.8	13.4	18.0 / 18.1	12.1	17.3	23.6	27.5	...	...	...
D Manufacture of paper and paper products, printing and publishing	23.6	19.2	20.8	26.3	32.5 / 32.6	38.6	54.7	50.0	73.3	...	...	...
E Manufacture of chemicals and chemical petroleum, coal, rubber and plastic products	58.3	77.3	137.3	110.9	112.6 / 112.9	123.8	162.5	155.5	219.2	...	...	...
F Manufacture of non-metalic mineral products except products of petroleum and coal	125.9	93.5	57.9	58.5	48.9 / 49.1	46.8	35.5	103.3	81.3	...	...	...
G Basic metal industries	7.6	6.0	9.1	10.6	10.5 / 10.6	9.6	16.2	10.0	5.3	...	...	...
H Manufacture of fabricated metal products, machinery and equipment	134.5	165.4	193.2	192.7	176.5 / 177.1	162.6	193.4	269.5	241.3	...	...	...
I Other manufacturing industries	...	...	...	...	... / ...	...	...	...	...	...	...	...
4 Electricity, gas and water	193.4	318.1	338.3	256.3	197.7 / 197.7	155.7	177.5	122.6	156.3	208.4	234.9	309.4
5 Construction	133.4	88.7	82.1	75.4	88.6 / 88.6	66.6	71.1	108.7	118.4	99.9	80.4	69.0
6 Wholesale and retail trade, restaurants and hotels	149.3	117.5	143.7	153.3	180.3 / 180.3	179.3	218.4	289.4	348.4	278.1	246.0	228.5
A Wholesale and retail trade	149.3	117.5	143.7	153.3	180.3 / 180.3	179.3	218.4	289.4	348.4	278.1	246.0	228.5
B Restaurants and hotels [a]	...	...	...	...	... / ...	...	...	...	...	...	...	...
7 Transport, storage and communication	287.0	530.5	506.4	432.2	440.9 / 440.9	457.8	469.7	603.5	724.9	716.2	652.6	794.5
A Transport and storage	159.5	332.4	289.6	314.5	304.4 / 304.4	333.9	338.7	453.4	567.1	547.0	517.9	641.3
B Communication	127.5	198.1	216.8	117.7	136.5 / 136.5	123.8	131.0	150.1	157.8	169.1	134.7	153.2
8 Finance, insurance, real estate and business services	705.2	923.4	999.9	987.2	1027.7 / 1065.9	1084.4	1020.9	1234.2	1403.8	1352.2	1504.5	1531.4
A Financial institutions	127.2	137.3	143.3	141.8	146.0 / 146.0	173.9	209.7	269.3	315.7	231.6	209.8	227.9
B Insurance	...	...	...	...	... / ...	...	...	...	...	...	...	...
C Real estate and business services	578.0	786.1	856.6	845.4	881.7 / 919.9	910.5	811.2	964.9	1088.2	1120.6	1294.8	1303.5
Real estate except dwellings	...	...	...	...	... / ...	...	...	...	...	...	...	...
Dwellings	578.0	786.1	856.6	845.4	881.7 / 919.9	910.5	811.2	964.9	1088.2	1120.6	1294.8	1303.5
9 Community, social and personal services [b]	270.2	426.0	382.1	421.9	435.4 / 435.4	449.7	415.9	393.8	410.1	579.6	594.6	589.0
A Sanitary and similar services [a]	153.0	255.5	228.8	232.3	257.2 / 257.2	263.4	271.3	257.0	285.9	443.6	425.9	411.7
B Social and related community services	117.2	170.5	153.2	189.6	178.2 / 178.2	186.3	144.6	136.8	124.2	136.0	168.7	177.3

Ireland

2.11 Gross Fixed Capital Formation by Kind of Activity of Owner, ISIC Divisions, in Current Prices
(Continued)

Million Irish pounds

	1980	1983	1984	1985	1986	1987	1988	1989	1990	1991	1992	1993
Educational services	64.6	94.7	84.1	99.5	93.0 / 93.0	87.4	55.1	45.2	52.4	76.5	105.2	113.1
Medical, dental, other health and veterinary services	52.6	75.8	69.2	90.1	85.2 / 85.2	98.9	89.5	91.6	71.8	59.5	63.5	64.1
C Recreational and cultural services [a]	...	...	...	...	...	...	...	...	...	...	...	...
D Personal and household services [a]	...	...	...	...	...	...	...	...	...	...	...	...
Statistical discrepancy	-	-	-	-	-	...	...	...	...	...	...	...
Total Industries	2620.4	3338.7	3431.9	3293.8	3297.7 / 3335.9	3367.3	3551.4	4221.8	4740.9	4505.3	4622.4	4695.9
Producers of Government Services [c]	56.8	80.3	84.5	92.7	95.8 / 95.8	102.2	118.4	141.9	202.5	155.8	138.5	123.5
Private Non-Profit Institutions Serving Households [b]	...	...	...	...	...	...	...	...	...	...	...	...
Total	2677.2	3419.0	3516.4	3386.5	3393.5 / 3431.7	3469.5	3669.8	4363.7	4943.4	4661.1	4760.9	4819.4

a) Items 'Restaurants and hotels', 'Recreational and cultural services' and 'Personal and household services' are included in item 'Sanitary and similar services'.
b) Item 'Private non-profit institutions serving households' is included in item 'Community, social and personal services'.
c) Item 'Producers of Government Services' includes public administration and defence only. All other activities of government are included in the corresponding industries.

2.12 Gross Fixed Capital Formation by Kind of Activity of Owner, ISIC Divisions, in Constant Prices

Million Irish pounds

	1980	1983	1984	1985	1986	1987	1988	1989	1990	1991	1992	1993

At constant prices of:1985

All Producers

	1980	1983	1984	1985	1986	1987	1988	1989	1990	1991	1992	1993
1 Agriculture, hunting, forestry and fishing	...	332.2	320.8	300.9	244.7 / 244.7	301.4	364.4	443.5	493.3	382.0	398.7	286.7
A Agriculture and hunting	...	305.0	291.0	274.1	220.0 / 220.0	257.4	340.2	401.7	452.9	347.4	369.5	262.6
B Forestry and logging	...	3.4	2.9	2.8	2.8 / 2.6	2.4	2.1	22.5	20.1	19.8	17.4	15.9
C Fishing	...	23.8	26.9	24.0	21.8 / 22.1	41.6	22.0	19.3	20.3	14.8	11.8	8.2
2 Mining and quarrying	...	43.7	21.7	18.1	26.9 / 24.9	33.8	37.7	42.1	53.4	28.8	26.6	20.7
3 Manufacturing	...	669.4	679.7	648.6	651.8 / 653.6	626.1	676.7	785.0	857.2	679.8	676.3	635.1
A Manufacturing of food, beverages and tobacco	...	222.2	199.1	198.6	222.7 / 223.3	205.9	192.5	215.7	231.5	...	...	...
B Textile, wearing apparel and leather industries	...	27.4	21.8	37.6	30.8 / 30.9	29.0	37.6	35.7	40.2	...	...	...
C Manufacture of wood, and wood products, including furniture	...	16.1	21.8	13.4	18.0 / 18.0	12.1	16.1	20.6	24.8	...	...	...
D Manufacture of paper and paper products, printing and publishing	...	21.4	21.8	26.3	32.5 / 32.6	38.4	51.0	43.6	66.4	...	...	...
E Manufacture of chemicals and chemical petroleum, coal, rubber and plastic products	...	86.3	143.4	110.9	112.4 / 112.7	123.0	151.3	135.7	198.4	...	...	...
F Manufacture of non-metalic mineral products except products of petroleum and coal	...	104.4	60.5	58.5	48.8 / 48.9	46.5	33.0	90.1	73.6	...	...	...
G Basic metal industries	...	6.7	9.5	10.6	10.5 / 10.6	9.6	15.1	8.7	4.8	...	...	...
H Manufacture of fabricated metal products, machinery and equipment	...	184.8	201.9	192.7	176.1 / 176.6	161.7	180.1	235.0	217.6	...	...	...
I Other manufacturing industries	...	...	...	...	...	...	...	...	...	...	...	...
4 Electricity, gas and water	...	354.4	353.1	256.3	194.5 / 194.5	155.0	161.1	105.9	133.0	174.2	196.9	258.1

Ireland

2.12 Gross Fixed Capital Formation by Kind of Activity of Owner, ISIC Divisions, in Constant Prices
(Continued)

Million Irish pounds

	1980	1983	1984	1985	1986	1987	1988	1989	1990	1991	1992	1993
					At constant prices of:1985							
5 Construction	...	98.1	84.9	75.4	88.8 / 88.8	65.6	65.4	93.9	106.6	84.9	71.1	58.0
6 Wholesale and retail trade, restaurants and hotels	...	134.4	152.0	153.3	173.2 / 173.3	164.1	191.3	241.4	283.8	224.3	198.2	177.3
A Wholesale and retail trade	...	134.4	152.0	153.3	173.2 / 173.3	164.1	191.3	241.4	283.8	224.3	198.2	177.3
B Restaurants and hotels	...	...	...	...	... / ...	...	...	...	...	...	...	...
7 Transport, storage and communication	...	588.0	558.2	432.2	426.1 / 426.1	433.1	425.2	522.0	617.2	593.6	534.0	633.5
A Transport and storage	...	369.0	334.5	314.5	293.2 / 293.2	314.2	304.6	389.7	477.7	447.8	418.6	502.6
B Communication	...	219.0	223.7	117.7	132.8 / 132.8	119.0	120.6	132.2	139.5	145.8	115.5	131.0
8 Finance, insurance, real estate and business services	...	978.8	1012.9	987.2	968.8 / 1028.3	1005.4	919.7	1061.6	1147.7	1057.2	1125.6	1092.4
A Financial institutions	...	138.3	137.0	141.8	146.1 / 146.1	172.9	195.8	236.4	282.1	199.4	180.4	190.7
B Insurance	...	...	...	...	... / ...	...	...	...	...	...	...	...
C Real estate and business services	...	840.5	875.9	845.4	822.7 / 882.2	832.5	723.9	825.2	865.5	857.8	945.3	901.7
Real estate except dwellings	...	...	...	...	... / ...	...	...	...	...	...	...	...
Dwellings	...	840.5	875.9	845.4	822.7 / 882.2	832.5	723.9	825.2	865.5	857.8	945.3	901.7
9 Community, social and personal services	...	475.9	399.1	421.9	424.4 / 424.1	432.1	379.3	336.6	344.3	477.2	484.8	466.9
A Sanitary and similar services	...	286.9	238.7	232.3	251.7 / 251.4	255.2	247.9	219.7	239.4	364.6	349.4	328.6
B Social and related community services	...	189.0	160.4	189.6	172.7 / 172.7	176.9	131.3	116.9	104.9	112.6	135.4	138.4
Educational services	...	105.9	88.0	99.5	89.4 / 89.4	82.2	49.4	38.6	43.2	62.9	84.4	88.9
Medical, dental, other health and veterinary services	...	83.1	72.5	90.1	83.2 / 83.2	94.7	81.9	78.3	61.7	49.7	51.0	49.5
C Recreational and cultural services	...	...	...	...	... / ...	...	...	...	...	...	...	...
D Personal and household services	...	...	...	...	... / ...	...	...	...	...	...	...	...
Total Industries	...	3674.9	3582.4	3293.8	3199.2 / 3258.3	3216.6	3220.7	3632.0	4036.4	3702.0	3712.3	3628.8
Producers of Government Services	...	89.4	87.1	92.7	92.7 / 92.7	96.3	106.4	121.4	169.0	126.9	111.7	97.0
Private Non-Profit Institutions Serving Households	...	...	...	...	... / ...	...	...	...	...	...	...	...
Total	...	3764.3	3669.5	3386.5	3291.9 / 3351.0	3312.9	3327.1	3753.4	4205.4	3828.9	3824.0	3725.8

2.17 Exports and Imports of Goods and Services, Detail

Million Irish pounds

	1980	1983	1984	1985	1986	1987	1988	1989	1990	1991	1992	1993
				Exports of Goods and Services								
1 Exports of merchandise, f.o.b.	4004.4	6812.7	8696.0	9526.8	9180.7 / 9180.7	10447.1	12073.0	14358.3	14100.5	14675.2	16386.8	19437.4
2 Transport and communication [a]	352.3	549.0	632.0	693.6	678.6 / 704.4	844.0	905.6	1027.4	1145.3	1278.4	1371.1	1342.9
A In respect of merchandise imports [b]	37.1	73.0	80.9	84.8	69.1 / 69.1	69.9	61.4	64.5	66.8	68.8	68.7	65.5
B Other	315.2	476.0	551.1	608.8	609.5 / 635.3	774.1	844.2	962.9	1078.5	1209.6	1302.4	1277.4
3 Insurance service charges	...	...	...	...	... / ...	...	...	...	...	...	...	...

Ireland

2.17 Exports and Imports of Goods and Services, Detail
(Continued)

Million Irish pounds

	1980	1983	1984	1985	1986	1987	1988	1989	1990	1991	1992	1993
4 Other commodities	...	...	...	...	...	...	...	...	...	...	...	...
5 Adjustments of merchandise exports to change-of-ownership basis	...	...	...	...	...	...	...	...	...	...	...	...
6 Direct purchases in the domestic market by non-residential households	281.9	390.0	442.0	518.0	492.2 / 492.2	564.0	655.0	751.0	870.0	939.0	949.0	1091.0
7 Direct purchases in the domestic market by extraterritorial bodies	...	...	...	...	...	...	...	...	...	...	...	...
Total Exports of Goods and Services	4638.6	7751.7	9770.0	10738.4	10351.5 / 10377.3	11855.1	13633.6	16136.8	16115.8	16892.6	18706.9	21871.4

Imports of Goods and Services

	1980	1983	1984	1985	1986	1987	1988	1989	1990	1991	1992	1993
1 Imports of merchandise, c.i.f.	5346.1	7334.2	8892.6	9390.2	8745.5 / 8745.5	9137.0	10047.6	12114.4	12286.1	12688.3	13019.7	14622.7
2 Adjustments of merchandise imports to change-of-ownership basis	...	...	...	...	...	...	...	...	...	...	...	...
3 Other transport and communication [a]	270.4	467.0	544.5	604.7	603.8 / 747.1	1087.3	1346.8	1679.7	1654.5	1817.0	2034.0	2128.6
4 Other insurance service charges	...	...	...	...	...	...	...	...	...	...	...	...
5 Other commodities	...	...	...	...	...	...	...	...	...	...	...	...
6 Direct purchases abroad by government	...	...	...	...	...	...	...	...	...	...	...	...
7 Direct purchases abroad by resident households	283.4	363.0	378.0	401.7	511.1 / 435.9	457.1	526.5	565.4	573.4	566.8	664.3	690.6
Total Imports of Goods and Services	5899.9	8164.2	9815.1	10396.6	9860.4 / 9928.5	10681.3	11920.9	14359.5	14514.0	15072.1	15718.0	17441.9
Balance of Goods and Services	-1261.3	-412.5	-45.1	341.8	491.1 / 448.8	1173.8	1712.7	1777.3	1601.8	1820.5	2988.9	4429.5
Total Imports and Balance of Goods and Services	4638.6	7751.7	9770.0	10738.4	10351.5 / 10377.3	11855.1	13633.6	16136.8	16115.8	16892.6	18706.9	21871.4

a) Item 'Transport and communication' includes all services.
b) Item 'Direct purchases in the domestic market by non-residential households' refers to governmental and other services.

3.11 General Government Production Account: Total and Subsectors

Million Irish pounds

	1990					1991				
	Total General Government	Central Government	State or Provincial Government	Local Government	Social Security Funds	Total General Government	Central Government	State or Provincial Government	Local Government	Social Security Funds
					Gross Output					
1 Sales	...	...	...	...	4.4	...	...	...	...	2.3
2 Services produced for own use	4082.2	2064.5	...	1939.1	78.7	4480.3	2269.7	...	2126.1	84.5
3 Own account fixed capital formation	...	...	...	...	...	...	...	...	...	...
Gross Output	...	...	...	...	...	...	...	...	...	...
					Gross Input					
Intermediate Consumption	...	...	...	...	...	...	...	...	...	...
Subtotal: Value Added	...	...	...	...	...	...	...	...	...	...
1 Indirect taxes, net	...	...	...	...	...	...	...	...	...	...
2 Consumption of fixed capital	...	...	...	...	...	...	...	...	...	...
3 Compensation of employees	2738.4	1603.2	...	1089.5	45.7	3014.8	1761.8	...	1202.6	50.4
4 Net Operating surplus	119.7	-36.8	...	156.5	...	140.6	-11.1	...	151.7	...
Gross Input	...	...	...	...	...	...	...	...	...	...

Ireland

3.11 General Government Production Account: Total and Subsectors

Million Irish pounds

	1992 Total General Government	Central Government	State or Provincial Government	Local Government	Social Security Funds
Gross Output					
1 Sales	...	...	...	...	16.5
2 Services produced for own use	4842.4	2453.0	...	2295.6	93.8
3 Own account fixed capital formation	...	...	...	...	...
Gross Output	...	...	...	...	...
Gross Input					
Intermediate Consumption	...	...	...	...	...
Subtotal: Value Added	...	...	...	...	...
1 Indirect taxes, net	...	...	...	...	...
2 Consumption of fixed capital	...	...	...	...	...
3 Compensation of employees	3255.9	1893.4	...	1307.2	55.3
4 Net Operating surplus	150.0	-8.2	...	158.2	...
Gross Input	...	...	...	...	...

3.12 General Government Income and Outlay Account: Total and Subsectors

Million Irish pounds

	1990 Total General Govt	Central Govt	State or Provincial Govt	Local Govt	Social Security Funds	1991 Total General Govt	Central Govt	State or Provincial Govt	Local Govt	Social Security Funds
Receipts										
1 Operating surplus	119.7	-36.8	...	156.5	...	140.6	-11.1	...	151.7	...
2 Property and entrepreneurial income	345.6	335.2	...	87.5	4.4	407.0	392.2	...	88.5	2.3
3 Taxes, fees and contributions	9796.1	8142.4	...	373.2	1280.4	10324.0	8545.1	...	394.3	1384.6
A Indirect taxes [a]	4144.4	3904.3	...	240.1	...	4178.7	3927.9	...	250.8	...
B Direct taxes	3775.5	3775.5	...	...	...	4120.3	4120.3	...	...	...
Income	3655.8	3655.8	...	...	...	3970.8	3970.8	...	...	...
Other	119.7	119.7	...	...	...	149.5	149.5	...	...	...
C Social security contributions	1876.2	462.6	...	133.1	1280.4	2025.0	496.9	...	143.5	1384.6
D Fees, fines and penalties [a]	...	...	...	...	...	...	...	...	...	...
4 Other current transfers	215.0	214.9	...	1981.7	76.1	366.2	366.1	...	2184.9	148.3
A Casualty insurance claims	...	...	...	...	...	...	...	...	...	...
B Transfers from other government subsectors	...	-	...	1981.7	76.0	...	-	...	2184.9	148.3
C Transfers from the rest of the world	215.0	214.9	...	...	0.1	366.2	366.1	...	...	-
D Other transfers, except imputed	...	...	...	...	...	...	...	...	...	...
E Imputed unfunded employee pension and welfare contributions	...	...	...	...	...	...	...	...	...	...
Total Current Receipts	10476.4	8655.7	...	2598.9	1360.9	11237.8	9292.3	...	2819.4	1535.2
Disbursements										
1 Government final consumption expenditure [a]	4082.3	2064.5	...	1939.1	78.7	4480.3	2269.7	...	2126.1	84.5
2 Property income	2125.3	2114.4	...	92.5	...	2146.2	2123.1	...	99.1	...
3 Subsidies	303.4	303.4	...	-	...	277.0	277.0	...	-	...
4 Other current transfers	4341.4	4360.5	...	702.4	1336.2	4781.0	4908.2	...	757.5	1448.5
A Casualty insurance premiums, net	...	...	...	...	...	...	...	...	...	...
B Transfers to other government subsectors	...	2057.7	...	-	...	...	2333.2	...	-	...
C Social security benefits	1336.2	...	...	...	1336.2	1448.5	...	...	...	1448.5
D Social assistance grants	2500.3	1847.1	...	653.3	...	2752.7	2044.1	...	708.6	...
E Unfunded employee pension and welfare benefits	...	...	...	...	...	...	...	...	...	...
F Transfers to private non-profit institutions serving households	448.7	399.5	...	49.1	...	479.2	430.2	...	48.9	...
G Other transfers n.e.c.	...	...	...	...	...	...	...	...	...	...
H Transfers to the rest of the world	56.2	56.2	...	...	...	100.7	100.7	...	...	...
Net saving	-376.0	-187.0	...	-135.0	-53.9	-446.7	-285.7	...	-163.2	2.2
Total Current Disbursements and Net Saving	10476.4	8655.8	...	2599.0	1361.0	11237.8	9292.3	...	2819.5	1535.2

Ireland

3.12 General Government Income and Outlay Account: Total and Subsectors

Million Irish pounds

	1992 Total General Government	Central Government	State or Provincial Government	Local Government	Social Security Funds
Receipts					
1 Operating surplus	150.0	-8.2	...	158.2	...
2 Property and entrepreneurial income	425.3	405.0	...	89.3	16.5
3 Taxes, fees and contributions	11119.0	9214.2	...	420.1	1484.7
A Indirect taxes [a]	4455.4	4187.9	...	267.5	...
B Direct taxes	4489.1	4489.1	...	...	...
Income	4308.5	4308.5	...	...	...
Other	180.7	180.7	...	...	...
C Social security contributions	2174.5	537.2	...	152.6	1484.7
D Fees, fines and penalties [a]	...	...	...	...	...
4 Other current transfers	337.3	337.1	...	2437.9	160.0
A Casualty insurance claims	...	...	...	...	...
B Transfers from other government subsectors	...	-	...	2437.9	159.7
C Transfers from the rest of the world	337.3	337.1	...	...	0.3
D Other transfers, except imputed	...	...	...	...	...
E Imputed unfunded employee pension and welfare contributions	...	...	...	...	...
Total Current Receipts	12031.6	9948.1	...	3105.5	1661.2
Disbursements					
1 Government final consumption expenditure [a]	4842.4	2453.0	...	2295.6	93.8
2 Property income	2116.5	2101.2	...	100.7	...
3 Subsidies	315.9	315.9	...	-	...
4 Other current transfers	5225.1	5416.8	...	843.6	1562.4
A Casualty insurance premiums, net	...	...	...	...	...
B Transfers to other government subsectors	...	2597.6	...	-	...
C Social security benefits	1562.4	...	...	...	1562.4
D Social assistance grants	3023.9	2241.6	...	782.3	...
E Unfunded employee pension and welfare benefits	...	...	...	...	...
F Transfers to private non-profit institutions serving households	529.1	467.8	...	61.3	...
G Other transfers n.e.c.	...	...	...	...	...
H Transfers to the rest of the world	109.7	109.7	...	...	...
Net saving	-468.1	-338.8	...	-134.4	5.1
Total Current Disbursements and Net Saving	12031.8	9948.1	...	3105.5	1661.3

a) Item 'Fees, fines and penalties' is included in item 'Indirect taxes' or is offset against item 'Final consumption expenditure'.

3.13 General Government Capital Accumulation Account: Total and Subsectors

Million Irish pounds

	1990 Total General Government	Central Government	State or Provincial Government	Local Government	Social Security Funds	1991 Total General Government	Central Government	State or Provincial Government	Local Government	Social Security Funds
Finance of Gross Accumulation										
1 Gross saving	-199.4	-111.1	...	-34.3	-53.9	-261.8	-206.8	...	-57.2	2.2
A Consumption of fixed capital	176.6	75.9	...	100.7	...	184.9	78.9	...	106.0	...
B Net saving	-376.0	-187.0	...	-135.0	-53.9	-446.7	-285.7	...	-163.2	2.2
2 Capital transfers [a]	179.5	-301.5	...	481.0	...	294.6	-224.5	...	519.2	...
A From other government subsectors	...	-333.3	...	333.3	...	...	-377.8	...	377.8	...
B From other resident sectors	-69.4	-217.1	...	147.7	...	-56.9	-198.3	...	141.4	...
C From rest of the world	249.0	249.0	...	...	...	351.5	351.5	...	...	...
Finance of Gross Accumulation	-19.9	-412.6	...	446.7	-53.9	32.8	-431.3	...	462.0	2.2
Gross Accumulation										
1 Gross capital formation	559.2	128.0	...	431.2	...	613.6	120.6	...	493.0	...

Ireland

3.13 General Government Capital Accumulation Account: Total and Subsectors
(Continued)

Million Irish pounds

	1990					1991				
	Total General Government	Central Government	State or Provincial Government	Local Government	Social Security Funds	Total General Government	Central Government	State or Provincial Government	Local Government	Social Security Funds
A Increase in stocks	...	...	...	...	...	...	...	...	...	...
B Gross fixed capital formation	559.2	128.0	...	431.2	...	613.6	120.6	...	493.0	...
2 Purchases of land, net	...	...	...	...	...	...	...	...	...	...
3 Purchases of intangible assets, net	...	...	...	...	...	...	...	...	...	...
4 Capital transfers [a]	...	...	...	...	...	...	...	...	...	...
Net lending	-579.0	-540.6	...	15.6	-53.9	-580.7	-551.9	...	-31.0	2.2
Gross Accumulation	-19.8	-412.6	...	446.8	-53.9	32.9	-431.3	...	462.0	2.2

	1992				
	Total General Government	Central Government	State or Provincial Government	Local Government	Social Security Funds
	Finance of Gross Accumulation				
1 Gross saving	-276.0	-257.5	...	-23.6	5.1
A Consumption of fixed capital	192.1	81.3	...	110.8	...
B Net saving	-468.1	-338.8	...	-134.4	5.1
2 Capital transfers [a]	236.9	-291.9	...	528.8	...
A From other government subsectors	...	-406.0	...	406.0	...
B From other resident sectors	-122.0	-244.8	...	122.8	...
C From rest of the world	358.9	358.9	...	...	...
Finance of Gross Accumulation	-39.1	-549.4	...	505.2	5.1
	Gross Accumulation				
1 Gross capital formation	623.8	113.5	...	510.3	...
A Increase in stocks	...	...	...	...	...
B Gross fixed capital formation	623.8	113.5	...	510.3	...
2 Purchases of land, net	...	...	...	...	...
3 Purchases of intangible assets, net	...	...	...	...	...
4 Capital transfers [a]	...	...	...	...	...
Net lending	-663.0	-662.9	...	-5.1	5.1
Gross Accumulation	-39.2	-549.4	...	505.2	5.1

a) Capital transfers received are recorded net of capital transfers paid.

3.51 External Transactions: Current Account: Detail

Million Irish pounds

	1980	1983	1984	1985	1986	1987	1988	1989	1990	1991	1992	1993
	Payments to the Rest of the World											
1 Imports of goods and services	5899.9	8164.2	9815.1	10396.6	9860.4 / 9928.5	10681.3	11920.9	14359.5	14514.0	15072.1	15718.0	17441.9
A Imports of merchandise c.i.f.	5346.1	7334.2	8892.6	9390.2	8745.5 / 8745.5	9137.0	10047.6	12114.4	12286.1	12688.3	13019.7	14622.7
B Other	553.8	830.0	922.5	1006.4	1114.9 / 1183.0	1544.3	1873.3	2245.1	2227.9	2383.8	2698.3	2819.2
2 Factor income to the rest of the world	832.1	1745.4	2342.9	2772.9	2705.1 / 2768.8	2899.4	3690.1	4577.6	4770.2	4627.3	4937.4	5352.3

Ireland

3.51 External Transactions: Current Account: Detail
(Continued)

Million Irish pounds

	1980	1983	1984	1985	1986	1987	1988	1989	1990	1991	1992	1993
A Compensation of employees	-	-	-	-	-	-	-	-	-	-	-	-
B Property and entrepreneurial income	832.1	1745.4	2342.9	2772.9	2705.1 / 2768.8	2899.4	3690.1	4577.6	4770.2	4627.3	4937.4	5352.3
3 Current transfers to the rest of the world	123.4	251.6	283.1	312.5	373.7 / 373.7	378.5	363.1	372.0	381.5	452.5	467.8	568.6
A Indirect taxes by general government to supranational organizations	99.0	213.3	238.7	237.2	283.8 / 283.8	328.8	293.7	318.0	301.5	335.4	325.2	385.6
B Other current transfers	24.4	38.3	44.4	75.3	89.9 / 89.9	49.7	69.4	54.0	80.0	117.1	142.6	183.0
By general government	23.4	37.0	36.6	43.5	67.4 / 67.4	25.7	18.0	19.1	53.0	60.7	70.7	70.7
By other resident sectors	1.0	1.3	7.8	31.8	22.5 / 22.5	24.0	51.4	34.9	27.0	56.4	71.9	112.3
4 Surplus of the nation on current transactions	-1101.0	-1016.7	-952.5	-700.5	-540.2 / -642.0	-46.8	-	-419.8	-182.4	551.2	974.9	2088.5
Payments to the Rest of the World, and Surplus of the Nation on Current Transfers	5754.4	9144.5	11488.6	12781.5	12399.0 / 12429.0	13912.4	15974.1	18889.3	19483.3	20703.1	22098.1	25451.3

Receipts From The Rest of the World

	1980	1983	1984	1985	1986	1987	1988	1989	1990	1991	1992	1993
1 Exports of goods and services	4638.6	7751.7	9770.0	10738.4	10351.5 / 10377.3	11855.1	13633.6	16136.8	16115.8	16892.6	18706.9	21871.4
A Exports of merchandise f.o.b.	4004.4	6812.7	8696.0	9526.8	9180.7 / 9180.7	10447.1	12073.0	14358.3	14100.5	14675.2	16386.8	19437.4
B Other	634.2	939.0	1074.0	1211.6	1170.8 / 1196.6	1408.0	1560.6	1778.4	2015.3	2217.4	2320.1	2433.9
2 Factor income from the rest of the world	474.0	561.5	704.1	807.2	748.1 / 752.2	787.0	1028.3	1344.8	1638.9	1762.2	1642.8	1625.4
A Compensation of employees	9.4	12.4	12.0	13.4	16.0 / 16.0	16.0	16.0	16.0	16.0	15.3	15.8	15.8
B Property and entrepreneurial income	464.6	549.1	692.1	793.8	732.1 / 736.2	771.0	1012.3	1328.8	1622.9	1747.0	1627.0	1609.7
3 Current transfers from the rest of the world	641.8	831.3	1014.4	1235.9	1299.5 / 1299.5	1270.3	1312.1	1407.7	1728.7	2048.1	1748.4	1954.4
A Subsidies to general government from supranational organizations	384.4	463.1	676.8	864.2	918.3 / 918.3	798.9	906.3	1012.2	1306.3	1360.8	1147.5	1319.4
B Other current transfers	257.4	368.2	337.6	371.7	381.2 / 381.2	471.4	405.8	395.5	422.4	687.3	600.9	635.0
To general government	91.1	96.8	38.9	57.2	55.9 / 55.9	80.0	64.5	62.0	69.5	193.7	162.1	189.3
To other resident sectors	166.3	271.4	298.7	314.5	325.3 / 325.3	391.3	341.2	333.5	352.8	493.6	438.9	445.6
Receipts from the Rest of the World on Current Transfers	5754.4	9144.5	11488.5	12781.5	12399.1 / 12429.0	13912.4	15974.0	18889.3	19483.4	20702.9	22098.1	25451.2

4.1 Derivation of Value Added by Kind of Activity, in Current Prices

Million Irish pounds

	1990 Gross Output	1990 Intermediate Consumption	1990 Value Added	1991 Gross Output	1991 Intermediate Consumption	1991 Value Added	1992 Gross Output	1992 Intermediate Consumption	1992 Value Added
			All Producers						
1 Agriculture, hunting, forestry and fishing	...	...	1986.5	...	...	1928.3	...	...	2155.1
2 Mining and quarrying	...	...	⎫	...	...	⎫	...	...	⎫
3 Manufacturing	...	...	8264.9	...	...	8721.6	...	...	9236.4
4 Electricity, gas and water	...	...	⎭	...	...	⎭	...	...	⎭
5 Construction	...	...	1290.3	...	...	1364.7	...	...	1406.2
6 Wholesale and retail trade, restaurants and hotels	...	...	3149.6	...	...	3063.5	...	...	3025.8
A Wholesale and retail trade	...	...	2609.4	...	...	2466.4	...	...	2380.1
B Restaurants and hotels	...	...	540.2	...	...	597.2	...	...	645.6
7 Transport, storage and communication	...	...	1392.8	...	...	1466.0	...	...	1518.6
A Transport and storage	...	...	756.0	...	...	811.4	...	...	840.9

Ireland

4.1 Derivation of Value Added by Kind of Activity, in Current Prices
(Continued)

Million Irish pounds

	1990 Gross Output	1990 Intermediate Consumption	1990 Value Added	1991 Gross Output	1991 Intermediate Consumption	1991 Value Added	1992 Gross Output	1992 Intermediate Consumption	1992 Value Added
B Communication	...	...	636.8	...	...	654.5	...	...	677.7
8 Finance, insurance, real estate and business services	...	...	1531.6	...	...	1744.1	...	...	2200.8
9 Community, social and personal services	...	...	3881.9	...	...	4143.1	...	...	4137.4
Total, Industries	...	...	21497.5	...	...	22431.2	...	...	23680.3
Producers of Government Services	...	...	3730.7	...	...	3990.5	...	...	4382.8
Other Producers	...	...		...	...		...	...	
Total	...	...	25228.2	...	...	26421.7	...	...	28063.1
Less: Imputed bank service charge	...	...	1006.0	...	...	1114.6	...	...	1139.0
Import duties	...	...	902.6	...	...	869.9	...	...	883.6
Value added tax	...	...	1968.9	...	...	2012.0	...	...	2179.3
Total	...	...	27093.7	...	...	28189.0	...	...	29987.0

4.3 Cost Components of Value Added

Million Irish pounds

	1990 Compensation of Employees	1990 Capital Consumption	1990 Net Operating Surplus	1990 Indirect Taxes	1990 Less: Subsidies Received	1990 Value Added	1991 Compensation of Employees	1991 Capital Consumption	1991 Net Operating Surplus	1991 Indirect Taxes	1991 Less: Subsidies Received	1991 Value Added
					All Producers							
1 Agriculture, hunting, forestry and fishing	187.9	369.7	1792.9	53.3	417.3	1986.5	190.5	378.4	1649.3	54.6	344.5	1928.3
2 Mining and quarrying												
3 Manufacturing	3824.8	588.1	3368.7	973.4	490.1	8264.9	4005.8	666.8	3396.6	1032.6	380.2	8721.6
4 Electricity, gas and water												
5 Construction	993.0	30.6	264.9	1.8	-	1290.3	1062.6	32.4	267.8	1.9	-	1364.7
6 Wholesale and retail trade, restaurants and hotels	1625.4	240.2	1667.7	141.8	525.5	3149.6	1806.0	230.8	1626.0	147.8	747.1	3063.5
A Wholesale and retail trade	1330.7	181.7	1510.3	112.2	525.5	2609.4	1470.1	166.5	1459.3	117.6	747.1	2466.4
B Restaurants and hotels	294.7	58.5	157.4	29.6	-	540.2	335.9	64.3	166.7	30.3	-	597.2
7 Transport, storage and communication	810.2	260.6	396.6	38.8	113.5	1392.8	852.4	283.7	403.8	38.9	112.9	1466.0
A Transport and storage	525.4	121.1	188.0	35.0	113.5	756.0	557.0	128.1	204.0	35.2	112.9	811.4
B Communication	284.8	139.5	208.6	3.9	-	636.8	295.4	155.6	199.8	3.7	-	654.5
8 Finance, insurance, real estate and business services	988.5	200.8	232.8	109.5	-	1531.6	1025.1	248.1	368.1	102.8	-	1744.1
9 Community, social and personal services	1284.4	691.5	1723.3	243.4	60.8	3881.9	1370.8	697.8	1881.0	244.3	50.8	4143.1
Total, Industries	9714.2	2381.5	9446.9	1562.0	1607.1	21497.5	10313.2	2538.0	9592.6	1622.9	1635.6	22431.2
Producers of Government Services	3543.4	176.6	-	12.8	2.1	3730.7	3798.6	185.0	-	9.4	2.5	3990.5
Other Producers												
Total	13257.6	2558.1	9446.9	1574.8	1609.2	25228.2	14111.8	2723.0	9592.6	1632.3	1638.1	26421.7
Less: Imputed bank service charge	...	...	1006.0	...	...	1006.0	...	...	1114.6	...	...	1114.6
Import duties	...	...	...	902.6	...	902.6	...	...	...	869.9	...	869.9
Value added tax	...	...	...	1968.9	...	1968.9	...	...	...	2012.0	...	2012.0
Total	13257.6	2558.1	8440.9	4446.3	1609.2	27093.7	14111.8	2723.0	8478.0	4514.2	1638.1	28189.0

	1992 Compensation of Employees	1992 Capital Consumption	1992 Net Operating Surplus	1992 Indirect Taxes	1992 Less: Subsidies Received	1992 Value Added
			All Producers			
1 Agriculture, hunting, forestry and fishing	201.9	369.0	1951.0	51.5	418.2	2155.1
2 Mining and quarrying						
3 Manufacturing	4156.3	737.4	3765.9	1069.8	493.1	9236.4
4 Electricity, gas and water						
5 Construction	1075.2	30.5	298.5	2.0	-	1406.2
6 Wholesale and retail trade, restaurants and hotels	1902.0	254.3	1081.2	161.6	373.4	3025.8
A Wholesale and retail trade	1535.1	190.5	900.6	127.3	373.4	2380.1
B Restaurants and hotels	366.9	63.8	180.6	34.3	-	645.6
7 Transport, storage and communication	873.7	301.0	413.8	41.9	111.8	1518.6
A Transport and storage	577.1	137.4	200.3	38.0	111.8	840.9

Ireland

4.3 Cost Components of Value Added
(Continued)

Million Irish pounds

	1992					
	Compensation of Employees	Capital Consumption	Net Operating Surplus	Indirect Taxes	Less: Subsidies Received	Value Added
8 Communication	296.6	163.6	213.5	4.0	-	677.7
8 Finance, insurance, real estate and business services	1153.1	296.0	640.8	110.9	-	2200.8
9 Community, social and personal services	1537.6	698.1	1701.4	264.8	64.5	4137.4
Total, Industries	10899.8	2686.3	9852.6	1702.5	1461.0	23680.3
Producers of Government Services	4178.2	192.1	-	15.4	2.9	4382.8
Other Producers						
Total	15078.0	2878.4	9852.6	1717.9	1463.8	28063.1
Less: Imputed bank service charge	...	...	1139.0	...	...	1139.0
Import duties	...	...	...	883.6	...	883.6
Value added tax	...	...	...	2179.3	...	2179.3
Total	15078.0	2878.4	8713.6	4780.8	1463.8	29987.0

Israel

General note. The preparation of national accounts statistics in Israel is undertaken by the Central Bureau of Statistics, Jerusalem. The official estimates are published annually by the Bureau in the 'Statistical Abstract of Israel' and in the May Supplement to the Monthly Bulletin of Statistics. A detailed description of the sources and methods used for the national accounts estimates is found in 'Israel's National Income and Expenditure 1950-1962' published in 1964. Another edition of this publication for the years 1950-1968 published in 1970 included a description of the principal changes made in the methods of estimation. The estimates are generally in accordance with the classifications and definitions recommended in the United Nations Systems of National Accounts (SNA). Input-output tables have been published in 'Input-Output Tables 1988'. The following tables have been prepared from successive replies to the United Nations national accounts questionnaire. When the scope and coverage of the estimates differ for conceptual or statistical reasons from the definitions and classifications recommended in SNA, a footnote is indicated to the relevant tables.

Sources and methods :

(a) Gross domestic product. Gross domestic product is estimated mainly through the expenditure approach.

(b) Expenditure on the gross domestic product. The expenditure approach is used to estimate government final consumption expenditure and exports and imports of goods and services. This approach, in combination with the commodity-flow approach, is used for private final consumption expenditure and gross capital formation. General government consumption expenditure is estimated on the basis of activity reports of the Accountant-General and the Budget Provision supplemented by data from the Ministry of Finance. Expenditure of the local authorities and national institutions is estimated on the basis of financial statements and budget proposals. Private expenditure estimates on food, beverages and tobacco are based on data concerning quantities produced and marketed and on consumer prices, while estimates of expenditure on housing and business services, consumption of industrial products and other food products are based on family expenditure surveys held every five or six years. For the intervening years, estimates are computed by extrapolating year-to-year changes by the commodity-flow approach. Estimates of increase in stocks in agriculture, fuel and government strategic stocks are prepared by multiplying inventory stocks by their average prices. Regular quarterly and annual surveys are used to estimate inventory changes for industry and wholesale trade. The data obtained are adjusted to approximate the value of the physical change in stocks. Building and construction works are estimated either from financial data on investment in building carried out by General Government and major enterprises or by multiplying data on the areas under construction by the average cost per square meter for each type of construction. The estimates of imported machinery and equipment are based on the foreign trade statistics using the customs tariff description to identify the relevent items, while estimates of locally produced goods are based on a monthly report of sales by product obtained from a sample of the producers. The estimates of exports and imports of goods and services are based on foreign trade statistics and balance-of-payments data. Data pertaining to trade with the Administered Territories are a gross evaluation based on a sample enumeration of movement of goods through the official transit points. For the constant price estimates, government wages and salaries are extrapolated using changes in the number of employees. Government purchases of goods and services are deflated by relevant components of the consumer or wholesale price index. Price deflation is also used for most of the items of private expenditure, gross fixed capital formation and exports and imports of goods and services. For private food consumption and inventory changes in agriculture, fuel supplies, and government strategic stocks, estimates are computed by multiplying current quantities by prices in the base year.

(c) Cost-structure of the gross domestic product. The estimates of wages and salaries are based either on surveys of the industrial and construction branches, surveys of parts of the transportation branch and surveys of government and private non-profit institutions and services or on employers' reports to the National Insurance Institute and estimates of supplementary payments. The estimate of consumption of fixed capital was calculated at replacement cost. Estimates of indirect taxes are based on the financial reports of the government and the local authorities. Operating surplus is obtained as a residual.

(d) Gross domestic product by kind of economic activity. The table of GDP by kind of economic activity is prepared in net factor values. Net indirect taxes are estimated as totals only and not by industry. The production approach is used to estimate value added of the agricultural sector, the mining, quarrying and manufacturing sectors and the construction industry. For other sectors, the income approach is used. Estimates for recent years have been extrapolated by using the production approach. For the agricultural sector, data on output and input are based on the agricultural statistics series prepared by the Central Bureau of Statistics. For mining and quarrying and manufacturing, estimates are based on industrial surveys carried out annually. For years not covered by industrial surveys estimates are interpolated and extrapolated using current production indices. The Israel Electric Corporation and the Water Authority Commission supply data for their respective utility. For the construction industry a fixed ratio is assumed between input and output at constant prices and differences between the price movements of inputs and outputs are taken into account. Bench-mark estimates for wholesale and retail trade have been based on a survey held in 1976/77. Extrapolation for other years is based on changes in sales to final users. The value added of the hotel industry is estimated by changes in revenue and inputs using data obtained from special surveys. For transport and communication, estimates are based on annual reports of the concerned establishments and on surveys of the trucking industry. Estimates for the financing and insurance industries are based on consolidated reports prepared by the Supervisor of Banks and the Supervisor of Insurance. Bench-mark estimate for residential rent for 1986 has been based on the family expenditure survey, extrapolated by the change in the value of inventories of dwellings. Estimates of government services are based on reports of the Accountant-General, the national institutions and local authorities as well as on data obtained from the Budget Provisions, and from the Ministry of Finance. For other services, estimates are derived from a sample of income tax files, indirect tax data, manpower data and data on qibbutz personal services. GDP by kind of economic activity is not estimated at constant prices.

1.1 Expenditure on the Gross Domestic Product, in Current Prices

Million New sheqel

		1980	1983	1984	1985	1986	1987	1988	1989	1990	1991	1992	1993
1	Government final consumption expenditure	45	545	2918	10413	13724	19427	22393	25424	31458	39623	44881	53010
2	Private final consumption expenditure	59	903	4128	16487	27824	36373	44311	53256	64894	81725	97889	116317
	A Households	57	880	4013	16077	27158	35504	43257	51952	63184	79651	95428	113484
	B Private non-profit institutions serving households	2	23	115	410	666	869	1054	1304	1710	2074	2461	2833
3	Gross capital formation	25	368	1677	5466	8742	11171	12838	14534	20685	33671	39203	44204
	A Increase in stocks	1	5	100	103	759	29	190	223	721	1580	1461	2589
	B Gross fixed capital formation	25	363	1577	5363	7983	11143	12648	14311	19963	32092	37742	41615
	Residential buildings	10	117	511	1462	2136	2959	3625	4618	6476	13134	14356	11334
	Non-residential buildings	3	33	145	469	690	978	1258	1559	1944	2527	3438	4932
	Other construction and land improvement etc.	2	30	108	362	612	913	1145	1353	1894	2712	3655	5029
	Other	9	183	813	3070	4545	6293	6620	6781	9649	13719	16293	20320
4	Exports of goods and services	46	505	2864	12054	16756	21429	23729	30348	34827	39789	49105	61347
5	Less: Imports of goods and services	59	683	3567	14065	19135	26812	27944	33858	41582	52337	61066	79081
	Equals: Gross Domestic Product	116	1638	8020	30355	47911	61588	75327	89704	110282	142471	170012	195797

Israel

1.2 Expenditure on the Gross Domestic Product, in Constant Prices
Million New sheqel

	1980	1983	1984	1985	1986	1987	1988	1989	1990	1991	1992	1993
			At constant prices of:									
			1980				1986			1990		
1 Government final consumption expenditure	45	43	45	47	43 / 13724	16176	15789	14516	15225 / 31457	32762	32819	34668
2 Private final consumption expenditure	59	78	73	73	84 / 27824	30275	31665	31771	33520 / 64894	69631	75324	81140
A Households	57	77	71	72	82 / 27158	29600	31028	31129	32872 / 63184	67879	73469	79223
B Private non-profit institutions serving households	2	2	2	2	2 / 666	675	638	641	648 / 1710	1752	1854	1917
3 Gross capital formation	25	30	28	25	28 / 8741	9048	9006	8631	10960 / 20686	29379	31205	32118
A Increase in stocks	1	-	1	1	3 / 759	-38	27	-15	327 / 721	1492	1559	2416
B Gross fixed capital formation	24	30	27	25	25 / 7983	9086	8979	8647	10633 / 19964	27887	29646	29702
Residential buildings	10	10	9	8	7 / 2136	2317	2367	2530	2981 / 6477	11256	11192	8160
Non-residential buildings	3	3	2	2	2 / 690	781	791	837	934 / 1944	2113	2582	3446
Other construction and land improvement etc.	2	2	2	2	2 / 612	746	788	767	935 / 1894	2296	2772	3534
Other	9	16	13	13	13 / 4545	5243	5033	4513	5783 / 9650	12223	13100	14562
4 Exports of goods and services	46	48	55	60	63 / 16756	18606	18340	18997	19420 / 34827	34291	39236	43350
5 Less: Imports of goods and services	59	71	71	70	77 / 19135	22805	22175	21140	22795 / 41582	47385	51206	59072
Equals: Gross Domestic Product	116	129	130	135	141 / 47910	51300	52625	52775	56330 / 110282	118678	127378	132204

1.3 Cost Components of the Gross Domestic Product
Million New sheqel

	1980	1983	1984	1985	1986	1987	1988	1989	1990	1991	1992	1993
1 Indirect taxes, net [a]	11	180	718	4253	8242	10848	12195	13476	17773	24684	30301	34221
A Indirect taxes	20	311	1403	6111	10195	13337	15207	16539	21076	28483	35202	38922
B Less: Subsidies [a]	9	131	685	1858	1953	2489	3012	3063	3303	3799	4901	4701
2 Consumption of fixed capital	17	233	1210	4744	7136	8882	10513	13135	15772	19307	22407	26908
3 Compensation of employees paid by resident producers to:	57	834	4119	14361	23341	31167	38941	46596	55632	69327	82703	96448
A Resident households	55	808	3993	13925	22573	30008	37774	45173	53889	67481	80233	94575
B Rest of the world	2	26	126	436	768	1159	1167	1423	1743	1846	2470	1873
4 Operating surplus	31	391	1973	6997	9192	10691	13678	16497	21105	29153	34601	38220
Equals: Gross Domestic Product	116	1638	8020	30355	47911	61588	75327	89704	110282	142471	170012	195797

a) Beginning 1975, item 'Subsidies' includes subsidy component in government loans to industries.
In 1975, subsidy was 0.2 million new sheqel.

1.4 General Government Current Receipts and Disbursements
Million New sheqel

	1980	1983	1984	1985	1986	1987	1988	1989	1990	1991	1992	1993
					Receipts							
1 Operating surplus	...	...	...	...	...	...	...	...	...	...	...	...
2 Property and entrepreneurial income	7	72	275	482	1122	985	1334	2087	3287	4083	4637	4957
3 Taxes, fees and contributions	47	665	2792	12494	20430	25670	30144	33113	40506	51732	63372	73656
A Indirect taxes	20	311	1403	6111	10195	13337	15207	16539	21076	28483	35202	38922

Israel

1.4 General Government Current Receipts and Disbursements
(Continued)

Million New sheqel

	1980	1983	1984	1985	1986	1987	1988	1989	1990	1991	1992	1993
B Direct taxes	19	254	955	4522	7335	8842	10795	11597	13404	15989	19930	25041
C Social security contributions	8	96	419	1776	2714	3188	3773	4505	5461	6605	7403	8676
D Compulsory fees, fines and penalties	-	4	15	85	186	303	369	472	565	655	837	1017
4 Other current transfers	12	155	1215	5860	6688	5881	6023	7126	8865	11558	12239	13317
Total Current Receipts of General Government	66	892	4282	18836	28240	32536	37501	42326	52658	67373	80248	91930
Disbursements												
1 Government final consumption expenditure	45	546	2918	10413	13724	19427	22393	25424	31458	39623	44881	53010
A Compensation of employees	21	280	1437	4571	7008	8925	11719	14336	17396	22148	25544	29454
B Consumption of fixed capital	2	25	127	480	737	955	1176	1442	1654	2054	2328	2608
C Purchases of goods and services, net	22	241	1354	5362	5979	9547	9498	9646	12408	15421	17009	20948
D Less: Own account fixed capital formation	...	...	...	...	...	...	...	...	...	...	...	...
E Indirect taxes paid, net	...	...	...	...	...	...	...	...	...	...	...	...
2 Property income [a]	11	163	974	3754	5387	6091	6838	8212	9720	11446	12579	14245
3 Subsidies	9	131	685	1858	1953	2489	3012	3063	3304	3799	4901	4701
4 Other current transfers	9	126	597	2425	4072	5307	6652	8454	11070	14155	16676	19539
5 Net saving	-8	-74	-892	386	3104	-778	-1394	-2827	-2894	-1650	1211	435
Total Current Disbursements and Net Saving of General Government	66	892	4282	18836	28240	32536	37501	42326	52658	67373	80248	91930

a) Item 'Property income' relates to interest on public debt.

1.7 External Transactions on Current Account, Summary

Million New sheqel

	1980	1983	1984	1985	1986	1987	1988	1989	1990	1991	1992	1993
Payments to the Rest of the World												
1 Imports of goods and services	59	683	3567	14065	19135	26812	27944	33858	41582	52337	61066	79081
A Imports of merchandise c.i.f.	49	531	2757	11319	15429	21998	22484	26541	32749	41650	48546	62166
B Other	10	152	810	2746	3706	4814	5460	7317	8833	10687	12520	16915
2 Factor income to the rest of the world	11	169	973	3588	4504	5073	5397	6555	7271	7722	8726	8657
A Compensation of employees	2	26	126	436	768	1159	1167	1423	1743	1846	2470	1873
B Property and entrepreneurial income	9	143	847	3152	3736	3914	4230	5132	5528	5876	6256	6784
By general government	3	60	379	1618	2000	2186	2401	2570	2733	3069	3389	3968
By corporate and quasi-corporate enterprises	6	84	468	1532	1736	1728	1829	2562	2795	2807	2867	2816
By other												
3 Current transfers to the rest of the world	1	14	57	131	164	312	294	271	380	540	719	1002
4 Surplus of the nation on current transactions	-1	-85	-22	1879	2227	-1421	-367	2054	622	-1566	-344	-4419
Payments to the Rest of the World and Surplus of the Nation on Current Transactions	70	781	4575	19663	26030	30776	33268	42738	49855	59033	70167	84321
Receipts From The Rest of the World												
1 Exports of goods and services	47	505	2864	12054	16756	21429	23729	30348	34827	39789	49105	61347
A Exports of merchandise f.o.b.	30	327	1927	8019	11664	14742	16434	21215	24475	27445	32830	41953

Israel

1.7 External Transactions on Current Account, Summary
(Continued)

Million New sheqel

	1980	1983	1984	1985	1986	1987	1988	1989	1990	1991	1992	1993
B Other	17	178	937	4035	5092	6687	7295	9133	10352	12344	16275	19394
2 Factor income from rest of the world	7	89	378	1155	1374	1520	1758	2645	3220	4050	3785	3407
A Compensation of employees	1	7	36	103	144	179	166	209	202	258	320	467
B Property and entrepreneurial income	6	82	342	1052	1230	1341	1592	2436	3018	3792	3465	2940
By general government	2	25	105	324	431	458	574	884	1198	1732	1532	1073
By corporate and quasi-corporate enterprises	4	57	237	728	799	883	1018	1552	1820	2060	1933	1867
By other												
3 Current transfers from rest of the world	16	187	1333	6454	7900	7827	7781	9745	11808	15194	17277	19567
Receipts from the Rest of the World on Current Transactions	70	781	4575	19663	26030	30776	33268	42738	49855	59033	70167	84321

1.8 Capital Transactions of The Nation, Summary

Million New sheqel

	1980	1983	1984	1985	1986	1987	1988	1989	1990	1991	1992	1993
Finance of Gross Capital Formation												
Gross saving	23	283	1655	7345	10968	9750	12471	16588	21306	32105	38858	39785
1 Consumption of fixed capital	17	233	1210	4744	7136	8882	10513	13135	15772	19307	22407	26908
A General government	2	25	128	480	737	955	1176	1442	1654	2054	2328	2608
B Corporate and quasi-corporate enterprises	15	208	1082	4264	6399	7927	9337	11693	14118	17253	20079	24300
C Other	...	...	...	...	...	...	...	...	...	...	...	...
2 Net saving	6	50	445	2601	3832	868	1958	3453	5534	12798	16451	12877
A General government	-9	-71	-892	386	3104	-778	-1394	-2827	-2893	-1650	1211	435
B Corporate and quasi-corporate enterprises	15	121	1337	2215	728	1646	3352	6280	8427	14448	15240	12442
C Other												
Less: Surplus of the nation on current transactions	-1	-85	-22	1879	2227	-1421	-367	2054	622	-1566	-344	-4419
Finance of Gross Capital Formation	24	368	1677	5466	8741	11171	12838	14534	20684	33671	39202	44204
Gross Capital Formation												
Increase in stocks	1	5	100	103	759	29	190	223	721	1580	1461	2589
Gross fixed capital formation	23	363	1577	5363	7982	11142	12648	14311	19963	32091	37741	41615
Gross Capital Formation	24	368	1677	5466	8741	11171	12838	14534	20684	33671	39202	44204

1.10 Gross Domestic Product by Kind of Activity, in Current Prices

Million New sheqel

	1980	1983	1984	1985	1986	1987	1988	1989	1990	1991	1992	1993
1 Agriculture, hunting, forestry and fishing	5	45	250	1048	1519	1778	1885	2119	2549	2648	3312	3197
2 Mining and quarrying	15	260	1403	4795	7079	9675	11617	14455	16898	19917	24698	29007
3 Manufacturing												
4 Electricity, gas and water	2	25	113	362	515	672	826	1072	1290	1561	1943	2263
5 Construction	7	86	347	889	1561	2307	2959	3583	4870	7762	9549	9678
6 Wholesale and retail trade, restaurants and hotels	11	147	744	3028	4464	5744	6411	7471	8861	10485	12987	15581
7 Transport, storage and communication	6	85	402	1701	2595	3446	4443	5107	6068	7385	9129	10238
8 Finance, insurance, real estate and business services	19	250	1289	5273	6969	9986	12357	15445	18702	24513	29421	34906
9 Community, social and personal services	2	39	169	646	1241	1822	2287	2824	3410	4069	4893	5683
Statistical discrepancy	6	45	227	551	630	794	705	571	572	581	520	474
Total, Industries	74	982	4944	18293	26573	36224	43490	52647	63220	78921	96452	111027
Producers of Government Services	21	286	1471	4688	7216	9244	12152	15009	18136	22875	26438	30482

Israel

1.10 Gross Domestic Product by Kind of Activity, in Current Prices
(Continued)

Million New sheqel

	1980	1983	1984	1985	1986	1987	1988	1989	1990	1991	1992	1993
Other Producers	...	...	...	...	...	...	...	...	...	...	...	...
Subtotal	95	1268	6415	22981	33789	45468	55642	67656	81356	101796	122890	141509
Less: Imputed bank service charge	7	68	243	1414	1600	2614	3289	3817	3958	4988	5273	5480
Plus: Import duties	...	...	...	...	...	...	...	...	...	...	...	...
Plus: Value added tax	...	...	...	...	...	...	...	...	...	...	...	...
Plus: Other adjustments [a]	1	25	-80	-209	343	-996	264	-747	-662	1671	-314	-1362
Equals: Gross Domestic Product [b]	89	1225	6092	21358	32532	41858	52617	63092	76736	98479	117303	134667

a) Item 'Other adjustments' includes errors and omissions.
b) Net domestic product in factor values rather than gross domestic product.

1.12 Relations Among National Accounting Aggregates

Million New sheqel

	1980	1983	1984	1985	1986	1987	1988	1989	1990	1991	1992	1993
Gross Domestic Product	116	1638	8020	30355	47911	61588	75327	89704	110282	142471	170012	195797
Plus: Net factor income from the rest of the world	-6	-80	-595	-2433	-3130	-3553	-3639	-3911	-4051	-3672	-4941	-5250
Factor income from the rest of the world	6	89	378	1155	1374	1520	1758	2644	3220	4050	3785	3407
Less: Factor income to the rest of the world	12	169	973	3588	4504	5073	5397	6555	7271	7722	8726	8657
Equals: Gross National Product	110	1558	7425	27922	44781	58035	71688	85793	106231	138799	165071	190547
Less: Consumption of fixed capital	17	233	1210	4744	7136	8882	10513	13135	15772	19307	22407	26908
Equals: National Income	93	1325	6215	23178	37645	49153	61175	72658	90459	119492	142664	163639
Plus: Net current transfers from the rest of the world	15	173	1276	6323	7736	7515	7487	9474	11428	14654	16558	18565
Current transfers from the rest of the world	16	187	1333	6454	7900	7827	7781	9745	11808	15194	17277	19567
Less: Current transfers to the rest of the world	1	14	57	131	164	312	294	271	380	540	719	1002
Equals: National Disposable Income	108	1498	7491	29501	45381	56668	68662	82132	101887	134146	159222	182204
Less: Final consumption	103	1448	7046	26900	41548	55800	66703	78680	96352	121347	142770	169325
Equals: Net Saving	5	50	445	2601	3833	868	1959	3452	5535	12799	16452	12879
Less: Surplus of the nation on current transactions	-1	-85	-22	1879	2227	-1421	-367	2054	622	-1566	-344	-4419
Equals: Net Capital Formation	6	135	467	722	1606	2289	2326	1398	4913	14365	16796	17298

2.1 Government Final Consumption Expenditure by Function, in Current Prices

Million New sheqel

Fiscal year beginning 1 April

		1980	1983	1984	1985	1986	1987	1988	1989	1990	1991	1992	1993
1	General public services	3	43	239	684	997	1287	...	...	...	...	...	...
2	Defence	33	407	2589	6345	7696	10983	...	...	...	...	...	...
3	Public order and safety	2	24	133	413	605	795	...	...	...	...	...	...
4	Education	9	127	708	1857	2604	3307	...	...	...	...	...	...
5	Health	5	61	351	932	1308	1630	...	...	...	...	...	...
6	Social security and welfare	1	10	57	158	222	305	...	...	...	...	...	...
7	Housing and community amenities	1	12	73	215	310	414	...	...	...	...	...	...
8	Recreational, cultural and religious affairs	1	18	91	239	323	412	...	...	...	...	...	...
9	Economic services	1	16	83	250	353	431	...	...	...	...	...	...
	A Fuel and energy	-	-	2	6	9	11	...	...	...	...	...	...
	B Agriculture, forestry, fishing and hunting	-	5	30	83	109	124	...	...	...	...	...	...
	C Mining, manufacturing and construction, except fuel and energy	-	1	4	13	18	27	...	...	...	...	...	...
	D Transportation and communication	1	6	26	81	118	163	...	...	...	...	...	...
	E Other economic affairs	-	4	21	67	99	106	...	...	...	...	...	...
10	Other functions	2	35	186	569	802	1035	...	...	...	...	...	...
	Total Government Final Consumption Expenditure	58	753	4510	11662	15220	20599	...	...	...	...	...	...

Israel

2.5 Private Final Consumption Expenditure by Type and Purpose, in Current Prices

Million New sheqel

	1980	1983	1984	1985	1986	1987	1988	1989	1990	1991	1992	1993
Final Consumption Expenditure of Resident Households												
1 Food, beverages and tobacco [a]	18	234	1121	4738	7615	9574	11614	14173	16389	19896	23342	26480
A Food	16	204	977	4166	6705	8335	10042	12259	13894	16682	19587	21828
B Non-alcoholic beverages	1	16	86	329	523	786	971	1196	1528	1839	2064	2501
C Alcoholic beverages	1	7	27	107	167	210	261	294	411	544	664	793
D Tobacco	1	12	57	227	390	433	506	624	785	1119	1380	1668
2 Clothing and footwear	3	55	215	1011	1956	2802	2960	2939	3310	3914	4886	6239
3 Gross rent, fuel and power	13	197	953	3778	5407	6684	8212	11027	14427	18751	22044	26617
A Fuel and power	2	22	100	431	544	613	736	1094	1362	1669	2173	2367
B Other	11	175	853	3347	4863	6071	7476	9933	13065	17082	19871	24250
4 Furniture, furnishings and household equipment and operation	7	110	431	1579	3137	4173	4930	5547	6796	8392	9880	11683
A Household operation	2	28	135	489	843	1261	1651	1938	2335	2728	3084	3578
B Other	5	82	296	1090	2294	2912	3279	3609	4461	5664	6796	8105
5 Medical care and health expenses	3	50	258	891	1570	2216	2782	3622	4323	5508	6672	7828
6 Transport and communication	6	106	471	1931	3262	4435	5563	5737	7291	9739	12996	15186
A Personal transport equipment	1	38	123	377	889	1322	2056	1393	1860	2798	4394	4742
B Other	5	68	348	1554	2373	3113	3507	4344	5431	6941	8602	10444
7 Recreational, entertainment, education and cultural services	4	60	269	1164	1967	2748	3305	4005	4635	5752	7318	9099
A Education	2	25	113	446	756	1090	1362	1749	2105	2669	3279	3959
B Other	2	35	156	718	1211	1658	1943	2256	2530	3083	4039	5140
8 Miscellaneous goods and services	6	92	423	1724	2733	3724	4611	5713	6477	7824	9632	11014
A Personal care	2	29	127	512	837	1144	1409	1715	1915	2267	2656	3197
B Expenditures in restaurants, cafes and hotels	2	33	163	722	1094	1500	1767	2154	2324	2610	3454	3781
C Other	2	30	133	490	802	1080	1435	1844	2238	2947	3522	4036
Total Final Consumption Expenditure in the Domestic Market by Households, of which	59	903	4142	16809	27648	36355	43975	52764	63647	79776	96772	114146
Plus: Direct purchases abroad by resident households [b]	3	42	211	706	1148	1550	1735	2364	2785	3368	3868	5723
Less: Direct purchases in the domestic market by non-resident households	5	65	340	1437	1638	2401	2453	3176	3248	3493	5212	6384
Equals: Final Consumption Expenditure of Resident Households	57	880	4013	16078	27158	35504	43257	51952	63184	79651	95428	113484
Final Consumption Expenditure of Private Non-profit Institutions Serving Households												
1 Research and science	-	1	3	11	18	21	32	32	39	50	64	75
2 Education	-	2	13	49	80	103	128	156	197	251	296	348
3 Medical and other health services	1	5	27	94	161	171	185	213	389	385	467	554
4 Welfare services [c]	-	5	24	82	135	179	220	275	350	463	548	639
5 Recreational and related cultural services	-	4	20	71	117	154	195	267	324	406	469	527
6 Religious organisations [c]	...	...	...	...	...	...	...	...	...	...	...	...
7 Professional and labour organisations serving households	1	6	28	103	155	241	294	361	411	519	617	690
8 Miscellaneous	...	...	...	...	...	...	...	...	...	...	...	...
Equals: Final Consumption Expenditure of Private Non-profit Organisations Serving Households	2	23	115	410	666	869	1054	1304	1710	2074	2461	2833
Private Final Consumption Expenditure	58	903	4128	16487	27824	36373	44310	53256	64894	81724	97889	116317

a) The sum of the components of item 'Food, beverages and tobacco' is greater than the totals shown because the sum has been adjusted for the expenditure included in other items of the national accounts.
b) For the years 1983-1990, the estimates for this item include taxes on purchase of foreign currencies by residents for travel abroad.
c) Item 'Religious organisations' is included in item 'Welfare services'.

Israel

2.6 Private Final Consumption Expenditure by Type and Purpose, in Constant Prices

Million New sheqel

	1980	1983	1984	1985	1986	1987	1988	1989	1990	1991	1992	1993
			At constant prices of:									
			1980				1986				1990	

Final Consumption Expenditure of Resident Households

	1980	1983	1984	1985	1986	1987	1988	1989	1990	1991	1992	1993
1 Food, beverages and tobacco [a]	18	21	21	22	23 / 7615	8227	8650	8762	9191 / 16389	17280	17984	19340
A Food	16	19	19	19	20 / 6705	7142	7327	7370	7684 / 13894	14696	15367	16384
B Non-alcoholic beverages	1	1	1	1	2 / 523	658	715	756	867 / 1528	1643	1551	1810
C Alcoholic beverages	1	1	1	1	1 / 167	162	170	165	194 / 411	392	454	513
D Tobacco	1	1	1	1	1 / 390	419	561	594	572 / 785	799	883	881
2 Clothing and footwear	3	4	3	4	5 / 1956	2468	2344	2228	2425 / 3310	3571	4058	4896
3 Gross rent, fuel and power	13	14	15	15	16 / 5407	5556	5725	5895	6043 / 14427	14865	15893	16614
A Fuel and power	2	2	2	2	2 / 544	587	650	704	723 / 1362	1444	1771	1859
B Other	11	12	13	13	14 / 4863	4969	5075	5191	5320 / 13065	13421	14122	14755
4 Furniture, furnishings and household equipment and operation	7	11	8	9	12 / 3137	3405	3480	3437	3864 / 6796	7278	7965	8823
A Household operation	2	2	2	2	2 / 843	913	953	934	986 / 2335	2374	2483	2735
B Other	5	9	6	7	10 / 2294	2492	2527	2503	2878 / 4461	4904	5482	6088
5 Medical care and health expenses	3	4	4	4	4 / 1570	1708	1773	1908	2044 / 4323	4690	5125	5501
6 Transport and communication	6	10	9	8	10 / 3262	3771	4187	3832	4069 / 7291	8383	10403	10575
A Personal transport equipment	1	4	2	2	2 / 889	1113	1379	880	1086 / 1860	2714	4010	3452
B Other	5	7	7	7	7 / 2373	2658	2808	2952	2983 / 5431	5669	6393	7123
7 Recreational, entertainment, education and cultural services	4	5	4	5	5 / 1967	2192	2228	2246	2264 / 4635	4907	5596	6230
A Education	2	2	2	2	2 / 756	834	839	884	898 / 2105	2229	2450	2683
B Other	2	3	2	3	3 / 1211	1358	1389	1362	1366 / 2530	2678	3146	3547
8 Miscellaneous goods and services	6	7	7	7	8 / 2734	2975	3035	3209	3277 / 6477	6789	7523	7794
A Personal care	2	2	2	2	3 / 837	907	946	1005	1027 / 1915	2007	2179	2438
B Expenditures in restaurants, cafes and hotels	2	2	2	3	3 / 1094	1213	1176	1212	1206 / 2324	2220	2635	2523

Israel

2.6 Private Final Consumption Expenditure by Type and Purpose, in Constant Prices
(Continued)

Million New sheqel

	1980	1983	1984	1985	1986	1987	1988	1989	1990	1991	1992	1993
			At constant prices of:									
			1980				1986			1990		
C Other	2	3	2	2	2 / 803	855	913	992	1044 / 2238	2562	2709	2833
Total Final Consumption Expenditure in the Domestic Market by Households, of which	60	77	72	74	83 / 27648	30303	31424	31510	33178 / 63647	67764	74546	79771
Plus: Direct purchases abroad by resident households b	3	5	4	3	4 / 1148	1229	1310	1503	1464 / 2785	2901	3007	3858
Less: Direct purchases in the domestic market by non-resident households	5	5	5	6	4 / 1638	1932	1707	1884	1770 / 3248	2786	4085	4406
Equals: Final Consumption Expenditure of Resident Households	57	77	71	72	82 / 27158	29600	31028	31129	32872 / 63184	67879	73469	79223

Final Consumption Expenditure of Private Non-profit Institutions Serving Households

	1980	1983	1984	1985	1986	1987	1988	1989	1990	1991	1992	1993
1 Research and science	-	-	-	-	18	20	27	27	29 / 39	42	48	52
2 Education	-	-	-	-	80	83	84	83	88 / 197	206	218	224
3 Medical and other health services	-	-	-	-	161	145	117	107	96 / 389	350	375	383
4 Welfare services c	-	-	-	-	135	142	145	148	165 / 350	393	420	447
5 Recreational and related cultural services	-	-	-	-	117	121	109	120	124 / 324	335	345	359
6 Religious organisations c	...	...	...	...	...	...	...	...	...	...	...	...
7 Professional and labour organisations serving households	-	-	-	-	155	163	155	156	147 / 411	426	447	452
8 Miscellaneous	...	...	...	...	...	...	...	...	...	...	...	...
Equals: Final Consumption Expenditure of Private Non-profit Organisations Serving Households	2	2	2	2	2 / 666	674	637	641	649 / 1710	1752	1853	1917
Private Final Consumption Expenditure	59	78	73	73	84 / 27824	30275	31665	31771	33520 / 64894	69631	75324	81140

a) The sum of the components of item 'Food, beverages and tobacco' is greater than the totals shown because the sum has been adjusted for the expenditure included in other items of the national accounts.
b) For the years 1983-1990, the estimates for this item include taxes on purchase of foreign currencies by residents for travel abroad.
c) Item 'Religious organisations' is included in item 'Welfare services'.

2.11 Gross Fixed Capital Formation by Kind of Activity of Owner, ISIC Divisions, in Current Prices

Million New sheqel

	1980	1983	1984	1985	1986	1987	1988	1989	1990	1991	1992	1993
					All Producers							
1 Agriculture, hunting, forestry and fishing	1	17	70	264	272	362	357	317	384	474	626	769
2 Mining and quarrying	4	62	314	1331	1825	2347	2172	2582	3394	4743	5633	7167
3 Manufacturing												
4 Electricity, gas and water a	2	17	87	255	406	537	729	990	1557	1682	1993	2897

Israel

2.11 Gross Fixed Capital Formation by Kind of Activity of Owner, ISIC Divisions, in Current Prices
(Continued)

Million New sheqel

	1980	1983	1984	1985	1986	1987	1988	1989	1990	1991	1992	1993
5 Construction [b]	-	5	13	26	46	88	115	113	243	680	551	782
6 Wholesale and retail trade, restaurants and hotels [c]	4	76	329	1193	1778	2316	2699	3191	4091	5344	6631	8648
7 Transport, storage and communication	3	65	251	833	1520	2532	2952	2498	3820	6034	7956	10017
8 Finance, insurance, real estate and business services	10	117	511	1462	2136	2959	3625	4618	6476	13134	14356	11334
9 Community, social and personal services [c]	...	...	...	...	...	...	...	...	...	...	...	...
Total Industries	24	360	1577	5363	7983	11143	12648	14311	19966	32092	37746	41615
Producers of Government Services	...	...	...	...	...	...	...	...	...	...	...	...
Private Non-Profit Institutions Serving Households	...	...	...	...	...	...	...	...	...	...	...	...
Total	24	360	1577	5363	7983	11143	12648	14311	19966	32092	37746	41615

a) Item 'Electricity, gas and water' includes water projects.
b) Item 'Construction' includes construction equipment only.
c) All services are included in item 'Wholesale and retail trade, restaurants and hotels'.

2.12 Gross Fixed Capital Formation by Kind of Activity of Owner, ISIC Divisions, in Constant Prices

Million New sheqel

	1980	1983	1984	1985	1986	1987	1988	1989	1990	1991	1992	1993
		At constant prices of:										
	1980				1986				1990			
					All Producers							
1 Agriculture, hunting, forestry and fishing	1	1	1	1	1 / 274	297	260	197	212 / 385	410	491	558
2 Mining and quarrying	3	5	5	6	5 / 1825	1964	1683	1696	1983 / 3395	4091	4393	5165
3 Manufacturing												
4 Electricity, gas and water	2[a]	1[a]	1[a]	1[a]	1[a] / 406	423	517	605	832 / 1557[a]	1456[a]	1565[a]	2080[a]
5 Construction	-[b]	-[b]	-[b]	-[b]	-[b] / 46	75	91	77	148 / 243[b]	597[b]	437[b]	567[b]
6 Wholesale and retail trade, restaurants and hotels	4[c]	6[c]	5[c]	5[c]	5[c] / 1777	1815	1901	1922	2238 / 4091[c]	4574[c]	5103[c]	6137[c]
7 Transport, storage and communication	3	6	4	4	4 / 1520	2193	2158	1621	2234 / 3819	5503	6465	7034
8 Finance, insurance, real estate and business services	10	10	9	8	7 / 2136	2317	2367	2530	2981 / 6477	11256	11192	8160
9 Community, social and personal services	...	...	...	...	... / ...	...	...	...	... / ...	...	...	...
Total Industries	24	30	27	25	25 / 7983	9083	8979	8647	10627 / 19966	27887	29646	29702
Producers of Government Services	...	...	...	...	... / ...	...	...	...	... / ...	...	...	...
Private Non-Profit Institutions Serving Households	...	...	...	...	... / ...	...	...	...	... / ...	...	...	...
Total	24	30	27	25	25 / 7983	9083	8979	8647	10627 / 19966	27887	29646	29702

a) Item 'Electricity, gas and water' includes water projects.
b) Item 'Construction' includes construction equipment only.
c) All services are included in item 'Wholesale and retail trade, restaurants and hotels'.

Israel

2.17 Exports and Imports of Goods and Services, Detail

Million New sheqel

	1980	1983	1984	1985	1986	1987	1988	1989	1990	1991	1992	1993
Exports of Goods and Services												
1 Exports of merchandise, f.o.b.	30	327	1927	8019	11664	14742	16434	21215	24475	27445	32830	41953
2 Transport and communication	7	75	409	1483	1881	2388	2658	3328	3944	4911	5770	6893
A In respect of merchandise imports	1	18	90	355	529	670	712	846	1047	1390	1642	1969
B Other	6	57	319	1128	1352	1718	1946	2482	2897	3521	4128	4924
3 Insurance service charges	-	1	-15	16	19	25	26	-31	-2	27	-44	38
A In respect of merchandise imports	-	-	2	12	15	18	21	22	28	48	52	68
B Other	-	1	-17	4	4	7	5	-53	-30	-21	-96	-30
4 Other commodities	5	37	201	1094	1538	1850	2120	2593	3067	3801	5207	5944
5 Adjustments of merchandise exports to change-of-ownership basis	-	-	-	-	-	-	-	-	-	-	-	-
6 Direct purchases in the domestic market by non-residential households	5	65	340	1437	1638	2401	2453	3176	3248	3493	5212	6384
7 Direct purchases in the domestic market by extraterritorial bodies	-	-	2	5	16	23	38	67	95	112	130	135
Total Exports of Goods and Services	47	505	2864	12054	16756	21429	23729	30348	34827	39789	49105	61347
Imports of Goods and Services												
1 Imports of merchandise, c.i.f.	49	531	2757	11319	15429	21998	22484	26541	32749	41650	48546	62166
A Imports of merchandise, f.o.b.	46	496	2577	10582	14318	20568	20951	24715	30492	38675	45029	57793
B Transport of services on merchandise imports	3	34	173	699	1056	1359	1446	1717	2128	2819	3332	4132
By residents	1	18	90	355	529	670	712	846	1047	1390	1642	1969
By non-residents	2	16	83	344	527	689	734	871	1081	1429	1690	2163
C Insurance service charges on merchandise imports	-	-1	7	38	55	71	87	109	129	156	185	241
By residents	-	-	2	12	15	18	21	22	28	48	52	68
By non-residents	-	1	5	26	40	53	66	87	101	108	133	173
2 Adjustments of merchandise imports to change-of-ownership basis	-	-	-	-	-	-	-	-	-	-	-	-
3 Other transport and communication	6	57	319	1128	1352	1718	1946	2482	2897	3521	4128	4924
4 Other insurance service charges	-	1	13	131	131	180	131	206	379	220	393	222
5 Other commodities	1	45	236	725	961	1215	1470	1990	2355	3017	3420	4617
6 Direct purchases abroad by government	-	4	22	100	108	139	145	168	244	313	402	545
7 Direct purchases abroad by resident households	3	45	220	662	1154	1562	1768	2471	2958	3616	4177	6607
Total Imports of Goods and Services	59	683	3567	14065	19135	26812	27944	33858	41582	52337	61066	79081
Balance of Goods and Services	-12	-178	-703	-2011	-2379	-5383	-4215	-3510	-6755	-12548	-11961	-17734
Total Imports and Balance of Goods and Services	47	505	2864	12054	16756	21429	23729	30348	34827	39789	49105	61347

Italy

General note. The preparation of national accounts statistics in Italy is undertaken by the instituto Central di Statistica, Rome. The official estimates are published in the 'Annuario Statistico Italiano' and in 'Compendio Statistico Italiano'. The latter publication is also published in English under the title 'Italian Statistical Abstract'. The following presentation on sources and method is based mainly on information prepared by the Statistical Office of the European Communities in 1976 in a report entitled 'Basic statistics needed for the ESA accounts and tables: present situation and prospects for improvements'. The estimates are generally in accordance with the definitions and classifications recommended in the United Nations System of National Accounts (SNA). Input-output tables have been published in 'Supplemento Straordinario al Bolletiono Mensile di Statistica'. The following tables have been prepared from successive replies to the United Nations national accounts questionnaire. When the scope and coverage of the estimates differ for conceptual or statistical reasons from the definitions and classifications recommended in SNA, a footnote is indicated to the relevant tables.

Sources and methods:

(a) Gross domestic product. GDP is estimated mainly through the production approach.

(b) Expenditure on the gross domestic product. The expenditure approach is used to estimate government final consumption expenditure, increase in stocks and exports and imports of goods and services. This aproach, in combination with the commodity-flow approach is used to estimate private final consumption expenditure and gross fixed capital formation. For central government, the estimates are based on data obtained from the Bilancio dello Stato. Complete accounts for tHe other bodies of the general government are available after 39 months and for social security funds, after 27 months, Household consumption expenditure is primarily based on the quarterly surveys of family budgets suplemented by estimates based on commodity-flows. The surveys cover 36,000 households by rotation with 9000 new families each quarter. Surveys carried out by the Banco d'Italia provide consumption data for non-resident households on the domestic market and for residents abroad. The main statistical source used for estimating changes in stocks is the value-added surveys conducted for all enterprises in the industrial construction, trade and transport sectors that employ more than 20 persons. The stocks relate to industrial products only. Data for estimating gross fixed capital formation are obtained through a questionnaire attached to the value-added survey. Government capital expenditure are obtained from government accounts. For construction and building, the Istituto Central di Statistico conducts specific surveys such as surveys on residential buildings and on public works. The estimates of exports and imports of goods and services are based mainly on the balance-of-payments and foreign trade statistics. For the constant price estimates, most of the items of GDP by expenditure type are deflated by appropriate price indexes. Government building depreciation is estimated as a certain percentage of the stock value at constant prices. Private consumption of own-produced food and stock increases of agricultural products are revalued at base-year prices. Gross rent is extrapolated by the number of dwelling units.

(c) Cost-structure of the gross domestic product. Compensation of employees is estimated through use of the value-added survey and a survey carried out by the Ministry of Labour and Social Security for the industrial sector, minimum contractual wages and survey of the compensation of permanent employees for the agricultural sector, surveys and inquiries carried out by other institutes for the service sector and other indirect evaluation for sectors not covered by surveys. Information on operating surplus is obtained from the value-added surveys and from actual interest received and paid by the various sectors. Depreciation is valued on the basis of time series of gross fixed capital formation at constant prices by product and by branch of economic activity. Constant prices of 1970 are estimated by using the perpetual inventory method, assuming that the devaluation of the product is constant during its economic life. Estimates of indirect taxes and subsidies are obtained from government sources. Taxes linked to production and imports are broken down by branch according to the type of tax. Data on subsidies are classified by branch on the basis of the recipients indicated in the government budgets.

(d) Gross domestic product by kind of economic activity. The table of GDP by kind of economic activity is prepared at market prices, i.e., producers' values. The production approach is used to estimate the value added of most of the industries. This is supplemented by the income approach for industries to which the value-added surveys are applied. The income approach alone is used for the producers of government services. Statistics on agricultural production prices, etc. are derived from current agricultural surveys. A new survey was carried out in 1975, covering 6,000 farms with complete accounts which produce about 10 percent of the total output. Crop surveys of major products are conducted annually. Information on gross marketable livestock production is available separately for major items. For forestry, a quarterly survey supplies data on production and prices. Monthly surveys of products unloaded in Italian ports are used for estimating value added of fishing. For the industrial activity sector, the estimates are based on value-added surveys and the product surveys. In addition to these surveys, the rapid surveys of large enterprises are also used for manufacturing. The annual value-added survey, which covers all enterprises employing more than 20 persons and is available after 15 months, includes transactions in goods and services, distributive transactions and employment data. The survey does not allow product-by-product analysis. The product survey which covers all enterprises employing more than 50 persons and is available after 24 months, is used for compiling input-output tables and is linked with the European Community surveys on industrial activity. The annual rapid survey, covering all enterprises employing more than 250 persons is available within 3 months. This survey provides information similar to that obtained in the value-added surveys. The surveys used for the manufacturing sector are also used for construction. In addition construction estimates are based on the results of surveys on the number of residential buildings, surveys of public works and sample surveys of work in progress on bUilding sites. For the trade sector, the main source is the value-added survey. However, to cover enterprises employing less than 20 persons, an indirect method, which consists in constructing an index of traded consumer goods, capital goods and goods for export, is used for estimating gross output of the trade sector. The value-added surveys are also used for the transport sector. Additional information is supplied directly by the relevant firms and public agencies. For the financial institutions, annual surveys are carried out which covers 97 percent of the activity. Special calculations are made for institutions not covered. Estimates of government services are based on surveys conducted by the social security funds and on data compiled by the Ragioneria generale dello Stato and the Istituto Centrale de Statistic. For other services, the Istituto Central di Statistica carries out a single direct survey of public hospitals. Other market services are valued indirectly, mostly on the basis of the results of family budgets surveys. For the constant price estimates, price deflation is used for community, social and personal services. Double deflation is used for all the other sectors. Output is either deflated by apropriate indexes or is extrapolated by quantum indexes while input is deflated by price indexes.

1.1 Expenditure on the Gross Domestic Product, in Current Prices

Thousand Million Italian lire

	1980	1983	1984	1985	1986	1987	1988	1989	1990	1991	1992	1993
1 Government final consumption expenditure	57013	103568	118034	133265	145960	163880	184291	198517	228375	249585	264149	275966
2 Private final consumption expenditure	236603	387170	443268	498048	551868	606889	670883	740267	806593	884753	946937	965390
A Households	235561	385566	441289	495811	549472	604429	668215	737407	803386	881111	943208	961579
B Private non-profit institutions serving households	1042	1604	1979	2237	2396	2460	2668	2860	3207	3642	3729	3811
3 Gross capital formation	104522	138190	166498	182558	188376	206499	234661	254800	275368	292117	291563	263448
A Increase in stocks	10460	3348	13895	14965	10722	12397	15409	13777	9422	10222	4855	-3179
B Gross fixed capital formation	94062	134842	152603	167593	177654	194102	219252	241023	265946	281895	286708	266627
Residential buildings	25991	42833	46733	49316	50171	51005	55691	60044	68237	76087	80389	81916
Non-residential buildings	23620	33146	35741	40141	44639	47330	52498	58435	66849	71835	71965	65586
Other construction and land improvement etc.												
Other	44451	58863	70129	78136	82844	95767	111063	122544	130860	133973	134354	119125
4 Exports of goods and services	84953	140016	165197	185022	181961	192273	210046	243047	272868	279974	300707	365442
5 Less: Imports of goods and services	95422	135508	167237	188313	168262	185738	208044	243169	271138	276976	299033	310132
Equals: Gross Domestic Product	387669	633436	725760	810580	899903	983803	1091837	1193462	1312066	1429453	1504323	1560114

Italy

1.2 Expenditure on the Gross Domestic Product, in Constant Prices

Thousand Million Italian lire

	1980	1983	1984	1985	1986	1987	1988	1989	1990	1991	1992	1993
					At constant prices of: 1985							
1 Government final consumption expenditure	116074	126053	128874	133265	136674	141425	145449	146629	148301	150558	151998	153170
2 Private final consumption expenditure	458153	472973	483229	498048	519789	542939	567825	588427	605500	621264	631927	612929
A Households	456128	470867	481021	495811	517486	540602	565441	585985	602945	618615	629260	610245
B Private non-profit institutions serving households	2025	2106	2208	2237	2303	2337	2384	2442	2555	2649	2667	2684
3 Gross capital formation	193050	164640	179418	182558	185138	193730	205944	210766	218570	218458	216720	178876
A Increase in stocks	17918	3897	12902	14965	13834	13856	13579	10102	10342	8933	11410	-3680
B Gross fixed capital formation	175132	160743	166516	167593	171304	179874	192365	200664	208228	209525	205310	182556
Residential buildings	51152	51008	50749	49316	48295	47151	47743	48896	50259	51795	51934	51512
Non-residential buildings	45311	39643	39171	40141	42898	43368	44888	47107	49061	48948	46709	41017
Other construction and land improvement etc.												
Other	78669	70092	76596	78136	80111	89355	99734	104661	108908	108782	106667	90027
4 Exports of goods and services	154839	166755	179521	185022	187106	195637	205057	221144	240355	239899	252763	279401
5 Less: Imports of goods and services	165919	161051	181006	188313	194445	213309	228878	245252	271339	277493	293594	270930
Equals: Gross Domestic Product	756197	769370	790036	810580	834262	860422	895397	921714	941387	952686	959814	953446

1.3 Cost Components of the Gross Domestic Product

Thousand Million Italian lire

	1980	1983	1984	1985	1986	1987	1988	1989	1990	1991	1992	1993
1 Indirect taxes, net	22496	39303	44520	49811	56778	69155	84485	95395	112952	129570	138834	155932
A Indirect taxes	35846	62084	72097	77636	89071	101141	117823	132464	148938	170552	178166	198956
B Less: Subsidies	13350	22781	27577	27825	32293	31986	33338	37069	35986	40982	39332	43024
2 Consumption of fixed capital	44581	77966	88456	100188	107966	116849	128252	140567	154252	168419	179939	191681
3 Compensation of employees paid by resident producers to:	184063	300156	334994	374051	404065	438837	482553	528340	592391	646776	680008	687163
A Resident households	183828	299659	334423	373323	403326	437920	481255	525937	589516	644702	678112	684893
B Rest of the world	235	497	571	728	739	917	1298	2403	2875	2074	1896	2270
4 Operating surplus	136529	216011	257790	286530	331094	358962	396547	429160	452471	484688	505542	525338
A Corporate and quasi-corporate enterprises	22818	29345	47030	56584	65979	69739	81755	88042	83889	75760	72016	91576
B Private unincorporated enterprises	113310	185666	209592	228626	263530	287439	312464	338373	365665	406075	429709	429723
C General government	401	1000	1168	1320	1585	1784	2328	2745	2917	2853	3817	4039
Equals: Gross Domestic Product	387669	633436	725760	810580	899903	983803	1091837	1193462	1312066	1429453	1504323	1560114

1.4 General Government Current Receipts and Disbursements

Thousand Million Italian lire

	1980	1983	1984	1985	1986	1987	1988	1989	1990	1991	1992	1993
					Receipts							
1 Operating surplus	401	1000	1168	1320	1585	1784	2328	2745	2917	2853	3817	4039
2 Property and entrepreneurial income	4054	6730	7478	9548	10787	10547	10902	12072	13762	14636	15048	13680
3 Taxes, fees and contributions	115301	215515	245654	275241	308804	344839	388149	444318	497542	553268	588167	647273
A Indirect taxes	33522	57987	67283	72661	81743	93240	109076	123867	139465	159022	167026	186026
B Direct taxes	37291	78402	91416	105466	115683	130611	145720	170697	189124	207054	221310	250459
C Social security contributions	44488	79126	86955	97114	111378	120988	133353	149754	168953	187192	199831	210788
D Compulsory fees, fines and penalties	-	-	-	-	-	-	-	-	-	-	-	-
4 Other current transfers	9340	18276	20696	25941	31494	29797	31876	35479	40682	48101	54457	60766
Total Current Receipts of General Government	129096	241521	274996	312050	352670	386967	433255	494614	554903	618858	661489	725758
					Disbursements							
1 Government final consumption expenditure	57013	103568	118034	133265	145960	163880	184291	198517	228375	249585	264149	275966
2 Property income	21858	50104	61012	68543	79754	82039	93240	111294	131802	151911	177851	191812
A Interest	21772	49933	60829	68312	79531	81779	92952	110946	131431	151464	177343	191259
B Net land rent and royalties	86	171	183	231	223	260	288	348	371	447	508	553

Italy

1.4 General Government Current Receipts and Disbursements
(Continued)

Thousand Million Italian lire

		1980	1983	1984	1985	1986	1987	1988	1989	1990	1991	1992	1993
3	Subsidies	11068	18381	22446	22878	27693	26093	26577	29837	29577	32554	31187	34504
4	Other current transfers	57354	113979	127036	145617	162554	178745	199155	224084	250642	276617	307391	322857
	A Social security benefits	54696	109355	121556	139055	154826	170500	189065	209963	238585	261320	290526	301620
	B Social assistance grants												
	C Other	2658	4624	5480	6562	7728	8245	10090	14121	12057	15297	16865	21237
5	Net saving	-18197	-44511	-53532	-58253	-63291	-63790	-70008	-69118	-85493	-91809	-119089	-99381
	Total Current Disbursements and Net Saving of General Government	129096	241521	274996	312050	352670	386967	433255	494614	554903	618858	661489	725758

1.5 Current Income and Outlay of Corporate and Quasi-Corporate Enterprises, Summary

Thousand Million Italian lire

		1980	1983	1984	1985	1986	1987	1988	1989	1990	1991	1992	1993
	Receipts												
1	Operating surplus	22818	29345	47030	56584	65979	69739	81755	88042	83889	75760	72016	91576
2	Property and entrepreneurial income received	76634	125507	140227	153038	153232	149574	164070	198135	225151	244324	279055	271867
3	Current transfers	15966	23784	26587	30103	32318	35441	39461	47091	53603	59851	64141	67050
	Total Current Receipts	115418	178636	213844	239725	251529	254754	285286	333268	362643	379935	415212	430493
	Disbursements												
1	Property and entrepreneurial income	84712	144859	158850	170009	167692	164553	182274	221660	250669	271349	304749	290140
2	Direct taxes and other current payments to general government	4933	12378	14395	18053	22168	29275	25112	37970	41502	45386	43658	54355
3	Other current transfers	10865	20249	21774	26513	28248	33497	36884	42887	50205	57529	61461	67642
	Statistical discrepancy	5325	5575	6860	7933	8029	6581	7443	8617	8424	9473	6921	5287
4	Net saving	9583	-4425	11965	17217	25392	20848	33573	22134	11843	-3802	-1577	13069
	Total Current Disbursements and Net Saving	115418	178636	213844	239725	251529	254754	285286	333268	362643	379935	415212	430493

1.6 Current Income and Outlay of Households and Non-Profit Institutions

Thousand Million Italian lire

		1980	1983	1984	1985	1986	1987	1988	1989	1990	1991	1992	1993
	Receipts												
1	Compensation of employees	185672	302452	337537	376681	406738	440993	484497	529420	592890	647133	680093	687218
	A From resident producers	183828	299659	334423	373323	403326	437920	481255	525937	589516	644702	678112	684893
	B From rest of the world	1844	2793	3114	3358	3412	3073	3242	3483	3374	2431	1981	2325
2	Operating surplus of private unincorporated enterprises	113310	185666	209592	228626	263530	287439	312464	338373	365665	406075	429709	429723
3	Property and entrepreneurial income	35832	74804	85619	91264	98253	102454	117942	142655	161655	181076	208529	214697
4	Current transfers	66731	130771	145457	166692	184245	204374	226979	252655	287011	314741	348596	368800
	A Social security benefits	58583	117344	129798	148667	164573	182196	202076	224011	254556	277914	310091	324655
	B Social assistance grants	...	...	...	...	...	...	...	...	...	...	...	...
	C Other	8148	13427	15659	18025	19672	22178	24903	28644	32455	36827	38505	44145
	Statistical discrepancy	6979	7274	8515	9897	10090	9286	10307	11496	11514	12877	10169	9878
	Total Current Receipts	408524	700967	786720	873160	962856	1044546	1152189	1274599	1418735	1561902	1677096	1710316
	Disbursements												
1	Private final consumption expenditure	236603	387170	443268	498048	551868	606889	670883	740267	806593	884753	946937	965390
2	Property income	10802	18647	20803	23396	24446	24965	27005	31560	34399	37464	45959	44098
3	Direct taxes and other current transfers n.e.c. to general government	77122	145448	164306	184883	205293	222747	254425	282953	317127	349561	378229	407718
	A Social security contributions	44764	79424	87285	97470	111778	121411	133817	150226	169505	187893	200577	211614
	B Direct taxes	32358	66024	77021	87413	93515	101336	120608	132727	147622	161668	177652	196104
	C Fees, fines and penalties	...	...	...	...	...	...	...	...	...	...	...	...
4	Other current transfers	22433	36676	41741	48866	56752	56726	62237	71273	81017	93840	103555	112964
	Statistical discrepancy	1654	1699	1655	1964	2061	2705	2864	2879	3090	3404	3248	4591
5	Net saving	59910	111327	114947	116003	122436	130514	134775	145667	176509	192880	199168	175555
	Total Current Disbursements and Net Saving	408524	700967	786720	873160	962856	1044546	1152189	1274599	1418735	1561902	1677096	1710316

Italy

1.7 External Transactions on Current Account, Summary

Thousand Million Italian lire

	1980	1983	1984	1985	1986	1987	1988	1989	1990	1991	1992	1993
Payments to the Rest of the World												
1 Imports of goods and services	95422	135508	167237	188313	168262	185738	208044	243169	271138	276976	299033	310132
A Imports of merchandise c.i.f.	87170	122469	150887	168791	149542	163692	181264	211316	219313	227894	234374	234033
B Other	8252	13039	16350	19522	18720	22046	26780	31853	51825	49082	64659	76099
2 Factor income to the rest of the world	5662	13422	16445	18600	18594	18157	20568	28612	38676	47840	58377	68680
A Compensation of employees	235	497	571	728	739	917	1298	2403	2875	2074	1896	2270
B Property and entrepreneurial income	5427	12925	15874	17872	17855	17240	19270	26209	35801	45766	56481	66410
3 Current transfers to the rest of the world	4007	6870	8359	9580	12900	13540	14831	18619	18162	25329	24282	30199
A Indirect taxes to supranational organizations	...	...	...	...	...	...	...	...	...	...	...	...
B Other current transfers	4007	6870	8359	9580	12900	13540	14831	18619	18162	25329	24282	30199
4 Surplus of the nation on current transactions	-8645	2167	-4662	-7403	4127	-2071	-8069	-15550	-18257	-26429	-33122	17476
Payments to the Rest of the World and Surplus of the Nation on Current Transactions	96446	157967	187379	209090	203883	215364	235374	274850	309719	323716	348570	426487
Receipts From The Rest of the World												
1 Exports of goods and services	84953	140016	165197	185022	181961	192273	210046	243047	272868	279974	300707	365442
A Exports of merchandise f.o.b.	66987	110747	131026	146059	144675	151114	166639	193013	203885	211126	220635	265236
B Other	17966	29269	34171	38963	37286	41159	43407	50034	68983	68848	80072	100206
2 Factor income from rest of the world	6452	9226	11709	13222	11687	11435	13018	18116	22975	27668	32658	43036
A Compensation of employees	1844	2793	3114	3358	3412	3073	3242	3483	3374	2431	1981	2325
B Property and entrepreneurial income	4608	6433	8595	9864	8275	8362	9776	14633	19601	25237	30677	40711
3 Current transfers from rest of the world	5041	8725	10473	10846	10235	11656	12310	13687	13876	16074	15205	18009
A Subsidies from supranational organisations	...	...	...	...	...	...	...	...	...	...	...	...
B Other current transfers	5041	8725	10473	10846	10235	11656	12310	13687	13876	16074	15205	18009
Receipts from the Rest of the World on Current Transactions	96446	157967	187379	209090	203883	215364	235374	274850	309719	323716	348570	426487

1.8 Capital Transactions of The Nation, Summary

Thousand Million Italian lire

	1980	1983	1984	1985	1986	1987	1988	1989	1990	1991	1992	1993
Finance of Gross Capital Formation												
Gross saving	95877	140357	161836	175155	192503	204428	226592	239250	257111	265688	258441	280924
1 Consumption of fixed capital	44581	77966	88456	100188	107966	116849	128252	140567	154252	168419	179939	191681
A General government	862	1437	1681	1988	2334	2735	3223	3799	4481	5270	6223	7256
B Corporate and quasi-corporate enterprises	18670	32877	37273	41739	44737	48134	52133	57028	62450	68355	72322	76750
C Other	25049	43652	49502	56461	60895	65980	72896	79740	87321	94794	101394	107675
2 Net saving	51296	62391	73380	74967	84537	87579	98340	98683	102859	97269	78502	89243
A General government	-18197	-44511	-53532	-58253	-63291	-63790	-70008	-69118	-85493	-91809	-119089	-99381
B Corporate and quasi-corporate enterprises	9583	-4425	11965	17217	25392	20848	33573	22134	11843	-3802	-1577	13069
C Other	59910	111327	114947	116003	122436	130521	134775	145667	176509	192880	199168	175555
Less: Surplus of the nation on current transactions	-8645	2167	-4662	-7403	4127	-2071	-8069	-15550	-18257	-26429	-33122	17476
Finance of Gross Capital Formation	104522	138190	166498	182558	188376	206499	234661	254800	275368	292117	291563	263448
Gross Capital Formation												
Increase in stocks	10460	3348	13895	14965	10722	12397	15409	13777	9422	10222	4855	-3179
Gross fixed capital formation	94062	134842	152603	167593	177654	194102	219252	241023	265946	281895	286708	266627
Gross Capital Formation	104522	138190	166498	182558	188376	206499	234661	254800	275368	292117	291563	263448

Italy

1.10 Gross Domestic Product by Kind of Activity, in Current Prices

Thousand Million Italian lire

	1980	1983	1984	1985	1986	1987	1988	1989	1990	1991	1992	1993
1 Agriculture, hunting, forestry and fishing	22305	33265	33823	36327	38604	40053	39330	41605	42133	47847	47300	45459
2 Mining and quarrying	107810	156159	176975	196473	213181	229201	256317	279628	293813	301423	308527	314939
3 Manufacturing												
4 Electricity, gas and water	15053	28957	33809	37479	43607	48109	52480	57543	67008	76819	86320	89086
5 Construction	28458	42563	47008	50987	54007	56664	61874	67782	76702	83818	87425	86824
6 Wholesale and retail trade, restaurants and hotels [a]	70274	119978	137446	154755	171302	188176	206244	222337	241124	264370	277407	284534
7 Transport, storage and communication	20026	33292	38578	43609	51277	55223	61820	67765	74344	83303	90693	98649
8 Finance, insurance, real estate and business services	74480	129411	154892	177559	206193	225602	252264	281092	319071	349598	386241	410647
9 Community, social and personal services												
Total, Industries	338406	543625	622531	697189	778171	843028	930329	1017752	1114195	1207178	1283913	1330138
Producers of Government Services	42791	76317	86593	96007	105652	118064	133205	143800	169020	184249	193738	200201
Other Producers	2939	5175	5860	7102	7862	7872	8733	10156	11571	13402	14867	15735
Subtotal	384136	625117	714984	800298	891685	968964	1072267	1171708	1294786	1404829	1492518	1546074
Less: Imputed bank service charge	16471	26510	30119	34373	39853	40215	44870	52004	61911	67359	79400	79231
Plus: Import duties	20004	34829	40895	44655	48071	55054	64440	73758	79191	91983	91205	93271
Plus: Value added tax	...	...	...	...	...	...	...	...	...	...	...	...
Equals: Gross Domestic Product [b]	387669	633436	725760	810580	899903	983803	1091837	1193462	1312066	1429453	1504323	1560114

a) Item 'Wholesale and retail trade, restaurants and hotels' includes repair services.
b) The branch breakdown used in this table (GDP by kind of activity) is according to the classification NACE/CLIO.

1.11 Gross Domestic Product by Kind of Activity, in Constant Prices

Thousand Million Italian lire

	1980	1983	1984	1985	1986	1987	1988	1989	1990	1991	1992	1993
	\multicolumn{12}{c}{At constant prices of: 1985}
1 Agriculture, hunting, forestry and fishing	35637	37876	36046	36327	37027	38412	37177	37608	36509	39159	40054	38787
2 Mining and quarrying	185999	182150	190177	196473	201383	209475	224875	233259	237742	237224	237163	232644
3 Manufacturing												
4 Electricity, gas and water	40848	37507	37667	37479	39655	40461	41190	42173	43912	44495	46020	46078
5 Construction	54532	52715	50961	50987	51310	52038	53386	55265	56667	57328	56808	54185
6 Wholesale and retail trade, restaurants and hotels [a]	143684	147727	152600	154755	157863	164138	171181	174796	178256	180407	181774	178121
7 Transport, storage and communication	38296	39866	41463	43609	45738	47397	50709	53378	55423	57114	59723	62497
8 Finance, insurance, real estate and business services	151168	161483	168998	177559	185757	191072	197302	205354	212483	215361	219613	226390
9 Community, social and personal services												
Total, Industries	650164	659324	677912	697189	718733	742993	775820	801833	820992	831088	841155	838702
Producers of Government Services	89882	93495	94736	96007	97426	98845	100160	101031	101821	102481	102897	103127
Other Producers	5545	6539	6694	7102	7321	6949	7063	7166	7460	7771	8187	8233
Subtotal	745591	759358	779342	800298	823480	848787	883043	910030	930273	941340	952239	950062
Less: Imputed bank service charge	30520	31905	32352	34373	35587	36888	38813	41800	43704	44951	49224	50974
Plus: Import duties	41126	41917	43046	44655	46369	48523	51167	53484	54818	56297	56799	54358
Plus: Value added tax	...	...	...	...	...	...	...	...	...	...	...	...
Equals: Gross Domestic Product [b]	756197	769370	790036	810580	834262	860422	895397	921714	941387	952686	959814	953446

a) Item 'Wholesale and retail trade, restaurants and hotels' includes repair services.
b) The branch breakdown used in this table (GDP by kind of activity) is according to the classification NACE/CLIO.

1.12 Relations Among National Accounting Aggregates

Thousand Million Italian lire

	1980	1983	1984	1985	1986	1987	1988	1989	1990	1991	1992	1993
Gross Domestic Product	387669	633436	725760	810580	899903	983803	1091837	1193462	1312066	1429453	1504323	1560114
Plus: Net factor income from the rest of the world	790	-4196	-4736	-5378	-6907	-6722	-7550	-10496	-15701	-20172	-25719	-25644
Factor income from the rest of the world	6452	9226	11709	13222	11687	11435	13018	18116	22975	27668	32658	43036
Less: Factor income to the rest of the world	5662	13422	16445	18600	18594	18157	20568	28612	38676	47840	58377	68680
Equals: Gross National Product	388459	629240	721024	805202	892996	977081	1084287	1182966	1296365	1409281	1478604	1534470
Less: Consumption of fixed capital	44581	77966	88456	100188	107966	116849	128252	140567	154252	168419	179939	191681

Italy

1.12 Relations Among National Accounting Aggregates
(Continued)

Thousand Million Italian lire

	1980	1983	1984	1985	1986	1987	1988	1989	1990	1991	1992	1993
Equals: National Income	343878	551274	632568	705014	785030	860232	956035	1042399	1142113	1240862	1298665	1342789
Plus: Net current transfers from the rest of the world [a]	1034	1855	2114	1266	-2665	-1884	-2521	-4932	-4286	-9255	-9077	-12190
Current transfers from the rest of the world	5041	8725	10473	10846	10235	11656	12310	13687	13876	16074	15205	18009
Less: Current transfers to the rest of the world	4007	6870	8359	9580	12900	13540	14831	18619	18162	25329	24282	30199
Equals: National Disposable Income	344912	553129	634682	706280	782365	858348	953514	1037467	1137827	1231607	1289588	1330599
Less: Final consumption	293616	490738	561302	631313	697828	770769	855174	938784	1034968	1134338	1211086	1241356
Equals: Net Saving	51296	62391	73380	74967	84537	87579	98340	98683	102859	97269	78502	89243
Less: Surplus of the nation on current transactions	-8645	2167	-4662	-7403	4127	-2071	-8069	-15550	-18257	-26429	-33122	17476
Equals: Net Capital Formation	59941	60224	78042	82370	80410	89650	106409	114233	121116	123698	111624	71767

a) Item 'Net current transfers from the rest of the world' excludes indirect taxes, net to EEC.

2.1 Government Final Consumption Expenditure by Function, in Current Prices

Thousand Million Italian lire

		1980	1983	1984	1985	1986	1987	1988	1989	1990	1991	1992	1993
1	General public services	8747	15297	17033	20279	22033	25576	28875	31266	36704	41024	43018	47334
2	Defence	6430	12421	14366	16748	17751	20121	22820	24300	25177	26772	27712	29334
3	Public order and safety	5208	9460	11278	12542	13890	15663	17804	18956	22563	24453	26524	29017
4	Education	16419	29988	33881	37505	41596	45741	51352	55887	64261	67316	72132	72572
5	Health	11522	20218	22657	24938	27132	31719	35573	38709	45899	53070	55805	57396
6	Social security and welfare	2518	4454	5111	5797	6435	6968	7667	8142	9776	10541	11048	11512
7	Housing and community amenities	1506	3322	3777	4244	4490	4831	5355	5746	6462	7197	7233	7785
8	Recreational, cultural and religious affairs	739	1534	1765	1905	2060	2271	2596	2740	2985	3585	3868	4103
9	Economic services	3747	6721	7871	8871	10018	10708	11699	12536	14117	15116	15949	16426
	A Fuel and energy	384	764	854	953	1020	1122	1296	1357	1503	1575	1558	1613
	B Agriculture, forestry, fishing and hunting	753	1392	1625	1798	2041	2137	2425	2709	3185	3236	3379	3484
	C Mining, manufacturing and construction, except fuel and energy	251	515	706	759	895	959	979	957	1132	1160	1209	1248
	D Transportation and communication	2022	3362	3855	4248	4735	5088	5540	5917	6535	7014	7433	7738
	E Other economic affairs	337	688	831	1113	1327	1402	1459	1596	1762	2131	2370	2343
10	Other functions	177	153	295	436	555	282	550	235	431	511	860	487
	Total Government Final Consumption Expenditure	57013	103568	118034	133265	145960	163880	184291	198517	228375	249585	264149	275966

2.2 Government Final Consumption Expenditure by Function, in Constant Prices

Thousand Million Italian lire

		1980	1983	1984	1985	1986	1987	1988	1989	1990	1991	1992	1993
		At constant prices of: 1980 / 1985											
1	General public services	13955 / 27652	30192	31282	32821	34035	35560	36547	37339	38438	39522	40354	41257
2	Defence	6430 / 14478	15907	16306	16748	17203	17794	18034	18162	18199	18429	18405	18638
3	Public order and safety	... / ...	...	...	...	...	...	...	...	...	...	...	...
4	Education	16419 / 34394	36342	36665	37505	38202	39587	41131	41551	41647	41937	42007	41953
5	Health	11522 / 21232	23509	24114	24938	25485	26377	26955	27021	27155	27299	27565	27765
6	Social security and welfare	2518 / 5163	5637	5676	5797	5841	5963	6014	6036	6074	6204	6234	6330
7	Housing and community amenities	1506 / 3770	4059	4112	4244	4334	4468	4531	4536	4557	4658	4657	4745
8	Recreational, cultural and religious affairs	739 / 1568	1722	1797	1905	1977	2073	2121	2161	2217	2279	2326	2368
9	Economic services	3747 / 7504	8504	8604	8871	9053	9337	9620	9624	9670	9844	9834	9782
10	Other functions	177 / 313	181	318	436	544	266	496	199	344	386	616	332
	Total Government Final Consumption Expenditure	57013 / 116074	126053	128874	133265	136674	141425	145449	146629	148301	150558	151998	153170

Italy

2.3 Total Government Outlays by Function and Type

Thousand Million Italian lire

	Final Consumption Expenditures Total	Compensation of Employees	Other	Subsidies	Other Current Transfers & Property Income	Total Current Disbursements	Gross Capital Formation	Other Capital Outlays	Total Outlays
1980									
1 General public services	8747	6215	2532	-	3320	12067	963	139	13169
2 Defence	6430	3913	2517	-	-	6430	42	-	6472
3 Public order and safety	5208	4537	671	-	106	5314	82	-	5396
4 Education	16419	14685	1734	75	566	17060	1403	13	18476
5 Health	11522	8071	3451	-	8588	20110	788	724	21622
6 Social security and welfare	2518	1941	577	-	48404	50922	185	12	51119
7 Housing and community amenities	1506	920	586	-	477	1983	2557	864	5404
8 Recreation, culture and religion	739	480	259	29	486	1254	419	38	1711
9 Economic services	3747	1961	1786	10964	1961	16672	5410	2586	24668
A Fuel and energy	384	247	137	79	270	733	765	14	1512
B Agriculture, forestry, fishing and hunting	753	478	275	567	331	1651	976	688	3315
C Mining (except fuels), manufacturing and construction	251	121	130	1782	370	2403	755	643	3801
D Transportation and communication	2022	919	1103	7482	882	10386	2258	914	13558
E Other economic affairs	337	196	141	1054	108	1499	656	327	2482
10 Other functions	177	9	168	-	14011	14188	429	27	14644
Total	57013	42732	14281	11068	77919	146000	12278	4403	162681
1985									
1 General public services	20279	13717	6562	-	8119	28398	2918	5339	36655
2 Defence	16748	9654	7094	-	-	16748	89	-	16837
3 Public order and safety	12542	10695	1847	-	245	12787	312	-	13099
4 Education	37505	32718	4787	147	1149	38801	2170	191	41162
5 Health	24938	17126	7812	-	17912	42850	1063	18	43931
6 Social security and welfare	5797	4212	1585	-	123461	129258	223	71	129552
7 Housing and community amenities	4244	1846	2398	-	1382	5626	8220	1368	15214
8 Recreation, culture and religion	1905	1166	739	294	1065	3264	959	132	4355
9 Economic services	8871	4430	4441	22437	3387	34695	11986	9599	56280
A Fuel and energy	953	535	418	387	403	1743	1992	68	3803
B Agriculture, forestry, fishing and hunting	1798	1177	621	1359	453	3610	1591	1957	7158
C Mining (except fuels), manufacturing and construction	759	307	452	3783	569	5111	1143	3011	9265
D Transportation and communication	4248	1952	2296	16055	1709	22012	5938	4074	32024
E Other economic affairs	1113	459	654	853	253	2219	1322	489	4030
10 Other functions	436	73	363	-	54197	54633	2354	951	57938
Total	133265	95637	37628	22878	210917	367060	30294	17669	415023
1990									
1 General public services	36704	24893	11811	-	13216	49920	4099	1018	55037
2 Defence	25177	16629	8548	-	-	25177	118	-	25295
3 Public order and safety	22563	19501	3062	-	296	22859	356	-	23215
4 Education	64261	56228	8033	294	2020	66575	3454	270	70299
5 Health	45899	30627	15272	-	34307	80206	2576	79	82861
6 Social security and welfare	9776	7427	2349	-	207486	217262	681	75	218018
7 Housing and community amenities	6462	2698	3764	-	1704	8166	8681	1907	18754
8 Recreation, culture and religion	2985	1883	1102	698	1713	5396	1828	366	7590
9 Economic services	14117	7008	7109	28585	3265	45967	18121	17423	81511
A Fuel and energy	1503	777	726	340	75	1918	1364	717	3999
B Agriculture, forestry, fishing and hunting	3185	1968	1217	2585	402	6172	1810	2710	10692
C Mining (except fuels), manufacturing and construction	1132	438	694	4416	545	6093	1853	4381	12327
D Transportation and communication	6535	2996	3539	20294	1611	28440	10858	8999	48297
E Other economic affairs	1762	829	933	950	632	3344	2236	616	6196
10 Other functions	431	164	267	-	113350	113781	3137	1709	118627
Total	228375	167058	61317	29577	377357	635309	43051	22847	701207

Italy

2.3 Total Government Outlays by Function and Type
(Continued)

Thousand Million Italian lire

		Final Consumption Expenditures Total	Compensation of Employees	Other	Subsidies	Other Current Transfers & Property Income	Total Current Disbursements	Gross Capital Formation	Other Capital Outlays	Total Outlays
	1991									
1	General public services	41024	27868	13156	-	17846	58870	4740	1190	64800
2	Defence	26772	18025	8747	-	-	26772	165	-	26937
3	Public order and safety	24453	20950	3503	-	303	24756	394	-	25150
4	Education	67316	58408	8908	394	2366	70076	3905	408	74389
5	Health	53070	35635	17435	-	38177	91247	2634	62	93943
6	Social security and welfare	10541	7973	2568	-	227306	237847	756	79	238682
7	Housing and community amenities	7197	2771	4426	-	1797	8994	9234	1911	20139
8	Recreation, culture and religion	3585	2111	1474	1217	1746	6548	1650	415	8613
9	Economic services	15116	7765	7351	30943	3181	49240	19414	12374	81028
	A Fuel and energy	1575	785	790	290	25	1890	1425	175	3490
	B Agriculture, forestry, fishing and hunting	3236	2093	1143	2304	402	5942	1656	3043	10641
	C Mining (except fuels), manufacturing and construction	1160	494	666	5376	707	7243	1874	4688	13805
	D Transportation and communication	7014	3316	3698	21621	1540	30175	12247	3595	46017
	E Other economic affairs	2131	1077	1054	1352	507	3990	2212	873	7075
10	Other functions	511	249	262	-	130221	130732	3629	1967	136328
	Total	249585	181755	67830	32554	422943	705082	46521	18406	770009
	1992									
1	General public services	43018	28703	14315	-	19400	62418	4813	1626	68857
2	Defence	27712	18668	9044	-	-	27712	160	-	27872
3	Public order and safety	26524	22149	4375	-	350	26874	386	-	27260
4	Education	72132	62739	9393	416	2848	75396	4228	636	80260
5	Health	55805	36766	19039	-	39010	94815	2264	63	97142
6	Social security and welfare	11048	8269	2779	-	255830	266878	737	80	267695
7	Housing and community amenities	7233	2676	4557	-	1918	9151	8975	1775	19901
8	Recreation, culture and religion	3868	2205	1663	1300	2026	7194	1623	413	9230
9	Economic services	15949	7892	8057	29471	3762	49182	19699	13812	82693
	A Fuel and energy	1558	760	798	328	29	1915	1424	481	3820
	B Agriculture, forestry, fishing and hunting	3379	2128	1251	2730	508	6617	1630	2919	11166
	C Mining (except fuels), manufacturing and construction	1209	490	719	5810	971	7990	1929	4429	14348
	D Transportation and communication	7433	3364	4069	19520	1780	28733	12436	5085	46254
	E Other economic affairs	2370	1150	1220	1083	474	3927	2280	898	7105
10	Other functions	860	353	507	-	154898	155758	2342	682	158782
	Total	264149	190420	73729	31187	480042	775378	45227	19087	839692
	1993									
1	General public services	47334	29895	17439	-	22705	70039	4925	1731	76695
2	Defence	29334	19697	9637	-	-	29334	166	-	29500
3	Public order and safety	29017	24009	5008	-	390	29407	384	-	29791
4	Education	72572	63021	9551	493	3320	76385	4229	633	81247
5	Health	57396	37716	19680	-	37544	94940	2133	59	97132
6	Social security and welfare	11512	8432	3080	-	268246	279758	606	79	280443
7	Housing and community amenities	7785	2690	5095	-	2092	9877	7522	2018	19417
8	Recreation, culture and religion	4103	2338	1765	1391	2579	8073	1476	521	10070
9	Economic services	16426	7898	8528	32620	4762	53808	17774	17189	88771
	A Fuel and energy	1613	777	836	428	28	2069	1199	887	4155
	B Agriculture, forestry, fishing and hunting	3484	2178	1306	2984	578	7046	1498	3038	11582
	C Mining (except fuels), manufacturing and construction	1248	476	772	5195	1020	7463	1861	5568	14892
	D Transportation and communication	7738	3321	4417	22876	2583	33197	11118	6684	50999
	E Other economic affairs	2343	1146	1197	1137	553	4033	2098	1012	7143
10	Other functions	487	269	218	-	168705	169192	1946	8247	179385
	Total	275966	195965	80001	34504	510343	820813	41161	30477	892451

Italy

2.5 Private Final Consumption Expenditure by Type and Purpose, in Current Prices

Thousand Million Italian lire

	1980	1983	1984	1985	1986	1987	1988	1989	1990	1991	1992	1993
				Final Consumption Expenditure of Resident Households								
1 Food, beverages and tobacco	67658	105169	115680	126157	134156	141017	148064	158140	168018	179980	189343	195191
A Food	59156	90771	100041	109121	115589	121561	127366	135994	144422	154349	162468	165132
B Non-alcoholic beverages	705	1220	1363	1523	1813	2090	2383	2662	3131	3556	3867	4099
C Alcoholic beverages	3940	5826	6150	6624	7199	7545	7760	8132	8752	9402	9771	9970
D Tobacco	3857	7352	8126	8889	9555	9821	10555	11352	11713	12673	13237	15990
2 Clothing and footwear	26964	39736	44871	51507	56584	64327	70875	77452	81056	87957	93099	91090
3 Gross rent, fuel and power	32391	56881	69127	74572	81119	88949	97339	107043	120073	138839	150712	161182
A Fuel and power	9363	16973	19399	21163	20339	21319	22537	24706	27936	35941	36667	39060
B Other	23028	39908	49728	53409	60780	67630	74802	82337	92138	102898	114045	122122
4 Furniture, furnishings and household equipment and operation	22413	35492	39812	45387	51041	55851	62212	69881	75819	83965	88550	88353
A Household operation	6445	10220	11558	12759	14606	15713	16969	18443	20040	21858	23292	23034
B Other	15968	25272	28254	32628	36435	40138	45243	51438	55779	62107	65258	65319
5 Medical care and health expenses	10862	21023	23689	27921	31058	36362	41878	46570	54138	59722	64637	69007
6 Transport and communication	28747	48395	54678	62707	68727	75616	83642	92620	99262	106724	115199	113837
A Personal transport equipment	9321	13681	16007	19007	21638	25333	29530	33745	35328	36962	39066	32896
B Other	19426	34714	38671	43700	47089	50283	54112	58875	63934	69762	76133	80941
7 Recreational, entertainment, education and cultural services	19162	30314	36162	41691	47855	51599	59289	67515	73190	78651	84132	86166
A Education	1015	2033	2568	3320	3989	4500	5093	5762	6237	7029	7333	7749
B Other	18147	28281	33594	38371	43866	47099	54196	61753	66953	71622	76799	78417
8 Miscellaneous goods and services	33161	59128	68412	77864	89009	100299	112883	125324	138902	153729	163605	168356
A Personal care	5252	9403	11168	13255	15581	18126	20273	22624	25211	27350	28916	30241
B Expenditures in restaurants, cafes and hotels	19212	35793	41206	46089	51408	57633	64128	70074	77579	86759	91879	93252
C Other	8697	13932	16038	18520	22020	24540	28482	32626	36112	39620	42810	44863
Total Final Consumption Expenditure in the Domestic Market by Households, of which	241358	396138	452431	507806	559549	614020	676182	744545	810459	889567	949277	973182
Plus: Direct purchases abroad by resident households	1901	2579	3363	4023	4694	6296	8261	9310	16591	14479	20409	20648
Less: Direct purchases in the domestic market by non-resident households	7698	13151	14505	16018	14771	15887	16228	16448	23664	22935	26478	32251
Equals: Final Consumption Expenditure of Resident Households	235561	385566	441289	495811	549472	604429	668215	737407	803386	881111	943208	961579
				Final Consumption Expenditure of Private Non-profit Institutions Serving Households								
Equals: Final Consumption Expenditure of Private Non-profit Organisations Serving Households	1042	1604	1979	2237	2396	2460	2668	2860	3207	3642	3729	3811
Private Final Consumption Expenditure	236603	387170	443268	498048	551868	606889	670883	740267	806593	884753	946937	965390

2.6 Private Final Consumption Expenditure by Type and Purpose, in Constant Prices

Thousand Million Italian lire

	1980	1983	1984	1985	1986	1987	1988	1989	1990	1991	1992	1993
				At constant prices of:1985								
				Final Consumption Expenditure of Resident Households								
1 Food, beverages and tobacco	121253	124662	125577	126157	127179	128320	129709	130549	130659	131184	131224	131393
A Food	104520	107707	108655	109121	109776	111341	112704	113413	113726	114219	114654	114519
B Non-alcoholic beverages	1319	1455	1470	1523	1716	1909	2087	2246	2430	2541	2638	2708
C Alcoholic beverages	6888	6817	6625	6624	6612	6561	6438	6334	6246	6168	6032	5911
D Tobacco	8526	8683	8827	8889	9075	8509	8480	8556	8257	8256	7900	8255
2 Clothing and footwear	51904	49212	49659	51507	52530	56244	58652	60175	59516	61348	62025	58434
3 Gross rent, fuel and power	69472	72668	73613	74572	76295	78366	79730	81295	83585	86842	87358	88606
A Fuel and power	20897	20804	20895	21163	21455	22115	22139	22380	23108	25061	24102	24402
B Other	48575	51864	52718	53409	54840	56251	57591	58915	60477	61781	63256	64204
4 Furniture, furnishings and household equipment and operation	42438	42693	43500	45387	48048	50022	52815	55502	56900	59431	59756	57139
A Household operation	12579	12497	12605	12759	13706	13953	14394	14851	15335	15920	16279	15599

Italy

2.6 Private Final Consumption Expenditure by Type and Purpose, in Constant Prices
(Continued)

Thousand Million Italian lire

	1980	1983	1984	1985	1986	1987	1988	1989	1990	1991	1992	1993
					At constant prices of: 1985							
B Other	29859	30196	30895	32628	34342	36069	38421	40651	41565	43511	43477	41540
5 Medical care and health expenses	23828	27086	27147	27921	29790	32336	33561	35573	39015	40576	42101	42092
6 Transport and communication	56364	58317	59038	62707	65582	69134	73735	77866	79330	80748	83559	78266
A Personal transport equipment	16307	16049	17044	19007	20699	23089	25867	28119	28326	28491	28951	22727
B Other	40057	42268	41994	43700	44883	46045	47868	49747	51005	52257	54608	55539
7 Recreational, entertainment, education and cultural services	36260	36993	39566	41691	44482	46189	49695	53490	55237	56419	57628	56579
A Education	2282	2567	2879	3320	3680	3848	4053	4261	4294	4438	4395	4410
B Other	33978	34426	36687	38371	40802	42341	45642	49229	50943	51981	53233	52169
8 Miscellaneous goods and services	65998	71990	75067	77864	82712	87965	93556	97236	102102	106467	107806	105455
A Personal care	11073	11640	12308	13255	14315	15496	16261	17054	18039	18410	18463	18372
B Expenditures in restaurants, cafes and hotels	40857	44797	45969	46089	47006	49636	51508	52212	53618	55613	54990	52702
C Other	14068	15553	16790	18520	21391	22833	25787	27970	30445	32444	34353	34381
Total Final Consumption Expenditure in the Domestic Market by Households, of which	467517	483621	493167	507806	526618	548576	571453	591686	606345	623015	631457	617964
Plus: Direct purchases abroad by resident households	3472	3148	3689	4023	4816	6352	7918	7585	14554	11959	15791	13319
Less: Direct purchases in the domestic market by non-resident households	14861	15902	15835	16018	13948	14326	13930	13286	17954	16359	17988	21038
Equals: Final Consumption Expenditure of Resident Households	456128	470867	481021	495811	517486	540602	565441	585985	602945	618615	629260	610245

Final Consumption Expenditure of Private Non-profit Institutions Serving Households

	1980	1983	1984	1985	1986	1987	1988	1989	1990	1991	1992	1993
Equals: Final Consumption Expenditure of Private Non-profit Organisations Serving Households	2025	2106	2208	2237	2303	2337	2384	2442	2555	2649	2667	2684
Private Final Consumption Expenditure	458153	472973	483229	498048	519789	542939	567825	588427	605500	621264	631927	612929

2.11 Gross Fixed Capital Formation by Kind of Activity of Owner, ISIC Divisions, in Current Prices

Thousand Million Italian lire

	1980	1983	1984	1985	1986	1987	1988	1989	1990	1991	1992	1993
					All Producers							
1 Agriculture, hunting, forestry and fishing	6600	9076	10170	11153	11825	12355	14901	15310	14901	15266	15935	...
2 Mining and quarrying	20953	23761	27749	27582	29726	34617	40463	46733	49650	...	...	...
3 Manufacturing										...	...	...
A Manufacturing of food, beverages and tobacco	1914	2430	2929	2766	2999	3484	4100	4488	4544	...	...	...
B Textile, wearing apparel and leather industries	2965	3172	4072	4031	3988	4335	5017	5315	6022	...	...	...
C Manufacture of wood, and wood products, including furniture	...	...	...	...	...	...	...	...	...	...	...	...
D Manufacture of paper and paper products, printing and publishing	...	...	...	...	...	...	...	...	...	...	...	...
E Manufacture of chemicals and chemical petroleum, coal, rubber and plastic products	...	...	...	...	...	...	...	...	...	...	...	...
F Manufacture of non-metalic mineral products except products of petroleum and coal	2049	2208	2563	2276	2140	3021	3652	4739	4694	...	...	...
G Basic metal industries	1592	1825	1887	2271	2455	2182	2026	2707	4120	...	...	...
H Manufacture of fabricated metal products, machinery and equipment	7053	8420	9557	9053	10005	12116	14465	16581	17081	...	...	...
I Other manufacturing industries	...	...	...	...	...	...	...	...	...	...	...	...
4 Electricity, gas and water	4210	6750	7440	8993	11079	11061	10729	11596	12350	...	...	...

Italy

2.11 Gross Fixed Capital Formation by Kind of Activity of Owner, ISIC Divisions, in Current Prices
(Continued)

Thousand Million Italian lire

	1980	1983	1984	1985	1986	1987	1988	1989	1990	1991	1992	1993
5 Construction	3336	3753	4330	5215	4828	5012	5373	6509	6561	...	...	...
6 Wholesale and retail trade, restaurants and hotels [a]	7084	9917	11851	13567	15336	15192	18740	21457	22902	...	...	...
A Wholesale and retail trade	5674	8005	9699	11329	12801	12459	15045	16590	18127	...	...	...
B Restaurants and hotels	1410	1912	2152	2238	2535	2733	3695	4867	4775	...	...	...
7 Transport, storage and communication	8182	13087	15913	16570	17378	21832	24818	28555	34034	...	...	...
A Transport and storage	5322	8307	10691	10702	11704	15133	16991	18880	21094	...	...	...
B Communication	2860	4780	5222	5868	5674	6699	7827	9675	12940	...	...	...
8 Finance, insurance, real estate and business services	34162	55384	60204	66419	69056	72941	82940	87544	99645	...	...	...
9 Community, social and personal services										...	...	...
Total Industries	84527	121728	137657	149499	159228	173010	197964	217704	240043	254796	261423	...
Producers of Government Services	9535	13114	14946	18094	18426	21092	21288	23319	25903	27099	25285	...
Private Non-Profit Institutions Serving Households	...	...	...	...	...	...	...	...	...	...	...	...
Total	94062	134842	152603	167593	177654	194102	219252	241023	265946	281895	286708	...

a) Item 'Wholesale and retail trade, restaurants and hotels' includes repair services.

2.12 Gross Fixed Capital Formation by Kind of Activity of Owner, ISIC Divisions, in Constant Prices

Thousand Million Italian lire

	1980	1983	1984	1985	1986	1987	1988	1989	1990	1991	1992	1993
					At constant prices of:1985							
					All Producers							
1 Agriculture, hunting, forestry and fishing	12243	10896	11114	11153	11160	11047	12595	12154	11058	10560	10446	...
2 Mining and quarrying	37738	28514	30295	27582	28364	31609	35646	39080	39611	...	...	...
3 Manufacturing										...	...	...
A Manufacturing of food, beverages and tobacco	3428	2911	3195	2766	2857	3167	3592	3732	3600	...	...	...
B Textile, wearing apparel and leather industries	5344	3803	4448	4031	3807	3961	4413	4436	4776	...	...	...
C Manufacture of wood, and wood products, including furniture	...	...	...	...	...	...	...	...	...	...	...	...
D Manufacture of paper and paper products, printing and publishing	...	...	...	...	...	...	...	...	...	...	...	...
E Manufacture of chemicals and chemical petroleum, coal, rubber and plastic products	...	...	...	...	...	...	...	...	...	...	...	...
F Manufacture of non-metalic mineral products except products of petroleum and coal	3687	2650	2802	2276	2040	2753	3206	3955	3745	...	...	...
G Basic metal industries	2874	2184	2057	2271	2351	2010	1800	2289	3346	...	...	...
H Manufacture of fabricated metal products, machinery and equipment	12723	10141	10432	9053	9495	10971	12679	13796	13504	...	...	...
I Other manufacturing industries	...	...	...	...	...	...	...	...	...	...	...	...
4 Electricity, gas and water	7805	8084	8136	8993	10618	10126	9333	9685	9734	...	...	...
5 Construction	6002	4477	4741	5215	4635	4594	4705	5416	5192	...	...	...
6 Wholesale and retail trade, restaurants and hotels [a]	12667	11767	12957	13567	14844	14121	16625	18019	18371	...	...	...
A Wholesale and retail trade	10168	9510	10616	11329	12354	11529	13283	13873	14464	...	...	...
B Restaurants and hotels	2499	2257	2341	2238	2490	2592	3342	4146	3907	...	...	...
7 Transport, storage and communication	14885	15366	17283	16570	17007	20526	22050	24115	27614	...	...	...
A Transport and storage	9679	9828	11662	10702	11321	14003	14754	15508	16544	...	...	...
B Communication	5206	5538	5621	5868	5686	6523	7296	8607	11070	...	...	...
8 Finance, insurance, real estate and business services	65620	65947	65584	66419	66757	68068	72585	72677	76469	...	...	...
9 Community, social and personal services										...	...	...
Total Industries	156960	145051	150110	149499	153385	160091	173539	181146	188049	189604	187412	...
Producers of Government Services	18173	15692	16406	18094	17919	19783	18826	19518	20179	19921	17898	...
Private Non-Profit Institutions Serving Households	...	...	...	...	...	...	...	...	...	...	...	...
Total	175133	160743	166516	167593	171304	179874	192365	200664	208228	209525	205310	...

a) Item 'Wholesale and retail trade, restaurants and hotels' includes repair services.

Italy

2.17 Exports and Imports of Goods and Services, Detail

Thousand Million Italian lire

	1980	1983	1984	1985	1986	1987	1988	1989	1990	1991	1992	1993
Exports of Goods and Services												
1 Exports of merchandise, f.o.b.	66987	110747	131026	146059	144675	151114	166639	193013	203885	211126	220635	265236
2 Transport and communication	...	...	...	...	...	...	...	...	...	...	...	...
3 Insurance service charges	...	...	...	...	...	...	...	...	...	...	...	...
4 Other commodities	...	...	...	...	...	...	...	...	...	...	...	...
5 Adjustments of merchandise exports to change-of-ownership basis												
6 Direct purchases in the domestic market by non-residential households	7638	13151	14505	16018	14771	15887	16228	16448	23664	22935	26478	32251
7 Direct purchases in the domestic market by extraterritorial bodies	...	...	...	...	...	...	...	...	...	...	...	...
Total Exports of Goods and Services	84953	140016	165197	185022	181961	192273	210046	243047	272868	279974	300707	365442
Imports of Goods and Services												
1 Imports of merchandise, c.i.f.	87170	122469	150887	168791	149542	163692	181264	211316	219313	227894	234374	234033
2 Adjustments of merchandise imports to change-of-ownership basis												
3 Other transport and communication	...	...	...	...	...	...	...	...	...	...	...	...
4 Other insurance service charges	...	...	...	...	...	...	...	...	...	...	...	...
5 Other commodities	...	...	...	...	...	...	...	...	...	...	...	...
6 Direct purchases abroad by government												
7 Direct purchases abroad by resident households	1901	2579	3363	4023	4694	6296	8261	9310	16591	14479	20409	20648
Total Imports of Goods and Services	95422	135508	167237	188313	168262	185738	208044	243169	271138	276976	299033	310132
Balance of Goods and Services	-10469	4508	-2040	-3291	13699	6535	2002	-122	1730	2998	1674	55310
Total Imports and Balance of Goods and Services	84953	140016	165197	185022	181961	192273	210046	243047	272868	279974	300707	365442

3.11 General Government Production Account: Total and Subsectors

Thousand Million Italian lire

	\multicolumn{5}{c}{1980}	\multicolumn{5}{c}{1985}
	Total General Government	Central Government	State or Provincial Government	Local Government	Social Security Funds	Total General Government	Central Government	State or Provincial Government	Local Government	Social Security Funds
Gross Output										
1 Sales	2480	1114	...	1230	182	6329	2665	...	3091	573
2 Services produced for own use	57059	30785	...	23833	2395	133265	72450	...	57243	3572
3 Own account fixed capital formation	...	...	...	...	...	...	...	...	...	...
Gross Output	59539	31899	...	25063	2577	139594	75115	...	60334	4145
Gross Input										
Intermediate Consumption	15133	6072	...	8373	688	39520	15780	...	22305	1435
Subtotal: Value Added	44406	25827	...	16690	1889	100074	59335	...	38029	2710
1 Indirect taxes, net	411	411	...	-	-	1129	1129	...	-	-
A Indirect taxes	411	411	...	-	-	1129	1129	...	-	-
B Less: Subsidies	-	-	...	-	-	-	-	...	-	-
2 Consumption of fixed capital	862	433	...	391	38	1988	980	...	936	72
3 Compensation of employees	42732	24831	...	16143	1758	95637	56737	...	36673	2227
4 Net Operating surplus	401	152	...	156	93	1320	489	...	420	411
Gross Input	59539	31899	...	25063	2577	139594	75115	...	60334	4145

	\multicolumn{5}{c}{1990}	\multicolumn{5}{c}{1991}
	Total General Government	Central Government	State or Provincial Government	Local Government	Social Security Funds	Total General Government	Central Government	State or Provincial Government	Local Government	Social Security Funds
Gross Output										
1 Sales	11853	5246	...	5372	1235	13073	5279	...	6346	1448
2 Services produced for own use	228375	124039	...	98331	6005	249585	132215	...	111002	6368
3 Own account fixed capital formation	...	...	...	...	...	...	...	...	...	...
Gross Output	240228	129285	...	103703	7240	262658	137494	...	117348	7816
Gross Input										
Intermediate Consumption	63328	23122	...	38133	2073	70042	24404	...	43305	2333

Italy

3.11 General Government Production Account: Total and Subsectors
(Continued)

Thousand Million Italian lire

	1990					1991				
	Total General Government	Central Government	State or Provincial Government	Local Government	Social Security Funds	Total General Government	Central Government	State or Provincial Government	Local Government	Social Security Funds
Subtotal: Value Added	176900	106163	...	65570	5167	192616	113090	...	74043	5483
1 Indirect taxes, net	2444	2444	...	-	-	2738	2738	...	-	-
A Indirect taxes	2444	2444	...	-	-	2738	2738	...	-	-
B Less: Subsidies	-	-	...	-	-	-	-	...	-	-
2 Consumption of fixed capital	4481	2216	...	2101	164	5270	2605	...	2472	193
3 Compensation of employees	167058	100497	...	62535	4026	181755	107128	...	70496	4131
4 Net Operating surplus	2917	1006	...	934	977	2853	619	...	1075	1159
Gross Input	240228	129285	...	103703	7240	262658	137494	...	117348	7816

	1992					1993				
	Total General Government	Central Government	State or Provincial Government	Local Government	Social Security Funds	Total General Government	Central Government	State or Provincial Government	Local Government	Social Security Funds
Gross Output											
1 Sales	15561	6612	...	7372	1577	16281	6977	...	7661	1643
2 Services produced for own use	264149	142903	...	114494	6752	275966	150006	...	118908	7052
3 Own account fixed capital formation	...	...	...	...	...	...	...	...	...	...
Gross Output	279710	149515	...	121866	8329	292247	156983	...	126569	8695
Gross Input											
Intermediate Consumption	75623	26950	...	46067	2606	81038	29688	...	48497	2853
Subtotal: Value Added	204087	122565	...	75799	5723	211209	127295	...	78072	5842
1 Indirect taxes, net	3627	3627	...	-	-	3949	3949	...	-	-
A Indirect taxes	3627	3627	...	-	-	3949	3949	...	-	-
B Less: Subsidies	-	-	...	-	-	-	-	...	-	-
2 Consumption of fixed capital	6223	3080	...	2915	228	7256	3589	...	3402	265
3 Compensation of employees	190420	114739	...	71427	4254	195965	118469	...	73208	4288
4 Net Operating surplus	3817	1119	...	1457	1241	4039	1288	...	1462	1289
Gross Input	279710	149515	...	121866	8329	292247	156983	...	126569	8695

3.12 General Government Income and Outlay Account: Total and Subsectors

Thousand Million Italian lire

	1980					1985				
	Total General Government	Central Government	State or Provincial Government	Local Government	Social Security Funds	Total General Government	Central Government	State or Provincial Government	Local Government	Social Security Funds
Receipts											
1 Operating surplus	401	152	...	156	93	1320	489	...	420	411
2 Property and entrepreneurial income	4054	1730	...	1314	1010	9548	4749	...	2231	2568
A Withdrawals from public quasi-corporations	...	...	...	...	...	...	...	...	...	...
B Interest	3677	1614	...	1054	1009	8435	4203	...	1668	2564
C Dividends [a]	...	...	...	...	...	...	...	...	...	...
D Net land rent and royalties [a]	377	116	...	260	1	1113	546	...	563	4
3 Taxes, fees and contributions	115301	68729	...	2940	43776	275241	170761	...	9969	94882
A Indirect taxes	33522	32367	...	1155	-	72661	68951	...	3710	-
B Direct taxes	37291	35672	...	1763	...	105466	99630	...	6207	...
Income	37291	35672	...	1763	...	105466	99630	...	6207	...
Other	-	-	...	-	...	-	-	...	-	...
C Social security contributions	44488	690	...	22	43776	97114	2180	...	52	94882
D Fees, fines and penalties	-	-	...	-	-	-	-	...	-	-
4 Other current transfers	9340	19659	...	36312	16353	25941	54526	...	83805	48655
A Casualty insurance claims [a]	...	...	...	...	...	...	...	...	...	...
B Transfers from other government subsectors	...	13586	...	33649	15749	...	38533	...	76486	46026
C Transfers from the rest of the world	143	69	...	74	...	431	103	...	328	...
D Other transfers, except imputed	4192	1540	...	2193	459	12394	4013	...	6124	2257
E Imputed unfunded employee pension and welfare contributions	5005	4464	...	396	145	13116	11877	...	867	372
Total Current Receipts	129096	90270	...	40722	61232	312050	230525	...	96425	146516

Italy

3.12 General Government Income and Outlay Account: Total and Subsectors
(Continued)

Thousand Million Italian lire

	1980					1985				
	Total General Government	Central Government	State or Provincial Government	Local Government	Social Security Funds	Total General Government	Central Government	State or Provincial Government	Local Government	Social Security Funds

Disbursements

1 Government final consumption expenditure	57013	30785	...	23833	2395	133265	72450	...	57243	3572
2 Property income	21858	18430	...	2379	1049	68543	61275	...	6379	889
A Interest	21772	18410	...	2314	1048	68312	61231	...	6195	886
B Net land rent and royalties	86	20	...	65	1	231	44	...	184	3
3 Subsidies	11068	8128	...	2940	...	22878	16656	...	6222	...
4 Other current transfers	57354	52066	...	9654	58762	145617	146333	...	22391	138309
A Casualty insurance premiums, net	...	...	...	...	...	...	...	...	...	...
B Transfers to other government subsectors	...	44391	...	5486	13251	...	122492	...	1313	37611
C Social security benefits			...					...		
D Social assistance grants	54696	6877		2471	45348	139055	20667		18003	100385
E Unfunded employee pension and welfare benefits			...					...		
F Transfers to private non-profit institutions serving households	706	170	...	428	108	1729	888	...	658	183
G Other transfers n.e.c.	1585	261	...	1269	55	3098	551	...	2417	130
H Transfers to the rest of the world	367	367	...	-	-	1735	1735	...	-	-
Net saving	-18197	-19139	...	1916	-974	-58253	-66189	...	4190	3746
Total Current Disbursements and Net Saving	129096	90270	...	40722	61232	312050	230525	...	96425	146516

	1990					1991				
	Total General Government	Central Government	State or Provincial Government	Local Government	Social Security Funds	Total General Government	Central Government	State or Provincial Government	Local Government	Social Security Funds

Receipts

1 Operating surplus	2917	1006	...	934	977	2853	619	...	1075	1159
2 Property and entrepreneurial income	13762	7416	...	2138	4208	14636	8180	...	2048	4408
A Withdrawals from public quasi-corporations	...	...	...	...	...	...	...	...	...	...
B Interest	12034	6614	...	1212	4208	12757	7288	...	1061	4408
C Dividends [a]	...	...	...	...	...	...	...	...	...	...
D Net land rent and royalties [a]	1728	802	...	926	-	1879	892	...	987	-
3 Taxes, fees and contributions	497542	309629	...	24146	164590	553268	344516	...	27275	182582
A Indirect taxes	139465	130963	...	8502	-	159022	149299	...	9723	-
B Direct taxes	189124	174399	...	15548	...	207054	190714	...	17445	...
Income	189124	174399	...	15548	...	207054	190714	...	17445	...
Other	-	-	...	-	...	-	-	...	-	...
C Social security contributions	168953	4267	...	96	164590	187192	4503	...	107	182582
D Fees, fines and penalties	-	-	...	-	...	-	-	...	-	...
4 Other current transfers	40682	83073	...	129296	69638	48101	88250	...	154490	68743
A Casualty insurance claims [a]	...	...	...	...	...	...	...	...	...	...
B Transfers from other government subsectors	...	58534	...	116425	66366	...	59092	...	138732	65558
C Transfers from the rest of the world	294	66	...	228	...	516	86	...	430	...
D Other transfers, except imputed	20032	5852	...	11566	2614	24823	8024	...	14273	2526
E Imputed unfunded employee pension and welfare contributions	20356	18621	...	1077	658	22762	21048	...	1055	659
Total Current Receipts	554903	401124	...	156514	239413	618858	441565	...	184888	256892

Disbursements

1 Government final consumption expenditure	228375	124039	...	98331	6005	249585	132215	...	111002	6368
2 Property income	131802	122480	...	9051	271	151911	141839	...	9780	292
A Interest	131431	122405	...	8764	262	151464	141760	...	9424	280
B Net land rent and royalties	371	75	...	287	9	447	79	...	356	12
3 Subsidies	29577	20442	...	9135	...	32554	23348	...	9206	...

Italy

3.12 General Government Income and Outlay Account: Total and Subsectors
(Continued)

Thousand Million Italian lire

	1990					1991				
	Total General Government	Central Government	State or Provincial Government	Local Government	Social Security Funds	Total General Government	Central Government	State or Provincial Government	Local Government	Social Security Funds
4 Other current transfers	250642	223996	...	42392	226402	276617	250653	...	46362	244089
A Casualty insurance premiums, net	...	...	...	...	...	...	...	...	...	...
B Transfers to other government subsectors	...	182787	...	866	58495	...	204287	...	732	59468
C Social security benefits	238585	36469	...	34889	167227	261320	39510	...	37757	184053
D Social assistance grants										
E Unfunded employee pension and welfare benefits										
F Transfers to private non-profit institutions serving households	3487	960	...	2141	386	3912	967	...	2568	377
G Other transfers n.e.c.	5814	1024	...	4496	294	6641	1145	...	5305	191
H Transfers to the rest of the world	2756	2756	...	-	-	4744	4744	...	-	-
Net saving	-85493	-89833	...	-2395	6735	-91809	-106490	...	8538	6143
Total Current Disbursements and Net Saving	554903	401124	...	156514	239413	618858	441565	...	184888	256892

	1992					1993				
	Total General Government	Central Government	State or Provincial Government	Local Government	Social Security Funds	Total General Government	Central Government	State or Provincial Government	Local Government	Social Security Funds

Receipts

1 Operating surplus	3817	1119	...	1457	1241	4039	1288	...	1462	1289
2 Property and entrepreneurial income	15048	7748	...	2385	4915	13680	5974	...	2569	5137
A Withdrawals from public quasi-corporations	...	...	...	...	...	...	...	...	...	...
B Interest	12807	6796	...	1096	4915	11848	5489	...	1222	5137
C Dividends [a]	...	...	...	...	...	...	...	...	...	...
D Net land rent and royalties [a]	2241	952	...	1289	-	1832	485	...	1347	-
3 Taxes, fees and contributions	588167	363466	...	30881	195029	647273	403090	...	40017	205735
A Indirect taxes	167026	155917	...	11109	-	186026	168636	...	17390	-
B Direct taxes	221310	202866	...	19653	...	250459	229524	...	22504	...
Income	221310	202866	...	19653	...	250459	229524	...	22504	...
Other	-	-	...	-	...	-	-	...	-	...
C Social security contributions	199831	4683	...	119	195029	210788	4930	...	123	205735
D Fees, fines and penalties	-	-	...	-	-	-	-	...	-	-
4 Other current transfers	54457	90502	...	159044	77481	60766	96143	...	146042	76075
A Casualty insurance claims [a]	...	...	...	...	...	...	...	...	...	...
B Transfers from other government subsectors	...	58100	...	140958	73512	...	59458	...	126534	71502
C Transfers from the rest of the world	476	82	...	394	...	464	59	...	405	...
D Other transfers, except imputed	27615	7823	...	16610	3182	32249	10401	...	17977	3871
E Imputed unfunded employee pension and welfare contributions	26366	24497	...	1082	787	28053	26225	...	1126	702
Total Current Receipts	661489	462835	...	193767	278666	725758	506495	...	190090	288236

Disbursements

1 Government final consumption expenditure	264149	142903	...	114494	6752	275966	150006	...	118908	7052
2 Property income	177851	167524	...	10017	310	191812	181567	...	9993	252
A Interest	177343	167441	...	9619	283	191259	181483	...	9550	226
B Net land rent and royalties	508	83	...	398	27	553	84	...	443	26
3 Subsidies	31187	21318	...	9869	...	34504	23923	...	10581	...

Italy

3.12 General Government Income and Outlay Account: Total and Subsectors
(Continued)

Thousand Million Italian lire

		1992				1993			
	Total General Government	Central Government	State or Provincial Government	Local Government	Social Security Funds	Total General Government	Central Government	State or Provincial Government	Local Government	Social Security Funds
4 Other current transfers	307391	266224	...	48380	266566	322857	258334	...	47944	275642
A Casualty insurance premiums, net	...	...	...	...	...	...	...	...	...	...
B Transfers to other government subsectors		214467	...	842	58470		198028	...	1153	59882
C Social security benefits			...					...		
D Social assistance grants	290526	44596	...	38359	207571	301620	49395	...	37069	215156
E Unfunded employee pension and welfare benefits			...					...		
F Transfers to private non-profit institutions serving households	4531	1105	...	3000	426	5263	1269	...	3540	454
G Other transfers n.e.c.	7176	898	...	6179	99	8268	1936	...	6182	150
H Transfers to the rest of the world	5158	5158	...	-	-	7706	7706	...	-	-
Net saving	-119089	-135134	...	11007	5038	-99381	-107335	...	2664	5290
Total Current Disbursements and Net Saving	661489	462835	...	193767	278666	725758	506495	...	190090	288236

a) Items 'Dividends' and 'Casualty insurance claim' are included in item 'Net land rent and royalties'.

3.13 General Government Capital Accumulation Account: Total and Subsectors

Thousand Million Italian lire

	1980					1985				
	Total General Government	Central Government	State or Provincial Government	Local Government	Social Security Funds	Total General Government	Central Government	State or Provincial Government	Local Government	Social Security Funds
Finance of Gross Accumulation										
1 Gross saving	-17335	-18706	...	2307	-936	-56265	-65209	...	5126	3818
A Consumption of fixed capital	862	433	...	391	38	1988	980	...	936	72
B Net saving	-18197	-19139	...	1916	-974	-58253	-66189	...	4190	3746
2 Capital transfers	5686	745	...	4580	361	20659	1801	...	18858	-
Finance of Gross Accumulation	-11649	-17961	...	6887	-575	-35606	-63408	...	23984	3818
Gross Accumulation										
1 Gross capital formation	12278	4407	...	7496	375	30294	8811	...	18679	2804
A Increase in stocks	...	...	...	...	...	...	...	...	...	...
B Gross fixed capital formation	12278	4407	...	7496	375	30294	8811	...	18679	2804
2 Purchases of land, net	31	2	...	29	-	58	8	...	50	-
3 Purchases of intangible assets, net	-	-	...	-	-	-	-	...	-	-
4 Capital transfers	9056	5355	...	3701	-	36002	30072	...	5930	-
Net lending [a]	-33014	-27725	...	-4339	-950	-101960	-102299	...	-675	1014
Gross Accumulation	-11649	-17961	...	6887	-575	-35606	-63408	...	23984	3818

	1990					1991				
	Total General Government	Central Government	State or Provincial Government	Local Government	Social Security Funds	Total General Government	Central Government	State or Provincial Government	Local Government	Social Security Funds
Finance of Gross Accumulation										
1 Gross saving	-81012	-87617	...	-294	6899	-86539	-103885	...	11010	6336
A Consumption of fixed capital	4481	2216	...	2101	164	5270	2605	...	2472	193
B Net saving	-85493	-89833	...	-2395	6735	-91809	-106490	...	8538	6143
2 Capital transfers	22948	2833	...	20115	-	23981	4647	...	19334	-
Finance of Gross Accumulation	-58064	-84784	...	19821	6899	-62558	-99238	...	30344	6336
Gross Accumulation										
1 Gross capital formation	43051	10883	...	29446	2722	46521	12854	...	30289	3378
A Increase in stocks	...	...	...	...	...	...	...	...	...	...
B Gross fixed capital formation	43051	10883	...	29446	2722	46521	12854	...	30289	3378
2 Purchases of land, net	90	4	...	86	-	66	3	...	63	-
3 Purchases of intangible assets, net	-	-	...	-	-	-	-	...	-	-
4 Capital transfers	42339	34393	...	7946	-	37133	28150	...	8983	-
Net lending [a]	-143544	-130064	...	-17657	4177	-146278	-140245	...	-8991	2958
Gross Accumulation	-58064	-84784	...	19821	6899	-62558	-99238	...	30344	6336

Italy

3.13 General Government Capital Accumulation Account: Total and Subsectors

Thousand Million Italian lire

	1992					1993				
	Total General Government	Central Government	State or Provincial Government	Local Government	Social Security Funds	Total General Government	Central Government	State or Provincial Government	Local Government	Social Security Funds
Finance of Gross Accumulation										
1 Gross saving	-112866	-132054	...	13922	5266	-92125	-103746	...	6066	5555
A Consumption of fixed capital	6223	3080	...	2915	228	7256	3589	...	3402	265
B Net saving	-119089	-135134	...	11007	5038	-99381	-107335	...	2664	5290
2 Capital transfers	53201	32004	...	21197	-	35286	12645	...	22641	-
Finance of Gross Accumulation	-59665	-100050	...	35119	5266	-56839	-91101	...	28707	5555
Gross Accumulation										
1 Gross capital formation	45227	12425	...	29248	3554	41161	11586	...	27166	2409
A Increase in stocks	...	...	...	...	...	...	...	...	...	...
B Gross fixed capital formation	45227	12425	...	29248	3554	41161	11586	...	27166	2409
2 Purchases of land, net	-84	3	...	-87	-	42	3	...	39	-
3 Purchases of intangible assets, net	-	-	...	-	-	-	-	...	-	-
4 Capital transfers	38627	30248	...	8379	-	50203	41999	...	8204	-
Net lending a	-143435	-142726	...	-2421	1712	-148245	-144689	...	-6702	3146
Gross Accumulation	-59665	-100050	...	35119	5266	-56839	-91101	...	28707	5555

a) Net lending of the capital accumulation account and the capital finance account have not been reconciled and are different due to different statistical sources.

3.21 Corporate and Quasi-Corporate Enterprise Production Account: Total and Sectors

Thousand Million Italian lire

	1980				1985				1990			
	\multicolumn{3}{	c	}{Corporate and Quasi-Corporate Enterprises}	ADDENDUM: Total, including Unincorporated	\multicolumn{3}{	c	}{Corporate and Quasi-Corporate Enterprises}	ADDENDUM: Total, including Unincorporated	\multicolumn{3}{	c	}{Corporate and Quasi-Corporate Enterprises}	ADDENDUM: Total, including Unincorporated
	TOTAL	Non-Financial	Financial		TOTAL	Non-Financial	Financial		TOTAL	Non-Financial	Financial	
Gross Output												
1 Output for sale	339095	330413	8682	...	716258	695790	20468	...	1071300	1038070	33230	...
2 Imputed bank service charge	16471	...	16471	...	34373	...	34373	...	61911	...	61911	...
3 Own-account fixed capital formation	...	...	...	...	...	...	...	...	...	...	...	...
Gross Output	355566	330413	25153	...	750631	695790	54841	...	1133211	1038070	95141	...
Gross Input												
Intermediate consumption	213969	192192	21777	...	456770	408751	48019	...	669657	580004	89653	...
1 Imputed banking service charge	16471	-	16471	...	34373	-	34373	...	61911	-	61911	...
2 Other intermediate consumption	197498	192192	5306	...	422397	408751	13646	...	607746	580004	27742	...
Subtotal: Value Added	141597	138221	3376	...	293861	287039	6822	...	463554	458066	5488	...
1 Indirect taxes, net	3278	1722	1556	...	5759	2586	3173	...	28583	22314	6269	...
A Indirect taxes	12661	11103	1558	...	26035	22770	3265	...	55246	48930	6316	...
B Less: Subsidies	9383	9381	2	...	20276	20184	92	...	26663	26616	47	...
2 Consumption of fixed capital	18670	17668	1002	...	41739	39479	2260	...	62450	59099	3351	...
3 Compensation of employees	96831	85465	11366	...	189779	168032	21747	...	288632	254524	34108	...
4 Net operating surplus	22818	33366	-10548	...	56584	76942	-20358	...	83889	122129	-38240	...
Gross Input	355566	330413	25153	...	750631	695790	54841	...	1133211	1038070	95141	...

	1991				1992				1993			
	\multicolumn{3}{	c	}{Corporate and Quasi-Corporate Enterprises}	ADDENDUM: Total, including Unincorporated	\multicolumn{3}{	c	}{Corporate and Quasi-Corporate Enterprises}	ADDENDUM: Total, including Unincorporated	\multicolumn{3}{	c	}{Corporate and Quasi-Corporate Enterprises}	ADDENDUM: Total, including Unincorporated
	TOTAL	Non-Financial	Financial		TOTAL	Non-Financial	Financial		TOTAL	Non-Financial	Financial	
Gross Output												
1 Output for sale	1114071	1076143	37928	...	1164438	1121677	42761	...	1209807	1149102	60705	...
2 Imputed bank service charge	67359	...	67359	...	79400	...	79400	...	79231	...	79231	...
3 Own-account fixed capital formation	...	...	...	...	...	...	...	...	...	...	...	...
Gross Output	1181430	1076143	105287	...	1243838	1121677	122161	...	1289038	1149102	139936	...
Gross Input												
Intermediate consumption	689678	589643	100035	...	727960	607241	120719	...	748340	616857	131483	...
1 Imputed banking service charge	67359	-	67359	...	79400	-	79400	...	79231	-	79231	...
2 Other intermediate consumption	622319	589643	32676	...	648560	607241	41319	...	669109	616857	52252	...
Subtotal: Value Added	491752	486500	5252	...	515878	514436	1442	...	540698	532245	8453	...

Italy

3.21 Corporate and Quasi-Corporate Enterprise Production Account: Total and Sectors
(Continued)

Thousand Million Italian lire

		1991 TOTAL	1991 Non-Financial	1991 Financial	1991 ADDENDUM: Total, including Unincorporated	1992 TOTAL	1992 Non-Financial	1992 Financial	1992 ADDENDUM: Total, including Unincorporated	1993 TOTAL	1993 Non-Financial	1993 Financial	1993 ADDENDUM: Total, including Unincorporated
1	Indirect taxes, net	32950	25623	7327	...	40916	32582	8334	...	44578	34826	9752	...
A	Indirect taxes	62273	54943	7330	...	68450	60114	8336	...	75642	65888	9754	...
B	Less: Subsidies	29323	29320	3	...	27534	27532	2	...	31064	31062	2	...
2	Consumption of fixed capital	68355	64809	3546	...	72322	68660	3662	...	76750	72904	3846	...
3	Compensation of employees	314687	276771	37916	...	330624	288574	42050	...	327794	283986	43808	...
4	Net operating surplus	75760	119297	-43537	...	72016	124620	-52604	...	91576	140529	-48953	...
	Gross Input	1181430	1076143	105287	...	1243838	1121677	122161	...	1289038	1149102	139936	...

3.22 Corporate and Quasi-Corporate Enterprise Income and Outlay Account: Total and Sectors

Thousand Million Italian lire

		1980 TOTAL	1980 Non-Financial	1980 Financial	1985 TOTAL	1985 Non-Financial	1985 Financial	1990 TOTAL	1990 Non-Financial	1990 Financial	1991 TOTAL	1991 Non-Financial	1991 Financial
	Receipts												
1	Operating surplus	22818	33366	-10548	56584	76942	-20358	83889	122129	-38240	75760	119297	-43537
2	Property and entrepreneurial income	76634	8692	67942	153038	16105	136933	225151	28731	196420	244324	30600	213724
A	Withdrawals from quasi-corporate enterprises	...	...	...	...	...	...	...	...	...	...	...	...
B	Interest	74775	7050	67725	147811	11539	136272	216163	21582	194581	234031	22141	211890
C	Dividends	1547	1331	216	4598	3937	661	7970	6131	1839	8694	6860	1834
D	Net land rent and royalties	312	311	1	629	629	-	1018	1018	-	1599	1599	-
3	Current transfers	15966	7900	8066	30103	15402	14701	53603	24219	29384	59851	26506	33345
A	Casualty insurance claims	2281	1361	920	4119	2468	1651	7370	4757	2613	8140	4862	3278
B	Casualty insurance premiums, net, due to be received by insurance companies	4047	...	4047	9717	...	9717	20857	...	20857	24068	...	24068
C	Current transfers from the rest of the world	...	...	...	...	...	...	...	...	...	...	...	...
D	Other transfers except imputed	424	196	228	934	724	210	1675	1365	310	2203	1815	388
E	Imputed unfunded employee pension and welfare contributions	9214	6343	2871	15333	12210	3123	23701	18097	5604	25440	19829	5611
	Total Current Receipts	115418	49958	65460	239725	108449	131276	362643	175079	187564	379935	176403	203532
	Disbursements												
1	Property and entrepreneurial income	84712	35628	49084	170009	72435	97574	250669	121988	128681	271349	131504	139845
A	Withdrawals from quasi-corporations	4323	4323	...	10651	10651	...	16471	16471	...	18182	18182	...
B	Interest	76884	28371	48513	148686	53198	95488	216038	91512	124526	232764	97035	135729
C	Dividends	2821	2253	568	8404	6327	2077	12832	8692	4140	14125	10025	4100
D	Net land rent and royalties	684	681	3	2268	2259	9	5328	5313	15	6278	6262	16
2	Direct taxes and other current transfers n.e.c. to general government	4933	3960	973	18053	13257	4796	41502	33492	8010	45386	35298	10088
A	Direct taxes	4933	3960	973	18053	13257	4796	41502	33492	8010	45386	35298	10088
B	Fines, fees, penalties and other current transfers n.e.c.	...	...	...	...	...	...	...	...	...	...	...	...
3	Other current transfers	10865	4868	5997	26513	12976	13537	50205	23124	27081	57529	26258	31271
A	Casualty insurance premiums, net	2322	1368	954	4382	2600	1782	8349	5514	2835	8869	5336	3533
B	Casualty insurance claims liability of insurance companies	4047	...	4047	9717	...	9717	20857	...	20857	24068	...	24068
C	Transfers to private non-profit institutions	876	...	876	1418	...	1418	2496	...	2496	2790	...	2790
D	Unfunded employee pension and welfare benefits	-	...	...	-	...	...	-	...	...	-	...	...
E	Social assistance grants	2778	2658	120	7174	6554	620	12774	11881	893	15017	14137	880
F	Other transfers n.e.c.	842	842	...	3822	3822	...	5729	5729	...	6785	6785	...
G	Transfers to the rest of the world	-	...	...	-	...	...	-	...	...	-	...	...
	Statistical discrepancy	5325	3733	1592	7933	5802	2131	8424	6458	1966	9473	6004	3469
	Net saving	9583	1769	7814	17217	3979	13238	11843	-9983	21826	-3802	-22661	18859
	Total Current Disbursements and Net Saving	115418	49958	65460	239725	108449	131276	362643	175079	187564	379935	176403	203532

Italy

3.22 Corporate and Quasi-Corporate Enterprise Income and Outlay Account: Total and Sectors

Thousand Million Italian lire

	1992 TOTAL	1992 Non-Financial	1992 Financial	1993 TOTAL	1993 Non-Financial	1993 Financial
Receipts						
1 Operating surplus	72016	124620	-52604	91576	140529	-48953
2 Property and entrepreneurial income	279055	28443	250612	271867	24805	247062
A Withdrawals from quasi-corporate enterprises	...	...	...	...	...	...
B Interest	271919	22957	248962	265786	20433	245353
C Dividends	5540	3891	1649	4596	2887	1709
D Net land rent and royalties	1596	1595	1	1485	1485	-
3 Current transfers	64141	28451	35690	67050	29357	37693
A Casualty insurance claims	8631	5750	2881	8888	6355	2533
B Casualty insurance premiums, net, due to be received by insurance companies	26098	...	26098	27955	...	27955
C Current transfers from the rest of the world	...	...	...	...	...	...
D Other transfers except imputed	2451	2035	416	3210	2750	460
E Imputed unfunded employee pension and welfare contributions	26961	20666	6295	26997	20252	6745
Total Current Receipts	415212	181514	233698	430493	194691	235802
Disbursements						
1 Property and entrepreneurial income	304749	141471	163278	290140	128621	161519
A Withdrawals from quasi-corporations	18711	18711	...	18101	18101	...
B Interest	263393	104889	158504	253590	97466	156124
C Dividends	16462	11705	4757	12357	6983	5374
D Net land rent and royalties	6183	6166	17	6092	6071	21
2 Direct taxes and other current transfers n.e.c. to general government	43658	33266	10392	54355	41184	13171
A Direct taxes	43658	33266	10392	54355	41184	13171
B Fines, fees, penalties and other current transfers n.e.c.	...	...	...	...	...	...
3 Other current transfers	61461	28492	32969	67642	32507	35135
A Casualty insurance premiums, net	8942	5775	3167	9208	6355	2853
B Casualty insurance claims liability of insurance companies	26098	...	26098	27955	...	27955
C Transfers to private non-profit institutions	3321	...	3321	3938	...	3938
D Unfunded employee pension and welfare benefits	-	...	...	-	...	...
E Social assistance grants	16659	16276	383	18080	17691	389
F Other transfers n.e.c.	6441	6441	...	8461	8461	...
G Transfers to the rest of the world	-	...	...	-	...	...
Statistical discrepancy	6921	4720	2201	5287	2927	2360
Net saving	-1577	-26435	24858	13069	-10548	23617
Total Current Disbursements and Net Saving	415212	181514	233698	430493	194691	235802

3.23 Corporate and Quasi-Corporate Enterprise Capital Accumulation Account: Total and Sectors

Thousand Million Italian lire

	1980 TOTAL	1980 Non-Financial	1980 Financial	1985 TOTAL	1985 Non-Financial	1985 Financial	1990 TOTAL	1990 Non-Financial	1990 Financial	1991 TOTAL	1991 Non-Financial	1991 Financial
Finance of Gross Accumulation												
1 Gross saving	28253	19437	8816	58956	43458	15498	74293	49116	25177	64553	42148	22405
A Consumption of fixed capital	18670	17668	1002	41739	39479	2260	62450	59099	3351	68355	64809	3546
B Net saving	9583	1769	7814	17217	3979	13238	11843	-9983	21826	-3802	-22661	18859
2 Capital transfers	2013	2013	-	12469	7628	4841	15942	15942	-	13313	13313	-
Finance of Gross Accumulation	30266	21450	8816	71425	51086	20339	90235	65058	25177	77866	55461	22405

Italy

3.23 Corporate and Quasi-Corporate Enterprise Capital Accumulation Account: Total and Sectors
(Continued)

Thousand Million Italian lire

	1980 TOTAL	1980 Non-Financial	1980 Financial	1985 TOTAL	1985 Non-Financial	1985 Financial	1990 TOTAL	1990 Non-Financial	1990 Financial	1991 TOTAL	1991 Non-Financial	1991 Financial
						Gross Accumulation						
1 Gross capital formation	36366	34928	1438	62045	58845	3200	122699	116384	6315	133731	127753	5978
A Increase in stocks	3073	3073	-	5736	5736	-	7190	7190	-	7692	7692	-
B Gross fixed capital formation	33293	31855	1438	56309	53109	3200	115509	109194	6315	126039	120061	5978
2 Purchases of land, net	10	24	-14	172	127	45	276	271	5	247	243	4
3 Purchases of intangible assets, net	545	545	-	956	956	-	1882	1882	-	1608	1608	-
4 Capital transfers	361	288	73	663	361	302	920	622	298	2595	2032	563
Net lending [a]	-7016	-14335	7319	7589	-9203	16792	-35542	-54101	18559	-60315	-76175	15860
Gross Accumulation	30266	21450	8816	71425	51086	20339	90235	65058	25177	77866	55461	22405

	1992 TOTAL	1992 Non-Financial	1992 Financial	1993 TOTAL	1993 Non-Financial	1993 Financial
			Finance of Gross Accumulation			
1 Gross saving	70745	42225	28520	89819	62356	27463
A Consumption of fixed capital	72322	68660	3662	76750	72904	3846
B Net saving	-1577	-26435	24858	13069	-10548	23617
2 Capital transfers	12871	12871	-	23362	21312	2050
Finance of Gross Accumulation	83616	55096	28520	113181	83668	29513
			Gross Accumulation			
1 Gross capital formation	122791	116739	6052	108340	104431	3909
A Increase in stocks	3222	3222	-	-2335	-2335	-
B Gross fixed capital formation	119569	113517	6052	110675	106766	3909
2 Purchases of land, net	402	400	2	278	276	2
3 Purchases of intangible assets, net	1738	1738	-	2049	2049	-
4 Capital transfers	15852	14264	1588	5270	4358	912
Net lending [a]	-57167	-78045	20878	-2756	-27446	24690
Gross Accumulation	83616	55096	28520	113181	83668	29513

a) Net lending of the capital accumulation account and the capital finance account have not been reconciled and are different due to different statistical sources.

3.31 Household and Private Unincorporated Enterprise Production Account

Thousand Million Italian lire

	1980	1983	1984	1985	1986	1987	1988	1989	1990	1991	1992	1993
						Gross Output						
1 Output for sale	309672	511255	559717	617771	679595	741087	822496	896424	972604	1062009	1120736	1147242
2 Non-marketed output	...	...	...	...	...	...	...	...	...	...	...	...
Gross Output	309672	511255	559717	617771	679595	741087	822496	896424	972604	1062009	1120736	1147242
						Gross Input						
Intermediate consumption	128010	211896	225210	245781	260611	283492	321989	354747	380183	408907	427583	432306
Subtotal: Value Added	181662	299359	334507	371990	418984	457595	500507	541677	592421	653102	693153	714936
1 Indirect taxes net liability of unincorporated enterprises	-1197	-2538	-2595	-1732	-2861	-403	1008	-135	2734	1899	3086	14134
A Indirect taxes	2770	4828	5419	5817	6640	7656	9608	10285	12057	13558	14884	26094
B Less: Subsidies	3967	7366	8014	7549	9501	8059	8600	10420	9323	11659	11798	11960
2 Consumption of fixed capital	25049	43652	49502	56461	60895	65980	72896	79740	87321	94794	101394	107675
3 Compensation of employees	44500	72579	78008	88635	97420	104579	114139	123699	136701	150334	158964	163404
4 Net operating surplus	113310	185666	209592	228626	263530	287439	312464	338373	365665	406075	429709	429723
Gross Input	309672	511255	559717	617771	679595	741087	822496	896424	972604	1062009	1120736	1147242

3.32 Household and Private Unincorporated Enterprise Income and Outlay Account

Thousand Million Italian lire

	1980	1983	1984	1985	1986	1987	1988	1989	1990	1991	1992	1993
						Receipts						
1 Compensation of employees	185672	302452	337537	376681	406738	440993	484497	529420	592890	647133	680093	687218
A Wages and salaries	136307	220899	247959	275692	294576	321106	...	378273	...	...	...	...
B Employers' contributions for social security	33324	56665	61718	69401	78978	84477	...	107660	...	...	...	...
C Employers' contributions for private pension & welfare plans	16041	24888	27860	31588	33184	35410	...	43487	...	...	...	...

Italy

3.32 Household and Private Unincorporated Enterprise Income and Outlay Account
(Continued)

Thousand Million Italian lire

	1980	1983	1984	1985	1986	1987	1988	1989	1990	1991	1992	1993
2 Operating surplus of private unincorporated enterprises	113310	185666	209592	228626	263530	287439	312464	338373	365665	406075	429709	429723
3 Property and entrepreneurial income	35832	74804	85619	91264	98253	102454	117942	142655	161655	181076	208529	214697
A Withdrawals from private quasi-corporations	4273	7692	9141	10464	11560	12508	13774	14568	16034	17695	18279	18098
B Interest	30009	64065	72887	76134	81110	83560	97550	119644	137055	154364	181063	187748
C Dividends	1104	2729	3027	3854	4741	5279	4988	5004	4638	4871	4700	4036
D Net land rent and royalties	446	318	564	812	842	1107	1630	3439	3928	4146	4487	4815
3 Current transfers	66731	130771	145457	166692	184245	204374	226979	252655	287011	314741	348596	368800
A Casualty insurance claims	2603	4823	5883	7118	8305	9662	11451	13265	15816	18899	19942	21129
B Social security benefits	58583	117344	129798	148667	164573	182196	202076	224011	254556	277914	310091	324655
C Social assistance grants	...	...	...	...	...	...	...	...	...	...	...	...
D Unfunded employee pension and welfare benefits	...	...	...	...	...	...	...	...	...	...	...	...
E Transfers from general government	...	...	...	...	...	...	...	...	...	...	...	...
F Transfers from the rest of the world	1059	1727	1963	2062	1796	1574	1587	1929	1447	1076	835	932
G Other transfers n.e.c.	4486	6877	7813	8845	9571	10942	11865	13450	15192	16852	17728	22084
Statistical discrepancy	6979	7274	8515	9897	10090	9286	10307	11496	11514	12877	10169	9878
Total Current Receipts	408524	700967	786720	873160	962856	1044546	1152189	1274599	1418735	1561902	1677096	1710316

Disbursements

	1980	1983	1984	1985	1986	1987	1988	1989	1990	1991	1992	1993
1 Final consumption expenditures	236603	387170	443268	498048	551868	606889	670883	740267	806593	884753	946937	965390
2 Property income	10802	18647	20803	23396	24446	24965	27005	31560	34399	37464	45959	44098
A Interest	10206	18229	20477	23046	24086	24610	26530	30926	33569	36374	44525	42212
B Net land rent and royalties	596	418	326	350	360	355	475	634	830	1090	1434	1886
3 Direct taxes and other current transfers n.e.c. to government	77122	145448	164306	184883	205293	222747	254425	282953	317127	349561	378229	407718
A Social security contributions	44764	79424	87285	97470	111778	121411	133817	150226	169505	187893	200577	211614
B Direct taxes	32358	66024	77021	87413	93515	101336	120608	132727	147622	161668	177652	196104
Income taxes	...	...	...	...	...	...	...	...	...	...	...	...
Other	...	...	...	...	...	...	...	...	...	...	...	...
C Fees, fines and penalties	...	...	...	...	...	...	...	...	...	...	...	...
4 Other current transfers	22433	36676	41741	48866	56752	56726	62237	71273	81017	93840	103555	112964
A Net casualty insurance premiums	2529	4540	5545	6765	7895	8874	10206	12552	14735	18011	19508	20702
B Transfers to private non-profit institutions serving households	208	320	396	447	479	492	534	572	641	728	746	762
C Transfers to the rest of the world	-	-	-	-	-	-	-	-	31	110	199	243
D Other current transfers, except imputed	3655	6928	7940	10066	15194	11950	12983	14662	16516	21057	23656	28478
E Imputed employee pension and welfare contributions	16041	24888	27860	31588	33184	35410	38514	43487	49094	53934	59446	62779
Statistical discrepancy	1654	1699	1655	1964	2061	2705	2864	2879	3090	3404	3248	4591
Net saving	59910	111327	114947	116003	122436	130514	134775	145667	176509	192880	199168	175555
Total Current Disbursements and Net Saving	408524	700967	786720	873160	962856	1044546	1152189	1274599	1418735	1561902	1677096	1710316

3.33 Household and Private Unincorporated Enterprise Capital Accumulation Account

Thousand Million Italian lire

	1980	1983	1984	1985	1986	1987	1988	1989	1990	1991	1992	1993

Finance of Gross Accumulation

	1980	1983	1984	1985	1986	1987	1988	1989	1990	1991	1992	1993
1 Gross saving	84959	154979	164449	172464	183331	196494	207671	225407	263830	287674	300562	283230
A Consumption of fixed capital	25049	43652	49502	56461	60895	65980	72896	79740	87321	94794	101394	107675
B Net saving	59910	111327	114947	116003	122436	130514	134775	145667	176509	192880	199168	175555
2 Capital transfers	2341	3242	4101	5082	4949	4961	5398	6126	6623	4866	5831	6707
Total Finance of Gross Accumulation	87300	158221	168550	177546	188280	201455	213069	231533	270453	292540	306393	289937

Gross Accumulation

	1980	1983	1984	1985	1986	1987	1988	1989	1990	1991	1992	1993
1 Gross Capital Formation	57475	74150	91293	99608	98285	102650	111751	120213	124310	129649	141435	130231

Italy

3.33 Household and Private Unincorporated Enterprise Capital Accumulation Account
(Continued)

Thousand Million Italian lire

	1980	1983	1984	1985	1986	1987	1988	1989	1990	1991	1992	1993
A Increase in stocks	7387	2354	7246	9229	7242	6716	6316	4169	2232	2530	1633	-844
B Gross fixed capital formation	50088	71796	84047	90379	91043	95934	105435	116044	122078	127119	139802	131075
2 Purchases of land, net	-41	-137	-201	-230	-150	-231	-481	-442	-366	-313	-318	-320
3 Purchases of intangibles, net	-596	-832	-1222	-900	-422	-685	-861	-573	-1453	-316	-567	-668
4 Capital transfers	409	3355	1572	932	869	1114	1300	1678	1190	1309	15871	6788
Net lending [a]	30053	81685	77108	78136	89698	98607	101360	110657	146772	162211	149972	153906
Total Gross Accumulation	87300	158221	168550	177546	188280	201455	213069	231533	270453	292540	306393	289937

a) Net lending of the capital accumulation account and the capital finance account have not been reconciled and are different due to different statistical sources.

3.51 External Transactions: Current Account: Detail

Thousand Million Italian lire

	1980	1983	1984	1985	1986	1987	1988	1989	1990	1991	1992	1993
Payments to the Rest of the World												
1 Imports of goods and services	95422	135508	167237	188313	168262	185738	208044	243169	271138	276976	299033	310132
A Imports of merchandise c.i.f.	87170	122469	150887	168791	149542	163692	181264	211316	219313	227894	234374	234033
B Other	8252	13039	16350	19522	18720	22046	26780	31853	51825	49082	64659	76099
2 Factor income to the rest of the world	5662	13422	16445	18600	18594	18157	20568	28612	38676	47840	58377	68680
A Compensation of employees	235	497	571	728	739	917	1298	2403	2875	2074	1896	2270
B Property and entrepreneurial income	5427	12925	15874	17872	17855	17240	19270	26209	35801	45766	56481	66410
3 Current transfers to the rest of the world	4007	6870	8359	9580	12900	13540	14831	18619	18162	25329	24282	30199
A Indirect taxes by general government to supranational organizations	...	...	...	...	...	...	...	...	...	...	...	...
B Other current transfers	4007	6870	8359	9580	12900	13540	14831	18619	18162	25329	24282	30199
By general government	367	951	1223	1735	2500	2320	3036	5772	2756	4744	5158	7706
By other resident sectors	3640	5919	7136	7845	10400	11220	11795	12847	15406	20585	19124	22493
4 Surplus of the nation on current transactions	-8645	2167	-4662	-7403	4127	-2071	-8069	-15550	-18257	-26429	-33122	17476
Payments to the Rest of the World, and Surplus of the Nation on Current Transfers	96446	157967	187379	209090	203883	215364	235374	274850	309719	323716	348570	426487
Receipts From The Rest of the World												
1 Exports of goods and services	84953	140016	165197	185022	181961	192273	210046	243047	272868	279974	300707	365442
A Exports of merchandise f.o.b.	66987	110747	131026	146059	144675	151114	166639	193013	203885	211126	220635	265236
B Other	17966	29269	34171	38963	37286	41159	43407	50034	68983	68848	80072	100206
2 Factor income from the rest of the world	6452	9226	11709	13222	11687	11435	13018	18116	22975	27668	32658	43036
A Compensation of employees	1844	2793	3114	3358	3412	3073	3242	3483	3374	2431	1981	2325
B Property and entrepreneurial income	4608	6433	8595	9864	8275	8362	9776	14633	19601	25237	30677	40711
3 Current transfers from the rest of the world	5041	8725	10473	10846	10235	11656	12310	13687	13876	16074	15205	18009
A Subsidies to general government from supranational organizations	...	...	...	...	...	...	...	...	...	...	...	...
B Other current transfers	5041	8725	10473	10846	10235	11656	12310	13687	13876	16074	15205	18009
To general government	143	227	297	431	220	305	256	266	294	516	476	464
To other resident sectors	4898	8498	10176	10415	10015	11351	12054	13421	13582	15558	14729	17545
Receipts from the Rest of the World on Current Transfers	96446	157967	187379	209090	203883	215364	235374	274850	309719	323716	348570	426487

Italy

3.52 External Transactions: Capital Accumulation Account

Thousand Million Italian lire

	1980	1983	1984	1985	1986	1987	1988	1989	1990	1991	1992	1993
Finance of Gross Accumulation												
1 Surplus of the nation on current transactions	-8645	2167	-4662	-7403	4127	-2071	-8069	-15550	-18257	-26429	-33122	17476
2 Capital transfers from the rest of the world	348	620	858	917	886	1020	1196	1791	1586	1713	2487	3991
Total Finance of Gross Accumulation	-8297	2787	-3804	-6486	5013	-1051	-6873	-13759	-16671	-24716	-30635	21467
Gross Accumulation												
1 Capital transfers to the rest of the world	134	235	229	304	956	461	385	558	522	590	934	897
2 Purchases of intangible assets, n.e.c., net, from the rest of the world	-51	-8	13	56	418	332	180	494	429	1292	1171	1381
Net lending to the rest of the world [a]	-8380	2560	-4046	-6846	3639	-1844	-7438	-14811	-17622	-26598	-32740	19189
Total Gross Accumulation	-8297	2787	-3804	-6486	5013	-1051	-6873	-13759	-16671	-24716	-30635	21467

a) Net lending of the capital accumulation account and the capital finance account have not been reconciled and are different due to different statistical sources.

3.53 External Transactions: Capital Finance Account

Thousand Million Italian lire

	1980	1983	1984	1985	1986	1987	1988	1989	1990	1991	1992	1993
Acquisitions of Foreign Financial Assets												
1 Gold and SDR's	-163	-367	25	-385	442	165	-137	...	...	...	...	...
2 Currency and transferable deposits	446	2783	2055	-5595	4333	5214	7628	...	...	...	...	...
3 Other deposits	...	...	...	...	...	...	...	...	...	...	...	...
4 Bills and bonds, short term	507	6354	2633	-7282	-838	1238	2305	...	...	...	...	...
5 Bonds, long term	-3	-231	-93	667	2000	3848	7990	...	...	...	...	...
6 Corporate equity securities	1394	3894	4148	4583	5984	4613	8400	...	...	...	...	...
7 Short-term loans, n.e.c.	4651	11197	9390	15050	-777	-926	11268	...	...	...	...	...
8 Long-term loans	821	907	1639	1966	1894	1053	1363	...	...	...	...	...
9 Prporietors' net additions to accumulation of quasi-corporate, non-resident enterprises	...	...	...	...	...	...	...	...	...	...	...	...
10 Trade credit and advances	2368	2464	4176	-1159	155	196	3045	...	...	...	...	...
11 Other	427	487	550	546	-179	-130	-1193	...	...	...	...	...
Total Acquisitions of Foreign Financial Assets	10449	27488	24522	8391	13013	15271	40668	...	...	...	...	...
Incurrence of Foreign Liabilities												
1 Currency and transferable deposits	-196	-355	-338	-419	-143	754	-74	...	...	...	...	...
2 Other deposits	-2	1	1	-	-	-	-	...	...	...	...	...
3 Bills and bonds, short term	-	190	-131	352	36	1722	4719	...	...	...	...	...
4 Bonds, long term	2	-29	389	1530	4988	-2113	513	...	...	...	...	...
5 Corporate equity securities	60	2249	2544	2154	-3303	819	11200	...	...	...	...	...
6 Short-term loans, n.e.c.	11893	16577	19426	3353	3726	1468	19089	...	...	...	...	...
7 Long-term loans	5652	4071	3800	7130	5100	12414	11272	...	...	...	...	...
8 Non-resident proprietors' net additions to accumulation of resident quasi-corporate enterprises	...	...	...	...	...	...	...	...	...	...	...	...
9 Trade credit and advances	1571	2462	3145	1393	-1193	2147	728	...	...	...	...	...
10 Other	...	...	...	...	...	...	...	...	...	...	...	...
Total Incurrence of Liabilities	18981	25165	28836	15493	9211	17211	47447	...	...	...	...	...
Net Lending [a]	-8532	2323	-4314	-7102	3802	-1940	-6779	...	...	...	...	...
Total Incurrence of Liabilities and Net Lending	10449	27488	24522	8391	13013	15271	40668	...	...	...	...	...

a) Net lending of the capital accumulation account and the capital finance account have not been reconciled and are different due to different statistical sources.

4.1 Derivation of Value Added by Kind of Activity, in Current Prices

Thousand Million Italian lire

	1980			1985			1990			1991		
	Gross Output	Intermediate Consumption	Value Added	Gross Output	Intermediate Consumption	Value Added	Gross Output	Intermediate Consumption	Value Added	Gross Output	Intermediate Consumption	Value Added
All Producers												
1 Agriculture, hunting, forestry and fishing	...	...	22305	...	...	36327	...	...	42133	...	...	47847
A Agriculture and hunting	...	...	21426	...	...	34661	...	...	39859	...	...	45398
B Forestry and logging	...	...	428	...	...	530	...	...	555	...	...	642
C Fishing	...	...	451	...	...	1392	...	...	1719	...	...	1866

Italy

4.1 Derivation of Value Added by Kind of Activity, in Current Prices
(Continued)

Thousand Million Italian lire

	1980 Gross Output	1980 Intermediate Consumption	1980 Value Added	1985 Gross Output	1985 Intermediate Consumption	1985 Value Added	1990 Gross Output	1990 Intermediate Consumption	1990 Value Added	1991 Gross Output	1991 Intermediate Consumption	1991 Value Added
2 Mining and quarrying [a]	...	...	...	...	...	...	...	...	...	...	...	...
3 Manufacturing [a]	...	...	107810	...	...	196473	...	...	293813	...	...	301423
A Manufacture of food, beverages and tobacco	...	...	10521	...	...	20884	...	...	30438	...	...	32685
B Textile, wearing apparel and leather industries	...	...	17599	...	...	34208	...	...	46728	...	...	48530
C Manufacture of wood and wood products, including furniture	...	...	6196	...	...	10743	...	...	15924	...	...	17042
D Manufacture of paper and paper products, printing and publishing	...	...	5830	...	...	10970	...	...	18120	...	...	18819
E Manufacture of chemicals and chemical petroleum, coal, rubber and plastic products	...	...	11958	...	...	23780	...	...	38126	...	...	38622
F Manufacture of non-metallic mineral products, except products of petroleum and coal	...	...	8243	...	...	12667	...	...	21744	...	...	21938
G Basic metal industries	...	...	5536	...	...	8493	...	...	12444	...	...	11435
H Manufacture of fabricated metal products, machinery and equipment	...	...	40584	...	...	72421	...	...	107060	...	...	108978
I Other manufacturing industries	...	...	1343	...	...	2307	...	...	3229	...	...	3374
4 Electricity, gas and water	...	...	15053	...	...	37479	...	...	67008	...	...	76819
A Electricity, gas and steam	...	...	15053	...	...	37479	...	...	67008	...	...	76819
B Water works and supply	...	...	...	...	...	...	...	...	...	...	...	...
5 Construction	...	...	28458	...	...	50987	...	...	76702	...	...	83818
6 Wholesale and retail trade, restaurants and hotels [b]	...	...	70274	...	...	154755	...	...	241124	...	...	264370
A Wholesale and retail trade	...	...	59523	...	...	130048	...	...	201096	...	...	221061
B Restaurants and hotels	...	...	10751	...	...	24707	...	...	40028	...	...	43309
7 Transport, storage and communication	...	...	20026	...	...	43609	...	...	74344	...	...	83303
A Transport and storage	...	...	15940	...	...	32168	...	...	56086	...	...	62091
B Communication	...	...	4086	...	...	11441	...	...	18258	...	...	21212
8 Finance, insurance, real estate and business services	...	...	74480	...	...	177559	...	...	319071	...	...	349598
9 Community, social and personal services	...	...		...	...		...	...		...	...	
Total, Industries	...	...	338406	...	...	697189	...	...	1114195	...	...	1207178
Producers of Government Services	...	...	42791	...	...	96007	...	...	169020	...	...	184249
Other Producers	...	...	2939	...	...	7102	...	...	11571	...	...	13402
Total	...	...	384136	...	...	800298	...	...	1294786	...	...	1404829
Less: Imputed bank service charge	...	...	16471	...	...	34373	...	...	61911	...	...	67359
Import duties	...	...	20004	...	...	44655	...	...	79191	...	...	91983
Value added tax	...	...	...	...	...	...	...	...	...	...	...	...
Total [c]	...	...	387669	...	...	810580	...	...	1312066	...	...	1429453

	1992 Gross Output	1992 Intermediate Consumption	1992 Value Added	1993 Gross Output	1993 Intermediate Consumption	1993 Value Added

All Producers

	1992 Gross Output	1992 Intermediate Consumption	1992 Value Added	1993 Gross Output	1993 Intermediate Consumption	1993 Value Added
1 Agriculture, hunting, forestry and fishing	...	...	47300	...	...	45459
A Agriculture and hunting	...	...	43732	...	...	...
B Forestry and logging	...	...	678	...	...	...
C Fishing	...	...	1959	...	...	...
2 Mining and quarrying [a]	...	...	...	...	...	...

Italy

4.1 Derivation of Value Added by Kind of Activity, in Current Prices
(Continued)

Thousand Million Italian lire

	1992 Gross Output	1992 Intermediate Consumption	1992 Value Added	1993 Gross Output	1993 Intermediate Consumption	1993 Value Added
3 Manufacturing [a]	...	...	308527	...	...	314939
A Manufacture of food, beverages and tobacco	...	...	34966	...	...	38310
B Textile, wearing apparel and leather industries	...	...	49586	...	...	51585
C Manufacture of wood and wood products, including furniture	...	...	17552	...	...	18125
D Manufacture of paper and paper products, printing and publishing	...	...	19494	...	...	20982
E Manufacture of chemicals and chemical petroleum, coal, rubber and plastic products	...	...	39956	...	...	39610
F Manufacture of non-metallic mineral products, except products of petroleum and coal	...	...	22919	...	...	21203
G Basic metal industries	...	...	10742	...	...	11143
H Manufacture of fabricated metal products, machinery and equipment	...	...	109835	...	...	110418
I Other manufacturing industries	...	...	3477	...	...	3563
4 Electricity, gas and water	...	...	86320	...	...	89086
A Electricity, gas and steam	...	...	86320	...	...	89086
B Water works and supply	...	...	...	...	...	...
5 Construction	...	...	87425	...	...	86824
6 Wholesale and retail trade, restaurants and hotels [b]	...	...	277407	...	...	284534
A Wholesale and retail trade	...	...	230982	...	...	236793
B Restaurants and hotels	...	...	46425	...	...	47741
7 Transport, storage and communication	...	...	90693	...	...	98649
A Transport and storage	...	...	66356	...	...	70777
B Communication	...	...	24337	...	...	27872
8 Finance, insurance, real estate and business services	...	...	386241	...	...	410647
9 Community, social and personal services	...	...		...	...	
Total, Industries	...	...	1283913	...	...	1330138
Producers of Government Services	...	...	193738	...	...	200201
Other Producers	...	...	14867	...	...	15735
Total	...	...	1492518	...	...	1546074
Less: Imputed bank service charge	...	...	79400	...	...	79231
Import duties	...	...	91205	...	...	93271
Value added tax	...	...	...	...	...	...
Total [c]	...	...	1504323	...	...	1560114

a) Item 'Mining and quarrying' is included in item 'Manufacturing'.
b) Item 'Wholesale and retail trade, restaurants and hotels' includes repair services.
c) The branch breakdown used in this table (GDP by kind of activity) is according to the classification NACE/CLIO.

4.2 Derivation of Value Added by Kind of Activity, in Constant Prices

Thousand Million Italian lire

At constant prices of: 1985

All Producers

	1980 GO	1980 IC	1980 VA	1985 GO	1985 IC	1985 VA	1990 GO	1990 IC	1990 VA	1991 GO	1991 IC	1991 VA
1 Agriculture, hunting, forestry and fishing	...	...	35637	...	...	36327	...	...	36509	...	...	39159
A Agriculture and hunting	...	...	...	...	...	...	...	...	34773	...	...	37403
B Forestry and logging	...	...	...	...	...	...	...	...	458	...	...	465
C Fishing	...	...	...	...	...	...	...	...	1278	...	...	1369
2 Mining and quarrying	...	...	...	...	...	...	...	...	...	...	...	...

Italy

4.2 Derivation of Value Added by Kind of Activity, in Constant Prices
(Continued)

Thousand Million Italian lire

	1980 Gross Output	1980 Intermediate Consumption	1980 Value Added	1985 Gross Output	1985 Intermediate Consumption	1985 Value Added	1990 Gross Output	1990 Intermediate Consumption	1990 Value Added	1991 Gross Output	1991 Intermediate Consumption	1991 Value Added
				At constant prices of: 1985								
3 Manufacturing	...	...	185999	...	...	196473	...	...	237742	...	...	237224
A Manufacture of food, beverages and tobacco	...	...	20608	...	...	20884	...	...	24978	...	...	26218
B Textile, wearing apparel and leather industries	...	...	34310	...	...	34208	...	...	38727	...	...	39323
C Manufacture of wood and wood products, including furniture	...	...	10245	...	...	10743	...	...	11580	...	...	12044
D Manufacture of paper and paper products, printing and publishing	...	...	10284	...	...	10970	...	...	13745	...	...	13504
E Manufacture of chemicals and chemical petroleum, coal, rubber and plastic products	...	...	17087	...	...	23780	...	...	31849	...	...	31463
F Manufacture of non-metallic mineral products, except products of petroleum and coal	...	...	13747	...	...	12667	...	...	16903	...	...	15979
G Basic metal industries	...	...	7963	...	...	8493	...	...	8414	...	...	8234
H Manufacture of fabricated metal products, machinery and equipment	...	...	69031	...	...	72421	...	...	89034	...	...	87948
I Other manufacturing industries	...	...	2724	...	...	2307	...	...	2512	...	...	2511
4 Electricity, gas and water	...	...	40848	...	...	37479	...	...	43912	...	...	44495
A Electricity, gas and steam	...	...	40848	...	...	37479	...	...	43912	...	...	44495
B Water works and supply	...	...	...	...	...	...	...	...	...	...	...	...
5 Construction	...	...	54532	...	...	50987	...	...	56667	...	...	57328
6 Wholesale and retail trade, restaurants and hotels [a]	...	...	143684	...	...	154755	...	...	178256	...	...	180407
A Wholesale and retail trade	...	...	118679	...	...	130048	...	...	151633	...	...	153721
B Restaurants and hotels	...	...	25005	...	...	24707	...	...	26623	...	...	26686
7 Transport, storage and communication	...	...	38296	...	...	43609	...	...	55423	...	...	57114
A Transport and storage	...	...	30475	...	...	32168	...	...	40283	...	...	40738
B Communication	...	...	7821	...	...	11441	...	...	15140	...	...	16376
8 Finance, insurance, real estate and business services	...	...	151168	...	...	177559	...	...	212483	...	...	215361
9 Community, social and personal services	...	...		...	...		...	...		...	...	
Total, Industries	...	...	650164	...	...	697189	...	...	820992	...	...	831088
Producers of Government Services	...	...	89882	...	...	96007	...	...	101821	...	...	102481
Other Producers	...	...	5545	...	...	7102	...	...	7460	...	...	7771
Total	...	...	745591	...	...	800298	...	...	930273	...	...	941340
Less: Imputed bank service charge	...	...	30520	...	...	34373	...	...	43704	...	...	44951
Import duties	...	...	41126	...	...	44655	...	...	54818	...	...	56297
Value added tax	...	...	...	...	...	...	...	...	...	...	...	...
Total [b]	...	...	756197	...	...	810580	...	...	941387	...	...	952686

	1992 Gross Output	1992 Intermediate Consumption	1992 Value Added	1993 Gross Output	1993 Intermediate Consumption	1993 Value Added
	At constant prices of: 1985					
	All Producers					
1 Agriculture, hunting, forestry and fishing	...	...	40054	...	...	38787
A Agriculture and hunting	...	...	37918	...	...	...
B Forestry and logging	...	...	496	...	...	...
C Fishing	...	...	1331	...	...	...
2 Mining and quarrying	...	...	...	...	...	...

Italy

4.2 Derivation of Value Added by Kind of Activity, in Constant Prices
(Continued)

Thousand Million Italian lire

	1992 Gross Output	1992 Intermediate Consumption	1992 Value Added	1993 Gross Output	1993 Intermediate Consumption	1993 Value Added
			At constant prices of: 1985			
3 Manufacturing	...	...	237163	...	...	232644
A Manufacture of food, beverages and tobacco	...	...	26479	...	...	26919
B Textile, wearing apparel and leather industries	...	...	39545	...	...	39495
C Manufacture of wood and wood products, including furniture	...	...	11959	...	...	11709
D Manufacture of paper and paper products, printing and publishing	...	...	13633	...	...	14404
E Manufacture of chemicals and chemical petroleum, coal, rubber and plastic products	...	...	32165	...	...	30722
F Manufacture of non-metallic mineral products, except products of petroleum and coal	...	...	16077	...	...	15160
G Basic metal industries	...	...	7954	...	...	7872
H Manufacture of fabricated metal products, machinery and equipment	...	...	86766	...	...	83949
I Other manufacturing industries	...	...	2585	...	...	2414
4 Electricity, gas and water	...	...	46020	...	...	46078
A Electricity, gas and steam	...	...	46020	...	...	46078
B Water works and supply	...	...	...	...	...	...
5 Construction	...	...	56808	...	...	54185
6 Wholesale and retail trade, restaurants and hotels [a]	...	...	181774	...	...	178121
A Wholesale and retail trade	...	...	155354	...	...	152712
B Restaurants and hotels	...	...	26420	...	...	25409
7 Transport, storage and communication	...	...	59723	...	...	62497
A Transport and storage	...	...	41321	...	...	41923
B Communication	...	...	18402	...	...	20574
8 Finance, insurance, real estate and business services	...	...	219613	...	...	226390
9 Community, social and personal services	...	...		...	...	
Total, Industries	...	...	841155	...	...	838702
Producers of Government Services	...	...	102897	...	...	103127
Other Producers	...	...	8187	...	...	8233
Total	...	...	952239	...	...	950062
Less: Imputed bank service charge	...	...	49224	...	...	50974
Import duties	...	...	56799	...	...	54358
Value added tax	...	...	...	...	...	...
Total [b]	...	...	959814	...	...	953446

a) Item 'Wholesale and retail trade, restaurants and hotels' includes repair services.
b) The branch breakdown used in this table (GDP by kind of activity) is according to the classification NACE/CLIO.

4.3 Cost Components of Value Added

Thousand Million Italian lire

	1980 Compensation of Employees	1980 Capital Consumption	1980 Net Operating Surplus	1980 Indirect Taxes	1980 Less: Subsidies Received	1980 Value Added	1985 Compensation of Employees	1985 Capital Consumption	1985 Net Operating Surplus	1985 Indirect Taxes	1985 Less: Subsidies Received	1985 Value Added
				All Producers								
1 Agriculture, hunting, forestry and fishing	6470	...	17123	129	1417	22305	10928	...	28309	332	3242	36327
A Agriculture and hunting	...	...	...	...	...	21426	...	...	...	...	...	34661
B Forestry and logging	...	...	...	...	...	428	...	...	...	...	...	530
C Fishing	...	...	...	...	...	451	...	...	...	...	...	1392
2 Mining and quarrying [a]	...	...	...	...	...	...	...	...	...	...	...	...

Italy

4.3 Cost Components of Value Added
(Continued)

Thousand Million Italian lire

	1980						1985					
	Compensation of Employees	Capital Consumption	Net Operating Surplus	Indirect Taxes	Less: Subsidies Received	Value Added	Compensation of Employees	Capital Consumption	Net Operating Surplus	Indirect Taxes	Less: Subsidies Received	Value Added
3 Manufacturing a	61676	...	45431	2971	2268	107810	109314	...	85659	6662	5162	196473
A Manufacture of food, beverages and tobacco	4419	...	4821	2487	1206	10521	8220	...	10052	5387	2775	20884
B Textile, wearing apparel and leather industries	9699	...	7933	95	128	17599	17554	...	16606	231	183	34208
C Manufacture of wood and wood products, including furniture	3025	...	3190	33	52	6196	5319	...	5412	83	71	10743
D Manufacture of paper and paper products, printing and publishing	3475	...	2447	31	123	5830	6469	...	4722	74	295	10970
E Manufacture of chemicals and chemical petroleum, coal, rubber and plastic products	7307	...	4602	109	60	11958	13315	...	10367	226	128	23780
F Manufacture of non-metallic mineral products, except products of petroleum and coal	4034	...	4223	41	55	8243	7078	...	5594	102	107	12667
G Basic metal industries	3260	...	2265	28	17	5536	5594	...	3336	63	500	8493
H Manufacture of fabricated metal products, machinery and equipment	25784	...	15277	140	617	40584	44613	...	28415	479	1086	72421
I Other manufacturing industries	673	...	673	7	10	1343	1152	...	1155	17	17	2307
4 Electricity, gas and water	3669	...	4317	7146	79	15053	7959	...	14834	15074	388	37479
A Electricity, gas and steam	...	...	...	...	...	15053	...	...	...	...	...	37479
B Water works and supply	...	...	...	...	...	...	...	...	...	...	...	...
5 Construction	12326	...	16421	253	542	28458	22117	...	29410	520	1060	50987
6 Wholesale and retail trade, restaurants and hotels	17466	...	53351	579	1122	70274	39872	...	114828	1427	1372	154755
A Wholesale and retail trade	14413	...	45710	498	1098	59523	33413	...	96582	1261	1208	130048
B Restaurants and hotels	3053	...	7641	81	24	10751	6459	...	18246	166	164	24707
7 Transport, storage and communication	15940	...	11326	242	7482	20026	31434	...	27643	587	16055	43609
A Transport and storage	11908	...	10718	200	6886	15940	23162	...	23115	495	14604	32168
B Communication	4032	...	608	42	596	4086	8272	...	4528	92	1451	11441
8 Finance, insurance, real estate and business services	21688	...	48710	4522	440	74480	51121	...	118605	8379	546	177559
9 Community, social and personal services		...						...				
Total, Industries	139235	...	196679	15842	13350	338406	272745	...	419288	32981	27825	697189
Producers of Government Services	42064	...	727	...	...	42791	94311	...	1696	...	...	96007
Other Producers	2764	...	175	...	...	2939	6995	...	107	...	...	7102
Total	184063	...	197581	15842	13350	384136	374051	...	421091	32981	27825	800298
Less: Imputed bank service charge	...	...	16471	...	...	16471	...	...	34373	...	...	34373
Import duties	...	...	...	20004	...	20004	...	...	...	44655	...	44655
Value added tax	...	...	...	...	...	...	...	...	...	...	...	...
Total bc	184063	...	181110	35846	13350	387669	374051	...	386718	77636	27825	810580

	1990						1991					
	Compensation of Employees	Capital Consumption	Net Operating Surplus	Indirect Taxes	Less: Subsidies Received	Value Added	Compensation of Employees	Capital Consumption	Net Operating Surplus	Indirect Taxes	Less: Subsidies Received	Value Added
					All Producers							
1 Agriculture, hunting, forestry and fishing	13938	...	32331	565	4701	42133	14214	...	38446	632	5445	47847
A Agriculture and hunting	...	...	...	...	...	39859	...	...	...	...	...	45398
B Forestry and logging	...	...	...	...	...	555	...	...	...	...	...	642
C Fishing	...	...	...	...	...	1719	...	...	...	...	...	1866
2 Mining and quarrying a	...	...	...	...	...	...	...	...	...	...	...	...

Italy

4.3 Cost Components of Value Added
(Continued)

Thousand Million Italian lire

	1990						1991					
	Compensation of Employees	Capital Consumption	Net Operating Surplus	Indirect Taxes	Less: Subsidies Received	Value Added	Compensation of Employees	Capital Consumption	Net Operating Surplus	Indirect Taxes	Less: Subsidies Received	Value Added
3 Manufacturing a	162880	...	126871	10697	6635	293813	174216	...	123871	11022	7686	301423
A Manufacture of food, beverages and tobacco	11983	...	14088	8051	3684	30438	13072	...	15458	8158	4003	32685
B Textile, wearing apparel and leather industries	24543	...	21889	495	199	46728	26170	...	22081	533	254	48530
C Manufacture of wood and wood products, including furniture	7158	...	8636	253	123	15924	7768	...	9155	273	154	17042
D Manufacture of paper and paper products, printing and publishing	10041	...	8341	177	439	18120	10830	...	8131	193	335	18819
E Manufacture of chemicals and chemical petroleum, coal, rubber and plastic products	22048	...	15834	402	158	38126	23605	...	14737	436	156	38622
F Manufacture of non-metallic mineral products, except products of petroleum and coal	12046	...	9611	211	124	21744	12365	...	9486	228	141	21938
G Basic metal industries	7017	...	5734	89	396	12444	7334	...	4416	91	406	11435
H Manufacture of fabricated metal products, machinery and equipment	66391	...	41176	983	1490	107060	71296	...	38820	1071	2209	108978
I Other manufacturing industries	1653	...	1562	36	22	3229	1776	...	1587	39	28	3374
4 Electricity, gas and water	12620	...	18161	36567	340	67008	13738	...	21320	42051	290	76819
A Electricity, gas and steam	...	...	...	...	...	67008		...	...	...	...	76819
B Water works and supply	...	...	...	...	...	...		...	...	...	...	...
5 Construction	33496	...	42907	1003	704	76702	36828	...	46811	1116	937	83818
6 Wholesale and retail trade, restaurants and hotels	60935	...	179091	3301	2203	241124	67515	...	196105	4034	3284	264370
A Wholesale and retail trade	51502	...	148480	3076	1962	201096	57323	...	163033	3780	3075	221061
B Restaurants and hotels	9433	...	30611	225	241	40028	10192	...	33072	254	209	43309
7 Transport, storage and communication	47651	...	45818	1169	20294	74344	51689	...	51908	1328	21622	83303
A Transport and storage	34869	...	38319	1025	18127	56086	37875	...	42081	1164	19029	62091
B Communication	12782	...	7499	144	2167	18258	13814	...	9827	164	2593	21212
8 Finance, insurance, real estate and business services	84340	...	219395	16445	1109	319071	95718	...	237212	18386	1718	349598
9 Community, social and personal services		...						...				
Total, Industries	415860	...	664574	69747	35986	1114195	453918	...	715673	78569	40982	1207178
Producers of Government Services	165103	...	3917	...	...	169020	179613	...	4636	...	...	184249
Other Producers	11428	...	143	...	...	11571	13245	...	157	...	...	13402
Total	592391	...	668634	69747	35986	1294786	646776	...	720466	78569	40982	1404829
Less: Imputed bank service charge	...	...	61911	...	...	61911		...	67359	...	...	67359
Import duties	...	...	...	79191	...	79191	...	...	...	91983	...	91983
Value added tax	...	...	...	...	...	...	...	...	...	...	...	...
Total bc	592391	...	606723	148938	35986	1312066	646776	...	653107	170552	40982	1429453

	1992						1993					
	Compensation of Employees	Capital Consumption	Net Operating Surplus	Indirect Taxes	Less: Subsidies Received	Value Added	Compensation of Employees	Capital Consumption	Net Operating Surplus	Indirect Taxes	Less: Subsidies Received	Value Added
					All Producers								
1 Agriculture, hunting, forestry and fishing	15684	...	37061	627	6072	47300	15043	...	36821	1051	7456	45459
A Agriculture and hunting	...	...	...	...	...	43732	...	...	...	...	...	...
B Forestry and logging	...	...	...	...	...	678	...	...	...	...	...	...
C Fishing	...	...	...	...	...	1959	...	...	...	...	...	...
2 Mining and quarrying a	...	...	...	...	...	...	...	...	...	...	...	...

Italy

4.3 Cost Components of Value Added
(Continued)

Thousand Million Italian lire

		1992					1993					
		Compensation of Employees	Capital Consumption	Net Operating Surplus	Indirect Taxes	Less: Subsidies Received	Value Added	Compensation of Employees	Capital Consumption	Net Operating Surplus	Indirect Taxes	Less: Subsidies Received	Value Added
3	Manufacturing a	178393	...	125200	11457	6523	308527	176229	...	129636	15040	5966	314939
	A Manufacture of food, beverages and tobacco	13649	...	15768	8459	2910	34966	13915	...	16602	10457	2664	38310
	B Textile, wearing apparel and leather industries	26463	...	22846	556	279	49586	25984	...	25123	803	325	51585
	C Manufacture of wood and wood products, including furniture	7813	...	9630	286	177	17552	7634	...	10310	375	194	18125
	D Manufacture of paper and paper products, printing and publishing	11371	...	8302	206	385	19494	11576	...	9466	306	366	20982
	E Manufacture of chemicals and chemical petroleum, coal, rubber and plastic products	25071	...	14578	458	151	39956	24914	...	14184	734	222	39610
	F Manufacture of non-metallic mineral products, except products of petroleum and coal	12882	...	9940	245	148	22919	13173	...	7835	388	193	21203
	G Basic metal industries	7357	...	3447	94	156	10742	7108	...	3892	269	126	11143
	H Manufacture of fabricated metal products, machinery and equipment	71996	...	39013	1112	2286	109835	70166	...	40443	1648	1839	110418
	I Other manufacturing industries	1791	...	1676	41	31	3477	1759	...	1781	60	37	3563
4	Electricity, gas and water	14553	...	25019	47146	398	86320	14299	...	27370	47845	428	89086
	A Electricity, gas and steam	...	...	...	...	...	86320	...	...	...	...	...	89086
	B Water works and supply	...	...	...	...	...	...	...	...	...	...	...	...
5	Construction	38809	...	48920	1168	1472	87425	37237	...	49362	1513	1288	86824
6	Wholesale and retail trade, restaurants and hotels	72498	...	204142	4317	3550	277407	75340	...	206179	6080	3065	284534
	A Wholesale and retail trade	61438	...	168851	4036	3343	230982	63789	...	170367	5488	2851	236793
	B Restaurants and hotels	11060	...	35291	281	207	46425	11551	...	35812	592	214	47741
7	Transport, storage and communication	54358	...	54416	1439	19520	90693	54224	...	64809	2492	22876	98649
	A Transport and storage	40067	...	41114	1254	16079	66356	40146	...	49525	1943	20837	70777
	B Communication	14291	...	13302	185	3441	24337	14078	...	15284	549	2039	27872
8	Finance, insurance, real estate and business services	102760	...	264471	20807	1797	386241	105452	...	275476	31664	1945	410647
9	Community, social and personal services		...						...				
	Total, Industries	477055	...	759229	86961	39332	1283913	477824	...	789653	105685	43024	1330138
	Producers of Government Services	188266	...	5472	...	...	193738	193799	...	6402	...	...	200201
	Other Producers	14687	...	180	...	...	14867	15540	...	195	...	...	15735
	Total	680008	...	764881	86961	39332	1492518	687163	...	796250	105685	43024	1546074
	Less: Imputed bank service charge	...	...	79400	...	...	79400	...	...	79231	...	...	79231
	Import duties	...	...	...	91205	...	91205	...	...	...	93271	...	93271
	Value added tax	...	...	...	...	...	...	...	...	...	...	...	...
	Total bc	680008	...	685481	178166	39332	1504323	687163	...	717019	198956	43024	1560114

a) Item 'Mining and quarrying' is included in item 'Manufacturing'.
b) The branch breakdown used in this table (GDP by kind of activity) is according to the classification NACE/CLIO.
c) Column 'Consumption of fixed capital' is included in column 'Net operating surplus'.

Jamaica

Source. Reply to the United Nations National Accounts Questionnaire from the Department of Statistics, Kingston. Official estimates, together with information on concepts, sources and methods of estimation utilized are published annually by the Department in 'National Income and Product'.
General note. The estimates have been prepared in accordance with the United Nations System of National Accounts so far as the existing data would permit.

1.1 Expenditure on the Gross Domestic Product, in Current Prices

Million Jamaican dollars

	1980	1983	1984	1985	1986	1987	1988	1989	1990	1991	1992	1993
1 Government final consumption expenditure	966.2	1406.2	1541.5	1741.5	2136.3	2491.6	3028.1	3241.1	4308.3	5554.3	6878.1	12575.9
2 Private final consumption expenditure	3146.8	4874.2	6277.1	7771.7	8890.2	10366.5	12277.0	15598.2	18912.5	26901.3	43325.0	57978.7
3 Gross capital formation	759.2	1556.6	2163.8	2837.3	2574.0	3704.8	4998.2	6726.1	8514.0	12045.9	20694.5	33267.2
A Increase in stocks	69.1	120.2	183.2	256.1	142.2	160.1	132.9	188.0	152.1	221.4	200.3	454.4
B Gross fixed capital formation	690.1	1436.4	1980.6	2581.2	2431.8	3544.7	4865.3	6538.1	8361.9	11824.5	20494.2	32812.8
Residential buildings	333.5	690.2	941.9	1101.2	1146.2	1598.2	2330.0	3274.6	3415.2	...	...	...
Non-residential buildings a										...	...	...
Other construction and land improvement etc.	28.0	56.5	59.2	53.9	87.3	83.3	274.0	126.7	176.5	...	...	...
Other	328.6	689.7	979.5	1426.1	1198.4	1863.2	2261.6	3136.7	4770.2	...	...	...
4 Exports of goods and services	2425.8	2621.1	4955.5	6521.4	7294.0	8404.5	9167.8	11036.0	15856.3	25109.6	51086.7	57049.7
5 Less: Imports of goods and services	2524.9	3465.0	5579.6	7669.3	7001.3	8344.2	10040.9	13259.2	17114.2	25452.8	49444.8	65086.8
Equals: Gross Domestic Product a	4773.1	6993.1	9358.3	11202.6	13893.2	16623.2	19430.2	23342.2	30476.7	44158.4	72539.5	95784.7

a) Data in this table have not been revised, therefore they are not comparable with the data in other tables.

1.2 Expenditure on the Gross Domestic Product, in Constant Prices

Million Jamaican dollars

	1980	1983	1984	1985	1986	1987	1988	1989	1990	1991	1992	1993
	\multicolumn{8}{c}{At constant prices of:1974}				
1 Government final consumption expenditure	444.7	466.7	434.0	419.8	422.2	444.3	484.3	457.2	...	...	...	...
2 Private final consumption expenditure	1155.9	1310.8	1353.4	1328.9	1294.5	1423.1	1552.0	1635.2	...	...	...	...
3 Gross capital formation	233.4	311.2	280.4	282.0	238.4	300.3	350.8	417.0	...	...	...	...
A Increase in stocks	26.5	33.4	37.7	42.0	21.2	19.8	15.2	17.8	...	...	...	...
B Gross fixed capital formation	206.9	277.8	242.7	240.0	217.2	280.5	335.6	399.2	...	...	...	...
4 Exports of goods and services	648.8	634.9	747.0	830.5	886.3	967.4	930.7	993.5	...	...	...	...
5 Less: Imports of goods and services	695.2	747.6	884.7	1014.1	982.3	1103.9	1282.5	1363.1	...	...	...	...
Statistical discrepancy	41.4	-33.8	-4.4	-9.9	10.5	-47.8	-22.7	-35.3	...	...	...	...
Equals: Gross Domestic Product	1828.8	1942.2	1925.6	1836.1	1869.8	1983.4	2012.6	2104.4	...	...	...	...

1.3 Cost Components of the Gross Domestic Product

Million Jamaican dollars

	1980	1983	1984	1985	1986	1987	1988	1989	1990	1991	1992	1993
1 Indirect taxes, net	387.1	591.8	934.1	1036.3	2041.5	2531.3	2776.8	...	...	...	...	...
A Indirect taxes	493.8	802.3	1028.1	1079.5	2155.3	2669.7	2954.0	...	...	...	...	...
B Less: Subsidies	106.7	210.5	94.0	43.2	113.8	138.4	177.2	...	...	...	...	...
2 Consumption of fixed capital	421.6	627.1	867.9	1082.3	1148.4	1312.6	1371.2	...	...	...	...	...
3 Compensation of employees paid by resident producers to:	2428.5	3554.9	4308.9	4891.2	5580.1	6703.2	8012.1	...	...	...	...	...
A Resident households	2416.0	3516.9	4249.6	4738.0	5411.8	6505.7	7809.7	...	...	...	...	...
B Rest of the world	12.5	38.0	59.3	153.2	168.3	197.5	202.4	...	...	...	...	...
4 Operating surplus	1535.8	2219.3	3247.6	4192.7	4618.5	5455.1	6587.9	...	...	...	...	...
A Corporate and quasi-corporate enterprises	970.3	1393.1	2238.4	3015.6	3272.9	3845.2	4761.9	...	...	...	...	...
B Private unincorporated enterprises	565.5	826.2	1009.2	1177.1	1345.6	1609.9	1826.0	...	...	...	...	...
C General government	...	...	...	...	...	...	...	...	...	...	...	...
Equals: Gross Domestic Product	4773.0	6993.1	9358.5	11202.5	13388.5	16002.2	18748.0	...	...	...	...	...

1.4 General Government Current Receipts and Disbursements

Million Jamaican dollars

	1980	1983	1984	1985	1986	1987	1988	1989	1990	1991	1992	1993
	\multicolumn{12}{c}{Receipts}
1 Operating surplus	...	...	...	...	...	...	...	...	...	...	...	...
2 Property and entrepreneurial income	63.4	98.1	174.4	197.7	243.6	293.6	423.3	444.4	...	...	...	...
3 Taxes, fees and contributions	1280.6	1774.0	2456.3	2510.0	4148.7	5073.7	5604.9	6659.4	...	...	...	...
A Indirect taxes	493.8	802.8	1028.1	1079.5	2155.3	2669.7	2954.0	3555.7	...	...	...	...

Jamaica

1.4 General Government Current Receipts and Disbursements
(Continued)

Million Jamaican dollars

	1980	1983	1984	1985	1986	1987	1988	1989	1990	1991	1992	1993
B Direct taxes	726.4	876.8	1314.7	1308.2	1858.1	2251.4	2476.1	2908.7	...	...	...	...
C Social security contributions	48.0	73.4	73.6	79.1	81.2	85.2	99.8	98.1	...	...	...	...
D Compulsory fees, fines and penalties	12.4	21.0	39.9	43.2	54.1	67.4	75.0	96.9	...	...	...	...
4 Other current transfers	2.3	6.1	16.4	164.9	111.5	62.0	64.3	72.6	...	...	...	...
Total Current Receipts of General Government	1346.3	1878.1	2647.1	2872.6	4503.8	5429.3	6092.5	7176.3	...	...	...	...

Disbursements

	1980	1983	1984	1985	1986	1987	1988	1989	1990	1991	1992	1993
1 Government final consumption expenditure	966.2	1406.2	1541.5	1741.5	2121.1	2436.0	3015.6	3150.0	...	...	...	...
A Compensation of employees	667.7	994.7	1108.8	1152.1	1279.9	1423.5	1660.6	1842.9	...	...	...	...
B Consumption of fixed capital	...	...	...	...	...	...	...	...	...	...	...	...
C Purchases of goods and services, net	298.4	411.4	432.7	589.4	841.2	1012.5	1355.0	1307.1	...	...	...	...
D Less: Own account fixed capital formation	...	...	...	...	...	...	...	...	...	...	...	...
E Indirect taxes paid, net	0.1	0.1	-	-	-	-	-	-	...	...	...	...
2 Property income	349.2	599.5	1118.7	1547.8	2065.9	2686.2	2941.7	3342.7	...	...	...	...
3 Subsidies	106.7	210.5	94.0	43.2	113.8	138.4	177.2	199.7	...	...	...	...
4 Other current transfers	73.8	119.4	136.8	185.0	200.9	227.1	302.9	320.1	...	...	...	...
A Social security benefits	18.7	43.2	45.0	47.8	49.2	68.5	98.3	97.9	...	...	...	...
B Social assistance grants	26.9	38.5	39.1	77.6	80.3	82.4	120.5	126.6	...	...	...	...
C Other	28.2	37.7	52.7	59.6	71.4	76.2	84.1	95.6	...	...	...	...
5 Net saving	-149.6	-457.6	-243.9	-645.1	2.0	-58.4	-345.0	163.9	...	...	...	...
Total Current Disbursements and Net Saving of General Government	1346.3	1878.1	2647.1	2872.6	4503.8	5429.3	6092.5	7176.3	...	...	...	...

1.5 Current Income and Outlay of Corporate and Quasi-Corporate Enterprises, Summary

Million Jamaican dollars

	1980	1983	1984	1985	1986	1987	1988	1989	1990	1991	1992	1993

Receipts

	1980	1983	1984	1985	1986	1987	1988	1989	1990	1991	1992	1993
1 Operating surplus	970.3	1393.1	2238.4	3015.6	3272.8	3845.2	4761.9	5177.1	...	...	...	...
2 Property and entrepreneurial income received	550.4	1315.8	1932.3	2500.8	2790.6	3476.9	4018.1	5016.0	...	...	...	...
3 Current transfers	8.5	20.9	19.0	23.6	17.9	28.6	1715.5	984.1	...	...	...	...
Total Current Receipts	1529.2	2729.8	4189.7	5539.9	6081.3	7350.6	10495.4	11177.2	...	...	...	...

Disbursements

	1980	1983	1984	1985	1986	1987	1988	1989	1990	1991	1992	1993
1 Property and entrepreneurial income	712.6	1289.1	2276.4	3188.1	3165.3	3901.9	4379.2	5561.5	...	...	...	...
2 Direct taxes and other current payments to general government	528.4	461.7	789.9	704.0	1079.0	1254.2	1246.6	1432.3	...	...	...	...
3 Other current transfers	21.7	50.2	33.5	31.2	56.6	52.9	1722.7	1013.4	...	...	...	...
4 Net saving	266.5	928.8	1090.0	1616.6	1780.4	2141.6	3146.9	3170.0	...	...	...	...
Total Current Disbursements and Net Saving	1529.2	2729.8	4189.7	5539.9	6081.3	7350.6	10495.4	11177.2	...	...	...	...

1.6 Current Income and Outlay of Households and Non-Profit Institutions

Million Jamaican dollars

	1980	1983	1984	1985	1986	1987	1988	1989	1990	1991	1992	1993

Receipts

	1980	1983	1984	1985	1986	1987	1988	1989	1990	1991	1992	1993
1 Compensation of employees	2498.7	3639.7	4446.4	5034.3	5722.6	7027.7	8286.1	10106.0	...	...	...	...
A From resident producers	2428.5	3554.9	4308.9	4891.2	5580.1	6703.2	8012.1	9822.7	...	...	...	...
B From rest of the world	70.2	84.8	137.5	143.1	142.5	324.5	274.0	283.3	...	...	...	...
2 Operating surplus of private unincorporated enterprises	565.5	826.2	1009.2	1177.1	1345.6	1609.9	1826.0	2210.7	...	...	...	...
3 Property and entrepreneurial income	162.5	363.2	523.0	776.7	913.0	1064.5	1199.0	1355.8	...	...	...	...
4 Current transfers	293.3	617.2	684.9	1257.4	1252.8	1072.8	2797.0	2229.8	...	...	...	...
A Social security benefits	18.7	43.2	45.0	47.8	49.2	68.5	98.3	97.9	...	...	...	...
B Social assistance grants	26.9	38.5	39.1	77.6	80.3	82.4	120.5	126.6	...	...	...	...
C Other	247.7	535.5	600.8	1132.0	1123.3	921.9	2578.2	2005.3	...	...	...	...
Total Current Receipts	3520.1	5446.3	6663.5	8245.5	9234.1	10775.0	14108.2	15902.2	...	...	...	...

Disbursements

	1980	1983	1984	1985	1986	1987	1988	1989	1990	1991	1992	1993
1 Private final consumption expenditure	3146.8	4874.2	6277.1	7771.7	8400.7	9801.0	11458.4	13609.7	...	...	...	...

Jamaica

1.6 Current Income and Outlay of Households and Non-Profit Institutions
(Continued)

Million Jamaican dollars

	1980	1983	1984	1985	1986	1987	1988	1989	1990	1991	1992	1993
2 Property income	94.1	203.1	266.5	347.2	378.2	454.0	516.5	611.6	...	...	...	...
3 Direct taxes and other current transfers n.e.c. to general government	258.5	509.4	638.4	726.4	914.4	1149.9	1404.2	1671.3	...	...	...	...
A Social security contributions	48.0	73.4	73.6	79.1	81.2	85.2	99.8	98.1	...	...	...	...
B Direct taxes	198.9	416.3	528.2	609.0	785.2	1004.9	1237.9	1487.3	...	...	...	...
C Fees, fines and penalties	11.6	19.7	36.6	38.3	48.0	59.8	66.5	85.9	...	...	...	...
4 Other current transfers	71.5	117.8	132.2	405.5	359.6	285.3	227.1	243.8	...	...	...	...
5 Net saving	-50.8	-258.2	-650.7	-1005.2	-818.7	-915.2	502.0	-234.2	...	...	...	...
Total Current Disbursements and Net Saving	3520.1	5446.3	6663.5	8245.5	9234.1	10775.0	14108.2	15902.2	...	...	...	...

1.7 External Transactions on Current Account, Summary

Million Jamaican dollars

	1980	1983	1984	1985	1986	1987	1988	1989	1990	1991	1992	1993
Payments to the Rest of the World													
1 Imports of goods and services	2524.9	3465.0	5579.6	7669.3	7001.3	8344.2	9929.8	12133.9	...	...	...	...
A Imports of merchandise c.i.f.	2086.6	2846.4	4513.6	6152.6	5331.0	6802.0	8220.4	10686.6	...	...	...	...
B Other	438.2	618.6	1066.0	1516.7	1670.3	1542.2	1709.4	1447.3	...	...	...	...
2 Factor income to the rest of the world	424.4	484.8	1366.6	1956.9	1921.2	2460.8	2498.7	2983.9	...	...	...	...
A Compensation of employees	12.5	38.0	59.3	153.2	168.3	197.5	202.4	209.4	...	...	...	...
B Property and entrepreneurial income	411.9	446.8	1307.3	1803.7	1752.9	2263.3	2296.3	2774.5	...	...	...	...
By general government	151.4	167.5	527.2	912.5	1187.5	1347.1	1221.6	1291.4	...	...	...	...
By corporate and quasi-corporate enterprises	260.5	279.3	780.1	891.2	565.4	916.1	1074.6	1483.1	...	...	...	...
By other	...	...	...	...	...	...	...	...	...	...	...	...
3 Current transfers to the rest of the world	69.3	111.7	115.8	240.6	248.1	223.3	162.8	171.2	...	...	...	...
4 Surplus of the nation on current transactions	-271.4	-717.0	-1100.6	-1788.6	-461.9	-1224.3	-331.8	-2203.7	...	...	...	...
Payments to the Rest of the World and Surplus of the Nation on Current Transactions	2747.0	3344.5	5961.4	8078.2	8708.6	9803.9	12259.5	13085.3	...	...	...	...
Receipts From The Rest of the World													
1 Exports of goods and services	2425.8	2621.1	4955.5	6521.4	7294.0	8404.5	9197.0	10637.4	...	...	...	...
A Exports of merchandise f.o.b.	1715.0	1392.0	2732.5	3128.3	3225.9	3873.6	4829.7	5746.6	...	...	...	...
B Other	710.8	1229.1	2223.0	3393.1	4068.1	4530.9	4367.3	4890.7	...	...	...	...
2 Factor income from rest of the world	106.2	236.5	464.5	490.7	369.1	562.9	532.0	524.5	...	...	...	...
A Compensation of employees	82.7	122.8	196.7	296.3	310.8	522.0	476.4	492.6	...	...	...	...
B Property and entrepreneurial income	23.5	113.7	267.8	194.4	58.3	40.9	55.6	31.9	...	...	...	...
By general government	1.8	4.5	7.9	11.1	12.6	15.4	7.7	8.0	...	...	...	...
By corporate and quasi-corporate enterprises	21.7	109.1	259.9	183.3	45.7	25.5	47.9	23.8	...	...	...	...
By other	...	...	...	...	...	...	...	...	...	...	...	...
3 Current transfers from rest of the world	215.0	486.9	541.3	1066.1	1045.6	836.6	2530.6	1923.5	...	...	...	...
Receipts from the Rest of the World on Current Transactions	2747.0	3344.5	5961.4	8078.2	8708.6	9803.9	12259.5	13085.3	...	...	...	...

1.9 Gross Domestic Product by Institutional Sectors of Origin

Million Jamaican dollars

	1980	1983	1984	1985	1986	1987	1988	1989	1990	1991	1992	1993
Domestic Factor Incomes Originating													
1 General government	...	...	...	...	...	...	...	...	...	...	...	...
2 Corporate and quasi-corporate enterprises	970.3	1393.1	2238.4	3015.6	3272.8	3845.2	4761.9	5177.1	...	...	...	...
A Non-financial	1056.9	1465.9	2335.6	3176.5	3602.2	4257.2	5229.7	5879.3	...	...	...	...
B Financial	-86.6	-72.8	-97.2	-160.9	-329.4	-412.0	-467.8	-702.2	...	...	...	...

Jamaica

1.9 Gross Domestic Product by Institutional Sectors of Origin
(Continued)

Million Jamaican dollars

	1980	1983	1984	1985	1986	1987	1988	1989	1990	1991	1992	1993
3 Households and private unincorporated enterprises	2994.0	4381.1	5318.1	6068.3	6925.7	8313.1	9838.1	12033.4	...	...	...	...
A Owner-occupied housing	42.6	64.4	73.7	87.1	93.8	100.9	110.6	120.2	...	...	...	...
B Subsistence production	2951.4	4316.7	5244.4	5981.2	6831.9	8212.2	9727.5	11913.2	...	...	...	...
C Other									...	...	...	...
4 Non-profit institutions serving households	...	...	...	...	...	...	...	...	...	...	...	...
Subtotal: Domestic Factor Incomes	3964.3	5774.2	7556.5	9083.9	10198.5	12158.3	14600.0	17210.5	...	...	...	...
Indirect taxes, net	387.1	591.8	934.1	1036.3	2041.5	2531.3	2776.8	3356.0	...	...	...	...
A Indirect taxes	493.8	802.3	1028.1	1079.5	2155.3	2669.7	2954.0	3555.7	...	...	...	...
B Less: Subsidies	106.7	210.5	94.0	43.2	113.8	138.4	177.2	199.7	...	...	...	...
Consumption of fixed capital	421.6	627.1	867.9	1082.3	1148.4	1312.6	1371.2	1748.4	...	...	...	...
Gross Domestic Product	4773.1	6993.2	9358.4	11202.6	13388.5	16002.1	18748.0	22314.9	...	...	...	...

1.10 Gross Domestic Product by Kind of Activity, in Current Prices

Million Jamaican dollars

	1980	1983	1984	1985	1986	1987	1988	1989	1990	1991	1992	1993
1 Agriculture, hunting, forestry and fishing	392.2	450.5	544.2	671.5	1048.8	1276.3	1392.6	1622.6	1973.1	3072.9	5777.4	8043.2
2 Mining and quarrying	678.0	283.7	664.2	569.3	901.8	1146.7	1727.3	2199.3	2831.3	4816.6	6845.0	6961.2
3 Manufacturing	794.1	1398.5	1731.5	2240.9	2959.5	3473.4	3804.6	4576.3	5922.9	8445.2	14239.2	17666.7
4 Electricity, gas and water	75.2	169.6	287.7	357.6	569.1	612.1	600.8	531.3	809.3	810.2	1836.1	2193.3
5 Construction	279.1	597.7	841.5	1014.2	1086.1	1405.0	2021.1	2672.4	3586.8	5564.7	9381.8	12341.2
6 Wholesale and retail trade, restaurants and hotels	996.4	1543.0	2125.3	2682.9	2794.2	3471.1	3967.0	4783.5	6419.0	9284.7	17137.8	22706.5
7 Transport, storage and communication	244.3	417.7	693.5	931.3	1309.8	1553.5	1742.0	2076.6	2641.3	3537.9	5581.5	7630.2
8 Finance, insurance, real estate and business services	635.1	1216.1	1398.8	1642.3	2022.0	2366.6	2803.9	3386.0	4284.9	5603.2	9017.1	10771.6
9 Community, social and personal services	166.8	237.3	282.9	343.9	596.7	712.6	766.8	933.5	1220.8	1713.4	2869.2	3838.0
Total, Industries	4261.2	6314.1	8569.6	10453.9	13288.0	16017.3	18826.1	22781.5	29689.4	42848.8	72685.1	92151.9
Producers of Government Services	667.8	994.8	1108.8	1152.2	1238.2	1407.1	1646.4	1908.8	2570.2	3445.6	4406.3	9062.5
Other Producers	...	...	...	...	111.3	117.9	148.2	181.5	229.2	273.8	427.5	505.2
Subtotal	4929.0	7308.9	9678.4	11606.1	14637.6	17542.3	20620.7	24871.8	32488.8	46568.2	77518.9	01719.6
Less: Imputed bank service charge	155.8	315.8	320.2	403.5	744.4	919.1	1190.5	1529.7	2012.1	2409.9	4979.5	5934.9
Plus: Import duties	...	...	...	...	...	...	...	...	...	...	...	...
Plus: Value added tax	...	...	...	...	...	...	...	...	...	...	...	...
Equals: Gross Domestic Product	4773.2	6993.1	9358.2	11202.6	13893.2	16623.2	19430.2	23342.2	30476.7	44158.4	72539.5	95784.7

1.11 Gross Domestic Product by Kind of Activity, in Constant Prices

Million Jamaican dollars

	1980	1983	1984	1985	1986	1987	1988	1989	1990	1991	1992	1993
	\multicolumn{4}{At constant prices of: 1974}					1986			
1 Agriculture, hunting, forestry and fishing	152.7	154.2	169.7	163.7	160.3 / 1048.8	1102.9	1065.3	968.5	1080.2	1078.3	1217.0	1323.8
2 Mining and quarrying	162.7	117.7	118.5	95.4	101.6 / 901.8	955.8	913.0	1238.1	1520.5	1606.7	1566.0	1575.2
3 Manufacturing	281.4	310.8	297.8	299.0	306.1 / 2959.5	3127.7	3296.3	3537.5	3668.3	3378.2	3410.2	3312.6
4 Electricity, gas and water	23.6	26.8	26.8	27.5	31.3 / 569.1	615.1	617.2	685.4	732.6	745.5	778.2	809.3
5 Construction	98.6	122.4	113.7	104.3	107.4 / 1086.1	1240.6	1424.6	1680.5	1707.2	1718.2	1725.5	1716.9
6 Wholesale and retail trade, restaurants and hotels	310.5	342.5	341.0	314.9	335.1 / 2794.2	3100.9	3131.1	3237.1	3387.3	3462.1	3645.3	3791.2
7 Transport, storage and communication	124.3	133.7	137.8	140.5	154.0 / 1309.8	1465.0	1532.2	1592.5	1647.2	1718.7	1802.9	1939.1
8 Finance, insurance, real estate and business services	324.6	376.4	360.1	346.6	372.4 / 2022.0	2154.2	2374.4	2648.8	2889.6	3258.6	3449.5	3493.9
9 Community, social and personal services	72.5	75.8	76.6	78.9	80.9 / 596.7	649.6	627.4	675.8	721.5	701.2	709.1	746.7

Jamaica

1.11 Gross Domestic Product by Kind of Activity, in Constant Prices
(Continued)

Million Jamaican dollars

	1980	1983	1984	1985	1986	1987	1988	1989	1990	1991	1992	1993
			At constant prices of:									
			1974						1986			
Total, Industries	1550.9	1660.3	1642.0	1570.8	1649.1 13288.0	14411.8	14981.4	16264.1	17354.4	17667.5	18303.7	18708.7
Producers of Government Services	351.5	370.0	354.4	333.8	321.6 1238.2	1243.3	1286.6	1270.4	1243.7	1222.3	1226.7	1217.3
Other Producers	...	...	...	...	... 111.3	114.9	119.2	113.6	121.4	114.3	102.8	88.3
Subtotal	1902.4	2030.3	1996.4	1904.6	1970.7 14637.6	15770.0	16387.2	17648.1	18719.5	19004.1	19633.2	20014.3
Less: Imputed bank service charge	73.5	88.2	70.9	68.5	103.7 744.4	804.0	989.5	1197.5	1371.0	1565.9	1954.0	2123.6
Plus: Import duties	...	...	...	...	...	...	...	...	...	...	...	...
Plus: Value added tax	...	...	...	...	...	...	...	...	...	...	...	...
Equals: Gross Domestic Product	1828.9	1942.1	1925.5	1836.1	1867.0 13893.2	14965.9	15397.7	16450.7	17348.6	17438.2	17679.0	17890.6

1.12 Relations Among National Accounting Aggregates

Million Jamaican dollars

	1980	1983	1984	1985	1986	1987	1988	1989	1990	1991	1992	1993
Gross Domestic Product	4773.1	6993.2	9358.4	11202.6	13388.5	16002.1	18748.0	22224.1	...	...	...	...
Plus: Net factor income from the rest of the world	-318.2	-248.3	-902.1	-1466.2	-1552.1	-1897.9	-1966.7	-2459.4	...	...	...	...
Factor income from the rest of the world	106.2	236.5	464.5	490.7	369.1	562.9	532.0	524.5	...	...	...	...
Less: Factor income to the rest of the world	424.4	484.8	1366.6	1956.9	1921.2	2460.8	2498.7	2983.9	...	...	...	...
Equals: Gross National Product	4454.9	6744.9	8456.3	9736.4	11836.4	14104.2	16781.3	19764.7	...	...	...	...
Less: Consumption of fixed capital	421.6	627.1	867.9	1082.3	1148.4	1312.6	1371.2	1748.4	...	...	...	...
Equals: National Income	4033.3	6117.8	7588.4	8654.1	10688.0	12791.6	15410.1	18016.3	...	...	...	...
Plus: Net current transfers from the rest of the world	145.7	375.2	425.5	825.5	797.5	613.3	2367.8	1752.3	...	...	...	...
Current transfers from the rest of the world	215.0	486.9	541.3	1066.1	1045.6	836.6	2530.6	1923.5	...	...	...	...
Less: Current transfers to the rest of the world	69.3	111.7	115.8	240.6	248.1	223.3	162.8	171.2	...	...	...	...
Equals: National Disposable Income	4179.0	6493.0	8013.9	9479.6	11485.5	13404.9	17777.9	19768.6	...	...	...	...
Less: Final consumption	4113.0	6280.4	7818.6	9513.2	10521.8	12237.1	14474.0	16997.2	...	...	...	...
Equals: Net Saving	66.0	212.6	195.3	-33.6	963.7	1167.8	3303.9	2771.4	...	...	...	...
Less: Surplus of the nation on current transactions	-271.5	-717.0	-1100.6	-1788.6	-461.9	-1224.3	-331.8	-2203.7	...	...	...	...
Equals: Net Capital Formation	337.5	929.6	1295.9	1755.0	1425.6	2392.1	3635.7	4975.1	...	...	...	...

2.5 Private Final Consumption Expenditure by Type and Purpose, in Current Prices

Million Jamaican dollars

	1980	1983	1984	1985	1986	1987	1988	1989	1990	1991	1992	1993
	Final Consumption Expenditure of Resident Households
1 Food, beverages and tobacco	1551.7	2264.4	3110.2	3922.4	4473.5	5127.3	5644.9	...	...	...	...	...
A Food	1222.0	1743.3	2388.3	2988.6	3448.4	3883.8	4334.1	...	...	...	...	...
B Non-alcoholic beverages	33.2	71.3	85.1	120.7	169.2	185.3	189.4	...	...	...	...	...
C Alcoholic beverages	132.9	195.9	293.2	354.6	402.1	481.9	509.0	...	...	...	...	...
D Tobacco	163.5	253.8	343.6	458.5	453.8	576.3	612.3	...	...	...	...	...
2 Clothing and footwear	107.4	192.6	248.2	349.9	459.9	586.5	655.3	...	...	...	...	...
3 Gross rent, fuel and power	425.5	664.1	950.8	1190.4	1289.7	1431.7	1486.2	...	...	...	...	...
A Fuel and power	154.6	233.4	409.0	530.4	612.3	703.6	689.0	...	...	...	...	...
B Other	270.9	430.7	541.9	660.0	677.5	728.0	797.2	...	...	...	...	...
4 Furniture, furnishings and household equipment and operation	189.1	371.9	464.7	540.2	579.0	679.3	774.1	...	...	...	...	...
A Household operation	94.8	192.5	238.1	292.6	333.0	388.4	445.4	...	...	...	...	...
B Other	94.2	179.5	226.6	247.6	246.0	290.8	328.7	...	...	...	...	...
5 Medical care and health expenses	76.7	125.1	167.4	225.8	269.6	330.0	400.5	...	...	...	...	...
6 Transport and communication	508.2	743.8	1023.5	1345.5	1419.1	1551.4	1746.3	...	...	...	...	...
A Personal transport equipment	298.8	441.8	597.8	769.8	786.0	830.8	932.5	...	...	...	...	...

Jamaica

2.5 Private Final Consumption Expenditure by Type and Purpose, in Current Prices
(Continued)

Million Jamaican dollars

	1980	1983	1984	1985	1986	1987	1988	1989	1990	1991	1992	1993
B Other	209.4	302.0	425.7	575.7	633.1	720.6	813.9	...	...	...	...	...
7 Recreational, entertainment, education and cultural services	123.5	196.4	221.2	240.2	257.9	280.9	317.9	...	...	...	...	...
A Education	8.8	12.4	15.2	13.8	17.3	19.8	28.4	...	...	...	...	...
B Other	114.7	184.0	206.0	226.4	240.6	261.1	289.5	...	...	...	...	...
8 Miscellaneous goods and services	573.2	1061.9	1554.1	1956.2	2222.0	2647.8	2756.9	...	...	...	...	...
A Personal care	115.9	196.8	249.2	347.7	389.0	455.7	504.9	...	...	...	...	...
B Expenditures in restaurants, cafes and hotels	267.5	516.4	863.3	1138.4	1371.6	1596.0	1553.6	...	...	...	...	...
C Other	189.8	348.7	441.6	470.1	461.4	596.1	698.4	...	...	...	...	...
Statistical discrepancy	4.1	93.4	100.1	145.9	193.3	235.9	326.0	...	...	...	...	...
Total Final Consumption Expenditure in the Domestic Market by Households, of which	3558.8	5713.6	7840.1	9916.5	11164.1	12870.7	14108.0	...	...	...	...	...
Plus: Direct purchases abroad by resident households	26.4	88.3	109.4	210.0	228.3	294.3	362.0	...	...	...	...	...
Less: Direct purchases in the domestic market by non-resident households	438.4	927.7	1672.4	2354.8	2895.2	3316.0	3081.7	...	...	...	...	...
Equals: Final Consumption Expenditure of Resident Households [a]	3146.8	4874.2	6277.1	7771.7	8497.2	9849.0	11388.3	...	...	...	...	...

Final Consumption Expenditure of Private Non-profit Institutions Serving Households

	1980	1983	1984	1985	1986	1987	1988	1989	1990	1991	1992	1993
Equals: Final Consumption Expenditure of Private Non-profit Organisations Serving Households	...	...	...	.	...	...	...	...	...	...	...	...
Private Final Consumption Expenditure [b]	3146.8	4874.2	6277.1	7771.7	8497.2	9849.0	11388.3	...	...	...	...	...

a) Item 'Final consumption expenditure of resident households' includes consumption expenditure of private non-profit institutions serving households.   b) Data for this table have not been revised, therefore, data for some years are not comparable with those of other tables.

2.6 Private Final Consumption Expenditure by Type and Purpose, in Constant Prices

Million Jamaican dollars

	1980	1983	1984	1985	1986	1987	1988	1989	1990	1991	1992	1993

At constant prices of:1974

Final Consumption Expenditure of Resident Households

	1980	1983	1984	1985	1986	1987	1988	1989	1990	1991	1992	1993
1 Food, beverages and tobacco	519.5	560.0	607.3	616.7	583.5	638.3	649.7	...	...	...	...	...
A Food	401.6	451.8	490.7	501.7	481.7	522.0	537.1	...	...	...	...	...
B Non-alcoholic beverages	8.6	11.5	11.3	13.2	15.1	14.0	13.5	...	...	...	...	...
C Alcoholic beverages	46.9	42.8	48.0	44.8	41.1	46.3	46.8	...	...	...	...	...
D Tobacco	62.3	53.9	57.4	57.0	45.6	56.0	52.3	...	...	...	...	...
2 Clothing and footwear	34.7	46.2	52.8	63.2	69.0	78.4	81.3	...	...	...	...	...
3 Gross rent, fuel and power	184.2	199.6	217.1	216.9	216.6	229.5	234.1	...	...	...	...	...
A Fuel and power	43.0	43.9	47.9	48.3	50.2	56.6	54.2	...	...	...	...	...
B Other	141.2	155.7	169.2	168.7	166.4	173.0	179.9	...	...	...	...	...
4 Furniture, furnishings and household equipment and operation	65.0	95.4	89.2	82.4	82.7	91.3	96.8	...	...	...	...	...
A Household operation	42.4	66.7	60.4	56.6	58.6	65.9	70.5	...	...	...	...	...
B Other	22.6	28.7	28.8	25.9	24.1	25.4	26.3	...	...	...	...	...
5 Medical care and health expenses	41.6	38.6	39.7	39.7	42.8	46.1	50.4	...	...	...	...	...
6 Transport and communication	147.3	178.4	197.7	209.6	218.7	237.6	257.7	...	...	...	...	...
A Personal transport equipment	84.3	102.5	109.3	110.8	112.1	116.5	122.2	...	...	...	...	...
B Other	63.0	75.9	88.3	98.8	106.6	121.1	135.5	...	...	...	...	...
7 Recreational, entertainment, education and cultural services	59.7	86.6	93.6	96.7	98.3	102.1	110.3	...	...	...	...	...
A Education	4.9	5.8	3.9	2.1	2.6	2.9	4.2	...	...	...	...	...
B Other	54.8	80.8	89.7	94.6	95.7	99.2	106.1	...	...	...	...	...
8 Miscellaneous goods and services	227.0	279.1	314.0	290.8	306.1	341.6	326.5	...	...	...	...	...
A Personal care	39.6	43.5	42.7	45.9	43.4	47.1	47.2	...	...	...	...	...
B Expenditures in restaurants, cafes and hotels	90.9	132.0	163.8	149.2	170.1	194.1	175.8	...	...	...	...	...
C Other	96.6	103.6	107.5	95.7	92.6	100.4	103.5	...	...	...	...	...

Jamaica

2.6 Private Final Consumption Expenditure by Type and Purpose, in Constant Prices
(Continued)

Million Jamaican dollars

	1980	1983	1984	1985	1986	1987	1988	1989	1990	1991	1992	1993
					At constant prices of:1974							
Statistical discrepancy	1.3	22.0	18.4	21.3	24.6	28.1	35.9	...	...	...	...	...
Total Final Consumption Expenditure in the Domestic Market by Households, of which	1280.2	1505.8	1629.9	1637.5	1642.2	1793.1	1842.7	...	...	...	...	...
Plus: Direct purchases abroad by resident households	8.2	20.8	20.1	30.6	29.0	35.1	39.9	...	...	...	...	...
Less: Direct purchases in the domestic market by non-resident households	132.5	215.8	296.6	339.2	376.7	398.1	340.0	...	...	...	...	...
Equals: Final Consumption Expenditure of Resident Households [a]	1155.9	1310.8	1353.4	1328.9	1294.5	1430.0	1542.5	...	...	...	...	...
	Final Consumption Expenditure of Private Non-profit Institutions Serving Households											
Equals: Final Consumption Expenditure of Private Non-profit Organisations Serving Households	...	...	...	...	...	...	...	...	...	...	...	...
Private Final Consumption Expenditure [b]	1155.9	1310.8	1353.4	1328.9	1294.5	1430.0	1542.5	...	...	...	...	...

a) Item 'Final consumption expenditure of resident households' includes consumption expenditure of private non-profit institutions serving households.

b) Data for this table have not been revised, therefore, data for some years are not comparable with those of other tables.

Japan

General note. The preparation of national accounts statistics in Japan is undertaken by the Economic Research Institute of the Economic Planning Agency, Tokyo. The official estimates are published in 'Annual Report on National Accounts'. The following presentation of sources and methods is mainly based on information from 'A System of National Accounts in Japan' published by the Economic Planning Agency. The estimates are generally in accordance with the classifications and definitions recommended in the United Nations System of National Accounts (SNA, 1968). Input-output tables have been published by the Management and Coordination Agency (former Administrative Management Agency). The following tables have been prepared from successive replies to the United Nations national accounts questionnaire. When the scope and coverage of the estimates differ for conceptual or statistical reasons from the definitions and classifications recommended in SNA, a footnote is indicated to the relevant tables.

Sources and methods:

(a) Gross domestic product. Gross domestic product is estimated mainly through the production approach.

(b) Expenditure on the gross domestic product. Using the commodity flow method, output, intermediate consumption by industry, household final consumption expenditure, gross capital formation, exports and imports are estimated for each of approximately 2,200 commodities. Shipments estimates are derived directly or indirectly from the statistics such as 'Crop Survey', 'Census of Manufactures', 'Current Production Statistics Survey', 'Establishment Census' and 'Census of Commerce'. The distribution channels and the constant coefficients such as the distribution ratios, the transportation fee rates and the trade margin rates are decided for each of the commodities based on the information of the 'Input-output Table'. Services produced and consumed by the producers of government services and private non-profit services to households are estimated separately based on the settlement of accounts of governments, 'Survey of Private Non-profit Institutions' and so on. Gross domestic expenditure is obtained by adding up final consumption expenditure, gross capital formation, increase in stocks and current external transactions. Exports and Imports are estimated by the estimation method for external transactions, which rearranges the 'Balance of Payments' in consideration of its consistency with the 'Balance of Payments'. For final consumption expenditure of households, calendar-year figure is estimated by the commodity flow method. Each commodity is classified into one of the elements of a 43-objects x 5-uses matrix. Each element of the matrix corresponds to one of the 4 types of expenditure. Quarterly figures are estimated by distributing the calendar-year figure through expenditure approach which uses 'Survey of Farm Household Economy', 'Family Income and Expenditure Survey' and 'National Survey of Family Income and Expenditure'. For gross capital formation, quarterly and sectorial figures are estimated by breaking down the calendar-year figure estimated by the commodity flow method, on the basis of the quarterly and sectorial figures estimated through expenditure approach which uses settlements of accounts of government, 'Financial Statements of Corporations by Industry' and so on for gross fixed capital formation. For increase in stocks, special accounts for food administration, 'Financial Statements of Corporations by Industry' are used. GDP at constant prices is estimated mainly using price indexes called basic unit deflators which correspond to the approximately 400 commodities aggregated from the approximately 2,200 commodities used for the commodity flow method. Series at constant prices are obtained by dividing the nominal values of the 400 commodities by the basic unit deflators for each demand item. In other words, constant value is estimated using Paasche-type deflator weighted by 400 commodities. Government services and private non-profit services to households are estimated using deflators by activities which correspond respectively to 6 activities of government services and 3 activities of private non-profit services to households.

(c) Cost-structure of the gross domestic product. Wages and salaries are estimated separately for the three groups of agriculture, forestry and fisheries, government services, and other industries. Concerning the other industries, quarterly cash allowances to employees by industries are calculated by multiplying the per head wage by the number of employees. In this case, the number of employees is based on the 'Population Census' conducted every five years and is interpolated in the mid-year of a five-year period by trends observed from the 'Labor Force Survey', while the cash allowances per head is mainly based on the 'Monthly Labor Survey'. Cash allowances to officers are estimated by multiplying the number of officers by the difference between the per head allowances of both officers and regular employees, which are obtained from the 'Financial Statements of Corporations by Industry', and the per head allowances of regular employees. Employers' contributions to social security schemes are estimated on the basis of the operational reports of these schemes. Employers' contributions to others and payments in kind are estimated on the basis of settlements of accounts of the central government and local governments data on taxation, business and housing survey data on payments for housing. The operating surplus is estimated through production approach (value-added method), and is distributed to each institutional sector according to the ratios of operating profits to the total by kind of income-earning subject (after inventory valuation adjustment). The ratios are estimated on the basis of statistical data such as 'Financial Statements of Corporations by Industry'. Consumption of fixed capital consists of loss from wear and tear (depreciation) and estimated damage from fire, typhoons, floods and other accidents. Depreciation is estimated on the basis of 'Financial Statements of Corporations by Industry', 'Financial Statistics of Local Public Enterprises' and so on. Accidental damage is estimated making use of settlements of accounts of insurance companies and so on. Indirect taxes and subsidies are estimated on the basis of settlements of accounts of central and local governments.

(d) Gross domestic product by kind of economic activity. The gross domestic product by kind of economic activity is prepared at market prices, i.e. producers' values. The output of each of the 82 industry groups is estimated from the V table --- a make matrix for commodity by activity --- of which the control total is given as the output of the 2200 commodities estimated by the commodity flow method. The intermediate input of each industry group is estimated from the U table --- a use matrix for commodity by activity in the base year which is compiled from 'Input-output Table' and the V table, and from the U table in the mid year which is separately compiled from the information of the cost structure estimated for about 4 or 15 items every year. The value-added and its component items by industry are estimated by substracting the intermediate input from the output. The output, intermediate input, value-added and its component items by the producers of government services and by the producers of private non-profit services to households are separately estimated using the settlement of accounts of government, 'Survey of Private Non-profit Institutions' and so on. Gross domestic product by industry at constant prices is estimated by the double deflation technique. The output by industry is estimated from the V table at constant prices which is obtained by dividing the output of each commodity by its output deflator. The intermediate input by industry is estimated from the U table at constant prices which is obtained by dividing the intermediate input of each commodity by its input deflator.

1.1 Expenditure on the Gross Domestic Product, in Current Prices

Thousand Million Japanese yen

		1980	1983	1984	1985	1986	1987	1988	1989	1990	1991	1992	1993
1	Government final consumption expenditure	23568	27996	29449	30685	32388	32975	34184	36275	38807	41232	43258	44666
2	Private final consumption expenditure	141324	169687	178631	188760	195969	204585	215122	228483	243628	255084	264824	270919
	A Households	139506	167509	176267	186235	193308	201973	212237	225427	240493	251540	261201	267125
	B Private non-profit institutions serving households	1818	2179	2364	2525	2661	2612	2885	3056	3135	3544	3623	3795
3	Gross capital formation	77434	79067	84262	90198	92953	99850	113705	125855	139054	146700	143838	139476
	A Increase in stocks	1613	186	1011	2159	1643	690	2630	3089	2322	3271	1631	661
	B Gross fixed capital formation	75821	78881	83251	88040	91310	99160	111074	122766	136733	143429	142207	138815
	Residential buildings	16205	15049	14983	15446	16568	20301	22927	23912	26146	24850	24040	25173
	Non-residential buildings	13631	14112	14583	15170	15123	15210	16514	19955	22618	25954	27473	25978
	Other construction and land improvement etc.	21257	21410	21845	22057	22967	24447	26903	28266	30651	33173	33595	33918
	Other	24727	28309	31840	35366	36652	39202	44730	50633	57318	59453	57099	53746
4	Exports of goods and services	32886	39275	45066	46307	38090	36210	37483	42352	45920	46810	47409	44244
5	Less: Imports of goods and services	35036	34258	36865	35532	24791	25195	29065	36768	42872	38529	36184	33333
	Equals: Gross Domestic Product	240177	281767	300542	320419	334609	348425	371428	396197	424537	451297	463145	465972

Japan

1.2 Expenditure on the Gross Domestic Product, in Constant Prices

Thousand Million Japanese yen

	1980	1983	1984	1985	1986	1987	1988	1989	1990	1991	1992	1993
	\multicolumn{12}{c}{At constant prices of:1985}
1 Government final consumption expenditure	26628	29320	30107	30623	31986	32124	32815	33482	34113	34650	35602	36201
2 Private final consumption expenditure	161925	177661	182529	188703	195079	203336	213983	223174	231948	237027	241024	243484
A Households	159968	175466	180199	186243	192525	200837	211283	220420	229270	234046	238020	240294
B Private non-profit institutions serving households	1958	2196	2330	2459	2554	2499	2700	2754	2678	2982	3003	3190
3 Gross capital formation	80344	80049	84614	90239	94051	101970	116126	127336	137210	143307	139683	136489
A Increase in stocks	1421	130	973	2160	1780	876	2979	3692	2627	3763	1701	947
B Gross fixed capital formation	78923	79919	83641	88079	92271	101094	113147	123644	134583	139544	137981	135541
Residential buildings	16917	15512	15154	15446	16646	20137	22432	22516	23587	21755	20533	21169
Non-residential buildings	14638	14564	14773	15179	15176	15237	16169	18572	20104	22317	23288	22000
Other construction and land improvement etc.	23052	21972	22003	22070	23068	24510	26395	27612	29190	30463	30278	30473
Other	24316	27871	31711	35385	37381	41210	48151	54943	61701	65008	63882	61900
4 Exports of goods and services	32235	38358	44035	46426	44153	44191	47295	51575	55343	58203	61216	62022
5 Less: Imports of goods and services	34410	32687	36098	35594	36453	39305	46652	54858	59572	57150	56902	58430
Equals: Gross Domestic Product	266722	292701	305187	320397	328816	342316	363567	380709	399043	416038	420622	419765

1.3 Cost Components of the Gross Domestic Product

Thousand Million Japanese yen

	1980	1983	1984	1985	1986	1987	1988	1989	1990	1991	1992	1993
1 Indirect taxes, net	14095	16664	19137	21250	21535	24961	27469	29058	30568	31116	33996	33724
A Indirect taxes	17688	20631	22943	24900	25213	28379	30878	32162	35212	34968	37301	37199
B Less: Subsidies	3593	3968	3806	3650	3678	3419	3409	3104	4644	3852	3304	3475
2 Consumption of fixed capital	30701	38426	40778	43615	46170	48861	52306	57941	62820	68387	72622	73348
3 Compensation of employees paid by resident producers to:	130398	157357	166120	173892	181959	189069	200111	214850	233374	251690	260792	266951
A Resident households	130154	156946	165718	173505	181703	188789	199880	214576	233060	251340	260430	266632
B Rest of the world	244	411	401	387	256	281	232	274	313	350	362	319
4 Operating surplus	64757	69233	74395	81501	84787	86625	93250	96390	99797	100680	94240	89188
A Corporate and quasi-corporate enterprises	31555	33521	37043	40610	42695	42723	47960	50703	53172	53122	44395	42645
B Private unincorporated enterprises	33202	35712	37352	40890	42092	43901	45290	45687	46626	47559	49845	46543
C General government	...	...	...	...	...	...	...	...	...	...	...	...
Statistical discrepancy [a]	225	88	114	161	159	-1091	-1708	-2041	-2022	-576	1495	2762
Equals: Gross Domestic Product	240176	281767	300543	320419	334609	348425	371429	396197	424537	451297	463145	465972

a) Item 'Other adjustments' refers to inventory valuation adjustment.

1.4 General Government Current Receipts and Disbursements

Thousand Million Japanese yen

	1980	1983	1984	1985	1986	1987	1988	1989	1990	1991	1992	1993
	\multicolumn{12}{c}{Receipts}
1 Operating surplus	...	...	...	...	...	...	...	...	...	...	...	...
2 Property and entrepreneurial income	4626	6686	7464	8369	9346	10009	11112	11617	13188	15119	14582	14640
3 Taxes, fees and contributions	61338	76426	82823	89909	93970	103111	110997	119874	132987	138965	140754	137811
A Indirect taxes	17688	20631	22943	24900	25213	28379	30878	32162	35212	34968	37301	37199
B Direct taxes	25876	32605	35291	38485	40639	44615	48329	53901	58367	62253	59519	54757
C Social security contributions	17513	22896	24270	26184	27761	29694	31363	33387	38957	41264	43436	45331
D Compulsory fees, fines and penalties	261	294	319	338	357	423	426	424	452	480	498	524
4 Other current transfers	250	393	421	487	543	603	665	749	846	939	1035	1069
Total Current Receipts of General Government	66214	83505	90707	98764	103860	113723	122774	132240	147021	155023	156370	153521
	\multicolumn{12}{c}{Disbursements}
1 Government final consumption expenditure	23568	27996	29449	30685	32388	32975	34184	36275	38807	41232	43258	44666

Japan

1.4 General Government Current Receipts and Disbursements
(Continued)

Thousand Million Japanese yen

	1980	1983	1984	1985	1986	1987	1988	1989	1990	1991	1992	1993
A Compensation of employees	19077	21973	23083	24172	...	...	...	...	...	...	...	...
B Consumption of fixed capital	1393	1892	2012	2078	...	...	...	...	...	...	...	...
C Purchases of goods and services, net	3068	4096	4318	4399	...	...	...	...	...	...	...	...
D Less: Own account fixed capital formation	...	...	...	...	...	...	...	...	...	...	...	...
E Indirect taxes paid, net	30	35	36	36	...	...	...	...	...	...	...	...
2 Property income	7569	11944	13337	14318	14912	15346	15671	16023	16820	17377	17733	17724
A Interest	7500	11848	13229	14212	14797	15225	15537	15871	16645	17180	17512	17489
B Net land rent and royalties	69	96	108	106	115	121	134	151	175	198	221	235
3 Subsidies	3593	3968	3806	3650	3678	3419	3409	3104	4644	3852	3304	3475
4 Other current transfers	25269	33081	34426	36456	39163	42136	44089	45813	51063	52115	55937	59574
A Social security benefits	18919	25883	27596	28960	31478	34235	35922	37389	42370	42954	46229	49380
B Social assistance grants	5250	5764	5349	5957	6073	6185	6313	6377	6453	6633	6913	7157
C Other	1100	1434	1480	1539	1615	1716	1854	2047	2240	2528	2794	3037
5 Net saving	6214	6516	9690	13655	13718	19848	25420	31025	35688	40447	36138	28081
Total Current Disbursements and Net Saving of General Government	66214	83505	90707	98764	103860	113723	122774	132240	147021	155023	156370	153521

1.5 Current Income and Outlay of Corporate and Quasi-Corporate Enterprises, Summary

Thousand Million Japanese yen

	1980	1983	1984	1985	1986	1987	1988	1989	1990	1991	1992	1993
					Receipts							
1 Operating surplus	31555	33521	37043	40610	42695	42723	47960	50703	53172	53122	44395	42645
2 Property and entrepreneurial income received	59808	79574	87628	93248	95839	100099	108846	127152	152406	161128	146887	135867
3 Current transfers	3074	3801	3972	4111	4030	3832	3926	4054	4648	6055	6064	6420
Total Current Receipts	94437	116896	128643	137969	142564	146654	160733	181910	210226	220304	197346	184932
					Disbursements							
1 Property and entrepreneurial income	72721	92399	100033	105751	109776	112061	120891	142131	171055	183571	165366	153556
2 Direct taxes and other current payments to general government	11082	13246	15095	17381	17790	19690	22247	26168	25199	24785	22657	20070
3 Other current transfers	3793	4705	4946	5207	5220	5131	5397	5610	6224	7858	7930	8579
4 Net saving	6840	6545	8568	9630	9778	9773	12198	8001	7748	4089	1393	2727
Total Current Disbursements and Net Saving	94437	116896	128643	137969	142564	146654	160733	181910	210226	220304	197346	184932

1.6 Current Income and Outlay of Households and Non-Profit Institutions

Thousand Million Japanese yen

	1980	1983	1984	1985	1986	1987	1988	1989	1990	1991	1992	1993
					Receipts							
1 Compensation of employees	130368	157299	166026	173815	182006	189125	200192	214957	233507	251781	261046	267152
A From resident producers	130154	156946	165718	173505	181703	188789	199880	214576	233060	251340	260430	266632
B From rest of the world	214	354	308	311	303	336	312	381	447	441	616	520
2 Operating surplus of private unincorporated enterprises	33202	35712	37352	40890	42090	43901	45290	45687	46626	47559	49845	46543
3 Property and entrepreneurial income	24880	30201	31356	32551	34108	33275	33358	37603	44809	50043	46557	44059
4 Current transfers	41593	52806	54611	57685	61363	65112	68937	70948	77843	81395	86454	89838
A Social security benefits	18919	25883	27596	28960	31476	34235	35922	37389	42370	42954	46229	49380
B Social assistance grants	6214	7274	6866	7691	7930	8228	8545	8677	8844	9146	9429	9370
C Other	16460	19649	20149	21034	21957	22649	24470	24882	26629	29295	30797	31088
Total Current Receipts	230043	276019	289346	304942	319568	331413	347777	369194	402785	430778	443902	447592
					Disbursements							
1 Private final consumption expenditure	141324	169687	178631	188760	195969	204585	215122	228483	243628	255084	264824	270919

Japan

1.6 Current Income and Outlay of Households and Non-Profit Institutions
(Continued)

Thousand Million Japanese yen

	1980	1983	1984	1985	1986	1987	1988	1989	1990	1991	1992	1993
2 Property income	9071	11750	12479	12886	13424	13977	14534	15476	19730	22242	20913	19107
3 Direct taxes and other current transfers n.e.c. to general government	32568	42549	44784	47627	50967	55042	57872	61544	72576	79212	80796	80542
A Social security contributions	17513	22896	24270	26184	27761	29694	31363	33387	38957	41264	43436	45331
B Direct taxes	14899	19470	20323	21248	22995	25098	26268	27925	33354	37650	37039	34865
C Fees, fines and penalties	156	183	192	194	211	251	240	232	265	298	321	346
4 Other current transfers	16108	19458	19871	20873	21775	22652	24397	24662	26393	28714	30092	29686
5 Net saving	30971	32575	33580	34796	37434	35156	35852	39029	40458	45525	47277	47338
Total Current Disbursements and Net Saving	230043	276019	289346	304942	319568	331413	347777	369194	402785	430778	443902	447592

1.7 External Transactions on Current Account, Summary

Thousand Million Japanese yen

	1980	1983	1984	1985	1986	1987	1988	1989	1990	1991	1992	1993
Payments to the Rest of the World												
1 Imports of goods and services	35036	34258	36865	35532	24791	25195	29065	36768	42872	38529	36184	33333
A Imports of merchandise c.i.f. [a]	29153	27902	30328	28856	19356	18708	21330	26906	31598	27670	25374	23481
B Other	5883	6356	6538	6676	5435	6487	7735	9863	11274	10859	10810	9852
2 Factor income to the rest of the world	2898	3900	4448	4631	4108	5553	7822	11911	15588	16577	14784	13001
A Compensation of employees	244	411	401	387	256	281	232	274	313	350	362	319
B Property and entrepreneurial income	2654	3489	4047	4244	3853	5272	7590	11637	15275	16227	14422	12681
3 Current transfers to the rest of the world	342	359	373	355	292	463	497	475	491	462	584	660
A Indirect taxes to supranational organizations	...	...	...	...	...	...	...	...	...	...	...	...
B Other current transfers	342	359	373	355	292	463	497	475	491	462	584	660
4 Surplus of the nation on current transactions	-2481	5083	8467	11660	14306	12697	10364	8100	5638	11171	15089	14780
Payments to the Rest of the World and Surplus of the Nation on Current Transactions	35794	43600	50153	52177	43497	43908	47748	57254	64589	66740	66640	61774
Receipts From The Rest of the World												
1 Exports of goods and services	32886	39275	45066	46307	38090	36210	37483	42352	45920	46810	47409	44244
A Exports of merchandise f.o.b.	29022	34964	40381	41555	34575	32490	33398	37372	40651	41438	42049	39133
B Other	3865	4311	4685	4752	3515	3720	4085	4980	5269	5372	5361	5111
2 Factor income from rest of the world	2820	4211	4953	5768	5337	7607	10124	14761	18520	19767	19052	17381
A Compensation of employees	214	354	308	311	303	336	312	381	447	441	616	520
B Property and entrepreneurial income	2606	3858	4646	5458	5035	7271	9811	14380	18073	19326	18436	16861
3 Current transfers from rest of the world	87	114	134	102	70	92	141	142	149	163	179	149
A Subsidies from supranational organisations	...	...	...	...	...	...	...	...	...	...	...	...
B Other current transfers	87	114	134	102	70	92	141	142	149	163	179	149
Receipts from the Rest of the World on Current Transactions	35794	43600	50153	52177	43497	43908	47748	57254	64589	66740	66640	61774

a) Imports of merchandise c.i.f. is not estimated in the Balance of Payments in Japan. Therefore, valuation basis is f.o.b.

1.8 Capital Transactions of The Nation, Summary

Thousand Million Japanese yen

	1980	1983	1984	1985	1986	1987	1988	1989	1990	1991	1992	1993
Finance of Gross Capital Formation												
Gross saving	74727	84062	92616	101697	107100	113638	125777	135996	146714	158448	157431	151494
1 Consumption of fixed capital	30701	38426	40778	43615	46170	48861	52306	57941	62820	68387	72622	73348
A General government	1392	1892	2012	2077	2144	2245	2325	2458	2508	2525	2624	2779
B Corporate and quasi-corporate enterprises	18682	23745	25301	27467	29445	31385	33832	38125	41698	45954	49070	48917
C Other	10626	12788	13464	14071	14581	15232	16150	17358	18614	19908	20928	21652
2 Net saving	44026	45636	51838	58082	60930	64777	73470	78056	83894	90061	84809	78146

Japan

1.8 Capital Transactions of The Nation, Summary
(Continued)

Thousand Million Japanese yen

	1980	1983	1984	1985	1986	1987	1988	1989	1990	1991	1992	1993
A General government	6214	6516	9690	13655	13718	19848	25420	31025	35688	40447	36138	28081
B Corporate and quasi-corporate enterprises	6840	6545	8568	9630	9778	9773	12198	8001	7748	4089	1393	2727
Public	-176	-1737	-1947	-2024	-2161	-1414	-784	2481	3716	-14	-1671	-3521
Private	7016	8283	10516	11654	11940	11187	12981	5520	4032	4103	3064	6249
C Other	30971	32575	33580	34796	37434	35156	35852	39029	40458	45525	47277	47338
Less: Surplus of the nation on current transactions	-2481	5083	8467	11660	14306	12697	10364	8100	5638	11171	15089	14780
Statistical discrepancy	225	88	114	161	159	-1091	-1708	-2041	-2022	-576	1495	2762
Finance of Gross Capital Formation	77434	79067	84262	90198	92953	99850	113705	125855	139054	146700	143838	139476
Gross Capital Formation												
Increase in stocks	1613	186	1011	2159	1643	690	2630	3089	2322	3271	1631	661
Gross fixed capital formation	75821	78881	83251	88040	91310	99160	111074	122766	136733	143429	142207	138815
1 General government	14685	15475	15164	15168	16048	17536	18860	19808	21549	23125	26449	30803
2 Corporate and quasi-corporate enterprises	38003	41456	46109	50006	51537	54235	61842	71154	81750	87410	82592	74937
A Public	8203	8105	7942	6480	6223	6194	6187	6074	6556	7164	8711	9685
B Private	29800	33351	38167	43526	45314	48041	55656	65080	75194	80245	73881	65252
3 Other	23133	21950	21979	22865	23726	27389	30372	31805	33433	32894	33166	33075
Gross Capital Formation	77434	79067	84262	90198	92953	99850	113705	125855	139054	146700	143838	139476

1.9 Gross Domestic Product by Institutional Sectors of Origin

Thousand Million Japanese yen

	1980	1983	1984	1985	1986	1987	1988	1989	1990	1991	1992	1993
Domestic Factor Incomes Originating												
1 General government	19077	21973	23083	24172	25357	26061	26952	28346	30136	31654	...	...
2 Corporate and quasi-corporate enterprises	172131	199845	212283	225760	235527	243590	259904	275979	295759	312997	...	...
3 Households and private unincorporated enterprises											...	...
4 Non-profit institutions serving households	3947	4772	5150	5461	5864	6044	6506	6915	7276	7719	...	...
Subtotal: Domestic Factor Incomes	195155	226590	240515	255393	266746	275694	293361	311240	333171	352370	355032	356138
Indirect taxes, net	14095	16664	19137	21250	21535	24961	27469	29058	30568	31116	33996	33724
A Indirect taxes	17688	20631	22943	24900	25213	28379	30878	32162	35212	34968	37301	37199
B Less: Subsidies	3593	3968	3806	3650	3678	3419	3409	3104	4644	3852	3304	3475
Consumption of fixed capital	30701	38426	40778	43615	46170	48861	52306	57941	62820	68387	72622	73348
Statistical discrepancy	225	89	114	161	159	-1091	-1708	-2041	-2022	-576	1495	2762
Gross Domestic Product	240176	281767	300543	320419	334609	348425	371429	396197	424537	451297	463145	465972

1.10 Gross Domestic Product by Kind of Activity, in Current Prices

Thousand Million Japanese yen

	1980	1983	1984	1985	1986	1987	1988	1989	1990	1991	1992	1993
1 Agriculture, hunting, forestry and fishing	8847	9516	9957	10214	9975	9768	9754	10132	10553	10520	10178	9977
2 Mining and quarrying	1363	1071	1008	958	992	976	1058	1054	1279	1304	1329	1235
3 Manufacturing	70232	81748	89245	94673	96262	99297	106649	114455	123443	131336	129594	124878
4 Electricity, gas and water	6580	8792	9542	10305	11332	11337	11387	11279	11489	12328	12943	13458
5 Construction	22506	23273	23993	25381	26886	30129	34009	37985	42127	45021	46596	47865
6 Wholesale and retail trade, restaurants and hotels [a]	36792	41556	41977	42836	43567	45540	48010	50377	54501	57830	59279	58389
7 Transport, storage and communication	14787	18238	19958	21087	21910	22871	24220	26301	27100	28618	28902	29390
8 Finance, insurance, real estate and business services	35095	42779	45646	49330	52443	56962	61668	67005	69529	72026	74308	75346
9 Community, social and personal services [a]	28063	37286	40622	46391	49787	51881	54993	60562	67313	71949	75761	76218
Total, Industries	224266	264260	281948	301175	313154	328761	351749	379150	407334	430932	438890	436756
Producers of Government Services	20499	23899	25131	26285	27535	28342	29314	30847	32688	34222	35661	36812

Japan

1.10 Gross Domestic Product by Kind of Activity, in Current Prices
(Continued)

Thousand Million Japanese yen

	1980	1983	1984	1985	1986	1987	1988	1989	1990	1991	1992	1993
Other Producers	4285	5342	5824	6218	6653	6923	7425	7905	8354	8830	9294	9638
Subtotal	249051	293502	312903	333678	347342	364027	388488	417902	448377	473983	483845	483206
Less: Imputed bank service charge	10413	13010	13811	14773	13938	15677	16568	20450	22322	22670	23061	20720
Plus: Import duties	1313	1187	1337	1353	1046	1166	1217	2252	2713	2872	2887	2549
Plus: Value added tax	...	...	...	...	...	...	...	-1467	-2208	-2312	-2021	-1825
Plus: Other adjustments [b]	225	88	114	161	159	-1091	-1708	-2041	-2022	-576	1495	2762
Equals: Gross Domestic Product	240176	281767	300543	320419	334609	348425	371429	396197	424537	451297	463145	465972

a) Restaurants and hotels are included in item 'Community, social and personal services'.
b) Item 'Other adjustments' refers to inventory valuation adjustment.

1.11 Gross Domestic Product by Kind of Activity, in Constant Prices

Thousand Million Japanese yen

	1980	1983	1984	1985	1986	1987	1988	1989	1990	1991	1992	1993
	\multicolumn{12}{c}{At constant prices of:1985}
1 Agriculture, hunting, forestry and fishing	9135	9863	10242	10214	10006	10325	9995	10328	10381	9595	9806	9361
2 Mining and quarrying	1182	1103	1009	958	996	937	960	890	1117	1097	1075	1030
3 Manufacturing	71482	81521	88426	94673	92113	98860	107999	116619	125492	133421	130809	127510
4 Electricity, gas and water	8181	9433	9570	10305	10437	10684	11431	11953	12731	13640	13983	14391
5 Construction	26326	24750	24714	25381	26297	29124	32071	33623	35641	36500	36691	37138
6 Wholesale and retail trade, restaurants and hotels [a]	38069	41861	42020	42836	44251	46963	49685	51484	55256	57255	58971	59060
7 Transport, storage and communication	16999	18706	19976	21087	21368	21937	23274	24637	25355	26256	26216	26830
8 Finance, insurance, real estate and business services	39493	43136	46349	49330	52511	56306	60162	64338	64922	65420	66060	65266
9 Community, social and personal services [a]	34686	40812	42835	46391	47808	47992	49711	52738	56913	58836	59659	58640
Total, Industries	245552	271185	285140	301175	305787	323129	345287	366611	387807	402020	403270	399225
Producers of Government Services	23487	25360	25864	26285	26503	26779	27000	27163	27262	26948	27309	27538
Other Producers	5065	5679	5969	6218	6439	6626	6917	7128	7213	7398	7695	7956
Subtotal	274103	302224	316973	333678	338729	356534	379205	400901	422282	436367	438274	434719
Less: Imputed bank service charge	10414	11981	13706	14773	14833	17105	18127	21948	23539	23794	24429	22390
Plus: Import duties	1274	1134	1317	1353	1583	1830	2044	2707	2505	3213	3665	3544
Plus: Value added tax	...	...	...	...	...	...	...	...	...	...	...	...
Plus: Other adjustments [b]	1758	1324	603	139	3337	1056	445	-951	-2205	253	3112	3892
Equals: Gross Domestic Product	266722	292701	305187	320397	328816	342316	363567	380709	399043	416038	420622	419765

a) Restaurants and hotels are included in item 'Community, social and personal services'.
b) Item 'Other adjustments' refers to inventory valuation adjustment.

1.12 Relations Among National Accounting Aggregates

Thousand Million Japanese yen

	1980	1983	1984	1985	1986	1987	1988	1989	1990	1991	1992	1993
Gross Domestic Product	240176	281767	300543	320419	334609	348425	371429	396197	424537	451297	463145	465972
Plus: Net factor income from the rest of the world	-77	311	505	1137	1229	2054	2302	2849	2932	3190	4268	4381
Factor income from the rest of the world	2820	4211	4953	5768	5337	7607	10124	14761	18520	19767	19052	17381
Less: Factor income to the rest of the world	2898	3900	4448	4631	4108	5553	7822	11911	15588	16577	14784	13001
Equals: Gross National Product	240098	282078	301048	321556	335838	350479	373731	399046	427469	454487	467413	470353
Less: Consumption of fixed capital	30701	38426	40778	43615	46170	48861	52306	57941	62820	68387	72622	73348
Equals: National Income [a]	209172	243564	260157	277780	289508	302708	323133	343147	366671	386676	393296	394243
Plus: Net current transfers from the rest of the world	-254	-245	-239	-253	-222	-372	-356	-333	-342	-299	-405	-511
Current transfers from the rest of the world	87	114	134	102	70	92	141	142	149	163	179	149
Less: Current transfers to the rest of the world	342	359	373	355	292	463	497	475	491	462	584	660
Equals: National Disposable Income	208918	243319	259918	277527	289287	302337	322777	342814	366329	386376	392891	393732
Less: Final consumption	164892	197684	208080	219445	228357	237560	249306	264758	282435	296316	308082	315586
Equals: Net Saving	44026	45636	51838	58082	60930	64777	73470	78056	83894	90060	84809	78146
Less: Surplus of the nation on current transactions	-2481	5083	8467	11660	14306	12697	10364	8100	5638	11171	15089	14780
Statistical discrepancy	225	88	114	161	159	-1091	-1708	-2041	-2022	-576	1495	2762
Equals: Net Capital Formation	46733	40641	43485	46583	46783	50989	61398	67915	76235	78314	71215	66128

a) Item 'National income' includes a statistical discrepancy.

Japan

2.1 Government Final Consumption Expenditure by Function, in Current Prices

Thousand Million Japanese yen — Fiscal year beginning 1 April

		1980	1983	1984	1985	1986	1987	1988	1989	1990	1991	1992	1993
1	General public services [a]	6461	7496	7859	8137	8859	8934	9108	9793	10614	11257	11855	12264
2	Defence	2066	2560	2744	2961	3093	3219	3415	3643	3944	4105	4237	4224
3	Public order and safety [a]	...	...	...	...	...	...	...	...	...	...	...	...
4	Education	8991	10367	10845	11262	11655	11961	12417	12922	13693	14206	14694	14895
5	Health	908	1154	1276	1212	1230	1267	1362	1513	1691	1873	2006	2126
6	Social security and welfare	1208	1457	1562	1726	1819	1888	1931	2155	2338	2498	2671	2826
7	Housing and community amenities	1397	1654	1697	1796	1857	1936	2036	2225	2431	2663	2858	3037
8	Recreational, cultural and religious affairs	472	624	670	718	758	800	860	934	1023	1110	1202	1295
9	Economic services	2532	2890	3034	3108	3162	3116	3228	3375	3592	3748	3947	3956
10	Other functions	88	103	121	119	125	121	208	174	194	210	217	365
	Total Government Final Consumption Expenditure	24122	28304	29808	31038	32560	33241	34565	36734	39520	41671	43686	44987

a) Item 'Public order and safety' is included in item 'General public services'.

2.2 Government Final Consumption Expenditure by Function, in Constant Prices

Thousand Million Japanese yen — Fiscal year beginning 1 April

At constant prices of: 1985

		1980	1983	1984	1985	1986	1987	1988	1989	1990	1991	1992	1993
1	General public services [a]	7240	7813	7943	7990	8880	8614	8587	8847	9121	9199	9529	9724
2	Defence	2279	2602	2668	2821	3045	3161	3325	3380	3524	3541	3560	3524
3	Public order and safety [a]	...	...	...	...	...	...	...	...	...	...	...	...
4	Education	10104	10943	11172	11304	11412	11575	11763	11744	11786	11676	11857	11812
5	Health	1039	1285	1417	1346	1219	1248	1323	1410	1520	1625	1722	1823
6	Social security and welfare	1349	1524	1588	1707	1778	1831	1835	1957	2019	2056	2163	2263
7	Housing and community amenities	1528	1716	1725	1797	1871	1942	2028	2115	2209	2349	2497	2652
8	Recreational, cultural and religious affairs	517	636	666	699	755	796	847	879	922	964	1029	1101
9	Economic services	2764	2934	2999	3005	3097	3040	3112	3117	3163	3168	3279	3253
10	Other functions	99	108	123	117	121	117	211	167	178	187	189	303
	Total Government Final Consumption Expenditure	26917	29559	30300	30786	32178	32323	33030	33618	34443	34766	35825	36454

a) Item 'Public order and safety' is included in item 'General public services'.

2.3 Total Government Outlays by Function and Type

Thousand Million Japanese yen — Fiscal year beginning 1 April

		Final Consumption Expenditures Total	Compensation of Employees	Other	Subsidies	Other Current Transfers & Property Income	Total Current Disbursements	Gross Capital Formation	Other Capital Outlays	Total Outlays
	1980									
1	General public services [a]	6461	5248	1213	46	...	...	859	...	...
2	Defence	2066	1133	934	-	...	...	-	...	...
3	Public order and safety [a]	...	...	...	...	...	...	...	...	...
4	Education	8991	7397	1594	1	...	...	2005	...	...
5	Health	908	1636	-728	150	...	...	419	...	...
6	Social security and welfare	1208	1173	35	126	...	...	297	...	...
7	Housing and community amenities	1397	824	573	387	...	...	2746	...	...
8	Recreation, culture and religion	472	250	222	11	...	...	462	...	...
9	Economic services	2532	1647	885	2933	...	...	8134	...	...
10	Other functions	88	74	14	-	...	...	18	...	...
	Total	24122	19380	4742	3654	34031	61807	14938	2514	79259
	1985									
1	General public services [a]	8137	6507	1630	73	...	...	840	...	...
2	Defence	2961	1470	1491	-	...	...	-	...	...
3	Public order and safety [a]	...	...	...	...	...	...	...	...	...
4	Education	11262	9255	2007	5	...	...	1420	...	...
5	Health	1212	2222	-1010	164	...	...	353	...	...
6	Social security and welfare	1726	1525	202	96	...	...	265	...	...
7	Housing and community amenities	1796	1056	740	610	...	...	3048	...	...
8	Recreation, culture and religion	718	359	359	16	...	...	454	...	...
9	Economic services	3108	2019	1089	2733	...	...	8964	...	...
10	Other functions	119	98	20	-	...	...	13	...	...
	Total	31038	24511	6528	3697	51939	86674	15358	2744	104776

Japan

2.3 Total Government Outlays by Function and Type
(Continued)

Thousand Million Japanese yen
Fiscal year beginning 1 April

		Final Consumption Expenditures Total	Compensation of Employees	Other	Subsidies	Other Current Transfers & Property Income	Total Current Disbursements	Gross Capital Formation	Other Capital Outlays	Total Outlays
	1990									
1	General public services a	10614	8281	2333	120	...	...	1773	...	...
2	Defence	3944	1781	2163	...	...	...	...	...	...
3	Public order and safety a	...	...	...	...	...	...	...	...	...
4	Education	13693	11323	2370	17	...	...	1308	...	...
5	Health	1691	2858	-1167	217	...	...	516	...	...
6	Social security and welfare	2338	2015	323	212	...	...	423	...	...
7	Housing and community amenities	2431	1328	1103	661	...	...	4819	...	...
8	Recreation, culture and religion	1023	488	535	20	...	...	1006	...	...
9	Economic services	3592	2358	1234	2154	...	...	11870	...	...
10	Other functions	194	80	114	-	...	...	116	...	...
	Total	39520	30511	9009	3401	66701	109622	21831	4713	136166
	1991									
1	General public services a	11257	8697	2560	131	...	...	1715	...	...
2	Defence	4105	1835	2270	...	...	...	...	...	...
3	Public order and safety a	...	...	...	...	...	...	...	...	...
4	Education	14206	11788	2418	19	...	...	1945	...	...
5	Health	1873	3047	-1174	239	...	...	591	...	...
6	Social security and welfare	2498	2137	361	146	...	...	495	...	...
7	Housing and community amenities	2663	1409	1254	687	...	...	5410	...	...
8	Recreation, culture and religion	1110	527	583	26	...	...	1057	...	...
9	Economic services	3748	2448	1300	2039	...	...	12457	...	...
10	Other functions	210	86	124	-	...	...	130	...	...
	Total	41671	31973	9698	3286	70491	115449	23800	5322	144571
	1992									
1	General public services a	11855	9017	2838	118	...	...	2136	...	...
2	Defence	4237	1927	2310	...	...	...	...	...	...
3	Public order and safety a	...	...	...	...	...	...	...	...	...
4	Education	14694	12107	2587	21	...	...	2217	...	...
5	Health	2006	3226	-1220	255	...	...	716	...	...
6	Social security and welfare	2670	2257	413	129	...	...	625	...	...
7	Housing and community amenities	2858	1469	1389	727	...	...	6627	...	...
8	Recreation, culture and religion	1202	563	639	30	...	...	1244	...	...
9	Economic services	3947	2576	1371	2036	...	...	14326	...	...
10	Other functions	217	89	128	-	...	...	141	...	...
	Total	43686	33231	10455	3317	74301	121304	28033	6077	155414
	1993									
1	General public services a	12264	9346	2918	120	...	...	2168	...	...
2	Defence	4224	1954	2270	...	...	...	...	...	...
3	Public order and safety a	...	...	...	...	...	...	...	...	...
4	Education	14895	12228	2667	22	...	...	2334	...	...
5	Health	2126	3343	-1217	275	...	...	923	...	...
6	Social security and welfare	2826	2333	493	158	...	...	733	...	...
7	Housing and community amenities	3037	1521	1516	767	...	...	7695	...	...
8	Recreation, culture and religion	1295	596	699	33	...	...	1330	...	...
9	Economic services	3956	2521	1435	2048	...	...	15850	...	...
10	Other functions	365	209	156	...	...	...	158	...	...
	Total	44987	34051	10936	3423	77923	126334	31191	6320	163845

a) Item 'Public order and safety' is included in item 'General public services'.

Japan

2.5 Private Final Consumption Expenditure by Type and Purpose, in Current Prices

Thousand Million Japanese yen

	1980	1983	1984	1985	1986	1987	1988	1989	1990	1991	1992	1993
				Final Consumption Expenditure of Resident Households								
1 Food, beverages and tobacco	34045	39037	40193	41537	42043	42825	43888	46090	48877	51213	52327	52636
2 Clothing and footwear	10126	11458	11925	12490	12873	13374	13549	14289	15287	16123	15703	15272
3 Gross rent, fuel and power	25033	30949	32994	35082	36113	37919	40036	42751	45952	49080	52095	54975
4 Furniture, furnishings and household equipment and operation	8112	9939	10675	11478	11819	12329	12939	13591	14659	15484	15634	15620
5 Medical care and health expenses	13778	17683	18438	19549	20737	22053	23126	24056	25472	26775	28420	29763
6 Transport and communication	14072	17049	17582	18120	18620	19351	20904	22560	24370	25027	25187	25588
7 Recreational, entertainment, education and cultural services	12221	15624	17031	18259	19303	20069	21115	22351	23881	25323	26667	28210
8 Miscellaneous goods and services	21198	24893	26546	28819	30818	32784	34628	37030	38877	39721	42192	42439
Total Final Consumption Expenditure in the Domestic Market by Households, of which	138585	166632	175383	185335	192327	200704	210185	222719	237375	248746	258225	264503
A Durable goods	8184	10106	10846	11443	12568	13551	15176	15916	16790	17656	16675	16627
B Semi-durable goods	18192	20650	21396	22562	23157	23804	24470	26058	28402	29647	29789	29545
C Non-durable goods	46194	54524	56466	58361	58006	58595	59849	62886	67235	70100	71908	72647
D Services	66015	81352	86675	92969	98595	104753	110691	117859	124949	131344	139853	145685
Plus: Direct purchases abroad by resident households	1089	1100	1144	1196	1247	1591	2439	3158	3651	3274	3443	3028
Less: Direct purchases in the domestic market by non-resident households	167	223	260	297	266	322	387	450	533	480	468	
Equals: Final Consumption Expenditure of Resident Households	139506	167509	176267	186235	193308	201973	212237	225427	240493	251540	261201	267125
			Final Consumption Expenditure of Private Non-profit Institutions Serving Households									
Equals: Final Consumption Expenditure of Private Non-profit Organisations Serving Households	1818	2179	2364	2525	2661	2612	2885	3056	3135	3544	3623	3795
Private Final Consumption Expenditure	141324	169687	178631	188760	195969	204585	215122	228483	243628	255084	264824	270919

2.6 Private Final Consumption Expenditure by Type and Purpose, in Constant Prices

Thousand Million Japanese yen

	1980	1983	1984	1985	1986	1987	1988	1989	1990	1991	1992	1993
				At constant prices of: 1985								
				Final Consumption Expenditure of Resident Households								
1 Food, beverages and tobacco	39112	41158	40706	41537	41863	43023	43941	45413	46572	46714	47323	47102
2 Clothing and footwear	11582	12055	12256	12490	12632	12952	13024	13223	13499	13574	12851	12447
3 Gross rent, fuel and power	29668	32526	33796	35082	35703	36992	38471	40173	42018	43666	45269	46726
4 Furniture, furnishings and household equipment and operation	8603	10049	10721	11478	11835	12438	13087	13642	14827	15695	15629	15840
5 Medical care and health expenses	16024	19571	19923	19549	20216	21036	22007	22637	23623	24691	25129	25835
6 Transport and communication	15874	17366	17757	18120	18904	19626	21349	23043	24699	25024	25072	25177
7 Recreational, entertainment, education and cultural services	13916	16227	17353	18259	19193	20193	21631	22539	23337	24682	25048	26229
8 Miscellaneous goods and services	23852	25586	26773	28819	30697	32395	34042	35515	36376	36087	37475	36835
Total Final Consumption Expenditure in the Domestic Market by Households, of which	158630	174539	179286	185335	191041	198655	207553	216186	224950	230133	233796	236192
A Durable goods	8107	9947	10724	11443	12967	14496	16962	18363	19503	21164	20034	20639
B Semi-durable goods	20294	21451	21855	22562	22896	23362	23847	24762	26222	26396	26041	25618
C Non-durable goods	52248	56535	56910	58361	58502	60025	61457	63515	65893	66252	67483	67697

Japan

2.6 Private Final Consumption Expenditure by Type and Purpose, in Constant Prices
(Continued)

Thousand Million Japanese yen

	1980	1983	1984	1985	1986	1987	1988	1989	1990	1991	1992	1993
					At constant prices of:1985							
D Services	77980	86605	89796	92969	96676	100772	105287	109546	113332	116322	120237	122237
Plus: Direct purchases abroad by resident households	1528	1159	1178	1205	1749	2504	4114	4670	4822	4348	4643	4462
Less: Direct purchases in the domestic market by non-resident households	191	232	265	296	265	321	384	436	502	436	419	360
Equals: Final Consumption Expenditure of Resident Households	159968	175466	180199	186243	192525	200837	211283	220420	229270	234046	238020	240294
	Final Consumption Expenditure of Private Non-profit Institutions Serving Households
Equals: Final Consumption Expenditure of Private Non-profit Organisations Serving Households	1958	2196	2330	2459	2554	2499	2700	2754	2678	2982	3003	3190
Private Final Consumption Expenditure	161925	177661	182529	188703	195079	203336	213983	223174	231948	237027	241024	243484

2.7 Gross Capital Formation by Type of Good and Owner, in Current Prices

Thousand Million Japanese yen

	1980				1985				1990			
	TOTAL	Total Private	Public Enterprises	General Government	TOTAL	Total Private	Public Enterprises	General Government	TOTAL	Total Private	Public Enterprises	General Government
Increase in stocks, total	1613	1913	-300	...	2159	1810	349	...	2322	2244	78	...
1 Goods producing industries	2080	...	...	...	820	...	...	...	1817	...	...	...
A Materials and supplies	141	...	...	...	-226	...	...	...	194	...	...	...
B Work in progress	1193	...	...	...	347	...	...	...	1055	...	...	...
C Livestock, except breeding stocks, dairy cattle, etc.	...	...	...	...	...	...	...	...	...	...	...	...
D Finished goods	746	...	...	...	698	...	...	...	568	...	...	...
2 Wholesale and retail trade	-467	...	...	...	1339	...	...	...	505	...	...	...
3 Other, except government stocks	...	...	...	...	...	...	...	...	...	...	...	...
4 Government stocks	...	...	...	...	...	...	...	...	...	...	...	...
Gross Fixed Capital Formation, Total	75821	52933	8203	14685	88040	66391	6480	15168	136733	108628	6556	21549
1 Residential buildings	16205	15317	889	...	15446	14633	813	...	26146	25218	929	...
2 Non-residential buildings	13631	...	...	...	15170	...	...	...	22618	...	...	...
3 Other construction	17415	...	...	...	17751	...	...	...	24342	...	...	...
4 Land improvement and plantation and orchard development	3843	...	...	...	4307	...	...	...	6308	...	...	...
5 Producers' durable goods	24727	...	...	...	35366	...	...	...	57318	...	...	...
A Transport equipment	5906	...	...	...	6648	...	...	...	13433	...	...	...
B Machinery and equipment	18822	...	...	...	28718	...	...	...	43885	...	...	...
6 Breeding stock, dairy cattle, etc.	...	...	...	...	...	...	...	...	...	...	...	...
Total Gross Capital Formation	77434	54846	7903	14685	90198	68201	6829	15168	139055	110872	6634	21549

	1991				1992				1993			
	TOTAL	Total Private	Public Enterprises	General Government	TOTAL	Total Private	Public Enterprises	General Government	TOTAL	Total Private	Public Enterprises	General Government
Increase in stocks, total	3271	3499	-227	...	1632	1681	-50	...	661	854	-193	...
1 Goods producing industries	2180	...	...	...	1055	...	...	...	223	...	...	...
A Materials and supplies	129	...	...	...	13	...	...	...	109	...	...	...
B Work in progress	1002	...	...	...	385	...	...	...	171	...	...	...
C Livestock, except breeding stocks, dairy cattle, etc.	...	...	...	...	...	...	...	...	...	...	...	...
D Finished goods	1048	...	...	...	657	...	...	...	-58	...	...	...
2 Wholesale and retail trade	1091	...	...	...	576	...	...	...	438	...	...	...
3 Other, except government stocks	...	...	...	...	...	...	...	...	...	...	...	...
4 Government stocks	...	...	...	...	...	...	...	...	...	...	...	...
Gross Fixed Capital Formation, Total	143429	113139	7164	23125	142207	107047	8711	26449	138815	98326	9685	30803
1 Residential buildings	24850	23839	1011	...	24040	22808	1232	...	25173	23765	1408	...
2 Non-residential buildings	25954	...	...	...	27473	...	...	...	25978	...	...	...

Japan

2.7 Gross Capital Formation by Type of Good and Owner, in Current Prices
(Continued)

Thousand Million Japanese yen

	1991 TOTAL	1991 Total Private	1991 Public Enterprises	1991 General Government	1992 TOTAL	1992 Total Private	1992 Public Enterprises	1992 General Government	1993 TOTAL	1993 Total Private	1993 Public Enterprises	1993 General Government
3 Other construction	26347	...	...	...	26708	...	...	...	27007	...	...	...
4 Land improvement and plantation and orchard development	6826	...			6887	...	...	...	6911	...	...	...
5 Producers' durable goods	59453	...	...	...	57099	...	...	...	53746	...	...	...
A Transport equipment	13924	...	...	...	14242	...	...	...	13707	...	...	...
B Machinery and equipment	45529	...	...	...	42857	...	...	...	40040	...	...	...
6 Breeding stock, dairy cattle, etc.	...	...	...	...	...	...	...	...	...	...	...	...
Total Gross Capital Formation	146700	116638	6936	23125	143838	108728	8661	26449	139476	99180	9493	30803

2.8 Gross Capital Formation by Type of Good and Owner, in Constant Prices

Thousand Million Japanese yen

	1980 TOTAL	1980 Total Private	1980 Public Enterprises	1980 General Government	1985 TOTAL	1985 Total Private	1985 Public Enterprises	1985 General Government	1990 TOTAL	1990 Total Private	1990 Public Enterprises	1990 General Government
	At constant prices of:1985											
Increase in stocks, total	1421	1781	-361	-	2160	1822	338	-	2627	2534	93	...
1 Goods producing industries	1935	...	...	...	820	...	...	...	2028	...	...	...
A Materials and supplies	138	...	...	...	-225	...	...	...	256	...	...	...
B Work in progress	1128	...	...	...	347	...	...	...	1173	...	...	...
C Livestock, except breeding stocks, dairy cattle, etc.	...	...	...	...	...	...	...	...	...	...	...	...
D Finished goods	669	...	...	...	698	...	...	...	599	...	...	...
2 Wholesale and retail trade	-514	...	...	...	1340	...	...	...	599	...	...	...
3 Other, except government stocks	...	...	...	...	...	...	...	...	...	...	...	...
4 Government stocks	...	...	...	...	...	...	...	...	...	...	...	...
Gross Fixed Capital Formation, Total	78923	54624	8770	15529	88079	66419	6484	15176	134583	108684	6154	19745
1 Residential buildings	16917	15969	948	...	15446	14633	813	...	23587	22755	832	...
2 Non-residential buildings	14638	...	...	...	15179	...	...	...	20104	...	...	...
3 Other construction	18876	...	...	...	17760	...	...	...	23530	...	...	...
4 Land improvement and plantation and orchard development	4177	...	...	...	4309	...	...	...	5661	...	...	...
5 Producers' durable goods	24316	...	...	...	35385	...	...	...	61701	...	...	...
A Transport equipment	5964	...	...	...	6652	...	...	...	14593	...	...	...
B Machinery and equipment	18353	...	...	...	28734	...	...	...	47108	...	...	...
6 Breeding stock, dairy cattle, etc.	...	...	...	...	...	...	...	...	...	...	...	...
Total Gross Capital Formation	80344	56406	8409	15529	90239	68241	6822	15176	137210	111218	6247	19745

	1991 TOTAL	1991 Total Private	1991 Public Enterprises	1991 General Government	1992 TOTAL	1992 Total Private	1992 Public Enterprises	1992 General Government	1993 TOTAL	1993 Total Private	1993 Public Enterprises	1993 General Government
	At constant prices of:1985											
Increase in stocks, total	3763	3969	-206	...	1701	1758	-57	...	947	1112	-164	...
1 Goods producing industries	2447	...	...	...	1042	...	...	...	345	...	...	...
A Materials and supplies	156	...	...	...	-116	...	...	...	189	...	...	...
B Work in progress	1122	...	...	...	446	...	...	...	211	...	...	...
C Livestock, except breeding stocks, dairy cattle, etc.	...	...	...	...	...	...	...	...	...	...	...	...
D Finished goods	1168	...	...	...	712	...	...	...	-55	...	...	...
2 Wholesale and retail trade	1316	...	...	...	659	...	...	...	602	...	...	...
3 Other, except government stocks	...	...	...	...	...	...	...	...	...	...	...	...
4 Government stocks	...	...	...	...	...	...	...	...	...	...	...	...
Gross Fixed Capital Formation, Total	139544	112436	6526	20583	137981	106716	7881	23384	135541	99116	8845	27580
1 Residential buildings	21755	20878	877	...	20533	19480	1053	...	21169	19973	1196	...
2 Non-residential buildings	22318	...	...	...	23288	...	...	...	22000	...	...	...

Japan

2.8 Gross Capital Formation by Type of Good and Owner, in Constant Prices
(Continued)

Thousand Million Japanese yen

	1991				1992				1993			
	TOTAL	Total Private	Public Enterprises	General Government	TOTAL	Total Private	Public Enterprises	General Government	TOTAL	Total Private	Public Enterprises	General Government
		At constant prices of:1985									
3 Other construction	24568	...	...	...	24419	...	...	...	24573	...	...	...
4 Land improvement and plantation and orchard development	5896	...	...	...	5859	...	...	...	5900	...	...	...
5 Producers' durable goods	65008	...	...	...	63882	...	...	...	61900	...	...	...
A Transport equipment	15214	...	...	...	15639	...	...	...	15121	...	...	...
B Machinery and equipment	49794	...	...	...	48244	...	...	...	46779	...	...	...
6 Breeding stock, dairy cattle, etc.	...	...	...	...	...	...	...	...	...	...	...	...
Total Gross Capital Formation	143307	116405	6319	20583	139683	108474	7825	23384	136489	100227	8681	27580

2.13 Stocks of Reproducible Fixed Assets, by Type of Good and Owner, in Current Prices

Thousand Million Japanese yen

	TOTAL		Total Private		Public Enterprises		General Government	
	Gross	Net	Gross	Net	Gross	Net	Gross	Net
		1980							
1 Residential buildings	...	133622	...	...	...	...	...	...
2 Non-residential buildings	...	116240	...	...	...	...	...	...
3 Other construction	...	186076	...	...	...	...	...	...
4 Land improvement and plantation and orchard development a	...	...	...	...	...	...	...	...
5 Producers' durable goods	...	90726	...	...	...	...	...	...
A Transport equipment	...	17490	...	...	...	...	...	...
B Machinery and equipment	...	73236	...	...	...	...	...	...
6 Breeding stock, dairy cattle, etc.	...	...	...	...	...	...	...	...
Total	...	526664	...	325549	...	65376	...	135738
		1985							
1 Residential buildings	...	159174	...	...	...	...	...	...
2 Non-residential buildings	...	156335	...	...	...	...	...	...
3 Other construction	...	252748	...	...	...	...	...	...
4 Land improvement and plantation and orchard development a	...	...	...	...	...	...	...	...
5 Producers' durable goods	...	119124	...	...	...	...	...	...
A Transport equipment	...	19352	...	...	...	...	...	...
B Machinery and equipment	...	99772	...	...	...	...	...	...
6 Breeding stock, dairy cattle, etc.	...	...	...	...	...	...	...	...
Total	...	687381	...	434084	...	66147	...	187151
		1990							
1 Residential buildings	...	217809	...	...	...	...	...	...
2 Non-residential buildings	...	214899	...	...	...	...	...	...
3 Other construction	...	359751	...	...	...	...	...	...
4 Land improvement and plantation and orchard development a	...	...	...	...	...	...	...	...
5 Producers' durable goods	...	183179	...	...	...	...	...	...
A Transport equipment	...	32381	...	...	...	...	...	...
B Machinery and equipment	...	150798	...	...	...	...	...	...
6 Breeding stock, dairy cattle, etc.	...	...	...	...	...	...	...	...
Total	...	972257	...	638120	...	70500	...	263638

Japan

2.13 Stocks of Reproducible Fixed Assets, by Type of Good and Owner, in Current Prices
(Continued)

Thousand Million Japanese yen

		TOTAL Gross	TOTAL Net	Total Private Gross	Total Private Net	Public Enterprises Gross	Public Enterprises Net	General Government Gross	General Government Net
				1991					
1	Residential buildings	...	230406	...	...	...	...	...	...
2	Non-residential buildings	...	234732	...	...	...	...	...	...
3	Other construction	...	391627	...	...	...	...	...	...
4	Land improvement and plantation and orchard development a	...	...	...	...	...	...	...	...
5	Producers' durable goods	...	198522	...	...	...	...	...	...
	A Transport equipment	...	36454	...	...	...	...	...	...
	B Machinery and equipment	...	162069	...	...	...	...	...	...
6	Breeding stock, dairy cattle, etc.	...	...	...	...	...	...	...	...
	Total	...	1049957	...	696958	...	69359	...	283641
				1992					
1	Residential buildings	...	236818	...	...	...	...	...	...
2	Non-residential buildings	...	248429	...	...	...	...	...	...
3	Other construction	...	414156	...	...	...	...	...	...
4	Land improvement and plantation and orchard development a	...	...	...	...	...	...	...	...
5	Producers' durable goods	...	209149	...	...	...	...	...	...
	A Transport equipment	...	39286	...	...	...	...	...	...
	B Machinery and equipment	...	169863	...	...	...	...	...	...
6	Breeding stock, dairy cattle, etc.	...	...	...	...	...	...	...	...
	Total	...	1101763	...	725882	...	72595	...	303286
				1993					
1	Residential buildings	...	244701	...	...	...	...	...	...
2	Non-residential buildings	...	258623	...	...	...	...	...	...
3	Other construction	...	434251	...	...	...	...	...	...
4	Land improvement and plantation and orchard development a	...	...	...	...	...	...	...	...
5	Producers' durable goods	...	211869	...	...	...	...	...	...
	A Transport equipment	...	40722	...	...	...	...	...	...
	B Machinery and equipment	...	171147	...	...	...	...	...	...
6	Breeding stock, dairy cattle, etc.	...	...	...	...	...	...	...	...
	Total	...	1141493	...	741416	...	76331	...	323746

a) Item 'Land improvement and plantation and orchard development' is excluded from this table.

2.14 Stocks of Reproducible Fixed Assets, by Type of Good and Owner, in Constant Prices

Thousand Million Japanese yen

		TOTAL Gross	TOTAL Net	Total Private Gross	Total Private Net	Public Enterprises Gross	Public Enterprises Net	General Government Gross	General Government Net
				At constant prices of: 1985					
				1980					
1	Residential buildings	...	142549	...	...	...	...	...	...
2	Non-residential buildings	...	124818	...	...	...	...	...	...
3	Other construction	...	201613	...	...	...	...	...	...
4	Land improvement and plantation and orchard development a	...	...	...	...	...	...	...	...
5	Producers' durable goods	...	85429	...	...	...	...	...	...
	A Transport equipment	...	17144	...	...	...	...	...	...
	B Machinery and equipment	...	68285	...	...	...	...	...	...
6	Breeding stock, dairy cattle, etc.	...	...	...	...	...	...	...	...
	Total	...	554409	...	...	...	...	...	...

Japan

2.14 Stocks of Reproducible Fixed Assets, by Type of Good and Owner, in Constant Prices
(Continued)

Thousand Million Japanese yen

		TOTAL Gross	TOTAL Net	Total Private Gross	Total Private Net	Public Enterprises Gross	Public Enterprises Net	General Government Gross	General Government Net
		\multicolumn{8}{c	}{At constant prices of:1985}
		\multicolumn{8}{c	}{**1985**}
1	Residential buildings	...	159174	...	...	...	...	...	...
2	Non-residential buildings	...	156335	...	...	...	...	...	...
3	Other construction	...	252748	...	...	...	...	...	...
4	Land improvement and plantation and orchard development a	...	...	...	...	...	...	...	...
5	Producers' durable goods	...	119124	...	...	...	...	...	...
	A Transport equipment	...	19352	...	...	...	...	...	...
	B Machinery and equipment	...	99772	...	...	...	...	...	...
6	Breeding stock, dairy cattle, etc.	...	...	...	...	...	...	...	...
	Total	...	687381	...	...	...	...	...	...
		\multicolumn{8}{c	}{**1990**}
1	Residential buildings	...	192714	...	...	...	...	...	...
2	Non-residential buildings	...	190096	...	...	...	...	...	...
3	Other construction	...	308880	...	...	...	...	...	...
4	Land improvement and plantation and orchard development a	...	...	...	...	...	...	...	...
5	Producers' durable goods	...	193700	...	...	...	...	...	...
	A Transport equipment	...	33779	...	...	...	...	...	...
	B Machinery and equipment	...	159922	...	...	...	...	...	...
6	Breeding stock, dairy cattle, etc.	...	...	...	...	...	...	...	...
	Total	...	885391	...	...	...	...	...	233816
		\multicolumn{8}{c	}{**1991**}
1	Residential buildings	...	198110	...	...	...	...	...	...
2	Non-residential buildings	...	200571	...	...	...	...	...	...
3	Other construction	...	322124	...	...	...	...	...	...
4	Land improvement and plantation and orchard development a	...	...	...	...	...	...	...	...
5	Producers' durable goods	...	212089	...	...	...	...	...	...
	A Transport equipment	...	37475	...	...	...	...	...	...
	B Machinery and equipment	...	174614	...	...	...	...	...	...
6	Breeding stock, dairy cattle, etc.	...	...	...	...	...	...	...	...
	Total	...	932894	...	...	...	...	...	244297
		\multicolumn{8}{c	}{**1992**}
1	Residential buildings	...	202068	...	...	...	...	...	...
2	Non-residential buildings	...	211375	...	...	...	...	...	...
3	Other construction	...	334573	...	...	...	...	...	...
4	Land improvement and plantation and orchard development a	...	...	...	...	...	...	...	...
5	Producers' durable goods	...	224629	...	...	...	...	...	...
	A Transport equipment	...	40344	...	...	...	...	...	...
	B Machinery and equipment	...	184285	...	...	...	...	...	...
6	Breeding stock, dairy cattle, etc.	...	...	...	...	...	...	...	...
	Total	...	972646	...	...	...	...	...	256908

Japan

2.14 Stocks of Reproducible Fixed Assets, by Type of Good and Owner, in Constant Prices
(Continued)

Thousand Million Japanese yen

		TOTAL		Total Private		Public Enterprises		General Government	
		Gross	Net	Gross	Net	Gross	Net	Gross	Net

At constant prices of: 1985

1993

		Gross	Net	Gross	Net	Gross	Net	Gross	Net
1	Residential buildings	...	206344	...	...	...	...	...	...
2	Non-residential buildings	...	220235	...	...	...	...	...	...
3	Other construction	...	346858	...	...	...	...	...	...
4	Land improvement and plantation and orchard development [a]	...	...	...	...	...	...	...	...
5	Producers' durable goods	...	231909	...	...	...	...	...	...
	A Transport equipment	...	41950	...	...	...	...	...	...
	B Machinery and equipment	...	189959	...	...	...	...	...	...
6	Breeding stock, dairy cattle, etc.	...	...	...	...	...	...	...	...
	Total	...	1005347	...	...	...	...	...	272778

a) Item 'Land improvement and plantation and orchard development' is excluded from this table.

2.17 Exports and Imports of Goods and Services, Detail

Thousand Million Japanese yen

		1980	1983	1984	1985	1986	1987	1988	1989	1990	1991	1992	1993
	Exports of Goods and Services												
1	Exports of merchandise, f.o.b. [a]	29022	34964	40381	41555	34575	32490	33398	37372	40651	41438	42049	39133
2	Transport and communication	2447	2460	2635	2607	1732	1738	1860	2313	2377	2396	2362	2126
	A In respect of merchandise imports	...	...	...	...	...	...	...	...	...	...	...	...
	B Other	2447	2460	2635	2607	1732	1738	1860	2313	2377	2396	2362	2126
3	Insurance service charges	71	1	22	2	27	42	31	28	9	-2	6	34
	A In respect of merchandise imports	...	...	...	...	...	...	...	...	...	...	...	...
	B Other	71	1	22	2	27	42	31	28	9	-2	6	34
4	Other commodities	938	1195	1293	1324	1107	1318	1537	1901	2100	2265	2284	2264
5	Adjustments of merchandise exports to change-of-ownership basis [a]	...	...	...	...	...	...	...	...	...	...	...	...
6	Direct purchases in the domestic market by non-residential households	167	223	260	297	266	322	387	450	533	480	468	407
7	Direct purchases in the domestic market by extraterritorial bodies	241	432	476	522	383	300	270	288	250	233	240	279
	Total Exports of Goods and Services	32887	39275	45066	46307	38090	36210	37483	42352	45920	46810	47409	44244
	Imports of Goods and Services												
1	Imports of merchandise, c.i.f. [b]	29153	27902	30328	28856	19356	18708	21330	26906	31598	27670	25374	23481
	A Imports of merchandise, f.o.b. [a]	29153	27902	30328	28856	19356	18708	21330	26906	31598	27670	25374	23481
	B Transport of services on merchandise imports	...	...	...	...	...	...	...	...	...	...	...	...
	C Insurance service charges on merchandise imports	...	...	...	...	...	...	...	...	...	...	...	...
2	Adjustments of merchandise imports to change-of-ownership basis [a]	...	...	...	...	...	...	...	...	...	...	...	...
3	Other transport and communication	2915	2777	2832	2773	2018	2414	2648	3215	3582	3637	3539	3287
4	Other insurance service charges	171	129	158	129	142	172	171	174	194	64	204	288
5	Other commodities	1698	2323	2376	2542	1996	2288	2452	3286	3810	3843	3581	3211
6	Direct purchases abroad by government	11	28	29	36	32	22	25	30	37	42	43	38
7	Direct purchases abroad by resident households	1089	1100	1144	1196	1247	1591	2439	3158	3651	3274	3443	3028
	Total Imports of Goods and Services	35036	34258	36866	35532	24791	25195	29065	36768	42872	38529	36184	33333
	Balance of Goods and Services	-2149	5017	8200	10775	13299	11015	8418	5584	3048	8280	11226	10911
	Total Imports and Balance of Goods and Services	32887	39275	45066	46307	38090	36210	37483	42352	45920	46810	47409	44244

a) Item 'Adjustment of merchandise export/import to change-of-ownership basis' is included in item 'Exports/Imports of merchandise, f.o.b.'.
b) Imports of merchandise c.i.f. is not estimated in the Balance of Payments in Japan. Therefore, valuation basis is f.o.b.

Japan

3.11 General Government Production Account: Total and Subsectors

Thousand Million Japanese yen

	1980					1985				
	Total General Government	Central Government	State or Provincial Government	Local Government	Social Security Funds	Total General Government	Central Government	State or Provincial Government	Local Government	Social Security Funds
Gross Output										
1 Sales	...	...	...	...	...	...	...	...	...	...
2 Services produced for own use	23568	5676	...	18107	339	30685	7489	...	22953	597
3 Own account fixed capital formation	...	...	...	...	...	...	...	...	...	...
Gross Output a	27712	...	...	...	...	36454	...	...	...	...
Gross Input										
Intermediate Consumption	7213	...	...	...	...	10170	...	...	...	...
Subtotal: Value Added	20500	...	...	...	...	26285	...	...	...	...
1 Indirect taxes, net	30	...	...	...	...	36	...	...	...	...
A Indirect taxes	30	...	...	...	...	36	...	...	...	...
B Less: Subsidies	...	...	...	...	...	...	...	...	...	...
2 Consumption of fixed capital	1393	...	...	...	...	2078	...	...	...	...
3 Compensation of employees	19077	...	...	...	...	24172	...	...	...	...
4 Net Operating surplus	...	...	...	...	...	...	...	...	...	...
Gross Input a	27713	...	...	...	...	36454	...	...	...	...

	1990					1991				
	Total General Government	Central Government	State or Provincial Government	Local Government	Social Security Funds	Total General Government	Central Government	State or Provincial Government	Local Government	Social Security Funds
Gross Output										
1 Sales	...	...	...	...	...	...	...	...	...	...
2 Services produced for own use	38807	9436	...	29325	759	41232	9768	...	31007	796
3 Own account fixed capital formation	...	...	...	...	...	...	...	...	...	...
Gross Output a	46475	...	...	...	...	49126	...	...	...	...
Gross Input										
Intermediate Consumption	13787	...	...	...	...	14904	...	...	...	...
Subtotal: Value Added	32688	...	...	...	...	34222	...	...	...	...
1 Indirect taxes, net	44	...	...	...	...	43	...	...	...	...
A Indirect taxes	44	...	...	...	...	43	...	...	...	...
B Less: Subsidies	...	...	...	...	...	...	...	...	...	...
2 Consumption of fixed capital	2508	...	...	...	...	2525	...	...	...	...
3 Compensation of employees	30136	...	...	...	...	31654	...	...	...	...
4 Net Operating surplus	...	...	...	...	...	...	...	...	...	...
Gross Input a	46475	...	...	...	...	49126	...	...	...	...

	1992					1993				
	Total General Government	Central Government	State or Provincial Government	Local Government	Social Security Funds	Total General Government	Central Government	State or Provincial Government	Local Government	Social Security Funds
Gross Output										
1 Sales	...	...	...	...	...	...	...	...	...	...
2 Services produced for own use	43258	10227	...	32608	837	44666	...	...	...	...
3 Own account fixed capital formation	...	...	...	...	...	...	...	...	...	...
Gross Output a	51651	...	...	...	...	53637	...	...	...	...
Gross Input										
Intermediate Consumption	15991	...	...	...	...	16825	...	...	...	...
Subtotal: Value Added	35661	...	...	...	...	36812	...	...	...	...
1 Indirect taxes, net	46	...	...	...	...	47	...	...	...	...
A Indirect taxes	46	...	...	...	...	47	...	...	...	...
B Less: Subsidies	...	...	...	...	...	...	...	...	...	...
2 Consumption of fixed capital	2624	...	...	...	...	2779	...	...	...	...
3 Compensation of employees	32991	...	...	...	...	33986	...	...	...	...
4 Net Operating surplus	...	...	...	...	...	...	...	...	...	...
Gross Input a	51651	...	...	...	...	53637	...	...	...	...

a) The subsectors of general government, central government, local government, and social security funds refer to fiscal year beginning 1 April.

Japan

3.12 General Government Income and Outlay Account: Total and Subsectors

Thousand Million Japanese yen

	1980					1985				
	Total General Government	Central Government	State or Provincial Government	Local Government	Social Security Funds	Total General Government	Central Government	State or Provincial Government	Local Government	Social Security Funds

Receipts

1 Operating surplus	...	...	...	...	...	...	...	...	...	...
2 Property and entrepreneurial income	4626	1310	...	664	2933	8369	1726	...	1029	5841
3 Taxes, fees and contributions	61338	29118	...	16555	18184	89908	40493	...	23947	27130
A Indirect taxes	17688	8397	...	9714	...	24900	10926	...	13455	...
B Direct taxes	25876	20592	...	6712	...	38485	29390	...	10329	...
Income	24954	...	...	...	...	37081	...	...	...	...
Other	921	...	...	...	...	1404	...	...	...	...
C Social security contributions	17513	...	...	...	18177	26184	...	...	...	27121
D Fees, fines and penalties	261	129	...	129	7	338	177	...	163	9
4 Other current transfers	250	413	...	13424	5779	487	541	...	16078	8244
A Casualty insurance claims	6	3	...	3	-	10	5	...	5	-
B Transfers from other government subsectors	...	198	...	13418	5733	...	103	...	16070	8184
C Transfers from the rest of the world	10	14	...	-	...	12	11	...	-	...
D Other transfers, except imputed	227	194	...	...	46	457	417	...	...	60
E Imputed unfunded employee pension and welfare contributions	6	4	...	3	...	8	5	...	3	...
Total Current Receipts [a]	66214	30840	...	30642	26896	98764	42759	...	41054	41215

Disbursements

1 Government final consumption expenditure	23568	5676	...	18107	339	30685	7489	...	22953	597
2 Property income	7569	5853	...	2162	-	14318	11121	...	3509	-
A Interest	7500	...	...	...	...	14212	...	...	...	...
B Net land rent and royalties	69	...	...	...	...	106	...	...	...	...
3 Subsidies	3593	2846	...	809	...	3650	2830	...	867	...
4 Other current transfers	25269	21147	...	4337	19880	36456	25935	...	5665	30067
A Casualty insurance premiums, net	6	3	...	3	-	11	5	...	5	-
B Transfers to other government subsectors	...	18900	...	229	220	...	23360	...	875	123
C Social security benefits	18919	-	...	-	19571	28960	-	...	-	29760
D Social assistance grants	5250	1750	...	3580	...	5957	1975	...	4021	...
E Unfunded employee pension and welfare benefits	6	4	...	3	-	8	5	...	3	-
F Transfers to private non-profit institutions serving households	1003	416	...	521	...	1430	509	...	761	...
G Other transfers n.e.c.	...	...	...	...	...	...	...	...	...	...
H Transfers to the rest of the world	84	74	...	-	...	90	81	...	-	...
Net saving	6214	-4680	...	5227	6677	13655	-4615	...	8059	10552
Total Current Disbursements and Net Saving [a]	66214	30840	...	30642	26896	98764	42759	...	41054	41215

	1990					1991				
	Total General Government	Central Government	State or Provincial Government	Local Government	Social Security Funds	Total General Government	Central Government	State or Provincial Government	Local Government	Social Security Funds

Receipts

1 Operating surplus	...	...	...	...	...	...	...	...	...	...
2 Property and entrepreneurial income	13188	2995	...	2253	8366	15119	2999	...	2541	9376
3 Taxes, fees and contributions	132987	61916	...	34474	39331	138965	63451	...	36144	42218
A Indirect taxes	35212	16548	...	18496	...	34968	17523	...	19476	...
B Direct taxes	58367	45144	...	15754	...	62253	45675	...	16438	...
Income	56495	...	...	...	...	60299	...	...	...	...
Other	1872	...	...	...	...	1954	...	...	...	...
C Social security contributions	38957	...	...	...	39323	41264	...	...	...	42210
D Fees, fines and penalties	452	225	...	224	8	480	253	...	230	8

Japan

3.12 General Government Income and Outlay Account: Total and Subsectors
(Continued)

Thousand Million Japanese yen

	1990					1991				
	Total General Government	Central Government	State or Provincial Government	Local Government	Social Security Funds	Total General Government	Central Government	State or Provincial Government	Local Government	Social Security Funds
4 Other current transfers	846	935	...	22565	10437	939	1048	...	23484	11245
A Casualty insurance claims	10	5	...	5	-	10	5	...	5	-
B Transfers from other government subsectors	...	166	...	22557	10341	...	190	...	23476	11145
C Transfers from the rest of the world	11	11	...	-	...	8	17	...	-	...
D Other transfers, except imputed	817	747	...	...	96	912	830	...	...	100
E Imputed unfunded employee pension and welfare contributions	9	6	...	3	...	9	6	...	3	...
Total Current Receipts a	147022	65847	...	59292	58134	155023	67498	...	62169	62839

Disbursements

	1990					1991				
1 Government final consumption expenditure	38807	9436	...	29325	759	41232	9768	...	31107	796
2 Property income	16820	13080	...	3909	4	17378	13379	...	4095	4
A Interest	16645	...	...	...	...	17180	...	...	...	...
B Net land rent and royalties	175	...	...	...	...	198	...	...	...	...
3 Subsidies	4644	2265	...	1135	...	3852	2151	...	1136	...
4 Other current transfers	51063	34266	...	6985	41523	52115	36071	...	7427	44325
A Casualty insurance premiums, net	11	6	...	6	-	12	6	...	6	-
B Transfers to other government subsectors	...	31445	...	1437	183	...	33082	...	1519	210
C Social security benefits	42370	-	...	-	40969	42954	-	...	-	43684
D Social assistance grants	6453	1963	...	4513	...	6633	1935	...	4756	...
E Unfunded employee pension and welfare benefits	9	6	...	3	-	9	6	...	3	-
F Transfers to private non-profit institutions serving households	2070	732	...	1026	371	2367	890	...	1142	432
G Other transfers n.e.c.	...	...	...	...	...	...	...	...	...	...
H Transfers to the rest of the world	149	114	...	-	...	139	152	...	-	...
Net saving	35688	6800	...	17937	15849	40447	6129	...	18404	17714
Total Current Disbursements and Net Saving a	147022	65847	...	59291	58135	155023	67498	...	62169	62839

	1992					1993				
	Total General Government	Central Government	State or Provincial Government	Local Government	Social Security Funds	Total General Government	Central Government	State or Provincial Government	Local Government	Social Security Funds

Receipts

1 Operating surplus	...	...	...	...	...	...	...	...	...	...
2 Property and entrepreneurial income	14582	3045	...	1959	10518	14640	...	...	...	...
3 Taxes, fees and contributions	140754	58103	...	35614	44953	137811	...	...	...	...
A Indirect taxes	37301	17983	...	19242	...	37199	...	...	...	...
B Direct taxes	59519	39860	...	16141	...	54757	...	...	...	...
Income	57516	...	...	...	...	52717	...	...	...	...
Other	2003	...	...	...	...	2041	...	...	...	...
C Social security contributions	43436	...	...	...	44944	45331	...	...	...	...
D Fees, fines and penalties	498	261	...	232	9	524	...	...	...	...
4 Other current transfers	1035	1100	...	24709	11580	1069	...	...	...	...
A Casualty insurance claims	11	5	...	5	-	11	...	...	...	...
B Transfers from other government subsectors	...	187	...	24701	11458	...	...	...	...	...
C Transfers from the rest of the world	19	12	...	-	...	16	...	...	...	...
D Other transfers, except imputed	996	889	...	...	123	1033	...	...	...	...
E Imputed unfunded employee pension and welfare contributions	10	7	...	3	...	10	...	...	...	...
Total Current Receipts a	156370	62248	...	62283	67051	153521	...	...	...	...

Disbursements

| 1 Government final consumption expenditure | 43258 | 10227 | ... | 32608 | 837 | 44666 | ... | ... | ... | ... |
| 2 Property income | 17733 | 13254 | ... | 4281 | 4 | 17724 | ... | ... | ... | ... |

Japan

3.12 General Government Income and Outlay Account: Total and Subsectors
(Continued)

Thousand Million Japanese yen

		1992					1993				
		Total General Government	Central Government	State or Provincial Government	Local Government	Social Security Funds	Total General Government	Central Government	State or Provincial Government	Local Government	Social Security Funds
	A Interest	17512	...	...	...	...	17489	...	...	...	...
	B Net land rent and royalties	221	...	...	...	...	235	...	...	...	...
3	Subsidies	3304	2117	...	1202	...	3475	...	...	...	...
4	Other current transfers	55937	37386	...	8060	47533	59574	...	...	...	...
	A Casualty insurance premiums, net	12	6	...	6	-	13	...	...	...	...
	B Transfers to other government subsectors	...	34396	...	1730	219	...	...	...	...	...
	C Social security benefits	46229	-	...	-	46845	49380	...	...	...	...
	D Social assistance grants	6913	1842	...	5061	...	7157	...	...	...	...
	E Unfunded employee pension and welfare benefits	10	7	...	3	-	10	...	...	...	...
	F Transfers to private non-profit institutions serving households	2604	961	...	1259	469	2830	...	...	...	...
	G Other transfers n.e.c.	...	...	...	...	...	...	...	...	...	...
	H Transfers to the rest of the world	168	175	...	-	...	184	...	...	...	...
	Net saving	36138	-736	...	16132	18676	28081	...	...	...	...
	Total Current Disbursements and Net Saving [a]	156370	62248	...	62283	67051	153521	...	...	...	...

a) The subsectors of general government, central government, local government, and social security funds refer to fiscal year beginning 1 April.

3.13 General Government Capital Accumulation Account: Total and Subsectors

Thousand Million Japanese yen

		1980					1985				
		Total General Government	Central Government	State or Provincial Government	Local Government	Social Security Funds	Total General Government	Central Government	State or Provincial Government	Local Government	Social Security Funds
		Finance of Gross Accumulation									
1	Gross saving	7608	-4442	...	6426	6686	15732	-4316	...	9835	10567
	A Consumption of fixed capital	1393	238	...	1199	9	2077	299	...	1776	15
	B Net saving	6215	-4680	...	5227	6677	13655	-4615	...	8059	10552
2	Capital transfers [a]	-1125	-6148	...	5158	-147	-465	-4787	...	4583	-266
	A From other government subsectors	...	-5889	...	5895	-6	...	-5129	...	5175	-46
	B From other resident sectors	-1029	-259	...	-737	-141	-322	342	...	-592	-220
	C From rest of the world	-96	...	...	...	...	-141	...	...	...	...
	Finance of Gross Accumulation [b]	6483	-10590	...	11584	6539	15267	-9104	...	14418	10301
		Gross Accumulation									
1	Gross capital formation	14685	2276	...	12611	51	15168	2482	...	12808	68
	A Increase in stocks	...	...	...	...	...	...	...	...	...	...
	B Gross fixed capital formation	14685	2276	...	12611	51	15168	2482	...	12808	68
2	Purchases of land, net	2396	386	...	2121	8	2703	228	...	2497	19
3	Purchases of intangible assets, net										
4	Capital transfers [a]	...	...	...	...	...	...	...	...	...	...
	Net lending [c]	-10599	-13253	...	-3147	6480	-2603	-11813	...	-887	10214
	Gross Accumulation [b]	6482	-10591	...	11585	6539	15267	-9104	...	14418	10301

		1990					1991				
		Total General Government	Central Government	State or Provincial Government	Local Government	Social Security Funds	Total General Government	Central Government	State or Provincial Government	Local Government	Social Security Funds
		Finance of Gross Accumulation									
1	Gross saving	38196	7114	...	20121	15862	42972	6452	...	20595	17729
	A Consumption of fixed capital	2508	315	...	2184	14	2525	323	...	2192	15
	B Net saving	35688	6800	...	17937	15849	40447	6129	...	18404	17714
2	Capital transfers [a]	224	-4854	...	4011	-381	-1357	-3403	...	4174	-505
	A From other government subsectors	...	-4786	...	4838	-51	...	-5203	...	5264	-61
	B From other resident sectors	659	-68	...	-826	-330	47	1800	...	-1090	-443
	C From rest of the world	-435	...	...	...	...	-1404	...	...	...	...
	Finance of Gross Accumulation [b]	38420	2261	...	24132	15482	41615	3049	...	24769	17224

Japan

3.13 General Government Capital Accumulation Account: Total and Subsectors
(Continued)

Thousand Million Japanese yen

	1990					1991				
	Total General Government	Central Government	State or Provincial Government	Local Government	Social Security Funds	Total General Government	Central Government	State or Provincial Government	Local Government	Social Security Funds

Gross Accumulation

1 Gross capital formation	21549	3215	...	18534	83	23125	3419	...	20293	87
A Increase in stocks	...	...	...	...	...	...	...	...	...	...
B Gross fixed capital formation	21549	3215	...	18534	83	23125	3419	...	20293	87
2 Purchases of land, net	4530	446	...	4249	18	5164	458	...	4838	26
3 Purchases of intangible assets, net	...	...	...	...	...	...	...	...	...	...
4 Capital transfers [a]	...	...	...	...	...	...	...	...	...	...
Net lending [c]	12342	-1401	...	1349	15381	13326	-829	...	-363	17111
Gross Accumulation [b]	38421	2260	...	24132	15482	41615	3049	...	24769	17224

	1992					1993				
	Total General Government	Central Government	State or Provincial Government	Local Government	Social Security Funds	Total General Government	Central Government	State or Provincial Government	Local Government	Social Security Funds

Finance of Gross Accumulation

1 Gross saving	38762	-416	...	18476	18691	30860	...	...	...	...
A Consumption of fixed capital	2624	320	...	2344	15	2779	...	...	...	...
B Net saving	36138	-736	...	16132	18676	28081	...	...	...	...
2 Capital transfers [a]	404	-4878	...	5491	-453	-228	...	...	...	...
A From other government subsectors	...	-6747	...	6807	-59	...	...	...	...	...
B From other resident sectors	590	1869	...	-1316	-393	-60	...	...	...	...
C From rest of the world	-186	...	...	...	...	-168	...	...	...	...
Finance of Gross Accumulation [b]	39166	-5294	...	23966	18239	30632	...	...	...	...

Gross Accumulation

1 Gross capital formation	26449	4242	...	23575	120	30803	...	...	...	...
A Increase in stocks	...	...	...	...	...	...	...	...	...	...
B Gross fixed capital formation	26449	4242	...	23575	120	30803	...	...	...	...
2 Purchases of land, net	5883	570	...	5561	39	6272	...	...	...	...
3 Purchases of intangible assets, net	...	...	...	...	...	...	...	...	...	...
4 Capital transfers [a]	...	...	...	...	...	...	...	...	...	...
Net lending [c]	6834	-10105	...	-5170	18079	-6443	...	...	...	...
Gross Accumulation [b]	39166	-5294	...	23966	18239	30632	...	...	...	...

a) Capital transfers received are recorded net of capital transfers paid.
b) The subsectors of general government, central government, local government, and social security funds refer to fiscal year beginning 1 April.
c) Net lending of the capital accumulation account and the capital finance account have not been reconciled and are different due to different statistical sources.

3.14 General Government Capital Finance Account, Total and Subsectors

Thousand Million Japanese yen

	1980					1985				
	Total General Government	Central Government	State or Provincial Government	Local Government	Social Security Funds	Total General Government	Central Government	State or Provincial Government	Local Government	Social Security Funds

Acquisition of Financial Assets

1 Gold and SDRs [a]	...	...	...	...	...	...	...	...	...	...
2 Currency and transferable deposits	-153	37	...	-744	-913	-106	2	...	80	56
3 Other deposits	1563	-10	...	716	781	2243	37	...	474	1689
4 Bills and bonds, short term	-834	136	...	-	-	1193	457	...	-	4
5 Bonds, long term	2337	1152	...	-	857	118	-105	...	-	1049
6 Corporate equity securities	-	-	...	-	-	5	-6	...	2	9
7 Short-term loans, n.e.c.	1207	500	...	242	497	906	606	...	174	161
8 Long-term loans, n.e.c.			...					...		
9 Other receivables	...	...	...	...	...	...	...	...	...	...
10 Other assets [a]	7169	4392	...	62	5342	7489	1460	...	54	8523
Total Acquisition of Financial Assets [b]	11289	6207	...	276	6564	11846	2451	...	783	11490

Incurrence of Liabilities

1 Currency and transferable deposits	...	...	...	...	...	...	...	...	...	...
2 Other deposits	...	...	...	...	...	...	...	...	...	...
3 Bills and bonds, short term	1873	3460	...	...	...	-757	-1041	...	...	...

Japan

3.14 General Government Capital Finance Account, Total and Subsectors
(Continued)

Thousand Million Japanese yen

	1980					1985				
	Total General Government	Central Government	State or Provincial Government	Local Government	Social Security Funds	Total General Government	Central Government	State or Provincial Government	Local Government	Social Security Funds
4 Bonds, long term	14709	14275	...	1015	...	12855	12730	...	-159	...
5 Short-term loans, n.e.c.	3974	1039	...	2764	150	3922	763	...	3461	32
6 Long-term loans, n.e.c.			...					...		
7 Other payables	...	...	...	...	...	...	...	...	...	...
8 Other liabilities	143	636	...	4	...	197	1877	...	2	...
Total Incurrence of Liabilities	20699	19410	...	3783	150	16216	14329	...	3305	32
Net Lending c	-9409	-13203	...	-3507	6414	-4369	-11878	...	-2522	11458
Incurrence of Liabilities and Net Worth b	11290	6207	...	276	6564	11846	2451	...	783	11490

	1990					1991				
	Total General Government	Central Government	State or Provincial Government	Local Government	Social Security Funds	Total General Government	Central Government	State or Provincial Government	Local Government	Social Security Funds

Acquisition of Financial Assets

1 Gold and SDRs a	...	...	...	...	...	...	...	...	...	...
2 Currency and transferable deposits	190	-3038	...	-257	-530	-78	18	...	475	812
3 Other deposits	10590	4040	...	4096	1768	8596	3906	...	1997	2558
4 Bills and bonds, short term	-51	784	...	-	18	1094	1488	...	...	...
5 Bonds, long term	3046	79	...	-2	342	-800	-702	...	-2	558
6 Corporate equity securities	37	31	...	7	3	80	62	...	13	5
7 Short-term loans, n.e.c.	1268	1373	...	461	113	2092	1466	...	745	438
8 Long-term loans, n.e.c.			...					...		
9 Other receivables	...	...	...	...	...	...	...	...	...	...
10 Other assets a	18384	5849	...	288	11734	15786	4758	...	308	13374
Total Acquisition of Financial Assets b	33464	9118	...	4593	13448	26769	10995	...	3536	17726

Incurrence of Liabilities

1 Currency and transferable deposits	...	...	...	...	...	...	...	...	...	...
2 Other deposits	...	...	...	...	...	...	...	...	...	...
3 Bills and bonds, short term	2805	-2010	...	...	...	-4360	-699	...	...	...
4 Bonds, long term	6199	3688	...	147	...	5453	5373	...	-817	...
5 Short-term loans, n.e.c.	7034	4886	...	3675	38	8324	4953	...	4546	15
6 Long-term loans, n.e.c.			...					...		
7 Other payables	...	...	...	...	...	...	...	...	...	...
8 Other liabilities	471	1307	...	20	...	-36	-193	...	12	...
Total Incurrence of Liabilities	16508	7871	...	3842	38	9381	9433	...	3741	15
Net Lending c	16955	1246	...	751	13410	17388	1562	...	-205	17711
Incurrence of Liabilities and Net Worth b	33463	9118	...	4593	13448	26769	10995	...	3536	17726

	1992					1993				
	Total General Government	Central Government	State or Provincial Government	Local Government	Social Security Funds	Total General Government	Central Government	State or Provincial Government	Local Government	Social Security Funds

Acquisition of Financial Assets

1 Gold and SDRs a	...	...	...	...	...	...	...	...	...	...
2 Currency and transferable deposits	111	769	...	158	-80	-43	...	...	...	...
3 Other deposits	6465	204	...	-274	1936	8027	...	...	...	...
4 Bills and bonds, short term	2358	1225	...	...	...	-3688	...	...	...	...
5 Bonds, long term	614	365	...	-1	956	1048	...	...	...	...
6 Corporate equity securities	68	53	...	13	2	35	...	...	...	...
7 Short-term loans, n.e.c.	1133	-298	...	631	213	3348	...	...	...	...
8 Long-term loans, n.e.c.			...				...	...	...	...
9 Other receivables	...	...	...	...	...	...	...	...	...	...
10 Other assets a	17471	2873	...	378	13406	17260	...	...	...	...
Total Acquisition of Financial Assets b	28219	5192	...	905	16430	25987	...	...	...	...

Incurrence of Liabilities

1 Currency and transferable deposits	...	...	...	...	...	...	...	...	...	...
2 Other deposits	...	...	...	...	...	...	...	...	...	...
3 Bills and bonds, short term	1585	721	...	...	...	1588	...	...	...	...

Japan

3.14 General Government Capital Finance Account, Total and Subsectors
(Continued)

Thousand Million Japanese yen

	1992 Total General Government	1992 Central Government	1992 State or Provincial Government	1992 Local Government	1992 Social Security Funds	1993 Total General Government	1993 Central Government	1993 State or Provincial Government	1993 Local Government	1993 Social Security Funds
4 Bonds, long term	8841	6634	...	3511	...	12036	...	...	...	...
5 Short-term loans, n.e.c.	13634	9358	...	3497	-	13477	...	...	...	...
6 Long-term loans, n.e.c.			...				...	...	...	...
7 Other payables	...	...	...	...	...	...	...	...	...	...
8 Other liabilities	117	561	...	-5	...	296	...	...	...	...
Total Incurrence of Liabilities	24176	17274	...	7003	-	27397	...	...	...	...
Net Lending c	4043	-12082	...	-6098	16430	-1410	...	...	...	...
Incurrence of Liabilities and Net Worth b	28219	5192	...	905	16430	25987	...	...	...	...

a) Item 'Gold and SDRs' is included in item 'Other assets'.
b) The subsectors of general government, central government, local government, and social security funds refer to fiscal year beginning 1 April.
c) Net lending of the capital accumulation account and the capital finance account have not been reconciled and are different due to different statistical sources.

3.21 Corporate and Quasi-Corporate Enterprise Production Account: Total and Sectors

Thousand Million Japanese yen

	1980 TOTAL	1980 Non-Financial	1980 Financial	1980 ADDENDUM: Total, including Unincorporated	1985 TOTAL	1985 Non-Financial	1985 Financial	1985 ADDENDUM: Total, including Unincorporated	1990 TOTAL	1990 Non-Financial	1990 Financial	1990 ADDENDUM: Total, including Unincorporated
Gross Output												
1 Output for sale	...	...	...	...	...	...	...	...	...	...	...	...
2 Imputed bank service charge	10413	...	...	...	14774	...	...	...	22322	...	...	...
3 Own-account fixed capital formation	...	...	...	...	...	...	...	...	...	...	...	...
Gross Output	...	...	...	...	...	...	...	...	...	...	...	...
Gross Input												
Intermediate consumption	...	...	...	...	...	...	...	...	...	...	...	...
Subtotal: Value Added	...	...	...	...	...	...	...	...	...	...	...	...
1 Indirect taxes, net	...	...	...	...	...	...	...	...	...	...	...	...
2 Consumption of fixed capital	18682	18077	605	...	27467	26607	860	...	41698	40102	1596	...
3 Compensation of employees	...	...	...	...	...	...	...	...	...	...	...	...
4 Net operating surplus	31555	37315	-5760	...	40611	49750	-9139	...	53172	68573	-15401	...
Gross Input	...	...	...	...	...	...	...	...	...	...	...	...

	1991 TOTAL	1991 Non-Financial	1991 Financial	1991 ADDENDUM: Total, including Unincorporated	1992 TOTAL	1992 Non-Financial	1992 Financial	1992 ADDENDUM: Total, including Unincorporated	1993 TOTAL	1993 Non-Financial	1993 Financial	1993 ADDENDUM: Total, including Unincorporated
Gross Output												
1 Output for sale	...	...	...	...	...	...	...	...	...	...	...	...
2 Imputed bank service charge	22670	...	...	...	23061	...	...	...	20720	...	...	...
3 Own-account fixed capital formation	...	...	...	...	...	...	...	...	...	...	...	...
Gross Output	...	...	...	...	...	...	...	...	...	...	...	...
Gross Input												
Intermediate consumption	...	...	...	...	...	...	...	...	...	...	...	...
Subtotal: Value Added	...	...	...	...	...	...	...	...	...	...	...	...
1 Indirect taxes, net	...	...	...	...	...	...	...	...	...	...	...	...
2 Consumption of fixed capital	45954	44425	1529	...	49070	47413	1657	...	48917	47398	1519	...
3 Compensation of employees	...	...	...	...	...	...	...	...	...	...	...	...
4 Net operating surplus	53122	69493	-16372	...	44395	62261	-17866	...	42645	60103	-17458	...
Gross Input	...	...	...	...	...	...	...	...	...	...	...	...

3.22 Corporate and Quasi-Corporate Enterprise Income and Outlay Account: Total and Sectors

Thousand Million Japanese yen

	1980 TOTAL	1980 Non-Financial	1980 Financial	1985 TOTAL	1985 Non-Financial	1985 Financial	1990 TOTAL	1990 Non-Financial	1990 Financial	1991 TOTAL	1991 Non-Financial	1991 Financial
Receipts												
1 Operating surplus	31555	37315	-5760	40610	49750	-9139	53172	68573	-15401	53122	69493	-16372
2 Property and entrepreneurial income	59808	7348	52461	93248	8524	84723	152406	14913	137493	161128	16127	145000
A Withdrawals from quasi-corporate enterprises a	...	...	...	...	...	...	...	...	...	...	...	...
B Interest	57143	5827	51317	88802	6436	82366	142232	8675	133557	150521	9469	141052

Japan

3.22 Corporate and Quasi-Corporate Enterprise Income and Outlay Account: Total and Sectors
(Continued)

Thousand Million Japanese yen

	1980 TOTAL	1980 Non-Financial	1980 Financial	1985 TOTAL	1985 Non-Financial	1985 Financial	1990 TOTAL	1990 Non-Financial	1990 Financial	1991 TOTAL	1991 Non-Financial	1991 Financial
C Dividends	2318	1174	1144	3961	1603	2357	9274	5338	3936	9603	5654	3948
D Net land rent and royalties	347	347	-	485	485	-	900	900	...	1004	1004	...
3 Current transfers	3074	857	2217	4111	1139	2972	4648	1274	3374	6055	1724	4331
A Casualty insurance claims	874	806	68	1157	1092	65	1159	1195	-36	1653	1637	16
B Casualty insurance premiums, net, due to be received by insurance companies	2148	-	2148	2906	-	2906	3406	...	3406	4311	...	4311
C Current transfers from the rest of the world [b]	...	...	...	...	...	...	...	...	...	...	...	...
D Other transfers except imputed [b]	...	...	...	...	...	...	...	...	...	...	...	...
E Imputed unfunded employee pension and welfare contributions	52	50	1	48	47	1	83	79	4	90	86	4
Total Current Receipts	94437	45519	48918	137969	59413	78556	210226	84760	125466	220304	87344	132960
Disbursements												
1 Property and entrepreneurial income	72721	29563	43159	105751	33628	72122	171054	50045	121009	183571	55991	127580
A Withdrawals from quasi-corporations [a]	...	...	...	...	...	...	...	...	...	...	...	...
B Interest	65439	24894	40545	94855	28006	66849	152333	41349	110984	164856	46961	117895
C Dividends	5725	3190	2535	8840	3698	5142	15357	5597	9759	15154	5744	9410
D Net land rent and royalties	1558	1479	79	2056	1924	132	3365	3099	266	3561	3286	276
2 Direct taxes and other current transfers n.e.c. to general government	11082	9264	1819	17381	13823	3558	25200	20765	4435	24785	20712	4073
A Direct taxes	10977	9175	1802	17237	13707	3530	25012	20610	4402	24603	20559	4044
On income	10930	9132	1798	16968	13473	3495	24663	20316	4347	24232	20231	4001
Other	47	42	4	269	234	35	349	294	55	371	328	43
B Fines, fees, penalties and other current transfers n.e.c.	106	89	17	144	116	28	188	155	33	182	154	29
3 Other current transfers	3793	1326	2467	5207	1846	3361	6224	2548	3676	7859	3049	4809
A Casualty insurance premiums, net	856	787	68	1149	1082	66	1144	1179	-35	1629	1611	18
B Casualty insurance claims liability of insurance companies	2148	-	2148	2906	-	2906	3406	...	3406	4311	...	4311
C Transfers to private non-profit institutions [b]	...	...	...	...	...	...	...	...	...	...	...	...
D Unfunded employee pension and welfare benefits	52	51	1	48	47	1	83	79	4	90	86	4
E Social assistance grants [b]	737	488	249	1105	717	388	1591	1290	301	1828	1351	477
F Other transfers n.e.c. [b]	...	...	...	...	...	...	...	...	...	...	...	...
G Transfers to the rest of the world [b]	...	...	...	...	...	...	...	...	...	...	...	...
Net saving	6840	5367	1473	9630	10116	-485	7748	11402	-3654	4089	7592	-3502
Total Current Disbursements and Net Saving	94437	45519	48917	137969	59413	78556	210226	84760	125466	220304	87344	132960

	1992 TOTAL	1992 Non-Financial	1992 Financial	1993 TOTAL	1993 Non-Financial	1993 Financial
Receipts						
1 Operating surplus	44395	62261	-17866	42645	60103	-17458
2 Property and entrepreneurial income	146887	13287	133599	135867	11760	124107
A Withdrawals from quasi-corporate enterprises [a]	...	...	...	...	...	...
B Interest	136629	6828	129801	124244	5480	118764
C Dividends	9181	5382	3799	10448	5105	5343
D Net land rent and royalties	1077	1077	...	1175	1175	...

Japan

3.22 Corporate and Quasi-Corporate Enterprise Income and Outlay Account: Total and Sectors
(Continued)

Thousand Million Japanese yen

	1992 TOTAL	1992 Non-Financial	1992 Financial	1993 TOTAL	1993 Non-Financial	1993 Financial
3 Current transfers	6064	1590	4474	6420	1510	4910
A Casualty insurance claims	1603	1499	105	1567	1415	152
B Casualty insurance premiums, net, due to be received by insurance companies	4366	...	4366	4754	...	4754
C Current transfers from the rest of the world [b]	...	...	...	...	...	...
D Other transfers except imputed [b]	...	...	...	...	...	...
E Imputed unfunded employee pension and welfare contributions	95	92	4	99	95	4
Total Current Receipts	197346	77139	120208	184932	73374	111559

Disbursements

	1992 TOTAL	1992 Non-Financial	1992 Financial	1993 TOTAL	1993 Non-Financial	1993 Financial
1 Property and entrepreneurial income	165366	50111	115255	153556	44873	108684
A Withdrawals from quasi-corporations [a]	...	...	...	...	...	...
B Interest	147465	40849	106615	134051	35521	98530
C Dividends	13968	5604	8364	15483	5607	9876
D Net land rent and royalties	3934	3657	277	4022	3745	277
2 Direct taxes and other current transfers n.e.c. to general government	22657	18187	4470	20070	15969	4101
A Direct taxes	22480	18044	4436	19892	15826	4066
On income	22096	17701	4394	19500	15477	4023
Other	384	343	42	393	350	43
B Fines, fees, penalties and other current transfers n.e.c.	177	143	34	178	143	35
3 Other current transfers	7930	2770	5160	8579	2307	6272
A Casualty insurance premiums, net	1585	1479	106	1544	1390	154
B Casualty insurance claims liability of insurance companies	4366	...	4366	4754	...	4754
C Transfers to private non-profit institutions [b]	...	...	...	...	...	...
D Unfunded employee pension and welfare benefits	95	92	4	99	95	4
E Social assistance grants [b]	1884	1200	684	2182	821	1361
F Other transfers n.e.c. [b]	...	...	...	...	...	...
G Transfers to the rest of the world [b]	...	...	...	...	...	...
Net saving	1393	6070	-4677	2727	10225	-7498
Total Current Disbursements and Net Saving	197346	77139	120208	184932	73374	111559

a) Item 'Withdrawals from quasi-corporate enterprises' is not included in the income and outlay accounts of the corporate and quasi-corporate enterprise table and household and private unincorporated enterprise table.
b) Unrequited current transfers are recorded on a net basis, so that those net estimates are included in item 'Social assistance grants'.

3.23 Corporate and Quasi-Corporate Enterprise Capital Accumulation Account: Total and Sectors

Thousand Million Japanese yen

	1980 TOTAL	1980 Non-Financial	1980 Financial	1985 TOTAL	1985 Non-Financial	1985 Financial	1990 TOTAL	1990 Non-Financial	1990 Financial	1991 TOTAL	1991 Non-Financial	1991 Financial
Finance of Gross Accumulation												
1 Gross saving	25523	23444	2078	37097	36723	374	49446	51504	-2058	50043	52017	-1974
A Consumption of fixed capital	18682	18077	605	27467	26607	860	41698	40102	1596	45954	44425	1529
B Net saving	6840	5367	1473	9630	10116	-485	7748	11402	-3654	4089	7592	-3502
2 Capital transfers [a]	1602	1602	-	1456	1456	-	1692	1692	...	2050	2050	...
Finance of Gross Accumulation	27125	25047	2078	38553	38179	374	51138	53196	-2058	52094	54067	-1974
Gross Accumulation												
1 Gross capital formation	39546	38665	881	52058	50989	1069	84047	80992	3055	90583	87588	2995

Japan

3.23 Corporate and Quasi-Corporate Enterprise Capital Accumulation Account: Total and Sectors
(Continued)

Thousand Million Japanese yen

	1980 TOTAL	1980 Non-Financial	1980 Financial	1985 TOTAL	1985 Non-Financial	1985 Financial	1990 TOTAL	1990 Non-Financial	1990 Financial	1991 TOTAL	1991 Non-Financial	1991 Financial
A Increase in stocks	1543	1543	...	2052	2052	...	2297	2297	...	3174	3174	...
B Gross fixed capital formation	38003	37121	881	50006	48937	1069	81750	78696	3055	87410	84414	2995
2 Purchases of land, net	1242	1126	117	2795	2614	182	12985	12429	556	5012	4458	554
3 Purchases of intangible assets, net	...	...	...	...	...	...	...	...	...	...	...	...
4 Capital transfers [a]	...	...	...	...	...	...	...	...	...	...	...	...
Net lending [b]	-13664	-14744	1080	-16300	-15423	-876	-45894	-40225	-5669	-43502	-37979	-5523
Gross Accumulation	27125	25047	2078	38553	38179	374	51139	53197	-2058	52094	54067	-1974

	1992 TOTAL	1992 Non-Financial	1992 Financial	1993 TOTAL	1993 Non-Financial	1993 Financial
Finance of Gross Accumulation						
1 Gross saving	50463	53484	-3020	51644	57623	-5979
A Consumption of fixed capital	49070	47413	1657	48917	47398	1519
B Net saving	1393	6070	-4677	2727	10225	-7498
2 Capital transfers [a]	2481	2481	...	3101	3101	...
Finance of Gross Accumulation	52944	55965	-3020	54745	60724	-5979
Gross Accumulation						
1 Gross capital formation	84195	81462	2733	75546	73214	2332
A Increase in stocks	1603	1603	...	610	610	...
B Gross fixed capital formation	82592	79859	2733	74937	72605	2332
2 Purchases of land, net	1781	1483	298	-1930	-2132	202
3 Purchases of intangible assets, net	...	...	...	...	...	...
4 Capital transfers [a]	...	...	...	...	...	...
Net lending [b]	-33031	-26980	-6052	-18871	-10358	-8513
Gross Accumulation	52944	55965	-3020	54745	60724	-5979

a) Capital transfers received are recorded net of capital transfers paid.
b) Net lending of the capital accumulation account and the capital finance account have not been reconciled and are different due to different statistical sources.

3.24 Corporate and Quasi-Corporate Enterprise Capital Finance Account: Total and Sectors

Thousand Million Japanese yen

	1980 TOTAL	1980 Non-Financial	1980 Financial	1985 TOTAL	1985 Non-Financial	1985 Financial	1990 TOTAL	1990 Non-Financial	1990 Financial	1991 TOTAL	1991 Non-Financial	1991 Financial
Acquisition of Financial Assets												
1 Gold and SDRs [a]	...	...	...	...	...	...	...	...	...	...	...	...
2 Currency and transferable deposits	-417	-1473	1056	1009	1128	-119	4065	3328	739	8155	9204	-1049
3 Other deposits	4777	4777	-	12347	12347	-	-4261	-4261	...	-16968	-16968	...
4 Bills and bonds, short term	2393	-35	2429	-1788	2	-1790	2740	447	2293	-5637	-447	-5190
5 Bonds, long term	13018	1677	11342	18561	1145	17416	8871	3584	5287	14931	1181	13751
6 Corporate equity securities	1584	481	1104	5356	212	5144	9005	3122	5883	-158	-1219	1061
7 Short term loans, n.e.c.	34220	-	34221	50679	-	50679	67964	-	67964	59963	-	59963
8 Long term loans, n.e.c.												
9 Trade credits and advances	9977	9977	...	2977	2977	...	15157	15157	...	12808	12808	...
10 Other receivables	...	...	...	...	...	...	...	...	...	...	...	...
11 Other assets [a]	-1197	-2769	1571	21154	5744	15410	33143	17659	15484	...	...	5163
Total Acquisition of Financial Assets	64356	12634	51722	110295	23553	86741	136686	39036	97650	...	...	73699
Incurrence of Liabilities												
1 Currency and transferable deposits	-1241	-	-1241	2893	-	2893	5388	...	5388	11286	...	11286
2 Other deposits	33231	...	33231	43002	...	43002	49318	...	49318	32695	...	32695
3 Bills and bonds, short term	-303	-303	-	142	142	-	-132	-132	...	-158	-158	...

Japan

3.24 Corporate and Quasi-Corporate Enterprise Capital Finance Account: Total and Sectors
(Continued)

Thousand Million Japanese yen

		1980			1985			1990			1991		
		TOTAL	Non-Financial	Financial	TOTAL	Non-Financial	Financial	TOTAL	Non-Financial	Financial	TOTAL	Non-Financial	Financial
4	Bonds, long term	5537	2777	2761	11550	5628	5922	16426	8603	7822	14690	13797	893
5	Corporate equity securities	1976	1858	118	2389	2018	371	6242	4438	1804	1437	1278	160
6	Short-term loans, n.e.c.	19928	18855	1074	39258	26138	13120	37128	41552	-4424	40010	29094	10916
7	Long-term loans, n.e.c.												
8	Net equity of households in life insurance and pension fund reserves	5622	-	5622	11460	-	11460	21404	...	21404	18998	...	18998
9	Proprietors' net additions to the accumulation of quasi-corporations	-	-	-	-	-	-	...	...	...	...	...	...
10	Trade credit and advances	6243	6243	-	1399	1399	-	9644	9644	-	7661	7661	-
11	Other accounts payable	...	...	...	...	...	...	...	...	...	...	...	...
12	Other liabilities	3570	-4446	8016	11633	1167	10466	41534	23727	17807	-1027	40	-1067
	Total Incurrence of Liabilities	74563	24984	49579	123725	36491	87234	186951	87833	99118	125591	51711	73880
	Net Lending b	-10207	-12349	2142	-13431	-12938	-493	-50267	-48799	-1468	...	...	-181
	Incurrence of Liabilities and Net Lending	64356	12634	51722	110295	23553	86741	136684	39034	97650	...	...	73699

		1992			1993		
		TOTAL	Non-Financial	Financial	TOTAL	Non-Financial	Financial

Acquisition of Financial Assets

1	Gold and SDRs [a]	...	...	...	...	...	...
2	Currency and transferable deposits	1938	2858	-920	3934	4038	-105
3	Other deposits	-8829	-8829	...	-7297	-7297	...
4	Bills and bonds, short term	-952	773	-1725	5047	27	5021
5	Bonds, long term	265851	-558	27143	34302	2417	31885
6	Corporate equity securities	-6437	-748	-5690	2863	-2851	5714
7	Short term loans, n.e.c.	39250	-	39250	25337	2	25335
8	Long term loans, n.e.c.						
9	Trade credits and advances	-13927	-13927	...	-7383	-7383	...
10	Other receivables	...	...	...	...	...	...
11	Other assets [a]	...	...	6233	...	...	-6252
	Total Acquisition of Financial Assets	...	...	64290	...	...	61598

Incurrence of Liabilities

1	Currency and transferable deposits	4845	...	4845	9656	...	9656
2	Other deposits	25934	...	25934	26609	...	26609
3	Bills and bonds, short term	-164	-164	...	-224	-224	...
4	Bonds, long term	15124	5628	9497	9915	3959	5956
5	Corporate equity securities	583	465	118	1279	823	456
6	Short-term loans, n.e.c.	20283	17181	3102	4879	13388	-8509
7	Long-term loans, n.e.c.						
8	Net equity of households in life insurance and pension fund reserves	20836	...	20836	23106	...	23106
9	Proprietors' net additions to the accumulation of quasi-corporations	...	...	...	...	...	...
10	Trade credit and advances	-12522	-12522	-	-4213	-4213	-
11	Other accounts payable	...	...	...	...	...	...
12	Other liabilities	-776	2485	-3261	1847	-4014	5861
	Total Incurrence of Liabilities	74143	13073	61070	72853	9718	63135
	Net Lending b	...	...	3220	...	...	-1537
	Incurrence of Liabilities and Net Lending	...	...	64290	...	...	61598

a) Item 'Gold and SDRs' is included in item 'Other assets'.
b) Net lending of the capital accumulation account and the capital finance account have not been reconciled and are different due to different statistical sources.

Japan

3.32 Household and Private Unincorporated Enterprise Income and Outlay Account

Thousand Million Japanese yen

	1980	1983	1984	1985	1986	1987	1988	1989	1990	1991	1992	1993
Receipts												
1 Compensation of employees	130368	157299	166026	173815	182006	189125	200192	214957	233508	251781	261046	267152
A Wages and salaries	115990	137697	145380	151291	157803	162580	172235	184623	200094	215836	225420	229879
B Employers' contributions for social security	8922	11615	12360	13437	14610	15376	16258	17759	20067	21421	22556	23521
C Employers' contributions for private pension & welfare plans	5457	7987	8286	9087	9593	11169	11699	12575	13347	14524	13070	13752
2 Operating surplus of private unincorporated enterprises	33203	35712	37352	40890	42092	43901	45290	45687	46626	47559	49845	46543
3 Property and entrepreneurial income	23920	29074	30141	31317	32837	32141	32316	36560	43415	48419	45157	42841
A Withdrawals from private quasi-corporations [a]	...	...	...	...	...	...	...	...	...	...	...	...
B Interest	19424	23549	24378	24938	25843	23881	23409	23857	30936	35875	33067	30630
C Dividends	3166	3977	4207	4765	5292	6387	6819	10427	10006	9864	9178	9106
D Net land rent and royalties	1330	1548	1556	1614	1702	1873	2088	2276	2473	2680	2912	3105
3 Current transfers	38607	48952	50650	53365	56759	60238	63543	65073	71500	74614	79310	82403
A Casualty insurance claims	1261	1573	1663	1726	1790	1807	1932	2012	2218	2617	2726	3151
B Social security benefits	18919	25883	27596	28960	31478	34235	35922	37389	42370	42954	46229	49380
C Social assistance grants	6214	7274	6866	7691	7931	8228	8545	8677	8844	9146	9429	9370
D Unfunded employee pension and welfare benefits	60	76	62	58	65	70	81	87	94	103	109	112
E Transfers from general government	...	...	...	...	...	...	...	...	...	...	...	...
F Transfers from the rest of the world	...	...	...	...	...	...	...	...	...	...	...	...
G Other transfers n.e.c.	12153	14145	14463	14929	15498	15898	17063	16908	17973	19795	20818	20390
Total Current Receipts	226098	271037	284170	299387	313693	325405	341340	362277	395049	422373	435358	438939
Disbursements												
1 Final consumption expenditures	139506	167509	176267	186235	193308	201973	212237	225427	240493	251540	261201	267125
2 Property income	8465	10972	11599	11985	12499	13045	13612	14511	18529	20832	19547	17750
A Interest	8125	10591	11217	11587	12079	12651	13186	14061	18038	20329	19042	17222
Consumer debt	751	1005	1116	1219	1360	1420	1629	1901	2451	3167	2904	2560
Mortgage	7374	9586	10101	10367	10719	11230	11558	12160	15587	17162	16139	14662
Other												
B Net land rent and royalties	340	382	383	399	420	394	426	450	491	503	505	528
3 Direct taxes and other current transfers n.e.c. to government	32568	42549	44784	47627	50967	55042	57872	61544	72576	79212	80796	80542
A Social security contributions	17513	22896	24270	26185	27761	29694	31363	33387	38957	41264	43436	45331
B Direct taxes	14899	19470	20323	21248	22995	25098	26268	27925	33354	37650	37039	34865
Income taxes	14025	18466	19222	20113	21806	23848	24933	26499	31832	36066	35420	33217
Other	875	1004	1101	1135	1189	1250	1335	1426	1522	1583	1619	1648
C Fees, fines and penalties	156	184	192	194	211	251	240	232	265	298	321	346
4 Other current transfers	15132	17929	18334	19119	19897	20589	22145	22340	23977	26168	27545	27442
A Net casualty insurance premiums	1275	1571	1661	1729	1801	1822	1946	2023	2230	2639	2740	3170
B Transfers to private non-profit institutions serving households	1701	2220	2291	2526	2694	2820	3129	3429	3673	3839	4022	4155
C Transfers to the rest of the world	...	...	...	...	...	...	...	...	...	...	...	...
D Other current transfers, except imputed	12095	14062	14320	14806	15338	15876	16989	16802	17980	19587	20675	20005
E Imputed employee pension and welfare contributions	60	76	62	58	65	70	81	87	94	103	109	112
Net saving	30426	32079	33185	34421	37022	34755	35475	38454	39473	44621	46269	46080
Total Current Disbursements and Net Saving	226097	271037	284170	299387	313693	325405	341341	362276	395049	422373	435358	438939

a) Item 'Withdrawals from quasi-corporate enterprises' is not included in the income and outlay accounts of the corporate and quasi-corporate enterprise table and household and private unincorporated enterprise table.

Japan

3.33 Household and Private Unincorporated Enterprise Capital Accumulation Account

Thousand Million Japanese yen

	1980	1983	1984	1985	1986	1987	1988	1989	1990	1991	1992	1993
\multicolumn{13}{c}{**Finance of Gross Accumulation**}
1 Gross saving	40761	44346	46025	47782	50860	49159	50761	54881	57073	63484	66053	66597
A Consumption of fixed capital	10335	12267	12840	13361	13838	14403	15286	16428	17600	18863	19784	20518
B Net saving	30426	32079	33185	34421	37022	34755	35475	38454	39473	44621	46269	46080
2 Capital transfers [a]	-1152	-1497	-1623	-1730	-2066	-2474	-2788	-2660	-3082	-2817	-3845	-3860
Total Finance of Gross Accumulation [b]	39607	42848	44401	46051	48794	46685	47973	52222	53991	60667	62208	62738
\multicolumn{13}{c}{**Gross Accumulation**}
1 Gross Capital Formation	22400	21033	20861	21860	22868	26312	29097	30444	31887	31378	31540	31563
A Increase in stocks	69	112	27	107	205	107	63	82	25	98	28	52
B Gross fixed capital formation	22330	20921	20833	21753	22663	26205	29035	30362	31862	31281	31512	31512
2 Purchases of land, net	-3808	-3610	-3178	-5649	-5902	-8766	-12543	-14534	-17529	-10320	-7710	-4466
3 Purchases of intangibles, net	...	...	...	...	...	...	...	...	...	...	...	...
4 Capital transfers [a]	...	...	...	...	...	...	...	...	...	...	...	...
Net lending [c]	21016	25425	26719	29840	31827	29139	31418	36311	39634	39609	38378	35640
Total Gross Accumulation [b]	39607	42848	44401	46051	48794	46685	47973	52222	53992	60667	62208	62738

a) Capital transfers received are recorded net of capital transfers paid.
b) Private non-profit institutions serving households are included in household and private unincorporated enterprises.
c) Net lending of the capital accumulation account and the capital finance account have not been reconciled and are different due to different statistical sources.

3.34 Household and Private Unincorporated Enterprise Capital Finance Account

Thousand Million Japanese yen

	1980	1983	1984	1985	1986	1987	1988	1989	1990	1991	1992	1993
\multicolumn{13}{c}{**Acquisition of Financial Assets**}
1 Gold [a]	...	...	...	...	...	...	...	...	...	...	...	...
2 Currency and transferable deposits	-749	291	3836	2042	5729	6418	6056	10160	1041	3099	2685	5609
3 Other deposits	22546	22773	19850	22185	19285	21812	24853	35291	40917	39235	26813	25768
4 Bills and bonds, short term	...	...	...	...	...	...	...	...	...	...	...	...
5 Bonds, long term	3451	6567	7094	1484	3281	6294	-656	5508	2982	-3110	-1426	-6899
6 Corporate equity securities	-76	-619	596	-567	-1554	4607	-1575	-1257	2144	-2904	-252	-1115
7 Short term loans, n.e.c.	...	...	...	...	...	...	...	...	...	...	...	...
8 Long term loans, n.e.c.	...	...	...	...	...	...	...	...	...	...	...	...
9 Trade credit and advances	...	...	...	...	...	...	...	...	...	...	...	...
10 Net equity of households in life insurance and pension fund reserves	5358	7466	9672	10799	14489	17217	20890	22273	18111	15840	15029	18080
11 Proprietors' net additions to the accumulation of quasi-corporations	...	...	...	...	...	...	...	...	...	...	...	...
12 Other [a]	678	1118	1156	2223	2229	1680	430	1825	2209	361	710	517
Total Acquisition of Financial Assets [b]	31209	37595	42204	38166	43458	58028	49998	73800	67404	52520	43559	41960
\multicolumn{13}{c}{**Incurrence of Liabilities**}
1 Short term loans, n.e.c.	10975	10359	9319	7572	12070	25784	19915	31047	23362	12211	5180	9601
2 Long term loans, n.e.c.	...	...	...	...	...	...	...	...	...	...	...	...
3 Trade credit and advances	3488	2484	4245	1385	1080	587	2076	8085	5441	5028	-1537	-3390
4 Other accounts payable	...	...	...	...	...	...	...	...	...	...	...	...
5 Other liabilities	...	...	...	...	...	...	...	...	-	-	-	-
Total Incurrence of Liabilities [b]	14463	12843	13564	8957	13150	26371	21991	39132	28803	17240	3644	6212
Net Lending [c]	16745	24753	28639	29209	30308	31656	28007	34669	38600	35281	39915	35748
Incurrence of Liabilities and Net Lending [b]	31209	37595	42204	38166	43458	58028	49998	73801	67403	52520	43559	41960

a) Item 'Gold and SDRs' is included in item 'Other assets'.
b) Private non-profit institutions serving households are included in household and private unincorporated enterprises.
c) Net lending of the capital accumulation account and the capital finance account have not been reconciled and are different due to different statistical sources.

3.41 Private Non-Profit Institutions Serving Households: Production Account

Thousand Million Japanese yen

	1980	1983	1984	1985	1986	1987	1988	1989	1990	1991	1992	1993
\multicolumn{13}{c}{**Gross Output**}
1 Sales	...	...	...	...	...	...	...	...	...	...	...	...
2 Non-marketed output	...	...	...	...	...	...	...	...	...	...	...	...
A Services produced for own use	1832	2245	2435	2548	2638	2677	2845	2953	3056	3544	3623	3795
B Own account fixed capital formation	...	...	...	...	...	...	...	...	...	...	...	...
Gross Output	...	...	...	...	...	...	...	...	...	...	...	...

Japan

3.41 Private Non-Profit Institutions Serving Households: Production Account
(Continued)

Thousand Million Japanese yen

	1980	1983	1984	1985	1986	1987	1988	1989	1990	1991	1992	1993
					Gross Input							
Intermediate consumption	2861	3179	3418	3595	3740	4037	4340	4660	4910	5135	5547	5579
Subtotal: Value Added	...	...	...	...	...	...	...	...	...	...	...	...
1 Indirect taxes, net	...	...	...	...	...	...	...	...	...	...	...	...
2 Consumption of fixed capital	292	522	624	710	743	828	861	930	1014	1044	1144	1135
3 Compensation of employees	3947	4772	5150	5461	5864	6044	6504	6942	7276	7719	8081	8430
4 Net operating surplus	...	...	...	...	...	...	...	...	...	...	...	...
Gross Input	...	...	...	...	...	...	...	...	...	...	...	...

3.42 Private Non-Profit Institutions Serving Households: Income and Outlay Account

Thousand Million Japanese yen

	1980	1983	1984	1985	1986	1987	1988	1989	1990	1991	1992	1993
					Receipts							
1 Operating surplus	...	...	...	...	...	...	...	...	...	...	...	...
2 Property and entrepreneurial income	960	1127	1215	1235	1271	1134	1043	1043	1394	1624	1400	1218
A Withdrawals from quasi-corporations	...	...	...	...	...	...	...	...	...	...	...	...
B Interest	915	1067	1148	1164	1178	1015	911	844	1211	1445	1244	1068
C Dividends	19	33	36	37	57	81	91	160	145	141	118	110
D Net land rent and royalties	26	28	31	34	36	38	40	39	38	38	38	40
3 Current transfers	2986	3855	3961	4321	4604	4874	5394	5875	6343	6781	7144	7435
A Casualty insurance claims	7	12	13	13	13	14	14	14	19	31	26	24
B Current transfers from general government	838	1063	1089	1129	1193	1267	1341	1418	1546	1718	1850	1982
C Other transfers from resident sectors	...	...	...	...	...	...	...	...	...	...	...	...
D Current transfers received from the rest of the world	2139	2776	2857	3177	3396	3590	4037	4441	4775	5029	5265	5425
E Imputed unfunded employee pension and welfare contributions	2	2	2	2	2	2	3	3	3	3	3	4
Total Current Receipts	3947	4982	5176	5555	5875	6008	6437	6918	7737	8404	8544	8653
					Disbursements							
1 Final consumption expenditures	1818	2179	2364	2525	2661	2612	2885	3056	3135	3544	3623	3795
A Compensation of employees	...	...	...	...	...	...	...	...	...	...	...	...
B Consumption of fixed capital	292	522	624	710	743	828	863	930	1014	1044	1144	1135
C Purchases of goods and services, net	...	...	...	...	...	...	...	...	...	...	...	...
2 Property income	606	778	879	901	925	932	922	964	1201	1410	1366	1356
3 Direct taxes and other transfers to general government	...	...	...	...	...	...	...	...	...	...	...	...
4 Other current transfers	977	1530	1537	1754	1877	2063	2252	2322	2415	2547	2547	2244
A Net casualty insurance premiums	11	17	18	19	18	18	17	19	21	31	28	27
B Social assistance grants	964	1511	1517	1734	1857	2043	2232	2300	2391	2512	2516	2213
C Unfunded employee pension and welfare benefits	2	2	2	2	2	2	3	3	3	3	3	4
D Current transfers to the rest of the world	...	...	...	...	...	...	...	...	...	...	...	...
E Other current transfers n.e.c.	...	...	...	...	...	...	...	...	...	...	...	...
Net saving	546	495	396	376	412	401	378	576	985	904	1008	1259
Total Current Disbursements	3947	4982	5176	5555	5875	6008	6437	6918	7737	8404	8544	8653

3.43 Private Non-Profit Institutions Serving Households: Capital Accumulation Account

Thousand Million Japanese yen

	1980	1983	1984	1985	1986	1987	1988	1989	1990	1991	1992	1993
					Finance of Gross Accumulation							
1 Gross saving	838	1017	1020	1086	1155	1229	1241	1506	1999	1948	2152	2393
A Consumption of fixed capital	292	522	624	710	743	828	863	930	1014	1044	1144	1135
B Net saving	546	495	396	376	412	401	378	576	985	904	1008	1259
2 Capital transfers	579	569	613	597	610	625	640	668	731	719	774	819
Finance of Gross Accumulation	1417	1586	1633	1683	1765	1854	1881	2174	2729	2667	2927	3212

Japan

3.43 Private Non-Profit Institutions Serving Households: Capital Accumulation Account
(Continued)

Thousand Million Japanese yen

	1980	1983	1984	1985	1986	1987	1988	1989	1990	1991	1992	1993
					Gross Accumulation							
1 Gross capital formation	803	1029	1145	1112	1062	1184	1337	1443	1572	1613	1654	1563
A Increase in stocks	...	...	...	...	...	...	...	...	...	...	...	...
B Gross fixed capital formation	803	1029	1145	1112	1062	1184	1337	1443	1572	1613	1654	1563
2 Purchases of land, net	170	119	49	150	159	192	277	334	15	145	46	124
3 Purchases of intangible assets, net	...	...	...	...	...	...	...	...	...	...	...	...
4 Capital transfers	...	...	...	...	...	...	...	...	...	...	...	...
Net lending [a]		444	438	438	421	544	477	266	397	1143	909	1226	1525
Gross Accumulation	1417	1586	1633	1683	1765	1854	1881	2174	2729	2667	2927	3212

a) Net lending of the capital accumulation account and the capital finance account have not been reconciled and are different due to different statistical sources.

3.44 Private Non-Profit Institutions Serving Households: Capital Finance Account

Thousand Million Japanese yen

	1980	1983	1984	1985	1986	1987	1988	1989	1990	1991	1992	1993
					Acquisition of Financial Assets							
1 Gold	...	...	...	...	...	...	...	...	...	...	...	...
2 Currency and transferable deposits	78	163	83	-52	-46	-62	-92	73	93	110	112	156
3 Other deposits	1150	857	488	984	1199	1289	1375	1510	1490	1595	1279	1238
4 Bills and bonds, short term	...	...	...	...	...	...	...	...	...	...	...	...
5 Bonds, long term	129	132	145	114	159	133	158	126	145	133	160	166
6 Corporate equity securities	5	12	15	11	11	11	32	17	11	5	5	8
7 Short-term loans, n.e.c.	487	372	92	152	184	31	-79	-193	114	244	181	296
8 Long-term loans, n.e.c.												
9 Other receivables	...	...	...	...	...	...	...	...	...	...	...	...
10 Proprietors' net additions to the accumulation of quasi-corporations	...	...	...	...	...	...	...	...	...	...	...	...
11 Other assets	40	46	35	92	102	94	136	-42	129	121	160	76
Total Acquisition of Financial Assets	1889	1581	858	1301	1609	1496	1529	1491	1982	2208	1896	1941
					Incurrence of Liabilities							
1 Short-term loans	1036	878	702	985	1178	1059	1080	1077	1822	1755	1467	1023
2 Long-term loans												
3 Other liabilities	268	169	-273	208	168	105	273	117	246	166	262	326
Total Incurrence of Liabilities	1304	1047	429	1192	1346	1164	1353	1194	2068	1920	1728	1350
Net Lending [a]	585	534	429	109	263	332	177	297	-86	287	167	591
Incurrence of Liabilities and Net Lending	1889	1581	858	1301	1609	1496	1529	1491	1982	2208	1896	1941

a) Net lending of the capital accumulation account and the capital finance account have not been reconciled and are different due to different statistical sources.

3.51 External Transactions: Current Account: Detail

Thousand Million Japanese yen

	1980	1983	1984	1985	1986	1987	1988	1989	1990	1991	1992	1993
					Payments to the Rest of the World							
1 Imports of goods and services	35036	34258	36866	35532	24791	25195	29065	36768	42872	38529	36184	33333
A Imports of merchandise c.i.f. [a]	29153	27902	30328	28856	19356	18708	21330	26906	31598	27670	25374	23481
B Other	5883	6356	6538	6676	5436	6487	7736	9863	11274	10859	10810	9852
2 Factor income to the rest of the world	2898	3900	4448	4631	4108	5553	7822	11911	15588	16577	14784	13001

Japan

3.51 External Transactions: Current Account: Detail
(Continued)

Thousand Million Japanese yen

	1980	1983	1984	1985	1986	1987	1988	1989	1990	1991	1992	1993
A Compensation of employees	244	411	401	387	256	281	232	274	313	350	362	319
B Property and entrepreneurial income	2654	3489	4047	4244	3853	5273	7590	11637	15275	16227	14422	12681
3 Current transfers to the rest of the world	342	359	373	355	292	463	497	475	491	462	584	660
A Indirect taxes by general government to supranational organizations	...	...	...	...	...	...	...	...	...	...	...	...
B Other current transfers	342	359	373	355	292	463	497	475	491	462	584	660
By general government	84	111	107	90	80	88	104	148	149	139	168	184
By other resident sectors	257	248	266	265	212	375	393	327	342	323	416	476
4 Surplus of the nation on current transactions	-2481	5083	8467	11660	14306	12697	10364	8100	5638	11171	15089	14780
Payments to the Rest of the World, and Surplus of the Nation on Current Transfers	35795	43600	50154	52178	43497	43908	47748	57254	64589	66739	66640	61774
Receipts From The Rest of the World												
1 Exports of goods and services	32887	39275	45066	46307	38090	36210	37483	42352	45920	46810	47409	44244
A Exports of merchandise f.o.b.	29022	34964	40381	41555	34575	32490	33398	37372	40651	41438	42049	39133
B Other	3865	4311	4685	4752	3515	3720	4085	4980	5269	5372	5361	5111
2 Factor income from the rest of the world	2820	4211	4953	5768	5338	7607	10124	14761	18520	19767	19052	17381
A Compensation of employees	214	354	308	311	303	336	312	381	447	441	616	520
B Property and entrepreneurial income	2606	3858	4646	5458	5035	7271	9811	14380	18073	19326	18436	16861
3 Current transfers from the rest of the world	87	114	134	102	70	92	141	142	149	163	179	149
A Subsidies to general government from supranational organizations	...	...	...	...	...	...	...	...	...	...	...	...
B Other current transfers	87	114	134	102	70	92	141	142	149	163	179	149
To general government	10	12	13	12	7	9	9	14	11	8	19	16
To other resident sectors	78	102	122	90	63	82	132	128	138	155	160	134
Receipts from the Rest of the World on Current Transfers	35794	43600	50153	52177	43498	43909	47748	57255	64589	66740	66640	61774

a) Imports of merchandise c.i.f. is not estimated in the Balance of Payments in Japan. Therefore, valuation basis is f.o.b.

3.52 External Transactions: Capital Accumulation Account

Thousand Million Japanese yen

	1980	1983	1984	1985	1986	1987	1988	1989	1990	1991	1992	1993
Finance of Gross Accumulation												
1 Surplus of the nation on current transactions	-2481	5083	8467	11660	14306	12697	10364	8100	5638	11171	15089	14780
2 Capital transfers from the rest of the world a	-96	-123	-117	-142	-127	-156	-172	-247	-435	-1404	-186	-168
A By general government	-96	-123	-117	-142	-127	-156	-172	-247	-435	-1404	-186	-168
B By other resident sectors	-	-	-	-	-	-	-	-	-	-	-	...
Total Finance of Gross Accumulation	-2577	4960	8350	11518	14179	12541	10192	7853	5203	9767	14903	14613
Gross Accumulation												
1 Capital transfers to the rest of the world a	...	...	...	...	...	...	...	...	...	...	...	...
2 Purchases of intangible assets, n.e.c., net, from the rest of the world	...	...	...	...	...	...	...	...	...	...	...	...
Net lending to the rest of the world	-2577	4960	8351	11518	14179	12541	10192	7853	5203	9767	14903	14613
Total Gross Accumulation	-2577	4960	8351	11518	14179	12541	10192	7853	5203	9767	14903	14613

a) Capital transfers received are recorded net of capital transfers paid.

3.53 External Transactions: Capital Finance Account

Thousand Million Japanese yen

	1980	1983	1984	1985	1986	1987	1988	1989	1990	1991	1992	1993
Acquisitions of Foreign Financial Assets												
1 Gold and SDR's a	13	-47	-16	75	39	58	51	-66	98	-62	-188	51
2 Currency and transferable deposits	...	...	...	...	...	...	...	...	...	...	...	...
3 Other deposits	...	...	...	...	...	...	...	...	...	...	...	...
4 Bills and bonds, short term	...	...	...	...	...	...	...	...	...	...	...	...

Japan

3.53 External Transactions: Capital Finance Account
(Continued)

Thousand Million Japanese yen

	1980	1983	1984	1985	1986	1987	1988	1989	1990	1991	1992	1993
5 Bonds, long term	...	...	...	...	...	...	...	...	...	...	...	...
6 Corporate equity securities	...	...	...	...	...	...	...	...	...	...	...	...
7 Short-term loans, n.e.c.	...	...	...	...	...	...	...	...	...	...	...	...
8 Long-term loans	...	...	...	...	...	...	...	...	...	...	...	...
9 Proprietors' net additions to accumulation of quasi-corporate, non-resident enterprises	...	...	...	...	...	...	...	...	...	...	...	...
10 Trade credit and advances	...	...	...	...	...	...	...	...	...	...	...	...
11 Other	3456	8046	14017	19287	24609	25039	21240	24954	16348	15288	7433	10928
Total Acquisitions of Foreign Financial Assets	3469	7999	14001	19362	24648	25097	21291	24888	16446	15225	7245	10979

Incurrence of Foreign Liabilities

	1980	1983	1984	1985	1986	1987	1988	1989	1990	1991	1992	1993
1 Currency and transferable deposits	...	...	...	...	...	...	...	...	...	...	...	...
2 Other deposits	...	...	...	...	...	...	...	...	...	...	...	...
3 Bills and bonds, short term	...	...	...	...	...	...	...	...	...	...	...	...
4 Bonds, long term	...	...	...	...	...	...	...	...	...	...	...	...
5 Corporate equity securities	...	...	...	...	...	...	...	...	...	...	...	...
6 Short-term loans, n.e.c.	...	...	...	...	...	...	...	...	...	...	...	...
7 Long-term loans	...	...	...	...	...	...	...	...	...	...	...	...
8 Non-resident proprietors' net additions to accumulation of resident quasi-corporate enterprises	...	...	...	...	...	...	...	...	...	...	...	...
9 Trade credit and advances	...	...	...	...	...	...	...	...	...	...	...	...
10 Other	6047	3038	5651	7844	10469	12556	11099	17035	11243	5459	-7658	-3633
Total Incurrence of Liabilities	6047	3038	5651	7844	10469	12556	11099	17035	11243	5459	-7658	-3633
Net Lending	-2577	4960	8351	11518	14179	12541	10192	7853	5203	9767	14903	14613
Total Incurrence of Liabilities and Net Lending	3470	7998	14002	19362	24648	25097	21291	24888	16446	15225	7245	10979

a) Item 'Gold and SDRs' excludes initial allocations of SDRs by IMF.

4.1 Derivation of Value Added by Kind of Activity, in Current Prices

Thousand Million Japanese yen

	1980 Gross Output	1980 Intermediate Consumption	1980 Value Added	1985 Gross Output	1985 Intermediate Consumption	1985 Value Added	1990 Gross Output	1990 Intermediate Consumption	1990 Value Added	1991 Gross Output	1991 Intermediate Consumption	1991 Value Added
All Producers												
1 Agriculture, hunting, forestry and fishing	16411	7563	8847	18400	8186	10214	18026	7473	10553	17920	7400	10520
2 Mining and quarrying	2621	1258	1363	1936	978	958	2286	1007	1279	2331	1028	1304
3 Manufacturing	242496	172264	70232	287810	193138	94673	348072	224629	123443	366078	234742	131336
A Manufacture of food, beverages and tobacco [a]	24059	16146	7913	32419	21285	11134	36017	22619	13398	37591	23624	13967
B Textile, wearing apparel and leather industries [b]	8759	6224	2535	8023	5478	2545	7561	5200	2361	7550	5157	2393
C Manufacture of wood and wood products, including furniture	...	...	...	...	...	...	...	...	...	...	...	...
D Manufacture of paper and paper products, printing and publishing [c]	8041	6032	2009	8411	6021	2390	9982	6622	3360	10059	6571	3488
E Manufacture of chemicals and chemical petroleum, coal, rubber and plastic products [d]	37733	29770	7963	39663	28707	10956	39441	24907	14534	40596	25215	15382
F Manufacture of non-metallic mineral products, except products of petroleum and coal	8236	5501	2735	8572	5124	3448	10273	5736	4536	10647	5990	4657
G Basic metal industries	41407	32523	8885	35424	27559	7865	38301	28678	9623	38769	28787	9982
H Manufacture of fabricated metal products, machinery and equipment	84568	56729	27839	118861	76536	42325	159126	102642	56485	170688	109844	60844
I Other manufacturing industries	29693	19338	10355	36436	22428	14008	47373	28225	19148	50178	29555	20624
4 Electricity, gas and water	13452	6872	6580	18425	8119	10306	19068	7579	11489	20369	8041	12328
5 Construction	55168	32662	22506	57660	32279	25381	89190	47063	42127	94514	49493	45021
6 Wholesale and retail trade, restaurants and hotels	55396	18604	36792	65896	23060	42836	84913	30411	54501	90286	32456	57830
7 Transport, storage and communication	25546	10760	14787	34095	13009	21086	42982	15882	27100	45264	16646	28618
8 Finance, insurance, real estate and business services	42343	7249	35095	60782	11451	49331	89425	19895	69529	91825	19799	72027
9 Community, social and personal services [e]	52796	24733	28063	81696	35306	46390	122921	55609	67313	132324	60375	71949

Japan

4.1 Derivation of Value Added by Kind of Activity, in Current Prices
(Continued)

Thousand Million Japanese yen

	1980 Gross Output	1980 Intermediate Consumption	1980 Value Added	1985 Gross Output	1985 Intermediate Consumption	1985 Value Added	1990 Gross Output	1990 Intermediate Consumption	1990 Value Added	1991 Gross Output	1991 Intermediate Consumption	1991 Value Added
Total, Industries	506229	281963	224266	626700	325525	301175	816882	409548	407334	860910	429979	430932
Producers of Government Services	27712	7213	20499	36454	10170	26284	46475	13787	32688	49125	14904	34222
Other Producers	7147	2861	4286	9814	3595	6219	13264	4910	8354	13965	5135	8830
Total	541087	292037	249050	672968	339290	333678	876621	428244	448377	924001	450017	473983
Less: Imputed bank service charge	...	-10413	10413	...	-14774	14774	...	-22322	22322	...	-22670	22670
Import duties	1313	...	1313	1353	...	1353	2713	...	2713	2872	...	2872
Value added tax	...	...	...	...	...	...	-2208	...	-2209	-2312	...	-2312
Other adjustments f	225	...	225	161	...	161	-2022	...	-2022	-576	...	-576
Total	542625	302449	240176	674482	354063	320419	875103	450566	424536	923984	472687	451297

	1992 Gross Output	1992 Intermediate Consumption	1992 Value Added	1993 Gross Output	1993 Intermediate Consumption	1993 Value Added
			All Producers			
1 Agriculture, hunting, forestry and fishing	17257	7079	10178	16754	6778	9977
2 Mining and quarrying	2351	1022	1329	2171	936	1235
3 Manufacturing	351407	221813	129594	331358	206480	124878
A Manufacture of food, beverages and tobacco a	38632	23819	14813	38438	23293	15145
B Textile, wearing apparel and leather industries b	7196	4644	2553	6245	3840	2405
C Manufacture of wood and wood products, including furniture	...	...	...	...	...	...
D Manufacture of paper and paper products, printing and publishing c	9772	6332	3440	9335	5822	3513
E Manufacture of chemicals and chemical petroleum, coal, rubber and plastic products d	40044	24135	15909	38144	22417	15727
F Manufacture of non-metallic mineral products, except products of petroleum and coal	10341	5798	4543	9793	5402	4391
G Basic metal industries	33429	24262	9167	30754	22256	8498
H Manufacture of fabricated metal products, machinery and equipment	163004	104748	58256	151945	97032	54913
I Other manufacturing industries	48989	28074	20914	46704	26418	20286
4 Electricity, gas and water	20977	8034	12943	21511	8054	13458
5 Construction	95458	48862	46596	95180	47315	47865
6 Wholesale and retail trade, restaurants and hotels	92150	32871	59279	90821	32432	58389
7 Transport, storage and communication	45606	16705	28902	46183	16793	29390
8 Finance, insurance, real estate and business services	95498	21190	74308	95548	20202	75346
9 Community, social and personal services e	137522	61761	75762	138466	62247	76218
Total, Industries	858225	419335	438890	837993	401237	436756
Producers of Government Services	51651	15991	35661	53637	16825	36812
Other Producers	14842	5547	9294	15218	5579	9638
Total	924718	440873	483845	906848	423641	483206
Less: Imputed bank service charge	...	-23061	23061	...	-20720	20720
Import duties	2887	...	2887	2549	...	2549
Value added tax	-2021	...	-2021	-1825	...	-1825
Other adjustments f	1495	...	1495	2762	...	2762
Total	927080	463934	463145	910334	444361	465972

a) Item 'Manufacture of food, beverages and tobacco' excludes tobacco.
b) Item 'Textile, wearing apparel and leather industries' refers to textile only.
c) Item 'Manufacture of paper and paper products, printing and publishing' excludes printing and publishing.
d) Item 'Manufacture of chemical and chemical petroleum, coal, rubber and plastic products' excludes rubber and plastic products.
e) Restaurants and hotels are included in item 'Community, social and personal services'.
f) Item 'Other adjustments' refers to inventory valuation adjustment.

Japan

4.2 Derivation of Value Added by Kind of Activity, in Constant Prices

Thousand Million Japanese yen

	1980 Gross Output	1980 Intermediate Consumption	1980 Value Added	1985 Gross Output	1985 Intermediate Consumption	1985 Value Added	1990 Gross Output	1990 Intermediate Consumption	1990 Value Added	1991 Gross Output	1991 Intermediate Consumption	1991 Value Added
	\multicolumn{12}{c}{At constant prices of:1985 — All Producers}											
1 Agriculture, hunting, forestry and fishing	16771	7636	9135	18400	8186	10214	18075	7694	10381	17219	7624	9595
2 Mining and quarrying	2542	1361	1181	1936	978	958	2189	1072	1117	2184	1087	1097
3 Manufacturing	241707	170225	71482	287810	193138	94672	370691	245199	125492	389792	256371	133421
A Manufacture of food, beverages and tobacco [a]	26517	16226	10291	32419	21285	11134	35458	23856	11602	36131	24537	11594
B Textile, wearing apparel and leather industries [b]	8906	6161	2745	8023	5478	2545	7870	5698	2173	7645	5571	2074
C Manufacture of wood and wood products, including furniture	...	...	...	...	...	...	...	...	...	...	...	...
D Manufacture of paper and paper products, printing and publishing [c]	7626	5720	1906	8411	6021	2390	10105	6872	3233	10158	6970	3188
E Manufacture of chemicals and chemical petroleum, coal, rubber and plastic products [d]	37041	29837	7204	39663	28707	10956	46369	33979	12390	47117	34689	12428
F Manufacture of non-metallic mineral products, except products of petroleum and coal	8347	5658	2689	8572	5124	3448	10172	5969	4204	10215	6087	4128
G Basic metal industries	39668	31402	8266	35424	27559	7865	39336	30066	9270	40715	31554	9160
H Manufacture of fabricated metal products, machinery and equipment	83582	56717	26865	118861	76536	42325	175029	109976	65053	189956	117418	72539
I Other manufacturing industries	30021	18505	11516	36436	22428	14008	46350	28782	17569	47856	29545	18311
4 Electricity, gas and water	15393	7212	8181	18425	8119	10306	22740	10009	12731	24017	10377	13640
5 Construction	58933	32607	26326	57660	32279	25381	79821	44180	35641	81660	45160	36500
6 Wholesale and retail trade, restaurants and hotels	58269	20200	38069	65896	23060	42836	85139	29883	55255	88463	31208	57255
7 Transport, storage and communication	28561	11562	16999	34095	13009	21086	41541	16187	25355	42799	16543	26256
8 Finance, insurance, real estate and business services	47300	7807	39493	60782	11451	49331	83754	18832	64922	83685	18264	65420
9 Community, social and personal services [e]	60864	26178	34686	81696	35306	46390	111546	54633	56913	117062	58225	58836
Statistical discrepancy	...	...	...	...	...	...	...	...	...	...	...	-1
Total, Industries	530340	284788	245552	626700	325525	301175	815496	427689	387807	846879	444859	402020
Producers of Government Services	31217	7730	23487	36454	10170	26284	41254	13992	27262	41782	14833	26948
Other Producers	7921	2856	5065	9814	3595	6219	12213	5001	7213	12580	5182	7398
Total	569477	295374	274103	672968	339290	333678	868963	446681	422282	901241	464874	436367
Less: Imputed bank service charge	...	-10414	10414	...	-14774	14774	...	-23539	23539	...	-23794	23794
Import duties	1274	...	1274	1353	...	1353	2505	...	2505	3213	...	3213
Value added tax	...	...	...	...	...	...	...	...	...	...	...	...
Other adjustments [f]	1758	...	1758	139	...	139	-2205	...	-2205	253	...	253
Total	572509	305787	266722	674460	354063	320397	869263	470220	399043	904706	488668	416038

	1992 Gross Output	1992 Intermediate Consumption	1992 Value Added	1993 Gross Output	1993 Intermediate Consumption	1993 Value Added
	\multicolumn{6}{c}{At constant prices of:1985 — All Producers}						
1 Agriculture, hunting, forestry and fishing	17184	7378	9806	16511	7151	9361
2 Mining and quarrying	2156	1081	1075	2025	994	1030
3 Manufacturing	379421	248612	130809	367660	240150	127510
A Manufacture of food, beverages and tobacco [a]	36457	25161	11297	36450	25148	11302

Japan

4.2 Derivation of Value Added by Kind of Activity, in Constant Prices
(Continued)

Thousand Million Japanese yen

	1992 Gross Output	1992 Intermediate Consumption	1992 Value Added	1993 Gross Output	1993 Intermediate Consumption	1993 Value Added
	\multicolumn{6}{c}{At constant prices of: 1985}					
B Textile, wearing apparel and leather industries [b]	7466	5193	2273	6870	4540	2330
C Manufacture of wood and wood products, including furniture	...	...	...	...	...	...
D Manufacture of paper and paper products, printing and publishing [c]	10041	6918	3123	9804	6674	3129
E Manufacture of chemicals and chemical petroleum, coal, rubber and plastic products [d]	49016	34918	14098	48808	35337	13470
F Manufacture of non-metallic mineral products, except products of petroleum and coal	9971	5941	4031	9597	5636	3961
G Basic metal industries	37480	29191	8289	36575	28651	7923
H Manufacture of fabricated metal products, machinery and equipment	182438	112760	69678	174970	106869	68100
I Other manufacturing industries	46552	28530	18022	44587	27293	17294
4 Electricity, gas and water	24620	10637	13983	25146	10755	14391
5 Construction	81028	44337	36691	80479	43341	37138
6 Wholesale and retail trade, restaurants and hotels	89955	30984	58971	89294	30235	59060
7 Transport, storage and communication	42796	16580	26217	43546	16716	26830
8 Finance, insurance, real estate and business services	85296	19236	66060	83565	18299	65266
9 Community, social and personal services [e]	119099	59440	59659	118837	60197	58640
Statistical discrepancy	...	...	-	...	...	...
Total, Industries	841555	438285	403270	827062	427837	399225
Producers of Government Services	43083	15774	27309	44145	16607	27539
Other Producers	13288	5593	7695	13630	5674	7956
Total	897926	459652	438274	884837	450117	434719
Less: Imputed bank service charge	...	-24429	24429	...	-22390	22390
Import duties	3665	...	3665	3544	...	3544
Value added tax	...	...	...	...	...	...
Other adjustments [f]	3112	...	3112	3892	...	3892
Total	904703	484081	420622	892272	472507	419765

a) Item 'Manufacture of food, beverages and tobacco' excludes tobacco.
b) Item 'Textile, wearing apparel and leather industries' refers to textile only.
c) Item 'Manufacture of paper and paper products, printing and publishing' excludes printing and publishing.
d) Item 'Manufacture of chemical and chemical petroleum, coal, rubber and plastic products' excludes rubber and plastic products.
e) Restaurants and hotels are included in item 'Community, social and personal services'.
f) Item 'Other adjustments' refers to inventory valuation adjustment.

4.3 Cost Components of Value Added

Thousand Million Japanese yen

	1980 Compensation of Employees	1980 Capital Consumption	1980 Net Operating Surplus	1980 Indirect Taxes	1980 Less: Subsidies Received	1980 Value Added	1985 Compensation of Employees	1985 Capital Consumption	1985 Net Operating Surplus	1985 Indirect Taxes	1985 Less: Subsidies Received	1985 Value Added
	\multicolumn{12}{c}{All Producers}											
1 Agriculture, hunting, forestry and fishing	2103	1754	5152	-161	...	8847	2379	1866	5835	134	...	10214
2 Mining and quarrying	403	297	654	9	...	1363	479	200	261	18	...	958
3 Manufacturing	35561	9220	18339	7112	...	70232	47925	12001	24561	10185	...	94672
A Manufacture of food, beverages and tobacco [a]	2837	662	2133	2281	...	7913	4112	647	2772	3603	...	11134

Japan

4.3 Cost Components of Value Added
(Continued)

Thousand Million Japanese yen

	1980						1985					
	Compensation of Employees	Capital Consumption	Net Operating Surplus	Indirect Taxes	Less: Subsidies Received	Value Added	Compensation of Employees	Capital Consumption	Net Operating Surplus	Indirect Taxes	Less: Subsidies Received	Value Added
B Textile, wearing apparel and leather industries b	1604	290	526	115	...	2535	1799	272	334	140	...	2545
C Manufacture of wood and wood products, including furniture	...	...	...	...	...	...	...	...	...	...	...	...
D Manufacture of paper and paper products, printing and publishing c	906	344	662	98	...	2009	1224	456	576	135	...	2390
E Manufacture of chemicals and chemical petroleum, coal, rubber and plastic products d	2436	1419	1987	2122	...	7963	3176	1527	3831	2422	...	10956
F Manufacture of non-metallic mineral products, except products of petroleum and coal	1688	484	436	127	...	2735	1845	475	943	184	...	3448
G Basic metal industries	2443	1697	4375	369	...	8885	3077	1275	3068	446	...	7865
H Manufacture of fabricated metal products, machinery and equipment	16635	3174	6463	1567	...	27839	23948	5782	9941	2656	...	42325
I Other manufacturing industries	7012	1153	1758	432	...	10355	8747	1565	3097	600	...	14008
4 Electricity, gas and water	1776	1473	2580	751	...	6580	2234	3399	3380	1292	...	10306
5 Construction	13340	2212	6390	562	...	22506	15584	2054	7018	725	...	25381
6 Wholesale and retail trade, restaurants and hotels	20080	2233	12920	1560	...	36792	26910	2967	10922	2037	...	42836
A Wholesale and retail trade	...	...	...	...	...	...	...	...	...	...	...	...
B Restaurants and hotels e	...	...	...	...	...	...	...	...	...	...	...	...
7 Transport, storage and communication	11121	2695	1174	-201	...	14787	14529	3813	2672	73	...	21086
8 Finance, insurance, real estate and business services	8080	6938	18932	1146	...	35095	11410	9513	25933	2476	...	49331
9 Community, social and personal services e	14911	2195	9027	1931	...	28063	22810	5016	15692	2873	...	46390
Total, Industries f	107374	29017	75170	12706	...	224266	144260	40828	96274	19814	...	301175
Producers of Government Services	19077	1393	-	30	...	20499	24172	2078	-	36	...	26284
Other Producers	3947	292	-	46	...	4286	5461	710	-	47	...	6219
Total f	130398	30701	75170	12782	...	249050	173892	43615	96274	19897	...	333678
Less: Imputed bank service charge	...	...	10413	...	...	10413	...	...	14773	...	...	14774
Import duties	...	...	...	1313	...	1313	...	...	...	1353	...	1353
Value added tax	...	...	...	...	...	...	...	...	...	...	...	...
Other adjustments g	...	...	...	...	...	225	...	...	...	...	...	161
Total f	130398	30701	64757	14095	...	240176	173892	43615	81501	21250	...	320419

	1990						1991					
	Compensation of Employees	Capital Consumption	Net Operating Surplus	Indirect Taxes	Less: Subsidies Received	Value Added	Compensation of Employees	Capital Consumption	Net Operating Surplus	Indirect Taxes	Less: Subsidies Received	Value Added
						**All Producers**						
1 Agriculture, hunting, forestry and fishing	2299	1783	6245	226	...	10553	2374	1859	6209	79	...	10520
2 Mining and quarrying	463	240	516	60	...	1279	482	280	483	58	...	1304
3 Manufacturing	61794	16996	31221	13433	...	123443	66312	17856	33838	13330	...	131336
A Manufacture of food, beverages and tobacco a	5463	937	2848	4150	...	13398	5904	967	3279	3817	...	13967

Japan

4.3 Cost Components of Value Added
(Continued)

Thousand Million Japanese yen

		1990					1991					
		Compensation of Employees	Capital Consumption	Net Operating Surplus	Indirect Taxes	Less: Subsidies Received	Value Added	Compensation of Employees	Capital Consumption	Net Operating Surplus	Indirect Taxes	Less: Subsidies Received	Value Added
	B Textile, wearing apparel and leather industries [b]	1862	203	85	211	...	2361	1911	180	82	219	...	2393
	C Manufacture of wood and wood products, including furniture	...	...	...	...	...	...	...	...	...	...	...	...
	D Manufacture of paper and paper products, printing and publishing [c]	1570	763	776	250	...	3360	1656	728	845	259	...	3488
	E Manufacture of chemicals and chemical petroleum, coal, rubber and plastic products [d]	4009	2140	5164	3220	...	14534	4285	2197	5690	3210	...	15382
	F Manufacture of non-metallic mineral products, except products of petroleum and coal	2422	592	1190	333	...	4536	2619	561	1130	347	...	4657
	G Basic metal industries	3596	1631	3624	771	...	9623	3757	1707	3711	808	...	9982
	H Manufacture of fabricated metal products, machinery and equipment	31464	8701	12909	3410	...	56485	33899	9502	13898	3545	...	60844
	I Other manufacturing industries	11407	2029	4625	1087	...	19148	12281	2014	5204	1125	...	20624
4	Electricity, gas and water	2979	4872	2567	1070	...	11489	3166	4965	3120	1077	...	12328
5	Construction	22501	3381	14334	1912	...	42127	24821	3698	14536	1966	...	45021
6	Wholesale and retail trade, restaurants and hotels	36385	4284	10110	3723	...	54501	39476	5216	9445	3692	...	57830
	A Wholesale and retail trade	36385	4284	10110	3723	...	54501	39476	5216	9445	3692	...	57830
	B Restaurants and hotels [e]	...	...	...	...	...	...	...	...	...	...	...	...
7	Transport, storage and communication	18489	4889	2589	1133	...	27100	19588	5487	1744	1798	...	28618
8	Finance, insurance, real estate and business services	16480	14000	35832	3218	...	69529	17218	15133	36430	3245	...	72027
9	Community, social and personal services [e]	34571	8855	18707	5179	...	67313	38880	10324	17544	5202	...	71949
	Total, Industries [f]	195961	59298	122120	29955	...	407334	212318	64817	123350	30447	...	430932
	Producers of Government Services	30136	2508	-	44	...	32688	31654	2525	-	43	...	34222
	Other Producers	7276	1014	-	65	...	8354	7719	1044	-	67	...	8830
	Total [f]	233373	62820	122120	30063	...	448377	251690	68387	123350	30557	...	473983
	Less: Imputed bank service charge	...	...	22322	...	...	22322	...	...	22670	...	...	22670
	Import duties	...	...	...	2713	...	2713	...	...	...	2872	...	2872
	Value added tax	...	...	...	-2209	...	-2209	...	...	...	-2312	...	-2312
	Other adjustments [g]	...	...	...	...	...	-2022	...	...	...	...	...	-576
	Total [f]	233373	62820	99798	30568	...	424536	251690	68387	100680	31116	...	451297

		1992						1993					
		Compensation of Employees	Capital Consumption	Net Operating Surplus	Indirect Taxes	Less: Subsidies Received	Value Added	Compensation of Employees	Capital Consumption	Net Operating Surplus	Indirect Taxes	Less: Subsidies Received	Value Added
						All Producers							
1	Agriculture, hunting, forestry and fishing	2357	1797	5707	317	...	10178	2357	1637	5644	339	...	9977
2	Mining and quarrying	472	272	528	57	...	1329	485	249	434	67	...	1235
3	Manufacturing	68235	18911	28085	14363	...	129594	68839	19441	22351	14247	...	124878
	A Manufacture of food, beverages and tobacco [a]	6060	1035	3243	4475	...	14813	6205	1065	3353	4522	...	15145

Japan

4.3 Cost Components of Value Added
(Continued)

Thousand Million Japanese yen

	1992						1993					
	Compensation of Employees	Capital Consumption	Net Operating Surplus	Indirect Taxes	Less: Subsidies Received	Value Added	Compensation of Employees	Capital Consumption	Net Operating Surplus	Indirect Taxes	Less: Subsidies Received	Value Added
B Textile, wearing apparel and leather industries [b]	1978	181	149	245	...	2553	1951	191	24	239	...	2405
C Manufacture of wood and wood products, including furniture	...	...	...	...	...	...	...	...	...	...	...	...
D Manufacture of paper and paper products, printing and publishing [c]	1704	752	708	275	...	3440	1729	766	740	278	...	3513
E Manufacture of chemicals and chemical petroleum, coal, rubber and plastic products [d]	4430	2406	5682	3391	...	15909	4553	2467	5248	3459	...	15727
F Manufacture of non-metallic mineral products, except products of petroleum and coal	2737	602	834	370	...	4543	2805	633	590	363	...	4391
G Basic metal industries	3852	1756	2714	846	...	9167	3813	1831	2038	817	...	8498
H Manufacture of fabricated metal products, machinery and equipment	34695	10008	9983	3569	...	58256	34577	10204	6720	3412	...	54913
I Other manufacturing industries	12779	2172	4771	1193	...	20914	13206	2285	3638	1156	...	20286
4 Electricity, gas and water	3262	5028	3479	1175	...	12943	3462	5072	3739	1184	...	13458
5 Construction	25830	4291	14380	2094	...	46596	27249	4689	13821	2106	...	47865
6 Wholesale and retail trade, restaurants and hotels	41003	5476	8723	4077	...	59279	41287	5245	7773	4084	...	58389
A Wholesale and retail trade	41003	5476	8723	4077	...	59279	41287	5245	7773	4084	...	58389
B Restaurants and hotels [e]	...	...	...	...	...	...	...	...	...	...	...	...
7 Transport, storage and communication	20264	5645	912	2081	...	28902	20921	5288	1061	2122	...	29390
8 Finance, insurance, real estate and business services	17683	16359	36832	3433	...	74308	17768	17095	37051	3432	...	75346
9 Community, social and personal services [e]	40615	11074	18656	5417	...	75762	42168	10718	18035	5297	...	76218
Total, Industries [f]	219720	68854	117301	33015	...	438890	224535	69434	109908	32879	...	436756
Producers of Government Services	32991	2624	-	46	...	35661	33986	2779	-	47	...	36812
Other Producers	8081	1144	-	70	...	9294	8430	1135	-	73	...	9638
Total [f]	260792	72623	117301	33130	...	483845	266951	73348	109908	32999	...	483206
Less: Imputed bank service charge	...	...	23061	...	...	23061	...	...	20720	...	...	20720
Import duties	...	...	...	2887	...	2887	...	...	...	2549	...	2549
Value added tax	...	...	...	-2021	...	-2021	...	...	...	-1825	...	-1825
Other adjustments [g]	...	...	...	...	...	1495	...	...	...	...	...	2762
Total [f]	260792	72623	94240	33996	...	463145	266951	73348	89188	33724	...	465972

a) Item 'Manufacture of food, beverages and tobacco' excludes tobacco.
b) Item 'Textile, wearing apparel and leather industries' refers to textile only.
c) Item 'Manufacture of paper and paper products, printing and publishing' excludes printing and publishing.
d) Item 'Manufacture of chemical and chemical petroleum, coal, rubber and plastic products' excludes rubber and plastic products.
e) Restaurants and hotels are included in item 'Community, social and personal services'.
f) Column 4 refers to indirect taxes less subsidies received.
g) Item 'Other adjustments' refers to inventory valuation adjustment.

Jordan

General note. The preparation of national accounts statistics in the Hashemite Kingdom of Jordan is undertaken by the Department of Statistics, Amman. The annual official estimates together with methodological notes are published in a series of publications entitled 'National Accounts'. A comprehensive description of the concepts and definitions underlying the various tables is contained in 'The National Accounts 1970-1974', published in 1976 by the Department of Statistics. The estimates are generally in accordance with the classifications and definitions recommended in the United Nations System of National Accounts (SNA). Input-output tables were published for the first time in 1963 and followed up annually until 1969 in 'The National Accounts and Input-Output Analysis'. The following tables have been prepared from successive replies to the United Nations national accounts questionnaire. Tables of the period 1960-1966 cover both the West Bank and the East Bank of Jordan, while tables of the period 1967 and onward cover only the East Bank of Jordan. When the scope and coverage of the estimates differ for conceptual or statistical reasons from the definitions and classifications recommended in SNA, a footnote is indicated to the relevant tables.

Sources and methods:

(a) **Gross domestic product.** Gross domestic product is estimated mainly through the production approach.

(b) **Expenditure on the gross domestic product.** All components of GDP by expenditure type are estimated through the expenditure approach except private consumption expenditure and investment in machinery and equipment which are estimated by using the commodity-flow approach. The estimates of government final consumption expenditure are obtained from the records of the Ministry of Finance, National Planning Council and municipalities. The estimates of private final consumption expenditure are built up from studies of the origin and use of the country's economic resources and from the input-output analysis made for the years 1960-1969. Estimates of gross fixed capital formation of the private sector are based on building licence statistics, a special survey and on imports of machinery and equipment, while that of the government sector are mainly obtained from records of the Ministry of Finance. Estimates of increase in stocks are approximate and in most cases based on inquiries in the manufacturing industry. Imports and exports of goods and services are mainly estimated from the external trade statistics. GDP by expenditure at constant prices is not estimated.

(c) **Cost-structure of the gross domestic product.** The sources and methods applied in estimating the cost-structure components of GDP are based on income estimates. Separate estimates are made for income of agricultural workers, income of skilled labourers, and for income from property and capital assets. Gross operating surplus (i.e. including consumption of fixed capital) is arrived at as a residual.

(d) **Gross domestic product by kind of economic activity.** The table of GDP by kind of economic activity is prepared at factor costs. The production approach is used to estimate the value added of most industries, such as agriculture, forestry and fishing, mining and manufacturing, wholesale and retail trade, while the income approach is used for a number of service sectors. Annual agricultural sample surveys are undertaken on a country-wide basis providing production estimates for crops. The quantities obtained from these surveys are valued at farm prices which are assumed to be a certain percentage of the relevant wholesale or retail prices. Livestock estimates are obtained from the municipalities and the Ministry of Reconstruction and Development, adjusted to arrive at a total number of slaughtering for the country. The estimates of industrial production are based on the 1967 and 1974 Industrial Censuses, balance sheets and income and expenditure statements in 1970, and on analysis of large industrial companies and industrial sample surveys for the remaining years. Value added of private building construction is calculated from cost estimates obtained from special inquiries, while value of public construction is obtained from the records of the Ministry of Finance, National Planning Council and municipalities. Special sample surveys of wholesale and retail trade were conducted in the years 1967-1971 and supplemented by a systematic study of the origin and use of all goods imported and produced in the economy for the year 1975. For passenger and freight transport, the source of information is mainly the records of the authority or the corporation concerned. As for road transport, estimates are based on a survey undertaken in 1974 and on special inquiries. The estimates for banking are based on returns sent to the Department of Statistics by the various banks. Information on the operation of insurance companies has been collected by means of special surveys undertaken during 1970-1974, covering also information on the activities of foreign exchange dealers. The income arising from ownership of dwellings represents the net rental value of all dwellings based initially on the assessments of the Ministry of Finance. For other services, data are provided by the Ministry of Finance or by the institutions concerned. GDP by kind of economic activity at constant prices is not estimated.

1.1 Expenditure on the Gross Domestic Product, in Current Prices

Million Jordanian dinars

	1980	1983	1984	1985	1986	1987	1988	1989	1990	1991	1992	1993
1 Government final consumption expenditure [a]	...	461.3	522.8	527.2	561.9	582.4	600.3	615.4	657.6	736.8	771.0	...
2 Private final consumption expenditure	...	1448.7	1521.4	1785.0	1717.1	1680.2	1672.4	1766.3	2380.7	2540.1	3021.6	...
3 Gross capital formation	...	601.9	561.4	426.8	447.9	544.6	569.1	602.3	751.5	667.9	1039.4	...
A Increase in stocks	...	53.4	31.0	41.6	37.6	76.2	60.9	54.9	60.1	59.2	59.2	...
B Gross fixed capital formation [a]	...	548.5	530.4	385.2	410.3	468.4	508.2	547.4	691.4	608.7	980.2	...
Residential buildings	...	158.6	163.0	112.7	100.2	125.3	224.6	229.5	297.8	327.7	396.8	...
Non-residential buildings	...	188.6	177.8	189.4	187.7	201.8	146.7	146.1	135.6	146.7	177.7	...
Other construction and land improvement etc.	...											...
Other	...	201.3	189.6	83.1	122.4	141.3	136.9	171.8	258.0	134.3	405.7	...
4 Exports of goods and services	...	637.2	743.2	733.5	587.0	675.2	896.3	1150.2	1296.9	1196.2	1399.7	...
5 Less: Imports of goods and services	...	1421.0	1481.2	1502.7	1199.3	1319.7	1519.7	1804.4	2474.3	2362.6	2974.7	...
Equals: Gross Domestic Product [b]	...	1728.1	1867.6	1969.8	2114.6	2162.7	2218.4	2329.8	2612.4	2778.4	3257.0	...

a) Government final consumption expenditure includes pension payments less employees' pension contributions. Some non-capital development expenditure of the central government is included in other construction of gross domestic fixed capital formation. b) Data in this table have not been revised, therefore they are not comparable with the data in other tables.

1.3 Cost Components of the Gross Domestic Product

Million Jordanian dinars

	1980	1983	1984	1985	1986	1987	1988	1989	1990	1991	1992	1993
1 Indirect taxes, net	...	222.6	213.9	237.3	342.4	330.3	317.4	262.1	337.2	360.3	474.6	...
A Indirect taxes	...	251.7	263.8	265.6	349.0	341.1	332.9	274.4	342.9	365.2	474.6	...
B Less: Subsidies	...	29.1	49.9	28.3	6.6	10.8	15.5	12.3	5.7	4.9	-	...
2 Consumption of fixed capital	...	144.2	162.1	197.3	187.7	193.8	211.9	228.3	221.1	292.3	344.4	...
3 Compensation of employees paid by resident producers to:	...	680.3	732.4	758.8	809.8	844.7	896.6	937.5	986.5	1064.7	1192.8	...
4 Operating surplus	...	681.0	710.3	776.4	774.7	793.9	792.5	901.9	1067.6	1061.1	1245.2	...
Equals: Gross Domestic Product [a]	...	1728.1	1818.7	1969.8	2114.6	2162.7	2218.4	2329.8	2612.4	2778.4	3257.0	...

a) Data in this table have not been revised, therefore they are not comparable with the data in other tables.

Jordan

1.4 General Government Current Receipts and Disbursements

Million Jordanian dinars

	1980	1983	1984	1985	1986	1987	1988	1989	1990	1991	1992	1993
					Receipts							
1 Operating surplus	...	...	...	...	... ...	...	...	...	...	...	...	...
2 Property and entrepreneurial income	11.1	9.4	23.0	24.0	16.0 / 139.0	126.2	...	...	...	...	...	...
3 Taxes, fees and contributions	203.9	334.3	348.3	352.0	348.1 / 484.5	478.6	...	...	...	...	...	...
A Indirect taxes	147.1	234.6	234.2	242.5	221.6 / 344.9	338.0	...	...	...	...	...	...
B Direct taxes	28.3	52.9	64.1	69.5	79.0 / 47.9	45.4	...	...	...	...	...	...
C Social security contributions	3.6	5.8	6.5	7.0	7.5 / 45.0	43.5	...	...	...	...	...	...
D Compulsory fees, fines and penalties	24.9	41.0	43.5	33.0	40.0 / 46.7	51.7	...	...	...	...	...	...
4 Other current transfers	388.8	289.6	257.9	288.7	200.0 / 258.0	254.2	...	...	...	...	...	...
Total Current Receipts of General Government	603.8	633.3	629.2	664.7	564.1 / 881.5	859.0	...	...	...	...	...	...
					Disbursements							
1 Government final consumption expenditure	243.8	348.3	376.9	410.5	461.0 / 546.5	566.3	...	...	...	...	...	...
A Compensation of employees	167.6	227.5	233.4	257.0	288.6 / ...	...	...	...	...	...	...	...
B Consumption of fixed capital	2.6	4.5	4.3	5.5	6.1 / ...	...	...	...	...	...	...	...
C Purchases of goods and services, net	73.6	116.3	139.2	148.0	166.3 / ...	...	...	...	...	...	...	...
D Less: Own account fixed capital formation	...	...	...	...	...	...	...	...	...	...	...	...
E Indirect taxes paid, net	...	...	...	...	...	...	...	...	...	...	...	...
2 Property income	...	...	...	...	... / 59.8	77.2	...	...	...	...	...	...
A Interest	...	...	...	...	... / 59.8	77.2	...	...	...	...	...	...
B Net land rent and royalties	...	...	...	...	... / -	-	...	...	...	...	...	...
3 Subsidies	56.0	37.1	50.8	37.1	8.2 / 6.6	10.8	...	...	...	...	...	...
4 Other current transfers	45.2	149.2	168.7	178.6	190.7 / 102.6	112.8	...	...	...	...	...	...
A Social security benefits	...	...	...	...	... / 7.4	9.1	...	...	...	...	...	...
B Social assistance grants	...	...	...	...	3.0	2.6	...	...	...	...	...	...
C Other	...	...	...	...	... / 92.2	101.1	...	...	...	...	...	...
5 Net saving	258.8	98.7	32.8	38.5	-95.8 / 166.0	92.0	...	...	...	...	...	...
Total Current Disbursements and Net Saving of General Government	603.8	633.3	629.2	664.7	564.1 / 881.5	859.0	...	...	...	...	...	...

1.7 External Transactions on Current Account, Summary

Million Jordanian dinars

	1980	1983	1984	1985	1986	1987	1988	1989	1990	1991	1992	1993
				Payments to the Rest of the World								
1 Imports of goods and services	...	1421.0	1481.2	1502.7	1199.3	1319.7	1519.7	1804.4	2474.3	2362.6	2974.7	...
2 Factor income to the rest of the world	...	55.0	73.6	85.6	94.6	101.8	137.3	250.3	317.4	329.6	320.0	...
A Compensation of employees	...	8.6	11.5	11.0	10.2	7.4	6.7	6.1	5.5	4.9	6.9	...
B Property and entrepreneurial income	...	46.4	62.1	74.6	84.4	94.4	130.6	244.2	311.9	324.7	313.1	...

Jordan

1.7 External Transactions on Current Account, Summary
(Continued)

Million Jordanian dinars

	1980	1983	1984	1985	1986	1987	1988	1989	1990	1991	1992	1993
3 Current transfers to the rest of the world	...	66.1	89.8	84.5	78.8	62.0	60.1	54.2	46.4	39.7	58.4	...
4 Surplus of the nation on current transactions	...	-161.6	-122.4	-208.9	-111.3	-278.1	-237.9	-241.4	-887.1	-815.0	-1018.0	...
Payments to the Rest of the World and Surplus of the Nation on Current Transactions [a]	...	1380.5	1522.2	1463.9	1261.4	1205.4	1479.1	1867.5	1951.1	1916.9	2335.1	...

Receipts From The Rest of the World

	1980	1983	1984	1985	1986	1987	1988	1989	1990	1991	1992	1993
1 Exports of goods and services	...	637.2	743.2	733.5	587.0	675.2	896.3	1150.2	1296.9	1196.2	1399.7	...
2 Factor income from rest of the world	...	104.1	87.2	80.8	77.3	51.6	48.9	59.0	78.1	108.5	133.8	...
A Compensation of employees	...	40.3	47.5	40.3	41.5	31.8	33.6	35.8	33.2	30.6	57.3	...
B Property and entrepreneurial income	...	63.8	39.7	40.5	35.8	19.8	15.3	23.2	44.9	77.9	76.5	...
3 Current transfers from rest of the world	...	639.2	691.8	649.6	597.1	478.6	534.0	658.3	576.1	612.2	801.6	...
Receipts from the Rest of the World on Current Transactions [a]	...	1380.5	1522.2	1463.9	1261.4	1205.4	1479.1	1867.5	1951.1	1916.9	2335.1	...

a) Data in this table have not been revised, therefore they are not comparable with the data in other tables.

1.9 Gross Domestic Product by Institutional Sectors of Origin

Million Jordanian dinars

	1980	1983	1984	1985	1986	1987	1988	1989	1990	1991	1992	1993

Domestic Factor Incomes Originating

	1980	1983	1984	1985	1986	1987	1988	1989	1990	1991	1992	1993
1 General government	167.6	227.5	233.4	257.0	288.6	302.3	...	...	...	...	...	...
2 Corporate and quasi-corporate enterprises	663.2	887.3	940.4	969.8	943.3	983.4	...	...	...	...	...	...
A Non-financial	572.0	780.4	826.8	847.3	817.4	855.2	...	...	...	...	...	...
B Financial	91.2	106.9	113.6	122.5	125.9	128.2	...	...	...	...	...	...
3 Households and private unincorporated enterprises	...	...	...	...	...	...	...	...	...	...	...	...
4 Non-profit institutions serving households	14.7	22.5	22.1	26.7	27.8	28.7	...	...	...	...	...	...
Subtotal: Domestic Factor Incomes	845.5	1137.7	1195.9	1253.5	1259.7	1314.4	...	...	...	...	...	...
Indirect taxes, net	91.1	180.4	183.4	210.2	229.4	239.0	...	...	...	...	...	...
A Indirect taxes	147.1	216.7	233.9	247.3	237.6	247.3	...	...	...	...	...	...
B Less: Subsidies	56.0	36.3	50.5	37.1	8.2	8.3	...	...	...	...	...	...
Consumption of fixed capital	47.7	104.6	120.1	138.7	142.3	132.9	...	...	...	...	...	...
Gross Domestic Product	984.3	1422.7	1499.4	1602.4	1631.4	1686.3	...	...	...	...	...	...

1.10 Gross Domestic Product by Kind of Activity, in Current Prices

Million Jordanian dinars

	1980	1983	1984	1985	1986	1987	1988	1989	1990	1991	1992	1993
1 Agriculture, hunting, forestry and fishing	...	97.2	79.6	84.4	96.2	126.6	114.5	131.7	179.6	174.3	204.0	...
2 Mining and quarrying	...	40.6	60.8	65.6	68.3	66.9	82.4	154.5	158.8	124.9	116.1	...
3 Manufacturing	...	197.6	233.7	205.4	193.9	213.6	197.0	254.7	345.2	343.7	426.0	...
4 Electricity, gas and water	...	22.1	32.0	40.1	44.2	48.5	50.6	52.8	53.3	62.0	70.9	...
5 Construction	...	188.0	177.6	155.7	144.3	126.0	118.0	106.3	111.5	125.7	152.4	...
6 Wholesale and retail trade, restaurants and hotels	...	241.3	252.3	289.4	273.5	269.1	257.2	180.6	207.9	254.7	269.9	...
7 Transport, storage and communication	...	190.5	191.1	265.4	274.7	277.4	294.5	359.1	362.0	365.5	428.0	...
8 Finance, insurance, real estate and business services	...	245.3	268.4	275.9	285.9	293.3	348.0	378.7	374.5	456.1	518.7	...
9 Community, social and personal services	...	30.9	35.8	38.4	39.4	40.3	46.1	45.6	51.2	66.2	67.8	...
Total, Industries	...	1253.5	1331.3	1420.3	1420.4	1461.7	1508.3	1664.0	1844.0	1973.1	2253.8	...
Producers of Government Services	...	266.1	289.5	323.8	365.1	383.7	415.0	427.8	444.9	469.3	555.0	...
Other Producers	...	17.8	18.9	24.7	25.5	26.3	27.2	31.2	26.2	29.4	35.0	...
Subtotal [a]	...	1537.4	1639.7	1768.8	1811.0	1871.7	1950.5	2123.0	2315.1	2471.8	2843.8	...
Less: Imputed bank service charge	...	31.9	34.9	36.3	38.8	39.3	49.5	55.3	39.9	53.7	61.4	...
Plus: Import duties	...	...	...	...	...	...	...	...	...	...	...	...
Plus: Value added tax	...	...	...	...	...	...	...	...	...	...	...	...
Plus: Other adjustments [b]	...	222.6	213.9	237.3	342.4	330.3	317.4	262.1	337.2	360.3	474.6	...
Equals: Gross Domestic Product [c]	...	1728.1	1818.7	1969.8	2114.6	2162.7	2218.4	2329.8	2612.4	2778.4	3257.0	...

a) Second series, gross domestic product in factor values.
b) Item 'Other adjustments' refers to indirect taxes net of subsidies.
c) Data in this table have not been revised, therefore they are not comparable with the data in other tables.

Jordan

1.11 Gross Domestic Product by Kind of Activity, in Constant Prices

Million Jordanian dinars

	1980	1983	1984	1985	1986	1987	1988	1989	1990	1991	1992	1993
				At constant prices of:								
			1975					1985				
1 Agriculture, hunting, forestry and fishing	68.0	59.1	64.9	71.4 / 84.4	86.7	116.1	140.4	113.4	149.8	129.7	142.7	...
2 Mining and quarrying	47.3	57.5	77.9	86.2 / 65.6	72.4	75.5	70.0	77.4	67.6	54.1	53.8	...
3 Manufacturing	79.8	95.0	110.9	109.1 / 205.4	197.1	203.6	164.8	204.4	224.0	218.3	249.5	...
4 Electricity, gas and water	8.2	12.6	14.5	15.0 / 40.1	60.8	64.7	63.1	69.4	53.3	56.2	61.7	...
5 Construction	54.2	83.5	81.7	72.4 / 155.7	152.6	135.2	150.9	123.3	128.1	141.5	164.0	...
6 Wholesale and retail trade, restaurants and hotels	109.7	125.8	131.0	140.2 / 289.4	271.5	264.2	228.6	77.5	54.3	70.2	71.7	...
7 Transport, storage and communication	44.9	62.6	68.8	70.0 / 265.4	275.1	290.4	288.8	279.9	270.2	247.8	280.1	...
8 Finance, insurance, real estate and business services	74.9	75.4	82.0	86.2 / 275.9	289.5	293.4	330.5	322.3	308.9	358.5	386.3	...
9 Community, social and personal services	7.6	10.6	13.2	16.8 / 38.4	37.6	37.8	40.1	29.8	30.9	40.1	38.2	...
Total, Industries	494.6	582.1	644.9	667.3 / 1420.3	1443.3	1480.9	1477.2	1297.4	1287.1	1316.4	1448.0	...
Producers of Government Services	105.0	112.7	115.8	115.7 / 323.8	348.6	376.4	401.5	385.5	383.6	390.0	414.6	...
Other Producers	8.8	13.2	14.4	15.8 / 24.7	25.6	26.5	26.4	24.5	18.2	19.9	22.5	...
Subtotal [a]	608.4	708.0	775.1	798.8 / 1768.8	1817.5	1883.8	1905.1	1707.4	1688.9	1726.3	1885.1	...
Less: Imputed bank service charge	7.3	13.0	15.4	20.6 / 36.3	38.9	39.6	48.3	44.5	29.1	37.5	40.7	...
Plus: Import duties	...	...	...	...	...	...	...	...	...	...	...	...
Plus: Value added tax	...	...	...	...	...	...	...	...	...	...	...	...
Plus: Other adjustments [b]	46.8	48.0	47.5	56.9 / 237.3	343.6	332.4	309.6	210.5	246.0	250.7	314.6	...
Equals: Gross Domestic Product	647.9	743.0	807.2	835.1 / 1969.8[c]	2122.2[c]	2176.7[c]	2166.3[c]	1873.4[c]	1905.8[c]	1939.5[c]	2159.0[c]	...

a) Gross domestic product in factor values.
b) Item 'Other adjustments' refers to indirect taxes net of subsidies.
c) Data in this table have not been revised, therefore they are not comparable with the data in other tables.

1.12 Relations Among National Accounting Aggregates

Million Jordanian dinars

	1980	1983	1984	1985	1986	1987	1988	1989	1990	1991	1992	1993
Gross Domestic Product	...	1728.1	1867.6	1969.8	2114.6	2162.7	2218.4	2329.8	2612.4	2778.4	3257.0	...
Plus: Net factor income from the rest of the world	...	49.1	13.6	-4.7	-17.3	-50.2	-88.5	-191.3	-239.4	-221.1	-186.2	...
Factor income from the rest of the world	...	104.1	87.2	80.8	77.3	51.6	48.9	59.0	78.1	108.5	133.8	...
Less: Factor income to the rest of the world	...	55.0	73.6	85.6	94.6	101.8	137.3	250.3	317.4	329.6	320.0	...
Equals: Gross National Product	...	1777.2	1881.2	1965.1	2097.3	2112.5	2129.9	2138.5	2373.0	2557.3	3070.8	...
Less: Consumption of fixed capital	...	144.2	211.0	197.3	187.7	193.8	211.9	228.3	221.1	292.3	344.4	...
Equals: National Income	...	1633.0	1670.2	1767.8	1909.6	1918.7	1918.0	1910.2	2151.9	2265.0	2726.4	...
Plus: Net current transfers from the rest of the world	...	573.1	602.0	565.0	518.3	416.6	473.9	604.1	529.7	572.5	743.2	...
Current transfers from the rest of the world	...	639.2	691.8	649.6	597.1	478.6	534.0	658.3	576.1	612.2	801.6	...
Less: Current transfers to the rest of the world	...	66.1	89.8	84.5	78.8	62.0	60.1	54.2	46.4	39.7	58.4	...
Equals: National Disposable Income	...	2206.1	2272.2	2332.8	2427.9	2335.3	2392.0	2514.3	2681.6	2837.5	3469.6	...
Less: Final consumption [ab]	...	1910.0	2044.2	2312.2	2279.0	2262.6	2272.7	2381.7	3038.3	3276.9	3792.6	...
Equals: Net Saving	...	296.1	228.0	20.6	148.9	72.7	119.3	132.6	-356.7	-439.4	-323.0	...
Less: Surplus of the nation on current transactions	...	-161.6	-122.4	-208.9	-111.3	-278.1	-237.9	-241.4	-887.1	-815.0	-1018.0	...
Equals: Net Capital Formation [ab]	...	457.7	350.4	229.5	260.2	350.8	357.2	374.0	530.4	375.6	695.0	...

a) Government final consumption expenditure includes pension payments less employees' pension contributions. Some non-capital development expenditure of the central government is included in other construction of gross domestic fixed capital formation.
b) Data in this table have not been revised, therefore they are not comparable with the data in other tables.

Jordan

2.1 Government Final Consumption Expenditure by Function, in Current Prices

Million Jordanian dinars

	1980	1983	1984	1985	1986	1987	1988	1989	1990	1991	1992	1993
1 General public services							...	...	...	...	...	...
2 Defence	171.9	224.6	228.6	261.1	302.1	292.1	...	...	...	...	...	...
3 Public order and safety							...	...	...	...	...	...
4 Education	39.1	57.7	59.6	65.4	72.4	77.6	...	...	...	...	...	...
5 Health	12.0	17.6	18.3	21.5	24.8	26.0	...	...	...	...	...	...
6 Social security and welfare	1.5	2.8	2.3	2.4	2.5	2.5	...	...	...	...	...	...
7 Housing and community amenities	...	...	...	...	...	...	...	...	...	...	...	...
8 Recreational, cultural and religious affairs	...	...	...	...	...	...	...	...	...	...	...	...
9 Economic services	8.4	13.5	24.2	19.0	21.5	23.6	...	...	...	...	...	...
A Fuel and energy	...	...	...	...	...	...	...	...	...	...	...	...
B Agriculture, forestry, fishing and hunting	...	...	...	...	...	...	...	...	...	...	...	...
C Mining, manufacturing and construction, except fuel and energy	...	...	...	...	...	...	...	...	...	...	...	...
D Transportation and communication	8.4	13.5	24.2	18.7	20.0	18.7	...	...	...	...	...	...
E Other economic affairs	...	...	...	...	...	...	...	...	...	...	...	...
10 Other functions	10.3	18.6	19.7	22.3	17.7	19.3	...	...	...	...	...	...
Total Government Final Consumption Expenditure	243.8	348.3	376.9	410.5	461.0	459.8	...	...	...	...	...	...

2.5 Private Final Consumption Expenditure by Type and Purpose, in Current Prices

Million Jordanian dinars

	1980	1983	1984	1985	1986	1987	1988	1989	1990	1991	1992	1993
Final Consumption Expenditure of Resident Households												
1 Food, beverages and tobacco	387.1	561.9	571.4	570.7	504.0	...	...	...	...	...	...	...
A Food	356.6	515.6	523.3	525.6	464.4	...	...	...	...	...	...	...
B Non-alcoholic beverages	13.9	20.0	20.7	18.7	16.1	...	...	...	...	...	...	...
C Alcoholic beverages						...	...	...	...	...	...	...
D Tobacco	16.6	26.3	27.4	26.4	23.5	...	...	...	...	...	...	...
2 Clothing and footwear	68.5	83.0	83.7	80.2	69.3	...	...	...	...	...	...	...
3 Gross rent, fuel and power	55.4	89.5	91.5	92.0	80.5	...	...	...	...	...	...	...
4 Furniture, furnishings and household equipment and operation	44.4	69.0	70.0	68.6	60.7	...	...	...	...	...	...	...
5 Medical care and health expenses [a]	32.8	55.2	57.2	58.0	50.7	...	...	...	...	...	...	...
6 Transport and communication	55.3	81.3	82.9	83.6	73.1	...	...	...	...	...	...	...
7 Recreational, entertainment, education and cultural services	53.1	86.0	87.7	89.9	79.2	...	...	...	...	...	...	...
A Education	25.0	46.8	47.2	48.3	42.1	...	...	...	...	...	...	...
B Other	28.1	39.2	40.5	41.6	37.1	...	...	...	...	...	...	...
8 Miscellaneous goods and services	179.8	355.2	362.6	409.5	352.0	...	...	...	...	...	...	...
Total Final Consumption Expenditure in the Domestic Market by Households, of which	878.4	1381.1	1407.0	1452.5	1269.5	...	...	...	...	...	...	...
Plus: Direct purchases abroad by resident households	107.8	149.1	141.1	166.4	155.2	...	...	...	...	...	...	...
Less: Direct purchases in the domestic market by non-resident households	154.9	183.1	173.2	204.2	186.3	...	...	...	...	...	...	...
Equals: Final Consumption Expenditure of Resident Households [b]	829.3	1347.1	1374.9	1414.7	1238.4	...	...	...	...	...	...	...
Final Consumption Expenditure of Private Non-profit Institutions Serving Households												
Equals: Final Consumption Expenditure of Private Non-profit Organisations Serving Households	...	...	...	...	...	...	...	...	...	...	...	...
Private Final Consumption Expenditure	829.3	1347.1	1374.9	1414.7	1238.4	...	...	...	...	...	...	...

a) Personal care is included in 'Medical care and health expenses'.
b) Item 'Final consumption expenditure of resident households' includes consumption expenditure of private non-profit institutions serving households.

Jordan

2.17 Exports and Imports of Goods and Services, Detail

Million Jordanian dinars

	1980	1983	1984	1985	1986	1987	1988	1989	1990	1991	1992	1993
Exports of Goods and Services												
1 Exports of merchandise, f.o.b.	171.5	210.6	290.7	310.9	256.0	315.7	...	...	...	...	...	...
2 Transport and communication	76.5	108.8	137.9	156.0	91.0	117.0	...	...	...	...	...	...
3 Insurance service charges		29.5	37.4	33.3	22.4	21.1	...	...	...	...	...	...
4 Other commodities	65.9	105.2	104.0	73.8	74.6	103.3	...	...	...	...	...	...
5 Adjustments of merchandise exports to change-of-ownership basis	...	...	...	...	...	...	...	...	...	...	...	...
6 Direct purchases in the domestic market by non-residential households	154.9	183.1	173.2	204.1	186.3	196.5	...	...	...	...	...	...
7 Direct purchases in the domestic market by extraterritorial bodies	...	...	...	...	...	...	...	...	...	...	...	...
Total Exports of Goods and Services	468.8	638.2	743.2	778.1	630.3	753.6	...	...	...	...	...	...
Imports of Goods and Services												
1 Imports of merchandise, c.i.f.	714.8	1102.0	1069.2	1072.5	847.8	915.6	...	...	...	...	...	...
2 Adjustments of merchandise imports to change-of-ownership basis	...	...	...	...	...	...	...	...	...	...	...	...
3 Other transport and communication	42.2	78.3	116.6	121.6	69.6	86.5	...	...	...	...	...	...
4 Other insurance service charges	...	...	...	...	...	...	...	...	...	...	...	...
5 Other commodities	96.9	108.3	148.9	108.4	91.2	102.0	...	...	...	...	...	...
6 Direct purchases abroad by government	...	...	...	...	...	...	...	...	...	...	...	...
7 Direct purchases abroad by resident households	107.8	132.4	146.5	166.4	155.2	150.7	...	...	...	...	...	...
Total Imports of Goods and Services	961.7	1421.0	1481.2	1468.9	1163.8	1254.8	...	...	...	...	...	...
Balance of Goods and Services	-492.9	-782.8	-738.0	-690.8	-533.4	-501.2	...	...	...	...	...	...
Total Imports and Balance of Goods and Services	468.8	638.2	743.2	778.1	630.3	753.6	...	...	...	...	...	...

كيفية الحصول على منشورات الأمم المتحدة

يمكن الحصول على منشورات الأمم المتحدة من المكتبات ودور التوزيع في جميع أنحاء العالم . استعلم عنها من المكتبة التي تتعامل معها أو اكتب إلى : الأمم المتحدة ، قسم البيع في نيويورك أو في جنيف .

如何购取联合国出版物

联合国出版物在全世界各地的书店和经售处均有发售。请向书店询问或写信到纽约或日内瓦的联合国销售组。

HOW TO OBTAIN UNITED NATIONS PUBLICATIONS

United Nations publications may be obtained from bookstores and distributors throughout the world. Consult your bookstore or write to: United Nations, Sales Section, New York or Geneva.

COMMENT SE PROCURER LES PUBLICATIONS DES NATIONS UNIES

Les publications des Nations Unies sont en vente dans les librairies et les agences dépositaires du monde entier. Informez-vous auprès de votre libraire ou adressez-vous à : Nations Unies, Section des ventes, New York ou Genève.

КАК ПОЛУЧИТЬ ИЗДАНИЯ ОРГАНИЗАЦИИ ОБЪЕДИНЕННЫХ НАЦИЙ

Издания Организации Объединенных Наций можно купить в книжных магазинах и агентствах во всех районах мира. Наводите справки об изданиях в вашем книжном магазине или пишите по адресу: Организация Объединенных Наций, Секция по продаже изданий, Нью-Йорк или Женева.

COMO CONSEGUIR PUBLICACIONES DE LAS NACIONES UNIDAS

Las publicaciones de las Naciones Unidas están en venta en librerías y casas distribuidoras en todas partes del mundo. Consulte a su librero o diríjase a: Naciones Unidas, Sección de Ventas, Nueva York o Ginebra.

Litho in United Nations, New York
93143—October 1996—3,170
ISBN 92-1-161381-7

United Nations publication
Sales No. E.96.XVII.5
ST/ESA/STAT/SER.X/22, Part I

DOES NOT CIRCULATE

WITHDRAWN

WITHDRAWN

DOES NOT CIRCULATE

WILLIAM F. MAAG LIBRARY
YOUNGSTOWN STATE UNIVERSITY